THE

ENCYCLOPEDIA OF MANAGEMENT

THE ENCYCLOPEDIA OF MANAGEMENT

THIRD EDITION

Edited by

CARL HEYEL

Management Counsel

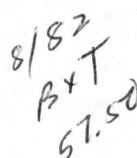

VNR
VAN NOSTRAND REINHOLD COMPANY
New York Cincinnati Toronto London Melbourne

Library of Congress Catalog Card Number: 81-16467
ISBN: 0-442-25165-3

Manufactured in the United States of America

Published by Van Nostrand Reinhold Company
135 West 50th Street, New York. N.Y. 10020

Van Nostrand Reinhold Limited
1410 Birchmount Road
Scarborough, Ontario M1P 2E7, Canada

Van Nostrand Reinhold Australia Pty. Ltd.
17 Queen Street
Mitcham, Victoria 3132, Australia

Van Nostrand Reinhold Company Limited
Molly Millars Lane
Workingham, Berkshire, England

15 14 13 12 11 10 9 8 7 6 5 4 2 1

Library of Congress Cataloging in Publication Data

Main entry under title:

The Encyclopedia of management.

Includes index.
1. Industrial management—Dictionaries.
I. Heyel, Carl, 1908-
HD30.15.E49 1981 658'.003'21 81-16467
ISBN 0-442-25165-3 AACR2

To Miriam Elizabeth Heyel

ACKNOWLEDGMENTS

The accompanying listing of individual contributors—203 in all—to this completely revised edition of THE ENCYCLOPEDIA OF MANAGEMENT indicates the high level of authoritativeness which can be attached to the finished work. Additionally, the editor has had the active cooperation of the leading professional societies and trade associations in the fields covered, both in reviewing texts in their areas of interest, and in arranging for qualified editorial contributors from among their memberships. . . . The editor also wishes to pay tribute to the highly competent support given by the publisher's editorial staff, especially the untiring assistance of the Managing Editor, Mrs. Alberta W. Gordon, and her associate, Mrs. Anne Dempsey.

SENIOR EDITORIAL ADVISORS

HAROLD LAZARUS, Ph.D., Professor of Management and former Dean of the School of Business, Hofstra University, Hempstead, N.Y. Editorial consultant for the Encyclopedia in the general area of management, and coordinator of the group of six editorial advisors drawn from the Hofstra faculty, whose names are included in the accompanying list of Editorial Advisors.

WILLARD A. LEWIS, Ph.D., LL.B., Professor Emeritus of Management and Industrial Relations, Graduate School of Business Administration, New York University, New York; Visiting Professor, Polytechnic Institute of New York, Brooklyn, N.Y. Senior advisor on a broad spectrum of the work as a whole, and responsible for securing the participation of recognized authorities as contributors of numerous entries. Author of the entries on collective bargaining and labor legislation.

MELVIN MANDELL, Editor, *Computer Decisions,* Rochelle Park, N.J. Editorial advisor on numerous Encyclopedia entries, especially in the areas of electronic data processing and management information systems, and responsible for securing the participation of recognized authorities as contributors.

DAVID VALINSKY, Ph.D., Professor of Statistics and Chairman, Department of Statistics and Computer Information Systems, Bernard M. Baruch College, City University of New York, N.Y. Advisor on mathematical entries in general, and author of the very extensive Encyclopedia treatment of statistics.

EDITORIAL ADVISORS

COLIN BARRETT, Transportation Consultant, Reston, Va., formerly editor of *Transportation and Distribution Management,* advisor on entries pertaining to transportation, distribution, and materials management. Author of entries on protective packaging, materials management, physical distribution management, traffic management, and warehousing.

L. J. BENNINGER, Ph.D., Professor Emeritus of Accounting, University of Florida, Gainesville, Fla., advisor on entries pertaining to accounting and financial control. Author of entries on cost accounting (managerial accounting), cost control, flexible budgeting, and standard costing.

BARRY BERMAN, Ph.D., Professor of Marketing, Hofstra University, Hempstead, N.Y., advisor on the areas of marketing and pricing. Co-author of the entries on pricing policy and sales statistics.

PATRICK CASABONA, Ph.D., Professor of Finance, Hofstra University, Hempstead, N.Y., advisor on the areas of business forecasting.

THOMAS C. CATTRALL, JR., Marketing and Refining Division, International Management Sciences Department, Mobil Oil Corporation, New York, N.Y., advisor on entries pertaining to mathematical programming and management sciences in general. Author of the entries on goal programming, linear programming, and mathematical programming.

ROBERT L. CRAIG, Vice President, Government and Public Affairs, American Society for Training and Development, Washington, D.C. office, advisor on all entries having to do with training and human resources development. Author of the entry on human resources development.

JOEL R. EVANS, Ph.D., Chairman, Marketing and International Business Departments, Hofstra University, Hempstead, N.Y., advisor on the areas of marketing and pricing. Co-author of the entries on pricing policy and sales statistics.

WILLIAM M. FOX, Ph.D., Professor of Industrial Relations and Management, University of Florida, Gainesville, Fla., advisor on the areas of behavioral science developments in management. Author of the entries on decision making and organizational effectiveness, and on "Taylorism" in scientific management.

ARABINDA GHOSH, Ph.D., Associate Professor of Finance, Hofstra University, Hempstead, N.Y., advisor on the areas of corporate finance and economics. Author of the entries on corporate capitalization and economics.

ROBERT N. HOGSETT, President, Hogsett Associates, Inc., Binghampton, N.Y., advisor on management techniques. Author of the entry on the application of control theory to management.

STEPHEN LANDEKICH, Research Director, National Association of Accountants, New York, N.Y., advisor on all areas of accounting. Author of the entry, Accounting.

DAVID C. LEAMAN, Director, Professional Development, American Society for Quality Control, Milwaukee, Wisc., responsible for reviewing and updating, on behalf of the Society, the Encyclopedia's extensive treatment of quality control. Co-author of the entry on quality control and quality assurance.

MAXWELL LEHMAN, Professor of Political Governmental Communication, Fairfield University, Fairfield, Conn., formerly City Administrator, City of New York, advisor on public administration, and co-author of the Encyclopedia entry on that subject.

ANITA LOEBER, Consultant to Management, San Diego, Calif., advisor on a broad range of Encyclopedia entries. Author of the entries on management societies and associations, supervisory training, and work measurement in the office.

BELDEN MENKUS, CPM., Management Consultant, Middleville, N.J., consultant on a wide range of Encyclopedia entries. Author of the entries on disaster recovery, forms design, records management, and records protection.

JOSEF P. SIREFMAN, Ph.D., JD., Professor of Business Law, Hofstra University, Hempstead, N.Y., advisor on legal aspects of management. Author of the entries on the legal structure of business organization, and the legal duties and responsibilities of directors.

WILLIAM D. STEVENS, Ph.D., Professor of Marketing, College of Business Administration, University of South Florida, Tampa, Fla., advisor on the areas of marketing research. Author of the entries on consumer behavior research and marketing research.

JACK YURKIEWICZ, Ph.D., The School of Business, Hofstra University, Hempstead, N.Y., advisor on the areas of advanced quantitative techniques. Author of the entries on dynamic programming, integer programming, and nonlinear programming.

PREFACE

Continuing rapid advances in management concepts and techniques, and changes in the climate in which business, government, and institutional enterprises must operate, call for an updated and revised edition of THE ENCYCLOPEDIA OF MANAGEMENT.

Almost a decade has passed since the second edition of the work appeared. While the general thrust of the core subjects remains intact, and while the organization of the material and the format for indicating additional sources of information have withstood the test of time (the first edition appeared in 1963 and in a short time established itself as a standard reference work), it is obvious that recognition must be given to new developments and innovative approaches. In addition to rapid advances in information processing and communications technology, the intervening years have brought changes in legislation in the areas of labor relations, taxation, and mergers and acquisitions, enhanced social consciousness regarding environmental responsibilities and acceptable norms of business ethics, heightened awareness of consumer and employee rights, sharpened mathematical techniques, and new insights of the behavioral sciences into human motivations and group effectiveness.

Every one of the three-hundred-odd entries in the second edition has been carefully reviewed by the original author or, where he or she was not available, by someone of equal standing and competence. The hundreds of contributors—all of recognized authority in their fields—have provided easily referenced, to-the-point articles on modern business practice, of direct and immediate pertinency no matter what the reader's field of specialization.

All entries are arranged alphabetically from ACCOUNTING through ZERO DEFECTS, and are presented, as the complexity of the subject matter demands, from concise, half-page statements to more elaborate discussions ranging in size to as many as twenty-five or thirty pages. The reader is further directed to additional information sources, and the entries themselves are cross-referenced for complete coverage of any area of interest.

Entries carried over from the previous edition have, of course, been updated, and some were totally rewritten or drastically revised because of developments in the past decade. Important new entries in this edition are:

ALTERNATE WORK SCHEDULES
ASSESSMENT CENTERS
BEHAVIOR MODELING IN TRAINING
BUSINESS ETHICS
BUSINESS-GOVERNMENT RELATIONS
CONTROL THEORY: Application to Management
COPYRIGHT
CORPORATE STRATEGY AND BUSINESS POLICY
DISASTER RECOVERY
DISTRIBUTION PLANNING AND RESEARCH
DYNAMIC PROGRAMMING
EMPLOYEE PRIVACY
ENGINEERING MANAGEMENT
FIFO/LIFO INVENTORY ACCOUNTING
FRANCHISING: Legal Aspects
GOAL PROGRAMMING
HUMAN RELATIONS IN INDUSTRY: An Overview
INTEGER PROGRAMMING
INTERNATIONAL MANAGEMENT: Management of the "World Enterprise"
MANAGEMENT EDUCATION: Professional Certification
MANAGEMENT PRACTICE: Learning from Foreign Management
MANAGERIAL EFFECTIVENESS: Climate for Organizational Results
MARKETING RESEARCH: Competitive Analysis
NONLINEAR PROGRAMMING
OCCUPATION SAFETY AND HEALTH ACT OF 1970
OFFICE SAFETY
ORGANIZATIONAL PLANNING: Q-Charts
PACKAGING: Legal and Ethical Considerations
QUALITY CONTROL CENTERS
QUALITY OF WORKING LIFE
ROBOTS IN INDUSTRY
SECURITY: Protection of Trade Secrets and Proprietary Information
TECHNOLOGICAL CHANGE: Union-Management Agreements
TECHNOLOGICAL FORECASTING
TERRORISM: Protective Measures
TRADEMARKS: International Protection
TRANSACTIONAL ANALYSIS IN MANAGEMENT

Unemployment Insurance
Uniform Commercial Code
Women in Management
Zero-Base Budgeting

All entries, to the extent appropriate as dictated by subject matter, follow the editorial formula laid down for the first and second editions, namely: to tell the executive or management staff person not versed in a given specialty just what the subject is all about . . . what kinds of business or operating problems it helps solve . . . the kinds of specialists required to put it to use in a given organization . . . the possibilities for the future as the subject undergoes further development . . . and sources of additional information.

For suggestions as to how to secure the maximum value from the wealth of authoritative information brought together in this single volume, the reader is referred to the section, immediately following the list of contributors, entitled "How to Use the Encyclopedia of Management."

CARL HEYEL, Management
Counsel, Manhasset, New York

CONTRIBUTORS

ROBERT A. ABBOTT, Director, Technical Services, American Society for Quality Control, Milwaukee, Wisc. (Quality Control and Quality Assurance)

LEE ADLER, President, Lee Adler & Company, New York, N.Y. (Marketing)

ADMINISTRATIVE MANAGEMENT SOCIETY, Willow Grove, Pa. (Office Management and Administrative Services; Office Space Planning: The "Open Plan")

WILLIAM M. AIKEN, President, H. B. Maynard and Company, Inc., Pittsburgh, Pa. (Incentive Systems)

PETER S. ALBIN, Professor, Department of Economics, City University of New York, John Jay College, New York, N.Y. (Econometrics)

JOE ALEXANDER, Consultant to Management, Apos, Calif. (Transactional Analysis in Management)

AMERICAN BUSINESS PRESS, INC., New York, N.Y. (Advertising Media: Magazines)

AMERICAN ASSOCIATION OF CERTIFIED PUBLIC ACCOUNTANTS, New York, N.Y. (Certified Public Accountant)

AMERICAN NATIONAL STANDARDS INSTITUTE, New York, N.Y. (Industrial Standardization)

AMERICAN SOCIETY FOR QUALITY CONTROL, Vendor-Vendee Technical Committee, Milwaukee, Wisc. (Vendor Rating)

A. JAMES ANDREWS, Director of Publications, Association for Systems Management, Cleveland, Ohio (Organization Analysis and Planning; Systems Management)

ANDERSON ASHBURN, Editor, *American Machinist,* New York, N.Y. (Automation)

ASSOCIATION OF NATIONAL ADVERTISERS, INC., New York, N.Y. (Advertising Measured Results)

AUERBACH PUBLISHERS, INC., Editorial Staff, Pennsauken, N.J. (Electronic Data Processing; Electronic Data Processing: Computer Peripherals; Electronic Data Processing: Equipment Classification)

K. S. AXELSON, Executive Vice President, J. C. Penney Company, Inc., New York, N.Y. (Responsibility Reporting)

LINDSAY L. BAIRD, Jr., Management Consultant, Mountan Lakes, N.J. (Security)

JAMES J. BAMBRICK, Labor Economist, The Standard Oil Company (Ohio), Cleveland, Ohio (Labor Unions)

BENNY BARAK, Ph.D., Assistant Professor of Marketing, Baruch College, City University of New York, New York, N.Y. (Sales Promotion)

RALPH M. BARNES, Professor of Engineering and Production Management Emeritus, University of California at Los Angeles, Calif. (Motion and Time Study)

COLIN BARRETT, Transportation Consultant, Reston, Va. (Freight Forwarders; Materials Management; Packaging, Protective: The Systems Approach; Physical Distribution Management; Traffic Management; Traffic and Transportation: Structure of the Transportation Industry; Warehousing)

O. WILLIAM BATTALIA, Battalia and Associates, New York, N.Y. (Executive Recruitment; Executive Selection)

CLIFFORD M. BAUMBACK, Professor of Production Management, University of Iowa, Iowa City, Ia. (Production Planning and Inventory Management—Concepts and Objectives)

HRACH BEDROSIAN, Ph.D., Professor of Management and Organization Behavior, New York University, New York, N.Y. (Personnel Administration)

MOSHE BEN-HORIM, Lecturer, School of Business, Hebrew University, Jerusalem, Israel, and Visiting Associate Professor, College of Business Administration, University of Florida, Gainesville, Fla. (Inflation)

EUGENE J. BENGE, Management Consultant, Boca Raton, Fla. (Job Evaluation)

L. J. BENNINGER, Ph.D., Professor Emeritus of Accounting, University of Florida, Gainesville, Fla. (Cost Accounting (Managerial Accounting); Cost Control; Flexible Budgeting; Standard Costing)

MURRAY BERDICK, Ph.D., formerly Director of Applied Research, Chesebrough-Pond's, Inc., Trumbull, Conn. (Outside Research)

B. J. BERKOWITZ, General Electric Company, Santa Barbara, Calif. (Game Theory)

GEORGE BERKWITT, Editor, *Industrial Distribution* (Materials Handling: Equipment Types)

BARRY BERMAN, Ph.D., Professor of Marketing, Hofstra University, Hempstead, N.Y. (Pricing Policy; Sales Statistics)

George N. Biggs III, President, American Society of Corporate Secretaries, Inc., New York, N.Y. (Corporate Secretary)

Serge A. Birn, Chairman, The Birn Organization, GmbH., Frankfort on Main, West Germany (Linear Responsibility Charting)

Lester R. Bittel, formerly Editor, *Factory*, New York, N.Y. (Manufacturing Management)

Horatio Bond, Consulting Engineer, Hyannis Port Mass., formerly Chief Engineer, National Fire Protection Association, Boston, Mass. (Fire Loss Protection)

Leland P. Bradford, formerly Executive Director, National Training Laboratories (now NTL Institute), Arlington, Va. (Sensitivity Training)

Thomas A. Budne, Statistical Engineering Consultant, Great Neck, N.Y. (Reliability Engineering)

Frederic E. Bulleit, Vice President and Director, Materials Management, Armstrong Cork Company, Lancaster, Pa.; past International President, American Production & Inventory Control Society; past Chairman, Curricula and Certification Council, APICS (Production Planning and Inventory Management—Production Planning (Manufacturing Resources Planning))

Ruth Burger, Director of Human Resources Research, Research Institute of America, New York, N.Y. (Alcoholism and Drug Abuse in Industry)

Samuel L. H. Burk, dec. formerly Vice President, Sherwood, Smith, and Associates, Inc., Philadelphia, Pa. (Job Evaluation)

W. V. Burnell, William V. Burnell & Associates, Boston, Mass. (Appraisal (of Property))

Paul W. Burton, Director of Public Relations, Norden Systems, Inc., subsidiary of United Technologies Corporation, Norwalk, Conn. (Public Relations)

William E. Camp, Management Consultant, Watertown, Pa. (Gantt Chart)

John Capozzola, Professor of Public Administration, New York University, New York, N.Y. (Public Administration)

Peter J. Carroll, Hayes/Hill Incorporated, New York, N.Y. (Marketing Strategy: Competitive Analysis)

Phil Carroll, P.E., dec., Industrial Engineer, Maplewood, N.J. (Method Improvement; Overhead Assignment)

Thomas C. Cattrall, Jr., Marketing and Refining Division, International Management Sciences Department, Mobil Oil Corporation, New York, N.Y. (Goal Programming; Linear Programming; Linear Programming: A Case Example; Mathematical Programming)

F. R. Cawl, Jr., Publisher, *The Buyers Guide to Outdoor Advertising*, Searsport, Me. and New York, N.Y. (Advertising Media: Outdoor Advertising)

Ya-Lun Chou, Ph.D., Department of Quantitative Analysis, St. John's University, New York, N.Y. (Business Forecasting)

Jesse L. Clark, Paperwork Systems, Newton, Mass. (Forms Design Instructions)

Lawrence Connell, Administrator, National Credit Union Administration, Washington, D.C. (Credit Unions)

Donald W. Conover, Vice President (ret.) Man Factors, Inc., San Diego, Calif. (Human Engineering (Human Factors Engineering))

A.V.C. Cook, Secretary, International Accounting Standards Committee, London, England (International Accounting Standards Committee)

Frederic W. Cook, Frederic W. Cook & Co., Inc., New York, N.Y. (Venture Management)

John Coughlan, CPA., Partner, La France, Waker, Jackley, and Saville, Washington, D.C.; Adjunct Professor, Loyola College, Washington, D.C. (Return on Capital)

Richard B. Countess, Manager, International Training, Westinghouse Electric Corp., Power Generation Division, Philadelphia, Pa., and Adjunct Professor of Management, MBA School, Widener University Center, Chester, Pa. (New Product Development)

Robert L. Craig, Vice President, Government and Public Affairs, American Society for Training and Development, Washington Office, Washington, D.C. (Human Resources Development)

Graef S. Crystal, Vice President, Towers, Perrin, Forster & Crosby, Inc., New York, N.Y. (Executive Compensation)

Samir P. Dagher, Ph.D., Chairman, Department of Business and Managerial Science, Marywood College, Scranton, Pa. (Business Ethics)

Robert F. DeLay, President, Direct Mail/Marketing Association, New York, N.Y. (Advertising Media: Direct Response Marketing)

GEORGE C. DEVOL, President, Devol Research Associates, Fort Lauderdale, Fla. (Robots in Industry)

W. J. DICKSON, formerly Personnel Research, Western Electric Company, Inc., New York, N.Y. (Hawthorne Experiments; Personnel Counseling)

J. WALTER DIETZ, dec., formerly President, Training Within Industry Foundation, Summit, N.J. (On-the-Job Training; Training Within Industry Program (TWI))

DIRECTORY OF INTERNAL PUBLICATIONS, Chicago, Ill. (House Magazines)

JOHN P. DORY, Professor of Management, Pace University, New York, N.Y. (Corporate Strategy and Business Policy)

JEROME L. DREYER, Executive Vice President, Association of Data Processing Service Organizations, Arlington, Va. (Computer Service Industry)

PETER F. DRUCKER, Clarke Professor of Social Sciences, Claremont Graduate School, Claremont, Calif. (Management Practice: Learning from Foreign Management)

DANIEL J. DUFFY, Professor of Business Administration, Loyola College, Baltimore, Md. (Industrial Engineering; Work Measurement)

DUN & BRADSTREET INC., New York, N.Y. (Credit Reporting)

MARVIN D. DUNNETTE, Professor of Psychology, University of Minnesota, Minneapolis, Minn. (Personnel Testing)

JULIUS E. EITINGTON, Director of Training and Research, BNA Communications Inc., Rockville, Md. (Personnel Management: Pioneers)

ESTHER E. ESPENSHADE, Manager, Employment Security Research, Illinois Bureau of Employment Security, Chicago, Ill. (Unemployment: Concepts and Measurement; Unemployment Insurance; Women in Business and Industry; Women in Management)

IRVIN B. ETTER, Director, Occupational Safety & Loss Control Consultant, National Safety Council, Chicago, Ill. (Safety and Health in the Workplace)

JOEL R. EVANS, Ph.D., Chairman, Marketing and International Business Department, Hofstra University, Hempstead, N.Y. (Pricing Policy; Sales Statistics)

DOROTHY FEY, Executive Director, The United States Trademark Association, New York, N.Y. (Trademarks)

FINANCIAL EXECUTIVES INSTITUTE, New York, N.Y. (Controllership; Treasurership)

SEYMOUR H. FINE, Ph.D., Marketing Associates, Glen Rock, N.J. (Marketing Research: Sources of Information)

STEVEN N. FISCHER, CPA, Adjunct Professor, Russell Sage College, Troy, N.Y.; Shareholder, Urbach, Kahn & Werlin, Albany, N.Y. (Taxation)

THOMAS FORD, Attorney at Law, Benesch, Friedlander, Coplan, & Arnoff, Cleveland, Ohio (Antitrust Legislation)

J. W. FORRESTER, Professor of Management, Massachusetts Institute of Technology, Cambridge, Mass. (Industrial Dynamics)

WILLIAM A. FOWLER, Executive Director, National Home Study Council, Washington, D.C. (Correspondence Schools)

WILLIAM M. FOX, Ph.D., Professor of Industrial Relations and Management, University of Florida, Gainesville, Fla. (Decision Making and Organizational Effectiveness; Scientific Management: "Taylorism")

ROBERT F. FROEHLKE, President, American Council of Life Insurance, Washington, D.C. (Group Life Insurance)

PAUL O. GADDIS, Dean, School of Management and Administration, The University of Texas at Dallas, Texas (Project Management)

NEWELL GARFIELD, Jr., President, Newell Garfield Company, Inc., New York, N.Y. (Management by Objectives)

LAURENCE N. GARTER, Partner, Touche Ross & Co., New York, N.Y. (Marketing: Patterns of Consumer Goods Distribution)

CHARLES E. GEARING, Professor and Dean, College of Management, Georgia Institute of Technology, Atlanta, Ga. (Decision Theory)

ARABINDA GHOSH, Ph.D., Associate Professor of Finance, Hofstra University, Hempstead, N.Y. (Corporate Capitalization; Economics)

CHARLES P. GIEL, M.D., Medical Director, Joseph E. Seagram and Sons, Inc.; Associate Professor of Clinical Medicine, New York University College of Medicine; Associate Attending Physician, University and Bellevue Hospitals; New York, N.Y. (Occupational Health)

JOHN J. GLASER, formerly Polaris Division, Sperry Gyroscope Co. Division of Sperry Rand Corp., Great Neck, L.I. (Critical Path Method; Integrated Project Management)

ARNOLD GOLDENBERGER, Security Consultant, Great Neck, N.Y. (Security)

WILLIAM M. GOLDSMITH, FIDSA, Goldsmith Yamasaki Sprecht, Inc., Chicago, Ill. (Industrial Design)

ROBERT T. GOLEMBIEWSKI, Department of Political Science, University of Georgia, Athens, Ga. (Motivation)

ROBERT D. GOODWIN, Executive Vice President, National Association of Credit Management, New York, N.Y. (Credit Management)

C. E. GRAESE, CPA, Partner, Peat, Marwick, Mitchell & Co., New York, N.Y. (Statistical Accounting)

CHARLES H. GRANGER, Hayes/Hill Incorporated, New York, N.Y. (Long-Range Corporate Planning)

FRANK K. GRIESINGER, President, Frank K. Griesinger and Associates, Inc., Cleveland, Ohio (Leasing of Industrial Equipment)

VINCENT F. GUERRIE, C.P.E., Chief Engineer, Johns-Manville World Headquarters, Denver, Colo. (Maintenance)

DENISE R. GUILLET, *Administrative Management,* New York, N.Y. (Information Data Banks, On-Line)

JOHN W. HAEFELE, Ph.D., formerly Research Scientist, Procter & Gamble Company, Cincinnati, Ohio (Brainstorming; Creativity)

OLIVER S. HALLETT, Executive Secretary, National Association of Suggestion Systems, Chicago, Ill. (Suggestion Systems)

ROBERT HAMPTON III, Partner, Price Waterhouse & Co., New York, N.Y. (International Accounting)

FRED C. HART, President, Fred C. Hart Associates, Inc., New York, N.Y. (Environmental Controls)

HARRY P. HATRY, Director, State and Local Government Research Program, The Urban Institute, Washington, D.C. (Cost-Benefit and Cost-Effectiveness Analysis)

ROBERT G. HAWKINS, Vice Dean and Professor of Economics and Finance, New York University Graduate School of Business Administration, New York, N.Y. (International Management: Management of the "World Enterprise")

HEIDRICK AND STRUGGLES, INC., Chicago, Ill. (Directors: Characteristics of Boards)

J. L. HESKETT, 1907 Professor of Business Logistics, Harvard University Graduate School of Business Administration, Boston, Mass. (Business Logistics; Business Logistics: Case Example—Using the "Distribution Solution")

CARL HEYEL, Management Counsel, Manhasset, N.Y. (Assessment Centers; Executive Development: Away-from-Company Programs; Executive Traits; Human Relations in Industry: An Overview; Industrial Research and Development; Management Movement: Leaders in Thought; Organization: Line-Staff Relationships; Scanlon Plan of Group Incentives; Standard Minute System; Supervisory Training; Technical Forecasting; Zero-Base Budgeting; Zero Defects)

WILLIAM E. HILL, Hayes/Hill Incorporated, New York, N.Y. (Long-Range Corporate Planning)

L. CLINTON HOCH, Executive Vice President, The Fantus Company, Millburn, N.J. (Industrial Districts; Plant Location)

DR. HAROLD L. HODGKINSON, President, NTL Institute, Arlington, Va. (Sensitivity Training)

DOROTHY HOGAN, Director of Communications, American National Standards Institute, Inc., New York, N.Y. (Standardization, Company)

ROBERT N. HOGSETT, President, Hogsett Associates, Inc., Binghamton, N.Y. (Control Theory: Application to Management)

DONALD J. HORTON, Attorney, Andrews, Kurth, Campbell & Jones, Houston, Tex. (Employment: Antidiscrimination Legislation)

WINFIELD HUTTON, Hunter College of the City of New York, New York, N.Y. (Break-Even Analysis)

INDUSTRIAL DISTRIBUTOR NEWS, Philadelphia, Pa. (Industrial Distributors)

THE INSTITUTE OF INTERNAL AUDITORS, Altemonte Springs, Fla. (Internal Auditors)

JOHN W. JOHNSON, Executive Vice President, American Collectors Association, Minneapolis, Minn. (Collection Services)

ANDREW KALMYKOW, Consultant, American Insurance Association, New York, N.Y. (Workers' Compensation)

DR. PETER KARES, Chairman of Finance, College of Business Administration, University of South Florida, Tampa, Fla. (Mergers and Acquisitions)

JOSEPH KAUFMAN, Manager, Value Program, Cooper Industries, Inc., Houston, Tex, (Value Engineering (Value Analysis))

W. E. KENDALL, Ph.D., Industrial Psychologist, Rye, N.Y. (Industrial Psychology; Personnel Testing: Types of Tests)

JAMES H. KENNEDY, Editor and Publisher, *Consultants News,* Fitzwilliams, N.H. (Management Consulting)

YUI KIMURA, MBA, University of Washington, Lecturer in International Management, New York University, New York, N.Y. International Management: Management of the "World Enterprise")

WALTER A. KLEINSCHROD, editor of *Administrative Management* and editorial director of *Word Processing & Information Systems* magazine, New York, N.Y. (Office Automation)

FRANK M. KNOX, Courier-Citizen Company, New York, N.Y. (Forms Control)

RICHARD S. KRASHEVSKI, Department of Economic Research, AFL-CIO, Washington, D.C. (Guaranteed Annual Wage)

H. E. KROLL, Dun & Bradstreet, Inc., New York, N.Y. (Financial Ratios)

DONALD J. KULICK, Associate Regional Administrator, U.S. Department of Labor, Employment and Training Administration, New York, N.Y. (Training and Development (Government Sponsored))

GEORGE H. KUPER, Associate, Production Resources Staff, General Electric Company, Bridgeport, Conn.; formerly Director, National Center for Productivity and Quality of Working Life. (Productivity: Concepts and Measures)

STEPHEN LANDEKICH, Research Director, National Association of Accountants, New York, N.Y. (Accounting)

THEOS A. LANGLIE, Industrial Psychologist, Southbury, Conn. (Executive Appraisal: Diagnostic Performance Appraisal; Performance Appraisal (Merit Rating))

DAVID C. LEAMAN, Director, Professional Development American Society for Quality Control, Milwaukee, Wisc. (Quality Control and Quality Assurance)

JERRY LEATHAM, President, American Warehousemen's Association, Chicago, Ill. (Warehousing: The Public Warehouse)

MAXWELL LEHMAN, Professor of Political Governmental Communications, Fairfield University, Fairfield, Conn.; formerly City Administrator, City of New York (Public Administration)

WILL J. LESSARD, Chairman of the Board, American Institute of Management, Boston, Mass. (Management Audit)

ROBERT E. LEWIS, Vice President, Citibank N.A., New York, N.Y (Marketing Research: Patterns of Population Growth)

WILLARD A. LEWIS, Ph.D., LL.B., Professor Emeritus of Management and Industrial Relations, Graduate School of Business Administration, New York University; Visiting Professor, Polytechnic Institute of New York, Brooklyn, N.Y. (Collective Bargaining; Labor Relations Legislation)

PHILIP A. LINK, Production Control Manager, Automatic Electric Company, Northlake, Ill. (Production Planning and Inventory Management—Measurement of Effectiveness)

DAVID F. LINOWES, Boeschenstein Professor of Political Economy and Public Policy, University of Illinois at Urbana-Champaign, Ill. (Employee Privacy; Social Audit)

IRA A. LIPMAN, Chairman of the Board and President, Guardmark, Inc., Memphis, Tenn. (Security: Protection of Trade Secrets and Proprietary Information)

GORDON L. LIPPITT, Ph.D., Professor, School of Government and Business Administration, The George Washington University, Washington, D.C.; President, Organization Renewal, Inc., Washington, D.C. (Group Dynamics)

ARTHUR D. LITTLE, Chairman of the Board, Narragansett Capital Corporation, Providence, R.I. (Venture Capital)

EDWIN A. LOCKE, Ph.D., College of Business and Management and Department of Psychology, University of Maryland at College Park, Md. (Goal Setting)

ANITA LOEBER, Consultant to Management on Organization, Systems, and Measurement, San Diego, Calif. (Management Societies and Associations; Supervisory Training; Work Measurement in the Office)

DR. J. R. LONGSTREET, Professor of Finance, College of Business Administration, University of South Florida, Tampa, Fla. (Mergers and Acquisitions)

J. KEITH LOUDEN, President, The Corporate Director, Inc., New York, N.Y. (Directors: Legal Duties and Responsibilities)

ROBERT L. MCCULLOUGH, Staff Writer, *Ohio Monitor,* monthly industrial safety publication of The Industrial Commission of Ohio, Division of Safety and Hygiene, Columbus, Ohio (Office Safety)

WALTER B. MCFARLAND, Ph.D., formerly Director of Research, National Association of Cost Accountants, New York, N.Y. (Cash Flow Analysis; Direct Costing (Variable Costing); Industrial Research Accounting; Industrial Research Budgeting; Management Accounting)

E. PATRICK MCGUIRE, Project Director, Management Research, The Conference Board, New York, N.Y. (Franchising)

MACHINERY AND ALLIED PRODUCTS INSTITUTE, Washington, D.C. (Fixed-Asset Investment Analysis: The MAPI Formulas and Procedures)

MAGAZINE PUBLISHERS ASSOCIATION, New York, N.Y. (Advertising Media: Magazines)

JOHN F. MAGEE, President, Arthur D. Little, Inc., Cambridge, Mass. (Operations Research in Marketing Decisions)

BERNARD F. MAJOR, formerly Manager, Package Development Laboratory, Ortho Pharmaceutical Corporation, Raritan, N.J. (Packaging: Organizing for Package Development)

RICHARD K. MANOFF, Chairman, Richard K. Manoff, Inc., New York, N.Y. (Advertising)

JULIUS J. MANSON, Professor or Emeritus and former Dean, Bernard M. Baruch School of Business and Public Administration, City University of New York; formerly Executive Director, New York State Board of Mediation. (Mediation)

HOWARD N. MANTEL, Director of Government Programs, Institute of Public Administration, New York, N.Y. (Public Authorities)

LEONARD S. MATTHEWS, President, American Association of Advertising Agencies, New York, N.Y. (Advertising Agencies)

H. B. MAYNARD, dec., formerly President, Maynard Research Council, Incorporated, Pittsburgh, Pa. (Materials Management: Material Handling Equipment Types; Operation Analysis; Process Analysis)

JOHN F. MEE, Ph.D., LL.D., Mead Johnson Professor Emeritus of Management, Indiana University, Bloomington, Ind. (Management Movement; Matrix Organization; Scientific Management)

BELDEN MENKUS, CPM., Management Consultant, Middleville, N.J. (Disaster Recovery; Forms Design; Records Management; Records Protection)

BERT L. METZGER, President, Profit Sharing Research Foundation, Evanston, Ill. (Profit Sharing)

DOROTHY J. MIAL, former Director, Education Division, National Training Laboratories (now NTL Institute), Arlington, Va. (Sensitivity Training)

ROBERT W. MILLER, Director of Management Sciences, Raytheon Company, Lexington, Mass. (PERT (Program Evaluation and Review Technique))

JAMES P. MITCHELL, Administrator, Bureau of Apprenticeship Training, U.S. Department of Labor, Employment, and Training Administration, Washington, D.C. (Apprenticeship Programs)

ALFRED JAY MORAN, Jr., The TJM Corporation, New Orleans, La. (Forms Control)

DR. STANLEY H. MULLIN, Vice President, University Alumni Relations, Pace University, New York, N.Y. (Public Relations Research)

G. T. MUNDORFF, Rear Admiral, U.S. Navy, ret.; Assistant to the President, Information Systems Group, General Precision, Inc., Glendale, Calif. (Line of Balance; Line of Balance: Day Control)

JOSEPH S. MURPHY, Vice President, ret., American Arbitration Association, New York, N.Y. (Labor Arbitration)

H. W. NANCE, President, Serge A. Birn Company, Louisville, Ky. (Pre-determined Motion Times)

BURT NANUS, Systems Development Corporation, Santa Monica, Calif. (Management Development Techniques)

NATIONAL ASSOCIATION OF BROADCASTERS, Washington, D.C. (Advertising Media: Broadcasting)

NATIONAL ASSOCIATION OF PERSONNEL CONSULTANTS, Washington, D.C. (Employment Agencies)

NATIONAL CABLE TELEVISION ASSOCIATION, Washington, D.C. (Advertising Media: Cable TV)

THOMAS A. NELSON, Manager, Office of Government Services, Price Waterhouse & Co., Washington, D.C. (Business-Government Relations)

BENJAMIN J. NIEBEL, Professor Emeritus of Industrial Engineering, The Pennsylvania State University, University Park, Pa. (Process Engineering)

NEWSPAPER ADVERTISING BUREAU, New York, N.Y. (Advertising Media: Newspapers)

BLAKE T. NEWTON, President, American Council of Life Insurance, Washington, D.C. (Employee Benefit Plans)

JOHN F. O'BRIEN, Assistant Regional Director, New York Regional Office, Federal Trade Commission, New York, N.Y. (Pricing: Legal Aspects)

JOHN F. O'CONNOR, Editorial Director, *Purchasing,* Boston, Mass. (Purchasing)

D. F. O'Donnell, P.E., O'Donnell Sales & Engineering Company, Buffalo, N.Y. (Depreciation)

George S. Olive, Jr., Geo. S. Olive & Co., Indianapolis, Ind. (Certified Public Accountant: Role in Management Services)

John W. Oliver, formerly Senior Vice President, The Linen Thread Company, Inc., New York, N.Y. (Taxation: Organization for)

David L. Olsson, Ph.D., Professor, Department of Packaging Science, Rochester Institute of Technology, Rochester, N.Y. (Packaging: Legal and Ethical Aspects; Packaging: Organizing for Package Development)

William Olsten, Chairman and Chief Executive Officer, The Olsten Corporation, Westbury, L.I., N.Y. (Temporary Personnel Services)

John C. O'Mara, Executive Director, Computer Security Institute, Northboro, Mass. (Computer Security/Automated Office Security)

Edward Patroski, Director of Investigations, Pinkerton's, Inc., New York, N.Y. (Terrorism: Protective Measures)

John R. Paulsen, Ph.D., IBM Education, Lexington, Ky. (Behavior Modeling in Training)

Vito F. Pennacchio, Coffin & Richardson, Boston, Mass. (Appraisal (of Property))

Stanley Peterfreund, President, Stanley Peterfreund Associates, Inc., Closter, N.J. (Employee Attitude Research: Attitude Surveys)

H. H. Peterson, President, OSR, Inc., Honolulu, Hawaii (Waiting Line Theory (Queueing Theory))

John Polastak, Executive Director, Transit Advertising Association, New York, N.Y. (Advertising Media: Transit Advertising)

Saul Poliak, President, Clapp & Poliak, Inc., New York, N.Y. (Trade Shows and Exhibits)

J. T. Powers, Peat, Marwick, Mitchell & Co., New York, N.Y. (Break-Even Analysis)

Kenneth Purdy, Senior Associate, Roy W. Walters and Associates, Mahwah, N.J. (Job Enrichment and Work Effectiveness)

Harold J. Raphael, Ph.D., Director, Department of Packaging Science, Rochester Institute of Technology, Rochester, N.Y. (Packaging: Legal and Ethical Considerations)

Erwin Rausch, Didactic Systems, Inc., Cranford, N.J. (Management Games; Managerial Effectiveness: Climate for Organizational Results)

Nyles V. Reinfeld, Director, National Institute of Management, Inc., Bath, Ohio (Production Planning and Inventory Management—Inventory Control)

Richard W. Reynolds, Senior Systems Analyst, Space Technology Laboratories, Redondo Beach, Calif. (Organization Analysis and Planning)

Markley Roberts, Economist, Department of Research, American Federation of Labor and Congress of Industrial Organizations, Washington, D.C. (Technological Change: Union-Management Agreements)

Simcha Ronen, Ph.D., Associate Professor of Management and Organizational Behavior, Graduate School of Business Administration, New York University, New York, N.Y. (Alternative Work Schedules)

Herbert C. Rosenthal, President, Graphics Institute, Inc., New York, N.Y. (Annual Reports)

Dr. Michael Rosow, Director, The Productivity Forum, Work in America Institute, Scarsdale, N.Y. (Quality of Working Life)

Albert H. Rubenstein, Professor of Industrial Engineering and Management Sciences, Northwestern University, Evanston, Ill. (Organization Theory)

Richard S. Sabo, Manager, Educational Services, Lincoln Electric Company, Cleveland, Ohio (Lincoln Incentive Management Plan)

Konrad Sadek, World Vision International, Monrovia, Calif. (Human Resources Requirements Planning; Management Information Systems)

Sales & Marketing Management, New York, N.Y. (Industrial Purchasing Power: The S&MM Annual Survey)

Henry F. Sander, Executive Director, American Production and Inventory Control Society, Inc., Washington, D.C. (Production Planning and Inventory Management—Introduction)

Albert V. Santora, CMfgE., Vice President, Operations, Visual Graphics Corp., Tamarac, Fla. (Production Planning and Inventory Management—Production Control)

Raymond Sarch, Senior Editor, *Data Communications,* New York, N.Y. (Data Communications)

Francis M. Schauer, Jr., Fellow, Society of

Actuaries; Actuary, The Wyatt Company, Washington, D.C. (Retirement Plans)

MICHAEL SCHIFF, Ph.D., Professor of Accounting, Graduate School of Business Administration, New York University, New York, N.Y. (Marketing Cost Analysis)

HOMER J. SCHNEIDER, Attorney, Leydig, Voit, Osann, Mayer & Holt, Ltd., Chicago, Ill. (Patents)

JAMES SCHWEITZER, Xerox Corporation, Stamford, Conn. (Computer Security/Automated Office Security)

R. C. SCOTT, Vice President, Eddy-Rucker-Nickels Company, Cambridge, Mass. (Rucker Plan of Group Incentives)

ALLEN H. SEED II, Management Consultant, Arthur D. Little, Inc., Cambridge, Mass. (Inflation Accounting)

BARNARD SELIGMAN, Graduate School of Business Administration, Pace University, New York, N.Y. (Money and Banking)

EDWIN SHADE, Editor, *Geyer Dealer Topics,* New York, N.Y. (Information Storage and Retrieval (non-Computer))

PHILIP W. SHAY, formerly Executive Vice President, Association of Consulting Management Engineers, Inc. (now ACME, The Association of Consulting Management Firms), New York, N.Y. (Innovation: The Management of Change)

GORDON D. SHELLARD, formerly Associate Actuary, New York Life Insurance Company, New York, N.Y. (Operations Research)

LEONARD J. SILVER, C.P.C.U., ARM, President, First Risk Management Company, Wincote, Pa. and First Risk Management (PR) Inc., San Juan, Puerto Rico (Insurance Management; Risk Management)

DR. LEONARD C. SILVERN, President, Education and Training Consultants, Co., Sedona, Ariz., (Teaching Machines, Programmed Instruction, and Computer-Aided Instruction)

JOHN D. SIMMONS, Financial Consultant, New York, N.Y. (Break-Even Analysis; Cost-Volume-Profit Analysis; Long-Range Corporate Planning; Long-Range Planning: Financial Aspects)

GILBERT SIMONETTI, Jr., Partner, Office of Government Services, Price Waterhouse & Co., Washington, D.C. (Business-Government Relations)

JOSEF P. SIREFMAN, Ph.D., J.D., Professor of Business Law, Hofstra University, Hempstead, N.Y. (Business Organization: Legal Structure; Directors: Legal Duties and Responsibilities)

LAWRENCE SLOTE, Eng. Sc.D., P.E., New York University; Director, The Center for Safety, New York, N.Y. (Occupational Safety and Health Act of 1970)

CHARLES W. SMITH, Consultant, Distribution by Design, Roslyn, N.Y. (Distribution Planning and Research)

RICHARD D. SMITH, Manager-Public Affairs, Norden Systems, Norwalk, Conn. (Publicity)

ALFRED SMOKE, Executive Director, New York Consumer Assembly, Inc., New York, N.Y. (Consumer Protection)

PETER M. SPADER, Ph.D., Associate Professor of Philosophy, Marywood College, Scranton, Pa. (Business Ethics)

JOHN L. SPAFFORD, President, Associated Credit Bureaus, Inc., Houston, Texas (Credit Bureaus)

LEO SPECTOR, Editor, *Plant Engineering,* Barrington, Ill. (Plant Engineering)

D. F. STANIC, Corporate Systems Manager, Alcan Aluminum Corporation, Cleveland, Ohio (Data Communications: A Case Example)

DANIEL STARCH, Ph.D., Founder of Daniel Starch & Staff, Mamaroneck, N.Y. (Advertising Research)

STARCH INRA HOOPER, INC., Mamaroneck, N.Y. (Advertising Research)

JOEL M. STERN, President, Chase Financial Policy, The Chase Manhattan Bank N.A., New York, N.Y. (Financial Analysis: Earnings)

WILLIAM D. STEVENS, Ph.D., Professor of Marketing, College of Business Administration, University of South Florida, Tampa, Fla. (Consumer Behavior Research; Marketing Research)

MORRIS STONE, Vice President, ret., American Arbitration Association, New York, N.Y. (Arbitration)

ROBERT W. TAFT, Senior Vice President, Hill and Knowlton, Inc., New York, N.Y. (Financial Public Relations)

WILLIAM H. TANKERSLEY, President, Council of Better Bureaus, Inc., Washington, D.C. (Better Business Bureaus)

JOHN PAUL TAYLOR, President, The John Paul Taylor Company, St. Joseph, Mich. (Manufacturers' Representatives)

CRAIG S. TEDMON, Jr., Staff Executive, Power

Systems Technology Operation, General Electric Company, Schenectady, N.Y. (Basic Research: Management Aspects)

CLAYTON J. THOMAS, Assistant for Operations Research, ACS Studies and Analysis, Headquarters, U.S. Air Force, Washington, D.C. (Operational Gaming and Monte Carlo Simulation)

JOHN M. THOMPSON, Vice President, Index Systems, Cambridge, Mass. (Computer Installations: Top Management Planning and Follow-Through)

STEPHEN TINGHITELLA, Editorial Director, *Traffic Management,* New York, N.Y. (Shippers' Associations)

ANTHONY R. TOCCO, Manager, Manufacturing Engineering, TRW Mission Mfg. Company, Houston, Tex. (Value Engineering (Value Analysis))

EDWARD TOMESKI, Ph.D., Consultant and Professor of Management, Barry College, Miami, Fla. (Human Resources Requirements Planning; Management Information Systems)

DR. DAVID VALINSKY, Professor of Statistics and Chairman, Department of Statistics and Computer Information Systems, Bernard M. Baruch College, City University of New York, New York, N.Y. (Statistics)

PAUL WACHTEL, Professor of Economics, New York University Graduate School of Business Administration, New York, N.Y. and Visiting Professor, School of Business Administration, Hebrew University, Jerusalem, Israel (Inflation)

WILLOUGHBY ANN WALSH, Executive Editor, *Word Processing & Information Systems,* New York, N.Y. (Word Processing)

ROY W. WALTERS, President, Roy W. Walters and Associates, Inc., Mahwah, N.J. (Job Enrichment and Work Effectiveness)

VERNON WEAVER, Administrator, Small Business Administration, Washington, D.C. (Small Business Administration)

EDGAR WEINBERG, Consulting Economist, Bethesda, Md., formerly Assistant Director, National Center for Productivity and Quality of Working Life (Productivity: Concepts and Measures)

ELI WERLIN, CPA, Professor and Chairman of Accounting, Russell Sage College, Troy, New York; Partner, Urbach, Kahn & Werlin, Certified Public Accountants, Albany, N.Y. (Taxation)

HARRY R. WHITE, formerly Executive Director, Sales Executive Club of New York, New York, N.Y. (Sales Management; Sales Training)

KENNETH W. WHITE, Vice President and General Manager, Health Insurance Institute, Washington, D.C. (Group Health Insurance)

LAWRENCE S. WICK, Attorney, Leydig, Voit, Osann, Mayer & Holt, Ltd., Chicago, Ill; member representing franchising industry, State of Illinois Franchise Advisory Board (Copyright; Franchising: Legal Aspects; Trademarks; Trademarks: International Protection)

C. WOODY WILLIAMS, Information Systems and Services Administration, Texas Instruments Incorporated, Dallas, Tex. (Management Information Systems: A Case Example)

FRED E. WILLIAMS, Associate Professor and Chairman of Graduate Program, College of Management, Georgia Institute of Technology, Atlanta, Ga. (Decision Theory)

MERRITT A. WILLIAMSON, Orrin Henry Ingram Distinguished Professor of Engineering Management, Vanderbilt University, Nashville, Tenn. (Engineering Management; New-Product Development)

WESLEY E. WOODSON, President, Man Factors, Inc., San Diego, Calif. (Human Engineering (Human Factors Engineering))

ED. YAGER, President, Consulting Associates, Inc., Novi, Mich. (Quality Control Circles)

GORDON YATES, Vice President—Administration, McCormick & Co., Inc., Hunt Valley, Md. (Multiple Management)

JACK YURKIEWICZ, Ph.D., The School of Business, Hofstra University, Hempstead, N.Y. (Dynamic Programming; Integer Programming; Nonlinear Programming)

W. CLEMENTS ZINCK, dec., Industrial Engineer, formerly Vice President—Operations, Arbogast & Bastion, Inc., Allentown, Pa. (Work Simplification)

HOW TO USE THE ENCYCLOPEDIA OF MANAGEMENT

The ENCYCLOPEDIA OF MANAGEMENT is more than an A to Z reference work, although it is that, of course. It is in addition presented as a *systematic reading course*—a "programmed" reading of entries in a planned sequence, in accordance with a prescribed subject listing. In essence, it is the "Great Books" idea in the field of management, between a single set of covers. It offers in one volume an authoritative treatment of the entire field.

The field is broad indeed, for management is the single discipline that has transformed the findings of all of the physical and social sciences into the towering achievements of our age. Without the genius and industry of the *manager,* the scientist and engineers would be mere dilettantes, engaging in intellectual pastimes with no necessary relation to the world of action.

THE PROVINCE OF MANAGEMENT

Like the domain of the ancient philosophers, "all mankind" is management's province. Management art and science must be brought to bear wherever effort must be organized on a significant scale—in government, the cultural arts, sports, the military, medicine, education, scientific research, and religion—as well as in the profit-making pursuits of manufacture and commerce.

Management takes appropriate advantage of technical developments in *all* of the fields it serves when it administers and controls any *one* of them. Small wonder, then, that if we have had "explosions" in the physical and social sciences, there must also have been an "explosion" in the discipline of management, which embraces all of them.

THE DANGERS OF SPECIALIZATION

The result of any explosion is fragmentation. While this can be accepted as the price of advance in any discipline, resulting perforce in ever-increasing specialization in component parts, it presents a peculiar problem in a discipline whose very reason for being is the exact opposite—the resolution of the complexity and diversity of many specialties into orderly patterns for planning and control. Here is the danger, then, that confronts management: the specialties with which it is concerned have proliferated to such an extent as to make it difficult for any single manager to know what management is all about. So rapid have the strides been in recent years in such subjects as mathematical techniques in decision-making, new insights of the behavioral sciences, integrated data processing and integrated information flow, and the like, to say nothing of proliferating legislative and governmental regulations, that heroic measures are required by the "older" executive (one who has been out of school all of fifteen years!) just to keep abreast. At the same time, continuing advances have been made in the traditional management subjects—accounting, production control, sales management, and the like—so that here, too, the alert executive needs a finger-tips reference source to update his or her concepts and skills.

The dilemma of management today is that in an age of specialists we face a growing dearth of generalists. The normal experience of a manager in business (at least in America) is to spend the formative years of his or her career in developing a great familiarity and proficiency in a relatively specialized field, such as a branch of engineering, or sales, production, procurement, personnel administration, or accounting. The manager thus develops only a peripheral knowledge of advances in other areas of management. Yet at the first promotion from a department-head or specialist type of position into one of truly administrative scope, the person with enlarged responsibilities suddenly finds that his or her horizon must extend beyond the four walls of a given specialty. It must now include more than only a superficial understanding of *all* aspects of managing—finance, purchasing, manufacturing, advertising and selling, industrial and public relations, research and development, and long-range planning. And the same is in a measure true in governmental and institutional administration as well as in private enterprise.

Moreover, as an executive attains successively higher rungs of management, he or she finds that many decisions of a far-flung enterprise must be made from the perspective of a broad liberal education which the demands of our technically oriented society may in many instances have precluded. Throughout the years spanned by the previous editions of this Encyclopedia, the cry has come from many quarters that top business leadership calls for more than the specialized training and narrow proficiencies of most of those who form the available pool of talent . . . that what is needed in addition is the grounding in history, literature, and philosophy that is the hallmark of the truly educated person.

A Help Toward a Solution

This Encyclopedia proposes to help solve at least the first half of the problem here stated. It does not presume to bridge the liberal-education gap. For information on philosophy, history, the arts, and letters, the reader must go elsewhere. But it *does* propose to bridge the other gap—to offer every executive, executive-aspirant, management consultant, and teacher and student of business administration, comprehensive and authoritative information on all arts, sciences, and techniques that impinge directly upon the executive job. It proposes to make the industrial research scientist aware of the thinking that goes on in top management, finance, and marketing; to make the salesmanager understand the problems of production and finance; to make the financial executive knowledgeable about production and plant engineering; and to give the top manager or administrator who occupies the generalist position new insights into the work of the specialists whom he or she must manage or draw upon in the management of others.

In addition, the Encyclopedia proposes to make all such practitioners aware of the exploding advances in the newer management sciences—the tools of linear programming, game theory, applied probability theory—and in the behavioral sciences—motivation, group dynamics, human engineering, and the like. These disciplines touch upon all areas of specialization, because they concern the pervasive problems of decision-making and interpersonal relations.

Reference, Plus a Planned Reading Program

The information herein is accessible in two forms: *First,* through the traditional A-Z compilation for the quick answer to an immediate question or concise background information on any aspect of the whole broad field. *Second,* and of more lasting importance, as a planned reading program for pursuit in depth of any of twenty-eight "core subjects" in management—the reader's own "Master's program" in business administration. (This program is set forth in the "Guide to 'Core Subject' Reading" immediately following this foreword.)

The arrangement of the book as a whole on a strictly alphabetic basis, rather than by categories of subjects, makes for extremely rapid and convenient information retrieval. At the same time, cross-referencing makes it easy to pursue a major area of interest in whatever depth desired. Cross references to related entries are listed at the end of each article; in addition, a term or name appearing within the text that is also the title of a separate entry is set in capital and small-capital type. It is emphasized, however, that each subject is treated in essay form and "stands on its own feet," so that the reader will obtain all essential information on a given subject without being continually shunted from one entry to another.

Every effort has been made to achieve comprehensiveness in choice and coverage of subject matter. The three-hundred-odd articles (i.e., exclusive of the biographical sketches) go far beyond mere definitions and referrals to other sources. They are in-depth treatments, giving background, subject branchings, "schools of thought," current applications, and potentials. All major subjects are covered in the form of signed articles by recognized authorities.

While appropriate emphasis is given to advanced techniques and tools such as linear programming, game theory, electronic data processing, sensitivity training, management games, and automation, all traditional subjects with which modern executives must deal are included. On all of these the reader will be able to get a quick picture of the basics of the subject, what the important developments have been since, roughly World War II, and what directions future developments may be expected to take.

Authoritativeness

Authoritativeness has been assured by the calibre of the individual contributors. In addition to the editor's own contacts among those professionally engaged in the subjects treated, which made possible original contributions by top-flight authorities, the work has benefited from the active cooperation of the leading professional societies active in the areas covered. For many subjects, these organizations either took on the responsibility of developing the entries, or secured authors from among their memberships. In the latter case, most of the entries were prepared not merely as signed, individual contributions, but as monographs carrying the imprimatur of the society. In many cases, the author of an entry is also the author of a recognized text on the subject, or editor of the leading trade magazine or professional journal in the field.

The Editorial Formula

The authors of all entries, especially those covering advanced techniques and new schools of thought, have to the extent feasible followed the editorial formula laid down, namely telling the executive not versed in the specialty just what the subject is all about . . . what kinds of management problems it helps solve . . . the kinds of specialists that are required to put it to use in a given organization . . . the degree of current acceptance . . . the possibilities for the future as the subject undergoes further development.

The editorial formula makes it possible to assert that if the reader starts out completely innocent of any substantive knowledge of a subject, he or she will, after referring to this Encyclopedia, be in possession of the basics of the subject—objective, scope, mode of attack, potentials with respect to the reader's own business or government/institutional organization, sources of further information, and the like. Such a reader will then be in position *to ask the right kind of questions* of specialists and technicians in his or her own organization, to make sure that the firm or department (or government agency, or institution) is taking full advantage of the opportunity the subject presents.

For Continuing Study

A feature of the subject development, in addition to the core reading program, is the listing of Information References at the end of each entry. These give the names of the important professional associations and societies active in the subject under discussion, the journals specializing in the field, and the names of certain important texts and articles bearing on the subject. Thus the reader is given a start on continuing study should he or she so desire—the door is opened to further *live* information.

C.H.

A GUIDE TO "CORE SUBJECT" READINGS

For the reading program mentioned in the preceding section, it is important that a planned sequence be followed. Thus for any major "core" of management the reader is interested in pursuing, the entries should be read *in the order in which they are listed below,* to develop the subject in logical sequence. In addition, the Information References at the end of each Encyclopedia entry will open the door to as many further avenues as interest and persistence will encourage the reader to explore.

I—Basic Management Concepts

Management Movement
Scientific Management
Scientific Management: "Taylorism"
Production: Large-Scale
Automation
Organization Theory
Human Relations in Industry: An Overview
Motivation
Managerial Grid
Incentive Systems
Profit Sharing
Guaranteed Annual Wage
Rucker Plan of Group Incentives
Scanlon Plan of Group Incentives
Lincoln Incentive Management Plan
Multiple Management
Business Ethics
Social Audit
Quality of Working Life

II—Pioneers in Management

Scientific Management: "Taylorism"
Management Movement: Leaders in Thought
Personnel Management: Pioneers
Smith, Adam
Boulton, Matthew Robinson
Owen, Robert
Babbage, Charles
Marx, Karl
Fayol, Henri
Gompers, Samuel
Halsey, F.A.
Taylor, Frederick W.
Barth, Carl G.L.
Gantt, Henry L.
Ford, Henry
Kimball, D.S.
Gilbreth, F.B. and Lillian E.M.
Follet, Mary Parker
Rowntree, B. Seebohm
Green, William
Babcock, George de Albert
Dennison, Henry S.
Hathaway, H.K.
Clark, Wallace
Lewis, John L.
Knoeppel, C.E.
Hopf, H.A.
Keynes, John Maynard
Meaney, George
Lincoln, James F. (in Lincoln Incentive Management Plan)
McCormick, Charles P. (in Multiple Management)

III—Management and the Economic Environment

Business Organization: Legal Structure
Economics
Econometrics
Money and Banking
Inflation
Income, Expenditures, and Wealth
Labor Force, Employment, and Earnings
Unemployment: Concepts and Measurement
Unemployment Insurance
Statistical Abstract of the United States
U.S. Economic and Business Censuses
Marketing Research: Patterns of Population Growth
Taxation
Value Added Tax (VAT)
Business-Government Relations

Technological Forecasting
Business Forecasting

IV—Corporate Planning

Business Organization: Legal Structure
Corporate Strategy and Business Policy
Long-Range Corporate Planning
Long-Range Planning: Financial Aspects
Marketing Strategy: Competitive Analysis
Technological Forecasting
New-Product Planning: Profitability Projections
Return on Capital
Fixed-Asset Investment Analysis: The MAPI Formulas and Procedures
Break-Even Analysis
Venture Capital
Venture Management
Mergers and Acquisitions
Antitrust Legislation
Management Audit
Social Audit

V—Legal Problems in Management

Business Organization: Legal Structure
Uniform Commercial Code
Business-Government Relations
Securities and Exchange Commission
Corporate Capitalization
Corporate Secretary
Directors
Directors: Legal Duties and Responsibilities
Antitrust Legislation
Arbitration
Franchising: Legal Aspects
Taxation
Patents
Trademarks
Trademarks: International Protection
Copyright
Labor Relations Legislation
Employee Privacy
Occupational Safety and Health Act of 1970
Packaging: Legal and Ethical Considerations
Pricing: Legal Aspects
Records Protection

VI—Organization

Organization Theory
Organization—Traditional Types
Management Levels: Definitions
Organization Analysis and Planning
Organizational Planning: Q-Charts
Linear Responsibility Charting
Managerial Effectiveness: Climate for Organizational Results
Organization: Line-Staff Relationships
Matrix Organization
Project Management
Engineering Management
Basic Research: Management Considerations
Organization: AMA's "Ten Commandments"
Organization: Urwick's Ten Principles
Women in Management

VII—Innovation

Innovation: The Management of Change
Creativity
Brainstorming
Suggestion Systems
Technological Forecasting
Industrial Research and Development
Basic Research: Management Aspects
Industrial Research Budgeting
Industrial Research Accounting
Outside Research
New-Product Development
New-Product Development: A Check List for Management Decisions
New-Product Planning: Profitability Projections
Patents
Copyright
Marketing Research
Marketing Research: Sources of Information
Venture Capital
Venture Management

VIII—Decision Making and the Quantitative Management Sciences

Management Sciences
Mathematical Programming
Statistics
Operations Research
Operations Research in Marketing Decisions
Goal Programming
Dynamic Programming
Linear Programming
Linear Programming: A Case Example
Nonlinear Programming
Integer Programming

Game Theory
Operational Gaming and Monte Carlo Simulation
Waiting Line Theory (Queueing Theory)
Business Logistics
Business Logistics: Case Example
Industrial Dynamics

IX—Financial Management

Corporate Capitalization
Securities and Exchange Commission
Venture Capital
Venture Management
Franchising
Franchising: Legal Aspects
Treasurership
Controllership
Return on Capital
Financial Ratios
Financial Analysis: Earnings
Fixed-Asset Investment Analysis: The MAPI Formulas and Procedures
Leasing of Industrial Equipment
Depreciation
Operating Margin Analysis
Long-Range Planning: Financial Aspects
Risk Management
Insurance Management
Appraisal (of Property)
Taxation
Taxation: Organization for
Value-Added Tax (VAT)
Cash-Flow Analysis
New-Product Planning: Profitability Projections
Break-Even Analysis
Cost-Volume-Profit Analysis
Credit Management
Credit Reporting
Credit Bureaus
Collection Services
Internal Auditing
Certified Public Accountant
FIFO/LIFO Inventory Accounting
Annual Reports
Financial Public Relations

X—Business Logistics

Business Logistics
Business Logistics: Case Example
Plant Location
Industrial Districts
Purchasing
Vendor Rating
Materials Management
Materials Management: Material-Handling Equipment Types
Physical Distribution Management
Packaging, Protective: The Systems Approach
Traffic Management
Traffic and Transportation: Structure of the Transportation Industry
Freight Forwarders
Shipper's Associations
Warehousing
Warehousing: The Public Warehouse

XI—Project Management

Project Management
Matrix Organization
Integrated Project Management
Gantt Chart
Critical Path Method (CPM)
PERT (Program Evaluation Review Technique)
Line of Balance (LOB)
Line of Balance: Day Control

XII—Manufacturing

Manufacturing Management
Production: Large-Scale
Production Planning and Inventory Management
Plant Engineering
Maintenance
Automation
Robots in Industry
Operation Analysis
Process Analysis
Process Engineering
Materials Management
Materials Management: Equipment Types
Cost Accounting (Managerial Accounting)
Standard Costing
Direct Costing (Variable Costing)
Overhead Assignment
Flexible Budgeting
Quality Control and Quality Assurance
Quality Control Circles
Job Enrichment and Work Effectiveness
Zero Defects
Reliability Engineering

Safety and Health in the Workplace
Occupational Safety and Health Act of 1970
Occupational Health
Environmental Controls

XIII—Industrial Engineering

Industrial Engineering
Control Theory: Application to Management
Systems Management
Work Measurement
Work Measurement in the Office
Ratio Delay
Process Analysis
Process Engineering
Operation Analysis
Method Improvement
Work Simplification
Motion and Time Study
Predetermined Motion Times
Incentive Systems
Standard Minute System
Industrial Standardization
Standardization, Company
Standards Engineering

XIV—Accounting Control

Controllership
Accounting
Management Accounting
Responsibility Reporting
Cost Accounting (Managerial Accounting)
Cost Control
Standard Costing
Overhead Assignment
Cost-Volume-Profit Analysis
Cash-Flow Analysis
Marketing Cost Analysis
Direct Costing
FIFO/LIFO Inventory Accounting
Statistical Accounting
Flexible Budgeting
Zero-Base Budgeting
Depreciation
Internal Auditing
Industrial Research Budgeting
Industrial Research Accounting

XV—Marketing Research

Marketing Research
Business Forecasting
Marketing Strategy: Competitive Analysis
Technological Forecasting
Standard Metropolitan Statistical Areas
Standard Industrial Classification System
Distribution Planning and Research
U.S. Economic and Business Censuses
Business Intelligence: Sources of Information
Marketing: Patterns of Consumer Goods Distribution
Statistical Abstract of the United States
U.S. Census of Manufacturers
Marketing Research: Patterns of Population Growth
New-Product Development
New-Product Development: A Check List for Management Decisions
New-Product Planning: Profitability Projections
Operations Research in Marketing Decisions
Marketing Research: Sources of Information
Industrial Purchasing Power: The S&MM Annual Survey

XVI—Advertising

Advertising
Publicity
Consumer Behavior Research
Advertising Media
Advertising Research
Advertising Agencies
Advertising: Measured Results
Advertising Yardsticks
Industrial Design
Packaging: Legal and Ethical Considerations
Trademarks
Trademarks: International Protection
Copyright

XVII—Selling

Marketing
Business Forecasting
Marketing Strategy: Competitive Analysis
Franchising
Franchising: Legal Aspects
Packaging: Organizing for Package Development
Packaging: Legal and Ethical Considerations
Pricing Policy
Prices: Legal Aspects
Prices: Statistics

Sales Statistics
Marketing: Changing Patterns of Consumer Goods Distribution
Industrial Distributors
Manufacturers' Representatives
Sales Promotion
Trade Shows and Exhibits
Sales Training
Marketing Cost Analysis
Credit Reporting

XVIII—Administrative Services

Office Management and Administrative Services
Systems Management
Word Processing
Records Management
Records Protection
Forms Design
Forms Control
Work Measurement in the Office
Office Space Planning: The "Open Plan"
Office Parks (Section in Industrial Districts)
Office Automation
Automated Office Security (Section in Computer Security)
Temporary Help Services
Office Safety

XIX—Security

Security
Security: Protection of Trade Secrets and Proprietary Information
Terrorism: Protective Measures
Fire Loss Prevention
Disaster Recovery
Records Protection
Risk Management
Computer Security/Automated Office Security

XX—Automatic Data Processing

Electronic Data Processing
Electronic Data Processing: Equipment Classification
Electronic Data Processing: Computer Peripherals
Computer Installations: Top Management Planning and Follow-Through
Data Communications
Data Communications: A Case Example
Management Information Systems
Management Information Systems: A Case Example
Computer Service Industry
Computer Security/Automated Office Security

XXI—Labor Relations

Collective Bargaining
Labor Unions
Technological Change: Union-Management Agreements
Labor Relations Legislation
Occupational Safety and Health Act of 1970
Labor Arbitration
Mediation
Incentive Systems
Profit Sharing
Guaranteed Annual Wage
Gompers, Samuel
Green, William
Lewis, John
Meaney, George

XXII—Personnel Administration

Personnel Administration
Human Resources Requirements
Employment: Antidiscrimination Legislation
Job Evaluation
Personnel Testing
Personnel Testing: Types of Tests
Performance Appraisal (Merit Rating)
Executive Compensation
Incentive Systems
Alternative Work Schedules
Temporary Help Services
Safety and Health in Industry
Occupational Health
Occupational Safety and Health Act of 1970
Alcoholism and Drug Abuse in Industry
Executive Compensation
Workers' Compensation
Employee Benefit Plans
Group Health Insurance
Group Life Insurance
Retirement Plans
Unemployment Insurance
Credit Unions
House Magazines
Personnel Management: Pioneers

XXIII—Human Resources Development

Apprenticeship Programs
On-the-Job Training
Training-Within-Industry Programs
Training and Development (Government Sponsored)
Teaching Machines, Programmed Instruction, and Computer-Aided Instruction
Behavior Modeling in Training
Correspondence Schools
Performance Appraisal: Merit Rating
Assessment Centers
Personnel Counseling
Supervisory Training

XXIV—Executive Development

Management Levels: Definitions
Executive Traits
Executive Recruitment
Executive Selection
Management Development Techniques
Executive Appraisal: Diagnostic Performance Appraisal
Management by Objectives
Executive Development: Away-from-Company Programs
Executive Development: Selection Guide
Management Games
Sensitivity Training
Managerial Grid
Multiple Management
Managerial Effectiveness: Climate for Organizational Results
Women in Management
Management Education: Professional Certification

XXV—Management and the Behavioral Sciences

Behavioral Sciences
Human Relations in Industry: An Overview
Motivation
Motivation: Maslow's Basic Needs
Motivation: McGregor's "Theory X" and "Theory Y"
Hawthorne Experiments
Personnel Counseling
Industrial Psychology
Personnel Testing
Personnel Testing: Types of Tests
Group Dynamics
Sensitivity Training
Transactional Analysis in Management
Behavior Modeling in Training
Job Enrichment and Work Effectiveness
Managerial Grid
Employee Attitude Research: Attitude Surveys
Consumer Behavior Research
Human Engineering (Human Factors Engineering)

XXVI—Public Relations

Public Relations
Public Relations Research
Publicity
Financial Public Relations
Annual Reports
House Magazines
Environmental Controls
Consumer Protection
Business Ethics
Social Audit

XXVII—Public Administration

Public Administration
Public Authorities

XXVIII—Foreign Operations

International Management: Management of the "World Enterprise"
Operating Margin Analysis
Management Practice: Learning from Foreign Management
European Economic Community
European Free Trade Association
International Accounting
International Accounting Standards Committee

THE ENCYCLOPEDIA OF MANAGEMENT

A

ACCOUNTING

Accounting is the process of identifying, measuring, and communicating economic information to permit informed judgments and decisions by users of the information [1]. This process is usually organized as a system of techniques and procedures which covers an entity (business enterprise, governmental unit, etc.) and generates information on resources that are susceptible to measurement in financial terms. The purpose is to meet the need for such information by managers (owners) and others (investors, creditors, government, etc.). Consequently, there are two basic sets of accounting reports—*internal* and *external.*

Internal reports are prepared for management. They are designed in accordance with directly identifiable and specific management requirements. External reports are issued as general-purpose financial reports in accordance with "generally accepted accounting principles," and are designed to disclose information that is useful for decision making by investors, creditors, and others [2].

Two major fields of accounting practice may be distinguished: (1) *management accounting* and (2) *public accounting.* The management accountant performs accounting services as an employee or officer of the enterprise. The public accountant's primary functions are independent auditing and reporting on financial statements. Most public accountants have met statutory requirements for practice as a Certified Public Accountant (CPA). (See CERTIFIED PUBLIC ACCOUNTANT). Each CPA has the responsibility for conducting his examination in accordance with generally accepted auditing standards and for stating in his report, among other things, whether the financial statements of an enterprise are in conformity with generally accepted accounting principles applied on a consistent basis.

STEPHEN LANDEKICH, Research Director, National Association of Accountants, New York

References Cited

[1] *A Statement of Basic Accounting Theory,* Evanston, Ill., American Accounting Association, 1966.

[2] Statements of Financial Accounting Concepts: No. 1, "Objectives of Financial Reporting by Business Enterprises," November, 1978, and No. 2, "Qualitative Characteristics of Accounting Information," May, 1980; both issued by the Financial Accounting Standards Board, Stamford, Connecticut.

Cross References: *Break-Even Analysis; Budgeting; Cash Flow Analysis; Certified Public Accountant; Controllership; Cost Accounting; Cost Control; Cost-Profit-Volume Analysis; Depreciation; Direct Costing; FIFO/LIFO Inventory Accounting; Financial Accounting Standards Board; Financial Analysis; Earnings; Financial Ratios; Flexible Budgeting; Industrial Research Accounting; Industrial Research Budgeting; Internal Auditing; International Accounting; International Accounting Standards Committee; Management Accounting; Marketing Cost Analysis; Operating Margin Analysis; Overhead Assignment; Responsibility Reporting; Return on Capital; Statistical Accounting; Treasurership.*

ADVERTISING

Advertising is only one of the tools of marketing, playing a greater or lesser role than product policy, pricing, packaging, distribution, personal selling, or sales promotion, dependent upon the goods or services offered. Its function is to inform and enhance the value of the thing avertised.

How it Works. While most effective advertising to some degree encompasses both, advertising is usually strategically designed to accomplish one of two objectives: (1) *inform* or (2) *persuade.*

Informational advertising is used to introduce new products, services, or ideas, announce events or sales, or to remind people of existing products or services.

Persuasion advertising is used to convince the target audience to prefer the product or service advertised over alternatives. The approach may be rational, offering a logical reason based upon an evaluative scale that supports the superiority of the product or service offered. It may also be either emotional or humorous.

Advertising Accountability. There is, of course, no room for dishonesty in advertising, and advertisers should be prepared fully to document any statements of fact they make about their product or service. Critics of advertising usually concede the importance of informational advertising, but attack persuasion strategy on the grounds that it talks people into buying things they don't want or need or that it misrepresents the benefits one actually receives.

To gain an understanding of the value of persuasion advertising, one must recognize that human needs are often conceptual in nature, not materialistic. Quoting Theodore Levitt: "The human audience *demands* symbolic interpretation in everything it sees and knows. . . . Without symbolism life would be even more confusing and anxiety-ridden than it is with it. . . . The product is not what the engineer explicitly says it is, but what the consumer implicitly demands that it shall be. Thus, the consumer consumes not things but expected benefits—not cosmetics, but the satisfactions of the allurements they promise; not quarter-inch drills, but quarter-inch holes; etc." [1]

Thus, rather than misrepresenting products or services, persuasion advertising should enable the consumer to perceive products and services as fulfilling various needs he might otherwise overlook.

Client/Agency Relationships. *Compensation.* For the most part, clients compensate their advertising agencies on an illogical basis. Although the agency reports to the client and must gain client approval of all its recommendations, and is very often held responsible for the sales performance, the agency is paid for its services by the media. Furthermore, this compensation fluctuates with the media budget—typically 15% of space and time billings—which may or may not have anything to do with the agency's performance.

The agency fee system is a more logical answer to this obviously unstable 15% media-commissioned system. The fee is a negotiated contract, usually based upon the historical compensation that the agency has expected, and is related to the tasks to be accomplished. Working under the fee system, the agency is free objectively to analyze a given marketing problem without biasing its judgment in favor of increased advertising spending. (For the agencies' position in defense of the commission system, see the section, *Sources of Agency Compensation,* in the entry, ADVERTISING AGENCIES.)

How to Work with Your Agency. Effective advertising is a unique combination of business science and art form. The agency will perform most effectively when the business aspects are highly disciplined by the client and the creative execution is left to the agency. This means that your agency should demonstrate a thorough knowledge of your business. The client, on the other hand, must make this happen by freely discussing both short- and long-range marketing plans and sharing all sales data regarding performances and projections.

The agency is then held responsible for a written statement of what the advertising should accomplish and how it will be done. This document is usually called the *Creative Strategy* and should contain the *Objective* of the advertising, the *Target Audience,* the *Buying Incentive* (or "*Reason Why*") and the *Tonality* of the advertising.

When this statement has been agreed to by the client and agency, all creative submissions should be evaluated only by the criteria of the written statement. Creative judgments should be left to the agency. In a similar manner the agency should prepare written strategies for media and sales promotion.

Less Fragmentation of Agency Services. Since the earlier discussion of this subject in the 2nd edition of THE ENCYCLOPEDIA OF MANAGEMENT (1973), there has been a lessened interest in so-called "a la carte" offering of agency services, i.e., the selling of agency services separately—particularly the creative service, as well as specialized advertising/marketing services such as "new product workshops." Interest in "a la carte" is more a function of the economy and the need to keep costs in line. Agencies to a greater extent have succeeded in helping advertisers control costs by hastening the growth and acceptance of the fee system of compensation, diminishing the need for advertisers to buy "a la carte."

Rather than a fragmentation of agency services there has been a consolidation as a result of the many mergers of agencies. Agency mergers that are set up to avoid product conflicts, establish new profit centers, or assume specializations not affordable within the parent agency are more in the news than fragmentation.

Competitive pressures will continue to force the advertising business away from the straight commission compensation and toward a negotiated fee. This fee system will allow the small, low-overhead shops to compete effectively against the large, high-overhead, multi-service agencies. If an advertiser needs only some marketing advice and a few ads and commercials, he can get high-caliber work at a reduced cost. However, most large advertisers will continue to require the range of services offered by large agencies.

In addition, the international advertiser will most often find his needs best served by the large international agency that can coordinate worldwide marketing efforts through a network of offices and local agency affiliations.

(See also ADVERTISING AGENCIES.)

Development of Advertiser In-House Capabilities. Over the years, a number of advertisers, motivated by cost consciousness, developed in-house capabilities to perform services traditionally handled by advertising agencies—media, research, and creative. An extreme form of this development is the so-called "house agency."

This trend originally gained impetus from cost-cutting needs, as well as from the adoption of the brand-management system. However, disaffection with the idea stemmed from the difficulty of attracting outstanding creative talent from the more stimulating agency environment.

The in-house agency phenomenon is still extant, but analysis by the 4-A's (American Association of Advertising Agencies) shows that the trend has peaked. Only the largest advertisers with the volume to support the additional overhead (e.g., Lever) can afford to bring the entire advertising function in-house.

"Consumerism." "Consumerism" will certainly continue to affect the future of advertising. While Consumer-Research and other organizations representing consumer interests have been active for many years, the current highly publicized phase began with the publication of Ralph Nader's book, "Unsafe At Any Speed." The timing was right. People's needs for products and services were becoming sated. Now they could afford to become critical.

In terms of its impact on advertising, consumerism has given rise to, or has strengthened, existing watchdog agencies, particularly the Food and Drug Administration and the Federal Trade Commission. Product labeling and product advertising claims are being questioned not merely on a factual basis, but also in terms of product presentation. (See *"Creative" vs. "Selling" Messages,* below.)

Another aspect of the impact of consumerism on advertising is the considerable concern over the quantity and quality of advertising directed at children, since children are assumed to be less able to discriminate between advertising claims of competitive products.

Advertising Research. The function of advertising research is first to provide maximum input to the creative people, and then to reduce the number of alternative strategies which inevitably develop as the creative process unfolds.

Development of Creative Strategy. In the first stage, research can provide basic intelligence about motivations and needs. The research techniques used include *qualitative analysis* of competitive advertising, *focus-group* and *individual depth interviews* among consumers representative of the users of the product category, and thorough research of existing secondary source material.

Once alternative creative strategies have been developed, research aids in isolating the one strategy likely to have the greatest leverage with the consumer. The techniques typically include individual or group interviews, concept tests with or without advertising roughs, etc.

Pretesting Individual Advertisements. The objective is to determine the strongest execution of a given creative strategy. For print advertisements, this is frequently accomplished through the placement of the test ad(s) in a portfolio of control advertisements, or in a dummy magazine. A sample of consumers is exposed to the portfolio or magazine, and subsequently questioned on a variety of criteria.

For television commercials, pretesting can be accomplished by substituting test commercials for regularly scheduled commercials in a number of markets, and then conducting telephone interviews with a sample of viewers of the respective television programs. Alternative techniques include the screening of test commercials with sample groups in theaters, in mobile vans or storefronts located in shopping centers, or by screening the commercials on portable movie projectors in respondents' homes.

Frequently, tests conducted in shopping centers include the added refinement of distributing "cents off" coupons to the consumers exposed to the various test commercials. Subsequent coupon redemptions provide a behavioral measure of the relative effectiveness of the commercials tested.

(See also ADVERTISING RESEARCH.)

Media. In recent years, media planning and media buying have become increasingly important and complex. During the past decade audience data have proliferated—specifically magazines and television. The major services, American Research Bureau (ARB) and Nielsen for TV, and Simmons and Brand Rating Index (BRI) primarily for magazines, have made it possible more clearly to pinpoint demographic target audiences and product users through media selection.

Thanks to computerization, it is now possible to retrieve these data and analyze them to select media. The computer has been used not only for the purpose of data retrieval, but also for simulation techniques (setting up a model that simulates the universe) and optimization in media selection (the combination of media elements that best satisfy the objectives). Because the costs of media are increasing, planning is critical to ensure a minimum of wasted advertising effort.

There are five major media, all of which have experienced major changes during recent years:

Television. Television trends are:

(1) TV is a mature medium, with penetration of 98%. The percentage of homes owning color TV sets has now increased until it is almost 83% of TV homes. The total number of TV stations exceed 750.

(2) Greatest growth is expected in cable. There are over 4,000 cable systems now serving 14 million homes (19% of all TV homes). By 1990, cable penetration is expected to be 45%.

(3) New technology like communication satellites that feed programming from distant points has already spurred the development of satellite networks and alternative program suppliers in competition with the currently existing three networks (CBS, NBC, and ABC).

(4) TV is moving to a more personalized medium with growing acceptance in the future of programming supplied on video cassettes and video discs. Pay cable may erode network TV viewing levels by 1990 by an estimated 10%.

(5) Despite pressure of increased costs to use TV, the basic advertising unit continues to be a 30-second commercial. No trend is discerned in the use of shorter length commercials because of fear of erosion of effectiveness.

Magazines. Magazine trends are:

(1) Magazines increase cover prices to consumers and continue escalating space rates to advertisers because of inflationary costs of paper, printing, and subscription mailing.

(2) Increased availability of small-circulation specialized consumer magazines to reach and segment upscale selective audiences. These consumer magazines fall within three categories:

(a) Avocational magazines: *Ski, Golf, Popular Photography.*

(b) General Editorial: *Harper's, Atlantic, Saturday Review, Reader's Digest.*

(c) Metropolitan: *New York, Chicago, L.A.*

In addition to the above of course are the traditional specialized trade and professional publications.

(3) Advertising flexibility in terms of shorter closing, regional and demographic flexibility to continue as magazines offer greater availability of standard size 7-in. by 10-in. page.

(4) Trend toward reducing charges for bleed as more magazines move toward computerized printing using offset and gravure reproduction on lighter paper.

(5) Cost experimentation with alternate distribution methods, e.g. newspaper carriers, to help keep advertising costs down and in line with other media efficiencies. Greater reliance on newsstand and supermarket distribution.

Newspapers. Basic trends in the newspaper industry are:

(1) Daily newspaper circulation during the past ten years has grown at a much slower rate than the general population.

(2) Non-dailies (i.e., weekly suburban and shoppers) have increased circulation at a faster pace than metro dailies.

(3) Ability to utilize color via ROP (Run of Press), Spot Color, HiFi, Spectacolor, is growing, but fastest growing segment of the newspaper medium is the pre-printed insert which now totals about 30 billion.

(4) Newspapers are providing more opportunity to provide greater reader selectivity through special editorial sections on living, food, sports, etc., greater reliance on features, and emphasis on state and local news. Geographic flexibility via availability of zoned editions.

(5) Newspapers, in an effort to increase national advertiser usage, are now offering continuity rates and standardized fixed size ads to avoid increased production costs of material required by different newspaper formats.

Radio. Trends in radio are:

(1) Radio has become a highly personalized

medium because of the emergence of the portable transistor radio.

(2) Radio has shifted from the all-family/all-entertainment medium to a "casual listening" background medium.

(3) Eight thousand radio stations have become highly selective in appealing to different consumer demographic audiences by programming varied music offerings from disco, rock to classical music preferences, and all news.

(4) FM radio has exploded into a mass audience medium with listening levels now exceeding AM.

(5) Technological developments on the horizon for radio include satellite transmission (RKO radio network), stereophonic (AM), and quadrophonic sound (FM).

Outdoor—Posters (Billboards) and Painted Bulletins. Trends are:

(1) The 1965 Highway Beautification Act severely limited the growth of poster locations. There are approximately 235 thousand posters today and they are not expected to be much more by 1985.

(2) Growth in use of painted bulletins (currently 20% of total boards). Paints are generally 14 ft. by 48 ft. They can be purchased for less than a year and rotated every 60 days to a new location to increase coverage.

(3) Tendency in outdoor to extend geographic flexibility by pinpointing locations to cover ethnic, supermarkets, etc. Special short-term contracts, for example, allow advertisers to schedule posters for a month or less.

(4) Future technological developments are on computerization in production of paints (i.e., use of computer to standardize reproduction quality rather than hand painted) and use of solar lighting to illuminate boards and posters.

In addition, out-of-home media also includes all transit, taxi, bus stop shelters, "8-sheets," criterion boards, etc.

((See also ADVERTISING MEDIA.)

Media Buying Services. Media buying services buy broadcast time for an advertiser or an agency's client(s) and receive remuneration in the form of an agreed-upon fee, or the difference between an advertiser's planned expenditures versus actual expenditures by the buying service in satisfying a client's advertising support levels. The services' degree of success is dependent upon a number of factors:

(1) The ability of their personnel to negotiate for broadcast time.

(2) The inability of agency media departments to get the most for their money.

(3) The emergence of small agencies, specializing in creative output, that are unwilling to assume the financial overhead required by an in-house media stff.

The buying service phenomenon, like that of the in-house agency, has crested. Agencies have increased their buying capability and controls. The greater sophistication of advertisers and more agency accountability have enabled agencies to help sell their media expertise to advertisers. Additionally, financial failures such as those by Media Corporation of America and Air Time have served to remind advertisers of the fiscal responsibility of agencies and the risk of double liability.

"Creative" vs. "Selling" Messages. With the proliferation of products (and ad messages), it became apparent that success in the market depended heavily on the ingenuity of the creative minds in advertising agencies. Headlines are written, visuals are drawn. The result is a rough layout of an ad. How to evaluate it? Is it interesting? Believable? Readable? Understandable? Factual? Does it meet the marketing strategy?

The communications tools available to creative departments are many and varied: humor, emotion, demonstration, testimonial, emulation, animation, live action, color, sound, photography, illustration (even *smell* coming up). All must be considered.

As ad budgets expanded during the last half of the 1960s, a certain creative "carelessness" crept into advertising. Television advertising, in particular, was carried to excess. The advertiser's product was often left behind as commercials became mini-movies in which the most important criterion was "Is it entertaining?" rather than "Is it *selling*?" Some commercials tried to become 60-second Hollywood musical extravaganzas. Other commercials tried to establish their creative reputations by using incredibly expensive production techniques or talent. (Without being identified, Orson Welles was used simply as a narrator in one costly campaign.) Production costs rose precipitously. An average 60-second commercial produced in New York during 1968 cost $20,000. It was not uncommon for an advertiser to pay $60,000, $80,000 or over $100,000 to produce a single commercial.

The recession that ushered in the 1970s changed this situation dramatically. Budgets were cut. Creative staffs were pared down to a professional hard core. And media cost efficiencies all but doomed the 60-second TV commercial as the 30-second length became the popular buy.

Exhibit I shows current distribution of commercial lengths.

Advertisers, feeling the recession's pinch, began to demand ads that could move products off shelves quickly. Creative departments also faced with low production budgets and the "no-time-for-Hollywood-musicals" discipline of the 30-second length—turned naturally to product-oriented commercials. After the creative splurges of the 1960s, advertising during the early 1970s rediscovered the idea that good ads should be *about* the product, with a persuasive "reason why" the consumer should buy.

Another development will further the move toward total candor in product-oriented advertising: the FTC is attempting to eliminate, or at least restrict, many present forms of advertising.

Under attack are the non-supportable claim (e.g., an out-and-out untrue statement), the partially supportable claim (FTC will require that extensive research be submitted to back up controversial statements about products), and the preemptive claim (there is presently an FTC prejudice against allowing a product in what it considers a generic category—e.g., beer, bread, aspirin—to make any claim at all. A notable case involved a bread manufacturer whose ads make the true, non-competitive statement that his enriched bread "helps build strong bodies twelve ways." FTC contended that this claim is unfair because it implies uniqueness in a generic category.)

Exhibit I

Distribution of Number of Commercials by Length

Commercial Length (Seconds)	Non-Network %	Network %
10	8.2	0.6
20	0.2	—
30	83.9	83.3
45	—	0.8
"Piggybacks"	*	12.3
60	7.6	2.8**
Total	99.9	99.8

* Less than 1% of total commercials.
Not shown separately but counted as 2-30".
** Includes 60" and longer.
Totals do not add up to 100 due to rounding.

SOURCE: Television Bureau/Bureau of Advertising Research

The FTC's insistence that *all* advertising carry some factual information upon which consumers can base their purchases will undoubtedly continue to influence the marketing and creative execution of ads. There will be less pure persuasion and puffery, more hard information.

RICHARD K. MANOFF, Chairman, Richard K. Manoff, Inc., New York, New York

Information References

Associations:

American Advertising Federation.
American Association of Advertising Agencies.
Advertising Research Foundation.
Association of National Advertisers.
Bureau of Advertising, American Newspaper Publishers Association.
Magazine Advertising Bureau.
National Cable Television Association.
Radio Advertising Bureau.
Television Bureau of Advertising.
Institute of Outdoor Advertising.

Periodicals:

Advertising Age.
Radio/TV Age.
Editor & Publisher.
Broadcasting.
Media Decisions.
Standard Advertising Register.
Agency List.

Texts:

Barton, Roger, ed., "Handbook of Advertising Management," New York, McGraw-Hill, 1970.
Kleppner, Otto, "Advertising Procedure," 7th ed., Englewood Cliffs, N.J., Prentice-Hall, 1979.
Ogilvy, David, "Confessions of an Advertising Man," New York, Atheneum Press, 1963.

References Cited

[1] Levit, T., "The Morality (?) of Advertising," *Harvard Business Review,* July–August, 1971.

Cross References: *(See accompanying entries with Advertising prefix.)*

ADVERTISING: Measured Results

Every advertising message has different results among its receivers. Each ad plays many different roles, simultaneously contributing to many of the firm's goals. Exhibit I depicts a way of thinking about the roles of advertising as a means of attaining certain desired ends in a business enterprise. In this example, top management's principal end is to increase prof-

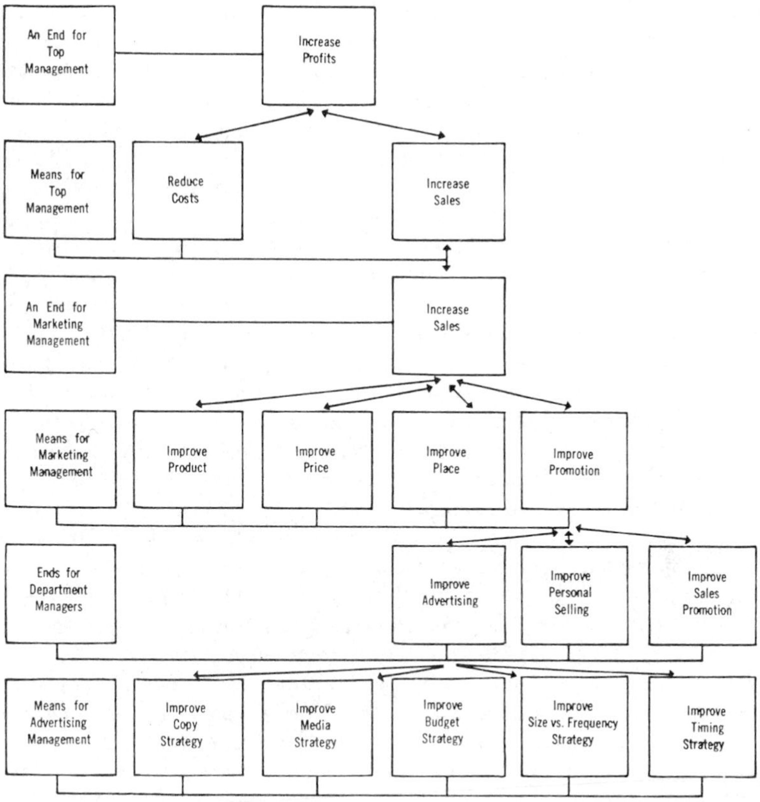

EXHIBIT I
A MEANS-END CHAIN FOR ADVERTISING

its by reducing costs or increasing sales. Here we shall concentrate on "increase sales."

Marketing Means. Marketing has four alternative means for reaching its end: the "Four Ps of Marketing"—*product, price, place,* and *promotion.* Our concern is with the fourth P.

The marketing means of improving promotion automatically become an end for the sales manager, the sales promotion manager, and the advertising manager. Translated into their own areas of responsibility, the three ends are (1) improve personal selling, (2) improve sales promotion, and (3) improve advertising. Five strategy areas are available to improve advertising: (1) copy, (2) media, (3) budget, (4) size vs. frequency, and (5) timing.

Copy as used here refers to all of the physical elements in the finished advertisements—not only the words in headline, text, and script, but also layout, artwork, photographic and film techniques, animations, and sound effects. *Media strategy* variables are the alternative offerings of magazines, newspapers, broadcast stations or networks, outdoor and car-card representatives, and direct-mail services. *Budget* strategy may be varied in absolute amounts or by share of product-class or industry advertising expenditures. Within a given media mix at a given cost, the advertiser must decide such size-frequency strategy questions as: Shall he use ten daytime sixty-second TV commercials per week, or fewer, more expensive commercials in prime evening time? Double spreads every other issue, vs. a full page in each issue? *Timing* or continuity strategy determines the period within a year during which the advertising shall be exposed, e.g., heavy department-store advertising between Thanksgiving and Christmas, canned fish advertising concentrated during Lent.

Goals for Advertising. It is impossible to assign to advertising specific communications tasks that are separate from marketing goals. Thus, rather than having its own goals, advertising has a continuing responsibility to learn more about the ability of advertising to serve as a means of attaining higher-order company goals. For example, can advertising be used to increase distribution? Will a consumer contest increase market share? Is it possible to change the coverage or frequency of the media schedule to increase incremental profit? For every product or brand there are literally hundreds of unanswered questions such as these.

A complete marketing plan calls for an integrated marketing attack, with advertising, personal selling, and sales promotion all striving for the same goals (e.g., more distribution, more displays, more shelf facings) as a means for marketing management to attain its end of increased sales.

Marketplace Outcomes. One of the ways of varying promotion strategy is to vary advertising strategy. The resulting marketplace outputs may be conveniently classified under the following "response" headings: (1) Advertising Memory, (2) Brand Image, (3) Marketing Environment, (4) Sales, and (5) Profit.

Advertising Memory Response. The most frequently measured result of advertising is the memory of the advertisement itself. This may be measured by the recognition method in which the ad itself is used to stimulate memory of it, or measurement may be by the limited-exposure tachistoscopic technique or the aided-recall method. (A tachistoscope is an apparatus used in psychological testing for exposing colors, figures, or other visual stimuli for short intervals—a fifth of a second or less.)

Brand Image Response. The differing mental pictures of the company, brand, product, or service form a continuum running from awareness through beliefs to intention. A prospective customer can have brand awareness of high or low saliency. High saliency is thought to be indicated by the response to a question of the type, "What brand do you think of when I mention 'cigarettes'?" This response, or top-of-mind awareness, is a composite effect of all previous messages received about the brand, plus the experience of use, if any.

Beliefs may be expressed as specific product attributes stated by respondents or classified by the interviewer's assessment of the amount of information possessed by respondents. Beliefs can also be expressed as semantic differentials along a pleasant-unpleasant scale. Intention may be defined as a "predisposition to act"—to buy or recommend a product.

Marketing Environment Response. It is in the changing of the surrounding conditions or influences that lead to sales, that advertising can often make its greatest contribution. Sales miracles can occasionally happen when a product is offered for a *different end use* (as occurred dramatically when Listerine advertising was switched from offering the product as a household antiseptic, to advertising it as a mouthwash to prevent "halitosis.") Similarly, pricing, packaging and display strategies, and the advertising of special offers can often cause larger units of sale, with a consequent increase in *consumption rate.* Advertising can affect *timing of purchase.* Consumer desire for the newest model or current fashion is a powerful environmental effect. *Upgrading* is an important response to advertising, e.g., buying the new car with accessories that have been made essential. Other environmental responses affected by advertising are increased *distribution,* increased *product display* and *dealer promotion,* and increased *store traffic.* (Examples of the last-named are sweepstakes which only require visiting a dealer to qualify for a chance to win a prize, and contests which call for getting entry blanks at the point of sale.) *Inquiries* developed through advertising are important sales leads.

Sales Response. Variations in total sales *volume* and in sales *share* are widely used measures of marketing success. Two specific sales effects of particular interest are variations in *trial purchases* and *repeat purchases.* The former should be a focal point for advertising management's attention. Repeat purchases are primarily the result of satisfactory product experience, although the reminder effect of advertising does influence rebuying.

Profit Response. The profit contribution of advertising expenditures is, of course, the most difficult to measure of all marketplace outcomes. The most appropriate measure is some form of incremental profit caused by advertising, i.e., the difference in the firm's total profits with and without the advertising cost. This is difficult to do, but not always impossible.

Field Measurement of Advertising Results. Any method of measuring advertising results would necessarily include: (1) at least one finished or rough advertisement, (2) a sample or samples drawn from the target market population, (3) a means of exposing the advertisement to the samples, and (4) a survey of the samples so that their responses to the advertisement can be inferred.

Pre-advertising surveys can be either in the laboratory or in the field. For example, in one type of syndicated TV theater, the questions are asked while the audience is in the theater; in another, the questions are asked by telephoning to the respondents' homes the next day. Post-advertising surveys are, of course, all field surveys. Pre-advertising measurements are in most cases limited to advertising memory and brand image responses. Post-advertising measurements can isolate advertising memory, or brand image, or marketing environment, or sales or profit responses. Pre-advertising measurements can only secure the responses to variations in copy strategy. Post-advertising can be used to appraise the response to variations in copy or media or budget, or size vs. frequency, or timing strategies.

Advertising measurements may also be classified as *standard* or *custom.* A standard measurement is a repetitive procedure in which the means of exposure and the survey of responses are the same in each case. Standard advertising measurements, both pre- and post-, are widely offered as syndicated services.

In custom field measurements, although outside services may be employed to survey the marketplace outcomes, the management of the undertaking is by the advertiser or agency. Each custom field measurement is different—decisions have to be made on whether to conduct an audit, or test, or experiment, and in what markets, with what survey technique, with what samples.

Advertising Audits. There are two kinds of advertising audits: the *advertising theme* audit, and the *advertising performance* audit. In the first, respondents are questioned by face-to-face or telephone survey to determine their remembrance of the current advertising claims of the sponsor and of his competitors. The advertising performance audit uses multiple questions such as: (1) "What brand do you think of when I mention cigarettes?" (2) "What brand of cigarette did you buy last?" (3) "About how many packs of cigarettes do you smoke a day?" Question No. 3 on usage may be applied to weigh the responses to the first two, thus permitting the calculations of a weighted brand awareness response from No. 1, and estimated market share from No. 2.

Advertising Experiments vs. Advertising Tests. The necessary and sufficient conditions for an advertising *field experiment* are: (1) two or more advertising treatments, (2) random assignments of treatments to market units, or vice versa, (3) a probability sample drawn from each market unit, (4) a survey of each sample's marketplace responses, and (5) two or more applications of each ad treatment.

An advertising *test* is any field measurement of advertising results with at least one new advertising treatment, which lacks one or more of the necessary conditions for an advertising experiment—usually lacking two or more replications of each advertising treatment.

Randomized Block Experiments. Advertising field experiments usually use a "randomized block design." The word "block" refers to a group of markets, chosen at random, which are to receive a single replication of each treatment. Market units in a given block are grouped so that the units to which one treatment is applied are closely comparable with those to which another treatment is applied.

Blocking may be accomplished by stratifying the good test cities by brand market shares, by median family income, by percent of families with income of $10,000 and over, by climate, or retail sales. Each advertiser will have some expert judgment on the environmental factors which have the strongest effect on his sales. Then he will block by the one with the greatest effect for which data are available. An industrial advertiser, for example, might stratify by census data on establishments in his prospects' industries.

Multiple Response Measurements. For some years an argument raged as to whether attitudinal measures or behavioral measures should be taken. This has now been largely resolved by a growing recognition that both are needed. The preponderance of evidence shows that attitude measures do predict purchase behavior. Sales response should be the primary marketplace outcome surveyed, but as many secondary responses as possible should also be measured.

Other Field Measurements. *Split Runs.* This refers to the 50-50 or A-B split offered by most newspapers and magazines. Every other copy carries ad A, with ad B in the alternate copies. In split-run tests, the two ads have keyed coupons or buried offers, and the relative effectiveness of the two ads is judged by the mail response to each.

Regional Editions. Virtually all consumer and business magazines offer regional editions which are excellent for use in advertising tests and experiments. The publishers furnish random samples of subscribers' names and addresses. Telephone surveys may be conducted, usually after the advertisement has appeared in four or more issues.

Mail-order Advertising. Mail-order advertising is continuously measured by keyed addresses. Some mail-order advertisers run their best proved ad in a long list of publications without change, but also continuously test it against new ads by split-run tests in a few publications.

Direct Mail. Direct-mail advertising is often used to test advertising that will appear in other media. Book publishers test the pull of various book offers by direct mailings to from 10,000 to 20,000 homes. Cents-off store coupons are also pretested by sending them through the mail to a limited list before they are put into wide circulation. These direct-mail tests are always keyed so that the offer producing the greatest response can be identified.

Advertising Frequency. All significant studies of the relationship between frequency and advertising effectiveness were appraised and summarized in a 1979 report by the Association of National Advertisers, Inc. [1]. Following is an itemization of the twelve conclusions reached:

(1) One exposure of an advertisement to a target group consumer within a purchase cycle has little or no effect in most cases.

(2) Since one exposure is usually ineffective, the central goal of productive media planning should be to place emphasis on enhancing frequency rather than reach.

(3) The weight of evidence strongly suggests that an exposure frequency of two within a purchase cycle is an effective level.

(4) By and large, optimal exposure frequency appears to be at least three exposures within a purchase cycle.

(5) Beyond three exposures within a brand purchase cycle, or over a period of four or even eight weeks, increasing frequency continues to build advertising effectiveness at a decreasing rate, but with no evidence of a decline.

(6) The frequency-of-exposure data strongly suggest that wearout is not a function of too much frequency per se.

(7) Very large and well-known brands—and/or those with dominant market shares in their categories and dominant shares of category advertising weight—appear to differ markedly in response to frequency of exposure from smaller or more average brands. In general, the smaller, less well-known brands will virtually always benefit by frequency of exposure, while very large brands may or may not.

(8) Perhaps as a result of the differing exposure environments of television dayparts, frequency of exposure has a differential effect on advertising response by daypart.

(9) In general, the greater the share of category exposure, the more positive the effects of frequency.

(10) Nothing in the studies suggests that frequency response principles or generalizations vary by medium.

(11) Although there are general principles with respect to frequency of exposure and its relationship to advertising effectiveness, differential effects by brand are equally important. There must be experimentation with each brand to find the right answer for its frequency equation.

(12) The leverage of different equal-expenditure media plans in terms of frequency response can be substantial.

Effectiveness of Advertising Measurement. Audits, tests, and experiments each have their uses. Audits of marketplace outcomes indicate the current marketplace responses to the cumulative effects of all marketing input variables, controllable and uncontrollable, without isolating advertising's contribution. But they can be used diagnostically to signal when more discriminate measurements of advertising results are indicated. However, advertising tests are *not* appropriate (1) under conditions of dynamic competition, and (2) under conditions of relatively homogeneous brands within a product class.

SOURCE: Association of National Advertisers, Inc., New York, New York

Information References

Campbell, Roy H., "Measuring the Sales and Profit Results of Advertising," New York, Association of National Advertisers, Inc., 1969.

Manville, Richard, "Advertising Research and Measurement," Chap. 10, Sec. 6 in Buehl, Victor and Heyel, Carl, eds., "Handbook of Modern Marketing," New York, McGraw-Hill, 1970.

Ramond, Charles, "Advertising Research: The State of the Art," New York, Association of National Advertisers, Inc., 1976.

Reference Cited

[1] Naples, Michael J., "Effective Frequency: The Relationship Between Frequency and Advertising Effectiveness," New York, Association of National Advertisers, Inc., 1979.

Cross References: *(See accompanying entries with Advertising prefix.)*

ADVERTISING AGENCIES

Four dynamic activities stimulate buyers to buy: personal selling; display; sales promotion; and advertising. Selling, display, and promotion are done either entirely or to a large extent by the seller himself, but most of his advertising—especially that of the manufacturer—is entrusted to an **Advertising Agency.**

History. In the 1800s there were fewer than a dozen advertisers who spent as much as $100,000 a year. The largest magazine was the *Century* with a circulation of 186,257, and the leading advertisers were sellers of patent medicines. There was at that time no "advertising agent" (he was principally a space broker). In some four generations we have seen the development of America's mass markets, the development of a multitude of media, and the development of today's advertising agencies which in 1980 handled about $20 billion of annual advertising volume.

In those early days, publishers found that their white space was not particularly salable. Prospective advertisers were inclined to say, "I might buy some space, but what would I say?" The need for another service—planning of a comprehensive campaign, writing copy, creating layouts, etc.—became apparent. However, publishers found that they could not successfully prepare advertising for competing manufacturers. Two soap manufacturers, for example, found it impracticable to go to one publisher and each rely on him to prepare an effective competitive campaign. Similarly manufacturers discovered that they could not prepare their own advertising most efficiently. This required specialized talent, an outside objective viewpoint to appraise sales opportunities, and experience with many advertising problems on which to base decisions.

As a result, around 1880 the advertising service agency began to evolve, and it developed rapidly during the next 20 years. By 1900, the service agency was offering expert and specialized services both in planning the advertising program and in executing it. Its services had reached the professional stage. Creative activities were stressed, and the role of the agency had become that of increasing the effectiveness of the client's advertising. Today there are some 8,100 advertising agencies.

Approaches and Techniques. The agency must justify itself in dollars and cents: It must produce for the client a more profitable return on his advertising expenditure, usually in the form of sales, than he can secure through any other means—spending the money on other dynamic activities, handling the advertising himself, or delegating it to a competing advertising agency. The primary function of the advertising agency is to convert the white space of print media and the blank time of broadcast media into advertising influence to help sellers find customers for their goods and services.

Nearly all of the advertising of products and services seen and heard on television and radio, in magazines, on outdoor posters and painted bulletins, on car cards, and in newpapers (except the display advertising of retail stores, most classified advertising, and much direct mail) is created and placed in these advertising media by advertising agencies.

What Advertising Agencies Are. An advertising agency can be described as:

(1) An *independent* business organization

(2) composed of *creative and business* people

(3) who *develop, prepare, and place advertising* in advertising media

(4) for *sellers seeking to find customers* for their goods and services.

It is emphasized that an advertising agency is an *independent* business organization—independently owned, and not owned by advertisers or media or suppliers—which brings to the clients' problems an outside objective point of view made more valuable by experience with other clients' sales problems in other fields. It is independent of the clients so as to be always an advocate of advertising (seeking to apply advertising to help clients grow and prosper); it is independent of media and suppliers so as to be unbiased in serving its clients (the sellers of goods and services).

An advertising agency is composed of creative and business people—the writers and artists, showmen and market analysts, media analysts, merchandising and research people, advertising specialists of all sorts. But with all this, they are business people, running an independent business, financially responsible, applying their creative skills to the business of helping to make their clients' advertising succeed. These people develop, prepare, and place advertising in advertising media, seeking in every way they can to apply advertising to advance their clients' business. Everything that goes before and everything that comes after the advertisement is preparation for advertising follow-up to help make it succeed. The agency does this, not for itself, but for sellers seeking to find customers for the sellers' goods and services. To prepare and place advertising—successful advertising for the advertiser—is the primary purpose of the advertising agency.

What Advertising Agencies Do. The work that advertising agencies do is described in the "Agency Service Standards" of the American Association of Advertising Agencies. These Service Standards, a delineation of fundamentals of successful agency operation, enable advertisers and media to know what to demand and agencies to know what may be expected of them in dealing with the problems of advertising. Agency service, according to the "Agency Service Standards," consists of interpreting to the public, or to that part of it which it is desired to reach, the advantages of a product or service. This interpretation (as directly quoted from the Standards) is based upon:

(1) A study of the client's product or service in order to determine the advantages and disadvantages inherent in the product itself, and in its relation to competition.

(2) An analysis of the present and potential market for which the product or service is adapted:

(a) As to location.
(b) As to extent of possible sale.
(c) As to season.
(d) As to trade and economic conditions.
(e) As to nature and amount of competition.

(3) A knowledge of the factors of distribution and sales and their methods of operation.

(4) A knowledge of all the available media and means which can profitably be used to carry the interpretation of the product or service to consumer, wholesaler, dealer, contractor, or other factor. This knowledge covers:

(a) Character.
(b) Influence.
(c) Circulation:
Quantity.
Quality.
Location.
(d) Physical requirements.
(e) Costs.

Acting on the study, analysis, and knowledge as explained in the preceding paragraphs, recommendations are made and the following procedure ensures:

(5) Formulation of a definite plan and presentation of this plan to the client.

(6) Execution of this plan:

(a) Writing, designing, illustrating of advertisements, or other appropriate forms of the message.

(b) Contracting for the space, time, or other means of advertising.

(c) The proper incorporation of the message in mechanical form and forwarding it with proper instructions for the fulfillment of the contract.

(d) Checking and verifying of insertions, display, or other means used.

(e) The auditing and billing for the service, space, and preparation.

(7) Cooperation with the client's sales work, to insure the greatest effect from advertising.

With the exception of the word "time" under 6(b) and one or two other minor changes, the "Agency Service Standards" of A.A.A.A. are exactly as they were first adopted on October 9, 1918, some 63 years ago. These are the elements of agency service, whether all of the functions above are shared by a few persons or each function is carried on separately by a specialized department. Into this pattern fit account executives who contact the client, art directors, copywriters, space and time buyers, researchers, production people, and others who work in advertising agencies.

Additional Agency Service. In addition to the advertising services described above, there is a willingness among many agencies today to assist the client with his other activities of distribution. Thus they do special work for the manufacturer in such fields as package designing, sales research, sales training, preparation of sales and service literature, designing of merchandising displays, public relations and publicity. But always the agency must justify such work by doing it more satisfactorily than can either the manufacturer himself or a competing expert.

The agency must be prepared to handle advertising in any medium for a client, even though he has never used it, if the agency deems the medium best for the client's purposes. It must be prepared to serve a client whenever and wherever his advertising should run—as for example, advertisers having seasonal peaks. The agency must therefore have adequate personnel with specialists in many fields. The expense of the "readiness to serve" is an important factor in agency costs. In general, the advertising agency is a hazardous business.

Sources of Agency Compensation. Nearly all major media—newspapers, magazines, television, radio, business publications, outdoor plant owners, and transit advertising companies—allow commissions to advertising agencies, which the media recognize individually.

Larger advertising agencies receive, on the average, about 75% of their income in the form of commissions allowed by advertising media, 25% from the agencies' own percentage charges on purchases (which they specify and/or supervise for their clients) and fees of various kinds for special services. Among medium sized agencies the corresponding figures are 70% and 30%, and among smaller agencies 50% and 50%. Agency service charges and fees are arrived at individually by agreement between each agency and client.

The principle of media allowing commissions to agencies is the sparkplug incentive for agencies. It makes advertising agencies dynamic. More than anything else, it is a great incentive principle, and the principle has benefited all business. The agency business has attracted a high type of businessman, a particularly enterprising type, one who is willing to take the risk that his agency will not get paid at all if the creative work is not used.

Because the agency is rewarded in proportion to the use made of its creative work, the agency owner is encouraged to hire the best creative people he can find. He is not led to stint on staff or to take too much out of profits for himself. This means that the finest possible creative organization is put behind the service and development of advertising. It is the main reason why American advertisers have available to them some of the most skilled advertising agencies in the world. In uncounted instances, advertising agencies have enabled small companies to prosper and grow into large ones. Today, there is scarcely a sizeable advertiser who does not rely on an advertising agency for expert, objective counsel and unique creative skills.

Statistics of the Advertising Agency Business. According to the 1972 Census of Business, there were 6,751 advertising agencies in the United States. Most of the agencies were very small, with 5,817, or 86.2%, reporting billings of less than $1 million annually, and with an average of four or five employees for each agency. According to preliminary results of the 1977 Census of Business, there were 8,089 agencies, with an annual gross income of $3.2 billion or capitalized billings of $21 billion. According to the Census Bureau, advertising agencies employed 82,515 people during the test week of March 12, 1977.

Of agencies' gross income (commissions, percentage charges, and fees), about 61% is paid out in salaries and other compensation to those who work in the business. The remaining 39% covers rent, traveling, taxes, and other costs, and with good fortune and sound management, a reasonable profit. [1]

The American Association of Advertising Agencies is the national organization of the advertising agency business, organized in 1917 to be a responsible spokesgroup of the country's agencies. Agencies must be elected to membership after demonstrating that they meet the A.A.A.A. qualifications. The qualifications require that the agency be independently owned, adequately staffed, operated on ethical principles, and soundly financed. As of June 30, 1980, A.A.A.A. agencies handled about three-fourths of all agency-placed advertising in the United States. They operated some 950 offices in 223 U.S. cities and employed about 50,000 people.

LEONARD S. MATTHEWS, President, American Association of Advertising Agencies, New York, New York

Information References

Advertising Age

American Association of Advertising Agencies, Inc.

References Cited

[1] *Advertising Age* statistics reported by Robert Coen, McCann-Erickson, Inc., New York, N.Y.

Cross References: *(See accompanying entries with Advertising prefix.)*

ADVERTISING MEDIA

BROADCASTING

Broadcasting is the newest method of selling goods and services through advertising. Commercial radio began in the early 1920s and commercial television has been with us just over three decades. Yet in this short period of time, radio and television have established themselves as a dynamic tool of merchandising which reaches vast audiences of potential customers. More importantly, to a greater degree than any prior medium of communication, they have become a part of the lives and habits of the American people.

Organization of the Industry. The *radio* industry consists of almost 4,600 commercial AM stations and nearly 3,300 FM stations, as well as 6 nation-wide networks. From the advertiser's point of view, this means that there is a local radio station in nearly every city and town of over 5,000 population (and a good many in smaller towns than this) in the United States. Radio is thus ideally suited for advertising which seeks to get to the grass roots on a local basis. There are almost 450 million radios in working order in the United States and nearly every American home has one or more sets. Most automobiles are equipped with radios. The development of portable transistor receivers means that radios may be taken to the beach, camping, and on picnics. In short, radio reaches everywhere.

The *television* industry consists of over 760 commercial television stations and three nationwide television networks. (Regional networks are also available to the advertiser in both radio and television.) There are about 145 million television sets in use. Though the television industry is less than 35 years old, 97% of all the households in the United States have one or more television sets.

In both radio and television, local stations are affiliated with networks under business contracts. The stations guarantee that they will carry a certain amount of network programming at certain hours, for which the network will compensate them. Thus, it is possible for the networks to offer a national advertiser a simultaneous network hookup which will carry its message throughout the entire United States. Stations provide their own programming if they are independent or during those hours when they are not carrying network programs. These programs may be locally developed or they may be purchased from outside sources. Thus the local station, whether affiliated or independent, can offer advertising time on a local basis.

How Broadcast Advertising Is Sold. Broadcast advertising can be defined as the use of commercial broadcast facilities, AM radio, FM radio, and television, by advertisers to promote and sell their services and products to the consumer. Commercial broadcasting is thus an advertising medium like newspapers and magazines, but with a substantial difference. Unlike these media, which make a charge to the customer, broadcasting's only source of revenue is the advertiser or sponsor.

The single most important characteristic of broadcast advertising is its flexibility. That is, the ability of an advertiser to purchase any amount of advertising and to distribute that advertising geographically in a manner which best suits his purposes. The advertiser can purchase announcements which vary in length from ten to sixty seconds, and they can be purchased in any quantity from one to several hundred or more. Such announcements may fall between programs or may be a part of a program in which other advertisers also participate. The client company may also sponsor an entire program and associate itself with it. Announcements or programs can be purchased in any combination of geographic areas up to and including national coverage. The advertising campaign can run at various times and can reach audiences of varying composition.

There are three basic methods of purchasing such advertising:

(1) *Network Advertising.* A network consists of a large number of stations geographically dispersed to provide national coverage and generally connected by microwave, satellite, or coaxial cable so that they simultaneously carry programs to a nationwide audience. Normally these programs are produced and transmitted from the production centers in New York, Hollywood, and Washington. The network produces the program itself or purchases it from an outside program source. An advertiser who purchases a program, a portion of a program, or announcements pays the network, and the network in turn pays its affiliated stations for carrying these programs at a specific rate which has been agreed upon in the business contract between them. The network thus undertakes the cost of production, distribution, and station compensation. Those sponsors who desire simultaneous national impact for their campaigns may purchase network advertising.

Years ago networks sold largely full program sponsorships. In an effort to accommodate the smaller advertiser, networks have devised various types of advertising such as participating shows in which several sponsors join. This makes it possible for the advertiser with the smaller budget to make good use of network advertising.

(2) *National Spot Advertising.* A promotion campaign can be planned to use "spot" radio or television. Advertising can be purchased on a station-by-station basis which enables an advertiser to tailor a campaign to specific needs by varying the markets and the stations used, the frequency of exposure, the time periods and duration of the campaign. Spot advertising is often used by regional advertisers because it can be closely tailored to a limited distribution pattern. It is also frequently used by national advertisers who have various reasons for wanting to advertise their product heavily in a particular area or particular combination of markets. Through spot advertising, an advertiser can move in and out of markets as his sales strategy dictates. In purchasing spot advertising the advertiser can use various programs which have been developed by the local station. Also

available are various combinations of announcements.

Most stations retain a national spot representative. These organizations have offices in cities where most of the national spot buying is done, and they represent groups of stations, serving as their out-of-town sales force for national advertising.

(3) *Local advertising.* Advertising may, of course, also be purchased from a single local station. All stations have a variety of programs which are suitable for local advertisers who may purchase an entire program, a participation in a program, or announcements between programs. The writing of this business is handled by the local salesmen employed by the station. The local advertiser often relies on the station to develop commercials, which may include writing, artwork, and recording. Local advertising is designed especially for local business such as car dealers, drug stores, movie exhibitors, supermarkets, banks, department stores, etc.

Advertising Costs. As in most advertising, costs are determined by the size of the audience reached by the commercial message. In broadcasting, this audience varies substantially by time of day, the appeal of a particular program, and the popularity of a particular station. Thus, in radio and television the cost of advertising varies substantially, based upon these factors. For example, television reaches its largest audiences in the evening time period, and these time periods therefore carry the highest rates. This applies to network programs and to the cost of local announcements which are available between network programs. Radio typically reaches its greatest audience in the driving times of early morning and evening, and radio rates are thus highest during those time periods.

Most stations give discounts to advertisers on volume purchases. An advertiser who purchases a "package" of ten or twenty announcements per week will pay less for each announcement than if he purchased a single announcement. An advertiser willing to contract to advertise on a program for thirteen or twenty-six weeks or longer will also benefit from substantial discounts by making this commitment. The flexibility of broadcast advertising is nowhere better illustrated than in the price structure. An advertiser can purchase a single announcement on a small radio station for as little as $3.00, whereas a minute of network television time may run $150,000. Any combination of amounts in between is feasible. Stations usually classify blocks of time by the amount of audience. In television, the blocks are called Daytime, Fringe Time, Prime Time, and Late Night. In radio, the times are called Morning Drive Time, Daytime, Evening Drive Time, and Nighttime. A radio station may also offer rotating plans which play the sponsors advertisement in every time block for a flat rate per spot. Rates for broadcast advertising are listed by the call letters of every station by the *Standard Rate and Data Service* which is available for purchase.

Advertisers measure the value of broadcasting time by a formula which establishes the cost-per-thousand figure. Rating services estimate the number of people who are listening to a particular program on a particular station. This is accomplished by various methods. The most common are:

(1) Attaching a device to the set which records the precise usage of the receiver.

(2) Providing the viewer or listener with a diary which is filled out to record programs which have been seen or heard.

(3) Telephoning at the time the program is on the air to determine how many people are listening or watching.

(4) Interviewing after the program has been on to determine how many people listened or watched.

This basic tool is supplemented, of course, by additional information and studies which provide data on viewers such as audience composition, including age and sex, family income, education, purchasing power, and product usage categories such as the amount of soap or beer consumed per thousand.

Normally this information, called demographics, is used by the advertiser when making a broadcast buy. In other words, by looking at the rating history of the station and the particular program, it is possible not only to estimate the probable size of the audience but also its characteristics. On this basis, the advertiser can measure his costs of reaching 1,000 people and weigh it against the cost of using other stations as well as other advertising media. Cost per thousand is, of course, not the only consideration for many advertisers. To many of them an important factor is whether or not the program is of a type which will provide the proper climate for presenting the advertiser's product or service. Many advertisers for example, prefer to associate themselves with prestige programs even though the audience may be smaller and the cost relatively higher.

SOURCE: Station Services Department, National Association of Broadcasters, Washington, D.C.

Information References

Associations:

National Association of Broadcasters.
American Association of Advertising Agencies.
Association of National Advertisers.
Radio Advertising Bureau.
Television Bureau of Advertising.
Station Representatives Association.

Periodicals:

Advertising Age.
Billboard.
Broadcasting Magazine.
Broadcasting Yearbook.
Media Decisions.
Standard Rate and Data Service.
Television Factbook.
Television/Radio Age.

Texts:

Quaal, Ward L. and Martin, Leo A.,"Broadcast Management—Radio and Television," 2nd ed., revised, New York, Hastings House, 1976.

CABLE TV

Cable Television was developed to meet the needs of people who, because of geographical locations, could not receive conventional broadcast signals. In areas where the "line-of-sight" television broadcast signal is obstructed by mountains, tall buildings, or bridges, a sensitive antenna, at an unobstructed site, receives the signals. These signals are then fed through a network of coaxial cables to the homes of viewers.

The first cable systems were constructed in 1948 in eastern Pennsylvania. Little development occurred in the industry during its first decade. However, as viewers demanded more viewing options, cable operators began to offer more diverse programming than simply retransmitting network programs.

This program diversity took the form of "distant signals" transmitted via microwave, a high frequency signal, from the closest city receiving conventional television, and locally originated programming. Program diversity continued to grow dramatically with the advent of satellite communications in 1975.

Growth. The cable industry continues to evolve at an amazing rate. As reported by the National Cable Television Association, the major trade association for the cable industry, as of June 1, 1980, there were approximately 4,300 cable systems serving 17.2 million homes. The rate of cable subscribers is growing at over 10% a year. Cable television reaches 10,200 communities, in all fifty states as well as Guam, the Marianas, Puerto Rico, and the Virgin Islands. In addition, most major American cities are expected to be wired for cable television during the 1980s.

Technology. Early cable systems received from one to three signals. Then the five-channel system became the standard. Since 1953, most new construction has utilized 12-channel or better equipment. The technology of the 80s will provoke the construction of 36-105 channel systems and encourage the upgrading of current 12-channel systems.

Much new construction in the industry has the capacity for two-way communications, fire, burglar and medical alarms, shop-at-home services and at-home banking. These services will be added to the list of cable's current offerings of automatic time and weather information, news wire reports, stock ticker quotations, and diversified programming.

Cable systems carry both very high frequency (off-air channels 2–13) and ultra-high frequency (those channels above 13). In addition to the retransmission of these broadcast signals, cable provides local programming—usually tailored to address the specific needs of the community. Another option for cable viewers are the pay services, which offer news, sports, and entertainment programming on more than 50% of all cable systems.

Regulation. The burgeoning development of cable was halted by the Federal Communications Commission in the late 1960s. The FCC effectively froze cable development by the imposition of stiff signal carriage regulations, but these were eased somewhat in 1972 with the establishment of a framework of rules governing the cable industry.

Regulations were imposed on the cable industry to protect the broadcasters, particularly UHF broadcasting, against adverse economic impact by cable that would endanger the viability of the broadcast service as a whole. Following the completion of an "Economic Inquiry" into the impact of cable to broadcast television, it was determined that cable television does not harm the broadcast industry.

The cable television industry is represented

before the FCC, Congress, state regulatory bodies, and in various programs of the television industry by the National Cable Television Association (NCTA). Forty-seven state and regional cable television associations serve the industry in matters of mutual interest.

Potential. The NCTA foresees cable playing an important part in concerns in which the home TV set will be utilized for far more than entertainment. This will include wide-spread electronic reproduction of newspapers and books, data transmission, armchair shopping, and the delivery of telegrams and mail.

SOURCE: National Cable Television Association, Washington, D.C.

DIRECT RESPONSE MARKETING

Direct Response Marketing also called direct marketing, uses one or more media to elicit a direct response. Action oriented, its purpose is to make a sale or obtain a sales lead or inquiry. Thus, its objective is unlike that of the general marketer whose aim is to condition the consumer for future sales. The Direct Mail/Marketing Association (DMMA) endorses the following definition:

> Direct Marketing is the total of activities by which products and services are offered to market segments in one or more media for informational purposes or to solicit a direct response from a present or prospective customer or contributor by mail, telephone, or other access.

Other terms frequently used in describing direct marketing are "mail order" and "direct mail." *Mail order* is the sale of products by means of a catalog or direct mail package, advertising one or more items. *Direct mailers* send promotional material through the mail, directly to the individuals' homes or offices. *Direct response marketing,* is a broader concept. Direct response marketers not only use the advertising medium of mail, but also use space (primarily newspapers and magazines), radio, television, and telephone.

Origins. Montgomery Ward's first mail order catalog in 1872 marked the beginning of direct marketing. Since that time, direct marketing has grown in scope and in sophistication. DMMA, initially called the Direct Mail/Advertising Association, was founded in 1917. By then, many marketers were using the direct marketing technique.

Recent Developments. Several important developments occurred in the 1960s which acted as catalysts for direct response marketing. This was a period of great technological and communication advances. The Postal Service introduced the ZIP code, which enabled direct marketers to reach specific groups of people through market segmentation. Computers were used to generate lists based on market segments. Detailed response analyses became feasible with the help of the computer. Credit cards were introduced in the sixties and their mailing lists recognized as a potentially great source of customers for direct marketing. Telephone support for direct marketing began at this time, too.

Social and political upheavals during the 1950s and 1960s changed traditional lifestyles and the marketplace. One major shift was the increased number of working women. Direct marketing responded to the changing needs of these women by offering the convenience of shopping by mail. Since then there has been a multimedia explosion in direct marketing. Direct mail campaigns are now supported by telephone, television, radio, and other print media.

Rising postal costs have given impetus to development of alternative delivery systems. Competition from private industry has encouraged the Postal Service to devote more resources to research electronic communication systems. To speed mail delivery, the Service also proposed a nine-digit zip code, at this writing scheduled for limited implementation in 1981.

Governmental agencies such as the Federal Trade Commission will undoubtedly seek to impose regulations on the industry, and the future of direct marketing will depend in great measure on how direct marketers deal with consumerism. In this connection, DMMA has established guidelines for ethical business practices. The association's watchdog committee is alert to keep the Government from enacting what the industry conceives to be unfair standards, and monitors the direct marketing field to guard against abuses.

Volume. In 1979, an estimated $99 billion of total goods and services was sold in the United States through direct response marketing.

It is only since the early 1970s that efforts have been made by most of the media to break out direct response marketing's share of advertising expenditures. Exhibit I shows a breakdown by DMMA for the year 1979, showing

EXHIBIT I

TOTAL ESTIMATED DIRECT RESPONSE ADVERTISING EXPENDITURES—1979

	(in millions)
Coupons	72.0
Direct Mail (postage, paper & production)	8,876.7
Magazines (mail order merchandise only)	123.0
Business Magazines (industrial products only) (1977 figure)	47.
Newspapers	54.4
Newspaper Preprints	1,779.5
Radio	23.0
Telephone	8,555.6
Television	217.0
GRAND TOTAL	19,748.2

Note: Creative costs not included in any of the above figures.

that of the total of $19.7 billion, $8.8 billion was accounted for by postage, paper, and production (exclusive of creative costs).

Potential. Direct response marketing is a rapidly growing discipline, and the coming years are expected to see the field explode with new ways to reach the consumer directly. Currently there already is much experimentation with interactive television services, home computer terminals, video cassettes, and electronic funds transfer. The future will see much more in the way of media specialization and multimedia support for direct marketing.

Direct marketing yields measurable responses. This capability enables marketers to project profitability based upon variables such as cost per inquiry, cost per sale, income returned per advertisement, and the weights, timing, and frequency of campaigns. Computers are now used for generating these figures, for market segmentation, and for personalized direct mail solicitations.

Specific Advantages. Kobs [1] lists the following four key factors that set direct response marketing apart:

(1) *Advertising and Selling Combined.* Direct marketing combines the advertising and sales functions into a single ad, mailing, or commercial.

(2) *Built-in Result Feedback.* The reply cards, coupons, and phone calls that come back—the inquiries, orders, and payments—provide the opportunity to measure virtually every element of the marketing program.

(3) *Service Concept Adds Value to Products.* For example, the sale of individual books at retail can become a book club when offered by mail. Even a merchandise offer becomes somewhat of a service by offering convenient monthly terms or a free home trial.

(4) *Action-Oriented for Impulse Sales.* While the general advertiser specializes in "conditioning" for future sales, the direct response advertiser specializes in selling *now.* His effort is geared to make it as easy as possible for the prospect to place an immediate order.

Copy Writing Formulas. Over the years, a number of formulas or guides have been developed to help make direct advertising copy as effective as possible. Among those which have received wide use are the following:

A-I-D-A. This is the oldest of the formulas. AIDA means (A) attract *attention;* (I) arouse *interest;* (D) stimulate *desire;* (A) ask for *action.*

D-D-P-C. This says the message should start by being *dramatic,* continue by being *descriptive* of the product or service, be *persuasive,* and end by *clinching* the sale.

Egner's Nine Points. The late Frank Egner, one of the nation's greatest copywriters, listed these nine points:

(1) Write a lead to create desire as well as get attention.

(2) Give an inspirational beginning.

(3) Give a clear definition of the product.

(4) Tell a success story about the use of the product.

(5) Include testimonials and endorsements from satisfied customers.

(6) List the special features of the product.

(7) Make a statement of the value to the purchaser.

(8) Devise an action closer that will make the reader want to buy immediately.

(9) Conclude with P.S. rephrasing the headline.

Picture-Promise-Prove-Push. According to this precept, you start by painting a word *picture* of what the product or service will do for the reader; then *promise* that the picture will come true if the product is purchased; offer *proof* of what the product has done for others; and end with a *push* for immediate action.

Jack Lacy's Five Points. This formula is actually a basis for all selling:

(1) What will you do for me if I listen to your story?

(2) How are you going to do this?

(3) Who is responsible for the promises you make?

(4) Whom have you done this for?

(5) What will it cost me?

To the above, DMAA has added:

(6) How do I order from you?

Robert Stone's Seven Steps. The following seven-step formula was advanced by Robert Stone, nationally known authority on copy:

(1) Promise a benefit in your lead or first paragraph—*your most important benefit.*

(2) Immediately *enlarge* upon this benefit.

(3) Tell the reader *specifically* what he is going to get.

(4) Back your statements with *proofs* and endorsements.

(5) Tell the reader what he might lose if he does not act.

(6) *Rephrase* prominent benefits in closing offer.

(7) Incite action NOW.

ROBERT F. DELAY, President, Direct Mail/Marketing Association, Inc., New York, New York

Information References

Association:

Direct Mail/Marketing Association, Inc.

Texts:

Hodgson, Richard S., "Direct Mail and Mail Order Handbook," 4th ed., Chicago, Dartnell, 1974.

Smith, Charles W., "When and How to Market Direct to Users," Ch. 8, Sec. Four, in Buell, Victor, and Heyel, Carl, eds., "Handbook of Modern Marketing," New York, McGraw-Hill, 1970.

References Cited

[1] Kobs, Jim, "Profitable Direct Marketing," Chicago, Crain Books, 1979.

MAGAZINES

About 1,500 general consumer and farm magazines are published in the United States. In addition, specialized business publications reach selective audiences in every field of economic activity. *Standard Rate and Data* lists upward of 4,000 publication titles in classifications ranging from Advertising & Marketing, Air Conditioning, Amusements, and Appliances to Water Supply & Sewage Disposal, Welding, Wire & Wire Products, and Woodworking.

In 1979, advertisers spent well over $2.7 billion in general consumer magazines, according to Magazines Publishers Association. In addition, American Business Press, Inc. estimates that advertisers in 1979 spent some $1.75 billion in the business press, including farm magazines with a business orientation.

Since the mid-Seventies, magazines have enjoyed a resurgent interest among both readers and advertisers. Circulation has been growing at twice the rate of the general population, and advertising revenues have more than doubled since 1975. Circulation growth is attributable to the growth in upscale demographic segments of the market—better educated, younger, more affluent households—which account for the bulk of magazine purchasers.

Advertising revenue growth can be accounted for, in part, by magazines' ability to reach these market segments with increasing efficiency. Another related factor in revenue growth has been the result of magazines' ability to hold their cost increase to the advertiser well below those of other media while shifting a greater proportion of their overall cost to the reader in the form of increased newsstand and subscription prices.

Diversification. New magazines have been a major source of the magazine industry's growth. An acceleration of growth in the number and types of magazines published has resulted in part from the increasing financial good health of the industry in general. Regional and city magazines, in-flight magazines, and a host of new single-interest magazines are contributing. Science, cultural interest, health, careers, sports, and women's interests have sparked dozens of new titles.

The new launchings, currently from 200 to 300 a year, come from established companies and young hopefuls. Many of the latter flounder through undercapitalization, but net growth is evidenced by an ever increasing number of listings in *Standard Rate and Data,* a trade publication listing advertising costs and other pertinent information.

Audience. As with other media, magazine advertising is sold on the basis of people reached—with audited figures on controlled or paid circulation, and with further documentation to back up claims of readers over and above the actual recipients. Circulation audits are made by Audit Bureau of Circulation, Chicago, and Business Publication Audits of Circulation, New York. Most magazines will supply information on the size and characteristics of their audience—income, education, type of position held (in the case of business publications), and even attitudes and motivations.

Special Techniques. Technology on the presses and at the bindery make possible increasing selectivity of editorial and advertising material. Some magazines are already publishing hundreds of different geographic and demographic advertising editions. For these and foreign editions, satellites are beginning to beam prose and pictures to printers around the world. The use of computers at the bindery could conceivably ultimately result in a reader selecting an edition with editorial content designed specifically for him or her. Cost, not technology, is the roadblock to immediate use of the newest technologies.

Outlook. Favorable demographic changes that will take place in the 1980s are grounds for long-term optimism. Increasing levels of education, growing affluence and concentration of affluence, as well as the growth of World War II babies to maturity, mark prime magazine growth markets.

Profits in the magazine industry have grown modestly, but remain well below those in television. This is mainly a result of rapidly accelerating postal and paper costs.

SOURCE: Magazine Publishers Association, New York, New York, and American Business Press, Inc., New York, New York.

Information References

Audit Bureau of Circulation, Chicago, Ill.
Business Publications Audit of Circulations, Inc., Chicago, Ill.
Canadian Circulations Audit Board, West Toronto, Canada.
Magazine Publishers Association, Inc., New York, N.Y.
Selected Market Audit Division of BPA, New York, N.Y.
Society of National Association Publications, Evanston, Ill.
Standard Rate and Data Service, Inc., Skokie, Ill.
Verified Audit Circulation Corporation, Santa Monica, Calif.

NEWSPAPERS

Some two-thirds of U. S. households have a **Newspaper** delivered to their door every day. As of 1979, there were 1,760 daily weekday and approximately 720 Sunday newspapers published in 1,553 cities and towns across the U. S., selling 62.2 million daily and 54.4 million Sunday copies, in addition to 9,000 weekly. Despite suspension of some major-city dailies, the number of newspapers has remained remarkably steady since World War II because of the increase in suburban papers. The bulk of the $14.5 billion newspaper advertising in 1979 was black and white, although color advertising revenues continue to grow.

Surveys reported by the Newspaper Advertising Bureau show that the great majority of readers are regular readers. In the course of a Monday-through-Friday week the daily newspaper reaches 89% of the total adult population, or approximately 139 million people. Coverage is even higher among "upscale" population segments. Two thirds of the readers go through the paper from the beginning, page by page.

Flexibility as to frequency, continuity, copy, and creative approach is a significant advantage in newspaper advertising. An advertiser can tell his story in a two-page spread for the "big sell," or in a "blitz" series of 17- to 25-line ads. Advertising can be tailored to local level appeals, and run on a cooperative basis with local dealers and retail outlets.

Costs. Newspaper advertising falls into six classifications: retail (local); general (national); automotive (national); financial; classified; and legal. Each has its own rate structure, primarily based on audited circulation. The retail rate, which is lower than the national, usually applies only when an advertiser sells directly to consumers through retail stores he owns or controls. The national rate applies to general and automotive advertising other than that of bona fide retailers. Various forms of volume and frequency discounts are offered, and today there is a trend toward adoption of a single rate for both local and national advertisers.

National advertising is handled by newspaper representatives, almost always exclusively for a given paper. These may be independents, ranging from two- or three-man sales offices to large firms with salesmen in major cities; or they may be part of the organization of a newspaper chain or of a single large paper. The representatives' commission is paid by the newspaper. A well-staffed firm of this sort will provide extensive market information on areas served by its papers, although it will not provide copy or perform other advertising agency functions. Cooperative advertising is handled through the advertising department of the retailer. Sunday is the most important day of the week for department store advertising; many national advertisers using Sunday newspapers advertise in Sunday magazine and comics sections, since those are among the most widely read sections of the Sunday paper.

Extensive newspaper research services are performed by Advertising Checking Bureau,

Inc., Media Records, Inc., and George Neustadt Co., all of New York.

SOURCE: Newspaper Advertising Bureau, New York, New York

Information References

Ayer Directory of Publications (yearly).

OUTDOOR ADVERTISING

Many people think that any sign with a commercial message which appears out of doors is **Outdoor Advertising.** Actually, only about 250,000—less than 5%—of such signs belong to the standardized medium. They include *poster panels* displaying 24- and 30-sheet posters, and *painted bulletins* of standard sizes and proportions. The standardized outdoor advertising structures are owned and maintained by the outdoor advertising companies—known as "plants"—and are built on private land owned or leased by the plants. The plants sell advertising space on the structures for specified periods.

There are one or more outdoor advertising plants in most cities and towns, and most are members of the Outdoor Advertising Association of America and subscribe to its Code of Practices. Advertisers can buy outdoor advertising nationally, regionally, or in any individual local market.

Posters. Standard outdoor advertising poster panels throughout the country are approximately 12 ft. high and 25 ft. long. Standardization enables advertisers to print posters in quantity, with the assurance that they will be displayed uniformly on the structures of any plant in any area. About 2.5 million 24- and 30-sheet posters are produced annually in the United States.

The terms "24-sheet" and "30-sheet" do not mean that posters are made up of that many individual sheets, although they were many years ago. Today, with larger presses, they are usually printed in ten to fourteen sections, centered within the panel area, and surrounded by white blanking paper.

The 24-sheet poster measures 8 ft. 8 in. by 19 ft. 6 in.; the 30-sheet measures 9 ft. 7 in. by 21 ft. 7 in. The "bleed" poster, extends the artwork to the panel frame. Size averages 40% larger than the 24-sheet poster, but there is no additional space charge for the larger size.

Market Coverage. For poster advertising, market coverage is expressed in Gross Rating Points (Grps) on a daily basis for four standard intensity levels, e.g., 100 Grps, 75 Grps, 50 Grps, and 25 Grps. Basic intensity, 100 Grps, includes the number of posters required to provide a daily effective circulation equal to the population of the defined market. A 50 Grps intensity includes the number of posters required to deliver a daily effective circulation equal to half the total population of the market and so on. Obviously, the number of posters required to deliver 100 Grps in a large market will be greater than in a smaller market. In either case, the intensity of market coverage will be about the same.

The standard intensity units of market coverage are normally sold for a period of 30 days. Posters are located on the main traffic arteries within a market, in those areas which are zoned for or used for commerce and industry. Many outdoor plants offer specialized coverages to meet the particular needs of individual advertisers, e.g., ethnic groups, income levels, supermarkets, etc.

Painted Bulletins. The dramatic painted bulletins represent less than 14% of all standard outdoor structures, although they account for about 45% of outdoor billing. Their greater cost is due to their dominant size and maximum traffic locations. For dramatic effect, they are frequently embellished with cut-out letters and three-dimensional effects which may extend beyond the frame, but are limited by OAAA standards to a maximum of 5 ft. 6 in. at the top, and 2 ft. at either side. In the "Tri-Vision," or "Multi-Vision," units, a portion of the face of the board is made of vertical sections of triangular cross-sections, which turn at intervals, showing successively three different messages on the same panel. New techniques, such as plastic-faced, back-lighted units, moving messages, unusual treatments of light and color, and the like are constantly being developed. The message is hand-painted directly on the face of the bulletin in the plant's paint shop, and the sections are assembled on the site.

Painted bulletins are generally sold for periods of a year or more on the basis of individual locations, which can be fixed or rotating. On a rotating or rotary plan, the entire design is transferred from structure to structure at specified intervals.

Audience Reach and Frequency. Numerous studies of the outdoor medium by Nielsen, W. R. Simmons & Associates, Target Group Index, etc. have uniformly shown high levels of reach and frequency. The Simmons Market Research Bureau 1979 report on Outdoor Advertising shows, nationally, for 100 Grps intensity, a reach of 87.2% with a frequency of 24.9 times for all U.S. adults eighteen years of age and over. The levels of both reach and frequency rise as income and educational levels rise. The highest level of frequency of exposure is among younger, upper socioeconomic people.

Traffic Audit Bureau, Inc. (TAB), sponsored jointly by advertisers, agencies and the outdoor industry, audits circulation of outdoor panels by actual counts of traffic. It also evaluates visibility on factors such as length of approach, speed of travel, angle of panel, etc., and assigns a Space Position Value Rating.

F. R. CAWL, JR., Publisher, *The Buyers Guide to Outdoor Advertising,* Searsport, Maine and New York, New York.

Information References

The Outdoor Advertising Association of America Inc.
The Institute of Outdoor Advertising, Inc.
The Traffic Audit Bureau, Inc.
The Buyers Guide to Outdoor Advertising, containing rate and market data for more than 8,000 Outdoor Markets.

TRANSIT ADVERTISING

Transit Advertising is carried by more than 70,000 vehicles (buses, subways, rail, and commuter trains) throughout U.S. and Canadian urban areas. Advertisers currently invest an estimated $70 million per year in it. Each month about 40 million different adults ride in transit vehicles, and they are counted by the most rigid audit available—paid fares, about 10 billion a year. In addition to these potential exposures are the even greater exposures to outside poster ads on vehicles.

Transit advertising is regularly scheduled, publishes prices, and can be bought nationally. Increased transit use builds the size of the inside audience, and new vehicles provide attractive media for outside ads. Posters on the walls of subway and commuter stations are also a major factor.

Newer techniques include *backlighted display* (full color on translucent sheets, lighted from behind to give the impact of a giant color slide, both inside and outside vehicles); *king-size posters,* 2½ by 12 ft. (with changeable portions and constant basic display, e.g., a food manufacturer promotes brand identity on the basic panel, and seasonal dishes on the variable one); *"take-ones"* (brochures or coupons at inside transit displays, so that the advertiser can, in effect, conduct a "direct-mail" campaign without postage); and a *merchandise bus* (a regular transit vehicle converted into a mobile showcase for displays, samples, and demonstrations).

A recent development is the introduction of attractive vinyl, frameless displays on the exteriors of buses. Also, in the new subway systems currently emerging, there is a trend to backlighted displays in subway stations.

Reach and Costs. Highly selective geographic coverage is provided, with individual exposures as long as 25 minutes during a ride, and high repetition. On a national basis, costs average 15 to 20 cents per thousand inside exposures; outside transit posters average less than seven cents per thousand exposures. Some 100 companies purvey transit advertising space, for single or multiple markets. They have exclusive contracts with transit companies, and see to it that the ads are properly serviced. (The advertiser or the ad agency provides the cards.) The medium normally pays a 15% commission to recognized agencies on billings for space. Transit ads can be scheduled in one or in any combination of 380 U.S. markets and across Canada. Rates are generally quoted on the basis of monthly showings. The Transit Advertising Association reports members' estimated "ridership."

JOSEPH PALASTAK, Executive Director, Transit Advertising Association, New York, New York

Cross References (all sections): *(See accompanying entries with Advertising prefix.)*

ADVERTISING RESEARCH

Mass production requires mass selling by means of advertising. These two, mass production and mass selling, grew up together during the last sixty years. Both came full scale with the large volume manufacture of automobiles after 1910. **Advertising Research** grew out of the necessity for a better understanding of mass distribution and mass marketing.

Beginnings of Advertising Research. The beginnings of Advertising Research go back to

1900 when Harlow Gale in the psychological laboratory of the University of Minnesota inquired into the problem of *relevant* and *irrelevant* words and pictures in advertisements. Gale used a rapid exposure method with actual advertisements. He reported that relevant words as headlines ranked highest in attention value and increased in attention value in successive exposures. Next in value came relevant pictures, then irrelevant pictures, and finally irrelevant words. Gale inferred that as soon as the novelty of irrelevant material had worn off, the advertisement lost in interest, whereas the strictly relevant material maintained interest.

In 1903 Walter Dill Scott, psychologist at Northwestern University, published this book "The Theory of Advertising" [1], a landmark in the analysis of advertising processes. In 1908 he followed it with his "The Psychology of Advertising" [2]. In it he reported his study of size of advertisements. He found that the average advertisement in *Century Magazine* increased four fold from 1872 to 1913, from 38 lines to 169 lines. He further studied the attention value of advertisements by having readers look through a magazine for ten minutes and immediately thereafter list all the advertisements they recalled having seen in the issue. His findings indicated that, per page occupied, full page and half page advertisements attracted about the same number of readers, whereas quarter page and smaller advertisements attract substantially fewer readers.

The present writer in 1908 at the University of Wisconsin and Edward K. Strong in 1912 at Columbia University also made studies regarding size and repetition of advertisements.

These early studies dealt mainly with physical characteristics of advertisements. Subsequently and particularly after 1920, investigators began to inquire into the *motivation* and *content* aspects of advertisements, and especially into marketing processes. Managements began to plan advertising programs as parts of the entire distribution and marketing process.

The Association of National Advertising Managers, changed (1913) to Association of National Advertisers, was formed in 1910. While it is primarily a trade association, it has fostered over the years various research projects, notably the early study of size and frequency by Strong mentioned above. In 1911 The Curtis Publishing Company under the direction of Charles C. Parlin established its research department to study markets for various major products.

The year 1914 must be set down as a landmark in advertising history because in that year the Audit Bureau of Circulations was established through the cooperation of the three chief interests concerned with advertising—publishers, advertisers, and advertising agencies. From that day on reliable circulation figures have been provided. Circulation figures in themselves are not research, but they are essential for many kinds of research projects.

In 1917 the American Association of Advertising Agencies was founded. While it too is primarily a trade organization, it subsequently (1924) established a research department under the direction of the present writer and over the years has fostered many research projects.

Around 1919 R. O. Eastman operated possibly the first independent marketing research organization. At that time also Percival White and Daniel Starch and soon thereafter Archibald Crossley formed independent research organizations.

In 1925 men interested in these research activities began to meet at regular intervals to discuss problems of common concern. This was the beginning of the Market Research Council in New York. In 1929 this Council appointed a committee to formulate plans for the establishment of a National Marketing Association. The association thus inaugurated was combined in 1938 with the Association of Teachers of Advertising started years before (around 1915), to form the American Marketing Association.

Mention must also be made of the contribution of the U. S. Department of Commerce. When Herbert Hoover was Secretary of Commerce, he greatly enlarged, in the mid 1920s, the statistical and fact gathering activities of the Department. The statistical data and continuing series have been of great value to business managements.

Research Methods. Over the years certain research methods have been devised and used as standard procedures for continuing studies and reports to the advertising industry. As advertising was being used increasingly, it became urgent for business managements to know more fully how advertising performs.

The Recognition Method for Measuring Readership. To what extent are advertisements seen and read? The present writer, while on the faculty of the Harvard Graduate School of Business Administration, devised, in 1922, the

"Recognition Method" for measuring the readership of advertisements and editorial articles. At that time there was only printed advertising. Radio was in the "earphone" stage and television was not even thought of. The recognition method in one form or another had been used previously by Scott and Strong. Their use, however, was with dummy sets of advertisements and tests under laboratory conditions. The recognition method involved a procedure for ascertaining normal day-to-day reading of advertisements as they actually appear in publications and as read by the usual readers of a given publication. Under this method, readership is measured by ascertaining in personal interviews which advertisements readers of an issue recognized having seen and read previously in the normal course of reading that publication. In 1932 the continuing Starch measurement and reporting of readership of advertisements in leading publications was undertaken.

The Case Method. In the middle 1920s and thereafter, the Harvard Business School under the direction of Neil H. Borden compiled extensive case studies of advertising procedures employed by various companies. This was part of a larger program of compiling cases in various aspects of business management for study by students in business schools. Professor Borden published a compilation of advertising cases for use by business schools and colleges. The development of the case method has been a landmark in business education. While the case method is primarily a teaching device, it has nevertheless contributed materially toward a better understanding of business operations.

Inventory Studies. In the early 1930s, A. C. Nielsen inaugurated a continuing program of measuring the flow of brands through retail outlets. These reports, periodically available, furnish the basis for various studies in marketing processes.

Probability Sampling Procedures. As demand increased for advertising and marketing information, it became essential to devise techniques for obtaining reliable cross sections of households throughout the United States. Over the years the sampling process has been greatly improved and refined. In 1927, when radio was becoming an important advertising medium, the National Broadcasting Company requested the writer to determine how many families in the United States had radios, and to what extent they were being used. This was before more refined probability sampling procedures had been devised, and a "home made" probability sample was designed. It consisted of 19,000 households scattered according to best judgment across the country so as to represent in approximate due proportion various segments of the population. This study was repeated on a smaller scale in 1929 and projected as of 1930. The findings of this early "probability" sample were within 4% of the number of radios found by the 1930 United States Census, which for the first time included a count of radios.

In the late 1940s more refined probability sampling methods were introduced in some aspects of advertising research, namely in research on audiences of magazines and newspapers. These sampling methods provided greater reliability of measurable results, and attained wide application during the 1950s and thereafter.

Coincidental Telephone Method. In the middle 1930s, C. E. Hooper employed the coincidence telephone procedure for ascertaining the listening to radio programs and commercials. It was called coincidental because respondents, when called on the telephone, were asked whether they were listening to radio and what programs.

Audimeter Method. After some years of technical development and pilot operation, A. C. Nielsen Company put its Audimeter to commercial use with the launching of the Nielsen Radio Index in 1942. The Audimeter also became the sole source of set tuning information for Nielsen Television Index, commercially launched in 1950. The Audimeter is a mechanism which is attached to a radio or television set to record when the set is turned on and to what station and program it is tuned.

Diary Method. To determine brand purchase and frequency of purchase, the diary method has been employed. This procedure consists of arrangements with households to keep a continuous diary of brands purchased day by day over a designated period. It is being used by the Market Research Corporation of America for continuing studies and reports.

Syndicated Studies of Magazine Audiences. In response to demand for joint data about the sizes and characteristics of the audiences of a large number of publications, Starch started its series titled Consumer Magazine Reports in the 1930s. This provided periodic data about the primary audiences of many consumer magazines. During the 1960s other services reporting on magazine audiences were started, dealing with total audiences (primary and secondary combined). It is customary to include in the studies not only data for demographic and socio-economic descriptions of audiences, but also information about consumption of a wide variety of products and services.

Research Findings. For convenience, the findings of various studies may be grouped under three headings: Findings regarding *markets, media,* and *advertising messages.*

Markets. An essential area of information regarding markets is the economic status of households. Over the years, much more precise and complete information has been developed. For example, there is now fairly common agreement and uniform practice in income groupings.

Next, criteria for classifying households into the various income brackets are more specific. The meaning of correlated characteristics of economic status is better understood—characteristics such as type of home, rental value of home, occupation of head of household, appliances in the home, and automobile ownership. Furthermore, respondents themselves upon being asked will classify themselves with fair reliability into the appropriate income brackets.

In the third place, more is known about family composition, the number, age, and sex of persons in the family unit, and the number employed.

Fourth, more is known today about purchases made by households at various stages in the life cycle. Certain products are bought more frequently at certain times of a family's life cycle or by households composed of various numbers of persons.

Fifth, there is much more information today about the frequency of purchase of specific brands, about the ages of appliances in the home, and about first time purchases or purchases for replacements.

As an example of demographic information available, Exhibit I shows an estimated distribution of U. S. households by number of members in 1979 [3].

EXHIBIT I

SIZE OF U. S. HOUSEHOLDS—1979

One or two persons	52.9%
Three or four persons	32.8
Five or more persons	14.3

As another example of market data, Exhibit II presents some estimates of home ownership and type of location [3].

EXHIBIT II

HOME OWNERSHIP, REMODELING AND LOCATION OF U.S. HOUSEHOLDS—1979

65% owned their dwelling
23% remodeled in past year
31% live in metro central cities
43% live in metro suburbs
27% live in non-metro

Media. Much of the same kind of information available regarding markets is now also available regarding media, i.e., avenues of communication by which to reach people constituting various markets. To illustrate figures regarding ages of magazine readers, two examples are given in Exhibit III, showing primary female readers age eighteen years or older [3]. While about one-third of the primary female readers of *National Geographic* are eighteen to thirty-four years old, almost three-quarters of primary female readers of *Playboy* are in this age group.

EXHIBIT III

EXAMPLES OF AGE GROUPINGS OF FEMALE PRIMARY READERS OF MAGAZINES

	18–34 years %	35–54 years %	55 and over %
National Geographic	33	39	28
Playboy	74	23	4

Exhibit IV illustrates data regarding ownership of home appliances in magazine-buying households [3].

Thus from data on markets and media, media can be selected for advertising specific brands to indicated markets.

Advertising Messages. Much concrete information has become available and some general principles have been formulated regarding the perception of advertising messages.

One of the significant findings brought out by readership studies 50 years ago was that advertisements differ enormously in their ability to attract readers and that these wide differences are due chiefly to two sets of factors: (1) differences in the inherent interests of people in different products, and (2) differences in the

EXHIBIT IV

EXAMPLES OF APPLIANCE OWNERSHIP OF MAGAZINE-BUYING HOUSEHOLDS

	Have a room air conditioner %	Bought new in last 12 months %	Have a microwave oven %	Bought new in last 12 months %
Family Circle	36	2	17	5
T.V. Guide	38	3	9	3

content and form of advertisements themselves. Thus, twice as many men will read automobile advertisements as food advertisements, and twice as many women will read refrigerator advertisements as tire advertisements.

Possibly the most significant finding is that with due recognition of other factors (see ADVERTISING), over the long pull dollars of sales can be related to dollars of advertising cost.

DANIEL STARCH, Ph.D., Founder of Daniel Starch & Staff (1883–1979) Revised by Starch INRA Hooper, Inc., Mamaroneck, New York

Information References

Associations:

American Marketing Association.
Advertising Research Foundation.

Periodicals:

Journal of Advertising Research (Advertising Res. Foundation).
Journal of Marketing (Amer. Marketing Assn.)

References Cited

[1] Scott, Walter Dill, "The Theory of Advertising," Boston, Small, Maynard & Co., 1903.
[2] Scott, Walter Dill, "The Psychology of Advertising," Boston, Small, Maynard & Co., 1908.
[3] Starch Primary Readership Study, 1979 Mamaroneck, N.Y., Starch INRA Hooper, Inc.

Cross References: *(See accompanying entries with Advertising prefix.)*

ADVERTISING YARDSTICKS

Since 1956, the publication *Advertising Age* has annually compiled and published statistics on advertising expenditures by the 100 top advertisers in the United States. The figures toward the end of the year cover the preceding

EXHIBIT I

100 LEADING NATIONAL ADVERTISERS

(TOTAL AD DOLLARS IN MILLIONS: 1979)

1	Procter & Gamble Co.	$614.9	33	Pillsbury Co.	$131.5	66	Mattel Inc.	$66.0
2	General Foods Corp.	393.0	34	American Cyanamid Co.	127.0	68	Trans World Corp.	62.0
3	Sears, Roebuck & Co.	379.3	35	Gillette Co.	126.9	69	Campbell Soup Co.	60.5
4	General Motors Corp.	323.4	36	Richardson-Merrell	123.8	70	Squibb Corp.	60.0
5	Philip Morris Inc.	291.2	37	Colgate-Palmolive Co.	122.5	71	Liggett Group	59.0
6	K mart Corp.	287.1	38	J. C. Penney Co.	122.0	72	Warner Communications	57.6
7	R. J. Reynolds Industries	258.1	39	Kraft Inc.	119.7	73	American Express Co.	55.4
8	Warner-Lambert Co.	220.2	40	Chrysler Corp.	118.0	74	Union Carbide Corp.	55.1
9	American Telephone & Telegraph Co.	219.8	41	B.A.T. Industries Ltd.	116.4	75	Volkswagen of America	55.0
10	Ford Motor Co.	215.0	42	Ralston Purina Co.	108.0	76	Greyhound Corp.	53.8
11	PepsiCo Inc.	212.0	43	SmithKline Corp.	107.7	77	UAL Inc.	52.5
12	Bristol-Myers Co.	210.6	44	Chesebrough-Pond's	107.3	78	Polaroid Corp.	50.5
13	American Home Products	206.0	45	Consolidated Foods Corp.	105.0	79	Brown-Forman Distillers Corp.	50.0
14	McDonald's Corp.	202.8	46	Time Inc.	102.4	80	MortonNorwich	49.2
15	Gulf + Western Industries	191.5	47	Revlon Inc.	101.0	81	Wm. Wrigley Jr. Co.	48.5
16	General Mills	190.7	48	Transamerica Corp.	95.0	82	Beecham Group Ltd.	46.7
17	Esmark Inc.	170.5	49	Sterling Drug Co.	92.0	83	American Motors Corp.	44.6
18	Coca-Cola Co.	169.3	50	Kellogg Co.	91.6	84	North American Philips Corp.	44.2
19	Seagram Co.	168.0	51	Nabisco Inc.	91.3	85	American Honda Motor Co.	44.0
20	Mobil Corp.	165.8	52	DuPont	89.4	86	Pfizer Inc.	43.7
21	Norton Simon Inc.	163.2	53	Eastman Kodak Co.	87.8	87	ABC Inc.	42.0
22	Anheuser-Busch	160.5	54	Quaker Oats Co.	86.6	88	Eastern Air Lines	40.4
23	Unilever U.S. Inc.	160.0	55	Nestle Enterprises	86.0	89	Noxell Corp.	40.2
24	RCA Corp.	158.6	56	American Brands	83.5	90	S. C. Johnson & Son	40.2
25	Johnson & Johnson	157.7	57	Toyota Motor Sales U.S.A.	80.3	91	Borden Inc.	39.0
26	Heublein Inc.	155.0	58	Schering-Plough Corp.	78.0	92	Levi Strauss & Co.	38.6
27	Beatrice Foods Co.	150.0	59	Miles Laboratories	77.8	93	A. H. Robins Co.	37.0
28	CBS Inc.	146.1	60	Clorox Co.	72.6	94	Scott Paper Co.	36.8
28	U.S. Government	146.1	61	CPC International Inc.	72.0	95	Standard Brands	36.4
30	Loews Corp.	144.5	62	Jos. Schlitz Brewing Co.	71.6	96	American Airlines	35.0
31	General Electric Co.	139.4	63	H. J. Heinz Co.	71.5	97	Delta Air Lines	33.5
32	International Telephone & Telegraph Corp.	132.4	64	Mars Inc.	69.5	98	Milton Bradley Co.	31.3
			65	Nissan Motor Corp.	66.1	99	International Business Machines	31.1
			66	MCA Inc.	66.0	100	Mazda Motors of America	28.4

Exhibit II

100 Leaders' Advertising as Per Cent of Sales

Covering total 1979 ad expenditures, including measured and unmeasured media

Airlines

AD RANK	COMPANY	ADVERTISING	SALES	ADV. AS % OF SALES
68	Trans World Corp.	$61,994,900	$4,334,000,000	1.4
77	UAL Inc.	52,461,900	3,831,523,000	1.4
88	Eastern Air Lines	40,400,000	1,881,526,000	1.4
96	American Airlines	35,039,800	3,252,532,000	1.1
97	Delta Air Lines	33,500,000	2,654,026,000	1.3

Appliances, Tv, Radio

AD RANK	COMPANY	ADVERTISING	SALES	ADV. AS % OF SALES
24	RCA Corp.	158,600,000	7,454,600,000	2.1
31	General Electric Co.	139,407,500	22,460,600,000	0.6
84	North American Philips Corp.	44,179,375	2,409,003,000	1.8

Automobiles

AD RANK	COMPANY	ADVERTISING	SALES	ADV. AS % OF SALES
4	General Motors Corp.	323,395,900	66,311,200,000	0.5
10	Ford Motor Co.	215,000,000	1,409,003,000	0.5
40	Chrysler Corp.	118,000,000	12,000,000,000	1.0
57	Toyota Motor Sales U.S.A.	80,256,200	13,460,000,000	0.6
65	Nissan Motor Corp.	66,082,900	13,079,598,000	0.5
75	Volkswagen of America	44,611,600	3,117,049,000	1.4
83	American Motors Corp.	44,611,600	3,117,049,000	1.4
85	American Honda Motor Co.	44,000,000	3,619,000,000	1.2
100	Mazda Motors of America	28,365,600	900,000,000	3.2

Chemicals

AD RANK	COMPANY	ADVERTISING	SALES	ADV. AS % OF SALES
34	American Cyanamid Co.	127,000,000	3,186,998,000	4.0
52	DuPont	89,380,700	12,572,000,000	0.7
74	Union Carbide Corp.	55,100,000	9,176,500,000	0.6

Communications, Entertainment

AD RANK	COMPANY	ADVERTISING	SALES	ADV. AS % OF SALES
29	CBS Inc.	146,118,000	3,729,701,000	3.9
46	Time Inc.	102,360,000	2,504,060,000	4.1
48	Transamerica Corp.	95,048,300	4,044,647,000	2.3
66	MCA Inc.	66,000,000	1,266,400,000	5.2
72	Warner Communications	57,600,000	1,648,027,000	3.5
87	ABC Inc.	42,049,500	2,053,570,000	2.0

Drugs

AD RANK	COMPANY	ADVERTISING	SALES	ADV. AS % OF SALES
36	Richardson-Merrell	123,800,000	1,090,546,000	11.4
43	SmithKline Corp.	107,737,000	1,351,145,000	8.0
49	Sterling Drug Co.	92,000,000	81,180,000	11.2
58	Schering-Plough Corp.	78,000,000	1,434,022,000	5.4
59	Miles Laboratories	77,822,800	595,218,000	13.1
70	Squibb Corp.	60,000,000	1,452,712,000	4.1
86	Pfizer Inc.	43,731,200	1,196,900,000	3.7
93	A. H. Robins Inc.	36,955,900	386,425,000	9.6

Food

AD RANK	COMPANY	ADVERTISING	SALES	ADV. AS % OF SALES
2	General Foods	393,000,000	5,959,600,000	6.5
14	McDonald's Corp.	202,807,500	5,385,000,000	3.8
16	General Mills	190,746,500	4,170,278,000	4.6
17	Esmark Inc.	170,547,000	6,771,883,000	2.5
21	Norton Simon Inc.	163,187,830	2,755,934,000	5.9
27	Beatrice Foods Co.	150,000,000	8,290,509,000	1.8
33	Pillsbury Co.	131,549,400	3,032,000,000	4.3
39	Kraft Inc.	119,653,600	6,432,935,000	1.9
42	Ralston Purina Co.	108,028,200	4,600,000,000	2.3
45	Consolidated Foods Corp.	105,000,000	5,000,000,000	2.1
50	Kellogg Co.	91,645,700	1,850,000,000	5.0
51	Nabisco Inc.	91,295,000	2,362,000,000	3.9
54	Quaker Oats Co.	86,640,000	1,966,300,000	4.4
55	Nestle Enterprises	85,978,600	1,433,000,000	6.0
61	CPC International Inc.	72,000,000	3,698,700,000	1.9
63	H. J. Heinz Co.	71,469,335	2,924,774,000	2.4
69	Campbell Soup Co.	60,524,400	2,248,692,000	2.7
80	MortonNorwich	49,209,800	731,984,000	6.7
91	Borden Inc.	38,958,600	4,312,533,000	0.9
95	Standard Brands	36,400,000	2,613,274,000	1.4

Gum and Candy

AD RANK	COMPANY	ADVERTISING	SALES	ADV. AS % OF SALES
64	Mars Inc.	69,523,000	887,600,000,000	7.8
81	Wm. Wrigley Jr. Co.	48,452,400	505,399,000	9.6

Photographic Equipment

AD RANK	COMPANY	ADVERTISING	SALES	ADV. AS % OF SALES
53	Eastman Kodak Co.	$ 87,751,300	$ 8,028,231,280	1.1
78	Polaroid Corp.	50,480,300	1,361,454,000	3.7

Retail Chains

AD RANK	COMPANY	ADVERTISING	SALES	ADV. AS % OF SALES
3	Sears, Roebuck & Co.	379,312,500	17,514,000,000	2.1
6	K mart Corp.	287,095,100	12,731,145,000	2.3
38	J. C. Penney Co.	122,000,000	11,274,000,000	1.1

Soaps, Cleansers (and Allied)

AD RANK	COMPANY	ADVERTISING	SALES	ADV. AS % OF SALES
1	Procter & Gamble	614,900,000	10,772,186,000	5.7
23	Unilever U.S. Inc.	160,000,000	2,124,000,000	7.5
37	Colgate-Palmolive Co.	122,500,000	4,494,000,000	2.7
60	Clorox Co.	72,590,000	565,400,000	12.8
90	S. C. Johnson & Son	40,204,000	650,000,000	6.2

Soft Drinks

AD RANK	COMPANY	ADVERTISING	SALES	ADV. AS % OF SALES
11	PepsiCo Inc.	212,000,000	5,090,567,000	4.2
18	Coca-Cola Co.	169,271,000	4,961,400,000	3.4

Telephone Service Equipment

AD RANK	COMPANY	ADVERTISING	SALES	ADV. AS % OF SALES
9	American Telephone & Telegraph	219,756,300	45,408,078,000	0.4
32	International Telephone & Telegraph	132,400,000	17,197,423,000	0.8

Tobacco

AD RANK	COMPANY	ADVERTISING	SALES	ADV. AS % OF SALES
5	Philip Morris Inc.	291,201,500	8,302,892,000	3.5
7	R. J. Reynolds Industries	258,115,100	8,935,200,000	2.9
41	B.A.T. Industries Ltd.	116,396,600	1,440,000,000	8.1
56	American Brands	83,549,200	5,845,985,000	1.4
71	Liggett Group	59,000,000	1,055,487,000	5.6

Toiletries, Cosmetics

AD RANK	COMPANY	ADVERTISING	SALES	ADV. AS % OF SALES
8	Warner-Lambert Co.	220,242,500	3,217,208,000	6.8
12	Bristol-Myers Co.	210,600,000	2,752,777,000	7.7
13	American Home Products Corp.	206,000,000	3,649,476,000	5.6
35	Gillette Co.	126,960,200	1,984,722,000	6.4
44	Chesebrough-Pond's	107,342,000	1,174,274,000	9.1
82	Beecham Group Ltd.	46,704,500	2,300,000,000	2.0
89	Noxell Corp.	40,216,285	179,700,000	22.2

Wine, Beer and Liquor

AD RANK	COMPANY	ADVERTISING	SALES	ADV. AS % OF SALES
19	Seagram Co. Ltd.	168,000,000	2,554,096,000	6.6
22	Anheuser-Busch	160,524,000	3,263,744,000	4.9
26	Heublein Inc.	155,000,000	1,769,074,000	8.8
62	Jos. Schlitz Brewing Co.	71,551,000	894,156,000	8.0
79	Brown-Forman Distillers	50,000,000	675,823,000	7.4

Miscellaneous

AD RANK	COMPANY	ADVERTISING	SALES	ADV. AS % OF SALES
15	Gulf + Western Industries	191,500,000	6,507,000,000	2.9
20	Mobil Corp.	165,840,600	48,241,000,000	0.3
25	Johnson & Johnson	157,700,000	2,372,128,000	6.6
28	U.S. Government	146,121,273	—	—
30	Loews Corp.	144,468,300	4,065,475,000	3.6
67	Mattel Inc.	66,000,000	805,064,000	8.2
73	American Express Co.	55,431,800	4,666,500,000	1.2
76	Greyhound Corp.	53,800,000	4,708,594,000	1.1
92	Levi Strauss & Co.	38,563,200	2,103,109,000	1.8
94	Scott Paper Co.	36,834,000	1,908,107,000	1.9
98	Milton Bradley Co.	31,328,000	360,059,605	8.7
99	International Business Machines	31,073,800	22,862,776,000	0.1

year. Exhibit I shows the ranking of the leaders in terms of total ad dollars. Exhibit II shows advertising as a per cent of sales for the same companies.

The data on "measured media expenditures" in the AA report come from various statistical services and associations. These include Leading National Advertisers, the Publishers Information Bureau, Radio Advertising Bureau, Radio Expenditure Reports, Agricultural Marketing Information Service (Agricom), LNA-Broadcast Advertisers Reports, Media Records, Institute of Outdoor Advertising, and the Outdoor Advertising Association of America. All of the estimated expenditures are estimates by *Advertising Age.* (Reprinted from *Advertising Age,* September 11, 1980, by permission. Copyright 1980 by Crain Communications, Inc., publishers of *Advertising Age.*)

ALCOHOLISM AND DRUG ABUSE IN INDUSTRY

There is no shortage of figures documenting the alarming size and cost of the **drug problem** in all its forms: percentage in relation to the total adult population, man-hours lost on the job, dollar cost of loss in productivity, impact on increase in accidents, correlation with fraud and theft . . . The list is endless. Unfortunately, most of the so-called statistics reflect more emotion than solid fact, especially where hard drugs are concerned.

Statistics on **drinking** are somewhat more reliable. The National Council on Alcoholism claims that alcoholism is "the fourth major health problem in the United States." It estimates that one out of every thirteen Americans is alcoholic, and that 60 out of every 1,000 employees are handicapped in some way by alcohol. The Department of Health, Education, and Welfare estimates the cost to business (via loss in productivity, motor vehicle accidents, and direct medical costs) at close to $25 billion annually.

The *relevance* of the most reliable statistics, however, from industry's point of view is marginal. For the individual company, the problem is not so much *how many* or how high the *cost,* but the *degree of involvement* that management can realistically assume.

Moral and emotional issues aside, the broad question of corporate responsibility has undergone radical change in the past decade. For the smaller company, much of the burden of responsibility accepted by the industrial giants would be an impossible load. But on some questions, like alcohol and—more recently—drugs, a small company may eschew a formal program, but it cannot function effectively without a policy.

Background. The growth of the so-called "drug culture" during the Sixties and Seventies inevitably forced business to confront the problem on the work scene. But with little agreement on basic definitions, causes, or cures—even among the experts—business has found it difficult to develop a realistic policy for handling the use and abuse of drugs on the job.

Not much more than a decade ago, management was wrestling with a similar problem with regard to alcohol. Some companies conceded that a "problem" existed, but felt that a man's drinking habits were his own private affair and that it was best for management not to become involved. Most took the old Navy attitude of "shape up or ship out" and handled the matter strictly as a disciplinary problem. A handful of companies—most of them industrial giants—began to develop an elaborate program aimed at rehabilitation. But success stories were rare.

The real shift in attitude—and in industry's acceptance of responsibility—was based on the redefinition of alcoholism as a *medical* problem. Today, it is generally acknowledged to be an illness, and even the Federal Government has guidelines for treating absences as "sick leave"—a far cry from the moral stigma that blocked rational search for solutions earlier.

Today, most companies recognize that the best approach to alcoholism is in terms of its effect on job performance. If a man's drinking causes his performance or that of others to deteriorate, then management will take action. But the action—whether a warning, reprimand, discipline or counseling—is taken on the basis of the performance itself. In other words, the focus on personnel policy is not cure, but the more realistic goal of keeping the man *functioning effectively* on the job.

With the return of the Viet Nam veterans, industry was finally forced to face the parallels between alcohol and drugs. To some extent, companies with clearcut policies on drinking found it easier to confront the question of drugs. Certainly, the fundamental test of "effect on job performance" provides the soundest possible basis for any personnel policy with regard to drugs as well as alcoholism. But the drug problem has facets that make the question of involvement a tougher one for business.

First of all, unlike alcohol, many drugs are *illegal.* Secondly, the fog of emotion and misinformation still surrounding the subject makes rational discussion difficult, at best. The distinction between so-called hard and soft drugs, the confusion between "use" and "abuse," the disagreement over psychological dependence versus addiction—all these and more frustrate any company's efforts to write hard-and-fast rules. Moreover, the typical business organization is not equipped to cope with the severe drug problems without the use of experienced medical facilities.

Even the industrial giants with their own medical facilities have found it valuable to work out cooperative arrangements with local agencies and rehabilitation centers. Companies located in metropolitan areas have a great advantage in finding such facilities nearby.

A Five-step Policy on Drinking and Drugs. The absence of well-defined guidelines leads to *ad hoc* decisions down-the-line, opening the risk of legal complications or union problems. Experienced personnel people point out that sooner or later the drug problem presents itself, not in terms of an abstract question, but in the very personal shape of a specific employee. It is essential to have firm guidelines in each of these areas: (1) selection and hiring; (2) detection and reporting; (3) discipline; (4) suspension and termination; and (5) rehabilitation.

1. *Selection and Hiring.* The hiring procedure is the first line of defense in any program. Unfortunately, there are no air-tight tests that will screen out all users of drugs or excessive users of alcohol.

Alcoholics. Despite claims to the contrary, there are no standard tests available that can spot potential or actual alcoholics. Industry has relied, for the most part, on evidence obtained from previous employers or pieced together from personal sources. However, if the law which is applicable to Government employees, should be extended to all of industry, then discrimination against former alcoholics would be illegal.

The Hughes-Javits-Moss bill, officially called the "Comprehensive Alcohol Abuse and Alcoholism Prevention, Treatment, and Rehabilitation Act of 1970," was signed into law on January 2, 1971. It established the National Institute of Alcohol Abuse and Alcoholism within NIMH (National Institute of Mental Health) and is, in effect, a bill of rights for alcoholics. Not only does it provide for treatment and rehabilitation, it forbids the Federal Government to fire or to refuse to hire anyone *solely on the grounds of former drinking habits,* except where national security is involved.

While legislation extending similar provisions to industry is still a long way off, the passage of the Hughes-Javits-Moss bill represented a giant leap forward in public attitude toward alcohol. As such, it can safely be viewed as a signal of the direction in which things are moving.

Drug Risks. Many personnel people delude themselves that they can spot a drug user by his appearance or behavior. Pressed for telltale signs, they cite bloodshot eyes, trembling hands, unsteady gait—all symptoms that are just as commonly caused by other medical or emotional problems. What is more, they stem from a distorted picture of who and what a "drug user" is.

All the evidence indicates that marijuana, commonly known as "pot," is by far the most likely candidate for an encounter with business. To date, no technique has been developed to detect marijuana use. Even medical sources suggest that the only possible method of screening out pot smokers is through questioning of previous employers. And with the all-but-universal acceptance of marijuana as "the equivalent of a cocktail," it is increasingly unlikely that a previous employer will be inclined to pass along such information, even if he has it.

Far more serious is heroin. Some companies claim to screen out many of the potential problems related to heroin addiction by including a urinalysis in the pre-employment medical examination. These tests are not only costly and time-consuming, but drug users can evade detection by staying off the drug for seventy-two hours before submitting to examination.

Personnel people advise that unless medical examinations are a standard part of a company's existing screening procedure for all applicants, it may be impractical to institute them for the sole purpose of screening out drugs. Odds are, the potential risk will not warrant either the time or the expense involved.

In some highly sensitive spots, urinalysis may be a procedure worth remembering as a way of double-checking. Management ranks are not immune to drug risks. If a candidate balks at the suggestion of a medical examination, some companies check his record and his references carefully for other signs of a drug problem.

2. *Detection—Some Caveats.* Detection presents some touchy problems. It cannot be too strongly emphasized that supervisory personnel should not be permitted to become engaged in a witch-hunt. This is the strongest argument against circulation of a list of symptoms, or encouraging supervisors to "be on the look-out" for specific behavior. Management can minimize the potential for trouble by following these precautions, recommended by the Research Institute of America:

(1) Discourage supervisors from attempting to diagnose. Caution them against jumping to conclusions on the basis of physical symptoms.

(2) Designate a well-qualified person with whom all front-line personnel may consult in connection with any suspected case of alcoholism or drug abuse.

(3) Demonstrate an objective and unemotional attitude toward drugs by keeping disciplinary actions consistent with *other* infractions of work rules.

3. *Discipline.* The earliest successes with alcoholism were based on a policy of "constructive coercion," that is, a medical acceptance coupled with a disciplinary procedure. The company would issue a policy statement clearly stating that it regarded alcoholism as a health matter. However, if the employee failed to cooperate in going for help, it was also clearly understood that disciplinary penalties would be enforced. Medical authorities agree that the alcoholic *needs the discipline* that a company can exert on him.

Companies with formal alcoholism programs adjust their methods to the individual, usually depending upon how valuable the person is and how long he or she has been with the company. In the words of one big-company executive, "Save your real efforts for the life-time employee with hard-to-replace skills." The usual procedure is to step up the pressure: first, to *remind* the employee that help is available if he wants it; second, to *insist* that the employee see a doctor; finally, to *compel* the alcoholic to seek medical help as a *condition of employment.* Again, it is worth mentioning that the step-discipline method works best when it conforms to company policy for *other* work infractions, such as gambling or insubordination.

In general, the same procedure is followed in the case of drug use on the job. Where firms have taken a harsh, inflexible stand such as immediate dismissal for a first offense, the policy has tended to boomerang. A supervisor simply will not report what he considers "harmless" pot smoking if he knows it means automatic dismissal. He will just look the other way.

4. *Suspension and Termination.* The test of *effect on job performance* will usually dictate the point at which dismissal is unavoidable. The performance test not only removes the emotion from the final decision, but it is management's best defense against later charges of discrimination.

Drugs, however, present a touchier *legal* problem. Some companies deliberately turn their backs on the possession of marijuana rather than become entangled in the legal question. One major employer, for example, makes a distinction in its policy between legal and illegal drugs. If an employee is suspected of possession of narcotics, the company turns full information over to a local narcotics law enforcement agency. If the suspicion is confirmed, and the employee is arrested, his employment is automatically terminated.

One West Coast firm solves the problem by providing that any employee suspected of being under the influence of a drug must be referred to the company doctor. The doctor may, of course, recommend dismissal if he finds it appropriate. Refusal to visit the doctor is considered "grounds for release for insubordination."

The strictest policy was spelled out by a major metropolitan bank in a statement which reads, in part, as follows:

> Unlawful possession or sale of a dangerous drug by an employee on company premises or engaged in company business makes that employee subject to release. Use of a dangerous drug by an employee is potentially dangerous to himself and others. Any employee found to be on company premises under the influence of a dangerous drug is subject to release.

"Sensitive" industries, such as airlines, banks and retailers, take the position that the risk to their public image is too great to justify any but the strongest position against drugs. For some manufacturing plants, the motivating factor is safety. The obvious risk of accidents is reason enough for work rules against use of judgment-impairing drugs by anyone who operates high-speed or potentially dangerous machines.

But employers must be in a position to demonstrate that such risk of danger does indeed exist. In one case where an employee under the influence of marijuana was fired on the grounds that he was endangering the lives of others, a labor arbitrator ruled that there must be "*specific evidence* of actual or probable future detriment to the employer's interests above and beyond . . . understandable fears of such consequences" [1].

Whereas companies differ on where to draw the line on the possession and/or use of drugs on the job, most follow a very hard line with regard to the *sale* of drugs. No company can afford to take a lenient attitude toward the pusher. In addition to the legal considerations involved, most employers feel a responsibility to protect their workforce from the pressure and temptation which the pusher opens up. While the employer is not under legal obligation to report the pusher to law-enforcement authorities, most companies feel a moral obligation to do so.

5. *Rehabilitation.* Policies vary on how many lapses to allow a problem drinker and when the company should cut bait. The National Council on Alcoholism requires two years of sobriety before hiring ex-alcoholics on its own staff. Most companies give a man extra leeway if he is making a sincere attempt to reform. The best sign of such sincerity is membership in Alcoholics Anonymous. If he quits AA, the prognosis for rehabilitation is poor.

Realistic Objectives of Company Policy. The most successful programs are those in which the companies have designed their policy in terms of measurable standards of job performance. For management to approach either drinking problems or drug abuse on *moral grounds*—in the hope of rehabilitation and cure or, the other side of the coin, in righteous disapproval—is to doom the program from the start.

Medical and other authorities who have been working with alcoholics for years agree that neither discipline, medicine, nor psychotherapy will guarantee a solution. Many authorities prefer to use the word "control" instead of "cure" [2]. They suggest that realistic objectives should be limited to making the alcoholic behave on the job. They unanimously recommend working in cooperation with Alcoholics Anonymous, but not with the prime objective of cure. Over-optimistic expectations lead both employer and employee to frustration.

Where and how to draw the line with drugs is a more complex matter. By and large, most companies have been reluctant to acknowledge the presence of addicts on their workforce. Some, with sophisticated personnel and medical services, have recently been trying to cooperate with rehabilitation centers. Usually, seeking the help of a rehabilitation program is a condition of continued employment. No company even attempts to deal with a known addict without the full cooperation of a qualified rehabilitation agency. And most policies provide for immediate termination if the employee discontinues treatment. Evidence of long-term cures, however are rare in industry.

Need for Research. One of the roadblocks hindering the development of a rational company policy is the lack of scientific evidence of the effect of drug abuse. Even medical authorities disagree about what marijuana does to the smoker physiologically. A medical journal recently reported that: "the only two effects universally agreed on are an increase in the pulse rate and reddening of the eyes" [3]

One point often discussed but not yet adequately researched is the effect of pot smoking on driving ability. The only available controlled study, made by the Motor Vehicle Department of the State of Washington, indicated that pot smokers did as well as nonsmokers, and that alcohol drinkers made more errors than the other two groups. Yet some experts feel that driving on a marijuana "high" is potentially dangerous because marijuana induces perceptual distortions.

Studies conducted under a grant package from the National Institute of Mental Health and the Department of Transportation, probing the effects of alcohol, marijuana, Librium, and amphetamines—alone and in combinations—on driving and on attention span have been far from conclusive [4]. Dr. Sydney Cohen, Director of the Council on Alcoholism and Drug Addiction, UCLA, concedes that methadone is the best available treatment at the moment for heroin addicts. But even methadone is the focus of much controversy among medical and drug experts [5].

Until research provides clearcut evidence, the business community will find itself under increasing pressures as social acceptance of drugs grows. As facts replace biases (for and against), the problem of establishing sound company policy will be resolved.

Where to Obtain Help. Few companies are equipped to deal with alcohol or drug problems single-handed. The personnel problems are only one facet, and many medical and legal questions may require outside assistance.

Not only are the Federal laws dealing with drugs undergoing change, but state laws vary widely. Any company concerned about the possibility of drug use would be well advised to secure legal counsel and check the laws in the states in which it operates. In certain states possession of two ounces or less can bring a $1,000 fine and up to 180 days in jail; in other states, possession carries a lower penalty than a parking ticket.

In some states, company property could be in danger. In California, for example, any vehicle used in the transport of drugs is subject to confiscation.

In many communities the local police are the best source of information and assistance. Regional offices of the Bureau of Narcotics and Dangerous Drugs of the U.S. Department of Justice should be consulted in situations involving narcotics. Facilities vary from community to community, but, in general, a good starting place is word-of-mouth recommendations of business executives with experience in the problem, or medical specialists.

RUTH BURGER, Director of Human Resources Research, Research Institute of America. New York, New York

Information References

Organizations:

Alcoholics Anonymous, New York, N.Y.

National Clearing House for Alcohol Information, Rockville, Md.

National Council on Alcoholism, Inc., New York, N.Y.

Christopher D. Smithers Foundation, Inc., New York, N.Y.

Veterans Administration, Alcohol and Drug Dependent Service, Washington, D.C.

(The above agencies have regional affiliates in many cities. Check local telephone book.)

For information and assistance in handling drug problems, consult phone book for regional offices of the Bureau of Narcotics and Dangerous Drugs. Local hospitals may also suggest qualified help. Community Action groups may be able to provide information, if not direct assistance.

Texts and Special Publications:

"Alcohol and Alcoholism," Public Health Service Publication No. 1640. National Institute of Mental Health, Chevy Chase, Md. 20015, for single copies. Quantity copies, Government Printing Office, Washington, D.C. 20402.

Blume, Sheila B., "Confidentiality of Medical Records in Alcohol-Related Problems "New York, National Council on Alcoholism, 1976.

"Dealing with Alcoholism in the Workplace," *Report No. 784,* New York, The Conference Board, 1980.

Follmann, Joseph F., Jr., "Alcoholics and Business (Problems, Costs, Solutions)," New York, Amacon Div. American Management Association, 1976.

"Manual on Alcoholism," Chicago, American Medical Association,

National Clearing House for Drug Abuse Information, publications, Chevy Chase, Md.

"A Company Program on Alcoholism—Basic Outline," New York, Christopher D. Smithers Foundation, rev., 1974.

Trice, Harrison M., "Alcoholism in Industry—Modern Procedures," New York, Christopher D. Smithers Foundation, rev., 1974.

———, and Roman, Paul M., "Spirits & Demons at Work: Alcohol and Other Drugs on the Job," ILR Paperback No. 11, Ithaca, N.Y., "What to Do About the Employee with a Drinking Problem?," Long Grove, Ill.,

New York State School of Industrial & Labor Relations, Cornell University, 1978.

References Cited

[1] Vulcan Materials Co., John C. Shearer, Arbitrator, March 18, 1971.

[2] "Treating Alcoholism," OHEW Publication No. (ADM), Washington, D.C., reprinted 1979.

[3] *Medical World News.* July 16, 1971.

[4] Trice, Harrison M., and Roman, Paul M., "Spirits and Demons at Work: Alcohol and Other Drugs on the Job, (*See above*).

[5] *Human Behavior,* January, 1973.

Cross Reference: *Occupational Health.*

ALTERNATIVE WORK SCHEDULES

The concerns of managers, legislators, economists, and psychologists over productivity and QUALITY OF WORKING LIFE issues have been reflected in the increased interest in work scheduling innovations. **Alternative Work Schedules,** it is felt by many, address both issues of organizational effectiveness and individual satisfaction, and as such have been incorporated into theories currently popular in the literature. For example, researchers have included alternative work schedules in their theory-building for quality of work life models (Ronen [1], Rosow [2]), career development models (Van Maanen and Schein [3]), and life-cycle stages within the context of the organization (Cohen and Gadon [4]).

Although the consideration of alternative work schedules may be limited in some cases by factors such as production processes and task interdependence, union contracts, and Federal and state legislation, creative managers not bound by the constraints of traditional management philosophy have found sufficient space for manipulating the fixed work schedule. The more accepted and popularized alternatives include the compressed, or four-day week, part-time work, and job sharing, and the many variations of flexible work hours. Each of these schedules represents variations in one or both of two dimensions of work scheduling. The first is the *number* of hours worked during a given period of time—usually a day. The second is the *timing* of these hours of work—that is, when the required number of hours are scheduled within the work period.

The number of hours required is a decision that is rarely left to the individual employee; it is dictated either by a provision of law or a particular organizational policy. Timing, on the other hand, is the dimension which allows sufficient flexibility to enable the individual some freedom of choice. Organizational constraints and task characteristics will determine the alternative work scheduling variations along these dimensions which are feasible.

The Compressed Work Week. The compressed work week (CWW) is an alternative work schedule designed to allow employees to work the standard number of weekly hours in less than five days. The most common compressed schedule is a ten-hour day, four-day week, often designated as the 4/40, although the number of hours worked per day and days worked per week can vary considerably.

The basic concept behind the compressed week is a trade-off between the number of days worked per week and the number of hours worked per day: for the opportunity to work *less* days per week, the employee agrees to work more hours per day. However, beyond the designation of the total number of hours worked per week, and the number of days in which the employee reports to work, there can be many variations in scheduling. For example, if a firm remains open five or six days per week for customers, employees on a compressed week must be assigned to staggered schedules, where different groups work different days, in order to ensure full coverage. One group of employees may work Monday through Thursday, while a second group may report to work on Tuesday through Friday. In general, it should be kept in mind that the compressed work week describes the employee's timetable, which will probably differ from the firm's hours of availability for interfacing with its environment.

For the employee, the CWW does not offer a choice of schedule, although it does offer the potential for better utilization of leisure time for recreation, personal business, and family life. On the job, the extended workday and possible reduction in the work force present on a given day have the potential for creating changes in job aspects such as the delegation of authority and task responsibility, cooperation, and increased job knowledge.

For managers, the fact that only a portion of the work force is available on certain days has implications for maintaining coverage and supervision, delegating authority, and disseminating information.

The concept of the compressed work week first gained acceptance in the late 1960s and early 1970s in the United States, and experienced a period of rapid growth in the early 1970s, leveling off by 1974. The Bureau of Labor Statistics reported approximately 650,000 employees working under some sort of compressed schedule in 1974, 750,000 in 1975, and about the same number in 1976. This represents roughly one per cent of all full-time nonfarm employees (Bureau of Labor Statistics, in 1977). Figures issued for mid-1977 indicate no further increase (*The New York Times,* 1977).

Despite the potential appeal of the CWW, certain environmental factors have limited its rate of adoption. For example, state and Federal legislation designed to protect the worker's right to overtime payments have limited the number of hours which can be worked per day without overtime. (Recent legislation has relaxed these laws for Civil Service employees, in order to allow experimentation with alternative work schedules.) Some unions have also been negative toward the CWW, viewing it as a threat to overtime payments. Others, however, have been more receptive to the system, regarding it as a step toward a further reduction in work hours and an eventual four-day, 32-hour work week.

Data on the Compressed Work Week. The data described here are based on a review by Ronen and Primps of studies published during the last decade [5]. In general, it appears that the compressed work week influences those extrinsic job facets which contribute to satisfaction with the work environment and the organization. There was also evidence that employees with low job satisfaction are more positive in their attitudes toward the CWW. Within the context of a compensatory model, the

CWW can be considered in terms of its ability to compensate for negative job aspects through a provision for additional or rearranged leisure time. The perception of a favorable trade-off is dependent upon the employee's leisure orientation: whether it is preferable to have an additional day per week of leisure in exchange for hours per day of work.

The impact of the CWW on performance and productivity is unclear, mainly because of the lack of objective measurements in the studies conducted thus far. When employees report their opinions concerning the impact of the CWW on performance, they tend to report favorable results. The few objective reports available, however, are less conclusive, indicating no changes associated with the schedule in this area.

In terms of membership behavior, there is stronger evidence to conclude that absenteeism is decreased. However, serious attention should be given to fatigue, since it was found to be a problem in all of the studies measuring this aspect. The decreases in absenteeism may not be sustained over the long term because of problems associated with fatigue. Further evidence is provided by the finding that employees in jobs making low physical demands tend to hold more favorable attitudes to the CWW.

Some clarification as to potential CWW outcomes can be provided when demographic variables are considered in the context of life cycle theory. For instance, there was some evidence that women, who tended to use their extra day off for home and family-oriented activities, were less satisfied with the new schedule than men, who were more likely to pursue leisure and recreational outlets.

From these study results, it is clear that the CWW influences the individual's work domain, particularly in terms of its effects on work attitudes, and attitudes toward the schedule itself. However, there were also cases in which the implementation of the CWW represented more than a change in work scheduling and became, in addition, an inducement for substantive changes in work process associated with supervisory styles.

With respect to the non-work domain, the impact may be substantial as well: we already have evidence that there are differences in attitudes toward the schedule based on differences in leisure orientation. The impact on organizational effectiveness is less conclusive, although there is little evidence of a decrease in productivity and substantial support for a decrease in absenteeism.

Part-Time Work. Part-time employment cannot be considered a recent innovation in work scheduling since it has been an accepted and popular alternative work schedule for many years. As of May, 1977, part-time workers constituted 22% of the non-agricultural work force—that is, 13 million employees worked less than a full-time schedule. However, the increased demand associated with the influx into the labor force of working mothers, older adults, students, and other groups with special needs has required employes to evaluate the availability and the nature of part-time work.

Part-time employment can be considered regular employment in which the employee works less than the full-time schedule. The schedule is not temporary, intermittent, or casual. Part-time employment is most common among sales, clerical, and laborer jobs, and in the trade and service industries. It is less common in areas such as management and the trades (Nollen [6]). A recent innovation in the part-time sector is the notion of job sharing. Job sharing can be defined as a situation where two employees are responsible for fulfilling the duties of one job.

There are four main categories of part-time workers which should be differentiated, as they represent different populations and fill different needs. First, one must distinguish between temporary and permanent part-time workers. Temporary part-time workers would include former full-time workers who have decreased their hours of work for a period of time. Typical would be a working mother who has temporarily decreased work hours to facilitate child-rearing responsibilities. Alternatively, an individual may enter the work force on a temporary part-time basis, such as students holding part-time jobs. Permanent part-time workers are those who have chosen part-time work as the optimal fit between work and non-work domains.

The second area of distinction is that between voluntary and involuntary part-time work. Involuntary part-time workers are those who would prefer full-time work, but are unable to find full-time employment, based on skills and education levels. Members of this group are typically young and often members of minority groups.

Of the total part-time work force, 64% are

regular, voluntary part-time employees. Further, there is competition for part-time permanent positions—these jobs are clearly desirable or necessary for many who wish to work. Despite the competition for such jobs, however, part-time workers are often perceived by managers as extrinsically or economically motivated, less than committed to their jobs, and lacking in career-orientation. This has been reflected in the lack of benefits and the paucity of professional or managerial level jobs available to this sector of the labor force. Recent legislation in the Federal government requiring the Office of Personnel Management to make available part-time jobs at all levels and the pressure from many professionals (especially women) for part-time opportunities should help to improve these attitudes.

In terms of differences in attitudes and effectiveness associated with part-time workers, there are virtually no systematic studies available which attempt to measure such aspects.

Flexitime. Flexitime is an alternative work schedule which grants the employee a certain freedom to choose the times of arrival and departure. The degree of variation possible is usually defined by the organization. The simplest variation of the system allows the employee to determine starting and finishing times within a certain time range set by the employer, provided that the employee works the contracted daily attendance hours. Conditions governing the degree of flexibility may include the total number of hours the company is operative during the day, the hours an employee is required to be present, and the level of interdependence between job, between departments, and with suppliers and customers.

It should be emphasized here that the choice given to the employee is restricted to variations in times present at work and the distribution of working hours, but does *not* apply to the total number of working hours required by the employment contract. This condition remains unaltered and is mandated by the organization. Further, flexitime will not alter current management policies regarding vacations or sick leave allowances.

By allowing the employee to create, through scheduling, a better fit between individual needs and the work environment, many other aspects of the work experience can be affected. Flexitime has the potential to influence the degree of autonomy experienced by the employee through increased participation in decision making and responsibility for maintaining coverage for absent employees. Group cohesiveness and orientation toward the organization's objective may be enhanced, as employees find it necessary to interact in a cooperative mode to maintain work processes. In addition to its potential to improve the quality of work life, flexitime can help to improve the fit between the work and personal domains of the employee.

Despite the many benefits of flexitime associated with improved quality of work life and of life in general, the actual reason for the adoption of flexitime in Europe was a practical organizational need created by the external environment. A serious traffic problem arose in the Ottobrunn Research and Development plant of the German Messerschmitt Bolkow Blohm aerospace company in 1967, due to congestion on the local routes connecting the major highways to the plant. A personnel manager invented the concept of flexible working hours to alleviate this problem.

Data on Flexitime Implementation. It is difficult to estimate exactly how many employees in organizations are currently using flexitime systems because of its rapid rate of adoption. As of 1979, however, at least 400,000 employees in the United States were on some version of flexible scheduling. Almost half of these were public sector employees. A 1978 study by Nollen and Martin [7] indicated that an estimated 13% of all non-government organizations have some type of flexitime program for 50 or more employees. These authors projected a national usage rate of 17% in 1979.

A compilation by Ronen [1] of data from twelve private-sector and 25 public-sector organizations on various forms of flexitime schedules indicated the following:

(1) There is some evidence that the organization, as a unit, can improve its level of effectiveness through flexitime implementation. Objective data on productivity, and subjective data on performance and interpersonal relations, support this conclusion. However, more systematic data collection is necessary in this area before the full effects are known.

(2) Individual employees have reported improved control over work scheduling and work process, as well as an increase in uninterrupted work periods. These benefits contribute to improved organizational as well as individual effectiveness.

(3) With respect to membership behavior,

absenteeism can be significantly reduced and tardiness virtually eliminated following the implementation of a flexitime schedule.

(4) Employee attitudes toward the job and the work environment are improved, although supervisors/managers tend to be somewhat less positive.

(5) Employees experience an improvement in the interrelationship between their work and non-work domains—specifically, the impact of work on personal life. This includes increased flexibility in allocating time for recreation and leisure, and educational and community activities, as well as the opportunity to take a more active role in family life and child rearing.

(6) Flexitime has the potential to improve commuting conditions and the employee's state of relaxation upon arrival. However, the data accumulated thus far is inconclusive. Additional studies are necessary to confirm this hypothesis.

Conclusions. Alternative work schedules are becoming more important as organizations focus on ways to maintain and increase productivity levels, and individuals attempt to cope with economic pressures by returning to or remaining in the labor force. Although the outcomes associated with alternative work schedules are positive, both for the individual and the organization, there are a few problem areas associated with this change which can be avoided through rigorous planning and well-thought-out implementation. Organization change techniques should be utilized—especially for the training and preparation of first-line supervisors. Often, this particular group is less receptive toward the concept and needs special attention.

In general, *all* levels of employees are more receptive to a new concept if they have had the opportunity to be included during the planning stages, and to contribute their ideas. Useful insights may be obtained which might be overlooked at higher levels of management. In the same context, it is important to design *each* alternative schedule installation around the demands of the immediate work environment. This may mean different designs within an organization, or even within a department.

SIMCHA RONEN, PH.D., Associate Professor of Management and Organizational Behavior, Graduate School of Business Administration, New York University, New York, New York

References Cited

[1] Ronen, S., "Flexible Working Hours: An Innovation in Quality of Work Life," New York, McGraw-Hill, 1981.

[2] Rosow, J. M. and Kerr, C., eds., 'Work in America—the Decade Ahead," New York, Van Nostrand Reinhold, 1979.

[3] Van Maanen, J. and Schein, E. H., "Career Development," in Hackman, J. R. and Suttle, J. L., eds., "Improving Life at Work," Santa Monica, Calif., Goodyear, 1977.

[4] Cohen, A. R. and Gadon, H., "Alternative Work Schedules: Integrating Individual and Organizational Needs," Reading, Mass., Addison-Wesley, 1978.

[5] Ronen, S. and Primps, S. B., "The Compressed Work Week as Organizational Change: Behavioral Attitudinal Outcomes," *Academy of Management Review,* 1981. vol. 6, 61–74.

[6] Nollen, S., "New Patterns of Work," New York, Work in America Institute, 1979.

[7] Nollen, S. and Martin, Virginia H., "Alternative Work Schedules: Flexitime," New York, AMACOM, 1978.

Cross Reference: *Personnel Administration.*

ANNUAL REPORTS

The Borden Company is credited with publishing, in 1858, the first **Annual Report** to give stockholders more information than balance sheet and income statement figures. AT&T followed suit in 1885. But the first really illustrated and comprehensive annual report was issued by U.S. Steel, under the presidency of Judge Elbert H. Gary, in 1902. In the same year, Monsanto Chemical and Swift & Company also began issuing informative annual reports.

However, these were the exception in corporation practice. Many companies made no reports to stockholders at all, while issuing the bare minimum of figures. In 1895, the New York Stock Exchange recommended to the companies listed on the Exchange that they issue annual reports. In 1900 it requested all companies applying for listing to publish a yearly statement. Since that time, there has been a gradual but considerable improvement in corporation annual reports, but there is still a long way to go.

The magazine, *Financial World,* holds a yearly contest for the best annual reports in 100 industries. A recent contest drew 5,000 entries—annual reports of which corporation managements were proud. Yet only 1,918 of these—less than 40% of the entrants—met the minimum requirements for modern annual reports: a comprehensive text, adequate financial information, and good design.

One of the problems seems to be that many executives involved in producing annual reports still see their primary audience as a combination of a sophisticated financial analyst and

"Aunt Jane"—a stockholder with no financial background. They are concerned to get across their message to this audience but are oppressed by the short, frantic production time available between the accountants' releasing final figures and the oncoming annual meeting. However, in this haste the fact should not be overlooked that the audience for annual reports has been changing—and reports must be shaped to meet its tastes.

The Stockholder Audience. According to the Shareowner Census by the New York Stock Exchange, the stockholder audience numbered 25,200,000 in 1980. This is down from a peak of 32,500,000 in 1972—but still twice as large as it was in 1960. The typical shareholder is 53 years old, works in a professional or technical occupation, had a household income of $19,000 in 1975, and has had four years or more of higher education.

A recent SEC survey of small stockholders (owning less than 1,000 shares in a company) shows some of the problems in reaching this audience. The survey found that 70% of these stockholders owned shares in six or more companies, while almost half (49%) owned shares in eleven or more companies. With most of these companies having December 31 fiscal years, and issuing their reports between March 1–31, this means stiff competition for the average stockholder's attention.

How are annual reports getting across to stockholders today? A survey by Graphics Institute of a thousand women stockholders revealed that only about one third of the women read thoroughly the annual reports they received. The vast majority of them leafed through their reports or just read parts. And 6% did not bother to read the annual report at all. The SEC survey produced quite similar results. About 5% of the stockholders stated that they didn't bother to read the reports they received, and only 26% claimed to read their annual reports thoroughly.

One should not take a defeatist attitude that this large stockholder audience will not read any type of report. Research shows that financial management can compete successfully with the mass media for the attention of the stockholder audience if it will use the communication tools developed by the mass media.

Approaches and Techniques. What is called for is the use of such devices as getting a lot of the story across visually, with good photographs and charts . . . captioning these visual elements crisply . . . summarizing and highlighting the text with newsy information-packed headlines, subheads, and callouts . . . and putting the whole package together in a professionally well designed format.

Many corporations are still issuing reports with conservative, all-type front covers. But a survey by Opinion Research Corporation has shown that a pictorial cover treatment scores widely, giving the overwhelming majority of stockholders a favorable impression of the company. Audience reaction shows over 60% using words such as *progressive . . . sound investment . . . active,* to describe their impression of a company based on a pictorial front cover. But where a concern uses an all-type front cover, it produces no impression, or a negative impression, in a majority of stockholders: 52% vote *no impression,* while only 14% say *progressive* and 15% say *conservative . . . dignified.*

Inside Matter. Once inside the covers of the annual report, the audience wants good writing. (The survey of a thousand women stockholders showed that 34% of them said the quality of writing influences the amount of attention they give to a company's report.) But an astonishing 70% said that the use of illustrations, charts and photos, was the prime influence in the amount of attention they gave a company's annual report. This agrees with a General Motors stockholder survey which showed that 71% of the stockholders welcome charts and diagrams—while only 5% do not.

Graphs and Charts. If charts are used, they should be made as pictorial as possible, especially if the report is intended for employees. A survey by The Borden Company set up an experiment which involved presenting financial data to employees via six different types of charts and tables. A chart incorporating illustrative symbols was found to be the most successful; the symbols seem to help the employee remember the charted facts, according to Borden's Public Relations Department.

Color. Occasionally a management official reports that he reversed the trend and went back to "the good old, simple black and white report"—and that his stockholders have not objected. But 68% of the women queried in the survey previously mentioned stated that color adds to the interest and readability of the annual report.

The Employee Audience. Surveys have shown that the great majority of employees definitely want to receive the company's annual report. A good many corporations meet this wish of employees for copies of the company report by distributing or making it available to all employees. Others follow the practice of issuing special annual reports to employees. Although these can be tailored to the special needs of the employer audience—and the special points management wants to make to them—this procedure also raises a question in some employee's minds as to whether management is withholding information from them that it is giving to stockholders, or perhaps patronizing them by sugar-coating their information.

The Financial Management Audience. It is sometimes alleged for financial analysts that graphics are a waste of time, that all they are interested in are the figures and perhaps the President's Letter. However, a much different point of view has been expressed by well known institutional investment managers, who are now responsible for 70% of the public volume on the New York Stock Exchange. Speaking at recent Annual Report Workshops conducted by Graphics Institute, Monte Gordon, vice president and director of the Dreyfus Group of Mutual Funds and Loren Ross, intreasurer and investment manager of the Russell Sage Foundation, made the point that good design and graphics give them a feeling for company/management style, and enable them to absorb a company's story more quickly. Burt Greenwald, vice president, marketing services of National Securities & Research Corp., cited comments such as the following from his security analysts about specific reports: ". . . photography is superb" (Northrop) . . . "meaningful graphics" (General Dynamics) . . . pictorial display and financial data are excellent" (American Standard) . . . "pictures and employment of Board members are presented. I think that a presentation like this is important for the shareholders" (FNMA).

HERBERT C. ROSENTHAL, President, Graphics Institute, Inc., New York, New York

Information References

American Institute of Certified Public Accountants.
S.D. Scott Printing Company, "Speaking Out on Annual Reports," New York, 1977.
U.S. Security & Exchange Commission, "Individual Investor Opinion Survey."

Cross Reference: *Financial Public Relations.*

ANTITRUST LEGISLATION

Antitrust Legislative Provisions in the United States generally have as their purpose the improvement and encouragement of competition. The principal antitrust provisions are encompassed in certain Federal statutory provisions. In addition, there are also state enactments in the antitrust area which in some cases provide extensive additional coverage. The implications of these antitrust provisions make it mandatory that businessmen be familiar with and abide by their strictures.

Antitrust regulation in the United States is substantially different from that found in other countries. As such, antitrust, in addition to governing competition in this country, may by its presence have an effect on competition between United States and foreign business. Foreign antitrust regulations have different coverage than is the case with United States laws. Businessmen doing business in Europe should be generally familiar with the antitrust provisions of the Treaty of Rome which was adopted in connection with the establishment of the EUROPEAN ECONOMIC COMMUNITY. And, if doing business in Japan, Australia, Canada or certain other foreign countries, businessmen should also be aware of the presence of antitrust regulations in these countries.

In other words, antitrust in the United States is unique because of its pervasive coverage. This coverage is not reflected in extensive detailed regulations. The Internal Revenue Code and, perhaps to a lesser extent, the Federal securities laws and regulations, provide extensive and detailed provisions to govern their respective areas. Not so with antitrust. The Federal antitrust provisions are really quite brief. The real meaning and implications of these provisions may only be gleaned from a careful review and understanding of their judicial interpretations. Interpretation of the Federal antitrust provisions is the work of the Federal district courts. Hence, there often are varying interpretations, and so the vagueness and uncertainty of the statutory provisions continue in the court interpretations. This vagueness is normally only resolved by the Supreme Court of the United States—unless, as is sometimes the case, its own decisions raise further questions and uncertainties.

Although the antitrust laws focus on the protection of competition, there has been frequent disagreement as to the meaning of competition, whether the laws are designed to protect competition or competitors, and whether the laws really do anything to improve the role of competition in United States business.

Historical Background. An understanding of

the antitrust regulations today requires an appreciation of their development. Generally, there have been three major merger movements in the United States. In each of these periods, the attitudes of the public and Congress have differed on how extensive antitrust regulation should be. The first movement developed in the late 1800s and early 1900s. At about that time, so-called trusts were being organized in the sugar, whiskey, oil, and other industries. The trust was generally an all-inclusive term used to refer to pools (whereby a number of companies informally agreed that certain aspects of their business could be regulated by a committee or by some other group), voting trusts, or holding companies. While there were differences in form, trusts had the purpose of combining the management of numerous companies for certain purposes, such as pricing decisions.

The trusts aroused the intense criticism of business, farm, and labor groups. These three groups claimed that the trusts prevented price competition and often stifled innovation. Although the basic antitrust statute—the Sherman Act—had been enacted in 1890, it really had not been enforced. This criticism brought about increasing enforcement. Many trusts were found to be illegal under that Act, including ones involving the Standard Oil Company of New Jersey and the American Tobacco Company. This public clamor, along with the enforcement by President Theodore Roosevelt (who became known as the "Trust Buster") under the Sherman Act, started antitrust enforcement as it is known today.

In 1914, Congress enacted the Clayton Act and the Federal Trade Commission Act—two statutes designed to include areas not covered by the Sherman Act. Surprisingly, it was at about this time that the second major movement commenced. This movement ran from approximately the beginning of World War I to the end of the 1920s. There seemed at this stage to be a more favorable attitude toward mergers; there was special emphasis on stability rather than on free competition. As in the first merger movement period, mergers in the second movement were largely of a horizontal type, although the diversification trend seemed to have a start in this period.

During this period, the merger-minded firms seemed to have the aim of achieving a dominant position in a particular product market. However, in the second period, acquisitions began to be made outside of a particular product or industry market. The business depression starting at the end of the 1920s appeared to cause a rethinking of the oft-mentioned efficiency of large corporations, and the impact of the concentration of firms was beginning to be recognized. This questioning of the advantages of bigness, and the appreciation of the dangers of the increasing level of concentration, caused the merger pendulum to swing in the opposite direction.

The third major merger movement began during World War II and continues today. During World War II—as was the case during World War I—there was the feeling that large business and stability were essential. Although the Clayton Act was amended in 1950 to close certain existing loopholes, the third movement continued largely unabated. The principal feature of this movement was the widespread development of the conglomerate merger. While conglomerate mergers accounted for less than 40% of all mergers in the late 1940s, more than 80% of mergers in recent years have been conglomerate mergers. This movement really has three phases. The first was the modest period during World War II and the 1950s, the second was the booming period in the mid and late sixties, reaching its peak in 1969 when 6,107 mergers or acquisitions were announced, and the third continues through today, marked by a decline in the total number of mergers (2,128 in 1979) but an increase in large acquisitions, as illustrated by the number of mergers involving a purchase price in excess of $100 million. In 1975, there were 14 such mergers. By 1976, there were 39, 41 in 1977, 80 in 1978, and 83 in 1979.

Antitrust and Economics. Antitrust, to an extent not found in any other area of law, is a combination of law and economics. As discussed further below, certain conduct and activities are *per se* unlawful, and no resort to any factual or economic analysis of competitive injury is required. However, in all other cases this analysis is essential. Perhaps one hindrance to the full cooperation between law and economics in this analysis is nomenclature. For example, it is important to separate the legal and economic meanings of terms such as "competition," "monopoly," and "discrimination." Economic monopoly would not necessarily indicate a violation of law. Whether absence of competition is contrary to the interests of the antitrust laws would depend not only on the way this absence of competition developed, but also on whether this was competition in the "perfect," "pure," "workable," or "effective" sense.

Another obstacle is that the law deals with activities and conduct which may impair competition, while economics deals with results of certain models or circumstances. There are certainly other differences in approach which may present obstacles to this cooperation. However, greater communication between the two professions can nevertheless be useful in improving antitrust policy and enforcement if the differences in approach are better understood.

Characteristics of Size. As evident from the foregoing, any discussion of antitrust, its background, and policy involves initially a review of the major merger movements. Each of these merger movements has brought about extensive dialogue as to the significance of size, and its advantages and disadvantages. The size of firms has a direct bearing on price competition which is a concern of the Sherman Act in nonmerger contexts. And, of course, pricing is the principal concern of the Robinson-Patman Act, which was adopted in 1936 as an amendment to the Clayton Act. (See PRICING: LEGAL ASPECTS.)

For years economists and others have probed the strengths and weaknesses of size. Generally, this probing has been caused by a concern about the growing concentration of firms, and has focused on size and its relation to pricing, innovation, and efficiency. It should be noted initially that economists' views differ on the definition of concentration, and on exactly how this should be measured. In other words, should concentration be defined in terms of assets, sales, financial resources, employment, or output? Despite this disagreement, the Bureau of Census reports concentration ratios for manufacturers in terms of value added by manufacture, and these reports have been utilized by Congressional committees responsible for antitrust matters. In addition, concentration, at least when measured in terms of assets, has increased. By the end of 1979, the 90 largest industrial corporations controlled over 60% of the total assets held by all manufacturing corporations. In 1968 this share was held by the 200 largest corporations, while in 1941 this share was held by the 1,000 largest firms.

With respect to size and pricing, some economists regard size as being pro-competitive. They feel that size does not stifle price competition and that it does not bring about price rigidity. Pricing policy of large firms, they feel, remains sensitive to market influences. For example, a large firm can better provide market leadership of a pro-competitive nature by making periodic price reductions. The contrary view, of course, is that size does cause price rigidity and, in some cases, administered pricing. Further, some economists say that periodic pricing reductions are often only for the purpose of further entrenching the dominance of the large firm and often result in the elimination of smaller competitors. Certain other economists, in taking a more impartial view, emphasize the difficulty of ascertaining the real influence of size on the pricing by large firms.

Similar disagreement is found in the area of size and innovation. Some economists regard large firms as being better able to finance innovations to the marketplace. They also feel that more "mature" pricing of new products will result from their development by large firms. Others disagree. They say that innovation by large firms begets integration and further concentration, and that in some cases innovation by large firms may not occur. For example, they say, large firms may resist innovation because it may lead to obsolescense of expensive existing facilities.

Finally, perhaps the most difficult inquiry is the one relating to size and efficiency. While there are some who regard size as bringing efficiency because of the economic ability to remove inferior managers, to stimulate superior managers properly and, in the case of conglomerate corporations, to coordinate inter-corporate functions, others stress that large firms do not seem to be outperforming small firms by any tests now available, while gaining inordinate and repressive power. Hearings involving economic concentration before the Senate Subcommittee on Antitrust and Monopoly heard testimony that the third major merger movement was causing the disappearance of healthy medium-sized firms—the so-called "viable middle tier"—which for the most part had consisted of healthy firms making good profits. While one view states that such disappearance inhibits the entry of new small companies into the marketplace and could lead to a major change in our concept of the free enterprise system, the opposing view points to such acquisitions as encouraging small companies by providing them with the incentive of having opportunities to sell successful enterprises and reap the benefits of their efforts.

Federal Antitrust Provisions. Generally, the Federal antitrust provisions consist of the Sherman Act, the Clayton Act, along with its Robinson-Patman Act amendment, and the Federal

Trade Commission Act. In addition, there are a multitude of statutory provisions governing specific areas such as the regulation of mergers in the transportation, aviation, broadcasting, power, and securities industries. For example the Webb-Pomerene Export Trade Act of 1918 grants domestic export associations a qualified exemption from the Sherman Act, to encourage exports and to permit domestic manufacturers to join together and effectively compete with foreign cartels.

Sherman Act. Section 1 of the Sherman Act forbids contracts, combinations, and conspiracies in restraint of trade or commerce. This general language of the statute can only be fully understood on the basis of its judicial interpretation. For example, an early decision concluded that the language was intended to reach only unreasonable restraints. Over the years, decisions of the courts have delineated certain forms of activities which violate the statute, and which are deemed unreasonable without any showing of additional facts. No showing of any adverse impact on competition is required; it is presumed. This category would include agreements or undertakings between competitors (i.e., of a horizontal nature) relating to price fixing, allocation of customers, division of territories, and group boycotts. These are called *per se* offenses. Other horizontal activities may violate the Act upon a showing of unreasonableness. The Sherman Act also applies to relations between a seller and his customer (i.e., of a vertical nature). These would include the requirement by the seller that the customer confine its sales efforts to a designated territory, the seller's determination of the customer's resale price and certain forms of tie-in arrangements. The last two examples are *per se* offenses while the first example violates the Act upon a showing of unreasonableness.

In recent instances, Section 1 has been utilized to strike down certain reciprocal dealing arrangements (generally a sales technique used to increase sales by virtue of purchases or purchasing potential). Enforcement with respect to reciprocity has been especially widespread in the steel and motion picture theater industries. In addition, at the present time, Sherman Act rules are being re-examined in their application to the patent and know-how licensing areas. Section 1 also has particular significance in its application to a wide variety of trade association activities.

The Sherman Act's other important provision—Section 2—pertains to monopolization and attempts and conspiracies to monopolize. While the mere possession of monopoly power is not unlawful, monopoly power combined with a "willful acquisition or maintenance of that power" violates the Sherman Act. (At the present time, many leading authorities have recommended that this "conduct requirement" for proving monopolization under Section 2 of the Sherman Act be eliminated in cases attacking "persistent and substantial monopoly power.") The most common form of relief granted in a Section 2 case has been injunctive relief designed to increase access to the monopolized market, thereby allowing the natural marketplace forces to slowly eliminate the monopoly position. In an extreme case, dissolution has been granted.

Clayton Act. The Clayton Act, aside from the Robinson-Patman amendment, is important generally because of Sections 3 and 7. Section 3 deals with tie-ins and exclusive dealing arrangements. Except with respect to certain tie-in arrangements, these activities are forbidden only if they are found to have the requisite adverse impact on competition. Section 3, in dealing with exclusive dealing arrangements, also sets the permissible ambits for requirements contracts.

Section 7 of the Clayton Act governs the legality of certain mergers and acquisitions. To be barred by the Act, they must have the requisite adverse effect on competition in a particular product and geographic market. The Act is applicable to horizontal (between competitors or potential competitors), vertical (between customers and suppliers), and conglomerate (involving no horizontal or vertical contacts) mergers. Of critical importance in any Section 7 proceeding is the determination of the relevant product and geographic market. This concept of the market is essential; the tests of competitive impact must have a context in which to be applied. In determining whether a product market is segmented, consideration will usually be given to the product's peculiar characteristics and uses, whether it has distinct customers and pricing, and different physical characteristics, and the extent to which other products should be regarded as interchangeable with the product. In many cases, the product market definition will be especially difficult to resolve.

Enforcement in the horizontal and vertical merger areas has been extensive, and this may be part of the reason for the large number of conglomerate mergers in the 1960s and 1970s.

Although the Act was always thought to be applicable to conglomerate mergers, the tests of illegality were vague and untried prior to the late 1960s. Also, the government's lack of success in challenging conglomerate mergers may be part of the continued attractiveness of this form of merger. Since 1974, the Government has been unsuccessful in all of its twelve challenges of conglomerate mergers.

The booming conglomerate merger trend of the mid and late Sixties could be explained by the normal merger incentives, such as efficiency, increased research and technology benefits, greater opportunity for profitability, better utilization and lower cost of capital, and the like. (See MERGERS AND ACQUISITIONS.) In addition, acquiring firms in this period clearly had their eyes on increasing earnings per share. Utilization of the pooling of interests method of accounting provided the opportunity of reporting substantial increases in earnings per share. In addition, an acquiring firm's earnings per share could be increased by acquisition of a firm where the price paid for the acquired firm per dollar of its earnings was less than the price-earnings ratio of the acquiring firm. These incentives for merger were aided by favorable tax laws and by large available financing during this period. As the conglomerate period advanced into the late Sixties, large established firms found themselves being threatened with takeovers by small firms, wherein their shareholders would receive in exchange stock, warrants, or debentures (sometimes called "funny money") of the smaller "raiding" firms. These take-overs were normally followed by substantial changes in management and employee relations—all of which some felt represented substantial adverse social effects of these transactions.

Generally, the mere institution of proceedings and the settlement favorable to the Government of certain of these actions probably has done much to curtail and dampen the conglomerate merger activity. However, a falling stock market, revised tax and accounting rules, and the slackening of available funds for financing these transactions had much to do with slowing the conglomerate boom.

The mergers of the 1970s were viewed more as a normal function of the business than the mergers in the boom of the 1960s. More and more, the objects of tender offers became publicly held companies. This was made possible by the same falling stock market that helped end the "boom" days. With stock prices for a publicly held company falling or remaining depressed, the company's stock became undervalued relative to the book value of the company's assets, making the tender offer more attractive. Also, in the 1970s, fewer companies used their own stock, warrants, or debentures to effect the acquisition. In 1969, approximately 32% of all acquisitions were for cash. By the end of the 1970s, more than 45% of all acquisitions were for cash.

Toward the end of the 1970s, new attempts were made in Congress to adopt new legislation to fight the tendency toward merger. One of the major motivations behind these attempts was the growth, importance, and increased consumer awareness of the oil industry. The high visibility of that industry, combined with extensive internal expansion in the oil companies, attracted Congress's attention. Indeed, one proposed bill was directed solely at the oil industry, in an attempt to gain a foothold in the area of merger reform.

Of course, Section 7 is not intended to reach the large existing established firm which over the years has secured a dominant position largely through internal growth. Challenge in this area must be by way of Section 2 of the Sherman Act, or through new legislation.

Robinson-Patman Act. In response to widespread views that the buying power of large purchasers had to be curtailed, in 1936 Congress enacted the Robinson-Patman Act as an Amendment to the Clayton Act. Generally, this Act seeks to eliminate the giving and inducement of discriminatory prices which would tend to have an adverse impact on competition. Although intended to curtail the power of buyers, the Act's principal impact has been on the pricing practices of sellers. Buyers' liability under the Act has been circumscribed with various pre-conditions which often are not satisfied.

The Robinson-Patman Act is one that is especially vague and difficult to understand. In fact, its constitutionality has been challenged simply because of this vagueness. Most businessmen and many lawyers have trouble fathoming its terms. The Acts seeks to rule out price discriminations having the requisite adverse impact on competition—either on the primary level (between the seller and its competitors) or on the secondary level (between the seller's customers and its competitors). The Act permits defenses to a prima facie discrimination case if the price was given in good faith to meet competition, or if the lower price was simply the passing along of the cost savings of the seller. Over the years, difficult questions have arisen, such as what is "price," when is there discrimination in interstate commerce, what is "like grade and quality," what factors point up the requisite adverse competitive effect, and the like. Similarly, the meeting competition and cost savings defenses are hedged with uncertainties. Competition must be met, not beaten. To rely on the cost defense, one must understand what costs are recognized by the defense, and how the savings are allocated to the product involved—an extremely difficult task.

The uncertainties of the statute have not been clarified by the interpretations given it by the Federal Trade Commission and the courts. These interpretations, when added to the vague provisions of the Act, make it clear that this is definitely confused legislation. In addition to these drawbacks, the Act may seek ends which run counter to the aims of the Sherman Act. The Robinson-Patman Act certainly curtails competition that the Sherman Act might welcome. Further, compliance with one Act may run afoul of the other Act. For example, when confronted by a customer's claim that he is receiving a lower price from the seller's competitor, the seller, to claim a basis for the meeting competition defense, might otherwise verify this with the competitor. However, because of Sherman Act prohibitions, he probably will be reluctant to do so.

Federal Trade Commission Act. The third important antitrust statute is the Federal Trade Commission Act which, in general, relates to unfair methods of competition. The Federal Trade Commission has practically limitless power in the enforcement of this Act. This power was broadened in 1973 when Congress included in the Trans-Alaska Pipeline Authorization Act provisions raising civil penalties, lowering standards of proof for injunctions, and extending investigatory powers. No statutory provision or regulation defines what is an unfair method of competition. The Commission has challenged deceptive advertising and practices in such diverse industries as over-the-counter drugs, funeral homes, and products designed for sale to children. The Commission also has challenged acts or activities that may or may not also violate the Sherman or Clayton Acts, including monopolization, "shared monopolies," price fixings, and vertical restraints. In some cases, it has used this Act to cover matters not within the ambit of the Robinson-Patman Act. Also, in the area of consumer protection, Congress amended the Federal Trade Commission Act in 1975 by passing the Magnuson-Moss Warranty Federal Trade Commission Improvement Act. Under these provisions, not only were minimum standards established for consumer product warranties, but also the Federal Trade Commission's powers were expanded again to investigate and prosecute manufacturers and to protect and seek redress for injury for consumers.

Difficulties with Existing Federal Legislation. In summary, the Federal antitrust provisions present rather unbelievable legislation. The provisions are overly general, in some respects vague and contradictory, and have not been aided by consistent interpretation by the courts. As a result, businessmen face severe uncertainties in knowing just what the laws require. Few efforts have been made to reduce this uncertainty. One significant step in the direction of greater certainty was taken through the issuance of Merger Guidelines in June, 1968. Here, the Department of Justice issued guidelines as to which mergers the Department might challenge. These guidelines detailed rather specific tests for horizontal and vertical mergers. Although the terms of the guidelines were criticized in certain respects, the Department's clarifying efforts were applauded. More recently, Congress enacted Title II of the Hart-Scott-Rodino Antitrust Improvements Act of 1976. Title II, together with interpretive rules and regulations issued jointly by the Federal Trade Commission and the Antitrust Division of the Department of Justice, specifies premerger notification and waiting period requirements on large corporations which are considering either mergers or acquisitions. Perhaps a continuing effort will be made to reduce uncertainty further through laws, rules, and regulations.

Antitrust Sanctions and Remedies. The pattern of antitrust in this country is made more complex because of different sanctions and multiple enforcement groups. Sections 1 and 2 of the Sherman Act have both civil and criminal sanctions. Generally, the other sections of the antitrust laws—except Section 3 of the Robinson-Patman Act—provide for only civil enforcement. Section 3 prohibits sales at unreasonably low prices and has been infrequently used. Civil remedies may include damages, but from the Government's standpoint refer principally to injunctive relief and divestiture. The criminal sanctions of the Sherman Act include fines and possibly jail sentences. Relatively few criminal antitrust defendants have been sent to jail; probably the most notable are those individuals who served sentences in connection with the electrical conspiracy cases.[1] However, the Department of Justice has shown increased interest in pursuing criminal actions and this is an area of antitrust that should become more active in the future.[2]

Antitrust Enforcement. The criminal features of the antitrust laws are enforced only by the Department of Justice. The Federal Trade Commission, which usually is responsible for enforcement of the Robinson-Patman Act, relies on the Department for enforcement of Section 3 of that Act. The Department of Justice enforces the Sherman Act and has concurrent jurisdiction with the Commission in the enforcement of the Clayton Act, other than its Robinson-Patman Act amendment. The Commission has sole responsibility for enforcement of the Robinson-Patman Act and the Federal Trade Commission Act.

In addition to proceedings by the Department and the Federal Trade Commission, private parties who have been injured in their business or property are entitled to sue for treble damages. Private actions in recent years have been at least as significant as Government enforcement.[3] The impact of private enforcement and its tremendous implications were probably first felt subsequent to the Government's actions in the electrical industry. Since then, practically every Government civil or criminal antitrust proceeding has generated its progeny of private actions.

In July, 1966, the Federal procedural rule permitting class actions was completely amended. The amendment permits actions to be instituted on behalf of huge classes having a common interest, and allows class members to be included within the class unless they affirmatively take action to withdraw. This amendment, the full implications of which caught some observers by surprise, is now producing massive litigation producing multiple procedural difficulties. Its purpose is to achieve remedies for those whose injuries are so small that individual suit would be impracticable. However, at this stage it may be questionable whether this is the most satisfactory means for providing relief for the small claimant.

To enable further enforcement on behalf of persons who might otherwise be unable to proceed individually, Congress passed Title III of the Hart-Scott-Rodino Antitrust Improvements Act of 1976. Title III specifically provides that a state may sue on behalf of its injured citizens to recover antitrust damages. These recent procedural developments have opened a new area of antitrust enforcement in which the consumer may successfully litigate a claim against a large corporation or even an entire industry.

Antitrust and the Future. Developments in the antitrust area are extremely difficult to predict. However, it is possible to say that antitrust for many years will be a substantial area of law with which businessmen will have to comply. Especially in the consumer products and warranties areas, increased pressure from the public should lead to an increase in Federal and state enforcement proceedings and private actions. Although more and more companies have instituted formalized antitrust compliance

1 In the early 1960s, Federal grand juries indicted certain large electrical companies, including General Electric, Westinghouse, Allis-Chalmers, and McGraw Edison, and certain of their executives, for fixing prices on various lines of electrical equipment. The tremendous impact of private treble damage litigation, as discussed below, was perhaps for the first time fully appreciated. In one of the many private treble damage actions following these indictments, the plantiffs were awarded the sum of approximately $29,000,000 in treble damages. See *Philadelphia Elec. Co. v. Westinghouse Elec. Corp.*, 1964 Trade Cas. ¶71,123 (E.D. Pa. 1964).

2 In 1976, Congress enacted the Antitrust Procedures and Penalties Act, increasing the maximum penalties under the Sherman Act to include 3 years in jail and a $100,000 fine for individuals and up to a $1,000,000 fine for corporations. In 1977, the Antitrust Division of the Department of Justice issued Guidelines for Sentencing Recommendations in Felony Cases Under the Sherman Act, stressing use of prison sentences rather than mere fines for individuals and stating that an 18-month sentence was deemed a "base sentence." Also, as recently as January 23, 1980, Sanford M. Litvack, the chief of the Antitrust Division of the Department of Justice, while speaking to the Antitrust Section of the New York State Bar Association, pledged to increase criminal antitrust enforcement and more actively seek jail sentences and larger fines.

3 The availability of treble damages has led to an ever-increasing amount of private enforcement action. In 1960, 228 such suits were filed; in 1978, over 1,400 private suits were filed and over 3,000 were pending in Federal courts. Recent suits have resulted in recoveries in excess of $1.8 billion. See, e.g., *MCI Communications Corporation v. American Telephone and Telegraph Company,* No. 74C 633 (N.D. Ill., June 16, 1980).

programs, such compliance, as the above discussion illustrates, is quite often fraught with uncertainties. Increased clarity in the law and a clearer picture of likely enforcement would help immeasurably. The Department of Justice Merger Guidelines and the Premerger Notification requirements were certainly a laudable step in the direction of clarity. The Federal Trade Commission should certainly do something to define its enforcement policy in the Robinson-Patman area. And its wide-ranging efforts in the prohibition of matters of unfair competition should at least have some guidelines. It seems unlikely, however, that these clarifying measures will be undertaken, and businessmen had best, therefore, adjust to antitrust uncertainty because it is here to stay.

THOMAS FORD, Attorney at Law, Benesch, Friedlander, Coplan, & Aronoff, Cleveland, Ohio.

Information References

"Antitrust Advisor," Colorado Springs, Shepard's/McGraw-Hill, 1978.

Areeda, Phillip and Turner, Donald, "Antitrust Law," Boston, Little, Brown and Company, 1980.

Austin, Arthur, "Antitrust: Law, Economics, and Policy," Colorado Springs, Shepard's/McGraw-Hill, 1976.

Clark, John M., "Competition as a Dynamic Process," Washington, Brookings Institution, 1961.

Galbraith, J. K., "The New Industrial State," New York, Houghton Mifflin Co., 1967.

"Investigation of Conglomerate Corporations; A Report by the Staff of the Antitrust Subcommittee of the Committee on the Judiciary, House of Representatives," June 1, 1971.

Kaplan, A. D. H., "Big Business in a Competitive System," Washington, Brookings Institution, 1964.

von Kalinowski, Julian O., "Antitrust Laws and Trade Regulation," New York, Matthew Bender & Co., Inc., 1969.

Kaysen, Carl and Turner, Donald F., "Antitrust Policy," Boston, Harvard University Press, 1965.

Kintner, Earl W., "An Antitrust Primer," New York, Macmillan, 1964.

Singer, "Antitrust Economics; Selected Legal Cases and Economic Models," Englewood Cliffs, N.J., Prentice-Hall, 1968.

Sullivan, Lawrence A., "Handbook of the Law of Antitrust," St. Paul, West Publishing Co., 1977.

Cross References: *Mergers and Acquisitions; Pricing: Legal Aspects.*

APPRAISAL (OF PROPERTY)

Management of a business enterprise includes the responsibility for whatever property may be employed in that business. The amount of the actual investment in physical property at any time is a factual matter of accounting. Likewise, the periodical provisions made for physical and functional deterioration and the cumulative amount of such provisions at any time are also factual matters of accounting.

By the process of accounting, the balance sheet of an enterprise, at any time, discloses the "net book value" of its physical property. It does not purport to represent any conclusion as to the "present worth" in any economic sense, which may vary widely one way or the other from such "net book value." Nor does the "net book value" under ordinary circumstances purport to include any consideration of the "present worth," if any, of the "Organization and Business" which may have been developed by the management.

Even though it is true in respect to the "book value" of property, that many accounting entries are necessarily the result of the exercise of judgment from time to time, their summation constitutes a matter of fact.

In contrast with the *factual* record of how much has been invested in physical property and of the amounts that have been recorded as provisions for its depreciation (discussed separately below), the present value of that same property, or property and business, is a matter of *judgment and opinion* in the form of an **Appraisal**, presumably by an agent whose qualifications entitle his conclusions to respect.

Definition. By definition (Webster), "to appraise," in the sense applicable here, is to "set a value on; to estimate the worth of, especially by persons appointed for the purpose" of which the result is characterized as an appraisal.

In the present context, perhaps the most significant suggestion indicated by the above definition is that appraisals in these days are usually made by "persons appointed for the purpose," which can be reasonably construed to imply that such "persons" are *especially* qualified in respect to the type of property to be appraised.

History. Historically, it is obvious that the making of appraisals must have begun long before the existence of money where exchanges were made only by the process of barter (so many of this for so many of that), the result being, unless compulsion was involved, a voluntary meeting of minds.

With the introduction of a monetary medium of exchange came a yardstick by which to measure the value of those things which, hitherto, were bought and sold only by the crude process of barter. Even there, however, the process of buying and selling must have proceeded for untold centuries before there was any great need for the services of a third party to determine the "value" of anything. The exchanges made during that long period, for the most part, were of what we today would speak of as "consumption goods," produced or gathered by hand without benefit of production facilities.

Present Practice. All of the above was a prelude to the gradual development, over the years, of the special need for the services of third parties to place values, not so much on consumption goods, but, more especially, on the capital facilities employed in their production. Thus, more and more, it has become one of the important functions of management, among its many responsibilities, to seek the advice of professional appraisers who are qualified by experience and reputation, each in his own field.

There is a wide variation in the types of property which come within the scope of management. So also there is a wide variation in the technique of their evaluation.

The property may be a group of dwelling houses, one or more residential apartments or office buildings. Or it may be an entire public utility property whose rates for service are subject to regulation; or an industrial manufacturing plant.

It may be a case where an agency of government is exercising its privilege of acquisition by the process of "eminent domain," requiring the fixing of the amount to be paid for the property. Almost always such property is taken only because the bare land is required for some other than the present usage.

Occasion for an appraisal often arises in connection with the settlement of estates involving a valuation of personal property, as well as real estate, sometimes of valuable antiques, works of art, and precious stones.

Lending institutions require appraisals of property upon which they contemplate, or have already made, mortgage loans.

Insurance companies which issue policies to protect the owners of property from losses incurred from fire and other physical damage, whether such losses turn out to be total or only partial, must rely on appraisals. The loss may consist only of a specific piece of machinery or it may be that an entire manufacturing plant is destroyed.

The competence of a professional appraiser for a particular assignment depends upon a wide variety of considerations related to the nature of the particular task. If the property is of a type that would require the services of engineers to design a plant to serve the same purpose at the time of the appraisal, it follows that the employment of a *valuation engineer* is called for.

That valuation engineer, moreover, is expected to be informed as to the relative costs of operation between the existing plant and a hypothetical modern substitute. It is by this approach that the effect of obsolescence is evaluated.

Even if the property should be a church or school house, the appraiser should either be an architectural specialist or have access to the advice of such a specialist so that he can be in a position to translate the pertinent technical aspects of the case into terms of present value.

In the matter of rental real estate, whether it be residential, commercial, or industrial, local statistics concerning purchases and sales have great significance and the appraiser should be well informed thereon.

The value of real estate for the purpose of local tax assessments is a subject of special concern to the professional appraiser who operates in that field and who must take into account the extent of the tax burden on such property and the necessarily depressing effect on the value of excessive taxation.

In the field of real-estate taxation, there is always present the vital distinction to be made between the God-given bare land and what has been added to it by human effort. How much a prospective purchaser of a building site can reasonably pay for land is related to what can be done with it, within the limitations of whatever zoning restrictions may apply. What happens to have been erected on the site often falls far short of its potentialities. The market value of a site may thus exceed by a wide margin any value that could be reached on the basis of present income. The competent appraiser must realize, in such cases, that the so-called "improvements" may be worth even less than nothing, to the extent of the prospective cost of demolition. He must be well aware of the implications of such situations, and embody them in his conclusions.

One of the categories of property to be appraised is often characterized as *income property* to denote that its objective is to produce a periodical return of net revenue for the owner, such as an office building, its value bearing a direct relationship to such revenue. By contrast, the property may consist of a collection of rare works of art yielding no revenue whatever but still of great value in terms of satisfaction to the present owner and, likewise, of potential satisfaction to some prospective buyer.

In both cases it may be said that the value bears a relation to the benefit which the present or prospective owner may derive from the ownership of the property, either during the period of ownership or by its eventual sale to others.

If the benefit of ownership can be reasonably estimated in terms of dollars per year, the process of appraising is fairly simple. If the value resides only in what would be yielded by sale, the problem is largely one of having a knowledge of the "market" for such property, a much more speculative basis of valuation.

A dwelling house occupied by the owner may not be regarded, ordinarily, as income property. In fact, however, it may properly be so classified because of its rental potentiality. For this class of property a knowledge of actual transactions between willing buyers and sellers is obviously important.

In connection with public utilities whose rates are subject to regulation, the special need for the services of the *valuation engineer* is indicated. The valuation engineer, although he is not expected to be an expert accountant or a lawyer, is expected to be somewhat familiar with the accounting and legal aspects that are applicable in the given location of the property he is called upon to appraise. His judgment may differ in some respects from the regulatory practices in some jurisdictions, but it is encumbent upon him to be informed as to what those practices are.

Approaches to Value. There are three general approaches to determination of present value: (1) comparative sales; (2) capitalization of earnings; and (3) reproduction or replacement cost new, less depreciation.

The *comparative sales approach* is just what it implies. A reasonable number of arms-length sales of property comparable to that which is being appraised are reviewed and analyzed. From this data, a value can be ascribed directly to the subject property. The comparable sales should have occurred as near as possible to the appraisal date for the subject property. This method is most appropriate for items such as residential property where significant numbers of similar property are bought and sold during a relatively short period of time.

Capitalized earnings are most appropriate for valuation of commercial income-producing enterprises. In this process, an appropriate annual net income is determined; and this net income is then capitalized by dividing by an appropriate capitalization (interest) rate for the type enterprise being appraised. In determining the appropriate annual net income, the appraiser must consider the potential future net income as well as that of the recent past. The selection of a capitalization rate is most important in this method. The cost rate of capital for similar enterprises or enterprises with similar risks is most relevant. (See RETURN ON CAPITAL.)

Reproduction cost new, less depreciation is the process of establishing the cost to reproduce the same item of property new as at the appraisal date, and reducing this result by the depreciation represented by the age and condition of the actual property as compared to the property when new. Replacement cost is used when the property being appraised is no longer made or in common use. The replacement cost thus is the cost to replace the subject property with something that will perform as closely as possible the same function as the subject property. The age and condition of the subject property are also used to determine the depreciation applicable to its replacement cost. This method is most appropriate for special-use property where the comparable sales and the capitalization of income methods may be inappropriate.

It is considered good practice to determine present value on as many bases as possible. The final opinion as to value is then based upon a weighting of all the various results with the most weight being given to the method or methods considered to be more appropriate for determining the value of the subject property for the purpose for which the property is being appraised.

Depreciation of Property. In the above discussion, the distinction was emphasized as between the factually available information concerning the *cost* of property and the *value* thereof, and that the determination of the latter must, in great measure at least, be a matter of informed judgment and opinion.

The same distinction is applicable to the factor of *depreciation.*

Whatever has been set aside over a period of

time as a provision against the ultimate complete loss in value of a property, and no matter how much judgment has been exercised in its determination, the "net book value" of the property is still a fact. How much that same property may be worth at any given time during the course of its useful life, that is to say its *present value,* is a proper matter for the consideration of a qualified professional appraiser.

Such an appraiser, after taking into account the many factors involved, may find a present value which falls far short of the net book value, or which greatly exceeds it. In the process of estimating present value, the first and primary task of the appraiser or valuation engineer is not at all to find an amount to be deducted from the book value of a property or its original cost. The difference between the one and the other is only the result of his *conclusion* of present value, and that conclusion is not reached by first making an estimate of the amount to be deducted for depreciation.

The qualified appraiser of residential or commercial property is well aware of the fact that the "original cost" or "book value" of a structure built many years ago has little or no bearing on its present value, and that any attempt to arrive at an estimate of depreciation to be deduced from such a figure would be to put the cart in front of the horse.

The valuation engineer, confronted with the task of evaluating an industrial or public utility plant, is equally aware that his conclusion in respect to present value must take account of the availability of facilities of more modern and efficient design, if such there are, as well as the *cost to reproduce new* the existing plant, if its design continues to be suitable. He then makes due allowance for the existing physical deterioration. Such an allowance, however, would not be properly deductible from the book cost but from the *reproduction cost.*

The essential distinction to be made between the two concepts of depreciation is that the one is an allowance more or less related to calendar time, while the other is a determination of the effect of what has actually transpired up to the date of the determination and may bear little or no mathematical relation to the passage of time.

Accrued depreciation is not normally a factor in the comparable sales approach or the capitalized income approach. Annual depreciation, however, should be included as an operating expense in the capitalized income approach. Annual depreciation for this purpose should be on a replacement cost basis. Accrued depreciation, however, can be important if the income producing property is old and in poor condition. This underscores the need of reproduction cost new less depreciation appraisals in such cases.

Inflation. Inflation is a significant problem to the appraiser. Comparable sales are more difficult to obtain, particularly for residential property. During periods of rapid inflation, sales made more than six months before or after the appraisal date may be incomparable, whereas in stable times sales as much as three to five years before or after the appraisal date can be valid comparisons.

The capitalized income approach is not without its problems. Incomes tend to vary considerably during inflationary times, making it difficult for the appraiser to select a reasonable income level. More importantly, money rates are extremely volatile, making it difficult to select an appropriate capitalization rate.

The valuation engineer must be more careful to obtain the correct cost applicable to the property being appraised as of the appraisal date. A price change just before the appraisal date could be significant if missed. A price change just after the appraisal date would be inappropriate if used.

In summary, the appraisal of the present value of property is a difficult task during times of relatively stable costs. During periods of extreme inflation, the appraiser must be on his toes to obtain data which are meaningful not only to the property being appraised but to the period of time for which the appraisal is to apply.

W.V. Burnell, William V. Burnell & Associates, Boston, Massachusetts, and Vito F. Pennacchio, Coffin & Richardson, Inc., Boston, Massachusetts, for American Society of Appraisers

Information References

There are a number of nationally organized societies, composed primarily of professional appraisers, which sponsor various publications relative to their activities, including rosters of their professional membership.

Specializing in the field of Real Estate are: American Institute of Real Estate Appraisers, and Society of Real Estate Appraisers.

The American Society of Appraisers has a membership which includes active professional appraisers in a wide variety of fields, each in his or her own, and including the important category of Valuation Engineers.

APPRENTICESHIP PROGRAMS

Apprenticeship as a means of thoroughly learning the intricacies of a trade has been well adapted to modern industry to meet workforce needs. Even with all the innovations in industry, experience has shown that the worker masters a skilled trade only by diligently repeating job operations under capable supervision until they are fully mastered.

Management is recognizing more and more its responsibility to provide the individual worker with the proper training. In many instances, this is a matter of self-preservation for the company if it is to obtain the skilled workers it needs. Trade unions are equally aware that apprenticeship is the lifeblood of their organizations. They strongly urge their members to encourage the establishment of such programs and to take part in them.

It must be emphasized that apprentices are not only students, but *employed workers.* They learn on the job and produce during their learning period. They are paid wages, because what they produce is sold. Apprenticeship, simply defined, is the preparation of youth for those occupations referred to as skilled crafts or trades that require a wide and diverse range of skills and knowledge as well as both maturity and independence of judgment.

History. Apprenticeship is not a new system of training skilled workers. It reaches back through the 18th- and 19th-century journeyman system of Western and Northern Europe, the guild system of medieval Europe, and the artisan system of ancient Greece and Rome to the Babylonian Code of Hammurabi which, 4,000 years ago, adjured masters to teach their craft to youth.

In the United States, apprenticeship has been rooted long enough to qualify as a *traditional* system of skill training. Several of the better known companies in the machine-tool, railroad, and shipbuilding industries have conducted outstanding apprenticeship programs continuously since the last two decades of the 19th century. Many craft unions have for generations placed special emphasis on apprenticeship as a means of entering their trades, among them the Bricklayers, Masons and Plasterers' International Union of America; the United Brotherhood of Carpenters and Joiners of America; the International Union of Operating Engineers; the International Association of Machinists and Aerospace Workers; the United Association of Journeymen and Apprentices of the Plumbing and Pipe Fitting Industry of the United States and Canada; and the Graphic Arts International Union.

However, American industry generally bypassed apprenticeship, largely because of the continuous supply of foreign-trained mechanics migrating to this country. The drastic retrenchment in all forms of industrial activity in the early and middle 1930s further delayed emphasis on apprenticeship, since it was almost impossible to justify carrying large numbers of apprentices on the payrolls.

Although the National Apprenticeship Act was approved in August, 1937, to promote standards of apprenticeship and to help formulate programs of apprenticeship, World War II caused another postponement. Specialization of production workers, rather than broad training, became the byword, in the need for speed at whatever cost, and the draft also had a crippling effect on apprenticeship.

The Bureau of Apprenticeship and Training, Employment and Training Administration, U.S. Department of Labor, is charged with the responsibility of promoting apprenticeship programs in industry. Its chief concern is for the employed worker who is learning a trade and who will at the conclusion of his training reach *journeyman status* and be recognized as a craftworker.

The Act under which the Bureau operates specifically empowers it to promote the furtherance of labor standards necessary to safeguard the welfare of apprentices, to extend the application of such standards by encouraging the inclusion of them in contracts of apprenticeship, and to bring together employers and labor for the formulation of programs of apprenticeship. In addition, the Bureau of Apprenticeship and Training is instructed by the law to cooperate with state agencies engaged in the formulation and promotion of standards of apprenticeship and to cooperate with the Office of Education in so doing.

The Federal Committee on Apprenticeship. The Federal Committee on Apprenticeship is one of the oldest public advisory committees in the Federal Government, established in 1934 by the Secretary of Labor to carry out an Executive Order issued by President Franklin Delano Roosevelt. As currently constituted, the Committee has 25 members, appointed by the Secretary of Labor for two-year terms. Ten of its members represent labor, ten are from management, and five represent the public. In addition, there are three exofficio members, the current president of the National Association of State and Territorial Apprenticeship Directors, a representative of the U.S. Office of Education, and the Assistant Secretary of Labor for Employment and Training. The Committee is chaired by a public member selected by the Secretary of Labor.

Committee members receive no compensation but may receive authorized expenses. Meetings, open to the public, are held at least twice a year, and summary reports on the proceedings are distributed to Committee members and other interested persons. Between meetings, Committee members work on subcommittees concerned with particular aspects of apprenticeship. Subcommittee sessions are also open to the public.

The Committee's recommendations to the Secretary of Labor concern a broad range of activities to improve and extend apprenticeship. Among them are proposals on such matters as:

- Expanding apprenticeship and journeyman training in all sectors of the economy.
- Increasing the effectiveness of equal opportunity programs.
- Promoting labor standards to protect apprentices and including them in apprenticeship contracts.
- Identifying research needs and planning projects to test new approaches to apprenticeship and other skill training.
- Strengthening cooperative relationships with State apprenticeship and training agencies.

Standards for Certification. Since 1937 the Bureau of Apprenticeship and Training has worked closely with employers, labor, vocational schools, and others concerned with apprenticeship in almost every industry, most recently the mining, energy-related, and health occupations. Through 1977, over 1,056,000 workers have become journeymen in more than 540 apprenticeable occupations as a result of programs promoted by the Bureau.

The Bureau of Apprenticeship and Training requires that apprenticeship programs meet the Labor Standards for the registration of apprenticeship programs. Twenty-two standards must be met before a program can be registered with the Bureau or a State Apprenticeship Council (SAC), and before the BAT or SAC will award a certificate of completion to an apprentice at the conclusion of their apprenticeship term. These standards of apprenticeship are:

(1) The employment and training of the apprentice in a skilled trade.

(2) A term of apprenticeship, not less than 2,000 hours of work experience, consistent with training requirements as established by industry practice.

(3) An outline of the work processes in which the apprentice will receive supervised work experience and training on the job, and the allocation of the approximate time to be spent in each major process.

(4) Provision for organized, related and supplemental instruction in technical subjects related to the trade. A minimum of 144 hours for each year of apprenticeship is recommended. Such instruction may be given in a classroom, through trade or industrial courses, or by industrial or correspondence courses of equivalent value, or through other forms of self-study approved by the registration/approval agency.

(5) A progressively increasing schedule of wages to be paid the apprentice consistent with the skill acquired. The entry wage shall be not less than the minimum wage prescribed by the Fair Labor Standards Act, where applicable, unless a higher wage is required by other applicable Federal law, State law, respective regulations, or by collective bargaining agreement.

(6) Periodic review and evaluation of the apprentice's progress in job performance and related instruction; and the maintenance of appropriate progress records.

(7) The numeric ratio of apprentices to journeymen consistent with proper supervision, training, safety, and continuity of employment, and applicable provisions in collective bargaining agreements, except where such ratios are expressly prohibited by the collective bargaining agreements. The ratio language shall be specific and clear as to application in terms of jobsite, workforce, department, or plant.

(8) A probationary period reasonable in relation to the full apprenticeship term with full credit given for such period toward completion of apprenticeship.

(9) Adequate and safe equipment and facilities for training and supervision, and safety training for apprentices on the job and in related instruction.

(10) The minimum qualifications required by a sponsor for persons entering the apprentice-

ship program, with an eligible starting age not less than 16 years.

(11) The placement of an apprentice under a written apprenticeship agreement as required by the State apprenticeship law and regulation, or the Bureau where no such State law or regulation exists. The agreement shall directly, or by reference, incorporate the standards of the program as part of the agreement.

(12) The granting of advanced standing or credit for previously acquired experience, training, or skills for all applicants equally, with commensurate wages for any progression step so granted.

(13) Transfer of employer's training obligation when the employer is unable to fulfill his obligation under the apprenticeship agreement to another employer under the same program with consent of the apprentice and apprenticeship committee or program sponsor.

(14) Assurance of qualified training personnel and adequate supervision on the job.

(15) Recognition for successful completion of apprenticeship evidenced by an appropriate certificate.

(16) Identification of the registration agency.

(17) Provision for the registration, cancellation and deregistration of the program; and requirement for the prompt submission of any modification or amendment thereto.

(18) Provision for registration of apprenticeship agreements, modifications, and amendments; notice to the registration office of persons who have successfully completed apprenticeship programs; and notice of cancellations, suspensions, and terminations of apprenticeship agreements and causes therefor.

(19) Authority for the termination of an apprenticeship agreement during the probationary period by either party without stated cause.

(20) A statement that the program will be conducted, operated, and administered in conformity with applicable provisions of 29 CFR Part 30, as amended, or a State EEO in apprenticeship plan adopted pursuant to 29 CFR Part 30 and approved by the Department.

(21) Name and address of the appropriate authority under the program to receive, process, and make disposition of complaints.

(22) Recording and maintenance of all records concerning apprenticeship as may be required by the Bureau or recognized state apprenticeship agency and other applicable law.

The foregoing are criteria for a *program.* An *apprenticeship occupation* is one which:

(1) Is customarily learned in a practical way through a structured, systematic program of on-the-job supervised training.

(2) Is clearly identified and commonly recognized throughout an industry.

(3) Involves manual, mechanical, or technical skills and knowledge which require a minimum of 2,000 hours of on-the-job work experience.

(4) Requires related instruction to supplement the on-the-job training.

The apprenticeship agreement must explicitly set forth the number of hours to be spent by the apprentice in work on the job, and the number of hours to be spent in related and supplemental instruction, recommended to be not less than 144 hours per year. There must also be a statement setting forth a schedule of the work processes in the trade or industry division, and the approximate time to be spent at each process. Also explicitly set forth must be the graduated scale of wages to be paid, and whether or not the required school time will be compensated. Further, there must be a provision for a specified period of probation during which the apprenticeship agreement may be terminated by either party to the agreement upon written notice to the registration agency.

Operation. The functions of the Bureau of Apprenticeship and Training are carried out by some 435 employees, with 30 in the national office in Washington and the remainder throughout ten regions with representatives in 160 major cities in the fifty states. These functions are:

(1) To urge management and labor, not only nationally but locally, to recognize the need for apprenticeship.

(2) To stimulate management and labor to analyze their own special and individual skilled workforce needs, not only currently but in the future, in the full expectation that they will do something to meet these needs.

(3) To provide technical assistance, aids, and materials to industry where it is necessary and within the Bureau's available resources.

(4) To conduct research studies to determine the demand for specific skills which in turn familiarize the public with the need for apprenticeship.

(5) To encourage national employer and labor organizations to adopt policies and proce-

dures to create a favorable climate for the development of apprenticeship and skill improvement systems.

(6) To work with management and labor, state apprenticeship agencies, the schools, and community groups to develop the organizational machinery for apprenticeship systems.

(7) To ensure that the standards of every apprenticeship program approved and registered with the Bureau or with state apprenticeship agencies conform to the Federal regulations governing equal employment opportunity in apprenticeship.

The Bureau of Apprenticeship and Training does not administer or conduct apprenticeship programs. It does no actual training, but serves as a *programmer.* Its work is that of promoting apprenticeship programs and improving existing programs.

Joint Apprenticeship Committees. The most successful programs are usually operated and administered by joint apprenticeship committees composed of equal representation of management and labor where workers are organized. The joint apprenticeship committee formulates the program, often helps select the apprentices, and sees that the objectives of the program are carried out. Job experience is obtained under journeyman supervision, and related training is usually received in evening vocational classes at local schools, community colleges, and, in some locations, correspondence courses.

The Bureau is constantly working with industries to encourage them to establish joint apprenticeship committees not only at the local level but at the national level. Such national committees function in a promotional as well as a policy-making capacity in the trades they represent. With the assistance of the Bureau of Apprenticeship and Training, they formulate national standards of apprenticeship for the guidance of local employer and labor groups. Through 1979, over 140 such national standards were adopted in trades utilizing the apprenticeship system of skill training. These have been developed by labor unions, national trade associations, and, as joint standards, by management and labor together, along with the various Federal agencies that have registered operating apprenticeship programs meeting the requirements of both BAT and the Office of Personnel Management.

Financing Apprenticeship Programs. The setting up of adequate financing for apprenticeship programs is encouraged by the Bureau. This is done by management and labor. Some of the trades, recognizing the need for additional funds to provide necessary training to meet today's constantly changing technologies, particularly in the construction industry, impose a payroll deduction tax for this purpose. Through this means some trades even provide their own training and retraining facilities. Some trust funds are organized and operated at the local union level, others at state, regional and national levels.

The United Association of Journeymen and Apprentices of the Plumbing and Pipe Fitting Industry, through its International Training Fund, has benefited local groups and encourages local joint apprenticeship committees to seek grants for training purposes.

Apprenticeship Coordinators. Financed from training trust funds established by the various industries, apprenticeship coordinators carry out the policy of joint apprenticeship and training committees in administering and conducting apprenticeship and other training programs.

The coordinators assist the committees by screening apprentice applications, arranging for apprentice interviews and tests, indenturing selected applicants, maintaining apprentice record files, arranging various meetings, and performing many other duties connected with administering and promoting the apprenticeship program.

The Bureau has developed a promotional pamphlet to aid industries in selecting apprenticeship coordinators and to assist coordinators in setting up their budgets and planning their work. The Bureau recommends that all committees fully explore the benefits that would accrue from the employment of apprenticeship coordinators.

Prior Education. The Bureau supports "Stay in School" campaigns. Until World War II, a high school diploma was practically a "must" for the apprentice applicant. Subsequent shortages of workers influenced letting down the bars. Nevertheless, some trades still consider it a prerequisite while others consider it desirable. However, no one recognizes more clearly than the young apprentice how much he or she needs the fundamentals of a high school education to cope with the stringent requirements of the related instructional work.

Comprehensive Employment and Training Act. Under the Comprehensive Employment and Training Act (Public Law 95–524, Oct. 27, 1978) CETA prime sponsors are encouraged to expose trainees to apprenticeship through two introductory programs:

Pre-apprenticeship. The immediate demand for production sometimes makes it necessary that an apprentice have some knowledge of the trade when he or she enters on duty. Pre-apprenticeship training provides this basic knowledge (e.g., a pre-apprentice automobile mechanic would learn the identification and use of parts and tools before going on the floor as an apprentice mechanic).

Apprentice-entry. Some employers need apprentices, but are unable to bear the expense of the apprentice's nonproductive time which occurs largely during the early stages of training. In these instances, the employer may be reimbursed for this nonproductive training time. After apprentice-entry training, the apprentice would continue to complete the full apprenticeship term, and the time spent in training would be credited toward the full term (e.g., six months of apprentice-entry training in a four-year apprenticeship term would leave a balance of three and one-half years following completion of apprentice-entry training.).

Minority-Group and Female Apprentices. The participation of minority groups and women in apprenticeship programs has been a source of great concern to the Department of Labor. Their rate of representation in the ranks of apprentices has been no match for their proportionate population rate. In 1963, the Secretary of Labor issued regulations on "Equal Employment Opportunity in Apprenticeship and Training" (Title 29 Code of Federal Regulations, Part 30). These regulations were revised and strengthened in 1971 and again in 1978. The regulations require that sponsors develop and implement a written affirmative action program which includes procedures for the identification, positive recruitment, training, and motivation of present and potential minority-group and female (minority and nonminority) apprentices. If the sponsor has deficiencies in terms of underutilization of minorities and females, it must develop percentage goals and timetables for the selection of minority-group and female apprentices or for the admission into an eligibility pool as part of its affirmative action program. The Bureau of Apprenticeship and Training is charged with the implementation of these regulations.

In another complementary effort to increase the participation of minority-group workers in apprenticeship, the Employment and Training Administration developed its *Targeted Outreach Program* (e.g., the Urban League LEAP and the RTP). These have two major objectives: to prepare minority youth to pass apprentice entrance examinations and place them as apprentices in the building and construction trades; and to provide experienced construction workers with the additional training and experience they need to qualify for journeyman status and union acceptance. In 1980, such programs were operating in more than 100 geographic areas throughout the country, with more planned for additional areas.

Veterans. For those returning to civilian life following completion of their military service obligations, apprenticeship may have a special attraction. Veterans are accustomed to the disciplines of training and in a great many cases the training they have received in the service lends itself to an apprenticeship in the skilled trades. To encourage them to move toward apprenticeship and to facilitate their transition into the world of work as an apprentice, the Veterans Administration provides a training allowance over and above their earnings as an apprentice. For the first six months of an apprenticeship, a veteran without dependents would receive $226 monthly; with one dependent, $254; with two or more dependents, $277. This allowance schedule is graduated downward every six-month period of the apprenticeship term as the apprentice-veteran's wages rise every six months, until the apprenticeship is completed. (These dollar figures are as of 1981.)

Apprenticeship in the Armed Services. To "arm the armed forces for civilian life," the Bureau of Apprenticeship and Training has registered apprentice programs with the Departments of Army, Navy, and Marine Corps. (Initial meetings have at this writing been held with the Air Force.) As of December, 1980, some 19,000 men and women were registered in the Army's program, and it is estimated that as many as 250,000 will eventually be eligible for the program. The Navy had approximately 267 apprentices in five occupations, and program standards are being developed for another 12 occupations. The Marine Corps had 478 apprentices with programs registered for four school commands.

The Future of Apprenticeship. The population of the United States is expected to increase from 222 million to 244 million between 1980 and 1990. By the middle of that decade employment in the skilled workforce category is expected to rise to more than 13.7 million. In the construction trades alone, the mid-decade will see about 4.3 million jobs. These projections, coupled with the fact that jobs in craft skills are increasingly well rewarded financially, reflect a continuing need for highly skilled workers in the economy. Moreover, these projections do not include another 2.6 million workers who will be needed to replace experienced persons who retire or die, while hundreds of thousands of openings will be created by the transfer of skilled workers into other occupations.

To meet the country's new industrial requirements for skilled craftsmen in all trades during this decade, qualified candidates for Certificates of Completion should be turned out at the rate of 250,000 a year. Some of the needed journeymen will reach that status in the trade without the benefit of planned apprenticeship, since some looseness is allowed by both management and labor. However, experience shows that the ideal is to have all journeymen come through sound apprenticeship.

In taking a forward look at apprenticeship, the further training of craftworkers to keep them abreast of changing technologies affecting their trades cannot be ignored. Some journeymen did not have the advantage of a complete apprenticeship and need additional training to round out their skills. Other programs are desirable to prepare some journeymen for supervisory positions and to fill vacancies in that category due to deaths and retirements.

The Bureau of Apprenticeship and Training continues to urge wide acceptance of apprenticeship because waste is inefficient, because the welfare and safety of this country need skilled craftworkers, and because the prolonged process of picking up a trade is an onerous burden on the individual citizen as well as an impediment to an improved economy.

James P. Mitchell, Administrator, Bureau of Apprenticeship and Training, U.S. Department of Labor, Employment and Training Administration, Washington, D.C.

Information References

Numerous publications are available from the Bureau of Apprenticeship and Training, U.S. Department of Labor, Employment and Training Administration, Washington, D.C. 20213.

Cross References: *Training and Development (Government Sponsored); see also cross references under Human Resources Deveopment.*

APTITUDE TESTS. See Personnel Testing; Personnel Testing: Types of Tests

ARBITRATION

Arbitration is the reference of a dispute by voluntary agreement of the parties to an impartial person who renders a decision, called an award, after hearing evidence and arguments presented by those parties. Although private in nature and less formal in procedure than a court of law, arbitration is usually governed by established rules and by standards of impartiality prescribed by law. Awards resulting from such proceedings are enforceable in all states under common law, and are more specifically enforceable through expedited procedures under arbitration laws of the United States and 40 individual states.

Arbitration is very widely practiced in labor relations, where it is generally held to be an alternative to strikes and work stoppages. (See Labor Arbitration.) Arbitration of disputes growing out of business transactions, or other non-labor relationships, between individuals or organizations is usually referred to as "commercial arbitration," and thought of as an alternative to civil litigation. With very few exceptions, any matter that could be the subject of a law suit may be resolved by arbitrators, if the parties so desire.

History. Some writers have traced arbitration to the dawn of civilization and have even found evidence of early use in mythology (the judgment of Paris as to the relative charms of Juno, Pallas Athene, and Venus, and in King Solomon's unusual procedure for determining the true mother of an infant). But it is doubtful whether a tribunal conducted by sovereigns who had life and death power over their subjects had much in common with modern arbitration, which is founded upon the consent of the parties concerned.

Perhaps a more direct precursor of modern, voluntary arbitration were the informal courts through which merchants in pre-industrial England resolved disputes over the quality of merchandise offered for sale at the fairs. "The time and precise manner in which law and free-will arbitration became identified are obscure," wrote Frances Kellor. "We know that out of the trade fairs and guild systems of England there developed principles and standards that came to be known as the Law Merchant, and that through its practice they settled into precedents and prerogatives which the courts perpetuated, thus creating the common law" [1].

The English tradition of arbitration was naturally carried over into the American colonies. One of the first arbitration tribunals in the New World was that of the New York Chamber of Commerce in 1768 [2]. Records of that organization tell of disputes over a reasonable fee for hiring a horse to make a trip from what is now lower Manhattan to Yonkers, and a fair wage to workmen hired to forge a chain intended to keep the British fleet from sailing up the Hudson River. Further evidence of early use of arbitration is seen in George Washington's last will and testament, which provided that in case of dispute among his heirs over division of his estate, the decision was to be made by "three impartial men known for their probity and good understanding," whose award was to be "as binding on the parties as if it had been given in the Supreme Court of the United States."

The attitude of the courts and the legal profession to arbitration was also strongly influenced by the English tradition. In 1609, Lord Coke had held that because arbitration "ousted the courts of their jurisdiction," courts would not enforce agreements to arbitrate future disputes [3]. Out of this there developed the common law rule that an agreement to arbitrate could be revoked at will, and that only those awards would be enforced which resulted from the participation of both parties.

This doctrine of revocability naturally had a deterrent effect on the use of arbitration clauses, but it did not prevent parties from choosing to arbitrate, rather than litigate, on a case-by-case basis. And the courts often showed sympathetic awareness of the reasons that motivated this choice. "Arbitrators are judges chosen by the parties to decide the matter submitted to them, finally and without appeal," wrote the U.S. Supreme Court in 1854. "As a mode of settling disputes, it should receive any encouragement from courts of equity. If an award is within the submission, and contains the honest decision of the arbitrators, after a full and fair hearing of the parties, a court of equity will not set it aside for error, either in law or in fact. A contrary course would be a substitute of the judgment of the chancellor in place of the judges chosen by the parties" [4].

Modern Practice. The common law doctrine of revocability was first challenged in New York in 1920, when a group of businessmen, led by the Chamber of Commerce of the State of New York, persuaded the Legislature to enact what became the first modern arbitration law in the United States. The future-dispute arbitration clause was given equal status with other contractual provisions, as far as enforcement through the courts was concerned. Other states soon followed the new pattern, as did the Federal Government with the enactment of an arbitration law governing maritime transactions and business disputes arising out of interstate commerce. In 1955, the National Conference of the Commissioners on Uniform State Laws and the House of Delegates of the American Bar Association approved a Uniform Arbitration Act, which has since been adopted by most of the states. The 40 modern arbitration laws in effect in the United States in 1980 [5] differ in some respects, but they are alike in that they permit enforcement of agreements to arbitrate future disputes, as well as of the awards themselves. They also establish expeditious procedures for such enforcement, so that the presumed intention of the parties to bring their controversies to quick determination may be given effect. By the same token, modern arbitration laws establish minimum standards of fair procedure, and permit judges to vacate awards where the rights of parties are violated in any substantial way.

The modern attitude of the judiciary to arbitration has had the anticipated effect. Most arbitration in the United States is now statutory arbitration, occurring in states where laws facilitate enforcement of the results. Many trade associations and commodity exchanges have established their own procedures for resolving disputes among members, or between members and non-member firms. Arbitrations outside these organized bodies are mostly conducted under the rules of the American Arbitration Association, a private, not-for-profit membership group organized in 1926. The Association also conducts a publication and educational program, to advance knowledge of the uses of arbitration to dispose of disputes of all kinds.

To serve the business community with arbitrators representing every specialized field, the American Arbitration Association maintains a National Panel of Arbitrators, numbering at this writing some 60,000 men and women in 2,500 communities in the United States. When selected by parties to disputes, or when appointed to a case by the Association in accordance with the arbitration agreement of the parties, these commercial arbitrators usually serve without fee, as a contribution to the public welfare. In unusual cases, where considerable time away from their regular professions may be involved, a fee is paid by the parties.

Overwhelmingly, voluntary arbitration practice in the United States now results from arbitration clauses in contracts which provide for this method of resolving disputes that may arise in the future. A typical arbitration clause reads: "Any controversy or claim arising out of or relating to this contract, or the breach thereof, shall be settled by arbitration in accordance with the Rules of the American Arbitration Association, and judgment upon the award rendered by the Arbitrator(s) may be entered in any court having jurisdiction thereof." To a lesser extent, arbitration is also conducted under the agreements of parties who have an existing dispute, but who either were not in a contractual relationship with one another or whose prior contract did not contain a future disputes clause.

During 1980, the American Arbitration Association administered over 45,000 arbitration cases of all kinds. Impressive as this figure is, it does not reflect the true impact of arbitration on business practice, for only a small proportion of arbitration clauses ever need to be invoked. Many business firms use standard arbitration clauses not only to provide for quick, inexpensive, and private resolution of disputes, but to build goodwill and to demonstrate an intention to apply the highest standards of fair dealing in the performance of contracts.

MORRIS STONE, Vice President (Retired), American Arbitration Association, New York, New York

References Cited

[1] Kellor, Frances, "Arbitration and the Legal Profession," a report prepared for the Survey of the Legal Profession. Published by the American Arbitration Association, 1952. Page 3.

[2] Kellor, Frances, "American Arbitration, Its History, Functions and Achievements," p. 7, New York, Harper & Bros., 1948. *See also* Gwynne, Charles T., in *The Arbitration Journal,* Vol. 1. No. 2, p. 117, 1937.

[3] 8 Co. 80a 81b (1609), decided by Lord Coke.

[4] *Burchell v. Marsh,* 17 Howard 344 (1854).

[5] Alaska, Arizona, Arkansas, California, Colorado, Connecticut, Delaware, Florida, Georgia, Hawaii, Idaho, Illinois, Indiana, Kansas, Louisiana, Maine, Maryland, Massachusetts, Michigan, Minnesota, Missouri, Nevada, New Hampshire, New Jersey, New Mexico, New York, North Carolina, Ohio, Oklahoma, Oregon, Pennsylvania, Rhode Island, South Carolina, South Dakota, Texas, Utah, Virginia, Washington, Wisconsin, Wyoming. United States Arbitration Act.

Cross Reference: *Labor Arbitration.*

ASSESSMENT CENTERS

The **Assessment Center** is a standardized selection procedure for the identification of management potential. Developed because thus far no single set of easily applied psychological tests has been devised that will produce the reliable prediction needed, the assessment center uses a variety of different techniques, including tests, interviews, and situation simulations. From these it is determined whether a person possesses a behavior pattern previously identified as important to success in a particular kind of management position.

The term assessment center does not necessarily refer to a physical facility, but rather to the method of evaluation. A number of successful managers, usually not including the candidate's immediate superior (where the issue is promotion rather than hiring from the outside), observe the candidate's performance. They later pool their observations and make recommendations. A number of candidates are processed at the same time.

The candidate's adjudged suitability for a specific position is typically set forth in a two- or three-page report pointing out areas of strengths and weaknesses.

The Assessment Center Process. As described by Kelly [1], the assessment center process in its complete form follows five sequential steps:

(1) *Identification of Job Dimensions.* This requires the identification and definition of the behavioral variables relevant to success in the position. Obviously, this can come only from management.

(2) *Determination of the Instruments of Measurement.* This requires the selection of the various psychological instruments, such as the interview, the simulation, the in-basket exercise (see MANAGEMENT DEVELOPMENT TECH-

NIQUES), and applicable psychological and personality tests.

(3) *Observation and Reporting.* In a typical center, up to twelve participants who have been recommended by their immediate superiors take part in the various exercises. They may play a business game, complete an in-basket exercise, participate in group discussions, and be interviewed. The assessors observe and evaluate the candidates' behavior and take notes on specially prepared observation forms.

(4) *Evaluation Process.* The exercises may go on for two or three days. The assessors spend two or more days comparing observations and making a full evaluation of each participant.

(5) *Feedback.* A summary report is developed on each participant, outlining potential, and, where appropriate, identifying training needs. This information is relayed to the candidate by the person (probably the personnel director) in charge of the assessment center administration.

T-group techniques may be used in the assessment center. (See SENSITIVITY TRAINING.)

The Assessment Center in Practice. When J.C. Penney Company embarked on a program of rapid expansion of its Product Service Division, it was confronted with the need to choose managers for its many new service centers from existing service personnel. As reported by Dr. William C. Byham [2] then in charge of the selection and appraisal programs for the company, an assessment center was designed to identify employees with managerial aptitude and to determine the training needed to prepare them for the jobs.

Six management assessors met in a nearby motel to observe twelve participants while they went through two and half days of different exercises designed to bring out behavior determined as important to success. The participants were service technicians or field representatives recommended by their supervisors for possible promotion. The assessors were two or more levels above them. Here are the highlights of what the candidates were rated on:

Manufacturing Company Game: In teams of four, the candidates had to organize and operate a "company" to manufacture toys. Each team was given starting capital, parts lists, and models of the toys to be assembled. They had to determine the most effective allocation of their resources, the relative profit margin of each toy, and how best to organize. The goal was to maximize profits. Prices of raw materials and finished products changed for each of the three 20-minute periods comprising the game. The assessors could observe their planning, organizing, and controlling skills, and their adaptability to change.

Irate Customer: The participants were told to expect a phone call in their rooms, and to answer as a product service manager. The caller followed a carefully prepared script as an irate customer who wanted immediate satisfaction on a number of complaints. An evaluation was made of the candidate's ability to handle a stressful situation. Was he polite and sympathetic? Was he able to get the information needed to make a correct decision?

In-Basket: Each candidate was given a pile of letters, notes, requests, and problems such as might be found in a service center manager's in-basket. He was also given background on the service center, the employees, and the former manager's activities. Within a specified number of hours, the candidate had to decide on priorities, organize the material, plan, delegate, make decisions, and seek information. Later he was interviewed by an assessor on how he handled the in-basket.

Simulated Appraisal: The participant had to conduct an appraisal of performance with a "service center technician." He first had to complete an appraisal form and prepare for the interview. (He had been given an entire evening to read instructions about the form, and on how to prepare for and conduct an interview.)

Job Applicant: Acting as a service center manager, the participant interviewed an applicant for the job of service center technician. He was given half an hour to study the application form and resumé before the interview, and after the interview he had to present an oral evaluation of the applicant and make a recommendation on hiring.

Small Business Financial Analysis: As an evening's assignment, each participant was given descriptive and financial information about a small business. He was told to act as a management consultant: to analyze the material provided and prepare answers to questions posed by the owner about ways of increasing profit, adding personnel, and whether to open a new branch. The "consultant" had to prepare a five-minute oral presentation of his recommendations.

Discipline Cases: Brief histories of four disciplinary cases were presented to participants. They had to resolve each case and make recommendations in writing within one hour.

Background Interview: In addition to the foregoing exercises, the personal and business background of each participant was explored in a one-and-a-half hour interview with an assessor.

Rating: Candidates were rated on a scale of one (lowest) to five (highest) to indicate whether in the assessors' opinions the candidate should remain in his present job, had limited or average potential, above-average potential, or further potential to be a regional or national manager.

Note: A rating of one did not mean the candidate was to be discharged. It merely meant that he was considered as having more strengths in technical areas than in managerial ones. A high rating, on the other hand, could have considerable positive effect on the candidate's chance for promotion to management.

CARL HEYEL, Management Counsel, Manhasset, New York

Information References

Cohen, Stephen L., "Pre-Packaged vs. Tailor-Made: The Assessment Center Debate," *Personnel Journal,* December 1980.

Hart, Gary L. and Thompson, Paul H., "Assessment Centers: For Selection or Development?" *Organization Dynamics,* Spring 1979.

References Cited

[1] Kelly, Joe, "How Managers Manage," Englewood Cliffs, N.J., Prentice-Hall, 1980.

[2] Byham, William C., "How a Scientific Assessment Center Works," a chapter in Marrow, Alfred J., ed., "The Failure of Success," AMACOM, 1972.

Cross References: *Executive Appraisal (Diagnostic Performance Appraisal); Executive Traits; Performance Rating (Merit Rating).*

ATTITUDE SURVEYS. See Employee Attitude Research: Attitude Surveys

AUDITING. See Certified Public Accountant; Internal Auditing.

AUTOMATIC DATA PROCESSING. See Electronic Data Processing and accompanying entries with that prefix; Management Information Systems; Management Information Systems: A Case Example.

AUTOMATION

Automation embraces a number of concepts, some new and some not so new, ranging from the automatic manufacturing of a product to the application of electronic devices to problem solving. In practical application today, automation involves three separate but related developments:

(1) The melding of production operations with handling and control operations to tie separate pieces of automatic equipment into continuous automatic production through a series of operations, an entire line, or a complete plant.

(2) Automatic control of variables in a machine or plant to produce a product within specified tolerances.

(3) Information processing and reporting on an automatic basis.

These three fields can be briefly described as *Detroit Automation, Process Control,* and *Data Handling.* (For the last-named, see ELECTRONIC DATA PROCESSING.)

Formal Definition. No general agreement on a definition for automation has been possible. The basic argument is between those who feel that automation is only a new word for mechanization and those who feel that automation connotes elements not involved in mechanization. Among the second group there are individual schools supporting different elements considered essential, such as feedback, the presence of electronic elements, or the use of computers. In general application, automation can be defined as doing things in a way that is "significantly more automatic" than they were done before.

To some, automation implies changes in methods, and is likely to be used to describe those changes that are on the advancing edge of manufacturing practice. In this sense, automation in the 1950s usually meant special machinery; in the 1960s it meant numerical control; in the 1970s it meant computers; and in the 1980s it means microprocessors.

Feedback, which is intimately associated with automation, can be defined as a way of measuring the results of some operation that is performed and feeding these results back to the control of the equipment performing the operation so that an adjustment is made automatically when needed.

History. As a word, and to some extent as a concept, automation had its origin in Detroit. It began at the Ford Motor Co. late in 1946 when Del S. Harder, then Vice President of

Manufacturing, was reviewing plans for a new plant and said, "Let's see more mechanical handling between these transfer machines. Give us some more of that—that 'automation.'" Within a short time an Automation Department had been established at Ford.

The original definition of automation, in the first report on the pioneering work at Ford, was "the art of applying mechanical devices to manipulate workpieces into and out of equipment, turn parts between operations, remove scrap, and to perform these tasks in timed sequence with the production equipment so that the line can be wholly or partially under pushbutton control at strategic stations."

Later this same task force produced the first Ford Cleveland Engine Plant, introducing new elements of selection and control. The work from two machines might be distributed to three (or combined in one) for the next operation. Just as the word automation caught the fancy of those who first heard it, the word caught on with others who read it and in a short period it had become popular and began to develop its present elastic meaning.

The elements of automation have their roots much further back, but the new elements of combining and controlling, the increased ability to control, and the application of the term all came at about the same time in the years following World War II.

Approaches and Techniques. All automation of manufacturing operations must start with a machine that has some form of automatic operating cycle. From this beginning the first step is to apply automatic loading and unloading devices. The next step is to add transfer devices between machines that connect the unloading device of one machine with the loading device of the next one. The steps to this point can be undertaken in easy stages to produce a *linked line,* or the entire job can be done at once with a *transfer machine.*

Transfer machines can be compact, with four or five working stations placed around a rotating table, or they can have the stations in a straight line. In either case, the work is "transferred" automatically from station to station within the machine.

The next step in automation is to apply automatic gaging or inspection of the work at desired points in the sequence. Then it is possible to have the production line stop if work is not going according to specifications, or go one more step and add feedback so that the necessary adjustments are made automatically and the line stops only when tools have been adjusted to the limit and must be replaced.

An auxiliary development that can be added at any point after the linking of operations begins is the inclusion of automatic in-process storage units. These maintain banks of parts at various stages so that a shutdown need affect only part of the production line, with preceding and following sections feeding into and out of these storage units.

Processing lines for painting, heat-treating, assembly, plating, welding, brazing, or forging can be automated by following much the same steps that are used with machining and pressing lines.

Assembly operations are usually performed by hand or with the aid of hand or power tools, but automatic assembly machines have come into wide use in the electronic industry and are a growing factor in the production of automobiles, appliances, and other high-volume products.

Numerical control of machine tools is a method of control by which numerical values fed to the machine are converted into physical values such as dimensions or quantities. Numerical control of machine tools first offered a form of automation to the plant producing many different things in small quantities (job shops) just as the transfer machine and mechanical handling have provided automation for mass-production plants.

Computers can store the programs and feed them to numerical control systems at the machines, bypassing the tape readers on the machines. Computers can also replace the conventional control, take over its computations, and feed operating pulses directly to the machines. Development of mini-computers and microprocessors also make it possible to incorporate them in individual machine controls.

Computer controls, whether for a single machine or for a group of machines, have more flexibility, and simplify the task of program changes. This makes it easier to correct program errors or to make changes that optimize the program timing.

With CNC systems it is possible for the operator to prepare programs at the machine, or to modify existing programs, and to record these for later reuse. For more complex operations, however, programming is normally done off the machine. Sometimes CNC control systems are now chosen for long production runs in high-volume production with no operator access to the program.

Fixed automation is also beginning to yield to adjustable or programmable mechanical devices that are more easily changed to suit a redesign or to handle different, but similar, parts in successive batches. Robots, with their own separate controls, can be used for loading and unloading, or the units can be built into the machine and operate from the machine's control system.

In all of these techniques management is faced with a wide latitude in the amount of automation that can be undertaken. In addition, choices must be made as to whether to modernize and upgrade the existing plant or start fresh on a new plant site.

Automatic Controllers. Control of continuous processes probably started with the steam-engine governor and has progressed to the stage of computer-controlled petroleum and chemical plants. This field of automation begins with a wide variety of instruments for reporting conditions in the process, feeds this information to a computer to analyze the data, and ends with instructions from the computer to various "servomechanisms" that make adjustments in valves and other controls.

Computers are also being applied in various data handling projects, ranging from production control in plants, the handling of payrolls and accounts, to the processing of checks by banks.

Most such applications are developed jointly with the firms developing and manufacturing the computers.

Application. Three major problems have arisen in applying automation:

(1) Cost of obsolescence, if the product changes, is greatly increased. This problem has been met in two ways. First, by trying to anticipate the nature of product changes and planning the original equipment so it will handle such changes. Second, by making use of standard components (modules, or "building blocks") in special equipment so that surplus lines can be broken up and the components used as the basis for new lines.

(2) A work stoppage at any point for a tool change or repair forces shutdown of the entire production line. This problem has been met by breaking transfer machines or linked lines up into short segments with banks of parts between segments.

(3) The need for "debugging": When a standard machine is placed on the market it has normally had enough development and field testing to eliminate the small errors in design and manufacture that are inevitable with a new product. However, with most one-of-kind special production equipment, it is natural that some things will have been done wrong and some overlooked. The process of detecting and correcting these ("debugging") will usually take weeks and may take months. Use of standard components will reduce, but not eliminate, this problem.

All three of these problems may be reduced when automation is by NC machine rather than by special machine. However, properly designed and debugged mechanical systems are usually considered more economical and reliable for most high-volume production.

The three reasons that are the biggest factors in deciding to invest in automation are (1) to reduce direct-labor costs, (2) to increase output, and (3) to improve product quality. These reasons introduce a dual economic standard: If it is necessary to automate to produce a product of acceptable quality, cost is not necessarily the controlling factor. If automation is considered only to maintain price competition, cost is the critical factor.

Technically, it is usually possible to provide any desired degree of automation, but the costs vary widely. Some operations are fairly easy to automate, others are extremely difficult. In planning for automation, close coordination of design, manufacturing, and sales is essential. Most of the problems that arise today can probably be traced to too much haste and too little coordination in the early planning stages.

Acceptance. The *12th American Machinist Inventory* (1978) reported that 5% of metalworking plants were using about 18,000 transfer machines, and 7% were using automatic assembly machines (also about 18,000).

In 1979, 20% of the value of new metal-cutting machine tools shipped consisted of transfer machines and 31% of NC machines. Thus, over half (by value) of new metal-cutting machine tools were automated. In addition, an unknown portion of the other machines (such as gear-cutting machines going into linked lines in auto plants) were also automated.

Potential. The initial period for the introduction of the Detroit automation was from about 1950 (when the impact of the first installations began to sink in) to about 1958 (when it became clear that there was a good deal of excess production capacity in most of the metalworking industries). Down sizing of automobiles in the 1980s involved replacing much of this early automation with newer, more flexible transfer lines, more automated welding lines, and with banks of NC machines. However, there are still large areas for application in other industries. Applications of both numerical control systems and of digital computers continue to increase each year.

There is much less talk, however, of "plants without people" than there once was. But there is general recognition that automation usually causes some displacement of labor. Potential is therefore limited not only by the ability to engineer particular applications and the availability of investment funds, but by the ability of management to deal with the complex labor problems often created.

Impact on Employment. Concern over growing foreign competition and the need to increase productivity to meet it have reduced the concern of both workers and government about the impact of automation on employment. There are now some factories in other countries where automation is more extensive than in the United States. There is also worry about the "export of jobs" by American manufacturers and retailers who produce goods overseas in order to meet the competition of imports.

Most people now recognize that without automation they would not be enjoying such a high standard of living and such a wide variety of choice in goods. Also recognized is the fact that the production of automation equipment, including computers, is a significant source of employment and a major earner of foreign exchange in export.

Another reason for the declining impact of automation on employment is the way in which the issue is being treated in some labor negotiations. This approach got its start many years ago when the United Mine Workers withdrew opposition to mechanization of coal mining in return for the establishment of a pension fund supported by a royalty paid on coal mined thereafter. More recently, shipping companies and the longshoremen reached a similar agreement on the use of containerized shipments that lend themselves to mechanical handling equipment.

As the United States economy has shifted more to a service than a production base, the concern has become whether automation can be introduced rapidly enough in the manufacturing sector to provide enough productivity growth to sustain the service sector (including government) where productivity growth is negligible.

ANDERSON ASHBURN, Editor, *American Machinist,* New York, New York

Information References

Associations:

Machinery and Allied Products Institute. National Machine Tool Builders' Association. Society of Manufacturing Engineers.

Periodicals:

American Machinist.
Control Engineering.
Manufacturing Engineering.
Production.

Texts:

"AM on Computers—Their Role in Manufacturing," reprint collection from *American Machinist,* New York, 1971.

"Automation Management: The Social Perspective," Athens, Ga., The Center for the Study of Automation and Society, 1970.

Buckingham, Walter, "Automation—Its Impact on Business and People." New York: Harper & Bros., 1961

Diebold, John, "Automation: The Advent of the Automatic Factory," New York, D. Van Nostrand (now Van Nostrand Reinhold), 1952.

Foster, David, "Automation in Practice," London, New York, McGraw-Hill, 1968.

Leone, William C., "Production Automation and Numerical Control," New York, Ronald, 1967.

Niland, Powell, "Management Problems in the Acquisition of Special Automatic Equipment." Boston, Harvard Graduate School of Business Administration, 1961.

Cross References: *Electronic Data Processing and accompanying entries with that prefix; Robots in Industry; Technological Change: Union-Management Agreements.*

B

BABBAGE, CHARLES

Charles Babbage (1792–1871) was not an industrialist or manager, although his work has had a profound influence on management concepts and practices. Mathematics professor at Cambridge University, England, from 1828 to 1839, he achieved fame as a mathematical scientist, and his invention of a "difference engine" to speed mathematical calculations was the forerunner of today's electronic computers. In the course of working on his device, Babbage became much interested in workships and factories both in Great Britain and in Europe, and visited many of them. His observation of their methods led him to conclusions regarding management which in many respects anticipated some of the most important findings of FREDERICK W. TAYLOR, although the latter was quite unaware of his work. These were embodied in Babbage's book "On the Economy of Machinery and Manufactures," 1832, later published in the United States. He noted common principles "that pervaded many establishments," and advanced the premise that principles of management exist, can be determined by experience, and can be broadly applied. He also anticipated modern practice in analysis of processes and manufacturing costs, use of time study, use of printed standard information blanks for investigation, and study of comparative practices of business firms in the same field.

Information Reference

Urwick, L., "The Golden Book of Management," edited for the International Committee of Scientific Management (CIOS), Newman Neame, Limited, London, 1956.

BABCOCK, GEORGE DE ALBERT

George D. Babcock (1875–1942) pioneered in introducing the Taylor system of management into the American automobile industry between 1908 and 1912. This work, begun by CARL BARTH as a consultant, and continued by Babcock as plant executive, was the first application of Scientific Management in a major American industry. Babcock is credited with several original contributions to the Taylor methods: an employee counseling program of the kind later made famous by Elton Mayo; an improved formula for base wage rates, which automatically adjusted the base wage rate with changes in the cost of living and the employee's personal record; and an integrated planning system visualized from a single control board. The latter installed at the Franklin Automobile Manufacturing Company, Syracuse, N.Y., made use of a board showing the exact location of every project in the plant, and introduced such features as pneumatic tubes for issuing and returning orders, and preservation of progress records by photography. In his work for the Rural Electrification Administration, 1937–39, he codified a very large number of government construction projects on a single sheet of paper, producing the first clear picture of this heterogeneous field. His writings include the book, "Taylor System in Franklin Management," Engineering Magazine Company, New York, 1917.

Information Reference

Urwick, L., "The Golden Book of Management," edited for the International Committee of Scientific Management (CIOS), Newman Neame, Limited, London, 1956.

BARTH, CARL G. L.

Carl George Lange Barth (1860–1939) was the earliest, closest, and by many considered the ablest associate of F. W. TAYLOR (see also SCIENTIFIC MANAGEMENT: "Taylorism"). He is famous for his development in 1899 of the Barth Slide-Rule, in connection with his formula of twelve variables used in analysis of the voluminous data accumulated by Taylor at the Bethlehem Steel Company. This slide-rule enabled the person preparing the instruction card for the machine operator easily to utilize the formla in the set-up of a machine, for the best performance of any operation within the capacity of the machine. The new slide-rule proved to be the solution to most of Taylor's metal-cutting problems. Many other standardized tools on which Taylor's system depended were the results of Barth's ingenuity. Barth also rendered much service in Taylor's other researches into time study, fatigue study, and the like, and in introducing scientific management into manufacturing concerns. Notable with respect to the last-named was his supervision of the application of new methods in the Link-Belt Philadelphia plant in 1903, the first of many assignments which Barth undertook to install the Taylor methods either in part or as a complete system of management. He worked with Taylor until the latter's death in 1915, although he established his own consulting firm, Carl G. Barth & Son, in 1912. He continued consulting work during his semi-retirement, 1923–1929.

Information Reference

Urwick, L., "The Golden Book of Management," edited for the International Committee of Scientific Management (CIOS), Newman Neame, Limited, London, 1956.

BASIC RESEARCH: Management Aspects

Research is a term that is often used to describe a broad spectrum of scientific endeavor ranging from fundamental investigation of the secrets of nature ("pure" research) to modest evolutionary improvements in common consumer products. Here we focus on *industrial* research, and use the term **Basic Research** to describe a body of technical activity aimed at achieving a quantitative understanding of natural phenomena, with the proviso, however, that unlike academically based "pure" research the activity is seen as having a recognized relationship to commercially exploitable results.

Basic research encompasses both scientific and engineering disciplines, and the distinction between a research scientist and a research engineer becomes blurred. The immediate objectives of the research scientist and the research engineer may be different, since the latter may be more closely associated with a specific new-product development, but both of them perceive the need to extend fundamental understanding of natural laws in order to achieve their ends.

Why Basic Research in Industry. Since this article examines the management of basic research in industry, it may be instructive to analyze the motivations or reasons for conducting such activities in the first place. Industrial basic research can be done for largely "defensive" purposes, i.e., to assure that a corporation has within its organization a competent, up-to-date technical resource that can solve problems. These problems can, and do, range from difficulties arising in production all the way to problems that arise in products many years after they have been in service.

A second motivation for a company to sponsor basic research is the anticipation that new products and services will result from the research, thereby providing new opportunities for future corporate growth. The new products and services may derive directly from discoveries in basic research, or they may be evolutionary extensions of existing product lines. Examples of the former category include many new types of plastics, or industrial diamonds (first produced in General Electric laboratories in 1955 and introduced commercially in 1957). In these cases, new materials, having properties superior to competing substances, became commercially available as a result of basic research that provided new understanding about chemical bonding and structures, processing, and in the specific case of diamonds, from breakthroughs in high-pressure physics and chemistry.

Although the development of brand new products from basic research is dramatic and is the dream of every research director, no less important is the wide variety of improved products and services that are made available from basic research. Basic research on semiconducting materials led to the discovery of the transistor, which in turn led to major improvements in an enormous number of familiar products, including radios, television sets, and all sorts of other communication devices. Basic research in high-temperature materials, aerodynamics, engineering mechanics, and numerous other fields led to the development of the aircraft gas turbine, which in turn greatly increased the speed, comfort, and economy of air travel.

These few examples illustrate some of the reasons why industry sponsors basic research. What are the mechanisms by which research is done?

Operating Considerations. The organization of laboratories in a decentralized company is a problem not confined to only a few large companies. For example, the choice of having a central research laboratory, or several decentralized laboratories, or both, will depend in large part on the diversity of a company's product line as well as its technological complexity.

Some scientific and technical operations have

a "critical size" imposed by the requirement of a close working relationship among a great variety of technical skills or specialized facilities. Analytical laboratories illustrate this case: today, a modern, well equipped analytical laboratory having the capability of performing detailed physical and chemical analyses of materials requires the skills of highly trained chemists, physicists, metallurgists, and electronics specialists, all working with millions of dollars of complex and sophisticated equipment. If the analytical laboratory has facilities for biological specimens, the size and expense increase even further.

Thus, certain types of research facilities, such as analytical laboratories, may operate most effectively and economically on a pooled basis. In a technically diverse, decentralized company, however, it is frequently desirable to establish product-oriented laboratories within the major business components, under the management control of the cognizant general manager. These laboratories are closely coupled with the immediate and near-term needs of the business, thereby providing direct technical support at the operating level required by the business. In turn, these laboratories or technical centers could be supported by a central research facility, which would have responsibility for the longer-range technical needs of the entire corporation, and for the basic research programs to implement those needs.

Reporting and Communications. Industry has developed extensive and frequently quite sophisticated procedures for reporting and communicating results from the traditional functional organizations of engineering, manufacturing, finance, and marketing. Learning how to report and communicate the results of basic scientific research poses a different, and in some respects, a more difficult challenge. Inventions and discoveries obviously cannot be scheduled. In many areas of basic research, experiments will often be unsuccessful, and reporting negative results could appear to be a difficult and onerous task. However, it is important that scientists and engineers conducting basic research be required to report the status of the investigations on a regular basis, regardless of whether or not the results are positive. Progress reports are an important tool for the research manager, enabling him to assess the rate of progress, to determine if more resources are needed, and ultimately to help determine whether to abandon or accelerate a program. Regular progress reports are a key input to the research manager in the determination of when to start transitioning the results of a successful research program to a business component.

Communication from one step to the next is a minimum requirement in a successful transition, and the steps must not be so large that people have difficulty in communicating. Frequent and regular communication between the research laboratory and the business component that will receive the transition is a powerful tool in overcoming inherent institutional barriers such as the "not-invented-here" syndrome. It is not unusual for technical personnel working in a business component to feel that they are in competition with their peers in the basic research laboratory. Yet, the technical people in business operations have a critical role in seeing that the technical results generated in the research laboratory are successfully implemented into their business. Thus, it is imperative upon management to ensure that frequent and regular communication take place in the corporate technical community, and to initiate the technical transition at the earliest feasible point in the project.

It is important that the basic scientist and his management at the starting end of this chain of events provide the "translation" of the discoveries; that is, that they explain and interpret the findings in a manner that is understandable to the people who wish to utilize the new knowledge. At this critical point experience indicates that the demonstration of technical feasibility is generally the key step in industrial scientific communication, to establish the validity of a new process or concept, or to illustrate the experimental form of a new material or the embodiment of an idea. It is the *visible* evidence of new knowledge, without which the road to practical utilization is difficult or impossible to follow.

Planning Basic Research. If basic research is "an adventure into the unknown," one might reasonably ask whether or not it is possible to plan such an adventure. Is it possible to plan discoveries or breakthroughs? The answer is clearly no—but, it *is* possible to plan basic research in areas that are *likely* to produce discoveries, breakthroughs, and inventions. Also, it is possible to plan for the results of success; that is, plan for the implementation and consequences of success. At any point in time, some areas of technology are moving faster than others; for example, the areas of microelectronics, automation and control, and power electronics, are all very fast moving, and it is reasonable to assume that these areas will yield more discoveries and inventions than a more mature area of technology. Thus, examining the various arenas of research and their relative rates of advancement provides the research manager with an important qualitative tool for making decisions of resource allocation.

A second tool for this purpose is, as stated, to examine the consequences of success. That is, what is the impact on the business if the research is successful? Will it yield a product improvement; a brand new product; or a whole new business? Is there a logical home for the new product in the business, and does the company have the resources successfully to engineer, manufacture, and market the product? Management methodologies that address these questions provide another important and essential aid in determining resource allocation. (See NEW-PRODUCT PLANNING: Profitability Projections.)

Measurement. The measurement of industrial research output and impact is important not only to the manager of this function, but of course, to the general manager of the entire enterprise.

Measurements available to the research manager include parameters of individual achievement and productivity, such as patents and publications. However, these are far from complete measurements of a scientist's productivity; patents and papers both differ greatly in quality. The value of a patent may depend upon time in an unpredictable manner. Furthermore, whether a novel idea is patentable or not depends on factors outside of the control of the inventor, such as Patent Office actions. Valuable new ideas may end up not being patentable, yet be of great value to the corporation, which may choose to exploit the idea in its product lines with the anticipation of protecting the idea as a trade secret. (See PATENTS.)

Consider scientific publications: although we do not know how to measure the value of scientific papers directly, it is certain that they differ greatly in their contribution to science. Some measure of the latter can be obtained by reference to Citation Indices, to ascertain the number of times a technical paper is cited by later scientific authors during a given period of time.

Other elements of individual scientific quality and productivity are qualitatively evident, such as leadership in technical societies, peer recognition, and the like.

The general manager of the entire business enterprise would like to be able to assess the value and impact of scientific research as he makes decision for investing the company's resources. Management is faced with numerous resource tradeoffs, such as investing in additional manufacturing capacity, new or expanded marketing programs, or research. In all but the last of these alternatives, it is generally possible to forecast the intended result with sufficient accuracy to permit decision-making with a satisfactory degree of confidence. The calculation of the future return on present research expenditures, on the other hand, involves more intangibles and hence is generally much more speculative. However, the combination of a first-rate research organization and farsighted management who view research as an important investment can lead to new discoveries, inventions, products, and processes that benefit not only their corporation, but society as a whole.

CRAIG S. TEDMON, JR., Staff Executive, Power Systems Technology Operation, General Electric Company, Schenectady, New York.

Information References

Drucker, Peter F., "Managing in Turbulent Times," New York, Harper & Row, 1980.

Heyel, Carl, ed., "Handbook of Industrial Research Management," New York, Van Nostrand Reinhold, 2nd ed., 1968.

Steele, Lowell W., "Innovation in Big Business," New York, Elsevier, 1975.

Cross References: *Industrial Research Accounting; Industrial Research Budgeting; Industrial Research and Development: National Patterns; New-Product Development; Outside Research; Technological Forecasting.*

BEHAVIOR MODELING IN TRAINING

Behavior Modeling is a term that designates a systematic way of developing the skills needed in human interactions, utilizing well-established learning principles. The basic ideas were developed by Arnold P. Goldstein and Melvin Sorcher, and are lucidly described in their book "Changing Supervisor Behavior" [1]. They term the process "Applied Learning." Another commonly used term is "Interaction Modeling." The American Telephone and Telegraph Company calls its supervisory training program which incorporates this process "Supervisory Relationships Training." Development Dimensions, Inc., of Pittsburgh, which markets a training system utilizing these principles, terms it "Interaction Management."

The process employs the use of a video tape or film model with associated learning points, practice in simulated situations, the reinforcement of correct behavior, and, finally, transfer of the learned behavior to real on-the-job situations. The specific objective in utilizing this process in supervisory training is to improve the way managers handle manager-employee interactions.

The reaction of many training people to their first exposure to these ideas is that there is really nothing new here, and in a sense they are correct to question the novelty of this approach. In fact, we are surrounded with examples of this kind of training. We have all experienced it, both as trainers and trainees. This is the way we were taught to drive a car; this is how a typist learns to type. It is so common to us that it might be called the common sense approach to training. It is, after all, nothing more than showing someone how to do something, getting them to try it, coaching them, and having them apply what they have learned. What is new is that these common sense steps have been formalized, and this training method has been adapted to the development of human interaction skills, particularly in the area of teaching supervisory skills.

In training new managers we have primarily relied, heretofore, on lecture or prescribed reading, discussion groups, or other similar means which are quite effective at teaching *concepts.* However, these methods leave a great deal to be desired where our objective is to develop specific *skills.* For example, a thorough understanding of the company's policies of nondiscrimination may be needed by all supervisors, but this understanding alone is seldom sufficient to prepare the supervisor to deal properly with an employee who has a discrimination complaint. Dealing with such a problem calls for interaction skill—skill in effectively handling a particular kind of human interaction.

The kinds of situations which are dealt with in supervisory behavior modeling programs are such regular occurrences as welcoming a new employee to the department, giving the employee verbal recognition, discussing communications problems, and handling employee complaints. It has been found that by training supervisors to handle a series of such interactions in specified ways, the trainees not only learn to perform these specific tasks in an acceptable fashion, but the trainees actually transfer this style of interaction with subordinates to other situations.

Procedure. The model employed in training managers via behavior modeling is typically a TV tape showing a good manger handling the specified interaction in an effective way. Associated with the tape are a number of learning points which are the specific behavioral steps the manager employs in handling the situation. The model clearly demonstrates the utilization of these points. Tapes or films have of course been widely utilized in supervisory training in the past, but most typically these tapes are not designed to demonstrate how specific learning points are effectively followed, but are more often used to provide *information,* which it is hoped will result in changed behavior on the part of the observer.

Practice consists of role playing. Each trainee is given the opportunity to display his ability to follow the learning points, handling a situation similar to that displayed on the tape. The practice continues until the trainee has shown that he can behave in the prescribed manner. Here again it is important to differentiate between role playing as it is employed here—better called "skill rehearsal"—and role playing as frequently used elsewhere. Here, the trainee has quite specific instruction (in the form of the learning points) as to what he is to accomplish, and he practices the specified skill until he "gets it right." Leading the trainee through the proper set of behaviors makes application of these skills back in the job situation relatively well assured.

Reinforcement is provided by the trainer who encourages the trainee with praise when he performs correctly and provides corrective coaching when he fails to behave appropriately. Reinforcement also comes from the "employee" role player as well as from his fellow trainees who are observing the role playing.

Transfer is accomplished primarily by requiring the trainees to apply on the job what they have learned in the classroom. In a subsequent class meeting, usually a week later, the trainee is required to report back to the class what transpired when the newly learned behavior was tried out in a real situation. This provision for transfer of training built into behavior modeling programs is virtually unique.

The process involves very little lecture, and no reading assignments. The discussion which takes place in the classroom is concerned almost entirely with the behavior displayed by the trainees in the role plays. Remarks by the trainer are restricted to those required to assure understanding on the part of the trainees of the learning points involved.

Behavior modeling has been shown to be effective as a means of training managers to behave differently in their dealings with their subordinates. It must be emphasized, however, that a training program can in a pure sense be called behavior modeling only if all four elements—*model, practice, reinforcement,* and *transfer*—are included. This is not to say that a program which uses a taped model, lecture, and demonstration will not be effective, but, properly speaking, it is something other than behavior modeling.

Proper attention to each of the four elements is essential if a program is to be successful, and each element presents unique challenges to the program developer. For instance, the model itself cannot be created without first developing the learning points which the model is intended to demonstrate, and there is no simple, systematic way of creating these points; this particular piece of the building of a total program calls for considerable creativity.

It is suggested that the writer begin by assembling some *general* learning points—statements which describe behavior deemed desirable over a wide variety of situations. These general learning points are not intended to provide specific instruction to the trainee, but are used as a framework within which the specific learning point can be developed. For example, a general learning point might be: "Maintain good communications." Specific learning points associated with this general learning point could be: "Express your concern about manager/employee communications. State your acceptance of the major responsibility for improvement. Ask the employee for help and ideas."

Some commonsense guidelines which should be borne in mind in writing specific learning points are these:

- Keep the number of learning points small. Three or four can be considered ideal, seven is too many.
- State the learning points in positive terms wherever possible.
- Use language easily understood by all trainees.
- Keep the learning points simple—one specific behavior per learning point.

Potentials. The utilization of behavior modeling is not limited to supervisory training, but can be employed in any situation in which the objective is to improve the interaction skills of employees. For example, one company has used the technique in training its plant security officers to handle such common interactions as "answering the telephone," "handling telephone complaints," and "confrontation at the time of a rule infraction."

In addition to these one-on-one interactions, the process has been used to train managers in "one-on-many" situations. "Conducting the Opinion Survery Feedback Meeting" was a program which prepared managers to handle the interactions likely to be experienced with their subordinates in a specific kind of department meeting.

Nor is the process necessarily restricted to face-to-face interactions. The administrators of a suggestion system were trained to handle the delicate matter of writing effective letters rejecting suggestions, using an adaptation of behavior modeling training.

Training programs utilizing interaction modeling, properly designed and carried out, will produce results. Several interesting studies were reported in an American Psychological Association symposium chaired by A. I. Kraut in 1975 [2]. In this symposium Dr. William Byam reported that employees managed by trained supervisors indicated that, following training, their supervisors responded to a variety of interaction situations in ways taught in the training program more frequently than they had done before training. Dr. Joel Moses, in the same symposium, showed how the American Telephone and Telegraph Company had evaluated the effectiveness of their Supervisory Relationships Training Program by utilizing an assessment technique. Dr. Robert Burnaska of General Electric, using an evaluation method similar to that employed by Moses, showed similar results in a study of trained professional salaried employees. Dr. Preston Smith of IBM showed how the training of field service managers to hold opinion survey feedback meetings resulted in improvement in their conducting of such meetings, but in addition the training was associated with an improvement in morale level of the employees, when compared with a control group.

Similar results were shown in a study by Dodd and Pesci [3]. Survey feedback training using behavior modeling techniques resulted in better meetings, better action programs, and ultimately better employee morale.

A study by Latham and Saari [4] demonstrated that a behavior modeling training program designed to improve supervisors' interpersonal skills was not only effective in test situations, but was also apparently instrumental in improving the supervisor's job performance, as reflected in performance ratings collected one year after training.

One concern of many people in the field is that the apparent simplicity of the approach may lead the uninitiated to believe that here, at last, is a training device that not only works, but can be adapted to any situation by any training manager, with hardly any effort at all. Here we have a scheme that will allow us to package our program into a neat TV tape and send it out to all our branch offices and, miraculously, our training problems will be solved. Would that if it were so! It works, and it works well—carried out correctly in appropriate situations—but the uninitiated are advised to proceed with care. The process appears to be simple, but much attention needs to be given to the development and execution of programs utilizing behavior modeling if successes such as those reported here are to be realized.

JOHN R. PAULSEN, PH.D., IBM Education, Lexington, Kentucky

References Cited

[1] Goldstein, A.P. and Sorcher, M., "Changing Supervisor Behavior," Elmsford, N.Y., Pergamon Press, 1974.

[2] Kraut, A.I., "Behavior Modeling Symposium: Developing Managerial Skills via Modeling Techniques: Some Positive Research Findings," *Personnel Psychology,* 1976, 29, 325–369.

[3] Dodd, William E. and Pesci, Michael L., "Managing Morale through Survey Feedback," *Business Horizons,* June 1977.

[4] Latham, Gary P. and Saari, Lise M., "Application of Social Learning Theory to Training Supervisors through Behavior Modeling," *Journal of Applied Psychology,* 1977, 64, 239–246.

Cross References: *Human Resources Development and cross references there indicated.*

BEHAVIORAL SCIENCES

The **Behavioral Sciences** include any science that studies the behavior of man (and of the lower animals) in their physical and social environment, by methods of experiment and observations in the manner of other natural sciences. The recognized behavioral sciences include psychology, sociology, social anthropology, and those parts of other sciences similar to these in outlook and method. These disciplines have in the past two decades been increasingly applied to the study of human behavior in a working environment.

BETTER BUSINESS BUREAUS

Better Business Bureaus—151 in the United States, 16 in Canada, 2 in Israel, and 1 in Venezuela, as of 1980—have a dual mission: to be an effective national self-regulatory force for private enterprise, and to demonstrate a sincere and visible concern for consumers. The BBB movement began in 1911 with "Vigilance Committees for Truth in Advertising" in local advertising clubs. These committees later became Bureaus, and expanded into the broader sphere of monitoring, investigating, and correcting misleading and deceptive advertising and business practices.

For nearly 70 years, the Bureaus have been virtually the only place a consumer could find information and help. The Bureaus have more contact with consumers than any private organization addressing itself to these problems. Primarily through telephone calls and the mail, over 6½ million consumers contacted Better Business Bureaus in 1980. Of this number, more than 5 million were inquiries from consumers seeking to determine the reliability of individual companies and various offers before investing. Another 1½ million requests were received from consumers with complaints about purchase or service transactions.

Better Business Bureaus also develop trade practice codes with business groups and cooperate with city and state consumer protection agencies and regional offices of the Federal Trade Commission. Advertisements are checked, and correction of misleading advertising is sought. Where voluntary compliance is not obtained, offenders are referred to appropriate law enforcement agencies.

All recognized Bureaus are part of the Council of Better Business Bureaus, Inc., which was organized in August 1970 by a consolidation of the National Better Business Bureau and the Association of Better Business Bureaus International. Offices of the Council of Better Business Bureaus are maintained in Washington, D. C. and New York City. The headquarters in Washington coordinates the activities of member Bureaus, issues advertising standards on the national level, administers the BBB arbitration program, disseminates information about charitable solicitations, and performs consumer education and public information functions. The Washington office also works closely with Government regulatory agencies and trade associations, and keeps abreast of Government activities that concern business and consumers. The New York office monitors and investigates complaints against national advertising.

WILLIAM H. TANKERSLEY, President, Council of Better Business Bureaus, Inc., Washington, D. C.

Cross Reference: *Consumer Protection.*

BOULTON, MATTHEW ROBINSON

Matthew Robinson Boulton (1770–1842) was, with **James Watt, Jr.,** partner of Boulton, Watt and Co., producers, from 1796 to 1849, of letter-copying presses and steam engines at the Soho Engineering Foundry near Birmingham, England. This foundry has been credited with the first illustration of scientific management in action. Boulton and Watt were the sons of Matthew Boulton and James Watt, pioneers in the development of the steam engine and founders of the firm. The following management techniques were applied by the sons, on a small scale, but systematically: market research and forecasting; planned site location; planned machine layout and work-flow; production planning; production process standards; standardization of product components; statistical records; advanced cost-accounting; workers' training; advanced division of labor; work study and payment by results based thereon; provision for personnel welfare, with a sickness benefit scheme administered by an elected committee of employees; an executive development program. In his introduction to Erich Roll's "An Early Experiment in Industrial Organization," 1930 (Longmans Green, London), Prof. J. G. Smith wrote: "There is in fact nothing in the details of the most progressive factory practice today that the two sons had not anticipated. Neither Taylor, Ford, nor other modern experts devised anything in the way of plan that cannot be discovered at Soho before 1805; and the Soho system of costing is superior to that employed in very many successful concerns today."

Information Reference

Urwick, L., "The Golden Book of Management," edited for the International Committee of Scientific Management (CIOS), Newman Neame, Limited, London, 1956.

"BRAINSTORMING"

In recent years, certain formal systems for group creation, with organized rules, have gained prominence. The best known of these is **Brainstorming.** The brainstorming method was developed by Alex Osborn and is described in his book. "Applied Imagination" [1], probably the most widely used single text for creative thinking courses. In brainstorming sessions, a group of individuals, usually five to twelve, develops ideas concerning a problem for a period of a few minutes to an hour, under the leadership of a chairman. The chairman announces the problem as succinctly as possible. The group then generates ideas, subscribing to these rules:

(1) Criticism of an idea is absolutely barred.

(2) But its modification or combination with another idea is encouraged.

(3) Quantity of ideas is sought.

(4) Unusual, remote, or wild ideas are sought.

It is emphasized that a wild and apparently unworkable idea expressed by one participant may spark in another either the way to make it work, or a workable modification. The simple rules are also recommended for *individual* brainstorming of a difficulty. The wild ideas, of course, are useful because they open up new directions of exploration.

The chairman must enforce the rule to bar criticism; must thwart "idea selling"; must restrain the comedian. If the session begins to run down, he must stimulate with an idea or new direction of his own. He closes the session when fatigue comes.

All contributions are welcome, and great stress is placed on the barring of criticism. "Hitch-hikes" on others' ideas are welcomed, and, indeed, are given right of way.

The principal function of a brainstorming session is to feed new, pertinent, perhaps remote associations to the one or two high-creatives in the group under prime conditions of motivation, permissiveness, and opportunity for achievement. Quantity is wanted, in the hope that in much quantity there may be some quality. The question should therefore be so structured that it will have many answers, usually rather specific. Examples are a name for, a slogan for, ways to use, or to do, something. For example, it is required to name a new face cream, provide a slogan for a safety campaign, invent different ways to use Scotch tape or aluminium foil, imagine opportunities to use an extension phone, or think of how to interest new groups of consumers in a given product. For questions of this type, brainstorming is relatively more effective than are other methods.

Charles S. Whiting gives a transcript of a brainstorming session in his "Creative Thinking" [2]. The problem before the group of eleven was to develop new uses for a resealable plastic bag, an item which could be resealed simply by pressing two specially prepared edges together with the fingers, and used primarily as a container for small parts in manufacturing processes. Sample ideas were:

"Use it for wet bathing suits."

"How about album covers for phonograph records?"

"How about taking something down when you go skin diving?"

"Put fish in it after you catch them."

"How about for bait? Live bait, you could put that in this."

"How about using it to contain paint or coloring material?"

. . . and so on for 99 suggestions.

Evaluation of the ideas produced can be conducted either by the brainstorming group itself or another group or individually. Usually if the same group evaluates the idea, it is done several days after the session.

Over the years, numerous variations of the basic technique have evolved, suitable for different sizes of groups and types of problems to be attacked. All, however, stress the need for freedom from criticism of comments made in the sessions.

The Gordon Method. One significant deviation from brainstorming was introduced by William J. Gordon of Arthur D. Little, Inc. He organized a six-member design-synthesis group to invent machines. This group learned to work together with him as leader. Gordon alone knew the real problem at the start of a meeting. At the beginning, he would extrapolate from the problem all the way back to the extremely general and abstract case of which it was a concrete and mechanical example. For example, wanting a new lawn mower, he would simply say, "The question today is separation." As discussion proceeded, he would watch for opportunities to narrow and guide it, meanwhile developing a vast association field to be channelled to the specific job when announced. Development in detail would then follow, the process often requiring several sessions of more than three hours.

Pros and Cons of Brainstorming. After a continued interest over many years, and some deliberate scientific study, the advantages and limitations of the brainstorming procedure may be evaluated.

Pro. First, it should be remembered that "brainstorming" is not a method for solving problems, but a technique for stimulating ideas that will lead to problem solutions. Brainstorming creates a situation where this can happen under discipline such as might be absent in individual work. It sparks a good man's ideas, and *makes* him think under tension. There is a stimulating and vitalizing ego-satisfaction as the group launches into unknown territory.

Brainstorming works best on specific and limited but open-ended questions. It serves to supply a plenitude of ideas on a restricted subject when that is what is needed. The principle of reserving judgment in accumulating these is most important to learn, both for brainstorming sessions, and for individaul creative thought. In this atmosphere, one learns to lose the fear of offering ideas.

With a limited definition, brainstorming is successful, more so than usual "conferences," in accomplishing its objective—a long list of ideas of more or less equal weight on a problem of modest scope.

Con. The criticisms of brainstorming come mainly where the method is extended beyond the scope indicated above. New combinations in advertising and business, where brainstorming was developed, are different from those in science or art in that few are foolish, many are good, several are almost equally acceptable, and judgment cannot really determine the best one—only trial. For example, let 100 names be brainstormed for a new product. Ten may remain in the final evaluated list. Who knows whether the one finally selected and used is actually better than another of the ten?

The group brainstorming procedure restricts the stages of creativity. It allows for little or no preparation or incubation, and in that alone automatically consigns itself to the superficial problem. This does not mean brainstorming is not useful. It does provide a way to build a list of things to consider, to try, or to aid in planning, that is more complete than one man could put together on his own. That is the most important function of brainstorming—a complete list.

Brainstorming does not provide for recognition and reward of the creator—a creative basic. A man will toss off a few names for a box of cereal without requiring credit. He will not put forth a major industrial invention quite so casually.

Taylor [3] compared individual creation with group brainstorming in one of the few experimental studies of this method and found:

(1) Not surprisingly, a group can produce more ideas than an individual.

(2) But a group of individuals working separately can produce more ideas than when working as a group.

(3) The group working as individuals also produce ideas of higher average quality.

Individuals working alone produce more and better ideas. A significant departure derives from one mind. In group work, others then add the fairly obvious until a new, significant thrust in another direction appears. Then the pack takes off on the new trail, with further superficial and trivial additions. But it is also true that occasionally a remark or suggestion sparks the new-direction idea in a participant.

In brainstorming, the newly formed group is not jelled. In a creative team, as in the Gordon technique, people know each other, learn to communicate through a common language, and soon understand the type of response others will give when a new idea or direction of thought is advanced. Such a rapport is missing in the casually formed brainstorming groups.

Current View. Brainstorming has continuing importance because it relates so closely to CREATIVITY TRAINING. Creativity is problem solving, which is accomplished by formulating fruitful alternatives, each one a new combination, until an elegant and workable one is found. This means, to initiate creation to a realized problem, one begins to brainstorm. Usually, one stops with two or three alternatives, instead of seeking many. In attacking a problem, one begins to add, subtract, multiply, divide, substitute, modify, seek new directions, etc. For example, to improve a Bandaid: add antiseptic, modify the adhesive to be less skin irritative, adjust the size to the site of application, or confer water resistance. Therefore, brainstorming is fundamental to creation and is used *routinely*. It pays to extend the list of alternatives in either individual or group ideation.

New modifications of the brainstorming method have been proposed [4] to improve group rapport, enlarge the scope of problems, allow incubation, and pave the way for a degree of recognition. Experiments have shown that the later ideas in a brainstorming series are more remote or original, and have possibly higher quality. They come after slowdowns, or complete stops, when ideation is forced to seek new directions, or to force-fit to new material. Therefore, it is now proposed not to stop the session when the initial spate runs down, but to pursue the session in spite of pauses.

Additions to the brainstorming list are often seen to be force-fitted connections to objects or pictures in the room. It is reasonable to plant props, pictures, or photographs deliberately for the session. Since in the new method there is no pressure of time, ideas can be sought by leafing through magazines, or getting help from a thesaurus through the use of some of the more exotic connotations to key words in the problem statement. Brainstorming can become a more formal, and more powerful method by extending the sessions, by using props and other trigger mechanisms, and finally, by employing repeat sessions, which would allow opportunity for incubation, and for projects of greater size.

JOHN W. HAEFELE, PH.D., formerly Research Scientist, Procter & Gamble Company, Cincinnati, Ohio

Information References

Haefele, John W., "Creativity and Innovation," New York, Van Nostrand Reinhold, 1962.

Articles in *The Journal of Creative Behavior,* State University College at Buffalo, New York.

References Cited

[1] Osborn, Alex, "Applied Imagination," New York, Scribner, 1957.

[2] Whiting, Charles S., "Creative Thinking," New York, Van Nostrand Reinhold, 1958.

[3] Taylor, C. W., "Some Variables Functioning in Productivity and Creativity," in C. W. Taylor

(Principal Investigator), Second University of Utah Research Conference on the Identification of Creative Scientific Talent, Salt Lake City, University of Utah Press, 1958.
[4] Haefele, John W., lecture, Creative Problem Solving Institute, State University College at Buffalo, N.Y., June, 1977.

Cross References: *Creativity Training; New-Product Development; New-Product Development: A Check List for Management Decisions; Suggestion Systems; Work Simplification.*

BREAK-EVEN ANALYSIS

Break-Even Analysis, a method for studying the relationships among sales revenue, fixed costs, and variable expenses to determine the minimum volume at which production can be profitable, is a useful technique in business decision-making. The basic break-even model can be adapted to three specific situations that often arise in business analysis:

(1) Multi-product operations.

(2) Variation in selling price, with the related problem of price-output determination.

(3) Mechanization decisions.

The general break-even function is as follows:

$$S = F/(1-V)$$

where S is the break-even sales volume, F is total fixed costs, and V is the ratio of total variable costs to expected dollar net sales volume.

Multi-product Operations. Most companies produce more than one product. Thus, there is frequently a need to adapt break-even analysis to multi-product operations and to changes in product mix. As might be expected, the break-even volume varies with the product mix. The greater the proportion of total sales accounted for by the products with above-average margins, the lower the break-even volume.

A specific example illustrates how variation in product mix can be represented graphically without introducing undue complexities. Assume that a company produces five products (A, B, C, D, and E) with variable cost per cents (V) of 60, 65, 70, 75, and 80, respectively, and total fixed costs (F), of $100,000.

Substitute these different variable cost percentages in the general break-even equation, and calculate five different break-even volumes, assuming successively that each of the products is the only one sold. Plot these five points on a chart (see the lower curve in Exhibit I), with

EXHIBIT I

APPLICATION OF BREAK-EVEN ANALYSIS TO MULTI-PRODUCT OPERATIONS

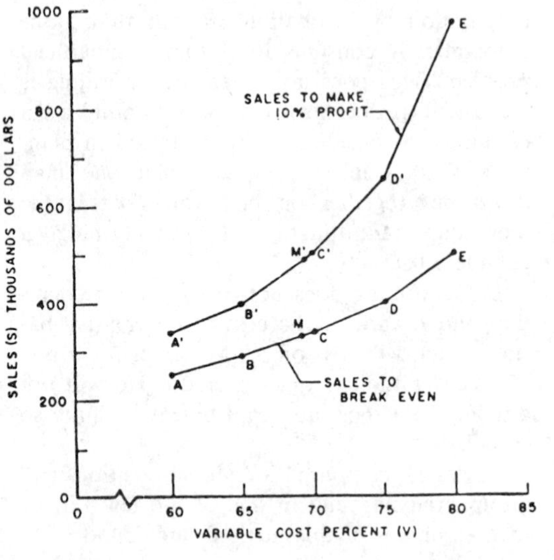

the horizontal axis representing variable cost per cents and the vertical axis representing sales dollars. The resulting curve is a *break-even zone* for product mixes representing all possible combinations of the five products. The break-even zone for this company will be between $250,000 (assuming product A is the only one sold) and $500,000 (assuming product E is the only one sold).

The break-even volume for a particular mix of these products will lie on the break-even zone formed by the lower curve in Exhibit I at a point depending upon the average variable cost per cent (V) for the product mix. The average variable cost per cent for the product mix is determined (see table, Exhibit II) by weighting the variable cost per cent for each product by its percentage of total sales dollars, adding

EXHIBIT II

DETERMINATION OF AVERAGE VARIABLE COST PER CENT FOR A HYPOTHETICAL PRODUCT MIX

Product	*Variable Cost %*	*% of Total Sales*	*Cross-Product*
A	60	20	0.120
B	65	20	0.130
C	70	20	0.140
D	75	30	0.225
E	80	10	0.080
Sum	—	100	0.695

the cross-products, and substituting their sum for V in the general break-even equation.

The average variable cost per cent (V) for this product mix is 69.5%. The break-even volume (point M in Exhibit I) would be around $328,000:

$$\frac{\$100{,}000}{1 - 0.695} = \$327{,}869$$

This is the ordinate on the vertical axis of Exhibit I that corresponds with the abscissa variable cost per cent of 69.5 on the horizontal axis.

A profit curve can be added to enhance the analysis in Exhibit I. This curve represents the total sales required to obtain a specified profit margin. Add the desired profit per cent to each variable cost per cent, and substitute in the general break-even equation to calculate the points through which the profit curve (the upper curve in Exhibit I) will pass. For example, assuming a desired 10% profit margin, point A′ is calculated as follows:

$$\frac{\$100.00}{1 - (0.60 + 0.10)} = \$333{,}333$$

The upper curve in Exhibit I shows the sales required to make a 10% net profit (before taxes) at each average variable cost per cent level for all possible combinations of the five products. Assuming the same product mix in Exhibit II, sales would have to be approximately $488,000:

$$\frac{\$100{,}000}{1 - (0.695 + 0.10)} = \$487{,}805$$

to make a 10% net profit. This point is M' on Exhibit I, the sales volume on the profit curve corresponding to an average variable cost per cent of 69.5.

Selling Price Variations. Business analysts often must determine the effect of price changes on volume-cost-profit relationships. Locating the price and output at which profit would be maximized under a given set of circumstances is one of the main problems of traditional microeconomic analysis. Break-even analysis can be used for both these calculations if the basic break-even model is modified to include variations in selling price. The following example illustrates the method.

The variable cost per cent (V) and hence the break-even volume (S) decrease as the unit sales price increases. For example, if the unit variable cost is 60 cents and the unit sales price is one dollar, the variable cost per cent is 60 (or $0.60 divided by $1.00), while if the unit sales price were 90 cents with a unit variable cost of 60 cents, the variable cost per cent would be 67 ($0.60 over $0.90).

The curve in Exhibit III indicates how the break-even volume changes as the unit sales price is varied between 75 cents and one dollar, given total fixed costs of $100,000 and a variable unit cost of 60 cents.

To derive a function depicting the relationship between selling price and break-even volume, select, say, five different units sales prices, calculate the variable cost per cents, and substitute in the general break-even equation to obtain the break-even volume at each selling price. The break-even volume curve connecting these points (as in Exhibit III) will always be a rectangular hyperbola because of the nature of the general break-even function ($y = k/x$).

Exhibit V shows how to determine by break-even analysis the price and output at which profit would be maximized. Using the data in Exhibit IV, subtract "Break-Even Volume" (col. 6) from "Total Revenue," (col. 3) and from "Total Costs" (col. 4), and put the remainders in columns 7 and 8 respectively. Then plot data from columns 7 and 8 (as is done in Exhibit V) in terms of the corresponding "Unit Sales Price" (col. 1 of Exhibit IV). Profit will be maximized at that price (and corresponding

EXHIBIT III

RELATION OF BREAK-EVEN VOLUME TO SELLING PRICE

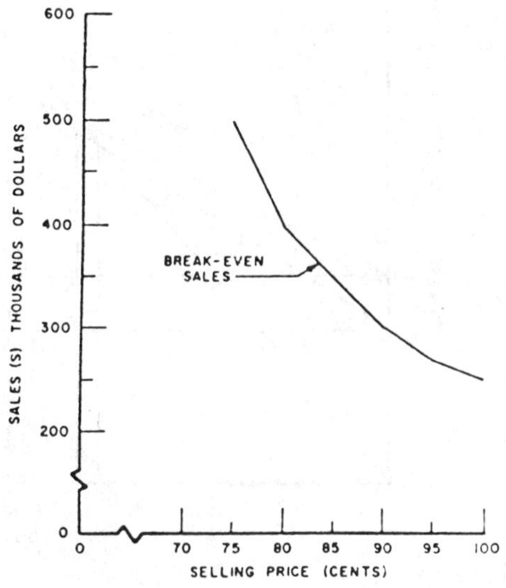

EXHIBIT IV

HYPOTHETICAL DATA INVOLVED IN DETERMINING, BY BREAK-EVEN ANALYSIS, THE PRICE AND OUTPUT AT WHICH PROFIT WOULD BE MAXIMIZED

Unit Sales Price (1)	*Anticipated Unit Sales* (2)	*Total Revenue* (3)	*Total Costs* (4)	*Profit* (5)	*Break-Even Volume* (6)	*Total Revenue minus Break-Even Volume* (7)	*Total Costs minus Break-Even Volume* (8)	*Difference* (Col. 7 minus Col. 8) (9)
$0.75	700,000	$525,000	$520,000	5,000	$500,000	$ 25,000	$ 20,000	$ 5,000
0.80	650,000	520,000	490,000	30,000	400,000	120,000	90,000	30,000
0.90	575,000	517,500	445,000	72,500	300,000	217,500	145,000	72,500
0.95	500,000	475,000	400,000	75,000	270,000	205,000	130,000	75,000
1.00	400,000	400,000	340,000	60,000	250,000	150,000	90,000	60,000

EXHIBIT V

APPLICATION OF BREAK-EVEN ANALYSIS TO PRICE-OUTPUT DECISIONS

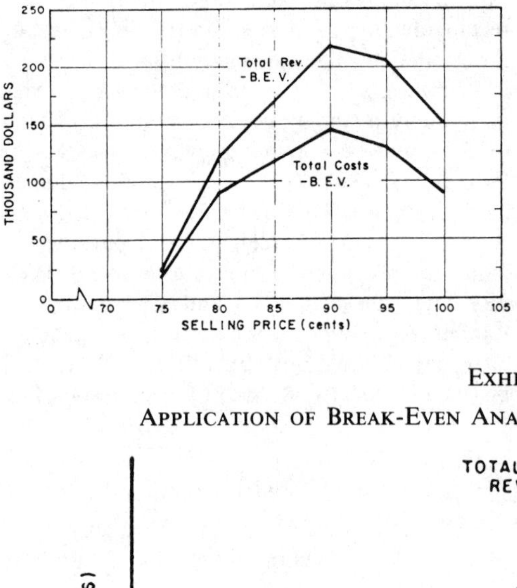

unit sales, or output, volume) where the spread between the curves is greatest. By inspection of Exhibit V (verified by columns 5 and 9 of Exhibit IV), the selling price that will maximize profit is approximately 95 cents, which corresponds to an anticipated sales (hence output) volume of 500,000 units in Exhibit IV. Note that the spread between the two curves in Exhibit V shows dollars of profit and the relative magnitude of profits at different selling prices.

Mechanization Decisions. Mechanization decisions arise with increasing frequency in the current era of automation. The basic break-even model also can be adapted to their solution. For example, if further mechanization

EXHIBIT VI

APPLICATION OF BREAK-EVEN ANALYSIS TO MECHANIZATION DECISIONS

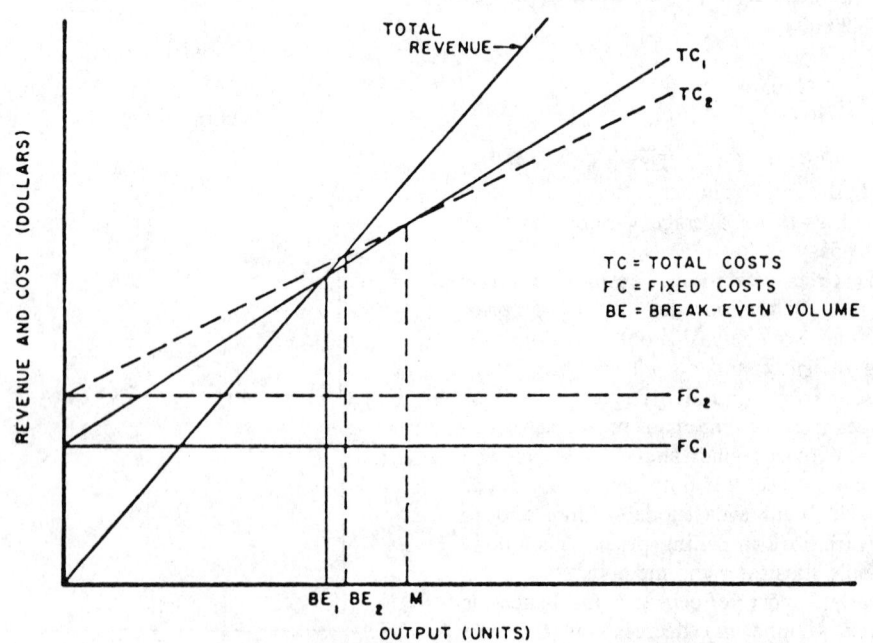

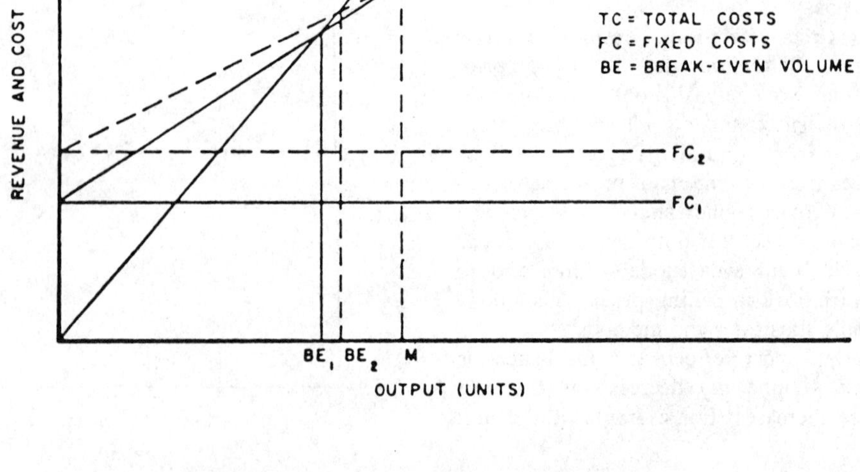

would increase fixed costs by $200,000 and reduce variable costs by 30%, would it be wise to mechanize? Exhibit VI shows the application of break-even analysis in solving this problem. The solid lines represent the existing situation before mechanization, and the dashed lines represent the relationships that would result from mechanization.

Mechanization would obviously be unprofitable if forecasted sales were less than the new break-even volume (BE_2). At outputs between BE_2 and M the company would not lose money by mechanizing, but it would not make as much profit as before mechanization. The company definitely should mechanize if forecasted sales are greater than M, for it would then clear a larger unit profit than under the old production function.

WINFIELD HUTTON, Hunter College of the City University of New York, New York
J. T. POWERS, Peat, Marwick, Mitchell & Co., New York, New York
JOHN D. SIMMONS, Financial Consultant, New York, New York (for third edition)

Information References

Anthony, Ted F. and Watson, Hugh, J., "Probabilistic Breakeven Analysis," *Managerial Planning,* November-December, 1976.
Harris, Clifford C., "The Break-Even Handbook," Englewood Cliffs, N.J., Prentice-Hall, 1978.
Hutton, Winfield and Powers, J.T., "Three Applications of Break-Even Methods in Economic Analysis," *The Engineering Economist,* publication of the Engineering Economy Division, American Society for Engineering Education, No. 1, Fall, 1961. (The above entry is based upon this article, incorporating some changes.)
Klipper, Harold, "Breakeven Analysis with Variable Product Mix," *Management Accounting,* April, 1978.
Smith, August W. and Kenneth R., "The Effects of Variable Costing in Break-Even Analysis," *National Public Accountant,* July, 1976.
Tucker, Spencer A., "Profit Planning Decisions with the Break-Even System," New York, Van Nostrand Reinhold, rev. ed., 1980.

Cross References: *Budgeting; Cost Accounting; Cost-Volume-Profit Analysis; Direct Costing; Flexible Budgeting; Operating Margin Analysis; Return on Capital; Standard Costing; Zero Base Budgeting.*

BUDGETING

Budgeting is an important—and, in any operation of significant size and complexity, an indispensable—part of management planning and control. Its objectives are three-fold: (1) to determine the input of planning, in terms of the costs of agreed upon activities and expectable levels of those activities, as well as expected revenues, if any, resulting from those activities; (2) to warn decision-makers and responsible managers when significant departures from planned cost inputs and revenues occur; and (3) to develop a responsive, cooperative work force in the matter of fiscal control.

A comprehensive budget may be defined as a forecast of all of the transactions of an organization for a stipulated period, organized in such a way as to bring to the attention of specific managers the financial results of those activities over which they have control, and to enable the preparation of financial statements such as the budgeted income statement, balance sheet, and cash flow statement.

The budgeting process itself is an extensive one, and consists of the preparation of individual budgets by those departments (or persons) best in a position to do so—for example, the sales budget by the sales department, the production budget by the production department, the purchases budget by the purchasing agent, and so on. The preparation of some of these budgets, for example, the manufacturing overhead and selling expense budgets, is expedited by a well developed system of flexible budgets. (See FLEXIBLE BUDGETING.) Standard cost data are also of help in providing information as to hours or quantities needed for manufacture at any given level of activity. (See STANDARD COSTING.) In turn, the budgeting process itself may lead to the revision of flexible budgets and the updating of standard costs.

A relatively recent development that has attracted wide attention is ZERO-BASE BUDGETING.

The timing and detailed preparation of each of the various budgets which in total form the master budget are usually the responsibility of a budget director, who in turn may have the help and authoritative back-up of a budget committee. The budget committee may be composed of the top executives of the firm, including the president, controller, and budget director.

Cross References: *Flexible Budgeting; Zero Base Budgeting.*

BUSINESS CYCLES. See Business Forecasting.

BUSINESS ETHICS

Webster's New World Dictionary defines **Ethics** as "the study of standards of conduct and moral judgment." Others define it as the study of human actions in respect to being right and wrong. But ethics is not simply a descriptive study of what we habitually accept: it is an attempt to discover what *ought* to be. Thus, ethics forms a critique both of the ultimate values and goods we seek, and the means we use in trying to achieve them. Therefore, a specification of responsibility for deciding and doing what is needed to be done is part of ethics.

History of Business Ethics. The history of business ethics displays a growing recognition of the need to examine our habitual modes of business conduct in the light of the social transformations that have impacted organization, management, and society.

The public continually hears about improper business practices involving poor product quality, bribery, misuse of internal corporate information, etc. People have always thought that the primary purpose of business is to serve society. After listening to corporate executives making excuses for their abuse of conventional moral and legal standards, they wonder about the motives and integrity of business leaders. In the light of such abuses, the shift in public thinking is leaning toward understanding the cause of such abuse as an unbridled search for increased corporate profits—simply reflecting the executive's egoistic empire-building approach.

It is, of course, not this simple. The need to provide goods and services efficiently for an ever-growing world population strains both our physical and our social environment; and the attempts to meet the new challenges raise new, sometimes unforeseen, moral quandaries for executives. The desire to take advantage of the "economies of scale," for example, has led to a growth in the size of organizations which jeopardized the traditional moral standards of the dignity and value of the individual human being. As the sense of individual responsibility has diminished, we have also seen a rise in an egoistic attitude which can undermine the kind of mutual trust and dependence that is basic to any business transaction.

The attempt to use governmental legal constraint has not helped to alleviate the problems created by growth. Although it has focused the attention of business executives on the legal aspects of rule interpretation in their attempts to justify corporate decisions, it nevertheless has not encouraged the kind of comprehensive examination dealing with the meaning of the executives' actions which might lead them to a better way. Such examination is crucial, considering the present problems. The kind of ethical questioning that might once have been left to philosophers and theologians now must be part of the decision-making process of even the most practical minded executives.

Business Ethics: What It Is. Ethics is the study of what ought to be, of what is the ultimate "good" and how we ought to achieve it. *Business* ethics is thus the study of business activity in light of such judgment. An advertising manager who is trying to decide whether or not to use deceptive but psychologically persuasive techniques, or to be scrupulously truthful, can make a fully informed choice only if his decision procedure includes awareness of the ultimate good his action serves and of the means appropriate to this ultimate good. Without such awareness, his procedure may well have to rest upon the rules his society provides. As useful as these rules often are, all too often they are unclear or contradictory. In this case the manager may well sense both an obligation to use the most effective techniques available and an obligation to be truthful at all times. Since this conflict in obligations is rooted in conflicting ideas about the good and how we ought to achieve it, it can be resolved only by study and decision on that level.

Such decision is not easy. Some argue, for example, that the ultimate goal of human activity is pleasure, and those acts (or types of acts) which have the consequence of producing the greatest amount of pleasure for the greatest number of people affected by this act are morally right. Taking this approach, if using deception leads to the production of more pleasure than pain, deception ought to be used. But other experts disagree with using the consequences of an act to judge its moral worth, believing instead that acts are *intrinsically* right or wrong regardless of their consequences, and that we have a "duty" to do or not do them accordingly. Being always truthful, regardless of the consequences, is often one of the "duties" in this approach, and so deceptive advertising, no matter how productive of general "pleasure," would not be approved. Given the present stage of human wisdom, it is often hard to choose between such competing and sometimes incompatible moral principles, but unless such fundamental questions are raised, the roots of even the most practical of moral dilemmas may well stay obscured.

It is difficult to raise such questions, however. No morality can condemn all business activity and so there is sometimes a tendency within business to take the internal, instrumental, measures of success (profits, for example) to be ultimate ends in themselves. As understandable as this is, it makes it hard to step back and see the conflicts between the instrumental goals of business and other, perhaps more ultimate, ends. But such investigation is necessary.

Business is a practical activity, but it need not be simply a practical art. Systematic and even scientific approaches are appropriate, even in moral matters. Although our economic system is based on free competition, we should not accept arbitrary standards for the morality expected in our operation of business relations. Adam Smith, in setting economics as a field for systematic inquiry, emphasized the large societal framework and the fact that the pursuit of profit is only one element of human activity.

The problems facing business ethics do not end with disputes over ultimate goods and basic moral principles. After corporate policies are established, they must be made operational. This is not an easy task. If, for example, the executive decides to use consequences as a way of judging the moral worth of an act, he/she must be able to project what those consequences are, and decide which consequences are acceptable. If, on the other hand, he looks to "corporate policy" as a way of judging actions, he must judge which policy is appropriate in each specific situation.

Codes of Ethics. A question that arises is how to utilize the adopted policies wisely. Formal Codes of Ethics are one traditional method, but even here there are difficulties. The authors' recent survey of attitudes of chief executive officers (CEOs) revealed that although many felt an international Code of Ethics would not hinder the decision-making process, there were serious questions raised about such a code. For example, who would create the code? Would it apply to all multinational corporations? Would both private and governmental agencies be included? And could such a code be kept strictly to matters of moral rather than non-moral economic policy?

Codes must be realistically achievable or they become merely ink on paper. Without the proper spirit, codes can be "met" without actually behaving in a truly moral manner. An executive can verbally subscribe to a code of ethics, yet set unachievable operational goals for subordinates. This kind of executive in no way encourages moral behavior. Therefore, the effectiveness of any code of ethics rests upon the integrity of the executives who make the decisions and live with the outcomes.

Resources. Given the persuasive nature of the concern that business ethics must deal with, it is difficult to pinpoint specialists as one might in a more narrowly technical area. However, an increasing number of individuals specializing in the theoretical problems of ethics are turning their attention to the problems of business ethics. And more executives are sharing with them both their practical experience and their theoretical insights. A Society for Business Ethics has been organized (at this writing under the direction of Professor Thomas Donaldson of Loyola University of Chicago), and there are a growing number of Centers engaged in sponsoring conferences, studies, and publications.

The Centers include the Center for Business Ethics at Bentley College, presently sponsoring annual conferences and reports; the University of Delaware's work on the teaching of business ethics; the "Values in Business Management" program at the C. W. Post Center of Long Island University; the studies being done at the Hastings Center in New York; Rensselaer Polytechnic Institute's *Business and Professional Ethics Newsletter,* and the work of the Darden School of Business at the University of Virginia. Such activity is growing and developing at virtually every major School of Business, and shows signs of continuing growth. Local colleges can be contacted for information concerning resources currently available to the public. In addition to the Centers are a growing number of books and articles appearing in scholarly and popular forums. Appended is a list of recent general texts and anthologies devoted especially to business ethics. Much material appearing under the rubric "Business and Society" is relevant as well.

SAMIR P. DAGHER PH.D., Chairman, Department of Business and Managerial of Science, and PETER H. SPADER, PH.D., Associate Professor of Philosophy, Marywood College, Scranton, Pennsylvania

Information References

Bibliographies:

Gothie, Daniel L., "A Selected Bibliography of Applied Ethics in the Professions: 1950–1970," Charlottesville, Va., University Press of Virginia, 1973.

Jones, Donald G., "A Bibliography of Business Ethics, 1971–1975,"Charlottesville, Va., University Press of Virginia, 1977.

Texts and Reports:

Barry, Vincent. "Moral Issues in Business," Belmont, Calif., Wadsworth, 1979.

Beauchamp, Tom and Bowie, Norman, "Ethical Theory and Business," Englewood Cliffs, N.J., Prenttice-Hall, 1979.

"Criteria for Decision Making" and "Case Narratives," Greenvale, N.Y., C. W. Post Center, Long Island University, 1979.

Dagher, Samir P. and Spader, Peter H., "Improving Business Ethics . . . ," *Management Review,* March 1980.

De George, Richard and Pichler, Joseph, "Ethics, Free Enterprise and Public Policy," New York; Oxford University Press, 1978.

Donaldson, Thomas and Werhane, Patricia, "Ethical Issues in Business," Englewood Cliffs, N.J., Prentice-Hall, 1979.

Garrett, Thomas. "Business Ethics," Englewood Cliffs, N.J., Prentice-Hall, 1966.

Missner, Marshall, "Ethics of the Business System," Sherman Oaks, Cal., Alfred Publishing Co., 1980.

Powers, Charles W. and Vogel, David, "Ethics in the Education of Business Managers," Hastings-on-Hudson, N.Y., The Hastings Center, 1980.

"Report of the Committee for Education in Business Ethics," Newark, Del, CEBE, American Philsophical Association, University of Delaware, 1980.

Cross References: *Better Business Bureaus; Consumer Protection; Public Relations.*

BUSINESS FORECASTING

Business action taken today must be based on yesterday's plan and tomorrow's expectations. Plans for the future cannot be made without forecasting events and their relationships. And not only may forecasting be made for a given type of activity independently, the forecast of one type of event may also be based on other forecasts. Thus, the projection of population growth for the next decade is an element in the forecast of future demand for steel which, in turn, is the basis for plans for expanding plant capacities. Similarly, forecasts of national income are used by the Government to estimate its future revenue, and by industries to predict their national market demand. Needless to say, an individual firm can base its forecast of sales on the forecasts of sales for the whole industry.

While management has long recognized the importance of **Business Forecasting** in rational decisions and action, the activity itself has remained an inexact science. Those who recall the forecasts by Government economists of mass post-war unemployment for the spring of 1946, or the conflicting pronouncements of early 1980 as to whether or not we were in a recession, and if so, whether it would be severe or mild, may dispute the assertion that it is a science at all. But despite such misgivings, forecasting must be done. The question is not, "Forecast or no forecast?" but rather, "What kind of forecast?" Moreover, for management the value of a forecast is not merely its relative accuracy, but the fact that making it requires a balanced consideration of all ascertainable factors which might influence future developments.

The fact that the past can never be a perfect guide to the future warns us that forecasting should not be thought of as a routine application of some techniques or theoretical ideas to a list of unchanging variables. Successful forecasting requires expert blending of economic theory and thorough familiarity with the relevant statistical data. It should utilize both quantitative and qualitative information. The forecaster must have the ability to distinguish between new facts that are important and those that are not. He must be competent to judge under what conditions past relationships can be relied upon and when they cannot. He must be able to appreciate the effects of nonmeasurable socioeconomic and political forces upon business activities.

Types of Forecasting Techniques. Numerous forecasting techniques with varying degrees of complexity have been devised during the past few decades. Most of these fall into one of three broad categories: the *naïve* method, the *barometric* method, and the *analytical* method.

A forecasting method is said to be naïve if it lacks rigid theoretical basis. As a method of forecasting, it ranges from simple coin tossing to decide on an upward or a downward movement, to mechanical projection of a time series into the future. A frequently used naïve device is the simple but not necessarily useless method of assuming that things will not change. Using this technique, plans are made on the assumption that, in so far as the particular events are concerned, the future will resemble the present. It is predicted, for example, that sales of the next quarter will be the same as those for this quarter, or sales of the next quarter will increase by the same amount as they did in the last quarter. For most short-term decisions, this is exactly what is done. Of course, this type of forecast becomes more questionable as the forecast period becomes longer. The naïve method, in general, and the time series analysis in particular, assume that the future is some kind of extension of the past.

The barometric method implies that past historical patterns tend to repeat themselves in the future, and it embraces the idea that the future can be predicted from certain happenings of the present. Thus past statistical behavior that seems to be associated regularly with fluctuations in particular series or general business conditions is discovered and used as the basis for forecasting. Foreshadowing series are searched to provide an advance reading of what is expected to follow in the series to be forecasted.

The search for foreshadowing series is not based on the leads actually revealed by historical data alone. Theoretical considerations as to the leads and lags in various series are also employed. Cross-checking between empiricism and theory in the search for leading series is the best hope for establishing the thesis that the future does not represent a break from the past but that changes are largely determined by present conditions. The foreshadowing or leading series selected serve as barometers of future changes in specific series or general business conditions.

The analytical method entails detailed analyses of causative forces operating currently on the variable to be predicted. Relationships of cause and effect disclosed by analyzing current data are used to judge the future course of the causative forces and their effects on the future behavior of the variable to be predicted. Analytical techniques may be non-mathematical, such as the rather naïve factor-listing method or the more sophisticated method of opinion polling; or mathematical, such as econometric models (See ECONOMETRICS) and regression analysis.

The analysis of current forces at work by no means excludes the employment of past statistical relationships to make the forecast. As a matter of fact, historical patterns are often used to estimate the constants contained in the mathematical models. Although the analytical method can be used to forecast the activity of a firm or an industry, its greatest advance in recent years has come from its use in forecasting the framework of the national income accounts.

The following forecasting techniques will be discussed in this article:

(1) The method of forecasting with time-series models.
  (a) The economic rhythm method, or method of forecasting a series by itself
  (b) Exponential smoothing
  (c) The Box-Jenkins approach
(2) The barometric method
  (a) Statistical indicators
  (b) Diffusion index
(3) The analytic method
  (a) Regression analysis
  (b) Econometric models
  (c) Opinion polling

The Economic Rhythm Method. This is one of forecasting a time series by itself. A time series may be defined as a collection of readings belonging to different time periods, of some variables or composite of variables, such as production of steel, per capita income, gross national product, or index of industrial production. It thus portrays the variations of the variable through time.

The behavior of a time series is caused by a variety of factors, some economic, some natural, and some institutional. Some of these factors affect only the long-run movement of the series, while others tend to produce short-run fluctuations. Thus different kinds of changes are contained in a time series, the four main ones being *secular trend* (the long-run general drift), *seasonal variations, cyclical movements,* and *irregular movements.* These components are assumed to be related to each other in many possible ways. By far the most popular assumption is the so-called "multiplicative model." This model assumes that the value of the original data is the product of the values of the four components, that is,

$$E = T \times S \times C \times I$$

where T = secular trend,
S = seasonal variation,
C = cyclical movement, and
I = irregular movement.

Under such an assumption, the measurable components, T, C, and S, can then be decomposed by appropriate statistical methods and used for forecasting purposes.

The economic rhythm method is often used by an individual firm or industry to forecast sales, production, need for plant facilities, and the like.

A firm or industry experiencing a steady and substantial rate of growth must make forecasts of future trends for planning the construction of costly facilities in anticipation of the future activity. A forecast of long-run growth will help the business managers to determine whether an increase in current demand is permanent (secular) or temporary (cyclical). When a cyclical expansion is mistaken for a secular growth, unneeded capacity may be built. When secular growth is incorrectly interpreted as a temporary expansion, a share of the market may be lost forever to competitors. A forecast of secular trend leads to the purchase or construction of equipment and plant at the most advantageous time, which is usually when the demand for the firm's output is below its peak, or when the producers of fixed assets are temporarily in a depressed stage of their activity.

Needless to say, in the forecast of secular trend, the first step is the measurement of the trend in the immediate past. The forecasting of trend can be made by extrapolation; that is, projection of the fitted trend into the future. It may be noted that projecting a trend into the future assumes that forces producing the change in secular trend will continue to have the same effects in the future as in the past. This implies that the further a fitted trend is projected into the future the more questionable the forecast becomes. However, judging from the fact that secular trend is a type of change that is quite persistent, it is fairly safe to project a series sufficiently into the future for planning purposes.

Forecasts in seasonals are necessary for such activities as budgeting and production scheduling, for example, which are planned on a monthly basis.

The seasonal index, where it can be constructed, is usually an adequate forecast of the seasonal variations for the next year. If the seasonal is undergoing a gradual change, it is often sufficient to use the specific seasonal index of one year as the forecast for the seasonal of the year that follows. Or, if the seasonal changes assume a clearly defined trend, the projected monthly trend values may serve as the forecasts. With an abruptly changing seasonal, the seasonal index computed after the change should be used as the forecast. Forecasts based on seasonal indexes are made by taking an annual forecast based on trend or other device and combining it with seasonal indexes, thus producing monthly forecasts that take account of seasonal fluctuations. (Thus, if January is traditionally only 80% of the monthly average, the forecast for January will be 80% of 1/12 of the forecast for the whole year.)

A forecast of actual value merely on the extension of trend line and the seasonal indexes may be adequate for many types of decisions. Nevertheless, we must recognize these limitations for such a forecast:

(1) The type of trend equation selected may not be appropriate.

(2) The trend constants and, therefore, the trend values are subjected to sampling errors.

(3) The forces influencing the trend may change after the trend equation has been selected.

(4) The seasonal may not remain the same as it has been in the past, or it has been changing and the change has not been adequately described.

(5) The forecast is made under the assumption that it is not influenced by cyclical and irregular effects.

Among these limitations, the first and the last are by far the most important. When selecting an appropriate trend equation, we must see to it that the selection is supported by economic theory or logical reasoning, or we may try alternative forms of trend curves in order to discover which one gives the best fit. In connection with the latter, logic would also play an important role in the final analysis. Consider, for example, the state and local government expenditure data, SLGE, in Exhibit I. For this series we have

a. the arithmetic linear trend:

$$y_t = 16.057 + 1.545x;$$

b. the semilog trend:

$$\log y_t = 1.242 + 0.0236x.$$

(Y = SLGE in billions of 1954 dollars; time unit = 1 year; origin = 1946.)

As can be seen from Exhibit I, both trends

EXHIBIT I

ALTERNATIVE PROJECTIONS OF STATE AND LOCAL GOVERNMENT EXPENDITURES

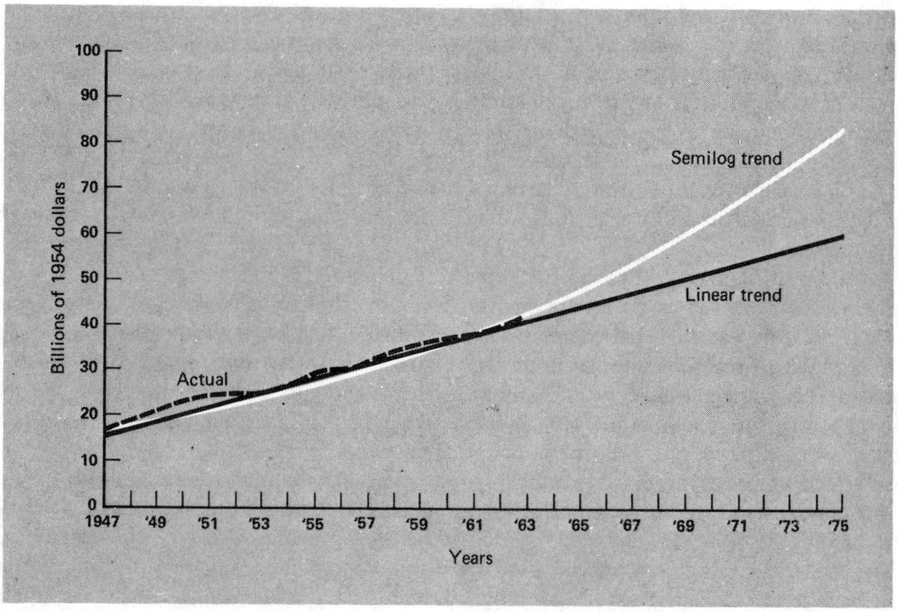

seem to fit the original data equally well. However, the difference between projected values becomes more and more pronounced over the long term. For instance, the projected trend value of 1975 for SLGE is 60.9 billion by the arithmetic linear equation but is 84.4 billion by the semi-log trend equation. The latter forecast is almost 140% as large as the former. This being the case, which trend line should one select?

Clearly, the selection can be made only on the basis of logic and reasonableness of the forecasted values. In the present case we have reason to believe that SLGE depends, among other things, upon the size of the population which, from past empirical evidence and theoretical considerations, has been growing at a constant rate through time. This leads us to the conclusion that SLGE should be growing at a constant rate rather than at a constant amount per unit of time and that the semi-log trend seems to be more appropriate than the arithmetic linear trend for forecasting in this case.

Next, while nearly every time series contains cyclical and irregular components, it may be discovered that a large number of products, such as the demand for motor fuel, for shoes, or for paperboard for food, have been experiencing ever-expanding markets with only mild responses to cyclical forces. Except for irregular factors, such as wartime restrictions and strikes, these products have considerable regularity in their growth over time, even though there are shifts in their growth rates. For such products, projections of the statistical normal can be considered as useful forecasts for both short-term and long-term planning.

However, for those series, such as consumers' durable goods and investment goods, which are greatly affected by the cyclical factor, projecting the cyclical movement becomes the most important part of forecasting a series by itself. This is so because nearly all types of short-run activities of the firm—ordering supplies of raw materials, scheduling production, advertising, hiring workers, arranging for a line of credit, or the like—are influenced by cyclical fluctuations. Unfortunately, accurate forecasts of both cyclical turning points and amplitude are extremely difficult if not impossible because there is simply no objective way of extending cyclical relatives or residuals into the future. Nearly all the methods of forecasting discussed in this Encyclopedia entry are concerned with cycles, but they are primarily for predicting general business conditions rather than specific cycles. Whatever method is used to project the cycle, the forecast of the actual value of a series equals projected trend times projected seasonal times projected cycle.

Exponential Smoothing. Among recent developments, the most exciting procedure of forecasting the cycle of a series by itself is the method of "exponential smoothing." It is an outgrowth of attempts to maintain the smoothing function of moving averages without their corresponding drawbacks and limitations. The technique, a kind of weighted moving average, is found to be useful in short-term forecasting of inventories and sales.

Under the moving-average process, with the running average over, say, a six-month period, the actual for the latest experienced period would be added to the previous six-month total, the earliest month would be subtracted, and a new average computed. One serious drawback is that you have to keep track of the past values, adding new information and dropping the old. Also, it is not responsive to a sudden unforeseen spurt in the latest period.

Exponential smoothing is a special kind of moving average that does not require keeping a long historical record. Like other moving averages, it has a stable response to changes, but the rate of response can be adjusted readily. Furthermore, the method can be extended to computation of trends, changes in trend, and the distribution of forecast error, with very little additional data processing effort. And errors in the computation are gradually washed out.

The basic principle and application are quite simple. If we wish to forecast the value of a time series for the period $t + 1$ on the basis of information available just after period t, the forecast is best considered as a function of two components: the *actual* value of the series for period t, and the *forecasted* value for the same period computed in the previous period $t - 1$. The use of both realized and estimated values available now for establishing future values is better than the use of either alone, since the actual value in period t might have been unduly influenced by random factors, and (or) the conditions that led to the forecast for period t may not hold any longer. Without going into mathematical derivation, we offer the following conceptual description. (For following through the mathematical reasoning, the reader is referred to "Statistical Forecasting for Inventory Control," by the developer of the exponential smoothing method, Robert G. Brown, McGraw-Hill, New York, 1959.):

The essence of exponential smoothing is, as stated, that it bases a forecast on the difference between the estimate for the period just passed, and the actual value experienced in that period. Say we are dealing with a demand series, and suppose that in our record we had stored only the average demand computed last month, but had not stored the moving total. This month we have a new demand, an actual figure, and we want to get a new value for the average to use in our forecast. It seems logical that if the demand this month was higher than the old average, we ought to increase our estimate. (Conversely, if the demand was below our previous estimate, the new estimate should be lower.) Furthermore, if the difference was small, the adjustment ought to be small, but if the actual demand was far above the average, we ought to increase our new estimate by a sizable amount.

The exponential smoothing rule is this: To get a new estimate of the average demand, add to the previous estimate a fraction of the amount by which this month exceeds that estimate. (If the demand is below estimate, you obviously subtract.)

The fraction is called a "smoothing constant," and is conventionally represented by α, the Greek letter alpha. Thus:

New estimate = old estimate + α (new actual demand minus old estimate).

By rearranging the terms:

New estimate = α (new demand) + $(1 - \alpha)$ (old estimate)

Assigning the Greek letter Beta, β, to the quantity $(1 - \alpha)$, and designating it the second "smoothing constant," we can write the equation for simple exponential smoothing as follows:

$$S_t = \alpha y_t + \beta S_{t-1},$$

where α and β are each greater than 0, and

$$\alpha + \beta = 1.$$

In the above equation S_t is the estimated *smoothed value* for the period ahead, $t + 1$. It is obtained as a weighted average of y_t, the *actual* value of the series for the period t, and S_{t-1}, the smoothed forecast value for the period t, which, of course, was made in the previous period $t - 1$.

Obviously, the question arises, what value should be assigned to α (which would also automatically determine β)?

It can be shown mathematically that if all estimates for a forthcoming new period had been made by the exponential smoothing formula going back for a given number of periods, say k periods, the latest new estimate, S_t made for the period ahead, can be represented (using our previous symbols) as:

$$S_t = \alpha y_0 + \alpha\beta y_1 + \alpha\beta^2 y_2 + \alpha\beta^3 y_3 \ldots + \alpha\beta^k y_k + (1 - \alpha)^k \cdot \text{(estimate made } k \text{ months ago)}$$

If we were to continue the process long enough, the factor $(1 - 1\alpha)^k$ would become so small that the estimate made that long ago would have no appreciable effect on the present estimate of average demand. The larger the value of α, the faster past responses are dampened out from the smoothed values. This provides a rule of thumb for determining the value of α. When the magnitude of random variations in the series is large, we would like to average out the random effects quickly. Thus we should select a small α, so that the smoothed value S_t will reflect S_{t-1} to a greater extent than it reflects y_t. When we have a moderately stable process, a large α should be selected. In practice, the value of α often falls within the range 0.10–0.60.

Note now that S_t as defined in the exponential smoothing equation may be considered as the forecast of a series for the period $t + 1$. If there is a significant trend in the series, exponential smoothing, like any other moving average, lags behind the systematic trend. Such a trend must therefore be estimated and adjusted for S_t in order to provide a final forecast for period $t + 1$.

As a final note, a point made earlier should be repeated: exponential smoothing is of special usefulness in short-term forecasting of inventory and sales, but the usefulness of the forecasts is questionable if they are projected too far into the future.

The Box-Jenkins Approach. The Box-Jenkins approach to forecasting is one of model building with time series. It is difficult to understand and quite expensive to implement; and there is no good way of presenting it in understandable summary form in a brief article such as this. However, the method has become increasingly popular, and its influence in the future will undoubtedly be widespread. Therefore we provide here a brief note on the nature of this modern and powerful technique, referring interested readers to the Granger-Newbold, Nelson, and Box-Jenkins listings in the appended Information References.

Unlike most forecasting methods, Box-Jenkins does not assume a particular pattern in the past data of the series to be forecast. It employs, instead, an iterative procedure of identifying a possible model from a general class of models. The models used are usually moving average models, providing a smoother series than the original "white noise" or purely random series; autoregressive models, providing a series with more structure than the white noise; and mixed autoregressive-moving-average models, which can generate a wider class of models than the first two.

When a model is selected, it is checked against the data to determine if it adequately describes the behavior of the series. The standard of a satisfactory model in each case is that the residuals, or errors, between data points and the forecasting equation be small, randomly distributed, and free of significant serial correction. If the selected model is judged to be satisfactory, it is used for forecasting. Otherwise, the process is repeated by using a different model designed to modify and improve the original one . . . and repeated again until an adequate model eventually is found.

It should be mentioned that the Box-Jenkins approach is entirely different from the classic time-series decomposition methods, which are purely descriptive in nature. Instead, it is like the regression model in that it has the advantage of specifying statistically the confidence one has in a forecast.

Statistical Indicators. It is of great importance for government economists and business managers to predict the turning points of cyclical swings in the economy—for example, the advance and decline of GNP. In general, the determination and prediction of turning points are difficult tasks, mainly because a series such as GNP not only consists of trends plus long swings, but also contains many ups and downs of shorter duration and milder amplitudes which obscure the picture. This is especially true in this country since the 1940s, because of institutional changes and more active government intervention in the private sector of the economy.

There has been continuing evidence since

EXHIBIT II

CROSS-CLASSIFICATION OF CYCLICAL INDICATORS BY ECONOMIC PROCESS AND CYCLICAL TIMING

A. Timing at Business Cycle Peaks

Economic Process / Cyclical Timing	I. EMPLOYMENT AND UNEMPLOYMENT (18 series)	II. PRODUCTION AND INCOME (10 series)	III. CONSUMPTION, TRADE, ORDERS, AND DELIVERIES (13 series)	IV. FIXED CAPITAL INVESTMENT (18 series)	V. INVENTORIES AND INVENTORY INVESTMENT (9 series)	VI. PRICES, COSTS, AND PROFITS (17 series)	VII. MONEY AND CREDIT (26 series)
LEADING (L) INDICATORS (62 series)	Marginal Employment adjustments (6 series) Job vacancies (2 series) Comprehensive employment (1 series) Comprehensive unemployment (3 series)	Capacity utilization (2 series)	New and unfilled orders and deliveries (6 series) Consumption (2 series)	Formation of business enterprises (2 series) Business investment commitments (5 series) Residential construction (3 series)	Inventory investment (4 series) Inventories on hand and on order (1 series)	Stock prices (1 series) Commodity prices (1 series) Profits and profit margins (7 series) Cash flows (2 series)	Money flows (3 series) Real money supply (2 series) Credit flows (4 series) Credit difficulties (2 series) Bank reserves (2 series) Interest rates (1 series)
ROUGHLY COINCIDENT (C) INDICATORS (23 series)	Comprehensive employment (1 series)	Comprehensive output and real income (4 series) Industrial production (4 series)	Consumption and trade (4 series)	Backlog of investment commitments (1 series) Business investment expenditures (5 series)			Velocity of money (2 series) Interest rates (2 series)
LAGGING (Lg) INDICATORS (18 series)	Duration of unemployment (2 series)			Business investment expenditures (1 series)	Inventories on hand and on order (4 series)	Unit labor costs and labor share (4 series)	Interest rates (4 series) Outstanding debt (3 series)
TIMING UNCLASSIFIED (U) (8 series)	Comprehensive employment (3 series)		Trade (1 series)	Business investment commitments (1 series)		Commodity prices (1 series) Profit share (1 series)	Interest rates (1 series)

B. Timing at Business Cycle Troughs

Economic Process / Cyclical Timing	I. EMPLOYMENT AND UNEMPLOYMENT (18 series)	II. PRODUCTION AND INCOME (10 series)	III. CONSUMPTION, TRADE, ORDERS, AND DELIVERIES (13 series)	IV. FIXED CAPITAL INVESTMENT (18 series)	V. INVENTORIES AND INVENTORY INVESTMENT (9 series)	VI. PRICES, COSTS AND PROFITS (17 series)	VII. MONEY AND CREDIT (26 series)
LEADING (L) INDICATORS (47 series)	Marginal employment adjustments (3 series)	Industrial production (1 series)	New and unfilled orders and deliveries (5 series) Consumption and trade (4 series)	Formation of business enterprises (2 series) Business investment commitments (4 series) Residential construction (3 series)	Inventory investment (4 series)	Stock prices (1 series) Commodity prices (2 series) Profits and profit margins (6 series) Cash flows (2 series)	Money flows (2 series) Real money supply (2 series) Credit flows (4 series) Credit difficulties (2 series)
ROUGHLY COINCIDENT (C) INDICATORS (23 series)	Marginal employment adjustments (2 series) Comprehensive employment (4 series)	Comprehensive output and real income (4 series) Industrial production (3 series) Capacity utilization (2 series)	Consumption and trade (3 series)	Business investment commitments (1 series)		Profits (2 series)	Money flow (1 series) Velocity of money (1 series)
LAGGING (Lg) INDICATORS (40 series)	Marginal employment adjustments (1 series) Job vacancies (2 series) Comprehensive employment (1 series) Comprehensive and duration of unemployment (5 series)		Unfilled orders (1 series)	Business investment commitments (2 series) Business investment expenditures (6 series)	Inventories on hand and on order (5 series)	Unit labor costs and labor share (4 series)	Velocity of money (1 series) Bank reserves (1 series) Interest rates (8 series) Outstanding debt (3 series)
TIMING UNCLASSIFIED (U) (1 series)							Bank reserves (1 series)

SOURCE: Business Condition Analysis, Jan., 1980.

World War II that the amplitude of business cycles has been greatly reduced, and that a fairly smooth growth can be achieved. This means that the turning points in general business activity, as measured by GNP or the index of industrial production occur less frequently and are more difficult to define. For this reason, in recent years, turning points are effectively searched in changes in the growth rate rather than in the absolute level of general business activity; and the main forecasting strategy for detecting turning points is the use of "statistical indicators" based on a study of the lead-lag relationships among different time series.

The lead-lag approach attempts to determine the approximate lapse of time between the movement of one series and the movements of general business conditions. This approach, for a very natural reason, has received more attention in the history of forecasting than has any other. If one or more series can be found such that their turning points lead by a number of months with substantial regularity the turning points of general business in the past, it is only logical to use these leading series to predict what is going to happen to general business activity.

The most important list of statistical indicators in modern times originated during the 1937–1938 sharp business contraction. Henry Morgenthau, at that time Secretary of the Treasury, requested the National Bureau of Economic Research (NBER) to devise a system that would signal when the depression was nearing an end. NBER economists, under the leadership of Wesley Mitchell and Arthur F. Burns, selected 21 series that, on their past performance, some dating as far back as 1854, promised to be fairly reliable indicators of business revival. Since then the Bureau has revised the list several times. Since its origin, series have been classified as leading, rough coincident, and lagging. In 1966, 72 indicators had been selected by NBER, 35 of which were classified as leading, 25 as coincident, and 11 as lagging. The most recent list at this writing, issued in 1977, shows 111 indicators, classified under various economic headings. As shown in Exhibit II, a number of series are considered to lead at peaks and lag at troughs.

Leading indicators are mainly those series which are concerned with business decisions to expand or to curtail output. Time is required to work out their effects, and so they tend to move ahead of turns in business cycles. Leading indicators signal in advance a change in the basic performance of the economy as a whole. Early warning signals provided by leading indicators aid in forecasting short-term trends in the coincident series. *Coincident indicators* are those whose movements coincide roughly with, and provide a measure of, the current performance of aggregate economic activity. Hence, they inform us whether the economy is currently experiencing a slowdown, a boom, or whatever. Movements of *lagging indicators* usually follow, rather than lead, those of the coincident indicators. In general, lagging indicators move in directions opposite to those of the leading indicators throughout various phases of business cycles.

The statistical-indicator approach to forecasting attempts to derive the broad general framework of what the whole economy is doing from what its sections are doing and then moves on to evaluate any particular segment within this framework. The use of this approach requires careful analysis of the underlying data, since the indicators are by themselves merely mechanical summaries. Furthermore, a good deal of confusion may arise from the fact that most indicators have behaved contrary to their usual fashion from time to time. A leading indicator, for example, may on occasion coincide with or even lag behind the turning points of general business cycles. (See Exhibits II and III.)

In 1963, the U.S. Department of Commerce, through its Office of Business Economics (renamed the Bureau of Economic Analysis in 1972), inaugurated the monthly publication, *Business Condition Digest,* which presented the data for cyclical indicators, including those listed in Exhibit II. The large number of indicators shown in the exhibit actually furnishes an excess of information for the purpose of predicting turning points. Thus the NBER specified a "short list" of 25 indicators to provide a convenient summary of the current situation. With the addition of "GNP in current dollars," one obtains the 26 series, 12 leading, 8 roughly coincident, and 6 lagging. Weekly plottings of these series, called SIA indicators, are made available to subscribers by Statistical Indicator Associates, North Edgremont, Mass. (See Exhibit III.)

Exhibit III shows that "general business activity" from month to month cannot be found in any single statistical series. Gross national

Exhibit III

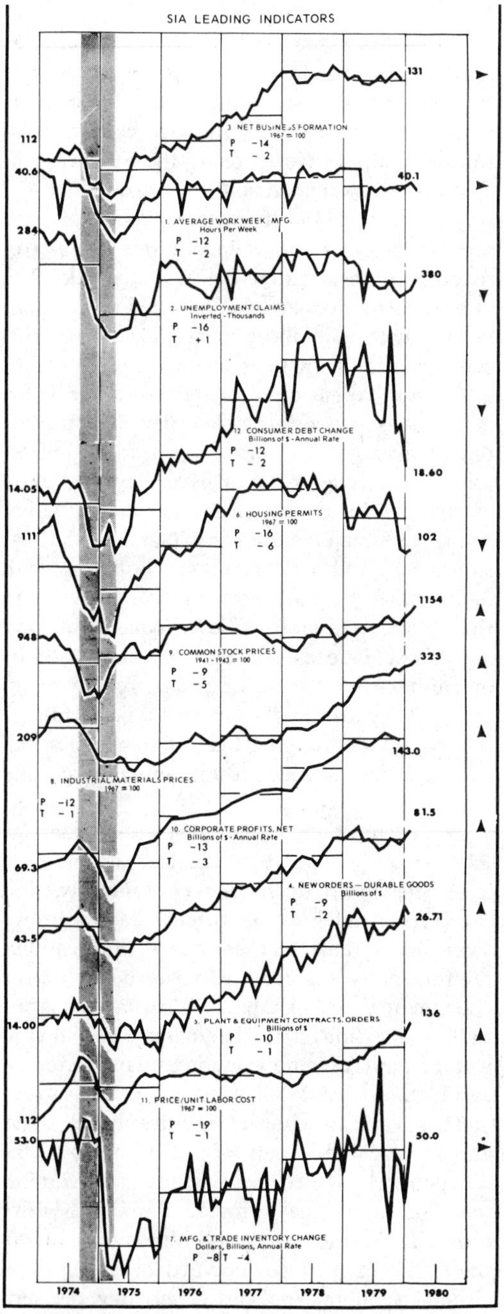

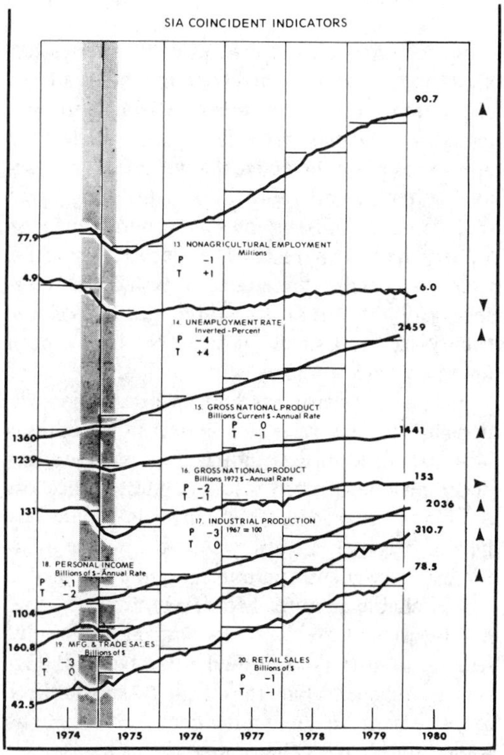

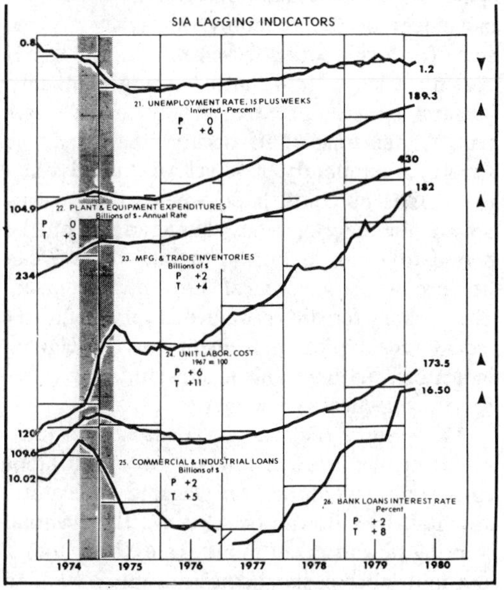

SOURCE: Weekly report to subscribers by Statistical Indicator Associates, North Egremont, Massachusetts, March, 12, 1980.

Explanatory Notes

Original sources of data are: Department of Commerce-indicators 4, 5, 6, 7, 10, 11, 15, 16, 18, 19, 20, 22 and 23; Department of Labor—1, 2, 8, 13, 14, and 21; Standard & Poor's—9; Dun & Bradstreet—3; Federal Reserve Board—12, 17, 25, and 26. Indicator 24 is the ratio of Dept. of Commerce manufacturing wages and salaries to FRB manufacturing production.

Unemployment claims (2) and the two unemployment rates (14 and 21) are inverted on the charts; they tend to rise when business falls and vice versa.

Estimates are indicated in the table by a letter "E". Revisions and new data are shown by an asterisk (*). Arrows in the charts illustrate prevailing trends. A change in trend is shown by an asterisk (*) over the arrow in the chart.

All series are seasonally adjusted except indicators 8 (industrial raw materials prices), 9 (common stock prices), and 26 (bank rates).

Only indicators 3, 6, 8, 9, 11, 17, and 24 are indexes. Base years and units for all indicators can be found by reference to the specific chart titles. Indicators 1, 3, 7, 11, 12, 13, 14, 21, and 24 are on an arithmetic scale because monthly changes are too small to be seen on a ratio scale, or because the ratio scale is inappropriate. All others are on a ratio scale; thus, equal vertical distances in the same direction represent equal percentage changes.

Thin horizontal lines represent annual levels.

Average monthly leads (minuses) and lags (pluses) at peaks (P) and troughs (T) are shown in the charts for each indicator. The averages cover the 5 business cycles preceding the latest 1974–5 recession.

product comes closest, but even this series has limitations. From its investigation of hundreds of different series of business statistics and contemporary business records, the NBER decided upon those months when the weight of the various statistics and other information suggested that definite highs or lows in general business activity had been reached. It is these months, technically called "reference peaks" and "reference troughs," that the three groups of the twenty-six statistical indicators have been found to lead, coincide with, or lag.

No one indicator has had an invariable relationship to the reference months. Exceptions have occurred often enough to make dependence on one or even a few of these indicators especially hazardous. This danger is avoided by having recourse to all twenty-six, where reinforcing movements permit the emergence of a more reliable picture. Moreover, analysis does not begin and end with looking at the twelve leading indicators. The dual role of the six laggers is indispensable: they help to substantiate a movement in the coincident indicators as something more than merely a temporary movement of the economy, and they set the stage for a subsequent reversal.

It must be realized that a turning point in a business cycle is an "event" only to the historian. At the time of its occurrence, it may be simply a temporary reversal of business activity. It is not until later, when we have witnessed the development characteristic of the period following a turning point, that we can be sure a major cyclical turn has occurred. These characteristic movements very definitely include the typical movements of the lagging indicators. Without them, substantiating a reversal as cyclical is tenuous.

As to setting the stage for a subsequent turning point, the levels of interest rates, unit labor costs, and inventories (all lagging indicators) are vital. In a downturn (upturn), the eventual working down (up) of money rates, inventories, and unit labor costs is instrumental in evoking a subsequent recovery (recession). To overlook the extent of these downturns (upturns) in the belief that the lagging indicators are of value only after a business reversal is to ignore the full value of the indicator approach.

It is important to realize that these critical levels do not usually precede the actual turning point of activity. The primary value is to provide confirmation of the cyclical nature of a turn in business activity within a few months after the turn has occurred.

To facilitate the reading of cyclical indicators, NBER has innovated a broader type of summary of the overall situation. This consists of constructing an index for each class of indicators. In the construction of these indices, indicators are weighted and adjusted in such a way so that all the indicators would have the same opportunity to influence the index irrespective of their differences in amplitude. The indices themselves are also adjusted in a similar fashion with a resulting magnitude of one percent per month in their average swings. Thus, if the most recent monthly increase in an index is 1.5, it is increasing 50% faster than its historical average. The index for leading indicators is further adjusted to have the same trend as that of the index for the coincident series. Thus, the major difference that remains, as shown by Exhibit IV, is in cyclical timing, with fluctuations of the three indexes moving in their typical fashion of lead, coincident, and lag. These indexes are easy to read, and the magnitudes of their swings are readily compared. They are thus a superior type of indicator, but close study of the components is still essential for understanding and interpreting their movements.

For example, in Exhibit IV we see that for the last quarter of 1979, the leading indicator index has been decreasing continuously, and the lagging index seems to have started an upswing even much earlier. These observations, reinforced by the fact of a slowdown of the coincident index in late 1979, seem to suggest that a recession is in the making and that it will perhaps become evident by late spring or early summer of 1980.

These are of course tentative conclusions, and more careful study of the behavior of the components of these indices and other important indicators may provide a more positive forecast. Furthermore, the directions of all these indices may be modified or changed by Federal economic policies concerning the seriously high rate of inflation and rather depressed economic activities in late 1979 and early 1980.

Note that the indices used in Exhibit IV included twelve leading indicators, four coincident indicators, and six lagging ones. Different series have been selected for the construction of these indices from time to time, and they can be identified in various issues of *Business Condition Digest.*

The indicators to be selected for the indices are evaluated according to six major character-

Exhibit IV

Composite Indices for Cyclical Indicators

Numbers entered on this chart indicate length of leads (−) and lags (+) in months from reference turning dates. Shaded area indicates recession. At top, P indicates end of expansion and beginning of recession, as designated by National Bureau of Economic Research. T indicates trough of cycle, i.e., end of recession and beginning of expansion as designated by NBER. The number 12, at right, shows latest month for which data are plotted (December). "Scale L-1" indicates a logarithmic scale with one cycle in a given distance.
SOURCE: *Business Conditions Digest,* Jan. 1980.

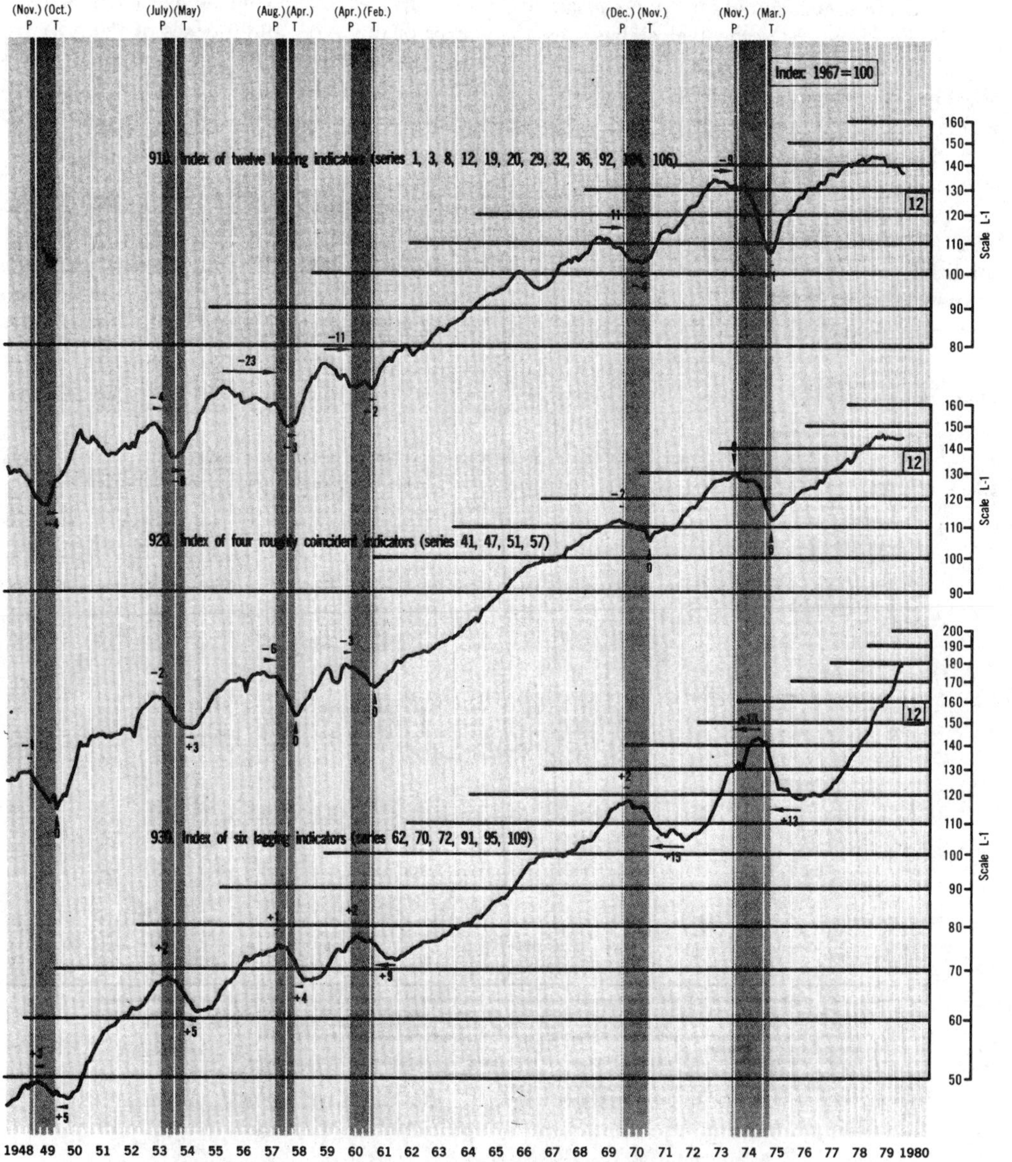

istics: (1) economic significance, (2) statistical adequacy, (3) consistency of timing at business cycle peaks and troughs, (4) conformity to business expansion and contraction, (5) smoothness, and (6) prompt availability.

The record of the NBER indicators in forecasting turning points has been quite good. However, statistical indicators are of little help in forecasting cyclical amplitude, although they can be used to secure an early and approximate judgment of how intensive a recession is likely to be. For this, the magnitude of declines in the leading series during the first few months is taken to indicate the severity of the full contraction. Such a judgment, however, may be so speculative and rough as to be of hardly any value for decision making.

One limitation of the indicators is that they are selected mainly in accordance with their historical performance. Their relationship to aggregate economic activity is not causal, although there may be some logical basis as to why a series tends to lead or to lag. These relationships, therefore, cannot be considered as stable ones. Their timing patterns will change with changes in the structure of the economy, in consumer's preferences, in managerial decision procedures, and in the reactions of business and government to changing business conditions.

The Diffusion Index. To handle the problem of variability of the individual statistical indicators, the NBER has worked with the movements of broad groups of the series instead of with each separately. The device employed is called the *diffusion index,* which shows the percentage of a given set of time series as expanding from month to month or in any other time interval. The Bureau has constructed many indexes of this type, and indexes of this sort have also been developed by The Conference Board, City Bank, and others; a number of such indexes are published in *Business Conditions Digest.*

The concept is well illustrated by Exhibit V, covering the period of the pronounced business depression of 1929–1933. This exhibit also shows vividly the difference between the amplitudes of cycles before and after the 1940s, as mentioned earlier. The diffusion index reflects

EXHIBIT V

DIFFUSION INDEX AND THE MOVEMENT OF BUSINESS ACTIVITY

SOURCE: G.H. Moore, "The 1957–58 Business Contraction: New Model or Old?" *American Economic Review,* Vol. 49, May 1959, p. 298.

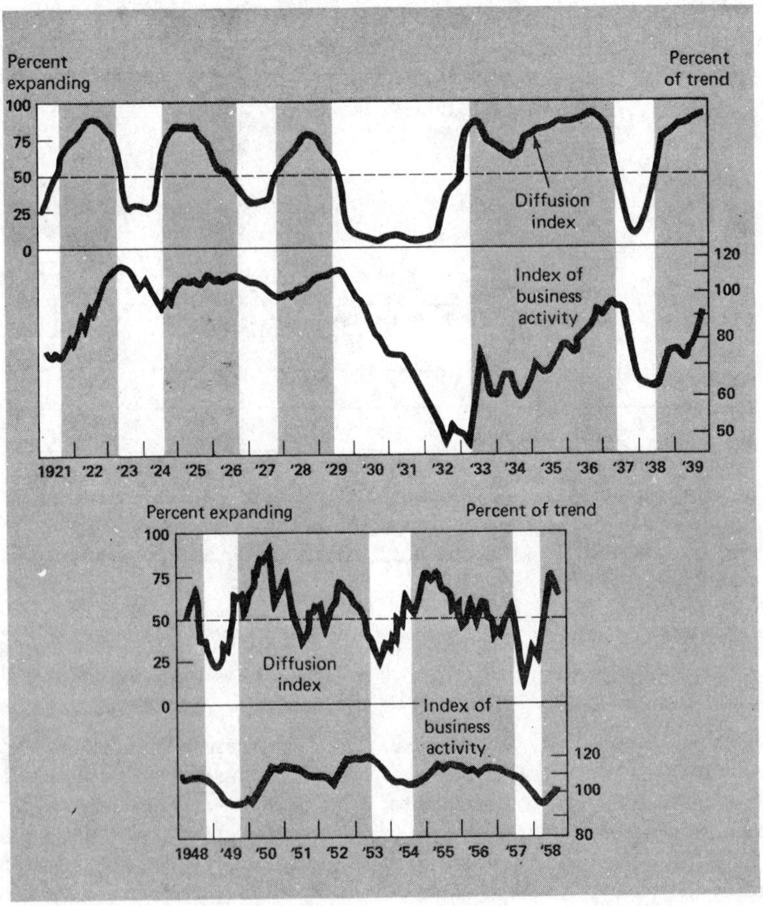

the tendency of all sectors of the economy to respond to aggregate demand at different time sequences. At any given time, some series are expanding while others are contracting; some are reaching their peaks while others are moving toward their troughs. However, after an upswing of general business activity gets into full force, almost all sectors of the economy will be expanding with it. After a certain period of time some sectors, and then more and more, will run into difficulties and thus start to contract.

The movement of the diffusion index is evidently related to that of general business activity. But it is important to note and understand that the peaks and troughs of the diffusion index are not the peaks and troughs of business cycles. It is easy to see that as long as more than 50% of the series are expanding, the economy as a whole is in a process of expansion. Consequently, it is not until the diffusion index has crossed the 50% line from above that the peak of business cycle is reached. Similarly, as long as less than 50% of the series are expanding, general business must be in a state of contraction. As a result, the aggregate economy itself reaches its trough and starts to expand only when the diffusion index has crossed the 50% line from below.

The white areas of Exhibit V are periods of business-cycle contractions. It can be seen there is a lead and lag relationship between the movements of the diffusion index and those of business activity. When the diffusion index reaches its peak and begins to turn down, the whole economy continues to expand until the diffusion index, decreasing, crosses the 50% line. Now, more sectors of the economy are contracting, and downswing of general business commences.

The diffusion index, comprising several hundred series, provides perfectly persistent leads, though of irregular durations, to the index of business activity. Thus, it seems to be an excellent device for forecasting the turns in business cycles. But the reader should not rush to conclude that we have now discovered an infallible predicting device. The leads are by no means regular. There are occasional false signals, such as those in 1951 and 1956. Waiting to date the turns until the diffusion index has risen or fallen to the 50% line may involve important delays. Further delays are also unavoidable because many of these series are not available for months. In forecasting we are not so much concerned with where the economy has been as with where the economy is and what its future course may be.

Despite these shortcomings, the diffusion-index approach to forecasting is now widely recognized as a supplementary device for observing the scope and vitality of cyclical movements. While diffusion indices are no substitute for more judgmental or less mechanical forecasting methods, they do furnish an interesting and informative continuing guard against the possibility that the forecaster's judgment may be carrying him away from the raw facts underlying trends in business data.

Regression Analysis with Time-Series Data. Most of the foregoing forecasting techniques have been presented in connection with broad economic forecasts. Such forecasts are of value to the businessman only indirectly, as a basis from which he can forecast for his own industry or his own firm. Demand forecasting on this microeconomic level is the most important type of business forecasting, since it obviously aids management directly in planning for additional plant capacity, establishing employment policies, setting sales and advertising budgets, making financing and purchasing arrangements, and the like.

Demand forecasting for an industry or a firm can be made in some fashion by every method discussed herein. However, the general procedure that has been receiving increasing attention is regression analysis. (The statistical concept of regression and correlation analysis is covered in the entry, STATISTICS, and will not be gone into here.) In forecasting, regression analysis is usually applied to time-series data. While this application presents no new computational problems, it should be pointed out that problems of a theoretical nature do arise. The mathematical techniques for the solution of the more frequently encountered regression difficulties are beyond the scope of the present treatment, and for them the interested reader is referred to the text cited at the end of this article. Suffice it to say that mathematical approaches are available to correct for errors, such as those, for example, introduced by so-called "serial correlation" and for distortions in the relationships between series caused by wartime or other unusual dislocations. The following conceptual explanation will show what is involved:

In many statistical applications, for example in quality control, the observations are as likely to occur in any particular sequence as in any other. It is exactly as likely (and no more likely) that the smallest and largest observation will be consecutive as that the two largest or two smallest, or any other two, will be consecutive. No light is thrown on the value of an observation by knowing the value of adjacent observations. But with most time series, observations that are consecutive or near together are correlated. In stock market reports, for example, it is almost impossible that consecutive days will see the all-time high and all-time low level of prices—or even the year's high and low.

The fact that methods of tackling these difficulties are not gone into here should not be allowed to create the impression that there are no such methods. Using techniques discussed in STATISTICS, and treated in detail in the text previously cited, the standard error of the mean of correlated observations can be tested if the amount of the correlation can be computed.

Presence of serial correlation can be tested, and its amount estimated, by comparing the standard deviation of the differences between consecutive observations with the value this standard deviation would be expected to have if the same observations were arranged independently at random.

The presence of significant trends in time series introduces dependence between successive observation and tends to produce serial correlation in the regression residuals. To correct for this, the trends for the original series are determined, then trends are eliminated from the original sets of data, and finally the method of least squares as described in STATISTICS is applied to deviations from trends in establishing the regression equation.

The other problem alluded to above has to do with unusually large distortions in the relationship between two series introduced by such influences as war, inflation, and recession. Consider, for example, the scatter diagram, Exhibit VI, of personal savings on personal income in the United States from 1935 to 1949. Wartime savings (circles in the diagram) are clearly at a much higher level than peacetime savings (dots in the diagram) corresponding to various levels of personal income. During wartime, because of rationing (tending to reduce consumption) and patriotism (tending to increase the purchase of government savings bonds), a greater proportion of personal income is saved. To isolate the effect of such influences and to improve the forecast, a so-called "dummy variable" is introduced for the wartime years into the basic regression line (the lower one in the exhibit) whose slope, in the parlance of economics, is the *marginal propensity to save.* The dummy variable causes this regression line to shift upward to reflect the general increase in savings due to rationing and patriotism. The device of introducing dummy variables can also be employed to make adjustments for seasonal fluctuations.

Forecasts for the Industry and the Firm. In regression analyses, the level of industry sales is usually forecast first, and the company forecast is then made on the basis of the predicted behavior of the whole industry.

The first step in forecasting the sales of an industry by regression analysis involves the selection of factors that are considered to affect the demand for the industry's output. The demand for many commodities often depends upon a multiplicity of aggregate economic variables, such as the GNP, real disposable income, industrial production, population, employment, and prices. As a rule, the factors to be selected for analysis should be kept to a minimum, even to a single one if it is believed to be adequate. This is because danger of seriously imprecise results is multiplied as correlations are made more complex, or if curvilinear relationships are used. If, for instance, a product is used by both consumers and producers, there is reason to believe that both real consumer disposable income and industrial pro-

EXHIBIT VI

REGRESSION LINES OF SAVINGS ON PERSONAL INCOME FOR PEACE AND WAR

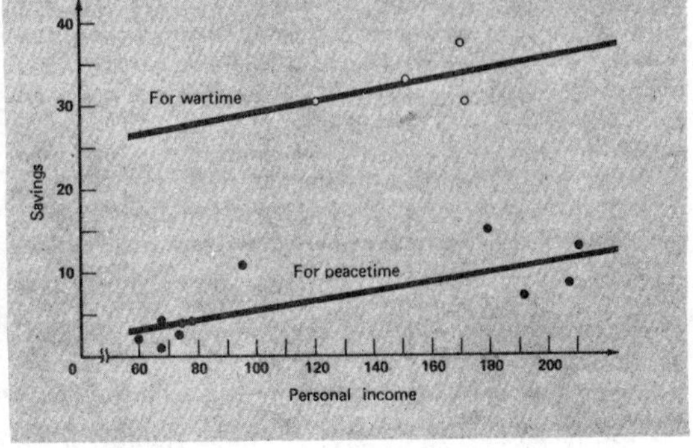

two factors are positively correlated themselves. Consequently, it would be quite sufficient to use either one of them for analysis. The one to be chosen, of course, should be that which has the best correlation with the past sales of the product.

The second step involves the development of a guide for appraising the industry's prospects of future sales. This is done by establishing a regression line for the industry's past sales (the dependent variable) and the past behavior of the selected demand factor (the independent variable) either by the freehand method or mathematically by the "least squares" method. The regression equation thus obtained will serve as the first approximation of the forecasting equation of sales on the basis of the independent variable.

Very often, by employing the most important independent variable for analysis, a reasonably good fit is obtained. However, residuals unexplained by the independent variable may still remain for three reasons: (1) inaccuracies may exist in the data used; (2) erroneous regression curves, time lag relationships, and other types of technical errors may have been introduced into the analysis; and (3) other factors that affect sales may have been excluded.

But if the investigator is convinced that his (her) analysis is reasonably free from the first two types of error, and that the residuals are mainly attributable to the third one, then he can acount for the omission of the minor independent variables by employing a *net time trend* as a "catchall" variable. This is accomplished by plotting the residuals from the regression line as a time series and fitting to it a trend line. Such a trend is in effect a regression line since "time" is treated as an additional independent variable that represents the combined effects of all demand factors not explicity determined.

The estimated trend (regression) equation may now be used to improve the accuracy of prediction. This is done by incorporating the regression equation for the explicit independent variable and for time. This is the third step of the general procedure.

The use of a single independent variable and a time trend factor is one of the simplest forms of multiple correlation. Although there are many correlations where the estimates may be considerably improved by fitting a trend to the residuals from the basic regression line, this device should not be used without discrimination. A net time trend is properly used in situations where the omitted factors are themselves highly correlated and where it may not be possible to determine directly their particular effects upon demand. Otherwise, multiple relationships may have to be called upon to explain and predict sales.

After sales of the whole industry are determined, a forecast of company sales may be based on the industry forecast. This involves the additional step of discovering the position of the firm's business in relation to the industry of which it is a part. Once the company has determined the percentage of its sales to the total market, it can project this percentage to correspond to the forecast for the industry. Sometimes the company's sales may be forecast by relating them directly to national or regional economic variables.

The use of regression analysis for forecasting involves a number of additional considerations that must be observed in order to provide results of maximum reliability:

First of all, time series employed in a given regression may need some prior adjustment or transformation in order to provide comparability, to avoid spurious correlation, and to improve the accuracy of forecasts. For example, if we are regressing the sales of beef on disposable income, we may note that both variables are positively correlated with the growth of population. When population increases, both sales of beef and disposable income will increase. Thus, a more realistic procedure should be the correlation of per capita beef consumption to per capita disposable income. Again, if we are dealing with value series, the original data should be deflated by appropriate price indices before regression is applied.

Second, a firm or an industry may produce several different products whose sales are subject not only to the influences of different factors but also to differences in the shifts of their relationships with general economic activity over time. It is therefore often desirable to break down the industry's total sales into homogeneous groups of output and carry out a separate regression study for each group.

Third, the independent variable or variables selected are either those whose estimates are logically obtained at an earlier stage in the analysis or those that lead or lag in time with the variable to be predicted. The employment of leads and lags, however, must be confined only to cases where some clear-cut reason underlies the relationship.

Finally, in establishing the regression line for two time series, it is often desirable that it fit the more recent years better than it fits the whole range of data. It is also better to ignore irregular disturbances produced by wars or strikes that affect particular years. When these irregular influences are taken into the analysis, dummy variables must be introduced. In general, to establish the best relationship possible requires that information other than statistical considerations be brought to bear on the problem. It is important to realize that the final purpose of a regression function is to provide the best set of future estimates of the variable to be forecast, not to minimize the average error of estimate in the past.

Econometric Models. Econometrics attempts to express economic theories in mathematical terms in such a way that they can be verified by statistical methods, and to measure the impact of one economic variable upon another so as to be able to predict future events. It views the behavior of an economic system as guided by numerous economic magnitudes whose interrelationships can be expressed by a set of simultaneous equations. The variables in these equations are either "endogenous" or "exogenous." Endogenous variables are determined within the economic system itself, and include, among others, income, production, money stock, employment, prices, rent, and interest. Exogenous variables are determined by such noneconomic forces as nature, politics, customs, or institutions. For the sake of simplicity and to avoid a vicious circle in which everything seems to depend upon everything else, the exogenous variables are first estimated on whatever information is available and these estimates are then used to determine the endogenous variables. Econometrics seeks to discover and measure the quantitative aspects of the actual operation of the economic system in order to forecast the course of certain economic magnitudes with a specific level of probability.

The appropriate procedure in forecasting by econometric methods starts with *model building,* or *specification.* It involves the theorizing of the interrelationships between the variables under investigation and expresses the theory in mathematical terms. A *model* is, then, a set of mathematical relations (usually in the form of equations) expressing an economic theory. (For a more detailed discussion, see ECONOMETRICS.)

If econometric methods are to yield useful forecasts, the models must be constructed with built-in flexibility in order to facilitate the absorption of shifting relationships. It may also be observed that although econometrics, to a greater degree than any other forecasting method, is analytical in nature, its successful use still requires a great deal of skill, scientific knowledge, and personal judgment. However, the development of models has made possible the quantification of predictions that can be readily checked, and it may be said that model building is the only logically suitable method with which to incorporate the best features of all forecasting techniques.

Econometric models may be constructed to predict future levels of some aggregate economic variables, such as national income, price level, or employment. They can also be employed for a particular industry or firm, to forecast sales, price, costs, or other related variable. The procedure used is the same. For instance, we may try to hypothesize that the demand for gasoline as a motor-vehicle fuel in the United States depends upon (1) the number of gasoline-consuming vehicles in use, which includes passenger cars, trucks, airplanes, busses, and so forth; (2) the average number of miles per consuming vehicle, which, in turn, depends on disposable income, prices of motor fuel, and so on; (3) the average number of miles driven per gallon; and (4) a time trend that is supposed to serve as a measure of the influence of other variables not included in the first three. On the basis of the empirical evidence available, we may then try to combine all these variables into a forecasting equation for the sales of gasoline used as motor fuel. To construct econometric models on the microeconomic level, the investigator, in addition to having technical competence, must also have experience with and knowledge of the particular industry or firm.

Opinion Polling. Opinion polling is a subjective device for forecasting that utilizes reports or surveys of opinions. Present plans about future actions are obtained by asking businessmen in strategic positions or individual decision makers such as heads of households for their estimates. Forecasts based on polls are simple in principle but quite useful in a number of situations. One such type of forecast made by business is the sales forecast, which can be made by the combined views of top management, by the prediction of the sales force, or by sample surveys of buying intentions.

Executive polling implies that the combined judgment of the group is better than the forecast of any single individual. This variation of the technique of opinion polling, without careful analysis of relevant information, can easily lead to a mere guessing game producing nothing more than sloppy and useless predictions. However, executive polling can yield a fairly reliable sales forecast if the forecast is based on thorough evaluation of market reports, sales data, and formal economic forecasts. Firms that employ this method often supplement it with the economic rhythm method of forecasting. Statistical measures of trends, seasonals, and cycles are adjusted in accordance with the results of executive polling.

The alternative of forecasting sales by asking the sales force is employed with the assumption that salesmen are good forecasters because of their constant contact with customers. Frequently, the forecast merely involves a totaling of the individual estimates. More appropriately, however, the salesmen's reports are evaluated and adjusted in the light of the judgment and data of the research staff and the expectations of people who are directly involved in planning.

To forecast sales by surveying intended actions, the salesmen may ask their customers what they intend to do with respect to a particular product. The answers are then tabulated and totaled to form the forecast.

Since World War II, by far the most important development of forecasting by opinion polling has been in general economic forecasting, particularly in plant and equipment anticipations. Valuable surveys of this kind include the following: The McGraw-Hill Survey of Business Plans for New Plants and Equipment; The Annual Survey of Business Anticipations of Plant and Equipment Expenditures by the Securities and Exchange Commission and the Department of Commerce; and The Conference Board's Quarterly Survey of Capital Appropriations of the 1,000 Largest Manufacturing Firms. The fundamental hypothesis of these anticipatory surveys is that investment expenditures always lag the basic decisions for such action by a considerable length of time. Consequently, by asking those who are responsible for investment decisions about their expectations as to future outlays for plant and equipment, a rough forecast of future actual investment expenditures can be derived in advance of the event.

A large number of survey forecasts are also continuously being produced by professional forecasters in business and government, and in the academic community. A survey of the opinions of some forecasters about future behavior of certain variables will give not only a consensus of expectation, but also a measure of the degree of disagreement that exists. A great deal of this type of survey data has been collected, but the findings are often not made public. For example, during the 70s, almost 100 different anticipation and expectation surveys by professional forecasters in more than 30 countries were conducted, although it is impossible to detail the availability of the data.

Another development has been the use of opinion polling to obtain anticipatory data on consumer spending. An example is the quarterly survey of consumer finances and buying plans conducted by the Survey Research Center of the University of Michigan. Using the method known as multistage area probability sampling, 2,300-odd dwelling units are randomly chosen to represent the nation's households. A field staff conducts personal interviews, using a fixed-question, open-answer technique.

Answers to the questions polled have been used since 1952 to construct what is called an "Index of Consumer Sentiment." Historically, the SRC's index has displayed a tendency to swing quite dramatically—with a high of over 100 in 1965 and a low of about 55 in 1974. To date, the index has succeeded in predicting the turning points of business cycles with an increasing lead—because of answers to such questions as, "Looking ahead, do you think that a year from now you will be better off financially, or worse off, or just about the same as now?" However, the major purpose of the index, according to SRC, is to anticipate consumer spending. On this score, the value of the index is controversial, since the plot of consumer spending against this index fails to suggest a clearcut or simple relationship. Here again, the expectation data are less clearly useful if used alone than if used to improve forecasts by consideration together with other information sets.

It should be mentioned that the Department of Commerce publishes quarterly data on anticipated consumer buying of new and used cars, houses, and fifteen selected categories of household durables, by income, age, race, and region. The anticipated levels are not simply the reported mean probabilities multiplied by the number of households, but are derived from regression equations. The regressions are estimated over the period 1960 to the present, with those quarters dominated by strikes in the automobile industry eliminated.

Comments on Long-Term Forecasting. Our previous discussion of forecasting for aggregate business activity was mainly concerned with cyclical fluctuations—that is, short-term forecasting. Before closing, we should comment briefly on long-term economic forecasting of economic aggregates. In many situations, projections of broad economic aggregates, such as GNP, for a decade or longer into the future are necessary. Long-term economic projection amounts to forecasts of aggregate supply or potential output at full employment capacity. Such projections serve a number of useful purposes in planning. In the first place, they indicate how fast aggregate demand has to grow in order to make possible a continuous high level of employment. They also suggest specific measures required to sustain the desired growth rate of aggregate demand. The measures may include, for instance, the stimulation of consumption or some particular type of investment. Finally, such projections are necessarily the first step in making long-range projections for particular industries and firms by the regression technique alluded to in the preceding discussion.

Real gross national product is the most important and comprehensive indicator of economic activity, and it is usually projected first over the long term. A working forecast of GNP can be simply made by assuming that the past trend will continue. Considering only peacetime years of a high level of employment, GNP has been growing, on the average about 3.5% per annum during the past fifty years. The stability of this growth rate serves as an indicator of its reliability.

A more detailed projection of aggregate supply is often made, in addition to this stable statistical growth rate, on assumptions of population growth, the proportion of the population in the labor force and its distribution between civilian labor and the armed forces, estimates of unemployment, productivity, number of hours worked per year per man, and so forth. Projected figures for these detailed factors are available from a variety of sources. Population and labor force projections are furnished by the Bureau of the Census and the Department of Health, Education, and Welfare. Other studies, such as *Potential Economic Growth of the United States During the Next Decade* by the Staff of the Joint Economic Committee and *Long-Range Economic Projection* by the Conference on Research in Income and Wealth, are available on trends in productivity and other factors. It may be noted that technological advances, more efficient use of raw materials, more efficient distribution methods, a more highly skilled labor force, and so on, have led to a continuous increase in labor productivity. During the past fifty years output per manhour, in both manufacturing and agricultural output, has increased at an annual rate of about two to three per cent.

YA-LUN CHOU, Ph.D., Department of Quantitative Analysis, St. John's University, New York, New York

(The foregoing presentation follows the treatment, updated and revised, in Chapter 21 of Ya-lun Chou, "Statistical Analysis: With Business and Economic Applications," 2nd ed., Holt, Rinehart, and Winston, New York, 1975.)

Information References

Publications of the National Bureau of Economic Research.

Publications of The Conference Board.

Publications of Statistical Indicator Associates, North Egremont, Mass.

Business Conditions Digest, Bureau of Economic Analysis, U.S. Department of Commerce.

Armstrong, J. Scott, "Long Range Forecasting, from Crystal Ball to Computer," New York, Wiley, 1978.

Box, G.E.P., and Jenkins, G.M., "Time Series Analysis: Forecasting and Control," San Francisco, Holden-Day, 1970.

Gilchrist, W., "Statistical Forecasting," New York, Wiley, 1976.

Granger, C.W.J., and Newbold, P., "Forecasting Economic Time Series," New York, Academic Press, 1977.

Kahn, H., "The Next 200 Years: A Scenario for America and the World," New York, Morrow, 1976.

Moore, G.H., "The Analysis of Economic Indicators," *Scientific American,* Jan., 1975.

Nelson, C.R., "Applied Time Series Analysis for Managerial Forecasting," San Francisco, Holden-Day, 1973.

Ya-lun Chou, "Statistical Analysis with Applications to Business and Economics," 2nd ed., New York, Holt, Rinehart & Winston, 1975.

Cross References: *Econometrics; Economics; Sales Statistics.*

BUSINESS-GOVERNMENT RELATIONS

To assure proper **Business-Government Relations,** effective representation in Washington has become extremely important. Legislative and regulatory actions have increased greatly in volume and complexity. While highly regulated industries, such as energy or health care, may have to make a greater commitment to Washington liaison, it is difficult to think of any business that is not affected in some way by the Federal Government, or that would not benefit from expressing its viewpoints to government. Members of Congress and officials in Federal departments and agencies benefit as well. Because of the diverse and often highly technical subject areas they must deal with, they need information and opinions from knowledgeable persons in order to properly fulfill their responsibilities.

There is no set formula which will ensure effective representation of management's views and problems before Federal government policy-makers. The strategy and level of activity necessary will vary according to the size and nature of the business as well as the amount of resources management may wish to devote.

This section provides generalized guidance on how to go about making a company's views known. The first step is to determine objectives. Management should decide whether it wants to influence or monitor policy-makers. Neither of these activities is mutually exclusive, and neither necessarily requires that a company have a corporate office in Washington.

Communicating with Congress. A number of avenues are open to those wishing to impact the legislative process, either individually or as members of an interest group. Here are some of the more important:

Individual members of Congress. Senators and Representatives (hereafter the term "Representative" will apply to both members of the Senate and House of Representatives) make every effort to be responsive to their constituents for the very practical reason that they will be held accountable to them at election time.

If a company wishes to establish meaningful communication with its Congressional Representatives, or generate positive action from them, it can start with the following checklist:

• Keep track of your Representatives' voting records and policy positions. Information of this sort may be available from associations or journals and newsletters that monitor Congressional activities. Also, most Representatives send out regular newsletters and releases to constituents. Be sure you are receiving one.

• Know your Representatives' priorities. Are issues of special concern to you receiving sufficient attention? Identify, specifically, whether a staff person has been assigned responsibility for such issues. Representatives' local offices should be able to supply names of members of the local and Washington staffs. As a general rule, the staff dealing directly with legislative issues will be located in Washington.

• Know your Representatives' Committee and Subcommittee assignments. Try to determine how much influence they have in their Committees. Do they chair any Committees or Subcommittees or serve as the ranking minority member?

• Establish regular, ongoing contact. This means not only with Representatives, but with members of their staffs, both at the district level and in Washington. Such contact will help "raise the profile" of specific issues for those Representatives appearing to have little interest in them.

Personal contact is important, but it need not be in Washington. Keep track of Representatives' scheduled visits to their districts or states. Letters are important. Representatives receive an immense volume of mail each day. Most letters request help or advocate a general point of view. Knowledgeable, articulate letters make an impact that is remembered.

Contact with your Representatives' staffs is important. Staff people can have significant influence over viewpoints and positions.

• Request commitment. Take any available opportunity to get your Representatives to support legislation you favor—and then hold them accountable. Try to arrange to give them public recognition if they follow through on a proposal. Remind them through calls and letters of promises they have made. Show knowledge of their voting records, their records of introducing legislation, and their Committee activities.

• Practice good public relations. Utilize local media (newspapers, radio, television, community magazines) to marshall community support for specific issues and display such support to your Representatives. Most pay close attention to their local media.

• Form issue advisory task forces. Most Representatives do not prefer to "go it alone." Frequently they will test the waters in their districts before deciding how to vote on important legislation or before introducing legislation. They also like to keep current on the concerns of their constituents. Many accomplish these objectives by forming constituent advisory task forces. In attempting to form such groups, Representatives may contact prominent citizens or local or regional business or civic associations. These groups should be aware of the possibility that their Representatives may be very receptive to the idea of forming a task force.

• Get legislation introduced. Work actively with Representatives and staffs in the drafting stages of legislation, or present draft legislation for consideration and introduction.

Efforts such as the above need not be confined to one's own Representatives. Contact should also be maintained with any member of Congress identified as having special interest in issues of concern to a given company. Many Representatives, especially those of long tenure, have developed reputations for expertise and interest in specific issue areas: energy, housing, banking, transportation, social services, health care, small business, etc. It is also advisable to identify and communicate with key members of Committees dealing with issues a company considers important.

House and Senate Committees. Committees are the "workhorses" of Congress. As the legislative burden on the House and Senate has increased in magnitude and complexity, so Congressional Committees have grown in numbers and importance. Contact with Committees is important for two reasons:

First, Committees are an excellent source of information. Testimony at hearings, which are held on general issues as well as to consider legislation, conveys the positions of interested parties.

Second, and most important, Committees are where the "legislative action" is. Often, legislation is initially developed in the Committees before being introduced in either the House or Senate. Legislation prepared by the Administration may be changed considerably in Committee. Committees set their own priorities and schedules, although they do respond to "calls" from the Administration and Congressional leadership. They can thus, within limits, bury unpopular bills and expedite popular ones.

When legislation of particular interest to a company is pending, the company should communicate with its own Representatives, whether or not they are on the Committee, as well as with Committee members. They may be effective intermediaries, depending on their personal or political relationship with the Committee members involved.

Importance of Staff Contacts. The importance of maintaining ongoing contacts with the personal staffs of Representatives, and especially with the staffs of Committees and Subcommittees, cannot be emphasized too strongly. These persons, especially those acting as staff directors, counsel, administrative assistants (generally the head of the personal staff) and legislative assistants, can have significant influence over the course and content of legislation. The Representative is the decision-maker, but quite naturally with so many issues to consider, staff is needed for assistance.

Communicating with the Administration and the Executive Branch. Communicating with Congress is only part of the battle in getting Washington to listen to company positions. Communication with the incumbent Administration and with Executive Branch departments and agencies is equally crucial.

The Administration is responsible for setting overall policy direction and priorities for the Executive Branch and for developing legislative proposals supporting its positions. The sources of real influence and decision-making will vary from President to President, and will shift during the course of an Administration. Care should be taken to locate these sources and establish contact with them.

Input into the Regulatory Process. Executive Branch departments and agencies implement the programs and policies legislated in Congress, primarily through developing regulations. This regulatory process, particularly during the first stage when new regulations are being drafted, can have significant influence over how well or how poorly those programs and policies work in the real world.

Affected individuals should try to have as much input into the rulemaking process as possible. There are two stages where this can be effective: Initial drafting of new regulations; and comments on proposed regulations, either in writing or at hearings held for that purpose. Notice of proposed rulemaking, and the proposed regulations, must be published in the *Federal Register.*

Contrary to popular belief, regulators are often responsive to the views of the regulated. Significant changes have been made in proposed regulations as a result of the active participation of interested parties during the course of the drafting and rulemaking proposal process.

Organized Interest Groups. Organized associations (business, trade, professional, or public interest groups, for example), whether broad-based or highly specialized, have become increasingly important entities for communicating with government decision-makers. In addition, they can often provide other types of assistance to their members in coping with the Federal bureaucracy. An increasing number of these associations have either relocated their headquarters to Washington or at least have a Washington office.

Washington offices of special interest groups may provide the following types of service to their members:

- Maintaining systematic contacts with the White House, Congressional Committees, Representatives and their staffs, and Federal departments and agencies.
- Developing long-range, "futurist," legislative, regulatory, and administrative programs, and working with Congressional, departmental, and agency staffs to get them implemented.
- Tracking the content and progress of significant legislation and regulations and reporting to members.
- Organizing "grass roots" support when an important issue is being considered by Congress or the Executive Branch.
- Canvassing their membership for views on specific issues, whom to support for elected office, etc.
- Demonstrating the importance, contributions, or needs of their membership through research studies, publications, speeches, etc.
- Acting as a clearinghouse of information on governmental services and programs of special interest to their membership (i.e., grants and procurements, information sources, etc.).
- Setting up appointments with Representatives and their staffs, or Executive Branch officials, for members visiting Washington.

GILBERT SIMONETTI, JR., Partner, and THOMAS R. NELSON, Manager, Office of Government Services, Price Waterhouse & Co., Washington, D.C.

Information References

The above entry is based on a 1980 Price Waterhouse publication, "Getting Your Point Across in Washington." Other documents published by Price Waterhouse dealing with government interaction with its citizens and ways in which it can be improved, include:

"Small Business in the '80s: A Call to Action."

"Monitoring Compliance with Control Systems Under the Foreign Corrupt Practices Act."

"The Value Added Tax."

Other References:

"Redefining Corporate-Federal Relations," New York, The Conference Board, 1979.

"Business and Public Policy," Cambridge, Mass., Harvard Graduate School of Business Administration, 1980.

"U.S. Government Manual," Washington, D.C., U.S. Government Printing Office.

Cross References: *Antitrust Legislation; Consumer Protection; Employment: Antidiscrimination Legislation; Environmental Controls; Occupational Safety and Health Act of 1970; Small Business Administration; U.S. Department of Commerce; U.S. Department of Labor.*

BUSINESS INTELLIGENCE: Sources of Information

GOVERNMENT SOURCES

The principal sources of statistical data on **Business Enterprises** abstracted in THE STATISTICAL ABSTRACT OF THE UNITED STATES are the *Survey of Current Business,* published by the Department of Commerce, Bureau of Economic Analysis (BEA); the *Federal Reserve Bulletin,* issued by the Board of Governors of the Federal Reserve System; the annual *Statistics of Income* reports of the Internal Revenue Service (IRS); *The Failure Record Through (Year),* issued by Dun & Bradstreet, Inc., New York; and *Fortune* and *The Fortune Directory,* issued by Fortune, New York. Other sources are publications of the Securities and Exchange Commission (SEC), and the Federal Trade Commission (FTC).

Corporate Assets and Liabilities. In its annual report, *Statistics of Income, Corporation Income Tax Returns,* the IRS presents balance sheet and income estimates for all active United States corporations. The FTC issues two current reports, the *Quarterly Financial Report for Manufacturing, Mining and Trade Corporations,* which presents quarterly income account and balance sheet data for manufacturing industries, and the *Working Capital of U.S. Nonfinancial Corporations,* which presents data on components of current assets and liabilities of all nonfinancial U.S. corporations. Until 1978, the latter was issued by the SEC. Broker-dealer financial data are detailed in the *Annual Report* of the SEC.

Corporate Income, Profits, Dividends, and Taxes. Several agencies, among them IRS and BEA, compile corporate income account data. These data, however, are not comparable because of differing methods of compilation. A reconciliation of the two can be found in *National Income and Product Accounts,* published by BEA.

The IRS publishes financial data for all business enterprises, based on a sample of income tax returns filed by sole proprietorships, partnerships, and corporations. These data appear in *Statistics of Income—Business Income Tax Returns* and *Corporation Income Tax Returns.* Supplemental reports published periodically present data on international income and taxes reported by United States corporations.

The corporate data issued by the BEA are a part of its national income and product accounts and are defined as required for purposes of national income estimation. The primary sources for BEA estimates of profits, taxes, dividends, and undistributed profits are the original corporate tax returns submitted to the IRS. Various adjustments of the IRS data are required by the national income treatment, particularly with respect to profits which would be disclosed if all tax returns were audited, depletion, capital gain or loss, treatment of bad debts, measurement of income received from abroad, and intercorporate dividends to make the figures comparable with other entries in the national income accounts. BEA's corporate profits data also include net earnings of Federal Reserve banks, credit unions, private noninsured pension funds, and several Federally sponsored credit agencies not included in *Statistics of Income.*

Sources and Uses of Corporate Funds. These data show capital requirements of corporations and the manner in which they are financed. Sources of funds should be equal to their uses. Certain discrepancies, however, interfere with this equality due to omission of such factors as (1) money accruing to corporations from an excess of sales over purchases of used plant and equipment, (2) transactions in securities held as permanent investments except public offerings, and (3) net purchases of land. Also, the balance sheet data upon which many of the financial flow estimates are based are not fully comparable with the tax-return based estimates of internal sources, or the establishment series underlying the figures on inventory change.

Plant and Equipment Expenditures. Estimates of actual and planned expenditures for new plant and equipment in the United States by most private, nonagricultural business firms are based on quarterly sample surveys conducted jointly by the Bureau of Economic Analysis and the Interstate Commerce Commission.

The sample was designed for complete coverage of all companies with gross assets of $50 million or more, and a random selection of companies with assets of less than $50 million. There are approximately 10,000 firms in the sample, with response rates varying from 70 to 75%. Published data are adjusted to reflect the expenditures of all companies. In 1972, the responding companies accounted for 68% of total capital expenditures in the United States.

For quarterly data, see current issues of the *Survey of Current Business;* for discussion of coverage, concepts, and methodology, see the January 1970 issue for actual expenditures and the February 1970 issue for planned expenditures.

Sales and Inventories. Sales are estimated aggregate values, and inventories are book values at the end of the period. Sales signifies sales or shipments for retail and wholesale trade and billings or shipments for manufacturing. Trade inventories are valued at cost of merchandise on hand, while manufacturers' inventories are valued at approximate current costs or at book values, as reported by the manufacturer. Inventories figures are based on data from censuses (conducted every five years, for years ending in "2" and "7") and annual surveys. Monthly data for manufacturing appear in *Manufacturers' Shipments, Inventories, and Orders,* published by the Bureau of the Census in its Current Industrial Reports, series M3–1; data for retail and wholesale trade appear in *Monthly Retail Trade, Sales Accounts Receivable and Inventories,* and *Monthly Wholesale Trade, Sales and Inventories.*

GUIDES TO OTHER SOURCES

Trade Associations, Excellent sources of background and statistical information are the thousands of professional, trade, business, and commercial associations and societies in the

United States. A comprehensive listing of these by field of interest, and cross-indexed alphabetically, is the "Encyclopedia of Associations," brought out yearly by *Gale Research Company, Detroit.* Gale also acts as distributor for "World Guide to Trade Associations," published by Verlag Dokumentation, Munich, Germany.

Data Bases. A relatively recent development in business information is the machine-readable data base. This refers to an organized collection of information in a particular subject area. A number of computer-based searching services are offered by the larger university libraries, as well as by commercial firms providing interactive data. Publications from some of these data bases, such as *Predicasts,* Cleveland, Ohio, which are primarily geared to business information, are found in "Business Books and Serials in Print 1977," published by *R.R. Bowker, Inc.,* New York. Commercially available on-line data bases applicable to business subjects are listed in "Encyclopedia of Business Information Sources," 4th ed., 1980, *Gale Research Company,* Detroit. The great majority of these are available through one or more of the three major commercial vendors: *Bibliographic Retrieval Services, Inc.* (BRS), Scotia, N.Y., *Lockheed Information Systems* (DIALOG), Palo Alto, Calif., and *SDC Search Service,* Santa Monica, Calif. (See also INFORMATION DATA BANKS: ON LINE.)

Business and Financial Services. A comprehensive information source on some 37,000 corporations, including Canadian businesses and major international corporations, providing names of officers, directors, and other principals, type of business, annual sales and number of employees, and more, is the annual three-volume "Standard & Poor's Register of Corporations, Directors, and Executives," *Standard & Poor's Corporation,* New York. "Moody's Industrial Manual," and "Moody's OTC [Over-the-Counter] Industrial Manual," *Moody's Investors Service, Inc.,* New York, supplemented by twice-a-week News Reports, provide up-to-date information of interest to investors on thousands of companies, with other services providing ratings on securities of governmental bodies, public utilities, and transportation companies. In addition to its credit reporting service (See CREDIT REPORTING), *Dun & Bradstreet, Inc.,* New York, (which is also the parent company of Moody Investors Service) provides an array of business information services. Through its National CSS it furnishes software and on-line computer services, image storage and retrieval technology, and computer systems for business information applications.

Also to be mentioned are the special services and publications of American Management Associations, New York, and The Conference Board, New York.

Information References

American Management Associations.
"Business Books and Serials in Print," New York, Bowker, 1977.
Dun & Bradstreet, Inc., New York.
"Encyclopedia of Associations," Detroit, Gale, annual.
"Moody's OTC Industrial Manual," New York, Moody's Investors Service, Inc.
"Standard & Poor's Register of Corporations," New York, Standard & Poor's Corporation.
"Statistical Abstract of the United States," Washington, Department of Commerce, annual.

Cross References: *Credit Reporting; Industrial Purchasing Power: The S&MM Annual Survey; Information Data Banks: On-Line; Innovation: The Management of Change; Labor Force, Employment, and Earnings; Marketing Research: Sources of Information; Prices: Statistical Abstract of the United States; Statistics; Technological Forecasting; U.S. Economic and Business Census; U.S. Census of Manufacturers; U.S. Department of Commerce.*

BUSINESS LOGISTICS

Business Logistics comprises a number of activities for which responsibility traditionally has been fragmented in the operation of business firms. These activities deal with control of incoming and outgoing materials. They include separately identified activities of inbound and outbound transportation, warehousing, materials handling, order processing, inventory control, and supply scheduling. These activities make up more than 20% of the value of tangible goods produced in the United States.

Formal Definition. The basic function of business logistics is to create "place and time utility" in goods, locating them at the right place at the right time and in the right quantities to meet customer demand. Thus, business logistics can be said to embrace: (1) the management of all activities that facilitate movement, and (2) the coordination of supply and demand, in the creation of time and place utility in goods. The first element of the task, movement control, requires coordinated management of transportation, materials handling, and storage. The second, demand-supply coordination, deals with order processing, supply scheduling, and inventory control. Each element of the overall task has profound implications for the others. Their planning, activation, and control must be integrated and carried out concurrently.

History. Business logistics has emerged as a recognized field since World War II. There are several reasons for this. Early emphasis on efficiency in manufacturing and sales left logistics as the last major area of operations in the business firm which had not received concentrated attention. Many feel that the field currently offers potential cost savings greater than either manufacturing or promotion. Second, the logistics systems of business firms have been greatly complicated by product diversification, the development of new sources of products, components, and raw materials, and the extension of markets geographically. Third, the field lends itself well to the use of quantitative techniques which have been developed in the past twenty years. Fourth, the recent availability of electronic data processing equipment in quantity has facilitated the growth of business logistics by providing the opportunity to mechanize the gathering and analysis of information. Fifth, the development of new methods of moving goods in containers, on pallets (see MATERIAL MANAGEMENT: Material Handling Equipment Types), by air or by coordinated systems of two or more modes of transportation has expanded the alternative methods available to the firm in accomplishing its logistics task. Sixth, proponents of the recently-developed *marketing concept* have placed emphasis on a greater attention to customer wants. This in turn has led to broadened product lines and more stringent customer service standards, both of which have created pressures for improved approaches to the management of logistics activities.

Professor Howard T. Lewis of Harvard was one of the first to recognize the potential of a coordinated approach to problems of business logistics in the firm. Early efforts dealt with the establishment of the subordinate field of material management. It first gained acceptance in the air-frame industry, primarily concerning itself with the integrated planning and control of transportation, warehousing, inventories, and often purchasing, of component parts and raw materials. Professor Lewis' study, "The Role of Air Freight in Physical Distribution," co-authored with James W. Culliton and Jack D. Steele and published in 1956 by the Division of Research of the Harvard Graduate School of Business Administration, was the first full-scale attempt to present currently accepted concepts. It has since been widely adopted by many business firms. One of the earliest advocates of what has come to be known as business logistics was Rudolph C. Waehner, responsible for developing one of the early model functions in the American subsidiary of one of the world's largest firms.

Early development of concepts of business logistics occurred in the distribution of grocery products, biologicals, pharmaceuticals, chemicals, cleaning agents, toilet preparations, and other products. Common characteristics of such industries are the production and distribution of products which require (1) balance between sizeable charges for logistics services and (2) high customer service standards.

Subject Branchings. Business logistics is made up of an amalgam of management activities and organizational functions which have existed for many years. At the heart of these is MATERIAL MANAGEMENT, PHYSICAL DISTRIBUTION MANAGEMENT, and TRAFFIC MANAGEMENT. In addition, INDUSTRIAL ENGINEERING has supplied some of the approaches through its attention to materials handling in production, transportation, and storage of goods. Other specific branches of the subject are *order processing, production scheduling,* and *inventory scheduling.* (See PRODUCTION PLANNING AND INVENTORY CONTROL, and WAREHOUSING.)

Approaches and Techniques. Basic to the field of business logistics is the *movement system concept.* Its underlying principles include: (1) viewing the movement of goods not as an activity carried on by or for one firm, but by and for all firms in a channel of logistics; (2) analyzing all costs resulting from the use of one of many methods of accomplishing a logistics task; and (3) designing a system involving men, machines, and information in such a way that the parts are closely integrated to create greater productivity in the system than that claimed for the sum of its parts.

The first of these principles recognizes that the price of a product to an ultimate consumer includes the cost of the sum of a number of logistics operations repeated over and over in a channel of logistics. Thus the separate healths of all firms in a channel are interrelated, requiring that any one firm in the channel analyze a movement system in terms of the logistics techniques employed by its suppliers and consumers as well as itself.

Second, business logistics calls for the appraisal of *all* costs of transportation, storage, materials handling, order processing, and the carrying of inventory under all practicable alternatives. This may involve trading one cost for another. For example, a decision to use rapid, premium transportation (such as air freight) might increase a firm's direct costs of transportation and yet give it a lower overall cost by eliminating certain warehouses, reducing inventory levels, and offering lower packaging and packing outlays. A basic objective of total cost analysis, then, is the measurement of *cost trade-offs.*

The concurrent design of all movement system components is rarely possible because of previous commitments and heavy emphasis on sunk costs. However, the third underlying principle of the concept advocates, to the extent possible, the avoidance of *sub-optimization* of system components—that is, the optimization of one system component to the detriment of total system cost or performance.

Logistics System Analyses. Any analysis of a logistics system will emphasize certain areas of study more than others, based on the definition of the system, the goal of the study, the nature of constraints imposed, the analyst's familiarity with the relative importance of system components, and the likely nature of cost trade-offs. Most analyses to date have been limited to a portion of the product items, product lines, or company divisions of a company under study. Thus, system definition in terms of product, geographical territory, or company division is an important first step in any analysis.

Next, the goal of the analysis should be determined. Is it to cut costs? Is it to improve physical service to customers? Must recommendations result in both? What are the time periods under consideration for goal achievement?

The early identification of constraints on a given study can save much wasted effort. Can plant and/or warehouse locations be altered? Can marketing territories be added, or more especially, can they be eliminated? Does competition require a given level of customer service? Can service levels be adjusted? Will pricing recommendations based upon costs of logistics for varying quantities of product be entertained?

More or less of the following types of information may be required for a given analysis: First, vital data on a company's markets should include the number, location, and size of customers. Service requirements imposed by competition, company policy, or both should be determined for those segments of the market most important to the company. Sales records and interviews can generate much of this type of information.

What is the nature of the product or products for which logistics systems are being analyzed? Important characteristics include: (1) product value, (2) weight, both unpacked and packed for shipment, (3) cubic measurements, both packed and unpacked, (4) the substitutability, in the customer's mind, of competing products for the product in question, and (5) the likelihood of product obsolescence—among others. Products frequently purchased or sold simultaneously can often be treated as one product to simplify analysis.

What is the nature of inventory fluctuations? First, what are sales patterns over a particular period of time (usually a year)? Are these caused totally by fluctuations in demand, or are patterns induced by company actions such as promotional efforts, seasonal back-order situations, or product design changes? What production patterns have been followed in the past? In what kinds of procurement patterns has this resulted? What types of inventory fluctuations of both finished goods and raw materials do these patterns typically produce? Are these fluctuations avoidable? Or are they the price of constant production levels or a high level of customer service?

What is the nature of the inventory on hand? Is it balanced with likely demands for various items over order cycle lead times? Or does it conceal dead stocks made obsolete by past inventory control decisions? What purpose does the inventory on hand serve? What portion of it is insurance against short-run back order situations? What portion is necessitated by seasonal demand over longer periods of time?

In order to answer many of the questions associated with inventory control, one needs to estimate the costs of ordering, storing, and transporting various items or product groups. What is the average cost to process a purchase order? What inventory holding costs are associated with raw materials? How do these affect order quantities for various item groups? What effect does the volume transportation rate, when combined with quantity purchase discounts, have on the order quantity inventory policy? How rapidly do suppliers respond to company orders, in terms of order cycle length? What level of transportation service can be expected between various sources of supply and the point of use? How does this affect the reorder point for goods stocked on a fixed reorder point inventory policy? What is the cost to process a sales order?

In addition to those questions associated most directly with inventory policy, others are related to specific areas of activity. How does the price for the purchase of speed, through increased technology in transportation, warehousing, or order processing, compare with the likely savings in decreased inventory and increased sales? What is the comparative dependability of various purchased services, or of company-owned and -operated transportation and warehousing facilities? What levels of accuracy do current order processing systems provide? What costs result from inaccuracy? To what extent can this trade-off be optimized by improved order processing equipment or methods?

Mathematical programming has lent itself effectively to the analysis of movement systems. One widely used application of mathematical programming has come to be known as the Transportation Problem, referring to the use of either the *distribution* method or the *simplex* method of MATHEMATICAL PROGRAMMING in pairings of origins and destinations for shipments moving between them. This has resulted in more effective allocation of: (1) production to alternative producing sites, (2) storage to warehousing alternatives, (3) purchases to alternative sources of supply, and (4) finished products to alternative markets. A case example of the Transportation Problem, using the distribution method, follows this article.

Queueing theory has aided in materials handling. It has been utilized in the design of conveyors, the scheduling of pickup and delivery vehicles into loading and unloading facilities, and other problems of materials flow. It is likely that the use of *mathematical models* to simulate logistics systems will continue to grow. Other techniques related to the field of OPERATIONS RESEARCH may profitably be used.

Acceptance. Business logistics is sometimes referred to as *physical distribution management,* or *physical supply management.* Some experts in the field have variously defined the subject as *distribution management, movement control,* or *rhocrematics.* However, there is a growing trend to consider the field as: (1) encompassing both physical supply and physical distribution management, and (2) the essential link between production and marketing.

Firms recognizing the potential of improved management of business logistic activities have reported annual savings in costs of up to 3% of sales, with no deterioration of customer service. In addition, the expansion of marketing territories by more effective use of logistics services has led to increased sales. In many companies, improved customer service is the primary objective.

The National Council of Physical Distribution Management was organized in 1962 in response to the growing interest in integrated management approaches to logistics problems. The growth and success of this organization has mirrored the increased emphasis placed on the "systems approach" to the management of logistics activities in numerous organizations.

Potential. The primary deterrent to growth of the field is the lack of fully qualified personnel to deal with logistics problems. A background adequate for the job would generally include some knowledge of the following subjects: mathematics, statistics, traffic management, industrial engineering, purchasing, inventory control, and production planning. In addition, the candidate would have to demonstrate the breadth of viewpoint to take an overall, total cost approach to problems with which he might be confronted.

Major emphasis has been placed to date on problems of physical distribution. The less-popularized area of physical supply management, through universal application of logistics in the operations of a business enterprise, will likely come in for its share of attention in future years. Although its growth will vary from industry to industry, the underlying importance of business logistics is too great to be neglected. As a result, the management of logistics activities which link a firm externally to its suppliers and customers, and which ties the firm's internal functions of purchasing, manufacturing, and sales together, will improve.

J. L. HESKETT, 1907 Professor of Business Logistics, Harvard University Graduate School of Business Administration, Boston, Massachusetts

Information References

Associations:

Groups emphasizing study and discussion of various aspects of the field include:

American Management Associations.
American Material Handling Society.
American Production and Inventory Control Society.
American Society of Traffic and Transportation.
Delta Nu Alpha Transportation Fraternity.
National Council of Physical Distribution Management.
Society of Logistics Engineers.

Periodicals:

Distribution Worldwide.
Handling and Shipping Management.
International Journal of Physical Distribution & Materials Management.
Logistics and Transportation Review.
Traffic Managment.
Traffic World.
Transportation Journal.

Texts:

Bowersox, Donald J., "Logistical Management," New York, Macmillan, 1978.
Heskett, James L., Glaskowsky, Nicholas A., Jr., and Ivie, Robert M., "Logistics," New York, Ronald Press, 1973.
VanBuijtenen, ed., "Business Logistics," Boston, Kluwer, 1976.

Cross References: *Business Logistics: Case Example—The Transportation Problem (Using the "Distribution Solution"; Freight Forwarders; Industrial Distributors; Linear Programming; Linear Programming: A Case Example—The Simplex Solution Method; Material Management; Physical Distribution; Traffic Management; Traffic and Transportation: Structure of the Transportation Industry; Warehousing; Warehousing: The Public Warehouse.*

BUSINESS LOGISTICS: Case Example—The Transportation Problem (Using the "Distribution Solution")

The so-called **Transportation Problem** refers to a specific dilemma which requires the allocation of effort to various segments of an operation. As such, it has much broader application than to the problems discussed here. Its early usage in connection with the optimization of transportation costs earned it its name, and it has continued to enjoy its greatest amount of practical use in connection with problems involving transportation and logistics in the allocation of effort. A solution of allocation problems by "linear programming" techniques may require a knowledge of elementary or advanced mathematics, depending on the technique employed.

The "distribution solution" to the problem discussed here, assumes the former (as opposed to the "simplex solution" to an allocation problem, for an example of which see LINEAR PROGRAMMING).

The linear programming approach to problems assumes that the most important relationships are exactly or approximately linear in nature. For example, the most common assumption in a shipping point allocation problem is that the transportation costs are linear in relation to volume. That is, it costs twice as much to transport two items as to transport one. It is important to keep this assumption in mind because it offers opportunities for scientific solution at the same time that it imposes important limitations on the ultimate solution it provides.

Organization of Information. The best way of setting forth the information needed for the distribution approach to the transportation problem is in matrix form. Information for an example situation involving Store Display Equipment, Inc., is shown in Exhibit I. Store Display operates four plants producing the same item, store display units, for shipment to four distribution warehouses.

Information necessary for the solution is the prospective cost of production at each plant, plant capacities, demands at each warehouse for a given period of time, and the cost to transport a unit from each plant to each distribution warehouse. The latter, when added to production costs, provides the total cost to land a unit at each warehouse from each plant. An analysis of every origin-destination pair is necessary because no constraints are typically placed on origin-destination pairs at the outset of the solution.

The goal of solutions to the transportation problem is either to maximize or minimize some element of the problem, in this case costs. Whichever is the case, it will determine the way in which information is presented and manipulated in the matrix. The goal in the example discussed here is to minimize total landed costs at the sum of the locations in the distribution system.

In Exhibit I, cost to produce a unit of product at each of the four plants is shown below the plant location. Transportation costs per unit and the total landed costs from each plant to each warehouse are indicated in the approximate matrix squares.

The amounts of capacity and demand in the matrix must balance if a solution is to be achieved. Because capacity and demand rarely balance in real situations, it is often necessary to force a balance by adding a "dummy warehouse" (when capacity exceeds expected demand) or a "dummy plant" (when demand exceeds capacity). The former has been done in Exhibit I.

The amount of product assigned to a dummy will never be produced or shipped. Products demanded by a dummy warehouse, for example, will reduce the actual production level of the plant designated to ship to it. The assignment of production to a dummy plant will determine customers who will or will not be served.

When the goal is to maximize something, usually profits, the values for shipments involving dummy plants or warehouses should be set unrealistically low. When the goal of the solution is to minimize costs, as in this case, the cost of shipping to dummy warehouses, or from dummy plants, should be set at an arbitrarily-chosen, unrealistically high level. Since actual dummy costs are unknown, they are usually set equal to one another.

The Initial Allocation. To establish a starting point, it is necessary to match up origins and destinations in some manner. This can be done haphazardly. Or one can assign as much product as possible to the matrix square with the lowest cost, the next lowest cost, on until all product has been assigned. Another method is to begin at the "northwest" (upper left hand) corner, assigning as much as possible to matrix square M_{11} and succeeding squares in the first row, then dropping down to the first available square in the second row to continue assignments.

Any system of initially matching origins and destinations should be designed to shorten subsequent work in effecting the distribution solution to the transportation problem. The best short cut to solving the problem is provided by the "least cost differential" method of assignment. The steps to be carried out are as follows (they are illustrated in Exhibits II and III):

(1) Compute the difference between the least

EXHIBIT I

DEMAND AND SUPPLY PATTERN, LANDED COST PER UNIT, JANUARY, 19—, STORE DISPLAY EQUIPMENT, INC.

		Column				
		C_1	C_2	C_3	C_4	
		Plant				
Row	*Warehouse*	*Jersey City* (21)	*Hershey* (26)	*Richmond* (24)	*Cleveland* (24)	*Warehouse (Market) Demand (In Units)*
R_1	Philadelphia	[23] <u>2</u> M_{11}	[27] <u>1</u> M_{12}	[29] <u>5</u> M_{13}	[29] <u>5</u> M_{14}	30
R_2	Richmond	[26] <u>5</u> M_{21}	[31] <u>5</u> M_{22}	[24] <u>0</u> M_{23}	[31] <u>7</u> M_{24}	20
R_3	Cincinnati	[27] <u>6</u> M_{31}	[32] <u>6</u> M_{32}	[30] <u>6</u> M_{33}	[27] <u>3</u> M_{34}	20
R_4	New York	[22] <u>1</u> M_{41}	[27] <u>1</u> M_{42}	[30] <u>6</u> M_{43}	[30] <u>6</u> M_{44}	90
R_5	Dummy	[40] M_{51}	[40] M_{52}	[40] M_{53}	[40] M_{54}	50
Plant Capacity (In Units):		40	90	30	50	Total 210

KEY: Number in circle = Production cost at each location (dollars).
Number underlined = Transportation cost from each plant to each warehouse (dollars).
Number in box = Total landed cost from each plant to each warehouse (dollars).

cost and the second to least cost square in each row and column, placing it in the least cost differential column outside each row and column. (See Exhibit II.)

(2) Assign as much product as possible to the least cost square in the row or column with the greatest least cost differential. Enter the amount in the matrix square.

Where there are two differentials with the same value (as in R_4 and C_3 in the first step of the example, shown in Exhibit II), "secondary differentials" must be computed. They consist of a consideration of the amount of extra cost incurred by accepting the second least cost in a row or column if the least cost alternative is made unavailable. Thus, the least-cost market supplied from the Jersey City plant is New York at \$22 per unit. But if it is decided that it is more economical to supply New York from some other plant, the second alternative is to send Jersey City production to Philadelphia at \$23 per unit. The secondary differential of R_4 is said to be 1. By the same process, the secondary differential of C_3 is 2, the difference between M_{23} and M_{21}. In those cases where there are "ties" in least cost differentials, allocation should be made to the matrix square with the greatest secondary differential, in this case M_{23}.

Exhibit II

First Step in the Allocation of Demand and Supply, January, 19—, Store Display Equipment, Inc., by the Least Cost Differential Method of Assignment

			C_1	C_2	C_3	C_4	
	Least Cost Differential, First Step		23 − 22 = 1	27 − 27 = 0	29 − 24 = 5	29 − 27 = 2	*Unallocated Warehouse (Market) Demand (In Units)*
			Plant				
	Least Cost Differential, First Step	*Warehouse*	*Jersey City*	*Hershey*	*Richmond*	*Cleveland*	
R_1	27 − 23 = 4	Philadelphia	23 M_{11}	27 M_{12}	29 M_{13}	29 M_{14}	Before and after assignment = 30
R_2	26 − 24 = 2	Richmond	26 M_{21}	31 M_{22}	24 20 ↙ M_{23}	31 M_{24}	Before assignment = 20 After assignment = 0
R_3	27 − 27 = 0	Cincinnati	27 M_{31}	32 M_{32}	30 M_{33}	27 M_{34}	Before and after assignment = 20
R_4	27 − 22 = 5	New York	22 M_{41}	27 M_{42}	30 M_{43}	30 M_{44}	Before and after assignment = 90
R_5	40 − 40 = 0	Dummy	40 M_{51}	40 M_{52}	40 M_{53}	40 M_{54}	Before and after assignment = 50
		Unallocated Plant Capacity (In Units):	Before and after assignment = 40	Before and after assignment = 90	Before assignment = 30 After assignment = 10	Before and after assignment = 50	

KEY: Number in box = Cost of shipping one unit between a pair of points indicated by column and row headings (dollars).
M_{11} = Matrix square with coordinates of R_1 (Row No. 1) and C_1 (Column No. 1).
↙ = Matrix square to which first allocation is made.

The amount allocated is 20 units, total demand at Richmond.

(3) Deduct the amount supplied and demanded from plant capacity and warehouse demand, respectively. The amount remaining will be unallocated supply or demand. If a plant's capacity is totally exhausted and/or a warehouse's demand is totally filled by the action, cross out the appropriate row or column to eliminate it from further consideration. In Exhibit III, for example, this has been accomplished by placing an "x" in the least cost differential notation for R_2 opposite step number two.

(4) Recompute least cost differentials and make the second assignment of product to an origin-destination pair.

(5) When all plant capacities and warehouse

EXHIBIT III

COMPLETED INITIAL ALLOCATION OF DEMAND AND SUPPLY, 19—, STORE EQUIPMENT, INC., BY THE LEAST COST DIFFERENTIAL METHOD OF ASSIGNMENT

			C_1	C_2	C_3	C_4	
		Least Cost Differential (See Key a)	1-1 5-x 2-1 6-x 3-x 7-x 4-x	1-0 5-13 2-0 6-x 3-0 7-x 4-0	1-5 5-11 2-1 6-x 3-1 7-x 4-1	1-2 5-11 2-2 6-x 3-2 7-x 4-1	*Unallocated Warehouse (Market) Demand (In Units)* (See Key a)
	Least Cost Differential (See Key a)	*Warehouse*	*Plant* *Jersey City*	*Hershey*	*Richmond*	*Cleveland*	
R_1	1-4 5-2 2-4 6-x 3-2 7-x 4-2	Philadelphia	23 M_{11}	27 (5) 30 M_{12}	29 M_{13}	29 M_{14}	1-30 5-30 2-30 6-x 3-30 7-x 4-30
R_2	1-2 5-x 2-x 6-x 3-x 7-x 4-x	Richmond	26 M_{21}	31 M_{22}	24 (1) 20 M_{23}	31 M_{24}	1-20 5-x 2-x 6-x 3-x 7-x 4-x
R_3	1-0 5-x 2-0 6-x 3-3 7-x 4-x	Cincinnati	27 M_{31}	32 M_{32}	30 M_{33}	27 (3) 20 M_{34}	1-20 5-x 2-20 6-x 3-20 7-x 4-x
R_4	1-5 5-x 2-5 6-x 3-3 7-x 4-3	New York	22 (2) 40 M_{41}	27 (4) 50 M_{42}	30 M_{43}	30 M_{44}	1-90 5-x 2-90 6-x 3-50 7-x 4-50
R_5	1-0 5-0 2-0 6-0 3-0 7-x 4-0	Dummy	40 M_{51}	40 (6) 10 M_{52}	40 (6) 10 M_{53}	40 (6) 30 M_{54}	1-50 5-50 2-50 6-x 3-50 7-x 4-50
		Unallocated Plant Capacity (In Units)	1-40 2-40 3-x 4-x 5-x 6-x 7-x	1-90 2-90 3-90 4-90 5-40 6-10 7-x	1-30 2-10 3-10 4-10 5-10 6-10 7-x	1-50 2-50 3-50 4-30 5-30 6-30 7-x	Total 210

KEY a: 1-2, 2-x, etc. = Results of successive calculations of least cost differentials, unallocated plant capacity, and unsatisfied warehouse demand for each row and column (number before dash indicates step; number after dash indicates results of calculation).

x = Capacity totally accounted for or demand fully satisfied, thereby eliminating the need to compute a least cost differential for the respective row or column.

Number in box = Cost of shipping one unit between a pair of points indicated by column and row headings (dollars).

M_{11} = Matrix square with coordinates of R_1 (Row No. 1) and C_1 (Column No. 1).

Number in circle = The order of the initial allocation of supply to demand. Underlined quantities indicate the amounts so allocated.

EXHIBIT IV

TOTAL COST OF FIRST ALLOCATION, JANUARY, 19—, STORE DISPLAY EQUIPMENT, INC.

Origin-Destination	*Landed Cost Per Unit*	*Units*	*Total Landed Cost*
Richmond-Richmond	$24	20	$480
Jersey City-New York	22	40	880
Cleveland-Cincinnati	27	20	540
Hershey-New York	27	50	1,350
Hershey-Philadelphia	27	30	810
Hershey-Dummy	40	10	Not Shipped
Richmond-Dummy	40	10	Not Shipped
Cleveland-Dummy	40	30	Not Shipped
		210	$4,060

demands have been exhausted except those in the dummy row (or column), allocate the remaining capacity and demand in the final step (step number seven in the example).

The completed initial allocation of demand and supply by the least cost differential method of assignment is shown in Exhibit III. The total cost of the first allocation is computed in the table, Exhibit IV. It is $4,060. To determine whether or not it is the lowest that can be found, it is necessary to check the matrix.

Matrix Check. We must create an artificial set of values for the purpose of checking the matrix. To do this, we can set any row or column matrix check value equal to any amount we wish. Generally, to simplify matters, R_1 is set equal to zero. The remaining matrix check values are set relative to it by equating each matrix square value (cost) to which items have been allocated to the sum of matrix check values for its row and column. In Exhibit V, this is achieved by the following process:

$$R_1 = 0$$
$$R_1\ (0) + C_2\ (?) = 27;\ C_2 = 27$$
$$C_2\ (27) + R_4\ (?) = 27;\ R_4 = 0$$
$$R_4\ (0) + C_1\ (?) = 22;\ C_1 = 22$$
etc.

Matrix check values were obtained by using the "stepping stones" (squares to which items were allocated in the theoretical body of water represented by the remaining unoccupied squares in the matrix. The values are next checked against "water" squares to determine if the first allocation is optimum (least cost). In each case, the sum of R and C matrix check values should not exceed the value of the matrix water square defined by each row and column. Saying it another way, we must ask ourselves:

$$\text{Is } R_1 + C_1 > M_{11}\ ?$$
$$0 + 22 > 23? \quad \text{No.}$$

If not, as in this case, we proceed to the next set of R and C values, and their matrix square. The matrix square (M_{11}) in question indicates no reallocation is necessary to optimize the solution.

Whenever a matrix square is encountered that has a cost value less than the sum of its R and C matrix check values, a lower cost solution could be obtained by allocating some product to it. Even after encountering such a situation, it is best to check all of the "water" squares in the matrix first. For the one whose cost value is the greatest amount less than the sum of its R and C matrix check values will offer the greatest cost reduction through the reallocation of freight to it. It thus provides us with a starting point in optimizing the final allocation.

Reallocation. There are no set rules in making an initial allocation of supply to demand; one need only adhere to restrictions imposed by facility capacities and demand quantities. The modified distribution method outlined above is only an approach which helps eliminate further reallocation and adjustments to produce an optimum solution. We could have just as well employed a technique which produced an allocation such as that shown in Exhibit V. How do we go about making necessary adjustments to optimize it, assuming we have no previous knowledge of information in Exhibit III?

First it is necessary to perform the same check on "stone" and "water" squares as described above. Our check reveals negative water values for matrix squares M_{23} and M_{34}. One need not check all matrix squares; instead, the first negative square encountered can provide the focal point for the first reallocation effort. However, the square with the most negative difference between matrix check value sums and total cost will produce the greatest savings

EXHIBIT V

MATRIX CHECK OF ALTERNATIVE INITIAL ALLOCATION, JANUARY, 19—, STORE DISPLAY EQUIPMENT, INC.

	Matrix Check Values	$C_1 = 22$	$C_2 = 27$	$C_3 = 27$	$C_4 = 27$	
		Plant				
Matrix Check Values	*Warehouse*	*Jersey City*	*Hershey*	*Richmond*	*Cleveland*	*Warehouse Demand*
$R_1 = 0$	Philadelphia	23 +1[a] M_{11}	27 0 30[b] M_{12}	29 +2 M_{13}	29 +2 M_{14}	30
$R_2 = 4$	Richmond	26 0 M_{21}	31 0 M_{22}	24 −7 − M_{23}	31 0 + 20 M_{24}	20
$R_3 = 3$	Cincinnati	27 +2 M_{31}	32 +2 M_{32}	30 0 20 M_{33}	27 −3 M_{34}	20
$R_4 = 0$	New York	22 0 40 M_{41}	27 0 50 M_{42}	30 +3 M_{43}	30 +3 M_{44}	90
$R_5 = 13$	Dummy	40 +5 M_{51}	40 0 10 M_{52}	40 0 + 10 M_{53}	40 0 − 30 M_{54}	50
	Plant Capacities	40	90	30	50	210

[a] Numbers in the upper right-hand corner of each matrix square denotes the relationship of the square's value to the sum of matrix check values for its row and column coordinates.
[b] Underlined quantities indicate the amounts (in units) allocated to each destination from each origin.

and progress if reallocation is based upon it. In Exhibit V, square M_{23} yields the highest negative value of −7.

From the most negative water square, trace a path on the matrix using only stone squares as points at which to make 90-degree angles. The path will resemble a series of moves that might be made by a chess rook with the provision that the rook must come to rest only on stone squares and proceed at a 90-degree angle on its next move. The object is to trace a path back to the starting water square. Stone squares can be passed over by a given move. There is no specified number of moves necessary to return the pathmaker to his "home" water square. Because of its resemblance to the technique employed by a person crossing a bridgeless creek, this method of reallocation is referred to as the "stepping stone" method. The path resulting from the application of this technique to the above problem is shown also in Exhibit V.

Because of the requirement that the path include only 90-degree turns, there will always be an even number of moves in any path. In the example, there are four. Each of these moves should next be assigned alternate plus and minus signs beginning from the first. Next, subtract the smallest quantity allocated to a stone square in which a positive move is terminated from all other stone squares at which positive moves are terminated. Likewise, add this same quantity to each square, be it stone or water, at which a negative move is terminated. In Exhibit V, this results in a reallocation of ten units from squares M_{53} and M_{24} to squares M_{54} and M_{23}. In terms of dollar savings, this can be translated as \$70. (Ten units supplied at a cost of \$24 per unit rather than \$31.) A second matrix check would tell us that this is not yet an optimum solution to the problem.

Two more iterations of the reallocation procedure would be required to produce the same result shown in Exhibit III. The first of these would result in the deduction of ten units each from squares M_{24} and M_{33} and the addition of the same amounts to squares M_{23} and M_{34}. The second iteration would reallocate ten units from squares M_{54} and M_{33} to squares M_{34} and M_{53}. (The reader may wish to carry out these subsequent reallocations in order to check his understanding of the procedure.) Based on this example, the importance of initial care in allocating supply to demand should be clear.

Introduction of Constraints. Constraints such as "Always work the Hershey plant to capacity, regardless of cost," "Never ship to Cincinnati from Cleveland," or "Always meet the demands of the New York warehouse" (or more typically a given customer), are sometimes introduced into allocation problems. They require only minor alterations in the initial formulation of data to solve a problem. Consider the second of the constraints imposed above on the Store Display Equipment, Inc., example.

In order to discourage the allocation of goods to Cincinnati from Cleveland, we need only to set the cost value of square M_{34} in Exhibit III arbitrarily and artificially high and proceed to solve the matrix once again. Any high number might be chosen, although theoretically there is no absolute minimum quantity that will guarantee compliance with the constraint. Therefore, the safest recommendation would be to assign the largest possible value, designated by any symbol (Z will do), to M_{34} and solve as if it were a number, albeit a very large one. Other adjustments of a similar type can be made to meet any of the above limitations which might be imposed for either rational or irrational reasons.

Alternate Solutions. A given optimum solution may be undesirable for a number of reasons. But most allocation problems have several optimum (basic) or near-optimum solutions offering an alternate operating plan at little or no cost over minimum. Whether or not a problem has more than one basic solution can be determined by a check of the water squares similar to that performed to determine optimality. For every water square with a cost value equivalent to the sum of its R and C matrix check values (i.e., a water square check value = 0), there will be an alternate optimum or basic solution. (If there are two or more of these, it can be demonstrated that there are an infinite number of quantities in which goods can be allocated to the several routes, all of which yield an optimum total result.)

Degeneracy. For any given matrix there is an exact number of stone squares which will allow a solution. It is one less than the sum of the number of rows and columns in the matrix, or $R + C - 1$. There is no guarantee that an initial allocation, even by a formal method, will produce the desired number of stone squares. There may be either too many or too few. They should be counted after the initial allocation and before solution. If not discovered, however, an incorrect number will soon halt the solution procedure after some wasted effort on the part of the analyst.

When an initial allocation produces too many stone squares, alternatives will be introduced in the assignment of matrix check values to rows and columns, obscuring the one best method. When this is the case, stone square allocations should be combined to produce the desired number before any attempt is made to check the solution for optimality.

Degeneracy results from the presence of too few stone squares in a matrix, either after an initial allocation or as the result of allocation procedures. In either case, a degenerate situation will not allow matrix check values to be assigned to all rows and columns. It can be corrected by arbitrarily allocating 0 units to any matrix square, thus creating the necessary stone or stones to facilitate the establishment of matrix check values. The actual square to be selected will have to fall in one row or one column of the matrix. The best of the possible squares to convert from water to a stone is that which best accomplishes the objective of the solution. In the Store Display Equipment, Inc., example it would be the one with the lowest cost value. Once a new stone square has been created, the problem should be solved in the normal manner, regarding the matrix square with 0 units assigned to it as one would any other stone square.

Occasionally, a deficiency of stone squares is created during solution. This will occur when reallocation converts one more stone square to water than vice-versa. It requires the allocation of 0 units, as above, to one of the stone squares eliminated by the allocation. The one to select for conversion from water back to a stone is once again the one which best accomplishes the desired goal. Once this has been achieved, the solution can proceed as before.

Solution by Computer. Rarely does a problem lend itself to a manual linear programming analysis. Because the complexity of the calculations required to solve larger matrices grows geometrically in relation to the increase in size of the matrix, computers invariably are employed to carry out such calculations. Nevertheless, it is useful to understand the logic underlying such calculations, and to be aware of the assumptions implicit in the use of linear programming by the transportation method.

J. L. Heskett, 1907 Professor of Business Logistics, Harvard University Graduate School of Business Administration, Boston, Massachusetts

Cross Reference: *Business Logistics.*

BUSINESS ORGANIZATION: Legal Structure

Broadly speaking, there are three principal kinds of business:

(1) *Proprietorship,* which is the easiest to begin and end, can have the most flexible purpose for its operations, needs no Government approval, has business profits taxed as personal income, and makes the owner personally liable for debts and taxes.

(2) *Partnership,* which is the simplest for two or more people to start and terminate, has the same flexibility of objective, has partners taxed separately, and makes all except limited partners personally liable for debts and taxes. Both the single proprietorship and partnership are relatively free of government regulation and therefore provide a high degree of privacy.

(3) *Corporation,* which is the most formal of structures, operates under state laws, has continuous and separate legal life, has its scope of activity and name restricted by a charter, has the business' profits taxed separately from earnings of executives and owners, and makes only the company (not the owners nor managers) liable for its debts and taxes.

(There are other types of legal structure such as syndicates, joint stock companies, Massachusetts trusts, and pools. However, these are specialized and rare.)

In organizing a company, advice and guidance of legal counsel are essential. It is worthwhile for the top executive to be familiar with the highlights of six main points on legal structure in addition to tax considerations: (1) costs and procedures in starting; (2) size of risk—that is, amount of investors' liability for debts and taxes; (3) continuity of the concern; (4) adaptability of administration; (5) influences of applicable laws; and (6) attraction of additional capital.

Costs and Procedures in Starting. *Single proprietorships* are the easiest to get started. The costs of formation are low. Basically all that is necessary is to find out whether a license is needed to carry on a particular business, and whether a state tax or license fee must be paid.

A *general partnership* is also started quite simply. It can be set up by having the executives in the business sign what is called a partnership agreement. A written document, however, is not necessarily a prerequisite, since an oral agreement can be equally effective. Moreover, a partnership may even be implied by actions which the managers of an unincorporated business have taken—even though no agreement of any kind, oral or written, exists.

In the absence of a partnership agreement, the partnership law of the state will determine how matters are to be handled. For example, partnership law generally provides that profits are to be shared equally and that losses are to be shared by the partners in the same proportion as profits. If the partners intend a different ratio of profits and losses this should be covered in a written agreement, which can also deal with such matters as the firm name, nature and extent of the business, duration, capital contributions, the amount of time each partner will devote to the enterprise and their respective duties, salaries and partnership draws, restrictions on individual partners, continuation after the death or withdrawal of a partner, distribution on dissolution, the liquidating partner(s), disposition of the firm name, arbitration, and other topics of importance.

Limited partnerships are somewhat more difficult to set up. To form one, the organizers must file with the proper state official a written contract drawn according to certain legal requirements. This contract permits them to limit the liability of one or more of the partners to only the amount which they invested. But, at least one general partner must be designated in addition to the limited partners. And all limited partners must have actually invested in the partnership. According to the Uniform Limited Partnership Act, those investments may be either cash or tangible property, but not services. Lastly, the business must conform strictly to the laws of the particular state in which it is organized; otherwise the business will be considered as a general partnership.

Corporations are more complicated to form than any of the other types of organization, and are subject to more intensive regulation, particularly if the stock is publically traded. They can be created only by following strictly the legal procedures of the particular state in which the corporation is being set up. First, certain responsible people are needed to organize and become officials in the new corporation. Next, they must file with the designated state official a special document, the "articles of incorporation." Then they must pay an initial tax and certain filing fees. And finally, in order to do the business for which the corporation was formed, various official meetings must be conducted to deal with specified details of organization and operation.

It is important to distinguish between two different types of corporations, the publicly traded and the closed or closely held, the latter being by far the most common corporate format. The stock of the publicly traded corporation is readily traded in the securities markets, whether it is listed on stock exchanges or sold over the counter. A closed corporation is characterized by a small number of stockholders who, unlike shareholders in publicly traded corporations, both work for and have their principal investment in the corporation; and there is no ready market for their shares, stock being transferred on an *ad hoc* basis.

Because the formalities of running a large publicly traded corporation are to a great extent unnecessary to the operations of a small closely held corporation, several of the industrialized states have modified their corporation laws to permit greater freedom in structure more akin to that found in partnerships without foregoing limited liability. For example, in New York State, stockholders may, in the Articles of Incorporation, dispense with directors and officers and run the business themselves, or hire a general manager.

Many states now permit a hybrid type of corporation for licensed professionals (e.g., doctors, lawyers, accountants, architects, engineers, certified shorthand reporters) known as a "PC," professional corporation. The professionals retain their full personal liability for professional activities but can use the corporate form to conduct their professions, purchase real estate, and make investments. Stockholders are generally limited to those licensed to practice the profession. Generally the fees of patients or clients are paid to the corporation, which in turn pays salaries to the stockholders. There are tax and pension advantages to this arrangement.

The Size of the Risk. The degree to which investors in the enterprise risk legal liability for the debts of the business is a cardinal consideration. Regardless of legal structure, creditors are always entitled to be paid out of business assets before any equity capital may be withdrawn. In cases where those assets are insufficient, the extent to which owners can be compelled to meet creditors' claims out of their own pockets varies with the type of organization.

A *single proprietor* is personally liable for all debts of his business—to the extent of his entire property. He cannot restrict his liability in any way. Likewise, each member of a *general partnership* is, himself, fully responsible for all debts owed by his partnership—irrespective of the amount of his own investment in the business. In a *limited partnership,* however, the limited partners are protected; they risk only the loss of the capital they have invested. But the general partners in a limited partnership are liable jointly and severally for all debts just like any other general partner. And, as stated, there must be at least one general partner in any limited partnership.

Corporations have a definite advantage, as far as risk goes, over other legal structures. Creditors can force payment on their claims only to the limit of the company's assets. Thus while a shareholder may lose the money he put into the company, he cannot be forced to contribute additional funds out of his own pocket to meet business debts. This is true even though the corporate assets may be insufficient to meet creditors' claims. Two exceptions are that leading stockholders may be personally liable for the corportion's failure to pay withholding taxes on payroll, and under some state labor laws, e.g., New York, these stockholders may be sued by employees for back wages after suit against the corporation leads to an unsatisfied judgment.

Continuity of the Concern. Although *single proprietorships* have no time limit on them by law, they are not fundamentally perpetual. Illness of the owner may disrupt the business and his death ends it. *Partnerships* are perishable in the same general sense—since they are terminated by the death or withdrawal of any one of the partners, or by bankruptcy of the partnership or a partner.

Corporations have a separate continuous life of their own. The withdrawal, insolvency, injury, illness, or death of a person officially concerned in a corporation does not mean its finish. Moreover, the certificates of stock, which represent investments and ownership in the business, may be transferred from one person to another without hampering the concern's operations.

It should be noted, however, that in the closely held corporation, operating for all intents and purposes as a "partnership," the death or incapacity of any stockholder may have the practical effect of terminating the business.

Adaptability of Administration. In the *single proprietorship,* policy and operations rest, of course, in one individual. This situation can be both good and bad. On the one hand, concentration of management avoids the problems of opposing factions and divided responsibilities. The fact that the chief executive is in full charge, and is in complete control of profits, can be an incentive to careful management. On the other hand, many persons cannot handle all management jobs by themselves. To be sure, an owner can, and often does, employ assistants to whom he assigns various details. But he still reaps the rewards or the penalties of what they do. It is also worth noting that after incorporating, the owner of a small business does not necessarily lose control of the enterprise. In many small, closely held corporations, the former sole owner can and often does retain control of the ownership of a majority of the stock in the newly formed corporation.

In *general partnerships,* each partner typically has an equal role in administration, with the various operating functions divided among them. The combined abilities and knowledge of several executives gives the partnership an advantage over the single proprietorship. But the division of functional responsibility among the several partners may lead to fundamental policy disagreements. Compared with corporations, partnerships have the following administrative features: Decisions may be taken and changes adopted simply by oral agreement among the partners. In limited partnerships, the limited partners may not engage in management functions; if they do, they may be held fully liable as general partners. They are, however, entitled to inspect the books and obtain full and complete information regarding the business.

In many medium and large *corporations,* the stockholders do not necessarily participate either in operations or in policy formulation, but they may. Often, however, those functions are centralized in a relatively small group of executives who own only a small percentage of the shares. Although corporations can get away from the shortcomings of the limited ability or knowledge of one person, they do run some risk of inefficient management where those in control have little or no direct financial interest. Corporations have an advantage over partnership in that in partnerships, each partner can act as general agent for the business; but in corporations, the stockholders cannot bind the firm by their acts simply because they have invested capital in it.

As their investment in the closely held corporation generally represents an individual stockholder's major or sole holding and sole source of income and employment, management and policy-making require a different technique from that of the medium or larger sized corporation in which ownership and management are usually separated. Thus, stockholders will have an interest in exploring any device which will provide them with a greater impact and influence on corporate decisions than the usually transient and relatively powerless stockholder in a publicly traded corporation possesses.

Over the years a number of such devices have been developed, e.g., qualified majorities (making the number of votes needed to adopt proposals either higher or lower in the Articles of Incorporation than are required by statute), pooling agreements, irrevocable proxies, voting trusts, and pre-incorporation stockholders agreements. All of the tools have advantages and drawbacks and should be employed only after consultation with counsel. The pre-incorporation stockholders agreement is the most versatile as it can cover the structure of the corporation (its purpose and capitalization), the subscription to stock by the shareholders-to-be, the details of employment if, as is most likely, the shareholders will also be the principal employees, the governance of the enterprises, e.g., who will be directors and officers, the method of dissolution, and, most importantly, restrictions on the transfers of stock.

Unlike the partnership, which requires the mutual consent of all partners to each other's ownership interest, the common law theory of the corporation is that stockholders should be free to come and go and there can be no absolute restriction on who can be a stockholder imposed by the other shareholders. However, in states which permit such arrangements, the stockholders and the corporation may agree that stock which becomes available because of death, disability, or withdrawal of a shareholder, should first be offered to the corporation to be purchased as treasury stock to maintain the other shareholders proportionate interests (cf. pre-emptive rights), then to other shareholders pro rata, and/or to the shareholders without regard to their proportionate holdings. Finally, if after these three steps there is still stock left unpurchased by the "insiders," the offering can be made to the public at large. It should also be noted that these so-called "buy-sell" or "cross-option" agreements are also available in partnership agreements, and that innovative use of life insurance can provide the immediate resources the corporation or a stockholder (or a partner) would require to buy out the estate of a deceased shareholder (or partner).

Agency. Corporations being legal but not natural persons must act through agents to bind third parties to contracts. Each partner is an agent for the other partners, and a single proprietor may engage agent(s) to make contracts for him or her in the marketplace. In short, one of the most important legal relationships applicable to business organizations is that of principal and agent. Here, again, we are dealing with a specialized and technical area of the law, and management must be ready to seek counsel on such matters as creating and terminating an agency relationship, the various legal theories of scope of the agent's authority, and the mutual duties and obligations of the principal and agent to each other.

Influences of Applicable Laws. *Single proprietorship* is the oldest and most widespread legal structure of business. As a result, little doubt remains as to the influences of laws regulating its legal rights and obligations. Likewise the relationships are clear between a sole owner, his agents, his creditors, and others with whom he deals in business. A private citizen working in Iowa, can carry on business in Kansas without paying any greater taxes or incurring any more obligations in Kansas than local Kansas businessmen have.

Broadly speaking, this same situation is also true for a *partnership.* Of course, a state may require the purchase of a license to carry on a particular kind of business. But the license will be equally available to businessmen of any state so long as they conform to prescribed uniform standards. (This equality of opportunity derives from the United States Constitution which guarantees to citizens of each state "all privileges and immunities" provided to citizens of the other states.) Thus, the legal structures which do not involve any artificial entity (as a corporation does) provide a freedom of action in all states which corporations cannot match.

Corporations owe their legal life solely to the states in which they are organized. No other state is required to recognize them. To be sure, all states do permit out-of-state corporations to function inside their boundaries. Nevertheless, out-of-state corporations must always comply with special in-state obligations such as (1) filing certain legal papers with the proper state officials; (2) appointment of a representative in the state to act as agent in serving process on the "foreign" corporation; and (3) payment of specified fees and taxes.

Also, corporations are regulated by numerous state laws which vary considerably. Even when the language is similar, these laws can be, and have been, interpreted differently in different places. Therefore, in running a corporation effectively, competent legal counsel is virtually indispensable. The normal course of business, for example, can easily involve statutes and court decisions of a state other than the one where the corporation was founded. Nevertheless, the essential feature of limited liability of stockholders is preserved in every state.

Attraction of Additional Capital. Every business may require additional funds from time to time to carry on operations, and inability to obtain adequate capital may well result in failure. It is important, therefore, in deciding upon legal structure to take into account the means for attracting new money.

In *single proprietorships,* the owner may raise additional money by borrowing, by purchasing on credit, and by investing additional amounts himself. Since he is personally liable for all the debts of his business, banks and suppliers will look carefully at his personal wealth. Consequently, the funds he can get will always be limited by his own circumstances. For this reason alone, a business requiring large amounts of capital for successful operation should probably not be organized as a single proprietorship.

Partnerships can often raise funds with greater ease, since the resources of all partners are combined in a single undertaking. Like single proprietors, partners must accept full personal liability for business debts; for this reason, a partnership may be able to borrow on better terms than some corporations. In addition, outsiders may be willing to extend credit because of the security deriving from the individual partners' full liability.

Corporations are usually in the best position of all to attract capital. They may, for example, acquire additional funds by borrowing money by pledging corporate assets. Also, they may sell securities to the public and attract a wide range of investors. A shareholder's investment in a corporation will not subject him to any financial risk beyond the amount of his holdings. In addition, as a part owner, he has the prospect of sharing directly, through dividends and rising value of the securities, in any profits the concern makes.

Nevertheless, the principal stockholder in a closed corporation may be required to place his (her) personal signature, in addition to corporate liability, on leases and loan agreements in order to secure space or financial support. Although not a legal requirement, the practical experience of the landlord and financing source is to treat the closed corporation as a "glorified partnership" and to seek to fix personal liability for these transactions.

JOSEF P. SIREFMAN, PH.D., JD., Professor of Business Law, Hofstra University, Hempstead, New York

Cross References: *Corporate Capitalization; Securities and Exchange Commission; Taxation.*

C

CASH FLOW ANALYSIS

Cash Flow Analysis is concerned with the cash phase of the capital turnover cycle. In a going business, the turnover of capital follows a continuous cycle which proceeds from cash to assets such as plant, equipment, and inventory; to receivables; and back to cash. Significant figures which describe the cash phase are (1) cash balance at any given time, (2) rate of cash flow (inflow, outflow, net increase or decrease) per unit of time, and (3) financial ratios which relate cash and cash flow figures to other associated indicators of financial position and performance.

Reasons for Cash Flow Analysis. A company must have enough cash to meet obligations as they mature, and management has customarily met this problem by carrying cash balances supplemented by sources of credit which experience has shown to be adequate for the purpose. In recent years, emphasis has been placed on cash flow to guide management in deploying its liquid capital resources most effectively. Financial management has become increasingly aware that, while capital in the form of cash or equivalent assets can earn a return, this rate of return is generally much below the rate that can be earned from investments in other types of business assets. Also, in a period of inflation, holding cash entails a loss of purchasing power. Hence cash balances are held at minimum levels consistent with anticipated requirements in order that cash in excess of such requirements can be promptly invested.

Cash flow has also come into widespread use by investors as an indicator of credit worthiness, as an index of management's opportunity to shift a company's capital into areas offering the most attractive rates of return, and as a measure of ability to pay dividends when undivided profits are available. Interest in cash flow analysis reflects a business environment characterized by rapid technological change and growth. It also reflects wider divergence between cash flow and periodic net profits as accounting methods have become increasingly affected by tax considerations.

N.A.A. Research Report No. 38 ("Cash Flow Analysis for Managerial Control," p. 3) defines cash as "capital in the form of cash or equivalent assets available at management's discretion for meeting obligations as they mature or for investment in operating assets." Usually included are temporary investments made to hold cash, provided such investments can be converted to cash without material delay or loss when needed for disbursements. Excluded are assets such as plant, equipment, and inventories which cannot be converted into cash for making current disbursements without impairing future revenues.

The definition above reflects the intent to measure funds available for disbursement in the immediate or near future. Somewhat different definitions are used for other purposes. For example, when the purpose is to measure funds available for capital expenditures, the relevant figure is net cash flow after deducting outlays for current operating costs and other recurring disbursements. In statements prepared to describe the flow of funds through a business over a period of time, cash is not always distinguished from other current assets, and certain transactions in which no cash changes hands (e.g., issue of capital stock for assets) may be reported as cash flows. Like many other accounting concepts, cash flow needs to be defined and measured in relation to the purpose for which the resulting data are intended.

Cash Forecasts. Management needs reliable information about cash balances and cash flow to guide financial planning and current administration of cash assets. Since decisions relate to the future, forecasts of cash movements constitute the principal sources of data for the purpose. Historical data are useful only insofar as they give an insight into the future. Some of the information needed in management of cash may be developed in the processes of budgeting and accounting, but additional procedures are required.

Three distinct patterns are distinguishable in cash forecasts:

(1) Forecasts of cash receipts and disbursements by days or weeks for periods ranging from one to six weeks ahead. These forecasts show adequacy of cash balances to meet disbursements, guide transfers of cash between

company locations and bank accounts, and show how much cash is available for temporary investment on a day-by-day basis. Anticipated cash collections and scheduled disbursements constitute the basic data for these short period forecasts. Ordinarily they are used only by financial management.

(2) Forecasts of cash flows and balances for the coming year by months and quarters. The principal purposes served by monthly forecasts are to disclose periods of cash shortage in time for loans to be arranged and to show when excess cash will be available for temporary investment. Knowing when cash will be available and when it will be needed, investment media and maturities can be selected to obtain the best available yields together with the desired degree of liquidity. Forecasting proceeds by scheduling receipts and disbursements, or, more commonly, by adjusting budgeted income to an approximate cash basis. Exhibit I shows, in summary form, a typical annual forecast of cash receipts and disbursements. Annual cash forecasting is usually a phase of annual budgeting.

(3) Long-range forecasts of cash flow covering periods of several years in advance. Such forecasts serve primarily to indicate amounts and timing of internally generated cash available for capital expenditures or the amounts of additional cash which must be provided to support a given program. The long-range cash forecast is an aspect of over-all long-range financial planning.

Cash Flow Reports. Detailed and frequent reports giving actual bank balances, receipts, disbursements, and transfers are used by financial management as a guide to need for decisions and for revising current forecasts. Top executives responsible for coordinating all functions usually receive frequent summary reports of cash position.

Summary statements intending to show the periodic flow of funds through the reporting entity are commonly included with both internal and external financial reports. These statements vary considerably in form and specific conduct.

In funds statements accompanying published financial reports, the term "funds" most commonly denotes working capital or net current assets. However, the N.A.A. study previously cited found that management tends to visualize funds flows as cash flows and prefers state-

Exhibit I

CASH FORECAST

Fiscal Year 19

	November	December	January	February	March	April	May	Totals for Year
Gross Shipments	1200	1987	2063	1387	2363	2325	1575	21000
Cash Balance Beginning of Month	375	396	222	150	257	160	192	375
Add: Cash Receipts								
Collections of Accounts Receivable	1380	1350	1605	1635	1680	2055	2205	19305
Miscellaneous Receipts	66	81	70	105	105	97	97	1050
Total Receipts	1446	1431	1675	1740	1785	2152	2302	20355
Total Cash Available	1821	1827	1897	1890	2042	2312	2494	20730
Less: Cash Disbursements								
Operating Expenses	810	915	1035	885	975	1020	960	10830
Raw Materials Purchases	503	570	1050	600	607	555	345	7140
Taxes		60	412	13		395	3	1310
Dividends	112			135			135	517
Pension Contribution		210						247
Total Disbursements	1425	1755	2497	1633	1582	1970	1443	20044
Cash Balance or (Deficiency) End of Month Before Bank Loans or (Repayments)	396	72	(600)	257	460	342	1051	686
Bank Loans or (Repayments)		150	750		(300)	(150)	(450)	900 (900)
Cash Balance End of Month	396	222	150	257	160	192	601	686

(From "Cash Flow Analysis for Managerial Control," *N.A.A. Research Report 38*)

ments which relate financial transactions to cash balances rather than working capital balances (see Exhibit II), In these statements, sources of funds received during the period (e.g., earnings, sales of assets, loans, issue of capital stock) are shown as additions to the opening cash balance and applications of funds listed by major categories (e.g., income taxes, interest, dividends, investment in long-lived assets, additions to current assets, repayment of loans) as deductions to arrive at the closing cash balance. Statement form is flexible and may be designed to emphasize desired aspects (e.g., funds available for capital expenditures).

Funds flows so reported are not all cash flows in a narrow sense, but include some transactions (e.g., earnings represented by receivables, property acquired on credit in which cash did not actually change hands). However, these items do reflect purchasing power availabe for disposition by management and inclusion in the statement helps show how the business was financed during the period.

Financial Ratios are used in financial analysis as numerical presentations of relationships between financial items which are associated to each other analytically. Two financial ratios commonly used in cash-flow analysis are the quick ratio, which relates cash to current liabilities, and the ratio of cash flow to debt (debt coverage). The former is viewed as a significant measure of short-term liquidity, while the latter is an important indicator of long-term repayment capability. (See FINANCIAL RATIOS.)

N.A.A. research report, "Financial Reporting and Business Liquidity" (1978), traces the trends in the liquidity related ratios for U.S. manufacturing companies and shows that there has been a continual decline in both the quick ratio and debt coverage. Much of the decline in the quick ratio is attributable to the development of more effective cash-flow forecasting, analysis and control. As to the decline in debt coverage, the report states (p. 53): "American manufacturing corporations display a dwindling capacity to liquidate outstanding debts

EXHIBIT II

Sources and Uses of Funds

Year ended December 31, 19__

(thousands of dollars)

Cash and marketable securities -- beginning of period	$ 156,109
Funds were made available from:	
Net income before taxes	$ 210,373
Charges against income not requiring current cash outlays (depreciation, depletion, property abandoned, accrued expenses, provision for deferred income taxes)	138,487
Funds generated by operations	$ 348,860
Bank loans	5,260
Capital stock issued	135,360
Miscellaneous -- net	1,282
Total funds made available	$ 490,762
Funds were used for:	
Acquisition, construction and replacement of property, plant, and equipment	$ 243,815
Income taxes	56,070
Dividends	82,870
Investments and advances -- subsidiary companies	7,405
Interest payments and reduction of long-term debt	20,617
Increase in inventories, receivables, and prepaid expenses less amounts payable for purchases, payrolls, taxes, etc.	25,624
Total funds used	$ 436,401
Increase in cash and marketable securities	$ 54,361
Cash and marketable securities -- end of period	$ 210,470

(From "Cash Flow Analysis for Managerial Control," *N.A.A. Research Report 38*)

without curtailment of capital expenditures. The latter action can result only in declining productivity and an inferior stance in world trade competition."

WALTER B. MCFARLAND, PH.D., formerly Director of Research, National Association of Accountants.

Information References

Arnett, Harold E., "Proposed Funds Statements for Managers and Investors," New York, National Association of Accountants, 1979.

Backer, Morton and Martin L. Gosman, "Financial Reporting and Business Liquidity," New York, National Association of Accountants, 1978.

Bechler, Paul J., "Contemporary Cash Management," New York, J. Wiley, 1978.

"Cash Flow Analysis for Managerial Control," *NAA Research Report 38,* New York, National Association of Accountants, 1961.

Hartley, W.C.F. and Meltzer, Yale L., "Cash Management: Planning, Forecasting, and Control," Englewood Cliffs, N.J., Prentice-Hall, 1979.

Heath, Lloyd C., "Financial Reporting and the Evaluation of Solvency," *Accounting Research Monograph #3* New York, American Institute of Certified Public Accountants, 1978.

Hunt, Alfred L., "Corporate Cash Management," New York, AMACOM, Div., American Management Associations, 1979.

Cross References: *Accounting (and cross references there given).*

CERTIFIED PUBLIC ACCOUNTANT

Until nearly the close of the nineteenth century, there were no generally recognized standards for the professional practice of accounting in the United States. Accounting in its earlier days had depended largely on practical experience to train the apprentice. However, in the 1880s a group of leading public accountants joined together to establish standards of practice in accounting. The result was the enactment in New York State in 1896 of the first law setting qualifications for the use of the title, **Certified Public Accountant.** Within thirty years, similar laws had been enacted in every state and territory. In 1900, there were only 243 certified public accountants in the United States. The total in 1980 was closer to 200,000.

Today, CPAs are unique in belonging to the only profession which has a uniform examination used to judge the fitness of candidates. However, while the CPA examination is uniform throughout the United States and its territories, eligibility requirements for taking the examination vary from state to state.

The examination is given twice a year, in May and November, in all states, the District of Columbia, and possessions. It occupies one afternoon and two all-day sessions. Essentially the test measures judgment and intelligence in applying accounting principles and auditing procedures to practical problems. There are four parts to the examination: *Accounting Practice, Theory of Accounts, Auditing,* and *Commercial Law.* A few states have additional tests in such subjects as *Ethics, Economics, Taxation,* or *Governmental Accounting.* The examination is uniformly graded at the offices of the American Institute of Certified Public Accountants. The actual license to practice as a CPA is issued by the states.

CPAs are subject to discipline under the regulations and codes of ethics of the state Boards of Accountancy. The American Institute of Certified Public Accountants and the state professional societies have similar codes of ethics governing the professional standards of their members.

As in other professions, there is an increasing tendency toward specialization, although the need for the general practitioner has not diminished. There is no such person as a "typical CPA," nor do all CPAs do the same kind of work. A CPA may have a salaried position with a single business enterprise, he may teach accounting, or work for the government. In these cases he is said to be in "private practice." Or he may provide accounting services to many clients as a staff member or principal of a public accounting firm. Then he is said to be in "public practice." A CPA practicing in a town of 20,000 people is subject to the same professional standards, requires the same kind of training and experience, and deals with problems of the same type as the CPA in a large city firm.

New machines and new techniques have somewhat reduced the need for routine manual bookkeeping, but better records have expanded opportunities for using the analytical services of trained accountants in dealing with more and more transactions and a larger variety of items. Thus, services to small businesses which cannot afford to hire full-time accountants as controllers or treasurers offer one of the most rapidly expanding opportunities in public accounting today.

Auditing. This is the unique function of the

independent public accountant and is the one in which his special training, skills, and judgment are most often called upon. Today, the conduct of an independent annual audit is a normal practice for most well-run businesses. In addition, some companies have quarterly or even monthly audits. An audit may be for the benefit of stockholders or creditors who want an independent opinion of a company's financial position and the results of its operations. However, even when no outside interests are involved, progressive business executives find it well worthwhile to obtain the opinion of an independent certified public accountant on their financial statements. All publicly traded corporations are required by law to have independent audits.

An audit is an examination of a client's financial statements and of the facts on which such financial statements are based. In such an examination, the CPA must determine among other things whether the financial reports have been prepared in accordance with generally accepted accounting principles, on a basis consistent with that of the preceding year. In order to do this, the CPA utilizes audit standards and procedures which have been generally accepted by his profession and the economic community in general.

The profession's authority on accounting principles is the FINANCIAL ACCOUNTING STANDARDS BOARD, which issues official statements for the guidance of the business community and independent auditors. The AICPA's Auditing Standards Board issues guidelines on auditing standards.

When the audit is completed, the independent certified public accountant expresses a formal opinion as to whether the financial statements fairly present the financial position of the client, the results of its operations, and changes in its financial position in conformity with generally accepted accounting principles.

The word *opinion* is important, because accounting is not and never can be an exact science. No one can say that the figure showing the income of a business for any given length of time is precisely correct; but the independent CPA, after a careful examination of the facts behind the figures, can say with confidence whether or not the figures may be relied upon for all practical purposes.

The CPA's opinion is no casual matter. Whenever his (her) name is associated with a financial statement, he must either give his opinion on the statement or indicate that he is unable to express an opinion, and state why he cannot do so. This is necessary because some engagements which a CPA undertakes are not sufficient to enable him to express an opinion on the financial statements as a whole.

The value of the CPA's opinion depends in large measure upon his reputation for independence, thoroughness, and integrity. He stakes his reputation on every opinion he expresses. For this reason the CPA's opinion will follow one of five well-recognized forms—depending on the circumstances:

(1) He may give an unqualified opinion, which means that he has no reservations about the financial statements.

(2) He will give a qualified opinion when he disagrees with accounting treatment in certain particulars. He will then state his exceptions as a qualification of his opinion.

(3) He states an adverse opinion if the matters to which he takes exception are of sufficient importance.

(4) He will disclaim an opinion if he has not done enough work to form an over-all opinion on the financial statement.

(5) In some types of engagements, no audit is made, but the CPA reports on the limited procedures undertaken without expressing an opinion. These are known as accounting and review services. The AICPA's Accounting and Review Services Committee issues guidelines on standards for these services.

Tax Services. Ever since 1909, when Congress imposed the first modern tax on corporate income, and especially since the Sixteenth Amendment to the Constitution in 1913 on taxation of individual income, certified public accountants have occupied a prominent place in the field of tax practice. Congress has consistently recognized, with a few specified exceptions, that taxable income should be determined in accordance with generally accepted accounting principles.

Naturally, there can be honest differences of opinion about complicated tax returns. Sometimes these have to be adjudicated by the courts, but more often they are settled by conferences with Internal Revenue Service officials. Certified public accountants often represent their clients in such conferences. CPAs, like lawyers, may be admitted to practice before the United States Treasury Department without further examination by that Department.

In addition to other factors, it is important

for businessmen to know the probable tax consequences of a transaction before a final decision is made. For example, what would the tax effects be if a new business is formed as a partnership as compared to a corporation? The difference in probable tax liability should be studied before deciding whether to buy a building or rent one; whether fringe benefits would be more desirable than a salary increase; etc. Businessmen often consult their CPAs before making such decisions.

Management Advisory Services. CPAs have historically served as business advisors and consultants. The term the AICPA adopted some years ago to describe this function is "management advisory services" (MAS). The governing Council of the AICPA has encouraged all CPAs to perform a range of management advisory services consistent with their professional competence, ethical standards, and responsibility.

In general, management advisory services performed by CPA firms consist of advice and assistance concerning such matters as an organization's management, structure, planning, finances, operations, systems, controls or other facets of current or proposed activities. MAS helps a client improve the use of its capabilities and resources to achieve its objectives. Such services are often closely related to the auditing, accounting and review, or tax services that CPA firms provide.

In performing the MAS function, CPAs may become involved in activities such as:

- Counseling management in its analysis, planning, organizing and controlling functions.
- Conducting special studies, preparing recommendations, proposing plans and programs, and providing advice and technical assistance in their implementation.
- Reviewing and suggesting improvement of policies, procedures, systems, methods, and organizational relationships.
- Introducing new ideas, concepts, and methods to management.

Some of the more common management advisory services involve: accounting systems, client financing, corporate strategy, financial forecasts, cash management, operating budgets, information systems and other computer operations, production operations, and human resources. The CPA may also be asked to act as an expert witness in the arbitration of commercial disputes, to give testimony in courts, and to assist a receiver or trustee in bankruptcy or in the reorganization of a company. (See following entry.)

SOURCE: American Institute of Certified Public Accountants, New York, New York

Information References

American Institute of Certified Public Accountants: "What Does a CPA Do?"; "How to Choose and Use a CPA"; also statements on Standards for Management Advisory Services; MAS Practice Aids; Management Advisory Services by CPAs.

Accountants' Handbook, 6th ed., Section 3, "Accounting Authorities and Organizations," and Section 9, "Independent Auditors and Audit Reports," New York, Ronald, 1980.

Cross References: *Accounting; Certified Public Accountant: Role in Management Services; Financial Accounting Standards Board; Taxation.*

CERTIFIED PUBLIC ACCOUNTANT: Role in Management Services

The CPA always served to some extent as advisor to management. This advisory service tended, in the early days, to be rather informal. Later recognition of **Management Advisory Services** (MAS) as a separate and proper activity tended toward more precise delineation of objectives of an MAS engagement. In addition, the CPA has, by evolution, come to offer such services to his clients rather than perform them only when requested.

Background. The profession of accounting as it developed in England in the late 18th century was based on an aid-to-management concept. This concept was later subordinated as the professional accountant's independence was recognized and he was cast in the role of a protector to third parties and owners (particularly in the corporate form). In the United States, during the 20th century, this role became increasingly important with the emergence of Federal regulatory and supervisory agencies during each of the World Wars and the depression years.

After World War II, with rapid increases in the rate of change of management techniques brought about by the advent of the computer and the scientific approach to planning and problem solving, consciousness of the need for professional advisory services grew rapidly. The CPA found himself being called upon more often to render assistance and advise upon matters of planning and control. Interest within the profession was reflected by the organization of separate MAS departments within public accounting firms, by the establishment in 1953 of a Committee on Management Services by the American Institute of Certified Public Accountants, and by the subsequent creation of a Management Advisory Services Division within the Institute.

Nature of Management Advisory Services. "Management advisory services by independent accounting firms can be described as the function of providing professional advisory (consulting) services, the primary purpose of which is to improve the client's use of its capabilities and resources to achieve the objectives of the organization." [1] All such services are categorized by AICPA as either MAS engagement or MAS consultations. Each of these two forms of MAS will be considered separately in future AICPA Statements on Standards for Management Advisory Services.

Since any functional area of a business requires analysis, organization, planning, and control, the scope of management services activity is as broad as the scope of management itself. In practice, however, a large proportion of the services rendered by CPAs has been in the finance and control areas. Personnel, marketing, production, inventory control, data processing, and general management are other areas in which CPA firms have rendered advisory services. Not-for-profit organizations and governmental bodies, as well as companies in the private sector, have used CPAs to perform MAS engagements. Techniques used in the work include system design and implementation, planning and control, statistical analysis and forecasting, quantitative methods, and many applications of the management sciences, including computer-based modeling.

Competence of the CPA in performing management services has increased with time, and with the improvement in university curricula in management techniques and quantitative methods.

Coordination. The Management Advisory Services Division of the American Institute of Certified Accountants currently has committees on MAS education and professional development, MAS practice and standards, and MAS small business consulting. All of these work through an executive committee of the division.

George S. Olive, Jr., Geo. S. Olive & Co. Indianapolis, Indiana, for American Institute of Certified Public Accountants.

Information References

Publications of the American Institute of Certified Public Accountants (AICPA).

Roy, Robert H. and Mac Neill, James H., "Horizons for a Profession—the Common Body of Knowledge for Certified Public Accountants," 1967.

Summers, Edward L. and Knight, Kenneth E., "Management Advisory Services by CPA's," 1976.

Scope of Services by CPA Firms, 1979.

Statements on Management Advisory Services, 1974.

Management Advisory Guideline Series #1–#7, 1968–1977.

References Cited

[1] Statements on Management Advisory Services, as above.

Cross References: *Certified Public Accountant; Management Consultants.*

CIVIL RIGHTS. See Employment: Antidiscrimination Legislation.

CLARK, WALLACE

Wallace Clark (1880–1948), management consultant (he headed Wallace Clark and Company, 1920–48) is recognized as having made perhaps the greatest single contribution of any American toward making American management methods known in other countries. For many years he counseled private and public organizations in Europe, and his writings have been translated into many languages. In 1934 the Gantt Medal was awarded to him by the American Society of Mechanical Engineers and the Institute of Management "in recognition of his distinguished service in the development and promotion of scientific management in the United States and abroad." On his death, four leading American management bodies (American Society of Mechanical Engineers, American Management Association, Society for Advancement of Management, and Association of Consulting Management Engineers) established the Wallace Clark International Management Award for "a distinguished contribution to scientific management in the international field." The basis of Clark's philosophy of management was the principles and methods of Henry L. Gantt, on whose consulting staff he had served 1915–1920, but he added contributions of his own. His "industrial gospel" for Europe was to "remove all obstacles to a free flow of work, starting from the bottom up, considering nothing as static or impossible." In 1952 his wife, Pearl Clark, long his business partner, established at New York University the Wallace Clark Institute of International Management, where reports and other records incorporating his international experience are available for use in research and education in the international management field. His books include "Foremanship" (as a contributing author), 1921 (Association Press), "The Gantt Chart," 1922 (Ronald Press), translated and published in fourteen other countries, and "Production Handbook" (contributing editor), 1944 (Ronald Press). In addition, he published numerous articles in technical and management journals and society proceedings.

Information Reference

Urwick, L., "The Golden Book of Management," edited for the International Committee of Scientific Management (CIOS), Newman Neame, Limited, London, 1956.

CLAYTON ACT. See Antitrust Legislation.

CLERICAL WORK MEASUREMENT. See Work Measurement in the Office.

CLOSED SHOP

The **Closed Shop** in industry refers to a situation where it is required of management to hire none but union members in good standing, and to discharge an employee who is no longer a union member in good standing. Such an agreement with a union is now outlawed by the Labor Management Relations Act, known as the Taft-Hartley Act. (See the section, *Labor Management Relations Act,* in the entry, LABOR RELATIONS LEGISLATION.)

COLLECTION SERVICES

A **Collection Service** may be defined as a system of methods and procedures employed to obtain payment of past-due consumer accounts receivable. As our credit economy has expanded over the past several decades, it has become increasingly important for businesses and the professionals to have available a competent, effective third party to continue the collection activities begun by their own staffs. Therefore, a collection office is generally considered an auxiliary arm of the creditor's credit department. The modern collection service must meet exacting professional standards which insure creditor and debtor of ethical and efficient procedures.

History. In the early stages of the use of consumer credit in the United States, it was found that no set of policies and procedures could be totally effective in eliminating difficulties in collecting money due on accounts receivable. During this period, many collection methods were devised. Some of these were crude and not in keeping with good business practice and good community relations. As a result, professional collection services came into being to serve the needs of the consumer credit community in a businesslike and ethical manner.

Modern Practice. Today, the collection service is a permanent business organization, adequately financed and properly equipped, under stable management, and staffed with collectors fully trained in approved collection methods. Collection offices may be privately owned or merchant-owned.

Many collection offices hold membership in national and international professional associations which require that members meet the highest possible standards of ethics and business practice. Members of the American Collectors Association, Inc., provide specialized services related to credit and collections. ACA members represent more than 2,800 of the approximately 4,500 firms that collect accounts receivable for the 2.6 million credit grantors in the United States. All association members are bonded as required by their state or through ACA. To retain membership, ethical conduct is required and competent business operations are encouraged.

ACA member collection offices provide a variety of services to the business and professional community including complete accounts receivable management, training in credit granting and collection, and consultation work, as well as a full range of collection activities. Although their prime responsibility is to serve credit grantor clients, ACA members also serve debtors by helping them solve their money management problems. This is done through counseling over the phone or in their offices or in cooperation with community nonprofit counseling agencies.

Through ACA, member collection services have access to an international network of collection offices, enabling them to forward accounts for collection anywhere in the world. In 1980, ACA members forwarded over $300 million worth of past due accounts.

The consumer credit system is based on the premise that every mentally competent wage earner is capable of assuming full responsibility for his actions. How well-founded this premise is can be determined from the frequently quoted statistic that out of every hundred consumer credit users, seventy can be sold anything they want and will pay as agreed; twenty-five will be slow-pays because of some unforeseen business or personal reverse but can be rehabilitated with understanding, competent counsel, and a little time. The remaining 5% includes consumers who do not respond well to their credit obligations and, in fact, often avoid payment altogether.

The modern collection service approaches the problem from the viewpoint that those who are slow in paying will pay, given a little assistance, and many of those who are chronically in credit difficulties can be persuaded to pay through patient, sound collection methods. Telephone, mail, and personal contacts with the debtor are all called into play when necessary.

The success of such techniques is evident from the fact that in 1980, ACA members handled nearly $5 billion in past due accounts and returned over $1¼ billion to creditor clients. While collection specialists are involved in less than one per cent of all collection activity, the money they recover can represent as much as 100% of the profit to many businesses, and the difference between success and failure for others.

Credit granters throughout the United States and Canada, as well as in other parts of the free world, have recognized that maintaining a collection operation as part of their credit departments is both expensive and time-consuming. They have, therefore, turned to reliable professional collection services for assistance in collecting their past-due accounts receivable. With the ever-increasing use of consumer credit, collection services will continue to grow in importance as an aid in holding credit losses to a minimum, thereby contributing to more economical prices for goods and services sold to consumers.

JOHN W. JOHNSON, Executive Vice President, American Collectors Association, Inc., Minneapolis, Minnesota

Information References

Associations

American Collectors Association, Inc.
Associated Credit Bureaus, Inc.

Periodicals

The Collector, publication of American Collectors Association, Inc.
Management, publication of Associated Credit Bureaus, Inc.

Texts

"Credit Management Year Book," annual edition, New York Credit Management Div., National Retail Merchants' Association, New York, N.Y.
Cole, Robert H. and Hancock, Robert S., "Consumer and Commercial Credit Management," Homewood, Ill., Irwin, 1964.

Cross References: *Credit Bureaus; Credit Management; Credit Reporting.*

COLLECTIVE BARGAINING

Under developing Federal and state labor relations legislation since the 1920s, employees have been granted the rights "to form, join, or assist labor organizations, to bargain collectively through representatives of their own choosing, and to engage in concerted activities, for the purpose of **Collective Bargaining** or other mutual aid or protection." The process of mutual negotiations between representatives of management and the recognized representatives of the company's employees (the labor union) comprising *an appropriate collective bargaining unit* has become part of our national labor policy for conflict resolution in the area of labor disputes.

This quest for stabilization of employer-union relations through collective dealings is reflected in the provision of the broad Federal Labor Management Relations Act of 1947, which established a Joint Committee to study the "methods and procedures for best carrying out the Collective Bargaining process." As a means of reducing interruptions in business operations due to strikes and lockouts, and for permitting a more predictable environment on the one hand, and as a means of providing job security and union security on the other, collective bargaining has also found its way into the public sector in the handling of government-employee controversies.

Despite the decades of experience in its practice, however, collective bargaining continues to be an unfinished business of an emotional kind. It may be properly said that "the type of industrial warfare with which the nation is concerned occurs mainly during the negotiation of the collective agreement" [1].

Background. Early in this century, the usually delineated organic functions of the business enterprise, namely, the finance function, the production function, and the sales function were supplemented by that of the personnel function. Concern with employees as members of the plant labor force and plant community incubated under the pressures of radical technological and managerial innovations, multiproduct, multiplant organizational complexity, highly effective union membership drives, war period demands, diffusion of social scientists' techniques and knowledge into the industrial culture, and the forging of a national labor policy by newly oriented Federal and state governments, judiciaries, and legislatures.

With the Railway Labor Act of 1926, the amendment to the Federal Judicial Code of 1932, and the national industry recovery acts (for the National Labor Relations Act was such), the practice of collective bargaining began to impinge directly upon the personnel-industrial-relations function. Under the impact of unionization and threats of unionization, large employers operating in industries "affecting interstate commerce" turned toward employee representation plans and other forms of company-dominated or company-assisted labor organizations as bulwarks, adapting the Works Councils of World War I to their apparent needs. Such efforts, sometimes involving contractual agreements, led to a greater delegation to specified company managers of the function of conducting employee relations with workers collectively, through the latters' representatives. More emphasis was placed on the one hand, upon detecting and handling grievances, and on the other, upon approaching the employee as a member of a group.

At the same time, attention to problems of employment and the labor market was forced upon management by war-time shortages and "freezes." Acute scarcities of workers, together with income and wage acceleration trends, led to governmental measures to control wage and price increments and to reduce labor mobility. The management response was to centralize what we now recognize to be subfunctions within personnel and industrial relations. Wage administration, governmental compliance, safety, employment (recruiting and selection, induction, indoctrination and placement), employee discipline, and the especially critical areas which came to the fore, such as industrial engineering, employee and supervisory training, and applied industrial psychology, were recognized as necessary subjects of management policy.

Organization. Centralized, away from the authority of first-line supervision, these subfunctions found their way increasingly into the hands of staff organizational specialists. With the passing decades, management preoccupation with manpower problems, cost minimization, employee motivation, and intraplant rationalization of personnel administration persisted and grew. Not the least of such growth is to be found in the area broadly denoted as labor relations, under which is properly subsumed the collective bargaining process. A result was the placing of an impossible load upon managers at the lowest levels of company operations in their dealings with production and maintenance workers. This led to functionalization and departmentalization, with the result that industrial relations and personnel departments, and corresponding titles of personnel manager, industrial relations director, vice president for personnel and industrial relations, and the like, sprang up. As trade and industrial unions forced their attentions upon employer organizations, a further differentiation of personnel subfunctions began to take place.

"Labor relations," an expression newly minted for general currency in the 1930s, made its way into the organization chart as the more generic term for that portion of the personnel or industrial relations function concerned with union-management matters. Hence the titles of labor relations manager, labor relations director, or vice president of labor relations, as heading up the labor relations department, rare in the 1930s, became more common in large business enterprise during the 1940s. And, with the statutory validation of collective bargaining followed up by Board and court decisional law defining such bargaining to include the requirement that the terms of negotiations be reduced to writing, collective bargaining necessarily became the core function of the labor relations departments.

The phenomenal rise of private and public binding arbitration, voluntarily agreed upon, added to the pressure for expertise in labor relations. Neither the personnel executive nor the legal officer of the company could achieve a proper balance of legal and plant experience. The legal department ceased to provide the necessary techniques, restricted as it was to adversary proceedings, to the drafting of protective and uniform language, and to advice regarding available rights and remedies. Personnel and industrial relations managers were fully occupied with administration and were for the most part untrained and unoriented in collective dealings. Antagonisms with plant-experienced production-, cost-, and sales-minded line executives, who often carried residual anti-union animus, impaired the efficacy of labor relations performance where no clear-cut delegation of authority, no frank top management communication, no planned and coordinated policy-making, and no special staff personnel existed.

Not surprisingly, the specialization of the collective bargaining subfunction devolved more and more upon staff labor relations executives (and labor relations attorneys and consultants) who could devote full time to such distinct subphases as preparation for bargaining, strategy and tactics, contract interpretation and administration, compliance with government regulations, contract simplification, supervisory training, grievance-arbitration analysis, labor relations audits, and labor relations research and statistics. Information retrieval and processing through use of the computer provided another tool for both employers and unions [2].

The need for contract uniformity (while preserving requisite differentials) and for coordination of contract negotiations and expiration dates, and above all the need for company labor relations policy, have accelerated both specialization and centralization of the labor-relations collective bargaining function. This has become true particularly where decentralization of authority accompanied product line or territorial reorganization, succeeding the simpler functional structure of business management and organization. Yet in many management structures, an accompanying restoration to the line executive of the labor relations function, as one form of decentralization of authority, took place. Another development has been the labor relations committee as a means of coordinating staff expertise with control and relating it to the realities of plant, office, and shop practices within and without multiple bargaining units.

Obligation to Bargain. The statutory duty to bargain collectively in good faith is, under the Federal Labor Management Relations Act, required of both the employer and the labor union if the latter is the certified or duly designated representative of an uncoerced majority of the employees constituting an appropriate collective bargaining unit (for example, production and maintenance, office and clerical, technical, or professional workers). That duty includes the obligation to meet at reasonable times and to confer, with the intention of reaching a written agreement with respect to wages, hours, rates of pay, or other terms and conditions of employment. Court decisions reviewing labor relations board rulings have distinguished among mandatory, permissive, and non-mandatory subjects for bargaining. They have also ruled on the employer's duty to produce wage and other employment information relevant and necessary to the carrying on of intelligent negotiations.

Where there is an existing collective contract, notification of proposed modification or termination must be served upon the other party, under Federal law, within 60 days prior to the expiration date of the contract. Within 30 days thereafter, if a controversy remains, a notice of labor dispute must be filed with the Federal Mediation and Conciliation Service and with any parallel state agency. Additionally, unilateral changes by management in terms or conditions of employment made without prior consultation with the incumbent union may be grounds for the unfair labor practice charge of "refusal to bargain." Neither party, however, may be compelled to accept a proposal nor to make a concession in the course of bargaining.

Nonprofit hospitals and health care institution employees were extended coverage of the Labor Management Relations Act by Congressional amendment in 1974, and the above notification time requirements were changed to 90 days and 60 days, respectively, for such contract modifications or terminations.

Issues. Developing issues and problems in collective bargaining not only include such subjects as salaries for "blue collar" workers, merit increases, intra- and inter-industry "portable" pensions, plans for profit sharing, and contractual obligations of successor corporations, but also relate to wildcat strikes, union membership rejection of negotiated agreements, impasse lockouts, and changing bargaining structures. The concept of coalition (coordinated) bargaining, for example, is a newer form of structure—a response to the corporate conglomerate whereby groups of different locals and international unions negotiate with multi-plant, multi-union, multi-product market employers on a joint basis for all employees represented by such unions.

Changing frameworks of economic conditions, technological developments, international and national competition, and statutory and decisional law have given rise to newer bargaining demands and counter demands. Cost-of-living improvement clauses, deferred wage increases, more paid time and new forms of job security and supplementary benefits along with pressures for increased productivity have emerged. Earlier retirement, with more liberal payments, increases in payments to retirees, expanded insurance coverage for dental, hearing, and vision disabilities, prepaid automobile and legal insurance, and establishment of day-care centers are examples.

Bargaining techniques have become complicated in the area of pensions benefits following the enactment in 1974 of the Federal Employee Retirement and Income Security Act (ERISA). Under the Act, minimum vesting and eligibility requirements, changes in benefit formulas, and more stringent funding regulations together with provision for employee coverage in the event of pension plan terminations have introduced rigidities within contract negotiations. A trend toward enlarging work and pay opportunities in the direction of the four-day work week, began in 1976 in the automobile (Big Three) contract with the United Auto Workers' Union, with thirteen added days of personal leave, flex-time, alternative work scheduling, and more paid time off. Protection against subcontracting threat and against loss of jobs because of plant closings has been reflected in relocation allowances and job-search assistance. Extended supplementary unemployment benefits (SUB), special pension supplements, and additional fringe benefits are exemplified in the United Steelworkers Union steel industry contract of 1977. Seniority continues as a key subject of bargaining, but in a context of the Federal Civil Rights Act of 1964 and similar state laws. Under these laws, training, apprentice programs, and the establishment and administration of seniority systems must be carried out in a nondiscriminatory equal opportunity manner, as interpreted by administrative and judicial law.

Employer demands for productivity bargaining have developed in the face of established work rules and practices as a means of cost minimization and overcoming resistance to technological change. Joint labor-management programs or direct and indirect wage and salary "buy-backs" are two avenues that have opened up. Productivity has been linked to work-improvement and quality-of-work programs. (See QUALITY OF WORK LIFE.) Labor-employer experimentation had been encouraged during the 1970s through the National Commissions on Productivity and Work Quality. Two other areas for both adversary collective bargaining and for cooperative union-management efforts are those of the external and internal hazards to the work environment, where Federal and state laws (e.g., OCCUPATIONAL SAFETY AND HEALTH ACT of 1970) have concentrated attention on protecting against and compensating for injuries and illnesses created directly, or indirectly, through stress-related conditions.

The cost of settlements arising out of collective bargaining is becoming more difficult to estimate in an inflationary period where, for example, hospital and health care protection rates tend to be unpredictable. With fringe benefit packages proliferating in kind and amount, and compliance with regulatory requirements increasing, "rolling up" wage-related benefits and indirect expenditures suggests that supplemental non-wage improvements will increase in significance at the bargaining table.

The private law of "industrial jurisprudence," that is, the body of awards and opinions of labor arbitrators, has widened the definition of collective bargaining to cover grievance processing and past plant and office practices as expressions of the intent of the parties to the collective agreements. Indeed, grievance-arbitration clauses, when viewed together with the management rights' clause and the "no-strike, no-lockout" clause, have become the heart of the administration of the labor-management contract. Significant United States Supreme Court decisions in these areas have fixed attention upon the need for care in the drafting of contract language where there has been a voluntary submission by the parties to arbitration of "rights" over the meaning and application of the terms of a collective bargaining agreement. However, as demonstrated by the basic Steel-United Steelworkers' experimental contract discussed below, the acceptance of voluntary arbitration of "interests," where the arbitrator or panel is called upon to "write" the disputed terms and provisions of a new or renegotiated agreement, has emerged. Other instances include hospital and airline labor disputes. (See LABOR ARBITRATION.)

Creative Collective Bargaining. Creative experiments in collective bargaining directed at problem solving and the avoidance of "crisis-bargaining" have taken place in steel (joint Human Relations Research Committee and tripartite Kaiser Long Range Committee), in meat packing (tripartite Automation Committee), and in West Coast longshore industry (Mechanization and Modernization Agreement) [3]. The establishment of the Labor-Management Institute within the American Arbitration Association and the Institute of Collective Bargaining in Group Relations, both in New York City, represent additional forums for investigation of newer modes in collective bargaining.

An important break with past collective bargaining occurred in 1974, following a 116-day nation-wide strike in the basic steel industry. The innovation was the Experimental Negotiating Agreement (ENA) entered into between the ten basic steel companies and the United Steelworkers of America. The union agreed to forego striking over industry-wide contract disputes and to submit deadlocked issues to binding interest arbitration while retaining the right to strike over local issues and over such fundamental matters as union security. In exchange, the employers gave up the right to lockout and granted a guaranteed 3% annual wage increase during the three-year term of the agreement, an anual cost-of-living adjustment (COLA), and a fixed dollar amount "bonus" for each covered employee as a kind of sharing in managements' gains.

The three-year cycle built into the initial joint labor-management experiment has continued with positive effects associated with national strike avoidance. Unstabilizing strike threats with accompanying stockpiling actions and consequent layoffs have been eliminated. A landmark in management-union joint participation was marked by the Chrysler Corporation and the United Automobile Workers Union collective bargaining which resulted in an agreement by the Union and employees to invest pension funds in the corporation's survival, and by the company to make the President of the UAW a member of Chrysler's board of directors. Interest in encouraging free collective bargaining through consultative and participative joint employer-union cooperation in local and national committee actions supported by Federal assistance has been expressed in such problem areas as occupational safety and health. The Labor-Management Cooperation Act of 1978 is a public expression, as spelled out in its declared legislative purposes, of the above trend toward new initiatives in collective bargaining.

WILLARD A. LEWIS, PH.D., LL.B., Professor Emeritus of Management and Industrial Relations, Graduate School of Business Administration, New York University, New York; Visiting Professor, Polytechnic Institute of New York, Brooklyn, New York

Information References

Bureau of National Affairs, Inc., Washington.
"Basic Patterns in Labor Contracts."
"Collective Bargaining Negotiations and Contracts, 1975."
"Labor Relations Yearbook"
The Conference Board, New York:
Bargaining Surveys.
Freedman, Audrey, "Managing Labor Relations," 1979.
U.S. Department of Labor, Bureau of Labor Statistics, Washington.

References Cited

[1] Aaron, Grodin, and Stern (eds.), "Public-Sector Bargaining," Washington, D.C., The Bureau of National Affairs, Inc. 1979.
[2] Bok and Dunlop, "Labor and the American Community," New York, Simon and Schuster, 1979.
[3] Kochan, Thomas A., "Collective Bargaining and Industrial Relations," Homewood, Ill., Irwin, 1980.
[4] Oberer and Hanslow, "Labor Law: Collective Bargaining in a Free Society, St. Paul, Minn., West Publishing Co., 1972.

Cross References: *Labor Arbitration; Labor Relations Legislation; Labor Unions; Lewis, John L.; Meany, George.*

COMMERCE DEPARTMENT. See U.S. Department of Commerce.

COMMON MARKET. See European Economic Community.

COMMUNICATION. See Advertising; Advertising Research; Annual Reports; Data Communications; Data Communications: Case Example; Employee Attitude Research: Attitude Surveys; House Magazines;

Management Information Systems; Management Information Systems: Case Example; Personnel Counseling; Public Relations; Public Relations Research; Publicity; Transaction Analysis in Management.

COMPUTER INSTALLATIONS: Top Management Planning and Follow-Through

While the use of **Computers** in American corporate life has been widely accepted for some time, the involvement of top management in planning and monitoring the computer resource has been less well understood and accepted. Senior managers are often confused and perturbed by the cost, confusion, and technical jargon which surround the data processing function within their companies, and are often concerned about what their involvement should be. As the use of computers has grown since the early 1950s, the applications to which they have been put have changed. Whereas, in the first wave of computerization, the objective was automation of clerical activity so as to stabilize costs, a clearly discernable second wave is seeking to use the computer to support decision making and support management control [1]. From the perspective of the senior manager, three different attributes of the use of computers command some attention:

(1) *The Business Depends on Them.* In most industries, the basic day-to-day transaction processing has been computerized. (See ELECTRONIC DATA PROCESSING.) Just as most manufacturing companies maintain their order entry and inventory control systems on a computer, so too most banks have their customers' accounts on a computer system. The benefits of reducing clerical activities, providing immediate customer service, and maintaining accurate records has been realized in most businesses, but there is a consequent vulnerability which ensues: If, for some reason, the computers one day should cease to function, so too, would the business.

(2) *They Are Useful for Management Control.* The basic cornerstone of any management information system—the regular report of performance against plan, of expenses against budget or of shipments against inventory—provides the manager with timely and accurate information about the activities of the business. Further, desirable decentralization of the business's activity can be supported by a distributed network of computers, all of them communicating with central computers at the home office. This allows management of the far-flung enterprise to stay in touch at all times with the activities of the geographically disbursed corporation. (See DATA COMMUNICATIONS.)

(3) *They Can Provide Information to Support Decision Making.* With the enormous capacity for storing large amounts of data, the potential exists for the manager to reach into the computer system and extract whatever information may be relevant in support of the decision-making process. (See MANAGEMENT INFORMATION SYSTEMS.) The availability of technology which allows on-line terminal networks, making available data in easy-to-use systems for nontechnical users, provides an intriguing scenario for the senior manager seeking to get whatever information he or she can to help make better decisions in a complex, changing business environment.

Corporate managers, who have long insisted on a ten-year strategic business plan and five-year plans for their marketing and production operations, have rarely required similar projections from their data processing departments. Yet information-processing budgets are now growing as large as those of other corporate operations and, more important, the function they perform is rapidly becoming critical to large companies. Data processing has been considered merely a support function that was part of administrative overhead. But the move to interactive systems that process orders, maintain inventories, and perform other financial transactions is making computers an integral part of doing business.

For the most part, top management has not moved to correct the lack of planning. Data processing strategy has been considered separate from the business strategy of an organization; a gap exists between the two cultures. Over the years, data processing people have depended on the vendors to determine their equipment needs, and computer manufacturers' efforts to educate the users have been aimed primarily at computer personnel who were often technicians bent on proving how good the machines were, rather than on managing them.

Systems Planning. Successful planning begins with a view of the computer center as a small business within a business, in the same way that operating divisions and other corporate profit centers are looked upon. This requires the involvement of top management so that the culture gap between management and the technology may be bridged, and so that assistance can be given in understanding change management and RISK MANAGEMENT. Despite the growing recognition of the need for more sophisticated planning for information processing, developing detailed strategies for computer configurations remains very much a "black art." The techniques are relatively limited, and data processing management is just starting to borrow techniques from other management disciplines.

Planning is more difficult and more essential when computers are being applied to operations of an enterprise for the first time. This is primarily because exact costs and data processing loads cannot be determined. The computer changes the company's entire mode of operating, so that extrapolation from past experences is useless. Making the planning process especially arduous is the large number of subjective questions that must be answered: How much money should be spent on data processing? . . . Is the manager competent? . . . Is the data processing organization properly matched to that of the corporation? It is not just the capacity of machines, but also the capacities of the people and procedures that must be planned.

Assessment. The process of planning begins with assessment of the current situation. Top management involvement should focus on six questions:

(1) The level of operating costs as compared to the quality and quantity of services offered. (Am I getting my money's worth?)

(2) The value of current EDP services in terms of strategic business priorities and operational control. (Are we doing the right things?)

(3) The degree to which the company is taking advantage of business opportunities made possible through new or improved EDP services. (Are we exploiting the resource?)

(4) The adequacy of current organizational structures and controls for developing and delivering EDP services. (Are we properly organized?)

(5) The technical and leadership quality of current senior and middle level EDP managers and the processes for management development. (Do we have the right people?)

(6) The level of risk exposure in EDP activities and the adequacy of current security controls. (Are we going to get any nasty surprises?)

To collect and analyze data for answers to the above questions, methodologies have been borrowed from strategic business planning and developed for the specific needs of data processing planning. Graphical models representing the state of EDP within the organization can be developed and presented to give top management a clear picture. No organization is static; each goes through its own stages of growth and maturity in EDP [2].

Planning. Out of the assessment process, top management will be able to focus on the parts of EDP operation that require their attention. Top management's involvement in the assessment will have ensured that it was not purely technical, and that attention was given to the alignment of the EDP direction with the strategic business thrust of the company. Thus, the assessment will highlight for managers those points which, being of a technical nature, require action by the data processing staff and monitoring attention by management—but it will also point out those places where top management's attention needs to be given to integration of the data processing resource into the direction of the business. The opportunity is then presented for a detailed examination of how short- and long-range plans for data processing will support the short- and long-range plans of the company.

Top Management Follow-Through. There are three major areas of EDP management about which top management should be constantly aware and which merit continued attention:

(1) *Definition of Needs.* If the EDP department is to service and support the company, it must understand the company's needs.

(2) *Project Management.* Industry is full of sad examples of projects which, because of lack of adequate control, ran late and over budget.

(3) *Communications and Perceptions.* Top management should constantly monitor the relations between the DP department and the line operations of the company. Three areas are potentially responsible for the three major areas of risk about which top management should be constantly aware:

- *Technical risk.* It will not work.
- *Functional risk.* It will not do what it is supposed to do.
- *Economic risk.* It will cost more than planned.

Definition of Needs. The user who is to be served by the computer system typically does not know what he (she) wants, and does not have the background to be able to specify what is meant in terms which the data processing professional will understand. For the DP professional this means the frustration of trying to pin down the user to think through what is required and to stop him from continually changing his mind. From the user's point of view, it is tiresome to have to explain to the data processing professional the language and the nature of the business. It is difficult to visualize what a system will be like by reading a detailed functional specification produced by the data processing department. Consequently, communications can be difficult and ineffective. The detailed functional specification is produced showing confusing screen layouts and report formats and the user is asked to "sign-off."

Even more difficult is the specification of the decision support system for managers. Increasingly, management is requesting of its data processing department on-line systems which allow them to access information about the company's operations in meaningful ways to support the decision-making process. Since, very often, the decision-making process is very unclear, it is usually impossible to specify what is needed without experiencing a prototype system first. However, for DP professionals to understand the needs of the manager for a decision-support system, they must understand very clearly the nature of the business decisions to be supported.

Top management's involvement in this process should be one of discouraging either side from trying to be "right." The DP professional does not understand the user's business and the user does not understand how to specify a system. It is important to discourage the setting up of mechanisms in which either side can be proved "wrong," for in such an environment little communication can take place.

One of the most important symptoms against which top management should be on guard in the specification of need is that of "pile-it-on." What starts out as a simple idea for a computer system seems inevitably to become complicated as all who are involved with defining the need feel compelled to "pile-on" every conceivable need that might be envisaged, however obscure. The simple system rapidly becomes extremely complicated, cost and time estimates escalate, and project risk is greatly increased. Even without direct understanding of the system being planned, top management can play a vital role in making sure that all those involved in explicating the need are focusing on the original purpose of the system and not overcomplicating it.

Project Management. Methodologies exist and are in place in most data processing installations for the life-cycle of a system development project. Top management should ensure that such methodology is in place to provide adequate control mechanisms, milestones, decision points, and reporting on the progress of any project. Nowhere is risk more manifest in the management of data processing than in the development of application software systems. (See INTEGRATED PROJECT MANAGEMENT.)

Besides being sure that adequate control mechanisms are in place, top management can play a vital role in assessing and managing this risk. Professor F. Warren McFarlan, of the Harvard Business School has defined three important measures of risk in any project: Size of the project, structuredness of the application, and familiarity with the technology to be applied [3]. Five rules of risk for top management to consider in reviewing application system development projects have also been suggested [4]:

(1) Understand the risk/return relationship; there is no sense in volunteering for risk unless the potential return is appropriate.

(2) Balance your "risk portfolio"; avoid too many high-risk activities at the same time, whatever the potential return of each.

(3) Understand the risk you are taking *before* you take it; get all the information you can to assess the major components of risk early.

(4) Plan the elimination or reduction of the major components of risk as early in the game as possible in order to minimize losses.

(5) Install control mechanisms to manage the risk as you proceed.

Finally, top management should be aware that it is a common experience for system development costs to be underestimated. This may reflect optimism, lack of detailed planning, or technical ignorance. More insidiously, it may reflect the perception of the recommender that if the true cost of the system were exposed to top management, the project would never be approved. Senior managers should put themselves through the exercise of asking themselves whether they would still approve the project if they knew in advance that it would cost two or three times the estimate submitted at the time the project is proposed, and should encourage recommenders to present "worse case" scenarios.

Communications and Perceptions. It is a common phenomenon in a company for line managers to feel that the data processing people are unresponsive or even inept. Such feelings are usually reciprocated by data processing staff who feel that users are fickle and lack understanding of the complexity of the computer systems they are demanding. When such perceptions exist within an organization and communications become guarded or even hostile, an intangible, but nevertheless powerful, dimension of risk of failure is introduced. Well-designed and well-controlled computer systems will fail in an environment of mistrust between the DP provider and the client user. Only top-management involvement can monitor and prevent such an environment typically festering at the middle-management level. It is common to find that the DP analysts and users work well together but their respective managers seek opportunities to score off each other. If the senior executive who observes this feels that he or she cannot get involved because a lack of technical background precludes an understanding of the problem, a situation may develop which will breed disaster.

Diagnostic techniques can be used to measure this risk. Methodologies are available to assist in the assessment of risk which do not deal with the technology of the project—but rather with the organizational behavior of those senior people taking the risk. Whether such methodologies are used or not, it is incumbent on top management in any company constantly to monitor the communications and perceptions which exist between the data processing staff and their user clients.

Trends for Top Management Attention. Two major trends are discernable in the 1980s about which senior executives should be aware:

(1) *Proliferation of Microcomputers.* The introduction in the late 1970s of the personal computer obtainable at retail stores at modest cost provides the opportunity for any department in a company to justify having its own computer to support small applications such as financial planning. Such proliferation raises the question of what the extent of control by the data processing organization should be. Historically, data processing power has been centralized; authority has resided in the senior data processing executive to decide about all acquisition of hardware, guidelines for software, and data-processing expenses. Now that independence is more within the reach of user budgets, top management must decide whether to try to continue that centralization of authority or whether to allow users to make their own decision about computer support. The best guideline for this decision is to see whether the user is truly willing to accept responsibility for the system he or she wishes to acquire.

(2) *Expansion from DP Management to Information Management.* As the information overload continues to escalate and tools for office automation become more available, top management should be encouraged to widen the scope of its thinking, so that planning and follow-through for data processing can include management of *all* the information resources of the company. This includes written and printed information in reference libraries and file drawers—not just the information which can be extracted from transaction-processing data.

JOHN M. THOMPSON, Vice President, Index Systems, Cambridge, Massachusetts

References Cited

[1] Thompson, John M., "The Computer Revolution: Insurance Investment Departments in the Second Wave," *Best's Review,* September 1980.

[2] Gibson, Cyrus F. and Nolan, Richard L., "Managing the Four Stages of EDP Growth," *Harvard Business Review,* January-February, 1974.

[3] McFarlan, Warren F., "Effective EDP Project Management," Boston, Mass., Harvard Business School, #9-173-207, 1973.

[4] Thompson, John, "Information Technology: Growing Risks at Thrifts," *American Banker,* January 31, 1980.

Cross References: *Computer Security/Automated Office Security; Computer Services Industry; Data Communications; Electronic Data Processing; Management Information Systems.*

COMPUTER SECURITY/AUTOMATED OFFICE SECURITY

THE COMPUTER SYSTEM

Management has a long record of failing to recognize one of its most serious risks—loss or disruption of its electronic data processing capability. Computer processed information has become the lifeblood of many organizations, an asset as valuable as cash, accounts receivable, and plant and equipment. Its loss, or the inability of management to use it, would severely restrict the firm's productivity.

Computer Security Institute surveys show that the degree of dependence varies considerably. Obviously, the more critical the operation, the more dangerous downtime becomes and the more important the need to assure **Computer Security.** For the typical manufacturing plant, the incremental cost of downtime runs between $1,000 and $10,000 per day; for a large bank or insurance company it is $100,000 per day. Extended downtime would significantly increase this rate, to say nothing of lost business and customer good will. Results also show that the primary reason for the lack of proper EDP safeguards can be traced to top management's lack of awareness of the need to protect these critical assets. With indifference at the top, it is understandable that adequate precautions have not been implemented.

Lack of Awareness. Although there is no simple answer to this lack of awareness, several causative factors are obvious. First, it is generally true that top management is uncomfortable in a computer environment. Most senior officers rose through the ranks before computers became familiar business tools. Most never had the opportunity to work with them in school or on the job. Even after installing their own facility, there is a reluctance to get close to the data-processing function; to do so would expose a lack of understanding. An almost blind dependency evolved preventing senior management from asking the right questions and effectively monitoring the EDP function. It has failed to scrutinize EDP with the same evaluative standards traditionally applied to manufacturing, finance, marketing, and other functions. To accentuate further the communications gap, EDP management has done a poor job in trying to "educate" upper management, thus promoting the mystique of the "black box." The net result is often a lack of awareness of the importance of the data processing function, not only in terms of its cost-effectiveness, but more importantly, in terms of its criticality to the firm's overall operational capability.

Establishing a Computer Security Program. Following is a useful, although somewhat simplified description of the major steps in establishing a computer security program:

Assign Responsibility. Choose an individual to serve as EDP systems security officer with full responsibility. A small or medium size company may not have someone to do this full time, but assignment of the role is essential.

Perform a Risk Analysis. Before corrective action can be taken, make a thorough analysis of your risk exposures:

- Identify vulnerabilities and threats. What effect would a disruption of EDP operations have on your company? What would be the effect of loss or destruction of vital records? What about the disclosure of trade secrets or other proprietary data? After all loss potentials are identified, evaluate the threats that could produce those losses . . . fire, power failure, flood, communication and air conditioning malfunctions, unethical employees, unintentional errors by loyal employees.
- Estimate probabilities of occurrence. What are the chances of these hazards occurring? For some threats, estimating can be relatively easy e.g., fire, tornado, power outage. Others can be more difficult e.g., fraud and sabotage.
- Quantify and prioritize loss potential. This final exercise attaches dollar values to the loss potentials previously identified, thus making it easier to evaluate, compare, and prioritize.

Conduct a Cost/Benefit Analysis. The risk analysis output ties directly into the evaluation of various risk reducing alternatives. How do you determine whether a proposed security system or procedure is cost-effective? By comparing the cost of the alternative to the potential loss it is expected to reduce or eliminate. Rational decisions can now be made as to the appropriateness of physical access control systems, back-up power, fire protection, and other remedial alternatives.

Determine Insurance Requirements. When protection systems and control procedures do not reduce the risk to an acceptable level, the residual risk is transferred to an insurance underwriter. With the results of the risk analysis, you will be in a position to make an intelligent judgment on the amount of insurance required.

Establish a Disaster Recovery Plan. Even after prudent measures have been taken, there exists the possibility of a breach in security. You need a contingency plan to establish a state of preparedness, and a capability to react immediately in a controlled and methodical way. Tasks should be clearly defined, rank-ordered in terms of priority, and they should be well documented and well practiced.

Monitor the Safeguards. Once you have accomplished all of the above tasks, a monitoring mechanism should be instituted. It should verify that control procedures are operable and the various automatic security systems are in working order and capable of performing when called upon.

The "Big Picture" in Focus. Keeping the "big picture" in focus requires a clear understanding of the role data processing plays in supporting day-to-day operations . . . and an understanding that its loss could be catastrophic. Prudent measures must be taken to assure smooth and uninterrupted operation of the EDP function. When management is dealing with hundreds of thousands or millions of dollars worth of assets, the patchwork, piecemeal approach to computer security is not good enough. An effective program does not happen by chance. It requires detailed, time-consuming planning, funding, and a commitment from all levels within the organization. However, if done conscientiously, and with the blessing of top management, it will result in the most efficient use of resources and minimal surprises.

Here is a list of useful security questions, to get a feel for how well a computer security program is doing:

• Is access to the computer room, tape-disk library, and forms storage areas denied to personnel other than those who have a business need to enter?

• Does at least one person function as librarian on each shift, and is that person responsible for maintaining up-to-date library records and enforcing data file access controls?

• Are external labels affixed to all tapes and disk packs, and random samples periodically taken to verify that the label properly identifies the contents?

• Are data processing employees prohibited from initiating original accounting transactions, adjustments, corrections?

• Has EDP management identified individual programmers or other technical personnel who are in a position to inflict significant harm to the organization or on whom the organization is excessively dependent?

• Is there a formal change procedure requiring dual signature authorizations to control systems applications software and modifications?

• Would management prosecute employees found guilty of a serious premeditated criminal act against the organization?

• Is an automatic fire extinguishing system installed in the computer room, forms storage room, tape-disk library?

• Is the internal audit function well versed in computer controls and security, and does it work closely with computer security personnel to improve the overall security program?

• For all major financial applications, is there an audit trail diagram and/or description clearly indicating how a transaction may be traced through the system?

• Does internal auditing and/or the security function receive standardized reports of cash and inventory differences, high-dollar transactions, large inventory usages, and other unusual, inconsistent or suspicious activity?

• Do customer files contain decoy names and addresses for the purpose of detecting unauthorized use of those files?

• Does backup planning include the identification of all critical data, programs, and documentation that would be necessary to support essential tasks during a disaster recovery period?

John C. O'Mara, Executive Director, Computer Security Institute, Northboro, Massachusetts

OFFICE OPERATIONS

Security Risks in the Automated Office. The 1980s will see increasing use of sophisticated office equipment—much of which will employ powerful computers, often imbedded in the office device itself. The security risks are similar to those traditionally encountered in the business data processing environment, that is, unauthorized exposure, modification, or destruction of information. In the past, the security community has been concerned with computer security in terms of the business data processing environment. However, the risks in the "automated office" have several important implications for the data security officer. These new dangers result from characteristics of the equipment and information to be found in the automated office. Thus:

(1) The use of digital electronics, the result of miniaturization, and favorable economics, brings computer power to the individual employee's work station. And once information is in electronic form, it becomes accessible in new ways. It becomes highly transferable among machines, is invisible, and through communication systems, offers clandestine access without physical entry.

(2) The originator of the information has in

mind some finite audience; that is, a certain group for whom the information is intended. Restricting information to the appropriate audience is fairly easy to achieve with paper-based information. But the rule that "all electronic systems require maintenance, whether hardware or software," means that unidentified people (to the information originator, at least) will have potential access, in the process of performing that maintenance.

(3) Information in the business data processing center is usually unintelligible raw data, requiring trained analysis and consolidation before use. Information in the office environment, by comparison, tends to be unprotected letters and memos. And, many of these contain ready-to-use business intelligence of a strategic nature. (Consider the computer-driven word processor and storage device in the office of a corporation president.)

Investment in office automation is soaring as businesses, large and small, install word-processing systems, secretarial/administrative mini-computer systems, and communicating typewriters. These devices have many of the attributes of the traditional business computer, in terms of hardware, software, magnetic storage media (tapes, disks, cartridges) on-site vendor maintenance, data transmission over public utility lines, and very significantly, susceptibility to unauthorized access via software faults or hardware modification.

Recommendations. Security managers should be taking prudent steps as follows, to minimize the risk of the above potential dangers.

- Establish and promulgate office procedures defining individual employee responsibility for protecting sensitive information created, received, or stored on automated office equipment.
- Encourage employees to be security conscious when ordering equipment/services—ask them to specify security features when appropriate, e.g., encryption capability for transmitting sensitive information.
- Develop and install effective controls for the identification and storage of magnetic tapes and disks in the office environment.
- Assure security for remote printers outputting sensitive information.
- Establish a record-keeping system which will allow review of accesses to sensitive information.

James Schweitzer, Xerox Corporation, Stamford, Connecticut

Information References

Associations:

Computer Security Institute.

Text:

Enger, Norman L. and Howerton, Paul W., "Computer Security: A Management Audit Approach," New York, American Management Association, 1980.

Hsiao, David K., "Computer Security," New York, Academy Press, 1979.

Cross References: *Electronic Data Processing; Office Automation; Security; Security: Protection of Trade Secrets and Proprietary Information; Word Processing.*

COMPUTER SERVICES INDUSTRY

The **Computer Services Industry** is comprised of companies that deal solely in, or divisions of corporations that market, information products and services to clients for profit. The industry is made up of more than 6,000 companies that sell professional services, software products, processing services, and integrated hardware and software systems. Computer services represents the "intelligent" side of the new information technology explosion by making the computer more accessible to a wide variety of users.

The computer services companies have built their businesses on the theory of supplying the user with a multiple of different products, services, and skilled personnel to deliver information to the client to solve business problems. The user can purchase as much or as little assistance as may be needed at reasonable cost. Service companies can provide total facilities management or processing services that give the user all the advantages of the current confluence of communication and computer technologies without having to own a computer, commit personnel to data processing activities, or change operations to accomodate the equipment. On the other hand, users that own their own computer installation can purchase a single software package; receive consultation and recommendations on a hardware, software or system purchases; have a custom-made software program developed; or find any of a number of limited services they may need to buttress their data processing operation.

The United States computer services industry produced $13.5 billion in products and services in 1979, a far cry from the $2 billion generated in 1970. Industry growth is expected to accelerate in the next five years, becoming a $36 billion enterprise by 1985.

The reason for this growth is simple—people have come to realize that the computer equipment is the vehicle, and the information produced provides the opportunity, to increase efficiency, effectiveness, and productivity in their operations. The computer services industry develops the tools and services to better meet its client's information needs. It is moving to meet changing societal and economic challenges—revising the way we operate our various enterprises, and improving the decision-making processes, by supplying more timely and worthwhile information.

SOFTWARE PRODUCTS

The **Software Products** firms of the computer services industry provide "off-the-shelf" pre-packaged software that can be purchased by a computer user in ready-to-operate form. Although the industry was born with early computer technology, it did not grow and prosper as a separate entity until 1969, when IBM "unbundled" its software from its computer hardware, offering each component individually for sale with separate prices. Since that time the industry has grown by leaps and bounds, and in 1979 United States software products revenues topped $1.2 billion. There are currently more than 1,000 software firms operating in the United States, marketing more than 6,000 products. Prepackaged software products sales are now increasing by more than 30% a year.

The prepackaged software products are programs that are developed, written, and tested by the software products company and marketed to computer users who own or lease a computer. Software products firms develop both applications packages that perform specific functions, and systems products which enable the computer to hold the data, and perform its basic functions. Applications products consist of cross-industry and single-industry products. Cross-industry products are general-purpose applications such as financial planning, payroll, bookkeeping, mailing lists, and inventory control that are used by many different types of enterprises. Single-industry products include specialized programs developed to service more narrow fields such as engineering, banking, real estate, mining, chemistry, petroleum, etc., and are designed to handle particular industry problems and needs.

There are three types of systems products that enable computer and computer/communications systems to perform their basic functions. *Systems operations* products function during applications program execution to make the computer operate more efficiently and effectively. Examples include data base management systems and operation systems.

Systems utilization products, used by operations personnel, improve the efficiency and effectiveness of the computer. Examples include performance measurement, job accounting, and computer operations scheduling.

Systems implementation products are used to assist programmers in designing, programming, and testing software products. Examples include computer programming languages, sorts, productivity aids, data dictionaries, program library management systems, and retrieval systems.

The reasons users purchase prepackaged programs are many and varied. Certainly, a major factor is cost savings. As *Business Week* pointed out in its September 1, 1980 cover story, "It (software products) is much cheaper to buy than custom software because the development cost is spread over a large number of users." Richard P. Daly, President of Comserv Corporation, a computer services firm that sells software packages, was quoted in the same article as saying, "Customers are buying something (software products) for $100,000 that would cost them several times that to develop themselves."

Another factor is time-savings. Prepackaged software can be put in operation much more quickly than waiting to develop the product. A further advantage is that prepackaged software suppliers handle the updates and improvements to the program and allow the user's programmers to develop new software specific to the user's needs, rather than spending time handling enhancements to existing programs.

With the continuing and increasing shortage of qualified data processing professionals, prepackaged software products are becoming more and more popular. Although these standard "off-the-shelf" products may sometimes cause a user to change business operations marginally to conform to the program, the trade-offs of this accommodation in time and money saved more than make up for the limited inconvenience. Further, many software products firms are now holding users' meetings to determine what the clients' needs are in terms of enhancements to existing programs and new product development. Users of a particular product line generally have similar needs, allowing customers to band together to achieve the next best thing to custom programming at a fraction of the cost.

In recent years, more and more effort has gone into developing software that will increase productivity, efficiency, and cost effectiveness of programmers by accelerating the development process for new software. Yet, software development is still in its infancy, and computer-aided software design has not reached a break-through comparable to the improvements in computer hardware design that have gone from the vacuum tube, to transistors and circuits, to computer silicon chips, each increasing efficiency, and lowering costs. But as the computer is becoming more available to more users, the software products firms will continue to grow in terms of revenues and importance to computer users.

PROFESSIONAL SERVICES

The **Professional Services** component of the computer services industry is made up of companies that provide clients with systems management; systems design and consultation; custom design and consultation; custom/contract programming; and education and training. The professional services contingent is comprised of more than 800 firms, employing 43,000 people, that generated more than $1.5 billion in revenues in 1979.

Systems management entails *business evaluation* to determine the needs of the client; purchasing the necessary equipment; working with the client's staff to get the systems operating properly; and training the client's employees to operate the system. The systems management employee works for and is paid by the service firm. However, the individual reports to work at the client's site and may be involved in working or training others to handle data entry, management of the system scheduling, maintenance, custom programming, program enhancement, computer operation, etc. A systems management individual or team may work with a client from a few days to a number of years depending on the needs of the customer.

Systems management can provide the client with the ultimate in computer service by providing as much or little assistance as the client needs. The client does not have to be as concerned about computer personnel employee turnover and is guaranteed a large pool of expertise from the professional service firm to deal with any particularly challenging problem that may arise. Further, the client knows that if the workload increases, the professional services firm has ready additional resources to commit to the project on short notice.

A second type of professional service is *systems design and consultation.* This service provides the potential user of computers or a company looking to change its computer operation with a professional or team of professionals to evaluate the client's business and computer needs. The professionals then recommend a services firm, hardware and software system, particular hardware configuration, or whatever management solutions are necessary to solve the information/information processing concerns of their client.

The third type of professional service available is *custom/contract programming.* The professional services company consults with the client on the specific problem to be solved, the availability of data, the function of the particular software program within the entire data processing system, and the potential impacts on business operations. The professional services firm then develops the program to the client's specifications, tests it, and installs it in the user's system.

A fourth example of professional service offered is *education and training,* where the professional service firm trains personnel of the client to improve their data processing skills and capabilities. With today's shortage of trained and qualified computer programming and technical personnel, the professional services firm can be crucial to the data processing manager, providing a trained and competent staff to handle any specific needs. In addition, the services firm represents a back-up resource for overburdened data processing staffs and a greater pool of expertise than most users can afford to have as full-time employees.

PROCESSING SERVICES

The **Processing Services** component of the computer services industry is made up of interactive remote computing services, remote batch processing, batch processing and total facilities management services. (See ELECTRONIC DATA PROCESSING.) In 1979, more than 2,000 companies offered processing services in the United

States, providing $6.7 billion in services to their clients. The actual industry growth from 1978 to 1979 was 20%.

Interactive remote processing services provide the client with a telecommunications "tie-in" to a computer on the processing company's site, so that the user may "call-up" a main-frame computer hundreds of miles away. Utilization of a keyboard, cathode ray tube (CRT) terminal and a high-speed printer, allows the data processing client to enter the data, make changes, request printouts, and perform the same operations available to a person with an "on-site" computer. The user can see the operation on his or her CRT (cathode-ray tube) terminal and receive a printout of any information necessary for permanent records.

This form of remote processing gives the user the feeling of simultaneous use of the computer while many other users are also on the line. However, the "simultaneity" is actually an illusion, since the process of feeding information into the computer by the user is at a much slower rate than that at which the computer is able to operate. Therefore, the computer can handle more than one operation concurrently, by handling parts of another operation during a given user's pauses. Thus it performs functions for many different users in a given time interval.

Remote processing networks now stretch internationally through use of telecommunications and satellites. Many companies offer the client the opportunity to "call-up" a computer halfway across the world with a local phone call through the use of an 800 toll-free number. These international teleprocessing networks are particularly useful for corporations doing business around the world. (See DATA COMMUNICATIONS.)

Remote batch processing is similar to remote interactive, except that the processing of the information takes place at a later time. This "after-the-fact" processing can be accomplished through a telecommunication link, and entering the information, data entry or changes desired. The remote batch company can then process the information in non-peak hours and have it delivered to the client either through a communications link to a terminal, or delivered by mail or by messenger. Frequently, processing service companies also market a mini- or micro-computer turnkey system to interact with the data processing network, or to act independently for smaller job functions.

Batch processing allows the user to have basic type processing done without having a computer terminal or any type of computer hardware at the user's site. The client company telephones in, or writes a letter to the batch company to make changes in its data base, or to request processed information. The batch company handles all data entry, processes the information, and delivers the finished information such as accounts payable and receivable, budgets, mailing lists, payroll checks, etc., by mail or messenger.

Processing service companies provide a wide variety of applications to their users and can frequently customize some part of their services. The processing companies can provide general business services, such as payroll, accounting, personnel management, or budget modeling systems. The general business services include the remote processing with software provided by the vendor in a complete package. Most business processing is repetitive and transaction-oriented, to supply the user with immediate and straightforward information.

Many processing companies also offer scientific and engineering services involving a variety of problems such as mathematical equations that might be utilized in architectural design, chemical engineering, or environmental protection. The scientific and engineering services provide the user with the tools to solve similar, but not identical problems.

Many processing services companies also provide *industry specialty-type programs* that are confined to a specific type of enterprise such as aeronautical applications for developing and testing design of aircraft; applications to cover insurance programs such as property and casualty insurance administration; electrical and electronic engineering applications such as drafting systems to develop diagrams for mechanical drawings; banking administration such as applications to handle loan administration or demand deposit accounts; etc.

A fourth type of processing service available is *utility services,* where the vendor provides access to a computer and communications network with the basic software, enabling a user company to develop its own solutions and processing system. The basic tools available would include terminal handling software, language compilers, data dictionaries, information retrieval software, and systems software to hold the data. The applications to be used with the system would be developed by the user and fed into the vendor's computer, along with the data necessary to make the system functional.

Many processing service companies also offer *facilities management.* This service is a "total management" approach to data processing. The computer services firm provides the user company with long-term total management of its entire data processing operation. The client does not have to be concerned about computer personnel problems, including turnover and training, because the employees of the computer services firm report to work at the user's site daily, and handle the entire operation. The client company has the ability to concentrate on the information it needs to improve its productivity and efficiency without worrying about the method of delivery. Further, the client knows that the computer services firm handling the management of its data processing facility has the back-up resources to handle peak workloads or particularly challenging problems.

There have been many exciting advances in the area of processing services as they have led the way toward convergence of technologies, enabling greater utilization of computer power. Computing, information, and communications are being brought together to provide users with delivered information systems. Here the user has access to information collected by the vendor in a data base system, enabling clients to access the information through a communications link utilizing computer power. Many corporations that are in the "information business" are acquiring companies involved in processing services and computer services, in order to disseminate their information to customers through computer technology and communications in the future. Examples include the acquisition of National CSS by Dun and Bradstreet; McGraw-Hill's acquisition of Data Resources; and On-Line Systems' purchase by United Telecommunications. All three of these acquisitions occurred in the late seventies and signal a change in the utilization of processing services.

AT&T is also, at this writing moving to enter the computer services marketplace in an attempt to merge its communications network with computer services. The Federal Communications Commission moved in 1980 toward allowing AT&T to participate in computer services, but it appears at this writing that its decision will not be finalized at least until 1982. It is entirely possible that AT&T will be required to offer computer services through a totally separate subsidiary, using entirely separate management, facilities, resources, and personnel.

Looking Ahead. Advances in communications technology, through the use of satellites and earth stations, are also improving the communications link for processing services, providing the end user with greater opportunity for utilization of the computer, particularly in areas where the telephone system is not reliable, or access is limited by government policies in foreign nations. Many companies currently use dedicated and/or leased telephone lines. The price of earth stations (large dishes capable of bouncing digital impulses off satellites to other earth stations) is dropping dramatically, making utilization of this technology more and more feasible.

We are also facing a convergence of television and computer technology through such enterprises as the Qube system in Columbus, Ohio, made popular on the television show, "Speak Up America," which makes possible answering back by viewers. The Canadians and English are also making use of this technology in terms of Viewdata, whereby they are establishing interactive communications through telephone lines, TV sets, and a converter to allow two-way communication and data processing. The ultimate utilization of this technology will enable persons in their homes to access data and information from a variety of sources, including magazines, newspapers, and other data bases. This will be the method for establishing the delivered information systems in the American home of the future.

Banks are currently making use of electronic funds transfer systems for their internal operations. In the near future, we may move closer to a cash-less, check-less society with all monetary transactions taking place through the use of remote processing computers to report our point of sale transactions.

Electronic mail services are also in their infancy. These systems allow an individual to type a letter into a personal terminal and have it delivered immediately to the receiving party terminal. The letter would be held until the receiving party got to his or her terminal, entered a code number, and received the "mail."

The use of remote computing power will increase in our society in the coming decade, revising our method of communications and utilization of computer technology, with an even greater impact on our daily lives.

SYSTEMS INTEGRATORS

Systems Integrators provide a total hardware and software integrated system to their clients. The systems integrator company purchases or manufacturers hardware and develops software to sell to clients as a complete "ready-to-go" system. Standard or customized systems may be purchased and may include hardware maintenance, system maintenance, and software "add-ons," or they may be a single integrated product sale. In essence, systems integrators supply their customers wishing to purchase and own a computer with "one-stop" shopping. The customer avoids the problems and time delays that can occur when purchasing hardware and software separately and having to bring the components together in a workable fashion.

Various types of support are available to clients purchasing a total system. Some companies offer remote processing "back-up" for their customers to use at peak-time periods or for handling particularly complex, seldom addressed problems. Other systems integrators offer a total facilities management system as part of their service, supplying not only the hardware and software, but the personnel to operate the entire system as well. Many systems suppliers also provide software updates and enhancements to their clients. In 1979, the computer services industry sold more than $4.1 billion dollars in integrated hardware and software systems and related support services. Currently 4,500 companies are marketing total systems packages, with 800 of those companies involved in other phases of the computer services industry as well.

The systems business continues to grow as the cost of computer hardware goes down, computing power increases, and there is a greater variety of software available to handle different problems.

SUMMARY

The computer services industry has come of age in the eighties.

Through access to hardware, software and processing services and products, management is receiving the opportunity to make sound judgments. As the industry grows and prospers by serving the needs and desires of the public, the service and product offerings will become more diversified and have an increasing impact on our daily lives.

Jerome L. Dreyer, Executive Vice President and Secretary, Association of Data Processing Service Organizations, Inc. (ADAPSO), Arlington, Virginia

Information References

Blankenship, A.S., "Computer Services Industry: 'Riding A Flood of Growth,' " *The Office Magazine,* January 1980.

"Bucking The System—The Computer Services Industry Expects Not Only to Survive in the Recession, But to Thrive in it," *Datamation,* July 1980.

"Computers 1980," *Dun's Review,* August 1980.

"Computerworld Extra! Dawn of the Software Decade Issue," Framingham Mass., CW Communications Inc., September 17, 1980.

"Don't Make—Buy! Support from Timesharing Services," *Computer Decisions,* July 1980.

"Missing Computer Software," *BusinessWeek,* September 1, 1980.

The Association of Data Processing Service Organizations' Annual Computer Services Industry Report 1980, Palo Alto, California: Input, Inc., July 1980.

Associations:

The Association of Data Processing Service Organizations (ADAPSO).

Cross References: *Data Communications; Electronic Data Processing.*

CONCILIATION. See Mediation.

CONSUMER BEHAVIOR RESEARCH

Research into consumer motivation, attitudes, and behavior is one of the most important yet controversial aspects of marketing research. It is important because consumer satisfaction is at the heart of the new marketing concept; controversial because there are conflicting theories about human behavior generally (and how to find out more about it).

Formal Definition. There is probably no formal definition of **Consumer Behavior Research,** but operationally it is the attempt to find out what satisfactions people want out of life, how they use products and services to achieve these satisfactions, how they perceive products and especially various brands, what kinds of product and promotional activities will lead to successful marketing, and how to assess the effects of such activities.

For example, why do people buy automobiles and why a particular brand or type? Beyond the obvious pleasure in having available individual transportation, there are factors of prestige and status, and individual expression of personality. Some makes of cars have been found to express high status and accomplishment. Some express a conservative and sound approach to life. Foreign cars especially may be bought in an attempt to express greater individuality. With the advent of the gasoline crunch, however, people in the U.S. may at last truly desire a small, sensible, economical auto. This is a clear change from the time when people professed on surveys a desire for such a car, but instead regularly bought large, expensive, prestigious gas guzzlers.

Approaches and Techniques. The same can be said for the majority of brands of products which are very similar in objective function (the various brands are largely interchangeable for all practical purposes), but which have been largely differentiated through the use of marketing symbolism. Cigarettes are an example. For many years their primary appeal was in terms of youth, prestige, masculinity, packaging, names, and the types of persons associated with brands through advertising. And then the obsessive tar and nicotine concern developed, wherein most brands strove to be the lowest, or lowest but with satisfactory taste. Other brands then relinquished the tar derby, and sought to position themselves anew as masculine, stylish, and even as symbols of women's liberation.

The techniques associated with consumer behavior research are often subsumed under the general field of *motivation research.* This approach attempts to determine, usually by indirection, how a product or brand is perceived and used in its normal cultural context. Indirect approaches are used because people are usually unable or unwilling to reveal their real reasons for their product selection and behavior.

One of the most common techniques is the depth interview. In contrast to fully structured questions, asking for direct and simple answers, the depth interview is a relatively loose conversational procedure wherein especially skilled interviewers get respondents to talk naturally about products or brands. During these conversations, respondents reveal in detail (often fifteen to twenty typed pages) their experience with products, feelings and associations, and the ways they use products to express their own particular mode of living.

Other techniques are borrowed even more directly from clinical psychology. These are usually called *projective techniques* and can be illustrated by word associations, sentence completions, and cartoons.

The word-association technique requires that people respond to a stimulus (perhaps a brand name) with the first word or words that come to mind. Sentence completion requires that respondents complete a sentence started by the interviewer, for example as follows: "It always seems that women who use Revlon———."

Cartoons can be of many varieties. For example, to find out how women react to cigar smoking, a cartoon can be drawn showing a young man and girl on a date, where the young man asks if he may smoke a cigar. Respondents shown this cartoon are asked to imagine what the young lady says and then what she thinks.

All of these techniques (and many more) are intended to catch people off guard and get them to project their true feelings which under more direct circumstances they would not reveal.

Typical consumer motivation studies usually start with a thorough job of introspecting about the probable meanings of products. Consulting behavioral scientists will usually be able to develop many hunches which can serve as working hypotheses to be investigated.

Then specially trained interviewers make unstructured individual depth interviews (no specific questions in a rigid sequence) with perhaps ten or fifteen people, trying to develop or refute the hunches. Frequently, group interviews are a productive part of this early diagnostic investigation. From ten to twenty appropriate respondents are gathered together for a series of loosely structured conversations about health products, banking practices, cooking or cleaning or whatever the topic. Usually the group interview is led by a skilled person, and the contents are recorded and analyzed subjectively. About ten to fifteen groups around the country are usually enough to reveal the principal problems and/or stereotypes about nearly any consumer activity or product.

After a series of such sets of interviews and analyses of the data (questions and areas of investigation change as insight develops), the important issues become clearer and the questions more pointed. Projective techniques are often used to get at additional hidden ideas.

Some of the terms commonly associated with consumer behavior research are *product, brand image, self image, subconscious,* and *social class.*

It is widely accepted that people have differing self images (feelings about themselves) which they attempt to express through the various products and brands which have their own images or personalities developed by marketing symbols—advertisements, names, colors, packages, etc. A drab woman may associate herself with sexually loaded cosmetic brands; an uncertain man with a very masculine cigarette.

Subconscious feelings and aspirations are assumed to cause people to feel and act in certain ways. A man may be only vaguely aware if at all that he buys a very expensive Scotch whiskey to bolster his self image. He will almost always rationalize the purchase entirely in terms of taste and quality.

Social class concepts and findings indicate the presence of five or six social classes in American society which differ widely in prestige, values, and behavior. These differences are reflected and expressed in products and brands purchased.

One of the curiosities which caused excitement in the late 1950s and early 1960s was *subliminal advertising.* This involved the possibility of broadcasting TV commercials which could not be seen but which could implant certain facts or ideas about products in the minds of viewers. Mechanically this would be achieved by flashing commercial messages very quickly on TV screens at a low contrast level continuously during programs so they could not be distinguished from the program pictures.

Early commercial subliminal experiments which seemed to show promise have not been substantiated—claimed effects on viewers were not achieved under more rigorous experimental conditions. Nevertheless, the possibility of such a technique caused both advertising excitement and moral indignation.

An even more novel approach suggests that the very structure and appearance of certain print advertising illustrations can cause effects of which the viewer is entirely unaware. For example, an amorphous sexual content is photographed or engraved into the glass and ice reflections in a liquor advertisement. Without being aware of it the viewer reacts to this unrecognized yet perceived image. Although casual inspection of representative illustrations does seem to allow such projections of figures, faces, heads, and animals, the degree and kind of deliberate causation and effectiveness has not been demonstrated satisfactorily.

Acceptance. Many differences of opinion exist about consumer motivation and behavior, and the research procedures appropriate to develop knowledge in this area. Behavioral scientists themselves do not agree on the degree to which behavior is motivated by conscious vs. subconscious drives. Advertising specialists do not agree about the relative effectiveness of logical vs. emotional appeals. Research specialists do not agree about the efficacy and validity of motivation research techniques used. Some contend that limited qualitative data (few interviews) are sufficient; others feel that much more extensive and representative sampling is necessary. Perhaps the most exciting controversy involves the degree to which industrial purchasing (as contrasted to consumer buying) involves emotional or irrational elements.

Despite these and many other controversial issues, consumer behavior research (in the sense described here as contrasted to completely conventional marketing research) is widely accepted at an operational level. Marketing and especially advertising executives almost overuse the concept of brand image. Market segmentation (dividing potential customers into categories) based on individual personality structure and social groupings is widespread. For example, a headache remedy for complaint hypochondriacs; or a small automobile for those who want to show inverse snobbery.

Research practitioners are also achieving a synthesis of sound behavioral science techniques with sound conventional marketing research procedures. Almost all marketing research survey questionnaires are now loaded with simplified and modified prospective questions designed to obtain more meaningful data on soundly projectable samples of respondents.

A further example of this synthesis of qualitative and quantitative has come to be known as lifestyle or psychographic research. Instead of a few depth or group interviews plus some projective tests, interpreted subjectively, hundreds of appropriately sampled interviews can be made, where respondents are asked merely to agree or disagree with an array of simple statements about their attitudes, values, and interests as measured by their activities, interests, and opinions. These data can of course be analyzed objectively using normal sampling statistics.

Toothpaste segments thus emerge as groups most concerned about taste and aesthetics; extra whitening and polishing; or decay prevention.

Liberated young women choose "liberated" type answers in sufficient numbers on the activities, interests, and opinions scales and soon find themselves part of a liberated woman-marketing segment perceiving a liberated cigarette advertisement in a liberated magazine, and perhaps at least giving the brand a trial.

Intelligent, health-conscious people are taught that orange juice is not just for breakfast anymore, but an integral part of an active lifestyle. If, however, frozen or chilled juice can't be found at all times, canned orange juice in small cans, in vending machines and convenience stores, once virtually written off, can find rebirth as an adequate substitute.

Inexpensive candy does hard battle against a health and weight conscious populace, while super expensive chocolates ($10.00 to $40.00) per pound explode in the marketplace. A segment lately known as the "me" generation, purchasers of the "best" of everything—the most expensive labels in autos, clothing, perfumes and liquors—obviously recognizes its chocolates.

On a verbal level there is less complete acceptance. Many businessmen (and researchers) make fun of motivation research, not recognizing the evolution which has taken place. This is an unfortunately stereotyped response which, while appropriate during the early days of exaggerated claims for motivation research, is no longer appropriate and will probably diminish.

The Future. The future for a science of consumer behavior is bright. The motivational movement has broadened into what is now termed the *interdisciplinary approach to marketing management.* Under this concept the insights of sociology, psychology, anthropology, semantics, communications, philosophy, experimental design, and operations research are combined with the more traditional disciplines. As this synthesis develops further, real progress will probably be made in understanding the intricate relationships that exist between peoples, products, and services in all the cultures of the world.

It is probable that recent business school graduates will have adequate perspective on the facts and theories and uses of consumer behavior research. These younger executives have been exposed to consumer behavior courses, and to most relevant concepts as they apply in communication, advertising, and management problems.

Consumer behavior courses became established in business schools during the late 1950s. A professor, then, had to refer to his own experience or to cases personally developed in neighboring business establishments.

Today, hundreds of articles and cases have been examined, culled, and assembled into a variety of consumer behavior books available not only to professors but to marketing practitioners. These books reflect a continuing interdisciplinary approach, e.g., models of consumer behavior, individual personality factors, social and cultural influences, perception, learning, research techniques, and case studies of applications to a variety of marketing problems or situations.

An examination of published research reports of behavioral scientists in business schools indicates a growing concern with exact problem definition, research methodology, and validity. Many of the earlier generalizations (for example, the precise relationship between personality of product and person) have not held up as well as expected under more rigorous investigation. Clinical and subjective research techniques seem somewhat less acceptable than standard survey and experimental methodology, reflecting a similar trend in most social science departments in most universities.

WILLIAM D. STEVENS, PH.D., Professor of Marketing, College of Business Administration, University of South Florida, Tampa, Florida.

Information References

Periodicals:

Harvard Business Review.
Journal of Advertising Research.
Journal of Marketing.
Journal of Marketing Research.
Public Opinion Quarterly.

Texts:

Engel, James F., Blackwell, Roger D., and Kollat, David T., "Consumer Behavior," New York, Hinsdale, Ill., Dryden Press, 1978.

Runyon, Kenneth E., "Consumer Behavior and the Practice of Marketing," Englewood Cliffs, N.J., C. Merrill, 1977.

Berkman, Harold W. and Gilson, Christopher C., "Consumer Behavior, Concepts and Strategies," Belmont, Calif, Dickenson, 1978.

Cross References: *Advertising: Measured Results; Advertising Research; Marketing Research; Marketing Research: Sources of Information.*

CONSUMER PROTECTION

With the tremendous growth of our industrial society during the twentieth century, a need arose for government to act as a protector of consumers against exploitation by producers. Initially, the primary concern was the health and safety of consumers. But as industrialization developed and merchandising and marketing practices grew more complex, the consumer needed to become better informed and protected.

Among the first pieces of important **Consumer Protection** legislation was the Food and Drug Act of 1906, to meet the need for regulation of drugs, poisonous preservatives and dyes, and food additives. Later Federal laws were passed dealing with antitrust practices, defective and unsafe products, pollution of air and water, and deceptive business practices. Consumer protection laws were also passed on state and local levels, creating public consumer protection agencies.

In recent years, business has strongly protested the degree of regulation, citing unnecessary interference with business practices and increased costs. It has effectively lobbied against such new regulatory proposals as the creation of a Federal agency for consumer advocacy.

Various commissions and committees have been created to deal with the problem of providing guidelines for adequate consumer protection. Also, public and private consumer agencies expanded their consumer education services in such important areas as health, housing, energy, food, legal services, and credit counseling. Modern consumer education focuses on the handling of consumer problems [1], information on the quality of products [2], and approaches for countering inflation [3].

It was Ralph Nader who projected consumer protection into the headlines in the early 1960s. He came into prominence when he attacked the automobile industry for failure to provide adequate safety standards [4]. Nader was in turn attacked by General Motors, and won a large award for damages. He utilized this money to develop several Washington-based consumer organizations which in turn encouraged the development of private state and local consumer groups.

CONSUMER ORGANIZATIONS

On the national scene in Washington, D. C. are the Consumer Federation of America, the National Consumers League, Congress Watch, the Environmental Defense Fund, Center for Science in the Public Interest, and a number of others. Their major activities are lobbying for consumer legislation, stengthening and protecting existing consumer laws, presenting and publicizing national consumer issues, and assisting state and local consumer groups.

State Organizations. On the state level, as in New York, there is the New York Public Interest Research Group, POWER, and the New York Consumer Assembly. In addition, there are numerous groups concerned with special issues such as pollution of air and water, utility rate increase hearings, cooperative consumer societies, and many small community groups.

FEDERAL REGULATORY AGENCIES

The three major regulatory agencies dealing with consumer problems are the Food and Drug Administration, Federal Trade Commission, and Consumer Safety Product Commission. The various Federal departments have consumer divisions, in accordance with Executive Order 12160 issued by President Carter in September 1979. The intent of this order was to ensure that consumers have an opportunity to be heard on proposals affecting them. Consumers can then participate in such programs and associated regulations.

As an illustration, the Transportation Department was involved in public hearings in rulemaking involving pipeline safety and transportation of hazardous materials. Procedures were established for the direct interaction and liaison with national, state, and local consumer organizations to respond to their concerns on transportation issues. The Department also assigned a senior affairs specialist to be a member of the Departmental Consumer Policy Coordinating Council (CPCC) to maintain liaison with other administrations. The Department required that a Notice of Proposed Rulemaking (NPRM) be published in the *Federal Register* and that public comments be solicited. After hearings are held, the proposal is promulgated with appropriate revisions, or rescinded.

Food and Drug Administration. The FDA [5] is responsible for enforcement of four major consumer laws.

(1) *Food Drug and Cosmetic Act.* The Act requires that food be safe and wholesome, that drugs and medical devices be safe and effective,

that cosmetics be safe, and that all these products be properly labeled.

(2) *Fair Packaging and Labeling Act.* This Act requires that labeling be honest and informative so that consumers will know what they are buying and how to use the product properly. (Limited to food, drugs, cosmetics, and medical devices.)

(3) *Radiation Control for Health and Safety Act.* This Act protects consumers from unnecessary exposure to radiation from electronic products such as x-ray machines, microwave ovens, and color television sets.

(4) *Public Health Service Act.* This Act provides the FDA with authority over vaccines, serums, and other biological products.

Federal Trade Commission. *Division of Food and Drug Advertising* is concerned with deceptive and false advertising.

Division of Product Reliability deals with warranties (Moss-Magnuson Act of 1975) on mobile homes and used cars. It polices warranties to ensure that the information is clear and complete and that warranties are not used deceptively.

Division of Professional Services covers occupation deregulation, involving trade and professional association rules that have the effect of impeding the operation of the marketplace, such as restraints of advertising.

The FTC was instrumental in permitting the advertising of drug prices and eyeglasses. It was unsuccessful in trying to compel the funeral industry to provide public disclosure of costs of services. The Insurance Program staff is studying several aspects of life insurance to see whether consumers are getting the most coverage and best return for their investments. The Division is seeking a law to permit pharmacists to select lower-cost bioequivalent drug products instead of the generally more expensive brand-name drugs often prescribed by physicians.

Division of Marketing Abuses, through its Land Sale Program, polices abuses in the sale of subdivision lots to consumers. The Housing program investigates the substantial defects in new houses and builders' failures to remedy those defects.

The Point of Sale Practices Program polices deceptive and unfair marketing techniques used by retailers. This includes the "three-day cooling off rule" which gives consumers the right to cancel most contracts from door-to-door salespersons.

The Franchising and Business Opportunities Program enforces the franchise rule. It provides buyers with pre-sale disclosure of information about the franchise, the franchise business, and the terms of the franchise relationship.

The Advertising Substantiation and Monitoring Program polices national advertisements to make sure their claims are substantiated.

The Cigarette Advertising and Labeling Program reports to Congress on the effects of cigarette labeling and promotion. It operates a tobacco testing laboratory to measure tar and nicotine content.

Division of Credit Practices, through its Fair Credit Reporting Program enforces the Fair Credit Reporting Act which ensures consumers the right to see, challenge, and correct information distributed about them to creditors, insurance companies, and employers.

The Credit Billing Program polices unfair and deceptive credit billing practices under the Fair Credit and Billing Act.

The Truth and Lending Program enforces the Truth-in-Lending Act which requires creditors to give consumers written disclosures of credit information before they enter into a credit transaction. It enables consumers to compare the costs and terms of credit available from different sources.

The Division's Holder in Due Course rule protects consumers by preserving their legal rights when they purchase goods and services on credit.

The Division also enforces the Fair Debt Collection Practice Act which prohibits deception, invasion of privacy, and overcharging.

Consumer Product Safety Commission. The CPSC was established by Congress in 1973. Its regulations are concerned with dumping of toxic wastes, toxic products in factories which affect the health of workers (asbestos fibers causing lung disease), flame-retardant night clothes for children, dangerous toys, child-resistant closures on drug containers, and aerosol propellants made of vinyl chlorides.

The CPSC works with the Organization for Economic Cooperation and Development (OECD) to improve international protection of consumers from imported and exported products.

REGULATION VERSUS DEREGULATION

While the consumer movement strongly favors the supporting and strengthening of these regulatory agencies, the private sector is battling for reducing regulatory powers. The fight is centered in Congress and has important implications for the future of the economy. Congress has now clearly indicated that it wants some veto power over new regulatory proposals. A recent example was the proposal by the FDA to ban saccharin as a sweetener because laboratory tests found it carcinogenic. Not only did the saccharin industry protest, but so also did many consumers who use saccharin. Congress placed a moratorium on such a ban. When the FDA proposed a ban on nitrites as an additive for cured meats, another moratorium was declared.

The major question is whether or not regulation is good for consumers and the economy. The universal answer by the consumer movement is that regulation which affects the health and safety of consumers is essential. On the other hand, regulation which results in monopoly of a service or product is harmful if it results in higher costs to the consumer and industry. An example was the deregulation of air-flight prices by the Civil Aeronautics Board. Also, the recent deregulation of the trucking industry permits greater competition and reduction in the cost of trucking.

Industry's demand for less regulation is illustrated by the automobile industry's demand for more time to meet emission control and safety standards. The pharmaceutical industry wants greater freedom to market its products. The oil industry's fight for decontrol of oil and gasoline prices resulted in legislation providing for a phaseout and gradual decontrol of prices by 1985.

Environmental Standards. Environmental standards, a major regulatory issue, involves establishing adequate standards for prevention of the pollution of air and water and the disposal of toxic industrial waste products. Chemical wastes and chemical dumps have become increasingly environmental and industrial problems. According to a Presidential panel, toxic substances are causing a greater number of illnesses and deaths. The Environmental Protection Agency stated in June, 1980, that conditions at many of the chemical dumps posed a serious threat to the health of about 600,000 people. Special consumer groups have organized to fight this growng menace. In May 1980, the EPA issued regulations establishing standards for dump operations. Under the rules, those not meeting the standards promulgated by the Resource Conservational Recovery Act of 1976 would be closed. (See Environmental Controls.)

The building of nuclear power plants is being severely restricted in numerous areas because of potential health hazards. The Nuclear Power Regulatory Commission is revising standards and ordering stricter supervision of existing power plants.

PRIVATE RIGHT OF ACTION

Consumer groups are increasingly seeking redress by instituting court action. Only a few years have passed since class action suits by consumers became legalized in many states. Previously, if a consumer wished to sue a corporation for damages, he or she would have to institute a private lawsuit. Such action was both expensive and time consuming. The passage of state legislation permitting class action suits made it possible for consumers to participate in a single court action. It could be an action seeking reimbursement for the cost of a defective product or for overpricing of a product or a service.

Small Claims Courts. Individual lawsuits have become easier to initiate by the creation of the State Small Claims Courts. In New York State, a consumer can initiate action in a Small Claims Court at very little cost. No lawyer is necessary but claims cannot exceed $1,000. However, while this court helps aggrieved consumers, it frequently lacks efficient enforcement powers to help consumers collect on judgments it has issued. Consumer groups are lobbying for legislation to increase the jurisdiction and enforcement powers of the Court.

Deceptive Business Practices. Until July 1980, consumers in New York State were not permitted to institute court action for cases involving deceptive business practices and false advertising. Such action was reserved for the Attorney General's Office, which before proceeding, would determine the merits of the case. In New York State, consumer groups lobbied over ten years for such private right of action legislation until its passage in 1980. The ceiling on such action is limited to $1,000.

Warranty Protection. Warranty of manufactured products remains a battleground for consumer protection. While the Federal Moss-Magnuson Warranty Act was an important step forward in warranty protection, it left many loopholes. Consumers find that most warranties are limited. When they purchase an automobile that is not functioning properly, they generally find that only warranted parts can be replaced, and only for a limited time. Long delays are common in having defective merchandise repaired. Since the retailer does not provide an express warranty, the product is frequently returned to the factory for repair or to a designated repair shop. As a result, consumers are seeking legislation that provides for retailer responsibility when the manufacturer provides a warranty.

PRODUCT LIABILITY

An area of growing debate is on product liability. Product liability refers to the manner in which consumers are to be compensated for injuries sustained from unsafe and defective products. Business interests have sought to avoid product liability laws on the basis that the cost factor has become prohibitive. They claim that multi-million dollar jury verdicts are a common occurrence. In response to the demands of business for reform, Congress conducted an investigation in 1975. It established an Interagency Task Force on Product Liability. After an eighteen month study, it issued an "Option Paper" outlining possible Government responses to the problem.

The final report of the Congressional Task Force issued November 30, 1977, cast doubt on certain industry claims. The most significant finding was that the product liability "crisis" was highly exaggerated. It was determined that in most industries, average cost of product liability insurance is less than 1% of sales. Even in the high-risk product industries, such as pharmaceuticals, automotive parts, and medical devices, the average cost of product liability coverage barely exceeded 1% in 1976. The report concluded that the burden of proof would appear to fall on the insurers to justify increases of 200% or 300% in premiums where they did not have data based on claims experience.

The Task Force further stated that an additional cause in the rise of product liability suits is "consumerism." Consumers are increasingly aware of their rights and are less likely to allow product-related injuries to go uncompensated.

Another area of concern is the marketing of products which do not cause any injury until many years after their purchase or use. There are drugs and chemicals whose toxic impact only becomes visible after an extended period of years. The response to the problem by the U. S. Department of Commerce has been the adoption of a program designed to abate rising product liability premiums. The program provided for the drafting of a model uniform product liability law for use by state legislatures. In addition, an amendment to the Internal Revenue Code allows businesses to carry back losses attributable to product liability incurred after September 30, 1979 and apply them against income for ten years, as opposed to the usual three years for most business losses.

There has also been some activity on the state level, leading to amended or new product liability state laws. As long as unsafe products are being marketed and consumer injuries continue to occur, meaningful product liability laws remain justified.

ALFRED SMOKE, Executive Director, New York Consumer Assembly, Inc., New York, New York

References Cited

[1] "Consumer's Resource Handbook," The White House Office of the Special Assistant for Consumer Affairs.
[2] *Consumers Reports,* Mt. Vernon, N.Y., Consumers Union of the United States, Inc.
[3] "People Power, What Communities are Doing to Counter Inflation," Washington, U.S. Office of Consumer Affairs.
[4] Nader, Ralph, "Unsafe at Any Speed," New York, Pocket Books, 1965 (extended ed. New York, Grossman, 1972).
[5] "A Consumer Guide to FDA," Washington, Food and Drug Administration.

Cross References: *Business-Government Relations; Environmental Controls.*

CONTROL THEORY: Application to Management

The need to control physical processes of operations has existed since the beginning of manufacturing. Such control takes the form of encouraging desirable action and inhibiting undesirable action, with the objective of maintaining operations within certain predetermined ranges. Central to this is the early recognition of loss of equilibrium or out-of-range performance and application of suitable restorative force. This **Control Theory** can profitably be applied to management.

Control of physical processes is often achieved by the application of ingenious mechanisms, exemplified by the household thermostat for maintaining an approximately constant level of temperature. The thermostat senses its surrounding atmosphere continually. If the temperature falls below the lower set limit, it "decides" to act and makes connection to a heating unit to supply additional heat. When the thermostat senses that the temperature has risen to the proper level, it switches off the heating unit. The "decision-making" is entirely physical and mechanical, and is built into the thermostat.

Transferring the above control principle to the area of management involves the following steps:

(1) Establish a direction, plan, or range, or level of operation.

(2) Sense operations to detect the amount and direction of departure from desideratum.

(3) Decide if change is significant.

(4) If not significant, decide to continue sensing.

(5) If change is significant, decide on direction and amount of correction.

(6) Apply correction.

(7) Continue sensing of status.

(8) Repeat as required.

The exercise of control is thus a *loop-type process,* repeating its steps as needed, with more or less continuous sensing of status. The difference, in management application, is that at least in some cases human intervention is required in the decision-making process. To some extent minor matters can be controlled by reference to pre-established policy, to be applied by subordinates and dealt with by upper management only when exceptions occur. Rarely can completely automatic controls be built into a management system, although theoretical and experimental work is going on in this regard.

When operating properly, *negative feedback* control, as this process is called, tends to damp out oscillations and variations from the desired path. Its ability to do so, however, depends upon the speed of operation of the sensing-decision-correction loop relative to the amount and speed of variation from the planned course. If the control loop operates more slowly than the variation rate, corrective action may become variation-reinforcing rather than variation-dampening, which can become disastrous. Such a result is often seen where decision making is in the hands of slow-moving deliberative bodies where a consensus of large numbers is required before action is taken.

Positive feedback is often applied under certain circumstances. In this case, the action is accelerative. Sensing of desired action results in added encouragement to continue and to increase that action. Such control is often effectively applied in behavior modification, to encourage and continue to increase desirable behavior. Examples are praise, financial incentives, and the like. However, this type of control is unidirectional, and it should be recognized that there can be a hazard of accelerating to the point of being counterproductive, or of having the cost of the incentives outrun the gains achieved. (See BEHAVIOR MODELING IN TRAINING and GOAL SETTING.)

The two types can be combined under certain conditions: applying positive feedback to encourage change when the need for it develops, then using continued sensing and the application of negative feedback to keep the process from going out of control.

Management by Exception. Managerial time is a precious and limited resource. The doctrine of "management by exception" says simply that this resource should be devoted to matters of major concern outside the routine of day-to-day operation, and not devoured by trivialities, no matter how annoying they may be.

Management's action under this doctrine should be to separate the important from the trivial, and to develop priorities for allocation of time. An important aid in this respect is to make use of the manufacturing idea of *tolerances.* In manufacturing, nothing is ever made exactly to the specified dimensions. There is always a certain amount of variation from any specified dimension which can be accepted or tolerated without harm to the function of the part or product. This principle can be transferred to the domain of management, in that there exists a level of problem or abnormality of operation that can be permitted to exist—tolerated—without real harm to the business. In many cases suitable tolerances can be established by appropriate policies, or by statistical means.

ROBERT N. HOGSETT, President, Hogsett Associates, Inc., Binghamton, New York

Cross References: *Break-Even Analysis; Budgeting; Standard Costing.*

CONTROLLERSHIP

Controllership is the function of business management which combines the responsibility for accounting, reporting, budgeting, measurement, operating controls, auditing, taxes and related areas. It is based on the word "control"—not in the direct sense of the control exercised by stockholders, corporate presidents, or operating executives, but in the indirect or "functional" sense that it provides and coordinates the mechanism for controlling action and making decisions with profit objectives in mind. Budgetary control is perhaps the purest example of the controllership principle in ordinary practice, but the latter includes all forms of measurement and appraisal. The function is typically performed by an executive with the title of Controller, but is frequently assigned, totally or in part, to a financial vice president or a treasurer, or divided in various ways between executives with other titles. It is closely allied to the planning function.

Formal Definition. An authoritative definition has been published for many years by the Financial Executives Institute (formerly Controllers Institute of America). The Institute's concept of the function of controllership is:

(1) *Planning for Control.* To establish, coordinate, and administer, as an integral part of management, an adequate plan for the control of operations. Such a plan would provide, to the extent required in the business, profit planning, programs for capital investing and for financing, sales forecasts, expense budgets, and cost standards, together with the necessary procedures to effectuate the plan.

(2) *Reporting and Interpreting.* To compare performance with operating plans and standards, and to report and interpret the results of operations to all levels of management and to the owners of the business. This function includes the formulation of accounting policy, the coordination of systems and procedures, the preparation of operating data, and of special reports as required.

(3) *Evaluating and Consulting.* To consult with all segments of management responsible for policy or action concerning any phase of the operation of the business as it relates to the attainment of objectives and the effectiveness of policies, organization structure, and procedures.

(4) *Tax Administration.* To establish and administer tax policies and procedures.

(5) *Government Reporting.* To supervise or coordinate the preparation of reports to government agencies.

(6) *Protection of Assets.* To assure protection for the assets of the business through internal control, internal auditing, and assuring proper insurance coverage.

(7) *Economic Appraisal.* To appraise continuously the economic and social forces and government influences, and to interpret their effect upon the business.

History. Controllership grew from the increased demands on accountants in the decade of the twenties. The accounting science, which had received strong impetus from the first U.S. income tax law (1913), was challenged during the depression of 1930–33 to contribute directly to profit planning. Controllers Institute of America was founded in 1931, to offer controllers of medium and large size companies a means for exchanging ideas and developing the science of controllership in business management. This group was primarily responsible for establishing the title of Controller as a recognized corporate office. In 1962, recognizing the integration with capital procuring, investment, and other money management functions which had progressively been identifying the interests of controllers, treasurers, and financial vice presidents, the organization changed its name to Financial Executives Institute. By 1980 it had grown to a membership of 11,000, with 79 chapters throughout the United States, Puerto Rico, and Canada.

Controllership principles, organizationally centered in a single executive, have come to be widely used (though with considerable variations in practice) in the United States and Canada, and are now beginning to command attention in other countries.

Related Techniques. Controllership is most closely related to accounting—particularly cost accounting—and to budgeting, subjects which have their own individual development, literature, and professional organizations. At management level, these, together with auditing and taxes, are commonly treated as segments of the controllership responsibility. The techniques of money management (embracing capital procurement, investment and so on) are also closely allied, though properly the concern of TREASURERSHIP. Controllers are often involved in the techniques of ELECTRONIC DATA PROCESSING, and more recently in the development of MANAGEMENT INFORMATION SYSTEMS (MIS) to provide selected decision-oriented information needed by management to plan, control, and evaluate the activities of the corporation. They are also involved in the SYSTEMS AND PROCEDURES function, in the sense of designing, installing, and coordinating paperwork flow and the like, although this group of functions may be assigned elsewhere so long as the needs of control are served.

A specialized management function is planning, which is vital to controllership since there can be no control without planning. However, most informed opinion holds that controllers should not be responsible for planning, although its modus operandi is their major concern. The term "management planning and control" emphasizes the involvement of controllership with planning.

Spelling. The terms "controller" and "comptroller" are identical in meaning. The former is the more modern form and is gradually becoming universal, although the by-laws of many large corporations still provide the older title. The word "comptroller" is associated by lexicographers with the French word *compte,* (account) or with *compt,* the keeper of a counterroll or check list.

FINANCIAL EXECUTIVES INSTITUTE, New York, New York

Information References

Association:

Financial Executives Institute (formerly Controllers Institute of America).

Periodicals:

Financial Executive (a monthly magazine published by FEI); and various research studies published by Financial Executives Research Foundation, an arm of FEI.

Cross References: *Accounting; Budgeting; Cost Accounting; Standard Costing; Treasurership.*

COPYRIGHT

Copyrights are limited monopolies which are granted under the U.S. Constitution and the Copyright Act, and similar laws in other countries, to persons who create original works of authorship, such as literary, musical, dramatic, pictorial, graphic, and audiovisual works. The owners of copyrights generally have the exclusive right for a certain period of time to control the reproduction, distribution, and sale of the copyrighted works—and in some situations may also control their use.

The first U.S. Copyright law was enacted on May 31, 1790 [1], and laid the framework of protection which has been followed ever since. The most recent Federal copyright law, the Copyright Revision Act of 1976 [2], generally became effective on January 1, 1978. The new law is considered to have strengthened the rights of authors and copyright owners, and reflects technological developments since the last comprehensive copyright law was adopted in 1909.

What Is Protectible. Virtually any original work of authorship is copyrightable, if it has been fixed in some stable or permanent form which can be communicated to another person—such as on paper, records, tapes, photo negatives or metal. Examples in the *general business area* include catalogs, directories, advertisements, sales promotional materials, instructions, plans, drawings, charts, diagrams, models, photographs and slides, product labels, prints, commercial and industrial films, videotapes, computer data bases and programs, and many others. Trademarks, trade names, titles, and slogans are not copyrightable; nor are ideas, concepts, methods of operation or inventions. (See TRADEMARKS and PATENTS.)

Why Copyright Is Important to All Business. The copyright laws are of obvious value to publishers, motion picture and recording companies, and other businesses which, it may be said, are in the business of creating or selling copyrighted works. However, it is less often recognized that the copyright laws are a valuable marketing tool for businesses of all kinds—both for the protection of copyrightable works which are made and used in the ordinary course of business and for preventing unfair competition or infringement of a company's proprietary rights. In a competitive economy, copyright can be used to help strengthen a company's intangible assets and to prevent their unfair use. While most competitors are honorable and will compete fairly, failure to obtain copyright protection for copyrightable works could allow a competitor or any other person to use a company's published works lawfully and without economic obligation, even though they may have been prepared at great cost.

How to Obtain a Copyright. Under the U.S. Copyright Act of 1976, a copyright automatically exists from the moment a copyrightable work is created. The copyright initially is owned by the author of the work. In the case of a "work made for hire," such as a work prepared by an employee within the scope of employment, the employer is considered to be the author, unless there is a written agreement to the contrary.

When a copyrightable work is published, the law provides that a copyright notice shall be placed on all copies at some place on the work where it can be perceived visually. The notice has three elements:

(1) ©, the word "Copyright" or "Copr." (for sound recordings, use ℗ instead); and

(2) The year of first publication (which may be omitted from certain pictorial, graphic, or sculptural works reproduced on or in certain items, such as stationery, jewelry, toys, or useful articles); and

(3) The name of the copyright owner (or a recognizable abbreviation or generally known alternative designation).

An example of proper notice is: Copyright 1981 Joseph R. Smith.

Omission of a copyright notice from a published work does not automatically forfeit a copyright if: not many copies have been distributed publicly; or if registration is obtained within five years after publication and the notice is added to all future copies; or if the omission was contrary to the copyright owner's written requirement.

An application for registration may be filed anytime, but to avoid the loss of certain remedies in infringement cases, ordinarily it is best to file within three months after publication. Application forms, instructions, and additional information may be obtained from the U.S. Copyright Office, Washington, D.C. The filing fee as of 1981 is $10.00. Registration is neither costly nor complicated, but it is important to follow the requirements precisely. Faithful use of the notice and registration procedures ensures that a company receives the maximum protections of the law and creates a public record of the company's property rights claims.

Extent of Rights. Works which have been created after December 31, 1977, receive copyright protection for the life of the author and an additional 50 years. Works made for hire are protected for 75 years after publication, or for 100 years after creation, whichever is less. Renewal requirements have been eliminated under the new law. After a copyright has terminated, the work enters the "public domain" and can be used by anyone.

The owner of a copyright is given the exclusive rights under U.S. law to (and to license or authorize others to): reproduce the work; prepare derivatives, such as translations, abridgments, condensations, and editorial revisions; distribute copies to the public by sale, some other form of transfer, rental, lease or lending; and in many situations, to perform and display the work publicly. Certain "fair uses" by nonowners are allowed under the law, such as for nonprofit, educational teaching or research.

Buying and Selling Copyrights. Copyrights may be bought and sold like other personal property. The exclusive rights, or any portion of them, can be transferred by a written document signed by the owner or authorized agent, which should be recorded in the Copyright Office.

Enforcement of Copyrights. Usually proper use of the copyright notice and subsequent registration are sufficient safeguards to prevent misuse of a company's copyright property interests by others. However, there may be instances of innocent or even intentional misuse by others of copyrighted works. In situations where a simple demand is not sufficient to stop an infringement (which simply is a violation of any of the copyright owner's exclusive rights), the Copyright Act provides extensive remedies for the owner. With limited exceptions, however, the copyright claim must be properly registered before an infringement complaint may be filed. The U.S. district courts have exclusive original jurisdiction over copyright cases, which generally must be filed within three years after the infringement began.

Copyright litigation can be expensive and time-consuming, although in its basic simplicity, there are only two essential questions to be answered: Is there a valid copyright in the owner (plaintiff)? Has a valid copyright been infringed by the accused (defendant)? In answering the first question, a court will look to such factors as: whether or not the work was copyrightable; whether or not it was original; whether or not the notice and registration requirements were complied with; and whether or not other legal formalities have been complied with, such as for any assignments or other transfers of ownership. To answer the second question, the court usually tries to determine if the defendant had access to the copyrighted work and if there is a substantial similarity between that work and the defendant's work. No infringement can be found where the copyright is invalid or there has been no copying; or generally where the defendant can prove statutory fair use or abandonment of the copyright; or in certain other limited situations. "Innocent intent" will not avoid liability, however.

Relief. The Copyright Act provides a strong arsenal of remedies for infringement. In addition to injunctions against further infringements, the court may order: the impoundment and destruction of infringing copies; a monetary award of either the copyright owner's actual damages plus the infringer's profits, or statutory damages of up to $10,000 for each single infringement of a single work, which in a case of willful infringement can be increased to $50,000; and full costs of the litigation, including reasonable attorney's fees. In certain circumstances, awards of statutory damages and attorney's fees are not allowed. There are criminal penalties for willful infringement of a copyright for commercial advantage or private gain.

Although routine copyright notice and registration procedures usually do not require an attorney, it is important to ensure that the legal requirements are complied with. A qualified attorney should be consulted in infringement matters.

International Protection. There is no international copyright registration procedure. Copyright protection for U.S. companies in foreign countries depends upon the laws in those countries and any applicable international treaties. The United States as of 1981 has international copyright understandings with more than 75 countries under the Universal Copyright Convention or other treaties. If international use of copyrightable material is anticipated, it is advisable to determine the existence of and requirements for copyright protection in each country, if possible, prior to publication [3].

Lawrence S. Wick, Attorney, Leydig, Voit, Osann, Mayer & Holt, Ltd., Chicago, Illinois

Information References

Register of Copyrights, Library of Congress, Washington (for publications, application forms, and instructions; also for list, "Publications of the Copyright Office").

Currently available literature on copyright for businessmen generally is out-of-date because of the revision of the copyright laws.

References Cited

[1] First Congress, Second Session, Chapter 15, "An Act for the Encouragement of Learning", enacted pursuant to Article I, Section 8 of the U.S. Constitution.

[2] Public Law 94–553 (94th Congress), 90 Stat. 2541, 17 United States Code, Sections 101–810, et al.

[3] As of July 31, 1979, the United States did not have copyright relations with such countries as Afghanistan, Albania, Bahrain, Ethiopia, Iran, Iraq, Jamaica, Oman, Saudi Arabia, Tonga, Turkey, and Yemen.

Cross Reference: *Trademarks.*

CORPORATE CAPITALIZATION

At the time of incorporation, the total amount at which the enterprise is to be **capitalized** is determined, based on the nature and size of the proposed operations. In addition to fixed capital requirements for buildings, equipment, etc., funds will be required for promotion and development work, and for working capital sufficient to maintain operations to the point where sales income and earnings will be sufficient to carry the project. Capitalization may take into account the value of patents, secret processes, trade-marks, and similar intangibles, but in a new enterprise there may be no basis for assigning more than nominal values to these items.

State and Federal legal requirements must be taken into consideration, since they affect franchise fees, taxation, security sales, and similar items. Initial capitalization may include plans for future expansion and future marketing of corporate securities.

Classification of Stock. Authorized capital stock of a company may be issued in a single classification, *common stock,* or it may include various types of *preferred stock.*

Common Stock carries no special rights or privileges, and bears the full risk of the enterprise. Common-stock holders are the legal owners of the enterprise, and usually exercise control over the business through the voting power of their stock.

Preferred Stock. This class of stock may be preferred as to dividends and assets; it may be convertible into common stock on special terms; a sinking fund may be set up to guarantee safety of the investment; and it may have other rights. However, it may have limited or no voting power, since preferred stockholders do not partake of the same risk as common stockholders.

The division between common and preferred stock is determined by such considerations as who is to control the enterprise, the feasibility of burdening earnings with obligations to pay fixed dividends, tax advantages, ease of sale of securities, and the like. In terms of other gradations of rights and privileges, stocks may be further classified as A and B common, or first preferred, second preferred, and the like.

Par- and No-par-value Stock. Common and preferred stock may have a *par value* ($10, $100, etc.) stated in the stock certificate to fix the unit of investment. However, the *real* value of the share is determined by the net assets and earning power of the company, and the *market* value is determined by what investors are willing to pay for the stock, which may or may not be greater than the net asset or book value.

Issued, Unissued, and Treasury Stock. After the enterprise is chartered, part of the stock is issued to pay for property transferred to the company, and part is sold to provide capital funds. The balance of the stock constitutes *unissued* stock to be used in subsequent financing. The latter is not to be confused with *treasury stock,* which is stock lawfully issued by the company and reacquired by it.

Bond Issues. Bond issues are borrowings based on company promises to repay the loan at stated periods and are backed by a mortgage on all or part of the company's property. They take the form of *bonds, debentures, certificates,* or *notes of issue,* based upon a trust agreement or indenture which contains all the rights and obligations between the company as borrower, the bankers who are to market the issue, the prospective bondholders (represented by the trustee) and the general public. The relationship between the company and bondholders is that of debtor-creditors. While the bondholders have no ownership interest in the company, their rights have priority over those of the stockholders. A temporary failure to pay interest charges or amortization may throw the company into receivership.

Differences Between Debt and Equity Capital. The basic difference between debt and equity capital are maturity, claims on corporate income and assets, and voice in management. While the long-term debts have a stated maturity date on which the principal amount borrowed must be repaid, equity has no such maturity since its life is presumed to be infinite. Again, the bond holder has a prior claim on both the income and assets of a corporation while the equity holder generally has no such claim, and payments to equity holders are not mandatory. Typically, the bond holders have no say in the management of a company so long as all the debts are paid, but the equity holders (the true owners of the corporation) have the only voice in the selection of the board of directors through their voting power.

The use of a high ratio of debt to equity capital (financial leverage) may be beneficial in that it increases the firm's earnings per share (EPS) when its earnings before interest and taxes (EBIT) are increasing, but the danger of a sharp decline in EPS is all too real when EBIT is falling. The reason for this is that with high leverage there is a high fixed charge in the form of the interest the firm *must* pay, no matter what its earnings are.

In order to understand the capital structure of a firm, the debt-equity ratio, the debt-to-total-capitalization ratio, the "times interest earned" (TIE), and total debt coverage must be calculated and analyzed, taking into consideration the record of past years as well as comparisons with the ratios of the industry to which the firm belongs. While neoclassical economists take the position that there is an optimum point in the cost-of-capital curve up to which the debt-equity ratio can be increased, critics of this point of view assert that the total risk for all security holders of a firm is not altered by changes in the capital structure, and that therefore the total value of the firm must be the same regardless of the financing mix.

Laws Affecting Financing. Complex Federal and state laws regulate the issuance of securities, to protect investors and the general public, and in every security issue process there will normally be an attorney charged with supervising its legal aspects. In general, every state prescribes conditions which must be complied with by companies incorporated within the state, doing business in the state even if incorporated elsewhere, or selling securities within the state.

Chief among Federal laws enacted under the interstate-commerce clauses of the Constitution are the Securities Act of 1933, the Securities Exchange Act of 1934, the Public Utility Holding Company Act of 1935, the Trust Indenture Act of 1939, the Investment Company Act of 1940, and some aspects of the Small Business Investment Act of 1958. In addition, bankruptcy laws deal with the reorganizations of corporations, to protect investors. Other legislation, such as banking and monetary laws, also give the Federal Government power to regulate and control securities operations.

ARABINDA GHOSH, Associate Professor of Finance, Hofstra University, Long Island, New York.

Cross References: *Business Organization: Legal Structure; Securities and Exchange Commission; Venture Capital; Venture Management.*

CORPORATE SECRETARY

The **Corporate Secretary** is a key executive officer in his or her corporation. The laws of practically all states require that there be a corporate secretary of each corporation. Further, the corporation's by-laws, as well as the disclosure regulations of the U.S. Securities and Exchange Commission, specify the corporate secretary as an officer.

The corporation's by-laws define in very broad general terms the corporate secretary's basic duties and responsibilities, usually tracking the requirements of applicable state law which devolve upon the corporate secretary. As in the case of most other officers, however, the duties and responsibilities of the position will vary from company to company, depending upon the officer's education, training, and experience, as well as on the size, complexity of operation of the company, and the historical development of various functions within the company. Also, as is true of all officers, many of the major responsibilities of the corporate secretary are those delegated to him or her by senior management and by the company's board of directors.

A corporate secretary's responsibilities have a direct relationship to the laws of the state in which the company is incorporated, to the company's charter, by-laws, and other regulations (if any), to the resolutions adopted by its stockholders and directors, and to the listing agreement with each stock exchange on which any of the company's securities may be listed. More and more, the corporate secretary of companies registered pursuant to the U.S. Federal securities laws must be familiar with the disclosure provisions of such laws and the rules and regulations thereunder, and many secretaries become involved in the development and filing of certain reports with the Securities and Exchange Commission and the dissemination of required disclosure documents to stockholders.

As may be seen from the above, because the function of the corporate secretary is grounded in legal requirements, many, but by no means all, corporate secretaries have a legal background. Often the corporate secretary is a member of the legal function of the corporation and in a number of instances may be the company's general counsel or associate or assistant general counsel or hold some other legal title. The corporate secretary usually reports to a senior executive officer of the company, usually the chairman of the board or the president, and is often an officer and/or director of subsidiary companies.

The corporate secretary occupies an important position as a key liaison between the board of directors and the stockholders of the company, as well as between the board of directors and the company's management.

Corporate Matters. As to corporate matters, the corporate secretary's responsibilities customarily include:

(1) Giving notices of meetings of stockholders, the board of directors, and committees of the board, the preparation and distribution of agenda, the dissemination of information relating to matters to be considered at such meetings, and advising and assisting in the general conduct of the meetings.

(2) Recording, securing approval of, and preserving the minutes of meetings of stockholders, the board of directors and committees of the board, and reporting action taken at such meetings to the appropriate management personnel and others.

(3) Co-ordinating the efforts of the company, management, staff, all agents of the company and printers in preparing for, holding and the follow-up to annual and special meetings of stockholders, insuring that all notice and other requirements of applicable state law, the company's by-laws, SEC and exchange or similar requirements are met. The corporate secretary also usually prepares and distributes the post-meeting report to stockholders, and may be involved in the preparation of all or parts of the annual report to stockholders.

(4) Assembling data for, preparing and mailing proxy statements and forms of proxies to the stockholders, soliciting proxies, tabulating returned proxies, and reporting the results to the meeting of stockholders. The solicitation and tabulation of proxies may be performed directly by the corporate secretary's office or through an outside agent, in which case the corporate secretary provides overall direction to such agent.

(5) Issuing and transferring the company's securities, maintaining stockholder ledgers and other records, and handling dividend disbursements, either in his or her own department or

through an outside agency; overseeing the company's escheat and abandoned property program and compliance with various state laws pertaining to the surrender of unclaimed dividend and interest payments and in some instances the underlying security certificates themselves; preparing and certifying lists of stockholders for various purposes, such as voting at stockholders' meetings, payment of dividends and stock splits, etc.; and replacing lost, stolen, or destroyed stock certificates upon being furnished satisfactory affidavit and indemnity bond. In many cases the actual work is performed by a professional transfer agent, such as a bank. The corporate secretary, however, acts as liaison with the company's transfer agent(s) and registrar(s) if these functions are performed outside the company.

(6) Maintaining a sound stockholder relations program, including answering or directing response by appropriate departments within the company of stockholder inquiries, the issuance of quarterly or other reports to stockholders, handling stockholder proposals, and advising and assisting in the establishment and development of other programs and communications aimed at the stockholders of the company.

(7) Listing the securities of the company on national securities exchanges, filing periodic notices and reports with such exchanges, ensuring that notification of dividend and other required actions is properly given, and otherwise complying with the listing and other requirements of such exchanges. If the company's securities are not listed on a securities exchange, the corporate secretary has similar responsibilities in the company's relations with the National Association of Securities Dealers, Inc.

(8) If counsel, or if not counsel by and with the advice of counsel, the corporate secretary is often involved in the registration of the securities of the company with the Securities and Exchange Commission and with the preparation and filing of annual and periodic reports with the Commission, such as the proxy statement, Forms 10-K, 10-Q, and 8-K.

(9) Advising the directors and officers as to the potential liabilities and limitations imposed upon them with respect to transactions in securities of the company and the requirements for reporting to the SEC the changes in their beneficial ownership of the company's securities.

(10) Acting as the normal channel for providing information and giving assistance to the company's directors, both during the orientation procedure for new directors and during these persons' tenure on the board.

(11) Handling the incorporation, qualification, reorganization and/or dissolution of the company and certain subsidiaries in various states and maintaining them in good standing therein.

(12) Assisting in the development of and monitoring compliance with various corporate policy statements and guidelines, e.g., conflicts of interest, standards of conduct, timely disclosure, etc.

(13) Overseeing and coordinating the corporate secretarial activities of some or all subsidiary companies and retaining copies of minutes and other corporate documents for such subsidiaries.

(14) Executing certifications of various official reports, resolutions adopted by directors and stockholders, amendments to by-laws, and other documents, etc.

(15) Being aware of developments affecting the foregoing functions, and advising and assisting the chairman of the board, president, and other members of senior management on the broad range of matters relating to the function of and relations with the board of directors and stockholders, and on federal and state corporate and securities matters.

Administrative Matters. As to administrative matters, the corporate secretary:

(1) Is custodian of corporate files and records, including minute books, stock record books, contracts, licensing agreements, agency agreements, employment agreements, patents, titles and trademarks, and other valuable corporate records.

(2) Usually determines corporate policy on the safekeeping, retention, and destruction of company records.

(3) Has custody of the corporate seal and attests to the powers of the officers and the regularity of corporate acts. (By impressing the seal on a document, the secretary attests that it is a valid corporate document.)

(4) Occasionally is responsible for relations with the financial community, especially security analysts.

(5) Frequently administers and/or interprets questions arising under stock option, stock appreciation right and stock purchase plans, and occasionally administers and/or interprets pension, profit-sharing, and group insurance programs. Also, on occasion directs and

administers overall company insurance program. Is particularly concerned with directors' and officers' liability insurance matters, as well as issues related to insurance under the Employee Retirement Income Security Act of 1974.

(6) Sometimes is designated to accept service of legal process and subpoenas regarding the company and certain subsidiaries, and the taking of proper action to see that their interests are protected.

(7) Occasionally is responsible for developing and administering the company's policies and programs in various other unrelated areas, such as corporate contributions and real estate.

GEORGE N. BIGGS, III, President, American Society of Corporate Secretaries, Inc., New York, New York

Information Reference

American Society of Corporate Secretaries, Inc.

Cross References: *Annual Reports; Business Organization: Legal Structure; Corporate Capitalization; Directors: Characteristics of Boards; Directors: Legal Duties and Responsibilities.*

CORPORATE STRATEGY AND BUSINESS POLICY

Corporate Strategy and Business Policy define and shape the success and character of an organization. Corporate strategy describes a firm's primary performance objectives, product-market scope, and major operating policies. Formulating strategy involves analyzing and synthesizing the environment and resources of a firm with the values of its managers and external constituents. Implementing strategy involves designing and administering the formal organization to elicit individual and collective behavior required by the strategy. Managing strategy involves orchestrating and influencing organizational renewal and growth through strategic change over time.

Strategic decisions are major resource commitments which affect a firm over long time periods. These commitments determine how the parts of a firm relate to one another and how a firm postures itself toward the environment. The pattern of resource commitments reflects a firm's priorities and establishes its level of risk. The sequence and timing of strategic decisions determine the efficiency and effectiveness with which a firm obtains, transforms, and deploys its resources.

History. Business policy as an academic subject began at the Harvard Business School in 1912. Throughout its early history, the course and the field involved successful top executives and senior faculty who discussed their problems and experiences with advanced students. The course had three characteristics which remain with the field today: it integrated the other areas of business; it adopted the viewpoint of top management; and it solved problems of importance. The field was descriptive and unstructured.

Following World War II, the field began to utilize a process of "Policy Formulation and Administration" articulated by George Albert Smith and C. Roland Christensen [1]. The process involved six steps: sizing-up a situation, formulating policies and planning programs of action, organizing administrative personnel, putting plans into action, controlling behavior and results, and reappraising previous actions in light of unfolding events.

The concept of strategy began to provide the field a conceptual structure and normative orientation in the 1960s. From his business history research about "Strategy and Structure," Alfred Chandler [2] concluded that environmental shifts induced strategy reformulation which required organizational change to implement it. Building on Chandler's work and on a decade of collaborative research, Kenneth Andrews [3] first articulated "The Concept of Corporate Strategy," and prescribed an analytical approach to its formulation and implementation. Simultaneously, Igor Ansoff [4] developed a normative methodology for formulating "Corporate Strategy" based on his corporate experience and on available management theory.

Over 75 books and numerous published articles built on the work of Andrews and Ansoff by providing theory, methodology, and examples which were useful in developing an analytical process of strategy. However, recent work has begun to explore an organizational and political process of strategy that reflects the increasing complexity of business organizations. Described in "Strategic Management" [5], this view of corporate strategy is less well developed, but has attracted the attention of both practitioners and researchers.

By 1980, corporate strategy was well accepted as a concept useful to the managers of a firm. The concept is most valuable in helping sophisticated and complex organizations anticipate and respond to their turbulent environment satisfactorily. Business policy is part of the curriculum in most schools of business, suggesting that future managers will rely on it increasingly.

Defining Strategy. Corporate strategy describes a firm's primary performance objectives, product-market scope, and major operating policies. Primary performance objectives state the criteria by which management judges the success of the firm and expects others to judge it. Product-market scope limits the firm's range of activities and therefore sets some of its environmental boundaries. Major operating policies stipulate how the firm conducts its activities, uses its resources, and faces its environment. Business policy indicates how managers should define, formulate, implement, and manage corporate strategy.

Primary performance objectives describe what the firm wants to accomplish. As economic entities, firms often focus on financial performance objectives. However, as societal entities, firms increasingly espouse objectives for their impact on the broader environment. (See SOCIAL AUDIT.) These objectives can include many dimensions from employee welfare or community improvement to political impact or philanthropic contribution. All objectives constrain the selection of other strategic choices and thereby guide the search for strategic alternatives as well as provide criteria for evaluating a strategy retrospectively.

Good strategic objectives have four common characteristics: they should be measurable, temporal, comprehensive, and realistic. *Measurable* objectives need not be quantitative; however, they should permit observers to agree on their meaning both when set and when reviewed. *Temporal* objectives specify a deadline for achievement, although appropriate horizons may vary by industry. *Comprehensive* objectives enable the firm to specify a small number of objectives that reflect the overall performance of the firm while permitting considerable latitude in how they are to be accomplished. *Realistic* objectives are achievable, even if challenging, and fully utilize the resources available to the firm.

The product-market scope of a firm describes the range of products it provides and customers it serves. This scope highlights two different types of firms and strategies. An integrated firm is one business, usually comprised of major organization units responsible for stages or functions in the development and delivery of a single product line to a market. Its scope is the breadth or focus of its product line and customer base. The objectives for integrated firms often relate to their industry positions and conditions.

By comparison, a diversified firm (and often a multinational firm) operates several distinct businesses, each as a separate organizational unit. For a diversified firm, product-market scope specifies the kinds of businesses it enters or exits, nourishes or starves. This specification may include criteria such as size, minimum profitability, potential growth, desired market share position, and other statistical criteria. In addition, it may specify commonalities among its businesses, such as common technology, raw materials, customer characteristics, or geographic coverages. In some cases it specifies the resources shared among businesses.

The major operating policies of an integrated firm define its approach to competition. Some of these policies guide the major functional areas of the business, such as marketing, production, research and development, personnel, and finance. Functional policies are guidelines or decision rules for the managers of these functions. They shape decisions that develop and deploy the resources of the firm by changing its capabilities and limitations over time. Other operating policies guide the timing and sequencing of changes in functional policies or define priorities in interfunctional decisions such as resource allocations. These policies also indicate the kind of coordination required among functional areas to compete effectively. Finally, operating policies indicate how some of the nonfinancial objectives of the firm will be achieved.

Operating policies in a diversified firm usually indicate how corporate management relates to its businesses or divisions, and how the businesses relate to one another, rather than how the businesses themselves compete. They address how the firm is financed and organized, how businesses are entered or exited, and how resources are allocated and shared among the divisions. Businesses are acquired, internally developed, or created by dividing existing businesses; they can be divested, liquidated, or consolidated. The policies can define the roles of businesses in the firm, such as providing growth, profitability, stability, or resources. They also stipulate what functions or decisions belong to corporate management and which belong to the businesses, such as accounting and planning systems, research and development, or personnel.

Formulating Strategy. Formulating strategy involves distinct steps of analysis and decision. Since the steps are interactive and repetitive, people disagree about the content and sequence of the steps. The content of the steps is somewhat different for integrated firms than for diversified firms. The sequence does influence the effectiveness and efficiency of formulation. Two early steps generally are to identify the current strategy and to select preliminary performance objectives for the future.

The next steps for most firms are to assess the major conditions and trends in the environment, to evaluate the capabilities and limitations of the firm, and to articulate the values of key managers and external constituencies. A firm scans the environment to identify social values, customer needs, technological changes, governmental regulations, economic movements, and competitor shifts, and to estimate their potential impacts on its future strategy and performance. These suggest opportunities or risks for the firm. A firm also evaluates its capabilities and limitations in absolute terms, both current condition and future potential. These suggest areas of strength or weakness relative to the environment. Values are inherently difficult to articulate and categorize; however, they often have significant impact on the assessment of environment, the evaluation of resources, and the choice of strategy.

The next three steps are to generate major alternative strategies, to forecast the likely performance results of each (including the current strategy), and to evaluate the resource utilization and risk associated with each alternative. Major strategic alternatives include changes in performance objectives, product-market scope, or operating policies. They are usually ways to seize opportunities, reduce risks, utilize capabilities, or overcome limitations either by changing the resource configuration or the arena in which it is deployed. A major impetus for generating alternatives is a realization that the future performance of a firm will not meet its objectives without strategic change. Alternatives seek to fill the gap. A second impetus is the realization that an existing strategy does not fully utilize the firm's resources. Alternatives seek to improve performance through their better or different utilization.

Finally, the firm compares the forecast performance results against the objectives and either selects one of the alternative strategies, searches for additional strategies, or revises the objectives. These steps are all iterative as analysis proceeds and repetitive as more information becomes available. Many techniques are useful for each of the steps; specific techniques depending on the situation. Before fully committing to a new strategic alternative, the firm should reassess the consistency among its strategic elements and the major factors which should be considered in its formulation. One of these factors is the firm's ability to implement a new strategy.

Recapitulating the steps:

(1) Identify the current strategy.

(2) Select preliminary performance objectives for the future.

(3) Assess major conditions and trends in the environment.

(4) Generate major alternative strategies.

(5) Forecast the likely performance results of each alternative, including the current strategy.

(6) Evaluate the resource utilization and risk associated with each alternative.

(7) Select an alternative strategy, or search for additional strategies, or revise objectives.

Implementing Strategy. Implementing strategy is making strategy an accurate description of a firm by transforming a statement of its strategy into decisions, activity, and performance. This transformation involves directing and motivating individual and group behavior toward the successful accomplishment of the tasks implied by the strategy. Organizational design and political leadership help managers implement strategy. Organization is important in implementing strategy because through it, senior executives can influence many people continuously and pervasively. Organization design influences behavior in at least two important ways: (1) it directly influences people's jobs and their perceptions of what the firm expects them to do and (2) it partially shapes the informal organization or corporate culture. Political leadership provides further opportunities to shape the informal organization of managers near the top of the formal organization.

Implementing strategy involves designing the structure and systems of the organization. Structure is the formal framework of job definitions, authority relationships, and communication channels which specifies how the work of the organization is divided and coordinated.

Dividing work and defining jobs can focus attention and activity on the key tasks required by strategy. Authority relationships and communication channels influence the independence or coordination among those tasks as required by strategy. The formal authority of specific positions in the organization provides one basis for the development and use of power by their encumbents.

Organizational systems further influence strategic behavior. These systems include those of planning and control, measurement and evaluation, reward and restraint, recruitment and selection, and training and development. Collectively, the pattern of these systems provides the knowledge, skills, and attitudes of job encumbents and determines how they use these attributes to contribute to the accomplishment of objectives through their behavior. Some of these systems may be pervasive throughout an organization, and others may be tailored to the specific requirements of parts of the organization. Through experience, people perceive what the organization expects of them and develop patterns of behavior reflecting those perceived expectations. Implementing strategy involves shaping those responses to conform to strategic needs. (See ORGANIZATION ANALYSIS AND PLANNING and ORGANIZATION THEORY.)

Political leadership recognizes that many business decisions are the outcome of an influence process. Managers with varying degrees of authority and power bring their influence to bear on decisions that are important to them. The political leadership of senior management utilizes, develops, and influences this process so that decisions support the selected strategy. Organization design and political leadership partially shape the social and political structure of the firm. This helps to stabilize and routinize continuing activity, to establish and reinforce norms of acceptable behavior, and to highlight and resolve important conflicts.

Managing Strategy. Strategic management refers to the roles of various executives in formulating and implementing strategy. The role of senior executives is process-oriented in firms that confront broad and turbulent environments and that adopt complex and decentralized organizations. In these firms, formulating and implementing strategy requires the continual involvement of many managers throughout the organization. Through new information, they perceive changes in environment, resources, and values. They each gather this fragmented information incrementally. Each manager brings a different organizational, political, and personal perspective to the information processing. Therefore, managers with different perceptions and perspectives prepare and support different proposals for strategic and organizational change.

Senior executives increasingly recognize that correctly managing the process of organizational renewal through strategic change is more important than critically evaluating the substance of proposals for strategic change. They argue that if the process is appropriate, the substance will be likewise. Managing the process involves analytical, organizational, and political skills to understand, structure, and administer it.

One way senior executives manage the process is by providing broad statements of corporate strategy which provide a framework for other executives to challenge or detail. Senior executives can articulate areas of particular interest or concern which strategy should address, and they can establish criteria for selecting strategy proposals submitted by others. These criteria stimulate and guide lower level managers who formulate and advocate strategic proposals. Since proposals often emerge incrementally, top management can maintain the continuity and consistency among them over time by selecting and rejecting proposals. Senior executives can also interrogate the analyses which support proposals and review the reliability of executives who propose them.

Senior executives also manage the process of formulating and implementing strategy through organizational design and political leadership, the same factors used to implement strategy. These factors provide a context within which proposals are generated, advocated, and adopted. This creates a tension between the use of organization as a way to stabilize operating behavior and implement strategy on one hand and to promote desirable strategic change on the other. In this sense, formulating and implementing strategy are inseparable processes which senior executives must manage through organizational design and political leadership. The future development of business policy will include a better understanding of these relationships.

JOHN P. DORY, Professor of Management, Pace University, New York, New York, and Management Consultant

Information References

Associations:

Academy of Management, Business Policy and Planning Division.

North American Society for Corporate Planning.
Planning Executives Institute.

Periodicals:

California Management Review.
Harvard Business Review.
Journal of Business Strategy.
Strategic Management Journal.

Texts:

References cited below are also valuable information sources.

Ansoff, H. Igor, "Strategic Management," New York, NY, Wiley, 1979.

Bower, Joseph L., "Managing the Resource Allocation Process," Boston, Div. of Research, Graduate School of Business Administration, Harvard University, 1970.

Hofer, Charles W. and Schendel, Dan E., eds., "West Series in Business Policy and Planning," St. Paul, Minn., West Publishing (beginning 1979).

Paine, Frank T. and Naumes, William, "Organizational Strategy and Policy," 2nd ed., Philadelphia, Saunders, 1978.

Quinn, James Brian, "Strategies for Change: Logical Incrementalism," Homewood, Ill., Irwin, 1980.

Stiner, George A. and Miner, John B., "Management Policy and Strategy," New York, Macmillan, 1977.

Uyterhoeven, Hugo E. R., et al., "Strategy and Organization: Text and Cases in General Management", rev. ed., Homewood, Ill., Irwin, 1977.

References Cited

[1] Smith, Jr., George Albert, and Christensen, C. Roland, "Policy Formulation and Administration: A Casebook of Top-Management Problems in Business," Homewood, Ill., Irwin, 1951.

[2] Chandler, Jr., Alfred D., "Strategy and Structure: Chapters in the History of the American Industrial Enterprise," Cambridge, Mass., MIT Press, 1962.

[3] Learned, Edmund P., Christensen, C. Roland, Andrews, Kenneth R., and Guth, William D., "Business Policy: Text and Cases," Homewood, Ill., Irwin, 1965; a revised version of the text appears in Andrews, Kenneth R., "The Concept of Corporate Strategy," rev. ed., Homewood, IL, Irwin, 1980.

[4] Ansoff, H. Igor, "Corporate Strategy: An Analytic Approach to Business Policy for Growth and Expansion," New York, McGraw-Hill, 1965.

[5] Hofer, Charles W. and Schendel, Dan E. (eds.), "Strategic Management: A New View of Business Policy and Planning," Boston, Little, Brown, 1979.

Cross References: *Decision Theory; Long-Range Planning; Long-Range Planning: Financial Aspects; Marketing Strategy: Competitive Analysis; Operating Margin Analysis; Social Audit.*

CORRESPONDENCE SCHOOLS

Correspondence Schools, also referred to as home study schools, are an important part of industrial and business training programs, and according to records of the National Home Study Council, more than 3,000 companies are helping their employees develop themselves through courses offered by accredited home study schools. NHSC estimates that some 3.5 million persons in this country are currently enrolled in study programs covering accounting, engineering, management, writing, etc. In 48 states the schools are subject to license and regulation by the state education department.

NHSC makes a distinction between "correspondence schools" and schools which merely provide educational and lesson material for self-study without instructor, counseling, and examining features. For its accreditation, it defines correspondence schools as those "which provide lesson materials prepared in a sequential and logical order for study, upon completion of which the student returns the assigned lesson to the school for correction, grading, and comment by qualified instructors." The instructors immediately return the corrected lessons to the student. After courses have been completed, vocational counseling and continuing information are furnished for as long as the student requests help. Research by the University of Wisconsin, University of Michigan, and others has shown that people learn as well through structured home study as in classrooms, and actually retain more. For example, students must learn *every* part of the subject matter, and respond *in writing* to *every* part of the lesson. On the other hand, not everyone in a classroom has a chance to participate at all times.

Types of Programs. Company participation varies from simple encouragement of employees to enroll in study programs on their own, to partial or total tuition reimbursement, and even to completely controlled sponsored programs. Special courses may be designed for a specific industry. Some schools offer terminal laboratory work following correspondence instruction.

Almost every conceivable subject connected with business and industry is taught by one or more of the more than 80 accredited correspondence schools. (See partial list in Exhibit I.)

Do students stick with the courses? Where tuition assistance is given and management and supervisors show a personal interest and keep student motivation high, the experience has been that completion rates range between 50% and 70%. This probably surpasses the record of

Exhibit I

A Partial List of Subjects Taught by Accredited Correspondence Schools

Accounting . . . Appliance Servicing . . . Architecture . . . Audio-Electronics . . . Automation . . . Auto Mechanics . . . Banking & Finance . . . Blueprint Reading . . . Bookkeeping . . . Broadcast Engineering . . . Broadcast Journalism . . . Building Construction, Estimating, and Maintenance . . . Business Insurance . . . Business Law . . . Chemistry . . . Commercial Art . . . Communications Technology . . . Computer Programming . . . Computer Repair Technician . . . Cost Accounting . . . CPA Preparation . . . Electricity . . . Electronics . . . Estate Planning & Protection . . . Food Service Administration . . . Health Insurance . . . Heating & Ventilation . . . High School Equivalency Examination Preparation . . . Hotel Operations . . . Industrial Security . . . Insurance License Examination Preparation . . . Interior Decorating . . . Journalism . . . Labor-Management Relations . . . Life Underwriting . . . Machine Shop Practices . . . Marketing Research . . . Materials Handling . . . Medical Transcription . . . Metallurgy . . . Minicomputers . . . Management Development . . . Office Practices and Management . . . Personnel Management . . . Plant Layout . . . Power Plant Engineering . . . Quality Control . . . Radio/TV Commercial Writing . . . Real Estate . . . Refrigeration . . . Retailing . . . Safety Training . . . Salesmanship . . . Sound Technician . . . Stock Market Science and Techniques . . . Supervisory Development . . . Surveying & Mapping . . . Systems and Procedures . . . Tax Procedures . . . Television . . . Traffic Management . . . Travel Agent Training . . . U.S. Air Force Career Specialties . . . U.S. Army Career Specialties . . . U.S. Marine Corps Career Specialties . . . U.S. Coast Guard Specialities . . .

Harvard and Yale! If proper records are kept, these can be used in considering pay increments and advancement.

Apprenticeship Programs. Some correspondence schools provide the related training in apprenticeship programs set up to meet the requirements for registration with the Bureau of Apprenticeship and Training of the U.S. Department of Labor. (See Apprenticeship Programs.) The correspondence school will provide all text and training materials, render instruction, and evaluate written examinations and drawings.

Costs. Correspondence courses (as of late 1981) can run from about $300 to $3,500, depending upon the subject matter selected, number of assignments, and type of instruction materials and tools or kits provided. Typically, a course will be in the $300–$1,000 range. Individual courses with relatively few lessons, that can be completed in six months to a year, may be had for half of the lower amount mentioned, plus an initial registration fee. High school diploma courses usually cost $500 to $750 and take two and a half to three years. A typical apprentice program involving 144 hours of related training per year will cost from $125 to $200 per apprentice per year.

Selection. The Accrediting Commission of the National Home Study Council has been designated by the U.S. Dept. of Education as a "nationally recognized accrediting agency under the terms of Public Laws 82–550 and 85–864." Accreditation may be important in connection with veterans' benefits. The National University Continuing Education Association, founded in 1915, consists of institutions of higher education, public or private, accredited by their regional accrediting agencies and active in continuing education of all sorts.

It is well to check with the state department of education. In some states, licensing means that a course has been reviewed by an expert in the field covered.

In its 1980–1981 *Directory of Accredited Home Study Schools,* the National Home Study Council lists 80 schools. Since NHSC is a voluntary association, the fact that a school is not accredited by it does not necessarily imply below-standard quality. However, accreditation does signify evaluation by competent educators. NHSC schools must be reaccredited every five years. Many non-NHSC correspondence course programs in business, engineering, and management subjects are offered by colleges and universities, notably those of the Universities of Michigan, Wisconsin, and St. Louis. More than 30 business and industry trade associations teach their members via the correspondence method.

Pointers. Here are important pointers provided by NHSC to pass along to an employee who is seriously considering a home study course:

• Investigate the merits of the school you are considering. Try to get in touch with someone who has taken the course. Check the accreditation.

• Are you equipped to assimilate the course? Do you have the experience and background to profit from it? Don't sign up for a course that is over your head.

• Do you have enough stick-to-it-iveness to complete the course?

• Act on facts, not impulse. Take time to consider. Make a decision based on information, not emotion. Don't buy a sales talk—buy an education!

• Don't sign any contract unless you intend and expect to keep it. You can't break the contract any time you want to, or just because you have fallen behind in your study, or because it is difficult.

WILLIAM A. FOWLER, Executive Director, National Home Study Council, Washington, D.C.

Information References

National Home Study Council.
National University Continuing Education Association (issues "A Guide to Correspondence Study in Colleges and Universities").

Cross References: *Human Resources Development (and cross references there given)*

COST ACCOUNTING (MANAGERIAL ACCOUNTING)

Although evidences of the practice of **Cost Accounting** exist as far back as the Medieval period, it is, both with respect to problems encountered and concepts employed, essentially a product of the twentieth century.

The years between 1880 and 1920 represent a period of tremendous ferment in this area. Traditional accounting processes had failed to meet the needs of the post-Industrial Revolution era in providing information concerning the manufacturing costs of products and departments. An enthusiastic and expanding group of people with backgrounds in engineering and factory record keeping, attempted to fill the void. For a time, widespread experimentation with cost systems occurred, but with the acceptance and integration of the cost accounts into the general and financial accounting structure around 1910, systems became more standardized in scope, and cost accounting took on an appearance within the accounts quite similar to its format in present-day cost systems.

In its beginnings cost accounting represented simply a procedure by which prime costs of manufacture were traced to products or processes. What to do with the newer costs associated with power-driven machinery represented an enigma. These costs, called *factory indirect expenses, manufacturing expenses,* or *manufacturing overhead,* gradually took on a position of significance in the triumvirate of manufacturing costs. A solution to the handling of these costs was found with the introduction of *overhead rates.* By means of these, a way was found to relate a vague body of manufacturing costs to a diverse group of products undergoing manufacture. Bases such as direct labor hours or machine hours were substituted for output as expressed by a variety of different product units.

Dividing manufacturing overhead cost by a common denominator of output made it possible to state the manufacturing overhead costs of individual products. This device, at first applied casually at year-end, evolved later into a careful and objective computation of overhead rates made before operations began, based upon expected production and forecasted costs. It made possible the costing of products for manufacturing overhead as operations progressed. This completed an orderly procedure by which all manufacturing costs are currently traced to products contained in inventory, and subsequently to cost of goods sold.

Formal Definition. Since cost accounting has been in a period of continuing development, any general definition attempting to present its meaning in a few words will tend to be incomplete, depending upon the particular interest of the user. Many textbook writers emphasize a definition describing cost accounting as an extension of financial accounting, having to do with the ascertainment of the cost of a product or a service. That such definitions minimize today's importance of cost accounting is well evidenced by the ensuing pages of texts which commence with such definitions. Subsequent content usually has a declining relevance to the definition posed, as each of the remaining chapters unfold.

In its modern application, cost accounting may be defined as a phase of management controls integrated in part with the general financial records, which attempts to provide management with the cost of a variety of objects of interest, such as product, service, operation, area, plan, problem, or decision. In its initial impetus at the beginning of this century, as has been observed, cost accounting stressed the ascertainment of aggregate costs of manufacturing a product or rendering a service in a form suitable for incorporation into financial statements. Techniques for achieving this, particularly in the more complex areas of general overhead, material overhead, and labor overhead were well developed by 1945; and certain aspects of these were developed considerably earlier.

More recently, as indicated below, in the discussion of *Managerial Decision Making,* emphasis in cost accounting has shifted to encompass a wide variety of approaches to cost control, and to provide for a wide range of special data required for the solution of managerial decision-making problems. Consequently, differences between the terms *cost accounting* and *managerial accounting* have become blurred, and the terms are coming to be used interchangeably.

Standard Cost Accounting, with its emphasis upon "should be" costs determined prior to the incurrence of actual costs, was partly an outgrowth of the use of standards in connection with factory machines and operations, and partly an expansion of the concept of overhead rates into materials and labor accounting. Although ideas concerning standard costing had been advanced earlier, standard costs for manufacturing did not reach relative maturity until the decade beginning in 1930. In standard manufacturing accounting, a comparison is made between actual and standard costs by elements of expense for both products and departments. This is done with a view towards analyzing differences into controllable and noncontrollable causes and directing management's control efforts toward departments most needful of correction. (See STANDARD COSTING.)

Marketing Costs. Cost accounting for marketing operations in contrast to manufacturing made little headway within formal accounting routines, and has over the years remained much in the process of development and experimentation. The subject received little consideration from accountants during the first forty years of this century, and such costing in the accounts proper has often been simply a matter of classifying expense items relating to distribution activities, either under one general marketing classification or under several subclassifications such as warehousing, delivery, and sales promotion costs. Although recommendations in the right direction have been made sporadically since the 1930s, only recently have accountants generally recognized the usefulness of flexible budgeting and standard costs to problems of marketing cost control and cost allocation. Today it is possible to compare within the accounts the actual and standard marketing costs of a variety of functions, to trace some of the distribution costs to products, and finally to obtain a knowledge of the standard marketing costs of various objects of managerial interest, such as a function, district, channel of trade, and class of customer. (See MARKETING COST ANALYSIS.)

Expanded Applications. Standard costing as it developed from 1920 to 1940 accustomed the accountant to deal with a variety of costs on a statistical basis, rather than upon the basis of costs recorded in the accounts according to generally accepted principles of accounting. Because standard costing requires a detailed analysis of costs and objective studies concerning their behavior, it laid the groundwork for the expansion in usefulness of cost accounting. This is evidenced by the development of DIRECT COSTING and the application of cost analyses to the managerial decision-making area in recent decades.

The subject of fixed-variable cost analysis had received only isolated consideration at the beginning of this century. So had the concept of the break-even chart. (See BREAK-EVEN ANALYSIS.) An analysis of costs into their fixed and variable elements is essential to the construction of overhead rates and an adequate accounting for overhead cost. As interest in volume-variation studies intensified during the 1940s, accountants took a more sophisticated view towards the fixed-variable cost classification. Statistical and mathematical techniques of least squares analysis and interpolation came into use to determine the reaction of costs to changes in operational activity. This made possible the categorization of an organization's or a department's costs into a formula which identified fixed and variable costs applicable to a range of output levels. Both direct costing and flexible budgeting rest upon this distinction.

Not only did the accountant arrive at a more precise means of analyzing costs into their fixed and variable elements, but he came to a mature understanding of fixed costs. He came to understand that the term "fixed costs" has validity only in the short run; most costs are variable over the long run. A number of costs classified as fixed are actually discretionary in nature, for example, costs of frequent repainting or certain types of grounds maintenance. Finally, in recent decades, the accountant recognized that the particular composition of fixed costs has relevance only to the problem posed. Annual costs of space may be pertinent to the problem of ascertaining costs for profit determination purposes; however, its cost (at least in the current year) may be irrelevant to the problem of utilizing such space.

Variable Costing. By 1950 the idea of "direct costing"—now more commonly referred to in the literature as "variable costing"—had gained prominence in accounting and management circles. Direct costing is partly a method of cost assignment applicable to financial accounting problems wherein manufacturing costs designated as "direct" (variable costs) are traced to specific items produced, and are therefore subdivided in the accounting process between inventories and cost of goods sold; also, variable selling and administrative expenses are separated from fixed selling and administrative expenses. Direct costing is also a method of analysis attempting to identify for a variety of managerial purposes those costs which vary by products, operations, departments, and branches. Focus of attention on direct costs is believed to provide a better basis of managerial control over the operation of areas of responsibility and also to provide management with a better basis for decisions in the short run concerning profitable products and departments. (See DIRECT COSTING.)

The Cost Accounting Standards Board. The Cost Accounting Standards Board (CASB) is a creature of the Congress of the United States (1970), established to "promulgate cost accounting standards designed to achieve uniformity and consistency in the cost accounting principles followed" under certain cost-basis, negotiated Federal contracts. The Board consists of five members including the Comptroller General of the United States and four of his appointees. Of the latter, two are chosen from the accounting profession, one from industry, and a fourth from some branch of the Federal Government. The CASB is assisted by a prescribed staff of 25 professional members.

Initially, the standards of the Board applied to defense contracts of $100,000 and over. By 1975, standards of the Board had been extended to all negotiated Federal contracts, defense and non-defense, where the initial contract amounted to $500,000 or more.

To date, the Board has promulgated the following standards [1]:

401 Consistency in estimating, accumulating and reporting costs.

402 Consistency in allocating costs incurred for the same purpose.

403 Allocation of home office expense to segments.

404 Capitalization of tangible assets.

405 Accounting for unallowed costs.

406 Cost accounting period.

407 Use of standard costs for direct material and direct labor.

408 Accounting for costs of compensated personal absence.

409 Depreciation of tangible capital assets.

410 Allocation of general and administrative expenses.

411 Accounting for acquisition costs of materials.

412 Composition and measurement of pension costs.

413 (Withdrawn) Adjustment of historical depreciation costs for inflation.

414 Cost of money as an element of the cost of capital.

415 Deferred compensation costs.

A significant aspect of the CASB's work is its promulgation of Disclosure Statement regulations. Certain contractors subject to the Board must complete statements which bring to light whether or not they are consistently following practices certified by the Board. These statements also provide information helpful to the Board in studying the need for new standards.

Managerial Decision Making. Although the results of the first fifty years' effort in cost accounting in this century are apparent in modern cost finding and cost control systems, the dynamic area of cost accountancy today lies in an *opportunity* and *incremental* approach toward determining costs essential to a variety of managerial decisions. Relative to the problem of expansion or contraction of operations, for example, only variable and incremental fixed costs may be considered. With regard to the decision on whether to drop a product, a host of opportunity and incremental revenue and cost factors will be studied, such as revenues lost and costs avoided by the discontinuance, and effects upon sales and profit contributions of other products. Capital budgeting studies pose the "opportunity costs" of one investment possibility as contrasted to an alternative one. An infinite variety of cost concepts such as incremental, variable, sunk, replacement, discretionary, and imputed costs will be used as contrasted to the application of aggregate historical costs when costing manufacturing inventories.

Not only does modern cost accounting array and analyze costs on an individual basis with respect to products, branches, or alternative investments, it also supplies cost data relevant to overall planning, scheduling, and control of projects involving numerous complex and alternative operations. Here it furnishes the needed underlying information for linear programming and operations research applications, and for techniques such as CRITICAL PATH METHOD (CPM), PERT (PROGRAM EVALUATION AND REVIEW TECHNIQUE), and others. These techniques provide an overall guide to the cost minimization of a project as a whole prior to its commencement, as well as after it is under way and problems arise involving alternative procedures and operations.

Both the need for increased precision and the newer uses of cost accounting have called for consideration of an increasing application of statistics and higher mathematics to cost accounting procedures. Excursions in this direction are apparent in fixed-variable cost analysis, minimum order point and economic lot size computations, cost allocation, capital budgeting decisions, analysis of variance, and linear programming. Today's more innovative cost textbooks [2] [3] commonly present discussions on single and multiple regression analysis, application of the theory of probability to a variety of cost/management problems, and the use of probabilistic managerial decision models as possible alternatives to standard cost accounting.

L. J. BENNINGER, PH.D., Professor Emeritus of Accounting, University of Florida, Gainesville, Florida

Information References

Associations:

American Accounting Association.
American Institute of Certified Public Accountants.
Society of Industrial and Cost Accountants of Canada.
Financial Executives Institute.
National Association of Accountants.

Periodicals:

The Accounting Review.
Cost and Management.
Management Accounting.

References Cited

[1] Interested readers can obtain explanatory rulings in full concerning standards promulgated and their effective dates from The Cost Accounting Standards Board, 441 G Street N.W., Washington D.C. 20548.

[2] Dopuch, Nicholas and Birnberg, Jacob B., "Cost Accounting: Accounting Data for Management Decisions," New York, Harcourt, Brace & Jovanovich, 2nd ed., 1974.

[3] Horngren, Charles T., "Accounting for Management Control," 4th ed., Englewood Cliffs, N.J., Prentice-Hall, 1977.

Cross References: *Accounting; Break-Even Analysis; Budgeting; Cost-Benefit and Cost Effectiveness Analysis; Cost Control; Cost-Volume-Profit Analysis; Depreciation; Direct Costing; Flexible Budgeting; Overhead Assignment; Responsibility Reporting; Standard Costing; Statistical Accounting.*

COST-BENEFIT AND COST-EFFECTIVENESS ANALYSIS

Cost-Benefit and Cost-Effectiveness Analysis are the quantitative examination of alternative ways to accomplish public goals as to their benefits, or effectiveness, to be gained and the costs to be incurred—for the purpose of identifying the preferred alternative.

In cost-benefit analysis, benefits are primarily expressed in monetary, dollar, values. In cost-effectiveness analysis, benefits are primarily left in non-monetary units.

These analyses are of principal concern to managers of public agencies—whether Federal, state, or local. Private, for-profit, firms use their own version of cost-benefit analysis when they analyze alternative investment opportunities to maximize profits. (See COST-VOLUME-PROFIT ANALYSIS.) The more complex cost-benefit and cost-effectiveness analysis approaches are needed for choices in the public sector because of the considerably more complex problems of determining benefits. Some private firms, however, are required to do these studies, for example, as part of their design of military hardware, or contract to do these types of studies for government agencies. Managers of such firms, thus, also need a basic understanding of them.

The term "cost" is used in the definition in its broad sense: Although dollars are the units most generally used in this type of analysis, any economic resource might, for a given problem, be the limiting factor—e.g., personnel.

History. Though evaluations of public projects have doubtless occurred throughout history, the modern use of cost-benefit analysis (CBA) can be said to have begun in the 1930s with the United States Flood Control Act of 1936. Congress declared that benefits "to whomsoever they may accrue" of Federal projects should exceed costs. In the 1950s, the Inter-Agency Committee on Water Resource issued "Proposed Practices for Economic Analysis of River Basin Projects," known as the "Green Book." It suggested specific procedures that provided the seed for future work in water-resource projects. Key publications in the 1950s were Otto Eckstein's (1958) "Water Resources Development: The Economics of Project Evaluation" and Roland McKean's (1958) "Efficiency in Government Through Systems Analysis." As these titles indicate, the first major application of CBA was to aid in the selection of water-resources projects. This application continues to the present time with the Corps of Engineers as one of the major performers of CBA. Probably the second major application of CBA has been to the selection of major transportation projects, e.g., highways, but applications can be found in almost all areas of the public sector.

Cost-effectiveness analysis (CEA) blossomed at the RAND Corporation in the late 1950s and gained considerable momentum when the Secretary of Defense (Robert McNamara) appointed Charles Hitch, of RAND, as comptroller of the Department of Defense at the beginning of the 1960s. The just-published book of Hitch and McKean, "Economics of Defense in the Nuclear Age," became a best-seller and formed the basis for a major effort at the regular use of CEA in the Defense Department. In the mid-1960s President Lyndon Johnson mandated the use of the DOD analysis approach for non-defense agencies as part of the introduction of the Planning-Programming-Budgeting System (PPBS). (See PUBLIC ADMINISTRATION.) Variations of CEA and CBA have since been used periodically by Federal agencies. These procedures have spread to state and local public agencies, though slowly. The more limited use in state and local agencies is due in large part to the more limited analytical resources available to those governments.

CEA has been used, particularly in military applications, to help determine the preferred "configuration" for specific equipment or systems, as well as to help determine which particular system is preferrable.

Procedures. Cost-benefit and cost-effectiveness analyses are composed of six principal steps:

(1) *Description of Alternatives.* Each alternative must be identified and examined to identify the major characteristics that affect over-all system performance and generate costs. The major equipment, though of primary interest, should not be examined in isolation. All components of the system necessary to perform the desired mission (including facilities, equipment, personnel, and maintenance needs) should be included in the analysis.

(2) *Identification of Pertinent Measures of Effectiveness, ie., Benefits.* The mission for which alternatives are being considered should be translated into specific quantifiable evaluation criteria. Sufficient attention to this vital step is necessary to avoid selections based upon inadequate criteria. The "criterion problem" is a particularly difficult one in these studies because of the usually ill-defined nature of public programs. Generally, for public sector programs, there will be multiple impacts, and so multiple evaluation criteria are needed. In addition, to be comprehensive, the analysis should consider possible unintended effects as well as those intended, for example, pollution resulting from a transportation system or displacement of families resulting from a housing program.

(3) *Expression of Both Mission Performance and Cost as Functions of the Characteristics of Each Alternative.* A mathematical model is developed to reflect the major relationships. The model will consist of both cost and performance relationships. Where the analysis involves alternatives that are only in conceptual or preliminary design states, the major elements determining these relationships will be the physical or performance specifications of the system. The primary cost and performance tradeoffs should be derived from the model. The mathematical formulation of the model

may involve any of a number of quantitative techniques, such as computer simulation or mathematical programming.

(4) *Estimation of the Costs and Benefits for Each Alternative.* Using the mathematical relationships developed in Step (3), the analysts then make estimates of the benefits and costs of each alternative. In analyzing public programs, an additional complication arises. Most programs affect different groups of citizens in different ways. Some programs will benefit different age groups, or different income groups, differently. Some programs will affect residents of some geographic areas in special ways but not residents of other areas. And so on. It is, therefore, necessary also to assess the "distributional" effects of each alternative program being considered.

(5) *Valuation of the Benefits and Costs (for Cost-Benefit Analysis Only.)* Cost-benefit analysis requires that dollar values be assigned to the benefits. For some benefits, such as added revenues that may occur with some of the alternatives being examined, this is relatively easy; however, in most cases the dollar values of benefits of public goods are by no means clear. For example, the value of improvements in client health, employment, faster and safer travel, added recreational opportunities, and so on, are difficult to determine. Various methods of *imputing* values to such benefits have been used, such as estimating the change in earnings that families would incur if mortality or mobidity rates were reduced, or using travel costs as an estimate of the value of an added recreational opportunity. With the highly subjective and intangible nature of many benefits, such imputations must generally be treated with some skepticism. (For example, in the example given earlier, what about the value of extending the life of a retired person, with no added earning power? Surely it has value!)

(6) *Analysis and Presentation of Results.* For cost-benefit analyses, the time flow of the costs and monetarized benefits are generally translated into "present-values" using an appropriate "discount" rate—to reflect the time value of money. (See RETURN ON CAPITAL for a description of this procedure, which is common in private sector investment analysis as well as in cost-benefit analyses). For each alternative examined, the present value of the benefits can be compared to that of the costs, perhaps in the form of cost-benefit ratios.

For cost-effectiveness analysis, for each alternative, the values for each evaluation criteria (e.g., the estimated reduction in morbidity rates, or amount of reduction in travel time and number of persons affected) are displayed along with the estimated costs.

A highly simplified example of the outputs of a cost-effectiveness analysis is shown in Exhibit I. The problem in this hypothetical study is to select a system that will provide nationwide weather observations. The Government is interested in determining which system it should put into development to get the most for its money. (An industrial concern might perform such a study to determine which of the alternatives it should emphasize in its internal research and development activities.) The graph on the left in Exhibit I plots, for each of the three alternatives, total system cost against a single measure of effectiveness—the number of weather observations per week. Considerable information is provided even on such a simplified graph as this. First, the graph indicates for each effectiveness level (that is, for each number of achievable observations per week) which of the three systems is least costly and by approximately how much. Second, the graph can be used to indicate for any specified budgetary limitation, what levels of effectiveness can be achieved. Third, it indicates the cost penalties associated with choosing an alternative other than the low-cost system. This would be of interest if, as frequently happens, other factors not included quantitatively in the analysis need to be considered.

It must be recognized that in a realistic situation more than one effectiveness criterion will probably have to be considered. In addition, various considerations may be involved that are difficult to quantify. The quantitative information must, of course, be placed in a proper perspective with the over-all requirements of the decision maker's problem.

The graph on the right in Exhibit I indicates the manner in which each of the curves in the graph on the left might have been developed. In order to compare the three alternatives, it was necessary to determine for each alternative the "optimum" characteristics (that is, those characteristics that yield minimum cost) of the alternative for each effectiveness level. In this example, alternative No. 3 is a satellite system, and the satellite's weight is the primary characteristic that needs to be optimized. The graph

EXHIBIT I

RESULTS OF HYPOTHETICAL COST-EFFECTIVENESS ANALYSIS: SATELLITE WEATHER OBSERVATION SYSTEM

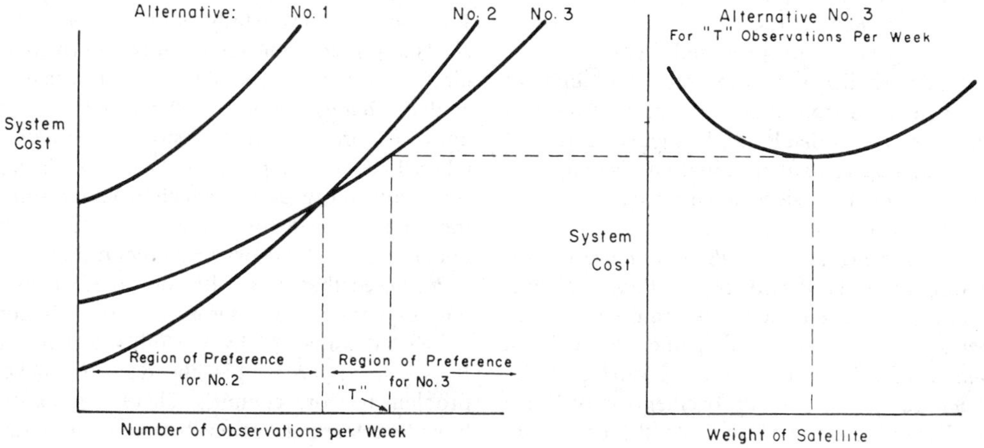

indicates the preferred (i.e., lowest cost) weight of the weather satellite of alternative No. 3 for one specified level of effectiveness.

Cost-benefit analysis has the advantage of greatly simplifying (at least on the surface) the decision-maker's choice: for each alternative, the output of the analysis is a cost-benefit ratio or is the difference between dollar benefits and dollar costs. The choice becomes simply a matter of choosing that alternative with the best cost-benefit value. In cost-effectiveness analysis, especially those analyses with multiple evaluation criteria, the product of an analysis is a display presenting the cost and the various values of the evaluation criteria for each alternative. It is left completely up to the decision-maker how to value the various criteria. The disadvantage of cost-benefit analysis is that this very simplicity can hide, or at least mask, the many assumptions and judgments used to impute monetary values to each evaluation criteria.

Major Applications. The information that can be obtained from these analyses has the following major uses:

(1) To aid decision makers, in situations where funds or other economic resources are a significant constraint, in making improved choices among alternative systems. (That is, information such as is indicated in the left graph of Exhibit I is provided.)

(2) To indicate the preferred characteristics of the alternative systems. (That is, the analysis, requires "sub-optimization" of the major characteristics of each alternative. In the example of Exhibit I, information was provided as to the preferred weight of the satellite.)

(3) To provide indications as to specific areas for further study or research in which funds might be applied to bring over-all system savings or to reduce critical areas of uncertainty. (For example, in the weather satellite illustration, the analytical results might indicate the over-all savings that would probably result from improved reliability of the major satellite components. The amount of such savings would suggest the magnitude of effort that could profitably be expended to improve component reliability.)

(4) To suggest, in certain situations, additional alternatives that would fare well in the face of the major difficulties of the examined alternatives and that, therefore, might be preferable.

(5) To indicate, for industrial users, the magnitude of the potential business for major components of the preferred system—at least, for specific effectiveness levels.

Subject Branchings. Two areas of special-technique development have been given impetus by cost-benefit and cost-effectiveness analysis: *cost analysis,* and *analysis of uncertainty.*

Cost Analysis. With dollar cost normally being used as one of the main selection criteria, accuracy in cost estimation becomes of considerable importance. Cost analysis, or cost estimation, has developed into a field, and perhaps a profession, of its own, especially for analyzing military weapon systems. Special techniques in addition to those traditionally used in corporate product cost estimating are needed. Some of the techniques in use are:

(1) *Statistical Regression Analysis.* For use in estimating costs for proposed items that are generally similar but have somewhat different characteristics from those on which direct cost experience is available. A distinctive feature of the resulting estimating equations is that they relate selected physical or performance characteristics of the item to cost.

(2) *Learning Curve Analysis.* For use in estimating future hardware costs in those instances where varying the quantity requirements appears likely to produce a significantly different *unit* cost. (The terms "learning curve," "progress curve," and "improvement curve" are used synonymously to indicate the cost-quantity relationship. The basic shape of this curve is generally represented as a downward sloping straight line where both the vertical and horizontal axes, representing respectively unit costs and cumulative quantity, are logarithmic scales.)

(3) *Engineering Analysis.* To provide the basic information for describing the cost-generating characteristics of any new or future components.

The primary concern of cost analysis is the development of relationships between a system's cost (to include research and development, investment, and operating costs as appropriate) and its physical and performance characteristics.

Analysis of Uncertainty. There are inherent uncertainties in the information and in the resulting data used in these analyses. Careful investigation may reduce this uncertainty somewhat, but can never eliminate it. Therefore, it appears desirable for decision makers to be aware of the approximate nature and magnitude of the uncertainties in order to evaluate the risks inherent in their decisions. Two approaches to this problem can be identified. The first is most frequently referred to as *sensitivity analysis.* In this approach, those equation parameters believed to be subject to the greatest uncertainty and to be of the most significance to the study are given more than one value. The calculations called for by the model are performed for each value of the parameter. The results indicate the sensitivity of the selection criteria to the value of the parameter. The computational problem, unfortunately, soon becomes great as more alternate values are examined. This greatly restricts the amount of sensitivity analysis that can be performed.

The effect of applying sensitivity analysis to a cost-effectiveness study is shown in Exhibit II. This presents the same study shown in Exhibit I, but with the addition of sensitivity analysis. Bands are now used rather than single lines to express the cost versus effectiveness relationships. The upper boundary of each band represents those events which would result in the most expensive conditions; the lower boundary, the least expensive conditions. It is to be noted that even with the range of uncertainties considered, alternative No. 1 is completely "dominated" by the other alternatives. It is also apparent that the decision maker's problem is more complex. There now exists a large overlapping region between alternatives No. 2 and No. 3. In addition to considering specific levels of effectiveness and cost, it is now also necessary to consider the likelihoods of the various conditions that determine the uncertainty.

It must be emphasized that the basic problem itself has not been made more complex. *Uncertainties that were always present have merely been explicitly and quantitatively expressed.* The complexity of the problem reflected in Exhibit II is probably much closer to

Exhibit II

A Cost-Effectiveness Analysis with sensitivity Analysis Applied: Weather Observation System

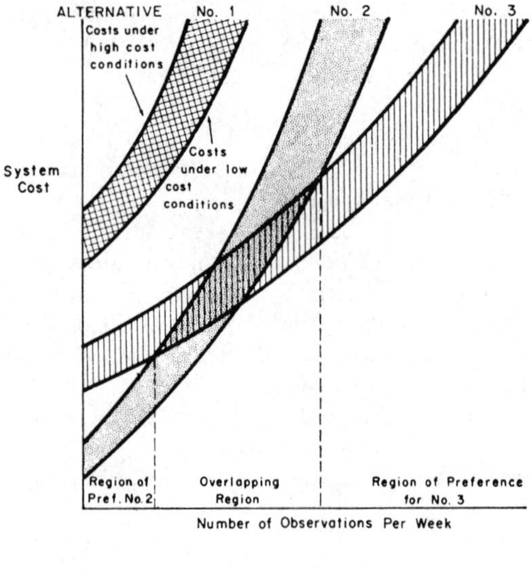

"reality" than the more simplified analysis of Exhibit I.

Exhibit II illustrates a primary consideration of cost-benefit and cost-effectiveness analysis—namely, to seek "dominant" solutions or, at least, solutions that are preferred over a wide range of possible conditions.

The second approach to analyzing uncertainty can be described by the term *subjective confidence limits.* This statistical technique serves to complement sensitivity analysis. Whereas sensitivity analysis indicates the impact of a change in the value of a parameter, it says nothing about the *likelihood* of occurrence of the various values. In the subjective confidence limits technique, the analyst provides a range of values for any parameter whose value is considered to be subject to significant uncertainty. These ranges of values are somewhat subjective, thereby giving rise to the use of the terms "subjective" in describing the procedure. The range of values for each such parameter is assumed to conform to a particular probability distribution. The statistical expected value and variance for each parameter can then be calculated and combined as called for by the equations of the model in order to estimate an expected value and variance for the total system. This is done for each alternative system to provide an expected value with confidence limits for each. This approach is similar to that used in PERT analyses in estimating the time requirements for a given network of activities.

Acceptance and Potential. The application of cost-benefit and cost-effectiveness analysts by industry and Government to assist in the evaluation of military and other Government-sponsored projects has been considerable. These approaches appear likely to continue to be used on a wide scale to help make choices of Federal programs. They are likely to gain more usage by state and local public agencies, especially as public agencies are increasingly required to justify their programs and as staff becomes more familiar, through education, with these approaches.

HARRY P. HATRY, Director, State and Local Government Research Program, The Urban Institute, Washington, D.C.

Information References

Dorfman, Robert, ed., "Measuring Benefits of Government Investment," Washington, D.C., The Brookings Institution, 1965.

Hatry, Blair, Fisk, and Kimmel, "Program Analysis for State and Local Governments," Washington, D.C., The Urban Institute, 1976.

Hitch, Charles J. and R. N. McKean, "The Economics of Defense in the Nuclear Age," Harvard University Press, 1960 (paperback ed. 1965).

McKean, R.N., "Efficiency in Government through Systems Analysis," New York, Wiley, 1958.

Mishan, E.J., "Cost-Benefit Analysis," New York, Praeger," 1976.

Quade, E.S., "Analysis for Public Decisions," New York, American Elsevier, 1975

Sassone, Peter G. and Schaffer, William A., "Cost-Benefit Analysis: A Handbook," New York, Academic Press, 1978.

Cross References: *Cost-Volume-Profit Analysis; Public Administration; Return on Capital.*

COST CONTROL

The term **Cost Control** as used in a larger and more general sense is applicable to all actions of management designed to accomplish objectives relative to the cost phase of profit maximization. In this context, then, cost control would embrace all activities designed to influence costs in planning and policy determination and costs applicable to all phases of operations management: research, production, marketing, and financial.

COST ACCOUNTING in this larger sense plays an active role in providing costs pertinent to contemplated policy moves, costs associated with plant expansion or contraction, and, at the operational level, providing cost data relative to special problems of management: inventory minimum order points, economic lot size, cost of auditing vendor invoices, costs of alternative wage incentive plans, cost of alternative capital investment decisions, and a host of other special problem and decision-requiring situations.

Formal Definition. Even though all of the above activities expedite control in a very real and fundamental sense, the term cost control as employed in cost accounting does not ordinarily refer to the foregoing, and is used in a more restricted fashion. Cost control as commonly used in cost accounting might better be called "performance control." It has to do with securing compliance with a prescribed plan or policy.

Approaches and Techniques. The term "cost control" is applied to a variety of techniques and procedures, including underlying concepts, employed by the accountant to assist management in achieving the cost phase of profit maximization at particular responsibility levels. Typically this methodology involves some form of cost comparison. Schiff and Benninger [1], in discussing the term "cost control," stress an analysis of cost by persons, provision of information concerning the manager's role relative to a plan or budget, the establishment of cost standards and the reporting of deviations thereof. Most writers on the subject present three phases of cost control: (1) comparison of present performance with predetermined standards; (2) taking corrective action if feasible; and (3) incorporation of the results of steps (1) and (2) into planning (utilization of cost feedback or cost "feedforward").

Use of departmental, process, or branch systems of cost accounting, particularly in connection with standard costs or budgets, epitomizes the service of cost accounting in furthering managerial cost control. Such systems premise control guidance upon a comparison of historically accumulated costs of an area of supervision with past, budgeted, or standard costs. Differences between historically accumulated costs and the benchmark chosen are studied as a guide to remedial action. In both FLEXIBLE BUDGETING and STANDARD COSTING, such differences play a major and positive role in directing individual efforts toward minimizing costs. Managerial incentive pay systems are sometimes premised upon the achievement of standard costs and the elimination of unfavorable variances.

Similar techniques are applied to accounting for company divisions in an effort to assure efficient divisional performance and control. Not only is control attempted by means of comparisons of costs with standards and budgets, but costs are matched against divisional revenues to secure a divisional profit and loss figure. Measurement of divisional income may be used as a basis of control, or, instead, the computation of rate of return on divisional investment may be attempted.

Divisional rates of return may be compared, one division to the other, or the rate of return may be compared with a separately constructed benchmark for each division. David Solomons presents a comprehensive discussion of divisional control techniques in his book "Divisional Performance: Measurement and Control" [2].

Human Relations Studies and Cost Control. As a consequence of behavioristic studies in business, a subtle but significant change has taken place in the prevailing philosophy of cost control, especially since 1960. Although such thinking has affected the mechanics of cost control, particularly in the establishment of accounts which cover a more carefully defined and delimited area of managerial responsibility, its most cogent effect has been in the area of account data utilization.

Construction of budgetary and cost standards in the new milieu are thought of more as phases of planning and are developed where feasible with the cooperation of the supervisor of the area to which the standards apply. The ideal is to have the manager set his *own* goals within the framework of the broader company objectives, with the hope that he will develop a feeling of responsibility for achieving them. When budgets or standards are not achieved, the comparisons carry less the connotation of the odious and more of the need to study and explain changes which have affected their achievement. (See RESPONSIBILITY REPORTING.) Thus the thrust of this approach is to substitute the more positive profit-generating goals and measures for the psychologically negative cost incentives and controls traditionally applied to production executives and supervisors.

L. J. BENNINGER, PH.D., Professor Emeritus of Accounting, University of Florida, Gainesville, Florida

References Cited

[1] Schiff, Michael and Benninger, L. J., "Cost Accounting," 2nd ed., New York, Ronald Press, 1963.

[2] Solomons, David, "Divisional Performance: Measurement and Control," New York, Financial Executives Research Foundation, 1965.

Cross References: *Cost Accounting (and cross references there given).*

COST OF LIVING. SEE PRICES: STATISTICS.

COST-VOLUME-PROFIT ANALYSIS

Cost-Volume-Profit Analysis is a microeconomic technique used for measuring the functional relationships between the major factors affecting profits, and for determining the profit structure of the firm. The basic methodology involved is fundamental to the use of financial data to guide managerial decision-making in a wide variety of business situation.

Fixed and Variable Costs. An understanding of cost-volume-profit relationships is predicated upon the acceptance of certain basic concepts of cost behavior regarding the manner in which costs respond to changing volume. Some costs vary quite closely with changes in volume whereas others remain unchanged in total amount regardless of changes in rate of activity. Costs which vary with volume are ordinarily called *variable costs* while those costs which do not vary with volume are called *fixed costs.* Inherently, costs are neither fixed nor variable, but acquire such characteristics as a result of management policies and decisions. They are classified as "fixed" or "variable" for analytical purposes.

Typically, fixed costs originate from the provision of capacity in readiness to do business, and in the short run they tend to remain constant in total amount irrespective of fluctuations in production or sales volume. Since such costs are fixed for a given period of time they are also termed *period, standby,* or *capacity* costs. Rent, depreciation, property taxes, insurance, and the salaries of key executive and supervisory personnel, are all typical examples of fixed costs. Conversely, the variable costs usually represent the factors of cost which increase or decrease proportionately with actual volume of production or sales. Usually raw materials and certain kinds of labor, supplies, and services are variable costs (also called *direct costs*), because the amount of total cost varies directly with volume of activity. (See DIRECT COSTING.)

In analyzing cost-volume-profit relationships, the first step is to study the behavior of costs under conditions of changing volume, and to divide costs into fixed and variable components. The next step is to determine the total amount of fixed cost and the rates at which variable costs and profit change in response to volume. Within the context of given conditions, these figures are constants, and together they describe the profit structure of the company and measure the functional relationships between costs, volume, and profit.

Volume is a key factor in profit planning, because most managerial decisions are affected, in part at least, by the changes in costs and sales income which accompany changes in volume. Therefore cost-volume-profit analysis is a highly useful management technique for studying business problems, and has many practical applications in connection with planning and control. The information derived from this type of analysis provides a suitable basis both for projecting profits under alternative proposed combinations of costs and volumes, and also for evaluating the profit consequences of alternative decisions. In particular, the principles of cost-volume-profit relationships have been implicitly accepted and systematically applied in connection with direct costing, profit planning, break-even analysis, marginal analysis, flexible budgeting, and pricing policy.

Marginal Analysis. Derived from economic theory, marginal analysis is an analytical technique for measuring the financial consequences of a given action. For the purposes of marginal analysis, only those cost and revenue elements affected by the action are considered: all others are irrelevant and therefore excluded. What matters here are only the amounts of change in the totals of these elements, i.e., the difference or increments to total cost or revenue that stem from the action. For this reason the technique has also been termed *incremental cost (or profit) analysis, differential cost (or profit) analysis,* or *marginal cost (or income) analysis.* Irrespective of the term used, the concept is the same: namely, to identify and quantify the financial effect of the action or forward decision. This analysis can be applied to a variety of situations, involving either past or future actions. However, it is most commonly used in industry in connection with profit planning and for guiding managerial decision-making involving alternative choices.

Some typical applications requiring the evaluation of alternative courses of action and the measurement of potential results include:

(1) Make-or-buy decisions.
(2) Capital investment decisions.
(3) Product-mix problems.
(4) Adding or deleting a product.
(5) Expanding or contracting sales volume.
(6) Pricing decisions.

It should be remembered that while marginal analysis does represent a considerable advance in the methodology of modern management, it should not be treated as the sole and infallible basis for decision making. While it provides a reliable means for measuring and comparing the economic worth of proposed projects, or alternative courses of action, there are often other important factors which management must take into consideration before reaching a decision. Since some factors, such as public relations, customer good will, or risk, are seldom susceptible to accurate measurement, the results of the analysis should be used with sophistication. (See also OPERATING MARGIN ANALYSIS.)

Break-Even Analysis. This is a technique of financial analysis for investigating the functional relationships between the rate of activity and costs, revenue, and profits. Specifically, BREAK-EVEN ANALYSIS focuses attention on an-

EXHIBIT I

BREAK-EVEN CHART

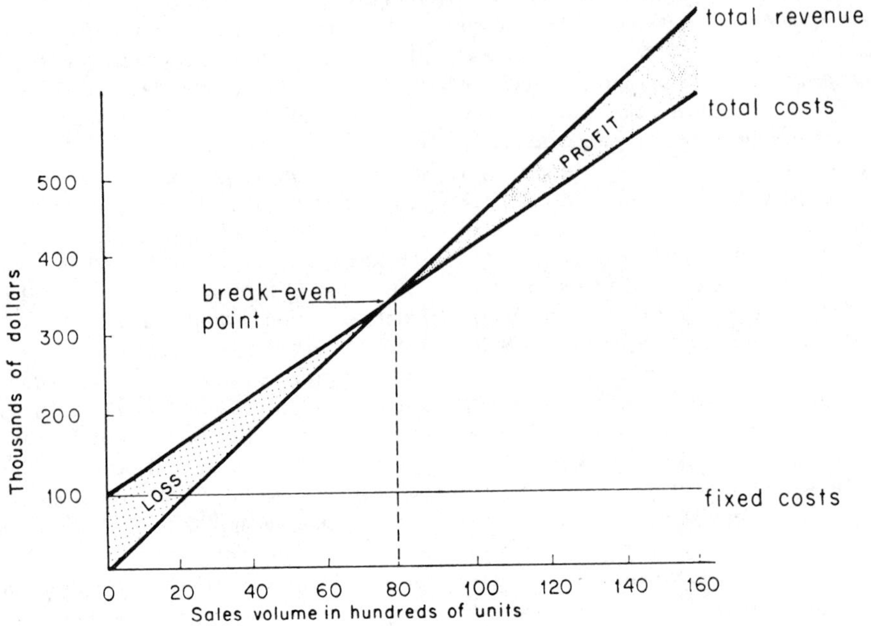

ticipated profit behavior in response to changes in underlying conditions by predicting the profit consequences of changes in sales volume, rate of output, selling prices, or product costs, etc.

A specialized form of profit graph, called the break-even chart, is frequently used to present diagrammatically significant cost-volume-profit relationships; relating total costs at various sales volumes to the expected revenue and profit (or loss) at each alternative volume. The break-even chart is also used for determining the break-even point. Since the break-even point identifies the volume of activity where revenue exactly equals total costs, both fixed and variable, it thus indicates that combination of sales (i.e., the volume) at which operations "break even" and yield neither a profit nor a loss. At sales levels below the break-even point, operations will result in a loss; and above this point they will contribute profits; as illustrated in Exhibit I.

The chart has been known to accountants for a long time prior to widespread discussions in industrial engineering and manufacturing-management literature, as evidenced by the appearance of an illustration and an explanation of methods for preparing such a chart in the "Encyclopedia of Accounting" edited by George Lisle and published in Edinburgh and London in 1904.

Knowledge of the break-even point and the underlying functional relationships between costs, volume and profit is particularly useful for the purposes of profit forecasting and planning. Some typical managerial application of this technique would include:

(1) Predicting profits at alternative sales volumes.

(2) Predicting costs and revenues at alternative levels of output.

(3) Measuring the effect of price changes on total profit.

(4) Measuring the effect on total profit of changes in product-mix.

(5) Measuring the effect of cost changes on break-even point.

(a) Changes in amount of total fixed cost (e.g., increasing advertising expenditures from $1,000,000 to $1,500,000).

(b) Changes in unit variable cost (e.g., increase in the unit cost of labor).

JOHN D. SIMMONS, Financial Consultant, New York, New York.

Information References

"The Analysis of Cost-Volume-Profit Relationships," Research Reports 16-17-18, New York, National Association of Accountants, 1950.

Cohen, Jerome B. and Robbins, Sidney M., "The Financial Manager," Ch. 5, pp. 160–191, New York, Harper & Row, 1966.

Livingston, John Leslie, "Management Planning and Control: Mathematical Models," Ch. 3, pp. 280–435, New York, McGraw-Hill, 1970.

"Managerial and Cost Accountants Handbook," Black and Edwards, eds., Ch. 1, "Concepts of Cost"; and Ch. 2, "Cost Components and Cost Behavior," Homewood, Ill., Dow-Jones-Irwin, 1979.

Moore, Brian and Talbot, John, "An Application of Cost-Volume-Profit Analysis," *Cost and Management,* March-April, 1978.

Richardson, A.W., "Some Extensions in the Application of Cost-Volume-Profit Analysis," *Cost and Management,* September-October, 1978.

Riggs, James L., "Economic Decision Models for Engineers and Managers," Ch. 2, pp. 41–81, New York, McGraw-Hill, 1968.

Cross References: *Break-Even Analysis (and cross references there given).*

CREATIVITY TRAINING

Formal programs for **Creativity Training** to enhance creative thinking by employees have been reported by such companies, as General Motors, Dow Chemical, Bell Telephone, B.F. Goodrich, and Eastman Kodak; and courses in creativity have been organized in such institutions as Battelle Memorial Institute, California State College at Long Beach, Xavier University, Cincinnati, and the U.S. Army Management School at Fort Belvoir.

In addition, innovative behavior is emphasized in the MANAGERIAL GRID and organizational development programs of many companies, as well as in creativity seminars offered by such organizations as the American Chemical Society and the American Management Association.

Synectics, a specialized technique for group creativity, has recently come to the fore, and training in synectics leadership is offered on a fee basis. In this method, as described by Prince [1], the leader guides the group along a tenuous trail from the problem area to an entirely different "world," for example, the "world" of microbiology, the "world" of professional football, or the "world" of modern tribal customs. Extensive material, developed on the framework of analogies in the new world area, is then force-fitted back to the problem to suggest unusual avenues of solution.

An early effort in creativity training is that of the General Electric Company, initiated in 1937. Men showing creative promise during the first months of employment have had the opportunity to join the company's creative engineering group. The methods of this group have been described by its leaders in the *General Electric Review* and elsewhere. Throughout the course, both theoretical and practical aspects are emphasized. In the first six months, creative theory is presented. Homework problems deal with engineering fundamentals, with design questions of interest to the company, and with specific model work.

The curriculum as it has existed in recent years at G.E. may be cited as a general pattern where training is to be done in depth:

(1) *Orientation.* Course administration and history, policy, procedures, facilities.

(2) *Creative philosophy.* Using Osborn's "Applied Imagination," plus lectures and reading, students see, hear, practice idea-building.

(3) *Engineering fundamentals.* Emphasis on physical laws of engineering, empirical equations, electronics, measurements, and control systems.

(4) *Unusual materials and processes.* Experts tell students about such things as radioisotopes and nucleonics so that these factors may be included in idea creation.

(5) *Useful basic components and devices.* Knowing how certain devices work (like thyratrons, thermistors) broadens the brain storehouse.

(6) *Company services and organizations.* This tells how to use staff assistance from the patent, purchasing, and traffic departments.

(7) *Presentation of ideas.* "One of the weakest points of young engineers is their inability to describe effectively and to sell ideas, whether in writing or orally." This course gives practice in this area.

(8) *Human relations.* An understanding of human relations and some of the techniques of handling people are woven into the course.

(9) *Homework problems.* About fifteen to twenty hours of each week. Aim is to get at least eight workable solutions to each problem presented.

(10) *Model-building project.* This five-week project completes the first phase of the course. In a way, it is like a thesis for a master's degree.

In the second phase of the course, lasting eighteen months, the development of ideas to final form is studied and practiced, according to this sequence:

Recognize
Define
Search
Evaluate

Select
Make preliminary design
Test and evaluate

Follow through.

There is constant association on the job with creative senior engineers. Emphasized are such tenets as, get eight solutions to the problem; use the input-output technique.

The "input-output technique" puts the problem in the form of a dynamic system comprising input, output, and specifications. These are generalized, and questions are asked about all three in such a way as to suggest variant approaches to answers. As an example, if an improved electric clothes dryer is the problem, the input is electricity, the output dry clothes; or by finer analysis, the input is electric heat, the output is evaporated water, or water vapor. The specifications are according to the objective, which might be a faster machine. Can the output solve the problem directly? Let the evolved water vapor be conducted over an indicator which switches the machine off when the vapor reaches a predetermined low concentration. Thus, in this method, the output is utilized as a new input aimed toward the specified objective.

In a creativity program developed by AC Spark Plug Company, the trainee is tested, then given the creativity course, then tested again. In the creativity test, the person has 80 minutes to answer twenty-five questions split into five groups, including the familiar "uses or improvement of a common object," or the "consequences of a described situation." The subsequent course includes:

History and objectives.
Judicial vs. creative thinking.
Factors affecting creativity.
Factors promoting or inhibiting creativity.
Training the mind to think.
Gathering data and developing hypotheses.
Restating the problem and rectifying.
Effect of effort, motivation.
Values in self-questioning.
Supervising creative people.
Review.
Re-test with new questions.

The program also uses Osborn's book, "Applied Imagination," for its stimulation and training exercises. The dual purposes are to maximize creativeness in the employees taking the course, and identify extra-creative participants. These persons are then judiciously distributed through the organization to catalyze progress on all fronts; some of them can be concentrated where progress has been stalled, or a break-through is needed.

Results. For AC Spark Plug, the average increase in total number of ideas was 40%. For GE, after training, participants averaged over double the number of patents of those who had not had the same training; and they won more than a proportional share of company awards for individual contributions. (But it is necessary to point out that they were also preselected for creative ability.)

University Courses. Many universities offer courses in creative thinking. One of the earliest was Professor John Arnold's at MIT. Students learn the basics of creativity, with emphasis on the different kinds of blocks to creativity. As indicative of the imaginative approach used, students in one class designed equipment for the hypothetical Methnanian people of a cold, heavy planet near Arcturus. This was described in *Astounding Science Fiction,* May 1953:

> Arturus IV is the fourth planet out from the sun α Bootis (Arcturus), 33 light-years from our solar system. It was first contacted by a member of the Solar and Galactic Explorers' Union on January 22, 2951. It is a large planet, 12×10^6 meters in diameter, having a mass of 60×10^{27} grams, and the acceleration of gravity at the surface is 11,000 centimeters per second squared. It is a distance of $1{,}800 \times 10^6$ miles from α Bootis and its sidereal period is 49.4 Earth-years. The length of day is 159 hours; the atmosphere is largely methane; and the mean temperatures range from $-50°$ C in the summer to $-110°$ C in the winter.

A program developed at Rutgers University contained features of special interest for group creativity: instruction and practice in basic research techniques; the creative process and its mental blocks and how to overcome them; and a group problem. As an example, one class chose solar energy. They subdivided this, and assigned segments to class members on the basis of individual skills. The intention was to read, think, confer, and fuse all experience toward solution.

Other courses have been based on the view of creativity as developed, in each case, by the professor, in his own text. Early examples were those by C. E. Gregory at California State College [2] and J. W. Haefele at Xavier University [3]. The aim of such courses is to present the theoretical basis of the creative process, and to utilize practical exercises in individual and group development of problem situations.

As of 1980, the Creative Education Foundation of the State University College at Buffalo, New York offered full-week seminars to teach and study creativity four times a year in different areas of the United States. The most important meeting is the Creative Problem Solving Institute held in Buffalo each year in June.

JOHN W. HAEFELE, PHD, formerly Research Scientist, Procter & Gamble Company, Cincinnati, Ohio

Information References

Barron, Frank, "The Creative Person and the Creative Process," New York, Holt, Rinehart & Winston, 1969.

Clark, Charles H., "The Crawford Slip Writing Method," 1978, and "How to Brainstorm for Profitable Ideas," 1966, Kent, Ohio, Yankee Ingenuity Programs.

Clark, Charles H., "Idea Management: How to Motivate Creativity and Innovation," New York, AMACOM Div., American Management Associations, 1980.

Haefele, John W., "Creativity and Innovation," New York, Van Nostrand Reinhold, 1962.

Osborn, Alex, "Applied Imagination," New York, Scribner's, 1957.

Articles in *The Journal of Creative Behavior,* State University College at Buffalo, N.Y.

References Cited

[1] Prince, George M., "Practice of Creativity: A Manual for Dynamic Group Problem Solving," New York, Harper & Row, 1970.

[2] Gregory, Carl E., "The Management of Intelligence," New York, McGraw-Hill, 1967.

[3] Haefele, John W., "Creativity and Innovation," New York, Van Nostrand Reinhold, 1962.

Cross References: *Basic Research: Management Aspects; Brainstorming; Innovation: The Management of Change; Technological Forecasting.*

CREDIT BUREAUS

Credit Bureaus are business service organizations which fill a specific need for retail and professional persons in their trade areas. They also benefit consumers who are able to obtain credit privileges rapidly and efficiently. The primary function of a credit bureau is to gather, assemble, file and report credit history and facts on individuals in order to assist credit grantors in determining the worthiness of consumers who apply for credit.

More specifically, credit bureaus can be described as business organizations that systematically collect and file identification data (name, social security number, address, etc.), pay habits (whether payments are current in the time period reviewed by other creditors), and public record (civil judgments, bankruptcy filing, etc.). Factual, impartial reports are then available to credit grantors who have a business need for such information.

History. In 1803, the very first "credit bureau" was organized by merchant tailors in London. Fifty-seven years later, the idea came to the United States and a bureau was formed in Brooklyn, New York. From these modest beginnings grew an industry which serves credit grantors and consumers throughout most of the free world.

Practice. The consumer credit system is based on the theory that the majority of consumers are responsible individuals who can be sold the goods and services they need today on their promise to pay tomorrow. That this is correct is borne out by statistics which reveal that approximately 70% of credit users will pay promptly. Another 25% will become slow-payers, and will require some follow-up activity. Of the remaining 5%, some may eventually pay, but many will never pay at all.

Credit grantors are interested in making profitable credit sales and holding credit losses to a minimum. Since losses due to extension of credit to consumers who do not pay must be passed on to all consumers by increasing the price of goods or services, it is in the public interest that credit grantors have a reliable, unbiased central source for the credit history of applicants.

The Fair Credit Reporting Act, which became law in 1971, governs the operation of all consumer credit bureaus. It requires, among other things, that credit grantors certify that they have a permissible purpose for each credit report they obtain. These purposes are listed in the law. In order to ensure that all the requirements of the Federal law are observed, credit bureaus in the United States require a contractual agreement with each credit grantor before they will furnish reports.

The bureau gathers its information from several sources. Information on paying habits is secured from credit grantors who furnish the data. Some creditors generally provide information only in response to a specific request. For example, the credit bureau in a small town may call a tire store, state that a consumer has given it as a credit reference, and ask how payments were made. Computerized credit bureaus have the capability of being able to accept complete accounts receivable tapes from automated credit grantors. Credit bureaus which are members of the trade association, Associated Credit Bureaus, Inc., have access to the data of many national and regional credit grantors through ACB's Trade Verification System. Data are processed by zip code and made available in tapes or in a format that non-automated bureaus can use.

Employment information is verified by contacting the consumer credit applicant's employer when requested to do so by the credit grantor. Public record information is obtained from the courthouse records and district courts. Bureaus generally obtain data regarding civil court judgments, divorce actions, tax liens, and bankruptcy filings. Some bureaus gather real estate data, chattel mortgages, marriage license filings, and other data affecting a person's ability to pay.

The information is held in strict confidence in compliance with the Fair Credit Reporting Act. This law also gives consumers the right to learn the nature and substance of all information about them on file in a credit bureau. Consumers also have the right to dispute data and request that they be re-checked. Credit bureaus are required by law to interview consumers about their files and to provide trained personnel to conduct these interviews.

Each individual file, whether on a computer or in a file jacket in a manual bureau, contains only items that are pertinent to his or her credit history. Every entry must be of the type that can be verified by documentation somewhere. This may be a creditor's ledger, an employer's records, or a file in the county clerk's office. Credit bureau files may contain no hearsay or statements of opinion. Adverse information is reported only as long as permitted by the Fair Credit Reporting Act (generally seven years) or a lesser time, if the bureau management chooses.

Credit reports are furnished in several ways. Computerized credit bureaus offer their largest credit grantor users the privilege of installing a terminal in their offices so reports may be produced quickly. Security safeguards are built into such arrangements to ensure that reports are drawn only for authorized reasons. Oral reports, read from the bureau's terminal or from the manual file in a non-automated bureau, comprise the bulk of reports furnished. Typewritten reports or "hard copies" from computers are produced when the credit grantor has a need for a permanent record of the report, such as home mortgage loan and car purchase applications.

In 1977, Associated Credit Bureaus, Inc., in cooperation with major credit grantors, developed a new format for the standard written report. Its purpose was to provide a format that was objective, factual, and easy to understand. In addition, the Equal Credit Opportunity Act had imposed new requirements on credit reports used by credit grantors as to the designation of responsibility for each account. All this was developed into a format known as "Crediscope," which replaced a format that was less objective.

In addition to providing reports on a local level, ACB member credit bureaus exchange information upon request for two purposes: (1) to transfer the credit records of individuals who apply for charge accounts in other communities, and (2) to transfer the credit records of those who move to other communities. To facilitate this exchange, the ACB Inter-Bureau Reporting System was founded in 1906. The majority of credit bureaus in the United States are members of Associated Credit Bureaus, Inc., an international trade association.

John L. Spafford, President, Associated Credit Bureaus, Inc., Houston, Texas

Information References

Associations:

Associated Credit Bureaus, Inc. (publishes the bimonthly, *Management*).

International Consumer Credit Association (publishes the monthly, *Credit World*).

Texts:

"Credit Management Year Book" (annual editions), New York, Credit Management Division, National Retail Merchants Association.

Cole, Robert H., and Hancock, Robert S., "Consumer and Commercial Credit Management," Homewood, Ill., Irwin, 6th ed., 1980.

Cross References: *Collection Services; Credit Management; Credit Reporting.*

CREDIT MANAGEMENT

Credit Management is one of the most crucial areas of financial management, for it controls the equivalent of company assets which are made temporarily available to outside interests. The credit manager must integrate internal financial policy and company profit planning with market strategy, the sales effort, and customer development.

It has become a business aphorism that no sale is complete until the money has been collected. The sale itself is only half of the transaction. The credit manager's job is to complete it, by a variety of special techniques and skills, and within a company credit policy which credit management determines, together with the company's other policy-making executives.

Definition. Credit involves three components: an exchange of values, futurity, and trust. It is usually defined as the ability of an individual or enterprise to obtain economic value, on faith, in return for an expected payment of equivalent economic value, usually at some specified future time.

Short-term credit extended by suppliers to commercial buyers for the purchase of goods or services is known as *commercial, trade,* or *business* credit. A high proportion of outstanding trade credit is *open-book credit,* appearing as purchase orders and sales invoices. Mutual trust and successful experience are the basis of the wide use and current availability of open-book credit, the primary concern of credit management in business.

Scope of Credit Management. Credit transactions, in some form, have probably been a business practice since men first did business with each other. Credit has certainly been part of the American business scene since the early colonists. The Plymouth settlement was financed by a seven-year loan from London merchants. Credit, in part, financed the American Revolution, the extension of the frontier, and later, the nation's industrial growth.

But since World War II, business credit management has become a more precise and imaginative managerial tool for fiscal control, market expansion, customer development, and profit building. Like other business functions, it has changed with the impact of automation and the forces of an increasingly competitive and expanding market.

Credit is a dynamic force in the total business economy. Analysis of U.S. Department of Commerce data indicates that approximately 90% of manufacturing sales, and more than 92% of wholesale sales are credit rather than cash transactions.

Although often overlooked, commercial credit is of immense importance to the economy. At midyear, 1980, the volume of trade accounts receivable outstanding amounted to $464.2 billion. This total, which was for all corporations (except banks and insurance companies), considerably surpassed the volume of consumer credit (excluding home mortgages) of $402.3 billion. That businesses rely heavily upon commercial credit for much of their financing is pointed up by the fact that commercial and industrial loans outstanding in our nation's banks in the second quarter of 1980 amounted to $256.8 billion. Commercial credit is much more widely used than bank credit. Almost every business depends to some extent on commercial credit to meet its needs.

In recent years the growth of commercial credit has been remarkable. It has grown by 70% since 1975. This matches the 33% increase in commercial and industrial loans at banks during the same period.

During recent years manufacturers have invested greater amounts of funds in their receivables as they have extended ever more credit to meet competitive conditions. In many companies, particularly smaller ones, receivables are now the largest single concentration of assets. In the second quarter of 1980, receivables of manufacturers accounted for 17.2% of all corporate assets, but in small companies they accounted for a much larger share. For instance, in manufacturing companies with assets $250 million to $1 billion, receivables were 19.5% of total assets in the second quarter of 1980, while for manufacturers with assets under $5 million, the comparable figure was 27.8%. Small companies rely a great deal upon their suppliers for financing.

Credit Responsibility. The credit management function is handled at a variety of management levels, usually depending on the size of the company. An analysis of the membership of the 44,000-member National Association of Credit Management indicates that 23.5% of those charged with credit responsibility carry the title of President, Owner, Partner, or Vice President. General Managers and other titled officers account for 15.8% and credit managers for 41.4%. In other companies the credit function is sometimes handled by the controller, the office manager, and the branch manager, among others.

Policies. Four basic, alternative credit policies are available to business, individually determined in relation to company goals and such specific factors as market, business function, size, and the current state of the economy:

(1) A liberal credit policy with a liberal collection policy.

(2) A liberal credit policy with collection strictly enforced.

(3) A strict credit policy with a liberal collection policy.

(4) A strict credit policy with a strict collection policy.

The first policy offers the advantage of savings in credit administration costs. But it might result in bad debts and slow collections that would more than offset the savings. Few companies would find this policy profitable, but might institute it to attract customers, providing that profit margins could be set high enough to offset potential loss.

A liberal credit policy with strict collection enforcement fills all customer orders but closely follows up on payments. This type of policy is most common in lines which sell relatively small orders of high mark-up, low unit-price goods. Analysis costs are low. But collection costs may be unusually high.

A strict credit policy with a liberal collection policy concentrates on pre-selecting customers who will be good credit risks, but does not exert pressure for payment. This policy assumes that carefully picked customers will tend to pay their bills within or close to terms.

A strict credit and strict collection policy goes one step farther. It pre-selects the most desirable credit accounts, and strictly enforces payment terms. Bad debt losses are minimized. But the detailed analysis of customer risk is expensive, as is the administration of collection effort. Sales potential may also be curtailed.

In practice, most companies will establish credit policies that mix these elements, and will periodically subject any policy to scrutiny in terms of current marketing strategy, economic and industry conditions, and company objectives.

The credit executive's primary function is to maintain the company's cash flow within the company's realistic financial expectations. He does this by checking prospective customers to be sure that they will pay on time, or by calculating the area of marginal risk in which sales can be profitably made.

Successfully selling this "calculated risk" area of business, for most companies, spells the difference between loss or gain at the close of the fiscal year. Most companies must rely on some marginal accounts for business. It is particularly in this vital area that skilled credit strategy can and does materially contribute to company profits.

Collections. The best-planned managerial strategy, judgment, and control cannot provide for every eventuality. Sometimes customers don't pay, won't pay, or can't pay. The collection effort, under such circumstances, then becomes of vital importance to both company profits and customer goodwill. In a company operating on a net profit of 5% of sales, it will take $2,000 in new sales to recoup a single charge-off of $100 (omitting the tax factor).

It is normal practice for the Credit Department to be responsible, as well, for the collection function. This becomes a full-time specialization whenever the volume of accounts is large enough to warrant it.

The Sales Department should be informed of the collection effort, since Sales has made the initial contact with the account, and continues this contact through further placement of orders. In some companies, salesmen assist in the collection effort; in others, they are asked to make initial collection contact with a delinquent account, then delegate the later follow up to the Credit Department or collection specialist. In a large company, collections may be the responsibility of the Accounts Receivable Department. This department is the first to know when an account becomes past due. Notification can be made immediately to the Credit Department, treasurer, and other concerned.

Collection techniques are a highly detailed area of special knowledge and skill. From top management's point of view, the results of the many specialized procedures are what count: (1) the collection of delinquent money in full, if possible, (2) the maximum possible collection of money from problem accounts, businesses in difficulty, or bankruptcies, and (3) the maintenance of continued customer goodwill.

Through its collection and credit analysis functions, the Credit Department becomes a major source of information on the company's customers. In the postwar years, practical and imaginative use has increasingly been made of these resources.

To make initial credit approval, the Credit Department has collected customer data directly from the customers themselves or from outside sources such as banks, commercial credit reporting agencies, credit association industry credit groups, and trade payment data interchange services.

Credit records on the customer usually include such minimum essentials as: business history and method of operation, the customer's financial statement and profit-and-loss statement, the amount the customer owes, what and when he has bought, when payments are due, the names of delinquent accounts (with amount and length of time past due), and his payment record among other suppliers.

This information is available to the company for customer analysis and sales research. Particularly in companies with electronic data processing facilities, it is possible to analyze sales by territory size, customer characteristics and demand, customer quality and potential, and market penetration, to name some of the areas to which credit departments now can and do contribute.

In recent years, Credit Management and Sales Management have coordinated their efforts more closely. The credit manager may conduct a credit orientation for the sales staff. If each salesman clearly understands the type of credit accounts that the company considers desirable and that have proved profitable, sales time can be allotted more productively. Accounts which would yield little profit potential can be by-passed, and more time spent on selling the higher-potential, higher-profit customers. Pre-analysis of prospects can be a productive sales function of the Credit Department.

Personnel. The development of qualified credit management personnel will improve the company's chances of realizing the full potential of the Credit Department. Many of the qualifications are, of course, technical, and can be developed at the credit subordinate level through in-company training programs, outside workshops, executive development courses, and college training. Educational programs of this kind are readily available to every company from the National Association of Credit Management through the correspondence courses of its National Institute of Credit and its Graduate School of Credit and Financial Management, as well as directly from schools and universities when the company is located in areas where these are available.

Technical qualifications for credit management include knowledge of financial analysis, commercial laws under which credit functions, and such usual general management requirements as skill in human relations, organizational ability, and communication techniques.

Research among successful credit executives indicates that personal requirements include: (1) initiative, adaptability, and resourcefulness in meeting new situations; (2) emotional stability to handle customer and internal relations diplomatically and firmly when required; (3) ability to analyze problems thoroughly and constructively; (4) perseverance in handling difficult situations; (5) ingenuity in developing confidential information; (6) fairness in dealing with people; (7) ability to absorb and retain details; and (8) a willingness to take considered risks for profitable company growth and development of sales potential.

Performance and Yardsticks. The credit executive's role as financial counselor has had increasing emphasis in recent years. Wise counseling helps strengthen new businesses or those whose condition may have become precarious. He is uniquely qualified to provide financial advice. He knows intimately the financial pattern of many other customers in similar lines of business. Often he has made or obtained operating ratios of the industry. He sees financial trends immediately reflected in the credit department's operation areas, and may recognize these before customers do. In many businesses today, competitive products and services are relatively equal in price and quality, and such personal service as customer counseling can become the deciding factor in the continuance of the seller-customer relationship.

Credit departments share in the preparation of cash flow forecasts through periodic estimates of cash collections from receivables. EDP equipment also enlarges the applications of Credit Department data to over-all company operational analysis and profit planning. Simulation techniques, for example, can project the probable effects of altered selling terms and cash flow, in relationship to such areas as warehousing, distribution, and production scheduling. The results of revisions in basic credit policy can be more precisely predicted in terms of their over-all effect on the dynamics of total company operations.

The effectiveness of the Credit Department is difficult to measure. A number of indices are used by management, of which the principal ones may be listed as follows:

Number of accounts offers an absolute measure, with annual comparisons yielding a rough measure of the company's credit business potential.

Total accounts receivable may be compared with prior years to indicate the extent and pattern of the company's accounts receivable investment.

Volume of credit sales is an indicator of the volume of business approved by the Credit Department.

Total collections, depending on the volume and speed of collections, may reveal a change in the company's financial position.

Proportion of inactive to total accounts may be a measure of the marketing effort and be used to identify, through periodic review, desirable sources of business for sales effort.

Rejection percentage is a ratio of disapproved accounts against total credit applications within any given period, and can indicate the effects of a strict vs. liberal credit policy.

Customer turnover reflects the rate at which customers change, and may lead to a reappraisal of credit and sales policies.

Delinquency percentage, computable in either dollars or numbers of accounts, can be used to analyze the concentration or size of delinquent accounts.

Aging of receivables, by length of time overdue (usually 30, 60, 90 days or more), discloses accounts requiring further review and follow-up.

Average collection period is useful as a complementary indicator in conjunction with the other measures.

Collection percentage is a proportion between amounts collected and amount outstanding during the month, and serves as a composite gauge of changes in the above three measures.

Bad debt loss percentage, for any given period, can be used to check the results of a liberal vs. a strict credit policy and to review the policy in relation to sales objectives.

ROBERT D. GOODWIN, Executive Vice President
National Association of Credit Management,
New York, New York

Information References

"Credit Management Handbook," compiled by National Association of Credit Management, 1981.

"Credit Manual of Commercial Laws," published annually by NACM since 1908.

Credit and Financial Management (monthly).

Many research and other publications, available from the National Association of Credit Management, New York.

Cross References: *Collection Services; Credit Bureaus; Credit Reporting; Financial Ratios.*

CREDIT REPORTING

Credit Reporting agencies provide to business and industry the information needed to reach credit, sales, financial, and general management decisions.

The seller can make his own inquiry. He can talk with people who know the prospective buyer, examine records to determine whether there are any liens or whether assets are pledged, and even go to the buyer himself and ask for figures which will show his financial condition. However, as business has become more complex, sellers have found it quite expensive to make their own investigations. If for example an apparel retailer in Texas orders $300 worth of goods from a New York manufacturer, it becomes prohibitive in cost for the latter to make inquiries at such a distant point, without some form of clearing house for information. Buyers would thus be restricted to purchasing in their own limited areas where they are known. This prompted the establishment of agencies to gather and supply the required information.

Development of Reporting Agencies. Credit reporting in the United States received its first impetus in the economic dislocations of the 1830s. Granting credits in those days was a haphazard procedure, and most risks were accepted on a strictly personal assay of character. A trader from the West carried letters of reference from the local banker or clergyman, and his purchases were often limited to the one source of supply where he was known. Terms, nominally at six months, often ran from eighteen months to two years.

It was a period of wasteful plenty, until the demand of the Jackson administration for specie payment on Government lands brought with it a severe punishment of guilty and innocent alike. The withdrawal of specie from normal channels of trade and collapse of the entire banking structure of the country left business prostrate. Lack of a supported money and the resultant lack of credit robbed the axles of trade of an indispensable lubricant. The Government's cure for the mania of land speculation was almost as ruinous as the disease. Small retailers were reduced to the ancient device of barter, and commerce stood still, at least for a year or two, until credit once more relaxed.

Continental practices based on the personal relationship of buyer and seller were outmoded. Business in a vast, expanding nation needed a new framework, one suited to its problems of geography, communication, and climate. Certain wholesale merchants, seeing the frailty of the "reference system" in granting credits, attempted to support their judgments by the employment of traveling reporters either by assuming the entire cost, or through a cooperative arrangement with other merchants. Lewis Tappan, of the firm of Arthur Tappan & Co., silk merchants, was one of these credit-minded executives who saw the necessity of designing a new order out of chaos. Arthur Tappan & Co. had struggled through the travails of insolvency between 1839 and 1841, a condition due first to large inventories and secondly to receivables frozen in sales to country storekeepers.

It was in this atmosphere that The Mercantile Agency (later known as R.G. Dun & Co.) was formed in 1841, "for the purpose of obtaining, in a proper manner, intelligency of the responsibility of merchants visiting the market from different parts of the country to purchase goods from time to time—the same to be imparted with proper limitations and restrictions, to such merchants and others, as may be disposed to patronize the Agency, and become subscribers thereto."

Meanwhile John M. Bradstreet, a Cincinnati retailer who later practiced law, also established the Bradstreet's Improved Commercial Agency. The name was changed later to the Bradstreet Company which was merged with R.G. Dun & Co. in 1933. The corporate name of the consolidated enterprise was changed to Dun & Bradstreet, Inc.

There are a number of credit reporting agencies, some operating on a national scope, and many more working on a regional or local basis. Their services frequently include rating books and individual reports. The Jewelers Board of Trade provides information and other assistance on credit matters to those dealing in jewelry. The Credit Exchange Inc. provides a credit-checking service to the apparel trades. Lyon Furniture Mercantile Agency publishes the "Lyon Red Book" and supplements. Lumberman's Credit Association, Inc., and Produce Reporter Co. are other examples of agencies providing credit information to their members in specialized lines. In addition there are others which collect and distribute ledger experiences.

Since the widely used business reports and the reference book of Dun & Bradstreet, Inc. are in many ways similar to those of other agencies, the rest of this discussion is based on the Dun & Bradstreet service.

Business Reports. Credit reporters prepare reports on all commercial enterprises listed in the Dun & Bradstreet Reference Book and on other, non-commercial enterprises. A subscriber contemplating doing business with a concern sends in an inquiry, and a report is sent to him, varying from one to five or six pages, and containing the essential elements needed in making a management or credit decision.

A Summary Section at the beginning, giving the highlights of the report, is followed by a Payments Section which gives a record of the ledger experience of suppliers. Then comes the Financial Section, usually including a balance sheet. The balance sheet figures are normally supplemented by profit-and-loss details, plus information regarding leases, insurance coverage, and other data. Comments by the reporter who prepared the report are then devoted to further explanation of the figures and a description of sales and profits trends. Then follows a section which describes what a concern does, that is how it operates: the lines of merchandise sold or services rendered, price range, class of customers, selling terms, and the like. Finally there is a statement as to the business organization, whether proprietorship, partnership, or corporation, and the business history of the principals of the business.

The Credit Reporter. The information for the reports is gathered by a trained group of credit reporters or investigators, working from the branch offices in principal cities. In country regions, travelers visit a town and call upon all the commercial enterprises.

The reporter has a number of sources of information open to him. He will generally first make a direct call on the owner or owners of the business. If the business is new, he will inquire as to the background of the owners, what they intend to do, and ask for the source and amount of capital with which they are starting.

The reporter will inquire as to how the capital is to be invested, that is, how much is planned to go into inventory, how much into fixed assets, and what type of operation is contemplated. If a business has been in existence for some time, he will ask for current financial condition and strive for a description of any material changes which have occurred since the last revision of the report. In addition to such direct interviews, he may call on the banks and suppliers of merchandise, and check court records for liens, mortgages, suits, and judgments.

Ratings. After the reporter has analyzed the above information, he assigns a *Rating* to the business. This becomes part of the listing in the Reference Book which contains close to three million business listings in the United States and Canada.

The rating presents an overall evaluation of the credit standing of a business concern. After using a standardized key for ratings in its Reference Book for many years, Dun & Bradstreet adopted a key to ratings as shown in Exhibit I. Essentially, the new key makes it possible to

EXHIBIT I

Key to Ratings

ESTIMATED FINANCIAL STRENGTH			COMPOSITE CREDIT APPRAISAL			
			HIGH	GOOD	FAIR	LIMITED
5A	$50,000,000	and over	1	2	3	4
4A	$10,000,000 to	49,999,999	1	2	3	4
3A	1,000,000 to	9,999,999	1	2	3	4
2A	750,000 to	999,999	1	2	3	4
1A	500,000 to	749,999	1	2	3	4
BA	300,000 to	499,999	1	2	3	4
BB	200,000 to	299,999	1	2	3	4
CB	125,000 to	199,999	1	2	3	4
CC	75,000 to	124,999	1	2	3	4
DC	50,000 to	74,999	1	2	3	4
DD	35,000 to	49,999	1	2	3	4
EE	20,000 to	34,999	1	2	3	4
FF	10,000 to	19,999	1	2	3	4
GG	5,000 to	9,999	1	2	3	4
HH	Up to	4,999	1	2	3	4

GENERAL CLASSIFICATION

ESTIMATED FINANCIAL STRENGTH			COMPOSITE CREDIT APPRAISAL		
			GOOD	FAIR	LIMITED
1R	**$125,000**	**and over**	**2**	**3**	**4**
2R	**$50,000 to**	**$124,999**	**2**	**3**	**4**

EXPLANATION

When the designation "**1R**" or "**2R**" appears, followed by a 2, 3 or 4, it is an indication that the Estimated Financial Strength, while not definitely classified, is presumed to be in the range of the ($) figures in the corresponding bracket, and while the Composite Credit Appraisal cannot be judged precisely, it is believed to fall in the general category indicated.

"INV." shown in place of a rating indicates that the report was under investigation at the time of going to press. It has no other significance.

"FB" (Foreign Branch). Indicates that the headquarters of this company is located in a foreign country (including Canada). The written report contains the location of the headquarters.

ABSENCE OF RATING, expressed by two hyphens (--), is not to be construed as unfavorable but signifies circumstances difficult to classify within condensed rating symbols. It suggests the advisability of obtaining a report for additional information.

EMPLOYEE RANGE DESIGNATIONS IN REPORTS ON NAMES NOT LISTED IN THE REFERENCE BOOK

Certain businesses do not lend themselves to a Dun & Bradstreet rating and are not listed in the Reference Book. Information on these names, however, continues to be stored and updated in the D&B Business Information File. Reports are available on such businesses and instead of a rating they carry an Employee Range Designation (ER) which is indicative of size in terms of number of employees. No other significance should be attached.

KEY TO EMPLOYEE RANGE DESIGNATIONS

ER 1	1000 or more	Employees
ER 2	500 - 999	Employees
ER 3	100 - 499	Employees
ER 4	50 - 99	Employees
ER 5	20 - 49	Employees
ER 6	10 - 19	Employees
ER 7	5 - 9	Employees
ER 8	1 - 4	Employees
ER N		Not Available

indicate a number of grades of estimated financial strength up to "$50,000,000, and over," instead of the former "over $1,000,000," and, to conform to the needs of electronic data processing equipment, eliminates the plus (+) signs in the estimated financial strength rating, and fractions from the composite credit appraisal.

The financial strength of a business is a combination of size and stamina. A good little business, of course, can be a more desirable credit account than a weak big business, but by and large a business becomes stronger as it grows and as the dollar investment in the business increases. Thus the letter envisions relative strength through size.

The number is a *Composite Credit Appraisal.* As shown in the Key to Ratings, there are four credit appraisals: *High, Good, Fair,* and *Limited.* To arrive at what the reporter believes to be the proper appraisal, he forms a judgment based on the following seven credit factors:

Proper organization according to law, and clear identification of ownership

Length of time in business

History of management—successful or unsuccessful

Balance of management experience

Financial condition

Trend—going ahead or going backward

Manner of payments

Application. The Reference Book is a simple and dependable checking tool. A manager has from it the facts to make a Yes, No, or Hold decision.

Credit Departments use it to set up credit lines based on ratings, check new and unsolicited orders, check small and sample orders, make preliminary credit checks, and keep up-to-date with customers' and prospects' businesses.

Purchasing Departments use the Reference Book to locate sources of supply, and to verify credit standing and stability of suppliers.

Sales Departments use it to give salesmen information on accounts before calls are made; to build and revise prospect files; to determine number and quality of outlets; to classify prospects; to revise sales potential estimates; to select prospects in a given area or analyze accounts receivable; and to set up sales objectives.

Change Notification. A "Change of Notification" service alerts subscribers on a weekly basis to certain changes that can affect the creditworthiness of their accounts. The subscriber supplies Dun & Bradstreet with a list of customer names and addresses. Dun & Bradstreet screens these names against the three million U.S. and Canadian commercial businesses in its data bank, which is updated by some 20,000 significant credit changes every week.

The subscriber's names that match or are substantially similar to the names in the data bank are registered for Change Notification service. The subscriber receives a printout "List of Registrations" confirming those names on which Change Notification service will be supplied. This list also contains the so-called D-U-N-S Number, a unique nine-digit identifying number which has many computer uses for identification, for processing bills, purchase orders, market analyses, and the like.

SOURCE: Dun & Bradstreet, Inc., New York, New York

Cross References: *Collection Services; Credit Bureaus; Credit Management.*

CREDIT UNIONS

Credit Unions (CUs) have become an important segment of the economy of the United States since these self-help cooperatives were introduced into this country in 1908. One out of every five Americans belongs to a CU. A growing number of employers have found that CUs help solve some of the personnel management and human relations problems caused by financial insecurity.

Basic objectives of CUs are:

(1) To promote thrift among their members through systematic regular savings.

(2) To mobilize the savings thus accumulated to provide credit for their members at reasonable rates of interest.

(3) To help people learn how to manage their financial and business affairs wisely through organizations they own and control.

Definition. A credit union is a cooperative corporation, chartered by a state or the Federal Government, with powers basically limited to promoting thrift and extending credit to members. The field of membership is restricted to a specific group of people by the charter and bylaws. These groups must have a common bond of occupation, association, or residence in a well-defined neighborhood, community, or rural district.

CUs are owned and controlled by their members, and each member has one vote, regardless of the number of shares owned.

History. The first CU organized in the United States was established in 1908 in Manchester, New Hampshire, with the help of Alphonse Desjardins, a French-Canadian journalist who had established the first People's Bank in Canada, at Levis, Quebec, in 1900. In most countries CUs serve more rural than urban people. In the United States, however, more than 80% operate among groups of employees of industry and government.

The first CU law in the U.S. was enacted in Massachusetts in 1909, upon the recommendations of Pierre Jay, Massachusetts Bank Commissioner, with the support of Edward A. Filene, Boston merchant, and the advice of Desjardins. This legislation has since become the basic pattern for other state laws and for the Federal Credit Union Act. Delaware, South Dakota, and Wyoming have no state laws at this writing (1980). The District of Columbia Credit Union Act was repealed in 1964, and all its CUs were converted to Federal charters.

Early Development. Between 1909 and 1921 only about 190 CUs were organized. However, in 1921 Filene took what was perhaps the most important action in the development of the movement by establishing the Credit Union National Extension Bureau. A young lawyer, Roy F. Bergengren, was hired as managing director. Bergengren carried on a vigorous campaign for the passage of state and Federal legislation to permit organization of CUs, and organized CUs and state CU leagues. By 1934 there were 39 state CU laws and more than 2,400 CUs had been organized. In June of that year, passage of the Federal Credit Union Act made it possible for people in any part of the United States to organize CUs.

With fulfillment of its objectives, the Credit Union National Extension Bureau, a philanthropically supported organization, was discontinued, and its functions were taken over by the dues-supported Credit Union National Association (CUNA), organized at Estes Park, Colorado, in June 1934. Roy F. Bergengren was first managing director, and Edward A. Filene was first president of CUNA, which was made up of state CU leagues composed of dues-paying CUs.

Accelerated growth followed passage of the Federal Credit Union Act. The responsibility for administration of the Act was placed in the Farm Credit Administration because of its experience with farmer cooperatives. The first director of the Federal Credit Union program was Claude R. Orchard, Personnel Director of Armour and Company of Omaha, Nebraska. Before heading the Federal Credit Union program, Orchard had organized about two hundred CUs in his own company and in others throughout the nation. Under his leadership chartering policies were established, standard bylaws developed, and an accounting manual, director's handbook, and manuals for the credit committee, supervisory committee, and education committee were published.

The rapid growth of the Federal CU program from 1935 to 1941 stimulated growth of state-chartered CUs. By the end of 1941, there were 9,891 active CUs, 5,663 state and 4,228 Federal. Although the number of CUs has fluctuated in the past decade, CU assets have increased every year since 1932.

In May 1942, responsibility for the Federal CU program was transferred to the Federal Deposit Insurance Corporation where it remained until July 1948, when Congress created the Bureau of Federal Credit Unions in the Federal Security Agency (later to become the Department of Health, Education, Welfare). On March 10, 1970, Public Law 91-206 established the National Credit Union Administration (NCUA) as an independent agency in the Executive Branch of the Government to supervise Federal Credit Unions.

Post-War Growth. About 58% of existing CUs are now Federally chartered, and their post war growth has been greater than that of any other type of financial institution. By the end of 1979, some 43 million members owned over 22,000 CUs with $66 billion in assets and more than $52 billion in loans outstanding. CUs held 15.5% of the outstanding consumer installment credit and almost 5% of personal savings in financial institutions.

Current Trends. There is a current decline in the number of new CUs organized each year. However, more than one million new members are added annually, and the total net savings of members have expanded by $3 to $7 billion a year. Credit unions extended approximately $36.8 billion in consumer installment credit in 1979.

Government Supervision. Each CU operates in accordance with the state or Federal law.

Federal CUs are chartered, supervised, and examined by National Credit Union Administration. State-chartered CUs are supervised by a state agency, usually the banking department. Federal CUs are required to keep their books in accordance with forms and procedures prescribed in an accounting manual. Some states do not prescribe accounting procedures, but CUs in these states generally have adopted the Federal procedure.

The NCUA prescribes standard bylaws which may be amended with the approval of the NCUA Board. CUs are required to carry surety bonds against dishonesty and to insure faithful performance of duties.

To obtain a charter for a Federal CU, an occupational group should have at least 200 persons; associational groups, 300 members; religious groups, 300 families; community groups, 1,000 population. Seven subscribers to the Organization Certificate are required.

Management. CUs are managed by a Board of Directors elected by the members at the annual meeting of members. The Board elects from its number a president, one or more vice presidents, a secretary, and a treasurer. Most laws provide that the treasurer shall be the general manager. Most laws and bylaws provide that the treasurer is the only officer that may be compensated. Directors may not be compensated for their services as directors.

The responsibility for approving loans is placed with a credit committee, also elected by the members, under most laws. The credit committee is not compensated for its work. Another committee, the supervisory or audit committee, is required to make certain audits each year and report to the director, members, and to the government authority. Under the Federal law, the supervisory committee is appointed by the Board of Directors while under most state laws, the supervisory or audit committee is elected by the members.

Source of Funds. The principal source of funds is equity capital represented by savings which are accepted in amounts as small as 25 cents. In a few states CUs may accept deposits, but even in most of these states, deposits are not extensively used. Some state laws limit the amount of shares any one member may own; the Federal Act does not. Average savings in all CUs amount to a little over $1,300, and this is increasing every year. Federal CU regulations limit dividends on members' shares to 7%. In some states dividends are limited by statute. However, a higher rate may be paid on share certificate accounts.

Savings in Federal CUs are insured to $100,000 per member account by NCUA. Qualified state CUs may also become insured by the National Credit Union Administration, but application is voluntary for these CUs. Massachusetts, Rhode Island, and Wisconsin have state-administered share insurance plans.

Federal CUs may borrow from any source in amounts up to 50% of their paid-in and unimpaired capital. Borrowing power of state CUs is limited by statute or bylaws or by approval of the supervising authority. Principal sources for borrowed funds are commerical banks and other CUs.

In 1978 Congress established a Central Liquidity Facility within the National Credit Union Administration. This mixed ownership government corporation provides for the short-term and protracted adjustment as well as seasonal liquidity needs of member CUs.

Loans. Loans may be made only to members, for provident or productive purposes, such as education, medical bills, residential mortgages, funeral expenses, consumer durables, and the like, not excluding vacations and other recreational expenses. Loan limitations vary from state to state, with unsecured loan limitations ranging from $300 to $1,000. A few states have no statutory limit. Some states limit the maximum secured loan to a fixed dollar amount, others to a percentage of the total share capital of the CU. The Federal Credit Union Act, as amended in 1980, permits Federal CUs to fix the limits on unsecured and secured loans to members provided the total loans outstanding to any one member does not exceed 10% of capital. Losses from bad loans have been only a third of one percent for Federal CUs, and experience of state CUs is comparable.

Cost of Installment Loans. Cost of CU loans is, on the whole, the lowest available to the average person from financial institutions. Interest rates are limited by law to an annual percentage rate of 15%, inclusive of all charges. (Under certain conditions, specified in law, the NCUA Board can lift the 15% ceiling for 18-month periods. CUs may not exact a greater rate by adding investigation fees, service fees, minimum fees, or insurance premiums. Many CUs charge lower rates on all or certain classes of loans, and make refunds to borrowers of a part of the interest paid by them when net income exceeds the requirements for reserves and dividends.

Other Services. The vast majority of CUs insure the lives of borrowers for the amount of their loans at no charge to the borrower. Many also insure the lives of savers in an amount equal to their savings up to $1,000 or $2,000 with no charge to the members. Some provide check cashing, and some sell money orders and travelers checks. An increasing number provide family financial counseling. Consumer education programs for members are common. CUs in employee groups frequently render a valuable service to the employer by helping employees who are harrassed by creditors and garnishments solve their financial problems.

Investments. Federal CUs may invest in obligations of the United States or fully guaranteed by the United States, loans to other CUs, and in savings and loan associations whose shares are insured by the Federal Savings and Loan Insurance Corporation. State-chartered CUs generally have broader investment powers. For example, they may invest in securities which are legal investments for trust funds or savings banks.

Reserves. Reserves must be established from net earnings before payment of dividends to the shareholder members. Federal CUs must set aside 10% of gross earnings until the reserve amounts to 7.5% of total loans outstanding and "risk assets," then 5% of gross earnings until the reserve amounts to 10% of loans and "risk assets."

State laws vary as to the required reserve, or guaranty funds, as it is often called. Experience indicates that the statutory reserves have generally been adequate. The National Credit Union Administration Board and some of the state supervisory authorities have the power to order special reserves for losses when the financial condition of the CU is threatened by potential losses, or when the amount of delinquent loans exceeds the prescribed standards.

Potential. Millions of people have no savings accounts in financial institutions; millions either do not have available, or do not use, legalized consumer credit facilities, and usury still flourishes among low income people. Existing CUs serve about half of their potential members in the aggregate; therefore, about 40 million more potential members are already eligible. Increased use of consumer credit will challenge the management of CUs to attract sufficient personal savings to meet future demands for low cost consumer credit.

LAWRENCE CONNELL, Chairman, National Credit Union Administration Board, Washington, D.C.

Information References

The National Credit Union Administration (NCUA) is an independent agency of the Executive Branch of the Federal Government. It assists eligible groups to organize CUs, and publishes information.

The Credit Union National Association, the industry's largest trade group, also publishes information and assists groups to organize.

Dublin, Jack, "Credit Unions: Theory and Practice," Detroit, Wayne State University Press, 1966.

Francis, Kent W., "Credit Union Dynamics," Madison, Wis., CUNA International, Inc., 1968.

International Credit Union Yearbook, Madison, Wisc., CUNA International, yearly.

Melvin, Donald J., "Credit Unions and the Credit Union Industry: A Study of the Powers, Organizations, Regulation, and Competition," Philadelphia, Pa., Temple University, 1977.

Moody, J. Carroll, and Fite, Gilbert C., "The Credit Union Movement, Origins and Development, 1850–1970," Lincoln, Neb., University of Nebraska Press, 1971.

National Credit Union Administration, Annual Report.

Cross References: *Employee Benefit Plans.*

CRITICAL PATH METHOD (CPM)

The **Critical Path Method** (CPM) is a mathematically ordered system of planning and scheduling for program management, often using electronic data processing, which makes possible a balanced, optimum, time-cost schedule to assure timeliness and minimum use of resources. One of the newer famiy of planning and control techniques, it is in many respects very similar to (PERT) PROGRAM EVALUATION AND REVIEW TECHNIQUE. (For an overview discussion of the various control techniques currently in use, see INTEGRATED PROJECT MANAGEMENT.)

Background. CPM was first used in 1957 by E. I. du Pont de Nemours & Co., to improve the planning, scheduling, and coordination of its new-plant construction effort. The development of the method is credited to James Kelley of Remington Rand, Univac, and Morgan Walker of du Pont. CPM caught on almost immediately in the construction industry. One of the biggest early users was Olin Mathieson

EXHIBIT I

CPM SCHEDULE/COST NETWORK PLAN

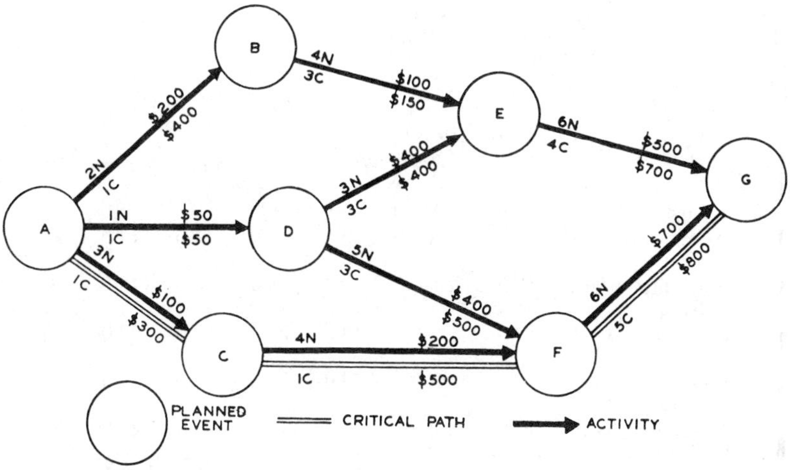

Chemical Corp. which scheduled $70 million worth of construction with CPM. Other early applications were developed at du Pont, Union Carbide Corp., large construction companies, and others, for research and development processes, building construction, plant maintenance, and the like.

What CPM Is. CPM, like PERT, is based on the network principle. *Events* are shown by circles in the network (Exhibit I), and *activities* are designated by arrows leading from one event to its successor event or events. An event represents a specified program accomplishment at a particular instant in time. An activity represents the time and resources required to progress from one event to the next.

Cost and Scheduling. After the arrow diagram is established, two time and cost estimates are applied to each activity and referred to as *normal* and *crash.* With the normal estimate, the primary consideration is minimum *cost,* and the time associated with it. Since attempts will be made later to reduce it, normal time is considered to be maximum time; a speed-up would presumably be accomplished only by more outlay for labor. Costs associated with normal times are assumed to be a minimum cost.

The "crash estimate" for a job is defined as the absolute minimum time and the cost associated with it—the maximum cost. (See Exhibit II.) It is assumed that a linear cost relation exists between normal and crash estimates for each activity.

EXHIBIT II

CPM TIME-COST RELATIONSHIP

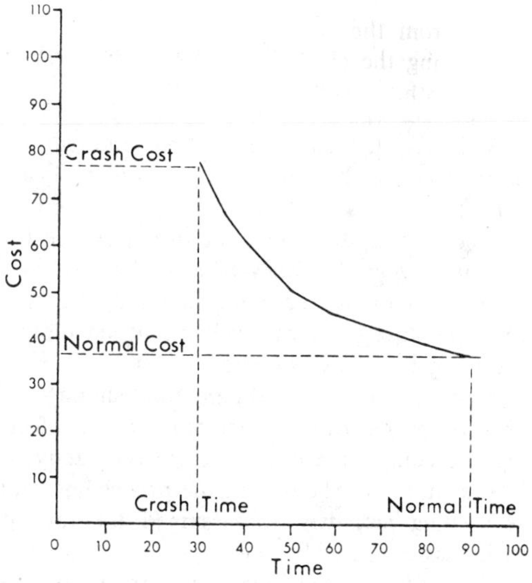

The *critical path* is that sequence of activities, as indicated by the double-ruled sequence in Exhibit I, which will require the greatest normal time to accomplish.

Based on the normal times for each activity, *earliest start dates* are computed for all activities along any path, by working forward from the beginning of the path, and allowing for elapsed times for each successive activity. *Latest start dates* are computed by working back-

EXHIBIT III

FIRST SCHEDULE DEVELOPMENT, (CPM)

Time Unit—Weeks	Schedule	0
Cost Unit—Dollars	Direct Cost	17250.0
Activity Count—8	Duration	42.0
Event Count—7		

Prec. Event	*Succ. Event*	*Description*	*Dura-tion*	*Direct Cost*	*Earliest Start*	*Earliest Finish*	*Latest Start*	*Latest Finish*	*Total*	*Float Free*	*Indep.*
1	2	Design	6.0	2000.0	0	6.0	0	6.0	0	0	0
1	4	Advertising Analysis	4.0	1000.0	0	4.0	13.0	17.0	13.0	0	0
2	3	Fabricate Test Samples	12.0	2000.0	6.0	18.0	6.0	18.0	0	0	0
3	5	Field-Test Samples	9.0	1500.0	18.0	27.0	18.0	27.0	0	0	0
3	7	Prepare Manufacturing	6.0	1000.0	18.0	24.0	30.0	36.0	12.0	0	0
4	5	Develop Sales Campaign	10.0	1250.0	4.0	14.0	17.0	27.0	13.0	13.0	0
5	8	Conduct Sales Campaign	15.0	6000.0	27.0	42.0	27.0	42.0	0	0	0
7	8	Manufacture Initial Commercial Quantities	6.0	2500.0	24.0	30.0	36.0	42.0	12.0	12.0	0

wards from the end of the path, successively subtracting the elapsed times for each activity in the path.

Similarly, the *latest finish date* and *earliest finish date* for all activities in a given path are computed.

It is obvious that this leeway is possible for any path *other than the critical path.*

Float. With the foregoing in mind, the concept of "float" can be readily grasped (corresponding to "slack" in PERT).

Free Float is the maximum time slippage of an activity that can be tolerated without affecting the completion date of any other activity, in the situation where both the proceeding and succeeding activities are assumed to start at their earliest possible times.

Total Float is the maximum slippage of an activity that can be tolerated without affecting the completion date of the overall project. This is computed assuming that all preceding activities start as early as possible, and all succeeding activities start as late as possible.

Independent Float is the maximum slippage of an activity that can be tolerated without affecting the latest completion date of any other activity, under the situation where all preceding activities are completed as late as possible, and all succeeding activities are started as early as possible.

Computer Runs. Initially, the computer analyzes the normal times of each activity on the critical path and computes a maximum time schedule, as shown in a simplified example in Exhibit III. Then the activity in the critical path is selected which offers the smallest cost increase in relation to time decrease, after which a new schedule is computed, with the selected activity crashed. (This may produce a new critical path, if the crashed time represents a substantial reduction.) The computer continues to "buy time" along the latest critical path as cheaply as possible. The last computation is based on a "total crash" assumption, and is the most expensive. Lastly, a summary is tabulated which lists all the schedules computed, time durations, and necessary costs (Exhibit IV).

EXHIBIT IV

CPM SCHEDULE COMPARISONS

Schedule number	*Optimal direct cost*	*Project duration*	*Critical activities*
0	17250.0	42.0	4
1	18750.0	35.0	4
2	20083.4	29.0	6
3	22583.4	24.0	8
4	24107.1	21.0	8
5	27732.1	17.0	8
6	31562.5	14.0	8

Once a final schedule has been decided, management is provided with sufficient information to insure dynamic control over costs. Comparisons of per cent complete to per cent expended, and man-hours consumed to planned final man-hours, pinpoint areas or activities which require remedial action.

The Optimum Schedule. The project cost curve reflects only the direct costs involved in executing a project. However, there are other costs which contribute to total project cost, such as overhead and administrative expenses. These indirect costs may vary with the duration of the job, and must be taken into account when deciding upon an optimum schedule, as indicated in Exhibit V.

EXHIBIT V

DETERMINATION OF OPTIMUM SCHEDULE, CPM

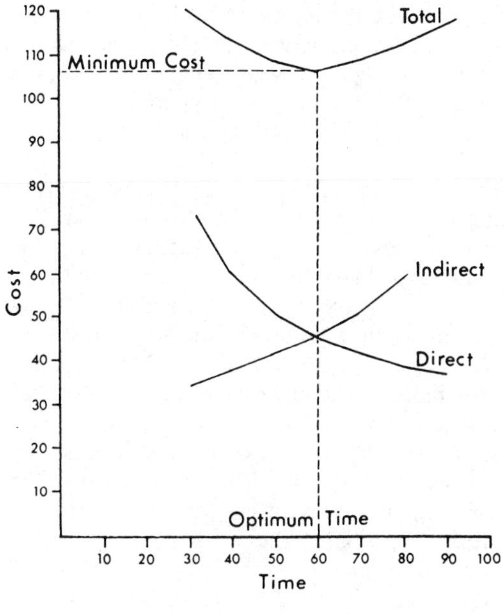

Application. Both CPM and PERT are, as stated, based on the same network principle. However, an immediate and major difference is in the time estimates. The manager using PERT is required to express his timing uncertainty in a range of "optimistic," "pessimistic," and "most likely," from which statistical determination of the "expected time" is made. The CPM user is assumed to be on less uncertain ground, and to have had some prior experience with the activities comprising the project. His estimates of "normal" and "crash" are assumed to be quite specific, and made with a good degree of confidence. Similarly, it is assumed that the cost estimates accompanying those of time can be based with a good degree of confidence on prior experience. Thus present application is found in the fields of construction, development projects, and new product introduction, where definite costs are available, and approximate times are known from past history. The outstanding feature is the time-cost relationship, which enables the manager to economize on time at a minimum cost, and to determine when diminishing returns make further time-saving uneconomical. It should be emphasized, however, that the assumption of a linear relationship between the crash and normal cost estimates implies a restriction of which the user should remain aware. If gross departures from linearity are to be assumed, refinements in the calculations must be introduced.

JOHN J. GLASER, formerly Polaris Division, Sperry Gyroscope Co., Division of Sperry Rand Corp., Great Neck, New York

Information Reference

Martino, R.L., "Critical Path Networks," New York, McGraw-Hill, 1970.

Cross References: *Integrated Project Management (and cross references there given).*

D

DATA COMMUNICATIONS

Data Communications is, as the name indicates, the means of communicating data—as opposed to communicating analog (telephone) voice. It comprises communications between digital computers, between terminals and these computers, and between terminals themselves. Thus, it is the means of tying together coherently all local and far-flung computerized devices.

Strictly speaking, data communications has existed as long as data processing, but its growth was severely restrained by the tariff restrictions imposed on and by the telephone industry. Telephone networks were the major means of connecting a remotely located terminal user to a centrally located mainframe computer. However, on June 26, 1968, the ground rules were drastically changed, and a "new" industry was spawned. On that date, the Federal Communications Commission rendered its landmark Carterfone Decision permitting direct interconnection to the telephone network of non-telephone company devices. Although the telephone companies remained free to maintain standards for the protection of their networks, this proved no deterrent to the growth of the newly liberated data communications applications. This growth is a major reason for the increasing computer orientation of our society.

Besides the telephone companies—especially AT&T—the other major influence affecting this growth has been and is IBM. This company is primarily known for its computers, typewriters, and other business machines, but its impact on data communications is twofold: in the interconnection of its own products, and in the connection of other manufacturers' "plug-compatible" products to IBM computers and other devices. The company's extremely strong position in the large-computer industry, and its strong position in other business-equipment areas, has enabled it to establish de facto standards for both the EDP and data communications fields.

Networks. The user realizes the full potential of data communications in the application of networks. The most elementary connection method of a remote terminal to a computer is via a leased line, point-to-point. When there are several terminals at a remote location requiring connection to the computer, instead of leasing an individual line for each terminal, it is possible and less costly to use only the one line in combination with a "multiplexing" (line-sharing) device. The multiplexer, representing an elementary form of networking, is commonly available today in several forms and variations of "intelligence."

As terminals from different remote sites require access to the centrally located computer, the network grows in complexity. Waystations, called nodal processors or nodes, become necessary within the network to interact with the terminals and the computer, storing, forwarding, and controlling the network's data flow. As more computers and terminals are added, the network design becomes ever more complex to provide the capability for any terminal to reach any computer or any other terminal.

The user firm is faced with a major design and implementation effort to provide a private network—which yields many control and security benefits—or it can avail itself of a public network to move its data. Among the different types of network designs are circuit-switching, which involves a straighforward transfer of data from one path onto another. Message-switching, on the other hand, adds a store-and-forward function: the message is stored at a network node, possibly checked for errors, then transferred onto another circuit (path). Depending on the distances involved and the network complexity, these nodal "stops" may occur from one to several times.

A variation of the message-switched network, growing in popularity, is the packet-switched network. Here, as the message enters the network, it is divided into discrete segments, called packets. Each packet travels the network independent of the others, with suitable identification. A packet is routed over the "free-est" path, node by node, until it reaches its exit node. There, all the packets are reassembled in their proper order, and presented to the destination device as the entered message.

An increasingly important element of the data communications network is the satellite—

particularly, the geostationary satellite. Its orbit matches the earth's angular rotation, and it is positioned over the equator. To an observer on the earth, it appears stationary in space. In this position, it acts as a relay and disseminating station for all forms of electrical signals. When a firm's network requires satellite use, "dish" antennas may be positioned on building roofs, to minimize land-line use. The increasing use of digital data—as typified by Satellite Business Systems' recent entry—makes the satellite of growing importance in data communications. SBS is a consortium of IBM Corp., Comsat General Corp., and Aetna Life and Casualty Co.

One drawback in the application of satellites to data transmission is the inherent propagation delay of this technique. There are several schemes to negate the delay's effect—especially noticeable in interactive (inquiry-response) applications—but the user must balance their cost against that of transmission via cable and normal microwave links. For non-interactive transmission, such as batch data, video, and facsimile, the delay is more readily absorbed.

Among the established public packet-switched networks in the United States are those of GTE-Telenet and Tymnet. Each interconnects internationally to Canada's Datapac, and via international record carriers to Europe and Japan. A private network that meets the interface requirements of one of the public ones could establish an economical combination of the two network types. International and overseas access is also available to the private network, with the proper interface.

The Terminal. The most ubiquitous data communications device is the operator's terminal. Commonly, it has a typewriter-like keyboard, and either a cathode-ray-tube (CRT) screen or a hard-copy capability (the two are not mutually exclusive). It permits the user to gain access to a wide range of data bases (information sources), including business, training, entertainment, and interactive applications. These services are usually available on a timeshared basis—meaning accessible to many users "simultaneously" (i.e., it appears so to the user).

The business office is where the terminal and all its attendant peripherals find their potential increasingly realized. OFFICE AUTOMATION—sometimes referred to as the "office of the future"—is driven by the need for higher office productivity. Until recently, this drive has been fueled by the replacement of discrete office equipment with electronic counterparts. But significantly higher productivity is gained by the application of data communications concepts.

One of these concepts is the local network. In its most common form, it consists of a loop of coaxial cable interconnecting offices in adjacent buildings, operating at megabit/second data rates. This is about two orders of magnitude greater than what is available over common leased lines. Ideally, the local network enables the user to attach any communicating office device to the loop, automatically gaining access to all the other devices so connected. This idea is rapidly reaching technological feasibility, as exemplified by Xerox's Ethernet offering. The user thus gains one of the most significant elements toward productivity improvement: resource sharing. Each office terminal device may readily access common data bases, rather than having to maintain its own. Also, with the advent of digitized voice transmission, the office network becomes the common shared medium for all office transmissions, thus avoiding the need for separate, costlier facilities.

Standards for local networks are being established by such groups as the Institute of Electrical and Electronics Engineers (IEEE) and the International Federation of Information Processing Societies (IFIPS). To enable resource sharing on a global scale, by allowing local networks to connect to each other, standards bodies are specifying the functions of the internetwork interface, called a gateway. These functions include responsibility for end-to-end accountability, data routing, and traffic flow control. With gateway availability, local networks will interconnect and will also gain access to existing long-haul networks.

The business-office terminal is evolving into a multifunctional device. Depending on the amount of intelligence its owner is willing to purchase, it can not only handle interoffice message communications—such as "electronic mail"—but also do a considerable amount of data processing. With today's integrated-circuit chip technology, the terminal will include microprocessors—each with its own designated function. The information processing power is limited only by the imagination and ability of its designers and programmers.

Facsimile terminals are also evolving. New digital techniques enable scanning in seconds the material to be transmitted. Among these techniques is the terminal scanner's ability to skip over or "compress" redundant characters, including "white space." Of course, the receiving machine interprets the received compression codes and restores the original material in its entirety.

The Network Minicomputer. One "older" device still much in evidence in network applications is the minicomputer. As a communications processor, it "front-ends" a mainframe computer to handle the network traffic, thus freeing its host for the "number-crunching" tasks it handles more efficiently. The communications processor also functions as a switch, connecting terminals to each other as required. When a user desires access to the host's data base, the front end opens a path to the mainframe.

Other network functions of the minicomputer are as a stand-alone message switch, as a cluster controller (directly controlling a group of terminals), as a gateway processor, and as a distributed processor. In the latter role, the mini may operate totally independent of a host computer, in conjunction with other minis. The resultant distributed data processing (DDP) network thus has no one element—such as a mainframe—that can make the network fail. Instead, if any of the DDP units becomes inoperative, only those functions it controls become unavailable. Of course, the coordination and programming tasks required by a DDP network are considerable, and the distributed data-base techniques are still evolving.

Network Control. A network does not run itself. For greatest efficiency, a control function is part of the basic network design. And the primary purpose of network control is to minimize—or better, avoid—downtime. The method used requires some specialized equipment, proven cost-effective, to acquire and interpret operational statistics. In this way, as a variable such as response time approaches its tolerance limit, the preprogrammed control mechanism apprises the network supervisor terminal of the condition. Depending on the control's complexity, corrective action may be automatic as the tolerance limit is reached, or the supervisor may key in suitable instructions to alleviate the condition.

When a network component experiences an outage, before the condition can be corrected, it must first be located and diagnosed. A properly designed network, with sufficient detection devices and diagnostic routines, and with built-in redundancy of critical components, will have minimum downtime. The problem will be located quickly, its extent readily evaluated, and the proper corrective measures promptly taken. The lesson to be learned is not to wait for trouble to decide how to handle it, but to anticipate and design for it at a very early stage of the overall project.

Protocols. The rules under which data communications devices communicate with each other are called protocols. They range from the simple, one-way-only simplex transmission to the packet-network high-level data link control (HDLC). They include transmission modes such as half duplex (one direction at a time), full duplex (both directions simultaneously), and multilayered interfaces. The more complex the protocol, the more intelligence required of the terminal/computer device and of the network. To the operator, protocols are "transparent," i.e., not visible, requiring minimal or no user reaction. As these protocols become standardized, the programming efforts needed to formulate them become susceptible to production methods such as solid-state chip technology, which makes the protocol a less-expensive hardware function.

An example of this protocol standardization sequence is the access to packet-switched networks. After much negotiation, the International Consultative Committee for Telegraphy and Telephony (CCITT) formulated its Recommendation X.25. Chips are becoming available that implement packet-network access. As the standard is further refined, access implementation will require even less software as the functions are increasingly handled by hardware.

Software. Some firms specialize in software packages to optimize network design. The number of network alternatives is growing so fast that the demand for optimization—both in private-network design and in the interface to, and use of, public-network facilities—can be satisfied only through computer aids. These aids range from simple memory systems that compile and store network statistics to complex data traffic simulators, network design configurators, and software for data-distribution modeling. Much time and effort can be spared by computer modeling of a proposed network prior to implementation. The effects of traffic variables and equipment changes may be examined in the model, leading to network design optimization.

Other data communications software is concerned with accessing of mainframe computers by remotely located terminals. For example, among the software packages implementing this function are IBM's Virtual Telecommunications Access Method (VTAM) and Telecommunications Access Method (TCAM), two of the more common ones. A software product that is designed to manage access methods and protocols is the teleprocessing (or telecommunications) monitor. The TP monitor optimizes a computer's processing time by off-loading the data communications software functions from the mainframe's operating system. The monitors are available from many software firms, as well as from computer vendors.

A software-related function of increasing importance to the network planner and user is data-base management, especially in DDP networks. A data-base management system (DBMS) provides users with a method of readily accessing data no matter where the data reside in a network. The aim of DBMS designers is to approach the ideal concept of totally distributed network processing. In this DDP environment, the user accesses a data base by subject, and the network connects the user terminal to the proper computer. The user is completely unaware of this network operation. Common communications-related DBMS problems are contention, deadlock (simultaneous access), and recovery in a distributed environment.

To facilitate DBMS development, computers are needed that are capable of storing and retrieving information in an efficient manner. Ideally, they would handle these functions by information content, rather than by the customary techniques of physical addressing. To achieve the greater efficiencies of a computer architecture dedicated to information storage and retrieval, a device such as the data-base computer is needed. In its most efficient application, the data-base computer acts as a network node, totally decoupled from the data processing functions of the other network computers. The ideal data-base machine is still to be a reality, but when its role is more fully understood, it will be a significant part of DBMS and networking.

Current Trends. Spurred on by technological advancements, and enjoying an increasingly competitive climate, the data communications industry's influence on business will be considerable. With the recent FCC rulings, AT&T is free to enter the computer field. And with that other industry giant, IBM, well into the data communications field, the considerable research and development capabilities of the two companies are expected to respond to the competitive pressures of each other and of the growing number of "outsiders" with more and more technical breakthroughs.

Another giant business, the United States Postal Service, intends to pursue its electronic computer-originated mail (ECOM) plans. Fallout from this and the enhanced services expected from Satellite Business Systems will be far ranging. Access to SBS' satellite network is scheduled to be made available to both large and small companies early in 1982. Such access will provide computer-to-computer links, high-speed document communications, video teleconferencing, and telephone communications. SBS will offer two forms of service: one dedicated to a sole user, the other to be shared among smaller user firms.

The pace of local-network growth is accelerating. One recently developed by Ungermann-Bass Inc. of Santa Clara, California, is believed to be the first over which traditionally incompatible computer equipment can communicate. As expected, the key to this network—as to so many recent computer-related developments—is the microprocessor. In the Ungermann-Bass local network, the network interface unit is microprocessor-equipped to manage data-packet processing, circuit connection, and error detection.

Another notable business-office development is the digital private branch exchange. As an office's communications interface to the outside world, the PBX is undergoing considerable transformation. Besides handling both data and voice, more recent versions of the device integrate the two by digitizing the voice signals. Digitized information from word processors, "intelligent" typewriter terminals, facsimile equipment, and other devices are all funneled through the digital PBX. Its own memory and switching functions, and interfaces to analog and digital networks (including packet-switched types) are all made possible by the application of microprocessor and chip technology.

The Future. One data communications technology showing extremely encouraging results in ongoing field tests and initial implementations is lightwave transmission. The medium in greatest use is glass, in the form of optical fibers. Using a light-emitting diode (LED) or a laser beam as the light source, data rates in the multimegabit-per-second range have been achieved. Other advantages are the material's ready availability, light weight (lighter than copper), and narrow gauge (less than coaxial cable)—all made available in a sufficiently strong packaged product.

Speech recognition and voice response technology are being applied to data-communications devices in several areas. One is voice mail, where a computer synthesizes messages for the user who dials up his "mailbox." Another is the voice-activated typewriter terminal (both with and without a data communications interface), which at this writing is expected by 1983. In its ultimate form, the operator will speak to it, and the machine will print the words as spoken and correctly spelled, and the text will appear as typical typed material. Companies expected to lead with this development are IBM, Xerox, Matsushita, and Exxon. The first commercial versions are expected to recognize correctly about 95% of "typical" business English as spoken by the "average" executive.

A growing phenomenon outside the United States, but starting to appear here in several versions, is interactive home TV, called videotex. Services expected are electronic mail, timeshared computing, remote shopping and banking, and travel and event reservations, besides the already vast array of home entertainment modes.

Of less visibility outside the data communications industry, but of tremendous importance, are the efforts of standards bodies to formulate specifications permitting interconnection of devices no matter which company is the manufacturer. Called Open Systems Interconnection (OSI), considerable progress is reported, but much work remains.

The increasingly competitive climate that evokes more and more advanced versions of data communications devices is starting to meet the productivity needs of inflation-plagued corporations. Just as standalone computers were seen as an aid in earlier troubled times, distributed data processing and allied data communications techniques are seen as the vehicles to help overcome the problems of more recent and near-future financially anxious eras.

RAYMOND SARCH, Senior Editor, *Data Communications,* McGraw-Hill Inc., New York, New York

Information References

Associations:

American Federation of Information Processing Societies.
American National Standards Institute.
Electronic Industries Association.
Institute of Electrical and Electronic Engineers.
International Consultative Committee for Telegraphy and Telephony.
International Federation of Information Processing Societies
International Standards Organization.
International Telecommunications Union.

Periodicals:

Data Communications
(See also periodicals listed under ELECTRONIC DATA PROCESSING.)

Texts:

"Data Communications Buyers' Guide," New York, McGraw-Hill, issued annually.
"Datacomm for the Businessman," Cherry Hill, N.J., Management Information Corp., 1978.
Doll, Dixon R., "Data Communications Facilities, Networks, and Systems Design," New York, Wiley, 1978.
Folts, Harold C. and Karp, Harry R., ed., "Data Communications Standards," New York, McGraw-Hill, 1979.
Karp, Harry R., ed., "Basics of Data Communications," New York, McGraw-Hill, 1976.
Karp, Harry R., ed., "Practical Applications of Data Communications," New York, McGraw-Hill, 1980.
Liebowitz, Burt H. and Carson, John H., "Distributed Processing," Silver Spring, Md., IEEE Computer Society Press, 1978.
McQuillan, John M. and Cerf, Vinton G., "A Practical View of Computer Communications Protocols," Silver Spring, Md., IEEE Computer Society Press, 1978.

Cross References: *Data Communications: A Case Example; Electronic Data Processing (all entries with that prefix); Information Data Banks: On Line.*

DATA COMMUNICATIONS: A Case Example

The following represents one of a number of possible system configurations for **Data Communications.**

Alcan Aluminum Corporation has, as of this writing, recently begun operating a new message switching system called ALCANET that has boosted transmission capacity about 60 times at no additional operating costs. The new system, employing IBM's Systems Network Architecture (SNA) is the first element of a streamlined communications system for the company's operations in the United States.

Alcan's purpose is to serve many company

communications requirements. The message switching system provides efficient communications and is the first step in establishing a complete United States network for all applications. It enables the company to exploit technology and prepare for digital and, eventually satellite transmission.

Display terminals replace 45 teleprinters. Further, six new 4800 baud Synchronous Data Link Control lines are able to service the network where fourteen were previously required because the equipment has increased transmission speeds from 10 to 600 characters a second.

Alcan, the United States' fourth ranking manufacturer of aluminum products, is one of 90 subsidiaries of Alcan Aluminium Limited, Montreal. United States operations, employing 4,800 persons in 27 states, comprise 5 divisions, 21 fabricating plants, 24 metal service centers, and more than 20 service facilities for building- and other products.

The new network not only provides 60 times faster message transmission and more effective message entry, but has also provided a vehicle for an order processing system for Alcan's Metal Goods Division. Metal Goods had plans for a new online inventory inquiry communications network, but instead was able to have ALCANET accept an inquiry program and perform the function without any other software or communication lines.

Alcan's communications had included its private line and a teleterminal network, as well as facsimile, public telex and TWX, and three separate teleprocessing networks. The system included point-to-point lines, dial-up lines, and low-speed and high-speed lines. The company was using hardware for communications in some cases and software in others. It was clear that if it progressed with its communications network in this fashion, the system would become unworkable.

The solution was to break from the one-application, one-network pattern and move into "multifunctionality"—the ability to perform several applications on the same terminal. It was determined that IBM's Systems Network Architecture and Synchronous Data Link Control could increase transmission throughput and provide for system growth.

Previously, Alcan had separate terminals with different procedures for messages, program development, and remote job entry. Under SNA, it is possible to sign on a terminal and perform any of these activities.

The message switching network operates under the control of an IBM processor in Warren, Ohio. The goal is to reduce the number of leased lines currently used for interactive or batch processing. Every time the company incorporates a line under SNA, it effects a saving.

Users at 55 United States ALCANET stations can now send or receive messages among the locations over Synchronous Data Link Control lines and under SNA. They can also connect to a network in Canada and international locations, and there are interface provisions to Telex and TWX service. Terminals can be used from 7 A.M. to 8 P.M. five days a week and can be used at other times by special arrangement.

Messages may be sent to one or more stations at a time simply by identifying the stations. Or, with one code, the message will go to all stations in the network. The system automatically records date and time of sending and receipt on the messages, so operators do not have to be concerned with that detail.

The processor uses the VS1 operating system and the Virtual Machine/Conversational Monitor System which provide separate machine environments for separate processing requirements as well as the interactive mode support. Message processing is done by the Advanced Communication Function/Telecommunications Access Method which can queue messages, store and forward, provide and audit trail of mesages, keep accounting information, and record billing data.

In addition to transmitting messages and sending manufacturing orders to various plants, the Metal Goods Division also uses ALCANET, so 120 terminals can access product availability files on the computer. The inventory inquiry system is the first phase of a larger inventory control system that will facilitate production ordering as well as communications with customers.

The IBM Development Management System was used to design screen formats to simplify browsing through the product list. Operators can determine locations at which a particular item is warehoused, the number of items on hand or on order, and the current prices of products.

ALCANET has provided a number of benefits for the company. Point-to-point message transmission turn-around time is virtually instantaneous now, compared with minutes or even hours that it previously took. The company also has better control of network traffic. Message logging is automatic, and transaction data are collected by the system. These data will help determine line use and facilitate system improvements.

Users like the format that can be provided for certain kinds of standard messages. For example, one user sends 200 messages a week at Alcan's Sheet and Plate Division plant in Warren, Ohio. Working with the screen format has greatly simplified his work. Formerly, if he made a mistake, he would not know it until the message was printed. With the screen, he can see the message and have a chance to correct errors. He can stop in the middle of sending a message—say, to answer a phone call—and not worry about losing the message or not knowing where he left off, because it is there on the screen. There is no paper tape to jam or tear, and it is possible to get immediate answers to urgent messages.

Alcan plans to add new applications to its communications network and bring existing systems under SNA.

D.F. STANIC, Corporate Systems Manager, Alcan Aluminum Corporation, Cleveland, Ohio

Information Reference

The above entry follows the treatment in the article, "SNA Talks Business," *Data Processor,* December, 1980.

Cross References: *Electronic Data Processing and entries with that prefix; Management Information Systems; Management Information Systems: Case Example.*

DECISION MAKING AND ORGANIZATIONAL EFFECTIVENESS: The Systems Approach

Certain concepts and check questions coupled with the systems approach are of value in improving **Organizational Effectiveness.**

System Defined. *A system is that particular combination of elements and relationships which is associated with the effects to be studied at a given level of fineness, and is isolated from a larger or more complex environment by a concept of diminishing effects.* The first half of this definition stresses the point that what we call a system is governed by what we conceive to be the interaction between "what is there" and "what we wish to look at" in terms of *what is important, achievable, and/or economical for our purpose.* One may take a particular automobile as an example. A suburbanite may be primarily interested in how it rides and handles for use around town as a second car. A research engineer, on the other hand, may be interested in characteristics which would enable it to meet minimum efficiency and safety requirements under widely varying conditions of operation and environment. He would therefore be concerned with many different and probably more numerous system elements than would the suburbanite, who would be willing to rely on his subjective judgments and do without extensive laboratory tests under controlled conditions.

The phrase "is isolated from a larger or more complex environment by a concept of diminishing effects" means that for any given purpose it is not worth the effort or expense to define the boundaries of a system beyond a certain point; though, ultimately, every system is part of some larger system. The organization is part of the state. A rank-and-file technical job is a subset of all of the jobs in the organization; yet, analysis of its key elements and processes, as a practical matter, would probably require inclusion of few, if any, of the other jobs. The conceptualization of a plant-wide incentive system would include more jobs within the organization, but it would not require as much information about each as would the individual job study. The model of a decision process that determines which products to make would go beyond the organization's boundaries to include consideration of factors such as the market, competitor activity, and anticipated government regulation.

The Systems Approach. The term "systems approach" is applied to the formulation of systems and subsystems as discussed above, and the relating of changes in any part of a system to total performance. It makes the study of modern, complex organizations conceptually manageable in the same way as medical researchers have made their study of the complex human system manageable (without oversimplfication) by focusing upon various subsystems separately as well as interactionally. The systems approach utilizes specialized knowledge from management science and industrial engineering as well as from the areas of organization theory and organizational behavior.

Diagnosis under the systems approach focuses upon the formulation of effectiveness criteria for each subsystem, as well as for the overall organizational system and upon the effective resolution of conflict where subsystems interface. Clear definition of different roles for different subsystems provides especially valuable guidance for those organizational members who must work in or with more than one system.

Effectiveness Criteria. Effectiveness criteria are the specific weighted standards against which achievement relative to the organization's goals is measured. Often too little attention is devoted to this basis for determining what will constitute success and failure. What this can lead to is dramatized by Morse and Kimball in an example from the Second World War [1]:

> Certain authorities were pushing for the removal of scarce antiaircraft guns from merchant ships, even though their presence had made the crews feel safer, because only 4% of attacking planes had been shot down. However, someone suggested that the number of planes downed was not the most important effectiveness criterion, but rather that the criterion should be the protection of the ship. Re-analysis of the data showed that the presence and use of the guns had reduced the accuracy of attackers, had reduced damage, and often had been responsible for saving a ship.

Additionally, there is need to recognize and resolve *conflicting goal situations.* For example, those who pass on the extension of credit often operate with implicit effectiveness criteria which are incompatible with those assumed by sales managers and their men in the field. Similarly, quality control and safety specialists have different basic objectives from those of production people.

By weighting goals we accomplish the following: We make them more congruent with the purposes of an organization or one of its subsystems, we discourage undue attention to particular goals based on ease of accomplishment or personal preference, and we have the opportunity to indicate absolute constraints as well as relative importance. To illustrate the last point: we might set a goal of decreasing the response time to phoned inquiries 10%, but specify that response time *must* decrease 5% to match our competition, and performance against other criteria must not drop below certain levels as a result of this.

Identification of Subsystems. A useful approach for identifying an organizational subsystem is to determine first the process it carries out, and then to identify its structure in terms of the arrangement of components required by that process. The same components may be utilized by several systems, and there is reciprocal influence (mutual causation) between a system's process and its structure [2].

Each process or subsystem accommodates a purpose or purposes, and one or more goals related to each purpose. For example, we might observe that a boy has the *purpose* of keeping his body temperature in the proper range, and so he may have the *goal* of finding and putting on a sweater [3]. In the example of the antiaircraft guns on merchant ships, we might say that the primary *purpose* of the gun was to protect the ship from damage, and that a secondary purpose was to contribute to the morale of the crew. As it turned out, it may have been more appropriate for a gun crew to have the *goals* of opening fire as soon as possible and maintaining a high rate of fire in the general direction of an attacking plane, rather than to delay opening fire, and then to fire slowly with the *goal* of getting the most hits possible.

Often the stated purpose of a system is not its actual purpose. We may be able to infer the true purpose of a system by observing the specific values for whose maintenance it expends resources. An important sign of trouble in an organization is provided by detection of incompatible purposes and/or incompatible goals.

In a business organization we can identify many possible subsystems for purposes of analysis and refinement in design. First, we might divide all of the work of the organization into major subsystems which involve the creation of salable values, the distribution of salable values, and the preparatory and support activities which are required to make the first two possible. We might then define planning subsystems and control subsystems to go with each of the above, and various motivational subsystems for top-level executives, foremen, rank and file workers, clerical help, and so on. Then, we might find it useful to define special subsystems for such things as the management of change, conflict resolution, technological specialization, innovation, integration, and special projects such as a merger or a unique defense contract. It would be useful then to define and study the information-flow and data-processing subsystems required for all of the above, and to compare critically what has informally evolved for them in the organization with what was formally prescribed.

We have no choice about the subsystems of an organism, for they are given. We do have choices, however, about organizational subsystems, for they are contrived by man. As an example of the kinds of choices involved, which, if any, of the following subsystems should be integrated into a materials system: production control, inventory control, traffic, transportation, receiving, shipping, purchasing? Is the establishment of decentralized product division profit centers appropriate? What degree of overall integration will be necessary, and how should it be achieved?

If a building or machine serves as a component of several systems, it is unlikely that its multiple roles will ever be in conflict with one another. Quite the contrary is true of a human component. He (she) usually belongs to a "getting ahead in the organization" subsystem (likely part of a political subsystem) and one or two active family subsystems, in addition to his regular work subsystem. There may also be professional activities. There is no assurance that the personal goals associated with each of these subsystems will be compatible. The problem is more pronounced for new employees, and for personnel at an organization's boundary (such as salesmen) who are more subject to external influences [4].

Part of the answer lies in the appropriate organization of work; part lies in good selection and placement; part lies in the functioning of positive informal social systems; and a larger part lies in the operation of carefully planned and properly integrated reward-penalty systems.

Lawrence and Lorsch [5] have identified differences in the following factors as likely causes of misunderstanding and conflict between personnel of differentiated subsystems:

Rates of change or innovation.
Certainty of information.
Time span of feedback.
Complexity of tasks.
Activity focus (e.g., on the extension of credit rather than the making of sales, or vice versa).

Among other things, these factors influence the "tightness of control" appropriate to any area of operation. Consequent differences in accountability which result can easily breed resentment. Also, such differences tend to accentuate even further the "parochial loyalties" which develop quite naturally from common work assignments and common concerns . . . loyalties which tend to encourage interdepartmental intrigue and infighting.

Understanding on the part of personnel involved as to the unavoidability of these forces which work against harmony can do much to neutralize their effects. Special orientation programs and use of integrating committees or staff personnel can help to develop and maintain such understanding.

Use of Simulation Models. A simulation model is a representation of a system which can be operated through time to reflect the effects of on-going system processes, i.e. to *simulate* them. System operating effects are determined experimentally through the simulation, rather than analytically through mathematical manipulation. The representation of a system can be either physical or mathematical. For example, the flight characteristics of a missile may be determined by observing the behavior of a scale model in a wind tunnel, or by observing how its mathematically noted characteristics interact with various mathematically noted environmental factors (such as wind conditions during a "flight" on the computer.

The validity of an organizational simulation model is crucial. It is determined by the model's ability to reproduce historical characteristics and outputs of the system being modeled and to predict its future effects. Research has produced principles which relate the structure of complex, nonlinear systems to their behavior, and the pace of such research is accelerating [6], [7]. Jay Forrester, a pioneer in systems dynamic research, describes provocative recent findings:

> The problem is not the shortage of data, but rather our inability to perceive the consequences of the information we already possess. . . . Time after time we have gone into a corporation that is having severe difficulties. The difficulties can be major and obvious, such as a falling market share, low profitability, or instability of employment. . . . Generally speaking we find that people perceive correctly their immediate environment. . . . They know the crises that will force certain actions. They are sensitive to the power structure of the organization, to traditions, and to their own personal goals and welfare. . . . In a troubled company, people are usually trying in good conscience to solve the major difficulties. . . . One can combine the company's policies into a computer model to show the consequences of how the policies interact with one another. In many instances it then emerges that the known policies describe a system that actually causes the troubles [8].
>
> Most planning criteria are derived from intuitive judgment, which will often be wrong because of the counter-intuitive nature of complex systems. Furthermore, when planning appears to be effec-

tive it may at the same time be developing the conditions for longer-term degradation. This is likely as a result of the common reversal that occurs between the short-run and the long-run consequences of a policy change in a complex system [9].

Forrester presents an extensive, detailed case study to illustrate how commonplace structure, time lags, and amplification effects combine to cause a typical information-feedback system to behave in unexpected ways [10]. (See also INDUSTRIAL DYNAMICS.)

Some Specific Questions and Related Considerations. With the foregoing general overview of the nature of the systems approach, let us consider some specific questions and concepts which help to make it useful in the field.

1. Has provision been made for the development and refinement of subsystem simulation models, where feasible, which planners may use to pre-test the effects of differing assumptions and tentative plans upon operations (e.g., as represented by forecast of financial statements and other indexes)?

When computerized, such models save time and effort in the otherwise difficult work of trying to assess the impact of various sets of alternatives, while taking all necessary constraints into account.

2. Have we achieved an adequate level of agreement among all concerned as to what our purposes are? Or the nature and ordering of the effectiveness criteria? Can we combine adequately defined effectiveness criteria for all subsystems of the organization without apparent conflict? Do we agree as to what are the significant constraints and risks involved, and as to the nature of the decisions which must be made?

Overall objectives, in addition to being based upon realistic premises about strengths and resources of the organization and the external environment in which it must operate, should be congruent whenever possible with what Ackoff refers to as the "stylistic objectives" of the management team [11]. He feels that by making explicit the emotionally based preferences about what the company should be doing and should not be doing (without regard to the test of profitability), the air may be cleared for more consistent and enthusiastic rational pursuit of both preferred and economically appropriate goals.

A useful test for agreement as to the nature of a given subsystem is provided by requesting that all who work in it or with it prepare independently written statements as to the specific objectives, responsibilities, and kinds of authority associated with each position in the system.

3. Does a particular system work as predicted? If not, why not? Will it recognize and respond to serious distress or malfunction signals . . . and do so in appropriate time? Does it handle maximum levels of informational or operational overload and underload in ways which are acceptable? Will the system handle unique or first-time demands upon it in acceptable ways?

4. Has adequate provision been made for sensing external information vital to the organization's internal decision-making? Which system's outputs are another system's inputs? Are input data for one or more systems generated independently of the same data being available as output from other systems? Has aggregation of decision-making occurred which is consistent with authority-accountability requirements when there are overlapping informational requirements? Has adequate provision been made to assure the continued supply of necessary information to respective users in the format desired, and with appropriate timeliness?

It is easy to lose sight of the reality that information, *per se,* is not always a blessing. Information is a "tool," not a "solution." As decision makers we cannot really understand our valid information needs until we understand the decision processes in which we are involved. Though clear identification of the key factors in decision processes will help to define information needs, it does not provide assurance that we are focusing on the *right* key factors in the *best* decision processes, given certain basic purposes.

To test the speed and accuracy of an organization's information system, issue a precise policy statement on the basis of normal procedure, then determine via interviews when the message was delayed and where distortion occurred, and attempt to pin-point the reasons.

5. What would happen if a particular system of control did not exist? If we could start from scratch, how would we design it? Could any of the control activities now performed by people be more economically performed by machines which exist, or which could be designed? What informal controls have been developed by groups and individuals and how congruent are they with those which are formally prescribed?

Feedback (modification of input to a system on the basis of assessments of output variations against some criterion or criteria) is an essential factor in *control:* making events conform to plans. Rapidity of response can be a problem. Too rapid a response to error signals can lead to over-adjustment, and—under certain conditions—oscillation. Too slow a response can lead to unnecessary cost or damage. Other important factors to consider with regard to feedback are: its relevance and inclusiveness, its validity (as to error introduction at source and message distortion), and the adequacy of provisions for recording and storing details of its occurrence for future reference.

Determination should be made as to whether or not it is the most *appropriate* system for the conditions at hand.

From a behavioral viewpoint, it is unrealistic to require an agency or person performing consulting or counseling functions for other people to audit or "check-up-on" these same people. Either the audit role or the supportive role will be neglected. One cannot view a person as a helper when he is rewarded for ferreting out and reporting one's deficiencies and mistakes.

The assignment of both audit and supportive roles to managers vis-à-vis their subordinates is inescapable. However, the impact of the audit role may be moderated through the use of means for facilitating the setting and acceptance of individual and group goals. (See GOAL SETTING.)

The net impact of the reward-penalty system should be geared to *all* of the behaviors which are important to a given function. Frequently the reward system (more pay, advancement, perquisites, status) may overlook a whole set of behaviors which are actually basic to optimum performance. Thus in academic circles, the "publish or perish" syndrome may be the determining factor in advancement, rather than conscientious teaching and counseling of students. In business, monetary recognition and promotion may be geared to immediate profits, penalizing the manager who seeks to take the long view (as in fact called for by his position description) in terms of research and development and modernization of facilities. There is a strong pull for most of us to give a system what it actually pays for, rather than what it "says" it wants.

Conclusion. The usefulness of the "systems approach" in a given situation is determined by the degree to which assumptions about factors, effects, and diminution of effects are correctly related to properly specified purposes. It is the search for significant system elements and regular patterns that has primary diagnostic value.

This discussion will end with a question: *Has adequate provision been made to assure the periodic review and up-dating of all systems as well as knowledge about systems?*

WILLIAM M. FOX, PH.D., Professor of Industrial Relations and Management, University of Florida, Gainesville, Florida.

References Cited

[1] Morse, P.M., and Kimball, G.E., "Methods of Operations Research," New York, Technology Press and Wiley, 1951.
[2] Miller, James G., "Living Systems," New York, McGraw-Hill, 1978.
[3] Ibid.
[4] Katz, Daniel, and Kahn, Robert, "The Social Psychology of Organizations," 2nd ed., New York, John Wiley, 1978; and Burns, Tom, "On the Plurality of Social Systems," in "Operational Research and the Social Sciences," Lawrence, J.R., ed., New York, Tavistock Publications, 1966.
[5] Lawrence, Paul R., and Lorsch, Jay W., "Organization and Environment," Homestead, Ill., Irwin, 1969.
[6] For example, Forrester, Jay W., "Principles of Systems," Cambridge, Mass., Wright-Allen Press, 1968.
[7] Forrester, Jay W., "Industrial Dynamics," Cambridge, Mass., M.I.T. Press, 1961.
[8] ———, "Collected Papers of Jay W. Forrester, Cambridge, Mass., Wright-Allen Press, 1975.
[9] Ibid.
[10] ———, "Industrial Dynamics."
[11] Ackoff, Russell L., "A Concept of Corporate Planning," New York, Wiley, 1970.

Cross References: *Control Theory: Application to Management; Goal Setting; Industrial Dynamics; Managerial Effectiveness: Climate for Organizational Results; Organization Theory.*

DECISION THEORY

Decision Theory is a methodology for structuring and analyzing risky or uncertain decision situations. It is primarily prescriptive rather than descriptive. That is, it is much more likely to be useful in prescribing the actions a decision maker should take in a given situation than in describing how decision makers actually behave, although it has been used for both purposes.

Although decision theory can be applied in many contexts, this discussion concerns prescriptive use in management decision situations. (See also the section, *Decision Theory,* in the entry, STATISTICS.) Risk and uncertainty pervade management problems, particularly those of a strategic nature. Some problems of this type are suggested by the following questions. Should we market that product? Should we test market it before deciding? What should we bid on that job? Should we continue developing that advanced product design? Should we build a pilot plant or launch a full-scale production?

But risk and uncertainty are also significant in many tactical decisions, like those suggested by another series of questions. What production process should we use? Which of several competing suppliers should we use? Should our vehicle fleet be commercially insured, and if so, what deductible should be selected? How many of the last shipment of transistors should be tested before the lot is accepted or rejected? How many transactions should be audited before we publicly attest that our client's financial statements are in good order?

Although these examples seem very diverse, decision theory provides a common unifying conceptual framework and associated methods for structuring and analyzing each of them. A decision-theoretic analysis abstracts the situation into a structured decision problem facing a single individual called the decision maker (for brevity, DM). DM is assumed to come to the situation with (1) some subjective judgments about relative likelihoods of uncertain events and (2) some well-defined preferences for outcomes or consequences. Decision theory combines these judgments and preferences, along with the available objective data, in a structured, systematic, quantitative analysis of the problem, an analysis that permits DM to evaluate the consequences of alternative decisions and to identify "good" or "best" decisions.

The "single decision-maker" abstraction presents no difficulty when the DM actually is a single individual or a group that must act as a single DM (e.g., a board of directors), provided the individuals' preferences and judgments are in reasonable agreement. However, the single DM assumption is inappropriate for situations with two or more agents who can act independently and whose preferences might lead them to do so. These problems belong not to decision theory, but to the closely related field of GAME THEORY.

Origins. Decision theory is known by several names. The more common include decision analysis, statistical decision theory, Bayesian decision theory, decision theory analysis, and decision trees. Decision theory's modern origins are in statistical decision theory and game theory. Both of these areas developed rapidly in the 1940s with the appearance of Abraham Wald's seminal work on statistical decisions and von Neumann and Morgenstern's classic book "Theory of Games and Economic Behavior." The subsequent two decades witnessed rapid advances in these areas, and decision theory seemingly acquired a more or less distinct identity, although in reality most of the basic ideas remain unchanged.

The Elements of Decision Theory. While the actual details vary, all decision-theoretic analyses share a common structure and have common basic elements. In the simplest case, DM must choose exactly one *act* from a set of available courses of action. That act combines with an unknown *state of nature* (or event) to produce a well-defined *outcome* that has consequences for DM. Although the act must be chosen without knowledge of the true state of nature, DM knows the relative likelihoods of the states. These are represented by a probability distribution on the set of possible states. That distribution, called the *prior distribution,* can be objectively specified by historical data or subjectively determined by DM on the basis of judgment, experience, and intuition.

To illustrate these ideas consider the problem of deciding about introducing a new product. Pricing strategy has been set and the major remaining decision concerns the scale of the production facility if the product is launched. DM has narrowed the set of available acts to three:

A1 - build a large facility
A2 - build a medium-sized facility
A3 - don't build a facility (i.e., don't introduce the product)

The major uncertainty stems from the unknown strength of demand for this product which, for simplicity, will assume one of the following three values (states), with the probabilities shown:

S1 - high demand	P(S1) = .3
S2 - medium demand	P(S2) = .4
S3 - low demand	P(S3) = .3

The outcome associated with any state-act combination in our illustration is calculated using known cost figures for the values assumed, with established sales prices, and is summa-

Exhibit I

Data for the New Product Problem
(Dollar outcomes in millions of dollars)

P(S)	STATES	ACTS A1	A2	A3
.3	S1	$2	$1	$0
.4	S2	.5	.4	0
.3	S3	−1	−.2	0

PRIOR DISTRIBUTION — PROFITS IN $ MILLIONS OUTCOMES

rized by a dollar profit or loss. These summary data are provided in Exhibit I.

The data in Exhibit I can be conveniently represented by the *decision tree* in Exhibit II. This decision tree is simply a convenient graphical representation of all possible combinations of acts and states that might materialize in this situation. Starting at the left-most node of this tree, DM chooses one of three acts. At one of the next nodes (precisely which one depends on DM's choice) a state of nature is randomly chosen according to the probabilities shown, and DM receives the outcome shown.

The square node represents a decision or choice, a point at which DM must choose one act from the available alternatives. The round nodes represent random events or points at which some random event is determined according to a known probability distribution.

This decision tree clearly shows that DM's choice of an action is essentially the choice of a lottery or probability distribution on the possible outcomes. For example, Al clearly yields lottery L1 (Exhibit III).

Exhibit II

A Decision Tree for the
New Product Problem

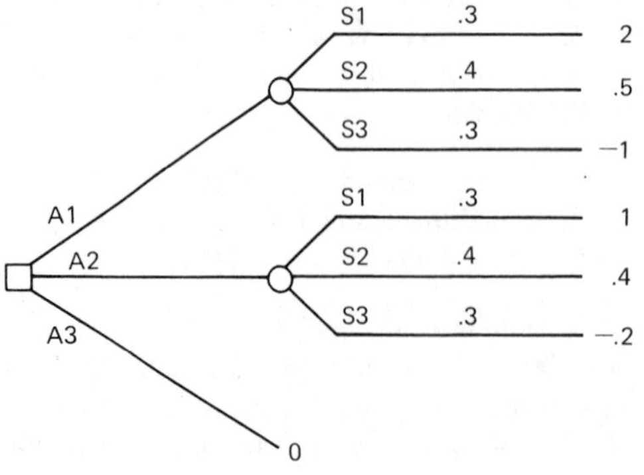

In addition to data in Exhibits I and II, then, one final element is required. DM must specify some consistent, well-behaved preferences among outcomes and lotteries on outcomes.

Preferences among outcomes are simple in this example; most decision makers prefer more profit to less. Preferences among lotteries can be more complex, but for expository convenience, assume DM's preferences among lotteries are determined by *expected monetary value* (EMV). For a lottery L that yields profit x with probability $P(x)$, EMV(L) is defined as follows:

$$\text{EMV(L)} = \sum_x xP(x)$$

For the example

$$\text{EMV(L1)} = .3(2) + .4(5) + .3(-1) = .5$$
$$\text{EMV(L2)} = .3(1) + .4(.4) + .3(-.2) = .4$$
$$\text{EMV(L3)} = .3(0) + .4(0) + .3(0) = 0$$

Thus, using the EMV criterion, DM strictly prefers L1 to either L2 or L3, and A1 (build a large facility) is the optimal act. The expected value of profit is .5 or $500,000.

Basic Structure When Experimentation or Testing Is Possible. Suppose the example is complicated by the possibility of conducting a test market before deciding on A1, A2, or A3. The test market costs $50,000 ($.05 million) and yields one of two outcomes:

Z1 = test market demand is high
Z2 = test market demand is low.

The conditional probabilities of these outcomes, given the state of nature, are shown in Exhibit IV.

A decision tree is shown in Exhibit V. The top half of the tree is precisely that shown in Exhibit II. The bottom half corresponds to conducting a test market. The test market demand is observed, and then DM chooses A1, A2, or A3 based on this test market information.

Exhibit III

Lottery L1:

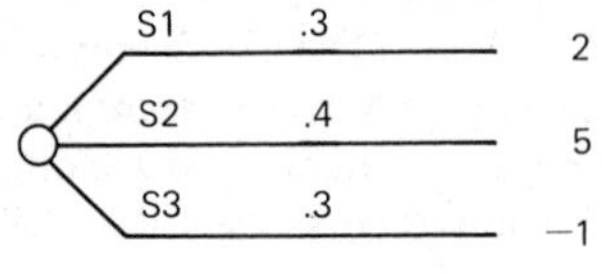

Exhibit IV

Conditional Probabilities for Test Market

S \ Z	TEST MARKET DEMAND Z1	Z2
S1	.9	.1
S2	.6	.4
S3	.2	.8

P(Z|S)

Note that the probabilities of S1, S2, and S3 depend on the test market outcome and, for either outcome, differ from the prior probabilities. For example, if the test market is used and the result is Z1, the relevant probability is P(S|Z1), that is, the *conditional probability of S given Z1.* These conditional distributions, called *posterior distributions,* are quite different from the conditional distributions in Exhibit IV. The probabilities in Exhibit IV describe inherent features of the test market. For example, if the test market is conducted, P(Z1|S2) is the probability of high test-market demand (Z1) *given* that the underlying, unknown strength of demand is medium (S2).

On the other hand, the posterior distributions describe the relative likelihoods of the states of nature *given* that the test market has yielded a particular outcome. P(S2|Z1), then, is the probability that the unknown strength of demand is medium (S2) *given* that the test market demand is high (Z1).

The posterior distributions are completely determined by the prior distribution and the conditional distributions in Exhibit IV, and are easily computed using Bayes' Theorem:

$$P(S|Z) = \frac{P(S,Z)}{P(Z)} = \frac{P(S)\ P(Z|S)}{\sum_{S} P(S)P(Z|S)}$$

Exhibit V

Decision Tree with Test Market

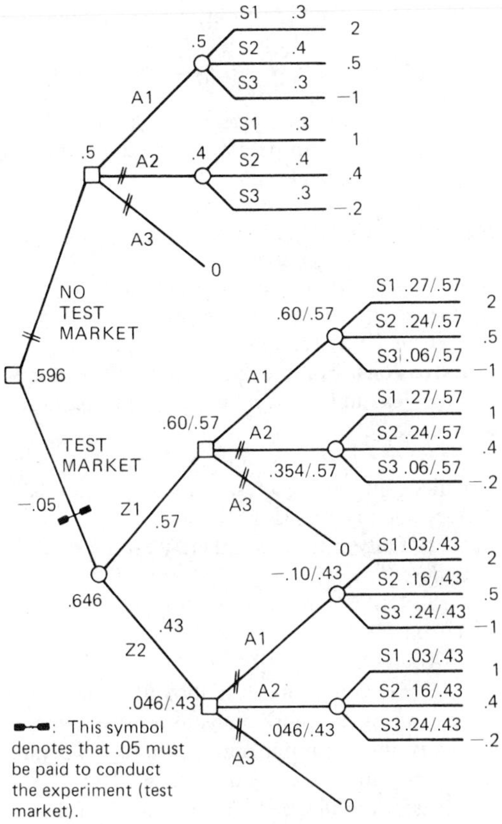

The numerator of the left-hand fraction, P(S,Z), is called the *joint probability* of S and Z and is easily computed by forming the product P(S)P(Z|S). Thus, the prior distribution and the conditional distributions in Exhibit IV combine to produce a *joint probability distribution* on the set of state-test outcome pairs. These joint probabilities are shown in the body of the left-hand table in Exhibit VI.

The numerator of the left-hand fraction, P(Z), is called the marginal or unconditional probability of test outcome Z. It is calculated using the denominator of the right-hand fraction. In tabular form this expression is found by summing the entries of the appropriate column of the left-hand table in Exhibit VI. The posterior probabilities in the right-hand table of Exhibit VI are found by forming the appropriate ratios from the table of joint and marginal probabilities.

A brief description of the computations should clarify the tree in Exhibit V. The EMV of each lottery is written by the appropriate node. Thus, in the top half, .5, .4, and 0 are the same EMVs that were calculated earlier. Backing up to the decision node in the top half, DM clearly prefers A1 (as before), so the A2 and A3 paths are marked with a double slash (||) to denote that they are inferior to A1. The EMV for A1, .5, is written beside the decision node. Computations in the lower part of the

EXHIBIT VI

PROBABILITY CALCULATIONS FOR DECISION TREE

JOINT PROBABILITIES

S \ Z	P(S,Z) = P(S)P(Z∣S) Z1	Z2
S1	.27	.03
S2	.24	.16
S3	.06	.24
P(Z)	.57	.43

POSTERIOR PROBABILITIES

S \ Z	P(S∣Z) = P(S,Z)/P(Z) Z1	Z2
S1	.27/.57	.03/.43
S2	.24/.57	.16/.43
S3	.06/.57	.24/.43

tree proceed similarly. If the test market demand is Z1 and DM chooses A1 the resulting lottery has EMV:

$$EMV = 2(.27/.57) + .5(.24/.57) - 1(.06/.57) = .60/.57$$

By a similar computation, the lottery at Z1, A2 has EMV=.354/.57. Thus, if Z1 is the test market demand, A1 is the preferred action with EMV = .60/.57. Similarly, if Z2 is the test market demand, A2 is the preferred action with EMV=.046/.43. Backing up to the random event node for the test market, DM faces another lottery, with P(Z1) = .57 probability of obtaining an EMV of .60/.57 and P(Z2) = .43 probability of obtaining an EMV of .046/.43. The EMV of this lottery is

$$EMV(test) = .57(.60/.57) + .43(.046/.43) = .646.$$

Backing up to the left-most node DM faces the following choice: choose NO TEST MARKET for an EMV of .5, choose TEST MARKET and pay .05 for an EMV of .646 or a net EMV of .596. Thus the preferred strategy is TEST MARKET: if test market demand is high, build a large facility (A1); if test market demand is low, build a medium-sized facility (A2).

Value of Information. The test market is clearly the best choice if its cost does not exceed (.646 −.5) = .146 or $146,000. It is natural to call this value the expected value of sample information (EVSI) for this particular test market. In a similar fashion the EVSI of any specific test market or similar experiment can be calculated.

A convenient upper bound on the value of *any* test or experiment is provided by the expected value of perfect information (EVPI). The EVPI is essentially the maximum amount DM would be willing to pay for perfect information. It is most easily understood by returning to Exhibit I and considering DM's expected profit were (s)he given access to a costless crystal ball which faultlessly reported the state of nature. If, for example, S1 were true, DM would know and, of course, choose A1 for a profit of 2. If the state were S2, A1 is preferred and the outcome is .5. If S3 is true, A3 is chosen and the profit is 0. With the prior probabilities in Exhibit I and a costless crystal ball, DM's expected profit, EMV*, would be

$$EMV^* = .3(2) + .4(.5) + .3(0) = .8$$

Since, by using the prior distribution alone, DM can attain an EMV of .5, the expected value of the crystal ball is

$$EVPI = EMV^* - EMV = .8 - .5 = .3$$

or $300,000. Under very reasonable conditions it can be shown that EVPI provides an upper bound on EVSI for any test or experiment.

Extensions. For expository purposes the new product example is deliberately oversimplified in five ways:

(1) There is a small number of vaguely-specified acts and states. (Precisely what is a "large" facility or "high" demand?)

(2) Only one experiment (test market) is considered.

(3) DM's preferences for lotteries are based on EMV.

(4) All probabilities are known.

(5) Outcomes are described as dollar profits instead of the more realistic time streams of sales revenues, capital and operating expenditures, market shares, employment levels, etc. But these simplifications are not necessarily re-

quired. They can be relaxed in principle and, frequently, in practice. A discussion of each follows.

Proliferating the states, acts, and possible experiments simply increases the data processing task. Although the computational burden increases, much larger problems can be analyzed in this fashion.

Basing preferences among lotteries on EMV characterizes one particular attitude toward risk, called risk neutrality, an attitude some DMs might reject. Consider the following two lotteries:

L1: 50% chance of a $2,000,000 profit
50% chance of a $1,000,000 loss
L2: 50% of a $1,000,000 profit
50% chance of a $0 profit.

A conservative DM might strictly prefer L2 to L1 despite the fact that EMV(L1) = EMV(L2). That preference illustrates risk aversion, a conservative attitude thought to characterize many DMs. Conversely, a more adventurous, risk-seeking DM might prefer L1 to L2 because L1 offers a higher possible profit.

Different risk attitudes and preferences among lotteries can be accommodated through the application of *preference* or *utility theory,* a well-developed topic that addresses the role of risk attitudes in decision making.

In many situations, precise objective probabilities are not known. In such cases DM, perhaps with the aid of others, must specify probabilities subjectively. An area called *judgmental* or *subjective probability theory* has been developed to guide this process.

When outcomes are described as time streams of cash flows, straightforward computations will reduce them to equivalent net present values (see section, *Net Present Value,* in RETURN ON CAPITAL) which can be treated like the dollar profits in the previous example. If, however, DM wishes to describe outcomes along several dimensions, other methods are required. *Multiattribute utility theory* is a new and rapidly growing field dealing with these situations.

Strengths and Weaknesses of Decision Theory. Decision theory's most important strength lies in the capability it provides for structuring and systematically analyzing very complex decision situations. To begin a decision analysis, the analyst or DM must explicitly identify the available acts, states, and outcomes, and if the analysis proceeds, the DM must carefully consider the relevant probabilities and attitudes toward risk. In fact, many users report that the exercise of structuring an appropriate decision tree frequently uncovers an optimal stategy without extensive computation. However, should a complete analysis be required, decision theory's explicit methods and straightforward computational procedures facilitate repeated analyses using several alternate assumptions.

But some of these sources of strength also can produce frustration and difficulty. Many important management decision problems arise in ill-structured situations involving more than one decision maker. Under these conditions, structuring an appropriate decision tree and obtaining the required judgmental inputs can be a formidable task. Short lead times can exacerbate any difficulties. And even if a problem can be structured, decision theoretic analyses require time and resources, and these requirements obviously increase with the complexity of the situation.

On balance, decision theory offers a potentially powerful and practicable approach for analyzing important management decision situations. It has been successfully applied in a variety of management contexts, and as the trend toward formal analysis of management problems continues, decision theory is very likely to be more frequently and routinely applied.

FRED E. WILLIAMS, PH.D., Associate Professor and Chairman of Graduate Program, College of Management, and CHARLES E. GEARING, PH.D., Professor and Dean, College of Management, Georgia Institute of Technology, Atlanta, Georgia.

Information References

Associations:

American Institute for Decision Sciences.
American Statistical Association.
Operations Research Society of America.
The Institute of Management Sciences.

Periodicals:

Decision Sciences.
Journal of the American Statistical Association.
Management Science.
Operations Research.

Texts and Articles:

Brown, Rex V., "Do Managers Find Decision Theory Useful?" *Harvard Business Review,* May-June 1970.

Hammond, John S. III, "Better Decisions with Preference Theory," *Harvard Business Review,* November-December 1967.

Holloway, Charles A., "Decision Making Under Un-

certainty: Models and Choices," Englewood Cliffs, N.J., Prentice-Hall, 1979.
Keeney, Ralph L. and Raiffa, Howard, "Decisions with Multiple Objectives: Preferences and Value Tradeoffs," New York, Wiley, 1976.
Raiffa, Howard, "Decision Analysis," New York, McGraw-Hill, 1968.
Raiffa, Howard and Schlaifer, Robert, "Applied Statistical Decision Theory," Division of Research, Graduate School of Business Administration, Harvard University, Boston, 1961.
Savage, Leonard J., "Foundations of Statistics," New York, Wiley, 1954.
Schlaifer, Robert, "Analysis of Decisions Under Uncertainty," New York, McGraw-Hill, 1969.
Von Neumann, J. and Morgenstern, Oskar, "Theory of Games and Economic Behavior," Princeton, N.J., Princeton Univ. Press, 2nd edition, 1947.
Wald, Abraham, "Statistical Decision Functions," New York, Wiley, 1950, and London, Chapman & Hall, 1950.

Cross References: *Decision Making and Organizational Effectiveness: The Systems Approach; Long-Range Corporate Planning; Long-Range Planning: Financial Aspects; Management Sciences (and cross references there given).*

DENNISON, HENRY

Henry Sturgis Dennison (1877–1952), an American industrialist, became known for making the management of his own medium-sized manufacturing company among the most progressive in America. He pioneered in profit-sharing plans, installing one in the Dennison Manufacturing Company in 1911. In the 1920s he pioneered with an unemployment insurance scheme and with an extensive executive development program. In 1924 he initiated the Manufacturers' Research Association, headquartered in Boston, a group of non-competing firms which established a small research staff for the exchange of detailed information on their management methods. Dennison was active in the organized management movement in America, particularly in the Taylor Society and the American Management Association. He was also a strong supporter of the International Management Institute. He authored many papers and delivered many lectures on management subjects. His books include "Profit Sharing and Stock Ownership for Employees" (with others), 1926 (Harper & Bros.), "Organization Engineering," 1931 (McGraw-Hill), "Modern Competition and Business Policy" (with others), 1938 (Oxford University Press), and "Toward Full Employment" (with others), 1938 (McGraw-Hill).

DEPRECIATION

Depreciation concepts in business take cognizance of the fact that plants, machinery, equipment, and all types of physical assets lose value with the passage of time. There has always been a wide divergence of opinion on the subject of how rapidly equipment should be depreciated from its original installed cost to its final salvage value at the time it is to be replaced as worn out or obsoleted. Final decisions are made by experienced engineers, financial executives, and tax experts who are familiar with the particulars of the equipment and its uses.

Engineering Concepts. The investment in any project is determined on the basis of the amount needed for new plant and equipment, plus the cost of installing new machinery, making suitable allowances for the cost of existing machinery obsoleted by the new, as well as presently available equipment which can be transferred to the new project. Capital reserves and other temporary provisions necessary during the construction of the project should be included.

However, the decision cannot be made without careful consideration of the continuing costs of the venture. These are computed on the basis of three items: (1) interest on the money used to finance the project; (2) depreciation, the cost of equipment wearing out and becoming obsolete; and (3) expenses, including labor costs, maintenance, power, supplies, insurance, direct overhead, taxes, engineering and administrative overhead, and others.

These three items are calculated for a period of time, usually many years ahead. The resulting annual cost will be proportionally lower if depreciation is spread over a greater number of years.

The engineer's basic objective is to design and install machinery that will deliver the goods day after day, year in and year out, under severe use and abuse. His method of handling depreciation reflects this approach. If his equipment can deliver over a long life, he can claim a smaller annual cost, hence a more profitable operation.

In certain industries, there are serious dangers of forced obsolescence due to changes in types of products produced, or new methods of production, causing even unworn equipment to be abandoned to salvage. But although it is possible for the life of machinery suddenly to be cut short by forced obsolescence, it is also probable that many machines will be used long after they have depreciated completely on the accountants' books either in their original application and location or after they have been sold, salvaged, rebuilt, and reinstalled. Somewhere between the extremes of forced obsolescence and extended lives of old equipment under restricted ratings is the *true life,* and this is allocated by management decision, varying with the business cycle and the type of business.

Engineers commonly use *Sinking-Fund* depreciation, *Straight-Line* depreciation, *Fixed-Percentage* depreciation, *Machine Hours* (which would be the total running time measured by an odometer fixed to the equipment), and *Rate per Unit Output,* which is used for tools, dies, and certain manufacturing machinery which can produce only a definite number of parts before it must be replaced. (Formulas are discussed below). Sometimes an annual rate is set up, a constant amount per year which covers the cost of depreciation and maintenance, so that as more maintenance is performed, less depreciation is taken.

When the usage of equipment will vary from year to year, depreciation may be taken in proportion to use. This permits a business to estimate its total income from a particular piece of equipment or income-producing item such as motion picture film, and take depreciation each year in proportion to income produced.

Accounting Concepts. Accountants and financial experts take a point of view that is sometimes directly opposite to that of the engineers, and recommend that physical assets be written off (depreciated) as rapidly as possible. More or less depreciation can be charged "on the books" without affecting the usefulness of the plant or equipment. Thus it is possible to have the "expense" without any outlay of funds to meet the expense because the depreciating items have been paid for in past years, and additional funds are provided for the enterprise. Funds provided by depreciation charges can be invested in inventory, accounts receivable, or whatever other investments seem to encourage the greatest return on investment until again needed for replacement of equipment or other purposes.

Depreciation of physical assets is considered an expense of running the business and is therefore deducted before taxes. A corporation pays 17% on the first $25,000 of earnings in a year, 20% on the next $25,000, eventually going to 46%, approximately, for large corporations in the United States (fiscal 1980). Therefore a tax deduction produces almost the same increase in income remaining after taxes as a corresponding increase in income before taxes.

EXHIBIT I

	Company A	*Company B*
Profit before depreciation	$100,000	$100,000
Depreciation	10,000	None
Other tax deductions	60,000	60,000
Taxable Income	30,000	40,000
Tax at 46%	13,800	18,400
Profit after taxes	$ 16,200	$ 21,600

Some accountants would say that no expense, depreciation or other, can lead to increase in income after taxes. For example, consider Exhibit I. Company A, which claims depreciation, has reduced net profits. On the other hand, many accountants point out that depreciation, which is lawfully claimed as tax deduction, might be higher "on the books" than in actual loss of performance or value of the equipment. So the above example might be considered another way, as shown in Exhibit II.

In this case the depreciation is an expense but not an expense involving outlay of funds. Yet it is a tax deduction and so does increase funds remaining after taxes.

Accountants may depreciate items individually, also by groups according to lives or by classes, according to use, or according to any other composite accounts. Each has its own depreciation reserve account, which is based upon the total amount invested in the group, in many cases including fully depreciated items. The value of the account and the life remaining is regularly adjusted for the retirement of assets or the acquisition of new assets, and depreciation for the group is taken according to one of the methods discussed below. It is permissible to claim accelerated deduction for tax pur-

EXHIBIT II

	Company A	*Company B*
Income	$100,000	$100,000
Expenses, less depreciation	60,000	60,000
	40,000	40,000
Taxes (compilation in Exhibit I)	13,800	18,400
Funds remaining after taxes	$26,200	$21,600

poses, yet keep separate books for internal business use.

Depreciation Formulas. In the depreciation formulas here discussed, the following symbols are used:

ΔD	Depreciation per year.
D_x	Depreciation after x years.
ΔD_x	Depreciation during xth years.
D	Total depreciation after n years.
n	Life of asset or group of assets, years.
P	Original price, total amount invested.
L	Lesser value, value less cost of disposing of asset after n years.
B_x	Book value at year x where $B_x = P - D_x$.
$B_{(x-1)}$	Book value at beginning of year x.
f	Depreciation factor or rate.
R	Future replacement value.

Straight-Line Depreciation assumes uniform yearly depreciation from original investment, first deducting the salvage value. The formula is:

$$\Delta D = (P - L)/n$$

For example, $15,000 invested in equipment will depreciate to $5,000 salvage value in ten years.

$$\Delta D = (15{,}000 - 5{,}000)/10$$
$$\Delta D = \$1{,}000 \text{ per year}$$
$$D = \$10{,}000$$

Fixed-Percentage Depreciation uses a depreciation percent or factor. When the difference between 100% and the factor is multiplied by itself n times (i.e., raised to the nth power), the original investment is converted to salvage value.

$$P(1.00 - f)^n = L$$

To determine the rate or factor f, the equation can be rewritten as:

$$f = 1 - (L/P)^{1/n}$$

where

$$\Delta D_1 = f \cdot P$$

and

$$\Delta D_x = f \cdot (B_{x-1})$$

EXHIBIT III

Year	B_{x-1}	f	D	B_x
1	$16,000	.2421	3,874	$12,126
2	12,126	.2421	2,936	9,190
3	9,190	.2421	2,225	6,965
4	6,969	.2421	1,687	5,278
5	5,278	.2421	1,278	4,000

Exhibit III shows the use of these formulas in an example where $P = \$16{,}000$, $L = \$4{,}000$ and n is 5 years.

Needless to say, when determining f, small salvage value must be handled with care since as L approaches zero, L/P ratio becomes indeterminate. Notice, salvage value is not deducted before depreciation is taken.

Accountants prefer to call the fixed-percentage method the *Declining Balance,* since the rate is applied to the remaining balance each year. Internal Revenue Service limits this method to twice the Straight-Line Depreciation rate, which becomes a special case called *Double-Declining Balance.* In a previous example we depreciate from original investment of $15,000 to $5,000 in ten years. The rate of depreciation was therefore $1,000 per year ÷ $10,000 total amount, or 10%—and so the double rate is 20%.

Double-Declining Balance takes double straight line rate and applies this to each year's balance as shown in Exhibit IV.

Since it is not permissible to depreciate below the salvage value, the amounts in parentheses, theoretically correct, are not allowed. The fifth-year depreciation is therefore limited to $1,144. Notice that the double rate is applied directly to original cost, and this rapid depreciation as shown above is permitted by IRS under specified conditions.

Sum of the Years (Digits, Integers) Method numbers each year, lists the numbers in inverse

EXHIBIT IV

Year	B_{x-1}	f	D	B_x
1	$15,000	.20	$3,000	$12,000
2	12,000	.20	2,400	9,600
3	9,600	.20	1,920	7,680
4	7,680	.20	1,536	6,144
5	6,144	.20	(1,229)	(4,915)
6	None permitted			

EXHIBIT V

Year	Digit	Sum of Digit Ratio	$P - L$	D	B_x
1	7	7/28	$12,000	$3,000	$9,000
2	6	6/28	12,000	2,573	6,427
3	5	5/28	12,000	2,143	4,284
4	4	4/28	12,000	1,714	2,570
5	3	3/28	12,000	1,285	1,285
6	2	2/28	12,000	857	428
7	1	1/28	12,000	428	0000
Total	28			12,000	

order, and determines the depreciation for a particular year by dividing that year's number by the sum of the digits. Exhibit V illustrates the computation. There, $14,000 is depreciated over seven years with a salvage value of $2,000. Salvage is deducted first. The sum of the digits is 28, with the digits listed in inverse order. Thus, for the first year, the depreciation is 7/28 of $12,000, or $3,000—and similarly for the other years.

Years of Life Remaining is an alternate method which takes the sum of the digits for any remaining years, on the balance remaining. Exhibit VI illustrates the computation, for a $15,000 investment depreciated over five years, with a salvage value of $5,000. Here, for example, the depreciation for the second year is determined by applying the sum of digits to the four years remaining, against the balance of $6,667 remaining after the depreciation for the first year has been deducted. As before, the salvage value is deducted first.

Sinking Fund Depreciation is used by engineers when it is not desirable to depreciate rapidly. It reflects the condition of a firm which is retiring indebtedness and therefore, by paying off part of the principal today, achieves the same effect as with a larger future payment. In another way we must say it anticipates that each credit to depreciation reserve will accumulate at compound interest to a larger future value.

Since business firms do make every effort to keep such funds working in the business to make a return, one might expect to find this method commonly used. However, business is ever changing, forced obsolescence is usually a danger, and tax considerations influence the thinking of businessmen, and so sinking-fund depreciation is rarely used, and might apply more appropriately to public works and tax-free institutions. In addition, most types of equipment tend to depreciate rapidly in early years and less as time goes by.

The formula is a variation of the compound interest formula:

$$D = \Delta D \left[\frac{(1 + i)^n - 1}{i} \right]$$

Values for the expression in brackets are normally listed in engineering handbooks and greatly simplify the calculation.

For example, ΔD of $1,000 which resulted from a $15,000 investment and $5,000 salvage under straight line now becomes:

$$15{,}000 - 5000 = \Delta D \left[\frac{(1.15)^{10} - 1}{.15} \right]$$

$$10{,}000 = \Delta D \times (3.046/.15)$$

$$\Delta D = \$492.52$$

This clearly shows how smaller credits to depreciation reserve under assumed conditions of 15% compounded annually over ten years, produce the same effect as $1,000.00 credits and no interest assumed. Exhibit VII compares methods of depreciation graphically.

Depreciation as a Tax Deduction. Since most investments are made by tax-paying firms, the consideration of depreciation usually involves its value as a tax deduction. However, this should not completely eclipse its value to engineers as an estimate of the future life of engineering projects.

Early in World War II, the U.S. Treasury Department published a schedule of acceptable useful lives, *Bulletin F*, which remained the acceptable depreciation guide for twenty years. During the tenure of this Bulletin practically every concern involved in manufacturing or similar activity using substantial capital equipment reached an agreement with IRS on spe-

EXHIBIT VI

Year	Digit				f	Unrecovered $P - L$	D	B_x
1	5				5/15	10,000	3,333	11,667
2	4	4			4/10	6,667	2,688	9,000
3	3	3	3		3/6	4,000	2,000	7,000
4	2	2	2	2	2/3	2,000	1,333	5,667
5	1	1	1	1	1/1	667	667	5,000
Total	15	10	6	3				

EXHIBIT VII

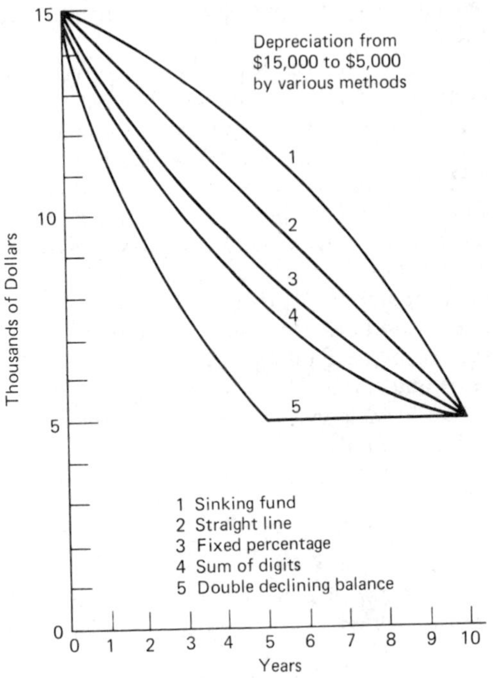

cial depreciation considerations, including forced obsolescence, sudden loss, abnormal retirements, and factors peculiar to the industry.

In July 1962, recognizing that useful life varies considerably with the type of usage, and also to encourage the sale of capital equipment as a stimulus to the economy, the Treasury Department published "Depreciation Guidelines and Rules" *Publication No. 456,* also called Revenue Procedure 62-21, which grouped properties and equipment into types of business. This shortened depreciable life from an average of nineteen years under the old *Bulletin F* to thirteen years for all manufacturing industry. It was still optional for a taxpayer to group his assets into the guideline classes. The guidelines contained a reserve ratio test to permit depreciation allowances to exceed the newly published rules. The ratio was the depreciation reserve times 100, divided by the cost of all assets, then multiplied by a rate of growth calculated as present assets divided by their value in the original or base year.

In 1965 the Federal Government conducted a computer simulation which attempted to determine if the reserve ratio test was indeed an accurate check showing that the depreciation tax deductions taken by the taxpayers were accurately reflecting their actual investments in new equipment, and were serving the intended purpose of stimulating economic growth in this country. In general, taxpayers tended to claim depreciation deductions without corresponding investment. Also, a problem developed when the new guidelines were used together with certain methods of depreciation (sum of digits), giving some taxpayers unjustified benefits. Because of this, Revenue Procedure 65-13 extended the moratorium on the reserve ratio test, and Revenue Procedure 72-10 in 1971 permitted the new ADR system, described below, with no reserve ratio test at all.

Because of the faster rates negotiated individually by businessmen under the old rules, these rates were greeted with some degree of skepticism, but the Treasury Department estimated that it would lose $1½ billion in tax revenue during the first full year of operation under these rules. In subsequent years the stimulation of tax relief could result in greater prosperity and subsequently greater tax revenues. Each purchase of capital goods contains a multiplier effect. As business picks up for the seller of capital goods, he in turn purchases more resources, and a chain reaction, the "multiplier effect," sets in, subject to taxes at every step. Theoretically, the multiplier is small but the psychological implications are great.

Interest on indebtedness is also a tax deduction, and it might appear that it would be equally advantageous to operate under increased debt, but unlike depreciation, interest payments must be met. It is possible for depreciation to take place on the books, often an accelerated depreciation taken for tax purposes only, while the true decline in value of the machinery or equipment may require no payments whatsoever, or deferred payments. Sudden losses and rapid retirements are handled by additional deductions if the situation so permits.

Depreciation allowances and allowances for interest paid on indebtedness may take place at the same time for the same taxpayer, resulting in a greater combined tax saving.

Many items lose value rapidly in the first year simply because they enter the "used" category. IRS permits an extra 20% depreciation allowance up to $2,000 maximum deduction ($10,000 maximum expenditure) during the first year, in addition to the normally calculated depreciation.

The entire 20% allowance may be taken in

the first year regardless of salvage, providing the item was tangible property having a useful life of at least six years and in use for part of the year. The usual depreciation methods, including the rapid double declining balance, can be used at the same time but only for the fractional part of the year that the item or group of items was in use.

The fast double declining balance method is limited to new equipment purchased after 1953, whereas 150% (wherein f equals $1\frac{1}{2}$ times straight line percentage) is the limit for used assets or assets purchased in 1953 or earlier. In the case of real estate other than low-income housing, the date is July 26, 1969 rather than 1953.

How is it an advantage for a business to claim tax savings from depreciation in present years rather than in the future? Highly competitive businessmen, concerned about the ever present dangers of obsolescence and the uncertainty of future business, consider today's income vital. Any savings made today results in funds that can be reinvested at compound interest, and in many concerns the best reinvestment is to carry additional assets in inventory, accounts receivable, property and equipment, or whatever makes the operation more efficient.

Consider the savings of $100,000 depreciation in chemical equipment. Under *Bulletin F* the life was fifteen to twenty-two years. Under *Guideline* classes, the life became eleven years. Using straight line depreciation the amounts are (100,000/15) = $6,660 per year, and (100,000/11) = $9,090 per year. The difference, $2,430, is additional tax deduction, and at a 46% tax rate, the saving is $1,117.80 per year. If the project were simply operated to the end of its useful life and abandoned, the total depreciation would seem to be the same in either case. However, consider the time value of money:

The formula to compare present values of yearly investments is:

$$P = R \left[\frac{1 - (1 + i)^n}{i}\right]$$

where i = interest or rate of return, the R rent or yearly amount. The present value of $6,660 per year for fifteen years at 10% (after taxes) is $50,000, while for $9,090 per year for eleven years it is $59,000; and 46% of the difference is $4,140, today's value of the accumulated savings. Of course, if future values are used, the amount is correspondingly greater, as a result of the compound interest effect. In the above case, the amounts after fifteen years compounded at 10% would be $210,500 and $245,800; and 46% of the difference would be $16,238.

In the same way, the advantage of accelerated depreciation over slower methods could be demonstrated to produce a saving, both in the long run and in the short run.

Exceptions are rare, but occasionally a firm may expect greater future earnings, and in such case it would be an advantage to take less depreciation at present so as to save tax deductions for future periods when income is higher. IRS permits users of declining balance depreciation to switch over to the slower straight line method on the remaining balance whenever they so elect, without permission.

The advantage of rapid depreciation almost seems to be lost when assets are grouped, since the older items in the group depress the group average. Nevertheless, the amount to be gained in the early life of the asset should, by virtue of compound interest, have a greater long-run effect.

When items are grouped into an average life class, the taxpayer may lose the advantage of a fast write-off on some items in the group. For example, consider one group of four machines. These depreciate $2,500 each per year on a straight-line basis. The group life is four years. On a straight-line basis, the first year's depreciation would be $10,000. Now, what happens when we do not group these items? Let us assume the actual lives of these four items are three, four, four, and five years. The respective depreciation amounts would be $3,333, $2,500, $2,500, and $2,000. In the latter case the depreciation is a total of $10,333 per year for the first three years, whereas it was only $10,000 per year for the same items when they were grouped.

For all of the methods of depreciation described here (excepting the sinking fund), the principle holds true, all else being equal, that grouping the items results in less depreciation in the early years.

Asset Depreciation Range (ADR). This is a system adopted in 1971 by the Internal Revenue Service which allows the taxpayer to group his assets by year placed in service (vintage accounts), or to keep them in item accounts and to base his depreciation on any period of years selected by the taxpayer within a range specified for designated classes of assets. The range, approximately "guideline lives" plus and minus 20%, has been published in Revenue Procedures as contained in Section 109 of the Revenue Act of 1971, and generally liberalized over the years. Taxpayers may elect the new ADR system (which requires no reserve ratio test at all) only on assets acquired in 1971 or later. The acquisitions must be scheduled with the taxpayers' return, so that IRS can decide if they properly belong to that particular asset group. The approved group then can be depreciated according to the life range published for that particular group.

Each asset group is entitled to an allowance for repairs which is tax deductible in the same period of time, as an "expensed" item.

Salvage values are set and not adjusted unless actual practice is too far off target, i.e., more than 10% low. Salvage value is not taken into account in establishing the annual depreciation deduction for an asset or class of assets, but no assets may be depreciated below their salvage value. Grouping for depreciation is a simple, effective way of handling things, but once a grouping is established as approved by IRS, then it is "all or none." IRS will not permit exceptions, although certain real estate properties have special rules in this regard.

Bonus Depreciation. This depreciation is allowed during the first year in which depreciation is claimed on any item or group of items considered "tangible personal property." The bonus allows the taxpayer an additional deduction in the amount 20% of the cost of the investment to a maximum amount of $2,000 tax deduction. Twenty per cent of the total "costs" is permitted, regardless of any expected future salvage values and regardless of the life of the items claimed (six year minimum). The remaining cost, after reduction for the bonus depreciation, may be depreciated under any of the methods acceptable to the Federal Government.

Replacement Accounting. Changes in the marketplace for assets cause historical costs to become untrue; for example, an older established industry with minimal changes over the years which is pricing its product based on historical cost data may be unknowingly liquidating its manufacturing facilities because it will not be able to replace them. In 1976, after years of rapid changes, the Securities Exchange Commission required for the first time that a corporation's annual report must reflect the replacement value of the corporation's physical assets.

While the S.E.C. asked for an evaluation of assets at current price levels, an engineer would calculate replacement value by obtaining an up-to-date price for the asset and adding current installation costs, considering possible salvage value or demolition costs as part of the installation cost. If the asset is currently useful, the years of remaining life are estimated and the total future replacement value is "brought back" to today's replacement value by the compound interest formula, $B = R/(1 + i)^{n-x}$ where $n-x$ is the years remaining. The interest rate, i, may or may not be corrected for the effects of inflation and alternate uses for funds.

In periods of high inflation it is not unusual that some assets actually appreciate in value rather than depreciate. But at the same time the attrition in normal usage of other assets, coupled with inflation of replacement prices, is causing a significant spread.

The law of supply and demand affects each particular asset's replacement value. For one example, a production machine price may increase severalfold if it was once a mass produced item but now becomes a specialty because of lack of demand. Technological innovations, as in the field of electronics and calculators, can cause prices to tumble, as when circuitry is improved and manufacturing breakthroughs develop. Competitive innovations may obsolete a manufacturing process which can only be effectively replaced by an investment much different from what historical costs might have indicated.

Considering these facts, we can conclude that a statement of replacement value is more of an art than a science and is a reflection of management's honest and considered opinion of predicted values in the field served by each corporation. The engineering estimate would be accurate only where the effects of obsolescense, supply and demand, innovations, governmental incentives, etc. are minimal, but is always a useful tool for managerial purposes.

Investment Credit. The Revenue Act of 1962 included a measure to stimulate the economy by tax relief on capital equipment, not including property and buildings. A businessman would calculate his income tax by the usual method, and then deduct from his tax an amount equal to 7% of his current investment.

Investment credit at the present time is 10% for items with seven years of life, two thirds of that for items with five to seven years, and one third for items with three to five years. This amount is a permissible deduction from income tax due, instead of being deducted before taxes are calculated, but may be taken only once for each investment.

Tax considerations are an important reason why depreciation is usually treated from an accounting standpoint in business literature. However, it should not be neglected as an engineering tool to help understand the effect of equipment life upon the annual cost or capitalization required of engineering projects such as public works which may be exempt from tax considerations.

Energy Credits. Energy credits were brought into effect by the Revenue Act of 1978 to encourage taxpayers to conserve scarce natural resources of oil and natural gas. In general, the credit applies to items that reduce heat lost from buildings, improve the efficiency of building space heaters, or items that switch from useage of scarce fuels (gas and oil) to common fuels (coal and wood). Energy sources that are renewable (solar, wind, waterpower, and geothermal) are also available for energy credit if they have an expected life of 60 months or longer.

The Revenue Act of 1978 has, at this writing, not yet been interpreted into specific and detailed Internal Revenue Service regulations, but it is currently in use to permit tax credit, and these are in addition to the investment credits, which are in addition to depreciation allowances. The final result is that the taxpayer will find for example, that 40% or more of his investment in solar energy is recovered in less tax paid.

D. F. O'Donnell, P.E., O'Donnell Sales & Engineering Co., Buffalo, New York

Information References

"Income Tax Depreciation and Obsolescence Estimated Useful Lives and Depreciation Rates," U. S. Treasury Department Internal Revenue Service Bulletin F, January 1942.

"Depreciation Guidelines and Rules," U. S. Treasury Department, Internal Revenue Service Publication No. 456 (7-62), July 1962.

Grant, Eugene L. and Ireson, W. Grant, "Principles of Engineering Economy," New York, Ronald Press, 1960.

"New Depreciation Rule Detailed; Change will Aid Businessmen in 70s," U. S. Dept. of Commerce, *Commerce Today,* Feb. 22, 1971.

"Tax Guide for Small Business," U. S. Treasury Department Internal Revenue Service Pub. No. 334, 1962.

1972 U. S. Master Tax Guide, Chicago, Commerce Clearing House, Inc., 1971.

"Internal Revenue Procedure 65-13," U. S. Treasury Dept. Internal Revenue Bulletin 1965-20, May 17, 1965.

"Internal Revenue Procedure 72-10," U. S. Treasury Dept. Internal Revenue Bulletin 1972-8, 13, February 21, 1972.

"Internal Revenue Procedure 77-3," U. S. Treasury Dept. "Internal Revenue Bulletin 1977-3," January 17, 1977.

Cross References: *Cost Accounting (and cross references there given); Fixed-Asset Investment Analysis: The MAPI Formulas and Procedures; Long-Range Corporate Planning; Long-Range Planning: Financial Aspects; Return on Capital.*

DIRECT COSTING (VARIABLE COSTING)

Direct Costing (also referred to in the literature as **Variable Costing**) is an accounting technique for implementing the economic theory of marginal analysis to guide the making of short-run business decisions. Underlying direct costing is the classification of costs recorded in the accounts and reported in the income statement into (a) *direct* or *variable* costs which tend to vary directly and proportionately with the current rate of activity, and (b) *period* or *fixed* costs which tend to persist unchanged in total amount within the usual range of activity fluctuations. The direct costing income statement characteristically displays relationships between costs, sales volume, and profits for the period covered by the statement. Knowing these relationships, costs, and profit margins can be readily projected for other volumes within the range for which cost-volume relationships remain stable.

In *absorption costing,* which is the alternative to direct costing, no distinction is made between direct (or variable) and period (or fixed) costs in the accounts and income statement. Production is costed at rates including a proportionate share of period manufacturing costs, a characteristic which has given rise to the term absorption costing. Where absorption costing is in effect, resort must be had to supplementary statistical analysis to disclose relationships between costs, volume, and profits.

Direct costing is not a complete cost accounting method, but rather is a feature introduced into standard or actual process or job order cost systems to make them more useful. Neither is it a reversion to primitive costing methods which determined only prime manufacturing cost of products, for direct costing implies analysis and classification of all costs (including selling and administrative costs) into direct and period components. Users of direct costing do allocate period costs to products for purposes such as pricing, but these allocations are made statistically and by methods flexible with the purpose instead of routinely in the accounts. In practice, many cost systems combine features of both direct and absorption costing.

Historical Background. Early cost accountants attempted to stabilize unit costs under conditions of fluctuating volume by charging production with overhead rates predicated on a so-called normal or standard volume. Since volume cannot be controlled to a standard level, under or overabsorbed cost balances arise in the accounts. These volume variances enter into the reckoning of periodic profit or loss, but they are not easily associated with the specific increments in output or sales which are the subject of many management decisions. Moreover, the practice of absorbing fixed costs in inventory causes reported profit or loss to be influenced by changes in the inventory of manufactured goods even when sales and other factors remain constant. As a consequence, under absorption costing, increased sales may be accompanied by lower profit if the inventory is reduced in the same period. Conversely, reported profit can be increased by producing goods for inventory in the face of declining sales.

Relationships between net profit determined by the direct costing method and by the absorption costing method are illustrated by Exhibit I. In this illustration, changes in profits from period to period are attributable solely to changes in volume of sales and production, because other factors which would affect profits are assumed to be constant.

It is seen that sales in the second quarter are lower than in the first quarter, but the absorption costing method shows an increase in net profit. The situation is reversed in the third quarter when, despite a sales volume larger than that in either of the preceding periods, the profit reported by absorption costing is lower than in the preceding periods. Sales volume is identical in the third and fourth quarters, but profit reported by absorption costing differs. On the other hand, it can be seen that profits have a consistent relationship to sales volume when direct costing is used. When sales and production are in balance (as in the first quarter and for the year as a whole), profits reported by the two methods are identical. Differences between profits reported by the two methods are explained by the amount of fixed cost deferred in inventory by absorption costing, as shown by the reconciliation at the bottom of Exhibit I.

Absorption costing tends to accentuate profit fluctuations in companies which experience cyclical swings in sales and profits because these companies usually increase inventories of manufactured products during periods of rising activity and reduce inventories during periods of recession. Growing companies find that a portion of current fixed cost is capitalized indefinitely because larger inventories are needed to support an expanded volume of sales. As a result, periodic profits tend to be over-stated. Under direct costing, decisions to increase or decrease inventory of manufactured goods do not affect profits.

The development of direct costing was motivated by the desire to have incremental cost and profit data to guide decisions and by the desire to clarify the income statement in order that management might better understand the interaction of volume, costs, and profits. An N.A.A. research study ("Direct Costing," *Research Report No. 23*) showed that early applications of direct costing were made independently in a number of different companies. A second N.A.A. research study, conducted to ascertain how direct costing is being used, summarized the experience of fifty companies ("Current Applications of Direct Costing," *Research Report No. 37*). Since publication of the foregoing N.A.A. study, interest in direct costing has grown rapidly, and applications now exist in many companies. However, for reasons stated subsequently, applications of direct costing are, with a few exceptions, limited to internal records and reports.

The term *marginal costing* generally replaces direct costing in British accounting terminology. In the U.S., *contribution margin reporting* is used, particularly where analysis of individual product and market contributions to profit is the objective.

Theory of Direct Costing. Under direct costing, determination of income proceeds by first deducting from sales revenues all of the direct costs of making and selling goods represented by sales revenues of the period. The resulting difference, termed *marginal income* or *contribution margin,* measures the amount contributed by the period's sales toward period costs and

Exhibit I

Comparison Between Absorption Costing and Direct Costing Methods

Quarterly Budget (In absorption costing form with fixed and variable costs separated)

	Total	*Per Unit*
Sales (30,000 units)	$30,000	$1.00
Cost of Goods Sold		
Variable Costs	19,500	.65
Fixed Costs	6,000	.20
Total	25,500	.85
Gross Margin	4,500	.15
Selling and Administrative Costs (fixed)	2,100	.07
Operating profit	$ 2,400	.08

Actual Production and Sales in Units

	1st Quarter	*2nd Quarter*	*3rd Quarter*	*4th Quarter*	*Year*
Opening Inventory	—	—	6,000	2,000	—
Production	30,000	34,000	28,000	30,000	122,000
Sales	30,000	28,000	32,000	32,000	122,000
Closing Inventory	—	6,000	2,000	—	—

Income Statement by Quarters and for Year

1. Using *Absorption Costing* with Fixed Manufacturing Cost Charged to Production at Predetermined Overhead Rate of $0.20 per Unit Based on Budgeted Volume and Budgeted Overhead Cost.

	Quarters				*Year*
	1	*2*	*3*	*4*	
Sales	$30,000	$28,000	$32,000	$32,000	$122,000
Cost of Goods Manufactured	25,500	28,900	23,800	25,500	103,700
Add Opening Inventory	—	—	5,100	1,700	
Cost of Goods Available	25,500	28,900	28,900	27,200	
Deduct Closing Inventory	—	5,100	1,700	—	
Cost of Goods Sold	25,500	23,800	27,200	27,200	103,700
Under or (Over) Absorbed Overhead	—	(800)	400	—	(400)
Total	25,500	23,000	27,600	27,200	103,300
Gross Margin	4,500	5,000	4,400	4,800	18,700
Selling and Administrative Costs	2,100	2,100	2,100	2,100	8,400
Net Operating Profit	$ 2,400	$ 2,900	$ 2,300	$ 2,700	$ 10,300

2. Using *Direct Costing* with Fixed Manufacturing Costs Treated as Period Costs.

Sales	$30,000	$28,000	$32,000	$32,000	$122,000
Cost of Goods Manufactured	19,500	22,100	18,200	19,500	79,300
Add Opening Inventory	—	—	3,900	1,300	
Cost of Goods Available	19,500	22,100	22,100	20,800	
Deduct Closing Inventory	—	3,900	1,300	—	
Cost of Goods Sold	19,500	18,200	20,800	20,800	79,300
Marginal Income	10,500	9,800	11,200	11,200	42,700
Fixed Costs					
Manufacturing	6,000	6,000	6,000	6,000	24,000
Selling and Administrative	2,100	2,100	2,100	2,100	8,400
Total	8,100	8,100	8,100	8,100	32,400
Net Operating Profit	$ 2,400	$ 1,700	$ 3,100	$ 3,100	$ 10,300

EXHIBIT I (con't)

Reconciliation of Differences in Reported Profits

	Quarters				*Year*
	1	2	3	4	
Absorption Cost Profit	$2,400	$2,900	$2,300	$2,700	$10,300
Direct Cost Profit	2,400	1,700	3,100	3,100	$10,300
Difference	$ —	$1,200	$(800)	$(400)	—
Change in Inventory (in units)	—	6,000	(4,000)	(2,000)	—
Change in Amount of Fixed Cost in Inventory*	—	$1,200	$(800)	$(400)	—

* Calculated by multiplying change in number of units by $0.20
SOURCE: "Direct Costing," N.A.A. *Research Report No. 23*

profit. Inventory is costed at direct cost because only these costs are causally associated with inventory in the sense that they were incurred specifically because the goods were produced in the current period and, to the extent that goods are carried forward in inventory, the same costs will be avoided in the future.

In a second step, period costs are deducted from marginal income to arrive at net profit. Period costs arise from provision of capacity to make and sell in the form of facilities and organization which remain relatively constant through ordinary fluctuations in production and sales. The full amount of period cost recognized in each period is deducted from income of the same period because the opportunity to use this capacity tends to expire with time whether or not it is fully utilized.

An illustration appears in Exhibit II. It may be noted that period costs specific to the product are shown separately because these period costs would be eliminated if the product were dropped. In practice, repetitive allocations of common period costs may be omitted because these allocations are unavoidably subjective and unreliable.

Scope of Direct Costing. Attention is called to the following characteristics of the direct costing income statement.

(1) Total marginal income varies directly and proportionately with sales within the range for which period costs remain constant. Hence unit marginal income can be used to project the contribution to profit from increments in sales and to evaluate *relative* profitability of products and other segments of the business.

(2) Significant figures such as sales volume required to break even or to earn a target rate of return on capital employed, selling price required to break even or to earn a target rate of return from a given volume, and effect on profits of changes in direct and period costs are readily estimated from data appearing in the income statement itself.

(3) Net profit varies with sales and is not affected by buildup or liquidation of inventory.

The foregoing characteristics make direct costing particularly useful in profit planning, budgeting, and pricing. The same characteristics facilitate analysis and explanation of reported operating results because they bring accounting for past events into conformity with patterns of thinking which management follows in planning for the future. Rapid spread in internal application of direct costing is attributable to its uses for these purposes.

An NAA mail survey conducted in 1979 shows that manufacturing firms formally identify fixed and variable expenses almost exclusively for internal management purposes, more often for planning, and less often for decision-making and evaluation. Data on fixed and variable expenses are rarely provided in the annual financial statements, but they are somewhat more frequently provided to governmental agencies, creditors, and financial analysts. ("Report on Fixed and Variable Expense Research," *Management Accounting,* June, 1980.)

Direct costing also has usefulness in controlling current costs, although it is not primarily a tool for cost control. This usefulness stems from the fact that knowledge of how individual cost items should respond to changes in volume is helpful to managers responsible for controlling these costs. An additional advantage may be gained from having the amounts of period costs collected and reported in the income statement instead of having these costs lost to

EXHIBIT II

PRODUCT LINE INCOME STATEMENT USING DIRECT COSTING

	Total		Product Lines					
			No. 1		No. 2		No. 3	
	Amount	Pct.	Amount	Pct.	Amount	Pct.	Amount	Pct
Net Sales	*$600,000*	*100.0*	*$300,000*	*100.0*	*$200,000*	*100.0*	*$100,000*	*100.0*
Direct Costs								
Manufacturing								
Direct Materials	$150,000	25.0	$ 75,000	25.0	$ 55,000	27.5	$ 20,000	20.0
Direct Labor	90,000	15.0	30,000	10.0	30,000	15.0	30,000	30.0
Direct Overhead	60,000	10.0	30,000	10.0	20,000	10.0	10,000	10.0
Selling								
Freight Out	12,000	2.0	9,000	3.0	3,000	1.5	—	—
Salesmen's Commissions	24,000	4.0	12,000	4.0	8,000	4.0	4,000	4.0
Total Direct Costs	$336,000	56.0	$156,000	52.0	$116,000	58.0	$ 64,000	64.0
Marginal Income	$264,000	44.0	$144,000	48.0	$ 84,000	42.0	$ 36,000	36.0
Period Costs Specific to Product Lines								
Depreciation	$ 40,000		$ 20,000		$ 10,000		$ 10,000	
Property Taxes and Insurance	20,000		10,000		2,000		8,000	
Advertising	24,000		20,000		—		4,000	
Total	$ 84,000		$ 50,000		$ 12,000		$ 22,000	
Margin after specific period costs	$180,000	30.0	$ 94,000	31.3	$ 72,000	36.0	14,000	14.0
Allocated General Period Costs								
Manufacturing	$ 40,000		$ 20,000		$ 13,320		$ 6,680	
Selling	30,000		15,000		10,000		5,000	
Administrative	30,000		15,000		10,000		5,000	
Research & Development	20,000		10,000		6,666		3,334	
Total	$120,000		$ 60,000		$ 39,986		$ 20,014	
Profit (loss) before taxes	$ 60,000	10.0	$ 34,000	10.3	$ 32,014	16.5	($ 6,014)	(6.0)

SOURCE: "Current Application of Direct Costing," N.A.A. *Research Report No. 37.*

sight by allocation between cost of sales and inventory.

Applications of direct costing are usually confined to internal reports prepared for management use, although there is no theoretical reason why some of the same advantages gained by management should not extend to outside shareholders and creditors. However, the use of direct costing in external financial reports has often been opposed by certified public accountants because it represents a change from established conventions in external reporting. Direct costing has not been accepted for determining taxable income, presumably because losses of tax revenue would result from write-off period costs in inventories in the change-over period and subsequently from current deduction of period costs which would otherwise be deferred as a business grows and its inventories increase.

For these reasons, external financial reports are usually prepared on the conventional absorption costing basis. The difference between profit determined by the two methods is explained by the change in the amount of period costs deferred in inventory. Where cost accounts are on a direct costing basis, an adjusting figure can be computed by relatively simple procedures at the end of each period to convert inventory and cost of goods sold to an absorption costing basis. Adjustments are applied to summary figures only and not to component details which appear in the internal records and reports.

W. B. MCFARLAND, formerly Director of Research, National Association of Accountants, New York, New York

Information References

The literature on Direct Costing is voluminous and items listed below are selected to give a broad view of the subject.

Publications of National Association of Accountants:

Direct Costing, *Research Report No. 23.*

Current Application of Direct Costing, *Research Report No. 37.*

Articles in NAA's Management Accounting:

Grinnell, D. Jacque, "Product Mix Decisions: Direct Costing Versus Absorption Costing," August 1976.

Schulte, R. Gregg, "One More Time: Direct Costing Versus Absorption Costing," November 1975.

Williams, Bruce R., "Measuring Costs: Full Absorption Cost or Direct Cost?" January 1976.

Texts:

Böer, Germain, *Direct Cost and Contribution Accounting: An Integrated Management Accounting System.* Wiley, New York, N.Y., 1974.

Lere, John C., *Pricing Techniques for the Financial Executive,* Wiley, New York, N.Y., 1974.

Cross References: *Cost Accounting (and cross references there given.)*

DIRECTORS: Characteristics of Boards

As of the end of 1980, six out of ten major companies had increased compensation of board members in the past year, and one director in five was receiving at least $18,000 annually, according to a study by the executive recruiting firm of Heidrick and Struggles [1]. The year before, only 11% of the board members were paid as well. These and other findings resulted from a questionnaire sent to board chairmen of the nation's 1,000 leading industrial companies and 300 leading non-industrial organizations in commercial banking, diversified financial services, insurance, retailing, transportation, and utilities.

Board Composition. Surveys conducted by Heidrick and Struggles over the past nine years have evidenced a steady increase in the proportion of outside directors on leading boards. In the 1980 survey, for the first time, organizations were asked to separate board members into three categories: (1) management directors, or officers of the corporation; (2) affiliated non-management directors, including family members, retired corporate officers, and lawyers and commercial or investment bankers doing business with the corporation; and (3) independent outside directors without ties as supplier or family member. As of this writing, independent directors constitute a majority of the typical board. Forty-five per cent of the companies reported that their boards will have a greater proportion of independent directors in the future.

Non-industrial boards are less homogeneous by race and sex than are those of industrial companies. The degree of diversity on industrial boards correlates with size of organization. Only 38% of the companies in the $2 billion and up category have exclusively white male directors, while 81% of firms under $500 million lack any female or minority board members.

Candidate Criteria. Sources most helpful in identifying director candidates remained relatively unchanged over the past four years. Present directors are still favored, although the nominating committee in particular has replaced non-director corporate officers in second place.

Selection of Directors. In 1976, the chief executive officer was most frequently the initial decision-maker in approving board prospects. At that time, the entire board acting as a group ranked a distant second, followed by the executive committee. The nominating committee served as initial decision-maker in only 8.2% of the companies. As of this writing, the nominating committee leads the chief executive officer acting alone, and all other alternative decision-makers, in 45.5% of the organizations. This committee holds sway in 69.2% of the premier-size companies.

Board Compensation. The annual cash compensation of outside directors attending all regular board meetings (excluding committee meetings) continues to advance. Sixty per cent of the companies are paying more than one year ago. As stated above, currently one in five directors receives at least $18,000 a year for board service. Two years ago, only 8% were compensated at this rate.

Only 10% of the organizations pay outside directors a meeting fee if they fail to attend. At 71% of the companies the basis of payment for outside directors is an annual retainer and regular meeting fee, while 8% pay an annual retainer only, and the remainder employ other plans.

Board Retirement Policy. Nearly 62% of the organizations have a retirement policy. This practice becomes less prevalent as company size decreases. In overwhelming majority of cases, the policy is based on age. The range is 65 to 75, although 70 represents the mean and modal average as well as the median figure. Most common consideration other than age is retirement from principal occupation; however, several companies base retirement on years of board service. Only 6.5% of outside directors receive retirement income. The average retirement pay is $12,600.

Evaluation of Chief Executive Officer. In about a third of the companies, the board has developed an objective, quantitative means of evaluating the chief executive's performance. Little variation in appraisal methodology exists among different sizes and kinds of companies. In every case, a substantial proportion indicates that a more formal approach to chief executive officer evaluation is being considered.

Audit Committee. The Heidrick and Struggles report did not include the question of audit committees. However, a 1979 study by The Conference Board [2] reports a rapid and widespread increase in the incidence of such committees in recent years. As recently as 1972, only a minority — 45% — of 855 companies surveyed by The Conference Board on directorship practices had an audit committee. Only five years later, in 1967, in a similar survey by the Board covering 753 companies, a mere 19% of manufacturing companies and 31% of non-manufacturing companies had audit committees. But 97% of the member companies of the American Society of Corporate Secretaries that responded to a 1978 Society survey on this question (on behalf of the New York Stock Exchange) had such a committee.

The CB report states that there can be little doubt that many of today's audit committees are exercising stronger authority than they used to. This is most easily observable in situations where there is a suspicion that improper payments or questionable practices have occurred. Company executives have stated that audit committee members have become more demanding than they used to be. They require more information and fuller cooperation from management, probe deeply if they have questions, and otherwise do business under the assumption that they have whatever authority they need to cope with their responsibilities. And this seems to be true whether or not the committee is backed up by a strong and specific charter, although a charter with teeth in it can definitely bolster the committee's position.

References Cited

[1] "The Changing Board, 1980 Update: A Profile of the Board of Directors," Chicago, Heidrick and Struggles, Inc., 1980.

[2] "Corporate Directorship Practices: The Audit Committee," New York, The Conference Board Report No. 766, 1979.

Cross References: *Directors: Legal Duties and Responsibilities.*

DIRECTORS: Legal Duties and Responsibilities

I—LEGAL STANDARDS

This presentation describes in summary form the general legal standards with respect to internal management and securities sales that apply to **Directors** of all business corporations, regardless of size of the corporations, the businesses in which they are engaged, or how they are internally organized. Application of these standards in a specific case or controversy will, of course, depend upon the particular circumstances, including size, the nature of the business, the corporation's internal organization, whether the director is or is not an "outsider," etc. Although the precise scope of the director's duties is still unfolding through court decisions, the trend toward widening liability continues, e.g., liability under Federal Civil Rights laws for racial discrimination in the sale or rental of property, and liability for improper political and foreign payments under the Foreign Corrupt Practices Act of 1977.

The overall legal duty and responsibility of the board of directors is to manage the corporation and to do so with due care and in good faith. The shareholders look to the board of directors for the proper conduct of the corporate business, and the directors, in turn, in running the company, are obliged to be guided by what is in the best interests of the shareholders. In addition, special obligations are imposed in certain areas on the directors and corporate management by state or federal law; e.g., to protect the investing public generally.

In theory, the board of directors has all the powers of business management except to do what is illegal, to do unilaterally what requires shareholders approval, and to act contrary to the charter and by-laws. Thus, directors could be subject to stockholders' derivative suits on behalf of the corporation for improper distribution of dividends and sales of stock, illegal distribution of assets, and *ultra vires* acts, i.e., acts beyond the powers of the corporation as set forth in its charter (Certificate of Incorporation) which damage the business [1].

In actual practice, however, the board delegates extensive authority to the corporate officers who carry on the day-to-day management of the corporate business; it generally confines itself to dealing with basic policies and the most important business questions and to generally supervising the management. Certain kinds of decisions, however, must be made by the board and cannot be delegated. These are decisions where the law requires that only the judgment of the board of directors decides. The list of such decisions varies somewhat from state to state, but usually includes declaring dividends and appointing and removing officers. In recent years, changes in corporation laws have considerably increased the extent to which the board of directors can delegate its responsibilities to committees of its members. State laws vary in this area, and directors should review carefully the laws that apply to their corporation before making important delegations to a committee.

Due Care. The standard of due care that the law imposes on directors is frequently referred to as "the business judgment rule." That is, directors have the duty in their actions to use their business judgment in a manner that is reasonable under the circumstances. One way of stating the standard of due care is that the director should exercise his (her) authority with the same energy, diligence, enterprise, and carefulness that the director gives (if ordinarily prudent) to his or her own personal affairs.

One of the most recent comprehensive revisions of state corporation law, "The Business Corporation Law of New York," effective September 1, 1963, describes the standard of due care as "that degree of diligence, care, and skill which ordinarily prudent men would exercise under similar circumstances in like positions." The new New York statute also expressly provides that: "In discharging their duties, directors . . . when acting in good faith, may rely upon financial statements of the corporation represented to them to be correct by the president or the officer of the corporation having charge of its books of accounts, or stated in a written report by an independent public or certified public accountant or firm of such accountants fairly to reflect the financial condition of such corporation."

Directors will not be legally liable for honest mistakes in business judgment—that is for acts taken in good faith which were not unreasonable under the particular circumstances as they then appeared to be. In other words, where they act in good faith, directors are generally liable only where their behavior was negligent.

It must be stressed, however, that the concept of "ordinary prudence" is constantly being widened, and outside directors are cautioned, despite such state statutes, to read every document before approving, and to question more and rely less on information furnished by "insiders." Regardless of intent, a failure to investigate independently may be deemed culpable ignorance and a breach of duty to stockholders.

Although prompted more by concern for violations of Federal statutes than general corporation law, the New York Stock Exchange has recognized the need in general for outside directors to have access to independently gathered corporate information. As of June 30, 1978 each domestic company listed on the NYSE must maintain "an Audit Committee comprised solely of directors independent of management and free from any relationships, that, in the opinion of the Board of Directors, would interfere with the exercise of independent judgment as a committee member. Directors who are affiliates of the company or officers or employees of the company or its subsidiaries would not be qualified for Audit Committee membership."

As a practical matter, the courts, and properly so, are reluctant to "second-guess" the business decisions of directors made in good faith. The courts are well aware that business decisions have to be taken on the basis of how things look at the time, and that there may have unavoidably been unpredictable or uncertain factors in the picture. The courts also know that their own business judgment may not be as good as that of the directors whose acts they are reviewing. Hence, the courts are properly reluctant to impose liability even though hindsight clearly indicates that some particular decision turned out to be a mistake. In short, the courts recognize that running a business necessarily involves taking calculated risks, and directors will therefore not be held liable for what are no more than honest mistakes of business judgment or honest failures to act.

Minutes should be kept of board meetings, showing who attended and the actions taken. It may also often be appropriate to include in the minutes references to the particular circumstances and the directors' evaluation thereof that constitute the background and explanation for the actions taken.

Ordinarily directors should act collectively (i.e., as a board). In other words, their actions should be taken at board meetings. Individual directors, absent Board authorization, have no power to bind the corporation to transactions with third parties. Directors should attend board meetings and should keep informed about company affairs. Directors should not be "dummies" or "fronts." A director is likely to be deemed to have concurred in an action taken at a board meeting he attended or subsequently learned about unless he indicates his dissent (either right at the meeting, if he was there; or within a reasonable time after learning of the action, if he was absent).

To keep properly informed, a director, during his term in office, has a right to inspect the corporation's books and records.

Good Faith. The law requires that directors be loyal to their corporations. Directors are sometimes called "fiduciaries" and are said to have a "fiduciary relationship" to their corporation. What this means is that the relationship is one of the highest trust and confidence where one side (here the shareholders) places trust and confidence in the other side (here the board of directors). This is why courts sometimes liken directors to trustees and guardians.

The basic legal significance of being a fiduciary (i.e., of being trusted and given authority to discharge the trust) is that the fiduciary must not take personal advantage of his authority. Doing so would be a breach of trust. But in the complex and interrelated business world, it is sometimes difficult for a conscientious businessman to be certain as to just where his proper loyalties are. For example, a director might get into a situation where his own interests might be adverse to those of his corporation in the following ways: (1) where he is dealing directly with the corporation; e.g., by selling it something or buying from it; (2) where he buys claims against his corporation; e.g., bonds, promissory notes; (3) where he learns or knows of some business prospect or development that would or might be opportune for the corporation but exploits it himself (this is the so-called "corporate opportunity" problem); and (4) where he is the director of two corporations that deal with each other.

It is impracticable to try to generalize a standard of loyalty and good faith that would apply to all combinations of circumstances. The real guide for most cases is probably what businessmen would generally regard as honorable behavior. Two common problems should be emphasized:

(1) The "interested director," who will be involved, directly or through another corporate connection, in a business transaction being considered by the board of which he is a member. Modern corporation law recognizes the frequent business necessity for such transactions and provides guidelines which should be followed. The interested director should make full disclosure of any adverse interest, abstain from voting on the proposal (some states will liberalize quorum requirements for such votes), and where appropriate obtain stockholder ratification. It should, however, be noted that even where these steps are taken some courts may still review the transaction to determine if it is fair and reasonable to the corporation [2].

(2) Converting corporate property or a corporate opportunity to one's personal use. Whereas courts are reluctant to "second guess" the director's exercise of pure business judgment, they are properly severe in dealing with cases where they find a deliberate breach of trust or dishonorable behavior and the legal theories of interference with contract relations, diversion of corporate opportunities, and breach of the duty to be loyal to the corporation, are highly developed. The fiduciary who is disloyal or who acts in bad faith must account to the corporation for whatever profit he makes or causes the corporation to lose. Therefore, a director should not use for personal gain "inside" or confidential information that belongs to the corporation [3].

Other Legal Duties. Both state and Federal laws impose criminal penalties on corporate officials who are responsible for the publication of reports about the corporation which are false or deliberately misleading. Directors who personally committed such acts or knowingly acquiesced in them would, of course, be subject to such laws. Other kinds of law violations which are usually crimes are: taking bribes, stock frauds, illegal dividends, illegal distribution of capital, and various kinds of improper property transactions.

Congress has enacted a great variety of laws which affect what directors should and should not do. A few that are of special importance will be stated here:

Under the Securities Exchange Act of 1934, directors of corporations whose equity securities are registered on a stock exchange must submit to both the stock exchange and the Securities and Exchange Commission: (1) an initial report of all holdings of the corporation's equity securities; and (2) further reports of any changes in those equity security holdings, within ten days after the close of any month in which any change has taken place.

The Securities Exchange Act of 1934 also requires—Section 16(b)—that such directors must turn over to the corporation any profit realized from trading in the corporation's equity securities where there has been a purchase-and-sale or sale-and-purchase of the corporation's equity securities within any period of less than six months. The corporation—or, if it fails to do so, any stockholder—can sue the director to enforce the profit recovery. This law is what is often referred to as the ban on "short-swing" profits of "insider trading." Certain kinds of "short-swing" transactions are exempted from this no-profit rule, either by express statutory provision or by rule of the Securities and Exchange Commission.

The regulation of "insider trading" by the Securities Exchange Act of 1934 includes a prohibition against "short sales" by directors. Section 16(c) provides that:

"It shall be unlawful for any such beneficial owner, director, or officer, directly or indirectly, to sell any equity security of such issues (other than an exempted security), if the person selling the security or his principal (1) does not own the security sold, or (2) if owning the security, does not deliver it against such sale within twenty days thereafter, or does not within five days after such sale deposit it in the mails or other usual channels of transportation; but no person shall be deemed to have violated this subsection if he proves that notwithstanding the exercise of good faith he was unable to make such delivery or deposit within such time, or that to do so would cause undue inconvenience or expense."

In addition, some states prohibit sales of stock by corporate officers and directors unless the shares are actually owned at the time of the sale.

Directors also have the obligation, under the Securities Act of 1933, to make reasonable investigation as to the truth of factual representations in registration statements. Failure to discharge this obligation may lead to both criminal penalty and personal liability to any security buyers who suffered losses because of the untruths for which the director is chargeable. The principal case is *Bar-Chris* [4], which imposed liability on two new outside directors under Federal Securities Law for failure to make an adequate independent adversary investigation of financial statements furnished to them by internal management. *Caveat:* The Court held that there could be *no* absolute reliance on financial statements under the state corporation laws discussed above when federal regulation is involved. The process of sorting out those experts that outside directors can properly rely on, as contrasted to non-expert information, is continuing, and consultation with counsel is recommended.

Significant responsibilities regarding use of inside information are outlined in the following statement by William L. Cary, then Chairman of the Securities and Exchange Commission [5].

> What are the responsibilities of insiders with respect to securities transactions? Where an insider has possession of facts that are known to him by virtue of his status and that, if known generally, would tend materially to affect the price of the security, the law requires that the insider disclose these facts to those with whom he deals or *forego the transaction.* Here the law is now beginning to crystallize. It is a fraud on the other party to a security transaction not to speak if there is a duty to do so. This duty may arise: (1) because of a relationship to the corporation, such as that of an officer or director, and (2) by reason of the inherent unfairness involved where a person takes advantage of information knowing it is unavailable to those with whom he is dealing.
>
> A manager should receive corporate information not for his own personal emolument, but to assist the corporation in its operations. The use of inside information by a director or other manager to trade in shares is the securing of additional compensation in a covert fashion and should be condemned. (It further, of course, infects the integrity of the market.) Since a director or manager is usually not in a position to discuss confidential information about his corporation, his alternative—and properly so—is to stay out of the market. In the recent case of *Cady, Roberts & Co.,* (SEC Securities Exchange Act Release No. 6668, Nov. 8, 1961) the Securities and Exchange Commission, for the first time, said that the duty of insider disclosure or—in the alternative—of abstinence applied in an exchange market and that it was a fraudulent practice to sell a security while in possession of inside information in a faceless transaction as well as face-to-face.

JOSEF P. SIREFMAN, PHD., JD., Professor of Business Law, Hofstra University, Hempstead, New York

II—RECENT DEVELOPMENTS

The corollary of widening the scope of a director's liability as a result of the Penn Central Bankruptcy, *Bar-Chris* [4], and similar developments is an emphasis on the vast powers that directors are expected to exercise. This has prompted considerable discussion of the type of director best equipped to handle these responsibilities, and the extent of independent legal and financial counsel responsible only to the board [6]. However, since 1978, "a director who resigns or decides not to seek re-election because of dissatisfaction with the way the company is run may force management to file a Form 8-K with the S.E.C., describing the reason for resignation. Management may add its own explanation if it wishes. This information also must be given in the next proxy statement" [7].

Inevitably, increasing potential for liability increases the demand by directors for indemnification or for insurance against claims [8]. This is governed by state corporation laws which vary considerably in the protection permitted. For example, where a successful defense may be the basis for the corporation's paying a director's outlays, a settlement may be interpreted by some jurisdictions as similar to an adverse judgment barring recovery from the corporation. In addition to specific statutory exclusions from indemnification or insurance, public policy prohibits a corporation from waiving a director's intentional or criminal misconduct or negligence.

Increasingly, companies are taking steps to bring their boards of directors into focus and to make them a viable unit in a professionally managed company. The fact of legal responsibility cannot be negated by weak excuses such as, "We didn't have the facts."

Setting aside such obvious wrongdoings as fraud, use of privileged information for personal gain, violation of antitrust and SEC laws and regulations, conflicts of interest, and gross negligence, the following are steps that can be taken to bring the board to a level of competence and effectiveness consonant with its role:

(1) Define the role of the board. Develop a position description not only for the board, but also for each of its committees.

(2) Prepare standards of performance to measure and evaluate the effectiveness of the board and its committees.

(3) Make the membership of the board predominantly outsiders. Carefully select men and women whose experience provides the required contribution potential.

(4) Clarify definitions and separation of those elements which constitute board matters, and those which constitute management matters.

(5) Have board meetings that are frequent enough and long enough to keep the board members informed and active.

(6) Prepare specific and detailed agenda for each meeting and send to directors well in advance of the meeting.

(7) Prepare a carefully thought-out "advance information package" and send to directors well in advance of the meeting.

(8) Recognize that one of the major responsibilities of the board is to set the course of the business.

(9) Compensate directors adequately so that they may be called upon for aid and counsel, without restraint.

(10) Replace directors who no longer can or do not contribute. Establish mandatory retirement ages for both inside and outside directors.

The foregoing ten points will be implemented only if the chief executive officer really wants a strong board and honestly seeks its advice and counsel.

When all is said and done, the best "insurance" the individual members of the board can have is to let the record speak that:

(1) Prudent business judgment was exercised at all times.

(2) There was no lack of due diligence.

(3) Board meetings were adequately attended.

(4) There were no conflicts of interest or misuse of priviledged information.

(5) There was good participation through the asking of discerning and penetrating questions.

(6) Each director recognized his responsibility to think about the business and to make recommendations that will aid the business, and to bring to the board and to management experience and judgment that probably could not be available to them in any other way.

The Audit Committee. The increasing recognition of the role of the board in corporate governance and oversight has led to a more careful examination of the true role of the board and its committees, particularly the audit committee.

The audit committee now sees its role as not only to review the year-end financial statements with the outside auditors, but also to satisfy itself as to the adequacy of the audit procedures and the thoroughness of the audit itself. It reviews, in detail, the Management Letter with the auditors and, in turn, discusses management's response to the letter with both the auditors and management. In addition, the committee meets with the internal audit group, in effect to approve the latter's program and review its findings. Again, this effort has been enlarged to include close scrutiny as to adherence to corporate policy and procedures, as well as to the accuracy and adequacy of financial statements and controls.

The matter of managerial oversight is best conducted by the board itself, but in more specific detail by the audit, executive, compensation, and organization committees. Boards are now intimately involved, and must recognize that they are accountable for managerial conduct and effectiveness.

J. KEITH LOUDEN, President, The Corporate Director, Inc., New York, New York

III—CO-DETERMINATION

For some time since World War II, German and other European union leaders have been directors on the boards of corporations in their countries. Although unionism and the involvement of government in the private sector have had a different history in Europe than in the United States, the question of union representation on boards, termed **co-determination,** has been a perennial one in this country.

New impetus was furnished by the election of Douglas Fraser, UAW president, to the Chrysler board. However, this clearly was not the portent of a new trend; rather, it reflected the economic difficulties of that company. Just as a major creditor of a financially vulnerable business may get a seat or two on the board to protect its investment, Mr. Fraser was admitted to the Chrysler board because the union, in experiencing huge layoffs and in agreeing to lower wages and benefits during the crisis, was in the same position as the creditor referred to. It demanded participation in future decisions that would protect the union's "investment."

At the present juncture it would appear that the only prospects in the near term for union members on corporate boards would be in situations of ailing companies or under employee stock option plans (E.S.O.P.) where the employees' ownership interest in the corporation has become substantial.

JOSEF P. SIREFMAN, PHD., JD., Professor of Business Law, Hofstra University, Hempstead, New York

Information References

Brown, Courtney C., "Putting the Corporate Board to Work," New York, Macmillan, 1976.

Juran, J. M. and Louden, J. Keith, "The Corporate Director," New York, American Management Associations, 1966.

Louden, J. Keith, "The Effective Director in Action," New York, AMACOM Div., American Management Associations, 1975.

"The New World of Corporate Directors," New York, Touche Ross & Co., 1980.

Nicolson, Miklos S., "Duties and Liabilities of Corporate Officers and Directors," Englewood Cliffs, N.J., Prentice-Hall, 1972.

References Cited

[1] In a ruling unfavorable to directors, the U.S. Supreme Court, *Ross v. Bernhard,* 396 U.S. 531 (1970) held that stockholders' derivative suits may involve jury trials.

[2] For a detailed discussion, see Section 21: 2040:01, "Interested Director Transactions and Consideration of Fairness," a note in 58 *Nebraska Law Review* 891 (1979).

[3] See Bruce, William C., "Theft of Business Opportunity: The Legal Basis for a Claim Against the Thief," 53 *Connecticut Bar Journal* 164 (1979).

[4] *Escott v. Bar-Chris Construction Corp.,* 283 F. Supp. 643 (S.D.N.Y. 1968).

[5] Cary, William L., "Corporate Standards and Legal Rules," 50 *California Law Review* (1962), pp. 415–416.

[6] Estes, Robert M., "Outside Directors: More Vulnerable Than Ever, *Harvard Business Review,* Jan.-Feb., 1973.

[7] Mace, Myles L., "Directors: Myth and Reality—Ten Years Later," 39 *Rutgers Law Review* 293 (1979), at p. 300.

[8] For a survey of many sources of potential liability and the status of indemnification, see Shaneyfelt, Donald L., "The Personal Liability Maze of Corporate Directors and Officers," 58 *Nebraska Law Review* 793 (1979).

[9] See note 7, *supra.*

Cross References: *Business Organization: Legal Structure; Directors: Characteristics of Boards; Multiple Management.*

DISASTER RECOVERY

Disaster Recovery has a single goal: assuring that an organization—its employees, its assets and its operations—effectively survive the impact and consequences of a disastrous event. By its very nature, a disaster creates an emergency environment. The disaster recovery effort should help the duration of that environment and minimize its after effects.

And, because of the atmosphere in which the disaster recovery process typically must be carried out, the organization involved must be prepared to draw primarily upon its own people and resources during this recuperation period. Assuring that they are available when and where needed requires careful and intensive planning and preparation. The exact nature of what must be done will be determined by the nature of the disaster—or disasters—to which the organizations could be exposed.

Development. The idea of creating a structured organizational response to a disaster emerged from World War II Civil Defense activities. The concept was broadened during the next 25 years to provide a means for assuring the *continuity* of essential industrial and governmental units after an enemy attack or natural disaster. However, the concept was refined into what appears to have become its generally accepted scope and form beginning about 1973. The catalyst for this change was a rapidly spreading recognition of the crucial role that computer system survival would play in the future ability of an organization to survive the impact of a disaster. This general renewal of corporate management concern for assuring organizational survival has led to the introduction of many procedural refinements of the disaster recovery process, and to the creation of numerous new products and services designed to assist in resolving the effects of several contingencies.

Definitions. *Disaster recovery* encompasses both "contingency response planning" and "emergency operations management." This effort is designed primarily to assure "operation continuity" in the post-disaster period. The emphasis is on minimizing adverse effects to employees and customers—to avoid loss of assets and disruption of business activities. Because of the need to act immediately to recuperate, "making the organization *whole*" (a principal goal of insurance-oriented loss/risk management efforts) is a secondary concern, though it is not ignored during the recovery process.

Disasters may be considered in two categories—natural and manmade. Those in the first category are fire, flood, earthquake, and hurricane. Those in the second category are explosion, civil disorders (including acts of civil disobedience, strikes, demonstrations, and terrorism activities), and utility or government service loss. (These distinctions are somewhat arbitrary at best. There is some overlap between the categories; for example, an explosion is "manmade" when it results from an industrial accident or bomb detonation, but it can be considered to be "natural" when it results, say from a lightning strike igniting a volatile chemical store or shorting out an exposed electrical generator or transformer.)

Responsibility. Administration of the disaster recovery process is considered to be a basic organizational risk management/loss prevention/security task. Its successful accomplishment requires positive support by senior management, since preparing an organization to survive effectively during an emergency requires an advance commitment of key employee time and other resources that cannot be related directly to a contribution to increased profits. Disaster recovery is a cost/loss avoidance process; unfortunately, its value can be demonstrated only under the most adverse of circumstances.

Generally, the person with overall accountability for maintaining the security of the organization's operating facilities—plants, warehouses, and office buildings—is charged with coordinating the development and periodic testing of the emergency operating plan and with activating it when a disaster occurs. (An alternate or "understudy" is selected to function if—and/or when—this person is not available when an emergency arises.)

Risk Analysis. The *Disaster Recovery Coordinator* (DRC) begins by determining the nature, likelihood of occurrence, and probable impact of each type of disaster that the organization might experience. Data used in this risk analysis are drawn from a variety of sources: these include, but are not limited to, local weather and law enforcement agency records, standard maps of flood plains and other hazard-prone areas, and reports by labor/community relations specialists. (This data collection/analysis process should be repeated periodically; that portion of it dealing with civil disorders, at times, for example, may have to be reviewed monthly, or even weekly.)

If the organization has multiple operating locations, the DRC will most likely discover that the nature—and the likelihood of probable occurrence—of particular disaster types will vary from location to location. And, the DRC should not discount the probability and impact of feasible, but unlikely, disasters, say the collapse of an abandoned main that runs under the organization's main building.

After this risk analysis is complete, the DRC identifies the level of recovery that is economically and operationally desirable for each risk possible, should it occur. (In recovering from a disaster it is not always essential that all of the organization's functions be restored immediately, or fully. However, what should be restored, and when it should be restored, will vary from facility to facility and over time. This set of priorities is just one aspect of the overall disaster recovery planning process that makes their thorough review at least annually desirable.)

Response Plans. The DRC next designates a key individual in each organizational unit/facility who participates as part of a DRC team in the development, implementation, and periodic review of a disaster recovery plan. (This person acts, in effect, as the DRC for that unit/facility.)

Within the constraints imposed by the already established priorities, the DRC team creates a comprehensive disaster recovery plan. The local needs and organizational practices will define its full content, but typically such a plan has at least these nine phases:

(1) Designation of management continuity. This section identifies by job title who decides/acts about specific processes, functions, or policies when other managers are unable to function in an emergency situation.

(2) Maintenance of an employee skills data base. While their basis job assignments may not call for the use of these skills, experience, and talents, many employees will have abilities that can prove essential to the success of the recovery process. This section of the plan deals with the establishment and operation of such a skills bank. (Safeguarding of this information should be one of the elements of the organization's records protection activity. This will assure that the needed information will be readily available during the post-disaster period.)

(3) Location of emergency operations sites. This section identifies secure space that will serve, in effect, as the organization's "command post" during the disaster recovery period. An alternative off-premises site should be available if access to the organization's regular facility is not possible during the recovery period.

(4) Arrangements for cooperating with the appropriate local government agencies. What is needed will vary with the differences in local situations. In some instances, for example, the organization's security staff may be able to support the local police force in restoring order after a disaster. But, in another situation, the organization may require special help from surrounding fire departments in dealing with a particular type of disaster. In this instance, this section should detail the nature of the help needed and the basis for securing it.

(5) Establishment of a records-protection program. The scope and operation of the program, detailed in this section, should include the organization's EDP materials, as well as its paper records.

(6) Provision of necessary communications capabilities. There are two aspects to be considered in this section: (1) prompt emergency notification of key organization employees needed on-site during the immediate post-disaster period, and (2) immediate restoration of essential voice and data communications capabilities to the organization. The ability of the organization to function independently in this regard will compensate for any delays or other difficulties encountered by the local common carrier in restoring communications services.

(7) Identification of—and arrangements for—the special services and resources required during the disaster recovery process. Depending upon individual organization/facility needs, this section will describe a wide variety of things that may be required. These could range, for example, from such things as on-site medical services to earth-moving equipment and portable sump pumps for draining electrical service vaults on the premises.

(8) Designation of sources for possible replacement of key equipment, tools, and raw material stocks. This section should tell the DRC how and from whom to secure, say, a replacement supply of a particular industrial-grade chemical needed before production of the facility can resume.

(9) Clarification of the role of the organization's security forces in the recovery process. Details in this section will include the special equipment and training that members of this force will need to carry out that role. The decisions and plans made will depend upon the organization's relations with local government agencies (as previously noted) and upon the force's basic status—employed by the organization or provided to it under contract by a third party.

Plan Tests. A major likely disaster should be simulated at least twice a year, and the organization's ability to respond to it demonstrated. With minimal advance notice, key employees should be required to carry out their duties assigned under the previously developed plan. This exercise will provide much needed training and offer an exceptional opportunity for appraising the likely effectiveness in a "real-world" situation of the plan itself.

Mutual Aid. Where a number of organizations are located near each other it may be feasible for them to share in a joint disaster recovery effort. While it has been most effective where the organizations involved are in essentially the same industry, these aid agreements have been developed successfully in a variety of environments since World War II. An independent operating committee functioning under the provisions of a formal contract seems to be essential to that success.

Disaster recovery can be carried out successfully. However, it will be no more successful than the quality of the advance preparation for recovery.

BELDEN MENKUS, CRM, Management Consultant, Middleville, New Jersey

Cross References: *Computer Security/Automated Office Security; Fire Loss Prevention; Risk Management; Security; Security: Protection of Trade Secrets and Proprietary Information; Terrorism: Protective Measures.*

DISTRIBUTION PLANNING AND RESEARCH

For any company to maintain its position in any industry, its distribution system must be cost effective whether distribution costs are relatively high or low as a percentage of sales volume. That is why every distribution system should be audited periodically to make sure it is providing competitive service at the lowest possible cost. That basically is the job of **Distribution Planning and Research.** The role that is played in any company by distribution planning and research tends to reflect the views top management holds regarding "distribution." In some companies, distribution is considered to be simply the physical movement and storage of products. In others, however, it is viewed as the total complex of activities required to create and supply ultimate demand for an entire product line.

In their classic book "Does Distribution Cost Too Much?" published by The Twentieth Century Fund in 1939, researchers Paul W. Stewart and J. Frederick Dewhurst offered the following definition:

> Distribution includes the transportation of goods from the point of original or intermediate production to the place of sale or further fabrication, the storage of goods until they are needed, and finally the merchandising, display, and advertising of goods and their actual sale or transfer into the possession of the ultimate buyer.

The conclusion of their study was that the total cost of distribution—so defined—accounted for over 50¢ of every consumer's dollar. What the relevant figure might be today is a matter of conjecture since the study has never been updated. But in view of rising energy costs and the inflation of labor costs—both major cost factors in any distribution system—it seems clear that total distribution costs are still high. So despite the streamlining of distribution methods in the United States during the last 40 years, the need for effective distribution planning and research is probably as great, if not greater, today than it was in 1939.

Goals and Types of Studies. Viewed in the larger "total" context, distribution planning and research basically involves two types of projects: (1) distribution system structure studies, and (2) operating efficiency or effectiveness studies.

System structure studies are made to determine the advisability of changes in the basic design of a distribution system long term. Questions that have sparked this type of study include:

- Should our direct-to-retail system be changed to a wholesale system?
- Do we have the right number of distribution centers properly located to provide competitive service at lowest cost?
- Should we consider developing a consolidated distribution system, or should we continue to encourage each product division to build and maintain its own system?
- Are there certain types of accounts that our sales people should no longer be assigned to contact on a regular basis?
- Should we change the amount of advertising and promotion we are doing in certain types of market areas?
- Are we using incentives to best advantage in every phase of our distribution system?

Most system structure studies, because of their broad scope, are initiated by top management and often involve participation by outside consultants. They also may involve the use of special company task forces. They are directed by a senior staff executive at corporate level. In many cases, their findings and recommendations are given only to a limited audience.

Operating efficiency or effectiveness studies are made to find ways to cut the cost, or to increase the effectiveness, of particular functional activities short term. Senior line executives responsible for the activities being studied usually initiate such studies. While the studies may involve the participation of outside specialists, they usually are conducted by staff personnel familiar with the details of day-to-day operations. Questions that have sparked this type of study include:

- Are present sales territories properly defined? Should the number be increased or decreased?
- Is delivery service fully competitive and cost effective in each market area? Should certain accounts be serviced from a different point?
- How complete is our coverage of key accounts and prospects in each market area? What should be done to improve our coverage?
- Should we change the mix of expenses in certain market areas? In which areas should we be using more special promotions?

Needed Facts. Whether a distribution research project is broad in scope or narrow, long term or short term, it requires the development of certain basic facts to determine how well distribution activities are being performed in some defined geographic area. The required facts typically include answers to such questions as:

- Where are customer accounts and prospects concentrated, by type and size of market area?
- Which accounts are being served by which distribution centers?
- What costs are being incurred to serve the customers in each market area?
- What market penetration is being achieved on each major product in each market area?
- What contribution to total company profit results is being made by each market area?

Anyone who has participated in a distribution system study knows the difficulties that can arise in developing solid answers to such questions even when company records are well organized and carefully maintained. One problem stems from the fact that distribution systems evolve over a period of time in response to constantly changing competitive conditions in specific market areas. As a result, company records tend to reflect the requests that operating units have made to resolve problems in one or another part of the distribution system (selling, advertising, traffic, handling and storage, etc.). Second, the market penetration and advertising cost information furnished by outside marketing service organizations is often reported by market areas that do not conform exactly to company market areas. Finally, multi-division companies typically use more than one distribution system, with each product division maintaining its own set of sales and cost records and its own set of market areas. The development of a clear picture of a company's total distribution system on an area-by-area basis under these conditions requires more than a little effort and a considerable amount of expertise.

The Location Coding Problem. One problem encountered in matching sales and cost figures on an area-by-area basis has been the absence of any universal system of geographic location coding. Cities and counties have provided the base units for the most widely used systems. But because they are politically determined, they do not provide a completely satisfactory basis for market area analysis. New York City, for example, is made up of only five counties, and yet accounts for over 5% of the entire country, while many rural counties have almost no commercial importance.

Various systems have been devised over the years to group cities and counties into marketing areas, such as the STANDARD METROPOLITAN STATISTICAL AREAS (SMSAs) of the Bureau of the Census and the marketing areas of research companies such as Nielsen and Arbitron. Other systems have been devised to break down large cities, notably the Census Enumeration Districts (CEDs) of the Bureau of the Census. These systems, all of which use strictly numeric codes, have one problem in common, namely, no automatic way to spot incorrectly assigned or invalid codes in a sales record file.

A New Coding System. A universal geographic location coding system known as LOKATE$_{TM}$ has been devised by Nabisco Brands, Inc., the large food-products manufacturer. It provides a computer tape file of place locations, a program for computer distance calculations between key locations, and documentation required to apply the system [1].

Nabisco's system is based on three developments during the past fifteen years:

(1) The establishment of the Zipcode system.

(2) The creation of the PICADAD system in connection with the Census of Transportation. (The acronym stands for Point Identification Characteristics of Area, Distance, And Direction.) [2]

(3) The increase in computer storage capac-

ity that has made it possible to hold all of a company's sales and cost data in a single data base file.

The 60,000 place name and five digit Zip-code area location records in the Nabisco system base file enable any company to locate every shipment to any account in the United States precisely at one of the 24,000 keypoints established by the PICADAD system. The advantages of LOKATE$_{TM}$ over previously available location coding systems are:

(1) Every file location is a commercially significant mail or freight delivery point.

(2) The codes are entered automatically into a sales record as a by-product of the billing procedure, so no special clerk training is needed to ensure entry of correct codes.

(3) When invalid codes are entered into a sales record by misspelling a location name or inverting a number in a ZIP code, the invalid locations can be identified by simply having the computer match them against valid locations in the base file. This feature resolves one of the major problems of distribution research by preventing entry of erroneous location codes into a sales data file.

(4) Every file location has been established by a Federal Government agency, so maintenance of the file to keep it current and accurate is clearcut and inexpensive.

(5) Every location record includes a latitude-longitude intersect code (or keypoint) that enables a computer to calculate direct distance in miles between any two locations. This feature provides the basis for calculating ton-mile flows in either an existing or a proposed distribution system. It also enables the computer to select from a coded sales record file all records located within a given defined area (for example, a sales territory) so that accounts can be listed or sales can be tabulated.

(6) Each location record includes a set of area codes commonly used in distribution system studies. The file format in Exhibit I shows a list of the codes in the file. These codes make it possible for a computer to group all records in the data base in any particular area or group of areas, or to bring together data from two or more data bases for the same areas. This facilitates the matching of sales and cost data with outside market data.

(7) The file structure allows entry of either (a) additional place locations, or (b) special area codes, without any need to restructure the file. This feature ensures continuity of records that are coded with base files codes, an important factor in using a data base to analyze area sales trends over extended time spans. In this connection it should be noted that the system includes all the additional five-digit ZIP code established by the United States Postal Service as of March 2, 1980, in preparation for implementing an expanded nine-digit ZIP code system in 1981 [3]. It has been estimated by USPS that the nine-digit system will provide ultimately for the assignment of about twenty million codes nationwide. With LOKATE$_{TM}$, a company will be able to maintain a central file of only those nine-digit codes out of the twenty million that are actually important in its business. Additions or deletions of address locations can be tracked, ensuring comparability of geographic area data over long-time periods.

(8) The base file design facilitates the entry of outside market data into working files when

EXHIBIT I

LOKATE$_{TM}$ BASE FILE FORMAT

Field	*Record Length*
Keypoint	5
ZIP Code	5
Location Name	20
FIPS County Code	3
State Abbreviation	2
State Name	20
FIPS State Code	2
Census State Code	2
Longitude	7
Latitude	6
SMSA Number	4
SMSA Size	1
Production Area	2
BEA Economic Area	3
Record Type	1
Keypoint Type	1
Place Code	1
Place Type	1
Place Description	1
Place Size	1
Arbitron - ADI Code	3
Arbitron ADI Name	19
Neilsen DMA Code	3
SAMI Area Code	4
Beale Metro Adjacency Code	1
Arbitron State Code	2
Nielsen State Code	2
Beale State Code	2
Congressional District Code	2
Index	6
Open (for Special Codes)	110
Total (including fillers)	256
Block Size	1,280
Records	60,000

EXHIBIT II

SOURCES OF COMPUTERIZED SMALL GEOGRAPHIC AREA DATA

Source (1)	*Location*
Data User Services Division-Bureau of the Census	Washington, DC
National Center for Health Statistics	Hyattsville, MD
All State Research and Planning Center (2)	Menlo Park, CA
Applied Urbanetics	Washington, DC
CACI (2)	Arlington, VA
Claritas Corporation (2)	Rosslyn, VA
Call Data Systems	Woodbury, NY
Consumer Direct (2)	Northbrook, IL
Data Resources (2)	Lexington, MA
Datamap, Inc.	Eden Prairie, MN
Decision Research Services	Ambler, PA
Demographic Research Company (2)	Santa Monica, CA
Donnelly Marketing (2)	Stamford, CT
Dun's Marketing Services	Parsippany, NJ
Economic Information Services	New York, NY
The Fantus Company	South Orange, NJ
International Data & Development, Inc.	Washington, DC
Market Science Associates	Pittsburgh, PA
Market Statistics, Inc.	New York, NY
Marketing Economics Institute, Inc. (2)	New York, NY
Marketing Information Systems, Inc.	San Diego, CA
Metro-Mail	New York, NY
National CSS	Wilton, CT
National Decision Systems, Inc.	San Diego, CA
National Planning Association	Washington, DC
National Planning Data Corporation (2)	Ithaca, NY
Old American Insurance Company (2)	Kansas City, MO
R.L. Polk & Co. (2)	Washington, DC
Population Reference Bureau, Inc.	Washington, DC
Rand McNally & Co. (2)	Chicago, IL
Rapidata (2)	Fairfield, NJ
Thomas E. Ryan, Inc. (2)	Hastings-on-Hudson, NY
Sophisticated Data Research (SDR)	Atlanta, GA
Survey Sampling, Inc. (2)	Westport, CT
Survey Tabulation Services, Inc.	Cambridge, MA
Urban Data Processing, Inc.	Burlington, MA
Urban Decision Systems, Inc. (2)	Los Angeles, CA Westport, CT
Westat (2)	Rockville, MD
Yuan Liang Marketing Service (2)	Chicago, IL

(1) From advertisements or listings in Demographic Research.
(2) Reportedly offering zipcoded data as part of services.

matching with company data. This feature is of particular interest in view of the increasing availability of outside market information being published by five digit zipcode areas. A list of services reporting information by counties and by zipcode areas is shown in Exhibit II.

Needed Skills. Emphasis placed on data collection and analysis to this point should not be allowed to obscure the importance of other expertise involved in doing effective distribution planning and research. Executives who direct distribution planning and research projects should be able to do three things well: (1) communicate with senior managers; (2) use computers for simulation; and (3) think conceptually.

Effective communication with senior managers is basic to the funding of research projects because every manager has to understand the objectives and the scope of any project that is going to impinge in any way on his or her division's operations. Managers must also accept any findings before recommendations will be implemented. Many proposed studies have not been undertaken, and many that have been conducted have failed to produce actionable results, simply because of a breakdown in communications between managers and researchers. Effective communication can be achieved only when there is rapport and cooperation between line managers and staff researchers based on mutual respect for each other's responsibilities and expertise.

Computer simulation is growing in importance as a tool of distribution planning and research because it is so difficult to reverse any steps to change the basic structure of a distribution system once they have been taken. It is much safer to test out the results expected from proposed system changes before they are either recommended or approved. One simulation model used in distribution planning known as LREPS (Long Range Environmental Planning Simulator) developed at Michigan State University for Johnson & Johnson, Inc. has been licensed to a number of companies.

Conceptual thinking is important to the development of realistic simulation models because such models require visualization of the possible. Practical experience—coupled with first-hand knowledge of developments that offer the possibility of a new approach to the solution of an old problem—are the keys to proper structuring of any simulation model.

CHARLES W. SMITH, Consultant, Distribution by Design, Roslyn, New York

References Cited

[1] LOKATE$_{TM}$ software package, Nabisco copyright; distributor: Distribution by Design, Roslyn, N.Y.
[2] PICADAD system documentation is provided in "Description and Technical Documentation of the PICADAD File," U.S. Department of Commerce, March, 1978. Place size codes in the file reflect population figures from the 1970 Census of Population. No plans are at this writing being made to revise the place codes to reflect 1980 Census of Population figures.
[3] A 14-page document, "Highlights of the Expanded Nine-Digit ZIP Code Program," issued by the Office of ZIP Code Expansion, Research, and Technology Group, U.S. Postal Service, Washington, DC 20260 provides an explanation of the structure of the new 9-digit codes. These will be established by adding four digits following a hyphen to existing 5-digit codes. This means that LOKATE$_{TM}$, based on existing 5-digit codes—will not have to be revised when the 9-digit system is implemented. It will provide a way to enter any new 9-digit codes into a company's basic location coding "library file" by using four digits in the "Open" part of the system's base file to insert the last four digits of the 9-digit code.

Cross Reference: *Marketing Research.*

DYNAMIC PROGRAMMING

Dynamic Programming is a mathematical technique particularly applicable to solving certain types of sequential decision problems. A sequential decision problem is one in which a sequence of decisions must be made, with each decision affecting the future decisions. Each decision changes the current situation into a new situation. Thus, the sequence of decisions made will result in a sequence of situations. Dynamic programming is a procedure for determining the set of sequential decisions that optimizes some measure of value. This sequence of decisions is called an *optimal policy.*

Unlike LINEAR PROGRAMMING, there is no standard mathematical formulation of the dynamic programming problem. At best, it is possible to classify dynamic programming problems into prototypes, with each prototype having its own computational procedure. Thus, dynamic programming is a general approach to solving these sequential decision problems, with different formulations and models appropriate to different individual situations.

History. Dynamic programming is largely due to Richard Bellman's work in the early 1950s. Bellman first postulated his now famous "Principle of Optimality," described below, and with great ingenuity and cleverness, used it to analyze hundreds of optimization problems in mathematics, OPERATIONS RESEARCH, economics, engineering, and other fields. Many of these contributions can be found in his two books on dynamic programming [1], [2]. Since then much research has been done, especially since the publication of Ronald Howard's work on policy improvement in 1960 [3]. As a result, dynamic programming has been applied to a wide variety of managerial problems, such as production scheduling, inventory control, capital budgeting, equipment maintenance and replacement, allocation of development funds, and long-run corporate planning, to name but a few.

Methodology. While it is impossible to delve even marginally into dynamic programming here, there is a certain structure common to many dynamic programming problems which can be mentioned. Relatively few concepts are involved; some are unique to dynamic programming, while others are shared with other models.

Dynamic programming problems are frequently divided into certain points in time called *stages.* A policy decision is made at each stage. Each stage in the problem has a number of *state variables* associated with it. These state variables completely specify the instantaneous situation of the process, giving the various possible conditions in which the process might be at that stage of the problem. The values of all these state variables is called the *state* of the system and tell the user all he needs to know about the system in order to make decisions about it.

As a policy decision is made at each stage, the current state is transformed into a state that is interrelated to a state associated with the next stage of the process. This transformation may be achieved via deterministic relationships or by probabilistic distributions.

Bellman's Principle of Optimality is invoked. This states that an optimal policy has the property that whatever the initial state and initial decision are, the remaining decisions must constitute an optimal policy with regard to the state resulting from the first decision. It is this principle of optimality that is shared by a host of optimization problems whose mathematical formulations are so very disparate, thus making dynamic programming such a theoretically powerful analytical technique.

At each stage of the process, given the current state, an optimal policy for the remaining stages is independent of the policy chosen in the earlier stages of the decision process. The decision maker models the process with a *recursive relationship,* or mathematical formula.

The solution procedure usually begins by finding the optimal policy for each state of the last stage of the process, that is, finding the optimal policy with one stage to go before completion. The next step involves moving backward one stage and, from the recursive relationship, finding the optimal policy for each state with two stages to go before completion. The solution procedure thus continues, moving backward, stage by stage, each time finding the optimal policy for each state of that stage, until it finds the optimal policy when starting at the first stage. At this point the problem is solved, because the optimal policy at the beginning of the process is thus known.

One serious disadvantage of dynamic programming is the computational difficulties that may be encountered. It is possible to characterize a state by any number of state variables, but as additional variables are incorporated into the definition of a state, the computational aspect of the problem grows exponentially. Thus a fairly large problem cannot be solved by even the most sophisticated computer. This unfortunate aspect of dynamic programming has been dubbed the colorful term, the *curse of dimensionality.*

In conclusion, it can be said that dynamic programming is perhaps the most powerful analytical technique available in management science, with vast areas of applications. However, the curse of dimensionality currently limits its use because of the computational problems, although advances in computer technology may lift this limitation. It may be compared to linear programming by saying it is conceptually more powerful but computationally more formidable.

JACK YURKIEWICZ, PH.D., The School of Business, Hofstra University, Hempstead, New York

Information References

Bellman, R., "Dynamic Programming," Princeton, N.J., Princeton University Press, 1957.

Bellman, R. and Dreyfus, S., "Applied Dynamic Programming," Princeton, N.J., Princeton University Press, 1962.

Denardo, E., "Dynamic Programming: Theory and Application," Englewood Cliffs, N.J., Prentice-Hall, 1981.

Dreyfus, S. and Law, A., "The Art and Theory of Dynamic Programming," New York, Academic Press, 1977.

Howard, R., "Dynamic Programming and Markov Processes," Cambridge, Mass., M.I.T. Press, 1960.

Ross, S., "Applied Probability Models with Optimization Applications," San Francisco, Holden-Day, 1970.

Hillier, F. and Lieberman, G., "Introduction to Operations Research," 3rd ed., San Francisco, Holden-Day, 1980.

Wagner, H., "Principles of Operations Research," 2nd ed., Englewood Cliffs, N.J., Prentice-Hall, 1975.

References Cited

[1] Bellman, R., first reference above.

[2] Bellman, R. and Dreyfus, S., second reference above.

[3] Howard, R., above.

Cross References: *Management Sciences (and references there given).*

E

ECONOMETRICS

Econometrics may be defined in the broad sense as the scientific methodology involved in the quantitative analysis of actual economic phenomena. Typically, the econometrician in investigating the characteristics of an economic relationship represents or *specifies* the relationship in the equations of a mathematical model and uses available data to estimate statistically the parameters or constants of the equations. Inferences as to the nature of the relationship are based on the observed values of the parameters and frequently the model can be adapted to forecast economic magnitudes or predict the effects of specific policy actions.

Research in the field has led to the development of a body of statistical and mathematical methods that are tailored to handle the special characteristics of data obtained from direct observation of the economy and economic units. With the advent of modern high-speed data processing, a large inventory of experience in the use of econometrics has been accumulated, and the reliability of many procedures has been established. The econometric approach is widely used in academic empirical research, and has many important applications in business and public policy areas. Of particular importance to management are procedures for forecasting product demand, and analyzing firm and industry cost structures.

History and Development. Empirical studies in economics are as old as economics itself; however the econometric method is comparatively new, drawing on the developments in modern mathematical statistics that are associated principally with R. A. Fisher and his school [1]. A widespread recognition of the need to examine the statistical properties of economic data was first evidenced in the late 1920s with the publication of a number of significant and germinal articles that mark the birth of the econometric method. Noteworthy are the essentially modern studies of production by P. Douglas [2] and demand by H. Schultz [3], and the theoretical contribution of E. Working [4] in elucidating the *identification* problem, the problem of isolating a specific relationship under study from others that "look alike" to impersonal statistical estimating procedures. Progress continued through the 1930s with the publication of a number of significant empirical studies including the pioneering cost studies of T. Yntema [5] and J. Dean [6], and the business cycle research of J. Tinbergen [7].

Methodology was enormously advanced during the 1940s, as the field became systematized and new procedures were developed that could handle interactions between specific sectors and the economy as a whole. This work, associated principally with the staff of the Cowles Commission (then in Chicago) developed into a general approach that now characterizes most research. It is now generally accepted as necessary to consider specific relationships (i.e., demand equations) within the context of *a simultaneous equation model* representing the *structure* of the entire related economic system, since bias, inefficiency, and ambiguity in estimation result from the algebra and stochastic characteristics of the structure [8].

In the years since World War II, with the development of electronic data processing, these methods have been applied to a wide variety of problems, including many of great complexity. Of particular importance is the estimation of a number of large-scale simultaneous-equation models of the entire economy by L. R. Klein and others [9]. Econometric analysis using such models is standard in governmental budgeting and forecasting. Still larger models are used to predict the international impacts of policy. Smaller models giving sectoral detail are used routinely for simulating the implications of new programs in nearly all fields of public activity. At this writing, energy policy has attracted considerable attention on the part of econometricians.

Econometrics is now recognized as a regular field of specialization in university graduate programs in economics, and the resultant increase in the number of graduate economists with competence in this area points to a future of continuing development and progress.

Econometric Forecasting. Probably the most interesting business applications of the econometric method are those of forecasting specific product demand and general economic conditions. Although a considerable degree of technical sophistication may be required to construct and estimate an adequate forecasting model, the actual application and implementation of such a model in the business situation is a matter entirely within the competence of most modern managers. In this regard the nontechnical reader is strongly urged to read the discussion of the accuracy and flexibility of econometric forecasting by D. B. Suits, involving a detailed examination of a model large enough to be accurate, yet compact enough to be comprehensible [10]. The model was constructed specifically to forecast major economic aggregates. Although the actual model is now obsolete in certain technical respects, Suits' presentation still stands as an introduction to the richer systems given in reference [9].

The model explored by Suits represents the U. S. economy by a system of thirty-two simultaneous equations that interrelate and explain such critical magnitudes (among others) as gross national product, employment, automobile consumption, expenditures for plant and equipment, residential construction, and corporate profits and dividends. Each equation reflects a presumably stable relationship, and is based upon observation of key variables in earlier years. Furthermore, the system is constructed with a number of built-in *lags.* (Lags are functional relationships that tie future values of variables to currently observable values, i.e., the change in plant and equipment expenditure is related to the previous year's change in corporate profits, and the previous year's total stock of plant and equipment.) The built-in lags and the interrelationships make forecasting possible. Current data and projections of labor force and Government expenditure are entered into the system, and the equations are solved to yield the forecasts. (Intuitively, the *predetermined* forces propagate themselves through the system to generate the forecast.) Each November since 1953, forecasts for the subsequent year have been published, thus allowing objective evaluation of the accuracy of the method. The worst results were errors of 4%, 6%, and 2% in respectively, the 1955, 1959, and 1960 forecasts of GNP. In all other years the error in the forecast was less than 1%, and in many years the error was less than 0.1%.

Forecasts applying to individual sectors and subsectors of the economy were significantly less accurate, but a virtue of this and many other models is a "component" design that allows the forecaster to increase accuracy at specific points by refining individual equations or by introducing additional equations to obtain more detail (at a possible cost of ambiguity or less accuracy elsewhere in the system). Thus, if the prediction of plant and equipment expenditure was unsatisfactory (and a supplier of industrial machinery would desire an extremely accurate forecast) it might be possible to improve accuracy in this equation by bringing in additional variables (age of existing stock, depreciation expense, etc.). It might also be possible to obtain a breakdown of the total expenditure according to industry groups or type of product by adding new equations to the system.

Costs and Benefits of Econometric Forecasting. A large model such as the above would be required where the forecasted variable is influenced by, and in turn itself strongly influences, major economic magnitudes. In many cases it is possible to produce satisfactory product forecasts using only simple one- or two-equation models. Even where a large model is desirable, it will usually be possible to work up to the large system by stages, patching detailed equations for the most critical variables into a system constructed with the use of previously published results.

Econometric forecasting is most appropriate in cases where product or industry demand is not expected to be peculiarly sensitive to style or fashion. Of course, the method is feasible only if an inventory of data exists. The benefits of reduced uncertainty due to superior market knowledge can be extremely valuable; the costs of econometric research would be comparatively slight.

At this time many private consulting firms provide econometric services to industry. Along with provision of data bases and development of models for special projects, the larger firms (including DRI, Wharton, Chase Econometrics, and Citibank) provide continuous access to full-scale models, so that economic forecasters within client firms can "patch" in-house models incorporating local knowledge and data onto larger systems. The rapid growth of the econometric consulting industry attests to the value of this service; and the major firms are continuing to expand their offered ranges of special sectoral and regional models.

Their forecasts and studies are widely reported in the financial press and have become an actual component of the nation's structure of expectations. It should be noted, finally, that despite the scientific discipline that enters model construction, the public forecast is a different sort of exercise entirely. Ultimately, the forecast will depend on political insight (regarding policies to be enacted during the period forecast) and judgment (regarding emerging developments unanticipated at the time the model was constructed).

Other Applications. Using similar methods it may be possible to forecast long-term industry or firm costs. Other interesting applications are the analysis of a firm's short-term costs for cost accounting or OR programs; analysis of regional costs or growth for locational decisions; analysis of the impact of marketing strategies; and the analysis of credit policies to improve the grading and selection of risks [11].

The Econometric Method. The subject matter of econometrics is data generated by actual economic processes as opposed to data artificially created in controlled experimental environments. In this sense, econometrics has been described as a "way of studying history" [12]. The problems faced by the econometrician can be likened to those of the historian in that both must cope with the problems of isolating the processes or relationships of interest from the background confusion of simultaneously occurring events, and both may have selective vision as to the phenomena and relationships to highlight. Additionally, both must reason on the basis of limited, frequently fragmentary, and possibly erroneous evidence with no opportunity to go back and alter circumstances to provide the additional evidence required for a full exploration of the problem. Some of the important problems encountered in the analysis of economic data will be outlined below, with a brief discussion of the appropriate countermeasures. It is quite likely that in many empirical studies a number of these data problems will appear, and that in almost all studies at least one will crop up. (It is taken for granted that in all but a few cases the data will be limited and the investigator will be forced to use methods adapted to small statistical samples.)

Cross-Sectional vs. Time-Series Data. Economic data can be in the form of *cross-section* observations of different entities or activities at a single moment in time; or they can be in the form of a *time series* of observations of a single variable at different times. Generally, studies using cross-sectional data (e.g., across a census sample, or across the Standard and Poor's sample of firms) test behavioral hypotheses such as conjectures regarding the behavior of firms in different industries. For obvious reasons, time-series data are basic in forecasting applications.

Using cross-section methods, a sample of 50 firms might be considered separately in ten different years, and the model would relate individual firm dividend payments to the firm's earnings level and previous dividends. The cross-section method is quite plausible for this sort of problem, but in others it might not be appropriate even if data exist. It may be difficult to interpret and generalize cross-section results for policy prescriptions or to adapt a cross-section model for forecasting purposes, since many important "policy" variables (e.g., aggregate prices and incomes) do not vary during the instant of time in which the sample is taken.

Although statistical routines are blind to the labeling of data, there are characteristic-problems associated with data of each type and in special models where types are mixed [13]. The problems noted below occur frequently but not exclusively in the context of time-series studies.

Identification Problems and Structural Relationships. A straightforward but unfortunately naive method of estimating the demand function for a product would be to compute a least squares regression (or line of fit) for price and quantity data. However, the equation thus obtained might be of little value as a basis for policy decisions; for if the supply function is also a function in the same variables (as is probably the case), the derived equation may be an ambiguous mixture of demand function and supply function. The two functions look alike statistically, and there is nothing in the method of least squares that automatically takes account of the intent of the investigator.

A situation such as the one just described, in which the relationship under investigation is not statistically isolated from the economic system to which it belongs, is generally termed *underidentification* [14]. It is possible in many cases to choose variables so that underidentification can be eliminated, but the possibility of underidentification must be discovered first, so that it is a cardinal rule in econometric practice to develop and investigate a model in the context of the related background economic system or *structure* in order to determine the proper choice of variables and estimating methods. (The opposite and far less serious condition, *overidentification,* also requires a structural approach but it is susceptible to a variety of treatments.)

Interactions Between Sectors of the Economy and Structural Estimation (Simultaneous Equation Methods). The establishment of exact identification does not end the analyst's concern with the overall structure. In many situations, particularly where economic aggregates are considered, interactions between sectors of the economy will be reflected in the equations representing these sectors, and errors of unknown size will bias the results. The concept is not difficult to grasp intuitively: Consider, for example, the problem of estimating expenditure on automobiles, where the demand for automobiles is dependent upon consumers' income, while such income is, in turn, dependent upon production levels in the automobile industry. It is clear that income determination and automobile demand must be considered *simultaneously,* and this may necessitate the use of special estimating procedures that involve formidable computations and a number of dangers. The most costly method and potentially the most accurate involves the simultaneous estimation of all structural equations *(full information, maximum likelihood estimation).* Other methods utilize only part of the structural information and are correspondingly less costly and accurate *(limited information, maximum likelihood; instrumental variables; reduced form, least squares; two- (or three)-stage least squares; ordinary least squares)* [15].

Serial Correlation. Consider an industry in which sales contracts commit a firm to production and deliveries spaced over several years (e.g., manufacturers of heavy equipment). It is clear that, since monthly, quarterly, or even yearly observations of the firm's activity will not be independent of one another, successive observations will be correlated, and results obtained in estimating equations incorporating these data will be in error. This situation, due to multiple observation of a single phenomenon, can also occur if data are used that are constructed by interpolation (yearly population statistics), or with the use of certain averaging methods which allow some overlap between successive observations (many production and price indices). Problems of this sort are usually classified together in the technical literature under the heading of *serial correlation* (alternates: *autoregressive errors, non-independent disturbances*). The terms refer to the statistical property. Imperfect but generally satisfactory procedures that test and correct for serial correlation exist.

Dynamics, Forecasting — Autoregression. Special problems come up in models used for forecasting, and in models where variables in one time period are related to variables in another. The likelihood of bias in such models is quite high as errors in early periods tend to be "inherited" all through the later years. The econometrician is compelled to sacrifice a good deal of the potential usefulness of his model if he is to eliminate such bias entirely, and delicate compromises are required.

The modeler's art is seriously tested in the use of *distributed lag* methodology, wherein the effect of a variable at an earlier time is presumed to be spread out over a succession of time periods, e.g., the population ultimately consumes $90 from a $100 tax cut in 1970, but the $90 is spread (distributed) over the next N periods. The distribution of the effect is expressed as a first-degree or higher exponential form. A distributed-lag scheme can permit simultaneous estimates of the consumption fraction, the coefficients of the exponential form, period of distribution, and other parameters of the equation. Needless to say, such estimates are highly sensitive to errors in specification.

Errors in Variables. Many economic observations are inaccurate. In some cases the statistical discrepancies are known (national income accounts provide an example). In other cases little is known about the magnitude or direction of possible error. Known methods (e.g., *weighted regression*) used to correct for errors in the variables entering estimating equations are difficult to apply, and preclude the use of other corrective methods outlined above. In practice, possible errors in variables are usually not taken into account in the estimation process, but considered in a final evaluation of the creditability of the results.

Econometricians are frequent users of *systems-modeling* approaches and have adapted and developed a wide range of statistical techniques. Of particular importance are the estimation of *constraint systems,* the compression of data sets and elimination of *multicolinearity* through *principle-components* analysis, and the analysis of dichotomous or probablistic variables through *probit* and *logit analysis,* the detection of structure through *pattern analysis.* New applications emerge continuously.

Related Fields. Econometrics is clearly linked to *mathematical economics* in that the expression or *specification* of economic or business problems in mathematical terms is a prerequisite to econometric analysis. Similarly, econometrics is dependent upon *mathematical statistics* for many of the estimating procedures in current use, and of course for the probability foundations of the discipline. Many leading econometricians have also made substantial contributions to these other fields.

Two other important and successful schools of empirical economics are frequently distinguished from econometrics proper, *input-output analysis* and the *time series decomposition* approach to business cycle analysis. Neither of these approaches involves a detailed concern with the probability characteristics of economic data and structure.

Input-Output Analysis. This approach was developed by W. Leontief immediately before World War II [16]. The method involves the use of actual data to estimate constants that represent the proportion (presumed to be fixed) of product inputs from all industries that are required to produce a particular industry's output. The collection of constants for all industries and all products can be put together to form a model of the entire economy, the *input-output matrix.* The approach is quite useful in finding bottlenecks that would hamper the achievement of a particular national production or growth goal, or in testing the effects of general policies on production within specific industries. Extremely large systems can be estimated as the method has a number of computational virtues. The method is closely related in its underlying mathematical structure to LINEAR PROGRAMMING and GAME THEORY, and is frequently grouped with them under the general heading of *Activity Analysis.*

Decomposition Approach. This is particularly identified with the National Bureau of Economic Research, and involves the breaking down of time series of raw economic data into separate components of seasonal variation, long-term trend, and cycle variation [17]. A purpose of the analysis is to discover cyclical patterns, *reference cycles,* that are common to wide groups of data. Series that tend to reach cyclical turning points before the rest of the economy are developed into *leading indicators.* In fact, many of the well known forecasting indices are formed in this way. (See BUSINESS FORECASTING.)

The approach has been criticized by econometricians for its lack of statistical rigor in that rule of thumb methods have been applied simplistically to any and all situations, and many observed cycles could be generated by the decomposition methods alone without having an underlying economic reality [18]. This criticism applies to indiscriminate application of the method. The decomposition approach is accepted as having definite value in short-term forecasting and has recently been given a new breath of life with the introduction of *spectral analysis* and powerful computer-based techniques [19]. These techniques offer unusual flexibility in uncovering periodicities, and provide a means for forecasting extremely short-term phenomena such as daily price changes and inventory variations.

PETER S. ALBIN, Professor, Department of Economics, City University of New York, John Jay College, New York, New York

Information References

Associations:

The Econometric Society.

Periodicals:

The primary source for materials pertaining to methodology is the journal of the Econometric Society, *Econometrica.* Studies involving econometric analysis regularly appear in virtually all of the professional economic journals.

Texts:

Gujarati, Damodar, "Basic Econometrics," New York, McGraw-Hill, 1978 (introductory).

Hood, W. and Koopmans, T., eds, "Studies in Econometric Methods," New York, Wiley, 1953. (Collection of pioneer Cowles Commission methodological studies; this is a standard reference.)

Kennedy, Peter, "A Guide to Econometrics," Cambridge, Mass., MIT Press, 1979 (basic).

Malinvaud, E., "Statistical Methods of Econometrics," Amsterdam, Netherlands, North Holland Publishing, 1966.

Pindyck, R. and Rubinfeld, D., "Econometric Models and Economic Forecasts," New York, McGraw-Hill, 1976 (applications).

Theil, Henry, "Principles of Econometrics," New York, Wiley, 1971 (advanced).

References Cited

[1] See in particular Fisher, R. A., "Statistical Methods for Research Workers," Edinburgh, Oliver & Boyd, 1938 (8th edition).

[2] Douglas, P. H., "Theory of Wages," Toronto, Macmillan, 1934 (recapitulates earlier studies with C. W. Cobb).

[3] Schultz, H., "The Theory and Measurement of Demand," Chicago, University of Chicago Press, 1938.

[4] Working, E. J., "What do Statistical Demand Curves Show?" *Quarterly Journal of Economics.* (Reprinted in American Economic Association, "Readings in Price Theory," Chicago, 1952.)

[5] Yntema, T. O., "Steel Prices, Volume and Cost," in TNEC *Papers,* Vol. 1, New York, 1940. (Discussed by H. Staehle, *American Economic Review,* 1940).

[6] Dean, Joel, "Statistical Cost Functions of a Hosiery Mill," *Studies in Business Administration,* Vol. 11, No. 4, University of Chicago, School of

Business, Chicago, 1941. (Also discussed by Staehle, reference 5, above.)

[7] Tinbergen, J., "An Economic Approach to Business Cycle Problems," Hermann (Paris), 1937.

[8] The Cowles Commission approach is expressed in Hood and Koopmans, above.

[9] Klein, L. R. and Goldberger, A. S., "An Econometric model of the United States, 1929–1952," Amsterdam, 1955. Duesenberry, James S., Fromm, Garry, Klein, Lawrence R., and Kuh, Edwin, eds., "A Quarterly Econometric Model of the United States Economy," Chicago, Rand-McNally, 1965. "Chase Econometric Model," Chase Manhattan Bank, New York. Larger models, today, incorporate international interaction of economic variables, and are capable of general forecasting.

[10] Suits, D. B., "Forecasting with an Econometric Model," *American Economic Review,* March 1962.

[11] See references and comments in Staehle (reference 5) and Tintner, G., "Econometrics," New York, Wiley, 1952.

[12] Klein, L., "A Textbook of Econometrics," Evanston, Ill., Row, Peterson, 1953.

[13] Technical problems associated with cross-section analysis are covered in Christ, C. F., "Econometric Models and Methods," New York, Wiley, 1966.

[14] The technical terms are indexed and discussed rigorously in Klein (reference 12), and the other texts cited above.

[15] In many cases a single equation model is sufficient to test a hypothesis on a relation among economic variables. However, the forecasting capabilities of the equation might be quite low, because of complex interrelationships among economic variables. In this case an econometrician might want to sacrifice simplicity and cost efficiency of computations for the forecasting advantages of multi-variable, multi-equation models. Extensive treatment of simultaneous models can be found in Malivand, 1966, Theil, 1971, and Christ, 1966 (reference 13).

[16] Leontief, W., "The Structure of the American Economy," Cambridge, Mass., Harvard University Press, 1941.

[17] Burns, A. F. and Mitchell, W. C., "Measuring Business Cycles," New York, National Bureau of Economic Research, 1946.

[18] Koopmans, T. C., "Review of Burns and Mitchell," *Review of Economics and Statistics,* 1947.

[19] Box, G. E. P. and Jenkins, G. M., "Time Series Analysis, Forecasting, and Control," San Francisco, Holden-Day, 1970.

Cross References: *Business Forecasting; Economics; Statistics.*

ECONOMICS

Economics is the body of knowledge dealing with the manner in which man uses the scarce and limited resources at his command to satisfy his wants. Its content embraces the production, distribution, and consumption of goods and services, and the institutions society has developed to facilitate such activities. Its primary concern is the maximization of useful output at a minimum cost of human and capital inputs (the so-called *minimax* principle).

The two terms, *macroeconomics* and *microeconomics,* are often used in defining the field of economics. The first concerns studies or statistics that consider aggregates of individual or groups of commodities: for example, total consumption, employment, or income. The second concerns studies or statistics that consider particular individuals or single commodities: for example, the demand for wheat, or for employment in the automotive industries.

The scarce resources involved in the economic process consist not only of human labor but also of land, capital, and management (technically, the entrepreneur). These four major inputs—termed "the four factors of production"—have been supplemented increasingly by the services of government—sometimes regarded as the fifth factor of production. The degree of scarcity of the various factors of production varies over time and among nations but is always present, since the wants or aspirations of man at all times exceed the ability of society to meet them. Every society, whatever its political form, is confronted with this inescapable element of scarcity and the choice of alternative uses of the existing limited factors of production available to it. Economics is the study of how to improve the ability of all concerned—the wage-earner, the consumer, the businessman, the public-policy maker—to make better use of these various alternatives.

These alternatives range over the entire spectrum of human activity. By command or by market determination, choices must be made as to what shall be produced, by whom, and at what price. How much of the current output shall be consumed and how shall it be saved; i.e., how much shall be set aside and invested for purposes of future growth in the form of plant, homes, equipment, and inventory? In what form and through what incentives can sufficient savings be provided to finance the desired capital formation—and how shall the available savings be rationed among business, government, individuals and foreign countries, all seeking to employ it? At what wage shall labor be employed and what profit, if any, shall ultimately be offered to the producer to assure his participation? What degree of personal freedom shall be exercised in the choice of competitive alternatives? Which choices shall be made by individuals; which, by government?

Historic Development of Economics. The scope and coverage of economic thought have been altered over time to accord with the changing institutions under which business has been conducted. Over the long sweep of history, various forms of economic organizations have evolved, flourished, and declined; among them were the ancient agricultural societies, feudalism, the manorial societies, and guilds. Modern-day economic theory of an industrialized society, however, finds its origin in the works of ADAM SMITH ("The Wealth of Nations," 1776) and the basic ideas he advanced on the essential functions performed by the free market mechanism.

The "invisible hand" of economic self-interest, Smith theorized, would guide the allocation of resources to yield far higher returns than mercantilism or the monopolies sanctioned by royalty against which he opposed his philosophy of *laissez faire,* or non-interference. ("Mercantilism" was the dominant economic concept of the sixteenth and seventeenth centuries which sought to maintain, by various regulations, an excess of exports over imports and to collect the difference in the form of precious metals for use in increasing the power and prestige of the state.) The invaluable rationing functions performed by a competitive market system, as Smith first described them in the early stages of the Industrial Revolution, became the basis for the expanded body of "classical" economic theory subsequently developed by David Ricardo, John Stuart Mill, Alfred Marshall, and other historic figures of the eighteenth and nineteenth centuries. Through the use of deductive reasoning, the economic philosophers of that era formulated a body of knowledge covering almost every phase of human activity. Questions of monetary policy, taxation, government expenditures, and international trade were explored and resolved largely on the basis of the abstractions of this body of theory, in terms of a highly competitive, individualistic economy.

In the writings of the classical economists, the "economic man" acting always in his self interest is assumed, and man's economic behavior is generalized in the form of principles or laws which are believed to be universally applicable. The general principle that both individuals as such and society as a whole prosper most without government intervention in economic life is indicated in one form or another in the writings of the classical school. A belief in economic freedom and private property is one of its fundamental doctrines.

Smith was a strong opponent of all forms of state interference with industry and commerce, holding that the natural balance of motives is most effective in economic affairs. Every individual, he contended, is most anxious to obtain the greatest profit for himself; this search for profits leads to division of labor, which in turn leads to dependence upon others, and this dependence leads to the need to consider the self-interest of others—leading in turn to paths ordained by the natural social order. Government, he held, should refuse to set up any special economic privilege, and should take positive action against any monopolistic position, whether by capital or labor. He saw preservation of free competition, by state action if necessary, as the principal duty of economic policy.

Not all observers accepted the emergence of capitalism and the factory system with equanimity. Hours of work were long, working conditions poor, and wages abysmally low judged against modern standards. Even David Ricardo (1772–1823), the outstanding exponent of classical political economy and as great a free-trader and believer in competition as Adam Smith, did not, like Smith, believe that the pursuit of self-interest by economic classes would necessarily lead to a harmony of social interests. He saw the interests of the landlords as opposed not only to those of labor, but also to those of the industrialists, since he considered rent a "surplus" and not a contributor to value. It was to the landlord's advantage that the price of food should continually rise, while the capitalists and workers desired a low cost of subsistence. Although the classical theory had held that the economic system automatically achieved full employment and equilibrium through time, and that severe fluctuations of economic activity or prolonged stagnation were impossible, Ricardo's analysis drew a pessimistic view of the future, expressed in a "law of diminishing returns." In spite of improvements in agriculture, he saw a progressive decline in the fertility of land and a continued increase in the price of food. Money wages, he thought, would have to go on rising in order to keep up with the rising cost of subsistence, although real wages would not rise. Rent would go up steadily and profits would steadily decline.

Karl Marx, writing in the milieu of mid-nineteenth century, passionately argued that the limited yields of early capitalism stemmed from the concerted exploitation of the propertyless by the propertied, rather than from the low levels of productivity then prevailing. His "Communist Manifesto" (1848) proposed sweeping institutional changes for the emerging industrialized society.

The main problems of the Marxian economics are the "transformation problem" of converting value into price, the increasing "organic composition of capital" over time in the capitalist production process, the "law" of falling rates of profits, and his principle of the increasing misery of the working class. According to Volume I of Marx's "Capital," the "values" of good are proportional to the labor embodied directly and indirectly in the goods, while in Volume III of "Capital," actual competitive "prices" are relatively lowest for those goods of highest direct-labor intensity and highest for those goods of low-labor intensity (or in Marx's words, for those with highest "organic composition of capital"). This contradictory position Marx tried to resolve with his famous "transformation procedures" in Volume III, which was theoretically unsatisfactory because Marx attempted to transform values into prices while at the same time transforming "surplus values" into "profits." But both cannot be attained at the same time.

Also, J. Gillman has shown that the organic composition of capital (i.e., capital/labor ratio) for the U.S. economy has not shown any sustained tendency to rise since about 1920 [1]. Also, the so-called Marxian "law" of the falling rate of profit along with the falling real wage rate (i.e., increasing misery of the working class) cannot be maintained at the same time. If R is the rate of profit, S is surplus value, V is variable capital, and C is constant capital, then:

$$R = \frac{\Sigma S}{\Sigma C + \Sigma V}$$

$$= \frac{\Sigma S}{\Sigma V} \cdot \frac{\Sigma V}{\Sigma C + \Sigma V}$$

= Rate of Surplus Value × (1 − Organic Composition of Capital)

$$(1).....\mathrm{R} = SV\,(1-K)$$

where K = organic composition of capital.

Obviously, if SV stays constant and K rises, it is a tautology that R must fall. But in those cases where unchanged rate of surplus value can be identified with the unchanged real wage, the only reason why a profit-maximizing firm may embark on higher capital-intensive production process is that such new technologies would provide it with *extra* rather than unchanged surplus value. Even in those instances where inventions do force a reduction in the rate of profit, it is mainly because the cheapening of goods' prices is greater than the subsequent increase in money wage rates, i.e., a falling down of the profit rate is the concomitant of the increase in real wage rate. Thus the improvements in technology cannot, despite the formula (1), drive down the rate of profit without increasing the real wage rate.

In "Capital," Marx formalized his theory of the motion of capitalist development and predicted the ultimate breakdown of the capitalist system because of "inner" contradictions. But history has not dealt kindly with Marx. Not only has the Western world grown unprecedently after World War II in economic prosperity, but also both the absolute and relative positions of the working people have improved significantly as compared to the socialist countries which have followed the Marxian precept of state control of production and distribution processes. With all the problems of recession and inflation, the capitalist system has been proved resilient enough to bounce back on the track and continue to progress forward.

Growth of the American Economy. The period following the mid-1800s was characterized by the expansion of the factory system in the United States, and by 1890 industry exceeded agriculture as the dominant economic activity here. The growth of industry during this period was marked by technological developments, the application of science to industrial processes, greater specialization, and the widespread application of the principle of interchangeable parts. Native population increase, augmented by large-scale immigration, provided a growing labor force to meet the demand for goods. Invested capital grew enormously, more and more of it being generated by the economic activity within the country, with less reliance upon foreign capital. The period from 1890 to the present witnessed a tremendous growth in per capita production and consumption, the further transformation of industrial production by the introduction of new sources of power and revolutionary technologies, the application of scientific methods to management processes, and the integration of manufacturing and distribution accompanied by large-scale combinations of business organizations.

World War I greatly stimulated industrial development in the United States, but it also resulted in imbalances between production and consumption and a decline in agricultural income, which, with a speculative rise in securities, combined in 1929 with an accumulation of other factors to bring about the severe Depression of the early 1930s. With the Depression came intervention in the economy by the Federal Government on an unprecedented scale—in industry, agriculture, finance, and local affairs. Billions of dollars were spent on programs of relief and recovery.

Keynesian Economics. The deep worldwide Depression of the 1930s provided fruitful climate for the economic theories and policies advanced by the British economist, JOHN MAYNARD KEYNES (1883–1946) and his followers, or attributed to them, and these are still subject to considerable controversy. Among the important assertions of the Keynesian school is the view that if savings are not offset by investments in new capital formation, unemployment will follow. It is argued that people decide how much of their income to spend and how much to save, and this is termed *propensity to consume.* Then they decide whether to hold their savings in wholly liquid form, as in cash or its equivalent, or to sacrifice complete liquidity for some form of investment, and this is termed *liquidity preference.* But such decisions may result in a failure to invest any of the savings. In that event the Keynesians hold that if the more severe depression phases of the business cycle are to be prevented, and if the economy is not to stagnate and mass unemployment become chronic, government must stimulate spending or create investments (public works) to assure full employment. In other words, after the economy has reached a certain low level, as was the case in the early 1930s, there is according to this view no automatic mechanism that will make corrective forces come into play.

Two additional terms used in Keynesian economics are the so-called *acceleration principle* and *multiplier principle.* The former is used to explain how an increase or decrease in consumer expenditures may cause changes in new capital formation. For example, a sufficient increase in consumer demand for a commodity may result in added facilities for producing it, and, conversely, a sufficient decrease may result in failure of producers to replace worn-out equipment. The acceleration factor, or *coefficient of acceleration,* is the ratio of change in investments to change in consumer expenditures. Thus, if increased consumer expenditures of $5,000,000 cause increased capital investments of $2,000,000, the associated coefficient of acceleration is two-fifths.

The multiplier principle is used to explain the way in which an increase or decrease in new capital formation can cause cumulative effects in national income through consumer expenditures. For example, a $5,000,000 increase in new capital formation will normally yield a like increase in the national income in the form of wages, interest, profit, rent, etc. The recipients will spend this income according to the existing marginal propensity to consume. Assuming this to be, say, 65%, then $3,250,000 will be spent for consumer goods. This will increase income in the consumer goods industry by that amount. The recipients will, in turn, spend 65% of this, or $2,112,500. This also becomes income, of which 65% will be spent, and so on. It can be shown that the total of the converging series thus formed will be $C/(1-R)$ where C is the original increase in new capital formation and R the marginal propensity to consume. The result in the example given would be $14,286,000. The multiplier is the ratio between the increase or decrease in income and the increase or decrease in new capital formation, or 2.86 in our example.

According to Keynes, the neoclassical assumption of automatic full-employment was wrong, as the economy can function indefinitely at under-employment equilibrium where there would be excess supply of labor, or what Keynes called "involuntary unemployment." To the neoclassical economist, this would not be possible because a fall in money wage rate will lead to a fall in real wage rate if the price level remains constant, so that the level of employment will increase until the market is cleared. But Keynes argued that a fall in money wages may lower production costs, but will also decrease the effective demand as the marginal propensity to consume is less than unity, resulting in unintended inventory accumulation. Prices will fall, so the real wage, on which the demand for labor depends, will eventually remain unchanged.

However, to a neoclassical economist, as

long as there is an uncleared labor market and as long as competition puts pressure on wages and prices, the real value of the money supply will increase, and this will force down interest rates, raise the level of investment, and increase the level of income and employment until unemployment is eliminated. Keynes rebutted this argument with his theory of *liquidity preference* where increase in the real value of money supply would not affect the interest rate because of the existence of a "liquidity trap" where the demand for money is infinitely elastic at the existing rate of interest. Also, as labor suffers from "money illusion" and as money wages tend to be sticky in the downward direction, the restoration of full employment can come only through a real wage fall resulting in an increase in aggregate demand and price level. Hence, Keynes' advocacy for active fiscal policy and for government intervention to stimulate aggregate demand in the economy.

Emergence of Empiricism and Institutional Economics. In contrast to the almost complete dependence earlier upon economic theory deductively derived, the twentieth century has been marked by increasing reliance upon the inductive method to derive conclusions and by intensive statistical study of the institutions shaping the response of the market. The most significant contributions have been drawn from analytical use of the "system of national or social accounts," built upon a conceptual framework developed earlier in this century, primarily by such American economists as Wesley C. Mitchell, Willford I. King, Simon Kuznets, and Wassily Leontief, as well as Britain's John Maynard Keynes.

Slowly but steadily an integrated statistical system of economic intelligence has been constructed, first in the United States and then globally, with the assistance of the League of Nations and the United Nations.

Shortly after World War I such eminent economic research institutions were brought into being as the National Bureau of Economic Research, the National Industrial Conference Board (now renamed as The Conference Board), the Brookings Institution, and the Twentieth Century Fund, and they have done much to clothe this system with meaning. This emerging body of economic intelligence was first used to illuminate the past, thereby shedding much needed light on factors contributing toward business cycles and economic growth. Later in the period between World War I and World War II, many new measures were devised to assist in determining the current position of business. Monthly measures of industrial production were developed, also of employment and unemployment, consumer and wholesale prices, etc. Most of the indicators now used by business and Government to determine current position of the national economy were introduced during this interwar period.

A System of National Accounts. In the mid-thirties the official measurement of national income was begun by the United States Department of Commerce, to which estimates of personal income were subsequently added. Later in World War II, annual measures of gross national product and its disposition were inaugurated. These highly valuable tools of analysis are also now available in deflated terms (with the influence of price change removed) and for personal income on a regional, state, and localized basis.

This system of national accounting, embracing as it does such vital areas as consumption, saving, business investment, foreign trade, and Government expenditures and taxes, has become the framework around which modern-day economic theory is not only built, but also verified. To it has been added, postwar, a growing system of related accounts designed to throw even more light on other aspects or sectors of the economy. Input-output tables explore specifically what commodities and how much of each are involved in the production of any given final product; e.g., the input of steel, coal, copper, glass, etc. required in the production of motor vehicles. Turning to the area of money and credit, a whole new series of "money-flow" accounts has been devised by the Federal Reserve Board designed to highlight changes in debt and saving that underlie the expenditures of individuals, business, and government in the national accounts.

As in the case of business accounts, knowledge of change in the structure and composition of the national balance sheet is essential in analyzing change in the gross national product and other variants of the national operating statement. Within the past decade progress has been made in measuring national wealth, including both the nation's physical assets as well as the sum of its financial claims and liabilities. The newly-developed measures of national physical output can then be related to such inputs as units of labor and of capital, another set of recently derived measures. As a result, much progress has been made in measuring output per unit of input—termed national productivity—and determining the respective contributions of manhours, capital, education, technology and government to economic growth.

Emergence of Foreshadowing Statistics. Following the passage of the Employment Act of 1946, interest intensified in the development of *foreshadowing* measures or statistics that would, when assembled, throw light on the future operations of the economy. Under the Employment Act of 1946, the full resources of the United States were to be harnessed to assure that ample job opportunities would be forthcoming for all seeking employment. Accordingly, both the President's Council of Economic Advisers and the Joint Senate-House Economic Committee became concerned with economic-model building and with the construction of bodies of data that would be useful in determining the size and composition of the labor force of the future and the potential dimensions of the economy employing this expanded manpower.

At the same time, there was a growing concern to gauge the upturn and downturn of the economy beforehand through the estimation of economic indicators. Under the leadership of famous economists such as Wesley C. Mitchell, Arthur Burns, and Geoffrey Moore working with the National Bureau of Economic Research (NBER), three kinds of indicators were developed, namely, leading economic indicators, coincident indicators, and lagging indicators, as schematically indicated in Exhibit I.

EXHIBIT I

LEADING, LAGGING, AND COINCIDENT INDICATORS

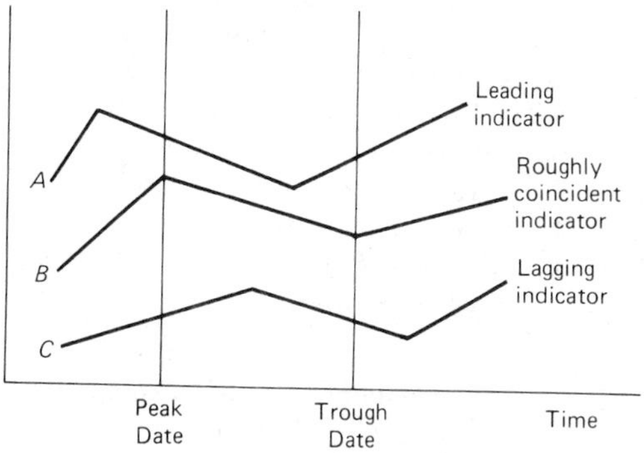

SOURCE: Roger K. Chisholm and Gilbert R. Whitaker, Jr., *Forecasting Methods* (Homewood, Ill.: Richard D. Irwin, Inc., 1971), p. 42.

The current "long list" includes 88 U.S. series: 72 monthly and 16 quarterly. Of these, 36 are classified as leading indicators, 25 are roughly coincident, 11 are lagging, and 16 are unclassified by timing. The "short list" is a subset of the long list and includes 25 U.S. series—12 leading, 7 coincident, and 6 lagging. Four of these are quarterly; the remainder are monthly. Through a composite *diffusion index,* economists in NBER try to estimate the timing and the extensiveness of an expansion or contraction. (See BUSINESS FORECASTING.)

Econometrics: Economic Models. Economists have aided everyone concerned with more efficient use of limited resources, not only by building an integrated system of statistical inference, but also by applying advanced mathematics to the interpretation of these statistics. Decision-making has been increasingly formalized through a growing number of mathematical devices. In fact, a highly specialized field of economics, ECONOMETRICS, now deals specifically with the mathematical analysis of empirical data. It aims to give specific formal content to much of the *a priori* reasoning incorporated earlier in economic theory in such areas as demand analysis, cost and production functions, and particularly the forecasting of gross national product (GNP).

One of the earliest econometric models of the U.S. economy was constructed by Lawrence R. Klein of the University of Pennsylvania in 1950. It was followed by the Klein-Goldberger model, which in turn led to the 32-equation forecasting model used in the early 1960s at the University of Michigan. In such models, alternative estimates of government receipts and expenditures can be "cranked" into the model and their ultimate impact upon gross national product and employment can be derived, as broad guides to such public policy questions as tax relief and the economic impact of prospective deficits.

A simple macro-model of an economy can be stated as follows:

$$(1)\ Y = C + I + G + X$$
$$(2)\ C = a + bY + dC_{-1}$$
$$(3)\ I = e + fi$$
$$(4)\ G = G'$$
$$(5)\ X = X'$$
$$(6)\ i = i'$$

where

Y = Gross National Product (GNP)
C = Consumption expenditure with C_{-1} denoting consumption expenditures in the previous period
I = Investment expenditures
G = Government expenditures
i = Interest rate
X = Net foreign exports
a, b, d, e, and f are unknown parameters or constants.

The above equations are either behavioral equations or identities. The behavioral equations are those which contain unknown parameters (i.e., equations 2 and 3), while the other equations are identities, either equilibrium conditions (1) or definitional identities (4, 5, and 6). In these equations there can be two kinds of variables—endogenous, which are determined with the system of equations (such as GNP, consumer expenditures, and investment expenditures), or exogenous, which are specified from outside the system (such as government spending, net exports, or interest rate).

The first step in econometric model building is that the model must be *specified,* i.e., appropriate functional relationships must be spelled out. Second is the *estimation* of unknown parameters, such as the values of *a, b, d, e,* and *f.* The third step is *simulation* where the forecaster "plugs in" values for the exogenous variables to get forecasts of the endogenous ones. Finally, the model must have internal *consistency,* and the error terms must be calculated. An *ex post* comparison must be made between the actual values and the predictive values of the model which will help to improve its predictive power in the future.

Today, macroeconomic model building is a "growth industry." Companies like Data Resources Inc. (DRI), Chase Econometrics, Wharton, and a few others now regularly calculate quarterly econometric models of the U.S. economy and market them to various firms and government agencies. But how good are they? The evidence for the period 1953–1970 in GNP forecasting disclosed substantial correspondence between the forecasts and the realizations. The predicted changes approximate the actual ones well in each period covered, the changes of the former being generally less than one percentage point smaller than the averages of the latter. The evidence supports the conclusion that the end-of-year forecasts of current dollar GNP for the next year had a reasonably satisfactory record of accuracy since 1953. But the forecasts of GNP in constant dollars (RGNP) and the implicit price deflator (DIP) which is a proxy for inflation rate, are less accurate. The former suffer from large turning point errors, the latter from large underestimation errors.

It should be understood that econometric forecasting is still both an art and a science. It needs better data and information, and the "fine tuning" to make adjustments in the constant terms of various equations, and to make possible value judgments regarding the magnitude and directions of these parametric changes.

Monetarist Position and the Emergence of "Supply-Side" Economics. The principal drawback of the Keynesian Revolution is that it was born as a challenge to the complacency of the orthodox economics in the face of high unemployment and economic retardation of the Great Depression era. When the Western economies moved into the post-World War II period, the crucial problem became the phenomenon of creeping inflation. Against this the Keynesian prescription of activist fiscal policy proved ineffective, while downplaying the role of monetary policy in the economy. To the Keynesians, the existence of the so-called Phillips curve which sought to establish the inverse correlation between the rate of unemployment and the rate of inflation, gave a choice to the economy as to how much inflation was to be tolerated vis-a-vis the unemployment rate. (See INFLATION.) But during the severe recession of 1974–1975 when it was found that *both* unemployment rate and the rate of inflation increased at a precipitous rate (a condition termed *stagflation*), the Keynesians replied that the Phillips curve had shifted forward, resulting in a higher trade-off between inflation and unemployment.

The monetarist counter-revolution, under the leadership of Professor Milton Friedman of the University of Chicago, challenged this position and pointed out that there could be no long-run trade-off between inflation and unemployment. As a matter of fact, the monetarists do not believe in the existence of long-run Phillips' curve, and talk of the "natural" rate of unemployment. The latter, they say, is embedded in the economic system and depends on the real phenomena such as market frictions, real income, tax rate, and unemployment insurance. According to Friedman's view, as soon as inflation begins to rise, people begin adjusting their expectation of it, causing the Phillips curve to shift forward. If raising the rate of inflation once and for all only lowers the unemployment rate temporarily, then the only way to keep the unemployment rate permanently below the natural rate is by continually increasing the rate of inflation. This would be particularly true under the "rational expectation hypothesis," which is based on the inflation psychosis of the general population and on changes in their expectation functions following the increased impact of inflation.

With the apparent failures of demand-managed incomes policy, there is today an emergence of "supply-side" economics which emphasize mainly the policy of economic stimulus to production and economic growth. One of the principal weapons for this stimulation is periodic and substantial cuts of income and other taxes. The income effects of an income tax cut would increase the work efforts of both lower and higher income groups since the disposable income would be higher. This, coupled with the substitution effects of people working more instead of seeking more leisure, would increase the total production of the economy.

The principal rationale for the tax cuts is the so-called Laffer curve named after Professor Arthur Laffer of the University of Southern California. This states that if tax rates on individuals or businesses are cut, this will spur them to greater efforts, with the result that total output and income will rise; hence tax revenues, out of higher income, will not fall and may even be greater at lower than at higher tax rates. The Laffer curve (Exhibit II) is a bell-shaped curve which shows that when tax rates fall to zero, tax revenues obviously fall to zero, but when tax rates rise to 100%, tax revenues also fall to zero because of lack of any incentive to work. Between these two extremes lies the maximum revenue point such as *C* in the exhibit. But the problem with the Laffer curve is that the tax cut that increases revenue must lie on the right-hand side of the above curve; any cut from *B* to *A* will decrease the tax revenues. Also, cutting tax rates from *D* to *B* or from *E* to *A* would decrease revenues. This is mainly because no one knows the true shape of the Laffer curve, or where we are on it.

Exhibit II

The Laffer Curve

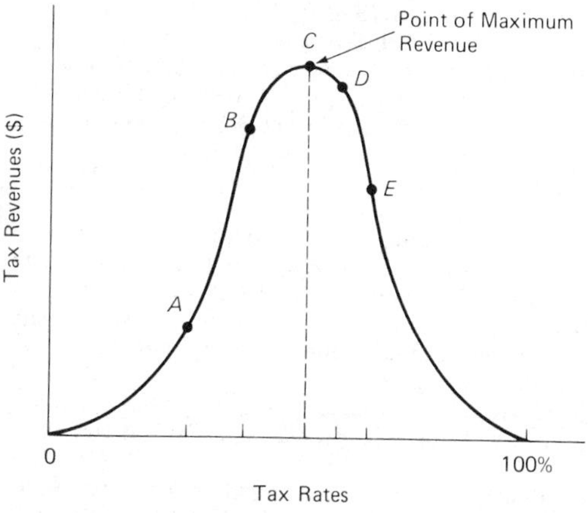

Economic science is at the cross-roads now. The problems of inflation and unemployment are as important today as are the problems of water and air pollution, congestion, and business cycle oscillation for tomorrow. At the same time, Adam Smith's "hidden hand" to keep the economy in equilibrium is not working well. This is mainly because the capitalist system has lost its principal strength and flexibility, because of government and other sundry controls over the economy. But a way has to be found which will turn Ruskin's castigation of "dismal science" into a science which, in Professor Kenneth Boulding's words, shows the mechanism of economic prosperity and well-being with freedom, justice, and equality.

Arabinda Ghosh, Ph.D., Associate Professor of Finance, Hofstra University, Hempstead, New York

Information References

Acknowledgment is made to the late Martin R. Gainsbrugh, former Senior Vice President, The Conference Board, New York, N.Y., for inputs to the above article relating to historical developments and portions of the treatment of Keynesian economics as presented in this entry in the second edition of The Encyclopedia of Management.

Associations:

American Economic Association.
American Statistical Association.
American Enterprise Institute.
The Brookings Institute.
Committee for Economic Development.
The Conference Board.
National Bureau of Economic Research.
National Planning Association.
Twentieth Century Fund.

Periodicals:

American Economic Review (American Economic Association).

Journal of the American Statistical Association.

Quarterly Journal of Economics (Harvard University).

(Publications of a general nature include *Journal of Political Economy, Harvard Business Review,* and other economic journals of leading colleges and universities).

Texts:

Bach, George Leland, "Economics: An Introduction to Analysis and Policy," 10th ed., Englewood Cliffs, N.J., Prentice-Hall, 1980.

Dernberg, Thomas F., and Duncan M. McDougall, "Macroeconomics," 6th ed., New York, McGraw-Hill, 1980.

Gould, John P. and C. E. Ferguson, "Microeconomic Theory," 5th ed., Homewood, Ill., Irwin, Inc., 1980.

Haynes, W. Warren, "Managerial Economics: Analysis and Cases," 4th ed., Dallas, Texas, Business Publications Ltd., 1978.

Roll, Eric, "A History of Economic Thought, 3rd ed., Englewood Cliffs, N.J., Prentice-Hall, 1956.

Samuelson, Paul A., "Economics: An Introductory Analysis," 10th ed., New York, McGraw-Hill, 1976.

Reference Cited

[1] Gilman, Joseph M., "The Falling Rate of Profit," London, D. Dobson, 1957.

Cross References: *Business Forecasting; Business Intelligence: Sources of Information; Econometrics; Income, Expenditures, and Wealth: Concepts and Measures; Inflation; Information Databanks: On Line; Money and Banking; Prices: Statistics; Productivity: Concepts and Measures; Statistical Abstract of the United States; Statistics; U.S. Census of Business; U.S. Census of Manufactures.*

ELECTRONIC DATA PROCESSING

Electronic Data Processing (EDP) refers to the use of electronic and associated electromagnetic devices for the communication, manipulation, and storage of data. The term is generally used when the data manipulations are in support of commercial, industrial, and business administrative or management areas, as well as simulation modeling, scientific calculations, and engineering design work. The application of electronic devices to the direct control of production facilities is usually called *Process Control* or *Automation.*

The need to process data is nearly as old as society itself. The keeping of records and the performing of computations to assist business can be traced back to the days of Babylon and Egypt. The use of popularly accepted mechanical devices to aid in this data processing starts with the introduction of bookkeeping machines about 1880, and continues with the advent of the tabulating or punched card device in the 1930s. The application of electronic techniques to data processing, however, dates essentially from 1948 when the IBM 604 Electronic Calculator was introduced. These techniques were an outgrowth of the use of electronics during World War II and of the development of computers for engineering and scientific calculations.

Data manipulations performed in a data processing application may be classified into four groups. The first group, *order issuance,* is the filing, processing, and output preparation related to the necessary information manipulations for issuing orders to other parts of an organization or to the outside world. This area includes such activities as billing, payroll, shop order issuance, and insurance premium notice preparation.

The second group of processing activity involves *feedback* data. Information is recorded about the present status of the organization's activities, and these recorded data are filed, manipulated, and reported to appropriate managers. Almost all accounting activities, including cost accounting and general accounting are classified in this area. The feedback area includes most phases of production control, inventory control, sales statistics and other marketing data reporting, and many activities of governmental organizations.

The third area is that of *decision making.* This area covers a wide range of necessary decisions, including shop scheduling, distribution planning, and assistance in the selection of strategy and tactics through modeling.

The fourth area is *scientific and engineering problem solving.* In addition to such computations as required to put a man on the moon, this includes calculations and displays in support of engineers in designing structures such as bridges, mechanical devices, and electrical equipment.

Fortunately, with the advent of the "general-purpose" computer, essentially the same equipment and manipulation methods can be used to process data for any of these groups of applications. However, some computers are better suited to business applications, while others are designed more specifically for scientific and engineering calculations. Throughout the remainder of this article, the basic electronic data processing system applicable to any of these applications will be discussed.

Formal Definition. Electronic data processing is the use of digital electronic devices with appropriate peripheral equipment, for the processing of data in support of the administration and management of an organization, or for the solution of scientific problems, including engineering design.

Care must be taken to distinguish among the following: the collection of *equipment* used to process the data, the *procedures* and computer *programs* required to process the data, the *administration* of the data processing center, and the *organization* which the EDP system supports. The term "EDP" includes the equipment, and the procedures and programs necessary to make the equipment do the jobs required. (The terms "ADP," for automatic data processing, "DP," for data processing, are used interchangeably with EDP in the literature of the subject.)

History. The basis for electronic data processing techniques goes back to the abacus, which is an elementary arithmetic unit, and to the work of Pascal, 1642, Leibniz, 1694, and Babbage in 1833, all of whom attempted to build mechanical data manipulation units. Real progress, however, had to await the development of electronic techniques, since the mechanical devices were too slow, bulky, and unreliable to be of general use. The transition from mechanical to electronic was realized in the Mark I computer completed in 1944, by Howard Aiken at Harvard University (supported by International Business Machines Corporation) and by the general development of the Hollerith or tabulating device using punched cards. The first truly electronic system was the ENIAC, built at the Moore School of Pennsylvania and completed in 1946. This electronic computer was designed to perform the computation of ballistics tables for the U. S. Army. Simultaneously, IBM developed an electronic calculator for general business use known as the IBM 604. Deliveries of this unit began in 1948. More than 4,000 of these were built and used for performing additions, multiplications, comparisons, and other processing related to a wide variety of business applications from payroll to statistical analysis.

The true flexibility of electronic data processing results from the concept of the "general-purpose" computer, that is, a computer which stores its instructions in the same memory as it stores data, and can therefore manipulate its instructions as if they were data. This permits the computer to perform a process repetitively on vast quantities of data by virtue of only a few procedural steps. It permits, in technical language, "address modification" and "program loops." These facilities were first realized in the EDVAC, built by the Moore School between 1947 and 1950, the SEAC, built by the Bureau of Standards between 1948 and 1950, and Whirlwind I, built by Massachusetts Institute of Technology (under contract with the Office of Naval Research) between 1947 and 1951.

The first system designed specifically for business applications was the UNIVAC I built by Presper Eckert and John Mauchly between 1947 and 1951. The UNIVAC I is a direct descendent of the ENIAC and EDVAC on which Eckert and Mauchly had worked at the University of Pennsylvania.

The group which built the UNIVAC I was also among the first to develop "automatic programming" techniques, programs which assist in writing other programs. These early computers gave rise to the now bewildering variety of computers available.

Equipment Basics. Digital computer equipment ("hardware") consists essentially of input devices, a central processing unit (CPU), auxiliary file storage equipment, and output devices. Programs ("software") supplied in part by the manufacturer, tell the computer what to do.

For the CPU to function, machine-readable media must be used for input. Examples are punched cards, punched paper tape, magnetic tape, diskettes, and fixed magnetic disks; documents printed in special font for optical character recognition (OCR); or documents printed in special ink for magnetic ink character recognition (MICR). These media are used for recording data to be read by the input devices and operated upon by the CPU as well as for initially recording the computer program, which is also read into the CPU by input devices. Information generated by the CPU may also be recorded on such media by output devices, or printed at high speeds on a continuous, tear-apart form. Input and output (I/O) devices interconnected by cables to the CPU are said to be "on line."

Circuits and controls in the CPU enable it to perform functions (operations) such as: read, add, subtract, multiply, divide, move, compare, branch, write, stop, and so on, at extremely high speeds. A CPU may have the capability of performing a few dozen or several hundred of such operations, depending on its design.

The CPUs primary internal storage (memory) stores the program and data. Such storage may consist of many small magnetic cores, but more recently of semiconductor materials. Under control of the program, these can be "set," (magnetized or not magnetized) in given locations to represent a number, letter, or symbol, coded in *binary form,* i.e., combinations of "on" or "off" (conducting or non-conducting). While data are manipulated internally by the computer only in terms of binary representation, translation into binary equivalents is done by the machine circuitry, and the user need not write instructions in that form.

File storage equipment, or auxiliary memory units, are used to store the large files of data processed by the CPU, since it would be impractical and prohibitively expensive to store them in the machine's internal memory. Under program control, the CPU draws blocks of data from external storage for processing and transfers those data to an output unit or back to auxiliary storage. Once data are removed from storage, the storage area is erased.

Magnetic reels were initially the only type of auxiliary memory. Although relatively inexpensive, they have the disadvantage of storing items serially. Serial storage is time-consuming when one needs to find a specific item. Therefore there have been developed highly efficient direct-access auxiliary memories (earlier called random-access memories) in the form of magnetized "bits" on the surfaces of rotating magnetic drums, bits on stacked revolving disks (similar in appearance to a phonograph record), on short magnetic tape strips, and on cartridges of magnetic cards.

The "Generations" of Computers. The designation *first-generation* is given to computers that were installed roughly in the period 1955–1960. They were relatively large-scale, used vacuum-tube circuitry, and had the limitations of small, slow cores of the mille-second cycle type, limited registers and accumulators, heavy reliance on punched-card input/output, and slow and troublesome peripherals. The machines were cumbersome and highly sensitive to environment, requiring air conditioning. So-called "machine language" was used, rather than the later, high-level, simplified languages, and there was little or no major "software" (i.e., computer programs).

The *second-generation* were the first solid-state transistorized computers that began to come into installation between 1960 and 1965. They were more user oriented, and improved circuitry and technology made them less sensitive to the environment. The central processors had expanded, higher speed memories. Magnetic tape began to be used heavily, and peripherals were improved. Random-access storage devices came into use. Smaller computers and modular systems broadened the areas of application.

The *third-generation* computers were widely announced in 1964 and 1965, and began to come into installation in late 1965. Integrated circuitry made miniaturization possible. Real-time access and "time-sharing" capabilities were features of many central processors, providing the capability of access from remote terminals.

The price of third-generation computers, because of their increasing miniaturization, has been steadily decreasing. It has been suggested that a "fourth generation" of computers has arrived with the advent of the mirocomputer. Today, miniaturization allows computer manufacturers to configure a CPU on a silicon wafer that is smaller than a human thumbnail.

The Place of EDP in Management. Since EDP is a basic tool, it relates to a variety of topics. Almost every management procedure can be automated through the use of an EDP system. This includes: accounting in all of its phases, the procedures derived from OPERATIONS RESEARCH, the automation of systems and procedures, computations required for engineering and scientific research, the data processing related to all phases of manufacturing control, and the mechanization of office procedures. (See *Cross-References* at the conclusion of this article.)

An EDP system's design is, of course, essentially a sophistication of the design of any data processing system and, therefore, is in a sense a part of systems and procedures or office management system techniques. (See SYSTEMS MANAGEMENT.) On the other hand, the EDP tool is so powerful that major advances in systems design have been made possible through it, and many of the techniques used in the "classical" systems and procedures work (that is, until about 1955), are no longer directly applicable. EDP systems can also be used as a tool for studying business management, particularly through the use of simulation. EDP systems form the basis of the broadly-conceived MANAGEMENT INFORMATION SYSTEMS (MIS), systems which collect information about the status of a business and present it promptly (often on demand) and concisely, thereby improving management decisions.

An EDP effort is of sufficient magnitude to present organizational problems in most firms. Decisions must be made as to where, organizationally, to locate the methods and systems analysts, the computer programmers, and the data processing center. Because data processing is such an integral part of all phases of a business, the most successful installations have reported directly to the vice-presidential level, to the Vice President of Finance, the Vice President of Administration, or the Controller or Treasurer. Below this level, there are generally two groups: the systems analysts and programmers in one, and the data processing center in the other. Because the boundary between systems analysis and programming is difficult to distinguish, it has been found most effective to combine these two skills into one methods or systems and procedures group whose responsibility is to define the requirements and complete the programming, including testing. The data processing center is then responsible for processing data on a day-to-day basis, using the tested programs. The data processing center may have a few programmers to make minor changes and improvements in the operating programs as required. The methods group is usually also responsible for making feasibility studies and for selecting the equipment for new EDP installations.

Data Processing: Approaches and Techniques. A data processing system involves the following functions:

(1) *Data recording.* The process of transcribing the input data or measurements into a form which data processing machines can manipulate.

(2) *Data communication.* This refers to both local and long-distance transmission of data.

(3) *Data storage or filing.* The retention of data in an organized form so that they may easily be retrieved. Data may be stored temporarily to help level data flow and, more permanently, as files for record-keeping.

(4) *Data retrieval or access.* The withdrawal of information from files.

(5) *Data processing.* The manipulation of data for arithmetic operations and logical operations, such as comparisons, editing, formatting. Processing includes file maintenance (keeping files up-to-date) and computation.

(6) *Data reporting.* The preparation of the printed reports or graphical displays which permit a human being to interpret the data in the system.

Exhibit I summarizes the various techniques which are available for performing these functions. Those along the bottom row, the electronic-magnetic techniques, are the ones generally included in an EDP system. However, many present-day systems actually use a mixture of techniques, and a system is referred to as an EDP system if the central processing, that is, the filing, the file retrieval, processing, and at least some of the report preparation are performed on an electronic data processing system.

Designing an electronic data processing system requires determining which technique to use to perform the various functions of the system, and then specifically designing or programming each unit to perform the data processing tasks required. The procedures for designing an EDP system are briefly reviewed below.

The design of an EDP system usually starts by choosing one or more applications which could be processed more efficiently. The cost of processing without automation may be high, the time required to get the desired results may be long, or the error rate may be higher than acceptable. Under these circumstances, one asks: Can electronic techniques help improve the data processing in these particular applications?

The first step is to make a feasibility study. For this, an EDP system to perform the job is designed roughly, in order to get a preliminary estimate of the equipment required and the processing times involved. This information permits an evaluation of data processing costs and the cost of converting from the present system to the new system. If the feasibility study indicates that an EDP system is justified, the following design steps are required:

(1) *Systems analysis.* The present data processing system, whether manual, tabulating, or mixture, must be carefully analyzed to determine exactly what steps are involved in processing the data. There are practically no situations in which the current procedures are documented sufficiently for the EDP system design. In addition, since the EDP system will be asked to do more than the present system,

Exhibit I

Data Processing Techniques

Function / Level	*Data Recording (Measuring)*	*Communication*	*Temporary Storage*	*File Storage*	*File Access*	*File Maintenance*	*Calculating*	*Printing*	*Display*
MANUAL	EYEBALL, WRITTEN RECORDS	MAIL, MESSENGER	PAPER	PAPER, TUB FILES	MANUAL	POSTING MANUALLY	HUMAN BRAIN	WRITTEN REPORTS	BOARDS & GREASE PENCIL
MACHINE-AIDED MANUAL	TYPEWRITER	PNEUMATIC TUBES, TEL-AUTOGRAPH	PAPER	MOTORIZED TUB FILES	KEYSORT	BOOK-KEEPING MACHINES	ADDING MACHINES, CALCU-LATORS	TYPE-WRITERS, BOOK-KEEPING MACHINES	SLIDE PROJECTORS
ELECTRO-MECH-ANICAL	PRE-PUNCHED CARDS MARK SENSE PAPER-TAPE PRODUCING TYPEWRITER	TELETYPE TELEPHONE	TAB CARDS	COLLATORS, SORTERS, MAGNETIC STRIP LEDGER-FILES	ACCOUNTING MACHINES (TAB)				PLOTTERS, FILM-PROJECTOR DISPLAYS
AUTOMATIC (ELECTRONIC MAGNETIC)	MAGNETIC & OPTICAL CHARACTER READERS, AUTOMATIC PICKUPS, SOURCE DATA RECORDERS	DATA LINKS, AUTOMATIC SWITCHING CENTERS, TELEPHONE LINES ELECTRONIC MAIL	INTERNAL MEMORY, DRUMS, DISCS, TAPES	MAGNETIC DRUMS, TAPES, DISKETTES	ELECTRONIC COMPUTERS			HIGH SP. PRINTERS, ELECTRO-MECHAN. PLOTTERS, C.O.M.* A.P.C.**	ELECTRONIC DISPLAYS, CATHODE RAY TUBE DEVICES

*Computer Output Micro-filmers.
**Automatic Photocomposers.

in most cases, the additional requirements on the EDP system must be determined.

(2) *System design.* The EDP system must be designed. (Going to EDP is too large a change to evolve spontaneously, as have previous systems.) Design is a combination of art and science in which the available EDP equipments are evaluated to determine which combination of equipment, with appropriate computer programming, will perform the desired job at the least overall cost. To accomplish this, available equipment and programming techniques must be known. This step obviously requires the skills of a person with considerable experience and talent in the application of EDP equipment to a specific data processing job. Several of the key design choices are described below.

(3) *Programming.* When the equipment is chosen and perhaps on order, the next major and expensive step is the preparation of the computer programs. An electronic computer by itself is merely a potential. It can be made to do a specific job only by being fed a large number of specific instructions. These steps must be prepared by analyzing the data processing requirements carefully and translating them into logic charts, program flow charts, and finally into specific computer codes which the machine will understand.

To help reduce the costs of this programming effort and to eliminate many of the clerical steps involved, techniques known as "automatic programming" have been developed. Among the principal automatic programs are: *translators* (also called *compilers*), which translate the program from a form easily written by a human being to the form required by the machine; *service routines,* which assist in the loading, unloading, and operating the computer; and *diagnostic routines,* which assist in testing programs and in analyzing the equipment performance.

A number of *problem-oriented* programs are available from manufacturers, universities, and other groups active in the field. Examples are automatic programs which generate programs for sorting, for file maintenance, for report generation. The general area of computer programs and especially automatic programs is known as *software,* in contradistinction to the familiar term given to the equipment—*hardware.*

The most powerful of these programming aids is the translator. This permits the programmer to express his procedures in a highly-stylized English "process-oriented" language such as shown in Exhibit IIa, for COBOL ("Common Business Oriented Language"). A

EXHIBIT IIa

COMPUTER PROGRAM WRITTEN IN A TYPICAL USER LANGUAGE: COBOL

PORTION OF COBOL VERSION OF "COMPUTE-FICA"

```
• MULTIPLY gross-pay BY 0.030 GIVING weekly-fica.
• IF weekly-fica PLUS annual-fica EXCEEDS 126.00 THEN COMPUTE
  weekly-fica FROM 126.00 MINUS annual-fica.
• SUBTRACT weekly-fica FROM adjusted-pay.
• ADD weekly-fica AND annual-fica.
• ADD weekly-fica AND quarterly-fica.
• ADD weekly-fica AND monthly-fica.
```

(*Courtesy International Business Machines Corporation*)

computer program, the translator (also called a compiler), usually supplied by the manufacturer, then translates these procedural statements into the language which the machine can understand. An example of machine language is shown in Exhibit IIb. Machine language is more difficult for a human being to use and to find errors in.

With the development of the proprietary software industry, numerous application packages are available for the more common problems such as payroll, accounts payable, etc. These should be studied for applicability to the particular problem at hand. Often a proprietary package can be found that will be satisfactory or that can be readily modified. While, in general, such a package will not be exactly what is desired, its cost will be less than one-fifth that of a custom-designed program for little compromise in design.

In addition to application software packages, many programs are available which make computer operation more efficient. Called *system utility packages,* these include sorters, communications aids, and data base management systems (DBMS). DBMS software packages create a logical pattern for filing and accessing large amounts of information on auxiliary storage devices. These packages are especially significant because they allow companies to put all operating data on the computer and access those data quickly.

(4) *Test.* When the programming is complete, each program and the entire system must be carefully tested, using both test data and actual data from previous operations.

(5) *Conversion.* Finally, the system is implemented. This often involves conversion of files from their present paper or punched card form to magnetic tape or other magnetic form. The system then goes into operation.

Organization and Operation. The operation of a data processing center is much like that of a small-job shop. Each data processing run must be carefully scheduled so that the work flows evenly through the shop, the data pro-

EXHIBIT IIb

PART OF THE SAME PROCEDURE WRITTEN IN A TYPICAL MACHINE LANGUAGE

PART OF THE MACHINE PROGRAM FOR PROCEDURE IN II-a

LOC	OP	SU	ADDRESS		PGLIN	SER	REF
09524	9	05	21215	JS/5	20540		*A62
09529	9	05	21215	JS/5	20550		*A62
09534	9	05	21215	JS/5	20560		*A62
09539	2		00500	0500	20570		
09544	R	00	00300	0300	20580		AA03
09549	R	00	21295	J295	20590		*A75
09554	1		09279	9279	20600		AY46
09559	B	00	00005	0005	20605		
09564	F	00	05356	5356	20610		AL27

(*Courtesy International Business Machines Corporation*)

EXHIBIT III

PRICE RANGES OF DATA PROCESSING SYSTEMS

TYPE	Price Range $ per month[1]	Equipment Characteristics	Basic Add time, micro-seconds	Principal Uses
MECHANICAL				
Bookkeeping	to 100	limited, one job units, not internally programmed.		very small business applications.
Tabulating	to 5,000[2]	functions performed on separate units, calculator unit not internally programmed.		small business, some very limited engineering.
ELECTRONIC				
Minicomputer	to 1,200+	physically small, fast, fixed word-length, elaborate interrupt system, can accommodate full range of peripherals.	0.3 to 2.0[3]	OEM, dedicated special purpose computing, scientific computation, time sharing, and process control.
Small Business	500 to 1,500	card input/output, diskette storage, some magnetic tape.	20 to 300	small business applications.
Medium	1,500–10,000	full range of peripherals including tapes and disk.	10 to 40	medium to large business and scientific applications.
Large	Over 10,000	same, faster, larger internal storage.	0.1 to 10.0	medium- to very large-scale business computation, scientific computation and time sharing.

NOTES
(1) Multiply by fifty to obtain approximate purchase price.
(2) Larger tab installations exist but most have been or are being converted to computers.
(3) These operations are not character-oriented, but typically act on one full word as a fixed-point number.

cessing equipment is utilized as effectively as possible, and the jobs are completed on time. This is true whether the system is to perform batch processing under direct control of the computer room operations staff, or in a time-shared mode under control of scheduling algorithms incorporated in the systems programs.

The design and operation of an EDP system involve a number of new skills. First, the broadly oriented EDP systems analyst is required to assist those who know the business application to determine the feasibility of EDP and to do the systems analysis and design. These steps are usually performed by a team headed by an EDP expert who also has some knowledge of the particular business field. The team consists of EDP experts and experts in the particular business involved. The detailed system design and programming must be done by people knowledgeable in computer programming. (Training in programming is supplied by the manufacturer of the equipment.) At least some of the programmers must be capable of assisting in the system design work, and must know, in detail, the computer on which the application is to be realized. Standard procedures skills are required to prepare the manual procedures related to the EDP system. This includes the procedures involved in data preparation, report distribution, and also the procedures to be utilized in the EDP center. Given several years, it is possible to develop these experts from within a given organization. In a program with a normal schedule, it has been found most effective to have at least one EDP analyst and one senior programmer (knowledgeable in automatic programming techniques) in the group from the outset of the EDP program.

Equipment Characteristics. The computers available today may be conveniently classified into four overlapping price ranges, as indicated below. The first two ranges—minicomputers and small business computers—overlap in price but are oriented toward difficult kinds of markets. The ranges given are as of 1980. Purchase prices can be estimated by multiplying the monthly rental price by fifty. This classification is summarized in Exhibit III.

To give some idea of the systems that are currently available, typical minicomputer, small business, and medium-scale computer systems are shown schematically in Exhibit IV a, b, and c.

(1) *Minicomputers.* Basic purchase price is around $15,000 to $25,000, with monthly rentals up to about $1,200+ per month in expanded configurations. Minicomputers are fast, physically small, low-cost computers with typical cycle times and fixed-point add times

word- and byte-oriented machines aimed largely at sophisticated users; minicomputer manufacturers have largely ignored the small business computer market because of the extensive sales support required, but are now penetrating this market by packaging business versions of their computers with appropriate software.

While many minis are used in dedicated, special-purpose installations (for example, process control or data communications), minicomputers with relatively large complements of

EXHIBIT IV a

TYPICAL EDP EQUIPMENT SYSTEMS TYPICAL $450/MONTH MINICOMPUTER FOR SMALL-SCALE COMPUTATION

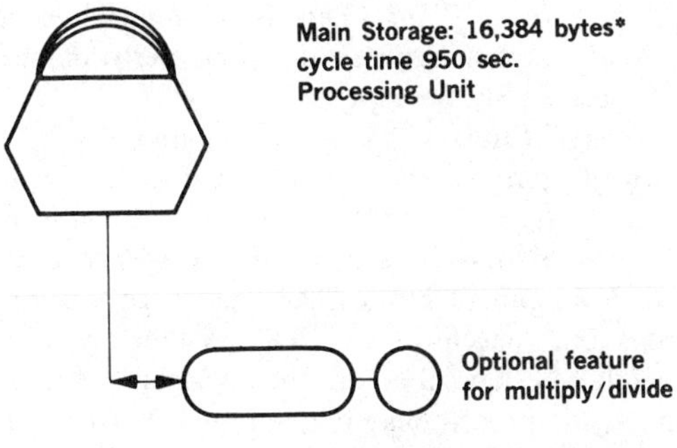

* Byte= a sequence of adjacent binary digits operated upon as a unit and usually shorter than a word.

EXHIBIT IV b

TYPICAL EDP EQUIPMENT SYSTEMS TYPICAL $2600/MONTH SMALL BUSINESS COMPUTER

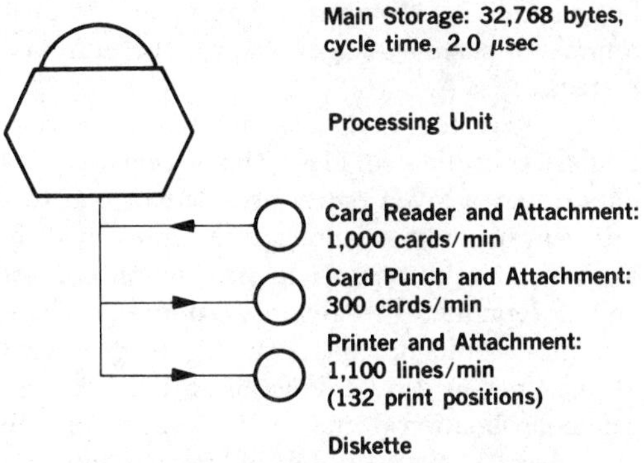

(Adapted from "AUERBACH Standard EDP Reports").

EXHIBIT IV c

TYPICAL EDP EQUIPMENT CONFIGURATIONS TYPICAL $7757/MONTH MEDIUM-SCALE COMPUTER

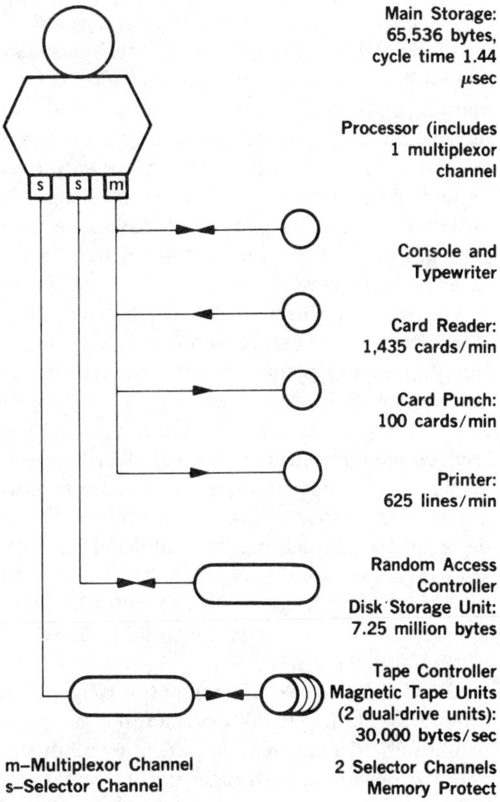

(Adapted from "AUERBACH Standard EDP Reports").

peripheral equipment are used for small-scale scientific computing and time sharing. Minicomputers are designed modularly, and the system shown in Exhibit IVa can be used as the basis either for some kind of real-time process-control or other dedicated system, or as the nucleus of a more extensive system for scientific computation and time sharing. A wide range of peripheral devices is available for most minicomputers; in addition to all the conventional computer peripherals and data communications interfaces, remote sensing and digital/analog converters are available for process control.

As an example of a more extensive minicomputer system for scientific computation, the system shown in Exhibit IVa can be extended by adding a 300 character-per-second paper tape reader, a 50 character-per-second paper tape punch, and an additional 10K words of main memory for an approximate additional rental of $200 per month. Minicomputer configurations are available with memory sizes ranging from 16K words to 1M words of memory.

(2) *Small Business Computers.* Basic rental is up to around $1,500 per month. Small business computers have cycle times around one to four microseconds with character-oriented arithmetic operations having execution times measured in tens of microseconds. Card input/output is limited; disk or diskette storage is always available. Small business computers have extensive software support for the unsophisticated small-scale business user.

The small business computer shown in Exhibit IVb is typical of many such systems. Many of these systems can be extended by the addition of peripheral devices and main memory to bring them near the range of medium-scale computers; magnetic tape, however, is unavailable for some of the small business computers. The system shown in Exhibit IVb can be extended by adding two replaceable disk storage drives with a capacity of 2.7 million bytes each, and a further 8,192 bytes of main memory for an approximate additional rental of $1,300 per month.

(3) *Medium-scale Computers.* Rental is around $1,500 to $10,000 per month. This price includes the small general-purpose computers with tape and disk storage and typical cycle times around one to two microseconds. Extensive systems software for business and scientific computation is provided.

(4) *Large-scale Computers.* Rentals can be over $10,000 per month. In this price range lie the larger and more extensive general-purpose computing and time-sharing installations. It is difficult to subdivide this price range, since these systems are built in a modular fashion; that is, they are specifically designed so that a user can start with a basic, relatively inexpensive system and add modules of memory, of additional or faster file storage, of random access storage, and other features, so that the equipment can grow as the needs grow.

Medium- and large-scale computers can be extended upward in the same way as small computers, subject to inherent limitations such as those imposed by the maximum allowable size of main memory or the maximum allowable input/output data rate. Exhibit IVc is a typical configuration falling in the range for medium-scale computers. Equipment configurations can be upgraded in other ways besides adding further peripheral devices and memory capacity. Examples include the replacement of one peripheral device by another of the same type with a higher performance, the addition of such central processor options as further instructions, and the addition of units available optionally for some computers to enhance the amount of peripheral simultaneity attainable.

Because of the variety of computer applications, overall computer performance is not necessarily directly related to the total system cost—an application involving large amounts of computation, for example, may be better performed on a minicomputer than on a medium-scale computer costing several times as much. Each of the classes of computer discussed here is suitable for particular types of application; the computer market has now developed to the point where no straightforward, overall tradeoff between cost and performance can reasonably be expected.

Design Choices. There are a number of divergent opinions in EDP, as would be expected in any dynamic field. One of the most basic is the *step-by-step* vs. the *integrated* approach to the development of an EDP system. In the former, one develops an EDP system by first merely mechanizing, on the electronic equipment, the procedures now being used. Then the system is allowed to evolve to the extent made feasible by the power of the electronic techniques. Alternatively, one can go directly to the more "integrated" EDP system. Experienced opinion in the field is that the initial system design should be based on an integrated approach which takes full advantage of the EDP facilities. However, the implementation may involve a series of steps, the first of which is a mechanization of existing procedures with perhaps minor improvements. The system is then improved stage-by-stage toward the ultimate system.

An integrated EDP system implies, in particular, consolidated files. The various bits of data about a given entity are filed in one record. An inventory would not be represented by a physical inventory file in production control and a separate cost file in accounting. These two files would be consolidated and processed at one time, as can be done on an EDP system. The consolidation of files reduces the error rate and permits more powerful decision-making procedures, since all of the information about an item is available at one time to incorporate into the decision process.

Having developed a file structure, response time must be considered. If the outputs are required within seconds or minutes of an input or a request for data—for example, in an air traffic control application—then an *on-line* or even a *real-time* system is required. *On-line* means that the equipments are interconnected (usually electronically) so data may be passed through the system without manual intervention and without batching. In a *real-time* system, the processing is performed fast enough to keep up with events in the real world. Where response time requirements are longer, off-line systems can be used, and inputs can be batched, rather than processed as they occur.

To obtain a rapid response, on-line system, *random-access* data stores are required. In these, the access-mechanism can proceed directly to the required record, whereas tape must be reeled or unreeled to get at specific data. Magnetic disk systems are the most common large-volume random-access stores in use. *Sequential-access* devices, such as magnetic tape, are best used by sorting batches of file requests into the file-key sequence. Sequential-access systems, therefore, have longer overall processing times, but are usually more economical.

A question arises as to the level of programming. Should programmers produce their work in a form which is essentially directly convertible to machine language, or should they program in a "process-oriented" language such as COBOL? The "process-oriented" language is easier for the human being to use and learn, but must be translated by a translator program into the machine language. This involves additional computer time and makes the "debugging" or testing of programs somewhat more difficult. The ability of process-oriented languages to reduce the cost of training personnel and to reduce the probability of error in defining the detailed data processing tasks makes these languages quite attractive. Almost every manufacturer of EDP equipment is providing the translators from COBOL or equivalent business-oriented languages to its machine language.

Another question of design is whether to employ one very-high-speed processor which performs all of the data processing, or whether to use a number of separate, slower processors. A common configuration of equipment, at the present time, is one large processor to do the basic file maintenance and computations, and a separate processor to obtain data from the files, to perform editing, to generate report formats and control a high-speed printer, and to execute other routine tasks.

Finally, there is the design choice concerning the extent of automation; or conversely, what procedures should remain manual steps? Usually the system grows in this respect. At first the human being handles not only all of the decisions, but many of the occasional or exceptional items, such as errors or situations which do not arise frequently. As the systems designers and programmers have time to incorporate these into the system, the computer takes over more and more of the exceptions and finally even some of the decisions. Where Operations Research studies have been performed successfully, entire decision-making areas can be mechanized.

Acceptance of EDP. EDP is probably the most rapidly and extensively accepted technological development. Starting in 1948 with the first delivery of an IBM 604 (which was a calculator, and not a complete computing system), computers are now being used in almost every conceivable place where data are manipulated, in small firms and large.

Almost every business manager realizes that his firm should think about EDP. If his business is too small to acquire equipment of its own, he will be considering the use of a service bureau, a place where computer time may be rented, or he may subscribe to a commercial data-processing service bureau or time-sharing service. (See COMPUTER SERVICE INDUSTRY.)

A time-sharing service is one in which each subscriber is provided with one or more input/output terminals, usually typewriters or alphanumeric display with a keyboard device. The terminals are connected via communication lines to a large computer system located on the premises of the time-sharing company. When a subscriber wishes to use the computer, he signals it by activating his terminal. He is charged a monthly rental for the terminal and the data transmission lines, a fee for the amount of permanent storage maintained in the computer, and a rental fee for the time he spends actually using the computer. The rental fee is usually relatively low, since the computer may be used simultaneously by a number of subscribers, so that the stipulated fees distribute the actual cost.

Potential for EDP. In addition to the classical data processing applications, the powerful electronic tools are now being considered for some very sophisticated areas. Among these is the automation of technical (and ultimately general) libraries to improve our ability to retrieve information. Sophisticated decision-making areas, ranging from automatic diagnosis in medicine to long-range allocation of funds in a business, are possible future EDP applications. Most challenging is current research into machines that perform "thinking" or creative acts. This research area is variously termed "artificial intelligence," or "self-organizing machines," "adaptive systems," "learning devices," or "heuristic devices or programs." All these efforts are intended to design a machine with some element of judgment. This would, for example, eliminate the need for writing a program, in exhaustive detail, which foresees every possible combination of events.

EDITORIAL STAFF, AUERBACH PUBLISHERS, INC.,
Pennsauken, New Jersey

Information References

Associations:

American Federation of Information Processing Societies.
Association for Computing Machinery.
International Federation for Information Processing.

Periodicals:

Communications of the Association for Computing Machinery (Association for Computing Machinery).
Computerworld
Computer Decisions
Computer Journal (The British Computer Society).
Data Processing Digest.
Datamation.
EDP Weekly.
Journal of the Association for Computing Machinery (Association for Computing Machinery).
Proceedings of the Fall Joint Computer Conference and *Spring Joint Computer Conference* (American Federation of Information Processing Societies), successor publications to *Proceedings of the Eastern Joint Computer Conference* and *Western Joint Computer Conference* (Association for Computing Machinery).

Texts:

"Auerbach Standard EDP Reports," Pennsauken, N.J., Auerbach Publishers, Inc., (updated monthly).
"Auerbach Minicomputer Reports," (updated monthly).
The Diebold Group, "Automatic Data Processing Handbook," New York, McGraw-Hill, 1977.
Diebold Research Program reports, New York, The Diebold Group.
Halstead, Maurice H., "Machine Independent Computer Programming," Washington, D.C., Spartan Books, 1962.
Heyel, Carl, "Computers, Office Machines, and the New Information Technology," New York, Macmillan, 1969 (spec. for historical information).

Cross References: *(See accompanying entries with Electronic Data Processing prefix); Computer Security/Automated Office Security; Computer Service Industry; Data Communications; Data Communications: A Case Example; Information Databanks: On Line; Management Information Systems; Management Information System: Case Example.*

ELECTRONIC DATA PROCESSING: Computer Peripherals

Although the fast-moving technology of the digital computer has bred a steadily growing list of new devices that perform computer-related functions, certain **Computer Peripherals** actually were created by quite unrelated technologies that flourished in the nineteenth century and even earlier. Punched paper tape, for example, was devised to expedite encoding and decoding communications not long after Morse's invention of the telegraph in 1884.

The concept of the punched card traces back even further. In 1798 the Frenchman Joseph Jacquard fashioned sets of holes in pieces of cardboard and with them controlled a loom to weave predesignated patterns automatically. The modern punched card and its accessories were developed in the 1880s by Herman Hollerith, who helped the United States Census prepare for the 1890 census.

The early digital computers had no peripherals in the modern sense except for an input punched-card reader and an output card punch. The output cards were inserted into tabulators not essentially different from those used before the era of computers for sorting and printing.

Although revolutionary in speed, the first digital computers were quite slow when compared with the ones that began to appear in the mid 1950s. With their application to business processing, large masses of data began to be involved. The result was massive output, which called for corresponding improvements in input and output peripherals.

The digital magnetic tape transport was the first device expressly created to provide auxiliary backup storage to main memory. It was also utilized as a buffering agent (i.e., a peripheral) between the computer and the low-speed electromechanical equipment. Even today the tape drive harmonizes the high-speed of the computer with the slow speed of such mechanisms as impact printers, automatic plotters, non-impact printer-plotters, and photocomposition systems.

By 1952, magnetic drums were introduced as internal storage media with acceptable random-access capabilities. Even after the perfection of magnetic core elements, magnetic drums continued to be used extensively as auxiliary storage devices.

With the shift in computational emphasis from scientific problems to accounting and other commercial applications in the early 1950s, a need for substantially faster printers soon arose, along with an urgency for faster computers. Many companies joined IBM and UNIVAC (then Remington Rand) in this field, and machines employing various printing concepts were developed, achieving speed ranges from 300 to 1,000 lines per minute.

Meanwhile, beginning in the early 1950s, developments were also forthcoming on the input side of the computer. Improvements were made in the action of keypunches, with card-to-tape converters and key-to-tape devices. The latter, at first slow and error-prone, were the forerunners of key-to-tape encoders introduced in 1965. These have evolved into multiple-station, shared-processor systems.

Optical character recognition (OCR) in its present form emerged in the early 1950s, in response to the need for preparing input faster than by keypunching. The first paying commercial installation of an optical character reader was made at Reader's Digest in Pleasantville, New York. The first page reader was delivered to the U. S. Air Force in Rome, N.Y., in 1959. It read a full upper- and lower-case alphanumeric font. The first document reader was delivered early in 1960.

To effect faster computer output, MIT utilized cathode-ray tube displays on the output of a computer. At the same time, the University of Illinois installed CRT outputs to the first ILLIAC computer for problems requiring the computer user to enter into a process of trial and error to find a solution. The most significant early computer-driven CRTs were developed at MIT in the mid-1950s, in cooperation with Stromberg-Carlson, as part of the SAGE system, a real-time computer system to track aircraft in America's first large computer-oriented air defense system. It was not until fifteen years later that this degree of interaction was generally available for commercial applications.

Graphic displays have been available since the early and mid-1960s. These provide the facility of drawing short line segments (vectors) or short curved segments and from them synthesizing some kind of graphical plot.

Automatic digital plotters, which produce hard-copy graphic output from computer-generated digital data, have been developed for a wide range of applications. From small beginnings as output devices for graphical representation of the results of mathematical calculations, they now cover such diverse applications as management information, automatic drafting, preparation of printed-circuit artwork, verification of input programs prepared for numerically controlled machine tools, and cloth cutting for tailoring.

A useful peripheral is the computer output microfilmer (COM). As long ago as the late 1950s and early 1960s, prototypes of today's COM devices were built by a number of companies active in the field. In the beginning, COM was simply a marriage of convenience between existing graphic terminals and photo-optical systems that had been developed during World War II. Today new cameras, new imaging techniques, and new indexing retrieval have created a wide technological gulf separating recent models from their ancestors of the early 1960s.

Present-day communications equipment has been designed to interrelate data communications and data processing devices. Today, almost all of the data transmission devices create, or can be adapted to, a medium which can be used as direct input to a computer. One such device transmits information from punched cards and recreates the card at the receiving end. Another permits perforated-tape-to-perforated-tape transmission, while yet another utilizes magnetic tapes or disks at both ends of the circuit.

Teletypes, one of the early mainstays of communications, are slow and inflexible, although convenient to use. In high-speed applications they have been supplanted by the automatic equipment previously mentioned, and by alphanumeric terminals, which print almost instantaneously. These terminals can also interact directly with the computer, so that editing and reformatting of the message can be effected. A prevalent technique today is batch transmission, i.e., accumulating a store of related information and then transmitting it continuously to completion at very high speeds. This transmission method is extremely cost-effective for large volumes of information that do not require response from the viewing device.

A Glossary of Computer Peripherals

Alphanumeric display. A device for visual representation of letters, numbers, and symbolic data on a cathode-ray tube (CRT) screen. Can be directly connected to a computer for on-line operation, or to an independent storage unit for off-line operation; and can be remotely located via communication facilities ranging in technical quality from low-speed telephone lines to high-speed (wideband) links. Today, there are several A/N displays that offer some data processing capabilities. These are known as "intelligent terminals." Used as a means of providing computer power at the user's site, the intelligent terminals have expanded to compete in some use-areas with the capabilities of small business computers, and can provide programming facilities as well as support for diskette storage.

Audio (voice) response terminal. A device, such as Touch-Tone telephone (registered trademark of the Bell Systems), which converts key depression into tone-coded data for transmission over telephone lines to an audio response unit front-ending a computer. Tone-coded data at the computer are converted into digital form and processed. The computer returns the answer to the audio-response unit, which converts it into a spoken message and transmits it to the originating terminal—either to the handset receiver or to a loudspeaker.

Automatic photocomposers. These systems were originally designed not as computer peripherals, but as independent devices, and were themselves special-purpose computers. The operator keyboarded unformatted copy in, and received justified (straight right-hand margin) output copy, photographically produced on film or paper, convenient starting points for the makeup of book and newspaper pages and preparation of printing plates. Type size, type style, line length, spacing, etc., were easily changed in the machine.

Although photocomposers are still manufactured, the determinations made by a keyboard operator can be advantageously performed by modern EDP equipment, and automatic photocomposers that operate as computer peripherals have been devised, serving not only printers and publishers, but also the computer center as print-out peripherals.

Badge reader. A device that reads data (e.g., an employee number on a plastic card) converting them into electrical signals. The card identifies the employee and may additionally carry access or authorization codes. Although encoding is generally in the form of punched holes, it may also be embossed characters, magnetically encoded stripe, or one of a number of nontamperable proprietary encoding schemes.

Card punch. A device that punches cards under control of a processing system's program. Popular enhancements include punching on previously punched cards, stacking cards selectively, printing the punched output on the card performing system-to-card code translations, and buffering (receiving the data for an entire card and storing it). Card punch output is frequently used for mailed invoices, etc.

Card reader. A device that collects data from punched cards and transmits them to a computer system. Reading techniques include electrical contact brushes and optical sensing. Popular enhancements include buffering (ability to store the data from a card), card-to-system code translation, selective card stacking, on- or off-line card sorting and collating, pencil-mark reading, and card punching (card read punches). Can also read system control cards or data into a system. Frequently used to read "stub" cards, e.g., the tear-off portion of a mailed punched-card bill.

Computer output microfilmer. Converts coded digital output of a computer into an image composed of alphanumeric characters, graphic forms, or a composite, and reduces the image to a prescribed format on microfilm. One purpose of COMs is to transform computer output data directly into a microformat without the need to photograph documents in a separate operation. A second is to capitalize on their high speed, reproducing computer output at a much faster rate than does any mechanical printer. Finally, the cost of a report page produced by a COM on microfilm is much less than the cost of corresponding paper when large quantities of duplicates are involved.

Data collection system. An integrated network of remotely located specialized source data entry or source data recording devices with provisions for assembling the data at a central location. Remote devices usually provide for entry of variable data via keyboard or dials and prepared data via card, badge, or ticket. The two principal types of data collection systems are those for industrial use (recording time and attendance, production progress, tool usage, etc.) and for retail merchandising use (recording inventory changes, customer account use, salesperson and department activity, etc.). Many systems have their own provisions for performing limited inquiry, analysis, and reporting function on the collection data.

Electromechanical plotter (automatic digital plotter). A device that generates hard-copy graphical output from digital data. Hard-copy can take the form of drawings on paper, mylar, or other drafting media; or on other peeled, scribed, or cut media for which special plotting tools are provided. Uses include presentation of computer-generated graphic output for business and scientific applications; examples include preparation of engineering working drawings, maps, and master plots for the production of business forms. Applications used with special-purpose plotting tools include preparation of photographic masters for electronics artwork preparation, chemical die-cutting, and cutting of cloth for the garment industry.

Graphic display. A device which displays

graphic data on a screen. Data can be modified whether by the operator or by a computer. Typical operator input includes keyboard, "joystick control," and light pen.

High-speed printer (line or matrix printers). Converts digitally coded electrical signals to alphanumeric printout. Typical output speeds range from 600 to 12,000 lines per minute, but some electrostatic printers claim much higher speeds. Line printer prints an entire line as a block rather than individual serial characters. Nonimpact printers use technologies such as electrographic, electrostatic, or laser printing, providing quietness, exceptional speed (in some cases), or intermingling of graphic and alphanumeric information. Their major limitation is an inability to produce carbon copies. Impact printers, on the other hand, print up to six carbon copies.

Image digitizer. A device which converts to digital form the shape of the path followed by some kind of sensor. Sensors may be a hand-held cursor, remote controlled TV camera with cross-wires centered in its field, or automatic line follower. Digitizers may operate in one, two, or three axes. Single-axis units are used to digitize data plotted on strip charts; two-axis units digitize maps and engineering drawings; three-axis units digitize the shapes of three-dimensional models, and are used primarily in automotive and aircraft design. An important application area is automatic drafting systems, in which a digitizer and an electromechanical plotter form a complete system for computer input, processing, and output of engineering drawings.

Magnetic disk devices. Usually, multiple magnetically coated disks mounted on a single shaft. Data are recorded on concentric tracks, generally on both faces of the disks, and almost always in bit-serial form. Removable disk packs are commonly used so that the platters and shaft form a modular unit. Disk-pack devices always have movable read/write heads mounted on an access mechanism. Nonremovable units have ganged heads which can cover all tracks in a few discrete movements for fast accessing of information, or one head per platter side for greater economy.

When disks serve as files, information is expected to be accessed with reasonable rapidity, but much information is expected to be recorded sequentially as well. Accessing from disks acting as a data base is substantially more random. The ultimate in accessibility is attained in auxiliary storage disks, which must freely exchange information with information in core memory.

An important use of disk files is as an intermediary from which data are transferred to magnetic tape, often selectively. The tape is then used to drive off-line equipment, such as other computers, electromechanical plotters, and computer output microfilmers.

Magnetic tape drive. The portion of a magnetic tape subsystem that moves, records upon, and reads magnetic tape. Information is stored on the tape by magnetizing particles embedded in the tape, and read by sensing that magnetism. Recording techniques vary, each with cost and performance advantages and disadvantages. Generally, 0.5 inch tape is used, but other widths are available. Speeds commonly vary from 25 to over 200 inches per second. The density (number of data rows per inch) of tape ranges from 200, 556, 800, or 1,600 to 6,250. Seven or nine data tracks are common. Enhancements include multi-format or multi-technique reading/writing; sharing by different controllers, systems, or channels; seeking a particular record (uncommon); and reading (but never writing) with the tape moving in reverse direction. Drives are most commonly used for data files or intermediate storage of data to be transcribed to printer or punched output.

MICR readers. These devices are slightly different from OCR and printed-code readers (see below) in that they analyze the magnetic waveform of characters. Each character is printed in ink containing iron-oxide particles, and then magnetized before reading. All three categories—MICR, OCR, and printed-code—can sort the input documents based on the data read, and translate the data into a form of computer input. MICR is most commonly used in banking. Printed-code readers and OCR vie for applications that involve preprinting of bills or forms that will later be read into a system, perhaps with one or two added items of data. OCR is the best method for handling large applications with a volume of semicontrolled types, printed, or numeric handprinted data.

OCR (optical character readers). Readers that identify printed characters through the interaction of light-sensitive scanners and scored recognition logic for shape identification, with transmission in code to an output device or computer. (See also MICR.)

Paper tape punch. A device to translate binary coded digits into holes/no-holes in paper or mylar tape. Industry-standard tape is nine channels wide: Eight channels store data; the ninth channel, located in the center of the tape, is a sprocket channel that contains a hole for each tape row. Paper tape punches operate as output devices from digital computers, both directly and indirectly (via data communication lines). The output can be programs or data.

Paper tape reader. A device to translate holes/no-holes in paper or mylar tape into binary coded digits (a hole is binary one, a no-hole is binary zero). Modern readers use a row of photoelectric sensors to detect the presence of holes in a tape row. Paper tape readers operate as input devices to computers, both directly and indirectly (via data communications lines). Input can be programs, data, or control commands.

Point-of-sale register. Output in the form of OCR printed characters or magnetic tape cassettes, or communications interface to a host computer system, may be processed by a computer system to derive inventory, sales activity, customer account status, and other reports. Many electronic cash registers can function as point-of-sale terminals and can be configured as part of a data collection system. Advanced capabilities include automatic multiple item, discount, and tax calculations; preprogrammed transaction-dependent operating sequences that illuminate instruction messages, prevent miskeying, and perform proper calculations at proper times; automatic reading of merchandise tags, credit cards, and employee badges; on-line credit authorization; and immediate summary reporting.

Printed-coded readers. These devices employ essentially the same principle as OCR readers (see above) except that the presence or absence of printed or penciled code marks in predefined locations or patterns is analyzed. These readers require less complicated scanning and logic circuitry than do OCR devices. (See also MICR.)

Remote batch terminal. A device which permits batch processing from a remote location, input/-output of *all* data for a specific task such as a payroll. Typical of these units are medium-speed peripherals such as card readers and/or magnetic tape transports and line printers, along with the necessary logic to perform conversion functions (code, speed, etc.), communications functions, and in some cases editing and formatting functions, as well as limited data processing functions.

Ticket (or tag) reader. A device that reads data encoded into a small paper document usually attached to some article for identification, and converts the data into electrical signals. Most common type is the merchandise ticket (or tag), which normally codes inventory data as punched holes, but can also encode data by magnetic striping, printed bars, or printed characters. Usually punched tickets must be removed and inserted into a reader, but the last-named three types may remain on the merchandise, where they are scanned optically or mechanically with a hand-held, cable-connected probe.

Video image systems. These systems store video information by defining an image on a magnetic disk and reproducing the image on a cathode-ray tube. The scanning method is essentially that of commercial television. Thus, an image is originally formed on a cathode-ray screen from digital information supplied by a computer and converted into an electrical analog that is recorded on the disk. The disk can then be used as an information file. To facilitate retrieval, a method for addressing a particular record or document must be devised. In addition, the disk can function as a storage element from which the image, once constructed on a CRT screen, can be refreshed. Graphic displays of this type are much less expensive than conventional systems that store the image digitally in a region of computer core memory.

EDITORIAL STAFF, AUERBACH PUBLISHERS, INC., Pennsauken, N.J.

Information References

Auerbach Plug-Compatible Peripheral Reports.

Auerbach Financial/Retail System Reports.

Auerbach Standard EDP Reports.

Diebold Research Program Reports, New York, The Diebold Group.

The Diebold Group, "Automatic Data Processing Handbook," New York, McGraw-Hill, 1977.

Cross References: *(See accompanying entries with Electronic Data Processing prefix.)*

ELECTRONIC DATA PROCESSING: Equipment Classification

Computers are classified by speed, type of system architecture, throughput capability, and fundamental systems configuration. The combinations of these parameters reflect their cost and application.

Speed of internal memories ranges from microseconds (thousandths of seconds) to nanoseconds (millionths of seconds), with gradations of memories, the fast small feeding the larger and slower. The faster "scratch-pad" memories are the more expensive solid state, and their slower counterparts are the less expensive magnetic cores. Thin-film, plated wire, and laser memories are vying for their rightful place, the thin-film and plated wire being used as internal memories, and the read-only laser memory now being developed as mass-storage medium.

Two basic types of system architecture employed by computer designers are the traditional serial concept and the more advanced parallel array approach. The basic serial machine fetches one instruction at a time and executes it before proceeding to the next. A sophisticated improvement to this approach is called "pipe-lining," i.e., interleaving the stages of execution of a stack of instructions, thereby accelerating the throughput of data. Parallel-array processors, on the other hand, allow for the simultaneous execution of a number of instructions. Pipe-lining is a more general approach to a wider variety of applications, while parallel-processing is highly problem-oriented.

The throughput of a computer is measured in MIPS (millions of instructions per second), indicating the volume of instruction it can execute following a given initialization such as the filling of a "pipeline." This measure can be used to provide comparative data on the speed of a sophisticated system that employs a number of specialized processors for fetching, parsing, and executing instructions both serially or in parallel from striated memories. Another relative measure of the speed of a computer is its bits per microseconds, but this measure weighs more heavily the direct speed of internal memory and does not reflect the built-in optimization and total system use.

Fundamental systems configuration is a bounding parameter which helps narrow down the computer's most basic applicability. Thus an "8-bit, 32K memory, 8-tape system without 'floating point' " must immediately be regarded as a general-purpose computer for application in a business environment. Consequently, the following hardware characteristics are a measure of the computer's applicability to a class of problems as well as of its sophistication: word size; memory capacity and speed; availability and number of accumulators and index registers; levels of indirect addressing; floating-point precision; number of operation codes (i.e., "instruction repertoire"), particularly the availability of byte manipulation (a byte being a sequence of adjacent binary digits operated upon as a unit and usually shorter than a word), and instructions for floating-point, hardware multiply and divide, and list processing; number of input/output channels and their transfer rate; and standard configuration of peripheral devices.

EDITORIAL STAFF, Auerbach Publishers, Inc, Pennsauken, New Jersey

Information References

American Federation of Information Processing Societies, *Proceedings* and other publications.

Association for Computing Machinery, *Proceedings* and other publications.

"Auerbach Computer Technology Reports" and other publications, Pennsauken, N.J., Auerbach, Inc.

Business and Automation (particularly, directory issues).

Datamation (particularly, directory issues.)

GML Corporation, Lexington, Mass.;
"Computer Review."
"Computer Terminals Review."
"Mincomputer Review."
"Minicomputer Peripherals Review."
"Computer Terminals Review."
"Computer Terminals Price Index."

EMERSON, HARRINGTON

Harrington Emerson (1853–1931) was an American engineer who had independently developed concepts along the lines of SCIENTIFIC MANAGEMENT, applying them in the reorganization of the workshops of the Santa Fe Railroad. When called by L. D. Brandeis as a principal witness for the shippers in the 1910–1911 "Eastern Rates Case," he was the only one who testified with first-hand experience of railroad transport. He stated on oath that the railroads could "save a million dollars a day" on their operating costs—a claim which hit the headlines, making Scientific Management news across America. He was a popularizer of Scientific Management in his consulting and in his writings and lectures, and early expounded the concepts of standard times, standard costs, and preventable waste. (He advocated the application of his scientific methods to many activities, even to potato growing, where he stressed the importance of the psychological factor in influencing workers to increase output.) He also was among the first to call attention to the lessons which business management could learn from the military. Although he was in close touch with the Taylor group (see SCIENTIFIC MANAGEMENT: "Taylorism") he was not a part of it. In addition to his many articles and lectures, his books include: "Efficiency as a Basis for Operation and Wages," (1900), "The Twelve Principles of Efficiency" (1912), and "The Scientific Selection of Employees" (1913).

EMPLOYEE ATTITUDE RESEARCH: Attitude Surveys

The Employee Attitude Survey is a systematic method used by many corporations both to assess the thinking and feelings of employees about their employment situation and to solicit worker ideas for possible improvements to be made in all aspects of the organization's operations.

Managers in most organizations agree that their employees should have dignity and meaning in their work, should be respected as individuals, have equality of opportunity, and be given recognition and rewards appropriate to their performance. However, most organizations, especially large ones, do not have such a free and open flow of information and such mutual respect and trust that management really knows how its employees feel about the company's performance in providing these kinds of conditions in their jobs. Often, management secures its impressions only from those who are especially outspoken (either pro or con) but never gets a balanced view about the attitudes of the population as a whole.

The traditional hierarchical organization of most corporations often produces a climate that inhibits the participation of their employees. The complaint of many workers is that they do not feel a bona fide part of the system in which they work. They are unsure of their role, status, and job circumstances; they see barriers, real or imagined, between them and the rest of the organization.

As companies have grown, sheer size and the number of layers between the top manager and lowest graded employee have made both communication and program and policy implementation slower, more cumbersome, than current operating conditions require. Further, universally applicable directions from the top are less likely to be effective than action generated and initiated locally. Utilization of survey research speeds up the process of problem-solving, and can effect better company performance by transferring the responsibility and accountability for results closer to where the action is. Also, problems that look ponderous—and, somehow, more abstract—at the top, are likely to be much more identifiable, tangible, and manageable at the local level. To summarize, employee attitude surveys can be used:

(1) As an integral part of an action process aimed at improving organizational effectiveness.

(2) As a means not only of measuring organizational climate, but an important force in shaping the climate.

(3) As a way of evaluating the state of communication in an organization, but equally importantly, as an effective channel of upward communication.

(4) As a means of recognizing the importance of the individual, by seeking his or her opinions and ideas, and demonstrating that management is interested in the jobholder's views.

(5) As a device to raise the degree to which people feel involved, feel they are really participants in an organization's operations.

(6) As a method of securing good ideas, both generating them (by inducing people to think in terms of solutions as well as the problems), and by bringing latent ideas to the surface.

How Surveys Are Typically Conducted. Many large corporations such as E. I du Pont, Citibank, Weyerhaeuser, Sears Roebuck, General Electric, AT&T, and IBM have an inhouse professional staff to survey employees on a regularly scheduled basis in company units, or to assist unit managers who want to survey their employees on an "as needed" basis. However, companies of this size often utilize the services of outside professionals as well. Management in companies of any size can obtain professional help in the conduct of a survey through management consulting or survey research firms specializing in the personnel field, through universities, or in some cases from trade associations serving their particular industry.

Qualifications of the Survey Staff. Company management, planning a survey of employees, should seek help from professionals who: (1) are experienced in the conduct of surveys—an ineptly conducted survey can create more problems than it solves; (2) have evolved procedures for conducting surveys that encourage employees to say what is really on their minds (effective procedures should differ depending on such factors as employees' job level or nature of the subject matter to be explored); (3) have the capability to handle data *rapidly* whether obtained by qualitative or quantitative methods—findings should be reported within weeks, while they are current, not months later when they have become history; (4) have insights for discussing clearly with management the implications of survey findings; and (5) are prepared to assist management in developing constructive follow-up actions.

Perhaps most important, company management should seek professionals who are business-oriented, interested in contributing to the growth and development and profitability of the companies they serve—in contrast to testing management theories or writing articles for professional publication.

What Is Involved in a Survey. The conduct of a survey of employee thinking and feeling involves a number of steps, as follows:

(1) *Clarification of the overall purpose and specific objectives of the survey.* Surveys may cover all aspects of employee relations or only specific elements. Whatever the objectives, it is important that management be committed in advance to taking action based upon the expressed feeling and thinking of employees. Studies of change in employee attitudes between initial surveys and resurveys have shown that in situations in which management does take action, attitudes most often have improved. But, in instances in which management does not take action, there tends to be an increase in the amount of dissatisfaction. It is important that the survey staff learn as much as possible about the organization's characteristics, background, and goals. If change is required, the successful management of change requires a clear understanding of the base from which it is being launched.

(2) *Decision as to who will be included in the survey, and techniques to be used.* A sampling of employees may provide the "answers" management seeks, but when economically feasible to do so a survey should cover *all* employees so that each has the satisfaction of participating and expressing his or her individual point of view. Also, if a census rather than a sample approach is used, managers at each organizational level can receive and go to work on those findings of singular importance to their own people. If sampling is done, employees should be *randomly* chosen for participation on some impartial basis.

A concurrent decision has to do with the technique to be utilized, e.g., questionnaire, interview, or combination. Interviewing, properly conducted, tends to yield information in greater depth but is more expensive than the questionnaire method and is far more difficult to quantify. One approach is to use a "mini-questionnaire" in conjunction with group interviews, to produce quantified data on a limited number of key indicators, bolstered by the insights from face-to-face discussions.

(3) *Tailoring the questionnaire or interview guide.* Preliminary, unstructured interviews with a small cross-section of employees will aid in constructing a suitable questionnaire or interview procedure. The specifics brought out in these interviews can also serve later to assist those who have the responsibility for interpreting the more general questionnaire data. Questions included in the questionnaire or interview should be phrased in such manner that employees feel free to express whatever they may wish about the topics under discussion.

There are some traditional personnel-related items which almost inevitably appear on surveys of employee attitudes. They include questions about communication, compensation, physical working conditions, and supervisor-employee relations. However, there is a growing recognition that work-related issues concern employees even more, i.e., pressures on the job, work standards, roadblocks to operating efficiency, systems breakdowns, and the management of change. For this reason, employee attitude surveys in recent years have become progressively more oriented to questions about work-place or other corporate issues. In any case, each survey should be geared to the organization's singular objectives and environment. Standardized, off-the-shelf questionnaires are useful, on occasion, in permitting comparisons to be made with other organizations, but too often they are so general and broad that they fail to come to grips with the singular issues of a given organization.

(4) *Announcement of the survey to employees, to assure their frank and candid participation.* Before the entire work force is notified of the forthcoming survey, management at all levels should be alerted to the process so they can be conditioned to recognize their responsibility for responsive action, and so that they can identify information objectives most important to themselves. Also, if there is a union, notification to the union in advance and seeking its involvement and cooperation early is just good business, even though it is management's prerogative to conduct surveys (as long as participation is voluntary).

The announcement to employees should state purpose, who will be included in the survey, emphasize the anonymity of responses, when and where the individual employee will be given the opportunity to participate, and what is expected of him/her. As noted, each employee should be assured that participation is voluntary.

(5) *Facilities and scheduling to enable all employees to participate without major interruption of work load.* In scheduling meetings with individual employees or groups of employees, adequate time should be provided to review the purpose of the survey and answer questions participants may have concerning the process. In general, it is desirable to conduct a survey in as brief an overall time period as possible. When possible, surveys should be conducted on the job to convey management's commitment to the process and to assure maximum participation.

If a questionnaire is used, the most effective procedure in most instances is to administer it in proctored groups. If this is not possible, the questionnaire might be distributed to individual employees at their work places with instructions to supervisors to grant time to fill it out. Thirdly, there may be situations in which the best method is to route questionnaires to employees if they are in widely dispersed geographical locations and ask that they return them by mail.

(6) *Analysis of data and reporting.* Although a formal written record of survey results is usually required, effective communication of the results should occur in meetings and discussions so that questions can be answered and

explanations of the data explored. While it is necessary for a skilled professional to synthesize the survey data, it is also advisable for people knowledgeable about the organization to be involved in relating the findings to the Company's present situation and future goals.

(7) *Presentation of survey outcomes to employee participants.* Feedback can be an important communication channel in its own right. Obviously, surveys serve as a channel of upward communication; the feedback of results provides an opportunity to establish dialogue, so sorely needed, between managers of different levels and different departments, and between supervisors and their employees. But, as importantly, they set the tone and provide the base from which the entire employee constituency can address the problems identified. When results are presented in small groups of like functions, employees can best be encouraged to participate in the beginning steps toward problem solution.

(8) *Realistic action program based on results.* Doing something about the findings from a survey typically involves both short-term and long-range planning. Some actions are obvious as a result of survey findings whereas other matters may require further investigation and analysis. As is the case in initial steps toward problem solving, one of the most important ways to achieve continued improvements in operations and relationships is to secure the fullest involvement of all personnel in on-going efforts to achieve change.

(9) *Continuity.* The trouble with too many applications of survey research is that they produce a massive set of data which by its sheer weight may cloud issues and inhibit response. Further, too often the results are a still picture, a "slice of life" at one point in time. Though there are occasions when special-purpose surveys, administered once only, can serve a useful purpose, the value of the approach is multiplied when the surveys become part of an ongoing system, a continuing feedback process. In that way, management can have an always-current picture of conditions as they are, as well as a means of program evaluation to measure progress (or lack of it) in addressing specific situations. Often the trends are as significant to note as are the results in an absolute sense.

Further, in today's employee relations climate, many companies are seeking to improve QUALITY OF WORKING LIFE in cooperation with their employees or through collaboration with unions. Employee attitude research can, and often should, be an important part of a continuous process designed to encourage greater worker involvement in the decisions and operations of any organization.

Additional Benefits of a Survey. Often, management experiences a very special impact from reading verbatim comments generated in a survey. In many instances, these responses provide graphic illustrations and examples of the feelings of employees which may be only generally described by the statistical data. They tend to represent a composite of "a lot of little things" about which employees may feel strongly. For this reason, it is vital that "check-list" questions be balanced with sufficient opportunity for employees to express themselves in their own words.

Survey results also provide management with the opportunity to see themselves as others see them; they act as mirrors of supervisory-management behavior. In essence, they indicate whether or not supervisory-management personnel are showing a high degree of sensitivity in interpersonal relations and in setting the proper working climate. For an organization to succeed, its philosophies, practices, and operating systems must function with consistency at all levels; surveys are an extremely useful means of spotting any discontinuity and highlighting spots where the gaps must be closed.

Decision to Conduct a Survey. Many executives are prone to say, "We know what the problems are." Whether this is true or not is academic. The emphasis of the survey approach is to seek out opportunities for improvement, to understand why the problems exist and what, if anything, blocks solution. In fact, problem persistence is often as debilitating as the problem itself. The survey process can frequently get an organization off dead center by focusing attention on even long-standing needs. The basic requirement for the successful outcome of a survey is management's sincere intention to take positive and contructive action on the survey findings.

STANLEY PETERFREUND, President, Stanley Peterfreund Associates, Inc., Closter, New Jersey

Information References

Davidson, W. L., "How to Develop and Conduct Successful Employee Attitude Surveys," Chicago, Dartnell, 1979.

Dunham, R. B. and Smith, F. J., "Organizational Surveys," Glenview, Illinois, Scott Foresman, 1979.

Holms, Sandra L., "What to Expect from your First

Survey of Employee Morale," *Personnel,* March/April 1979.

Loffreda, Robert, "Employee Attitude Surveys: A Valuable Motivating Tool," *Personnel Administrator,* July 1979.

Miller, Ernest C., "Attitude Surveys: A Diagnostic Tool," *Personnel,* May/June 1978.

Mirvis, Philip H. and Lawler, Edward E., "Measuring the Financial Impact of Employee Attitudes," *Journal of Applied Psychology,* February 1977.

Morano, Richard A., "Opinion Survey: The How-To's of Design and Application," *Personnel,* September/October 1974.

Peterfreund, Stanley, "Managing Change: Regarding the Use of Attitude Surveys to Improve Organizational Effectiveness," Englewood Cliffs, N.J., Stanley Peterfreund Associates, Inc., 1980.

Cross References: *Hawthorne Experiments; Personnel Administration; Personnel Counseling; Quality of Working Life.*

EMPLOYEE BENEFIT PLANS

Employer-granted compensation to employees which are not directly a part of salary payments are generally classified as **Employee Benefits,** and they can run a wide range from vacations with pay to subsidy of the plant softball team. However in its most widely used sense, employee benefit plans relate to programs insuring against the expenses of old age, death, accident, illness, and loss of wages.

RETIREMENT PLANS, GROUP LIFE INSURANCE and GROUP HEALTH INSURANCE, and WORKMEN'S COMPENSATION plans are the four major elements providing protection against these expenses.

Retirement plans in industry had their begining in the latter part of the nineteenth century, and in the early decades of the current century formal programs were installed in several large industries. Group life insurance was first introduced in 1911, and the third major factor in employee benefits, group health plans, first appeared in the thirties, but their growth is almost entirely a product of the post World War II era.

The World War II economic climate fostered the beginning of the phenomenal growth achieved in all three areas of employee benefit planning over the ensuing 40 years. At that time, Government regulation of wages as an anti-inflation measure so restricted wage increases that other methods of compensation were necessary to attract and keep competent civilian workers during a period when manpower was at a premium. To most employers and employees, family security programs seemed the most attractive means of benefit compensation.

The depression years of the 1930s and the introduction of the Social Security program in 1935 had already resulted in a growing national emphasis on personal security and protection programs. Therefore, the introduction of retirement programs and group insurance at places of employment was well received. Employers credited these programs with increasing efficiency and employee morale. Employers also were allowed Federal tax deduction for contributions to "qualified" pension and group insurance programs.

In 1949, the U.S. Supreme Court upheld the decision of the National Labor Relations Board in the Inland Steel Case, ruling employee benefit plans subject to collective bargaining, further strengthening the position of employee benefit plans. Such plans were ruled to come within the meaning of "wages" and "conditions of employment" as defined under the Wagner Act, and became almost as important an issue in collective bargaining as wages, hours, and other conditions of work.

In the ensuing years there has been a marked development of employee benefit plans in all industries and business, and among government workers. Nearly one-half of all workers in commerce and industry in the United States and three-fourths of all government civilian personnel are now enrolled in retirement plans other than Social Security. This compares with fewer than one-fifth of employees in commerce and industry and fewer than one-half of government workers in 1940. Group life insurance, protecting the family should the worker die, also covers more than three-quarters of the work force as compared to about one-third in 1950 and less than one-tenth in 1930.

Even faster growth in employee benefit planning has been experienced in the health insurance area. About three quarters of all earners now have some form of group health insurance protection for themselves and their families. These plans include insured, self-insured, and Blue Cross-Blue Shield coverages. Over 169 million people under age 65 are protected against hospital expenses, mostly through group health plans. Nearly 145 million of these individuals are also protected against major medical expenses, primarily through insurance company coverage. Protection against the temporary loss of wages due to illness or injury is afforded more than 84 million workers.

Recent innovations in the health insurance area of employee benefit planning have been such added services as dental and vision care.

The impact of employee benefit plans on the national economy can be judged from the following comparisons. Private pension plans, which include both insurance company plans and non-insurance company plans, had $362.6 billion in assets and reserves at the start of 1980, compared with $52.0 billion in 1960. The flow of retirement benefit payments under private pension plans amounted to $14.9 billion, going out to 7.1 million retired persons in 1975. Comparable statistics for 1960 were $1.7 billion in pension benefits paid to 1.8 million persons.

Immediately following World War II, 11.5 million group life insurance certificates were issued under 31,000 master group life insurance policies, representing nearly $22.2 billion of life insurance in force in the United States. This averaged about $1,930 of life insurance per certificate. The group certificate is an employee's evidence of guaranteed insurance. At the start of 1980, group life insurance protection was provided under 114.9 million certificates by 559,000 master group life insurance contracts, for total coverage of $1.4 trillion. Average ownership per certificate increased to about $12,350.

The cost of employee benefit plans continues to grow. Through the years benefits have become more comprehensive, with the result that the cost of providing these programs has risen faster than wages in the past decade.

For the employer, administration of these plans has become an important budget factor. Administrative services can be sizeable and costly, and in larger business organizations especially, technically competent staffs are necessary to provide these services for employees.

In the past, employers and employees generally shared the costs of insurance and pension benefits. In recent years there has been a gradual shifting to the point where a considerable number of plans are now entirely paid for by the employer. Full contributions by employers enable them to have greater flexibility in determining the future course of the employee benefit programs.

The end results of this vast planning for economic security are the benefits realized in the time of need. A majority of American families are now receiving protection against the economic losses of death, disability, retirement, and unemployment through plans originating at their places of employment.

Progressive management today accepts employee benefit plans as a corporate responsibility whereby the uncertain and unknown economic burdens of our working population are assisted ably through the private sector of our economy.

Three particuar factors are often considered by management in the development of employee benefit plans. They are: (1) the social trend; (2) the area of industry practice relating to benefit programs; (3) the general economic climate.

These factors blend into the basic and long-range objectives of management in furthering its own performance through a more satisfied and secure work force.

Blake T Newton, Jr., President, American Council of Life Insurance, Washington, D.C.

Information References

Associations:

Council on Employee Benefits, American Council of Life Insurance.

Periodicals:

Employee Benefit Plan Review, (monthly) Charles D. Spencer Associates, Chicago.

Texts:

"Employee Benefits," Chamber of Commerce of the United States, Washington, D.C.

Cross References: *Credit Unions; Guaranteed Annual Wage; Group Health Insurance; Group Life Insurance; Occupational Safety and Health Act of 1970; Profit Sharing; Quality of Working Life; Retirement Plans; Workers' Compensation.*

EMPLOYEE COUNSELING: See Personnel Counseling.

EMPLOYEE PRIVACY

Ever-increasing information needs of business and government, combined with the miracles of computer and telecommunications technology, are having a profound impact on all of us as citizens of a relatively free society. In a sense, all citizens have become victims of a data dominated environment. What schools they go to . . . what jobs they are offered . . . what promotions they are given . . . what mortgage loans they are granted . . . what insurance policies are issued to them . . . even what apartments they can rent or homes they are permitted to buy—all is covered in information contained in their files—information which is now being stored in computer data banks, perhaps never to be destroyed, and retrievable in a few seconds. And the opportunities the world holds for them for the rest of their lives may be based on this information.

The single source holding more personal information of this sort than does any other is the corporate employer. Not only does the employer have the basic data furnished on the original employment application forms, together with the results of various employment-related actions and interviews, but the company files also contain the findings of consumer credit-reporting bureaus, information furnished by reference sources, and reports of supervisors, among others.

The U.S. Privacy Protection Commission, created by Congress during the Ford Administration, presented its report to President Carter and the Congress in July 1977, urging legislation on individual privacy in the areas of banking, insurance, consumer credit, investigative reporting, Internal Revenue Service, and education, among others. However, in the area of **Employee Privacy** as regards employment records, the Commission, at the urging of business leaders, recommended that industry be given a reasonable opportunity to adopt appropriate privacy safeguards voluntarily. In April 1979, President Carter formally endorsed the substance of the Commission's recommendations.

Guidelines for Action. Following are guidelines which the Commission determined to be necessary if the privacy rights of employees are to be protected:

(1) An employee should have a right to see, copy, and correct if necessary, the record an employer has about him or her.

(2) An employer should not transfer information about an employee to another without the employee's permission, or at least without his or her knowledge.

(3) An employer should not maintain secret records about an employee. (An employer might find it necessary to maintain a confidential record for security purposes, but the employee should know that such a record exists.)

(4) Information about an employee should not be obtained under false pretenses, or through pretext interviews.

(5) An employer should only obtain personal information about an employee or applicant which is relevant for proper administration or decision making.

(6) An employer or prospective employer should use individually identifiable employee data only for the purpose for which it was collected.

Current Practice. The Commission recommended that if voluntary employer action was not forthcoming after a reasonable period, appropriate legislation be enacted. Two years was suggested as a "reasonable time."

Two years after the submission of the report to the President, a research study by the University of Illinois, under the direction of the present writer who had served as chairman of the U.S. Privacy Protection Commission, was undertaken to determine the degree to which industry had followed through on the Commission's recommendations—at least for the 20 million persons employed by the largest industrial corporations in the country—the Fortune 500 companies.

With reference to giving the employee a right to see, copy, and correct if necessary his (her) record, it was found that although about three-fourths of the companies allowed the individual to have access to his or her personnel record, less than half gave the employee the right to copy the record. Some 79% of the companies permitted employees to place corrections in the record, but three out of four companies did not forward these corrections to anyone who had received the incorrect information from them.

Most employees still are not being told much about their own records. Over two-thirds of the companies do not inform their personnel of the types of records maintained on them, how they are used, what they have access to, and what the company's routine disclosure practices are. Apparently secret records continue to exist.

Over two-thirds (69%) of the corporations surveyed did not inform the individuals that they gave personal information to credit grantors; 85% of the companies disclosed such information to credit grantors without subpoena, as compared to 49% to landlords and 22% to charitable organizations.

Three out of four companies used medical information in their files for making employment-related decisions; yet 83% of the organizations did not allow their personnel to see it.

Two out of five companies did not have a

policy concerning which records are routinely disclosed to government agencies.

It would seem that the research findings do not indicate widespread voluntary adoption of privacy safeguards in the employment systems of the country's largest corporations. This, in spite of the fact that almost four out of five companies indicated that they had appointed an executive-level individual to be responsible for maintaining privacy safeguards in employment records.

Continued exposure to possible abuse of an individual's privacy rights chips away at the personal freedoms of workers and executives alike, with the hazard of further weakening our democratic free-enterprise way of life.

David F. Linowes, Boeschenstein Professor of Political Economy and Public Policy, University of Illinois at Urbana-Champaign, Illinois; former Chairman, U.S. Privacy Protection Commission, Washington, D.C.

Cross Reference: *Employment: Antidiscrimination Legislation.*

EMPLOYMENT: ANTIDISCRIMINATION LEGISLATION

The Civil Rights Act of 1964—Title VII

Title VII of the Civil Rights Act of 1964 is the most important piece of legislation in the employment discrimination area. Title VII prohibits an employer from discriminating against an employee or applicant for employment on the basis of race, color, religion, sex, or national origin. The Act is administered by the Equal Employment Opportunity Commission (EEOC) which has the right to sue to enforce the Act after exhausting administrative attempts to resolve alleged discrimination. Additionally, after exhaustion of EEOC procedures, an aggrieved individual may bring suit.

Title VII covers employers engaged in an industry affecting commerce with fifteen or more employees. The phrase "engaged in an industry affecting commerce" has been defined so broadly that almost every employer with fifteen or more employees is covered.

Not only does Title VII cover almost every employer, but the discrimination prohibitions cover the entire range of employment practices. It is unlawful for an employer to discriminate against an individual because of his race, color, religion, sex, or national origin with respect to compensation, terms, conditions, or privileges of employment. It is also illegal to discriminate with regard to apprenticeship, training, or retention programs, to indicate in employment advertisements a preference based on race, color, religion, sex, or national origin, and to segregate or classify employees in any way that would deprive any individual of employment opportunities or otherwise adversely affect his status as an employee because of his race, color, religion, sex, or national origin.

Not only is disparate treatment of employees or applicants for employment on account of their race, color, sex, religion, or national origin unlawful, but employment practices that have a disparate impact may also be illegal. Thus, an employment practice that may be innocent, or seem to be innocent, may be prohibited by Title VII where the practice adversely impacts members of a protected class and cannot be justified by business necessity. For example, a facially neutral employment test may be discriminatory if it results in blacks being accepted at a lower rate than whites, and the test cannot meet strict validation requirements and/or cannot be demonstrated to be job-related. Similarly, high school diploma requirements have been held unlawful because such a requirement had a disparate impact upon blacks and could not be shown to be job-related. The disparate impact approach to discrimination by the EEOC and the courts make it extremely difficult to employ standardized tests and to use many formerly accepted means of screening applicants for employment or promotion. Further, there is no requirement that *intent to* discriminate exists in order for an employment practice with a disparate impact to be held unlawful.

Race Discrimination. Aside from the obvious and overt acts of race discrimination being unlawful, a number of other practices have been held to discriminate against blacks because of their adverse impact:

(1) Educational and diploma requirements.

(2) Inquiries into arrest and conviction records.

(3) Disqualification because of receiving a less than honorable discharge.

(4) Refusal to hire or termination because of garnishments.

(5) Dress or grooming codes that adversely affect blacks.

(6) Practices that perpetuate the effect of past discrimination, such as departmental seniority where there were previously "black" departments.

Sex Discrimination. *Pregnancy.* The definition of sex discrimination was broadened by the 1978 Pregnancy Disability Amendment to Title VII. The amendment requires an employer to treat pregnancy and childbirth the same as other causes of disability under fringe benefit plans; prohibits terminating or refusing to hire or promote a woman solely because she is pregnant; bars mandatory leaves for pregnant women arbitrarily set at a certain time in their pregnancy and not based on their inability to work; and protects the reinstatement rights of women on leave for pregnancy-related reasons, including credit for previous service and accrued retirement benefits and accumulated seniority.

The Amendment expands the definition of sex discrimination to include discrimination on the basis of "pregnancy, childbirth or related medical conditions." Only discriminatory treatment is prohibited and an employer is not required to treat pregnant women in any particular manner with respect to hiring, forbidding them to continue work, providing sick leave, furnishing medical and hospital benefits, providing disability benefits, or any other matter. The Act simply requires that pregnant women be treated the same as other employees on the basis of their ability or inability to work.

The Amendment prevents employers from treating pregnancy, childbirth, and related conditions in a manner different from treatment of other disabilities. Women who become disabled due to pregnancy, childbirth, or other related conditions must be provided the same benefits as those provided to other disabled workers. This would include temporary and long-term disability insurance, sick leave, and other forms of employee benefit programs.

The only time an employer is required to allow pregnant workers to use their disability leave is during the time they are medically unable to work, during the same period and in the same terms applicable to other employees. For example, if a woman wishes to stay home to take care of a child, no benefit must be paid because this is not a medically-determined condition related to pregnancy. If an employer has a temporary disability program, that does not mean a pregnant worker can receive benefits for all the weeks allowable under the program unless other employees suffering from other disabilities are also permitted to do so. If, however, medical complications arise, these complications should be covered by the same time limits or dollar amounts otherwise provided disabled workers.

The Amendment requires an employer who provides medical benefits for its employees to cover the medical and hospital costs of pregnancy, childbirth, and related medical conditions under the same terms and conditions of coverage for other medical conditions. For example, if the medical plan covers all medical and hospital costs of employees, all the costs related to pregnancy, childbirth, or related medical conditions must be fully covered. Furthermore, there can be no special conditions placed on the number of days or dollar amounts unless these limitations apply to all disabilities covered by the medical benefits plan.

An employer is prohibited from requiring women who become pregnant to take mandatory maternity leave, and is also prohibited from setting arbitrary time limits within which disabled women must return to work, or before which they may not return to work, if no such limits exist for other disabled employees. Employers are also required to credit women with accumulated seniority after pregnancy disability leave on the same terms applicable to other persons absent from work for other disabilities. Finally, an employer will not be able to refuse to hire or promote women simply because they are pregnant.

Sexual Harassment. The definition of sex discrimination has been expanded to include sexual harassment of employees as a violation of Title VII. The EEOC has issued detailed guidelines on this aspect of sex discrimination. It defines sexual harassment as:

> "Unwelcome sexual advances, requests for sexual favors, and other verbal or physical conduct of a sexual nature constitute sexual harassment when (1) submission to such conduct is made either explicitly or implicitly a term or condition of an individual's employment, (2) submission to or rejection of such conduct by an individual is used as the basis for employment decisions affecting such individual, or (3) such conduct has the purpose or effect of unreasonably interfering with an individual's work performance or creating an intimidating, hostile, or offensive working environment.

This broad interpretation of sexual harassment will certainly lead to increased charges of sex discrimination and may expose employers to liability for acts by its supervisors and management employees whether or not the specific acts were authorized or even forbidden by the employer, and regardless of whether the employer knew or should have known of their occurrence.

Equal Pay. In additional to the prohibition against sex discrimination contained in Title VII, the **Equal Pay Act** prohibits dual-standard compensation for males and females performing the same or substantially the same jobs. The Equal Pay Act is enforced under the Fair Labor Standards Act.

National Origin Discrimination. Title VII prohibits an employer from discriminating on the basis of national origin. As in the area of sex and race discrimination, violations have been found where the employment practice appears neutral on its face but has a discriminatory effect on persons of a particular national origin. The following employment practices have been held to be in violation of the prohibition against national origin discrimination:

(1) Requiring the ability to speak English where the employer could not establish business necessity for the requirement.

(2) Requiring that English only be spoken on the job.

(3) Job assignment based on national origin.

(4) Minimum height and weight requirements—minimum height and weight requirements have been found to discriminate particularly against Spanish-surname American males.

(5) Derogatory epithets or stereotype images—allowing fellow employees to make an employee's ancestry the butt of jokes, permitting insults and "kidding" based on national origin by fellow employees, condoning ethnic jokes, and derogatory ethnic statements.

Religious Discrimination. The EEOC takes the position that an employee's beliefs are protected as religious even if they are not recognized by a particular religious establishment if they are "as deeply and sincerely held as more conventional religious convictions." Of course, overt discrimination because of someone's religion is prohibited by Title VII. However, most religious discrimination issues center around whether or not an employer has made "reasonable accommodation" to the religious needs of an employee. Under current court decisions, an employer need not incur more than minimal cost in order to accommodate an employee's religious practices, and it need not take steps inconsistent with an otherwise valid seniority system. Frequently, the issue of accommodation focuses around an employee's desire to observe his Sabbath. Another area of frequent litigation revolves around accommodating employees who, because of religious reasons, seek to maintain a dress or physical appearance that varies from the norm approved by the employer. In determining whether or not an employer has made efforts to accommodate employees' religious practices, the following factors have been deemed important:

(1) The nature of the job.

(2) The size of the employer's establishment.

(3) The effects of transferring the employee to a different job.

(4) The effects of accommodation upon the morale of other employees.

(5) The employee's efforts in reaching accommodation.

Enforcement. The Equal Employment Opportunity Commission is primarily responsible for enforcement of Title VII. Typically, the enforcement process begins with a charge being filed with the Equal Employment Opportunity Commission by an individual. The charge must be filed within 180 days of the discriminatory act. After the charge has been filed, the Equal Employment Opportunity Commission notifies the employer of the charge and then begins its investigation. The employer will be requested to provide the EEOC with information relating to the charge and answer specific questions prior to attending the "Fact Finding Conference." In addition, the employer is requested to provide the EEOC with its Statement of Position on the charge.

The Fact Finding Conference is an investigative forum intended to define the issues, to determine which elements are undisputed, to clarify issues, to obtain evidence, and to ascertain whether there is any basis for a Negotiated Settlement of the Charge. While the employer is permitted to have a legal representative at the Fact Finding Conference, the role of the legal representative is limited to advisory, and he (she) is not permitted to cross-examine the charging party. The EEOC has the power to subpoena witnesses and documents.

After the EEOC has completed its investigation, it will issue its Determination in which it will either find that there is reasonable cause to believe that the allegation in the charge is true, or will find no reasonable cause to believe there has been a violation of the Act. At the time the EEOC issues its Determination, it will issue a statutory Notice of Right to Sue after a finding of no reasonable cause or after a finding of reasonable cause, failure of conciliation, and a determination that the case will not be litigated by the EEOC as a party plaintiff. After receiving the Notice of Right to Sue, the charging party must file a civil action with the Federal District Court within 90 days. A statutory Notice of Right to Sue may also be issued prior to Determination if the EEOC finds it has no jurisdiction or upon the request of a charging party before completion of administrative process. If the EEOC decides to sue for enforcement, the charging party has the right to intervene. If the Court finds that an employer is guilty of prohibited discrimination, it may order that the unlawful practices be enjoined and may order the aggrieved employee reinstated with back pay. If the suit is a class action, the class-wide relief can be granted.

The Age Discrimination in Employment Act (ADEA)

The Age Discrimination in Employment Act of 1967, as amended, prohibits job discrimination against workers between 40 and 70 years of age. The ADEA's prohibitions parallel those in Title VII in that employers are forbidden to fail or refuse to hire, to discharge, or otherwise discriminate against any individual with respect to compensation, terms, conditions, or privileges of employment because of such individual's age. The Act forbids an employer to operate a seniority system or employment benefit plan that requires or permits the involuntary retirement of an employee under age 70.

Enforcement of the ADEA was transferred from the Department of Labor to the EEOC in 1979. Prior to suing in Federal District Court, an employee must now file a charge within 180 days of the alleged discriminatory act and 60 days prior to instituting any civil action.

The Vocational Rehabilitation Act

Section 503 of the **Rehabilitation Act of 1973** requires employers with Federal contracts over $2,500 to take affirmative action for the employment of handicapped people. The affirmative action requirements are enforced by the Office of Federal Contract Compliance Programs (OFCCP).

The Government's approach to affirmative action for the handicapped is similar to that for women and minorities. However, no specific numerical goals must be set. As in the area of religious discrimination, an employer must make reasonable efforts to accommodate an employee's handicap. The Government's affirmative action requirements emphasize recruiting, outreach, and communication of the company's policy to hire and promote the handicapped.

Executive Order 11246 and the OFCCP

Executive Order 11246 requires that every Government contract contain provisions against discrimination in employment on the basis of race, color, religion, sex, or national orign. In addition, contractors are required to take affirmative action to ensure that applicants and employees are employed without regard to such factors. Contractors are also required to furnish required information to the OFCCP. In the event of noncompliance with the Executive Order or Rules and Regulations promulgated thereunder, a contract may be cancelled, terminated, or suspended, and the contractor may be declared ineligible for future Government contracts.

The affirmative action plans required under Executive Order 11246 and the rules and regulations promulgated thereunder require, among other things, that the contractor perform a utilization analysis which consists of a work force analysis, identification of job groups, an availability analysis, and an underutilization analysis. Finally, the contractor is required to establish goals and timetables to correct any underutilization of minorities and women that may exist.

The requirement that covered employers initiate a written affirmative action program is a major tool in promoting the goals of Executive Order 11246. It is hoped that the self-analysis involved in preparing an affirmative action program will make the employer aware of its equal employment deficiences and will lead to voluntary actions to remedy any problem in that area.

The Office of Federal Contract Compliance conducts compliance reviews to determine if an employer is striving for a goal of equal opportunity and meeting its affirmative action requirements. Such a review could lead to sanctions against an employer which could include loss of Government contracts, being barred from future contracts, and damages in the form of back pay to affected classes.

Donald J. Horton, Attorney, Andrews, Kurth, Campbell & Jones, Houston, Texas

Information References

Title VII of the Civil Rights Act and the Age Discrimination Act:

The Regional Offices of the Equal Employment Opportunity Commission.

Equal Pay Act:

Wage and Hours Division of the Area Office of the Department of Labor

General References:

"Fair Employment Practices Manual" Washington, Bureau of National Affairs.

Schlei, Barbara L. and Grossman, Paul, "Employment Discrimination Law," Washington, Bureau of National Affairs, 1976 ed. with 1979 Supplement.

Cross References: *Personnel Testing; Personnel Testing: Types of Tests.*

EMPLOYMENT AGENCIES

Over 10,000 **Employment Agencies** in the United States—not counting about 2,500 state employment offices operated as part of the U.S. Employment Service—provide recruiting services covering every class of industrial and commercial employment: skilled and unskilled workers, technical and professional specialists, executives and administrators. The services are by no means confined to rank-and-file help, and the placements of personnel in the $25,000-and-over salary range are not uncommon.

Many large corporations make use of employment agencies regularly, finding them more effective in time and money spent per hire and in calibre of placements than their own personnel departments in advertising and initial screening. Such companies find the services especially advantageous when they are actively engaged in programs of expansion, diversification, plant relocation, and the like.

Operations. Some of the private employment agencies are small, perhaps two- or three-man operations. On the other hand, some are heavily staffed organizations with offices in many cities. In addition, there are networks of franchised offices or associated agencies, which can make available to a using company the facilities of all locations at no extra cost. However, it should be noted that a large agency may be recruiting largely for clerical or routine jobs, while a small office may represent a specialized firm handling only highly technical or executive personnel. Some agencies, also, may specialize in particular industries or crafts.

In practically all states, as well as Puerto Rico and the District of Columbia, there are laws regulating employment agencies. However, these laws vary widely, running the gamut from mere prohibition of misleading advertising, to licensing and strict regulation, to specifying maximum permissible fees and the kind of references required for certain classes of positions.

Some firms perform retainer-search, but most work on a contingency basis, in which case a placement fee is charged only if a job is actually obtained. This may be paid by the employee, with the employer sometimes reimbursing all or part after a probationary period.

In recent years, however, there has been a trend to "fee-paid" jobs, with the employer paying. The National Association of Personnel Consultants, Washington, D.C., numbering some 2,200 agencies, has published a Code of Ethics covering service charges and collections, relations with applicants and employers, advertising, etc. It publishes an annual Membership Directory which includes a listing of the special services of each office.

Selection. The following pointers are recommended to a company selecting an employment agency: Does the agency's advertising indicate that it is active in the company's field? An agency cannot screen effectively if it does not understand or have a "feel" for the types of jobs involved. Does the agency have specialists for the kinds of jobs to be filled, and affiliates who can help fill the company's needs in other locations? Experiences of other users should be checked. Size in terms of numbers of offices operated or numbers of franchised or associated offices may not be meaningful in an area dominatd by a powerful independent, or an area where there is an agency geared to the company's special needs.

SOURCE: National Association of Personnel Consultants, Washington, D.C.

Cross References: *Executive Recruitment; Executive Selection; Temporary Personnel Services.*

EMPLOYMENT AND UNEMPLOYMENT. See Unemployment: Concepts and Measurement

ENGINEERING MANAGEMENT

Engineering Management is the name given to the area of engineering and management concerned with managing technical work and technical people in a predominantly technical environment. This type of management is as old as technology itself, but only recently has it been recognized as an area deserving of a separate name and a separate educational preparation. The adjective "engineering" in this context is used to describe activities based on mathematics and the physical sciences, and is not narrowly restricted to the traditional engineering disciplines. Persons engaged in "Engineering Management" may have educational backgrounds other than engineering, but they must be qualified by education and/or experience to make sound decisions involving technical work.

Formal Definition. As with any area still seeking to define itself, no universally accepted definition has yet evolved. However, the most commonly accepted definition is: *Engineering Management is the art and science of planning, organizing, allocating resources, directing and controlling activities which have a technological component.*

This definition identifies a management specialty and also identifies specific activities which are integral to the full practice of the various engineering and scientific disciplines. The practitioners of engineering management, known as "Engineering Managers," generally claim an identification with some field of engineering or science or some related area which is also rooted in mathematics and the physical sciences. Engineering Management differs from INDUSTRIAL ENGINEERING to which it is most closely related on the engineering side, by its greater focus on "people" problems rather than on system design, which, of course, also includes people along with materials and equipment. On the management side, it differs from general management in its requirement that practitioners be competent in some technical field. Engineering managers may be found occupying top, middle, and supervisory management positions. (See MANAGEMENT LEVELS.) They may be found working wherever a blending of managerial and technical knowledge is required, which may be in any organization, whether or not its primary business is technological.

History. The management of technical activities by technically competent persons represents nothing new. It has been customary, however, for practitioners to identify themselves as either engineers or managers depending on their work environment. The establishment of engineering management as a separate branch of academic study is a post World War II development. Graduate level courses in Research Administration were offered at Illinois Institute of Technology, New York University, and the University of Pennsylvania in the 1940s and early 1950s. Engineering management graduate programs leading to the Master's degree were started during this same period at several institutions, including George Washington University, New Jersey Institute of Technology, Rensselaer Polytechnic Institute, and the University of California in Los Angeles. It was also in the 1950s that the first engineering society, the Institute of Electrical and Electronics Engineers (IEEE) organized a unit to be concerned with engineering management.

Since 1965, however, there has been a rapid growth of both educational programs and society committees or divisions concerned with engineering management. The American Society for Engineering Education in 1972 established its present Engineering Management Division. The first real move toward recognition as a separate profession took place in 1979 when a group of interested people from government, industry, and universities organized the American Society for Engineering Management. The rapid growth of this society in its first year is indicative of the widespread interest in this field.

Education. Although education alone does not qualify one for the responsible practice of management or engineering, there has been a growing recognition that engineers need a more extensive knowledge of management. Survey data from the Engineering Manpower Commission collected in 1969 showed that more than 80% of all the engineers surveyed were regularly assigned managerial duties [1]. Its Bulletin stated: "If management is an inherent part of the work of so many engineers, that fact should receive greater recognition in the education and career development of members of the profession. . . . Not only do engineers need more education in the arts and techniques of management, but they must be made more aware of the ways in which their duties will change during their professional careers."

Universities and colleges have responded by offering classes and establishing programs leading to degrees. In addition, short courses, seminars, and workshops are being offered in increasing numbers. As of 1980, students in over 30 institutions may enroll as candidates for the Bachelor's degree in Engineering Management studies. (Most of these curriculums are known by other names such as Engineering Administration, Engineering Operations, Management Engineering, etc.) This diversity of name, which is also found, but to a lesser extent, in programs at the post-baccalaureate level, is a reflection of the recent application of a suitable name to distinguish this important area of professional practice.

As of 1980, two of the baccalaureate curriculums have been accredited by the Accreditation Board for Engineering and Technology (ABET). Undergraduates receive an education in engineering fundamentals and in management-related subjects. A more extensive response to needs has been the establishment of Master's and Doctor's programs. In 1980, these programs numbered over 80. Many of these are offered on a part-time basis. Most of them prefer and many require applicable work experience prior to entry.

Relationship to MBA Programs. Business and Management Schools offer programs leading to the Master of Business Administration (MBA) degree. These programs usually require two academic years to complete, and impose no requirement of prior work experience. Some of them provide for specialization in such areas as accounting, banking, marketing, etc. Engineering Management graduate programs usually require one year of formal study following a technical undergraduate education. This year of academic study may be taken on a full or part-time basis. The curriculum is usually a Graduate School offering, but administered within the Engineering School, and is designed to provide additional studies of particular importance to those who aspire to managerial responsibility where technical knowledge is also required. The MBA and Engineering Management programs are in no way competitive, because they are designed to meet entirely different needs.

Acceptance and Potential. Recognition of this blend of engineering and management as a separately identifiable profession is being achieved. Most of the present engineering managers are probably not yet informed about the identification and emergence of this field. Most are not graduates of engineering management programs because these have not been in existence long enough nor numerous enough to have provided large numbers of graduates. They are not yet widely known to personnel managers and recruiters. It is too early to assess the impact of the newly formed American Society for Engineering Management, but it is expected to be influential in advancing engineering management in theory and practice and maintaining a high professional standard among its members. The existence of this society should in time lead to increased recognition of engineering management as an important profession in the future.

MERRITT A. WILLIAMSON, Orrin Henry Ingram Distinguished Professor of Engineering Management, School of Engineering, Vanderbilt University, Nashville, Tennessee

Information References

Associations:

Academy of Management.
American Society for Engineering Education (Engineering Management Division).
American Society for Engineering Management.
Institute of Electrical and Electronics Engineers, Inc. (The Engineering Management Society).
The Institute of Management Sciences (College of Engineering Management).
Management Committees and Divisions of various Engineering Societies.

Periodicals:

Engineering Management International.
Engineering Management Review.
R & D Management.
Research Management.
Transactions on Engineering Management.

Texts:

Amos, John M. and Sarchet, Bernard R., "Management for Engineers," Englewood Cliffs, N.J., Prentice-Hall, 1981.
Blanchard, B. S., "Engineering Organization and Management," Englewood Cliffs, N.J., Prentice-Hall, 1976.
Gray, Irwin, "The Engineer in Transition to Management," New York, Wiley, 1979.
Karger, D. W. and Murdick, R. G., "Managing Engineering and Research," rev. 3rd ed., New York, Industrial Press, 1980.
Shannon, R. E., "Engineering Management," New York, Wiley, 1980.

Reference Cited

[1] Engineering Manpower Commission, *Bulletin No. 25,* September 1973.

Cross References: *Basic Research: Management Aspects; Management Education: Professional Certification; Project Management.*

ENVIRONMENTAL CONTROLS

The **Environment** has become one of the major factors affecting capital management decisions today. The past decade has produced many Federal and state laws, as well as a public awareness and sophistication that makes adherence to these laws not only a legal requirement but also a public image one as well.

Environmental laws today focus on the control of specific chemicals for which there is considered to be evidence that they could damage the public health or the environment. While the "environment" is defined many ways, we include the air, surface water, and groundwater. Most recent attention has been addressed to toxics or poisonous materials. While toxicology, the study of poisons, is an old science, there are few cases where much data exists of the impacts on the environment and the public of small quantities of these materials. Most available data come from animal or other tests believed to represent their effects on humans, and as a result there are disagreements as to the scientific basis for some standards. On the other hand, when the public is subjected to direct contact with these materials, such as occurred at Love Canal, New York—where housing was constructed over a chemical waste dump—the results can be horrifying (cancer, brain damage, birth defects). Given these risks, environmental regulations have broad support and do not seem to be going away. Rather, the controls are tightening.

Air Pollution Control. The Clean Air Act, passed in 1970, controls air pollution both by direct controls of the sources of pollution—industry processes, motor vehicles, etc.—and by controls of growth in a region. Source control includes establishing "new source performance standards" in which standards are set for various pollutants emitted by a specific industry process. For old sources, allowable pollutant levels are generally set so that the regional air quality can be within ambient air quality standards—levels established by the Environmental Protection Agency (EPA) as those necessary to protect public health.

New regulations have been developed to regulate growth by controlling pollution in areas of the country which are currently in compliance with the ambient air quality standards. The prevention of significant deterioration or "PSD" regulation establishes environmental limits for new pollution which any new facility could produce. Other regulations have been developed to control pollution and allow some economic growth in areas of the country which do meet the clean air standards. The "bubble concept" allows a company to reduce emissions in one part of its facility in order to allow increased emissions from a new operation.

New regulations are being developed which relate to regulating the effects of air pollution, including visibility standards and control of acid rain.

Water Pollution Control. The Federal Water Pollution Control Act, passed in 1972, established significant controls on direct discharges of waste into the nation's waterways. The Act established three phases of nationally uniform industrial effluent limitations:

BPT—Best Practicable Technology (to be achieved by 1977).

BAT(EA)—Best Available Technology Economically Acheivable (to be met by 1984—as changed by the 1977 Clean Water Act).

NSPS—New Source Performance Standards (to be achieved when a new source commences operation).

In addition, the Act established special controls of toxic pollutants which were confirmed in a 1976 court decision setting out new controls on industrial discharges of 65 families of toxic chemicals. The Act created a permit system for controlling discharges of pollution. This program, the National Pollutant Discharge Elimination System (NPDES), requires permits to be renewed and upgraded at least every five years. An NPDES permit establishes limitations on the volume and characteristics of the wastewater to be established by the permittee. Finally, river basin and regional water quality planning was set in motion through other provisions of the Act.

Congress amended the 1972 FWPCA by passage of the Clean Water Act in 1977. The Clean Water Act requires control of conventional pollutants (BOD, Suspended Solids) from industry using Best Conventional Technology (BCT) by July 1, 1984. It requires control of toxic discharges (the list of 65) by July 1, 1984, or not later than three years after a substance makes the list using Best Available Technology Economically Available (BATEA). BCT and BATEA vary by industry.

In addition to standards applicable to industries which discharge directly to a receiving body of water, a separate set of standards will be established for industries discharging into publicly owned treatment works (POTW). There are standards to be set for 34 industry groups addressing the 65 toxic pollutants.

Drinking Water Control. The Safe Drinking Water Act (SDWA) of 1974 aims to protect the quality of drinking water in the United States. The SDWA applies to the quality of all drinking water sources including both surface and groundwater supplies.

The SDWA establishes National Interim Primary (and Secondary) Drinking Water Regulations. The Primary Drinking Water Standards establish standards for all public water supply systems designed to protect the public health. Industry discharges into bodies of water intended as a public drinking water cannot cause these Standards to be violated. The Secondary Drinking Water Standards are similar in their effect on industry except the standards are not Federally enforceable but serve as guidelines for the states.

A major part of the SDWA is directed to protect groundwater supplies from contamination. The regulations (the Underground Injection Control Program Regulation) are intended to govern state programs to regulate wells into which fluids (primarily waste fluids) are injected underground in order to preclude damage to present or future sources of drinking water. As of 1980, 22 states were expected to have underground injection control programs.

The final major portion of the SDWA is the requirement that areas underlain by an aquifer (a body of underground water) which is the sole or principal drinking water source for an area, be designated by USEPA as a "sole source aquifer" if damage to the aquifer would create a significant hazard to public health. Any action in the area of a sole source aquifer is subject to review under the SDWA and, if the activity could endanger the water quality of the underground drinking water source, mitigative matters would be required before the activity could proceed.

Solid/Hazardous Waste. The Resource Conservation and Recovery Act (RCRA) passed in 1976 regulates both industrial and municipal solid waste. Industrial waste under this law can be considered hazardous or non-hazardous. If the waste is non-hazardous, it is controlled in the same way as a municipal landfill. While these controls are less severe than for hazardous waste, they are nonetheless costly.

The controls of hazardous waste are having a dramatic effect on costs. Hazardous waste, which received wide interest from such tragedies as Love Canal, is controlled by comprehensive regulations which regulate the waste from "cradle to grave." The regulations not only increase the direct costs of disposal, but close the environmental regulatory loop so that onetime solutions to other environmental problems—like air pollution control and water pollution abatement such as land disposal—become more costly, if they are possible at all.

In the regulations, a list of hazardous waste processes as well as other hazardous compounds were identified for control. Over the next few years, there will be routine identification of new materials and they will be identified as hazardous when warranted and thus to be controlled.

Generators of these wastes must prepare manifests to accompany the waste to final disposal, indicating the quantity, type, and composition of all hazardous material. Those industries which treat, store waste for more than 90 days, or dispose of it, are subject to new design and operating standards. The design standards are expected to be very costly and will increase costs above present levels by over twenty times. Operating standards include the need to train all operating personnel, provide emergency plans, and develop plans to analyze incoming waste as to its compatability for treatment in the plant.

In the future, management should expect RCRA to be the major environmental law, with specific standards established for control of wastes for each industry. RCRA likely will follow the Clean Water Act in its move to compliance. The Water Act standards have changed twice in ten years (each time being more restrictive) with the standards being much less general and much more industry specific.

RCRA primarily addressed the problems of future disposal sites, but had provisions for dealing with old sites where waste was dumped and now had created an "imminent hazard." It is under this provision and other laws that enforcement is occurring at Love Canal and other locations. In the acquisition of property, management should be careful to assess adequately the environmental condition of that property and conduct an environmental audit of it (see remarks on environmental audit under *Environmental Disclosure,* below).

Toxic Substances Control Act (TSCA). Congress in 1976 reached the conclusion that existing Federal environmental laws which controlled residues during, and after a product was manufactured, were not adequate to *eliminate* the danger to the public health and environment. It believed that ultimate control would occur if production of certain chemicals was controlled, and mechanisms to do this were established through the Toxic Substances Control Act (TSCA).

Under TSCA, the USEPA has the authority to (1) gather certain levels of basic information on chemicals to identify harmful substances and (2) control those substances whose risk of injury outweighs the benefits to society and the economy when other environmental laws cannot control the specific sources of exposure. This Act allows EPA to control every facet of industry—product development, testing, manufacturing, processing, distribution, use, and disposal.

A section of TSCA imposes testing requirements to determine the health effects of manufactured chemical substances. Advisory bodies established in the Act provide the input as to the types of tests to be conducted on each chemical, and the quality control measures which must be taken. The section which goes the furthest in controlling chemicals coming on the market is that which requires the submission of a "premanufacturing notification" by an individual who intends to: (1) manufacture or import a "new chemical substance" in commerce, or (2) manufacture, import, or process in commerce a chemical substance for a "significant new use." The information will be used to perform "risk assessments" of the chemical substances proposed for manufacture, import, or significant new use and determine if the material should be restricted under other provisions of the Act. The material could be prevented from coming in the market.

The last important section of the Act delineates the scope of regulatory authority in protecting public health against the unreasonable health or environmental risks posed by hazardous chemical substances and mixtures. These restrictions which apply to new and existing chemicals can include a manufacturing ban, labeling, limits on use, etc. At this writing two classes of substances are controlled—polychlorinated biphenyls (PCBs) and chlorofluorocarbons (CFCs).

Other Environmental Laws. Management should be aware that other environmental laws exist at the Federal level which can have a significant impact on operations including the Surface Mining Control and Reclamation Act (SMCRA), Marine Protection, Research, and Sanctuary Act of 1972, and the Coastal Zone Management Act of 1972.

State laws are equally important and there is no provision in Federal laws which prevent states from being more restrictive in establishing their standards. While most state laws parallel Federal laws, some states are much more demanding.

Permits. The description of the standards is a crucial part of any environmental review, but the real-world problem is obtaining permits. A review of current Federal and state requirements shows that it could require up to seven years to obtain all the necessary environmental permits for a synthetic fuel development in several key energy states.

The Federal Government is attempting to bring order to its portion of the permitting process. It developed "consolidated permit regulations" which allow a single filing by industry for permits under the following:

Hazardous waste management program (RCRA).

Underground injection control program (Safe Drinking Water Act).

NPDES or national pollutant discharge elimination system (Clean Water Act).

PSD or prevention of significant deterioration program (Clean Air Act).

Section 404 (dredge or fill) programs (Clean Water Act).

This program is designed to streamline the permitting process over which EPA has control. Standard information is only provided once while specific program data are collected on the program's form. Also EPA may consolidate draft permits, public notice, public hearings, and administrative records for the permits.

Environmental Assessments. The National Environmental Policy Act (NEPA) in 1969 established the need for evaluating the environmental impacts of "major Federal actions" and their alternatives. Passage of NEPA began a wave of laws at all levels of government designed to develop a process for considering environmental issues for any project or program. While there are exceptions, these laws are procedural in nature, designed to ensure that issues affecting the environment are considered, alternatives to the proposed action are examined, and the public is allowed to be heard. In the past, most environmental assessments were quite subjective. Increasingly, as technical standards are developed under other environmental laws, and experience is gained in estimating social, economic and other factors, assessments require much more concrete analysis.

Management must recognize that NEPA and similar laws require early consideration of environmental factors in developing a project. The laws do not seek an examination of environmental issues *after the project is developed,* but rather expect environmental issues to be considered *from the beginning,* as all others such as economics and technical feasibility are considered. As a result, early environmental involvement in projects is essential.

Environmental Disclosure. In a number of ways non-environmental regulatory bodies are forcing consideration of environmental factors in business decisions. As an outgrowth of a 1979 acquisition attempt, the SEC began an investigation of a major company as to its disclosure of the financial liabilities resulting from current and past environmental practices facing the company. The registration statement prepared for the acquisition attempt, in the judgment of the SEC, did not adequately consider these liabilities. The company was forced to have an outside consultant do a corporate-wide environmental audit of the financial liabilities in the environmental area. The SEC has established this concept as a regulation to be met by all public companies.

Management Approaches. Environmental control can no longer be accomplished as the last item in the checklist of management actions. These considerations must be part of the management process for all new projects and even on-going operations.

(1) *Zero Discharge.* One way of accomplishing environmental control is not creating environmental problems in the first place. The 3-M Company aims to develop new products with "zero discharges" or with limited air, water, or solid residuals. Management must assume that the environmental requirements will expand, and that environmental controls will be costly. Obviously, then, the fewer residuals, the less long-term exposure a company has in this area.

(2) *Purchasing Department.* Environmental control in the future will be more pollutant specific. The toxic materials will receive much more regulatory attention than nontoxic nuisance materials. If toxic raw materials can be replaced by nontoxic raw materials, the long-term costs and controls can be reduced. A purchasing department trained to consider the environmental implications of its actions can be an effective management resource.

(3) *Risk Management Within The Plant.* Environmental control should be approached as a risk-management problem. Risk management is defined here as creating approaches and strategies which give a company the flexibility and resistance necessary to decrease its vulnerability. Companies are today combining the environmental, health and safety, and insurance activities into one organization. Too often, environmental controls have been the "black box" at the end of the process with little thought as to new raw materials, process modifications, or any other factor which might produce the same environmental benefit. Just as such managers use internal changes to keep insurance claims cost down, risk managers can also keep environmental costs down.

Conclusion. Environmental factors continue to be critical elements in both product cost and plant siting. This will continue into the foreseeable future and can be expected to remain a major management problem. New approaches must be taken in resolving these new corporate problems that result, but analysis must be done early in the game without expecting a magical black box to solve the problems at the end of the stream. These regulations will not go away and, in fact, may intrude even more into the way business is conducted.

FRED C. HART, President, Fred C. Hart Associates, Inc., New York, New York

Cross Reference: *Business-Government Relations.*

EQUIPMENT REPLACEMENT. See Fixed-Asset Investment Analysis: The MAPI Formulas and Procedures.

EUROPEAN ECONOMIC COMMUNITY

The **European Economic Community,** informally called the Common Market, is an economic organization consisting originally of France, West Germany, Italy, Belgium, The Netherlands, and Luxembourg. It was established by treaty at Rome on March 25, 1957, and began operations on Jan. 1, 1958. Great Britain, Denmark, and Ireland joined as of Jan. 1, 1973. On January 1, 1981, Greece became the tenth member.

Member nations plan gradually to reduce and ultimately eliminate all barriers to trade among them, and to adopt common tariffs on goods imported from the rest of the world. In addition to integrating economies, the objective is to develop political affinity.

Functioning. The EEC creates a free trade area such as exists among states in the United States. Before its establishment, duties were imposed on 30,000 commodities traded among member nations. The Common Market calls for the free flow of investment capital, industries, and workers from one member to another.

After the formation of the EEC, several other nations entered into various types of association agreements with the Common Market. Greece and Turkey signed agreements providing for imports to the EEC on the same terms as EEC imports within the Common Market. The treaty admitting Greece was negotiated in 1981. Spain and Portugal have also applied for membership, but are not expected to join until the late 1980s.

Several agreements between developing nations and the EEC (principally the Arusha and the Yaoundé) were superseded by the Lomé pact of 1975 between EEC and 46 developing nations of Africa, the Caribbean and the Pacific, by which these countries were exempted from EEC tariffs, and ACP countries were required to give most-favored-nation treatment to the EEC.

The establishment of common EEC tariffs, together with the rapid economic growth of the EEC Community market, materially affected U.S. investment patterns. Many U.S. businesses, anxious to sell in the EEC, but wishing to avoid the tariff wall, established subsidiaries in EEC countries. This has a detrimental effect on the U.S. balance of payments, but tends to promote U.S. control over European business, including economic slowdown or inflation.

The expansion of the EEC in 1973 made the organization a most imposing economic power. In 1975 its production and exports totalled $1,349 billion compared with that of the U.S. of $1,513 billion and the USSR's $760 billion. Its economic growth has been very rapid during the early 1970s, although economic and monetary crises and rampant inflation curtailed this growth and have given rise to many problems and frictions. These were influenced and accelerated by energy shortages and costs.

Originally the EEC, the European Coal and Steel Community, and the European Atomic Energy Community each had its own Council of Ministers and a Commission. Since 1967 the three communities have shared a single Commission and a single Council of Ministers. The Commission is the principal executive body, and its fourteen members are appointed by agreement between the EEC governments. The European Parliament is consulted about important actions of the Commission and the Council, but lacks direct control over the executive functions. Since 1976 the Parliament consists of 410 representatives elected by the ten member nations. In July 1979, the Parliament elected a woman, Simone Veil of France, as its President.

In 1977 the EEC adopted a Four-Year Plan aimed at full employment and cutting inflation through more adequate investments, restrained wage increases, and a boosting of worker participation in decision making. In July 1977, EEC became a "free-trade" area, in that customs duties on industrial goods traded between the EEC member countries ended, although agricultural and other barriers still exist. In 1978 EEC unveiled its Five-Year Plan for monetary and economic union. The EEC is the world's largest trader and the major importer from developing countries.

Cross References: *European Free Trade Association; International Management: Management of the "World Enterprise."*

EUROPEAN FREE TRADE ASSOCIATION

The **European Free Trade Association (EFTA),** is an economic organization somewhat similar to the EUROPEAN ECONOMIC COMMUNITY. It originated in 1959, when seven of the nations unwilling to participate in the EEC, established the European Free Trade Association, with its own free-trade area but without common outside tariffs.

EFTA began operation in 1960 with Britain, Sweden, Norway, Denmark, Switzerland, Austria, and Portugal as members. Finland became an associate in 1961 and Iceland became a full member in 1970. Liechtenstein is represented by Switzerland in EFTA.

Unlike the EEC, the EFTA sets up no common tariff against non-member nations. It is strictly an economic organization with no plans for political integration. EFTA is designed to promote trade among members in industrial, agricultural, and marine products. It eliminated tariffs and quota restrictions on industrial goods by the end of 1966. Trade in agricultural products remains restricted, but a number of bilateral agricultural agreements have been negotiated. Internal trade was regulated by the Stockholm Convention, which established EFTA.

Although trade among members of EFTA, especially among the Scandinavian countries, expanded considerably during the first years of its existence, it became clear that the organization could not compete with the increasingly powerful European Economic Community. Two members, Britain and Denmark, left EFTA and joined EEC.

Treaties between EEC and EFTA provide for a wide industrial free-trade area in Europe. Under the provisions of the agreements, tariffs between the EFTA countries and the EEC countries were eliminated between the years 1973 and 1977. This stimulated trade increases of significant proportions.

A seven-member council made up of one delegate from each country administers EFTA. The council makes decisions for the entire Association and enforces EFTA's constitution. Each member is chairman of the council for six months. The association's headquarters are located in Geneva, Switzerland.

Cross References: *European Economic Community; International Management: Management of the "World Enterprise."*

EXECUTIVE APPRAISAL: Diagnostic Performance Appraisal

The following presentation illustrates an analytic, detailed approach to **appraising the performance and essential characteristics of a manager.** It does not involve scoring, or assignment of an index number or letter, although this can be done as a final summary conclusion. The objective here is to identify needs for improvement and special strengths, and to plan individualized development programs. This approach can be used by the appraisee's superior alone, or by several appraisers in conference discussions.

There are four parts to this method:

Part I—Appraisal in terms of *Technical Competence*

Part II—Appraisal in terms of *Operational Competence*

Part III—Appraisal in terms of *Judgmental Competence*

Part IV—A *Summary and Projection*

Part I—Technical Competence. Technical competence, for these purposes, is defined as the sum of the knowledge acquired from formal education, practical experience, specialized training, self-teaching, and other learning processes which provides a manager with the "know-how" required in carrying on the activities involved in his position.

The first step in appraising a man's technical competence, as defined above, is to determine or define the management activities required by the position in question. Exhibit I shows the first part of an Appraisal Form on which are to be listed the various activities applicable to the position involved. So long as position content or scope remains unchanged, the selected activities can be used for all future appraisals of incumbents of the position.

The selected activities applicable to the position are to be entered as shown. In Column A will be entered a number indicative of the minimum degree or amount of detailed "know-how" required for the successful discharge of the position. The degrees are as follows:

(1) Expert and detailed specialized knowledge in the specific area.

(2) General knowledge of principles, terminology, practices, and/or procedures.

(3) Sufficient familiarity with the activities involved to enable incumbent to cooperate with specialists in the area in order to discharge the incumbent's own duties effectively.

(4) Sufficient familiarity with the area involved to direct, control, or coordinate the work of specialists in that area with the work of those in other areas.

Column B provides for an evaluation of the individual's technical competence as compared with the degree of competence required for the

EXHIBIT I

TECHNICAL COMPETENCE APPRAISAL FORM

*Code**	*Applicable Management Activities Description*	*A Job*	*B Man*
10.B.2	Establish policies and procedures		
11.B.11	Determine personnel requirements		
11.C.1	Establish objectives for organizational components administered		
11.C.4	Make forecasts and budgets etc.		

* A checklist of Management Activities may be used for reference, in which case each item should be preceded by its Code designation.

job in question. If his current or past performance with respect to duties in any area indicates that he has the degree of competence indicated by the number entered for that area in Column A, a check mark (✓) will be entered in Column B. If the individual has more than the degree indicated, a plus sign (+) will be entered in Column B. If, however, the individual's performance indicates any deficiency in technical competence in that area, *as compared to the job requirements,* a minus sign (−) will be entered in Column B. Should the individual's technical competence in any area be unknown, or should there be an appreciable degree of uncertainty concerning his competence, a question mark (?) will be entered in Column B.

All minus signs signal the need for analysis and all practical and immediate remedial actions when applicable to performance in the current position. When applicable to appraisals for purposes of transfer or promotion, they are indicative of the need for developmental activity perferably prior to but, in any case, at the earliest possible date after a transfer or promotion is made.

Plus signs can have many varied meanings and are to be interpreted in the light of each individual man-job situation. Among the various interpretations are: the job is not calling on a man's full technical competence: the man has progressed to a position in which his technical competence is no longer so important as competence in different fields; the man may be a likely candidate either for promotion or greater responsibility in his present position; etc. In the case of questioned entries indicating uncertainty as to competence, the uncertainty can usually be resolved by an exploratory interview or examination given by a person who is more expert in that area, preferably at a higher organization level.

It is essential to remember that within the limits of an individual's mental and physical capacity, technical competence is fully acquirable. In any individual case, however, there may be many situations where the acquiring process will present many practical difficulties.

Part II—Operational Competence. Operational competence, for these purposes, is defined as the sum of the characteristics of an individual which, given adequate technical competence and the required mental and physical capacity, enable him to *do* the various things and take the many actions necessary to carrying out his duties with better than average effectiveness. The ability to do any one of these things well usually results from a combination of many complex traits and characteristics. Since no one has yet been able to isolate these traits to determine their respective contributions to success in any one or any group of operational duties, or to measure satisfactorily how much of any trait any individual may have, we must use a less scientific but yet satisfactorily systematic approach.

Exhibit II shows Part II of the Appraisal Form. On it are brought together a partial list of the things that have to be done by most administrative, executive, or professional workers. Recognizing that a fully comprehensive list could not be held to a workable length, only the most common duties are listed. Space is provided for listing the less common duties that may apply in any special job situation.

The first step in this part of the appraisal is to rate the importance of each duty to the specific position. Opposite each listed or written-in duty, a number is to be placed in Column C which will indicate that duty's importance to the successful performance of the position, on the basis of the following scale:

EXHIBIT II

OPERATIONAL COMPETENCE APPRAISAL FORM

Duty List	*C* *Job*	*D* *Man*
1. Communicate by word of mouth to individuals inside the organization.		
2. Communicate by word of mouth to individuals outside the organization.		
3. Communicate in writing to individuals inside the organization.		
4. Communicate in writing to individuals outside the organization.		
5. Lead conferences to give out information.		
6. Lead conferences to get participation in group action or thinking.		
7. Lead conferences to get information.		
8. Take part in conferences aimed at securing group thinking or action, or at information gathering.		
9. See that subordinates receive and understand essential information.		
10. See that superior is informed of appropriate matters.		
11. etc.		
12.		

EXHIBIT III

JUDGMENTAL COMPETENCE APPRAISAL FORM

Characteristics	*E Job*	*F Man*
1. A keen sense of profitability: knowledge of what makes or will make for profitable operations and how to obtain them— a. Currently b. In the future.		
2. Ability to master the details of a business situation easily, then plan, organize, delegate and/or control so that he can concentrate on only the most important phases of the situation while remaining alert to and aware of other situations.		
3. Willingness and ability to weigh problem situations, decisions, and actions on the basis of the over-all viewpoint rather than solely that of his own position, function, self-interest or specialized background.		
4. Requires a minimum of direction and supervision; given the end results desired and told "why," seldom asks or must be told "how;" proceeds soundly and effectively on his own.		
5. Accepts and reaches for responsibility; refuses to stay within a comfortable "safety zone" within his assignment, but at the same time recognizes and acts within established policy limits.		
6. Recognizes need for policy determination or change and strives for it with all the strength of his convictions.		
7. Is sound, logical and quick in reasoning and judgment; anticipates long- as well as short-range effects of decisions.		
8. Makes dependable generalizations; whenever possible or practical, makes certain that he has all available and importantly pertinent facts but is willing and able to make decisions based on sometimes incomplete or not fully reliable data.		

(1) Essential and critical to success in the position.

(2) Makes a substantial contribution to success in the position.

(3) Of minor importance to success in the position.

(4) Of little or no importance to success in the position.

When all of the duties have been rated for importance to success in the position, the appraiser should rate, by entry of the appropriate number in Column D, the ability of the individual *based on observation of actual performance* and in accordance with the following scale: (If unable to rate on the basis of observed actual performance the appraiser should leave that square temporarily blank.)

(1) Outstandingly strong in ability to do this.

(2) Has better than standard but not exceptional or outstanding strength in this field.

(3) Is at or below standard strength, but has some recognizable capacity in this area.

(4) Has little strength in or no capacity for this type of duty.

When the individual's capacities have been appraised on the basis of observation of actual performance, the appraiser should go back over the list and consider those duties for which no individual appraisal entries have been made. If he (she) believes he can make a reasonably sound assumption or deduction, even though he has no performance evidence, he should enter the appropriate number and put a circle around it. Note, however, that it is not required that every square be filled in; it is better that ability to perform a duty go unappraised than to create a false impression that might cause serious consequences for the individual, the company, or both.

Given technical competence and physical and mental capacity, ability to perform in these activities, where not present, can be partially acquired. Most people can be guided in improving their abilities if they are interested and motivated in doing so. However, different individuals have different limitations in each of these duty categories. This is the area in which matching the man to the job is at one time the most essential and the most difficult. It is also the area in which a sound and constructive superior-subordinate relationship is most important to effective improvement in performance.

Part III—Judgmental Competence. Judgmental competence, for these purposes, is defined as the capacity for learning and for critical observation as well as for implementing what has been learned and critically observed in such a way that decisions made and actions taken are, in the highest possible percentage of cases, the *right* decisions or actions *from the viewpoint of the company's best interests.* It is based to some extent on technical competence, but is not limited to or by what has been learned from formal education or business experience. It is used to some degree in nearly all activities involved in operational competence.

It is limited by both mental and physical capacities of the individual. These limits are both inherent and environmental, but marked improvement in judgmental competence, *per se,* is rarely if ever acquired through training or development activities of the individual or his mentors.

The above factors are brought together in Part III of the Appraisal Form, as shown in Exhibit III. The importance of the characteristics to the specific position, and the abilities of the individual, are rated respectively in Columns E and F, using the numerical scales given for Exhibit I.

Part IV—Summary and Projection. With the foregoing pages as "work sheets," Part IV of the Appraisal Form can be completed. This develops the final, over-all appraisal in the following terms:

SUMMARY AND PROJECTION

A. Does the manager's education or recent experience indicate the possession of strong or outstanding technical competence in activities not required in his present position? If so, name them.
B. In the light of foreseeable promotional or position expansion possibilities, what types of technical competence need to be acquired or strengthened and how may this be done?
C. What practical steps can be taken by the Company and the executive to strengthen fields of operational competence required either by his or her present position or by foreseeable future positions:
   a. through supervisory guidance and counsel?
   b. through other means (name suggested method)?
D. Are there any items of either operational or judgmental competence in connection with which the incumbent has not had sufficient recent opportunity to prove his or her capacity, and which are or may be an essential or significantly important element in a future assignment? If so, name such items. (Note: Relatively reliable testing and interviewing techniques can be made available to determine the individual's capacities in many of these areas.)
E. What practical plans or programs can be established to provide an opportunity for the individual to demonstrate his (her) operational or judgmental competence in the above items?
F. Agreed upon program of action, with scheduled dates for interim or final accomplishment.

Remarks. The foregoing approach to the appraisal of executive personnel demands much care and the exercise of sound, objective judgment for best results. It has value in direct proportion to the thoroughness of the analyses of the demands of the job and the qualifications of the executive. Having been done once, however, a follow-up review can be accomplished more quickly. Even such review must, however, be as conscientious as the original analysis.

The listing of items and the analysis of their importance to the job can be initiated by the executive appraisee. He (she) may also find it worthwhile to appraise himself and his performance. His self-ratings can then be compared with the analytic observation of his superior. Objectivity on the part of both appraiser and appraisee is a *sine qua non.* Since a company's performance is dependent upon good executive performance, the time required from management for an occasional objective diagnosis by methods such as those outlined above is time well spent.

THEOS A. LANGLIE, Industrial Psychologist, Southbury, Connecticut

Information References

Heyel, Carl, "Appraising Executive Performance," New York, American Management Association, 1958.

Johnson, Robert G., "The Appraisal Interview Guide," New York, Amacom Div., American Management Associations, 1979.

Kellogg, Marion S., "When Man and Manager Talk . . . A Casebook," Houston, Tex., Gulf, 1969.

——— "Supervisory Appraisal," Ch. 6, Sec. 8, in Heyel, Carl, ed., "Handbook of Modern Office Management and Administrative Services," Huntington, N.Y., Krieger, repr. 1980.

Cross References: *Assessment Centers; Executive Development: Selection Guide; Executive Traits.*

EXECUTIVE COMPENSATION

Some time ago, it was quite acceptable—and even considered good form—to pay an individual only a salary. Gradually, however, pay began to take on added dimensions, to become a package rather than a single entity. In today's complex business world, we find this trend most marked in the way executives—a company's upper-middle and top managers—are paid. The elements which collectively comprise the **Executive Compensation** package of these individuals include: base salary, incentives for short-term performance, incentives for longer-term performance, perquisites, and fringe benefits.

This entry discusses all of these compensation elements except fringe benefits. (The latter, being offered to all of a company's employees, are not a form of executive compensation *per se*; see EMPLOYEE BENEFIT PLANS.)

BASE SALARY

The salary an executive receives is influenced by at least seven major factors:

Type of Responsibilities. Here are considered the skills and experience necessary to do the job, and the types of output desired.

Level Within the Organization. The less the number of intervening management levels between the executive and the CEO, the higher is likely to be the salary.

Scope of Responsibilities. Two company CEOs may have the same type of responsibilities, and both occupy the same level within the organization. But the one with the greater sales volume to manage is apt to receive the higher salary. Sales volume, profits, assets, number of employees and other similar factors measure the scope of the executive's job. Many correlation studies show that about 40% to 50% of the variance in executive salary levels can be accounted for by differences in position scope.

Type of Industry. Differences in pay among various industries, while once pronounced, are gradually eroding as talented executives from one industry move to another. It is more often the case today that pay differences cut across industry lines, being associated more with company performance, management challenge, and governmental regulation. Thus, high-performing companies in two different industries may pay more like each other than high-performing and low-performing companies in the same industry. And running a highly diversified, multinational company generally involves more challenge than running a company engaged in a single industry servicing only United States customers. Finally, heavy government regulation has a dampening effect on executive pay, as witnessed by the pay levels in most power utilities.

Presence of Incentives. Companies with executives bonus plans tend to pay lower base salaries than those without such plans, but the combination of base salary and bonus in the bonus-paying companies almost always exceeds the lone salary paid by the other companies.

Supply/Demand Factors. In many ways, the "career executive" is becoming a contradiction in terms. Executive talent is essentially a free market commodity, and its price therefore varies according to the classic laws of supply and demand. For example, marketing executives were typically paid more than production and financial executives during the Depression, since an ability to move goods in a ravaged economy was highly prized. During World War II and the early 50s, however, it was the production man who was the highest paid, reflecting the fact that a company could sell virtually anything if it could only make it. Today, we see the financial man emerging as the compensation "star," owing to the stress being placed on capable asset management, and in controlling diversified, decentralized global enterprises.

Performance. The outstanding executive is apt to receive more than the mediocre one, but this is not always the case, since base salaries go up but hardly ever down, and therefore most managements see that they don't go up very fast. It is hard to reward performance properly when the compensation device being utilized contains a good deal of inertia.

INCENTIVES FOR SHORT-TERM PERFORMANCE

Because of the problem mentioned in connection with performance, the great majority of companies offer their executive personnel an opportunity to earn extra money based on the performance of the company, the unit in which the executive is employed, his personal performance—or all three factors.

Eligibility and Size of Awards. Eligibility for participation in executive bonus plans is typically limited to about the top 1% to 2% of total employment, depending on company size and type of industry. Awards range from zero all the way up to 300% of salary, although it is more common to "cap" bonuses at 100% of the base salary. There is a distinct tendency for bonuses, expressed as a percentage of salary, to rise as the salary level rises. Thus, the average bonus for an individual earning $50,000 per year is around 20% of salary, but the comparable figure for one earning $150,000 per year is about 50% of salary.

There are two reasons for this trend, but one is no longer markedly valid. The first involves risk vs. reward. By discounting a senior executive's total cash compensation opportunity by a higher percentage than is utilized for a less senior executive, the former ends up with a lower base salary in relation to his/her total cash compensation opportunity than the latter. Hence, if the company performs poorly, the senior executive will experience relatively more pain than the less senior one. But fair is fair: if the company performs brilliantly, the former will also experience more joy.

The second reason involves taxes. When a tax structure is steeply progressive, it is necessary to give a more senior executive a larger bonus percentage if his/her *after-tax* total compensation is to exhibit the same percentage increase as is the case for a less senior executive. Today, however, the United States tax structure is not very "progressive." Maximum marginal tax rates on salaries and bonuses, which once ranged as high as 91%, have remained at 50% for about the past ten years. Given inflation, this means that almost anyone worthy of being called an executive will be at the same marginal tax rate as the CEO. Hence, the tax argument for differential bonus percentages is now moot. But since the risk vs. reward argument is not, the pattern of accelerating bonus percentages will likely continue.

Funding Formula. The funds required for bonus purposes are sometimes voted by the board of directors on an *ad hoc* basis, but more often, they are generated by a specially designed formula which is applied to the company's income statement and balance sheet. Although numerous formulas are used, a typical one would be as follows:

> 5% of pre-tax profits which are in excess of an amount equal to a 14% return on stockholders' equity but are less than a 21% return; plus 10% of pre-tax profits which are in excess of an amount equal to a 21% return on stockholders' equity.

This formula has several major features:

Performance Parameter. It rewards, not for raw profits per se, but for an increasing return on the stockholders' investment. Thus, it "incents" the company's executives to give the stockholders a better return than they could receive from alternative sources.

Elimination of Tax Effect. It is based on pre-tax, rather than after-tax, earnings, since changes in Federal income tax rates are essentially beyond the control of the company's executives.

As of 1980, a number of companies were beginning to have second thoughts regarding the non-controllability of income taxes. First, an executive faced with the need to build a new plant or other facility can elect to switch operations to another state with a lower tax rate, or even to another country. Second, the U.S. Government is itself in the incentive compensation business. Among other things, it offers companies a tax credit for making new investments. Finally, even though an executive may not be able to counter the effects of a tax increase, he/she can adopt other strategies (raising prices, cutting costs) to deliver the same bottom-line result to the shareholders. Because of these factors, the majority of newly adopted bonus plans are geared to rewarding after-tax, not pre-tax, profits.

Deductible. It reserves all of the first portion of company profits for the stockholders. In our example, incentive funds are created only when the return on stockholders' equity is at least 14%.

Accelerator. It recognizes that it is harder to move from above average to outstanding performance than it is from mediocre to average performance. Thus, the executives get 5% of the middle slice of corporate profits, but 10% of the top slice.

Allocating the Bonus Fund. Having created an over-all incentive fund, the company must then decide how it should be apportioned among the executive group. Here, several methods are available. If the company is divisionalized, chunks of the over-all fund may be distributed to each division based on its particular performance achievements for the year. That approach may certainly motivate individual division performance, but it may also unwittingly create a certain divisiveness among the various division managers—especially when it comes to allocating scarce capital resources and to transferring good people. As a result, many companies will distribute most, but not all, of the fund based on divisional performance, and will distribute the remainder based on over-all corporate performance. In this manner, division general managers are given an incentive, admittedly often symbolic, to play ball on the corporate team to the extent required.

In distributing its own fund, a division in turn may employ one of three methods. It may apportion all awards pro rata to salary, it may distribute awards based solely on individual executive performance, or it may utilize a combination of these approaches. The first method obviously encourages a maximum degree of teamwork, but it certainly gives no incentive for individual excellence. The second method does that, but it may possibly squire a group of "prima donnas" as well. The combination approach, on the other hand, seeks to achieve the best of both worlds: some team work and a large amount of individual initiative.

Payment Methods and Media. Awards, once decided upon, are typically paid in cash and in a lump sum shortly after the close of the fiscal year on which they are predicated. Sometimes negotiable company stock is used, or a combination of cash and stock, with perhaps enough cash to pay the taxes on the entire award. Other companies employ forcible deferrals, where, for example, the award is paid out in five annual installments, with the individual forfeiting any subsequent installments if he voluntarily resigns.

This approach is supposedly justified on the grounds that it will hold down the executive's tax payment and will also help to retain good executives. In fact, it is likely to do neither. With lower marginal income tax rates and an income-averaging provision built into the tax law, there is little advantage in spreading bonus payments over a series of years. And from a motivational standpoint, forced deferrals—derisively called the "golden handcuffs" approach by many executives—are uniformly resented. If they hold anyone, they are likely to hold a company's mediocrity, since the best performers can be bought off by a competitor. Indeed, this is unwittingly made easier, as the following example illustrates, since the executive's cash flow income under a stream of deferred compensation payment is often less than his purported income:

> Assume that the executive has a base salary of $40,000, and that the company awards him a $20,000 bonus. His nominal compensation for that year is therefore $60,000, but under the "golden handcuffs" approach, with the bonus spread over five years, his cash flow in the first year of his eligibility for a bonus award is actually only $44,000. Assume that he receives another $20,000 bonus the next year and continues with a salary of $40,000. His cash flow compensation increases to $48,000, since he is receiving one installment from each of two bonuses. Obviously, it is not until five years have passed that he actually receives $60,000. During the sensitive build-up period, he is therefore more vulnerable to a competitor who says, "Come with me, and I'll give you $60,000 [or probably more] all at once."

Still other companies offer optional, as opposed to forced, deferrals. The executive can take his award in cash, or he can defer any part or all of it. He can choose the length of the deferral period, the number of years over which the award will be paid, the types of securities in which it will be invested, and even the disposition of dividends and interest. Although there is relatively little tax advantage in deferred compensation payments, there is some motivational appeal in giving each executive what he wants, when he wants it.

Incentives for Longer-Term Performance

Not too long ago, the results of most executive decisions were realized in the very same year in which the decisions were made. Now however, technological complexity has created a situation where the results of major decisions are often not known for many years. To illustrate, an oil company may decide to build a giant petrochemical facility, whose cost will be $500 million. Just designing the plant may take one or two years; three or four years more may be required for it to be built. And perhaps a one- or two-year period is needed to break in the plant and bring it up to peak efficiency.

All told, five to eight years will thus have elapsed between the time the decision to build the petrochemical complex was made and the time that the profit results of that decision could be judged. Meanwhile, the company incurred significant costs for engineering talent, interest charges on $500 million of debt, and so on. During that period, its profits would have been increased had it not decided to build the facility. And if its profits had been increased, the incentive bonuses payable to its executives for short-term performance would also have increased. Yet not to build the facility might have meant parlous times for the company five years later.

Thus, incentives to maximize the current years' profits, although satisfactory as far as they go, do not go far enough in motivating optimum business behavior. What are needed are *additional* incentives for performance, not in a single year, but over the longer term. Once monolithic in their design (all companies used to employ the qualified stock option, a device that has now been killed by Congress), long-term incentives today fall into a number of categories, as indicated below.

Plans Based on Increasing the Market Price of the Stock. The plan of choice in this category is the *non-qualified stock option.* Although the plan designer can call for any option price he/she likes and any length of exercise period, it is almost always the case that the option price will be equal to 100% of the fair market value (FMV) of the stock on the date of the grant, and that the option will have a term of ten years. The underlying theory here is that if the company does well over a series of years, its performance will be reflected in a higher stock price, thereby creating a "spread" between the option price and the FMV at exercise. From a tax standpoint, the executive incurs no tax until exercise takes place, and then the "spread" is taxed at personal service income rates (maximum of 50%).

Should the executive hold the stock past exercise, any further gain or loss between the date of exercise and the date of eventual sale is treated as a capital gain or loss. For its part, the company is granted a tax deduction in the year of exercise and for an amount equal to the option "spread." What is more, if the company follows the plan design discussed above, it need not charge its earnings with the option "spread." However, this does not mean there is no cost to an option, as some believe. Rather, the cost is buried in the balance sheet and is not so visible as would be the cost of a comparable amount of cash.

Options create problems for corporate officers, however. Being subject to the "insider trading" provisions of the Securities Exchange Act, these executives are effectively barred from selling their option stock for six months. As a result, they are saddled with interest costs to carry stock purchase loans and, worse, should the stock decline during the six-month holding period, they can end up receiving no gain but still paying the taxes attributable to the gain on exercise.

Because of these problems, many companies have added so-called *stock appreciation rights* (SARs) to their option arrangements. Under current SEC rules, a company can, under certain circumstances, permit the executive to receive a cash payment equal to his/her option "spread" in lieu of exercising the option itself. This cash payment would not be considered to be in violation of SEC "buy-sell" provisions. But it would have to be charged to earnings, which is why SARs are typically extended only to the most senior executives (Assuming the option shares are registered and that there is no formal or informal pressure applied to hold shares past exercise, a non-insider can create his/her own "do-it-yourself SAR" simply by selling the shares as soon as they are exercised. The individual gains the same cash payment as the insider, but the company is not forced to take a charge to its earnings.)

Plans Based on Internal Performance Measurements. While one cannot deny the validity of the argument that excellent corporate performance will, sooner or later, be validatd by an increasing FMV (else the stock would eventually sell for less than its earnings per share!), the stock market, at least at this writing, seems bent on proving the proposition that the FMV will rise later, and never sooner.

The fact is that one major component of the FMV—the price/earnings multiple—is simply outside the control of any executive. To be sure, a well-aimed PR campaign might have some effect on the P/E multiple, but the effect will be transitory. It is sad but true that the Chairman of the Federal Reserve and, indeed, the Chairman of the Soviet Union can have more effect on the P/E multiple of a given company's stock that that company's own chairman. Because of this, some companies have eliminated the FMV incentive in their long-term incentive programs and have instead geared payouts to *long-term corporate performance achievements.* Thus, one company might offer its executives a large bonus opportunity for achieving, say, a 15% compounded annual increase in earnings per share (EPS) over a five-year period. Or another company might offer the same payout for delivering, say, a 20% average return on equity over the same period. In either event, the executive is being rewarded for performance that is truly in the shareholders' interest and that is more under his/her control. Plans for this type are generally called "performance unit" plans.

Combination Plans. Although few companies have seen fit to remove entirely the FMV component in their long-term incentive plans, and to move to pure performance unit plans, a large and growing number of companies have decided to adopt a *combination plan,* whereby an executive receives a lesser number of option shares than was the case in the past, together with a number of performance units. In this manner, the executive is being simultaneously "incented" to deliver excellent long-term internal performance and to do what he/she can to raise the FMV.

Other Plans. In a few companies, the executive is granted the same number of option shares as he or she would be granted were the company to employ only options. Then the executive is also granted the same number of performance units as would be granted were the company to employ only performance units. At the end of the performance period, usually four or five years, the executive is then permitted to take whichever of the incentive devices—the options or the units—has the most economic benefit. The device not chosen is then cancelled.

Under such a plan, the executive really ends up with the best of both worlds. If the company performs brilliantly, but the P/E multiple has sagged, the executive ends up with the same economic benefit as he/she would have received from a company offering only performance units. And if the company performs in only a mediocre manner but the P/E multiple unaccountably rises, the executive ends up with the same economic benefit as he or she would have received from a company offering only stock options. Small wonder that executives love this sort of plan. Equally small wonder that informed shareholders do not.

In some other companies, although happily not too many, the executive is given free shares of stock. The shares carry restrictions such that they cannot be sold for, say, five years. During the five-year period, the executive receives dividends and may vote the shares. However, if he or she quits before the restrictions lapse, the shares are forfeited back to the company.

To gain an economic benefit under a performance unit plan, the executive must deliver solid, long-term performance achievements. To gain an economic benefit under an option plan, the FMV of the stock must rise. But to gain an economic benefit under the plan we are now discussing, the executive need only breathe in and out aproximately seventeen times a minute for five years and exhibit a positive pupil reflex. After all, if the executive remains with the company, the only way he or she can gain nothing under the plan is if the FMV plummets to zero—an event that makes any long-term incentive plan an academic matter.

Eligibility. If there are few people in an organization who have a significant impact on annual operating results, there are even fewer who impact long-term results. Hence, eligibility for long-term incentive plans is typically more restrictive than that for annual bonus plans. However, companies employing stock options tend to be more liberal than those employing performance unit plans. The reason, of course, lies in the earlier discussed fact that most stock option plans do not carry a charge to the earnings.

Frequency of Awards. Most companies follow the practice of making annual long-term incentive grants. Thus, in 1981, an executive will receive a contingent grant based on performance to be delivered during 1982 through 1985. And in 1982, he or she will receive another contingent grant based on performance to be delivered during 1983 through 1986.

Size of Awards. Perhaps reflecting the necessity to look more to the long-term than the short-term, many companies now offer their senior executives more in the way of long-term incentive opportunity than they do in annual bonus opportunity. Among the larger companies, it is not at all uncommon to find that the annualized value of long-term incentive opportunities significantly exceeds 100% of the base salary. Thus, if the company's performance is excellent over a series of years, the executive will receive more of his total compensation through long-term incentive payments than through any other medium.

PERQUISITES

Lastly, we come to a rather shadowy group of compensation elements, which, taken together, are called perquisites. These include such things as: lavishly furnished offices; company cars; chauffeured limousines; luncheon club memberships; country club memberships; corporate jets; extra medical insurance coverage; extra life insurance coverage; enhanced pensions; and personal financial counseling. Perquisites, such as these, are typically offered for one or both of the following reasons:

Status. Any item, whether of high value or virtually no value, that is given to those generally perceived to be high-ranking and that is not given to those generally perceived to be of lesser rank carries instant status implications. Increasingly, companies are discovering, as armies have known for millenia, that the need for status is never dead, no matter how ostensibly democratic is the sociey. Executives are often apt to denigrate the value of status symbols ("It's what's in the little old paycheck that counts"), but if actions speak louder than words, they crave them deeply.

Tax Considerations. Many perquisites can be offered to the executive on a wholly or at least partially tax-free basis. This is one reason why perquisites are rampant in countries such as England, where the maximum marginal tax rates border on the confiscatory. It should be noted, however, that the Internal Revenue Service is taking an increasingly stringent view towards perquisites, and most are therefore short-lived from the standpoint of producing any significant tax advantage. And in any event, perquisites constitute a very small fraction of the executives's *total* compensation package.

Summary

The executive compensation package in progressive companies has grown very complex, owing to convoluted tax laws and a rapidly changing, highly technological business environment. In addition to salary, the executive is apt to receive an incentive to produce optimal results in the current year and another incentive to produce optimal results over a period of years combined. He/she is also likely to receive one or more perquisites. If properly designed, these compensation arrangements will motivate the executive to produce results that are directly beneficial to the company's stockholders. And that, after all, is the acid test of any viable executive compensation program.

Graef S. Crystal, Vice President, Towers, Perrin, Forster & Crosby, Inc., New York, New York

Information References

Crystal, Graef S., "Executive Compensation: Money, Motivation, Imagination," 2nd. ed., New York, American Management Associations, 1978.
Executive Compensation Service, New York, American Management Association.
"Executive Compensation and Tax Coordinator," New York, Research Institute of America, Inc.
Washington, George T. and Rothschild, V.H., "Compensating the Corporate Executive," 4th ed., New York, Ronald, 1981.

Cross Reference: *Retirement Plans.*

EXECUTIVE DEVELOPMENT: "Away-from-Company" Programs

A significant aspect of business education is the great interest in programs for the development of experienced managers for greater responsibilities. The MIT Executive Development Program initiated at the Massachusetts Institute of Technology by Professor Erwin H. Schell in 1931 was the forerunner of the present activity in developing mature executives in especially designed, intensive courses given away from the job.

These courses are given by academic institutions, management associations and societies, consultants, and small and large private organizations formed not for consulting but solely for the offering of executive development programs. Courses today range from one-day seminars costing several hundred dollars to the twelve-months MIT Alfred P. Sloan Fellows program leading to the Master of Science in Management degree, for which tuition alone for the 1981–1982 year was $15,250.

Widespread participation developed shortly after World War II, and by the mid-1960s there were well over a hundred formally recognized executive development programs with away-from-company residence requirements. Attendance at programs of all types continued to increase until the business recession of the early 1970s. During that slowdown, attendance slipped sharply, and many one-, two-, and three-day seminars were cancelled for lack of registration. Some of the seminar companies went out of business, and some of the sponsoring groups showed heavy losses. But as of this writing there has been a significant resurgence, and James L. Hayes, president of American Management Associations, has estimated that as of 1980 some 500,000 American managers a year take a formal management-education course [1]. AMA alone, as indicated below, enrolls some 100,000 managers a year, up from 60,000 in the early 1970s. The University of Pennsylvania's Wharton School has reported [1] that enrollment in short courses for executives as of 1980 rose to 7,800 a year, six times the figure of six years earlier, and six times the 1980 enrollment of full-time MBA candidates.

Definition. The American Management Associations has made the following distinctions: *Course*—an integrated but broad educational program, usually lasting more than two weeks (either on consecutive days, or as a series of sessions spread over a longer time), limited in enrollment, and utilizing a coordinated staff for instruction; *Seminar*—an intensive discussion meeting oriented around a single topic lasting from a few days to a few weeks, limited in enrollment, and usually guided by discussion leaders rather than instructors or lecturers; *Conference*—a meeting with a large number in attendance, usually lasting longer than a week, with papers or formal addresses on a variety of topics; *Class*—a series of meetings on a single topic, usually held in the evenings over several weeks, for people in the immediate locality.

The remainder of the present discussion is confined to *courses,* as defined above, and does not consider the briefer seminars, conferences, and classes. Also, the management-development programs here discussed do not, by definition, include those designed to give training in specialized skills or techniques. Rather, they cover those directed to *conceptual* skills, for managers as "generalists." And they do not include on-location development programs (for which see MANAGEMENT DEVELOPMENT TECHNIQUES).

Background. The need for this broader training for mature, seasoned men who have already attained positions of responsibility in specific functional areas is attributable to the greater spectrum of managerial skills demanded by the growing size and scope of industrial activity, the rise of unions, the growing interest in a scientific approach toward business problems, the increasing pressures from government and international competition, and the emergence of conglomerate and worldwide enterprises. Additionally, greater emphasis on human relations—the satisfaction of human needs and motivations—and on the need for social awareness demands more from the high-ranking manager today than formerly: it calls for the *professional* manager.

In the post-war era, leaders in industry and in the universities, recognizing these increased demands, came to see the need for some formal approach, either in a "return to the campus" movement, or in intensified post-graduate work. Initial steps were taken by the Harvard Business School, with its Advanced Management and Middle Management programs, inaugurated in 1943, and by Columbia University, with its Executive Program in Business Administration, at Arden House in Harriman, New York. As of 1981, the latter is in its thirtieth year. Following these, many universities and colleges have instituted programs. Examination of the various offerings shows that they range from one week up to one year, although about half are four to five weeks; they involve managers at all levels—some are structured for top management only, others for middle managers, and others for first levels of supervision. Some special programs have been developed for governmental administration, notably by the Brookings Institution in Washington, D.C.

Several companies have set up their own in-company programs, patterned after the university types, but conducted solely for the company's own executives. They are included in this discussion of "away-from-company" programs, because they involve the establishment of separate facilities where the executive takes in-residence courses, in an academic-oriented environment.

University Programs. Space will not permit description of the university courses in detail, but some discussion of the leading programs for middle and higher management is given below, to provide an insight into this type of executive development.

Massachusetts Institute of Technology. The Alfred P. Sloan School of Management's *Sloan Fellows Program* comprises a twelve-month program of study designed for a limited number of able young executives whose past performance has been outstanding, and whose promise for the future, in the judgment of their corporate managements, can be enhanced by a full year of study of the fundamentals underlying sound management action. The full-year program affords the opportunity for a Master's degree. Participants are those who ". . . have the will to manage and to risk, who can deal with complete systems, who have insight into themselves as well as others, who understand the total environment in which they live, and who continue to learn."

Approximately 50 Sloan Fellows are selected each year. Typically they are in mid-career with some ten to fifteen years of successful experience behind them and expectably many years of significant contributions to their organizations ahead of them. Nominations are welcomed from both large and small companies, and from a variety of industrial, nonprofit, and government backgrounds. The program of study covers a wide range of subjects including marketing, finance, organizational psychology, and a wide variety of seminars. A highlight of each spring term is an "international management field trip" lasting three weeks. The Program fee (1981–1982) is $15,250. The sponsoring organization normally pays this fee, continues the Fellow's usual compensation, and provides some necessary extra living and moving costs. Books and other study materials cost about $800.

The MIT Program for Senior Executives is a twice-a-year nine-week, intensive interdisciplinary study of management and the economic, social, and technological environment of the organization. The program, which emphasizes new knowledge, current research, and future trends, is conducted by the faculty of the Sloan School of Management and the Department of Economics. The format includes seminar discussions, lectures, and substantial reading assignments.

Participants are United States and international senior executives with substantial experience in decision making at the policy level, and responsibility for resources that affect the future of their companies or major segments of them. Fee for the program (1980 sessions) is $12,200, which includes tuition, all instructional materials, accommodations, all meals, and daily private-car transportation between Dedham and Cambridge. Spouses customarily join the participants for the last three days of the program.

Columbia. Each year over 1,600 executives participate in the 27 various executive programs offered by Columbia University. Participants represent more than 600 organizations and come from throughout the United States and over 65 foreign countries.

The *Executive Program in Business Administration,* the largest of the programs, has been offered annually since 1952. Twice a year, 80 men and women convene at Arden House—the Harriman, New York campus of the University—for six weeks of intensive work designed to equip them with the skills and knowledge to perform more effectively as top-level general managers.

There is no adherence to a single teaching approach or concept. Extensive use is made of case studies, but instructional methods include lectures, discussions, simulations, and work projects. Total cost for each six-week session is $6,750 (as of 1981), including tuition, all instructional materials, accommodations, meals, and gratuities.

Also offered is a four-weeks *Executive Program for International Managers,* at $5,000, and a two-weeks *Executive Program in Business Strategy,* at $2,800. A number of one-week programs at fees of under $2,000 cover such subjects as marketing, sales management, transportation management, marketing research, production and operations management, commercial bank management, and consumer credit management. While criteria vary for each program, most programs are targeted for senior and top-level managers.

Harvard. Harvard's Advanced Management Program, inaugurated in 1943, is the oldest of the senior development programs. It is aimed specifically at the concerns and responsibilities of top management. Offered three times a year, the duration of each program is thirteen weeks. (A split summer session is held beginning every even year.) Elective courses are offered during the later weeks of the program. Instruction relies primarily on the case method, based on class participation in the discussion of typical business situations. Participation is emphasized through small group discussions. Participants are mature executives, men and women with considerable management experience. A four-day program for spouses and their guests is scheduled the last week of the program. Tuition is $11,100 (1980), including room and meals except Saturday and Sunday dinners.

Also offered is a Program for Management Development, Inaugurated in 1960, given twice a year for a duration of fourteen weeks. Tuition is $9,575 (1980), including room and meals except for Saturday and Sunday dinners. Main areas of concern are implementation of organizational policy, decision making, marketing, and related subjects. Included is one week of short elective courses. The case method is heavily used, plus small-group exercises, lectures, and video presentations. A sophisticated business game is played. Included is a special program for spouses in the final three days.

A number of smaller programs are also offered, lasting from two to three weeks, plus one of nine weeks, covering business, government, and the international economy, financial management, corporate planning, computer resources, manufacturing strategy, and, in the case of the nine-week program, smaller-company management problems.

Company-Sponsored Residence Programs. The broad-gaged approach of large-scale company-sponsored programs situated in separate management centers is exemplified in its advanced form by the following program of *International Business Machines Corporation.*

IBM has had a residential, company-sponsored executive development program since 1956. This activity had been located at an IBM executive development facility in Sands Point, Long Island, for over twenty years, but recently was relocated within a new Management

Development Center in Armonk, New York. The company's development strategy calls for selected middle management and higher executive personnel to attend an alternating sequence of internal and out-company programs on a career-long basis. This sequence includes three internal, IBM-focused executive development activities, and four categories of external programs.

The internal programs include:

(1) The three-week *Advanced Management School* designed for high-potential middle managers. The curriculum focuses on the IBM Company, the managerial process, and the business environment.

(2) The one-week *Executive Seminar,* for higher-level executives, covers IBM's strategic issues as well as external economic, social, and political developments.

(3) The two-week *International Executive Program,* for senior United States and foreign-national IBM executives, concentrates on strategic international issues facing IBM.

The internal programs feature small classes (twenty persons) and a faculty composed of top IBM executives as well as selected outside speakers.

The out-company executive programs can be classified as follows:

(1) "General Management" programs, usually offered by graduate schools of business at major universities.

(2) "Leadership" programs, concentrating on interpersonal effectiveness at the executive level.

(3) "Public Affairs" programs, dealing with Federal Government operations and national policy issues.

(4) "Humanities" programs which provide courses of study on man, society, and values.

The above mix of internal and out-company programs has been designed to provide IBM executives with opportunities to hone skills, augment knowledge, enhance perspectives, and, it is hoped, increase effectiveness in carrying out their managerial responsibilities.

American Telephone and Telegraph Company. AT&T's *Bell Advanced Management Program (BAMP)* completed its fourth year in 1981. It provides a developmental experience for high-potential Bell System fourth- and fifth-level managers viewed by their companies as having officer-level potential. Two four-week programs, one in spring and one in fall, are conducted each year at the University of Illinois in Champaign/Urbana. The method of instruction includes lectures, case studies, and simulations that generate test conditions approximating operational conditions. The initial course design was determined from interviews with 23 Bell System officers, and continuing development is guided by a six-member officer-level steering committee chaired by a Bell company president.

The stated design of the program is to help the participants accomplish four objectives:

(1) The acquisition of relevant information concerning the current and anticipated major issues facing the business.

(2) The development of appropriate techniques and concepts for analyzing and understanding the impact of external forces on the business.

(3) The sharpening of strategic decision-making skills and the formulating of integrated responses.

(4) An increased awareness of the need for more flexible, risk-oriented approaches to the development and implementation of business strategies.

The current BAMP concept, contrasted with the earlier Bell System Humanities Program terminated in 1960 after running for seven years, typifies the swing in concept of executive development which has taken place. The Humanities Program was perhaps the broadest based of the individual-company programs for executive education in intellectual fields far removed from immediate operating problems.

The program was conducted for the Bell System by the University of Pennsylvania. Every year Bell companies sent two dozen young district and department managers, with their families, to the Penn campus for ten months of intensive study of art, music, literature, and philosophy. The objective, as reported by Wilford D. Gillen, then president of Bell Telephone Company of Pennsylvania which administered the program for the Bell System, was to assure the telephone companies of a supply of executives "with breadth and depth, with a broad knowledge of the world in which business exists and operates, and with an understanding of people and their motivations." To this end the participants covered such subjects as "the philosophy of ethics" and "practical logic." They read Freud and Huxley and Dante and Cervantes, Flaubert and Dostoyevsky and Camus and T.S. Eliot. They attended chamber music concerts and poetry readings, and heard guest lectures by behavioral scientists, economists, and journalists. Bell did not impute the 1960 termination to failure of the program, stating simply that it represented a changing phase in the continuing "experiment" of training [2].

Association Programs. By far the most active nonacademic institution in the field of management education is *American Management Associations.* Its conferences, seminars, and courses cover the whole range of functional and conceptual subjects of interest to executives. In its 58th year, fiscal 1980–1981, attendance at more than 4,000 AMA meetings totaled over 100,000. In addition, the Associations carries on extensive publishing activities in the form of periodicals, research reports, and hard-cover books on management.

Of interest in the present context is the AMA Management Course inaugurated in 1952. This consists of four one-week units of advanced study and practice in the principles, skills, and tools of management geared to the needs of participants who already have a considerable depth of management experience. This course, with a focus on problems of upper-level management, has been attended by more than 25,000 executives. Subjects included in the units are: *Unit I* - operational and strategic planning, organizing, controlling, decision making, and problem solving; *Unit II* - financial management; *Unit III* - human resources staffing, development, and management; self-development and management of stress; and time management; *Unit IV* - social, economic, and political issues; managing conflict and change; negotiating; and team building. Teaching aids include microcomputer-assisted business simulation, cases, projects, role playing, and in-basket exercises. (For specifics on such techniques see SUPERVISORY TRAINING.)

Units are offered throughout the year at the AMA headquarters in New York, and AMA locations in Chicago, Atlanta, San Francisco, Dallas, and Washington, D.C. As of 1981, the fee for the course is $2,100 for AMA members and $2,350 for non-members.

AMA also offers many other executive development courses, ranging from a management course for presidents to courses in the specific fields of marketing, production, personnel, EDP systems, R&D, purchasing, and international operations.

NTL Institute Programs in Sensitivity Training. The ST-Group (ST for sensitivity training), also termed the T-Group, is the central training unit in the "laboratory approach" to human relations training. Under this program, executives meet for one to three weeks with a staff team of behavioral scientists. While lectures and other structured activities are part of the laboratory training, the T-Group itself is unstructured, with no imposed agenda or leadership. This method of self-development is the outgrowth of the work in group dynamics pioneered by Kurt Lewin in the early 1930s. (For details on the concept and methodology, see the entries GROUP DYNAMICS and SENSITIVITY TRAINING.) Sessions are regularly held at Bethel, Maine, in the summer and the year 'round all over the country.

Acceptance. Executive development of the broad "conceptual" type has gone through the typical "new movement" curve over the past thirty years. At first, acceptance was slow, and major pioneering effort was made by some universities and individual companies, often at great expense. Then enthusiasm for the activity developed (as when something becomes "the fashion" to do), and courses of varying degrees of excellence proliferated. In the earlier years some companies, as already mentioned, developed elaborate programs, some of which concentrated entirely on the humanities with no direct relation to management. In the past decade, which witnessed a period of tightened business, many managements have taken a closer look at the expense of all development programs in terms of direct dollars-and-cents results in their companies' operations.

No conclusive method of evaluation has been found, and the results of this form of executive education must still rest largely on the intuitively accepted but not demonstrable premise that such broadening experience will reflect favorably in the executive's later job performance. Suspensions of programs by individual companies are not necessarily due to disenchantment with results. The situation may simply be that the turnover rate in higher-echelon positions is not large enough to justify programs on a continuing basis without recesses. The alternative would be to extend the programs increasingly to lower levels of managers, which would dip into areas where local and specific-technique training is still the basic need. And if broader education is desirable at these levels, managements can adopt a policy of all or partial defrayment of tuition expenses for educational opportunities, in the evenings or over weekends, at local universities and colleges.

CARL HEYEL, Management Counsel, Manhasset, N.Y.

References Cited

[1] "Back to School: More Executives Take Work-Related Courses to Keep Up, Advance," *The Wall Street Journal,* March 3, 1980.

[2] "No More Humanities for Brass," *Business Week,* June 8, 1960.

Cross References: *Executive Development: Selection Guide; Management Development Techniques; Management Games; Sensitivity Training.*

EXECUTIVE DEVELOPMENT: Selection Guide

In its discussion with managements concerning the use of its Advanced Management Course in **Executive Development Programs** the Society for Advancement of Management found that few companies had a standardized procedure for deciding just what sort of management training or development an executive needs. Despite the considerable expenditures involved, the majority of corporations apparently made selections for management training in an informal manner. The Society accordingly developed the Selection Chart for Management Development shown in Exhibit I. The chart and explanatory notes are based on the composite observations of hundreds of businessmen who have authorized, planned, conducted, attended, or appraised various kinds of management training and development programs.

For each person being considered, the superior, after consultation with others in a position to judge (but not with others on the person's own level), fills in the circle on the appropriate point on the scale in each column on the rating chart. The circles can then be connected by lines to form a "profile." The following key is to be used:

A—Management Level: This man is . . .

(1) A technical worker with no present management responsibility, but may have management potential.

(2) Supervisor or foreman/forelady.

(3) In middle management, supervising two or more people in level #2.

(4) In functional management, responsible for an entire department or plant, with at least two levels of management below him/her.

(5) In top or general management, with policy level responsibility reaching across several functions, departments, or plants. (For staff personnel not in line management positions, but serving or advising managers, S.A.M. suggests rating at the management level of the executive he or she advises or helps, or at one level below that.)

B—Motivation: The person under consideration . . .

(1) Goes through the motions adequately; is interested in making a living.

(2) Is willing to learn more than the present job, in hope of promotion.

(3) Consistently looks and works beyond the job; has strong motivation to advance.

(4) Has real loyalty to the company and a sense of teamwork, in addition to the #3 qualification.

(5) Shows a sense of responsibility to the community and the American way of life, in addition to #4 qualifications.

C—Potential: The person under consideration . . .

(1) Is probably at his/her ceiling now in salary and range of responsibility.

(2) May have added potential, but is currently held back by heath, family trouble, or other difficulty that may be straightened out later.

(3) Has probably one more promotion ahead: then will be near his or her limit.

(4) Has potential to move at least as far as department head or plant manager.

(5) Exhibits no apparent long-range limitations to his or her development.

D—Likelihood of Higher Opening: For this person . . .

(1) No opening is likely in the near future.

(2) No opening is likely inside of two years.

(3) No opening is apparent inside of one year.

(4) Could be promoted now, if he (she) had breadth of experience and viewpoint.

(5) Must assume heavier responsibility very soon, even though (we think) he (she) is not quite ready for it.

E—Degree of Specialization: This person . . .

(1) Has had experience in only a single function or department and has shown no disposition to look at or understand other functions.

EXHIBIT I

SELECTION CHART FOR MANAGEMENT DEVELOPMENT

Name & Job		A Management Level	B Motivation	C Potential	D Likelihood of Higher Opening	E Degree of Specialization	F Creative Ability	G Useful Years Available	CONCLUSIONS (Circle)
	5	o	o	o	o	o	o	o	NO
	4	o	o	o	o	o	o	o	INCO
	3	o	o	o	o	o	o	o	WAIT
	2	o	o	o	o	o	o	o	RES
	1	o	o	o	o	o	o	o	AMC
									(other)
	5	o	o	o	o	o	o	o	NO
	4	o	o	o	o	o	o	o	INCO
	3	o	o	o	o	o	o	o	WAIT
	2	o	o	o	o	o	o	o	RES
	1	o	o	o	o	o	o	o	AMC
									(other)
	5	o	o	o	o	o	o	o	NO
	4	o	o	o	o	o	o	o	INCO
	3	o	o	o	o	o	o	o	WAIT
	2	o	o	o	o	o	o	o	RES
	1	o	o	o	o	o	o	o	AMC
									(other)
	5	o	o	o	o	o	o	o	NO
	4	o	o	o	o	o	o	o	INCO
	3	o	o	o	o	o	o	o	WAIT
	2	o	o	o	o	o	o	o	RES
	1	o	o	o	o	o	o	o	AMC
									(other)
	5	o	o	o	o	o	o	o	NO
	4	o	o	o	o	o	o	o	INCO
	3	o	o	o	o	o	o	o	WAIT
	2	o	o	o	o	o	o	o	RES
	1	o	o	o	o	o	o	o	AMC
									(other)
	5	o	o	o	o	o	o	o	NO
	4	o	o	o	o	o	o	o	INCO
	3	o	o	o	o	o	o	o	WAIT
	2	o	o	o	o	o	o	o	RES
	1	o	o	o	o	o	o	o	AMC
									(other)

(Society for Advancement of Management)

(2) Has worked in only a single function or department, but seems to have picked up a good idea of what goes on in related areas.

(3) Because of chance assignments and changes in jobs, has had experience in several functions or aspects of business.

(4) Has made an effort to move around and gain different types of experience within the company (as distinguished from a "job hopper").

(5) Has had a wide range of experience and attempts to keep posted on the development of other functions and problems outside his own responsibility.

F—Creative Ability: This person . . .

(1) Likes routine, resists change, does not innovate.

(2) Likes routine, resists change coming from others, but has some new ideas himself.

(3) Jumps too fast on his/her own and other new ideas, before they are carefully thought out.

(4) Is open-minded in accepting ideas and adequately thorough in utilizing and making them work.

(5) Is a real "idea person"; uses both own and others' new ideas with outstanding effectiveness and profit.

G—Useful Years Available: This person has . . .

(1) Less than 5 years to retirement.

(2) 5 to 10 years to retirement.

(3) 10 to 15 years to retirement.

(4) 15 to 25 years to retirement.

(5) Over 25 years.

In the *Conclusions* column at the right hand side of the chart, S.A.M. suggests the following code:

NO: Applies with equal logic to someone who is already a first rate manager, or someone who has limitations so evident and unchangeable that he or she at the ceiling and is not likely to profit from further training.

INCO: This person will profit most from the company's inside training program which focuses sharply upon the company's own history, products, policies. This is a broader view of other functions in the company before moving to a more responsible post.

WAIT: This person may have potential, but has probably not been long on the present assignment. Management should watch him (her) a while longer before reaching any conclusion.

RES: This person has been under pressure for so long that he or she and the company will profit by a change of pace and scene. The company can spare the person for a few weeks before he/she goes on to the next assignment. The cost of a residence course away from the job will be well spent.

AMC: The company can't spare this person from the job. Or for some reason the company is not justified in spending more on residence courses, tuition, travel, and time away from the job. Yet, this employee could do better if he/she had a broader perspective and realized that other companies make a profit by doing some things differently from the way the company does them. Needs to rub shoulders with people from other companies and other lines of business.

WALTER MITCHELL JR., formerly Executive Director, Society for Advancement of Management, New York, New York

Cross References: *Assessment Centers; Executive Development: "Away from Company" Programs; Executive Traits.*

EXECUTIVE RECRUITMENT

Executive Recruitment involves: (1) making the position opening known to protential applicants, (2) screening applicants, (3) face-to-face interviewing of qualified candidates, (4) selection, (5) offer of employment, and (6) acceptance of the offer. Only when this entire process is completed has an actual placement been made. Placement thus refers to the actual matchup of a candidate's education, work experience, skill, and personality with the specific requirements of the position to be filled. (See EXECUTIVE SELECTION.)

Recruitment of competent personnel at any level is becoming increasingly difficult. To attract properly qualified candidates, a company must establish a personnel policy that is competitive and that will serve the best interests of both the potential executive and the company. Such a policy is properly based on research done by the wage and salary administrator, employee benefits administrator, and other specialists. An organization must decide what its needs are, and create a "climate" in keeping with those needs, covering compensation, promotional opportunities, benefits and privileges, and the like. For executive and professional personnel, climate is also dependent upon freedom to be creative, true responsibility for decision-making, and good communications.

Manpower Planning. Effective executive recruitment depends upon effective HUMAN RESOURCES REQUIREMENTS PLANNING. One cannot recruit properly on a crisis basis—long-range personnel planning is essential.

Organization charts and manning tables were at one time the primary basis for plotting manpower needs and determining action. For small and medium sized companies this may still be the most effective approach. However, in the past ten years more sophisticated means have been developed through the use of the computer. Here management has at its fingertips a "personnel inventory bank" able to identify in a very short time existing personnel according to length of service, year of retirement, current responsibilities, or any other category management may choose for its personnel profile. Such an inventory bank enables management to forecast how many replacements will be needed because of retirement, how many for unsatisfactory performance, how many for normal turnover (including health casualties), and additions needed for planned expansion.

To help establish whether a legitimate need for a new position exists, the personnel department should assist in the drawing up of a job description and man specifications. In this way responsibilities can be clearly delineated to avoid overlapping and misunderstanding. Three factors should be covered:

(1) *Job Description:* Title, reporting relationship, summary of objectives and purposes, and listing of responsibilities and authority.

(2) *Man/Woman Specifications:* Desired years of experience, training, and other special qualifications required.

(3) *Brief One-Page Summary:* For information of applicants and sources, this highlights

the duties and specifications as described in the job description and man specifications.

College Recruiting. Some large companies employ full-time college recruiters. Their primary task is to persuade college graduates or M.B.A. students to enter management training programs in their companies. This is done to ensure a constant influx of young, new talent into the company—men and women who would be trained in the management philosophy and in the specific product or service of that company. The understanding is that there will be an opportunity to move rapidly into management positions.

During the 1960s college recruiting ran into opposition from students protesting the Viet Nam War and opposing the participation of these large corporations in the war effort. Toward the end of the 60s and the beginning of the 70s, college recruiting faltered still more because of the cutback in defense spending and because of the general business recession. With the unemployment rate in 1969 and early 1970 at the highest point in many years, there was an influx into the job market of highly skilled and experienced personnel.

The 1973–74 recession continued this trend. In the mid-1970s, college recruiting took off again and reached a feverish pitch by 1980. Cultivation of favorable college relations is important. This involves getting acquainted with the placement officer and the department heads, inviting them to the company location, and mutually cooperating on equipment and facilities, grants in aid, and, where appropriate, consulting assignments for faculty.

It is important that the company representative be mature, articulate, personable, persuasive, and sincere. He/she should be equipped with adequate information about the company and the positions. A simple fact sheet is often as good as an overelaborate booklet. Overselling should be avoided. The counseling approach to students—helping them think about their development and goals—is highly effective.

It is not unusual to have to interview 20 students to recruit one person, and rarely will more than one or two acceptances be forthcoming from a single college. If the quota is twelve, it may be necessary to visit from 10 to 20 colleges and to interview around 250 students.

Summer Recruitment. A well-recommended practice is summer employment of students one or two years prior to receipt of final degree. This gives an inside track to employers, and an opportunity to get a line on capable graduates, try them out, and offer them permanent employment if mutually interested.

Military Recruitment. Officers and technical men leaving the armed services represent a source of well-educated, disciplined personnel that many corporations are tapping for executive talent. Some of this recruitment is done by the companies themselves. However, more and more companies are relying on employment agencies and executive recruiting firms to identify potential executives well before their last day in uniform. After identifying potential candidates, screening and relating of military experience to corporation needs are the most difficult tasks.

Outside vs. Inside Recruiting. Before a company looks outside for an executive, it should look inside the organization to see if there is someone in-house deserving and capable of filling the opening. (A company utilizing the personnel inventory bank mentioned earlier will know quickly if such a candidate is available.)

Advertising. If the decision is to look outside for an executive, the company may first want to try on its own to attract new talent. Advertising is the principal way of accomplishing this. To be effective such an ad should: (1) be straightforward and honest in representing the opening, (2) be specific as to the opening and the type of candidate wanted, and (3) underscore the critical qualifications to avoid many unqualified candidates.

Such ads are effectively placed in the Financial and Business Section of the Sunday edition of *The New York Times,* or midweek in *The Wall Street Journal.* When the opening is less critical and it is believed that such talent can be obtained from the local market, classified or display advertising in local papers will draw a sufficient number of candidates for a decision to be made. In certain instances, trade papers and magazines are useful, although they are slower and do not pull as well as the newpapers. Advertising agencies specializing in employment advertising can be consulted for proper wording, layout, and placement in newspapers.

Colleges and Universities. Some companies may also want to use colleges and universities as sources of executive talent. Most of the larger schools have effective divisions of alumni placement.

Employment Agencies. EMPLOYMENT AGENCIES are another means of recruiting executive talent. Such agencies usually handle executives earning $40,000 or less. They work primarily for the individual looking for work and, therefore, usually charge him a fee upon placement. However, the practice in some areas is for the company to pay the fee, especially for the higher-salaried people. The fee is normally restricted by law, and agencies are licensed by the states. Most states have a state employment service, at least in the larger cities, and these may also be helpful.

Executive Search Consultants. Finally, the company can turn to the executive search consultant. This is usually done for positions commanding $40,000 and above—and when the company wants to preserve confidentiality or is not able to approach all the qualified candidates in a certain discipline. A Conference Board survey has indicated additional significant reasons for using a search firm: (1) to assist personnel department staff without adding permanent overhead; (2) to obtain complete and broad coverage of the market; (3) to save time (and time is money); (4) to introduce third-party objectivity that is not biased nor influenced by historical conditions or internal politics.

The first professional executive search firm started in business some 50 years ago, and it is estimated that today there are over 1,000 search businesses in this country alone. The current American Management Association's listing of executive recruiting consultants lists over 100 member firms. In spite of this number, the Association of Executive Recruiting Consultants has admitted only 60 firms as meeting its professional standards. It is estimated that executive search is at least a $500 million-a-year business.

Initially, the executive search consultant, after receiving an assignment, spends time with the company representatives to obtain all the necessary information for conducting a thorough search: company history, current financial status, and goals for the immediate and distant future. The searcher visits the company to gather firsthand knowledge of the product and the place where the executive is to work. The consultant wants to know the history of the particular job opening—its function, how long it has been in existence, who was the incumbent. He/she wants to know what the reporting lines are, and to meet the people to whom the incumbent will report. Additionally, the outside recruiter can help define more specifically the job responsibilities and the position specifications.

Most search consultants have contacts in various industries and keep exhaustive files on people they have contacted in the past or who have written to them. These files are coded according to skills and speed the identifying process.

The candidates who pass extensive screening by resumés and interviews and checking of references are then presented to the client company through an in-depth written report and evaluation. The client then may choose to bring several of these persons in for interview. Before the final selection is made, some companies also want the candidate to undergo physical and/or psychological tests to make certain of the prospective executive's soundness before the placement is finally made.

Fees. The consultant firm typically bases its retainer fee upon 25% to 30% of the annual salary of the position. Some consultants charge on a regular retainer basis and others on a per diem or hourly basis. Search firms also charge out-of-pocket expenses for major items, such as long-distance calls, travel, hotel, and advertising.

Unlike employment agencies who are paid only upon "delivery" and whose fee structure is controlled by state law, the consultant bills a portion of the fee each month until the position is filled, providing it does not exceed the predetermined fee. As indicated earlier, the main difference between the employment agent and the search consultant is that the latter represents the client employer exclusively and, in a sense, is an extension of the latter's staff during the assignment, whereas the employment agent represents the individual seeking employment from whom the agent derives his or her fee unless the company has agreed to pay it.

O. WILLIAM BATTALIA, Battalia & Associates, Inc., New York, New York

Information References

A listing of firms rendering executive search services may be secured through:

American Management Associations.

Association of Executive Recruiting Consultants.

Publications:

Consultants News, Fitzwilliam, N.H. (publishes a directory of executive recruiters).

Executive Search Consultants in the U.S., National Survey Information Co., Lake Bluff, Ill.

Cross References: *Executive Selection; Executive Traits.*

EXECUTIVE SELECTION

The person-to-person interview is the primary tool of **Executive Selection.** Too much emphasis is frequently placed on the resumé which merely supplies basic information for initial screening.

The interview is the key step in the information-gathering process for selection. It is here that solid flesh is put on the outline contained in the resumé. But the really crucial step is in the *evaluation* of the information gathered by the interviewers. This evaluation process is the best measure of the person. For this reason, the people conducting the interview must not only be trained in the techniques of interviewing, but, most important, must be competent and open-minded enough to evaluate the information they secure.

The initial interview does much to set the tone or image of the company in the mind of the candidate. The interview area should be private, and properly lighted and ventilated. The atmosphere should be comfortable, since the candidate and interviewer will be in one place for an hour or more. The interviewer must create a climate of mutual trust and confidence, so that the candidate will speak openly.

The interviewer should be thoroughly knowledgeable about the company and the position for which the recruitment is being done. He (she) will have at hand the candidate's resumé or application and questions drawn up beforehand to be explored with the candidate. The interviewer should make detailed notes and leave nothing to memory. The candidate should be given sufficient time to relate his or her experience and offer any explanations that might be required.

After the interview, the interviewer should go over his (her) notes and *immediately* put in writing an evaluation of the candidate. If the candidate is not acceptable, he or she should be notified as soon as possible. If the assessment is favorable, another meeting should be arranged at which time the candidate will be interviewed by the supervisor to whom he will report and also by the person in charge of the department or division. These interviews should be arranged as soon as possible, because many qualified candidates are lost through excessive delay. On the occasion of the second visit, the candidate should be given a tour of the facilities.

After this second meeting the interviewers (there should be several) should meet to discuss their individual evaluations and arrive at some decision regarding the candidate. If the candidate is still considered a definite prospect for the position after this evaluation, a check of the references should be made.

Reference Checking. Reference checking will verify information given by the candidate on quality of performance, personality, and relationship with people. Remember that references submitted by a candidate will usually not develop negative information. The telephone check with former employers is more effective than written requests for information; but a personal visit is probably the most effective and should be used for special situations. Former employers may also be asked to suggest others who can speak authoritatively about the candidate.

For a comprehensive investigation it is well to use a reference-check guide, making sure that questions are added that may pertain to the particular situation in question. A sample of a guide is shown in Exhibit I.

Many a well-qualified candidate has been lost because of the negative attitude of the spouse toward a change in jobs or toward relocating. More and more companies are seeing the wisdom of involving the candidate's wife (or husband) in the interviewing process. A spouse's contentment goes a long way to removing additional pressure from the executive. Some executive positions call for a good deal of social involvement on the part of both marriage partners. For these reasons it is of great value to interview both and to acquaint each with the proposed new position.

Psychological Assessment. Psychological testing can be a very useful instrument in the selection of executive talent. A person's effectiveness in a particular company will depend to a large degree on the "chemistry" of the situation. How one relates to other people will determine whether or not policy changes are accepted or rejected or whether a new marketing technique is tried or not. Psychological

Exhibit I

Sample Reference Check List
(Telephone Use)

REFERENCE CHECK FORM

RE:
VIA:

Introductory Statement: a) We plan to make an offer. Seek aid in proper placement.
b) Don't want to put him over his head or underrate his potential.

I. a) Have you personally been responsible for his work?
b) Supervised him during his entire tenure?

II. What did he do? (Compare with resume.)

III. a) How well does he perform? - 1. very persevering?
2. fairly persistent?
3. in spurts?

b) Does he - 1. accept responsibility?
2. contribute without any push?
3. need some prodding?

c) Is he mature .... or, rather, has he made adequately sound adjustment for his age?

d) Does he cooperate very well with others or display ordinary depth of cooperation?

e) Does he have exceptional ability of clear expression in writing and orally or average ability?

f) Does he grasp ideas readily or poorly?

g) Does he exercise good judgment?

h) Is he more a leader or led?

i) Does he follow through without follow-up?

IV. How would you rank him with others in your department?

V. Would you rehire?

VI. Why did he leave?

VII. Does he have any areas that need strengthening? - a) What impressed you most?
b) What impressed you least?

VIII. Verify earnings.

IX. Is his personal life clear? Sincere and honest character? Drinking habits? Community relations - good?

Battalia & Associates, Inc.

tests can be effective in highlighting personality traits that might indicate whether or not a person should be hired. If testing is employed for the first time, members of the current staff should also be tested to help provide a better match when new people are brought in.

Such testing should only be administered and interpreted by completely trained personnel. Most tests will require the services of a psychologist. However, some may be administered by people trained in the administration of tests. Large companies maintain a staff of professional people for this purpose. Smaller companies, whose needs may not be as great, use outside consultants. An individual psychologist or psychological testing firm's competence or

EXHIBIT II

RBH STANDARDIZED BACKGROUND QUESTIONS (EXPERIMENTAL FORM B)

Please choose the one answer which is most nearly true for YOU, even though you may feel that none of the answers describes you exactly. Cross out the letter in front of it.

Mark only ONE answer for each question unless you are told to mark more. If there is any question which you consider too personal, cross out the whole question.

171. Which characteristic have you liked most in leaders or supervisors under whom you have served?
   a. Advancing subordinates who show ability
   b. Maintaining adequate supplies and equipment in good condition
   c. Getting along with employees
   d. Knowing the policies of management
   e. Being able to take justified criticisms from their subordinates

172. How much time do you spend in the usual week with those whose work you are responsible for?
   a. Less than ¼ of your time
   b. Between ¼ and ½
   c. About ½
   d. Between ½ and ¾
   e. Over ¾

173. In the past year, what has been the major factor in your recommending an employee for an increase or a promotion?
   a. Ability to get the work out
   b. Quality of work or technical competence
   c. Ability to get along with people
   d. Ability to sell ideas and express himself
   e. Something else

174. Which was the second most important factor in your recommending an employee for an increase or promotion?
   a. Ability to get the work out
   b. Quality of work or technical competence
   c. Ability to get along with people
   d. Ability to sell ideas and express himself
   e. Something else

175. Which has been the least important factor in your recommending an employee for an increase or promotion?
   a. Ability to get the work out
   b. Quality of work
   c. Ability to get along with people
   d. Ability to sell ideas and express himself
   e. Something else

176. How often have you had to turn down an invitation from one of your subordinates to have lunch together?
   a. Very rarely; always try to fit it in
   b. Rarely; only when it is unavoidable
   c. Sometimes; when you think he has an ulterior motive
   d. Frequently; your schedule doesn't permit it
   e. Most of your luncheon appointments are with people from other companies

177. About how much of your business time is spent with people from outside your own company?
   a. Less than ¼
   b. ¼ to ½
   c. About ½
   d. ½ to ¾
   e. Over ¾

178. About how much of your working time is spent with people higher than you are in the company organization?
   a. Less than ¼
   b. ¼ to ½
   c. About ½
   d. ½ to ¾
   e. Over ¾

Sample page from RBH Experimental Form, showing questions typical of those in RBH Individual Background Survey. (Copyright Richardson, Bellows, Henry and Co., New York.)

ethical standing can be ascertained by contacting the American Psychological Association in Washington, D.C.

Total reliance should not be placed on the psychological evaluation. This should be only one of several factors to be taken into consideration.

Recent legislation has affected the selection process significantly. Not only must applications not be discriminatory by asking certain questions as to race or sex, but the tests used to select candidates must meet rigid standards, and companies using them must be prepared to validate their lack of bias, particularly racial bias. Because of the complexity and legal implications of these new requirements, special consultants have been retained by many firms to evaluate their selection process in light of the new legislation.

Types of Tests. A complete review of applicable and available tests is impossible here. However, to give the reader an insight into types of tests used, illustrative examples of representative tests are offered below, together with supporting information used in executive assessment. (Not all of these would be used in any one situation.)

Background Information: Biographical Information Blank. This instrument is presented in the multiple-choice format, and covers such areas as early life experiences, education, parents, and self-evaluation. Additionally, it contains about 125 questions designed to answer such queries as, "What are the personal history characteristics of the effective manager?" "How do effective managers differ from the less effective?" "What, if any, biographical characteristics can be found to identify young persons with management potential?"

Traditionally, the Biographical Information Blank is the first instrument that is examined in the establishment of a selection battery. This is done for two reasons. First, because of its lengthy, complex nature, it must be carefully scrutinized with special techniques to locate meaningful trends. Second, it has proven in many situations to be the most predictive instrument in the test battery.

The success of this instrument has been attributed mainly to the fact that past performance is the best predictor of future performance. The objective in scoring a Biographical Information Blank is to develop a weighing system for the items that yield a total score that best differentiates between the successful and the nonsuccessful.

Standardized Test Data. The information gathered from the Biographical Information Blank should be supplemented by information derived from standardized test data. The Biographical Information Blank provides useful information concerning the life styles and early life experiences of effective managers; the standardized test battery will help explain the basic abilities and attitudes underlying these general life styles.

The usual battery of tests is designed to measure the two basic aspects of the managerial personality: the intellectual system and the motivational system. Following are examples of tests used by Lopez & Associates, psychological consultants, Port Washington, N.Y. to measure both of these. (See also PERSONNEL TESTING: Types of Tests.)

The Primary Mental Abilities Test (PMA) published by Science Research Associates measures five factors found to be the basic dimension of human intelligence:

(1) *Verbal Meaning.* The ability to understand ideas expressed in words. This ability is essential to activities in which information is obtained by reading or listening.

(2) *Space.* The ability to visualize objects in two or three dimensions and to see the relations of an arrangement of objects in space. This ability is also referred to as a measure of the fluid intelligence thought to be most closely associated with creative, problem-solving, and decision-making behaviors. (See Exhibit II.)

(3) *Reasoning.* The ability to solve logical problems. It is one of the most important mental abilities. The person with good reasoning ability can analyze a situation on the basis of past experience and make and carry out plans according to recognizable facts.

(4) *Number.* The ability to work with figures; to handle simple quantitative problems rapidly and accurately.

(5) *Word Fluency.* The ability to produce words easily. It differs from verbal meaning in that it concerns speed and ease with which words can be used rather than with the degree of understanding of verbal concepts.

Supervisory Practices Test. This test is designed to aid in appraising supervisory ability and potential. It is basically a test of awareness of modern principles of supervision and management.

Sales Comprehension Test. This test is designed to aid in the appraisal of sales ability and know-how. It provides an objective measure of the understanding and appreciation of basic principles of selling.

Motivational System Analysis: Holland Vocational Preference Inventory (V.P.I.). The V.P.I. is a personality inventory composed of 160 occupational titles, each of which the respondent is asked to indicate whether he likes or dislikes. By clustering these occupations into categories, the scoring procedure yields a broad range of information in two separate areas: occupational type and behavioral patterns. The first set of scales consists of six classes into which people can be placed according to their occupational preferences. The second set of scales indicates the respondent's coping behavior, interests, values, and self-regard.

Edwards Personal Preference Schedule (E.P.P.S.). This was designed primarily to provide measures of a number of relatively independent normal personality variables. The instrument yields scores on fifteen scales that reflect the manifest needs of people for certain personal satisfactions. Because the need is the basic element in a motive, responses to this instrument give, in a real sense, a picture of the respondent's primary motivations. Knowing a person's motivations reveals a good deal about his or her behavior which would make it possible to predict with some accuracy the future pattern of behavior.

Guildford-Zimmerman Temperament Survey. This survey yields scores on ten personality factors identified and conceptualized on the basis of factor analysis procedures which have amply demonstrated their uniqueness and their utility in clinical applications, in counselling, and in placement.

Physical Examinations. Most companies follow the standard practice of pre-employment physical examinations. The medical history and health record of an applicant can affect performance, insurance programs, and workmen's compensation. This examination is recommended as the final step before an offer of employment is made.

Placement and Introduction to the Company. When the candidate passes all pre-employment tests and the offer is extended and accepted, the placement is made. However, the Personnel Department's responsibility should carry over to the proper introduction of the new executive into the company. The newcomer should meet key people and associates with whom he or she will work. The ground rules, written and unwritten, and the policies and practices of the company and the department should be explained. In this way, the new executive's entrance into the company will be a pleasant experience that could well set the tone for his or her entire stay.

O. WILLIAM BATTALIA, Battalia & Associates, Inc., New York, New York

Information References

For information on specific types of tests, and sources of tests: American Psychological Association. See also references under entry, PERSONNEL TESTING: Types of Tests.

Cross References: *Executive Recruitment; Executive Traits; Personnel Testing; Personnel Testing: Types of Tests.*

EXECUTIVE TRAITS

Researchers have been able to isolate certain **Executive Traits** that are found in significant amounts in successful executives. These basic characteristics generally needed for business competence are considered far more important than any differences that may exist. The latter usually have to do with the technical nature of particular industries, rather than with the skills and abilities needed by managers. Since the common element found in the administration of all enterprises is the influencing of human behavior, a skillful manager should be able to manage anything with equal success.

In studying 3,000 men, Randle [1] found thirty such qualities "significantly present in executives who had been judged promotable, and significantly absent in those who had been judged inadequate." Randle was able to isolate eight traits which he says distinguished promotable men: *Position Performance, Drive, Intellectual Ability, Leadership, Administrative Ability, Initiative, Motivation,* and *Creativeness.* Randle calls these "universals."

Professors Gordon and Howell [2] in their study of higher education for business, also found similar basic characteristics which are generally needed for business competence.

Marshall E. Dimock points out that the elements in administering any large scale enterprise are "90% the same," whether it be a governmental or private organization. Ordway Tead recognized this in 1935. Gantt touched on it in 1916, when he remarked that "administration means administration of human affairs, and . . . the one common element in all enterprises is the human element" [3], [4], [5].

In his American Management handbook on executive appraisal [6] Heyel lists eight factors of appraisal of management skills, in making a decision regarding promotion, all but the first of which would come under the head of "traits":

(1) As perspective, determine the amount of background technical knowledge and skill called for by the position, and the extent to which the candidate qualifies.

(2) Evaluate the ability to plan in long-range terms.

(3) Evaluate the ability to make decisions.

(4) Evaluate the ability to organize and plan current operations.

(5) Evaluate the ability to coordinate and direct operations.

(6) Evaluate the ability to delegate and assign.

(7) Evaluate the willingness to check up and follow up.

(8) Evaluate the ability to develop people.

The above eight factors are related by Heyel

to the specific result factors desired on each job, established by prior careful job evaluation.

Common Denominators. Managements are not always in agreement on which characteristics are most desirable in executives. Part of the difference of opinion seems to stem from semantic difficulties, owing to the necessity for distinguishing the subtle variations in human behavior. This was apparent in the replies given by the companies in a study by Sands [7] to the question: Which five man-specifications do you consider universally important in any executive position? Twenty-eight traits were mentioned, many so similar as to suggest that the respondents themselves had the ability to discriminate among the fine distinctions. This in itself is considered a measure of executive competence.

Ability to Get Along with People, including various aspects of human relations, social graces, tact, poise, and appearance was mentioned most frequently, mainly by banks, merchandising companies, life insurance, and manufacturing companies, in that order. Utilities did not note these traits at all. Second most popular were *Knowledge of the Work,* or experience, and *Skill in Leading.* (The utilities did not appear among those to whom leadership ability was important, either.) *Integrity* and *Good Character* were a close third in popularity, especially with banks and insurance companies.

Ability to Plan and Organize was given less frequently, though other aspects of administrative skill were also mentioned. *Drive, Intellectual Ability,* and *Imagination* were also named, as were such characteristics as *Initiative, Judgment,* and *Analytical Ability.* Mentioned least often were such traits as *Courage, Energy, Perseverance,* and *Ability to Make Decisions,* but some of these are contained within the broad definitions of other previously named characteristics.

In studying common denominators in executive specifications. Sands concluded, on the basis of her questionnaires and interviews with top corporations in the country, that it is possible to subsume under the following heads most of the factors considered important in executive selection: (1) *the leader type personality;* (2) *specific intellectual capacities;* (3) *highly developed social sensitivity;* (4) *certain physical characteristics;* and (5) *mode of living.* (Nos. 4 and 5 are not, of course, "traits," but they are executive selection factors established by managements, differing in accordance with specific requirements.)

In the foregoing, No. 1, the "leader-type personality," is perhaps least susceptible of being pinned down. The successful business leader usually has a clear sense of duty and responsibility to his organization. He sets himself a high standard of performance toward which he continually drives himself. He can organize a job and be a long way toward completing it while others are still thinking about how to tackle it. In addition to the moral obligation the leader-type feels to get the job done, he is usually found to be striving toward a definite goal which he envisions. These forceful traits, however, must be tempered with integrity. The presence or absence of this quality is quickly discovered by a man's subordinates whose willingness to be led is directly affected by their respect for him. The kind of personal relationship that exists between the manager and those who report to him determines the effectiveness of the leadership he provides.

A Top Executive Appraisal. People who have made it to the top reported in a *Wall Street Journal/Gallup* survey of 782 chief executives [8] that the three most important personal traits needed to advance are rather simple virtues: integrity, industriousness, and the ability to get along with people. To be promoted, the heads of U.S. corporations of all sizes said employees should demonstrate personal ambition and a commitment to the company and its goals. Many cited imagination, leadership, good judgment, and the ability to motivate other people, but few mentioned technical experience or educational background among the most important qualifications.

Results were based on interviews with heads of 282 of the country's largest corporations (including 102 Fortune 500 companies), heads of 300 medium-sized companies, and owners of 200 small firms. Asked about the weaknesses they noticed most often in subordinate executives, the respondents cited narrow-mindedness and inability to work with and understand others.

The strong consensus among chief executives of companies of all sizes was that "inner" character strengths matter most for success and advancement. In particular, respondents mentioned honesty, good judgment, self-reliance, and hard work. Six of every ten executives in the largest U.S. corporations mentioned at least one of these qualities, as did half of the executives in medium-sized companies and more than 40% of small-company heads. Such "people skills" as leadership and the ability to motivate others were mentioned by half the chiefs of the large and medium-sized companies and by nearly as many small-company heads.

The Million-Dollar Executive. In discussing the "million-dollar executive" (the "Midex" as he terms him), John Wareham [9] founder and president of an international executive search and management consulting firm, enumerates his special characteristics as:

Sensitivity—a synthesis of intuition, creativity, and judgment—at the tips of the fingers: "the Midex touch." (He encapsulates this in the vivid German expression, *Fingerspitzengefühl.*) Such intuition, says Wareham, is a faculty of the unconscious that comes very close to clairvoyance or extrasensory perception: it is the ability to *divine* an insight into reality without using rational thought; the Midex makes his decisions on the basis of what he may call his "gut reactions." Since the whole process is subconscious, he is unable to tell you why he is doing what he is doing. He only knows, *feels* that he is right. The "archives of his subconscious," rich with ideas as a result of an active life, enable him to sift, compare, and synthesize a rich pattern of perceptions in order to solve complex problems that cannot be encompassed rationally.

Wareham points out that creativity and intuition are double edges of the same sword and a particular trait of the creative individual is his ability to "disappear inside his head." A creative executive, he says, can sometimes seem as deaf and distraught as Beethoven when, stone deaf, he created the Ninth Symphony. Such a gift is not always endearing or readily recognized, and the early life of the Midex commonly reveals a history of unwillingness, sometimes an inability, to submit to authority or to conform.

An abnormally high level of psychic energy. The Midex mostly functions in the manic phase of the manic-depressive cycle, and sometimes seems to be on a "high." Says Wareham, "The Midex can maintain several conversations on different levels more or less simultaneously, his words coming in torrents, his thoughts cascading in a stream of consciousness. He seldom seems to listen to what people are saying. In fact, he absorbs almost every idea into his id, which may process an answer for him to spit out later during the same conversation but on another subject."

An almost desperate need to prove something. Wareham's analysis: While the Midex functions almost perfectly under stress, he is "commonly boxing unconscious childhood shadows, surpassing the achievements of an outstanding father; or he may feel he began "from the wrong side of the street," and must erase the humiliation. Yesterday's performance, however great, is not enough for him.

Persuasive powers. The Midex has the capacity to "intoxicate" anyone who comes within his influence. He has a commanding presence, and can communicate on several levels, intuitively choosing words to stroke the unconscious needs of his followers. He offers not just a job and a paycheck, but *fulfillment.*

CARL HEYEL, Management Counsel, Manhasset, New York

Information References

This entry represents an updating of the entry appearing in the second edition of the Encyclopedia, by Edith Sands, based on her findings referenced in (7), below.

Relevant to the discussion of executive traits are the periodically published "Profiles" by the search firm, Heidrick and Struggles, Inc., New York, N.Y. Recent titles:

"Profile of a Chief Executive Officer" (1980, 1977).
"Company Chief Executive Officer" (1980).
"Profile of a Woman Officer" (1980).
"Profile of a Black Executive" (1979).
"Profile of a Chief Research and Development Executive" (1978).
"Profile of a Mobile Executive" (1980).

References Cited

[1] Randle, C. Wilson, "How to Identify Promotable Executives," *Harvard Business Review* May–June 1956.

[2] Gordon, Robert A. and Howell, James E., "Higher Education for Business," New York, Columbia University Press, 1959.

[3] Dimock, Marshall E., "A Philosophy of Administration," New York, Harper & Bros., 1958.

[4] Tead, Ordway, "The Art of Leadership," New York, Whittlesey House, McGraw-Hill, 1935.

[5] Gantt, H. L., "Industrial Leadership," New Haven, Conn., Yale University Press, 1916.

[6] Heyel, Carl, "Appraising Executive Performance," New York, American Management Association, 1958.

[7] Sands, Edith S., "Selecting Executive Personnel: An Empirical Study in which the Practices of Eighty-two Billion Dollar Corporations are Analyzed and Compared with Theory in order to Investigate the Existence and Use of Quality Standards in Selecting Executive Personnel." Un-

published dissertation, Graduate School of Business Administration, New York University, 1961. (*Cf.* also her "How to Select Executive Personnel," New York, Reinhold, 1963.)

[8] "Bosses List Main Strengths, Flaws, Determining Potential of Managers," *The Wall Street Journal,* November 14, 1980.

[9] Wareham, John, "Secrets of a Corporate Headhunter, " New York, Atheneum, 1980.

Cross References: *Assessment Centers; Executive Appraisal: Diagnostic Performance Appraisal; Executive Development: Selection Guide; Executive Recruitment; Executive Selection.*

F

FACTORY MANAGEMENT. See Industrial Engineering; Manufacturing Management; Production: Large-Scale; Production Planning and Inventory Management.

FAYOL, HENRI

Henri Fayol (1841–1925) was one of the most distinguished figures which Europe contributed to the management movement. For thirty years (1888–1918) he was chief executive of the great French mining and metallurgical combine, Commentry-Fourchambault-Decazeville ("Comambault"). When he took charge, this operation was on the verge of bankruptcy. When he retired, its financial position was impregnable, it had made a valuable contribution to the national effort in the first World War, and it had an administrative and technical staff famous throughout France.

Fayol attributed his practical success to the application of certain simple principles which could be taught, his Theory of Administration. "This isolation and analysis of administration as a separate function was his unique and original addition to the body of management theory. It paved the way for the evolution of the whole modern approach to problems of higher management by way of functional analysis. It exercised . . . a profound influence on all efforts to clarify and to organize thinking as to the qualities required for, the nature of, and the correct analysis of 'top management' " [1]. Fayol's principles included division of work, authority, discipline, unity of command, unity of direction, subordination of individual interests, remuneration, line of authority, order equity, stability of personnel tenure, initiative, and esprit de corps. This "essence of management" has stood the test of time.

After his retirement, at the age of seventy-seven in 1918, he devoted the remaining seven years of his life to spreading an understanding of his theory and pointing out its application to fields other than business—military, naval, and governmental.

While at first Fayol was inclined to be unsympathetic toward F. W. Taylor's work, he later saw it as complimentary to his own field of study. Taylor had merely started at the worker level, whereas Fayol had started at the opposite end of the scale—the chief executive. (See SCIENTIFIC MANAGEMENT; SCIENTIFIC MANAGEMENT: "Taylorism.")

In 1925 there was effected a union of the "Centre d'Etudes Administratives" which Fayol had founded, and the "Conference de l'Organisation Française" which had been established to introduce Taylor's ideas to France, the new organization being termed the "Comité National de l'Organisation Française." With the founding of "CNOF," France became the first country with an institution equipped to promote the study and application of scientific methods to business and other institutions *regarded as a whole.*

Fayol was the author of many papers and articles on administration. His books include "Administration Industrielle et Générale—Prévoyance, Organisation, Commandement, Coordination, Contrôle," 1916. (Republished in 1925 by Dunod, Paris; first English translation, "General and Industrial Administration," 1929, International Management Institute, J. A. Conbrough, Geneva; second English translation, "General and Industrial Administration," by Constance Storrs, London, Pitman, 1949, with a foreword by L. Urwick.) "L'Incapacité Administrative de l'Etat—Les Postes et Télégraphes," 1921 (Dunod, Paris). 'L'Eveil de l'Esprit Public," 1927 (Dunod, Paris).

References Cited

[1] Urwick, L., "The Golden Book of Management," edited for the International Committee of Scientific Management (CIOS), London, Newman Neame, Limited, 1956.

FIFO/LIFO INVENTORY ACCOUNTING

FIFO ("First In, First Out") and **LIFO** ("Last In, First Out") are two forms of inventory accounting. Under the FIFO concept, costs are assigned to units sold in the same order as the costs entered in the inventory. As a result, during periods of rising prices, the older, and therefore lower, costs are subtracted from revenues when determining reported, and therefore taxable, earnings. Under LIFO, the newest costs are "removed from the top" and assigned to units sold. Unless the "bottom layer" of costs is liquidated by sale of inventories, it can remain on the books indefinitely. Thus, during periods of rising prices, the older, and therefore lower, costs remain in the balance-sheet inventory account while the newer and higher costs are used in calculating earnings. Compared to FIFO, reported earnings under LIFO will in most cases drop—but so do taxes on earnings. Thus a company will have more cash available for operations or dividend distribution, but its published profits are lower.

Information Reference

National Association of Accountants.

Cross References: *Accounting; Certified Public Accountant; Financial Accounting Standards Board; Inflation Accounting; Internal Auditing; Production Planning and Inventory Management (Section on Inventory Control).*

FINANCIAL ACCOUNTING STANDARDS BOARD (FASB)

Since 1973, the **Financial Accounting Standards Board** has been the designated organization in the private sector for establishing standards of financial accounting and reporting. Those standards are, in effect, rules governing the preparation of financial reports. The FASBs function is important because decisions regarding allocation of capital (investment) are based on financial information, much of which is the product of the financial accounting/reporting process.

FASB standards are officially recognized as authoritative by the Securities and Exchange Commission (Accounting Series Release 150, December 1973) and the American Institute of Certified Public Accountants (Rules of Conduct, as amended May 1973 and May 1979).

The SEC has statutory authority to establish financial accounting and reporting standards under the Securities Exchange Act of 1934. Throughout its history, however, the Commission's policy has been to rely on the private sector for this function to the extent that the private sector demonstrates ability to fulfill the responsibility in the public interest. The FASB was conceived by a special study group headed by a former SEC Commissioner and was designed to carry out this responsibility.

The seven members of the Financial Accounting Standards Board have diverse backgrounds, but they must possess "knowledge of accounting, finance, and business, and a concern for the public interest in matters of financial accounting and reporting." They serve full time, are compensated, and are required to sever all previous business or professional connections before joining the Board. They are aided by a staff of 40 technical specialists plus administrative and other support personnel.

An Independent Tripartite Structure. The FASB is the operating part of a tripartite structure that is independent of all other business and professional organizations. The Board's 1981 budget was $7.9 million. Funds are obtained through contributions and sales of publications.

Contributions are received by the *Financial Accounting Foundation,* which is incorporated to operate exclusively for charitable, educational, scientific, and literary purposes within the meaning of Section 501(c)(3) of the Internal Revenue Code.

More than half the funding is provided by industry and the financial community, with the remainder coming from the public accounting profession and other private-sector sources. No single contribution of more than $50,000 can be accepted under the Foundation's by-Laws.

The Foundation also is responsible for selecting the members of the FASB and its Advisory Council and for exercising general oversight (except with regard to the FASB's resolution of technical issues).

The Foundation is separate from all other organizations. However, its Board of Trustees is made up of nominees from six sponsoring organizations whose members have special knowledge of, and interest in, financial reporting. The sponsoring organizations are:

- American Accounting Association (academe).
- American Institute of Certified Public Accountants (public accounting).
- Financial Analysts Federation (investors and investment advisors).
- Financial Executives Institute (corporate executives).
- National Association of Accountants (primarily management accountants).
- Securities Industry Association (investment bankers, brokers).

There also is a trustee-at-large whose election is endorsed by the principal national associations in the banking industry.

The *Financial Accounting Standards Advisory Council* has responsibility for consulting with the Standards Board as to major policy questions, technical issues on the Board's agenda, the assigning of priorities to projects, matters likely to require the attention of the FASB, selection and organization of task forces, and such other matters as may be requested by its chairman or the FASB chairman. The Council has 41 members who are broadly representative of preparers, auditors, and users of financial information.

Due Process. The Standards Board issues Statements of Financial Accounting Standards, Statements of Concepts, and Interpretations. Statements of Financial Accounting Standards establish new standards or amend those previously issued. Statements of Concepts do not establish new standards or require any change in existing accounting principles. They provide a guide to the Board in solving problems and enable those who use financial reports better to understand the context in which financial accounting standards are formulated. Interpretations clarify, explain, or elaborate on existing standards. The FASB staff issues Technical Bulletins to provide guidance on applying existing standards to certain financial accounting and reporting problems on a timely basis.

Before it issues a Statement, the Board is required by its rules to follow extensive "due process" procedures which in many ways are more stringent than the requirements of the Federal Administrative Procedure Act.

In connection with each of its major projects, the Board takes the following steps:

- Appoints a task force of technical experts representing a broad spectrum of preparers, auditors, and users of financial information to advise on the project;
- Studies existing literature on the subject and conducts such additional research as may be necessary;
- Publishes a comprehensive discussion of issues and possible solutions as the basis for public comment;
- Conducts a public hearing;
- Gives broad distribution to an exposure draft of the proposed Statement for public comment.

The FASB technical staff works directly with the Board and task forces, conducts research, participates in public hearings, analyzes oral and written comments received from the public, and prepares recommendations and drafts of documents for consideration by the Board.

The Board's deliberations are open to the public, and a complete public record is maintained.

Significant Issues Resolved. Among the significant and long-standing issues of financial accounting and reporting that have been resolved by the FASB are: accounting for research and development costs; self-insured losses; castastrophe losses incurred by property and casualty insurance companies; losses from expropriations of property by foreign governments; reporting by development stage companies; accounting for leases; segment reporting; capitalization of interest cost; and accounting for defined benefit pension plans.

In November 1978, the FASB issued a Statement of Financial Accounting Concepts on "Objectives of Financial Reporting by Business Enterprises," and in September 1979, a Statement on "Financial Reporting and Changing Prices." Exposure drafts on the elements and qualitative characteristics of financial statements also were issued in 1979, as was a discussion memorandum on reporting earnings.

Other important projects on the Board's agenda at this writing include: the effects of rate regulation on accounting for regulated enterprises, the objectives of reporting by nonbusiness organizations, including governmental units, and accounting by employers for pensions and other retirement benefits.

Pronouncements of Predecessor Bodies. Before the present independent standard-setting structure was created, financial accounting and reporting standards were established first by the Committee on Accounting Procedure of the American Institute of CPAs and then by the Accounting Principles Board, also an arm of the AICPA. Pronouncements of those two predecessor bodies remain in force unless amended or superseded by action of the FASB.

Cross References: *Accounting; Certified Public Accountant; Financial Analysis: Earnings; International Accounting Standards Committee.*

FINANCIAL ANALYSIS: Earnings

A glance through the price-earnings ratios distributed to newspapers by the Associated Press along with stock tables shows that the PE range on the New York Stock Exchange reaches from 2 to about 735. Thus if one knows that a company's earnings per share are $1, he can conclude with confidence only that the price of its stock will be between $2 a share and $735 a share!

Though even so cursory an examination might lead to the suspicion that there must be other important things, much of the financial and business world revolves around earnings per share, or EPS. Yet in fact determining the merit of corporate policies by their impact on per-share earnings is fraught with danger. EPS is too often a misleading indicator that can result in costly decisions that frequently shortchange the common shareholders.

The EPS criterion confuses investment decisions with financing policies. Substandard projects can appear desirable simply because of the way in which they are financed. Furthermore, a large body of empirical evidence indicates (as the range in PE ratios suggests) that the market is not primarily interested in earnings or in EPS per se.

There are many reasons why management and the financial community would be well advised to abandon EPS as an analytical tool. This is particularly true for acquisition pricing and financing and capital structure planning. Both executives and analysts need to take a closer look at the key elements that determine the price of a company's stock.

Acquisition Analysis. The rhetoric we read in many business publications about acquisition analysis is misleading. Commonly, for instance, we are told that companies should make acquisitions because of the "earnings leverage" that will result.

As an example, let us assume that company A sells at a price-earnings multiple of 20 and that company B sells at a PE of 10. Often, we are told that company A can offer B's shareholders a PE of, say, 15—a premium of 50%—and that A can still increase its EPS. For each dollar of earnings A is buying, it only has to give up shares earning 75 cents. Thus, if A uses its shares to buy B and form a new company, AB, AB's EPS will always exceed A's EPS. Hence, we are told that the acquisition of B is good for A's shareholders. And, obviously, it is good for B's shareholders since they obtain a 50% premium above the market price of their shares.

But if we turn the example around, the danger in using EPS becomes obvious. If B buys A to form BA, B will pay at least A's PE of 20. But now BA's EPS will be less than B's, because the company with the lower PE must offer more shares per dollar of acquired earnings.

The same people who tell us that AB is good for A's shareholders tell us that BA is bad for B's shareholders, even though AB and BA are the same company, most often with the same assets and earnings expectations and, even, the same management. Should we expect AB and BA to sell at different prices in the market when they are really the same company?

A's acquisition of B or B's acquisition of A is in fact good for the buyer's shareholders only if synergism is expected. And the synergism must be at least large enough to justify the premium paid above the seller's current share price. Thus, it is illogical to claim that IBM, for example, can afford to pay more for B than could the Chase Manhattan Bank because IBM sells at a much higher PE than Chase. If Chase can expect to generate larger synergism than IBM with the acquisition of B, shouldn't Chase be able to offer a greater price for B?

Furthermore, the business writer fails to realize that if IBM (or any firm selling at a high PE) were to acquire firms for which it paid full value (i.e., there is no added benefit to the buyer's shareholders), IBM's PE would fall to offset the gain in EPS. Empirical evidence supports this position.

Confusing Investment With Financing. Another pitfall in using EPS as a guide for acquisition policy is confusing investment with financing. In one case the president of a well-diversified manufacturer selling at 16 times earnings wanted to acquire a small, but exceptionally profitable, engineering consulting firm for a PE of 25. An equity swap would "dilute" the pro forma EPS. Facetiously, we suggested that he sell his company to the engineering firm, even though the latter was only about 10% as large as the manufacturer, so that the EPS would rise. He suggested an alternative: use debt to finance the acquisition. The anticipated profits from the acquisition would more than cover his company's out-of-pocket cost of interest on debt. Thus his company's income would rise while the number of outstanding shares would remain constant. He was right, the pro forma EPS would rise.

However, there is conceptual problem with his suggestion. Since the pro forma EPS can be enhanced simply by employing debt, bad investments can appear to be good invetments because the management can lever the firm and increase the EPS at the time the investment is undertaken. Furthermore, the management can increase the EPS without making any investment by borrowing to retire common shares. So there are many ways financing decisions can affect EPS, though they cannot change the intrinsic desirability of the acquisition, which is simply a multiplant decision. This means the invetment decision must be made independently of the financing decision, or in other words, on the basis of considerations other than the effect on EPS.

Thus, there are two distinct shortcomings to employing EPS as an analytical tool in acquisition pricing. First, the existing PEs of the buyer and seller determine the decision, so that synergism may be excluded from consideration. Second, EPS can lead the decision-maker to believe that bad investments are good investments; simply lever the firm sufficiently at the time an investment is undertaken and EPS can be enhanced to any level desired by management.

The Benefits of Debt Financing. An emphasis on EPS not only misdirects management in selecting and pricing acquisitions, it also leads to ridiculous conclusions on the balance between debt and equity in a company's financial structure. Depending on the PE multiple, mechanical dependence on EPS would lead to the expansion of debt to cover dubious projects, or to the elimination of all debt by issuing common shares. While in most cases an increase in the amount of debt in relation to equity will enhance EPS, in fact the benefits to a company's market value derived from its financing policies have nothing to do with EPS.

A company can use debt to increase its EPS so long as its after-tax return on fixed capital is larger than its after-tax interest costs. Today high-grade bonds cost the firm less than 4.5% after taxes. Thus, corporate investments in new plant and equipment yielding more than 4.5% after taxes would appear desirable to analysts emphasizing EPS. It is certainly not difficult to imagine the likely direction of IBM's share price if projects were undertaken earning a mere 5% on fixed capital, even if the EPS were rising.

The market will not ignore the fact that an increase in debt forces the common shareholder to assume greater financial risk, in the form of higher fixed costs due to interest expense. Without some factor to offset part of this new risk, the price-earnings multiple will decline. So the price of the common shares would remain unchanged despite the added EPS.

At the other extreme, the EPS criterion would dictate that high PE firms issue shares to retire debt. As it works out mathematically, EPS can be increased by issuing shares to retire debt so long as the price-earnings ratio is larger than the reciprocal of the after-tax borrowing rate. If a company's after-tax cost of borrowed funds is 4.5%, the reciprocal is one divided by 4.5% or 22.2. Whenever the PE exceeds 22.2, management can increase the EPS simply by issuing equity to retire debt. Hence, supporters of EPS maximization would recommend that companies selling at very high PEs be debt free, a policy that would hardly be beneficial to the common shareholders.

There is considerable evidence that debt financing does add to the market value of a firm's common equity. Of course, the reason is that there is a factor that reduces part of the financial risk created by the fixed interest expense. The Federal Government bears a large portion of the financial risk—up to 48%, the corporate income tax rate. The deductibility of interest expense in calculating taxable income means that the company's earnings are reduced by up to only 52% of the cost of debt.

A large body of empirical evidence clarifies our intuition about borrowed capital, namely, that investors do not expect management to reduce debt. As it comes due they expect management to refinance and, hence, maintain a particular target debt ratio. A target debt ratio implies that investors expect the annual tax saving to continue forever.

The present value of this perpetual stream is simply the corporate income tax rate multiplied by the amount of interest-bearing debt that is anticipated by the market. As long as the level of debt does not exceed prudent limits, the market value of a firm's common shares will rise 48 cents for each dollar of interest-bearing debt in its target capital structure. Thus, the real benefit of debt financing to the common shareholders is not the added EPS; it is the tax saving.

What Really Determines Prices? It is clear that an EPS criterion frequently misallocates valuable corporate resources and shortchanges the shareholders. Nor, to judge by market behavior, is EPS the criterion that impresses investors, especially the sophisticated investors who really determine share prices.

Investors do not discount earnings per se.

Consider two companies, X and Y. Assume that all we know is that their profits are expected to increase at identical annual rates of 15%. At this stage, a foolish question would be: which company should sell at a higher price, X or Y? Of course, the obvious answer is that we would expect X and Y to sell at an identical price, since, in the absence of additional information, X and Y are the same company!

However, with the addition of one other item about the two companies we must conclude that X would command the greater market value: X requires almost no investment in new capital to increase its profits 15% annually, whereas Y requires a dollar of additional capital for each incremental dollar of sales. X sells at the higher price and price-earnings multiple because it requires less capital to grow at a given rate despite the fact that X and Y are expected to have identical future profits. That is, X has a larger expected rate of return on incremental capital. The key determinant of market value in this case is the expected return on incremental capital.

The implication we can draw from this example is that investors do not simply discount expected earnings; rather, investors discount anticipated earnings net of the amount of capital required to be invested in order to maintain an expected rate of growth in profits. This concept can be referred to as the expected future "Free Cash Flow." It is expected cash flow that is above and beyond the anticipated investment requirement of the business.

The key to successful acquisition analysis and capital structure planning is to focus on the determinants of market value that are employed by sophisticated investors. The pricing mechanism is to calculate the current value of the expected future free cash flow. The resulting EPS is unimportant.

JOEL M. STERN, President, Chase Financial Policy, The Chase Manhattan Bank, N.A., New York, New York

Cross References: *Financial Ratios; Return on Capital.*

FINANCIAL PUBLIC RELATIONS

Financial public relations is an important part of a corporation's total public relations effort. The purposes of financial public relations are:

- To generate interest in the stock among potential investors.
- To strive for a fair market-place appraisal of the stock as an investment.
- To keep pace with the market progress of the industry group as a whole.
- To keep the investment community informed of both short- and long-term prospects and developments of the company.
- To cultivate the good will (and, when necessary, the support) of those who have invested in the company, and who are its real owners.
- To broaden the public ownership of shares.
- To facilitate raising new equity capital on favorable terms when necessary.

To achieve these goals companies engage in two very different activities, both termed "financial public relations" and both necessary components of any publicly traded corporation's communications effort. The first involves a communications effort directed toward security analysts and other financial professionals on Wall Street. The second is more general in character and is directed at shareholders, potential investors, brokers, and other corporate audiences. Although these activities are commonly spoken of together and often handled by the same individual at a corporation, we discuss them separately here.

The Security Analyst. Security analysts conduct research on public companies to identify and report on their investment appeal. Analysts who work for brokerage firms are called "sell-side" analysts. They make investment recommendations to individuals ("retail customers") and/or large pools of managed money, such as insurance companies, mutual funds, and pension funds ("institutional clients"). Analysts who are employed by the institutional clients themselves are called "buy-side" analysts.

Typically, security analysts follow some or all of the companies in a single industry group, such as nonferrous metals, banking, etc. They are intimately familiar with the mechanics of the business and the dynamics of the market place. They know what is happening in the industry as a whole, so what they want is detailed information about what is going on individually, with the companies they follow, including information about the companies' future plans and the companies' own assessment about probable future developments.

The Security-Analyst Contact. Most larger

companies assign a single individual to deal with security analysts. The security-analyst contact communicates with the security analyst directly and continuously. He (she) may identify a group of from 5 to 50 or more security analysts (depending on the industry group) who are "key" analysts, widely recognized for their knowledge and ability to select companies that have solid investment potential. To be successful, he must discuss the company in relatively sophisticated terms and must address the interests of these security analysts.

An effective analyst contact must have access to all information available to a company's management. The job requires access to the company's top executives, and dotted-line access to all areas of the company. He need not, nor should he, share all this information with security analysts. But he must never mislead analysts and should never be surprised by, or surprise an important analyst with corporate information inconsistent with what he has been discussing previously with the analyst. Credibility is a precious commodity and easily destroyed. A security-analyst contact without credibility cannot be effective.

The security-analyst contact typically uses the following tools in his (her) work:

(1) *Telephone.* The analyst contact is on the telephone a great deal, either answering questions or telling analysts about new developments at the company and what they mean. Most analyst contacts maintain careful logs of all calls and conversations. One measure of the success of a financial public relations program is the growth, over time, in telephone activity.

(2) *Face to Face Meetings.* The analyst contact should have a regular program of travel to meet and get to know key analysts and to build interest among new analysts. Although many analysts are located in New York City, a company with national activities should expect to visit several other financial centers each year.

(3) *Written Communications.* Most companies maintain current mailing lists of analysts to insure that press releases on all essential corporate information reach this key audience promptly. In addition, more elaborate programs involve preparation of special materials for security analysts (see below).

(4) *Periodic Group Meetings.* Most companies meet regularly with groups of security analysts either as guests of a city's Society of Security Analysts (directories of these societies are available through the Financial Analysts Federation, New York City), as guests of a "splinter group" (an informal association of several analysts who follow the same companies or industries—for example, the "chemical splinter group"), or at meetings which the company itself calls and pays for. A growing number of companies sponsor their own meetings with analysts on a quarterly basis in New York City.

(5) *Fact Book.* A widely used tool of financial public relations is the security analyst fact book. In it is collected in one place all the essential information an analyst is likely to be interested in. Some of this information may duplicate information available in the company's annual report or Form 10-K filed with the Securities and Exchange Commission. But it may also include such varied information as a history of price fluctuations of commodity products, detailed biographical information about several levels of management, technical descriptions of particular products, elaborately developed financial ratios commonly used in security analysis, and information about the industry as a whole, about competitors, or about the company's position in an industry.

(6) *Other Materials.* Beyond the above essentials, a security-analyst contact is free to develop any ideas he considers necessary to catch wider attention or provide more and better information. Newsletters, special meeting reports, copies of company materials, facilities tours, and extensive financial publicity in national business publications are all widely used.

Perhaps the most important element in the security-analyst contact's success is his personality, his intelligence, and his willingness to serve the needs of the security analyst quickly and completely.

Shareholder Relations: Present Shareholders. The shareholder relations function at most companies is the responsibility of the public relations department. It includes such activities as preparation of the annual and quarterly reports to shareholders, conduct of the annual meeting, and continuing distribution of financial press releases to the news media. These activities are widely understood and accepted at most companies.

The major issues in this area of communications today are (1) finding ways for a company to hold on to what is generally a declining number of individual shareholders and (2) building sufficient loyalty among shareholders to increase the possibility of affirmative shareholder actions which support the present management in the face of a hostile tender offer. We focus here on some newer developments in the field which address these problems.

(1) *Dividend Reinvestment.* More than 500 companies have adopted dividend reinvestment programs in recent years. The terms vary, but in general they permit shareholders to reinvest dividends in additional shares of company stock at little or no cost (or at a modest discount), and to make additional cash purchases of shares under the plan on a regular basis. Originally these programs created an inexpensive means for a corporation to raise capital on a continuing basis. Today even companies with no capital needs have such programs.

In most plans, the company buys shares on the open market to fulfill purchase requests. A smaller number of companies issue new shares of stock, resulting in some dilution over time. While these programs are desirable, there is very little evidence that they either attract investors (those who would make an initial investment simply because of the existence of a reinvestment program) or hold investors who have made an independent decision to sell their stock. Participation by 20% of a company's shareholders is considered excellent.

(2) *Shareholder Information Meetings.* An increasing number of companies are holding meetings in various parts of the country each year to meet with shareholders and answer their questions. These meetings omit the tedious official business which makes most annual meetings formal and difficult forums. The success of such informal meetings varies widely and depends a great deal on the personal effectiveness of management.

(3) *Shareholder Attitude Research.* Companies of all sizes are using traditional research techniques (mail questionnaires or telephone interviews) to learn more about who owns the company's stock and what motivates these individuals to buy, hold, or sell. Such surveys can also test the effectiveness of the annual report and other corporate communications to determine whether they are read and what message they convey.

(4) *Supplemental Information.* Corporations are making available a great deal more corporate information to interested shareholders. For example, AT&T devotes a page in its annual report to publications which shareholders may send for. In addition, more company annual reports now include a shareholder's page which summarizes all the information of interest to shareholders with more information on whom to contact with questions about lost shares and other matters.

(5) *Political Action.* Many companies, particularly in the petroleum industry, are organizing shareholder constituencies to support corporate positions with Federal or state officials. While these groups are primarily concerned with rebutting special-interest activities on particular issues, they serve the secondary benefit of involving interested shareholders in important ways with the future of the company.

There is growing interest in these and other activities to capture the attention and loyalty of existing shareholders. The climate of tender offers and takeovers has made companies painfully aware that they must pay continuing attention to their present shareholders.

Shareholder Relations: Potential Shareholders. Most companies continue to spend more money on attracting new shareholders than on any other part of financial public relations. The effort is largely a marketing activity. The New York Stock Exchange estimates that there are about 25 million investors in the United States. It has prepared extensive information on the known demographic characteristics of investors for use by its member firms. For most companies the audience is so large and so diffuse that only advertising or various types of financial publicity are considered cost effective tools to market a company to this audience.

Although efforts continue, there is still no valid data to support the proposition that advertising alone can trigger a potential investor's decision to purchase shares in a particular company. Probably because less dollars are involved, far less effort has been made to determine the impact of financial publicity on a potential investor's buy decision.

Because of these problems and others, companies have begun direct-mail and other efforts to reach brokers. Brokers are a smaller audience (about 36,000 individuals) and surveys suggest they play an important role in the investment decision process of a substantial percentage of potential investors. The recent availability of a mailing list of stock brokers (registered representatives) and the emergence of several publications aimed at this group, have opened the way for experimentation in novel communications programs. Here are some of the new activities in the field:

(1) *Broker Mailings and Materials.* Since brokers are salesmen, companies are assisting them in their work by preparing sales material for customers. This material may highlight a few key facts that make a company an attractive investment. Brokers may use this material on the phone or in mailings to customers.

(2) *Stockbroker Societies.* These organizations have patterned themselves along the lines of analyst societies. However, most are run for profit and charge companies to appear. They are controversial and vary widely in quality and impact.

(3) *Broker Service Programs.* These activities involve helping a broker do his customer relations work more effectively. Generally a broker is overworked and lacks adequate secretarial assistance. These programs seek to help him by assuming responsibility for mailing company materials directly to customers. At this writing, it is too early to tell whether these programs are cost effective over the long run.

(4) *Meetings with Brokerage Firms.* Increasingly companies send representatives to meet with groups of sales people in brokerage firm offices. This strategy can be particularly effective in cases where the firm's research department has recently published a research report on the company.

(5) *Broker Magazines.* There are at least three magazines written specifically for, and distributed without charge to, all brokers. They offer an advertising vehicle for companies aggressively marketing their shares.

(6) *Research for Pay.* Some companies are either too small or too new to attract any serious written analysis by research professionals. Some former analysts and some public relations people will prepare, for a fee, a "research" report on the company for circulation to brokers and others. While in some cases the quality of this work may be good to excellent, there is an inherent conflict of interest problem that erodes the credibility of this advice.

(7) *Television.* There is a good deal of experimentation with television programming on cable, cassettes, and VHF and UHF stations. No pattern of success has emerged. The field of broker communications is still in the experimental phase. There are no activities which have yet become widespread.

International Investor Relations. An increasingly important part of many companies' financial public relations is an international investor relations program. Primarily, these programs are oriented toward the European investor, by far the largest investing segment internationally. Their impact on the U.S. securities market can be shown by the fact that at this writing an estimated 12% of the total gross activity on the New York Stock Exchange is believed to be accounted for by European investors.

Largely institutional in nature, the European investor has the highest degree of concentration after the U.S. institutional investor. Approximately 450 firms in twelve countries manage the investment of securities totalling nearly $300 billion in value. In all but the largest of these firms, one or two individuals will have responsibility for following all U.S. companies of interest.

The main goal of a European investor-relations program is to contact these U.S. securities specialists in the major European financial institutions and to familiarize them with the company's operations. Ideally, ongoing contact with these specialists will be maintained over a period of years, building trust, credibility, and a regular following. The program itself generally consists of three parts:

- Formal presentations to groups of analysts and portfolio managers in European money centers;
- Follow-up mailings of earnings releases and significant company announcements; and
- Individual follow-up meetings with the investor relations managers in these key financial institutions.

The formal company presentations are usually given by the chief executive officer and the chief financial officer. Other officers, such as the CEO of European operations, may also be present. Having the CEO in a country for a presentation often provides an excellent opportunity to maximize the financial story by arranging press interviews in major publications.

Follow-up mailings to analysts and portfolio managers can also be combined with an ongoing European financial advertising and publicity program. More companies today supplement these analyst communications with information to leading officers at European financial institutions.

Additional Background and Research. The burgeoning field of research and services tailored expressly to financial public relations is one measure of the recognition that the function is valid corporate activity. There is now a trade association of individuals engaged in financial relations, The National Investor Relations Institute, based in Washington, with chapters in most large cities. It currently has about 800 individual members. A section of The Public Relations Society of America is also devoted to investor relations.

Seminars on financial relations now are conducted at least annually by such organizations as The Public Relations Society of America, The National Investor Relations Institute, and Opinion Research Corporation, as well as by independent seminar sponsors.

Research designed to provide information for those in the field of financial relations is offered by such organizations as Yankelovich, Skelly and White, Greenwich Research, and Opinion Research Corporation, as well as by numerous firms which evaluate shareholder attitudes and motivation for individual companies.

Major suppliers to the field, such as Technimetrics (analyst mailing lists), can offer a wealth of practical information. In addition there is a monthly column on investor relations in the magazine *Institutional Investor,* and at least three monthly newsletters devoted exclusively to reporting new ideas and trends in the field.

All these sources are readily accessible and, with the exception of research, free or inexpensive starting points for a company interested in undertaking a financial public relations program for the first time or upgrading an existing program. (For addresses, see Appendix B.)

Legal Restraints. Omitted from this summary of financial public relations is any discussion of the numerous legal restraints which govern corporate communications. Anyone engaged in the field must be aware of the extensive ramifications of Rule 10b-5 of the Securities and Exchange Act of 1934, the concept of materiality, the philosophy of timely disclosure and the mechanics of disclosure outlined in the New York Stock Exchange's *Company Manual.*

Special rules limit communications in tender offers, in offerings of shares to the public, and other activities. In general, a person engaged in any aspect of financial public relations should work with the advice and counsel of a competent securities lawyer to protect both himself and his company.

ROBERT W. TAFT, Senior Vice President, Hill and Knolton, Inc., New York, New York

Cross References: *Annual Reports; Public Relations; Securities and Exchange Commission.*

FINANCIAL RATIOS

Financial Ratios portray relationships that exist between various items appearing in balance sheets and income accounts and occasionally other items. They may be expressed in simple mathematical terms (e.g., two to one), in percentages, or in other terms which make them more readily comprehensible (e.g., sales per square foot of selling space). They are used to measure and evaluate the financial condition and operating effectiveness of a business.

Many different ratios are commonly used and new ones are constantly being devised to serve specific purposes. Some of those most commonly used portray the following relationships:

Net profit on sales.

Net profit on tangible net worth.

Current assets to current liabilities.

Current liabilities to tangible net worth.

Net fixed assets to tangible net worth.

Sales to inventories.

Sales to receivables (expressed in days' sales).

Operating profits to interest charges.

Need of Standards. In order to have significance, the ratios of a specific company must be compared with a norm, just as a golfer compares his score with par. Since different lines of industry have different characteristics, the typical ratios in one line of business tend to be different from those in another and, therefore, sets of typical ratios for each line of industry are desirable. These sets are becoming available in a steadily increasing number of lines, particularly as more and more trade associations develop statistics for their members.

Sources of Standards. The Robert Morris Associates, Philadelphia, an organization of bank credit men, has been compiling Financial Ratios since 1920. Dun & Bradstreet, Inc., New York, has issued annually since 1931 a set of fourteen ratios in seventy-two lines of business in manufacturing and construction; thirty-two in wholesaling, and twenty-two in retailing. Leventhal, Krekstein, Horwath and Horwath,

C.P.A.s, New York, compile and publish ratios in the hotel and restaurant lines. Seidman & Seidman, C.P.A.s, New York, do the same in the furniture manufacturing industry. The First National Bank of Chicago issues annually twenty-six ratios pertaining to the installment sales finance and consumer finance industries.

Ratios and Financial Analyses. Techniques of use vary somewhat and some skill is desirable. Even without training, however, a businessman can usually arrive at some worthwhile conclusions regarding the financial condition and operating effectiveness of a concern by the use of ratios, provided a set of standard ratios of that line is available. A comparison of the ratios of the company being analyzed with the appropriate standard ratios shows in what respects that company is typical of, superior to, or inferior to representative companies in its industry.

The *financial condition* (as distinguished from the operating effectiveness) can be determined basically from five ratios:

(1) *Net Fixed Assets to Tangible Net Worth.* When this ratio is significantly above the norm, it indicates a potentially topheavy investment in fixed assets, possibly an excessively high breakeven point in sales, and is frequently accompanied by a shortage of working capital.

What the proper ratio should be depends, of course, on the line of business. Near one extreme are such concerns as finance companies and wholesalers, which generally operate in leased quarters, do no manufacturing, and have no need of fixed assets beyond necessary office equipment. Such concerns rarely have more than about 10% of their tangible net worth invested in net fixed assets. At the other extreme will generally be found the public utilities, which must have large investments in plant assets. Such concerns may have an investment in net fixed assets equivalent to 300% of tangible net worth. Despite these extremes, it is generally true in most lines of business that the investment in net fixed assets tends to range between 30% and 60% of tangible net worth.

The business which invests too high a proportion of its capital in fixed assets may easily find itself with insufficient money left over with which to conduct operations. This rule applies to every concern, whether a small retailer or a giant manufacturer. So long as the company is adequately equipped for its operational needs, there is no danger in too small an investment in net fixed assets. Generally speaking, a low fixed investment leaves the greater part of the invested capital free for other purposes.

(2) *Sales to Net Working Capital.* This measures the adequacy of working capital for the volume transacted. A ratio which is significantly higher than the norm indicates inadequate working capital and reflects an excessive risk of financial embarrassment.

Simply stated, this ratio is important because it takes capital to finance the day-to-day operations of a business. Again, what the relationship should be depends on the line of business. Near one extreme are such concerns as wholesalers of cigarettes and confectionery, which are usually close to their sources of supply so that they can obtain frequent and quick replenishment of their inventories. They are not required to process their inventories except to break large incoming lots into smaller quantities for delivery to their customers. And since selling terms are either cash or on a load-to-load basis, collections are prompt. As a result, cash is received sufficiently rapidly to meet obligations punctually.

Generally speaking, those industries in which inventory turnover is relatively rapid and in which selling terms are short can and usually do have a higher turnover of net working capital than others not so situated. Dealers in perishables and style goods particularly have a high turnover of net working capital—and among such lines, an annual sales volume equivalent to from eight to fifteen times net working capital is typical.

Near the other extreme are industries in which the inventory turnover is necessarily low or in which selling terms are long. Thus, net working capital in substantial amounts is required for meeting maturing obligations while the company waits for its inventories to be processed or aged, as the case may be, before they are delivered to customers, and while it waits for collections on its receivables. Here annual sales may be equivalent to only once or twice the net working capital. Distillers of whiskey and manufacturers of tobacco products, for example, must age their merchandise for extended periods. Furniture retailers and others selling on installment terms require substantial amounts of net working capital to carry their receivables.

The lines of industry in which the extremes of either a high or a low net working capital turnover appear are in the minority. In the great majority of cases, sound financial policy requires that management provide net working capital equivalent to at least one sixth to one fourth of annual sales. Failure to preserve this ratio usually indicates that the company is undercapitalized, and that it must "overtrade." It will be straining its resources and undergoing the risk that maturing obligations may not be met promptly, that creditors may take temporary control, or, worst of all, that the company will be in too weak a condition to withstand any unexpected loss without going into bankruptcy.

(3) *Inventory to Net Working Capital.* With the exception of relatively few lines of business (e.g., retail shoes, retail drugs) inventories typically are equivalent to less than 100% of net working capital and are generally in the 60%–80% range. The importance of this ratio comes from the fact that as long as inventories are equivalent to less than 100% of the net working capital, it is simultaneously true that cash and receivables cover the current liabilities. Above 100%, cash and receivables fail to cover the current debt. In times of economic stress the ability to meet maturing obligations promptly is predicated largely on the liquidity of the current assets, and the so-called "acid test" of liquidity is met when cash and receivables cover the current debt. Inventories are unlike cash and receivables in that the former are worth only what they will bring when they are sold, whereas the latter are already in definite dollar amounts. The desirability of maintaining cash and receivables at least equivalent to the current liabilities is thus apparent, and this objective is always attained so long as inventories are less than net working capital.

A high ratio of inventory to net working capital does not necessarily indicate that inventories are excessive. The basic weakness may be that net working capital is inadequate. Whether the latter is true can be determined by studying the net working capital turnover, as discussed above in connection with Ratio No. 2.

(4) *Sales to Receivables.* This ratio is commonly expressed in number of days' sales represented by the receivables. The number of days is called the *collection period,* and measures the liquidity of the receivables. Cash sales are eliminated in making this calculation, since cash sales do not generate receivables.

A quick method to determine the over-all quality of the receivables is to examine the receivables in the light of credit terms extended by the company. For example, if the terms of sale provide for payment in thirty days, then, barring seasonal factors, there should be approximately thirty days' credit sales in receivables at any given time. The analysis calls for dividing annual credit sales by 365 to determine average credit sales per day. The resulting figure is then divided into total receivables, the answer being the numbers of days' sales in receivables or the average collection period. If the collection period is substantially longer than the period provided by the terms of sale, the company faces a potentially serious financial situation.

(5) *Sales to Inventory.* By indicating the rapidity with which the inventory turns, this ratio indicates its liquidity. A low ratio suggests slow-moving items and a lack of inventory control.

Other Ratios. Because the five ratios discussed above are basic, they tend to control other balance sheet ratios. If these five are normal, other ratios such as *Current and/or Total Debt to Tangible Net Worth* and the *Current Ratio* (current assets to current liabilities) will likewise be normal. Conversely, a heavy debt-to-worth ratio or a low current ratio is invariably caused by the fact that one or more of the five basic ratios are out of line.

Whatever may be the real cause of business failures, there is one thing which is common to them all, and that is debts—debts which could not be paid. One of the best means of telling whether debts are excessive is to compare them with the tangible net worth. The relationships vary considerably from one line of industry to another, but a dependable rule of thumb is that current liabilities should generally not exceed 50% or 60% of tangible net worth. Generally, most financially sound enterprises operate with current liabilities equivalent to not much more than 40% of the tangible net worth, except for those concerns in certain lines (e.g., finance companies, wholesalers of cigarettes) in which wide seasonal fluctuations are inevitable. Total debts, including both current liabilities and funded debt, should generally be not more than 70% or 80% of the tangible net worth; and another good general rule is that a funded debt should not be greater than net working capital.

There has long been a widespread idea that a current ratio of $2 of current assets for every $1 of current liabilities is indicative of financial soundness. It is true that many companies with a current ratio of 2 to 1 are indeed financially sound; but when they are, it is invariably because sound management policies which resulted in the first five ratios being in line were followed. Actually, many companies with current ratios of 1.25 or 1.50 to 1 are sounder financially than others with current ratios of 5 to 1. The current ratio should be recognized for what it is—a guide of some value, but by no means an all-inclusive answer. The current ratio, like many others, is a result of other, more basic factors.

Operating Effectiveness can be determined by the use of ratios developed from items in the income statements. The simplest are those of net profits in relation to sales and to tangible net worth. When these are low, a more detailed analysis is required to determine the cause, which may be one or a combination of things. Causes of low earnings may be found in inadequate gross profit margins, excessive rent, excessive salaries, raw material costs, or any of the other items of expense. (For more detailed discussion of this point, see RETURN ON CAPITAL.)

Analysis by means of financial ratios becomes more valuable when a comparison is made between specific ratios in successive years. For example, a steady reduction in gross profit margin should constitute a warning of potential danger. Or a steady reduction in turnover of receivables or inventory may point out the need for prompt remedial steps. Conversely, a reduction in the ratio of debt to net worth or an increase in the current ratio would suggest that the financial condition is becoming stronger.

H. E. KROLL, Dun & Bradstreet, Inc., New York, New York

Information References

Foulke, Roy A., "Practical Financial Statement Analysis," New York, McGraw-Hill, 6th ed., 1968

Gibson, Charles H. and Boyer, Patricia A., "Financial Statement Analysis," Boston, 1978.

McMullen, Stewart Y., "Financial Statements," Homewood, Ill., 7th ed., 1979.

Cross References: *Accounting; Financial Analysis: Earnings; Return on Capital.*

FIRE LOSS PREVENTION

Many properties, including manufacturing industries with severe fire hazards, have excellent records so far as loss of life or property from fire is concerned. The good record is the result of good management, particularly in regard to **Fire Loss Prevention.** On the other hand, all serious fires in industry, as elsewhere, reflect failure to provide proper management procedures. Loss-*prevention* is an essential phase of management.

Organization. The plant manager cannot reasonably be relieved of the ultimate responsibility for fire safety even though he may have staff specialist assistants, and even though the responsibility for the accomplishment of fire safety is extended down the organization line. There should be a fire loss prevention manager in the central management and in each plant when needed. This manager is a staff assistant to the plant manager. He normally develops the planning, policies, and procedures which the plant manager, upon his approval, issues and makes effective through the organization line. His normal place in the organization is on a par with the plant engineer and other division or department superintendents with whom he must deal. His relationships with other department superintendents are on a staff planning and advisory basis. His interests and work must necessarily cut across all lines in the organization.

There is still considerable difference in practice. In the early industrial plants, it was fairly common that the fire loss prevention man would be on the staff of the plant engineer, since his duties were principally maintenance of fire protection equipment. The fire loss prevention manager's duties are sometimes included in the duties of a security manager. This arrangement is characteristic of plants in the aircraft and electronic industries, where the companies have contracts with the Federal Government which require attention to security. An interesting organizational set-up is that of a number of companies which have a "loss prevention" manager who is a fire protection engineer in charge of safety, security, insurance, and fire protection, with staff assistants for each of these functions. This general setup is being used as management seriously studies its needs. Engineers who meet the qualifications for membership in the Society of Fire Protection Engineers are available now with appropriate experience to make such an arrangement effective and practical.

The fire loss prevention manager should have responsibility to establish the necessary schedules for periodic inspection of plant fire protective equipment—both fixed and portable—and to see that these inspection schedules are properly carried out. He should assist in establishing the necessary relationships with the public fire departments and with the area industries for mutual aid.

He should act as the coordinating person for insurance company contacts. In this connection he should make arrangements for routine insurance company inspections and for special inspections as needed; guide (or see that necessary escort is provided for) the insurance company representative during his plant visit; see that the insurance company representative gets the information that he needs to evaluate the risk or to provide the desired advice; see that a necessary "exit interview" is provided between the proper management members and the insurance company representatives so that all recommendations and their intent are properly understood by the plant persons involved; and coordinate the scheduling of accepted insurance company proposals and recommendations. In plants requiring fire brigades, he should see that they are established and trained.

In the average industrial plant, the greatest importance of the guards' (or watchmen's) rounds is their connection with fire protection, rather than plant "security" as such. It is therefore important that patrolmen's rounds be laid out with full consultation with the fire loss prevention manager.

Systems and Procedures. Systems and procedures having to do with fire safety should be selected and developed by the fire loss prevention manager, with the full participation of all concerned members of plant management. Some of the fundamental systems and procedures would cover the following items:

Engineering design review.
Work order review.
Hot work permit.
Outside contractor relationships.
Insurance company relationships.
Fire protection equipment inspection.
Fire brigade organization.
Fire and damage investigation and reports.
Notification of protection impairment.
Emergency procedures.

Standards for Methods and Equipment. The items selected for standardization, established on the basis of the particular property's need, should be assigned for first drafting to the plant specialist who knows most about the subject. Generally, of course, the preparation of the first drafts will fall to the responsibility of the fire loss prevention manager. The first draft of any standard should have wide circulation among all responsible members of plant management for comments and contributions. Important standards for plant fire safety include:

Identification and mounting of first-aid fire extinguishers.
Hose standards.
Nozzle standards.
Bulk storage of flammable liquids.
Storage and handling of flammable liquids—drum sizes and smaller.
Tank car loading and unloading of flammable liquids.

New Design. As soon as a new process, layout, or structure is contemplated, it should be the responsibility of the company engineering department to notify the fire loss prevention manager so that there can be necessary consultation in the early stages. It should be made the responsibility of Engineering to know the company's fire safety standards and to apply them in all new design and in all plant changes. It is their further responsibility to know all laws and statutes applying, and to see that such legal requirements are complied with.

Contractor Relationships. When projected work is to be done by an outside contractor, it should be Engineering's responsibility to contact the fire loss prevention manager and to determine from him exactly what special requirements must be met by the contractor. These requirements will vary with the job and ordinarily they would contemplate such items as: possible isolation of the contractor's work site, notification to the contractor of special hazards to be encountered in the plant processes or stored materials at or near the job site; the possible hazard which his work might present to the plant equipment, property, and personnel; smoking restrictions; use of hot work permits; control of contractor's employees and vehicles on the plant property; movement and storage of construction equipment and materials as far as fire safety is concerned; contractor's waste disposal. For relatively minor undertakings, the contractor should be instructed to see that a proper person is delegated to take care of this matter at individual plant locations.

Major Emergencies. In an emergency, particularly where loss of life is involved, management of an industrial plant has to take actions which include the following. (These are not listed in order of relative importance or in the order in which the actions will be taken):

(1) Account for every person on the payroll and rescue any who may be trapped in the plant.

(2) Call the public fire department and get the plant fire brigade into action.

(3) Issue releases to the press, radio and television news services immediately, giving the facts so far as they are known and are properly of public interest, but asking these services to withhold notifying the families of employees injured or killed until management can do it.

(4) Ask the police not to notify the families, but have this work done by appropriate teams of employees organized by the management.

(5) Report to top management the extent of damage and the possible time the plant will be shut down, so that necessary arrangements for transferring business to other plants and other adjustments in operations can be made promptly.

(6) The plant manager must decide the nature of an emergency; that is, he has to define the scale of operations which will be undertaken. Of course, the best management is one in which the scope or stages of a possible emergency have been visualized in advance, and a series of stages set up within which a predetermined pattern of operation will be followed.

Technically, the plant manager or ranking manager present is always in charge of the actual emergency.

Some operating functions must be preformed in some emergencies which have no exact counterpart in a day-to-day industrial operation, or which require additional personnel and equipment. This has sometimes led to the erroneous assumption that emergencies require a new all-encompassing operating organization. A special plant organization should not be set up to direct general operations in an emergency inconsistent with the operating organization.

In an emergency involving areas or people outside of the plant, there are additional management problems. Many managements recognize the principle of having well-worked-out procedures for dealing with the managements of neighboring industrial plants affected or exposed by the immediate fire or emergency and with all of the public agencies. Less well understood are principles of management action in an emergency outside the plant, in a neighboring plant, or in other property in neighboring communities.

For the handling of this type of situation the commonsense principle is that the manager's own plant should get his first attention. Its needs and requirements must not be overlooked in any gestures which are made to give assistance elsewhere. A manager who weakens his own plant fire or other defenses unreasonably may contribute to a much more serious disaster.

Physical Arrangements. Fire protection in large plants is principally a matter of physical arrangements. For example, spacing and cutoffs between buildings or units, automatic sprinkler systems, water supplies, and specially designed protection for certain items for process or storage. Such features as are fixed and local to the plant itself are not facilities which could be shared with other plants.

A large plant will have a technical staff which deals with fire safety and with employees assigned to a plant fire department or brigade. Of course, every industrial plant, whatever its size, should have fire extinguishers for promptly fighting small fires. Employees trained and assigned to use extinguishers are sometimes described as members of a plant fire brigade or fire department. However, the term "fire brigade" or "private fire department," as used here, refers to a fire department organization additional to the employees assigned to use extinguishers for the fighting of small fires. The majority of plants need have only first-aid fire fighters who would be under the direction of their usual foremen or departmental managers.

Relations with Public Fire Department. No matter how self-sufficient a manager may feel his plant is, he cannot ignore the services of the public fire department even where the public fire department is designed for the protection of the surrounding community rather than the plant. Unless there has been prior agreement as to their respective responsibilities, the chief of the public fire department might be considered to have the responsibility for dealing with a fire in the plant rather than the plant manager himself. This is because of a principle of common law in which very broad authority is given a fire department in case of fire. Where a plant has special fire hazards because of materials and processes with which the community fire department cannot be expected to be familiar, it is especially important to have prior agreement on the details of the types of emergency each will handle.

Traffic. The within-plant traffic problem will generally be assigned to a plant exit drill organization or plant police. Individual buildings should be provided with exits arranged in such a manner as to allow personnel to get from a dangerous to a safe location in minimum time. Such procedures should be developed with the public police agencies who deal with traffic outside the plant in case of emergency.

The movement of public utility and transportation agency employees is particularly important. Both the plant and the public interest demand also that representatives of newspaper, radio, and television news services be able to move to the emergency area so as to be properly informed as to matters which should be passed on to the public through these news media.

Public Relations. A big fire or other emergency requires an effective procedure for informing people associated with the plant who need to know what the situation is, and to inform the public generally. Public announcements cannot be well considered if they have to be thought up at the time of an emergency. Much of the planning for the handling of public relations matters must be done before an emergency develops.

Definite public relations responsibilities for each plant must be made in advance. The individuals assigned to this work should be ones not likely to be seriously involved in actually dealing with the emergency. These news or public relations people on the plant staff should be made well known in advance to representatives of all news services. The plant manager must give someone the responsibility of seeing that news representatives get information they should have, yet at the same time not violate local plant security regulations nor put themselves in an unnecessarily dangerous position.

The management should be available or be represented for reasonable questioning by news representatives if the conditions of the disaster make this at all possible. In some cases it may be extremely important for public relations for the plant manager to make an appropriate statement.

Evaluation of Fire Possibilities. Two specific figures are useful for management appraisal of the fire problem. The first is the *largest percentage of the property value likely to be affected by fire, heat, smoke, and water damage.* This figure would show the extreme possibilities of loss of physical plant facilities. This determination may also help to indicate probable loss of life of people associated with the plant, including the management.

The second figure is *probable loss.* This will be smaller than the first figure, and takes into account the facilities for firespread limitation and fire fighting.

Similar calculations can be made, not only for fire potential, but for the effects of other disaster factors.

HORATIO BOND, Consulting Engineer, Hyannis Port, Massachusetts, formerly Chief Engineer, National Fire Protection Association

Information References

A principal source of information is the National Fire Protection Association, with services and publications as indicated below. Insurance companies, their service organizations and brokers, and also consulting fire protection engineering firms, can provide useful services on loss prevention and also make useful publications available to management. Principal fire insurance organizations serving industrial property include the Factory Mutual System, the Industrial Risk Insurers, the American Mutual Insurance Alliance and the Improved Risk Mutuals, although this listing is not offered as comprehensive. Mechanical equipment used should conform to listings by Underwriters Laboratories or the Factory Mutual System.

Publications and Services:

The National Fire Protection Association will furnish lists of its numerous periodicals and publications, and descriptive material on a number of useful services. Important publications include "Industrial Fire Hazards Handbook," "Fire Protection Handbook," "National Fire Codes," "NFPA Inspection Manual," "Industrial Fire Brigades Training Manual." It can provide slides, cassette tapes and manuals for training in dealing with hazardous materials emergencies, and educational films on fire subjects. It holds regular meetings devoted to fire loss prevention matters and supplements these with workshops for industrial emergency forces and seminars on industrial fire protection in various cities of the United States and Canada.

In addition to the sources mentioned above, fire loss prevention matters are treated in trade and technical periodicals (although as a side interest to their main fields).

Cross Reference: *Disaster Recovery.*

FIXED-ASSET INVESTMENT ANALYSIS: The MAPI Formulas and Procedures

The Machinery and Allied Products Institute (MAPI) has long been a leader in developing formulas and procedures for analyzing **Fixed-Asset Investment** proposals and providing management with policy guidelines regarding such investment. Studies undertaken in 1948 resulted in the publication of a series of volumes including a basic theoretical analysis, "Dynamic Equipment Policy" (1949), a general guide to application, "MAPI Replacement Manual" (1950), and a more detailed guide, "Company Procedural Manual on Equipment Analysis," (1951). These were followed by a series of revisions and refinements, culminating in the definitive volume of 1967, "Business Investment Manual," by MAPI research director George Terborgh. (This is the extant volume as of 1981.)

The Institute stresses that the new system in no way repudiates or discredits the earlier ones.

EXHIBIT I

PROJECT NO.__________ SHEET I

MAPI SUMMARY FORM

(AVERAGING SHORTCUT)

PROJECT____________________

ALTERNATIVE____________________

COMPARISON PERIOD (YEARS) (P)__________

ASSUMED OPERATING RATE OF PROJECT (HOURS PER YEAR) __________

I. OPERATING ADVANTAGE

(NEXT-YEAR FOR A 1-YEAR COMPARISON PERIOD,* ANNUAL AVERAGES FOR LONGER PERIODS)

A. EFFECT OF PROJECT ON REVENUE

		INCREASE	DECREASE	
1	FROM CHANGE IN QUALITY OF PRODUCTS	$	$	1
2	FROM CHANGE IN VOLUME OF OUTPUT			2
3	TOTAL	$ X	$ Y	3

B. EFFECT ON OPERATING COSTS

4	DIRECT LABOR	$	$	4
5	INDIRECT LABOR			5
6	FRINGE BENEFITS			6
7	MAINTENANCE			7
8	TOOLING			8
9	MATERIALS AND SUPPLIES			9
10	INSPECTION			10
11	ASSEMBLY			11
12	SCRAP AND REWORK			12
13	DOWN TIME			13
14	POWER			14
15	FLOOR SPACE			15
16	PROPERTY TAXES AND INSURANCE			16
17	SUBCONTRACTING			17
18	INVENTORY			18
19	SAFETY			19
20	FLEXIBILITY			20
21	OTHER			21
22	TOTAL	$ Y	$ X	22

C. COMBINED EFFECT

23	NET INCREASE IN REVENUE (3X−3Y)	$	23
24	NET DECREASE IN OPERATING COSTS (22X−22Y)	$	24
25	ANNUAL OPERATING ADVANTAGE (23+24)	$	25

* Next year means the first year of project operation. For projects with a significant break-in period, use performance after break-in.

It points out that companies that have gone to the trouble of installing the second MAPI system—no small undertaking—and have their work sheets and procedures set up accordingly, will probably find no sufficient reason to change over, but that others, starting *de novo*, would probably prefer to install the new one.

"Business Investment Manual" presents and explains the application of a detailed specimen or suggested form. The first section of this form (Exhibit I) deals with *operational analysis*, and the second section (Exhibit II) deals with *investment and return calculations.* The form is designed for relative-return analysis—the comparison of a project with a stated alternative,

EXHIBIT II

SHEET 2

II. INVESTMENT AND RETURN

A. INITIAL INVESTMENT

26 INSTALLED COST OF PROJECT $ ______
MINUS INITIAL TAX BENEFIT OF $ ______ (Net Cost) $ ______ 26
27 INVESTMENT IN ALTERNATIVE
CAPITAL ADDITIONS MINUS INITIAL TAX BENEFIT $ ______
PLUS: DISPOSAL VALUE OF ASSETS RETIRED
BY PROJECT * $ ______ $ ______ 27
28 INITIAL NET INVESTMENT (26–27) $ ______ 28

B. TERMINAL INVESTMENT

29 RETENTION VALUE OF PROJECT AT END OF COMPARISON PERIOD
(ESTIMATE FOR ASSETS, IF ANY, THAT CANNOT BE DEPRECIATED OR EXPENSED. FOR OTHERS, ESTIMATE OR USE MAPI CHARTS.)

Item or Group	Installed Cost, Minus Initial Tax Benefit (Net Cost) A	Service Life (Years) B	Disposal Value, End of Life (Percent of Net Cost) C	MAPI Chart Number D	Chart Percent-age E	Retention Value $\left(\frac{A \times E}{100}\right)$ F
	$					$

ESTIMATED FROM CHARTS (TOTAL OF COL. F) $ ______
PLUS: OTHERWISE ESTIMATED $ ______ $ ______ 29
30 DISPOSAL VALUE OF ALTERNATIVE AT END OF PERIOD * $ ______ 30
31 TERMINAL NET INVESTMENT (29–30) $ ______ 31

C. RETURN

32 AVERAGE NET CAPITAL CONSUMPTION $\left(\frac{28-31}{P}\right)$ $ ______ 32
33 AVERAGE NET INVESTMENT $\left(\frac{28+31}{2}\right)$ $ ______ 33
34 BEFORE-TAX RETURN $\left(\frac{25-32}{33} \times 100\right)$ % ______ 34
35 INCREASE IN DEPRECIATION AND INTEREST DEDUCTIONS $ ______ 35
36 TAXABLE OPERATING ADVANTAGE (25–35) $ ______ 36
37 INCREASE IN INCOME TAX (36×TAX RATE) $ ______ 37
38 AFTER-TAX OPERATING ADVANTAGE (25–37) $ ______ 38
39 AVAILABLE FOR RETURN ON INVESTMENT (38–32) $ ______ 39
40 AFTER-TAX RETURN $\left(\frac{39}{33} \times 100\right)$ % ______ 40

* After terminal tax adjustments.

EXHIBIT III

MAPI CHART NO. 1A

(ONE-YEAR COMPARISON PERIOD AND SUM-OF-DIGITS TAX DEPRECIATION)

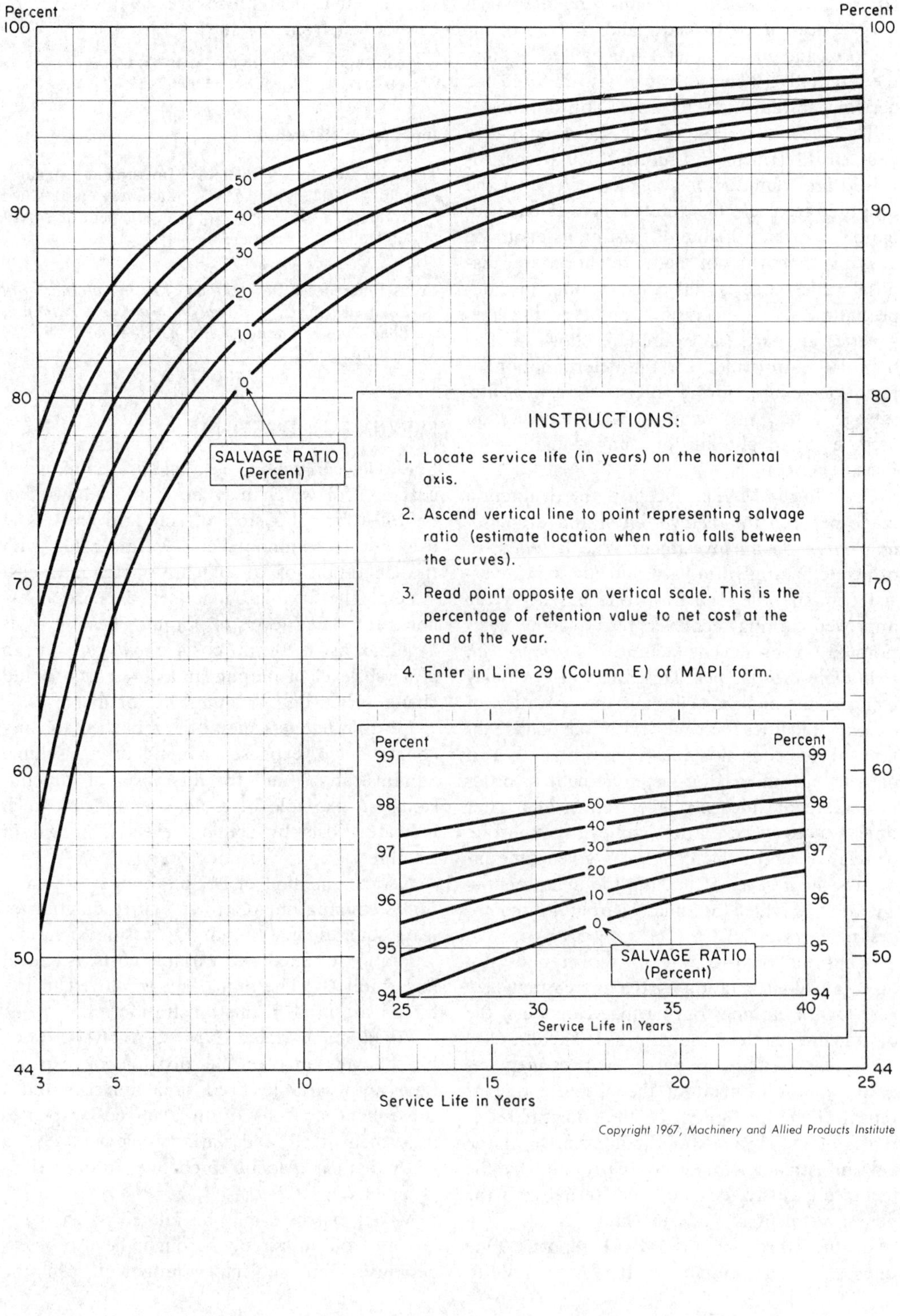

i.e., the cost of going on without the new investment. For this reason it calls for estimates of the operating *differences* between a proposed project and an alternative. The increases and decreases for specific items (direct and indirect labor, fringe benefits, tooling, maintenance, floor space, property taxes and insurance, inventory, and many others) are figured against the alternative. (The form can also be used for deriving absolute returns where appropriate.)

The second section of the form embodies detailed investment and return calculations. Involved are computations on the net cost of the proposed project, the limited investments required to extend the life of existing assets if the new investment is not made, retention and disposal values, net capital consumption, tax, depreciation, interest computations, and the like. A series of charts (an example is shown as Exhibit III) is provided for the determination of retention values, giving effect to service life, salvage ratio, and form of tax depreciation used, e.g., straight line or, sum-of-digits. (See DEPRECIATION.)

Basic to the MAPI concept is the distinction made between the *relative return* and the *absolute return* on an investment. The latter is, in principle, a straightforward and non-controversial computation. The former is based on the improved earnings achieved by replacing deteriorated or obsolescent facilities, *compared with continuing with the old.* This rate will obviously increase, the more uneconomic the operation of existing facilities becomes with the elapse of time. That does not mean, however, that it pays to put off making an investment in order to achieve the higher rate of return at a later time. It does mean that a significantly high rate of relative return calculated at a given time indicates the *urgency* of making the investment—an urgency which becomes sharper as the investment is put off.

What the relative rate of return does not take into consideration is the increasingly severe loss of earnings during the years when the old facilities are continued in use. Therefore, to determine the best *timing* of an investment requires the adjustment of the absolute rate of return of the investment by the computed sacrifices of the earnings of the alternative, if the new investment is made too early, and by the incurred excessive costs of the alternative if the new investment is made too late.

In the words of the MAPI report, "One thing should be evident . . . It is impossible to make sound investment decisions without a clear comprehension of the distinction [between the two rates of return]. It is the beginning of wisdom in the art of investment analysis. Once it is grasped, it is at least *possible* to develop rational analytical procedures; without it, the case is lost from the start."

SOURCE: MACHINERY AND ALLIED PRODUCTS INSTITUTE, Washington, D.C.

Information Reference

Terborgh, George, "Business Investment Management," Washington, D.C., Machinery and Allied Products Institute, 1967 (plus supplementing MAPI publications).

Cross References: *Depreciation; Leasing of Industrial Equipment; Long-Range Corporate Planning; Long-Range Planning: Financial Aspects; Return on Capital.*

FLEXIBLE BUDGETING

Flexible Budgeting is a major technique of cost control which may be employed whether or not a formal system of standard costs is in use, but is commonly closely integrated with the operation of a company's standard cost system. The flexible budget sets expense allowances for stated levels of output. These serve as a guide as to what costs *should be* at an *achieved* level of output, and how costs should change when output diminishes or increases.

Flexible budgets may be established for any component of expense—manufacturing, selling, administrative—and for any level of supervision. An example of a flexible budget which indicates costs by activity levels is shown in Exhibit I.

Another method of flexible budget presentation stemming out of either scatter diagram or least squares analysis, and stressing a careful separation of fixed and variable costs, is shown in Exhibit II. (The same data employed in Exhibit I are used in this illustration.)

Fixed and Variable Expense Analysis. Flexible budgets involve the division of expense items into variable, fixed, and "mixed," and a subsequent analysis of the "mixed" expenses into their fixed and variable elements by a study of their reaction to changes in operational activity.

Mixed expenses may be related to changing levels of output simply through the use of experienced but subjective judgment. On the

EXHIBIT I

FLEXIBLE BUDGET SHOWING COSTS BY LEVELS OF OUTPUT
Department No. 16

	Direct Labor Hours					
Expense	*40,000*	*50,000*	*60,000*	*70,000*	*80,000*	*90,000*
Indirect Materials	$1,000	$1,250	$1,500	$ 1,750	$ 2,000	$ 2,250
Power	400	500	600	700	800	900
Indirect Labor	1,800	2,200	2,600	3,000	3,400	3,800
Maintenance	300	350	400	450	500	550
Supplies	550	650	750	850	950	1,050
Miscellaneous	950	1,100	1,250	1,400	1,550	1,700
Depreciation	500	500	500	500	500	500
Space Occupancy	400	400	400	400	400	400
Supervision	1,000	1,000	1,000	1,000	1,000	1,000
Totals	$6,900	$7,950	$9,000	$10,050	$11,100	$12,150

other hand, a study may be made of these expenses by means of scatter diagram or least squares analysis. In either of the latter cases, past experience in terms of dollars spent at actual levels of output achieved is arrayed and studied, non-random variations are eliminated, and the behavior of the remaining items are generalized on a straight-line basis.

Scatter Diagram Analysis of a Mixed Expense. The data in Exhibit III represent a company's historical experience with indirect labor cost. These figures are plotted graphically in Exhibit IV to illustrate the use of scatter diagram analysis to effect the separation of a mixed expense into its fixed and variable elements.

Note that the cost curve intersects the vertical axis at about $51,000, indicating the fixed element of indirect labor cost. Once this amount is known, total indirect labor cost for some one particular level of output is estimated from the cost curve, for example, indirect labor cost at 10,000 direct labor hours totals $54,000. To obtain the variable rate per direct labor hour, fixed indirect labor cost of $51,000 just noted is subtracted from the $54,000 total indirect labor cost, and divided by 10,000 direct labor hours. The variable rate for indirect labor cost is therefore $0.30 per direct labor hour. These data may be summarized and generalized into a formula for indirect labor cost, where Y represents indirect labor cost, a, the fixed element in indirect labor cost, b, the rate in dollars and cents at which indirect labor

EXHIBIT III

HISTORICAL DATA FOR MIXED EXPENSE ANALYSIS

Month	*Direct Labor Hours*	*Indirect Labor Cost*
January	65,000	$70,000
February	70,000	68,000
March	40,000	62,000
April	40,000	63,000
May	50,000	67,000
June	75,000	75,000
July	66,000	65,000
August	65,600	69,300
September	70,000	74,000
October	90,000	78,000
November	82,000	74,000
December	75,000	70,000

EXHIBIT II

FLEXIBLE BUDGET SHOWING COSTS BY FIXED AND VARIABLE ELEMENTS
Department No. 16

	Fixed Amount (if any)	*Variable Rate*
Indirect Materials		$0.025
Power		.010
Indirect Labor	$ 200	.040
Maintenance	100	.005
Supplies	150	.010
Miscellaneous	350	.015
Depreciation	500	
Space Occupancy	400	
Supervision	1,000	
Totals	$2,700	$0.105

EXHIBIT IV

SCATTER DIAGRAM ANALYSIS OF INDIRECT LABOR COST

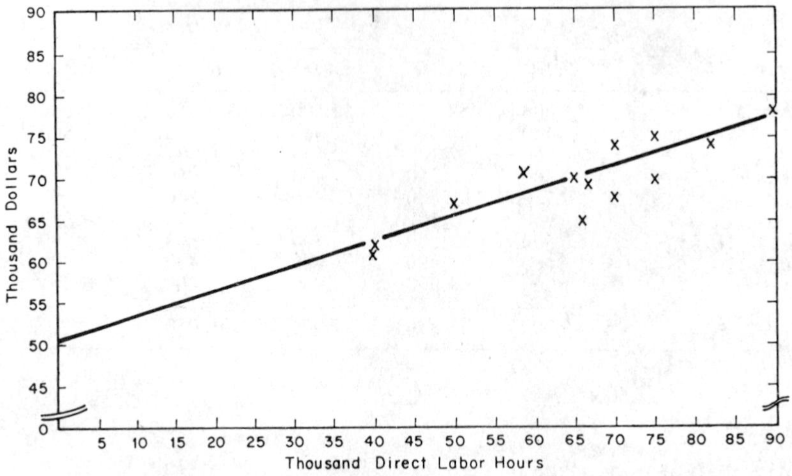

cost varies with changes in activity, and x the measurement of activity:

$$Y = a + bx$$

Indirect labor cost data as analyzed in the foregoing example may be shown therefore as:

Indirect labor cost = \$51,000 + \$0.30x

Horngren, in "Cost Accounting," Chapter 25 presents a comprehensive discussion of the application of least squares analysis, a mathematical and statistical approach to the separation of mixed expenses into their fixed and variable elements [1]. A sophisticated discussion concerning a wide variety of cost behaviors expressible in cost equations is given by Dopuch and Birnberg, "Cost Accounting" [2].

Flexible budgeting may be used as a basis for performance control over any specified area of business operations. For example, if Department No. 16 referred to in Exhibits I and II incurred \$10,600 expenses when operating at 60,000 direct labor hours (DLH), the flexible budget given in either Exhibit I or II is used as a basis for determining variations in expense items from that allowed by the budget. Exhibit V presents the actual and budgeted costs of Department No. 16 for the month of November.

Control procedures would call for an explanation of the variance of \$1,600. Such an explanation is facilitated when (1) the budget is separated into expense items controllable by the supervisor and those which are not, with correction efforts directed toward controllable items, or (2) fexible budgeting for overhead costs is integrated into either overhead accounting or standard costing, and the overhead variance is analyzed into controllable and noncontrollable variances.

Flexible Budgeting and Overhead Accounting. When a flexible budget is employed in conjunction with overhead accounting, the budget is used to construct overhead rates which are in turn used to apply overhead costs to production. Differences between actual and ap-

EXHIBIT V

ACTUAL AND BUDGETED COSTS OF DEPARTMENT NO. 16 NOVEMBER, 19—

	Budget for 60,000 DLH	*Actual Costs*	*Variance*
Indirect Materials	\$1,500	\$ 2,000	\$ 500
Power	600	550	(50)
Indirect Labor	2,600	3,000	400
Maintenance	400	700	300
Supplies	750	950	200
Miscellaneous	1,250	1,500	250
Depreciation	500	500	
Space Occupancy	400	400	
Supervision	1,000	1,000	
Totals	\$9,000	\$10,600	\$1,600

plied overhead may in such instance be analyzed into (1) a variance deemed *controllable by the supervisor,* called a budget, performance, or expense variance, and (2) a variance denoting the *inability of top management to provide work,* called a capacity, volume, or activity variance.

To illustrate the computation and use of these variances, assume that the fixed overhead rate is based on an average monthly output of 60,000 DLH. Dividing the $2,700 fixed overhead cost obtained from Exhibit II by 60,000, the fixed cost rate per DLH becomes $0.045. The variable overhead rate obtainable from the same Exhibit II is $0.105 per DLH. During November, when Department No. 16 works 50,000 DLH, manufacturing overhead incurred and overhead costs applied to production are pictured in the "T" accounts given in Exhibit VI.

In the 2-variance method of analysis (in a non-standard cost system), the analyst would separate the difference between the $8,200 spent and the $7,500 taken to inventories into two variances. He would first turn to the budget of overhead cost allowed for 50,000 DLH, $7,950 (see Exhibit I), and subtract it from the actual manufacturing overhead costs of $8,200. The resulting variance of $250 would ordinarily be typed as a *controllable* budget variance and, if considered significant, would require explanation from the supervisor and subsequent efforts at correction.

In turn, the analyst would compare the $7,950 allowed overhead cost with the $7,500 applied to output (see "T" accounts, Exhibit VI), and compute a capacity variance of $450. (To check: multiply 10,000 DLH worked below average capacity times the fixed cost rate of $0.045.) This variance is ordinarily interpreted as resulting from management's inability to obtain sufficient orders to keep the department busy, and, if so, it would be charged as a cost

EXHIBIT VI

OVERHEAD ACCOUNTS

Mfg. Oh. Dept. No. 16	
Actual $8,200	

Work in Process	
From Mfg. Oh. Applied $7,500	

Mfg. Oh. Dept. No. 16 Applied	
	To Work in Proc. (50,000 × $0.15) $7,500

of general administration rather than a variance controllable by the supervisor of Department No. 16. However, alternatively, failure to utilize facilities at normal in Department No. 16 may have been due to inefficiency and work stoppages in previous departments, requiring lay-offs in Department No. 16. In this latter instance, therefore, the variance becomes the responsibility of supervision taking place prior to Department No. 16.

Flexible Budgeting and Standard Costing. If carefully developed, the flexible budgets described in Exhibits I and II could also be used in standard costing. In standard costing, under a 2-variance method of analysis, a subtle change would take place in the construction of the fixed overhead rate. Normal capacity would refer to good output achieved, not actual hours worked. In addition, standard overhead rates would be applied to hours *allowed* for good output achieved rather than actual hours. For example, assume that in the preceding illustration, 60,000 *actual* direct labor hours had been worked, but that only 50,000 "standard direct labor hours of output" were earned. The 25,000 units of product manufactured were allowed only 2 hours of direct labor time each at standard. Despite the fact that 60,000 DLH were worked, all figures to be shown in "T" accounts and the derivation of resulting variances would remain the same as in the foregoing illustration based upon 50,000 DLH. The budget allowance of $7,950 would be based upon 50,000 DLH earned, and the capacity variance would be computed by comparing the 50,000 DLH earned with the stated normal of 60,000 DLH.

In discussing defects in commonly used methods of overhead variance analysis when used in connection with flexible budgeting, critics have complained that so-called controllable budget variances are often caused by a variety of dissimilar events having little relationship to one another. The magnitude of the budget variance, for example, is often affected by prices paid for expense factors not always controllable by a supervisor, by inefficient use of expense items such as supplies and power, and, in standard costing, by excessive use of time calling for increased operating expenses. If the "T" account data in Exhibit VI were based on standard costs and 60,000 DLH had been operated, one might argue that the supervisor of Department No. 16 did quite well. If the budget allowance were based upon the 60,000 actual hours worked, the supervisor would have been allowed $9,000 overhead cost (see Exhibit I), and he had only spent $8,200. Furthermore, the capacity variance of $450, often termed uncontrollable by lower level supervision, is in this instance indicative of the use of excessive time in the achievement of output.

Improvement in Variance Analysis Through Use of the 3-Variance Method. When flexible budgeting is utilized in connection with standard costing, use of a 3-variance method of analysis overcomes some of the objections noted in the use of the 2-variance method. The budget is based on actual hours worked, and the effect of the excessive use of time or saving in time on the total overhead variance is separated into a variance called an "efficiency" variance. Normal capacity continues to be based upon standard hours earned.

To illustrate, using the same data employed in the "T" accounts in Exhibit VI, actual manufacturing overhead cost for November is $8,200, and standard overhead cost applied to products is $7,500. A revised budget variance is computed on the basis of 60,000 actual direct labor hours worked ($8,200 actual overhead − $9,000 overhead allowed), and a favorable budget variance of $800 results. The efficiency variance is computed by multiplying the 10,000 extra hours taken (60,000 DLH actual − 50,000 DLH allowed) by the variable overhead rate of $0.105. This would give an unfavorable efficiency variance of $1,050. In accountancy, the $1,050 unfavorable amount would be carried as a debit variance. Were less hours utilized than were allowed, the efficiency variance would denote a favorable use of time, and the variance would be shown as a credit. The capacity variance would be computed as under the 2-variance method above to be $450. In this illustration, therefore, the total variance of $700 ($8,200 actual less $7,500 standard) has analyzed into a favorable budget variance of $800, an unfavorable efficiency variance of $1,050, and an unfavorable capacity variance of $450.

It should be emphasized at this point that none of the variances calculated are self-explanatory. They require further investigation to determine their cause. As was pointed out earlier, changes in factor prices may affect the amount of the budget variance. Excessive use of time as expressed by an efficiency variance may be laid to lack of control in the current department; but on the other hand, it may be indicative of defective or off-grade materials and delays due to difficulties in other departments.

L.J. Benninger, Ph.D., Professor Emeritus of Accounting, University of Florida, Gainesville, Florida

References Cited

[1] Horngren, Charles T., "Cost Accounting," Englewood Cliffs, N.J., Prentice-Hall, 4th ed., 1977.
[2] Dopuch, Nicholas, and Birnberg, Jacob G., "Cost Accounting: Accounting Data for Management Decisions," New York, Harcourt, Brace & Jovanovitch, 2nd ed., 1974.

Cross References: *Budgeting; Cost Accounting (and references there given); Zero-Base Budgeting.*

FOLLETT, MARY PARKER

Mary Parker Follett (1868–1933) was a political and social philosopher whose contribution to management was to apply psychological insight and the findings of the social sciences to industry. "It was her special merit to turn from the traditional subjects of study [of political or social scientists]—the state or the community as a whole—progressively to concentrate on the study of industry. In this context she not only evolved principles of human association and organization specifically in terms of industry, but also convinced large numbers of businessmen of the practicality of these principles in dealing with their current problems. Her approach was to analyze the nature of the *consent* on which any democratic group is based by examining the psychological factors underlying it. This consent, she suggested, is not static, but a continuous process, generating new and living group ideas through the interpenetration of individual ideas" [1]. Well in advance of her time, she contended that the final authority inhering in the chief executive should be replaced by an authority of function in which each individual has final authority for his own allotted task. By this means, personal power gives place to "the law of the situation," in which a decision, though it may appear to crystallize in an act of the chief executive, is only a "moment in a process" which may have started with the office boy.

From 1924 onwards she was lecturing to business audiences in both the United States and England, and many businessmen sought her advice on organizational problems. Her books include "The New State," 1920, (Longmans, Green, New York and London); "Creative Experience," 1924 (Longmans, Green); "Dynamic Administration: The Collected Papers of Mary Parker Follett," ed. by Metcalf, H. C., and Urwick, L., 1941 (Pitman, London); "Freedom and Co-ordination: Lectures in Business Organization by Mary Parker Follett," ed. Urwick, L., 1949 (Pitman, London).

Reference Cited

[1] Urwick, L., "The Golden Book of Management," edited for the International Committee of Scientific Management (CIOS), Newman Neame, Limited, London, 1956.

FORD, HENRY

Henry Ford (1863–1947), the American automobile manufacturer, formed the Ford Motor Company in 1903, in partnership with James Couzens, later a United States Senator, the Dodge brothers, and others. Following two unsuccessful ventures—His Detroit Automobile Co., organized in 1899, had dissolved in bankruptcy in 1901, and the successor Henry Ford Co. had ended in a disagreement between Ford and his associates—the new company, which was launched with only $28,000 paid into its treasury, was immediately successful. By 1919, Ford and his son, Edsel B. Ford, were able to acquire the interests of all minority stockholders for $75,000,000.

Ford pioneered modern large-scale assembly-line operations when in 1913 he implemented that revolutionary labor-saving concept in his mammoth new Highland Park (Detroit, Michigan) plant—a manufacturing complex that in time spread over 278 acres, with 105 acres of floor space under one roof. This form of mass production was instrumental in enabling Ford to become the world's largest automobile producer, and one of the world's wealthiest men.

Under the assembly-line concept, side feeder lines and overhead and other types of conveyors, all tightly integrated, fed Ford car parts and components to a waist-high moving line. Workmen were stationed along the line, each performing a single specialized operation the nature of which had been determined and synchronized by scientific study. The worker did not have to step away from his station to get a tool or a part to affix to the gradually materializing car passing before him. At the end of the production sequence, the completed Ford car rolled off the assembly line.

With the demand for Ford cars, trucks, and tractors continuing to soar, the Ford Motor Co. acquired a 1,000-acre tract on the River Rouge, a few miles west of Detroit, for an even larger plant. Eventually this became the world's largest single industrial unit, extending over 1,200 acres. Within the complex were a foundry, power plant, rolling mills and blast furnaces, and plants producing tires, glass, cement, paper, and other materials going into Ford products, with raw materials (from Ford-owned mines and forests) and finished products transported by Ford-owned freighters, and, for a number of years, over a Ford-owned railroad. At the peak of operations during Ford's lifetime, the company had 35 manufacturing and assembly lines in the United States and 28 in Europe, Asia, Africa, Australia, and South America.

Ford pioneered in many aspects of industrial construction and layout, and in manufacturing planning and control. He is credited with being the first to construct large manufacturing spaces without dividing walls and the first to recognize the economies in the one-story as opposed to the multistory factory. Every Ford plant was dedicated to achieving the utmost in efficiency, with waste of time, labor, and materials reduced to the absolute minimum.

In 1914, Ford created a sensation when he announced that the minimum wage at Ford plants would be $5 for an eight-hour day—at a time when unskilled labor was receiving $1 and skilled workmen were getting $2.50 a day. In the same year he inaugurated a profit-sharing plan that would distribute up to $30 million annually among his employees. (The minimum wage was increased to $6 a day in 1922 and to $7 in 1929. Because of the worldwide Depression, the figure was reduced to $4 in 1932, but in 1935 the $6 minimum was restored.) In 1926 the company adopted a five-day, 40-hour week.

Over the years Ford instituted a thoroughly equipped medical department and a welfare department with a trained staff to provide visitation and counsel; and it was his policy to give employment in his factories to disabled war veterans and to the blind, the infirm, and the aged. However, he incurred considerable antagonism because his paternalistic attitude toward his employees was coupled with a strong—his critics said "stubborn"—resistance to unionization of his factories. For years, he successfully fended off the efforts of the United Automobile workers to organize his employees.

However, in 1941 the UAW called a general strike in the Ford factories. When a National Labor Relations Board election revealed that 70% of the workers favored the UAW, Ford promptly signed a contract with the union granting all its demands, including the closed shop and a dues checkoff system. He was the last of the big automobile manufacturers to yield to union pressure.

Ford's efficiency extended to assuring a continuous stream of competent workers to build his cars. Starting with six boys and one instructor, he established a trade school at the Highland Park plant in 1916. By 1932 this school had an enrollment of 2,800 students and 400 instructors. Subsequently other Ford trade schools were opened in Michigan, Massachusetts, and Georgia, and in England and South America.

Ford's business sagacity was demonstrated in the economic depression of 1920–1921. He had large sums of money tied up in raw materials and was faced with maturing notes for $33,000,000 given in 1919 when he and his son, Edsel, bought out the minority stockholders. However, he rejected offers of loans by New York bankers since their terms would have given them a voice in management. Instead, he shut down Highland Park for two months, persuaded Ford dealers to take $25,000,000 worth of cars off his hands for cash, and made other drastic economies. By these moves he realized many millions more than he needed to meet all his obligations.

Ford's international reputation made him a continuing object of attention by the press, and some of his activities not connected with automobile production brought him prominently into public notice. A sincere pacifist, he entered upon an ill-fated venture in 1915 in an attempt to bring about the end of World War I. Having received what he considered reliable intimation from abroad that the belligerents would be receptive to peace overtures, he personally chartered the ocean liner "Oskar II" and embarked for Europe accompanied by a large group of educators, clergymen, representatives of American peace societies, and a number of American newsmen. The intent was to hold a peace conference in some neutral country, but Ford left the ship when it reached Christiana, Norway, at the strong urgings of his colleagues at home, and the expedition failed miserably.

In 1918, at the request of President Woodrow Wilson, Ford accepted the Democratic nomination for United States senator from Michigan, but was defeated. In 1916, Ford sued *The Chicago Tribune* for $1,000,000 libel over an editorial headed "Ford is an Anarchist," and which alleged that he had been pro-German during World War I. In 1919 a jury gave him a favorable verdict, but awarded him only six cents in damages. The suit led to an examination by the *Tribune* attorney that highlighted Ford's lack of formal education. Later, anti-Semitic articles in a Ford-owned paper, *The Dearborn Independent,* brought more legal action, and Ford was forced to apologize for the articles. His relations with others in the business community were not of the best: he was openly hostile to bankers and financiers, and steadfastly refused to allow outside investment in Ford enterprises.

In addition to numerous philanthropies, Ford in 1936 established the Ford Foundation for receiving and administering funds for scientific, educational, and charitable purposes, and gave it as an endowment all the nonvoting stock of the Ford Motor Co.

Henry Ford's son, Edsel, had assumed the presidency of the Ford Motor Co. in 1919, with the elder Ford becoming chairman of the board. Upon the death of Edsel in 1943, Henry Ford again assumed the presidency, although nearly 80 years old. He continued in that capacity until 1945, when he finally retired and was succeeded by his grandson, Henry Ford II. Henry Ford died in Dearborn, Michigan, April 7, 1947.

Information References

Ford, Henry (in collaboration with Samuel Crowther), "My Life and Work," New York, Arno, repr. 1922.

Nevins, Allan and Hill, Frank E., "Ford," 3 volumes, New York, Arno, repr., 1976

Wik, R.M., "Henry Ford and Grass Roots America," Ann Arbor, Mich., University of Michigan Press, 1973.

FORECASTING. See Business Forecasting; Production Planning and Inventory Management (Section on Production Planning).

FOREIGN OPERATIONS. See International Accounting; International Accounting Standards Committee; International Management:

Management of the "World Enterprise"; Management Practice: Learning from Foreign Operations

FOREMEN: See Supervisory Training.

FORMS CONTROL

Correct design of forms is important, but mere attention to design must not be mistaken for control over business forms.

There are two main means of communication in an organization: oral and written. Oral communication breaks down into two subcategories: person-to-person and telephone. If two people in an organization are unable to communicate, management becomes aware and will attempt to correct the problem. The same holds true for telephone system problems, because management uses the telephone frequently.

The problem with written communication is that a major means of data communication in an organization is business forms, and management never fills out a business form. As a result, the lack of **Forms Control** is a major source of low productivity and unnecessary cost. The problem is magnified by the fact that the business forms industry salesmen are volume/commission incentived, and therefore the industry is generally interested in more forms, not better forms. Likewise, the purchasing function in most organizations is unit price oriented and not concerned with the efficiency of the business forms system.

The total market for business forms in the United States for 1980 was $4.3 billion. A 10% savings via a forms control program would save $430,000,000, and could well save 40 times that amount in clerical efficiency, or $17.2 billion annually.

A lack of forms control usually manifests itself in problems such as:

(1) Stocking out of forms.
(2) "Rush" printing.
(3) Lack of written specifications.
(4) Inaccurate forms inventory control.
(5) No typewriter calibration.
(6) Wasted paper.
(7) Many forms doing the same job.
(8) Possible combinations.
(9) No interdepartmental communication on forms.
(10) Excess copy and duplicating of forms on copy machines.
(11) No forms control policy.
(12) No recessive ink colors.
(13) No forms control procedures.

Factors of the Forms Control Problem. When a person picks up a piece of blank paper and draws lines and puts words on the paper, leaving blank spaces in which someone will later insert data, he becomes the author of a form. Obviously, forms control must take into account the interests of persons who originally start the process which will ultimately result in a printed form—but it can readily be seen that unless some degree of integrated control is exercised, forms will proliferate in numbers, and in differences of shapes, sizes, format, type design, and paper. (See FORMS DESIGN.)

Too often the purchasers of forms force the printers to do much of their work not only in a rush, but also in a haphazard manner, without proper specifications and without the knowledge of how a given form fits in the overall system. The form authors, who may spend days, weeks, or even months working out the design of their form, usually want the purchasing department to get the forms overnight, and there is theoretically no time for the writing of specifications. This practice can be paid for dearly by discovering later that the forms have not been printed in the way the author meant them to be, or that clerks in other departments are filling out duplicate information.

Both form control and form design entail a detailed study of the clerical and machine operations involved in the filling out and use of the form, and the relationship of the form to the flow of other paperwork in the systems and procedure in effect. Forms control is impossible without studying the forms system as a whole. Piecemeal study is useless. Such an examination may lead into methods and procedures analysis, WORK SIMPLIFICATION, personnel training, and other activities resulting in the reduction of office expense.

Basic Steps in a Forms Control Program. There are six basic steps in setting up a forms control program:

(1) The establishment of forms control as a company policy.

(2) The collection of samples of all forms used in the company.

(3) The building of a Functional Index to the forms, with a Numerical Work File.

(4) The integration of the forms control program in the company organization.

(5) The scientific design of all forms.

(6) The coordination of forms control with systems and procedures studies.

Forms control suffers because most managements do not take the matter of forms and paperwork seriously enough. Forms are apt to go unnoticed and ignored until they begin to cause trouble, and then to its surprise, management becomes aware of their existence. It should be realized that $100 saved in office expenses can represent almost a clear $100 profit, whereas it may take $1,000 or more of additional sales to produce the same dollar profit. The average office can actually save thousands of dollars in clerical expense through intelligent control of paperwork.

(1) *Forms Control as a Company Policy.* Forms control must be established as a policy, and the notice to that effect must spring from the policy-making level of management. All departments must be made aware of the program and what it will mean to them, and what they must do to make it work.

(2) *Collection of Samples of All Forms.* At the outset of the control program, a collection must be made of every form in use in the company. Before this can be done, however, the word "form" must be defined to mean every piece of paper containing information, printed or reproduced by whatever means, with blank spaces left for the entry of additional data or information to be used for subsequent clerical operations, or for information and decision-making purposes. The definition includes all temporary as well as permanent forms: numbered as well as unnumbered forms; those purchased from commercial suppliers as well as those reproduced internally on office duplicating equipment; those used in the smallest as well as in the largest quantities; letterheads, envelopes, tags, and all specialty forms. The only satisfactory method is to ignore the stock room completely and to send out a collection letter to all departments and branches, requesting several samples of every form used by that department or branch.

(3) *The Functional Index and Numerical Work File.* The Forms Control Program requires a complete set of all forms, analyzed and classified in a way to furnish correct, positive, and quick answers to all questions of location and use. One sample of each form should be put in the Numerical Work File. Each form should be put in a separate folder with the identifying number entered on the tab of the folder. All extra samples of that form and all related correspondence and working papers should be kept in this folder.

Experience has shown that the second file, the Functional Index, which is a classification on what the form *does,* is much more practicable than a classification based on *who uses* the form, or by *name* of form. Filing by who uses is usually a departmental classification, all forms used in a given department being filed together. This does not readily yield answers to major questions, and poses problems where forms are used interdepartmentally.

Classification by name may use the title appearing on the form, or in some cases, key words in the title or in the body of the form itself. However, titles are often quite meaningless, and many forms will be found to have no titles at all.

The Functional Classification, if properly carried out, answers all questions and provides a permanent, flexible classification which can readily be kept up to date. The main difficulty here is the looseness or misuse of terms and the lack of any standard terminology in the field of office forms and procedures. The term "check" is an example. In the hotel business, one finds not only bank checks, but checks dealing with the coatrooms and parcel room, as well as checks which the waitress gives to the patron of the dining room. True, they are all checks, but the check dealing with the hats or parcels will probably be classified in the Functional Index under the subject "Personal Property," and the function, "to identify." (In this case, no operation or condition is involved.) The dining-room check, on the other hand, is found upon analysis to be an invoice for food consumed, and it would be classified under the subject "Food," the operation, "sale of," and the function "to notify."

Many forms are self-explanatory, and can be easily analyzed. Many will be misleading because of the carelessness of design. Experience has shown that the Functional Index analysis, if properly done, takes about one month for two persons for each thousand forms analyzed, including the coordination of the Functional Index with the Numerical File. This assumes that at least one of the analyzers is experienced in this work, and can train the other person in the new methods of thinking about forms as the work progresses.

(4) *Integration of the Forms Control Program with the Company Organization.* The majority of forms are interdepartmental. Hence, if forms

control is to be effective, it must be done on an interdepartmental level, and should be established as a staff function, usually heading up under the office of the Controller. The forms control function thus organized will partake of the three normal functions of any staff operation: control, coordination, and service.

Control means that no new forms may be established for interdepartmental use without clearance by the forms control group, and this must be a procedure strictly adhered to. As to forms for purely internal use or convenience, of a temporary nature, within a small organizational unit, the requirement for clearance may not be that strict, and the forms control group may be called upon primarily for advisory assistance.

The point about clearance should be understood to be that of a staff operation, and not an interference with line authority. The forms control group cannot countermand a line decision to establish a given form—but if it feels that such a form is detrimental to the program, it must seek to correct the situation first by persuasion, and if that fails, by calling the facts of the situation to the attention of its own superior executive for management resolution. Thus forms control personnel should be good salesmen. Much of this selling can be done by the simple means of letting the line departments have the credit for the accomplishments of forms control within their units.

Liaison is important. It is advisable for each department to assign to some one person the responsibility for controlling forms and paperwork within the department, and to work closely with the central forms control group. This person should have a thorough knowledge of the paperwork problems and routines within the department, with within-department staff control over the creation of forms, and forms use. Formal programs designate such persons as "forms contact representatives."

It is imperative that the integration of the forms control program be extended to include the relationship with the purchasing department. The requisite to good forms purchasing is the creation of an efficient form design, incorporating the desired standards of printing efficiency and economy, and the writing of complete and correct specifications for manufacturing the form. This is the duty of the forms control unit.

(5) *Provision for the Scientific Design of Forms.* Since the focal point of forms control is the correct design of forms, it is obvious that management must provide the training, professional assistance, and facilities for this work.

(6) *Integration for Forms Control with Methods and Procedures Control.* Forms control and the control of office methods and procedures are two parts of the same thing. The end use of forms determines the flow of office work. (See SYSTEMS MANAGEMENT.) By going to the spread sheet of the Functional Index one can quickly determine which subjects, which operations, which conditions, and which functions apply to the procedures to be studied, and the pertinent forms will be found in the Functional Index.

Results. Actual case studies show substantial savings from a program of Forms Control. Examples:

National Bus Company: 119 locations. Management supplied 610 known forms. Study uncovered an additional 580. Remote locations would produce forms on photocopy machines when stockout of forms occurred. Photocopy savings alone were $288,000 annually. Total savings for all reasons were $1,800,000 annually, in addition to increased clerical efficiency.

Mining Service and Equipment Company. Sales $32,000,000. Company spent $30,000 on business forms annually. It used 587 forms. Of these forms 126 had no numbers; 159 had no revision date; 24 projected a poor public image; 90 were produced by photocopy; 154 had poor printing; 25 were poorly designed; 137 were printed on improper paper; 3 should have been designed with window envelopes; 37 were not typewriter calibrated; 63 could have been combined; 34 could have been eliminated. The company experienced a 50% reduction in forms cost by establishing a forms control program.

Single Plant, Heavy Industry: 5,000 employees. Had a record of 510 known forms; the program uncovered 2,157 more that were being produced in local areas and unknown to the central control. Of the 2,667 forms, 81% were not under control. In the first month of the control plan, the direct savings were $6,762, and the first year's savings were over $60,000.

Multi-plant, light industry, 28,000 employees: Had a record of 1,680 forms; the program uncovered 5,998 more, for a total of 7,678, of which 78% were uncontrolled. In the first year of operation, the program showed direct savings of $50,995 and the estimated annual savings thereafter were $111,000. This was more than double the entire cost of installing the program, including professional services.

Small Health Insurance Company: 400 employees: Had an effective program with 368 forms under control. However, the new program uncovered 158 additional forms in the single home office. Direct savings in the first month of the new program were $7,945, which was more than the cost of the program.

In each of the above cases, the direct savings were stated by management to be only one of the benefits derived from the program. Added "dividends" were better paperwork and greater clerical efficiency.

FRANK M. KNOX, Courier-Citizen Company, New York, New York, and ALFRED JAY MORAN, JR., The TJM Corporation, New Orleans, Louisiana

Information References

Knox, Frank M., "Design and Control of Business Forms," New York, McGraw-Hill, 1965.

Lovecchio, John B., "Forms Management," Chap. 3, Sec. 5, in Heyel, Carl, ed., "Handbook of Modern Office Management and Administrative Services," Huntington, N.Y., Kruger, repr., 1980.

Menkus, Belden, "The Forms Control Handbook," New York, Graphic Arts, 1973.

Moran, Alfred Jay, Jr., "Forms Management—A Primer—1981," The TJM Corporation, New Orleans, Louisiana.

Nygren, William V., "Business Forms Management," New York, AMACOM Div., American Management Associations, 1980.

Cross References: *Forms Design; Records Management; Systems Management.*

FORMS DESIGN

Forms are so much a part of all that an organization does that management tends to take these documents for granted. This is not wise. Each form must be challenged continually to prove that (1) it is contributing to company operating efficiency and profits, and (2) its future use is warranted by the extent of that contribution. Ideally, management will in every case continually be seeking an *effective* form.

Forms Design, properly done, is the purposeful creation of that effective form—one that is an adequate information processing tool. Three things identify the effective form:

(1) It is an integral part of the information processing system in which it is used. The system will not function properly unless this form is used with each transaction in the right way at the right time.

(2) If facilitates the recording, analysis, and complete a particular transaction; it does not contain excess or extraneous data. Another form is not required to supplement or facilitate its use.

(3) It can be used with a minimum of special knowledge or training. The nature, meaning and significance of the data to be entered are clearly indicated in the form itself.

A special type of person is required if this effective form is to be designed. The skills and knowledge of the graphic designer must be wedded to a comprehensive understanding of the information accumulation/processing/transmission cycle. The ideal candidate for this assignment will have some artistic skill, have demonstrated some analytical ability, and be able to work with minimum supervision and to communicate effectively with others. This person need not be a potential manager; but he or she should not be a glorified clerk.

How does the forms designer's work differ from that of the systems analyst? The forms designer is responsible for planning and devising a particular type of information processing tool. His task begins with *forms analysis.* It involves questioning the plans, ideas, and work of others. The process can be summarized this way:

- Challenge the need for the form.
- Challenge every copy of the form.
- Challenge every data item on the form.

At the close of this questioning process the forms designer should be familiar with the function that the form is to perform, the data items it must include, and the physical circumstances of its preparation and use—including the number of copies required, the source and destination of this information, as well as related forms and information processing routines.

If the form is to be used to provide input to an automated data processing system or to capture output from it, the forms designer must be aware of the specific performance characteristics of the equipment on which the form is to be processed. This knowledge may include such things as its operating speed, the various tolerances within which it must operate, and the physical pressures and tensions to which the form may be subjected while it is being processed.

Then, the forms designer begins what almost might be termed an *engineering* task:

(1) Data item caption terminology must be reviewed to assure that any possible ambiguity is avoided.

(2) Data item captions must be organized into a pattern that logically aids understanding by the persons who must prepare and use the form.

(3) A preliminary sketch of form layout must be prepared to provide adequate space for data item entry, and to assure proper use of all available typographic devices to identify and organize data items on the form. Exhibit I provided by Jesse L. Clark, a consultant in paperwork systems, illustrates some of the possible uses of these devices. (See pp. 340–341.)

(4) Physical limitations, operating speed, and other performance characteristics of the equipment on which the form will be prepared must be reviewed along with the need for creating form copies at the time it is prepared, or at different points in the processing routine.

(5) Form content must be refined and its physical aspects defined in a design sketch; paper weights, fastening methods, and other considerations must be resolved. (Ideally, by this time a formal written instruction covering the use of this form will have been drafted, possibly by the forms designer.)

It may be necessary for the forms designer to repeat this process several times before the requirements of the form specifier and user are fully met, and the design sketch and specifications can be released to the printer.

Following are standard form sizes and paper sizes for economic cutting and for meshing with standard file sizes (in inches):

Cards
3 × 5
5 × 8

Paper
8½ × 11 (standard letter size)
8½ × 14 (legal only)
11 × 17 (B size in Engineering Drawings)
17 × 22 (C size in Engineering Drawings)
22 × 34 (D size in Engineering Drawings)
11 × 14¾ (Computer continuous)
11 × 15¾ (Computer continuous with tear-off tractor strips)

Layout of a form calls for consideration of the means of preparation. Forms which are to be hand-written are more useful if light guidelines are provided for the entries.

BELDEN MENKUS, Management Consultant Middleville, New Jersey.

Information References

Periodicals:

Business Forms Management.
Business Forms Reporter.

Texts:

"How to Design Business Forms," Arlington, Va., International Business Forms Institute, 1971.
Kish, Joseph, Jr., "Business Forms: Design and Control," New York, Ronald, 1971.
Knox, Frank, "The Knox Standard Guide to Design and Control of Business Forms," New York, McGraw-Hill, 1965.
General Services Administration, Washington, National Archives and Records Service:
"Forms Analysis and Design," 1980.
"Forms for Automation," 1981.

Cross References: *Forms Control; Records Management; Systems Management.*

FRANCHISING

Franchising is a method of distribution open to a manufacturing or service firm that becomes feasible when the products or services can support the full-scale distributive operations of owners/managers in many different locations. Franchising dates back at least a hundred years, but its most widespread application in the United States came primarily since the 1950s.

The company adopting franchised distribution is faced with many of the problems of product selection, market fit, and the like that any company must deal with in launching a new product or service. It must also consider such factors as the deployment, control, motivation, and profitability of its franchisees. In effect, the company designs every element of a model business, which must then be reproduced and sustained in large numbers in many different areas.

The grantor—the *franchiser*—gives the grantee—the *franchisee*—the rights to do, use, or sell something that is the property of the grantor. In exchange, the franchisee may pay an initial fee (although this is not always the case). For some franchisers, such fees are a primary source of income in their expansion period. Franchisees, in some cases, receive continuing revenue from franchisors' payments of royalty or license fees, lease charges, and the like.

The franchise contract spells out the responsibility of each of the partners. To the extent that it fails to do so, it can provide the basis for future conflict. The contract normally contains clauses describing the obligations of the franchisee, with particular reference to such matters as product quality, territorial responsibility, and sources of supply.

EXHIBIT I

GENERAL FORMS DESIGN INSTRUCTIONS

All forms will be designed in accordance with the format shown below when feasible.

To standardize on design specifications the following type fonts should be used where practicable. It will be necessary at times to deviate from established design where the nature of some forms would make it impracticable to follow these standards. In such cases type fonts may be used as the need dictates.

Form Title

Vari-Type font 670-12A

Sub Titles should be at least one point size smaller than main title.

Sub Headings

Vari-Type font 670-8C, 660-8C, 660-7D, 2000-4D, or 2000-3D (as space allows).

Box Titles

Vari-Type fonts 2000-2D, 2000-3D, and 2000-4D

Body

Copper plate gothic should be used throughout the body of the form. Upper and lower cases should not be combined unless absolutely necessary.

Ruling

Double line top and bottom - every 4th or 5th line bold on forms with 12 or more continuous ruled lines as a guide for easy reading.

All check blocks and columns will be aligned vertically and horizontally to provide minimum number of tab stops and eliminate loss typewriter motion.

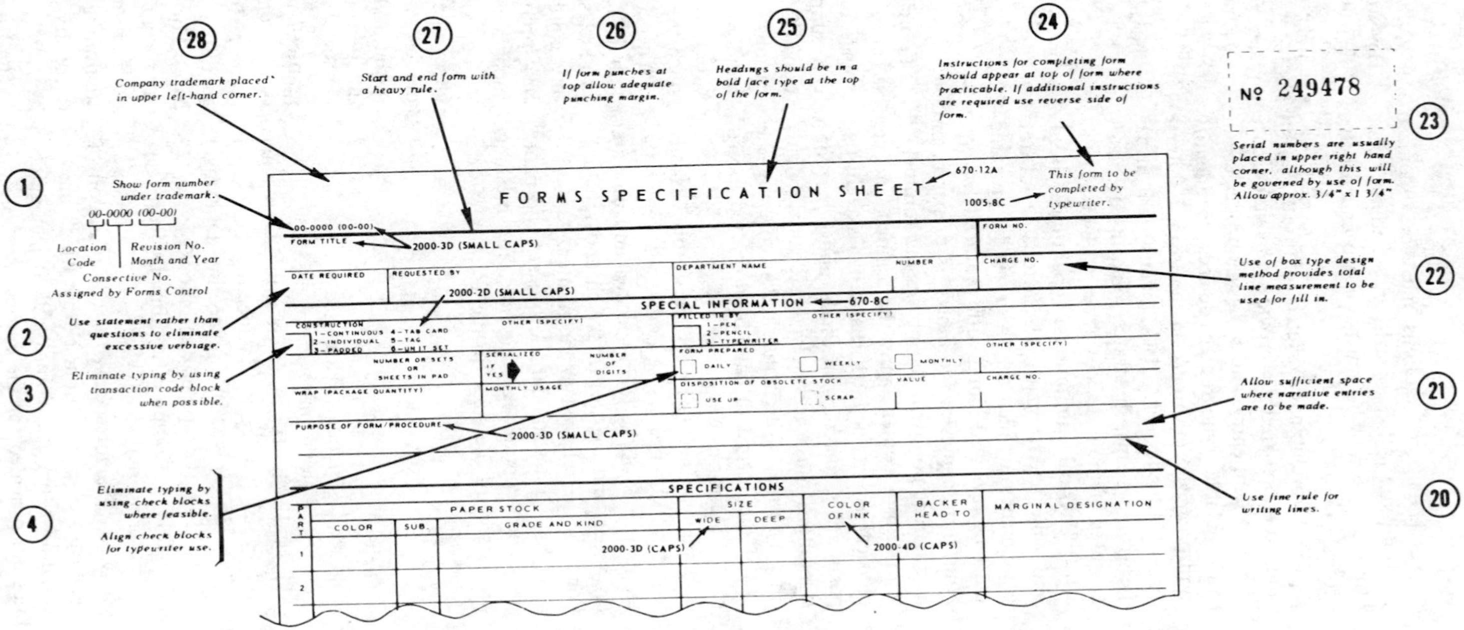

28
Company trademark placed in upper left-hand corner.
27
Start and end form with a heavy rule.
26
If form punches at top allow adequate punching margin.
25
Headings should be in a bold face type at the top of the form.
24
Instructions for completing form should appear at top of form where practicable. If additional instructions are required use reverse side of form.
This form to be completed by typewriter.
№ 249478
23
Serial numbers are usually placed in upper right hand corner, although this will be governed by use of form. Allow approx. 3/4" x 1 3/4"
1
Show form number under trademark.
00-0000 (00-00)
Location Code
Revision No. Month and Year
Consective No. Assigned by Forms Control
2
Use statement rather than questions to eliminate excessive verbiage.
3
Eliminate typing by using transaction code block when possible.
4
Eliminate typing by using check blocks where feasible.
Align check blocks for typewriter use.
22
Use of box type design method provides total line measurement to be used for fill in.
21
Allow sufficient space where narrative entries are to be made.
20
Use fine rule for writing lines.
FORMS SPECIFICATION SHEET
670-12A
1005-8C
00-0000 (00-00)
FORM TITLE
2000-3D (SMALL CAPS)
FORM NO.
DATE REQUIRED
REQUESTED BY
2000-2D (SMALL CAPS)
DEPARTMENT NAME
NUMBER
CHARGE NO.
SPECIAL INFORMATION
670-8C
CONSTRUCTION
1—CONTINUOUS 4—TAB CARD
2—INDIVIDUAL 5—TAG
3—PADDED 6—UNIT SET
OTHER (SPECIFY)
FILLED IN BY
1—PEN
2—PENCIL
3—TYPEWRITER
OTHER (SPECIFY)
NUMBER OR SETS OR SHEETS IN PAD
SERIALIZED IF YES
NUMBER OF DIGITS
FORM PREPARED
DAILY
WEEKLY
MONTHLY
OTHER (SPECIFY)
WRAP (PACKAGE QUANTITY)
MONTHLY USAGE
DISPOSITION OF OBSOLETE STOCK
USE UP
SCRAP
VALUE
CHARGE NO.
PURPOSE OF FORM/PROCEDURE
2000-3D (SMALL CAPS)
SPECIFICATIONS
PART
PAPER STOCK
COLOR
SUB.
GRADE AND KIND
SIZE
WIDE
DEEP
COLOR OF INK
BACKER HEAD TO
MARGINAL DESIGNATION
2000-3D (CAPS)
2000-4D (CAPS)

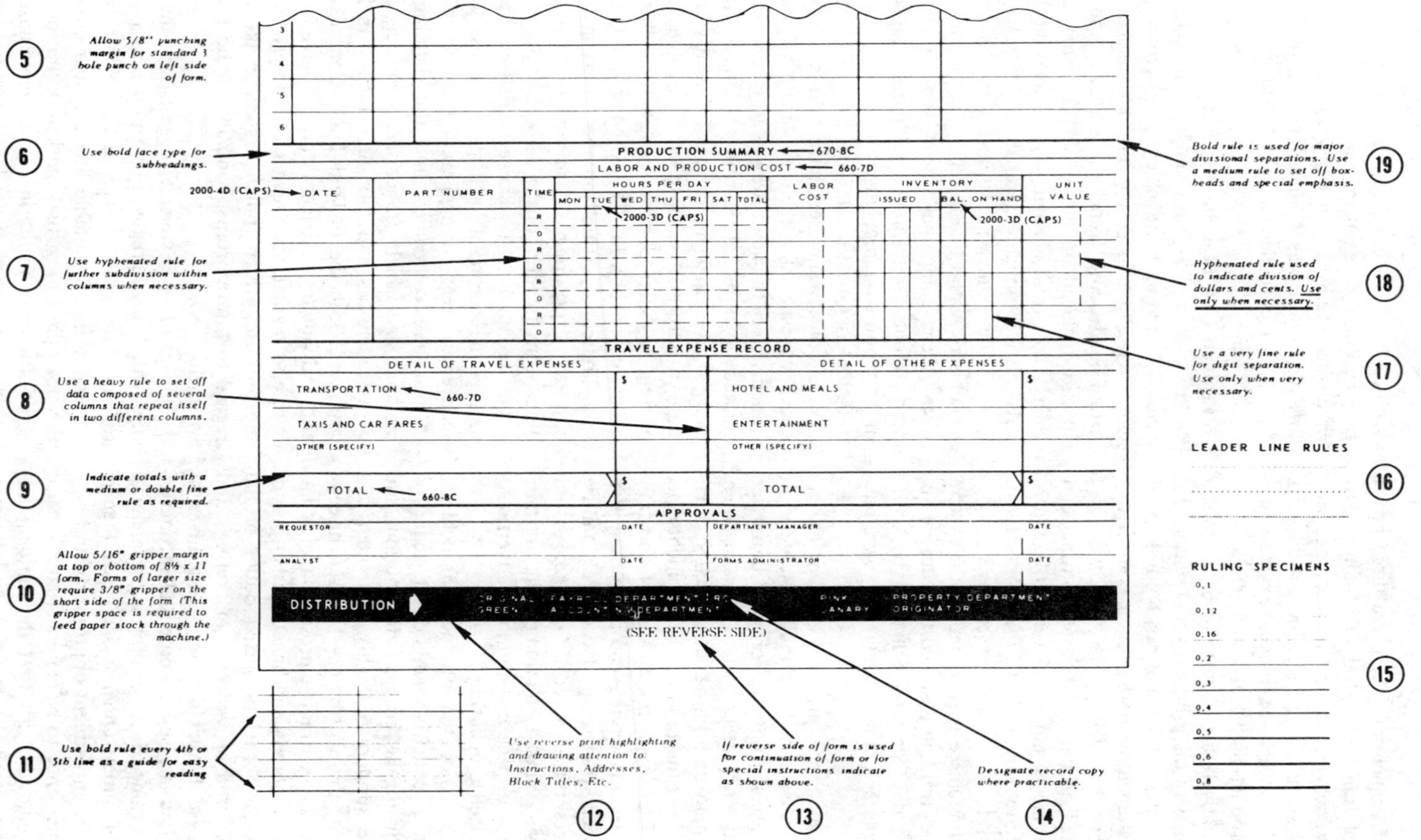

5
Allow 5/8" punching margin for standard 3 hole punch on left side of form.
6
Use bold face type for subheadings.
2000-4D (CAPS)
7
Use hyphenated rule for further subdivision within columns when necessary.
8
Use a heavy rule to set off data composed of several columns that repeat itself in two different columns.
9
Indicate totals with a medium or double fine rule as required.
10
Allow 5/16" gripper margin at top or bottom of 8½ x 11 form. Forms of larger size require 3/8" gripper on the short side of the form (This gripper space is required to feed paper stock through the machine.)
11
Use bold rule every 4th or 5th line as a guide for easy reading
PRODUCTION SUMMARY
670-8C
LABOR AND PRODUCTION COST
660-7D
DATE
PART NUMBER
TIME
HOURS PER DAY
MON
TUE
WED
THU
FRI
SAT
TOTAL
2000-3D (CAPS)
LABOR COST
INVENTORY
ISSUED
BAL. ON HAND
2000-3D (CAPS)
UNIT VALUE
TRAVEL EXPENSE RECORD
DETAIL OF TRAVEL EXPENSES
DETAIL OF OTHER EXPENSES
TRANSPORTATION
660-7D
TAXIS AND CAR FARES
OTHER (SPECIFY)
HOTEL AND MEALS
ENTERTAINMENT
OTHER (SPECIFY)
TOTAL
660-8C
TOTAL
APPROVALS
REQUESTOR
DATE
DEPARTMENT MANAGER
DATE
ANALYST
DATE
FORMS ADMINISTRATOR
DATE
DISTRIBUTION
PROPERTY DEPARTMENT
ORIGINATOR
(SEE REVERSE SIDE)
12
Use reverse print highlighting and drawing attention to: Instructions, Addresses, Block Titles, Etc.
13
If reverse side of form is used for continuation of form or for special instructions indicate as shown above.
14
Designate record copy where practicable.
19
Bold rule is used for major divisional separations. Use a medium rule to set off box-heads and special emphasis.
18
Hyphenated rule used to indicate division of dollars and cents. Use only when necessary.
17
Use a very fine rule for digit separation. Use only when very necessary.
LEADER LINE RULES
16
RULING SPECIMENS
0.1
0.12
0.16
0.2
0.3
0.4
0.5
0.6
0.8
15

Types of Franchises. There are three principal types of franchises: straight product distribution, product license, and trade name. Most franchise systems involve straight product distribution. The franchisee in such a system markets the product in his assigned territory and exercises relatively little control over the mix or characteristics of his products (or services). The growing number of franchisees holding product-license franchises have greater control over these factors. Frequently, the franchisee in a system based primarily on uniform trade identification alone is subject to very little control and may have very little further contact with the franchiser.

Once a franchisee is recruited to the system, he undergoes training designed to acquaint him with the product or service he will be selling and to prepare him to manage his own business.

Most franchisers provide both initial or start-up services and continuing services to their franchisees. Common forms of initial services include: operating manuals, management training, employee training, site selection, facility design, lease negotiation, and franchise fee financing. The depth and quality of the franchiser's continuing services can mean the difference between franchisee success or failure. Such services often include: field supervision, merchandising and promotional help, retraining, quality inspection, national advertising, and centralized purchasing.

Advantages. For the producer, franchising may afford a potential method for acquiring capital, reducing his costs of distribution, and gaining the support of highly motivated distributors. For the distributor—the franchisee—it promises the continuing protection of a national-brand umbrella and benefits arising from transfer to the local franchised outlet of the franchiser's product concept, marketing, and other expertise. Franchisers' recruiting advertising most often stresses the potential income or profit to be gained from owning and managing a franchised outlet. Other widely used themes emphasize the investment opportunity and personal independence to be gained from franchise ownership, and the fact that the national advertising campaigns provide a promotional thrust that individual entrepreneurs would be incapable of attaining.

For many franchiser firms, adoption of the franchised method of distribution has provided an avenue to remarkable growth. Sales of the average franchise company surveyed in a Conference Board study increased 350% during the preceding five years. In many cases, growth of this dimension was financed largely by initial franchise fees collected from newly recruited franchisees.

Problems of Franchisees. Apart from difficulties common to most small business enterprises, franchisees are chiefly concerned with employee problems, low profit margins, competition, inadequate franchiser support, and restrictions placed on them by their franchisers. Energy costs and changing auto travel patterns have also complicated franchisees' futures. In general the Conference Board survey showed, franchisees would like to receive more guidance from their companies' field representatives, more frequent retraining, and more assistance in promotional campaigns.

Practices Questioned. The accounting practices of some franchisers have been called into question, especially their reporting of initial franchise fees in such a way as to give an exaggerated picture of earnings. Critics have charged, too, that franchisers frequently overstate to prospects the income possible from owning an outlet. Serious abuses in franchising, bordering on or actually involving fraud, have been limited to a small number of companies; but their exposure has tarnished the image of other firms in the industry as well.

Out of all this have come increasing efforts to regulate certain franchiser practices. Most such efforts seek the registration and licensing of franchise companies, and the defining of methods by which franchisers can negotiate with franchisees and terminate their franchise contracts. Both the Federal Trade Commission and individual state legislatures have enacted laws and regulations which more closely define the promises which franchisers can make with regard to future profits, company support, and so forth.

Opportunities. Evidence suggests that the future will bring: greater protection and power for the franchisee: greater difficulty for franchisers in finding suitable sites for their outlets; the possibility of virtual market saturation for a few franchise firms; increased repurchase of franchises by some of the larger and most successful firms; increased application of service franchising; and increased consideration of franchised distribution for both consumer and industrial products by established manufacturers who have never before used it.

Sales of goods and services through franchise outlets have continued a steady rise, despite the depressing effect in recent years of a dropoff in sales by automobile and truck dealers, which account for nearly half of all franchised sales. A survey by the U.S. Department of Commerce showed an estimated sales of $338 billion for 1980, compared to $312 billion in 1979 and $287 billion in 1978 [1]. The number of franchised outlets in the United States for the same years were estimated at 488,000, 463,000, and 452,000, respectively.

The survey showed real estate to be the fastest growing sector of franchising in both sales and units. Sales of all types of franchised restaurants continued to be the second fastest growing category. Data from the survey also indicate the growing importance of U.S. franchising in world markets. In 1978, 266 franchisors reported 17,156 outlets in foreign countries, a rise of 21% over the previous year. Based on data collected from all franchisors, 4.5 million persons were employed.

E. PATRICK MCGUIRE, Project Director, Management Research, The Conference Board, New York, New York

Information Reference

The foregoing presentation is essentially the findings in McGuire, E. Patrick, "Franchised Distribution," a research report of The Conference Board, Inc., New York, 1971, as summarized in the "Highlights for the Executive" section of that study, updated here by the author.

Jacoby, Julian E. and McGowan, Lynn, "Franchising Today: A Whole New Ballgame!," *Perspective*, Laventhol & Horwath, New York, N.Y., Spring/Summer, 1980.

Reference Cited

[1] "Franchising in the Economy, 1978–80," prepared by the Bureau of Industrial Economics, U.S. Department of Commerce, available from U.S. Government Printing Office, Washington, DC 20402. The report contains data on 22 business categories and includes tables on sales, number of establishments, average sales volume per franchise operation, and other data.

Cross References: *Franchising: Legal Aspects; Marketing: Patterns of Consumer Goods Distribution.*

FRANCHISING: Legal Aspects

During the last decade, the **Franchising** method of distribution of goods and services in the United States has grown dramatically. By 1979 franchise sales had exceeded $300 billion and accounted for nearly one-third of all retail sales [1]. This growth in franchise activity has been followed by a proliferation of Federal and state laws and regulations. Where franchise regulation once had been largely a matter of Federal antitrust law, since 1970 Federal and state franchise registration, disclosure, trade regulation, and other franchise laws have developed.

Any company executive or manager who is considering business format, product license, or trade name franchising, whether as a franchisee or particularly as a franchisor, will need to develop some familiarity with these complex franchise laws. And any prospective franchisor, in the decade ahead, will require substantial financial resources, experienced management, qualified marketing, accounting and legal consultants, and a demonstrable market success record before undertaking a franchise program.

Although a considerable investment in time and money ordinarily is required, franchising can be a profitable marketing system. Most day-to-day management and operation responsibilities usually are assumed by the franchisee; most business start-up costs and usually all operation costs are paid by the franchisee, who also ordinarily pays a periodic franchise royalty or fee; and responsibility for compliance with business qualification, license, state and local income, sales and use tax, employment and other laws usually is assumed by the franchisee.

Federal Franchise Disclosure. Since October 21, 1979, a Federal Trade Commission Rule [2] has required all franchisors involved in two types of marketing relationships to give a securities-type disclosure statement to prospective franchisees anywhere in the United States before the sale of a franchise is completed. The two types covered by the FTC Rule are:

(1) Where a franchisee sells goods or services meeting the franchisor's quality standards under a trademark, service mark, tradename, or other commercial symbol, for a payment of at least $500, and the franchisor has "significant control" over the franchisee or provides "significant assistance"; and

(2) Where a franchisee sells goods or services supplied by a franchisor, for a payment of at least $500, and the franchisor either secures accounts or provides rack or vending locations for the franchisee.

Single trademark licenses, retailer-owned co-ops, leased departments, "fractional" franchises (those where franchise sales won't exceed 20% of gross) and a few other arrangements are excluded. It is not altogether clear in all marketing situations whether or not the FTC Rule applies, but under these definitions many traditional licenses and distributorships are franchises.

For businesses which fall within the Rule, prospective franchisees must be given detailed, current information on twenty different subjects, such as: the business experience of the franchisor's executives and directors; litigation and bankruptcy history of the franchisor, executives and directors; details of all franchise royalties, commissions and costs; the franchisor's financial information; the franchisor's obligations to the franchisee; restrictions on the franchisee; termination, cancellation and renewal provisions; and the like. Actual or potential sales, income, or profit representations are prohibited unless detailed accounting and substantiation guidelines are followed; and any such statements must be relevant to the local franchisee's geographic market.

FTC registration or approval of the franchise documents is not required, although the FTC may undertake compliance investigations or impose reporting requirements.

The FTC Rule provides that it is an unfair or deceptive act or practice within the meaning of Section 5 of the Federal Trade Commission Act for any franchisor to fail to give such disclosure statements and copies of form franchise agreements to prospective franchisees. Each violation may bring up to a $10,000 civil penalty. The FTC has been encouraging franchisees also to seek private remedies.

A number of companies have challenged the FTC's Franchising Rule [3] and, while the outcome of that litigation is uncertain at this publication, the issues presented are certain to be expanded upon in franchise litigation and legislation during the 1980s.

State Registration and Disclosure. In 1970 California enacted the first state franchise registration and disclosure law and thirteen other states have followed with similar laws [4]. Generally, these laws require separate registration in each state, often with the State Securities Commissioner, of a statement which is similar to that required for use by the FTC Rule discussed above, before any franchisor may offer or sell franchises in these states.

The state laws coexist with the FTC Rule, and Federal "pre-emption" is limited to a number of rather technical situations. Moreover, although these state laws are similar to each other and to the FTC Rule in many respects, not every state now accepts the FTC documents and none automatically accepts a registration from another state.

Other State Franchise Relationship Laws. Some states have separate franchise laws regulating special franchise industries, such as gasoline, auto, farm implement, and beer distributors. Others prohibit various unfair practices, restrict rights of franchise termination and nonrenewal, or affect other aspects of franchise relationships, such as franchise trade association rights and sources of supply.

Many state franchise registration and relationship statutes provide criminal penalties. Criminal trials of franchisors have occurred in Illinois [5] and New Jersey [6].

Trademark and Other Intellectual Property Considerations. The franchisor's trademark and trade name have been referred to as the "cornerstone of a franchise system" by one U.S. District Judge [7] and nearly all franchise agreements will include a license to use the franchisor's mark, name, or other commercial symbols. A trademark functions in a franchise system to identify the source and signify the quality of the products and services of the franchise and, moreover, has obvious marketing value in helping to develop and maintain buyer acceptance and demand.

The franchisor who owns a Federally registered trademark is required by law to exercise adequate quality control over the products and services of the franchisee under the mark, such as by specifications, testing, and inspection. The quality control requirement necessarily gives a franchisor greater freedom under the antitrust laws, although no exemption exists. For example, certain restrictions on sources of supply, handling competitive or other products, and the like are permissible.

The use of copyrighted works or patented inventions often is licensed as part of the franchise arrangements and is subject to usual licensing considerations. Consideration also should be given to protection of any trade secrets and other confidential information of the franchisor, such as processes, formulas, ingredients, or products. Ordinarily, such secrets will not be revealed to a new franchisee until after execution of a franchise agreement, which should include provisions defining the trade secrets and binding the franchisee to secrecy both during and following termination of the franchise. Covenants not to compete, where valid, often increase protection against misuse of trademarks, patents, copyrights, and trade secrets in such situations. (See also TRADEMARKS.)

Antitrust Considerations. Federal and state antitrust laws impose restrictions on franchise operations, just as they restrict all other forms of market distribution in the United States. Among the most important for franchising are:

Territory and Customer Restrictions. Horizontal allocations of customers or territories, such as by franchisees, are prohibited. Usually, a franchisor can agree with a particular franchisee to limit the number of franchises to be sold in a specific territory and encourage the franchisee to emphasize market development in that territory by use of primary responsibility, location, or pass-over payment clauses.

Price Fixing. Suggested resale prices are the limit, *period.* No minimum, maximum, price range, or set price may be imposed by a franchisor on a franchisee.

Sources of Supply. "Tying sales," which require a franchisee over its objection to purchase one product in order to acquire another more desirable or necessary product, are condemned. A number of courts have found that the trademark can be a tying item in some franchises; but others have held the opposite. This law is at this writing in a state of change, and caution is recommended. Generally, it is possible for a franchisor to design approved supplier, product specification, or other supply systems, whereby it may require franchisees to purchase certain items from certain sources or perform other acts, such as contribute to national advertising, in the operation of the franchise, provided that those restrictions are essential to the franchise operation or to its legitimate quality control program, or are part of its "bundle of benefits."

Price Discrimination. Franchisors may not discriminate against similar franchisees with regard to prices or allowances, unless justified by differences in costs of manufacture, sale, or delivery. All allowances and services must be made available to franchisees on a proportionately equal basis.

Liability for Franchisee's Acts. In some situations, such as wage and tax collection cases, a franchisor may be liable for a franchisee's acts or omissions, if it is found that the franchisee is an actual or implied agent of the franchisor. This risk usually can be avoided by clearly fixing the franchisee's responsibility in the franchise agreement and acting to avoid the appearance of an agency or employer-employee relationship. With regard to franchisor liability for injuries to franchisee customers, however, the law is not settled, and in some product liability cases, franchisor liability has been found [8].

The Franchise Agreement. Under the FTC Rule, as well as the disclosure laws of fourteen states, a franchisor now must have a form franchise agreement to present to prospective franchisees along with the required disclosure statement, either at their first meeting or at some other early time. A new product-line franchise agreement may be no more than a trademark license coupled with the franchisee's agreement to advertise, promote, sell, and perhaps service the new product. In situations where new businesses are being started by franchisees, among the franchisor's legal considerations in drafting an agreement will be:

(1) A description of the franchise system, products, services, and benefits, and the marks and symbols associated with it.

(2) A license to use the franchisor's marks, names, symbols, copyrights, patents, and trade secrets, with adequate quality controls and post-termination safeguards.

(3) Requirements for adequate compensation to the franchisor, in light of the probable tax and accounting consequences, including such possibilities as: a uniform or negotiable start-up or initial fee, based on potential franchisee sales, earnings, or other considerations; deposits for real estate, inventory, or other costs; periodic royalty payments; costs of equipment, inventory, supplies, or accounting and other services provided by the franchisor; and cooperative or other advertising and promotion charges.

(4) Dispute settlement procedures, such as private arbitration of such typical issues as royalty computations and quality control compliance.

(5) Provisions for liability insurance, and wage and tax payments, collection, and reporting.

(6) Quality controls on the franchisee's operations, within antitrust limitations, including such factors as: primary areas of sales responsibility; site selection; appearance of building, business premises, etc.; product specifications and/or approved sources of supply; restrictions

on other products and services; advertising specifications; inspections and testing; product sample and advertising submissions; bookkeeping and accounting procedures; and the like.

(7) Provisions for termination or transfer of the franchise, subject to state law restrictions, such as upon termination for cause (bankruptcy, death, material breach of agreement, etc.), post-termination non-competition clauses, and provision for franchisor's consent to any sale.

International Franchising. United States franchisors have franchise operations in over twenty countries, principally in Europe, Canada, Japan, the Middle East, and Australia. Foreign franchising generally is less complicated for United States companies, although not only foreign law but also the international reach of United States antitrust laws must be taken into consideration.

In Canada, for example, where franchising also accounts for about a third of all retail sales, franchise laws are in effect in Alberta and Quebec, and have been under consideration in Ontario. Various national laws impose antitrust restraints. The Canadian Trade Marks Law is similar in many respects to the U.S. law, but requires registration of franchisees as "registered users."

LAWRENCE S. WICK, Attorney, Leydig, Voit, Osann, Mayer & Holt, Ltd., Chicago, Illinois; member representing the franchisor industry, State of Illinois' Franchise Advisory Board

Information References

Associations:

American Institute of Certified Public Accountants (franchise accounting, finance and taxation).

Federal Trade Commission (FTC rule, guidelines, opinions).

International Franchise Association (franchisor services).

National Franchisee Association Coalition (franchisee services).

Texts:

"Business Franchise Guide," Chicago, Commerce Clearing House, 1980.

Glickman, G., "Franchising," New York, Matthew Bender & Co., 1980.

U.S. Department of Commerce, "Franchising in the Economy," 1979.

References Cited

[1] U.S. Department of Commerce, "Franchising in the Economy," 1979.

[2] FTC Disclosure Requirements and Prohibitions Concerning Franchising and Business Opportunity Ventures, Title 16 Code of Federal Regulations, Section 436; see 44 *Federal Register* No. 246, Dec. 21, 1978, pages 59,614 through 59,753 for complete discussion.

[3] *In re FTC Franchise Disclosure Rule Review,* No. 78–3680 et al., U.S. Court of Appeals, 9th Circuit, 1980.

[4] Hawaii, Illinois, Indiana, Maryland, Michigan, Minnesota, New York, North Dakota, Rhode Island, South Dakota, Virginia, Washington, and Wisconsin. Oregon requires disclosures but not registration. Registration legislation was under consideration during 1980 in Florida, Massachusetts, Oklahoma and other states.

[5] *People* vs. *Dale M. Carter* (Chairman, The Pie Tree, Inc.), No. 79C–2158, Cook County Circuit Court, 1980. (Three year sentence for sale of unregistered franchises in Illinois.)

[6] *State of New Jersey* vs. *Lawn King, Inc. and Joseph Sandler,* 150 N.J. Super. 204 and 152 N.J. Super. 333, Law Div., 1977. (Restraint of trade convictions), reversed 169 N.J. Super. 346 (Appellate Div., 1979), acquittals affirmed ___ N.J. ___ (Supreme Court, No. A–129, 1980).

[7] *Susser* vs. *Carvel Corp.,* 206 Fed. Supp. 636, S.D. N.Y., 1962.

[8] For example, *Kosters* vs. *Seven-Up Co.,* 595 F.2d 347, U.S. Court of Appeals, 6th Circuit, 1979 (franchisor's liability for injuries caused by explosion of bottle packaged by franchisee).

Cross References: *Franchising.*

FREIGHT FORWARDERS

A **Freight Forwarder** performs all facets of transportation except the actual, physical line-haul movement. For the latter it employs the services of "underlying" air, motor, rail, and water carriers.

Most forwarder business in the United States is handled by *surface freight forwarders*—those that make use of rail and motor exclusively for line-haul transportation. They handle relatively low-weight shipments which would fall into the category of less-than-truckload (LTL) or less-than-carload (LCL) traffic. They assess rates closely comparable to the motor carriers' LTL and the railroads' LCL rate levels; their profit comes after they consolidate the freight they receive and turn it over to line-haul rail or motor carriers for physical transportation, from the difference between LTL/LCL rates they charge their customers and the truckload/carload rates they pay the underlying line-haul carriers. Thus, the entire forwarder industry is built on the transportation industry's economies of scale, which dictate reduced rate levels for larger quantities of freight.

In all respects except the actual physical haulage of goods, the freight forwarding company acts in the capacity of carrier. It assumes full origin-to-destination responsibility for the shipments tendered it, issues a through bill of lading, provides (either itself or through local drayage companies) pickup-and-delivery service, handles any required tracing of shipments while in transit, and otherwise maintains full control of the entire origin-to-destination movement. In the event of in-transit loss or damage, the shipper legally looks only to the forwarder for settlement of claims; it is up to the forwarder to obtain such settlements as it can, for its own account, from the line-haul carrier(s).

Surface freight forwarders must obtain operating authority from the Interstate Commerce Commission for any interstate service they provide. Air freight forwarders, which provide similar services by use of underlying airlines and are known as "indirect air carriers," require no regulatory authority under a 1977 law deregulating air cargo traffic, and operate on a strict market-competition basis.

Freight forwarders generally offer direct through transportation service between major industrial and commercial centers, consolidating shipments at the point of origin and distributing them at the destination. Their personnel are highly skilled in transportation procedures, and can often secure for the shipper faster and better transportation service than he can obtain through his own independent efforts. They also relieve the shipper of the burden of considerable documentation. Many forwarders specialize in certain types of traffic, or particular types of service. For example, some forwarders deal almost exclusively in "piggyback" (trailer-on-rail-flatcar) transportation; their capabilities in these areas of specialization are usually broader than those of the individual shipper. A number of forwarders also operate private communications systems to facilitate the tracing and expediting of shipments.

Foreign Freight Forwarders. Foreign freight forwarders operate in essentially the same fashion as domestic forwarders, except that they generally offer export-import services in connection with documentation, consular invoices, etc. Ocean freight forwarders differ in that they actually receive fees from the shippers they serve, and are permitted to serve as brokers for shipping lines, receiving a commission from the latter in addition to the shipper's fee. For the small shipper exporting or importing via ocean carrier, the services of a foreign freight forwarder in documentation, credit, export packing, and Customs requirements are particularly valuable.

To the extent that they perform operations within the United States, ocean forwarders are regulated by the Federal Maritime Commission (and are classed as "NVOs"—"non-vessel operators").

COLIN BARRETT, Transportation Consultant, Reston, Virginia

Information References

Air Freight Forwarders Association.
Freight Forwarders Institute.

Cross References: *Shippers' Associations; Traffic and Transportation: Structure of the Transportation Industry; Traffic Management.*

G

GAME THEORY

The Theory of Games is a branch of mathematical analysis dealing with abstract models of conflict situations or games of strategy. Such games are characterized by the fact that their outcomes are dependent on the joint action of the participants and, frequently, by chance effects as well. Game theoretic analysis presents a fundamentally conservative view which treats as optimal not the best that a player might achieve (as by boldness, intuition or luck), but the best that he can *guarantee* himself through his own actions. While best exemplified by the well-structured systems of parlor-games, games of strategy find their real-life analogues at the heart of economic, military, and political conflicts. Although game theory in its present state is generally incapable of affording rigorous solutions to these problems, it does provide useful concepts and an improved understanding of the factors involved in real conflicts.

The proof of the fundamental theorem of game theory, the *minimax principle,* was first obtained by John von Neumann in 1928. Widespread interest in the concepts of the theory, however, dates from the publication in 1944 of "Theory of Games and Economic Behavior" by von Neumann and Morgenstern. The growth of the management sciences since World War II has given additional impetus to the development and application of the theory.

Definitions. From the game theoretic viewpoint, a *game* is defined as a model of a conflict situation. The competing players are referred to as *persons* whether they are individuals, teams, or any other aggregation representing a single set of interests. A *play* of a game is a single exercise of the conflict model according to the *rules;* it consists of one or more *moves* by each player and may involve moves left to chance. The outcome of the game is represented by the *payoff,* a gain or loss of some utility to each of the players as a result of the positions reached at the end of the game. The *solution* of a game comprises the identification from among all the possible, alternative courses of action of that which ensures the player's expected payoff at a quantity called the *value* of the game.

For example, in a business situation, the competition between two firms manufacturing the same kind of product may be structured in game-theory terms. The "persons" are the firms, the "play" may be taken as an arbitrarily determined period of time, the "rules" are the discipline of the marketplace. Within these rules, the firms' managements may make a wide variety of specific business decisions on which particular actions will be taken. These are the "moves." As indicated below, the master plan which unifies the moves is the "strategy," and in our example a selected strategy would describe the firms' general decisions regarding such things as retooling, advertising outlay, new product lines, merger, etc. The results of the interactions among the strategic choices made by the two firms is manifested by the "payoff," which could be chosen to be annual gross sales or net profit, etc. Only when this sort of situation is rigorously structured and quantified (see *Normal Form,* below), is it meaningful to speak of a "solution" and "value" for a game; moreover, it is not generally possible to obtain the solution by direct means.

Extensive Form of a Game. The rules of a game normally specify: (1) a progression of steps, each consisting of one or (usually) more alternatives, originating from a unique starting point; (2) the identification at each step of either the person to select the alternative to be followed, or chance, if the step is a stochastic, i.e., a probabilistic or randomly determined, one; (3) for each stochastic step, the appropriate probability distribution; (4) a criterion for recognizing the terminal positions of the game; and (5) a payoff function defined over the set of terminal positions for each person.

These requirements are satisfied by a tree-like network, in which each branch-point or node is assigned either to a player as a decision point or to chance, and each link corresponds to a move which advances the game situation. Every path through the network eventually reaches a terminal point with which is associated a value of the payoff function for each player. This network is referred to as the *extensive form* of the game. If the rules of the game make available complete information regarding past actions, then all players know precisely which node of the network describes the game position at any time; such a game is characterized as possessing *perfect information.* If, on the other hand, certain information is available to only some of the players and, as a result, the opponent(s) can know only that the game situation is at one or another of a set of nodes, the game is characterized as having *imperfect information* and the network must be refined to indicate the grouping of nodes into such *information sets* with an indication of the correspondence among the related links arising from each node of the set.

Exhibit I is an example of such a network. The numerals associated with each node or information set (nodes grouped within a dotted line) identify the player whose turn it is to choose among the lettered links arising from that node or set. In the latter case, the correspondence among related links is indicated by single and double priming. The nodes from which no links arise are terminal points and are associated with statements regarding the payoff to be awarded each player.

Strategy. The extensive form of a game allows a clear visualization of the meaning of a *strategy:* a plan of action for one player indicating the link to be selected from every node or information set calling for his move which can possibly be reached in the course of a play. Since a single strategy dictates the alternative to be chosen for every contingency which can arise, the number of component statements in a single strategy as well as the number of different strategies can be astronomical even for relatively simple games. The concept of a strategy, however, is one of the important contributions of game theory, since it focuses attention on the fundamental decision involved rather than on the details of its execution.

EXHIBIT I

NETWORK OF ALTERNATIVES

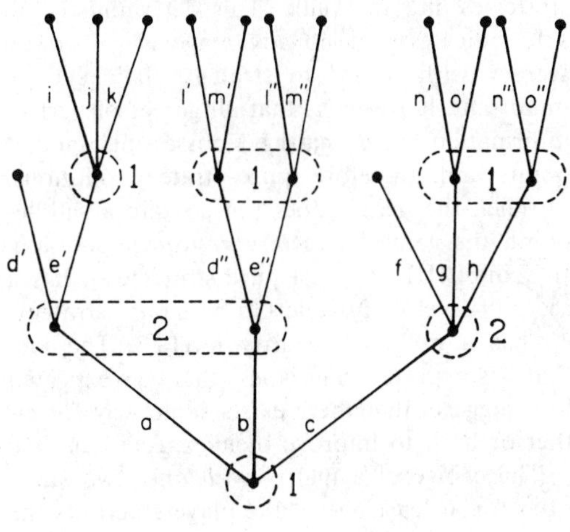

Normal Form of a Game. A two-person game may be represented in tabular form by listing all the strategies available to one player, let us call him R, the row player, down the left side, and all the strategies available to the other player, C, the column player, across the top. At the intersection of each row and column is entered the payoff to be awarded each player as a result of the joint selection of that row and column. This table is called the *payoff matrix* or the *normal form* of the game. R's strategy selection problem is thus the choice of a row; C's, the choice of a column.

Classification of Games. Finite games, games in which each player has available a finite number of strategies, may be classified according to number of persons, relationships among the payoffs, and whether cooperation among the players is allowed. The simplest case is the *two-person, zero-sum* game, zero-sum indicating that the sum of the payoffs to the two players is zero; what one player gains, the other loses. This is of necessity a *strictly competitive* game, there being no opportunity for mutual gain by any form of cooperation. Game theory provides a satisfactory analysis and concept of solution for all possible games of this type.

Passing to the two-person, *non-zero-sum* game, the total payoff is dependent upon the joint decisions of the players, thus creating the possibility in this *non-strictly-competitive* case of gain by each player greater than that which he could achieve by uncoordinated strategy choices predicated on self-interest alone. It therefore becomes important to investigate whether *cooperation* is permissible or whether, as in the *non-cooperative* case, the players must arrive at their solutions independently. Two-person, non-zero-sum games correspond more closely to real (economic or military) situations than do the simpler zero-sum games, but the theory is unable to provide satisfactory general solutions for this more complicated case. The analysis of *more-than-two-person* games depends upon the fact that they present an opportunity for *coalition* formation. While this leads to a number of significant results, new difficulties, as well as those encountered in the two-person case, are present and preclude the formulation of an adequate general theory.

Analysis of the Two-Person Zero-Sum Game. By convention, the payoff matrix of this game is expressed in terms of the payoff to R; C's payoffs are the negative of R's, thus satisfying the condition that their sum be zero. Positive matrix entries represent payments by C to R; negative ones, payments by R to C. In addition to identifying the value of the game, the solution can take either of two forms: in the *pure strategy* case, a single strategy will be indicated as optimal; in the *mixed strategy* case, two or more strategies will appear along with the relative frequencies with which they must be employed.

An example of a two-person zero-sum game in normal form which leads to a pure strategy solution is presented in Exhibit II. R's problem is to choose one of his four strategies; C's, one of his three. For example, the independent choices of r_2 and c_2 result in the payment by C to R of 3 units, while r_4 and c_3 lead to the payment by R to C of 2 units.

Consider first R's analysis of his problem. It is apparent that r_1 is a weak strategy since it nets R less than does the equally available strategy r_2, regardless of C's choice. We say that r_1 is *dominated* by r_2, and on this basis will drop r_1 from further consideration. Continued similar reasoning by R, however, is of no avail; choosing r_4 in an effort to realize the payoff of 10 units at r_4 and c_1 could result in the loss of 2 units if C selects c_3; similar dilemmas exist for the other choices. In general, fixing attention on the possible gains does not help resolve the situation. Suppose now that R takes a conservative point of view and examines the *least* that his choice could produce: a gain of 2 for r_2, a gain of 5 for r_3, and a loss of 2 for r_4. Of these options, r_3 and its consequence appear most satisfactory; the 5 unit gain represents an assured *security level* to R since he cannot be driven below this point by any action available to C. To summarize, R has examined the *minimum* gain that each row strategy could produce and, wishing to maximize his gain, has selected the *greatest* of these. This is referred to as R's *maximin strategy,* r_3 in Exhibit II.

EXHIBIT II

MATRIX OF A TWO-PERSON ZERO-SUM GAME

		C's strategies			
		c_1	c_2	c_3	Row minima
R's strategies	r_1	0	−1	7	−1
	r_2	2	3	8	2
	r_3	9	5	6	5*
	r_4	10	4	−2	−2
Column maxima		10	5*	8	

Following an analogous line of reasoning, player C examines the *greatest loss* he might sustain as a result of his strategy choice: 10 units for c_1, 5 units for c_2, and 8 units for c_3. Of these, c_2 inflicts the smallest loss on C and establishes his security level by guaranteeing that no action of R's can force his loss beyond 5. Summarizing, C has examined the *maximum* loss that each column strategy could produce and, wishing to minimize his loss, has selected the *least* of these; this is referred to as C's *minimax strategy.* The essential feature of this result is the independently arrived at agreement on the part of the players as to their security levels, and is a direct consequence of the fact that the matrix of Exhibit II possesses a *saddle-point,* an element which is simultaneously the greatest of the row minima and the least of the column maxima: the entry 5 at r_3 and c_2. Its special significance lies in the fact that if either player deviates from this choice, it will result in either decreased gain or increased loss. The selected strategies thus represent an *equilibrium pair,* a pair of strategies each of which is best against the other member of the pair. The complete solution is that R always employs r_3, C always employs c_2, and the value of the game is 5. Of course, as it stands, this is not a *fair* game since R wins 5 units at each play. It can be made fair, however, simply by requiring R to pay 5 units to C each time to induce C to play, or, what is the same thing, reducing each element of the game matrix by 5.

In general, the presence of a saddle-point immediately identifies the equilibrium pure strategies and the value. This deterministic result indicates that no advantage is gained by secrecy with regard to strategy choice. More important, however, is that all games of perfect information have matrices possessing saddle-points and, therefore, pure strategy solutions.

When the matrix does not contain a saddle-point, the game has a *mixed strategy* solution. In Exhibit III, R's best pure strategy, r_2, has a security level of 2 while C's best pure strategy, c_1, has a different security level, 3. The fact that R's expected gain is less than C's expected loss suggests that there exists some way for either or both to improve their expectations.

The choice of a matrix with only two strategies for at least one of the players permits the

EXHIBIT III

MATRIX OF A GAME WITH MIXED-STRATEGY SOLUTION

	C's strategies c_1	c_2	Row minima
R's strategies r_1	3	1	1
r_2	2	4	2*
Column maxima	3*	4	

two-dimensional, graphical representation of Exhibit IVa. Let x_1 be the relative frequency of playing r_1, and x_2 that of r_2; since $x_1 + x_2 = 1$, any mixed strategy (x_1, x_2) can be represented as a point on the unit length baseline. Plotting R's payoff by using r_2 against each of C's strategies at the left ($x_2 = 1$), and by using r_1 against C's strategies at the right ($x_1 = 1$), and then connecting the appropriate points, two graphs representing the payoffs of all possible mixes of r_1 and r_2 are obtained.

The security levels of all of R's strategies, both pure and mixed, are represented by the heavy line segments; R's maximin strategy,

EXHIBIT IVa

GRAPHIC REPRESENTATION OF STRATEGIES

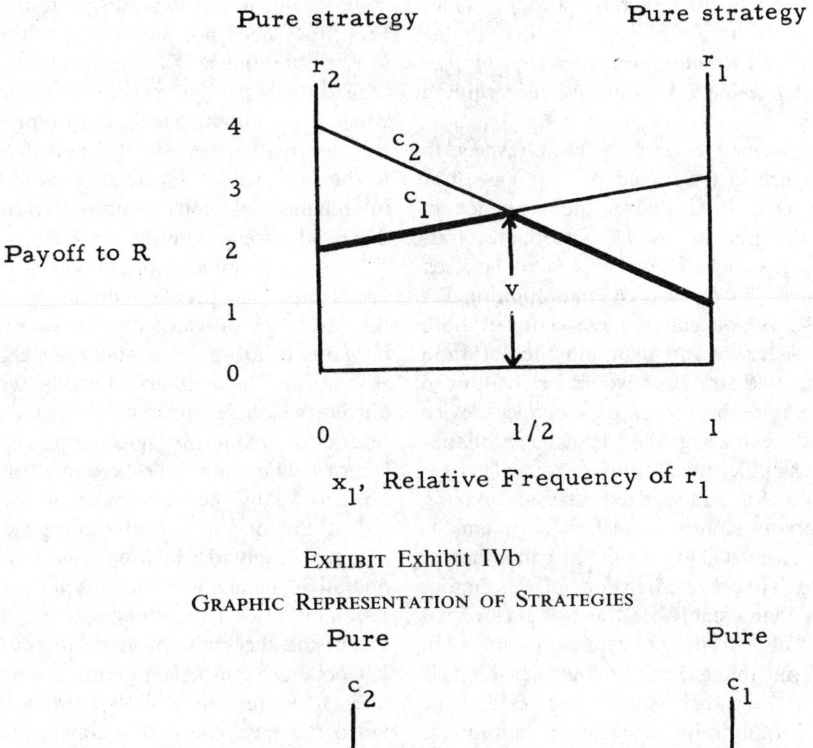

EXHIBIT Exhibit IVb

GRAPHIC REPRESENTATION OF STRATEGIES

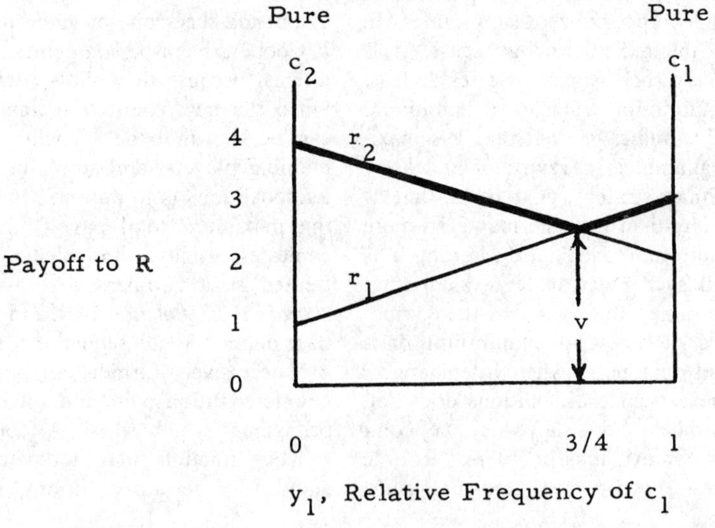

which maximizes his security level, is therefore $x_1 = 1/2$, $x_2 = 1/2$.

Exhibit IVb is a similar graph, drawn to emphasize C's point of view. Here we have again plotted the payoff *to R,* but this time as a function of y_1, the relative frequency of using strategy c_1, against both of R's choices, r_1 and r_2. In this form, C's maximum security level corresponds to the minimum payoff which he must anticipate; as shown by the heavy line segments, this is at the point $y_1 = 3/4$ and corresponds to a value, v, of $2 1/2$.

Finally, note that the solutions ($x_1 = x_2 = 1/2$) and ($y_1 = 3/4$, $y_2 = 1/4$) are in equilibrium, since both yield the same value, and that value is a better result than either player could have achieved by using his best pure strategy. Thus, r_1 and r_2 in the ratio 1:1 and c_1 and c_2 in the ratio 3:1 are an *equilibrium mixed strategy pair* and, with the value $2 1/2$, comprise the required solution.

The importance of secrecy with respect to strategy choice in the mixed strategy case may easily be seen. If C knows the sequence in which R will play his equally probable strategies, he can choose c_2 when r_1 is to be used and c_1 when r_2 is to be used, thus limiting R's gain to $1 1/2$. A convenient method for R both to preserve secrecy and maintain the 1:1 ratio between his two strategies would be for him to make the choice by means of a chance device capable of generating the requisite probabilities; for example, by flipping a coin. This rationalization for randomized decision-making in appropriate strategy selection problems is one of the more striking results of game theory.

Minimax Theorem. The proof of this fundamental theorem establishes the *existence* of solutions for all two-person zero-sum games. In particular, in the mixed strategy sense, it is shown that every such game possesses at least one pair of equilibrium strategies (maximin and minimax) and a value, v, such that R's maximin strategy guarantees a return of at least v and C's minimax strategy guarantees that R will gain no more than v. There may exist more than one equilibrium pair; in this event it is shown that all such pairs are equivalent, that all lead to the same value, and that the component strategies of any two equilibrium pairs produce equilibrium pairs when interchanged.

Proof of the existence of solutions does not, in general, indicate how they may be computed. In this context, it is of interest to note that every finite, two-person zero-sum game can be reduced to a LINEAR PROGRAMMING problem and solved in that form. Other techniques more directly related to the concepts of game theory have been developed, but all involve significant computational effort for even medium-sized matrices.

Non-Zero-Sum Games. The concept of equilibrium sets of mixed strategies is central to the analysis of non-zero-sum games, whether of the two-person or n-person (n greater than 2) variety. Equilibrium sets are characterized by the fact that if all players but one adopt strategies drawn from the set, then the last player's optimal strategy is also a member of the set. For non-cooperative games, equilibrium sets always exist; their properties, however, differ markedly from those of the two-person zero-sum game. First, they need not be optimal solutions in the sense of allowing the players collectively to realize the maximum gain possible; second, when more than one equilibrium set exists, they are neither necessarily equivalent (i.e. lead to the same value) nor do they indicate that the interchange of corresponding strategies produces additional equilibrium sets.

The two-person cooperative case, with its opportunity for preplay communication, opens the structure of game theory to problems of bargaining, arbitration, and the negotiation of *side-payments,* auxiliary payoffs among the players which redistribute the game payoffs in return for previously agreed upon strategy selections. The main issue here involves the criteria for fixing the side payment in order to reflect the players' relative strategic strengths and the extent to which each benefits from cooperative behavior. The resolution of these problems leads to matters generally considered as outside the scope of game theory proper.

Cooperative n-person games are of particular interest because they allow *coalition* formation. Since the best counter to any given coalition can be shown to be a coalition of all the remaining players, and since the purpose of the two coalitions is to optimize the distribution of the maximum total payoff, the situation becomes essentially a duopolistic one and may be treated as a two-person zero-sum game. The *characteristic function* of the n-person game is then defined as the sequence of values obtained by successively forming all possible coalition-countercoalition pairs and solving the two-person games which result. Although the characteristic function may indicate the potential stability of certain coalitions, it is inadequate as a solution since it does not provide a basis for apportioning the coalition's gain among its members. The assignment of payoffs to each member of a coalition is called an *imputation* if it satisfies the conditions of *individual rationality* (each member's payoff must equal or exceed the security level which he can achieve alone), and *group rationality* (the sum of the individual payoffs must equal the maximum amount which a single, grand coalition of all the players can obtain). Since *essential games,* games in which coalition formation serves a purpose, have infinitely many imputations, some dominance concept is required. One imputation is said to dominate another if the former affords each of its members a greater payoff than the latter and, in addition, if its members can prevent the formation of a coalition based on the latter imputation. A solution of an n-person game is considered to be a set of imputations which dominate any imputation not in the set, but none of which dominates another in the set. Difficulties with this treatment lie in the fact that solution sets are not unique and that it has not been proven that all such games have such solution sets. Efforts to resolve these problems have led to additional criteria imposed on the imputations of a solution set, but a generally satisfactory treatment has not been achieved.

Conclusion. It is seen that game theory has proven to be a conceptually rich structure and has made possible the precise and rigorous analysis of some aspects of decision making in conflict situations. At the same time, the intractability of many kinds of conflict models and the inherent difficulty of establishing well-structured strategic alternatives and of quantifying conflict outcomes have severely limited its application.

B. J. BERKOWITZ, General Electric Company
Santa Barbara, California

Information References

Brams, Steven J., "Game Theory and Politics," New York, Free Press, 1975.

Case, James H., "Economics and the Competitive Process," New York, New York University Press, 1979.

Davis, Morton D., "Game Theory: A Nontechnical Introduction," New York, Basic Books, 1973.

Hamburger, Henry, "Games as Models of Social Phenomena," San Francisco, W. H. Freeman, 1979.

Rapoport, Anatol, "N-Person Game Theory: Concepts and Applications," Ann Arbor, University of Michigan Press, 1970.

Von Neumann, John, and Morgenstern, Oskar, "Theory of Games and Economic Behavior," 2nd ed., Princeton, N.J., Princeton University Press, 1947.

Cross References: *Management Sciences (and cross references there given).*

GANTT CHART

The Gantt Chart is a visual management control device developed during World War I by HENRY L. GANTT, one of the pioneers in SCIENTIFIC MANAGEMENT. It is a linear calendar on which future time is spread horizontally and work to be done is indicated vertically.

In any activity, the only constant is time, and therefore the scale of the Gantt chart is time—future time—the calendar spread horizontally across a sheet. Any suitable divisions and subdivisions of time can be used—months, weeks, days, or hours.

The Planning Chart. There are two basic types of Gantt chart. In the first form, the "planning" chart, the things to be done are entered in symbols and descriptions under the portions of the calendar in which it is planned to do them. (See Exhibit I.) (The standard symbols are described in Exhibit Ia.)

It should be noted that the heavy progress line always starts at the opening angle and never runs beyond the closing angle. The heavy progress line does not necessarily bear any relationship to the *amount* of time actually spent or to *when* it was spent. The chart has no value as a historical record and is usually thrown away after all operations are completed. The important thing in reviewing progress is the position of the ends of the progress lines in relation to the current date (V).

The Progress Chart. This form is used in production control to show cumulative work against time in relation to schedules. In Exhibit II, for example, figures in the upper left-hand corners are outputs in units scheduled for that particular period (in this case charting is done by five-day weeks). Figures in the upper right-hand corners show the cumulative schedule. As work progresses, a light bar is drawn in each period, its length proportional to the percentage of the work scheduled for that period completed in that period. (Note that for week 8–4, 20% more work was done than was scheduled for that week, represented by the double light line.) In this illustration, "today" is the end of Week 8–4. A vertical chain or weighted string can be suspended from hooks at the top of a

Exhibit I

Development Engineer's Project Planning Chart

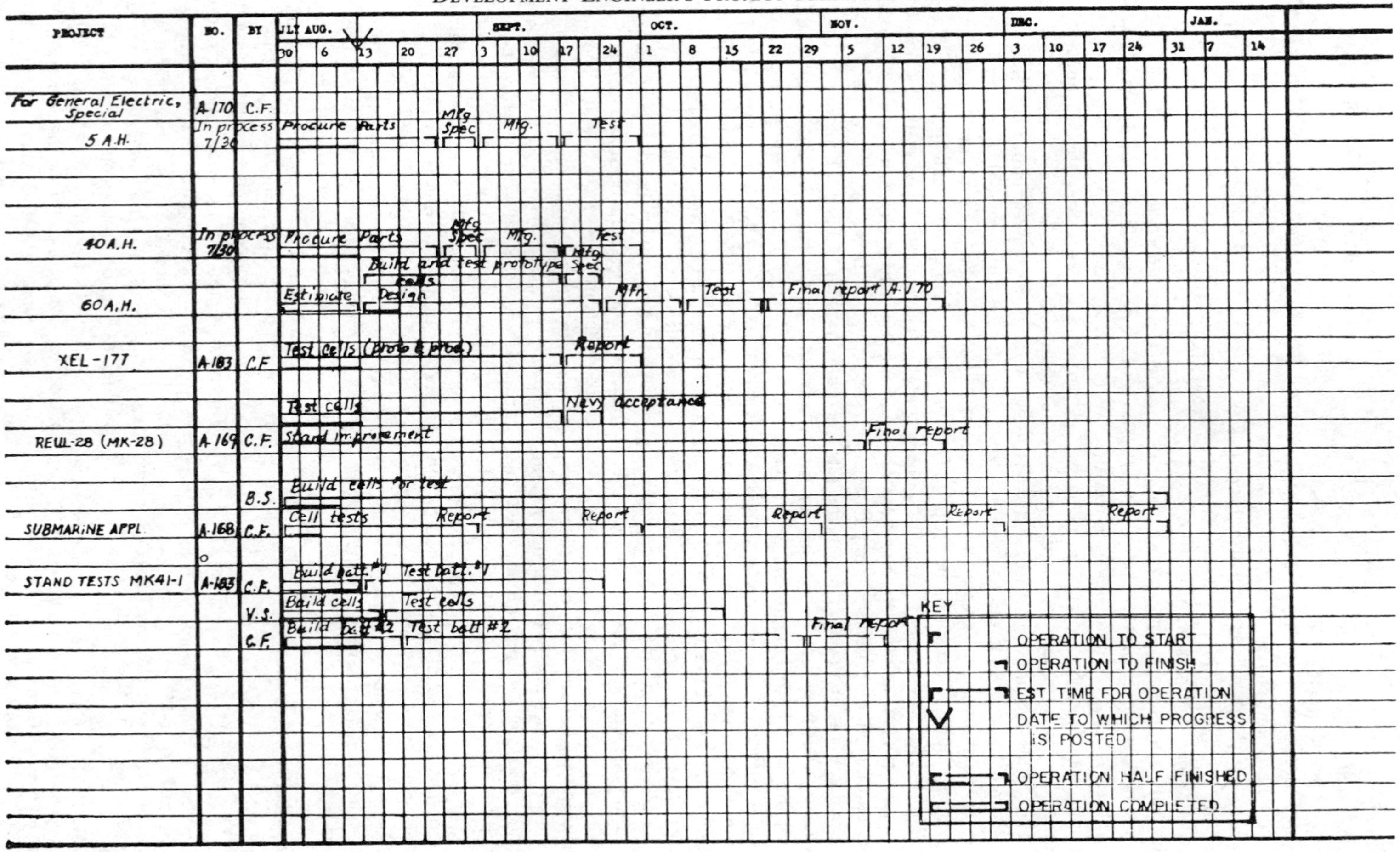

Planning chart of development engineer in laboratory of a battery manufacturer. Some operations are done by others, but he has allowed time for them and is responsible for follow-up. At the end of the week of Aug. 6, 60 A.H. is a week ahead of schedule in the design department, and A 168 (second item from bottom) is a week behind schedule.

Exhibit Ia

Standard Symbols for Gantt Planning Chart

 = the "opening angle," entered under the date when an operation is planned to start.

 = the "closing angle," entered under the date when an operation is planned to finish.

 = the time span during which the operation is to be active.

 = the state of progress, as shown by the length of the heavy line compared to the planned. In R&D, the length of the heavy line is determined by reestimating the time still needed for completion and then measuring back (toward the left) from the closing angle—in other words, the open space between the end of the heavy line and the closing angle is the time still needed to complete the work.

 = the date when progress was posted, and is entered at the top of the calendar columns.

Gantt wall chart and readily moved to today's date to show status at any time.

Opening and closing angles are not used. The heavier bar at the bottom shows *cumulative amount finished.* This line is posted at the scale of the week through which it passes.

On individual projects, the chart can be used to show *and watch* expenditures of man-days or dollars in relation to budgets. A project budget might be $1,000 per month, but it can (and probably does) build up to a period of greatest activity and then taper off—e.g., $500 in the first month, $750 in the second, three months at $1,500, then down to $1,000 or $500.

Actual figures are not shown on the chart but are included in an accompanying tabulation, usually bound facing the chart. The actual figures are of little consequence and need not be referred to, except in cases of significant overrun or underrun (end of heavy line to the right or left of the V).

When this form is used for presenting load, the figures represent capacity in man-days or man-weeks. The V is not used here, because all time is future (the chart is redrawn periodically with the first future month at the left.) The light lines show overloads or unused capacity, *in the months in which they will occur.* The heavy line indicates the date when a department or section would be "out of work" if no new work came in. Experience usually leads to discovery of a normal or optimum total load—one in which adequate service can be rendered without idle staff or equipment. Exhibit III, for example, shows how far into the future machine tools in a certain shop will be kept busy by orders in the plant at the time it is drawn up. The heavy bars show the total amount of work ahead of the machines. "Z" indicates months in which no work is scheduled.

On Gantt planning charts, new work can readily be added without erasure to take prece-

Exhibit II

Gantt Chart, Production Control

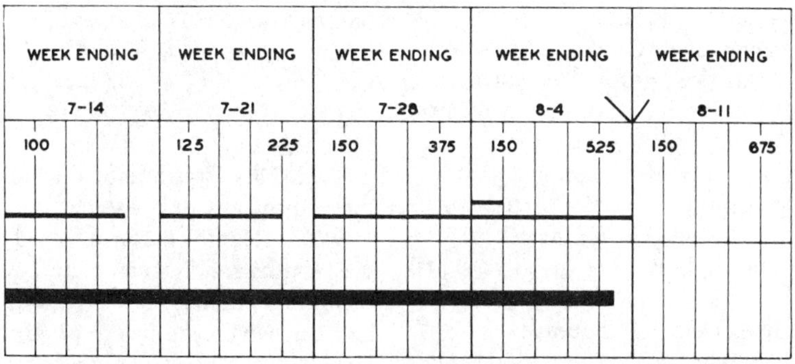

Figures in upper left are schedules for the week shown; figures in upper right are cumulative schedules. Light bars are actual production. Heavy bar is cumulative production as of end of week 8-4. Complex schedules covering large numbers of parts and assemblies can readily be controlled.

EXHIBIT III

GANTT LOAD CHART

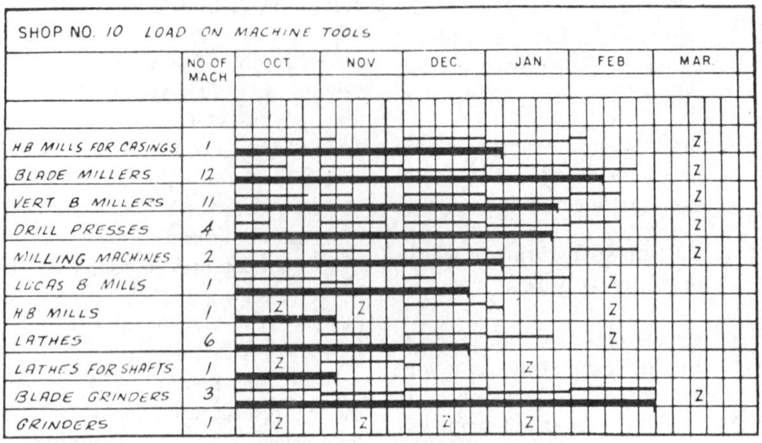
SHOP NO. 10 LOAD ON MACHINE TOOLS
NO OF MACH
OCT
NOV
DEC.
JAN.
FEB
MAR.
HB MILLS FOR CASINGS 1
BLADE MILLERS 12
VERT B MILLERS 11
DRILL PRESSES 4
MILLING MACHINES 2
LUCAS B MILLS 1
HB MILLS 1
LATHES 6
LATHES FOR SHAFTS 1
BLADE GRINDERS 3
GRINDERS 1
Z

Light lines indicate portion of month machines are scheduled to be utilized as of day chart was drawn. Heavy bars are cumulative load ahead of machines. "Z" means no work scheduled for that month. (Cf. Clark, Wallace, "The Gantt Chart.")

dence over work already planned—in fact, no erasing is ever required. The charts are "self-adjusting" for delays or inaccurate time estimates.

The use of the Gantt chart makes a definite plan for each project necessary. This is one of its advantages. It forces the thinking through of the things that will be encountered and must be provided for.

Percentage-Complete Progress Measure. The most common method of measuring progress is estimating the percentage complete. If one is dealing with the production of common units—the fabricating of a quantity of identical machines or machine parts—the numerator and denominator for the percentage are readily at hand. A project in research or development, however, is not composed of a number of identical parts—there is no common denominator applicable to both the portion completed and the portion uncompleted. Lacking any recourse other than a "blue-sky" guess, the tendency is to assume that the project is moving in relation to the allotted time plan—until the allotted time is nearly exhausted. Successive periodic reports of "percentage complete" sometimes appear like this: 25, 33, 50, 75, 90, 91, 92, 93, 94, etc. Since the figures were given at equal periods of time, it is fair to assume either that the earlier figures were too optimistic or that unforeseen difficulties have arisen in the later periods. At best, management has no assurance that the next reports may not be 94.5, 95, 95.25, etc.; and it cannot forecast *when* the project will be completed.

Where man-days or man-hours can be pre-estimated, hours can be used as units of measurement, and the percentage complete can be calculated:

$$\frac{\text{Hours spent to date}}{\text{Total hours estimated}} = \%$$

This does, however, require a timekeeping and reporting system. Also, it is accurate only when the original total estimate is accurate. This objection can be overcome by using the formula:

$$\frac{\text{Hours spent to date}}{\text{Hours spent to date} + \text{Hours estimated necessary to complete}} = \%$$

Re-estimating Progress Measure. The status or position versus plan is also secured in another way where Gantt planning charts are in use. This method is: first, to estimate the *time still necessary to complete;* and second, to subtract this time from the planned date of completion. This gives a date, on the plan, to which the project has progressed.

Where Gantt charts are used, the estimated weeks necessary to complete are counted back from the planned "closing angle" (⌐) to a point at which the heavy progress line is to be terminated. The advantage of this method is that it does not, in itself, alter the original plan, but compensates for inaccuracy in it (based on latest knowledge). Progess is indicated ahead of or behind the plan, and by how much.

Rescheduling. Where formal methods of planning have been introduced, the tendency has been to change schedules almost as soon as performance fails to meet the schedules. It is obvious that this will lead to complacency with any performance. It is possible to be "on schedule" always, if the schedule is changed to conform with current progress. The habit of frequently revising schedules also leads to lack of thoroughness in thinking through the original plan for a project.

Of course, a change in direction, objective, area of investigation, or general method requires a new plan. However, changing schedules because of overoptimism in the original planning or failure to pursue the plan with vigor destroys the very usefulness of planning: It accomplishes nothing—that is, it does not expedite the project; and it weakens the confidence of management in information furnished for its plans.

WILLIAM E. CAMP, Management Consultant, Watertown, Pennsylvania

Information References

Camp, William E., "Executive Direction of Projects," Ch. 8 in "Handbook of Industrial Research Management," Heyel, C., 2nd ed., New York, Reinhold, 1968.

Clark, Wallace, "The Gantt Chart," 3rd ed., London, Pitman, 1952.

Clark, Mrs. Wallace, "The Gantt Chart," Ch. 7-3, in "Industrial Engineering Handbook," Maynard, H. B., ed., 2nd ed., New York, McGraw-Hill, 1963.

Cross References: *Integrated Project Management (and cross references there given).*

GANTT, HENRY L.

Henry Laurence Gantt (1861–1919), a pioneer American industrial and management engineer, taught natural sciences and mechanics, worked as a draftsman, and held a succession of increasingly responsible technical and executive positions in industry from 1887 through 1901. From 1902 until his death he served as a consultant. In 1917 he relinquished his private activity to accept a Government assignment in the Frankford Arsenal, and later in the building of ships for the Emergency Fleet Corporation. A contemporary of Taylor in the MANAGEMENT MOVEMENT, Gantt was one of the earliest to give major attention to human-relations aspects in industry, as distinguished from Taylor's primary emphasis on financial incentives. At the Midvale Steel Co. in Philadelphia (1887–93) he became Assistant to the Chief Engineer (F. W. Taylor) and then Superintendent of the Casting Department. There he made his first original contribution to management with his "task and bonus" system wage payment, which worked successfully at Midvale Steel earlier than Taylor's differential piece-rate system, and won acceptance long afterwards because it was simple, generally applicable, and less severe than Taylor's when the worker failed to attain standard.

The GANTT CHART, now so widely known, was a revolutionary improvement in the planning and control of production in terms of time as well as quantity. But more enduring than his techniques is the new outlook he brought to bear upon industrial leadership. "In his later years, his influence in bringing American industry, and particularly the American engineering profession, to accept the new concepts of management was enhanced by his success in insisting that the training of workers should become a responsibility of management. In 1908 he was putting forward views not generally accepted until the end of the First World War. By then he was already thinking further ahead, to 'democracy in industry' and the humanizing of the science of management. In his later writings he rose to philosophical stature in his proposals for equality of opportunity in industry, and for the identification of the interest of employers and employed on the basis of scientifically ascertained facts" [1]. Gantt's books include "Work, Wages, and Profits," 1910 (Engineering Magazine Co.): "Industrial Leadership," 1916 (Yale Univ. Press); and "Organizing for Work," 1919 (Harcourt, Brace, and Howe, New York). Important among the papers he read before the American Society of Mechanical Engineers are, "A Bonus System of Rewarding Labor," 1902 (*Transactions,* vol. 23); "A Graphical Daily Balance in Manufacture," 1903 (*Transactions,* vol. 24); "Training Workmen in Habits of Industry and Cooperation," 1908 (*Transactions,* vol. 30); "The Relations Between Production and Costs," 1915 (*Transactions,* vol. 37); and "Efficiency and Democracy," 1918 (*Transactions,* vol. 40). Gantt was a prolific writer and active speaker. Over 150 titles are listed in the official biography by Alford [2].

Information Reference

Rathe, Alex W., ed., "Gantt on Management," American Management Association, New York, 1961 (jointly with ASME in commemoration of the hundredth anniversary of the birth of Henry L. Gantt).

References Cited

[1] Urwick, L., "The Golden Book of Management," edited for the International Committee of Scientific Management (CIOS), Newman Neame, Limited, London, 1956.
[2] Alford, Leon P., "Henry Laurence Gantt, Leader in Industry," New York, Harper & Bros., 1934.

GILBRETH, F. B., AND LILLIAN, E. M.

Frank Bunker Gillbreth (1868–1924), American engineer, building contractor, and management consultant, a contemporary of TAYLOR and GANTT, made his most distinctive contribution to scientific management in his development of motion study, although this should not overshadow his substantial work in the wider field of general management. In his "Field System" and "Concrete System" (1908) he described the lines of authority and the responsibility of different jobs within his own business as a building contractor. "His unique contribution was, however, his emphasis on human effort and the methods he devised for showing up wasteful and unproductive movements. He felt that if the 'one best way to do work' could be discovered for each and every element in a worker's movements and surroundings, the resulting gains in productivity could add significantly to the gains which Taylor was making by revising the system of management in the productive unit as a whole" [1]. Gilbreth simplified the motions used in brick laying, reducing their number from 18 to 5, increasing the number of bricks laid per hour from 175 to 350. He had similar success during World War I in training recruits and rehabilitating disabled men. In 1912 he gave up his contracting business and turned to "management engineering," specializing in physical working methods, and, until his death in 1924, devoting himself to the further development of the science of motion study. He was the first to apply the motion picture camera to the recording and analysis of operations, the first to classify the elements of human motions or "therbligs" (Gilbreth spelled backwards). From this work grew the laws of motion economy, looking to the systematic elimination of inefficiencies and waste, and the techniques of estimating performance times as the sum of times normally taken for the elementary motions in an operation.

While Taylor's emphasis had been primarily on the external factors affecting the worker, Gilbreth looked at the worker first, applying the knowledge available from the social sciences to broaden the worker's capacity to contribute to productivity. "Gilbreth's particular contribution was therefore to develop management as a social science, with the human being the center of interest, round which research and experiment revolve, and towards whose development they are directed" [1]. In 1916 he and his wife, Lillian E. M. Gilbreth (see below) jointly contributed a significant paper to the American Academy of Political and Social Science, on their "Three Position Plan of Promotion," outlining, far ahead of their time, a procedure for developing personnel through a "man in charge of promotion," utilizing a "master promotion chart," and "individual promotion charts," and calling for regular meetings between the promotion man and the worker to discuss the latter's aims and progress.

Frank Gilbreth's books include "Concrete System," 1908 (Engineering News Publishing Co., New York); "Field System," 1908 (Myron C. Clark, New York); "Bricklaying System," 1909 (Myron C. Clark, New York); "Motion Study," 1911 (D. van Nostrand, New York); the following in collaboration with Lillian E. M. Gilbreth: "Primer of Scientific Management," 1912 (D. van Nostrand, New York); "Fatigue Study," 1916 (Sturgis & Walton, New York); "Applied Motion Study," 1917 (Sturgis & Walton, New York); and "Motion Study for the Handicapped," 1920 (Macmillan, New York). He was the author of numerous papers on motion study and scientific management in collaboration with Lillian Gilbreth.

Lillian Evelyn Moller Gilbreth (1878–1972), wife of Frank B. Gilbreth, carried on the latter's management engineering work as President, Gilbreth, Inc. after 1924. A psychologist and a teacher at the time of her marriage, Dr. Lillian Gilbreth had always been an active collaborator in her husband's work and writings. She became widely known in her own right, and was an active teacher and lecturer at numerous institutions in this country and abroad, and a member of U.S. Government committees on civil defense, as well as of state and local committees. In later years, much of her writings and lectures were directed to increasing the efficiency of physically handicapped women as home-makers. In addition to works on which she collaborated with her husband, her writings include "Psychology of Management," 1912 (Macmillan, New York); "Living With Our Children," with Edna Yost, 1928 (rev. 1951, Norton, New York); "The Foreman and Manpower Management," with Alice Rice Cook, 1947 (McGraw-Hill, New York); and "Management in the Home," with O. M. Thomas and Eleanor C. Clymer, 1954 (rev. ed. 1959, Dodd, New York).

Reference Cited

[1] Urwick, L., "The Golden Book of Management," edited for the International Committee of Scientific Management (CIOS), Newman Neame, Limited, London, 1956.

GILBRETH PRINCIPLES OF MOTION ECONOMY

The twenty-two **Principles of Motion Economy,** as originally developed by Frank B. Gilbreth may be profitably applied to all types of work situations. Although not all of these principles are applicable to every operation, they do form a basis for improving the efficiency and reducing fatigue in manual work.

Use of the Human Body

(1) The two hands should begin as well as complete their therbligs at the same instant. (A *therblig* is Gilbreth's elementary subdivision of a cycle of motions thought to be common to all work; see MOTION AND TIME STUDY.)

(2) The two hands should not be idle at the same instant except during rest periods.

(3) Motions of the arms should be in opposite and symmetrical directions, instead of in the same direction, and should be made simultaneously.

(4) Hand motions should be confined to the lowest classification with which it is possible to perform the work satisfactorily.

(5) Momentum should be employed to assist the worker wherever possible, and it should be reduced to a minimum if it must be overcome by muscular effort.

(6) Continuous curved motions are preferable to straight-line motions involving sudden and sharp changes in direction.

(7) Ballistic (rhythmic) movements are faster, easier, and more accurate than restricted (fixation) or "controlled" movements.

(8) Rhythm is essential to the smooth and automatic performance of an operation, and the work should be arranged to permit easy and natural rhythm wherever possible.

Arrangement of the Work Place

(9) Definite and fixed stations should be provided for all tools and materials.

(10) Tools, materials, and controls should be located around the work place and as close to the point of assembly or use as possible.

(11) Gravity feed bins and containers should be used to deliver the material as close to the point of assembly or use as possible.

(12) Drop deliveries should be used wherever possible.

(13) Materials and tools should be located to permit the best sequence of therbligs.

(14) Provisions should be made for adequate conditions for seeing. Good illumination is the first requirement for satisfactory visual perception.

(15) The height of the work place and the chair should preferably be so arranged that alternate sitting and standing at work are easily possible.

(16) A chair of the type and height to permit good posture should be provided for every worker.

Design of Tools and Equipment

(17) The hands should be relieved of all work that can be performed more advantageously by the feet or other parts of the body.

(18) Two or more tools should be combined wherever possible.

(19) Tools and materials should be prepositioned wherever possible.

(20) Where each finger performs some specific movement, such as in typewriting, the load should be distributed in accordance with the inherent capacities of the fingers.

(21) Handles such as those used on cranks and large screw drivers should be designed to permit as much of the surface of the hand to come in contact with the handle as possible. This is particularly true when considerable force is exerted to use the handle. For light assembly work, the screw-driver handle should be so shaped that it is smaller at the bottom than at the top.

(22) Levers, crossbars, and handwheels should be located in such positions that the op-

erator can manipulate them with the least change in body position and with the greatest mechanical advantage.

Information Reference

Zinck, W. C., "Dynamic Work Simplification," New York, Van Nostrand Reinhold, 1962.

Cross References: *Human Engineering (Human Factors Engineering); Method Improvement; Motion and Time Study; Work Simplification.*

GOAL PROGRAMMING

Goal Programming is a newly emerging variation of linear programming. First proposed by Charnes and Cooper [1] it was subsequently extended by Ijiri [2] and more recently developed by Lee [3] for practical application.

Whereas Linear Programming provides for optimization of a single objective function subject to a set of constraints, Goal Programming allows for multiple goals which may be conflicting and which may or may not have the same units of measurement. Goals must be rank ordered by the problem formulator. The solution method proceeds by finding a solution which most closely satisfies each goal in turn. There are no trade-offs. Achievement, or proximity to achievement, of higher priority goals is not sacrificed to permit closer attainment of lower priority goals.

A Goal Programming problem then is:

$$\text{Minimize:} \quad P_1 d_1^+ + P_1 d_1^- \;\ldots\ldots\; + P_n d_n^+ + P_n d_n^-$$

Subject to:

$$\begin{array}{lllllllll}
\text{Goals:} & a_{11}X_1 & + \; a_{12}X_2 & + \; a_{13}X_3 \;\ldots\; + & d_1^- & - \; d_1^+ & \cdot \quad \cdot \quad \cdot & & = b_1 \\
 & \vdots & \vdots & \vdots & \vdots & \vdots & \vdots & & \\
 & a_{n1}X_1 & a_{n2}X_2 & + \; a_{n3}X_3 \;\ldots\; + & \cdot & \cdot & + \; d_n^- \; - \; d_n^+ & \cdot & = b_n \\
 & \vdots & \vdots & \vdots & \vdots & \vdots & \vdots & & \\
\text{and} & & & & & & & & \\
\text{Constraints:} & a_{i1}X_1 & + \; a_{i2}X_2 & + \; a_{i3}X_3 \;\ldots\; + & \cdot & \cdot & \cdot & \cdot \; + \; a_{ij}X_j & \leq b_i
\end{array}$$

Where:

$P_1 \ldots P_n$ = ranked priorities

$d_1 \ldots d_n$ = amounts by which goals are exceeded (d^+) or underachieved (d^-)

a_{ij} = relational coefficients

X_j = alternate activities

fining Division, International Management Sciences Department, Mobil Oil Corporation, New York, New York

References Cited

[1] Charnes, A. and Cooper, W. W. "Management Models and Industrial Applications of Linear Programming," New York, Wiley, 1961.
[2] Ijiri, Y., "Management Goals and Accounting for Control," Chicago, Rand McNally, 1965.
[3] Lee, S., "Goal Programming for Decision Analysis," Philadelphia, Auerbach, 1972.

Cross Reference: *Linear Programming.*

GOAL SETTING

The first scientific approach to **Goal Setting** as a means of improving employee productivity was developed by Frederick W. Taylor, the founder of Scientific Management, in the early 1900s. Based on the results of time and motion studies, he assigned blue-collar workers daily goals or *tasks.* Work quantity and quality were measured daily and workers were given feedback indicating whether or not they attained their assigned tasks. Bonuses were paid for task accomplishment. Taylor's ideas, especially his ideas on cost accounting, were later adapted by Pierre Dupont for use with managers at the

Dupont Powder Co. and later at General Motors by Dupont, Donaldson Brown and Alfred P. Sloan [1]. This was the probable origin of the practice of MANAGEMENT BY OBJECTIVES (although it was not so labeled until 1954 by Peter Drucker, based on work done at General Electric.)

The Goal-Setting Process. Goal setting is the key element in MANAGEMENT BY OBJECTIVES, and, in addition to application in wider management systems, can raise the productivity of a single work unit or department, and even of individual employees. Extensive research in recent years has yielded new insights about the goal-setting process and what makes it work [2].

Goal Attributes. It is generally accepted that to be effective goals should be *specific* (preferably quantitative, e.g., "Reduce costs by 5%"). There has been less agreement, however, on the issue of goal *difficulty.* One popular view is that goals will produce the highest performance if they are of moderate difficulty, since low goals will produce low effort and high goals allegedly will produce discouragement and apathy as a result of repeated failures. Actually, some 50 research studies have found that hard goals lead to better performance than either moderate or easy goals, while about the same number have found that setting specific hard goals leads to better performance than telling individuals simply to "do their best" [3]. Thus, goals are most effective when they are both specific and challenging.

Goal Mechanisms. There are four major mechanisms by which goals affect task or work performance. Knowledge of these mechanisms will enable the manager to monitor the goal-setting process more effectively.

First, goals direct attention and action. If a manager is given a goal to cut costs, then he or she will focus on this activity rather than on tasks with lower priority (e.g., recruiting, new product development). If goals are not being achieved, one possibility is that activity is not being directed to the goal in question. This could be due to lack of goal clarity or lack of clear priorities.

Second, goals mobilize effort and energy. Thus, people will work harder to attain a challenging goal than to attain a moderate or easy one (e.g., to increase sales by 20% vs. to increase sales by 10% or 1%). If hard goals do not produce high effort, again lack of clarity or of clear priorities may be the problem. Another possibility is that the employee has not fully accepted the goal.

Third, challenging goals increase task persistence. If goal commitment is adequate, people will keep working until the goal is reached. For example, more persistent effort will be required to reduce the error rate from 5% to 0% than to reduce it from 5% to 4%.

Finally, goals may indirectly motivate the development of new strategies for goal attainment. Goals can't always be achieved simply through hard work and persistence; often it is necessary to "work smarter" rather than harder [4]. Thus, for example, to increase sales may require a new marketing strategy or new product development rather than more effort to sell existing products. This mechanism, of course, ties goal setting in with the general area of decision making and strategy formulation. Problems in this realm may not be due to lack of motivation so much as to lack of knowledge.

Goal Choice. How is a manager to decide what specific goals to set? Frederick W. Taylor developed the most scientific system for repetitive manual work, namely, MOTION AND TIME STUDY; it allows a reasonably precise calculation as to what constitutes a "fair day's work." However, all jobs (e.g., managerial jobs) do not allow for such exact estimates. Furthermore, employees sometimes resist such methods. An easily calculated and readily accepted alternative to motion and time study is to set as a goal the average previous performance of the individual or unit. This technique has been used successfully in a number of studies. Sometimes, however, the proper goal level is simply a matter of judgment; competent employees can be allowed to set their own goals through delegation, or the goals can be set by joint agreement of supervisor and subordinate through participation. (See JOB ENRICHMENT AND WORK EFFECTIVENESS and MANAGEMENT BY OBJECTIVES.)

Often there are external constraints such as contract deadlines or competitors' actions which dictate what goals must be set. Under a management by objectives system, of course, the formal goals of the organization, however derived, are the basis for setting the goals for each employee.

Goal Commitment. Once goals have been set, managers often assume that commitment can be taken for granted. Unfortunately, this is not always the case. Thus, managers must consider what methods to use to ensure that goal commitment will be achieved. The theory of management by objectives is that joint participation by superior and subordinate in setting goals is the best way to achieve goal acceptance. Surprisingly, some recent research studies have not produced strong support for this assumption. A recent review of over 60 studies of participative decision making found that while participation often led to higher satisfaction than unilateral decision making, participation was no more effective than unilateral decision making in motivating productivity [5]. Studies of participative decision making have shown a median performance improvement of only 0.5% [6]. Individual studies, however, have shown performance increases as high as 47%, indicating that participation can be highly effective. It appears that while participation can be effective, it is not *necessary* to achieve goal acceptance. In many successful goal-setting installations, the employees have simply been assigned goals by their supervisors [2]. When goals are reasonable and when the supervisor acts in a supportive manner [7], assigned goals are typically accepted by subordinates.

Acceptance is often facilitated by spontaneous competition that arises among employees performing similar tasks, especially when performance feedback is provided. (Deliberately encouraging competition is a risky procedure, however, since the focus may become more on beating the other employees than on getting the job done and on the success of the organization as a whole. Also chronic losers often give up, which they would not do if they were trying for a fixed standard that was suited to their level of experience and ability.) Money bonuses for goal accomplishment are a very effective method of facilitating goal commitment [3], since most people value money and want recognition in a tangible form. Once employees have a history of success in reaching their goals, acceptance of future goals is more easily attained.

In sum, there are a variety of techniques for obtaining goal commitment. Instead of being tied to a single method, managers who use goal setting (whether they are under an MBO system or not) can be *flexible* in their approach to obtaining goal commitment. Employees who are both highly competent and highly motivated might be allowed to set their own goals without management intervention. Those who need or will accept direction could simply be assigned goals. Employees who require tangible incentives could be offered bonuses. Those who need to have some control over goal setting but are not ready to be on their own could be allowed to participate in the process. Ironically, while there is evidence that participative goal setting does not necessarily enhance goal commitment, occasional studies have shown that some employees set *higher* goals participatively than their supervisors would have assigned to them [3]. This may be especially true of unskilled employees at the lowest job levels. Participation at higher job levels may be more useful as an information exchange or communication device than as a motivator of performance [5].

An important distinction must be made between participation in setting goals and participation in implementing goals (and other organizational changes). While participation in setting goals has not been found in recent research to have consistent effect, participation may be quite beneficial in developing action plans to achieve the goals. If employees have task-relevant knowledge, they may be able to come up with more creative and effective action plans than their supervisors could develop on their own. In this sense the cognitive benefits of participation may be far more substantial than its motivational effects [5].

Resistance to Goal Commitment. Employees resist goal commitment typically for one of three reasons. They may feel that they cannot attain the goal because it is too difficult. Additional training and skill development plus encouragement will often overcome fear of failure. Of course, the goal actually may be too difficult, in which case it should be lowered. Some employees do not accept goals because they do not trust their bosses. Allowing such employees to participate in setting goals may overcome some of their distrust and give them a greater sense of control over their fate.

Goals may also be rejected because employees do not believe that goal accomplishment is really considered important by the organization. They may believe that setting goals is "just a lot of paper work" that will be put into the files and forgotten. (In some cases, of course, they are correct; a good example is the recent fad toward the use of "instructional objectives" in the public schools. Typically teachers simply fill out the forms which are then filed, never to be seen again.)

A good way to convince employees that their goals are to be taken seriously is to base the employee's performance appraisal and rewards (e.g., pay) partly on goal attainment. The term "partly" is used deliberately here. If tangible rewards are based *solely* on goal accomplishment, employees will have a vested interest in setting easy goals, since this will ensure success. For example, the new Civil Service bonus system inaugurated under the Carter administration is almost certain to fail, in part, because rewards will be based on the degree to which goals are reached and exceeded. There is no control for differences in the difficulty of the goals employees set. Thus, managers who think that MBO or other goal-setting systems will completely solve the problem of rewarding people for their performance will be disappointed. While MBO is a substantial improvement over systems which entail no specific goals, managerial judgment is still required in allocating rewards.

Support Elements. While setting goals and getting employees committed to reaching them is necessary to motivate improved performance, a number of support elements must be provided to ensure that this heightened motivation is translated into successful action. First, the employees must have the *ability* to attain their goals. Simply motivating untrained, incompetent employees will not make them effective. Managers must ensure that their selection techniques and training systems yield able and knowledgeable employees. One indication that employees may lack the ability or knowledge to attain their goals is that they will not be able to develop effective strategies or action plans for achieving them. Specifying action plans in advance will enable the manager to uncover knowledge deficits and may have the added benefit that methods which involve inappropriate short cuts can then be avoided. It was noted earlier while goals may *motivate* strategy development, this is no guarantee that a sound plan will actually be developed. In addition to the manager's input, suggestions from co-workers (as in team problem-solving) may also be valuable.

Second, it has been found that goal setting only works when individuals are provided with *feedback* regarding their progress in relation to their goals. Without such feedback employees will not know if they are working hard enough or if the strategies they are using are appropriate. Feedback frequency should be based on need. For nonmanagerial jobs, daily feedback may be both appropriate and useful. For managerial jobs it may be practical only to provide feedback weekly, monthly, or quarterly. It should be added that feedback in the absence of goals is no more effective than goals without feedback. Feedback must be *combined with* performance standards or objectives if performance is to improve, although, as noted earlier, feedback often leads to spontaneous competition even without any formal goal-setting process.

Third, management must provide sufficient resources to get the job done. This may involve additional equipment, people, time, money, and/or expertise.

Fourth, *company policies* must not block goal attainment. For example, rigid rules may prevent action plans from being implemented. Failure to give a degree of responsibility commensurate with the complexity of the goals to be attained may prevent the goals from being reached.

Benefits and Pitfalls. When the goal-setting process is carried out properly, numerous benefits can result. Productivity and performance quality should increase. Costs may decline. Role clarity may increase while role ambiguity is reduced. If goals are achieved, there will be increased satisfaction, pride in accomplishment, and self confidence on the part of employees.

But goal setting is not without its hazards. For example, if hard goals are combined with high management pressure and low supportiveness, employees may be tempted to take short cuts and even resort to dishonest practices. This is just what happened recently in a large national corporation. When middle managers failed to attain their growth targets, upper management responded by firing some and putting increased pressure on the rest. In desperation, the middle managers resorted to false bookkeeping and created millions of dollars of false profits until the deception was discovered. Also, aspects of the job which have not been translated into goals will typically be ignored. This, of course, is the purpose of setting goals: to direct action toward certain ends at the expense of others. But sometimes the ignored aspects of the job are still important to the organization. One way to solve this problem is to formulate goals for such previously ignored aspects. Finally, as already indicated, striving for goals entails the risk of failure. Employees who fail to reach their goals can become discouraged and dissatisfied. However, this problem can be mitigated somewhat by emphasizing *progress* toward the goals and by developing more appropriate action plans.

Implementation. Goal-setting programs should be administered by an individual well versed in the goal-setting literature. If no goal-setting programs currently exist in an organization, hiring an outside consultant is advisable. Based on subsequent experience, organizations may then develop their own in-house capability for operating goal-setting programs. However, if such programs are to succeed on a wide scale (as opposed to in a single unit or department) extensive support is needed from the highest levels of management.

Costs. Goal-setting programs are extremely cost effective. For example, one such program, developed by Dr. Gary Latham of the University of Washington involved truck drivers at a forest products company [8]. These drivers, who transported wood from the field to the mill, were only loading their trucks to about 60% of capacity and knew from feedback given at the time of weigh-in that they were doing this. After being trained in goal-setting techniques, supervisors assigned the drivers the goal of loading their trucks to 94% of capacity (a suggestion which higher management considered ludicrously simple-minded). Performance improved immediately and within three months the truckers were regularly exceeding 90% of load capacity. This improvement has been maintained to the time of this writing, more than seven years later [2]. Company accountants estimated that the cost of buying new trucks to carry the extra load which the almost fully loaded trucks were now carrying would have been at least $250,000.

Conclusions. In the last eleven years alone there have been over 100 published studies on the effects of goal setting on performance in both laboratory and organizational settings. In 90% of the studies goal setting was found to be effective in improving task performance [6]. This makes it one of the most effective and reliable motivational techniques known. The average goal-setting program in an organizational setting achieves a 16% improvement in task performance; some achieve much more. In combination with money incentives, goal setting has been found to achieve performance improvements in excess of 40% [6].

EDWIN A. LOCKE, PH.D., College of Business and Management and Department of Psychology, University of Maryland at College Park, Maryland

(Preparation of this entry was facilitated by Contract No. N00014-79-C-0680 from the Organizational Effectiveness Research Program of the Office of Naval Research.)

References Cited

[1] Wren, Daniel A., "The Evolution of Management Thought, 2nd ed., New York, Wiley, 1979.

[2] Latham, Gary P. and Locke, Edwin A., "Goal-Setting: A Motivational Technique That Works," *Organizational Dynamics,* Autumn 1979.

[3] Locke, Edwin A., Shaw, Karyll N., Saari, Lise M., and Latham, Gary P., "Goal Setting and Task Performance: 1969–1980," *Psychological Bulletin,* in press.

[4] Vough, Clair F., "Tapping the Human Resource," New York, Amacom, 1975.

[5] Locke, Edwin A. and Schweiger, David M., "Participation in Decision-Making: One More Look," in Staw, B.M., ed., "Research in Organizational Behavior," vol. 1, Greenwich, Conn., JAI Press, 1979.

[6] Locke, Edwin A., Feren, Dena B., McCaleb, Vickie M., Shaw, Karyll N., and Denny, Anne T., "The Relative Effectiveness of Four Methods of Motivating Employee Performance," in Duncan, K., Gruneberg, M., and Wallis, D., eds., "Changes in Working Life: Proceedings of the NATO International Conference," London, Wiley, in 1980.

[7] Latham, Gary P. and Saari, Lise M., "Importance of Supportive Relationships in Goal Setting," *Journal of Applied Psychology,* vol. 64, 1979, 151–156.

[8] Latham, Gary P. and Baldes, J. James, "The 'Practical Significance' of Locke's Theory of Goal Setting," *Journal of Applied Psychology,* vol. 60, 1975, 122–124.

Cross References: *Job Enrichment and Work Effectiveness; Management by Objectives; Motivation.*

GOMPERS, SAMUEL

Samuel Gompers (1850–1924), born in a London tenement, emigrated to America with his family as a boy of thirteen, in 1863. His formal schooling ceased at the age of ten, but through his own readings and attendance at evening lectures in New York's Cooper Union, he attained a broad education; and achieved great and respected prominence as a leader in the American labor movement, becoming active in the Cigar Makers Union. In 1881, with Adolph Strasser of the Cigar Makers Union, he formed the Federation of Organized Trades and Labor Unions. In 1886 this became the

American Federation of Labor, with Gompers as its president. He was repeatedly re-elected to that office until his death in 1924, with the exception of only one year, 1895. (See LABOR UNIONS, section on *Samuel Gompers and the American Federation of Labor.*) Gompers' power within the organization steadily increased, and he was largely responsible not only for its victory over the Knights of Labor, but also for the general adoption of the "craft" principle in U.S. trade unionism of the time, his motto being "only one union for each trade in all North America." In 1894 he became editor of the A.F. of L. paper, *The American Federationist.* As such, in 1907, he was sentenced to twelve months' imprisonment for contempt of court in disobeying an injunction prohibiting the publication from blacklisting the Buck Stove and Range Co. of St. Louis, but the sentence was eventually set aside by the Supreme Court.

Gompers was in theory opposed to war, but after the outbreak of World War I he opposed any pacifist tendency in the trade unions, and organized the War Committee on Labor, composed of representatives of organized labor and employees. He was a member of the advisory commission of the U.S. Council of National Defense, 1917, and represented the A.F. of L. at the Paris Peace Confeence, 1918–19, where he was made chairman of the Peace Conference Commission on Labor Legislation. He was active in the organization of the Pan-American Federation of Labor, and was largely responsible for the decision of the A.F. of L. to hold aloof from the International Federation of Trade Unions in 1919.

Gompers consistently resisted socialistic movements among the unions, fought the I.W.W. (the radical Industrial Workers of the World), and consistently chartered craft unions (as opposed to industrial unions). He opposed compulsory arbitration in labor disputes. He enjoyed a worldwide reputation as a conservative labor leader, and exercised a powerful influence in American trade unionism, even though his policies aroused bitter opposition in some circles. Gompers' autobiography, "Seventy Years of Life and Labor," 1925 (2 vols., E. P. Dutton, New York, 1925; one-vol. edition with an introduction by Matthew Woll, Dutton, New York, 1943) is considered an indispensable source book for all students of labor. His other published works include, "Labor in Europe and America," 1910 (Harper & Bros. New York); "American Labor and the War," 1919 (Geo. H. Doran, New York); "Labor and the Common Welfare," 1919 (E. P. Dutton); and "Out of Their Mouths: A Revelation and an Indictment of Sovietism," with W. E. Walling, 1921 (E. P. Dutton).

GOVERNMENT RELATIONS. See Business-Government Relations.

GREEN, WILLIAM

William Green (1872–1952) was President, American Federation of Labor, from 1924 until his death. Called "the diplomat of the American Labor movement," Green was almost entirely self-educated, his formal schooling having stopped after the eighth grade. His father, who had been a miner in England, was a member of the Progressive Miners Union, forerunner of the United Mine Workers of America, and William went into the mines in Ohio at the age of sixteen. He immediately took an active interest in labor affairs, and at eighteen was secretary of the Coshocton (Ohio) Progressive Miners Union (later Local 273 of UMW). In 1900 he was elected subdistrict president of UMW, and in 1906 was made president of the Ohio District, UMW. In 1908 he gave up working in the mines to devote all of his time to union affairs. He served two terms in the Ohio State Senate, where, as Democratic Floor Leader, he won enactment of the Ohio Workmen's Compensation Law. In 1913 he was appointed a member of the executive council of the American Federation of Labor, and was elected president of A.F. of L. in December, 1924, and re-elected for many successive terms. Green continually emphasized the value of collective bargaining, pointing out "how much further we could be by using our heads than by using our fists," and urged upon his followers that "good times for the miners are bound up with prosperity for the mine operators." He got along well with businessmen, and did little to encourage the wave of labor militancy that swept the country in 1934 and 1935. In 1936 he came out against Government fixing of wages, and called for Congress to curb the power of the National Labor Relations Board.

In 1935 Green split with JOHN L. LEWIS after the latter formed the Committee for Industrial Organization (later the Congress of

Industrial Organization), over the question of industrial unionization, at a time when hundreds of thousands of unskilled workers were unorganized. Subsequently the C.I.O. broke away from the A.F. of L.

GROSS NATIONAL PRODUCT. See Income, Expenditures, and Health.

GROUP DYNAMICS

As organizations in the industrial society grow larger, there is more and more concern on the part of management over how personnel can most effectively be motivated for the accomplishment of individual and organizational goals. One of the most fruitful approaches is to increase the effectiveness of *face-to-face groups* at all levels of the organization.

In the development of such teamwork, an understanding by management of the complexity of group behavior is of prime importance. It has been estimated that the average executive spends up to 70% of his time in meetings and conferences of one kind or another, in addition to working within one unit of which he is a *member,* and overseeing another work group of which he is a *leader.* Most executives will be quick to indicate that many such group activities are ineffective and frustrating. However, the reasons for such negative feelings are not inherent in group behavior, but in the lack of understanding of the dynamics of the group, and inadequate carrying out of leader and member responsibilities in the group.

Group Dynamics is concerned with the multiple factors affecting the operation of a group. Whenever two or more persons get together, a set of complex interpersonal relations occurs which will determine its behavior. The interaction of these forces and their effects on the group constitute its dynamics. In this sense, as stated by Knowles [1], group dynamics is to groups what "personality dynamics" is to individuals.

The term group dynamics is also used to describe a field of research in the social sciences which attempts to discover why groups behave in the way they do. In the past thirty years a considerable amount of research has been done in this field through the contributions of social psychologists and sociologists. In fact, the field has developed a bridge between psychology and sociology.

The application of this knowledge has been evident in group leadership, conference techniques, organizational effectiveness through groups, group decision making, and related areas.

Management has been particularly interested in group dynamics because of the increasing recognition of the importance of the face-to-face functional work groups in the organization. Particularly significant here has been the research into productivity and morale conducted at the Institute for Social Research at the University of Michigan. Dr. Rensis Likert, the director of the Institute, describes the importance of organizational work units as follows [2]:

"Each of us seeks to satisfy our desire for a sense of personal worth and importance primarily by the response we get from people we are close to, in whom we are interested, and whose approval and support we are eager to have. The face-to-face groups with whom we spend the bulk of our time are, consequently, the most important to us. Our work group is one of the most important of our face-to-face groups, and one from which we are particularly eager to derive a sense of personal worth."

Studies in the fields of psychology, sociology, and psychiatry reinforce this statement. They clearly indicate that if an organization is to make the maximum use of its human resources and meet the highest level of man's needs, it must see to it that the individual relates effectively in the organization's groups of which he is a member, and particularly those in which he is a leader. Well-knit, effective face-to-face work units will develop out of conditions which provide effective relationship between leader and members.

Emphasis on the group is an aid to individual growth and development. "Social science, by discovering what happens in group situations and what causes different individual behavior, and by contributing to the recent growing movement of leadership and membership training, has aided materially in freeing and developing the individual rather than submerging the individual in the group" [3].

Man performs creative, rational, and organizational acts through the communication process with others. One cannot contribute to society without relationships with others. The important factor is to make these relationships as meaningful and helpful as possible.

History. The research emphasis in group dynamics began in the 1930s. One of the pioneers in this field was Kurt Lewin who came to the United States in 1932 as a lecturer at Stanford and remained in this country when Hitler's rise to power made his return to Germany impossible. Lewin and a committed group of students initiated a series of classic studies in leadership and group behavior at the University of Iowa. This group later moved to the Massachusetts Institute of Technology, and in 1947 to the University of Michigan, where it formed the Center for Group Dynamics as part of the Institute for Social Research. Dr. Lewin underscored the great value of group dynamics research for the Western world when he stated [4]: "In the field of Group Dynamics, more than in any other psychological field, are theory and practice linked methodologically in a way which, if properly handled, could provide answers to theoretical problems and at the same time strengthen that rational approach to our practical social problems which is one of the basic requirements of their solution."

Dr. Lewin died in 1947 and left behind a rich stimulus and heritage that continue today in the field of social science. The research work has now spread to research centers at Harvard University, New York University, Boston University, George Washington University, University of Chicago, Temple University, Ohio State University, University of Illinois, Columbia University, and others.

Dr. Lewin and his followers were committed to the integration of research, training, and action. Their work led to the establishment in 1947 of the National Training Laboratory in Group Development at the National Education Association, under the direction of Dr. Leland P. Bradford, to provide training in group relations and leadership. The National Training Laboratory (now named NTL Institute) has conducted sessions at its summer conference center at Bethel, Me., attracting leaders from all parts of the world. Following this lead, many companies are initiating similar training programs on their own. (See SENSITIVITY TRAINING.) Many universities, institutes, centers, and consulting firms provide services in group behavior, encounter groups, etc.

The University Associates, Adult Education Association, Project Associates, Inc., and NTL Institute of Applied Behavioral Development publications are some of the major sources of literature on group leadership. Many of the large publishing firms have brought out textbooks and research literature for those wishing to pursue the field in greater depth.

Factors in Group Behavior. Research, observation, and experience have identified certain factors which always occur in group behavior. They may be listed as follows, [5]:

(1) *Group Background.* Each group has a background consisting of previous experience and notions which individuals bring to the group. These bear directly upon the working of the group. The responses and feelings of the group which the group itself has generated in the past are also present—traditions, norms, goals, procedures, and activities. The group leader's effectiveness will depend upon how much he knows (and keeps in mind) about the group as to (a) how well the members were prepared for the group work; (b) the members' expectations about the group and their role in the group; (c) the backgrounds of the individual group members—prior experience, friendship patterns, etc.

(2) *Group Participation Patterns.* In every group situation, people interact in different ways and to differing degrees. Participation can be described in terms of who speaks to whom, and how much speaking is done and by whom. Participation patterns will tell something about the status and the power in the group, and often will indicate how effectively the group is using the resources of its members. Participation for participation's sake is not the goal, but rather participation appropriate to the task, the resources of the individual, and the readiness of the group. It is the leader's task to secure the most effective involvement: Who is doing the most talking? Are those who are silent showing interest and alertness?

(3) *Group Communication Patterns.* The way people communicate—how they talk, and the effect of what they say—is an important dimension of group behavior. However, much significant communication is non-verbal—in posture, facial expression, gesture, etc.—and our response is frequently primarily to this non-verbal level of communication. In verbal communication, the clarity of expression, the apparent honesty with which real feelings are expressed, and the ability to listen to others significantly influence group effectiveness.

(4) *Group Cohesion.* This relates to how attractive a group is to its members. Research indicates that this is important in individual commitment and group effectiveness. A variety of factors are involved in the cohesiveness of a group. For example, the ways in which members express likings for one another affect group cohesion. Fear of a common enemy or zeal for a common task can also affect cohesion. The most effective cohesion is that which is evidenced by members working together in an interdependent way, where each member feels free to express him(her)self and to make a contribution toward the work of the group, while retaining his or her individuality.

(5) *Group Atmosphere.* This defines whether the group is "accepting" or "defensive" in its "climate." In a defensive atmosphere members are unable to communicate freely, to disagree with other members, or to expose ideas and feelings which run counter to the direction in which the group is going. If the atmosphere is a controlling, rigid, punishing one, the group's behavior will tend to become conforming, dependent, or apathetic. But if the atmosphere is one of listening, understanding, trusting—in short, accepting—then the group will develop greater creativity, with more helpful relations among the members.

(6) *Group Standards.* These are the norms of behavior, which are set by the group itself; they affect both group morale and productivity. The standards are both formal and informal. They provide a framework or guide for adjusting individual needs and resources to the actions of the group. They help stabilize the group and contribute to its cohesion. Some examples of standards are: whether members speak out spontaneously, wait to be called on, or wait for "their turn" to talk; whether they sit at the same place each meeting or change places; etc. Group standards can be either implicit or explicit, with most groups operating on certain implicit standards which are rarely stated openly.

(7) *Group Procedures.* All groups must work with a certain set of procedures, of defined ways of getting work done. If a group is to achieve maximum effectiveness, it must be able to vary its procedures so that they are appropriate to the task to be done. Some group procedures are: how an agenda is prepared and used; how votes are taken (by ballot or by hand); how discussion is controlled or guided; etc.

(8) *Group Goals.* These are the targets for group accomplishment. Goals can be immediate and short-range or long-range; they can vary in their clarity and in the value which the group places upon them; they can emerge from the group or be imposed on it; they can be realistic in relation to the resources of the group, or completely unrealistic.

(9) *Group Leader Behavior.* This refers to the way in which the assigned or unassigned leadership acts are performed to aid in group locomotion. Leader behavior in a group can range from almost complete control of the decision-making by the leader to almost complete control by the group, with the leader contributing his resources like any other group member. A leader can assume most of the functions required to provide leadership for the group; or these functions can become the responsibility of the members as well.

(10) *Group Member Behavior.* One of the continuing problems management faces in attempting to increase the effectiveness of groups is that of becoming aware of the relation of the group's structure and dynamics to its task performance. Member behavior is "task centered," "group centered," or "self-centered." Thus every group operates at three levels:

(a) *Group Task Level:* Most groups have some task confronting them, and exist primarily to carry out that task. Frequently they are so conscious of the need to accomplish this task that they are unaware of the other levels of need which are operating simultaneously—the group maintenance level and the individual needs level.

(b) *Group Maintenance Level:* As people work together on a task, they are also doing something *to* and *with* each other. Consequently, a group consists of a constantly changing network of interactions and relationships. A group needs to have a growing awareness of itself as a group, and to face the need of maintaining the relationships within it if the task is to be accomplished. The maintenance level refers to what is happening to persons as the task is being accomplished.

(c) *Individual Needs Level:* Every individual member brings to a group a particular set of needs which impinge upon the group and its task. It is at this level that groups are most apt to be found wanting, for individual needs are frequently well hidden behind the task drive of the group, or behind well developed behavior patterns.

As a group operates to balance these three levels, it becomes more mature and thus more effective. When one or more of these levels is neglected, the effectiveness of the group is impaired.

Implications for Management. The research in group dynamics indicates that an effective group will maximally have the following characteristics:

(1) A clear understanding of its purposes and goals.

(2) Flexibility in selecting its procedures as it works toward its goals.

(3) A high degree of communication and understanding among its members. Communications of personal feelings and attitudes, as well as ideas, occur in a direct and open fashion because they are considered important to the work of the group.

(4) Ability to initiate and carry on effective decision-making, carefully considering minority viewpoints, and securing the commitments of all members to important decisions.

(5) Appropriate balance between group productivity and the satisfaction of individual needs.

(6) A sharing of leadership responsibilities—so that all members are concerned about contributing ideas, elaborating and clarifying the ideas of others, giving opinions, testing the feasibility of potential decisions, and in other ways helping the group work on its task and maintain itself as an effective working unit.

(7) A high degree of cohesiveness (attractiveness for members) but not to the point of stifling individual freedom.

(8) Intelligent use of the differing abilities of its members.

(9) No domination by its leader or by any of its members.

(10) Objectivity about reviewing its own processes. It can face its problems and adjust to needed modification in its own operation.

(11) A balance between emotional and rational behavior, channeling emotionality into productive group effort. Increasing importance of group behavior is seen by management's use of project groups, task forces, ASSESSMENT CENTERS, QUALITY CONTROL CIRCLES, "huddle" meetings, and other techniques manifesting the need for collaboration between persons in the complexity of modern management.

When management talks about the importance of *teamwork,* the understanding of group dynamics will be essential to be able to diagnose, measure, and improve such teamwork.

GORDON L. LIPPITT, PH.D., LL.D., Professor, School of Government and Business Administration, The George Washington University, Washington, D.C.; President, Organization Renewal, Inc., Washington, D.C.

Information References

Benne, K.D., Bradford, L.P., Gibb, J.R., and Lippitt, R.O., "The Laboratory Method of Changing and Learning," Palo Alto, Calif., Science and Behavior Books, Inc., 1975.

Dyer, W.G., "Team Building: Issues and Alternatives," Reading, Mass., Addison-Wesley, 1977.

Fisher, B.A., "Small Group Decision Making," New York, McGraw-Hill, 1974.

Kington, Donald Ralph, "Matrix Organization," New York, Harper & Row, 1973.

Lippitt, Gordon L., "Organization Renewal," 2nd ed., Englewood Cliffs, N.J., Prentice-Hall, 1981.

Merrell, V. Dallas, "Huddling," New York, Amacom, 1979.

References Cited

[1] Knowles, Malcolm and Hulda, "Introduction to Group Dynamics," New York, Association Press, 1962 (revision).

[2] Likert, R., "The Human Organization," New York, McGraw-Hill, 1967.

[3] Lippitt, G., "Team Building for Matrix Organizations," Washington, D.C., Project Associates, Inc., 1970.

[4] Lewin, Kurt, "Field Theory in Social Sciences," Cartwright, Dorwin, ed., New York, Harper & Row, 1951.

[5] Lippitt, Gordon L. and Seashore, Edith, "Leader Looks at Group Effectiveness," Washington, D.C., Leadership Resources, Inc., 1974 (revision).

Cross References: *Goal Setting; Hawthorne Experiments; Human Relations in Industry; Job Enrichment and Work Effectiveness; Management by Objectives; Managerial Grid; Motivation (and accompanying entries with Motivation prefix); Personnel Counseling; Sensitivity Training.*

GROUP HEALTH INSURANCE

Group Health Insurance, as the name implies, provides a means for insuring a group of people against the costs of ill health under one policy. It may be acquired through an employer or labor union, or professional or other association. Most such plans include dependents in their coverage.

When a person enters such a group he may be automatically covered immediately, or after a specified waiting period. Protection generally ends when he leaves the group, although it is possible to convert to an individual or family policy at that time.

The most usual group is made up of employees of a business organization insured without medical examination under a master contract issued to the employer. Such contracts generally help to pay for hospital, surgical, and medical expenses, and also help replace income lost when employees cannot work because of illness or injury (not caused by their work).

The principal characteristics of a group health insurance policy are:

Economy of Cost. This is possible because insurance companies, using mass marketing techniques, can administer these plans more economically.

Group Concept. The group contract holder (the employer or employee association) normally pays part or all of the premium—usually as agreed upon through union-negotiated contracts.

Physical Condition Waived. Individuals are eligible regardless of physical condition (except on some occasions in small groups).

Non-cancellable. The insurance cannot be cancelled—unless the plan itself is terminated, or the individual decides to leave it.

Today, payments under group plans amount to almost 87% of all health insurance benefits paid by insurance companies. They pay some four-fifths of the health care expenses incurred by the insureds and their dependents for items of health care against which the health insurance was purchased.

Group plans reimburse 92% of hospital charges for semi-private rooms; 84% of surgical charges; 74% of the charges for nonsurgical physicians' visits to the hospital; 83% of the charges for private duty nursing; and 64% of the charges for prescribed drugs. (Figures based upon a recent study of insurance company medical care benefits.)

In summary, over half of the claimants under group policies are reimbursed for 90% or more of their covered expenses, and nearly nine in ten are reimbursed for 70% or more.

Normally, the employer and employee share the cost of this insurance—the employees' portion being deducted (with their consent) from their salary or wages, and the balance of the premium being paid by the employer.

The Health Insurance Institute estimates that about 31% of workers covered by new group health insurance contracts have the total cost paid for by their employer. Only 7% of the workers pay the full cost of the insurance themselves.

To obtain coverage, employees receive what is known as a "Certificate of Participation," stating that they are insured for specified amounts under a master contract issued to the employer. These certificates are not policy contracts. The contract is between the employer and the insurance company or service plan providing the benefits.

History. The first group health insurance contract covered employees of Montgomery Ward & Co. for temporary disability income payments. It was written in 1910. But it was not until 1928 that the next plan, group hospital expense and surgical insurance, went into effect.

These plans were followed in 1940 by medical expense contracts, and in the latter part of the decade by major medical expense insurance.

By 1978, group health insurance premiums written by insurance companies had reached almost $33 billion—over three-and-a-half times more than was written by these companies ten years earlier. The increase is attributed to the awareness of most Americans of their health needs, and the efficiency of the employer-group method of providing health insurance.

Group programs can be set up today with as little as one employee and one employer. Meanwhile, the nation's largest voluntary health insurance plan, the Federal Employees Health Benefits Program, insures almost three million workers and their nearly six million dependents.

Approaches. There are generally four ways in which employee and union health plans can be set up:

(1) Benefits can be paid directly out of current operating income without setting up reserves of any type.

(2) A trust fund can be set up by an employer or a union, as its own program of putting aside monies to pay the claims that are currently occurring, but have not been repeated. This is a form of self-insurance.

(3) Self-insurance can be incorporated with insurance. Under this type of plan, the managers of the fund set a limit as to the total amount of claims they want to pay in a year, and purchase insurance to cover all claims above this amount. This is referred to as "self-insurance with stop-loss coverage."

(4) Health insurance plans made available by insurance companies (life, casualty, and health) or hospital-medical service plans. To-

gether these are the most widely accepted means of protection.

Basically, there are two forms of health insurance protection: (1) against medical expenses, and (2) against the loss of income because of inability to work.

Protection Against Medical Expenses. There are four major forms: hospital expense; surgical expense; medical expense; and major medical expense.

Hospital Expense Insurance. This provides benefits for care in the hospital for periods generally ranging from 70 to 365 days or longer. In general, these benefits help pay for two types of services:

(a) Daily room and board, routine nursing care, and minor medical supplies.

(b) Additional related services such as laboratory tests and X-rays, anesthesia and its administration, use of operating room, drugs and medications, and local ambulance service.

Hospital expense policies, too, usually provide a single lump sum payment toward hospital costs of a normal birth. Separate provisions exist for a Caesarian section and complications of pregnancy.

Over and above in-patient hospitalization, a growing number of plans provide specific benefits for out-patient care. There have also been an increasing number of plans that provide for diagnostic expense in and out of a hospital.

Surgical Expense Insurance. This coverage helps pay the cost of operations and often applies even if the operation is minor and is not performed in the hospital. These policies contain a list of surgical operations, and the maximum benefit amounts to be paid for each. Also, for operations not listed, benefits may be paid as specified by the policy.

Medical Expense Insurance. A wide range of coverages are available under medical expense insurance (usually written as a rider to hospital-surgical plans), from specified medical fees for hospitalized cases to coverages for medical services, including doctor calls to home and office visits. Also included is the coverage for diagnostic X-rays and laboratory examinations.

Major Medical Expense Insurance. This insurance is specifically designed to handle really serious illnesses and accidents, up to the disaster level. It covers in substantial part, the costs of medical catastrophes running from $10,000 on up to more than $250,000 or unlimited, depending on the agreement.

Major medical insurance is built around a system of "deductibles," a term familiar to every car owner. Just as one buys collision insurance in which the first $25 or $50 or $100 of damage is paid for by the policyholder, most major medical policies call for the insured person to pay the first $50 to $150 or more of the cost of the illness. This helps to keep premium costs at a reasonable level, while placing the protection on the major expenses rather than on the small initial costs. Beyond the deductible amount, the insurance company generally pays 75% to 80% of medical and hospital bills up to the limit of the policy.

Protection Against Loss of Income. In most business and industrial concerns across the nation, this form of protection has replaced the outmoded "sick leave pay" which was once prevalent, costly to the employer, and often inadequate for employees.

Short-Term Disability Insurance. This is usually paid in the form of weekly benefits covering non-occupational disability and paying up to 75% of an employee's weekly pay. The duration of payments varies, but may continue for up to two years. There is usually a waiting period for sickness benefit payments, normally around seven days, while accident benefits are payable from the first day. Provision may be made for continuance of coverage for a limited time in case of a temporary layoff or leave of absence where re-employment is probable. The extension will generally range from two weeks to three months.

Several states have laws requiring employers to provide temporary disability protection either through an insurance plan of their choice or through a state fund. Disabilities resulting from on-the-job accidents are covered under WORKER'S COMPENSATION plans.

Long-Term Disability Insurance. This can provide maximum monthly benefits for disabled employees as high as $1,000 or more, based on salary. Benefits of $100 to $150 a week are generally available. Usually the policy specifies benefit limits between 40% to 60% of the disabled employee's base salary after a period—often three months—of full pay, with the benefits continuing in many cases until age 65 and sometimes even for life.

Features of Plans. Group health insurance plans usually terminate when the employee leaves the job, retires, or discontinues payment of his (her) premiums (if under a contributory plan). Still, he generally has the option, at termination, to convert to an individual plan within thirty days with no evidence of insurability required.

Underwriting rules require that all employees, or all employees of a certain type, be covered under the plan if the employer pays all the premiums. A common practice is to make the plan available to everyone in an organization—shopworkers, office workers and executives alike—although the plan may vary in application between hourly rated and salaried employees.

If the plan is paid jointly by employers and employees, then at least three-quarters of those eligible must agree to participate.

Plans paid completely by the employer offer the following advantages: (1) it puts the entire premium under the income tax deduction privilege granted the employer (this reduces the overall cost of the protection); (2) it provides blanket coverage for all employees, regardless of their health; (3) it requires no salary deduction on the part of participating employees (to some of whom it might be a hardship).

Where both the employer and employees pay, the plan has the advantage of providing larger benefits than an employer might be willing to offer without sharing the cost. It also usually assures better employee understanding of the plan's cost, makes the employees more appreciative of the plan (if they share in its maintenance), and suggests the possibility of staying in force during slack-work periods, if employees carry part of the cost.

Trends. Broader and more expensive coverages continue to be introduced under group health insurance. Many company and union officials are studying these new plans, at the same time resurveying existing plans with a view to bringing their own plans into conformity with the increased cost of living and medical care:

Since 1968, the number of persons covered for hospitalization costs under group policies written by insurance companies had increased, at end of 1978, from 86 million to 103 million; for surgical costs, from 82 million to 96 million; for general medical expenses, from 66 million to 91 million; and for major medical expenses, from 68 million to 102 million.

Adding to these basic coverages is the widespread inclusion of more recently developed coverages such as dental care, the treatment of mental illness, and out-of-hospital and convalescent care.

The costs of providing better medical care have been steadily increasing. Advances in medical research, the rising cost of living, and the public's desire for comprehensive medical care are all clear indications that the rise will continue. The American public spent $128 billion on health care in 1978, 239% more than ten years earlier—and there is little indication that any slackening of this pace can be expected.

Before World War II, less than three million people had the protection of group health insurance through insurance companies. As of 1978, 92 million employees and their dependents were covered under plans that utilized the services of most of this nation's 381,000 private physicians, 117,000 dentists, 1,018,000 nurses, and more than 7,000 hospitals.

KENNETH W. WHITE, Vice President and General Manager. Health Inusrance Institute, New York, New York

Information References

Association:

Health Insurance Institute.

Texts:

Dickerson, O. D., "Health Insurance," 3rd ed., Homewood, Ill., Irwin, 1968.

Faulkner, Edwin J., "Health Insurance," New York, McGraw-Hill, 1960.

Gregg, Davis W., "Life and Health Insurance Handbook," 2nd ed., Homewood, Ill., Irwin, 1964.

"Private Health Insurance Plans in 1977," *Health Care Financing Review,* Fall, 1979.

"Source Book of Health Insurance Data," Health Insurance Institute, Washington D.C. Annual.

Cross References: *Employee Benefit Plans; Group Life Insurance; Workers' Compensation.*

GROUP LIFE INSURANCE

Group Life Insurance has been called the "keystone of employee benefit planning" by both employers and the insurance companies that write this protection. Under a master group life insurance policy or contract issued to an employer, the employees are individually provided with life insurance protection payable to the families of employees who die. Since the risk is spread among a large group of people, life insurance companies, which provide the greater percentage of survivor benefits, usually offer this protection without medical examinations and other underwriting restrictions necessary to individual life insurance policies.

The lower costs of sales, service, and administration of this "mass" coverage result in a lower premium to be paid by policyholders. Group life insurance premiums are calculated to cover the anticipated death and (where included) disability claims, plus current operating expenses. To calculate the premium rate initially, the life insurance company must be provided with personnel data indicating such factors as number of employees, age, sex, and possible job hazards.

Evidence of insurability is generally not required of workers coming under a group life insurance plan. Since they are physically able to work, they are, from a health standpoint, generally good insurance risks.

In underwriting employee group life insurance protection, the life insurance companies require that: (1) the group of persons to be insured are bound together by a common working relationship; (2) the amount of life insurance is predetermined for each person according to some formula or schedule, such as benefits related to a percentage of annual salary. Group insurance specialists advise corporate buyers of group life insurance to set basic and long-range objectives and determine how much money they have available to attain these objectives before establishing a group life insurance program.

Each group-insured employee receives an individual certificate and in most cases a booklet outlining benefits provided under the employer's master contract. The life insurance company has no direct contractual relationship with the employees, even where employees contribute to the plan. However, the benefits indicated in the employees' certificates are guaranteed and backed by the assets of the life insurance company.

A major percentage of group life insurance plans are paid for by employers, and all employees must be covered under such plans. If a plan is paid for by the joint contribution of employer and employees, only employees who agree to pay their share are insured. However, such a plan must have at least a minimum participation, usually 75% of the employees, when the plan is put into effect.

Frequently, in jointly financed group life insurance plans, the employers pay for the basic coverage, and individual workers have the option to take out additional coverage which they pay for themselves or which is jointly provided.

Nearly 117.8 million group life insurance certificates were in force in the United States at the start of 1980, with over $1.6 trillion of group life insurance protection provided under nearly 586,000 master contracts. As of 1980, nearly four out of five wage and salary workers were covered by group life insurance. Death payments in 1980 to the families of group policyholders were nearly $5.7 billion. Nearly one-half of the total annual death payments made by life insurance companies are under group life insurance policies.

By contrast, in 1945, following World War II, 11.5 million group life insurance certificates provided $22.2 billion of group protection under 31,000 master contracts. Death payments for that year were $171.1 million.

The current growth of group life insurance reflects for the most part the stepped-up increases in the amount of coverage per individual worker and the addition of new workers to already existing plans.

Average group life insurance ownership per certificate has climbed to over $13,400, or more than six times the immediate post-war average. There is a definite trend towards group life planning that calls for workers' protection equaling one or one and a half year's salary, and there has been considerable expansion in the plans of some industries to provide protection equal to two or two and one-half times annual salary.

Since 1911, when the first group life insurance plan was written by the Equitable Life Assurance Society on 121 employees of the Pantasote Leather Company, a small New Jersey firm, practically every business and industrial concern of material size has adopted a group life insurance program for its employees. A majority of the states now permit group life insurance policies to be issued on firms with as few as ten employees.

In the founding days of group life insurance, retirement from one's job was rare, and the emphasis was on providing death payments for the families of workers who died while still employed. It soon proved to be a more dignified and beneficial approach to the problem of immediately providing for families than the previously accepted outlook of "passing the hat" in the shop.

By 1979, with nearly 25 million persons at or beyond age 65, and with their ranks rapidly increasing, there was a growing tendency for employers to provide group life insurance to workers who retire. By the end of 1979, a study of 267 representative companies by the Bureau of National Affairs, Inc., showed that group life insurance was provided by more than half of the responding organizations.

Because of the high cost of maintaining group life insurance coverage among older people, pre-retirement benefits are in most cases reduced at retirement. Post-retirement group life insurance is usually either a "uniform benefit" where all retired persons receive the same amount of life insurance protection, or "salary-graduated" benefits, where the amount of group life insurance received is based upon the salary at retirement. The most common practice under this plan is to reduce the pre-retirement coverage by one-half, either at retirement or in a series of annual reductions.

The vast majority of group life insurance plans are on a yearly renewable term plan. Each year the premium is paid to cover the cost of protection for that year. There are no cash values or paid-up benefits after retirement.

Group plans with permanent insurance features usually provide a combination of accumulating units of single premium whole life insurance and decreasing units of group term life insurance. Employees usually contribute to the added cost of the permanent protection which assures them of paid-up cash value life insurance at their retirement.

There has been a long-term trend toward the "packaging" of group life insurance with group health insurance plans, provided by a single insurance company. This has been particularly beneficial to employers of small and moderate size because of coordinated administration and resulting cost savings.

Generally improved mortality among the nation's working men and women was reflected in the National Association of Insurance Commissioner's approved 1960 Standard Group Mortality Table, the first official table for group life insurance. Previously, the Ordinary Mortality Table was used as a guide for group insurance purposes.

If an employee leaves the job prior to retirement, his or her group life insurance is also terminated unless it has permanent provisions. However, the employee has the right to continue the insurance protection under a permanent form of ordinary insurance issued at the current age without evidence of insurability. This option must be exercised within 31 days after termination of employment.

Group life insurance written at places of employment accounts for the major share of this type of protection. Other forms include creditors' group life insurance, covering the lives of borrowers in the amount of their outstanding loans in a form of group life insurance that has kept pace with the greater growth in installment credit in the post World War II era. Trade associations, fraternal organizations, college alumni groups, credit unions, and professional associations are among the organizations that may set up group life insurance programs under the law of some states.

Forty-one states and the District of Columbia now permit the writing of group life insurance on the dependents of workers. The amount of coverage is usually limited to between $1,000 and $10,000 on wives, and $500 or $1,000 on each child.

Most group life insurance plans provide for waiver of premium or some other disability benefit should an employee become permanently disabled before age sixty. Such disability, resulting either from bodily injury or illness, must prevent the employee from engaging in any form of occupation.

Through low premium group insurance, workers are provided with life insurance protection at the lowest possible cost. It provides protection for the wage-earner during the working years when family obligations are most demanding. Group life insurance provides life insurance protection to a large number of people who otherwise would have a totally inadequate life insurance program. It also extends life insurance protection to workers who, by reason of health or occupation, would otherwise not qualify for life insurance.

Group life insurance, by providing a degree of security to employees, is a major factor in maintaining good industrial relations. However, viewing group life insurance ownership today from the measurement of social and economic adequacy, most workers under group plans are still underinsured.

Most students of family money management have found that group life insurance, while serving as an excellent foundation for meeting security needs during the working years, must be augmented by individual purchases of life insurance. Availability of group permanent life insurance works toward the solution of individual need. So do employer programs permitting allotment of salary towards life insurance purchases. However, individual planning is necessary to fit life insurance purchases to the particular family makeup, to its other resources, and to its financial objectives.

ROBERT F. FROEHLKE, President, American Council of Life Insurance, Washington, D.C.

Information References

Association:

American Council of Life Insurance.

Periodicals:

Life Insurance Fact Book, American Council of Life Insurance (annual).

Texts:

Eilers, Robert D. and Crowe, Robert M., eds., "Group Insurance Handbook," Homewood, Ill., Irwin, 1966.

Gregg, D. W., "Life and Health Insurance Handbook," Homewood, Ill., Irwin, 1973.

Greider, Janice C., and Beadles, William T., "Principles of Life Insurance, vol. 1," Homewood, Ill., 1972.

Huebner, Solomon S., and Black, Kenneth Jr., "Life Insurance," Englewood Cliffs, N.J. Prentice-Hall, 1976.

Mehr, Robert I., "Life Insurance: Theory and Practice," Homewood, Ill., Irwin, 1977.

Cross References: *Employee Benefit Plans; Group Health Insurance; Retirement Plans; Workers' Compensation.*

GUARANTEED ANNUAL WAGE

Guaranteed Annual Wage plans are designed to provide employees a steady annual income. Normally, these plans guarantee employees a specified number of hours per year at their regular pay. If the number of hours worked falls short of the annual guarantee, the employee generally receives the regular rate of pay for the difference between the hours guaranteed and the hours actually worked. The regular rate of pay generally includes the basic hourly wage plus job and shift differentials. Few companies have guaranteed annual wage or employment provisions, and there has been no significant increase or decrease in the number of these plans over the past fifteen years. For example, in their survey of agreements covering 1,000 or more workers, the Bureau of Labor Statistics found that only six collective bargaining agreements had annual wage or employment guarantees in 1978. The same number had annual guarantees in 1963.

Under most plans, an employee must have at least one to five years of seniority to be eligible for the annual guarantee. In some cases, however, employees with less than the minimum seniority are eligible for a partial income guarantee. Another frequent requirement is that an employee must work a minimum number of hours each year to be eligible for the income guarantee, although time lost due to illness, injury, or military service isn't usually deducted when determining eligibility.

Some guarantees protect only certain classifications or groups of employees. During layoffs, unprotected employees are laid off first and protected employees must be given preferential transfer rights. Eligibility for annual wage or employment guarantees generally terminates if an employee is discharged, quits, or declines a transfer.

A typical annual wage guarantee is provided by the collective bargaining agreement between the Wisconsin Public Service Company and the Operating Engineers. The company guarantees to provide 2,080 hours of work per year, less vacation and holidays, to workers who have completed five years of service. These hours are paid at regular rates. Employees not under the guaranteed work plan must be laid off first. If further reductions are necessary, employees with the least seniority under the guaranteed work plan may be transferred to other departments or plants where their services are required.

The Longshoremen have negotiated several well-known annual wage guarantee plans. These plans arose as a means of promoting the acceptance of operational and technological change that reduced the need for labor. Labor and management jointly control the size of the registered work force and of the employment guarantees. Workers are registered in order to establish a concentrated work force, and no employer that has signed the agreement may hire any longshoreman not included in the basic work force until all available men of the registered work force have been hired and then only as temporary fill-ins. Through normal attrition, the size of the registered work force has been reduced. Liberalized pension provisions, including voluntary early retirement, have assisted in these reductions. Because of the rapid drop in the number of hours worked, it was essential to introduce those guaranteed work or pay plans.

One such plan is provided by the agreement between the Longshoremen (ILA) and the Steamship Trade Association of Baltimore. The agreement guarantees an annual income of 1,900 hours per contract year at existing hourly straight-time rates to all employees who are properly registered. To be eligible for the guarantee, the employee must have worked at least 700 hours during one of the two previous contract years. Sickness, disability, or injury, however, is credited toward the 700 hours at a rate of twenty hours per week of absence. There can be no hiring of workers not qualified for the guaranteed annual income plan as long as qualified workers are available. Gross earnings received during the guarantee period are deducted from the guaranteed income, in order to determine payments due under the plan. In computing gross earnings, all hours worked are calculated at straight time rates. Payments made to the employee for vacations, holidays, and unemployment compensation are also deducted.

Procter & Gamble Company guarantees employment to employees of over two years' service for a minimum number of hours each week and for a minimum number of hours each year, less time lost by reason of holidays, vacation, disability, voluntary absence, and emergencies. However, employees may be subjected to reduced wage rates, and in the event of an extreme emergency, the company may revoke the guarantee. (The company prefers to refer to its plan as a "guaranteed annual employment plan," because strictly speaking it does not guarantee wages.)

Another well-known guaranteed annual income plan is provided by the Hormel Company (a meat packer). Because daily and seasonal receipts of livestock fluctuate widely, a plan of this type was needed to encourage the complete processing of each day's receipts. Employees may go home after completing the day's work load, regardless of the number of hours actually worked. Subject to the limitations in Section 7b (2) of the Fair Labor Standards Act, overtime on heavy days is balanced by shorter hours on light days. Workers are employed on an annual wage or income basis. Covered employees are guaranteed 52 regular weekly paychecks at their base rate for 36 to 40 hours, depending on their department.

RICHARD S. KRASHEVSKI, Department of Economic Research, AFL-CIO, Washington, D.C.

Cross References: *Incentive Systems; Lincoln Incentive Management Plan; Profit Sharing; Rucker Plan of Group Incentives; Scanlon Plan of Group Incentives; Standard Minute System.*

H

HALSEY, FREDERICK A.

Frederick Arthur Halsey (1856–1935) originated the first successful incentive wage system in American industry to improve upon the straight piece-work system, reporting upon it to the American Society of Mechanical Engineers in 1891. Ordinary piece-rates were unsatisfactory because they were so frequently associated with rate-cutting by employers as soon as a worker achieved a substantial rise in output.

The gain-sharing plan which had recently been introduced by H. R. Towne was deficient, Halsey showed, in that the increased output due to the efforts of the better workers provided rewards without distinction between good workers and bad. Halsey's "premium plan" was an original contribution, with the avowed aim of eliminating rate-cutting. It guaranteed a daily or hourly rate for a fixed quantity of work as agreed upon with the worker based on his customary performance, and then provided a premium payment for any additional work, of about one half to one third of the sum the employer would have paid for this work under the daily or hourly rate. The premium plan had great influence not only in the United States, but also in Great Britain, where it was, along with Taylor's piece-rate system, the model for many incentive plans. (See SCIENTIFIC MANAGEMENT: "Taylorism"; TAYLOR, FREDERICK W.)

In America Halsey influenced Taylor's work on incentives, and although the premium plan was overshadowed by Taylor's piece-rate system, it continued to be used where its advantages remained evident. The limitation of Halsey's premium plan was that it took the *customary* output of workers as the basis of calculation. Taylor's contribution was to show how the scientific measurement of work could do much more to increase and improve output than any methods of payment. Taylor's emphasis was on management planning; Halsey's was on the initiative and constructive cooperation of the individual worker, with greater use of suggestion schemes. Halsey was a graduate mechanical engineer. He was employed by the Rand Drill Company (later Ingersoll-Rand Company), 1880–90, rising to Chief Engineer; Engineer and General Manager, Canadian Rand Drill Co., Ltd., 1890–94; Associate Editor, later Editor, *American Machinist,* 1894–1911. His writings include "The Premium Plan of Paying for Labor," *Transactions,* ASME, 1891; "Administration of the Premium Plan," *American Machinist,* July 6, 13, and 27, 1899; "Experience with the Premium Plan of Paying Labor," *American Machinist,* March 9, 1899; "Economics of the Premium Plan," *American Machinist,* May 3, 1900; and "Origin of the Premium Plan: A Personal Statement," *American Machinist,* June 9, 1902.

Information Reference

Urwick, L., "The Golden Book of Management," edited for the International Committee of Scientific Management (CIOS), London, Newman Neame, Limited, 1956.

HATHAWAY, H. K.

Horace King Hathaway (1878–1944) was, with HENRY L. GANTT and CARL G. L. BARTH, one of the close associates with whom F. W. TAYLOR developed his system of management. He was outstandingly successful in applying scientific management to the Tabor Manufacturing Company, Philadelphia (machine shop and manufacturer of moulding). In 1910 this company's remarkable improvement from the time Hathaway took over in 1904 was used by Brandeis in the Eastern Rates Case hearings (see SCIENTIFIC MANAGEMENT) as the strongest argument for the efficiency of the Taylor system. Hathaway also assisted in the early installation of the Taylor System in the Philadelphia plant of the Link Belt Company. After holding high posts in industry, he engaged in private consulting practice in San Francisco, 1941–1944. He was the author of numerous articles on scientific management.

HAWTHORNE EXPERIMENTS

The experimental studies in human relations referred to as the **Hawthorne Experiments** have had a profound effect upon the whole "human relations movement." They were conducted at the Hawthorne Works of the Western Electric Company in Chicago during the period 1927 to 1932. These studies were preceded by and grew out of a series of experiments on the effects of illumination on employee efficiency which were conducted in cooperation with the National Research Council of the National Academy of Sciences from November, 1924 to April 1927.

Throughout the greater part of the time covered by the Hawthorne Studies, the Company enjoyed the close collaboration and guidance of Professor Elton Mayo, then Head of the Department of Industrial Relations Research of the Graduate School of Business Administration, Harvard University, and of F. J. Roethlisberger, Wallace Brett Donham Professor of Human Relations of the Harvard Business School. Professor C. E. Turner, Department of Public Health, Massachusetts Institute of Technology, collaborated in some of the earlier phases of the research. Other members of Professor Mayo's staff made valuable contributions, notably Professor T. N. Whitehead in his comprehensive statistical analysis of the Test Room data and Professor W. L. Warner in his methodological contributions to the study of the social structure of industry.

Three Types of Studies. The Hawthorne Studies can be divided into three general phases: (a) Test Room studies; (b) interviewing studies; and (c) observational studies. Each study grew out of the preceding one and built on what had been learned in the others. Thus the studies led step by step to an enlarged body of knowledge and to an improved understanding of worker behavior.

The test room studies were concerned with assessing the effects of single variables upon employee performance and were experimental in nature. The interviewing studies were concerned with improving employee attitudes and were psychological in nature. The observational studies were concerned with describing and understanding the factors influencing the informal organization of work groups and were sociological in nature.

The Test Room Studies. *Illumination Experiments (1924–1927).* The Test Room studies developed from a series of controlled experiments, extending over three winters (1924–1927), of the relationship between variations in the intensity of illumination and the efficiency of shop workers. In thse studies the company cooperated with the National Research Council by providing a site in which to carry out the experiments, and some technical assistance. The results were completely unexpected. In one study, as illumination was increased in the experimental group, output rose. But to everyone's suprise, output also rose in the control group. In another study, illumination was gradually reduced. Instead of decreasing, output began to rise in the experimental group and there was a corresponding rise in the control group. Other experiments yielded similarly unanticipated and seemingly contradictory results.

The conclusions from these findings were, first, that in the situations studied, illumination was only one and not the most important factor affecting output. Secondly, and more important methodologically, it was seen that there was no simple cause and effect relationship between the single variable, illumination, and operator efficiency. It was recognized that other factors had not been adequately controlled and, indeed, that experimental studies in the large groups of regular shop departments presented extreme difficulty of adequate control. It was with this recognition that the next study was organized.

The Relay Assembly Test Room (1927–1932). In April 1927, a second inquiry, known as the Relay Assembly Test Room study, was instituted in an attempt to observe the effects of various changes in the conditions of work. A small group of average, experienced women asemblers, who volunteered for the study, were moved into a separate room where arrangements were made to obtain exact measurements of their output and quality of work as well as of temperature and humidity changes and other factors. In separating the group from their department, they were constituted as a separate piece-work payment group. In an effort to assure that the girls' attitudes would remain constant and unaffected by experimental changes, considerable effort was made to gain their confidence in the objectives of the study and to assure their working in a "steady state," that is, without extra effort.

The women were given complete physical examinations before the experiments began, and thereafter every six weeks, to determine any effects of the changes introduced on their health. An observer was stationed in the test room throughout the experiments. His job was to keep accurate records of output and of other factors of possible significance, to create and maintain a friendly atmosphere, and to exercise a quasi supervisory function.

Over a period of the first two and a half years, a number of combinations of two variables, hours of work and rest periods, were introduced independently. None of these changes were cumulative—they were interspersed with check periods in which there was a return to previous arrangements.

Here as in the illumination studies there were some unexpected results. Ouput increased steadily during the first two and half years of the experiment irrespective of the experimental changes imposed. Total output for the group during this time increased more than 30% from what had been considered originally a high level, and was sustained throughout the remaining two and one-half years of the study. In the opinion of the examining physician the health of the girls improved and their attendance irregularities (lateness and absences) dropped from 15.2 to 3.5 on an annual basis. By their own testimony, they felt greatly increased satisfaction with their working lives.

Four hypotheses were considered in seeking an explanation for the marked improvement in performance of these operators: (1) relief from fatigue; (2) relief from monotony; (3) increased wage incentive; and (4) change in method of supervision.

Exhaustive statistical analysis of the output and other data compelled rejection of the fatigue hypothesis. The evidence on relief from monotony was not persuasive.

Subsequently two additional experiments with other groups were undertaken to investigate further the possible influence of pay incentives as distinct from changes in working conditions. The results of these studies tended to confirm that both incentives and working conditions were influential, but that the total improvement could not be attributed to either.

One further factor considered in explaining the results was the high degree of *esprit de corps* that developed in the group. The daily log kept by the observer indicated that a remarkable shift in the attitudes of these workers had occurred in the environment of the test room. This was manifested in a variety of ways such as making up in output for a girl who did not feel well, and by group social activities outside working hours. The principal factor accounting for this change was determined to be related to the freer atmosphere of the test room and the less authoritative, more personal, interest shown in them by the test room supervision and higher management.

Thus it appeared to be evident that conditions of work—lighting, hours, rest periods and even pay and supervision—could not be viewed as things in themselves affecting the work of people, but that these conditions take on meaning in terms of the perceptions, interpretations, and attitudes of those experiencing them. This recognition led the Hawthorne investigators away from further attempts to isolate simple relationships between environmental factors and the reactions of workers in terms of either productivity or morale.

Interviewing Studies (1928–1931). The findings of the Test Rooms led to a high degree of interest in the attitudes of the plant population toward their jobs, working conditions, and supervision. In pursuit of this interest, there was organized one of the first, and certainly a very extensive, morale survey. This project ultimately included interviews with 21,000 people. An initial assumption was that if attitudes toward those features of the work environment which workers liked and disliked could be determined, improvements might be instituted which would enhance their satisfaction and motivation.

In the attainment of this objective, the interviewing program was only partially successful. It was found that only in limited cases could the reason for an individual's dissatisfaction be identified objectively. In the greater number of cases, the source of dissatisfaction had to be sought in the complexity of the person's feelings and sentiments concerning what was appropriate work for him (her), good working conditions for him, fair pay for him, and reasonable supervisory behavior toward him. The source of these feelings under skilled interviewing could be readily traced to the previous life experience of the individual, and to his or her social situation at work and in the wider associations at home and in the community. It was clear that simple manipulation of features of the work environment provided no remedy for many of the dissatisfactions of this kind. Rather, they were matters with which the individual himself or herself had to deal.

In the process of developing an interviewing method adequate to the exploration of attitudes and sentiments, the investigators found that the individual could be materially assisted in better understanding his environment, his conflicts, and himself through talking things over with an interested listener. This interviewing method, subsequently called nondirective, has received ample confirmation of its value in the hands of clinical psychologists. It became the basis later for an extensive employee counseling program in the Western Electric Company. (See PERSONNEL COUNSELING.)

Observational Studies (1931–1932). It remained for the last phase of the investigations to bring into bold relief some of the social factors important in the motivation of workers. This study, referred to as the Bank Wiring Observation Room study, had as its subjects fourteen men and their associated supervision. It grew out of a recognition of the logical insufficiency of a merely psychological study of the individuals in a department: The persons who make up a working department are not isolated, they constitute a group within which individuals have developed routines of relationships to each other, to their superiors, and to their work. The study resembled in many respects the small group studies in industry which have been carried on by a number of research groups in recent years. It differed from the earlier test room studies at Hawthorne in that no experimental changes were planned. Instead every effort was made to study the group in its customary functioning. The method adopted was one derived from the cultural anthropologist in the field—a combination of observation and interviewing.

The findings of the study made clear that the work group constituted a complex social organization with well established norms of conduct and shared sentiments over and above those required by the formal organization of their work.

The norms of the group included prohibitions concerning how much and how little work should be done, communication with supervisors, and relations with "outsiders." For example, a well-established standard of a fair day's work was generally recognized by all members of the group. While somewhat short of the goals formally established, it was considered by management to represent creditable performance. It could readily be seen by the observer, and was affirmed and demonstrated by the operators, to be well below their capacity. This standard was maintained by the group through a variety of social pressures of varying degrees of subtlety. It was maintained despite the fact that in the process they were limiting their earnings accordingly.

The conclusions of the research staff as to the reasons for this behavior were complex and led to a consideration of the nature of industrial organization as a *social system.* It is sufficient to observe that for the individual in this group of workers, as for people everywhere, the importance of his relations with his fellows loomed large in his motivation. These relations, in the situations studied, were found to be influenced by sentiments engendered by the position of the group in the social structure of the plant. This position was characterized as one in which employees acted as though they continually needed to protect themselves from real or fancied changes emanating from elsewhere in the company structure. Thus this study, while of behavior in direct contrast with that of the Relay Assembly Group, served to reaffirm the importance of the informal organization in the motivation of workers, and directed attention to ways of bringing about a reorientation of group sentiments in support of a freer, more spontaneous, and, it may be said, more satisfactory system of interpersonal relations. From this quest there was developed within the company an approach to human relations which combined a system of nondirective counseling with an enlightened, people-oriented supervisory leadership designed to achieve this objective.

Summary. The Hawthorne Studies in their various phases served to call into serious question a number of prevalent assumptions as to the nature of the worker and his work. An example of this was the clear revelation that the worker is no mere "economic man" motivated solely by the pay check. A second recognition was that of the singular importance of individual attitudes in the determination of behavior. Third, was the demonstration of the importance of the supervisor's role in the equation of morale and productivity. Fourth, there was demonstrated the crucial importance to the accomplishment of organizational objectives and worker satisfaction of group spirit and teamwork. Finally, there was the illumination that little was known, on a systematic basis, about the informal structure of work groups and their effects upon organizational objectives.

Implications. The impact of the Hawthorne experiments over subsequent decades can only be suggested here. First, is the contribution of the studies to the growth and development of the human relations approach in personnel administration. This movement assumed overwhelming favor in industry, particularly during the post-war years. In its beginning, certainly as seen in the framework of the Hawthorne studies, this approach emphasized the importance of basing supervisory practice upon a direct, first-hand, intelligent understanding of the human situations under the supervisor's care. It emphasized the need for taking into account as an essential body of fact, the attitudes and sentiments of the worker and of instilling in him a sense of belonging as an important contributing member of the enterprise. This approach has lost some of its favor largely because of its identification by some with laxity in administration and "do-goodism." In actual fact, the Hawthorne research advocated a hardheaded factual approach to an area too often the scene of conflicting emotion and confusion in thought and purpose.

A second area to which the Hawthorne studies contributed was in the field of PERSONNEL COUNSELING. This movement, which also achieved considerable popularity during and after the war, stressed the values of the talking out process in alleviating personal stress and preoccupation and in bringing about cooperative relations within work groups.

A third area in which the Hawthorne studies pioneered was in the field of industrial sociology. Some authorities trace the development of this relatively new field of study to the descriptive studies of informal groups undertaken in the final phases of the Hawthorne research. The Bank Wiring Observation Group study, upon which the Hawthorne investigations ended, stands as a forerunner of a vast literature on methods, results and implications of small-group studies.

Finally, there must be mentioned the influence of the studies on the general teaching and practice of industrial management. The studies served to stimulate and provide course material and a focus for research to the many Industrial Relations Departments in major colleges and universities during the past quarter of a century.

W. J. DICKSON, formerly Personnel Research, Western Electric Company, Inc., New York, New York

Information References

To place the findings of the Hawthorne studies in proper perspective as regards continuing research into human motivation and behavior in industry and some later reassessments critical of the findings, the reader is referred to the overview entry, HUMAN RELATIONS IN INDUSTRY.

For the official account of the original study: Roethlisberger, F. J. and Dickson, W. J., "Management and the Worker," Harvard University Press, Cambridge, Mass., 1939.

For a detailed analysis of the test-room studies: Whitehead, T. N., "The Industrial Worker," 2 vols., Cambridge, Mass., Harvard University Press, 1938.

For an overview of the research and its implications for administration in a democratic society: Mayo, Elton, "The Human Problems of an Industrial Civilization," Boston, Mass., Division of Research, Harvard Business School, 1946 (first published 1933); "The Social Problems of an Industrial Civilization," Boston, Mass., Division of Research, Harvard Business School, 1945.

For summaries: "Fatigue of Workers," Report of the Committee on Work in Industry, National Research Council, Chap. 4, "Western Electric," Lt. Col. Lyndall and Brech, E. F. L., "The Hawthorne Investigations," Vol. 3, in "The Making of Scientific Management," London, Management Publishing Trust.

Cross References: *Human Relations in Industry (and cross references, there given).*

HOPF, HARRY A.

Harry Arthur Hopf (1882–1949), American management consultant was, with W. H. Leffingwell, a pioneer in applying scientific management methods to the office. He was born in London, and in 1898 emigrated as a penniless youth to the United States where he managed to complete his education by attending evening classes at New York University and Columbia. Before organizing his own consulting firm, he held responsible posts in life insurance companies, and at E. I. duPont de Nemours & Company. Between 1908 and 1917 he made some of the earliest studies and applications of techniques now part of scientific office management, e.g., procedures analysis, standardization of clerical work, production control, and job analysis; and later he made original contributions in the field of executive compensation. Toward the end of his career he achieved international repute in the broader areas of business administration and organization.

Hopf helped establish a number of management societies, and was instrumental in founding the National Management Council, serving as its first Chairman, 1933–36. He was one of the founders of CIOS (see MANAGEMENT SOCIETIES AND ASSOCIATIONS) and served as its Deputy President, 1935–38. Booklets published by him between 1915 and 1947 surveyed the whole field of management thought. His papers, "Adapting the Industrial Organization to Changing Conditions," 1946 (Rutgers University, New Brunswick) and "Evolution in Organization during the Past Decade," 1947 (*Proceedings,* VIII International Management Congress, Stockholm; Hopf Institute of Management Publication No. 10) are considered outstanding in the literature on organization. In 1938 he founded the Hopf Institute of Management, Ossining, New York, to serve as a center and clearing house for scholars in the field of management. He was the author of a great many articles and papers, and through his Institute he published and distributed many booklets on management subjects. Widely read and quoted is his "Soundings in the Literature of Management: Fifty Books the Educated Practitioner Should Know," 1945 (Hopf Institute of Management Publication No. 6; also, *Advanced Management,* September, 1945).

Information References

Urwick, L., "The Golden Book of Management," edited for the International Committee of Scientific Management (CIOS), London, Newman Neame, Limited, 1956.

HOUSE MAGAZINES

House Magazines or "house organs" may be defined as publications not supported by advertising, frankly devoted to promulgating the interests and point of view of their sponsors. They may be of magazine or newspaper format. Two basic types are recognized: the *internal* publication, distributed to employees (often mailed to their homes), and the *external* publication, distributed to customers, prospects, and/or dealers and distributors, or as a public-relations and institutional-advertising medium, for more general readership. Some, of course, are combination of these types.

Publications of this type are a continually growing means of communication, with a collective circulation of over 160 million—slightly over twice the combined circulation of all the daily newspapers in the U.S.! Estimates indicate that there are probably over 60,000 publications that would qualify under the definition given, but consider that there are probably some 4,000 which are substantial enough in content, and with definite publishing schedules, to be classifiable as publications, either in magazine or newspaper format.

Large companies may have weekly, bi-weekly, or monthly newspapers or slighter publications for specific plants or divisions, highlighting employee activities, supplemented with overall monthly magazines dealing with more general subjects. Smaller concerns publish internals bi-weekly or monthly, and combinations are usually monthly. Most successful publications which are strictly external publish monthly, bi-monthly, or quarterly. The preferred format is a 6- by 9-in. size for external magazines, and small internal "tabloids" for local plants.

The house magazine has a remarkable record of stability, the great majority continuing year after year, with only company failure or merger seeming to affect them. Today's modern house magazine is a "highly enlightened publication which draws its strength from a mixture of 'let's-put-the-facts-on-the-table' approach and an honest desire to forward the interests of both the employee and the company." Internal house magazines are, generally speaking, no longer preoccupied with "chit-chat and bowling scores," and are seeking to give employees a broader picture of the company—its history, its present, and its plans for the future.

Broader company information is also a development in externals, with a mixture of out-and-out company promotion and general interest material. Most successful publications of this type follow a proportion of roughly one-third direct company interest, one-third indirect company interest, and one-third with no company interest or connection.

In large companies, the pattern of responsibility is usually as follows: the Advertising Department for magazines going to dealers, salesmen, prospects, etc.; the Public Relations Department for externals, and the Personnel Department for internals.

SOURCE: *Directory of Internal Publications,* Chicago, Illinois

Information References

Association:

American Business Communication Association (ABCA).

Publication:

National Research Bureau, part of The Information Products Group of Automated Marketing Systems, Inc., Chicago, publishes "Directory of Internal Publications," which is Vol. 5 of "Working Press of the Nation," a media resource for public relations and communications professionals.

HUMAN ENGINEERING (HUMAN FACTORS ENGINEERING)

Human Engineering means engineering for human use. In a more philosophical sense, human engineering could be described as a point of view, an attitude or frame of reference within which the engineer approaches design problems. In describing the activity of the human factors specialist, an analogy commonly made is that of impedance matching between the human operator and the machine system of which he is an element.

Within the past fifteen years the term *Human Engineering* has been expanded to the more inclusive **Human Factors Engineering,** and it may be formally defined as "the application of social, biological, and psychological science or knowledge from other sources to the design, operation, and maintenance of man-machine systems and system components." The System Development Corporation, employing what is probably the largest single group of human factors engineers in this country, lists typical duties as follows: ". . . the human factors engineer designs and implements scientific experiments and other research methodology to study human factors areas as they pertain to the operation of man-machine, weapons, and other complex systems and concepts. Evaluates existing or proposed man-machine systems and sub-systems in terms of human physiological and psychological requirements so that optimum system reliability and durability from a human input standpoint are established. Consults with design engineers and other professionals prior to, during, and after design and development of systems to assure optimum operation in terms of human capabilities, limitations, and variables. Provides the most current state-of-the-art information in his particular field of specialization."

Approaches and Techniques. A human factors engineering group will generally include engineering psychologists, mathematicians, several types of engineers, physiologists, anthropologists, radiobiologists, physicians, and specialists from related fields who have worked together as a team long enough to have developed a common technical language and meaningful methods for the solution of man-in-systems problems. Some of the well-known tools and techniques now used in human engineering include the following: experimental design, mathematical modeling, game theory, linear programming, information theory, decision theory, simulation and testing, field testing, statistical sampling, and direct case history studies. The methodology of human factors engineering research and design relates in many ways to associated technical fields such as operations research, industrial engineering, weapons systems analysis, industrial design, life support engineering, and systems development engineering.

History. There is general agreement among specialists in this field that there have been at least three stages in the development of human factors engineering. The first, unrecognized and entirely informal, lasted from the beginning of mankind to approximately 1940. Next came what some workers in the field term the *man versus machine* stage; phasing in during the last decade is a stage which can be called *men and machines.* Perhaps the next stage may be called *man-machine symbiosis* by future historians.

The current stage is being derived from an abstraction and conceptualization based upon definitive systems principles, augmented by compatible data and theory contributed from supporting sciences. Cogent arguments by other recognized human factors specialists point out that human factors engineering is not systems engineering, nor is it part of systems engineering. They claim that the human factors specialist has a different job—that his responsibility is to see efficient utilization of people in systems, not to develop efficient systems. Whatever their point of view, the number of people classified as human factors specialists has shown a steady, if no spectacular, increase over the past four decades.

Beginning in the early 1940s individuals and groups were calling their work "aviation psychology" and the term "human engineering" was beginning to be associated with equipment design. Several Government and university programs were started toward the end of World War II which provided the foundation upon which human factors engineering would be built. By the mid-1950s several aircraft companies began to utilize human engineering contributions in equipment design, training programs, and in weapons system analysis.

Before 1949 there were only one or two human engineering groups doing recognized work in the field; by 1979 there were perhaps 500 industrial firms, government laboratories, and nonprofit institutions claiming to have active human factors efforts under way on a regular basis. It is roughly estimated that four to six thousand people are currently employed within business, industry, and government in work broadly describable as human factors research, bio-technology, and human factors engineering applications.

Acceptance. The functions and responsibilities of this discipline have continually broadened in scope, and participation by human factors specialists is virtually standard on most government-sponsored system development projects. In numerous other, non-government organizations such as the automobile industry, farm machine industry, and business machine industry, human factors staffs are becoming permanent parts of these organizations. And, of course, considerable industrial human factors effort is sustained through government contract requirements that impose human engineering specifications and standards on the products produced for the government.

Some of the notable indications of an increasing awareness of the need for human factors in industry are the recent development of in-house human factors staffs in such companies as The Bell Telephone Laboratories, IBM, NCR, Texas Instruments, General Motors, The Ford Motor Company, The John Deere Co, etc. Similarly, there has been an increase in the development of human factors staffs within government agencies that heretofore had not recognized this important discipline, e.g., U.S. Department of Transportation, U. S. Post Office, the Consumer Product Safety Commission, and OSHA.

Within parent organizations, the position occupied by the various human factors engineering programs ranges from a one- or two-man staff to fairly large groups of 50 or more specialists. Responsibilities vary from management to line organization, making it apparent that organizations are beginning to recognize the broad scope of human factors needs, and the value of applying human factors principles not only to design, but to management procedures and personnel and training.

Potentials. The decade ahead will see a widespread utilization of human factors engineering in the consumer goods and transportation industries, in architecture and civil systems, and some utilization by the agricultural machinery, heavy equipment, and machine tool makers. Until recently, there has been a shortage of trained specialists in the field, some of which has been relieved by entry into human factors of growing numbers of technical specialists from allied fields such as industrial engineering, computer technology, physiology, physics, electronics, reliability maintainability, industrial design, interiors design, and safety engineering.

Nearly 60 institutions of higher learning offer course work in human factors/bio-technology. Numerous universities have outstanding curricula in human factors engineering, many of them offering programs at the graduate level.

DONALD W. CONOVER, Vice President (retired) and WESLEY E. WOODSON, President, Man Factors, Inc., San Diego, California, for Human Factors Society.

Information References

Several professional organizations have developed either as an interdisciplinary group, e.g., Human Factors Society in the U. S. and Ergonomics Societies in other countries such as England, France, Germany, Sweden, Italy, Israel and Japan; or as divisions of recognized professional organizations, e.g., American Psychological Association, Society of Automotive Engineers, American Society of Mechanical Engineers, Institute of Electrical and Electronic Engineers, etc.

Among the most important human factors professional, technical information publications are *Human Factors Journal, Ergonomics* (published by the International Ergonomics Association), and the more applied journal, *Applied Ergonomics,* published by IPC Science and Technology Press Ltd, in cooperation with the Ergonomics Society of Great Britain.

Texts:

DeGreene, K. B., "Systems Psychology," New York, McGraw-Hill, 1970.

Gagne, R. M., et al, "Psychological Principles in Systems Development," New York, Holt, Rinehart & Winston, 1962.

McCormick, E. J., "Human Factors in Engineering and Design," New York, McGraw-Hill, 1976

Meister, David, "Human Factors: Theory & Practice," New York, Wiley, 1971.

Woodson, W. E. and Conover, D. W, "Human Engineering Guide for Equipment Designers, Berkeley, Calif., University of California Press, 1964.

Woodson, W. E., "Human Factors Design Handbook: Information and Guidelines for the Design of Systems, Facilities, Equipment, and Products for Human Use," New York, McGraw-Hill, 1981.

Cross Reference: *Industrial Robots.*

HUMAN RELATIONS IN INDUSTRY: An Overview

Human Relations in Industry is a broad term applied in an embracive way to a concern on the part of management for the welfare of workers—viewing them as human beings possessing dignity and worth, and not merely as units of production. The underlying concept, which recognizes enlightened self interest rather than sheer altruism, was early stated by ROBERT OWEN, a successful textile manufacturer in Scotland widely known as a social reformer. In his 1813 *Address to the Superintendents of Manufactories* he had this to say:

> If then due care as to the state of your inanimate machines can produce beneficial results, what may not be expected if you devote equal attention to your vital machines, which are far more wonderfully constructed? When you shall acquire a right knowledge of these, of their curious mechanism, of their self-adjusting powers; when their proper mainspring shall be applied to their varied movements, you will become conscious of their real value, and you will be readily induced to turn your thoughts more frequently from your inanimate to your living machines; you will discover that the latter may be easily trained and directed to procure a large increase of pecuniary gain, while you may also derive from them high and substantial gratification.

However, the term "human relations movement" as used in the literature today does not apply to earlier experiences with "paternalism"—which in many cases failed to achieve desired results, as indicated below—but rather covers the attempts to develop and apply a coherent and proven theory of worker motivation and behavior in order to channel the latter into desirable and productive patterns. The movement is based on the recognition that more than good physical working conditions and employee welfare programs, and more than money incentives alone operate in the development of a responsive work force.

The Precursing Paternalism. Under the philosophy of paternalism, managements sought to raise employee morale by providing good working conditions, fringe benefits, employee services, and often (but not always) high wages. The rationale as stated by Strauss and Sayles [1] takes two forms, "naive" and "subtle." The naive argument holds that if management is good to employees, they will work harder out of loyalty and gratitude. The more subtle argument ignores the question of gratitude; it holds that liberal benefits and good working conditions make for happy employees, and that happy employees work harder.

Naive paternalism had its heyday in the 1920s. In part, its fairly widespread adoption at that time was the result of a genuine concern on the part of employers for the welfare of their employees, but also to a significant degree a result of the rise of unionism during and immediately after World War I. In any case, as Strauss and Sayles point out, under the banner of the "New Industrial Relations," management became interested in a wide variety of projects, varying from cafeterias and recreation programs for employees to cooking classes for their wives. Some of the programs were designed to change the employees' personal lives as well as their on-the-job performance.

The early Ford Motor Company program embodied in its Sociology Department went farther than most, and is an example of the extreme form of such activity. Headed by a Protestant minister, the department at its peak was manned by 30 "investigators." Constructively, the latter functioned somewhat like the caseworker of a modern public welfare agency, visiting employees in their homes and giving advice on budgeting, hygiene, and home management. However, "hearsay as well as fact found its way into a card catalog where a record was kept of every worker's deviation, including 'earmarks of unwholesome living,' such as use of liquor, and reports of marital discord" [2].

Ford's program was shortlived, but somewhat similar if less extreme programs were developed in other companies. However, Strauss-Sayles point out that "there is little evidence that any of them were particularly successful in eliciting gratitude, in motivating workers to do a better job, or even in staving off the development of unions. In fact, some of the best companies with the best-known histories of paternalism later became scenes of bitter labor-management strife."

Modern Approaches. Ever since the mid-1920s, and especially as a concomitant of the social problems created by the Great Depression of the thirties, management has been increasingly preoccupied with the human side of its operations. It had seen that paternalism was not the answer to labor unrest, and began casting about for more effective answers to the problems of worker behavior. Important in this connection are the famous Hawthorne experiments of the Western Electric Company in 1923–1926 and 1927–1932, which triggered the human relations movement. (See HAWTHORNE EXPERIMENTS.) This research produced the first purported objective truth of a positive correlation between employee participation in the decisions affecting him (her) and the work output produced. A major conclusion of the study was that the factory was a social system and that informal groupings in the work situation vitally affected human behavior. The corollary was that the worker could no longer be viewed solely as a factor of production. Rather, the employee was a human being with wants, desires, attitudes, and feelings, all of which influenced his or her productive usefulness.

In addition to the Hawthorne experiments and the subsequent (and continuing) research of behavioral scientists into the question of human motivation, several other factors also contributed to the human relations movement. Employment departments (later called personnel departments) were established by many organizations to handle employee selection, training, and turnover, to cope with increasing problems of trade unionism, and to research new areas of employee relations.

Prior to the Hawthorne experiments, industrial engineers had been seeking most of the answers to efficient operation in improved production processes and more refined budgeting and cost controls. This engineering approach had been sparked by the work of Frederick W. Taylor and other pioneers of the "scientific management" movement at the turn of the century. (See SCIENTIFIC MANAGEMENT and SCIENTIFIC MANAGEMENT: "Taylorism.") Although the benefits of that movement are well known, it has nevertheless come in for increasing criticism in the intervening years on the grounds that in its emphasis on efficiency of operations it was not sufficiently concerned with problems of individual worker motivation beyond financial incentives.

In all fairness to Taylor and his associates, however, as pointed out by Heckman [3], the scientific management movement did not designedly overlook the human element in industry. In fact, a prime concern of these pioneers was to increase the productivity of the worker with a commensurate decrease in his or her effort, fatigue, and other detriments to physical welfare. (The slogan was to "work smarter, not harder.") What was overlooked, however, was the relationship of the individual to the work group of which he (she) was a part. In other words, the worker was viewed solely as a production unit, and little, if any recognition was given to the complex social network that comprises any organization of human beings. It therefore remained for later investigators to demonstrate the tremendous influence of interpersonal relationships upon human behavior, and hence upon individual productivity.

Following the Hawthorne experiments there was a tremendous swing by management to a deep preoccupation with the human and social aspects of work. In industrial relations literature and from the platforms of management gatherings, the Hawthorne findings were quoted extensively. This is not, of course, to say that the swing was due solely to this work—but the findings did provide an apparent scientific basis for the arguments that were increasingly being advanced by socially conscious spokesmen for government, business, and academic circles. These arguments held that human relations had been a neglected factor in productivity; that too much attention had been given to money incentives and to impersonally engineered standards of performance; that management in general and supervisors in particular had to be much more concerned with "what made people tick," with problems of informal organization in any working group, and with problems of *communication, participation,* and *understanding.*

This new trend in management thinking had a marked influence on the type and content of supervisory training programs—and in many cases the preoccupation with the human reactions on the job led to rather extreme emphasis on psychological and even near-psychiatric approaches. While there was later a justified reaction against "analyzing" and giving advice to subordinates on alleged personality defects and a concomitant swing back to stressing performance on the job, the net result was a salutary concern in getting managers and supervisors to think about what constitutes effective leadership on the job: about effective techniques of communication and teaching, overcoming resistance to change, instilling pride in work, and achieving identification with company objectives.

Evolving Insights into Motivation. In the years under review, a great deal of attention has been given to the question of human motivation and behavior. Social scientists have sought to develop theories and predictive laws about the motivations, attitudes, actions, and reactions of people at work. These have been based on observations in controlled industrial situations, reports by clinical psychologists, reactions under controlled conditions of non-industry groups such as school children and military units, and laboratory studies of the behavior of birds and animals subjected to various stimuli. Inputs also were congruent inferences drawn from "real-life" examples furnished by the practitioners of WORK SIMPLIFICATION, successful programs such as the LINCOLN INCENTIVE MANAGEMENT PLAN, and experiences in participation gained from programs such as MANAGEMENT BY OBJECTIVES and JOB ENRICHMENT AND WORK EFFECTIVENESS.

An outgrowth of the above activity has been a vast body of literature on worker motivation and behavior—shelves of books and reams of articles and papers in business and academic journals. (The diversity of subjects covered is indicated by the extensive cross references appended to this article.) Unfortunately, this wealth of literature does not add up to a coherent, internally consistent whole, as will be indicated presently. However, a direct result has been that human relations has been a continuing prominent part in supervisor and management training courses. "How to Get Along with People," "How to Motivate Employees," "How to Develop a Responsive Work Force," "Job Enrichment," and more latterly "Behavior Management (or Modification)," or their equivalent, have been recurring session titles in management seminars.

Important among the concepts that have attained wide prominence are:

Maslow's "Hierarchy of Needs." Dr. Maslow postulated five basic needs which, he said, are organized into successive levels. For example, hunger is a basic physiological need. But when there is plenty of food, higher needs emerge, such as safety needs, love needs (termed by some writers "social needs"), esteem needs, and the need for self-actualization, or self-fulfillment. (See MOTIVATION: Maslow's "Basic Needs.") When a higher need is satisfied, newer and still higher needs come to the fore, and so on. Thus, gratification becomes as important a concept in motivation as deprivation. A want that is satisfied is no longer a want.

Even if all of the first four needs are satisfied, we can still expect that a new discontent and restlessness will develop, unless the individual is doing what he is fitted for. People who are satisfied in all five levels of needs are basically satisfied people, and the theory states that it is from these that we can expect the fullest creativity and productivity. However, quite aside from the fifth level, the fourth, or esteem needs (also termed "egoistic" needs) are rarely completely satisfied in the typical industrial and commercial organization, and it is the recognition of this situation that has forced so much attention on ways to provide employees with a sense of participation.

The Maslow formulation is still frequently quoted in management literature despite the recent challenges indicated below.

McGregor's "Theory X" and "Theory Y." Douglas McGregor set forth six positive assumptions about worker attitudes, which he called "Theory Y." He contrasted these with commonly held negative assumptions about workers, which he termed "Theory X," the traditional view. The "X" assumption, he contended, form a block to constructive manager-employee relations. (See MOTIVATION: McGregor's "Theory X" and "Theory Y.")

Herzberg's Motivation-Hygiene Theory. This theory advanced by Dr. Frederick Herzberg underlies the development of the widely discussed and practiced technique of job enrichment. The motivation factors have to do with satisfaction from achievement and recognition, the task content of the job (variety of challenge, freedom of boredom), responsibility, and opportunities for growth and advancement. The "hygiene" factors (the term is borrowed from medical use as preventive and environmental), or potential dissatisfiers, are: salary, company policy and administration, working conditions, and interpersonal relations. A significant point made is that optimum hygiene factors merely *prevent dissatisfaction;* for *positive results,* the motivation factors, the *satisfiers,* must be brought into play. (See the section, *Motivation-Hygiene Theory,* in the entry, JOB ENRICHMENT AND WORK EFFECTIVENESS.)

The foregoing tie in with the continuing emphasis that has been given to the advantages of so-called "democratic" versus "authoritarian" supervision, and to the need for more "participative" management. A manager or supervisor who is "democratically oriented" is described as one who thinks of himself or herself as a coordinator of his group rather than "boss." He (she) believes subordinates should have more voice in running the department, listens to ideas and suggestions from them, and passes adequate explanations on to subordinates when changes are made. He or she is ready on occasion to give in to a subordinate if there is disagreement on how something should be done.

Countermovement. The cumulative effect, in some companies, of all the emphasis on human relations was to swing the pendulum pretty far—to a "do-gooder's" philosophy of personnel administration. Inevitably there were second thoughts. Was all the talk about the human factor in industry taking on the aspects of a fad? Was "democratic" supervision simply "soft" supervision? Were all the interesting cases studies nothing more than anecdotes—isolated casebook material without any general significance? Participative management is all well and good, but should girls really be allowed to set conveyor speeds? Are we overly concerned with patting workers on the head, giving them expressions of approval to bolster their self-esteem? Do engineered performance standards really rob a worker of human dignity? Moreover, is there any proof that satisfied and happy workers are more productive?

To seek answers to questions such as these, numerous attempts were made to put a somewhat firmer scientific base under all the admonitions to encourage participation, to provide scope for individual goal setting, to consider social relationships, and the like. By and large the attempts to provide hard evidence based on strictly controlled situations proved disappointing, despite the undeniably positive results obtained with job enrichment programs in such companies as Texas Instruments [4] and AT&T [5]. (The interpretation of these has, as indicated below, been challenged by advocates of "behavior management" based on Skinnerian psychology.)

In the search for hard evidence, even the famed Hawthorne experiments came under critical review. In 1953, twenty years after the original Hawthorne reports, a British social scientist, Michael Argyle, published a paper entitled "The Relay Assembly Test Room in Retrospect" [6]. He carefully re-examined all the reported results, subjecting them to tests for statistical significance, evaluated the types of controls that had been set up, and reconsidered all the possible influences on the final measurements. He flatly stated that there was no quantitative evidence for the conclusions for which the study is famous, namely, the claim that the increase in worker output was due not to physical factors, but to social changes, and in particular to the new attitude of the girls toward supervision.

The British paper apparently made no significant impression upon American management literature, considering the continued frequent non-critical references over the years to the Hawthorne findings. However, Lawrence M. Miller, who *is* skeptical of the conclusions drawn from Hawthorne, quotes in his book, "Behavior Management" [7] a report by H.M. Parsons documenting similar adverse findings from a re-examination of the Hawthorne studies [8].

Miller is an articulate representative of a school of thought that has come into prominence in recent years, which is in fundamental disagreement with the basic motivational assumptions of Maslow, Herzberg, McGregor, et al. Resting upon the theories propounded by the famed behavioral psychologist B.F. Skinner, the advocates of "behavior management" or "behavior modification" brush aside all interpretations of behavior that rely upon motivation. Knowledge of what goes on inside a person is in any event, they say, unavailable to another, and speculating upon it and hoping to change it is actually irrelevant to the problem of changing behavior. All that matters, they contend, is the outward observable behavior. Skinner's controlled laboratory experiments with rats and pigeons, they claim, show that desired behavior can be achieved by suitable positive or negative reinforcements (appropriate and appropriately timed rewards or the withholding of them), and by avoidance of "aversive" (threatening) controls.

As to job enrichment, Miller [7] points out that most descriptions of such programs portray complex changes in the environment, and contends that it is very difficult, if not impossible, in most of these experiments to identify what change caused what effect on performance. And he sharply disagrees with a statement by Robert N. Ford, one of the first and most thorough researchers in job enrichment, made in Ford's book, "Motivation through the Work Itself" [5]. There Ford says, "A business owes the employee the most satisfying work it can give him within the limits of staying in business." Commenting on this, Miller [7] clearly draws the line between the newer behaviorists and the earlier expounders of motivation and human relations theory:

> The implications of the concept that a "business owes the employee the most satisfying work it can give him within the limits of staying in business are profound. The manager who does accept this premise had best think this through to its logical conclusions, namely, that the business exists to provide satisfaction to the employee . . . Efforts to prove satisfying work have often proved ineffective because they have assumed that, if a state of satisfaction exists, employees perform well. This places satisfaction first and performance second. Systems that have succeeded in improving

performance and satisfaction have placed performance first, with satisfaction or rewards following and contingent upon the desired performance.

On Balance. Given the sharp differences of professional opinion regarding human motivation and behavior, how can the management practitioner arrive at a viable human relations philosophy as regards his own organization? The following observations may provide a workable rationale:

It must be remembered that the differing approaches and schools of thought highlighted in the foregoing do not mean that as one concept comes into prominence it completely negates all that went before. There is no succession of one "truth" following another. In real life, all the concepts live together; one approach is successfully applied in place A at the same time that another has been "proven" and is in successful operation in place B. Thus, a high degree of paternalism is still operative in many quarters—and is successful in preventing unionization—and management and employees may not even know about the theoretical and historical pitfalls involved. Job enrichment programs are flourishing in many companies where management is totally unaware that the advocates of behavior management have declared that the programs suffer from "inadequacies of theory." Many managers who have gone through a training seminar that stressed "Theory X" vs. "Theory Y" are as a result performing as better managers because they have a new confidence in the desire and ability of employees to take on new responsibilities and do a conscientious job without having to be driven or coerced, quite unaware that in some quarters the contention is that much of McGregor's Theory X does *not,* as he claimed, comprise assumptions widely held by management.

It should also be remarked that publications of conflicting approaches appear concurrently. At the same time that some books and academic papers report studies purportedly invalidating Hawthorne or job enrichment or participative goal setting, other books and articles appear that quote the Hawthorne findings or Herzberg or McGregor et al. as recognized authorities. Thus, in reading about any human-relations concept such as presented in the numerous relevant entries in this Encyclopedia—whether on Taylorism or the Hawthorne experiments or whatever—the reader should automatically make the following assessments:

- When was this approach advocated? During what period was this experiment conducted or these observations made? For example, Miller [7] referring to Theories X and Y, observes, "In defense of McGregor it must be said that he made his assumptions about X at a time when it was in vogue, particularly in academia, to assume all good things about anonymous individuals, workers in particular, and to assume all negative things about 'the system,' business and management."
- Can I use the practical-sounding parts of the concept without necessarily having to acquiesce in all of it? For example, a manager can profit from the Skinnerian thesis about changing behavior through positive reinforcement—which in any case accords with practical experience—without going "whole hog" into acceptance of Skinner's radical determinism which makes *all* of a person's behavior the result of environmental and genetic influences to the total exclusion of free will and an inner motivational and decision-making apparatus.
- Have contradictory or countervailing theories been advanced since the one here advocated was propounded? If there is a demonstrated contradiction, can insights on both sides of the contradiction nevertheless be usefully applied? For example, one can couple the constructive and commonsense prescriptions based on the behavior-psychology approach with the insights into motivation based on the Herzberg formulation (even though the behaviorists insist that one need not postulate motivation at all).
- Is there a good probability that more causes than the one(s) set forth in the account were contributory to the effect(s) described? This is one of the criticisms leveled against the report of the Hawthorne experiments, and is an explanation offered for the success of many job enrichment programs.
- Are research findings or case example results advanced to provide a basis for a particular motivation-behavior theory or a new approach to management-employee relations based on sufficient evidence? How valid are the generalizations inferred from the findings reported?
- Does the policy or procedure advocated involve management's abdicating the right to manage? For example, the concept of "democratic supervision" is sound—within limits. Yes, if it means careful indoctrination of the workers by the supervisor on what is expected of them, solicitation of suggestions, a voice by

employees *to the extent feasible* in work allocation. Yes, if the supervisor knows that his (her) people are ready for it. No, if the supervisor has green help, or if methods in the department have undergone a significant change, or if the quality record is poor.

The Bottom Line. In the last analysis, the "bottom line" in all of this is that the manager must in the end devise and define his own consistent and coherent human relations philosophy, formulating it over the years by continuous and compatible accretions from all credible sources available.

CARL HEYEL, Management Counsel, Manhasset, New York

Information References

Ford, Robert N., "Motivation Through the Work Itself," New York, American Management Associations, 1969.
Herzberg, Frederick, "One More Time: How Do You Motivate Employees?" *Harvard Business Review,* January-February 1968.
McGregor, Douglas, "The Human Side of Enterprise," New York, McGraw-Hill, 1960.
Myers, M. Scott, "Every Employee a Manager," New York, McGraw-Hill, 1970.
Miller, Lawrence M., "Behavior Management: The New Science of Managing People at Work," New York, Wiley, 1978.
Nye, Robert D., "What is B.F. Skinner Really Saying?" Englewood Cliffs, N.J., Prentice-Hall, 1979.
Skinner, B.F., "Beyond Freedom & Dignity," New York, Knopf, 1971.
Walters, Roy W. and Purdy, Kenneth L., "Job Enrichment Programs," in Heyel, C. ed., "Handbook of Modern Office Management and Administrative Services," Huntington, N.Y., Krieger, repr. 1980.

References Cited

[1] Strauss, George and Sayles, Leonard R., "The Human Problems of Management," Englewood Cliffs, N.J., Prentice-Hall, 1960.
[2] Sward, Keith, "The Legend of Henry Ford," New York, Rinehart, 1948.
[3] Heckmann, I.L., "Human Relations in Industry," entry in 2nd ed., "The Encyclopedia of Management," New York, Van Nostrand Reinhold," 1973.
[4] Myers, M. Scott, as above.
[5] Ford, Robert N., as above.
[6] Argyle, Michael, "The Relay Assembly Test Room in Retrospect," *Occupational Psychology,* Vol. 27, 1953.
[7] Miller, Lawrence M., as above.
[8] Parsons, H.M., "What Happened at Hawthorne," *Science,* March 1974.

Cross References: *Employee Attitude Research: Attitude Surveys; Goal Setting; Group Dynamics; Hawthorne Experiments; Human Engineering (Human Factors Engineering); Incentive Systems; Industrial Psychology; Job Enrichment and Work Effectiveness; Management by Objectives; Managerial Grid; Motivation; Motivation: Maslow's "Basic Needs"; Motivation: McGregor's "Theory X" and "Theory Y"; Organization Theory; Personnel Counseling; Quality of Working Life; Scientific Management: Taylorism; Sensitivity Training; Transaction Analysis in Management; Work Simplification.*

HUMAN RESOURCE DEVELOPMENT

Human Resource Development (HRD) has become an evolving concept for building work force performance to meet the needs of an organization. The essential elements of HRD are (1) on-going assessment of work force competency needs, (2) activities to fill those needs—employee education and training, organization development, "quality of work life" programs, or other efforts to serve the needs, and (3) evaluation to determine if the intended purpose has been met.

Developing the competence and productivity of the work force, in reality, is a multi-faceted and direct responsibility of management. The quality of human performance is integral to the quality of organization success. And while line management must bear a direct responsibility, HRD success is heavily dependent upon effective use of the growing body of available know-how. The prudent manager would do well, in his or her own interest to get the best available professional HRD support to help build human performance.

History. Human resource development in the world of work has grown through many stages, beginning thousands of years ago when artisans handed down knowledge and skills of the earliest crafts to younger generations, often through some kind of apprenticeship, which was known as early as 2100 B.C. [1].

Means of developing job competence have progressed through many forms, including major roles played by public and higher education. The need for industrial capacity during World War II was a powerful impetus to the formation of what we have come to know, more recently, as employee training and development, or HRD. The field has seen rapid evolution in the past decade or two with major application of the behavioral sciences, and with a strong emphasis on relating employee development directly to the needs of the organization. Employee training and development has come to encompass broader concerns of developing employee performance so that now the term *Human Resource Development* is commonly accepted as more descriptive of the function.

Approach. Basically, the line management responsibility for developing the work force is to ensure that the objectives of the organization are supported with work force competencies which can accomplish those objectives. Strategic organizational plans should be translated into manpower requirements and the manpower requirements translated into work force competency and training needs.

It is essential to recognize the need for a problem-analysis approach. Employee development must be directed to real needs to be effective. Without proper needs assessment, employee development can even be counterproductive. It is not uncommon that management requests (or demands) for a "training program" are inappropriate and misdirected. Reports from highly regarded HRD specialists have shown that as many as 80% of line managers' training requests have turned out not to be training problems at all when thoroughly analyzed.

Need analysis has become so prevalent as an HRD activity that some observers have noted that the HRD department is doing more job definition than the industrial engineers.

Implementation. After the need has been carefully established, the appropriate education or training or development effort must be designed and developed or selected/adapted from existing sources. If the need is broadly generic, the development program might be obtained from the vast array of materials and packages available nowadays from publishers and consultants and other resources that make up a large "training industry." In some instances, educational institutions can be used for employee education and training [2]. Community colleges have often been cited as the educational sector most responsive to employee education needs.

If the need is specific to one company only, the HRD department, or a consultant, usually designs and prepares the developmental activity to meet that need. In most cases, the program can be used time and again with similar groups of employees throughout the organization. Many employers have extensive "catalogs" of employee development activities. The Bell System is reported to have 12,000 employee training courses alone!

It is important to recognize that a major instructional resource for employee development is the organization itself. "In-house" managers and specialists are often the best source of job training knowledge. Getting them involved in formal training has many advantages including realistic carry over from classroom to the job and "ownership" of training results by line personnel.

Evaluation. The bottom line question for any HRD effort is to know if it has achieved the desired results. How does management, or the HRD function, know that supervisors are better supervisors after a training program?—that the employees in a job skill training program are better performers after their learning experience? Answering this question is impossible if the objectives for the learning experience have not been specified through careful needs analysis. A widely respected model for looking at training evaluation was first described some 20 years ago by Dr. Donald L. Kirkpatrick [3]. He set out four levels of employee training evaluation:

(1) *Reaction:* Did the participant like the experience? (This may or may not be relevant to better job performance.)

(2) *Learning:* Did the participant learn anything? (This can be determined by testing the knowledge of the participants before and after the experience, but still may not be evidence of better job performance.)

(3) *Behavior change:* Did the experience produce a change in the behavior of the participant? Learning experiences can produce behavior change but the new behavior may or may not be related to improved job performance.

(4) *Results:* Did the participant acquire the desired job performance as established in the needs analysis?

Evaluation of employee development, however, is often easier said than done. While the HRD field has a good deal of evaluation technology at its command, it is still very difficult to evaluate, with precision, some kinds of development, such as management training or continuing engineering education. And in some instances, where evaluation might be possible, with very sophisticated techniques, the cost of doing so may well negate the benefits. All HRD should be evaluated within technical and economic constraints, and approximations can often serve as adequate indicators.

Range. The range of Human Resource Development activities is broad. It can include *entry level education and training* to help with the transition from school to work for youth. Many employers must provide education in basic skills (reading, writing, basic math, etc.) since young people often come into the workforce lacking in these areas. Orientation training and apprenticeships also fall into the entry level.

Probably the largest area of human resource development in the world of work is *job-skill training*—crafts, technical training of all sorts, clerical and data-processing skills, and specialized training for the myriads of jobs we have today. Managers can call upon a wide range of external sources for training in these job areas. For example, members of the ASTD Technical and Skills Training Division can be reached through the American Society for Training and Development. Many trade and professional groups can provide good information about training resources in their special fields, and they may also have extensive training materials or programs themselves. (See Information Reference appended.)

A significant training resource is the Federal Government. (See TRAINING AND DEVELOPMENT (Government Sponsored).) The Bureau of Apprenticeship and Training of the U.S. Department of Labor is the prime source for apprenticeship information. (See APPRENTICESHIP PROGRAMS.) Proprietary schools and home-study courses can be good sources for training in technical and job skills. (See CORRESPONDENCE SCHOOLS and Information References appended.) The Industrial Management Society makes available a wide selection of management and industrial engineering films and video tapes, covering such subjects as performance rating, methods improvement and work simplification, electronic data processing, work sampling, quality control, office clerical and hospital operations, and others. Good sources of general information about programs—packaged training programs, audio-visual materials, schools and colleges, consultants, computer-assisted instruction, business games, seminars, etc.—are the publications, meetings, and information services of the American Society for Training and Development. ASTD purveys no management training products or services, and therefore has no bias and can refer inquirers to many sources, as well as offering its Buyers Guide and Consultants Directory.

Management development represents one of the most pressing need of HRD. As talented people are moved up from their areas of technical or professional specialty, and on upward through the managerial ranks, there is continuing need for them to acquire new managerial competencies. As a result, management training, in a wide range of forms, is widespread. A study by the Bureau of National Affairs [4] indicated that only a small portion of *management and supervisory training* is done on business school campuses. Employers must do most of it, often using outside resources such as trade and professional groups, consultants, and the like. (See MANAGEMENT DEVELOPMENT TECHNIQUES and SUPERVISORY TRAINING.) Large corporations and government agencies often have elaborate campus-like management training centers. (See EXECUTIVE DEVELOPMENT: "Away from Company" Programs, and Information References appended.)

High-technology firms are often faced with doing much of their own *continuing engineer and scientist education* "in-house." Often their own technological "state-of-the-art" is considerably ahead of most engineering schools, and sometimes the schools are not responsive to changing industry needs. However, many excellent continuing engineering and scientific education programs are offered by engineering schools and other sources. A good source of information is the American Society for Engineering Education, Washington, D.C.

For training in highly competitive fields—SALES TRAINING is a good example—companies will often insist on doing their own training in order to safeguard proprietary information and practices. Many consultants specialize in sales training. A source of information is the Sales Training Division, American Society for Training and Development, and the Sales Executive Club of New York.

Recent Developments. Increasingly, employers are providing more training for their women and minority employees to help integrate them into the work force and to provide them with opportunities for upward mobility as part of *affirmative action* initiatives. In this HRD activity, as with all employee development, managers should make certain that their selections and the developmental experiences offered are nondiscriminatory and can be shown to be job-related. (See EMPLOYMENT: Antidiscrimination Legislation.)

Organization development is a movement that has gained wide acceptance in the past decade and, in simplified terms, is directed to building "team" effectiveness, as distinguished from development directed to individual employees.

More information can be obtained from the Organization Development Division, American Society for Training and Development.

A newer movement that has developed widespread interest and increasing acceptance, as the U.S. productivity growth rate has dropped, is known by the broad term, QUALITY OF WORK LIFE. QWL programs are usually intended to increase job satisfaction for employees through involving the employees in the decision making of their work groups. It may include techniques variously labeled as participative decision making, autonomous work groups, industrial democracy, job redesign, and others. Invariably, an expected outcome of a QWL program is increased productivity. In fact, much of the credit for better productivity and better quality of product in Japan has been attributed to QWL practices such as QC CIRCLES. The ASTD Task Force on QWL has defined QWL as: "a process for a work organization which enables its members at all levels to participate actively in shaping the organization's environment, methods, and outcomes. This people-based process is directed to meeting the twin goals of enhanced effectiveness of the organization and improved quality of work life for employees."

It seems inevitable that HRD will become an even more vital concern for the manager in the future as the cost of labor escalates, as the international marketplace becomes more competitive, as technological change creates demands for new job knowledge and skills, as attitudes and demographics of the work force change, and as social change impacts the work place. A proficient work force will undoubtedly be a major factor in managerial success.

ROBERT L. CRAIG, Vice President, Government and Public Affairs, American Society for Training and Development, Washington Office, Washington, D.C.

Information References

Employee Training:

Association of General Contractors of America.
Bureau of Apprenticeship and Training, U.S. Department of Labor.
Industrial Management Society, specifically "Audio-Visual Library Catalog."
National Home Study Council.
National Tool, Die, and Precision Machining Association.

Management Development:

Bricker, George W., ed., "Bricker's International Directory of University-Sponsored Executive Development Programs," Chatham, Mass., Bricker Publishing, 1980.
"Directory of Management Education Programs," Management Development Resource Service of American Management Associations, New York, Amacom, 1978.
McNulty, Nancy G., ed., "Management Development Programs: The World's Best," New York, Elsevier North Holland, 1980.

Continuing Engineer and Scientist Education:

American Society for Engineering Education.

Sales Training:

Sales Training.
Sales & Marketing Management.

Re. All of the Above:

American Society for Training and Development.
Bureau of National Affairs.
Desatnick, Robert L., "The Expanding Role of the Human Resources Manager," New York, Amacom, 1979.
Industrial Management Society.
National Educational Media, Inc. (specifically "Management, Business, and Sales Educational Curriculum Guide," and "Catalog of Color/Sound Motion Picture Programs."

References Cited

[1] Craig, Robert L., ed., "Training and Development Handbook," Chap. 1., "The History of Training," New York, McGraw-Hill, 1976.
[2] ———, Chap. 45, Whitlock, G. H., "The Role of Universities and Colleges in Training and Development"; Chap. 46, Parry; S. B. and Ribling, J. R., "Using Outside Training Consultants"; and Chap. 47, in Cantwell, J. A. et al., "Using External Programs and Packages," 2nd. ed., New York, McGraw-Hill, 1976.
[3] Kirkpatric, D. L., "Techniques for Evaluating Training Programs," *Journal of the American Society for Training and Development,* November-December, 1959 and January-February, 1969.
[4] "Management Training and Development Programs," *PPF Survey 116, March, 1977,* Washington, D.C., The Bureau of National Affairs.

Cross References: *Apprenticeship Programs; Behavior Modeling in Training; Correspondence Schools; Creativity Training; Executive Development: Selection Guide; Management Development Techniques; Multiple Management; On-the-Job Training; Sales Training; Sensitivity Training; Supervisory Training; Teaching Machines, Programmed Instruction, and Computer-Aided Instruction; Training and Development (Government Sponsored; Training Within Industry Program (TWI); Transaction Analysis in Management; Work Simplification.*

HUMAN RESOURCES REQUIREMENTS PLANNING

Human Resources Requirements Planning deals with anticipating staffing requirements, taking into account current and likely future demands for skills, and the probable availability of individuals with such skills. The action part of the definition deals with the policies and programs that are used in coordinating supply and demand to attain the goals desired.

While it has frequently been stated that human resources are a nation's and an organization's most valuable asset, there has been, paradoxically, relative lack of attention to this critical resource. Financial planning, product planning, physical facilities planning, market planning, and the like are probably more advanced in most organizations than is manpower planning.

The recent trends to greater emphasis on human behavior and social awareness will probably accelerate interest in manpower planning, in both governmental, institutional, and business organizations. The bureaucratic and mechanistic emphasis on the nonhuman physical systems and economic goals will have to give way, partially, to concern about people as part of systems.

Macro-Level Planning. Essential to sound thinking about long-range staffing needs and policies is a realization of the variety of activities and actions, attitudinal and behavioral patterns, and formal and informal decisions by private individuals, organizations, and government which make manpower policies in a free and democratic society.

In a general sense, four major conditions account for much of our misuse of human resources: unemployment, underemployment, inadequate training and development, and arbitrary barriers to employment. The objective of a comprehensive manpower planning effort is to ameliorate these undesirable conditions.

At the national level, three pieces of legislation have particular significance in the human resources planning concept. First, the Employment Act of 1946 recognized the responsibility of the Federal Government to maintain a high level of employment. Second, the Manpower Development and Training Act of 1962 provided for logistical studies of manpower that will help the nation determine its needs and the priorities required to meet them. Third, the Comprehensive Employment and Training Act of 1973 was a beginning to implement programs to upgrade the skills of a large number of citizens.

In the United States, there has been a rather sharp separation between the agencies that influence the level of employment (the demand side) and those concerned with the use of manpower resources (the supply side). The Council of Economic Advisers, the Treasury, the Federal Reserve, and the Office of Management and Budget are mainly concerned with the creation of demand and the general level of employment. The Department of Labor and the Department of Health, Education, and Welfare have dealt chiefly with the supply side (education, training, counseling, and referral for placement). This segmented administration is reflected in the lack of integration of the President's Economic Report and his Employment and Training Report. At the Congressional level, this lack of integration continues: different committees receive and discuss the economic and employment and training reports. At the top policy level of the nation, there thus seems to be a need for greater integration of the supply and demand sides of the employment picture—since it so vitally affects the real wealth of our nation: our people.

To be effective, human resources planning must eventually be made at the local level, where the people live and work or are looking for work. This means that in addition to the Federal and state governments, local government must play a role. The Federal Government has a number of programs, some with the states and others with local governments, which are attacking specific manpower problems—many of which are related to assisting the underprivileged and unskilled groups. (See TRAINING AND DEVELOPMENT (Government Sponsored).)

An effective planning effort is, at least partially, dependent on the availability of a supporting information system that contains needed and timely data. On the macro-level in the United States, there is some deficiency in this area. One of the major problems in human resource planning has largely been the collection of masses of descriptive data without any scheme for relating and using them, and the use of aggregates and averages that are so general that they mask the useful characteristics of the data.

Our nation's pluralistic, free enterprise system places some obvious constraints on strong central planning and related information banks. In several other nations considerable progress has been made toward achieving a responsive, national manpower planning system with an accompanying information data bank [1]. (See Exhibit I.) Without such an approach,

EXHIBIT I

AN INTEGRATED MODEL OF HUMAN RESOURCES SUPPLY AND DEMAND

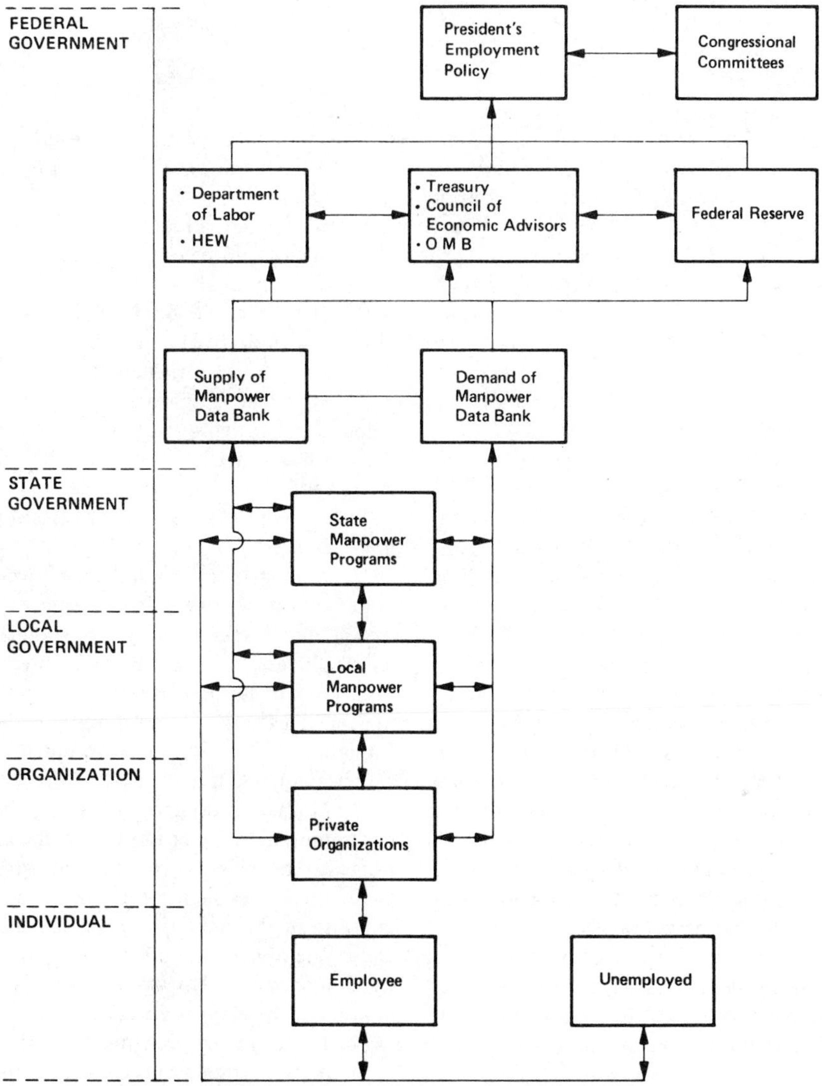

the impediments of a segmented and incomplete manpower planning system with an inadequate information base will undoubtedly constrain both macro- and micro-manpower planning in the United States.

One intergovernmental effort, in the United States, that is worthy of note is the establishment of several computerized job matching systems; these systems, at least partially funded by the Federal Government, have been installed in several states and metropolitan areas. The purpose of the systems is to facilitate the matching of available job openings with applicants having required skills. It is expected that this approach may one day be nation-wide, at minimum making information more readily available for those that want and need it. Also, such a system is a potential source of valuable micro-level data.

Micro-Level Planning. As recently as two decades ago, the personnel function was primarily engaged in providing largely uncoordinated services to the operating units in the organization. Personnel units are now beginning to have an overriding mission for dealing with the broad people-related activities, including the climate of motivation, and are increasingly geared to provide the services needed by top management for effective planning and control.

The nation's manpower requirements in the coming decade can be expected to reflect both the growth in demand for skills and the changes in occupations and their distribution arising out of emerging national goals in a technological dynamic and socially aware society. Even in a stable company, the normal replacement process usually requires some estimate of the organization's future work force. In a large and dynamic organization the needs become considerably more compelling, and the task more difficult.

Human behaviorists have indicated that large and bureaucratic organizations have characteristics that have been deleterious to human growth and development. Such characteristics are: impersonality of interpersonal relations, few avenues for improving skills, limited opportunity for expressing opinions, emphasis on conformity and regulations, inflexibility of organizations to change, etc. Part of a human resources planning concept involves an enlightened viewpoint as regards employees, including: treating each person as a unique and valuable individual, providing avenues for improving skills, encouraging the growth and maturation of each individual, primary concern with human rather than physical systems, flexibility within the organization, etc.

The adoption of human resources planning in an organization should not only be based on a desirable social goal, it should also facilitate the organization's economic goals related to:

(1) The need for greater, more creative contributions to productivity in the face of rising costs and stiffer competition.

(2) The need for more broadly skilled managers at the top of the organization, and stable executive succession.

(3) The need to plan and assimilate changes in status, work, and relationships of employees.

The kinds of questions to which staffing planning is usually addressed include the following:

(1) What number of employees, by type, are needed to meet objectives?

(2) Are such employees available within the organization?

(3) What number of people, by type, must be recruited by time period?

(4) How should these employees be allocated to the various components of the organization?

(5) What is the best way to recruit and select the required personnel to assure the best quality for the positions available?

(6) What type of education and training is required to satisfy the needs of the organization and the individual?

(7) What kind of career program is available for each individual?

(8) How can the work be designed to provide for a desirable balance between productivity and employee satisfaction?

(9) How can the work environment be developed to provide maximum motivation for the employee and to coincide with the organization goals?

From the above discussion, certain principles are suggested.

(1) Management should not overlook the qualifications of its existing employees to fill anticipated work openings. It should think of its employees in terms of their potential rather than only in terms of their existing skills.

(2) Education and training should be thought of as being continuing processes, rather than one-time or spasmodic events.

(3) Human resources planning itself is a continuing activity. It must be sufficiently long-range to be able to provide the proper manpower resources in the right place, in the right amount, at the right time. Because all planning should be approximate in view of uncertainties, the manpower plan should be flexible and adaptable to changes in conditions.

(4) Each organization must tailor its staffing plan to its particular needs and planning process and policies.

(5) Human resources planning is highly dependent on good information. Consequently, a first consideration of the development of a planning program for staffing is the establishment of the informational base which will permit meaningful forecasting.

(6) Planning should not be performed in an ivory tower, but should involve all those affected. Involvement is necessary to assure all meaningful inputs, and to obtain acceptance of the plans.

(7) The plan should be subject to appraisal to determine its effectiveness and to strengthen the planning process.

(8) The planning should be action-oriented to accomplish specific tasks and to attain specific goals.

(9) The plan should emphasize broad and comprehensive goals, rather than minute and excessive details.

Some efforts are currently being made to improve human resources planning by use of a variety of computerized mathematical models. It appears that these efforts have either been of a research nature or are still being evaluated for effectiveness in an operational sense. The Federal Government, as the largest employer, has done some development work with various manpower planning models. The primary emphasis here has probably been in the Defense Department, where the dimensions and the nature of the planning problem differ to some significant degree from those of most other organizations.

Approaches to Computerization of the Personnel Process

Fragmented Approach. An approach often taken is to computerize particular existing phases of the personnel process in relative isolation from the rest of the process. Exhibit II illustrates such compartmentalization. Unfortunately, this approach impedes coordination and the achievement of commonality of objectives. Moreover, it necessitates considerable searching and analysis by the personnel staff. Data are scattered through many files (e.g., employee records, recruitment, education and training, payroll, medical, benefits, etc.). Further, there are frequently both considerable overlap and duplication of data and, perhaps more important, a not infrequent disparity between data which should coincide or relate. Finally, the files are frequently not up-to-date. Studies have indicated that organizations may have hundreds of separate and distinct personnel documents, and may record hundreds or thousands of different items of data on documents; some of the items of data are reported time and time again on different documents. As a result, the personnel staff has difficulty in accurately and quickly searching for data to provide answers, and it neglects important personnel activities, including human contacts, because of the pressures of handling clerical work.

Experience in countless computer installations has shown that the human factors have been the major retardants of computerization (rather than the technical problems of computers). It is therefore ironic that the personnel function is perhaps the single area of organizations in which most remains to be done in applying the computer. Even in the Department of Defense (DoD), where a unification of the three services has been a major goal for some years, there are significant dissimilarities between the personnel systems of the Army, Navy, and Air Force. There is a lack of integration between the three services' personnel systems—and even considerable segmentation within any one service (e.g., lack of coordination between military and civilian records). It is interesting that in the DoD—which is the largest user of computers and where much sophisticated work has been done with computers—fragmented personnel applications still exist. Of course, one must realize that the DoD's data processing involves millions of active and inactive military personnel and civilians.

Systems Approach. The opposite approach to computerization is to develop an overall plan for a personnel MIS. As it proves economically and technically feasible, particular phases of the MIS can be computerized in a planned sequence.

A model of a personnel information system is presented in Exhibit III. The system is designed within an overall plan; consequently,

Exhibit II

Fragmented Personnel Data Processing

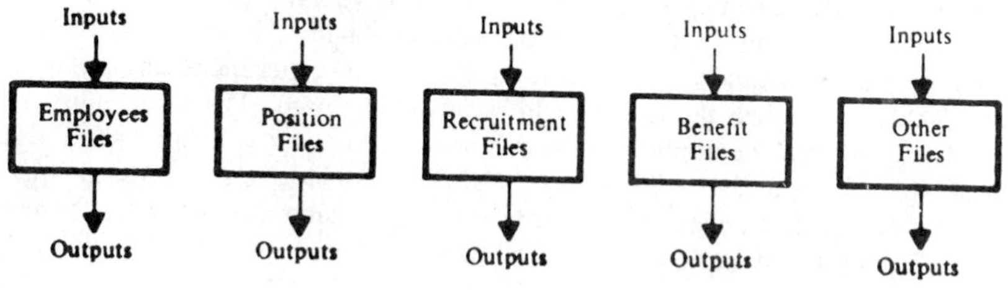

EXHIBIT III

INTEGRATED PERSONNEL INFORMATION SYSTEM

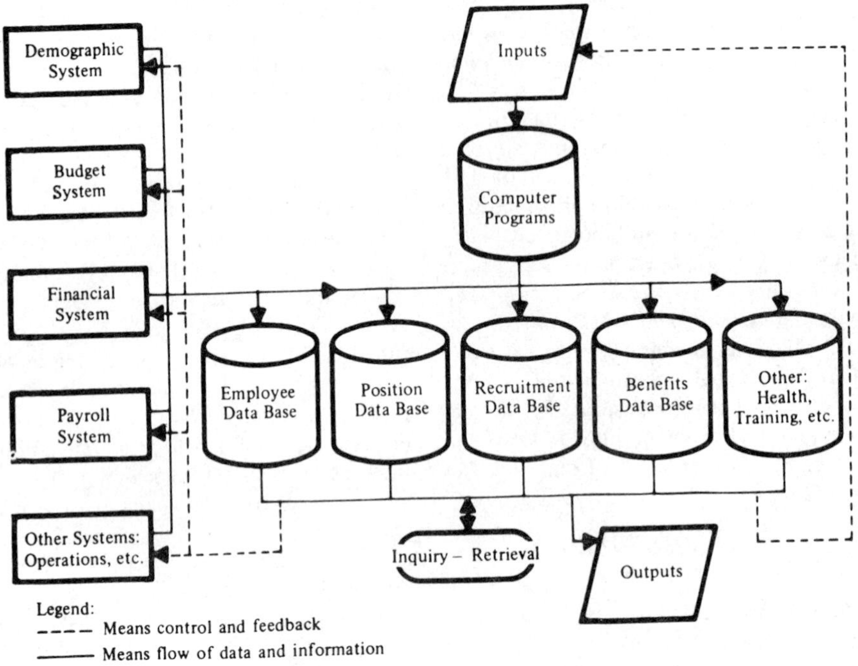

there is a high degree of coordination and commonality of goals. It is to be noted that there is a single stream of input data, through an array of appropriate programs. The several data bases are linked together for coordinated processing. Also, other related systems (such as the budget and financial systems) have clearly defined communication paths to and from the personnel system. Outputs from the system are available to administrators, personnel staff, and authorized employees. Provision is available for authorized personnel directly to interrogate and use the system via a remote data terminal.

There is need to view personnel within a total system, interrelated and interacting with the other systems—the financial and various operational systems. This approach entails integrating, by use of the systems approach, the multiple files (including employee records, recruitment, positions, benefits, etc.). It also aims at maintaining the records up-to-date, so that inquiries are answered with timely and accurate information. Such an approach should result in elimination of a great deal of duplication and inconsistencies in existing files.

If an effective computerized data system for personnel is to be developed, certain minimum essentials must be met. A personnel data base must be established which includes all data needs for making decisions, and for fulfilling legal and other report requirements. The data include facts about employees, such as: skills, personal history, employment record, benefits, etc. In addition, data about positions, the personnel budget (appropriations, authorizations, commitments, expenditures), as well as other relevant data can be included. Before inclusion in the data base, the data must be edited to assure accuracy, non-redundancy, and consistency. Provision must be made for updating the data, so that they reflect a status that is current and useful to the user. In addition, there must be adequate assurance that the data in the data base are available only to authorized individuals.

Since the data base usually entails consolidation and integration of formerly scattered and segmented files, it should provide information that is more pertinent and reliable than that previously used. Provision must be made to permit access to the integrated data base by those who formerly accessed the integrated files. The same data base can be tapped by all interested and authorized individuals, to serve their particular requirements. In addition, management can use the data base to monitor the personnel effort.

For the personnel manager, management-by-exception can be programmed for such ongoing problems as determining those employees for whom salary increases are overdue, determining which recommended pay changes are in excess of or below specified criteria, determining those employees whose pay levels are inconsistent with their performance appraisals, identifying personnel or organizational units that have excessive lost time, and indicating manpower requisitions that have remained unfilled for excessive periods of time, etc. In addition, management is in the position to make studies that were difficult, if not impossible, to make previously. Employee bargaining groups might want to know the specific costs if vacation allowances are extended an additional week for certain employees. It might be desirable to identify all jobs that will be open, in the next several years, due to retirements. Identification of recruiting sources that will lead to reduced costs and an increased quality and quantity of candidates could be facilitated.

Eventually, an organization's computerized data bank might be supplemented by having it interconnected with external data banks. For example, it would be possible to have computer communications with a cooperative industry-wide data bank, a network of public and private employment offices, or government entities. Such a broad computer network provides a basis for such operations as: a rapid job-man matching system, consolidation of manpower data, comprehensive salary surveys, etc.

The Federal Civil Service Commission (CSC) has made a study of the feasibility of developing a government-wide personnel system. The basic concept involves a central data bank for all Federal employees, doing away with the conventional personnel file folders in decentralized offices, and the use of remote data terminals for inquiry and answer purposes to personnel offices in the many Federal departments and agencies. The magnitude of such an effort is made clear by the Commission's estimate that it would take more than $50 million and five years' effort to implement such a comprehensive system. Of course, the system must provide for the millions of Federal civil servants, active and retired, as well as having provision for handling the thousands of job applicants. It was estimated that the current annual cost of about $75 million, for doing paperwork and preparing reports by current methods, would be reduced under the proposed new system to about $25 million per fiscal year. Thus, savings resulting from elimination of duplication and efficiencies in scale-of-operation were projected, which would recoup the implementation cost in the first year that the system was operative. At this writing, only limited progress has been made in moving towards such a grand-design system.

EDWARD TOMESKI, PH.D., Professor of Management, Fordham University, New York, New York and Barry College, Miami, Florida

KONRAD SADEK, MIS Consultant, World Vision International

Information References

"Employer Manpower Planning and Forecasting," Washington, D.C., U.S. Dept. of Labor, 1970.

Tomeski, Edward A. and Lazarus, Harold, "People-Oriented Computer Systems," New York, Van Nostrand Reinhold, 1975.

Tomeski, Edward A., Stephenson, George, and Man Yoon, B., "Behavioral Issues and the Computer," *Advanced Management Journal,* 1978.

Walker, James W., "Forecasting Manpower Needs," *Harvard Business Review,* March–April 1969.

Reference Cited

[1] Morton, J. E., "On the Evolution of Manpower Statistics," Kalamazoo, Mich., Upjohn Institute, 1969.

I

INCENTIVE SYSTEMS

The typical industrial employee on unmeasured day work is generally found to produce no more than 50% to 70% of what measurement would show to be a fair day's work. This low level of performance has provided management with a strong stimulus to establish **Incentive Systems** to increase productivity. As a result, a wide variety of systems and plans have been developed with the basic objective of increasing worker effectiveness and reducing unit labor costs. All of these plans can be classified into two major categories: (1) *non-financial plans;* and (2) *financial plans.*

Non-financial incentives are generally of a nature that appeal to an individual's emotions rather than his pocketbook. They include such things as pride in workmanship; recognition of achievement; patriotism; feeling of inclusion; gratitude; shame of poor performance; pride in superior performance; spirit of competition; and a host of other factors which tend to stimulate good performance. Certain of these motivating factors are inherently present in most industrial situations. By themselves, they cannot begin to create the strong pull of a financial incentive. However, they can help to make financial incentives more effective and palatable.

Financial incentive plans, in turn, may also be of two types—*indirect* or *direct.*

Indirect incentives include such things as equitable pay structures, merit increases, pension and profit-sharing plans, hospitalization programs, and other factors generally referred to as "fringe benefits." These indirect incentive benefits are definitely financial in nature. Unlike direct incentives, however, they apply on a company-wide basis and are not directly dependent upon the contribution of an individual or group.

Direct financial incentive plans provide an opportunity for higher pay through increased productivity or effectiveness. They are based upon the concept of plus pay for plus performance.

History. *Piece rates* constitute one of the oldest forms of direct financial incentives. This type of wage payment has been in existence for thousands of years and is still very commonly used today—particularly in the needle trades, foundries, and other specific industries. The modern concept of wage incentives, however, is closely associated with Frederick W. Taylor and his efforts in the late 1800s to develop a way of measuring "a fair day's work." While the principle of plus pay for plus performance is simplicity itself, the problem of measuring "normal performance" is extremely complex.

There is little question that direct financial incentive plans do provide a very strong incentive for increased productivity. A study made by the War Production Board during World War II showed that increases in productivity averaged about 60% when incentives were based upon engineered standards, and were applied on an individual basis [1]. Since many of these plans were installed somewhat hurriedly under the press of wartime production demands. it is likely that they underestimated the full increases to be obtained from incentives. It is not at all uncommon to find that productivity doubles when going from a straight hourly basis of payment to a soundly designed incentive plan.

The greatest single problem in the development of any wage incentive system is the determination of what constitutes a fair day's work. Up until late 1940s, the most commonly accepted means of establishing engineered time standards was the use of stop watch time study techniques. Other less objective methods include supervisory estimates and standards based on past performance. Since the early 1950s, the use of predetermined motion times and standard data based upon these systems has become quite general. Although predetermined time standards were almost unheard of prior to 1948, they were being used as a basis for work measurement by 72% of 302 companies surveyed by *Factory* magazine in 1959 [2]. (See PREDETERMINED MOTION TIMES.)

Application. Because of the difficulties encountered in developing fair and accurate time standards, most wage incentive plans were initially limited to the highly repetitive direct labor operations. As soon as some direct workers began to earn incentive bonuses, however, other direct workers on less repetitive jobs and indirect workers began to demand the opportunity to work on incentives as well. Unfortunately, a number of attempts were made by unqualified people to meet this strong demand for incentives on these types of activities. The loose standards and controls associated with these installations soon resulted in run-away earnings and this, in turn, led many managements arbitrarily to cut the rates. This, in turn, created many industrial relations problems. This was the era of the so-called "efficiency expert"—an era that industrial engineers are still trying to live down.

As work measurement techniques improved, however, along with improved incentive plans and wage administration practices, it became possible to extend the use of incentives to more and more of the jobbing types of operations and to a wide variety of indirect labor activities as well. In fact, incentives are now being applied to clerical, drafting, laboratory, and many other operations formerly thought to be too complex to measure with any degree of accuracy. Indeed, the decade starting in 1950 was characterized by a definite trend towards the application of incentives to all types of indirect labor activities.

Initial attempts to set up incentive plans for indirect labor frequently made use of indirect time standards for these activities. Material handlers, for example, were simply related to the number of production workers they served. Their incentive earnings were then tied to the incentive earnings of the production workers. In other cases, maintenance workers have received incentive bonuses based upon a minimum of equipment downtime. In actual fact, the maintenance men were busiest when the equipment was down and had little to do when everything was working smoothly. Paradoxes such as this, coupled with technical advances in work measurement techniques, have tended to result in indirect incentives based on the direct measurement of the work involved rather than the use of the ratios.

Types of Plans. There is a wide variety of incentive plans from which to choose. In the early days of wage incentive development, it was popular for individuals and consultants to develop unique incentive plans and then to associate their name with the plan. Some of the more widely known plans of this sort include the *Gantt* Task and Bonus, *Halsey* 50-50 Gain Sharing, *Rowan* Plan, *Bedaux* Plan, *Taylor* Differential Piece Rate Plan, and the like. The *Factory* survey previously referred to indicated, however, that by the beginning of the decade of the 1960s most of these unique plans had gradually passed out of the picture. Today, probably 80% of the employees covered by incentives are covered by one of two types—*piecework* plans or *standard minute (standard hour)* plans. The standard minute (hour) is by far the most popular. It covers 55% of all employees in the plants surveyed. Straight piecework plans cover 25% of all employees. Of the remaining 20%, 16% are covered by a plan that pays the worker less than one per cent bonus for each one per cent increase in production. The other 4% are covered by a variety of other plans.

In all of the early incentive plans, there was no provision for a minimum, guaranteed hourly rate of pay. The individual was simply paid whatever he earned. Today, however, all incentive plans make some provision for a minimum, guaranteed rate of pay.

Piecework Plans. A piece rate is usually expressed in dollars and cents per piece produced. Its great virtue is that it is easy to understand. By multiplying the number of pieces produced by the piece rate, the employee immediately knows how much he (she) has earned. Initially, rates were frequently set on the basis of estimates and past performance. As a result, the rates were set without regard to standard time as such. But, in fact, a piece rate is actually made up of two separate and independent factors. One is the *time* required to produce a unit of work—the other is the *base rate of pay.* When these two factors are multiplied together, a piece rate is obtained. Thus, two jobs that take exactly the same time to perform will have a different piece rate if one job is performed by a higher-rated class of labor and the other by a lower labor grade. Since every piece rate changes whenever a general wage increase is granted, this introduces an administrative problem.

Standard Minute Plans. In order to get away from these problems but still retain the simplicity of the piece-rate plan, a standard minute plan was developed. (Standard hour plans are also commonly used. The only difference between the two plans is the unit of measure—the use of hours in one and the use of minutes in the other.) Basically, a standard minute rate is a piece rate expressed in terms of time rather than in dollars and cents. The bonus earnings of an individual working under either plan are exactly the same. In both cases, they are directly proportional to output. By having the rates expressed in terms of minutes, it is possible to make better use of the standards for other purposes such as planning and scheduling the work and the like. A standard minute plan also helps to draw a clear distinction between the base rates of pay and the time standard for a job. Further, the rates are not affected in any way by wage rate increases or adjustments. (See STANDARD MINUTE SYSTEM.)

The Halsey Plan. This plan is typical of incentive plans that pay the worker something less than a one per cent increase in pay for a one per cent increase in production. A common version of the Halsey Plan paid the worker one half of one per cent for each additional one per cent increase in production over one hundred per cent. This plan was designed in the late 1800s when time standards were frequently established by estimates or past performance. Since estimating usually results in more liberal time standards, this plan tended to compensate for the looseness in the time standards. In addition, management also reasoned that when production was increased, the wear and tear on the equipment was increased. It was felt, therefore, that by sharing the increase in productivity, management would be compensated for the greater depreciation on the facilities.

Measured Day Work. This plan had long been used in the automotive industry and gradually attracted more attention from other industries. As the name implies, the workers under this plan work at a day rate or hourly rate of pay. The work they produce, however, is carefully measured and controlled. Individual or group performance indexes are determined in much of the same manner as they are under an incentive program. The basic difference, however, is that the workers are paid a fixed rate for the day, regardless of whether their performance is above or below one hundred per cent.

A variation of the measured day work plan does provide for changes in the base rate of pay for a given job based upon the performance index of the worker. For example, workers performing at a rate below 90% may receive the lowest base rate for the job. Workers performing between 90% and 100% receive the next highest rate; those between 100% and 110%, the third highest rate; and so on. The number of steps in the base rate usually varies from three to five. The performance index is calculated monthly or quarterly, and the base rates are changed whenever there is a change in the performance range. Used in this way, the plan definitely provides a financial incentive.

A more common application of the plan, however, does not provide for differential base rates keyed to performance. Under this version of the plan, the worker has no financial incentive to produce at a rate higher than 100%. However, since satisfactory performance is usually one of the conditions of employment, the worker has an incentive to maintain production at a satisfactory level to insure continuance of employment. In many cases where this plan is used, there is no strict definition of "satisfactory performance." In other cases, satisfactory performance is clearly defined as 100% of standard plus or minus 5%. In other words, the minimum acceptable performance is 95% of the established standard.

This type of plan appears to be best suited to progressive assembly line operations where the speed of the line is mechanically controlled. The line is then manned with the proper number of operators and each individual must keep up with the line or be replaced. This is one reason why the plan had such wide acceptance in the automotive industry. The plan has also had wide application to a variety of industries, however, and is not by any means limited to paced or controlled operations. The chief virtue of the plan is that it does provide management with a measure and control over the standard hours of work produced without tying this control to an incentive wage payment plan. In this way, management can obtain the advantages of work measurement and control without the disadvantages of wage inequities which incentive plans frequently produce.

Individual and Group Plans. Most early applications of wage incentives were made on an individual basis. An individual was paid in direct proportion to what he produced. He was, in effect, placed in business for himself. There is no question but that this form of incentive provides the greatest stimulus to production. There are, however, many cases where a job cannot be performed by a single individual but must be performed by a team. In other cases, team work is to be encouraged rather than individual performance. For these reasons, group systems of incentive payment have been developed.

A wage incentive group is made up of a number of workers who pool their production.

The method of computing and distributing the earnings of the group is known as the group system of incentive payment. The group system is not another type of incentive plan like the Halsey Plan, for example. Rather, it is a concept of incentive payment that can be used in conjunction with any of the common incentive plans.

The group system is most applicable under either one of the following conditions:

(1) There is a community of interest among the members of the group.

(2) The work is such that it is impossible to measure the contribution of the individual member accurately.

The most common example of community of interest is the assembly line. In this case, the work has been broken down into a number of equal and specialized tasks. By performing a particular part of the work well, each individual on the line permits the other members of the group to do their work well and the output of the group as a whole rises. In this case, individual incentives are impossible to apply since any one worker cannot proceed at a rate of production different from any other member of the group. They *must* work as a group.

In other cases, such as shipping and receiving operations, plant maintenance operations, and the like, it is difficult to measure the output of individuals separately since they work essentially as a team. The only practical method of incentive payment in these cases is a group basis. Following are some of the major advantages claimed for the group system of payment:

(1) Better cooperation between individual workers is achieved.

(2) Need for supervision is reduced.

(3) Operator training time is reduced.

(4) Indirect labor may be included and controlled by the group.

(5) Timekeeping is simplified.

(6) Quality of product is improved.

(7) Wages are fairly distributed.

The major disadvantages of the group are:

(1) Exceptional ability is penalized.

(2) It is difficult to handle jobs that are still incomplete by the end of the pay period.

(3) No check on individual performance is provided.

(4) No check on time standards for individual jobs is provided.

(5) It is difficult to find the right man for group leader.

Acceptance. Work measurement and wage incentives are, along with methods analysis, among the oldest techniques used in industrial management. To determine application trends, *Industrial Engineering,* the journal of the American Institute for Industrial Engineers, in collaboration with Patton Consultants, Inc., conducted a broad survey in 1977 among industrial companies in the United States and Canada. It then compared the results of its survey with the findings of one conducted by *Factory* magazine 18 years earlier, published in that magazine's April, 1959 issue [2]. A detailed report on its survey and the comparison with the earlier one was published in the July, 1977 issue of *Industrial Engineering* [3].

Of the nearly 1,500 usable responses to the IE-Patton Survey, 89% reported that they were using work measurement and 4% said they had wage incentive applications. The 785 respondents to the *Factory* survey reported 71% work measurement and 51% wage incentive applications. Twenty percent of the *Factory* respondents used work measurements for performance measurement only, while 53% of the IE-Patton respondents used work measurement to measure performance ony.

These data indicate a 25% increase in work measurement applications, largely for use in performance measure or measured day-work. Also indicated is a 7% decrease in wage incentive applications during the eighteen-year period—from 51 to 44% of those who participated in the surveys.

However, in the in-depth portion of its two-part survey [4], the IE-Patton study found that those plants that had wage incentives reported a balanced increase in coverage and in favorable attitudes toward incentives. In the words of the report, "The latter data tend to tell us that there is no significant trend toward disenchantment with wage incentives . . . A further significant related factor is that a shortage of industrial engineering personnel is the major factor in deterring an increase in wage incentive applications." Significant tables from the IE-Patton survey are reproduced as Exhibits I through IV.

The most significant variation in the use of incentives is by industry. Petroleum plants, for example, make little use of incentives. In these plants, the operators have little or no control over the quantity of product produced, which is largely fixed by the equipment and the process. On the other hand, textile and apparel

EXHIBIT I

EXTENT OF USE AND TYPES OF USAGE OF WORK MEASUREMENT

Total responses:	*Abbreviated survey*	*Depth survey*	*Total*
Use work measurement	88%	94%	89%
for direct labor	85%		
for indirect labor	37%		
for wage incentives	42%	56%	44%
Responses, manufacturing industries:			
Use work measurement	93%	95%	93%
for wage incentives	47%	59%	50%
for performance measurement	64%	41%	60%
for estimating and costing	75%	89%	78%
for production scheduling	56%	55%	56%

Source: *Industrial Engineering*

EXHIBIT II

USE OF WORK MEASUREMENT AND INCENTIVES BY SIZE OF COMPANY

How many are employed at this location?

Number of employees	*Percent using work measurement*	*Percent using wage incentives*
Up to 99	64%	55%
100–249	97%	48%
250–499	95%	60%
500–999	95%	55%
1000–2500	94%	57%
Over 2500	94%	59%
Not answered	100%	33%
Total	94%	56%

Source: *Industrial Engineering*

plants and fabricated metal products plants are extremely high in incentive applications. In manufacturing industries, in the IE-Patton findings, 95% use work measurement, and 59% have wage incentive applications. Among the non-manufacturing respondents, 69% reported work measurement aplications, but only one company in the in-depth group had a wage incentive plan. As shown in Exhibit II, with the exception of plants of less than 100 employees, work measurement is uniformly high among respondents to the in-depth questionnaire. However, the smallest size plants match the larger ones in applications of wage incentives.

Multiple-factor Incentives. In many process-industry plants, it is difficult to provide an incentive which is based upon increased individual productivity, for reasons mentioned in connection with the petroleum industry. However, the operators can have an important influence on the quality or the yield of the process. Therefore, instead of basing incentive solely on the single factor of production, or pieces produced, these plans give consideration to several factors. The most common factors are *quality, yield,* and *production quantity.* Yield standards may be established as a percentage of finished product weight to raw material

EXHIBIT III

PURPOSES FOR WHICH WORK MEASUREMENT IS USED

	Percent
Wage incentives	59%
Estimating and costing	89
Performance measurement only	41
Production scheduling	55
Machine loading	52
Short-interval control	18
Manning and capacity planning	2
Operations control	1.5
Budgeting	1
Machine and method justification	1
Labor control	1
Wage rate (merit increases)	1
All other	1

Percentages of uses add up to more than 100 because of multiple uses. Applications of wage incentives and of performance measurement only add up to 100%—59 and 41%, respectively. Source: *Industrial Engineering*.

weight. Quality may sometimes be measured not by the final product quality characteristics but by such measures as the variation permitted to take place in the temperature of the process. The different factors may also be allocated different degrees of importance. For example, yields are the most significant or controllable factor in many processes. In this case, the factor of yield may be assigned a weight of three, while quality and quantity are only assigned weights of one each. Obviously, many variations of factors and weights to be assigned to each factor can be developed to fit specific applications.

Another characteristic tending to discourage the use of incentives in such industries as petroleum is that the labor costs are generally a small portion of the total cost of manufacturing. Utilization of equipment may be far more important than utilization of labor.

In those industries where incentives are used to a high degree, labor costs normally form a very significant part of the cost of goods manufactured. In addition, the process is such that the workers can have a strong influence on the quantity of the product produced. A good example is the needle trades industry.

Plant Wide Plans. The idea of a plant-wide incentive plan applicable to all employees has had a great attraction to management for some time. The time required to establish and maintain the time standards required for a conventional incentive plan is quite sizeable, frequently equal to one per cent of the total labor cost. In addition, the time required to install a new plan often seems painfully slow to an impatient manager. For these and other rea-

EXHIBIT IV

CATEGORIES OF EMPLOYEES COVERED BY WORK MEASUREMENT

	Percent of Respondents			
% of hours worked that are measured	*Up to 10%*	*10–70*	*70–90*	*90–100*
Direct (production)	3%	20%	34%	43%
Indirect and service:				
Material handling	15	28	21	36
Receiving and shipping	8	28	26	38
Tool and die service	16	16	24	44
Quality control and inspection	19	29	16	36
Housekeeping	16	32	13	39
Maintenance	15	24	15	46
Clerical, shop	13	23	15	39
Clerical, general offices	44	31	12	13
Engineers and technicians	20	20	20	40
First-line supervisors	17	25	8	50
Assemble leaders and setup	100	—	—	—
Stores	—	—	—	100

Source: *Industrial Engineering*

sons, many attempts have been made in industry to develop simplified, overall incentive plans. Two of the best-known of this type are the Scanlon and Rucker plans. (See SCANLON PLAN OF GROUP INCENTIVES and RUCKER PLAN OF GROUP INCENTIVES.)

The Scanlon Plan. In essence, the Scanlon Plan can be reduced to three elements:

(1) Suggestion system.

(2) Plant-wide incentive scheme.

(3) Profit-sharing plan.

There are no individual suggestion awards, and this part of the plan is administered by a joint union-management committee. The Scanlon Plan bases the incentive scheme on the value added to production against an historically established labor cost ratio. As the labor percentage of the value added to production decreases, a plant-wide bonus is earned. A bonus reserve is established to help stabilize monthly fluctuations.

The profit-sharing feature differs from the usual profit-sharing plan in that the basis for the plan is cost reduction, over which the employees have some control, and not profits, which are heavily dependent upon prices and other factors beyond their control. As a result, workers may be receiving bonuses when the company is losing money or not receiving any bonus when profits are high. At the heart of the Scanlon Plan lies the principle of union-management cooperation. It has achieved some success in a few special cases where both union and management were desperate for a solution to keep a company in business.

The Rucker Plan. The Rucker Plan is quite similar to the Scanlon Plan in several respects. It is a program for group incentives that uses day-to-day employee participation and broad coverage to develop cost reductions and improve profits. It is backed by a precise measurement of productivity gains in money terms (not physical units). It recognizes and reinforces those gains with an equitable, automatic method of sharing them between the participants (added pay) and the company (added margin).

The measure of productivity used is called *economic productivity*—the output of *value added by manufacture* for each dollar of input of *payroll costs.* Value added by manufacture is the difference between sales income from goods produced, and the costs of the materials, supplies, and outside services consumed in the production and delivery of that output. Payroll costs are all employment costs paid to, because of, or on behalf of the employee group measured.

Thus, economic productivity may measure the financial effectiveness of a plant's hourly-rated employees, its total employment, or some blend of hourly and salaried people. Flexible extra pay programs may be designed, using the principles mentioned here for plant people only, for a mixture of plant and office people, for office people only, or for managers only.

Since the objective of the Rucker Plan is to maximize the output of value added for a given payroll input, opportunity for added earnings to the participants and added margin to the company comes from the following:

Improved use of materials.
Improved use of supplies.
Improved output per man-hour.
Improved product quality.
Improved production methods.
Improved machinery and equipment.
Improved service to customers.
Reduced absenteeism and turnover.
Better training of new employees.
Skill upgrading for older employees.
Improved safety performance.

Whereas the conventional "piecework" or "standard hour" type of individual or small group incentive based on physical productivity usually covers only 40–65% of a plant's work-force, this program is intended to cover *everyone*—including the indirect plant people, supervision, planning and scheduling people, etc.

Summary. The use of wage incentives will, no doubt, continue to be a somewhat controversial subject. More recently, a number of behavioral scientists have proposed alternative means for motivating employees and improving productivity. Worker participation, job enrichment, and job enlargement are some of the approaches advocated by McGregor, Herzberg, Gellerman and others, and, latterly, the Skinnerian reinforcement techniques advocated by strict behaviorists. All of these proposals have received a great deal of attention in management literature, because all managers clearly recognize the need for motivating workers and are familiar with the shortcomings of conventional techniques, such as wage incentives. While much has been written about theories of motivation, it would appear that limited pratical results have been accomplished to date. It is the present writer's position that until greater progress is achieved by the behavioral scientists in developing practical approaches to increasing productivity by improved forms of motivation, wage incentives will continue to be widely used. (See HUMAN RELATIONS IN INDUSTRY.)

The attitude of organized labor toward incentives varies. The United Automotive Workers (UAW) is generally against the use of incentives. The United Steelworkers (USW) generally favors incentives. A few years ago the latter recently won a major arbitration case which forced the steel companies to provide wage incentive opportunities for maintenance workers.

The major benefits of incentives from management's viewpoint are:

(1) Reduced labor costs.

(2) An aid to supervision.

(3) Improved employee morale.

(4) A basis for planning and scheduling work.

(5) Increasing plant capacity.

If a company does not have a good industrial engineering staff skilled in developing engineered time standards and in administering wage incentive plans, it would be well advised *not* to make use of wage incentive plans. In these cases, the gains to be made in productivity will probably be more than offset by runaway wages, inequities in earnings, poor quality, and increased grievances. On the other hand, companies with experienced industrial engineering staffs, sophisticated management, and labor-intensive products will find it exceedingly difficut to be competitive without the use of incentives.

The mistake most frequently made by management in the administration of a wage incentive plan is the failure properly to maintain the plan once it is installed. The major problem areas in connection with incentives are these:

(1) Keeping the time standards properly maintained to prevent inequities and loose rates.

(2) Eliminating grievances due to inequities in the standards.

(3) Maintaining a high incentive coverage.

(4) Keeping to a minimum the cost of administering the incentive plan.

WILLIAM M. AIKEN, President, H. B. Maynard and Company, Inc., Management Consultants, Pittsburgh, Pennsylvania

Information References

Maynard, H. B., "Industrial Engineering Handbook," New York, McGraw-Hill, 3rd ed., 1971.

Rath, Arthur, A., "The Case for Individual Incentives: Management's Most Potent Motivational Tool," *Personnel Journal*, October 1960.

Schwinger, Pinhas, "Wage Incentive Systems," New York, Halsted Press, 1975.

Society for Advancement of Management, relevant publications.

References Cited

[1] Hummel, Joseph O. P. and Nickerson, John W., in "Industrial Engineering Handbook," Maynard, H. B., ed., Sect. 6, Chap. 1, New York, McGraw-Hill, 1963.

[2] "Wage Incentives and Work Measurement Today," *Factory*, April 1959.

[3] Rice, Robert S., Professional Engineer, Atlanta, Ga., in collaboration with Patton Consultants, Inc., Des Plains, Ill. and the American Institute of Industrial Engineers, "Survey of Work Measurement and Wage Incentives," *Industrial Engineering*, July 1977, pp. 20–31.

[4] In essence there were two surveys. One, an "abbreviated" survey, asked only, "Are you using work measurement, and if so, for what purposes?" The second, the "in-depth" survey, asked the same questions and many more.

Cross References: *Guaranteed Annual Wage; Lincoln Incentive Management Plan; Motion and Time Study; Rucker Plan of Group Incentives; Scanlon Plan of Group Incentives; Scientific Management: "Taylorism"; Standard Minute System; Work Measurement.*

INCOME, EXPENDITURE, AND WEALTH: Concepts and Sources of Data

The "Statistical Abstract of the United States" presents data on gross national product (GNP), rates of economic growth, national and personal income, saving and investment, money income, poverty, national and personal wealth, and fixed business capital. The data on **Income and Expenditure** measure two aspects of the United States economy. One aspect relates to the national income and product accounts (NIPA), a summation reflecting the entire complex of the nation's economic income and output and the interaction of its major components; the other relates to the distribution of money income to families and individuals, or consumer income.

The primary source for data on GNP, national and personal income, gross savings and investment, and business capital is the *Survey of Current Business,* published monthly, with supplements, by the Department of Commerce, Bureau of Economic Analysis (BEA). Detailed historical data and a discussion of the conceptual framework of NIPA and of the statistical sources and methods used to derive the estimates appear in *The National Income and Product Accounts of the United States, 1929–74,* a Supplement to the *Survey of Current Business,* and Part I of the January 1976 *Survey.*

Sources of income distribution data are the decennial censuses of population and the Current Population Survey, both products of the Bureau of the Census. Annual data on income of families, individuals, and households, by income class, are presented in *Current Population Reports—Consumer Income,* series P–60.

Data on individuals' saving and assets are published by the Board of Governors of the Federal Reserve System in the quarterly *Flow of Funds Accounts;* and detailed information on personal wealth is published periodically by the Internal Revenue Service (IRS) in *Statistics of Income,* Supplemental Report, *Personal Wealth.*

Gross National Product is the total national output of goods and services valued at market prices. GNP can be viewed in terms of expenditure categories which comprise purchases of goods and services by consumers and government, gross private domestic investment, and net exports of goods and services. The goods and services included are largely those bought for final use (excluding illegal transactions) in the market economy. A number of inclusions, however, represent imputed values (estimates of "income in kind"), the most important of which is rental value of owner-occupied dwellings. GNP, in this broad context, measures the output attributable to the factors of production—labor and property—supplied by United States residents. GNP differs from "national income" mainly in that GNP includes allowances for depreciation and for indirect business taxes (such as sales and excise taxes). *Gross domestic product* is GNP minus gross product originating outside the United States. (See Exhibit I, top.)

National Income is the aggregate of labor and property earnings which arise in the current production of goods and services by the nation's economy. It is the sum of employee compensation, proprietors' income, rental income, net interest, and corporate profits. Thus, it measures the total factor costs of the goods and services produced by the economy. Earnings include direct taxes on earnings.

Capital Consumption Adjustment for corporations and nonfarm sole proprietorships and partnerships is the difference between capital consumption (i.e., depreciation charges and accidental damage to fixed business capital) claimed on income tax returns and capital consumption allowances that are measured at straightline depreciation, consistent service lives, and replacement cost. The tax return data are valued at historical costs and reflect changes over time in service lives and depreciation patterns as permitted by tax regulations. *Inventory valuation adjustment* represents the difference between the book value of inventories used up in production and the cost of replacing them.

Personal Income is the current income received by persons from all sources minus contributions for social insurance. Classified as "persons" are individuals (including owners of unincorporated enterprises), nonprofit institutions, private trust funds, and private noninsured health and welfare funds. Personal income includes transfers (payments not resulting from current production) from Government and business such as social security benefits, military pensions, etc., but excludes transfers among persons. Also included are important nonmonetary types of income—chiefly, estimated net rental value to owner-occupants of their homes, the value of services furnished without payment by financial intermediaries, and the value of food and fuel produced and consumed on farms.

Disposable Personal Income is personal income less personal tax and nontax payments. It is the income available to persons for spending and saving. Personal tax and nontax payments are tax payments (net of refunds) by persons (except personal contributions for social insurance) that are not chargeable to business expense, and certain personal payments to general government that are treated like taxes. Personal taxes include income, estate and gift, and personal property taxes. Nontax payments include passport fees, fines and penalties, donations, and tuitions and fees paid to schools, etc.

Distribution of Money Income to Families and Individuals. Money income statistics are based on data collected in various field surveys of income conducted since 1936. Since 1947, the Bureau of the Census has collected the data on an annual basis and published them in *Current Population Reports,* series P–60. In each of the surveys, enumerators interview representative samples of the population with respect to income received during the previous year. Money income as defined by the Bureau of the Census differs from the BEA concept of "personal income" (see above). Money income is

EXHIBIT I

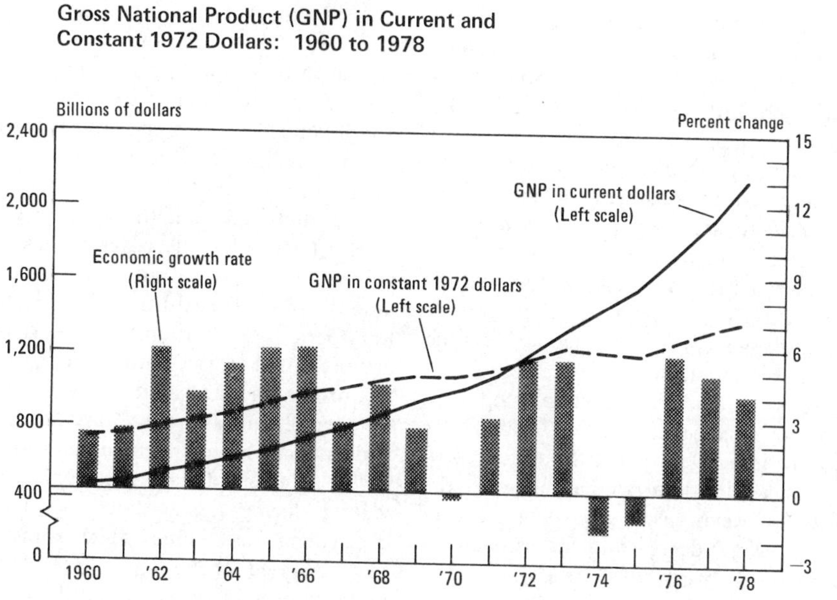

Source: Chart by U.S. Bureau of the Census. Data from U.S. Bureau of Economic Analysis.

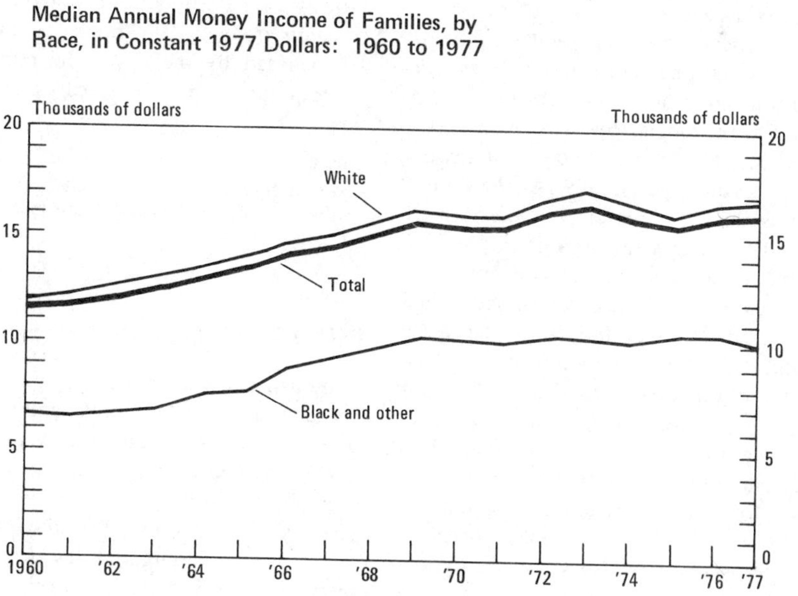

Source: U.S. Bureau of the Census.

SOURCE: Statistical Abstract of the United States

income before the deduction of income taxes and social security taxes unless otherwise specified in the individual tables. *Nonmoney items of income,* such as wages received in kind, the value of food and fuel produced and consumed on farms, the net rental value of owner-occupied homes, the property income received by life insurance companies, and the value of the services of banks and other financial intermediaries rendered to persons without the assessment of specific charges, *are not included.* None of the aggregate income concepts (gross national product, national income, or personal income) is exactly comparable with money income, although personal income is the closest. (See Exhibit I, bottom.)

In 1976, the method of collecting and processing money income data for 1975 and later years was revised. Data for 1974 were reprocessed to make the data comparable with the data for 1975. Revisions to the 1974 data resulted in an *overall* decrease in the estimate of persons living in poverty by 3.7% (24.3 to 23.4 million) and an increase in the estimate of median family income by 0.5% ($12,836 to $12,902). Differences within most subgroups, however, are more pronounced. For example, family money income for Black and other races (excluding White) increased by 3.8%.

Poverty. Unless otherwise specified, poverty-level statistics represent measures of *money income* and are based on a "poverty index" first developed by the Social Security Administration (SSA) in 1964 and modified by a Federal Interagency Committee in 1969. At the core of this index is the 1961 Economy Food Plan designed by the Department of Agriculture. This index provides a range of income cutoffs or "poverty income thresholds" adjusted by such factors as family size, sex and age of the family head, number of children under age eighteen, and farm-nonfarm residence. Until 1969, annual revisions of these levels were based on price changes of items in the economy food plan. In 1969, two changes were made: (1) SSA levels for nonfarm families were retained for the base year 1963, but annual adjustments in the levels were to be based on changes in the Consumer Price Index rather than on economy food plan costs, and (2) farm levels were raised from 70 to 85% of the corresponding nonfarm level.

Personal and National Wealth. Personal wealth estimates, issued by the IRS, are based on a sample of Federal estate tax returns which must be filed for deceased persons. Estimates are weighted to adjust for age, sex, and "social class" (as determined by IRS through insurance holdings). Gross estate is the gross value of all assets, including the full face value of life insurance (reduced by policy loans), before reduction by the amount of debts. Total assets are obtained by using the cash value of the insurance policy. Net worth is one's level of worth after all debts have been removed.

The national wealth data are intended chiefly to indicate the order of magnitudes involved and to permit rough comparisons among types of wealth and of the growth over long periods. Definitions and analytical details are presented in the source publication.

Current and Constant Dollars. Figures in a number of tables in the *Statistical Abstract* are expressed in both current dollars and constant dollars. Current dollar figures reflect prices prevailing during the specified period. Constant dollar figures are values which eliminate the effect of price changes and are derived from price indexes based on a specified period. The constant dollar values may be obtained by dividing current dollar values for a given period by related price indexes for the same period.

The implicit price deflator for GNP is the ratio of GNP in current dollars to GNP in constant dollars. The money income statistics are deflated by means of the consumer price index prepared by the Bureau of Labor Statistics.

Cross References: *Business Intelligence: Sources of Information; Economics; Statistical Abstract of the United States.*

INDUSTRIAL DESIGN

Industrial Designers are employed by industry, commerce, government, and institutions to plan and design products, very often their collateral marketing aids such as packaging, and even the environments in which products and services are marketed. For the purchaser and or the user, the industrial designer's objective is to create a design that provides maximum human satisfaction, both esthetic and functional. For the client, most often a manufacturer, the professional designer works to create a design that will achieve maximum consumer acceptance and commercial success.

Essentially, industrial designers are concerned with the *human* aspects of machine-made objects and mass services. Most obvious of these is visual appeal and appropriateness: the psychological effects of form, proportion, materials, finish, texture, and color. But equally important to the designer are such factors as convenience, utility, safety, maintenance, and cost to the manufacturer, distributor, and user. Thus, the designer must work closely with engineering, research, marketing, and other management units to achieve this coordinated result.

Product design was for many years, and continues to be, the basic activity of the profession. But today, more and more frequently, the industrial designer is called upon to consider all of a company's physical aspects that may be seen by its public and influence their use of its products and services. Corporations, institutions, and other organizations now recognize that good will and market success are influenced not only by the actual products and services, both consumer and industrial, but also by any or all of the following: packaging; graphics communications design including corporate identity; interiors of offices, showrooms, and retail outlets; displays; trucks; company signs; even stationery, office forms, and employee uniforms—and in addition to these, the very environment in which the company operates.

The purpose and end result of this increasingly comprehensive use of design—usually called a corporate design program—is to create a recognizable and consistent corporate personality which will inspire confidence in the company's products and services, as well as faith in the company itself. In effect, the cumulative impact of the company's presentations can be considerably increased. For these reasons, industrial design becomes both a vital tool of marketing, and a means to effect both short- and long-term planning.

The designer is modern society's version of the artist-craftsman who preceded the Industrial Revolution. Today, most industrial designers are graduates of degree programs in colleges, universities, or professional art schools. They sometimes have engineering training as well, and are increasingly adding marketing courses to their education, either during school or after graduation. Such training allows them to speak the language of management, engineers, and production and marketing people, to know materials and manufacturing processes, and to be pragmatically familiar with consumer needs and desires and marketing-distribution factors. Industrial designers like to think of themselves as the consumer's advocate in our industrial/marketing society.

History of Industrial Design. Industrial design as we know it was founded in the late 1920s on the eve of the Great Depression. Until that time, the artist/designer's role in commerce and industry was marginal and decorative. There were designers, working on their own, who had developed important products, but in the early days, paid-for design usually meant adding "tassels and ginger bread," painting flowers on products, or carving decorations into furniture.

Around that time, a small group of young men, trained in several different disciplines but fired with the urge to enter industry and influence public taste, foresaw the need for a more serious approach to design in a competitive marketing economy. Shortly before the crash of 1929, Walter Dorwin Teague, Henry Dreyfuss, Raymond Loewy, and a handful of other pioneers began to function as design consultants to industrial clients. The Depression, interestingly, did not stifle the new profession, but encouraged manufacturers to turn to design as a new marketing tool to improve sales. Results rewarded their hopes: the demand for salable design increased, and new industrial design talent appeared from related fields such as architecture, stage design, and advertising design.

The World Fairs of the 1930s gave an important boost to industrial design: widely publicized, these events gave designers a stage on which to display their talents. Another important boost came from the establishment of design departments in the large mail order houses and automobile companies.

Although World War II brought the development of industrial design to a temporary halt as American industry devoted its major effort to supply military needs, 1945 brought a new period of rapid growth. The return of peacetime production brought an economic boom and fierce competition in an exploding economy. New economic and cultural patterns emerged: more leisure time; more discretionary income; and greater public emphasis on good taste and the refinements of living. The mass communications media—and particularly the new visual medium of television—spread the news of these cultural changes. These powerful influences combined to create new patterns of consumption and new marketing potentials in which design played a more visible and prominent role.

Range and Scope of Industrial Design Practice. The practice of modern industrial design continues to place major emphasis on products, with consumer items ranging from fountain pens to small appliances to automobiles, while capital and industrial products are as diverse as milling machines and farm machinery.

The designer is responsible not only for the development of new products and the redesign of old products, but also for the conception of entire lines, where all units have a family resemblance and provide a range of functions, features, and costs to fill the various requirements of different consumers in a marketplace that continues to become more segmented each year.

More and more, too, many design projects are essentially the creation of programs or systems. Some programs, for example, will allow for the development of a continually evolving line of products, both for the present market and for future needs. Other systems designs will give architects and planners the basic components that permit a wide latitude in designs for store fronts or commercial buildings.

Military contracts frequently include provisions for the services of industrial designers, who function as specialists in human factors. (See HUMAN ENGINEERING (HUMAN FACTORS ENGINEERING).) Designers have participated in the development of military vehicles, naval combat vessels, and instrumentation for missile systems as well as other hardware and environments for the military establishment. In addition to this activity, other governmental agencies and departments have also utilized the designer's services in such projects as the design of foreign trade fairs and in technical assistance programs to expand the commerce and industries of underdeveloped countries.

Packaging, too, is involving industrial designers more today than before, for several reasons. Whereas package design originally involved graphic labelling of existing stock containers, today, shape, construction, and opening and closing and reuse functions are a vital part of the packaging solution, per se. Also, the package is now a significant marketing tool, integrated much more completely with the product or the service it contains, protects, communicates about, and functions for. These new industrial and consumer needs and requirements have dictated the use of new materials, manufacturing concepts and distribution methods. The industrial designers' capabilities fill this role with increasing frequency.

Many industrial design consulting offices are also active in architecture, interior design, and display. Stores, showrooms, offices, plants, and other corporate facilities that affect the marketing of products and the client's public image are often designed by industrial designers in collaboration with architects and space planners, to coordinate the total corporate look.

Organization of Industrial Design Offices. Today by far the greatest number of industrial designers work for organizations as members of internal staffs. Probably the majority of these internal organizations range from four to six (small) to fifteen to twenty (larger), with several major companies such as automobile companies and large manufacturers like GE having staffs that may total a hundred or more.

A few consultant offices also reach this figure, but most constultant offices have under ten professional people, and include a large number of one to three-person units. The number of internal staffs will probably continue to grow, but the role of the consultant will continue to be significant.

Advocates of corporate design departments list the following advantages: (1) Corporate design staffs develop maximum familiarity with their company's structure and operations; (2) build a more complete knowledge of their specific area of industry; (3) give their total attention to one company's problems; (4) maintain better communication with all units of the corporation; (5) inspire the confidence of management in a familiar staff; (6) encourage integration of the design function into the corporate structure; (7) may cost less if design requirements are constant and permit long-term budgeting.

Advocates of consultant industrial design services cite the following advantages: The consultant (1) brings to the client the broadest possible background, based on experience not in one manufacturing or distribution organization, but in a broad cross-section of industry; (2) takes a broader and more objective view of corporate problems, and is less likely to be influenced by internal politics; (3) brings a fresh point of view, unrestricted by traditional approaches to problems; (4) has wider, less parochial marketing experience; (5) can absorb extra workload, deadlines, and/or kinds of work the internal group cannot do (such as graphics), or is not staffed or scheduled to absorb; (6) allows a corporation to retain the services of a fully staffed, fully equipped and diversified design organization which the corporation often cannot afford to maintain within the company structure.

Design consultants are generally engaged on a flat-fee-per-project basis, but retainers—either monthly fees plus added-on charges for time and expenses, or an annual all-inclusive budget—are also frequent. Sometimes designers enter joint-ventures or work on a royalty arrangement based on a percentage of the gross income of the specific product's sales.

No matter how the design is managed, there is general agreement on two points: (1) Design must *not* be an afterthought, with the designer second-guessing management, marketing, or engineering groups after-the-fact. The earlier the designer participates in a project, the more effective the results. (2) Because design calls for policy decisions affecting the very existence of a business, industrial design must be a top management concern.

How the Design Process Operates. Design normally falls into three phases. The first phase is *fact-finding and the establishment of objectives:* Information is gathered on the nature of the market, consumer attitudes and the competitive situation, manufacturing capabilities and limitations, management policy and long-range goals, and all other factors that could or should influence the project's objectives and parameters.

The second phase is *design development.* Sketches and models explore various design directions, and the designers work closely with research and development, engineering, manufacturing, and marketing units, as well as with top management. Generally, also, the client's other consultants and resources, including advertising and public relations counsel, are involved.

In the final phase, *implementation,* the designer creates production drawings, working closely with production engineers to insure efficient manufacture within pre-set financial and technical limits, and to make sure that the design/marketing objectives are achieved.

Viewed as stylists only, the designer is principally a specialist in fashion and visual appeal and rarely steps beyond this territory. Viewed as a designer-in-depth, he moves into functional areas such as ease of use, maintenance, safety, marketing, and economy of production, as well as aiming for maximum contributions to human satisfaction and to the quality of our society.

Today, major industries, significantly the automotive and large appliance manufacturers, have rejected the "yearly model" or change for change's sake as a wasteful procedure. It is now recognized that a visual change in the product must reflect a significant functional change that benefits the consumer.

Acceptance and Future Directions. Industrial design is now generally recognized as a significant profession in our country, and perhaps even more so in some of the industrialized nations of Europe and Asia. The United States has been viewed as the profession's founder and leader, but today Britain, Japan, West Germany, France, the Scandinavian countries, and Canada are demonstrating new directions and concepts that merit attention. Considerable government support for the profession exists in these countries. For example, Britain has a "Design Council" which is supported by government to the tune of several million dollars a year to maintain a "Design Center" in Haymarket, as well as a periodical, *Design,* and a professional staff to help industry incoporate visual design into product development, especially for export sale. France's Pompidou Center has a large area devoted to an industrial design display, with no rent charged to the profession. Japan's government helped support the ICSID Congress held in Tokyo, and there is continuous cooperative effort between government and the design profession. There is nothing of comparative scope in the United States.

In the years ahead, designers will utilize computers and new sophisticated communications and photo printing and lettering systems more intensively. They will also continue to increase the degree of integration with management, R&D, and other departments and disciplines, as mentioned earlier.

Many supply and service organizations as well as a great number of small manufacturers who have not previously utilized design will be the new market for designers' skills.

The Industrial Designers Society of America estimates that there are 13,000 to 15,000 practicing professionals, with industrial-design schools turning out 400 to 500 new graduates a year. While economic slowdowns do somewhat affect this discipline, all evidence points to a widening horizon for the profession.

WILLIAM M. GOLDSMITH, FIDSA, Goldsmith Yamasaki Specht, Inc., Chicago, Illinois.

Information References

Associations:

American Institute of Graphic Arts (AIGA).
Industrial Designers Society of America (IDSA).
International Council of Societies of Industrial Design (ICSID).
Package Designers Council (PDC).
Society of Typographic Arts (STA).

Periodicals:

Abitare (Italy).
Design (Britain).
Design Industrie (France).
Domus (Italy).
Form (Germany).
Form (Sweden).
ID (USA).

Texts:

Bayley, Stephen, "In Good Shape," Washington, Design Council, 1979.
Heskett, John, "Industrial Design," New York, Oxford University Press, 1980.
Meikle, Jeffrey L., "Twentieth Century Limited," Philadelphia, Temple University Press, 1979.
Nelson, George, "George Nelson on Design," New York, Whitney Library of Design, 1979.
Pentagram, "Living by Design," New York, Whitney Library of Design, 1978.
Pile, John F., "Design: Purpose, Form, and Meaning," Amherst, Mass., University of Mass. Press, 1979.

Cross References: *Packaging: Legal and Ethical Aspects; Packaging: Organizing for Package Development.*

INDUSTRIAL DISTRIBUTORS

Industrial distributors are sometimes referred to as "The Supermarket for Industry." They are, for a large variety of industrial goods, the single most important channel of distribution from manufacturer to industrial user, performing functions of true utilitarian value. In the absence of distributors, these functions must be passed on to either the manufacturer or the industrial user. Thus industrial distributors serve to keep the lines of supply and distribution between industrial producers and industrial users from becoming hopelessly tangled.

Formal Definition. Industrial distribution concerns the marketing of industrial supplies and equipment. These goods are used by factories, mines, railroads, mills, utilities, and other facilities in the operation of their businesses. Industrial supplies and equipment do not include raw materials or assemblies (except for standard parts, such as fasteners), but do include small equipment, tools, parts, and other supply items used in daily production, operation, and maintenance. Today these items are more commonly referred to as maintenance, repair, and operating (MRO) supplies. Industrial distributors also stock and sell standardized shop equipment such as lathes, drill presses, pipe threading equipment, pumps and compressors, and the like.

Today's industrial distributor is a local independent businessman who sells and services supplies to industries in his market area. The reason for his existence is that he can perform a far more effective job than the manufacturer can in merchandising a particular line of industrial products at the local level. In fact, the service provided by the industrial distributor actually adds value to the product as sold. This "value added" concept is a key principle in industrial distribution.

A partial list of the varied products sold by industrial distributors includes: abrasives; cutting tools; saws and files; hand pumps, valves, and compressors; power transmission equipment; industrial rubber goods; material handling equipment; air and hydraulic equipment; precision measuring tools; tubing; tool steel; and bearing stock.

The industrial distributor keeps in constant contact with his customers' top management, purchasing managers, engineers, maintenance foremen, and stockroom and shop personnel. His awareness of their problems and needs makes him a logical distribution channel from manufacturer to user. He is known by a variety of names locally which perhaps best define who the industrial distributor really is: mill supply house; industrial distributor; factory, foundry, mill, mine, oil well, contractor, marine, railway or textile supply house; hardware wholesaler; automotive jobber; construction equipment distributor; plumbing and heating wholesaler; electrical wholesaler; aircraft supply distributor; machinery and equipment dealer.

History. The field of industrial distribution generally dates back a little more than 100 years. Before that time most industrial distributor firms were not much more than hardware peddlers operating out of covered wagons. But as many of these peddlers found they could serve the new industries then starting up, they settled down nearby and began concentrating their sales efforts in those directions. For a long period there were, however, few distributors, and those that did exist often sent their salesmen on extended trips of several months, calling on plants across the country.

Industrial distributors really came into their own with the advent of standardized parts and machinery. It must be remembered that in heavy engineered installations where total unit sales are large, it is often advantageous for the manufacturer to perform all the functions himself. But as regards standardized items, e.g. light machine tools and other forms of accessory equipment, perishable productions tools and many other maintenance items and industrial supplies, industrial buyers are in the habit of purchasing on a day-to-day basis. So the mill supply house was born, the one that carried everything.

A more recent development has been the emergence of the specialized distributor. This is a firm that concentrates on only one line or service, such as bearings, valves and fittings, fasteners, or mechanical power transmission equipment.

The limited lines or departmentalized distributor also exists. He is essentially a compromise between a specialized house and a general line, or mill supply, distributor.

Operations. Many general line houses are slimming down their lines and becoming more departmentalized. Limited line houses are either becoming specialists or general line houses. Specialized distributors are adding more lines. No discernable pattern is yet clear.

The industry has in recent years continued to experience a profit squeeze, with average net profit after taxes as low as one-third of one percent. A number of factors have been responsible for this profit squeeze. Vicious price cutting is one. Increasing operating costs another. Dual distribution, that is competition for sales from their manufacturer-suppliers, another. Consequently, many industrial distributors have gone in for profitability analysis of their lines and customers, weeding out and discarding those lines and customers which do not add to their profit picture.

A manufacturer selling through industrial distributors must realize that he not only is competing against other manufacturers who make the same product, but he is also competing for the distributor's time and attention against all the manufacturers whom the distributor represents. Therefore some understanding of what distributors want is in order. This is best stated in the "Statement of Policy" formulated by the National Industrial Distributors Association and the Southern Industrial Distributors Association:

> Manufacturers should firmly establish and clearly *state in writing* (italics supplied) their expected relationship with distributors. Distributors feel that selective distribution, limited by actual market potential, should be applied to those items requiring specialized sales training and/or heavy inventory investment. Distributors feel that manufacturer, distributor and consumer will all benefit by this through greater sales activity and interest, a better chance for a fair return on inventory investment, and more competent application of such products to the consumer's need.
>
> Appointment of distributors on a selective basis should be made only after a thorough study of the distributor's sales ability and financial responsibility. Contracts between manufacturer and distributor should contain a clause providing that upon termination by either party, all goods of current design in distributor's stock are returnable at distributor's cost, with return transportation cost to be paid by the cancelling party.
>
> Those manufacturers who, totally or largely, use industrial distributors as their sales and warehousing divisions should not weaken this important arm of their business by pricing their distributors out of the O.E.M. market or by reserving large volume industries or accounts to themselves.

The industrial distributor's single most important customer is the firm engaged in metalworking. Other important customer groups are woodworking industries, public utilities, governmental agencies, agriculture equipment industries, retail hardware stores, contractors, textile industries, mines and quarries, paper manufacturers, and petroleum refiners.

Trends. Several noticeable trends in industrial selling have been emerging. Most significant is systems contracts, also known as systems selling or blanket contracts or orders. Under this arrangement, a customer signs a blanket order for his requirements with his local industrial distributor. The distributor agrees that he will always have on hand the tools or materials needed by his customer. He relieves the latter of the need to be concerned with complex purchase order forms, warehousing, inventory-taking, and other costs of purchasing and possession. In return, the distributor is guaranteed a market for his products.

Leasing is another trend. Long-term leasing of production equipment by industry has established itself as a major new form of business financing among industrial distributors.

The trend to *specialization* will most likely

continue. The reason this branch of distribution should see sustained growth is that it is easier for new firms to start as specialists rather than as general line firms. Investment capital needed is considerably lower. A former mill supplies salesman may have specialized knowledge about one field which is in much demand in his territory and he can often enlist manufacturer support in setting up a specialized distributorship.

Potential. Industrial distributors who are members of the National and Southern Industrial Distributors Associations (NIDA/SIDA) reported approximately $3 billion in total sales during 1979. Most industrial distributors are small, independent businesses, although some are large-scale public corporations with many branches. The sales of an "average" industrial distributor will total about $4 million annually, according to NIDA/SIDA. Typical industrial distributors handling general lines will average from 20,000 to 30,000 different items in their inventory. This figure may range from 5,000 items for a distributor specializing in certain product lines to as many as 50,000 different items for the larger firms. NIDA/SIDA indicate that the gross margin has traditionally averaged between 22% and 24% of sales, and net profit as a percentage of net worth (return on investment, or ROI) averaged 15.24% for NIDA members during a recent year.

The market for sales through industrial distributors is not static, but only limited by the economic forces in the country. Industrial distributors are taking advantage of new markets. For instance, the interest in environmental quality control and energy conservation has opened a whole new market for industrial distributors. Enterprising distributors have set up divisions to handle pollution control equipment.

Industrial distributors have, like others, been subject to mergers and acquisitions. Many have merged to form large corporations. Others have been absorbed by venture-seeking conglomerates. The industrial distributor of the immediate future will be beset with higher operating costs, inflation, and a dwindling profit margin. His survival will depend on his ability to grow with the times.

SOURCE, *Industrial Distributor News,* Philadelphia, Pennsylvania

Cross References: *Franchising; Franchising: Legal Aspects; Manufacturers' Representatives; Marketing; Industrial Purchasing Power: The S&MM Annual Survey; Purchasing.*

INDUSTRIAL DISTRICTS

In older manufacturing centers, industry is plagued by cramped sites, traffic congestion, and inadequate parking facilities. Preference for single-story plants and the desire to avoid future congestion have directed attention to the planned **Industrial District.** This is a tract of land subdivided and promoted by a sponsoring managerial organization for industrial occupancy. While the term "industrial park" is used increasingly as a promotional device, it would be misleading to give any definitive status to that title.

Industrial districts vary considerably in their extent of planning, but the basic concept provides for the installation of streets, railroad tracks, and utilities before sites are sold (or leased) to industry. Building and zoning restrictions are frequently adopted to protect the character of the district and future real estate values. In its most advanced form, the planned industrial district may offer a full range of services: assistance in design, financing, and construction; fire and police protection; banking; restaurants; club rooms; computer time-sharing; etc.

Types of Districts. Characteristics of a planned industrial district will depend, in large measure, upon the promoting group and its objectives. Some general observations can be made, however, on the types of districts established by typical sponsors.

Railroad Districts. Railroads create industrial districts in an effort to increase freight revenues. Availability of land in districts of this type, therefore, may be limited to manufacturers or distributors who can guarantee substantial rail tonnage. Carriers are seldom interested in more than a break-even price on the land in their districts (and, were it not for I.C.C. restrictions, some would readily release land below actual development cost). With a few notable exceptions, railroads seldom exercise strict controls over the type of buildings which can be erected, setbacks, ratio of land coverage, or vehicular movements within their districts.

Entrepreneural Districts. Many planned industrial districts are owned and operated as private enterprises for profit by real estate corporations, building contractors, architects, real estate brokers, or syndicates comprising a combination of such interests. This type of district is generally the most highly developed from the standpoint of restrictions, as well as services to occupants. In direct contrast to the railroads seeking additional tonnage, private developers of industrial districts are vitally interested in return on investment. They aim to secure AAA-1 firms as occupants and, under present income tax provisions, they usually prefer to erect structures for long-term lease (rather than sale of raw land).

Community-Sponsored Districts. The basic motivation for community sponsorship of an industrial district is the attraction of new payrolls. Older urbanized areas may also use this type of district to discourage the migration of existing industry. Community-sponsored districts may be organized by the Chamber of Commerce, industrial foundations (profit or nonprofit), local or county governments, port commissions, airport authorities, redevelopment agencies, or special commissions. In some states, legislative approval has been obtained for industrial districts to be financed with statewide industrial development funds—including the erection of speculative buildings.

Industry-Sponsored Districts. Manufacturers themselves have been sponsoring an increasing number of planned districts. These projects may involve a speculative real estate venture on the part of the corporation. More frequently, however, the district represents an opportunity for the industrialist to recoup the costs of developing the site for his own new plant by selling off excess land. The industry-sponsored district may also be used as a marketing tool. In the case of chemical manufacturers, this procedure is adopted as a means of insuring an outlet for products, attracting potential customers for over-the-fence delivery at adjacent sites. Similar motivation has led to the establishment of sponsored districts by steel mills where occupancy is restricted to steel users.

Trends. While the concept of the planned industrial district predates the American Revolution, greatest growth has occurred in the United States since World War II. Prior to 1940, only 24 districts had been established; 87 were added between 1940 and 1954; and almost 4,000 are listed currently.

Size of the typical district has also been changing. Most developments created before 1950 contained less than 300 acres. Average size increased to 500 acres during the 1950–60 period, and some were announced which exceeded 1,000 acres. Current trends indicate a decline in average size, probably reflecting the more intensified land development of port authorities, inner city agencies, etc.

Considerable design changes can be observed. Increasing use of automobiles and trucks has required larger paved areas for parking and off-street loading ramps. Major thoroughfares within new developments are 60 to 80 feet wide in contrast to the 30-foot widths in older districts. Utility lines are increasing in size and some new districts have completely eliminated overhead wires. Rail crossings are being minimized, and lack of rail access is no longer considered a serious sales deterrent. The average size of buildings in industrial districts has held remarkably constant. Higher ceiling clearances and larger bay dimensions, however, are expanding the average cubic capacity of structures—particularly warehouses designed for modern material handling equipment.

Advantages. The typical occupant of an industrial district is a manufacturer or distributor having need for a small to medium size structure. For smaller projects, management is generally reluctant to develop an independent site which may involve a long rezoning procedure, costly extension of utilities, etc. In the industrial district, appropriate zoning has been obtained by the developer, and all necessary facilities are usually in place prior to construction.

Distinct economic advantages may be available in the form of centralized services: contract maintenance; security guards; restaurants; banking; etc. In addition, covenants may protect real estate investments against deterioration and also ensure a safe, pollution-free environment. Unquestionably, the availability of risk capital for a "package" or "turnkey" plan has also been an important factor in the growth of industrial districts.

Special advantages can be claimed by the district for warehouse operations. Since the geographic location of distribution facilities is more often dictated by service requirements than cost differentials, the industrial district usually represents a viable site. Moveover, it offers the flexibility of sale or sublease if market conditions or distribution policies are altered.

Disadvantages. The major objection to industrial districts involves land allocation. In order to pay out, developers of a district must insist upon a high ratio of land coverage, usually 50%. This 2-to-1 ratio of land to building contrasts sharply with the requirements of growing companies for sites having ample opportunity for future expansion. More open acreage may be made available in the district, but only at increased annual rentals equivalent to the income another plant on this land could provide to the developer.

Another major disadvantage of districts is the higher cost of land, whether for sale or lease. In some cases, this may represent an unreasonable price inflation by the owners. More frequently, however, it reflects an inherent problem of industrial districts: "overbuilding." Developers tend to install interior roads and utility lines meeting city specifications so that they may be deeded to the municipality (along with maintenance responsibility) when the district is fully occupied. An industrial company improving its own site, of course, would not attempt to meet such strict standards and could effectively reduce costs.

Similarly, construction costs in many industrial districts can be excessive. In some cases, this situation occurs in the absence of competitive bidding opportunities because the land is controlled by a firm of contractors. More frequently, however, it reflects an attempt by the new occupant to match the expensive design features of neighboring plants in the district. Elimination of "frills" unwarranted by the manufacturing process or warehouse function would reduce costs on an independent site.

By far, however, the most frequent objection to industrial district locations concerns labor, in all its ramifications. It is extremely difficult to establish (and maintain) wage patterns consistent with the needs of each individual firm in an industrial district. National companies operating warehouses or small plants in these development areas frequently offer the same wages and fringe benefits paid in their home plants—wherever they may be located. Consequently, the district may contain a hodge podge of wage structures which may prove disruptive for a manufacturer competing with other producers in his industry who do not face similar problems. For these and other reasons, occupants of industrial districts report comparatively unstable labor management relations. Labor problems can be extremely contagious in such industrial concentrations.

Some industrial districts have unintentionally introduced traffic congestion. Planning within the district may be excellent, but simultaneous release of employees by all occupants at shift change hours may cause congestion at main exits, backing up within the district itself. The concentration of industry also involves considerably more movement of rail cars at grade crossings and heavier truck traffic than would be encountered at an independent site.

Research and Development Districts. The concept of a planned district for R&D is a relatively recent innovation. Successful marketing by a few districts possessing locational attractions has prompted widespread imitation, and now almost 120 "research park" developments have been established throughout the United States. They range widely in size, from a few acres to over 10,000 acres. Research directors are virtually unanimous concerning the importance of orienting their laboratory facilities to leading universities. It is not surprising, therefore, to find that many planned districts are sponsored (directly or indirectly) by institutions of higher learning. However, a scientific complex of the Federal Government can also be considered a major attractor.

Site requirements for a research laboratory differ significantly from those sought for manufacturing, but these prerequisites can be met in an R&D district if it is planned intelligently. Freedom from noise, odor, smoke, dirt, and vibration is imperative for "controlled-condition" laboratories. Further, the district should be oriented to attractive residential areas, the local university, and a good commercial airport. Since research facilities are relatively expensive to build, the district must also offer prospects for retaining or improving real estate values.

Advantages of the planned R&D district over an independent site primarily involve the economic potentials of centralized services; contract maintenance, security, restaurants, conference auditoriums, etc. The most successful developments offer computer centers, pooling of scientific instrumentation, testing laboratories, technical libraries, and even atomic accelerators.

The primary disadvantage in many planned districts is a restrictive land coverage ratio. The R&D site must be capable of expansion because (1) the full extent of research activity cannot be predicted when the new laboratory is constructed; and (2) the demand for increased laboratory space is often quite abrupt. Research directors in established districts also complain about the noncompatibility of salary and fringe benefit levels in private and government laboratories, especially during periods when corporate budgets are subject to cost pressures.

The greatest danger, however, involves the

probability that sponsors will be forced to admit light manufacturing within the district in order to be financially successful. Such mixed use detracts from the R&D atmosphere and can introduce attendant problems of congestion, air pollutants, and higher wage rates for support labor.

Office Districts. Almost 400 "office park" developments have been established in the suburban sectors of major U.S. metropolitan areas since 1960. Their growth has coincided with the rapid expansion of white-collar employment and the accelerating trend toward decentralization of headquarters and administrative offices. As in the case of the suburban shopping center, a planned office district competes with both the downtown sector and a free-standing structure to be built by (or for) the prospective tenant. To be successful, the developer must offer more than reduced executive commutation, freedom from congestion, lower taxes, etc.—all of which are available at an independent suburban site. He must also be able to demonstrate operating convenience in a protected environment. Increasingly, therefore, developers of office districts offer such built-in services as: covered parking, restaurants, health club facilities, barber shops, retail stores, and helicopter shuttles to airports.

Occupants of planned office districts cite some disadvantages. Rentals, of necessity, are somewhat high in fully-serviced developments. Smaller firms feel a loss of identity in multitenant buildings, especially when the structure is renamed for a major occupant. Lower-paying companies report excessive clerical turnover, mostly defections to higher-paying companies in the same district. Among nonexempt employees, common complaints are inadequate public transportation, long walking distances between parking areas and building entrances, and lack of reasonably-priced luncheon facilities.

L. Clinton Hoch, Executive Vice President, The Fantus Company, Millburn, New Jersey

Cross Reference: *Plant Location.*

INDUSTRIAL DYNAMICS

Industrial Dynamics is a way of studying the behavior of industrial systems to show how policies, decisions, structure, and delays are interrelated to influence growth and stability. It integrates the separate functional areas of management—marketing, investment, research, personnel, production, and accounting. Each of these functions is reduced to a common base by recognizing that any economic or corporate activity consists of flows of money, orders, materials, personnel, and capital equipment. These five flows are integrated by an information network. Industrial dynamics recognizes the critical importance of this information network in giving the system its own dynamic characteristics. Analysis of information-feedback characteristics of industrial activity shows how organizational structure, amplification (in policies), and time delays (in decisions and actions) interact to influence success.

Since the concept was first formulated by the present author at the Massachusetts Institute of Technology in 1957, its scope and application have been broadened to embrace other social institutions, and those working in this field have adopted the term **System Dynamics** to describe their work [1]. Thus, applications by these investigators have been made to corporate policy, to the dynamics of diabetes as a medical system, to the growth and stagnation of an urban area [2], and to world dynamics representing the interactions of population, pollution, industrialization, natural resources, and food. The last-named application received world-wide publicity with the publication of "World Dynamics" and "The Limits to Growth" [3,4].

More recently, system dynamics has become the basis of a new approach to understanding economic behavior [5,6,7]. The System Dynamics National Model is being used to achieve a better understanding of inflation, energy policy [8], and the reasons for major depressions at about 50-year intervals.

Approach and Techniques. Four developments were necessary before industrial dynamics could be formulated: (1) the concept of the information-feedback system; (2) better understanding of the processes of decision making; (3) the experimental model approach (simulation); and (4) the digital computer.

Before industrial dynamics can be applied, goals must be clarified and the dynamic hypothesis must be identified. The result is a mathematical model which can be used to simulate operation of the actual system. Once the model is refined, it can be used to explore policy "redesign." Unlike real life, all conditions but one can be held constant in the model, and a particular sequence of events can be repeated to see the effect of that one change. Daring changes that would seem too risky to try in actuality can be investigated.

In the technique developed for industrial dynamics, the equations are written as collections of "words" that consist of the initial letters of the words making up a phrase. For example, SOF may stand for Shipping Orders at the Factory, and RFIF may mean Requisitions Filled from Inventory at Factory. These are combinations any businessman can understand, and the analyst can take an equation to the production shop foreman and make himself understood.

Model Structure. The first step in creating a formal mathematical model is to select an effective and fundamental logical structure for the representation. A very simple framework suffices. A particular system may be complex because of its size and wealth of detail, but its fundamental nature can still be represented in the form of alternating "levels" and "rates" as shown in Exhibit I, taken from the author's "Industrial Dynamics" [1]. The elements of the methodology are also described in "Principles of Systems" [9] and "Study Notes in System Dynamics" [10]. Exhibit I contains four essential features:

Several levels.

Flows that transport the contents of one level to another.

Decision functions (drawn as valves) that control the rates of flow between levels.

Information channels that activate the decision functions from the levels.

Levels represent the state of the system at any particular moment in time. The levels are the accumulations within the system. They are the inventories, goods in transit, bank balances, factory space, and numbers of employees. Levels also describe the so-called "intangible" states of a system dealing with knowledge, character, tradition, and attitude. Levels exist in all of the six networks listed later.

It is important to note that the units of measure of a variable do not serve to distinguish levels from rates, defined below. Some levels have the dimension of units over time (as units per week). This may cause confusion until the basic distinction between levels and rates is clear. If all activity, in the form of flows, were to cease, the levels would still exist. Thus, stopping the receiving and shipping of goods does

EXHIBIT I

BASIC MODEL STRUCTURE

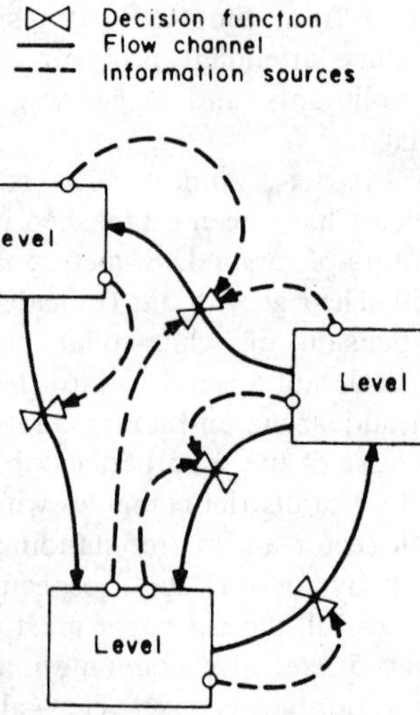

not affect the continued existence of inventory that is in a warehouse. If all activity in a system were momentarily stopped, rates would be unobservable; there would be no movement to be detected. However, the levels continue to exist and to be observable.

Average sales are often spoken of as a level—the level of sales or the level of business. The average sales *level* is obtained by summing the moment-by-moment actual sales *rate* over some period of time, as a year. By the test of bringing the system to a rest, it is seen that average sales for the last year is a level. One can stop all present sales and shipping activity without destroying the concept and numerical value of average sales for the preceding year.

Flow Rates define the present instantaneous flows between the levels in the system. The rates correspond to *activity,* while the levels measure the resulting *state* to which the system has been brought by the activity. Rates exist in all six networks that may constitute a system. The flow rates are the decisions in the system. These flows or decisions are governed by decision functions (or policy).

Decision Functions are the statements of policy that determine how the available information about levels leads to the decisions (current rates). All decisions pertain to impending action and are expressible as flow rates (generation of orders, construction of equipment, hiring of people). The decision functions pertain both to managerial decisions and to those actions that are inherent results of the physical state of the system. A decision function may appear as a simple equation that determines, in some elementary way, a flow in response to the condition of one or two levels (like the output of a transportion system that may often be adequately represented by the goods in transit, which is a level, and the average transportation delay, a constant). On the other hand, a decision function may be described by a long and elaborate sequence of computations that progresses through the evaluation of a number of intermediate concepts (e.g., a personnel hiring decision might involve the levels of: present employees, average order rate, employees in training, employee requisitions already initiated, backlog of unfilled orders, present inventory levels, available capital equipment, available materials, etc.).

In Exhibit I it is shown that the decision functions determining the rates are dependent only on information about the levels. Rates are not determined by other rates. This is always true in principle.

Policies are the rules which state how the incoming information about levels will be used to create the concepts of apparent and actual conditions and the action taken as a result of these.

Six Interconnected Networks. The basic model structure in Exhibit I shows only one network, with a rudimentary set of information ties from levels to rates. Several interconnected networks are needed to represent industrial activity.

EXHIBIT II

TYPICAL PICTORIAL REPRESENTATION OF VERBAL DESCRIPTION AND MATHEMATICAL EQUATION

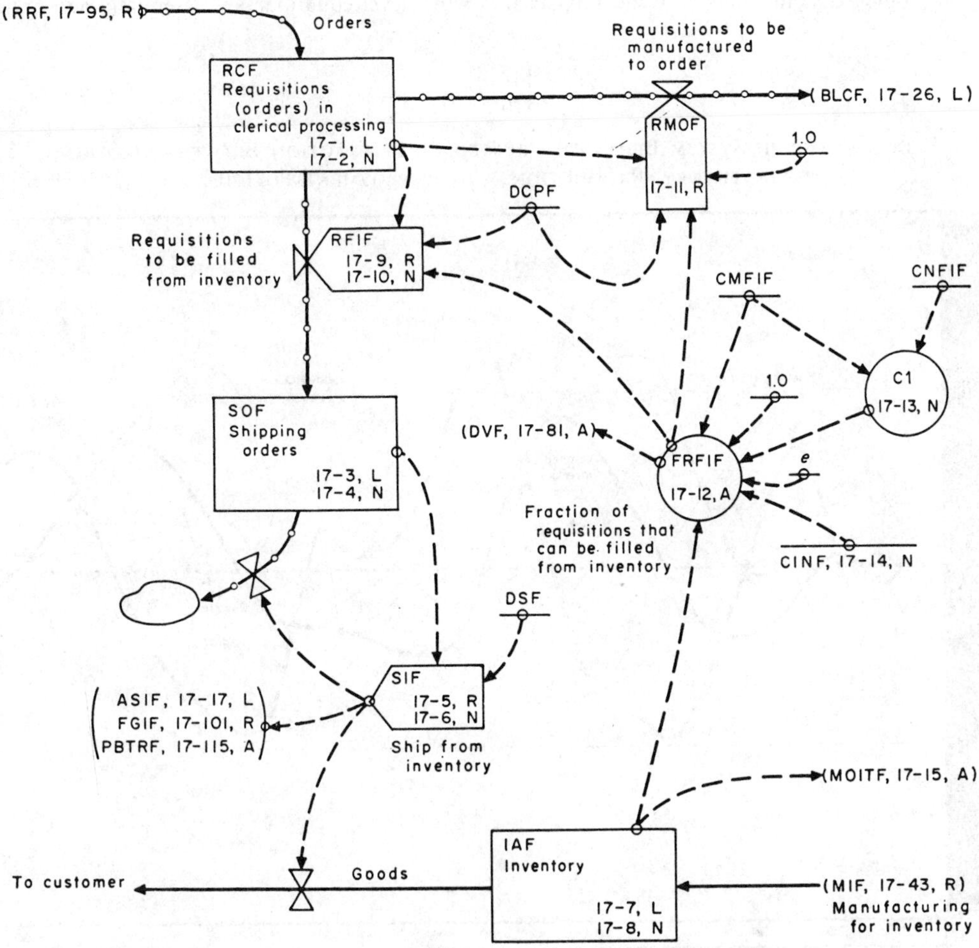

A system representation may consist of six interconnected networks each of which contains levels and rates. Five of these networks represent physical flows—*materials, orders, money, personnel,* and *capital equipment.* (Money is here used in the cash sense. Money flow is the actual transmittal of payments between money levels.) The sixth network is the *information network,* which is itself a sequence of alternating rates and levels. It is considered to be in a position superior to the other networks because it is the interconnecting tissue between all. In general, the information network starts at the levels in the other five networks and ends at the rate-generating decision functions in those five. It transfers information about the levels in the system to the decision points. The information network is usually the major fraction of a model. Information is the basis for decision making. It is the linkage that causes the other five networks to interact on one another.

The complexity and detail of the industrial dynamics approach can be seen from Exhibit II [1]. The illustration shows a small section of an order-filling system in which orders, goods, and information are interrelated. (The exhibit is offered only to show the nature of representation, and the underlying study is not discussed.) A level is shown by a rectangle, with symbol group identifying it in the upper left-hand corner, and equation number in the lower right-hand corner. Various types of arrows are used to represent the six types of flow systems. (Here, a broken line represents information, a solid line broken by small circles represents orders, and a solid line shows materials.) The pointed rectangles with "valves" represent decision functions (rate equations).

The correspondence between the verbal description of a system and the equations of an industrial dynamics model can be illustrated by selecting one of the level equations and one of the rate equations that are represented in Exhibit II.

All level equations are essentially accounting

EXHIBIT III

FLUCTUATIONS IN SYSTEM BEHAVIOR CREATED BY INTERACTION BETWEEN ORDERING, INVENTORY, PRODUCTION, AND EMPLOYMENT POLICIES

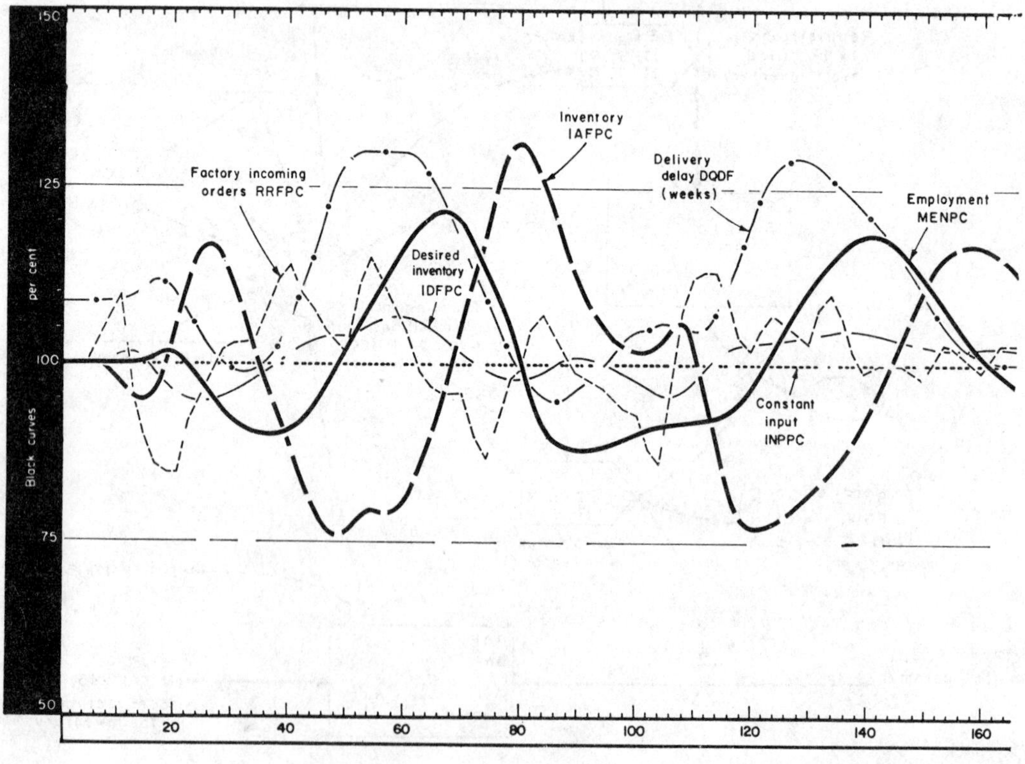

statements that integrate the inflow and outflow rates to determine the present content of a level. The specific equation 17-7 developed in the underlying study for inventory in the Exhibit would be written:

IAF.K = IAF.J + (DT) (MIF.JK − SIF.JK)

IAF — Inventory Actual at Factory (units)

DT — Delta Time, interval between equation solutions (weeks)

MIF — Manufacturing rate for Inventory at Factory (units/week)

SIF — Shipments from Inventory at Factory (units/week)

This equation states that the present inventory (at time K) equals the previous inventory (at time J) plus what has entered minus what has left in the interval between time J and time K. To calculate the amount which has been put into inventory, the manufacturing rate MIF is multiplied by the time interval DT between successive computations of values of the variables. Likewise, the amount removed is the shipping rate SIF times the interval DT.

A properly formulated closed model exhibits the essence of behavior of the system being studied. Its desirable and undesirable characteristics, like those of the real system, are generated by the interactions of the components within the model. By tracing through these interactions using a digital computer for the large amount of computation required, the model simulates the behavior of the real system. One can thereupon see how the interactions between the parts of the system result from how those parts were described in the earlier steps. Exhibit III [1] shows such a result. The figure shows employment, inventory, and backlog fluctuations within an industry, even though that industry is selling its product to the ultimate customers at a constant rate. The observed employment fluctuation is wholly a consequence of the interactions of the particular policies being followed by the participants within the industry.

Acceptance. System dynamics is now being used worldwide. Corporations apply system dynamics in choosing policies to improve stability of employment and market share. Universities are teaching system dynamics for analysis of social, environmental, corporate, economic, and medical systems [11–15]. Study units built around system dynamics for use in high schools serve as a unifying framework for integrating what would otherwise be disparate facts [16]. Governments are using system dynamics to analyze changes in population, economic behavior, agriculture, and political stability.

JAY W. FORRESTER, Professor of Management, Massachusetts Institute of Technology, Cambridge, Massachusetts

References Cited

[1] Forrester, Jay W., "Industrial Dynamics," Cambridge, Mass., MIT Press, 1961.
[2] Forrester, Jay W., "Urban Dynamics," Cambridge, Mass., MIT Press, 1969.
[3] Forrester, Jay W., "World Dynamics," Cambridge, Mass., MIT Press, 2nd ed., 1973.
[4] Meadows, Donella H. et al., "The Limits to Growth," New York, Universe Books, 1972.
[5] Mass, Nathaniel J., "Economic Cycles: An Analysis of Underlying Causes," Cambridge, Mass., MIT Press, 1975.
[6] Forrester, Jay W., "Changing Economic Patterns," *Technology Review,* vol. 80, no. 8, August–September 1978.
[7] Forrester, Nathan, "The Life Cycle of Economic Development," 2nd ed., Cambridge, Mass., MIT Press, 1973.
[8] Forrester, Jay W., "A Self-Regulating Energy Policy," *Astronautics and Aeronautics,* vol. 17, nos. 7 & 8, July–August 1979.
[9] Forrester, Jay W., "Principles of Systems," Cambridge, Mass., MIT Press, 1968.
[10] Goodman, Michael R., "Study Notes in System Dynamics," Cambridge, Mass., MIT Press, 1974.
[11] Forrester, Jay W., "Counterintuitive Behavior of Social Systems," *Technology Review,* vol. 73, no. 3, January 1971.
[12] Forrester, Jay W., "Collected Papers of Jay W. Forrester," Cambridge, Mass., MIT Press, 1975.
[13] Mass, Nathaniel J., ed., "Readings in Urban Dynamics" vol. 1, Cambridge, Mass., MIT Press, 1974.
[14] Schroeder, Walter W. et al., eds., "Readings in Urban Dynamics" vol. 2, Cambridge, Mass., MIT Press, 1975.
[15] Roberts, Edward B., ed. "Managerial Applications of System Dynamics," Cambridge, Mass., MIT Press, 1978.
[16] Roberts, Nancy, "Teaching Dynamic Feedback Systems Thinking: An Elementary View," *Management Science,* vol. 24, no. 8, April 1978.

Cross Reference: *Management Sciences.*

INDUSTRIAL ENGINEERING

Industrial Engineering applies systematic engineering methods to the solution of problems arising in the production of goods and services. Problems that have received special attention include: design, analysis, and implementation of work measurement, methods analysis, economic analysis, facility planning, incentive systems, job evaluation, equipment utilization, plant layout, materials management, material handling, quality control and quality assurance, human factors, production planning and scheduling, workplace design, systems management, and safety in industry. However, industrial engineering has not been limited to manufacturing, for industrial engineers are also assigned to work in such areas as banking, health care, and utilities.

The profession has changed substantially since its inception, and continues to be dynamic. More emphasis is now given to the use of quantitative techniques, electronic computers and controllers, and to consideration of the impact of the proposed solutions to all facets of an organization—the systems approach.

Formal Definition. The Institute of Industrial Engineers has defined industrial engineering as follows:

> *Industrial Engineering* is concerned with the design, improvement, and installation of integrated systems of people, materials, equipment, and energy; drawing upon specialized knowledge and skill in the mathematical, physical, and social sciences together with the principles and methods of engineering analysis and design, to specify, predict, and evaluate the results to be obtained from such systems.

History. While FREDERICK W. TAYLOR was not the first to consider factory management as an area where engineering techniques might be fruitfully applied, it was his work, begun at the close of the last century, that stirred widespread interest, and that initiated the SCIENTIFIC MANAGEMENT movement. An essential component of the scientific management concept was to divide work tasks into small components, timing the components, and then rearranging, combining, or eliminating them for more efficient combinations. World War II called attention to statistical quality control, a technique initiated by Walter Shewhart of the Bell Telephone Laboratories. Statistical control not only prompted an interest in statistics on the part of industrial engineers, but also offered them a tool of great practical importance in many areas, and profound insight into rational methods of inquiry. World War II also encouraged the development of more scientific industrial engineering through the emergence of Operations Research. Today's quantitatively oriented industrial engineer designs highly sophisticated, computer-controlled systems of machines, materials, and humans to produce goods and services. The profession is thus truly that of the "productivity engineer."

Approach and Techniques. Industrial engineering work has been and still is concerned with workplace design and redesign to solve problems such as poor quality or low productivity. The I.E. design approach has been found valuable in contriving and rearranging entire systems to minimize or eliminate inefficiencies.

Industrial engineering design uses models of many sorts. Graphic models such as plant-layout drawings, organization charts, Gantt charts, and critical path networks present information about a system in formats designed to emphasize the significant and eliminate unessential detail. Mathematical models such as those of mathematical programming, queueing, engineering economy, and reliability also concentrate on the relationships between significant factors. As systems and their components have become more complex and computers have become more sophisticated, industrial engineers have moved rapidly toward computer approaches to solve system design problems. Use of computers to control processes, incorporate industrial robots into the production system, and to process information greatly expanded the effectiveness of the I.E. approach in the improved utilization of energy, materials, machines, and people in the industrial process.

Acceptance. Acceptance of the profession is indicated by the growing number of industrial engineers holding top management positions, and a general widening of the responsibilities carried by chief industrial engineers. The industrial engineering department also continues to be, as in the past, a prime source of personnel for line management responsibilities.

Potential. The record of effective industrial engineering in manufacturing operations has been extended to other areas and will be further extended as the number of quantitatively trained and systems-oriented engineers increases. Realization of the potential will be speeded as managers encourage industrial engineers, through guidance and support, to view technical problems in terms of the criteria used by highly placed executives. Industrial engineering programs in colleges offer rigorous quantitative courses accredited by the Accreditation Board of Engineering and Technology. This educational process stresses design, mathematical modeling, computer capability, statistical analysis, and consideration of the human in the system. It is clear that top managers are increasingly aware of the industrial engineer and his potential contribution to problem solving in a diversity of areas.

DANIEL J. DUFFY, Professor of Business Administration, Loyola College, Baltimore, Maryland, for the Institute of Industrial Engineers

Information References

Association:

Institute of Industrial Engineers

Periodicals:

Industrial Engineering

Transactions of the Institute of Industrial Engineers

Text:

Hicks, Philip E., ed., "Introduction to Industrial Engineering and Management Science," New York, McGraw-Hill, 1977.

Turner, Wayne C., Mize, Joe H., and Case, Kenneth E., "Introduction to Industrial and Systems Engineering," Englewood Cliffs, N.J., Prentice-Hall, 1978.

Vaughn, Richard C., "Introduction to Industrial Engineering," Ames., Ia., Iowa State University Press, 2nd ed., 1977.

Cross References: *Break-Even Analysis; Cost Accounting; Gantt Chart; Fixed-Asset Investment Analysis; Gilbreth Principles of Motion Economy; Incentive Systems; Materials Management; Motion and Time Study; Process Analysis; Process Engineering; Production Planning and Inventory Control; Quality Control and Quality Assurance; Safety in Industry; Standard Minute System; Systems Management; Work Measurement; Work Measurement in the Office; Work Simplification. (For mathematical references, see cross references under Management Sciences.)*

INDUSTRIAL ESPIONAGE: See Security: Protection of Trade Secrets and Proprietary Information.

INDUSTRIAL PSYCHOLOGY

Industrial Psychology is the study of human behavior in the business, industrial, and military setting, and the application of psychological principles, knowledge, and theory in these settings. The industrial psychologist is an individual who has had formal training at the graduate level in psychological methods employed in the study of human behavior, and is familiar with important findings derived from relevant research. He (she) may be employed full time by a company, work as a consultant, or be engaged in teaching or research.

History. While the earliest work in industrial psychology predates the present century, most psychologists consider industrial psychology to have had its most rapid growth in the periods during and following the two world wars. In each case the tremendous problems of classifying and training large numbers of individuals in short periods of time led to the use of available psychological procedures and to the development of new means for dealing with the problems. The success of work in the development of testing during World War I was followed in World War II by development of a wide variety of methods for selection of individuals for specific military specialties, assessment of troop morale, and evaluation of military indoctrination and education.

The Division of Industrial and Organizational Psychology of the American Psychological Association has more than quadrupled its membership since the end of World War II. In addition, there are many psychologists affiliated with other divisions of the American Psychological Association who work part or full time as industrial psychologists. As recently as 1949 there were no more than 50 industrial psychologists employed full time in industry; yet by 1980 a single company or consulting firm could employ that many.

Terms Used in Industrial Psychology. Many terms commonly used in industrial psychology have precise meanings which differ substantially from the meanings of everyday speech. Some of these terms are defined as follows:

Aptitude is a condition or set of characteristics regarded as predictive of an individual's ability to acquire with training some knowledge, skill or set of responses, such as the ability to type, the ability to play the piano, or the ability to operate a milling machine.

Talent refers to a relatively high order of aptitude, especially of a creative nature.

Ability is the power to perform some responsive act, *e.g.,* to solve an intellectual problem or perform a complex coordinated movement.

Proficiency refers to the degree of ability already acquired, *e.g.,* typing 120 words per minute or solving quickly and accurately problems in celestial navigation.

Capacity refers to potential ability.

Skill refers to ease and precision in performing complex motor acts.

Intelligence, may be considered to be the ability to deal with new or novel situations by improvising novel adaptive responses.

Personality can be defined as the physical and affective qualities or attitudes of an individual as they attract or impress others.

Attitude is a disposition or readiness to respond to a situation with a prepared reaction.

Morale (high) may be considered to be an attitude of satisfaction with, desire to continue in, and willingness to strive for the goals of a particular group or organization.

Motivation refers to the inner directing processes which determine an individual's movement or behavior toward ends or goals.

Subject Branchings. Industrial psychology may be divided into four major branches: personnel research, employee counseling, human engineering, and marketing and survey research. Each of these major branches may, in turn, be subdivided into specialized areas in which the psychologist works.

Personnel Research includes work on recruiting, selection, placement, induction; performance evaluation; promotion, transfer, job evaluation, wage and salary administration, and incentive systems; organization of work; training, management development, business games; executive, management and supervisory methods; decision making; employee communication, employee motivation, employee attitudes and morale; absenteeism and turnover; individual and group behavior on the job; safety and accident prevention; collective bargaining, and labor relations.

Employee Counseling is oriented toward clinical evaluation of individuals and personal counseling in individual job adjustment problems, inter- and intra-group problems, supervisor-subordinate relationships, retirement, and the problems of industrial mental health such as alcoholism.

Human Engineering is concerned with the study and design of systems and equipment in terms of the capabilities and limitations of human operators, including man-machine systems, instrument design, color coding, dial arrangement, work space, decision making, and methods analysis.

Marketing and Survey Research is concerned with the broad field of external relationships which exist between an industrial organization and the many publics with which it deals. These publics may represent such diverse groups as present and potential customers, clients, competitors, suppliers, governmental personnel, special interest groups, or entire communities. The study of advertising and its effectiveness and the use of the various media forms—newspapers, magazines, radio, and television—as communication devices, are important areas of investigation.

Schools of Thought. Industrial psychology as it is presently developing does not represent a unified technical-scientific specialty. In practice, there are two somewhat different points of view which are characteristic of psychology generally: the objective, experimental, statistical-probability orientation to problem solving, versus the subjective, intuitive, *ad hoc* approach to dealing with a specific situation or individual. It should be understood, however, that although the individual industrial psychologist may have a basic orientation toward one approach, this does not preclude his use of either approach as the situation demands.

Approaches and Techniques. When approaching a new problem, the industrial psychologist attempts to formulate a statement of the problem in operational terms. Using this statement, he will then incorporate what are considered to be the important variables into a research design which will permit the study and evaluation of alternative solutions. Normally, he will develop a criterion against which experimental outcomes can be judged. Finally, when the study or studies are carried out as planned, the data are subjected to statistical analysis and a research report, and recommendations are prepared.

The industrial psychologist relies on the experimental method; on principles of research design; and on statistical methods, probability, and sampling theory. Specific techniques which may be employed when appropriate include psychological tests, rating scales, application blanks, evaluation forms; job analysis and job description, skill analysis, motion and time study, controlled observation; mail questionnaires, telephone, face-to-face, and depth interviewing; experimental manipulation of environmental and situational factors; psychophysical, sensory, and perceptual discriminations; programmed instruction, lecture and discussion training methods, role playing, and group dynamics.

Psychological Tests. A few comments on psychological testing should be made here because it is in the field of testing that the psychologist is best known. Most people when they think of testing think of paper and pencil tests; however, to the psychologist any sample of behavior obtained through a standard procedure is a test. In this sense, interviews carried out under standard conditions, or application blanks which have been developed as a result of research may be considered as tests.

There are a number of ways of classifying or categorizing tests. While any classification may be somewhat arbitrary, the following categories will be found to be useful: Tests may be described as achievement tests, aptitude tests, or as self-description inventories. An *achievement test* is one which attempts to measure present knowledge or skill. Thus, tests in history or mathematics or typing or shorthand tests are all achievement tests. Some of these measures of present level of skill are known as *psychomotor tests,* that is, they are performance tests which require the individual to perform certain operations, to manipulate controls or objects, or to assemble parts of a machine, as measures of reaction time, or of manual or physical coordination, or of dexterity. Other measures are known as *skill tests* or *trade tests,* that is, they are tests which relate the performance of an individual to others with respect to ability to perform a skilled or learned task; tests of typing, stenography, welding, or soldering illustrate skill or trade tests. *Aptitude tests* are tests which measure some present characteristic found to be predictive of future ability to perform some task given the necessary training. Since the best single predictor of how one will perform in the future is still past performance, it can be seen that an achievement test in sixth grade arithmetic might be used as an aptitude test of high school mathematics.

Self-description Inventory. The self-description inventory may be of several types. These include *interest inventories* which attempt to measure the amount of relative interest that an individual has in various vocational or avocational areas; *personality inventories* which are designed to elicit in their answers information about the way a person feels or behaves, the typical mode of thinking, social action, or areas of personal concern; and *background or biographical information inventories* which record, in either a multiple-choice or write-in format, background items many of which are similar to those found in application blanks.

Acceptance and Potential. Originally the industrial psychologist was viewed as a test technician of value primarily to the employment function. While he (she) continues to expand efforts in personnel selection and evaluation, he is called upon increasingly by management to aid in solving a variety of problems involving both individuals and groups. It is probable that major demands for his or her assistance come from those responsible for human engineering, consumer advertising, and training and development programs.

A number of research units have been established in industry for the purpose of studying basic problems of human behavior. These organizations, together with those operating at a dozen or more universities, are making significant contributions to the understanding of the psychology of business and to the practice of management.

W. E. KENDALL, PH.D., Industrial Psychologist, Rye, New York

Information References

Associations:

American Psychological Association.
American Marketing Association.
American Society for Training and Development.
American Association for Public Opinion Research.

Periodicals:

Journal of Applied Psychology.
Personnel Psychology.
Harvard Business Review.
Human Relations.

Texts:

Anastasi, A., "Fields of Applied Psychology," 2nd ed., New York, McGraw-Hill, 1979.

Dunnette, M. D., ed., "Handbook of Industrial and Organizational Psychology," Chicago, Rand McNally, 1976.

Lawler, E. E., III, "Pay and Organizational Effectiveness: A Psychological View," New York, McGraw-Hill, 1971.

Ronan, W. W. and Prien, E. P., ed., "Perspectives on the Measurement of Human Performance," New York, Irvington, repr. 1979.

Schultz, D. P., ed., "Psychology and Industry." New York, Macmillan, 1970.

Stone, C. H. and Kendall, W. E., "Effective Personnel Selection Procedures," Englewood Cliffs, N.J., Prentice-Hall, 1956.

Tyler, L. E., "Individual Differences: Abilities and Motivational Directions," Englewood Cliffs, N.J., Prentice-Hall, 1974.

Wexley, K. N., and Yukl, G. A., eds., "Readings in Organizational and Industrial Psychology," New York, Oxford University Press, 1971.

Cross References: *Motivation (and accompanying entries with that prefix); Personnel Counseling; Personnel Testing; Personnel Testing: Types of Tests.*

INDUSTRIAL PURCHASING POWER: The S&MM Annual Survey

The magazine *Sales & Marketing Management* publishes annually in April a **Survey of Industrial Purchasing Power.** It provides the latest data on manufacturing activity on all levels, and profiles of over 400 customer industries that buy goods and services from both consumer and industrial manufacturers. It also includes an evaluation of the top 50 manufacturing counties, showing industrial purchasing power by counties and S.I.C. codes.

Exhibit I and accompanying text from the 1980 Survey show how the survey results are organized and retrieved for use:

(A) All the 2,843 counties with at least one manufacturing establishment of twenty or more employees are included, listed alphabetically by state. In each county, individual industries whose establishments have an aggregate employment of 1,000 or more are listed. These industries are at the four-digit level of the Standard Industrial Classification (S.I.C.) system used by the Federal Government. (See Standard Industrial Classification System (S.I.C.))

(B) When a county is a part of a metropolitan area, it is indicated with a numerical code that refers to the 300 S&MM-designated metropolitan markets. To find out in which metropolitan area a county is included, the user consults an alphabetical listing of metro markets provided.

(C) The "All mfg." line that appears in boldface type refers to the overall totals for all the manufacturing plants in the county with twenty or more employees. The names of the four-digit S.I.C. industries appear in lightface type. The *Survey* has a few more four-digit industries than shown in the Government's "Standard Industrial Classification Manual" because it has retained certain industries that were merged by the Government into catchall groups.

(D) This is the total number of manufacturing plants with at least twenty employees.

EXHIBIT I

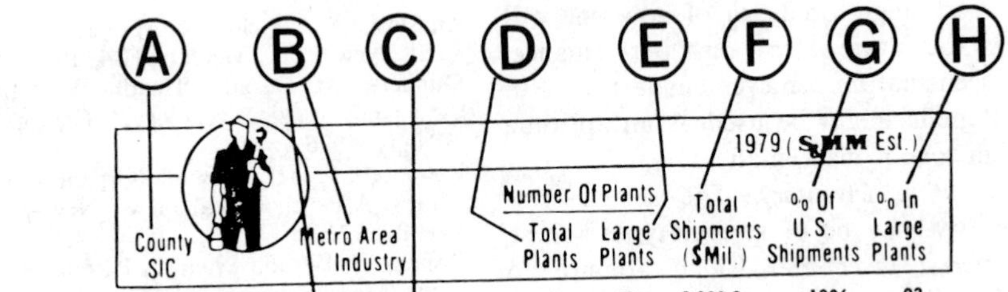

County SIC	Metro Area	Industry	Number Of Plants: Total Plants	Number Of Plants: Large Plants	1979 (S&MM Est.) Total Shipments ($Mil.)	1979 (S&MM Est.) % Of U.S. Shipments	1979 (S&MM Est.) % In Large Plants
Rock Island	**69**	**All mfg.**	**104**	**43**	**2,089.2**	**.1396**	**93**
2892		Explosives	1	1	222.7	29.0997	100
3321		Gray-iron foundries	3	2	72.6	.9058	96
3523		Farm machinery & equipment	4	4	1,076.4	10.4946	100
St. Clair	**240**	**All mfg.**	**107**	**32**	**1,442.2**	**.0964**	**81**
2011		Meat-packing plants	7	3	393.8	1.0162	87
2865		Cyclic crudes & intermediates	2	2	305.9	5.3377	100
Saline		**All mfg.**	**10**	**3**	**32.3**	**.0022**	**53**

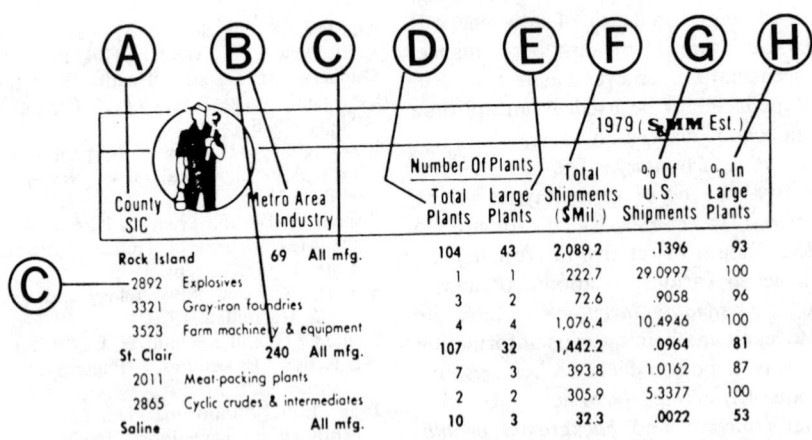

Total Plants: Establishments with 20 or more employees. **Large Plants:** Establishments with 100 or more employees. **Shipments:** Output of all establishments. % **Of U.S.:** Share of U.S. total shipments. **Average Shipments Per Plant:** Mathematical average computed by dividing total plants into total shipments. **Plant Index:** State's average shipments per plant as a ratio of all-U.S. average. **$10,670,** which represents par, or 100; number above or below 100 indicates degree by which state is above or below the U.S. norm. % **In Large Plants:** Share of shipments accounted for by plants with 100 or more employees.

Note: Details may not add up to total due to rounding.
SOURCE: *Sales & Marketing Management's 1980 Survey of Industrial Purchasing Power.*

Exhibit II

Regional and State Summaries of Manufacturing Markets

Region & State	Total Plants	Large Plants	1979 Shipments ($Mil.)	% Of U.S.	Average Shipments Per Plant ($000)	Plant Index U.S. = 100	% In Large Plants
NEW ENGLAND	**10,755**	**3,486**	**$89,659.7**	**5.9919%**	**8,337**	**78**	**80%**
Connecticut	3,006	919	26,931.7	1.7998	8,959	84	83
Maine	762	304	6,679.3	.4464	8,765	82	82
Massachusetts	4,977	1,534	40,347.1	2.6964	8,107	76	79
New Hampshire	759	277	5,891.2	.3937	7,762	73	80
Rhode Island	878	341	7,620.4	.5093	8,679	81	80
Vermont	373	111	2,190.0	.1464	5,871	55	69
MIDEAST	**28,798**	**8,604**	**271,532.2**	**18,1462**	**9,429**	**88**	**81**
Delaware	273	92	5,036.2	.3366	18,448	173	89
Dist. of Columbia	164	39	1,634.2	.1092	9,965	93	83
Maryland	1,544	587	19,512.8	1.3040	12,638	118	86
New Jersey	6,731	1,914	62,968.7	4.2081	9,355	88	79
New York	10,958	2,880	81,784.1	5.4656	7,463	70	77
Pennsylvania	9,128	3,092	100,596.2	6.7228	11,021	103	85
GREAT LAKES	**33,640**	**10,327**	**416,812.8**	**27.8552**	**12,390**	**116**	**85**
Illinois	10,220	3,170	106,968.3	7.1486	10,467	98	83
Indiana	3,713	1,421	56,954.3	3.8062	15,339	144	87
Michigan	7,105	1,809	103,984.3	6.9492	14,635	137	88
Ohio	9,074	2,843	109,002.7	7.2846	12,013	113	86
Wisconsin	3,528	1,084	39,903.2	2.6667	11,310	106	83
PLAINS	**10,275**	**2,948**	**115,296.6**	**7.7052**	**11,221**	**105**	**80**
Iowa	1,667	431	19,884.1	1.3288	11,928	112	75
Kansas	1,804	388	18,635.6	1.2454	10,330	97	78
Minnesota	2,508	838	29,773.3	1.9897	11,871	111	83
Missouri	3,149	964	34,242.1	2.2884	10,874	102	83
Nebraska	764	235	9,464.9	.6325	12,389	116	75
North Dakota	145	30	1,254.9	.0839	8,654	81	58
South Dakota	238	62	2,041.7	.1364	8,579	80	71
SOUTHEAST	**29,132**	**10,560**	**307,562.0**	**20.5541**	**10,558**	**99**	**83**
Alabama	2,331	939	25,362.3	1.6949	10,880	102	82
Arkansas	1,697	580	15,959.7	1.0666	9,405	88	77
Florida	3,694	908	26,009.1	1.7382	7,041	66	72
Georgia	3,751	1,280	34,832.5	2.3278	9,286	87	80
Kentucky	1,686	628	25,419.7	1.6988	15,077	141	87
Louisiana	1,490	525	27,939.1	1.8671	18,751	176	87
Mississippi	1,505	588	14,100.3	.9423	9,369	88	79
North Carolina	5,153	2,051	47,715.6	3.1888	9,260	87	83
South Carolina	1,824	857	21,732.9	1.4524	11,915	112	86
Tennessee	3,130	1,192	32,195.1	2.1516	10,286	96	84
Virginia	2,125	762	24,404.7	1.6309	11,485	108	85
West Virginia	746	250	11,891.0	.7947	15,940	149	88
SOUTHWEST	**9,562**	**2,804**	**119,784.2**	**8.0051**	**12,527**	**117**	**82**
Arizona	951	195	10,028.4	.6702	10,545	99	80
New Mexico	328	78	2,866.7	.1916	8,740	82	73
Oklahoma	1,477	382	18,081.2	1.2084	12,242	115	82
Texas	6,806	2,149	88,807.9	5.9350	13,048	122	83
ROCKY MOUNTAIN	**2,947**	**734**	**29,684.2**	**1.9838**	**10,073**	**94**	**76**
Colorado	1,281	306	11,531.8	.7707	9,002	84	75
Idaho	450	138	3,908.1	.2612	8,685	81	71
Montana	292	55	3,307.9	.2211	11,328	106	78
Utah	774	209	8,779.5	.5867	11,343	106	80
Wyoming	150	26	2,156.9	.1441	14,379	135	67
FAR WEST	**15,127**	**4,372**	**146,022.8**	**9.7586**	**9,653**	**90**	**80**
California	11,596	3,381	109,720.2	7.3325	9,462	89	81
Nevada	115	25	828.4	.0554	7,203	68	65
Oregon	1,678	486	13,782.8	.9211	8,214	77	73
Washington	1,738	480	21,691.4	1.4496	12,481	117	81
U.S.	**140,236**	**43,835**	**$1,496,354.5**	**100.0000%**	**$10,670**	**100**	**82%**

(E) Because of the economies of scale, large plants (100 or more employees) account for a greater share of a county's manufacturing activity than is indicated by their numbers. Hence, a separate total of such establishments is provided. They can be considered key selling prospects—the ones that merit special emphasis.

(F) This is the dollar value of all goods produced by the manufacturing type establishments. It is a reliable indicator of the county's buying potential because, overall, 58% of the dollar amount is expended on equipment, supplies, and materials (an additional 4% goes for new capital expenditures). However, the ratio will differ from industry to industry; an industry's particular ratio can be obtained from the 1977 *Census of Manufactures* report, *Selected Statistics for Industry Groups and Industries: 1977 and 1972;* MC77-2-1(P), available from Subscriber Services (Publications), Bureau of the Census, Washington, DC 20233. The shipments figure includes interplant shipments between establishments of a common ownership; however, they make up a very small share of the overall total. Also, where a four-digit S.I.C. industry is concerned, if a plant produces goods that fall into more than one classification, all its output is credited to the "primary" industry that describes the largest share of its output.

(G) The county's "All mfg." share of United States shipments indicates its importance relative to other counties. The comparable ratio is provided for four-digit industries, making it easier for the marketing executive to determine those counties that are the most important markets for his products. However, it should be borne in mind that the percentage figure in boldface type pertains to a county's share of total United States shipments, the percentage figure in lightface type to the county's share of the United States total of a particular industry. Thus the lightface percentages, when totaled, will not add up to the boldface percentage figure.

(H) The portion of a county's manufacturing output produced by the large plants will suggest the necessary level of sales coverage. Normally, the higher the percentage figure, the fewer salespeople required because proportionately fewer prospects will account for relatively more of the purchases.

Exhibit II shows a representative Survey highlight.

SOURCE: *Sales & Marketing Management, New York, New York*

Cross References: *Distribution Planning and Research; Patterns of Population Growth; Marketing Research: Sources of Information; Standard Met-*

INDUSTRIAL RESEARCH ACCOUNTING

Since Research and Development operations are largely non-repetitive and the end result is usable knowledge rather than a tangible product, the techniques applied in **Industrial Research Accounting** differ somewhat from those commonly applied to manufacturing operations.

Definition of Function. Specific definitions differ from company to company because the nature of the activities carried on and the manner in which they are organized differ. As stated in *NAA Research Report No. 29* [1]:

> Research and development comprises a variety of activities, including search for new products and new manufacturing processes; improvement of existing products, processes, and equipment; finding new uses for known products; solving technical problems arising in manufacture and application of products; and expanding general knowledge in basic scientific fields.

In the *FASB Statement No. 2*, "Accounting for Research and Development Costs," issued in 1974 [2] research and development are defined separately. These two definitions make use of the distinction between, "planned search or critical investigation aimed at discovery of new knowledge" (research) and "the translation of research findings or other knowledge into a plan or design" (development). Nevertheless, the FASB Statement No. 2 does not require that R&D expenditures be separately reported, but it does require that all firms, with some stated exceptions, must treat R&D expenditures for financial reporting purposes as charges against current income. The Statement also contains examples of R&D activities and of activities that should not be treated as R&D.

One of the findings of NAA research study, "Industrial R&D Management" [3] was that

Statement No. 2 had little, if any, effect on industrial planning for R&D. Most firms were expensing a substantial portion of R&D expenditures prior to Statement No. 2. Moreover, among a variety of factors taken into consideration by a company with a well-established R&D activity of primary concern is the need to maintain it at a relatively stable level in order to preserve continuity of R&D staff and avoid potential competitive disadvantages. It is, therefore, of minor importance whether R&D expenditures are expensed or deferred, though this probably is of greater importance to small firms.

Research and development are often included in the organizational structure of a company as a single R&D function. The role of this function in the attainment of company goals is well understood. Its general objectives are set forth largely by using managerial criteria common to all activities within the company. With regard to the process of achieving these objectives, it is recognized, however, that R&D is not fully susceptible to the analytical technology applied to the other company activities. It is also increasingly recognized that the effectiveness of R&D as a purposive activity can be enhanced by the judicious use of measurement and control devices designed to provide information for managerial decision-making. Conventional approaches have become practicable, by virtue of new information technology.

Some company organization plans assign to the research department responsibility for technical services applied to the elimination of manufacturing difficulties, routine testing of materials and products, and occasional production or sale of items requiring skills or equipment not available in the factory. While such functions are performed by research personnel, they are not necessarily looked upon as research activities. Consequently, costs of the work are often transferred to departments served. The research department in a small company usually performs a wider variety of tasks than it does in a large company where greater size permits more extensive subdivision of functions.

A dividing line between Research and Production often needs to be established by company policy because there is overlapping at the stage where new products or methods developed by Research are being transferred to Production. This stage may include production in a pilot plant, experimental production with regular factory equipment, and work by research personnel to eliminate difficulties which arise in the early stages of production.

In general, there are two main options regarding the place of R&D in the organization: (1) centralized R&D, segregated from the rest of the business, and (2) decentralized R&D, placed within divisions and/or other units of the company. It is not unusual to find some decentralized R&D efforts in a company with a corporate (centralized) R&D organization. Another alternative is to have a centralized administration of R&D, while the planning and operational control of R&D remain at the respective profit/responsibility centers.

A different way of looking at the organization of R&D is to distinguish a horizontal from a vertical structure. The former is composed of various groups working side by side on specific processes or products, or assigned to specific phases or stages of R&D projects, or formed for various disciplines, etc. The latter regulates the levels of authority, communication channels, roles, relationships, and responsibilities.

Classifying Research Costs. The plan of accounting realistically for research costs should provide classifications which permit desired reports to be prepared directly from the accounts. Provision should also be made for special analyses which may be desired from time to time.

NAA Research Report No. 29 states that plans for classifying research costs are designed to provide answers to the following principal questions:

(1) How much was spent for research and development?

(2) Who spent it? (i.e., classification by responsibility for control).

(3) For what were the expenditures incurred? (i.e., classification by nature of expense).

(4) How was the effort of the research and development organization applied? (i.e., classification by project and division).

In order that cost may be accumulated under appropriate headings to answer such questions, accounts are set up and code numbers are assigned to them to facilitate data-processing operations.

One or more control accounts are needed to ascertain the total amount spent for research. Multiple control accounts are used when more than one major class of research cost is recognized. For example, one company uses the three control accounts listed below.

(1) *Control Account 15300—Research Expense*

Includes cost of operating the Research and Development Center, pilot plants operated by the Research and Development Center, the cost of services of outside laboratories, and expenses incurred by the staff of the Research and Development Center.

(2) *Control Account 15400—Research Development Expense*

Includes costs incurred in and by the company's plants for tests made at the request of the Research and Development Center.

(3) *Control Account 15600—Engineering Development Expense*

Includes costs incurred in the development and application of a new or redesigned machine or facility.

Major categories of R&D expense and the corresponding control accounts differ from company to company according to activities carried on and preferences of top management in each company.

EXHIBIT I

TYPICAL RESPONSIBILITY CODES

Code Number	*Unit Name*	*Supervisor*	*Location*
6701	Plastic Research	C. Smith	Research center
6702	Ceramics Laboratory	E. Williams	Research center
6705	Motor Development Laboratory	O. Carlson	Chicago plant
6710	Project B Laboratory	E. Johnson	Cleveland
6713	Patent Department	J. Law	Research center
6714	Technical Library	A. Richards	Research center
6718	Research Administration	J. Keller	Research center

Responsibility for Cost Incurrence. Accumulation of R&D costs by responsibilities for control is accomplished by use of a responsibility code. This code should follow the company's organization plan for its research activities. While the units in such a code may be divisions, departments, or other similar units, each should be an actual organization unit headed by an individual in charge of activities within the unit. Otherwise, it is difficult or impossible to fix responsibility for costs.

Responsibility codes are illustrated in Exhibit I.

R&D costs incurred are accumulated by accounts represented by numbers in the responsibility code. This permits cost reports showing by whom costs were incurred. Charges to each responsibility are best limited to items which the corresponding executive or supervisor is authorized to incur, for responsibility cannot be maintained for costs which the individual has no authority to control. If, for any reason, costs not controllable within a given responsibility are included in the charges, controllable and noncontrollable items should not be merged, but reported separately.

Source or Item of Expense. Within each responsibility, costs should be classified properly by source or item of expenditure. Research and development expenditures arise from the same basic sources (e.g., salaries and wages, supplies, occupancy of space, etc.) as do costs of other functions, and a uniform, company-wide classification is often used. This makes possible summarization of costs by source or item of expense for the company as a whole.

However, in some cases, it may be desirable to have additional expense source accounts to catalog expenses peculiar to R&D activities. Under decentralized management, an R&D division is usually permitted to establish whatever accounts it considers helpful in guiding its operations. Accounts established should, however, be related to a general company chart of accounts so that accounts of the R&D division can be readily consolidated with those of other divisions.

Application of R&D Effort. Financial control over R&D activities is exercised primarily by controlling the application of effort and facilities to projects. A cumulative record of costs incurred as work progresses on each project is an essential aid in the process of financial control. The same record provides the basic information needed to allocate R&D expenditures to company divisions and to product lines benefited. If research is undertaken for customers or others outside the company, a knowledge of project cost is needed to ascertain profit or loss on each contract. A record of project cost is necessary for billing customers where research services are priced on a cost reimbursement basis.

Methods employed to determine costs of individual projects are much like those used in job-order costing of manufacturing orders. Each project is assigned a number, and costs applied to the project are accumulated on a cost sheet or other suitable record.

When an extensive R&D program is carried on, project codes may be designed to facilitate summaries of costs on a variety of desired bases. A chemical manufacturer, for example, classifies projects and summarizes project costs under the categories listed below:

(1) *Sales and Production Service Projects*

Include activities of laboratories designed to maintain and assist in the normal growth of established products.

Code Number.

1. Sales Service.
2. Quality Control.
3. Production Service.

(2) *Research and Development Projects*

Include all activities of laboratories designed to develop new products or to increase sales and profits on present business at an extraordinary rate.

Code Number.

5. Research and Development—Established Products.
6. Research and Development—Related New Products.
7. Research and Development—Unrelated New Products.

Another example from *NAA Research Report No. 29* illustrates the development of additional information and the purpose this information is intended to serve. (See Exhibit II.)

The code number shown in Exhibit II is entered on time sheets filled out by individual laboratory employees. The first six digits in the code (which are pre-printed on time sheets) identify the person who did the work, his division, and his department. The remaining digits (which are filled in by the individual) identify the product group and the item worked on, the purpose (that is, to improve the product), and the origin of the project. The project source code serves as a basis for accounting distribution of costs when projects are carried out as a service to responsibilities ouside of the research and development department. This plan for classifying projects accomplishes the following purposes:

(1) It furnishes a short-term record to R&D management, that is, to the department head, to the division head, and to the vice-president responsible for R&D, on how the effort of the scientific areas is being applied.

(2) It serves as a basis for projecting and preparing new budgets.

(3) It furnishes a long-time record of approximate expense by project.

(4) It furnishes a long-time record of the types of research effort expended.

EXHIBIT II

CODING SYSTEM FOR SUPPORTING INFORMATION

Employee	John Doe 0012
Division	1—Organic and Biochemical Research
Department	3—Microbiological Research
Group and Product	213—Antibiotics: Penicillin
Type of Effort	3—Improvement
Source of Problems	00—Scientific Area

W. B. McFarland, formerly Director of Research, National Association of Accountants, New York, New York

Information References

Batty, Joseph, "Accounting for Research and Development," London, U.K., Business Books, Ltd., 1976.

Francis, Philip H., "Principles of R&D Management." New York, American Management Association, Inc., 1977.

White, Percival A. F., "Effective Management of Research and Development," New York, Wiley, 1975.

References Cited

[1] "Accounting for Research and Development Costs," *Research Report 29,* National Association of Accountants, New York, 1955.

[2] "Accounting for Research and Development Costs," *Statement No. 2,* Stamford, Conn., Financial Accounting Standards Board, 1974.

[3] Gambino, A. J. and Gartenberg, M., "Industrial R&D Management," New York, National Association of Accountants, 1979.

Cross References: *Basic Research: Management Aspects; Industrial Research Budgeting.*

INDUSTRIAL RESEARCH BUDGETING

The nature of research and development must be kept in mind in designing a plan for cost control. Unlike manufacturing, neither the precise form of the end-result nor the exact procedures necessary to obtain this result can be predicted with certainty. Except for routine supporting functions, R&D involves training, skill, and judgment in a high degree. For this reason, reliable standards usually cannot be set for measuring efficiency of R&D operations as they can for repetitive manufacturing operations. Under these circumstances control over costs is concerned with the amount and direction of the work to be done rather than with the results obtained.

The R&D Budget. The principal financial control for R&D activities is the periodic budget. Through the budget, management can control the total amount of money spent for R&D and it can direct expenditures to make sure that funds are spent in the way management wants them to be spent.

This is accomplished by planning how available funds are to be used and by comparing current expenses with budgets to aid management in charge of research to keep actual expenditures within limits. The R&D budget is an appropriation type budget in which expense allowances are based upon preplanned activity rather than a flexible budget in which the experienced activity level determines the amount of allowable expense. However, when properly applied, the budget does not restrict R&D management's judgment as to how its resources can be best used, because individual budget allowances should always be subject to revision—either upward or downward—if new developments indicate that previously made plans should be changed.

Recognition should be given to the fact that the budget is a financial control tool, and not a device to measure the output of R&D operations. In many respects, budgetary control of R&D expense is similar to control of advertising expense. While the application of effort can be controlled through the control of expenditures, measurement of results obtained in relation to specific expenditures is usually uncertain and often impossible. Certain goals in the form of new knowledge may underlie the allocation of resources when the budget is prepared, but expenditures are not contingent upon realization of these goals. Budgetary control over R&D expenses should not be confused with budgetary control over variable manufacturing costs, where the amount of allowable expenditure can be based directly on output of a measurable product under standardized conditions.

The scope and objectives of an R&D program are determined by top management, and policy, once established, usually continues from year to year. Each year the amount to be spent is determined by a specific appropriation made by top executive management or the board of directors.

Detailed Budget for R&D Expense. In some companies a detailed budget covering projects proposed and facilities to carry out work entailed by these projects is prepared before the annual appropriation for R&D is made. In other companies, project planning at the annual budget stage is limited to projects to be continued from the prior period with, in addition, broad plans for new projects.

An NAA study of accounting for research and development costs [1] states that detailed budgeting of research costs generally starts with consideration of personnel and facilities that are expected to be available. These are then tentatively distributed to proposed projects. The reason for this approach is that a qualified scientific and technical staff cannot be expanded or contracted in accord with short-period shifts in research plans. Effective research requires long-range planning and stable employment for personnel. However, outside research organizations can often be used to supplement a company's own research facilities.

A more recent NAA study [2] states that usually the amount to be allocated to the entire R&D function is determined by the company management on the basis of its judgment as to the expenditures that the company can support as compared with the budget prepared by R&D management, including moneys that must be provided for contracted OUTSIDE RESEARCH. The amount for the corporate R&D program is determined on the basis of amounts needed for the projects that are supportable in accordance with established criteria such as the generation of sales and a standard minimum for return on investment. The amounts budgeted for specific projects are based on estimates of work hours, including supporting service personnel, cost of material, and travel. Variable and fixed overhead costs and consultant fees are estimated in accordance with the data for prior years as adjusted for expected changes in the level of activity, for inflation, etc. If new attractive opportunities arise during the year, a supplement to the budget is prepared.

Budgeting by Projects. In some cases the annual budget is completely built up by projects as well as by source of expense. In other cases capacity for R&D provided by costs budgeted is only partially assigned to specific projects when the annual budget is prepared. The detail in which project costs are prepared also varies according to nature of the planned projects and practices of the company. Detailed budgeting is desirable when the operations to be performed can be planned in advance and time requirements can be estimated with sufficient reliability to constitute a useful guide. Many product development or application projects fall in this class. On the other hand, projects in the field of "pure" or exploratory research of a broad character cannot be budgeted in detail because no one can predict what work will be necessary or what the outcome may be. In general, as a project moves closer to the stage of commercial application, costs are more closely controlled by pre-established estimates of costs to be incurred.

Detailed estimates of time applied to projects by classes of employees are prepared by research management because this work can be done only by persons who possess an understanding of the technical problems that will be encountered. The accountant assists by translating research plans expressed in man-hours into dollars of research expense. The accountant also applies overhead rates for charging projects with an appropriate share of indirect costs which cannot be identified with individual projects. However, throughout the budgetmaking process, decisions and plans for use of personnel and facilities are a responsibility of management in charge of R&D, and the accountant's function is to assist management to express these plans in financial terms.

Once the R&D budget has been prepared, it provides the basis for subsequent control to make sure that previously made plans are carried out. However, as the budget period progresses, research management reviews progress in projects under way and may make revisions in the budget. Unused funds may be shifted from one project to another, new projects introduced, and unpromising projects terminated.

Maintaining Current Control Over R&D Costs. Current control is concerned with keeping actual expenses in line with expenses budgeted. Reports showing actual expenses to date in comparison with budgeted expenses are needed to guide R&D management in maintaining control over costs.

The purposes of cost control in its application to R&D activities should be understood throughout the organization to ensure cooperation. These purposes are:

(1) To make sure that the plan expressed in the budget is followed by directing funds into projects of types desired.

(2) To avoid spending R&D funds on nonproductive or nonresearch activities.

(3) To stimulate an attitude of dollar-consciousness so that personnel will attempt to perform as much research as possible for the funds available.

(4) To keep the total spent within the limit set by the appropriation for the period.

To reduce the amount spent for R&D should not be an objective of cost control. On the contrary, the fact that expenditures are substantially less than budgeted is likely to indicate that planned work is not proceeding. If true, managerial attention is needed to prevent loss of profits in the future.

Variances from budget signal deviations from the planned application of funds. They have no significance as a measure of results accomplished by R&D personnel.

Project budgets are estimates prepared to guide application of funds rather than to set rigid limits to project costs. When actual expenditures approach the amounts estimated, a review of the project should be made. At this time, R&D management decides whether to recommend an additional appropriation or to discontinue the work. When a project promises a valuable outcome, it is unlikely to be closed because it could not be completed with the initial appropriation.

W. B. McFarland, formerly Director of Research, National Association of Accountants, New York, New York

Information References

Hill, Walter D., "Planning Investments in Research and Development," *Managerial Planning,* July–August 1970.

Mathews, Lawrence, "Practical Operating Budgeting," New York, McGraw-Hill, 1977.

Pattillo, James W., "Zero-Base Budgeting: A Planning, Resource Allocation and Control Tool," New York, National Association of Accountants, 1977.

Petersen, Gerald T., "Working R&D into Corporate Strategy," *The Conference Board Record,* January 1976.

Quinn, James B., "Budgeting for Research," Chap. 11 in "Handbook of Industrial Research Management," Heyel, C., ed., New York, Van Nostrand Reinhold, 2nd ed., 1968.

Rogoff, Donald, "Budgeting R&D—A Behavioral Approach," *Managerial Planning*, September-October 1976.

References Cited

[1] "Accounting for Research and Development Costs," *Research Report 29*, National Association of Accountants, New York, 1955.
[2] Gambino, A. J. and Gartenberg, M., "Industrial R&D Management," New York, National Association of Accountants, 1979.

Cross References: *Basic Research: Management Aspects; Budgeting; Industrial Research Accounting; Outside Research.*

INDUSTRIAL RESEARCH AND DEVELOPMENT

Each year the National Science Foundation (NSF) issues science resources reports that provide detailed information on various facets of the American scientific and technical personnel system and on the different modes of R&D funding and performance. Its publication, "National Patterns of Science and Technology Resources, 1980" [1], the initial volume of a new NSF series, presents an integrated summary overview of United States science and technology resources, with a detailed analysis of R&D resources viewed from a national perspective.

National Totals. For the four years preceding the issuance of the report in March 1980, United States financial support for research and development showed signs of renewed strength, comparable to the levels recorded during the first seven years of the sixties. In constant dollars, the nation's R&D expenditures increased each year since 1975, for a four-year total real growth of 18%. Non-Federal funding increased at almost twice the rate of Federal R&D funding.

Defense, energy, and space-related research and development, representing two-fifths of the $54.3 billion R&D total in 1979, were chiefly responsible for the growth in R&D activity, while inflation was the chief damping factor in the growth of real R&D support. For 1980, the total estimated expenditure was $60.4 billion; the overall increase is estimated at 11%, or 1% in constant dollars using the Office of Management and Budget's inflation estimate of 10% [1]. (See Exhibit I.)

The United States spends more than any other nation on R&D activities—twice the total amount spent by the other Western countries and Japan together. Relative to the gross national product (GNP), United States expenditures for R&D are equal to those of West Germany, with Japan a close third. Excluding defense and space expenditures and concentrating on "civilian" R&D activities, the resulting R&D-GNP ratio is 1.5% for the United States as compared with 2.2% for West Germany and 1.9% for Japan. These ratios for all countries have been leveling off since the early seventies (Exhibit II).

The search for solutions to the energy shortage has clearly affected the national R&D picture. Since 1975 the increase in both Federal and industry R&D expenditures for energy programs has accounted for three-tenths of the constant-dollar increase in all R&D expenditures in the United States. Industry's energy-related R&D spending has risen at an average annual rate of 26%, or 18% in constant dollars, since 1972. Defense R&D expenditures, while clearly the largest single item in the nation's R&D total (24% of the total in 1979), accounted for less than one-tenth of the real R&D dollar increase over the same period. Recent budgets, however, are reversing this situation, with significant increases in defense R&D funding.

Definitions. As defined by NSF [2], R&D activity includes the following:

Research and Development—Basic and applied research in the sciences and engineering and the design and development of prototypes and processes. This definition excludes quality control, routine product testing, market research, sales promotion, sales service, research in the social sciences or psychology, and other nontechnological activities or technical services.

Basic Research—Original investigations for the advancement of scientific knowledge not having specific commercial objectives, although such investigations may be in fields of present or potential interest to the reporting company.

Applied Research—Investigations directed to the discovery of new scientific knowledge having specific commercial objectives with respect to products or processes.

Development—Technical activities of a non-routine nature concerned with translating research findings or other scientific knowledge into products or processes. Does not include routine technical services to customers or other activities excluded from the above definition of research and development.

Basic Research, Applied Research, and Development. Within the research total, propor-

EXHIBIT I

THE NATIONAL R&D EFFORT

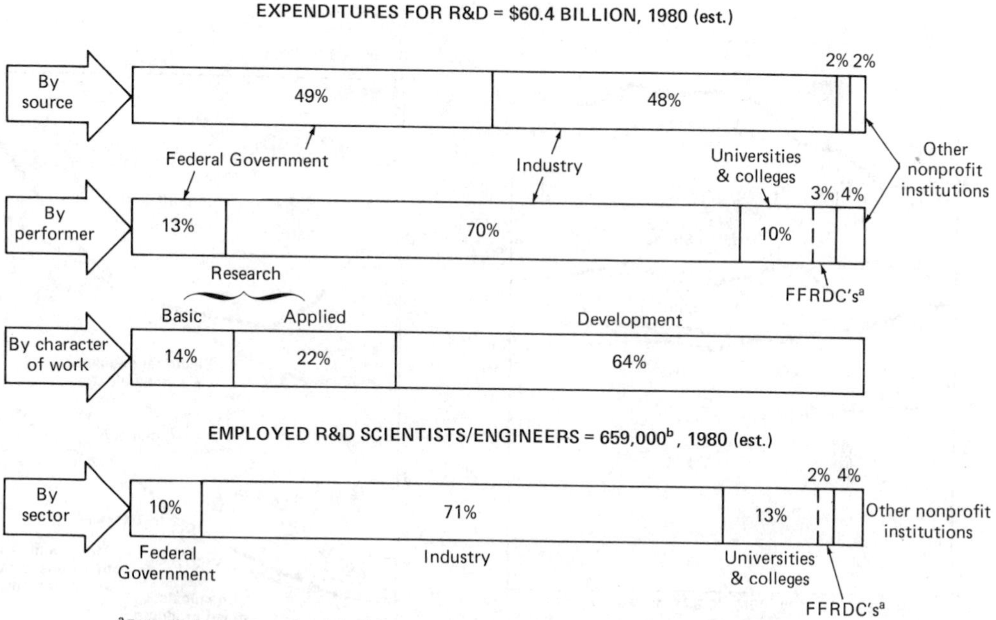

[a]Federally funded research and development centers administered by universities and colleges.
[b]Full-time equivalents.
SOURCE: National Science Foundation: appendix tables 5, 6, 7, 9, 11, and 14.

tionately more funds have been allocated to basic research—35% in 1975 and an estimated 40% in 1980. Between 1975 and 1979, Federal basic research obligations grew 24% in constant dollars. Because of fiscal restraints and inflation, final figures for real growth in Federal basic research support in 1980 is expected to be more moderate. Meanwhile, Federal expenditures for applied research and development increased in real terms between 1975 and 1979 at average annual rates of 2% each, compared with 4% each for the national total funding of these activities.

Federal R&D Support. Federal R&D expenditures, which dropped in constant dollars by more than 20% between 1966—the peak year—and 1975, have increased each year since 1975 at an average annual rate of nearly 3% in real terms. Moreover, the proportion to total Federal outlays allocated to R&D support increased in 1979 for the first time in a decade. Although significant increases occurred in defense, space, and energy, the greatest Federal R&D emphasis during the late seventies was in the energy area. Succeeding Federal R&D effort is expected to stress defense, the space shuttle, and selected energy projects.

The focus of Federal R&D obligations changed significantly between 1971 and 1979, with an increase in research activity relative to development. Within the research total, however, not all fields of science increased at the same rates. Since 1971, the fields growing most rapidly have been (1) the life sciences, (2) the environmental sciences, and (3) mathematics and computer science—in that order. The life sciences accounted for 36% of all Federal research obligations in 1979, engineering for 24%, the physical sciences for 17%, and the environmental sciences for 11%.

Industrial R&D. Since 1975, industrial R&D has been increasing at a faster constant-dollar rate—6% annually through 1979—than has Federal R&D support (3%). Within the industry sector, which provides about 95% of the non-Federal total, the growth in company R&D spending has closely paralleled sales increases. Interviews with industrial R&D executives indicate that this growth reflects in part a change in corporate strategy, which places

EXHIBIT II

INTERNATIONAL R&D/GNP

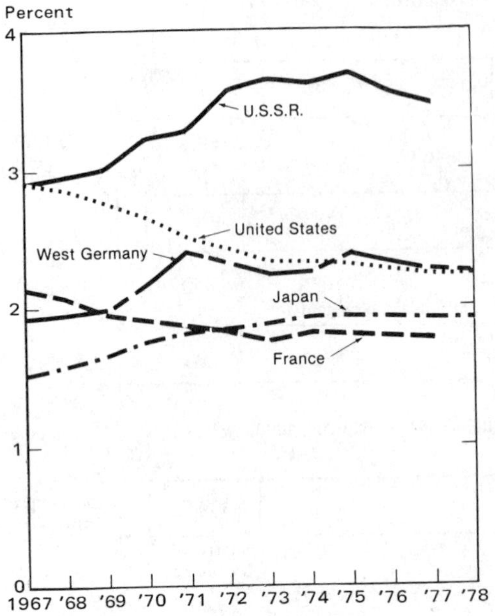

SOURCES: National Science Foundation, Organization for Economic Cooperation and Development, and Robert Campbell (Indiana University); appendix table 17.

Note: Data regarding the U.S.S.R. should be treated as rough estimates because differences in Soviet R&D definitions and GNP accounting make international comparisons involving the U.S.S.R. difficult.

EXHIBIT III

FUNDS FOR R&D PERFORMANCE BY THE FIVE LEADING INDUSTRIES.

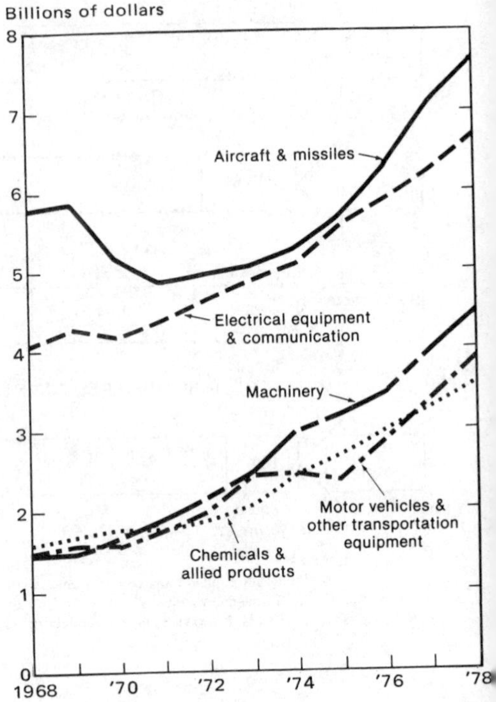

SOURCE: National Science Foundation; appendix table 37.

greater emphasis on R&D performance as a source of future growth and new market opportunities. The NSF report points out, however, that corporate strategy is only a partial explanation for recent increases in company R&D funding. The Federal Government provides almost 50 cents of every R&D dollar spent domestically, and industry provides 47 cents. But Federal policies influence industry's own expenditures through regulations and minimum standards in areas such as environmental pollution, food and drug production, and public safety.

R&D expenditures by industrial firms reached $33.4 billion in 1978, a 4% constant-dollar gain over the 1977 figure. Nearly 80% of these R&D funds are spent by companies in five industries—aircraft, electrical equipment, machinery, motor vehicles, and chemicals. NSF estimates that final 1980 figures will show industry's total expenditures to exceed $42 billion. (See Exhibit III.)

R&D directed toward pollution abatement rose 10% in real terms between 1977 and 1978. Greater emphasis on basic research has also occurred, particularly in energy-related work. Adjusted for inflation, industry reported a 20% increase in basic research funds between 1975 and 1979, following a decrease by a similar amount during the preceding nine years.

Academic R&D. Academic R&D expenditures have increased at rates significantly above the rate of inflation in every year since 1975. Universities and colleges spend more than one half of all basic research funds in the nation, with most of the financing being provided by the Federal Government. However, there has been a shift in emphasis away from basic research toward applied research. Basic research accounted for 69% of all academic R&D expenditures in 1978, compared with 77% a decade earlier, while the proportion allocated to applied research grew from 19% to 26%.

Innovation as a Corporate "Way of Life." Since World War II, the achievements of industrial research have been spectacular to a degree that makes the adjective itself almost an understatement. The strides in space technology, as one example, while perhaps foreshadowed in preceding technology, have emphatically borne out the point that management can only sense what may importantly affect its operations a mere year or two ahead. In 1945, television, jet travel, and digital computer industries were commercially nonexistent. A short two decades later these industries were contributing more than $13 billion to our Gross National Product, and an estimated 90,000 jobs.

The rapidity with which innovations became a familiar part of everyday life sometimes makes us lose sight of how sudden was the revolution they effected. In 1949, television had been out of the laboratory about three years,and there were a few thousand sets in use. Ten years later, the industry reported that television sets, tubes, components, and various materials going into components represented upward of $885 million in business, and in 1972 the figure based on estimates by *Merchandising Week* was approximately $2.6 billion (factory prices).

As of 1981, the new scientific breakthroughs that are exciting commercial and investment interest are in the field of "genetic engineering," with newly formed companies prominent in the news, carrying such names as Genetech Inc., Cetus Corp., and Genetics Replication Technologies. Well-established firms such as Becton, Dickinson & Co., New England Nuclear Corp., and the Ortho Pharmaceutical Corp., a subsidiary of Johnson & Johnson, are among those doing hybridoma research. (Hybridomas are "clones" of hybrid cells grown in the test tube; each hybridoma produces a unique antibody, a protein bit that can seek out and latch onto specific cells or microbes. The quality of selectivity gives antibodies great potential for new methods of diagnosis and treatment of disease.) Following earlier patterns, it can well be that in a short decade developments in the whole area of genetic engineering will burgeon into a multibillion dollar industry.

But innovation as a "corporate way of life" is not limited to "glamorous" scientific breakthroughs. A continuing program of developing new products has become a normal factor in business management. A McGraw-Hill survey of business plans and expenditures [3] indicates that for the manufacturing industries as a whole, managements in 1979 estimated that by 1983, 15% of their sales would be from new products—new products being defined as products not produced in 1979. The same 15% figure was reported in a Conference Board study [4] covering 148 medium- and large-sized manufacturers. Here the figure referred to current sales of products introduced over the preceding five years. (The survey dealt only with major new products, not with existing products which had been improved or modified.) Incidentally, the firms reported improvement in their ability to predict the sale of new products. Two-thirds of the surveyed firms said the accuracy of their first-year sales projections from major new products had significantly improved over the past five years. (See also NEW-PRODUCT PLANNING: Profitability Projections.)

The Challenge to Management. The foregoing discussion indicates the need to plan for and manage industrial R&D. The *need* is hardly questioned in any quarter. The *how* is a question that must be answered by every going concern—large, medium-size, or small—to avoid serious jeopardy of position. Indeed, for many companies the pressure of competition may make the question one of sheer competitive survival.

The problem is complicated by the fact that many types of research and development programs require almost back-breaking investment before payout. DuPont, as an example, has reported that it invested $27 million in research, development, and facilities for nylon before large-scale production was achieved. "Dacron" polyester fiber was an $80-million project.

Similarly, at Westinghouse the development of a superconducting generator has reportedly been under development for 30 years. As of this writing Westinghouse is finally building an experimental 300-megavolt-ampere superconducting generator which it plans to complete by 1983 and have running at a commercial power station by the middle 1980s [4]. And a Battelle Memorial Institute study of eight cases of technological innovation, out of which ten new products emerged, shows that each took an average of 19.2 years to move successfully from laboratory to marketplace [5].

The foregoing is not to say, of course, that planned research programs can be carried on only by industrial giants. It does emphasize the need for careful determination of commercial possibilities before extensive research projects are undertaken. This critical step is often overlooked or given too little emphasis. And it does mean that once research and development programs are established, management must give the same attention to review and control and judgment of results that it gives to any other aspect of the business.

Risks. Development work in durables, as seen from the above, is subject to intensified risk. If not as extreme as the Westinghouse and Battelle examples, a minimum of six to eight years may well be involved between the original concept of a new piece of equipment and the delivery of tested units to customers. In that period, much may have happened to the business climate in general, and to the target market in particular. In addition, concurrently with the rising costs of individual research projects, the profitable life span of many new equipment offerings seems to be foreshortened. The pressure of competition, expensive model revisions and improvements, if not total withdrawal from the market, are often called for within a relatively short time after the original introduction. For example, the history of commercially available business computers has witnessed one technological revolution after the other, resulting in four successive computer "generations." The risks in this industry were dramatized by RCA's traumatic bow-out in 1971 at a reported loss of $250 million.

Exhibit IV schematically portrays the concept of the life cycle of new products. The actual time scale will vary with different products and industries, but the figure is intended to illustrate that every product or product line, or even a system of interrelated products, traditionally goes through a cycle with the following periods (of varying lengths): a product development and introductory stage, during which there will more than likely be a loss; then a growth or market development period of sharply rising sales, with correspondingly rising profits. The peak in profit as a percentage of sales occurs at a point when acceleration changes to deceleration, and instead of exponentially rising, the sales curve begins to show lesser increases. This is the point at which the effects of competition begins to tell, and it ushers in a period of market maturity, during which sales reach a peak, as the product reaches practical saturation in the share of market it can achieve. This is followed by a period of decline, with diminishing profits.

What is required, then, is planning ahead for new products while profits on the existing products are still high, in order to provide future profits to compensate for the fall-off. In some types of products—cosmetics, for example—items in a line will have a relatively brief life cycle, and companies must continually plan

EXHIBIT IV

LIFE CYCLE OF NEW PRODUCTS

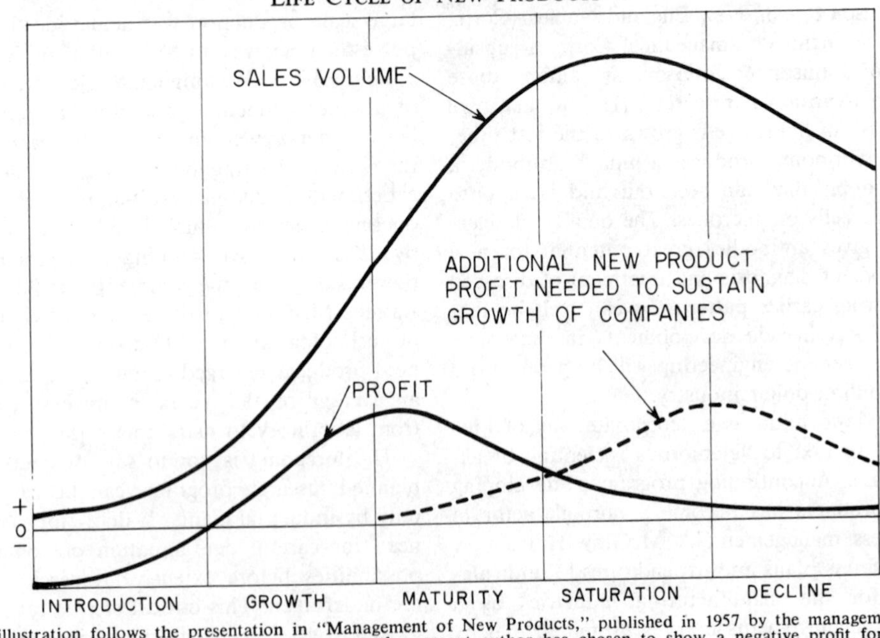

(This illustration follows the presentation in "Management of New Products," published in 1957 by the management consulting firm of Booz, Allen & Hamilton; however, the present author has chosen to show a negative profit for the introductory period.)

ahead, living, as it were, on a plateau of successive new-product peaks.

Developing the Specific Company Program. In focusing on its particular business, the starting point in any management's reasoning will be an attempt to establish bench marks by which to make a first approximation of the adequacy of its own program. While no standard formula can be cited, it is helpful to have industry bench marks by which to judge what companies in roughly similar situations are doing. A general measure often used is R&D spending as a percent of net sales. Exhibit V provides benchmarks from the 25th annual McGraw-Hill Survey of Business Plans and Expenditures (1980).

Attempts should, of course, be made to gauge competitive activity in R&D. Through its sales, purchasing, and engineering services departments, management can secure intelligence as to order of magnitude and trends of research by competitors; through their contacts, all of these departments can act as eyes and ears for R&D policy-making groups.

EXHIBIT V

R&D AS A PERCENT OF SALES
(1978 PLUS PROJECTIONS FOR 1979, 1982)

	1978	*1979*	*1982*
Iron and steel	0.43	0.50	0.49
Nonferrous metals	0.62	0.61	0.71
Electrical machinery[1]	3.66	3.73	4.06
Machinery	3.45	3.57	3.46
Aerospace	14.39	13.07	14.71
Autos, trucks and parts, and other transp. equipment	3.25	3.25	3.10
Stone, clay, and glass	0.79	0.81	0.86
Fabricated metals and instruments	1.60	1.61	1.54
Chemicals	2.90	2.88	2.90
Paper	0.66	0.68	0.67
Rubber	1.58	1.57	1.41
Petroleum	1.13	1.10	1.02
Textile mill products and apparel	0.21	0.20	0.18
Food and beverages	0.19	0.19	0.22
Other manufacturing	0.15	0.14	0.12
ALL MANUFACTURING	2.07	2.08	2.15

1. Excludes some electronic communications equipment.

To arrive at a reasonable business judgment as to the justifiable total R&D appropriation, the following probing questions are in order:

(1) Do our figures show a relationship between change in our ratio and sales gain? Is there a relationship between our R&D expenditures and our share of market?

(2) What has been the relationship between our R&D expense and selling and advertising expense?

(3) How many new ideas and marketable products have been forthcoming over a period, compared with the amount spent on research? How does our rate of innovations compare with what competition is doing?

(4) What has been our record as to "feast and famine" research support?

Finally, to keep the whole picture in perspective, it should be borne in mind that innovation is not simply R&D. In the words of the Panel on Invention and Innovation [6], "the path between an invention (or idea) and the marketplace is a hazardous venture, replete with obstacles and substantial risks."

Organization and Control. Organization of R&D involves, first, the place it should have within the company organization and structure and its relations with other departments, and second, its proper internal organization.

Organizational Relationships. Experience indicates that where a serious effort is projected, a status for Research on a par with other important segments—Manufacturing, Finance, Sales—is called for. This implies in most companies a vice-presidential level.

In final commercial product development as distinguished from the underlying research investigations, relationships, with other departments may present problems. Exhibit VI reproduces the substantive portions of a policy statement one company developed regarding the initiation of research projects. (Detailed statements in the company's procedural manual spell out the mechanics of authorizations, initiating projects, and so on.) The statement was drawn up after the company had had several experiences of expensive work being undertaken on products which were later found to have limited commercial potential. Some companies with active product diversification programs have separate product planning departments. Others have product development committees, composed of representatives from the major departments involved. No matter what the form, the organizational problem is

EXHIBIT VI

POLICY STATEMENT

New-Product and Improved-Product Development

(1) Policy Objective: The Company requires that continuing productive effort be directed toward adding new, profitable markets by developing new uses for existing products, adapting existing products as required, and creating new products. However, before committing significant funds to any of these types of development work, the Company requires that all reasonable precautions be taken to ascertain the practicability of entering the field, the commercial possibilities, and the probable investment involved.

(2) The Research Division is concerned with investigations into new products and processes. It carries such projects to the point where significant further appropriations would call for management review based on market potentials established by the Market Research Department.

(3) All suggestions for new product development, no matter where the idea originated, must first be reviewed by the Market Research Department. Management approval must be obtained by the Market Research Department before projects are undertaken by the Research Division, *with one important exception*:

(a) Research can "self-generate" ideas without individual management approval and without review by the Market Research Department, as long as the work done by Research is within its budgetary limitations for exploratory projects. On all developments of a promising nature, on which further work would call for large-scale appropriations, management authorization must definitely be obtained.

(4) Before any new-product project or extensive product-change project is approved by management, there must be, in addition to estimates as to feasibility rendered by Research, an estimate of sales, prices, and profit potentials developed by Market Research.

(5) The intent is to have the Market Research Department serve as the coordinator in assuring that proper divisions of the Company simultaneously develop the preliminary data on commercial possibilities, technical practicability, patent implications, and the like, to provide data needed for intelligent authorization of further expenditures.

one of coordination, communication, and follow-through.

Internal Organization. The internal organization will obviously be dictated by the size of the research activity. The principle to be stressed is that the administrative organization should be such as to free the director of research as much as possible from routine administrative preoccupations so that he may concern himself with the company's broad program for the future and keep up with the accelerating developments in his own and related fields. In most companies this means the establishment of an administrative-assistant function to take over the direction of the procedural and paperwork problems, and to supervise the necessary clerical and information support.

Project Control. The GANTT CHART, so effectively used in production, can profitably be applied to progress measurement and control of R&D projects. CRITICAL PATH METHOD (CPM), LINE OF BALANCE, and PERT (PROGRAM EVALUATION AND REVIEW TECHNIQUE) are more recent control methods especially suited to complex, nonroutine projects such as R&D. Important in the development stage is an effective communication and feedback procedure to provide management with go, no-go decision opportunities at suitable stages.

Evaluation of Research. A company's research effort is an area most difficult to evaluate in tangible terms. Even where a given program and expenditures have resulted in a specific product whose sales and profits are there for all to see, the allocation of credit in dollar terms can be done in only the roughest way. How much was due to sales effort, or advertising, or manufacture and servicing?

Index of Return. An "index of return" method originally advanced by Dr. Fred Olsten of Olin Industries assigns varying measures of return to be compared with the estimated cost of research, as follows:

I.R. = Summation of process savings, one year, + 3% of the sales value of new products each year for five years + 2% of the sales value of improved products each year for two years.

$$\text{Value of new products} = \frac{\text{Estimated I.R.} \times \text{Probability of Success}}{\text{Estimated Cost of Research}}$$

The value of measures of this sort is primarily as a trend indicator. The danger is in too literal interpretation. Experience has shown that it is important not to refer to this index of return as some sort of credit to the Research Department. There is no profit unless Manufacturing produces the new or improved product and Sales merchandises it. (See NEW PRODUCT PLANNING: Profitability Projections.)

The bench marks and bench-mark questions

previously presented can profitably be subjected to annual searching review. The time is past when it was thought best to "leave Research alone," trusting that if enough money is supplied, the scientists and engineers will somehow come up with a satisfactory flow of new products and an agreeable number of "firsts." The task of defining company goals, weighing and balancing alternatives, and establishing check points and controls remains the essence of sound management of R&D.

CARL HEYEL, Management Counsel, Manhasset, New York

Information References

Associations:

American Association for the Advancement of Science.
American Chemical Society.
Industrial Research Institute.

Periodicals:

Industrial Research.
Research & Development.

Texts:

Heyel, Carl, ed., "Handbook of Industrial Research Management," 2nd. ed., New York, Van Nostrand-Reinhold, 1968.

Publications of the National Science Foundation, specif., latest issues of "National Patterns of Science and Technology Resources" and "Research and Development in Industry."

Francis, Philip H., "Principles of R&D Management," New York, AMACOM, 1977.

References Cited

[1] National Science Foundation, Washington, D.C., "National Patterns of Science and Technology Resources, 1980."

[2] National Science Foundation, "Research and Development in Industry, 1978."

[3] McGraw-Hill, New York, "25th Annual McGraw-Hill Survey of Business Plans and Expenditures for 1980–82."

[4] The Conference Board, New York, "New Product Winners and Losers," January 1980.

[5] Mechlin, George F. and Berg, Daniel, "Evaluating Research—ROI Is Not Enough," *Harvard Business Review,* September–October 1980.

[6] "Technological Innovation: Its Environment and Management," U.S. Department of Commerce, January, 1967.

Cross References: *Basic Research: Management Aspects (and cross references there given).*

INDUSTRIAL STANDARDIZATION

Standardization is a basic, indispensable part of the industrial machine. It is a fundamental and natural concomitant of the mass production technique. The interchangeability required by assembly line production methods can be assured only through standardization, and at the same time the product itself must be standardized to the extent necessary to permit the desired amount of continuous production. Standardization thus is the seizure and consolidation of the latest knowledge and experience and the temporary fixation of the advances in technology in order that their benefits may be realized through quantity production.

However, standardization is not restrictive. It does not inhibit or stifle research or development or other means of advancement. It encourages such progress in fact by establishing the bases from which new developments can spring. Like the bricklayers' scaffold, standardization provides a temporary platform, a working level, from which new advances can be made and additional heights reached. New standards are established as soon as the action is warranted by further technologic progress and economic conditions, and from this new platform efforts toward still further advancement can be launched. Standardization thus also facilitates the extension of the mass production technique to more and more specialization and diversification and fosters continually greater precision, efficiency, and technologic and scientific progress.

There is no intent here to claim everything for standardization, but it does fill this basic requirement of modern industry and in doing so yields numerous incidental benefits as well. As a means of communication, standards serve to coordinate industrial operations and to integrate the entire industrial community. Standards of measure, tolerance, and gaging permit the expression of dimensional requirements in definite and certain known terms and the determination of performance or compliance with those requirements. Standard specifications have appropriately been called the language of industry.

As will be elaborated upon later, many diverse industry groups use the machinery of the American National Standards Institute to develop national standards under the designation "American National Standard." An American National Standard is a common national agreement on the one best way to do something . . . make something . . . measure or test or define something . . . or make it safer.

Some 11,000 American National Standards are in common use by multiple industry groupings and by government. Fields of application include electrical, mechanical, civil engineering and construction, photography and motion pictures, material handling, petroleum products, chemical, automotive, nuclear energy, and acoustics. Manufacturers of products in these areas have agreed upon common national standards, greatly simplifying purchasing procedures of companies using their products, and assuring uniform, specified dimensions.

There are numerous examples of industry's use of standardization to gain a voice in its own regulation. Thus in the operation and maintenance of its own equipment, the elevator industry enjoys national acceptance of the American National Standard Safety Code for Elevators, Dumbwaiters, and Moving Walks, and the American National Standard for Inspection of Elevators. These concern areas rigidly controlled by government, but the elevator manufacturers—voluntarily and in full cooperation with insurance, engineering, architectural, governmental, and other interests—helped write the code and "Inspector's Manual" upon which controls are based.

In the field of industrial safety, about 750 American National Standards form the core of many industrial safety and hygiene regulations and codes established in the 50 states. Also, the U.S. Department of Labor adopted or referenced (as of 1979), some 265 ANSI-approved national consensus standards under provisions of the OCCUPATION SAFETY AND HEALTH ACT OF 1970. Many of these American National Standards, plus additional ones, have also been adopted by the Labor Department in its Inspection Survey Guide Bulletin 326 [1]. This guide is used by Department of Labor safety engineers and industrial hygienists in making inspections of the contractor's work place.

Definitions. In relation to industrial standardization, the meaning of the word "standards" must be accepted and understood. For this purpose no objection is taken to one of the definitions given in Webster's new International Dictionary, "that which is established by authority, custom, or general consent, as a model or example; criterion; test; in general, a definite level, degree, material, character, quality, or the like, viewed as that which is proper and adequate for a given purpose." Many other definitions have been proposed, especially in recent years as standardization has been given greater recognition and standards engineering has become a profession of its own.

Considerable controversy has arisen in relation to the term "specification." There are those, including the Department of Defense, who wish to make a distinction between *standard* and *specification.* They restrict specification to a document used primarily for procurement purposes, and consider a standard to be a document intended primarily for engineering purposes or for restriction of application. This concept is considered erroneous, however, in that it limits standardization to practices and to the simplification process, whereas standardization can and does have much greater utility.

Dr. John Gaillard provided the answer to this controversy with these definitions with which there is strong agreement: "A *specification* is a statement of requirements to be met if a given objective is to be attained. A *standard* is a specification intended for recurrent use" [1]. The point brought out by these definitions is that a standard serves a repetitive purpose. A specification may serve or may originally be intended to serve only a limited purpose. If it finds repetitive use, it becomes a standard. If it is origially intended for recurrent use it is a standard.

In relation to standards used by industry, however, the concept of general acceptance is considered to be so important that its inclusion in the definition is necessary. Thus Webster's definition is helpful in that as the basic approach to industrial standardization, the idea of "general consent" to "that which is proper and adequate for a given purpose" is emphasized. The dictionary definition is also good in that it identifies all three methods by which standards in general and even standards affecting industry do come into existence. Standards are established by *authority* such as laws and other regulations or, as within the company, by management dictum. They are established by *custom* such as men's attire, or sizes of paper for correspondence, or implements for eating. By industrial standardization, however, is meant only that process by which the *general consent* of those concerned is actively obtained with respect to the provisions of the standards. To best serve the purposes of industry, standards are deliberately formulated by industry interests, and they become industrial standards only when and if there is general consent to their provisions on the part of industry which is interested in them or affected by them. The meaning of general consent varies with the status or level of the standard, but multilateral action of some degree or extent definitely is reflected.

Formal Definition. *Industrial standardization* then is the orderly and systematic formulation, adoption, application, and revision of industrial standards. An industrial standard is a generally accepted statement of the requirements to be met for the attainment of a recurrent objective.

History. Certain standards of quality of and for craftsmanship were fairly common before the Industrial Revolution, but only the advent of mass production and its refinement in assembly line technique dictated the absolute need for interchangeability and for the industrial standardization by which interchangeability can be obtained.

While industrial standardization is thus as old as the Industrial Revolution, its recognition as a specific function, its development as a planned process, and its extension to an organized, cooperative, and orderly activity are relatively new. Some standardization work had been under way before World War I—for example, in the American Society of Mechanical Engineers, founded in 1880, and in the American Society for Testing and Materials, incorporated in 1902. But the exigencies of that war period highlighted the problems created by non-standardization, and gave impetus to the initiation of work at several levels.

The American Standards Association (later renamed the American National Standards Institute) was founded in 1918. The World War II needs of the U.S. and Allied countries focused attention sharply on the lack of sufficient standardization, and thus sparked considerably increased activity. Subsequent military alliances and the growth of world trade have given added momentum, and numerous other influences have spurred and are still spurring still greater standardization effort.

Development of Standards. The development of standards for the benefit of industry takes place at a number of different levels and under a variety of auspices. At the corporation level, Company Standardization (see STANDARDIZATION, COMPANY), is a relatively clearly defined activity. It concerns only the particular company, and its benefits are expected to accrue only to that company. Below the corporation level, standardization is advantageously undertaken at the division, department, and even lower levels and is equally clearly defined.

Standardization at the next higher level however is another matter. There is a vast amount of industrial standardization activity, much of which is overlapping and duplicative and even competitive. While individual activities are well organized, standardization on the whole at this level is thus by comparison with that at other levels, uncoordinated and ill-defined. Most of this standardization takes place at what might be called the industry and technical level and is carried out under the auspices and procedures of technical societies, professional societies, trade and business associations, and other national or regional groups and agencies definitely including those of the Federal Government. Some idea of the extent of this activity can be gained from "An Index of U.S. Voluntary Engineering Standards," published in 1971 by the National Bureau of Standards. This publication lists more than 19,000 standards, specifications, test methods, and recommended practices of some 360 U.S. technical, trade, and professional organizations. Supplements issued in 1972 and 1975 augment these numbers.

The American Society for Testing and Materials (ASTM) stands out in the materials field and is probably the most productive and most widely recognized of these standardizing organizations. Except perhaps for Federal agencies, the ASTM is unique in its very broad interest in the entire materials field. Much of industry collaborates under the procedure of the Society for the development of needed standards on their materials, and those standards, the familiar ASTM specifications and test methods, are accorded a high standing.

The Society of Automotive Engineers is another organization with a broad standardization program. The SAE serves as the technical society of the automotive industry, its work being supported in substantial part by a grant from the Motor Vehicle Manufacturers Association. Its standards serve the motor vehicle, aircraft, airline, space vehicle, farm tractor, earthmoving and road building machinery, and other manufacturing industries using internal combustion engines.

Among the professional societies the American Society of Mechanical Engineers, with its widely used "ASME Boiler and Pressure Vessel Code" and other standards is noted for its standardization activity in the mechanical field, as is the Institute of Electrical and Electronics Engineers in its fields. In the field of fire protection the National Fire Protection Association maintains an extensive program which in 1980 produced more than 240 standards published as separate pamphlets and as a 16-volume set of National Fire Codes.

Trade associations with extensive standardization programs include the National Electrical Manufacturers Association, Electronic Industries Association, Aerospace Industries Associations, American Petroleum Institute, and Rubber Manufacturers Association.

Federal departments and agencies contribute importantly. The General Services Administration not only promulgates Federal Standards, but effects additional standardization through its broad Federal Specification program, such specifications often being accepted as the industry standards for the items covered. Similarly, the Department of Defense issues Military Standards and also contributes to additional standardization through its very extensive Military Specification activity.

American National Standards Institute (ANSI). The American National Standards Institute is a private, nonprofit federation of leading trade, technical, and professional organizations, government agencies, companies, and consumer and labor groups. Its principal functions are to coordinate development of voluntary standards, approve and promulgate nationally recognized and accepted standards, and represent U.S. interests in international standards work of nontreaty organizations.

As the coordinating and approval agency for voluntary national standards, the Institute:

Provides the means for determining the need for national standards.

Ensures that existing organizations competent to fill these needs undertake the development work.

Coordinates their activities to eliminate wasteful duplication and conflict.

Approves the results of their efforts as national voluntary standards when it is satisfied from evidence presented that the proposed standards have been recognized and accepted by national groups substantially affected.

The Standards Institute neither supplants nor duplicates the standardization efforts of trade organizations and professional and technical societies, but provides the facilities and methods to make their efforts most effective.

Participation in the Institute's programs protects an organization from working independently on a standard which is already under development, and frees its resources for other important projects. Questions of jurisdiction are worked out from the conception of the standard, so that each participant contributes to the area in which he or she is most interested and most knowledgeable.

The American National Standards Institute was originally organized as the American Engineering Standards Committee in 1918, and ten years later was expanded to become the American Standards Association. The Association was incorporated in 1948 under the laws of the State of New York. In 1966, under a new constitution and bylaws, it became the United States of America Standards Institute. In 1969 it changed its name to the American National Standards Institute.

Typical of American National Standards available are the following (a sample listing only):

Mechanical Engineering—for screw threads; bolts and nuts; bearings and gears; small tools and machine tool components; flanges and fittings; pipe and valves.

Safety—national safety codes for use of abrasive wheels; for washing windows; inspecting elevators; operating a power press; marking a compressed gas cylinder to identify contents; wiring building; installing gas piping and appliances; using industrial x-rays and radiation; for protective clothing; allowable concentrations of toxic gases.

Civil Engineering and Construction—standards for cements; identification of piping systems; gypsum plastering; reinforcing bars; industrial lighting; fire tests for door assemblies; paving brick; concrete; and design loads in buildings.

International Standardization. All industrial countries and many of the countries in the process of industrial development are also engaged in national standardization. Some of their work in fact antedates that in this country. The increase in world trade and the establishment of regional economic blocs have emphasized the need for closer agreement among these national standards, and thus at the international level there is also extensive standardization activity. Again there is confusion due to the number of international organizations, many of which sponsor some standardization activity as a part of their programs, and due also to the considerable interest of governments in standardization at this level.

Two international standards bodies are the International Organization for Standardization (ISO) and the International Electrotechnical Commission (IEC). The ISO came into existence following World War II as the successor of a prewar International Standards Association. By 1980 the standards bodies of 71 countries were members of this organization and the program consisted of more than 160 technical projects ranging in subject matter from steel and other materials to drawings, photography, computers and information processing, and products of various types. Also by 1980 nearly 4,000 ISO Standards had been approved.

The IEC is a much older organization, having been founded in 1904. It operates autonomously but is affiliated with the ISO as the Electrical Division. Its 1980 membership was comprised of 43 national committees and its program consisted of 82 projects ranging in subject matter from turbine-type generators to semiconductor devices. Published IEC Recommendations totaled 1,500.

In accordance with one of its own constitutional objects and with the constitution of the ISO and the IEC, the ANSI serves as the United States member body of these organizations. It provides the means by which American industry may cooperate with the industries of other countries and by which coordinated U.S. views may be brought to bear on the international work.

Although the ISO holds consultative status with the United Nations and is generally recognized as the international organization for standardization, considerable standardization activity is undertaken by various UN agencies as well as by other international governmental and non-governmental organizations. The specialized agencies of the UN are particularly active, although a substantial amount of standardization is also undertaken by the functional commissions of the Economic and Social Council, and especially by its regional economic commissions. Other inter-governmental activities also affect standardization, such as those related to conventions or other international agreements. Organizations such as the North Atlantic Treaty Organization also have strong influence on standardization among their members although they are not agencies for the issuance of standards as such.

American National Standards Institute, Inc., New York, New York

References Cited

[1] U.S. Department of Labor, Inspection Survey Guide, Bulletin 326, U.S. Government Printing Office, 1970. (Check with Occupational Safety and Health Administration for subsequent publications.)

[2] Gaillard, John, "Specifications and Standards," *The Magazine of Standards*, August 1959.

Cross Reference: *Standardization, Company.*

INFLATION

The term **Inflation** indicates a condition of generally rising prices, or a situation in which price increases are larger and/or more widespread than price decreases. This is usually applied to the average rate of increase of prices or movements in one of the standard indexes of the price level. In recent history the opposite process, deflation, has occurred infrequently. In fact, all economies have experienced episodes of inflation which can often be severe. The term *hyperinflation* is used for inflationary episodes where prices in terms of money or the unit of account are rising so rapidly that economic agents resort to primitive barter arrangements with great loss of economic efficiency.

Macro-Economic Theory

Economic theorists have sought explanations for change in the overall price level for centuries. For most of this time a great deal of emphasis has been on the role of the money supply. The "quantity theory" which was advanced as early as the eighteenth century suggested that the price level is determined by the money supply. *Monetarism* represents a contemporary version of the same approach. Although Keynesian economists in the postwar period tended to give much less emphasis to money supply changes, there is a current consensus among most economists that at least in the long run, inflation is a monetary phenomenon.

The Quantity Equation. The cornerstone of monetarist argument is the so-called "quantity equation," $MV = PY$, where M = the quantity of money, V = income velocity, P = the price level, and Y = real income. The equation is simply an identity that says that the supply of money is used in transactions (velocity) to support a given amount of nominal income (PY). The presumptions underlying classical quantity theory are that velocity, the rate at which the stock of money turns over, is fixed by institutional arrangements in the economy, and that real income is determined by supply and demand in the real sector. In this case, changes in the supply of money would impact solely on the price level.

In common language, an increase in the supply of money, when the quantity of goods is taken as fixed, represents "too much money chasing too few goods." Thus, the price of goods in terms of the money unit of account will increase.

Contemporary monetarists are more likely to present a dynamic version of the quantity equation. That is, we can write:

$$\%\Delta \text{ money} + \%\Delta \text{ velocity} = \%\Delta \text{ prices} + \%\Delta \text{ real income}$$

where $\%\Delta$ = "percentage change in."

In the past 25 years, improvements in the efficiency of the banking system have caused velocity to increase by about 3% per year. Also, productivity growth and increases in the labor force should allow real income to grow by about 3% per year. Since the money supply has grown by about 4% per year, we would expect that inflation has averaged 4% per year, as it has.

Although this approach provides a reasonable explanation of the relationship between prices and money supply over long time periods, it is important to note that short-run deviations from the quantity equation can be substantial. For example, in 1979, nominal GNP grew by 11.3% and the money supply by 5.5%. Thus, by implication, income velocity increased by almost 6%. It is difficult, if not impossible, to use the quantity equation to determine the effect of money supply growth on inflation in the short run.

Effect of Money-Supply Change. A change in the money supply can, depending on conditions in the real-sector labor and goods markets, affect either prices or real output. The quantity equation relates M to nominal income (PY). If the economy is not always producing at a full employment output level, a change in nominal income can be due to either a price change or real output change. The major drawback of the monetarist explanation of inflation is its inability to decompose monetary effects on nominal income into price and real output changes. In the long run this is not a problem because output grows with the economy's potential. However, in the short run, there are substantial and frequent deviations in output from its potential. In fact, these can often be induced by monetary growth.

The Keynesian View. The approach to macroeconomics by John Maynard Keynes emphasized short-run income determination. Only when output is at its capacity level will increases in demand have inflationary consequences. This can be termed *demand-pull inflation.* It emerges when expenditure policy or monetary expansion increases the demand for goods beyond the ability of the economy to produce, therefore generating inflation. Keynesians tend not to view the quantity equation as useful because they believe that velocity responds to economic conditions. That is, the financial sector can either use the stock of money more efficiently or utilize money substitutes more intensively and thus mitigate the effects of a low rate of growth of the money supply. Thus, inflation is not quite so clearly due to monetary expansion. As noted, Keynesian emphasis is on excess demand pressures that cause inflation.

Although the monetarist approach views inflation as a monetary phenomenon, its predictive powers are limited. An increase in the rate of growth of the money supply will affect nominal income but it is difficult and often impossible to determine whether prices or real output will be affected. In the short run, given available capacity and following the Keynesian emphasis on aggregate demand determination of output, the monetary impetus will fall on production. In the long run, where output growth is determined by the underlying structure of the economy, monetary growth determines inflation. Although the distinction between the long and short runs may be clear theoretically, they are often not empirically distinguishable.

The Phillips Curve. Keynesians and monetarists did not make this distinction between the long and short run until the 1970s. Thus, earlier theoretical discussions of inflation would pose a monetarist (long run) argument against a Keynesian (short run) argument. Much of this controversy centered around the notion of the Phillips curve, a post-Keynesian analysis that is usually associated with the Keynesians. It is named after A. W. Phillips, who examined the relationship between unemployment and changes in wage rates in Great Britain over nearly a century. He found a surprisingly stable trade-off—as if the attainment of a higher degree of price stability almost invariably entailed a social cost in the form of more severe unemployment.

The Phillips curve is consistent with the short-run (Keynesian) framework previously discussed. When the overall unemployment rate is low, the economy is operating near capacity and there will be many sectors of the economy with excess demand pressures and rising prices. As unemployment increases, the number of industries so affected will decrease.

Monetarists and other classically oriented economists have made several theoretical suggestions why the Phillips curve is only a short-run phenomenon. This has been borne out by empirical observation that indicates that the Phillips relationship has tended to shift over time. The most important reason for this is the role of inflationary expectations. Expectations are important both for understanding the Phillips curve and for understanding the acceleration and persistence of inflation.

The Effect of Expectations. Inflationary experience tends to generate expectations of future inflation as economic units learn from past behavior. However, when additional inflation is expected, such expectations will be built into every price and wage bargain with the outcome of higher inflation. Thus, any attempt to maintain the unemployment rate below a so-called "natural rate" that can be associated with the long run steady growth of the economy will lead to acceleration of the rate of inflation.

The effect of expectations can also be viewed as the primary source of *cost-push* in the inflation process. Even when excess demand is diminishing or unemployment is increasing, inflation may continue unabated if wage and price bargains are still being affected by expectations of increased inflation. This has occurred in recent cyclical episodes (1968–1969 and 1974–1975) where inflation continued to increase well into the recession. It was only after a prolonged period of recession that the inflation rate began to respond to the slack in the real economy.

A major problem for the modern economy is that the extent of economic slack required to diminish the inflationary spiral seems to be growing. This could be because economic units expect recessions to be short-lived and not very serious because of society's continuing attempts to reduce unemployment. Thus, it has become increasingly difficult to reduce the expectation of continued inflation.

In the 1950s, economists argued about the sources of inflation, whether it could be attributed to demand-pull or cost-push. Current thinking acknowledges that inflation must have some underlying roots in excess demand, which is often but not always due to monetary expansion. In addition, inflationary expectations can sustain cost-push influences in the economy even long after excess demand has disappeared.

Supply Inflation. In the 1970s, a new form of inflationary pressure emerged which can be termed *supply inflation.* It is associated with the rapid increases in the price of oil by the OPEC oil cartel since 1973. Supply inflation takes place when the price of certain goods is determined by forces not subject to the influences of the competitive market place. In addition, in order for increases in the price of certain goods to generate an aggregate inflationary spiral, it is necessary that the economy be unable readily to shift to alternative or substitute goods.

Clearly, oil fulfills the requirements for being a source of supply inflation. Prices have increased very rapidly and the economy will take decades to adjust fully to less energy use and/or alternative energy sources. Thus, the increased oil prices get passed through the structure of the economy to the prices of all of the goods that use oil as an input in production. Such price increases create expectations of future price increases, which strengthen the inflationary spiral. Since oil is such a pervasive element in all production processes, as well as in final consumption by automobile users, the spiral of inflationary pressures created by the OPEC price increases is very strong.

Supply inflation is very persistent because individuals have strong expectations of real income growth. Thus, when supply inflation erodes their ability to purchase the same basket of consumption goods purchased earlier, they expect wage increases to compensate. Although the oil price increases have made oil importing countries like the United States poorer, people expect to maintain their real earnings. Their attempts to do so in wage bargaining generates additional inflationary pressures. The existence of rapid inflation has reduced the willingness of firms to resist wage bargains because they expect to be able to pass on cost increases without losing customers to their competitors.

Thus it is possible that producers have begun to condone inflation because they feel that prices can be readily increased and labor peace is best not threatened. Although this conjecture is unproven, there is much casual evidence of an inflationary spiral which is accepted at increasingly higher rates. Such arguments have as much to do with the willingness of producers to risk larger price increases as with the power of labor unions to negotiate higher wages.

Effects of Inflation

In the past decade economists have come full circle from minimizing the real costs of inflation to finding inflation costs lurking in every nook and cranny of the economy. A 1978 survey of the real costs and effects of inflation by Stanley Fischer and Franco Modigliani [3] provides a useful outline of inflation effects. These effects can be cataloged as those which arise in or as a consequence of:

(1) A fully inflation-adjusted (indexed) economy.

(2) Nominal institutions and arrangements.

(3) Unanticipated inflation.

(4) Inflation-induced uncertainty.

Inflation-Adjusted Economy. Early discussions of inflation effects often assumed (implicitly, if not explicity) that economic institutions and agents were able to adjust fully to or protect themselves from inflation. In that case, the only cost of inflation is that it imposes a tax on nominal money balances. That is, money loses purchasing power at the rate of inflation. Other financial assets do not suffer this tax because interest adjusts to include an inflation premium. Even the tax on money balances disappears if a market interest is payable on demand deposits. Furthermore, inflation imposes certain resource costs on the economy—the cost of revising price lists, catalogs, etc. It is hard to imagine that either the tax on money or the cost of revising prices is the only reason why society seems to find inflation so distasteful.

More importantly, there are additional inflation costs which are often overlooked but are of farreaching consequences. They are the costs that arise because inflation erodes the value or usefulness of price information which is collected through experience by every agent in the economy. This increases the degree of economic uncertainty, particularly for those decisions which involve commitments over time and are contracted in nominal terms—i.e., most saving and investment decisions. Inflation imposes information costs and increases in price uncertainty, even in a fully inflation-adjusted economy. For example, because the costs of price change are not uniform, firms will differ in their frequency of price change even when inflation is fully anticipated, as a consequence the variability of relative price changes.

Nominal Institutions. Many of the effects of inflation on saving are due to institutions and institutional arrangements faced by savers and investors. Either by custom or by law, the institutional framework is usually specified in nominal terms and in such a way that precludes adjustment to inflation. As a consequence, inflation creates distortions in the return on saving, and in the relative income of different individuals. Of primary concern in this regard are the tax system and the regulation of financial institutions.

Inflation introduces distortions into the tax system in several ways. To begin with, because of the progressiveness of taxes levied on nominal incomes, real tax collections increase with inflation-induced increases in nominal incomes. Secondly, inflation alters the after-tax real return on saving even if pre-tax nominal returns fully adjust to inflation (so as to keep the pre-tax real return constant). This is because taxes are levied on nominal returns and thus inflation may lower the after-tax real return. Of course, borrowers are faced with the converse of this problem since nominal interest payments (which include an inflation premium) are tax deductible. Finally, taxes are levied on nominal capital gains and may often result in negative real after-tax returns on equities. This has led to substantial argument for the reform of capital gains taxation to allow the indexation of purchase prices.

There are also many private-sector nominal institutions where nominal arrangements lead to important inflation effects. These are particularly apparent in the financial sector where regulatory constraints often discourage the evolution of inflation-adjusted institutions and arrangements. For example, of particular importance to household-saving decisions are the regulatory constraints that limit nominal interest rates on the important outlets for household-sector saving (time deposits at various financial intermediaries). These constraints prevent a full inflation adjustment of nominal interest rates and may discourage saving. Of course, these constraints are not binding given opportunities for disintermediation, but available alternative assets are often unobtainable to the small saver, or less desirable because they are less liquid.

It is interesting to note that even in the absence of regulatory constraints, financial markets seem reluctant to develop instruments that are inflation-adjusted or indexed, with the exception of a few mortgage instruments. The preference for nominal certainty in financial contracts seems to be universal.

Unanticipated Inflation. Although theory often makes an important distinction between anticipated and unanticipated inflation, the practical difference is small if the economy prefers, as it seems to, not to adjust its contractual arrangements fully. We need only add that unanticipated inflation magnifies the distortions and uncertainties already noted.

When inflation is not correctly anticipated, economic decisions turn out to be non-optimal. Thus, unanticipated inflation increases the distortions due to decision-making under imperfect information. Furthermore, available survey measures of inflationary expectations indicate that errors in forecasting inflation are more frequent and larger when the inflation rate is higher. Thus, the distortions which arise from unanticipated inflation increase with the inflation rate. In addition, since forecast errors (unanticipated inflation) increase with inflation, uncertainty is also increased.

Unanticipated as well as anticipated inflation leads to a redistribution of income and wealth throughout the economy since institutions and markets do not fully adjust. Although such redistributions are substantial, they are for the most part nonsystematic and do not have a major effect on the shape of the income distribution.

Uncertainty. Inflation increases the extent of economic uncertainty (even, as noted earlier, in an indexed economy) in three ways. First, it increases the variability of relative prices. Second, higher inflation rates tend to be more variable. Third, higher inflation rates are more difficult to predict, which means that inflation is more likely to be unanticipated. These relationships have been established empirically.

Inflation and the Firm

Recent high and persistent inflation rates in the United States and elsewhere have had considerable effects on the financial positions of firms. Some of these effects were created by a discrepancy that exists between the firm's *economic* net income and its *reported* net income as a consequence of generally accepted accounting practices (GAAP). These practices are based on the traditional historical cost basis of accounting. A firm's economic income is defined as the income that it can distribute during the period so that at the end of the period it is left with sufficient physical assets to carry on the same level of activity as at the beginning of the period. This income is also referred to as "sustainable income," and it is often quite different from reported income by GAAP. The inflation-induced discrepancy between the two measures of income is due primarily to the measurement of the cost of goods sold (and the value of inventories) and the depreciation expense. These cost and expense items tend to be understated by GAAP in inflationary periods, leading to overstated profits and higher tax bills than otherwise would have been the case.

Inflation accounting is different from GAAP in that it attempts to reduce the discrepancy between the actual and reported cost expense items and between sustainable and reported profits. After years of debate, the Financial Accounting Standards Board (FASB) has, since 1979, required large public companies to report the effect of inflation on their financial statements. The Board requires these companies to supplement the traditional historical cost reporting with inflation accounting, using either one of two alternative principles: (1) the *constant dollar accounting* principle by which a general price level adjustment is applied, or (2) the *replacement cost accounting* principle by which price level adjustments are made using specific price indices for certain items. (See Inflation Accounting.)

At this writing, income for tax purposes is still measured by the traditional accounting. Under GAAP, the value of the firm's inventory and cost of goods sold may be calculated by using either the *first-in-first-out* (FIFO) or the *last-in-first-out* (LIFO) method. In inflationary periods, the cost of goods sold tends to be higher under LIFO than under FIFO. Consequently, reported earnings are lower under LIFO. While this is clearly a disadvantage at least to the extent that stockholders prefer higher to lower reported earnings, the advantage of LIFO is that lower reported earnings implies a lower tax bill for the firm. Conversely, the use of FIFO results in higher reported profits which are in part illusory "inflationary profits" and are subject to taxes. (See FIFO/LIFO Inventory Accounting.)

As already mentioned, the depreciation expense is an important source of the discrepancy between reported and sustainable income. During inflationary periods, historical cost depreciation could be substantially less than the real value of the depreciation expense. Although inflation-adjusted depreciation expense is not currently used in the United States for tax purposes, several investment incentives are offered to the firm, which provide some compensation for the erosion of the real value of allowed depreciation by inflation. These incentives are various *accelerated depreciation* methods and the *investment tax credit.* Although these incentives were not intended to compensate for inflation, but rather simply to induce investment, they have in recent years provided some compensation for the eroded value of the allowed depreciation expense for tax purposes.

Inflation and Investment. Inflation affects a firm's capital budget by changing the *net present value* (NPV) of its prospective investment projects. This is particularly true when depreciation expense for tax purposes is based on historical cost. To see this, denote the corporate tax rate by T, the before-tax cash flow of an investment project in year t by S_t, and the depreciation expense by D_t. The after-tax cash flow is given by $(1-T)(S_t-D_t) + D_t$, and the project's net present value (NPV) in the absence of inflation is

$$\text{NPV}_0 = -I + \sum_{t=1}^{n} \frac{(1-T)S_t}{(1+k)^t} + \sum_{t=1}^{n} \frac{TD_t}{(1+r)^t}$$

where I is the initial investment, n is the project's lifetime, k is the discount rate for risky cash flow, and r is the discount rate for nonrisky cash flow. With inflation at rate h per year, the cost of capital of risky flow changes from k to $(1 + k)(1 + h)-1$ and that of nonrisky flow changes from r to $(1 + r)(1 + h) - 1$. Assuming that the inflation is neutral and depreciation is based on book value, the cash flow S_t changes to $S_t(1 + h)^t$, but D_t is unaffected. Thus, the project's net present value with inflation (NPV*) is given by

$$\text{NPV}^* = -I + \sum_{t=1}^{n} \frac{(1-T)S_t(1+h)^t}{[(1+k)(1+h)]^t} + \sum_{t=1}^{n} \frac{TD_t}{[(1+r)(1+h)]^t}$$

$$= -I + \sum_{t=1}^{n} \frac{(1-T)S_t}{(1+k)^t} + \sum_{t=1}^{n} \frac{TD_t/(1+h)^t}{(1+r)^t}$$

so that NPV* < NPV, meaning that investment projects become less attractive under inflation if depreciation expense is based on historical cost. Furthermore, since inflation is never really neutral, the firm faces the risk that the prices for its products will lag behind the general price level. This added risk increases the firm's cost of capital and further reduces the attractiveness of investment projects.

Inflation creates nominal gains for firms holding assets whose nominal values increase. Such increases are not necessarily accompanied by an increase in the real value of the firm's net worth nor do they necessarily add to the firm's real profits. Inflationary holding gains add to the firm's real profit only if the firm is in a *net debtor position* and if the actual inflation rate exceeds the expected rate of inflation at the time the firm's debt was issued. If indeed the actual rate of inflation exceeds the rate which was expected at the time of the debt issue, the firm's liability in real terms will decrease and the firm's net worth will increase in real value. Clearly, the reverse situation will occur if the actual inflation rate is lower than what was expected at the time of the debt issue: the firm's liability will increase in real value and its net worth will decrease.

Inflation and Financial Markets

Inflation-induced changes in the real values of financial assets reduce their usefulness as stores of value. In particular, inflation affects interest rates and stock returns.

In the absence of inflation, interest rates on fixed-income securities should cover the required real rate of interest and a premium for default risk. The interest on short-term government-fixed income securities such as Treasury bills which are essentially default-free should in the absence of inflation be equal to the real rate of interest. When inflation is expected over the holding period, the nominal interest rate on a bill should cover the real rate plus an inflation premium that should provide a compensation to the bond-holder for the depreciation in the real value of his or her investment.

Thus, if the real rate of interest and the expected inflation rate over the period in question are r and h, respectively, then the nominal rate that compensates for the expected inflation and the real rate is $R = (1 + r)(1 + h) - 1$. For example, if expected inflation rate is 10% and the required real rate of return is 1%, then the nominal rate is $R = (1.01)(1.10) - 1 = 0.1110$, or 11.10%. That is, an investment of $1,000 at this nominal rate will provide the investor with a nominal amount of $1,111 at the end of the period, which is equal to $1,111/1.10 = $1,010 in real terms. The real return is then $10, or 1% on the investment.

When the actual inflation rate during the period in question is different from the expected inflation rate, the realized real interest rate is different from the expected real rate of interest. In the above example, if the actual inflation rate is 5% while the nominal rate is 11.10% (based on 10% expected inflation), the realized real investment value at the end of the period is $1,111/1.05 = $1,058.10, yielding a real return of 5.714% on the investment. If the actual inflation rate is 15%, the value of the investment at the end of the period is $1,111/1.15 = $966.09, yielding a negative real return of −3.30%.

Exhibit I presents the nominal and the realized real rates of return on Treasury bills for selected years 1926–1978. Examination of the data reveals that nominal rates tend in fact to rise with inflation rates, but real rates have tended to decline when inflation rates rise. Average real return on Treasury bills in the 10 deflationary years since 1926 was 5.3%, the average in the 13 years during which inflation exceeded 5% was negative: −4.37%. In theory, there is nothing to suggest this kind of inverse relationship. Rather, it is often assumed that the real rate of interest shoud be invariant to

EXHIBIT I

NOMINAL AND REAL TREASURY BILL RATES OF RETURN, SELECTED YEARS, 1926–78

	Nominal Return	*Inflation Rate*	*Real Return*
1926	3.27	−1.49	−4.83
1933	.30	.51	−.21
1940	.00	.96	−.95
1947	.50	9.01	−7.81
1954	.86	−.50	1.37
1961	2.13	.67	1.45
1968	5.21	4.72	.47
1975	5.80	7.01	−1.13
1978	7.18	9.03	−1.70

SOURCE: Ibbotson and Sinquefield.[1].

the inflation rate. Consequently, the fluctuations of realized real returns are explained by errors in predicting inflation rather than by changes in required real returns. During the 1960s, when inflation rates were rather stable and presumably predictable, the average real return was 1.3%, so that we can safely assume that the required real rate is within the range of 1% to 2%.

Inflation and Stock Prices. Since common stock represents investment in real assets, it is sometimes thought that common stocks are an inflation hedge. Furthermore, it is believed that the return on equity increases if actual inflation is higher than expected inflation and decreases if actual inflation is lower than expected inflation. In reality, this conclusion is only valid when the investment holding period is long. For short holding periods, the evidence is quite different. William F. Sharpe concludes from his study of common stock returns in many countries over a 30-year period [2] that "While it may be reasonable to expect capital assets as a whole to act as a hedge against inflation over the long pull, the fact that common stocks represent only part of the set of such assets, and the great uncertainty associated with such investments makes it impossible to guarantee that stock returns will neatly offset changes in the price level on an exact one-for-one basis, even when a holding period of many years is contemplated."

Recent empirical studies concerning the relationship between common stock returns and the rate of inflation show accumulating evidence that the relationship is significantly negative: other things being equal, the return on common stocks is lower, the higher the inflation rate.

INFLATION AND THE HOUSEHOLD SECTOR

Many inflation effects on business and financial markets also affect the household sector. In particular, the loss of valuable information and the increase in uncertainty associated with inflation are likely to affect household decisions. Also, households are often less able than firms to circumvent many nominal institutions and arrangements. The regulation of financial institutions that prevents them from paying market interest rates which include an appropriate premium for expected inflation affect the household sector profoundly.

Although it is difficult to say whether aged

or poor households suffer more from inflation, we do know that inflation has distributional effects. For example, households which are net holders of financial assets have been unable to maintain the real value of those assets in inflationary periods. On the other hand, many households with large mortgage debts have benefited from the erosion of the value of their debt and the increase in the value of their homes.

Without repeating arguments already presented, we can summarize the ways in which inflation can affect household consumption decisions. There are three basic issues—money illusion, intertemporal substitution, and uncertainty.

Money illusion occurs when inflation is not recognized. Consumers overestimate the purchasing power of their nominal income and decide to raise real consumption levels. Consequently, real consumption expenditure is increased, and saving is reduced.

Intertemporal substitution is the term applied to the argument that when price increases are expected, expenditures are advanced in time. Intertemporal substitution is relatively rare because rational behavior requires that the expected price increases be sufficiently large and certain to make it worthwhile to maintain goods inventories. However, such buying sprees do occur occasionally when households expect large price increases on certain items or when low real interest rates make saving unattractive and consumer credit borrowing relatively cheap.

If nominal incomes are more accurately forecast than inflation when the inflation rates are high, then inflation leads to real income *uncertainty*. With income uncertain, households will tend to reduce their expenditures. Of course, difficulty in predicting inflation rates also makes real return less certain, and often reduces real returns as well.

The overall effect of inflation on consumer behavior has probably changed as the inflationary environment has changed. The following scenario might be descriptive of the dominant patterns: at first inflation induces financial asset accumulation for precautionary purposes; over time, inflationary expectations induce a search for assets which are inflation hedges. A secondary reaction may then be the leveraged accumulation of tangible assets, and high credit extensions mainfested in low saving. Thus, although the uncertainty reaction of the 1960s was high saving rates, in the 1980s it might well result in low measured saving rates.

Inflation Measurement and Policy

Price Indexes. Several measures of inflation are used in the United States—the Consumer Price Index, the Producers Price Index (formerly known as the Wholesale Price Index), and the Implicit Price Deflators. Each has somewhat different characteristics and will be briefly described. (See also Business Forecasting.)

The Consumer Price Index prices a basket of goods purchased by a typical urban household. The market basket is updated about once a decade and currently uses purchase patterns based on a 1972–1973 survey. It is available monthly for the nation as a whole and for a number of large urban areas. The CPI may overstate inflation because the fixed weighting scheme fails to take account of the major way in which individuals cope with inflation. That is, substituting alternative purchases for those items which become relatively more expensive. In addition, the CPI has been criticized for failing to account adequately for improvements in the quality of consumer goods and for the calculation of the mortgage interest component which gives too much weight to the current mortgage interest rate.

The Producers Price Index provides a variety of information on prices paid for goods by the business sector. It is available monthly for the overall business sector as well as for a number of industries. The indexes are also available for goods at different stages of production—raw materials, intermediate goods, and final goods. These indices enable the analyst to trace where inflationary pressures are emerging.

The Implicit Price Deflators are constructed to deflate the National Income and Product Accounts into real dollars. They provide the broadest coverage, and weight individual components by their importance in current production. Unlike the CPI, such a current weighting scheme reflects all the substitutions made in response to inflation.

Indexation. Indexation refers to the linkage of payments in contractual agreements (e.g., mortgages, wage contracts) and other economic measures (e.g., depreciation expense, insurance premiums) to a price index such as the Consumer Price Index (CPI)/or the Producers Price Index (PPI). In the presence of inflation the interest on a loan, for example, depends on the default risk involved and on the inflation expectations of the borrower and the lender. Both of them know that in the period of rising prices the loan repayments will have lower purchasing power than otherwise. Therefore, the lender asks for a higher nominal interest rate so as to obtain a compensation for the decrease in the value of both the principal and the interest. The borrower is willing for the same reason to pay a higher interest rate than otherwise, so that the actual nominal rate of interest is likely to be higher the higher the expected rate of inflation.

As long as inflation is fully anticipated, accurate adjustment of the interest rate can be made in advance without hurting the borrower or the lender. However, the effectiveness of the adjustment of interest rates to future anticipated inflation, even in countries with fully developed money and capital markets, is lower the greater the uncertainty surrounding future inflation rates. In addition, this uncertainty is greater the longer the period of the agreement. Indexation is a way to avoid this uncertainty. By providing a linkage to a known index, a full compensation for realized inflation by the definition of the agreed upon index is given so that payments are guaranteed in real terms.

Indexation has been applied in various countries to a wide range of contracts and agreements, among them wage contracts, rents and leases, money and capital transactions, social insurance policies, tax liabilities, and more. It is particularly common in Brazil, Israel, and Finland. In these countries, as well as in the United States, many wage contracts include provision for the periodic revision of all or part of wages to reflect changes in the Consumer Price Index. In the United States, the most important set of payments which are index-linked are social security pensions. In the countries mentioned, but not in the United States, many financial assets (e.g., government bonds and saving deposits) are linked to changes in the overall price level.

The American Inflationary Experience. Awareness of the unfavorable consequences of inflation has made the avoidance of inflation a high-priority objective of public policy. Although policy restraint can combat inflation, the degree of restraint needed and the magnitude of the effects on employment and growth present policymakers with some cruel choices. In addition, the emergence in the 1970s of strong elements of supply-induced and expectations-sustained inflation may imply that return to stable prices will not be possible in the foreseeable future.

In the early postwar period, inflation in the United States was very moderate. The existence of economic slack and fears of a re-emergence of a depression served to mitigate inflation. More expansive fiscal policies in the 1960s improved the unemployment situation and had little effect on inflation rates because they were accompanied by wage-price guideposts and periods of monetary constraint.

The situation changed in the late 1960s as expenditures on the war in Vietnam led to widespread excess-demand pressures. Policy restraint was unduly delayed and as public dissatisfaction increased, the Nixon administration imposed a program of wage and price controls in 1970. It is widely acknowledged that controls impair the allocative efficiency of the price system and discriminatorily deprive affected sectors of their economic freedom. The controls program deferred some price increases until they were abandoned in 1974, but had no long-term effect on the upward path of prices.

Although policy makers professed to follow the policy of monetary and fiscal restraint in the 1970s that would reduce inflationary pressures gradually, this has not been the case. Recurrent fears of recession led to the easing up of policy, and since 1973 large doses of supply inflation from the energy and agricultural sectors have buffeted the economy.

The recessions of 1968–69 and 1973–75 did dampen inflationary pressures, but once inflation has taken a firm hold it becomes very difficult to return to a stable price path. Indeed, as the economy recovered in the late 1970s and another large runup of oil prices emerged in 1979, the inflation rate began to accelerate once again. A program of voluntary standards announced by the Carter administration in 1978 did not have any apparent effect. In October of 1979, the Federal Reserve Board made a major shift in its operating procedures and simultaneously imposed severe policy restraints. These policy changes and further constraints introduced in the spring of 1980 must be seen as contributing to the severity of the recession that emerged in 1980, and as being likely to affect the inflation rate over the next several years.

The increasingly common bouts with ever higher inflation rates in the 1970s and the apparent lack of success of policy constraint have suggested to many analysts that there are other factors at work as well. In particular, inflation is difficult to curb because the rate of growth of labor productivity in the United States has declined. (See PRODUCTIVITY: Concepts and Measures.) This has happened because of changes in the demographic structure of the work force, increased Government regulation of industry, and a possible decline in capital formation. These factors have contributed to lower productivity growth, which makes industry less able to control costs. In addition, policymakers have found it difficult to impose long-run constraints on the growth of the Government sector, and gradually to reduce monetary expansion, both of which are necessary to achieve lower inflation rates in the long run.

MOSHE BEN-HORIM, Lecturer, School of Business Administration, Hebrew University, Jerusalem, Israel, and Visiting Associate Professor, College of Business Administration, University of Florida, Gainesville, Florida

PAUL WACHTEL, Professor of Economics, New York University Graduate School of Business Administration, New York, New York, and Visiting Professor, School of Business Administration, Hebrew University, Jerusalem, Israel

Information References

Ben-Horim, Moshe and Levy, Haim, "Financial Management in an Inflationary Environment," in Altman, E., ed., "Financial Handbook," New York, Wiley, 1981.

Cagan, Phillip and Lipsey, Robert E., "The Financial Effects of Inflation," Cambridge, Mass., Ballinger, for National Bureau of Economic Research, 1978.

Modigliani, Franco and Cohn, Richard A., "Inflation and the Stock Market," *Financial Analysts Journal,* July–August 1979.

Sametz, Arnold W., "Financing the Business Sector, 1976–1985," in Sametz, Arnold W. and Wachtel, Paul, eds., "Understanding Capital Markets, Vol. II: The Financial Environment and the Flow of Funds in the Next Decade," Lexington, Mass., Lexington Books, 1977.

Wachtel, Paul, "Inflation and the Saving Behavior of Households: A Survey," in Von Furstenberg, George, ed., "The Government and Capital Formation," Cambridge, Mass., Ballinger, 1980.

References Cited

[1] Ibbotson, Roger and Sinquefield, Rex, "Stocks, Bonds, Bills, and Inflation: Updates," *Financial Analysts Journal,* July–August 1979.

[2] Sharpe, W. F., "Investments," Englewood Cliffs, N.J., Prentice-Hall, 1978, p. 173.

[3] Fischer, Stanley, and Modigliani, Franco, "Toward an Understanding of the Real Effects and Costs of Inflation," *Weltwirtschafliches Archiv,* 1978, 114 (4), pp. 810–33.

Cross References: *Business Forecasting; Econometrics; Economics; Inflation Accounting; Money and Banking.*

INFLATION ACCOUNTING

Inflation Accounting generally refers to current cost and constant dollar accounting methodologies used either to (1) measure the impact of inflation (by using current cost), or (2) eliminate the effect of inflation (by using constant dollar) on reported results. Both approaches are incorporated in Financial Accounting Standards Board *Statement No. 33* governing financial reporting by large publicly held United States companies. Current cost and constant dollar inflation accounting techniques are also used by management accountants and strategic planners for internal planning and control purposes.

This entry describes the current cost and constant dollar concepts, how they are applied as a result of FAS 33, how inflation affects the reported results of companies, and how these and other techniques are being used for internal planning and control purposes to cope with inflation.

Current Cost Accounting. Current cost accounting is based on the concept of updating balance sheet items to their estimated current value and adjusting the income statement to reflect these changes in value caused by inflation and other changes in price levels. This concept differs from the traditional historic costs methodology which is centered on the actual amount of each transaction without any adjustment for inflation or unrealized price level changes. To illustrate, assume a company paid $250,000 for a building, but could sell it today for $700,000 net of real estate commissions. Under historical cost accounting, it would show the building on its balance sheet at $250,000, but under current cost accounting it would show it at $700,000. Under historic cost accounting, any profit on the sale of the house (including profit resulting from inflation) would be recognized only when the building was sold. Under current cost accounting, the gain in value would be recognized as it occurs.

Current cost accounting is also referred to as "replacement cost" and "current value" accounting in accounting literature.

LIFO (last in, first out) inventory valuation may be viewed as another form of current cost. This method was conceived in the late 1930s to minimize taxation in an inflationary environment. The Internal Revenue code pertaining to LIFO requires that LIFO be used for financial reporting in order to be acceptable for tax accounting purposes. While the related conceptual accounting underpinnings of LIFO have been the subject of controversy, LIFO is being used more and more widely as a principal method of inventory valuation for historical purposes as well as a surrogate for current cost information for compliance with FAS 33.

In 1976 the Securities and Exchange Commission called for the current cost approach to inflation accounting. Its release ASR 190 document required certain publicly held companies to disclose replacement cost information about inventories, cost of sales, productive capacity, and depreciation.

Constant Dollar Accounting. Constant dollar accounting is based on the concept of converting all dollars to units of constant purchasing power. Elements of the income statement and balance sheets are adjusted by an inflation index so that a dollar shown in 1982 will be roughly comparable to a dollar shown in, say, 1977. Whereas the current cost concept focuses on "what an element is worth in today's dollars," the constant dollar concept is centered on "what the dollar will buy." Because purchasing power, and not specific values, are relevant in constant dollar accounting, general inflation indices, such as the consumer price index (CPI), are used to calculate constant dollar amounts.

Requirements of FASB Statement 33. In September 1979, the Financial Accounting Standards Board issued the long awaited and hotly debated *Statement 33,* "Financial Reporting and Changing Prices." This statement requires that publicly held companies include selected constant dollar and current cost information in their annual reports, when they have either (1) inventories and property, plant, and equipment amounting in aggregate to more than $125 million before deducting accumulated depreciation, depletion, or amortization; or (2) total assets amounting to more than $1 billion after deducting accumulated depreciation.

Two financial reports are required: (1) a comparison of information for the current year, (a) as reported in the traditional statements, (b) adjusted for general inflation (constant dollars), (c) adjusted for changes in current prices (current costs); and (2) a five-year summary of historical cost and current cost information in constant dollars.

Minimal financial data in units of current purchasing power (constant dollars) include:

(1) Net sales and other operating revenue. (CPI applied to historic sales.)

(2) Earnings (loss) from continuing operations. (CPI applied to inventory and property, plant and equipment.)

(3) Earnings (loss) per common share from continuing operations (by calculation).

(4) Net assets (shareholders' equity) at year-end. (CPI applied to inventories, and property, plant, and equipment.)

(5) Purchasing power gain or loss on net monetary items. (CPI applied to elements of net monetary assets and liabilities. Net monetary assets and liabilities are specific cash and equivalent amounts owned, receivable or payable.)

(6) Cash dividends declared per common share. (CPI applied to dividends.)

(7) Market price per common share at fiscal year-end. (CPI applied to market price.)

Effect of Inflation Accounting. The application of the current cost and constant dollar inflation accounting concepts prescribed by FAS 33 had a substantial effect on the 1979 results reported by 27 of 30 companies included in the Dow Jones Industrial Average as shown in Exhibit I. (Three companies were excluded from this sample because their fiscal year ended before FAS 33 became effective).

Cost of sales increased only slightly because of the wide application of LIFO inventory practices by most of the companies included in the sample. However, depreciation expense is substantially affected by the application of constant dollar and current cost accounting. This is the area of cost where inflation causes the most significant distortions.

Reported profits are torpedoed by both constant dollar and current cost accounting. The after-tax decrease is more pronounced than the pre-tax decline because the provision for income taxes is not affected by the rules prescribed for the different accounting methods.

The effective income tax rate is substantially increased by inflation. In the sample shown it is increased from a level of 47% of net income on a historic basis to 63% on a constant dollar basis and 65% on a current cost basis.

The monetary gain (loss) on purchasing power of net amounts owed offsets much of the earnings decline. This amount is shown as a separate figure because these gains are "unrealized." However, if depreciation based on replacement costs is deducted from earnings and cash flow from continuing operations, it may be equally appropriate to include these gains or losses in this calculation. This issue is the subject of debate.

Funds flow is also affected by inflation. As shown in the analysis (Exhibit II) of the 1979 results of 27 Dow Jones companies, funds available for growth were cut by more than half from 37% of cash flow from continuous operations to 15% to 11% of cash flow depending on which methodology is considered. Similarly, the dividend payout ratio (dividends - net earnings) increased from 48% of net earnings to 85%-94% of net earnings. In short, when aggregate reported results are adjusted for inflation, net earnings do little more than cover dividend requirements.

While the overall "message" delivered by constant dollar accounting is really not much different than the message delivered by current cost accounting, impacts vary by industry group and by company within each industry. These variations are caused by the capital intensity, age of assets, method of inventory valu-

Exhibit I

Summary of Aggregate 1979 Results Reported by 27 of 30 Companies Included in Dow Jones Industrial Average

($ Billions) 27 Companies			*(Percent Sales) 27 Companies*		*13 Companies (Reporting Current Cost)*	
Historic (As Reported)	Constant Dollar	Income Statement	Historic (As Reported)	Constant Dollar	Constant Dollar	Current Cost
449.2	449.2	Sales Costs and expenses:	100.0	100.0	100.0	100.0
301.0	303.9	Cost of sales	67.0	67.7	73.3	73.0
20.5	30.2	Depreciation	4.6	6.7	8.5	8.9
75.1	75.1	Other costs and expenses	16.7	16.7	7.0	7.0
396.6	409.2	Total Costs and Expenses	88.3	91.1	88.8	88.9
52.6	40.0	Profit before taxes	11.7	8.9	11.2	11.1
24.7	24.7	Provision for taxes	5.5	5.5	7.2	7.2
27.9	15.3	Net earnings	6.2	3.4	4.0	3.0
	10.1	Gain (Loss) on purchasing power of net amounts owed		2.2	3.6	

Exhibit II

Analysis of Aggregate 1979 Sources and Funds Available for Growth of 27 of 30 Companies Included in the Dow Jones Industrial Average

($ Billions) 27 Companies			*(Percent Sales) 27 Companies*		*13 Companies (Reporting Current Cost)*	
Historic (As Reported)	Constant Dollar	Income Statement	Historic (As Reported)	Constant Dollar	Constant Dollar	Current Cost
		Sources of funds:				
27.9	15.3	Net earnings	52	30	29	27
20.5	30.2	Depreciation	38	59	61	63
5.7	5.7	Other non-cash items	10	11	10	10
54.1	51.2	Cash flow from continuing operations	100	100	100	100
20.5	30.2	Provision for plant and equipment replacement	38	59	61	63
13.3	13.3	Dividends	25	26	27	26
20.3	7.7	Funds available for growth	37	15	12	11
	10.1	Gain on purchasing power of net amounts owed		20	26	
		Dividend payout ratio	47.7	86.9	91.8	94.3

ation, and financial structure of each company.

Management Accounting Practices. Current cost and constant dollar inflation accounting concepts are applied to only a limited extent for internal planning and control purposes. Very few companies, for example, measure performance on an inflation-adjusted basis. Instead, inflation causes increasing emphasis to be placed on (1) switching to LIFO inventory valuation (indeed, a variation of current cost), (2) updating plans, budgets, and product costs more frequently, (3) measuring and managing funds flow, and (4) measuring and managing productivity. These conclusions are based on an analysis of 282 responses to a questionnaire that was mailed to the chief financial executives of the *Fortune* 1,000 companies by the National Association of Accountants in March, 1980.

Current cost inflation accounting concepts are used by some companies in the strategic planning process to determine the acquisition costs of new businesses and the exit values of existing businesses. For example, a large oil company uses current cost techniques to determine which of its retail marketing operations should be disposed of.

Constant dollar techniques are also used in the strategic planning process. Historic results are sometimes restated by a business unit on a constant dollar basis in order to analyze "real" growth and profitability trends. Many companies project future operations on a constant dollar (inflation-free) basis so as to facilitate year-to-year comparisons and because managers are uncertain as to what inflation rate to assume. More sophisticated companies, however, tend to (1) establish inflation rate premises by year and element of cost, and (2) present projected financial information on *both* a nominal and constant dollar basis.

Practices vary for dealing with inflation in *capital expenditure evaluations.* Many companies project capital outlays on a nominal (current) dollar basis, and future cash flows and residual values on a constant dollar basis. However, constant dollar projections do not reflect increased working capital requirements resulting from inflation. Some large companies have developed their own construction cost indices which they revise periodically. They track cost escalation changes by project and type of cost.

Most companies adjust their capital expenditure hurdle rates for an inflation-adjusted cost of capital, but others do not. Sophisticated companies project all cash flows on an inflation-adjusted basis and compare the resulting internal rate of return with an inflation-adjusted cost of capital. While several different inflation rate assumptions may be applied, and a computer model may be required to process the data, this approach offers the benefit of factoring the reality of inflation into the capital expenditure decision-making process.

Many companies update their *plans, budgets, and product costs* more frequently as a result of inflation. Mid-year revisions of plans, budgets, and standards are becoming more common. Some companies maintain dual standard costs: A fixed standard is used for valuing inventory, and a current standard is used for measuring product profitability.

Price level adjusted flexible budgeting is an emerging technique that is used to separate the effect of inflation from other causes of variance for purposes of performance measurement. In this case the budget is "flexed" to adjust for noncontrollable price level changes in the same manner that budgets are flexed to accommodate variations in production volume in a plant.

Largely because of inflation, increasing emphasis is being placed on planning and controlling *funds flow.* ("Funds flow" is generally considered to be synonomous with "cash flow.") Most companies include a projection of funds flow in their strategic plans and budgets, and they monitor the flow of funds against budget monthly. Some companies base part of their managers' incentive compensation on funds flow.

Distributable funds measurement is a useful approach to financial analysis in an inflationary environment. A going concern has distributable funds available only after it makes provision to maintain that portion of its operating capability financed by equity.

Recent emphasis has been placed on *productivity measurement* and improvement. While productivity measurement is not considered to be an "inflation accounting" technique, as such, much of the attention that has been directed toward productivity measurement is caused by inflation because productivity measurements remove the influence of changing prices from the measurement of performance.

Meaningful productivity measurements are often difficult to develop because of complexities entailed in identifying uniform measures of output and related measurements of input that can be tracked over time.

Trend. Management accounting techniques are constantly evolving to reflect the effect of inflation. While current cost and constant dollar inflation accounting concepts have not been widely adopted to date, their continued use in external financial reporting is eventually bound to have an effect on internal planning and control practices.

ALLEN H. SEED, III, Management Consultant, Arthur D. Little, Inc., Cambridge, Mass.

Information References

Much of the material in this entry was abstracted from the National Association of Accountants research study, "The Impact of Inflation on Internal Planning and Control," 1981, and is reproduced with the permission of the National Association of Accountants.

Ingberman, Montrole, "The Evolution of Replacement Cost Accounting," *Journal of Accounting, Auditing, and Finance,* Winter, 1980.

MacGibbon, D.I., "Why Not Price-Adjust Your Budget?," *The Australian Accountant,* November 1979.

Rappaport, Alfred, "Measuring Company Growth Capacity During Inflation," *Harvard Business Review,* January-February, 1979.

Seed, Allen H. III, "Inflation: Its Impact on Financial Reporting and Decision-Making," New York, Financial Executives Research Foundation, 1978.

Sweeney, Henry W., "Stabilized Accounting," New York, Harper & Brothers, 1936; rev. by Holt, Rinehart and Winston, New York, 1969.

Financial Accounting Standards Board, FASB Statement No. 33, Stamford, Conn., September 1979.

Cross References: *Accounting; Certified Public Accountant; FIFO-LIFO Inventory Accounting.*

INFORMATION DATA BANKS, ON-LINE

Our modern society produces a never-ending flow of data on a wide variety of subjects of interest to administrators. To mention a few: ecology, energy, chemicals and metals, agriculture and forest products, technology and engineering, healthcare and life sciences, and finance and marketing. Having such facts on hand is important for effective decision making.

The demand for information, however, tends to outstrip the capabilities of most organizations. Few have the resources necessary to pinpoint, gather, and organize data in *all* areas of interest. Hence the growth of a new and sophisticated industry—**On-Line Data Banks.** High-speed computer technology helps make data bank information easily accessible.

The major benefit of using a data bank is the ability quickly to retrieve information at a central location. An information-seeker avoids spending endless hours locating material from random sources. Data bank vendors have taken care of that chore by collecting data on a vast range of subjects, all of which are stored in computer software. Access to the data is then offered to business, industry, and government for a fee.

The amount of data available is enormous. A *data base* is a comprehensive collection of information on a specific subject and its related areas. A *data bank,* however, is a storehouse of many different data bases on many different subjects. Computer technology also makes it possible for users to conduct an on-line search of a data base within a data bank. Information needed for a particular project can be located in a few seconds. Cathode-ray tube (CRT) terminals or other communicating tools make this procedure easy. Manual methods would take hours, even days, to produce the same results.

Presently, there are hundreds of data banks, in the public and private sector, creating and maintaining a wide scope of information in data-base form. Users can select a data bank for the type of A to Z information that it offers, and also for the form in which the data are provided.

Basically, there are two types of data base forms: reference or bibliographic, and source or nonbibliographic. Source data bases differ from reference data bases in that they provide users with complete documents to work with rather than just a notation or abstract as to where the data are.

Reference Data Bases. *Bibliographic data bases* contain citations (specific notations as to where information is located) and abstracts or brief synopses of original source literature.

Referral data bases contain descriptions of projects, institutions, activities, the expertise of individuals, and other nonprint document sources.

Reference data bases of both types are stored in sequential files which contain descriptive elements such as the title of a book, a particular institution, a project, or a person's name. Knowing only one of these elements enables a user to locate the required information.

Source Data Bases. *Numeric data bases* contain numerical data that have been summarized or statistically manipulated from original surveys only.

Textual-numeric data bases contain records from textual or numeric information, or both. For example, a user looking for a census on coal mines would receive data that are a combination of words and numbers.

Properties data bases contain dictionary or handbook-type chemical and physical data.

Full-text data bases contain records of the *complete* text of an item or primary source.

Make or Buy? When management discovers that specific subject matter is in great demand within its organization, it must decide whether to create its own data base or buy access to an existing one through a data bank vendor. There are certain conditions that should be considered before making the choice.

Managers should *compile* rather than buy data, if the following criteria exist:

(1) The data will be proprietary and valuable.

(2) The organization will make intensive use of the data.

(3) The staff has expertise on the subject matter.

(4) The data bank is small enough to be tractable.

(5) The data bank may be marketable to others, thereby permitting the organization to recoup part of its costs.

(6) No satisfactory alternative is available.

Managers should *buy or lease* the data when these conditions apply:

(1) The body of information is large and expensive to collect.

(2) The data bank requires frequent, expert updating.

(3) A large data bank, or an unpredictable subset of one, is needed only on a periodic or episodic basis.

(4) No competitive advantage will be lost, nor any significant security risk incurred, by relying on an outside source.

Another question for an organization to ask itself is whether to use its own in-house terminals with a data bank service, or employ a data bank "retailer" who will provide the hardware needed. (Data banks typically, do not, provide hardware, just *access* to data bases.)

If an organization already has terminals installed in its offices, it is a simple matter to hook up directly to one or more data banks. Terminals can be either video or printer types; however, they must be compatible with the data bank vendor's computers. Users can also access the data bases directly on a telephone dial-up basis. Here, the data bank vendor will set up training programs to familiarize the customer with search techniques and special features unique to its particular product.

If an organization does not have terminals, it can make use of a retailer or an information on-demand service. These companies have computer terminals hooked up to a variety of data bases. When using such a service, a user calls up one of the retailer's research professionals, who develops a strategy to see if the request can be fulfilled. Researchers plan and execute the search, select the appropriate data bases to use, and deliver the results by mail, usually within one to ten days.

Costs. The cost-effectiveness of data bank use must be evaluated when choosing an on-line system. An assessment of organizational needs enables the user to decide which type of service is appropriate.

Most data banks offer the following options: outright purchase, rental, subscription, one-time usage fee, fees per datum (one specific piece of information), and surcharges on time-sharing bills. For instance (based on 1980 prices), a user might buy unlimited time-shared access to a data bank for a maximum of $5,000 per year. One data bank retailer will search data banks on request and then edit, screen, and index the results. A user can expect to pay anywhere from $80 for a *single* data bank search to $400 or higher for a search of over 75 data banks of some seven time-sharing vendors. The New York Times Information Bank (abstracts of *The New York Times,* 13 other newspapers, and over 40 magazines) charges between $80 to $110 per hour of on-line use.

Following are some estimates of what a user might expect to pay for other services:

- Up to 50 cents for a single datum or small set of related data.
- $5 to $250 for a report that requires no computer programming to produce.
- $100 to $2,500 and up for a report or special study request.
- $200 to $10,000 and up for a complete data bank.

DENISE R. GUILLET, *Administrative Management,* New York, New York

Information References

American Society for Information Science.
Association of Data Processing Service Organizations.
Association of Time-Sharing Users.
"Directory of Online Databases," Santa Monica, Calif, Cuadra Associates.

Guillet, Denise R., "On-Line Databanks," *Administrative Management,* July 1980.
Information Industry Association.
"NTIS Directory of Computerized Data Files, Software, and Related Technical Reports," (gives offerings of over 100 Federal agencies), Arlington, Va., National Technical Information Service.

Cross Reference: *Management Information Systems.*

INFORMATION STORAGE AND RETRIEVAL (NON-COMPUTER)

Records and documents fall into two broad categories—transaction documents and reference documents.

Transaction documents are orders, invoices, checks, active correspondence with customers, services, suppliers, and the like. Records management consultants report that these comprise over 75% of the total records of most companies. Files for these can be arranged numerically or alphabetically, and usually present no special retrieval problem.

Reference documents are reports, research data, marketing information, books and brochures, legal documents, and the like. While comprising the smaller percentage of filed information, they represent by far the greater problem in terms of prompt and comprehensive information retrieval.

For both transaction and reference retrieval, significant improvements in mechanical, microfilm, micro-fiche, electronic, and cathode-ray display equipment and systems have been developed. A document may fall into both categories, or at one time may be looked upon as a transaction document, and at another time as a reference document; e.g., an insurance policy may be considered a reference document. However, it may have to be updated and otherwise changed fairly frequently, or be consulted in connection with related transactions, and may thus be considered also a transaction document.

Transaction and control *information,* as distinguished from actual documents or copies of documents, is today directly obtainable from computer systems by cathode-ray printers, or voice response. However, the demand for manual and mechanized filing systems for original documents and copies has continued to expand, since even the smallest companies must keep more and better records than ever before for their own operations and to comply with governmental regulations. And computer systems themselves have called for improved means of filing and retrieving information for inputs as well as for their own proliferating printouts.

Manual Systems. For manual systems, one can choose from a wide variety of filing cabinets, tub files, drawers, flat trays, "lazy Susan" files, open and closed shelf files, and the like. No-drawer, laterally suspended filing equipment, long in use in Europe, is now available in this country, and offers substantial space advantages. For records that must be worked on continuously, often by several people, the "lazy Susan" turntable file gives ready access and reduces wasted time and worker fatigue. Ready access is also achieved with rotary card files, available in mechanized as well as manual form.

For very active files, the *rotary systems* are considered the most practical. Ordibel's Roto-Scan uses wedge-shaped file folders, sequentially marked to prevent misfiling and provide to out-file control. Smaller rotary files are desk-top items for telephone numbers or frequently-used addresses. Rotary files are relatively expensive, but they provide a good space/capacity ratio.

Tub files, an adjunct to the open plan office system, are based on the hanging file concept, with files in tiers, open at top or sides. Units are frequently on casters for moving to other work stations. Some have desk surfaces built into the stand. Plastic trays such as Eldon's Hot File can be expanded to form a permanent desk side filing system.

Visible Records. Manual record keeping can be extremely effective with properly designed and applied visible records. Visible systems involving color-coded or tabbed hinged cards or pockets in horizontal trays, records in shingle binders, or shingled vertical records in tubs have long been available. In the system illustrated in Exhibit I, a few hundred or many thousands of records are all instantly available in a single motion from a seated position. Posting is done in the normal position on a flat surface.

Retrieval Techniques. *Transaction Records: Parallel Numbering and Alphabetizing:* A transaction record system, especially one associated with computer processing, will benefit by a numbering system that maintains true alphabetic access to operational files, while having all entries in numerical sequence. To achieve this, the DANS system (*D*iebold *A*lpha *N*u-

EXHIBIT I

VISIBLE-VERTICAL FILING SYSTEM

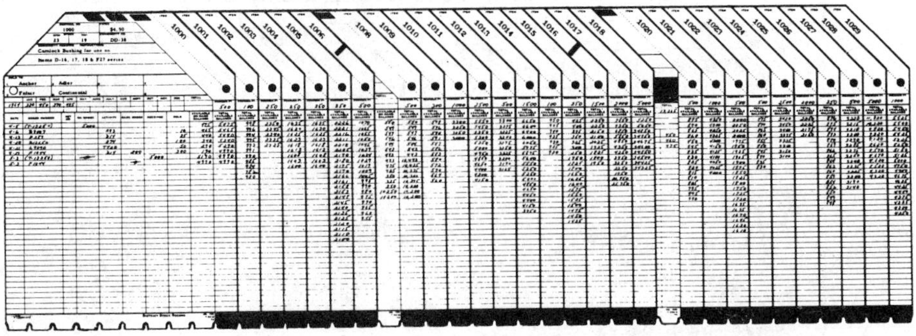

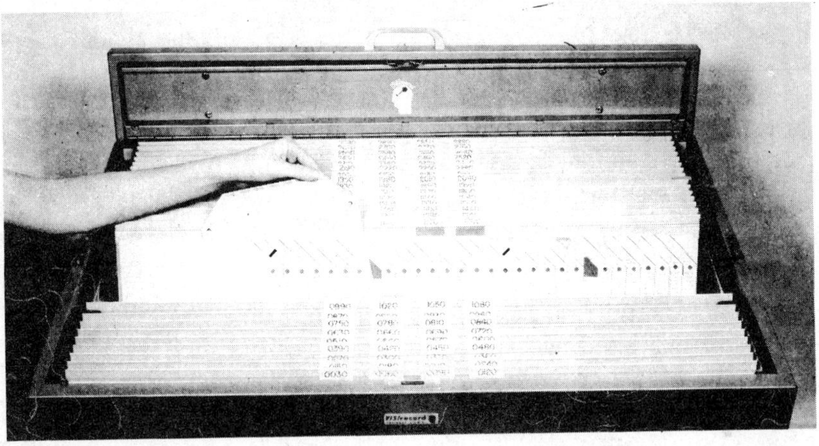

Forms can be accommodated for a wide range of size, shape, and visible margin.

(Courtesy VISIrecord, Inc.)

meric System), developed by Diebold, Inc., applies names to numbers, rather than numbers to names, through a zigzag arrangement of numbers preprinted on Diebold-supplied forms. Gaps are provided between numbers in prearranged blocks to permit alphabetic insertion of new names without disturbing the numerical order. The zigzag pattern of preprinted numbers visually locates the numerical midpoint between two previously assigned names when a new name must be entered. A check digit can also be assigned to make possible accuracy checks on input to automated systems.

The technique is illustrated in Exhibit II. Names in an existing file for conversion to the system are originally entered at the top of each column. In this example, say that between the two originally assigned names of Cable and Caldwell, you wish to assign in the following sequence of arrival, the names of Cain, Cade, Cahill, and Calabrese. Cain, which has to fit between Cable and Caldwell, would get No. 119, midpoint of the first column. Later, when Cade has to be assigned, he gets the midpoint between Cable and Cain, i.e., No. 111. Cahill has to fit between Cade and Cain, and gets No. 115. By the same process, Calabrese, which must fit between Cain and Caldwell, get No. 127.

The probability of there being no vacant number in the proper alphabetic sequence is small. When such a name appears, it is assigned to a set of prelisted numbers on the last register card in each thousand series, i.e., in the 900s.

Reference Documents: Inverted Indexing. Reference document files have always created indexing and retrieval problems. With conventional arrangement by broad subject, multiple cross-indexing proliferates as an at-

EXHIBIT II

DANS NUMBERING SYSTEM

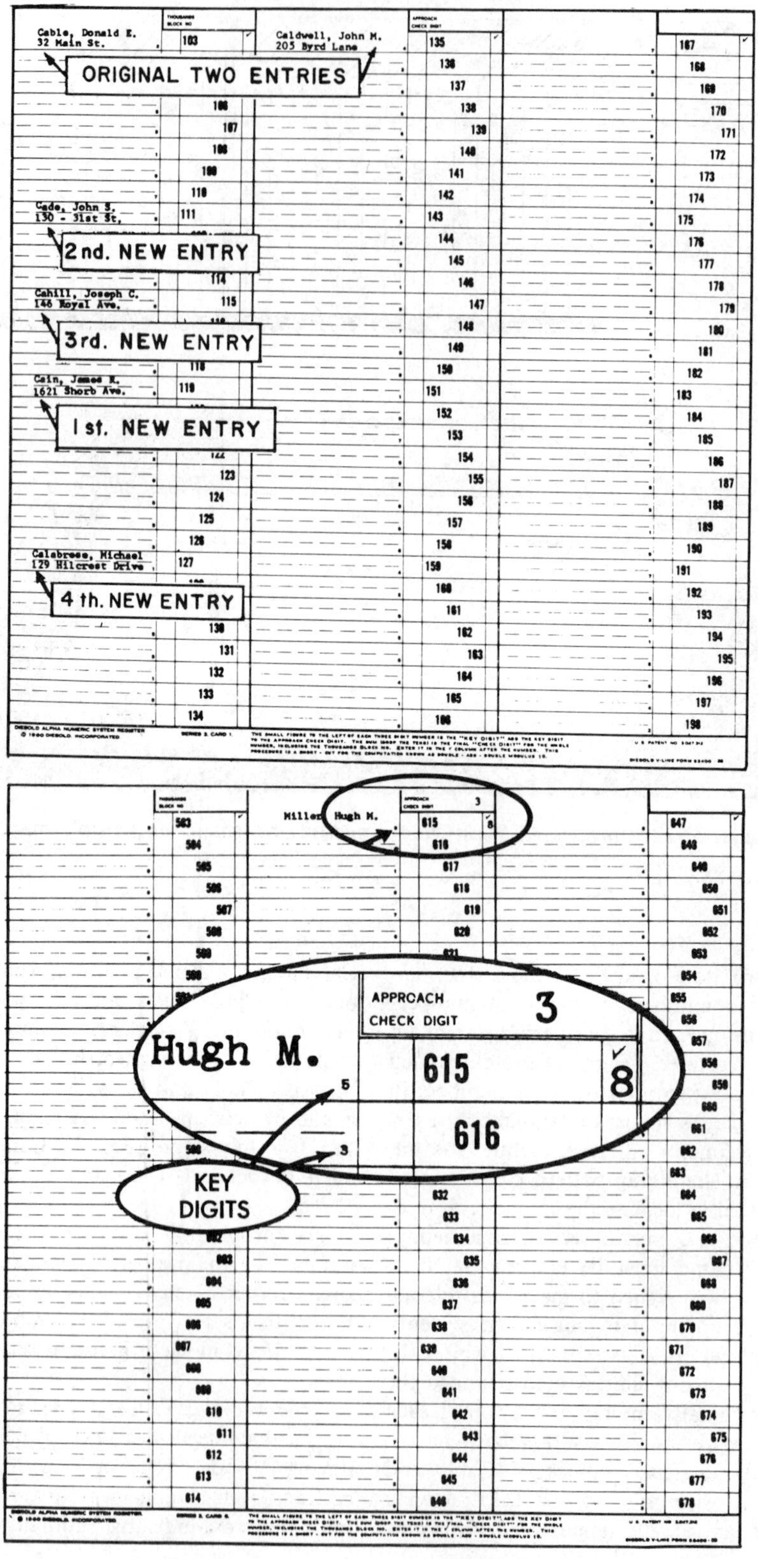

tempt is made to anticipate all possible look-ups. A single report or document could have as many as ten or twenty index cards. Thus 1,000 reports or documents could give rise to 10,000 to 20,000 index cards.

A powerful system for overcoming these handicaps, and one that lends itself to simple manual retrieval as well as being readily adaptable to punched-card or computerized search, is *inverted indexing,* also referred to as *concept coordination.* Here the flexibility and control are all in the indexing. The documents themselves are simply given consecutive address numbers and filed by those numbers. (For some subject areas it may be convenient to keep like documents together by assigning blocks of numbers.)

Instead of indexing and arranging the documents themselves, a limited number of appropriate *basic concepts* (also termed *descriptors* or *uniterms*) are developed, and these are placed on cards which are then filed alphabetically. Since the documents and reports are numbered and filed consecutively, there is no awkward problem of squeezing a new document in between others in a tight location.

The card for each descriptor or uniterm contains the addresses of *all* documents containing information on that particular concept. (In an automated sytem, the descriptors with their associated numbers can be in a computer's memory, or be in the form of punched cards.)

To see how the system works, assume that one has a large collection of reports, brochures, and documents, referenced by marketing and research personnel. Broad information retrieval will be handled by producing all the documents (or, more likely, preparatory to that, a list of their titles) available on one concept card, e.g., *Tires.* However, suppose that what is wanted is information on *automobile tires,* as distinguished from airplane tires, or other types of tires. Then only those documents (or titles) will be produced whose addresses appear on *both* the concept *Automobiles* and the concept *Tires.* If the request is narrowed to *Nylon Automobile Tires,* then only the smaller number of documents or titles will be produced whose addresses are on three concept cards, with *Nylon* added to the other two. (Of course, the setting up of concept cards will depend upon the nature of the file and the probable kinds of look-ups.)

Exhibit III illustrates the technique. A "trace card," shown at the top, is made for every document entered into the files. Here the document *Guide to Nylon Automobile Tires* has been given the address number 482. In the column, Locater Terms, the filing clerk or librarian has listed all the descriptors or uniterms which his scanning or reading of the document showed him were covered. The document number 482 is the posted on each of the separate descriptor or uniterm cards. Thus, in addition to being posted on the *Tires* card shown in the lower half of Exhibit III, it is also posted on the uniterm cards *Cords, Nylon,* and *Automobiles.* Note that at various times twenty-seven documents were posted on the *Tires* card. The numbers are posted in accordance with their *last* digit. In this way no more than ten columns are needed on each uniterm card.

EXHIBIT III

INVERTED INDEXING CONCEPT

GUIDE TO NYLON CORD AUTOMOBILE TIRES	Document Number 482 / Location
LOCATOR TERMS	**PROPER NAMES**
Tires	B. F. Goodrich Co
Cord	
Nylon	
Automobile	

Trace card

TIRES									
0	1	2	3	4	5	6	7	8	9
1490	231	482	1463	914	215	816	1157	1148	719
		1622	1623	1004	425	1626	1437	1778	819
				1464	555	1156	1697		1149
				1624	905				1159
					1625				

Uniterm card

Edge-punched cards, such as those of McBee Systems, can be used for quickly locating cards containing the trace-card information just described. McBee cards come with holes around the edges (Exhibit IV). Coding is accomplished by notching out holes in a specified coding pattern. Keysorting is done by aligning a stack of cards, and inserting a long needle through the holes corresponding to the code for a specific uniterm. When the needle is slightly raised, the desired cards will detach themselves, because the needle lifts only the cards with unnotched holes.

Still essentially manual is the "peekaboo" system originated by Jonker Corporation (now Termatrex Corp.) marketed under the name

Termatrex. A 9 by 11 inch card is made for each basic concept, or uniterm. The card is marked off by numbered vertical and horizontal coordinates, providing as many as 10,000 specific locations or addresses. Each of these addresses represents a specific document containing information on that uniterm. Holes are drilled into the locations indicated by the coordinates. Then when information on a given combination of uniterms is desired, all individual uniterm cards are pulled and superimposed. The packet of cards is placed against a light source, and the holes through which a beam of light is visible identify all the documents, and *only* those documents, pertinent to the search. (See Exhibit V.) For larger retrieval needs, the cards are supplanted by microfilm.

Movable Aisle Systems. Movable aisle filing systems decrease storage space requirements by eliminating all but one aisle per system. Sets of shelves are moved either manually or by motor, on carriages or on tracks in the floor. Access to

EXHIBIT IV

MCBEE EDGE-PUNCHED SORTING

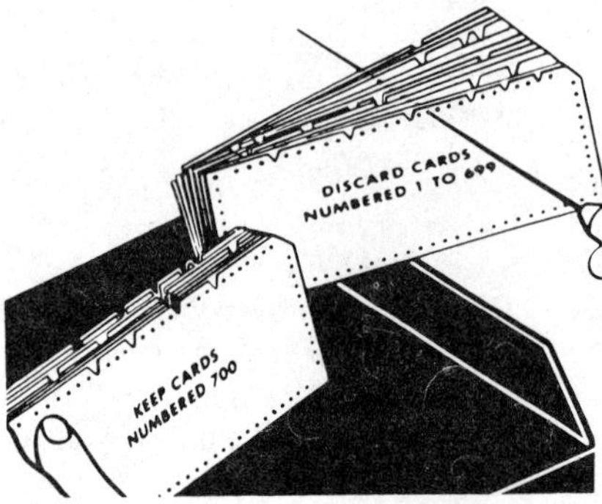

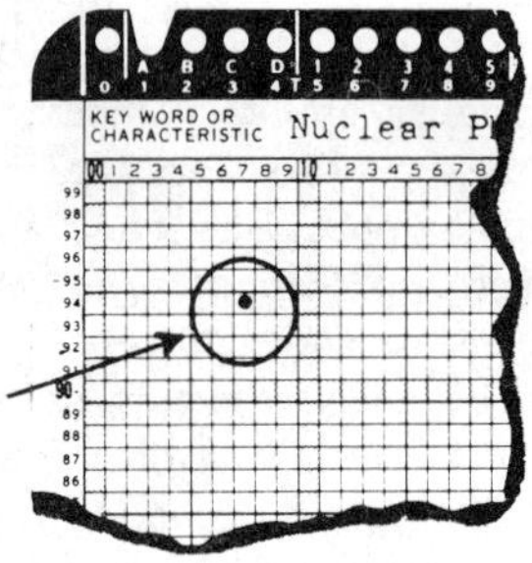

EXHIBIT V

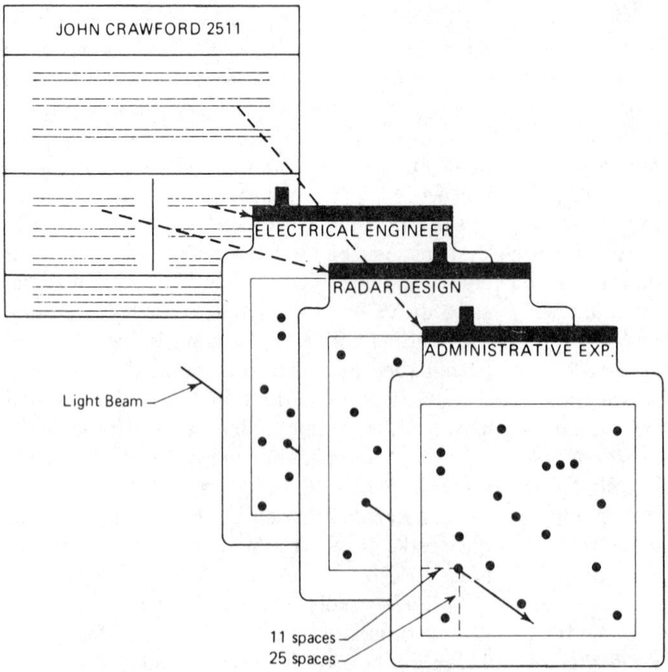

The Termatrex system. In a personnel file, to find electrical engineers with radar-design experience as well as administrative experience, superimpose cards *Electrical Engineer, Radar Design,* and *Administration Experience.* Coinciding holes, visible as light spots, represent employees (applicants) meeting *all* these requirements.

a desired file section is achieved by moving the single aisle until it reveals the chosen section.

Rollaway files are a variation on this technique, with a rear section that is stationary and a front section moves from right to left to allow access to the back row of files. Both systems tend to have rather high shelving, and offer an approximate 50% saving in space, i.e., giving twice the number of file rows in a given space as compared with conventional plans. They are cost-justified only where volume is large, since these systems are generally custom made.

Mechanized Systems. Many electromechanical pushbutton-operated systems are available to house and quickly retrieve documents and cards in their original form, or, in more elaborate systems, present them on cathode-ray screens. Electromagnetic card files, for example, cause a desired card or group of cards to jump up when a code is keyed in by pushbutton. Coded information on a thin row of metal teeth along the bottom edge of each card permits calling out a specific card by name, number, territory, billing date, and the like. An important time-saving feature is that a record can be refiled by placing it anywhere in the tray at random. In 1965, Wheeldex automated an 11-million-card record system for the Civil Service Commission in Washington, D.C., with a powered rotary file. The file operates somewhat like a ferris wheel, with rows of trays riding on cradles up, down, and around the interior of the machine. Operation is from a pushbutton keyboard, with the cradles rotating in either direction, automatically taking the shortest route from the position in which they happen to be at the signal.

In the realm of elaborate information retrieval is the Video-file information system of "electronic information management" developed by Ampex corporation, embodying television-type electronic images. This system combines television recording and computer techniques to reduce conventional paper files to compact magnetic recordings on video tape. Approximately 250,000 standard 8½- by 11-inch pages—the contents of 20 four-drawer cabinets—may be filed on a single 14-inch diameter reel.

Microfilm. Microfilm, now popular enough to justify its own association (National Micrographics Association), dates from the 19th century. In 1839, Louis Daguerre produced a photographic image which offered fine detail, and later the same year, John Benjamin Dancer produced the first microphotographs with Daguerre plates using a reduction of 160:1.

Microfilm has long been used as a space saver. Since the 1950s, continuous improvements in the convenience of operation and quality of image in microfilm viewers, including small battery-operated portable units, have expanded microfilm use beyond archival storage only. Now mechanized systems provide almost instant retrieval of images on microfilm combined with punched cards or in other forms. In recent years, microfilming has been combined with computer displays on cathode-ray tubes to eliminate the bottlenecks of conventional computer printout devices. Microfilm in forms other than reels can be placed in jacketed cards and subjected to rapid retrieval methods previously discussed.

Microfilm is used primarily for documents in serial form, e.g.: magazines, newspapers, books, voluminous reports, etc. Film is packed in reels, cartridges, and cassettes. Single frames are generally mounted in aperture cards, 3¼ × 7⅜″. Other options permit small groups of frames to be ganged into a multiple image card.

Rivaling microfilm in popularity, microfiche is a flat film which can store from 98 to 420 pages sized 8½ × 11, depending on the magnification chosen. Fiche may be inserted into edge-notched or magnetic carriers for retrieval, in special card carriers or in carousels. Storage units for fiche are conceptually identical to files for card systems, with adjustments for size and protection of the film surface.

There is also an extension of the system called ultrafiche, with a reduction of 90×, which allows 1,000 pages to be stored on a 3 × 5 area.

EDWIN SHADE, Editor, *Geyer Dealer Topics*, New York, New York

Information References

Associations:

Administrative Management Society.
Association for Systems Management.
National Micographics Association.

Publications:

Administrative Management.
Geyer Dealer Topics.
Information and Records Management.

Texts:

Dickinson, A. Litchard, "The Right Way to File," New York, Geyer-McAllister, 1971.

Heyel, Carl, "Handbook of Modern Office Management and Administrative Services," Chap. 11, Section 4, "Information Storage and Retrieval," Huntington, N.Y., Krieger, repr. 1980.
"Information Retrieval Systems," Washington, General Services Administration, National Archives and Records Service, Office of Records Management, Federal Stock No. 7610-181-7577, 1970.

Cross References: *Office Automation; Systems Management.*

INNOVATION: The Management of Change

Systematically planned **Innovation,** on a continuing basis, has become a central element in continued economic growth.

Economic growth is not a force of nature. It is the result of the purposeful, responsible, risk-taking action of entrepreneurs and managers. The immediate generator of economic growth is, or course, investment. Investment is set in motion partly by economic forces. But more basically, investment arises from new ideas, new knowledge, new developments in science and technology, and from research. Innovations—new products, new processes, new resources, new services—are the real needs of long-term economic growth.

These innovations need not be accidental and irregular. By a new emphasis on research and by systematizing innovation, industry and government now make regular provision for the occurrence of new and unpredictable developments. This process has taken significant hold in American business, though it still varies widely from industry to industry.

What Innovation Involves. The central fact about economic activity is that it commits present resources to an unknowable and uncertain future. In effect, it is a commitment to future expectations rather than to lines of action based on presently known facts. To take risks is, therefore, the essence of economic activity, and risk-making and risk-taking constitute the basic functions of enterprise. They define the role of innovation. *Innovation is purposeful, organized, risk-taking change introduced for the purpose of maximizing economic opportunities.* It is the generation and introduction of some new element which will give the business a new economic dimension.

Innovative ability is conceptual and creative rather than technical or scientific. It is the ability to look at the business as a system and to provide the missing element which will convert the already existing elements into a new and more productive whole. It involves the determination of what will change the customer's need-value-satisfaction relationship.

Innovation is non-specific. It applies to and discovers its particular shape and methodology from each specific area of activity. It occurs in two forms: (1) exploration and improvement within the various parameters of the business, and (2) the questioning, testing, and establishing of the parameters themselves. In relation to the other central tasks of managing, it cuts across all areas of a business. It is as important in the establishment of goals, objectives, organization, and the operating and procedural aspects of the business as it is in the technological areas of product and process. It may take the form of a change in design, in product, in packaging, in price, in service to the customer, or in the overall corporate or marketing strategy. Or it may involve the use of new materials or new automatic machinery, or the introduction of new knowledge, techniques, skills, organizational schemes, or policies into the business.

Thus there are two basic kinds of innovation in every business: innovation in *product or service;* and innovation in the various *skills and activities* needed to supply them. Since it extends across all functions, all activities of the business, every managerial unit should have clear responsibility and definite goals for innovation. Innovative performance should be built into the job and into the spirit of the organization, and be made an important criterion for personal progress in the company.

Innovation and Corporate Planning. Every business must have some kind of informal or formal corporate strategy. To a large extent, the success of the company depends on how clearly defined, how well understood, and how smoothly it is geared to the company's environment.

Many activities have recently emerged under such labels as long-range planning, corporate development, corporate planning, or corporate strategy. Corporate planning is deciding what the company ought to be and defining the major steps to reach and maintain that goal. A corporate strategy is an organized set of fundamental objectives, goals, and policies through which the purpose and missions of the corporation are realized. The effective strategic plan stresses what to do to preserve the long-term vitality of the business and to engineer its profitable growth. (See CORPORATE STRATEGY and BUSINESS POLICY and LONG-RANGE CORPORATE PLANNING.)

A systematic approach to corporate planning implies two key elements: (1) the imposition of a planning discipline on the present operations of the business (that is, the establishment of a planning system for each division of the organization and the maintenance of this system); and (2) a reappraisal of the business and of the direction in which it should be heading. The essence of corporate planning is the application of the company's resources and talents to the most profitable uses. *Innovation* is at the core of such planning for change. It is the critical element in the total process of planning which enables management to accomplish its marketing goals and objectives.

Innovation Strategy. Over-all innovation strategy involves the setting of objectives for technical innovation. Since technical innovation offers one of the best prospects for a company's growth and for achieving an expanding economy, top management should take an active, aggressive attitude toward it. Its most essential activities in this area should include (1) providing research with a clear understanding of company goals and strategies, and defining specific objectives for research within the context of these plans; (2) seeing that appropriate organizational arrangements are made (a) to assess carefully the major technological threats and opportunities the company faces, (b) to facilitate transfer of research technology into operations; and (3) developing a project evaluation procedure which results in a balanced package of projects to meet company objectives. From this point on, management must continuously evaluate its program of technical innovation to see that both research and operating units carry out their intended functions in developing and utilizing technology to support company goals. (See TECHNOLOGICAL FORECASTING.)

The need for innovation in the social area is just as important as it is in the technical area. For the explosive development of technological progress and change will be largely unproductive unless it is accompanied by major innovations in the social area. The most important need for such innovation is in marketing and distribution. Also urgently needed are real advances in methods, tools, and measurements for doing the managerial job, as well as improvements in the management and organization of knowledge workers and the structuring of their work. Obviously, objectives for social innovation should further and be closely correlated with those for technical innovation.

Social and technical innovation goals for the average business should include:

(1) New products or services needed to attain marketing objectives.

(2) Product improvements and new products or services needed to meet technological competition and offset technical and other forms of obsolescence.

(3) New resources, new materials, new equipment, new processes needed to keep pace with technology.

(4) Social innovations and improvements in all major areas of company activity.

While innovation does not lend itself to a magic formula, it should not be left to chance. If companies are to enjoy an increased rate of corporate growth, it is not enough to trust that random change, improvement, product development, invention, or research will do it. Management must itself take a hand in the process, giving full, vigorous, and continuous support to the work of technical and social innovation. Herein lies the key to an expanding economic system.

PHILIP W. SHAY, formerly Executive Vice President, Association of Consulting Management Engineers, Inc., New York, New York

Information Reference

Burgher, Peter H., "Changement, Understanding & Managing Business," Lexington, Mass., Lexington Books, 1979.

Cross References: *Basic Research; Brainstorming; Creativity Training; Industrial Research and Development; Long-Range Corporate Planning; Long-Range Planning: Financial Aspects; New Product Development (and accompanying entries with that prefix); Patents; Suggestion Systems; Technological Forecasting; Venture Capital; Venture Management.*

INSURANCE MANAGEMENT

All business and industry carried on for a profit pose important problems of risk taking. The risks assumed are "business" risks, the compensation for which is realized or potential profit. Business risks, or commercial risks, are generally self-assumed and are usually not transferrable to a professional risk carrier. However, no soundly managed business will venture upon a commercial risk unless, to the extent possible, practicable, and economic, its assets are secure and protected, and its earning potential safeguarded.

Through the machinery of RISK MANAGEMENT, the exposure to risks to which the assets and earning potential are exposed are defined, and then transferred very frequently to a professional risk carrier by the purchase of insurance policies. With the complexities of modern business and the intricacies of the insurance industry itself, it is no simple matter to purchase insurance in a way that satisfies the risk transferral needs of a company at the lowest premium cost. The problem is compounded by the numerous laws and regulations to which insurance is often the best answer (workers' compensation, automobile liability, temporary non-occupational disability). Add to this the vastness of the insurance market (international in scope), the apparent limitations at times of insurance companies to provide business with the specific protection they seek, and the cyclical ups and downs of the insurance marketplace resulting in cyclical increases in premium levels followed by extreme competitiveness. It is obvious that the result is highly technical and complex.

Insurance Management is that part of the risk management function that concerns itself, on a technically trained and professional level, with the post-evaluation of transferral of risk, or with the scientific self-insurance of the risk, and with the resulting effects of that transfer or self-insurance; it is the liaison between buyers of insurance for business needs and the sellers, i.e., the insurance industry; it is the maximizing of the insurance benefit by way of advantageous policy terms, premium levels, and, often, cash flow.

The categories of risk management that fall within the insurance management function are:

(1) Knowledgeable and aggressive negotiation with insurance carriers (or with agents or brokers), insurance commissions, rating bureaus, and state legislatures, by technically trained professionals whose prime interest is the benefit of the company. This means purchasing (rather than being sold) insurance protection, and the minimizing of existing and prospective risks.

(2) In conjunction with the legal staff or outside attorneys, the indemnification for damages sustained by the company through acts of others, and supervision of collection of claims from insurers.

(3) Maintenance of records of premium costs and loss statistics for astute negotiation of renewals of coverage and for periodic reviews to determine the soundness of buying insurance vs. self-insurance and vs. non-insurance.

(4) Continual surveillance of the part of the insurance industry dealt with by the company, to avoid over-insurance, under-insurance, human error, omission, and possible negligence.

(5) Continual awareness of developments in the entire insurance field which might afford the company better coverage, better rates, or better methods of reducing or eliminating risks.

(6) Where needed, development of sound self-insurance programs, and their supervision.

(7) Continued surveillance of the financial ability and stability of the firm's insurer.

(8) The rendering of complete, accurate, and concise reports to appropriate members of management concerning the company's insurance program.

Background. Modern insurance management came into being with the emergence of the insurance broker (and, to a lesser degree, of the insurance companies' agents). The function of the broker was to be familiar with the entire insurance market and to buy on behalf of his client only the policies the latter needed, and to provide him with necessary allied services.

However, to a large extent, the concept of the broker (and more so that of the insurance agent, whose principal was the insurance company and not the insurance buyer) was local in outlook and limited by such ulterior pressures as the need to retain working relationships with insurance companies, and commission considerations. During the latter half of the 1960s and the 1970s (and, it is expected, there will be similar periods in the 1980s, 1990s, etc.) the worldwide insurance market became very constricted.

During the latter half of the 1960s and the 1970s (and it is expected, there will be similar periods in the 1980s, 1990s, etc.) the worldwide insurance markets became highly constricted. This constriction was brought about by many factors occurring simultaneously, which may be summarized briefly as follows:

• Inflationary trends that brought about severe increases in values and the ensuing concentration of large values at risk.

• Severe increases in loss ratios and consequent reductions in insurance company profits.

• Growing social disorders throughout the world, as typified by many riots in the United States and elsewhere.

• Especially in the United States, the merger of insurance companies into conglomerates, so that insurance company surpluses, sidetracked to the interests of the parent company, became reduced to the point that underwriting commitments had to be curtailed.

• The ever increasing dependence of insurance on investment and interest income (subject to severe fluctuations in the financial marketplace) instead of on underwriting profit.

As a result of the curtailment not only of available insurance markets on a local level, but also of reinsurance markets on a worldwide level as well, both brokers and agents found the advantageous placement of their clients' insurance needs more and more difficult to accomplish. Previously existing leverage seemed to a large extent to evaporate in this period, and insurance buyers had to start taking notice of the fact that the producer was often as interested in protecting his markets as he was in looking out for the interests of his clients. Especially in some of the larger urban communities, the smaller brokers and agents found themselves in a distressing position in regard to their suppliers, and, of course, their own welfare, while the large insurance agencies and brokerage firms found that it was becoming more and more difficult to tailor coverage, terms, and conditions as closely to their clients' needs as hitherto. (The 1980s portend even greater possible problems in this area due to the movement of the large brokers to eliminate much local competition substantially by buying up significant local agencies and brokerage firms in great numbers.)

These factors of self-interest in commissions and preservation of relationships with the ever diminishing market are not mentioned in denigration of today's many highly professional insurance brokers and agents. However, it is true that the workings of the insurance industry to a great extent create the possibility of dual allegiance, where commission is related to premium volume, and where the producer's relationship with the insurance company determines the availability of his sources of supply for tomorrow.

The "local outlook" is a purely American development. Unlike his or her English colleagues, whose market was virtually centralized around Lloyd's and the many insurance companies in London, the insurance broker in the United States had to maneuver in an insurance market that was widespread, with many centers (e.g., Hartford, Boston, New York, Philadelphia, Dallas, Chicago, Los Angeles, and points between) and with many insurance companies operating in only limited areas.

In the early part of the twentieth century, several large firms whose insurance needs were becoming complex, whose premium expenditures were becoming substantial, and whose insurance handling detail was becoming overwhelming, delegated to one employee the responsibility of dealing with the insurance brokers, agents, and companies. By 1930, this contact with the insurance industry became more sophisticated, astute, and knowledgeable, and instead of being *sold* insurance, the designated staff member became an insurance *buyer* who established the specifications of the insurance needs and desires of his firm.

Gradually, and especially after World War II, the insurance buyer's position in many firms developed into the broader and more vital position of risk manager, and the insurance management function became but a part—although an important and highly technical part—of the larger risk management function.

Modern Practice. Today, insurance management may be implemented by staff executives of high professional training and experience, as is the case of over 3,200 American and Canadian firms (mostly of relatively large size), or by independent risk-managing consulting firms, who provide similar services to medium or small firms, and serve in an advisory capacity to the larger firms.

Recognized independent risk-management consulting firms sell no insurance; and as their compensation is not tied to premium value, but rather is obtained solely from preagreed fees paid by the client firm, complete objectivity is assured.

Generally, the insurance management function is limited to *property insurance, liability insurance, workers' compensation, marine insurance,* and *suretyship.* However, some firms include their programs for pension, group life, hospitalization, etc., within the duties of the insurance manager. This is especially true in recent years because of the growth of fringe benefits and the accompanying large sums of money involved. Consequently, some firms have established separate employee benefits management departments working closely with the financial office of the firm, while others, feeling that the importance of these areas relates more to employee and industrial relations, have these activities directed by their officer in charge of personnel.

Usually the insurance manager limits his work to the firm's needs, specifically avoiding the responsibility for the executives' or employees' insurance needs. Yet others allow this, and some even encourage the latter, in spite of the possible liability for error, omission, or malpractice.

Scope. The insurance manager must digest, weigh, and interpret a vast amount of data pertaining to many facets of his firm's operation. These include:

• Geographic and physical conditions that often contribute to the possibility of loss—such as earthquake, flood, power interruption, windstorm.

• Make-up of raw materials and finished products (including methods for promotion and advertising) that could contribute to product liability—one of the most rapidly growing areas of insurance problems at the moment, especially with the growing acceptance of strict liability concepts of law.

• The idiosyncrasies of courts and court-made law (further complicated by vastly different concepts if his firm does business on an international basis).

• Knowledge of worldwide insurance markets.

• Thorough understanding of his (her) firm's finances so that he can determine the financial expediency of insuring vs. non-insuring. (See RISK MANAGEMENT.)

• Full understanding of availability of raw materials and continued production sources—to determine the propriety and extent of business interruption insurance, etc.

Further, a good insurance manager (or risk manager) must be ever aware of constantly changing social, political, and economic climates both in the country of domicile and abroad (where the firm may have assets, operations, suppliers, and customers). Strikes, civil commotion, and rioting affect not only insurance policies but the decision base upon which self insurance decisions are made. TERRORISM has similar impact, plus the effect on the possible need for kidnap or extortion coverage, to say nothing of its possible impact on workers' compensation (and similar disability coverages) and loss ratios (and ultimate premium development). Breaks in diplomatic relations or war could prevent a damaged or destroyed plant in the U.S. or Canada from rebuilding and resuming proper operations because of inability to obtain machinery from or via (in case of blockage or embargo) a now not friendly supplier's nation—eventualities which could increase the amount of business-interruption insurance needed.

If a company spends large amounts on liability insurance—where there is a time lag between an accident and payment to the victims—an alternative type of policy structuring that might prove to be advantageous is the so called "cash flow" plans. This is a highly intricate arrangement that evolved in the mid to late 1970s.*

Though each such policy is acutely tailored to a specific firm's needs, substantially the insured gives the insurance company funds only to investigate, administer, and defend claims. Money to pay claims is given to the insurer *only* when it will be paid to the claimant. The insured firm often keeps the use of that money for several years. In as much as fees are attached by insurers, this is not a panacea plan for everyone. However, where a firm is expanding, or its outlook for future cash flow is otherwise negative, (e.g., impending economic downslide), this approach is often beneficial.

It is critical that the insurance manager keeps his finger on the economic conditions of his firm and the firm's territory. He must understand and negotiate an almost limitless number of forms of insurance of which the following are among the most important. (The list is by no means comprehensive and the reader is referred to "The Insurance Marketplace" mentioned in *Information References* at the end of this article.

Accounts Receivable Insurance. Provides virtually all risk coverage against the firm's inability to collect outstanding balances following

* During the past few years, the IRS has been attacking such programs on various basis, though such attacks—while growing in frequency—have been spotty. Some states, e.g. California and Texas as of this writing, have been attacking the legality of such insurance plans, with growing success. Before entering into such a plan, expert advice should be sought—other than from or via the proposed insurance company or insurance producer.

the destruction of the accounts receivable records, plus reasonable expenses incurred to reconstruct those records.

Advertisers' Liability Insurance. Protects a firm against liability arising our of libel (through advertising), slander, defamation of character, infringement of copyright, piracy, or the rights of privacy.

Aircraft Public Liability Insurance. Protects against bodily injury and property damage liability imposed by law for injury to or death of members of the public, or destruction of their property, arising out of the ownership, maintenance, or use of aircraft.

Aircraft Hull Insurance. Coverage against damage to the plane itself from physical causes; usually fire, theft, windstorm, crash, and many other perils.

Aircraft Non-Ownership Liability Insurance. Covers the firm for liability arising out of bodily injury or property damage, which in turn arise out of operations of aircraft not owned by the firm.

Aircraft Passenger Liability Insurance. Covers the firm against liability imposed by law, for bodily injury to passengers arising out of ownership, maintenance, or use of aircraft.

Automobile Bodily Injury and Property Damage Liability Insurance. Covers the firm against liability arising out of the ownership, maintenance, or use of automobiles owned by the firm, or by others.

Automobile Collision Insurance. Pays for the direct and accidental loss of—or damage to—insured vehicles caused by collision with another object, or by upset, usually on a deductible basis, although not necessarily so.

Automobile Comprehensive Liability Insurance. This is a standard form contract which covers the liability of the firm for ownership, maintenance, or use of automobiles regardless of ownership, combining all automobile liability protection into one contract, including automobile liability exposures not recognized at the inception date of the policy. When combined with a *Comprehensive Liability Policy,* it forms a *Comprehensive General—Automobile Liability Policy* that covers virtually all liability risks on a blanket basis, known and unknown.

Automobile Comprehensive Physical Damage Insurance. Covers insured vehicles against *any* direct and accidental damage to the vehicle, except collision (and a few other limited restrictions).

Automobile Non-Ownership Liability Insurance. Covers against liability from operation by others of automobiles not owned by the firm. Its principal application is to protect businesses against liability incurred by employees, agents, etc., operating their own vehicles on the business of the firm.

Blanket Crime Policy. A package form of policy which, with a single overall limit, provides coverages against infidelity (on the same basis as the *Commercial Blanket Bond*), *Monies and Securities Broad Form* coverage on premises, *Money Order* and *Counterfeit Paper Currency Insurance* and *Depositor's Forgery Insurance.* This coverage is substantially the same as the *Comprehensive Dishonesty Disappearance and Destruction Policy (DDD).* However, the Blanket Crime Policy is written at a single limit of liability.

Blanket Position Bond. A fidelity bond covering employees with a limit per employee. If two or more employees conspire, the limit of each is applicable.

Builder's Risk Insurance. Usually written by fire insurance companies, it covers a building in the course of construction as well as the tools and building materials on the premises. The forms are numerous and flexible, as are the perils that can be provided against.

Business Interruption Insurance. This coverage is often known as Use and Occupancy Insurance, and it provides protection for the loss of the operating income of a business, including loss of profits, continuing expenses, etc. In the case of non-manufacturing firms, it provides protection until the firm is in a position where it is physically able to provide the same service it provided just prior to the loss. In the case of a manufacturing firm, it provides that it will continue to cover until the firm is able to manufacture again, and until its goods in the course of manufacture are brought back to the same status that they had immediately preceding the loss. The forms are numerous and flexible, including actual cash value forms as well as valued forms (the latter being stated preagreed amounts of loss written into the policy, substantially avoiding the necessity of post-loss adjustment). In most business interruption policies, extra expenses that the insured spends to mitigate the loss by interruption of business is also covered. (See *Extra Expense Insurance,* below).

Commercial Blanket Bond. A form of fidelity bond coverage which provides a single limit per loss regardless of how many employees may have conspired to create the loss.

Comprehensive General Liability Insurance. A policy similar in principle to the *Comprehensive Automobile Liability Policy* and often combined with it, covering all liability of the insured except from automobiles (when combined with the *Comprehensive Automobile Liability Policy,* it of course does not so hold). The policy is broad enough to cover contractual liability and products liability as well as premises and operations. If a manufacturer, premium is usually computed based on payroll, otherwise on area. Products liability portions of such policies premium is based on sales, either dollar value of units sold.

Comprehensive Glass Insurance. Covers insured glass against all risk *except* fire, war risk, and nuclear reaction.

Consequential Loss Insurance. This is a form of *Power Plant Insurance* and provides coverage against *spoilage* of property due to the lack of power, heat, light, steam, refrigeration, etc., from a described accident in an insured object, both as defined by a *Power Plant Policy.* Though it primarily covers only property at the described location, it can also cover the liability of the insured for damage to property of others there and can be utilized by schools or institutions for loss of admission or tuition fees, caused by interruption of heat, light, etc.

Consequential Loss or Damage Insurance. Unlike the preceding *Consequential Loss Insurance,* this is primarily a fire insurance form and provides protection against spoilage, or other damage to property because of fire, or other insured damage to heating, refrigeration, and other apparatus. The same form is also used by garment manufacturers who send part of their work to other processors, to provide coverage for loss or value of the remainder of a suit should part of it be destroyed elsewhere.

Contingent Business Interruption Insurance. Also known as *Contingent Use and Occupancy Insurance* it protects the firm against interruption of its business due to fire, or other insured perils at another's premises, such as a supplier, or customer, and can be written on a scheduled peril form, or all risk form.

In most cases, *Contingent Business Interruption Insurance* also covers extra expenses to mitigate the interruption loss, e.g., where the location damaged (contributing location) is a supplier, it will cover the extra expense to buy the needed supplies elsewhere even at higher cost or transportation charges.

Contractor's Equipment Floater. Covers the equipment and materials of the contractor within the continental limits of the United States and Canada, against those perils specified, regardless of where the material or equipment may be at the moment.

Contractor's Protective Liability Insurance. This coverage is also known as *Contingent Public Liability Insurance* and protects a prime contractor, or the firm directly, against liability for injury to members of the public or damage of their property arising out of acts of subcontractors.

Contractual Liability Insurance. Provides coverage to the firm for bodily injury or property damage liability specifically assumed under contract, as opposed to the normal exposure to liability imposed solely by the law and the courts, which are based on the law and not upon assumed liability under contract. Such coverage is available as relates to a specific contract or on an automatic or blanket basis applicable to all contracts within certain categories or to *all* contracts.

Credit Insurance. Protects the firm against losses in excess of a deductible, known as a primary loss, caused by the insolvency of customers or delinquest claims, filed within a prescribed period. This coverage is not readily available to companies doing a retail business.

Deductible Fire Insurance. Provides fire insurance coverage (and other risks as scheduled in the policy) over and above a stipulated preagreed deductible per loss.

Depositor's Forgery Bond. Protects the firm against loss from forged or altered checks, or financial instruments, drawn or purported to have been drawn by the insured, his agent, or authorized employee. It also specifically includes situations where the instrument is drawn to the name of a fictitious person, we well as those obtained by someone impersonating the payee.

Difference of Conditions Insurance. This coverage is also known as *Parasol Insurance.* It is catastrophe protection on an all-risk basis. The policies generally are tailor-made. It covers specific property against virtually any peril, usually over and above standard fire insurance, extended coverage, etc.

Earthquake Insurance, Earthquake and Volcanic Eruption Insurance. Commonly written through earthquake "belts" as an endorsement to fire policies, or as specific policies (depending upon jurisdiction) and covers against physical property damage caused by earthquake, earth movement, and volcanic eruption, and can be extended to business interruption coverages as well.

Elevator Collision Insurance. Covers damage to elevators, shafts, machinery, equipment, as well as property on the elevator caused by anything going wrong with the elevator causing it to fall.

EDP (Electronic Data Processing) Insurance. A relatively new form of coverage that provides specially tailored property insurance coverage on virtually an "all-risk" basis. It covers the insured for his financial loss arising from damage to or destruction of his EDP equipment, his peripheral equipment, or his media. The policy covers not only the replacement of loss or damage to property, but can be tailored to cover the business interruption emanating from the damage, the extra expense brought about by the need to use substitute facilities or even revert to manual methods, and in certain instances, to cover the insured's liability resulting from the damage, i.e., the loss of other people's media or records, who might time-share the units.

EDP Errors and Omissions Insurance. This covers a firm for liability for error or omission when providing computer services to others.

Elevator Liability Insurance. Protects the firm against liability imposed by law for bodily injury or property damage liability caused by the ownership, use, or maintenance of elevators. (Elevator Liability Insurance is automatically covered in *Comprehensive Liability Policy*).

Employer's Liability Insurance. Provides protection for the firm against liability arising out of injury to employees apart from that imposed by the Workers' Compensation Laws.

Errors and Omissions Insurance. Covers liability exposure for *professional* error or omission. Intended for accountants, architects, lawyers, insurance agents/brokers/consultants, etc. (see *Professional Liability,* below).

Export Credit Insurance. Covers agreed percentages of loss sustained because of insolvency of firms to whom the assured has extended credit, and based on that credit, exported merchandise or services to them. The newer governmental sponsored forms also protect the insured for a substantial percentage of his exposed credit line, because of his inability to collect because of governmental interferences.

Extended Coverage Insurance. Usually an endorsement extending the standard fire insurance policy to cover the specific perils of windstorm, hail, explosion, riot and civil commotion, aircraft damage, vehicle damage, and smoke damage (and often further extended to include vandalism and malicious mischief).

Extra Expense Insurance. Coverage against the additional expense of operating a business under emergency conditions, because of fire or other insured perils. It is not the same as Business Interruption Insurance, for in the case of extra expense insurance, there is no recovery for the loss of operating income, but merely for the extra expense that the firm goes to in order to avoid interruption of operations.

Further, whereas many Business Interruption policies cover extra expense *to the extent that said extra expense mitigates the business interruption loss* (only), Extra Expense insurance has no such prerequisite limitation. Business Interruption (and Contingent Business Interruption) policies with extra expense coverage with no mitigation limitation can often be negotiated.

False Arrest Insurance. Protects the firm against liability that arises from erroneous arrest. (This is particularly important to retail stores.)

Fire Legal Liability Insurance. Coverage against liability of the firm for damage to property of others caused by the fire, including property in the care, custody, or control of the insured (usually excluded under general liability forms).

Hull Insurance. Insurance written on the hull, fittings, machinery, and equipment of ships for loss from perils of the sea and other specifically named perils. It is commonly referred to as Marine Insurance.

Kidnap/Extortion Insurance. This new form of insurance covers the firm for loss due to paying ransom to free an officer, director, other employee or kidnapped member of their family; or for extortion paid to prevent a threatened account. *(Note: Maintenance of such coverage should be kept very confidential and copies of the policy or written reference to it should be kept out of normal or accessible corporate files.)*

Landlord's Protective Liability Insurance. Covers owners of property who may lease the entire premises to others, or sell the property under conditional sales contract, with the party taking possesion assuming the responsibility for the property. This is a contingent form of liability insurance, and is intended to step in to protect the firm should the party occupying the property fail to do so.

Libel Insurance. Part of the package known as *Personal Injury Liability Insurance,* Libel Insurance is of ever-increasing importance. Though often written, in the past, for people in the radio business, advertising business, etc., it is commonly becoming more accepted today by firms in general because of high court decisions arising out of libel, slander, invasion of privacy, etc.

Malpractice Insurance. See *Professional Liability Insurance* below.

Manufacturer's Output Insurance. This is a flexibly designed form on a virtually all-risk basis that covers most all personal property of larger firms whose principal activity is manufacturing, as long as the property is away from the manufacturing premises; it is usually written in excess of a substantial deductible.

Mercantile Robbery Insurance. This is the official name of that which is commonly known as "inside holdup" and "outside holdup" insurance.

Mercantile Safe Burglary Insurance. Provides coverage against loss of property caused by forcible entry into safes or vaults and includes merchandise and monies stolen therefrom.

Monies and Securities Insurance—Broad Form. Protects the insured against loss of monies or securities within the premises and (depending on how the policy is written) outside the premises, and includes within the premises of a bank, the safe deposit vault; loss protected against may be caused by destruction, disappearance, or wrongful abstraction. The policy can be extended to cover Mercantile Open Stock Burglary Insurance in the same contract. It is among the broadest forms of protection where monies and valuable instruments are involved.

Motor Cargo Liability Insurance. Covers carriers transporting property of others by motor truck against liability for damage to the cargo and can be written on named perils, or all risk forms, as negotiated by the insured and the insurance company.

Motor Cargo Insurance. This coverage is substantially the same as the liability form, but it is intended for firms that carry their own merchandise on their own or leased vehicles.

Names Schedule Bond. A form of Fidelity Bond coverage which covers individual employees only as listed by name.

Ocean Cargo Insurance (Marine Insurance). Probably the oldest form of insurance. This covers merchandise being carried by ocean-going vessels on a per voyage basis, or an open form that covers all voyages and all shipments, blanket. The forms are multitudinous and subject to individual negotiation between client and insurer.

Officer's and Director's Liability Insurance. Suits by stockholders against corporate officers and directors are the primary reason for the development of this new type of insurance, currently being written on only a rather limited basis, but both insurance market for and utilization of this coverage have shown significant signs of rapid expansion since about 1978. Subject to a sizeable deductible, the policy covers the corporation for its loss, including defense costs, arising out of suits against it or its officers and directors by stockholders or others alleging improper or inadequate action and management by the officers or directors. Not only does it cover the corporation in regard to any judgment against it, but it also protects the officers and directors of the firm against judgments against them as individuals. It does not cover any suit or action predicated on the alleged commission of a crime by the corporation, its officers, or its directors. Though many corporate officers and directors insist that the corporation purchase the coverage, it is too new a form to be properly court-tested, although it is growing in importance.

Though there is a question as to the tax implication to the corporation purchasing insurance for the benefit of officers' and directors' protection, it is the opinion of many in the field that the expense is fully deductible by the corporation and need not be included in the earnings reports of the officer or director individually.

Open Stock Burglary Insurance. Provides coverage for loss of merchandise, and other property, from within the premises caused by burglary (forcible entrance, or forcible exit) or the robbery of a watchman. The coverage only applies when the premises are not open for business.

Owners, Landlords, and Tenants Liability Insurance. Covers premises and operations liability for bodily injury and property damage for risks other than manufacturers (where a premium base is payroll) and can also include on an optional basis, Elevator Liability, Products Liability, Contractual Liability and can be written on a *Comprehensive Liability Policy* form.

Paymaster Robbery Insurance. A limited form of inside and outside holdup insurance applying primarily to payroll funds.

Power Plant Insurance. This title applies to almost any type of power plant equipment or appliances including steam, electric, internal combustion, and refrigeration, and insures against accident, or breakdown. It is referred to in some quarters as *Steam Boiler Insurance* as well as *Boiler and Machinery Insurance.* It covers, generally, specified objects against specified accidents, i.e., steamboiler against the accident of explosion or rupture. In addition, it covers damage to property of others (as well as the insured), expediting charges, and can include bodily injury liability insurance.

Power Plant Use and Occupancy Insurance. The coverage is similar in principle to Business Interruption Insurance written on a fire insurance policy form, but protects against losses due to interruption of operations of specified premises because of an accident to an insured object as defined by the policy form.

Processors Floaters. Covers manufacturers for loss of property due to fire and other named perils while the property is on the premises of subcontractors doing processing as well as while in transit.

Products Liability Insurance (Including Completed Operations Insurance). This is a bodily injury and property damage liability form protecting the firm against liability incurred from the handling, use, or existence of any condition in goods or products manufactured, sold, handled or distributed by the firm, causing an accident away from the firm's premises, and after the firm has relinquished possession of the product. It also covers liability arising out of completed or abandoned operations. Products Liability Insurance and Completed Operations Insurance, today, are usually *not* mutually inclusive and are separately insured items in a liability insurance policy.

Professional Liability Insurance (Also known as Malpractice Insurance). An increasing claim-conscious public has caused the creation of both court law and statutory law holding professionals liable for losses arising out of their errors in judgment, technique, and practice. The medical malpractice environment in the mid 1970s came to near panic proportions with high verdicts against doctors and hospitals. Similar, but less publicized suits have been sustained against attorneys, architects, beauticians, undertakers, engineers, etc.

The insurance industry's response has been the making available to professionals Professional Liability Insurance (which comes in an infinite variety of forms to fit the needs of the various followings) which provides insurance protecting the professional against lawsuit for malpractice, errors or omissions. One of the prime features is the coverage for the technically intricate defenses often brought about by such litigation.

Property Damage Liability Insurance. Any form of insurance against legal liability due to the damage of property of others. It is usually part of the *Automobile Policy, Contractual Liability Policy, Elevator Liability Policy, General Liability Policies (Comprehensive Forms and Otherwise), Protective Liability Policies, Products Liability Policies and Umbrella Policies.* The form *usually* excludes property in the care, custody, or control of the insured.

Protection and Indemnity Insurance. A form of *Marine Liability Insurance* for those operating vessels.

Radioactive Contamination Insurance. Inasmuch as virtually all bodily injury liability and property damage liability policies in current use exclude loss caused by nuclear reaction, nuclear radiation, or radioactive contamination, specific insurance protecting a firm dealing in these hazards is available under this form.

Recapture or Product Recall Insurance. Covers a manufacturer against the expense of recalling a defective product which has gone into the market in a substandard condition, and can include the cost of replacing the merchandise with sound merchandise and the extra expenses necessitated therefrom.

Rent or Rental Value Insurance. Covers the owner of a building (in the first instance) against loss of rent from leased premises due to fire, or other perils insured against, while the rental value form usually covers premises occupied by the owner for the loss of rental value due to the same perils. Rental Value Insurance is sometimes used to designate coverage for loss of potential rent, even to vacant property, because of an insured peril (fire, etc.)

Replacement Costs Insurance (Depreciation Insurance). This is substantially an agreement added to an insurance policy to settle the loss on the basis of the actual costs of repairing or replacing, without deduction for depreciation. It is basically intended for real property, though more and more frequently, of late, due to the problems caused by inflation, used for insurance on non-real property as well.

Retrospective Penalty Premium Insurance. Covers a substantial portion of the excess of standard premium, which would have been developed on a risk under a standard rating plan that the insured may be called upon to pay under Workers' Compensation, General Liability, or Automobile Liability contracts established on retrospective rating basis.

Securities Blanket Forgery Bond. Covers financial institutions, and other organizations, against loss due to forgery or alteration of instruments, or papers giving rights or title or loan documents, etc.

Sprinkler Leakage Insurance. Usually added to a fire policy, though not always, it covers the damage to property involving discharge from a sprinkler system, as does it cover the system itself.

Sprinkler Leakage Liability Insurance. Covers a firm having a sprinkler system on the premises against liability for damage, caused by leaking sprinklers, to property of others.

Temporary Nonoccupation Disability Benefits Insurace. A compulsory state disability plan in Rhode Island, California, New Jersey, and New York providing temporary disability benefits within prescribed limits for disability arising through non-occupation activities. The plans are competitive between state funds and private insurance companies in all states, except Rhode Island, where the plan is operated through a monopolistic state fund.

Umbrella Insurance. Catastrophe protection which covers against all unexcluded sources of liability in excess of your normal liability insurance, or in the case of an uninsured loss in excess of a pre-agreed and self-sustained deductible.

Valuable Papers Insurance. Provides all risk coverage on valuable papers, often on an agreed amount basis. Valuable papers and records are defined as written, printed, or otherwise described documents and records including books, maps, films, drawings, abstracts, deeds, mortgages, manuscripts, but not monies or securities; and it covers either on an indemnity basis or the cost to reconstruct.

Water Damage Insurance. Covers the firm against loss to its property caused by accidental discharge, leakage, or overflow of water.

Water Damage Legal Liability Insurance. Inasmuch as most liability forms exclude water damage liability, this is a specific policy to cover the firm's liability as a result of property damage to others, caused by the leakage, overflow, or discharge of water from that portion of the building occupied by the insured. (New York only.)

Workers' Compensation Insurance. A form of insurance to comply with compulsory Workers' Compensation Acts. It is statutory in form and varies by state. Generally it provides coverage as per the state law and is usually obtained through a private insurance company, or an optional state fund. However, Nevada, North Carolina, Oregon, Washington, Wyoming, and Puerto Rico have a monopolistic state fund that does not permit self-insurance, or commercial insurance. Ohio has a monopolistic state fund and permits self-insurance, but not commercial insurance. In West Virginia there is a semi-monopolistic state fund. California, Colorado, Idaho, Maryland, Michigan, Montana, New York, Oklahoma, Pennsylvania, and Utah have competitive state funds. (See WORKERS' COMPENSATION.)

Trends. Insurance management, while growing in importance, is at the same time losing something of its individual identity within the RISK MANAGEMENT function among more and more firms, especially those of medium or larger size. Consulting firms selling no insurance are being utilized by firms of all sizes at an increasingly rapid rate, and many larger firms are using such independent firms to audit the activities of their insurance management or risk management departments.

In the mid 1960s, many of the independent risk and insurance management consulting firms in the United States and Canada organized the Insurance Consultants' Society. Their membership is limited to those professionals in the field of risk and insurance management who earn their income *solely* by professional fees. They sell no insurance and are affiliated with no insurance company, agency, or brokerage firm. The main purposes of the society are the maintenance of ethical practices of its members and to serve as a medium of continued education and exchange of experience and developments. Since the society has now admitted members from abroad, it has become an international society. This is further emphasized by the international experience of many of its members.

In 1975, another consultants' professional society, Institute of Risk Management Consultants, was formed. There are no substantial differences between the goals and the ethical and professional standards of the two organizations.

With the creation of the professional designation CPCU (Chartered Property Casualty Underwriters), CLU (Chartered Life Underwriter), the Insurance Institute of America's Risk Management program and diploma (Associate In Risk Management—ARM), the insurance industry has introduced professional status. Most important, insurance purchasers have become aware of the fact that not only is their year-to-year Profit and Loss Statement radically affected by their insurance management, but that the survival of their business may depend upon their ability to find a sure way through the complexities of forms of protection, and that the insurance management function is too vital and costly to be attacked in less than a thorough and objective manner.

LEONARD J. SILVER, C.P.C.U., ARM, President, First Risk Management Company, Wyncote, Pennsylvania, and First Risk Management (P.R.) Inc., San Juan, Puerto Rico

Information References

Associations:

American Institute for Property and Liability Underwriters.

American Management Association, Insurance Division.

Insurance Consultants Society.

Institute of Risk and Insurance Consultants.

Society of Chartered Property and Casualty Underwriters.

Texts:

Allen, Tom C., "Risk Management Methodology" (an anthology), New York *The Journal of Commerce,* 1974.

Blancard, Ralph A., "Risk and Insurance and Other Papers," Lincoln, Neb., University of Nebraska Press, 1965.

Gallagher, Russel B., "Auditing the Corporate Insurance Function," New York, American Management Associations, 1964.

Hart, Carole S., "Source Book of International Insurance and Employee Benefit Management, Vol. I—Europe," New York, American Management Associations, 1967.

"The Insurance Job: Technical and Managerial Aspects" (an anthology), New York, American Management Associations, 1964.

"The Insurance Market Place," 17th ed., The Rough Notes Co. Indianapolis, Ind., 1979–80.

"The Legal Environment of Insurance," Malverne, Pa., American Institute for Property and Liability Underwriters, 1978.

Mehr, Robert I. and Hedges, Bob A., "Risk Management: Concepts and Applications," Homewood, Ill., Irwin, 1974.

"Principles of Risk Management and Insurance," Malverne, Pa., American Institute for Property and Liability Underwriters, 1978.

Silver, Leonard J. and Sleeper, Richard C., "EDP Risk Management," New York, American Management Associations, 1966.

Wells, Robert, "Source Book on International Corporate Insurance and Employee Benefit Plans, Selected Countries of the World," New York, American Management Associations, 1968.

Cross References: *Appraisal (of Property); Risk Management.*

INTEGER PROGRAMMING

Integer Programming may be thought of as a special case of LINEAR PROGRAMMING. As described in the article on linear programming, a linear program is a mathematical model which is formulated to find a set of nonnegative numbers or decision variables which maximizes (or minimizes) a linear objective function while satisfying a system of linear constraints. The objective function is the mathematical expression describing the behavior of the variables affecting some process or situation which management desires to optimize.

However, there are many situations in which linear programming models are used, but the decision variables must have integer values. For example, it is impossible to ship 2.47 turbines, manufacture 6.91 office buildings, build 0.61 bridge, or bus 221.2 students. A linear program having all its decision variables integer constrained is called an *integer program* (IP). If some, but not all, of the decision variables of a linear program are integer constrained, it is called a *mixed integer program* (MIP). In many cases, the integer variables are only permitted to assume the values of zero or one. These cases are called *binary* or 0-1 *integer programs* and may be either of all integer or mixed integer type of linear program.

Applications. A few integer programming models have been found to represent a large number of real-world problems. As a result, they have been given special names, and much work has been and is being done on developing algorithms to solve them. (An algorithm is a set of arithmetic rules by which it is possible to start with an assumed answer to a problem, and then by following prescribed repetitive procedures, arrive as close as desired to the true answer based on the number of iterations performed.) Some of these classical models are mentioned here.

(1) *Facility Location Problems.* In such a problem there are a number of facility locations which produce a single commodity for a number of customers. Each customer has a certain demand for the product. If a particular facility is built, it has some fixed costs as well as a production capacity associated with it. This is true for each of the facilities. In addition, there is also a positive cost incurred for shipping a unit of the product from any facility to any customer. The problem is where to locate the facilities so that the capacities of the facilities are not exceeded, the demands of the customers are met, and the total cost is minimized.

(2) *Knapsack Problems.* Here the model is a hiker who carries all the supplies he needs for a hiking trip in a sack. The hiker sets the maximum weight the packed knapsack may have. Each of the potential items to be put in the sack has a known weight. The hiker is able to rank all the items so that he knows the relative value of each of them to him on the trip. The problem is to select the items to be taken in such a way as to maximize the total value of the items in the knapsack without exceeding its weight limitation.

Although knapsack problems are the simplest integer programs, they are representative of many industrial situations. For example, capital budgeting problems, in which decisions must be made on the selection of a number of potential investments so as to maximize the total investment return, subject to fixed amounts of resources available, are in actuality knapsack problems. Numerous loading problems (such as cargo loading), as well as some project selection and capital investment problems, and many budget control problems, can be modeled as knapsack problems. Finally the so-called cutting stock problems are knapsack models. These are situations in which a material comes in standard lengths and must be cut up according to requirements and costs. These include goods that come in rolls (e.g., paper, textiles, and sheet metals) as well as less flexible materials (e.g., glass, metal pipe, lumber, etc.).

(3) *Set Covering and Set Partitioning Problems.* Many sequencing, scheduling, and routing problems can be modeled as set covering or set partitioning problems. For example, suppose there are some available resources which must perform a number of tasks, where each resource can perform some or all of the tasks. It may be possible to list for each resource, subject to time, location, and other constraints, all the possible ways that resource can do the tasks. There is a known cost involved with each combination of task and resource performing that task. The problem is to choose those resources, at total minimal cost, so as to ensure that each task is done at least once. This is referred to as the set covering problem. In many problems it is necessary that each task is performed exactly once, and these are called set partitioning problems.

Numerous situations can be modeled as a set covering or a set partitioning problem. These include applications in the areas of airline crew scheduling, vehicle dispatching, political redistricting, circuit design, map coloring, network attack and defense, personnel scheduling, PERT/CPM analysis, general routing, and many other applications.

(4) *Traveling Salesman Problems.* Here the model is one of a traveling salesman, who starting from his home, wishes to visit several other cities and return home at minimal cost. He must visit each city exactly once, and the cost incurred traveling from one city to any other city is known. The problem is to select his route.

The traveling salesman model is used as a central component of many vehicular routing and scheduling models. It also arises in production scheduling. The machine scheduling problem is an example of this. Here the problem is to sequence a number of jobs on a single machine, and there is a cost involved for setting the machine up to perform a certain job, given the machine has just completed a known job. What must be found is a scheduling sequence for the jobs that gives the lowest total set-up costs. This can be modeled as a traveling salesman problem.

(5) *Network Problems.* Examples of these are the transportation and assignment problems, the shortest (or longest) route problem, the minimum-cost-flow problem, and the maximum-flow-through-a-network problem. These models have special structure, and many efficient algorithms exist which find the optimal solutions.

Approaches and Techniques. It has long

been known that certain integer programs, because of their special structure, may be solved as linear programs, using the simplex method. Examples of these are the transportation problem, the assignment problem, or the static maximum-flow-in-a-network. (See LINEAR PROGRAMMING: A Case Example—The Simplex Solution Method.) However, most integer programs do not have this integrality property, and thus the simplex algorithm, per se, will generally not solve mixed integer or integer programs.

In practice, a common approach to integer or mixed integer programming problems is to use the simplex method (thus ignoring the integer restrictions) and then rounding off the noninteger values to integers in the resulting solution. The procedure does, in many instances, produce a solution which may be "good enough." This is especially true for problems where the accuracy of the data is questionable, or when the integers can take on large values. For example, the effect of importing 1,256,312 barrels of oil rather than 1,256,312.6, or for that matter, 1,256,000, is negligible. On the other hand, the rounding procedure (either up or down) is not a good idea when the data of the problem are small, or when the variables are binary. In some such cases it is possible that the optimal linear programming solution is not feasible (i.e., it violates one or more constraints) after it is rounded off. If feasibility can be maintained, it is often difficult to see in which way the rounding should be done to maintain that feasibility. The following two examples illustrate the ideas.

Example 1: Consider the problem:

$$\begin{aligned}
&\text{maximize } x_1 + x_2 = z\\
&\text{subject to } 4x_1 - x_2 \geq 1\\
&\qquad\qquad 4x_1 + x_2 \leq 3\\
&x_1, x_2 \geq 0 \text{ and integer}
\end{aligned}$$

See Exhibit I for graph of the feasible region.

The linear programming feasible region is spanned by the extreme points ABC, so the feasible region is the shaded triangle. The optimal solution to the linear program occurs at point $C = (\frac{1}{2}, 1)$. However, it is impossible to round-off x_1 (either up or down) and still maintain feasibility. In fact, there are no integer points (x_1, x_2) inside the triangle ABC, so the integer program has no feasible solution.

EXHIBIT I

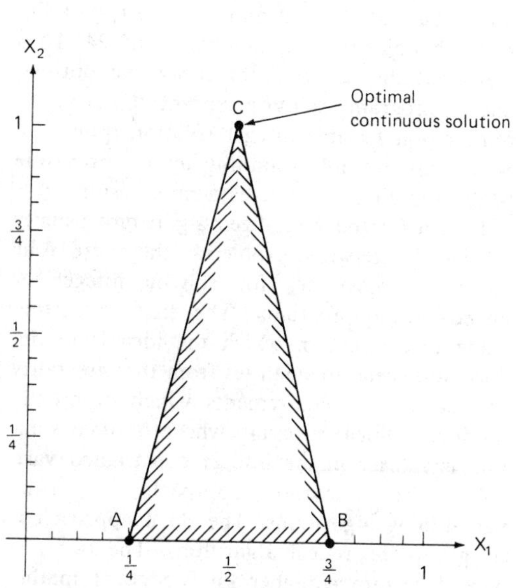

Example 2: Consider the problem:

$$\begin{aligned}
&\text{maximize } 2x_1 + 12x_2 = z\\
&\text{subject to } x_1 + 15x_2 \leq 30\\
&\qquad\qquad x_1 \leq 4\\
&\qquad\qquad x_1, x_2 \geq 0 \text{ and integer}
\end{aligned}$$

See Exhibit II for a graph of the feasible region.

The optimal linear program solution is $x_1 = 4$ and $x_2 = 26/15$ (point C), giving an optimal value of the objective function of 28.80. It is impossible to round off x_2 to 2 because the point (2,2) is not feasible. Rounding x_2 to 1 gives a feasible solution $x_1 = 4$ and $x_2 = 1$ (point B), with an objective function value of

EXHIBIT II

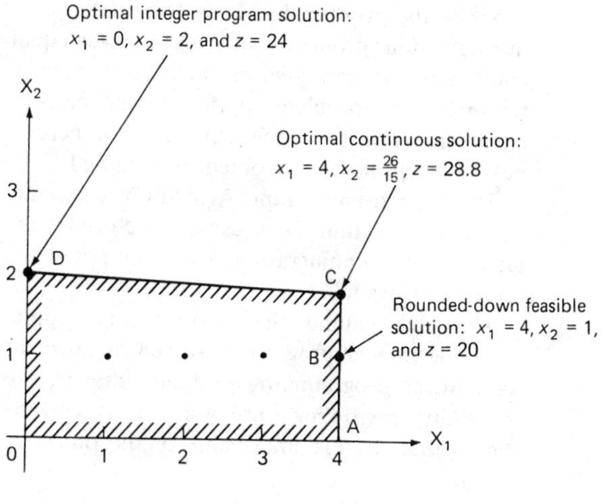

20. However, the optimal integer program solution occurs at $x_1 = 0$ and $x_2 = 2$ (point D), with an objective function value of 24. It is seen that this is far from either the optimal linear program solution (point C) or the rounded-off feasible integer solution (point B). So in this example rounding up is impossible while rounding down gives a poor result.

Except for the specialized algorithms usually applied to network problems, there are four principal approaches for solving integer or mixed-integer programs. The first is cutting plane techniques, in which the idea is to deduce additional inequalities from the integrality and constraint requirements which eventually produce a linear program whose optimal solution is integer in the integer constrained variables. The second approach is using partitioning algorithms. The third approach is by group theoretical algorithms. The two just named require a higher knowledge of mathematics.

The last approach is by enumerative methods. Here the idea is to enumerate, either explicitly or implicitly, all feasible solution candidates to the mixed integer or integer program. These are then examined in turn, and an optimal integer solution is chosen from those candidates which maximizes (or minimizes) the objective function. This is not as simple as it sounds. For example, if there are 10 variables and each one has 20 feasible values, there can be as many as 10^{20} feasible solutions. Examining each one and choosing the one that yields the best objective function value would involve a prohibitive amount of work. However, there is a special algorithm, called "the branch and bound algorithm," which is a clever enumerative method. The procedure examines only a small percentage of the potential solutions and chooses the best one. While it is not the best algorithm to use on every integer or mixed integer programming problem, it is perhaps the most popular and has shown good success on a large number of problems. Computer codes are readily available for it as well. It is this algorithm that will be discussed here.

The Branch and Bound Solution Method. When solving ordinary linear programs, the decision variables are said to be continuous, in the sense that they are allowed to be fractional. When fractional values are not permitted, the problem is an integer or mixed integer program. It can be written as

$$\begin{array}{llllllll}
\text{maximize} & c_1x_1 & + c_2x_2 & + c_3x_3 & + \ldots & + c_nx_n & = z \\
\text{subject to} & a_{11}x_1 & + a_{12}x_2 & + a_{13}x_3 & + \ldots & + a_{1n}x_n & \leq b_1 \\
 & a_{21}x_1 & + a_{22}x_2 & + a_{23}x_3 & + \ldots & + a_{2n}x_n & \leq b_2 \\
 & \vdots & \vdots & \vdots & & \vdots & \vdots \\
 & a_{m1}x_1 & + a_{m2}x_2 & + a_{m3}x_3 & + \ldots & + a_{mn}x_n & \leq b_m \\
 & & & x_j \geq 0 \ (j = 1,2,\ldots,n) & & & \\
 & & & x_j \text{ integer (for some or all } j = 1,2,\ldots,n) & & &
\end{array}$$

While the problem has been formulated as a maximization problem with less-than-or-equal constraints, it can just as well have been a minimization problem with greater-than-or-equal constraints. In the sequel, for concreteness, a maximization problem is assumed.

The Branch and Bound Algorithm is an enumerative algorithm. It is usually pictorially related to an enumeration tree composed of nodes and branches.

The idea behind the algorithm is simple. First the integer program is solved as an ordinary linear programming problem; that is, the integrality restrictions are ignored. It can be shown that the maximal value of the objective function to the mixed integer (or integer) program solved as an ordinary linear program is an upper bound on the value of the objective function of any mixed integer (or integer) program. Once the integrality constraints are added, the objective function value of the linear program will decrease, or at worst, remain the same. It cannot increase. If the optimal solution of the mixed (or integer) problem solved as a linear one is infeasible, then so is the mixed (or integer) program.

Once the linear programming problem has been solved (and assuming the solution is not integral in those variables that should be integral), it is postulated that the feasible region probably contains integer points. One (or more) of these will be the optimal solution to the integer programming problem. The feasible region is then partitioned into smaller subregions or subdivisions. These subdivisions are chosen so as eliminate nonintegral solutions but not the integral ones. There are a number of ways to divide the feasible region, so that there are different branch and bound algorithms. The one considered here is used most often and was first discovered by R. Dakin in 1965. The problem is then resolved over these subdivisions. The process continues until an optimal integer solution is found or it is concluded that none exists. The following simple example will show the details of the algorithm and give a geometric interpretation of it as well.

Example 3:

$$\begin{aligned} \text{maximize} \quad & 5x_1 + 3x_2 = z \\ \text{subject to} \quad & 16x_1 + 6x_2 \leq 96 \\ & 7x_1 + 11x_2 \leq 77 \\ & x_1, x_2 \geq 0, \text{ integer} \end{aligned}$$

Referring to Exhibit III, the feasible region is denoted by R_o and is bounded by OABC. The continuous optimal solution is given by $x_1 = 4.43$ and $x_2 = 4.18$ and the optimal value of the objective function is $z = 34.7$. This is point B in Exhibit III. Thus the optimal value of the integer program is at most 34.7. This information is summarized in node zero of the tree diagram in Exhibit IV. Since neither value x_1 or x_2 is integer, the branch and bound algorithm will be applied. One variable, say x_1, is chosen and since $x_1 = 4.43$, it is seen that in the integer programming solution, x_1 must be either an integer less than or equal to four, or an integer greater than or equal to five. So the feasible region R_o is subdivided into two smaller feasible regions, R_1 and R_2, reflecting the additional constraints $x_1 \leq 4$ and $x_1 \geq 5$, respectively. R_1 is bounded by ODGC and R_2 is bounded by EFA in Exhibit III. Notice that with this subdivision of R_0 into R_1 and R_2, a portion of R_0 containing the original continuous optimal solution has been eliminated.

The linear program is solved in turn once again with each of the additional constraints $x_1 \leq 4$ and $x_1 \geq 5$ (this is called *branching*). The optimal solution over region R_1 is $x_1 = 4$, $x_2 = 4.45$, and $z = 33.4$, and is point G in Exhibit III. The optimal solution over region R_2 is $x_1 = 5$, $x_2 = 2.67$, and $z = 33.0$, and is point F in Exhibit III. These results are summarized in nodes 1 and 2 in Exhibit IV.

Since R_1 did not yield an integer solution, it is subdivided further by realizing that an optimal integer solution must have either $x_2 \geq 5$ or $x_2 \leq 4$. Thus R_1 is subdivided into regions R_3, bounded by ODKL, and R_4, bounded by CJH in Exhibit III. That is, the linear program with the extra constraint $x_1 \leq 4$ is further branched into two new linear programs with additional constraints $x_2 \leq 4$ and $x_2 \geq 5$, respectively.

The optimal solution over region R_3 is given by $x_1 = 4$, $x_2 = 4$ and $z = 32$; this is point K in Exhibit III. The optimal solution over region R_4 is given by $x_1 = 3.14$, $x_2 = 5$, and $z = 30.7$, and this is point H in Exhibit III.

There is now no need to subdivide regions R_3 and R_4 further. This is because the optimal solution over R_3 is integer, and because the value of the objective function at point H of R_4 is 30.7, which is less than the current lower bound of the problem, which is 32. It is thus said both R_3 and R_4 have been *fathomed*. This is shown on nodes 3 and 4, respectively, in Exhibit IV.

Similarly R_2 is subdivided because an integer solution must have either $x_2 \leq 2$ or $x_2 \geq 3$, and so is branched into two new linear pro-

EXHIBIT III

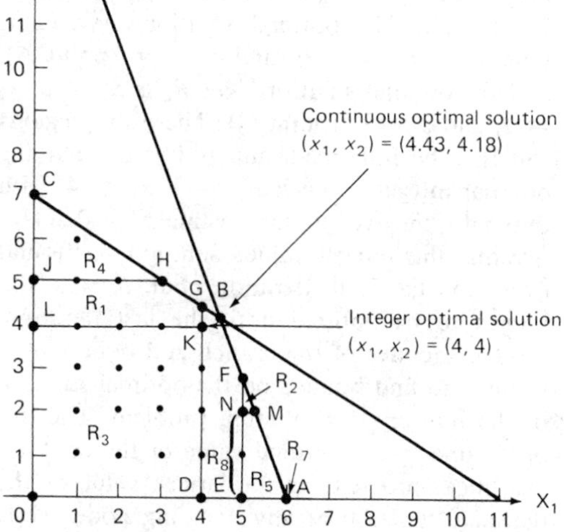

EXHIBIT IV

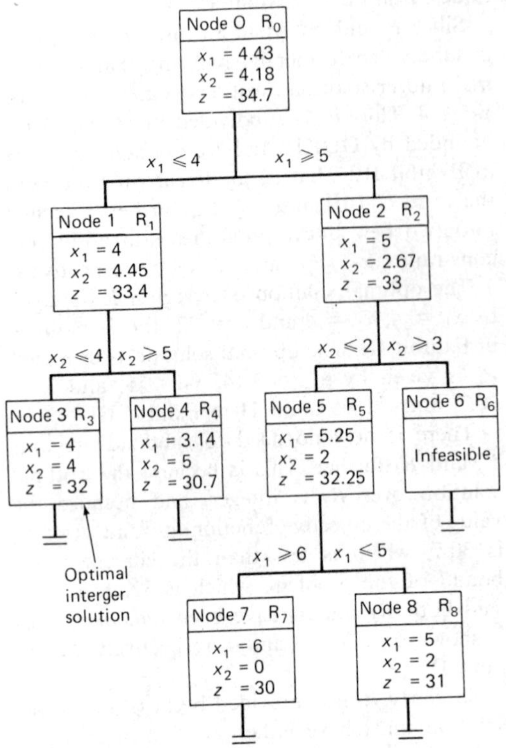

grams with the additional constraints $x_2 \leq 2$ and $x_2 \geq 3$. This yields region R_5, bounded by EAMN, and an infeasible region respectively. The optimal solution over R_5 is $x_1 = 5.25$, $x_2 = 2$, and $z = 32.25$, which is point M in Exhibit III. (See nodes 5 and 6, respectively, in Exhibit IV.) Now region R_5 is further subdivided into R_7 (by adding the constraint $x_1 \geq 6$) and R_8 (by adding the constraint $x_1 \leq 5$). R_7 is just point A and R_8 is the line segment EN in Exhibit III. The optimal solution over R_7 is thus $x_1 = 6$, $x_2 = 0$, and $z = 30$ (point A), and the optimal solution over R_8 is $x_1 = 5$, $x_2 = 2$, and $z = 31$ (point N). These two regions can thus be fathomed, and it is seen that the optimal integer value is $x_1 = 4$, $x_2 = 4$, with optimal objective function value $z = 32$. Notice that this integer valued solution was found prior to the final iteration, but it was not known to be optimal until the last iteration.

Thus the idea of the branch and bound algorithm is to find bounds on the optimal solution of the integer programming problem. The upper bound is the optimal value of the continuous linear program or the largest value of the objective function at any dangling node, while the lower bound is the largest value of the objective function found from a feasible integer point. The feasible region is subdivided in order to get these bounds. A region is fathomed if either the optimal solution over that region is integer, or the program is infeasible over the region, or if the optimal objective function value over the region is less than the current lower bound of the problem.

The flowchart of Exhibit V summarizes the algorithm.

Two final comments can be made about the algorithm. Once it is recognized that a subdivision must be made of the feasible region, which subdivision should be analyzed first? One branch rule says to select the subdivision having the most favorable bound (the largest upper bound in the case of maximization) because this subdivision would seem to be the most promising one to contain an optimal solution. Another branch rule says to take the most recently created subdivision that has not been fathomed, breaking a tie between subdivisions created at the same time by taking the one with the most favorable bound. This rule results frequently in easier bookkeeping. It can-

EXHIBIT V

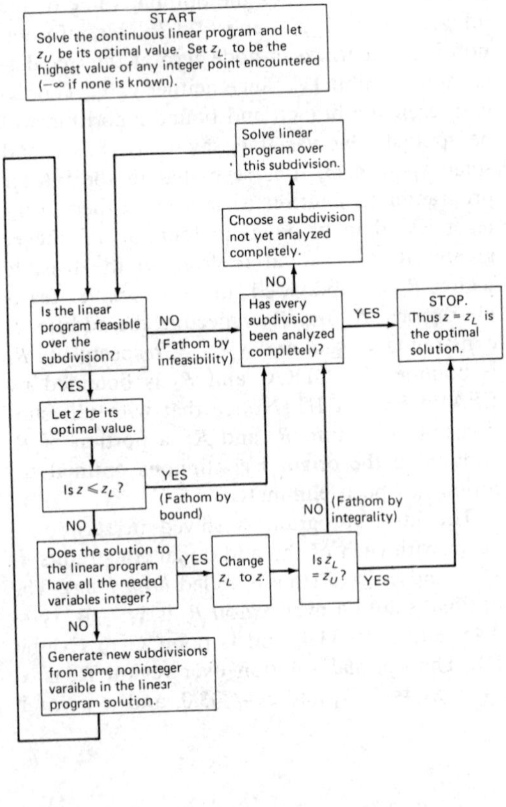

not be said with certainty that one rule is always better than the other.

The second comment is how to choose a noninteger variable to use in making a subdivision. There are many possible procedures, but a simple rule is to choose that variable with the largest fractional part.

Conclusion. As so many linear program formulations require integer solutions, and since the simplex algorithm does not guarantee such a solution will occur, the ideas of integer programming become very important. Many problems in business, health services, social sciences, etc. can be formulated as classical integer programs. While research is presently being done to find efficient algorithms, especially using group-theoretical ideas, the branch and bound algorithm seems to be the best general purpose algorithm for most integer programs.

JACK YURKIEWICZ, PH.D., The School of Business, Hofstra University, Hempstead, New York

Information References

Bradley, S., Hax, A., and Magnanti, T., "Applied Mathematical Programming," Reading, Mass., Addison-Wesley, 1977.

Garfinkel, R.S. and Nemhauser, G.L., "Integer Programming," New York, Wiley, 1972.

Geoffrion, A.M. and Marsten, R.E., "Integer Programming Algorithms: A Framework and State-of-the-Art Survey," *Management Science,* March 1972.

Salken, H., "Integer Programming," Reading, Mass., Addison-Wesley, 1975.

Taha, H.A., "Integer Programming: Theory, Applications and Computations," New York, Academic Press, 1975.

Cross Reference: *Management Sciences.*

INTEGRATED PROJECT MANAGEMENT

Management is continually seeking new and better control techniques to cope with the complexities, masses of data, and tight deadlines that are today characteristic of the defense industry and the highly competitive commercial field. We here subsume these techniques under the embrasive terms, **Integrated Project Management.** Coming into prominence after World War II have been PERT (Program Evaluation and Review Technique), CRITICAL PATH METHOD (CPM), and variations of them. Of somewhat earlier origin is LINE OF BALANCE (LOB), which was introducted in 1941; and, of course, the GANTT CHART has long been used in industry. (See separate entries on all of these.)

Most literature covering project control techniques lays almost sole stress on their advantages, since they are written by enthusiastic proponents of the particular technique described. Exhibit I (pp. 486–487) presents a bird's-eye-view, in the form of a factor comparison chart, of the four most widely used techniques, showing strengths *and* weaknesses as related to installation, operation, applicability for planning and scheduling, output information, suitability for control of specific types of applications, and actual usage to date.

JOHN J. GLASER, Polaris Division, Sperry Gyroscope Co., Great Neck, New York

Cross References: *Critical Path Method (CPM); Gantt Chart; PERT (Program Evaluation and Review Technique): Line of Balance (LOB); Line of Balance: Day Control.*

INTERNAL AUDITING

Internal Auditing is defined by The Institute of Internal Auditors as "an independent appraisal function established within an organization to examine and evaluate its activities as a service to the organization. The objective of internal auditing is to assist members of the organization in the effective discharge of their responsibilities. To this end, internal auditing furnishes them with analyses, appraisals, recommendations, counsel, and information concerning the activities reviewed.

"The members of the organization assisted by internal auditing include those in management and the board of directors. Internal auditors owe a responsibility to both, providing them with information about the adequacy and effectiveness of the organization's system of internal control and the quality of performance. The information furnished to each may differ in format and detail, depending upon the requirements and requests of management and the board" [1].

Internal auditing is concerned with the review of any phase of business activity where it may be of service to the organization. This involves going beyond the accounting and financial records to obtain a full understanding of the operations under review.

The function involves appraising:

- The reliability and integrity of information.

Exhibit I

Integrated Project Management—Factor Comparison of Current Techniques

Factors for Consideration		*Gantt Charts*	*LOB*	*PERT*	*CPM*
Installation	Training of personnel to operate and maintain.	No problem: only one or two persons usually required.	Involves some training of two to four specially qualified personnel.	Requires extensive training of four or more qualified personnel.	Requires extensive training of three or more qualified personnel.
	Orientation of personnel concerned.	No problem.	No problem.	Considerable amount required: procedural manual usually necessary	Brief orientation required.
	Records system required.	No problem: majority of records maintained at working level.	No problem.	Extensive: tends to be complicated.	Extensive.
	Special requirements.	None.	Minimum of outside help required.	Outside consulting services are required.	Outside consulting services are required.
Operation	Up-dating.	No problem: maintained on daily or weekly basis: up-dated by working level supervisors.	No problem: maintained on bi-weekly basis.	Voluminous input data required: but easily processed by computer.	Considerable input data required: normally processed by computer.
	Monitoring.	Good.	Good.	Very good.	Good.
	Need for computer.	Not required.	Not required.	Ordinarily required, especially with more than 100 events.	Required.
	Outputs.	Graphs: readily analyzed by inspection.	Easily understood graphic form.	Computer tab runs: require group presentation.	Computer tab runs: requires group presentation.
Applicability for Planning and Scheduling	For planning.	Excellent for manufacturing control; on R&D projects, effectiveness decreases as activity interrelationships increase.	Good.	Very good: networking presents all essential information.	Very good: networking presents all essential information.
	Cost-schedule alternates.	Poor.	Fair: but no provision for minimizing cost.	Good.	Very good.
	Provision for uncertainty in estimates.	None.	None.	Very good.	None.
	Flexibility.	Good: self-adjusting for delays and inaccurate estimates.	Fair.	Very good.	Very good.
	Usefulness for allocation of resources.	Fair.	Good.	Good.	Very good.

EXHIBIT I *Continued*

Factors for Consideration		*Gantt Charts*	*LOB*	*PERT*	*CPM*
Output Information	Management summary information.	Good: however, amount of details given calls for close examination.	Good: basic and not complicated: group presentation may be required.	Very good: available in variety of forms: adequate but complicated.	Very good: available in variety of forms, excellent for cost-minded management.
	Program status and progress reports.	Good.	Very good.	Good, but fails to show incremental activity progress.	Good, but fails to show incremental activity progress.
	Cost information.	Good.	Very good.	Good.	Very good.
	Timeliness and quality of danger signals.	Excellent for manufacturing control; not effective for detailed control of complex R&D projects.	Good.	Very good.	Very good.
	Availability of historical information.	Poor.	Poor.	Poor.	Poor.
Suitability for Control of:	Research projects	Fair.	Fair	Very good.	Good.
	Development projects	Fair.	Fair.	Very good.	Good.
	Production.	Very good.	Very good.	Poor.	Poor.
	Subcontracting.	Fair.	Very good.	Good.	Fair.
Usage to Date		Short period planning and continuous manufacturing planning. Widely accepted by many companies as a fundamental control technique.	Design and production, e.g., DEW line, control of subcontracting for Polaris Navigation Subsystem, followup production of preceding PERT and CPM efforts.	Research, Weapon-Systems, and other *large* complex government projects e.g., Polaris Project, Skybolt Program.	Commerical industries, fields of construction, development projects, and new product introduction.

• Compliance with policies, plans, procedures, laws and regulations.

• The safeguarding of assets.

• The economical and efficient use of resources.

• The accomplishment of established objectives and goals for operations or programs [1].

Development of Internal Auditing. Over the years, internal auditing has broadened materially in its objectives and scope. Originally an activity concerned primarily with the protection of cash, later reaching into the area of the verification of accounting documents and records, it is now a managerial control dealing with operations as well as with financial matters. This new concept does not eliminate the valuable and necessary services embodied in the earlier activities of internal auditing—protection of assets and accuracy and propriety of accounting entries. These services are still an important segment of any internal auditing program.

The growth of businesses and the accompanying decentralization of operating responsibility brought a trend toward the recognition and establishment of internal auditing as a distinct function. At the present time, virtually all large business enterprises and many governmental units maintain internal auditing staffs as an essential feature of their management control. This considerably broader field of activity calls for higher qualification standards for internal auditing.

In most companies, the constructive accomplishments of the internal auditor in the financial area have led to the extension of the scope of the internal auditor's responsibility to the operating departments. Some internal auditors cover all areas of their company operations; a majority include such functions as purchasing and sales in their regular audit programs.

Operational Controls and Auditing. The operational controls which are reviewed and analyzed by the internal auditor include; (1) Organization Structure, (2) Procedures, (3) Accounting and Other Records, (4) Reports, and (5) Standards of Performance (such as budgets and standard costs).

The extension of internal auditing to operating departments has led to the use of the term *operational* or *comprehensive auditing.* Since the operating controls and the techniques of the internal auditor are similar for all departments (both financial and operating), the terms *operational auditing, comprehensive auditing* and *internal auditing* should be considered synonymous.

Audit Procedures. An internal audit comprises four phases:

(1) *Planning.* This phase includes procedures such as establishing audit objectives and scope of work, obtaining background information about activities to be audited, determining the resources necessary to perform the audit, performing as appropriate an on-site survey to become familiar with the activities and controls to be audited, identifying areas for audit emphasis, inviting auditee comments and suggestions, and preparing an audit program.

(2) *Examining and Evaluating Information.* This phase includes collecting, analyzing, interpreting, and documenting information to support audit results. Here the internal auditor examines and tests to learn whether actual operations and assignments of responsibility follow the plans laid down by departmental management. The internal auditor then analyzes the findings and decides whether there appears to be some deficiency in operating controls. For example, the regular departmental reports may not present an adequate picture of operations to management.

(3) *Communicating Results.* This phase includes the reporting of audit findings and constructive recommendations where required. An essential of reporting is that the report be discussed with the management of the audited department before formal submission.

(4) *Following Up.* This phase includes determining that corrective action was taken and is achieving the desired results, or that management or the board of directors has assumed the risk of not taking corrective action on reported findings.

Limitations in Recommendation. In certain areas, such as financial control, the internal auditor will be qualified by background and experience to give a definite recommendation for improvement or correction of an unsatisfactory situation. In some operating areas, he may not have sufficient technical background to permit definite recommendations. In such areas, his analysis and study of management controls will be directed to making sure that these controls and his report bring to management's attention those situations which may require further study by qualified experts. For example, a physical inspection in the course of an audit of receiving operations might reveal that the receiving department appeared to be unduly congested with received materials. Possible corrective measures might include such measures as: (1) revised material handling; (2) revised production scheduling; (3) revised receiving procedures.

Organizational Responsibilities and Relationship. The scope and recognition accorded to internal auditing in a business are entirely dependent on the delegation of authority from management and the board. The usual trend is for scope and recognition to broaden when the internal auditor demonstrates his ability as a constructive analyst. A statement by the Institute of Internal Auditors reads as follows:

"The organizational status of the internal auditing function and the support accorded to it by management are major determinants of its range and value. The head of the internal auditing function, therefore, should be responsible to an officer whose authority is sufficient to assure both a broad range of audit coverage and the adequate consideration of and effective action on the audit findings and recommendations.

"Objectivity is essential to the audit function. Therefore, an internal auditor should not develop and install procedures, prepare records, or engage in any other activity which he would normally review and appraise and which could reasonably be construed to compromise his independence. His objectivity need not be adversely affected, however, by his determination and recommendation of the standards of control to be applied in the development of systems and procedures under his review" [2].

The Institute's latest pronouncement standards for the professional practice of internal auditing elevates the reporting status of internal auditing to include such additional guidelines as recommending that the director of internal auditing have direct communication with the board of directors and that the board concur in the appointment or removal of the director of internal auditing.

The majority of internal auditors report to a senior operating executive, such as an executive vice president or financial vice president. Also, recent studies show that internal auditors are beginning to have a greater dual reporting responsibility to both executive management and to the board of directors or its audit committee [3].

Internal Auditing and Internal Control. Management's responsibilities for maintaining an adequate system of internal control, particularly internal accounting control, have increased as a result of recent events. The most significant was the passage of the Foreign Corrupt Practices Act of 1977 (FCPA). The FCPA requires all entities registered with the Securities and Exchange Commission (SEC) to devise and maintain a system of internal accounting control sufficient to provide reasonable assurance that specified objectives are met.

Several groups have proposed that annual reports to shareholders include a discussion of the system of internal accounting control, which add to management's concern over the adequacy of such systems. The Commission on Auditors' Responsibilities recommended in its *Report, Conclusions, and Recommendations* that corporate management prepare a report to shareholders that would, among other things, disclose whether material weaknesses exist in the enterprise's system of internal accounting control.

The Financial Executives Institute suggested, in a position statement outlining the contents of a report by management, that the report include a discussion of the organization's system of internal accounting control. The SEC has also proposed that registrants be required to include a statement by management on internal accounting control in annual reports filed with the Commission and sent to stockholders [4].

The need to comply with the FCPA and the increasing likelihood that organizations will report on their internal accounting control system suggest that management will undertake explicit evaluations of the system. The internal audit function will most likely play a major role in that effort. Internal auditors may increasingly be looked to as evaluators (rather than providers) of internal control; as such, they will be asked to furnish assurance to management that the system is functioning effectively. The final report of the American Institute of Certified Public Accountants (AICPA) Special Advisory Committee on Internal Accounting Control recognized the importance of internal auditing in a control-conscious environment as follows [5]:

> An effective internal auditing function can serve as a high-level organizational control, as well as a constructive and protective link between policy-making levels and operating levels of an organization.

Professional Internal Auditing Standards. In June of 1978, The Institute of Internal Auditors Board of Directors approved the release of an official pronouncement titled: "Standards for the Professional Practice of Internal Auditing." In setting these *Standards,* the following developments were considered:

(1) Boards of directors are being held increasingly accountable for the adequacy and effectiveness of their organizations' systems of internal control and quality of performance.

(2) Members of management are demonstrating increased acceptance of internal auditing as a means of supplying objective analyses, appraisals, recommendations, counsel, and information on the organization's controls and performance.

(3) External auditors are using the results of internal audits to complement their own work where the internal auditors have provided suitable evidence of independence and adequate, professional audit work.

In the light of such developments, the stated purposes of these *Standards* are to:

(1) Impart an understanding of the role and responsibilities of internal auditing to all levels of management, boards of directors, public bodies, external auditors, and related professional organizations.

(2) Establish the basis for the guidance and measurement of internal auditing performance.

(3) Improve the practice of internal auditing.

The *Standards* differentiate among the varied responsibilities of the organization, the internal auditing department, the director of internal auditing, and internal auditors.

The *Standards* encompass:

(1) The independence of the internal auditing department from the activities audited, and the objectivity of internal auditors.

(2) The proficiency of internal auditors and the professional care they should exercise.

(3) The scope of internal auditing work.

(4) The performance of internal auditing assignments.

(5) The management of the internal auditing department.

In 1980, the Foundation for Auditability Research and Education, Inc. (FARE) published "A Framework for Evaluating an Internal Audit Function" [7]. This book provides guidelines to evaluate the performance of the department objectively against its assigned responsibilities and against the Institute's *Standards.* An evaluation of the internal audit function against the *Standards* should provide valuable information.

The book points out that "the audit function is not limited to meeting emerging responsibilities related to internal accounting control. The importance of an effective internal audit function has long been recognized both by organizations that are subject to the FCPA or to possible SEC requirements for reporting on internal control, and by those that are not—governmental agencies, nonprofit organizations, and privately owned firms. Managements and boards have for many years given specific charters to their internal auditors; only formally evaluating how those charters are being fulfilled is relatively new."

Qualifications and Promotional Opportunities. The role of a business analyst—a representative of top management—dealing with operating as well as financial affairs, has raised the qualification standards for an internal auditor. His initial qualifications, special training programs, acquaintance with management policies and plans, and knowledge of the detailed operations of many departments help to prepare the internal auditor for higher positions in his company. He gains knowledge of his company at the operating level—and at the same time gains experience in the constructive analysis of managerial controls. These factors combine to result in the use of the internal audit department as an executive training ground. In some companies, service on the internal audit staff for a specific period is preliminary to transfer to line executive positions in operating or financial areas. In a survey conducted by The Institute of Internal Auditors [6], it was found that 54% of the companies answering used internal auditing as a managerial training ground. This affirmative response was concentrated among the medium- and large-sized organizations surveyed.

Professional Recognition. The Institute's Certified Internal Auditor (CIA) designation is the professional credential for internal auditors. The CIA Program is open to internal auditors and to all others who meet certain educational and experience requirements. The program is governed by a Board of Regents, appointed by the board of directors of The Institute of Internal Auditors, Inc., and administered by a staff at The Institute's international headquarters.

In addition to possessing a baccalaureate degree and being of good character, qualified candidates must successfully pass all four parts of a written examination and satisfy a work experience requirement in order to attain the CIA designation. The CIA Examination measures the technical competence of the candidate, provides a foundation for granting professional recognition, and gives direction to all internal auditors who seek to further their professional development. Certified Internal Auditors are required to maintain their certificate in good standing by completing a designated number of hours of continuing professional development within a three-year period.

Relationship with Public Accounting. Because some of the verification and testing techniques of internal auditing are similar to those of public accounting, there is often an erroneous assumption that there is little difference between these two functions. In fact, the two are complementary, as will be seen by a consideration of the objectives.

The independent public accountant seeks to determine whether or not the financial statements issued by a company are true representations of its financial position—whether data are accurate and accounting nomenclature is proper; whether the statements are the end result of procedures which are generally accepted in accounting circles, and which are consistent with similar previous statements.

The internal auditor, however, is an employee of management. His status and interests are quite different from those of the public accountant. All of his studies are designed to assist the top management of his company by furnishing information as to whether operations are being conducted in accordance with management policies and plans, and whether performance is satisfactory. He is, therefore, an integral and important part of his company's scheme of managerial control.

The internal auditor is concerned not only with the historical accuracy of the statements but with investigating the possible existence of conditions which, if corrected, might result in increased profits or better operation in the years ahead. His activities go beyond the post-mortem aspects of operations; they point the way to future improvements.

He is charged with the responsibility for examining and appraising the effectiveness of the operating controls; whether company policies and programs have been followed; and whether operating waste has occurred. Beyond this, the internal auditor relates the controls to the physical operations of his company, makes recommendations for improvement of the business, and covers non-financial areas of his business as a regular part of his work.

THE INSTITUTE OF INTERNAL AUDITORS, Altamonte Springs, Florida

Information References

Association:

The Institute of Internal Auditors.

Periodical:

The Internal Auditor (bimonthly journal).

Texts:

"The Practice of Modern Internal Auditing," 1973.

"Modern Internal Auditing—An Operational Approach," 1973.

"The Manager and the Modern Internal Auditor," 1979.

"Understanding Management Policy and Making It Work," 1978.

"Computer Control and Audit," 1978.

"How to Save $14,500,000 Through Internal Auditing," 1975.

(The above represents a selection of texts published by The Institute of Internal Auditors, Inc.)

References Cited

[1] "Standards for the Professional Practice of Internal Auditing," Altamonte Springs, Fla., The Institute of Internal Auditors, Inc., 1978.

[2] "Statement of Responsibilities of the Internal Auditor," The Institute of Internal Auditors, 1976.

[3] *See:* "The Audit Committee Interface with the Internal Auditor," National Association of Corporate Directors and The Institute of Internal Auditors, Inc., 1980.
Mautz, R.K. and Neumann, F.L., "Corporate Audit Committees: Policies and Practices," The Institute of Internal Auditors, Inc., 1977.
"Internal Auditing," New York, The Conference Board, 1978.

[4] Securities and Exchange Commission Release No. 34–15772, "Statement of Management on Internal Accounting Control," April 30, 1979.

[5] "Report of the Special Advisory Committee on Internal Accounting Control," New York, American Institute of Certified Public Accountants, 1979.

[6] "Survey of Internal Auditing, 1979," The Institute of Internal Auditors, Inc., 1980.

[7] Glazer, Alan S. and Jaenicke, Henry R., "A Framework for Evaluating an Internal Audit Function," Foundation for Auditability Research and Education, 1980.

Cross Reference: *Certified Public Accountant.*

INTERNATIONAL ACCOUNTING

The **International Accounting** scene is a hodgepodge of widely differing national principles and practices, with no common body of accounting and reporting standards in general acceptance worldwide among preparers and users of financial reports. Accordingly, true "international accounting" is a goal rather than a reality, achievement of which depends on a successful global effort to harmonize the myriad variations that characterize multinational accounting.

Differences: Extent and Causes. A recent survey [1] of accounting principles and reporting practices in 64 countries, with respect to 267 propositions covering fundamental concepts, broad principles, and specifics of application, disclosed that no two of the countries had identical standards of financial reporting; and, further, that applications of all 267 propositions differ among countries.

These differences cover the spectrum: basic concepts of preparing financial reports (such as consolidation, consistency, and conservatism); specific accounting principles and varying applications in practice; the extent and quality of disclosure.

And for many reasons they are as persistent as they are pervasive. Thus:

(1) All nations have business-oriented law that codifies local custom and practice, and that influences (in some cases prescribes) local accounting. Where laws differ, so does the related accounting, and the resulting multinational differences are very stubborn.

(2) Local tax law also affects (sometimes determines) local accounting practice—witness the impact of LIFO tax rules in the United States, where financial accounting is otherwise largely unconstrained by the tax system. In some countries, accounting provisions of tax law fill a void left by absence of enunciated financial reporting standards. In other countries, minimization of income taxes takes precedence over fair presentation of financial results. Tax-oriented accounting differences among nations are highly resistant to harmonization.

(3) Formalization of local financial reporting is a natural concomitant of shared commercial activity and a general expectation of reliable public reporting by business. In countries with such a climate (e.g., the United States) recognized private-sector accounting standard-setting bodies promulgate authoritative standards, creating a structured accounting system coexistent with and separate from legal requirements. (See FINANCIAL ACCOUNTING STANDARDS BOARD (FASB).) Private-sector accounting pronouncements have often differed from nation to nation, resulting in embedded multinational differences.

(4) Finally, variances arise simply from differences in the national outlook as shaped by culture, history, and temperament. For example, deep concern for the protection of creditors is a hallmark of the continental European tradition. Countries in that tradition tend to tolerate, even encourage, creation of hidden reserves via understatement of assets and overstatement of liabilities. By contrast, the British tradition views overconservatism and underconservatism with equal distaste, as incompatible with "true and fair" reporting. Both traditions exist elsewhere in the world, giving rise to deep-rooted multinational accounting differences.

The Quest for Harmonization. Ever-increasing world trade and transnational investment have brought a growing awareness of and dissatisfaction with the fact that accounting, the traditional "language of business," is globally the parlance of Babel. As noted, there are good reasons why this is so, but in an era of internationally oriented financial decision making there is a strengthening consensus that it must not remain so.

EEC. Of great significance are events in the EUROPEAN ECONOMIC COMMUNITY (EEC or Common Market). The ten Common Market countries are pledged to the objective of trade and commerce as though they were a single nation, which calls for a measure of uniformity in business reporting.

Common Market membership entails a commitment to conform national law with directives duly issued by the EEC Council of Ministers, and formulating directives on accounting and reporting has been a slow process.

The EEC "Fourth Directive"—ten years in progress—was issued in July 1978, and the Company Laws of each member nation must be conformed with it, generally by 1982. Concerned primarily with format, it also affects content of annual financial reports, setting minimum standards that each member nation may exceed if it chooses.

The Fourth Directive will impact financial reporting in all ten countries to some degree, notwithstanding numerous options that reflect a basic compromise between the legalistic (German) and the judgmental (British) views. The specific effects will, of course, depend on the legislative actions of the member countries.

Still in the draft stage is another EEC accounting directive of great importance—the "Seventh Directive," which will require publication of consolidated financials complying with all requirements of the Fourth Directive. The Seventh Directive has controversial points, such as an "economic group" concept of consolidation and a proposal to require sub-consolidations of the EEC affiliates of entities based elsewhere. Final adoption (probably with some changes) is expected in 1981.

Common Market harmonization efforts involve only the member nations. Discussed next are harmonization initiatives with broader horizons.

IASC. The International Accounting Standards Committee (IASC) was formed in June 1973 by agreement among the professional accounting organizations in the four English-speaking nations, plus those in Mexico, Japan, Netherlands, France, and Germany, to assume leadership in promulgating worldwide accounting and reporting standards. Since then, Nigeria and South Africa have become voting members of IASC, and 32 other countries have joined as nonvoting members pledged to support IASC and take part in its work.

As of this writing, IASC has issued thirteen Statements of International Accounting Standards and has exposed for comment drafts of four others. These Statements all address significant problems and should help raise world standards of accounting and reporting, especially in the developing nations.

IASC is doing valuable work, but it has inherent limitations as a vehicle for international accounting. IASC has no power to enforce, relying solely on enforcement by its constitutent members, which to date has been spotty. Moreover, IASC is not yet a world organization: more countries do not belong than do. Now under discussion (1981) are closer ties with the International Federation of Accountants (IFAC), a more broadly based organization oriented to concerns of practicing auditors. A larger base might or might not strengthen IASC's position, depending upon its eventual role vis-à-vis IFAC.

Finally, regardless of its autonomy, IASC cannot as a practical matter harmonize differences that arise from conflicting national pronouncements. Attempting to do so would provoke no-win confrontations with national standard-setters. (See INTERNATIONAL ACCOUNTING STANDARDS COMMITTEE (IASC).)

Other organizations. Recent years have seen a groundswell of international concern over business conduct. Various government and supergovernment bodies are actively studying supervision and control of transnational business, which would necessarily require a variety of relevant financial information.

OECD. In June 1976, the 24 countries that compose the Organization for Economic Cooperation and Development (OECD) formally adopted a Code of Conduct for multinationals domiciled within each. Although voluntary, this Code is supported by each of the member governments, and compliance will tend to standardize important aspects of financial reporting by all multinational companies.

OECD has recently acted to form a task force on accounting standards comprising representatives of each member country, which will work with international business and labor interests, IASC, and Common Market advisors. This task force is not a standard-setting body. Its mission is to encourage exchanges of views on enhancing global comparability of reporting standards and to seek ways for OECD to augment harmonization.

UN. The United Nations Commission on Transnational Enterprises is also concerned with international accounting and reporting differences. In 1975 it authorized a study group to identify differences, study their causes, and suggest ways to harmonize them.

In October 1977 the group reported out with detailed recommendations for minimum disclosure, financial and nonfinancial, by transnational businesses. These recommendations were taken under advisement by the Commission, which decided to set up an ad hoc Intergovernmental Working Group to pursue the question of establishing international standards.

The Working Group first met in February 1980; participating were some 30 governments and representatives of OECD, EEC, the International Chamber of Commerce, IASC, and IFAC. The meeting produced a generalized statement on disclosures by transnational enterprises, reasonably consistent with the OECD guidelines.

The group has scheduled additional meetings, the agenda for which will probably include the 1977 study group report, current input from other international bodies, and the role of the developing countries in setting international standards.

These efforts of the U.N. may or may not

prove to be a constructive force for harmonization, depending upon the extent to which an international focus remains unblurred by nationalistic perspectives.

Prospects. At this writing, harmonization of multinational accounting differences is widely accepted as an important objective, and prospects for eventual success appear to be improving. Realistic near-term goals might be:

(1) Eliminating unnecessary variations among nations with highly developed accounting, by concentrating on matters of principle and eschewing details of implementation; and

(2) Raising the general level of transnational reporting by establishing basic standards of disclosure and basic principles of good accrual accounting that all nations can accept and will observe.

Both goals appear attainable, and attaining them would represent significant progress toward true international accounting.

ROBERT HAMPTON, III, Partner, Price Waterhouse & Co., New York, N.Y.

Information References

Associations and Governmental Bodies:

American Institute of Certified Public Accountants.
International Accounting Standards Committee.
International Federation of Accountants.
Organization for Economic Cooperation and Development.
United Nations Centre on Transnational Corporations.

Periodicals:

Hampton, Robert III, "A World of Differences in Accounting and Reporting," *Management Accounting*, September 1980.
Price Waterhouse, New York, *EEC Bulletin* (periodic newsletter).

Texts:

American Institute of CPAs, "Professional Accounting in 30 Countries," New York, 1975.
Price Waterhouse & Co., "Information Guides for Doing Business" (in numerous individual countries), New York, various dates.
Watt, G.C., Hammer, R.M., and Burge, M., "Accounting for the Multinational Corporation," New York, Financial Executives Research Foundation, 1977.

Reference Cited

[1] Price Waterhouse International, "International Survey of Accounting Principles and Reporting Practices," Scarborough, Ontario, Butterworths, 1979.

Cross References: *Accounting; International Accounting Standards Committee; International Management: Management of the "World Enterprise."*

INTERNATIONAL ACCOUNTING STANDARDS COMMITTEE

The **International Accounting Standards Committee** (IASC) was founded in 1973 by the professional accounting bodies of Australia, Canada, France, Germany, Japan, Mexico, the Netherlands, the United Kingdom and Ireland, and the United States. Other countries associated themselves with the work of IASC and as of the end of 1980 the membership consisted of 58 accountancy bodies from 44 countries.

The Board of IASC consists of the founder members and of two members (in 1980, Nigeria and South Africa) elected for a period not exceeding five years.

The aim of IASC is to formulate and publish in the public interest standards to be observed in the presentation of audited financial statements. The need for such standards arises because the user of financial statements is increasingly adopting an international perspective. Investors, business, labor, governments, and economic and social agencies all require information—often complex—that is relevant to their needs and presented in a common accounting language.

Content of Standards. An International Accounting Standard is a brief and, as far as possible, simple statement dealing with one aspect of financial statements and specifying (1) measurement rules to be applied in establishing certain items within the financial statement, and (2) disclosures appropriate to understanding the meaning of the financial statements in this respect.

Development. The development of an International Accounting Standard requires research, consultation, and debate over a period typically of two to three years. Complex subjects can take much longer. This process involves both accountants and non-accountants. Informal consultation is undertaken wherever possible with interested parties, and every proposed Standard is exposed in advance for public comment.

Implementation. Implementation of International Accounting Standards depends first on an undertaking by member bodies to use their best endeavors both as preparers and as auditors, to ensure that published financial statements comply with the Standards or that the extent of non-compliance is disclosed. The Standards, however, do not override local law, and they cannot always be framed to accord with existing legislation. Where appropriate, members seek to persuade governments and regulatory authorities to encourage compliance.

Publications. International Accounting Standards, exposure drafts, and discussion papers published by the IASC are available from the local IASC member bodies. Single copies may also be obtained from the IASC Secretariat.

A.V.C. Cook, Secretary, International Accounting Standards Committee, London, England

Information References

The Secretary, International Accounting Standards Committee, 49/51 Bedrord Row, London WCIV 6RL, England.

Board Members in Canada, the United States, and Mexico:

The Canadian Institute of Chartered Accountants, 250 Bloor Street East, Toronto, Ontario, Canada.

American Institute of Certified Public Accountants, 1211 Avenue of the Americas, New York, N.Y. 10036.

Instituto Mexicano de Contadores Publicos, A.C., Danubio 8050, piso, Mexico 5, D.F.

Cross References: *International Accounting; International Management: Management of the "World Enterprise."*

INTERNATIONAL MANAGEMENT: Management of the "World Enterprise"

One of the most dramatic trends of the post World War II era is the rapid and sustained expansion of **International Business.** Both in the form of traditional international trade and the newer multinational corporation, international business has grown to be a major influence on economic, political, and social affairs of nations.

Particularly, multinational corporations have emerged as the one form of economic organization best able to survive and prosper in an interdependent world of sovereign national states. Multinational corporations—MNCs—are companies with operating facilities, as opposed to sales offices, in several foreign countries. Such foreign facilities typically contribute a significant proportion to the company's worldwide sales and profits, so that the financial performance of the MNC system depends significantly on the firm's foreign operations. General Motors, ITT, Exxon, and the Bank of America of the United States, Nestle of Switzerland, Philips Lamps of the Netherlands, and Toyota and Matsushita of Japan are a few examples.

The fact that these companies operate across national boundaries in several foreign countries offers them opportunities, and poses them risks, which companies operating within a single nation state would rarely encounter. Opportunities arise from MNCs' ability to perceive the inter-country variability in resource availability, productivity, and useful knowledge, as well as the synergistic effects achieved through integration on a worldwide basis of the company's operations in production, marketing, management, and research and development. Risks arise from the fact that when MNCs operate across national boundaries, they are confronted with sovereign national entities with their own monetary standards, national goals, political systems, regulatory frameworks, social institutions, and cultures, each of which is different from that in their home country.

Confronted with the opportunities and risk inherent in international business, management must consider their impacts on each foreign operating unit as well as on the total multinational corporate system when arriving at major decisions. The need to incorporate these factors in their decision making exists for all types of MNCs. However, there are substantial differences among MNCs in management structure and process, often due to the different industry, market, product, and technology characteristics. But despite these differences, general patterns of behavior among MNCs can be observed.

Operating Characteristics of MNCs. Like management of national enterprises, the management of multinational enterprises must focus consistently on providing an adequate return on invested capital in the long run. Perceiving the inter-country variability in resource availability, productive efficiency, and useful knowledge, the MNC seeks long-range profit maximization and exploits the inter-country variability. This is where the opportunities lie which are not fully accessible to uninational corporations.

MNC management can be viewed as running an "information factory." Success depends upon achieving efficiency in the collection of information and its application in the use of available corporate resources at each production facility and optimal resource allocation among sites within its global logistic network. This involves intrafirm exchange or transfers of managerial and technical information, as well as processing of information on markets, raw materials, and other inputs. The information efficiency reduces reaction time on the part of the firm to shifts in market supply and demand factors.

With the information collected and processed efficiently on a global basis, the MNC is able to achieve efficiency in resource allocation by shifting, at the margin, the location of production internationally to reduce input costs of relatively immobile inputs—such as land, labor, or natural resources—and to improve the productive use of relatively mobile inputs, particularly capital and technology. Efficiencies are also made possible by economies of scale at individual plants, and in management service functions and research and development activities, by applying a consistent set of performance criteria across all production and distribution units.

Faced with the uncertainties and risk associated with multiple national environments with differing political, economic, and financial systems, MNC management requires a commensurately higher expected rate of return on capital invested abroad. To limit the risks associated with foreign operations, MNCs attempt to increase product-market control and reduce effective competition. As MNCs operate from a strong competitive base—with strength in financial resources, managerial and marketing skills, and technological advantages—MNCs have sometimes been successful in "oligopolizing" industry by increasing industry concentration, particularly in small national markets in developing countries with weak indigenous firms.

Finally, to achieve the above mentioned efficiencies, MNCs attempt to avoid governmental restrictions which hinder efficient operations and long-range profit maximization. For example, shifts in production and distribution patterns can be used to circumvent either tariffs and other barriers to market-access or restrictions on sources of raw material supplies. Financial operations may be modified to sidestep nations' restrictions on international capital mobility and to minimize the firm's tax burden or avoid foreign exchange regulations.

It should also be noted that realizing the above advantages depends on the firm's ability to control from the center the transfer of those specialized corporate resources to operating units located in foreign countries. Only with this ability is the system-wide coordination and integration feasible.

Obstacles to Global Efficiency. The obstacles which constrain MNCs in achieving system-wide global efficiency can be classified into three basic categories: international risks, multinational conflicts, and multiple operating environments.

International Risks. The MNC engages in operations in several countries with different monetary systems, all of which must be consolidated and accounted for in a single currency—the currency of the parent firm. Transactions in many currencies and the need to consolidate financial statements into a single currency is the source of *foreign exchange risk.* This risk stems from the fact that one or more host countries may experience a balance of payment crisis resulting in a depreciation of its currency, the institution of import taxes or other trade controls, or imposition of foreign exchange controls over earning repatriations and the like.

Currency depreciation may result in conversion losses in MNC transactions and/or translation losses from balance sheet items which MNCs are forced to record in their financial statements. Imposition of taxes on imports or other trade controls may increase the prices of components and raw materials that the affiliate may have to import from the parent or third country affiliate, or limit the absolute quantity of these imports, thus affecting operating profits. Imposition of foreign exchange controls may limit remission of profits and fees, thus harming the cash flow of the parent company.

MNCs also face *different national tax rates* which are not fully offset by tax treaties or allowable credits. This makes the location of profits within the MNC system a factor in determining its total tax bill. Planning for inter-affiliate transfers of products and services must incorporate these differences in effective tax treatment as well as exchange control systems.

Furthermore, *different national rates of inflation* in the cost of inputs to internationally traded products will affect relative profitability. Unless these price level changes are exactly offset by changes in exchange rates, the expected rate of return on investment will also depend on the relative rate of inflation in the host country relative to the nation of the parent.

Another type of risk is that stemming from *political* or *regulatory change.* The MNC is exposed to such risks in much greater degree than is the uninational firm. Not only does the MNC face a larger number of such changes due to its multinational character, but its managers or corporate planners are usually more familiar with their home country than with the foreign countries in which the MNC operates, and can generally predict more accurately the political and regulatory changes in the former than in the latter. Thus, MNC management must consider the possibilities of expropriation, change of tax treatment, blockage of profit and fee remissions, price controls, and similar policy actions.

Multinational Conflicts. Nation states have a wide range of national goals such as maintenance of sovereignty and autonomy, national security, and the economic welfare of the population. These often get translated into objectives relating to economic growth, improvement of balance of payment positions, growth of indigenous industries, achieving particular patterns of income distribution, and the like. Governments attempt to control the behavior of national groups and foreign enterprises which affect the nation's efforts to achieve its goals.

Indeed, multinational corporations contribute in several ways to the achievement of host country goals. With investment in a foreign affiliate, the MNC injects financial and human resources from abroad. It also contributes production technology, partly disembodied and partly embodied in imported capital equipment. Management and market know-how are also significant inputs. Continued access to markets and material supplies abroad through the MNC system, as well as permanent access to technical and managerial advances developed abroad, are typically important aspects of multinational corporate involvement in host national economies.

However, the main goals of MNCs may often come into conflict with some objectives of the host country. The MNC seeks to achieve long-run profit optimization in the worldwide perspective, to *direct* and *control* its affiliates from the center, and to *side-step* national regulations which may compromise its drive for global efficiency and profit optimization. So long as there are substantial areas in which possible incongruence may arise between MNC interests and those of host countries, the host government is prone to attempt to control the MNC through regulation.

To illustrate, MNCs may transfer resources in great need to host countries. But its operations in that country may require substantial imports of components and parts from abroad to ensure profitability, which has a negative impact on the host's balance of payments. The MNC goal to exploit the local market with imported inputs and the host country objective to preserve its balance of payments position collide, and the host country may find it politically convenient to limit the imports of the MNC affiliate. Many other examples of possible conflicts are possible.

Thus, in formulating its strategy for global operations, an assessment of the MNC's impact on the economic, political, and social environment in the host nation is needed to minimize conflicts which might trigger regulations limiting the MNCs operating freedom. Such an assessment is important for deciding whether to enter the market. It is also essential for reducing the risks to assets and profitability of future national controls over foreign firms. However, such assessments are problematic. The difficulty arises from the diversity in operating patterns of MNCs, and from the difficulty in developing the standard to which MNC impacts should be measured.

The diversity in operating patterns of MNCs complicates policy formulation by host countries, making general policies less than ideally effective in accomplishing the goals of the host country. From the MNC's viewpoint, the diversity of characteristics of host country markets also makes economic (or political) impact analysis of MNC investment projects difficult, since simple extrapolation of impacts and experiences from previous foreign investment projects may be misleading or erroneous because of the unique characteristics of the next host country. The post-entry assessment is also difficult because it involves the question of what things would have been like in the host country if MNC involvement had not occurred. Until an alternative assessment has been made, little can be convincingly said about the impact of the MNC.

Even though a plausible and objective impact assessment can be developed, it remains difficult to align the MNC mode of operations to host country interests because there is no coherent single set of host country interests. Host country interests are the collective preferences of pluralistic interest groups and individuals and are thus inherently unstable. Being politically determined, the host country interests may differ markedly over time and among countries. Some societal goals may be both stable and consistent, e.g., minimum unemployment, maximum level of real income per capita, and price stability. Others may differ widely from one country to the next, e.g., regional economic development objectives, the desired pattern of income distribution, the value placed on democratic institutions, and the treatment of racial and ethnic minorities. Still others may shift significantly over time, e.g., value placed on domestic ownership of production facilities, economic independence, consumer protection, and perceived vulnerability to foreign cultural and political influences. In addition, national decision-making systems differ, encompassing changing interrelationships and influence among political parties, social interest groups, the media, military, legislative and judicial organs of government, and the like.

Multiple Environments. Once a firm has become involved in operations in several countries, it must deal with several foreign currencies, differing rates of inflation in each country, regulations that differ from country to country and change over time, differing tax policies in each country and political environments which differ markedly from one nation to another. Another set of environmental variables is the diversity of the institutional setting. Labor unions are organized on a different philosophical principle and play varying roles from country to country. Patterns of economic policy formulation differ greatly in purpose, scope, and impact on business activities. Capital markets and financial institutions also differ in size, level of development, and roles.

Finally, cultural differences encompass such diverse dimensions as consumer behavior, human relations in an organization, and working hours. This aspect of international business creates a full range of communication problems arising from different languages, values, and attitudes.

Striking a Balance between Global Objectives and Constraints. Environmental complexity and diversity and the associated uncertainties and risk element require the MNC to rely on locally acquired experience and expertise to operate effectively in various locations. This creates a tendency for individual affiliates to aggrandize their own sphere of influence and act independently from other elements in the system. There is thus a strong centrifugal force in management of MNCs, and to reap the potential benefits for the MNC system requires centralization in management decisions, and tendencies toward fragmentation among foreign affiliates has to be controlled. MNCs have thus been compelled to establish formal planning and control systems.

The two forces, one toward fragmentation and another toward unification, are vectors running in opposite directions, and a balance must be struck between them. The degree to which one of the forces is or should be allowed to dominate the other depends primarily on the characteristics of the firm's operations—product diversity, product differentiation, sophistication of its technology, maturity of the technology, and the like. Important here is the choice of a particular organizational design.

Stopford and Wells [1] in their study of the evolution of the organizational structures of 170 American MNCs, identified the following three general forms of organization for foreign operations:

International Division. This is the unit in the parent company that provides an umbrella to cover all of the foreign activities of the MNC. Managers of individual foreign affiliates are responsible to the president of the corporation as a whole. Below the level of the international division there may be an intervening group of area or product subdivisions over the individual operating subsidiaries. The international division may provide certain staff or functional services in common for all of the international subsidiaries, such as finance and control. But responsibility for production and marketing resides with the individual affiliates. This structure is normally the first step in integrating foreign operations into the managerial processes of a domestic firm. It typically develops after foreign operations have become significant contributors to overall company performance, and frequently is the result of competitive challenges to the MNC's market share abroad or a crisis in control of previously independent subsidiaries.

Global Structure. A second common step in the evolution of organization design for foreign operations usually involves a structural reorganization, toward centralization, intended to facilitate a global perspective for management and control, especially for purposes of long-term planning. The "global structure" may involve organizations based on: (1) worldwide product groups; (2) regional or area divisions;

or (3) a mixture of the two. The structure of authority and control remains hierarchical in all three.

In the product-based global structure, the formal communication and control links take little cognizance of national boundaries. Lines of communication and control run across regions, but within the specific product group involved, and up the hierarchy to the product general manager. Aside from informal coordination within countries among product groups, the formal coordination among product groups is carried out at corporate headquarters. This organization structure is most frequently used by MNCs with relatively diverse product lines, those in which there is much interchange of goods among affiliates in the system, and those with relatively high technology and/or research and development activity.

The area-based organization form is frequently an elaboration of the international division phase, with its intervening layer of regional headquarters. In most instances, the functions of the international division are taken over by the region managers, who become directly responsible to corporate headquarters. This organizational form appears most prevalent in MNCs with relatively homogeneous, mature, and stable product lines, and in firms whose products are closely tied to local consumer markets and for which local marketing, servicing, and production are important requisites for maintaining market share. Moreover, this organizational structure is more prevalent where there is little commercial interchange among the affiliates in the system.

The mixed organizational form takes elements from both the product-based and area-based forms. Certain product lines which are particularly amenable to worldwide planning and coordination tend to be organized on that basis, while an area-based structure is retained for the other products.

Grid Structure. One of the more recent organizational concepts, designed to avoid some of the aforementioned weaknesses and improve communication and coordination, is the grid structure. This retains both the area and product structures, but imposes multiple reporting and responsibility requirements on individual managers. For example, a subsidiary manager in a given location may be under the direction of both a product-group manager and a regional manager. In addition, staff groups or management committees may be given responsibilities which cut across both the regional and product-group divisions. Although very few MNCs have instituted a formal grid organizational structure, various aspects of it have been taken over and utilized by firms within the organizational frameworks mentioned earlier.

In the late 1960s, most multinational firms still retained the lower level international division structure—a structure which is not conducive to integrated planning (Stopford and Wells). Only three of the MNCs surveyed had introduced a formal grid structure. The larger and more sophisticated of them relied most heavily on the various global structures, the worldwide divisional and the mixed structure being the most common. These structures are most amenable to centralization of decision making and for planning from the top down.

The organizational structure of the MNC tends to condition the style and form of corporate planning and management. There is a general tendency for geographically organized MNCs to be characterized by substantial decentralization in decision making, national (or local) orientation toward forecasting the economic environment, and bottom-up planning. This is characterized by planning targets being initiated at the subsidiary level, and passed up through the organization for approval, rejection, or amendment. There is little effort except at the corporate headquarters level, to integrate the plans of the various units.

Firms organized on a worldwide product basis tend to be more centralized, with decision-making power retained at the top, and with a global view taken of strategy and planning—sometimes at the expense of advice on the evolving business environment from local managers. The planning in this type of firm is frequently top down, as overall MNC targets are developed at corporate headquarters, and distributed across product groups where managers further subdivide the targets along subsidiary and individual product lines. Inputs originating at the subsidiary level occur during the negotiation over its share of the initial global plan, after which adjustments may filter back up the hierarchy.

The grid pattern, and to a lesser extent, the mixed pattern of organization, is characterized by intensive interactions, both horizontally and vertically, among managerial units in the structure. This permits not only centralized coordination, but also the free flow of information inputs from all levels including the local subsidiary. The formulation of plans in this context would, ideally, occur simultaneously in top-down and bottom-up directions so as to integrate all possible informational inputs. Thus, regional and product structures would be developed simultaneously in the planning process, to be integrated and made consistent at the headquarters level through several interactions of negotiations with groups of intermediate and lower-level executives.

Several investigators have argued—Lorange [2], Schwendiman [3], and Schollhammer [4]—that the grid structure and its associated planning process is the preferred form for large multinational firms. Yet, an apparent general tendency among MNCs, regardless of organizational form, is a definite centralization of the strategic planning process, even in regionally oriented management structures, as reported by Channon [5]. As noted above, this centralization in the planning and control process may be viewed as a response to the forces of decentralization that foreign operations carry with them, and a strong tool for regaining control over the subsidiary network to achieve the economies of centralized decision making.

ROBERT G. HAWKINS, Vice Dean and Professor of Economics and Finance, New York University Graduate School of Business Administration, New York, New York

YUI KIMURA, MBA, University of Washington, Lecturer in International Management, New York University, New York, New York

Information References

Professional Organizations:

Academy of International Business.
Business International.

Texts:

Bergsten, C.F., Horst, T., and Moran, T.H., "American Multinationals and American Interests," Washington, D.C., The Brookings Institution, 1978.

Eiteman, D.K. and Stonehill, A.I., "Multinational Business Finance," Reading, Mass., Addison-Wesley 2nd ed., 1979.

Fayerweather, John, "International Business Strategy and Administration," Cambridge, Mass., Ballinger, 1978.

Gladwin, T.G. and Walter, Ingo, "Multinationals Under Fire," New York, Wiley, 1980.

Hawkins, Robert G. ed., "The Economic Effects of Multinational Corporations," Greenwich, Conn., JAI Press, 1979.

Hood, N. and Young, S., "The Economics of Multinational Enterprise," New York, Longman, 1979.

Keegan, Warren, "Multinational Marketing Management," Englewood Cliffs, N.J., Prentice-Hall, 2nd ed., 1980.

Robock, S.H., Simmonds, Kenneth, and Zwick, Jack, "International Business and Multinational Enterprise," Homewood, Ill., Irwin, rev. ed., 1977.

Stopford, J.M. and Wells, L.T., Jr., "Managing the Multinational Enterprise," New York, Basic Books, 1972.

Vernon, Raymond, "Storm Over the Multinationals," Cambridge, Mass., Harvard University Press, 1977.

Vernon, Raymond, "Sovereignty at Bay," New York, Basic Books, 1971.

References Cited

[1] Stopford, John and Wells, Louis T., "Managing Multinational Enterprise," New York, Basic Books, 1973.

[2] Lorange, Peter, "Formal Planning in Multinational Corporations," *Columbia Journal of World Business,* Summer, 1973.

[3] Schwendiman, John S., "Strategic and Long-Range Planning for the Multinational Corporation," New York, Praeger, 1973.

[4] Schollhammer, Hans, "Long-Range Planning in Multinational Firms." *Columbia Journal of World Business,* September-October, 1971.

[5] Channon, Derek F., "Prediction and Practice in Multinational Strategic Planning," paper presented at the Second Annual European Seminar on International Business, 1974.

Cross References: *International Accounting; International Accounting Standards Committee.*

INTERNATIONAL MANAGEMENT CONGRESSES. See Management Movement (Section: Professional Management Associations); Management Societies and Associations.

INVENTORY MANAGEMENT. See Production Planning and Inventory Management.

J

"J" PROGRAMS (JIT, JMT, JRT): See On-the-Job Training.

JOB ENRICHMENT AND WORK EFFECTIVENESS

The term **Job Enrichment** designates a technique used by company managers to maximize in individual workers the internal motivation to work, which is the true source of job satisfaction. Basically a concept of the 1960s, founded on the work of Frederick Herzberg as described below, job enrichment has been significantly augmented by work done at Yale University under the direction of Dr. Richard Hackman. This later development is subsumed under the term **Work Effectiveness,** as outlined in the concluding section of this article.

JOB ENRICHMENT

The job-enrichment concept designates a production- and profit-oriented way of managing, as well as a means of making work experience meaningful for people. It is based upon the premise that people are not motivated by what is externally *done to them* by management with rewards, privileges or punishment, nor by the environment or context in which they perform their work. People develop lasting motivation only through their experience with the content of their jobs—the *work itself.*

Such factors as pay, fringe benefits, the work environment, working conditions, and the quality of supervision cannot be ignored or given only token attention. Dissatisfaction with these factors can have a severely debilitating effect on a work force. Caring properly for these needs can result in an absence of dissatisfaction. But generating motivation in workers requires doing something with what they do in their work.

Managers in recent years have been witnessing high-velocity change and turmoil in the patterns of employee behavior, and are forced to cope with a host of problems including: high turnover or quit rates, absenteeism, tardiness, union grievances and work stoppages, high training costs, poor production quality, and low rates of production. Job enrichment was designed to eliminate such problems, thereby benefiting both the employee and the employer.

The Motivation-Hygiene Theory. The keystone of job enrichment theory is the "motivation-hygiene theory," or the "two-needs theory," developed by Frederick Herzberg [1]. As a clinical psychologist. Dr. Herzberg had become interested in the relationship between meaningful experience at work and mental health. He began research to test his belief that man has two sets of needs: to avoid pain, and to grow psychologically. The motivation-hygiene concept grew out of the analysis of interviews with accountants and engineers concerning their reactions to work experiences which supported Herzberg's two-need theory. Thousands of subsequent interviews with people in all types of jobs corroborate the concept.

A duality of attitudes about work experience has been found in the responses of workers to their jobs. Job experiences which lead to good reactions most often are related in the *content* of the jobs, that is, the task content. The bad reactions are most often related to the *context* in which the job is performed, that is, the surroundings and factors on the periphery of task *content.* In addition, the factors causing bad responses are related to *avoidance of discomfort.* The factors causing good responses are related to *personal growth,* or fulfillment of psychological needs. Herzberg labelled the factors associated with growth and the task content of the job as *satisfiers.* Factors associated with pain avoidance and the "surround" of the job were labelled *dissatisfiers.*

The Satisfiers. The factors identified as satisfiers, which are the *motivators* in jobs, are as follows:

Achievement. The personal satisfaction of solving problems independently, completing a task, and seeing the results of one's effort.

Recognition. Positive acknowledgment of the task completed or other personal achievement, rather than generalized "human relations" expression of rewards.

Work Itself. The task content of the job and relative interest, variety, challenge, and freedom from boredom.

Responsibility. Being entrusted with full responsibility and accountability for certain tasks, or the performance of others, and having control over deciding how and when tasks are to be done.

Advancement. Advancement to a higher order of task to perform.

Growth. The sense of the possibility for growth and advancement as well the actual satisfaction from new learning; being able to do new things.

Dissatisfiers. The potential dissatisfiers, or "hygiene factors" (using an analogy to the medical use of the term, meaning preventive and environmental) are: salary, company policy and administration, supervision, working conditions, and interpersonal relations.

Key Principles. The three key principles at the heart of the motivation-hygiene theory are:

(1) *The factors involved in producing job satisfaction are separate and distinct from the factors that lead to job dissatisfaction.* Growth occurs with achievement, and achievement requires a task to perform. Hygiene factors are unrelated to tasks.

(2) *The opposite of satisfaction on the job is not dissatisfaction, it is merely no job satisfaction.* Satisfaction and dissatisfaction are discrete feelings. They are not opposite ends of the same continuum. Herzberg described them as "unipolar traits."

(3) *The motivators have a much longer-lasting effect on sustaining satisfaction than the hygiene factors have on preventing dissatisfaction.* The motivators in a work experience tend to be more self-sustaining and are not dependent upon constant supervisory attention. Hygiene needs, however, are related to things for which our appetites are never satisfied completely. Applications of hygiene improvement must be constantly reapplied, since the need for them always recurs, usually with increased intensity. Hygiene must always be replenished. Most all of the methods used in work-related organizations to "purchase" motivated behavior over the years have appeared to be ineffective, since the traditional motivation problems still exist. This is the inevitable result because only the things that surround the work itself were being improved, and these things have no lasting effect on motivation of workers.

To provide the motivation for people to perform work over the long term, the *content* of the work must be set up to deliver motivating experiences. The hygiene factors are no more than the stage and background for that process.

Job Loading. In attempting to enrich an employee's job, Dr. Herzberg contends [2], management often merely succeeds in reducing the man's personal contribution, rather than giving him an opportunity for growth in his existing job. He calls this "horizontal job loading," as opposed to "vertical loading," which provides motivator factors. Horizontal loading, in his view, is what has mostly been wrong with earlier programs centered on job *enlargement.* He gives some examples of this approach, with some tart observations:

- Challenging the employee by increasing the amount of production expected of him. If he tightens 10,000 bolts a day, see if he can tighten 20,000 a day. "If the job is already zero in motivation, multiplying zero by anything still equals zero."
- Adding another meaningless task to the existing one, usually some routine clerical activity. "The arithmetic here is adding zero to zero."
- Rotating the assignments of a number of jobs that really should be enriched. This means, for example, washing dishes for a while, then washing silverware. "The arithmetic is substituting one zero for another zero."
- Removing the most difficult parts of the assignment to free the worker to accomplish more of the less challenging assignments. "This traditional industrial engineering approach amounts to subtraction in the hope of accomplishing addition."

Dr. Herzberg concedes that all of the principles of motivating through job enrichment have not been worked out as yet, but he offers the seven-point checklist shown in Exhibit I as a practical guide for anyone who wishes to reexamine the motivator factors in the jobs over which he has control.

Opportunities in Job Enrichment. Robert N. Ford, personnel director, manpower utilization, for AT&T, has aptly described the job-enrichment process as "the art of reshaping jobs." [3] Quantitative measures of production rates, quality, and job attitude have been carefully made in many applications. Improvements have amply demonstrated the validity of changing job content to effect increased motivation. Space limitations preclude recounting application results in detail. However, the following brief examples cited by Ford will serve to indicate the possibilities:

A group of ten girls was responsible for getting out charges in toll bills on staggered dates through the month:

Exeter 2—due out February 1.
Exeter 5—due out February 8.
Exeter 7—due out February 13.
Exeter 9—due out February 17 . . . and so on.

EXHIBIT I

Vertical Job Loading Possibilities	Motivators Involved
1. Remove some controls while at the same time retaining accountability.	Responsibility and personal achievement
2. Increase the accountability of individuals for their own work.	Responsibility and recognition
3. Give a person a complete natural unit of work.	Responsibility, achievement and recognition
4. Grant additional authority to an employee in his activity; more job freedom.	Responsibility, achievement and recognition
5. Make periodic reports of output and progress to the worker himself rather than to his supervisor only.	Internal recognition
6. Introduce new and more difficult tasks not previously handled.	Growth and learning
7. Assign individuals specific or specialized tasks, enabling them to become experts.	Responsibility, growth, and advancement

The girls worked as a team: when they finished Exeter 2, they started Exeter 5 under the scheduling and direction of the supervisor. But productivity was bad, due dates were missed, costs of overtime were high, and so on.

A new young supervisor on one of his first assignments saw the answer: give *one girl* responsibility for getting out Exeter 2, another girl Exeter 5, and so on. She might or might not have to get help from another girl. But in either case, each girl in rotation had a *whole* piece of responsibility—all of Exeter 2 by 5 p.m. on a specified date. She had to organize the effort and succeed or fail by herself.

Results from the new setup were described by management as "dramatic." Note that a girl did not have more work to do, merely more immediate responsibility for the work she was going to do anyhow. Previously, the billing task had been automatic. The supervisor's orders amounted to: "Work on this pile of papers. When you are done, give them to so-and-so. Then we'll bring you more. We'll tell you when to stop." Under this system, actual accomplishment from her own efforts was hard for a girl to see. The supervisor improved performance and cut costs by *motivation through the work itself.*

In a factory application cited by Myers [4], when janitors and their supervisors became involved in a problem-solving-goal-setting program, they first established the criteria of building maintenance, and then took part in planning their own work. Definite improvements were noted in three areas: The work force was reduced from 121 to 76, the reductions being achieved through job bidding and normal turnover; quality of performance was increased; and turnover dropped from 100% per quarter to 20% per quarter.

The Process of Enriching Jobs. At the outset, a decision should be made as to whether the effort is to take the form of an *experimental project* or a *program.* An experimental project is essentially a scientific study complete with experimental groups, in which the job changes will be made, and control groups in which all conditions are controlled to keep them as constant as possible. In a project, great care is taken to make very little of the process known to the employees. The purpose is to reduce the chance of short-term improvements in results occurring solely because the employees are reacting to the attention heaped on them as an "elite" group.

The program, on the other hand, is a straightforward application affecting as large a population as possible without regard to control groups. The question of running a project or program is often decided by the nature of the management environment in the organization. If upper management attitudes are very hostile and skeptical about organizational change of this sort, then it is often necessary to provide indisputable proof of effectiveness by using a project model if the effect is to have any future.

Work Within a Department. One department or an identifiable functional group should be selected as the "client" group to work with, rather than attempting to redesign problem jobs in work groups across functional lines. This is suggested to gain the advantage of having a homogeneous management team participating in workshops and subsequent work on redesigning jobs.

Preferably, a *basic job* performed by a large number of people should be selected. Avoid the management, staff, and support jobs at first—let changes in *basic jobs* force changes at higher levels. Basic jobs are usually those which directly affect the product or service turned out, or they involve direct interface with the public or the customer.

Careful consideration should be given to the selection of the individual who is to act as the director for the project or program. This individual is best equipped for the job if he is highly respected and has a proven record of success as a line manager.

The Supervisor's Workshop. Once the problem job has been identified and the key man selected, a three-day workshop should be arranged at some location away from the work site that is suitable for live-in training. The effectiveness of workshops is greatly reduced if they are not isolated and are not free from interruptions. In a typical organization, the workshop might include first-line supervisors, section heads, manager, division head, and department head.

Middle and executive level managers should also attend. The commitment of managers at these levels may undergo some severe tests in months to follow, and personal exposure to the concepts and methods is of great value. In addition, the lower level supervisors will be very hesitant to carry out even the least of job changes if they feel that doing so will place them in jeopardy from executive levels.

The workshop should begin with a review of motivation research and the conceptual basis of job enrichment. The chasm between conceptual generalities and job changes can be bridged in the workshop through the process of brainstorming or so-called "greenlighting".

"Greenlighting" is a device used to remove the usual obstacles to free thinking. When the greenlight condition is announced, the group begins tossing out ideas for getting motivators into each job as fast as possible. Everyone is warned that no "red lights" or negative comments such as "We tried that before," "That won't work," or "This isn't a good time for that," are permitted. Worry about implementing the recommended changes should not be a concernduring greenlighting. There is plenty of time for that later.

A timetable can be set at the workshop for completing a detailed analysis of each proposed item for job change, and installation of items selected to start with. Then plans are made for additional meetings to continue greenlighting and evaluation of the items from the first greenlighting session.

Thorough greenlighting and evaluation in the authors' experience can profitably extend over a four to six week period, with the supervisors meeting two or three hours each week before they actually start with the items. A job-enrichment specialist or project director should assist in accomplishing changes which require higher approval. But the lower supervisors are the principal change agents. They should install the job changes with their subordinates.

The Module of Work and Vertical Loading of the Job. Among the best ways to set up individual responsibility is to seek natural modules of work which can be individually assigned. A work module can appear in many forms. In general, a module is a set of related tasks which contribute in sequence to the completion of some function or turning out some completed item. The module of tasks can be made more meaningful if it is related to some natural unit of work for which an individual has continuing responsibility.

Natural units of work may have geographic, alphabetical, or numerical grouping or other identity. That identity may also be related to serving some recipient or group of recipients. When a natural work module is first identified it may be performed by several people doing fragments of the full module with no one singly responsible for the whole. To the greatest degree that is practical each individual is given the full process to perform. In effect, a sense of "proprietorship" can and should be developed.

The responsibility is full and individual. In one keypunch job, for example, the operators were given a module of work by having them prepare all cards from a certain geographic area or for certain kinds of reports, rather than whatever cards happened to come along next.

The principle of vertical loading involves process-loading into a job additional tasks and responsibilities which can deliver more satisfaction than the tasks in the job to begin with. This is very different from adding more tasks which may be varied but have essentially no greater substance. The process is usually vertical because the tasks of greater interest and responsibility are most often found above in the supervisory job or a job at a higher level of complexity.

Direct Feedback. The process of feedback is highly important in the enriching process. It affects the recognition motivator and is the sophisticated area where, perhaps, most is yet to be learned about employee motivation. The most effective feedback occurs in the transaction between employee and the task rather than in the usual transaction between employee and supervisor. Effective feedback has these characteristics:

- It is related to task performance, not personal characteristics.
- It is given on an individual rather than group basis.
- It occurs at short intervals.
- It is given direct from the task to the employee, not through the supervisor.

This is not intended to imply that supervisory feedback is ineffective or a waste of time. Most people desire it, and such interpersonal feedback on performance can be of great value when done well. Direct feedback is not fettered with interpersonal problems and is less complicated.

Soon after completion of a task, a worker should be learning through task feedback how well he is doing, where he stands, and what he is worth. Then he should have the opportunity to do something about it himself. This is usually accomplished by making him responsible for changes and adjustments in his process and for correcting his own errors.

Once a new responsibility is given, the supervisor must give consideration to what his response will be if the employee fails with it. Some failure must be expected. The supervisor should help the employee correct the error, examine why it occurred, and assist in planning to prevent recurrence. This kind of individual coaching becomes a major supervisory function which ushers in a new way of life for many supervisors.

WORK EFFECTIVENESS

Building upon Herzberg's original theory, Drs. Richard Hackman and Greg Oldham, in conjunction with Roy W. Walters and Associates, have developed a model which identifies five items or "core job dimensions," crucial to the design of meaningful work [5]. These are *Task Significance, Skill Variety, Task Identity, Autonomy,* and *Feedback.* (See Exhibit II.) The first three relate to the meaningfulness of the work, the fourth to the experiencing of real responsibility, and the fifth to knowledge of the results of work activities.

The implementing concepts—*Content Analysis, Task Combination, Natural Work Units, Client Relationship, Vertical Loading,* and *Feedback Channels*—are action steps for redesigning the work. All impact on the core job dimensions in various ways, which in turn impact on the critical psychological states.

Referring to the model, the following notes elaborate upon the job-dimension and implementation components:

EXHIBIT II

THE WORK EFFECTIVENESS MODEL

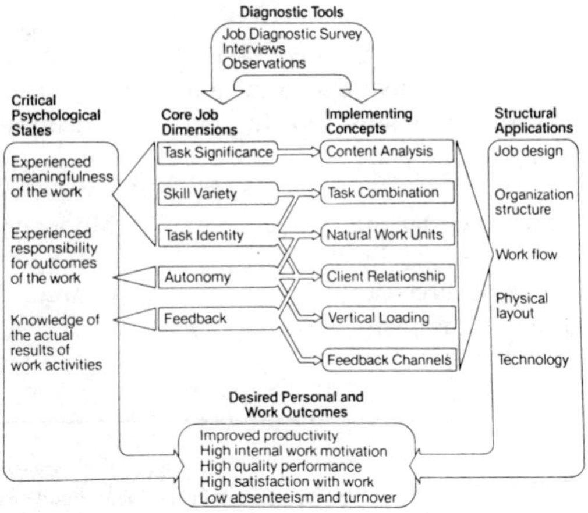

Core Job Dimensions. *Task Significance.* The degree to which the job has a substantial and perceivable impact on the lives of other people, whether in the immediate organization or the world at large. Most people in service organizations have a fairly high feeling of significance.

Skill Variety. The degree to which a job requires the worker to perform activities that challenge his or her skills and abilities.

Task Identity. The degree to which a job requires completion of a "whole" and identifiable piece of work—doing a job from beginning to end with a visible outcome. The route to experienced meaningfulness is important for workers' feelings and very important for behavior.

Autonomy. The degree to which the job gives the worker freedom, independence, and discretion in scheduling work and determining how to carry it out. This is the key to continuing responsibility for outcomes of the work. By combining the jobs, the manager allows for conditions to do this.

Feedback. The degree to which a worker, in carrying out the work activities required by the job, gets information about the effectiveness of his or her efforts. Feedback is most powerful when it comes directly from the work itself. This comes when the manager structurally puts separate jobs together by individual or team. Feedback becomes more meaningful when it is

Exhibit III

Job Diagnostic Survey

Section One

Circle the number which is the most accurate description of your job.

1. To what extent does your job require you to *work closely with other people* (either "clients", or people in related jobs in your own organization)?

1	2	3	4	5	6	7
Very little; dealing with other people is not at all necessary in doing the job.			Moderately; some dealing with others is necessary.			Very much; dealing with other people is an absolutely essential and crucial part of doing the job.

Section Two

Write a number in the blank beside each statement, based on the scale shown: How accurate is the statement describing your job?

1	2	3	4	5	6	7
Very Inaccurate	Mostly Inaccurate	Slightly Inaccurate	Uncertain	Slightly Accurate	Mostly Accurate	Very Accurate

_____ 1. The job requires me to use a number of complex or high-level skills.

_____ 2. The job requires a lot of cooperative work with other people.

Section Three

Indicate how *you personally feel* about your job. Write a number in the blank for each statement, based on the scale shown. How much do you agree with the statement?

1	2	3	4	5	6	7
Disagree Strongly	Disagree	Disagree Slightly	Neutral	Agree Slightly	Agree	Strongly Agree

_____ 1. It's hard, on this job, for me to care very much about whether or not the work gets done right.

_____ 2. My opinion of myself goes up when I do this job well.

_____ 3. Generally speaking, I am very satisfied with this job.

Section Four

How satisfied are you with each aspect of your job listed below? Once again, write the appropriate number in the blank beside each statement.

1	2	3	4	5	6	7
Extremely Dissatisfied	Dissatisfied	Slightly Dissatisfied	Neutral	Slightly Satisfied	Satisfied	Extremely Satisfied

_____ 1. The amount of job security I have.

_____ 2. The amount of pay and fringe benefits I receive.

_____ 3. The amount of personal growth and development I get in doing my job.

EXHIBIT III *Continued*

JOB DIAGNOSTIC SURVEY

Section Five

Now think of the *other people* in your organization who hold the same job you do, or the job most similar to yours. Indicate how accurately you think each of the statements describes the feelings of those people about the job. Write the number in the blank, as before.

1	2	3	4	5	6	7
Disagree Strongly	Disagree	Disagree Slightly	Neutral	Agree Slightly	Agree	Agree Strongly

____ 1. Most people on this job feel a great sense of personal satisfaction when they do the job well.

____ 2. Most people on this job are very satisfied with the job.

Section Six

Using the scale below, indicate the degree to which you would like to have each characteristic present in your job.

4	5	6	7	8	9	10
Would like having this only a moderate amount (or less)			Would like having this very much			Would like having this *extremely* much

____ 1. High respect and fair treatment from my supervisor.

____ 2. Stimulating and challenging work.

____ 3. Chances to exercise independent thought and action in my job.

Section Seven

For each question, two different kinds of jobs are briefly described. Indicate which of the jobs you personally would prefer—if you had to make a choice between them. For each question, assume that everything else about the job is the same.

Job A	Job B
1. A job where the pay is very good.	A job where there is considerable opportunity to be creative and innovative.

1	2	3	4	5
Strongly Prefer A	Slightly Prefer A	Neutral	Slightly Prefer B	Strongly Prefer B

Job A	Job B
2. A job where you are often required to make important decisions.	A job with many pleasant people to work with.

1	2	3	4	5
Strongly Prefer A	Slightly Prefer A	Neutral	Slightly Prefer B	Strongly Prefer B

an inherent part of the operation vs. an artificial situation imposed by supervision.

Implementing Concepts. *Content Analysis.* Examining the content of the job to determine that irrelevant, redundant operations are not present. This impacts on whether or not the job is seen as significant to the person performing the work.

Task Combination. Combining tasks to a complete task module has a high degree of potential. This will provide additional interest, challenge, and a feeling of responsibility for the whole piece.

Natural Work Units. Designing the work according to a logical group that is aligned with the mission allows for the personal feeling of responsibility. Workers start to identify with this group and behave accordingly.

"Client" Relationship. Where natural work units are groupings by customers—for example, billing or accounts receivable—the engendered sense of responsibility leads the workers to form a "client relationship" with the accounts. They start to call them "my customers" and take on a strong attitude of ownership.

Vertical Loading. This pushing of responsibilities down from higher levels and giving the workers more control make for increased responsibility. This should be done selectively according to individual competence.

Feedback Channels. Setting up conditions for feedback from the job is very important in the transition from a 100% checking job to a partial or full task module. Elimination of checking without feedback might hurt quality. Workers and supervisors must know how they are doing.

Job Diagnostic Survey. This survey instrument is given to job incumbents anonymously. The form developed [6] requires only 30 minutes to complete and produces scalar scores for each of the core dimensions, immediately defining the areas of weakness that require improvement. The nature of the questions is indicated in Exhibit III, showing fragments of each Section. (The exhibit shows only a sample of the complete questionnaire, which can be obtained from the authors as indicated in [6].)

The first section of the questionnaire asks the employee to describe the job as *objectively* as possible, by circling a figure on a numerical scale.

Section Two asks the employee to give a numerical rating as to the degree of accuracy of listed statements about the job.

Section Three asks for a numerical rating to indicate how the employee *personally feels* about given aspects of the job.

Section four asks for similar ratings on how *satisfied* the employee is with listed aspects of the job.

Section Five asks for numerical ratings on how the employee believes *other employees* who hold the same or a similar job feel about the job.

Section Six asks for ratings on the kinds of characteristics the employee would like to see as part of the job.

Finally, Section Seven lists twelve pairs of characteristics for a "Job A" and a "Job B" and asks the employee to consider each pair on the assumption that in all other respects the jobs are equal, and to indicate by circling a number the degree to which he (she) would prefer one job over the other.

Section Eight asks for certain biographical information, re sex, age, education, etc.

Guided by the survey findings, the implementing concepts (action steps) are then applied in order to improve the strength (quantity and quality) of the core job dimensions.

Structural Applications. Other structural applications require consideration in order to construct meaningful work effectiveness systems. The organizational structure is invariably affected, as are the work flow, the physical layout, and the technology.

ROY W. WALTERS, President, and KENNETH PURDY, Senior Associate, Roy W. Walters and Associates, Inc., Mahwah, New Jersey

Information References

Ford, Robert N., "Motivation Through the Work Itself." New York, American Management Association, 1969.

Gardner, John W., "No Easy Victories," New York, Harper & Row, 1968.

Hackman, J. Richard and Oldham, Greg R., "Work Redesign," Reading, Mass., Addison Wesley, 1980.

Herzberg, Frederick, "One More Time: How Do You Motivate Employees?" Harvard Business Review, January-February, 1968.

Herzberg, Frederick, "Work and the Nature of Man," Cleveland, World, 1966.

Snyderman, and Mausner, "The Motivation to Work," New York, Wiley, 1959.

Janson, Robert H., "Job Enrichment: Challenge of the Seventies," *AST Journal,* June, 1970.

Myers, M. Scott, "Every Employee a Manager," New York, McGraw-Hill, 1970.

Paul, William S., Robertson, Keith B., and Herzberg, Frederick, "Job Enrichment Pays Off," *Harvard Business Review,* March-April, 1969.

Walters, Roy W., and Purdy, Kenneth L., "Job Enrichment Programs," in Heyel, C., ed., "Handbook of Modern Office Management and Administrative Services," New York, McGraw-Hill, 1972.
Walters, Roy W., "Job Enrichment for Results," Reading, Mass., Addison Wesley, 1975.

References Cited

[1] Herzberg, Snyderman, and Mausner, "The Motivation to Work," New York, Wiley, 1959.
[2] Herzberg, Frederick, "One More Time: How Do You Motivate Employees?" *Harvard Business Review*, January-February, 1968.
[3] Ford, Robert N., "Motivation Through the Work Itself," New York, American Management Association, 1969.
[4] Myers, M. Scott, "Every Employee a Manager," New York, McGraw-Hill, 1970.
[5] Hackman, J.R. and Oldham, G.R., "Motivation through the Design of Work: Test of a Theory" (Tech. Rep. No. 6), New Haven, Conn., Yale University, Department of Administration Sciences, 1974.
[6] Hackman, J.R. and Oldham, G.R., "The Diagnostic Survey: An Instrument for the Diagnosis of Jobs and the Evaluation of Job Redesign Projects" (Tech. Rep. No. 4), New Haven, Conn., Yale University, Dept. of Administrative Sciences, 1974. The complete instruments, of which fragments are shown in Exhibit III, can be obtained from Roy W. Walters and Associates, Whitney Industrial Park, Mahwah 1, N.J. 07430.

Cross References: *Goal Setting; Human Relations in Industry; Management by Objectives; Motivation (and accompanying entries with that prefix).*

JOB EVALUATION

Job Evaluation in its broadest sense means determination of appropriate base salary or wage rates for specific combinations of duties that are called "jobs" or "positions" in business organizations. In this context, whenever two or more paid individuals are employed by any organization, job evaluation of some kind takes place. The employer tries to recognize, in terms of relative rates of payment, differences among the comparative values of contributions to organizational goals made by the jobs among which the total efforts of the enterprise are divided.

In the more limited context used here, "job evaluation" is the generic title applied to those approaches to job rate determination which attempt to systematize the processes that are essential to achievement of equity and employee satisfaction—in so far as wage or salary scales and position rate differentials are concerned. The claim that any "system" of job evaluation is "scientific" cannot be made with accuracy or assurance, despite the fact that many job evaluation systems use numbers in the process of comparing job values or in relating them to wage scales. The knowledgeable practitioner of the art recognizes that the best he can do is to introduce an optimum amount of order into making and recording the human judgments that are essential to construction of more effective wage and salary scales.

History. Although, undoubtedly, many individual employers had always sought to bring some order into their wage and salary structures, it was not until the twentieth century, coincident with the growth of increasingly complex business institutions, that general managerial attention has been accorded to systematic job evaluation. E. O. Griffenhagen set up a "job classification" plan for Chicago municipal employees in 1909–1910. The results of his participation in similar work for the Commonwealth Edison Company were published in 1912.

Westinghouse, General Electric, and Sperry Gyroscope developed practical systems for hourly paid employees prior to 1920. Also prior to 1920 the Pennsylvania Railroad established a clerical position classification plan. Additionally, the Philadelphia Electric Company, the Federal Reserve Bank of New York, and several other large companies in other fields experimented with and in some cases implemented similar practices during the 1920s. In the majority of these situations, clerical workers and their salary rates were the chief targets for the earlier "systematizers." The inaccurate and hence frequently misunderstood term "salary standardization" was applied to these attempts up to the time that the world was shaken by the Great Depression. During the early 1930s only a handful of dedicated individuals cared to continue their researches into an area of personnel administration that seemed to promise so little to righting a topsy-turvey economy.

The social, economic, and political climate of the middle and late thirties, including Federal encouragement of collective bargaining and the growth of labor unions, forced a majority of larger companies to seek a satisfactorily defensible method of justifying individual job or position rate differentials and the salary and wage scales that placed money values on those differentials. By the end of that decade, few professional personnel administration meeting programs were considered complete without at least one session on orderly salary and wage administration. Imposition of salary and wage controls in World War II and the Korean War intensified the need for and interest in systematic job evaluation. From the middle fifties to the present, there has been continuing research in evaluation methods by employers, educators, and consultants. Some of the resulting refinements have contributed to significant improvements in the art [1] [2] [3]. Unfortunately, too many of the allegedly improved systems call for unnecessarily complicated approaches which inhibit management and employee understanding and acceptance.

The extension of job evaluation up through the very highest positions in the organization was characteristic of the late sixties and early seventies, and this will undoubtedly continue. Professional managers have learned to recognize orderly salary and wage administration as a highly useful tool.

Approaches and Techniques. The process of job evaluation starts with the determination and recording of information about all of the jobs or positions to be covered, as such information is related to the appraisal of the difficulty and importance of such positions. This activity is usually referred to as *Job Analysis* and results in a Job Description or *Job Specification.* Essentially, such documents contain:

(1) Identifying details such as job title, job location, name of organizational component(s) in which the job is located, and the like.

(2) A brief but informative description of each major duty performed as well as a listing of minor duties assigned.

(3) Indications of the scholastic training or equivalent required, as well as of basic working experience expected for entry into the position.

(4) A description of the precision or decision limits within which the incumbent is required to produce.

(5) Special requirements related to ingenuity, initiative, resourcefulness, and creativity.

(6) Descriptions of elements of responsibility assigned, such as men, money, materials, equipment, methods, markets, and records.

(7) Statements as to the physical effort involved.

(8) Descriptions of the surroundings, hazards, and other unusual or adverse physical conditions under which the work must be performed.

It is essential to recognize that data descriptive of position content contain both fact and opinion. Items of fact can be checked objectively; for example, a worker does or does not perform a certain duty. However, determining what it takes in skill or training to qualify for performance of the duty can well be a matter of opinion. The best place to start gathering fact and opinion is, therefore, the person or an adequate sample of the people assigned to each position. Suitably trained job analysts then can prepare tentative descriptions and submit them for supervisory approval, and, when feasible after required modifications have been made, secure agreement from the employee or employees whose jobs have been described. *All job evaluation must start with general agreement on the accuracy of the job analysis.*

With respect to clerical employees and others accustomed to recording ideas in writing, questionnaires can be used advantageously to speed the job analysis process. However, these are not customarily used to the exclusion of an adequate sampling of personal interviews. Moreover, the analyst must assure himself that job incumbents who have the same titles actually have the same or similar duties. It is better to err at first on the side of preparing too many job descriptions than, during the evaluation stage, to realize that what are really different jobs have been combined because they happened to carry like titles.

Job Rating. When the preparation of job descriptions has been completed, the process of job rating or job comparison begins. This is the heart of job evaluation. Experience has shown that employees are usually more concerned with equitable comparison of their individual *job rates* with those of fellow workers than they are with the absolute amounts of their salaries or wages. Moreover, mal-alignment of *internal* position values can cause considerable difficulty when it comes to the next step of *external* market rate comparisons.

The actual pricing of the internal job comparison schedule is accomplished by a labor market survey that will reveal how much companies in the local area and in related industries are paying for comparable positions. For such a survey, a relatively few "key" jobs are selected which, it is expected, will have reasonably similar counterparts in other companies and which range from low to high on the comparison schedule. The assurance that the outside rate quotations are for comparable combinations of duties and requirements can be attained by personal interviews with knowledgeable persons from other companies or by membership in properly operated local or industry-wide labor market survey groups, or both.

The results of the "market survey" can be entered on a simple scatter diagram, using cross-section paper, with company key jobs identified at appropriate intervals along the "X," or horizontal, axis (in terms of points assigned to them), and rates paid by other companies for those same jobs entered in the intersecting squares in accordance with an hourly, weekly, or monthly dollar scale on the "Y," or vertical, axis. A regression line representing the central tendency of the rate comparisons can be drawn by inspection or determined by statistical methods. This line permits translation of point values to market rates; it is more likely to be curvilinear than straight.

Selection of a suitable company relationship between the indicated regression line for the "market" and the company wage schedule involves determination of company policy as to whether an average, higher, or lower general wage scale comparison is to be maintained (or bargained for collectively). Federal imposition of minimum wage rates distorts the ascertained values of the low-paid jobs, gradually changing a straight or curvilinear regression line to the shape of a hockey stick. Other aberrations occur if a company has a Federal contract, and must apply "going" rates, which generally become union rates.

Collective Bargaining. The process of collectively bargaining for job rate differentials and general levels of wage scales is fraught with hazards to rational or logical job evaluation installations. Most labor unions have, perhaps understandably, refused or been reluctant to commit themselves to accepting a management-installed evaluation plan or to joining with management in selecting and implementing such a plan. As a result individual job differentials determined by the internal job comparison schedule can be distorted by successive union attacks, over a long period, on single job rates, and by periodic bargaining positions that change the slope of the entire line representing the relationship between job difficulty and importance and the over-all wage scale.

Other Distortions. Another source of distortion of originally logical rate schedules stems from an otherwise sound practice adopted on installation. When an employer applies the new wage scale, he usually finds that some individuals are underpaid and some are overpaid. The usual practice is to increase the rates of the underpaid individuals to the new flat rates for their positions, or to the minima of their respective new salary ranges. On the other hand, rates of over-paid individuals are not reduced. The theory is that the latter will not participate in future general wage or salary scale increases until their over-payments are removed by the cumulative effects of successive general increases, or until they have been transferred to higher level positions. (These individually overpaid situations are frequently referred to as "red-circle" rates.) However, these inequalities are often perpetuated by collective bargaining provisions or perhaps by unilateral management action aimed at not denying some small pay consideration to holders of "red-circle" rates when most other fellow employees are receiving increases.

There are two sources of salary or wage plan distortion that can be avoided, however, namely, *failure to recognize changes in existing position content,* and *introduction of new jobs.* It is essential that any wage and salary administration activity include constant re-analysis and re-evaluation.

Outlines of Some Typical Methods of Job Rating. Many individual companies employ several variations of one or more basic methods in order better to satisfy the needs of quite different kinds of employees. On the other hand, no one company should assume, without further validation, that a plan that has been successfully applied in another company can necessarily be taken over and applied in its entirety to the company's own situation.

Ranking. The earliest methods involved simple ranking of all of a certain type of jobs (e.g. production and maintenance or clerical) into a pre-determined number of "grades" or "levels" that progressed from the least to the most difficult and important. For example, from office boy, at the lower end, to assistant bookkeeping supervisor, at the upper end. Individual combinations of duties were identified and placed in various intermediate grades in accordance with what, in the opinion of the evaluator, appeared to be the appropriate order of over-all ranking in difficulty and importance.

Point Plans. A logical improvement over the overall ranking method was the identification of all of the factors that might be considered in the ranking of positions, the assignment of numerical points to the various levels of each of the factors, and the summation of the points so assigned to arrive at total relative job values. In spite of the early application of job grading to clerical work, the first widely known "point rating systems" were applied to factory jobs. The National Metal Trades Association and the National Electrical Manufacturers Association pioneered in promulgating a method in which the major factors were broken down into sub-factors and the sub-factors assigned percentage weights in relation to other factors and sub-factors. Definitions were given for levels of the factors, and sub-factors were related to such matters as required education, years of experience, and the like. Exhibit I shows NEMA point assignments. Some companies have gone to great lengths in their manuals to assure assignment of points in as uniform a manner as possible. Exhibit II shows a representative "Rating Guide" for a program that assigns a maximum of 450 points to "Previous Training and Experience" [4].

Factor Comparison. Many companies have developed their own point systems or adapted NMTA and NEMA methods to their own needs. Eugene J. Benge developed a new approach to the construction and definition of point system scales which, when first practically applied by S. L. H. Burk to factory positions and later to office occupations, and then by E. N. Hay to banking positions, aroused considerable interest and gained broad acceptance under the name "Factor Comparison."

The distinctive features of the factor comparison approaches were:

(1) The use of an internal committee of operating executives in pooling their judgments to analyse the "going rates" *for a group of key jobs* to establish values for job factors so that the key jobs can be used as guides to the factor level and to the total evaluation of all other jobs.

(2) The use of key job factor titles to define each factor level, as against the use of verbal definitions in rating of new or changed positions.

(3) The elimination of any maximum number of points or maximum percentage weights. This is essential to the rating of jobs other than key jobs, as well as new jobs to be established in the future. Such jobs may well require either lower or higher factor ratings than those available from the current job comparison schedules or the original key job list.

(4) The detailed rating of key positions in other companies in the labor market on the basis of the inquiring company's evaluation method to assure accurate comparison for wage scale determination.

Summary Principles. In practice, predetermined point assignments are often used, confining detailed factor comparison only to a relatively few key jobs, which are then used as "benchmarks" in assigning points to all other jobs. Following are points which may serve as a guide for companies newly undertaking a job evaluation program:

(1) The pooled judgment of the largest practical, qualified group or groups should be used in the construction of scales and/or in their application.

(2) In selecting the factors (or job elements) to be used, use those that include in total, all of the considerations that make one position more or less difficult or important than another.

(3) The number of factors used should be kept to a minimum (perhaps five to eight) and should be so selected and defined as to reduce as far as possible the "halo" effect, that is, pyramiding or overlapping of credits among factors. As indicated in Exhibits V and VI, five

EXHIBIT I

MAXIMUM POINTS ASSIGNED TO FACTORS AND KEY TO GRADES

Factors	
Skill	
1. Education	70
2. Experience	110
3. Initiative and Ingenuity	70
Effort	
4. Physical Demand	50
5. Mental or Visual	25
Responsibility	
6. Equipment Process	25
7. Material or Product	25
8. Safety of Others	25
9. Work of Others	25
Job Conditions	
10. Working Conditions	50
11. Unavoid Hazards	25

Score Range	Grades	Score Range	Grades
162–183	10	272–293	5
184–205	9	294–315	4
206–227	8	316–337	3
228–249	7	338–359	2
250–271	6	360–381	1

EXHIBIT II

REPRESENTATIVE RATING GUIDE: SKILL IN TERMS OF PREVIOUS TRAINING AND EXPERIENCE

Training and Experience Required in	*Point Values Based on Time Required to Reach Maximum Requirements*							
	1 week or less	*1–3 mos*	*4–6 mos*	*7–12 mos*	*13–18 mos*	*2 years*	*3 years*	*4 years*
A. *Use of Equipment and Tools* . . . . Hand tools, drills, power saws, multiple control processing equipment, lathes, automatic screw machines, etc.	5	10	15	25	35	65	100	150
B. *Methods* . . . . Routine and sequence of working procedure; variety, detail, complexity.	5	10	15	25	35	65	100	150
C. *Use of Materials* . . . . Properties of metals, raw material formulae, stores stock, paints, lubricants.	5	10	15	25	35	65	100	150

The analyst should look to the training requirement of the typical individual under usual conditions. The training period should represent the total experience gained on previous jobs, and the breaking-in period required on the job under consideration. The total should reflect the cumulative weeks, months, or years required, assuming continuous progress under adequate instruction. The estimate of value for the length of training period should equal the total point value for A + B + C.

factors often used are "Mental Effort," "Skill," "Physical Effort," "Responsibility," and "Working Conditions."

(4) The degrees or levels of factors should be defined as objectively as possible by eliminating such relative terms as "rarely," "usual," "normal," "fair," "good," "frequent," and the like.

(5) Within the limits of human fallibility, the same degree of the same factor occurring in different jobs should always be given equal weight.

(6) The point method used should assure that jobs common to the employer and the outside market should carry employer total point ratings which are generally consistent with outside market rate differentials for the same or similar job duties (not necessarily the same job titles).

(7) The method selected and its related procedures should provide for valid, practical checks of results at each successive stage of the process, the check-points to be so arranged as to extend the basis of comparison to increasingly larger groups of positions and broader, pooled judgments.

Explanation of Exhibits. The exhibits are included for purposes of illustration only. They are not intended to represent ideal or suggested approaches to job analysis, job description, or job rating methods for any individual company's use. They have been developed by the company or companies using them and have been found satisfactory. There is no doubt, however, that they will be subject to further improvement from time to time in order to meet changed circumstances or as new ideas are introduced.

Exhibit III is a sample "Hourly Job Specification," and Exhibit IV is a sample "Salaried Job Specification." Perhaps the first thing to be noted is the printed reservation with respect to the purposes for which these completed specifications are to be used, namely: *This job description is not a duty list. It outlines only the general character of the work for comparison with other jobs to determine their relative ratings.* This warning prevents any impression that the activities described *limit* the duties that the incumbents may be called upon to do. It also establishes the fact that specifications for purposes of recruitment, selection, training, performance appraisal, merit rating, and the like, may be included on other special forms to be used for those different purposes.

On the reverse side of the forms, various factor headings and subheadings are inserted. Entries under such headings must be fully described in standardized terminology in a Job Analyst's Manual to assure that similar phrases are used to describe comparable abilities, activities, responsibilities, or conditions.

In the Hourly Job Specification, Exhibit III, the "Class," in this instance, 73, indicates that the job was placed in this class even though it was rated at 72. The scheme calls for jobs

EXHIBIT III A

THIS JOB DESCRIPTION IS NOT A DUTY LIST. IT OUTLINES ONLY THE GENERAL CHARACTER OF THE WORK FOR COMPARISON WITH OTHER JOBS TO DETERMINE THEIR RELATIVE RATINGS.

DATE ____________

HOURLY JOB SPECIFICATION

DEP'T Refinery — DIVISION Services — LOCATION Stores-Tools - 6886, Various Tools Locations

DESCRIPTION OF DUTIES

Under general supervision of Foreman is engaged in: issuing, receiving, inspecting and/or laying out tools, tool kits, protective clothing, etc.; and in handling laundry details where applicable. Exercises work guidance over 1-3 helpers as assigned.

Receives oral, written and phone orders from Foreman as necessary, but otherwise works in accordance with established practices. Works at permanent tool houses, or at temporary or portable tools locations as assigned.

Issues and exchanges tools, tool kits, protective clothing, etc., upon receipt of appropriate authorized tool replacement or various other purposes, checking against short list and adhering to established practices and procedures. Issues electric or other tools in accordance with special regulations. Checks off returned items and returns order to employee upon receipt of all items issued; where items were issued from another tools location, cancels by phone. Inspects condition and/or tests items before issuance and upon receipt; lubricates, makes minor repairs or replacements, etc., where applicable and sets aside non-repairable, damaged or worn items for disposition by others. Orders items as needed through Leaderman. Assembles items for delivery to other tool houses, job sites, portable units, etc. Prepares individual layouts as required.

Issues and exchanges wiping towels, and where applicable handles issuance and receipt of clothing and other matters related to laundry service, all in accordance with standard procedures; signs invoices, reports shortages, etc.

Takes and reports daily inventories of designated items; prepares and maintains short list and other activities. As required, on other than week-day day work may drive truck in connection with tools activities and may infrequently issue stores items from adjacent stores locations. May order stores materials as requested relative to near-by portable stores units. Observes security requirements at specific locations, locking toolhouse or skids, sealing designated lockers, etc., at end of working day. Maintains cleanliness of tools location and keeps tools in orderly condition. Exercises work guidance over 1-3 helpers as assigned.

99-5203-2 12/54

SPECIFICATION NUMBER	PAYROLL TITLE	ALTERNATE TITLE	☐ DAY ☐ SHIFT ☐	CLASS
12-037R	Toolhouseman			73

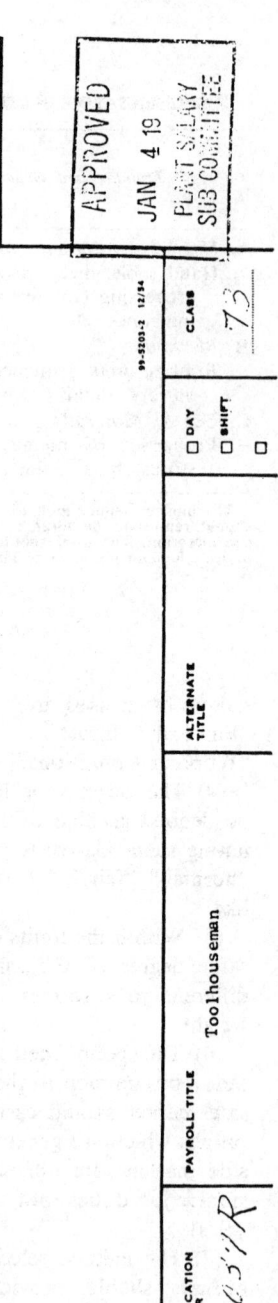

APPROVED
JAN 4 19
PLANT SALARY
SUB COMMITTEE

Exhibit III B

(Reverse of Exhibit III A)

MENTAL EFFORT	SKILL	PHYSICAL EFFORT	RESPONSIBILITY	WORKING CONDITIONS
EDUCATIONAL REQUIREMENTS OR EQUIVALENT Grade 8	EXPERIENCE REQUIRED TO START ON JOB Good knowledge of various tools group routines and of stocks carried in tools locations; use and condition of tools; knowledge of tools inspection procedures. PREVIOUS TIME TO ACQUIRE & WHERE 1 - 2 years in lower graded jobs in tools group. KNOWLEDGE ACQUIRED ON JOB AND TIME TO ACQUIRE 1 Month	ACTIVITY Standing, walking hauling, lifting; using hand tools. SPECIAL PHYSICAL REQUIREMENTS None	MEN Work guidance over 1-3 helpers as assigned. MATERIALS Care in handling laundry and wiping towel details EQUIPMENT Proper issuing, receiving, inspecting, storing and handling of tools; keeping tool house and stocks in order; setting aside defective tools for repair or scrapping. MARKETS None MONEY None METHODS Execution of established methods. RECORDS Preparation and maintenance of complete and accurate records.	PLACE Indoors; outdoors at portable units SURROUNDINGS Average and orderly; occasionally dirty and noisy. Occasional fumes; drafty in winter at certain locations. HAZARDS Cuts, falls, strains. HOURS 7:30-4:00 PM

SPECIAL REMARKS:

99-5203-2 REVERSE

EXHIBIT IV A

DAM

Name(s) Various

SALARIED JOB SPECIFICATION

Date
Rev.

Gr. 10 No. 231

Position Ledgerman Dep't. Accounting Div. Marketing

Sec., Loc., etc. 1442 DPC Accounts Rec. Title Immed. Supervisor: Supervisor (J. F. Murphy)

Under general supervision: maintains mechanically-tabulated accounts receivable records for wholesale, dealer, corporation and local government accounts; processes remittances, makes adjustments, releases statements and handles certain contacts with customers.

1-Processes daily remittances: pulls related charge cards from appropriate ledger trays; calculates discounts as applicable, referring doubtful discount cases to credit group and preparing debit memos as necessary; ascertains that remittances and related charges balance, including checking for discounts taken before deducting taxes, presence of credit memos, journals, etc., as indicated, and verifying pricing or extensions with appropriate persons; arranges to secure necessary explanations from customers of remittances failing to tie-in; prepares daily ledger control listings, posting individual remittances for which no corresponding charge cards are present, and ascertains that cash is in balance; is authorized to adjust differences under one dollar. As applicable, similarly maintains related notes receivable, escrow credit, etc., accounts. Receivable accounts are characterized by numerous transactions, large balances, varying credit and discount terms, and frequently involve several different delivery locations carrying different account numbers for same account which may be active in several different regions.

2-Handles adjustments to accounts: investigates discrepancies in detail, referring to various source records and contacting appropriate persons to secure explanations; prepares debit and credit journals, voucher requests, etc. to adjust accounts for errors, transfer accounts to suspense, return over-payments to customers, record bad debts and returned goods, make intra-ledger payment transfers, etc. Prepares statements and transfer accounts to notes or other miscellaneous accounts receivable.

3-Performs related duties: releases monthly statements to customers, pulling and developing statements carrying large credit balances for which charges are not present, statements to night delivery accounts, and other obviously unsuitable statements; periodically reviews outstanding charge cards to ascertain that charge belongs to the Region, is being carried in proper ledger, does not exceed specified credit limits, etc., and assembles information incidental to preparation of "switch" journals; handles routine correspondence with accounting offices of other regions concerning unidentifiable charges or remittances; answers customer telephone or correspondence inquiries relative to details of their accounts; prepares request forms for tab group to prepare new master cards for accounts; prepares special statements of accounts to accompany collection letters; prepares various regular and special reports relative to accounts handled; keeps credit and other interested persons informed of remittances received, over-collections on equipment accounts, changes in names and addresses, and other pertinent information, etc.

4- As assigned, participates in performing duties of other incumbents of this position during peak periods and absences, and may infrequently participate in performing duties of Sp. Ledgerman.

This job description is not a duty list. It outlines only the general character of the work for comparison with other jobs to determine their relative ratings.

Exhibit IV B

(Reverse of Exhibit IV A)

MENTAL EFFORT

Educational Requirements & General Knowledge:

High School 4

SKILL

Specific Knowledge to Start

General knowledge of regional sales accounting methods and procedures.

Where Acquired & Time to Acquire

2 years' experience in various lower-level sales accounting positions.

Knowledge Acquired on Job & Time for Minimum Proficiency

Knowledge of procedures relative to the processing of remittances, handling adjustments and performing related duties in connection with mechanically-tabulated accounts receivable records; familiarity with accounts handled, special terms applicable, etc.
3-4 months.

PHYSICAL EFFORT Sitting; some standing and walking

RESPONSIBILITY

Men None

Materials Using office supplies

Equipment Operating office equipment

Markets Telephone and correspondence contacts with customers relative to details of their accounts.

Money None

Methods Selecting and executing clerical methods.

Records Securing, transcribing, verifying and filing accounts receivable records.

WORKING CONDITIONS Reg. Working Hours 8:30-5:00, 5 days (38-3/4 hrs.)

Surroundings, Hazards, etc. Normal office conditions.

REMARKS

99-5203 (Rev.)

EXHIBIT V

PLANT JOBS—RATINGS AND TOTAL POINTS

Title	ME	SK	PE	WC	R	Total
Plant Janitor	3	4	30	8	4	49
Laborer	3	3	37	9	3	55
Drum Handler	5	5	35	8	4	57
Drum Filler	8	9	28	7	9	61
Truck Washer & Greaser	7	9	30	9	8	63
Boilermaker Helper	7	11	32	10	7	67
Furnace Cleaner	4	7	39	13	8	71
#1 Toolhouseman	15	16	22	6	13	72
Storekeeper	17	18	21	6	13	75
2nd Cl. Pipefitter	13	18	27	10	11	79
Pipecoverer	14	19	28	9	12	82
Spray Painter	11	19	31	12	12	85
Safety and Fire Insp.	19	17	23	9	19	87
1st Cl. Carpenter	20	24	25	8	14	91
1st Cl. Electrician	26	25	21	8	17	97
Toolmaker	23	32	21	6	17	99
Patternmaker	26	32	22	6	17	103

within a three-point interval to be placed at the midpoint of the interval. A job rated at 74 would also have been placed in Class 73. (The job illustrated was rated in a "Factor Comparison" plan, using joint values of the order of magnitude shown in Exhibit V.) Also in this scheme, salaried positions were assigned to "Grades" but the point ranges varied geometrically as the grade numbers progress upward from the lowest to highest. (Numbers of grades or classes, and their point assignments, will vary for different companies.)

Exhibits V and VI are classic examples, respectively, of an original hourly rated key job list and of an original weekly salaried key job list. In both cases, the jobs are shown ranked in terms of total points assigned, which are then translated into either hourly or weekly pay rates.

On the basis of these key job lists, all other jobs to be evaluated were rated for each factor and total factor points to establish complete Job Comparison Schedules. In this process, additional factor intervals were established which could be used in evaluating future new or changed jobs. (For a step-by-step description of this process, see references [5] and [6].) These exhibits indicate how the total numbers of job rating points (which represented actual hourly or weekly rates) were divided among the several factors.

In Factor Comparison installations, no consideration is given to maximum percentages of

EXHIBIT VI

OFFICE JOBS—RATINGS AND TOTAL POINTS

Grade	Title	ME	SK	PE	WC	R	Total
2	Messenger	9	7	14	3	5	38
3	Office Trainee	10	8	14	3	7	42
4	Addressograph-Graphotype Oper.	12	11	13	3	8	47
5	Keypunch Operator	15	13	13	3	8	52
5	Typist	16	14	13	3	7	53
6	Jr. Stenographer	17	16	12	3	10	58
6	Telephone Operator	16	14	13	4	9	56
7	Stenographer	19	17	12	3	12	63
7	Offset Press Operator	18	18	14	4	12	66
7	Tab Equipment Operator	18	18	13	3	14	66
8	Sr. Stenographer	22	20	12	3	15	72
8	Accounts Payable Clerk	24	18	11	3	18	74
9	Payroll Clerk	24	21	11	3	21	80
9	Sr. Tab Equipment Oper.	24	20	13	3	18	78
9	Accounting Clerk	28	20	11	3	19	81
10	Accounts Receivable Clerk	28	22	11	3	22	86
10	Industrial Nurse	28	20	13	6	19	86
11	Jr. Accountant	38	24	11	3	22	98
12	Time Study Engineer	38	28	11	4	22	103
13	Traffic Rate Clerk	42	37	11	3	28	121
14	Senior Accountant	46	41	11	3	31	132
15	Tax Accountant	50	45	11	3	34	143

factor or sub-factor points to total points. In very nearly all other point systems, a maximum number of total points is allowable and maximum percentages of factor and sub-factor points total are assigned. Exhibit VII shows four different successful point systems having different allowable point totals and different factor and sub-factor ratios to total points. If job evaluation were truly "scientific," only one of these approaches or perhaps none of them would be "right." Yet from a pragmatic viewpoint, each of these several approaches has served its user or users with satisfactory results. Because the factor comparison system is "open end," it can avoid the limitations of preset maximum point plans.

Further Development. There is still one area in which much new work must be done to undo a serious mistake that goes back to the quite early days of "Position Classification, Grading and Standardization." Until quite recently, too much weight has been placed on the number of employees supervised or directed through subordinate supervisors, especially as compared to the weight given to the part played by lone professional and scientific workers whose responsibility lies mostly in the areas of technology improvements, creativity, and individual imagination. Many management position evaluation plans have corrected this former failing. In an age of increasingly technical accomplishment we cannot afford to have valuable professional workers enticed away from their important work by inequitably disproportionate salaries awarded largely on the basis of responsibility for large numbers of subordinates.

Finally, it must be recognized that there is nothing permanent to job content, labor-market job differentials, and methods of determin-

EXHIBIT VII

COMPARISON OF FOUR POINT SYSTEMS IN SUCCESSFUL USE

Plan A	Plan B	Plan C	Plan D
Skill Education 70 (14%) Experience 110 (22%) Initiative & ingenuity 70 (14%) Total permitted 250 (50%)	Skill Mentality 100 (12½%) Skill 400 (50%) Total permitted 500 (62½%)	Skill Education 100 (18½%) Experience 100 (18½%) Aptitude 125 (28½%) Total permitted 325 (60½%)	Skill Skill 100 (10%) Dexterity 50 (5%) Accuracy 80 (8%) Education or mental development 100 (10%) Experience & training 120 (12%) Total permitted 450 (45%)
Effort Physical 50 (10%) Mental - visual 25 (5%) Total permitted 75 (15)	Effort Mental 50 (6¼%) Physical 50 (6¼%) Total permitted 100 (12½%)	Effort Physical 40 (7½%) Mental 40 (7½%) Visual 40 (7½%) Total permitted 120 (22½%)	Effort Mental 100 (10%) Physical 60 (6%) Total permitted 160 (16%)
Responsibility Equipment 25 (5%) Material or product 25 (5%) Safety of others 25 (5%) Total permitted 100 (20%)	Responsibility Responsibility 100 (12½%)	Responsibility Safety of others 25 (4½%) For product 25 (4½%) For equipment 25 (4½%) Total permitted 75 (13½%)	Responsibility Safety of others 50 (5%) Supervision 50 (5%) Materials 90 (9%) Machinery & equipment 50 (5%) Total permitted 240 (24%)
Job Conditions Working conditions 50 (10%) Hazards 25 (5%) Total permitted 75 (15%)	Job Conditions Working Conds. 100 (12½%)	Job Conditions Unusual features 20 (3½%)	Job Conditions Hazards 50 (5%) Surroundings 40 (4%) Connecting expense 10 (1%) Fatigue 50 (5%) Total permitted 150 (15%)
ALL 500 (100%)	ALL 800 (100%)	ALL 500 (100%)	ALL 1,000 (100%)

ing equitable wage and salary rates—except change. Managements must remain alert to the possibility or actuality of change, and, as necessary, revise the processes used in job evaluation to keep up to date with improved methods and new socio-economic conditions that affect sound wage and salary administration.

SAMUEL L. H. BURK, formerly Vice President, Sherwood, Smith and Associates, Inc., Philadelphia, Pennsylvania, and (for third edition) EUGENE J. BENGE, Management Consultant, Boca Raton, Florida

Information References

Benge, E. J., Burk, S. L. H., and Hay, E. N., "Manual of Job Evaluation," New York, Harper, 1941.

Britz, Matthew L., "Job Evaluation," in Heyel Carl, ed., "Handbook of Modern Office Management and Administrative Services," New York, McGraw-Hill, 1972.

McCormick, Ernest J., "Job Analysis," New York, AMACOM Div., American Management Associations, 1979.

Miner, Mary Green, "Job Evaluation Policies and Procedures," Washington, D.C., Bureau of National Affairs, 1976.

Roark, Robin, "Salary Administration," in Heyel, Carl, ed.) "Handbook of Modern Office Management and Administrative Services," New York, McGraw-Hill, 1972.

Rock, Milton L., "Handbook of Wage and Salary Administration," New York, McGraw-Hill, 1972.

References Cited

[1] Hay, E.N., "The Guide Chart-Profile Method of Job-Man Evaluation," *Management Report No. 1,* "Making the Most of Our Human Resources," New York, American Management Associations, 1957.

[2] Britz, Matthew L., as above.

[3] Roark, Robin, as above.

[4] Adapted, with slight simplification, from the Armstrong Cork Company Rating Guide.

[5] Ch. XII of Dooher, M.J. and Marquis, V., "The AMA Handbook of Wage and Salary Administration," New York, American Management Associations, 1950.

[6] Benge, as above.

Cross Reference: *Performance Rating (Merit Rating)*

K

KEYNES, JOHN MAYNARD

John Maynard Keynes (1883–1946), English economist and monetary expert served in the India Office of the British civil service (1906–1908), where he was concerned with the problems of Indian currency. In 1919 he was appointed principal British Treasury representative at the peace conference ending World War I. He resigned in protest over what he termed the inequitable and uneconomic provisions of the Versailles Treaty. Keynes stated his views in his book, "The Economic Consequences of the Peace" (1919), which won him world fame. In 1929 he signaled his departure from the classical concepts of a free economy by endorsing government spending on public works to promote employment. In the worldwide depression of the 1930s, Keynes's theories influenced governments in several nations to adopt spending programs, as exemplified by President Roosevelt's New Deal, designed to maintain a high level of national income. His concepts of large-scale government planning are set forth in his major work, "The General Theory of Employment, Interest, and Money" (1936). (For a discussion of Keynesian economics see the section, *Keynesian Economics,* in the entry, ECONOMICS.)

Cross References: *Economics; Inflation.*

KIMBALL, D.S.

Dexter Simpson Kimball (1865–1952), first dean of the unified College of Engineering, Cornell University (1920–36), Acting President, Cornell (1918 and 1929–30), and before that, professor of machine design and construction at Cornell, established at Cornell (1904) the first course in any American university to teach the principles of management. While there had been books and lectures on shop systems, costs, etc., this was the first effort to inform engineering students of the economic basis of modern production, and to give full attention to the pioneering work by FREDERICK W. TAYLOR. (Four years later, in 1908, the new Harvard School of Business Administration hesitated for some time before deciding to adopt the Taylor system as the basis of its teaching of shop management.) Kimball's book, which grew out of his lectures at Cornell, "Principles of Industrial Organization," 1913 (McGraw-Hill, New York) long remained a standard textbook. In 1941 he was Chairman, Tools and Equipment group, Priorities Division, Office of Production Management, Washington. His books include, in addition to the text mentioned, "Elements of Cost Finding," 1914 (Alexander Hamilton Institute, New York); "Plant Management," 1919 (Alexander Hamilton); "Industrial Economics," 1929 (McGraw-Hill, New York); and "I Remember," 1953, (McGraw-Hill).

Information References

Urwick, L., "The Golden Book of Management," edited for the International Committee of Scientific Management (CIOS), London, Newman Neame, Limited, 1956.

KNOEPPEL, C.E.

Charles Edward Knoeppel (1881–1936) was one of the exponents of the Taylor system of SCIENTIFIC MANAGEMENT in the years most immediately following the active period of Taylor and Gantt, adding several original contributions to the principles and methods already established. "By 1907 he had done much work in cost accounting, including development of standard costs in the foundry industry and elsewhere. By 1908 he had developed methods of factory organization and administration based on Taylor's system. He is credited . . . with probably the earliest use of the cross-over 'break-even' chart now a standard tool of management. He became the original exponent of 'profit engineering,' and coined the name 'profitgraph' as more descriptive of the purpose of the break even chart" [1]. Through his many publications, lucidly written and popular, Knoeppel focused attention on the science of management at the crucial time in the struggle for its acceptance by American industry. He played an important part in the Committee on Waste in Industry, organized under Herbert Hoover by the Federated Engineering Societies (1920–21), and was the author of the chapter in the Committee's report entitled "Purchasing and Sales Policies." Selected publications include: "Maximum Production in Machine Shop and Foundry," 1911 (Engineering Magazine Co., New York); "Installing Efficiency Methods," 1915 (same publisher); "Industrial Preparedness," 1916 (same publisher); "Organization and Administration," 1917 (Industrial Extension Institute, New York); "Graphic Production Control," 1920 (Engineering Magazine Co.); "Profit Engineering—Applied Economics in Making Business Profitable" 1933 (McGraw-Hill, New York); and "Managing for Profit," 1937, with E. G. Seybold, 1937 (McGraw-Hill).

Information References

Urwick, L., "The Golden Book of Management," edited for the International Committee of Scientific Management (CIOS), 1956, Newman Neame Limited, London.

L

LABOR ARBITRATION

Labor Arbitration is now a universally accepted method for resolving disputes between labor and management over interpretation and application of their collective bargaining agreements. Today, nearly 94% of all such agreements contain provisions, called arbitration clauses, by which the parties agree to resolve grievances through impartial machinery after having tried unsuccessfully to dispose of them by direct negotiation. Exact figures are lacking as to the total number of arbitration cases that take place every year, but a conservative estimate, based on reports of the American Arbitration Association, the Federal Mediation and Conciliation Service, and other agencies, was 60,000 cases in 1979 (as compared to an estimated 25,000 cases in 1962). The American Arbitration Association alone handled 16,580 labor arbitrations in 1979, with 11,174 in the private sector and 5,406 in the public sector [1].

Definition. Labor-management arbitration is the reference of a dispute by voluntary agreement to an impartial person for final and binding determination. It is basically different from other methods of dispute settlement, such as *mediation, conciliation* and *fact-finding.* (See MEDIATION.) The chief difference is that an arbitrator hears evidence and arguments from both parties and renders a decision representing his (her) judgment of the rights of parties under their collective bargaining agreement, or, occasionally, of the terms of the agreement, while the mediator's chief function is to assist both sides in coming to a compromise solution.

History. While arbitration in trade matters has many centuries of activity, historians of the labor movement have discovered no reference to labor arbitration until 1829, when it was found in a union constitution. The word was not used in its modern sense until collective bargaining became firmly established in American industrial life. During the entire half century between 1865 and 1914, according to the United States Department of Labor, there were only 54 arbitration cases officially on record [2].

The great railroad strikes in the latter part of the nineteenth century gave rise to legislation providing for arbitration, which eventually resulted in the compulsory arbitration of our present Railroad Adjustment Boards. At the turn of the century an arbitration agreement (1901) was entered into by the American Newspaper Publishers Association and the International Typographical Union, which remained in effect for over fifty years. The strikes in the needle trades in 1910 ended in the Hart-Schaffner and Marx Agreement in Chicago and the "Protocol of Peace" in New York. Both agreements provided for permanent arbitrators (called "impartial umpires"), and this system still remains in effect. The "Protocol of Peace" was negotiated largely through the efforts of Louis L. Brandeis who later became a Justice of the Supreme Court of the United States. Brandeis served as arbitrator of disputes for four years and established a record which inspired social reformers, labor leaders and government officials to adapt that experience to other industries. Like the "Protocol of Peace," the Hart-Schaffner and Marx agreement was soon extended to other cities.

The total volume of actual arbitration cases was nevertheless small in these early days. The period of rapid increase began with the First World War when organized labor was given official recognition by the United States Government. Unions were relatively weak, but representatives of labor organizations were appointed to Governmental boards, and the Wilson administration officially declared it to be in the public interest to resolve disputes by arbitration rather than by work stoppages. In 1918 the Secretary of Labor established the War Labor Conference Board which consisted of five representatives of the American Federation of Labor, five from the National Industrial Conference Board (an employers' organization, now named the Conference Board), and two cochairmen, former President Taft and Frank P. Walsh, who represented the public.

But the progress of arbitration was not uninterrupted. The post-war depression during the 1920s took its toll of the labor movement. Although the concept of arbitration still held the imagination of civic and political leaders, the opportunities for invoking arbitration procedures declined with the return in many areas to nonunion working conditions. Moreover, many union leaders whose experience with arbitration was slight at best were reluctant to risk wage cuts at the hands of men they regarded as "outsiders."

It was during the 1930s that collective bargaining, and therefore grievance arbitration, achieved a firm foundation. The National Labor Relations Act of 1935 affirmed labor's right to organize for collective bargaining, which was now not only *permitted*, but *advocated* as national policy. Employers were no longer permitted to use their superior economic power to frustrate the rights of employees to self-organization. By the time the United States entered the Second World War, an estimated ten million industrial workers were enrolled in labor unions.

Again, as during the First World War, there was a no-strike pledge by labor, and machinery was established for impartial resolution of disputes which in fact was a form of compulsory arbitration. Controversies were brought to the National War Labor Board and to its regional boards, all established on a tripartite basis: representative of labor, management, and the public. Over 20,000 decisions were rendered before the Board completed its work. By the time the war ended, thousands of employer and union representatives had acquired direct experience with arbitration. Furthermore, a new profession had been created, as hundreds of men had served the war effort as full-time, paid adjudicators of labor-management disputes. Companies and unions which may have been fearful of decisions rendered by "outsiders" now had confidence that the professional arbitrator had valuable insight into the problems of labor-management arbitration.

Modern Practice. While the war was in progress, no new contract terms could be put into effect in basic industries without the approval of the War Labor Board, and the Board required as a condition for approval that contracts contain arbitration clauses. When the war ended, however, and emergency restrictions were relaxed, the parties chose to continue arbitration on a voluntary basis. A conference of labor and management representatives was convened by President Truman in 1945 for the purpose of reaching an understanding on labor-management relations during the period of reconversion from a war economy. This conference reached complete agreement with respect to arbitration. It was recommended to all that "unsettled grievances or disputes involving the interpretation or application of the agreement" be finally determined by "an impartial chairman, umpire, arbitrator, or board" [3].

The systems of arbitration that have evolved since World War II have generally been of two kinds: *permanent* and *ad hoc*.

The *permanent arbitrator* is named in the contract as the final judge of all matters that may be properly brought before him. His term of office may be a few years or the life of the contract. This type of machinery is usually established by the large multi-plant corporations which deal with equally powerful international unions, or where a great deal of small industry is concentrated in a limited geographical area. The chief advantage of a permanent arbitrator lies in the fact that he can become intimately acquainted with all the details and problems that arise in the collective bargaining relationship. Moreover, he must render decisions in accordance with precedents established by himself or his predecessors. The *ad hoc arbitrator,* on the other hand, is selected on a case-by-case basis. Here the parties may anticipate too few actual cases to justify establishing full-time arrangements with any one arbitrator. Although the parties may choose to select the same arbitrator again and again, they make no commitment to do so. Each call to service concerns a specific grievance or a group of grievances which confront the parties at the time.

The next most popular system, in addition to the permanent arbitrator and *ad hoc* systems, are the various types of rotating panels that have been negotiated, whereby a specific number of arbitrators are selected for the duration of an agreement and serve on particular cases on a rotating basis, by lot, by type of grievance, or by geographical location.

In its 1953 study, the Bureau of Labor Statistics found that 76% of all collective bargaining agreements provided for *ad hoc arbitrators* [4]. In a 1966 study, the Bureau of Labor Statistics showed that 85% call for the *ad hoc* method of selecting arbitrators [5]. Since that date the percentage of impartial chairmanships has slowly increased. *Ad hoc* procedures were most commonly found in the following large industries: chemicals, petroleum and coal products, lumber and timber basic products, furniture and finished wood products, fabricated metal products, electrical machinery, mining, crude petroleum and natural gas production, communications, electric and gas utilities, and construction. Permanent arbitration machinery was most prevalent in apparel, automobiles and farm equipment, basic steel and aluminum, food and kindred products, rubber, hotels and restaurants, and services.

Selection of Arbitrators. Arbitrators are selected in a variety of ways. The American Arbitration Association is written into many collective bargaining agreements as the appointing agency. The Association and the Federal Mediation and Conciliation Service will, however, submit panels of arbitrators to both sides and invite the parties to make a mutual choice from such lists. Other contracts may provide for direct appointment of arbitrators in each case by the parties themselves or by a judge, mayor, or governor. State agencies vary with regard to appointment of arbitrators, and some provide arbitration by salaried staff members.

Although no Government license is required for one to serve as a labor-management arbitrator, the profession is not as open to all as it might seem. The most important restricting influence is the preference of the parties. Thousands of individuals have served from time to time, but there are probably no more than 500 who earn a substantial portion of their living as grievance arbitrators. Parties establish the kind of grievance machinery and arbitration that suits them best, and they call upon the arbitrators whose work is known to them and whose method of operation conforms to their needs. Furthermore, although collective bargaining agreements differ in many respects, they are all fashioned within a general framework of standard practices.

Companies and unions understandably want their contracts interpreted by those who are familiar with usages and traditions of the field. This, they believe, leads to predictable decisions which in a sense carry out the original intent of the parties.

The arbitration profession, therefore, is primarily made up of educators and labor attorneys. Knowledgeability in industrial relations, economics, law, or industrial engineering is clearly an asset. Moreover, educators, because of their academic environment, and attorneys, unless they have become identified solely as "union" or "management" attorneys, are viewed by the parties as being in a neutral position.

Arbitrated Issues. Most arbitration clauses today limit the jurisdiction of the arbitrator to disputes over "interpretation and application" of the contract. The arbitrator is usually specifically barred from "adding to or changing the terms of the agreement." Despite the limitation, however, the arbitrator's jurisdiction appears to have been broadened by recent Supreme Court decisions which widen aspects of the collective bargaining relations unless clearly restricted by specific contractual language.

The most important single issue referred to arbitrators involves discharge and lesser forms of disciplinary action, such as suspensions or reprimands. In view of the increasing value of an employee's job—now including vacations, holidays, medical benefits, pension rights, etc.—discharge cases are particularly hard-fought.

A second frequent issue in arbitration grows out of the dynamic American economy where products and methods of manufacture undergo constant change. The effect of these continual changes on job security, rates of pay, work assignments, incentive pay rates, and individual job changes produces numerous grievances.

The third most frequent issue brought to arbitration involves application of seniority rules. In negotiating collective bargaining agreements, labor usually favors the strictest application of seniority in such matters as promotion and retention of jobs during periods of reduction in force. Employers, on the other hand, very strongly favor ability as the chief criterion for such decision. An accommodation is frequently reached by a contractual formula requiring that both seniority and ability be taken into consideration. Whether a particular employee has the requisite ability to assert his seniority is a matter often left for the determination of the arbitrator.

With much less frequency, a wide variety of other issues are brought to arbitration, such as those involving premium pay, overtime, subcontracting, vacations, holidays, pension and welfare plans, management rights, union security, and health and safety issues related to the work environment.

While over 95% of the arbitration in the United States is grievance arbitration—that is, a determination of disputes over interpretation or application of existing contracts, sometimes called "arbitration of rights"—there is also a small practice of new contract arbitration, called "arbitration of interests." Although strikes which seriously inconvenience the public inevitably give rise to proposals that arbitration be made compulsory or that new contract terms be submitted voluntarily to arbitration, very little support of this practice has been found within the labor-management community. Such arbitration is often regarded as inconsistent with the obligation of the parties to make their own bargains. Furthermore, the consequences of a harsh or unworkable decision would be much more serious than in the case of a grievance arbitration.

Nevertheless, the practice of arbitration of new contract terms does exist in isolated areas. Chief among them is the public utility field. One reason for the incidence of wage and contract term arbitration here is that strikes would work an immediate hardship on the public and would lead to more government controls. Furthermore, rates of public utilities are governed by public agencies. Negotiators often believe that public boards would approve price increases based on wage improvements more readily when those increases were directed by impartial arbitrators than when they result from the direct negotiation of the parties.

Other areas where arbitration of wages has been more frequent than elsewhere are the textile industry, some segments of the retail industry, and certain service industries where neither labor nor management would find themselves able to recover fully from a strike.

Arbitration and the Law. Arbitration today is conducted within the framework of the law. The legal basis for the enforcement of an arbitration award and an arbitration agreement was originally dependent on individual state laws. As late as 1947 less than one-third of the states would enforce an agreement to arbitrate future disputes. Section 301 of the Labor-Management Relations Act (1947) provided, however, that either party might sue for violation of contracts, and relying on this provision, the U. S. Supreme Court ruled in the Lincoln Mills case that either side might sue for performance of the arbitration clause of the contract [6]. Later decisions by the Supreme Court (Enterprise Wheel and Car Corp., Warrior & Gulf Navigation Co., American Manufacturing Co.) affirmed the authority of the arbitrator to determine arbitrability questions unless the agreement clearly and unmistakably excludes an issue from arbitration. These decisions also indicate that the courts are not to consider the merits of cases or substitute their judgment for that of the arbitrator [7].

Recent developments in government employment indicate an increasing use of arbitration. Private arbitration is used in certain municipal transit systems, state-created bodies such as universities and authorities, and Federal missile and construction projects. A trend towards "advisory" arbitration (wherein the award may be rejected by either party) is seen in certain city, state, and Federal departments.

Beginning in the middle 1960s, a tremendous increase occurred in collective bargaining by public employees. By 1970, thirty-three states had passed some form of law authorizing the right of public employees to engage in collective bargaining with units of states, cities, or counties as employers. With the passage of these laws there has been a tremendous increase in arbitration in the public sector. In 1979, the AAA administered over 5,000 cases involving employment at the state, county, and city level, primarily in the field of public education.

In addition, certain states have passed compulsory arbitration laws for new contracts for certain segments of public employment. By 1979, 30 states, three counties, six municipalities, and the District of Columbia had provided for compulsory arbitration as the means of last resort for resolving disputes over the terms and conditions of new contracts for public employees [8]. Further, a number of states have passed laws providing for fact-finding with recommendations, or advisory arbitration. While recommendations or advisory arbitration awards are not binding, they are nevertheless accepted almost universally by the parties in dispute.

On the Federal level, the Kennedy Order No. 10988 was replaced by the Executive Order No. 11491 (amended in 1975). This order set up a United States Federal Service Impasse Panel for impasse settlement, and has given considerable importance to grievance arbitration in the Federal public sector.

Within the United States there is also provision for compulsory arbitration for private industry in some Federal and state laws. The 1934 amendments to the Railway Labor Act provide for compulsory arbitration features. These Railroad Boards of Adjustment have neutral referees who decide the grievance issues, which are not resolved by representatives of the railroads and unions involved. The Act also provides for the appointment of Emergency Boards in new contract situations, but the opinions of these Boards are merely advisory.

Certain state statutes provide for complete compulsory arbitration, usually in industries involving health and general welfare. The statutes usually specify the industry involved, among which are power, gas, electric and water utilities, transportation, and hospitals.

This aspect of compulsory arbitration in the United States is in complete contrast to arbitration in many foreign countries, where the size of the country, the nature and size of the working force, and the percentage of organization of employees are important factors. Even more important is the extent of government ownership, nationalization, and control of industry.

Potentials. Some students of labor-management relations maintain that public opinion and government pressures in strike situations will influence parties to greater use of voluntary arbitration in new contract or wage matters in basic industries or in those affecting the general welfare. Others maintain that the only solution to major strikes in American industry is a Federal law compelling arbitration. This position is frequently advanced in the face of crises in particular situations, even by adherents who object vigorously under more tranquil circumstances to Government fixing of wages and its natural complement, price control.

The great reduction in wildcat strikes since the early 1940s, the presence of the arbitration clause in virtually all of the collective bargaining agreements, and the steady increase in arbitration cases, would indicate that arbitration has become a universally accepted method of dispute settlement. There is general recognition of its contribution to industrial peace, and all educational levels have reserved a place in the curriculum for consideration of labor arbitration. The extensive educational programs of the American Arbitration Association, and the concentration of management and labor upon arbitration education in their training programs, appear to assure its continued usage in the next decade.

JOSEPH S. MURPHY, Vice President, ret., American Arbitration Association, New York, New York

Information References

Coulson, Robert, "Labor Arbitration: What You Need to Know," 3rd ed., New York, American Arbitration Association, 1981.

Elkouri, Frank and Asper, Edna, "How Arbitration Works," 3rd ed., Washington, Bureau of National Affairs, 1973.

Prasow, Paul and Peters, Edward, "Arbitration and Collective Bargaining," New York, McGraw-Hill, 1970.

Updegraff, Clarence M., "Arbitration and Labor Relations," 3rd ed. of "Arbitration of Labor Disputes," Washington, D.C., Bureau of National Affairs, Inc., 1970.

References Cited

[1] From the files of the American Arbitration Association.

[2] "Results of Arbitration Cases Involving Wages and Hours, 1865 to 1929," *Monthly Labor Review*, Nov., 1929.

[3] "The President's National Labor Management Conference, Nov. 5–30, 1945," United States Department of Labor, Division of Labor Standards, Bull. No. 77, 1946.

[4] "Arbitration Provisions in Collective Agreements, 1952," *Monthly Labor Review*, Mar., 1953.

[5] "Major Collective Bargaining Agreements—Arbitration Procedures," Bulletin No. 1425-6. June 1966, p. 36, United States Department of Labor, Bureau of Labor Statistics.

[6] Textile Workers Union of American vs. Lincoln Mills of Alabama, 353 U. S. 448 (1957).

[7] United Steelworkers vs. Enterprise Wheel & Car Corp., 363 U. S. 593 (1960); United Steelworkers vs. Warrior & Gulf Nav. Co., 363 U. S. 574 (1960); United Steelworkers vs. American Mfg. Co., 363 U. S. 564 (1960).

[8] Rehmus, Charles M., "Interest Arbitration: Portrait of a Process—Collective Negotiations in Public Employment." Fort Washington, Pa., Labor Relations Press, 1979.

Cross References: *Collective Bargaining; Labor Relations Legislation; Mediation.*

LABOR FORCE, EMPLOYMENT, AND EARNINGS

The STATISTICAL ABSTRACT OF THE UNITED STATES provides statistics dealing with the characteristics of the economically active segment of the population, the labor force; its distribution by occupation and industry affiliation; and the supply of, demand for, and conditions of labor.

The chief sources of these data are the Current Population Survey conducted by the U.S. Bureau of the Census; and the monthly *Employment and Earnings*, the *Monthly Labor Review*, the annual *Handbook of Labor Statistics*, and the periodic *Special Labor Force Reports*, published by the U.S. Bureau of Labor Statistics. Detailed data on the labor force are also available from the Census Bureau's decennial census of population.

Statistics are obtained by two methods: household interviews or questionnaires, and reports of establishment payroll records. Data based on households are obtained from a monthly sample survey of the population. The Current Population Survey (CPS) is used to gather data for the week including the 12th of the month, and provides current comprehensive data on the labor force. CPS provides information on the work status of the population without duplication since each person is classified as employed, unemployed, or not in the labor force. Employed persons holding more than one job are counted only once, according to the job at which they work the most hours during the survey week.

Monthly data from CPS are published by the Bureau of Labor Statistics (BLS) in *Employment and Earnings* and the related reports mentioned above. Data presented include national totals, by sex, race, and age, of the number of persons in the civilian labor force; the number employed, hours of work, and industry and occupational groups; and the number unemployed, reasons for, and duration of, unemployment.

In addition to monthly national data, CPS also produces annual estimates of employment and unemployment for each state and the 30 largest standard metropolitan statistical areas. These estimates are published by BLS in its annual *Geographic Profile of Employment and Unemployment.* More detailed geographic data (e.g., for counties and cities) are provided by the decennial population censuses.

Data based on establishment records are compiled by BLS and cooperating state agencies as part of an ongoing Current Employment Statistics Program. Data, gathered from a sample of employers who voluntarily complete mail questionnaires monthly, are supplemented by data from other government agencies and adjusted at intervals to data from government social insurance program reports. The estimates exclude proprietors of unincorporated firms, self-employed persons, private household workers, unpaid family workers, agricultural workers, and the Armed Forces. In March 1978, reporting establishments employed 11 million manufacturing workers (56% of the total manufacturing employment at the time), 11 million workers in nonmanufacturing industries (24% of the total in nonmanufacturing), and 10 million Federal, state and local government employees (68% of total government).

The establishment survey counts workers each time they appear on a payroll during the reference week (as with CPS, the week including the 12th of the month). Thus, unlike CPS, a person with two jobs is counted twice.

The establishment survey is designed to provide detailed industry information for the nation, states, and metropolitan areas on nonagricultural wage and salary employment, average weekly hours, average hourly and weekly earnings, and labor turnover. Establishment survey data are published in *Employment and Earnings* and *Monthly Labor Review,* cited above. Historical data, in geographic detail, are shown in BLS Bulletin No. 1370–13, *Employment and Earnings, States and Areas, 1939–78;* and in the *Handbook of Labor Statistics.*

Labor Force. According to CPS definitions, the total labor force comprises the Armed Forces and the civilian labor force, and the latter comprises all civilians classified according to the criteria below: Employed persons comprise (a) all civilians who, during the reference week, did any work for pay or profit (minimum of an hour's work) or worked 15 hours or more as unpaid workers in a family enterprise, and (b) all persons who were not working but who had jobs or businesses from which they were temporarily absent for noneconomic reasons (illness, bad weather, vacation, labor-management dispute, etc.). Unemployed persons comprise all civilians who had no employment during the reference week, who made specific efforts to find a job within the previous four weeks (such as applying directly to an employer, or to a public employment service, or checking with friends) and who were available for work during that week. Persons on layoff from a job or waiting to report to a new job within 30 days are also classified as unemployed. All other persons, 16 years old and over, are "not in the labor force." (See Exhibit I.)

Hours and Earnings. Average hourly earnings, based on establishment data, are gross earnings (i.e., earnings before payroll deductions) and include overtime premiums; they exclude irregular bonuses and value of payments in kind. Hours are those for which pay was received. Persons who worked 35 hours or more are classified as working full time; those working less than 35 hours are considered part-time workers.

EXHIBIT I

TRENDS IN THE LABOR FORCE: 1970 TO 1980

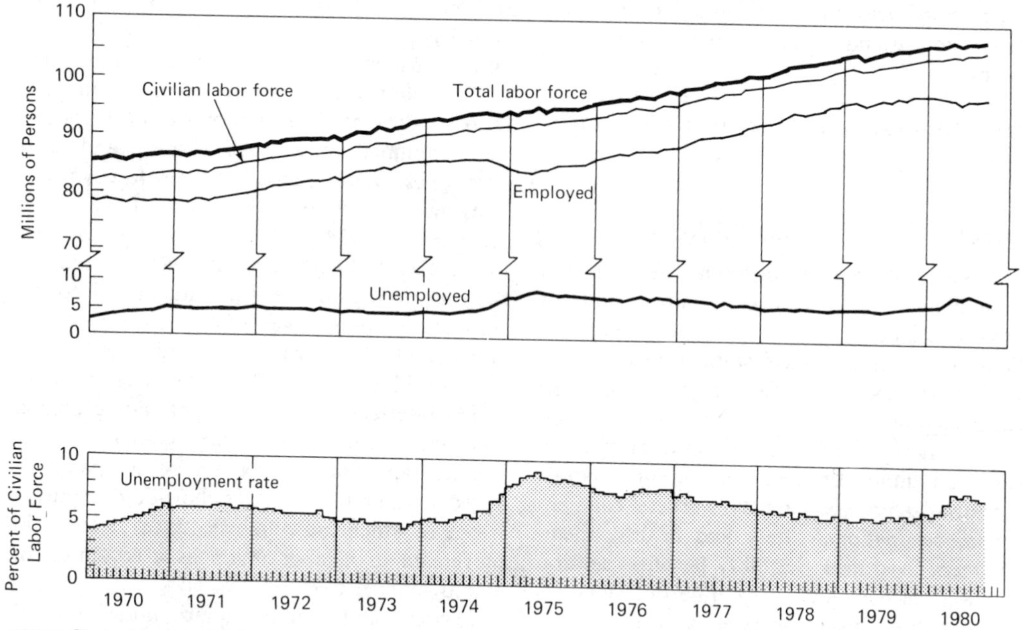

SOURCE: Chart prepared by U.S. Bureau of the Census.

Industrial and Occupational Groups. Establishments responding to the establishment survey are classified into industries on the basis of their principal product or activity (determined by annual sales volume) in accordance with the *Standard Industrial Classification* (SIC) *Manual,* Office of Management and Budget; 1972 is at this writing the latest issue.

Productivity. BLS publishes measures of productivity under two major programs which measure the relationship between production and one factor of input, labor time. The first program is concerned with measures relating to private business as a whole and its various subsectors; the second provides measures for selected specific industries and various functional areas of the Federal civilian government. Data for the first program are published quarterly in the BLS press releases, *Productivity and Costs: Private Business, Nonfarm Business,* and *Manufacturing Sectors,* and *Productivity and Costs: Nonfinancial Corporate Sector.* Data for the second program are published annually in the BLS Bulletin, *Productivity Indexes for Selected Industries.* Conceptual and background information concerning the Federal-sector measures appears in *Monthly Labor Review,* Nov. 1974. Detailed information on methods, limitation, and data sources for both programs appears in BLS *Handbook of Methods,* BLS Bulletin 1910 (1976), chapters 30 and 31.

Labor Turnover. Labor turnover is the gross movement of wage and salary workers into and out of employed status with respect to individual establishments. This movement, relating to a calendar month, is divided into two broad types: Accessions (new hires and rehires), and separations (quits, layoffs, and terminations). The data cover all workers, temporary or permanent, and full- or part-time.

Unions. Unions on which statistics are given include all affiliates of the AFL–CIO, all unaffiliated national unions, and all unaffiliated unions which are party to collective bargaining agreements with different employers in more than one state. The definition excludes unions whose activities are confined to a single locality or to a single employer. In addition, BLS accounts for all unions of Federal Government employees that have received exclusive recognition. Collective bargaining settlements data are available for unions of 1,000 members or more.

Work Stoppages. Work stoppages include all strikes and lockouts known to BLS and its cooperating agencies which last for at least one full day or shift and involve six or more workers. All stoppages, whether or not authorized by a union, legal or illegal, are counted. Excluded are work slowdowns and instances where employees report to work late, or leave early, to attend mass meetings or mass rallies.

Cross Reference: *Statistical Abstract of the United States.*

LABOR RELATIONS LEGISLATION

Labor Relations Legislation, Federal and state, includes within its scope both a body of protective labor laws and a body of labor relations laws. The protective statutes relate to the worker in the industrial environment, and cover such areas as factory inspection, child labor standards, restrictions on hours of employees, minimum wages, maximum hours, industrial safety and hazards, workers' compensation, occupational safety and health, unemployment insurance, disability benefits, pension and welfare benefits, voting time off, veteran's rights, anti-kickback remedies, anti-discrimination, old age and survivors insurance, employer liability, apprenticeship programs, and manpower development and training. An outstanding example of Federal legislation of this nature is the Fair Labor Standards Act of 1938, as amended.

Labor relations laws, however, have had a more pervasive effect on managerial decision-making. They pertain to union-management relations and to the rights of employees, labor organizations, union members, employers, and the government, within the context of union organizing and labor disputes. Areas covered by labor relations statutes include: conditions of employment, freedom of association, concerted employee activities, unfair practices, employee representation, employer payments, government-conducted elections, mediation, arbitration, collective bargaining, union security, dues-deduction authorizations, right to strike and to lock out, picketing, boycott, injunctions, health, welfare, and pension fund regulations, suits for breach of collective agreements, national emergencies, and the conduct of internal union affairs.

The Railway Labor Act. The first detailed statutory expression of Federal policy toward freedom of association, union recognition, company-assisted unions, unadjusted grievances, and national strike or lockout emergencies, containing enforceable provisions, was the *Railway Labor Act of 1926.* It had been preceded by such pieces of legislation as the Arbitration Act of 1888, Erdman Act of 1898, Newlands Act of 1913, Adamson Act of 1916, and Transportation Act of 1920, all directed toward labor dispute adjustment in the railroad industry. The Railway Labor Act of 1926, initially confined to railroad carriers and their employees, was expanded in 1936 to cover airlines and their employees as well. It had been amended in 1934, 1940, and 1951. Employees under the Railway Labor Act are guaranteed the right to organize and to bargain collectively through representatives of a majority of any craft or class. Railroad and airline employers are forbidden from labor practice conduct which interferes with such right. For example, so-called "yellow-dog" contracts may not be exacted, and unions may not be company assisted or dominated. (A "yellow-dog" contract is one in which the employee agrees not to join or remain in a labor union as a condition of employment.)

Carriers and employees are under mutual duty to enter into and maintain collective bargaining agreements and to follow the machinery for grievance adjustment and disputes settlement provided by the Act. A National Mediation Board composed of three members appointed by the President has authority over controversies concerning (1) designation of collective bargaining representatives, (2) negotiation of terms and conditions of collective agreements, and (3) interpretation of such agreements arrived at through mediation. A thirty-day notice of any contemplated change in contract terms is required and, if no agreement is reached, mediation and voluntary arbitration are made available. Where arbitration is refused and the differences remain unsettled, the President must be notified of any dispute which the National Mediation Board deems to be a substantial threat to interstate commerce. The President may then appoint an Emergency Board to investigate and report within thirty days. During such period, and for an additional thirty days after the Board makes its report, no change may be made in the conditions which gave rise to the dispute, except by mutual agreement of the parties.

The Railway Labor Act also established a National Railroad Adjustment Board of 36 members representing equally the carriers and the national railway labor organizations, and, through amendment, a comparable Air Transport Adjustment Board. The Boards are empowered to make final and binding awards in controversies growing out of grievances involving the application and interpretation of existing collective bargaining agreements.

Violations by a carrier of those sections of the Act which relate to selection of representatives, employee rights to organize and to bargain, "yellow-dog" contracts, and the duty to give notice of contract changes or to post required notices, are misdemeanors punishable by fine up to $20,000, imprisonment, or both. The enduring importance of the Railway Labor Act of 1926 is two-fold: the test of its constitutionality before the United States Supreme Court in 1930 sustained the power of the Congress to reach into labor relations regulation through the "commerce clause" of the Federal Constitution; its statutory provisions set up the framework which was to serve as a precursor for the embracing labor relations enactments that were to follow.

The Federal Anti-Injunction Act. In 1932 an Act to Amend the Judicial Code of the United States, generally to become known as the *Federal Anti-Injunction Act,* or Norris-LaGuardia Act, declared the same rights and freedoms granted to railroad workers earlier to be the overall Federal public policy. However, no such substantive enforceable rights were created by the policy statement of the Norris-LaGuardia Act. What that law did provide was limited to the following: (1) it sharply restricted the circumstances under which Federal courts could exercise jurisdiction as to the issuance and scope of labor injunctions in labor disputes, and then only after notice and open hearings; (2) it pronounced "yellow-dog" contracts to be contrary to public policy and unenforceable in the Federal courts; and (3) it limited the responsibility of union officials to acts committed, authorized, or ratified by them. Corresponding anti-injunction laws have been adopted by not less than twenty-five of the states.

One effect of the Norris-LaGuardia Act was to limit the use of injunctions against labor unions. Such relief had been made available to employers through judicial interpretations of the Clayton Anti-Trust Act. This latter law had been passed by Congress in 1914 as a substantial supplement to the Sherman Anti-Trust Act of 1890. Reflecting the long campaign of pressures by organized labor, the Clayton Act sought to withdraw the applicability of anti-trust regulation, with its treble damages and criminal provisions, from labor unions. It also sought curtailment of the wide powers of the Federal courts in enjoining union conduct in labor controversies.

United States Supreme Court decisions subsequent to 1914, however, through judicial construction, continued to hold labor unions vulnerable to anti-trust lawsuit, damages, and injunctions. It was a series of such court cases which led to mounting union demands for further Federal protection. These demands, following the passage of the Railway Labor Act, led to the Federal Anti-Injunction Act and the explicit denial of the use of anti-trust legislation as a basis for enjoining labor unions in labor disputes. It was not until 1937 that the constitutionality of the Anti-Injunction Act was sustained.

Although all four of these statutes referred to remain on the lawbooks, the two anti-trust laws are held to apply against bona fide labor unions only where there is proof of collusive combination with employers or nonlabor groups in conspiracies to control prices or output, or to pre-empt markets in restraint of competition for unionized operators.

The National Labor Relations Act. The year 1935 marked the dividing line in the history of American labor relations legislation. Prior to that date, except for the railroad industry, workers as trade-unionists had no affirmative enforceable rights that could be asserted against employers, aside from those arising from voluntary labor-management collective bargaining contracts. In that year, the *National Labor Relations Act* (Wagner-Connery Act) was passed, to be validated in the United States Supreme Court two years later. 1935 was a time of economic depression and of rising industrial unionization aimed at the mass of unorganized production workers in the economy. The new law was enacted as a successor to Section 7(a) of the National Industrial Recovery Act of 1933, a measure which had been struck down by the highest court.

The Wagner Act, as this legislation is most popularly called, was both an expression of the Administration's economic counter-depression strategy of raising purchasing power, and the Administration's recognition of union efforts to secure legislation favorable to their growth. A major effect was to reduce the number of work stoppages occasioned by the denial of union recognition. Re-enacted with substantial changes twelve years later, the National Labor Relations Act remains on the federal statute books as Title I of the *Labor-Management Relations Act of 1947,* as amended.

The Wagner Act may be viewed in three parts: (1) unfair labor practices; (2) representation machinery; and (3) administrative and enforcement provisions. The entire Act was derivative from Section 7: "Employees shall have the right of self-organization, to form, join, or assist labor organizations, to bargain collectively through representatives of their own choosing, and to engage in concerted activities for the purpose of collective bargaining or other mutual aid or protection."

To guarantee the rights proclaimed by Section 7, the NLRA listed five employer unfair labor practices which interfered with such employee rights and for which an employer could be charged. Management was obliged, under the Act, to bargain collectively with the duly designated majority representative of its employees in an appropriate collective bargaining unit. And such labor union had the right to demand a closed shop agreement in the course of its bargaining. The Act, which applied to employers engaged in industries affecting interstate commerce, established machinery for the determination of majority representation. Government-conducted elections led to certification of the union achieving such majority in secret balloting by employees eligible to vote in the appropriate collective bargaining unit. The employer was obligated to bargain in good faith with the majority union.

The NLRA is administered through the National Labor Relations Board consisting of five members appointed by the President. Violations are prosecuted by an independent General Counsel, also appointed by the President, and result in Board orders compelling employers or labor oganizations, or both, to cease and desist from engaging in unfair labor practices, to post notices of compliance, and, in appropriate situations, to reinstate employees with backpay or to follow other prescribed remedies. Enforcement of NLRB orders, or challenges to vacate, modify or set aside such orders are pursued through judicial review in the United States Courts of Appeal.

The Labor-Management Relations Act. Twelve years after the passage of the National Labor Relations Act, with a post-World War II business boom instead of the Great Depression of the 1930s, with public opinion against strike waves in peacetime conversion, and with labor unions having grown in size, power, and status, Congress enacted the *Labor-Management Relations Act of 1947,* known as the Taft-Hartley Act. This, the most extensive piece of Federal labor legislation, in its Title I re-wrote the Wagner Act with a view, this time, to restraining actions of labor unions. To the Wagner Act right to form, join, or assist labor organizations, the 1947 law added the right to *refrain* from so doing. To the five employer unfair labor practices of the earlier legislation, the LMRA, added five *union* unfair labor practices. Included in the latter were provisions which had the effect of prohibiting closed shop agreements, sympathy strikes, secondary boycotts, and jurisdictional strikes. Labor organizations were, in addition, made subject to the charge of refusal to bargain collectively in good faith. Employers were given a protected area of "free speech" opposing unions, and, when faced by union demands for recognition, employers were given for the first time the right to petition the NLRB for a representation election. As an exception to the Norris-LaGuardia Act limitations upon the courts, the Federal Government was given the power to seek injunctions in United States District Courts against union or employer violators, with the special provision making such Federal action mandatory as against secondary-boycott type of conduct by unions.

The definition of the obligation to bargain collectively was spelled out for the first time as requiring the parties to meet at reasonable times and to confer in good faith with respect to wages, hours, and other terms and conditions of employment, and to reduce such agreement to writing if requested, "but such obligation does not compel either party to agree to a proposal or require the making of a concession." Procedurally, where there is a collective contract in effect, it becomes an unfair labor practice for the party wishing to terminate or modify such contract to seek to do so without: (1) notifying the other party of such intention 60 days prior to the contract expiration date, (2) offering to meet and confer with the other party for the purpose of negotiating a new contract, (3) notifying the Federal Mediation and Conciliation Service and the State mediation agency of the dispute, and, (4) continuing in effect all of the terms of the contract and refraining from a strike or lock-out for the 60-day period. Any employee who engages in a strike during such period loses his employee status until rehired. By amendment in 1974, Congress extended coverage of the Act to employees of nonprofit hospitals and other health care institutions. Special provisions were added to minimize the interruption of patient care. For example, the procedural notification rules were changed to require a 90-day notice of intent to terminate or modify an existing agreement, and a 60-day notice to the mediation agencies. Where bargaining is demanded for an initial contract following recognition or certification, mediation services are to be given 30-day notices. Further, picketing, striking, or other concerted refusal to work at any health care institution, in general, requires notification to the employer and to the Federal Mediation and Conciliation Service not less than ten days prior to such action.

Title II of the Labor-Management Relations Act of 1947 provided for an independent Federal Mediation and Conciliation Service, and set up national emergency machinery for dealing with strike or lockout threats to the nation, outside of the railroad and airlines industries. Under this Title, the President is authorized to appoint an *ad hoc* Board of Inquiry where the national health or safety is threatened.

Upon receiving the Board's report, the President may direct the Attorney General to press for an 80-day injunction in the Federal courts. If the parties to the labor dispute have not adjusted their differences within 60 days following the issuance of the injunction, the Board of Inquiry will make a further report, this time with a statement of the employer's final position. Before another fifteen days elapse, the National Labor Relations Board is to be called in to conduct an election to determine whether the employees involved wish to accept the employer's last offer. Within five days after that balloting, the results must be certified to the Attorney General, who must then request the discharge of the injunction, and the Federal District Court must so act. Thereafter, the parties are free to strike or lockout, but if the controversy continues unsettled, the President must submit a report to Congress with recommendations, if any.

Title II of the LMRA of 1947 introduced the Federal right of either party to a collective labor agreement to bring suit for breach of contract in the Federal District Courts without reference to amount or diversity of citizenship. Thus labor unions may sue or be sued directly in such connection. Damage actions against labor unions were also expressly written into the law to correspond with each of the union unfair labor practices relating to secondary boycott, and sympathy and jurisdictional strike action which appeared in Title I. In addition, subject to criminal prosecution, it placed restrictions upon union dues-deduction authorizations ("check off"), and payments to employee representatives, particularly contributions to welfare, pension, and pooled vacation plans. For example, union-management negotiated welfare plans must be administered jointly by employer and employees under trust agreements with provisions for a neutral party in the event of a deadlock. Violations may lead to a fine of not more than $10,000, one year imprisonment, or both. Title III also forbids labor organizations, as well as corporations, from making contributions or expenditures in connection with elections to Federal office.

A new pension reform law, *The Employee Retirement Income and Security Act of 1974* (ERISA) repealed the *Pension Plans Disclosure Act of 1958* and provided an elaborate set of provisions to establish minimum standards and assure equitable distribution and financing in the establishment, operation, and administration of employee benefit plans. As defined by the Act, "employee organization" means any labor organization. As a result neither a labor union nor an employer may, through collective bargaining, agree upon conditions of eligibility or rules for employee vesting under pension plans which vary from those established by ERISA as administered through the U. S. Department of Labor.

Developing trends in Board and court rulings under the Labor-Management Relations Act include extension of employer-industry coverage (to educational institutions, for example), expansion of the subject matter for mandatory collective bargaining, revocation of union certification for failure to represent employees fairly because of racial considerations, growth of employer entitlement to privileged lockouts, addition of novel unfair labor practice remedies, and an increase in judicial recognition of the arbitration forum for alleged breaches of collective contracts. Coupled with the last has been the granting of injunctions despite the Norris-LaGuardia Act anti-injunction provisions, where unions have violated no-strike clauses of grievance- arbitration-worded agreements. Compulsory arbitration has found its way into final resolution of national emergency disputes, arising under the Railway Labor Act, for example, in the form of individual *ad hoc* acts of Congress.

The Labor-Management Reporting and Disclosure Act. A second 12-year span separates the Labor-Management Relations Act of 1947—the broadest expression of national labor relations policy—from the *Labor-Management Reporting and Disclosure Act of 1959*—the broadest expression of national union-membership relations policy. While both organized labor and management over the years sought changes in the 1947 Taft-Hartley Act (unions had dubbed it a "slave labor act"), the revelations of the Senate Select (McClellan) Committee on Improper Practices in the Labor and Management Field, together with the tide of criticism of undemocratic union affairs, led to the enactment of the new statute known also as the Landrum-Griffin Act, or the Labor Reform Act. Directed at eliminating or preventing "improper practices" on the part of labor organizations, employers, labor relations consultants, and their officers and representatives, which distort and defeat the policies of the Labor-Management Relations Act, 1947, as amended, and the Railway Labor Act, as amended, the Landrum-Griffin Act went on, in its Title VII, to amend the Wagner Act provisions of the LMRA as well. Thus, for example, Taft-Hartley Title I restrictions on union secondary boycott and sympathy and jurisdictional strike activities were made more stringent, and new unfair labor practices were added, including picketing for recognition under certain circumstances and joint employer-union "hot cargo" agreements to refuse to handle the products of any other employer, usually a nonunion company. However, economic strikers who are not entitled to reinstatement were granted eligibility to vote in elections held within one year after the strike began.

Title I of the Act constitutes a Bill of Rights for union members, protecting their exercise of the democratic process; Title II requires compulsory reporting by labor organizations, employers, and consultants; Title III regulates union trusteeships; Title IV sets statutory standards for union-membership elections; Title V prescribes safeguards for union finances against malfeasance and embezzlement, and restricts communists and criminals in their access to union and management posts. In general, these provisions are administered and enforced through the office of the United States Secretary of Labor, but for various violations, the Landrum-Griffin Act also contains remedies including suit by union members in the Federal District Court and substantial fines and prison sentences.

Other Legislation. In the body of labor relations legislation there are a number of statutes drafted expressly to remedy particular situations. The (Byrnes) *Anti-Strikebreaker Law of 1936,* as amended in 1938, makes it a felony to transport strike breakers in interstate commerce; the (Hobbs) *Anti-Racketeering Law of 1946* makes it a felony to obstruct movement of goods in commerce by robbery or extortion; the (Lea) (Anti-Petrillo) *Unlawful Practices in Radio Broadcasting Law* prohibits "featherbedding" practices in that industry.

The Federal *Civil Rights Act of 1964,* Title VII, establishes unlawful employment practices enforceable against employers and labor organizations when they discriminate against individuals because of race, color, religion, sex, or national origin. Although not a labor relations law, this particular civil rights legislation stimulated the National Labor Relations Board to recognize that racial discrimination practiced by a union also constitutes a breach of its statutory "duty of fair representation" under the Labor-Management Relations Act. Employers, similarly, commit unfair labor practices when they refuse to bargain over their racial policies or discriminate against employees because of race or national origin. Moreover, company appeals to race prejudice are grounds for invalidating NLRB-directed representation elections. [1].

State Laws. Because there are great numbers of workers employed by intra-state employers who are not subject to the reach of Federal labor relations legislation, it is important to emphasize that there also exists a body of state labor relations legislation. Such emphasis is necessary in view of the language of the Taft-Hartley Act of 1947 which left the permissible form of union security agreement between employers and labor unions to the law of the state where the agreement is to be in force. And such emphasis is all the more necessary in the light of the Title VII provision of the Labor-Management Reporting and Disclosure Act of 1959, which amended the Wagner Act in such fashion as to permit a state agency or a state court to take jurisdiction where the National Labor Relations Board declines to exercise its powers.

State laws covering public utilities and medical and hospital facilities employ a variety of procedures in dispute settlement, including investigation, mediation, voluntary arbitration, emergency boards, use of moderators, plant seizure, and compulsory arbitration.

In addition to state labor relations acts and state anti-injunction acts, as well as state anti-monopoly laws, there are laws restricting picketing, laws restricting wage assignments, fair employment practice statutes, union regulation laws, pension and welfare plan disclosure laws, mediation, arbitration, labor dispute settlement statutes, and so-called "right-to-work" laws. The last-named type of state law prohibits, as a condition of employment, membership in a labor union. Numerous states have legislated such enactments which declared closed shops, union shops and other types of union security, in varying degrees, to be unlawful, but many such laws have been repealed. In 1975 a landmark law, *The Agricultural Labor Relations Act,* was adopted by the State of California extending the rights of organization and collective bargaining to farm workers.

Labor Relations Laws for Government Employees. Acceleration of union organization among government employees, Federal, state, county, and municipal—and their concerted activities in labor disputes, have attracted attention to the traditional statutory prohibition against strikes and work stoppages in the public service. Newer legislation and administrative practices have provided for representation procedures, grievance handling, and collective bargaining, as well as fines and other penalties for job actions that interrupt operations. Effective in 1970, Executive Order 11491 established, as part of labor management relations in the Federal Service, a Federal Labor Relations Code, a Federal Services Impasses Panel, and a Code of Fair Practices.

WILLARD A. LEWIS, PH.D., LL.B., Professor Emeritus of Management and Industrial Relations, Graduate School of Business Administration, New York University, New York; Visiting Professor of Law and Management, Polytechnic Institute of New York, Brooklyn, New York

Information References

Periodicals:

United States Department of Labor:
Annual Digest of State and Federal Labor Legislation.
Federal Labor Laws and Agencies.
Monthly Labor Review.

Looseleaf Services:

Bureau of National Affairs, Inc., Washington, D.C.:
Labor Relations Reference Manual.
Labor Relations Yearbook.
Commerce Clearing House, Inc., Chicago, Ill.:
Labor Law Course.
Labor Law Reporter.

Texts:

Gregory, Charles O., "Labor and the Law," New York, Norton, 1979.

"Labor Relations Yearbook," Washington, D.C., Bureau of National Affairs.

Cross References: *Collective Bargaining; Employment: Antidiscrimination Legislation; Labor Arbitration; Labor Unions; Mediation; Occupational Safety and Health Act of 1970; Training and Development (Government Sponsored); Workers' Compensation.*

LABOR UNIONS

I—HISTORY

Organized Labor continues as a powerful influence in management-worker relations. The United States Department of Labor, Bureau of Labor Statistics, estimates that there are about 80,000 local unions chartered by national and international unions with headquarters in the United States. While the figure of 24.5% of the non-agricultural U.S. labor force enrolled in unions represents a decline of about nine percentage points in the past 20 years, there has been no significant diminution of the power of organized labor, as shown by continuing gains in terms of pay, shorter hours, and fringe benefits in key industries.

Early History. Soon after the American Revolution, trade unions composed of shoemakers, tailors, carpenters, printers, bakers and other skilled workers were organized. These early unions did not emerge in collective bargaining as we know it today by meeting with the employer to work out terms and conditions of employment. Instead, they posted the prices and conditions under which they would work. The employer either met these conditions or faced a refusal to work. Gradually, however, the idea of bargaining by employers and union leaders over the terms and conditions of employment took hold, and with it came an end to such unilateral posting.

In the early 1830s, idealistic union reformers came into vogue. Robert Dale Owen, for example, wanted to set up a "Utopia" where everyone would work for the good of all; a sort of heaven on earth. The realities of labor's needs soon separated Owen and his fellows from the more practical men of labor. The great depression of 1837 brought a rapid decline in a few unions then in existence. After this, the intellectuals never again made any serious inroads on labor unions in this country.

With the 1840s came the impact of the Industrial Revolution. The middle nineteenth century saw the rise of large factories, the concentration of wealth, and the widening of the gap between employees and employer. Unions of this period, however, were not aimed at organizing the expanding mass of unskilled workers, and appealed instead to the highly skilled worker. In 1852, the International Typographical Union, which still flourishes today, was founded. In the next dozen years some dozen other "craft unions" were established.

Rise and Fall of the Knights of Labor. In 1869 several tailors met in Philadelphia and formed the Order of the "Knights of Labor." The purpose was to unite all workers under one banner, regardless of race, nationality, or creed. The order was, at first, a secret society, as were many early labor unions. Because of the terroristic activities of some secret groups (particularly the "Molly Maguires," who went so far as to murder company officials) secrecy was, for the Knights, a liability.

In 1879, Terrence V. Powderly became head of the Knights of Labor, his title being "Grand Master Workman." Insisting that secrecy be abolished, Powderly won approval of the Roman Catholic Church for his organization. With the end of secrecy, the Knights grew rapidly. Powderly, a genial Irishman, had a keen sense of social justice and a firm belief in the American system of private property. Many of the figures around him were of a more radical bent, however, and under the constitution of the Knights they held the ruling hand.

The Knights of Labor attempted to weld together all the elements of the working classes. To do so, they permitted craft unions to join directly with their general assembly, or national organization. They also organized local groups, called "mixed assemblies," which took in workers on any basis under which they would enroll. Sometimes these came as craft unions, but at other times the local group would take in all workers in any industry, making no distinction between crafts. The Knights were thus one of the first large unions to attempt what is known as *industrial unionization.*

The Knights of Labor grew rapidly. In 1885 membership reached 100,000. Through a strike in 1886, Jay Gould, who controlled the Wabash, Missouri-Kansas-Texas, and Missouri Pacific Railroads, was forced to grant the Knights recognition. This helped to skyrocket the membership, which in one year—1886—grew, to 700,000.

The decline of the Knights was as rapid as the ascent. They lost a number of strikes, notably a resounding defeat when for the second time they struck the Missouri Pacific Railroad. They also lost many craft unionists to a new labor organization, later to be known as the American Federation of Labor. In 1888 the Knights declined to 222,000 members, in 1890 to 100,000, and in 1893 to a scant 75,000. Twenty years later, when they finally dissolved, they were only a paper organization.

Samuel Gompers and the American Federation of Labor. In 1881, Samuel Gompers and Adolph Strasser of the Cigar Makers Union helped form a group known as the Federation of Organized Trades and Labor Unions, which in 1886 changed its name to the American Federation of Labor. The AFL reflected Gompers' philosophy of trade unionism. He believed that skilled workmen should not submerge themselves in a mass labor movement such as the Knights of Labor, but rather should form their own craft unions.

Samuel Gompers set the American trade union movement on an entirely different road from that taken by the European labor movement. Unlike European Socialist, Communist, and Syndicalist union leaders, he did not believe that unions should try to achieve their goals through revolutionary upheaval. Rather, he believed that American unions should try to achieve their goals on a gradual basis. He felt that instead of looking forward to a socialist Utopia, American unions should strive for five cents an hour more in the pay envelope, an hour less per day of work. His motto for the American trade union movement was "More, now."

Samuel Gompers also strongly felt that American unions should not be the tail of any political party's kite, or be embroiled in splinter-party politics. His political counsel to the American workingman was "support your friends and punish your enemies" in the major political parties. Except for one year when a

Socialist was elected AFL president, the organization has always been headed by men who essentially believed in the American system of free, competitive enterprise.

The American Federation of Labor under Gompers grew slowly but steadily. Under its constitution, the national unions in the AFL were strictly autonomous, and had full control of their internal affairs. Rules for governing the AFL were made at yearly conventions, with policy and direction between conventions by a full-time president, secretary, and executive board. This board varied from five to thirteen members, and under the constitution held considerable power.

Except for a one-year period, Samuel Gompers served as AFL President from 1886 until 1924. The highest point of AFL membership under his leadership occurred in World War I, when its ranks shot up to 5,500,000. Immediately after the war, labor union membership declined because of a number of factors, chief of which were (1) a post-war depression; (2) a change in national administration; and (3) a tendency by employers to provide directly what the unions promised the workers. In 1923 union membership had declined to 3.5 million members.

AFL in the Twenties. Upon the death of Samuel Gompers in 1924, United Mine Worker president John L. Lewis secured the election of Mine Worker Secretary William Green as president of the AFL. Under Green, the AFL did not gain membership during the increased employment of the "Roaring Twenties" prosperity. Instead, unions only held their own or declined in membership. In 1929, at the height of prosperity, unions had no more members than they had in 1923. The Great Depression following the 1929 stock market crash brought further union membership losses. By 1933, union membership had declined to 2,973,000.

Early New Deal and Rise of the CIO. In 1933, during the early days of the Roosevelt Administration, Congress enacted the National Industrial Recovery Act, one section of which granted to labor the right of self-organization without employer interference (See LABOR RELATIONS LEGISLATION). At that time, John L. Lewis's UMW had only a few members, and was practically insolvent. Relying on Section 7(a) of the Act, which gave unions protection in their organizing activities, Lewis took the last bit of money in the union's treasury and hired scores of organizers. Under the protection of the new law, he signed up mine workers by the thousands. Other unions followed Lewis's example and conducted intensive organizing drives. Among these were the International Ladies Garment Workers, the Amalgamated Clothing Workers, the Oil Workers, and the Building Service Employees.

AFL craft unionism left large groups of workers in the mass production industries untapped by unions, and pressure for membership drives among such workers led to discontent in AFL circles. To exert pressure for organizing on an industrial union basis, John L. Lewis of the Mine Workers, David Dubinsky of the Ladies Garment Workers, Sidney Hillman of the Amalgamated Clothing Workers, and leaders of oil, textile, and metal unions formed within the AFL a Committee for Industrial Organizations, which the newspapers shortened to CIO. The governing body of the AFL, the Executive Council, ordered this committee disbanded. When the CIO member unions refused to disband the committee, the AFL Executive Council suspended the unions affiliated with the Committee for Industrial Organizations. These unions did not show up at the 1936 AFL convention, and the convention voted to expel them.

The expelled CIO unions changed the name of the committee to Congress of Industrial Organizations, and elected John L. Lewis as President. The new CIO immediately conducted whirlwind organizing drives in automobile, steel, meat-packing, and other mass production industries.

In organizing the steel industry, the CIO used as forums to sell the CIO's brand of unionism the independent unions established by the companies in the early twenties and thirties. By January, 1937, the CIO's Steelworkers Organizing Committee had largely unionized the big Carnegie-Illinois Steel plant of the United States Steel Corporation. Through the good offices of the White House, John L. Lewis and Myron Taylor, then Board Chairman of U.S. Steel, met and signed a contract for U.S. Steel's many plants. Heading up the Steelworkers Organizing Committee was Phillip Murray, Vice President of John L. Lewis's Mine Workers Union.

In organizing the automobile industry, the CIO's United Automobile Workers union conducted a series of sit-down strikes at General Motors and Chrysler. Both these companies recognized the United Automobile Workers in

1937. Ford held off the union that year, but signed a contract after a strike in 1941. This union succeeded in organizing the rest of the automobile industry and also organized a number of aircraft and agricultural implements companies.

Other CIO unions succeeded in organizing the "Big Three" rubber companies, many of the meat-packing companies, and the big producers of electrical appliances.

CIO Expulsion of Communist Unions. One of the basic weaknesses in the CIO organizing campaigns was that John L. Lewis permitted the Communist Party to supply organizers. While the Communists were effective union organizers, Lewis soon found that they had captured large CIO unions.

In December of 1940, John L. Lewis resigned as president, and CIO elected to the top office Phillip Murray, Vice President of the United Mine Workers and President of the United Steelworkers of America. Murray, after some delay, began a campaign to wean away the leadership of Communist-dominated unions and bring them into the anti-Communist camp. Under his leadership, the CIO in 1949 expelled the following unions on charges of Communist domination: (1) United Electrical, Radio and Machine Workers of America; (2) United Office and Professional Workers; (3) Food, Tobacco, Agricultural, and Allied Workers; (4) Mine, Mill and Smelter Workers Union; (5) Farm Equipment Workers; (6) Fur and Leather Workers; (7) United Public Workers; (8) International Longshoremen's and Warehousemen's Union; (9) National Union of Marine Cooks and Stewards; (10) American Communications Association; (11) International Fisherman and Allied Workers. Of the eleven unions expelled by the CIO on charges of Communist domination, only two unions, the United Electrical, Radio, and Machine Workers and the International Longshoremen's and Warehousemen's Union, survived as independent unaffiliated unions as of 1981. The other nine unions either merged with other unions or disbanded.

Formation of AFL-CIO. In the fall of 1952, AFL President William Green and CIO President Phillip Murray died. As Green's death occurred shortly after the AFL's convention, the responsibility of picking his successor devolved on the AFL Executive Council. This body elected George Meany, who the following year was elected by convention vote. Murray died a week before the scheduled CIO convention, and his successor was chosen by convention vote. The two nominees were the heir-apparent, Allan Heywood, CIO Executive Vice President and Walter Reuther, President of Automobile Workers. After a heated floor fight, Walter Reuther was elected CIO President by the slimmest of margins.

Immediately after his election as AFL President, George Meany announced his determination to reunite the divided labor movement. Abortive attempts at reunification of the AFL and CIO had been made in 1937, 1939, and 1942. These were resumed in 1947 and 1952, but it was under Meany, on December 5, 1955, that the AFL and CIO were once more together. The one vast organization encompassed some fifteen million workers: ten million from the AFL unions and five million from CIO unions.

Expulsion of Unions on Corruption Charges. In the December, 1955, merger convention, the AFL-CIO wrote into the new constitution Article 8, Section 7, which provided: "It is a basic principle of this Federation that it must be and remain free from any and all corrupt influences and from the undermining efforts of Communist, Fascist or other totalitarian agencies." Under this provision, the AFL-CIO Executive Council was given power to:

(1) Investigate corrupt unions.

(2) Give clean-up directions to unions involved.

(3) Suspend upon two-thirds vote, if the clean-up directions are not followed.

The suspended unions were given the right to appeal to the next AFL-CIO convention, but the Executive Council's decision was to stand until that time.

Hearings before the McClellan Senate Sub-Committee on Improper Activities in the Labor or Management Field, running from 1957 to 1959, revealed widespread corruption in AFL-CIO unions. At the AFL-CIO convention in December, 1957, unions indicated by the AFL-CIO Executive Council were heavily dealt with, following revelations of corruption and undemocratic practices. The Teamsters' Union, the Bakery Workers, the Laundry Workers, the United Textile Workers, the Brewery Workers, and the Jewelry Workers were all either expelled or suspended.

In 1959, with James R. Hoffa's Teamsters' Union threatening to become the nucleus for a new federation of the dishonorably discharged, the AFL-CIO Executive Council decided to abandon recourse to expulsion. It concluded that unions were not strong enough on their own to wipe out all corruption, and that what was needed was a law.

The Labor-Management Reporting and Disclosure Act introduced Government control of unions to a greater extent than union proponents of reform had anticipated. It sought to protect employees and the public from breach of trust and corruption by placing restrictions on the powers and qualifications of union officers. For decades, beginning in the thirties, the unions had enjoyed all the advantages of two legal worlds: Statutory authority bolstered their bargaining and organizing power on the one hand, while on the other, as voluntary nonprofit associations, they still held privileged status. Congress decided that internal union affairs could not be closed to regulation or inspection. (See LABOR RELATIONS LEGISLATION.)

Lane Kirkland Elected AFL-CIO President. George Meany's death on January 10, 1980, marked the end to an era. Beginning with Samuel Gompers in 1881 and continuing with William Green, John L. Lewis, Phillip Murray, Walter Reuther, and George Meany, organized labor in the United States had always been headed by self-educated men who rose from the ranks. In the 80s the picture changed and the AFL-CIO is at this writing led by two college-educated men—President, Lane Kirkland and Secretary-Treasurer, Thomas Donahue—whose work careers have largely been in labor relations.

AFL-CIO President Lane Kirkland graduated from the United States Merchant Marine Academy in 1942 and served during World War II as a deck officer aboard merchant vessels carrying munitions and other war materials. He was licensed near the end of the war as a Master Mariner to captain any vessel in any ocean. He entered the U. S. Navy's Hydrographic Office in Washington, D.C. as a nautical scientist while studying at night at Georgetown University's School of Foreign Service, from which he received a B.S. degree in 1948. He took further graduate courses at night at Georgetown's Graduate School. In 1948, he joined the research staff of the AFL, specializing in pensions. He joined the International Union of Operating Engineers in 1958 as Research Director. Two years later he returned to the AFL-CIO as executive assistant to George Meany, a post he held until his election as AFL-CIO secretary-treasurer in 1969. With George Meany's retirement, he was elected AFL-CIO president without opposition at the November 1979 convention. Upon his election to the AFL-CIO presidency, Lane Kirkland announced that one of his goals was the return of the 2-million member Teamsters, the 1.3-million member Auto Workers, and the United Mine Workers to the AFL-CIO fold.

II—LABOR UNION ORGANIZATION

Types of Unions. There are two types of unions: industrial unions and the craft unions. Industrial unions take in all workers in a plant or industry from top to bottom. For this reason they are called vertical unions. The same industrial union, for example, may bargain for unskilled production workers, highly skilled craftsmen, and professional and clerical employees. Craft unions, on the other hand, take in only members of a particular craft no matter where they are working in the local union's area. An International Association of Machinists' local union, for example, may take in as members and bargain for one to a dozen maintenance machinists at each of several hundred plants in an area. Since they bargain for only thin strata of workers in each plant, they are called horizontal unions.

In the building and construction trades, local craft unions in the northern states frequently control employment in their areas. Thus, for example, when the contractor reaches the stage in building where he needs bricklayers, he calls the Bricklayers Union hiring hall for the required number. As soon as the bricklayers are finished, he sends them back to the union hiring hall where the process is repeated again and again with other contractors. This is the "spigot" concept of labor: the union controls the pool of skilled labor and doles it out on an as-needed basis. Unions in such situations take on many characteristics of employers, and employers become subcontractors of labor.

Some large national unions take in members on both a craft and an industrial union basis. The International Association of Machinists, for example, has local unions made up strictly of highly skilled craftsmen; but it also has local unions made up for all workers, skilled and unskilled, at giant aerospace plants. The United Automobile Workers Union, which is the country's largest industrial union, has set up Skilled Trades Departments in the auto plants, which bargain separate and apart from the production workers.

Local Unions. When one talks about unions in a labor relations situation, one is generally talking about local unions. The unions may be small locals limited to one plant ard containing but 50 members. They may be giant one-plant locals such as Ford Local 600 at River Rouge with about 40,000 members. Or they may be area-wide organizations, such as Service Employees Union Local 32B in New York's Manhattan, with about 55,000 members—one of the largest local unions in the United States. While some local unions are limited strictly to workers of one company, or one plant of one company, most are chartered by national and international unions of workers in a particular industry, trade, or craft.

Locals Based on Nationality Lines. Some local unions are based on common nationality or language lines. The founding of unions along these lines is an outgrowth of the successive waves of immigration that have swept across the United States. There was and is continuing, for example, a wave of Italian immigration into the Eastern seaboard. A large number of Italians went to work in the ladies garment industry. They stuck together and spoke Italian, not English. The already established local Garment Unions were largely Jewish as a result of a previous immigration wave. When Italians went to local union meetings they found the members lapsing into Yiddish, which they did not understand.

To meet this situation, the officers of the International Ladies Garment Workers Union organized an Italian-American Dressmakers' Union. Now when members at local union meetings find that they cannot think of the right English word, they lapse into Italian and everybody at the meeting understands.

The newest wave of immigration is Spanish-speaking. Some national unions are setting up Spanish-speaking local unions. In Miami, Florida, many local union meetings are conducted on a bilingual basis, with Spanish the second language. The slogans and much of the literature of the United Farm Workers Union are in Spanish. Local unions founded on nationality or common language are fairly common. The International Typographical union, for example, has the Yiddish-American Typographical Union in New York, whose members set type for the Yiddish-language papers. Also in New York are locals of the Hebrew Actors Union and the Italian Actors Union. In a number of Midwestern cities, there are German-American, Polish-American, and Swedish-American local unions.

At one time, national unions set up "A" local unions for white members and "B" local unions for black members, with the "A" members getting the best jobs and the "B" members getting the dirty, heavy labor jobs, such as loading hides. With the advent of Federal and state laws banning discrimination, such "A" and "B" local unions ceased to exist.

Structure of AFL-CIO. The United States Bureau of Labor Statistics estimates the number of local unions chartered by national and international unions at approximately 80,000. More than three-quarters of the local unions are in AFL-CIO affiliates. The AFL-CIO resulted from the merger of the American Federation of Labor and Congress of Industrial Organizations in December, 1955. The structure of the AFL-CIO is set forth in the organization chart shown in Exhibit I. As can be seen from this chart, the principal member organizations of the AFL-CIO are:

(1) The affiliated national and international unions, which, in turn are made up of local unions.

(2) City Federations of Labor and State Federations of Labor, also made up of local AFL-CIO unions.

(3) Departments composed for the most part of a group of national or international unions in a particular trade or industry.

(4) Local trade unions and local industrial unions directly affiliated with the AFL-CIO and not chartered by any national or international union.

Government of AFL-CIO. A convention which is held every two years, is the AFL-CIO's supreme governing body. Each union attending the convention is entitled to representation based on the number of members on which it pays a per capita tax of 19 cents per member per month to the AFL-CIO. Between conventions, the affairs of the AFL-CIO are directed by the executive officers assisted by the Executive Council, the Executive Committee, and the General Board.

The function of the two top officers and of the three governing bodies are as follows:

Executive Officers. The AFL-CIO has two executive officers, President and Secretary-

EXHIBIT I

STRUCTURE OF THE AFL-CIO

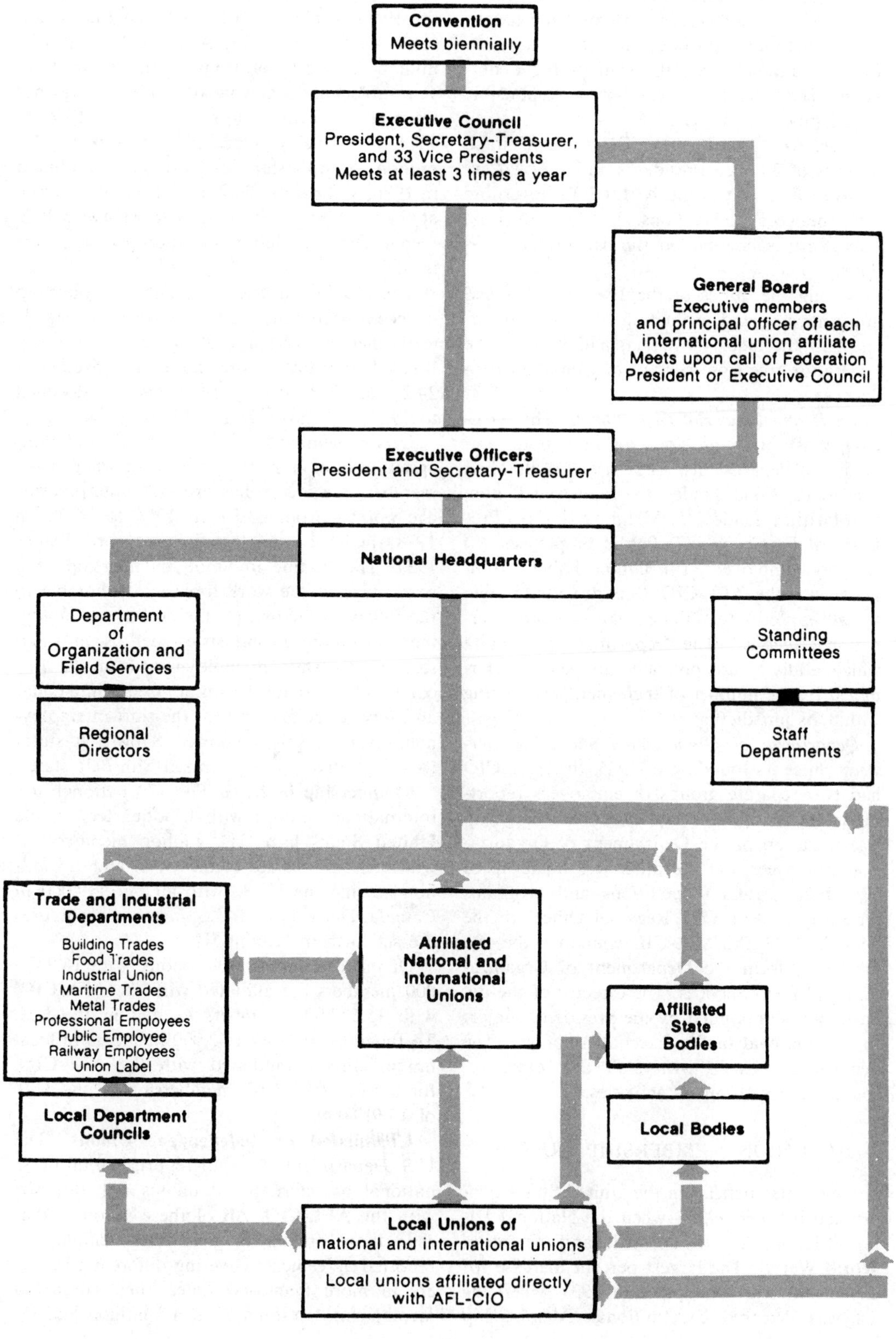

Treasurer. The President is the chief executive officer. He has authority to interpret the constitution between meetings of the Executive Council, and to direct the staff of the Federation. The Secretary-Treasurer is responsible for all financial matters.

Executive Council. The Executive Council consists of 33 Vice Presidents and the two executive officers. It is the AFL-CIO's governing body between conventions. It meets at least three times each year on the call of the President.

Among the duties of the Executive Council are proposing and evaluating legislation of interest to the labor movement and keeping the Federation free from corrupt or Communist influences.

Trade and Industrial Departments. The AFL-CIO constitution provides for nine trade and industrial departments. They are: (1) Building Trades, (2) Food Trades, (3) Industrial Union, (4) Maritime Trades, (5) Metal Trades, (6) Professional Employees, (7) Public Employees, (8) Railway Employees, (9) Union Label. Affiliation with the AFL-CIO Departments is open to "all appropriate affiliated national and international unions." The Department per capita which affiliates are obligated to pay is determined by the number of their members coming within its jurisdiction.

Department of Organization and Field Services. Since its founding in 1955, the AFL-CIO had two separate groups of employees reporting to its Washington headquarters: one group was made up of the Department of Organization employees and the other was made up of all other AFL-CIO operations and programs reporting to AFL-CIO Regional Offices in the field. In 1973, the AFL-CIO combined the two groups to form the Department of Organization and Field Services. The director of the department is appointed by the president, subject to the approval of the Executive Council. The department has its own staff and other resources to carry out its activities.

III—UNION MEMBERSHIP TRENDS

Union membership in the United States quadrupled between 1935—when the National Labor Relations Act was enacted—and the end of World War II. The largest percent increase for any single year took place in 1937, when the act was declared constitutional. Membership remained fairly constant in the second half of the 1940s, while the early 1950s saw many new entrants to union rolls. After peaking at 17.5 million, exclusive of Canada, union membership underwent a downward trend that was not reversed until the mid-sixties. From 1964 to 1974, membership increased to a peak of 20.2 million. Membership dropped to 19.6 million in 1976, and rose to 20.2 million in 1978, which at this writing is the latest year for which U.S. Department of labor membership data are available.

The absolute decrease in union membership in recent years must be viewed against a significant increase in the work force. The proportion of the total work force unionized was 24.2% in 1958, and by 1978 this had declined to 19.7%, as shown in Exhibit II.

Union membership as a proportion of nonagricultural employment, the sector where most members are found, has dropped nine percentage points—from 33.2% in 1958 to 24.0% in 1978, the lowest penetration rate recorded since 1937. The decline in union membership as a percentage of the work force is attributable to the following factors: (1) the decline in employment in unionized industries such as auto and steel, (2) the shift in employment from the blue collar sector to the less unionized white-collar and service sectors, and (3) the shift in employment from largely unionized Snow-Belt states to the relatively nonunionized Sun-Belt states.

Membership in U. S. The 174 national and international unions with headquarters in the United States have 21.7 million members, of which 20 million are in the U. S. and 1.7 million outside the U. S., with all but 119,000 in Canada. Derivation of U.S. membership figures are set forth in Exhibit III.

Of the 174 unions, 108 unions, with 16,982,000 members are affiliated with the AFL-CIO, with 15,577,000 members located in the U.S. To this must be added 42,000 members in local unions directly affiliated with the AFL-CIO, for a total AFL-CIO membership in the U.S. of 15,619,000.

Unaffiliated or Independent Unions. The U.S. Department of Labor reports a total of 63 national or international unions not affiliated with the AFL-CIO. All of these unions, other than those organizing government employees, reported agreements covering different employers in more than one state. Their combined membership is estimated at 4.7 million and in-

EXHIBIT II

UNION MEMBERSHIP AS A PERCENT OF TOTAL LABOR FORCE AND OF EMPLOYEES IN NONAGRICULTURAL ESTABLISHMENTS, 1930–1980

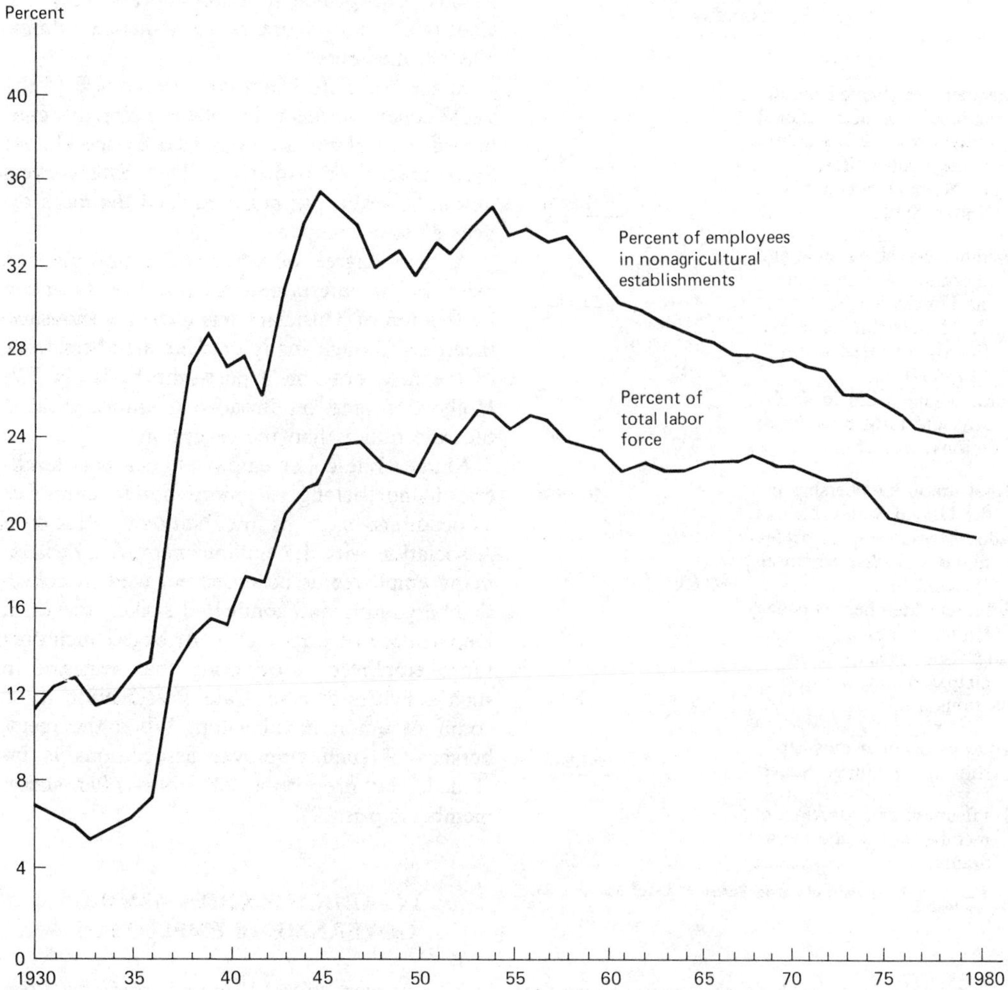

cludes members of long-established and well-known organizations such as the Brotherhood of Locomotive Engineers and the United Mine Workers of America. Approximately four-fifths of the membership in unaffiliated national and international unions are in unions once affiliated with the AFL-CIO or the former CIO. These include the United Automobile Workers and expelled unions such as the International Brotherhood of Teamsters, the United Electrical Workers (UE), the Longshoremen's and Warehousemen's Union, and the Distributive Workers.

In addition to independent national and international unions, there exists another type of independent union. This is a union whose membership is confined to a single employer, establishment, or locality. The U.S. Department of Labor estimates that such independent unions have a membership of approximately 332,000, which represents about 1.6% of total union membership in the U.S.

Professional and State Employee Associations. Many professional and state employee associations have taken on more and more characteristics of unions, including engaging in collective bargaining and in strikes. The U.S. Department of Labor estimates their total

EXHIBIT III

MEMBERSHIP OF NATIONAL UNIONS AND EMPLOYEE ASSOCIATIONS 1978
(In Thousands)

Membership claimed by all national and international unions with headquarters in the United States		21,742
Less: Number outside the United States		− 1,656
Membership of national and international unions in the United States		20,085
Add: Membership of locals directly affiliated with AFL-CIO	+42	
Add: Membership in single-firm and local unaffiliated unions	+332	+ 374
Total union membership in the United States		20,459
Add: Membership of professional and state employee associations	+2,635	
Subtract: Members outside United States	−22	
Add: Membership of municipal employee associations	+235	
Total association membership in the United States		+2,848
Total union *and* association membership in the United States		23,307

SOURCE: U. S. Department of Labor, Bureau of Labor Statistics, September 1980

membership at 2.6 million, the largest being the National Education Association with 1.7 million members.

White-Collar Union Membership. Of the 47.2 million white-collar workers, there are approximately 37.1 million in non-managerial jobs. Of these, unions have organized 4,067,000, or 11%. Despite continuing organizing efforts, this figure of 11% has been fairly constant for the past 18 years.

The 11% of the white-collar work force that unions have organized is not a uniform 11%. It ranges from practically zero for banks, insurance companies, and company home offices, to over 90% of railway white-collar employees who are members of the AFL-CIO Railway, Airline and Steamship Clerks International Union, with approximately 201,000 members.

In the telephone field, between 50% and 75% of the white-collar force is represented by unions. The principal union in this field, the Communication Workers of America, claims 508,000 members.

In the basic steel industry, about 50% of the white-collar workers in offices directly connected with plants are organized by the United Steelworkers of America. The Steelworkers union, however, has not organized the main offices of steel companies.

A high degree of white-collar unionization exists in the entertainment field. The American Federation of Musicians has over 330 thousand members, though many of their members work in the field only on a part-time basis. In TV, Hollywood, and on Broadway, unionization is the rule rather than the exception.

Many white-collar employees, such as teachers, do not belong to unions but to employee associations, such as the National Education Association with 1.7 million members. Because many employee associations engaged in collective bargaining and conducted strikes, the U. S. Department of Labor in 1970 began including those employee associations that engaged in such activities as a separate classification in its count of union membership. When the membership of such employee associations is included, the proportion of white-collar union membership is 17%.

IV—UNIONIZATION AMONG GOVERNMENT EMPLOYEES

Thirty years after Congress and the President passed the National Industrial Recovery Act and 27 years after they passed the Wagner Act, President John F. Kennedy issued Executive Order 10988 in 1963. This order gave the union winning a majority vote within a bargaining unit of Federal employees the sole collective bargaining right to represent these employees.

Previous to 1963, the European system prevailed. Government unions spoke only for their members. Two, three, and sometimes more unions could, and did, speak for Federal government workers who were its members in a particular department of location.

Under Executive Order 10988, by a vote much akin to the National Labor Relations

Board representation elections in industry, Government employees for the first time could choose an exclusive bargaining representative.

Executive Orders 11491, 12107, and Civil Service Reform Act. President Kennedy's Executive Order 10988 was followed up in 1969 by President Nixon's Executive Order 11491 and in 1978 by President Carter's Executive Order 12107. Congress subsequently enacted the Civil Service Reform Act whose Federal labor relations sections became effective in 1980. What these executive orders and the Civil Service Reform Act did in effect was to pick up almost *in toto* many sections of the Wagner Act as amended by the Taft Hartley Act and the Labor Management Reporting and Disclosure Act of 1959 (See LABOR RELATIONS LEGISLATION). Therefore, to a large extent Federal labor relations are much the same as in private industry in that the parties are required to meet and confer in good faith and execute written agreements or memoranda of understanding on items on which they reach agreement.

Federal employee labor relations laws differ theoretically from the laws affecting private industry in that excluded from the requirement to meet and confer are these items: wages, benefits, the number of employees needed, and technology of the work. The executive orders and the Civil Service Reform Act forbid unions to call or engage in a strike, work stoppage, slowdown, or picketing. Events show that such a ban may be more theoretical than real. Postal strikes, threatened postal strikes, and mass picketing of postal headquarters have taken place despite this ban. Police, firemen, teachers, and garbagemen engage in sick-call strikes despite similar bans under state and local laws. In Europe such strikes by public employees are frequent.

Extent of Government Employee Unionization. In 1962, a total of 1.2 million Federal, state, and local government employees were in government unions. By 1968 this number had grown to 2.2 million, and by 1978 to 3.6 million. Thus, during the 1962–1978 period, union membership among Federal, state, and local government employees tripled. Major public sector unions that more than tripled in size during this period are the Teachers Union, the Government Employees Union, and the State, County and Municipal Employees Union.

V—PROFESSIONAL ATHLETE UNIONS

A recent development has been the formation of unions by professional athletes. Among the earliest of such organizations is the Major League Baseball Players Association with a membership of 650 and 26 local unions, one each for the 26 major league teams. Its Executive Director, as of 1981, Marvin Miller, was previously Research Director and Assistant to the President of the Steelworkers' Union. Among the newer professional associations in athletics are the Major League Umpires Association, the National Basketball Players Association, the Football League Players Association, and the Hockey League Players Association. All are independent unaffiliated organizations.

VI—ANNUAL REPORTS OF UNIONS

As do all organizations, unions change. Helpful in keeping up to date with the changes in union officers, finances, and constitutions are the annual reports, called LM-2s, that unions are required to file under the Labor-Management Reporting and Disclosure Act. The law makes these reports public information. Interested citizens may examine them—and obtain copies at 10 cents per page—at the U. S. Department of Labor, Labor Management Services Administration (LMSA), Public Document Room, Frances Perkins Building, 2nd Street and Constitution Avenue, Washington, D.C. 20216, or at area offices in some 24 cities in the continental United States, and in Hato Rey, Puerto Rico, and Honolulu, Hawaii.

JAMES J. BAMBRICK, Labor Economist, The Standard Oil Company (Ohio), Cleveland, Ohio.*

* Opinions expressed in the foregoing article are the author's, and not those of The Standard Oil Company (Ohio).

Information References

Texts:

Bambrick, James J. "Collective Bargaining and Union Contracts," in "Handbook of Modern Personnel Administration," Famularo, Joseph J., ed., New York, McGraw-Hill, 1972.

Bambrick, James J. and Haas, George, "Handbook of Union Government, Structure and Procedures," *Studies in Personnel Policy, No. 150,* New York, The Conference Board, 1955.

Bellante, Don, "Labor Economics—Choice in the Labor Market," New York, McGraw-Hill, 1979.

Bloom, Gordon F. and Northrup, Herbert R., "Economics of Labor Relations," 8th ed. Homewood, Illinois, Irwin, 1977.

Bok, Derek C. and Dunlop, John T., "Labor and the American Community," New York, Simon & Schuster, 1970.
Bureau of Labor Statistics, "Brief History of the American Labor Movement," *Bulletin No. 1000,* 5th ed., Washington, D.C., *U.S. Dept. of Labor, 1978.* "Directory of National and International Unions in the United States, 1979," Washington, D.C., U.S. Department of Labor, 1980.
Burtt, Everett Johnson, "Labor in the American Economy", New York, St. Martin's Press, 1979.
Chamberlain, Neil W., "The Labor Sector," 3rd ed., New York, McGraw-Hill, 1980.
Commons, John R. and Associates, "History of Labor in the United States," New York, Macmillan, 1966.
Fink, Gary M., "Biographical Dictionary of American Labor Leaders," Westbury, Conn., and London, England, Greenwood Press, 1974.
Finley, Joseph E., "The Corrupt Kingdom—The Rise & Fall of the United Mine Workers," New York, Simon & Schuster, 1972.
Gompers, Samuel, "Seventy Years of Life and Labor," New York, Dutton 1957.
Holley, William H. and Jenning, Kenneth M., "The Labor Relations Process," Hinsdale, Ill., Dryden Press, 1980.
Hutchinson, John, "The Imperfect Union: A History of Corruption in American Trade Unions," New York, Dutton, 1970.
Marshall, F. Ray, "Labor Economics: Wages, Employment and Trade Unionism," 4th ed., Homewood, Ill., Irwin, 1980.
Phelps, O. W., "Introduction to Labor Economics," 4th ed., Huntington, N.Y., Kreiger, 1978.
Reynolds, Lloyd G., "Labor Economics and Labor Relations," Englewood Cliffs, N.J., Prentice-Hall, 1978.
"Who's Who in Labor," New York, Arno Press, New York Times Company, 1976.

Cross References: *Collective Bargaining; Labor Arbitration; Labor Relations Legislation; Mediation; Women in Business and Industry, Part IV, Section on Women and Unions.*

LEADERSHIP: See Hawthorne Experiments; Human Relations in Industry; Job Enrichment and Work Effectiveness; Managerial Grid; Motivation (and accompanying entries with that prefix); Supervisory Training.

LEASING OF INDUSTRIAL EQUIPMENT

Since the early 1950s users of many different kinds of chattel property have entered into leasing and rental arrangements for the equipment they need in their enterprise. While leasing existed in certain industries prior to 1950, this type of financing has had a steadily accelerating growth in recent years, due to the fact that the user has begun to recognize that an asset produces the same profit or cost reduction whether it is owned or leased. When a manufacturer wishes to modernize his productive equipment, he may be eager to conserve working capital so that it may be invested in acquiring inventories needed for increased production, or for the hiring of additional labor. The profitability of the enterprise is increased through the leverage of additional debt.

However, those contemplating long-term leasing contracts should keep in mind that other financing alternatives may be available, such as conditional sale contracts or purchase contracts secured by a chattel mortgage. The Government has liberalized depreciation rules to stimulate capital investment. And investment tax credit may apply to a lease transaction, although complex rules apply. Thus, substantial equipment acquisition should justify the study of all the alternative financing methods available. The sophisticated company will ask its financial officers to use the discounted cash flow method of analysis of these alternatives, or some similar analytical technique. (See RETURN ON CAPITAL)

Assets for which Leasing Service May Be Available. In general, a lease contract can be arranged for any asset which has sufficient value to justify the paperwork involved and sufficient durability to permit the lessor to realize salvage value should the lessee fail to fulfill his contract. It is difficult to find a lessor who will provide leasing service for an asset which retails at less than $500. It may be quite easy to find a lessor for an asset costing several million dollars. Assets which are commonly leased include aircraft, computers, business machines, material handling equipment, machine tools, trucks, automobiles, and railroad cars.

Definitions. In recent years, the word *lease* has come to mean a transaction of several years' duration which frequently approximates the depreciable life of the equipment leased. The term *rental* refers to short-term leasing, generally by the day, week, month, or perhaps for a year or less. A *pay-out* lease means that the lessor will collect rental payments which will be equal to his cost of purchasing the equipment so that it may be leased to the lessee. Naturally, his collected rentals will likewise include a factor which will cover his administrative expense and profit on the money he may have borrowed to finance his equipment purchase.

The *non-pay-out* lease means that the lessor will collect less than his equipment cost over the lease term. He then will take the equipment back and re-sell it, or re-lease it. The non-pay-out lease is not common, but it is sometimes used in leasing machine tools and material handling equipment when asset durability is high and resale values are well established on the used equipment market.

Manufacturers of computers and copying equipment may offer "rental" contracts which permit the lessee to cancel the contract on short notice without penalty. These contracts are common examples of the non-pay-out lease.

Sources of Lease Financing. As time goes on, more and more entrepreneurs have begun to recognize profit potential through offering leasing service. The potential lessee must use great caution in selecting his lessor, so that he can be sure that the lessor will continue in business during the lease term.

Manufacturers may offer a lease plan to their customers directly or through an associated captive finance company. If the manufacturer wishes to emphasize greater distribution of his product, he may be content with his normal profit margin on the "sale" to the lessor and thus price his leasing service at very reasonable rates.

The finance companies may offer leasing service as well as their standard services of accounts-receivable financing, chattel-mortgage financing, and conditional-sale financing. However, as competition from other lessors has intensified, many finance companies have been unable to secure their desired return on investment through offering leasing service, and this part of their operation has been de-emphasized.

Many leasing companies offer their services through direct mail, magazine, and newspaper advertising. They may work closely with a manufacturer, train salesmen in leasing techniques, and provide outside financing to carry the leases produced by the manufacturer's sales department. Where such liaison exists, the manufacturer may arrange to market used equipment returned from the leases.

Commercial banks now offer leasing service to their customers, since regulating authorities authorized them to become outright owners of leased equipment. The banks find that their return on investments in leased property may exceed that of mortgaged property. Sometimes banks furnish capital for leases to their customers; a leasing company may handle administration of the leases.

Lease brokers act as intermediaries between lenders, leasing companies, and leasing users. The broker determines the need of the prospective lessee and solicits bids from banks, leasing companies, and other financing sources. The broker is compensated for his services by the organization furnishing the financing, or he may be paid as a consultant by the lessee.

Investment bankers and the tax departments of large accounting firms may assist a prospective lessee in finding leasing service through private placement of the lease with syndicates of wealthy investors or with corporate customers with available cash reserves. Many limited partnerships have been formed which permit the partners to use depreciation on leased assets and the investment tax credit as deductions against taxable income. As income requirements of such investors may be minimal, the rates for this type of leasing service may be below those otherwise available. Similarly, the manufacturer wishing to lease equipment may form his own subsidiary leasing company which may secure financing on its own credit standing or on the guarantee of its parent. Careful legal work must be done to insure that such an organization is a separate entity for tax purposes.

Trends in the Leasing Industry. In earlier years, many small organizations with less than first-grade credit standing were successful in leasing assets, although the rates charged were very high. Such leasing service is now more difficult to locate, as lessors generally require a good credit standing for long-term leasing. There has been high mortality among smaller leasing companies which were unable to secure the needed capital for equipment puchasing as their marketing activities expanded. Many such companies were merged with larger firms. Thus, the trend in the industry is toward consolidation, with the larger firms surviving.

Banks are becoming more and more aggressive in direct leasing. As the smaller leasing companies secure their financing from banks, frequently banks used by their lessee, the banks control money costs to the lessor. When a bank enters the leasing industry directly, it eliminates the leasing company's mark-up on the cost of borrowed funds and thus decreases the cost of leasing to the user. Thus, growing bank leasing involvement is accelerating the consolidation of small leasing organizations into larger, well-financed firms.

As users of leasing have become more sophisticated, they have insisted that their financial officers solicit several bids for substantial leasing requirements. Rate competition among major lessors is very common. This competition has decreased the profitability of leasing achievable by the smaller leasing organization.

For several years, such specialized leasing companies offered computer leases at rates less than those charged by the computer manufacturers. These were non-pay-out leases. The lessor felt he could re-market the used computer at the end of the lease term. To offset this competition with their own leasing plans, manufacturers reduced rates and likewise removed "software" services from leases undertaken by the computer leasing companies.

While early leases may have averaged three years in length, there is a trend toward lengthening the lease to an approximation of a normal depreciable life of the asset as allowed by Government schedules. This is done to counteract the Government's effort to disallow short-term leases on the ground that they are disguised contracts of conditional sale.

Because of wide fluctuations in interest rates, there is a growing trend to negotiate a floating financing rate which is tied to the prime rate as set by major banks.

Advantages of Leasing to the User of Equipment. Advertising literature distributed by leasing companies frequently features claimed leasing advantages which may be illusory. At the same time there are many genuine advantages which leasing brings to the user.

Additional Credit Source. Those offering leasing service may have access to sources of financing which may not be available to the user. Insurance companies, pension trusts, syndicates, investors, and companies with excess cash may be willing to finance the organization offering leasing service. It may be difficult for the individual user of leasing to negotiate directly with such sources.

Cash Flow. A particular lease contract may permit the lessee to charge lease payments against business operating expenses in an amount which is more desirable than depreciation deductions for puchased assets. These increased expenses decrease profit, decrease taxes, and may improve the cash flow of the enterprise.

Investment Tax Credit. At times when the Government grants such a credit, a leasing transaction may offer opportunities to secure the credit, just as would be the case in a purchase transaction. However as stated above, complex rules apply. In leases entered into after September 22, 1971, individuals and noncorporate lessors can claim the ITC only if they manufactured or produced the leased property, or are in the business of offering "short"-term leases. There may be numerical tests which are difficult to meet.

The lessor has the option of passing the ITC along to the lessee, or retaining the credit. However, on leases entered into after November 8, 1971, the lessor can pass through the credit to the lessee only if the term of the lease is at least 80% of the "class life" of the asset. But this rule does not apply if the class life is 14 years or less, or if the lease is a net lease. In these cases, the lessor may pass through the credit to the first lessee, but the passed-through amount of the credit may be no greater than the part of the credit which the lease period bears to the class life of the property.

Thus, the lessee may wish to negotiate with the lessor for a pass-through of the credit. He may benefit by securing an immediate deduction from taxes without having made an outlay for the entire purchase price of the asset acquired.

If the lessee is operating at a loss, or has already accumulated all the investment tax credit which is allowable for deduction in a particular year, he can negotiate with his lessor so that the lessor may retain the credit, reducing the rental payments to compensate the lessee for the loss of the credit.

Offsetting "Asset Depreciation Range" (ADR). Government regulations may require a company to group several different assets in one class for which a specific ADR is specified. The asset user may find that his particular machine has a life expectancy which is much less than the required life specified by the Government. Under such circumstances, the asset may be leased on a contract which is tailored to actual experience. Such a lease could not be attacked by tax authorities when company records justify the shorter lease.

Off-Balance-Sheet Financing. In past years,

only a currently-due lease obligation was shown as a liability on the balance sheet. The leased asset did not appear on the asset side of the balance sheet. Accountants would mention the existence of the lease contract as a footnote to the financial statements. Thus, companies were able to acquire needed assets without risking disapproval of stockholders or committees entrusted with enforcement of capital budgeting requirements within the corporation itself. However, recent developments indicate that certified public accountants may require their clients to capitalize substantial leases on the balance sheet, so that investors and creditors will be informed of these long-term obligations.

Sale-Leaseback Considerations. Many organizations offering leasing service are willing to appraise assets already in use in a client's organization. The assets are then purchased and leased back to the user, thus providing additional working capital. Those interested in such transactions must be careful to clear them with legal advisors so there will be no difficulty with creditors claiming that a "bulk sale" has taken place.

Hedging Against Inflation. As lease contracts are being written for longer terms, an equipment user may be able to insure that his equipment usage cost is stabilized for a period of many years. The lessor likewise must be conscious of inflation factors which may increase his cost of money and the expense of administering the lease. At the same time, competition within the industry may prevent the lessor from adding this factor to protect himself against inflation.

Savings on Local Taxes. In some states, sales and use taxes are added to each rental invoice. If an asset should be returned to the lessor prior to the end of its useful life and a new lease contract is negotiated for a replacement asset, there may be a substantial saving in state taxes in comparison to having paid the full tax outright on purchase.

Simplified Asset Acquisition. When a user is contemplating leasing many different items of equipment over an extended period, an individual lessor may be willing to negotiate a master lease contract covering the entire series. Then as assets are added, simple documentation covers those additions, thus decreasing paperwork.

One Hundred Percent Financing. A creditworthy lessee can usually convince his lessor that no rental payment need be made until the equipment is delivered and accepted. If the lessor should require an advance payment of rental, that payment is frequently less than that required under normal conditional sale or chattel mortgage plans.

Hedge Against Obsolescence. If a lessor offers his lessee a contract which permits cancellation of the lease on short notice without penalty, the lessee can hedge against obsolescence in an industry which may be rapidly changing in its technology. However, most long-term leases will require full payment of asset value within the basic lease term, thus eliminating any hedge against obsolescence.

Leasing Payments Made with Before-Tax Dollars. This phrase sometimes appears in leasing literature as an inducement to the lessee. The lessee should remember that the Government is continuing to liberalize depreciation allowances. Those allowances may actually provide cash-flow advantages which will be equal to or greater than those furnished by leasing. Depreciation is also a "before-tax" deduction.

Simplified Automotive Acquisition. Leases offered covering automobiles and trucks are for much shorter terms because of shorter vehicle life. Specialized companies operating in this leasing field offer record-keeping services on fleet-operating expense which may be helpful. They may offer to market used cars and trucks. Executive time may be saved which otherwise might be spent on acquisition of new vehicles and disposal of used vehicles. Expensive specialized repair facilities for truck fleets may be eliminated by centralized facilities maintained by a truck lessor. Concentrated purchasing power of the vehicle lessor may produce lower cost on the vehicle, accessories, and tires, thus helping to offset cost of the leasing service.

Advantages to the Lessor of Equipment. *Increased Sales for Manufacturers.* As leasing service is widely available from the sources mentioned earlier, any manufacturer can offer a leasing plan to his customers without investment of his own capital in these long-term receivables. Consequently, his marketing is made more effective through his offering of the leasing plan.

Stabilizing Business Cycles. Lease receivables billed on a monthly or quarterly basis provide a determinable future income on which cash utilization projections can be made. A company which manufactures on a seasonal basis may find that leasing will assist in spreading sales income more evenly throughout the year.

Forced Obsolescence. As all lease contracts have a basic lease term, the manufacturer's or leasing company's marketing department has an opportunity to approach the lessee toward the end of the basic lease to suggest that an improved machine be leased to replace the current machine. Such a marketing program can have substantial impact on the regular introduction of new products.

Profit on Resale or Re-Lease of Used Equipment. Where there is residual value left in equipment at the end of a lease, it may be diverted to a secondary market at considerable profit to the lessor.

Profit on Financing. The lessor always has the opportunity to increase his financing rate sufficiently to return a profit on the financing of the lease, in addition to the profit to be realized on salvage value of the asset at the end of the lease.

Discount from Manufacturer. The lessor operating independently may be able to negotiate a purchase of the asset at a discount from the manufactuer, and then charge the lessee rentals based on the full retail price.

Profit on Renewals and Purchase Options. The lease may include such provisions, and if the lessee exercises them, additional profit comes to the lessor.

Retention of Investment Tax Credit. The lessor may have the right to retain the investment tax credit. Individuals and non-corporate lessors may claim the ITC only if they manufactured the leased assets, or are in the business of offering "short"-term leases, or are able to meet certain difficult-to-pass mechnical tests. Large lessors in a profit position may find the credit very useful in reducing income taxes.

The Lessor's Problem of Financing. As mentioned earlier, there has been considerable mortality among leasing companies because of cash flow problems. An aggressive marketing staff constantly brings new leases to the financial officer. He must constantly tap new sources of financing to secure the money required to purchase the equipment needed by the lessee. Organizations planning to enter leasing should enlist help from their accountants in charting anticipated cash requirements. Lessees selecting leasing organizations should be sure to choose one with proper financing and with the needed managerial skills.

Contractual Arrangements. Leases normally are written for a basic term of an agreed number of months or years. Renewal options may be negotiated by the lessee. Purchase options may likewise be negotiated. Some leases provide for substitution of later-designed equipment and return of original equipment. The rates for leasing service are usually expressed in percentages of total equipment cost paid on a monthly or quarterly basis. The effective add-on interest rate can be determined by multiplying the amount of the monthly leasing payment by the number of months in the basic period, and then comparing that total to the quoted retail purchase price of the asset being leased.

For leases of smaller dollar amounts to companies of less than first-grade credit standing, effective interest rates may range from 12% to 18%, or higher. For large companies, typical rates may be expressed as additions to the prime rate of interest, perhaps 2% to 3% above the prime rate. In special transactions, applicable financing rates may be less than the prime rate if the lessor is permitted to keep the investment tax credit and also expects to realize substantial income on residual or salvage value. Substantial leasing transactions such as those relating to jet aircraft may carry financing rates substantially below the normal equipment-leasing rate schedules.

Most leasing contracts provide that the lessee maintain the equipment. Normally the lessee is expected to insure the equipment in favor of the lessor as well as the lessee, and the lessee is expected to pay personal property and other taxes assessed against the leased equipment. In Ohio, for instance, if the lease contract permits the lessee to purchase the property at lease-end, the lessee must pay the property taxes. If there is no purchase option, the lessor must pay the property tax. If the lessee can contractually shift to the lessor the payment of taxes, the insurance of the leased assets and their maintenance, then the tax deductibility of the lease payments is more assured.

Legal Interpretation of Chattel Leases. A long series of court cases holds that the intention of the lessor and lessee should govern legal interpretation of the contract. Thus, if there is honest intent to lease, rather than to purchase, the lease is valid. The Internal Revenue Service has issued a number of administrative rulings governing leasing. The earliest rulings, 55-540-1-2, give valuable guidance to lessors and lessees. Here are some observations concerning interpretation of various IRS rulings:

In general, a "nominal" renewal option may be evidence that a lease is in reality a sale. Whenever possible, renewal options should be set at a rate which is comparable to established rates quoted in the open market for used equipment of the same type.

In Revenue Procedure 75-21, the IRS states that a purchase option at the end of lease term must approximate the fair market value of the leased assets. Thus it is dangerous to fix the purchase price of the assets at the beginning of the lease.

To qualify for a lease, the leased asset must still have substantial remaining value at the end of the lease term. The asset may not be "used up" during the lease term. Revenue Procedure 75-21 states that the asset at lease-end must have a remaining value of the longer of: (1) one year, or (2) 20% of the asset's total useful life.

Lessees should not permit the lessor to insert a clause indicating that the leased asset will be abandoned by the lessor to the lessee at the end of the lease term, as this would not permit classification under the "substantial remaining value" concept mentioned above.

Here are other characteristics which may result in classification of a transaction as a lease, not a sale:

(1) The legal documents state that the transaction is a lease.

(2) Title remains with the lessor at all times.

(3) There is no large amount of prepaid rent followed by much smaller payments.

(4) The equipment is removable and is not affixed to the property of the lessee.

(5) The tax accounting and ledgers of the lessee treat the transaction as a lease.

(6) The lessor does not have the characteristics of a "finance company" financing a sale, rather than a lease.

For these many reasons, lessees should be very careful about signing lease contracts prepared by the lessor. Legal documents should be carefully examined by the lessee's counsel so that a document can be designed which will result in tax treatment favorable to the objectives of both lessor and lessee.

Tie-in. In the early days of leasing, some manufacturers offered leasing service as an effort to ensure that the lessee was required to use consumable supplies manufactured by the same firm in addition to using a machine itself. The Government has prosecuted such arrangements as being in restraint of trade.

FRANK K. GRIESINGER, President, Frank K. Griesinger and Associates, Inc., Cleveland, Ohio

Information References

Publication:

Staff Recommendations: *Leasing vs. Buying: Decision Guidelines for the '80s,* New York, Research Institute of America, Inc., 1980.

Texts:

Clark, T. M., "Leasing," London, McGraw-Hill, 1978.

Contino, Richard M., "Legal and Financial Aspects of Equipment Leasing Transactions," Englewood Cliffs, N.J, Prentice-Hall, 1979.

Greenfield, Harvey and Griesinger, Frank E., "Sale-Leaseback and Leasing in Real Estate and Equipment Transactions," Cleveland, Frank K. Griesinger and Associates, Inc., reprint 1980.

National Association of Accountants and Society of Management Accountants (Canada), "The Lease Purchase Decision, 1980.

Pritchard, Robert E. and Hindelang, Thomas, "The Lease-Buy Decision," New York, AMACOM Div., American Management Associations, 1980.

Vancil, Richard F., "Leasing of Industrial Equipment," New York, McGraw-Hill, 1963.

Cross References: *Depreciation; Fixed-Asset Investment Analysis: The MAPI Formulas and Procedures; Long-Range Corporate Planning; Long-Range Planning: Financial Aspects; Return on Capital.*

LEWIS, JOHN L.

John Llewellyn Lewis (1880–1969), American labor leader (see LABOR UNIONS) began his union work in 1909 when, after early jobs in mining and other occupations, he became statistician for the United Mine Workers. He rose to the positions of Vice President (1917–18), Acting President (1919), and President (1920–60). Taking advantage of the Government's policy, established in 1933, of fostering collective bargaining, he built the UMW into the country's strongest union.

Lewis was convinced that labor's future lay in the organization of all wage earners in a given industry into one industrial union. This philosophy led him in 1935 to break with the leaders of the American Federation of Labor, who favored the traditional separate craft unions. He formed the Committee for Industrial Organization (CIO), composed of eight of the largest AFL unions, and became its first president. In September, 1936, the CIO unions were expelled by AFL. However, CIO continued to organize large portions of the automobile and other mass-production industries. In 1938 it changed its name to Congress for Industrial Orgnization, and began taking an active part in national politics.

Lewis supported Franklin D. Roosevelt for the presidency in 1936, but broke with other labor leaders in 1940 when, opposing a third term for Roosevelt, he supported the Republican candidate. Upon Roosevelt's victory, Lewis resigned as CIO president, and in October, 1942, led the UMW out of the CIO. In 1946, the AFL readmitted the UMW into its ranks, and unanimously elected Lewis as a vice president and council member.

Under Lewis' leadership the UMW strikes achieved for mine workers the $8.50/day wage, the union shop, the 35-hour week, and portal-to-portal pay. During these years, the mines were repeatedly seized by the Government to halt strikes. Settlements were invariably favorable to the workers. For example, the 59-day soft coal strike in the spring of 1946 ended with governmental seizure, but Lewis won an 18½¢ per hour increase, and a pioneering welfare and retirement fund, financed by a levy of 5¢ per ton of coal produced. However, later that year Lewis terminated the agreement, invoking a new strike. As a result he was fined $10,000, and the UMW $3,500,000, for contempt of court. He therefore called off the strike on December 7, 1946, for the first time yielding to a superior force.

Lewis became President emeritus of the United Mine Workers in 1960. His public work included membership on the Labor Advisory Board and National Labor Board of the National Recovery Administration, chairmanship of Labor's Non-Partisan League, and, during World War I, membership on the Coal Production Committee of the National Council of Defense. Self educated, he received honorary doctorates from West Virginia University (1957), and Georgetown University (1960).

LICENSING: See Franchising; Franchising: Legal Aspects; Patents.

LINCOLN INCENTIVE MANAGEMENT PLAN

The Lincoln Incentive Management Plan, instituted in 1934 by James F. Lincoln at the Lincoln Electric Company, Cleveland (welding equipment and supplies), is a combination profit-sharing and incentive plan. It has received wide publicity, not only because of the size of the extra payments made to workers, but also because of the way in which worker-management identification is achieved, resulting in continuing suggestions for method improvements, which in turn lower costs and prices while at the same time returning increased take-home pay. End-of-year bonuses attainable by employees are in the order of magnitude of 60% to 150% of basic pay, while at the same time basic wages and salaries are comparable to those of comparable jobs in the Cleveland area. Everyone but the president and the chairman of the board shares in these incentives.

Performance standards are set by the usual time-study techniques. However, the system differs from time-study-based incentives in the determination of the individual bonus, which is based on an over-all judgment of the worker's performance and attitude, and in the continuing stimulation of improvement ideas on the part of the entire organization. Management constantly hammers home the theme that there must be a continuing reduction in the price of Lincoln products, so that not only the management and employees share in the increased productivity, but the customers as well. In Lincoln's own words [1]:

> The man is rewarded for all the things he does that are of help, and penalized if he does not do as well as others in all these same ways. He is a member of the team and is rewarded or penalized depending on what he can do in all opportunities to win the game.
>
> The man is rated by all those who have accurate knowledge of some phase of his work . . . This program runs parallel to the write-ups following the playing of a game or the selecting of an all-American team. The best man gets the praise and the standing he warrants and craves.
>
> Each man is advanced or retarded in his standing by his current record. He is rated two times per year. The sum of these ratings determines his share in the bonus and advancement.

Exhibit I

Lincoln's Incentive Management Appraisal Forms

(1)

This is your merit rating for:

YOUR IDEAS AND YOUR COOPERATION

This rating is done by your department head jointly with the Time Study Department in the shop and with other department heads in the office and in engineering.

New ideas—new methods—new thinking are very important to you and your Company. This card credits you if you are using your initiative and intelligence to find new and better methods which may help the Company reduce costs, increase output, improve quality, or which may help the Company improve its relationship with customers and the public.

This card also evaluates your attitude towards your supervision, your co-workers, and your Company. "Cooperation" means teamwork. This card credits you for your willingness to meet emergencies by doing other jobs, in helping others do their jobs, or in making your expert knowledge available to others.

[*The employee is rated with respect to the above on a scale which permits selection of a point in a continuous range of "Fair," "Good," "Outstanding."*]

(2)

This is your merit rating for:

WORKMANSHIP AND ATTITUDE TOWARD QUALITY

It covers:

(1) The quality of work produced.
(2) The elimination of scrap.
(3) The elimination of errors.
(4) Your attitude toward improving the quality of our finished product.

This rating is done by your department head jointly with Inspection in the shop and with other department heads in the office and in Engineering.

[*The employee is rated with respect to the above on a scale which permits selection of a point in a continuous range of "Poor quality, too much scrap, too many errors, attitude needs improvement," "Quality sometimes unsatisfactory, makes scrap and errors," "Workmanship is of a fair quality, occasional errors, makes some scrap," "Slightly above fair quality," "Quality of work is good; tries to improve quality," "Work is superior, minimum quality supervision necessary," "Outstanding."*]

(3)

This is your merit rating for:

SUPERVISION REQUIRED

It covers:

(1) Knowledge of your job and helpfulness by imparting it to others.
(2) Your ability to supervise yourself.
(3) Your initiative and all-round skill.
(4) Your orderliness and care of equipment.

This rating has been done by your department head.

[*The employee is rated with respect to the above on a scale which permits selection of a point in a continuous range of "Requires additional training and experience, needs supervision regularly, apt not to take care of equipment," "Lacks required job knowledge, needs supervision; not orderly; may give equipment poor care," "Has required job knowledge, requires supervision, can do other jobs, is fairly orderly, gives equipment fair care," "Considerable job knowledge, requires some supervision, takes some initiative, orderly and careful of equipment," "Expert on job, does help others, requires little supervision, careful of equipment and orderly," "Unusual job knowledge on his and other jobs; helpful to others, requires no supervision, takes pride in equipment and work station," "Outstanding."*]

EXHIBIT I *Continued*

(4)

This is your merit rating for:

OUTPUT

It covers:

(1) Dependability; on the job, not absent, tardy, or waiting time.
(2) Putting out, not holding back.
(3) Willingness to do any job available.
(4) Teamwork and extra effort in case of absence of others or in emergencies.

This rating is done by your department head jointly with Production Control in the shop and with other department heads in the office and in Engineering.

[*The employee is rated with respect to the above on a scale which permits selection of a point in a continuous range of "Wastes time, holds back," "Wastes time occasionally, holds back some, does other jobs when out of work reluctantly," "Does a day's work, will try other jobs and occasionally helps in emergencies," "Usually dependable and on the job; does not hold back, fair teamworker," "Dependable, does not hold back, tries to maintain output by teamwork and extra effort when needed," "Very dependable, on the job, does all the work he can, very good in teamwork and meeting emergencies," "Outstanding."*]

At the time of giving each man his rating, any question he may want to ask as to why the rating is as it is and how it can be improved is answered in complete detail by the executives responsible.

The progress in new methods and techniques flows naturally from the desire of the worker to find . . . progressive ideas. It is obvious that lower cost will be the outcome.

Size of Bonus is determined as follows: At the end of the year, a fair return is paid to the stockholders as a dividend, which the workers are made to see as "the wages of capital." After the dividend is provided for, the company sets aside what it terms "seed money" for the future. The amount is determined by the directors on the basis of current operations. After these deductions from profits, all of the balance is divided as a bonus among the workers and management on the basis described, i.e., on the basis of the contribution of each person to the success of the company for the year. The size of the individual's bonus depends on three factors: his merit rating, his base salary, and the size of the total bonus pool. The actual bonus is computed by multiplying the base wage or salary times merit rating times the bonus factor. The bonus factor is obtained by dividing the dollars of total bonus pool by the dollars of total company payroll. It can be seen that for this system to work out, each department head must see that the merit ratings in his department average out at 100. Thus for each 120 that a supervisor awards, he must give out an 80, or perhaps two 90s.

Merit Appraisal of the individual worker is made in detailed fashion jointly by his immediate superior and others who are in a position to know what he has done. Appraisal occurs three times a year. Exhibit I shows the substance of the four rating cards filled in by the supervisor.

Results. As of 1980, Lincoln stated that the bonus distribution has slightly exceeded wages during the last 45 years. From management's point of view, one major criterion of the program's success is the company's productivity which has attained $150,000 annual sales per employee. This compares favorably with the average for all manufacturing. Another success indicator is employee stability. The company has a turnover rate of less than 1% per month. These results were accompanied by highly competitive prices for all Lincoln products.

That industry has not adopted the Lincoln plan in widespread fashion, despite the spectacular success achieved with it by its originator, perhaps testifies to the personal dedication of Mr. Lincoln himself to the furtherance of constructive employee motivation in industry. His philosophy may be summed up in the opening sentence of his pamphlet, "Intelligent Selfishness and Manufacturing" [2]: "Great as American industry is, it leaves largely untapped its greatest resources, the productive power, initiative, and intelligence latent in every person."

RICHARD S. SABO, Manager, Educational Services, Lincoln Electric Company, Cleveland, Ohio

References Cited

[1] Lincoln, James F., "Incentive Management," Cleveland, Lincoln Electric Company, 1951.

[2] Lincoln, James F., "Intelligent Selfishness and Manufacturing," a pamphlet published by Lincoln Electric Company, Cleveland.

Cross References: *Incentive Systems (and cross references there given).*

LINE OF BALANCE (LOB)

Line of Balance is a management control procedure for collecting, measuring, and presenting facts relating to time cost and accomplishment—all measured against a specific plan. It shows the progress, status, background, timing and phasing of intra-project activities, thus providing management with a means of:

(1) Comparing actual progress with forecast performance.

(2) Examining *only* the deviations from established plans, and gaging their degree of severity with respect to the remainder of the project.

(3) Receiving timely information concerning trouble areas and indicating areas where appropriate corrective action is required.

(4) Forecasting future performance.

The "Line of Balance" itself is a graphic device which enables a manager to see at a single glance which of many activities comprising a complex operation are "in balance"—i.e., whether those which should have been completed at the time of the review actually are completed, and whether any activities scheduled for future completion are lagging behind schedule. The Line of Balance chart comprises only one feature of the whole philosophy, which includes as well numerous danger-signal controls for all of the various levels of management concerned. (For comparison of LOB with other project control and scheduling techniques, see PERT: (PROGRAM EVALUATION AND REVIEW TECHNIQUE); CRITICAL PATH METHOD (CPM); and the "overview" discussion, INTEGRATED PROJECT MANAGEMENT.)

History. LOB was devised by the members of a group headed by George E. Fouch, established during 1941 to monitor production of the Goodyear Tire & Rubber Company at the commencement of the latter's war effort. It was successfully applied to the production planning and scheduling of the huge Navy mobilization program of World War II, and also proved to be a valuable tool for expediting production during the Korean hostilities, when it was used for a wide band of defense suppliers for the Armed Forces.

Since that time its applications have been further expanded, making it now suitable across a whole spectrum of activities ranging from research and development through job-shop and flow-shop operations. In recent years it was used to monitor design and construction of the early warning (DEW-line) defense system, and, for the Navy, the Type II periscope, and Star Tracker—both critical items in the Polaris program.

Specific forms and reports will be found to differ in detail, but the basic pattern and symbology are quite uniform throughout industry. Because of important differences, however, care must be taken to distinguish between the technique used for production efforts (repetitive operations) and the technique for monitoring R&D programs (one-time operations). Procedure for the first-named application is set forth in two manuals issued by the Department of the Navy, "Production Analysis" [1] and "Line of Balance Technology" [2]. The second is described in detail in the manual, "Managing a Development Program" [3].

Standard Symbols. All LOB charts use standard symbols, as shown in the lower right-hand corner of Exhibit I. They indicate the so-called "sensors" ("milestones"), i.e., readily identifiable stages of development or control points in the process, designating completion of specific activities or clusters of activities.

Application to Production. Exhibit I is a simplified example of an LOB chart for a hypothetical fabrication and assembly operation, demonstrating the original application in monitoring and controlling production. The finished LOB chart displays, first, the *Objective* (the required delivery schedule), as shown in the upper left-hand portion. Second, there is a clearly defined *Plan* for meeting that objective, indicating interrelationships, and how each major component fits into the assembly process, as well as the exact point in the cycle when

EXHIBIT I

LINE OF BALANCE CHART

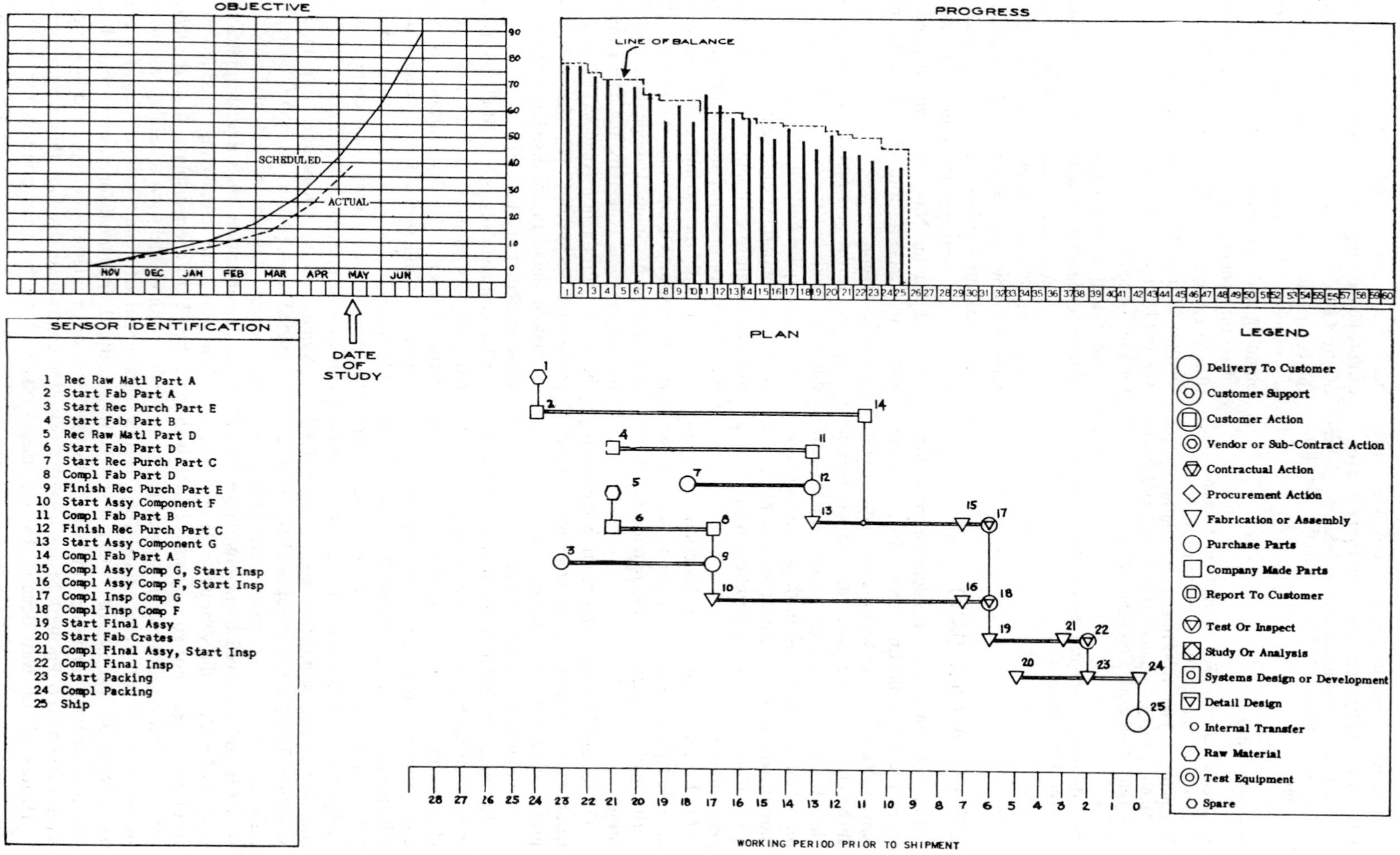

each one is required to be available. This is shown in the graphing of sensors, using standard symbols, in the lower half of the chart, the bottom scale being the number of working periods (in this case, the measure is in days), counting backwards from total completion, when each component must be finished. Third, there is an appraisal of the progress that has been achieved, given by the vertical bars in the *Progress* chart in the upper right-hand portion. Finally, also in the upper right-hand portion, there is the *Line of Balance,* i.e., a measure of the level of progress that must have been reached if the objective is to be met on schedule, in accordance with the established plan. These four basic elements are vital ingredients of any effective management system. Together they will provide for the continuous exercise of authority and create a balanced and integrated operation out of a large number of individual and uncoordinated transactions.

The Objective curve is a plot of scheduled cumulative deliveries against calendar dates. In this instance the curve tells us that a total of ninety units are scheduled for delivery between November 1 and June 30. The dotted curve indicates that actual deliveries have fallen below the required number, reaching only thirty-eight units by May 10, whereas forty-eight had been scheduled.

The Operating (manufacturing) Plan is represented by the series of interconnecting horizontal lines, seen in the lower portion of the Line of Balance chart. Along these lines are the sensors indicating identifiable stages of development and control points. These control points are numbered consecutively from left to right across the schematic diagram, and from top to bottom wherever two or more points have a common position along the horizontal scale. As will be seen later, each of these control sensors is keyed by corresponding number to a bar graph in the Progress portion of the LOB chart. The Operating Plan illustrated has an established cycle of twenty-four days per unit. It indicates the manner in which the several types and kinds of parts and components are joined together to form the completed product.

In order to restrict the number of sensor points to an optimum (about fifty), certain conventions have been introduced. One of these is to develop a separate chart for each of two or more categories of parts, such as purchased, company-made, major components, customer-furnished parts, etc. In any case, however, there always remains the requirement for a summary of the whole to indicate the over-all state of the program. A Summary Chart generally is made by selecting key control points from each of the supporting charts, and having each such point represent a number of subordinate sensors.

A similar device frequently is adopted in the treatment of complex products consisting of a large number of parts. This expedient calls for each sensor to represent an association of parts—for example, a so-called "family group" of items on an indented parts list. Under such conditions the symbol should be positioned for the earliest required of all such parts, and all other related data (such as stock status) should be representative of the least favorable condition obtaining within that particular family group at the time of the survey.

The next step in our example is to bring about a visual combination of the data displayed in the Objective and the Plan portions of the chart. This will be used to establish a gage for measuring the performance requirements that will be necessary to meet the prescribed delivery goal under operating conditions established by the Manufacturing Plan. This combination of elements is known as the *Line of Balance*—the feature that gives its name to the technique.

Deriving the Line of Balance. Referring to Exhibit I, note that the date of the progress review is May 10. This now becomes the date for all reference purposes. The delivery requirements at any time will be found by erecting a perpendicular at the point corresponding to the date in question, and extending it to intersect the cumulative delivery curve. The value of the ordinate at that point represents the required *total deliveries* for that time. In the case illustrated, the curve shows that by May 10 there should have been shipped a total of 48 units, the Line of Balance relating to sensors 24 and 25, the events which take place at the time of delivery.

For *current* needs to insure *future* deliveries, consider sensors Nos. 1 and 2. These actions initiate the manufacturing cycle and are slated for accomplishment 24 days prior to delivery of the finished unit. It is apparent that on May 10 we must have used not only the 48 end-item sets of items 1 and 2 required for delivery on that date, but must also have completed an additional quantity sufficient to meet the shipping needs 24 working days later. The precise level of this requirement can be found by erecting a perpendicular at the calendar date which is 24 working days after May 10, viz. June 13. The cumulative delivery curve at that point calls for 78 finished units, showing that a total of 78 end-item sets of items 1 and 2 should have been used (or have been available for use) on May 10. The Line of Balance is drawn at this level in the Progress Chart. Similarly, sensor 3, which is slated for 23 days prior to delivery date, must provide for requirements for June 12, namely, 76 units, which is its Line of Balance.

Now, consider sensors Nos. 4, 5, and 6, all of which are required 21 working days in advance of shipment. The May 10 level of requirements for these items is represented by the value of the ordinate at the point corresponding to June 10, 72 units. For sensor No. 7, scheduled for accomplishment 18 working days in advance of shipment, a requirement for 66 end-item sets is shown by the Objective curve value for June 5.

By following the same principle of construction, requirement levels for all other elements are established, culminating in a 48 unit delivery schedule by May 10, the date of the study, and providing for planned future deliveries.

The end result is the characteristic step-down contour of a Line of Balance. Properly constructed, this invariably will step downward from a high point on the left to the level indicated for cumulative deliveries on the date of the study. By comparing the Line of Balance with the record of used and available inventories of each item, management is afforded a graphic portrayal of program status and an accurate forecast of shipping capability.

The vertical bars in the Progress chart are a typical LOB representation of the progress being made on a program. As was mentioned earlier, each sensor in the Operating Plan is keyed by an identifying number to a bar-graph display. The length of this bar represents the number of end-item sets that have been used or are available for use, as read off the vertical scale used for the Objective curve. It will be noted that because of the manner in which the chart was constructed, the bar graphs with the lowest numbers relate to the events that occur earliest, automatically pointing out the priority of correction action. Also, by reason of the fact that progress is reported in terms of *end-item sets,* the inventory count is translated into capability of delivery of finished units. That is to say, if the end product is a bicycle, the bar graph for wheels will be of a length that is equivalent to the total number of wheels that have been used (or are available for use) divided by two. The result shows how many finished bicycles can be delivered out of the current stock level of wheels.

All of the sensors that are behind schedule are indicated by bar graphs that fail to meet the Line of Balance. The first of these is sensor No. 8, complete fabrication of Part D. Inasmuch as supporting sensors 5 and 6 are on schedule, it is evident that some problem exists in the fabrication process. The effects of this difficulty have been transmitted throughout subsequent operations as may be seen by the bar graphs for 10, 16, 18, 19, 21, 22, 23, 24 and 25. It may be concluded that the fault for shipping only 38 instead of 48 units lies almost entirely with the failure to complete the required quantity of Part D. The chart also reveals the presence of a problem area in the operation represented by sensors 13 and 15. Even if the trouble with Part D were cleared up, the deliveries would be limited to only 51 units as shown by the height of bar graph 15.

This rudimentary example serves to illustrate the application of this technique to a simple process of fabrication and assembly. Line of Balance can be applied to all other manufacturing or production operations—whether job shop or flow shop. Although more than some forty years have elapsed since Line of Balance was first introduced, it is still considered to be a most effective device for control of production.

Application to Research and Development. For development programs the mechanics of the technique differ slightly, but the standard symbols remain the same as shown in Exhibit I, and are used to designate specific points leading toward the completion of specific activities or clusters of activities.

Individual Flow Diagrams and Level III Integrated Flow Chart. After the over-all plan for a project has been established, usually in a conference of managers with their chief supervisors, Individual Flow Diagrams are prepared for the component tasks. The working level supervisors provide the information for the Individual Flow Diagrams, which:

EXHIBIT II

LEVEL III INTEGRATED FLOW CHART

LEVEL II REF. NO.	WORK DESCRIPTION	# TOTAL BUDGET	SCHED-ULED TO	ACTUAL TO.
	RECEIVER SYSTEM	272		
	R.F. SUB ASSEMBLY	144		
	R.F. INPUT CHASSIS	352		
	FILAMENT FILTER ASSY	328		
	CHASSIS ASSY	240		
	R.F. SUB ASSY FAB.	190		
	FINE FREQ. TUNER	112		
	F.F. OSCILLATOR	328		
	HOUSING ASSY	320		
	F.F. SUB CHASSIS	112		
	VARIABLE IF AMP.	112		
	TUNING ASSY	130		
	SLUG DRIVE ASSY	120		
	SLUG TABLE ASSY	104		
	FINE FREQ TUNER FAB	168		

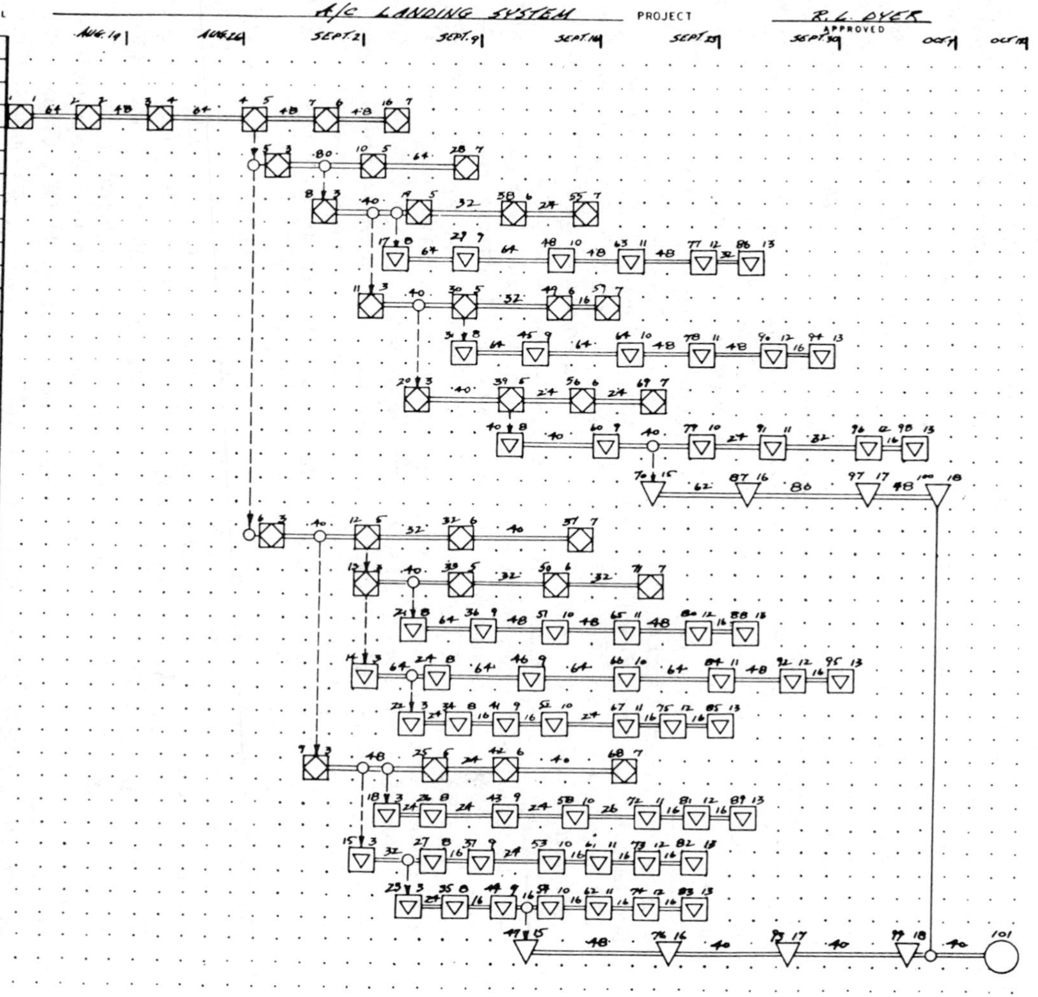

(1) Organize the individual sub-tasks into a time-phased plan.

(2) Identify the total budget assigned to the tasks.

(3) Show budget to date and budget expended to date.

(4) Indicate planned expenditures of man-hours and money for periods between sensors.

(5) Provide supervisors with a graphic picture of their responsibilities, and their progress and costs.

Related Individual Flow Diagrams are consolidated into a chart of similar format, termed the "Level III" Integrated Flow Chart, as illustrated in Exhibit II.

Manloading and Critical Capacities Form. This is a form (not reproduced here) used to verify the feasibility of a plan shown on a Flow Diagram. It shows, by working days, the number of man hours that will be required on a given contract or project over a twelve-month period. With slight modification, the same form can be used to summarize manpower requirements for several projects or for an entire organization. It provides a useful check on the availability of manpower for in-house or anticipated work. A discrepancy between man-hour requirements on the Flow Diagram or Manloading charts, and the actual manpower available, is a clear indication of the need for further study and adjustment.

"Level II" and "Level I" Charts, and Line of Balance. Integrated Flow Charts provide voluminous information about project status, needed for managers directly in charge of work. Higher levels of managment, however, require something more concise, with significant points highlighted. This is the purpose of the "Level II" and "Level I" Charts. Level II Charts condense the data from a series of Level III Charts; and Level I Charts further summarize the Level II Charts. In this way, successively higher levels of management view the picture on successively broader scales. A reasonable ratio for the number of charts to be summarized on the next higher level is 10:1.

The usual format (see Exhibit III) shows:

(1) *Objective:* Goal and performance in terms of dollar expenditures (see upper left-hand portion of Exhibit III).

(2) *Program:* Structure of the work plan scaled against time (see central body of Exhibit III). Included with the chart is a "Sensor Identification List" (Exhibit IV) which shows how sensors of underlying Level III Charts have been consolidated to form the Level II Chart illustrated, and how sensors of the Level II Chart combine to make the higher order Level I Chart.

(3) *Comparison of Program Progress:* Attainment of objective is gauged against a specific "Line of Balance" (upper right-hand portion of Exhibit III).

Construction and Use of the Line of Balance. The Objective section of the Line of Balance Chart in Exhibit III represents expected progress to completion of the entire collection of activities represented on the chart. Assume a date of "survey," i.e., today's date, when progress is being evaluated, as shown by the arrow at the bottom of Exhibit III. On the Objective chart, proceed perpendicularly from that date. From the point (here, 221.5) of intersection with the Objective curve, project a horizontal line to the Progress section of the Line of Balance Chart. Continue this horizontal line until it extends across all bars having reference to sensors which are scheduled for completion by the date of the survey. This constitutes the Line of Balance for sensors occurring *on or before* the date of the survey.

In the R&D procedure, the level of the Line of Balance for any sensor scheduled to occur *subsequent* to the date of survey is determined as follows: On the Objective chart, erect a perpendicular at the date of the sensor's occurrence. From the height of the perpendicular's intersection with the Objective curve, subtract the ordinate of the Objective curve at the date of survey, and in turn subtract the difference thus arrived at from the ordinate at the date of survey. The resulting ordinate is the level of the Line of Balance for the sensor date selected. By a similar procedure the LOB level for all other sensors is determined, following which the several segments are joined to form the Line of Balance for the entire project. This represents the *minimum level of accomplishment that will satisfy project requirements.* Deviations from planned progress are visually apparent in the bars that extend above or fail to meet the line of balance.

Construction of the Progress Bars. As shown, the vertical bars are keyed by identifying number to correspondingly numbered sensors. The height of the bar is determined as follows:

From the cross-reference list (Exhibit IV) identify the Level III sensors which correspond to the Level II sensor under consideration. From the Level III Chart, determine the num-

Exhibit III

Level II Line of Balance Chart

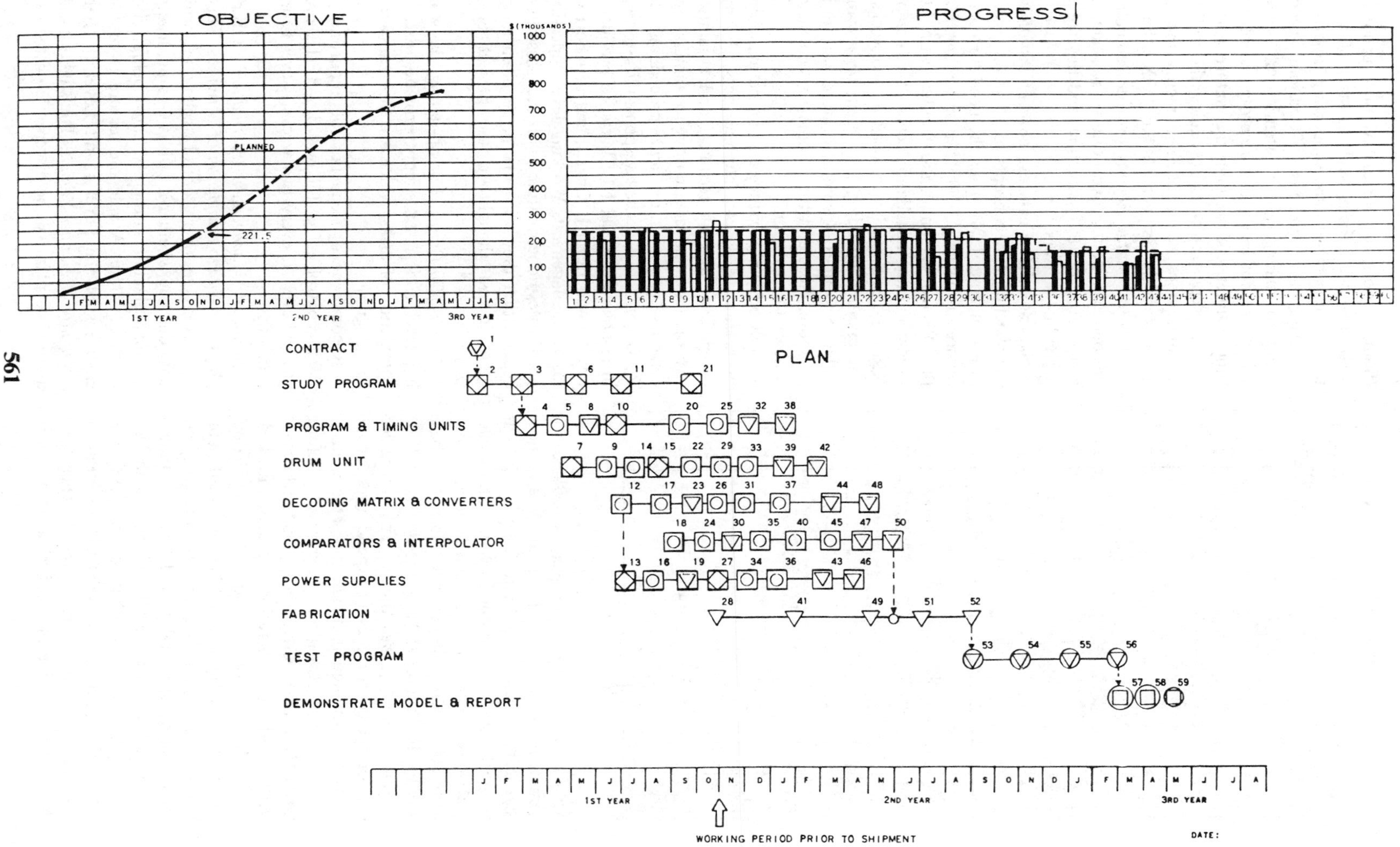

EXHIBIT IV

CROSS-REFERENCE LIST FOR LEVEL II CHART

LEVEL III	SENSOR IDENTIFICATION	LEVEL I
1.1 & 10	1.RECEIVE CONTRACT	1
2.1 & 5	2.START D.F.G. STUDY PROGRAM	2
2.4 & 8	3.COMPL. STUDY TIMING TECHNIQUFS	3
3.1 & 3	4.START STUDY PROGRAM TIMING UNIT SYS.	3
3.4 & 6	5.START MECH & ELEC DES. PROGRAM & TIME UNITS	5
2.6 & 9	6.COMPL. LOGIC SOLVING INTERPOLATION FORMULAS	4
4.1	7.START STUDY DRUM UNIT SYS.	4
3.7,8	8.START MECH & ELEC DES. PROGRAM & TIMING UNIT	5
4.3 & 5	9.COMPL. SYS. ROUGH SKETCHES, DRUM SYS.	16
3.10 & 13	10.COMPL. STUDY PROGRAM & TIME SYS.	5
2.11,12	11.COMPL. STUDY DATA REDUCTION	10
5.1	12.START DEVEL. MATRIX & CONVERTER UNITS	5
7.1	13.START POWER SUPPLY STUDY	6
4.6,16	14.COMPL. STUDY, CONFIGURATION	16
4.2 & 18	15.COMPL. FINAL SYS. DWGS, DRUM STUDY	16
7.2 & 10	16.START MECH & ELEC DES. PWR SUPPLY	7
5.2 & 4	17.START DES. MATRIX & CONVERTER UNITS	19
6.1	18.START DEVEL. COMPARATORS & INTERPOLATORS	8
7.11 & 21	19.START DET. DRFTG PWR SUPPLY	9
3.14 & 22	20.COMPL. ELEC. DES. PROGRAM & TIME UNITS	14
2.14 & 18	21.COMPL. STUDY PROGRAM FOR D.F.G.	10
4.7 & 39	22.COMPL. SYS. DWGS DRUM MAPPING	16
5.5.6	23.START DET. DES. MATRIX & CONVERTER UNITS	19
6.1 & 5	24.START DESIGN COMPARATORS & INTERPOLATORS	21
3.23 & 25	25.COMPL. MECH DES. PROGRAM & TIME UNITS	14
5.7 & 10	26.COMPL. DEVEL. MATRIX & CONVERTER UNITS	19
7.18 & 25	27.COMPL. STUDY POWER SUPPLY	11
8.1	28.START DET. FAB.	12
4.9 & 67	29.COMPL. FINAL SYS. DWGS MAGNETIC HEADS	16
6.6 & 10	30.START DET. DES. COMPARATORS & INTERPOLATORS	21
5.11 & 15	31.COMPL. ELEC DES. MATRIX & CONVERTER UNITS	19
3.26 & 39	32.AVAIL. TO MFG. DETAIL ELEC. DES. PROGRAM & TIME UNITS	14
4.16 & 78	33.COMPL. FINAL SYS. DWGS, HOUSING DES.	16
7.26 & 31	34.COMPL. ELEC DES. PWR SUPPLY	13
6.8 & 15	35.COMPL. DEVEL. COMPARATORS & INTERPOLATORS	21
7.29 & 35	36.COMPL. MECH DES. PWR SUPPLY	13
5.16 & 35	37.COMPL. MECH. DES. MATRIX & CONVERTER UNITS	19
3.28 & 44	38.AVAIL. TO MFG. DET. MECH DES. PROGRAM & TIME UNITS	14
4.23 & 91	39.AVAIL. TO MFG. DET. ELEC DES. DRUM UNIT	16
6.16 & 24	40.COMPL. ELEC DES. COMPARATORS & INTERPOLATORS	21
8.2 & 15	41.START SUB-ASSY FAB.	15
4.31 & 94	42.AVAIL. TO MFG. DETAIL MECH. DES. DRUM UNIT	16
7.36 & 55	43.AVAIL. TO MFG. DETAIL ELEC. DES. PWR SUPPLY	17
5.21 & 40	44.AVAIL. TO MFG. DETAIL ELEC. DES. MATRIX & CONVERTER UNITS	19
6.25 & 32	45.COMPL. MECH. DES. COMPARATORS & INTERPOLATORS	21
7.50 & 71	46.AVAIL. TO MFG. DET. MECH. DES. PWR SUPPLY	18
6.28 & 39	47.AVAIL. TO MFG. DET. ELEC. DES. COMPARATORS & INTERPOLATORS	21
5.38 & 62	48.AVAIL. TO MFG. DET. MECH. DES. MATRIX & CONVERTERS	19
8.13 & 32	49.COMPL. DET. FAB	20
6.40 & 52	50.AVAIL. TO MFG. DET. MECH DES. COMPARATORS & INTERPOLATORS	21
8.17 & 45	51.COMPL. SUB-ASSY FAB.	22
8.32 & 60	52.COMPL. FINAL ASSY UNIT	23
9.1	53.START TEST & ADJUST D.F.G.	24
9.2 & 21	54.COMPL. TEST POWER SUPPLIES	28
9.15 & 40	55.COMPL. TEST RACK UNITS	32
9.22 & 60	56.COMPL. TEST & ADJUST D.F.G.	38
10.1	57.START CUSTOMER ACCEPTANCE	42
10.2 & 15	58.COMPL. CUSTOMER ACCEPTANCE	42
10.12 & 25	59.SUBMIT DEVEL. REPORT	43

ber of these sensors that were scheduled for completion by the date of the survey, and those that were actually completed. Draw a solid bar whose length is determined by the ratio of actual completions to scheduled completions, with 100% being the distance from the base line to the Line of Balance for the sensor.

Representing Expenditures. The unshaded bars on the chart represent expenditures for the sensors, calculated in much the same manner as the bars representing progress. As before, Level III sensors corresponding to the Level II sensor under consideration are determined, as well as the sensors scheduled for completion, by the date of the survey. The budgeted man-hours and material dollars required to complete these sensors are totaled, and from the Financial Status Report (mentioned below) the actual expenditures are determined. As before, ratios of actual to budgeted are determined, and the bars drawn, against the distance from the base to the line of balance taken as 100%. (Some sensors, of course, have no expenditures associated with them, such as start of an action, or receipt of some supporting input.)

Management Reports. Deviation Reports bring to management's attention all sensors which are not being met according to planned time estimates, describing the nature and degree of departure from schedules, the problem existing, steps being taken to rectify the situation, and the impact on the LOB schedule.

Financial Status Reports provide tabulations on budgets, actual expenditures to date, approximate costs to completion, and the like, for individual sensors.

Salient LOB Features. *Ease of installation.* No startling new concepts must be understood in establishing LOB. Thus the need for outside services is usually held to a minimum. Once the affected personnel are familiar with LOB fundamentals, installation even for complex R&D projects can be achieved in two weeks to one month, depending on present organization (relative to lines of communication, accounting structure, etc.), and the complexity and magnitude of the program.

LOB on complex projects can be maintained by a team of two to four members who have competence in both technical and administrative matters, and are thoroughly familiar with company organization and procedures. For R&D control, it is their responsibility to assist in establishing Level III Charts, to produce all Level I and Level II Charts, and to report status to management. Working level supervisors need little indoctrination, with the possible exception that they may now be required to give more logical thought to the project before them.

Ease of Up-Dating. For up-dating, the working level supervisor simply provides data on completion of tasks, which are then transferred to bar graphs.

Recommended frequency of reporting for R&D control is as follows: Level III, every week; Level II, every two weeks; Level I, once a month.

Summary Management Information. LOB displays *percentage completion* of activities. This is an advantage over control techniques which only disclose whether a task is lagging, leading, or on schedule—progress thus being either black or white. A valuable feature is the succinctness of the Level I and Level II charts.

Quality of Danger Signals. The slightest deviation from plan will be discernible on the LOB charts. Once a slippage is evident, however, it also is important to know how it will affect the rest of the plan. On a production project, the danger signals provided by LOB are timely and of great help, because the question of over-all effect can be answered. But on projects where surplus time may exist within activities, LOB does not attempt to deal directly with the reallocation of spare time as do CPM and PERT.

Application. Line of Balance is best known for its application to industrial production, where it has been found so effective that organizations using PERT or CPM for R&D activities often switch to LOB for control of the related manufacturing processes. In general, the reverse is not true. Relatively recent extensions of the LOB technique have demonstrated its applicability as a controlling device in any operation that involves the consideration and integration of a number of time-phased elements. Its merit is the versatility of employing a single type of display and reporting technique for program control from genesis to completion, whether or not the process is repetitive or a one-time effort. LOB can be applied throughout the entire cycle—from inception, during development and engineering test, to the end of production.

G. T. MUNDORFF, Rear Admiral, U. S. Navy, ret.; Assistant to the President, Information Systems Group, General Precision, Inc., Glendale, California

References Cited

[1] "Production Analysis," Office of Naval Material, Department of the Navy, Mar., 13, 1953, NavExos Publication P–1171.

[2] "Line of Balance Technology," Office of Naval Material, Department of the Navy, Feb. 24, 1958, NavExos Publication P–1851.

[3] Mundorff, George T. and Bloom, William, "Managing a Development Program," General Precision, Inc., New York, 1960 (prepared under the direction of the Bureau of Research & Development, Federal Aviation Agency, and reissued as Department of Commerce Technical Publication # PB 171841).

Cross References: *Integrated Project Management (and cross references there given); Line of Balance; Day Control; Production Planning and Inventory Management.*

LINE OF BALANCE: Day-Control

To provide a management-type reporting medium readily reflecting schedules, inventories, and the progress of a program, **Day-Control** was developed in 1957 by the Sandia Corporation as an out-growth of experience with LINE OF BALANCE [1].

Users of this more recent derivative maintain that Day-Control gives better control throughout the course of a production program, is easier to interpret, and requires less maintenance time. The philosophy is the same in both cases, and the technique differs only as to the format of presentation; thus it may be questiond whether one system gives any better control than the other. It is true, however, that Day-Control requires less maintenance time than Line of Balance. This gain, perhaps has been obtained through sacrifice of simplicity in presentation and so is not entirely clear profit. Both will be found effective in giving an early warning of potential problems.

Production Flow Plan. As in the case of the parent technique, a Day-Control application starts with the preparation of a rough draft Production Flow Plan.

The next step is to convert the crude schematic into a time-scaled Production Flow Chart, using standard LOB symbols (often supplemented by a distinguishing color coding system) as shown in the lower portion of Exhibit I. (This exhibit is drawn for the same example described in the article, LINE OF BALANCE, so that the techniques may readily be compared.) The control stations, or sensors, are numbered in the same manner as for LOB, i.e., consecutively from left to right and from top to bottom where two or more points have a common position along the time scale. In addition, the *end-item sets* (a number of identical parts in a completed unit) are denoted by a number in parentheses adjacent to the sensor. Where duplication of parts occurs among two or more sensors, only that control station having the greatest lead time need be indicated on the chart.

Again, as in LOB, separate charts may be prepared for the various categories of parts (company-made, purchased, etc.) whenever it is desired to reduce the number of control stations appearing on a single chart. It is always desirable to report the overall status on a single Summary Chart in which subordinate control points are included in one symbol representing the least favorable condition in that family group.

Day-Control Chart. The third step is to lay out the Day-Control Chart, as shown in the upper portion of the exhibit. A vertical scale is selected which will accommodate the total

EXHIBIT I

DAY-CONTROL INDUSTRIAL PROGRAMMING CHART

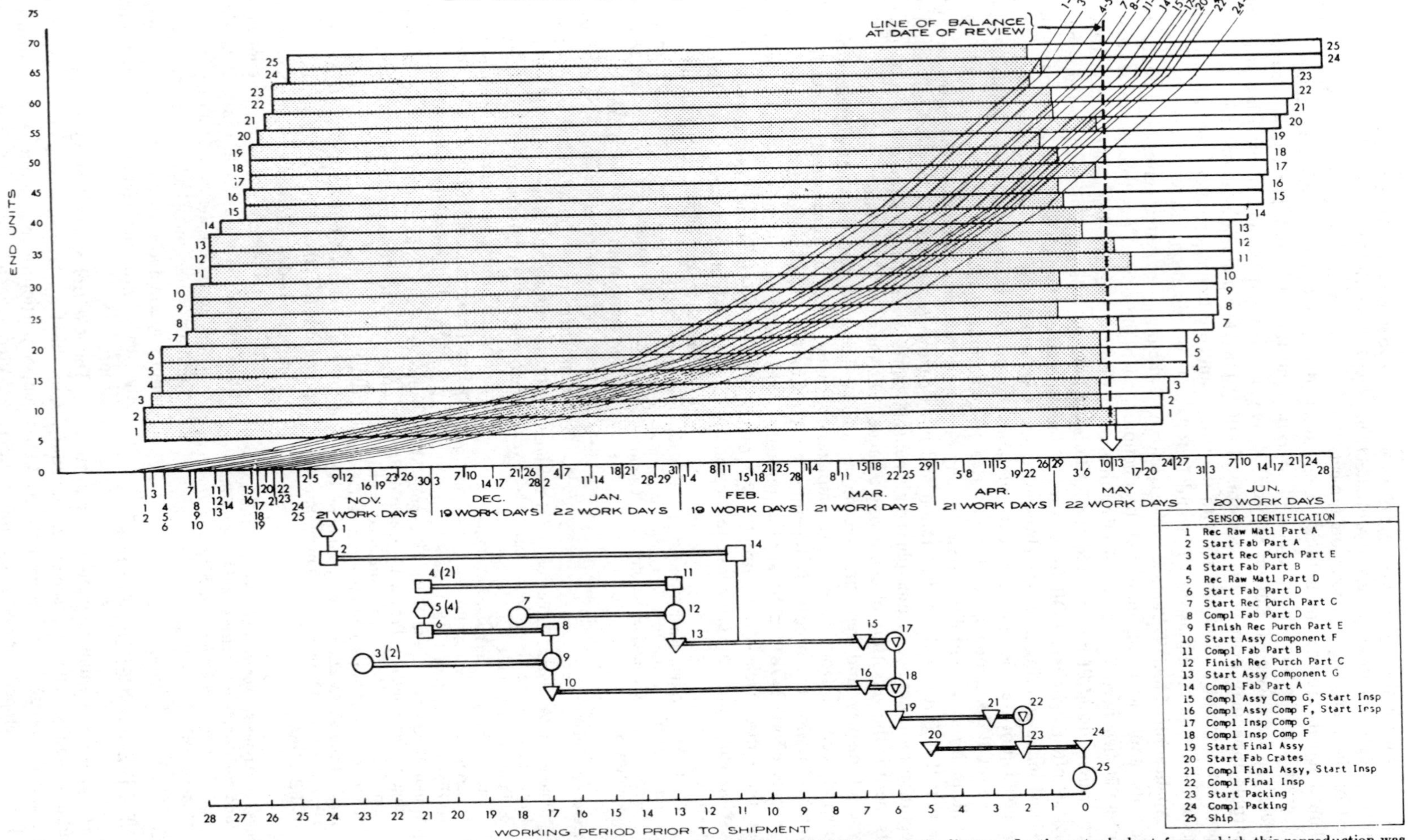

NOTE: This is the same example as charted in *Line of Balance* (*LOB*). Exhibit I, with the same symbols used in the schematic diagram. In the actual chart from which this reproduction was taken, the left-hand scale extends to 90, and the parallel curves extend correspondingly (here cut off to make larger-scale reproduction possible). To visualize the extension, refer to "Objective" chart of the other Exhibit I.

Erratum: Space between curves 24-25 and 22-23 should be equivalent to two days to conform to text discussion.

number of units on order. The abscissa is scaled in standard working days from the start of operations to completion of the order, but holidays, week-ends, and scheduled plant shut-downs are not included.

With this system of coordinates, plot the Contract Delivery Schedule (line 24–25 in the exhibit) for finished units. Next draw a parallel line for each of the sensors, spacing these lines to the left according to the number of working days that each sensor occurs in advance of shipment as plotted on the Flow Chart. Thus in this example, line 22–23 is spaced two working days to the left of line 24–25; line 21 is three days to the left, and so on. Note that sensors with the same point in time share a common line, viz., 24–25, 22–23, etc.

Inventory Bar Graphs. Inventory bar graph space is now provided horizontally across the parallel schedule lines just drawn. The beginning and end of the space to be taken by each bar graph must line up vertically with the start and finish of its corresponding schedule line. As is indicated in the exhibit, each bar graph space is keyed by a number corresponding to both the related sensor and its schedule line. Each of these is also identified by the name of the control station. (The reader must keep in mind that at this point we have not yet drawn in any shaded bars: we are simply talking about the total space provided for the bars.)

The next step is to obtain a cumulative inventory count of those piece parts, subassemblies, inspected units, etc., to correspond with each of the various control stations on the Flow Chart. This count should include all units which have passed through the station as well as those completed and currently awaiting transfer to the next following operation. As in LOB, *this count must be in "end-item sets"* and thus would be factored in all instances when two or more items are required per completed assembly. For example, at Station 3, two of Part E are needed for each assembly. The cumulative inventory at Station 3 should therefore be divided by two for the "end-item set."

The shaded inventory bar for each sensor is determined from its corresponding delivery schedule line as follows: Read the end-units completed on the vertical scale at the left. Proceed horizontally to the right, to point of intersection with the appropriate schedule line. The right hand edge of the inventory bar for that sensor must line up with this point. In effect, this is the same as saying that the number of end-units completed should have been completed at the date just determined, and this date may be to the right or to the left of the Line of Balance, the vertical broken line, drawn for the date at which the review was made. (Example: a horizontal bar drawn from 56 end-items for sensor 8, completed "today," May 10, intersects with line 8–9–10 at April 29. Thus, 56 end-items *should* have been completed on April 29.)

Analyzing the Chart. All inventory bars ending short of the Line of Balance indicate low inventories, while those bars at or extending beyond the vertical line represent surplus inventories. The status of the manufacturing situation can thus be appraised on a daily basis, if desired, or certain critical stations can be monitored daily to note their progress. In most cases, a weekly inventory taken at each control station and reflected on the schedule chart will be found to give the desired control. Once Day-Control has been established, it usually takes but a few minutes per reporting interval to bring a chart up to date.

G. T. MUNDORFF, Rear Admiral, U. S. Navy, ret.; Assistant to the President, Information Systems Group, General Precision, Inc., Glendale, California

Reference Cited

[1] Credited with the development of Day-Control are Q. D. Freyermuth, A. E. Kaping, R. R. Davies, and J. W. Benson of Sandia Corporation, Albuquerque, N.M. In 1959, Sandia issued a "Day Control Manual." (The Corporation, a prime contractor to the U. S. Atomic Energy Commission, designs, develops, tests, and monitors production of nearly all components and systems in U. S. nuclear bombs and warheads except the nuclear systems.)

Cross References: *Integrated Project Management (and cross references there given); Line of Balance.*

LINEAR PROGRAMMING

Linear Programming is the best known, and today is the most widely used, of all the techniques of mathematical programming. Here, programming means to plan for the best use of scarce resources in situations where there are many alternative uses for them, and therefore more than one possible solution to a management problem. The problem of choosing among alternative solutions is an ancient one. However, an efficient solution method was not discovered until 1947, when George Dantzig and his associates first stated the "linear programming problem" in mathematical terms and then developed a systematic method of solution which they named the "simplex method." Since 1951, when Dantzig's work was first published [1], the list of linear programming applications, and the volume of technical literature concerned with research into and development of the method, have grown at an explosive rate. Solution of the linear programming problem has, in the last twenty years, stimulated work in two related fields: industrial management planning, decision making and control [2], and in the area of "linear economics" [3].

The class of problems that George Dantzig solved is described by him as problems of "maximization of a linear function of variables subject to . . . [restraints that can be expressed in terms of these same variables as] . . . linear inequalities."

History. Linear programming was first formulated mathematically by George Dantzig and his associates in 1947 as a method for solving some of the U. S. Air Force's planning, programming, and budgeting problems. Dantzig's investigation of the interpretive potential of linear programming soon led him to the conclusion that "interrelations between [alternative] activities of a large organization [could] be viewed as a linear programming type model [of the organization] and the optimal program [of activities] could be determined by minimizing a linear objective function."

Early theoretical and applied interest in linear programming was confined mainly to its relationships with and applications to military problems, problems of inter-industry economics based on Leontief input-output type analyses, and theoretical problems concerning relationships between GAME THEORY and linear programming. In the past fifteen years the emphasis has shifted to management problems. It is not surprising to find management of industrial organizations turning to linear programming. Less sophisticated techniques for deciding how best to use scarce resources are inadequate in an era of highly complex operations conducted under conditions of intense competition.

The more completely interdependent each of a company's activities are, the more dangerous are any attempts to suboptimize each of the component operations without regard to the effect on the other activities. Operation of a large petroleum company, for example, is an exercise in the operation of a highly integrated set of activities which cover a range from crude producing in various parts of the world, through crude transportation, refining, and product distribution, to the final marketing activity. It should not surprise the reader, then, to find petroleum companies actively using advanced techniques such as OPERATIONS RESEARCH, MATHEMATICAL PROGRAMMING, and linear programming. It is from this industry that the illustrative sample problem in the accompanying article has been taken. (See LINEAR PROGRAMMING: A CASE EXAMPLE.)

Approaches and Techniques. Any manager is typically faced with problems that have a number of conditions or "restraints" concerning availability of resources, and he usually has several simultaneous production requirements, each of which competes, to some extent, with the others for the available supply of men, material, and money. There are a relatively large number of activities over which he has control, and he can choose combinations of these to obtain a solution to his problem. But, whatever the solution, it must satisfy all of the restraints and meet all of the fixed demand requirements. Since there always are many feasible solutions to his problem, he is further obliged to consider the cost or profit associated with each activity and to find the combination (i.e., feasible solution) that will produce the maximum profit or incur the minimum cost; in the parlance of linear programming, he wishes to optimize an objective function, subject to several restraints.

To express the relationship between activities, restraints, production requirements, and objectives in linear programming format, only "straightline" or linear algebraic expressions may be used. To the newly initiated, this requirement might seem severely to limit the application of linear programming to real-life problems, since so many real-life relationships are characteristically "non-linear." However, much art and ingenuity are demonstrated in the technical literature which describes methods of reducing highly curvilinear relationships to linear forms by changing scales (normalizing) or by approximation of curved relationships with a series of linear segments. (But see also NONLINEAR PROGRAMMING.)

The process of building a linear programming representation (model) of a management decision-making problem involves:

(1) Definition of the operating area in which choices (i.e., decisions) can be made, and identification of all the alternative choices available.

Preparation of a flow diagram is often useful in this process.

(2) Quantifying the economic and physical consequences of each alternative.

(3) Quantifying external, uncontrollable, circumstances that restrict freedom of choice.

(4) Quantifying the criteria for evaluating alternative choices, that is, defining the criteria for optimality.

Translating these relationships and restraints into a set of linear algebraic statements completes the process of building a model of some real-life operation in linear programming format. The generalized form for all LP models is shown in Exhibit I.

The restraints define limiting relationships among the variables. These relationships pertain to material balances at each decision point in the system (input equals output), process capacity limits, blended product quality specifications, and to uncontrollable restraints such as availability of resources and market demand volumes.

The Simplex Solution Method. The linear programming concepts are convenient terms in which to consider management decision-making problems. Managers are always faced with many more alternatives (in LP terms, many more unknowns) than are needed to satisfy some set of operating requirements (in LP terms, restraints). Therefore, a manager's problem is to apply some criterion (in LP, objective function) for evaluating alternative solutions, then compute a number of alternative solutions, evaluate each by the criterion that was previouly established, and pick the solution that looks best. In the past, alternate solutions were generated and evaluated by hand computation, and only rarely was an exhaustive study possible. Under these circumstances, the "best" solution obtained was rarely the optimal solution.

Linear programming models are characterized by a discrepancy between the number of restraints and the number of unknowns; most usually, there are several times as many unknowns as restraints. The algebraic consequence of the discrepancy is an infinite number of solutions that will satisfy all restraints simultaneously. George Dantzig's beautifully ingenious solution to this dilemma requires that we obtain a solution (any solution) to the problem in terms of only as many unknowns, called "basis" unknowns, as there are restraints. This device reduces the problem to one of solving a set of simultaneous equations by standard algebraic methods that depend on identifying as many unknowns as there are equations. For example, out of ten possible gasoline components, *three* components would have to be identified as elements of a finished gasoline if that product had to meet *three* simultaneous requirements. The requirements, each expressed as an algebraic equation, might typically be: a certain volume must be produced, an octane specification must be met, and a certain resistance to vapor-lock must be obtained. These three algebraic equations, involving three (components) unknowns, can be solved to determine how much of each of the three chosen components should be included in the blend so that all specifications are satisfied. If there are five requirements to satisfy simultaneously, then five unknowns, each representing a different component, will have to be identified in order to obtain a solution that indicates how much of each of the five components is required.

Proper evaluation of the solution according to the criteria defined by the objective function (e.g., cost of each available component, and

EXHIBIT I

GENERALIZED FORM FOR LINEAR PROGRAMMING MODELS

$$
\begin{array}{lllllllll}
\text{Optimize} & C_1X_1 & + C_2X_2 & + C_3X_3 & + \cdots & + C_nX_n & & \\
\text{Subject to 1)} & a_{11}X_1 & + a_{12}X_2 & + a_{13}X_3 & + \cdots & + a_{1n}X_n & = & b_1 \\
\text{Restraints: 2)} & a_{21}X_1 & + a_{22}X_2 & + a_{23}X_3 & + \cdots & + a_{2n}X_n & = & b_2 \\
\vdots & \vdots & \vdots & \vdots & & \vdots & & \vdots \\
m) & a_{m1}X_1 & + a_{m2}X_2 & + a_{m3}X_3 & + \cdots & + a_{mn}X_n & = & b_m
\end{array}
$$

where:

Unknowns, $X_1, X_2, \ldots, X_n$ are alternative choices available, and all are constrained to have values greater than or equal to zero.

Coefficients, $a_{11}, a_{12}, \ldots, a_{mn}$ are the physical consequences of choices.

"Cost" coefficients, $C_1, C_2 \ldots C_n$ are the economic (or other criteria) consequences of choices.

Constants, $b_1, b_2 \ldots b_m$ are the externally imposed physical limitations.

revenue for finished gasoline) will not only indicate the profit associated with the particular solution, but also will indicate which new unknown to introduce to the "basis" set and which unknown to remove from the "basis" set so that a new, more profitable solution can be computed. Each of the successive solutions produced by this method will be in terms of a set of basis unknowns that differs from the immediately preceding set by only one unknown component. And the profitability of each successive solution to the problem will be equal to or greater than the profitability of the immediately preceding solution. Finally, a solution will be obtained that cannot be changed in a way to increase profit. By definition, then, an optimal solution has been achieved. The optimal set of activities is specifically identified and a magnitude is indicated for each. Non-optimal unknowns represent rejected choices.

Sensitivity analysis is an important by-product of an optimal solution. It has two aspects: one shows the rate of decrease in profit that would accompany insistence that a rejected (non-optimal) activity be chosen; the other shows the rate of increase in profit that would accompany relaxation of one of the restraints. The first of these, called Δ_j, is the quantity that is used at each step of the simplex algorithm (solution method) to indicate which new unknown to bring into the basis so that the profit for each new solution will be greater (or at least equal) to profit for previous solutions. At optimal, the Δ_j (one for each unknown) indicate no profitable choices remain; their numerical values are, then, the relative unprofitability of the remaining activity choices.

The second of the sensitivity aspects is variously called "dual variable," "W," "π," "shadow price," "imputed value," or "marginal value." One such value exists for each restraint equation in an LP model. Each π_i is validly interpreted as the change in profit per unit change in the corresponding right hand side constant b_i while all other b_i remain unchanged. The real-life interpretation that corresponds to relaxing a particular b_i is usually obvious, but subtleties are sometimes encountered as a consequence of the "only-one-b_i-change-at-a-time" nature of the π values. (It has been a long-standing practice in the literature to use the Greek letter π to symbolize the dual variable. It is not to be confused with the familiar constant 3.1416+.)

In general, marginal values are useful indicators: of action to take in make-or-buy decisions, of incentives for bottleneck removal at specific locations in the operating system, of incentives to change product line composition and volumes, and of the effect on profit of decisions to change product quality specifications. These results also have important implications for managements of organizationally decentralized companies. In firms of this type, the various operating units are supplied by, and in turn are the suppliers for, other operating units. For example, these relationships typically exist between crude supply, transportation, refining, and product distribution functions in large international petroleum companies. The method for controlling a decentralized operation depends on establishing "control prices" or "transfer prices" for finished or semi-finished products that flow between departments. Individual department managers are expected to do as well as they can in view of these "prices." But, unless these prices are properly set, apparently optimal operation of a department may not be in the best corporate interest. But, "control prices" based on marginal values (π) from linear programs do constitute valid bases for decentralized corporate control. Of course, if unlimited open-market purchases or sales are permitted activities, marginal values (π) will respond appropriately by taking on the open-market price.

The relationships shown in Exhibit II exist between the various aspects of an optimal solution, and the coefficients and constants that represent input data to a linear program.

Parametric Linear Programming studies can be automatically and efficiently conducted by most existing computer programs for solving LP problems. For example, a manager might want to study the way his optimum operating and production volume patterns change as cost(s) of input material(s), or as revenue(s) for finished product(s), change. One way of forcing the computer to make the required series of computations is to instruct it to change one (or more) cost or revenue coefficients C_j over a range.

Another way of studying the same relationships involves setting the corresponding unknown(s) X_j equal to some starting constant(s) b_i, then systematically increasing the b_i and noting the changes in profit until no further changes are possible. In either of these two ways, the shape of an incremental cost (or revenue) versus production volume curve can be

Exhibit II

Relationships of an Optimal Solution

1) $\varphi = C_1X_1 + C_2X_2 + \cdots + C_nX_n$
and also
2) $\varphi = \pi_1 b_1 + \pi_2 b_2 \cdots + \pi_m b_m$
3) $\Delta_j = a_{1j}\pi_1 + a_{2j}\pi_2 \cdots + a_{mj}\pi_m - C_j$
4) $\delta\varphi/\delta X_j = \Delta_j$
5) $\delta\varphi/\delta b_i = \pi_i$
6) $\delta\varphi/\delta a_{ij} = -\pi_i X_j$
and all restraints
7) $\sum_{j=1}^{n} a_{ij}X_j = b_i$ (for $i = 1, 2, \ldots m$) are satisfied;

where:

- φ = Profit function value at optimal solution
- C_j = Cost coefficients (−) and revenue coefficients (+)
- X_j = Alternate activity choices
- π_i = Dual variables, or shadow prices, representing optimal effect on profit function per unit positive change in corresponding right hand side constant b_i
- b_i = Right hand side constant for restraint (i)
- Δ_j = Optimal rate of change in profit function per unit of any non-optimal activity (X_j) that is forced into the solution. Unknowns X_j included in optimal basis have Δ_j values of zero.
- $\delta\varphi/\delta X_j$ = Partial derivative of profit function with respect to a particular unknown X_j
- $\delta\varphi/\delta b_i$ = Partial derivative of profit function with respect to a particular right hand side constant b_i
- $\delta\varphi/\delta a_{ij}$ = Partial derivative of profit function with respect to a particular coefficient a_{ij}

obtained. For an example, suppose a petroleum refinery manager wanted to study the cost of producing a new grade of gasoline over a range of production volumes (barrels per day) from zero to maximum capacity while holding production of all other products constant. He would represent the new gasoline in an LP model of his refinery with a new unknown name (say X_{new}), and relate that unknown to appropriate blending components, and quality specifications. The cost of crude and other raw materials, processing costs and process capacity limits would, presumably, already be represented. A product demand restraint, $X_{new} = 0$ can be written and included.

An optimal solution for this circumstance represents the existing operation as a "base case." The optimizing program can then be caused to increase the right hand side from zero to some new value that is just enough to cause a change in the basic unknowns. At this point a new solution is given, and then by making another increase in right hand side, the cycle is repeated. The results obtained in this sort of parametric study of demand for X_{new} (actually a parametric study of changing a right hand side constant from zero to some maximum value) would produce a graph that economics students will recognize as a typical incremental cost-volume relationship. (See Exhibit III.)

The shape of this relationship runs counter to the conventional notion that "the greater the production volume, the lower the unit cost." However, readers are cautioned to note that only variable (out of pocket) costs are included as elements of incremental costs; no effort is made, because none is justifiable, to try to allocate continuing cost elements such as labor, overheads, taxes, or stockholder dividends. The economic rationale underlying linear programming considers these costs to represent available resources, or existing costs, whether any "new gasoline" is manufactured or not. But, if new gasoline is produced, it will result in costs for raw materials, processing, power, etc. The shape of an incremental cost curve may be better understood by considering the logical sequence involved. The first volumes of new product will be produced by using the most efficient processes available. When these process capacities are exhausted, less and ever less efficient processing methods will be used until

Exhibit III

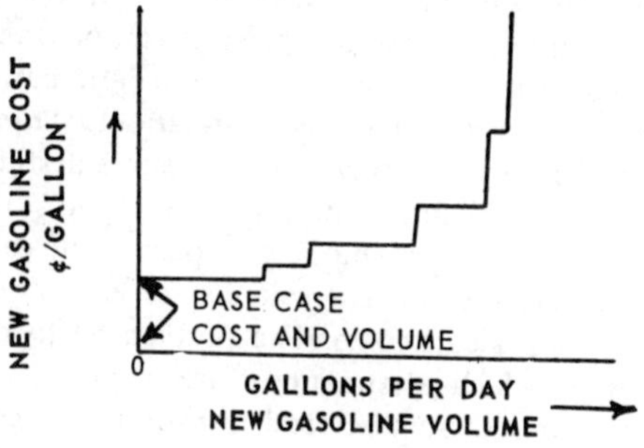

no further processing capacity of any type is available. At this point, expenditure of even an infinite sum will not produce additional product; only capital expenditures to remove processing bottlenecks will permit additional production.

Managers of companies engaged in other than the petroleum business will recognize parallels between their own problems and the illustrations used above. They will be concerned about how best to utilize their existing facilities to meet current or near-term forecasts of market demand for their products; i.e., for multi-plant, multi-product operations, which plants should produce how much of each of the products in the line? Or, for service industries, which pieces of equipment (e.g. aircraft, service trucks and crews, delivery trucks) should be assigned to which tasks? They will also be concerned about which facilities are bottlenecks in current or forecasted operations, and what the incentives are for making additional investment to relieve capacity limitations. They would like to have operating guide-lines that indicate the direction and approximate magnitude of changes in operations needed to accommodate unexpected changes in market demand, availability of raw material, availability of facilities (i.e., how to accommodate equipment failures or delays in delivery schedules), and how to respond to spot market buy-sell opportunities. And, if they are managing a decentralized corporation, executives will be interested in providing their field managers with information that will motivate them to control their individual operations in ways that are optimal from an *overall corporate view.* Manipulation of linear programming models, especially by parametric LP techniques, can provide information that will lead to answers to all these questions.

Linear Programming Applications. One of the earliest, and still most frequently encountered, applications of linear programming has been the solution of transportation problems. In the simplest cases, one product can be transported from any one of several alternative sources to each of many destinations. Transportation rates for each feasible source-destination combination are known, and the manufacturing or shipping capacity of each source and the demand volumes for each destination are also known. The problem is to determine which destinations are supplied by which sources so that total transportation cost is minimized. Transportation problems are a special case of the more general linear programming problem, and because of their special character, special solution methods have been devised that are more efficient than the simplex algorithm. Most commonly used of these special algorithms is the "stepping stone" method.

Linear programming techniques have also been adapted to the solution of a wide range of problems that incude:

(1) Allocation of Scarce Resources: including circumstances where demands are uncertain.

(2) Scheduling: production facilities, transportation equipment, maintenance programs, investments, where integer (i.e., discrete or "all-or-none") solutions are required.

(3) Inventory Control.

(4) Routing: e.g., deployment of aircraft, oil tankers, etc.

(5) Personnel Assignment: e.g., maintenance crew utilization over a period of time, toll collectors.

(6) Structural Design.

An exhaustive list of applications can be found in most of the texts listed below, especially [4].

Potential. The management function is to make decisions and to be responsible for the consequences of those decisions. Competent staff personnel, using linear programming techniques, can provide management with information on which their decisions can be based. The value of linear programming to management can be very great if skill and intelligence are exercised in building LP models, formulating problems for solution, and in analyzing the computed results. But, as it is with any powerful tool, incompetent and unskilled users will court disaster.

In general, linear programming techniques can be used to strengthen the management decision making process where allocation of resources is the problem. Allocation problems include long range (strategic) programming for a sequence of related decisions, evaluation of intermediate range capital budgeting decisions, and programming relatively short range operational response to forecasted circumstances. However, linear programming techniques are not (now) useful for improving the accuracy of forecasts or for solving many day-to-day scheduling problems. Other management science techniques described elsewhere in this volume are useful in this area. (See *Cross-References,* below.)

Linear programming is a tool. The techniques for handling the tool can be learned and understood by almost anyone. Whether or not something useful and valuable is produced depends on the ability of the individual practitioner. In this sense, linear programming (which implies a computer program and an electronic computer for making the particular arithmetic manipulations called the simplex method) is not unlike a desk calculator or a slide rule or any other computational aid. But it is a far more powerful tool than any of these. In general, it will not produce answers more quickly, but rather, it will produce very much more valuable information than available heretofore.

Managers of small companies need not be dismayed at the need for an electronic computer to solve problems by LP techniques. These managers usually employ technical assistants who perform a staff function, and who can become competent in LP techniques by various processes of self education or by attending short courses given by computer manufacturers and universities. Computer time and computer codes for solving LP problems are available from many computer service firms on a fee for service basis. In large companies today, planning and operations research staffs frequently include individuals who have considerable experience, competence, and imagination in LP applications. Some management-consulting firms are similarly staffed.

Caveat. Two recent new developments have created a situation which endangers the practical utility and management acceptance of the LP technique. The first was the development of special computer programming languages which were easily learned and used for automating the process of assembling linear programming models . . . particularly large ones. The second development was large, fast computer hardware and sophisticated mathematical programming codes which made it inexpensive to run very large LP models. The result was inevitable: huge models were built. Linear programs with 1,000 equations containing 1,500 different unknowns and a total of 10,000 data coefficients are not uncommon. The author knows of several which are twice that size.

The motivation behind this trend seems to be the notion that validity and utility of LP models will automatically be improved either by increasing the depth of detail for some particular process, or by increasing the scope of representation . . . even up to the ultimate limit of a physical and financial model of an entire firm. The peril lies in the difficulty of understanding, maintaining, and using such colossi. Managements will be reluctant to accept a model which contains too much data and too many assumptions to permit them confidently to judge the significance of results. In addition, the planning and technical staff effort to maintain, update, or change data for specific studies increases geometrically with model size as the probability rises rapidly for errors and omissions. Output data volume and the attendant job of interpreting results grow equally fast. And, finally, job rotations threaten the abandonment of complicated LP models. New managers and staffs are faced with the very difficult task of absorbing and understanding the thousands of details and relationships built into models which they inherit rather than sponsor and create.

The solution to these problems is either to avoid building large LP models, or to develop systems and computer programs which can very significantly reduce the complexity and effort. The choice depends on specific circumstances. In the author's opinion, the small LP models are more preferable than would be indicated by the trend toward large ones. There seems no *a priori* reason to believe that adding details necessarily improves reliability. Ill-structured intangibles which cannot be expressed quantitatively are simply ignored; yet these factors may be more important than any which might be included in the model.

A few systems to facilitate the use of large LP models have been built to date. Each one is tailored to the specific needs of the management and staff using it. These are generally expensive to build, and so commitments for large LP models and supporting systems can be made only for the relatively few problems where large incentives exist and justification is relatively obvious.

Thomas C. Cattrall, Jr., Marketing and Refining Division, International Management Sciences Department, Mobil Oil Corporation, New York, New York

Information References

Periodicals:

Operations Research, bi-monthly, Operations Research Society of America, Baltimore.

Management Science, monthly, Institute of Management Sciences, Providence, R.I.

Econometrica, quarterly, Econometric Society, Yale University, New Haven, Conn.
Naval Research Logistics Quarterly, Office of Naval Research, Washington, D.C.
International Abstracts in Operations Research, published quarterly by North Holland Publishing Co., Amsterdam, The Netherlands; available from Elsevier North Holland, Inc., New York.

Texts:

Danzig, G. B., "Linear Programming," Princeton, N.J., Princeton Univ. Press, 1963.
Frazer, J. Ronald, "Applied Linear Programming," Englewood Cliffs, N.J., Prentice-Hall, 1968.
Gass, S. I., "An Illustrated Guide to Linear Programming," New York, McGraw-Hill, 1970.
Hughes, Ann J. and Grawaig, Dennis E., "Linear Programming: An Emphasis on Decision Making," Reading, Mass., Addison-Wesley, 1973.
Naylor, Thomas H., Byrne, Eugene T., and Vernon, John M., "Introduction to Linear Programming: Methods and Cases," Belmont, Calif., Wadsworth, 1971.
Zionts, Stanley, "Linear and Integer Programming: International Series in Management," Englewood Cliffs., N.J., Prentice-Hall, 1974.

References Cited

[1] Dantzig, G. B., "Maximization of a Linear function of Variabes Subject to Linear Inequalities," in T. C. Koopmans, ed., "Activity Analysis of Production and Allocation," pp. 339–347, New York, J. Wiley, 1951.
[2] For a typical work in this area, see Gass, S. I., "Linear Programming Methods and Applications," 3rd ed., New York, McGraw-Hill, 1969.
[3] For typical works in this area see Dorfman, R., Samuelson, P. A., and Solow, R. M., "Linear Programming and Economic Analysis," New York, Mc-Graw-Hill, 1958; Baumol, W. J., "Economic Theory and Operations Analysis," Englewood Cliffs, N. J., Prentice-Hall, 1961; Coleman, R. F., "Linear Programming and Cash Management," Cambridge Mass., M.I.T. Press, 1968.
[4] Gass, S. I., "An Illustrated Guide to Linear Programming," New York, McGraw-Hill, 1970.

Cross References: *Goal Programming; Linear Programming: A Case Example—The Simplex Solution Method; Management Sciences (and cross references there given).*

LINEAR PROGRAMMING: A Case Example—The Simplex Solution Method

Imagine that the manager of a small section of a petroleum refinery is faced with the following problem: He is in complete charge of two processing operations (an unlikely event, but a necessary hypothesis if we are to keep this example manageably small). Each of the processes can be used to refine a naphtha "cut" produced by the distillation process at another location in the refinery. One of the processes produces high quality gasoline, and the other process produces jet fuel. The manager is told that he must accept exactly 300 barrels of naphtha per day which he can divide between his processes in any ratio he sees fit, or he may send the naphtha to the powerhouse to be burned. However, fifty barrels per day must be reserved for sale directly as paint brush cleaning fluid, and he must also meet certain marketing ratio requirements and product quality specifications in the event he decides to produce gasoline or jet fuel. Exhibit I is a flow diagram of his problem situation.

The manager has been informed that in the event gasoline is produced, it can be sold for \$4.00/barrel.* However, blending costs are \$1/barrel for the chemical additives. The gasoline process produces a high quality gasoline component (100 Octane) but costs \$2/barrel for operating the process; there is no volume loss as a result of processing, and the gasoline produced by this process automatically meets minimum quality specifications. Jet fuel can be sold for \$2.00/barrel, but the processing cost is \$1.50/barrel. Jet fuel produced by this process automatically meets minimum quality specification, and here again there is no volume loss as a result of processing. There will be neither credit nor cost for any naphtha sent to the powerhouse. No information is available concerning revenue per barrel for the paintbrush cleaner, or cost per barrel for the 300 barrels per day of raw material. But the manager realizes that since these volumes have been presented to him as "fixed," any total revenues or costs associated with them are also "fixed" and therefore have no bearing on his problem, which is to choose among the alternatives that *are* open to him in such a way as to "maximize profit."

The alternative activities have been labeled in Exhibit I as unknowns *(X_j),* where the subscripts *(j)* distinguish the specific activity; in this example, the activity X_1 represents processing some, not yet determined, number of barrels per day of naphtha to make high quality gasoline component for blending, and X_2 repre-

* Prices used here appeared in the original Encyclopedia of Management entry by Thomas C. Cattrall, and do not reflect intervening upward movement caused by OPEC action and inflation. Since the former are unpredictable, and since the argument presented does not depend upon actual figures, an editorial decision was made not to change the computations.—Ed.

EXHIBIT I

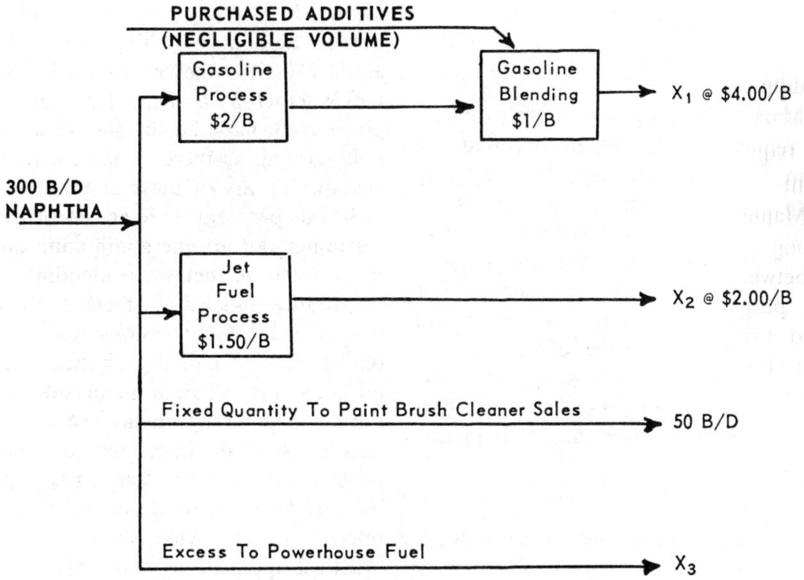

sents an unknown number of barrels per day of jet fuel produced.

Referring to the revenues and costs associated with each of the activities, the net profit for activity X_1 is:

Revenue	\$4.00/bbl.
minus blending cost	2.00/bbl.
minus processing cost	1.00/bbl.
Net profit for $X_1 =$	\$1.00/bbl.

Similarly, net profit associated with X_2 is \$0.50/bbl. There are no other profit or cost producing activities, so that the total profit for the combined operation, in dollars per day, can be written in the form of a linear algebraic expression containing only two terms:

$$\text{(I)} \qquad \text{"Profit"} = 1.00\, X_1 + 0.50\, X_2$$

The manager is motivated to maximize this specific definition of profit. But he realizes that he is constrained . . . certainly he cannot make infinite profit by producing an infinite volume of gasoline. In general, his maximum profit will be limited by the realities of life. He will want these represented in a linear program that the technical staff prepares.

There are material balances to observe . . . these simply state that one cannot get more out of a process than one puts into it.

There are process capacity limitations to observe . . . the total volume per day (per hour or any other convenient scale) passing through a process must be less than some stated maximum capacity.

There are quality specifications to meet when several components are blended to produce a final product . . . finished products can be better than specified, but economic disaster awaits the manufacturer who does not impose quality restraints on his objective of maximizing profit.

Finally, there are political and other arbitrary restraints . . . the petroleum industry is restrained by the Government from importing unlimited quantities of foreign crude oil; it is also restrained by consumer demand from making unlimited quantities of any one product. Every industrial manager's choice of alternative decisions is limited by restraints similar to these.

In our sample problem we are faced with only two restraints: a requirement to maintain material balance, and a market ratio requirement.

Material balance requires that the combined volume (per day) of naphtha used for gasoline, jet fuel, paintbrush cleaner, and powerhouse fuel be equal to the volume of naphtha available. This restriction is written in the following linear algebraic language.

$$\text{(II)} \qquad X_1 + X_2 + X_3 + 50 = 300$$

which can be rewritten in a form suitable for Linear Programming:

(III) $$X_1 + X_2 + X_3 = 250$$

Let us suppose, for purposes of this problem, that the Marketing Department imposed the following requirement on the Manufacturing Department . . . "We can sell any quantities that the Manufacturing Department can produce as long as a reasonable balance is maintained between product volumes. For marketing purposes, gasoline volume should not exceed twice the volume of jet fuel + paintbrush cleaner." In the language of linear algebra, this restriction will take the form of an inequality (i.e., a less-than-or-equal statement):

(IV) $$X_1 \leq 2\,(X_2 + 50)$$

Rewritten (normalized) for linear programming, this statement becomes:

(V) $$X_1 - 2X_2 \leq 100$$

But, in order to permit algebraic substitutions and manipulation, something has to be done about the inequality ($\leq$) in restraint (V), yet we want the restraint to permit the total quantity ($X_1 - 2X_2$) to take values less than 100. This can be accomplished if we define a new unknown, say S_1, that will measure how much less than 100 is any particular value of ($X_1 - 2X_2$).

(VI) $$X_1 - 2X_2 + S_1 = 100$$

Unknowns of this sort are called "slack" variables. A separately named slack variable is required for each inequality in a linear program. The coefficients are always +1.0 for less-than-or-equal slacks, and are always −1.0 for greater-than-or-equal slacks. And, true slack variables never appear with a positive or negative coefficient in the objective function. The reader's attention is drawn to the fact that unknown X_3 is really a slack variable, representing the amount by which ($X_1 + X_2$) does not equal 250. It makes no difference to the problem whether X_3 is defined as powerhouse fuel, given-away naphtha, or simply a "slack" variable so long as there is no cost or revenue assignable to any of these alternatives.

In this problem there are no process capacity restraints, nor are there minimum quality specifications to be met when blending components to produce finished products. If there were, the normalized LP expressions (i.e., all unknowns on left side of equality or inequality sign and all constants on right hand side) would have the same general form as restraints III and V above. Readers interested in the technical problems of reducing frequently complex quality specifications to linear algebraic forms are referred to the extensive literature describing practical applications of LP [1].

Taken together, the objective function (I) and two restraints (III and VI) are restated here as the linear programming model of the alternative refining operations, and of the corresponding decision-making problem facing our hypothetical manager:

(VII) Maximize:
$$1\,X_1 + \tfrac{1}{2}\,X_2$$

(VIII) Subject to:
$$1\,X_1 + 1\,X_2 + 1\,X_3 = 250$$

(IX)
$$1\,X_1 - 2\,X_2 + 1\,S_1 = 100$$

It is not necessary to assemble and solve a linear program in the "long hand" equation format used in VII, VIII, and IX above. The same data are more conveniently contained in matrix (tabular) format for input to an electronic computer which can be instructed to make the arithmetic manipulations required to find an optimal solution, shown in Exhibit II.

EXHIBIT II

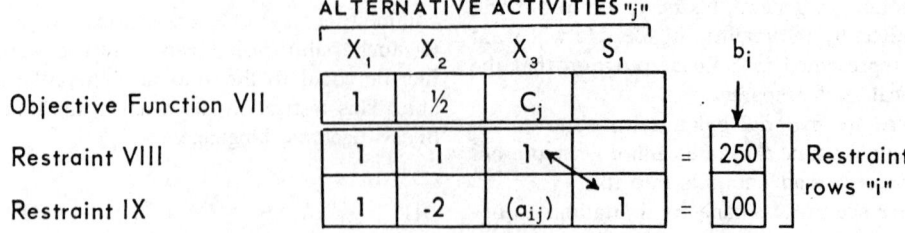

	ALTERNATIVE ACTIVITIES "j"						
	X_1	X_2	X_3	S_1		b_i	
Objective Function VII	1	½	C_j				
Restraint VIII	1	1	1		=	250	Restraint rows "i"
Restraint IX	1	-2	(a_{ij})	1	=	100	

Here, the general term C_j refers to the cost or profit coefficients in the objective function row, b_i refers to the "right hand side" constants for the restraint rows, and a_{ij} refers to the coefficients for each unknown *(j)* in each restraint *(i)*.

The Simplex algorithm requires a solution to the simultaneous linear equations as a place to start. The solution need not be optimal; it only must be a "basic" solution in the sense that it is given in terms of as many unknowns as there are restraints. In matrix format, a basic solution is indicated by a set of unknowns whose columnar tabulations of coefficients (vectors) can be put together (by re-arranging the left-to-right order if necessary) to form an identity matrix. An identity matrix is one where all but one of the a_i coefficients for each unknown *(j)* are zero. The single non-zero a_i has a value of 1, but no two of the unknowns included in an identity matrix can have a unit positive coefficient on the same row. Thus, the pattern of coefficients in an identity matrix will be a "diagonal of plus ones" in an $m \times m$ square when m is the number of restraint equations in the linear program. For a 5 restraint LP, an identity matrix would look like Exhibit III.

If all the non-basis unknowns are temporarily considered eliminated, the problem reduces to one of five equations in terms of five unknowns. The equations are of the simplest possible type; in fact they indicate the solution directly: $X_k = b_1$, $X_l = b_2$, etc.

EXHIBIT III

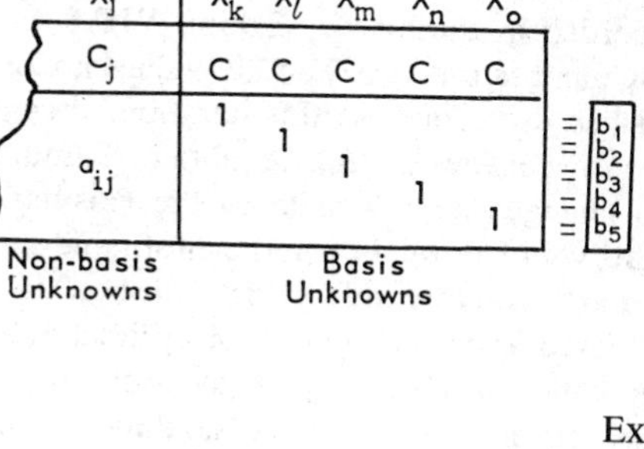

Xj
Xk Xl Xm Xn Xo
Cj
C C C C C
aij
1
1
1
1
1
=
=
=
=
=
b1
b2
b3
b4
b5
Non-basis Unknowns
Basis Unknowns

In the event that a basic starting solution cannot be obtained in terms of the unknowns and slack variables of the problem as formulated, artificial variables are introduced; one for each row not containing an element in the starting basis. Artificials are given large penalty coefficients in the objective function to insure their rejection from an optimal solution.

Fortunately, the refinery manager's problem includes unknowns X_3 and S_1 which can be made elements of an initial basis. The two simultaneous algebraic equations can be solved in terms of these two basis unknowns. If the reader will imagine for a moment that X_1 and X_2 do not even exist, then the initial solution to the problem is given directly if the matrix notation is translated back to more familiar algebraic notation: $X_3 = 250$, and $S_1 = 100$. The profit coefficients for both these choices (C_j) are zero dollars per barrel, so the total profit associated with this particular decision . . . to burn 250 barrels per day of naphtha and fall short by 100 barrels per day of making twice as much gasoline as distillate . . . is zero dollars per day. (See Exhibit IV.)

Now we begin the search for a better solution. Toward this end, the first step is to list the profit coefficients for the unknowns in the current basis. These are shown in Exhibit IV as C_i. Each row in the matrix is assigned a C_i coefficient depending on the variable "in the basis" on that row. For example, X_3 is in the basis on row 1 and since the profit coefficient for this unknown is zero, then $C_{i=1}$ is set equal to zero. Similarly $C_{i=2}$ is zero because the profit coefficient for S_1 is zero. These C_i coefficients are then used to calculate Z_j values for each unknown. Each of the coefficients in the column under one variable is multiplied by the C_i coefficient on the corresponding row. The resulting products are cumulatively added to obtain the column total called Z_j. This process is repeated to obtain Z_j column totals for all the unknowns in the matrix.

EXHIBIT IV

ROW	BASIS	C_i	C_j: 1 X_1	½ X_2	0 X_3	0 S_1	
1)	X_3	0	1	1	1		250
2)	S_1	0	①	−2		1	100
	$Z_j = \Sigma a_{ij} C_i$		0	0	0	0	Profit = 0
	$\Delta_j = Z_j - C_j$		−1	−½	0	0	

Δ_j is computed for one unknown column at a time by subtracting cost coefficients from the corresponding Z_j values.

Values of Z_j and Δ_j thus obtained are indicated in Exhibit IV. Δ_j values measure the net economic effect (actually rate of change in profit from current value) that will be obtained as a result of introducing one unit of the corresponding unknown X_j into the basis. This net effect is composed of two parts, C_j which measures the direct profit or cost contribution of the corresponding activity X_j, *and* Z_j which measures the economic effect of changes in the current basis that will be necessary to accommodate introduction of the new unknown. Because of the sign conventions chosen for calculation of Z_j and Δ_j, *the largest negative value of* Δ_j represents the most profitable change. As of this first solution, X_1 is the activity to bring into the picture next; it will increase profit at a net rate of \$1 per barrel.

The only remaining problem is to decide how many barrels of X_1 can be produced at this rate of profit without violating either of the two restraints. Dividing b_i for each row by the coefficient for X_1 on that same row will indicate the limiting value the particular restraint places on X_1. In this example the ratio for row 1 is 250/1, and for row 2 it is 100/1. That is, according to restraint 1, X_1 can be 250 barrels/day. But restraint 2 limits X_1 to 100 barrels per day (because the 2:1 product ratio limitation must be satisfied and, so far, only 50 barrels of paintbrush cleaner per day is being produced). Since restraint 2 is most limiting, X_1 will be defined by (that is, entered into the basis on) that row. In order to accomplish this, X_1 must be eliminated, by algebraic substitution, from all other rows. And it will remain, with its coefficient of + 1 on row 2 becoming a component of the "diagonal of ones." In matrix algebra, this is accomplished by identifying as a "pivot point" the coefficient at the intersection of X_1 and row 2 (circled in the matrix, Exhibit IV) and then multiplying the entire equation by whatever constant is required to convert the pivot coefficient to a value of + 1. Note that the process of multiplying an algebraic equation through by a constant is a legitimate manipulation that does not change the validity or meaning of the equation. In this case, the pivot coefficient is already + 1, so nothing need be done. But the + 1 coefficient for X_1 on row 1 must be removed: that is, X_1 must be removed from equation 1 by substitution. Subtraction of one equation from another is a legitimate algebraic process that will accomplish the same result as shown in Exhibit V.

The result is a valid, alternative way, of expressing restraint 1 in terms that do not include X_1. In matrix format, the new basis (i.e., new solution) in terms of X_3 and X_1 is as indicated in Exhibit VI. Now, X_3 equals 150 and X_1 equals 100 barrels per day, and profit has been increased by the expected rate of \$1 per barrel of X_1, over the previous solution, to a total of \$100 per day.

Z_j and Δ_j values are computed column by column as previously. The largest, and only, negative Δ_j indicates that the next solution will profitably involve X_2. The ratios b_i/a_i for X_2 are 150/3 for row 1 and 100/−2 for row 2. The negative ratio indicates restraint 2 imposes a limit only in the event that it is desirable to give X_2 some negative value, in which case −50 would be the limit. But the variables may not take negative values, so the search must be confined to the smallest positive values of the b/a ratio. In this case there is only one . . . 150/3 for row 1. Having defined X_2 as the unknown to come into the basis, and row 1 as the most limiting restraint, the pivot coefficient at this row-column intersection (+ 3 circled in Exhibit VI) is transformed to + 1 by dividing the entire equation 1 by 3. The new coefficients for row 1 are shown below. Unknown X_2 can be eliminated from row 2 if the new coefficients for row 1 are multiplied by two, and the result added to row 2 as shown in Exhibit VII.

This new expression for restraint 2 is also recorded in the matrix, Exhibit VIII.

Computations of Z_j and Δ_j values are accomplished as before. At this iteration, though, no negative values of Δ_j are obtained, indicating no change can be made to the existing basis that would result in a more profitable new solution. Therefore, an optimal solution has been achieved and computation of optimal values of the dual variables (π_i) is the only remaining task. (It has been a long-standing practice in

EXHIBIT V

	$(1\ X_1 + 1\ X_2 + 1\ X_3 + 0\ S_1) =$	250
Minus	$(1\ X_1 - 2\ X_2 + 0\ X_3 + 1\ S_1) =$	100
Equals	$0\ X_1 + 3\ X_2 + 1\ X_3 - 1\ S_1 =$	150

EXHIBIT VI

ROW	BASIS	C_i \ C_j	1 X_1	½ X_2	0 X_3	0 S_1	
1)	X_3	0	0	③	1	-1	150
2)	X_1	1	1	-2	0	1	100
$Z_j = \Sigma a_{ij} C_i$			1	-2	0	1	
$\Delta_j = Z_j - C_j$			0	-2½	0	1	Profit = 100

EXHIBIT VII

$$2 \times (0\,X_1 + 1\,X_2 + 1/3\,X_3 - 1/3\,S_1 = 50)$$
$$\text{plus } 1\,X_1 - 2\,X_2 + 0\,X_3 + 1\,S_1 = 100$$
$$\text{equals } 1\,X_1 + 0\,X_2 + 2/3\,X_3 + 1/3\,S_1 = 200$$

the literature to use the Greek letter π to symbolize the dual variable. It is not to be confused with the familiar constant 3.1416+.)

Since the relationship at optimal is:

$$\Delta_j = \Sigma_i(a_{ij})\pi_i - C_j$$

a set of m simultaneous equations can be written and solved for the π values that apply for each of the original *(m)* restraints. Because our sample problem contained a "slack" variable for each of the original constraints, π_i values will be the same as Δ_j for the "slack" variables on the respective rows. No such simple relationship holds for "tight" equations that are included in LP models. In these cases, π values must be computed from a set of simultaneous equations.

Optimal choices of the alternate activities, their values, Δ_j penalties for non-optimal choices, and shadow prices for our sample problem can now be tabulated as shown in Exhibit IX.

The rationale of these results will be readily apparent to the reader with the possible exception of the $1/6 per barrel value given to S_1 and π_2. The fog obscuring understanding usually lifts if one keeps clearly in mind that these values are appropriate for changing only the gasoline-distillate ratio while the total gasoline plus distillate volume remains constant.

The utility of sensitivity analysis can only be

EXHIBIT IX

Optimal Activity	*Unknown Name*	*Optimal Value*
Gasoline Volume	X_1	200
Kerosine Volume	X_2	50
Non-Optimal Activity	***Unknown Name***	***Δ_j Penalty for Choosing Activity***
Burn Naphtha	X_3	$5/6 per barrel
Produce less gasoline than 2:1 ratio	S_1	$1/6 per barrel of gasoline less than twice the distillate produced
Restraint	***Original RHS***	***Change in Profit per unit increase in RHS***
Naphtha Material Balance	250	π_1 = $5/6 per barrel of naphtha
Gasoline/Distillate ratio	100	π_2 = $1/6 per barrel of gasoline in excess of twice the distillate volume

EXHIBIT VIII

ROW	BASIS	C_i \ C_j	1 X_1	½ X_2	0 X_3	0 S_1	
1	X_2	½	0	1	1/3	-1/3	50
2	X_1	1	1	0	2/3	1/3	200
$Z_j = \Sigma a_{ij} C_i$			1	½	5/6	1/6	
$\Delta_j = Z_j - C_j$			0	0	5/6	1/6	Profit = 225

suggested here by pointing out that armed with these results, our refinery manager can return to his superior with the advice that additional naphtha would be worth $5/6 net profit per barrel, and unless some other foreman had more profitable use for naphtha the 300 barrel per day quota should be increased. Similar information should be conveyed regarding the market ratio.

THOMAS C. CATTRALL, JR., Marketing and Refining Division, International Management Sciences Department, Mobil Oil Corporation, New York, New York

References Cited

[1] See for example: Daellenbach, Hans G. and Bell, Earl J., "User's Guide to Linear Programming," Englewood Cliffs, N.J. Prentice Hall, 1970. Gass, Saul I., "Linear Programming: Methods and Applications," 4th ed. rev. New York, McGraw-Hill, 1975. Driebeek, N. J., "Applied Linear Programming." Reading, Mass., Addison-Wesley, 1969.

Cross Reference: *Linear Programming.*

LINEAR RESPONSIBILITY CHARTING

The **Linear Responsibility Chart** is a graphic method of analysis and recording (1) of organizational structure, job content, and functional operating responsibilities ("vertical" LRC); and (2) of a procedure and the distribution of responsibilities for this procedure, which usually crosses a number of departments ("horizontal" LRC; for example, the introduction of a new product). It compacts on a single sheet of paper information normally requiring dozens of pages of an organization manual, organization charts, operating or procedure flow charts, and job description write-ups recorded by traditional methods.

LRC replaces standard block type organization charts and particularly the unwieldy organization manuals, which normally become obsolete very rapidly. LRC does not replace *policy* manuals. (The top portion of the LR Chart is in essence a block type organization chart.) LRC allows any executive quickly to assess the actual relationships between management people, their functions, and their workloads.

Background. LRC, introduced in this country in the early 1950s by Serge A. Birn Company, is an outgrowth of the earlier, somewhat more complex *Hijmans Chart* developed by the Netherlands consultant Ernst Hijmans. The American firm had at that time discontinued preparing organization manuals for clients because they tended to be difficult to understand, and were often shelved, after brief usage, because of excessive upkeep cost. It enlisted the aid of Hijmans in developing the more simplified LRC.

How to Use LRC. Exhibit I shows a Linear Responsibility Chart which replaced a fifty-page organization manual. LRC uses the eight symbols shown to indicate eight relationships between executives and subordinates in any position or function they may handle as policy makers, supervisors, coordinators, or do-ers. The job titles are listed horizontally at the top. Their functions are listed vertically at the left. In the square where the job title and function meet, the relationship is indicated by the appropriate symbol. If the job has nothing to do with the function, the square is left blank.

Symbols. *Work Is Done:* The activity or function is actually performed by the individual designated.

General Supervision: Direction and control of the function involved where close supervision is not called for.

Direct Supervision Over Work Done: Close supervision of a subordinate's work.

Supervision with Coordination: Committee-chairman type supervision where coordination of the activities of two or more individuals or groups is essential.

Decision on Points Specially Submitted. This applies when an individual either delegates decisions on specific points to subordinates, or, in reverse, delegates *all* decisions to a subordinate, with the exception of decisions on specific points he keeps for himself.

Person Must Be Consulted.. The incumbent indicated *must be heard.*

Person Must Be Notified. The incumbent marked *must* be advised of a decision or action.

Person May Be Called in for Exchange of Views. Emphasis here is on "may." The incumbent decides whether he wishes consultation—he is under no obligation to do so.

With the above symbols, virtually any activity can be covered. New symbols are never required—provided the functions are correctly selected *and worded.* Utmost care in developing correct wording of the functions is absolutely essential. Also, the LRC analyst must make sure that all involved agree with and understand the contents of functions, and that no functions are omitted. Meetings of all concerned are needed to obtain general agreement.

Applications. Following are some of the more important LRC uses:

(1) To simplify and speed up the making of a management audit. Instead of making extensive notes on interviews with personnel, the LRC analyst charts the information received onto a blank LR chart.

(2) To simplify executive control and speed decisions. The at-a-glance picture of the exact distribution and degree of responsibility by function helps clarify communications and pinpoints who is to do what. It speeds and improves decision making.

(3) To spot organizational errors. The "before" chart highlights every fault in the organization—namely, overlapping of responsibility, responsibility not specifically assigned, authority not commensurate with responsibility, and the like.

(4) To facilitate changes in duties and authorities when a change in leading personnel occurs.. New executives brought into an organization usually handle their jobs quite differently from their predecessors, resulting in shifts in the distribution of responsibilities. (Here is where the maintenance of the unwieldy organization manual is apt to break down.)

(5) To analyze and improve procedures.. LRC gives quick and exact analysis of a given procedure which may cut through the entire organization. All faults and bottlenecks are automatically highlighted. Correct decisions can then be made with full knowledge of all facts.

(6) As a training tool. With LRC, new executives can be rapidly oriented in the exact extent and distribution of their responsibilities. When a new company is incorporated into a large multiplant organization, LRC is effective for quick training of executives in corporate staff-line type of organization. (See Exhibit II.)

Special Applications. Corning Glass Company developed an approach whereby administrative procedures of similar departments and their costs can be readily compared. Causes of excessive overhead costs are thus clearly pinpointed, and overhead is reduced accordingly.

Use of EDP. The Crane, Indiana, Naval Ammunition Depot coded LR symbols, functions and supervisory relationships, programmed them on EDP equipment, and thus produced LR charts by computer. Exhibit III shows the same chart in two forms—at the top, in the manual form, and at the bottom as a computer printout. Basic advantages of computerizing LRC are the speed of charting and the virtual elimination of human errors.

With EDP, the first step is to produce horizontal LR charts, one for *each* major activity in a given company department or group. Once this has been done and all the horizontal charts have been programmed, the computer will produce at will the vertical LR chart of that company or department. In simple terms, this means *producing the organization manual by computer.*

How are time savings achieved? It is obviously much easier and faster to analyze activities of a given organizational group *one-by-one,* than to analyze *all of them at the same time*—which is exactly what the organization specialist does—if he starts with vertical LR charting. Valuable time of a highly paid specialist is saved by breaking down the complex vertical organizational analysis into a number of easy-to-digest steps, i.e., into "horizontal" LR charts by activity. Thus the very tedious and error prone manual transfer of the information contained in several horizontal activity charts onto one "LRC Organization Manual" is completely eliminated.

LR job descriptions can also be used in connection with salary job evaluation much more effectively than conventional job descriptions. The LR job description not only describes the functions of the incumbent in one column, but also shows the exact degree of the responsibility and authority *for each function.* This technique greatly facilitates upkeep and adjustment of salaries in cases of shifts of responsibility. Finally, by using the salary (point) evaluation form as an appendix to the LR chart, a procedure can readily be developed to make sure that salary reviews take place in all such cases.

Acceptance. A pioneer user was General Shoe Corp. (Genesco). Others include such firms as Esso Research and Engineering, Morgan Manufacturing Co., Gamble Brothers, Woodworking Corporation of America, and Anglo-Newfoundland Development Co. Ltd. Applications have been in general management, finance, production, sales, research for solving problems or organizational bottlenecks, overload of individual executives, lack of organization and delegation, realignment of duties in times of expansion or contraction, reduction of

Exhibit I

Linear Responsibility Chart for a Cost Improvement Function

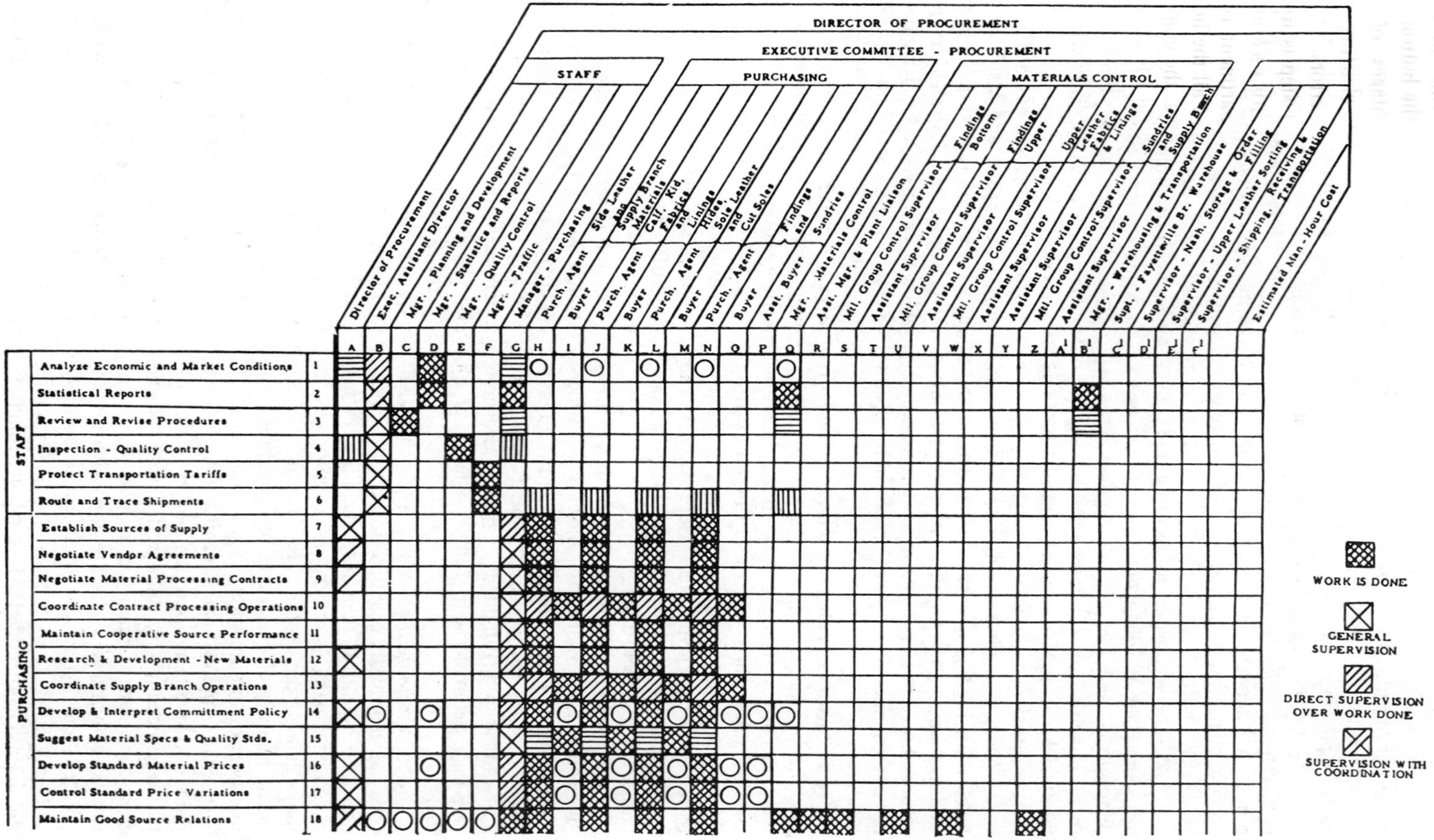

DIRECTOR OF PROCUREMENT
EXECUTIVE COMMITTEE - PROCUREMENT
STAFF
PURCHASING
MATERIALS CONTROL
Director of Procurement
Exec. Assistant Director
Mgr. - Planning and Development
Mgr. - Statistics and Reports
Mgr. - Quality Control
Mgr. - Traffic
Manager - Purchasing
Purch. Agent
Buyer
Side Leather and Supply Branch Materials
Calf, Kid, Fabrics and Linings
Hides, Sole Leather and Cut Soles
Findings and Sundries
Asst. Buyer
Mgr. Materials Control
Asst. Mgr. & Plant Liaison
Mtl. Group Control Supervisor
Assistant Supervisor
Findings Bottom
Findings Upper
Upper Leather Fabrics & Linings
Sundries and Supply Branch
Mgr. - Warehousing & Transportation
Supt. - Fayetteville Br. Warehouse
Supervisor - Nash. Storage & Order Filling
Supervisor - Upper Leather Sorting
Supervisor - Shipping, Receiving & Transportation
Estimated Man - Hour Cost
A B C D E F G H I J K L M N O P Q R S T U V W X Y Z A' B' C' D' E' F'
STAFF
Analyze Economic and Market Conditions 1
Statistical Reports 2
Review and Revise Procedures 3
Inspection - Quality Control 4
Protect Transportation Tariffs 5
Route and Trace Shipments 6
PURCHASING
Establish Sources of Supply 7
Negotiate Vendor Agreements 8
Negotiate Material Processing Contracts 9
Coordinate Contract Processing Operations 10
Maintain Cooperative Source Performance 11
Research & Development - New Materials 12
Coordinate Supply Branch Operations 13
Develop & Interpret Commitment Policy 14
Suggest Material Specs & Quality Stds. 15
Develop Standard Material Prices 16
Control Standard Price Variations 17
Maintain Good Source Relations 18
WORK IS DONE
GENERAL SUPERVISION
DIRECT SUPERVISION OVER WORK DONE
SUPERVISION WITH COORDINATION

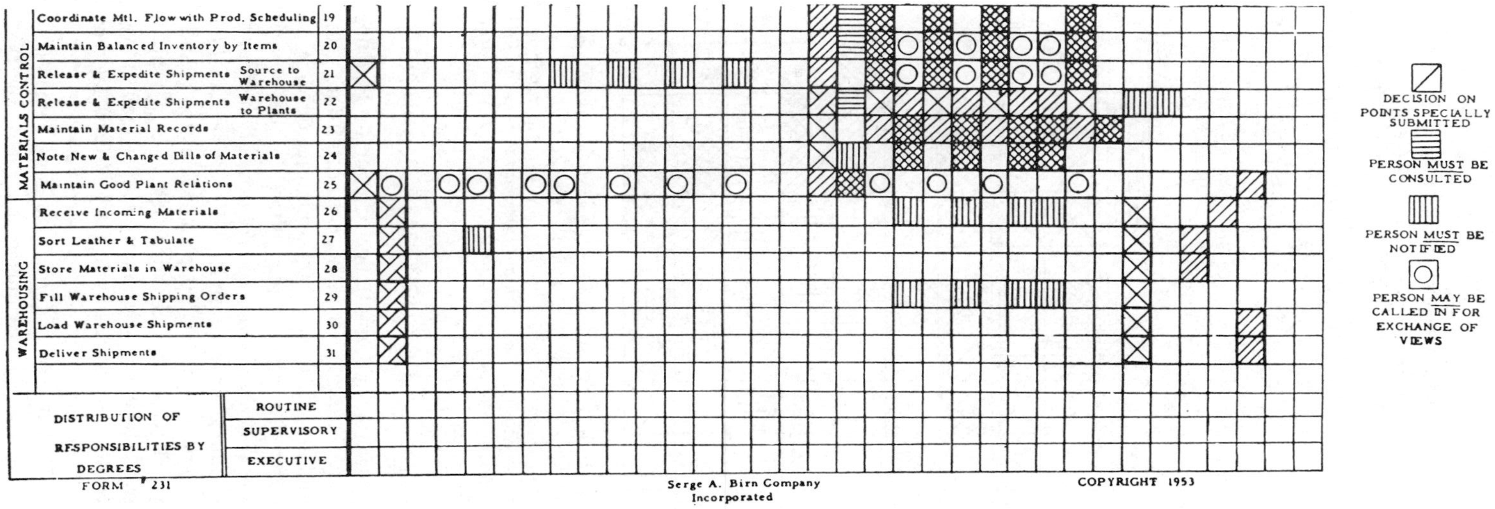

Typical Linear Responsibility Chart is this "single-sheet organization manual" of a large Purchasing Division. The study was aimed at (1) more clearly defining authorities and responsibilities; (2) reassigning present personnel to jobs that company experience and testing showed them best fitted for; (3) providing for an orderly progression of advancement; (4) pointing up where on-the-job training is needed to fit others for advancement. The bottom part of the chart is used with quantitative symbols to tally time or to make interplant comparisons of costs.

EXHIBIT II

LINEAR RESPONSIBILITY CHART FOR A COST-IMPROVEMENT FUNCTION

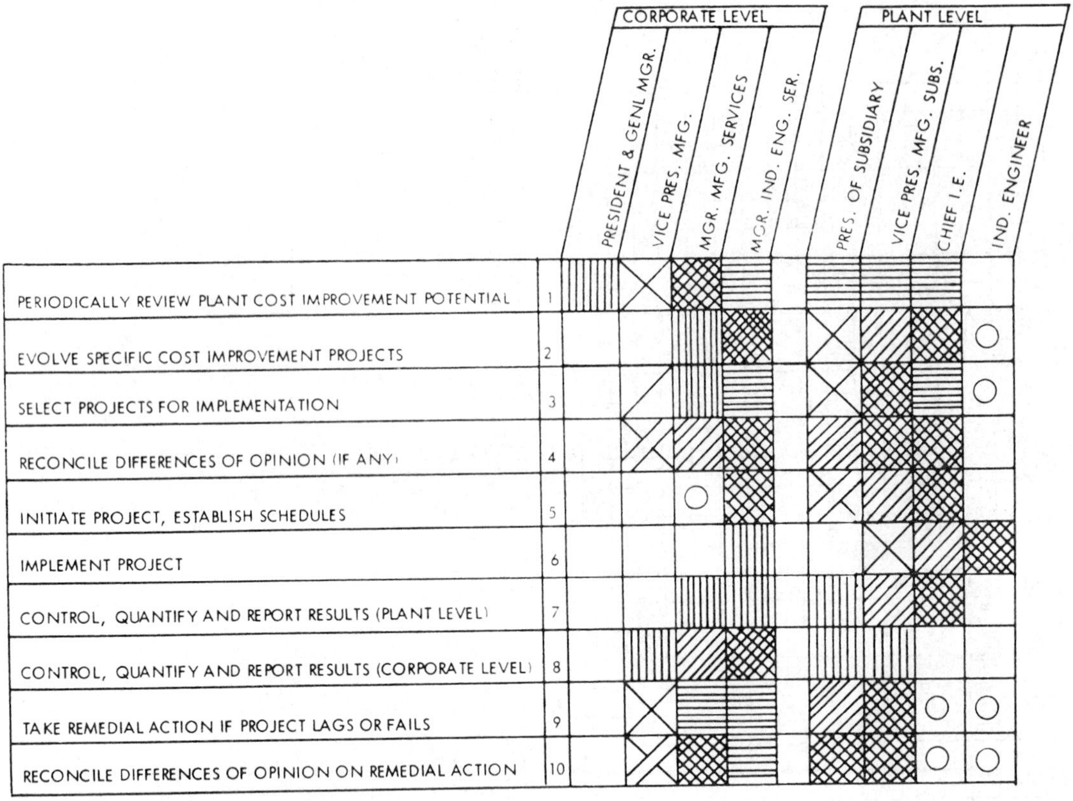
CORPORATE LEVEL
PLANT LEVEL
PRESIDENT & GENL MGR.
VICE PRES. MFG.
MGR. MFG. SERVICES
MGR. IND. ENG. SER.
PRES. OF SUBSIDIARY
VICE PRES. MFG. SUBS.
CHIEF I.E.
IND. ENGINEER
PERIODICALLY REVIEW PLANT COST IMPROVEMENT POTENTIAL 1
EVOLVE SPECIFIC COST IMPROVEMENT PROJECTS 2
SELECT PROJECTS FOR IMPLEMENTATION 3
RECONCILE DIFFERENCES OF OPINION (IF ANY) 4
INITIATE PROJECT, ESTABLISH SCHEDULES 5
IMPLEMENT PROJECT 6
CONTROL, QUANTIFY AND REPORT RESULTS (PLANT LEVEL) 7
CONTROL, QUANTIFY AND REPORT RESULTS (CORPORATE LEVEL) 8
TAKE REMEDIAL ACTION IF PROJECT LAGS OR FAILS 9
RECONCILE DIFFERENCES OF OPINION ON REMEDIAL ACTION 10

This chart was prepared as the result of a merger, in order (1) to insure effective and systematic cost improvement by exact pinpoint of the staff/line responsibility for that function, and (2) to train corporate and plant management in "who does what" in cost improvement. This became necessary because (1) the "merged-in" plant was previously privately owned, and its management was totally unfamiliar with the staff/line concept, and (2) the corporation which had acquired that plant had never faced that problem before.

overhead, training of executive and middle management in cases of mergers and acquisitions, and many others.

SERGE A. BIRN, Chairman, The Birn Organization, GmbH., Frankfurt on Main, West Germany

Information References

Birn, Serge A., "Clearing up Executive Confusion in Mergers and Acquisitions," *NAFM News*, September 1968.

Liptak, J. D., "Responsibility Charting—a Methods Tool," *NACA Bulletin*, May, 1956.

"Linear Responsibility Charting—Fast Way to Clear up Confusion," *Factory*, March 1963.

Cross References: *Human Resources Requirements Planning; Matrix Organization; Organization: Internal, Traditional Types (and accompanying entries with Organization prefix); Project Management.*

LONG-RANGE CORPORATE PLANNING

The term **Long-Range Corporate Planning** came into popular management use during the middle 1950s. By 1960, a minority of large industrial companies (e.g., those in the *Fortune 500* list) had some sort of formal long-range planning process under way. Some of these companies introduced planning on too grandiose a scale, and abandoned it after a year or two because it was more trouble than it was worth, only to re-install it a few years later on a more moderate, step-by-step basis.

The concept of formal planning gained continued acceptance during the 1960s. By 1980, probably 80% to 85% of the *Fortune 500* engaged in some form of long-range planning (not always of outstanding quality), as did perhaps half of the industrial companies down to

EXHIBIT III

MANUAL AND COMPUTER FORMATS FOR LRC

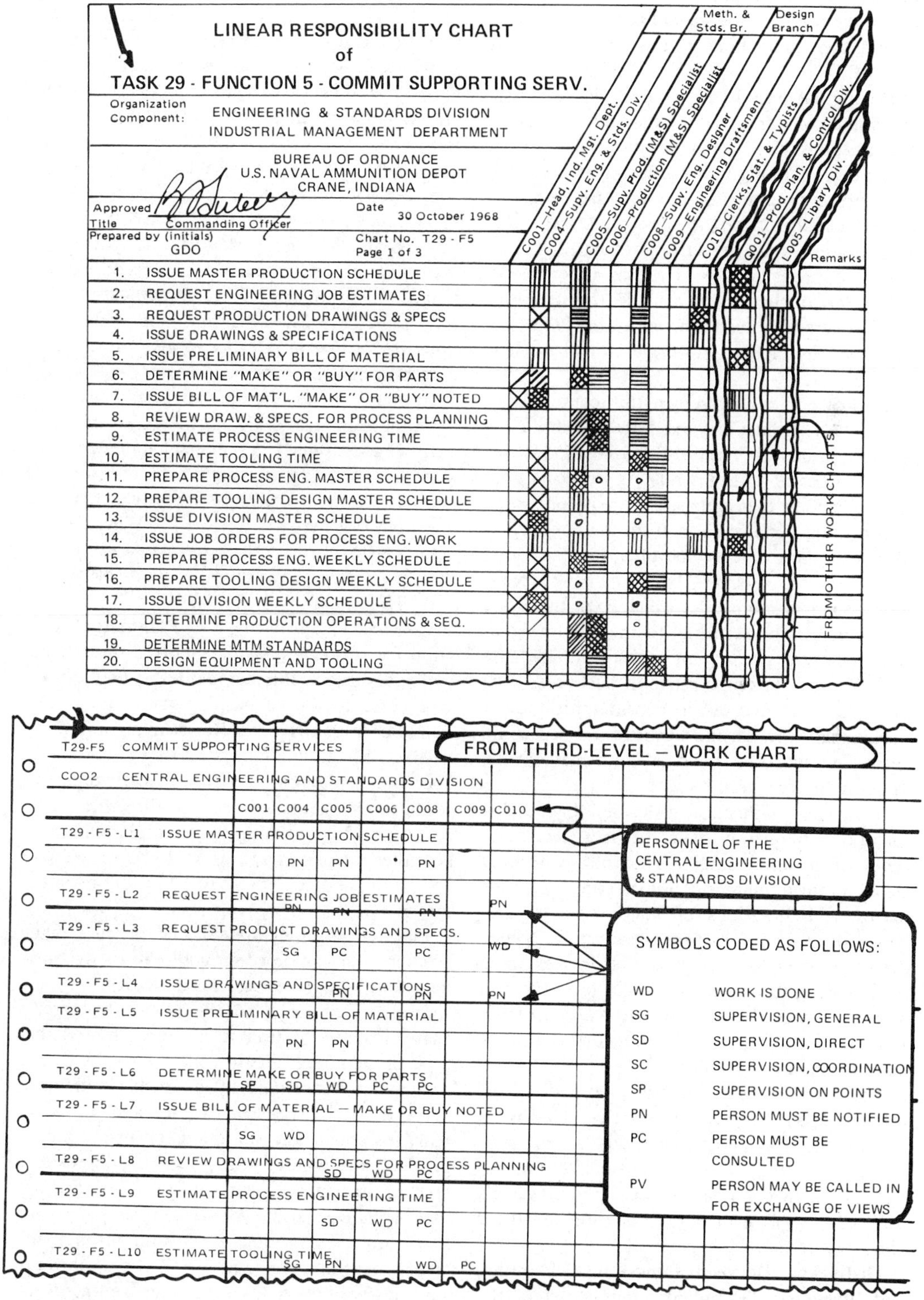
LINEAR RESPONSIBILITY CHART
of
TASK 29 - FUNCTION 5 - COMMIT SUPPORTING SERV.
Organization Component:
ENGINEERING & STANDARDS DIVISION
INDUSTRIAL MANAGEMENT DEPARTMENT
BUREAU OF ORDNANCE
U.S. NAVAL AMMUNITION DEPOT
CRANE, INDIANA
Approved
Title Commanding Officer
Date 30 October 1968
Prepared by (initials) GDO
Chart No. T29 - F5
Page 1 of 3
Meth. & Stds. Br.
Design Branch
C001—Head, Ind. Mgt. Dept.
C004—Supv. Eng. & Stds. Div.
C005—Supv. Prod. (M&S) Specialist
C006—Production (M&S) Specialist
C008—Supv. Eng. Designer
C009—Engineering Draftsmen
C010—Clerks, Stat. & Typists
Q001—Prod. Plan. & Control Div.
L005—Library Div.
Remarks
1. ISSUE MASTER PRODUCTION SCHEDULE
2. REQUEST ENGINEERING JOB ESTIMATES
3. REQUEST PRODUCTION DRAWINGS & SPECS
4. ISSUE DRAWINGS & SPECIFICATIONS
5. ISSUE PRELIMINARY BILL OF MATERIAL
6. DETERMINE "MAKE" OR "BUY" FOR PARTS
7. ISSUE BILL OF MAT'L. "MAKE" OR "BUY" NOTED
8. REVIEW DRAW. & SPECS. FOR PROCESS PLANNING
9. ESTIMATE PROCESS ENGINEERING TIME
10. ESTIMATE TOOLING TIME
11. PREPARE PROCESS ENG. MASTER SCHEDULE
12. PREPARE TOOLING DESIGN MASTER SCHEDULE
13. ISSUE DIVISION MASTER SCHEDULE
14. ISSUE JOB ORDERS FOR PROCESS ENG. WORK
15. PREPARE PROCESS ENG. WEEKLY SCHEDULE
16. PREPARE TOOLING DESIGN WEEKLY SCHEDULE
17. ISSUE DIVISION WEEKLY SCHEDULE
18. DETERMINE PRODUCTION OPERATIONS & SEQ.
19. DETERMINE MTM STANDARDS
20. DESIGN EQUIPMENT AND TOOLING
FROM OTHER WORK CHARTS
T29-F5 COMMIT SUPPORTING SERVICES
FROM THIRD-LEVEL – WORK CHART
COO2 CENTRAL ENGINEERING AND STANDARDS DIVISION
C001 C004 C005 C006 C008 C009 C010
PERSONNEL OF THE CENTRAL ENGINEERING & STANDARDS DIVISION
T29 - F5 - L1 ISSUE MASTER PRODUCTION SCHEDULE
PN PN PN
T29 - F5 - L2 REQUEST ENGINEERING JOB ESTIMATES
PN PN PN PN
T29 - F5 - L3 REQUEST PRODUCT DRAWINGS AND SPECS.
SG PC PC WD
T29 - F5 - L4 ISSUE DRAWINGS AND SPECIFICATIONS
PN PN PN
T29 - F5 - L5 ISSUE PRELIMINARY BILL OF MATERIAL
PN PN
T29 - F5 - L6 DETERMINE MAKE OR BUY FOR PARTS
SP SD WD PC PC
T29 - F5 - L7 ISSUE BILL OF MATERIAL – MAKE OR BUY NOTED
SG WD
T29 - F5 - L8 REVIEW DRAWINGS AND SPECS FOR PROCESS PLANNING
SD WD PC
T29 - F5 - L9 ESTIMATE PROCESS ENGINEERING TIME
SD WD PC
T29 - F5 - L10 ESTIMATE TOOLING TIME
SG PN WD PC
SYMBOLS CODED AS FOLLOWS:
WD WORK IS DONE
SG SUPERVISION, GENERAL
SD SUPERVISION, DIRECT
SC SUPERVISION, COORDINATION
SP SUPERVISION ON POINTS
PN PERSON MUST BE NOTIFIED
PC PERSON MUST BE CONSULTED
PV PERSON MAY BE CALLED IN FOR EXCHANGE OF VIEWS

Same LRP chart in two forms: Manual form (top) and computer print-out (bottom).

the $25 to $50 million sales range. Companies significantly smaller than this are usually subject to close, personalized management, under which the need for the formalized planning and formal communications discussed here is less evident.

During the past 10 to 15 years, large banks, insurance companies, and other non-industrial organizations also began to undertake formal long-range planning to a significant degree. Today, formal programs of this sort are being activated by universities, professional and trade associations, units of city governments, and other nonprofit groups. On the other hand, only a few of the largest firms in the securities and brokerage industry have, as of 1980, undertaken any significant formal forward planning.

Typically, "long-range" in this context may be five years, sometimes ten, with possibly even longer periods in natural-resources industries such as forestry and minerals. Typically, a time span is chosen that embraces at least one decision-making cycle, such as from the conception of a new plant or new line of products to getting them on stream. The "long-range planning" span is almost always longer than one year, but it is not unusual to find the designation "one-year profit plan" applied to the first year of the long-range plan. In such cases the first year is spelled out in considerably greater detail than the second, third, or succeeding years. The first-year financial data may be the same as the one-year budget.

In further clarification of terminology, a distinction is frequently made between two basic types of planning effort. The first is usually called *strategic* planning, and is concerned primarily with questions of major strategy and new growth directions for an enterprise. Major decisions may be involved, as for example those having to do with a merger or entry into a new business. (See CORPORATE STRATEGY AND BUSINESS POLICY and MARKETING STRATEGY: Competitive Analysis.)

The second type is frequently termed *operating* or *divisional* planning. Such planning is usually centered under the heads of the individual operating units or divisions of an organization. In contrast, strategic planning calls for the heavy involvement of the corporate chief executive.

Distinction Between Long-Range Planning and Budgeting. Documents coming out of the planning process differ significantly from budget documents, both in content and use. Budgets are prepared for financial and operating control. They typically aim for maximum accuracy in the dollar quantification of authorized activities rather than the formulation of imaginative new objectives. They usually concentrate on financial results, with little elaboration of the "whys" and with little background, descriptive analysis, or text material on programs. In contrast, planning documents covering more than one year tend to have somewhat ambitious goals, and good deal of analytical and text material, and discussion of impending programs. They are used for communication, setting policy, decision-making, and long-range thinking on resource allocations, rather than month-to-month controls.

In many cases the financial statements in planning documents are much more simplified than those found in budget statements or monthly operating statements. In one form or another the plans address themselves to the questions, "Where are we now?" "Where do we want to go?" and "How do we want to get there?"—the last including the items of "Who" and "How much will it cost?"

Reasons for the Growth of Planning. A program for *strategic planning* is often undertaken by highly successful companies simply to assure continuation of existing momentum. For example, both IBM and Xerox inaugurated extensive strategic planning efforts (in addition to operational planning) because of their desire to continue their outstanding growth records. The motivation for initiating strategic planning may be either offensive (e.g., to exploit an attractive opportunity) or defensive (e.g., to minimize future risk).

Planning is often inaugurated because management sees an upcoming threat to its business and recognizes the need to develop new sources of earnings to overcome the threat. Many defense contractors have attempted this type of planning, albeit with only spotty success, when threatened by cutbacks in defense spending. As a specific example, a paper company foresaw that its main profit-producing product line would undergo greatly intensified competition in the years ahead. Through formal, organized strategic planning it succeeded in adding new product lines both through internal development and acquisition, so that earnings are now many times the size they were when the threat to the one line was first recognized.

The growth of *operating* or *divisional* planning has received much of its impetus from the growing complexity of business (and also nonbusiness) organizations. The head of a moderate-size company with two or three divisions may in many cases have an adequate "feel" of the future of each, so that he can, for example, decide which unit should get the lion's share of new investment expenditures, without formal planning. In contrast, the head of a company with twenty or thirty divisions or major product groups cannot do this, and must use formal planning as a tool to help make such resource allocations rationally.

The complexity of far-flung international operations provides ready examples. Both Citicorp of New York, and Merck & Co., have extensive international operations in many foreign countries. They are widely recognized for their organized approach to formal planning of their international operations.

The growth of formal planning is often attributed to the acceleration of technological and social change, and to similar external and uncontrollable factors. While these may be underlying causes, it is usually something much more concrete that provides the actual impetus to more formal planning. For example, many companies have initiated formal planning because their banks or other financing institutions asked to see their long-range plans in connection with loan applications.

For completeness here, it should probably also be added that a small percentage of companies have undertaken long-range planning simply because it is the fashionable thing to do. However, unless such organizations can direct their planning in a way to provide tangible returns, it can be expected that they will soon abandon those efforts for resumption at a time when they can make them practical. In any event, long-range corporate planning can never be an "ivory-tower" undertaking. Guidelines for operational and divisional planning can be set in terms of the broad parameters of strategic planning—but constructive divisional involvement in a long-range planning program sponsored by corporate headquarters will only be secured if the divisions see "user benefits" in terms of their own operations.

Basic Steps in Operating Planning. Operating long-range planning (also referred to as divisional planning or profit improvement planning for present operations), typically begins with the generation of a series of forward plans by the individual operating units. They frequently have a three- to five-year time span. In concept, the head of the individual operating unit is responsible for executing it; however, he may receive assistance from his own staff or the staff of corporate headquarters.

It is quite common for the corporate headquarters staff to issue a five-year set of economic and other basic assumptions at the beginning of each year's planning cycle. This facilitates coordination so that each unit bases its planning on similar assumptions, in contrast to one unit's predicating its planning on more prosperous overall conditions than another. This planning cycle is undergone annually, adding a year on the future end and dropping a year gone by. It is not uncommon for the planning cycle to begin with the issuance of the aforementioned assumptions in the summer, followed by a month or two of compiling the plan by the operating units, a period of review by headquarters staff, and final approval or modification by headquarters line management toward the end of the year.

The budget for the upcoming year may be approved at the same time. Some organizations have found it useful to phase the long-range planning at a different time of year from the one-year budget preparations. The justification usually cited is that the attention to the details of the budget process overshadows the more conceptual thinking generally considered to be the hallmark of effective planning. Still other organizations engage in more or less continuous planning which plays down the prominence of the annual planning cycle. Such organizations may update long-range plans or introduce new long-range programs whenever circumstances warrant.

A representative table of contents of a division long-range plan is shown in Exhibit I. Myriad variations are of course used. However the concept of using a "market back" focus to the plan, as illustrated, has come into wide acceptance. It is also common to consider the past record as well as the future plans and outlook. There appears also to be a growing feeling that the financial summary should indeed be merely a financial representation of the previously discussed conditions. Many organizations have found that so-called long-range plans that deal only in financial material, or that lay too much emphasis on financial detail, tend to represent wishful thinking and may be rather shallow in coming to grips with the real issues in the business.

Robert W. Haigh in his capacity as a group vice president of Xerox Corporation, has put forward the idea that division plans can sometimes become so complex and detailed that fundamentals are lost sight of. He prefers, as an indication that his people are doing effective planning, that the head of a unit be able to cite without reference to notes the key factors in his business. These include such elements as:

- The few major trends in the business environment.
- The few major objectives of this business unit in fairly specific terms.
- The few major programs to be featured in achieving the objectives.
- How the foregoing relate to the short-term plan of the unit.

It is quite common for the divisional plans to be summarized or consolidated by headquarters planning staff into a total plan for the present units of a company. There may be negotiation between headquarters management and division management as to goals to be achieved and programs to be undertaken. In some cases (ITT is an example), negotiation and at least preliminary approval take place at the objectives-setting stage, so that the lengthy job of working out detailed programs does not have to be reworked because of changed objectives.

It is not uncommon for some headquarters managements to include a positive or negative "fudge factor" in their own private thinking to offset what they consider undue optimism or pessimism on the part of individual units. They may also add a factor for objectives or expectations from new sources of earnings, that is, new earnings coming from sources other than the present divisions, such as new acquisitions or ventures. (This is discussed further immediately below.) Thus the "corporate long-range plan" is born, although it may never exist as a single document in one place.

Basic Steps in Strategic Planning. The underlying concept of *strategic* long-range planning is that it provides the vehicle for the enterprise to reposition its business mix or basic pattern of doing business, in order to achieve superior objectives, i.e. results which would be superior to continuing on substantially an "as is" basis. Thus some textile organizations have successfully made a

EXHIBIT I

Table of contents of a market-oriented long-range plan as used in multi-division companies.

Table of Contents

Long-Range Plan—X Division

I. MARKET

1. For each major product line, graph of total industry volume in units and dollars for each of the past five years, forthcoming year, and projection for each of the next five years.
2. As above, for significant market segments (e.g. new versus replacement, or jobber sales versus direct, or high-price versus low-price).
3. Similar data for new product lines to be introduced.
4. Commentary on significant trends.
   (a) Growth trends in markets and segments.
   (b) Changing trends of customer requirements in quality, service, product types, distribution requirements, purchasing practices, etc.

II. COMPETITION

1. Listing of principal competitors and estimated share in each market segment.
2. Financial results (where available) on each significant competitor; graph of sales growth, profit on sales, return on investment.
3. Comment on new entrants: numerous smaller competitors, foreign competition, etc.
4. Strong and weak points of significant competitors.
5. For significant competitors, apparent strategy and prospects: segments of market emphasized, marketing and distribution practices, technical and new product strategy, resistance to price competition.
6. Graph of capacity versus consumption.
7. Graph of price structure for bellweather products.
8. Our strengths and weaknesses versus competition and market needs.

III. OUR PERFORMANCE PLAN

1. Commentary on what is apparently needed to achieve superior earnings in this industry. Alternate strategies we could select.
2. Outline of selected strategy: market segments, product and pricing ranges, marketing and distribution practices, production locations and strategies, new product and technical strategies.
3. Graph of volume, share and margin objectives for major product lines (lines and dollars) for each of past five years, forthcoming year, each of next five years.
4. Major assumptions; commentary on change in share of market.
5. Graph of major elements of cost, each of the past five years, forthcoming year, each of the next five years.
6. For direct and indirect labor: Average number of employees per unit of output, average hourly rate, comments on programs for control of labor costs.

EXHIBIT I

IV. SUPPORTING ACTION PROGRAMS

Commentary on step-by-step programs for achieving above performance by major activities:

1. Manufacturing.
2. Marketing.
3. Technical.
4. Organization.
5. Other.

V. REQUIRED INVESTMENTS IN CAPITAL FACILITIES, R&D, PERSONNEL, ADVERTISING, ETC.

1. R&D expenditures each of last five years, forthcoming year, each of next five years.
2. As above, machinery and equipment.
3. As above, buildings and land.
4. As above, advertising.
5. As above, changes in working capital.
6. Comment on purposes and timing of expenditures in above categories.
7. Outline of personnel requirements for each major department; comment on recruitment and training programs.

VI. FINANCIAL SUMMARY

1. Condensed P&L for each of last five years, forthcoming year, each of next five years.
2. As above, condensed balance sheet.
3. As above, cash flow data.
4. As above, for key ratios: profit on sales, profit on investment, capital turnover, inventory turnover, etc.

conversion from being primarily weavers of commodity greige goods to organizations which supply, say, fashion-oriented finished goods, knit as well as woven constructions, consumer end products, and other specialized items less vulnerable to low-price commodity import competition. Burlington Industries and Collins & Aikman are examples of textile companies which have used formalized strategic planning to help re-direct their corporate strategies along new lines. In contrast, the actual survival of some other large companies is in question because they have not succeeeded in developing a strategy that enabled them successfully to evolve out of their conventional business patterns.

In actual practice, formal strategic planning is often done on a more spasmodic basis than operational long-range planning. Thus a formal strategic plan is usually not redrawn in total annually, adding and dropping a year, as in formal operating long-range planning. Rather, parts of a strategic plan may be revised several times a year, for example as new studies disclose new areas of opportunity or possibly indicate the desirability of de-emphasizing some traditional areas. Other aspects of a strategic plan, for example to expand in certain European businesses through ventures and internal expansion, may continue without change in basic concept for some period of years.

Some writers on strategic planning have adopted a doctrinaire attitude, putting forth "cookbook recipes" as to how it should be done. In contrast, it is the writers' observation, based on consulting with companies which have had successful results in strategic planning, that effective planning of this sort may be carried out in many different ways, with various degrees of formality and with varying frequency of updating. However, the main factors to be considered as part of the overall strategic planning process include elements such as the following:

(1) *Establishing financial objectives.* For publicly-held companies, consistency of growth in earnings per common share is generally the overriding financial objective. Companies usually wish to do at least as well as their own past record, or at least as well as other companies in their field.

(2) *Measuring the earnings "gap."* In comparing the financial objectives with the outlook as portrayed by the sum of a company's operating long-range plans, it is frequently apparent that there is a gap between what is *desired* and what is *anticipated.* It is the job of the strategic planner to fill this gap by laying plans for developing new sources of earnings or redirecting present resources into more productive lines. As in operating planning, it is the line management (i.e. the chief executive) which has the ultimate responsibility for strategic planning decisions.

(3) *Appraising internal strengths, weaknesses, and issues.* In many organizations, strategic planners make an inventory from time to time to determine where there are strengths which can be capitalized or weaknesses to be circumvented or offset.

(4) *"Pullers-draggers" analysis.* The writers have coined this term to describe the process by which the strategic planner analyzes the component businesses within a company. This pinpoints the need to force-feed the "pullers" (businesses with attractive earnings and prospects) and lay specific plans for doing this, and to correct or withdraw from the "draggers" (components of the business with unattractive earnings or prospects). Thus we find for exam-

ple that IBM withdrew from its timeclock business, and W. R. Grace & Company sold off certain domestic operations and much of its traditional Latin American businesses, and merged its bank with a larger financial institution. In an analysis of this type, other segments of the business may be identified as cash "milk-cows" and still others may be identified as "comers," each requiring appropriate treatment.

(5) *Analysis of business environment.* Strategic planners will also from time to time attempt to portray future trends in their business environment. This includes their markets, their competition, their technologies, the social climate, trends in governmental regulation, and the like. It is the job of the strategic planner to see that a company capitalizes on such trends where possible, and avoids being trapped by surprise in disadvantageous trends.

(6) *Directional planning.* Selecting new growth directions for a company, when done on the most rational basis, involves setting criteria for evaluating new growth directions, screening the full range of possibilities against these criteria, and establishing priorities for implementation. Criteria can be based on three principal factors, each of which has sub-factors in turn. The first is *profit opportunity:* "Does this field give us an opportunity for the size, growth, consistency, and level of profits which we are seeking?" The second criterion relates to *compatibility:* "Is this a field which we can understand and to which we can make some unique contribution based on our marketing strength or technical strength, or the like?" The third criterion has to do with *feasibility* or *prospects for successful entry.*

Screening the full range of possibilities against the criteria is less difficult than it may at first sound. It is important that a variety of factors be considered, such as growth markets, growth business areas, horizontal and vertical integration and all possibilities which closely relate to a company's strengths, such as its own type of technology, as well as the screening of all acquisition candidates within certain established limits. By this process, it is possible for a strategic planning group to say truly it has considered all possibilities for new growth directions and has established priorities accordingly. Reorienting priorities as conditions change is more-or-less an ongoing job in many organizations.

(7) *Implementation.* Many strategic planning groups also have responsibility for acquisitions, divestitures, and setting up of ventures. If these activities are not housed organizationally within the planning group, there must obviously be a close liaison. Close liaison is also required with the technical people responsible for developing altogether new products for a company. This implementation stage, calling as it does for somewhat different activities than strictly planning, is sometimes referred to as the "development" or "planning and development" activity.

Departure from Theory. In the foregoing material, the authors have endeavored to spell out the practices typically employed in organizations which are well managed and experienced in the techniques of long-range planning. However, one common departure is frequently found in unquestionably successful companies (although it is now less common). This is an acquisition program to acquire new companies, based more on opportunism than on reasoned planning of suitable growth directions for the parent company. In other words, if an attractive "deal" can be made, the business the acquired company is in is not considered to be especially important. This may still be justifiable where the parent company is threatened with immediate disastrous prospects in its base business. However, many conglomerates spent the early years of the 1970s undoing the mistakes made through overly optimistic acquisitions in the late 1960s.

Planning theory says that objectives must be spelled out so that all concerned can be working toward a common goal. However, professional planners sometimes encounter chief executives who are reluctant to spell out the real objectives of the company. These company heads apparently feel that they had best keep their options open by articulating only vague or highly generalized goals—for example, "to maximize profits." Obviously, unless this attitude at the top is changed, the planner will have to develop proposed programs based on his own assessment of needs and opportunities, and secure separate approvals on an ad-hoc basis.

Another problem encountered by planners is a tendency for managements to be biased by existing conditions—i.e., to make overly optimistic plans in good times and overly pessimistic plans in poor times. Use of professional economists' inputs to the planning process will provide more objectivity in this regard.

Organization of the Planning Function. A competent planner should be a specialist in the techniques of planning, but he should also be a generalist who knows the requirements for success in his particular industry. The head of planning typically reports to the chief executive (or division head if the planner is on a division level). In large organizations having an "office of the president" the planning function may report there. In other large organizations the planner may report to the executive vice president for administration.

Planning staffs for operating planning are typically small, perhaps consisting of only a few people even in a large company. This is because their focus is to see that the operating planning gets done, rather than actually doing the actual planning. However, to the extent that there is major emphasis on *strategic* planning, study of new growth directions, acquisitions, and venture work, the planning staff can consist of a dozen or even several dozen persons.

New Developments in Planning. There has been considerable interest in the application of computer techniques to planning matters. Certainly computers have been used for many years in dealing with such "planning" problems as warehouse location and transportation networks; however, for most companies, matters of that nature are peripheral to the main issues of business planning.

Computer models have been constructed which provide helpful answers to "what if" questions which sometimes have to be faced in planning—for example, "What if we were to change our price . . . ?" or "What if we were to increase the size of our sales force . . . ?" Citibank of New York among others has developed a computer model for use with its customers which forecasts under certain assumptions the effect of a merger for five or more years ahead. Such techniques can be useful aids to planning decision making where many "what if" questions must be (or should be) answered. However, they are still only aids to decision-making. No one is yet "planning by computer" in the literal sense of the phrase.

Some interesting work has gone into developing massive econometric and corporate models as an aid to planning. While again these show signs of promise especially on peripheral matters, the fundamental planning decisions are still being made by seasoned executives on the basis of their conviction and judgment. It seems that this will continue to be the case.

MANAGEMENT BY OBJECTIVES, which can be described as medium-range personal planning by individual managers, has come into widespread use. However, where companies have both long-range corporate planning and management by objectives programs, the link between the two is generally indirect. In setting his own objectives, say for the forthcoming year, an individual manager must be guided by the immediate objectives of his unit of the company. Obviously, none of his objectives can run counter to long-range operational planning. However, they must be very specific for short term results in his segment. (See separate entry.)

In the coming years, formal long-range planning can be expected to continue to spread to industrial organizations which do not now practice it, and to an increasing degree to nonbusiness organizations.

Formal planning has already achieved a foothold in numerous educational institutions, charitable organizations, hospitals, and the like. Nevertheless many business executives who insist upon sophisticated long-range planning in their own business organizations, sit on the governing boards of nonbusiness organizations where formal long-range planning does not exist. However, the changing pressures of the times are beginning to work for the installation of formal long-range planning in such organizations.

The *strategic planning* aspect of long-range planning will undoubtedly play an increasingly prominent role. More effective strategic planning probably represents one of the greatest profit-improvement opportunities for business today.

WILLIAM E. HILL and CHARLES H. GRANGER, Hayes, Hill Incorporated, New York, New York, and (for third edition) JOHN D. SIMMONS, Financial Consultant, New York, New York

Information References

Ansoff, H. Igor, "Corporate Strategy: An Analytic Approach to Business Policy for Growth and Expansion," New York, McGraw-Hill, 1965.

Caves, Richard E., "Industrial Organization, Corporate Strategy and Structure," *Journal of Economic Literature,* March 1980.

"Corporate Guides to Long Range Planning," *Report 687,* New York, The Conference Board, 1976.

Ewing, David W., ed. "Long Range Planning for Management," New York, Harper & Row, 3rd. ed., 1972.

Roney, C. W., "The Two Purposes of Business Planning," *Managerial Planning*, November-December 1976.

Turk, Frederick J., "A Tool for Planning and Decision Making," *Management Focus*, Peat, Marwick, Mitchell & Co, New York, March-April 1980.

Vancil, Richard F., "Decentralization: Managerial Ambiguity by Design," New York, Dow-Jones-Irwin, 1979.

Association

North American Society for Corporate Planning

Cross References: *Business Forecasting; Corporate Strategy and Business Policy; Long-Range Planning: Financial Aspects; Marketing Strategy: Competitive Analysis; Operations Research in Marketing Decisions; Return on Capital.*

LONG-RANGE PLANNING: Financial Aspects

Long-Range Planning is a systematic process for purposefully directing and controlling the future activities of the enterprise for periods extending beyond one year. It does more than merely predict the future, for it is above all a program of intended action and desired result.

Unlike *forecasting* which is restricted to predicting the future, the fundamental aim of all business *planning* is to exercise some degree of control over the business and its environment in order to exert a favorable influence over future events.

The distinctive feature of long-range planning is the aim of imposing before-the-fact control over the results of events that may take place as much as 5, 10, or even 25 years ahead. The choice of the time span for the plan is often influenced by the special characteristics of the company and its industry. For example, a public utility company with a large investment in capital equipment may plan 25 years ahead; whereas a lumber company may have a 50 or 100-year reforestation program; and conversely, a small firm manufacturing consumer products may need to plan no more than two years ahead. But a cursory survey of actual practice indicates that the time span in long-range planning typically ranges from two to ten years, with a decided preference for a five-year period. A period longer than five or ten years is seldom used, apparently because of the extreme uncertainty inherent in planning for more extended time periods.

Ideally the long-range plan should be both an operational and a strategic plan, integrated with short-range planning so that each year the first year of the long-range plan becomes the basis for the current year's financial operating plan. The formal planning document expressing the actions and results that have been preplanned should be kept current, so that it will always correspond with corporate objectives. A suitable means for making changes in the plan is to put it on a "rolling base" so that it can be updated and extended every twelve months by dropping the immediately past year and replacing it with a further annual period.

For the conventional five-year plan, the key objectives are usually future profitability and company growth. But it should not be overlooked that in some instances the long-range plan may be, in effect, a plan for survival (as a necessary pre-condition to making profit in some later period).

The long-range plan is an *overall* plan for the company, which encompasses all areas of company activity (e.g. marketing, manufacturing, finance) and integrates the subordinate plans for each individual department, function or activity, etc. Therefore while there will be separate plans for research and development, capital facilities, acquisitions and diversifications, product development, etc., each is nonetheless only one aspect of the overall company plan. The financial long-range plan translates these other plans into the common language of finance, and quantifies the projected results in financial terms.

Acceptance. Over the past fifteen years or so, long-range financial planning has been rapidly accepted into the repertory of modern professional management. With its growing popularity, the enthusiasm of its proponents and a large body of professional literature on the subject, it is now widely used by many companies of varying size. In fact, it has successfully moved into the mainstream of management practice as a vital and highly regarded disciplinary tool to optimize long-term results.

There is a crucial need for long-range planning because a growing proportion of total costs now is of the *fixed* type and represents the *continuing costs* of having capacity and maintaining an organization in readiness to manufacture and sell. Greater expenditures for fixed investment in plant and equipment, an increasing number of persons employed on a salary basis, and continuing large-scale long-term commitments for research facilities, training centers, and headquarters staff, are indicative of this type of situation. It follows, then, that companies are typically faced with a situation where many of the day-to-day operating decisions are constrained within the framework of managerial decisions made long ago, because the earlier decisions involved forward commitments having long-term implications or payout. Under such circumstances long-range planning becomes not only desirable but mandatory if a company is to grow and prosper.

Processes and Techniques. Long-range planning comprises processes and techniques that are already known and understood: *forecasting, planning, analyzing, controlling,* and *coordinating* are not new in themselves. But in the past these techniques had often been treated as individual managerial tools to be used independently of one another, instead of being used in conjunction or combined in an integrated program for planning and controlling future operations. What is new is the concept of a comprehensive planning program, motivated by profit and geared to the long-term future, and making use of the other known managerial techniques as instruments to help in attaining specific planned objectives.

Stages of Long-Range Planning. *Stage I—Long-Range Economic Forecasting.* In order to have basic data that will serve as guides in setting company goals it is necessary to forecast the basic overall characteristics of the environment within which business operations will be conducted. It will be prudent to predict prospective *economic, political, sociological, technological, competitive* and other relevant conditions in order to formulate the key assumptions upon which long-range strategy and planning should be based. Some typical factors to be forecast include population, income levels, and buying habits. Such factors are analyzed to outline the prospective developments that will influence the market during the planning period. These long-range economic forecasts do not in themselves constitute firm plans, but serve instead as guides for planning and policy making, and in the preparation of plans and budgets. (See BUSINESS FORECASTING.) Company long-range strategic goals, financial objectives, and product strategy are all conditioned by and influenced by this prediction of the future and the eventual estimation as to what the *optimum attainable results* would be.

Stage II—Determining Long-Range Goals. Having determined the basic features of the future environment (including estimated size of the overall market, nature of competition, potential market share, etc.) management formulates overall company policy for the intended future development of the business; establishes long-range goals; and determines the basic strategies (e.g. diversification, acquisition, research) for achieving them. These goals, which are expressed in terms of markets to be served, products to be sold, and targets for sales and profit performance, etc., will be ultimately translated into specific objectives.

Stage III—Specific Planning Objectives and Sales Forecasting. The specific planning objectives identify the business operations, plus the key sales and profit results desired. The next stage therefore is the preparation of long-range sales revenue forecasts reflecting the planned level of operations. Such forecasts will specify and identify (both in total and by interim time segment) the dollar amount, physical volume, product mix, market mix, market share, and other relevant sales details.

It may also be necessary to translate the overall company plan into individual plans for the major components of company activity. Thus there will be separate but coordinated individual specialized plans for such areas as: *Marketing,* and related advertising, promotion, and distribution activities; *Production,* and related manufacturing, organization, and manpower activities; *Engineering,* and related design, styling and testing activities.

Stage IV—Organization and Facilities Planning. This stage involves the planning of the level and type of organization and facilities that will be needed. The principal purposes of the facilities plan are:

(1) Determination of the amount, type, and desired timing of future requirements for physical facilities, manpower, etc.

(2) Provision of the lead-time necessary to construct facilities, develop an organization, and arrange necessary financing.

(3) Determination of priorities for the allocation of funds.

(4) Provision of the proper capacity at a minimum of expense.

(5) Optimum use of capacity.

Since these requirements for facilities etc. imply expenditures for future years, the plans should be expressed in terms of the money needed to provide the facilities so that the capital budget may be prepared from these data.

Stage V—Capital Budgeting. Data prepared for the facilities plan form the basis for prepar-

EXHIBIT I

FORMATS, CASH BUDGETING AND LONG-RANGE CASH FORECASTS

CAPITAL BUDGET

		Historical Data			Five Year Outlook Data					
					Approved for Current Year	Budget	Planned			Total
Class	Capital Expenditures	1978 $	1979 $	1980 $	1981 $	1982 $	1983 $	1984 $	1985 $	1981-85 $
1	Land and Buildings									
1A	Expansion									
1B	Replacement									
2	Machinery and Equipment									
2A	Expansion									
2B	Replacement									
3	Patterns and Tools									
3A	Expansion									
3B	Replacement									
4	Automobiles and Trucks									
4A	Expansion									
4B	Replacement									
5	Furniture and Fixtures									
5A	Expansion									
5B	Replacement									
6	Other									
6A	Expansion									
6B	Replacement									
	Total									
	Expansion									
	Replacement									
	Grand Total									

1a

LONG RANGE CASH FORECAST

	Historical Data			Five Year Outlook Data					
				Approved for Current Year	Budget	Planned			Total
	1978 $	1979 $	1980 $	1981 $	$	1982 $	1983 $	1984 $	1981-85 $
Funds Generated from Operations									
Net Income									
Capital Recovery									
Assets Sold*									
Other									
Total Funds Generated									
Funds Required for Operations									
Capital Expenditures									
Investments and Advances									
Working Capital									
Total Funds Required									
Net Surplus (Deficit) From Operation									
Cash Dividends									
Net Surplus (Deficit) Before Financing									
Changes in Financing									
Sale of Capital Stock									
Long-Term Debt									
Short-Term Debt									
Total Changes in Financing									
Increase (Decrease) in Total Cash									
Opening Cash Balance									
Closing Cash Balance									

1b

ing a program of projected capital investments, and for drawing up the capital budget for the related capital expenditures. Planning and control of expenditures for investment in plant and equipment are achieved through the capital budget, which provides a means for the comparative evaluation of investment projects, the selection of those with the highest priorities, and the forecasting of cash disbursements. (See Exhibit Ia.)

Stage VI—Long-Range Cash Forecasting. Forecasts of cash flows are important in the financial planning of capital expenditures and for working capital for future operations because they have an important role in:

(1) Selecting investment projects.

(2) Determining the amount and timing of the cash needed.

(3) Forecasting the time when cash can be recovered for reinvestment, payment of debts, dividends etc.

(See Exhibit Ib.)

Stage VII—Other Financial Planning. Consistent with other areas of financial planning, and coordinated with all functions and activities that are planned, it is also necessary to plan company capital structure and financial position, profits and return on capital employed, etc. Expenses must be budgeted; shorter-range plans must be prepared and integrated with the long-range plan; financial results must be projected and measured; and all relevant financial aspects must ultimately find their expression in the long-range planning document.

JOHN D. SIMMONS, Financial Consultant, New York, New York.

Information References

"Aspects of Corporate Planning—A Collection of Four Papers," London, England, The Institute of Cost and Works Accountants, March 1970.

Henry, Harold W., "Long-Range Planning Practices in 45 Industrial Companies," Englewood Cliffs, N.J., Prentice-Hall, 1967.

Hiller, Robert W., "The Role of Finance in Strategic Planning," *Canadian Business Review* (Ottowa, Canada, Conference Board in Canada), Summer 1979.

Hilton, Peter, "Planning Corporate Growth and Diversification," New York, McGraw-Hill, 1970.

Hussey, D. E., "Corporate Planning: Theory and Practice," New York, Pergamon, 1974.

"Long Range Profit Planning," *Research Report 42,* New York, National Association of Accountants, 1964.

Michals, George F., "Does Formal Planning Stymie Initiative?," *Canadian Business Review* (Conference Board in Canada), Summer 1979.

Smith, Shea and Walsh, John E. Jr., "Strategies in Business," New York, Wiley, 1978.

Cross References: *Long-Range Corporate Planning (and cross references there given).*

M

MAINTENANCE

Maintenance is the corporate effort directed toward upkeep and repair of equipment and facilities. It requires management as well as technical skills. Industry figures cited by the Research Department of *Industrial Maintenance and Plant Operation* place the annual corporate bill for maintenance labor and materials in the manufacturing industries at $47 billion.

History. Until the 1920s, the emphasis was upon those physical aspects that limit or contribute to uninterrupted production. The function was mainly in the hands of craftsmen or engineers. They sought technical solutions to the problems of more reliable power transmission, better ways to lubricate shafts and bearings, materials that would prevent severe corrosion, etc. Management of the maintenance function was haphazard and neglected. Generally speaking, maintenance was ineffective and costly.

The first professional recognition of the maintenance function was in 1930 in Chicago when a 3-M Congress (Management, Maintenance, and Material Handling) was held. The depression years blocked further development, however, and the 1930s became notorious for "deferred maintenance." Maintenance "found itself" during World War II, when the goal for industry was production at any cost. With this goal came the realization that good maintenance was the key to high production, and required the same kind of effective management as did good production.

Following World War II, maintenance grew in stature and was highlighted in 1950 by the founding of the National Plant Maintenance Conference and Show, now attended yearly by over 2,500 maintenance and plant engineering managers. The function continues to grow steadily in total numbers of people employed, quality of its personnel, and identification with the profit goals of business enterprise. Influencing this development, five significant changes in the last three decades may be noted:

(1) Continuing transition from slow-speed to high-speed production equipment, which means more production and more wear on equipment.

(2) Continuing movement from man-controlled to automatically-controlled production equipment, which requires high-grade engineering talent for maintenance.

(3) Increased cost per-hour of productive labor, which adds to the cost of equipment downtime.

(4) Increased cost of productive equipment, which intensifies pressure for greater equipment utilization.

(5) Increased ratio of maintenance employees to production employees, which means fewer men on the *do* side of plant operations and more men on the *keep-ready* side.

Maintenance Management. To achieve optimum costs for upkeep and repair, the maintenance function must integrate five major factors. These factors are people, policies, equipment, practices, and performance evaluation.

Organization. Typically, maintenance is headed by a manager or superintendent assisted by various staff engineers and specialists. These assistants aid in work planning, job scheduling, and cost estimating, and also furnish engineering and technical guidance. The manager is supported by a staff of supervisors, generally organized on a craft or departmental basis. In turn, these supervisors manage a team of hourly employees in varying craft grades.

Policies. The quality of maintenance is greatly dependent upon the suitability of its organization to the technical problems arising in the plant. At the very outset, for instance, management must choose between centralized and decentralized (or area) maintenance. The former offers greater control, while the latter has the advantage of specialization and speed.

Other policy decisions involve the reporting level of the maintenance department—whether to the production manager, to a more general "plant engineering" department, or directly to the manager of operations. Practices vary about half and half between keeping maintenance separate from plant engineering or having it unified with that function. Another problem is the question of whether to subcontract various maintenance services (such as electrical or construction) or to perform these services by the plant's own permanent workforce.

Tools and Equipment. The maintenance force

should be as well equipped for its job as a production department. For example, it needs: (1) an up-to-date stores facility for supplies and spare parts, (2) a shop equipped with first-rate machine tools and welding and cutting equipment, (3) material handling equipment such as lift trucks, powered carts, hoists, etc., (4) a wide range of powered hand tools, and (5) effective communications equipment such as portable intercoms and the like.

Practices. Maintenance borrows heavily from Production in its development of management and control practices. A well-run maintenance department should have a systematic work order system, employ material and manpower controls, and maintain histories of equipment repairs and repair costs. It will work with budgets and use cost accounting procedures, check work activity by work sampling and measure work performance by standard time data, consider application of wage incentives, improve efficiency, and reduce costs through methods study, work simplification, statistical studies and the like. It will also provide for regular training of new craftsmen and updating of older men in new skills.

And like all operations, maintenance must face up to a regular, and realistic performance evaluation. This means (1) comparing trends in cost of maintenance per unit of product produced, (2) recording history of machine utilization, (3) examining state of backlogged work orders, and (4) making surveys of plant operating and housekeeping conditions.

A new form of keeping records, scheduling preventive maintenance, and controlling maintenance of buildings and equipment has been made possible by the computer. In the past few years, the mini-and microcomputers have been made available with software capable of controlling and reporting, and managing plant operation and maintenance. These units are adaptable to many and varied functions.

Integrated Maintenance. Probably the most significant advance in maintenance practices in the last 30 years has been the development of managed maintenance practices.

Preventive Maintenance (PM) contains two basic activities: (1) periodic inspection of plant assets and equipment to uncover conditions leading to production breakdown or harmful depreciation; and (2) upkeep of plant to rectify such conditions while they are still in a minor stage. Today, almost 80% of all companies conduct a PM program to some degree.

In the past few years, other aspects of managed maintenance have been developing. They are corrective maintenance and maintenance prevention.

Corrective Maintenance (CM) is a program of regular analysis of maintenance costs of equipment. Its purpose is to identify the high-repair cost items and find out the reasons for them. These items are then subjected to a program of corrective design directed at reducing or eliminating the condition that made maintenance frequent and/or costly.

Maintenance Prevention (MP) is a program that attempts, through good equipment and facility design, to minimize the amount of maintenance required by a machine component, the whole machine, a process, a utility service, or a building. It even attempts to eliminate the item, if possible, on the premise that if the item does not exist, it will need no maintenance. MP recognizes that maintenance is a continuous, year-after-year expense. Consequently MP can justify a high initial cost of an item by a greater return from yearly savings through lower maintenance costs. Often the savings in downtime alone will justify the choice of a superior valve, motor, drive, or instrument that wouldn't stand a chance in direct price competition.

The three techniques of PM, CM, and MP will undoubtedly become increasingly integrated as the management function of maintenance matures. A company first "engineers out" of the equipment as much maintenance as it can; next, takes good care of the equipment that it chooses to use; and, finally, bears down hard on any maintenance problems remaining.

Contract Maintenance Service has long been used for janitorial services: a maintenance firm will clean walls, floors, windows, laboratories, public rooms, etc. in all types of buildings, and provide attended services where desired, as in washrooms. In the past 20 years, however, a new form of contract maintenance has reached significant proportions, especially in the process industries. This is not the routine servicing of special equipment, long available from local contractors (e.g., maintenance of elevators, motors, sewing-machines, air conditioning and refrigerating equipment, etc.), but rather the maintenance of *all* equipment in a plant, sometimes even including the function of maintenance management, as well as the supplying of maintenance labor.

Maintenance contracts fall broadly into four

categories: (1) the mere supplying of temporary help, with no responsibility for supervision; (2) assumption of responsibility for preventive maintenance performed in a defined shut-down period, or "turnaround," in which the temporary forces used need not be integrated with the plant forces—the contractor provides shift and craft supervisors, but the planning and coordination of the turnaround may be done by either the company's or the contractor's staff; (3) the plant staff handles all routine maintenance, and the contractor meets the extra, seasonal demands; (4) the contractor assumes the *full* responsibility for planning, coordination, and supervision of the work, as well as the supplying of labor.

The concept of contracting for total maintenance, (4) above, has been confined largely to the process industries, in view of the complex maintenance problems prevalent there, the heavy cost of shutdowns, and special types of skills involved.

VINCENT F. GUERRIE C.P.E., Chief Engineer, Johns-Manville World Headquarters, Denver, Colorado, for American Institute of Plant Engineers

Information References

Periodicals:

Electrical Construction and Maintenance.
Industrial Maintenance and Plant Operation.
Plant Electrical Systems.
Plant Engineering.
Plant Services.

Texts:

Higgins, L. P. and Morrow, L. C., ed., "Maintenance Engineering Handbook," 3rd ed., New York, McGraw-Hill, 1979.
Newbrough, E. T., "Effective Maintenance Management," New York, McGraw-Hill, 1967.

Association:
American Institute of Plant Engineers.

Cross References: *Fire Loss Prevention; Plant Engineering.*

MANAGEMENT ACCOUNTING

Management Accounting is concerned with supplying financial data useful to management at all levels in planning and administering an enterprise. More specifically, three different areas can be distinguished in which management has need for financial data provided by the accountant, *viz:*

(1) In long and short range strategic planning there is need for evaluating alternatives in financial terms.

(2) In administering operations, management needs to know promptly when current results deviate significantly from planned results.

(3) In discharging management's obligation to report on the results of its stewardship to stockholders, creditors, and others having a legitimate interest in financial operations of the enterprise.

While management accounting has been most highly developed in profit-oriented businesses, there is need for reliable financial data to guide operation of any enterprise that employs economic resources.

The uses listed above cover a wide variety of individual purposes for which accounting data may be used. An equally wide range exists in the kinds of data relevant to these purposes and in the techniques employed to measure and to communicate the data. However, many of these techniques are comparatively recent.

Evolution of Management Accounting. In the past, the accountant's function was restricted to recording financial transactions and preparing periodic summaries of financial position and income. The resulting historical record served an important purpose, but it gave little assistance in planning future operations or in directing current operations toward realization of plans. This inadequacy was most serious at divisional and departmental levels, for accounting services were seldom available and the accountant's reports had little relevance to problems faced by management at these levels.

The SCIENTIFIC MANAGEMENT movement aroused a widespread demand for reliable quantitative data to guide management actions, and accounting was swept into the stream in the early years of the twentieth century. In the process, the management accountant's outlook has broadened to include the present and the future as well as the past, and accounting has become an integral part of modern management technology. While accounting is a staff function, the management accountant now exercises a substantial influence on decisions through selection and interpretation of data. As a result he is, in effect, an active participant in management.

The process began in COST ACCOUNTING, with the introduction of STANDARD COSTING. Every supervisor having authority to incur costs could be apprised of his current performance relative to pre-established standard costs.

With the development of budgeting, the same concept of forward financial planning was extended to cover *all* operations during a chosen period of time. In a complete application, a budget is a coordinated financial plan for operations summarized in statements of income and financial position for the budget period. Management is thus in a position to see in advance the expected results of its operating plans and to make changes in these plans if it believes the results can be improved.

In historical reporting, the accountant is concerned only with those events which have occurred; but in developing data to guide management *planning,* he must consider the entire range of alternatives from which management chooses in making decisions. Since volume or level of activity is usually a significant independent variable, techniques for measuring functional relationships between cost, volume, and profit have been extensively developed. (See COST-VOLUME-PROFIT ANALYSIS.) Continuing and systematic analysis of cost-volume profit relationships is obtained through FLEXIBLE BUDGETS and DIRECT COSTING. Special studies following the marginal approach are used in non-repetitive situations. Special cost and income constructions are also prepared to reflect changes in variables other than volume (e.g. prices of cost factors, production methods, mix, selling prices).

Analytical techniques for evaluating and comparing alternatives are now widely employed in conjunction with the preparation of budgets. Termed *profit planning,* the variable factors are manipulated to find a combination which promises an acceptable financial outcome. Criteria such as rate of return on capital employed, sales volume, and share of the market are used to judge acceptability of a proposed plan. (See RETURN ON CAPITAL.)

Organization of the Management Accounting Function. Within an enterprise, broad responsibility for the accounting function is usually assigned to the Controller, although other titles are common. In a large organization, sub-functions such as the following are recognized.

Financial Accounting. Accounting for revenues, expenses, assets, liabilities, and net worth together with the production of summary financial reports.

Cost Accounting. Accounting for current, standard, and prospective costs; analysis and communication of cost data at all levels of management within the organization.

Systems and Procedures design and installation.

Data Processing. Recording accounting data, performing repetitive operations with these data (e.g., payroll preparation), preparing reports from recorded data.

Internal Auditing. Review and appraisal of accounting procedures and records to ascertain their reliability, conformance with prescribed practices, and adequacy to protect against loss of assets by fraud, waste, and other causes.

Budgeting. Assembly and consolidation of budgets; assistance to management personnel in translating operating plans into financial budgets; reporting and analysis of budget variances.

Tax Reporting. Preparing reports required by Federal, state, and local tax authorities.

Financial Analysis. Interpretation of accounting reports: analysis in financial terms of proposed projects, plans, and procedures; assistance to management in interpretation and evaluation of financial data of all types.

WALTER B. MCFARLAND, PH.D., formerly Director of Research, National Association of Accountants, New York, New York

Information References

Anthony, Robert N. and Welsch, Glenn A., "Fundamentals of Management Accounting," rev. ed., Homewood, Ill., Irwin, 1977.

Benston, George J., "Contemporary Cost Accounting and Control," 2nd ed., Encino, Calif., Dickenson Publishing Company, 1977.

Horngren, Charles T., "Cost Accounting: A Managerial Emphasis," 4th ed., Englewood Cliffs, N.J., Prentice-Hall, 1977.

Louderback, Joseph G. and Dominiak, Geraldine F., "Managerial Accounting," 2nd. ed., Belmont, Calif., Wadsworth, 1978.

Shillinglaw, Gordon, "Managerial Cost Accounting," 4th ed., Homewood, Ill., Irwin, 1977.

Cross References: Break-Even Analysis; *Cash Flow Analysis; Cost Accounting (Managerial Accounting); Cost-Volume-Profit Analysis; Financial Ratios; Responsibility Reporting; Return on Capital; Statistical Accounting.*

MANAGEMENT AUDIT

Management Audit concepts were originally developed as a tool for investment appraisal.

Within the past twenty years, however, their use has been expanded to cover virtually all kinds and sizes of business organizations, as well as non-profit enterprises ranging from individual hospitals and colleges to the world-wide operations of the Roman Catholic Church. (While the term *management audit* is sometimes used to denote any evaluation of management, it is properly applied only to the systematic method of appraising administrative performance developed and validated by the American Institute of Management, and used by it in its evaluations of American businesses and other organizations.)

The management audit may be defined as a procedure for systematically examining, analyzing, and appraising a management's overall performance. To determine this overall performance, the management audit combines the evaluations of ten categories of appraisal, each a determination of the worth of the subject management in one category of the analysis, viewed historically and in comparison with other organizations.

As applied to a business organization, the management audit presents the qualities of the subject management relative to those of other managements in its particular industry, as well as in relation to the finest managements in other industries.

The ten categories of the management audit of business organizations are as follows:

(1) Economic function.
(2) Corporate structure.
(3) Health of earnings.
(4) Service to stockholders.
(5) Research and development.
(6) Directorate analysis.
(7) Fiscal policies.
(8) Production efficiency.
(9) Sales vigor.
(10) Executive evaluation.

These categories do not represent single functions of management, or pure variables.

In actual practice, preparation of a management audit of an organization consists of two distinct parts. The first is the compilation of data for analysis and evaluation. To insure completeness as well as comparability with data collected on other organizations, the American Institute of Management uses detailed prepared questionnaires covering management's performance in each appraisal category over a number of years. The information obtained through the Management Audit Questionnaire (questionnaires have been developed for a wide range of industries and types of business) is supplemented by interviews with members of management, directors, and a wide range of others associated with the company as employees, suppliers, competitors, customers, or investing owners. At the same time, material is assembled on the subject company's industry, to provide the comparative basis.

The second and significant portion of the management audit is the analysis of all information obtained. This results in the appraisal of individual categories and, from these, of the overall performance of management. It must be stressed that management appraisal, even with the systematic approach of the management audit, cannot be considered a science in the full sense of that word, since subjective judgment ultimately enters the appraisal. One of the values of the management audit, however, is the extent to which it permits judgment to rest on the widest possible base of substantive information, and on a uniform and general conceptual foundation. The most basic concept underlying the system is that management, wherever it is found, is *the art of purposeful action.*

(1) Economic Function. The category Economic Function in the management audit assigns to management the continuing responsibility for the company's importance to our economy. In effect, economic function determines the *public value* of the company. This value is based on what the company has chosen to do—what products or services it produces—and how it does these things in the moral and ethical sense. It comprises such intangibles as the company's reputation and management's view and enlargement of the purpose of the enterprise. The *public* as referred to in economic function includes not merely the consumers of the company's products or its shareowners, but a number of distinct groups, all with varying interests, which the business organization must seek to satisfy (among them, its employees, suppliers, distributors, and the communities in which it operates).

The fulfillment of economic function is cumulative, in the sense that time alone can test a company's public value. A new corporation may quickly become an important element in our national life, but until it has endured trade cycles, met competition over the years, developed and replaced its management teams, and earned its reputation among its various publics, it cannot have achieved maximum economic function. It is by such outstanding companies as Eastman-Kodak and Minnesota Mining and Manufacturing that the public value of new companies must be measured.

(2) Corporate Structure. The category Corporate Structure appraises the effectiveness of the structure through which management seeks to fulfill its aims. The organization structure of any company must expedite making and executing corporate decisions, must permit control of the enterprise, and must establish the areas of responsibility and authority of its executives. These are requirements that must be met regardless of the specific form of organization a company adopts.

In actual practice, the real form of organization of a company under study is seldom that of the nominal organization charts. Published organization charts are, in fact, often so inaccurate in depicting the actual relationships and relative authorities within the company that they are of little use to the management analyst.

Companies that have developed product-division or other forms of decentralized organization have maximized the delegation of responsibility and authority, but they have not reduced the need for clear understanding of them throughout the organization. For the most part, corporations decentralize after the lines of authority have been well established; but at times, even large corporations have suffered as the result of a breakdown in the acceptance or exercise of authority.

(3) Health of Earnings. The evaluation of earnings is concerned with the historical and comparative aspects of corporate income formation, not merely with the income itself. The category Health of Earnings must determine whether the profit potential of the corporation's assets has been realized in full. (By assets are meant not merely company-owned net equity but, in addition, the assets represented by whatever debt is included in capitalization—the net capital invested. These capital factors are represented in the production process by fixed assets in the form of land, plant, and equipment, or by more liquid assets including actual cash or, more remotely liquid, inventories. No matter what form they take, the paramount question is whether they have been employed at the optimum for the full realization of their potential.)

For both manufacturing and non-manufacturing companies the fruitfulness of capital can be determined by a study of the risk assumed in the employment of resources, in the profit returns upon their employment, and in the nature and distribution of the assets among various categories. Industrial enterprises are particularly suited to this analysis. Although the actual value of their assets (in particular, of their patents and processes) cannot always be determined exactly, one can at least trace the cost of their acquisition, the rates at which they have been depreciated, and the extent to which they have been employed profitably or unprofitably. While prepared information is seldom available for other categories of the management audit, the information required on health of earnings is usually on public record in a company's annual reports and in digests of its financial structure. Eastman-Kodak has the best of all records in this category.

(4) Service to Stockholders. Appraisal of a company's service to stockowners rests chiefly on a three-part mandate that stockholders give the board of directors of corporations: *first,* that their principal not be dissipated or exposed to unnecessary risks; *second,* that the principal be enhanced as much as possible through the sound use of undistributed profits, and *third,* that they receive a reasonable return on the principal in the form of dividends, while their ownership interest is protected through preemptive rights. How well a company satisfies these three requirements determines its *fairness* to stockowners.

In addition, the appraisal covers the obligation that every company has today to provide service to its shareowners—primarily, to keep them well enough informed so that they can evaluate the progress of their investment in the company and participate in decisions that are likely to affect that investment. Even the financially inexperienced shareholder can review his own relationship with the company to determine whether or not the essentials of stockholder service are present. And while stockholder relations are less vital than sound dividend policies, they indicate a management conscious of its responsibilities—a fundamental of excellent management in any company.

For the specifics of analyzing fairness to stockowners, companies and industries differ too widely in what earnings they can pay out as dividends to set optimum ratios of dividends to net income or other absolutes. Rather, the ultimate return and capital appreciation are the important determinants of fairness to stockowners, not any particular or current percentage. Xerox excels in this category.

(5) Research and Development. Because adequate research efforts over a period of years can assure company growth and improvement of its industry position, evaluation of company research policies is crucial to a management audit. Giant corporations, almost without exception, know the importance of research as a continuing activity, regardless of how well they pursue it. Too many smaller corporations, however, still look upon it with fear, and often do not undertake meaningful research at all. They could benefit immeasurably by greater boldness—if that boldness is based on a clear concept of what research is and can do and a realistic approach to budgeting and evaluating it.

Evaluating research results can show how well the research dollar has been employed, but it does not show whether or not management has realized the maximum from its research potential. For this reason, research must be examined comparatively and historically—in dollars expended, in the number of research workers employed, in the ratio of research costs and staff to total expenses and personnel, in new ideas, information, and products turned out. These expenditures, examined with past research results, provide an estimate of management's willingness to employ research for *future* growth and health.

Some companies establish an arbitrary payout period to evaluate their own research results. This arbitrary system focuses attention on the need for research profitability, but it may actually discourage future research. The Management Institute's analysis of research success depends on no formula; it attempts, rather, to determine what part of the company's past progress can properly be credited to research and how well research policies are preparing the company for future progress.

(6) Directorate Analysis. The company directorate selects and guides operating management in the interest of the business owners and the public. In appraising its effectiveness, three principal elements are considered:

(a) The quality of each director and the contribution he makes to the board.

(b) How well the directors work together as a team—whether they complement and stimulate each other. This, of course, is a principal test, since it is the board's actions as a group that affect the company.

(c) Whether the directors truly act as trustees for the enterprise.

The trusteeship responsibility of the directorate can best be examined in those areas in which a partial conflict of interest exists between a company's executives and the business owners and public. One of the clearest of these is the area of executive incentives. How well the directorate resolves compensation and other incentive problems provides an excellent key to its quality. American Telephone & Telegraph excels in this category.

(7) Fiscal Policies. While the fiscal history of a company—the result of all management activity expressed in measurable money terms—is appraised in the category Health of Earnings, past and present financial policies are appraised directly in fiscal policies. This category includes three areas of study: the company's capital structure; its organizations for developing fiscal policies and controls; and the application of these policies and controls in different areas of corporate activity. The key problems are providing, controlling, and husbanding funds. Eastman-Kodak excells in this category.

(8) Production Efficiency. Evaluating production efficiency has obvious importance in appraising a manufacturing company. What is not so widely understood is that production efficiency or its equivalent, *operating* efficiency, is equally vital to non-manufacturing companies, whether they are in banking, insurance, transportation, communications, electric or other power, or any other field in which the end product is not a tangible good. Virtually all companies which are not merely agents for other companies must obtain and process some good or service before marketing it. This is the field of a company's overall operation evaluated in the category Production Efficiency.

The analysis of present-day production management must be divided into two parts. The first of these may be terms the appraisal of *machinery and material management,* since it evaluates the mechanical production or processing of the company's products. This one part is often overemphasized, so that management's mastery of its machinery appears the major factor in production efficiency. However, a second aspect of production evaluation, that of *manpower management,* is equally important. This facet of operations properly includes all personnel policies and practices for non-sales and non-executive employees developed by management. Only when both aspects are analyzed can overall production in operating efficiency be appraised. General Motors excels in this category.

(9) Sales Vigor. Within single industries and even within single companies, sales practices can vary broadly enough to represent different marketing principles. Between different industries the variations are often still greater. Yet the comparative appraisal of sales vigor must encompass all the forms that marketing can take.

Sales vigor can, of course, be appraised despite these variations, but only after the marketing goals of each subject company have been determined and assessed. These goals, in turn, must be appraised in terms of the over-all goals of the entire organization. Then, as with other categories of the management audit, historical and comparative evaluations become possible—namely, how well past sales potential has been realized and how well present company sales policies prepare it to realize the future potential. The treatment of sales personnel usually belongs in this category. Procter & Gamble excels in this category.

(10) Executive Evaluation. Executive Evaluation is the most important single appraisal category of the ten that comprise the management audit. To a degree, of course, the other categories in this system of management appraisal also evaluate the organization's executives, since they appraise the results of executive thinking and action in each management function. But the quality of the executives themselves, their management philosophy, and the appropriateness of both to the purposes of the organization must still be appraised directly.

The American Institute of Management has found three personal qualities—ability, industry, and integrity—to be the essential elements for the business leader. These provide a framework for his evaluation in the management audit and should also be the criteria of the organization's leaders in selecting and advancing executives. Excellent management requires that executives work together in harmony, each with specific tasks contributing to the total effort, conscious that he is participating in this effort with men who command his respect. As a group, the executives must regard the continuity of the corporation as an important goal, assuring it by sound policies of executive selection, development, advancement, and replacement. A key problem is to assure sound succession in depth.

Universality of Evaluation. The principles of the management audit remain valid regardless of the nature of the enterprise. All human activity is confronted with the same management problems. When two or more individuals get together in any common endeavour, wanting the best possible result, they must ask, "What shall we do, and how shall we do it?" In order to get good results, whether they are aware of it or not, they must follow fundamental tenets of management, which can be appraised.

Social Function. Whatever the undertaking, its impact upon the public welfare must be helpful rather than harmful. In the affairs of a church society, for example, this value may be termed *social function.* In an educational institution, it is *academic function.* The principles of evaluation remain the same.

Organization. The activities of two or more individuals—members of a management team once they unite in a common venture—create lines of authority and responsibility. They may be adjusted as the organization grows in size and consequence and progresses with its undertakings, but the extent to which authority and responsibility are made clear provides a basis for evaluation.

Growth. The enterprise must exhibit growth of facilities, whether these come from gifts or profits derived from merchandising goods or services. The health of that growth can be appraised.

Membership. Members, shareowners, or proprietors of an enterprise are encouraged to cooperate and contribute, whether through dividends or less material rewards. How this is done is a matter of techniques peculiar to the kind of enterprise and varying with circumstances and time. But that it shall be done activates fundamental management principles and permits evaluation of its effectiveness.

Research. Management of whatever kind seeks the most reliable, comprehensive, accurate, and up-to-date information available. Research and development includes study of any phase of group activity, with a view to betterment of either principles or techniques.

Fiscal Policies. The financial and other resources of any group effort are the life blood of its activity. Where they are obtained—and obtained in proper quantity—the enterprise can continue to exist and grow. How well resources are found and used can be appraised. Fitting financial policies and practices to the immediate and long-term needs that experience indicates, and then altering them as the result of study or alertness, is a management principle closely related to survival.

Trusteeship. Whether called trustees, directors, or guardians, those overseeing an undertaking have the responsibility of determining its leadership. In this way they exercise the power of the organization. Appraisal can be made of how well they recognize that their authority needs the sanction of morality and creates obligations to assume responsibility for the welfare of the total enterprise, including the public and all individuals concerned.

Operations. The operation of an undertaking has a degree of effectiveness no matter what the product, service, or purpose. This is true even within the area of charitable, social, political, and spiritual endeavors. Every organization then, has production or operating problems, just as it has a research need; it must understand and solve these problems to be well managed.

Sales. Everyone must be able to persuade others to accept him (her), and his services, products, or ideas, whether doctor, lawyer, merchant, or priest. Every group activity must be sold or merchandized if the enterprise is to grow and prosper. The techniques to accomplish this vary with the enterprise, the occasion, and the purpose, but they can be assessed in terms of how well they persuade prospective purchasers, joiners, or whomever.

Leadership Quality. The quality of leadership in any enterprise is the most important single aspect of the activity. The success of the executive group and the activity may depend on their integrity, ability, and industry, their devotion to the enterprise, their acceptance of responsibility, and their foresight in providing continued leadership after themselves. These qualities, all of which can be appraised, are not limited to the profit making corporation—they are fundamental wherever individuals join together for a common purpose, whatever the inspiration and the motive.

In conclusion, administrative evaluation must recognize that for an organization to be well managed, it must have sound purposes and use good techniques. To be excellently managed, it must fit these techniques and practices within the framework of true administrative principles.

Acceptance. Within the past years, the American Institute of Management has conducted three separate management audits of the Roman Catholic Church, and two audits of Minnesota Mining & Manufacturing Company and Procter & Gamble Company. In addition, it has conducted at least one audit of hundreds of other well known companies, a number of audits of educational institutions, and industry and area audits.

WILL J. LESSARD, Chairman of the Board, American Institute of Management, Boston, Massachusetts.

Information References

Martindell, Jackson, "The Scientific Appraisal of Management," New York, Harper & Bros., 1950.

—"The Appraisal of Management," New York, Harper & Bros., 1962.

"Manual of Excellent Managements," 11th ed., New York, American Institute of Management, 1969

Cross References: *Corporate Strategy and Business Planning; Long-Range Corporate Planning; Marketing Strategy: Competitive Analysis; Social Audit.*

MANAGEMENT CONSULTING

Omnibus use of the term "management"—as evidenced by the scope of this Encyclopedia—makes it difficult to define, with any degree of exactitude, the term **Management Consulting.** Indeed, the field of management consulting is so broad that many who do not call themselves management consultants use the same skills, techniques, and knowledge to accomplish the same management goals and objectives (systems and methods experts, top executives, and staff specialists).

The Association of Management Consulting Firms (ACME, Inc.) defines management consulting as: "The service performed for a fee by independent and objective professional persons—or a group organized as a firm—who help managers analyze and diagnose management and operating problems." ACME further limits such counsel to upper management—goals, objectives, policies, strategies, administration, organization, and principal functional or operating areas—although this limitation would probably not be agreed to by most practitioners in the field.

The management consultant is concerned with change and improvement, not merely with facts, but people and systems . . . and the profession is as much art as science. And, though born in industry, management consulting has transcended its original boundaries to become accepted today in various institutions of society—from nonprofit organizations to those providing services to government itself.

History. Management consulting had its origins in the then new "industrial engineering" and "time and motion study" pioneered in the United States by FREDERICK W. TAYLOR in the 1890s. The fathers of this new "scientific" management thinking—Taylor, GANTT, FRANK and LILLIAN GILBRETH, HARRINGTON EMERSON, CARL BARTH, H. K. HATHAWAY, and others—were themselves the first management consultants. Their work was largely connected with straightening out production problems in factories, and the increasing demand for their services soon outgrew their ability to satisfy it. This void inevitably attracted many inept and unethical practitioners, and a number of self-styled "efficiency experts" of the World War I era, by their inexpert attempts to handle a variety of problems they did not truly understand, had an unfortunately adverse effect on the professional standing of all management consultants—a condition that in some measure still prevails today.

In the 1920s, consulting spread increasingly to other functional areas of business, though it was still far from widespread in application or acceptance. In the 1930s, however, another generation of management consultants evolved: the generalist who could put specialized services in perspective and provide manager-clients with needed objectivity. Thus, Edwin Booz (a psychologist), James O. McKinsey (a professor/accountant), and others like them built acceptance for the profession and broadened its scope. It was in this period, too, that a major new area of activity opened: financial reconstruction and reorganization of companies in difficulty because of the Depression. The role of consultant thus became associated with the saving of "sick" businesses. This association, too, still persists to some degree today, even though management consultants actually make their greatest contributions in furthering the objectives of essentially healthy and well-managed organizations.

Despite a return to specialization demanded by the exigencies of World War II, management consulting emerged in the early 1950s as a prime aid to organizations making the transition to a peacetime economy . . . and it was in this period that the profession experienced almost meteoric growth.

Emerging Professionalism. In the 1980s, management consulting, though still a generation behind the accounting profession, is increasingly recognized as a valid (though still sometimes controversial) service to managers in almost every environment. Firms have proliferated, individuals have entered by the thousands, and the professional associations are trying to self-regulate against the specter of bureaucratic control.

As the "Who's Who" of management consulting professional groups (Exhibit I) shows, eight organizations of varying impact and quality currently serve the management consulting profession. (Others, with similar or even more prestigious-sounding titles, have so far failed to achieve sufficient national acceptance or recognition to be mentioned.) While several of the professional groups have attempted over the years to define exactly what a management consultant is, or what he or she should know, perhaps the most concise presentation is the following summary prepared by the Institute of Management Consultants as a part of its Body of Knowledge for the accreditation of management consultants: [1]

All management consultants should possess certain knowledge in common, and they should also possess substantially greater amounts of knowledge in one or two of a group of specialties or functions.

Knowledge in common: (1) management consulting as a process and a profession, and (2) general knowledge. The first covers the processes by which consultants apply their knowledge in the context of real-life situations to the solution of their clients' problems. Sheer possession of knowledge about how organizations are managed and specific functions operate is not enough: the consultant's role as analyst, recommender, and implementer of change is often crucial.

The "general knowledge" expected of all consultants covers the nature of the management process and the principal technical and functional areas; the legal, political, and social backgrounds within which entities operate; and the major common and differentiating charac-

EXHIBIT I

A "WHO'S WHO" OF MANAGEMENT CONSULTING PROFESSIONAL GROUPS

	General Description	Current Membership Profile
ACME, Inc. (Association of Management Consulting Firms) 230 Park Ave., New York, N.Y. 10017 (212) 697-9693	Founded in 1929, ACME is the grandfather of all management consulting groups. Originally limited to larger firms, it is now more representative but still maintains strict entry requirements. ACME reaches beyond its membership, however, conducting surveys and maintaining an information center covering a wide segment of the profession.	48 member firms, of which 12 bill over $5 million per year and 8 have revenues of less than $1/4 million annually. Member firms have offices or affiliates in 60 cities of 31 states as well as 45 locations in 27 foreign countries. Member firms list over 130 separate areas of practice and several hundred more narrowly defined fields of expertise.
AMC (Association of Management Consultants) 331 Madison Ave., New York, N.Y. 10017 (212) 687-2825	AMC, founded in 1959, serves smaller firms and independents whose needs, interests, and service requirements are different from the large consulting organizations.	102 member firms with offices in 27 states and overseas. About half are solo practitioners, with the bulk of the remaining firms at up to 10 professionals.
IMC (Institute of Management Consultants) 19 W. 44th St., New York, N.Y. 10036 (212) 921-2885	A certifying body for individual management consultants, IMC grants the designation CMC (Certified Management Consultant) to those who qualify. It was founded in 1968 and represents a major self-regulating effort and commitment to professionalism.	760 regular members, 55 senior associate members, 48 associate members. Approximately a third of the members are consultants in the larger independent management consulting firms, a third are Management Advisory Service (MAS) practitioners in the larger CPA firms, and the rest are solo practitioners and consultants in smaller firms.
SPMC (Society of Professional Management Consultants) 205 W. 89th St., New York, N.Y. 10024 (212) 362-3068	Founded in 1959 and the oldest organization accrediting individuals in the management consulting profession. Special focus on the needs of the seasoned individual practitioner, the partner in a small firm, or the highly experienced manager, executive, or internal consultant moving into full-time consulting.	125 members offering a broad spectrum of services in a wide variety of disciplines and industries serving business, government, and associations.
MAS/AICPA (Management Advisory Services division, American Institute of Certified Public Accountants) 1211 Ave. of Americas, New York, N.Y. 10036 (212) 575-6363	AICPA is the professional society for CPAs who provide accounting, audit, tax, and management advisory (management consulting) services in public practice for clients, as well as CPAs in industry, government, and universities. The MAS division is an administrative hub coordinating the Institute's services for MAS practitioners.	Some 7000 CPAs working in MAS divisions (mostly with the Big Eight).
AM/MC (Academy of Management, Division of Managerial Consultation) Drawer KZ, Mississippi State, Miss. 39762	Since 1936 the Academy — largely B-school professors — has been furthering scholarly research in Management, and the Division of Managerial Consultation became a special interest group (there are more than a dozen others) in 1970. While primarily of somewhat theoretical thrust, it is of interest as a monitor of management research and as a window on the considerable world of academic consulting.	3800 Academy members, 630 in MC division. Non-academics (associate members) account for some 10%.
AIMC (Association of Internal Management Consultants) Box 472, Glastonbury, Conn. 06033 (203) 633-5826	AIMC is an association of individuals, not firms, and was formed in 1971 to provide a forum for exchange of information, to give formal recognition to the internal management consultant's role in modern business, to raise standards of professionals so engaged, and to establish some basis for evaluation of internal management consultants.	185 members, 40% in manufacturing firms, 20% insurance. Average size of consulting group is 13. Over half have responsibility for hiring external consultants and monitoring their work.
COMCO (Council of Management Consulting Organizations) c/o ACME, 230 Park Ave., New York, N.Y. 10017 (212) 697-9693	Founded in 1977, COMCO is an umbrella organization composed of the major management consulting groups. It functions as an information exchange for the various societies, associations, institutes, organizations and groups representing the management consulting profession in the U.S. It also provides a contact point with similar management consulting organizations abroad.	The following groups comprise COMCO: Association of Consulting Management Engineers (ACME), Association of Internal Management Consultants (AIMC), Association of Management Consultants (AMC), Institute of Management Consultants (IMC), and Society of Professional Management Consultants (SPMC).

SOURCE: Consultants News.

teristics of business, not-for-profit, and governmental institutions.

Knowledge of functional Areas of Management: These include (1) general management; (2) operations; (3) marketing; (4) logistics, materials management, and physical distribution; (5) research and development; (6) finance and accounting; (7) human resources; (8) electronic data processing and systems, (9) management science.

It should be noted that many experienced executives fail as consultants: the shades of difference in philosophy and approach between doing and advising far transcend the closest parallel, i.e., the normal difference between line and staff functioning.

Types of Management Consultants. Four basic types of management consultants may be identified:

1. *Independent consultants* function in large firms, mid-sized firms, small firms, and as individual practitioners. They have no connections with other business services or suppliers and can offer the ultimate in objectivity.

2. *Accounting-firm consultants.* These professionals, usually called MAS (Management Advisory Services), operate within a CPA firm (such a firm is typically organized into Audit, Tax, and MAS departments). While these MAS departments burgeoned in the 1970s, serious questions have arisen over possible conflicts of interest (or the appearance thereof), although critics have been hard-pressed to cite specific cases. (See CERTIFIED PUBLIC ACCOUNTANT: ROLE IN MANAGEMENT SERVICES.)

3. *Professor/consultants.* Literally thousands of business-school professors work part-time as management consultants. This enriches their experience and can make them better teachers, and it also enables them to supplement faculty salaries. Some universities are concerned about possible diversion from academic thrusts. Professors typically consult in "soft" areas such as organization and training, but this is not always the case. They are accused, too, of an "ivory tower" approach, but this criticism, too, is not always valid.

4. *Internal consultants.* Originally spurred by the high cost of consultants, many organizations have established their own management consulting departments. Little uniformity exists in these functions when viewed from the outside: in one firm it might be a glorified industrial engineering group, in another the thrust might be MANAGEMENT BY OBJECTIVES, in another an assemblage of systems and procedures specialists. Few mini-general management consulting operations are found, and the groups—because they are internal—are rarely called upon for really top-level organizational counsel. Increasingly, however, internals become the focal point for an organization's use of external management consulting assistance. In such cases the internals aid in selection, work with the externals during their assignment, and help to assure implementation of recommendations after the outsiders have gone.

Size of the Profession. The *Directory of Management Consultants* identifies 583 firms billing almost $2 billion. There are at least 2,000 additional individual practitioners, plus perhaps 5–10,000 parttimers. So the entire market is "upwards" of $2 billion, though difficult to quantify exactly. Large firms, however, dominate: the 30 largest firms have about half the market. Of the fifteen largest firms, seven are from the Big Eight CPA firms, showing their growth and dominance in management consulting (or MAS, as they call it).

How To Select a Management Consultant. (1) Prepare a statement outlining the nature, general scope, and purposes of the proposed assignment. Do this before contacting any consultants, but be ready to accept the outsider's redefinition of the "problem" in more objective terms later.

(2) Achieve a consensus within the organization that seeking outside assistance is a reasonable alternative. Nothing can destroy a management consultant's effectiveness faster than internal dissension on whether or not the outsider should have been retained.

(3) Make a "long list" of management consultants who appear to have the qualifications to assist you. Use the associations, directories, personal recommendations: spread your net wide. Then write to these individuals or firms and ask for literature describing their firm and their services. (Don't be too specific about your problem at this point, or the replies may become too "tailored.") Consider only the firms who respond as requested.

(4) Develop a "short list" of consultants and invite them in for preliminary discussions. Ask those who survive this step to submit proposals.

(5) Study the proposals carefully and check references. Consider the qualifications of personnel who will actually be working on the project.

(6) Ask for modifications of the proposal as necessary, and make your selection.

Fees and Billing Practices. Among the more common methods of compensation for professional management consulting services are: (1) per diem or hourly fee; (2) bracket quotation; (3) lump sum or fixed amount; and (4) retainer. Management should beware of consultants who attempt to secure assignments by offering free services, guaranteeing results or savings, or proposing a fee contingent upon the findings or results of services: such inducements are not compatible with sound professional practice. Reputable management consultants make their professional experience available to clients and serve them to the best of their ability and skill; those who promise more may be unfaithful to the best interests of clients.

Knowledgeable clients know that they really cannot get services for nothing, and that they make it difficult for the consultant to be objective when they request free surveys; for once the consultant has made an investment in free survey time, he (she) may well feel obligated to recommend the further use of his services whether needed or not in order to recover his investment. Additionally, many professional people and businessmen feel that the consulting services offered by equipment manufacturers should be viewed with caution, for obvious reasons of objectivity. On the other hand, when a professional management consultant works for a client, it may be part of his service to help the client evaluate competitive bids on equipment. The client can then expect effective implemenatation at a fair price.

Standards of Professional Conduct. The interplay of relationships between client and consultant brings into focus specific responsibilities to the client which have been set forth in the ACME standards of professional conduct and practice, covering the following points (among others): [2]

- Placing client interest first.
- Always being impartial and independent.
- Preserving confidential material.
- Not serving competitors without their knowledge.
- Not overstating competence.
- Accepting only engagements for which qualified.
- Performing each engagement in an individualized basis.
- Training client personnel.
- Maintaining appropriate files.
- Not reviewing another consultant's work without the latter's knowledge.
- Charging reasonable fees.
- Not paying commissions.

James H. Kennedy, Editor & Publisher, *Consultants News,* Fitzwilliam, New Hampshire

Information References

"Directory of Management Consultants," Fitzwilliam, N.H.

"UCN Register" (University Consultants Network), published by The Anderson Group, Madison, N.H., designed to put decision makers in business, government, and institutional administration in touch with college and university faculty consultants. Contains information on some 500 faculty members whose services cover all areas of management specialization. Published twice yearly, Spring and Fall, with Addenda updatings.

References Cited

[1] "A Body of Knowledge for the Accreditation of Management Consultants," New York, Institute of Management Consultants, 1979.

[2] "How to Get the Best Results from Management Consultants," New York, Association of Consulting Management Engineers, rev. ed., 1974.

Cross Reference: *Certified Public Accountant: Role in Management Services.*

MANAGEMENT DEVELOPMENT TECHNIQUES

In the learning process by which a manager is made aware of new relationships, as a result of which he modifies his behavior, he goes through the following phases:

(1) Awareness of a problem area and dissatisfaction with the status quo.

(2) Recognition of alternative solutions to the problem.

(3) Selection and practice of a new behavior.

(4) Feedback from a reliable source.

(5) Generalization and integration of the new behavior pattern into his established frame of reference.

The instructor plays a major role in the first, second and fourth phases. He often creates the initial dissatisfaction by making the participant aware of the need for change. This is particularly critical with experienced executives for whom a departure from existing habit patterns represents insecurity and the risk of disapproval or resentment from superiors, associates, and subordinates. After creating dissatisfaction with the status quo, the instructor may reveal alternative solutions, and then create an environment in which the executive-students can experiment with them. He is also in a position to offer feedback and to help the participants understand its meaning by analysis, synthesis, and interpretation. Thus, the essence of learning can be thought of as guided self-discovery.

Techniques in Management Development. Educational techniques should be chosen to create the best environment for this learning experience. Many techniques are available today, ranging from on-the-job methods such as job rotation, to classroom devices such as role playing and the case study. Advantages and disadvantages of the techniques in current use appear below.

The success of any single technique depends on its relevance to the subject matter discussed and the principles to be illustrated; its emotional and motivational impact; the assistance it can offer in providing an environment for testing and evaluating various approaches; the degree to which it relates training with the job situation; and its suitability for the particular caliber of the participants in the program. In the final analysis, however, the skill with which the instructor *uses* the techniques is obviously the greatest factor in its success. Sensitivity to the needs of the training group, flexibility and desire to help the learner discover himself or herself, and an understanding of the training process are critical to the success of any training technique. A lecture on human relations by an effective speaker may be more successful than a poorly structured role-playing session, although the latter provides certain unique benefits for such a subject when properly employed.

On-the-Job Teaching Techniques for Executives. Since the primary objective of business education is to modify behavior on the job, many companies feel that the most effective training must take place there. On-the-job techniques are relatively inexpensive since they involve little loss of productive time and rarely need the assistance of a professional training director. On the other hand, the pressure of daily operations, the lack of time for analysis and reflection, and the absence of skilled direction often make on-the-job training programs ineffective for many teaching purposes.

Three on-the-job techniques are in common use today:

The Coaching or Guided Experience Method. Many businessmen maintain that there is no instructor as effective as an inspiring superior. By delegating authority, counseling, building mutual confidence, evaluating performance, and assigning meaningful tasks, there is no doubt that an executive contributes greatly to the development of subordinates. However, it is rare for a manager to devote sufficient time to these obligations, and it is even rarer for him or her to convey effectively to subordinates a feeling for the complexities and interrelationships of decision areas, or some of the more theoretical aspects of economics and sociology.

Job Rotation. By enabling a manager to move from job to job according to a specially designed schedule, many companies endeavor to create a well-rounded individual who has proven adaptability. At the same time, the advocates of job rotation point out that the new incumbent often brings new ideas to the job, introduces an element of competition, broadens his or her contacts, and becomes better able to judge his (her) own abilities. On the other hand, when a successful manager is rotated out of a department, the move can disrupt operations and make the subordinates insecure. Also, the method may be costly in terms of the errors which the new manager may make, and the attention required of his or her immediate superior. As with the guided experience method, there is no guarantee that the lessons learned are correct or desirable and, even if they were, they are often learned much too slowly.

Multiple Managements, Junior Boards of Directors, and Problem-Solving Committees. Some managements consider the opportunity to participate in group discussions and decision-making conferences to be useful educational experiences. Certainly this experience may develop a sense of responsibility, broaden the scope of the individual by cooperation with his (her) associates, and give experience in decision making. However, the authority of such conferences is frequently ill-defined (or, of necessity, must be limited), and little attention is paid to the developmental needs of the participants. For example, a manager who communicates poorly or is misinformed is not given special attention, because the object of the conference is to achieve results rather than to learn. Since committees themselves are frequently poor mechanisms for decision making, their use in developing this ability should be discouraged.

Off-the-Job Teaching Techniques. Formal

educational programs off-the-job are increasing in scope and number because they seem to be the most effective way to develop the managers needed in industry today. They offer an escape from office pressures, eliminate in-breeding, enable participants to experiment with new ideas away from the critical eyes of their peers, and provide an opportunity for instruction by experts. The main problem with off-the-job training has always been insuring the transfer of the learning to on-the-job behavior. Motivation is often a problem since many managers resent the implication that a classroom instructor can teach them how to perform their jobs better. Off-the-job training also means lost productive time and the need for competent instructors and suitable facilities. (See EXECUTIVE DEVELOPMENT: AWAY-FROM-COMPANY PROGRAMS.)

To motivate managers in an off-the-job teaching session, and to involve them in the learning process, many companies seek techniques which involve a great deal of individual and group participation. Such participation helps trainees to select their own educational goals, teaches respect for other people's ideas, assists in self-analysis, helps them to forget their own immediate problems, and permits them to benefit from the breadth of experience of their classmates. By participating in describing and analyzing a problem situation, and by proposing, criticizing and defending solutions to it, the trainee usually carries away more new ideas and habit patterns than he or she could absorb by a passive experience such as listening to a lecturer. It is entirely possible for people to listen to lectures, and even take extensive notes, without ever reflecting upon what is being said. Worse than this is the fact that lectures offer the manager no opportunity to experiment with new behaviors in a safe environment.

BURT NANUS, Systems Development Corporation, Santa Monica, California

Information References

Associations:

American Management Association.
American Society for Training and Development.

Texts:

Derby, Elles M., "Supervisory Training," Ch. 4, Sec. 6, in Heyel, Carl, ed., "Handbook of Modern Office Management and Administrative Services," Huntington, N.Y., Krieger, repr. 1980.

Milgiore, R. Henry, "Blue Collar to Top Executive," Washington, D.C. Bureau of National Affairs, 1977.

Shaw, Malcolm, ed., "Assertiveness Training for Managers," Cambridge, Mass., Addison-Wesley, 1979.

Silber, Mark B. and Sherman, V. Clayton, "Managerial Performance and Promotionability: The Making of an Executive," New York, American Management Association, 1974.

Spitz, John, "Building Your Management Team," Los Angeles, University of California, 1976.

Stewart, Valerie and Stewart, Andrew, "Managing the Manager's Growth," New York, Halsted Press, 1979.

Watson, Charles E., "Management Development through Training," Cambridge, Mass., Addison-Wesley, 1979.

Cross References: *Human Resources Development (and cross references there given).*

MANAGEMENT EDUCATION: Professional Certification

Professional Management Degrees. Top managers of business, consulting, and engineering firms, and officials in the higher administrative ranks of government, health care, and institutional management, are increasingly holders of professional management degrees from graduate schools of business and administration. Similarly, corporate recruiters for management programs designed to develop potential top executives are increasingly showing preference for holders of such degrees. In recent years, university degree programs for Master of Business Administration, MBA, have been vying with medical and law schools for the attention of the brightest and most ambitious college graduates.

The Graduate Management Admission Council, Princeton, N.J., which sponsors the Graduate Management Admission Test (GMAT) required by most schools of higher education in business, recognizes the following graduate management degrees. *Master of Business Administration* (MBA), *Master of Science in Business Administration* (MSBA), *Master of Science in Management* (MSIM), *Master of Science in Administration* (MSIA), *Master of Management* (MM), *Master of Public and Private Management* (MPPM), and *Master of Public Administration* (MPA).

Most of the graduate programs requiring the GMAT for admission are described in the annual editions of the "Guide to Graduate Management Education." This publication, prepared for the Graduate Management Admission Council by Educational Testing Service, Princeton, N.J., also discusses many aspects of graduate management education and possible careers to which an MBA or similar degree might lead. In addition, it contains an authentic GMAT, including actual directions, time limits, and scoring instruction. The book also includes information about test-taking strategies, guessing, and the various types of questions that may appear in the test. It is sold in many university and commercial bookstores, or may be obtained directly from ETS at Princeton, N.J. 08541.

The *MBA program* provides a comprehensive foundation in basic subject areas: accounting, taxation, business law, computer application and information systems, economics, finance, management and organizational behavior, marketing, and quantitative analysis, and may require 68 credits. (See APPENDIX A for a listing of AACSB (American Assembly of Collegiate Schools of Business) accredited universities and colleges offering programs in business administration.)

The *MS in Management or Administration* provides a business base or management core for professionals in engineering, sciences, statistics, computer applications, and public policy, who may then wish to concentrate upon their area of interest. Up to 45 credits may be required.

Advanced Professional Certificates designed to meet the special professional and growth needs in business and government are also offered by graduate schools of business and management. A number of graduate business schools also offer doctorate programs.

Certified Administrative Manager Program. Twice yearly, in some one hundred cities throughout the United States and Canada, managers from virtually every field of industry and commerce demonstrate their managerial talent through written examinations administered by the Academy of Certified Administrative Managers, an arm of the Administrative Management Society. The C.A.M. Program allows a manager to write any two of five required examinations in one day, and for eight hours a candidate is engrossed in what is described as Master's level material. The five examinations cover Personnel Management, Financial Management, Administrative Services, Information Systems Management, and Management Concepts. In addition, a case study is undertaken by the candidate for 30 days, on which a dissertation must be submitted.

The examinations and case study are only one of the five program standards required for the C.A.M. designation. Other prerequisites include three years at the administrative management level, high standards of personal and professional conduct as attested by reference letters, and proof of significant leadership in at least two voluntary organizations. Finally, the candidate must produce evidence of having made contributions to effective management by means of speeches, articles, and/or books in the field of management.

Information References

Administrative Management Society, Willow Grove, Pa. 19090

Educational Testing Service, Princeton, N.J. 08541

Graduate Management Admission Council, Princeton, N.J. 08541

Cross Reference: *See Appendix A.*

MANAGEMENT GAMES

A **Management Game** is a dynamic training exercise utilizing a model of a work situation. Players, usually managers, grouped into teams representing a manager or the management of one of several competing organizations, make the same type of operating and policy decisions as they do in real life. The word "game" is perhaps an unfortunate one, since it has an implication of fun, and fun is seldom associated with education. Many prefer to speak of "simulation exercises" or "dynamic decision-making sessions." The term "game," however, has won currency. Management games, though serious in intent, *are* also fun.

Purposes. Management games are used for several training purposes. They provide practical experience and the opportunity to experiment. Because they bring rapid feedback on the results of a decision, they can sometimes show cause and effect relationships that may be blurred during the much longer period that elapses in real life situations. At the same time, management games provide opportunities for exchange of ideas with peers. All this can bring much heavier personal involvement, greater attention, and greater retention of new concepts or of ideas that have been acquired.

Preliminary research at the Western Behavioral Sciences Institute and more thorough work at the Center for Social Organization of Schools at the John Hopkins University have confirmed that games will indeed bring better retention, not necessarily of facts, but of concepts. There also is some evidence that learning with games will bring enhanced ability to relate concepts to one another and to the work environment.

Broader Perspective. Management games represent only one technique that has gained wide acceptance in the search for more effective training technologies. The original type of management game, the model-based business game will be described in greater detail in the remainder of this article. Other techniques (See also HUMAN RESOURCES DEVELOPMENT) include:

(1) Analysis of, and greater attention to the needs of the adult learner who wants to apply his or her experience immediately in the learning situation and who wants learning to be highly practical. This has led to much wider use of cases, to development of various methods of role playing and other simulations, as well as to the adaptation of pure games and toys such as three-dimensional tic-tac-toe and tinkertoys to serious learning designs.

(2) Programmed simulations, where one decision after another is presented to the learners in a structured, programmed form so that they must follow the steps that have been prescribed, and analyze one segment of the situation after another, in partial isolation, so that concepts can be seen or applied more precisely.

(3) Role plays, which are special forms of simulations. These have become more sophisticated with more precise direction and evaluation.

(4) Finally, pure games are used to dramatize topics such as careful planning, decision-making, and communication processes in groups.

It might be worthwhile, at this point, to clarify the distinction between certain words: (1) situation (or case); (2) simulation; (3) game.

(1) A *situation* or *case* is the description of an environment, either real or hypothetical. Obviously, such a description does not consider all the factors which influence reality, but it attempts to describe those that are most pertinent to the purpose for which the situation or case is to be used.

(2) A *simulation* occurs when somebody uses the case to ask questions like: "What would happen, if . . ." A simulation requires an analysis of what would happen to the situation if a particular variable were changed, such as if inventory were increased or computers were installed, or another facility were purchased. It also allows exploration of the impact of external events such as changes in the interest rate, or withdrawal of a competitor, or increased activity by competitors, or other changes in the market such as major new inventions. Tracing the impact of these decisions or events is a simulation of what would occur in a real situation.

(3) A *game* exists when an individual or teams of people are in competition either against one another or against the situation, or against both people and the situation. Games against people can either be win-win or win-lose. Win-win means that all teams can win, for example, in a game environment in which the market can grow if the actions of participating companies are appropriate. The game in which everyone can win could also be one in which everyone who completes a certain task by a certain time is a "winner." A win-lose game can be zero-sum or other than zero-sum. In a zero-sum game, one team wins exactly as much as another team or combination of teams loses. In a non-zero sum game, the winnings and the losses are not equal.

A Typical Game. It may be helpful at this point to give a brief description of a typical model-based game play. (The mechanics of play for most model-based games are somewhat alike.)

The game session begins with a briefing. At this time the instructor describes for the participants what they will do in the game, whether it is to manage an entire company, or a sales force, or build a bridge or tower. The scope of their authority, the decisions to be made, and the information they will receive are all discussed. In addition to the mechanics of play, the purpose of the exercise and the manner in which it relates to the entire educational program are covered.

After the briefing the participants meet with the other members of their management team. In a typical game, there would be two or more teams, each with four to eight members. The team members all play the same role, though sometimes a leader or "president" is chosen. In a well-run game, teams may be asked to decide on objectives such as achieving highest net profit, net worth, or ROI, of all playing teams, or building a bridge within a specified amount of time, or building a tower of a specific height.

Model-based games are played in periods,

each period being the equivalent of a day, week, month, quarter, or year, depending on the particular game. In a business game, using numerical information about inventory, market, or financial factors, participants receive operating reports for the past period and begin by making decisions for the next one.

The teams' decisions are processed by a computer or a staff member, and operating reports are then returned. In most model-based game sessions, teams have about a quarter hour to a half hour in which to make decisions. In this manner time is compressed, and many periods of operation are covered in a few hours.

In many games there are observers with each team to follow the proceedings so they can provide feedback on the human interactions evidenced. These observers may themselves be members of the training course, they may be "facilitators" (extra instructors), or specially invited social scientists. In some cases, elaborate facilities are used to observe and record the actions of the participants. This is especially the case when the game is used for evaluation of participant skills, as in assessment centers.

At the end of the game play, team decisions are compared during a discussion session. This "critique" session is held to focus attention on the ideas and concept which were to be learned. The participants have an opportunity to compare their performance with that of other teams, and to receive feedback from the game, the administrator, and observers. Very often the critique takes the form of a report and is guided along specific channels by a previously prepared check list.

The game experience itself provides many learning opportunities but, as an educational device, a well-run briefing and critique are essential for a participant to obtain the full benefit.

History of Management Games. The use of models of reality, instead of reality, has had extensive training applications, best typified by the Link Trainer in which many pilots learned to fly without leaving the ground. The military, of course, have been playing war games for centuries. Chess was early used as a form of war game, and many varieties of "war chess" have been created, the game being adapted to changing military concepts. Helwig, Master of Pages at the court of the Duke of Brunswick, developed a form of war chess in the eighteenth century which used a board made up of 1,666 squares, and had pieces representing battalions of fusileers, squadrons of dragoons, batteries of seige guns, and so forth.

War chess evolved, primarily as a result of the work begun by the Prussian War Counselor von Reisswitz for the Prussian Army in 1811, into the modern much-used map maneuvers, where actual maps of terrain are used instead of a checkered board. The Germans made extensive use of war games and map maneuvers, in preparation for both World War I and World War II.

Beyond use for training, business games even provided a vehicle for review of company policies and procedures in emergencies. For instance, one such simulation was conducted by the plant manager of a huge pharmaceutical facility. The outcome of that simulation was awareness of many potential obstacles to effective emergency measures such as traffic congestion that might prevent emergency vehicles from entering the plant, potential mushrooming effect of damage to critical utility distribution points, and elimination of bottlenecks. All this resulted in vastly improved emergency procedures and some physical re-arrangements.

Business games for management training purposes, even the model-based ones, are only a few decades young. It is difficult to assign credits and dates to any particular person or group. There is little doubt however, that many early game builders were influenced by either the computer game developed by the American Management Association or the manual game first described in the *Harvard Business Review* of March-April 1958, "Business Games—Play One," by G.R. Andlinger.

The last-mentioned game became widely known as a result of the publication of the article referred to above. Andlinger was with the management consulting firm of McKinsey and Company at that time, and the game has been variously known as the Andlinger Game, The McKinsey Game, and the *Harvard Business Review* Game. The computations are performed by "clerks" using desk calculators. Its widespread use was encouraged by its low cost (all necessary materials and instructions being available at the time for $2.00 from the *Harvard Business Review*). It has been translated into many languages, and has been modified in numerous ways by various groups.

Other organizations such as the University of California at Los Angeles, the University of

Washington, Carnegie Institute of Technology, the Pillsbury Company, Westinghouse, General Electric, and Remington Rand Univac, to name just a few, were building model-based management games in those early days.

IBM customer education groups also developed many games to demonstate the use of computers for simulation gaming purposes. Most of these games were of the type referred to in this article as model-based business games. They used simulated financial statement items or inventory characteristics, almost all in numerical form, for decision-making by teams and for feedback to them.

Use of Computers. While there were many attempts, particularly at the General Electric Company and by R. L. Sisson and Jay R. Greene, in addition to the one by Andlinger, to make games independent of computers, the early surge of business game development during the sixties was greatly aided and stimulated by the availability of computers. Computers brought to business games a vastly greater ability to include more variables, and even to include incidental events such as shut-down of individual plants, or fire, or strikes, or major competitive activities. They also made it much easier to simulate changes in business conditions such as the probable impact of additional marketing, research and development expenditures, or changes in inventories or production methods, or locations of plants and warehouses, etc.

However, while computers brought many benefits to simulation and games, they also brought with them the seeds for the decline of wide use of model-based business games in training and education, particularly for inhouse training in individual organizations.

There are three primary reasons for this decline:

(1) The trend sparked by business games, toward more involving training, led to evaluation of alternative methods. It was then found that extensive involvement of learners and the benefits of business games could be achieved in many other and often less costly ways than with model-based business games. As a matter of fact, business games diffuse, to some extent, the cause-and-effect relationship because of the many variables they present simultaneously. Programmed simulations, role plays, structured problem solving sessions, and incident process (where some of the information is withheld until needed and requested) all have taken over a large share of the potential use of model-based business games in education and training. (See SUPERVISORY TRAINING)

(2) The use of computers brought with it the potential for making simulation and business games so highly realistic that they would approximate reality. The lure of such realism is almost irresistible. Adult learners, particularly experienced adult learners, want to apply their knowledge and capabilities to situations with all the variables that exist in reality. Without that degree of realism, they frequently suspect the underlying model to be less than fully applicable and reject it as a foundation for a realistic learning experience. They may refuse to accept the assumptions of the model as appropriate, demanding consideration of more variables. Combined with the difficulty of tracing cause-to-effect when complexity increases, is the high cost of design. In the late sixties one game, supported by the Federal government gradually used up four successive allocations of $250,000 each.

(3) Besides the potentially huge costs of higher fidelity, one additional difficulty arises when a business simulation is made more complex in an attempt to make it more realistic. The amount of knowledge that is required to understand the situation and the skill needed for simultaneous consideration and evaluation of the impact of many variables is of such a high level that only very competent managers can effectively work on such a game. The less experienced members of the team therefore rely heavily on the more competent ones and fail to achieve significant new learning. In effect, the game is too challenging for it to be a useful learning experience. The more competent managers may gain something from it but for them the benefits of playing the game may not compensate for the amount of time they have to devote to it. Straight simulations, when needed to solve business problems, can be more productive learning experiences for such managers.

Games Today. Games have a tendency to go through cycles. While many different techniques were developed during the seventies, toward the end of that decade and going into the eighties there appeared to be a resurgence of interest in model-based business games. In view of the negative factors mentioned above, the cause of this renewed interest is a matter for speculation.

What at this writing appears to be happening is that managers charged with human resource development are making use of the participative learning techniques which were developed during the early sixties and seventies. They are now seeking ways to provide learners with comprehensive experiences that will enable the learners to apply, simultaneously, the principles or skills acquired or sharpened in preceding training experiences. This search often leads to more streamlined, more realistic games which serve as a supplement to other training. The development of such simulations is easier today because comprehensive data bases exist now as part of the more sophisticated management information systems in place, providing data that are more relevant to the success of the enterprise. These simulation games, therefore, represent a new generation of learning tools that are more economical than their precursors, but are nevertheless more useful as learning tools.

ERWIN RAUSCH, Didactic Systems, Inc., Cranford, New Jersey

Information References

Associations:

ABSEL (Association for Business Simulation and Experiential Learning), College of Business Administration, Illinois State University.
American Management Associations.

Texts:

Boocock, S.S. and Schild, E.O., "Simulation: Games in Learning" Beverly Hills, Calif., Sage Publications, Inc., 1968.

Buskirk, R., "Simulation Games and Experiential Learning in Action," Austin, Texas, Bureau of Business Research, University of Texas, 1976.

Carlson, E., "Learning Through Games," Washington, D.C., Public Affairs Press, 1969.

Didactic Systems "Catalog of Ideas for Results-Oriented Managers/Trainers/Communicators," Cranford, N.J., annual.

Gibbs, G. Ian, ed., "Handbook of Games and Simulation Exercises," Beverly Hills, Calif. Sage Publications, Inc., 1974.

Horn, Robert E., ed., "Guide to Simulations and Games for Education and Training," Cranford, N.J., Didactic Systems, Inc. 1976.

Cross References: *Human Resources Development (and cross references there given).*

MANAGEMENT INFORMATION SYSTEMS

Management Information Systems are planned and organized approaches to supplying executives with intelligence aids that facilitate the managerial process. Exhibit I contrasts the difference between conventional data processing and MIS. Increasingly, management information systems are designed to take advantage of modern tools (e.g. ELECTRONIC DATA PROCESSING, DATA COMMUNICATIONS, microfilm, WORD PROCESSING) and techniques (e.g., OPERATIONS RESEARCH, systems analysis). Fundamental to the concept is the tenet that information is a catalyst of management and is the ingredient that coalesces the managerial functions of planning, operating, decision making, and controlling.

EXHIBIT I

DATA PROCESSING AND MIS COMPARED

Data Processing	• Routinized • Accounting-Oriented • Historical • Internal Focus • Mechanistic • Basic Computations • Non-Managerial Output
Management Information System	• Non-Routinized and Novel • Intelligence-Oriented • Futuristic • External, as well as Internal, Focus • Behavioristic • Complex Computations • Managerial Output

Information is the symbolic representation of the real world (money, manpower, materials, machines, markets, etc.). Since decision-makers rely on information systems to supply them with intelligence that will influence the selection of particular means and ends, it is essential that the information system be an accurate representation of the real world. This underscores the need for a carefully designed and reliably operating information system; otherwise, a manager can be making decisions based on information that does not mirror the real world.

The constantly increasing complexity of society, the growth in size of many organizations, the expanding information demands, the shortage of specialized human skills—these and other factors have increased the interest in a disciplined and analytical approach to the gathering, storage, processing, selection, and dissemination of information.

A fundamental consideration in the design and development of management information systems is determining which is the vital information needed for maintaining and extending the organization at desired levels of stability and growth. The selection of the key information requirements, from the universe of information available, prevents information underload or information overload. Thus, there follows the requisite that management itself must be deeply involved, along with technicians, in the overall specifications of management information systems.

The management information system should be viewed as essentially dynamic and subject to continual review and renewal. This viewpoint is required to avoid the situation of an information system which is out-of-phase with the environment and the current needs of managers. It need not necessarily be constrained by accounting conventions or legal requirements and governmental regulations; rather, the MIS is a flexible instrument which often is futuristic-oriented and combines external information with the organization's internal information.

A significant trend is that of organizational data bases. The data base is a carefully planned structure of basic data elements of the organization; the data are usually stored in a device that can be interfaced with a computer which permits various combinations of the data elements to be used. Also, the data base can be interrogated from some remote points (e.g. an executive's office), by use of a variety of data terminals (e.g. video displays, printers) connected, by communications lines, to the computer. (See schematic, Exhibit II.)

The data base has several important implications for MIS. First, it normally assumes that the fundamental data elements, vital to the organization, have been rigorously identified. Second, the data files are so defined and structured as to assure reliability and integration of all data elements. Third, the accessibility of a variety of data elements permits increased flexibility and responsiveness of the system for unique as well as recurring informational requirements. The data base should preferably be developed to provide for a certain open-endedness; that is, the specifications should provide for orderly growth and the capacity to absorb data elements overlooked in the original design.

Cost-effectiveness must be an important consideration in the design of the system. High quality data, large quantities of data, and rapidly available data involve higher costs for the management information system; however, the cost of the information must be balanced

EXHIBIT II

MAN-MACHINE INTERFACE

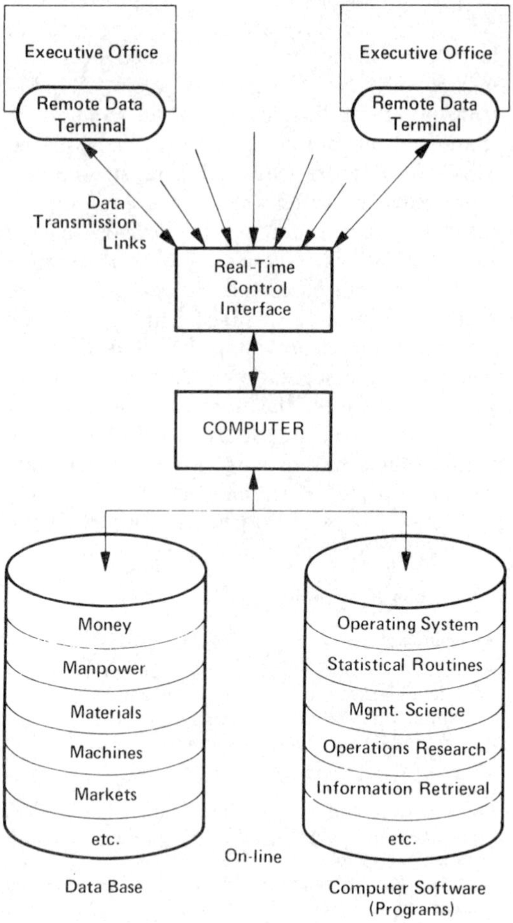

against the resulting reduction of uncertainty, increased predictability of events, and more responsive managerial decision-making.

The MIS appraoch usually provides management with new information that previously was not envisioned, or which could not reasonably be obtained (cost- or time-wise) by conventional means. For example, the MIS may involve:

(1) Analysis of the organization's performance (by product line, geographical area, etc.) compared to the best information about competitors.

(2) Use of several economic forecasts or econometric models to determine the likely conditions the organization will find itself in forthcoming time periods.

(3) Use of input-output models to determine under- or over-exploited markets.

(4) Quicker signals about operational variations from desired plans, so that managerial corrections can be taken before extensive degradation has taken place.

The success of MIS is, of course, highly dependent on the availability of particularly competent executives and technicians who are versed in the organization's policies and procedures and the new managerial technologies of computer, systems analysis, management sciences, etc. While the MIS promises significant benefits in providing management with improved knowledge aids for decision-making, there is the need for relatively substantial commitments of time and money for its design, development, and maintenance, including its related computer, communications, and other equipment. The organization must use sound methods of appraising the MIS approach, and of determining which kind of MIS best suits the requirements and resources of the organization.

DR. EDWARD ALEXANDER TOMESKI, Consultant and Professor of Management, Barry College, Miami, Florida

KONRAD SADEK, World Vision International, Monrovia, California

Information References

Burch, John G., Jr. and Strater, Felix R., Jr., "Information Systems," Santa Barbara, Calif., Hamilton Publishing Co., 1974.

Davis, Gordon B., "Management Information Systems," New York, McGraw-Hill, 1974.

Emery, James C., "Concepts of Management Information Systems," Sec. 3, Chap. 2, in Diebold Group, "Automatic Data Processing Handbook," New York, McGraw-Hill, 1977.

Martin, James, "Principles of Data Base Management," Englewood Cliffs, N.J., Prentice-Hall, 1976.

Mockler, Robert, "Information Systems for Management," Columbus, Ohio, Merrill, 1974.

Tomeski, Edward A. and Sadek, Konrad, "Future Challenges for MIS.," *Journal of Systems Management,* July 1979.

Tomeski, Edward A., ed., *"Fundamentals of Computers in Business,"* Chap. 15, San Francisco, Holden-Day, 1979.

MANAGEMENT INFORMATION SYSTEMS: A Case Example

Texas Instruments Incorporated (TI) is a highly diversified, multinational corporation, and a leader in today's "electronic revolution." This leadership position has resulted from 50 years of innovation and high technology developments.

TI Growth. The forerunner of today's Texas Instruments was established in 1930 as Geophysical Service. The company grew in two directions with two names: a parent company, the Coronado Corporation, was involved with oil production, and a subsidiary, Geophysical Service Inc., was involved with seismic exploration. With the onset of World War II, a new opportunity presented itself—magnetic airborne detection (MAD) systems which would locate enemy submarines. By taking advantage of this opportunity, the company entered a new field—military electronics.

In 1951, "Texas Instruments" became the company name; and in 1952 solid state technology in the form of the transistor opened the door for extraordinary growth and creativity. The invention of the integrated circuit in 1958 was a critical achievement that provided a base for future developments in electronics. In 1959, TI acquired Metals & Controls Corporation of Attleboro, Massachusetts, the company's only major merger. A key ingredient of TI's growth was the decision to expand manufacturing operations worldwide. Beginning with Bedford, England, in 1957, TI began operations in Europe. In 1968, TI began operations in the Far East with a plant in Tokyo. Today, TI employs more than 86,000 people and has a worldwide network of 50 major plants in 19 countries with worldwide sales and service offices (see Exhibit I).

The company has several major business groups which produce and market a wide spectrum of products from radar to hand-held calculators. In 1979, TI's net sales billed reached $3.2 billion (see Exhibit II). TI's goal for the late 1980s is $15 billion annual net sales billed.

According to J. Fred Bucy, TI President and Chief Operating Officer, at the 1980 Stockholder's Meeting, "One measure of TI's leadership in technology is our patent position. TI holds more than 5,200 patents worldwide, but it is quality that counts more than the numbers. . . . The ability of TI's innovators to think conceptually and bring concept to reality in the marketplace is TI's lifeblood." This philosophy is currently producing technological advances in semiconductor devices, solid-state software, speech synthesis, microprocessors and minicomputers, software technology, thermal printing, defense electronics, petroleum exploration, and in TI's solar energy system.

TI's growth, which has led to geographical dispersion of people and plant sites has pre-

EXHIBIT I

TI WORLDWIDE PLANT LOCATIONS

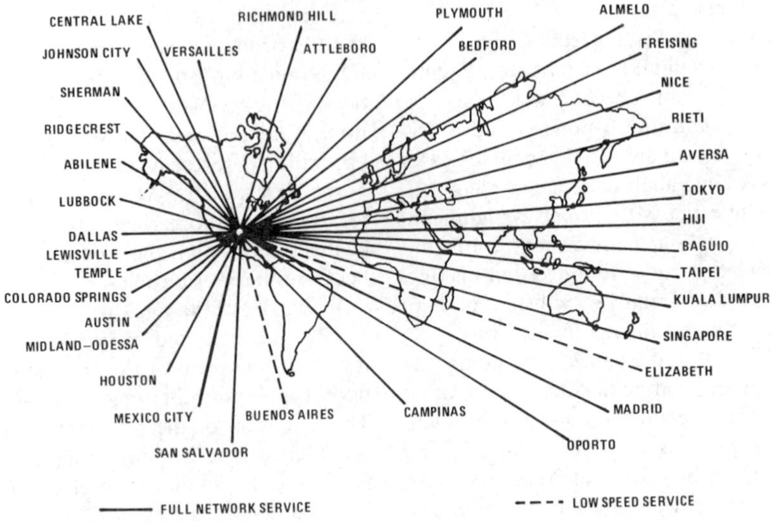

sented major challenges and opportunities for TI management. One of the greatest challenges has been to provide the necessary flow of information and provide adequate communications between numerous multinational sites, considering the social, economic, and legal implications of doing business. The development of a rapid and reliable computer-communications network became vital to TI's continued growth.

TI Computing History. TI established its first data processing center in Dallas, Texas, in 1955, with the traditional programmers, keypunch equipment, and IBM hardware. Evolutions of centralized vs. decentralized concepts were tried. What started as a handful of EDP personnel and a few pieces of hardware located at the Corporate headquarters has mushroomed into a worldwide Information Systems and Services (IS&S) organization of approximately 2,000 people.

IS&S Organization. Information Systems and Services is chartered to provide computer systems and communications capability to TI worldwide. It is responsible for operating the Corporate Information Center (CIC), operating the data and voice communications network; defining, developing, and maintaining the computer-communications network, and providing distributed processing capability to TI worldwide users. It defines, develops, and operates application systems for TI's engineering, manufacturing, marketing, and control and administration activities.

Information Systems and Services personnel are now embedded in each of the TI business groups and staff functions to ensure that all TI organizations have management information systems and computer-communications network capabilities at all levels of the company. The create, make, market, and control functions of business are all linked through one of the most technologically advanced computer-communications networks and array of business and engineering application systems in use by the private sector today.

The management systems made possible by this worldwide network are key factors in continuing the company's productivity improvements. Engineers are pioneering interactive graphics to develop new engineering information data bases to aid their design work. Global production planning, manufacturing automation and control, and tracking material in-transit between sites are now realities. Every organization in TI uses standard on-line systems for financial planning and control, general ledger, and a worldwide personnel data base.

TI's Computer-Communications Network. TI currently has 300 remote job-entry terminals, over 8,500 inquiry terminals, and almost 200 distributed computers connected to the network. These terminals and distributed computers, deployed as shown in Exhibit III, interface with the general purpose computers in the Corporate Information Center (CIC), TI's Dallas-based central computer facility, and with the

EXHIBIT II

TI NET SALES BILLED AND NET INCOME
(Millions of $)

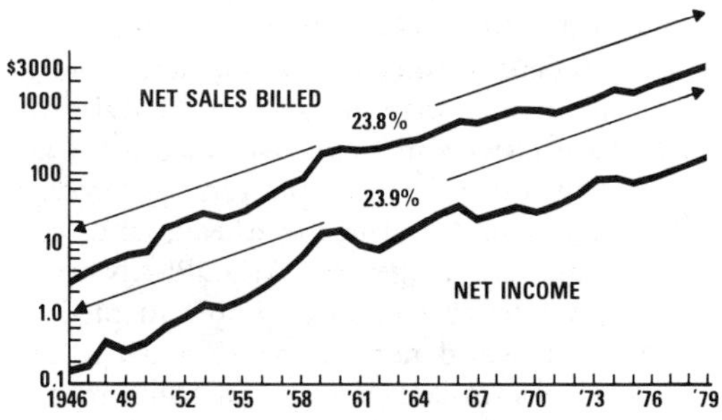

Scientific Computers located in Austin, Texas, which are used for seismic processing.

TI uses a significant number of distributed processors for interactive processing, having local data storage and terminal access to other distributed processors in the network and to the central computer facility. Programs and data are transferred to and from other processors in the network. Applications span engineering, manufacturing, marketing, control, and software development.

The Corporate Information Center is driven by six IBM 3033 computers. These computers have access to 376 disk drives and 80 tape drives. They operate in a loosely coupled multiprocessor environment managed by JES3 software. In order to maintain the high degree of realiability essential for TI's requirements, all software and hardware systems are fully tested on an IBM 4341 computer in a virtual machine environment prior to being placed into production.

TI's international communications network circuits are satellite based. A 56 kilobit circuit between Dallas and Singapore serves the plant sites in Singapore, Malyasia, Taiwan, and Australia. A 19.2 kilobit connection between Dallas and Tokyo serves the four plant sites in Japan. Serving Europe, TI has three 50 kilobit lines with lower speed circuits used for voice communcations and as emergency backup for the 50 kilobit links. Central America and South America are served with 9.6 kilobit links to El Salvador, Panama, and Brazil; and low-speed lines to Mexico and Argentina.

The communications network utilizes TI-developed Texas Instruments Communications Grid (TICOG) TI980/990 minicomputers, with TI-developed packet switching software to

EXHIBIT III

INFORMATION SYSTEMS AND SERVICES NETWORK

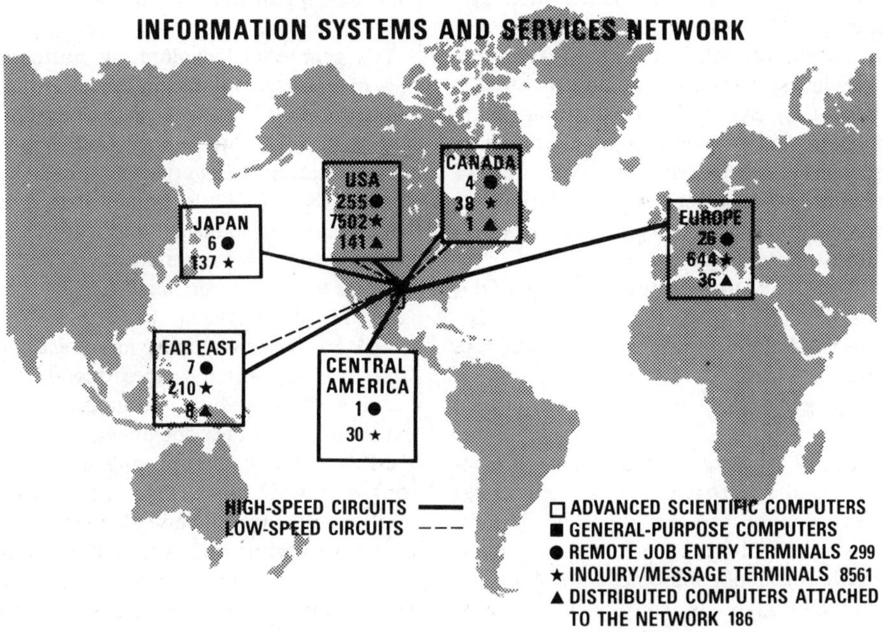

manage the data flow around the world. There are currently 32 TICOG's supporting this network.

This international network supports remote job-entry stations, distributed processors, and inquiry terminals. The network allows the multiplexing of these multiple devices and multiple functions such as Information Management System (IMS), Time Sharing Option (TSO), Job Entry System (JES), and distributed processor access over a single communications line. Alternate routing, used in cases of circuit outages, gives improved reliability to the communications network. By utilizing a continuous transmit/selective retransmit protocol, a 4 to 1 improvement in line utilization is realized over conventional protocols on these satellite links. Priority queueing for the interactive functions minimizes the impact of communications delays within the network.

This sophisticated network enables TI to process and store data in Dallas and at the various sites where distributed computers are located, from remote job entry and inquiry terminals at TI sites worldwide. In addition to processing an enormous volume of both batch and inquiry transactions each day, the network serves other requirements, such as electronic mailing and electronic filing.

Three Management Systems. TI's highly efficient computer-communications network has made possible the development of numerous systems which improve people effectiveness throughout the organization. Three such systems are: (1) MODPLAN, TI's planning and control system; (2) MSG, the company's electronic mailing system; and (3) TIOLR (TI On Line Reporting System), an electronic filing system. Office automation is a major thrust at TI, and these three systems used with the TI Office System word processor play a vital role in improving the productivity of managers, administrators, professionals, secretaries, and clerks throughout the company. The MODPLAN, MSG, and TIOLR systems are discussed in the following paragraphs to illustrate their impact on TI in solving the problems caused by geographic distances of multiple plant sites.

MODPLAN is used for the collection, manipulation, and interrogation of any numerical data which can be arranged by time periods, such as is commonly done in forecasting, planning, budgeting, reporting, and controlling activities. MODPLAN is composed of many diverse data bases which are three dimensional in terms of (1) line items, (2) time periods, and (3) organizational entities. There are currently 90 different data bases in MODPLAN using a total of 18,610 unique entities. MODPLAN is TI's standard financial planning and control tool. While the majority of the MODPLAN data bases deal with financial data, there are also many other applications such as product planning, manufacturing, overhead, and personnel analysis. In general, MODPLAN capabilities are flexible enough to be adapted to many numerical data-base applications and can provide both on-line inquiry and batch reporting.

The message system (MSG) permits video display or hard copy real-time communications to any point in TI's worldwide network. MSG is used for preparation, storage, distribution, and re-distribution of message text. The MSG system supports a broadcast capability allowing a message to be sent to multiple locations; security for storage, access, and distribution; and supports a direct interface to the public telex system. MSG permits messages to be inserted directly from other application systems for automatic distribution to predefined destinations, indicating such events as completion of processing cycles or the availability of computer-produced reports. It also provides the capability for individual "electronic post office boxes" for private and timely review of personal messages. MSG is used by engineers, secretaries, managers, planners, controllers, even ships at sea.

TI's geophysical exploration business has a fleet of marine exploration vessels which communicate via MARISAT, a satellite communications link, to the TI computer-communications network, and, thus, have access to the MSG electronic mailing system. Benefits to the manager and professional include the speed of communications and the privacy of the electronic mailbox. TI secretaries using TI Office System word processors connected to the computer-communications network can transmit messages directly from the word processor while continuing to perform text editing on other documents. A key benefit of MSG is the synchronization of communications worldwide. A message can be sent to any or all points in the network where it can be reviewed in prime time which may not coincide with the sender's prime time. The recipient can then respond on a timely basis. The members of the TI Operating Committee, who report to the President of TI, each have secure terminals which can access this system; the President of TI has three terminals which he uses for communications—one at his office, one at home, and a dial-up portable terminal which he uses when traveling.

The number of MSG transactions increased from 10,000 per day at year end 1977 to an average of 25,000 per day at year end 1979, with a volume at this writing of about 30,000 per day, and an average of four recipients per message. During this period the cost per copy has decreased from eight cents to four cents.

TI's system for electronic filing is referred to as TIOLR for TI On-Line Reporting. *The TIOLR system* is used for creating, storing, viewing, and retrieving information, and provides worldwide accessibility to this information from any inquiry or TI word processor terminal. Information stored on TIOLR is hierarchically structured by reports, generations, chapters, sections, and pages, and can be retrieved quickly. TI organizations use TIOLR to file standard policies and procedures, computer-generated reports, electronic newspapers, reference information, systems documentation, standards, schedules, and other data.

The TI On-Line Reporting capability was introduced in 1977 and its usage has increased dramatically. Currently, there are approximately 12,000 TIOLR reports on-line. About 170,000 transactions per day access this information. Cost per transaction has been reduced from 3.9 cents to 2.7 cents over the past two years.

Benefits of electronic filing for the secretary are that it reduces copying and messengering time, and permits the word processor to create files on central computers, thus making the information created by word processors globally accessible to other users within the network. Thus, a document can be viewed on-line simultaneously at several TI plant sites. Benefits to the manager or professional include accessibility to worldwide information on a timely basis, and selective display of desired information without the need for paper reports.

IS&S Management Philosophy. Ensuring that the TI business group and staff activities have a rapid, reliable, and efficient network is an on-going effort. The Information Systems and Services list of priorities in ranked order are as follows: (1) providing the company with *accurate, secure* information; (2) ensuring *availability* of computer-communications service to all TI organizations; (3) giving TI organizations *efficient service* by improving response time and cost. From 1967 to 1979, IS&S reduced user charges to 40% of 1967 prices. But if one gives effect to the 120% increase in price levels in view of inflation over the same period, user charges have been reduced to 18% of what the 1967 price would be in 1979 dollars. (See Exhibit IV.) IS&S introduces and implements new system and service capabilities only when data integrity, service availability, and system efficiency criteria have been achieved.

IS&S monitors operating systems performance closely to ensure that optimum service is provided to TI organizations on the worldwide computer-communications network. Performance information, including downtime reason and length of time for all major services, and response and turnaround time, are stored in data bases. Graphs are made weekly against goals and acceptable limits for major services. Tracking is done for mainframe computers, communications, distributed computers, and key information systems. Rigorous tracking has been done since 1974. About 250 parameters are reviewed weekly by Information Systems and Services.

To ensure that IS&S meets TI systems and services requirements, an IS&S strategic planning organization has been implemented. It includes strategies for engineering systems, manufacturing systems, marketing systems, control and administration systems, communications, distributed processing, central information services, and people/asset effectiveness. The strategic organization serves to centralize systems planning, design, and implementation for decentralized activities. Each TI business group has the same basic organizations-engineering, manufacturing, marketing, and control and administrative activites; therefore, the strategic organization concept promotes standardization of systems and services and reduces duplication of effort across groups, thereby improving productivity.

Distributed Network Architecture. The distributed processing strategy makes possible the decentralization of the create, store, process, and retrieval capabilities. The distributed processing-communications network is a four-level hierarchy of interconnected computer systems (see Exhibit V). Large central systems are referred to as Level I. At this writing, one center is operational in Dallas (the Corporate Infor-

Exhibit IV

Information Systems and Services CIC Discount Curve with Inflationary Factors

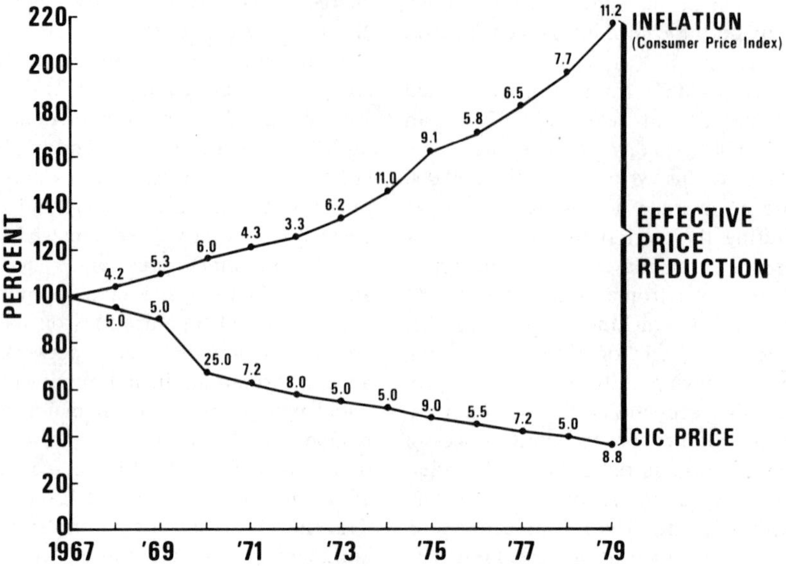

Exhibit V

Information Systems and Services Distributed Processing Network Concept

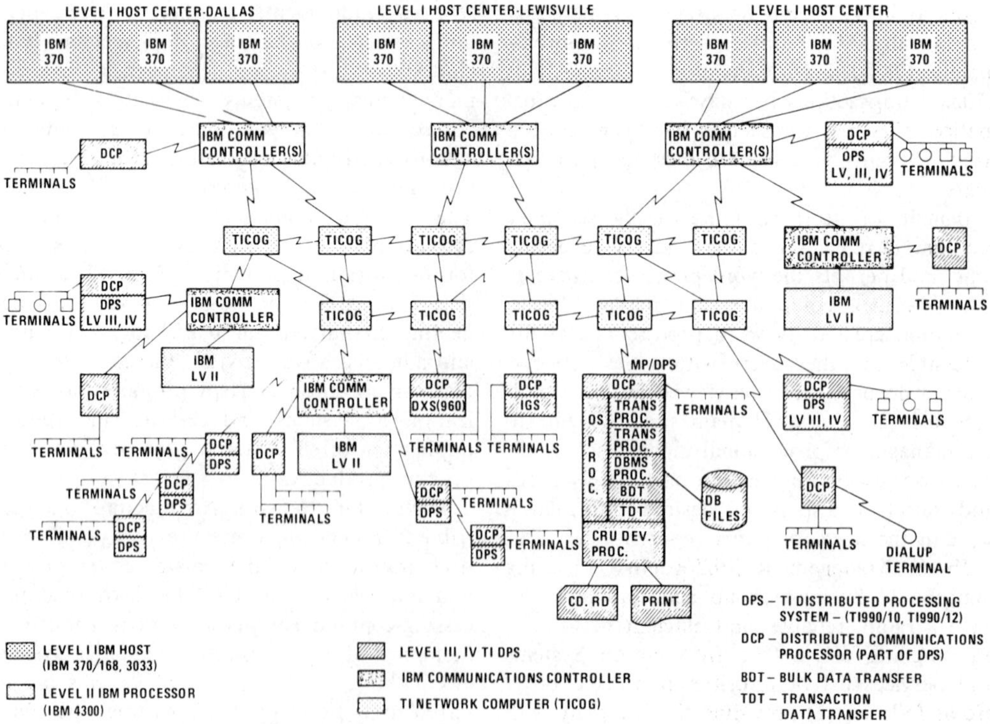

mation Center) and a second center is scheduled for Lewisville, Texas, in 1982.

At Level I, TI businesses are provided with standard worldwide application systems such as a personnel data base called Personnel File Management (PFM), MODPLAN, MSG, TIOLR, and many other systems used by all TI organizations.

At Level II, IBM 4341 computers are planned to support TI's major engineering, marketing, and manufacturing requirements, and to process these and other systems at the local level. Level II computers are connected to Level I and thus can also access the standard worldwide systems.

Level III and Level IV computers are TI990 minicomputers supporting functions for order entry, work-in-process, financial, and other systems that require extensive real-time interaction. The Level III computers contain the TI990 Distributed Processing System (DPS) software packages. The DPS/990 system was released for use in TI this year. It makes available several capabilities for IS&S application systems using the TI990 computer family. DPS provides an efficient transaction processing environment for both COBOL and PASCAL languages; a communications link to the IS&S worldwide network; communications support for a variety of video and hard copy terminals; and the ability to transfer data files between Level I and Level III computers and between Level II and Level III computers.

Level IV systems are primarily individual work station computers supporting such functions as interactive design in the engineering areas, and word processing in the administrative and clerical areas of TI, or in manufacturing process control.

Using the network, TI business groups can collect, store, and process data at local sites, and/or communicate with other levels in the network heirarchy. Thus, a Level III computer at a plant in Tokyo can access production planning information stored on a Level II or III computer at TI's plant in Bedford, England. This enables TI to operate from multiple geographic sites as if it were based at one location. Through innovative products brought about by the electronic revolution, TI organizations are no longer remote, except for their geographic location. The latest information is immediately available and is as close as the nearest terminal.

Changes Due to Computer/Communications Technology. As a result of these new computer communications capabilities and new product technology, TI is already experiencing some revolutionary changes in the way that TI and the many TI customers and vendors conduct their day-to-day business. Here are some examples of the future impact of these capabilities:

Engineers will be using the power of the computer to design products by accessing design data bases at other sites worldwide.

Manufacturing planners will act in harmony with planners at other worldwide sites by interacting with common data bases.

Computer-driven manufacturing lines will produce and test new products.

Product engineering will be enhanced with the ability to inspect parts produced in one part of the world from a distant terminal through digitized images transmitted through the computer network.

Automated warehouses operated from computer consoles will provide products for shipment.

Inventory systems of these products will have worldwide visibility to other sites.

Sales and service offices around the globe will have immediate access to shipment schedules, market trends, statistics, and other pertinent information.

Managers will hold multiple-site electronic conferences without loss of productivity and expense associated with travel time. TIers making trips will be accompanied by portable terminals to enable them to access pertinent computer-stored data associated with their business.

Administrators will in some cases prepare their own memos and correspondence, access data, and electronically communicate through the network from their office via an Office System word processor.

Secretaries will be receiving electronic mail while creating text, sending electronic mail, electronically filing, or inputting data to a system from an Office System word processor connected to the network.

Office hours will be more flexible since network capabilities will enable professionals and managers with terminals to do more work from their homes.

Home computing devices will enable TIers to access airline reservations, stock market exchanges, weather bureaus, library services, and other information at will, thus enabling them to be constantly informed.

Thus, while conquering geographical distances and multiplicity of plant sites, technology and innovation have provided the way of the future that will shape tomorrow's way of doing business. TI is uniquely positioned to "make it happen"—since most of the futuristic capabilities just described are already in place today in some part of TI.

C. Woody Williams, Information Systems and Services Administration, Texas Instruments Incorporated, Dallas, Texas

Cross References: *Electronic Data Processing; Management Information Systems.*

MANAGEMENT JOURNALS. See Management Movement, under heading, Magazines and Journals.

MANAGEMENT LEVELS: Definitions

Terms such as "top management," "middle management," and "supervisory management" are commonly used, but often there is no clear definition of them. Meanings attached to them sometimes differ from one company to another, so that care must be taken in interpreting discussions of management policy, compensation, and the like for various executive levels. And internally, while most managements seek to apply the same broad policies to all employees, the nature of tasks and measurements of performance change with increasing levels of responsibility, so that it is advantageous to classify jobs into well defined broad groups.

The following classification has been adopted by the Executive Compensation Service, American Management Associations:

Top Management. This is the policy-making group responsible for the over-all direction and success of all company activities. It is made up of the Board Chairman, President, Directors who are also officers, other officers, and key top management personnel. Positions other than the Chairman, President, and often Executive Vice President, or General Manager, are usually directly responsible for a major division or function of the business, but each also carries a responsibility for the performance of the business as a whole, participating in decisions of a company-wide nature and collaborating with others in the group in important matters affecting any or all phases of the company's operations.

Middle Management. This group is responsible for the execution and interpretation of policies throughout the organization, and for the successful operation of assigned divisions or departments. They have a high degree of responsibility for individual initiative and judgment, acting under policies and directives of top management. They have the responsibility for recommending new or revised policies and for establishing objectives of their assigned activities. They generally accomplish results through lower levels of supervision. Important staff functions may be assigned to this group.

Supervisory Management. This is the supervision directly responsible to the middle management group for final execution of policies by rank-and-file employees, and for attainment of objectives in assigned organizational units through practices and procedures approved and issued by top or middle management. It may include assistants to middle management positions and staff functions of a lesser nature than those in the two upper management groups.

Professional and administrative employees, exempt from the Federal Fair Labor Standards Act, may be included in any one of the three groups, depending on the importance of individual duties. For example, a consulting engineer could be a member of top management even though he is not responsible for the supervision of any company activity, provided he has the primary function of assisting other officers in important policy decisions. Likewise, engineers could be included in either the middle or supervisory group, depending upon the nature and importance of their duties. The term "management" is used for want of a more descriptive word, the purpose being to include in one of three broad groups all salaried positions that are exempt from Federal wage and hour regulations.

These definitions are further refined in some companies by reference to organization levels, job grade levels, or salary amounts, although this must be done with care and understanding because arbitrary limitations are not always applicable. For example, an assistant to the president is on the second level of an organization chart but the group in which the position would be included would depend on whether the duties are executive, administrative, or secretarial. Also, some companies use only two groupings for executive compensation purposes, combining the first two into one group.

Information References

American Management Associations, Executive Compensation Service.

Stessin, Lawrence, and Heyel, Carl, "The Encyclopedia of Managerial Job Descriptions," New York, Business Research Publications, Inc., 1979.

Cross References: *Linear Responsibility Charting; Matrix Organization: Organization: AMA's "Ten Commandments of Good Organization" (and accompanying entries with Organization prefix).*

MANAGEMENT MOVEMENT

During the nineteenth century, inventors of products and creators of technological advances furthered an industrial revolution which demanded skills, knowledge, and attitudes beyond those possessed by untrained owner managers of small enterprises. When the factory system became established, a concept of management emerged which in this country contributed to the development of the most productive economy in the history of the world, and influenced management thinking in all industrialized countries. Management came to be recognized as a distinct and identifiable discipline that achieved established objectives by emphasizing the most efficient utilization of human effort and facilitating resources. The resulting sequence of events and their impact on the economy became known as the **Management Movement.** Management *moved* into the affairs of men as a means for maximizing the total productivity of labor, land, and capital. As an important part of this movement, SCIENTIFIC MANAGEMENT emerged as a revolutionary concept which provided a mental attitude and a problem-solving framework for increased industrial efficiency and productivity.

The management movement expressed a new philosophy which conceived of conservation as the central motive in the conduct of industry. The definite pursuit of efficiency was believed to offer a cure for the cycle of increasing costs and rising prices. The goal in view was the elimination of waste and the apportionment of savings among all concerned.

Environmental Climate. The management movement was generated by certain cumulative forces in the United States and Western Europe. Modern management is a product of the twentieth century; but it received its initial momentum in the fertile environmental climate of the latter part of the nineteenth century. The desired result envisioned optimum productivity and profits to owners, increased wages to workers, and greater human satisfactions. During the nineteenth century, changes resulted in the political and economic climate which could accommodate the seeds of management thought for the subsequent management movement and modern management practices.

Cumulative Forces. The most stimulating concepts which generated the cumulative forces for the management movement were:

(1) The concepts of division of labor and a factory system instead of the "self sufficiency" concept of craft labor and commerce influenced the social and economic climates. It was discovered that the division of labor and specialization could facilitate productivity and the creation of wealth. Experience subsequently proved that someone in some manner must mesh and utilize the divided efforts of the specialists in a factory system for production. An awareness appeared of a need for the managers and administrators in the economy. The factory system developed from the need for: (a) large outputs of standardized products for expanded markets; (b) complex operations which necessitated sizeable investments in fixed plant, mechanized processes, and power; and (c) an assembly of workers under a definite organizational discipline.

(2) The Protestant or Puritan Ethic guided the behavior of American businessmen. For a struggling capitalist economy, the value system of the Protestant Ethic was most advantageous; it permitted the entrepreneurs to consider social good, personal gain, and God's will as one and the same. Consequently, they were motivated to risk their capital in an uncertain profit and loss economic system. Economic prosperity resulted from the opportunities for freedom of choice in private enterprise ventures.

(3) Belief in the concept of "Social Darwinism" permitted a system of ruthless competition which resulted in the success of the fittest who survived. The impact of the tenets of Social Darwinism on the decision making values of businessmen unleashed their "achievement motives" and produced a dynamic climate for innovation and change in the economy.

(4) The concept of organized labor was a logical reaction to the forces of social Darwinism and the Protestant Ethic which permitted the strong to exploit the weak, especially after

the 1890 census when the U.S. frontier was declared closed. Laboring personnel organized for survival and labor organizations forced employers to consider in the interests of employees as well as the owners.

(5) The concept of personal ownership incentives became established with the approval of Pope Leo XIII in the *Rerum Novarum* in 1891. He indicated approval for the right of every man to hold private property as his reward for engaging in remunerative labor. The personal ownership incentive has been a powerful force in motivating workers to participate in the management movement for increased productivity and a growing national product.

(6) The impact of technology produced necessary changes in management philosophies. Managers were challenged to find proper methods for augmenting human effort with technological aids. Industrial organizations increased in size, complexity, and productivity.

(7) The diversification of products within an enterprise and the decentralization of production operations resulted in the decentralization of management functions. There was an evolution from one-product types of industry to industries so complex that one-man management of an enterprise was no longer adequate. The authoritarian type of manager faded with the expanding scope of the management function, and the transition to the emerging professional type of manager took place.

(8) The concept of scientific management early in the twentieth century provided the trigger which released the composite forces in the environment to initiate and sustain the management movement. For the first time in history, entrepreneurial and professional managers had a logical conceptual framework for resolving problems and achieving the objectives set for business enterprises.

By the end of the nineteenth century, the cumulative forces and their companion concepts created the need for a different type of industrial manager and management philosophy.

Towne's Spark. If one desired to identify the spark that ignited the management movement in the United States, the presentation of Henry R. Towne's classic paper, "The Engineer as an Economist," could be cited. At a meeting of the American Society of Mechanical Engineers in 1886, he initiated the movement which gave impetus to the development of management as a discipline separate from engineering. Said Towne:

"The matter of shop management is of equal importance with that of engineering . . .

"The management of works is unorganized, is almost without literature, has no organ or medium for the interchange of experience, and is without association or organization of any kind . . .

"The remedy must not be looked for from those who are business men or clerks, or accountants only, it should come from those whose training and experience has given them an understanding of both sides (the mechanical and the clerical) of the important questions involved"

A young man by the name of Frederick W. Taylor had joined the ASME in 1885. He heard Towne's paper, and was motivated to respond. He and some of his contemporaries subsequently developed the body of practices, attitudes, and thought processes that have come to be known as "Scientific Management."

Awareness of Management. The potential benefits from a systematic, scientific way of thinking about management was early appreciated by some industrialists in this country, such as Henry Hathaway and James Mapes Dodge, in addition to Towne—and by the pioneering industrial engineers who included, in addition to Taylor, H. L. Gantt, Frank B. Gilbreth, Harrington Emerson, Carl Barth, Morris Cooke, A. H. Church, and others.

Shops, foundries, and factories grew in size, in importance, and in influence on the economy. Large-scale manufacturing became entrenched. With the growing size and complexities of factories, problems appeared that could not be solved without planning systematic relationships of work methods and effective organization. Waste control and methods of improving operating efficiency became essential to effective competition, along with improved cost accounting techniques.

However, the awareness of scientific management concepts and their potential to the economy on the part of a few enlightened industrialists and industrial engineers was not sufficient to generate a management movement of any consequence. By some means the benefits which could be realized had to be communicated to all who were responsible for the management of business enterprises, as well as public officials, labor union leaders, and even the general public. The advanced management philosophies were spread through the educational media of management conferences, professional management associations and management publications, and the curricula of educational institutions.

Three developments may be cited that had a great impact on the management movement. The first was the tremendous publicity attending the Eastern Rate Case hearings in 1911, when Harrington Emerson testified that by "scientific management" the railroads in this country could save $1,000,000 a day. (See SCIENTIFIC MANAGEMENT.)

The second was the formulation of the General Motors reorganization plan by Alfred P. Sloan, Jr., in 1920. Sloan advanced a new concept of organization which provided for organizational growth by means of decentralized administration with centralized policy control.

The third was the monumental series of studies in human relations conducted at the Hawthorne Works of the Western Electric Company in Chicago from 1927 to 1932. The Hawthorne studies provided a stimulus for the advancement of the human relations movement as a part of the total management movement, by providing a quantitive basis for conclusions about the attitudes and behavior of people in a working environment. (See HAWTHORNE EXPERIMENTS and HUMAN RELATIONS IN INDUSTRY.)

Management Conferences. Recognition was given to the developing management movement in April, 1911, at the Congress of Technology in Boston, and the first conference on scientific management was held at the Amos Tuck School of Administration and Finance in October, 1911. Subsequent schools of business and engineering were instrumental in disseminating information and knowledge about the nature and potential of the new ideas for management practices. A typical example was the Congress on Human Engineering held at Ohio State University in 1916.

At the first conference on scientific management, the spark which Henry Towne struck in 1886 for the management movement had developed into a kindling fire. For the first time, there were assembled the pioneers of the emerging management discipline, viz., Taylor, Gantt, Emerson, Kendall, Dodge, Cooke, Hathaway, Barth, Thompson, Person, and the Gilbreths. The influence of the conference itself and the published proceedings served to establish significant management concepts in the thinking of the industrialists of the time.

An explosion effect followed the first management conference. Professional management associations were organized. A literature of management ensued. Management courses were established in the universities and colleges. Management correspondence courses became popular. Management consultants were in demand. The concepts and techniques of scientific management were used with success throughout industry for increased productivity during World War I. The management movement continued with increasing momentum and impact on the economy.

Professional Management Associations. Much of the progress, success, and influence of the management movement can be attributed to the leadership and the programs of the professional management associations and allied societies. They were the launching pads for the creative management ideas and the media for the exchange and evaluation of management concepts and technical innovations.

The Society for the Advancement of Management has the first and oldest roots of all of the professional management associations. It was established in 1912 as The Society to Promote the Science of Management. The original society was reorganized in 1916 as The Taylor Society. The present SAM emerged in 1936 from the union of The Taylor Society and the Society of Industrial Engineers which had organized in 1917. Later the Industrial Methods Society merged with it, and in July, 1972 SAM itself became affiliated with the American Management Association. (The name has since been pluralized to American Management Associations.)

The American Management Association was formed in 1923. It developed from the National Personnel Association which was started in 1922 by combining the National Association of Corporation Schools and the Industrial Relations Association.

During the 1920s, the American Engineering Council contributed greatly to the initiation and development of improved management practices. Of special significance were the council's reports on *Waste in Industry, The Twelve Hour Shift,* and *Safety and Production.*

The flowering of other groups interested in improving the art and science of management occurred as follows: National Association of Foremen in 1918; National Office Management Association in 1919 (now named Administrative Management Society); National Association of Cost Accountants in 1919 (now named

National Association of Accountants); Management Division of the ASME in 1921; International Management Congress in 1923; and The Academy of Management in 1936. Closely allied groups were the American Marketing Association in 1930 and the Controllers' Institute in 1931 which in 1962 assumed the name, Financial Executives Institute.

Evidence of the world-wide spread of the management movement can be found in the initiation of the International Management Congresses in 1923 in Prague. Subsequent congresses, under the auspices of Comité International de L'Organization Scientifique (CIOS), Geneva, Switzerland, have been held as follows: Brussels (1925); Rome (1927); Paris (1929); Amsterdam (1932); London (1935); Washington, D.C., (1938); Stockholm (1947); Brussels (1951); Sao Paulo (1954); Paris (1957); Sidney (1960); New York (1963), Rotterdam (1966), Tokyo (1969), Munich (1972), Caracas (1975), and New Delhi (1978). Proceedings of all of these form an important body of management literature. As of this writing, the next Congress is scheduled for Nov. 16–19, 1981, at Lima, Peru.

In the programs and the journals of the professional management associations, business managers and educators found the means to learn about management, and became motivated to keep the management movement in a dynamic state of progress. Management concepts spread from manufacturing and production to office, personnel, marketing, and financial functions. (See MANAGEMENT SOCIETIES AND ASSOCIATIONS.)

Curricula and Publications. Since the turn of the century, a literature of management has been created which has changed management from a static mass of techniques and mechanics to a dynamic intellectual discipline that challenges both the professional managers in industry and the research scholars and educators in educational institutions. Although the first management books and journal articles were written and published by practicing industrial engineers and business managers, the college professors were quick to recognize the importance of the new discipline and prepare publications to support the management courses in schools of business and engineering. Starting in 1915, management courses grew in number and popularity in both residence and correspondence schools.

The American Association of Collegiate Schools of Business was organized in 1916. (The name has since been changed to the American Assembly of Collegiate Schools of Business, AACAB.) This association, which has been concerned with curricular affairs in addition to other academic and professional standards, took early action to include the requirement of management in the basic curriculum of schools admitted to membership. Inasmuch as about twenty per cent of college students are graduated from schools of business, the management movement has been facilitated by the management education received by their students.

Interest was generated in the proper content of courses in management because of the growth and acceptance of management in the educational programs of the engineering and business schools. On December 5, 1924, The Taylor Society sponsored the first meeting of the teachers of management in New York. This was the first occasion in which the management professors had an opportunity to explore the nature and content of management curricula and course titles.

Records of that first conference of management teachers state that:

> Both the schools of commerce and the schools of engineering took up the teaching of management as soon as a science of management came to be recognized, the schools of commerce earlier perhaps than those of engineering. They too have been moving toward each other, at least in this field, and a comparison of their catalogues shows an overlapping of courses reflecting the conditions in industry.

As a guide for the program, the first "Management's Handbook" was used. It had been published earlier in 1924, after its preparation by L. P. Alford, the editor. During the conference, the professors agreed that the introductory course in management should be titled *Organization and Management*.

The college professors soon after that historic meeting began to produce textbooks for basic management courses. Examples were: "Business Organization and Management" by H. P. Dutton in 1925; "The Principles of Factory Organization and Management," by R. C. Davis in 1928; and "Industrial Organization and Management," by W. B. Cornell in 1928. Previously, D. S. Kimball had published "Principles of Industrial Organization" in 1913 and R. H. Lansburgh had contributed "Industrial Management" in 1923.

The management education programs which received such impetus in the 1920s have been expanded today into graduate degree programs for students, and advanced management programs for practicing professional managers. (See MANAGEMENT EDUCATION: Professional Certification.)

Magazines and Journals. The pioneering magazines and journals which augmented the management movement include: *Engineering Magazine* (1891); *Factory* (1908); *Bulletin of the Taylor Society* (1916); *Administration* (1921); *Management Engineering* which combined into *Management and Administration* (1923); *American Management Review* (1923); and *Factory and Industrial Management* (the early *Factory*, later again called *Factory*, after having appeared variously as *Factory Management and Maintenance*, then *Factory*, then *Manufacturing Industries;* it is now no longer published.)

Some of the early journals have now been replaced by such publications as the *Academy of Management Review, Administrative Management, Advanced Management Journal, Administrative Science Quarterly, Business Horizons, California Management Review, Harvard Business Review,* and *Management Review.*

The Continuing Trend. The management movement which had begun to take hold in the early years of the century was firmly established in the 1920s. The trend of managerial practices and the progress of management were reported in 1929 in "Recent Economic Changes," (Vols. 1 and 2, McGraw-Hill Book Co., New York, 1929). Herbert Hoover was chairman of the committee which compiled the progress report of improved management concepts and practices pertaining to better forms of internal organization structure, better methods of coordinating manager and worker efforts, and better techniques of order giving. Special mention was made of improved planning for work and budgetary control.

Although the influence of the management movement permeated the area of public administration in the 1920s, the President's Committee on Administrative Management in 1937 submitted a report to Congress which generated interest in the application of newly established management fundamentals to the work of government. For the executive branch of the Federal government, a more efficient form of organization was conceived and implemented. (See PUBLIC ADMINISTRATION.)

During World War I, the concepts and techniques of scientific management were employed in the production plants of the nation with recognized success. During World War II, the momentum of the management movement was accelerated by the Engineering, Science, and Management War Training Program which was in force from 1940 until 1945. During this program, the trend gravitated from technical training toward the management aspects of personnel training for the most productive contributions to U. S. industrial mobilization. (See TRAINING WITHIN INDUSTRY PROGRAM.)

Experience from the program served as an impetus for the further refinement and development of management thought. There developed an appreciation of the value of management training in terms of a body of fundamentals of management in place of a description of procedures and routines. A general management viewpoint evolved, and the search for a universal philosophy of management added vitality to the continuing management movement.

During the 1950s, the concept of the "management process" received wide acceptance as the model for management education in the universities and practice in the business firms. The functions of management (planning, organizing, motivating, controlling, and innovating) were applied generally to the functions of business; principles-of-management textbooks appeared and enjoyed wide popularity. Concurrently, the trend of management thought and practice was influenced by research findings and theories from the behavioral sciences that extended the so-called "Human Relations Movement" (See HUMAN RELATIONS IN INDUSTRY); and developments in the area of MANAGEMENT SCIENCE advanced the techniques of the decision-making process for goal setting, planning, and controlling.

During the 1960s, the management movement was accelerated by knowledge and abilities stemming from innovations in the space industry as well as burgeoning research efforts of management scholars. The conceptual models for management thinking were oriented around MANAGEMENT BY OBJECTIVES and strategic planning for results, in addition to the operational planning for methods and activities used by the scientific management approach. The concept of management as a system of authority for organization and control evolved into a concept of management as a resource function for the attainment of specific, quantifiable, and realistic results through the participation of all members of the organization with the knowledge and abilities to contribute to the achievement of the objectives. Organizational discipline and effectiveness became more dependent upon self-commitment and self-control of personnel toward objectives than upon authoritarian methods. Management moved to a concept of results-oriented management as distinguished from activities-oriented management.

The systems concept with developments in the process of systems analysis and design became established by the close of the 1970s. Results-oriented management developed into a concept of "commitment," by goal-oriented people, to specific, realistic, quantifiable objectives in a changing environment. Although activities-oriented management characterized by "compliance" to a "one best way" from the decree of a hierarchical authority was much in evidence, there was increasing momentum in the trend toward a belief that managers could shape the future of an organization through commitment to a predetermined objective instead of reacting to changing environmental conditions.

The success of the Apollo Project, managed by the National Aeronautics and Space Administration, accelerated the management movement with new futuristic ways of thinking and more sophisticated techniques.

Actually, many of the innovative developments in the practice of management indicate the continuing trend of the basic concepts that evolved from the fundamentals of scientific management. However, the decade of the 1970s has been the scene of much differentiation in the concept and practice of management. The basic process of management that provided a logic of achievement for set objectives became surrounded by various approaches to management practices such as: decision theory approach, management science approach, social systems approach, applied systems approach, situational management approach, operational approach, group behavior approach, interpersonal behavior approach, et cetera.

The management movement continues to move toward the 21st century in a dynamic manner. As the environmental situation has changed, the management movement has adapted to meet the demands of society on the nation's managers. Management originated and flourished in an economic dominated society; the trend of the management movement rushes toward a merging social and economic oriented economy. The differentiated and fragmented approaches to the practice of management may be expected to move toward a more unified theory of management for practice, study, research, and teaching.

JOHN F. MEE, PH.D. LLD., Mead Johnson Professor Emeritus of Management, Indiana University, Bloomington, Indiana

Information References

George, Claude S., Jr., "The History of Management Thought," Englewood Cliffs, N.J., Prentice-Hall, 1968.

"Fifty Years of Progress in Management, 1910–1960, New York, American Society of Mechanical Engineers, 1960.

Mee, John F., "A History of Twentieth Century Management Thought," Ann Arbor, Mich., University Microfilms, Inc., 1961.

"Recent Economic Changes in the United States," Vols. 1 and 2, New York, McGraw-Hill, 1929.

"Technology and Industrial Efficiency," Proceedings of the Congress of Technology, New York, McGraw-Hill, 1911.

Towne, Henry R., "The Engineer as an Economist," No. 207, *ASME Transactions,* 8, New York, American Society of Mechanical Engineers, 1886.

Wren, Daniel A., "The Evolution of Management Thought," rev. ed., New York, Wiley, 1979.

Cross References: *Management Movement: Leaders in Thought; Personnel Management: Pioneers; Production: Large-Scale; Public Administration; Scientific Management; Scientific Management: Taylorism.*

MANAGEMENT MOVEMENT: Leaders in Thought

At about the beginning of the twentieth century, management thought began to be discernible as a separate discipline, with a growing body of applicable literature. Haynes and Massie [1] identify the following streams of thought which have been converging in the past few decades to form the corpus of the new discipline:

(1) The scientific management movement, with its origin in engineering.

(2) The development of organization theory, first in the form of traditional principles of management, and later as revolutionized by interdisciplinary contributions.

(3) The personnel, human relations, and behavioral science flow of thought. This stream, they point out, was early identified with scientific management, changed by experiments in the 1920s and 1930s, and cross-fertilized in the 1950s and 1960s.

(4) The quantitative approaches of mathematical models and statistical techniques.

(5) The accounting stream, with its separate channels of managerial accounting.

(6) The economics stream, with its separate channel of managerial economics.

To the above we may add, for our present purposes:

(7) The general management stream, the mode of thought and special skills required for the broad area of coordination, administration, and strategy.

Obviously, any attempt to indicate leaders in the streams of management thought within practicable compass will be subject to arbitrary selection and suffer from omissions. However, with some modification of the Haynes-Massie categorization, i.e., separating industrial engineering as a separate category as an outgrowth of the original scientific management movement, using as a single category managerial accounting and managerial economics (referring the general economics stream to the entry ECONOMICS), and adding our seventh suggested category, we may identify outstanding contributors as follows:

THE SCIENTIFIC MANAGEMENT MOVEMENT

For leaders of thought in this area, refer to the entries, MANAGEMENT MOVEMENT, SCIENTIFIC MANAGEMENT, and SCIENTIFIC MANAGEMENT: "TAYLORISM." In addition, for information on outstanding contributors to management thought who may be identified in a primary way with the early scientific management movement, consult the following entries:

BABCOCK, GEORGE DE ALBERT
BARTH, CARL G. L.
BOULTON, MATTHEW ROBINSON
EMERSON, HARRINGTON
GANTT, HENRY L.
GILBRETH, F. B., and LILLIAN, E. M.
HATHAWAY, H. K.
KNOEPPEL, C. E.
TAYLOR, FREDERICK W.

For contributions by others active in the broadening management movement, who later carried forward the work of the scientific management pioneers, consult the following entries:

CLARK, WALLACE
HOPF, HARRY A.

Lillian Gilbreth, whose long and active career extended to 1971, should receive special mention here.

Also worthy of mention in this connection is **William H. Leffingwell** (1876–1934). He was the first to demonstrate that the principles of scientific management as applied to production could be applied with equal success in the office. His first major contribution was his "Scientific Office Management," 1917. In 1925 he brought out "Office Management Principles and Practice," a comprehensive treatise which has earned a place in the general literature of management.

Among contemporaries, **Allan H. Mogensen,** the American industrial engineer, is inseparably linked with work simplification. As a member of the staff of *Factory* magazine in the 1930s, he pioneered the articles on work simplification that brought this hitherto little-used tool to the attention of business executives. His book, "Common Sense Applied to Motion and Time Study," appeared in 1932. In 1937 he launched the now famous Work Simplification Conferences, held annually at Lake Placid, New York.

The late industrial engineering consultant and manufacturing executive, **W. Clements Zinck,** became an enthusiast for work simplification after attending an early Mogensen Conference at Lake Placid. He wrote numerous articles on work simplification in the industrial press, lectured widely on the subject, and for many years conducted work simplification seminars in industrial plants for foremen and supervisors. These formed the basis for his book, "Dynamic Work Simplification," (1962) oriented to the foreman level. (He is author of the entry, WORK SIMPLIFICATION.)

With respect to scientific management abroad, note in the entry, SCIENTIFIC MANAGEMENT: "TAYLORISM," references to **Joseph S. Lewis,** England (1852–1901), **Karol Adamiecki,** Poland (1866–1933), and the **Michelin** brothers, France (**Andre,** 1853–1931 and **Eduard,** 1859–1940), who independently developed concepts and techniques similar to those of Taylor and his associates. Lewis's book, "The Commercial Organization of Factories," 1896, was the earliest comprehensive analysis published in Great Britain of the fundamentals of industrial administration, with special reference to the control function.

INDUSTRIAL ENGINEERING

Dexter Simpson Kimball (1865–1952) established at Cornell, in 1904, the first course in any American university to teach the principles of management. (See the entry, KIMBALL, D. S.) Also to be mentioned is **L. P. Alford** (1877–1942), first chairman of the American Society of Mechanical Engineers Management Division, created in 1920. He made original contributions to the literature of industrial economics, particularly in showing how engineers could bridge the gap between technology and business management. Best known of his writings are "Management Handbook," (ed.) 1924; "Cost and Production Handbook," (ed.) 1934; "Production Handbook," (co-ed., with J. R. Bangs) 1944; and "The Principles of Industrial Management," 1944. **Charles E. Knoeppel** (1881–1936), mentioned in connection with the scientific management movement, should be referred to here, also; he is credited with probably the earliest use of the "break-even" chart, now a standard tool of management. (See BREAK-EVEN ANALYSIS.)

Harold B. Maynard (1902–1975), the American industrial engineer widely known for his contributions to scientific work measurements and the application of motion and time study in American industrial plants, pioneered in establishing the concept of PREDETERMINED MOTION TIMES, specifically, MTM (Methods Time Measurement), and was instrumental in founding the MTM Association for Standards and Research. His published works include "Industrial Engineering Handbook," (ed.) 3rd ed. 1971; "Handbook of Business Administration," (ed.) 1967; "Methods Time Measurement," 1948; and "Time and Motion Study and Formulas for Wage Incentives," (with S. M. Lowry and G. J. Stegemerten) 1940.

Alexander Hamilton Church (1866–1936), spent his early career in England, before taking up permanent residence in the United States. While still in England, he published a series of articles in *Engineering Magazine* of New York, entitled "The Proper Distribution of Establishment Charges." These articles are recognized [2] as a pioneering reference work in cost-accounting literature both in Britain and the United States, helping to displace the rudimentary costing methods then in use for allocating overhead charges.

Among contemporary writers, **Ralph M. Barnes,** Professor of Engineering and Production Management, University of California at Los Angeles, should be mentioned for his difinitive "Motion and Time Study: Design and Measurement of Work," of which the new and revised edition appeared in 1980. (See his entry, MOTION AND TIME STUDY.) Also **Dr. Joseph M. Juran,** an industrial engineering consultant and chairman, 1945–1951, of the Department of Administrative Engineering, New York University, especially known for his work in statistical quality control. He is editor of the authoritative "Quality Control Handbook," rev. 3rd. ed., 1974, and has been instrumental in publicizing in this country the concept of QUALITY CONTROL CIRCLES applied so successfully in Japan.

ORGANIZATION THEORY

See the numerous contributors to organization theory cited in the entry, PERSONNEL MANAGEMENT: PIONEERS. See also the individual entries, FAYOL, HENRI and FOLLETT, MARY PARKER. Outstanding contributions to the literature of organization (as well as to the literature of our final category, general management) have been made by the following: **Luther H. Gulick** is the author of numerous pamphlets and books, including "Administrative Management in the Government of the United States," (with Louis Brownlow and Charles E. Merriam) 1937; "Administrative Reflections from World War II," 1948; "Modern Management for the City of New York," 1953; and "Papers on the Science of Administration," (ed., with L. Urwick) 1937, 1947, 1954. **Lyndall F. Urwick,** English consultant and educator, is recognized as an outstanding authority on management. His writings include "Papers on the Science of Administration," (with Luther Gulick), 1937, 1947, 1954; "Dynamic Administration," 1941; "The Elements of Administration," 1943; "The Pattern of Management," 1956. **Herbert A. Simon,** Professor of Computer Science and Psychology, Carnegie-Mellon University, Pittsburgh, is a recognized authority on organizational behavior, and author of "Administrative Behavior," 1957; "Models of Man," 1957; "Organizations," (with J. G. March) 1958; "Public Administration," (with D. W. Smithburg and V. A. Thompson) 1950; and "New Science of Management Decision," 1960 (latest ed. 1977).

In the category of organization theory there should also be mention of the writings of **John Diebold,** a leader in the fields of automation and the application of the electronic computer to data processing and managerial decision making. The thrust of his published works is directed to the effect of this new technology upon traditional concepts of organization. Among his books stressing this theme are "Automation: The Advent of the Automatic Factory," 1952, which attracted world-wide attention and has been translated into many languages; "Man and the Computer," 1969; "Beyond Automation," 1970; and "Business Decisions and Technological Change," 1970. Recurring in his writings is the theme that technological change and the social consequences of that change are the outstanding phenomena of our times, and that managements must "rethink" their business in the light of such change—in the process discarding traditional concepts of business organization, since modern information technology has obsoleted traditional divisional and departmental enclaves.

Personnel, Human Relations, and The Behavioral Sciences

See the entry, Personnel Management: Pioneers; and in connection with the reference there to **Elton Mayo,** see the entry, Hawthorne Experiments. To be mentioned in this category also is **Max Weber** (1864–1920), the German sociologist and political economist, who became Germany's leading social-science journalist until the advent of Hitler. His work greatly influenced twentieth-century socio-historical theories; his books include "The Protestant Ethic and the Spirit of Capitalism," 1904, and "Theory of Social and Economic Organization," 1924.

Along with **Douglas McGregor** and his "Theory X" and "Theory Y," referred to in the pioneers entry, mention should be made of psychologist **Abraham Maslow** (1908–1971) whose insights contributed greatly to our understanding of worker motivation. Among his books of interest here are "Motivation and Personality," 1954, rev. 1970, and "Dominance, Self Esteem, Self Actualization: Germinal Papers of A. H. Maslow," published posthumously. (For his hierarchy of needs, see the entry, Motivation: Maslow's Basic Needs.)

As indicated in the entry, Human Relations in Industry, in recent years there has been a swing to the concepts of "behavior management" which have challenged the preceding emphasis on worker satisfaction as a precursor to satisfactory performance, and have stressed performance first, with satisfaction or rewards contingent upon desired performance. Seminal work here is that of the Harvard psychologist **B. F. Skinner,** with his behavioral concept of the strengthening effect of reinforcement when operant behavior has certain desired consequences. His most widely quoted book is "Beyond Freedom and Dignity" (1971). Others of his writings relevant here are "Behavior of Organisms" (1938), "Schedules of Reinforcement" (1957), "Analysis of Behavior" (1961), and "About Behaviorism" (1974). An example of the recent work growing out of this approach is "Behavior Management: The New Science of Managing People at Work" (1978), by **Lawrence M. Miller,** and "Theories of Organizational Behavior" (1980), by **John Miner.**

Another contributor to behavioral insights has been **William Foote Whyte,** who has been professor of industrial relations at the New York State School of Industrial and Labor Relations, Cornell University, since 1948. Significant among his books are "Patterns for Industrial Peace," 1951, "Money and Motivation," 1955, "Men at Work," 1961, and "Organizational Behavior," 1969.

Important to personnel relations have been developing concepts of wage payment. For a discussion of contributions made by specific individuals in this connection, see: Halsey, Frederick A., on the man who originated the first successful incentive wage system in American industry to improve upon the straight piecework system; the discussion of the work of **Allan W. Rucker** in the *History* section of Rucker Plan of Group Incentives; and the accounts of the innovations by **James F. Lincoln** (1883–1965), in Lincoln Incentive Management Plan and by **Joseph N. Scanlon,** an official of the United Steelworkers of America and later on the faculty of M.I.T., in Scanlon Plan of Group Incentives.

In addition to James F. Lincoln, there have been numerous outstanding industrialists who left their stamp upon management thinking by putting into practice their philosophy of human relations and the need to be concerned about the welfare of their employees. See the entries, Owen, Robert (1771–1858); Rowntree, B. Seebohm (1871–1954), considered the British management movement's greatest pioneer; and Dennison Henry (1877–1952), who pioneered in profit-sharing plans, and became known for making his medium-sized manufacturing company among the most progressive in America.

Quantitative Approaches

Analysis and Decisions. One of the most significant of recent developments in management is the increased use of quantitative methods of analysis and decision making. For background, see the entry, MANAGEMENT SCIENCES, and the cross references there given. See also the individual entry, BABBAGE, CHARLES. Technical aspects are covered in the entries, STATISTICS, OPERATIONS RESEARCH, and RELIABILITY ENGINEERING, and cross-referenced entries.

Names that loom large in the development of statistical theory important in business analysis and decision-making are **R. A. Fisher,** in statistical inference; **George Snedecor,** in the analysis of variance; **J. Neyman,** in mathematical probability; **Karl Pearson,** in correlation analysis; **Claude E. Shannon,** in the mathematical theory of communication; **W. E. Deming,** in statistical sampling; and **W. A. Shewhart** in scientific quality control. (See the entry, STATISTICS.)

Of profound significance to management decision making was "The Theory of Games and Economic Behavior" 1944, by **John Von Neumann** and **Oscar Morgenstern;** as were the concepts of cybernetics introduced by **Norbert Wiener,** of M.I.T. (including the coining of the word). The latter provided the theoretical base for computer development, to which seminal contributions also were made by John Von Neumann. The bulk of Wiener's writings are for the specialist; however, of interest and profit for the business reader is his "The Human Use of Human Beings: Cybernetics and Society," 1950.

With regard to Operations Research and related concepts, the writings of **C. W. Churchman** are important, including "Introduction to Operations Research," (With R. L. Ackoff and E. L. Arnoff) 1957; and "Prediction and Optimal Decision," 1961. See also the remarks under *History and Development* in the entry, ECONOMETRICS, for references to important contributors to that discipline. A significant contributor to new mathematical techniques of analysis and decision-making is **Jay W. Forrester,** of M.I.T., best known, perhaps, for his work described in the entry, INDUSTRIAL DYNAMICS.

MANAGERIAL ACCOUNTING AND MANAGERIAL ECONOMICS

Attention was early focused on the importance of budgeting as a major instrument of management by **James O. McKinsey** (1889–1937), American professor, consultant, and business executive, who wrote the first standard book on the subject in 1922—"Budgetary Control." He communicated his concepts of management, which included emphasis on sound organization planning, through his writings, his teaching at the University of Chicago, and through extensive activity in the American Management Association, of which he was Chairman of the Board at the time of his death. Important works by contemporary authorities include those of: **Joel Dean,** a consultant and member of the faculty of Columbia University, specifically his "Managerial Economics," 1951, and "Capital Budgeting," 1961, and his chapter, "Techniques for Pricing New Products and Services," in Buell, Victor P., and Heyel, Carl, eds., "Handbook of Modern Marketing," 1970; **Eugene L. Grant,** "Statistical Quality Control" (with W. Ireson) 3rd ed., 1964, and "Principles of Engineering Economics," 5th ed., 1970; and **George Terborg,** research director for the Machinery and Allied Products Institute, "Business Investment Management," 1967. (See entry, FIXED-ASSET INVESTMENT ANALYSIS: The MAPI Formulas and Procedures.)

GENERAL MANAGEMENT

An outstanding figure in the management movement is Great Britain's **Oliver Sheldon** (1894–1951), author of the management classic, "The Philosophy of Management," 1923. He spent all of his working career in the service of Rowntree & Co., and was thus closely associated with the great advances in managerial practice being made there under B. SEEBOHM ROWNTREE [2]. In 1921 Sheldon emerged as one of the founders of the Institute of Industrial Administration and a contributor to its *Journal.* His 1922 paper, "The Case for the Institute," was an important document in the British management movement, and one of the earliest cases made for the establishment of professional standards in management. He was prominent as B. S. Rowntree's colleague in organizing in 1920 the Rowntree Lecture Conferences, the forerunners of the management conferences of today.

Another of the earlier figures that looms large in the history of modern management is **Ralph Courrier Davis** (1894–   ), who headed the management department at General Motors Institute, Detroit, 1927–1930, and was later professor of business organization at Ohio State University, 1936–1965. He was the first

American to identify and differentiate the functions of management, and his classic book, "The Fundamentals of Top Management" (with Alten W. Baker), 1951, is still being used. Many of the university advanced management programs in the 1950s used his approach. Significant among his other books are "Principles of Factory Organization and Management," 1928, 3rd ed., 1957; "The Principles of Business Organization and Operation," 4th ed., 1937, reprinted 1973; "Principles of Management," 1962.

Alvin E. Dodd (1883–1951), while not a contributor to the literature of management, was nevertheless an inspiring catalytic force as executive vice president of the American Management Association, 1933–1936, and president, 1933–1948. Taking over when AMA had been greatly set back by the Depression, he built it into an authoritative forum for collecting, analyzing, and disseminating management knowledge. However, it was **Lawrence A. Appley,** who succeeded Alvin Dodd as president of the American Management Association (now American Management Associations), 1948–1968, chairman, 1968–1974, and since then emeritus chairman, who built AMA to the towering organization it is today. (See MANAGEMENT SOCIETIES AND ASSOCIATIONS.) Appley had held vice presidential posts at Vick Chemical Company and Montgomery Ward, and during World War II served as Assistant to the Secretary of War and later as executive director and deputy chairman of the War Manpower Commission. He has been active in executive development work, and is author of a number of books on management, among them: "Management in Action," 3rd ed., 1956, and "Formula for Success: A Core Concept of Management," 1974.

Peter F. Drucker, Professor of Management of New York University from 1950 to 1971, and since then Professor of Social Sciences, Claremont Graduate School, Claremont, Calif., has written extensively on the theory and practice of management. Perhaps his most widely quoted work is "The Practice of Management," 1954. Others to be mentioned in our present context are include: "Concept of the Corporation," 1946; "Managing for Results," 1964; "The Effective Executive," 1967; "Technology, Management, and Society," 1970; "Management: Tasks, Responsibilities, Practices," 1974; and "Managing in Turbulent Times," 1980.

CARL HEYEL, Management Counsel, Manhasset, New York

References Cited

[1] Haynes, W. Warren and Massie, Joseph L., "Management: Analysis, Concepts, and Cases," Englewood Cliffs, N.J., Prentice Hall, 2nd. ed., 1969.

[2] Urwick, L., "The Golden Book of Management," edited for the International Committee of Scientific Management (CIOS), Newman Neame, London, 1956.

Cross References: *Management Movement (and cross references there given).*

MANAGEMENT BY OBJECTIVES

The term **Management by Objectives** has taken on a special meaning in the vocabulary of management. Typically it refers to a formal procedure in which each "manager pair," i.e., a manager at any level and his immediate superior, periodically reach mutual agreement on *specific* and *measurable* goals or objectives which the subordinate manager is expected to attain in the upcoming period—perhaps the next quarter or the next year. A written record is made of these objectives. Where a junior manager is involved, his superior may undertake to provide day-by-day on-the-job coaching during the period. In any event, personal development—participation in on-job training programs, enrollment in extension courses available locally, use of correspondence-school offerings, etc.—is included in the program.

At the end of the period, the management pair meets again to conduct a performance review of the subordinate manager's activities. (Here the great importance of having reached *mutual agreement* on the subordinate's objectives becomes apparent: He either achieved his objectives or he did not—and if he did not, he must be in a position to explain why not.) At this time further on-job or off-job training needs are considered, and then the manager pair sets objectives for the next period.

Alternative terms for the program described above are "work planning and review" (used by General Electric, which has pioneered in applying the concept), "management by results," and "performance assurance."

Development of the Concept. Management by objectives, or MBO, stems from several parallel developments occurring roughly from the mid-1950s to the mid-1960s. As early as 1954, Peter F. Drucker, in "The Practice of Management" [1], used the term "management by objectives" and recognized one of its main ingredients, the desirability of *self-set goals.* At the same time, spurred by Drucker and other management authorities, many organizations began to undertake formal LONG-RANGE-PLANNING, calling for overall corporate goals and in many cases goals for subunits of their organizations. A logical extension of this was the development of personalized business goals for individual managers.

Also during this period, behavioral scientists such as Douglas McGregor [2] and Rensis Likert [3], [4] were putting forth more evidence to support the idea that self-set controls and self-set objectives were frequently more effective than controls and objectives set by others. (See MOTIVATION: "THEORY X" AND THEORY Y.") Concurrently, many people engaged in very practical personnel and organizational development were experiencing increasing concern over the ineffectiveness of performance appraisal that was largely traits-oriented (leadership, initiative, etc.) or methods-oriented (organizing, delegating, etc.). However, they nevertheless were convinced that some sort of performance appraisal was necessary. They thus were receptive to the idea of *results-oriented* performance appraisal not only because of its logic, but because of the introduction of evidence that it helped improve performance. (See, for example, accounts of experiments at General Electric published under the title "Split Roles in Performance Appraisal," noted in *Information References* at the end of this entry.) On top of this, management consultants such as John W. Humble of Urwick, Orr & Partners, Limited, and professor-consultants such as George Odiorne of the University of Michigan, began to develop and extend an organized body of knowledge on management by objectives. Through their extensive writings, lectures, and consulting assistance, they brought the concept to a variety of organizations in all types of business and nonbusiness endeavors.

Thus, the rise of goals-oriented corporate planning came about during the 1960s, and management by objectives became an accepted and widely used set of management techniques. Influential in this development were the advocacy by behavioral scientists of personal goals as motivators, the dissatisfaction of personnel professionals with the conventional performance review, and the activity of management consultants in practical applications.

The 1970s became a period of modification and further experimentation with MBO as a management technique. One of the more active proponents was Hay Associates in Philadelphia. This consulting firm's long experience in compensation and background in behaviorial sciences was combined with research in businesses strategy. Out of this emerged a system for developing objectives for managers tied to changes required under specific business strategies. Existing management climate, corporate structure, and stage in the development of the business were incorporated into the process to facilitate realistic goal setting so often lacking and the cause of downfold in many MBO programs. This technique is known as "performance assurance" in a number of companies.

Mechanics. The mechanics of management by objectives are deceptively simple in concept. Every few months, typically three to twelve, each manager and his superior get together to review results for the period gone by, and to plan work and set goals for the coming period. Relatively few priority goals are set (typically two to ten), influenced by and linked with the general business plans.

These goals should be in *quantitative* terms where at all possible, so that their degree of accomplishment can be determined from readily available records. For example, an objective might be to reduce scrap on a certain operation from an existing 2% to a goal of 1.5% by September—with notes as to how this is to be accomplished. Sometimes records on the key measurement of a part of the business do not exist and must be established or revised.

As indicated earlier, consideration should be given to special areas where training may be needed, either for the present job or to prepare for promotion.

Principles and Pitfalls. When properly installed and functioning, management by objectives is actually a system for managing an entire enterprise. Following are basic principles and pitfalls, to provide the reader with a perspective for further research (see the references at the end of this entry):

(1) The subordinate manager should receive continuing encouragement and necessary coaching from his superior.

(2) An effective installation will avoid the pitfall of being thought of as simply another personnel-department device. True, management by objectives can be a valuable tool in performance appraisal, development of managers, and establishing proper compensation—all areas of interest to personnel specialists. But

these are also properly the major concerns of line managers. Thus management by objectives is a *management* program, rather than a *personnel* program. The specific objectives chosen must be consistent with the objectives of the organization's long-range plans—hence the program is clearly a concern of general management.

(3) The man in charge of a management-by-objectives program (whether chief executive, division head, or profit-center head) must be thoroughly sold on it and give it strong support. Since it may take about two years for this sytem to become ingrained, any relaxation of such support will lead to its abandonment at an early date.

(4) There will be a tendency of some managers not to come to grips with the real issues and the real profit-improvement opportunities in their business areas. In effect, they will state that they are already performing at a peak. This is a danger signal, a warning of shallow thinking.

(5) Management by objectives is particularly difficult to install in a crisis situation, where it may, in fact, be inappropriate. Where the continued existence of an organization is threatened, senior management may have to lay down certain goals by edict—contrary to normal management-by-objectives principles. However, management by objectives can still be useful in gaining ideas and support on *how* the goals are to be achieved.

(6) More and more practitioners are now linking MBO with compensation as a practical means of reinforcing performance. Typically, levels of performance on specific goals will be geared to a percentage of an individual's opportunity for increased compensation. Early practitioners debated such practices hotly, opponents claiming that little attention was paid to anything other than factors affecting compensation. Realistically, most management by objectives programs that prove successful are directly linked to compensation.

(7) It is again stressed that the MBO performance review should be used as a means of determining the individual's personal development, needs for further coaching, on-job or off-job training, or job rotation. This is often overlooked.

Acceptance and Prospects. The author, based on his consulting experience, estimates that between one half and three-quarters of the "Fortune 500" companies apply management by objectives to some degree or another. This may be limited to a single division or apply to a limited number of managers in a number of divisions. In a few instances, probably less than 10% of the Fortune 500, management by objectives is widely employed, covering most of the managerial jobs in the companies. An early Conference Board study [5] names five large companies in which MBO was in wide-spread use; however, experience has proved that meaningful objectives for lower levels of management are not always practical. While desirable from many points of view, MBO for lower levels of managment becomes ineffective because of a lack of organizational clarity and vitality, constraints on freedom to act, and peculiarities in the company's decision-making processes.

Typically, in times of recession, MBO systems are quickly put aside as management discontinues all but essential capital spending and concentrates decision making at the highest levels in the organization. This happened in each of the past recessions, 1970, 1974, and 1980, resulting in a slowing of the growth rate of MBO from the 1960s. Further modifications and innovations aimed at improving management performance will probably improve penetration of MBO during the 1980s. Few practitioners of MBO report complete satisfaction with their programs, but most continue to state that the use of these techniques has contributed to improved management performance.

Appropriate use of MBO has to some extent been impeded by the apparent simplicity of the concept. This has promoted installation of systems without appropriate grounding in the fundamentals, guarding against the pitfalls discussed above and gaining the required commitment of management. As a result, MBO becomes perceived as another management gimmick and abandoned after a short trial.

Proper MBO presupposes "Theory Y" or a participative style of management. (See MOTIVATION: McGregor's "Theory X" and "Theory Y," and MULTIPLE MANAGEMENT.) Equally important is a clearly articulated strategy, one which has been developed through substative evaluation with goals that stretch the capability of the organization and at the same time are perceived to be valid. Thus, it is clear that depending on whether the business is in an emergent, development, mature, or liquidation phase, a particular decision to invest or pull cash out of the business unit is appropriate. Another important element is organizational clarity and vitality; that is to say, there exist management processes and people with the characteristics suitable for implementing the indicated strategy. With these ingredients in place, MBO serves as a useful tool for implementing strategies.

NEWELL GARFIELD, JR., President, Newell Garfield Company, Inc., New York, New York

Information References

Albrecht, Karl G., "Successful Management by Objectives: An Operational Approach," Englewood Cliffs, N.J., Spectrum Books, 1977.

BNA Films Div., Bureau of National Affairs Rockville, Md. Series of films on Management by Objectives.

Heyel, Carl, "Appraising Executive Performance," New York, American Management Association, 1958.

Morrisey, George L., "Management by Objectives and Results for Business and Industry," Reading, Mass., Addison-Wesley, 2nd ed., 1977.

Ordiorne, George S., "Management by Objectives," New York, Pitman, 1965.

References Cited

[1] Drucker, Peter F., "The Practice of Management," New York, Harper & Row, 1954.

[2] McGregor, Douglas, "The Human Side of Enterprise," New York, McGraw-Hill, 1960.

[3] Likert, Rensis, "Human Organization," New York, McGraw-Hill, 1967.

[4] Likert, Rensis, "New Patterns of Management," New York, McGraw-Hill, 1961.

[5] The Conference Board, "Managing By and With Objectives," New York, 1968.

Cross References: *Executive Appraisal: Diagnostic Performance Appraisal; Goal Setting; Managerial Effectiveness: Climate for Organizational Results; Zero-Base Budgeting.*

MANAGEMENT PRACTICE: LEARNING FROM FOREIGN MANAGEMENT

"What can we learn from American management?" was the question asked all over the world as recently as the early 1970s. Now it is perhaps time to ask: "What can American management learn from others in the free world, and especially from management in Western Europe and Japan?" For as of 1980, Europe and Japan have the managerial edge in many of the areas which we used to consider American strengths, if not American monopolies.

Employee Responsibility. First, foreign managers increasingly demand responsibility from their employees, all the way down to the lowliest blue-collar worker on the factory floor. They are putting to work the tremendous improvement in the education and skill of the labor force accomplished in this century. The Japanese are now famous for their QUALITY CONTROL CIRCLES and their "continuous learning." Employees at all levels come together regularly, sometimes once a week, more often twice a month, to address the question: "What can we do to improve what we already are doing?" In Germany, a highly skilled senior worker known as the "Meister" acts as teacher, assistant, and standard-setter, rather than as "supervisor" and "boss."

Benefit Policies. Second, foreign managers have thought through their benefits policies more carefully. "Fringes" in the United States are now as wide as in any other country, that is, they amount to some 40 cents for each dollar paid in cash wages. But in this country, many benefits fail to help the individual employee. In many families, for instance, both husband and wife are docked the full family health insurance premium at work, even though one insurance policy would be sufficient. And we pay full Social Security charges for the married working woman, even though married working women under our Social Security system will never see a penny of their money paid back into their accounts.

By contrast, foreign managements, especially those of Japan and Germany, structure benefits according to the needs of recipients. The Japanese, for instance, set aside dowry money for young unmarried women, while they provide housing allowances to men in their early thirties with young families. In England, a married woman in the labor force can opt out of a large part of old-age insurance if her husband already pays for the couple at his place of employment.

Marketing. Third, foreign managers take marketing seriously. In many American companies marketing still means no more than systematic selling. Foreigners today have absorbed more fully the true meaning of marketing: knowing what is value for the customer.

Foreigners are increasingly thinking in terms of market structure, trying to define specific market niches for their products, and designing their business with a marketing strategy in mind. The Japanese automobile companies are but one example. Few companies are so attentive to the market as the high-technology and high-fashion entrepreneurs of northern Italy.

Profits. It is not correct, as is so often asserted in this country, that Japanese and Western European businesses subordinate profits. Indeed, the return on total assets is conspicuously higher today in a great many foreign businesses than it is in this country, especially if profits are adjusted for inflation. But the foreign manager has increasingly learned to say, "It is my job to earn a proper profit on what the market wants to buy." In this country, managements still, by and large, try to say, "What is our product with the highest profit margin? Let's try to sell that, and sell it hard."

Incidentally, when the foreign manager says "market," he tends to think of the world economy. Very few Japanese companies actually depend heavily on exports. And yet it is the rare Japanese business which does not start out with the world economy in marketing, even if its own sales are predominantly in the Japanese home market.

Obsolescence. Fourth, foreign managements base their marketing and innovation strategies on the systematic and purposeful abandonment of the old, the outworn and the obsolete. In every business plan of a major foreign company the writer has seen in recent years—Japanese, German, French, and so on—the first question is not: "What are the new things we are going to do?" The first question is: "What are the old things we are going to abandon?" As a result, resources are available for innovation, new products, new markets. In too many American companies, the most productive resources are frozen into defending yesterday.

Long-term Perspectives. Fifth, foreign managements keep separate and discrete those areas where short term results are the proper measurement and those where results should be measured over longer time spans, such as innovation, product development, product introduction, and manager development. The quarterly P & L is taken as seriously in Tokyo and Osaka as it is in New York and Chicago; and, with the strong role that the banks play in the management of German companies, the quarterly P & L is probably taken more seriously in Frankfurt than it is in the U.S. But outside the U.S., the quarterly P & L is increasingly being confined to the 90% or so of the budget that is concerned with operations and with the short term.

There is then a second budget, usually no more than a few per cent of the total, which deals with those areas in which expenditures have to be maintained over a long period of time to get any results. By separating short-term operating budgets from longer term investment or opportunities budgets, foreign companies can plan for the long haul. They can control expenditures over the long term and get results for long-term efforts and investments.

Business Management and Public Policy. Sixth, managers in large Japanese, German, and French companies see themselves as national assets and leaders responsible for the development of proper policies in the national interest. One good example was furnished by a delegation of the chief executive officers of the 40 largest Japanese companies that came to the United States to discuss how Japan should adjust to demographic changes.

"We don't want to discuss," said the leader of the group, "what we in Japanese business should be doing. Our agenda is what *Japan* should be doing and what the best policies are in the national interest. Only after we have thought through the right national policies, and have defined and publicized them, are we going to think about the implications for business and for our companies. Indeed we should postpone discussing economics altogether until we have understood what the right social policies are and what is best for the individual Japanese and for the country altogether. Who else besides the heads of Japan's large companies can really look at such a problem from all aspects? To whom else can the country really look for guidance and leadership in such a tremendous change as that of the age structure of our population?"

Any American executive, at all conversant with our management literature, may now say: "Every one of these things I have known for 30 years or so." But this is precisely the point. What we can learn from foreign management is not what to do. What we can learn is to *do* it.

American in Origin. Each of the foregoing six practices is American in origin. The foreigners have learned every one of them from us in the twenty years during which they have come to this country to find out how to manage.

The "quality circles" for productivity and quality improvement which are now being touted in American industry as the latest and most advanced "innovation" were brought to

Japan in the fifties and sixties by three Americans—Edwards Deming and Joseph M. Juran, both then at New York University, and A. V. Feigenbaum of General Electric.

The German "Meister" has ancient roots, but its present form dates back to the fifties and to unashamed imitation of the way IBM, first in this country and then in its European subsidiaries, had restructured the role and job of the first-line supervisor, converting him or her from a "foreman" into an "assistant" and "teacher."

The Japanese and Germans pratice in marketing what every American marketing textbook has been preaching for the last 30 years. The distinction between short-term and long-term budget goes back to Du Pont and General Motors in the twenties. Indeed each of these practices can be found in any management books written in the late forties and early fifties. We don't need to learn what the rules are—we invented them. What we need is to put them into practice.

PETER F. DRUCKER, Clarke Professor of Social Sciences, Claremont Graduate School, Claremont, California

This entry follows the treatment in Dr. Drucker's article, "Learning from Foreign Management," in *The Wall Street Journal,* June 4, 1980.

Cross References: *Quality Control Circles; Long-Range Corporate Planning; Social Audit.*

MANAGEMENT SCIENCES

The **"Management Sciences"** refers to the movement begun shortly after the end of the Second World War that applies the scientific method and advanced quantitative techniques to the study of management. The term may be used interchangeably with OPERATIONS RESEARCH, but it is not to be confused with SCIENTIFIC MANAGEMENT, a movement based on the techniques and philosophy of Frederick W. Taylor. (See MATHEMATICAL PROGRAMMING; OPERATIONS RESEARCH; SCIENTIFIC MANAGEMENT.)

Cross References: *Business Logistics; Business Logistics: Case Example; Cost Benefit (Cost Effectiveness) Analysis; Dynamic Programming; Econometrics; Game Theory; Goal Programming; Industrial Dynamics; Integer Programming; Linear Programming; Linear Programming: A Case Example; Mathematical Programming; Nonlinear Programming; Operational Gaming and Monte Carlo Simulation; Operations Research; Operations Research in Marketing Decisions; PERT (Program Evaluation and Review Technique); Statistics; Waiting Line Theory (Queueing Theory).*

MANAGEMENT SOCIETIES AND ASSOCIATIONS

Much of the progress, success, and influence of the management movement and of the advanced positions of many managements today can be attributed to the leadership and programs of the **Professional Management Societies** and allied groups. Mention of some of these, and of societies and associations with management divisions, is made in the entry, MANAGEMENT MOVEMENT, under the heading, *Professional Management Associations.*

The most active and influential of the professional management groups of the early 1980s are listed below.

Academy of Management. This is a professional organization of professors in American higher education who teach management in any of its aspects or applications, and also selected individuals in business and governmental administration who have made a significant written contribution to the theory and practice of management. It was initiated in 1936 by Professors C. L. Jamison (University of Michigan) and W. N. Mitchell (University of Chicago), and formally established in 1941. Regional and national meetings are held annually. Proceedings of the national meeting are distributed quarterly to libraries. Other publications are the quarterly *Academy of Management Journal,* the quarterly *Review,* and a *Newsletter*. The Academy is advisor to the American Association of Collegiate Schools of Business. Headquarters rotate among universities.

Administrative Management Society. The Administrative Management Society (AMS—formerly NOMA, National Office Management Association), is composed of more than 150 local chapters with over 12,000 members in the United States, Canada, and the free world. Areas of interest emphasized are management development, administrative services, personnel, systems, information management, and finance. Its Management Information Center in Willow Grove, Pa., services each year hundreds of requests by members for information on professional subjects. An international conference is held annually to project the latest thinking on administrative management problems and managerial techniques through seminars, workshops, and panel discussions.

AMS assists educational institutions in developing training programs and courses of study; encourages and participates in research; presents Merit Awards; sponsors professional accreditation for certified administrative managers. Publications include the monthly *IMPACT: Information Technology;* monthly *Management World; Yearbook; Guide to Management Compensation* (annual); and *Office Salary Surveys.* Its headquarters are Willow Grove, Pa. 19090.

American Association of Industrial Management. This association was founded in 1899 as National Metal Trades Association. Its purpose is the promotion of good employee-employer relations. Activities are directed to such matters as wage and salary administration, personnel practices, training, communications, etc. Members include manufacturing companies, hospitals, banks, universities, and municipalities.

AAIM's publications include the monthly *Consumer Price Index, The Executive Manager,* and *Signs of the Times.* Headquarters: 7425 Old York Road, Philadelphia, Pa., 19126.

American Institute of Management. The American Institute of Management is a nonprofit research and educational organization dedicated to the advancement of management. Its studies are concerned with the overall management function and corporate policy as a whole. Through its MANAGEMENT AUDIT the Institute rates the management function in the following categories: Economic Function, Corporate Structure, Health of Earnings, Service to Stockowners, Research and Development, Directorate Analysis, Fiscal Policies, Production Efficiency, Sales Vigor, and Executive Evaluation. It issues numerous publications, conducts work study courses and seminars in management and finance, and renders research and personal counsel to members. Headquarters: 607 Boylston St., Boston, Mass. 02116.

American Management Associations. The American Management Association was formed in 1923 from a group of management organizations. It traces its origins from two fields of organized industrial work: "corporate schools" and employment management. Groups active in the former organized nationally in 1913 as the National Association of Corporate Schools, incorporated in 1920 as the National Association of Corporate Training. The National Association of Employment Managers was organized in 1918, and in 1920 incorporated as the Industrial Relations Association of America. These two groups merged in 1922 as the National Personnel Association. The name of this organization was changed in 1923 to the American Management Association. The National Association of Sales Managers joined the American Management Association in 1925. (In 1973, AMA pluralized its name to American Management Associations.)

AMA is by far the most active non-academic institution in the field of management education in this country. Its conferences, seminars, and courses cover the whole range of functional and conceptual subjects of interest to executives. It numbers more than 8,100 members, and over 100,000 participants attended more than 2,000 AMA programs in 1971. In addition, the Association carries on extensive publishing activities, producing reports, periodicals, printed proceedings, and hardcover books.

AMA has Management Centers and offices in many U.S. and Canadian cities and through AMA International (see separate entry) in Europe and South America. It maintains extensive library, bookstores, and Management Information Service including films, cassettes, tapes and records covering all areas of management expertise.

AMA's Divisions: AMA International; AMACOM (publishing); Center for Entrepreneurial Management (see separate entry); Center for Management Development (seminars); Center for Planning and Implementation (long-range team planning); Extension Institute (study-at-home programs); In-House Development and Training; National Association of Corporate Directors; Presidents Association; Professional Institute; Society for Advancement of Management (see separate entry). SAM became an affiliated division of AMA in 1972, making it possible for AMA to offer its diverse membership a local and regional chapter base and to promote senior and college chapters internationally.

Publications: *AMA Management Digest,* monthly; *Compensation Review,* quarterly; *Compflash* (newsletter on compensation, monthly; *Health Services Manager,* monthly; *Management Review,* monthly; *Organizational Dynamics,* quarterly; *Personnel,* bi-monthly; *The President,* monthly newsletter; *Supervisory*

Management, monthly; and *Supervisory Sense,* monthly.

Headquarters: American Management Associations Building, 135 West 50th Street, New York, N.Y. 10020.

AMA/International. This division of AMA was founded in 1956 as a separate professional group to service the overseas management members and to provide educational and other organizational services to the international business community. It conducts over 500 meetings each year, adapting and extending AMA techniques in the Management Centers of Brussels, Sao Paulo, Mexico City, and Toronto. It was formerly the International Management Association. Its headquarters are based at AMA, New York.

American Production and Inventory Control Society. APICS was founded in 1957 to promote inventory management control for its members which in 1980 totaled 28,000. It conducts annual meetings in addition to local chapter activity and publishes the *APICS News,* monthly, and *Production and Inventory Management,* quarterly. Provides bibliographies, dictionaries, and training aids. It is headquartered at the Watergate Bldg., 2600 Virginia Avenue N.W., Washington, DC, 20037.

ASME Management Division. In 1920, the American Society of Mechanical Engineers, itself one of the oldest professional societies in the United States (founded in 1880), established its Management Division. This was a natural development, since the Society had provided the forum for the presentation of early papers on the science of management by Taylor, Towne, Gantt, and others (See SCIENTIFIC MANAGEMENT, and MANAGEMENT MOVEMENT.) Today the Division sponsors conferences on management subjects throughout the year, including an annual conference for invited top executives. It cooperates with other professional groups in conducting the annual conferences on engineering management which it initiated. The Management Division, directed by an executive committee of five ASME members, is composed of ASME members who designate it as one of five divisions in whose subject matter they are interested. (Over 30,000, some 34,000 from among ASME's 95,000 members, made such a designation.) Articles of management interest are carried in ASME's monthly publication. *Mechanical Engineering* or in its quarterly, *Journal for Industry.* It publishes papers and articles on management subjects which ASME sponsored. Headquarters: 345 E. 47th Street, New York, N.Y. 10017.

Association for Systems Management. This is an international professional organization for the advancement and self-renewal of information systems managers. Founded in 1947, ASM had a membership in 1980 of over 10,000, and more than 125 chapters. ASM publishes technical reference books and a monthly *Journal of Systems Management.* In cooperation with ASM International Headquarters, chapters and divisions develop and sponsor many educational seminars relating to current systems knowledge at basic, intermediate, and advanced levels. It makes available tape recordings of seminars papers presented at the annual conference. Headquarters: 24587 Bagley Road, Cleveland, Ohio 44138.

CIOS. Founded in 1926 under the leadership of Herbert Hoover and Thomas Masaryk, CIOS (pronounced "see-oss" in every language), the **Comité International de l'Organization Scientifique** is a nonpolitical, nonprofit international management organization with headquarters in Geneva. It has member affiliates in 40 countries. The basic purpose of CIOS is to promote internationally the principles and methods of scientific management, and thus to improve living standards in all nations. Its best known activity has been its sponsorship of the International Management Congresses. These are now held every three years in different host countries. The first Congress was held in Prague in 1924.

The Conference Board. Formerly the National Industrial Conference Board, this organization in 1970 changed its name, broadened its scope, and increased its international emphasis. Organized in 1916, The Conference Board is a nonprofit, fact-finding organization which conducts research in economics, business management, human relations, public affairs, and personnel policies. In addition to its numerous reports on these studies, the Board issues *Across the Board,* monthly; *Mergers and Acquisitions,* monthly, and *Antitrust Proceedings* and *Cumulative Index,* annually; also reports, bulletins, and statistics. Other CB publications are:

The Conference Board RECORD, Focus (for Associates), *Monthly Business Review, Statistical Bulletin, Library Bulletin,* and *Announcements of Mergers and Acquisitions;* semi-monthly *Road Maps of Industry and Consumer Attitudes and Buying Plans;* quarterly *Capital Appropriations*

Survey, Business Outlook Chartbook, and *World Business Perspective;* semi-annually *Investment Conditions;* and *Weekly Desk Sheet of Business Trends.*

Membership is composed of over 4,000 Associates, including business corporations in the U.S. and abroad, trade associations, labor unions, colleges and universities, U.S. government agencies, libraries, and individuals. U.S. headquarters: 845 3rd Avenue, New York, N.Y. 10022. Canada headquarters: 333 River Road, Ottawa, Ontario K1L8B9.

Data Entry Management Association DEMA was organized in 1976 to meet the specialized needs of data-entry managers and others involved in the data-entry profession. It promotes the individual development of its members through the exchange of ideas, national seminars, and regional workshop, and meetings. It publishes a *Newsletter* from its headquarters at 16 E. Weavers Hill, Greenwich, CT 06830.

Data Processing Management Association. DPMA is the largest organization serving the information processing and computer management community. Organized in 1951 under the name of National Machine Accountants Association, as of 1972 it had nearly 30,000 members in over 265 chapters located in the United States, Canada, Mexico, Japan, Okinawa and the Philippines. DPMA engages in education and research activities focused on developing effective programs for a broader understanding of the principles and methods of data processing as it relates to hardware, software, and management techniques. Membership is granted by the individual chapter board of directors to persons engaged as managerial or supervisory personnel in EDP installations, systems and methods analysts, research specialists, and computer programmers employed in executive, administrative, or consulting capacities; and staff, managers, educators, and executive personnel with a direct interest in data processing.

DPMA publishes *Data Management,* monthly; *Management Reference Series,* and EDP-oriented books and pamphlets. It holds an annual International Data Processing Conference and Business Exposition, and is the founder of the Certificate in Data Processing (CDP) examination program (now administered by an intersociety organization). DPMA presents the "Computer Sciences Man of the Year Award" for outstanding contributions to the profession. Headquarters: 505 Busse Highway, Park Ridge, Illinois 60068.

Industrial Management Society. IMS was organized in the mid-thirties to advance the profession of management, promote research in the various fields of management activities, and study problems of the social science as related to industry. *Industrial Management,* a monthly publication containing current reports of progress in the field, is distributed to members and is made available to public, business and educational libraries on subscription. The Society promotes the use of scientific management, techniques of measurement, analysis and evaluation, plant layout, work simplification and humanics. IMS holds spring and fall seminars on industrial engineering and management development. It maintains a film library, conducts conferences, seminars, and workshops, engages in cooperative programs with other leading organizations and societies, assists schools in planning pertinent courses, sponsors an annual methods improvement contest, and provides information service to members and the general public all over the world.

Proceedings of the Society's annual Management Clinic are distributed to members. Headquarters: 570 Northwest Highway, Des Plaines, Ill. 60016.

The Institute of Management Sciences. The Institute of Management Sciences (TIMS), is an international professional organization of managers, educators, and practicing management scientists occupying managerial, technical, and teaching positions in business, industry, government, and the universities. Its activities are aimed at the development and application of scientific methods and concepts in management.

Founded in 1953 by 69 chapter members, the Institute in 1980 had a membership of approximately 7,000, representing more than 77 countries. It publishes *Management Science* monthly in two series. Quarterly, it publishes *Interfaces,* whose primary goal is to encourage interaction between managers and management scientists. The Institute publishes *Proceedings* of Symposia on Planning and special issues on education, ecology, urban issues, game theory and gaming, and marketing management models.

TIMS also serves as a communications link among the various subdivisions of the Institute. The Institute also conducts local, regional, national, and international meetings. TIMS encourages research and publication in selected fields through grants, awards, and special symposia. Headquarters: 146 Westminster Street, Providence, R.I. 02903.

International Academy of Management. Membership in IAM is composed of leaders in management from six continents and 23 countries. Its purpose is to provide the members of CIOS (see separate entry) with a consultative organ at the international level for fundamental research in evolving and advancing theories of practical and philosophical management. It also provides a body to safeguard the objectivity and precision of the art and science of managing and the disciplined integration of new managerial trends. Fellows are elected annually on the basis of their achievements in management, particularly on an international context. It was founded in 1958 and holds conventions triennially. Its headquarters are in The Hague, Netherlands.

International Management Council. IMC has grown from its founding in 1935 to over 13,000 members in 1980. Its purpose is to help supervisory managers develop as leaders in their industries and communities. Divisions include Standards, Educations, Financial Development, Leadership Development, Public Relations and Management Development. It was formerly the National Council of Foremen's Clubs and the National Council of Industrial Management Clubs. Located at 291 Broadway, New York, NY 10007.

International Executives Association, Inc. Founded as the Export Managers Club of New York in 1917, IEA serves international business executives and the companies they represent. Services rendered consist of regular scheduled meetings, special meetings called to meet specific needs; social functions; educational programs; confidential personnel services; advisory services on business matters; a series of useful publications; and a unique "Questionnaire Service" issued whenever a member desires to have the entire membership polled on a specific problem or situation. IEAs 250 members are primarily executives of American firms in the field of international trade. It publishes a monthly bulletin, *International Trade Highlights*. Headquarters: 122 E 42nd Street, New York, NY 10017.

Management Consulting Professional Groups. Information on the following organizations will be found in the entry, MANAGEMENT CONSULTANTS:

Academy of Management, Division of Managerial Consultants.

Associaton of Consulting Management Engineers.

Association of Internal Management Consultants.

Association of Management Consultants.

Council of Management Consulting Organizations.

Institute of Management Consultants.

Management Advisory Services Division, American Institute of Certified Public Accountants.

Society of Professional Management Consultants.

National Management Association. Founded in 1925, NMA boasts 60,000 members from business and industrial management personnel. Most are from the supervisory level, but middle and upper management are also well represented. Its emphasis is on the free enterprise system and its promotion by the management profession. Chapter programs center around management policy and practice, communications, human behavior, industrial relations, economics, political education and productivity. Prior to 1956 it was the National Association of Foremen. Its major publication is *Manage*. Headquarters: 2210 Arbor Boulevard, Dayton, Ohio 45439.

Planning Executives Institute. The membership of this professional society is primarily corporate planners, budget directors, controllers, bankers, professors, and others dealing with planning. It was organized in 1951 and in 1980 had over 4,000 members. It was formed by the merger of several budget and management planning groups. Publications: research monographs and bimonthly *Managerial Planning*. Headquarters: 5500 College Corner Pike, Oxford, Ohio 45056.

Project Management Institute. Originally the Society of CPM Consultants and affiliated with SAM (see separate entry below), this group was founded in 1969 and currently has 2,500 members. Its primary objective is to foster recognition of the need for professionalism in project management and to provide a forum for the free exchange of project management problems, solutions and applications. It also coordinates industrial and academic research efforts and provides an interface between users and suppliers of hardware and software systems. It conducts programs for instruction and career development in the field of project management. Headquarters: P.O. Box 43, Drexel Hill, Pa. 19026.

Society for Advancement of Management (affiliated with the American Management Association). The Society for Advancement of Management (SAM) claims the oldest roots of all of the professional management societies. In 1912, the concept of professional management societies was realized first in the United States with the forming of the Society to Promote the Science of Management. This group changed its name in 1916 to the Taylor Society to honor FREDERICK W. TAYLOR. The Society for Advancement of Management was organized in 1936 by the union of the Taylor Society with the Society of Industrial Engineers, founded in 1917. Soon after, the Industrial Methods Society merged with SAM. As of 1980, over 200 SAM chapters covered cntinental United States and Canada, Hawaii, India, Japan, Puerto Rico, and South America.

The basic objectives of the Taylor Society and the Society of Industrial Engineers have been integrated and augmented. Local SAM chapters sponsor meetings, conferences, and other activities to help develop individual managers and improve management practices in their localities. Student SAM chapters are in operation in leading universities and colleges.

SAM gives national awards and citations each year for outstanding contributions in the functional areas of management, including the Taylor Key, the Gilbreth Medal, and the Emerson Trophy. Research reports and professional monographs are published on pertinent management subjects. SAM publishes *Advanced Management Journal* and *SAM News International.* Headquarters: 135 West 50th Street, New York, N.Y. 10020.

Effective December 31, 1972, all SAM members within the United States and internationally became members of the organization formed by the affiliation of SAM with the American Management Associations, ratified in mid-year.

Society for Management Information Systems. Members of SMIS, founded in 1968, numbered 1,400 in 1980, chiefly concerned with management information systems in the electronic data processing industry, including business systems designers, managers and educators. The Society serves as a clearing exchange for technical information about management information systems, including theory, applications, methodology, and techniques. It promotes improved communications between management information systems directors and the executives responsible for management of the business enterprise. SMIS offers educational and research programs, sponsors competitions, bestows awards, and maintains a speakers bureau. Headquarters: One Illinois Center, 111 E. Wacker Drive, Chicago, Ill. 60601.

Young Presidents' Organization, Inc. Founded in 1950, helps members become better presidents through local meetings, seminars, and area conferences. More than 70 chapters are located in the United States and in 45 countries throughout the world. Membership as of 1981 is over 3,300 successful young chief executives who have become presidents of sizable companies before the age of 40. Headquarters: 201 East 42nd St., New York, N.Y. 10017.

ANITA LOEBER, Consultant to Management (Organization, Systems, and Measurement), San Diego, California

MANAGERIAL EFFECTIVENESS: Climate for Organizational Results

This article describes a general blueprint which can serve as a foundation for developing higher levels of **Managerial Effectiveness.** It is based on the fundamental truism that a manager will not, by himself or herself, achieve organizational results but will rather, for most objectives require the cooperation, even enthusiastic support of staff members.

It is certainly obvious that an organization can achieve ambitious goals only if its people will contribute knowledge, skill, and effort, to the best of their ability. It is equally obvious that people will not continue to do so continuously if they are not rewarded appropriately for their contributions. Furthermore, "the best of their ability" will only be as much as it possibly can be if the organization helps individuals to develop to their maximum capabilities. All this requires several things:

(1) A climate which sets high expectations on individual performance and which supports individuals appropriately with the necessary knowledge and tools.

(2) An atmosphere of cooperation, which assures that each unit is aware of its functions and cooperates with other units.

(3) Tangible and psychological rewards which are perceived by the employees as fair,

or preferably, better than what they would obtain elsewhere.

Such a climate does not develop naturally. It requires capable leadership of people, and competent management of technical affairs.

Unfortunately, leadership and management have become very complex matters in the modern world. There are few comprehensive frameworks available which show the entire picture and can, therefore, serve as guides for the manager who wishes to achieve high level performance and a lasting achievement-oriented climate.

The Linking Elements Concept. Two diagrams, a simple one and a more elaborate one (Exhibits I and II), give an overview of what is termed here the "Linking Elements Concept" which can provide such a framework. Though the diagrams seem to concentrate on skills and strategies related to the management of people, they do not mean to imply that a competent manager does not also need a high level of personal imagination and creativity, as well as knowledge and skills in many diverse fields. Managers do need these. Much has been said, for instance, about the importance of intuitive judgment in determining the results which a manager achieves. That intuitive judgment, though, is also heavily influenced by the knowledge and skill base which the manager brings to bear on the problems and opportunities the organization faces.

The diagrams should also be seen as applying to the personal situation of the manager as well as to the other individuals in the organizational unit. The manager is also an individual who must bring alignment between his or her own needs and characteristics and those of the organization. For the manager, the diagrams, therefore, have a triple purpose:

(1) They provide a detailed road map to the analysis of the causes of organizational problems and opportunities.

(2) They provide a guide to the development of policies and procedures which will lead to the achievement of the highest possible level of performance.

(3) They are a device for analysis of personal strengths and weaknesses and for the development of self-improvement plans.

The two diagrams are closely related since the first one is merely a simplification of the second, more elaborate one. When their implications are understood, both can provide interesting insights into the skills a manager needs for outstanding performance. Both identify the *linking elements,* the skills and strategies which a manager must apply, with respect to the other people in the organization as well as with respect to himself/herself.

Exhibits I and II show what is commonly accepted: that an organization will achieve the performance it seeks—in other words, that it will be successful—if three conditions are met:

(1) It is in control of the situation. This means that it is making progress in the direction in which it wishes to go and no internal obstacles retard its progress.

(2) Its people have a high degree of technical competence for their jobs.

(3) Morale is good.

Control requires that:

(1) There are clear goals to show direction, and standards for gauging progress toward these goals.

(2) There are good systems and procedures to assure coordination so that conflict is avoided and each organizational segment properly supports the mission of the organization.

(3) Rules for personal behavior exist which help to assure that all individuals follow the same set of guidelines, and which at the same time, bring equitable treatment.

Technical competence speaks for itself. It cannot be universally defined. Every single position has a different set of skills and competencies that must exist if the position is to satisfy the role which the organization has assigned to it.

Morale can exist only if there are appropriate rewards for performance. These rewards are of two types: (1) tangible, contributing to the economic welfare of the individual, (2) psychological, contributing to a feeling of satisfaction with the job and with the organization.

In every organizational unit it is the manager's job to arrange for all of the above. He or she must look closely at individuals, at the characteristics and expectations which they bring to the organization because, in one way or another, these must be linked by the manager to the needs of the organization.

Referring to Exhibit II, the *characteristics and expectations* of individuals are:

(1) Personal performance standards which explain how much effort the individual is willing to devote toward the achievement of organizational goals.

(2) Willingness to cooperate, which determines, to a large extent, how well the individual will follow the coordination procedures.

(3) A personal behavior code, philosophy, and morality which guide adherence to, or lack of conformance with, the rules.

(4) Technical competence, and deficiencies relative to the technical knowledge/skill requirements of the position, and of other positions along the career path.

Two types of satisfactions concern the *needs* of individuals. These consist of:

(1) tangible ones, which seek fulfillment of economic needs.

(2) intangible ones, for the satisfaction of psychological needs.

Adapted from the findings of Abraham Maslow, the widely known behavioral scientist, these tangible and psychological needs are indicated in the right-hand portion of Exhibit II. (Cf. MOTIVATION: Maslow's "Basic Needs.")

Physiological needs include all the basic needs required for survival, such as food, clothing, and shelter.

Safety and security needs refer to the desire to see that these physiological needs are protected for the future. To the extent that it is not already covered under physiological needs, any danger to physical well-being is also included.

The desire for *comfort and luxury,* of course, expresses the human need for more than just bare existence.

Intangible needs relate to the feeling of security that comes from knowing that the organization is fair and reliable, that management is trustworthy. Included are the conviction that the organization will do its best to provide rewards for the individual as they are deserved or earned, and assurance that there will be no undeserved punishment.

Social and the esteem needs are the needs of people to be part of a group, to belong, and to be recognized as individuals, for accomplishments and for capabilities.

Finally, *self-realization,* is the highest of all psychological needs which drive people toward accomplishment. It brings self-satisfaction, personal confidence, and the feeling of having achieved what one is striving for.

Depending on the competence of the individual manager, employees in an organization unit will align their behavior to serve the unit's expectations for performance and they will feel appropriately rewarded in tangible and psychological ways. Conversely, also depending on the competence of the manager as leader and manager, many of the characteristics of the organizational units will be adapted to serve better the people who work in it, so that all aspects of the unit's internal environment are shaped into a smoothly functioning mechanism, with good directions, competence, and cohesiveness.

EXHIBIT I

ORGANIZATION

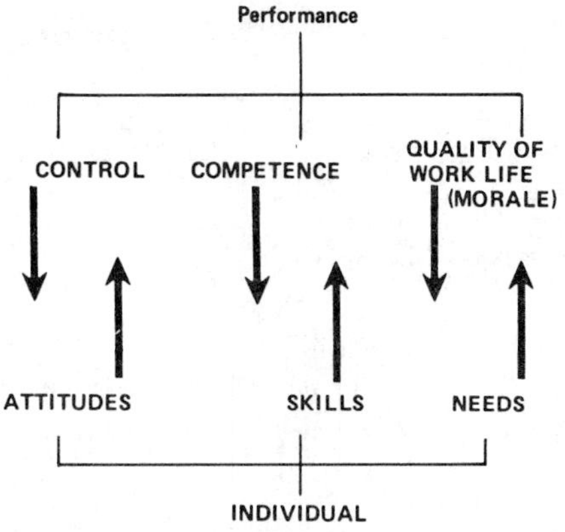

Linking Elements. Linking Elements describe the components of managerial competence. They have not been spelled out in the diagrams but are represented by the space between the misaligned arrows. Examples of appropriate skills and strategies for each set of arrows are listed below. These lists are not all-inclusive, nor are they the only way to look at the diagrams. They do provide an overview of the way the arrows could be brought into closer alignment.

For Control:

(1) Organizational Standards and Goals/Objectives

• Setting and communication of high quality goals and objectives

• Appropriate involvement and participation

• Regular progress reviews

• Meaningful placement of responsibility

• Avoidance of unnecessary paperwork and record keeping

(2) Coordination and Cooperation

• Relevant policies and procedures

• Appropriate counseling including competent use of questions and feedback

• Communication of procedures and policies

• Competent analysis of cooperation problems

EXHIBIT II

THE LINKING ELEMENTS CONCEPT

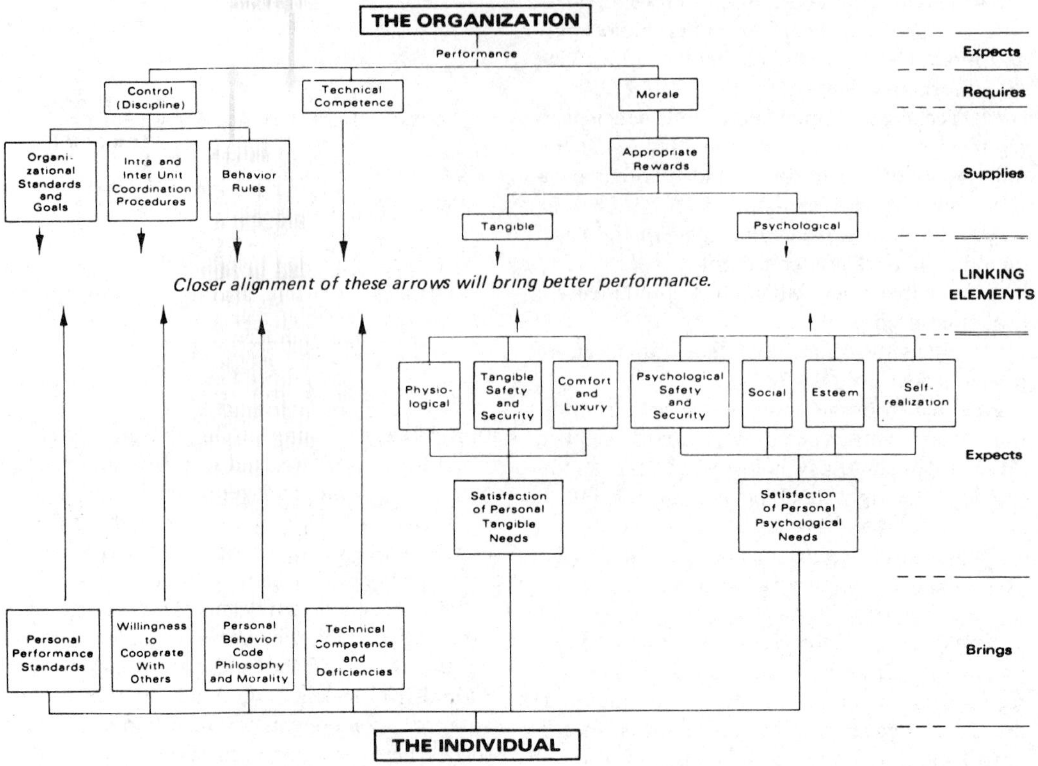

• Conflict management (prevention/recognition/resolution)

(3) Rules

• Relevant rules

• Communication, and reasonable and fair enforcement

• Personal observance by manager

For Technical Competence:

• Analysis of causes of performance problems

• Selection of candidates and applicants

• Competent training and development including individual needs analyses and individualized development plans

• Position management/organizational strategies

For Satisfaction of Tangible Needs:

• Appropriate compensation programs.

• Competent administration of compensation programs

• Competent administration of fringe programs

• Appropriate use of perquisites

For Satisfaction of Psychological Needs:

• Appropriate praise and recognition

• Elimination of inter- and intra-departmental frictions

• Establishment of trust and confidence

• Open two-way communications

When applying these skills and strategies, a manager must maintain a keen appreciation of the great interdependence of the individual linking elements and how each one contributes, or has the potential to detract from the positive, achievement-oriented climate.

ERWIN RAUSCH, President, Didactic Systems, Inc., Cranford, New Jersey

Information References

Laudicina, Mininberg, Nichols, Rausch, Scholz, and Weiss, "Management in Institutions of Higher Learning," Lexington, Mass., Lexington Books, 1980.

Rausch, Erwin, "Balancing Needs of People and Organizations," Washington, D.C., Bureau of National Affairs, 1978.

Cross References: *Motivation and entries with that prefix.*

MANAGERIAL GRID

The **Managerial Grid,** developed by Professors Robert R. Blake and Jane S. Mouton of the University of Texas and used in their executive leadership seminars, postulates two universal dimensions of management—a concern for *people* and a concern for *production.* As a logical extension of McGregor's theories (see MOTIVATION: McGregor's Theory X and Theory Y), they identify within this frame of reference five major styles of management. In their book, "The Managerial Grid," [1], they offer a thorough analysis of these styles, which reflect combinations of degrees of concern for production (plotted along the horizontal axis of a two-axis grid), and concern for people (plotted along the vertical axis). The grid is shown in Exhibit I.

A style described as 1,1 represents minimum concern for production and minimum concern for people. The 9,1 management represents a high concern for production and a low concern for people in the sense that human elements are not allowed to interfere to any great degree with production. Similarly, a 1,9 management style represents a high concern for people, coupled with a low concern for production. (The authors term this the "country-club" style of management, which makes for pleasant relationships until the need for competitive costs imposes more realistic work assignments and more rigid controls.) A 5,5 style represents a middle-of-the-road position. The ideal style is 9,9 in which concern for people is integrated with the goals of the organization.

The book offers a self-assessment rating guide with which the reader can compare his managerial style with norms developed from data collected by the authors. As an example, a description of the 9,9 style is offered here, as given in the self-assessment paragraphs:

> I place high value on getting sound, creative decisions that result in understanding and agreement. I listen for and seek out ideas, opinions, and attitudes different from my own. I have clear convictions but respond to sound ideas by changing my mind. When conflict arises, I try to identify reasons for it and resolve underlying causes. I rarely lose my temper, even when stirred up. My humor fits the situation and gives perspective; I retain a sense of humor even under pressure.

To bring a "moment of truth" into the proceedings, the executive seminars provide for

EXHIBIT I

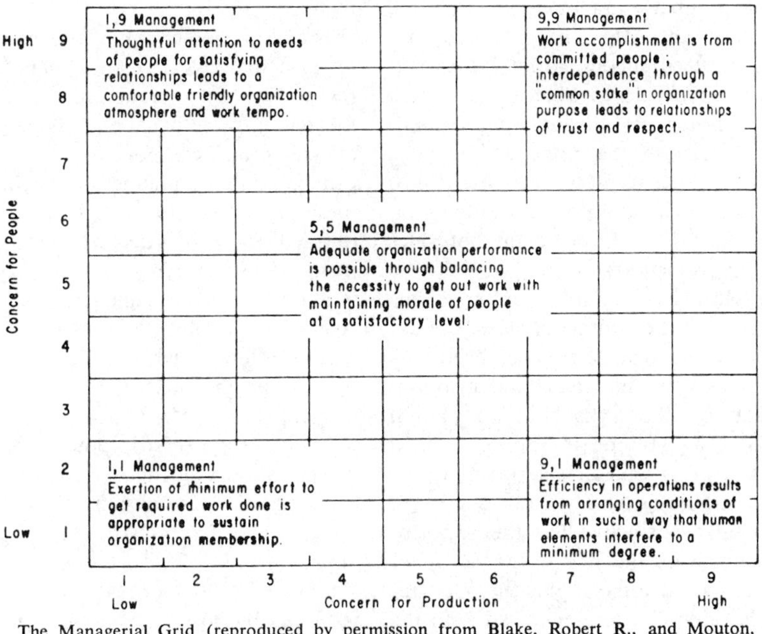

The Managerial Grid (reproduced by permission from Blake, Robert R., and Mouton, Jane S., "The Managerial Grid," copyright 1964, Gulf Publishing Company, Houston, Texas.)

assessment of each member by the other members of the group. Details given on all five managerial styles, and mixtures of them, provide a guide for self-improvement. Note that a high level of communication skills enters into the 9,9 elements that constitute the ideal style.

Reference Cited

[1] Blake, Robert R. and Mouton, Jane S., "The Managerial Grid," Houston, Texas, Gulf, 1964. (See also "The New Managerial Grid," same authors, Houston, Gulf, 1978.)

Cross References: *Hawthorne Experiments; Human Relations in Industry; Job Enrichment and Work Effectiveness; Managerial Effectiveness: Climate for Organizational Results; Motivation and accompanying entries with Motivation prefix).*

MANPOWER PLANNING. See Human Resources Requirements Planning.

MANUFACTURERS' REPRESENTATIVES

A **Manufacturers' Representative** is the independent sales representative for a group of manufacturers (referred to as the principals) in a defined sales territory. That territory may be defined geographically or by type of customer, or by both means.

Chief source of income to the MR is the commission paid by his principals upon the sale of their products and/or services in the sales territory of the MR. The MR does not receive a guaranteed income from his principals, except in special cases when for a limited time period a principal will guarantee a minimum income because the introduction of a product requires unusual initial expense. Thus, the income of the MR is dependent directly on the volume of gross sales made in that sales territory for his principals.

Since the selling expense for a principal thus varies directly with the volume of sales, the use of manufacturers' representatives has been particularly popular with the small- and medium-size manufacturer who lacks both the capital and potential sales volume to support a field sales force with its attendant salaries or drawing accounts and overhead costs. In addition to this advantage, the principal has the opportunity to make use of the MR's knowledge of and acceptance by customers, plus the opportunity to obtain "tie-in" sales connected with the sale of other products or services of the principals represented by the MR.

An MR represents from two to as many as 40 principals, depending upon the characteristics of the products and of the sales territory. No matter how few or how many, the guiding rule is that the products of all principals represented must be "related product lines." By the term "related product lines" is meant that the chief markets (defined by industry classification and also by the job responsibilities of those who specify and buy those products) must be the same. The established "sales call pattern" of MR salespeople, both as to companies called upon and the individuals called upon in those companies, should be such that the product lines of all the principals represented should have their major potential for sales within that "sales call pattern." Ideally, also, the products of the principals should be closely enough related in application so that the sale of the product for one principal will usually create the opportunity for the sale of the products of the other principals to fulfill customer's needs.

A manufacturers' representative can be one person or an organization of 20 or more salespeople and nearly as many clerical and inside engineering personnel. The trend in all fields has been away from the one- or two-man MR toward the development of sales organizations that fulfill in a sales territory the complete functions of field selling, sales analysis, sales promotion, and territory sales management.

Rates of Commission. The commission paid by principals to industrial manufacturers' representatives vary from only a few percent of the selling price to as high as 38%. In the field of electronic components, sold by the MR principally to manufacturers who incorporate these components in their own products (termed an OEM sale—to an "Original Equipment Manufacturer"), the average commission is about 5%. That same rate of 5% also is the customary amount of commission paid for a totally different type of sale—the sale at a high price when the MR's work is primarily contact and supplying information.

In the "engineered product" sale to industry, where salespeople must have the capability of assisting the customer to solve his problems, the average of commissions paid to the MR is approximately 17½%. The customary commission paid is 20% or 25%, but this average is reduced because the commission on repair parts is much less.

Many industrial MRs will carry in stock certain standard products from the product lines of their principals. They do not function then in the complete role of the distributor because they restrict their stocking to those items of their principals for which rapid delivery is desired by the customer. An MR who stocks, buys the products for his inventory from the principal and re-sells them to the customer, gaining his income from the discount at which the principal sells to him. Stated payment terms by the MR to the principal usually are 30 days net but in practice are extended to 60 and 90 days net.

In the consumer products market, such as "hardware" or "houseware," the commission ranges from 5% to 12%, with a mean of 10%.

The MR in this market usually sells to the wholesaler/distributor who sells to the dealer with the sales assistance of the MR. In some situations, the MR will sell direct to the distributor and/or to a chain and/or to a "dealer-owned organization" for whom the MR provides additional services such as demonstration clinics and other sell-through services.

Principals may pay higher commission rates than these on sales of a new product which has special features that require introduction and explanation and when probably the initial unit sale at any one time will be relatively low in dollars.

Special commission arrangements are made when an MR represents principals who provide service rather than a product. For example, an MR representing different principals who supply the services of gray iron castings and the like, is compensated relative to how much of a continuing contact and advisory service is rendered to the customer.

Some principals pay commissions to the MR upon receipt of the purchase order from the buyer, with provision for chargeback if the order should be cancelled or altered. Other principals pay commissions upon shipment of the order; still others do not pay commissions until they have been paid by the buyer.

Sales Promotion and Advertising. Direct mail is highly flexible and useful because the MR can control its distribution and tailor its sales appeal to the customers' needs. The promotion-minded MR uses the professional services of advertising agencies and direct-mail specialist.

One group of industrial manufacturers' representatives has worked together cooperatively for more than forty years in a scheduled direct-mail program wherein professionally-produced house organs are distributed for each manufacturers' representative in a sales territory over the latter's prospect list and identified as his (her) publication.

These customized house organs not only promote the sale of the product lines of the principals represented, but also present information on product application, product selection, news, and general engineering information. The costs of producing these publications are shared between the principals and the MRs, and they are produced, printed, and mailed at one time.

The local equipment show has been another growing method of local sales promotion. Again using the principle of sharing the costs between the principal and the MR, the local equipment show is set up usually in a rented hotel auditorium and attendance is by invitation only. These shows have been particularly successful where product lines of the principals represented are closely related.

A variation of the local equipment show is the traveling exhibit, using either a bus or a trailer as the mobile demonstration unit.

For customers for whom the potential purchase of the product lines is major, many industrial manufacturers' representatives assemble the product literature of principals into large binders that are presented to the buyers.

A related promotional activity is for the MR to have a catalog produced annually or biennially in which are included condensed descriptions of the products of the principals represented. These condensed catalogs are given wide initial distribution by mailing, and are also used by salespeople on their sales calls, for rapid review of the product lines represented.

Market Analysis. Some MRs make an extensive analysis of the prospective customers in their sales territory. This usually begins with classification according to industry by STANDARD INDUSTRIAL CLASSIFICATION (SIC). It then proceeds to detailed analysis, guided by information from principals as to market priorities of their major industries, followed by analysis of the buying influences within each of the major prospective customers within each industry. This analysis is made in recognition of the fact that approximately 80% of the sales of a given product will be made to approximately 20% of the prospective buyers.

From the foregoing studies, the MR plans

the sales-call pattern, frequency of calls, and sales promotion.

The established manufacturers' representative is an excellent means for field testing a product. He has a range of customer-friends from whom he can select a desired number to cooperate in using a new or changed product and reliably provide feedback information as to its qualities and deficiencies. This is done on a completely confidential basis.

Business Management. An increasing need has developed for knowledgeable business management by the MR. Working capital requirements have increased as the MR organization provides increasing amounts of back-up service to salespeople, enters into stocking arrangements, provides sales training and field supervision, and provides greater sales territory coverage and the development of salespeople by employing new representatives before product-line income is adequate for their support.

Contracts. The working agreement between a manufacturer and a manufacturers' representative varies from the informality of oral statements secured by a handshake to a formal contract supplemented by a written sales policy statement. In whatever form, it usually includes the following subjects:

> Definition of relationship (recognizing the independence of the principal and of the manufacturers' representative); territory and coverage; products to be sold; sales policy; prices; terms; customer, credit responsibility; product warranties; invoices; collections; cancellations; change orders; returns; commissions and methods of computation and division; servicing obligations of factory and representative; sales aids; and rights of principal and representative under consummation and termination.

Attempts are also made, sometimes, to include standards of performance for continuance of the contract. The majority of agreements in the past are cancellable upon thirty to sixty days' notice by either the principal or the representative without the need to show cause. However, recent agreements provide for extended notice of cancellation after the MR has represented the principal for a substantial time period.

Some principals establish quotas or targets, which the more progressive MRs welcome since these assist them in their planning and market analysis. In quota setting, each territory is evaluated by SIC classification according to the major markets of the principal's product line as determined by past performance and anticipated new product uses. The projected goal for the principal is then allocated to each territory. This evaluation requires a knowledge of other than the primary SIC classifications of larger companies. To provide additional incentive to reach targets or quotas, some principals provide a higher rate of commission when gross sales in a given territory exceed the target point. Frequently the target point is set at 80 to 85% of the quota.

Some manufacturers use the "trend-line" methods of evaluating the performance of each MR. The "trend-line" method takes into account the inertia effect, which is negative in regard to sales when an MR first handles the product lines of a principal and then has a positive effect after a number of years. The "trend-line" method also enables the manufacturer to recognize the need for improvement of a particular product or substitution for it even though sales continue to increase.

John Paul Taylor, President, The John Paul Taylor Company, St. Joseph, Michigan

Information References

Trade Association:

Since practices such as commission rates, splitting of commission advertising allowances, service requirements, billing procedures, etc., vary from industry to industry, the would-be principal will do well to secure information from a manufacturers' representatives' trade association if one exists in the industry concerned.

Material Marketing Associates, Inc., St. Joseph, Mich., is a so-called "closed" nonprofit trade association. The member MRs represent principals who market chemical materials and equipment to the chemical industry. By "closed" is meant that in each marketing area in the United and Canada, only one MR has been elected to membership. It communicates management information to its members and provides principals with such services as market research, selective mailing lists for direct mail campaigns, evaluation of new-product possibilities—all on a basis that is nationwide in scope or pinpointed to selected territories.

Professional Manufacturers' Agents, Inc., St. Joseph, Mich., is composed of members who sell principally to the paint sundry trade. Every marketing area throughout the United States has multiple PMA membership.

Industrial Marketing Associates, Inc., St. Joseph, Mich., has two types of members: manufacturers' representatives who sell industrial equipment to all industry, and manufacturers who sell through MRs as their principal marketing means. It provides a medium for the interchange of business management information, and brings together principals and MRs at national and regional meetings.

Manufacturers' Agents National Association, Irvine,

Calif., includes MRs for all types of goods and services, from costume jewelry to foundry facilities. Membership is not restricted or qualified. A principal activity is the publication of *The Agent and Representative,* as well as conducting an annual convention. The monthly magazine provides an advertising medium for manufacturers seeking representatives, and representatives seeking additional principals.

Hardware Affiliated Representatives, Inc., St. Joseph, Mich., is composed of manufacturers' representatives throughout the United States and Canada who market hardware lines principally to distributors, chains, and "dealer-owned" cooperatives.

Heavy Duty Representatives Association, Inc., St. Joseph, Mich., is composed primarily of manufacturers' representatives who market parts and accessories to the heavy duty vehicle and equipment market, both OEM and aftermarkets.

Cross References: *Industrial Distributors; Marketing; Marketing: Patterns of Population Growth.*

MANUFACTURING MANAGEMENT

Manufacturing Management is that portion of business management concerned with the planning, direction, and control of production and allied services performed in the manufacturing industry. Specifically it deals with the forming assembling, finishing, packaging, and shipping of a product. In terms of objectives, manufacturing management is charged with the responsibility to produce a product of specified quality at a competitive cost and to make it available for delivery to the customer at a time stipulated by the Sales Department. As such, its operations can be differentiated from other major management functions such as marketing, research and development, or finance.

Stated simply, manufacturing management is concerned with the production of a product within the limits of cost, quality, and time established by the marketing and financial policies of the total organization.

History. More than any other portion of management, manufacturing management finds its roots in SCIENTIFIC MANAGEMENT and the division of labor. Manufacturing management utilizes most fully the techniques of applied engineering fundamentals in the measurement and control of work and of human activity.

In its earliest form, manufacturing management was concerned mainly with production. Examination of ancient ruins gives evidence that the Egyptians systematically organized the efforts of many people in producing goods. However, it was not until the Industrial Revolution that the productive efforts of individuals were regularly organized in factories. The factory system was developed concurrently with the introduction of machinery and centralized power sources.

During the years prior to 1900 it was not uncommon to find the owner of a factory (the entrepreneur) subcontracting the production activities to a shop superintendent. This superintendent hired and directed his own employees in processing the materials of manufacture, which were generally supplied by the owner, on the owner's equipment, and in the owner's plant. As production processes grew more complex, the owners retained greater control over production operations—finally employing engineers and other production experts to manage this function. With the advent of scientific management in the early 1900s, management of production began to grow in scope to include all the functions related to manufacturing of a product.

Scope of Manufacturing. Over the years, many auxiliary management and engineering services have been introduced in the manufacturing industries to support production (or line) management. Rather than performing these auxiliary functions itself, in most companies the line management (while retaining ultimate accountability) depends upon the advice, guidance, or services of specialized staff departments. Most typically these services include:

Industrial Relations, directed toward employee retirement, job placement, and training. It is concerned with labor union negotiations, and aids in establishing and administrating pay practices. In general, its objective is to develop a cohesive, well motivated, and effective work force.

Costing and Budgeting may report either directly or indirectly to manufacturing management. The manufacturing manager employs it to plan the financially related aspects of his operation, such as the establishment of operating budgets, and to accumulate and control production and related costs.

Production Planning furnishes production schedules and machine loading programs, and expedites work as it flows through the plant.

Inventory Control works closely with Marketing and Finance to determine when, and how much, inventory should be accumulated.

Industrial Engineering is the means by which engineering principles are applied to manufacturing problems. Typically, this function deals with work measurement, work methods, wage incentives, and standard costs. In most plants it also encompasses materials handling, plant layout, production machinery specifications, and manufacturing engineering.

Plant Maintenance has to do with the upkeep and repair of production equipment, buildings, and plant services.

Plant Engineering is concerned with the design, construction, and installation of plant facilities and services.

Quality Control responsibility includes inspection and test of in-process and finished products, utilizing statistical techniques in order to control product manufacture within specified quality limits.

Purchasing. While manufacturing management does not always supervise the procurement function, it exerts considerable influence upon the purchase of materials, supplies, services, equipment, and facilities, as they facilitate or impede the production process.

Traffic is generally concerned with scheduling of raw materials into the plant and delivery of finished goods from the plant warehouse to either regional warehouses or the customer's facility.

Product Design normally lies between the realm of manufacturing and marketing, although each area exerts an influence.

Measures of Effectiveness. The measure of how well manufacturing management performs its function is often a simple comparison between the profits manufacturing generates as compared with the capital monies put into the manufacturing operation, namely the rate of return on capital investment. For instance, if an automatic lathe is purchased for $100,000 and it saves $25,000 per year as the result of its increased output, the rate of return is expressed as 25%. Conversely, this investment may be described as having a "four-year payback." (For a more sophisticated treatment of what has here been stated in simplified form, see FIXED-ASSET INVESTMENT ANALYSIS: the MAPI Formulas and Procedures, and RETURN ON CAPITAL.)

When this rate of return principle is applied to *all* input costs—labor, materials, machinery, utilities, building facilities—and compared to total value of product output, it is probably the most comprehensive measure of the effectiveness of manufacturing management performance.

Other performance measures include those of material- or equipment-utilization, delivery schedule conformance, budget adherence, extent of operating cost reduction, reduction in rejects, labor productivity, and state of employee morale (as indicated by attitude surveys, accident records, number of grievances, extent of tardiness and absenteeism, and strikes).

Productivity and Automation. Manufacturing management's continuous objective is that of improving productivity—of the capital invested in the operation, and of materials, machinery, and manpower. Traditionally, this improvement is achieved through (1) more effective utilization of present resources and (2) replacement or modernization of existing equipment and facilities with more efficient ones. Either approach has as an ultimate effect the increased productivity of the total manpower employed.

Attaining greater return from existing resources usually takes the form of METHOD IMPROVEMENT or WORK SIMPLIFICATION, designed to reduce *total* cost of operation or *net* cost per unit of production. Replacement of hand methods or obsolete equipment is dependent upon the investment of capital in new facilities that, compared with existing ones, produce at faster rates, perform new operations, finish to higher specifications, or provide any of a number of improved services.

Replacement of human activity by machinery is termed *mechanization.* As the rate of mechanization accelerates and becomes more complex, employing principles of *feedback* and highly sophisticated controls, it is called *automation.* But it is important that the label not obscure the fact that automation *and* cost reduction are both employed by management to reduce inputs or increase outputs, or both, in order to improve manufacturing productivity. (See AUTOMATION.)

Manufacturing Management Trends. Since 1950, manufacturing employment in the United States has remained relatively constant while declining in its ratio to the total American labor force. In part, this reflects management's success in raising direct-labor productivity. Productivity of the *entire* manufacturing workforce during this period has been considerably slower. This has been due to the rise in indirect-labor input into manufacturing. More supervision, larger maintenance forces, increased number of clerical employees and engineering staffs are some examples. Consequently, since the 1960s management has shifted its productivity efforts to include non-productive costs as well as producing costs.

The introduction of computers and advanced data handling systems has also brought a greater integration of manufacturing functions.

High priorities are being placed on coordinating production and inventory schedules with marketing information.

Development of machines with higher performance capabilities plus intensification of consumer demands for better products are bringing about renewed efforts to improve product quality and reliability.

Finally, economic and political factors have caused manufacturing management to become increasingly aware of the impact of its efforts beyond the factory. Unemployment, air and stream pollution, water consumption, are examples of the civic responsibilities it now is sharing with the general public.

LESTER R. BITTEL, formerly Editor, *Factory*, New York, New York

Information References

Associations:

American Institute of Industrial Engineers.
American Management Associations.
American Society of Mechanical Engineers.
National Association of Manufacturers.

Periodicals:

American Industry.
Industrial Maintenance & Plant Operation.
New Equipment Digest.

Texts:

Bethel, L. L., Atwater, F. S., Smith, G. H. E., and Stackman, H. A., Jr., "Industrial Organization and Management," 5th ed., New York, McGraw-Hill, 1971

Smith, M., "Manufacturing Controls," New York, Van Nostrand Reinhold, 1981.

Cross References: *Automation; Cost Accounting; Cost Control; Industrial Districts; Industrial Engineering; Maintenance; Materials Management; Materials Management: Material Handling Equipment Types; Method Improvement; Operation Analysis; Plant Engineering; Plant Location; Process Analysis; Process Engineering; Production: Large-Scale; Production Planning and Inventory Management; Purchasing; Work Simplification.*

MARKETING

The essence of **Marketing** can be distilled into two concepts: *customer orientation* and the *integrated use of all of a company's resources* to aid and abet the firm in supplying wanted goods and services at a profit to itself. As Peter Drucker has said: "Marketing is so basic that it cannot be considered a separate function . . . It is the whole business seen from the point of view of its final result, that is, from the customer's point of view" [1].

Marketing—trade distribution—erupted into a major national and business problem in 1946. The combination of a major depression and war—vast unfilled wants coupled with ability to pay and huge productive capacity—gave the nation the greatest potential it had ever known. Several significant changes resulted:

(1) Emphasis upon mass distribution along with mass production.

(2) New industries and products (electronics, chemicals, plastics, drugs, etc.).

(3) Huge sums spent on research and development.

(4) Importance and wide acceptance of marketing research (including motivation research and operations research).

(5) Consumer orientation—as opposed to production orientation—as part of the "new marketing concept."

(6) Profit orientation rather than sales orientation.

(7) Marketing management as a major company division.

(8) The development of product managers.

(9) Product innovation coupled with an increased rate of product obsolescence.

(10 Discounting as a retailing way of life.

(11) Large-scale retailing in terms of size of store, number of stores under one control, and amount and variety of goods carried.

(12) International selling.

Too little recognized—and, therefore, leading to confusion—is the fact that marketing may be looked at from both a macro and a micro point of view. At the national level, marketing is charged with the responsibility of moving our vast and growing gross national product. Concurrently, it is the delicate fulcrum balancing production with consumption. If marketing, in toto, does not operate efficiently, turmoil may result. Marketing may also be perceived as a vast communications system, giving information regarding product availability to consumers while feeding back data regarding consumers' wants to producers.

While philosophically the competitive market place regulates total activity, nevertheless, marketing managers (whatever their titles) of individual firms carry a heavy responsibility, for their cumulative actions lead to balance or imbalance in our economy. Within the firm (micro viewpoint), marketing managers share—perhaps carry the major portion of—the responsibility for profits. They recommend what to produce, when, at what price; they are responsible for informing consumers and moving the firms' goods through a network of salesmen, channels of distribution to consumers, *at a minimum cost* (profit rather than sales orientation).

But increasingly the controllable elements in the company's marketing plan (that is, controllable by the company) are being profoundly influenced by variables uncontrollable by the firm, and there must be factored into the formulation of marketing strategy. Among these variables are:

- Stabilized population growth.
- Shift to the so-called Sun Belt states.
- Continued institutional inflation.
- Continuing electronics explosion.
- Health care considerations; environmental control.
- Worldwide egalitarian push, by force if necessary.
- Changing customer social and psychological values.
- Uncertainties of commodity and raw material supply.
- Pressure for increased social responsibility.
- Increasing prominence of women as a marketing force.
- Increasing senior citizen power.
- Competitive compression, with everyone seemingly entering everyone else's business, and with quicker competitive response.
- Continuing blurring of traditional markets, marketing relationships, and marketing practice.
- Intensifying regulation-deregulation face-off.

Today's marketing manager is more analytical and sophisticated than the old sales manager. He must have more than a surface knowledge of psychology, sociology, and anthropology if he is adequately to forecast consumer wants and behavior and guide men; he must know statistics and mathematics in order better to solve the more complex and interrelated marketing logistical problems; he must know about electronic data processing to do better research , control inventories, and obtain information for decision-making.

Definition. Marketing is admittedly an elusive, all-embracing, and often confusing term. It has been described variously as a group of business activities, a trade phenomenon, a structure of institutions, and a frame of mind.

Marketing has been defined by the Committee on Definitions of the American Marketing Association as "the performance of business activities that direct the flow of goods and services from producer to consumer" [2]. This definition has been improved by McCarthy: "Marketing is the performance of business activities that direct the flow of goods and services from producer to consumer or user in order to best satisfy customers and accomplish the firm's objectives" [3].

Subject Branches. Perhaps a more fruitful way of appreciating marketing is to see what is involved in the activity:

(1) People (as buyers and sellers in a culture).
(2) Goods and services (product innovation).
(3) Channels of distribution (a complex of wholesaling and retailing institutions).
(4) Performance of functions:
  (a) Marketing information and research
  (b) Buying
  (c) Selling (personal, advertising, promotion, publicity)
  (d) Transportation
  (e) Storage
  (f) Financing
  (g) Risk-taking
  (h) Standardization and grading
  (i) Consumer services.
(5) Pricing.
(6) Laws and the governments.
(7) The environment, including competition.
(8) Marketing management (creativity, planning, control).
(9) Transfer of title.

Profitable, efficient marketing implies combining many interrelated variables in correct proportions in a dynamic system.

History. "Marketing"—as old as man—is now in its third stage. The first, up to the time of the Industrial Revolution in the United States in the middle of the nineteenth century, relegated marketing to a rather low status. Agriculture was all-important. Stage two thus started about 1850 and ended somewhere in the first quarter of the twentieth century. During this time, manufacturing superseded agriculture in importance; nevertheless, marketing was subjected to various investigations, first by theorists—economists such as Alfred Marshall, agricultural economists, and students of business cycles—and, increasingly since 1900, by marketing men themselves, as a formal area of study.

The third stage—the current one—reflects the dynamics of our economy, with more and more engaged in the service industries. Marketing is now studied by and uses the talents of statisticians, mathematicians, economists, historians, psychologists, sociologists, anthropologists, accountants, logicians, and lawyers, in addition to those directly engaged in marketing and management.

Concepts and Practices. Current concepts and practices of marketing are detailed elsewhere in the present work, and are cross-referenced below. Two terms bear mentioning here: The first is *new marketing concept.* While not uniformly defined, it implies: consumer orientation, management and profit orientation, and innovation orientation by marketing leaders. The second term, *marketing mix* refers to the combination of variables necessary for efficient, successful marketing. It does not imply any one correct combination, but rather an efficient combination changing over time.

Significant is the fact that an organization (Marketing Science Institute) was established in 1962 with the sole purpose of developing theoretical constructs of marketing with the use of highly developed scientific techniques.

As to organization, more and more companies are today establishing the post of Vice President—Marketing, with top responsibility for all functions having to do with selling and distribution in all of their aspects.

A good illustration of marketing as a system is the current impact "consumerism," an environmental factor, is having upon marketing practice. Today, consumer reaction to certain practices is now organized and has greatly influenced the establishment of special governmental offices at all levels designed to protect the consumer. In addition, there is much new legislation and the Federal Trade Commission and Congress have increased the number and rate of hearings dealing with this topic. (See CONSUMER PROTECTION.)

Finally, there have been significant changes in the area of international marketing. One such change has to do with the increased number of "common markets." (Cf. EUROPEAN ECONOMIC COMMUNITY; EUROPEAN FREE TRADE ASSOCIATION.) Another is the growth of multinational firms. (See INTERNATIONAL MANAGEMENT: Management of the "World Enterprise.")

Marketing Strategies. To cope with the myriad complexities of marketing, professionals in the field—with marketers of consumer packaged goods in the vanguard—have developed a number of fundamental strategies. To cite several of critical significance:

Market Segmentation. Identifying and concentrating on factions of a total market capable of yielding more than proportionate volume and profit in return for the gratification of the special needs of that segment.

Market Stretching. A series of actions to be utilized at various stages of a product's existence to sustain its sales and profit performance, rather than allowing the usual decline to occur.

Multi-brand Entries. Offering more than one brand in a given product category.

Brand Extension. Use of a successful brand name to bring out related products using that name.

LEE ADLER, President, Lee Adler & Company, New York, New York

Information References

Associations:

Advertising Research Foundation.
Marketing Division, American Management Association.
American Marketing Association.
Marketing Science Institute.
National Retail Merchants' Association.
National Association of Wholesalers.

Periodicals:

Advertising Age.
Harvard Business Review.
Industrial Marketing.
Journal of Business.
Journal of Marketing.
Journal of Marketing Research.
Journal of Retailing.
Sales and Marketing Management.

Texts:

Adler, Lee, "Plotting Marketing Strategy," New York, N.Y., Simon & Schuster, 1977.
Alderson, Wroe, "Marketing Behavior and Executive Action," Homewood, Ill., Irwin, 1964.
Bartels, Robert, "The History of Marketing Thought," 2nd ed., Columbus, Ohio, Grid, 1976.
Buell, Victor P. and Heyel, Carl, eds., "Handbook of Modern Marketing," New York, McGraw-Hill, 1970.
Kotler, Philip, "Marketing Management: Analysis, Planning & Control," 4th ed., Englewood Cliffs, N.J., Prentice-Hall, 1980.

Moyer, Rood, "Macro Marketing: A Social Perspective," New York: J. Wiley, 1972.

Webster, F.E., Jr., "Social Aspects of Marketing," Englewood Cliffs, N.J., Prentice-Hall, Inc., 1974.

References Cited

[1] Drucker, Peter F., "Management: Tasks, Responsibilities, Practices," New York, Harper & Row, 1973.

[2] "Marketing Definitions," American Marketing Association, Chicago, 1960.

[3] McCarthy, E. Jerome, "Basic Marketing, A Managerial Approach, 6th ed., Homewood, Ill., Irwin, 1979.

Cross References: *Advertising (and accompanying entries with Advertising prefix); Business Forecasting; Consumer Behavior Research; Distribution Planning and Research; Industrial Distributors; Industrial Purchasing Power: The SM&M Annual Survey; Manufacturers' Representatives; Marketing: Changing Patterns of Distribution (and accompanying entries with Marketing prefix); New Product Development (and accompanying entries with New Product prefix); Operations Research in Marketing; Prices: Statistics; Pricing: Legal Aspects (and accompanying entries with Pricing prefix); Sales Management; Sales Promotion; Sales Statistics; Sales Training; Standard Industrial Classification (S.I.C.); Standard Metropolitan Statistical Areas; U.S. Census of Manufacturers; U.S. Economic and Business Censuses.*

MARKETING: Patterns of Consumer Goods Distribution

When goods are scarce and demand is plentiful, marketing tends to be limited to, and synonymous with, **Distribution,** the *physical function of moving goods from place to place.* The emphasis in business firms is on *producing* a vast array of products which are readily accepted by a "hungry" marketplace. This continued emphasis on production implies huge research and development expenditures so that a constant stream of products may flow through the existing channels of distribution. Profits are turned into larger plants and the result is not unlike a science fiction monster, feeding on itself, and increasing its capacity until there is more product than demand. Then the shoe switches to the other foot and marketing assumes the rich role it has in our modern economy.

Oversimplified, and with the details omitted for the sake of clarity, the paragraph above describes the *evolution* which took place in the American economy as it grew from colonial times to the end of World War II. What happened after that can best be described by the word *revolution.*

Pent-up consumer demand of the Depression-World War II period exploded in the years that followed, greatly enlarging the capacity of the productive monster. Anything which could be produced was produced, and things which existed only as vague images in the minds of their creators were given substance and sent out into the marketplace. Products (and their packages) proliferated in a seemingly endless variety of sizes, shapes, styles, colors and grades. As the productive technology advanced and more and more products clogged existing channels, two things had to happen:

(1) *Producing* and *making* took a back seat to *marketing.* This occurred in the 1950s and is embodied in what is commonly referred to as "the marketing concept."

(2) Existing channels of distribution went through drastic changes to accommodate the volume of products moving through them.

Retail Outlets—End of the Channel. Discount stores (or mass merchants as they prefer to be called), door-to-door selling, vending machines, and franchises are but a few of the innovations that have occurred in retailing over the past thirty-five years to accommodate the increased output of the American production machine. As these new channels developed, existing channels expanded and contracted to adjust to the changing patterns of distribution.

There was a time when one knew what a store sold by virtue of the sign on the door. Today, auto supplies are sold in drug stores, drugs are sold in food stores, and food is sold in department stores. Moreover, retailers sell wholesale, wholesalers sell retail, soft goods are sold in hardware stores and discount stores sell everything! Confusing? Yes! Easy to manage? No!

Discounters ($55 billion volume in 1980—up from $2 billion in 1959) have set a furious pace for other retailers to follow. *Variety stores* have upgraded and widened their lines until they have become indistinguishable from discounters. Woolworth, historically a variety store operation, has expanded into discount (Woolco) operations. S. S. Kresge has likewise expanded into discount operations with K-Mart and Jupiter stores.

Traditional *department stores* joined the race by establishing or acquiring discount divisions. Examples, with discount divisions in parenthesis, are: Dayton-Hudson (Target and Lechmere), Federated (Gold Circle), Gamble-Skogmo (Tempo), May Company (Venture), Rich's (Richway). Supermarket and drugstore chains have gotten into the act by carrying more general merchandise items and by establishing separate divisions as Grand Union did with Grand-Way.

The *leased department operator* (really only a refinement and extension of the *rack-jobber*) brought detailed knowledge of displaying, selling, and servicing products unrelated to a store's primary merchandise lines. However, in some discount stores large percentages of the departments were leased, and the carnival atmosphere was not unlike that experienced in the fairs of medieval Europe. Today, however, the percentage of leased departments in most discount stores is negligible. But the 1980s may well bring an increase in specialty leased departments (optical, travel, insurance, beauty care) as the department stores and discounters stores alike seek new ways to improve sales productivity of selling space under severe pressure from declining population growth and a weakened economy.

The furious pace of the 1960s gave birth to the *retail conglomerate.* City Stores (department, specialty, furniture stores), Dayton-Hudson (department, discount, jewelry, book stores), Gamble-Skogmo (department, discount, specialty, food, drug, variety stores), Interco (department, discount, hardware, shoe stores), Interstate Department Stores (department, discount, toy stores), Zale Corporation (jewelry, variety, shoe, toy, furniture, sporting goods and drug stores) are but a few of the many companies which expanded their operations to sell a multitude of product lines in a variety of places. Just as the discount store has brought one-stop shopping to the consumer, the retail conglomerate resulted in one-stop selling for manufacturers and wholesalers.

For a variety of reasons, some of these conglomerates failed in the 1950s and 1960s as big cities began their deterioration. People moved to the suburbs and retailing followed. And when every grassy meadow became a shopping center parking lot, and the market was "overstored," there was no place left to go—unless one jumped across country and invaded another retailer's market area. Thus, Broadway-Hale stores, traditionally based in Los Angeles and its suburbs, in 1961 announced plans to buy New York's Bergdorf Goodman, and San Francisco-based I. Magnin stated that it would soon open a new store in Chicago. Lord & Taylor of New York, which had never before opened a store more than an overnight truck ride away in 1970 opened a store in Atlanta and began looking as far west as Houston. More examples of this retail leapfrog are being announced every day, and we can expect this trend to continue in the future as retail mobility tries to keep up with individual mobility.

In the mid-1970s the gasoline crisis slowed the exodus to the suburban malls. Retailers began rethinking their decisions about site location, and some began refurbishing their urban and downtown stores. While neither retailers nor consumers are abandoning the suburbs, the city will loom much larger in the plans of merchants in the 1980s.

Automatic Retailing. This form of distribution has not lived up to the expectations marketers had for it in the 1950s, largely because the technology involved has not kept up with other technologies. Except for food items and cigarettes, vending machines do not play a significant role in the distribution of goods. While the "vending industry" did an estimated $12.8 billion in food sales in 1979, much of this volume was accounted for by the fact that the giants of the industry, such as Canteen Corporation, Servomation Corporation, Interstate United Corporation, and Macke Company, have gone into such fields as restaurants, airlines catering, fast-food franchising, and the operation of hotels and recreation areas.

Door-to-door Selling. This form of distribution, despite well known individual successes such as Avon Products, is likewise not a significant factor. The crime problem in inner cities tends to preclude its use, and in rural areas the method is too expensive. In suburban areas the expansion of various types of retail outlets previously mentioned has tended to negate the effectiveness of door-to-door marketing programs.

Future of Retailing. After decades of expansion and diversification, the retail industry as of the early 1980s faces a time of reappraisal. Inflation, the energy squeeze, and a changing economy are altering the rules for all segments of retailing, affecting every aspect from store location to marketing strategies to productivity. Retailers, regardless of size, will face difficult adjustments during the 1980s. And survival—not to mention profitability or growth—will demand vision, wisdom, and adequate resources.

High inflation, high interest rates, and expensive energy are central challenges to both the consumer and the retailer in this decade. Devising successful strategies to meet these challenges depends on the degree of professionalism the retailer brings to bear on them.

In addition to dealing with high inflation, high interest rates, and expensive energy, the retailer of the eighties must adjust to the changes in his consumer profile, and to their effect on buying patterns. For example, the country's population as a whole is getting older, and the retailer must revise his marketing plans to correspond to that change. As population shifts toward the "Sunbelt" regions, retailers must follow. More women are joining the work force, and retailers must react to their new shopping schedules. Higher gasoline costs will reduce shopping trips, forcing retailers to accommodate a more efficient, better organized shopper. Changing credit rules, less discretionary income, and a heightened consumerism will demand more accountability from the merchant.

Caught in the middle between soaring costs and the shrinking consumer dollar, the retailer will continue to feel the pressure to keep prices down. To do so, he must find ways to improve efficiency and flexibility in areas such as scheduling sales help, improving the flow and turn of inventory, and modifying the merchandise mix. Traditional store hours may have to be reduced drastically to reduce costs. The number and locations of stores wil have to be scrutinized. The gasoline crunch may lead to the rebirth of the downtown store.

Successful retailers of the eighties will advance in their collection and use of information, extending the applications of technology. Electronic scanning, automated order entry, and universal vendor marking will make decision making more quantifiable. New offerings such as electronic shopping and payment, insurance, travel, banking, legal and dentistry services will be a part of retailing in this decade. The specialty store in apparel, food and other goods will take a greater market share because of its ability to economize while offering a depth of assortment in relatively limited lines and price points. Other retailing segments will, to some extent, follow the trend toward narrower and more limited lines.

Wholesaling—Turmoil in the Middle. As retail channels have gone through considerable transformation, keeping pace with a mobile consumer who demanded one-stop shopping, so too have wholesale channels expanded their horizons beyond "traditional" wholesaling functions. In the early 1950s there were some observers who predicted a gloomy future for the merchant wholesaler. Since retailers and manufacturers were getting larger and beginning to assume some of the wholesaling functions, wholesalers, they argued, would be caught in the middle and squeezed out of business.

In 1954, sales of *merchant wholesalers* were \$101.3 billion, or 28% of the Gross National Product. By 1968, sales of merchant wholesalers had more than doubled to \$219.9 billion, and then soared to \$883.3 billion in 1979. At worst, wholesaling has kept pace with other segments of the economy, and dire predictions about the uncertain future of the merchant wholesaler have not come true.

The survival (even growth) of the merchant wholesaler has not been accomplished without much turmoil. Those companies unable to adjust to the changing patterns of distribution brought about by the washing away of traditional product-line barriers in retail stores have withered and disappeared. Others have grown and prospered by continuing to provide essential services to manufacturers and retailers despite encroachment (through vertical integration) by these institutions.

"Conventional" marketing systems and relationships (i.e., many small, loosely aligned and independent manufacturers, wholesalers and retailers), have given way to vertical marketing systems (large vertically integrated manufacturers, wholesalers and retailers performing ancillary marketing functions through manufacturers' stores, voluntary chains, retailer cooperatives, franchises, etc.). Proliferating product lines by manufacturers and "scrambled merchandising" by retailers have forced the merchant wholesaler to:

(1) Abandon traditional concepts of "product lines" and instead adopt multiple marketing strategies so as to be able to satisfy the needs of a more diverse group of retailers.

(2) Take a hard look at the products and the merchandise lines carried in order to determine the most profitable mix.

No longer are sales the sole objective of the merchant wholesaler. The sheer magnitude of the number of suppliers and outlets in today's economy virtually assures that volume will be achieved. Instead, the merchant wholesaler must carefully select those product lines that he can *service* most effectively within the constraints presented by his business operations. Every item which the wholesaler carries must be identified, labeled, handled (perhaps two or three times), stacked, controlled, picked, packed, shipped, and invoiced. Multiply each of these operations by some very large number which represents the number of separate stock-keeping units he carries, and one has a very complex operation indeed.

The computer is being called upon more and more to assist both in the management of day-to-day operations and in the evaluation of the profitability of various lines of merchandise. New techniques which harness the power of the computer for inventory management, warehousing, transportation and location analysis, financial planning, and accounting and control, are rapidly being developed to help the merchant wholesaler keep in step with ever-changing markets, suppliers, and product lines.

Finally, merchant wholesalers have expanded the services they offer to retailers. Thus, maintenance of account records, merchandising support, inventory management, and product line profitability analysis are new services offered by some wholesalers to their retail accounts in an attempt to provide more useful service and bind them to their customers.

Conclusion. Distribution, like other business functions, is constantly changing to meet the challenges presented by a changing political, economic, and social world. Not every company will make equal progress in adapting its operations to these changes. But all will spend a lot of time trying. Some will fail and disappear. Others will succeed and be stronger for it because, like good halfbacks, they were able to change direction rapidly and with little notice. The outcome for our economy will be a stronger, more effective, and less costly distribution network.

LAURENCE N. GARTER, Partner, Touche Ross & Co., New York, New York

Information References

Buell, Victor P. and Heyel, Carl, "Handbook of Modern Marketing," New York, McGraw-Hill, 1970.

Publications of National Retail Merchants Association.

Stores

Publications:

Chain Store Age

Stores

Vending Times (sp. annual census).

Cross References: *Franchising; Marketing (and cross references there given)*

MARKETING COST ANALYSIS

Marketing Cost Analysis in its broadest sense is concerned with the study of the costs incurred from the time goods are manufactured to final delivery and payment, with a view toward providing the members of the marketing organization with useful quantitative financial information. The information is designed to aid in planning, decision making, and control at all levels of the marketing organization. The tools of analyses employed are derived from accounting and other related disciplines using quantitative methods.

It should be pointed out that the term *marketing* as used here is more than selling or order getting. It includes the activities of personal selling (field selling), impersonal selling (advertising, sales promotion, etc.), physical distribution (warehousing, order filling, and shipping), marketing research, and any other function assigned to a marketing department. The definition is particularly relevant in the light of the wide adoption of what is called the *marketing concept.* Progressive companies have accepted a changed view of the marketing function. Its task is no longer viewed as selling that which has been produced. Instead, marketing is placed at "the beginning" of the process. It is the function of marketing to ascertain market needs, present and future, as guides to research. By its forecast, marketing indicates what will be sold, when, to whom, and at what price. Manufacturing as well as research are then geared to the market needs. This has resulted in new and important responsibilities for the marketing executive. As an important member of the management team, he must be concerned with more than just sales volume. He is now concerned, as are his colleagues on the top management team, with maximizing the return on the investment in the business through effective planning, decision making, and control.

Marketing Cost Information — Defining Needs. In developing financial information for marketing management, the analyst must have a clear understanding of the specific responsibilities assigned to the members of the marketing management team. This provides knowledge on the types of problems faced, the kinds of information necessary in planning and decision making, and on the control areas delegated. This is the most important because of the inclination of accounting-oriented analysts to design information based on a limited perception of the marketing operation, resulting in reports and analyses which fail to meet the needs of marketing managers and as a result are rarely used. It has frequently been observed that the critical problem in marketing cost analysis is the difficulty of communication between financial executives and marketing people because of the limited perception of problems and capabilities.

Among others, information needs of marketing managers relate to problems of:

(1) Product mix (the quantities of the different products to be sold).

EXHIBIT I

A COMPARISON OF NATURAL AND FUNCTIONAL EXPENSE STATEMENTS, 19—

Natural Expense Statement

Salaries and wages	$272,996
Truck expenses	53,498
Traveling expense for salesmen	18,663
Depreciation—auto and trucks	8,618
Depreciation — building and equipment	3,134
Fuel and light	1,700
Repairs to building	7,542
Rent	65
Postage	1,938
Stationery and office supplies	7,167
Insurance	19,833
Telephone and telegraph	3,812
Administrative car expense	398
Advertising	2,071
Interest	9,936
Pensions	2,400
Bad debts	4,039
Taxes—state, county, and city	15,315
Taxes—federal old age, unemployment, excise	5,717
Amortization of premium on U.S. bonds	1,799
General expenses—legal, auditing, and contributions	7,654
Total	$448,295

Functional Expense Statement

Sales		
Floor selling	$ 937	
Telephone orders	644	
Mail orders	2,119	
Outside selling	68,494	$ 72,194
Office routines		
Salesmen's ledgers	$ 1,642	
Commission calculations	487	2,129
Advertising	$ 2,645	2,645
Credit		
Credit authorization	$ 8,664	
Accounts receivable	10,619	19,283
Order routine		
Packing department forms	$ 4,870	
Pricing and extensions	6,575	
Invoice typing	9,435	
Cashier	3,009	23,889
Buying		
Buying	$ 6,208	
Accounts payable	707	
Receiving	15,583	22,498
Storage	$ 35,750	35,750
Stamping	$ 2,899	2,899
Order filling		
Packing	$ 16,314	
Shipping	62,166	
Checking	5,039	
Loading	13,474	96,993
Delivery		
Routing	$ 2,619	
Delivery	124,815	127,434
Executive and general	$ 42,581	42,581
Total		$448,295

(From Longman and Schiff, "Practical Distribution Cost Analyses.")

EXHIBIT II

BASES OF ALLOCATION OF JOINT COSTS
(Summary of bases used by 28 companies)

Function	*Products*	*Customer Classes*	*Territories*
Advertising	Standard cost of goods sold.	Direct to products; to customers in terms of purchases.	Circulation by area. Direct to products, then to districts on units sold.
Promotion		Direct to products; to customers in terms of purchases.	
Personal Selling	Budget unit volume. Planned effort. Estimated time. Direct to dealer on time basis, then to products. Commissions, direct. Time log, test basis.	Estimated time, salary expense. Commissions direct.	Cases shipped.
Storage	Pallet units. Av. inventory vol. No. of invoice lines. Space reserved. Costs for storing specific products. Taxes, value of average inventory. Fixed costs, space used.	Allocated to products, then to customers on products purchased.	Allocated to product groups, then to districts on units shipped.
Order-Filling, Physical	Estimated time of warehousemen. Number of cases. Gallons handled. Standard handling units. No. of invoice lines. Performance standards for functions.	Allocated to products, then to customers on products purchased. Average cost per unit times billings.	Same as storage.
Delivery	Analysis of freight bills. Freight rates times product. Freight factor times weight. Mileage times rate per mile, by type of vehicle. Time times rate per time, and driver reports Fixed costs—stops, stop time, miles. Variable costs—miles.	Same as product. Same as product.	Average facility charge for fixed vehicle costs; other costs direct.
Order-Filling, Clerical—Sales Accounting	Budgeted units. Number of invoice lines. Cost per line for various forms. Number of invoices and average volume per invoice. Some direct, others cost per invoice times number of invoices.	Cost per line for various forms. Number of invoices and average volume per invoice.	Number of invoice lines.

EXHIBIT II—*Continued*

Function	*Products*	*Consumer Classes*	*Territories*
General and Administrative	Budgeted unit volume. Based on all other costs. Estimated effort. Projected sales dollars. Shipments. Production, assets, manpower. Detailed functionalization and multibases.	Based on all other costs.	
Product Management	Standard cost of goods. Estimated time.	Direct to products, then in terms of products purchased.	Direct to products, then to districts on sales dollars.
Research	Projects, direct. Basic, standard cost of goods sold as based on direct.		Direct to product groups, then to districts on sales dollars.
Credit	Allocated to class of customers, distribution to product groups on sales dollars of products.	Same as products.	To customers, then to territories in which located.

SOURCE: Schiff and Hellman, "Financial Management of the Marketing Function."

(2) Product addition or deletion.

(3) Marketing mix (the extent of utilization of different strategies—advertising, promotion, personal selling, etc.

(4) Sales personnel (performance, goals and evaluation, compensation plans).

(5) Customer volume or order size (the problem of the small order).

(6) Prices.

It is well to stress that marketing cost analysis stresses *profits* rather than mere *sales volume* as a goal, and is one of the indications of the transition from mere "selling" to marketing. In addition, costs are classified by marketing functions, and since functions are the responsibility of people, it leads to the adoption of RESPONSIBILITY REPORTING. Budgets and standards can thus be used for evaluating performance.

Functional Classification. The analyst abstracts raw data from accounting records, the latter oriented toward financial reporting for the entire enterprise. Accordingly, the costs of marketing operations are listed in so-called *natural classifications,* wherein the object of the expenditure (salaries, supplies, depreciation, insurance) is employed and is relevant for financial and tax reporting. However, for marketing cost analysis, these expenses have to be recast in terms of the functions performed by marketing. This means the assignment of portions of natural expenses to activities of the marketing organization and related to the delegation of authority therein. The two types of classification are illustrated in Exhibit I.

The determination of functional costs serves to associate costs with responsibilities and also provides the basis for assigning costs to segments of the marketing operation. Accordingly, costs may be assigned to product or product groups, to customers and groups of customers as channels of distribution, to geographic units of the full marketing organization (territories, districts, regions), to groups of orders by size of order, etc. Practices in assigning costs vary as is evidenced by the summary of the practices of twenty-eight large companies in Exhibit II. A useful test for the assignment of cost to segments is *causation* which requires that the factor controlling the occurrence of a cost and its variation be the basis used.

Product and Customer Costs. An alternate approach suggests the classification of marketing functions into three groups: product costs; customer costs; and other costs. *Product costs* are those costs which are related to products—their physical characteristics and related marketing activities. *Customer costs* are those which depend upon where the customer is located, how he buys, and when he buys. The rest of the costs not governed by either products or customers are classified as *other costs.*

A classification of marketing costs on this basis appears in Exhibit III, which also includes the bases used in allocating these costs to specific products and customer groups. This approach permits the preparation of reports showing the profit contribution by product before allocation of customer costs, and conversely the profit contribution by customer before allocation of product costs. It therefore follows closely the delegation of responsibility within the marketing organization. A product manager's report should focus on profit contribution after product costs—those costs which he can influence (Exhibit IV). Similarly, the

EXHIBIT III

MARKETING COST AND BASES OF ALLOCATION

Functional Cost Group	*Total*	*Basis of Allocation*
Customer Costs		
Outside Selling		
Personnel cost (commissions, etc.)	$254,820	Dollar Sales
Travel and auto costs	114,040	Call—Miles
Sales supervision	104,814	Calls
Sales Call Reports		
Sales Records (order review, traffic, postage and stationery for invoices)	61,458	Orders
Accounts Receivable Posting		
Invoice Typing (personnel costs, etc.)	19,556	Orders × 3 plus invoice lines
Credit Authorization		
Credit manager, etc.	15,614	Per customer
Bad debts	36,000	Direct
Collection	1,120	Direct
Accounts Receivable—Interest on borrowed funds	22,500	Average Balance
	$629,922	
Product Costs		
Advertising	$357,448	Direct
Finished Goods Storage		
(Interest on borrowed funds)	40,500	Average inventory value
(Space costs)	30,932	Space—sq. ft.
Packing—(supplies)	64,000	Direct
Packing, Trucking, Supervision	119,480	No. of units sold × handling unit
	$612,360	
Executive and General		
General Selling, Accounting, Executive, etc.	$314,048	

Derived from Longman and Schiff, *Practical Distribution Cost Analysis,* R. D. Irwin, 1955.

EXHIBIT IV

MARGINAL CONTRIBUTION ON SALES OF A PRODUCT

Net Sales		$2,100,000	100.00%
Cost of Goods Sold		1,702,800	81.09
Gross Profit		$ 397,200	18.91%
Product Costs:			
Inventory Carrying Costs	$ 10,733		
Inventory Space Costs	7,284		
Handling Costs	28,974		
Product Advertising	104,320		
Packing Supplies	19,000	170,311	8.11
Marginal Contribution for Customer Costs, General Administrative Overhead, and Profit		$ 226,889	10.80%

EXHIBIT V

MARGINAL CONTRIBUTION ON SALES IN A CHANNEL OF DISTRIBUTION

Net Sales		$160,000	100.00%
Cost of Goods Sold		121,200	75.75
Gross Profit		$ 38,800	24.25%
Customer Costs:			
Sales Salaries and Commissions	$ 5,096		
Traveling	18,535		
Invoice Typing and Sales Records	3,103		
Accounts Receivable Records	652		
Credit Authorization	780		
Collection	140		
Bad Debts	7,000	35,306	22.07
Marginal Contribution for Product Costs, General Administrative Overhead, and Profit		$ 3,494	2.18%

EXHIBIT VI

ACCOUNTING REPORTS FOR MARKETING

Control

1. Performance (control) reports giving (1) actual, (2) variance from budget (predetermined standard of performance), and (3) ratio of variance to budget (year-to-date and for month) for each:
   a. Salesman (sales and cost to gross profit).
   b. Sales district manager (sales, cost and expense to district operating profit).
   c. Product group (sales, cost and expense to gross profit or profit contribution).
   d. Division or department (sales, cost and expense to division operating profit).
2. Supervision of salesmen: (areas for improvement).
3. For any product, group of products or profit-investment center, the trend of merchandising profit and ratios to sales and investment over a period of years. (In this case investment includes cost of establishing territory [district or region] as well as allocation of working capital and manufacturing facilities.)
4. Sales vs. potential, trend for five-year period.
5. Customer analysis, by customer:
   a. Annual sales and total profit contribution.
   b. Annual sales and gross profit by products.
   c. Number and average size of orders.
   d. Payment and credit received.
   e. Reciprocity record.
6. Listing of customers (within districts) by:
   a. Type of selling or frequency of salesmen's calls.
   b. Importance (volume) for reciprocity purposes.
   c. Credit ratings.
7. Production vs. capacity.

Order Processing and Billing

1. Standard costs of order processing and billing:
   a. Per unit product,
   b. Variations due to complexity of orders, number of items, back ordering, and items on invoice.

Physical Distribution

1. Comparison of:
   a. Profit from shipments direct from plant, with
   b. Profit from shipments through a regional or district warehouse.
2. Studies of shipments from several plants to various markets considering variable costs.

Physical Order Filling

1. Receiving, handling, shipping: standard costs per unit of shipment.
2. Packing: standard costs per unit of shipment.
3. Other costs:
   a. Those variable with "in" and "out" activity
   b. Those variable with inventory size.
   c. Those variable with other specific factors.
   d. Fixed or Period costs.
4. Economic analysis of alternative packaging.
5. Economic analysis of alternative delivery methods including packing for shipment, shipping, transportation, and delivery.
6. Analysis of alternative warehousing plans.

Product Pricing

1. Variable costs, whole costs, variable (marginal) profit, gross profit, gross profit and merchandising profit per unit of each product.
2. Analysis of price elasticity of various products (response of change in sales to change in price); and change in net profit resulting from a change (up or down) in price of product.

Profitability Reports

1. Reports of product cost and profit:
   a. Variable cost (within specific production capacity): (1) pricing, short term; (2) to determine contribution to pool; (3) to secure costs quickly without allocating overhead; (4) buy or make decisions (short run); (5) allocation of production to plants.
   b. Whole cost (within specified production capacity): (1) long-range relative profitability; (2) long-range pricing; (3) long-range study of business; (4) long-range budgeting.

Salesmen's Compensation and Performance

1. For each salesman, for year:
   a. Sales and gross margin (or gross profit if variable costs to secure gross margin are not available for each salesman).
   b. Total compensation and ratio: (1) to sales; and, (2) to gross margin (or gross profit).
2. Studies to indicate increasing productivity of salesmen with experience (years of service).
3. Cost of turnover of salesmen:
4. Appraisal of performance (actual sales compared to potential, or after measure) with compensation paid.
5. Comparison of selling time to travel time.
6. Analysis of costs of alternative methods of providing transportation for salesmen.
7. Reports of performance of salesmen compared to specific budget items.
8. Reports for control of salesmen include:
   a. Sales volume vs. sales quotas and potential.
   b. Calls per day by class of customer.
   c. Number and average size of orders.
   d. Orders per call.
   e. Direct selling expense per call.
   f. Direct selling expense per order.
   g. Sales coverage, ratio of desired number of customers to total prospects in territory.
   h. Call frequency ratio.
9. Analysis of salesmen's compensation plans, considering whether they:
   a. Provide an incentive.
   b. Minimize the effect of windfalls and compensate when adverse conditions prevail.
   c. Reward or penalize the salesman only for factors over which he has control.
   d. Are easily understood, interpreted, and administered.
   e. Compensate for qualitative as well as quantitative results.
   f. Base incentive on volume, product or customer mix, or profit.
   g. Compensate for differences in territorial potential and competition.
   h. Place a ceiling on total earnings.
   i. Result in a maximization of the firm's return on its investment in the territory.
   j. Facilitate budgeting.

EXHIBIT VI *Continued*

Size of Orders

1. Determine for each unit of product intrinsic* "delivered" costs which vary with:
   a. Number of orders.
   b. Value of orders.
   c. Number of items per order.
   d. Number of invoice lines.
   e. Any other significant variable factors, or,
   f. Are unrelated to above factors (fixed).
2. Based on above costs, determine for each unit of product:
   a. "Delivered" cost, and
   b. Profit contribution (sales less "delivered cost") for various sizes of orders.

Special Studies

1. Analysis of profit with alternative patterns or channels of distribution, or with alternative choices of product mix or marketing mix.
2. Estimate of net added profit from additions to product line, after allowing for loss of profit due to decreases in volume of existing products as a result of selling the new line; also, return on added investment.
3. Estimate of difference in net profit between selling direct and selling through distributors, jobbers, or agents.
4. Estimate of minimum added sales required to provide sufficient earnings to offset cost of the following:
   a. Special services to customers.
   b. Product advertising.
   c. Sales promotion.
   d. A price cut of X per cent.
5. Analyses of trend of share of the market.
6. Evaluation of benefits from selling products with warranty vs. cost of warranty.

* Intrinsic delivered costs include product costs, packing and shipping, selling expense, order handling, billing, and transportation to customer (unless sold F.O.B. plant).

SOURCE. Schiff and Mellman, "Financial Management of the Marketing Function."

manager of sales to a channel of distribution (department stores, chain stores, supermarkets, etc.) should receive a report which shows profit contribution after those customer costs which he can influence (Exhibit V).

Variations in reporting financial information to marketing management occur in different firms because of differences in the market faced, strategies and tactics employed, and the organization of the marketing effort. A portion of a list of reports reviewed in a recent field study of practices in a number of large companies is shown in Exhibit VI.

Full Costing v. Marginal Costing. Apart from the problem of defining responsibilities and designing information about responsibilities, there is continuing difference of opinion among analysts on the desirability of reallocating fixed costs to segments of the marketing department. It is maintained by one group that no fixed costs should be allocated, because they are not relevant in evaluating specific product or market performance. The opposing group urges that failure to incorporate fixed costs ignores the availability of services reflected in fixed costs which may be shifted from less profitable to more profitable uses.

It is submitted here that most of the controversy stems from a failure to delineate clearly the objective for which an analysis is being made. Is it a product deletion or addition problem, a problem involving shifting of advertising effort, one of adding or deleting a territory, or a problem of alternate methods of delivery? Herein the relevant costs, fixed or variable, *those affected by the decision,* are the only ones to be considered. On the other hand, the evaluation of performance should relate the revenue and costs affected by a given level of management and the assets risked in the case of a revenue producing activity. Where revenue is not produced, then costs which are controllable should be related to activity and measured by output.

The change in marketing management's attitude toward profits and maximization of return on investment is reflective of the new responsibilities assigned. Profit *responsibility* is readily replacing profit *awareness,* and the tendency to deal with segments of the marketing organization as profit centers results in both a need for adequate financial information, as well as an understanding of the financial implications of decisions made. This is true of the vice president of marketing developing a long- or short-term marketing plan, as well as the salesman developing his approach in meeting a customer or a prospect. It also suggests the need for integrating financial information with information developed by marketing research and operations research. For example, an increase in sales *and* profits of a given product group beyond plan may be reported, but when associated with share of market information it may show a decline because of an increase in total market potential. Similarly, a decrease in warehousing cost below budgeted levels might not reflect increased efficiency if a study of operations reveals either poorer service rendered, or perhaps a more effective way of providing warehousing service which would result in improved service at a lower cost.

The challenge for additional effort and study in developing better coordinated information for marketing management is underscored by the huge expenditures for marketing functions. Here is a fertile area for creative work which will yield a sizeable return on the effort invested.

MICHAEL SCHIFF, PH.D., Professor of Accounting, Graduate School of Business Administration, New York University, New York, New York

Information References

Lambert, Douglas M., "The Distribution Channel Decision," New York, National Association of Accountants, 1979.

Longman, D.R. and Schiff, Michael, "Practical Distribution Cost Analysis," Homewood, Ill., Irwin, 1955.

Schiff, J.S. and Schiff, Michael, "New Sales Management Tool: ROAM," *Harvard Business Review*, July-August, 1967.

Schiff, Michael, "Accounting and Control in Physical Distribution Management," Chicago, National Council of Physical Distribution Management, 1971.

Schiff, Michael and Mellman, Martin, "Financial Management of the Marketing Function," New York, Financial Executives Research Foundation, 1962.

Cross References: *Marketing (and cross references there given).*

MARKETING RESEARCH

Marketing Research is not a new activity. However, it has been revitalized, enlarged, and formalized since World War II. With the development and recognition of the so-called "marketing concept" in recent years, having the objective of furnishing consumer satisfaction, marketing research has been recognized as one of the major marketing activities, co-equal in status with sales, advertising, new product development, pricing, distribution, and marketing services.

Formal Definition. Most formal definitions are similar to that adopted by the American Marketing Association: "Marketing research is the systematic gathering, recording, and analyzing of data about problems relating to the marketing of goods and services."

Operationally this means finding out facts about the market for goods, the numbers and types of consumers, the product itself, channels of distribution, and consumer motivation and behavior, plus developing advertising and sales promotion ideas, and eventually testing them.

Some of the commonly used names of marketing research are: market research, product or consumer research, distribution research, motivation research, copy research (in advertising), and sales planning and control research.

Approaches and Techniques. The approaches to marketing research can be characterized by four procedures. The *historical method* involves the gathering of past data so that comparisons and contrasts can be drawn and predictions made. The *observational method* gathers data by direct measurements of consumer and market phenomena as it is going on. The *experimental method* sets up experiments with proper control procedures so that the effects of specific marketing actions can be determined. The *survey method,* which is perhaps the most widely used, gathers data by asking questions of knowledgeable informants usually selected by some sampling technique.

The procedure in any one investigation usually includes at least the following steps: A *situation analysis* is made to orient the research and develop hypotheses. The researcher makes a *preliminary investigation* of the company, its products, the underlying channels of distribution, etc. The *informal investigation* extends the preliminary search by informal conversations with people who have special knowledge of the company or industry. *Definition of the problem* with great precision is then necessary so that effort can be focused only on the important problem areas. The *formal investigation* is then planned very carefully so that time and money will not be wasted, and the proper data actually gathered. Data must be collected and analyzed, and this is really the heart of the project. *Interpretations and recommendations* must be made in a form and manner most useful for those who requested the study.

The most interesting and widely known part of marketing research is the consumer survey with its attendant questionnaires and sampling procedures. The premise underlying marketing surveys is that people generally can and will give information of value to marketers, provided no "leading questions" are asked, and that in other ways the approach will not give biased results.

For example, people will tell interviewers which products they use, when, where, and how much. If asked, they will also try to express preferences and reasons for them. If a new flavor is developed for a food product, potential consumers (a consumer panel) will try the new flavor, compare it to the old one, and express a preference.

Actually, data from panels of people continue to grow in importance. Just as the company can now ask on-line questions of its internal data, just so a panel can be queried continuously on its changing perceptions and behavior. The data are especially valuable as an early warning signal.

A growing problem with individual interviews is the growing reluctance of people to be interviewed. Even the Census finds it necessary to mount an extensive public relations campaign to elicit compliance. Marketing research interviewers have an even more difficult job imposing on people's time and patience year after year. The continuing problem is that many door-to-door sales presentations are couched initially in the guise of a survey. It is difficult for a genuine interviewer to establish credibility and elicit cooperation from people who have been thus betrayed.

Sampling. Because it would be too expensive and impractical to question all consumers, samples of consumers are selected which for all practical purposes represent all the people from whom the sample was selected. The most accurate samples are *random* in nature and each person in the sampling universe has a known chance of being selected. For many purposes, as few as 1,500 people can accurately express the preferences of all American women for a certain food taste or appliance design. The principal advantage of random sampling is that the exact size of the sample needed to represent the whole population and the degree of certainty of the conclusions drawn from questioning people in the sample can be computed by probability statistics. These samples are extremely complex and require specially trained people to draw them up and administer them. (See STATISTICS.)

More commonly used are *judgment samples,* where a conscientious effort is made to include a certain proportion of the kinds of persons one wishes to question—men vs. women, various ages, areas, education, users vs. non-users, etc.

The principal disadvantage of judgment samples is that probability statistics cannot be used on the data because randomness has not been achieved. It is not possible to determine *mathematically* how accurately the obtained sample represents the total population, although this determination can be approximated by comparing results with census data.

These two methods are therefore not interchangeable. Quota or judgment sampling is more often used because it is simpler to develop and administer and less expensive. Random sampling requires lists of regions, areas, states, counties, cities, and often requires prelisting (interviewers call on dwellings and determine just exactly who does live there). The statistical manipulations involved require special training and much experience.

The simplest and most frequent means of sampling is often called *haphazard sampling.* Most of the selection of respondents is left to interviewers, who usually tend not to call on people who are hard to interview (the poor and the rich). Its only advantage is that it is quick and cheap; from a scientific point of view it is indefensible.

While many kinds of marketing research can be carried out by persons within the marketing department, it is often useful and even necessary to employ an outside independent marketing research firm for survey research.

Issues. Among the more important controversies in the field today are the following:

Should marketing researchers simply report the facts or should they go further and make marketing recommendations? The general tendency is toward the latter role, and with the further development of the research "generalist," who understands both research and marketing, more extensive involvement in marketing planning will probably develop.

Who should pay for marketing research—advertisers or advertising agencies? This problem becomes more acute as agencies offer more collateral services and become more marketing oriented. At present there is no general solution, but more and more advertising agencies are performing comprehensive research on a fee basis.

Should advertising agencies do research at all? This problem is perhaps most acute when it involves advertising effectiveness studies. The problem is complex and involves, as negatives, possible bias, sloppy work, and extra costs, as against the positives of deep product knowledge, research sophistication, and enlightened self-interest.

Qualitative vs. quantitative research? This problem became acute with the development of motivation research, which makes extensive use of the social sciences, such as sociology, psychology, and anthropology, in finding out how and why people react to products and advertising, and which in the beginning made little use of more accepted sampling techniques. The problem is less acute now as the qualitative and quantitative approaches resolve their differences and in many respects enrich each other. (See CONSUMER BEHAVIOR RESEARCH.)

One extreme form of quantification is the application of management science techniques to marketing management. Independent operations research firms may set up and manage computerized customized marketing models. Or a small number of operations research people, in a rather uneasy, even hostile, relationship to the regular marketing research department, may be employed by the firm as a separate unit. Whatever the manner of interaction, the estrangement and lack of communication between the two groups can be painful for all concerned. Usually, the estrangement develops when it becomes known that an operations research group has been called in to work on a project, notwithstanding excellent planning, field work, analysis, interpretation, and practical recommendations for marketing action on the part of the marketing research personnel. At the same time, it soon becomes obvious that the operations research group is setting up total business or marketing models, based on continuing discussions with top management, and is monitoring the allocation of resources and measuring results on a continuing basis. In effect it is managing by giving specific, continuing advice on what to do, when, and the probable consequences.

Top management has become used to such systems working miracles in production, refinery, distribution, and logistics problems, and expects to see similar results in the more esoteric realms of marketing. Reasonable progress has indeed been made in some of the more mechanical areas of marketing, e.g., media allocation and sales effort allocation. Less progress has been made in such areas as the measurement of specific results of certain kinds of creativity in advertising communications. Whether such operations research activity is marketing research or is not depends upon definition. Nevertheless, it is always a critical decision for a firm as to how to conceptualize and integrate orthodox, well executed marketing research with its more exotic cousin.

Whenever the company is not so large or sophisticated as to have such applications of operations research and models, it will probably resort to more obviously articulated, almost commonsense, "what if" or "what is the relationship of," kinds of questions to be answered from internally generated data. What if we collapsed this sales district with that; what if we reduced our promotional effort on that line; or combined this product with that, or added a new flavor?

Continuous monitoring of sales, especially at the retail level, is another example of greatly expanded speed and capacity. Virtually instantaneous retrieval of data from computer systems allows almost continuous access to sales by category and brand and almost immediate remedy of problems. Most of these studies are simple enough in principle and practice so that most executives can understand and participate fully rather than be made uneasy and alienated.

Acceptance. Marketing research has been accepted by the majority of large corporations, advertising agencies, and media. This is indicated by the rapid growth in formal departments, numbers and quality of people involved. and relative increase in status.

The marketing research operation is organized in many ways in such companies. Almost all large consumer goods companies have large, formally organized departments. These developed earlier and tend to be larger, more frequently found, and more sophisticated than in industrial goods companies.

In smaller companies of both types, the activity is often restricted to one or two persons, often attached to the sales manager, and in very small companies it may be a part-time activity of an inadequately trained person.

Some of the larger and more diversified research departments are in advertising agencies. There may be 100 or more persons including a director, manager, research account executives (research liaison and planning), plus functional departments for economic analysis, survey planning and administration, print media, TV and radio research, copy research, motivation research and operations research, plus communications, public relations, and sales consultants.

Most media—magazines, newspapers, TV and radio networks—have extensive marketing and media research departments.

While it is not yet predominant, the most logical organizational and reporting structure for marketing research is as a staff function reporting to the marketing manager. Under this concept the Marketing Research Department is co-equal to Advertising, Sales Promotion, Sales Management, New Product Development, Pricing, Distribution, and any other marketing functions. Reporting to the marketing manager, marketing research is the eyes and ears of all other marketing functions and can work effectively in helping them all.

If, as is still common, it is organized as part of one other marketing function—Sales, for example—its role is often restricted to that function's work, and it is not used at all by other marketing functions. A good general reporting principle is that marketing research should be independent from but available to any other marketing function.

On a less formally documented plane, however, acceptance is not so real, and very serious problems exist. Crash programs are probably still the norm as against systematic, long-range planning of research. Often, research results are not accepted if they conflict with marketing experience and judgement. There is serious controversy over the extent to which research inhibits creativity. In too many cases research is used as a status symbol, rather than as a marketing tool.

The future, however, looks relatively bright. It is probable that as marketing becomes more of a science than an art, depending more on long-range planning than intuition, marketing research will achieve high status and full integration.

Industrial vs. Consumer Marketing Research. While most of the above discussion is applicable to both industrial as well as consumer marketing research, there are some minor differences between the two, stemming from the differences between the markets for consumer and industrial goods.

Industrial markets in many cases are thin; that is, there may be very few companies that buy lathes, or certain chemicals. Sampling the attitudes of purchasing agents or engineers in the larger companies may be sufficient, whereas broader samples are necessary in consumer marketing.

Industrial marketing researchers must often be specialists of some type—chemists, engineers, technicians. Often they are as a consequence less well trained in marketing research theory and practice. They must at the same time be conscious of the varying buying influences within a company. That is, the attitudes of company presidents, financial executives, research personnel, maintenance, production and purchasing personnel must be investigated separately because they are different. There is less use of motivation research and of research to determine advertising appeals or check the effects of advertising.

As a consequence of these differences, industrial marketing research often seems to be less exciting, dynamic and glamorous than its consumer counterpart. It concentrates on locating the market—industrial and government customers—and estimating their demands. As industrial marketing research grows and as concepts of industrial marketing become more dynamic, it is probable that industrial marketing research will grow by further borrowing from consumer research and the development of its own special character.

William D. Stevens, Ph.D., Professor of Marketing, College of Business Administration, University of South Florida, Tampa, Florida

Information References

Associations:

American Marketing Association.

Advertising Research Foundation.

Professional Publications:

Journal of Advertising Research.

Journal of Marketing Research.

Significant articles on the subject also appear in *Harvard Business Review* and *Public Opinion Quarterly.*

Churchill, Gilbert A., "Marketing Research," Hinsdale, Ill., Dryden Press, 1979.

Wentz, Walter B. "Marketing Research," New York, Harper & Row, 1979.

Boyd, Harper W., Westfall Ralph, Stash, and Stanley F., "Marketing Research," Homewood, Ill., Irvin, 1977.

Cross References: *Marketing (and cross references there given)*

MARKETING RESEARCH: Patterns of Population Growth

The 1980 decenial Census tallied an estimated 227 million people in 86 million housing units located in over 20,000 villages, towns, and cities in this country. It provides not only a head count, but also a multidimensional portrait of the characteristics of each locality by age, sex, race, employment, income, etc.

The Census will determine how tens of billions of dollars are distributed each year under a multiplicity of Federal and state aid, grant and revenue-sharing programs. Unfortunately, the Census Bureau experiences its greatest difficulties in collecting accurate data in the very areas where the need for funds is greatest—localities with a high proportion of blacks, Hispanics, or illegal aliens. In the 1970 Census, about 2½% of the people were missed—more of them black than white. A barrage of publicity and numerous follow-up techniques are aimed at reducing the undercount as much as possible.

Counts, Estimates, and Projections. It is important to distinguish between the Census itself, Census Bureau estimates, and Census Bureau projections. A *Census,* such as the 1980 Census, counts the entire population every ten years. It provides the basis for reapportionment of the House of Representatives, as set forth in the Constitution. And in modern times it has also become an essential tool for all sorts of business and government activities.

In the decade between Censuses, the bureau provides more up-to-date *estimates* of population, household and family characteristics, income, and many other vital statistics by using reports of births and deaths and the results of sample surveys in conjunction with the basic Census data. The 1980 Census will provide a check on how accurate these estimates have been.

Census *projections* of population, age distribution, and family formation are the starting point for many planning and marketing efforts. The Census Bureau is always quick to emphasize that these projections are not forecasts of what *will* happen but calculations of what, under a certain set of assumptions, *could* result over the long run. They usually present three, four, or more sets of assumptions from which to choose. The unexpectedly violent swings in the birth rate—one of the key assumptions—during the postwar period have often made these projections outdated almost as soon as they were published.

This time, however, the demographers at the Census Bureau seem to be on the right track. Their middle-of-the-road projection of total population (Series II), published in 1977, has shown during the first three years a cumulative error of less than one-tenth of one per cent. As with most good forecasts, the closeness of the total results from compensating errors in the components. The 1977, Series II projections underestimated the number of births between mid-1976 and mid-1979 by only 0.8%, but they overestimated deaths by 4%. Altogether the natural increase (births minus deaths) was about 107,000 a year greater than projected, but over half of this was offset by legal immigration being 57,000 a year less than projected.

Immigration now accounts for over 20% of our annual population increase. But a major shortcoming of the Census estimates of total population and of annual changes is the lack of comprehensive information on immigration and emigration. Obviously, no accurate figures on illegal immigration exist, either for the total number or the annual inflow. The Immigration and Naturalization Service used to make estimates but, according to the magazine *American Demographics,* not only does it not make current estimates, but in 1976 all past estimates were destroyed. Nor does the service collect reliable figures on emigration from the United States.

Declining Deaths. In appraising the record of these projections for clues to their future usefulness, the most newsworthy aspect is the decline in the death rate. During the 1950s, '60s, and early '70s, the death rate appeared to have stabilized at about 9.5 per 1,000 population per year, but since 1975 the rate has dropped to about 8.6.

The almost continuous drop in the death rate during the first half of this century from 17.2 per thousand in 1900 to 9.6 in 1950 mainly represented progress against infectious and parasitic diseases and tended to reduce mortality among the young. The recent decline comes from medical progress in the treatment of high blood pressure and heart disease and cerebrovascular diseases such as stroke, and has mainly represented an improvement in life expectancy for older people.

If the death rates were adjusted to take account of the increasing proportion of older people in the population, the decline would be even more spectacular. Since the decline in death rates means the average person can expect to live two or three years longer than he might have anticipated a decade or so ago, it has important implications for funding Social Security, pension plans, and life insurance, and for the planning of medical facilities, nursing homes, and housing for the growing number of "senior citizens."

Declining Births. The other major variable in these projections in the last two decades was a tendency to underestimate the steepness and persistence of the decline in the birth rate. The total fertility rate—the estimated number of children an average woman would have in her lifetime—had jumped from a Depression low of 2.21 in 1936 to a high of 3.76 in 1957, but then dropped by more than half to 1.77 in 1976. The rate has not changed much since 1975, and the latest estimate, for 1978, is 1.80.

This is below the level needed to maintain the level of population, excluding the effects of immigration. For 1,000 women to produce 1,000 females in the next generation, it is estimated that they have to have 2,110 children, allowing for the slightly higher proportion of male babies born and for the females who die before reaching childbearing age. The Census, in its Series II projections, assumes that the total fertility rate will gradually move back up to 2.1 children per woman by the turn of the century.

To many this seems the most logical path. In the last three annual surveys of women aged 18–34, the number of lifetime births expected appears to have stabilized between 2.1 and 2.2. Among women under 25, however, expectations are still slightly below the 2.1 replacement rate.

Those who argue that a rise is due in the birth rate point out that the children from the small families of the depressed '30s tended to have large families in the '50s, while the children of the '50s had small families in the '70s. A return to large families in the '90s might logically follow. Cynics might attribute this to the natural perversity of the younger generation, doing the opposite of what their parents did. But Richard Easterlin of the University of Pennsylvania and others have argued that children born in periods of low birth rates face less competition for jobs, are able to improve their economic position faster, marry earlier, and raise larger families. The opposite is the case for the baby-boom generation who face greater competition in their careers and in many cases have been deferring both marriage and children.

Other demographers point out that the birth rate has been on the decline for the last 180 years. By the early '30s the birth rate was only one-third of what it had been in 1800. It is now back down below even the Depression levels. In long-range perspective, the baby boom was the abnormality and the subsequent decline in the birth rate was a return to trend.

Those who expect still further declines in fertility emphasize that the changing role of women in today's society makes the renewed decline more than a cyclical phenomenon. The desire of many women for careers and the incompatibility of large families with modern life styles has tended to delay the beginning of families as well as to reduce their eventual size.

The marked decline in births during the 1960s has been attributed primarily to a reduction in unplanned births owing to improved techniques and accessibility of contraception and the more widespread availability of abortion. The decline in the 1970s probably also includes a sizable reduction in planned births. In many cases, this represents voluntary postponement of childbearing, but inevitably it tends to reduce the eventual size of families. For the first time in this nation's history, fertility is greater among women 25–29 than among the younger age groups.

But a Baby Boom Nevertheless. But even if there is no great increase in fertility, another bumper crop of babies seems to be on the way. As the charts in Exhibit I show, the Census Bureau, in its Series II projections, assumes only a modest rise in the general fertility rate (the number of births divided by the number of women of childbearing age). Yet, in the latter half of the '80s the number of births is projected to rise above four million a year for the first time in over twenty years. This is an echo of the first baby boom and reflects the increased number of women aged 15–44. It would take a further sharp decline in fertility from the historically low levels of the late '70s to keep the number of births from rising in the years ahead.

This may be an echo, but it is an echo with a difference. The first baby boom was the result of women having more babies—a case of rising fertility. The coming surge in births will be the result of more women having babies—stable

EXHIBIT I

BABY BOOM—AN ECHO IN THE '80S?

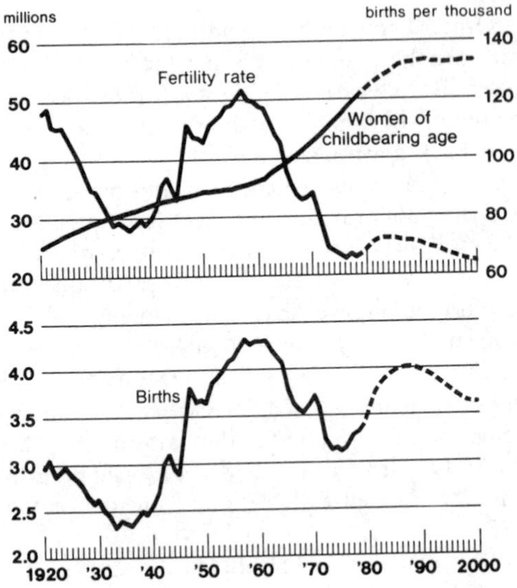

fertility, but more potential mothers.

The echo effect of an increase in the number of births will work its way through the economy during the decades ahead, just the way the effects of the original baby boom are doing now. The boom started in 1947 and crested in 1961 when a record 4,350,000 babies were born. Between 1947 and 1964, the last year of 4 million births, a total of 72.9 million babies were born in the United States, equivalent to about one-third of the present-day population. Thus, the baby-boom generation now ranges from 17 to 34 years old. In terms of labor-force growth, family formation, and the acquiring of the capital goods that surround a modern household, this group is a highly strategic force in the economy.

The way in which these surges and declines in births work their way through the various age categories is shown in the charts of Exhibit II. For the most part, little estimation is needed; the number of 30-year-olds is virtually the same as the number of 20-year-olds a decade earlier. But for those born after 1977, the Census Bureau's Series II projections have been used.

The top panel reflects the effects of the Great Depression of the '30s, which held down the number of births and produced the so-called "hollow generation." The second panel shows the beginning of the post-World War II baby boom. The number of children less than five years old was 55% greater in 1950 than it was a decade earlier. By 1960, this was reflected in an equally sharp increase in the number in their early teens.

These developments were reflected in the widespread pressures on the educational system and the housing market and in the growth of a youth-oriented culture. During the 1950s, there

EXHIBIT II

THE AGING OF AMERICA

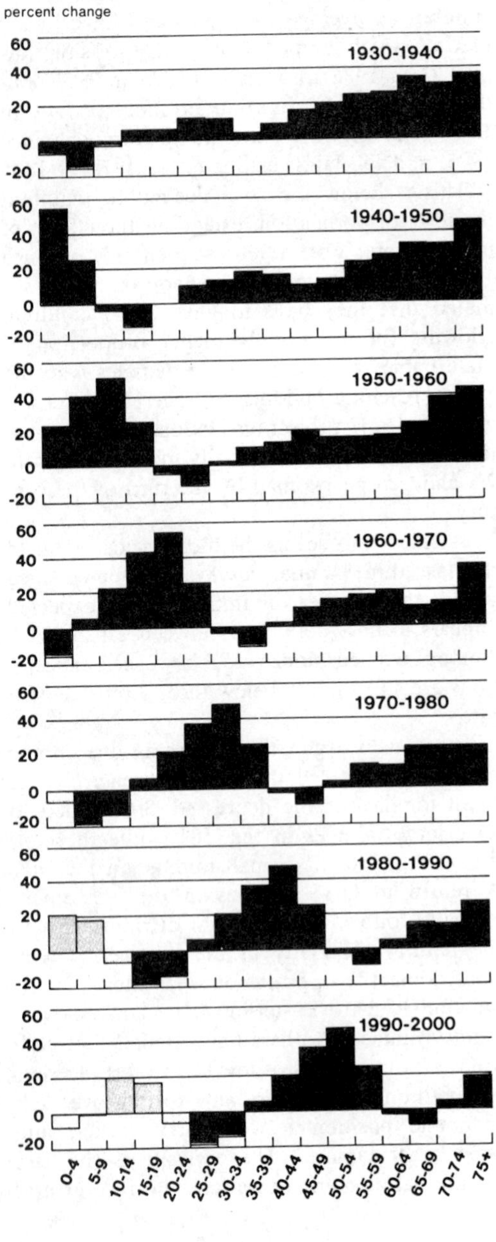

was actually a decline in the number of people in their twenties, but those who entered the job market at that time had an easier time getting established than did the group that followed them.

The fall in the birth rate during the '60s begins to be apparent in the fourth panel. By 1967, the number of children in elementary schools was greater than ever before or since. In 1973, the number in high school reached a similar high water mark. Meanwhile, the first groups from the baby-boom years were entering the labor market and meeting with intensified competition for jobs, just as they had encountered difficulties in getting accepted at the college of their choice.

In 1980, colleges may have admitted the last of their really big classes, from the over 4-million-births years of the early '60s. Meanwhile, the ranks of those in their twenties and thirties are swelling with the now-adult members of the baby-boom years. Since these are the years when families are formed and life styles are shaped, what this group does will be critically important to the markets of the '80s. Moreover, this generation has tended to break with precedent—from the rock-and-roll of the '50s to the campus uprisings of the '60s to the permissiveness and declining birth rate of the '70s.

The entry of large numbers of young workers into the labor force in recent years has been cited as a reason for the lack of productivity growth. In the '80s, however, these workers, an increasing proportion of whom are college trained, will be gaining skill and experience. As the rising numbers of women in the labor force pursue careers and gain experience instead of the part-time, intermittent, and unskilled jobs of earlier decades, overall productivity also should benefit.

But as the 1990s draw near, a second "hollow generation" will be entering the labor force. And by the turn of the century, the baby-boom generation—the first of them already in their fifties—will be approaching retirement. This will set the stage for a classic tug-of-war in which an increasingly large number of older people—with corresponding increases in voting power and political clout—seek to defend or enhance all the retirement and health-care benefits that a benevolent government has provided, while a relatively diminishing labor force seeks to protect its own standard of living against the rising costs of providing for those in the dependent generations. And by then, it will be time for another Census.

ROBERT E. LEWIS, Vice President, Citibank N.A., New York, New York

Information Reference

Lewis, Robert E., "The Nation Poses for its Family Portrait," *Monthly Economic Letter,* February 1980, Citibank N.A., New York, N.Y.

Cross References: *Marketing (and cross references there given).*

MARKETING RESEARCH: Sources of Information

In the following compilation, certain significant sources were included, even though they bear an early publishing date, for the benefit of those pursuing research in historical depth. The reader is advised to check with publishers to determine where later editions of the nonperiodical sources have been brought out.

SPECIFIC MARKETING AND ADVERTISING INFORMATION SOURCES

Advertising Age, Annual Feature Issue, Chicago, Advertising Publications. Reports sales, advertising expenditures by media, and other pertinent facts regarding the 100 leading advertisers.

Advertising Age, Annual Market Data Issue, Chicago, Advertising Publications, Inc. Lists over 1,500 market studies released by media during the immediate past year, many of which are available free of charge.

N. W. Ayer and Sons Directory of Newspapers and Periodicals. Philadelphia, N. W. Ayer and Sons, Inc. Lists newspapers and periodicals by state and county, giving information such as editor, publisher, when established, advertising rates and technical data, plus data in relation to the geographic areas in which the individual publications are issued. Annual, 1880 —.

Basic Bibliography on Marketing Research, Chicago, American Marketing Association, 1974. Annotated list of articles and some books arranged in 31 subject areas.

Bradford's Directory of Marketing Research & Management Consultants in the U.S. & the World, Fairfax, Va. Biennial report that gives a brief description of scope and activity for each listing, and, for many, names of top officers.

The Journal of Marketing, Chicago, American Marketing Association. Quarterly.

Journal of Marketing Research, Chicago, American Marketing Association. Statistically oriented articles on marketing topics.

Marketing Economics Guide, New York, Marketing Economics Institute. Gives information to assist in developing effective marketing strategies.

Standard Rate and Data Service, Skokie, Ill., Standard Rate and Data Service, Inc. Issued in eleven volumes: *A.B.C. Weekly Newspaper Rates and Data,* published every March 5 and September 15; *Business Publication Rates and Data,* monthly; *Canadian Media Rates and Data,* monthly; *Consumer Magazine Rates and Data,* monthly; *Consumer Markets,* annually in May; *Films for Television,* monthly; *National Network Radio and Television Service,* monthly; *Newspaper Rates and Data,* monthly; *Spot Radio Rates and Data,* monthly; *Spot Television Rates and Data,* monthly; *Transportation Advertising Rates and Data,* monthly.

STATISTICAL REFERENCES

Agricultural Statistics, Washington, D.C., U.S. Department of Agriculture (Historical Series). Reference book on agricultural production, supplies, prices, consumption, facilities, etc. Annual, 1936 —

American Statistics Index (ASI), Washington, D.C., Congressional Information Service, Inc., updated monthly. A two-volume index of Government publications. The first volume is a standard index, and the second contains abstracts of the indexed publications. First edition, 1974, contained *all* of the Federal Government statistical publications in print at that time, as well as the most significant publications since 1960.

Annual Survey of Manufacturers, Washington, D.C. Bureau of the Census, Department of Commerce. Annual report for intercensal years; provides statistics on manufacturing activity and employment for geographic regions, industry groups, and individual industries.

Commercial Atlas and Marketing Guide, Chicago, Rand McNally. Provides data on population, number of households, retail sales, etc. by Zip codes.

Current Population Reports: Consumer Income, Washington, D.C., Bureau of the Census, U.S. Department of Commerce Series 60. Distribution of families by family income, of unrelated individuals by income, and of persons 14 years and older. Several releases yearly.

Employment and Earnings, Washington, D.C., Bureau of Labor Statistics, U.S. Department of Labor. Current data on trends and levels of labor force, employment, hours worked, labor turnover, etc. Monthly, 1909 —.

Handbook of Women Workers, Washington, D.C., U.S. Department of Labor (Women's Bureau Bulletin #275). Gives summary figures on employment of women, women's income, family support, educational and vocational training, etc. Biennial, 1960 —.

The Farm Income Situation, Washington, D.C., Agricultural Marketing Service, U.S. Department of Agriculture. Estimates of cash receipts from farm marketing by commodity groups and Government payments. Monthly.

Market Share Reports, Springfield, Vt., National Technical Information Service, U.S. Dept. of Commerce, annual pamphlet. Provides product by product comparisons of exports from the U.S. and competing industrial nations.

Personal Income by States Since 1929: A Supplement to the Survey of Current Business. Washington, D.C., U.S. Department of Commerce. A breakdown of U.S. personal income series of the national income and product accounts and an elaboration of data on consumers. Annual.

Quarterly Survey of Consumer Buying Intentions—Federal Reserve Bulletin. Washington, D.C., Board of Governors of the Federal Reserve System. A study of consumer purchases, buying plans, family income expectations. Based on 17,000 samples on intentions to buy automobiles, T.V. sets, etc. Quarterly.

Sales and Marketing Management Survey of Buying Power, New York, *Sales and Marketing Management.* Reports current estimated figures on buying power. (See INDUSTRIAL PURCHASING POWER.)

Statistical Abstract of the United States, Washington, D.C. Bureau of the Census, U.S. Department of Commerce. A summary of statistics on industrial, social, political and economic organization of the United States. Refers to other statistical publications. Annual, 1878 —. (See STATISTICAL ABSTRACT OF THE UNITED STATES.)

Statistical Bulletin, Washington, D.C., Securities and Exchange Commission. Data on new securities offerings, registrations, underwriters, trading on exchanges, stock price indexes, etc. Monthly.

Statistics of Income, Washington, D.C., Internal Revenue Service, U.S. Department of the Treasury. Income deduction exemptions and other data for individuals grouped by source of income, size of source, etc. Annual.

United Nations Statistical Yearbook, New York, Department of Economics and Social Affairs, Statistical Office of the United Nations. Reports on population, income, hours, etc., for countries of the world. Annual, 1948 —.

U.S. Census of Business, Washington, D.C., Bureau of the Census, Department of Commerce. Covers businesses operated in the continental United States, Alaska, Hawaii, Guam, and the Virgin Islands. (See U.S. CENSUS OF BUSINESS.)

U.S. Census of Manufacturers, Washington, D.C., Bureau of the Census, Department of Commerce. Covers all establishments primarily engaged in manufacturing as defined in the STANDARD INDUSTRIAL CLASSIFICATION SYSTEM manual, in the continental United States, Alaska, Hawaii, Guam, and the Virgin Islands. (See U.S. CENSUS OF MANUFACTURERS.)

GENERAL REFERENCES: BUSINESS

Bibliographic Index (Cumulative Bibliography of Bibliographies), New York, H. W. Wilson. Alphabetic subject arrangement of separately published bibliographies, and bibliographies included in books and periodicals; 1,000–1,500 periodicals, many in foreign languages, are covered. Quarterly, 1938.

Business Periodicals Index, New York, H. W. Wilson. Monthly, except August, 1958 —.

Conference Board Cumulative Index, New York, The Conference Board. Annual subject and title index to Conference Board publications.

Directory of Special Libraries and Information Centers, Detroit, Gale Research Company, 1968 (vols. 1 and 2), 1970 (vol. 3, New Special Libraries). Details on 10,500 information units operated by business, government agencies, educational institutions, trade associations, professional societies, and research institutes.

Encyclopedia of Associations, Detroit, Gale Research Company, annual. Guide to organizations, trade and business associations, scientific and technical societies, clubs, unions, and groups. Describes purposes and membership, and whom to contact for information.

Funk and Scott Index of Corporations and Industries, Cleveland, Investment Index Company. Designed to help locate corporate and industrial analyses, opinions, forecasts, and newsworthy items, through coverage of all major business, financial and trade magazines, key newspapers, and the analytical reports of advisory services and stock brokers. Weekly, with monthly and annual cumulations.

Guide to American Directories, Detroit, Gale Research Company, 1971. Lists over 3,000 directories of individuals, institutions, and business firms in 250 fields. Includes directories of executives, scientists, government agencies, etc.

Middle Market Directory, 1964 —, and *Million Dollar Directory,* 1959 —. Both directories are annuals, with current business information such as management, products, and addresses of individual companies. New York, Dun & Bradstreet.

Standard & Poor's Industrial Survey, New York, Standard & Poor's Corporation. Financial information on over 6,000 companies, including detailed descriptions of background, financial structure, and securities. More concise coverage for over 6,000 additional smaller firms. Bimonthly, 1940 —, with daily supplement.

Standard & Poor's Register of Corporations, annual, New York, Standard & Poor's Corporation. Information on business activities, executive personnel, and directors of 32,000 companies in the U.S. and Canada. Annual, supplemented three times a year, 1928 —.

Trade Directories of the World, Croner, H. E., Queen's Village. N.Y., Croner Publications. Pages are sent monthly to update information. Lists all general trade, business, and professional directories of the U.S. and more than 60 foreign countries. Contains approximately 1,300 entries, most of which are annotated. 1952 —.

Industrial Outlook, a compilation of data and forecasts for 200 industries, Washington, Bureau of Industrial Economics, U.S. Department of Commerce, published annually. Includes one-year and five-year projections for each industry: shipments data, trends information and analysis, input-output charts, trade information, and statistical profiles. Superintendent of Documents, U.S. Gov't. Printing Office, Washington, D.C. 20401.

General References: Government

Catalog of U.S. Census Publications, Washington, D.C. Covers all Bureau of the Census publications. Quarterly. (See specific Census publications: *Census of Manufacturers; Census of Housing; Census of Population; Census of Agriculture.)*

Foreign Commerce Handbook: Basic Information and a Guide to Sources, Washington, D.C., Chamber of Commerce of the United States, 1976. Outlines function of U.S. Government, intergovernmental, and private organizations providing foreign trade sources outlined. Lists key addresses.

A Popular Guide to Government Publications, Leidy, W. Philip, New York, Columbia University Press, 2nd ed., 1963. First edition, 1940-50, covered 2,500 titles published. Second edition, 1951-62, covers 2,300 titles, mainly by U. S. Government Printing Office. Arranged by broad subject, with a detailed subject index.

Moody's Municipal and Government Manual, New York, Moody's Investors Service, Inc. Contains detailed essential financial data on national, state, and local governments throughout the world, with emphasis on the U.S. In addition, a number of special features draw together much of the data presented throughout the volume. Annual, with semiweekly supplement, 1909 —.

Standard Industrial Classification Manual, Washington, Office of Management and Budget. Defines industries in accordance with the composition and structure of the U.S. economy. (See STANDARD INDUSTRIAL CLASSIFICATION SYSTEM (S.I.C.))

Economics References

Business Conditions Digest, Washington, D.C., Bureau of the Census, U.S. Department of Commerce, U.S. Government Printing Office Presents in detail many of the economic time series—such as GNP, employment and unemployment, and money and credit—which arrange statistical information in such a way as to facilitate the analysis of the course and degree of well being of the U. S. economy. Monthly, 1961 —.

Business Indexes, Washington, D.C., Board of Governors of the Federal Reserve System. Indexes of physical volume of industrial production and the output of consumer durable goods. Monthly.

Business Plans for the New Plants and Equipment, New York, McGraw-Hill Economics Department. Summary of annual questionnaire, with figures giving actual plans for one year and preliminary plans for three years.

Economic Indicators, Washington, D.C., Council of Economic Advisors (prepared for the Joint Economic Committee). Has tables and charts on total output of economy, income, spending, prices, production, Federal finance, etc. Monthly.

Economic Indicators: Publications of the National Bureau of Economic Research. (See also, BUSINESS FORECASTING.)

Federal Reserve Charts on Bank Credit, Money Rates and Business, Washington, D.C., Board of Governors of the Federal Reserve System. Charts of significant indicators of financial and general business conditions. Covers bank reserves, deposits and currency, etc. Monthly.

International Bibliography of Economics, Chicago, Aldine. One of the annual series of *International Bibliography of the Social Sciences.* Extensive classified list of books, pamphlets, periodical articles, and official government publications, in various languages, including Slavic and Asian. Indexed by author and subject (in English and French). Annual, 1960 —.

Statistical Bulletin, monthly, New York, The Conference Board. Short-range forecasts for leading economic and business indicators.

Survey of Current Business, Washington, D.C., Office of Business Economics, U.S. Department of Commerce. Reports trends in industry, the business situation outlook, etc. Monthly, 1921 —.

SEYMOUR H. FINE, PH.D., Fine Marketing Associates, Glen Rock, New Jersey

Cross References: *Marketing (and cross references there given).*

MARKETING STRATEGY: Competitive Analysis

Competitive Analysis concerns itself with understanding past, present, and future positions of comparative advantage; frequently this means understanding relative delivered cost position. However, it is not as simple as making a comparison of current competitive pricing. First, price is a decision variable and may be used in a variety of ways independent of cost; second, product differentiation obscures and confuses the ability to make comparisons; third, current price or cost comparisons yield no trend information. Competitive analysis therefore must concern itself with actions which will affect relative position over a period of time.

Investment is the chief mechanism by which relative position is affected. Like cost, investment must be defined appropriately. For strategy purposes, investment includes all capitalized items plus all expensed items which are aimed at the development or expansion of the business. Thus, plant and equipment is one aspect of investment, market development is the other. The latter may include many expenses which appear as part of current cost of goods, but which relate in large part to future periods. Examples may be margin reductions to gain share, extra R&D effort, new product development costs, sales and marketing expansion costs.

Competitive analysis serves four functions:

(1) *Market Definition.* Market definition, like competitive analysis itself, is a discrete component of strategy development encompassing market size and growth, segmentation, participants and their share and financial performance, demand analysis, and related areas. Through competitive analysis the finer details of market definition, in particular by key participant, can be obtained. This is the easiest of the four functions to fulfill and in some cases may be the sole objective of a competitive analysis.

(2) *Inference of Competitors' Strategies.* It is essential to infer the strategies of competitors. These strategies represent competitors' attempts to influence relative delivered cost position in their favor. Some competitors announce strategies, other do not. Among those who do, not all then *follow* the strategy. Among those who do not, not all *have* a conscious strategy. Inferring competitors' actual strategies, whether they are consciously held or not, is therefore a function less easy to fulfill.

(3) *Determination of Actual Positions of Comparative Advantage.* The analysis of sources of comparative advantage is also an integral part of strategy development. It explores the fundamental economics of a business. All businesses reflect underlying characteristics unique to them. These characteristics describe the way in which some factor varies systematically with another: the cost of a ton of steel drops as the scale of the facility which produced it rises; the delivery charge is proportional to the distance from the facility; the propensity for a consumer to buy a given brand is a function of the last brand bought. Discovering these relationships and leveraging one or more of them into a strategy is the role of the analysis of sources of comparative advantage. This analysis is essentially an abstract or general one which may be done without reference to specific participants in the business (though it usually relies on data from at least one).

One of the functions of competitive analysis is to translate this abstract understanding of the business into a concrete appraisal of relative competitive position. At its simplest it determines relative delivered cost and explains any observed differences in terms of the underlying economics of the business. This function is difficult to fulfill.

(4) *Modification of Strategy.* Ultimately competitive analysis must result in the confirmation or modification of strategies developed by other means. If it did not it would be irrelevant. Learning more about competitors is valueless unless it affects our actions. Competitive

analysis will tend to modify strategies by calling for greater focus, for withdrawal, for attack, or for defense. This function is easy to fulfill, but it requires that the others be fulfilled first.

Information Base. Data are the starting point of competitive analysis. Most corporations do not even have a competitor file. Those which do may collect annual reports and 10Ks, and may require field salespeople to report on competitive activity that they experience. In some companies, files are maintained on competitive product offerings and their prices and may even involve an engineering and cost appraisal of such products. Most such data are more valuable at a tactical than at a strategic level.

Incorporation of data into the formulation of tactics or strategy is invariably subjective. There are four basic reasons for this: First, the need for systematic competitive analysis has only recently been acknowledged, so no person has the responsibility of accomplishing it. Second, there are no widely known and accepted techniques for incorporating competitive information into strategy or tactic decision-making. Third, the frequency of analysis (a major analysis is required only every few years) is such that it is difficult to motivate collection of the required data. Fourth, there is a stultifying tendency in all management decision-making to rely on data produced by the annual account cycle despite its capacity for misinterpretation.

There are two main sources of information for competitive analysis: secondary research and field research. Secondary research comprises all publicly available sources, such as annual reports, newspaper articles, and product literature. Field research comprises anything discovered purposefully from non-public sources. By far the majority of usable information is publicly available. Field research may provide unique information in its own right, but is more likely to enhance the interpretation of other material.

Secondary research sources include:

Annual reports, 10Ks.

Security analysts' reports and D&B reports.

Public relations materials.

Trade associations.

Ph.D. theses.

The publication *Advertising Age.*

Books on company histories.

Company organization charts.

Product literature.

Magazine and journal articles.

Newspaper articles.

Price lists.

Acquaintanceship with company directors.

Patents.

Standard Rate & Data service.

Local newspaper files.

Field research sources include:

Field interviews with:

Participants—Sales, Marketing, Production, R&D, Controller, CEO, Planning staff, Purchasing.

Suppliers—Key raw materials, key plant and equipment, process plant designers, key service vendors.

Past Employees.

Distributors.

Customers—Key accounts, marginal accounts.

Research Labs.

Consultants.

Engineering product break-down and costing.

Field interviewing, an essential part of competitive analysis, is usually undertaken by consultants, since it is not usually possible for company employees to undertake such a program.

In a sense, any information is interesting and valuable. But in a competitive analysis one should retain a sense of purpose and not seek information for its own sake. As outlined earlier there are four main functions of the analysis and each should be borne in mind during the data phase. An age profile of senior management, for example, is interesting and may be revealing. It is of secondary importance, however, compared to obtaining details of investment history by operating group. Following are some of the major items required both as point measurements and as trends.

Sales.

Financial performance.

Plant investment.

Personnel.

Organizational structure.

Geographical coverage.

Ownership.

Distribution.

Product information.

Advertising expenditures.

R&D Expense and direction.

Salesforce.

Statement of philosophy and strategy.

Capital structure.

Production technology.
Product technology.

The collection of this information via secondary research and field research, time-consuming though it is, is only the first step. It must be made to support each of the four functions of a competitive analysis.

Two of these functions are based largely upon analytical work of a different type. The first is the development of a full and proper market definition. The output of competitive analysis in this context is essentially a refinement of market definition by segment to incorporate competitive information. The second is the analysis of sources of comparative advantage. The output of competitive analysis enables an abstract understanding of potential sources of advantage to be translated into a statement of actual relative positions.

Strategy Inference. A competitors' strategy may be inferred from two separate sources: the analysis of investment patterns and the interpretation of feedback from the field. Neither can determine a competitor's strategy absolutely. Each must be used to modify the findings of the other. Some companies announce a planned set of moves, but subsequent analysis shows that they followed a quite different course. Normally this is not planned deception, but internal confusion or inadequate linking of theory and practice. It is therefore not sufficient to rely on statements of strategy. On the other hand we are concerned with the future, not the past, so a study of five or ten years' investment habits need not necessarily reflect forthcoming moves. We must combine the effects of both sources of input on competitive strategies.

The starting point is an analysis of investment in the competitive unit. Rate of investment in assets, both fixed and current, relative to real market growth is the key. This determines the competitor's basic investment strategy. Within this, bias toward different types of investment can exist. A company may invest in replacement capacity, incremental capacity, non-productive assets such as pollution control, or facilitating assets such as warehousing or inventory control equipment. Knowledge of these will help assess possible changes in the efficiency of manufacturing value added. Investment in market development is less easy to discern from published figures. By combining an analysis of financial accounts and information in the field it may be possible to find a pattern of investment, such as regional warehouse and sales expansion, or a commitment to more rapid customer service, more extensive sales coverage, or some other level of added cost designed to increase penetration at the expense of current profitability.

The assessment of the pattern of investment in the areas of basic capacity and market development as well as of qualitative factors relating to each form of investment is the best guide to a competitor's strategy. Field research will provide information to elaborate on this position as well as explicit statements of strategy by competitors which may need to be reconciled with the apparent strategy.

Estimating the competitor's ability to pursue this strategy is the next step of analysis. For a stand-alone competitor there exists a maximum sustainable growth rate which is determined from a consideration of capital structure, return on invested capital, and dividend payout. Basically, the maximum rate of growth is equal to return on capital multiplied by financial leverage (total capital divided by equity) multiplied by retention rate (one minus dividend payout). Only that which is financed can happen. In the absence of the ability to raise outside equity, this fact constrains a company's ability to grow. For members of a corporate portfolio, of course, this constraint may be relaxed by transfers of cash from other units, enabling a unit to exceed its purported maximum rate and outgrow the market and its competition.

Strategy inference therefore takes us into the world of corporate strategy. Indeed the same patterns of investment we wish to discern for units may be studied for competitors, who represent a portfolio of businesses. In this case the pattern of investments over time is studied for each element of a competitor's portfolio, and reconciled with field research findings concerning explicit statements of strategy for the corporation as a whole. Where a company has several multi-business competitors this analysis is an essential part of the strategy inference process.

The complete analysis of a competitor's portfolio, the rate of and type of investment in each element, and a reconciliation of management's expressed intentions with observed patterns is known as a Total Resource Analysis. It is, in a sense, a macro-analysis where analysis of one unit in depth is a micro-analysis.

Strategy Modification The end point of

competitive analysis is the modification of the strategy development process to take into account actual competitive positioning and its constraints upon courses of action. Relative size is a key determinant of competitive success. This is true *independently* of other factors which are themselves related to size, such as scale of facilities. However, relative competitive size is not a straightforward measure.

A competitive battle is waged over a long period. What matters is relative size over the period of the battle. One of the immediate outputs of the secondary research and field research phases of a competitive analysis is the ability to depict competitors by relative size.

In a competitive battle various resources will be brought to bear, all of them in some way scarce. Usually the limiting factor will be cash. For two companies in the same business, a basic measure of relative size would be invested capital. But if one company has no debt and the other has 50% debt, 50% equity, then the first has unused debt capacity. If one is, or feels itself to be, constrained to pay dividends while the other is not, its ability to bring resources to bear is further constrained. One company may enjoy a 1% lower cost position than the other. This will translate into extra resources over the five year span. One company may use its "profit" to invest in market development, thus reducing reported earnings, and tax. The other may report profit, pay taxes, and suffer further erosion in its net competitive "size."

If we assess all the ways that resources can be brought to bear over, say, a five year period, we may arrive at totally different estimates of resource size. In fact, two $100 million companies may be in the proportion of two or three to one as the result of the accumulation of ways each can bring resources to bear.

In practice there are usually innumerable ways that actual companies can affect the pool of resources available to them over a given period. Few companies are so dedicated to their immediate task that they have no disposable assets on the books, some holdover from an earlier time. Sale of these can realize extra resources. More significant, most businesses have the potential to enhance or diminish the flow of resources to one area by transfers of funds to and from separate businesses. In assessing the "size" of a unit for purposes of competition theory, it is therefore necessary to estimate the maximum additions to, or subtractions from, that unit's resources, represented by transfers from, or to, other parts of the parent corporation.

These maximum levels will not often be realized. An estimate of likely transfers is one of the primary outputs of the attempt to infer competitive strategies and of the process called Total Resource Analysis. This raises a subject which impinges on competitive behavior directly: that of psychology. The sheer resolve to allocate funds in a certain way, to focus efforts in a competitive move or in a defense against competition, may not be present. When all the analysis and strategy development have been done, competitive actions take on a poker-like aspect involving chips, bluffs, cards, folds and "pots." While this subject is interesting and relevant, it is not included in the present discussion. In any event, it in no way nullifies the need for sound competitive analysis.

PETER J. CARROLL, Hayes/Hill Incorporated, New York, New York

Cross References: *Corporate Strategy and Business Policy; Long-Range Corporate Planning; Long-Range Planning; Financial Aspects*

MARX, KARL

Karl Marx (1818–1883), the founder of modern international Communism, was born at Trier, Germany, the son of a Jewish lawyer. He studied law at Bonn and Berlin, but his interests led him to pursue history and philosophy. In 1842 he became editor of a democratic paper, *Rheinische Zeitung,* which was forced to suspend publication within a year because of his virulent articles against the government. He moved to Paris in 1843, where he engaged in a number of brief journalistic assignments. He was expelled in 1845 because of his writings, and settled in Brussels. There, in close collaboration with the German socialist Friedrich Engels, he reorganized the Communist League, which met in London in 1847. Marx and Engels jointly produced the famous *Communist Manifesto* in 1848, which proposed sweeping institutional changes for the emerging industrial society, and ended with the celebrated exhortation, "The workers have nothing to lose but their chains. They have a world to win. Workers of all lands, unite!" The manifesto attacked the state as a mere instrument of oppression, and religion and culture as propaganda of the capitalist class. Overproduction was seen as the inevitable cause of the latter's downfall. Publication of these views caused Marx's immediate expulsion from Brussels.

After participating in the revolutionary upheavals in the Rhineland in the late 1840s, Marx settled with his family in London. They lived there in grinding poverty while Marx spent long hours in the British Museum reading room, where he acquired a wide knowledge of economics. In this he benefitted from his collaboration with Engels, who was the son of a well-to-do Rhenish cotton manufacturer and had gained a first-hand knowledge of British industry by serving as his father's agent in Manchester, England.

In 1859 Marx published the first result of his economic studies, the book "Zur Kritik der politischen Okonomie." This was conceived as the first part of a much larger work, but Marx was dissatisfied with its structure, and, having altered his whole plan, he decided to rewrite the book. The result, eight years later, was the first volume of his *magnum opus,* "Das Kapital," 1867. This work was carried to completion by Engels, volumes II and III appearing, respectively, in 1885 and 1895.

Volume I of "Das Kapital" argues that capitalist expansion depends on "surplus value," the difference between the mere subsistence wage paid to labor and the much higher value produced by that labor. Capitalist competition, it contends, is only successful at the expense of the worker, who becomes poorer and more desperate. From this circumstance, revolution is claimed to be inevitable. After a short "dictatorship of the proletariat," the classless society would emerge, in which the state would have "withered away." The role of Communism was to hasten the inevitable by making the proletariat conscious of its historic role. (See the section, *Historic Development of Economics,* in the entry, ECONOMICS, for further comments on Marxism.)

Marx helped found the First International Workingmen's Association, which in 1873 broke up into Marxist and Bakunin factions, with the former surviving until 1876. He died on March 14, 1883, with "Das Kapital" unfinished.

Assessment by economic historians is that Marx contributed an original and persuasive analysis of the underlying social tensions of his time, but he failed to provide a political program because under his concept the eventual classless society would mean the end of politics. And he did not foresee the decisive role of the managerial class, for which he provided no place in his system.

Information Reference

Beer, Max, "Life and Teachings of Karl Marx," New York, International Publishers, rev. ed., 1929.

Cross References: *Economics, under heading, Historic Development of Economics.*

MASS PRODUCTION. See Production, Large-Scale.

MATERIALS MANAGEMENT

Materials Management is the name given to material handling functions as they pertain to the physical distribution chain.

There are, essentially, two distinct types of material handling functions in industrial operations: (1) those concerned directly with the manufacturing process, and (2) those concerned with physical distribution, i.e., the transportation, storage, inventory control, and so forth, of raw materials, finished or semifinished products, and the like.

Material handling in a manufacturing process becomes essentially a manufacturing process itself through integration into the production line. For that reason, it is almost invariably in the purview of production management and tends to become largely a matter of engineering compatibility with production machinery. In certain high-volume consumer goods industries such as food or liquor, nonproduction material handling and protective packaging functions tend to be integrated into the production processes as well, but these cases are the exception rather than the rule. And although certain types of handling equipment may be common to both production and nonproduction material handling operations—fork lift trucks and conveyors are two examples—by and large the two activities tend to be separate and distinct, both in their orientation and in their management.

An analysis of production-line material handling, therefore, belongs properly with appraisal of the manufacturing function. It is nonproduction material handling that is given the title materials management, in that it concerns itself with the physical distribution process.

Under the materials management concept, authority of material handling personnel extends to other related activities such as packaging, storage, and transportation. Further responsibilities relate to production, sales/marketing, customer relations and other areas. The goal of materials management cannot be defined independently; it must be considered in the light of its relationship to this wide range of other industrial functions.

Company executives and department heads with responsibilities in this area will vary from company to company, with a great deal depending on the departmental alignment of these three specific activities: shipping-receiving, loading-unloading, and warehousing. It is not uncommon, for instance, to have shipping-receiving under Production, loading-unloading under Traffic, and warehousing under Sales. Even further divisions will occur, as when shipping is under Traffic and receiving under Purchasing. Similarly, in the case of warehousing, one department may be responsible for locating warehouses, another for constructing and equipping them, a third for operating them and a fourth for securing full utilization.

Although there is a definite trend toward systemization of material handling throughout these segmented activities, there is little evidence that any one individual job function is consistently *the* prime mover. Instead, material handling problems tend to be bucked up to the various department managers concerned directly and indirectly with customer service, for group action at the point where there is an overview of the total movement system.

Trade-off. A pronounced shift away from the "hardware" approach to materials management—i.e., the installation of specific equipment to perform a specific task—has been recognizable in recent years. In its place there has evolved a systems approach to this function, exemplified by increasing emphasis on the concept of the "trade-off."

"Trade-off" implies throughput systemization of material handling, transportation, warehousing and protective packaging, with a marketing goal. Two fundamental questions are: "Can we render the same level of customer service at less cost?" and "Can we render a better level of customer service at no increase in cost?" In the process of answering these questions, it becomes clear, for instance, that added expense in material handling activities may be offset by even greater savings in transport costs, packaging, and storage space—and improved customer service.

Similarly, with an overview of the total movement system, it is possible to determine in what instances an increase in transport cost (by switching to premium transportation) will be justified by savings in handling, protective packaging, and warehousing.

An important factor in this trend has been the development of new containerized systems and unit loading techniques which present savings in handling, transportation, and storage. Even more important, however, are the new marketing opportunities they offer in the form of improved customer service and increased unit of sales. Recognition of this factor has led many companies to develop their movement systems—handling, packaging, containerization, transportation, etc.—to a point of maximum compatibility with their customers' receiving and production facilities. In companies with strong marketing orientation, this approach will extend to sending teams to the customer's facility to assist him in developing more efficient receiving and handling systems.

Responsibility for Equipment. This customer-service or marketing orientation is the most reliable clue to the identity of individuals actually responsible for purchases of material handling equipment for nonproduction line use. Although the actual number of departments involved may be as few as one or as many as six or seven, the functional responsibility of an individual for some aspect of the movement system is a far more accurate indication of his or her activity and influence than is the specific job title.

Studies show that these individuals carry titles in the following departments: Traffic/Transportation; Distribution; Sales; Warehousing; Production (where it includes responsibility for shipping-receiving functions); Engineering (where concerned with loading and unloading facilities); and Purchasing.

It should be noted that material handling engineers perform an important staff function, particularly in companies which produce uniform products like canned goods in large volume, and have opportunities for total integration of handling systems. However, operations of this type are relatively few in number, and since material handling engineers are in general attached to production staffs, their influence does not usually carry over very far into nonproduction handling activities.

COLIN BARRETT, Transportation Consultant, Reston, Virginia

Cross Reference: *Materials Management: Material Handling Equipment Types.*

MATERIALS MANAGEMENT: Material Handling Equipment Types

Material handling represents 35% to 40% of *all* production costs—in some basic industries, as much as 75% or even more. It is one of the few areas where costs can still be substantially reduced as shown by the fact that handling costs vary widely among plants with the same general volume of output, even in the same industry. The plant hampered by the limitations of old buildings, the plant that "just grew," the plant where material handling is regarded as not specially related to basic manufacturing, all these can often be helped to lower handling costs. However, lack of proper planning of buildings has in many cases made the task, if not impossible, at least impractical from an investment standpoint. Only when management becomes sufficiently alerted to this problem to pinpoint *actual* material handling costs and analyze the effect of efficient handling on other functions can their true significance in overall cost control be appreciated.

Where only warehousing operations are concerned, handling problems are usually more readily identifiable. It is in the complexity of manufacturing or processing areas that the handling factor often becomes obscured and must be isolated by careful operation analysis.

In the face of the increasing pressure on costs, the ultimate solution is of course the complete new facility. This calls for a true *integrated handling system,* based on the concept of a complete producing unit, planned with an eye on the full effect of each single function on all other functions. Production processes may even be modified to tie them in better with material handling. Actually, this kind of thinking goes even beyond the bounds of a plant facility. The scientific material handling system starts with the packaging of raw materials at the supplier's plant and ends only when the product reaches the customer's receiving dock.

The activities which comprise the *total* material handling system are many. The following list is generally accepted:

1. Packaging at vendor's plant.
2. Transportation from vendor.
3. Unloading.
4. Receiving.
5. Stores (indoors and out).
6. Issuing to production.
7. In-process handling.
8. In-process storage.
9. Workplace handling.
10. Intradepartmental handling.
11. Interdepartmental handling.
12. Intraplant handling.
13. Handling related to auxiliary functions.
14. Packaging (consumer).
15. Packaging (protective).
16. Finished goods warehousing.
17. Loading.
18. Shipping.
19. Transportation.
20. Record keeping.

Each of these areas may be studied and improved separately. Package design, for example, can have as much influence on handling methods as can more obvious factors such as floor capacities and the like. A significant increase in effective floor space can often be attained by slightly altering the dimensions or type of a shipping container. Such an approach requires an examination of raw material sources and the effect of their packaging and shipping methods on costs. At the other end, the handling costs of market distribution facilities must be considered.

"Processing on the Move". The *integrated material handling systems concept* seeks to eliminate material handling as such. The key word is "flow," that is, *processing on the move,* with coordinated flow lines extending from the raw material source, through receiving, processing, warehousing, and shipping, and ultimately to primary distribution centers.

Recent years have produced a number of outstanding examples of the effectiveness of this approach. Some are large-scale operations. But even in medium-size plants, the processing-on-the-move approach has been used with highly effective results.

The trend toward integrated handling systems is by no means confined to completely new plants. The approach has been used to modernize existing plants, at least to the extent permitted by building limitations. The highly competitive brewing industry, for example, has taken some noteworthy steps in this direction. In the most modern brewing operations, empty cans come from the supplier's plant in large, specially designed bulk bins from which they are fed by gravity directly to the filling lines. Intermediate handling has been eliminated, but this saving was made possible only by coordinating the shipping methods of the can supplier with the best system for the user.

Because an integrated handling system means lower costs, it has an important place in the planning of any new production facility. This calls for a free interchange of ideas. The architect, the industrial and process engineers, and the product designers, all must participate.

Terms like "integrated handling" and "systems concept" often conjure up a vision of highly specialized automatic equipment. This is a misconception. To be sure, strides have been made in the design of highly specialized handling equipment. But a wide variety of near-standard equipment can be fitted to a specific situation with the use of various accessories. In fact, about 400 different kinds, types, and varieties of material handling equipment are presently available. They are classified by the International Material Management Society and the American Society of Mechanical Engineers into nine major classifications as follows:

Either mobile or fixed

- 1.000 conveyors
- 2.000 cranes
- 3.000 positioning equipment

Mobile

- 4.000 industrial vehicles
- 5.000 motor vehicles
- 6.000 railroad cars
- 7.000 marine vehicles
- 8.000 air transports

Fixed

- 9.000 containers and supports

There may be as many as 1,000 pieces of equipment or devices in some of these classifications. The following paragraphs describe a representative few of the devices commercially available.

Monorail systems are a highly efficient means of handling loads on an intermittent basis. The advantages are: no rigid floor requirements, better use of overhead space, and little or no need for aisle space. However, routes and areas served must be more or less fixed, and auxiliary mobile equipment may be needed to supplement the system.

Conveyors are one of the mainstays for handling material in various forms, and some innovations in the conveyor field have still further increased their versatility. In the so-called "power and free" overhead conveyor system, loads are actually suspended from the "free" overhead conveyor line and are moved along by spring-loaded pusher bars connected to a parallel overhead power chain. Use of the sping-loaded pushers permits banking or backing up of loads when desired, thus providing storage for anticipated peak requirements at the production unit, and the flexibility of varying load speeds.

In the field of roller and belt conveyors, automatic control, combined with standard conveyor equipment, has produced mass-handling of high capacity with the advantages of en route storage, stop-offs for processing, and automatic package sorting.

Other interesting types of conveyor equipment have been developed in recent years. Thus a flexible steel belt conveyor can be made to go around turns in snakelike fashion, eliminating the roller curves required with a conventional belt conveyor; and the oscillating trough conveyor carries bulk materials along in a uniform, continuous forward movement (even upgrade) by vibration.

Conveyors are also being used as moving assembly benches which make for better control of workers' output and simplify inventory control because materials can move more directly.

Forklift trucks have been greatly improved in versatility and maneuverability, with direct bearing on effective use of floor space. Not so long ago, a ten-foot-wide aisle was the narrowest in which a conventional 4,000-pound forklift truck could turn 90 degrees, pick up a load, and return to its original position. Innovations have reduced required aisle widths considerably in the last few years. The trend now is to look upon the basic fork truck as a power source for various attachments or devices that can be changed quickly to meet varying needs.

Out of doors, forklift trucks are becoming bigger and more stable. The trend is toward greater maneuverability, and at the same time, better balance, plus (as an outgrowth of OSHA), all-weather driver protection and a full complement of safety features in relation to both the driver and the load.

The driverless tractor and train is a development that is commercially applicable. Such a system can be used to dispatch individual loaded cars to remote points, where they are dropped and empties are picked up—all without the need for a driver-operator. Guidance and motive power for the tractor come either from a single wire hung overhead or running in an inconspicuous groove in the floor, or from a line painted on the floor that reflects light rays to light-sensitive devices within the tractor which keep it "on the beam" as it moves along its path. Overall control of the system is handled from a central programming panel where routings, stopovers, and pickups may be preselected in a few seconds.

The unit load concept is becoming standard practice. The idea is not new, but as the full potential of integrated handling has become apparent, it has taken on new meaning. Materials and products are being moved in unit loads, not only in the plant and warehouse, but over highways and railroads and by air. Unit load is based, to a great extent, on modules (sizes in multiples) which coordinate carriers, pallets, package shapes and sizes, etc., so that they square off and fit with minimum wasted space and dunnage.

The idea of a container of full trailer-truck size, separate from the rolling stock, opens up tremendous possibilities not only for lowering loading and unloading costs, but for reducing breakage and spoilage. Full trailer-size, the cargo unit can be loaded and blocked for shipment at the output end of the production line, with a free choice of transportation media. The "packaged" cargo unit may be conveyed by railroad car to a seaboard point, picked up as a unit, and loaded aboard ship for over-water shipment. Each transfer between media is performed at a fraction of the cost of manual handling. Other outstanding advantages offered by these sealed cargo units are protection against pilferage and elimination of special export packing.

Modern pallet handling equipment has helped greatly to sell the "unit load" idea. Plant-wide pallet systems now include automatic stackers (palletizers), unstackers for depalletizing incoming loads, pallet conveyors, and automatic fast-acting floor-to-floor pallet elevators. The automatic pallet loaders available today can take many different packages from production lines, sort and stack them in any desired sequence, and forward the loaded pallet by conveyor to warehouse or shipping dock—all without manual effort. Systems like this can save as much as 90% of the cost of manual stacking.

Here again, the integrated handling system concept comes in. When all loading and unloading were done manually, the type of truck or railroad car was of minor consequence. The only requirement was manual labor—and plenty of it. For pallet handling, however, highway truck bodies must be suitable for handling pallet loads.

Pallet manufacturers are trying to develop standard pallet sizes, but the multiplicity of package sizes makes this difficult. Meanwhile, the concept of unit loading without pallets is growing. This can be accomplished by using a fork truck clamping arrangement for gripping and moving the assembled stack as a unit.

Automation Concepts. Computers are increasingly being used to control various aspects of material handling. Some of the computerized material handling systems do a remarkably complete job. In one plant, large component parts are placed on pallets on a conveyor. The computer then directs the movement of each pallet to an empty storage rack in a warehouse (unlighted because machines do not need to see). As a pallet is deposited in the storage rack, the computer notes its exact location. Later on, when the part on the pallet is needed for assembly or further processing, the computer brings it out of storage on command. Other automation concepts and components include ultrasonic or light-interrupted readers for filling containers to preset levels, photoelectric cells and read-color or other graphic codes for dispatching mixed loads on containers, and the like.

Planning, Pre-Planning, and Organization. An obvious corollary to the integration of material handling with plant design is the integration of the building and the handling system with all other related functions—for example, the production process and related equipment. Material handling, however, is a primary function, and in many situations, is almost as important to the success of an enterprise as the production process. It calls for extensive preplanning when new building construction is being considered. Preplanning, in this case, means that before actually planning a new plant or any sizable plant expansion, management must decide who will participate in the actual planning, and what factors are to be considered. At the preplanning stage, capital limitations are assessed, a team is chosen, and goals are established. The actual planning of technical and other aspects should proceed only after this groundwork has been laid.

The integration of the material handling

function with other parts of the modern industrial enterprise is no easy task. Experiences in recent years have dramatized the importance of material handling, and many companies have adopted the materials manager type of organization.

Education work has been going forward, with traveling clinics and related activities sponsored by the Material Handling Institute and the American Material Handling Society.

H. B. MAYNARD, President, Maynard Research Council, Incorporated, Pittsburgh, Pennsylvania
GEORGE BERKWITT, Editor, *Industrial Distribution*, New York, New York (for third edition)

Associations:

Conveyor Equipment Manufacturing Association.
Material Handling Institute, Inc.

Information References

Periodicals:

Handling & Shipping Management.
Material Handling Engineering.
Modern Materials Handling.

Texts:

Apple, James M., "Plant Layout and Materials Handling," 3rd ed., New York, Wiley, 1977
"Conveyor Terms and Definitions," CEMA Standard No. 102, Washington, D.C., Conveyor Equipment Manufacturing Association, 1975. (Also numerous other technical publications.)
"Material Handling Engineering Handbook & Directory," Cleveland, Ohio, Penton/IPC, published biennially.
Maynard, Harold B., ed., "Industrial Engineering Handbook," 3rd ed., New York, McGraw-Hill, 1971.

Cross Reference: *Materials Management.*

MATHEMATICAL PROGRAMMING

Mathematical Programming, a general term, connotes a number of mathematical techniques developed since World War II for the purpose of evaluating alternative operating programs (i.e., plans for future operations) in systematic ways that lead to selection of an optimal program. Mathematical programming methods have also been described as techniques for solving the economic problems of allocation, that is, assignment of scarce resources such as men, money, and materials, to the attainment of some goals in the best possible way.

Linear Programming, including the special cases of transportation problems, Dynamic Programming, analysis of Markov Processes, Inventory Control, PERT programming, and certain classes of problems to which Game Theory is applicable . . . all are generally considered as techniques of mathematical or scientific programming.

Other important and powerful mathematical methods used by the business world are not generally termed mathematical programming because manipulations of these mathematical models do not lead to optimal solutions. Results obtained by these techniques are descriptive, revealing the economic (or other) effects of complex interactions between a number of causal parameters. Waiting line theory (queueing theory), statistical sampling and quality control, Monte Carlo simulation, and statistical methods of data analysis to determine cause-effect relationships (regression analysis) are examples.

The mathematical research that led to the theories on which these techniques are based is generally considered part of an OPERATIONS RESEARCH function. Another operations research function is to apply these products of mathematical research to the solution of practical business problems. In this latter activity, problem identification is of primary concern, and the mathematical programming technique chosen for solution is only the means to a desired end.

The appropriate relative emphasis to place on mathematics research, and on applied research, development, and implementation is a matter of personal opinion or corporate policy. But only after implementation, usually by technical staffs, will the time and effort spent on research and development begin to pay.

THOMAS C. CATTRALL, JR, International Division, Management Sciences Department, Mobil Oil Corporation, New York, New York

Information References

Associations:

Operations Research Society of America.
The Institute of Management Sciences.
American Statistical Association.
The Institute of Mathematical Statistics.
American Institute of Industrial Engineers.
American Mathematical Society.

Texts:

Ackoff, Russell L., and Sasieni, Maurice W., "Fundamentals of Operations Research," New York, Wiley, 1968.
Duckworth, W. Eric, "A Guide to Operational Research," 2nd ed., rev. London, Methuen, 1974.
Eck, Roger D., "Operations Research for Business," Belmont, Calif. Wadsworth, 1976.
Di Roccaferrera and Ferrero, Guiseppe M., "Operations Research Models for Business and Industry," Cincinnati, South Western, 1964.
Miller, Ernest, "Advanced Techniques for Strategic

Planning," Research Study No. 104, New York, American Management Association, 1970.
Zaremba, Joseph, "Mathematical Economics and Operations Research," vol. 10, Gale Information Guide Library, Detroit, Gale Research Co., 1978 (an annotated bibliography of more than 1600 books).

Cross References: *Management Sciences (and cross references there given)*

MATRIX ORGANIZATION

Matrix Organization, evolved in the development of aerospace technology, is an organizational design used to establish a flexible and adaptable system of resources and procedures to achieve a series of project objectives. Exhibit I illustrates the coordinated or matrix system of relationships among the functions essential to the marketing, financing, and production of highly specialized goods or services.

The traditional divisional type of organization permits a flow of work to progress among autonomous functional units of a specific division. A division manager is responsible for total programs of work involving the products of his division. In a matrix organization, the divisional manager has the same responsibility, authority, and accountability for results. Differences occur in the division of work performed as well as in the allocation of authority, responsibility, and accountability for the completion of work projects.

If work performed by an operating division of a company is applied to standardized products or services with high volume, there is no need to consider a matrix organizational design. The total work can flow through the division with each functional group adding its value and facilitation to the completion of the production process. The total work can flow along and among the functional groups of production to a market. The emphasis is on the efficiency of the flow of work.

It is when work performed is for specific project contracts that a matrix organization can be used effectively. If the market for a product is a single customer such as the U.S. Air Force or an industrial firm with a prime Government contract, the production emphasis changes to the completion of action for a specific work project instead of a flow of work on production programs for product volume. In the illustration of the aerospace division, the emphasis is on the completion of specific work projects, namely, Venus project, Mars project, and Saturn project. Additional projects may be added as new contracts are signed by the marketing group. As projects are completed or abolished, they are deleted from the organization; it is a fluid organization.

A matrix type of organization is built around specific projects. A manager is given the authority, responsibility, and accountability for the completion of the project in accordance with the time, cost, quality, and quantity provisions in the project contract. The line organization under this concept operates solely in a *support relationship* to the project line organization.

The project manager is assigned the number of personnel with the essential qualifications from the functional departments for the duration of the project. Thus the project organization is composed of the manager and functional personnel groups. With responsibility and accountability for the successful completion of the contract, the project manager has the authority for work design, assignment of functional group personnel, and the determination of procedural relationships. He has the authority to reward personnel with promotions, salary increases, and other incentives while the project is in progress. He also has the authority to relieve personnel from the functional group assignments. Upon completion of the project, the functional group personnel return to the functional departments for reassignment, or transfer to other divisions or training programs to develop their skills and knowledge. The project manager himself is also available for reassignment by the division manager or company president.

It should be noted that some team members may remain administratively attached to their functional area, or may join and withdraw from the team assignment as they are needed. This organic adaptive feature is one of the primary differences between the matrix approach and the autonomous project group. (See PROJECT MANAGEMENT.) The project organization draws primarily on its own internal resources; a team working under a matrix structure "borrows" resources from the functional divisions, which, as stated, then assume a supporting relationship.

Management by Objectives. Management by project objectives or results is paramount to the way of thinking and working in a matrix type of organization. The group organizational personnel perform the line operational work to complete the project. The department functional personnel give support assistance to the line projects such as policy guidance, technical advice, and administrative services. In a matrix organization chart, the line operations may be illustrated horizontally as the functional groups are aligned to achieve a specific project. The support assistance from the functional departments appears vertically in relationship to the series of projects undertaken by the division.

The Matrix Concept. The concept of a matrix organization entails an organizational system designed as a "web of relationships" rather than a line and staff relationship of work performance. The web of relationships is aimed at

EXHIBIT I

MATRIX ORGANIZATION (AEROSPACE DIVISION)

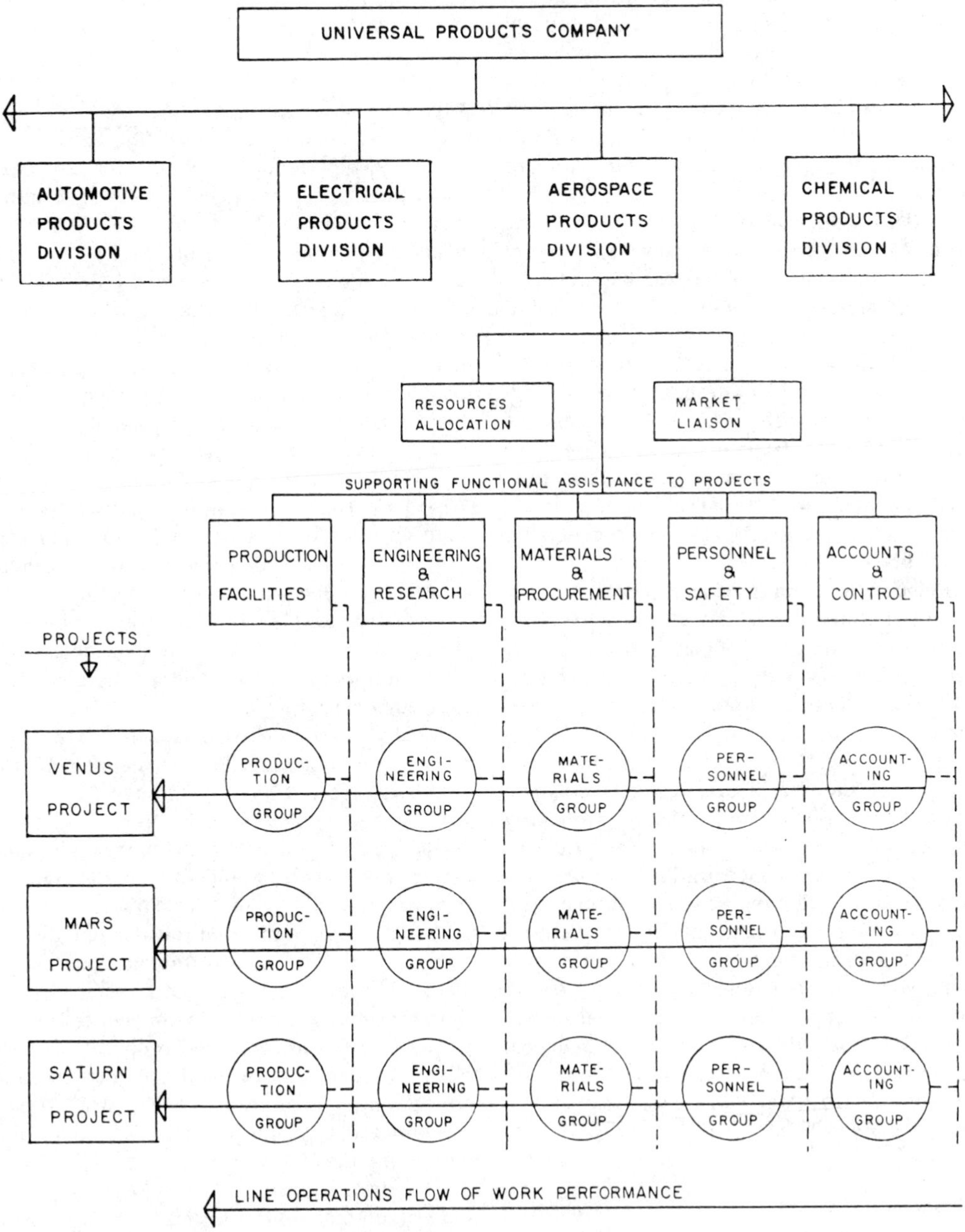

(After Mee, John F., [1])

starting and completing specific projects. An overall divisional function of resource allocation for multiple projects determines the priority of resources for specific projects and measures progress against contract requirements.

Matrix organization permits a higher degree of specialization for human talents, with maximum efficiency of operations. However, unless managers and operating personnel are educated and trained to work in the developing organizational designs, they can suffer frustrations, emotional disturbances, and loss of motivation. Working in an environment characterized by change as projects are started and completed is not as comfortable and secure as performing a continuing function in a more stable, standardized work flow situation.

Business organization structures have developed from the functional and divisional organizational charts in which clearcut hierarchies of authority are defined. As top managers encounter more complex organizational relationships resulting from market environments and diverse obligations, the traditional functional and product-line hierarchies become cumbersome. The use of a matrix organization focuses on a new arrangement among organizational functions oriented around the objective and designed to adjust to change and benefit from teamwork.

Relation to Project Management. The matrix organization grew out of PROJECT MANAGEMENT. Managers may use project management without a matrix organization; but a matrix organization requires project management as well as MANAGEMENT BY OBJECTIVES to enjoy the successful teamwork involved in the web of organizational relationships. Matrix organization offers a productive alternative to traditional hierarchical structures because it fosters concentration on the right persons and facilitating resources at the right place with the advantages of self commitment and self control. Managers may choose the best features of both functional and project forms. Research findings from both the areas of organizational behavior and systems management find ready application in matrix organizations.

JOHN F. MEE, PH.D., LLD, Mead Johnson Professor Emeritus of Management, Indiana University, Bloomington, Indiana

Information References

Davis, Stanley M. and Lawrence, Paul R., "Matrix," Reading, Mass., Addison-Wesley, 1977.

Galbraith, Jay R., "Matrix Organizational Designs," *Business Horizons,* February, 1971.

Hill, Raymond E. and White, Bernard J., "Matrix Organization and Project Management," Ann Arbor, Mich., Division of Research, University of Michigan, 1979.

References Cited

[1] Mee, John F., "Matrix Organization," *Business Horizons,* Summer, 1964.

Cross References: *Organization Theory (and cross references there given)*

MEANY, GEORGE

George Meany (1894–1980), termed the "iron-willed symbol of the American labor movement" for most of the 20th century, stepped down in November, 1979, after 25 years as the first president of the American Federation of Labor-Congress of Industrial Organizations (AFL-CIO). At the time of relinquishing his position, he had for long been a man of great political power who felt that he could even challenge the President of the United States as essentially an equal.

There was never any question about Meany's belief in free trade unions. That belief, said *The New York Times,* "kept him an enemy of Communism when détente was in fashion, and kept him on the outs with Presidents who expected him to make the unions in the federation jump at their wishes. George Meany knew, if Presidents did not, that he could conciliate, lean, urge, and persuade, but he could not make other union leaders jump."

Meany's basic job, as he saw it, was to promote the economic welfare of the 13.6 million members of the federation through free collective bargaining and signed contracts. On the legislative front, he supported higher minimum wages, health care, public works, the right to organize, and the protection of the picket line. Although conservative and anti-Communist on foreign policy, he was liberal on domestic issues. He threw the AFL-CIO's considerable power against conservative nominees to the Supreme Court, and supported proposals to curb business concentration and to increase and strengthen national health projects. He strongly supported a provision for equal job opportunities in the debates leading to the Civil Rights Act of 1964.

George Meany did not speak for all of organized labor. He led the fight to expel from the AFL-CIO the International Brotherhood of

Teamsters, the nation's largest union, contending that its leadership was corrupt; and the nation's second largest union, the United Automobile Workers, walked out to protest what it termed Meany's "rusty-bottom conservatism." However, Congressional committees learned to respect his presentations before them which were based on an impressive command of facts. In the late 1970s, labor's influence in Congress and in the White House began to wane, and critics within labor contended that he did not understand the changing times, and that his image was an obstacle to organizing younger workers.

Meany was born in Harlem, New York City, on August 16, 1894, the second son among ten children. His father was a plumber who headed a union local and dabbled in politics. When he was sixteen, Meany quit school to work as a plumber's helper for $1.50 a day. At age nineteen he qualified as a journeyman, earning $30 a day as a member of his father's union. His career in union office-holding began in 1923 when he was named secretary-treasurer of the New York Building Trades Council, and eleven years later he became state president of the AFL. In 1939 he moved to Washington as secretary-treasurer of the AFL, and became president in 1952 upon the death of WILLIAM GREEN.

As AFL president, Meany in 1952 undertook to unify the labor movement, which had been split since the formation of the CIO in the 1930s. In 1955 a formula was devised which made possible the merging of the two organizations, with Meany as head of the resulting AFL-CIO. Early in 1967, as a result of a rift between Meany and Walter Reuther of the United Auto Workers, the latter led his Detroit-based union out of the federation.

Cross References: *Gompers, Samuel; Green, William; Labor Unions.*

MEASURED DAY WORK. See Incentive Systems.

MEDIATION

Mediation is a method for solving labor disputes where an outsider persuades parties to reach a voluntary agreement. *Conciliation* is another word for mediation, with negligible variations.

Arbitration differs from mediation in the power of the outsider to make a binding decision. The parties have given him this authority to decide for them. The mediator has no such grant. He can only help the parties to decide for themselves. They are free to reject the mediator's advice and aid. (See LABOR ARBITRATION.)

Mediation, formerly used mainly to settle issues in foreign and domestic relations, has attained an expanding role in labor relations fostered through Federal, state and local agencies. The rise of government employee unions during the 1960s has opened a new area for the introduction of mediation techniques. Because of the public's concern to avoid breakdowns of vital private and public services, the government generally assigns a mediator to aid the parties in their pursuit of labor peace.

The governmental policy of peaceful adjustment of labor disputes flows along two main avenues in the United States. One road is paved with statutes, like the National and State Labor Relations Acts, since the 1930s, where the Government acts as an enforcement office, to secure compliance with statutory standards and procedures. These regulations commonly do not affect the substance of the labor-management contract, and do not rest on the joint consent of the principals. The second and more ancient road starts from the consent of the parties where they may invite the assistance of Federal, state, or city officials to help them shape their own solutions. Here, the heart of the activity reaches the substance of the agreement. Acceptance of mediation replaces the reference to force with the appeal to reason.

The neutral mediator can be any public or private individual who is acceptable to the disputants. He can only operate in a climate of assent. If the parties are bargaining, he acts to avoid a deadlock. If a deadlock happens, he seeks to restore negotiations. If a breakdown is imminent, he seeks to prevent it. If the break occurs, he seeks to end it. For each of these phases the consent of the parties is critical.

The basic steps in the mediation process are uncomplicated. The mediator invites the principals to meet with him for a rational statement of the issues. At the outset, the disputants rarely reveal exactly what each wants. Characteristically, the first mediation conference produces an outpouring of real and imagined grievances, punctuated by personality clashes, with the mediator almost a solitary listener. This capacity to listen permits him to define the chief areas in dispute. A seasoned mediator would note the psychological strands which are interwoven with the social, political, and economic facets in a difficult case. He has to determine the relative importance of the issues. The mediator then separates the parties, and consults with each group in private caucus. Here he can learn in confidence how far each side would move, what each would yield, what each would need. The barriers to agreement emerge plainly. It is from this point on that the mediator relies on his skills to find formulas for dissolving differences, in separate or joint conferences.

There are many other instances where the mediator is available, but invisible, ready to enter if wanted, and settlement is achieved because the parties were prepared to find common ground. Some doubts exist regarding the effectiveness of mediation in large disputes with sophisticated negotiators who are presumed to know what they are doing. Mediators in such cases may even be aware of the futility of their services, yet remain on the scene as a reminder of the public's concern. Yet many veteran negotiators agree that a positive contribution toward settlement could still be made by keeping mediation available for use as a channel of communication, through which each side makes private concessions until both sides are ready for full disclosure.

Mediation thus spans a wide range of maneuvers: at one end to keep the parties talking about their own proposals; at the other, to keep the parties exploring the mediator's proposals. The core of the mediator's role is to sustain intelligent discussion of lines of settlement.

History. The above type of modern mediation of labor disputes was practiced in England in the 1860s among the cotton weavers, and elsewhere. In the United States, formal state mediation agencies also appeared in the 1880s, preceding the organization of the United States Conciliation Service, within the newly established United States Department of Labor in 1913. In that year, the Congress empowered the Secretary of Labor

> ". . . to act as a mediator and to appoint commissioners of conciliation in labor disputes whenever, in his judgment, the industrial peace may require it to be done."

In 1947, the United States Conciliation Service was taken out of the United States Department of Labor by the Taft-Hartley Act, and given independent status under the new name of the Federal Mediation and Conciliation Service, (FMCS).

The earlier experience with the National Defense Mediation Board of 1941 and the National War Labor Board of 1942, both emergency measures, pointed the way for providing mediation service to facilitate uninterrupted retooling from a war-time to a peacetime economy.

As of 1980, forty-five states and Puerto Rico offer some type of Mediation service and more than half the states had one or more full-time mediators. Special laws authorize mediation in forty-five states, with statements of policy ranging from a declaration of intention to promote voluntary mediation, to a prescription for formal or permanent machinery. Out of all fifty states, only five as of 1980 have no agency to mediate general industrial disputes: Mississippi, New Mexico, Tennessee, Texas, and Wyoming. However, the Labor Commissioner of Tennessee and certain bureaus in other states may aid the parties in serious cases.

The decade ended with nine states in 1979 enacting laws which extended mediation services to teachers, firemen, policemen, and other sections of public employment. The concept of "final offer arbitration" may encourage subtle mediation gambits to minimize the risks implied under the new state laws which allow a third party to award the "last best offer."

Approaches. The timing of intervention differs among the agencies. Knowledge of a dispute does not automatically prompt an offer of mediation in all cases. Under Section 8(d)(3) of the Taft-Hartley Act a notice of a proposed contract termination or modification must be given to the other contracting party 60 days before contract expiration. Additionally, if there is no agreement within 30 days after such notice, existing state agencies as well as the FMCS must receive notice of the unsettled dispute. Under a 1974 amendment, timely notice must be given to FMCS where health-care institutions are involved.

The FMCS would intervene if the dispute threatens a substantial interruption of interstate commerce. Some agencies intervene immediately; others wait for a specific call from one or both sides. Several state laws set up guidelines plainly. For example, the laws of Connecticut, Illinois, Massachusetts, Ohio, Pennsylvania, and Puerto Rico require the agencies, upon learning of a lockout or a strike, to offer mediation service. Several laws require the agency to intervene when directed to do so by the Governor, or requested to do so by one or both parties. In some states, intervention may depend on the number of employees involved.

An example of a large permanent state agency is the New York State Board of Mediation, composed of three salaried members appointed by the Governor who designates one as Chairman. The professional staff consists of fourteen mediators and four supervising mediators, drawn from Civil Service, and an executive secretary, appointed by the Board. The Board, in its discretion, may, or at the direction of the Governor, must offer mediation in a labor dispute. New York State has engaged in mediation since 1886.

The major Federal agency is the FMCS. The director is appointed by the President, heading a staff of over 250 mediators who handle general industrial disputes. The scope, structure and function of the agency appear under Title II of the Labor Management Relations Act, 1947. The FMCS has eight regional offices serving all 50 states, the District of Columbia, Guam, Puerto Rico, and the Virgin Islands.

Other Federal agencies narrowly limit their mediation work to specific kinds of disputes. The National Mediation Board under the Railway Labor Act, for instance, tackles railroad and airline disputes only. The Board acts as an independent agency in the executive arm of the Government, with three full-time appointees of the President, and a small staff of mediators. The Atomic Energy Labor Relations Panel created by Executive action, offers its services in disputes at Atomic Energy plants after mediation efforts have failed to avoid a breakdown. A President's Executive Order in 1961 established the Missile Sites Labor Commission, a tripartite panel with authority to intervene after local mediation fails. The Commission was dissolved in 1967, after scheduled missile-site construction subsided.

The Federal Service Labor-Management and Employee Relations Law took effect in January 1979, setting up a Federal Services Impasses Panel which, among other duties, would seek to mediate disputes affecting employees in the Federal Executive Branch.

Mediation has been affected by the post-World War II developments in the statutes and substance of labor relations. The requirement under Section 8(d)(3) of the Taft-Hartley Act to give Federal and state mediation agencies advance notice of forthcoming contract modifications has expanded mediation activity. On occasion, two or more agencies with blurred jurisdictional lines offer mediation, with the parties choosing all, one, or more.

The bare issues of union recognition and wages have proliferated into a technical complexity of union security arrangements, job evaluation plans, collective pay systems, welfare and pension programs. These tend to become more elaborate as experiments are tried through collective bargaining to control the social hazards incidental to quickly-paced technological change and the economic climate. Moreover, contracts formerly running for a year or so now tend toward longer terms.

The work of the mediator has expanded to cope with the broadened band of issues and the extended contracts. He is required to have informed opinions on economics, law, insurance, accounting, and administration. He plainly needs an understanding of the mainsprings of human action to cope with the emotional outbursts which accompany mediation sessions.

Complexities which may baffle teams of negotiators may overwhelm one mediator, and there is a discernible tendency to use panels of three in hard cases. The increase in industry-wide negotiations has drawn attention to the probable impact on national health and safety of certain breakdowns in sensitive industries. Several cases in the early 1960s and late 1970s regarded as critical prompted the personal intervention of the Secretary of Labor. The involvement of a cabinet officer as a mediator is symptomatic of an enlarged White House concern of the public interest.

It has been suggested that mediators should generally provide guidelines to the parties to safeguard the public interest. The countervailing view is that many may differ on what constitutes the public interest; and until the public interest receives more precise formulation, the process of mediation must rest on consent. The extent to which labor and management may make or take a strike to compose their differences remains a measure of a free society.

To strengthen the contribution of mediation, the Association of State Mediation Agencies, now called the Association of Labor Mediation Agencies, organized in 1951, publishes the proceedings of its annual conference, dealing with the problems of policy, personnel, and techniques. Several mediators attained national renown. Among the outstanding names are William Leiserson, George Taylor, William H. Davis, Arthur Meyer, Cyrus Ching, David Cole, John T. Dunlop, and Theodor Kheel.

JULIUS J. MANSON, Professor Emeritus and former Dean, Bernard M. Baruch School of Business and Public Administration, City University of New York; formerly Executive Director, New York State Board of Mediation

Information References

Anderson, Arvid, Sovern, Eleanor, and O'Reilly, John F., "Impassee Resolution in Public Sector Collective Bargaining," *St. John's Law Review,* vol. 51, No. 3 (Spring 1977).

Getman, Julius G., "Labor Relations: Law, Practice, and Policy," Mineola, N.Y., Foundation Press, 1978.

Industrial Relations Research Association, *Proceedings, passim.*

Labor Law Journal, Proceedings of the Association of State Mediation Agencies (now Association of Labor Mediation Agencies), from 1955.

Levin, Edward and DeSantis, Daniel V., "Mediation: An Annotated Bibliography," Ithaca, N.Y., New York School of Industrial Relations, Cornell University, 1978.

Manson, Julius J., "Mediators as Arbitrators," Association of State Mediation Agencies (now Association of Labor Mediation Agencies, Proceedings of 4th Annual Conference, 1955, reprinted in *Labor Law Journal,* August 1955.

Robins, Eva and Denenberg, T. S., "A Guide for Labor Mediators," Honolulu, University of Hawaii, 1976.

Ross, Jerome H., "Federal Mediation in the Public Sector," *Monthly Labor Review,* vol. 99 February 1976.

Simkin, William Ed., "Mediation & the Dynamics of Collective Bargaining, Washington, Bureau of National Affairs, 1971.

Cross References: *Collective Bargaining; Labor Arbitration; Labor Relations Legislation; Labor Unions.*

MERGERS AND ACQUISITIONS

The terms **Merger, Acquisition, Consolidation** and **Amalgamation** are commonly used interchangeably. They all describe the event of two or more companies combining into one economic entity. In the technical jargon of finance, however, a *merger* is the absorption of one or more corporations by another with the acquiring firm retaining its corporate identify and the other firms disappearing from the corporate community. A *consolidation* occurs when all the combining firms disappear as distinct and separate corporate entities and a new consolidated corporate entity is created. Mergers also include the acquisition of the working control of an acquired firm that may leave the legal corporate entities undisturbed. The financial press tends to use the term merger for all types of combinations and we adopt that convention for the purpose of this article.

Types of Mergers. Business mergers are generally classified by the market relationship that exists between the merging parties. Mergers can be classified as *congeneric* or *conglomerate.* A congeneric merger occurs when firms combine in the same or related industries, while conglomerate mergers occur when firms in different or unrelated industries combine. *Horizontal* mergers and *vertical* mergers are both of the congeneric variety. A horizontal merger unites two or more firms engaged in the production or sale of the same or similar products. Horizontal mergers, in particular, are generally considered as eliminating competition and increasing the concentration of economic powers in surviving firms.

A *vertical merger* unites one or more firms engaged in the production of a given product at different levels or stages of the productive process. Frequently the merging parties have a buyer/seller relationship with one being a customer of the other. Vertical mergers are also classified as:

(1) Backward—merging toward earlier stages of production (i.e., toward raw material source).

(2) Forward—merging toward later stages of production (i.e., toward consumers of the final product).

Mergers that are not congeneric are conglomerate. Conglomerate mergers may involve the addition of new products, entry into a new industry, or the combination of different production technology, or marketing channels.

A *concentric merger* occurs when merging firms are in different product areas but are related in raw materials, production technology, or marketing channels. Concentric mergers are classified as a subset of conglomerate mergers.

History. Historically, mergers have played a central role in determining the level of concentration and the amount of competition in many U.S. industries. Merger activity has also been instrumental in determining the relative size and diversification of many large U.S. corporations and has left an indelible mark on the structure of the U.S. economy.

Historical data on merger activity are incomplete, but sufficient information is available to provide valuable insights concerning merger movements. Corporate mergers and acquisitions in the United States have occurred in three major "merger movements." The first merger movement occurred at the turn of the century, beginning with a trough in 1897, reaching a peak in 1899, and bottoming out with the stock market slump in 1904. The second merger movement occurred in the late 1920s, and extended from a trough in 1922 to a peak in 1929 and receded quickly after the stock market crash in 1929 to a trough in 1933. (A "mini-merger" wave occurred in the 1940s, peaking out in 1945.)

The third major merger movement began in the 1950s, continued through the 1960s, peaked in 1968–69, and receded to a trough in 1972. This movement is commonly called the merger wave of the 1960s. After the peak in 1968–69, merger activity fell to levels that existed in the first half of the 1960s. Substantial merger activity continued into the 1970s with the years 1976 and 1977 characterized as a "merger binge" of companies of large size [1]. A decision concerning the place of the merger activities of the late 1970s and early1980s will have to wait an historical perspective.

The first merger movement was preceded by the so-called "trust movement" of the 1890s. The major trust activity began with the organization of the Standard Oil Trust in 1879. The following decade ushered in substantial trust activity in many industries, including cottonseed oil, lead, and sugar. But merger and trust activity, although important prior to 1890, was almost insignificant when compared to the enormous activity in the 1890s. The turn-of-the-century merger movement was of relatively short duration, but the magnitude and the quickness of the movement had a profound and lasting effect on the structure of industry in our economy.

The magnitude of merger activity is exemplified by the 1895–1904 period, when 170 firms disappeared into the U.S. Steel Corporation, and 162 firms were absorbed by the American Tobacco Company, while 65 and 64 firms disappeared respectively into E. I. duPont de Nemours and the American Can Company. In the year 1899, at the peak of the merger movement, 1,028 firms disappeared from the corporate community. By 1903 it was estimated that there were 318 important industrial consolidations in the U.S., and that of this total, 236, or over 70% had occurred in the preceding five years. The economic impact is revealed by the fact that these large consolidations controlled about 40% of the total manufacturing capital in the U.S. economy at that time.

Horizonal mergers dominated the activity at the turn of the century. As a result, the first merger movement greatly increased the proportionate size and control of a few firms over production and marketing in many of the major industries in the U.S. This activity resulted in high levels of economic concentration in such industries as steel, tin cans, farm machinery, tobacco, copper, chemicals, and typewriters.

Primary factors contributing to the increase in merger activity at the beginning of this century were changes in state incorporation laws and the formation of larger and more efficient capital markets. Until the early 19th century, corporation laws usually did not permit mergers and did not allow corporations to hold stock in other corporations. New Jersey, starting in 1889, removed many of the typical restrictions on corporate acquisitions and consequently became the leading state of incorporation for merger activity. New Jersey corporations alone accounted for over 50% of mergers by dollar value in the period 1889–1920.

It is argued that good capital markets encouraged merger activity and were a necessary ingredient for the merger activity of this period. It is also argued that merger activity and subsequent security flotations provided the basis for the development of a healthy securities market. As with many economic phenomena, the growth of both variables occurred jointly and their respective growth was in part dependent upon the other's existence and condition.

Of significance at the turn of the century was the role of the professional promoter in merger activity. In many cases the compensation of the professional promoter was very large (i.e., up to 20% of the capitalized value of the merging firms), and evidence seems to indicate that it was the existence of promotional profits rather than operational efficiencies that motivated many mergers in this period.

In general the merger movement of the 1890s co-existed with and was an integral part of the times. Expansion of industrial activity and technological advances permitted large-scale production and resultant economies. The growth of the railroad system and the settling of the west expanded the markets for many products. The development of the New York Stock Exchange coupled with a bullish stock market and a rising economy provided the financial incentive and opportunity for new stock issues to finance mergers. These factors also provided the opportunity and the environment for large promotional profits and the feverish promotional activity of the period. While mergers increased at a feverish pace in the 1890s, the demise of the merger movement was equally rapid. In 1901 prices on the stock market started to fall. A great many mergers were not financial successes, and the disillusioned investor was not as easily enticed by the professional promoter. These factors ultimately ended the first merger movement, aiding and aided by the economic downturn of 1903.

The second major merger movement began in 1923, reached a peak in 1929, and declined rapidly after the stockmarket crash, to be finally choked off by the Great Depression. The merger wave in the "roaring 20s" resembled that of the turn of the century in many respects. It was coincident with a bouyant stockmarket and an increase in economic activity and general prosperity. As with the earlier merger movement, the merger wave of the 1920s was largely horizontal in nature; but the movement also included an increase in vertical integrations and in concentric types of mergers.

As with the earlier period, merger activity in the 1920s played an important role in creating and preserving the oligopolistic structure that prevailed in many industries, and in increasing the degree of concentration in our economy. Between 1925 and 1930, the largest 100 manufacturing corporations increased their share of corporate manufacturing assets from 26.1% to 43.3%. Merger activity accounted for nearly all of this increase. The second merger movement resulted in larger concentrations in major industries, including food manufacturing, public utilities, oil, commercial banking, motion pictures, hotels, and retail stores. The importance of the chain store movement should be singled out. The development of the chain store resulted in a change in retailing from small individually owned stores to the retail chain store that sold approximately one-fourth of all food, drugs, tobacco, apparel, and general merchandise by the end of the 1920s.

One important aspect of both the turn of the century and the 1920s movements was the important role of the professional promoters. Since merger activity generated a profitable activity for both investment bankers and brokers, some investment bankers employed commission men who did little else but search for potential merger candidates. Of course, the merger activity and promotional profits were again coincident with a strong and rising stock-market and a feeling of economic prosperity.

Mergers did provide economies for firms in many industries. Merchandising economies could be achieved through the chain store development, and economies of scale could be achieved through large scale production. Both real economies of scale and the opportunity for financial profits provided a stimulus for mergers in the 1920s.

Innovations in organizational techniques went hand in hand with merger activity in this period. Decentralized management and multidivisional organizational techniques provided managerial efficiencies that were used extensively by such firms as General Motors, DuPont, and Standard Oil. Other factors commonly cited as fostering and enabling the merger movement in the 1920s were the improvements in transportation and in communications (especially the growth of radio). The growth of a good transportation system and the advent of radio greatly enlarged marketing areas and provided the basis for large-scale distribution and production, and consequently the potential for economics of scale.

The merger wave of the 1960s was unprecedented in magnitude, in United States history, regardless of the measure used. It contributed to even further increase the concentration of control over economic activity in a relatively small number of corporations. This merger movement started in the early 1950s and grew steadily throughout the 1950s and 1960s to reach dizzy heights in 1967, 1968, and 1969. In 1968 alone approximately $15 billion of assets were acquired by firms in manufacturing and mining. In that single year nearly 10% of all independent manufacturing corporations of over $10 million in assets were acquired by other firms. After 1969, if activity is measured by the value of assets acquired, merger activity declined by one half in 1970 and continued to decline through 1972, to turn around, and return to the 1970 level by 1976. Available data indicate that the turnaround has continued through 1979. The most recent wave of mergers followed the trough of 1972 and has grown in size yearly through 1979.

The major distinguishing factor of the wave

of the 1970s is the size of the acquired company. In the 1970s well over 100 companies of over 100 million in asset size were acquired. Also, this period evidenced an unprecedented number of billion-dollar acquisitions. Toward the end of the decade of the 1970s, the 100 largest firms controlled about the same proportion of the nation's assets as the top 200 did in the 1940s. Additionally, the largest 200 manufacturing firms at this writing control over two thirds of corporate manufacturing assets, a greater amount of assets than did the largest 1,000 manufacturing corporations in 1941.

Although there has been some congeneric merger activity in the recent merger movement, the great bulk of merger activity through the 1960s and 1970s has been of the conglomerate variety. Congress has been investigating the possible adverse effects and suggested remedies of the recent conglomerate merger movement [2], and various government agencies responded by increasing their supervisory activities. In 1978, for example, the Federal Trade Commission established new rules under the Hart-Scott-Rodino Anti Trust Improvement Act of 1976 requiring increased disclosure for acquisitions of large size. It is clear that the effects and the possible impact and reaction to the merger activity in the last two decades will be felt for years to come and will probably result in further anti-merger legislation.

Reasons for Mergers and Acquisitions. The primary justification for a merger or acquisition is the "synergistic effect" of combining two or more firms. The combination is assumed to provide some real economies, a reduction in risk or both. Since any increase in earnings or reduction in risk has the effect of increasing the value of a going concern. the value of the firms combined is presumably greater than the sum of their values separately. The synergistic effect will occur when a merger produces economies in production costs or the elimination of duplicate facilities. It may also occur as a result of reductions in marketing costs. A reduction in marketing costs may result from either an expansion of product lines, or the easing of competitive pressures. Reduction of risk in the combined firm by virtue of diversification may also occur through merger. However, this reduction in risk may not result in a benefit to the stockholders. Stockholders can achieve comparable diversification through portfolio selection and therefore should not realize a gain from mergers specifically done for risk reduction. Finally, there may be economies in either the management or the financing of the firm.

The logic of economies of scale is persuasive: however, many recent studies designed to measure or identify the existence of such economics have failed to find statistically significant evidence of these benefits or have concluded with conflicting results.

Since expectations are not always realized, empirical data are an imperfect measure of motivations. Interviews in depth with officers of firms which have been involved in mergers or acquisitions also provide an indication of merger objectives. Specific motives indicated by acquiring corporations include the following:

(1) To obtain diversification.

(2) To offset product obsolescence.

(3) To acquire new customers or expand the market area.

(4) To offset an actual or threatened loss of market.

(5) To obtain a greater rate of growth.

(6) To add glamour to the company.

(7) To improve cyclical and seasonal stability.

(8) To exploit a product, a productive process, or a basic raw material.

(9) To improve the effectiveness of the marketing effort.

(10) To obtain cost reductions through elimination of duplicate facilities.

(11) To support increased product development work.

(12) To improve credit position.

(13) To secure or use a tax loss.

(14) To acquire management with specific technical competence.

(15) To enhance power and prestige of owner or management.

(16) To substitute efficient management for inefficient management.

Motives for Selling. Quite often, the small corporation with one or a few products comes to realize that its size is a handicap in a national market. The owners are then apt to decide that joining forces with a larger corporation would yield a better return on their accumulated capital than the yields they would receive through expansion with funds generated internally. Also, many small firms cannot generate sufficient internal funds or raise funds as rapidly as needed to finance their desired growth. Small firms lacking sufficient stature to raise funds advantageously in the capital markets often find that their principal alternative is to merge.

Reasons for selling are frequently personal as well as economic. Personal reasons are generally most important in small, closely-held firms and include the following:

(1) Retirement. Owner-manager wants to retire and does not have capable managerial talent available internally.

(2) Stock not listed on an exchange. Merger with firm listed on organized exchange would give seller a marketable security with greater liquidity and capital gains treatment on the subsequent sale of the security.

(3) Estate taxes. The reason most cited for sale or mergers of closely held firms is the anticipation of estate taxes. The problem of liquidity to pay estate taxes and the problem of valuation of the ownership interest are eased when the estate is in marketable securities.

Economic reasons cited for the sale or merger include the following:

(1) Financial problems.

(2) Inadequate distribution and incomplete product lines.

(3) Rapid change in technological product design and manufacturing processes.

(4) Lack of qualified managerial talent. The firm may be too small to afford a well staffed management group, but too large to be run efficiently by one or two men.

(5) Attractive offers. The price the acquiring firm is willing to pay may be too attractive to turn down.

Methods of Acquisition. Many of the fifty states have statutes spelling out procedures for merging two or more firms. These normally call for an exchange of common stock. Whenever a merger is executed in conformity with the statutes of the states in which the acquirer is incorporated, it is called a *statutory merger*.

The method of compensating the firms being acquired may involve cash, securities, or a combination of cash and securities. The securities offered may be common stock, preferred stock, or bonds. Convertible preferred stock and convertible debentures were particularly popular means of payment during the last half of the 1960s. While cash seems to have been the popular alternative in the 1970s.

Acquisition by Purchase of Capital Stock. The acquiring company may purchase all, or a majority, of the outstanding common stock from the owners of the company to be acquired. This may occur with the support of the management of the companies being acquired, or despite their opposition. Once the purchase of stocks has been accomplished, the company of the selling stockholders becomes a wholly or partially owned subsidiary of the acquiring firm.

Acquisition by Purchase of Assets. The acquiring company may purchase the tangible and intangible assets of a firm and make payment in either cash or securities. Frequently, all the liabilities of the selling company are assumed by the purchaser as a condition of sale. However, this is not mandatory. It is possible to purchase only a portion of the assets and to assume responsibility for only selected liabilities.

After the sale, the selling company may distribute proceeds of the sale to its shareholders and terminate its corporate charter. On the other hand, if the company continues as a legal entity it may invest the proceeds from the sale of its assets in a portfolio of marketable securities and become, in effect, an investment trust company. It may also use the proceeds to acquire new assets as an operating company in some new area of economic activity.

When the property and assets of a corporation are sold, formal approval of the sale by the stockholders of the selling corporation is required. Typically, holders of two-thirds of the shares entitled to vote must vote in favor of the sale. The percentage required for approval is set in the company's charter and/or in its bylaws. Dissenting shareholders generally have the right to receive a cash payment equal to an appraised value of their shares, but it is unlikely that the appraisal value of dissenting shares will exceed the pro rata distribution of the proceeds of sale if the transaction is arranged in good faith. Therefore, the right of appraisal becomes the right to receive cash in lieu of securities if the terms of acquisition provide for payment in securities.

Purchase of Control. The purchase of less than 100% of the outstanding common stock may occur as a matter of policy or strategy if the acquiring company is simply seeking corporate control. Such a transaction can have serious legal implications and should be approached cautiously by both buyers and sellers.

If a buyer limits his purchase of shares to the amount necessary to achieve control, and pays a premium for the control shares, the sellers can be held liable by the minority stockholders for the premiums they received. It is rather clearly indicated that control shares should not be acquired unless the buyer is willing and able to offer the same price and terms to the minority shareholders. Holders of control shares carry the responsibility of ascertaining the good faith of the buyer in order to avoid sale to a buyer who would proceed to loot the corporation, an act for which the sellers of control shares can be held liable.

Unfriendly and Friendly Mergers. When a merger is opposed by the management of the firm to be acquired, it is called an unfriendly merger while friendly mergers have the support of the management. In an unfriendly merger the potential acquirer may attempt to accomplish the merger by initiating a "proxy fight" or making a "take-over bid." In a *proxy fight,* the stockholders of the firm to be acquired retain their shares, but are asked to vote in favour of a slate of candidates that will favor the merger of the firms. If the insurgents win the proxy fight, the new Board of Directors can be expected to replace the management team that was opposed to the merger and the new management will work out the terms of the combination.

In the 1960s and the 1970s *take-over bids* replaced proxy fights as the dominant method of achieving mergers when there was management opposition to a combination. A take-over bid represents a direct offer by the acquiring firm to purchase all, or a majority, of the outstanding stock from the stockholders of the target company. If the offer to buy the stock is made for cash, the take-over bid is called a *tender offer.* If the offer to buy is made in terms of securities that will be exchanged for the shares of the target company, the take-over bid is called a *registered exchange offer*.

Requests to "tender for cash" are regulated by the Williams Bill which added Section 14(d) in 1968 to the Securities and Exchange Act of 1934. The Williams Bill makes it unlawful for a corporation to make a tender offer for any class of equity involving more than 5% of that security unless the offering firm has filed a statement with the Securities and Exchange Commission. This statement must include an identification of any position that the potential acquirer already has established in holding stocks of the target firm, disclosure of the source and amount of funds that will be used to acquire the shares tendered, and a statement of the purpose, or purposes, behind the tender offer. If the tender offer will result in transferring control, the statement must disclose any plans to liquidate the target firm or to sell any significant portion of its assets. The Williams Bill also places restraints upon the management of the target company. Before the management can make any recommendations to their shareholders either to accept or reject the tender offer they must file a supporting statement with the Securities and Exchange Commission justifying their recommendation.

Accounting Treatment. The Accounting Principles Board (see CERTIFIED PUBLIC ACCOUNTANT) recognizes two methods of recording business combinations—"purchase" and "pooling-of-interests." The earlier practice of using a mixture of techniques, part-purchase and part-pooling, is no longer acceptable [3]. In the 1950s and '60s the accounting treatment adopted was frequently determined by management's preferences based on the effect of the accounting procedure upon future income tax payments and/or the short-run impact on reported earnings per share. However, *Accounting Principle Bulletin #16* issued in 1970 establishes a series of criteria that must be met if a combination is recorded as a "pooling-of-interests." As a result, the accounting method for recording a merger is supposed to be based on the facts in the case rather than the preference of the parties.

The essence of "pooling-of-interests" consists of those combinations where two or more independent stockholder groups lose their individual identity and are combined by an exchange of common stock and thereafter share the same risks and rights. The essence of a purchase is found where all or a portion of the assets of the company being acquired are paid for with cash and/or securities other than the common stock of the acquiring firm.

The "pooling-of-interests" method records the value of assets and liabilities of the separate companies as they are reported on the books of the firms being combined. This treatment also results in the combining of stockholder equities. The new total equity is the sum of the equities of the combining firms and the new retained earnings account is the sum of the retained earnings of the companies involved.

No positive or negative goodwill is recognized under "pooling-of-interests." The financial statements for periods prior to the combination are restated as though the firms had been combined throughout the period being reviewed even though it may cover years when they were separate entities. The income statement in the year of the combination is reported as if the combination had occurred at the beginning of the year, even though it may have occurred on the last day of the year.

In accounting for a purchase, the acquired assets are recorded on the books of the acquiring corporation at the cost to the purchaser. Cost is measured by the amount of cash payment or of securities issued as consideration. If the acquisition is effected through issuance of securities, the fair market value of the securities delivered determines the cost of the assets acquired.

Frequently, the acquiring corporation will pay a price in excess of the net book value of the assets of the acquired firms. This excess must be recorded in some manner on the balance sheet of the acquiring firm. If, as is frequently the case, some of the assets being acquired have a market value well in excess of their book value, then those assets should be assigned a new cost basis equal to their current market value.

Restating the value of the assets acquired affects the tax position of the acquirer and the future earnings per share that will be reported after the merger. Writing up assets to market value can increase tax-deductible expenses for the purchaser. If fixed assets are restated, depreciation expense will change and if inventory is written-up, the next year's cost of sales will increase. This reduces future income tax liabilities but it also depresses the level of reported future net income and earnings per share. For the closely held acquiring company, the emphasis is clearly on minimizing income taxes and maximizing after-tax cash flows. However, the publicly owned firm may worry about how this treatment may affect the price of its common stock. If the market value of its common stock is a function of reported earnings, this treatment would depress stock prices.

To the extent that the seller's tangible assets cannot be written up to reflect a purchase price in excess of book values, the balance is recorded as "goodwill" on the acquirer's balance sheet. Companies subject to the regulations of the Securities and Exchange Commission must observe the requirement that goodwill be amortized over a period not to exceed 40 years. On the other hand, the Internal Revenue Code has ruled that the amortization of goodwill cannot be deducted as an expense for income tax purposes. This has the effect of reducing reported earnings without any compensating income tax benefits.

If patents of material value to the business are part of the acquired assets, they may be assigned an appraised value and amortized as a tax-deductible operating expense over their remaining lives. Similarly, if the seller agrees not to compete for a specified period of years with the acquirer of the business, such an agreement has a value which the acquirer should fix and amortize as an expense over the stated period.

The "pooling-of interest" accounting treatment became widespread after 1954 and was the primary method of reporting in the 1960s. This was a period when the purchase price was typically well in excess of the book value of the company being acquired and the method of payment was primarily via exchange of voting securities. In the 1970s, the purchase method of accounting dominated. Purchase prices, particularly in the last half of the 1970s, were frequently less than book value, and the acquisition was frequently accomplished by cash payments via a tender offer [4]. It is not clear whether the accounting treatment permitted by APB #16 affected the method of acquisition employed in mergers during the 1970s or whether the more rigorous standards of APB #16 were introduced in a period when the "pooling-of-interest" technique was no longer particularly attractive to corporate acquirers.

Tax and Legal Considerations. While tax considerations may not be a significant factor in deciding to execute a merger, tax problems will undoubtedly be important to both parties and may dictate the method of effecting the transaction. For the most part, the tax problems derive from Subchapter C of the Internal Revenue Code. This is one of the Code's most complex areas, and at an early stage both parties should retain competent tax counsel. The following discussion does not purport to interpret the tax laws, but merely outlines principal aspects of importance.

(1) *Taxable vs. Nontaxable Transactions.* Essentially, a taxable merger or acquisition is one under which the seller has a recognized gain or loss for tax purposes in the year the transaction is completed. A nontaxable transaction, usually referred to as a "tax-free" merger or exchange, is one in which there is no immediate recognition of gain or loss. In a tax-free transaction, the sellers realize a taxable gain or loss when they sell the securities received in payment. Buyers realize gains or losses as they dispose of, or amortize, the assets acquired. In a taxable transaction, the seller has a realized taxable gain or loss in the year of the transaction.

Taxable gains and losses are equal to the difference between the tax basis of the property disposed of and the fair market value of the consideration received.

(2) *Types of Nontaxable Mergers and Acquisitions.* Essentially, the Internal Revenue Code provides that a merger or acquisition may be "tax-free" if it is consummated

(a) As a statutory merger or consolidation.

(b) Through exchange of voting capital stock of one corporation for that of another if, immediately after the acquisition, the acquiring corporation has control of the acquired corporation.

(c) Through exchange of voting capital stock of one corporation for all, or substantially all, of the assets of another firm.

In "Type A" mergers the stock issued by the acquiring corporation does not have to be voting stock. Furthermore, a part of the consideration to the stockholders of the acquired corporation may be an obligation, such as notes or debentures, without disqualifying the transaction as tax-free. However, the use of debt securities, being an obligation and not an equity, will be treated as "boot" and regarded as a dividend taxable at ordinary income rates. In the exchange of stock for stock, designated as "Type B." the emphasis is on issuance of a voting stock, common or preferred, to effect the acquisition. The transaction may qualify as nontaxable to the shareholders of the acquired corporation even if less than all of the shares are exchanged. In the exchange of voting stock for properties of the other corporation, designated as "Type C," the acquiring corporation may assume the liabilities of the other or provide cash for their discharge.

(3) *Other Qualifications for Nontaxable Transactions.* In addition to statutory requirements, several doctrines derived from judicial decisions are important. Failure to observe these issues may negate the tax-free status of the merger.

(a) *Business Purpose.* It has been held that there must be a rational bona fide business purpose for the reorganization, not one "masquerading as a corporate reorganization." The usual type of merger or acquisition would have little difficulty satisfying this requirement, but it is an aspect which must not be overlooked in planning the transaction.

(b) *Continuity of Interest.* The courts have interpreted the law to mean that to secure the benefit of non-taxability, the stockholders of the acquired corporation must retain an equity interest in the new or surviving corporation consistent with the value of the stock or property transferred to it. This condition is generally satisfied by the issuance and exchange of voting stock. A serious question is raised, however, when a statutory merger involves a disproportionate amount of debt securities being delivered to the sellers.

(c) *Step Transactions.* In cases where the plan has been devised in the form of a series of transactions, each of which is designed to be tax-free under the Code, the courts have held that the net effect of all the steps becomes the determining factor.

(4) *Section 306 Stock.* Section 306 of the 1954 Code established severe restrictions on issuance of preferred stock in a corporate reorganization, as well as in transactions commonly referred to as the "preferred-stock bailout." "Section 306 stock," as it is termed in the Code, is defined to include preferred stock if the effect is substantially the same as receiving a stock dividend. Thus, as often occurs, if a portion of the earned surplus of the acquired corporation is capitalized as a result of issuing preferred stock, and if such stock is disposed of by the recipient shortly thereafter, the proceeds would constitute, in net effect, a cash distribution out of surplus. Consequently, although received in a non-taxable transaction, the proceeds of subsequent sale of "Section 306 Stock" may be subject to tax as ordinary income rather than as a capital gain.

Antitrust Factors. Corporate mergers and acquisitions involve compliance with, often interpretation of, Federal and state laws. Early discussions with legal advisors on the antitrust implications of proposed acquisitions is frequently essential.

Corporations entering into a merger transaction, particularly those of substantial size, or those holding a large share of a relatively small market, are confronted with the uncertainties of possibly violating one of more sections of the Sherman Act or the Clayton Act. Notwithstanding the many cases decided under these laws, attorneys still regard their provisions to be relatively undefined and subject to flexible interpretations, with the possible result of civil or criminal liability. (See ANTITRUST LEGISLATION.)

Management should be fully aware of the implications of Section 7 of the Clayton Act as amended in 1950 by the Celler-Kefauver Act; it provides that mergers and acquisitions are unlawful" . . . where in any line of commerce in any section of the country the effect of such acquisition may be substantially to lessen competition, or tend to create a monopoly." It should be noted that "substantially to lessen competition" has in recent actions been interpreted to include *potential* competition as well as competition already existing. Thus, management may expect counsel to examine aspects such as size, rate, and manner of growth (i.e., record of previous acquisitions), share of the market before and after the transaction, and how that market is defined, the pattern of distribution, the effect upon customer and supplier relationships, the relative ease of entry of new competitors into the pertinent market, and the question whether the acquirer possesses a " . . . dominant ability to produce and sell which threatens . . . extremely adverse competitive effects."

Congressional comment in the course of amending Section 7 in 1950 and in the 1978 hearings on mergers and industrial concentration was to the effect that the Section "applies to all types of mergers and acquisitions, vertical and conglomerate as well as horizontal." Further, even though the corporation to be acquired does not make products competitive with those of the acquiring corporation, the fact that it has facilities adaptable to such manufacture may be grounds for a charge that "potential competition" is lessened or precluded. [2].

Planning Mergers and Acquisitions. The planning phase starts with the task of defining the specific objectives of the firm. If objectives such as growth, stability diversification, product line improvement, etc., cannot be attained efficiently by internal development within the desired period of time, the merger route is a natural alternative. The reasons for seeking acquisitions establishes the criteria that should be used in selecting the firms to be acquired.

As a general rule, the best acquisitions are made among companies which are not openly available for sale or are being "shopped about." The soundest procedure is to search and predetermine the targets by deciding which companies will bring to the combination the desired assets, tangible and intangible, quickly ruling out those that fail to meet the acquiring firm's established criteria.

Approach to Negotiation. Formulating the strategy of approach is a critical step. Success or failure may hinge upon the initial and preliminary discussions. Data compiled in the early search procedures should be augmented by other published information about the company which could be useful in developing the reasons why the acquirer's proposition should be seriously considered. If the company is listed on a stock exchange, the Form 10-K reports to the S.E.C. are a valuable source of information on ownership of the stock, salaries of the highest paid executives, incentive compensation plan, and other pertinent information. The prospectus of any recent public offering of securities, the registration statement, and the attached exhibits on file with the Securities and Exchange Commission also provide information on takeover targets.

The age of the major stockholders, the probability of estate problems in a closely held company, the connections of the officers and directors, and the company's principal banking connections are valuable information in planning the strategy of approach. It is just as important to initiate merger discussions with the right individual as it is to present the merger idea effectively. (For example, if analysis of the company's financial statements indicates heavy current loans as well as long-term debt, a talk with the loan officers of the company's bank may lead to a better entree than a direct approach to the president.) In some situations, an unequivocal rejection may result from a direct approach to the president, who may be concerned primarily with protecting his position, whereas a more effective approach may be made through an "outside" director who is fully aware of his responsibility to the shareholders.

Essentially, the strategy is to identify a company's needs and problems, (e.g., capital shortage, inadequate distribution, lack of management succession, lack of marketability for its stock) and present the advantages of this merger in solving those problems. It is also appropriate to demonstrate that, through merger, the stockholders of the acquired company can improve their prospects for growth and market value appreciation for their shares.

An important factor is the determination of who should initiate the merger discussions. Sometimes it is inadvisable for the president of the acquirer to make the initial approach because his presence in the company's offices could set afoot rumors when secrecy is of utmost importance. Delegating the initial approach to an investment banker or to a consultant is a common tactic which has the added advantage that, should the proposal be rejected, the president of the acquiring corporation remains free to make another attempt by changing the strategy to meet the reasons given for rejection.

Use of a Business Broker. Commercial and investment bankers may act as intermediaries. This may include finding firms for acquisition, or simply handling the negotiations. After the reputation and reliability of the intermediary have been established, and as a prelude to his disclosure of a candidate, it is essential to confirm in writing: (1) the amount of the commission; (2) the conditions under which the commission becomes payable (usually only in the event the acquisition is consummated); (3) if negotiations are initiated by an intermediary representing a company seeking to sell, the authority of the intermediary to represent the seller (usually a letter from the president or controlling stockholder of the seller).

The fees of a business broker are negotiable and should be governed by the services performed and the amount involved. The seller may expect to pay 5% of the first million dollars, 3% of the second million, and 1.5% on the balance, with a further step down for large deals. If finding a buyer is difficult or if the negotiations are protracted and require the broker to maintain the continuity and equilibrium of the trading, the broker may justifiably bargain for a higher fee.

The fee is payable irrespective of whether the transaction involves cash or stock. Although the obligation to pay the fee commonly is that of the seller, the net effect often is that the total purchase price is increased by the amount of the fee, or that the net assets received are reduced by the fee payment.

Negotiation. The first few discussions are usually confined to generalities on why the two corporations should be combined. These discussions would include the firms' respective strengths, organizational structure, staffing, financial position, and economic prospects. Preliminary information exchanged will concern areas where economies from the merger are anticipated. The information would include marketing, manufacturing, and other expense and revenue data. It would also include the certificate of incorporation, the bylaws, copies of loan agreements and, frequently, an auditor's report.

The terms proposed by the acquirer are submitted subject to a full investigation of the corporation to be acquired, and consequently must be regarded as a preliminary indication of terms. On the other hand, the sellers may demand that the terms be final if the investigation does not disclose any material misrepresentations or any adverse factors not previously disclosed. Failure to resolve divergent views on price frequently is overcome by authorizing a consulting firm to make a comprehensive examination of both corporations and recommend an equitable ratio of exchange.

Not all negotiations are preceded by the planning, selection, and approach strategy just described. Frequently, a prospective acquirer is approached by an investment banker, a business broker, or other intermediary acting on behalf of the seller. Obviously, under these circumstances, the prospective acquirer is entering the negotiations without the benefit of previous investigation. There is then a tendency for top management of the acquirer to request opinions of middle management and sales personnel regarding the products and reputation of the seller. Such an approach inevitably results in rumors which can be adverse if not disastrous to the negotiations. Consequently, if is usually advisable to gain such information through a confidential survey by a professional firm or through the acquirer's commercial bank and its correspondents.

Preliminary Agreement. Upon reaching agreement, the negotiating officers of the two corporations generally will draw up a simple memorandum stating: (1) the basis of the agreement—i.e., the terms of the merger or acquisition: (2) that it is subject to approval by the respective boards of directors; (3) that it is subject to authorization by the shareholders of each corporation (in a cash purchase, the acquirer usually does not need approval of its own shareholders unless securities are to be issued); (4) that the acquirer shall have access to the business, properties, books, records, agreements, and operations of the corporation to be acquired and the right to examine them completely, and that the agreed upon terms are contingent upon a favorable finding in such examintion; (5) that the effective data of the merger or acquisition shall be on a specified day or as soon as practicable thereafter; and (6) that in the interim, until stockholder action is taken, neither corporation will make any substantial change in its operations or enter into unusual commitments unless the other is informed and gives prior approval.

Approved by the Board of Directors. The boards of both corporations should be kept informed of the progress of the negotiations. Each board must take formal action to approve the terms and conditions of the merger or acquisition as expressed in the preliminary agreement. Such approval, unless the terms were based upon a comprehensive examination made in the course of negotiation, would be a preliminary action providing authority to the respective managements to pursue the various procedural steps. If the terms and conditions are not subject to adjustment, the approval by the respective boards would be a definitive action followed by submission of the matter for shareholders' approval.

Announcement. Unless there are substantial reasons for withholding disclosure until the notice of the meeting of stockholders is sent out (assuming such action is required), it is advisable to make prompt announcement of the pending transaction, indicating advantages to both corporations, their employees, and customers. This is usually done by simultaneous letters from the president of each corporation to the stockholders, executives, key employees, distributors, customers, etc., by notices to clerical and plant employees, and by releases to the newspapers and trade publications.

Organizing the Procedural Activities. There are a great many tasks to be accomplished by the closing date. Here we can merely indicate the major procedural matters, since the detailed program will be different in individual situations.

(1) Final agreement of merger or contract of purchase—usually drafted by counsel for the acquirer but with participation by counsel for the seller.

(2) Investigation of the corporation to be acquired (unless this was performed previously)—sometimes by a task force of executives and key personnel of the acquirer, but generally by a consulting firm.

(3) Review of audited financial statements of the corporation to be acquired and a reconciliation of differences in accounting policies and practices to make its statements comparable with those of the acquirer—almost always performed by the certified public accountants of the acquirer.

(4) Examination of commitments and liabilities of the corporation to be acquired, whether or not reflected or reserved against in the balance sheet. Consideration must be given to undisclosed contingent liabilities for assessment of additional income taxes (for prior years not yet audited by the IRS), for patent infringement, for customer claims under product warranties, etc. It is also important to ascertain whether adequate reserves have been provided for future pension and retirement benefits to which the acquired corporation may be committed.

Post Merger Audit. When the corporate marriage has finally been consummated, a new set of problems arises that need attention if the long-run benefits of the combination are to be achieved. A suggested check list of some of the more important post-merger activities includes [5]:

(1) Effecting the merger by:
- completing legal arrangements (e.g., new corporate charters, transferring title on assets).
- designating agents of the new corporation for suppliers and vendors.
- changing corporate signs and logos.
- preparing necessary public-relations releases.

(2) Maintaining momentum immediately after the merger by:
- clarifying reporting relationships.
- ensuring the continuity of credit lines and insurance.
- making financial authorizations.

(3) Bringing the new organization into the corporate structure by:
- installing a reporting system for the new company.
- consolidating financial reporting, press relations, and stockholder communications.
- reviewing compensation and personnel policies of the acquired company.
- consolidating tax return preparation.
- reviewing accounting practices and policies, developing a new audit program.
- eliminating activities not appropriate to a division.

(4) Realizing short-term profit-improvement potential by:
- consolidating the headquarters staffs.
- closing down unnecessary facilities.
- eliminating redundant executive positions and unproductive personnel.
- centralizing functions (e.g., purchasing, insurance, data processing).
- cutting unnecessary frills (i.e., cars, planes, club memberships),
- consolidating banking relationships.

(5) Realizing long-term profit-improvement potential by:
- integrating operations (e.g., raw materials, manufacturing, distribution, marketing),
- and transferring technologies and methods.

Valuation of Company Being Acquired. The terms upon which an acquisition or merger is consummated may require a determination of the value of the acquired corporation or simply the relative value of the securities to be exchanged. There is no standard formula or set of rules for this evaluation: however, there are basic concepts which may be applied.

The management of the firms involved frequently have difficulty agreeing upon a fair price or a fair rate of exchange if the combination is accomplished by an exchange of securities. If the exchange ratio differs substantially from current market prices of the securities involved, it is not uncommon to seek the help of an impartial outsider. This role is frequently filled by either an investment banking firm or a consultant.

A variety of procedures may be used by outside experts to establish reasonable values of the firms involved in a merger. The basic principle is that the value of business assets is determined by their expected or potential earning power and the degree of risk or uncertainty associated with these expectations. Confirmation and application of this principle are found in numerous court decisions, one of the most succinct statements being by Mr. Justice Brewer of the Supreme Court of the United States who in 1894, said, "The value of property results from the use to which it is put and varies with the profitableness of that use, present and prospective, actual and anticipated."

The theoretical value of the acquired firm would be the present value of the incremental cash flows that would be attributed to the acquired firm discounted or adjusted for the risk of the acquired firm. The risk measure should consider the portfolio effects of the combination. The use of the capital asset pricing model and the evaluation of systematic risk has gained support as a possible approach to the valuation problem when risk is present [6].

The theoretical value of the combined firm would be the present value of the estimated future earnings of the combined firm discounted or adjusted for its risk. If synergism exists, the post-merger value of the combined firms should exceed the sum of the pre-merger values of the merging firms. A number of studies have attempted to investigate this concept (value additivity) as well as other real gains of merger activity [7]. Results of these studies are mixed, and although some studies indicate that there are real benefits accruing to stockholders of merged firms, most studies indicate little support for synergism. Yet, executives and managers cite many potential gains from these combinations, and actively seek acquisitions.

An appropriate evaluation method would estimate the expected future earnings stream of the combined firm, discounted at a discount rate that recognizes the risk associated with the combined firm. The maximum value of the acquisition would be the difference between the value of the acquiring firm with the acquisition, less the estimated value of the firm without the acquisition. The minimum value of the firm would be its value in liquidation. The final price or terms should be within this range and would depend upon the bargaining positions of the firms. If the synergistic effects exist, it is probable that stockholders of both firms would benefit from the combination.

It is not unlikely that the acquiring firm will offer an exchange ratio that represents a premium over the market price for the stock. This reflects the normal results of bargaining when the incentives to reach an agreement are not equally divided among the parties. Assuming there are "synergistic" possibilities in a business combination, the distribution of the increased economic values is not necessarily based on relative contributions, but rather on the relative bargaining powers.

The evaluation techniques that may be applied by impartial experts observing a business combination are many and varied. While the basic concepts of valuation can usually be agreed upon, the methods of measurement are subject to dispute. As a result, a fair ratio of exchange should be visualized as a range rather than a specific value.

Pros and Cons of Mergers. The bulk of the voluminous literature developed on the subject tends to be critical of corporate expansion through mergers and acquisitions. The basic criticism of merger activity rests upon the resultant reduction in competition or potential competition. The impact on competition may occur not only as a result of the reduction in the number of firms, but also through an increase in the frequency of "price leadership" or "conscious parallelism." Even though socially undesirable mergers may exist, there may also be economic benefits which result from mergers and acquisitions that should not be overlooked. Economic and technological innovations frequently demand larger and larger economic units in order to take advantage of economies of scale. In the absence of mergers and acquisitions, the economics of the market place would still create the needed economic size in surviving firms, but it would simultaneously increase the rate of business failures as smaller units were driven out of the market rather than being absorbed by other firms.

Mergers involving large publicly owned companies probably do not involve any significant economies of scale, but the threat of future take-over bids may well have a beneficial effect upon the activity and efficiency of entrenched management groups. The concept of corporate democracy is appealing, but it is not very compatible with the frequently expressed attitude that if a shareholder is unhappy with the performance of the management of his company he should simply sell his stock. The possibility of proxy fights and/or take-over bids represents potential corrective devices when the machinery of corporate democracy breaks down.

While the merger process may contribute to economic efficiency and growth, there is no doubt that some mergers and acquisitions may also be socially undesirable. However, such disadvantages and social costs should be controlled with appropriate legal restraints and supervision rather than by eliminating a process that can be both socially and economically valuable.

DR. PETER KARES, Chairman of Finance, College of Business Administration, University of South Florida, Tampa, Florida

DR. J.R. LONGSTREET, Professor of Finance, College of Business Administration, University of South Florida, Tampa, Florida

Information References

Bean, D. G., "Financial Strategy in the Acquisition Decision," New York, N.Y., Unipub, 1975.

Elgers, Pieter T., and Clark, John J., "Merger Types and Shareholder Returns: Additional Evidence," *Financial Management,* Summer 1980.

Federal Trade Commission, "Economic Report on Corporate Mergers," Washington, U.S. Government Printing Office, 1969.

Federal Trade Commission, Bureau of Economics, "Statistical Report on Mergers and Acquisitions," December 1978.

Gussow, Don, "The New Merger Game," New York, AMACOM, 1978.

Lewellen, Wilbur G., "A Pure Financial Rationale for the Conglomerate Merger," *Journal of Finance,* May 1971.

Nelson, Ralph I., "Merger Movements in American Industry 1894–1956," Princeton, N.J., Princeton University Press, 1959.

Scharf, Charles A., "Acquisitions, Mergers, Sales and Takeovers," Englewood Cliffs, N.J., Prentice-Hall, 1971.

Steiner, Peter O., "Mergers," Ann Arbor, Mich., University of Michigan Press, 1975.

U.S. Department of Commerce, "Mergers and Economic Efficiency," vol. I, Washington, D.C., Superintendent of Documents, U.S. Gov't. Printing Office, 1981.

References Cited

[1] Business Week, November 14, 1977, "The Great Takeover Binge".

[2] "Mergers and Industrial Concentration," Hearings before the Subcommittee on Antitrust and Monopoly of the Committee on the Judiciary, United States Senate Ninety-fifth Congress, U.S. Government Printing Office, Washington, D.C., 1978.

[3] American Institute of Certified Public Accountants, Opinions of the Accounting Principles Board, "Business Combinations No. 16," August, 1970.

[4] Hong, Kaplan, and Mandelker, "Pooling vs Purchase: The Effects of Accounting for Merger on Stock Prices." *The Accounting Review,* January, 1978.

[5] Serby, Frederick Wright, "Control Postmerger Change," *Harvard Business Review,* September-October, 1969.

[6] Rappaport, Alfred, "Strategic Analysis for More Profitable Acquisitions," *Harvard Business Review,* July-August, 1979.

[7] Copeland, Thomas E. and Weston, J. Fred, "Financial Theory and Corporate Policy," Chapters 17–18, Reading, Mass., Addison-Wesley, 1979.

Cross References: *Antitrust Legislation; Business Organization: Legal Structure; Long-Range Corporate Planning; Return on Capital; Securities and Exchange Commission.*

MERIT RATING. See Performance Appraisal (Merit Rating).

METHOD IMPROVEMENT

Method Improvement is an organized mental and physical process to get better results. As used in industry, the term includes changes made in materials, equipment, tooling, process, and layout. The objectives are to save time, reduce work, increase production, lower costs, and improve quality, or a combination of these. Sometimes one of these purposes is served at the expense of another—as when quality may be improved only through an increase in cost.

Manufacturing industries have been concerned with improving processes and flow of work ever since the factory system began. What is commonly referred to as mass production dates from 1798 when Eli Whitney originated interchangeable parts manufacture. This principle became applicable to industry in general when Carl Johansson standardized measurement in 1885 by creating "Jo-blocks," gauges which may be used as a standard of measurement with an error of less than one hundred thousandth of an inch.

Utilizing interchangeable parts manufacture, coupled with the idea of traveling racks borrowed from the meat-packing industry, Henry Ford "put America on wheels." He set out to make a car for the masses, and by repeated method improvement got the price for a Ford Touring Car to a low of $295, and for a Ford Runabout to $265 in 1924.

A related activity has been industry's efforts in standardization to reduce the numbers of sizes and varieties of materials and parts. Engineering societies and the American Standards Association, and individual companies, continue to seek and to adopt standards for interchangeability. (See entries on INDUSTRIAL STANDARDIZATION and STANDARDIZATION, COMPANY.)

History. Method improvement, in today's commonly accepted sense as a distinct function, began in 1881 at the Midvale Steel Company when FREDERICK W. TAYLOR pioneered detailed time study by dividing work into its elements and recording times taken. In this effort, he saw that "each elementary movement known in the trade" would repeat in other jobs. Thus he established the principle of determining standard element time data. His objective was ". . . to select the proper series of motions which should be used in making any particular article, and by summing the times of these movements . . . to find the proper time for doing almost any class of work" [1]. The fundamental concept of standard times that Taylor outlines is now called standard data. (See WORK MEASUREMENT.)

By dividing work into its elements, Taylor established the present approach to method improvement. His method, stated in his own words, was "Pick out all useless movements and discard them." He went on to prescribe, "Study, one after another, just how each of several workmen makes each elementary movement, and with the aid of a stopwatch select the quickest and best method of making each elementary movement known in the trade. The analysis of a piece of work into its elements almost always reveals the fact that many of the conditions surrounding and accompanying the work are defective: for instance, that improper tools are used, that the machines used in connection with it need perfecting . . ." [1].

Taylor's attempts to overcome the problems of "improper tools" led to the introduction of high-speed steel for machining and hence to increases in cutting speeds. With these improvements came Carl Barth's and Henry L. Gantt's special slide rules for computing machining times for use in setting job standards.

Henry L. Gantt helped Taylor make his work standards more effective by devising the "task and bonus" incentive plan, to reward operators and supervisors who met tasks set. The value here, as regards methods, lay in the follow-up. As Gantt describes it, ". . . the man's record . . . is the most complete analysis we can make of the workings of a plant, and the one that will help us most quickly to bring into their proper channels things that have gone haphazard. Such an analysis is far more important than an improved tool steel or a new set of piece rates, for it enables those in authority to see each day how their orders are being carried out" [2]. In trying to remove causes, Gantt stressed better engineering specifications, design standardization, store-keeping, cost and performance recording, scheduling, and employee training. These and other techniques were instituted to improve the management of work flow. In particular, he devised the GANTT CHART for production planning. He also invented and patented various types of equipment for more efficient processing.

Further progress in work analysis was made when Frank B. Gilbreth began in 1885 to study minutely the motions he and others made in laying bricks in the construction industry. He developed a complete set of specifications for all phases of the work, and published them in book form in 1909, "Bricklaying System." Before his book was published, Gilbreth turned his attention to motion study in general. His purpose was two-fold: first, to eliminate waste motion and establish the "one best way"; second to reduce fatigue. (See MOTION AND TIME STUDY.)

Gilbreth carried on extensive laboratory work to define the basic motions of work which he named therbligs (without, in his original paper describing them, calling attention to the fact that "therblig" is, phonetically, Gilbreth spelled backwards). He developed the process chart which, with greatly simplified symbols, is used extensively today to analyze the steps a part or product goes through in production. (See PROCESS ANALYSIS and OPERATION ANALYSIS.)

Later Developments. From Gilbreth's principle of stressing the method of doing work, Allen H. Mogensen subsequently evolved WORK SIMPLIFICATION. This procedure involves the study of work elements and distances moved, as well as the motions of individual operators and man-machine combinations, to reduce waste effort. Usually, such studies concentrate on specific jobs or processes, and rely heavily on stimulating supervisors and employees to suggest better methods of doing their work, after an indoctrination in basic principles of analyses by industrial engineering specialists.

A less detailed method is Work Sampling, an outgrowth of "ratio-delay" studies. In its simplest form, this is the determination of ratios of work time to idleness. Currently, studies are expanded to show also different types of work and lost time. Work sampling is primarily used to get over-all studies of group or department activities. (See RATIO DELAY.)

A broad approach, value analysis, was developed more recently. This started primarily as a purchasing endeavor to buy parts more cheaply than they are made internally. It is a form of method improvement that takes advantage of principles of standardization and mass production, but it basically is a process of analysis, of getting the simplest design that will perform the intended function. In such searches, all available talents are used, including the skills of outside specialists in the particular arts, and those of suppliers. The underlying fundamental is that no cost should be included in the product without adding a function either causing it to perform better or enabling it to be sold more competitively. (See VALUE ENGINEERING.)

Approaches. From the foregoing, it is apparent that there are many kinds and degrees of method improvement, and that the concepts involved need not be limited to factory operations. One important factor in results achieved is the initiating force. At one extreme are managers who act defensively. At the other extreme are managers who set quotas for cost reductions and maintain groups of skilled people to develop and install better methods. These groups are variously known as Timestudy Department, Industrial Engineering, Standards Department, or Methods Engineering. The kinds and degrees of method improvement carried on by these departments vary. At one end of the scale are departments which practically restrict their efforts to rate-setting for wage payment. At the other end are groups which work diligently to improve methods with little appreciation of the time-cost factors. A balanced approach is necessary.

Organizing Method Improvement. The first consideration in achieving best methods relates to the *proper place of method improvement in the organization.* Too often this function is assigned a relatively low place in the manufacturing organization, reporting to someone directly in charge of production. Conscientious as such an executive may be, when forced to choose he will get out production to meet delivery promises rather than cut costs. There are two additional reasons for placing the responsibility for method improvement higher in the organization. One is to spread the efforts into overhead cost reduction where relatively little attention has been given to either time-study or method improvement (See OVERHEAD ASSIGNMENT). The other is to have the influence of a high executive when efforts to make cost reductions require actions by other functions in the organization, especially when those actions will raise the latters' operating costs. Examples are the requirements for better engineering specifications, more precise production schedules, and earlier performance and cost reports.

A second consideration is to *organize the method improvement function itself,* so that it can operate effectively. An analysis leading to this objective is shown in Exhibit I, applicable where operations are large enough to permit sufficient personnel. (When this is not the case, the principles should nevertheless be applied by personnel "doubling up.") The chart portrays four sets of duties and functions directly related to method improvement. The division of the functions into two vertical sections is to emphasize the need for at least two distinct groups in each function. The reason is that when one group is expected to do both creative and maintenance work, very little of the creative gets done. Experience seems to show also that two different types of persons are needed to achieve results in each of these two fields.

The third consideration relates to the *economics of method improvement.* Costs should be returned, plus a profit. To do so requires effective operation in two details. The first is to recognize that there are almost as many ways of going about method improvement as there are individuals. Finding a better method is a creative process that takes place in the mind of an individual. The skill and experience of the innovator should be supplemented by those of others to give him more experience to think

Exhibit I

Chart of Duties of Time Study and Methods Personnel Related to Method Improvement, Showing Interrelations and Time Intervals

Time	Function: *Time-Cost Control*	Function: *Method Improvement*
Install	Make saving estimates	Learn about new methods
	Compute project costs	Review new designs, tools
	Determine rate return	Study new equipment
	Take new time-studies	Check new materials
Maintain	Set work standards	Extend method improvements
	Develop operation sheets	Maintain suggestion plan
	Utilize wage incentives	Solicit foremen ideas
	Survey performances	Aid employee training

Exhibit II

Each Method Improvement has its own break-even point —the number of repetitions of an improved method that are required to pay off the money invested in making the change.

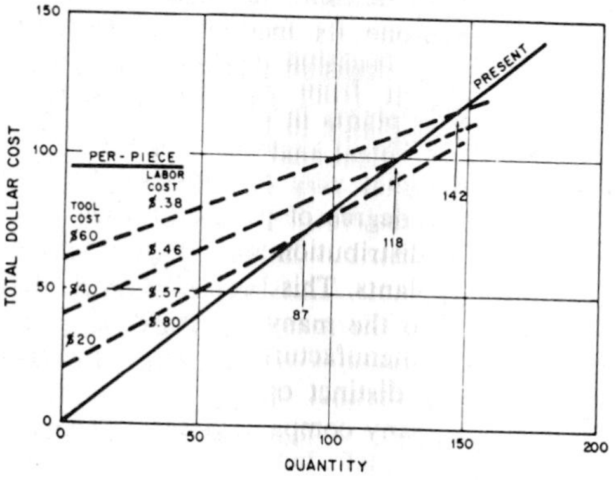

with. BRAINSTORMING is one way devised by Alex Osborn to generate more ideas. Such collaboration is helpful in developing the new idea which is more than simply the addition to previous ideas.

The second detail is to determine the rate of return on each proposed improvement. This depends upon the cost to make the change, and, in manufacturing, the quantity of repetition that will occur afterwards and the saving per unit anticipated. With predictions of new costs, results of specific suggested improvements may be shown graphically by break-even charts, as in Exhibit II. The method improvement portrayed there concerns new tools of varying cost, but the principle applies to any proposed improvement. Each has a different break-even point in terms of quantities, and different rates of return on the cost of the improvement, for anticipated quantities. Calculations such as these may show declining rates of return from further refinement of methods. Rates of return can be used to establish priority of projects to be worked on, thus making the best use of money available for method improvement.

The fourth consideration is suggested by the duty in Exhibit I, "Extend method improvements." This is stressed because there is a general tendency to improve one job at a time as though it were the only one in the plant. A factor here is the ever-present pressure to open up bottlenecks. In contrast, some engineers look for *repetition* of elements of work that go to make up many operations of a type. For example, the first element in most operations is called "Pick Up Piece"—a part, a tool, or a snap-out form. Viewed this way, method improvement made in elements of work may be applied wherever they occur in a plant. Methods personnel should organize procedures for multiplying the applications of the better methods they develop.

Improvements should be extended in other ways: Periodic audits should be made to keep abreast of ever-changing quantities caused by shifts in consumer demands. Future occurrences of costly methods should be avoided by reviewing proposed new designs, tools, equipment, plant layouts and the like while they are in the paper stage. Designers should be instructed in comparative costs of likely designs.

The fifth consideration concerns the *maintenance* of method improvements. Improvements can slip into disuse through changes in personnel, and through interferences by irregular working conditions. In manufacturing, both are largely prevented when sound measurement and incentives are used. Correct standards allow for only the work required by a prescribed method. Conversely, records of new or experienced people call attention to extra work caused by irregular conditions. The "Survey performances" duty listed in Exhibit I should uncover the problem.

When the organized attack on methods here

outlined is utilized, the cost reductions will be substantial. One reason is that the average company has done its method improvement work only when occasion demanded. Another reason is evident from surveys that report roughly half the plants in this country as having utilized the critical analyses of timestudy. A third reason is that very few companies have made the same degree of progress in studying overhead and distribution work as they have made in their plants. This latter reason applies generally also to the many types of work that lie outside of manufacturing. Thus, probably there are three distinct opportunities for cost reductions in many companies.

PHIL CARROLL, P.E., Industrial Engineer, Maplewood, New Jersey

Information References

Maynard, H. B., ed., "Industrial Engineering Handbook," 3rd ed., Section on Methods, New York, McGraw-Hill, 1971.

Niebel, Benjamin W., "Motion and Time Study," Homewood, Ill., Irwin, 1976.

References Cited

[1] Copely, Frank Barkley, "Frederick W. Taylor," New York, Harper Bros., 1923.

[2] Gantt, H. L., "Work, Wages, and Profits," New York, McGraw-Hill, 1913.

Cross References: *Brainstorming; Creativity; Gilbreth Principles of Motion Economy; Motion and Time Study; Operation Analysis; Process Analysis; Process Engineering; Ratio-Delay; Scientific Management; Scientific Management: "Taylorism"; Standardization, Company; Systems Management; Value Engineering (Value Analysis); Work Measurement; Work Measurement in the Office; Work Simplification.*

METHOD TIME MEASUREMENT (MTM).

See Predetermined Motion Study.

MONEY AND BANKING

Our modern economy is often referred to as a "money economy" implying that in our complex and interdependent economic system, money is the device which enables us to conduct trade more easily. Without the use of money, and credit instruments which represent a claim to funds, a barter system would prevail which would be both cumbersome and inefficient. Thus the use of money not only increases the feasibility of specialization, but also facilitates trade. In a modern economy its use is essential.

However the use of money and credit is much more than a passive instrument of the economic system, for the monetary system is the lifeblood of the circular flow of income and expenditure which characterizes all economies. A badly performing monetary system can be disastrous, while a properly functioning system can make a positive contribution to the goals of price stability, full employment, and economic growth.

THE CONCEPT OF MONEY

Money consists of anything which is generally acceptable in payment for goods, services, and debts. Historically many things have served as money, such as stones, slaves, cattle, and even cigarettes. Today, however, in all advanced countries, money consists primarily of paper currency and demand deposits of banks. To a lesser extent, precious metals circulate as a means of payment.

Money can also be defined in terms of the functions it performs. As a medium of exchange it frees us from the need to barter, but at times, because of the loss of confidence in the continued acceptability of money in exchange for goods and services, there has been a "flight" from money. This has occurred to varying degrees, when a significantly rising price level was threatened which in effect would lessen the purchasing power of money. Hence recipients of money dispose of it quickly to buy other assets before prices rise.

Another function of money is to serve as a standard for deferred payments; that is, to act as a future medium of exchange. Money thereby is used to link together the present and the future in definite terms and thus can be employed in financial contracts. Obviously, if the value of money changes significantly owing to inflation or deflation, its performance as a standard of deferred payments will be unsatisfactory.

A third function of money is to act as a standard of value, as a yardstick to measure the relative value of different goods and services.

Similarly, money serves as a store of value. Since it is the most liquid form of all assets, it is a convenient way to store wealth, but obviously the real value of this saving will vary with changes in the purchasing power of money. Finally, money serves to provide both liquidity and solvency to the economy, since it can be held to ensure that accruing debts and contingencies can be paid as they come due.

Kinds of Money. There is some variation in the monetary systems of the advanced countries, but the circulating media in most of these countries are mainly composed of checking deposits, paper currency issued by the government or central banks, and coin. In the United States the most significant form of money is checkbook money. However, a classification which is based on the relationship between the value of money as a medium of exchange and its value as a commodity is useful for analytical purposes, and is as follows:

(1) *Full Bodied Money.* This is a type of money whose value as a commodity is as great as its value as money. In the United States, for example, full bodied gold coins were in circulation until 1933, when all gold was called in by the Government. Prior to this time, the Federal Government would coin gold in unlimited quantities.

(2) *Representative Full Bodied Money.* This term refers to a receipt for full bodied coins or their equivalent. While the receipt is merely "paper" it represents in circulation an amount of metal with a commodity value in the market place equal to its value as money. Before their recall in 1933, the gold certificates which circulated in the United States were an example of this type of money.

(3) *Credit Money.* Credit money is a type of money which circulates at a value greater than the commodity value of the material from which it is made. The main varieties of credit money are paper money, checking deposits, and coins when the market value of the material in the coin is less than its monetary value. Paper money of this type is often referred to as "fiat money," inasmuch as it derives its value by government edict rather than by any intrinsic commodity value it may contain.

The Money System of the United States

Currency. While an object can become money because of its general acceptability, the legal code can improve and safeguard the monetary system. Legal tender is an attribute given to money by law which requires debtors to offer and creditors to accept when it is offered in payment of an obligation. The Banking Act of 1933 affirmed that all types of currency were legal tender. The following is a description of the currency system of the United States:

(1) *Federal Reserve Notes.* These notes are a liability of the Federal Reserve Banks. When the public withdraws currency from deposit accounts at a commercial bank, the bank meets these requests by holding an inventory of paper money. The commercial bank gets this paper money in the form of Federal Reserve Notes by drawing down on its deposit account at the Central Bank. Formerly, the notes were legally required to be collateralized by gold, but over time the "gold cover" was gradually reduced, and in 1968 all legal restrictions were dropped. Federal Reserve Notes are the predominant form of circulating currency now used in the United States.

(2) *Gold Certificates.* Since the Gold Reserve Act of 1934, these notes have not been used as a circulating medium in the United States. Instead, the Treasury has issued non-circulating gold certificates when gold was purchased, and with only minor exceptions, $35 of gold certificates have been issued for each ounce of monetary gold held by the Treasury. The certificates are deposited with the Federal Reserve Banks to restore the Treasury's account which was reduced because of the purchase of gold, and the Treasury receives a deposit credit equal to the amount of gold certificates. In the past, gold certificates provided the legal reserves for the Federal Reserve Banks, but since 1968 there is no such rule imposed by law.

(3) *Silver Certificates.* Throughout its earlier history, the United States has intermittently monetized silver, and in the 1930s the Silver Purchase Act monetized silver at $1.29 an ounce (far above its market price). The Treasury paid for the silver by issuing currency in the form of silver certificates. With World War II and the increased industrial usage of silver, however, free-market silver prices eventually rose over the monetary value, and now the Treasury no longer monetizes silver. The silver certificates are being replaced with Federal Reserve Notes.

(4) *Other Currency.*

(a) *U.S. Notes.* First issued in 1878, this currency represented an extension of the "greenbacks" introduced in the Civil War. Currently they are being replaced by Federal Reserve Notes.

(b) *National Bank Notes.* When the National Bank Act was passed in 1863, these notes issued by private national banks came into use. During most of their history they were secured by Government bonds. This type of currency was discontinued when the Banking Act of 1935 was passed.

(c) *Treasury Notes of 1890.* As a result of the Sherman Purchase Act of 1890, these notes were issued and were collateralized by silver. Since 1893 they have been in the process of retirement.

(d) *Federal Reserve Bank Notes.* Originally intended to serve as a transition currency when Federal Reserve Notes were to replace National Bank Notes, this medium was first issued in 1916. In 1933, and 1942–43, they were also used, but since 1945 no more notes of this type may be used.

Metallic Money. While metallic money is an indispensable part of our monetary system it is relatively unimportant. In all cases the coins are alloyed with metals other than the principal metal used in each coin. During most of their history, the monetary value has been greater than the market value of the commodity embodied in the coins.

Demand Deposits. Demand deposits are liabilities of banks, and are convertible into currency or are transferable from one owner to another without prior notice. In distinction to time deposits which primarily represent savings accounts and are subject to notice (usually thirty days), no interest can be paid on demand deposits by any commercial bank which is a member of the Federal Reserve System. Demand deposits are subject to check and constitute the major means of payment used in the United States, hence they constitute the major part of money in circulation.

Measurement of the Money Supply. Because of the legal restrictions on payment of interest on demand deposits, negotiable orders of withdrawal (NOW) accounts, share drafts, and automatic transfer systems (ATS) have been introduced. Essentially, these are checking accounts that pay interest. Furthermore, in response to high open-market interest rates, Money Market Mutual Funds that permit investors to write checks against their balances have become popular. In recognition of these changes in the financial system, early in 1980, the Federal Reserve announced the following new statistical definitions of the money supply.

M-1A—currency plus demand deposits at commercial banks, including holdings of foreign banks and official institutions.

M-1B—M-1A plus other "checkable deposits" including NOW, share drafts, and ATS accounts.

M-2—M-1B plus savings and small time deposits, money market mutual fund shares, overnight agreements by commercial banks to repurchase securities, and overnight Eurodollar deposits held by non-bank U.S. residents at Caribbean branches of U.S. banks.

M-3—M-2 plus large time deposits (over $100,000) in all depository institutions and term repurchase agreements at commercial banks and savings and loan institutions.

L—M-3 plus other liquid assets not included elsewhere, such as bankers acceptances, commercial paper, short-term U.S. securities and savings certificates, and term Eurodollars held by non-bank U.S. residents.

Monetary Standards. The ultimate means of payment is the standard money of a monetary system, and the system used is named after this money of ultimate redemption. Two basic types of monetary standards have been in existence: (1) a commodity standard whereby the ultimate means of redemption is some commodity such as gold or silver; and (2) a "fiat" or inconvertible paper standard, where the standard money is not redeemable into anything else.

When a commodity standard is practiced, the standard money has value both as a commodity and as money, and early monetary standards were of this type. With the passage of time, precious metals came to be used as standard money because of their desirable qualities as money, and metallic standards spread in usage. These were often monometallic standards where gold or silver was used, or bimetallic standards, where both metals were used concurrently. In past history, the United States has employed both types of metallic standards.

Besides legally defining the standard monetary units in terms of a metal, when a monometallic standard is adopted, it may be either a coin standard or a bullion standard. In the case of a monometallic coin standard, the standard money (gold, for example) circulates as money and all other forms of money are redeemable into the standard money. Under a monometallic bullion standard, however, the standard monetary metal is not coined and does not circulate as money. Rather, the circulating money is representative money or credit money which is redeemable into the standard money with certain restrictions.

Bimetallic standards are similar to monometallic standards except that two metals are used instead of one. Historically, gold and silver have been widely used under this arrangement. Since two metals are used in this system the standard money must be defined in terms of both metals, thus establishing a fixed ratio of value between them. This ratio is called the mint ratio. Whether this system will work well or badly in practice depends on whether the mint ratio and the ratio of values established for the metals in the market as commodities are identical. If the ratios are different, the metal which is undervalued will tend to disappear from circulation and only the overvalued metal will circulate. This tendency was first observed by Sir Thomas Gresham, and from this has come the principle known as Gresham's Law: that an overvalued money tends to drive an undervalued one out of circulation.

A fiat standard, often called an inconvertible paper standard or a managed currency standard, refers to a system whereby the circulating medium is also the standard money, and the money has no value as a commodity. Under this system, since the money in use has no intrinsic value, its worth is derived solely from its purchasing power or general acceptability.

The Monetary Standard of the United States. After the passage of the Gold Reserve Act of 1934, the U.S. monetary system basically became "fiat" in nature, and subject to management by the monetary authorities. Gold holdings are now unimportant as a source of credit creation by the central banking authorities.

Externally, however, sometimes gold is used to settle international balances, and prior to 1972, the U.S. purchased and sold monetary gold at $35 an ounce which in effect set the world price. After chronic unfavorable balances of payments extending over a period of years, plus the rise in price of gold in the free gold markets, the U.S. "closed the monetary gold window" in 1971. In 1972, and 1973, in two steps, the U.S. also raised the book value of its gold holdings from $35 to $42 an ounce.

Free gold markets, where the price of gold is determined by the interplay of supply and demand for the metal, should not be confused with monetary gold. Monetary gold is held by central banks and government institutions and priced at a legally set price—not an open-market price. In all developed economies, gold is unimportant as a basis for credit creation—the money supply is "managed" by governmental authorities.

Characteristics of the Banking System

Supervision. The commercial banking structure in the United States is characterized by a multiplicity of chartering, supervising, and examining agencies. This is a result of the dual banking system of both Federally and state chartered banks which rests on the separation of Federal and state powers in our legal code, as well as the diffusion of powers among different Federal agencies.

National banks receive their charter from the office of the Comptroller of the Currency. Each state, however, can also grant a charter to a bank which does not wish to be organized under Federal law. Thus, capital requirements, laws, and regulations on lending and investing, as well as on bank operations, may differ considerably from state to state and from Federal law.

All national banks are automatically members of the Federal Reserve System and hold stock in the Federal Reserve Bank in their area, and thus are subject to the jurisdiction of the Federal Reserve authorities as well as the Comptroller of the Currency. State banks, which are more numerous than national banks, can join the Federal Reserve System if they apply and are accepted for membership. Most state banks, however, have preferred to stay out of the system because of capital requirements, reserve regulations, and other restrictions placed on their operations, and in recent years there has been a drift out of the system. Currently, about 5,600 of the 19,700 commercial banks in the United States are members of the Federal Reserve, with around 73% of total bank deposits.

All banks which are members of the Federal Reserve System are also participants in the Federal Deposit Insurance Corporation and are subject to the regulation of this agency. State banks can join the Federal Deposit Insurance Corporation without joining the Federal Reserve System. Participants pay a premium based on their deposits, and currently deposits are insured up to $100,000. Only about 300 commercial banks are not members of the Federal Deposit Insurance Corporation.

Organization. Compared to other countries, the number of commercial banks in the United States—approximately 14,700—is relatively large, but the industry is quite concentrated; a small number of banks account for a relatively large proportion of the business. Through mergers too, the number of banks has been declining for years.

The number of branch banks, however, has increased. This development, though, has been uneven because of the restrictions imposed by law. Some states permit branch banking on a state-wide basis, while others restrict it to a limited area. Still other states prohibit it entirely. National banks follow state law on this matter.

Because of these restrictions, chain banking and group banking have evolved. Chain banking refers to the use of interlocking directorates to link banks together, while in group banking, a holding company is formed to control the stock of a number of banks. State law on multi-bank holding companies varies and some states prohibit them entirely.

In the last decade or so, most of the major banks have been reorganized as "one bank holding companies," and now about 70% of commercial bank deposits are controlled by this type of organization. The motivation behind reorganizing as a one-bank holding company was to expand financial services beyond the legal restraints imposed on banks, but in 1970 the Federal Reserve was given power to regulate the activities of one-bank holding companies. Generally, one-bank holding companies have been restricted to activities of a financial nature.

Foreign Banking in the United States. Foreign banks have a long history in the United States, but with the growth of multinational business in all the western countries since the 1960s, the movement by foreign banks into this country has accelerated. These banks are mostly located in New York City, Chicago, Los Angeles, and Miami, and there are about 250 foreign bank subsidiaries, branches, and agencies with close to $100 billion in U.S. assets.

Since 1978, with the passage of the Foreign International Banking Act, any foreign bank with assets of $1 billion or more is subject to Federal Reserve interest ceilings and reserve requirements, and if a branch holds at least $100 thousand in deposits it must be covered by FDIC insurance. Before the 1978 law, too, unlike domestic banks, foreign banks could set up branches across state lines, but now they are subject to the same rules as U.S. banks.

Services Performed. Commercial banks have constantly widened their scope of activities, but their major services include the acceptance of demand deposits subject to check, and the maintenance of time deposits which consist mainly of savings accounts and certificates of deposit, and legally are subject to prior notice before withdrawal. The providing of credit to business and government in the form of loans and investments are their major asset-producing activities. Other services include the servicing and collection of checks and debt instruments, the operation of trust departments and foreign departments, and other related banking functions.

Lending Activities. Somewhat over one half of the loans currently granted by commercial banks represent credit extended to business. Other major categories of loans consist of credit granted to farmers, consumers, homeowners, and foreign credits.

Business loans are generally written on a short-term basis with a maturity of less than one year, although term loans with a maturity date of over one year are often granted. These loans may be unsecured where they are extended on the basis of the credit rating of the borrower, or may be secured by collateral such as equipment, real estate, life insurance, securities, or other collateral. Bank loans are for the purpose of providing temporary working capital for business, such as seasonal needs or for a build-up of inventory or accounts receivable, and thus are self liquidating in nature. Capital loans are also granted for such purposes as the acquisitions of fixed assets or as a permanent addition to working capital of a business, and usually are placed on an amortized basis.

Interest rates on bank loans vary by the size of the loan, size and credit status of the borrower, and the size and location of the lending bank, as well as by the maturity of the loan. The rates on loans scale upwards from the so-called prime loan rate: i.e., the rate the largest banks charge the biggest and best rated short term borrowing customers.

Commercial banks generally establish a line of credit for a business customer. The line of credit is established after a credit analysis and is a statement of intent by the bank establishing a maximum loan limit with specified terms. In addition, borrowers are often required to maintain a certain compensating balance in their deposit account when a loan is outstanding. All loans, of course, must adhere to applicable state and Federal law.

Investment Policy. Because one of the major liabilities in a commercial bank is the demand deposits which are subject to immediate withdrawal, commercial banks must always consider the need for liquidity in their lending and investment program. Hence, their investments are confined to high-grade securities which are easily convertible to cash without significant loss. To a great extent the investments must be relatively short term in nature. U. S. Government issues, and to a lesser extent, state and municipal securities, meet this need for quality and liquidity as well as providing income.

Management Policy. The theory of bank management has gone through a number of distinct phases, and historically the emphasis was primarily on proper asset management. In recent years, however, large international "money market banks" have adopted the "liability management" policy of banking. Under this practice, banks protect their liquidity needs by offering certificates of deposits, buying Euro-dollars, and borrowing funds from other banks. Liquidity needs, thus, are met by "managing" the liability side of the balance sheet rather than by relying only on proper bank asset creation.

Creation of Deposits. When a bank makes a loan or buys securities, bank deposits are increased. Contrariwise, when the loan is paid or the security sold, deposits in the banking system decrease. Since deposits are tantamount to money, the lending and investing activities of the banks affect the volume of the money supply.

When a loan is consummated, a credit in favor of the borrower is created. When the proceeds of the loan are withdrawn by check, the recipient of the check redeposits the check in the banking system. Similarly when a bank buys securities, the seller of the securities receives a check from a bank, which is deposited in the banking system and thus creates a deposit. The seller of the securities can then issue checks against this credit which in time will create additional deposits.

Since banks are required to maintain reserves against deposits, the limitation on this potential deposit creation is the reciprocal of the reserve requirement. Thus if the reserve requirement were 20%, the banking system theoretically could expand deposits five times. Because of currency withdrawals and the movement of funds to time deposits which have lower reserve requirements than demand deposits, the actual multiplier tends to be much lower than the reciprocal of the reserve requirement.

Other Credit Institutions. In addition to commercial banks, there are other financial intermediaries which compete directly or indirectly with the commercial banks. Mutual savings banks, located mostly in the northeastern section of this country, accept deposits and invest primarily in mortgages and high-grade bonds. Unlike the savings banks, which are state chartered, savings and loan institutions are either Federally or state chartered, and confine their investment activity almost exclusively to mortgage financing. CREDIT UNIONS, which are mostly small organizations, primarily grant consumer credit exclusively to members. In addition to these organizations, life insurance companies, finance companies, government credit agencies, and other organizations all engage in some activities which are related to those of commercial banks.

Central Banking. In all the major countries, central banks have been established which operate in the public interest rather than for profit. Originally these banks were formed to function as bankers' banks, by supplying funds to banks and by protecting the liquidity and reserves of the banking system. Over time, they have gradually assumed more extensive responsibilities and now carry out monetary policy to help achieve high and stable levels of production and employment.

FEDERAL RESERVE SYSTEM

Background. After the charter of the Second Bank of the United States was not renewed in 1836, the United States had no central bank until 1913, when the Federal Reserve Act was passed. Originally intended to correct the defects of the National Banking System, the Act has been subject to amendments which have increased the powers of the monetary authorities.

Organization. *Board of Governors.* At the apex of the Federal Reserve System is the Board of Governors, consisting of seven members appointed by the President and confirmed by the Senate for fourteen-year terms. The term of one member terminates every two years. The President designates one of the members of the Board as Chairman.

In addition to formulating and executing national monetary policy, the Board represents the Federal Reserve System in its contacts with the agencies of the Federal Government. It supervises the operations of the Federal Reserve System, names three of the nine directors of each of the twelve Federal Reserve Banks, and appoints the Chairman and Deputy Chairman of each bank. It also has important powers in carrying out monetary policy, the more significant of which are listed below:

(1) To fix reserve requirements of member banks within the limits imposed by law.

(2) To determine amounts and kinds of loans Federal Reserve Banks can make.

(3) To approve discount rates established by the Federal Reserve Banks.

(4) To set margin requirements on loans made for the purpose of purchasing qualified securities.

(5) To fix maximum rates of interest paid on time deposits by member banks.

Federal Open Market Committee. Composed of the seven members of the Board of Governors and five presidents of the Federal Reserve Banks, the Open Market Committee is authorized to conduct purchases and sales of U. S. Government securities, for the purpose of influencing credit conditions. Transactions are supervised by an officer of the Federal Reserve Bank of New York and the holdings of securities are allocated to the Federal Reserve Banks according to the ratio of each Reserve Bank's assets to total assets of the Reserve Banks combined.

Federal Advisory Committee. The function of this committee is purely advisory, but it exerts influence because of the prestige of its members. It has twelve members, one from each Federal Reserve District elected by the Board of Directors of each Federal Reserve Bank, and usually is made up of bankers.

Federal Reserve Banks. Because of the fear of centralized economic power and because of the size and economic diversity of the country, twelve central banks were established, rather than one. Twelve Federal Reserve Districts were defined which were intended generally to follow economic areas rather than state lines. (See Exhibit I.)

EXHIBIT I

BOUNDARIES OF FEDERAL RESERVE DISTRICTS AND THEIR BRANCH TERRITORIES *

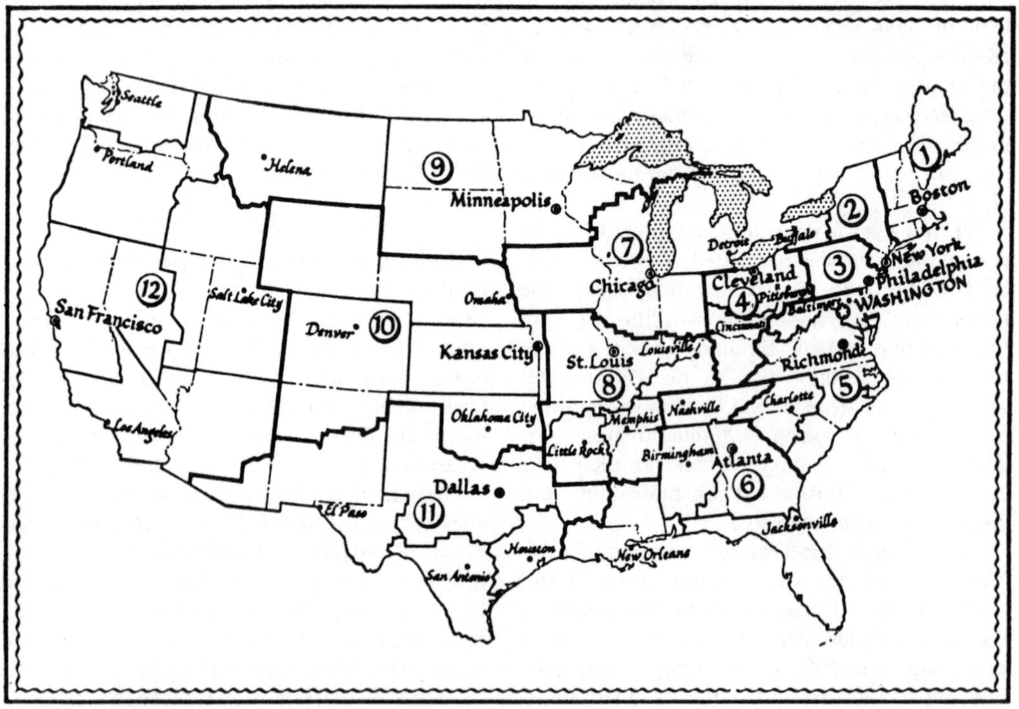

* Alaska and Hawaii are included in District 12.

Each of the twelve Federal Reserve Banks receives its charter from the Federal Government, but is owned by the member banks, since each member must subscribe for the stock of a Federal Reserve Bank equal to 6% of its capital and surplus. Dividends of 6% are paid on the stock.

Each Federal Reserve Bank has nine directors. The member banks elect the three Class A and the three Class B directors, but the Board of Governors selects the three Class C directors. Class A directors must be bankers, but the Class B and C are not connected with the banking industry. Thus non-bankers dominate the boards.

Major assets held by the Reserve Banks include gold certificates, held as cover for Federal Reserve notes and deposit liabilities, and U. S. Government securities. Major liabilities are Federal Reserve Notes and deposits of member banks, the U. S. Treasury, and foreign governments, and their central banks.

Member Banks. All national banks are required to join the system, but membership is optional for state banks. As stated earlier, most state banks have chosen to remain out of the system to avoid meeting the requirements of membership.

Methods of Monetary Control. The techniques of monetary control exercised by the central banking authorities can be divided into quantitative and qualitative controls. Quantitative controls affect the cost and availability of credit by their influence on bank reserves and interest rates, while qualitative controls are directed at a particular segment of the economy. The United States Treasury also has significant influence over credit conditions in its funding operations, its power over gold and silver purchases, and other activities.

Quantitative Controls. *Open Market Operations.* The buying and selling of United States obligations, particularly short term securities, by the Federal Reserve Open Market Account has been the most important technique used by the monetary authorities to control the cost and availability of credit. It is a flexible instrument and can be used for day-to-day operations.

When the Federal Reserve buys a security from a Government bond dealer, banks gain reserves upon deposit of the check received by the dealer. Similarly when banks sell a security to the Federal Reserve, they exchange an earnings asset for a credit to their reserve account. When the central bank sells from its portfolio rather than buying, the reverse effect takes place.

Change in Reserve Requirements. Since the Banking Act of 1935, the Board of Governors has been given power to change the reserve requirements of member banks. Recently the method of classifying banks was altered, and now member banks are classified either as Reserve City Banks or Other Banks. The range of reserve requirements for Reserve City Banks is now 10–22% of net demand deposits, and 7–14% of net demand deposits for Other Banks. The range on time deposits is 3–10% for all member banks.

Changes in reserve requirements are limited in their effect since only member banks come under the jurisdiction of the Federal Reserve. Furthermore, changes in the prevailing level of reserve requirements are made infrequently because of the difficulty of banks to adjust to the new requirements.

Discount Rate. The discount rate refers to the rate charged by the central banks for loans to member banks. Its usefulness, however, is limited since member banks may be reluctant to borrow, and because borrowing is a privilege, not a right, of member banks, and the monetary authorities may display reluctance to lend. Sometimes a change in the discount rate is regarded as a "signal" of a change in policy by the central banks.

Moral Suasion. Through its public pronouncements and influence, the Federal Reserve authorities have attempted to persuade the banking community to follow a certain policy at times. This has generally been regarded as ineffective by most students of banking, and is of minor importance today.

Qualitative Controls. *Margin Requirements.* The Board of Governors was given power to control the amount of credit being channeled into security markets by the Securities and Exchange Act of 1934. The Board limits the volume of credit on purchases of listed and other qualified securities by setting the margin, the difference between market value and the maximum loan value. Thus with a margin requirement of 70%, the maximum loan value is 30% of its purchase price.

Both long and short sales are covered under this procedure. Regulation T applies to brokers and dealers, and Regulation U applies to banks.

Other Qualitative Controls. During World

War II and for a time after the war as well as during the Korean War, the Board of Governors was able to exert some control over consumer credit. Under Regulation W, down payments and maturity dates on consumer loans were established to check the inflationary force of consumer spending. Similarly, under Regulation X, lending for purposes of residential and construction credit was controlled by establishing maximum loan values and minimum amortization terms.

Treasury Monetary Powers

In addition to the influence of the Federal Reserve authorities on the cost and availability of credit, the Treasury also possesses certain powers which affect monetary conditions. The size of a deficit and the method of financing, as well as the size of a surplus and how it is used, are important elements to consider, as is the system of taxation. Debt management policy, and the location and size of Treasury deposits, too, exert significant influence on monetary conditions.

Effects of Deficits and Surplus. Generally, cash deficits of the Treasury have an expansionary effect on the economy, since more spending is being added to the flow of expenditures than is being removed by taxation. Contrariwise, when the Treasury accrues a cash surplus, expenditures and income tend to be reduced inasmuch as a greater amount is being taken out of the circular flow of income than is being added to it.

The technique used in financing the deficit and the class of bondholders paid off in case of a surplus, too, has importance. If a deficit is financed by selling bonds to the public, no change in the level of bank deposits or reserves is experienced. On the other hand, if the debt is sold to the commercial banks, the money supply will increase. The most inflationary form of financing would be to sell obligations to the central banks, for then both deposits and reserves in the banking system would increase. If excess reserves are created, a multiple expansion of the money supply is possible.

Similarly to the preceding, the most deflationary use of a surplus to decrease debt would be to reduce the central banks' holding of securities. A reduction of the portfolio of United States obligations held by commercial banks would reduce deposits, and a retirement of the debt held by the public would cause no change in deposits or reserves in the banking system. Thus the technique employed in debt financing and the uses made of a surplus exert an important influence on the availability and cost of credit.

Taxation and Spending. The turnover of money (the *velocity* of money) is affected by the propensity to consume on the part of those taxed. If taxes are levied on those with a relatively high propensity for consumption, the dampening effect of the taxes will be greater than if the taxes were assessed on those with a relatively low propensity to consume. Similarly, if Government expenditures are channeled to groups with a relatively high rate of consumption, the expansion in demand will be greater than if the funds were expended on those with a relatively low level of consumption.

Debt Management. The power of the Treasury to change the maturity distribution of the national debt, as well as to determine the interest rate on Government securities, and eligibility for purchase, constitutes an important factor in monetary management. Although legislation, generally, restricts Treasury issues with a maturity of ten years or over to a ceiling of $4^1/_4\%$, the growth of the national debt has greatly enhanced the significance of debt management.

An increase in the short term debt, for instance, would raise the liquidity of the economy, while an increase in the long term sector of the debt would decrease liquidity. Furthermore, since security prices and yields on other forms of obligations reflect conditions in the Treasury bond market, the interest rate on Federal Government securities, and the marketability factor, are important in their influence on the money market and bond market.

Treasury Deposits. The Treasury maintains deposits in commercial banks and in the Federal Reserve Banks, as well as keeping some vault cash. A transfer of deposits from commercial banks to the central banks by the Treasury causes a contraction of the money supply as well as losses of reserves. Opposite action can, of course, be taken.

Other Government Powers. There are a multitude of Government corporations that lend funds, and others that guarantee or insure loans. Loans by Government corporations, for instance, are made for purposes such as assisting agriculture, foreign trade, small business, railroads and other industries. Guarantees and insurance are particularly important in mortgage financing, where the Veterans' Administration and the Federal Housing Authority are especially active.

Monetary Policy

Recent Central Bank Policy. During World War II, central bank monetary policy was subordinate to the needs of the Treasury to borrow vast sums of money at low rates of interest. The pattern of yield rates on government securities was established at 3/8 of 1% for the short term bills to 2½% for the long term bonds, and the Federal Reserve maintained this relationship in the market by open market operations.

Following the end of the war, the Treasury desired the policy of "pegging" Government bond prices to continue, maintaining that this would restrain the cost of servicing the Government debt, as well as preventing a loss of confidence in the economy if Government bond prices were allowed to decline. The latter, it was feared, would have an unfavorable effect on employment. Furthermore, it was alleged that allowing interest rates to rise would not halt the inflation that was threatening at the time.

The arguments in favor of removing the "peg" on Government bond prices centered on the belief that allowing interest rates to rise and the drop in bond prices which this would cause, would slacken investors' conversion of bonds to cash and thus act as an anti-inflation measure. Furthermore, it would allow the Federal Reserve freedom from control of the Treasury.

This argument was debated with great intensity, but finally in 1951 an agreement was reached whereby the Federal Reserve authorities gained the freedom to discontinue the practice of pegging Government bond prices. In effect the significance of this so-called "accord" lay in the fact that the central bank authorities were free to follow monetary policy as their judgement dictated, rather than be subservient to the needs of the Treasury.

Following the accord, the Open Market Committee adopted a policy of dealing only in the short term bills in their open market operations. This policy of "bills only" was defended on the grounds that any suspicion of pegging Government bond prices would be eliminated by following this practice and that a free market in government bonds would thus prevail. Opposition developed to this policy on the grounds that it restricted the power of the Reserve authorities and that a policy of dealing in all maturities would lessen the volatility of the bill rate. Finally, partly in response to the need to maintain short term interest rates because of the persistent deficit in the balance of payments, the "bills only" policy was abandoned in 1961.

In 1961, the economy fell into a recession, and the monetary authorities applied expansionary techniques to stimulate demand. In the following year, "growthmanship" became national policy as the administration attempted through fiscal policy to increase the growth rate of the economy and reduce unemployment. Depreciation rules were liberalized, an investment tax credit was passed, and income tax rates were decreased in both 1964 and 1965. By the mid-1960s, aggregate demand had responded to these measures, but Government deficits generated by spending programs and the cost of the Viet Nam War were piled on top of a fully employed economy. The result was an acceleration of inflation.

By 1969, the Federal Reserve authorities adopted a policy of restraining inflation by tightening up on money and credit conditions, interest rates rose to historic levels, and fears of a "liquidity crisis" developed. In the following year, the Federal Reserve apparently felt that its medicine had created the desired effect, and that inflationary expectations had been subdued, so credit was made more available, and interest rates fell in response to monetary management.

Monetary Policy. In the 1970s there was a basic change from fixed to floating rates on foreign exchange markets, the United States continued to pile up deficits both internally and externally, and double-digit inflation threatened economic stability. Clearly, confidence in the U.S. dollar eroded and debate over the proper "targets" for the money supply and interest rates intensified.

There was a recession in 1973–1974, and monetary policy was eased from its previous position. Later, this was reversed. By late 1979, the cost of living soared, gold and silver rose to record highs, confidence in Government attempts to stop inflation fell, and the monetary authorities had to face the problem of breaking inflation expectations. For the first time, restraints were put on credit-card operations and money-market funds. Interest rates moved sharply up to the highest levels ever recorded in American history as the central bank faced the task of breaking inflation.

The Effectiveness of Monetary Policy. Monetary policy can make a positive contribution toward achieving our welfare goals, by influencing the cost and availability of funds. Unlike fiscal policy, it is a particularly flexible instrument in that it can move quickly in either direction toward expansion or toward restraint of demand.

Monetary policy is generally regarded as more effective in curtailing inflation than as a recovery measure. With the powers it now possesses, the central bank authorities can curtail the money supply through means such as open market operations, raising reserve requirements, and by discount policy. Bank reserves can thus be reduced until the banking system cannot make any new loans, and unless offset by an increase in velocity, total demand will decline. Obviously, measures which are too strong can also produce a downswing rather than merely reduce inflationary pressures.

During recessions, reserves can be created by the monetary authorities, and interest rates forced down, but business may be reluctant to borrow, despite the cheap credit available, and banks may be afraid to lend because of a loss of confidence. Thus, while a policy of ease may be promoted by the monetary authorities, it may be ineffective in promoting recovery.

Besides acting as a countercyclical device, monetary policy can also aid economic growth. By providing a satisfactory level of the money supply, an acceptable and sustainable rate of economic growth may be fostered. In addition, by following a proper monetary policy, the social goal of full employment may more closely become a reality, by promoting credit conditions that not only create an atmosphere of confidence, but meet the credit needs of the economy.

BARNARD SELIGMAN, Graduate School of Business Administration, Pace University, New York, New York

Information References

Cargill, Thomas F., "Money, the Financial System, and Monetary Policy," Englewood, N.J., Prentice Hall, 1979.

Chandler, Lester V. and Goldfeld, Steven M., "The Economics of Money and Banking," New York, Harper Row, 1977.

Davis, Thomas E., "Issues in Monetary Policy," Kansas City, Mo., Federal Reserve Bank of Kansas City, 1980.

Luckett, Dudley G., "Money and Banking," New York, McGraw Hill, 1980.

Cross References: *Economics; Inflation.*

MOTION AND TIME STUDY

Motion Study and **Time Study** were essential parts of the SCIENTIFIC MANAGEMENT movement which came into prominence around the turn of the century. Time study, originated by FREDERICK W. TAYLOR, was mainly used for establishing time standards and piece rates. Motion Study developed by FRANK and LILLIAN GILBRETH was largely employed for the analysis and improvement of work methods. Gradually the combined use of motion study and time study has become widespread. Motion and time study provides a means for determining the preferred method of performing work and a means for measuring work, that is, determining what constitutes a standard day's work or determining the standard time required to perform a specific task [1].

The great expansion in business and industry has brought with it wider acceptance and greater use of motion and time study. Many practices in this field that once were accepted in only the most progressive companies have now become commonplace. Moreover, motion and time study is now applied to many different business activities and to areas far removed from industry itself. The caliber of the people engaged in this field has changed. Today, a large percentage are college graduates or are people from the shop or office who have been carefully selected and thoroughly trained for this work. This specialized staff has better equipment and facilities to work with, and is making greater use of mathematics and statistics and electronic data-processing equipment to aid in gathering, analyzing, and summarizing facts, and solving complex problems.

The same careful study and consideration that have been given to direct factory labor in the past are now being extended to indirect labor and to the evaluation and control of machines and processes. This includes the consideration of such factors as yield, quality, waste, and scrap.

Motion study was originally defined by the Gilbreths as the study of the motions used in the performance of an operation or an activity for the purpose of eliminating all unnecessary motions and building up a sequence of the most useful motions for maximum efficiency. Motion study not only includes the analysis of the movements used in performing work but it also involves consideration of the tools, equipment, and materials that the worker uses and the conditions surrounding the worker and the work place. The objective is to design the work method that will result in high operator productivity and low cost with the least fatigue possible.

Motion Study Techniques. Before a motion study application is undertaken it is desirable to make a preliminary analysis to determine the extent to which the study should be carried—how much is likely to be saved, how long the investigation will probably take, and how much it will cost.

The tools and techniques of motion study may be divided into three classes.

(1) Process Analysis.

(2) Equipment Utilization.

(3) Operation Analysis.

Process Analysis. The system or process of making a part or performing an activity should be studied before undertaking a thorough investigation of a specific operation in the process. Such an over-all study will ordinarily include the analysis of each step in the manufacturing process (See PROCESS ANALYSIS.)

Process Chart. The process chart is a device for recording a process in a compact manner as a means of better understanding it and improving it. The chart represents graphically the separate steps or events that occur during the performance of a task or during a series of actions. The chart usually begins with the raw material entering the factory and follows it through every step, such as transportation to storage, inspection, machining operations, assembly, until it becomes a finished unit itself or a part of a subassembly. The process chart might of course record the process through only one or a few departments.

A careful study of such a chart, giving a graphic picture of each step in the process through the factory, is almost certain to suggest improvements. It is frequently found that certain operations can be eliminated entirely or that a part of an operation can be eliminated, that one operation can be combined with another, that better routes for the parts can be found, or more economical machines used, delays between operations eliminated, and other improvements made, all of which go to produce a better product at a lower cost.

Flow Diagram. Sometimes a better picture of the process can be obtained by putting flow lines on a plan drawing of the building or area in which the activity takes place. This is called a flow diagram. Both a process chart and a flow diagram are sometimes needed to show clearly the steps in a manufacturing process, office procedure, or other activity.

Equipment Utilization. *Activity Chart.* Although the process chart and the flow diagram give a picture of the various steps in the process, it is often desirable to have a breakdown of the process or of a series of operations plotted against a time scale. Such a diagram is called an activity chart. The activity chart is of special value for analyzing maintenance work, jobs involving people working in groups, and operations where the work is unbalanced and where there is "necessary" idle time.

Man and Machine Chart. The operator and the machine may work intermittently on some types of work. That is, the machine is idle while the operator loads it and while he removes the finished work from it, and the worker is idle while the machine is in operation. Not only is it desirable to eliminate idle time for the worker but it is also important that the machine be kept operating at as near capacity as possible. (See PROCESS ANALYSIS.)

The first step in eliminating unnecessary waiting time for the operator and for the machine is to record exactly when each works and what each does. Much work consists of three main steps: (1) *Get Ready,* such as putting material in the machine; (2) *Do* (doing the work), such as drilling a hole; and (3) *Put Away* or clean up, such as removing the finished piece from the machine. Very often a clearer picture of the relationship of the operator's working time and the machine time can be obtained by showing the information graphically to scale.

Operation Analysis. The overall study of the process should result in a reduction in the amount of travel of the operator, materials, and tools, and should bring about orderly and systematic procedures. The man (woman) and machine chart often leads to ways of eliminating idle machine time and promotes a better balancing of the work of the operator and the machine.

After such studies have been completed it is time to investigate specific operations in order to improve them. The purpose of motion study is to analyze the motions used by the worker in performing an operation in order to find the most economical way of doing it. A systematic attempt is made to eliminate all unnecessary motions and to arrange the remaining necessary motions in the best sequence.

Operation Chart. For those who are trained in the micromotion study technique, that is, those who are able to visualize work in terms of elemental motions of the hands, the operation chart, or the "left-hand right-hand chart," is a very simple and effective aid for analyzing an operation. No timing device is needed, and on most kinds of work the analyst is able to construct such a chart from observations of the operator at work. The principal purpose of such a chart is to assist in finding a better way of performing the task, although this chart also has definite value in training operators.

Micromotion Analysis. Most work is done with the two hands, and all manual work consists of a relatively few fundamental motions which are performed over and over again. Frank B. Gilbreth, in his early work in motion study, developed certain subdivisions or events which he thought common to all kinds of manual work. He coined the word *therblig* (Gilbreth spelled backwards) in order to have a short word with which to refer to any of the elementary subdivisions of a cycle of work. (Example of therblig: *Grasp*—that part of the cycle during which the hand is taking hold of an object, closing the fingers around it preparatory to picking it up, holding it or manipulating it. Grasp begins when the hand or fingers first make contact with the object, and ends when the hand has obtained control of it.) Not all of these seventeen therbligs are pure or fundamental elements in the sense that they cannot be further subdivided, but they serve a useful purpose. The experienced analyst has no difficulty in using the therbligs in industrial applications.

Motion pictures are made of the operation or activity to be studied. A special clock is placed in the picture to indicate time on the film, or the camera is driven by an electric motor so that the time interval from one frame of film to the next is known. After the film has been processed it can be placed in a special analysis projector and the motions for the hands, arms or other body members can be determined and the time for each motion can be measured and recorded.

A *Simo Chart* (simultaneous motion-cycle chart) can be constructed showing graphically and to scale the movements of each member of the body. The simo chart is useful in finding the most efficient method of doing work and it can also be used to assist in training individuals to understand the classification of body motions.

Micromotion study was originally employed mainly for job analysis work but it is now also used (1) as an aid in obtaining motion-time data for synthetic time standards, (2) as a permanent record of the method and time employed in doing work, (3) as an aid in studying the relationship of the activities of two or more persons on group work, (4) as a means of timing short-cycle operations, and (5) for research in the field of motion and time study. As valuable as micromotion study is for these purposes, however, its two most important uses are: (1) to assist in finding the most economical method of doing work, and (2) to assist in training individuals to understand the meaning of motion study. It enables them to become proficient in identifying the motions used by the worker, to *see* the motions made by the operator's right hand and by his left hand, and even to note what the fingers of each hand do.

It is necessary to detect where one motion ends and another begins. The term *motion minded* has been used to describe this ability of the person who has trained himself (herself) to follow unconsciously the motions of the worker and to use this ability to aid in designing the preferred method of performing the operation.

Work Measurement. The object of work measurement is to determine the time in minutes that a qualified, properly trained, and experienced person should take to perform a specific task or operation when working at a normal pace. This time is called the *standard time* for the operation. In the early days such time standards were mainly used as a basis for wage incentives. Frequently the standard was converted into money value and was called a piece rate. Piece rates were usually expressed as so many dollars per hundred pieces, and these piece rates were used as a basis for paying workers. Today time standards still have wide use as the basis for wage incentives, but they are also used for planning and scheduling work, for determining standard costs, for preparing budgets, for cost control, for balancing assembly lines, and for determining the size of gangs.

Time Study. Although time study data may

be obtained with a motion picture camera, an electronic data collector, or by machines, the decimal minute stopwatch and the electronic timer are the most common means of obtaining such data. The operation to be studied is divided into small elements, each of which is timed with a stopwatch. A selected or representative time value is found for each of these elements, and the times are added together to get the total selected time for performing the operation. The speed exhibited by the operator during the time study is rated or evaluated by the time study observer, and the selected time is adjusted by this rating factor so that a qualified operator, working at a normal pace, can easily do the work in the specified time. This adjusted time is called the *normal time.* To this normal time are added allowances for personal time, fatigue, and delay, the total being the standard time for the task.

Standard Data. Standard data are forms of work measurement that consist of time values for specific elements of work. The manual part of a task is broken down into groups of hand motions or body movements that can be precisely defined and that are applied only in connection with a particular machine or a specific operation. The elemental time values usually take the form of tables, formulas, or graphs. Elemental time values for establishing standard data were originally determined by time study. Now predetermined time systems, either directly or from "elemental building blocks," simplify the procedure. The application of standard data by computer is widely used.

Predetermined Time Systems. Manual work can be divided into basic hand and body motions, and time values can be established for each motion. (See PREDETERMINED MOTION TIMES.) A predetermined time system consists of a set of time data and a systematic procedure which analyses and subdivides any manual operation or human task into motions, body movements, or other elements of human performance, and assigns to each the appropriate time value. Each system of time data was originally developed from extensive studies of all aspects of human performance through measurement, evaluation, and validation procedures. Tables of time data are compiled and may be used to determine synthetically the time required to perform any operation or activity covered by the data. The procedure is simply to make a list of the motions that are required to perform a manual task and then apply the appropriate time values to the motions. The sum of these values gives the time required to perform the operation.

The Work-Factor System and Methods-Time Measurement (MTM) are examples of two widely used systems. Both of these plans include the original detailed system as well as other systems such as those designed especially for use with machine tools; for use for clerical related work, including desk-top operations and such tasks as filing, typing, keypunching, and data entry; for manual assembly work performed under stereoscopic magnification; and for measuring mental processes such as inspection, proofreading, composing, color matching, calculations, and other repetitive or semi-repetitive mental operations. A number of the predetermined time systems have been computerized and utilize a data collection instrument and a desk-top computer.

Work Sampling. Work sampling, first used in the British textile industry, is a fact-finding tool. In many cases, needed information about the performance of men and machines can be obtained in less time and at lower cost by this method than by other means.

Work sampling has three main uses: (1) *activity and delay sampling*—to measure the activities and delays of workers or machines—for example, to determine the percentage of the day that a person is working and the percentage that he or she is not working; (2) *performance sampling*—to measure working time and non-working time of a person on a manual task, and to establish a performance index or performance level for the person during his or her working time; (3) *work measurement*—under certain circumstances, to measure a manual task, that is, to establish a time standard for an operation. This involves determining the pace or performance of the operator when he or she is observed to be working and by recording the number of units produced during the study. (See RATIO DELAY.)

Work Methods Design. The original design of work methods or the improvement of existing operations calls for the use of the problem-solving process. In the early days, greatest emphasis was placed on the improvement of existing methods. The use of process charts, flow diagrams, man and machine charts, and simo charts gave the analyst a clear picture of the existing work method. Then by applying principles of motion economy [2], using check lists, and by asking "why" questions about every aspect of the work, it was possible to develop improvements. However, in recent years greater emphasis has been placed on the original design of the system and methods. Moreover, this had gradually been recognized as a design problem and the general problem-solving process is now being used with great success.

Problem-Solving Process. The five steps described here are useful in the logical and systematic approach to solving almost any problem [3]. This approach has been found useful in the area of work methods design and methods improvement.

(1) *Problem Definition*—General statement of purpose, goal, or objective—formulation of the problem.

(a) Criteria—means of judging successful solution of problem.

(b) Output requirements—(1) Maximum daily output. (2) Seasonal variations. (3) Annual volume. (4) Expected life of product, shape of volume growth and volume decline curve.

(c) Completion date—Time available to: (1) design; (2) install and try out facilities; (3) bring output up to full production.

(2) *Analysis of Problem* (No evaluation is to be made at this step).

(a) Specifications or constraints including limits on original capital expenditures.

(b) Description of present method if operation is now in effect.

(c) Determination of activities that machine operator probably can do best and those that machine can do best, and establishment of man-machine relationships.

(d) Re-examination of problem—Determination of sub-problems.

(e) Re-examination of criteria.

(3) *Search for Possible Solutions*—Try the elimination approach—Use check lists—Apply the principles of motion economy—Apply creative imagination.

(4) *Evaluation of Alternatives*—Determine the preferred solution—Method that gives lowest cost or requires least capital—Method that permits product to be put into production most quickly.

(5) *Recommended Action*—Prepare written report—Make oral presentation—Have all supporting data available—Anticipate questions and possible objections.

Organization Patterns for the Use of Motion and Time Study. Although traditionally motion and time-study work has been performed by industrial engineers and staff specialists, there is a trend toward developing forms of work organization in which motion and time study and the problem-solving process are used by line managers and supervisors and by the employees themselves [4].

The ways in which motion and time study is used may be classified into three patterns:

Pattern A, used by industrial engineers and staff specialists: Taylor, Gilbreth, and their contemporaries worked largely as specialists providing services for the line or operating organization. Motion and time study and wage-incentive applications were the core of much of the work in industrial engineering in the early days, although the scope was much broader in some companies.

Pattern B, used by line managers and supervisors. L. P. Persing at the Fort Wayne works of the General Electric Company was one of the first to change drastically the way motion and time study was used. In 1928 he began conducting motion-study training programs for the foremen and supervisors. The supervisors took the initiative in studying their own problems, made improvements in methods in their own departments, and were recognized for their cost reduction accomplishments. Today, managers and supervisors in many companies receive training in motion and time study and the problem-solving process and follow a similar pattern. Industrial engineers may serve as teachers and consultants and may also work on special assignments for the line people.

Pattern C, used by workers themselves in teams or groups. Nonmanagement workers participate directly in the design and management of their jobs. They learn new skills, assume greater responsibilities, and receive higher pay. They are trained in motion and time study and the problem-solving process. Industrial engineers and the supervisors may serve as teachers and consultants and may also work on special assignments for the teams. This form of work organization requires a long period of time for full understanding and implementation. However, in a growing number of companies motion and time study provides a means of increasing human effectiveness and improving life satisfactions through work itself [5].

Motion and Time Study a Part of Industrial Engineering. The two important parts of industrial engineering have traditionally been (1) *work methods design* including motion study and methods improvement; and (2) *work measurement* and *labor cost control.* In many organizations the latter includes wage-incentive applications for direct and indirect labor. Motion and time study has brought great benefits to management in the form of increased productivity and lower unit costs and has benefited the worker by making his job easier and more satisfying.

RALPH M. BARNES, Professor of Engineering and Production Management Emeritus, University of California at Los Angeles, Los Angeles, California

Information References

Barnes, Ralph M., "Motion and Time Study—Design and Measurement of Work," 7th ed., New York, Wiley, 1980.

Carson, Gordon B., Bolz, H. A., and Young, H. H., eds., "Production Handbook," 3rd ed., New York, Wiley, 1972.

Ireson, W. G. and Grant, Eugene L., eds., "Handbook of Industrial Engineering and Management," 2nd ed., Englewood Cliffs, N.J., Prentice-Hall, 1971.

Maynard, H. B., ed., "Industrial Engineering Handbook," 3rd ed., New York, McGraw-Hill, 1971.

References Cited

[1] Barnes, Ralph M., "Motion and Time Study—Design and Measurement of Work," 7th ed., New York, Wiley, 1980.
[2] *Ibid.,* Chap. 15.
[3] *Ibid.,* Chap. 4.
[4] *Ibid.,* Chap. 2.
[5] *Ibid.,* Chaps. 39 to 43.

Cross References: *Gilbreth Principles of Motion Economy; Industrial Engineering; Method Improvement; Predetermined Motion Times; Process Analysis; Process Engineering; Ratio Delay; Work Measurement; Work Measurement in the Office; Work Simplification.*

MOTIVATION

Motivation must be at the heart of concern in the study and the practice of management. Organized effort—that is, getting work done through and with others—requires motivating promotively interdependent effort, as opposed to effort that is self-canceling. Agreement on this point is a dominant theme in the history of the study of management. Thus Henri Fayol, one of the early observers of organized effort, shares the contemporary opinion that motivation is the core of management [1,2].

Dramatic changes have occurred in our understanding of motivation. The periods following the two world wars saw cumulative breakthroughs in describing and influencing motivational states, and advances of the last few years promise far more striking results.

Formal Definition. "Motivation" often receives no precise conceptual designation; and implicit and explicit meanings of the term commonly differ. The concept, however, covers at least this area of meaning: "Motivation refers to the degree of readiness of an organism to pursue some designated goal, and implies the determination of the nature and locus of the forces inducing the degree of readiness." The necessity of considering all of these factors together must be underscored, particularly since the common emphasis has been upon motivating behavior with a specific direction, such as high satisfaction or high output. The danger is that all low producers be considered as unmotivated, when in fact they may be highly motivated toward goals other than, for example, high output. The point has a crucial practical significance, for changing the direction of intense motivation poses quite a different set of problems than motivating the phlegmatic. Relatedly, the locus of motivating forces often has been assumed to be in the formal organization or the individual. The assumption is too restrictive, as will become clear.

Contemporary views of motivation also emphasize an "expectancy" view. Thus, observers tend to agree that motivation will occur only under the specific conditions referred to by three key notions: *expectancy, instrumentality,* and *valence,* building upon the seminal work of Victor Vroom [3]. Thus, individuals will be motivated to the degrees that:

• They *expect* that their effort will lead to enhanced performance.

• They believe that enhanced performance will be *instrumental* in leading to their reward, both extrinsic and intrinsic.

• They value the expected reward which, in the terminology of expectancy theory, has a high *valence* for individuals.

In contrast, earlier approaches proposed a simpler linkage. In Maslow, for example, individuals were presumed to be motivated if work satisfied their "higher-level needs." (See MOTIVATION: Maslow's "Basic Needs.") This emphasized only valence, and assumed that expectancy and instrumentality also would be high. The assumptions do not apply in many cases. Consider job enlargement, which often will have a high valence for many employees but may not be instrumental in leading to an extrinsic reward because management views the program as a speed-up only, or because labor unions or employees have concerns about increasing productivity, especially during hard economic times. Expectancy views of motivation have become widely influential [4] because of such perceived deficits of earlier concepts.

History. The history of approaches to motivational phenomena may be summarized in terms of four emphases. Each continues to have some currency although the emphases are to varying degrees incompatible.

First, *fear and punishment* may be considered the main themes of the traditional approach to motivating effort. This emphasis cannot be relegated to some dim past, although such early massive organized efforts as the building of the Egyptian pyramids were sustained in large part by fear-punishment. More recent variants of this emphasis are not lacking. Indeed, the traditional theory of organization clearly reflects the influence of this first emphasis in coming to grips with motivational phenomena. Its "principles" emphasize a limited span of control, minute subdivision in assigning work, and complete dependence of subordinates. All of these characteristics are consistent with the limited range of motivational forces of the fear-punishment emphasis. Since the "principles" commonly guide attempts at organizing work, this first emphasis in understanding and controlling motivational states is significant indeed.

Second, an early emphasis upon *rewards* as motivators was manifested in programs which may be dubbed "naive paternalism" and "subtle paternalism." Strauss and Sayles distinguished these two forms of rewards as motivators in these terms: "The naive argument holds that if management is good to employees, they will work harder out of loyalty and gratitude. The more subtle argument ignores the question of gratitude; it holds that liberal benefits and good working conditions make for happy employees, and that happy employees work harder" [5]. The manifestations of such uses of rewards to motivate cover a broad spectrum. At an extreme, a "Sociology Department" at the Ford Motor Co. attempted to "Americanize" the Ford work force, with a zeal for reconstruction that sometimes precipitated attempts to influence employee attitudes, behavior, diet, drinking, and marital relations [6]. Such efforts were not uncommon. The expectation was that employees would be thankful for such concern and would express their gratitude in higher output. Hence the designation "naive paternalism." Less ambitious efforts of the same general type attempted to influence motivational states by inaugurating pension and retirement systems, employee recreation programs, and the like.

This second emphasis derived from an undigested interpretation of some pathfinding empirical demonstrations that fear-punishment left untapped a mother lode of motivational forces. The vogue of the second emphasis began in the late twenties, deriving momentum from studies such as those of the British Munitions Board during World War I and the famous American research at the Hawthorne Works. (See HAWTHORNE EXPERIMENTS.) These studies demonstrated the wide psychological and social bases of motivation that were neglected, if not turned against management, by such derivatives of the fear-punishment emphasis as the "speed-up." (See SCIENTIFIC MANAGEMENT: "TAYLORISM.")

The weight of such studies was not sufficient to replace the first emphasis, root-and-branch. The practice deriving from the second emphasis, that is, was to seek employee satisfaction outside of work while preserving the traditional organization of work. The intended balance of motivational emphases—the use of rewards external to tasks which were organized consistent with the fear-punishment emphasis—seems to have been achieved only in part. Thus employees might resent someone else providing for what someone else considered to be their needs, with consequent discontent rather than thankful docility. Or the benefits might come to be considered a matter of employee right rather than of management generosity.

Third, since World War II and particularly in the last few years, the study of motivation has moved toward what will be called a *reward-in-work emphasis.* This third emphasis stresses building rewards into work that is organized with broad motivational considerations in mind, rather than tacking rewards onto a pattern of work that admits only a narrow range of motivational forces.

This third emphasis derives from two overlapping lines of investigation. An enormous body of work has explored the power of "informal groups" in the control of behavior, with the primary goals being precise description and the formulation of theory to serve scientific and applied purposes. This work on "informal groups" is the sophisticated extension of the pioneering insights of the work of Mayo and Roethlisberger at Hawthorne, it profited from the seminal experimentation of the psychologist Kurt Lewin, and it receives its most massive and detailed expression in the small-group literature [7]. In a complementary line of work, considerable research demonstrated that the "formal organization" patterned on the "principles" of traditional organization theory was not particularly effective as a motivator of behavior under the prevailing social and technological conditions. In fact, solid research demonstrated that the "principles" often had consequences opposite those intended. In one case, for example, only 30% of the work units that experienced a style of supervision consistent with the "principles" were high producers [8].

A generation of students made the obvious connection. The well-documented observations that "social organizations" may be quite effective in controlling behavior, then, encouraged the effort to build these powerful informal motivational factors into the very formal organization of work. Drucker, Worthy, Argyris, and Likert, particularly, responded to the challenge in the late 1950s and early 1960s.

Fourth, and especially in the last few years, increasing attention has been directed toward building organizations that will have desired motivational properties. This is an extension of the third emphasis above, but it is an extension more of kind than of degree. The focus is on designing specific jobs so as to increase their motivating qualities, as well as on developing organization climates or atmospheres that will help unleash productive effort.

Approaches and Techniques. The above four emphases implied distinct approaches to motivational phenomena and characteristic techniques for inducing desired motivational states.

The fear-punishment emphasis straightforwardly implied an approach and techniques to achieve high motivation toward, for example, the goal of high output. The early work of Frederick W. Taylor with pig-iron handlers illustrates the marriage of techniques well suited to the fear-and-punishment approach [9]. Thus the task was chosen so as to maximize the isolation and dependence of the employee. Spatial isolation was achieved by dispersing the unloading sites; and social isolation was encouraged by the careful choice of employees who either had little taste for social interaction or who were social isolates, and was reinforced by differential rates of pay. Psychological dependence upon the instructions of the methods man was clearly the intention of Taylor's note that the job specifications for this task required an "ox of a man."

The conditions under which this approach would achieve the desired consequence of high motivation are rather special ones [10], and modern industrial development has moved increasingly away from these conditions. This is the case even during periods of relatively high unemployment in America, for example, given such cushions as liberal unemployment compensation benefits. In terms of Maslow's "hierarchy of needs," that is, the Taylor approach emphasized physiological and safety needs (see MOTIVATION: MASLOW'S BASIC NEEDS). These levels of needs, however, tend toward fulfillment under existing conditions. Therefore, such needs are likely to be ineffective motivationally, since a "satisfied need is not a motivator of behavior."

The two types of paternalism previously mentioned were encouraged by a general recognition that the extreme conditions required by the emphasis on fear-punishment were difficult to achieve and maintain, were undesirable, and did not have the advertised consequences. Early studies also demonstrated that the satisfaction of employees was a factor of some importance in high motivation reflected in high productivity, low absenteeism, and the like.

The second approach to inducing high motivation, however, was of the have-your-cake-and-eat-it variety in choosing an approach and techniques. The basic pattern of organizing work consistent with the fear-and-punishment approach was retained, but it was counter-balanced by many non-work features designed to make assuming the burdens of work worthwhile. In general, some structure to care for a worker's "social needs" was tacked on to the existing patterns of organizing work assumed to be universally determined by "technical needs." More specifically, the rewards in this approach tended to be outside the lines of work (as recreation programs), to have no clear relation to performance (as most retirement programs), and to be administered by officials who did not supervise the performance of the individuals receiving benefits (vide the phenomenon of the "personnel department" intended to fill "social needs" while the rest of the organization concentrates on "technical needs"). Consistent with this concern over the employee's non-work happiness, this second emphasis also was marked by a massive preoccupation with the techniques of opinion polling or "morale surveys." The general assumption, of course, was that as long as individual attitudes concerning the employment organization were favorable, motivation would be high and directed toward high output and satisfaction.

Compelling evidence demonstrates that the expectations of this second emphasis were over-enthusiastic. Thus, both earlier and recent comprehensive reviews of studies of the relation of employee attitudes and output did not reveal any consistent pattern [11,12]. Favorable opinion of the employing organization might be related to high output, but hardly in enough cases to justify confidence that the second emphasis had solved a major part of the motivational puzzle. The evidence was only a little more favorable when other possible indicators of high motivation with a favorable direction were considered, that is, low absenteeism, low turnover, and the like.

The inability to verify the expectations of the second emphasis gave added impetus to research demonstrating the power of the social group and the failure of the traditional theory of organization to yield the expected results in many cases. In general, the approach of the third emphasis involved the attempt to determine the loci of behavioral control in organizations. The first and second emphases, of course, assumed that the *formal organization* or the *individual* were the behaviorally-relevant loci. The third emphasis attempted in addition to isolate the techniques that would permit tying the power of these behaviorally-relevant centers to the *purposes of the formal organization.*

The combination of the approach and a technique of the third emphasis must be illustrated. Consider the approach which assumes that the membership groups are highly relevant for employees, and consider the group decision-making technique which attempts to trade participation for greater involvement and enforcement. A significant industrial experiment supports the approach through the social group and the group decision-making technique [13]. Exhibit I gives relevant data. Thus the "total participation" condition, in which all members of a formal work unit participated in a minor work change, proved more effective than the

EXHIBIT I

EFFECTS UPON PRODUCTIVITY OF SEVERAL DEGREES OF PARTICIPATION IN DECISIONS CONCERNING A MINOR CHANGE IN WORK

	Production (in units per hour) at Five-Day Intervals after the Change in Job					
	5	*10*	*15*	*20*	*25*	*30*
Total Participation	64	63	75	71	71	72
Representative Participation	50	53	60	68	64	66
No Participation	45	53	55	51	49	55

SOURCE: Coch and French [10].
SOURCE: Coch and French [13]

"representative participation" condition that involved only elected representatives of work units.

The significant differences illustrated do not reflect the effects of a "gimmick," as can be suggested by several lines of related research and experience. That is, group decision-making attempts to utilize at the work site higher levels of needs in motivating behavior than the fear-punishment emphasis, the supervisor's role is not as authoritarian as in the "principles," and so on. Relatedly, the group decision-making results are consistent with evidence about the value of goal-setting [14], both for individuals and groups, which has been reflected in a variety of management systems and practices. For example, MANAGEMENT BY OBJECTIVES as a system rests on the basic and pervasive usefulness of goal-setting [15]. (See also the entry GOAL SETTING.)

Other related techniques prove equally useful. Thus, the findings on group decision-making suggest that employees tend to prefer some self-determination. Consistently, "general supervision" was associated with high output more than twice as often as "close supervision" in one study, although the latter style of supervision patently stresses dependence upon the superior. Job enlargement, job rotation, "peer ratings" in the choice of workmates and supervisors, decentralization, and so on, illustrate other related techniques and approaches. These cannot be squared with the first two emphases in the study of motivation, of course.

Two particular limits of such techniques, however, have become clear. First, the relations outlined will not apply in every case; they reflect central tendencies only. Thus, *all* individuals will not respond favorably to "general supervision." For example, individuals who are highly "authoritarian" are not likely to welcome "general supervision." And even low scorers might reject the style under certain conditions. Second, and relatedly, it has become clear that such effects as those above will occur consistently only under rather specific conditions.

The growing realization of the limits on successful applications of techniques and approaches consistent with the third emphasis has led to the fourth and recent major emphasis. This fourth emphasis seeks to determine the specific conditions that increase the probability of successful applications, and it also seeks to innovate technologies capable of inducing those specific conditions at the worksite. Two broad sets of conditions have received attention: the structuring of organizations and of component jobs, and the development of climates or atmospheres.

Considerable attention has been given to the effects of structure on motivation. Much is known about guidelines for designing jobs [16] so as to increase their motivating capabilities (see JOB ENRICHMENT AND WORK EFFECTIVENESS). Firms such as Texas Instruments and AT&T have generated interesting experience on this score [17]. Less is known about the more complex problem of structuring large organizations, but certain basic elements of the required comprehensive theory seem clear enough [18, 19].

Creating organization climates or atmospheres that will have motivating properties has been a growing focus of much recent inquiry and some experimentation. Observers have pointed up the hamstringing qualities of the "pyramidal values" seen as typically influencing organization climate or atmosphere. Such climates may be called "mechanical and bureaucratic." Some experimental work has gone beyond such observations in attempts to induce the development of an alternative set of values in organizations that will sustain a climate or atmosphere that can be characterized as "adaptive and organic" [20]. The "laboratory approach" is the technology commonly underlying such efforts at organization development [21].

Acceptance and Potential. The approach and the techniques of the fourth and especially the third emphasis in understanding motivation have gained rather wide currency. Two major tasks remain, however. Thus considerable work must be directed toward spelling out the precise conditions under which various effects may be expected. The existing literature, in contrast, tends to concentrate upon central tendencies in large aggregates of data. In addition, the implications of the third and fourth emphases must be developed into a comprehensive theory of organization, both to facilitate rigorous testing and to guide applications.

ROBERT T. GOLEMBIEWSKI, Department of Political Science, University of Georgia, Athens, Georgia

Information References

Associations:

Bureau of Business Research, Ohio State University.
Industrial Relations Research Association.
Research Center for Group Dynamics and Survey Research Center, University of Michigan.
Tavistock Institute of Human Relations, London; professional societies in psychology, sociology, and business and public administration.

Periodicals:

Administrative Science Quarterly.
Human Relations.
Journal of Abnormal and Social Psychology.
Journal of Applied Behavioral Science.
Journal of Applied Psychology.
Personnel.

Texts (see also References Cited)

Chung, Kae H., "Motivational Theories and Practice," Columbus, Ohio, Grid, Inc., 1977.
Golembiewski, Robert T., "Approaches to Planned Change," New York, Marcel Dekker, 1979. (Parts 1 and 2).
Hackman, J. Richard and Oldham, Greg R., "Work Redesign," Reading, Mass., Addison-Wesley, 1980.
Lawler, Edward E., III and Rhode, John Grant, "Information and Control in Organizations," Pacific Palisades, Calif., Goodyear, 1976.
Vroom, Victor, "Work and Motivation," New York, Wiley, 1967, (see [9]).

References Cited

[1] Newton, Grant, ed., "Organization and Behavior," San Francisco, Canfield, 1978.
[2] Lawler, Edward E., III and Rhode, John Grant, "Information and Control in Organizations," Pacific Palisades, Calif., Goodyear, 1976.
[3] Vroom, Victor, "Work and Motivation," New York, Wiley, 1967.
[4] Ronen, J., and Livingstone, J. L., "An Expectancy Theory Approach to the Motivational Impacts of Budgets," *The Accounting Review,* October 1975.
[5] Strauss, George, and Sayles, Leonard R., "Personnel: The Human Problems of Management" (Englewood Cliffs, N.J.: Prentice-Hall, 1960), p. 11.
[6] Sward, Keith, "The Legend of Henry Ford," New York, Rinehart, 1948.

[7] Golembiewski, Robert T., "The Small Group," Chicago, University of Chicago Press, 1962.
[8] Katz, Daniel, and Kahn, Robert L., "Human Organization and Worker Motivation," in Tripp, L. Reed, ed., "Industrial Productivity," Madison, Wisc., Industrial Relations Research Association, 1951.
[9] Taylor, Frederick W., "The Principles of Scientific Management," New York, Harper & Bros., 1911.
[10] Zaleznik, A., Christensen, C. R., and Roethlisberger, F. J., "The Motivation, Productivity, and Satisfaction of Workers," pp. 394–404, Norwood, Mass., Plimpton Press, 1958.
[11] Brayfield, A. H., and Crockett, W. H., "Employee Attitudes and Employee Performance," *Psychological Bulletin,* **52,** 1955.
[12] Locke, Edwin A., and Schweiger, D. M., "Participation and Decision-Making: One More Look," in Staw, B. M., ed., "Research in Organizational Behavior," Vol. 1, Greenwich, JAI Press, 1979.
[13] Coch, Lester, and French, John R. P., Jr., "Overcoming Resistance to Change," *Human Relations,* Nov., 1948.
[14] Latham, Gary P., and Locke, Edwin A., "Goal Setting: A Motivational Technique That Works," *Organizational Dynamics,* **8,** Autumn, 1979.
[15] McConkie, Mark, "Clarifying and Reviewing the Empirical Work on MBO," *Group and Organization Studies,* **4,** December 1979.
[16] Hackman, J. Richard and Oldham, Greg R., "Work Redesign," Reading, Mass., Addison-Wesley, 1980.
[17] Ford, Robert N., "Motivation Through the Work Itself," New York, American Management Association, 1969 (based on the approach developed by Frederick Herzberg, *et al.,* "The Motivation to Work," New York, Wiley, 1959.)
[18] Golembiewski, Robert T. "Men, Management and Morality," New York, McGraw-Hill, 1965.
[19] Galbraith, Jay, "Organization Design," Reading, Mass., Addison-Wesley, 1977.
[20] Golembiewski, Robert T. and Stokes, B. Carrigan, "Planned Change in Organization Style Based on Laboratory Approach," *Administrative Science Quarterly,* **15,** pp. 79–93 and 330–40, March and September 1970.
[21] Golembiewski, Robert T., "Approaches to Planned Change," New York, Marcel Dekker, 1979. (Parts 1 and 2)

Cross References: *Employee Attitude Research: Attitude Surveys; Goal Setting; Group Dynamics; Hawthorne Experiments; Human Relations in Industry; Incentive Systems; Job Enrichment and Work Effectiveness; Lincoln Incentive Management Plan; Motivation-prefix entries; Personnel Counseling; Rucker Plan of Group Incentives; Scanlon Plan of Group Incentives; Sensitivity Training; Standard Minute System; Suggestion Systems; Work Simplification.*

MOTIVATION: Maslow's "Basic Needs"

Since World War I, and especially in the last three decades, social scientists have sought to develop theories about **Motivation** of people at work by means of observations in industrial situations, analyses of studies by clinical psychologists, studies of the reactions of non-industry groups such as school children and military personnel under controlled experiments, and the actual results obtained by the practitioners of WORK SIMPLICATION and by such programs as that of the Lincoln Electric Company. (See LINCOLN INCENTIVE MANAGEMENT PLAN.)

Significant in this connection are some ideas about motivation advanced by A. H. Maslow [1]. Dr. Maslow postulates five basic needs which, he says, are organized into successive levels. For example, hunger is a basic physiological need, but when there is plenty of food, higher needs emerge. When the higher needs are satisfied, newer and still higher needs come to the fore, and so on. It follows that gratification becomes as important a concept in motivation as deprivation. A want that is satisfied, Dr. Maslow points out, is no longer a want.

Below are given the levels of basic needs, starting with the lowest. However, it should not be assumed that a need must be entirely satisfied before the next one emerges. Most people are partially satisfied in all of their basic needs at the same time.

(1) *The Physiological Needs.* These are hunger for food, sexual gratification, and shelter. In most industrialized societies, chronic extreme hunger of the emergency type is rare, rather than common. Certainly, this is the case in the United States. The average American citizen is experiencing appetite rather than hunger when he says he is hungry. He is apt to experience sheer life-and-death hunger only by accident, and then only a few times in his entire life.

Obviously, says Dr. Maslow, a good way to obscure the "higher" motivations, and to get a lopsided view of human capacities and human nature, is to make the organism extremely and chronically hungry or thirsty. Anyone who attempts to make an emergency picture into a typical one, and who will measure all of man's goals and desires by his behavior during extreme physical deprivation, is certainly being blind to many things. It is quite true that man lives by bread alone—when there is no bread. But what happens to man's desires when there *is* plenty of bread and when his belly is chronically filled? Dr. Maslow contends that *at once other and higher needs emerge* and these, rather than physiological hungers, dominate the organism. And when these in turn are satisfied, there will emerge, as stated, newer and still higher needs.

(2) *The Safety Needs.* If the physiological needs are relatively satisfied, a set of needs emerges for protection against danger and threats. In an ordered society a person usually feels safe from extremes of climate, tyranny, violence, and so on. Expressions of safety needs are thus seen in preferences for job security, insurance, and the like. Other manifestations are preferences for the familiar rather than the unfamiliar, the known rather than the unknown. These are normal reactions. Arbitrary management actions giving rise to uncertainty can have an adverse effect at any level in the organization. The tendency toward resistance to change is human and universal.

The healthy, normal, fortunate adult in our society, says Dr. Maslow, is largely satisfied in his safety needs. The peaceful, smoothly running, "good" society ordinarily makes the citizen feel safe enough from wild animals, extremes of temperature, criminals, assault, and murder, etc. Therefore in a very real sense he no longer has any safety needs as active motivators. Just as a sated man no longer feels hungry, a safe man no longer feels endangered. If we wish to see these needs directly and clearly, we must turn to neurotic or near neurotic individuals, and to the economic and social underdogs. In between these extremes we can perceive the expression of safety needs only in such phenomena as, for instance, the common preference for a job with tenure and protection, the desire for a savings account, and for insurance of various kinds (medical, dental, unemployment, disability, old age).

(3) *The Love Needs.* (Some writers term these "social" needs.) If the physiological and safety needs are fairly well taken care of, the needs for love and affection, and "belongingness" (see HAWTHORNE EXPERIMENTS) will emerge, and the cycle will repeat itself with this new center. The person now seeks affectionate relations with people in general, a place in his (her) group. If deprived of these goals, he will want to attain them more than anything else in the world, and, as Dr. Maslow puts it, "he may even forget that once, when he was hungry, he sneered at love." In our society, the thwarting of these needs is the most common cause of severe psychological maladjustment.

Dr. Maslow stresses that love is not synonymous with sex. Sex may be studied as a purely physiological need. Ordinarily sexual behavior is multidetermined, that is to say, determined not only by sexual but also by other needs, chief among which are love and affection needs. Also not to be overlooked is the fact that the love needs involve both giving *and* receiving love.

(4) *The Esteem Needs.* Practically everyone has a need for self respect and for the esteem of others. This results in the desire for strength, adequacy, confidence, independence, reputation or prestige, recognition, attention, and appreciation. These "egoistic" needs are rarely completely satisfied. They are of special importance in our discussion because the typical industrial and commercial organization does not offer much opportunity for their satisfaction to employees at the lower levels. It is the recognition of these needs that has forced so much attention upon ways to provide employees with a sense of participation. Extreme advocates call for very broad participation indeed, covering even allocation of work and setting of the work pace, and criticize SCIENTIFIC MANAGEMENT as deliberately thwarting these esteem needs.

(5) *The Need for "Self-Actualization," for Self-fulfillment.* Even if all the needs mentioned above are satisfied, we can still expect that a new discontent and restlessness will develop unless the individual is doing what he is fitted for. Dr. Maslow writes: "A musician must make music, an artist must paint, a poet must write, if he is to be ultimately happy. What a man can be he must be. This need we may call self-actualization." The clear emergence of these needs rests upon prior satisfaction of the physiological, safety, love, and esteem needs. People who are satisfied in these needs are basically satisfied people, and it is from these that we can expect the fullest and healthiest creativeness.

Reference Cited

[1] Maslow, A. H., "A Theory of Human Motivation," *Psychological Review,* **50,** 1943.

Information References

To place the foregoing in proper perspective as regards continuing research into human motivation and behavior in industry, the reader is referred to the entries, MOTIVATION and HUMAN RELATIONS IN INDUSTRY.

Cross References: *Motivation (and cross references there given)*

MOTIVATION: McGregor's "Theory X" and "Theory Y"

In "The Human Side of Enterprise" [1], Douglas McGregor presents what he terms a new "Theory Y" with respect to the management of people, which has been widely quoted. He sets forth six assumptions about industrial behavior, contrasting them with the traditional view, which he terms "Theory X." Thus:

(1) *The expenditure of physical and mental effort is as natural as play or rest.* This is contrasted with *Theory X,* that the average human being has an inherent dislike of work, and will avoid it if he can.

(2) *Man will exercise self-direction and self-control in the service of objectives to which he is committed.* This is contrasted with *Theory X,* that most people must be coerced, controlled, directed, and threatened with punishment to get them to put forth adequate effort toward the achievement of organizational objectives.

(3) *Commitment to objectives is a function of the rewards associated with their achievement. The most significant of such rewards, e.g., the satisfaction of ego and self-actualization needs, can be direct products of effort directed toward organizational objectives.*

(4) *The average human being learns, under proper conditions, not only to accept but to seek responsibility.* This is contrasted with *Theory X,* that the average human being prefers to be directed, wishes to avoid responsibility, has relatively little ambition, and wants security above all.

(5) *The capacity to exercise a relatively high degree of imagination, ingenuity, and creativity in the solution of organizational problems is widely, not narrowly, distributed in the population.*

(6) *Under the conditions of modern industrial life, the intellectual potentialities of the average human being are only partially realized.*

Information References

To place the foregoing in proper perspective as regards continuing research into human motivation and behavior in industry, the reader is referred to the entries, MOTIVATION and HUMAN RELATIONS IN INDUSTRY.

Reference Cited

[1] McGregor, Douglas, "The Human Side of Enterprise," New York, McGraw-Hill, 1960.

Cross References: *Motivation (and cross references there given).*

MULTIPLE MANAGEMENT

Multiple Management is a system of participative management introduced at McCormick & Company, Inc., the Baltimore based international producer of seasonings, flavorings, and specialty foods. The system was introduced by Charles P. McCormick shortly after his election to the presidency of the concern in 1932 after the death of his uncle, Willoughby M. McCormick, who had founded the company in 1889. The plan proved highly successful, and has been adopted by numerous companies in this country and abroad.

From its inception until the founder's death in 1932, the company had been a "one-man organization." This statement implies no denigration of the elder McCormick, since individual leadership was in keeping with the spirit of his time. However, Charles McCormick recognized defects in the one-man system as applied to a company of the size to which McCormick & Company had grown. He saw it as tending to stifle imagination, originality, and ambition on the part of the organization as a whole. He therefore advocated giving the young men of the company not only more to say, but better opportunities for development and advancement. That idea was the first principle of Multiple Management.

The Junior Board of Executives. The first step was the formation of a Junior Board of Executives. Management called together seventeen of the younger men—assistant department heads, accountants, junior executives—who were considered the best prospects for future leadership. They were told that they were to be given direct participation in management within their own group, operating independently of the Board of Directors and line organization. They were to elect their own chairman and secretary, set up their own schedule of meetings, and draw up their own bylaws. They were given the right to discuss anything in the business which interested them, and were assured that top management would not look over their shoulders in the meetings, nor would there be any interference with their free discussions.

The members were at that time told that every recommendation from their board must be unanimous (currently, a three-fourths vote is necessary). If the original idea could not be sold to the Junior Board members, it was suggested that they revise it and amend it so that their finished idea was thoroughly thought out and sound.

Little, if anything, connected with the business escaped the searching eye of the Junior Board. In the first five years, 2,109 unanimous recommendations were made to the Senior Board and of this number only six were rejected. This ratio of acceptances has continued through the years. Aside from the fact that the Junior Board is a source of new ideas, able executives and department heads have, through experience on the board, developed from clerks, chemists, and others who normally would have had little opportunity to display management ability in their regular jobs. Board activity teaches men and women how to conduct meetings, gives them an understanding of people and of the problems of leadership and management, and provides them with an overall picture of the business.

The Factory Board of Executives. As success with the Junior Board developed, the McCormick management realized that the same plan adapted to the factory should provide means for solving employment problems and meshing all factory activities more firmly and harmoniously with those of other divisions of the business. A logical development therefore was the formation of a Factory Board of Executives along the same lines and with the same two directives. Supervisors and heads of departments of the factory were called together, and the plan to organize a factory board to cooperate with the senior and junior boards was explained to them. They were informed that, through the factory organization, they were to be given an opportunity to contribute ideas and plans for the improvement of the business.

As with the organization of the Junior Board, there were some slight misgivings as to the possibility of impracticable recommendations from the Factory Board of Executives. But, like the members of the Junior Board, they demonstrated immediately that they were surprisingly conservative. Moreover, it soon became evident that the board was sales minded, and the minutes of their meetings indicated that they were increasingly concerned with production improvements and with measures to create a more attractive atmosphere for visitors to the factory. In its first five years, this board, which is composed of men closely associated with factory operations—supervisors, foremen, and their assistants—increased production in the plant by more than one third with the same people and practically the same machines.

The Factory Board was later renamed the Plant Board, and the Junior Board was later renamed the Headquarters Board.

The Sales Board. A large number of recommendations from both boards concerned new products, advertising campaigns, merchandising aids, and displays and sales promotions. A great many of these recommendations were practical and proved to be profitable, but a just criticism of the majority was made in the vein that each had a weakness, because they were produced by individuals who were not sales minded by training or by occupation. Numerous suggestions for revision of advertising and sales methods failed to provide the means whereby results could be obtained. Others, while they appeared to be of value, would have necessitated changes in sales policies and would seriously have affected distribution. Much time was lost because members had no means of determining whether or not projects of this nature were worth while. Accordingly management created two (one East and one West) Sales Boards which would provide a valuable source for new merchandising ideas and a clearing house for all sales projects suggested by the other boards. As of this writing, however, there is only one Sales Board.

The Sales Board is composed of employees who are active in sales positions in the Grocery Products Division. Since they are scattered hundreds of miles apart, the board presented a special problem which was solved by arranging for week-long meetings twice a year. In the interim board committees carry on projects by correspondence.

Complete reports of each meeting go to every salesman in the division, and results have been extremely beneficial. All salesmen know that they are adequately represented in formulating and recommending company policies in which they are most interested. In addition, each salesman knows it is possible to obtain membership on the Sales Board, provided he or she can demonstrate the required ability.

In less than two years, the Sales Board established itself as a permanent part of the Multiple Management plan. Eventually the number of Multiple Management boards at McCormick grew to eleven. Membership at this writing totals about 150.

Multiple Management in Operation. The Senior Board of Directors is selected by the stockholders annually, with no limit on re-election, and corresponds almost identically with the board of directors of any average corporation. No member of the Senior Board of Directors may serve on Multiple Management boards, and they attend meetings of the subordinate boards by invitation only.

Subordinate board members are divided into two groups. The first includes the regular members, those who ranked highest on the merit rating chart—the men and women with proven talent for management. The second group includes the associates who did not rank sufficiently high on the merit rating chart to achieve regular membership and those who have yet to prove their management ability, either because they have recently joined the company or have not yet advanced to more responsible positions. The associate members take an active part in all board functions and discussions, but do not vote. All begin as associate members, and after one year associate members can become regular members if their ratings are sufficiently high.

At six-month intervals each Multiple Management board member, for example, rates every member except himself on a chart which provides points for each of several qualifications considered necessary for an executive, namely, originality, judgment, achievement, forcefulness, and human relations.

In a typical example, the six who rate highest, thereby becoming the membership committee, select by interview and discussions among themselves the additional members of the board for the next term; they rate on merit every potential eligible executive in the company. The lowest 20%, or a minimum of three, are dropped from the board; the reason is explained by the membership committee, and they are assured that there is a good chance of selection for return to the board six months later.

Popularity or pull cannot obtain board membership for an employee. He has to prove his merit and ability to his own contemporaries. This eliminates the mere politician, the handshaker, and the storyteller from merit membership.

The board structure has brought management closer to all McCormick employees. The result of this closer contact is an exchange of ideas which works both ways. A Plant Board member, for example, can communicate to plant employees some of the problems and difficulties facing top management, and the employees in the business, in the same way, can communicate to a board member their problems and desires. In this way suggestions and requests are passed along very rapidly in the next board meeting and reach management quickly for prompt action.

A feature of McCormick's plan is a profit-sharing system, in addition to the normal group life insurance, hospitalization, sick benefit, and pension plans. Each year, on an established formula basis, a certain per cent of the company's profits before taxes are deposited in a Profit Sharing Trust. All employees participate in the Trust after three years of employment, and their share of the deposits plus investment earnings is paid to them when they leave at retirement or for any other reason.

Bonuses equivalent to one to seven weeks' salary per year have been paid during the operation of Multiple Management. This is in addition to profit-sharing payments, vacation pay, paid holidays, and a week off between Christmas and New Year.

Results. McCormick & Company has obtained an invaluable return in spirit and morale, with very low labor turnover. The discovery of talent and the training of future leaders are valuable by-products. Employees have increased their earnings, management has received a direct return in the form of increased profits, and stockholders have benefited by the company's dividend record.

Many companies in this country and abroad have adapted the principles of Multiple Management to their organizations. McCormick & Company considers that it has demonstrated through its plan that a number of interested employees, from the principal divisions of a business and working in orderly cooperation, are best able to solve many of its problems by studying the relationship of the human factor to the progress of the business as a whole.

W. GORDON YATES, Vice President-Administration, McCormick & Co., Inc., Hunt Valley, Md.

Information References

Dudek, Daniel H., "Multiple Management," *Advanced Management Journal,* Spring, 1979.

McCormick, Charles P., "The Power of People," printed for McCormick by Penguin, 1973.

Murray, Thomas J., "More Power for the Middle Manager, *Dun's Review,* June, 1978.

Watson, Brantley K., "The Maturing of Multiple Management," *Management Review,* July, 1974.

N

NEW-PRODUCT DEVELOPMENT

New-Product Development is certainly not new. Its appearance on industrial organizational charts as a recognized area of responsibility is, however, a post World War II phenomenon. Also, sometimes called *New Product Planning,* this activity is generally considered to be part of the overall responsibility of Marketing Management. It does involve, however, an active relationship with the technical operations of the company located in the Research and Development and the Engineering organizations. New-product development is concerned with getting ideas for new products, screening them by a selective process, and, through technical research and development, translating them to tangible products ("hardware") which can be mass-produced and sold at a profit.

Companies depend on new-product development for many reasons, among which are: (1) to counteract a slowdown in company growth rate; (2) to replace short lived products; (3) to capitalize on surplus capacity, including both physical facilities and managerial time, ability, and desire; (4) to employ surplus funds or available borrowing power.

It is important to have a working definition of the term "new product." A noted writer on this subject, Peter Hilton, has defined a new product as "any product, which, regardless of the length of time it has been marketed, is still unknown by name or application to 75% of its potential users." He points out that "a new product need not, of necessity, employ a brand new concept. It can be an improved product or an established product with a new feature or a new application."

In this article, major emphasis is placed on the development and commercialization of those products that embody ideas or knowledge which are new to the company seeking product diversification.

History. From the beginning of our present industrial era (about 1770) to roughly the beginning of the twentieth century, there was little, if any, attempt on the part of the then existing industries to do any formalized planning for new products. Prior to the last decade of the nineteenth century, new products resulted from occasional discoveries by those working in the industry or by the fortuitous appearance of persons with inventions to peddle. Deliberate planning for new products as a recognized business activity is a product of this century.

From data on the establishment of organized research activities in American companies, it would appear that new product development as an assigned responsibility of an organized technical group made its appearance in the United States around 1893 at Eastman Kodak Company. As an important factor in company management, however, one must infer that it is still a young art, probably not yet quite four decades old, with the main impetus coming since World War II.

The Process. New-product development encompasses all activity from idea conception to full-scale introduction of the product to the market. The process is highly complex, requiring successful coordination of many individual activities. It may be looked upon as a sequence of six separate and distinct stages: Exploration, Screening, Business Analysis, Development, Testing, and Commercialization. The following description of the six stages is based on ideas presented in the references included at the end of this article.

(1) The *exploration* stage comprises the seeking of new ideas which may come from many sources, among which may be listed the sales force, which is in constant contact with customer needs and applications, and the personnel handling sales inquiries. Also useful is a study of the products of competitors and of products that are allied and substitutable. Ideas may originate with management, stockholders, or consultants, or may come from a study of foreign products and markets, reports from trade associations, Government or university laboratories, the Patent Office, trade journals, or from papers delivered at technical or trade meetings. Research and development organizations are expected to be alert to new product possibilities, and their effectiveness in this direction is directly related to the knowledge they possess of the marketing conditions. Engineering and manufacturing departments often get ideas from proving-ground tests, performance records, observing products in use, and from

other work. Suggestions systems, market analyses, cost studies, and feedback from service organizations may also prove to be fruitful sources of new product ideas. Emphasis in the exploration stage should be placed on quantity, not quality, of ideas.

(2) *Screening* is the selection of the most promising ideas for further consideration. If a company has good sales and research and development organizations, there will be no dearth of ideas to exploit. The greatest problem facing management is that of proper selection and rejection. Whereas in the past this was done by shrewd guesswork or by hunch, today every bit of quantitative and factual information is assembled and arranged to eliminate chance as much as possible from the decisions made by management.

Prerequisite to any successful screening procedure is a clear understanding of company objectives. These should be written down in an appropriate top-management policy statement. This should eliminate many suggestions, which although intriguing, are entirely unsuited to the production facilities or the sales organization.

Concerning the ideas that survive, many questions must be answered such as: Is there a market opportunity? Is the concept technically feasible? What is the patent position? What is the status of needed raw materials or supplies? How stable are the sources of supply? Are production facilities suitable? If not, how much will it cost to obtain them? Many companies have evolved specific written new product criteria which spell out such items as short-term and long-term profitability requirements, estimated profit margin, dollar volume of production each year for a period of time, estimated amount of new capital required, etc.

It is important that management prepare such questions and make certain that they are answered quantitatively, if possible. If not possible, then they should be answered qualitatively by the best informed and least biased persons available. A number of books and articles given at the end of this article offer lists of representative questions. (See also NEW PRODUCT DEVELOPMENT: A Check List for Management Decisions.)

Once these data are available (and they should be in writing), then the difficult job of decision making occurs. Screening at this point should not be exclusively logical; neither should it be whimsical. Too much logic leads to too safe a position which results in trivial new product advances. If there is too much whimsey, survival of the enterprise is possible only with continued good luck.

(3) The *business analysis* stage consists of establishing a project with manhours and funds budgeted to permit the analysis of the technical and economic factors in sufficient detail to evaluate the commercial feasibility of the idea. This may include some preliminary testing and analytical studies. The end result is usually a capital budget.

(4) The *development* stage determines the practicality of the idea by producing a working model embodied in a new product design. At this stage a preliminary study of acceptability to customers may be conducted.

(5) The *testing* stage comprises redesigning the working model into a production prototype, producing a limited quantity, and usually testing the market before proceeding to full-scale production.

(6) The final stage, *commercialization,* involves deciding whether to make or purchase component parts, developing mass production methods, and activating a distribution organization. New Product Development is completed when the new product is fully integrated into the company's normal operation and is achieving satisfactory sales volume and profit.

In proceeding successfully through the stages, the following are essential:

(1) An R & D organization with competence, interest, and enthusiasm to solve the problems involved.

(2) An engineering organization equal to its part of the job.

(3) A production organization oriented to new products.

(4) A marketing organization that is interested and motivated by the challenge of selling new things.

(5) A service organization that is capable and interested, should post-sales service be required.

The key words are *competence, interest, enthusiasm, capability.*

Mortality Rate. Published data show that it takes anywhere from 50 to 500 new product ideas at the exploration stage to result in one successfully introduced new product. Since each succeeding stage of the process is more expensive, it is imperative that only the most promising ideas be allowed to progress. Even the idea which survives and eventually leads to a new product on the market is subject to further mortality. Depending on the sample and the definition used, anywhere from 50% to 98% of new products introduced into the market fail for various reasons, and a large majority fail in the first year on the market. Some companies have estimated that 75% of the annual corporate expenditures for new products in the United States are unproductive. One company reported that, of the products that are considered successful, only one in four significantly contributes to company profits. To help reduce the high mortality in new products on the market, it is imperative to review periodically all planning for new products in the light of changing customer demands, introduction of competing products, increases in production costs, and general changes in the economic outlook.

Organization. It is generally conceded that it is the function of the president of the company to assume responsibility for the product line. Since the successful development of new products involves so many entirely separate operations of the company, there is a need for high-level coordination. Neither the president nor any of his immediate staff are apt to be competent on such a broad front as to be able to provide the best detailed supervision. Two methods to effect coordination have been used: either a committee has been appointed or a new department established to take responsibility for new product development. Before establishing either of these organizational devices there must be a clear definition of authority, responsibility, and functions assigned. The activity must be located within the company so that it can function effectively, and the selection of personnel must be carefully planned.

If a committee is appointed it should be clearly spelled out whether the committee is *advisory* or *action-taking*, and to whom it reports. If it is an action-taking committee with authority over some of the line officials, this should be clearly spelled out in a written charge or charter. It should be made very clear whether the president is prepared to accept the recommendations of the committee unless there is good reason to do otherwise, or whether he is seeking advice which he may or may not accept. If a committee is appointed, it must be provided with statements from the top management regarding company policies which serve as the first filter in the screening operation.

The persons selected for the committee must be chosen carefully and it must be made clear whether they are appointed for their personal abilities and experience, or because of their particular position in the company. This is important to know when it becomes necessary to replace anyone. Also it must be decided whether committee service is a full-time or part-time obligation. If it is full-time, some provision must be made to introduce new blood into the committee. This may be done by releasing persons for other duties and replacing them on some kind of schedule. Persons who possess the knowledge and abilities to be extremely valuable on such committees may not have the temperament to serve for long periods in an advisory and coordinating capacity. This is particularly true if the committee is set up as an advisory committee only.

If a department is established, the duties must be clearly defined so that it does not overlap the responsibilities of other departments. There appears to be a trend to establish the new-product development function in a separate department.

A department would usually consist of a small number of specialists who do not become involved with routine responsibilities. To this small nucleus there are generally added persons from other operating divisions to provide information and advice. Thus *ad hoc* task forces are formed with different membership, depending on the product being developed.

If a committee structure is used, the chairmanship may change as the product passes through different phases from research to final production. Selecting persons on a part-time basis from these different operations and keeping them as a team from start to finish has the advantage of acquainting all responsible people with the whole project. Their own operations may thus be more effectively integrated to save time and money. In a departmental structure, this technique might also be used, but generally the department supplies the chairman, and others are brought in as needed.

New-product development activities are controlled through appropriate reports, and through accounting-type data such as man-hours expended through budgets, but most importantly through the constant personal contact of responsible parties. The chairman of such efforts is, in effect, a little president with the responsibility of getting the product planned, developed, and marketed, making use of the organization existing in the company. He must constantly strive to minimize cost and time, and maximize the utilization of resources available. (See INDUSTRIAL RESEARCH ACCOUNTING and INDUSTRIAL RESEARCH BUDGETING.)

Potentials. New-product development is a very active and growing part of the management function. Experimentation is constantly being carried out to determine the most effective method of operation. There is no unique formula, since this depends on many company variables such as size, location, personnel, etc. The increased numbers of publications on new product development appearing in the business and trade journals provide ample evidence of the nation-wide concern of industry with these problems.

RICHARD B. COUNTESS, Manager, International Training, Westinghouse Electric Corp., Power Generation Division, Philadelphia, Pa., and Adjunct Professor of Management, MBA School, Widener University, Chester, Pennsylvania

MERRITT A. WILLIAMSON, Orrin Henry Ingram Distinguished Professor of Engineering Management, School of Engineering, Vanderbilt University, Nashville, Tennessee

Information References

Sources of Continuing Information:

American Management Associations.
American Marketing Association.
California Management Review.
The Conference Board.
Harvard Business Review.
Industrial Research Institute.

Texts:

Balachandran, Sarojini, ed., "New Product Planning," Detroit, Gale, 1980.
Karger, D. and Murdick, R., "New Product Venture Management," New York, Corden and Breach, 1972.
Peters, Michael P., and Hisrich, Robert D., "Marketing a New Product: Its Planning, Development, and Control," Menlo Park, Calif., Cummings div. of Addison-Wesley, 1978.
Scheuing, E. E., "New Product Management," Hinsdale, Ill., Dryden, 1974.
Spitz, E. A., "Product Planning," Van Nostrand Reinhold, 1977.

Articles and Reports

Block, R.G., "Ten Commandments for New Product Development," *Industrial Research/Development,* March 1979.
Hopkins, D.S., "New-Product Winners and Losers," *Report No. 773,* New York, The Conference Board, 1980.
Phelps, E. D., "Improving the Product Development Process," *Industrial Marketing Management,* vol. 6, No. 1, 1977.
Souder, W.E., "Effectiveness of Product Development Methods," *Industrial Marketing Management,* vol. 7, No. 5, October 1978.

Cross References: *Basic Research: Management Aspects; Brainstorming; Copyright; Creativity Training; Industrial Research and Development; Marketing Strategy: Competitive Analysis; accompanying entries with New Product prefix; Patents; Trademarks; Trademarks: International Protection.*

NEW-PRODUCT DEVELOPMENT: A Check List for Management Decisions

The following points are representative of the type of questions to which answers must be secured—factual or estimated—before extensive developmental commitments are made. On many of these the Research Department will be expected to have answers or opinions. In some companies, a director of planning, or of commercial development, will coordinate the gathering of facts and opinions needed for a decision. The check list can form a guide for a report to management.

(1) A brief description of the proposed product.

(2) At what broad market target areas would this product be aimed?

(3) With respect to our company, is this a new product, an extension of size or application of an existing line of products (i.e., additional model), or an optional accessory to an existing product?

(4) If a new product or model, start development of a "factor comparison" chart, comparing the proposed product features with competing products.

(5) A succinct statement as to possible "pluses":

  (a) Is this an entirely new invention, marking a new departure in terms of labor-saving or in the sense that it produces something not heretofore in existence?

  (b) Possible technological advantages over similar products of entrenched companies in the field.

  (c) Possible style appeal beyond that of potential competitors.

  (d) Possible company advantages in deliveries or service.

  (e) Are our background and standing *vis-a-vis* a product of this type such that our name would add special prestige?

(6) Into what price range does this product fall? Is there a chance that under our manufacture there will be a "plus" in price? (Include prices of comparable ex-

isting products in factor-comparison chart, item 4 above.)

(7) Bibliography of pertinent literature having to do with necessary descriptive information, market possibilities, etc., with possible excerpts or photostats of key items.

(8) Names and makers of all principal commercially available items of this type, including principal imported units, if any. Who dominates this field?

(9) As to existing competition:
   (a) Names of leading companies in the field, with estimate, if possible, of the share of the market each is apparently enjoying in the product in question.
   (b) What is the parent corporate control of key companies in the field?
   (c) Analysis of published financial figures of key companies, showing profit record in recent years, with possible analysis as to profits from the products in question.
   (d) Start a special library of catalog information, advertising brochures, annual reports, etc.

(10) Is this product seasonal in usage, and if so, how?

(11) What published data can be quoted (U.S. Dept. of Commerce, trade associations, directories, trade papers, etc.) as to *current business* being done? (If possible, assemble for five past years, with estimate for current year. If an authoritative source can be cited for future years, do so; if any estimate for future years is that of the Market Research or Planning Division, cite rationale behind it. In the foregoing, give units as well as dollars, if possible also, break down by domestic manufacture, exports, and imports.)

(12) List leading trade journals and trade associations in the field. Should any of these be contacted for possible surveys they may have conducted or know about, showing share of market by leading producers, etc?

(13) At what kind of expositions or trade shows are products of this type shown? What was the most recent? When and where will the next one be held?

(14) What data from the Sales Department and other contacts exist, that will throw light on opportunities in this product?

(15) What *potential business* (for all companies) is foreseeable?

(16) A "bird's-eye-view" of *potential market breakdown* (give sources for statistical information):
   (a) Classification of users—as by kinds of industries or companies, areas, income group, or other identifiable categories.
   (b) Analyze above for logical size breakdowns to use: numbers of employees, dollar sales, income group, or the like.
   (c) Give estimated numbers of establishments (or other logical unit) in above breakdowns.
   (d) Give rating as to prospective buyers ("Limited," "Fair," "Good," or "Excellent").
   (e) Are any of the above prospects for multiple sales?
   (f) Can an estimate be made of the frequency of purchase?

(17) Which of the foregoing are worth considering for any special surveys? Does the company have any special contacts in any of them? Should any of them be surveyed by an outside market research organization?

(18) What steps, if any, should be taken with respect to our own dealer or sales organization, in gathering information?

(19) Would the *sale* of this product be:
   (a) Largely through existing company sales organization and channels?
   (b) To users to whom we are quite well known, but who would require a different selling organization and approach?
   (c) To users to whom we are not well known?

(20) What sales channels are the leading factors in the field now using?

(21) What is the private-brand situation?

(22) What is the mail-order house situation?

(23) What are the customary discounts to dealers, markups, etc.?

(24) Would the manufacture of this product be classed as:
   (a) Mass-produced?
   (b) Semi-massed-produced (perhaps mass-produced parts, with relatively limited assembly)?

(c) Custom-built?

(25) If a model or drawings or samples have been submitted, what is R&D's report with respect to the product's technical feasibility and function?

(26) Does this type of product require special research and production-development know-how? If so, do we have it in our organization? If not, is it readily available on a consulting basis? If not on consulting basis, how difficult and expensive would it be to expand our own company staff?

(27) Are our research, engineering, and manufacturing know-how particularly applicable to this type of product?

(28) Are our present manufacturing facilities particularly suitable?

(29) Is a big plant investment involved, and/or is intricate equipment required to compete? (What leads can be obtained from suppliers of the type of equipment involved?)

(30) Can important components be subcontracted for?

(31) Does this product require extensive tooling investment?

(32) Are there existing "bugs" in the product? Is it possible to estimate the extent of additional development work which would have to be done?

(33) What is the patent situation?
- (a) Secure patent numbers on patents issued, if this is a new product brought to the company by the inventor.
- (b) Secure photostatic copies, when needed, of patent applications.
- (c) Arrange for a preliminary report on above by our patent department.
- (d) Does the company now dominant in the field have comprehensive basic patents? If so, are they approachable regarding licensing?

(34) Even if the product is to be manufactured by us, are important component parts to be purchased? If so, are these dominated by a single producer who might create problems later on?

(35) Is the principal material to be used a by-product of some large, unrelated operation (unrelated insofar as markets for the proposed product are concerned)? If so, would a company that is not in the first kind of business stand a chance against such a first company which, through a subsidiary, may have brought out a product of the type under consideration?

(36) Is the principal raw material subject to violent price fluctuation?

(37) What synthetic materials worth investigating have come to the fore?

(38) Is there a company in the field which may be acquired?
- (a) Check to see whether our company was in contact with it previously.
- (b) Is there a special line of contact through a present board member, official, or affiliated company?
- (c) Roughly what order of magnitude of investment would be involved?
- (d) Is this company in sound financial condition now? (Secure credit information—analyze last five years' financial statements.)
- (e) What is this company's reputation?
- (f) What can be said at this time about its physical facilities? Is a detailed engineering survey in order?
- (g) Does it have special research or engineering know-how worth acquiring?
- (h) Does it have special sales facilities worth acquiring?

Information Reference

Heyel, C., ed., "Handbook of Industrial Research Management," 2nd ed., Chap. 11, New York, Van Nostrand-Reinhold, 1968.

Cross References: *New-Product Development (and cross references there given).*

NEW-PRODUCT PLANNING: Profitability Projections

Numerous formulas and projection techniques have been developed to measure the **value of a proposed new product** or project in relation to others proposed. In discussing these, Asbury [1] points out that a note of caution must be raised in the application of formulas or equations. A prudent research director or management will not allow judgment and experience to be displaced by a premature economic analysis.

Indexes. An example of an equation quoted by Asbury for determining a project index for product development projects is reported by a chemical research organization [2]:

$$PVI = \frac{CTS \times CCS \times AV \times P \times \sqrt{L}}{TPC}$$

where:

PVI = project value index
CTS = chances for technical success, on an arbitrary rating scale, say 0 to 10
CCS = chances for commercial success, on an arbitrary rating scale, say 0 to 10
AV = annual volume (total sales of product in units)
P = profit, in dollars per unit—simply price minus cost
L = life of product in years
TPC = total project cost, in dollars.

A simple index formula has been advanced by the Industrial Research Institute. This is an index of net probable monetary return per research dollar. When it is properly developed, the elements of good judgment, experience, and intuition are reflected in the number itself:

$$I = (PN/C)$$

where:

I = Index of relative worth
P = overall probability of commercial attainment of the goal
N = estimated net return for an arbitrary five-year period
C = estimated future research cost.

Point System. A variation of the formula approach is a point system of weighted factors, cited by Blake [2]. In this system, chances of success are rated from 10 (good) to 2 (poor); pay-off in years (total costs divided by annual earnings) is rated from 20 to 2; and cash position in two years is rated from 10 to 2. Cash position is defined as one half the difference between ten years' gross earnings and the total investment in research and plant. In addition, the formula gives one point each to ten miscellaneous factors, such as good raw material position, etc. With this system, two proposed projects can be compared, or one project can be measured in relation to an acceptable minimum score or rating standard.

Graphs. Another system which uses no formulas but does use graphs and charts is described by Brozen [3]. In this method, up-to-date graphs are kept which chart for each of the company's products the percentage of the total market sold by the company. Further graphs are kept which chart the gross margin, in percentage, received on each product. If either of these graphs begins to drop for any single product, work is started to improve the product, reduce its cost, or find a new product which will do the job better or more cheaply.

Product Profiles. A technique involving a series of screenings of proposed new products has been developed by the New Products Study Committee of Dewey and Almy Chemical Company [4].

First appraisal is a preliminary screening as to probable suitability of the product for the company's type of business, and with relation to general policy. If the new product idea passes this preliminary test, the next step is a set of profiles, divided into three categories: *stability, growth,* and *marketability*. These are shown in the first three of the accompanying profiles. For each of the profiles, the new-product idea is rated on the scale as very good, good, fair, poor, or very poor.

The next step is a series of specific profiles (not illustrated here) but developed in similar vein, concerning the proposed product's suitability for the company's *manufacturing program,* and how it fits into or desirably augments the *research program.*

Next, a profile of *financial factors* is plotted, as shown in Profile IV.

Finally, the new-product idea is profiled on a series of *position factors.* These are shown in Profile V.

If the new-product idea has succeeded in clearing all of these analytical hurdles, more detailed analyses are made. If the new product is to be recommended to top management, the committee accompanies its report with a project evaluation. This is usually based on careful market research and on preliminary technical research, and includes a reasonably thorough estimate of the manufacturing cost and the projected profit-and-loss statement.

Dewey and Almy considers the ultimate measure of attractiveness of a new product to be the return on investment which can be expected from it. To give uniform evaluation to new product ideas, as well as to provide sound, recurrent re-evaluation of existing product

PROFILE I

Stability Factors — *Very Good* | *Good* | *Fair* | *Poor* | *Very Poor*

1. Permanence of market
2. Possibility of captive market
3. Stability in depression
4. Stability in war
5. Size of market
6. How difficult to substitute or copy

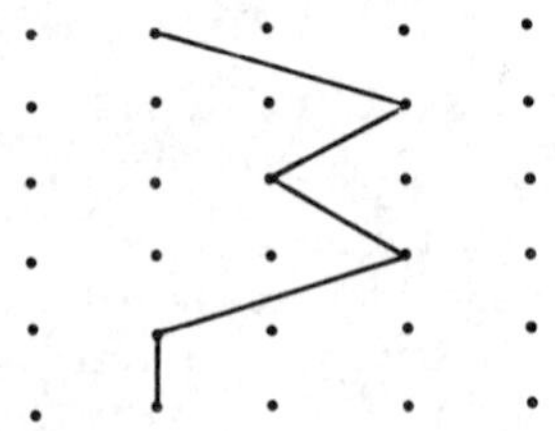

PROFILE II

Growth Factors — *Very Good* | *Good* | *Fair* | *Poor* | *Very Poor*

7. Chance of substantial future growth
8. Demand situation or need for additional suppliers
9. Export possibilities
10. Unique character of product or process
11. Is a change going on in this industry which this product can ride?

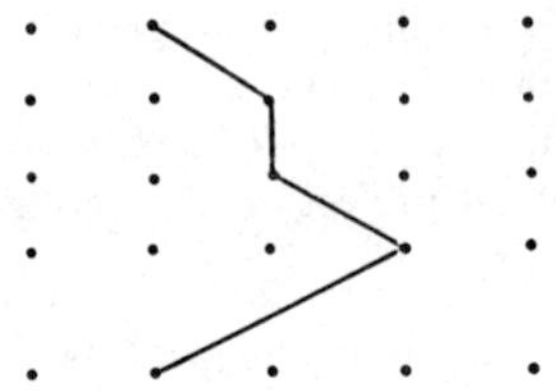

PROFILE III

Marketability Factors — *Very Good* | *Good* | *Fair* | *Poor* | *Very Poor*

12. Product does not compete with, imitate, or injure present customers
13. D&A's reputation in similar fields
14. Relation to markets we now sell
15. Customers' service requirements compared with D&A ability
16. Standing in relation to probable competition
17. Few variations or styles required
18. Large volume with individual customers

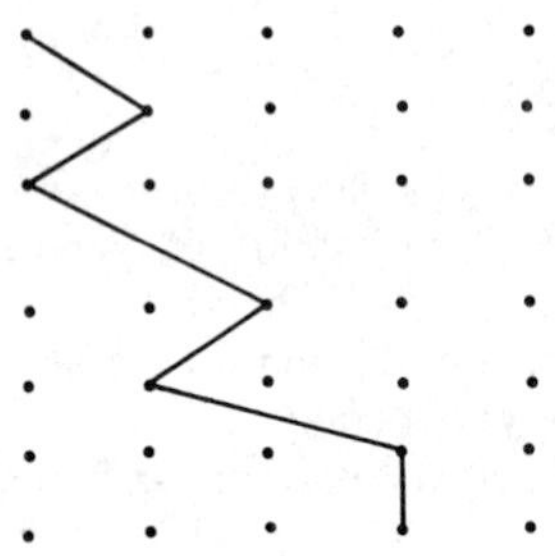

lines, the company has established certain principles and definitions:

The definition of "investment" includes working capital and fixed investment.

Working capital consists of accounts receivable and inventories. The company does not deduct accounts payable, because in its business the amount per plant would have to be estimated on an arbitrary basis and because the cash on hand is practically an exact offset. Inventories are evaluated at standard direct cost.

Fixed investment includes land, buildings and equipment (normally before depreciation). Occasionally a project arises contemplating converting existing unused equipment to new products. This calls for including only the current realizable value rather than the new value of the equipment involved. The company considers that it would be a mistake to use the original book value of such equipment blindly, or even its depreciated book value The true value of the equipment is determined by its alternate usefulness *other than* for the project under consideration. For example, if the equipment is otherwise useful only for junking, under this concept it should be evaluated into the new project at its junk value.

In calculating percentage return on total investment, the operating margin is normally used as the "return." This is the net earnings

PROFILE IV

Financial Factors — *Very Good* | *Good* | *Fair* | *Poor* | *Very Poor*

1. Return on investment
   a. Fixed capital
   b. Fixed and working capital
   c. Fixed and working and initial R&D cost
2. Investment required relative to competitive product
3. Investment required per dollar of sales

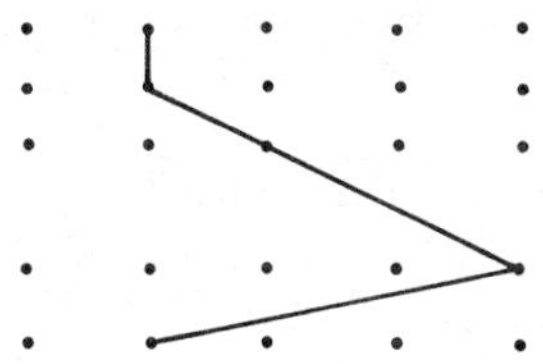

PROFILE V

Position Factors — *Very Good* | *Good* | *Fair* | *Poor* | *Very Poor*

1. Time required to become established and accepted
2. Effect on sales of other product lines
3. Value added by our processing
4. Chance of exclusive or favored purchasing position
5. Raw materials improve vertical integration
6. Raw materials improve position in other purchases

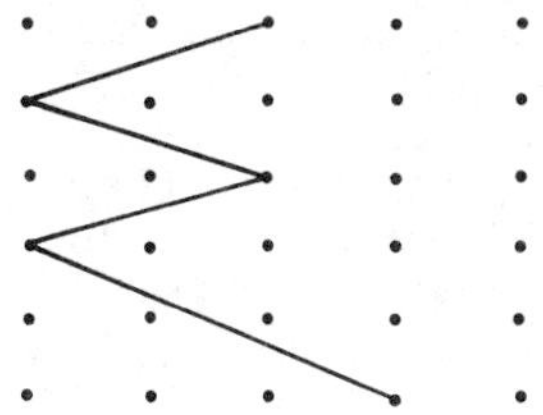

before deduction for income tax and interest expenses. However, the return *after* taxes is also estimated. This gives a better measure of the comparative attractiveness of two propositions, one of which can take heavy advantage of accelerated depreciation rates for tax purposes, while the other cannot.

As a third way of appraising an investment project, an estimated *cash flow* is projected—that is, operating margin after taxes, but with the depreciation write-offs added back in—and related to the time required for the original outlay in the project to be returned. This is an aid to long-range financial planning, because it indicates the future availability of cash for dividends, modernization, debt retirement, exploratory research, and reinvestment in other projects both as fixed capital and as new working capital.

In this case, the company includes in the original outlay what it terms the "grubstake." This is one half the cost of product development, start-up expenses, and market development, based on present corporate income tax conditions. (Obviously, this reasoning can be used safely only by a going concern operating at a profit.)

Cash Flow. James W. Russell, formerly Manager of Planning, American Machine & Foundry Company, has contributed the following discussion and Exhibit I on the assessment of tangible risks that can be defined and measured in terms of dollars, i.e., engineering cost estimates, production cost estimates, market forecasts of sales volume at various price levels, and organizational costs of getting into business. He points out, however, that the evaluation of a proposed new product necessarily includes the consideration of *intangible risks,* i.e., advantages and disadvantages that cannot be reduced to numerical terms. These include product fit with the present business, possibilities of future growth in lines allied to the proposed product, and probable reactions of competition. Such factors involve guesses, "feel," and judgment, as does an assessment of the general chances of success for the proposed program, although the latter may be expressed as a percentage, as in the first two formulas quoted.

A table such as Exhibit I can be used. One purpose of this table is to aid in the listing and analysis of the tangible factors. The goal is to arrive at a single figure that can be weighed against the intangible risks mentioned above. A second purpose is to recheck and re-evaluate the profit potential of the product as the estimates and forecasts are further refined during the development program.

The first 17 lines of the table constitute a

EXHIBIT I

FINANCIAL PROJECTION AND ANALYSIS FOR A PROPOSED NEW PRODUCT

(All figures in thousands of dollars except unit sales)	*Basis*	*1st Year*	*2nd Year*	*3rd Year*	*4th Year*	*5th Year*	*6th Year*	*7th Year*	*8th Year*	*9th Year*	*10th Year*	*Totals*
1. Unit Sales Penetration:	80%					50	300	450	500	400	300	2,000
2. Sales @ $10,000/unit	100%					500	2,000	4,500	5,000	4,000	3,000	20,000
3. Nor. Mfg. Cost @ $5,500/unit	55%					275	1,650	2,475	2,750	2,200	1,650	11,000
4. Normal Mfg. Profit	45%					225	1,350	2,025	2,250	1,800	1,350	9,000
5. Normal Marketing Expenses	15%					75	450	675	750	600	450	3,000
6. Normal Product Engineering	1%					5	30	45	50	40	30	200
7. Normal G. & A.	4%					20	120	180	200	160	120	800
8. Normal Profit	25%					125	750	1,125	1,250	1,000	750	5,000
9. Production Startup Expense					40	100						140
10. Marketing Startup Expense				10	50	150						210
11. Product Development		80	110	120	40							350
12. Tooling					150							150
13. Miscellaneous-Contingencies		20	30	40	50	10						150
14. Total Nonrecurring Expenses		100	140	170	330	260						1,000
15. Pretax Profit (Loss)		(100)	(140)	(170)	(330)	(135)	750	1,125	1,250	1,000	750	4,000
16. Income Tax Provision	50%	(50)	(70)	(85)	(165)	(67.5)	375	562.5	625	500	375	2,000
17. Profit Aft. Taxes (Line 15–16)		(50)	(70)	(85)	(165)	(67.5)	375	562.5	625	500	375	2,000
18. Cumulative Cash Flow		(50)	(120)	(205)	(370)	(437.5)	(62.5)	500	1,125	1,625	2,000	
19. Working Capital Requirements	50% of Sales					250	1,500	2,250	2,500	2,000	1,500	
20. Work. Cap. Charge	5%					12.5	75	112.5	125	100	75	500
21. "Criteria" Investment (Line 17–Line 20)		(50)	(70)	(85)	(165)	(80)	300	450	500	400	300	Discounted Rate of Return 31.5%

Courtesy James W. Russell, American Machine & Foundry Company.

pro forma profit-and-loss statement of the operation by year. Costs and expenses through line 7 are restricted to "normal" items, resulting in the "normal" profit of line 8.

The second section (lines 9 through 14) covers the non-recurring expenses required to get the enterprise started. Production and marketing start-up expenses are included, as well as product development and tooling. These one-time costs are separated from the "normal" costs to facilitate analysis as well as to accommodate later changes in the forecast.

The after-tax cumulative profit and loss is shown in line 18 to indicate the flow of speculative funds required for the program. At this point, the estimated working capital requirements are also shown (line 19), so that the actual funds tied up at any point in the program can be calculated. The speculative funds are not combined with working capital on this sheet, however, since working capital involves a relatively low order of risk and should not be confused with risk capital in evaluation of the program.

The fact that working capital will be tied up is recognized, however, by levying an artificial working capital charge against the enterprise (line 20). This change is deducted from the profit after taxes to give a "criteria" investment, which is used to calculate the discounted rate on the speculative investment. (For discussion of discounted rate, see RETURN ON CAPITAL.)

The example in Exhibit I shows a projection of a hypothetical new machine with a potential market of 2,500 units, and an attainable market of 80%, or 2,000 units, within ten years. The rate of sales build-up and decline of this particular unit is forecast at a selling price of $10,000. Estimates of all expenses necessary to build up and maintain a marketing organization are made and entered in the table.

Engineering development cost estimates, and costs of manufacturing, tooling, start-up, and production are also entered, together with normal product engineering and appropriate general and administration expenses. In this case, the product development and tooling expenses are burdened with a 30% miscellaneous and contingency allowance, arbitrarily spread over the first five years.

The working capital requirements are forecast at 50% of annual gross sales, and the charges on use of working capital are assessed at 5% after taxes.

Thus, the business estimated for the proposed machine amounts to $20 million gross sales over a six-year sales period. Preceding this is a four-year engineering development, testing, and tooling-up period which, together with initial marketing expense, will cost $1 million. Most of this money must be committed before any return can be anticipated.

In order to compare this investment with other investment possibilities, the "criteria" investment is obtained, and the discounted rate of return on investment is found to be 31.5%.

The discounted rate of return represents the rate at which compound interest would have to be earned by the outstanding investment in order for the interest plus the principal to provide sufficient funds to pay the cash flow-backs anticipated at the times predicted. This one figure can serve as a realistic measure of the desirability of the venture, and it is an important criterion in evaluating the proposal as a favorable or unfavorable company move.

As mentioned earlier, the table also serves as a measuring device during each succeeding stage of the product's evolution. As the development, testing, and commercialization stages proceed, the effect of changes or further refinements in each of the estimates and forecasts can be readily seen. The rechecking and reevaluation necessary throughout a new-product program are thus focused on the ultimate effect of each change on the overall business picture. Decisions made can be based on their net effect on the profit goals.

References Cited

[1] Asbury, W. C., "Establishing Research Projects," Chap. 7 in Heyel, C., ed., "Handbook of Industrial Research Management," 2nd ed., New York, Van Nostrand Reinhold, 1968.

[2] Blake, Walter T., "Project Selection," University of Wisconsin Engineering Institute Conference on Industrial Research Organization, December 13–14, 1956 (quoted by Asbury).

[3] Brozen, Yale, "The Economic Future of Research Development," *Industrial Laboratories,* December 1953 (quoted by Asbury).

[4] Miller, T. V., "New Product Profiles," Chap. 11 in Heyel, C., ed., "Handbook of Industrial Research Management," 2nd ed., New York, Van Nostrand Reinhold, 1968.

Cross References: *New-Product Development (and cross references there given).*

NONLINEAR PROGRAMMING

Nonlinear Programming is the branch of MATHEMATICAL PROGRAMMING concerned with finding optimal values of functions called *objective functions,* over some region, called a *feasible region.* As in LINEAR PROGRAMMING, the objective function is the mathematical expression describing the behavior of the variables affecting some process or situation which management desires to optimize. The feasible region is specified by a series of *constraint functions.* The problem is considered a nonlinear program if the objective function and/or any of the constraint functions are nonlinear. If the objective function and all the constraint functions are linear, the problem reduces to a linear programming problem. However, where for example the objective is to minimize costs or maximize profits, the operation may be highly complex, with numerous constraints having to do with quality standards, special customer needs, availability of materials and skills, and the like, so that the relationships involved are not necessarily linear. Hence nonlinear programming is more general than linear programming, and the latter is a special case of the former.

Unlike linear programming, which has the simplex algorithm or one of its variants, there is no single powerful algorithm for nonlinear programming. (An algorithm is a set of arithmetic rules by which it is possible to start with an assumed answer to a problem, and then by following prescribed repetitive procedures, arrive as close as desired to the true answer based on the number of iterations performed.) Since nonlinear programming problems are usually more difficult to solve than linear programming ones, researchers often try to "linearize" nonlinear objective functions and nonlinear constraints to take advantage of linear programming's ease of solution. This technique is not always possible, and so the need to develop efficient nonlinear programming algorithms is of paramount importance in current research.

History. Nonlinear programming, or optimization theory, as it is sometimes referred to, is the art of arriving at optimal policies to satisfy some objective while at the same time satisfying fixed requirements or constraints. Such problems date back to antiquity: the ancient Egyptians tried to find the best way to impose taxes on farms, at the same time taking into account that, with the annual flooding of the Nile River, farmlands may change in value. With the advent of the calculus by Newton and Leibniz in the seventeenth century, optimization theory took a new turn. Functions could be minimized or maximized and their optimal solutions obtained, so long as they were "well-behaved," i.e., followed smooth curves. Equality constrained optimization problems were solved with the help of so-called "Lagrange multipliers."

The theory was further developed, but it was the publication of papers by Karush in 1939 [1], John in 1948 [2], and Kuhn and Tucker in 1951 [3], that led to an explosion of theoretical advances. At about the same time, the introduction of high-speed electronic computers with their large memories and extremely rapid calculational ability enabled researchers to develop better algorithms to solve larger classes of nonlinear programs. Presently, there is still much work being done in the field, and more efficient and powerful results are being discovered frequently.

Applications. All the areas in which nonlinear programming problems arise are too numerous to list here. However, a few can be mentioned. Nonlinear programming problems appear in many engineering applications, especially in chemical engineering (in the form of geometric programs, among others), electrical engineering (in electrical network problems, power generation problems, etc.), mechanical engineering (in problems of mechanical design), and civil engineering (in the form of structural design problems and water resources systems analysis). In addition, nonlinear programs are found in control theory applications, advanced mathematical economic theory, and in many business applications. Among the latter are portfolio selection, location of facilities, production-inventory, and stochastic resource allocation. The list could seem almost endless, as new applications and problems are formulated and solved as nonlinear programs almost every day.

A few atypical examples can be mentioned. Nonlinear program models have been formulated which fine polluters who discharge waste into the environment, which develop offshore oil fields and minimize costs, which study relationships among finance, production, and marketing decisions, and which determine diets that are optimal in their protein composition. There are literally thousands of other examples.

Approaches and Techniques. The general nonlinear program problem is to find n decision variables $x_1, x_2, \ldots, x_n$ which will optimize (either minimize or maximize) a given objective function $f(x_1, x_2, \ldots, x_n)$ of the decision variables over some given feasible region defined by a series of constraint functions. The objective function and/or the constraint functions are nonlinear. For concreteness, a minimization problem will be considered. So the general nonlinear program is called *(P)* and is

$$(P): \quad \begin{array}{rl} \text{minimize} & f(x_1, \ldots, x_n) \\ \text{Subject to} & g_1(x_1, \ldots, x_n) \leq 0 \\ & g_2(x_1, \ldots, x_n) \leq 0 \\ & \vdots \qquad\qquad \vdots \\ & g_m(x_1, \ldots, x_n) \leq 0 \end{array}$$

where each of the m functions $g_1, g_2, \ldots, g_m$ as well as the objective function f is given.

For notational convenience the set of n decision variables $x_1, \ldots, x_n$ is usually denoted by the vector x. So the general nonlinear program *(P)* can be written as

$$(P): \quad \begin{array}{rl} \text{minimize} & f(x) \\ \text{subject to} & g_i(x) \leq 0, \quad i=1, 2, \ldots, m \end{array}$$

Notice that equality constraints are written as two inequality constraints. Also note that nonnegativity conditions on any of the solution variables are implicitly defined as part of the set of inequality constraints $g_i(x) \leq 0$, $i=1,2,\ldots m$. Any solution vector x which satisfies all the constraints is called a feasible solution.

A serious difficulty in solving nonlinear programs is that the optimal solution may occur at an interior point of the feasible region, or on the boundary of the feasible region which is not an extreme point, or at an extreme point of the feasible region. Because of this, techniques such as the simplex algorithm that investigate only extreme points of the feasible region may not find the optimal solution.

Another potential source of difficulty is the idea of a function having local or global minima. This is illustrated in Exhibit I.

A global minimum is a solution to the minimization problem over the entire feasible region. Its objective function value is as low as any other point in the feasible region. A local minimum, however, gives a minimum objective function value only with respect to feasible solutions close to that point. So in Exhibit I, the values of x at $a,b,c,$ and d yield local minima, while the global minimum occurs at $x=e$.

Local minima are important because of the general nature of algorithms seeking the global minimum of a function. These algorithms are frequently myopic and can only find local minima, depending upon the starting point of the algorithm. Thus, with the possibilities of multiple optima occurring at interior points or boundary points, the prognosis of finding the global optimum may seem bleak. However, if certain conditions and properties of all the functions in the program are satisfied, the characterization of the unknown optimal solution becomes relatively well defined. However the actual solution procedure might still be extremely complex.

Because of their appearance so frequently in model formulations and their special mathematical properties, certain functional forms predominate in mathematical programming. Linear functions is one such class. Another such class is convex functions. A *convex function $f(x)$* has the property that a linear interpolation overestimates its values; that is, for any points a and b, the line segment joining $f(a)$ and $f(b)$ lies above the function. *Concave functions* are the negative of convex functions; a linear interpolation underestimates its values.

EXHIBIT I

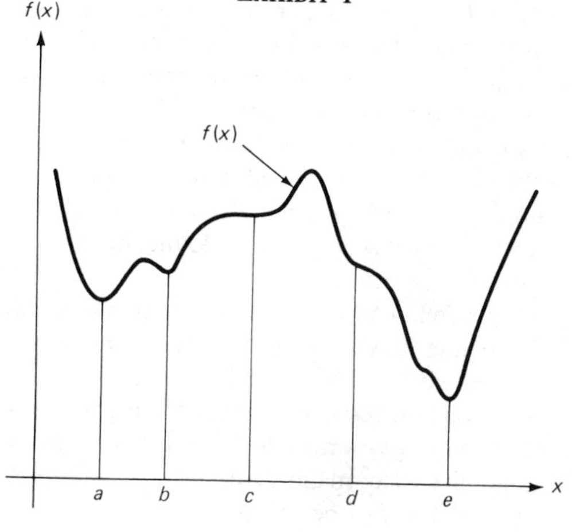

EXHIBIT II

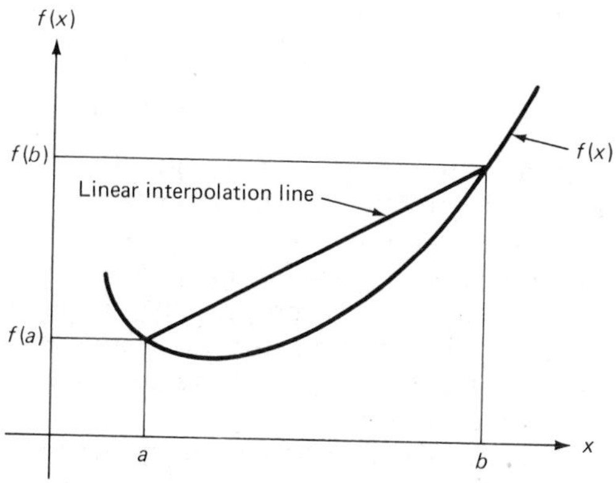

See Exhibit II for an illustration. A *convex set* of points has the property that for any two points in the set, the entire line segment connecting the two points lies in the set also. The reader is referred to the references for a more complete discussion of this special class of functions.

Convex functions have the useful property that on a convex feasible region, any local minimum is also a global minimum. That is, any feasible solution which minimizes the function over the feasible solutions in its immediate neighborhood also minimizes it over the entire set of feasible solutions. Thus, it is necessary to find only one local, and hence global, minimum. Nonlinear programs having the objective function and constraints convex are called *convex programs*. These play an important role in the sequel.

The following discussion is offered for the reader interested in pursuing some of the mathematical principles involved. (For detailed treatment, consult the references given at the end of this article.)

Before solving any nonlinear problem, it is important to know how to recognize an optimal solution. The so-called Karush-Kuhn-Tucker conditions will indicate such solutions. Rather loosely put, the following theorem gives the results.

Theorem. Consider the minimization problem *(P)*. Suppose the objective function and all the constraint functions are differentiable (i.e., smooth-curved) and convex. Let x^* be some feasible solution to the program *(P)*. Suppose also that a set of numbers $\lambda_1, \lambda_2, \ldots, \lambda_m$ can be found so that the following equations are seen to be true:

$$\frac{\partial f(x^*)}{\partial x_j} + \sum_{i=1}^{m} \lambda_i \frac{\partial g_i(x^*)}{\partial x_j} = 0, \; j=1,2,\ldots,n \quad (1)$$

$$\lambda_i g_i(x^*) = 0, \quad i=1,2,\ldots,m \quad (2)$$

$$\lambda_i \geq 0, \quad i=1,2,\ldots,m \quad (3)$$

then the feasible solution x* is a global optimal solution to problem *(P)*. Equations (1) − (3) are called the Karush-Kuhn-Tucker conditions.

It also can be shown that applying this theorem to ordinary linear programming problems results in the complementary slackness conditions, so that those conditions are just a special case of this theorem.

Example. To show how to apply the theorem, consider the following example. Consider the following nonlinear program:

$$\begin{aligned} \text{minimize } f(x) &= (x_1 - 5)^2 + (x_2 - \tfrac{1}{2})^2 \\ \text{subject to } g_1(x) &= (x_1)^2 + (x_2)^2 - 17 \leq 0 \\ g_2(x) &= \tfrac{1}{2}x_1 - x_2 - 1 \leq 0 \\ g_3(x) &= -x_1 \leq 0 \\ g_4(x) &= -x_2 \leq 0 \end{aligned}$$

EXHIBIT III

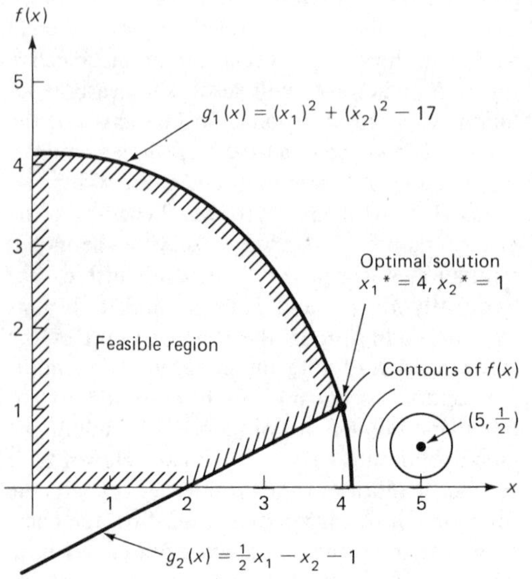

See Exhibit III for a graph of the feasible region. The point $x^* = (x_1^*, x_2^*) = (4,1)$ is postulated to be the optimal solution. All the functions involved are both convex and differentiable. The Karush-Kuhn-Tucker conditions must be verified. This yields

$$\begin{aligned} &2(x_1^* - 5) + \lambda_1(2x_1^*) + \lambda_2(\tfrac{1}{2}) - \lambda_3 = 0 \\ &2(x_2^* - \tfrac{1}{2}) + \lambda_1(2x_2^*) - \lambda_2 - \lambda_4 = 0 \\ &\lambda_1[(x_1^*)^2 + (x_2^*)^2 - 17] = 0 \\ &\lambda_2\,[\tfrac{1}{2}x_1^* - x_2^* - 1] = 0 \\ &\lambda_3 x_1^* = 0 \\ &\lambda_4 x_2^* = 0 \end{aligned}$$

Substituting $x_1^* = 4$ and $x_2^* = 1$, the above equations become

$$\begin{aligned} -2 + 8\lambda_1 + \tfrac{1}{2}\lambda_2 - \lambda_3 &= 0 \\ 1 + 2\lambda_1 - \lambda_2 - \lambda_4 &= 0 \\ 4\lambda_3 &= 0 \\ \lambda_4 &= 0 \end{aligned}$$

The solution of these equations yields $\lambda_1 = 1/6$, $\lambda_2 = 4/3$, $\lambda_3 = 0$, and $\lambda_4 = 0$. Since the Karush-Kuhn-Tucker conditions hold at $x^* = (4,1)$, then x^* is a global minimum of the problem.

The converse of the theorem is true with the additional proviso of a regularity condition called a constraint qualification. That is, under this regularity condition, if x^* is a local optimal solution to the problem *(P)*, then there exist numbers $\lambda_1, \lambda_2, \ldots \lambda_m$ which satisfy the Karush-Kuhn-Tucker conditions (1)−(3). It is not necessary for the functions to be convex in this case. For further details, including some different constraint qualifications, as well as some weakening of the hypotheses of the theorem to make it more flexible, the interested reader should consult the references.

Unfortunately, it is usually difficult, if not impossible, to derive an optimal solution directly from the Karush-Kuhn-Tucker conditions. The conditions will verify that a potential feasible solution is indeed optimal, but will not, in general, give that solution to the problem-solver. Hence algorithms must be used to get these optimal solutions.

Algorithms. It is impossible to go into the details of any of the literally hundreds of algorithms available to solve nonlinear programming problems. All that will be done here is to acquaint the reader with some of the more well known ones, with a brief idea of the types of problems they solve and also perhaps an indication of how they work. The details of the algorithms themselves can be found in the references.

In the following discussion, no special properties of the functions are assumed, unless otherwise noted.

For concreteness, the optimization problems will be minimization ones, although with some simple algebraic manipulations, maximization problems can also be solved.

Unconstrained Minimization Problems

Here there are no constraints of the type mentioned in our opening paragraph, but the objective function is nonlinear. The problem is to find a local minimum of the function. Studying unconstrained problems is useful because they are easier to solve than constrained problems, and many constrained problems can be transformed into unconstrained ones by "penalty functions" as described later herein. In the sequel, it is assumed that the objective functions are differentiable, unless otherwise noted.

Newton's Method. This classical method approximates the function to be minimized by a quadratic function. The objective function must be at least twice continuously differentiable. Since a necessary condition for a minimum of a quadratic function is that its gradient is equal to zero, this fact is used for the approximating quadratic function of the objective function. A drawback of Newton's method is that as the algorithm is applied to some chosen point, a successor point is found and the algorithm is then applied to this successor point, and so on. But the successor point may not decrease the objective function, and may actually increase it. In fact, it is possible that the sequence of points generated by the algorithm may converge to a maximum of the objective function. The starting point is thus extremely important. Another drawback is that if there are a large number of variables, the process is expensive and time consuming. However, the method does find the minimum of a quadratic objective function, starting at any point, in one iteration. So it is useful for quadratic unconstrained problems.

Steepest Descent Method. Here the idea is that the algorithm, starting from some point, finds a direction that will minimize the objective function most rapidly in an iteration; that is, find a direction of steepest descent. The method is a classical, first discovered by the famous French mathematician, Augustin Cauchy. Its chief disadvantage is that convergence to an optimal point may be quite slow, working well initially but poorer as the iterations continue.

Method of Conjugate Gradients. This is an example of a line search technique. The premise is that, given a point, find a direction vector and a suitable step size so that a new point, given by the sum of the original point and the product of the step size and the direction vector, can be found. Solving for a step size involves first solving a subproblem of minimizing the objective function evaluated at the new point as a function of the step size. This is a one-dimensional search problem of the step length. Once the step length is determined, the direction vector is found. The method uses directions that are conjugate to each other at each iteration. (A special case of conjugate directions is perpendicular directions.) It turns out that the method finds the minimum of a quadratic objective function in at most as many steps as there are variables. Thus, the technique is most useful for quadratic forms. There are several ways of generating conjugate directions. The rate of convergence is, in general, not worse than that of the steepest descent method.

Variable Metric or Quasi-Newton Methods. This is a conjugate direction method which combines the advantages of Newton's and the steepest descent methods. A search direction is found by an updating technique; the update varies at each iteration. There are many updating procedures, each giving a different search direction, and some are more powerful than others. Variable metric methods are widely used with much success. Because of this, researchers are extending the ideas to constrained minimization problems.

Constrained Minimization Problems

Here the problem is to minimize an objective function subject to either equality or inequality constraints or both.

Penalty Function Methods. The approach here is to convert the constrained minimization problem to an unconstrained one. This is accomplished by adding a so-called penalty function to the objective function. This penalty function is zero at any feasible point (a point which does not violate the constraints) and is very large at an infeasible point. So a point minimizes the sum of objective function plus the penalty function (an unconstrained problem) if and only if it minimizes the original constrained minimization problem. The powerful unconstrained-minimization-problem algorithms can thus be used. The method generates a sequence of infeasible points whose limit is an optimal solution to the original problem. Many different types of penalty functions are used. Perhaps the best known penalty function method is the Sequential Unconstrained Minimization Technique (SUMT), where, instead of giving every infeasible point the same large penalty, a penalty is imposed that increases the more a point becomes infeasible.

Barrier Function Methods. This approach is basically similar to the penalty function method. Once again the idea is to make the constrained problem an unconstrained one. Here a barrier term that prevents the points generated from leaving the feasible region is added to the objective function. The unconstrained-minimization-problem algorithms can thus be used. The technique generates a sequence of feasible points whose limit is an optimal solution to the original problem.

Method of Feasible Directions. Here the constraints are considered directly, in contrast to the penalty or barrier function methods which incorporate the constraints into the objective function. The idea is that a point is chosen, and then a direction and sufficiently small step length are found so that a new point, given by the sum of the old point plus the product of step length and direction vector, is found. The new point has the properties that it is feasible, and also that the objective function evaluated at this point is better than the objective function at the old point. The process is then repeated. There are many feasible direction methods, and a further discussion here is not practical. The references give many of the techniques.

Approximation Methods. Since linear programs are much easier to solve than nonlinear ones, researchers have devised methods in which the nonlinear functions are approximated by linear ones and then results from linear programming are used. For instance, cutting plane algorithms can be used for convex programs, reduced gradient methods use the ideas of basic and nonbasic variables from linear programs, etc. There are numerous approximation-type algorithms; some are discussed in the references.

Conclusion. More often than not, optimization problems are nonlinear in nature. There are numerous examples of formulating these nonlinear programs in the literature and in actual occurrence. In general, because of several local minima, they can be troublesome to solve, usually being much more difficult than linear programs as there is no single powerful algorithm to apply. The theory has enabled practitioners to recognize optimum points but rather sophisticated algorithms are usually needed to get these points in the first place. Some algorithms work better on certain classes of problems than others; hence there are many algorithms available to choose from. Much research is still being performed in obtaining more efficient and powerful algorithms, but no breakthroughs, analogous to the simplex algorithm in linear programming, are foreseen.

JACK YURKIEWICZ, PH.D., The School of Business, Hofstra University, Hempstead, New York

Information References

Avriel, M., "Nonlinear Programming: Analysis and Methods," Englewood Cliffs, N.J., Prentice-Hall, 1976.

Bazaraa, M.S. and Shetty, C.M., "Nonlinear Programming: Theory and Algorithms," New York, Wiley, 1979.

Beightler, C.S., Phillips, D.T., and Wilde, D.J., "Foundations of Optimization," 2nd ed., Englewood Cliffs, N.J., Prentice-Hall, 1979.

Gottfried, B.S. and Weisman, J., "Introduction to Optimization Theory," Englewood Cliffs, N.J., Prentice-Hall, 1973.

Zoutendijk, G., "Mathematical Programming Methods," New York, Elsevier North-Holland, 1976.

References Cited

[1] Karush, W., "Minima of Functions of Several Variables With Inequalities as Side Conditions," M.S. Thesis, Dept. of Mathematics, University of Chicago, 1939.

[2] John, F., "Extremum Problems With Inequalities as Subsidiary Conditions," *Studies and Essays,* 187–204, (Courant Anniversary Volume), New York, Interscience, 1948.

[3] Kuhn, H.W. and Tucker, A.W., "Nonlinear Programming," *Proceedings of the Second Berkeley Symposium on Mathematical Statistics and Probability,* Berkeley, Calif., University of Calif. Press, 1951.

O

OCCUPATIONAL HEALTH

Occupational Health is a collective term used to characterize all the various activities and disciplines devoted to maintaining and promoting the health, safety, and productivity of wage earners. This field, then, includes, but is not necessarily limited to, occupational medicine, occupational health nursing, industrial hygiene, industrial accident prevention or safety engineering, and occupational health education. The earlier, almost synonomous, term, "Industrial Health," which was used when these efforts were largely limited to factories, mines, railroads, and other large or "heavy" industries, is also still in use. As these activities have been extended to mercantile, financial, and other business institutions, and even to governmental agencies and other nonprofit organizations, such as hospitals, the more accurate and broader term, "Occupational Health," is replacing it.

Occupational Health Activities

The growth of occupational health activities within the traditional industries listed, and their extension into the other institutions mentioned, reflect fundamental economic and social changes which have been steadily accelerating in the 35 years since the end of World War II. The perceived value of individual workers has risen as ever more complex businesses and industries have needed people with higher levels of skill and training; the unskilled common laborer hired for his simple muscular strength has become a rarity. At the same time, increasing rates of pay, triggered by union demands, have made more organizations "labor intensive" and increased the perceived value of employees collectively.

As the purely economic needs of wage earners have been better met, other rewards and benefits have received greater emphasis. Employers are expected to provide safer and more healthful working conditions, and government is expected to require them to do so. These trends culminated in enactment of the Federal Occupational Safety and Health Act, establishing an Occupational Safety and Health Administration within the Department of Labor, in 1970. (See Occupational Safety and Health Act of 1970.) Briefly, the statute authorizes this new Administration to develop, encourage, and enforce uniform minimum national standards of health and safety in employment. The Act also created a National Institute of Occupational Safety and Health within the, then, Department of Health, Education and Welfare to provide scientific advice and assistance to the new Administration. The activities and achievements of both these agencies remain highly controversial at the end of their first decade, but there can be no question that the Act itself has had a stimulating effect on the whole field of occupational health. It seems reasonable to hope that its impact will ultimately be beneficial.

Nevertheless, as of this writing, most of the occupational health services, outlined below under "Employee Health Services," are still provided by private enterprises to their employees on a voluntary basis, in the sense that only a few of these services are required by law. However, as a result of the adoption of the Act, a number of new private businesses organized to provide employers with those services which *are* required by law have arisen. Most of them tend to concentrate on the environmental control of hazards to health and safety and to provide minimal medical services, but a few provide a full range of occupational health services. In addition, some state and local governmental units within the Departments of Health or Labor have long provided some service, mostly in the form of inspections of work places to detect and correct violations of legal minimum health and safety standards. A few such units have also provided consultative, analytic, and other laboratory services to employers to help them control hazardous conditions. The new Federal agencies are continuing and expanding both these functions.

Occupational health workers give priority to preventing those illnesses and accidents which are directly attributable to, or associated with, the work performed. A few well-known examples, in addition to the notoriously high accident rates in the construction and transportation industries, are lead poisoning, asbestosis, insecticide poisoning, leukemia from ionizing radiation, and loss of hearing from excessive noise. Occupational health workers foster the productivity and general well-being of employees by providing relief of minor symptoms of nonoccupational diseases and injuries during the work day.

Occupational health workers are also increasingly concerned with the prevention and control of diseases which, while not attributable to the work performed, affect the health and longevity of many workers in their most productive middle years, such as coronary heart disease, cancer, and off-the-job accidents. Efforts are also made to educate and motivate employees to develop better health habits and better utilize the services of their own doctors. Finally, there is increasing concern with certain diseases or conditions which are especially vulnerable to attack in a work setting. Alcoholism is the oldest example, but programs for the detection and control of high blood pressure, excessive weight, and cigarette smoking, are also being successfully developed.

Occupational Medicine. Occupational medicine may be defined as that branch of medicine which is concerned with the prevention and treatment of occupational injuries and diseases, and with the promotion of the optimal health, productivity, and social adjustment of gainfully employed people at all levels. It is the oldest discipline in occupational health, the others having developed as special non-medical skills were needed. It is also an ancient branch of medical knowledge in the sense that the relationships between certain diseases and certain kinds of work and between general health and productivity have been recognized and studied from earliest times—ancient writers from Hippocrates to Pliny described particular occupational diseases.

However, occupational medicine in the sense of a separate form of practice did not develop until the second decade of this century, with the passage of Workers' Compensation laws in every state. (See WORKERS' COMPENSATION.) These laws make employers responsible for treating injuries and illnesses associated with work, and for a significant part of any consequent loss of wages. Employers are required to carry insurance against both these costs. As some private doctors began to concentrate on the treatment of such injuries, and some larger companies hired doctors to provide treatment directly, "industrial surgery" was born.

Many employers and their insurance carriers made efforts to reduce the frequency, severity, and consequent cost, of work injuries. A new discipline of "safety engineering" within new "safety departments" appeared, and the National Safety Council was organized. (See SAFETY AND HEALTH IN THE WORKPLACE.). Safety programs have been so successful that most workplaces are now safer than the homes and recreational areas of workers. Industrial surgeons and company doctors gave these safety programs full support and cooperation from the beginning. However, they did not, and still do not, usually accept responsibility for their routine operation, but occupational safety and occupational rehabilitation remain vital concerns of occupational medicine.

As the administration of Workers' Compensation was refined and the safety movement became effective, occupational diseases, which were also covered under the compensation laws, drew more attention. They are, of course, far more complex than occupational injuries, and far greater efforts were required to establish their causes, understand their mechanisms, treat their effects, and ultimately prevent their occurrence. Older ones, such as silicosis, lead poisoning, and the "bends" or decompression sickness were studied in much greater detail.

With the growth in the size and complexity of industry, particularly during and immediately after World War II, many new potentially toxic materials, such as plastics and pesicides, and new noxious agents, such as ionizing radiation and laser beams, also needed study. In addition, some noxious agents which had been unthinkingly accepted in the past, such as excessive noise, came under scrutiny and attack. Similarly, newer criteria for safety margins began to develop: it was no longer considered sufficient to prevent obvious disease; rather, it became desirable to prevent any detectable biological change in an exposed person, if possible. The broader medical knowledge needed to study, treat, and prevent these diseases made the title "Industrial Physician" more appropriate than the older one of "Industrial Surgeon." As this knowledge has been applied to all kinds of employees in all kinds of employment the title "Occupational Physician" has become even more accurate.

Most of the knowledge about occupational diseases has been acquired by physicians employed by private companies, but physicians associated with the United States Public Health Service and some state labor or health departments, notably in New York, Massachusetts, Pennsylvania, and California, have also made vital contributions. Increasingly, in recent decades academicians affiliated with Occupational Medical Departments in medical schools have conducted important research. Since the measurement of toxic substances and noxious agents is essential in evaluating the quantitative exposure of workmen, chemists and physicists were needed. And since the elimination or reduction of the offending agents required modification of buildings, equipment, and operations, engineers were also needed. The application of these pure and applied sciences to the control of occupational disease created the new discipline of "Industrial Hygiene." (See ENVIRONMENTAL CONTROLS.)

By and large, industrial hygiene has been successful, especially in larger companies, in greatly reducing the exposure of workers and largely eliminating new cases of some of the worst of the older occupational diseases such as silicosis, decompression sickness, lead poisoning, and radium poisoning. As mortality and serious morbidity have decreased, more attention has been given to less dramatic agents, such as nuisance dusts and occupational skin diseases. As with industrial safety, occupational physicians do not usually accept direct responsibility for industrial hygiene, but occupational medicine remains concerned with its rationale, techniques, and effectiveness.

Second in priority only to the prevention and treatment of specific occupational diseases and injuries, occupational medicine is concerned with maintaining the immediate well-being and productivity of workers, as well as their long-term health. One way of doing so is the proper selection and placement of workers in terms of their physical, mental, and emotional capacities. Applicants for new jobs, people being transferred to other jobs, and those returning from absences due to illness can be evaluated in these terms by techniques similar to those of any diagnostic medical evaluation. Since nonoccupational illnesses and accidents cause many times more absence from work and ineffectiveness at work than occupational ones, another way to maintain productivity and well-being is to provide some general medical care in the work place. Other efforts to promote general health concentrate on the early diagnosis of disease in its most reversible stage.

Every contact of an employee with a physician also provides an opportunity to educate and motivate him or her to develop better health habits and to make better use of community medical resources. All these therapeutic, diagnostic, and educational efforts are discussed below under "Employee Health Services."

Occupational Medical Practice. This practice is less standardized than any other medical or surgical specialty or sub-specialty. Like other specialties, it has developed a large body of knowledge, ethical and scientific principles, and many specific techniques. Postgraduate training programs of varying duration and intensity are available in a number of medical schools, and shorter courses in particular areas within the field are available through specialty and general medical associations.

The American Board of Preventive Medicine certifies knowledge and competence in the subspecialty of occupational medicine. This certification is comparable to that in other subspecialties. An increasing number of young physicians complete formal postgraduate training in a medical school, usually adding a Master's Degree in Public Health to their basic degree of Medical Doctor early in their careers, and they obtain certification in the subspecialty shortly after they become active in the field. But many physicians still become interested in occupational medicine after training and practice in general medicine or another specialty.

Occupational physicians with each of these different educational backgrounds are found at every level of responsibility, achievement, and recognition. They usually seek full-time careers at a high level in private enterprise, an academic institution, or a government agency. However, a few establish, or participate as partners in, private practices, often called "Industrial Health Clinics" or "Occupational Health Clinics." These may provide a broad range of occupational medical services to a number of smaller employers, or to the smaller plants of larger employers in the nearby area. Some have office facilities in one or more large trailers which move from one industrial plant to another, operating as "mobile" industrial or occupational medical clinics. Private consulting practices in a special area of occupational medicine, such as epidemiology, toxicology, occupational skin diseases, or occupational lung diseases, are important, but rare.

Besides these certified specialists, there are even more physicians who work full time in occupational medicine without having sought formal training and certification. Some simply confine their private practices to the treatment of work injuries. Others may also examine candidates for employment or render some other limited employee health services.

Thus, the physicians who actually provide occupational medical services, and therefore may be said to practice occupational medicine, run a complete range from the general practitioner who occasionally treats a work injury, through the cardiologist who reads electrocardiograms on employees a few hours a week, to the highly trained and skilled Diplomate of the American Board of Preventive Medicine in Occupational Medicine, with a Master's Degree in Public Health.

The day-to-day activities of an occupational medical practice will also vary widely, depending on which of the many forms of practice described is involved. They differ from other forms of practice in that they may include a role in the environmental control of occupational injuries and diseases, in the treatment and rehabilitation of work injuries and diseases; in job placement in terms of health, and in health maintenance by means of early diagnosis and health education. They may also include a role in special employee health services such as alcoholic rehabilitation, "troubled employee" counseling, hypertension control programs, and others, discussed under "Employee Health Services."

As employee health insurance to defray at least partially the cost of medical care has become almost universal, and as employers (voluntarily or through collective bargaining) have assumed a greater share of the premiums, occupational physicians have become involved in determining the benefits to be provided and the most effective way of administering them. (See GROUP HEALTH INSURANCE.) They are also often asked for advice about other employee benefits, such as life insurance, supplemental sick pay, and pensions. (See GROUP LIFE INSURANCE and EMPLOYEE BENEFIT PLANS.) While they do not ordinarily actually administer these employee benefits, they often participate in efforts at cost containment. In fact, a whole new paramedical, parapersonnel specialty in "Health Care Cost Containment" is developing.

As consumer advocates, environmentalists, government agencies, and the general public have become more concerned about the health effects of commercial products, intermediate products, by-products, and waste products, occupational physicians have become involved in these matters as they affect the corporations for which they work. (See ENVIRONMENTAL CONTROLS.) They are frequently consulted, not only for their general knowledge of medicine and preventive medicine, but because the toxicology and epidemiology of substances in the workplace are so similar to those of substances in the general environment.

Finally, occupational physicians are often asked for advice about health-related corporate charitable contributions to local hospitals, local community funds, or local and national heart and cancer associations. They can be extremely useful in this area, helping to make sure that limited funds are wisely apportioned to the neediest and worthiest activity or organization.

Employee Health Services. Health services provided by employers in private business, government, and other nonprofit organizations are as variable as the practice of occupational medicine. Workers' Compensation coverage, so important in the history of occupational medicine, is the practical minimum. The vast majority of employers, who of course employ only a few people each, usually provide nothing more, especially in the absence of serious, readily recognized hazards to safety or health. The many small stores, offices, and providers of personal or home services which fall into this category employ very many people in the aggregate. At the other extreme, some large international companies, with thousands of employees at many locations all over the world, such as large oil, steel or electronics companies, provide all the services to be briefly described, on a large scale.

Every combination in between can be found, depending on the nature of the work, the likelihood of injury or disease associated with that work, the size and prosperity of the organization, and the attitudes of the employer, the employees, and their respective medical and legal advisers. The location at which services are given will depend on the location of the physician who provides them. Larger companies, especially at locations where they employ between one and five thousand people, are likely to provide them on the premises. Such "in-plant" facilities are still often referred to as the "Medical Department," but there is an increasing tendency to call them the "Health Service" to stress their preventive function. The chief services which may be included can be summarized as follows, in approximate order of importance and frequency:

(1) *Environmental Control.* The physician providing health services will frequently need the help of industrial hygienists and safety engineers, who may be company employees or outside consultants. He or she should also be generally familiar with minimum legal health and safety requirements. Many states have long enforced certain safety standards, and the "factory inspectors" who do so are familiar figures, not only in the United States, but in England and on the Continent. Some states, notably New York, Pennsylvania, California, and Massachusetts, have also long had a series of occupational disease codes which set minimum standards for environmental control. The newer Federal Occupational Safety and Health Administration has already promulgated new standards for some hazardous materials and agents, has proposed but not yet adopted standards for others, and has temporarily used those of the older governmental agencies for the remainder. The Federal Environmental Protection Administration, Transportation Administration, and Poisonous Substances Act may also be involved. (See ENVIRONMENTAL CONTROLS.)

(2) *Emergency and Palliative Treatment.* This treatment for both occupational and nonoccupational diseases and injuries, has become very common since the end of World War II in establishments of all kinds which employ more than 300 to 500 people. It is usually rendered by registered occupational health nurses. These nurses are usually provided with written standing orders by a physician for the treatment of common conditions. If there is a physician on the premises, he or she may supervise this activity more closely and will often amplify it. This is the kind of employee health activity which most employees most frequently encounter.

(3) *Definitive Treatment of Occupational Injuries and Diseases.* Relatively minor injuries are often treated on the premises, if nurses and doctors are employed to provide other services as well. However, few individual plants employ enough people to keep a nurse or doctor busy with such cases alone. More serious occupational diseases and injuries are usually treated elsewhere, most frequently by private practitioners, since they are likely to need hospital facilities and the care of specialists, and involve absence from work. These are most important, but fortunately not very frequent, services.

(4) *Medical Evaluations or Examinations.* "Examination," although a less exact term than "evaluation," is so well established that it will probably continue to predominate. "Examination" suggests primarily looking and touching, whereas "evaluation" is a broader term which also includes the history of current symptoms and prior illnesses and laboratory and X-ray determinations, as well as the interpretation of all the observations. The practical distinction is that 85% of diagnoses are very strongly suspected from the history alone, another 10% during the actual examination of the patient's body, and only a final 5% from laboratory studies. Many nonmedical people, including employers wishing to obtain such services, think that this order is just reversed and mistakenly judge the thoroughness of an evaluation by the number of laboratory tests. Having made this important point, the word "examination" will be used for simplicity.

(a) *Placement or Preplacement Examinations.* Examinations of applicants for employment or for transfer to other jobs, are performed to ascertain that they are able to perform the new job effectively and without danger to themselves or fellow workers. Examples of conditions which may prevent their doing so are a serious uncorrectable hearing defect in a receptionist, an inguinal hernia in a heavy laborer, or epilepsy in a crane operator. Job restrictions of this kind should be realistic in order not to restrict unnecessarily any individual's job opportunities or the recruitment of otherwise well-qualified applicants. The restrictions must be individualized and carefully documented. Generalizations, such as that women are unable to perform heavy work, must not be used.

Recent Federal, state, and local regulations against discrimination in employment reinforce these principles. (See EMPLOYMENT: Antidiscrimination Legislation.)

A placement examination may also reveal ways in which the new employee can improve his health, through alterations in his daily habits, such as weight control, or by seeking treatment for a newly discovered abnormality, such as high blood pressure. Finally, such examinations give the health staff an initial contact with each employee, and provide a baseline of the new employee's physical, mental, and emotional characteristics which can facilitate later contacts. Until quite recently these placement examinations were also sometimes used to exclude applicants who were likely to be excessively absent or to use a disproportionate share of employee benefits, but the new regulations forbid selection on this basis.

(b) *Hazard Examinations.* This type of examination, also called "medical surveillance," may be necessary at regular intervals of people actually or potentially exposed to dangerous materials or agents, lest any undetected or temporary break in environmental controls have produced excessive exposure, or temporary, or even permanent damage. Such examinations are often limited to the particular tests which are most likely to be affected by the particular agent involved, such as chest X-rays for workers exposed to silica or asbestos, or hearing tests on those exposed to noise.

There is an increasing trend toward utilizing "biological markers" which show the earliest detectable biological alteration, even before any permanent or even temporary dysfunction occurs. Hazard examinations have long been provided, and even made mandatory, by more enlightened employers. Some recent federal standards promulgated by OSHA include requirements for particular kinds of examinations at specific intervals for workers exposed to particular hazards.

(c) *Return to Work or Clearance Examinations.* These may be performed on employees returning to work after any extended absence due to illness, leave of absence, or lay-off, to ascertain that they are again able to perform their work. The scope of these examinations and the duration of absence for which they are required are extremely variable. Brief questioning by an astute nurse is often sufficient, but in some cases quite detailed examinations may be needed, and information from the employee's own physician may be essential.

(d) *Separation Examinations.* Examinations on termination are required by only a few employers, usually where the employee may have been exposed to a material, agent, or situation which could lead to a later claim. Testing the hearing of an airplane mechanic who is leaving his job, but who will continue to work near noisy engines elsewhere, is a good example.

(e) *Periodic Prevention Medical Examinations* are second only to placement examinations in frequency and importance. They are often provided only for executive or management personnel, but they may be provided for all employees in some instances. Eligible employees are usually examined every year after the age of 40, but often less frequently at earlier ages. The scope of the examination also frequently varies with age, and sometimes with job level.

An adequate periodic examination should lead to one of the three following conclusions, in decreasing order of frequency: (i) The individual is in good general health and needs no further medical study or treatment at the present time. (ii) The individual has certain definite diseases or conditions for which he should seek treatment from private physicians of his own choice. Or (iii) Certain abnormalities are detected which require additional medical study or consultation. These additional studies may also be provided in the Employee Health Service, but the employee is more often referred to his own private physician for them.

Most such periodic examinations are conducted by full-time occupational physicians in an Employee Health Service on the employer's premises, but some are performed by fixed or mobile occupational or industrial health clinics, and quite a few are done, especially at high executive levels, at sophisticated and prestigious medical centers. These are frequently connected with medical schools, sometimes at a considerable distance from the location of the business.

There is no evidence that these "fancier" examinations are more useful than the commoner kind. All kinds have become very popular with employers and employees, but recently their long-term value has been questioned by some physicians. Their value is difficult to measure; the critics may focus too strongly on mortality and serious morbidity, whereas the recognition and relief of minor conditions may contribute greatly to productive and satisfying daily living at work and at home. Certainly periodic examinations have more value if they can be reinforced by more frequent contacts in selected cases, as well as by continuing efforts to improve health, such as the programs in the control of excessive weight, high blood pressure, and cigarette smoking discussed below.

(5) *Rehabilitation.* Rehabilitation is an important employee health activity. Some large companies provide quite elaborate facilities and trained physical and occupational therapists on the premises to rehabilitate employees injured at work. These facilities may also be made available for nonoccupational cases when scheduling permits. More frequently rehabilitation of both occupational and nonoccupational cases is provided in community facilities. Even

more frequent and far more important, is the rehabilitation of employees recovering from any illness or injury by means of temporary adjustment of their work assignments.

Ideally, the occupational physician or the occupational health nurse should begin to plan with the employee and his or her treating physician for the eventual return to work as soon as it becomes apparent that the patient will be ill long enough to need readjustment after recovery. Most frequently, a simple gradual increase in hours worked each day permits the employee to readjust to his or her previous job, but sometimes responsibility and effort cannot be directly measured in time, especially for executives. In these cases the employee must only gradually resume full responsibility, regardless of the number of hours put in. In some cases only a completely different, temporary, assignment will permit gradual resumption of full responsibility.

All necessary job limitations should be prescribed as exactly as possible. Vague directions like "take it easy," "don't overdo it," or "pace yourself," while popular with many doctors, are not helpful. They tend to prolong the time for full recovery of a fearful person and encourage a more adventurous one to exceed his capacity.

(6) *Immunizations.* Protection against infectious diseases is frequently provided. Immunizations may be given for work-related purposes, such as tetanus toxoid for work injuries, or they may be provided for general purposes, such as recreational travel. They may also be given on a large scale to help control an epidemic, such as influenza. There is a trend in occupational medicine, as in general preventive medicine, to give only those "shots" which are clearly needed and effective. This more conservative attitude was intensified by the realization a few years ago that, with the worldwide eradication of smallpox, more people would become ill or die from smallpox vaccination than from the disease, if the old schedule of vaccination every three years were continued.

(7) *Hypertension and Other Specific Disease Control Programs.* Control programs are increasingly frequent employee health activities. An example of those controllable by drugs is high blood pressure. Lowering it with drugs has been clearly shown in recent years to avoid or delay complications and prolong life. Good control requires fairly frequent blood pressure determinations, and careful adjustment of the dosages of one, two, and sometimes more drugs which may produce inconvenient or even dangerous side effects. Once the diagnosis and need for control have been established, it is quite convenient for the patient to obtain the detailed observations and adjustments needed during brief visits to the Employee Health Service at his work place without absence from work, additional travel, or prolonged waiting.

It takes little additional time or expense for the occupational physician to conduct this preventive service. Some of the necessary observations can be made by occupational health nurses. The patient's own physician will usually welcome this help for his or her patient, provided that he (she) is initially consulted, kept regularly informed, and respectfully involved in all important decisions.

(8) *Alcoholism and Other Behavioral Disoders.* The Employee Health Service must work as an equal partner with other departments of the organization to achieve good results in this area. (See ALCOHOLISM AND DRUG ABUSE IN INDUSTRY.)

The existence of a drinking problem usually becomes apparent when the employee's attendance, or the quality and quantity of his work, or both, deteriorate. Once the supervisors and the personnel staff suspect alcoholism, the diagnosis should be confirmed medically, since excessive and compulsive drinking may be only a symptom of a more serious mental disorder which requires separate treatment. In addition, prolonged excessive drinking can produce physical disease, such as cirrhosis of the liver, which also requires active treatment.

Physicians can direct the alcoholic toward effective help, which almost always includes Alcoholics Anonymous. They can also help supervisors and the personnel staff monitor the employee's cooperation, which should always be made a condition of continued employment. The successful management of addiction to other drugs is analogous to that of alcoholism, but they are less frequently encountered in the work setting, and therefore formal programs are fewer and of lesser scope.

(9) *Troubled Employee Programs.* These are a relatively new activity in which the Employee Health Service participates with other departments. Most of them have grown out of alcoholism programs, as it became apparent that deterioration in attendance and quality and quantity of work of many employees was due, not to excessive drinking, but to some other

personal problem. Included are emotional disorders, family health problems, marital problems, child development and behavior problems, and financial problems.

Once the supervisor has established that an unexplained work deficiency exists, he or she, or a member of the personnel staff may suggest that the employee accept evaluation and counseling. In some programs the occupational physician then evaluates the problem, determining the presence and importance of medical factors, and recommends specific medical or psychiatric treatment, or some other kind of counseling. In other programs a counsellor interviews the employee first, using the occupational physician as a later consultant in developing a counseling program.

(10) *Health Education and Motivation.* Every contact of an employee with the Health Service presents an opportunity for health education and motivation. No other technique is so effective as this kind of timely individual teaching and persuasion. Also worthwhile are posters and booklets, motion pictures, and lectures. Discussion groups can be extremely valuable if they are structured, focus on taking action rather than simply giving information, and deal with a single specific problem. Thus, groups to achieve weight reduction or stop cigarette smoking verge on formal group therapy and can be very effective.

Occupational Health Nursing. There are about 22,000 registered nurses in this country who devote all or part of their time to occupational health activities. This nursing subspecialty began almost contemporaneously with industrial surgery just before World War I, grew rapidly with industrial medicine after World War II, and has entered the current era as the most important partner of occupational medicine in the occupational health field.

Like occupational medicine, it has developed a large body of knowledge, special techniques, and educational curricula. A Master's degree in Occupational Health Nursing is awarded for formal postgraduate study, and many shorter courses in particular areas of interest are offered by academic institutions, government agencies, and professional nursing associations, especially the American Association of Occupational Health Nurses. An independent and prestigious American Board of Occupational Health Nursing certifies knowledge and competence in the field.

Occupational health nurses participate in the detection and control of safety and health hazards in the work place. To do so they must visit work areas and be familiar with work materials and processes, and with the working organization and interpersonal relationships. They almost always treat minor job-related illnesses and injuries, and monitor the treatment and progress of more serious ones. They very frequently also provide similar treatment for injuries and illnesses which are not job related. They may assess the health of workers exposed to specific health hazards, making some of the observations needed for "medical surveillance," and may also assess the general health of employees.

The nurses do a great deal of individual health counseling and guidance, both in terms of helping employees develop more healthful daily habits, and advising them of the need for specific medical investigation and treatment. Many nurses also do group teaching.

The legal limits of their activities are defined by Nurse Practice Acts in each State. In general they may diagnose and treat injuries and illnesses only under the direction of a particular physician who accepts responsibility for their actions, but they may undertake the preventive activities listed, such as hazard detection and control, health assessment, and health counseling, without specific medical direction.

The approximately 22,000 nurses engaged in occupational health work in about 8,500 organizations, only 1,500 of which are large enough to employ more than eight nurses. These are obviously the larger employers, and the other 7,000 units usually employ far fewer people. About one-third of the nurses work in units without any doctor on the premises, relying on written standing orders and telephone consultation for medical guidance. A quarter work where there is at least one full-time doctor. The remaining 40% work in units where a doctor comes in a few hours a week.

Each of these forms of practice is useful and acceptable, if it is well suited to the health and safety problems encountered, and to the size and type of work unit involved. The occupational health nurse must of course be properly selected and trained, and management must understand and support her function. It is particularly important to obtain the services of a properly trained occupational health nurse in a smaller plant with fewer employees, where there will be no doctor on the premises, and where the doctors available for consultation and guidance may have little training or experience in occupational medicine. Unfortunately, it is under just these circumstances that the nurse is most likely to be selected on the basis of acquaintance and personal recommendation by someone in management or a local physican. Instead, management would be well advised to seek consultation with a nearby Federal, state, or local health agency or with one of the larger insurance companies, which frequently provide such service, both to determine the employee health activities needed and to select a well-qualified and preferably Certified Occupational Health Nurse.

Industrial Hygiene. This is the scientific discipline which seeks to ensure a safe and healthful work environment. Engineers and chemists began to participate in such efforts very early in this century, but the specialty was widely recognized and named only during the burst of industrial and business growth following World War II. Like occupational medicine and occupational health nursing, industrial hygiene has developed a large body of knowledge, many highly refined techniques, and educational prerequisites. An undergraduate degree in engineering, chemistry, physics, or one of the other basic sciences is essential. Master's degrees in Industrial Hygiene, Industrial Health, or Environmental Science are available from many academic institutions. There are also advanced courses available outside specific degree programs.

The American Industrial Hygiene Association is the principal professional association, but industrial hygienists in government agencies and academic institutions usually also belong to the American Conference of Governmental Industrial Hygienists. The American Industrial Hygiene Association has also established a special Board which certifies the knowledge and competence of individuals in this field.

Industrial hygienists follow three basic sequential procedures. The first is the *recognition* of hazards by detailed inspection of the work place, which requires a thorough familiarity with innumerable materials and processes and with their possible safety hazards and toxic effects. The second is *evaluation* of the extent or degree of the hazard, which frequently involves chemical and physical measurements, analysis of the duration and intimacy of contact between individual workmen and the offending agent, and an estimation of the exact quantitative extent of the exposure of the workmen. The third and final procedure is *control,* which means lowering the exposure of individual workers to a safe level. A safe level should be one-tenth to one-hundredth of that level which could produce any ill effect in order to provide a margin of safety.

Control is achieved through four basic approaches. *Elimination* of the offending material, process or agent is obviously the most effective control if it is feasible; an example would be the prohibition of explosive or inflammable ingredients such as gasoline from home dry-cleaning agents. *Substitution* of a less toxic *agent* is advantageous, but still requires continued monitoring; an example would be the substitution of perchlorethylene for carbon tetrachloride in commercial degreasing and cleaning processes. *Substitution* of one *process* for another may reduce the concentration of an offending substance to safe levels; an example would be the substitution of wet grinding for dry grinding. *Enclosure* is another means of reducing the exposure of the individual worker; one can enclose the machine to reduce the noise it produces, but the use of earplugs really "encloses" the worker's ear in a different way. *Ventilation* is, of course, one of the most widely used and effective means of reducing the air concentration of toxic substances.

There are presently about 5,000 industrial hygienists in the United States. About 20% of them work for the Occupational Safety and Health Administration, probably another 20% work in other governmental agencies, academic institutions, or private consulting firms, and the remaining 60% are directly employed by private enterprises, usually large corporations with many employees, extensive operations, and significant potential safety and health hazards, such as the larger oil, chemical, steel, mining and utility companies.

As stricter health and safety standards are adopted, and as more extensive environmental monitoring is required, more industrial hygienists will be needed in all these categories. A specific employer can get help in determining his need for an industrial hygienist, and in obtaining a well-qualified candidate, through the National Institutes of Occupational Safety and Health, his Sate Labor or Health Department, his insurance carrier, or one of the many private consulting firms in the field.

Other Occupational Health Disciplines. As the preceding discussion of occupational medical practice implies, some occupational physicians limit their interests and activities to special areas such as *Occupational Epidemiology, Toxicology, Radiation, Psychiatry, Dermatology,* as well as many others. Since these subspecialists almost always work with other general occupational physicians in larger, structured, employee health programs, detailed discussion of their fields appears unnecessary here.

"Physicians Assistants" and "Nurse Practitioners" have begun to enter the occupational health field during the last decade. These are people who have received limited medical training, almost always at a medical school, which qualifies them to perform simpler diagnostic and theraputic procedures under the supervision of a licensed physician. Many of them were nurses, medical corpsmen in military service, or medical technicians of various kinds. They are well trained in the more common and routine medical procedures, and particularly trained to recognize unusual illnesses or injuries which must be brought to the attention of a fully trained and licensed physician promptly. They have proven extremely useful in performing routine examinations, treating simpler illnesses and injuries at work, and conducting preventive programs, such as the control of excessive weight or high blood pressure. Since the necessary supervision is relatively easily arranged in the work situation, the number of such practitioners may be expected to grow.

"Health Physicists" are the equivalent of Industrial Hygienists who concentrate on the control of hazards due to physical agents, particularly ionizing radiation from X-rays or radioactive materials. "Health Educators" may be physicians, nurses, or specifically trained educators, who specialize in this area. "Administrators" in large Employee Health Services may have specific postgraduate training in medical or hospital administration. Finally, "Safety Engineers" and other safety workers, while of the greatest importance, have not developed so formal a discipline as other occupational health workers. Nevertheless, their efforts and their activities have undoubtedly prevented more discomfort, inconvenience, and disability among workers, and have saved more money for their employers and society, than any other group of workers in the field.

Administration

Costs and Benefits. Every employer must provide Workers' Compensation, and the number and scope of other occupational health services required by law are rapidly increasing. Management should provide as many other occupational health services as the company's size and resources permit, because it values its employees, wants their respect and cooperation, is genuinely concerned with their welfare, and wants the respect of business allies, competitors, and the community.

A company should not provide services in the expectation of any immediate financial benefit. Very few Employee Health Services can be shown to be cost-effective in the short-term accounting sense. They do reduce absence, increase productivity and morale, perhaps limit some employee medical benefits, and help attract and hold good employees, but so many of these factors are intangible, and there are such poor bases for comparisons, that any exact savings are difficult to measure.

Organizational Relationships. The Employee Health Service should serve as a staff function, providing information and advice to management in all matters relating to health and illness.

The individual in charge of the service, whether an occupational physician or an occupational health nurse, should have ready access to top management, such as the president of the company, a senior vice president, the local regional manager, another physician within the organization at a higher level, or some comparable official in other organizations. However, the occupational health worker should not accept direct responsibility for personnel, legal, or other management decisions.

Records. The results of all medical examinations, treatments, and other contacts of the health staff with each individual should be preserved in legible form and should be readily accessible at need. Medical details should be kept confidential and should not be revealed to management or anyone else without the employee's freely given permission.

However, the interpretation of the medical data may not be privileged if it is obtained outside a true doctor-patient relationship. For example, an applicant for employment understands that the physician will report his conclusions to management. Similarly, if an employee seeks authorization for absence, he knows that the physician will tell management whether he was indeed ill and whether he is able to work again. In other words, if an employee comes for a periodic preventive examination, or freely consults an occupational physician for some other reason, the information is confidential; but if the employee was sent to the physician for an administrative decision, the conclusion cannot be confidential.

Other records of individual employees, even though not purely medical, may be important for the health of the employee, and should be preserved with equal care. Job histories, especially with respect to actual or potential exposures to noxious agents, as well as environmental data on such agents, are very important. Finally, information about illnesses not actually seen in the Employee Health Service, or not even occurring during the period of employment, can be important.

All these quasi-medical observations can be especially valuable for statistical and epidemiological studies on the occupational diseases themselves, as well as on the individual employees exposed. For example, recent epidemiological studies on potential carcinogens draw on environmental data, complete work histories, and complete individual medical data, including illnesses after leaving employment, and the ultimate cause of death from Social Security files.

The volume of all these records becomes enormous, and systems for storing, sorting, and disposing of them when they become outmoded should be developed from the outset if they are to remain at all manageable. The automation of data, now common in larger companies, is of considerable help.

Until recently most records were made and kept by employers of their own volition, but OSHA now requires the keeping of certain records, and prescribes the content and format of some. The first requirement was only for records of all job injuries, but both environmental and medical data are now required for some occupational disease hazards too. The Agency has also, as of this writing, promulgated a rule that medical and environmental data on all exposed individuals and hazardous situations must be preserved and readily available for 30 years, even if the affected employees are no longer employed and the hazard has been eliminated. The rule also gives the employee or his (her) authorized representative access to medical and environmental data. It further gives the staff of the Agency and of the National Institute for Occupational Safety and Health access to both kinds of data, even without the employee's permission. It gives union representatives access to environmental data, but not to the medical data, without the employee's permission.

The ethical problem of confidentiality of those medical records which are not in any way related to hazardous exposures, and the practical problem of preserving so much data in a readily accessible way, are too complex for discussion here. It is to be hoped that compromise and court interpretation will preserve the objective of free access to the specific information needed to study occupational disease and protect exposed workers' health without significantly compromising the value of the many preventive medical activities discussed, such as periodic and other diagnostic examinations, the treatment of minor nonoccupational illnesses, and the control of diseases like alcoholism and hypertension, which seem to require confidentiality.

Reports to Management. Budgets, expense reports, staffing justifications, personnel evaluations, and special requests are the same for the Employee Health Service as for any other staff units. Specialized reports which may be needed at times include: (1) Environmental surveys of work areas in terms of existing potential hazards, the effectiveness of control measures, and recommendations for improvement. (2) Health and illness summaries in terms of illnesses or injuries observed, absences recorded, or diseases found during routine examinations. (3) Statistical summaries of services rendered. (4) Narrative comment on any of the above statistics or about special problems and recommendations.

Internal Organization. Every Occupational Health Service or Medical Department is different, but some organizational guidelines have been developed out of experience. The size, type, and location of the physical facilities required, the number and kind of professional and clerical staff needed, the number and types of activities to be undertaken, the record system and budget, will depend on the size, function, and location of the company or other institution. Advice and help can be obtained from the Council on Occupational Health of the American Medical Association, the American Occupational Medical Association, The National Institute of Occupational Safety and Health, the American Association of Occupational Nurses, some state and local health agencies, insurance carriers, and a number of private consultants.

CHARLES P. GIEL, M.D., Medical Director, Joseph E. Seagram and Sons, Inc.; Associate Professor of Clinical Medicine, New York University College of Medicine; Associate Attending Physician, University and Bellevue Hospitals; New York, New York

Information References

Associations (See Appendix A):

American Academy of Occupational Medicine.
American Association of Occupational Health Nurses.
American Conference of Government Industrial Hygienists.
American Industrial Hygiene Association.
American Medical Association, Council on Occupational Health.
American Occupational Medical Association.
American Public Health Association.
Health Physics Society.
Industrial Health Foundation.
National Institute for Occupational Safety and Health.

Periodicals:

American Industrial Hygiene Association Journal.
American Journal of Public Health.
Archives of Environmental Health.
British Journal of Industrial Medicine.
Health Physics.
Journal of Occupational Medicine.
Occupational Health and Safety.
Occupational Health Nursing.

Texts:

Brown, M. L., "Occupational Health Nursing; Principles and Practices," New York, Springer, in press.
Hunter, D., "Diseases of Occupation," Boston, Little Brown, 1975.
International Labor Organization, "Encyclopedia of Occupational Health and Safety," New York, McGraw-Hill, 1972.
National Institute of Occupational Safety and Health, "New Nurse in Industry," Washington, D. C., U.S. Gov't Printing Office, 017-033-00295-9, 1978.
Patty, F. A., "Industrial Hygiene and Toxicology," New York, Wiley; Vols. I & III, 1979; Vol. II, in press.
Plunkett, E. R., "Handbook of Industrial Toxicology," New York, Chemical Publishing, 1976.
Sax, N. I., "Dangerous Properties of Industrial Materials," New York, Van Nostrand Reinhold, 1979.
Schilling, R. S. F., "Occupational Health Practice," Ontario, Butterworth, 1973.
Zenz, C., "Occupational Medicine; Principles and Practical Applications," Chicago, Chicago Yearbook Publishers, 1975.

Cross References: *Alcoholism and Drug Abuse in Industry; Environmental Controls; Group Health Insurance; Occupational Safety and Health Act of 1970; Office Safety; Quality of Working Life; Safety and Health in the Workplace.*

OCCUPATIONAL SAFETY AND HEALTH ACT OF 1970

On December 29, 1970, the 91st Congress passed a bill which became a significant part of Federal labor law: Public Law 91-596, known as the William-Steiger **Occupational Safety and Health Act of 1970,** or OSHA, which became effective on April 28, 1971. This law resulted from a recognition of a significant deterioration in working conditions and practices, accompanied by a continuing heavy toll in occupational deaths and serious injuries. In terms of lost production and wages, medical expenses, and disability compensation, the burden on the nation's commerce was staggering. Human cost was beyond calculation.

Duties and Obligations of Employers and Employees. *Employer.* The term "employer" defined by the Act means a person engaged in a business affecting commerce who has employees, but does not include the United States or any State or political subdivision of a state. The Act states:

(a) Each employer—

(1) shall furnish to each of his employees employment and a place of employment which are free from recognized hazards that are causing or are likely to cause death or serious physical harm to his employees.

(2) shall comply with occupational safety and health standards promulgated under this Act. An employer can be cited for violation of this section and fined.

Employees. The term "employee" defined by the Act means an employee who is employed in a business of his employer which affects commerce. The Act states:

(b) Each employee—

(1) shall comply with occupational safety and health standards and all rules, regulations, and orders issued persuant to this Act which are applicable to his own actions and conduct. There are no citations or penalties for violations.

It should be noted that the word *shall* indicates mandatory adherence, as opposed to "may" or "should," which connote permission to comply if desired. The word "shall" occurs many times both in the Act and in the *Federal Register* which contains the specific detailed standards which must be obeyed.

OSHA'S Purpose. Under the provisions of the Act, the Occupational Safety and Health Administration (OSHA) was created within the Department of Labor. While OSHA continually reviews and redefines specific standards and practices, its basic purposes remain constant—to assure safe and healthful working conditions for every worker in the nation. OSHA strives to implement its Congressional mandate fully and firmly with fairness to all concerned by:

(1) Encouraging employers and employees to reduce hazards in the work place and to implement new or improve existing safety and health programs.

(2) Establishing "separate but dependent responsibilties and rights" for employers and employees for the achievement of better safety and health conditions.

(3) Establishing reporting and record-keeping procedures to monitor job-related injuries and illnesses.

(4) Developing mandatory job safety and health standards and enforcing them effectively.

(5) Encouraging the states to assume the fullest responsibility for establishing and administering their own occupational safety and health programs, which must be "at least as effective as" the Federal program.

The mandatory job safety and health standards mentioned in (4) above are detailed in a publication known as the *Coded Federal Register.* This document contains in its many volumes the details of enacted legislation and records of other transactions, amendments, and notices. As an example Part 1910, *Occupational Safety and Health Standards* pertains to general industry. These standards cover every employer in a business affecting commerce who has one or more employees. They do not affect self-employed persons or family-owned and operated farms. They do not affect work places covered under other Federal laws such as Coal Mine Health and Safety Act, the Federal Aviation Administration, Railway Safety, Gas Pipelines Safety, Atomic Energy Acts, or the Metallic and Non-metallic Mine Safety Act. However, Federal Government employees are covered under separate provisions of the Act.

Regulations for Part 1910 contain nineteen subparts, sixteen of which contain references to the equipment, practices, environment, materials and substances found in work places. These subparts include:

D- Walking-Working Surfaces.
E- Means of Egress.
F- Powered Platforms, Manlifts and Vehicle-Mounted Work Platforms.
G- Occupational Health and Environmental Controls.
H- Hazardous Materials.
I- Personal Protective Equipment.
K- Medical and First Aid.
L- Fire Protection.
M- Compressed Gas and Compressed Air Equipment.
N- Materials Handling and Storage.
O- Machinery and Machine Guarding.
P- Hand and Portable Powered Tools and Other Hand-Held Equipment.
Q- Welding, Cutting and Brazing.
R- Special Industries.
S- Electrical.

It is within these subparts that the specific procedures, mandatory inspections, prohibitions, and other applicable standards are detailed. It is the employers' responsibility to become familiar with the standards applicable to their establishments and to assure that employees have and use personal protective gear and equipment required for safety. Even in cases where OSHA has not promulgated specific standards, employers are responsible for following the intent of the Act's General Duty clause.

Establishing Standards. The Secretary of Labor establishes occupational safety and health standards. These are published in the *Federal Register* and have the effect of law. The Secretary is assisted by the National Institute for Occupational Safety and Health in the Department of Health and Human Services (formerly called the Department of Health, Education, and Welfare) and by special committees which he is authorized to establish.

Rule-Making Power. The Secretary is also given the power to make rules governing the administration of the Act. These rules are published in the *Federal Register* and once adopted also have the effect of law. They apply to such areas as: requirements for record keeping, posting of notices or citations for violations, informing employers and employees of their rights under the Act, requirements for recording and reporting of occupationally caused deaths, accidents and illnesses, notices of hearings, internal administrative procedures, and any interpretation of provisions that require publication of rules.

Inspection, Enforcement, and Penalties. The Secretary is responsible for conducting regular or special inspections of work places. He cites employers found in violation and recommends civil or criminal penalties. Contested citations dealing with imminent danger situations, compliance orders, or recommended penalties are referred by the Secretary to the Occupational Safety and Health Review Commission which will issue an order, based upon the record of a hearing.

The Secretary of Health and Human Services is also authorized to make inspections to carry out his duties as provided by the Act in the fields of research, special experiments, monitoring and recording of toxic materials surveillance, etc.

Approval of State Plans. The Secretary of Labor is directed to approve plans submitted by states that wish to assume responsibility for developing and/or enforcement of standards, and are able to meet the requirements of the Act. He may assist the states by making both planning and operational grants to them. The Secretary must monitor the operations of the state under an approved plan, and if there is substantial failure to comply with any of the provisions, he may then withdraw approval and assume Federal regulation.

Research. The Secretary of Health and Human Services in consultation with the Secretary of Labor and other agencies is directed to do research, experiments, demonstrations, publish a list of toxic materials, develop criteria (for development of occupational safety and health standards), make inspections, and require monitoring, measuring and physical examinations. These activities, to the extent feasible, will be carried out by the National Institute for Occupational Safety and Health (NIOSH) in the Department of Health and Human Services.

Training and Employee Education. The Secretary of Labor is authorized to conduct short-term training programs for his own personnel. In consultation with the Secretary of Health and Human Services, he is directed to establish training programs for workers and management to promote the purposes of the Act.

Both Secretaries are mutually responsible for informational and educational programs for both workers and management on means of preventing occupational accidents and illnesses.

Statistics. The Secretary of Labor, in consultation with the Secretary of Health and Human Services, is directed to develop and maintain a national reporting system on occupational deaths, illnesses, and injuries. This system is to cover all kinds of employment, whether or not subject to the provisions of the Act.

Workplace Inspections. Compliance inspections come under the supervision of the OSHA area director. He assigns compliance officers and industrial hygienists on the basis of the system of priorities as follows [1]:

(1) Imminent Danger.
(2) Catastrophes and other fatal accidents.
(3) Valid employee complaints.
(4) Special emphasis programs.
  (a) Target industries.
  (b) Target health hazards.
(5) General inspection (random).

Before making an inspection, the compliance officer or industrial hygienist becomes familiar with as many relevant facts as possible about the work place, taking into account such things as the history of the establishment and the nature of the business, and determines the particular OSHA standards most likely to apply. He (she) takes along the appropriate special equipment for testing for toxic substances in the air, for noise, etc.

The 1978 Supreme Court decision in the *Barlow* case affected OSHA enforcement nationwide. The Court found that Section 8(a) of the Act, which authorized unannounced warrantless inspections, was unconstitutional as violating the Fourth Amendment. Following the Court's decision, OSHA must obtain a warrant if requested by the employer before conducting an inspection. Though the Supreme Court did not hold OSHA to strict showing of probable cause that a violation existed, magistrates and lower courts have attempted to impose such a showing in subsequent enforcement proceedings.

Inspections are conducted during regular working hours of the establishment except in special circumstances. The Act and OSHA's regulations prohibit advance notice of inspections except in cases where such notice would serve to make the inspection more effective.

An inspection begins when the compliance officer arrives at the establishment. The compliance officer displays official credentials and asks to meet an appropriate employer representative. The compliance officer informs the employer of the purpose of the visit, scope of the inspection, and the standards that apply. The employer is given copies of applicable safety and health standards as well as a copy of any employee complaint that may be involved. If the employee has so requested, his or her name will not be revealed.

The employer is asked to designate his representative to accompany the compliance officer during the inspection tour. An authorized employee representative also is usually given the opportunity to accompany the compliance officer for the walk around. If the employees at the work place are represented by a recognized bargaining representative, the union will ordinarily designate the employee representative who will accompany the compliance officer. Where there are no employee groups, the employee representative may be selected by the employees themselves, but not by the compliance officer or the employer.

During the walk around, each work area is inspected for compliance with OSHA standards. Neither representative may harass or otherwise obstruct the inspection process. The compliance officer takes appropriate notes of conditions and discusses them with both representatives. He or she may take photographs (for record purposes), make instrument readings, and examine records to the extent considered appropriate. The compliance officer must take special care to protect the privacy of trade secrets or security matters.

The compliance officer also inspects records of deaths, injuries, and illnesses which the employer is required to keep. He or she will check to see that the annual summary of occupational injuries and illnesses has been posted. Where records of employee exposure to toxic substances have been required they are also examined.

Some apparent violations may be found that can be corrected immediately. These could include blocked aisles, unsafe floor surfaces, hazardous projections, unsanitary conditions, etc. The employer representative may, and usually does, direct that they be corrected at once. Such conditions are recorded to help in judging employer good faith in compliance. Even though corrected, the apparent violation may be the basis for a citation and/or proposed penalty.

After the walk around, a closing conference is held between the compliance officer and the employer, or the employer representative. The compliance officer discusses with the employer what has been found during the walk around and advises the employer of all apparent violations for which a citation may be issued or recommended. The compliance officer does not indicate any proposed penalties.

After the compliance officer reports to his or her OSHA office, the area director determines what citations, if any, will be issued, what penalties will be issued, and what penalties, if any, will be proposed. The employer will receive citations and notices of proposed penalties by certified mail.

OSHA citations and proposed penalties are similar to traffic violations. If contested, they are subject to final action by a separate authority—in this case the Occupational Safety and Health Review Commission.

Violations. If violations are found, citations may be issued and civil penalties proposed. In order of significance, following are the types of violations of standards normally considered on a first inspection:

- *De Minimis:* A violation that has no direct or immediate relationship to job safety and health. A notice is issued but citations and proposed penalties are not.
- *Nonserious Violation:* A violation that has a direct relationship to job safety and health, but probably would not cause death or serious harm. A proposed penalty of up to $1,000 is discretionary. A penalty for a nonserious violation may be adjusted downward by as much as 80%, depending on the severity of the hazard, the employer's good faith, history of previous violations, and size of the business. When the adjusted penalty amounts to less than $50 no penalty is proposed.
- *Serious Violation:* A violation where there is substantial probability that death or serious physical harm could result and that the employer knew, or should have known, of the hazard. A proposed penalty of up to $1,000 is mandatory. A penalty for a serious violation may be adjusted downward by as much as 50% based on the gravity of the violation, the employer's good faith, history of previous violations, and the size of business.
- *Imminent Danger:* A violation where there is reasonable certainty that a danger exists that can be expected to cause death or serious physical harm immediately or before the danger can be eliminated through normal enforcement procedures. If an imminent danger situation is found, the compliance officer will ask the em-

ployer to abate the hazard voluntarily, and to remove endangered employees from the area. Should the employer fail to to this, OSHA, through the regional solicitor, will apply to the nearest Federal district court for appropriate legal action to correct the situation (treated as a Serious Violation).

Citation also may be issued for violation of other OSHA regulations. Examples include:

• Failure to post requirements—$1,000 per violation.

• Failure to correct cited violation—$1,000 per day.

• False information—to $1,000 and/or up to six months imprisonment.

In addition, for any employer who willfully or repeatedly violates the Act, penalties of up to $10,000 for each such violation will be assessed. If an employer is convicted of a willful violation that has resulted in the death of an employee, the offense is punishable by a fine of not more than $10,000 or by imprisonment up to six months, or both. A second conviction doubles these maximum penalties.

Some Challenges to OSHA's Future. *Legislative.* On December 19, 1979, Senator Richard Schweiker (R-Pa) introduced a bill (S.2153) which posed the most serious threat to OSHA in the Act's decade-long history. It seeks to target OSHA's field resources on those plants with the most severe hazards. Under its provisions, employers would be able to qualify for exemptions from routine safety inspections and the majority of complaint inspections provided that they (1) had no occupational injuries during the year prior to the year of eligibility for the exemption, as reported by states' workers compensation agencies, or, (2) by filing an affidavit with the Secretary of Labor stating that they had no employee deaths and had a low lost-workday injury rate for the preceding year.

States' workers compensation agencies would provide the Secretary of Labor with a list of employers who had reported one or more occupational injuries during the preceding year. Any employer in the state who was not on the list would be exempt from routine OSHA inspections.

No employer would be exempt from inspections of serious accidents, occupational health hazards, imminent danger situations, or investigations aimed at protecting employees against discrimination in exercising their rights under the law. Any alleged safety violation found during the course of such inspections could be cited. The bill removes all penalties for serious and other than serious violations for businesses with ten or fewer employees, or for larger exempt employers who maintain a joint labor-management safety committee and a regular on-site consultation program. Even employers ineligible for the inspection exemption would still be eligible for reduced penalties for most safety violations as long as they could demonstrate that they had the labor-management safety committees and on-site consultation services.

Judicial. Concurrent with the legislative challenge on OSHA, judicial challenges to the law and its administration have been ever present. The U.S. Court of Appeals for the Fifth Circuit concluded that OSHA had failed to prove that the reduction in benzene exposure from ten parts per million to one part per million was reasonably necessary to protect worker health. Unless OSHA could show a definite risk of leukemia or other toxic effects resulting from exposure to ten parts per million, reduction in exposure at so great a cost could not be justified according to the Court.

In an appeal by the AFL–CIO Industrial Union Department to the U.S. Supreme Court, organized labor sought to overturn the Fifth Circuit Court's decision because of its effect on all carcinogen regulation. The U.S. Supreme Court struck down the OSHA benzene standard in a five-to-four decision upholding the Fifth Circuit. The plurality of justices found that OSHA failed to show that a significant risk of harm existed at the present ten parts per million standard and that available evidence did not justify a tenfold reduction in the permissible exposure level.

It appears that a quantitative assessment and demonstration of risk at existing levels may be required for all standards, though available scientific evidence does not permit meaningful assessment for most hazards. At this writing, the impact of this decision on OSHA's generic cancer policy and other health and safety standards yet to be promulgated remains to be seen.

LAWRENCE SLOTE, Eng.Sc.D., P.E., New York University; Director, The Center for Safety, New York, New York

Information Reference

The Occupational Safety and Health Act, Public Law 91–596.

Reference Cited

[1] "All About OSHA," U.S. Dept. of Labor, OSHA 2056, rev., 1980.

Cross References: *Environmental Controls; Group Health Insurance; Occupational Health; Office Safety; Safety and Health in the Workplace.*

OFFICE AUTOMATION

Office Automation is a popular term covering any major use of machines in office operations. The term first appeared in management literature in the late 1950s when computers entered the office as powerful tools for processing paperwork.

Today the term has several meanings, none of them precise, which go beyond the singular idea of "using computers." It can refer to the use of WORD PROCESSING equipment, for example, or of micrographics equipment, reprographics equipment, and more.

Increasingly, the term has taken on a future connotation. The automated office, "the office of the future," the integrated information system, and similar expressions are used interchangeably in casual business conversation. All refer to a basic concept in which various kinds of electronic office devices are tied together, or "integrated," by means of telecommunications linkages. Thus, functions which once operated more or less separately, in "stand-alone fashion," now interact with each other. They are components in a larger system no longer bounded by departmental lines or even office-wide limits. Through telecommunications, the automated office in this view can embrace an entire region, a nation, the globe.

While machines have "talked to each other" for some time, the automated future office carries the idea much further. In the past, machines of like kind did most of the talking. In the future—and even, within limits, in the present—systems of differing kinds can transfer information from device to device. Thus, text keyed on a word processing terminal could be sent to a computer for "merging" of certain data lately processed there; the combined message of words and numbers could then be printed out on a device located many miles away. The device might be a rapid ink-jet printer or an "intelligent" laser copier. Or the information might be displayed paperlessly on the screen of a terminal located, perhaps, on an executive's desk.

The benefits of office automation are potentially enormous. Like automation in the factory and in agriculture, the use of machines to accomplish work in the office can increase productivity and lower overhead. Because the end product of most office work is information, the use of powerful systems to process and transmit that information can greatly benefit decision makers and other knowledge workers. And because these systems can dispatch their informational products over telephone lines, and now via satellite, they can do in seconds what the older systems of messenger and mail took hours and days to perform. "Electronic mail" is thus one more concept embraced by office automation.

The difficulties with office automation are also potentially large. Already the computer and word processing have altered the ways offices operate. Word processing has greatly changed the role of the secretary—the single largest job category in the office. No one fully knows how the further expansion of office automation will change the nature and number of white-collar jobs. It seems probable that fewer clerks will be needed while the demand for knowledge workers and "information managers" will increase.

Technology can also pose some problems. While it is true in a general sense that the technological base of the automated office is "already here," several components of that base are not yet economically feasible or even openly on the market. One particularly vexing issue as more and more devices interact with others (or try to) is the lack of communicational compatibility among them. The data codes one device uses may not be understood by another. Transmissions across national borders may face political as well as technological barriers. These problems are much talked about but may never be universally solved. Systems specialists can usually come up with some kind of decoding device through which incompatible machines can converse, but these arrangements are never as efficient as direct terminal-to-terminal communication would be.

The ways in which managers plan for automation will also change from what this entailed in the past. Previously, administrative change could be episodic and selective: an improved system here, a new machine there. But the demands of future office automation are more far-reaching. They lead management into a complex change-process of interactive disciplines: the merging of functions, the counseling and retraining of personnel, the testing of systems through pilot projects, the planning over longer time spans for deliveries of new equipment and the expected obsolescence of the old. And much as each phase of the process must be planned and managed, so must also the change-process as a whole.

Office automation, in sum, is more than machinery. In its contemporary meaning, it is a multi-faceted concept. It involves new ways to process and transmit information and new understanding of what that elusive commodity, information, really is. It involves new ways to value our workforce, to configure our organizations, to assess productivity, and manage the ever-more-complex cycles of change.

WALTER A. KLEINSCHROD, editor of *Administrative Management* and editorial director of *Word Processing & Information Systems* magazine.

Information References

Connell, John J., "Office of the 80s: Productivity Impacts," *Business Week,* February 18, 1980.

Fronk, Robert L., Mayfield, Anne M., and Zimbel, Norman S., "The Emerging Real World of Office Automation," Cambridge, Mass., Arthur D. Little Inc.

Lodahl, Thomas M. and Meyer, N. Dean, "Pilot Projects: A Way to Get Started in Office Automation," *Administrative Management,* February, 1980; "Six Pathways to Office Automation," *Administrative Management,* March 1980.

"Managing the Process of Change," multi-article report, *Administrative Management,* January 1980.

"Office Automation, Personnel, and the New Technology," *Personnel Journal,* October, 1980. (Report on the first annual Office Automation Conference held in Atlanta, Georgia, 1980.)

Office Technology Research Group, various publications and reports, Pasadena, Calif.

Cross References: *Data Communications; Electronic Data Processing; Office Management and Administrative Services; Word Processing.*

OFFICE LANDSCAPING: See Office Space Planning.

OFFICE MANAGEMENT AND ADMINISTRATIVE SERVICES

In the decade of the Eighties, society is moving rapidly from an industrially labor-intensive orientation to an information services-intensive one, due to the impact of computerization on almost all aspects of conducting business. As a result, **Office Administrative Services Management,** which is heavily information-intensive, is becoming an increasingly important area in business, industry, government, and institutional operations. Today's office or administrative services manager is likely to control a significant budget covering computerized equipment to type, file, mail, and calculate the information needs of such integral functions as manufacturing and marketing. Because of the increased volume of such necessary information, OFFICE AUTOMATION is growing in importance as a means of handling work with greater speed and efficiency. This is impacting the role of the administrative office manager, who is being called upon to oversee the automation and coordination of various office systems such as WORD PROCESSING, DATA COMMUNICATIONS, and RECORDS MANAGEMENT.

Today, as in the past, there is no singular, clearcut definition of what comprises the administrative services office management function. Thus, persons responsible for administrative operations do not have one recognized title, such as ones given plant managers and sales managers. According to a survey of Certified Administrative Managers (C.A.M.s), conducted by the Administrative Management Society, the job titles most frequently carried are:

- Administrative Manager
- Manager of Administration
- Office Manager
- Manager of Administrative, Office, or General Services
- Controller
- Manager of Accounting
- Director of Administration or Administration Director
- Director of Personnel or Human Resources

These titles typically report to top management, such as the vice president-administration, executive vice president, or in smaller companies, to the president. Persons with any one of these many titles may have direct responsibilities for the supervision of office operatons and for the furnishing of administrative services. These may include most or all of the following functions, which have been developed by the editorial advisory board of the "Handbook of Modern Office Management and Administrative Services," in collaboration with the Administrative Management Society:

- Accounting
- Automated office systems and procedures
- Budgeting for office operations
- Cafeteria, dining room
- Computer input (planning)
- Copying, duplicating equipment
- Credit and collections
- General office equipment and supplies

- Internal auditing
- Library
- Mail and messenger services
- Management information systems
- Microfilm services
- Office maintenance
- Office security, space planning and decor
- Printing, in-house and out-of-house
- Records management
- Recruiting and training general office and clerical personnel
- Telecommunications
- Temporary help services

Computer operations of significant size plus the application of advanced information technology have traditionally been the responsibility of departments that report separately to top management. However, as automation enters the office, persons responsible for administrative services must be sufficiently familiar with developments in these areas to see that office operations are performed as efficiently as possible, which very often implies the use of computerized equipment. Furthermore, while company-wide financial planning, budgeting, and accounting operations are functions that have usually reported separately to top management, the manager of administrative services needs a sound working knowledge of these areas as well, since part of his/her duties involve input to accounting in the form of budgeting procedures and transaction records, and operations requiring accounting control.

As the various automated office operations, including word processing, data processing, telecommunications, and records management, begin to merge into one, unified information system, the administrative services manager will be called upon to assume the new role of *information manager* or *manager of information services.* In addition to a broad perspective of office information-handling functions, this new manager must also possess a keen awareness and knowledge of human resources. As office workers continue to work ever closer with sophisticated machines, the person in charge of information processing operations must strive harder for a smooth-running man/machine environment.

ADMINISTRATIVE MANAGEMENT SOCIETY, Willow Grove, Pennsylvania

Information References

Management World and Impact, monthly publications of the Administrative Management Society, Willow Grove, Pa.

Heyel, Carl, ed., "Handbook of Modern Office Management and Administrative Services," Huntington, N.Y., repr. 1980.

Cross References: *Office Management (and related entries with Office prefix); Temporary Help Services; Word Processing.*

OFFICE PARKS: See Industrial Districts.

OFFICE SAFETY

While it is true that office personnel usually are not exposed to such industrial hazards as moving machine parts, toxic chemicals and dust, or power hand tools, existence of other potential hazards should not be overlooked. Painful and disabling injuries can and do occur amid the papers, desks, and file cabinets, establishing the need for emphasis on **Office Safety**.

Management should see to it that office employees develop an awareness of office hazards; their vigilance will then help identify and eliminate potential accident situations. Unsafe conditions can also be prevented through scheduled inspection by supervisors or a safety committee.

Accident Categories. Office accidents can generally be classified in six categories: slipping, tripping, or falling; using equipment improperly or operating faulty equipment; collisions and obstructions; falling objects; fire and electricity; and horseplay and other freak accidents that defy classification or fall under more than one heading.

National statistics show that more than 50% of all disabling office injuries result from a slip or fall. Most could probably have been prevented by the exertion of a little more caution by office personnel and management.

Preventive Measures. Floor space, including storage areas, should be well lighted, clean, dry, and free of debris. Even a rubber band can cause an accident. In one case, an office supervisor slipped on a rubber band on the floor, breaking his arm in two places and crushing his elbow. He lost six weeks of work.

Spills should be cleaned up quickly, and when bad weather occurs, a slip-resistant mat should be placed in building entrances. Stairways should have anti-slip treads, and handrails should receive attention regularly to ensure dryness and cleanliness. Damaged areas in floors should be repaired or replaced immediately.

On a highly polished floor, such as linoleum or tile, a slip-resistant preparation should be used. (One secretary lost five weeks of work when she slipped on a waxed floor and broke her wrist and ankle.)

Carpeting can cause problems if allowed to deteriorate. Rugs and carpets should be secured to prevent slipping and creeping.

Desks and file cabinets should be arranged so that they do not open into aisles or walkways. Drawers should always be closed after materials have been pulled or filed. Also, materials should not be stored in corridors or other traffic lanes. If improperly stacked, they can fall over, causing additional problems.

Cords on telephones, typewriters, and other electrical equipment are obvious tripping hazards. They should be taped or secured, or shortened to appropriate lengths.

Office Machines. Many office machines are used by workers who may not be familiar with their mechanics, but know only what the machine does. While it is not necessary that the employees know how to repair a copier or an electric typewriter, it is important for them to know the hazards involved while operating them.

Most, if not all, of the moving parts of office machines, including belts, gears, pulleys, and rotating parts, are well guarded. Accidents are most likely to occur when an employee violates a safety rule by attempting to fix a machine without turning it off, or by trying to repair it without proper knowledge. An office employee tried to clean the cylinder of a multilith machine while it was running. Her bracelet caught in the cylinder and her thumb was pulled under the guard. Her broken thumb resulted in a week of lost time. Another employee's hair caught in the rollers of a duplicating machine. Fortunately, the machine jammed—but not before she was partially scalped. It may be a good idea to put a red tag on office machinery until all employees know the proper operating procedures.

Office Traffic. Busy corridor traffic is a hazard, especially when two people meet near a blind corner. A simple solution is to follow the same rules as in driving a car—stay on the right and approach intersections cautiously. Office workers should be made aware of the hazards of carrying bundles or stacks of material. If the material blocks vision, the chance for an accident increases.

Employees should watch floor surfaces for obstacles and obstructions. Anything that protrudes above the floor or into an aisle should be removed, guarded, or clearly marked. Pencil sharpeners should not extend beyond the edge of a desk, and wastepaper baskets and briefcases should be kept under the desk.

People have walked through unmarked glass doors and windows. Unlettered glass surfaces should be identified by placing a stencil or decal approximately 4½ feet above the floor. Also, partly opened doors create a greater hazard than those completely closed or open.

Office Overhead. Storing heavy materials like card files on top of cabinets represents a danger. Movable objects, such as flower pots, vases, and boxes should not be placed on window sills or ledges. Ceiling fixtures and fans should be checked periodically to assure safe operation, and also to assure that they are securely attached. Ceilings should be checked for defects; cords on Venetian blinds and drapes, as well as the operating mechanism for windows, should be in good repair.

File cabinets that are weighted toward the top can overturn when an upper drawer is opened. If the weight cannot be distributed within the cabinets, cabinets should be fastened together, or weight should be added to the bottom.

Fire Hazards. Office equipment such as copiers, typewriters, adding machines, space heaters, and coffeemakers should be properly grounded, and electrical connections should be checked regularly for frayed or damaged cords.

Other fire hazards exist. A secretary regularly replaced the fluid in a copier and tossed the empty containers into a wastebasket. Her supervisor, a heavy smoker, deposited his cigarette ashes in the same wastebasket. When the inevitable fire ensued, no one was injured, but damage to the office was extensive.

Miscellany. Tilt-back chairs and chairs on rollers can result in falls if used improperly. Common office tools can be hazardous if treated carelessly. Pencils should be stored with their points down; letter openers, scissors, and razor blades should be sheathed or placed out of the way when not used; thumbtacks and paper clips should be stored separately to avoid cuts and punctures; paper cutters should be left with the blade edge down.

Chipped and broken office furniture should be replaced or repaired as soon as the problem is discovered. If disposal of broken glass becomes necessary, it should be picked up with several thicknesses of wet paper towels, and the supervisor should make sure that the housecleaning crew is aware of its presence in the trash.

Back injuries continue to be a leading type of injury. Office personnel should know the proper lifting techniques, and be aware of their strength limitations. A key punch operator suffered a navel hernia when she lifted a large bag of bills from the mail rack to the floor.

Sometimes office employees may have to perform a job that requires going into the factory. In that case, they should be aware of the hazards in the area they are visiting.

Office safety is still one of the least publicized and most neglected aspects of an overall company safety program. Some experts say that the number of office accidents sustained each year is disproportionate to the hazards actually encountered. It follows that all employees should be inculcated with the proper safety attitude, and that all, especially supervisors, be made aware of existing hazards.

ROBERT L. MCCULLOUGH, Staff Writer, *Ohio Monitor,* monthly industrial safety publication of The Industrial Commission of Ohio, Division of Safety and Hygiene

Information Reference

The above entry is based on the author's article, "How Safe Is Your Office?" *Management World,* publication of the Administrative Management Society, March 1980.

Cross Reference: *Occupational Safety and Health in Industry.*

OFFICE SPACE PLANNING: The "Open Plan"

The term **Open Plan** refers to a relatively new approach to office space planning. It connotes an open space free of conventional walls, corridors, and private offices. Work areas are defined by free-standing, movable screens or dividers, and further flexibility is provided by modular work stations and storage units. Furniture is arranged at varied angles as dictated by the natural lines of workflow and communications, rather than in the conventional grid layout of row after row of desks.

The open plan has evolved from the "office landscape" concept, which was introduced in Europe in 1960 and became popular soon after in the United States. The landscape concept, which also featured absence of walls, was characterized by an emphasis on decorative appointments such as plants, statuettes, bright colors, etc.

In the open plan there are no private offices. However, status and privacy are achieved by location, space assigned, and type of furniture and appointments. Attention is given to such environmental factors as (1) air conditioning, humidity control, lighting, and acoustics, (2) functionally designed, modular furniture, and (3) aesthetically pleasing decor involving wall-to-wall carpeting, attractive use of color and plants. Dividers and wall-to-wall carpeting serve an important sound-absorption function. The immediately obvious advantage is maximum flexibility to accommodate changes in organization and workflow, since there are no fixed partitions. Experience has also shown that costs of initial installation and maintenance are significantly lower.

A survey of business executives, office designers, and office workers, conducted by Louis Harris & Associates for Steelcase, Inc., in 1978, found that in several ways the open plan answers the needs of the contemporary office. Office workers have become more mobile, and are being increasingly called upon to use computerized equipment that demands special wiring and spatial requirements. Today's office requires flexibility, efficient organization, and furniture that can accommodate a wide range of office equipment; an office, in other words, that can expand to facilitate ever-increasing paperwork and communications needs.

The survey confirms that the greatest immediate benefit of the open plan is the ability to change office layouts with a minimum of cost and dislocation. More efficient use can be made of increasingly expensive office space through flexibility in wiring, lighting, and furniture configurations. An additional advantage is that as furniture, open-plan components offer tax and depreciation advantages which fixed walls, which are considered real estate, do not. Drawbacks indicated by the Steelcase study include the loss of privacy, particularly conversational privacy, and a perceived loss of status to those used to traditional private offices.

According to the study, a large majority of the responding executives and office designers believe that within ten years the open plan will become more prevalent than the traditional office. Response from office workers, however, indicates that the occupants of traditional offices are unprepared for the kind of change that a widespread move to the open plan would involve. This, plus concern over loss of privacy and status, suggest that some resistance to the open plan should be anticipated.

ADMINISTRATIVE MANAGEMENT SOCIETY, Willow Grove, Pennsylvania

Information References

"The Steelcase National Study of Office Environments: Do They Work?", Grand Rapids, Mich., Steelcase, Inc., 1978.

Impact: Information Technology, a monthly newsletter of the Administrative Management Society, Willow Grove, Pa.

Cross Reference: *Work Measurement in the Office.*

OFFICE WORK MEASUREMENT: See Work Measurement in the Office.

ON-THE-JOB TRAINING

Learning by doing is the most widely used method of acquiring operating skill and necessary related knowledge immediately useful on the job. However, its greatest drawback is blind faith in assuming that simply telling, watching, or showing is enough. If the learner has not learned or acquired speed, or continues to make mistakes, it is easy to assume that he is just not suitable for the job, and never would become efficient: the instructor gave him a chance but he couldn't learn.

On-the-job training demonstrates that this is not true. The weakness is usually not in the learner but in the instructor, be he a skilled, experienced worker at the next machine or bench, a group leader, or a supervisor.

Concepts. Over the years, apprenticeship has demonstrated that when jobs are chosen to give experience in progressively more difficult work, versatility, speed, and confidence can be acquired. Related technical knowledge will need to be added to cover what can not be acquired on the job. On the other hand, upgrading, rotation, introduction of changes in work or processes, and transfers to different work are every-day situations which lean heavily on every-day experience at the job level. But experience is expensive when gained principally through mistakes, rejects, and accidents. It should be emphasized, then, that *education* deals with the acquisition of knowledge, whereas *training* is the acquisition of skill. Training may be manual or supervisory. To be most effective and continuously useful, coaching must be right on the job where all the factors of actual work situations have to be dealt with.

To improve results of on-the-job training, sound techniques have been developed to pass the know-how along. These avoid having beginners learning in the wrong way. They emphasize the essential key points which must be mastered or the work is unsatisfactory.

Sophocles, in 445 B.C., put it this way: "One must learn by doing the thing; for though you think you know it, you have no certainty until you try." Observing, watching, showing, telling, and looking at pictures are not enough. Here is the difference between gaining knowledge and acquiring skills. Skill can be acquired only by doing. Additional skill can be acquired by more difficult and varied doing. Additional speed is acquired through repetition and confidence.

History. To meet the tremendous demand of war industries for workers and supervisors during World War II, the War Manpower Commission established the TRAINING-WITHIN-INDUSTRY PROGRAM throughout the country. This program was designed to help supervisors and key men pass their know-how along to the great numbers of inexperienced men and women who had to be brought into production quickly. The objective was to impart the skill of instructing—to "teach men how to teach." The result was "Job Instruction Training," a set of practical techniques—largely developed by Glenn Gardiner, then with Forstmann Woolen Company, based on the original World War I work of Charles R. Allen, a vocational training pioneer—to be used by group chiefs, foremen, and supervisors in giving specific job skills quickly and uniformly to operators at the work level.

In addition, many skilled workers and newly made supervisors had never before been responsible for getting results through people. They needed on-the-job training in working with people. This was done through a "Job Relations Training" program.

A similar approach helped supervisors to be constructively critical of the way the job was being done. This was developed through "Job Methods Training," a program which also used the problem-solving approach in making better use of equipment, materials, and manpower.

The well organized, simple "four-step methods" of all three programs have stood the test of time, in world-wide use through Government, private consulting, and industrial promotion.

Job Instruction Training (J.I.T.). The J.I.T. program as then developed and as still used, was presented to groups of ten supervisors or key men using their own every-day jobs as practice demonstrations. The method was summarized on a pocket-size guide and reference card given to every one of the ten men in the group. On the front were listed points on "How to Get Ready to Instruct"; on the reverse was the four-step formula on "How to Instruct." (see Exhibit I.)

From experience in hundreds of plants it was demonstrated that this on-the-job training approach could be organized to contribute to improved every-day work relationships between worker and worker, worker and union representatives, and worker and supervisor.

Job Relations Training (J.R.T.). The J.R.T. program used the same "close-to-earth" every-day situation approach to helping supervisors in their human relationships. It was also so organized that the four-step formula could be summarized on a pocket size reference card. The card proved to be a valuable reminder as problems came up. (See Exhibit II.)

Exhibit I

Job Instruction Training

How to Get Ready to Instruct

HAVE A TIME TABLE—
How much skill you expect him to have, by what date.

BREAK DOWN THE JOB—
List important steps.
Pick out the key points. (Safety is always a key point)

HAVE EVERYTHING READY—
The right equipment, materials, and supplies.

HAVE THE WORKPLACE PROPERLY ARRANGED—
Just as the worker will be expected to keep it.

How to Instruct

1. PREPARE THE WORKER
   Put him at ease.
   State the job and find out what he already knows about it.
   Get him interested in learning job.
   Place in correct position.
2. PRESENT THE OPERATION
   Tell, show, and illustrate one IMPORTANT STEP at a time.
   Stress each KEY POINT.
   Instruct clearly, completely and patiently, but no more than he can master.
3. TRY OUT PERFORMANCE
   Have him do the job—correct errors.
   Have him explain each KEY POINT to you as he does job again.
   Make sure he understands.
   Continue until YOU know he knows.
4. FOLLOW UP
   Put him on his own. Designate to whom he goes for help.
   Check frequently. Encourage questions.
   Taper off extra coaching and close follow up.

IF THE WORKER HASN'T LEARNED
THE INSTRUCTOR HASN'T TAUGHT

Exhibit II

Job Relations Training

Foundations for Good Relations

Let each worker know he is getting along.
Figure out what you expect of him.
Point out ways to improve.

Give credit when due.
Look for extra or unusual performance.
Tell him "while it's hot."

Tell people in advance about changes that will affect them.

Tell WHY if possible.
Get them to accept the change.

Make best use of each person's ability.
Look for ability not now being used.
Never stand in a man's way.

PEOPLE MUST BE TREATED AS INDIVIDUALS

How to Handle a Job Relations Problem

1. GET THE FACTS.
   Review the record.
   Find out what rules and plant customs apply.
   Talk with individuals concerned.
   Get opinions and feelings.
   Be sure you have the whole story.
2. WEIGH AND DECIDE.
   Fit the facts together.
   Consider their bearing on each other.
   What possible actions are there?
   Check practices and policies.
   Consider objective and effect on individual, group, and production.
   Don't jump at conclusions.
3. TAKE ACTION
   Are you going to handle this yourself?
   Do you need help in handling?
   Should you refer this to your supervisor?
   Watch the timing of your action.
   Don't pass the buck.
4. CHECK RESULTS.
   How soon will you follow up?
   How often will you need to check?
   Watch for changes in output, attitudes, and relationships.
   Did your action help production?

The training is done entirely by solving problems presented by members of a group, and discussion of principles and procedures involved. There are no prepared lectures, no textbooks, no illustrative or entertaining pictures. The entire time is spent in practice in the use of principles until there has been some change in habits and attitudes, some more ready recognition of "who has a problem," as well as "what is the problem" and its underlying cause.

Job Methods Training (J.M.T.). The J.M.T. program was an approach to improvement of ways of doing the every-day job by helping supervisors be alert and constructively critical of the way the present job was being done. It was again developed through a four-step method, given on a reference pocket card, as shown in Exhibit III. A similar problem-solving approach was effective in making better use of equipment, materials, and manpower.

EXHIBIT III

JOB METHODS TRAINING

What Problems Should Be Tackled First?

Review production schedules and output records.
Check cost, rework, scrap, and accident records.
Consider "Unpleasant" Jobs.
"Ask the boss where improvement is needed most."

1. WHAT IS THE PRESENT METHOD?
   What is done?
   How is it done—What is used to do it?
   Have the worker help you get a complete picture.
2. CHALLENGE THE PRESENT METHOD.
   Identify possible unnecessary actions.
   Question necessary actions—Search for better ways.
   Write down each idea.
3. DEVELOP A NEW METHOD.
   Eliminate unnecessary action.
   Simplify necessary parts of the job—make it easier and safer.
   Use available manpower, machines, and materials.
4. PUT THE NEW METHOD TO WORK.
   Develop a proposal showing expected results.
   Give credit for help—Clear with all concerned.
   Tackle another problem.

Aids for Improvement

Consider "Where," "When," and "Who."
Combine and rearrange operations, tools, equipment.
Look at the workplace and layout.
Study the materials—the type and how handled.
Use gravity feed and drop delivery chutes —mechanical lifts—conveyors and holders.
Can both hands be used?
Use Good Job Relations.

J.M.T. is in no sense a substitute for a major plant engineering approach to introduction of new technical processes, department layouts, or application of new equipment. It is directed to the smaller repetitive operations right on the job. That is where much time and material are wasted. Attention to details at this level has a direct bearing on service, cost, and quality.

Acceptance. Acceptance and use of these simple and practical ways of improving on-the-job training by over 16,000 American plants during the war period established them as valuable tools of management in increasing production quickly and reducing costs. This systematic approach replaced costly trials and errors.

Further evidence of the soundness and adaptability of this approach is seen in its acceptance in foreign countries. The basic procedure has been translated into many foreign languages.

After the close of the War in 1946, a non-profit Training Within Industry Foundation was incorporated, with headquarters in Summit, New Jersey, to further these on-the-job training concepts and methods.

J. WALTER DIETZ, President, Training Within Industry Foundation, Summit, New Jersey

Information References

Training Within Industry Materials, September, 1945: Bulletins issued by TWI and "Outlines of the TWI Programs for War Plants and Essential Services"; also "The Training Within Industry Report, 1940–1945." Foregoing issued by Government Printing Office—out of print, but available in Library of Congress and public libraries of principal cities, and in many engineering colleges.

Editor's Note: Having rendered invaluable service in the postwar years in furthering the concepts and techniques of the "J" programs, the Training Within Industry Foundation suspended operations upon Mr. Dietz's retirement.

OPERATING-MARGIN ANALYSIS

Operating-Margin Analysis has been advanced by Hodgson and Uyterhoeven [1] as an effective technique for evaluating opportunities in foreign operations. However, it should provide useful insights in corporate planning where new industries are to be entered, whether in domestic or foreign markets.

Operating margin in a business is defined as the difference between sales price and the cost of materials purchased. For example, if a manufacturer pays $66 for materials going into a refrigerator which sells for $101, his operating margin amounts to $35. It is the margin within which he will have to operate, e.g., manufacture, sell, pay for research, conduct all other corporate activities, and make a profit.

Operating-margin analysis enables management to reconcile its basic manufacturing, marketing, and growth plans within the price-materials cost limits imposed by competitive environments.

The writers quoted express the operating margin as a percentage of the cost of materials purchased. Thus, the operating margin for the refrigerator in the above example would be $35/$66, or 53%.

The operating-margin concept is not new, for it is the economist's concept of "value added." However, it should not be confused with a common accounting usage, in which operating margin constitutes the difference between sales price and cost of goods sold. What is novel about the concept is the framework in which its proponents suggest that it be used: It defines the condition of an *industry* and not just an individual firm. The margin limits are almost identical for all competing participants in a given industry (or in a given country) because each sells his products competitively and buys his materials at approximately the same price. Variations in margin within the same product line do not hinder the approach, but invite investigation as to the reasons for the difference. Likewise, different degress of integration among companies can be reduced to a common denominator by using one of the least-integrated firms as a base, and segregating the additional activities of the other participants as separate "businesses."

The operating-margin concept is also helpful because it keeps management from placing excessive emphasis on the accounting statements of established firms. Accounting principles give companies great flexibility, especially in allocating expenses, thus making "true" profits a rather elastic notion. (The correct profit figure becomes even more elusive in foreign countries with their different accounting practices, tax laws, disclosure regulations, etc.) The operating margin as here conceived is highly exact because its two basic points always remain unobscured and untouched by either accounting convention or company practices. Both the selling price and the cost of materials purchased can be determined objectively. In most cases they are common knowledge. If not, they can readily be determined either through trade channels or with the help of an engineer familiar with the product requirements.

Treatment of Costs. Under operating-margin analysis, two totally different components are analyzed: *involuntary costs* and *discretionary expenses*. Involuntary expenses arise from the nature of a firm's business, its scale of manufacturing, the types of processes used, and the degree of product specialization or standardization achieved. They consist mainly of minimum manufacturing costs, and cannot be eliminated unless a firm cuts production. Therefore, they have to be insured by everyone in the industry.

Involuntary expenses normally constitute the difference between cost of goods sold and cost of materials purchased. However, there are exceptions: Tooling expenses, though usually included in the costs of goods sold, are in reality discretionary expenses. Manufacturing costs which are not absolutely necessary, but which may add desirable features to the product line, are also discretionary, even though included in the costs of goods sold.

Discretionary expenses allow a company to fulfill its marketing and development objectives. Within the framework of competitive conditions, a firm has a certain latitude in determining which and how many discretionary expenses it wants to incur. Thus one corporate strategy may call for large profit distributions to stockholders, or for retention to finance expansion or diversification. Another firm may direct discretionary expenses toward product development, upgrading of quality, and tooling for frequent model changes. Or it may strengthen its marketing position by establishing distribution outlets, creating brand loyalty, improving service to customers, etc. Still another firm may surrender discretionary money to reduce prices.

Discretionary expenses often qualify as true economic investments and should be considered as such even though they are entered into accounting statements as expenses and not as assets. In terms of a company's long-term competitive strength, money invested in building up the distribution position or in creating product differentiation may be no less important than money invested in fixed plant and machinery. During periods of rapid growth, management often emphasizes increases in productive capacity while ignoring discretionary expenses of an investment nature. With the maturity of an industry, however, the emphasis usually shifts from the "capacity to make" to the "ability to sell," thus penalizing companies which in earlier years ignored discretionary expenses for marketing.

Because discretionary expenses of an investment nature in a firm's income statement (in contrast to fixed-asset investment) reduce current profits substantially, a careful analysis of these costs is needed if low profits, or even accounting losses, in growth industries are to be interpreted correctly.

Appraising Competition. An enterprise must be able to live within the prices imposed by competition and still generate a sufficiently wide operating margin to achieve growth. For this reason, in determining entry and participation requirements of a foreign venture (or entry into a new domestic field) it is vital to analyze the company's probable position relative to the industry leaders. By considering the involuntary costs and discretionary expenses of the leaders, management can predict future price trends. It can then assess its relative capacity to compete and estimate its ability to pay for the necessary discretionary expenses of an investment nature that will be needed to achieve a strong position in the industry. Such an analysis will permit an estimate of the extent to which industry leaders may be able to cut prices. These reductions will primarily hinge on (1) the lowering of their involuntary costs; and (2) as an industry moves to maturity, the extent to which achievement of product and marketing objectives allows the leaders to lower their discretionary expenses.

Lowering Involuntary Costs. In a dynamic industry, volume is the prime determinant of the operating margin. Larger scales of production reduce involuntary costs, enabling industry leaders to lower prices. The extent as well as the timing of price reductions can be fairly accurately predicted by analyzing the leader's involuntary costs and by establishing a schedule of his costs for various increases in volume that can be anticipated with market growth. Price declines will often depend not only on increases in the scale of manufacture of a single product, but also on increased production volumes of similar products. In such cases an appraisal should include those products as well as the one of main concern.

A manufacturer contemplating entry into an industry in a less mature stage of development must anticipate the conditions under which he could be the victim of a price-cost squeeze. This contingency will occur if prices drop faster than a company's ability to lower costs, which could happen if the industry leaders grow faster than anyone else. Thus management may have to incur losses and match the price reduction in order to maintain its relative market share. Otherwise it may not achieve sales levels which justify increasing its plant scale to the point where this would ultimately bring the venture's costs in line with the costs of industry leaders.

It is therefore essential to establish entry goals, such as market-share objectives, and to decide what production and sales efforts are necessary to achieve them. This will help to ensure that the venture will generate adequate resources at least to sustain its position relative to the industry leaders.

Cuts in Discretionary Expenses. During rapid growth periods, companies are likely to make substantial discretionary expenses of an investment nature—e.g., outlays to establish the product, to strengthen distribution, and to finance expansion. As the growth slackens or its objectives are achieved, fewer discretionary expenses of this type will be required, thus freeing the money for price reductions. The magnitude of this drop can also be predicted through operating-margin analysis, although it is more difficult to foresee its timing. High discretionary margins are also vulnerable when competitors lower their profit margins or undertake less expensive marketing methods and resort to price cutting in order to gain a larger market share.

During periods of substantial excess capacity, the temptation may develop to make sales so long as these will cover out-of-pocket costs, resulting in a major price break. Such conditions, however, cannot last indefinitely. As demand catches up with capacity, prices will usually return to a level at which the most efficient industry leaders can still make a reasonable return on their investment.

Conditions of Entry into a Market. A wide operating margin indicates that a new venture can incur high levels of involuntary and discretionary costs. A margin tends to be wide when even the industry leaders have a comparatively low scale of output; when the industry leaders have high discretionary expenses or cash requirements for marketing, product development, construction of new capacity, or diversification programs; when there is insufficient competition; when the industry leaders have priced their products to maximize their profits even though this induces smaller competitors to use minor price reductions as a competitive weapon; or when the leaders are inefficient manufacturers or marketers.

A tight industry will be characterized by relatively low profits for the industry leader, while loose competitive conditions permit satisfactory profits to both leaders and followers. It is important to recognize, however, that both loose and tight conditions are possible under a wide as well as a narrow operating margin.

In sum, Hodgson and Uyterhoeven submit that opportunities and difficulties in *entering* an industry are more a function of the magnitude of the operating margin than of the profitability of industry members. A wide operating margin can provide a better opportunity for entry than a narrow operating margin *whether the industry leaders are profitable or not*. On the other hand, a profitable industry with narrow operating margins may be very difficult to enter.

Reference Cited

[1] Hodgson, Raphael W. and Uyterhoeven, Hugo E. R., "Analyzing Foreign Opportunities," *Harvard Business Review,* March-April 1962.

Cross Reference: *Long-Range Corporate Planning; Long-Range Planning: Financial Aspects; Marketing Strategy: Competitive Analysis.*

OPERATION ANALYSIS

The factors that surround even the simplest industrial operation are many and varied, and comparatively small progress toward improvement will be made if any job is studied as a whole. Therefore, the first step in seeking to reduce the cost of doing any job is to make a thorough analysis by resolving it into its component parts or elements. Each part or element may then be considered separately, and the study of the operation thus becomes a series of fairly simple problems.

During analysis, the operation is broken down into ten general factors as follows:

(1) Purpose of operation.

(2) Complete survey of all operations performed on part.

(3) Inspection requirements.

(4) Material.

(5) Material handling.

(6) Plant layout.

(7) Setup and tool equipment.

(8) Common possibilities for job improvement.

(9) Working conditions.

(10) Method.

Each one of these factors is then examined minutely and critically in order to discover possibilities for improvement. This kind of work is described by the term **Operation Analysis.**

Approach. To do analysis work successfully, industrial engineers have found it helpful to develop a distinctive mental attitude. They have found from experience that there are few established methods which cannot be improved if sufficient thought and study are given to them. Therefore, they do not speak of the "one best method" of doing a job, but "the best method yet devised," implying recognition of the fact that further improvement is undoubtedly possible, even if from an economic standpoint it may not be practical at the time to seek it.

This approach is fundamental to success in methods improvements work. When followed, it ensures an open mind. Such mental obstacles as "it won't work," "it can't be done," and "it was tried before and didn't work" are eliminated. Lack of success in improving any job is not interpreted to mean that the job cannot be improved, but rather that no way of improving it has yet been discovered.

An open mind is important, but it will not necessarily result in improved methods. The industrial engineer finds it necessary to adopt what is known as "the questioning attitude." By constantly asking questions and taking nothing for granted, he develops ideas for improvement which he then tries out and puts into effect if they are found to be practical. The importance of asking questions cannot be overstressed. The chief difference between a successful analyst and one who seldom accomplishes much is that the former has developed the questioning attitude to a high degree. The latter may be capable of making the same improvements as the former, but they do not occur to him because he accepts things as they are instead of questioning them.

Analysis Sheet. Questions should not be asked at random, although this would be better than asking no questions at all. Rather, the industrial engineer seeks to proceed systematically, questioning points in the order in which they should be acted upon. To aid in doing this, a form known as the Analysis Sheet is often used. Experience shows that wherever it is regularly used, suggestions for improvement increase. It ensures that none of the factors which should be considered are overlooked. By securing the information needed to fill out the form completely, the industrial engineer is forced to make a complete analysis. An analysis sheet properly filled in is shown by Exhibits I and II. A brief description of each of the factors considered during operation analysis follows.

(1) *Purpose of operation.* To design the best method of performing any operation, the analyst must determine why the operation is being done and the function the part will play in the

EXHIBIT I

ANALYSIS SHEET (FRONT)

Date 4-12- Dept. 5 Dwg. Sub.
Mould Die Style C-1 Item
Pattern Ins. Spec. L. Spec. Sub.
Part Description 11" x 12" Bank Calendar
Operation Glue calendar to bottom of picture Operator Smith

DETERMINE AND DESCRIBE | **DETAILS OF ANALYSIS**

1. PURPOSE OF OPERATION To position calendar to bottom of calendar for permanent stapling and to prevent slipping while stapling.

Can purpose be accomplished better otherwise?

2. COMPLETE LIST OF ALL OPERATIONS PERFORMED ON PART

No.	Description	Work Sta.	Dept.
1.	Lithograph picture	press	4
2.	Glue calendar to picture	bench	5
3.	Staple	stapling machine	5
4.	Wrap & pack		7
5.	Ship		7
6.			
7.			
8.			
9.			
10.			

Can oprn. being analyzed be eliminated? Yes
be combined with another?
be performed during idle period of another?
Is sequence of oprns. best possible?
Should oprn. be done in another dept. to save cost or handling?

3. INSPECTION REQUIREMENTS
a—Of previous oprn. Unmarred picture
b—Of this oprn. Calendar top must line up with guide line on picture.
c—Of next oprn. When stapled must still be aligned with guide line.

Are tolerance, allowance, finish and other requirements necessary? too costly? suitable to purpose?

4. MATERIAL Picture
Calendar
Glue pot with glue
Glue brush
Cutting compounds and other supply materials None

Eliminate glue and brush (Eliminated 5-1-)

Consider size, suitability, straightness, and condition.
Can cheaper material be substituted?

5. MATERIAL HANDLING
a—Brought by Hand in cartons
b—Removed by Hand in cartons
c—Handled at work station by Operator by hand

Should crane, gravity conveyors, totepans, or special trucks be used?
Consider layout with respect to distance moved.

6. SET-UP (Accompany description with sketches if necessary)
No regular - each operator lines material up on bench to suit own convenience

How are dwgs. and tools secured?
Can set-up be improved?
Trial pieces.
Machine Adjustments.

a—Tool Equipment
Present None

Suggestions Prepare fixture to line up calendar to fixture in stapling operation (Completed 5-1-)

TOOLS
Suitable?
Provided?
Ratchet Tools
Power Tools
Spl. Purpose Tools
Jigs, Vises
Special Clamps ✓
Fixtures ✓
Multiple
Duplicate

Methods Engineering Council
Form No. 101
ANALYSIS SHEET

Actual size, 8½ x 12 in. (From Maynard, H. B., "Reducing Costs through Methods and Time Study")

EXHIBIT II

ANALYSIS SHEET (BACK)

7. CONSIDER THE FOLLOWING POSSIBILITIES.

1. Install gravity delivery chutes.
2. Use drop delivery.
3. Compare methods if more than one operator is working on same job.
4. Provide correct chair for operator.
5. Improve jigs or fixtures by providing ejectors, quick-acting clamps, etc.
6. Use foot-operated mechanisms.
7. Arrange for two-handed operation.
8. Arrange tools and parts within normal working area.
9. Change layout to eliminate back tracking and to permit coupling of machines.
10. Utilize all improvements developed for other jobs.

RECOMMENDED ACTION

Operation eliminated – need not consider these items

8. WORKING CONDITIONS.

Unpleasant odor
Dirty

a—Other Conditions

Conditions made satisfactory 5-1- by eliminating gluing operation.

Light
Heat
Ventilation, Fumes
Drinking Fountains
Wash Rooms
Safety Aspects
Design of Part
Clerical Work Required (to fill out time cards, etc.)
Probability of Delays
Probable Mfg. Quantities

9. METHOD (Accompany with sketches or Process Charts if necessary.)

a—Before Analysis and Motion Study.

Position picture
Pick up calendar
Pick up glue brush
Apply glue to back of calendar
Line up calendar with line on picture
Press calendar on picture by hand

b—After Analysis and Motion Study.

Eliminated all above operations

Arrangement of Work Area
Placement of
Tools
Materials
Supplies
Working Posture
Does method follow Laws of Motion Economy?
Are lowest classes of movements used?

Saving .0083 × .50 × 200,000 = $ 830.00 per year

See Supplementary Report Entitled

Date 5-19-

OBSERVER R. H. Smith APPROVED BY Ed. Jones

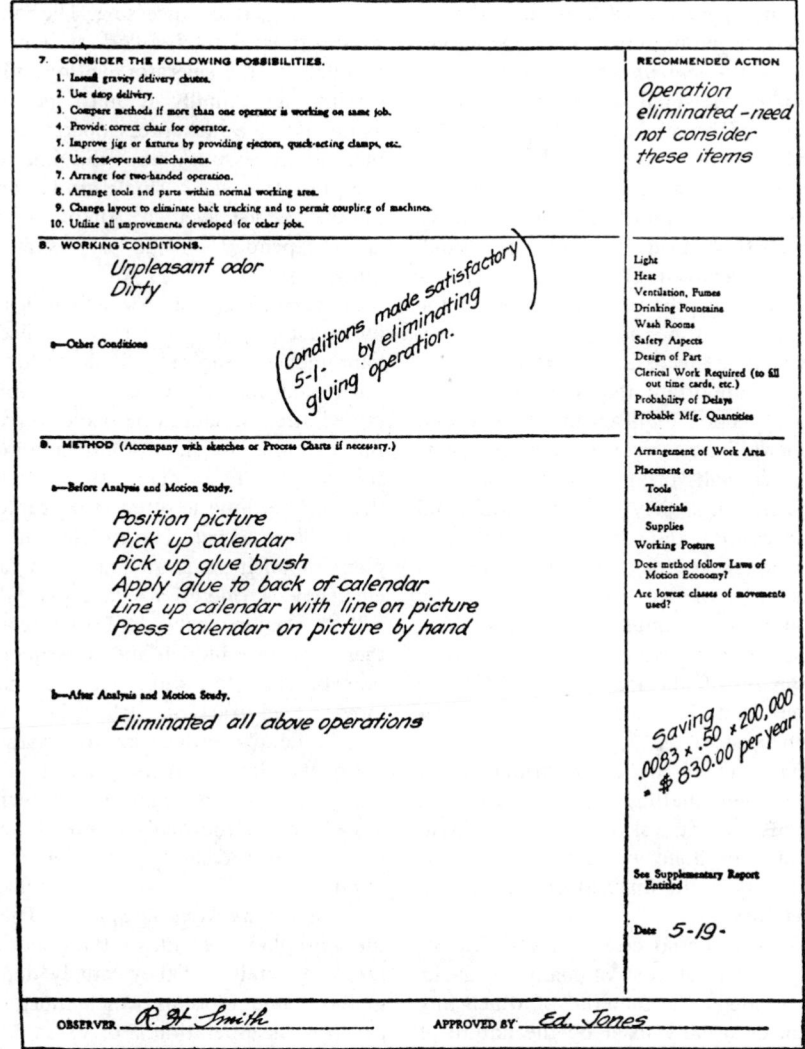

finished product. Sometimes asking the question "Why is the operation being performed?" will disclose the fact that the operation is altogether unnecessary or can be accomplished much more effectively in some other manner.

If analysis shows that the operation serves a useful purpose, then other means of accomplishing the same result should be considered to see if a better way can be found. The purpose of the operation should always be the first step of operation analysis to avoid the wasteful possibility of improving methods for doing unnecessary work.

(2) *Complete survey of all operations performed on part.* All operations performed on the part should next be listed, if Operation or Flow Process Charts have not previously been made. (See PROCESS ANALYSIS.)

This step of operation analysis often discloses that the operation being analyzed can be performed better in some other way. It also brings to light any unnecessary duplications of work which sometimes creep into complicated processes. No operation can be safely studied by itself, but must be regarded as a part of a more or less complex whole. The effect of any changes which are suggested must be considered in the light of the complete job. Only in this way can the analyst be sure that the improving of one operation will not be at the expense of one or more subsequent operations.

(3) *Inspection requirements.* The inspection requirements or the standards of quality, accuracy, finish, and so on which the operation must satisfy play an important role in the methods used to produce the part. In fact, in many cases, the requirements fix the method. The accuracy to which the diameter of a small shaft must be machined and the finish the machined surface must have will determine the machines that must be used, the number of cuts taken, and the feeds and speeds.

Hence, it is important that the analyst first knows the inspection requirements and second that he reviews them for correctness. Designers sometimes lose sight of the function of some features of the part they are designing, and specify unnecessary and costly accuracy. For example, a design specified that a groove in a milling machine table was to be machined to a tolerance of plus or minus .005″. Questioning revealed that the purpose of the groove was to drain surplus oil off the machine table. It was then obvious that the specified accuracy was entirely unnecessary.

Operation analyses are made primarily for the purpose of eliminating waste and reducing costs. It goes without saying, however, that nothing should be done which will impair the necessary quality of the finished product or impair its salability.

(4) *Material.* Material cost is a very important part of the total cost of many products. Therefore, although the material of which any part is made is usually fixed by the nature of the part and the service conditions it must withstand, and although the material is usually specified by the designer, engineer, stylist, or perhaps sometimes the purchasing agent, the analyst should nevertheless check the material at least briefly. The ever-present human element sometimes leads to the use of a wrong or a too costly material, and the analyst with his practical shop background, because of his close contact with all kinds of materials during manufacturing processes, may be able to suggest a better substitute.

(5) *Material handling.* The subject of material handling is so important that whole books are devoted to its discussion. The handling of material is costly, and therefore it should be eliminated or reduced as much as possible. (See MATERIALS HANDLING.) About 90% of all industrial activity is material handling, and the balance is actual processing. The material must be transported to the work station, it must be handled by the operator before and after processing, and finally it must be taken away again. On a punch press operation, for example, the processing time is the time required for the press to make a single stroke, about 1/100 minute on the average. All of the rest of the labor expended on the part is material handling.

In general, the part which is least handled by human labor is the best handled. Material handling adds nothing to the value of a part, but it does increase its cost. Therefore, a determined attempt should be made to reduce material handling to an absolute minimum. When sufficient study is made, the extent to which this can be done is often remarkable.

(6) *Plant layout.* The physical layout of the plant or business is an important factor in its efficiency of operation. Poor plant layouts result in major costs. Unfortunately, most of these costs are hidden and consequently cannot be exposed. The indirect labor expense of long moves, back-tracking, delays, and work stoppages due to bottlenecks are characteristic of antiquated layout. Although it is difficult and costly to make changes in arrangements that already exist, the analyst should review every part of every layout with improvement in mind.

(7) *Setup and tool equipment.* The set-up or the workplace, layout, or both should be analyzed in detail, for they largely determine the methods and motions which must be used to perform the operation. For example, the position in which materials are placed relative to the point of use will determine the length of the motions required to secure them.

Before any work can be done, certain preliminary or make-ready operations must be performed. These include such elements as getting tools and drawings, getting materials and instructions, and setting up the machine or positioning materials and tools about the workplace. When the operation has been completed, certain clean-up or put-away elements must be performed, e.g., put away tools tools and drawings, remove finished material, and clean up workplace or the machine. Make-ready and put-away element methods should be questioned closely, particularly on small quantity work, for these operations are usually fairly long. Many of them take the operator away from his workplace. This is undesirable, and the necessity for trips to other parts of the department should be minimized.

The tool equipment used to perform the operation may logically be considered at the same time as the setup, for the two are closely related. Where the work is at all repetitive, the possibilities of automation or at least a higher degree of mechanization should be considered.

(8) *Common possibilities for operation improvement.* Among the various things which may be done to improve methods, there are ten which are sufficiently important to justify separate consideration. They are:

(1) Install gravity delivery chutes.

(2) Use drop delivery.

(3) Compare methods if more than one operator is working on same job.

(4) Provide correct chair for operator.

(5) Improve jigs or fixtures by providing ejectors, quick-acting clamps, etc.

(6) Use foot-operated mechanisms.

(7) Arrange for two-handed operation.

(8) Arrange tools or parts within the normal working area.

(9) Change layout to eliminate backtracking and to permit coupling of machines.

(10) Utilize all improvements developed for other jobs.

These kinds of improvements are applicable to practically any kind of work. The list as given should therefore be gone over carefully on each operation analyzed. If each possibility is viewed open-mindedly, applications are almost certain to be found.

(9) *Working conditions.* Work is done most effectively under safe, comfortable working conditions. It is therefore part of the task of the analyst to seek to provide such conditions in so far as he is able. The various factors which have been considered up to this point have all been analyzed with the idea of providing the best tools, equipment, and work station possible. It requires human effort to do the prescribed task, however, unless the job has been fully automated. Therefore, the conditions which affect human effort must also be considered thoroughly.

The improvements which can be made in working conditions are many, and the more progressive companies are constantly making them.

(10) *Method.* All of the factors which are considered during operation analysis affect the method of performing the operation. When all of the improvements uncovered during operation analysis are combined and put into effect, the method will be improved as much as it can be by operation analysis alone. The improved method can usually be improved still further if the repetitiveness of the job justifies additional study time by making a detailed analysis of the motions used to do the work. This is done by motion study or with the aid of a predetermined elemental time system such as Methods-Time Measurement or MTM. (See MOTION AND TIME STUDY and PREDETERMINED MOTION TIMES.)

H. B. MAYNARD, formerly President, Maynard Research Council, Incorporated, Pittsburgh, Pennsylvania

Information References

Hammond, Ross W., "Industrial Engineering," sec. 10, chap. 2 in H. B. Maynard, ed., "Handbook of Modern Manufacturing Management," New York, McGraw-Hill, 1970.

Maynard, H. B., ed., "Handbook of Business Administration," sec. 7, New York, McGraw-Hill, 1967.

Niebel, Benjamin W., "Operation Analysis," Chaps. 3 and 4 in Niebel, B. W., ed., "Motion and Time Study," Homewood, Ill., Irwin, 1976.

O'Donnell, Paul D. and Martin, John C., "Developing Improved Methods," sec. 3, chap. 8 in H. B. Maynard, ed., "Handbook of Modern Manufacturing Management," New York, McGraw-Hill, 1970.

Stegemerten, G.J. and Geitgey, Duane C., "Operation Analysis," sec. 2, chap. 4 in H. B. Maynard, ed., "Industrial Engineering Handbook," New York, McGraw-Hill, 1971.

Cross References: *Gilbreth Principles of Motion Economy; Method Improvement; Motion and Time Study; Predetermined Motion Times; Process Analysis; Process Engineering; Work Measurement; Work Measurement in the Office; Work Simplification.*

OPERATIONAL GAMING AND MONTE CARLO SIMULATION

Operational Gaming and **Monte Carlo Simulation** refer to operations research techniques developed since World War II as extensions of early devices such as war gaming and statistical "model sampling." Essentially, these techniques simulate a real, often complicated, process by a simplified representation or model that retains much of the appearance of reality but permits more "experimentation." As a prototype, there is the representation of battle by a simple war game with rules for moving counters about a miniature battlefield according to players' choices and the roll of a die. The modern development of simulation techniques has been stimulated by the interest in military studies, the increasing emphasis on scientific studies of industrial processes and management, and the growing availability of user-oriented (i.e., problem-oriented) programming packages that facilitate construction of computer models. Regarding the last-named, online computer systems now facilitate interaction between model user and computer.

War games have been extended to study logistics management, politico-military relationships, and some aspects of resource allocation. There have been simulations of systems ranging from loading docks and job shops through airlines and communication networks to hemispheric weather patterns and the United States economy [1].

Definitions. The terms *simulation, Monte Carlo,* and *operational gaming* are similar enough in spirit and appeal that they are often used interchangeably. For serious discussion, however, it is desirable to distinguish them [2]. Used in a broad sense, *simulation* is any representation of a system or process by a model. Such a broad interpretation includes not only Monte Carlo computations and gaming, but also almost every technique for solving problems and many devices for training people. However it is usual to exclude simulation training devices, such as flight trainers, and mathematical models that can be solved by standard devices, such as algebraic manipulation, differentiation, and integration, from a definition of simulation. An important subset of what is left is *digital simulation,* in which the original process or system is represented by a program that is executed on a digital, electronic computer. Simulation may be performed with analogue computers, or even by hand computation, and it is perhaps the notion of a flow chart or set of rules for the computation that comes closest to the basic idea.

Monte Carlo, as most frequently used, denotes a computation involving a statistical sample for whose selection random numbers are generated according to some specified probability distribution or by a random device. (The thought of a roulette wheel or dice as generators of random number suggests the name Monte Carlo.) According to some usage, the term *Monte Carlo* is limited to computations in which the element of probability is artificially introduced as a device for solving a problem that is originally nonprobabilistic, or to computations in which special sampling techniques are used to reduce the variance of the results. Neither limitation is much used when Monte Carlo is applied to management problems. *Monte Carlo simulation,* then, is a simulation in which the original process or system has random elements that are represented.

Operational gaming may be defined [2] as the serious use of *playing* as a primary device to *formulate* a game, to *solve* a *game,* or to *impart* something of the solution of a *game.* Operational gaming is not to be confused with GAME THEORY, from which the formal notions of *game,* the *value* of a *game,* and the *solution* of a *game* are derived. Although operational gaming is included in the broad sense of simulation, it is convenient here to exclude it from the usual meaning of simulation as a special technique of operations research. Operational gaming involves human play and decision making during the play of a game (which may be computer-aided); a simulation, once formulated, can be accomplished by a computer with no further human decision making. Operation gaming often involves random elements and therefore methods of Monte Carlo as the term is used here, but not necessarily.

History. War games have been used for instruction in tactics for several hundred years. Prior to World War I and World War II, military planners of several nations also used games to explore strategy and test large scale plans [3]. After World War II many organizations began to use and extend war games in military operations research studies [4]. As their use increased further there was also terminological extension: "*Operational Gaming*—a name proposed by Ellis Johnson to describe the use of war gaming in a context broader than that of military situations alone" [5].

Many of the games of the previous century had elements in common with modern operational gaming. There were definite rules, sometimes as rigid as a computer program. There were random elements, clearly in the spirit of Monte Carlo methods. In practice, there was interest in realism combined with the recognition that complete reality is unattainable, just as in modern simulation.

Though the spirit of Monte Carlo was evident in early games, its direct antecedents were in statistics and computations of nuclear physics. The "model sampling" [1] that statisticians used to generate approximate histograms for difficult probability distributions was essentially Monte Carlo. The name, however, and most of its modern impetus came from nuclear physics. At the Los Alamos Project during World War II [4], finding that analytical work alone would often not give even qualitative answers to problems concerning elementary particles, Ulam and von Neumann began to consider fictitious "particles" treated by an electronic computer which could compute and record the random branchings in their "life histories."

That these techniques became tools for management as well as the scientist and military planner was due to a combination of new developments. The availability of ever more powerful computers made it possible to do what had been only a dream before. The introduction of game theory gave new concepts of strategy, optimization criteria, and solution. And the growth of industrial operations research, with strengthened interest in systematic decision making, led to a continuing search for ever better management tools.

Approaches and Techniques. The application of operational gaming to management problems has led to a large number of "business games." One of the earliest, and best known, is that developed for executive training purposes by the American Management Association [6]. Beyond training in decision making, the objectives of a business game may include simulation of business competition, and the suggestion of fruitful problems for such specialists as the mathematician, the economist, the industrial engineer, and the psychologist. (See MANAGEMENT GAMES.)

Typical of the situation simulated in a business game is that of a number of firms competing for a known consumer market. Each firm, which is represented by a team of players, knows its own past sales, prices, share of the market, inventories, production costs, and budget allocations, as well as the constraints on its future budget allocation. In addition it may know something of its competitors, such as prices and possibly share of the market. At each time period of play, on the basis of the available information, it must determine prices, production rates, and budget allocations. For that time period the decisions of all the teams are input to a computer, which then determines the status of each firm at the beginning of the next time period. This process continues, with each team seeking to optimize the status of its firm through its decisions, for a specified number of time periods. At the end of the play, each team is given the results, the previously unknown decisions of its competitors, and a chance to explain its own strategy, in a general critique.

Starting with such a basic pattern, one may vary the structure and purpose of business games in many ways. Different amounts and kinds of information may be made available to the players. Definite objectives for optimization may or may not be specified to the players. The detail of the simulation may be greatly varied, and the time of play may be compressed or expanded. The object of the game may be training, discovery of good strategies for a firm, or the identification of research problems for a management scientist. To different objectives there should correspond different structures.

In simulation also, as in operational gaming, there is a basic pattern with the possibility of variation in many directions. As a first step in building a simulation model, one must gain adequate intimacy with the real situation that he seeks to represent. Then one decides the scope of the simulation, the scale of the mapping of the "real world" onto the "model world." Given this decision, one determines the set of rules, the flow diagram, that governs happenings in the model world. This set of rules must then be tested for realism, and if found faulty, then corrected or "debugged." Once validated, the model is ready for use, for replication, in the common case of Monte Carlo simulation where an adequate statistical sample is required.

Before discussing some of the problems of simulation, it may be useful to outline an extremely simple example of Monte Carlo simulation. Consider a barber who has a one-man shop but things that he might enlarge his operation. He is almost always busy and often has potential customers who will not wait. Before undertaking any changes, however, he collects data on the arrivals of customers over many days. After some analysis of the data, he produces the array shown in Exhibit I. This will aid him to simulate what his business might be like if he expanded.

Although he can think of many potentially troublesome complications, the hypothetical barber begins with the bare essentials. Concentrating on the distribution of times between the arrival of consecutive customers, he draws up the table as indicated.

In order to generate a sample of arrival times, he needs a source of random numbers. Let us suppose that he uses one of the many tables available, starting with a page that yields the two digit numbers extracted in Exhibit II.

A set of random numbers like these may be thought of as arising from repeated throws of a fair, 100-sided die. The first hundred throws, for example, are likely to yield repetition, and so not give *all* the possible two-digit entries from 00 to 99, but if the throws were continued and the table extended, each of the 100 different possibilities would tend to constitute about 1% of the total entries.

By using such random numbers as a convenient substitute for throwing dice, the barber can represent "on paper" the chance arrival of customers to his shop. He does not know which time interval will occur next, but he knows the probability of each time interval, based on the analysis that led to Exhibit I. By using the table of Exhibit II for randomness and Exhibit I for the proper probability distribution of arrival times, as illustrated below, the barber can simulate the "real life" behavior of customers.

EXHIBIT I

DISTRIBUTION OF TIMES BETWEEN SUCCESSIVE ARRIVALS (MIN.)

Time Interval	*Probability*	*Time Interval*	*Probability*
1	.11	17	.02
2	.10	18	.02
3	.09	19	.02
4	.07	20	.02
5	.05	21	.02
6	.04	22	.02
7	.03	23	.02
8	.03	24	.02
9	.03	25	.02
10	.03	26	.02
11	.03	27	.02
12	.03	28	.02
13	.02	29	.01
14	.02	30	.01
15	.02	31	.01
16	.02	32	.01

If he is to use the tables in Exhibits I and II, he needs a convention as to which random numbers represent which times between successive arrivals. Since a time of 1 minute occurs with probability 11/100, he must let 11 of the 100 different two digit numbers correspond to 1 minute, say the two digit numbes 00, 01, 02, . . . , 10. Continuing in this way, he obtains the correspondences shown in Exhibit III.

Our simulator is now ready to generate arrival times. The first random number in Exhibit II is 38. According to Exhibit III, 38 corresponds to 5 minutes. Adding the 5 minutes to his starting time of 9:00, he gets 9:05 for the first arrival time. The next random number is 22, which corresponds to 3 minutes, which puts the next simulated arrival at 9:08. Proceeding in this way, he generates successive arrival times, some of which are shown in Exhibit IV.

Samples of times like those in Exhibit IV can now be used to try out various schemes of operation. Possibility A might be to continue operating a one-man shop. Possibility B could be, say, the employment of another experienced barber, and possibility C might be the employment of an inexperienced, less expensive barber. In order to simulate such possibilities, it is necessary to fix some rules and decide on some numerical values. Suppose that customer impatience is represented by the rule that if there are two customers already waiting *per barber,* then an arrival does not wait; if there is only one waiting, the arrival also waits. Suppose, moreover, that an experienced barber always takes 15 minutes to cut a head of hair, an inexperienced barber 20 minutes. Then, denoting the barbers by A (employer) and B (employee), the three possibilities, A, B, and C translate Exhibit IV into Exhibit V.

Given such a sample of case histories, the simulator should ask if the results simulated for possibility A seem realistic. The small sample shown in Exhibit V does seem consistent with the barber's initial impression—he is busy most

EXHIBIT II

TWO DIGIT RANDOM NUMBERS

38 22 85 24 63	39 21 20 44 65	97 24 28 42 53	61 23 08 77 11	43 47 03 50 37
74 57 25 65 76	59 29 97 68 60	71 91 38 67 54	13 58 18 24 76	15 54 55 95 52
16 90 82 66 59	83 62 64 11 12	67 19 00 71 74	60 47 21 29 68	02 02 37 03 31

EXHIBIT III

CORRESPONDENCES BETWEEN RANDOM NUMBERS AND TIMES

Time Interval	*Random Nos.*	*Time Interval*	*Random Nos.*
1	00. . .10	17	72, 73
2	11. . .20	18	74, 75
3	21. . .29	19	76, 77
4	30. . .36	20	78, 79
5	37. . .41	21	80, 81
6	42. . .45	22	82, 83
7	46. . .48	23	84, 85
8	49. . .51	24	86, 87
9	52. . .54	25	88, 89
10	55. . .57	26	90, 91
11	58. . .60	27	92, 93
12	61. . .63	28	94, 95
13	64, 65	29	96
14	66, 67	30	97
15	68, 69	31	98
16	70, 71	32	99

of the time and a significant number of customers turn away.

The results in Exhibit V are suggestive, but they do not solve the barber's problem by themselves. He would want to generate a larger sample of case histories, of course, but that still would not solve his problem. He must go further and apply costs and prices in order to evalulate the possibilities that he is considering. Exhibit V suggests, subject to confirmation from a larger sample, that two barbers are not kept busy all the time, even if one is inexperienced (slower), and that few customers would leave. Thus an inexperienced (cheaper) barber might be a better employee than an experienced barber. Actual costs would have to be used to determine whether either possibility B or C is economically desirable.

EXHIBIT IV

SIMULATED ARRIVAL TIMES

9:05	10:45	11:49
9:08	10:48	11:56
9:31	10:51	11:57
9:34	10:57	. . .
9:46	11:06	. . .
9:51	11:18	
9:54	11:21	
9:56	11:22	
10:02	11:41	
10:15	11:43	

One notes that even with prices and costs included, the barber's simultion would not be an optimizer. Simulation is an "if-then operator" [1]. Is one uses policy B, for example, then he gets the service times shown in Exhibit V, and the corresponding economic returns or losses. Optimization is approached through simulation only as a process of making repeated trials and noting the best policy tried.

On the other hand, one often has only an imperfect idea of what should be optimized, and then simulation can be especially helpful. By looking at detailed results of simulation, one may come to understand better what his criteria really are. The hypothetical barber, for example, in looking at results for possibility C might note the instances when he serves two consecutive arrivals and realize that this seems to him undesirable (or unrealistic). Or he might note that his calculations provide for no coffee break, and decide to elaborate his simulation.

Problems. Associated with the use of operational gaming and Monte Carlo simulation are three classes of problems. First, there are difficulties in describing and evaluating the operation that is to be simulated or "gamed." Second, there are the technical difficulties of executing a simulational approach. And third, there are problems and dangers that arise from the very successes of operational gaming and Monte Carlo simulation.

The first class of problems is by no means peculiar to simulation or gaming. There are still serious gaps in our knowledge of the basic sciences. It is often difficult to collect good data to characterize an operation. Often we may not know or agree on criteria for success. Taking the hypothetical barber as an example, it may be difficult for him to get relevant data if, say, his shop is in a neighborhood of rapidly changing character. Or he may not really know how customers would react in a multi-barber shop. And, as we have seen, he may not have found it easy at first to formulate just what his objectives are.

Many technical problems arise in the development and application of operational games and Monte Carlo simulations. Much progress has been made [7] in the development of computer languages for simulation and efficient techniques for computation, but the execution of simulatons still may require large amounts of calendar time and computer time. This puts a premium on simplifying models, but deciding

EXHIBIT V

SIMULATED CASE HISTORIES

Arrival Time	*Possibility A*		*Possibility B*			*Possibility C*		
	Cutting Starts	*Cutting Ends*	*Cutting Starts*	*Cutting Ends*	*Barber*	*Cutting Starts*	*Cutting Ends*	*Barber*
0905	0905	0920	0905	0920	A	0905	0920	A
0908	0920	0935	0908	0923	B	0908	0928	B
0931	0935	0950	0931	0946	A	0931	0946	A
0934	0950	1005	0934	0949	B	0934	0954	B
0946	1005	1020	0946	1001	A	0946	1001	A
0951	1020	1035	0951	1006	B	0954	1014	B
0954	Leaves		1001	1016	A	1001	1016	A
0956	Leaves		1006	1021	B	1014	1034	B
1002	Leaves		1016	1031	A	1016	1031	A
1015	1035	1050	1021	1036	B	1031	1046	A
1045	1050	1105	1045	1100	A	1045	1105	B
1048	1105	1120	1048	1103	B	1048	1103	A
1051	1120	1135	1100	1115	A	1103	1118	A
1057	Leaves		1103	1118	B	1105	1125	B
1106	1135	1150	1115	1130	A	1118	1133	A
1118	Leaves		1118	1133	B	1125	1145	B
1121	1150	1205	1130	1145	A	1133	1148	A
1122	Leaves		1133	1148	B	1145	1205	B
1141	1205	1220	1145	1200	A	1148	1203	A
1143	Leaves		1148	1203	B	1203	1218	A
1149	Leaves		1200	1215	A	1205	1225	B
1156	1220	1235	1203	1218	B	1218	1233	A
1157	Leaves		1215	1230	A	1225	1245	B

which details to include and which to exclude is still largely an art. Setting the size of the sample in Monte Carlo simulation is a problem in STATISTICS.

There are well known results like the rule [1] that errors tend to vary inversely as the square root of the sample size. But setting the sample size in operational gaming leads to difficult questions in GAME THEORY. Some simple examples [2] show that the required sample size tends to be much larger than intuition suggests. When used in optimization, operational games and Monte Carlo simulations tend to be clumsy unless supplemented [7] with analytic techniques.

The successes of operational gaming and Monte Carlo simulation themselves lead to some problems. The results of simulation are so plausible and the *appearance* of reality so convincing that special effort is required to seek out the essence of reality [2]. In the last several years renewed emphasis [9] has been placed on the validation of games and simulations. Past successes have led to great proliferation in operational gaming and simulation [8, 11]. These techniques are sometimes misused, or used when analytic methods would be better. Often the documentation of new techniques is inadequate, and occasionally there is redundant development. Currently, surveys [10] are being conducted to learn more about the state of present practice and the management improvements that may be indicated.

Potential. Despite their obvious difficulties, operational gaming and Monte Carlo simulation will be used increasingly in the coming decade. Past applications to such diverse areas as the factory, the firm, transportation networks, communication networks, the economy, international politics, etc., will intensify. To them will be added new applictions [8] to questions of urban development, ecology, etc., and the general problem of setting goals in a rapidly changing society. To control the proliferation [11] there will be new management techniques [10] and new combinations of technical methods [7, 8].

CLAYTON J. THOMAS, Assistant for Operations Research, ACS Studies and Analysis, Headquarters U.S. Air Force, Washington, D.C.

Information References

To keep abreast of the developing theory of simulation techniques one may use the journals, *Operations Research* and *Management Science.* Some of the computational problems may be discussed in *Journal of the Association for Computing Machinery,* and some of the statistical questions raised by Monte Carlo computation may be discussed in the *Annals of Mathematical Statistics.* For the details of specific simulation studies one may consult the various trade journals and business journals.

Emshoff, James R. and Sisson, Roger L., "Design and Use of Computer Simulation Models," New York, Macmillan, 1970.

Gibbs, G. Ian, ed., "Handbook of Games and Simulation Exercises," Beverly Hills, Calif., Sage, 1974.

References Cited

[1] Morgenthaler, G.W., "The Theory and Application of Simulation in Operations Research," in "Progress in Operations Research," 363–419, Ackoff, ed., New York, Wiley, 1961.

[2] Thomas, C.J. and Deemer, W.L., Jr., "The Role of Operational Gaming in Operations Research," *Opns. Res.,* 5, 1–27, 1957.

[3] Thomas, C.J., "The Genesis and Practice of Operational Gaming," *Proc. of the First Inter. Conf. on OR,* 64–81, ORSA, Baltimore, 1957.

[4] Thomas, C.J., "Military Gaming," in "Progress in Operations Research," 421–463, Ackoff, ed., New York, Wiley, 1961.

[5] Cushen, W.E., "Operational Gaming in Industry," in Operations Research for Management, Vol. 2, Joseph F. McCloskey and John M. Coppinger, eds., Baltimore, The Johns Hopkins Press, 1956.

[6] Bellman, R., *et al., "On the Construction of a Multistage, Multiperson Business Game," Opns. Res.,* 5, 469–503, 1957.

[7] Tocher, K. D., "The State of the Art of Simulation—A Survey," *Proc. of the Fourth International Conf. on OR,* IFORS, 1966.

[8] Thomas, C.J. and McNichols, G. R., "Why People Play Games—Report of a Survey," 35th National ORSA Meeting, Denver, June, 1969.

[9] Thomas, C.J., "Model Verification—Fighting the Unfightable Fight," TIMS College on Logistics, Washington, D.C., March, 1970.

[10] Shubik, M. and Brewer, G., "Questionnaire—Models, Computer Machine Simulations, Games and Studies," The RAND Corp, P-4672, July, 1971.

[11] Shubik, M., Brewer, G., and Savage, E., "Gaming Literature Review: A Critical Survey of Literature on Gaming and Allied Topics," The RAND Corp., R-620, (forthcoming).

Cross References: *Management Sciences (and cross references there given).*

OPERATIONS RESEARCH

Operations Research is a science devoted to describing, understanding, and predicting the behavior of man-machine systems. Thus operations research workers are engaged in three classical aspects of science:

(1) Describing the behavior of the systems.

(2) Analyzing this behavior by constructing theories (frequently called "models") that account for the observed phenomena.

(3) Using these theories to predict future behavior, that is, the effects that will be produced by changes in the systems or in their methods of operation.

Since the operating systems studied by operations research workers arise in a wide variety of practical industrial, military, and governmental environments, it follows that the results of their research frequently make important contributions to the solution of problems of choice, policy, and planning that arise in these environments; these contributions are characteristically made by presenting the research findings directly to the executives in charge of the operations that are studied. Thus an important goal of much operations research is assistance to executives in improving the operations under their control.

What particularly distinguishes operations research from other research and engineering is its emphasis on analysis of operations *as a whole,* and its bringing to bear the orderly, coordinated, intensive analysis of all the physical and social sciences involved—mathematics, chemistry, physics, biology, psychology, and the like. This "interdisciplinary" approach provided useful solutions to problems of military operations in World War II, and has since been found equally successful in application to problems of non-military operations.

Most present-day business applications are primarily concerned with mathematical and statistical analysis of the results of possible alternative actions. Often using techniques especially designed or refined for business problems, operations researchers have been able to provide companies such diverse benefits as improved inventory and reorder policies, minimum-cost production schedules, optimum location and size of warehouses, and guidance in sales and advertising policies. The basic pattern applied is clarification of the various courses of action open, estimation of the outcome to be expected from each, and evaluation of these in terms of the over-all goal desired.

Definition. Most definitions will be found essentially to parallel the following, by Pocock, which stresses that OR is an applied science: "Operations research is a scientific methodology—analytical, experimental, quantitative—which, by assessing the over-all implications of various alternative courses of action in a management system, provides an improved basis for management decisions" [1]. Morse and Kimball have stressed the quantitative approach of OR, and earlier proposed that "Operations research is a scientific method of providing executive departments with a quantitative basis for decisions regarding the operations under their control" [2].

History. The characteristic method and name of operations research came out of World War II. British scientists setting up the first field installations of radar during the Battle of Britain were able to observe air operations. Their analyses of these led to suggestions that greatly increased the effectiveness of British fighters, and contributed to the successful British defense. Operations research was then extended to anti-submarine warfare and to all phases of military, naval, and air operations, both in Britain and the United States, and was incorporated in the post-war military establishments of both countries.

The effectiveness of military operations research spread interest in OR to other governmental departments and to industry. In the United States in 1951 the National Research Council formed a Committee on Operations Research, and the first book on the subject, "Methods of Operations Research," by Morse and Kimball, was published. In 1952 the Operations Research Society of America was formed.

Today almost every large corporation in the United States has staff applying operations research, and in government the use of operations research has spread from the military to widely varied departments at every level. This general acceptance has come as managers have learned the advantages of the scientific approach on which OR is based, as computing facilities have become increasingly greater, faster, more flexible and available, and as the number of qualified OR professionals has increased. The growth of OR has not been limited to the United States and Great Britain. Indicative of this is that the International Federation of Operations Research Societies, founded in 1959, now comprises member societies from twenty-four countries on five continents.

Approach, Techniques, and Tools [3], [4], [5]. An OR team (in some companies this may be a single individual) consists of trained researchers utilizing the skills and tools of applicable sciences, without any preconceived idea of what the correct solution should be. The first step is to formulate the problem, after which a *mathematical model* is generally constructed to represent the system being studied. Mathematical models, or conceptual models, are usually equations or formulae developed to relate important factors of the operations studied. The factors can then be tested, and operated on mathematically to determine the effects of changing the values of the variables, with particular reference to the optimization of some *criterion.*

Optimization means achieving the best—highest or lowest—value of the criterion. *Suboptimization* occurs either when some criterion subordinate to the overall criterion is optimized, or when the overall criterion is optimized over only a portion of the total of all possible alternative actions. Any suboptimization may result in a value of the overall criterion other than its best possible value. A *criterion* is a measure by which results can be evaluated. It measures the effectiveness of the operations under study in terms of the ultimate object of the operations, and may be net profit, return on investment, cost, or other items appropriate to a particular study.

Operations research uses any suitable techniques or tools available. These frequently include common mathematical or statistical procedures, cost analyses, or electronic computers, but OR analysts have given special impetus to the development and use of the following: LINEAR PROGRAMMING; WAITING LINE THEORY (QUEUEING THEORY); GAME THEORY; *Design of Experiments;* AND OPERATIONAL GAMING AND MONTE CARLO SIMULATION.

In addition, the reader will hear in discussions of OR, and read in the literature of it, references to such specific tools as DYNAMIC PROGRAMMING, INTEGER PROGRAMMING, NONLINEAR PROGRAMMING, *Sequencing Theory, Replacement Theory, Symbolic Logic, Information*

Theory, and Utility (Value) Theory. These are briefly defined as follows [1], [3], [4], [5]:

Dynamic Programming is a method of analyzing multi-stage decision processes, in which each elementary decision is dependent upon those preceding it as well as upon external factors. It drastically reduces the computational effort otherwise necessary to analyze results of all the possible combinations of all possible elementary decisions. (See separate entry.)

Integer Programming methods may be used when one or more of the variables can take only integar values. Examples are the number of trucks in a fleet, the number of generators in a power station, and so on. Approximate solutions can be obtained without using integer methods, but the approximations generally become poorer as the numbers become smaller. The case in which only 1 and 0 can enter, 1 to indicate "yes" or "do," and 0 to indicate "no" or "do not do," is particularly important. (See separate entry.)

Nonlinear Programming methods may be used when either the objective function or some of the constraints are not linear functions. Nonlinearity may be introduced by such things as discount on price for purchase of large quantities, and graduated income tax. Linear assumptions may be employed to approximate non-linear conditions, but the approximations become poorer as the range is extended. Non-linear methods may be used to determine the approximate area in which a solution lies, in which area linear methods may then be used to obtain a more exact solution. (See separate entry.)

Sequencing Theory, related to Waiting Line Theory, is applicable when the facilities are fixed, but the order of servicing may be controlled. The scheduling of service or the sequencing of jobs is arranged to minimize the relevant costs.

Replacement Theory, the mathematics of deterioration and failure, may be used to estimate replacement costs and determine optimum replacement policies.

Symbolic Logic, the algebra of logic, substitutes symbols for words, propositions, classes of things, or functional systems. There have been only limited attempts to apply this technique to business problems; however, it has had extensive application in the logical design of computing machinery.

Information Theory, an analytical process transferred from the electrical communictions field to operations research, seeks to evaluate the effectiveness of information flow within a given system. Despite its application mainly to communications networks, it has had an indirect influence in stimulating the examination of business organizational structures with a view to improving information or communication flow.

Utility (Value) Theory is a process of assigning numerical significance to the worth of alternative choices. To date this has been only a theoretical concept, and is in the status of elementary model formulation and experimentation. When developed, this should be most helpful in the decision-making process in assessing the worth of various possible outcomes.

In addition to the foregoing, the term *Mathematical Programming* is often used. This is a general, embracive term, descriptive of a number of mathematical techniques developed since World War II for evaluation of alternative operating programs. (See MATHEMATICAL PROGRAMMING.)

Organization of an OR Group. The composition of an OR group and its place in an organization's structure are factors which may critically affect the group's contribution to the organization. Problems have generally been most successfully treated by well-balanced teams of a few researchers working in an advisory capacity for the executive in charge of the operations being studied.

At least one member should have good mathematical and statistical training, at least one should be familiar with the techniques and tools that have been found most useful in solving OR problems, and at least one should be familiar with the problem under study and the organization in which it is found. Most, if not all, should be "problem-oriented," with a knack for and a love of tackling and solving problems. Subject to such restrictions assuring that the pertinent knowledge is readily available, the size of the group studying any particular problem should be kept to a minimum.

It goes without saying that all members of an OR group should have sincere respect for all those with whom they work and have contact, and that all aspects of any problem should be considered in the light of the overall objectives of the organization concerned. The group should have ready access to all relevant data, including opportunity to observe the actual operations involved.

An organization wishing to employ OR may

feel that it lacks personnel with the necessary qualifications to set up its own OR group. In such a case the services of a consulting firm may be obtained, either to do the entire OR job or to aid in the formation of a company group. Many organizations have found it advisable to utilize a consulting firm in the early stages of developing their own groups. With one or more experienced men as a nucleus, others with appropriate background can be trained while working in the group.

In forming a group it is best to begin on a modest scale, both in the size of the group and types of jobs tackled [3], [6], [7]. Problems that are neither too difficult not too time-consuming, and which lead to demonstrable results, are best. Experience has shown that problems of production and inventory control are frequently of this nature. From such beginnings it is easy to develop into broader areas and problems of long term significance.

Growth. The "Encyclopedia of Management," in its first edition, cited a 1958 survey by the American Management Association showing that over half the companies responding to a questionnaire reported using OR at that time. No parallel current figures could be elicited, since the focus of surveys, with OR now generally accepted, has apparently shifted to identifying the areas in which it is most profitable to employ OR, especially in the area of strategic business planning.

Growth in acceptance has been matched by growth in educational facilities and professional personnel. Many universities offer OR courses at the graduate level. Membership in the Operations Research Society of America was reported to be over 11,000 as of 1979, with professional training heavily skewed to Master's and Doctorate degrees.

Indicating the growth of OR in industry and government, and its introduction into new areas, the Society now has special technical sections in the fields of cost-effectiveness, education, health applications, military applications, space, transportation, and urban affairs.

GORDON D. SHELLARD, for Operations Research Society of America, Baltimore, Maryland

Information References

Associations:

American Statistical Association.
Operations Research Society of America.
The Institute of Management Sciences.

Periodicals:

Management Science (The Institute of Management Sciences).
Operational Research Quarterly (Operational Research Society, London).
Operations Research (Operations Research Society of America).
International Abstracts in Operations Research (International Federation of Operational Research Societies).

Texts:

Zaremba, Joseph, "Mathematical Economics and Operations Research," vol. 10, Gale Information Guide Library, Detroit, Mich., Gale Research Co., 1978. (An annotated bibliography of more than 1,600 books.)
See also References Cited, below.

References Cited

[1] Pocock, John W., "Operations Research: A Challenge to Management," in "Operations Research," Special Report No. 13, New York, American Management Association, 1956.
[2] Morse, Philip M. and Kimball, George E., "Methods of Operations Research," New York, John Wiley, 1951.
[3] Phillips, Don T., Ravindran, A., and Solberg, James J., "Operations Research: Principles and Practice," New York, Wiley, 1976.
[4] Riggs, James L. and Inoue, Michael S., "Introduction to Operations Research and Management Science: A General Systems Approach," New York, McGraw-Hill, 1975.
[5] Thierauf, Robert J. and Klekamp, Robert C., "Decision Making Through Operations Research," 2nd ed., rev., New York, Wiley, 1975.
[6] Miller, Ernest C., "Advanced Techniques for Strategic Planning," Research Study No. 104, New York, American Management Association, 1970.
[7] Craft, Clifford J., "How to Organize Effectively for Operations Research," *Systems and Procedures Journal,* May-June 1961.

Cross References: *Management Sciences (and cross references there given).*

OPERATIONS RESEARCH IN MARKETING DECISIONS

The contribution of **Operations Research to Marketing Decisions** is based on three main points: (1) the systems concept; (2) the emphasis on experimentation; and (3) the model concept, and the search for models of consumer action. (The contributions considered in the present discussion are not limited to work done with an "Operations Research" label. However, the operations research approach provides a focal point, and a center of common interest.)

The Systems Concept. Marketing people often stress the marketing *function,* as distinct, for example, from manufacturing, finance, or other industrial functions. To be sure, it is important to build functional knowledge and skill in marketing. But it is also important to recognize that the systems skills and concepts of operations research are a useful complement to functional skills of marketing.

The systems concept is well illustrated in the field of inventory control and management. Marketing managers are interested in inventory management since most inventory investment, whether held by retailers, manufacturers, or others in between, is held for marketing purposes. Decisions on product line, promotions, or channels of distribution will seriously affect the requirements of inventory investment. So will customer demands and buying patterns. [1]

Exhibit I indicates that the inventories at each point serve as buffers between successive operations or functions. Any policy must take into account costs and problems of both the user and the supplier.

Planning the Distribution System. Four elements exist in a typical factory-to-customer distribution system: (1) local and regional warehouses, and the inventories stored in them; (2) production facilities and central storage; (3) transport facilities; and (4) the communications system.

Each one of these elements is essential, and the proper balance of interrelationships among them determines the efficiency of the distribution system. They break down into the following questions:

(1) What about the location and number of warehouses? With more or better located warehouses, we can get closer to the customer, perhaps give better service, cut local delivery costs. But with fewer, we can achieve greater "throughput" in each, afford more frequent replenishment, cut field stocks, or give more reliable delivery with the same stocks. It has been estimated that from about twenty distribution points, properly located, we can reach over 80% of the consumer market within one day. Is this the right number to meet any particular company's needs? What is the right balance?

(2) What items and in what quantities shall the local warehouses store to protect service? Study of the product lines of a wide variety of industries shows that these follow a common pattern (a so-called "Lorenz curve"), as shown in Exhibit II. The curves reproduced show the range within which the experience of most companies falls, depending on specific product line and market characteristics. The top 10% of the items account for as much as 80% of the sales volume; half of the items account for as little as 2% of the sales. In most businesses, these slow-moving items account for far more of their share of inventory investment, service headaches, and handling costs. Where shall these be carried to balance investment cost and ensure availability—at all field locations, a few regional distribution centers, or only at the producing plants? [2]

(3) What transport method shall be used to replenish inventories? To what extent can higher priced transport cut delivery time and the size of local inventories? The day when transportation decisions could be made strictly on a cost-per-ton-mile basis is gone. In today's competitive, diversified, nation-wide markets, fast, flexible and reliable transport is required for adequate distribution.

EXHIBIT I

TYPICAL DISTRIBUTION SYSTEM

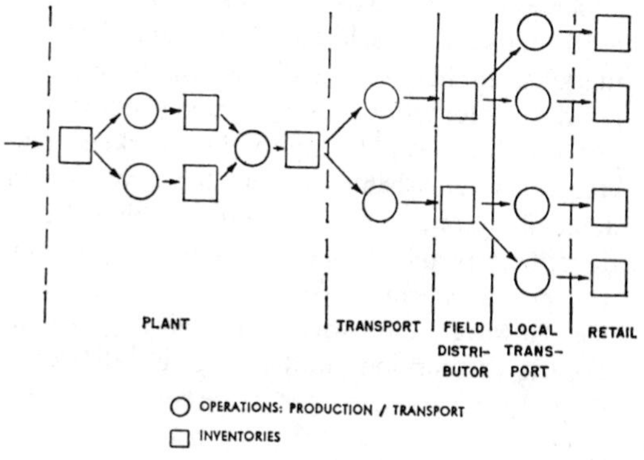

EXHIBIT II

TYPICAL SALES PATTERN

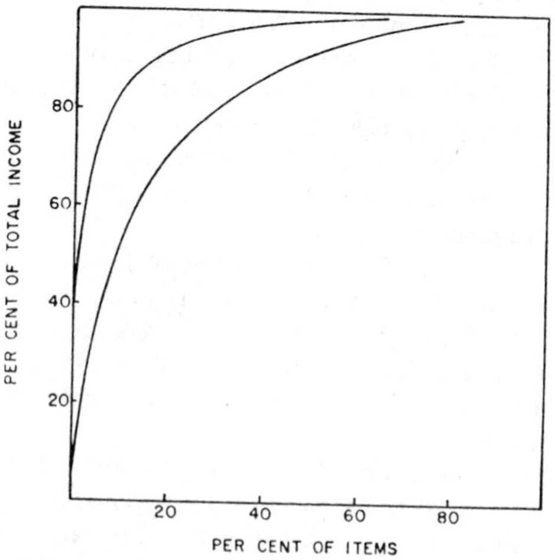

Per cent of total income drawn from high-volume items versus per cent of total items included.

(4) Can accelerated communications make possible better service and smaller inventories? The new technology of information handling must be properly integrated in production-distribution systems if these are to respond to the market challenge.

(5) With respect to the foregoing, what balance among service to the field, inventory investment, and production stability makes sense? Sales, promotion, and field-stocking policies have a tremendous impact on production stability. In industry after industry, consumers are using products at a stable rate, yet marketing practices generate major demand fluctuations on plant facilities. These fluctuations cost money—even ignoring the social effects—and thereby cut margins and make the marketing job more difficult.

These questions cannot really be answered in isolation; they are tightly interrelated. A sound answer for any business depends on a balance of costs and needs. The interests of no single function in the business are sufficient to get a sound answer. The whole production-distribution *system* must be examined.

Within the last fifteen years these systems have received considerable study in the operations research field, and so there is now a sizeable, growing body of theory and method to deal with them [3].

In the coming years, new, growing technologies in the handling of information, transportation, and materials, increased attention to distribution costs, and changes in manufacturing technology can be expected to have serious impact on product engineering, plant location, manufacturing organizations, logistics, and distribution cost. These are vital matters to the marketing function. The operations research discipline can assist in designing production-distribution systems to capitalize on changing technology to meet marketing needs.

Two other areas where operations research concepts and methods of dealing with systems have come to play a role are:

(1) The timing and location of facilities investment to meet anticipated forecast requirements. Here a key problem is to make sure that capital expansion plans are flexible enough to adapt to forecast inaccuracies or changing conditions.

(2) Allocation of marketing effort among media, markets, or products; between increased penetration and market expansion; and between immediate profits and future returns. Here progress is encouraging.

Emphasis on Experimentation. Experimentation, the method of scientific inquiry, must be one of the tools of marketing. Experiments are used to test hypotheses about the effect of a given factor and the extent of that effect. Surveys which may provide a representative picture of customers' characteristics or figures for control or market forecasting purposes, are at best only a limited form of experiment. For example, if we want to get a measure of the balance of different kinds of farm soil conditions in the United States, a probability sample might be the approach, perhaps biased or stratified to match concentration on agriculture. But if we want to measure the effect of fertilizer on crop growth, as influenced by soil conditions, a rather different experimental design would be used.

There is plenty of room in marketing for other kinds of experiments, designed to measure differences among customers, to test hypotheses about the effects of different marketing actions, and to measure purchasing characteristics of elements of the market. The design of such experiments is quite different from the typical "representative" survey; the objectives are different. Yet marketing literature, which places great emphasis on "representative" population surveys, contains relatively little on the design and operation of other types of tests.

The methods of experimental design have been highly developed by statisticians, biologists, and others. Today these methods are playing a vital role in such fields as medicine, space engineering, and chemical engineering, far from the original fields of agriculture, where the interest in experimental design was nurtured.

Here are some examples of such experimentation:

(1) One well-known distributor of consumer goods wanted to study the effectiveness of its allocation of advertising expenditures among local markets. It selected forty representative markets. In half of these, the marketing program was turned backward: heavy effort was put on the normally lightly hit markets, and vice versa. This campaign ran for a year, with detailed records of sales and customer reactions. Management knew that this test program was probably much worse than normal practice. However, the experiment was designed to test the assumptions underlying the allocation of promotion, and to get a measure of differences.

No doubt this was expensive, but the company has continued similar tests. The information gathered by experiments is just as valuable as and often more valuable than is information produced by surveys.

(2) In other articles by the present writer [4] are examples of experiments using classical methods of experimental design—Latin square, randomized block methods, etc.—and the related techniques of statistics, such as analysis of variance. These techniques have since been found extremely valuable in setting up meaningful marketing field experiments and getting sound interpretation.

Two Key Experimental Problems. Use of experiments in marketing is neither easy nor inexpensive. But it is hardly more difficult or more expensive than many modern experiments in other fields, such as chemical engineering or physics. Here are just two key experimental problems that need to be solved:

(1) How to measure *change* in individual customers. Most marketing-survey techniques give us a snapshot of the individual customer. For many purposes, we want a measure of change in purchasing, attitude, or whatever, as well. Indeed, change may be a key attribute [5].

Panels are valuable in giving us some measure of change, but their difficulties are well known.

(2) How to select experimental samples to balance low variance against experimental opportunity and cost. Experimental units do not have to be representative, but reasonable homogeneity within experimental blocks is certainly desirable.

Statistical methods of experimental design in marketing are used, and the use of these techniques is growing. Operations research people are contributing in two ways to this development. Characteristically they are trained in experimental and statistical techniques required; and their training leads them to press for use of these methods to get the measurements needed in systems studies and in building and testing models of customer activity.

Models of Customer Activity. There are many ways of describing customers. The use of psychological and sociological concepts has grown tremendously, for example. There is another method which is also of value—quantitative models of customer activity.

A simple example based on the "switching" or "transition" concept will illustrate how such models might look. Suppose we could classify the potential market for a product into two groups: *customers* and *noncustomers.* Then in time there will be some interchange. Exhibit III illustrates the situation where the "customer" group constitutes a third of the total: 20% leave in a period and are replaced by 10% of the noncustomers. This can be summarized in the two-way table, Exhibit IV.

Sales effort might be characterized in terms of its effect in changing the transition rates. This is a quite artificial concept. What evidence is there that it has any merit? In what directions is work going on to improve and expand it? What use is it?

Vidale and Wolfe published an article many years ago giving results of experimental work on evaluating advertising [6]. They proposed a model or description of advertising results based on this work. The "transition" concept gives exactly the same results they demonstrated.

The basic idea of class and intergroup transition can be expanded. The two-way table might encompass any number of groups: two as shown in Exhibit III, ten, fifty, hundred, or more. The basis for the groups may include social or economic condition, attitudes, use patterns, current brand usage, or other factors. This makes it possible to use the "transition" model to interpret attitude and survey data, and to study durable as well as nondurable goods.

Here are some of the ways such models are being used:

(1) To identify the characteristics that are most important to change in customers—for directing marketing action.

(2) To identify the numbers to be measured by survey or experiment.

(3) To interpret experimental results to work out sales budgets and allocation. For example, this switching concept can be used to choose advertising policy based on *long-term* payoff.

Work on the concept of consumer behavior as a Markov, or, alternatively, a learning process has continued, illustrative of an active interplay between experimental evidence and efforts at explanation in the form of a general theoretical model. For example, a classic article by Alfred A. Kuehn [7] attempts to address the questions: "What do we know about brand choice? What behavioral mechanisms appear to underlie this phenomenon? Is such behavior habitual? Is learning involved? Does repeated purchasing of a brand reinforce the brand choice response? . . . ." Kuehn shows how empirical data on brand choice in sequences of

EXHIBIT III

SWITCHES IN CUSTOMER PREFERENCE

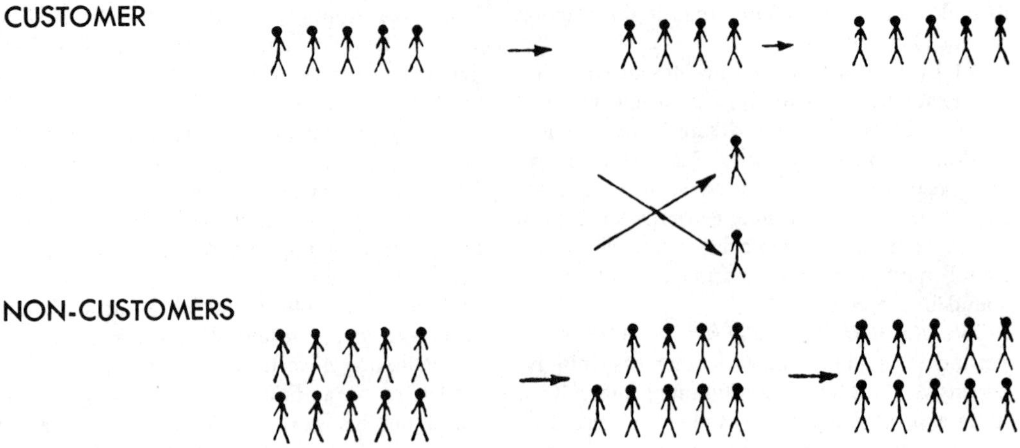

purchases can be interpreted in the light of stochastic learning models.

An alternative to the use of "learning theory" as an explanation of consumer behavior is described by Lawrence [8]. He suggests that the same results can be achieved by interpreting consumer data as resulting from a stable or stationary process subject to random shocks. Lawrence shows how a broad range of observed consumer behavior can be interpreted as a statistical process without need to rely on the concept of "learning."

Work on analysis of consumer choice and development of models of branch switching by consumers continues. Publication of results is inhibited by the highly proprietary nature of the work and the value of data that are obtained. Nevertheless, consumer brand preference and switching models, employing a combination of data obtained from studies of brand purchases, stated brand preferences from consumer surveys, and quality preferences derived from psychological and demographic studies have been shown to be useful in marketing strategy.

However, models based on the foregoing concept or others cannot be viewed as the *only* way to characterize customers. Such models are one useful way of looking at customers that operations research has introduced. They complement and support the usefulness of studies of customer attitudes and the bases for them.

JOHN F. MAGEE, President, Arthur D. Little, Inc., Cambridge, Massachusetts

EXHIBIT IV

Start of Period	*End of Period* Customer	Noncustomer
Customer	80%	20%
Noncustomer	10%	90%

Information Reference

See references in the entry, OPERATIONS RESEARCH.

References Cited

[1] For a detailed discussion of inventory management, see section, *Inventory Control,* in the entry, PRODUCTION PLANNING AND INVENTORY MANAGEMENT.

[2] See Brown, Robert G., "Statistical Forecasting for Inventory Control," New York, McGraw-Hill, 1959, for a discussion of the Lorenz curve and related lognormal distribution, and the significance of these to inventory control.

[3] For a detailed discussion, see Magee, John F., "Industrial Logistics," New York, McGraw-Hill, 1968.

[4] Magee, John F., "Operations Research in Making Marketing Decisions," *Journal of Marketing,* October 1960 (substantially reproduced, by permission of the *Journal of Marketing,* in the foregoing entry, and updated by the author).

[5] Magee, John F., "Some Approaches to Measuring Marketing Results," *Proceedings of the National Conferences, American Marketing Association, Philadelphia, December 1957.*

[6] Vidale, M.L., and Wolfe, H.B., "An Operations Research Study of Sales Response to Advertising," *Operations Research,* vol. 5, pp. 370–382, June 1957.

[7] Kuehn, Alfred A., "Consumer Brand Choice—A Learning Process?" in Frank, Ronald E., Kuehn,

Alfred A., and Massy, William F., eds., "Quantitative Techniques in Marketing Analysis," Homewood, Ill., Irwin, 1962.
[8] Lawrence, Raymon D., "Consumer Brand Choice—A Random Walk?," *Journal of Marketing Research,* August 1975.

Cross References: *Marketing Strategy: Competitive Analysis; Operations Research.*

ORGANIZATION: AMA's "Ten Commandments of Good Organization"

The "Ten Commandments of Good Organization" were formulated by M. C. Rorty, formerly a vice president of International Telephone & Telegraph Corporation, shortly after he became president of the American Management Association in 1934. In 1941, AMA issued these in commemorative form. They have been widely quoted in management literature.

(1) Definite and clear-cut responsibilities should be assigned to each executive, manager, supervisor, and foreman.

(2) Responsibility should always be coupled with corresponding authority.

(3) No change should be made in the scope or responsibility of a position without a definite understanding to that effect on the part of all persons concerned.

(4) No executive or employee, occupying a single position in the organization, should be subject to definite orders from more than one source.

(5) Orders should never be given to subordinates over the head of a responsible executive. Rather than do this, the officer in question should be supplanted.

(6) Criticisms of subordinates should be made privately. In no case should a subordinate be criticized in the presence of executives or employees of equal or lower rank.

(7) No dispute or difference between executives or employees as to authority or responsibility should be considered too trivial for prompt and careful adjudication.

(8) Promotions, wage changes, and disciplinary action should always be approved by the executive immediately superior to the one directly responsible.

(9) No executive or employee should be assistant to and at the same time a critic of the person he is assistant to.

(10) Any executive whose work is subject to regular inspection should, whenever practicable, be given the assistance and facilities necessary to enable him to maintain an independent check of the quality of his work.

Cross References: *Organization Theory (and cross references there given).*

ORGANIZATION: Internal, Traditional Types

Detailed Organization Structure varies widely from company to company, even in the same industry; and within a given company, especially if it is of large size, the relationships of functions and sub-functions usually undergo continuing change, to conform to changes in environment, objectives, and needs. Traditionally recognized, however, are five principal organization types: (1) line; (2) line and staff; (3) pure functional; (4) line and functional staff; and (5) line, functional staff, and committee.

Line Organization is the simplest form of structure, and is the framework on which a more complex organization may be built. It assumes a direct line of responsibility and control from the chief executive or general manager to intermediate "line" executives, to foremen and supervisors, to workers.

Line and Staff Organization developed in industry in recognition of the need for assistants to line executives in large and complex organizations, to handle specific advisory responsibilities, in connection with such functions as research, planning, distribution, public relations, industrial relations, and the like. As the activities of these assistants increased, other personnel were added to help them, these eventually forming *staff departments,* supplementing the line organization.

Pure Functional Organization is of historical interest only. Originally strongly advocated by F. W. Taylor, this concept involved the complete reorganization on a functional basis, removing the staff specialist from his "assisting," or "advising" role and giving him authority and responsibility for supervising his function. Under Taylor's "functional foremanship," one man, for example, was in charge of production, one for scheduling, one for inspection, one for maintenance, etc., all dealing directly with the workers. The scheme failed because of the practical difficulties in each worker's having not one, but many different bosses.

Line and Functional Staff combines the advantages of the line and staff organization, and the functional organization. Here functional staff departments are given responsibility and authority over specialized activities, such as inspection, time study, employment, purchasing, etc. These functions are performed by specialized personnel apart from the line operators, who are responsible to their own line supervisors. The staff department directs its function in the operating units, but if disagreement arises, the matter is taken up with the administrative head over both production and staff units. Large, multi-plant organizations may have decentralized staff functions, where separate operating units have their own staff departments responsible to the local operating head, with the central headquarters retaining staff departments serving in an advisory and resource capacity to the local staff functions.

Line, Functional Staff, and Committee involves the addition of committees (usually in large organizations) to facilitate coordination and cooperation. Committees are established for special duties, and may be permanent, or "standing" committees, or set up for a temporary need only.

Variants. Significant variants are MATRIX ORGANIZATION and PROJECT MANAGEMENT, discussed in separate entries.

Information Reference

Bethel, Lawrence L., Atwater, Franklin S., Smith, H. E., Stackman, Harvey A., Jr., and Riggs J., "Industrial Organization and Management," 5th ed., New York, McGraw-Hill, 1971.

Cross References: *Organization Theory (and cross references there given).*

ORGANIZATION: Line-Staff Relationships

Line and **Staff** are two terms that are often used in ways that are loose and unclear. Attempts have been made in some organizations to dispense with them, and thus "operating" is frequently substituted for "line," and "auxiliary" and "service" are common substitutes for "staff." Clarification will be achieved if we examine the terms in the light of work done and authority exercised.

A *line* or *operating* organization unit is one that is actually doing the work that represents the *primary mission* of the larger organization unit of which it is a part. Examples: an assembly department in the manufacturing division; a selling branch in the sales division.

A *staff* or *service* organization unit is any unit which is helping the line do its work, or making it possible for the line to do its work, but is not actually engaged in the work itself. Examples: a purchasing unit, a time-study unit, a payroll-preparation unit, an in-service training unit.

When Is it Line, and When Is it Staff? Misunderstandings arise from failure to realize that whether an activity is "line" ("operating") or "staff" ("service") depends upon whose shoes you are in when you are looking at the operation. Thus, the total organization headed up by a controller renders service to all of the other organization units in the entire company. Those other units therefore look upon this organization unit as staff or service. The controller, however, looking at his own operations, can consider the various units within his organization carrying out his primary mission as operating units as far as he is concerned. He may, however, within his organization, set up staff units (perhaps an economist to advise him, or a special analyst devoted solely to improving procedures in his own department).

Organizational Relations and Lines of Authority. It is frequently said that a member of a staff unit cannot tell a manager or a member of a line unit to do anything—he can only inform or suggest or advise, or offer his specific services. This is largely true, but there are exceptions. For example, a safety engineer may be empowered to shut down a line activity, as may a quality inspector. Similarly, it is often said that a line manager cannot issue direct orders to a staff or service man. This is an oversimplification, as indicated under (6) below.

Following are seven distinct types of line and staff relationships:

(1) *Advisory.* Here the staff unit is one that offers advisory help only—an operating manager may or may not avail himself of it. He may request it, but the staff unit cannot foist itself upon him. However, the staff unit may volunteer suggestions on the basis of observations made, even though uninvited.

(2) *Services requested.* This relationship is similar to (1) above, but involves services rather than advice or suggestions. The relationship of the staff personnel is similar to that of an outside contractors personnel—their "boss" is their own staff unit head.

(3) *Staff services rendered to an organization unit as part of fulfilling the unit's mission, supplied on a programmed basis.* For example, there may be certain periodic specialized technical services rendered by a headquarters engineering unit to customers served regularly by a customers' service department working out of a branch plant. There should be no question about lines of direct supervision—the direct chain of command of these specialists or technicians is to the head of the central staff unit, and the latter is responsible for the quality of their service and their mode of operating. The head of the customers' service department at the branch cannot attempt to supervise the specialists, he can communicate directly with the head of the central staff unit if he (she) questions the quality of their work, their adherence to schedules, etc. At the same time, the head of the central staff unit cannot dictate the degree of utilization of the services, since this is stipulated by an overall program previously authorized at a higher level.

(4) *Auxiliary services necessary to operations, routinely supplied.* Accounting and procurement are examples. The "supplying" organization unit has the right to insist that the operating organization follow officially specified rules having to do with reporting, requisitions, or other information necessary to rendering the service. If established procedures are not complied with, personnel of the service unit (after normal courtesies in the form of requests to the operating personnel) have the right to insist to the operating supervisor that corrective action be taken. Personnel of the "using" organization unit can communicate directly with the "supplying" unit to request service or information about service, as long as specified initiating or confirming paperwork is executed.

(5) *"Functional relationship" between a central staff unit and personnel in a counterpart staff unit attached to an operating organization unit.* Examples are a central quality control department which operates through a quality control department at each plant; and a central personnel department which operates through a personnel department at each plant. On organization charts, a "broken line relationship" is shown between such central staff units and the counterpart units in the operating organization. A solid line goes up from the operating organization's staff unit through the local operating chain of command, and its ultimate "boss" is the head of the local operating organization. However, the central staff unit has responsibility for the professional conduct of the work, and its personnel can make suggestions for improvement. They do not give direct orders to the counterpart professional people in the local operating organization's staff unit. If they have strong feelings about the way something is or is not being done, they can make strong suggestions to the head of the operating organization's staff unit, and, failing action, can only proceed higher in the operating chain of command.

(6) *Relationship between a department head and personnel assigned to him by a staff unit.* Specialized personnel are often assigned to an operating unit by a staff unit which is responsible for their training and for the quality of their professional work. They are considered as being permanently attached to their "home" staff unit, even though their assignment may be of relatively long duration. But they are under the "administrative command" of the head of the operating unit, and for accounting purposes may be on the operating unit's payroll. They are under the "professional command" of the head of their staff unit. The latter is their direct superior, and (a) he is the one who can deploy them from one location to another, with proper notification and as long as he supplies equivalent personnel to the using unit, (b) he determines their merit rating and makes recommendations for promotion or pay increases, and (c) he is responsible for their continuing professional development. "Administrative command" means that the head of the operating unit can deploy them on the job, has the power of approval regarding personal time off, and the like, and in general can direct them to follow his personnel rules. "Professional command" means that the staff unit head, and not the operating unit head, lays down the procedures and sets the standards with respect to their professional work. An example is a special project team composed of research and engineering personnel assigned to an operating unit for the duration of a specific project.

(7) *Relationship between an operating executive and an advisory or service staff person or unit directly reporting to him (her); and relationship between the staff personnel and other personnel in the organization units under the operating executive.* The staff person or unit supplies information, and advises and recom-

EXHIBIT I

SEVEN BASIC LINE-STAFF RELATIONSHIPS COMPARED

No.	*Type*	*Relationship of staff-unit employees to head of operating unit*	*Relationship of head of operating unit to staff unit and members of staff unit working in his department*	*Relationship of staff unit to employees of operating unit*
1	Advisory	May only volunteer suggestions . . . but may not necessarily have to wait to be invited.	May or may not have to avail himself of suggestions.	Do not give or receive instructions.
2	Service as requested	Similar to (1) but involves services, and the staff unit must be invited into the department.	Same as toward any outside contractor. The "boss" of the staff personnel is their own staff unit head.	Through operating unit's supervisors issue such requests as required to make service effective.
3	Staff services supplied on a programmed basis	Somewhat stronger than (2). Services are rendered on a programmed basis approved by higher authority, and cannot be refused by operating unit head.	The direct chain of command of the staff personnel is to the staff unit head. Operating unit head must work through head of staff unit if dissatisfied with mode of operation.	Same as (2).
4	Auxiliary services routinely supplied	Services are a routine part of operations, not on an "invited" or specially programmed basis.	Same as (3).	Staff-service personnel can insist on regular procedures being followed. Routine communications flow directly between staff and operating personnel except in cases of sharp disagreement.
5	Central staff and counterpart staff unit in operating department	Advisory and suggestive only . . . but does not have to wait to be invited.	May or may not have to avail himself of advice and suggestions of central staff unit. Through his own chain of command, head of operating unit is "boss" of the staff unit in his department.	"Functional" relationship between central unit and employees of the staff unit in operating department . . . on matters of professional standards, mode of operation, etc., "suggestions" from the central unit have strong force and are to be disregarded only under special circumstances and with approval of head of operating unit.
6	Personnel assigned to operating unit by staff unit	Assigned personnel are under administrative command of head of operating unit as to deployment on job, discipline, hours of works, etc., but their "boss" is the head of the staff unit.	In administrative command of the assigned personnel . . . Head of staff unit may, with notice to head of operating unit, withdraw them from the job if he can supply replacements.	Relationships are those of any employees under direct supervision of head of operating unit. They carry on their own activities and work through normal channels within department.
7	A staff unit which is part of an operating organization unit	Supply information and advise and recommend . . . Decisions are made by operating head, and he issues instructions to operating personnel.	Direct relationship, through chain of command.	Same as (6). Staff personnel do not issue direct instructions to operating personnel except under unusual circumstances (e.g., a safety man or quality inspector shutting down an operation where emergency does not permit normal working through channels.)

mends. The operating executive is the one who must make the decisions and take action. The staff unit can act only in the name of that executive—it cannot tell other employees what they must or must not do.

Exhibit I gives a bird's eye view of the seven basic line-staff relationships.

Carl Heyel, Management Counsel, Manhasset, New York

Cross References: *Organization Theory (and cross references there given).*

ORGANIZATION: Urwick's Ten Principles

The following principles are part of Lyndall F. Urwick's "Notes on the Theory of Organization," prepared originally in connection with Col. Urwick's addresses in an American Management Association unit dealing with "Organization Building." The "Notes" were published in booklet form at the request of teachers and students of organization, and the "ten principles" have been extensively quoted.

(1) *Principle of the Objective.* Every organization and every part of every organization must be an expression of the purpose of the undertaking concerned or it is meaningless and therefore redundant. You cannot organize in a vacuum; you must organize *for* something.

(2) *Principle of Specialization.* The activities of every member of any organized group should be confined, as far as possible, to the performance of a single function.

(3) *Principle of Coordination.* The purpose of organizing *per se,* as distinguished from the purpose of the undertaking, is to facilitate coordination, unity of effort.

(4) *Principle of Authority.* In every organized group the supreme authority must rest somewhere. There should be a clear line of authority from the supreme authority to every individual in the group.

(5) *Principle of Responsibility.* The responsibility of the superior for the acts of his subordinate is absolute.

(6) *Principle of Definition.* The content of each position, both the duties involved, the authority and responsibility contemplated, and the relationships with other positions should be clearly defined in writing and published to all concerned.

(7) *Principle of Correspondence.* In every position the responsibility and the authority should correspond.

(8) *The Span of Control.* No person should supervise more than five, or at the most, six, direct subordinates whose work interlocks.

[The key word here is "interlocks." Where there is no interlocking, the span of control can be greater. That is especially true of employees reporting to the lowest level of supervision. The span of control and the number of supervisory levels are interrelated. The smaller the span, the greater the number of levels. However, if the number of levels is too great, communication is slowed up and an organization tends to become slow-moving and inflexible. If the span of executive control is 5, and 20 workers report to the lowest level of supervision, then a division or department head with two levels of executives under him can head an organization of 500 rank-and-file employees. With another executive level, the working level would be increased to 2,500.]

(9) *Principle of Balance.* It is essential that the various units of an organization should be kept in balance.

(10) *Principle of Continuity.* Reorganization is a continuous process; in every undertaking specific provision should be made for it.

Information Reference

Urwick, Lyndall F., "Notes on the Theory of Organization," New York, American Management Association, 1952.

Cross References: *Organization Theory (and cross references there given).*

ORGANIZATION ANALYSIS AND PLANNING

The concept of an organization embraces a human system whereby source power is transferred from ultimate authority through various levels of human beings to achieve the results required by original objectives. **Organization Analysis and Planning** is the process of determining the most effective overall system to achieve the specific objectives of an organization. In a primitive sense, it is as old as the earliest tribes of human beings who first banded together for self protection and other advantages. More recently, it is used to maximize achievement of overall organizational objectives.

The transfer of creative power, that is, the transfer of power exercised to make things happen, has the highest priority among all basic factors that concern management. Analysis of the component parts of such a system is seldom practical, however, unless it includes the objectives involved, the human forces that are released to each component part (in the form of authority, motivation, and direction), the human, physical, and financial resources available to each component part, and the environment in which each component part operates.

Organization analysis and planning is a continual process because the environment and objectives of business, as well as other factors, change constantly. In most large companies there is at least a small staff engaged in this activity on a permanent basis. However, the success of the organization planning activity requires that top management participate actively.

Formal Definition. Organization analysis and planning is the analysis of the objectives, of the environment, and of the human, physical, and financial assets of an organization in order to arrive at the most effective design of a human system for the transfer of human creative power from the organization's ultimate authority to eventual accomplishment of its established objectives.

Background. Historical records indicate ancient forms of organization analysis and planning by priests in Mesopotamia, court philosophers in China, Roman public contract administrators, and various military organizations.

Modern applications began in the early 1900s when F. W. Taylor developed concepts of SCIENTIFIC MANAGEMENT which called for the careful planning of the human/physical/financial system, as well as for the coordination and control of it. Shortly thereafter, Henri Fayol concluded that all work in industry can be divided into the following six groupings: technical, commercial, financial, security, accounting, and managerial. Immediately prior to World War II, Robert W. Porter, a management consultant, published a thesis entitled, "Design for Industrial Coordination" [1]. Porter focused attention on the fact that the work at every level of the organization logically divides into three basic functions: planning, implementation (doing), and inspecting (controlling). By grouping all organizational tasks within these three functions at each level, the organizational design will be most conducive to the establishment of natural checks and balances. These are essential to the coordination of every system.

Approach and Techniques. World War II and the expansion of corporate organizations in the 1950s created unprecedented problems in organization design. The natural and concomitant result has been a more intent and permanent managerial attention to the function of organization analysis and planning. Such analysis and planning may be accomplished by a single executive in the smaller company, or by a staff man or team in the more complex organizations. Requisite to any detailed analysis is an overall perspective on the current organization, including the objectives, subobjectives, and problems of attainment at every level.

Detailed Analysis and Planning. Detailed analysis properly begins at the top levels, for any efficiencies that may be accomplished at the top may save more money than years of study at the bottom levels of the organization. Each level of authority is identified and evaluated for its effectiveness in delegation.

Failure to meet objectives is also identified within one or more of the human, physical, financial, or environment areas.

In planning a redesign of the organization, concentration is focused first on achieving transfer of human creative power. Therefore adequate provision is made to delegate authority, and to facilitate motivation and direction of personnel. To this end, adequate provision is made for the delegation of authority, and for the facilitiation of motivation and direction.

Secondly, concentration is focused on the grouping of the planning, implementation, and inspecting functions so as to provide effective check and balance forces. This is to reduce the possibility that the transfer of creative power at each level will be misdirected, or otherwise frustrated. Although coordination is facilitated by well designed checks and balances, the responsibility for effecting good coordination at any level is vested in the person holding the next higher position of authority.

A point is often reached when the objectives of the functional organization become so diversified that the accounting/communication phase of the system breaks down and coordination becomes excessively difficult. When this occurs the organization must be studied with a view to effective subdivision. Basically, subdivision is accomplished either by divisionalization (the grouping of functions along product or geographic lines) or by decentralization of near-maximum authority to levels where action takes place.

Line and Staff. It is now well agreed that there is very little area that is either straight line or straight staff. Line and staff proportions must be designed to meet the reality of the specific situation, and must be changed as the organizational environment changes. A 1962 report by the National Industrial Conference Board (now The Conference Board) [2] made the point that "'line' and 'staff' are two of the most perplexing, ambiguous, overworked, and overdefined terms in the lexicon of the organization planner. . . . Attempts have been made in some companies to dispense with these terms. 'Operating' is quite often substituted for 'line'; 'auxiliary' and 'service' are the most common substitutes for 'staff.' But substitution of terms is of doubtful value in clarifying the organizational relationships involved." In general usage, as pointed out in this article, the terms are used in two quite different settings: (1) to distinguish or characterize types of work, and (2) to distinguish or characterize types of authority. For a more recent clarification, the reader is referred to the entry, ORGANIZATION: Line-Staff Relationships.

Span of Control. The span-of-control "principle" is something that must be applied with utmost elasticity—and only after analysis of the capacities of the people involved, and of many other factors in the specific situation. While there is obviously a limit to the number of positions that can be supervised effectively by a single executive, there is no discernible justification for arbitrarily limiting the span to some number such as five. A large transportation company quoted in the NICB report cited above states the case succinctly: "There are no fixed rules for determining span of control; the number of subordinates reporting to one executive should be determined by the capacities of the individuals involved and the nature of their responsibilities."

Promulgation of Policy. In the more complex organizations, the planners are usually responsible for the publication, distribution, and maintenance of an organization manual. Ideally, the manual will clarify the authorities and responsibilities of each management individual to all other management individuals. It will further provide for the clarification of relationships and working methods between these individuals.

Acceptance. The acceptance of organization analysis and planning as a continual process is close to being universal among the larger companies where strangulation of communications and coordination is the acknowledged alternative. And in smaller companies, the competitive squeeze on profits has caused ever-increasing attention to this technique of improving efficiency in obtaining objectives. The potential for increased use of this technique appears to be considerable in light of the current potential for growth in both corporate and governmental organizations, as well as in the economy that nourishes them.

RICHARD W. REYNOLDS, Senior Systems Analyst, Space Technology Laboratories, Redondo Beach, California, and (for third edition) A. JAMES ANDREWS, Director of Publications, Association for Systems Management, Cleveland, Ohio

Information References

Associations:

American Management Associations.
Association for Systems Management.
The Conference Board.
Society for Advancement of Management.

Texts:

Biggs, Charles, Birks, Evan, and Atkins, William, "Managing the Systems Development Process," Englewood Cliffs, N.J., Prentice-Hall, 1980.
Chacko, George K., "Management Information Systems," New York, Petrocelli, 1980.
Fayol, Henri, "General and Industrial Management," London, Pitman, second translation, 1949, foreword by L. Urwick.
Galbraith, Jay R., "Organizational Design," Reading, Mass., Addison-Wesley, 1977.
Stanford, Melvin J., "Management Policy," Englewood Cliffs, N.J., Prentice-Hall, 1979.

References Cited

[1] Porter, R. W., "Design for Industrial Coordination," New York, Harper & Bros., 1941.
[2] Stieglitz, Harold, "Corporate Organization Structures," New York, The Conference Board, 1962.

Cross References: *Organization Theory (and cross references there given).*

ORGANIZATION THEORY

Organization Theory, as a distinct area of study and research, has emerged from a combination of several academic disciplines. It is not yet sufficiently mature for the content and research methods to have jelled into a coherent, readily apparent whole. Deeply rooted in the behavioral sciences, this new field represents an attempt to explain and predict human behavior in organizations. It is linked with application—attempts to influence such behavior—through activities such as organizational design.

People involved in management and administration—as teachers and as practioners—have thought and written about "organization" for many years. Some of the earliest works on the subject predate ancient Rome. The distinguishing feature of *modern* organization theory is the attempt to make the study of organizational behavior more scientific, drawing upon the ideas and research methods of fields such as psychology, sociology, anthropology, applied mathematics, operations research, and economics.

It has become a field for the scientific study of how organizations and people in organizations *do* and *can* behave. This is in contrast with the huge volume of literature on how they *should* behave, based primarily on the intuition and specific experiences of the writer.

The following headings may serve to indicate the range of subjects which are currently being studied by people engaged in research which has potential relevance to Organization Theory: Organization Structure and Process; Leadership and Morale; Communication; Control and Evaluation; Decision-Making; Interaction Theory; Bureaucracy and Complex Organization; Work Flow; Small Group Behavior (a vast field of research which encompasses many of the other topics as they relate to small groups); Game Theory and Coalition Formation; Productivity and Performance Measurement; Growth of Organizations; Incentives; Creativity; Attitudes; Status; Prestige, Power, Role Definition; Effects of Socio-Cultural Environment on Behavior; Formal vs. Informal Organization; Unanticipated Consequences of Control Systems.

Most current research in this field can be described along the following dimensions:

(1) *Focus* or *Level.* This can range from primary concern with the behavior, feelings, attitudes, etc. of *individuals* to primary concern with whole *organizations* or classes of organizations.

(2) *Research Methods.* This can range from primarily speculative work or formal theorizing, through experimental laboratory work, to field studies and experiments in operating organizations.

(3) *Kind of Data.* This can be confined to consideration of only the outward manifestations of behavior—particularly those things which can be counted or measured in some way—or it can include "internal" data such as feelings, attitudes, needs, motivations, etc.

(4) *The Specific Phenomena.* This may include decision-making, morale, communication, influence relationships, leadership, or any of the topics listed earlier.

(5) *Degree of Abstraction.* This can range from primary verbal description to highly mathematical descriptions or mathematical models.

With respect to research in this field, several promising "new" tools or techniques might be mentioned, some of which have been in wide use for as long as 50 years, some for only 10 to 20. Most of them have not as yet been fully exploited as research tools to develop organizational theories which can help us to explain, predict, and eventually systematically to influence organizational behavior. These five tools are:

(1) The small group experimental laboratory.

(2) Simulation of behavior on computers and in "almost-real-life" situations.

(3) Mathematical models.

(4) The field study methods of the anthropologist.

(5) Field experiments.

The first of these research tools is perhaps the best known. It is also the only one that may be conceived as equipment or hardware, analogous to that used in the natural sciences. The small group laboratory, in its pure form, is a specially designed facility for establishing experimental conditions and providing observations of the experiment in progress. One of the earliest such laboratories was the one at Harvard in the Department of Social Relations, designed and built under the direction of R. F. Bales over 30 years ago. An important feature was a one-way mirror for observing the members of small groups without, in turn, being observed.

The second research tool or method is partly hardware and partly experimental design. It is the simulation of organizational behavior. This simulation is being performed in two ways: on high-speed computers and in organizational laboratories. Simulation of organizational behavior by computer has progressed slowly with only a few actual studies in the literature. One of the earliest of these was the simulation of small group decision-making in the summer of 1951 at the Rand Corporation. With the increased availability of high-speed computational facilities all over the country and increased access to them for behavioral research, this method holds tremendous promise for breakthroughs in the field. The major obstacles encountered by the Rand experimenters, however, still persist. The computer can approach reality only in relation to our systematic knowledge of reality. That is, nonsense instructions on human behavior, fed into a simulation, will produce nonsense results. Computer simulation, despite its great promise, cannot stand alone without adequate formal—that is, mathematical—theory and good empirical or experimental data. The advantage of simulation experimentation, of course, is its economy of time and money (depending on whether one can get computer time free). Organizational parameters such as growth rates, size, status relationships, decision rules, etc. can readily be changed to see what *would* happen, or what *might* happen. One can start with very simple models and gradually increase their complexity so as to approach "real" life.

The other major method of simulation involves controlled experiments on organizations in an almost-real-life situation. This is about the closest we can come to "real" real life, because in real, real life there are no experimenters, at least none that we are aware of. Again, one of the earliest and still the largest scale simulation of this type was done at the Rand Corporation in the 1950s. The salient feature of this kind of simulation is that actual people are involved, with all of the richness of perception and behavioral potential that is human. The control is achieved through control over the inputs to the system (i.e., information, assigned tasks, etc.), the reward and penalty system, and the ability to manipulate certain other environmental constraints and inter-personal relations. For example, communication patterns can be systematically varied, alternative decision rules can be tried, and so on.

The third and perhaps most powerful research method in Organization Theory has been in general use less than twenty years. It is the employment of mathematical models to describe and represent organizational behavior. It is also, perhaps, the most controversial. This controversy is well exemplified by Abraham Kaplan, in his paper "Sociology Learns the Language of Mathematics" [1]. In it he criticized the vast amount of pseudo-mathematics and non-applicable mathematics that had entered the literature. There have been attempts prior to the recent upsurge in mathematical modeling to apply directly the mathematical methods and specific mathematical models from various fields of science and engineering to the study of organizational behavior. Most of them have not been very useful so far in advancing the field. Their major effect has been stimulatory and in some cases of help in building an abstraction of real life situations. It is possible that as simulation techniques and other data collection and experimental methods advance, some of these models and analytical tools such as servomechanism theory, information theory, game theory, etc., may produce important insights or breakthroughs about actual organizational behavior.

The fourth tool is the field study method of the anthropologist. With proper interplay between the other research methods and this one, rigorous field studies—not mere data collection exercises or cases studies of current practice—provide the greatest hope for increasing our understanding of organizational behavior. There are two common categories of such field studies, each with its own advantages and procedural difficulties. The traditional method, borrowed directly from social anthropology, uses an observer who is clearly a researcher—an outsider to the group or organization being studied. The second kind, which is rather hazardous both methodologically and physically at times, is the participant-observer method, in which the researcher is actually part of the organization being studied, either through design or by chance.

Included in the repertoire of the field study researcher are many interviewing and questionnaire techniques as well as methods of analyzing documentary information and making unobtrusive measures without contacting the respondents. Some of these techniques are used exclusively by some researchers or as the dominant mode of data collection. For example, *survey research* may employ standard questionnaires or interview schedules to obtain large quantities of data that may be subjected to rigorous statistical analysis.

A fifth method, combining the richness of the field study approach and the potential control aspect of the small group laboratory, involves *field experiments, natural experiments,* or *administrative experiments* in field sites. The distinction between varieties of field experimentation methods in the behavioral sciences and management rest, among other things, on the degree of involvement of the people primarily concerned with the outcome—at the field site this is generally the manager—in establishing the effects to be achieved, or the conditions to be assessed.

Where management or its representatives or the members of an organization participate heavily in the development and design of the experiment and the selection of the effects they want to achieve or assess (the dependent variables), one might characterize such efforts as "administrative experiments." This classification helps to distinguish this kind of study from "controlled field experiments" done for primarily scientific reasons with the participation of field site people limited to that of subjects in the experiments or informants about the organization and the impacts of the experiment. "Natural experiments" may involve rigorous experimental design and data collection, but the events occurring or the situations prevailing which serve as independent variables are not manipulated by the experimenter or the experimental team (which may include members of the field site). Essentially, the independent variables "happen" and are observed by the "experimenter" within a quasi-experimental framework.

What is needed for the future is more direct use by management of the methods and results achieved by the behavioral scientists who are contributing to our knowledge of organizational behavior. Some of the specific problems with which management is frequently concerned involve organizational variables and relationships very similar to the ones studied by organizational theorists. In the installation of new information-handling systems, new decision rules, and new work systems, questions and problems such as the following (among many others) arise continually:

(1) The effects of incentives on motivation and behavior.

(2) Reactions to changes in the pattern of communication and decision-making among managerial personnel.

(3) Criteria for control and evaluation of non-routine activities.

(4) Response to organizational changes and changes in objectives.

(5) Needs for and uses of information by various executives.

(6) Decision and estimation criteria in activities such as capital investment, advertising, and R&D.

(7) Trade-offs between efficiency and effectiveness of organizational units.

It is particularly disturbing for a specialist in organizational theory, acquainted with some of the material available in this growing field, to observe many practitioners attempting to deal with problems such as those indicated above without making any attempt to examine or use the literature of the field. Many poor experiences resulting from bad organizational design and inadequate consideration of some of the above questions can be traced to a lack of interest in or knowledge about the methods and content of organization theory.

ALBERT H. RUBENSTEIN, Professor of Industrial Engineering and Management Sciences, Northwestern University, Evanston, Illinois

Information References

Argyris, Chris, "Understanding Organizational Behavior," Homewood, Ill., Irwin-Dorsey, 1960.

Blau, Peter M. and Schoenherr, Richard, "The Structure of Organizations," New York, Basic Books, 1971.

Galbraith, Jay R., "Organizational Design," Reading, Mass., Addison-Wesley, 1977.

Katz, Daniel and Kahn, Robert L., "The Social Psychology of Organizations, 2nd ed., New York, Wiley, 1978.

Lorsch, Jay and Morse, John J., "Organizations and Their Members: A Contingency Approach," New York, Harper & Row, 1974.

Perrow, Charles, "Organizational Analysis: A Sociological View," Belmont, Calif., Wadsworth, 1970.

Rubenstein, A.H. and Haberstroh, C.J., eds., "Some Theories of Organization," Homewood, Ill., Irwin-Dorsey, 1960.

Simon, Herbert A., "Models of Man," New York, Wiley, 1957.

Stan, Barry and Salancik, Gerald R., eds., "New Directions in Organizational Behavior," Chicago, St. Clair, 1975.

Periodicals:

Administrative Science Quarterly.

American Behavioral Scientist.

American Sociological Review.

Behavioral Science.

Human Organization.

Journal of the Academy of Management.

Journal of Management Studies.

Transactions on Engineering Management, Institute of Electronic and Electrical Engineers.

Reference Cited

Kaplan, Abraham, "Sociology learns the Language of Mathematics," *Commentary,* Vol. XIV, September, 1952.

Cross References: *Decision Making and Organizational Effectiveness; Linear Responsibility Charting; Managerial Effectiveness: Climate for Organizational Results; Matrix Organization; Organization prefix entries; Organizational Planning; Q-Charts (Quantitative Charts); Project Management; Public Administration.*

ORGANIZATIONAL PLANNING: Q-CHARTS (QUANTITATIVE CHARTS)

So-called **Q-Charts,** or quantitative charts, are an innovative form of organization charting that assigns quantitative values to each subunit found in traditional charts, and displaying those values by means of proportionally sized boxes. Fraser [1] has described the technique in terms of the charts shown in Exhibits I and II, prepared at Westinghouse Electric Corporation to highlight and compare the relative communication and analytical potentials of traditional and quantitative charts.

Shown is a hypothetical corporate line organization with four manufacturing divisions, scheduled to add a fifth five years hence. Sales, investment, and after-tax income shifts are to be planned during the five-year span to meet the unit's overall operating goals at the end of the period.

Under traditional charting, despite the reassigning of duties and responsibilities among the boxes and rearranging hierarchical relation-

EXHIBIT I

TRADITIONAL ORGANIZATION CHARTS

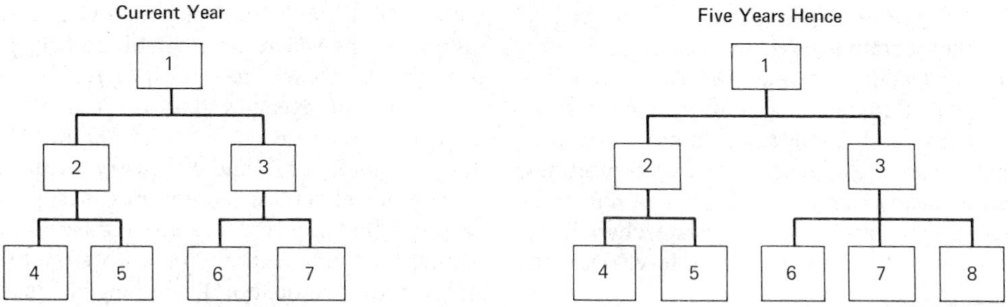

EXHIBIT II

QUANTITATIVE CHARTS

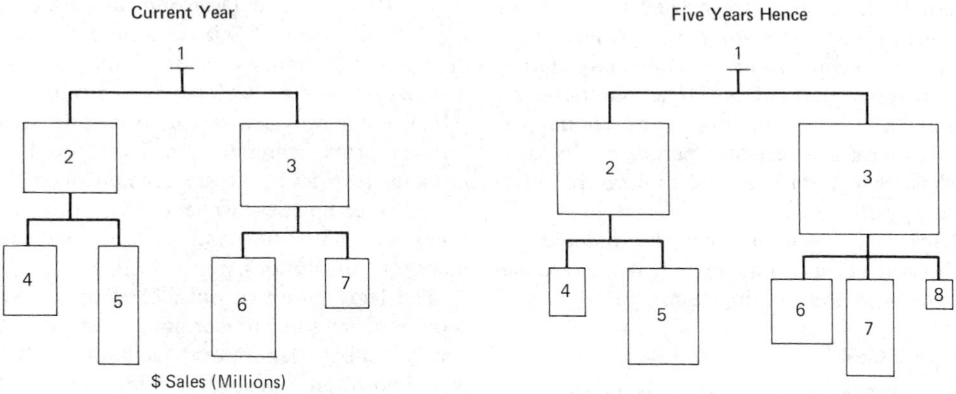

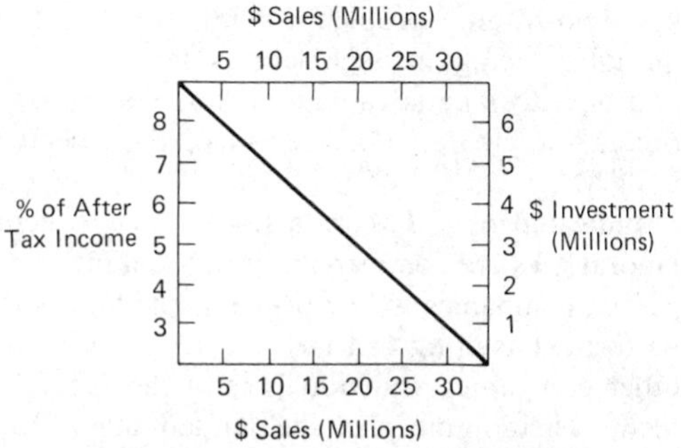

Legend

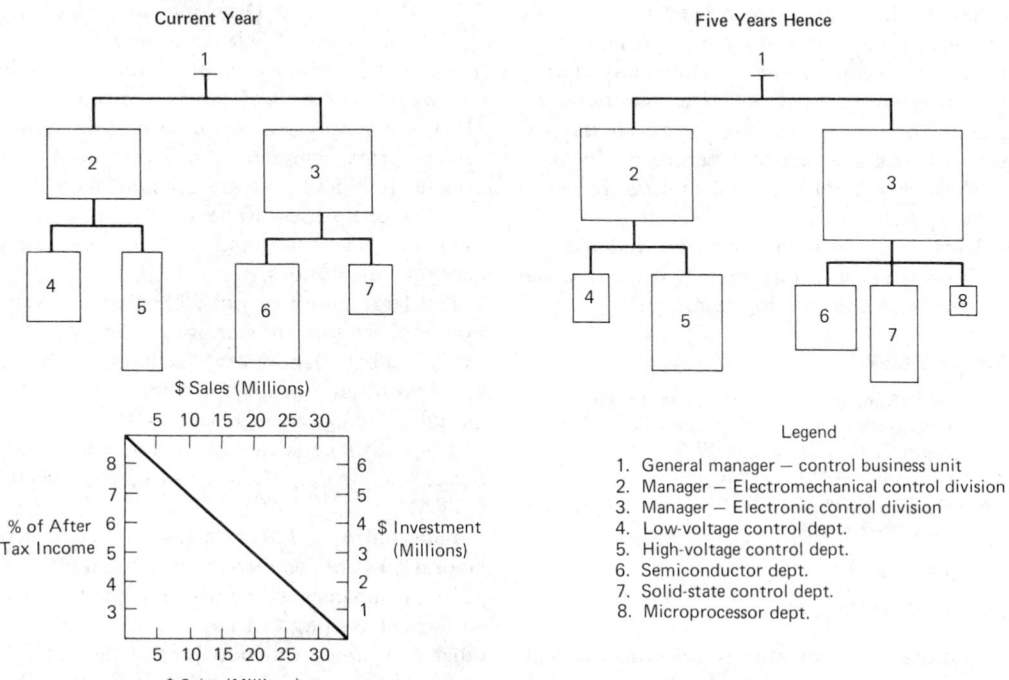

1. General manager – control business unit
2. Manager – Electromechanical control division
3. Manager – Electronic control division
4. Low-voltage control dept.
5. High-voltage control dept.
6. Semiconductor dept.
7. Solid-state control dept.
8. Microprocessor dept.

Reprinted, by permission of the publisher, from "Q-Charts: How to Give New Perspective to the Organizational Picture," by Ronald Fraser, *Management Review,* December 1979, p. 38,

ships among the subunits, the new organization chart usually looks strikingly like the chart it was meant to replace. In Exhibit I, the addition of box 8 is the only visible change effected in the five years.

Exhibit II shows schematically how Q-charts can convert a host of decisions into a concise plan, including intended goals and magnitude of change. Information is provided on investment versus sales for corporate divisions and on after-tax income versus sales for the operating departments. As indicated in the legend, vertical lines represent percentage of after-tax income for the departments, and investment dollars for the divisions. Horizontal lines represent sales dollars for both departments and divisions.

At the operating level, the charts in Exhibit II can provide a flexible tool for stimulating individual thinking, focusing group strategy workshops, and conducting routine organizational reviews. At general manager meetings, division heads can use variations of the technique to help assess and translate charted expectations into internal division-level decisions for income and sales goals.

Department level managers, with wider multidivision performance responsibilties, can use Q-charts to help determine what changes in the external relationships are needed to attain the five-year plan. Contrasting division-level market environments—some growing, some declining—become part of a larger multidivision picture. A series of interim progress charts, presented over a five-year-plan period, can be used to show changing trends and to measure movement toward stated goals.

Obviously, Q-charts must be tailored for each company use. Imagination is an essential ingredient in the charting technique.

Reference Cited

[1] Fraser, Ronald, "Q-Charts: How to Give New Perspective to the Organizational Picture," *Management Review,* December 1979.

Cross References: *Organization Theory (and cross references there given).*

OUTSIDE RESEARCH

Outside Research means scientific, technological, and engineering work carried out for a company by personnel who are not employees, using facilities not owned by the company. The terms "contract" or "sponsored" are often used to refer to essentially the same type of research activity. Since the bulk of outside research is oriented toward practical objectives, the term will be used here to mean both research and development.

The principal agencies available to industry for sponsored research are about 1,000 independent industrial laboratories which engage in research to a greater or lesser extent; about a dozen research institutes whose principal activity is contract research, and several hundred academic institutions which will undertake scientific and engineering research programs sponsored by the Federal Government and by industry. Supplementing these facilities are thousands of individual consultants and consulting groups which are available to help plan, execute, and control research programs. A second group of agencies that is available, but used to a lesser extent, includes about 300 endowed foundations, and "industry institutes," plus technical service laboratories of suppliers, "captive" laboratories of some industrial companies, trade association laboratories, and state and territory agricultural and engineering experiment stations.

Outside research is a multibillion dollar, continually growing activity. In its 1979 publication, "Research and Development in Industry, 1977," the National Science Foundation states that in 1977 industry reported that 3% of its company-financed R&D total expenditures of $19.4 billion was contracted to outside organizations. This represents an increase of 12% over its 1976 level. Of this amount, most went to other companies, while a lesser proportion went to universities and colleges and other nonprofit institutions.

The large group of outside research organizations represents an enormous reservoir of scientific talent, laboratory facilities, technical know-how, and problem-solving ability. The question facing management is when, where, and how to take advantage of this reservoir to obtain the greatest mileage out of the research budget.

Independent Laboratories. Independent laboratories are commercial, profit-making, taxpaying companies whose primary function is to perform consulting and laboratories services for other companies, individuals, and the Government. Their number in the United States has been estimated to be as high as 2,300, but many of these restrict their activities solely to testing, analysis, inspection, and sampling. Out of the total, perhaps as many as 1,000 engage in research and development activities. These laboratories are scattered across the country, but they tend to concentrate in industrial centers, and the majority are in New York, California, Illinois, Massachusetts, New Jersey, and Pennsylvania.

To assist industrial organizations seeking help on specific problems, some 250 independent laboratories (and the number is growing) belong to the American Council of Independent Laboratories, Inc., Washington, D.C., which issues a directory of member laboratories, giving details about the staff and the scope of activities. The directory is indexed to simplify the selection of laboratories qualified to perform work in different areas of technical specialization. (ACIL has taken a vigorous public stand against what it sees as unfair tax-favored competition from government bodies, nonprofit organizations, colleges, and universities.)

Many independent laboratories offer testing and analytical services which are sometimes valuable in support of research programs. The "Directory of Testing Laboratories—Commercial and Institutional," (available from the American Society for Testing Materials, Philadelphia), lists over 600 commercial testing laboratories and their branches, as well as some 700 to 800 laboratories of institutions that are prepared to do testing under certain conditions. This directory classifies the laboratories according to the commodities tested and the types of tests performed. However, it is far from complete, since there are probably more than 1,600 commercial testing laboratories in this country. In seeking such services, geographical location is often very important—which means that the local classified telephone directory can be a valuable source of information.

The 1980 ACIL directory has 231 major headings, many of them divided into eight or ten subheadings, covering areas such as agricultural testing, air pollution, antibiotics, brewing, catalysis, dyes, electrochemistry, enzymes, fertilizers, gamma ray field laboratory, hormones, market research, perfumes, printing inks, resins, starch, tobacco, vitamins, and welding.

Research Institutes. Out of about 300 multidisciplinary nonprofit research institutes in the United States, there are about a dozen major laboratories that are essentially independent of university connection and whose principal activity is research sponsored by industry and Government. Some were originally set up as endowed institutions, and others were founded with industrial support, usually to provide technical facilities for a specific area of the country. Most of them use the income from sponsored projects to self-sponsor research in their own fields of interest.

The principal scientific fields of interest to the research institutes are chemistry, physics, and metallurgy; their activities also include geology, geophysics, and other earth sciences; and medical, agricultural, biological, engineering, and social sciences. The research institutes are usually large, compared to the average independent laboratory.

Prominent organizations of this type that accept industrial sponsorship of projects on a confidential basis are Battelle Memorial Institute, Columbus, Ohio; Carnegie-Mellon Institute of Research, Pittsburgh, Pa.; Franklin Institute, Philadelphia, Pa.; Midwest Research Institute, Kansas City, Mo.; Research Triangle Institute, Research Park, N.C.; and Southwest Research Institute, San Antonio, Tex.

Information on these and other not-for-profit research organizations will be found in "Research Centers Directory: A Guide to University-Related & Other Nonprofit Research Organizations," published by Gale Research Co., Detroit. The 6th edition, 1979, contains 6,268 listings. These include research institutes, centers, foundations, laboratories, bureaus, experiment stations, and similar nonprofit research facilities and organizations. Excluded are departmental laboratories and facilities used primarily in instructional programs and internship activities, with research merely of incidental concern. The directory interprets research broadly, and its seventeen categories cover fundamental, applied, and developmental studies, as well as programs of data gathering, analysis, and synthesis.

Academic Institutions. All technological institutes, most universities, and many colleges and professional schools operate research programs as part of the educational system. Wherever people are being *trained* to do research, they must be *doing* research; no substitute for this approach has ever been found. Therefore, every such institution is a center of research activity.

Traditionally, these research activities have been centered on the idea that there should be no restrictions on the nature of the inquiry.

Thus, universities have been a major source of important basic and fundamental research. In fact, the term "academic research" has come to mean almost the same thing as "pure," "basic," or "fundamental" research. However, the pressures of World War II made many of the schools shift their emphasis to much more practical research objectives, thus creating a large number of applied-research centers at these institutions, which in many cases were continued as a regular operation after the war.

Information about the facilities available at many technical institutions can be found in the "Annual Directory of Engineering College Research and Graduate Study," published by the American Society for Engineering Education, Washington, D.C.

Consultants. Consultants normally do not conduct any research themselves, but act in an advisory capacity. The ways in which industry employs consultants are varied: They may merely lecture on a regular basis to the technical staff; come to the research laboratory on a regular schedule for individual conferences with staff members who have troublesome problems in their areas of specialization; be called in on a one-time basis to try to give some new ideas to the research staff on a specific problem; or be retained to advise on, or act as liaison with, a research project going on in outside facilities.

One source of information about consultants is "Consulting Services," a directory of the Association of Consulting Chemists and Chemical Engineers, Inc., periodically updated. Another source is "Who's Who in Consulting: A Reference Guide to Professional Personnel Engaged in Consultation for Business, Industry, & Government," published by Gale Research Co., Detroit.

Foundations and Institutes. Generally, foundations and institutes may be separated into four types. (Two have already been discussed under "Research Institutes," and "Academic Institutions.") A third group consists of those institutes and foundations that operate under endowment or with Government support and do not accept industrially sponsored research (though some may accept research grants in the same way that universities do). A number of such organizations operate in medical research, and others are organized to deal only with problems of direct interest to the Government in national defense.

The fourth type might be called the "industry institute," which deals primarily with problems of concern to specialized industries. A number of these are supported by funds contributed from the industry, and the results of the research are available to the entire industry. Some of these institutes enter into individual contracts with their members for research projects on a confidential basis.

Trade Associations. There are more than 3,000 national trade, business and commercial associations in this country, and upwards of 1,000 scientific, engineering, and technical associations and societies. The former are nonprofit, cooperative organizations of business competitors who have grouped together to aid themselves and their industry in mutual business problems. Among these problems is industrial research, and a number of these trade associations have sponsored substantial programs of industrial research and development, with the results becoming generally available to the industry. The areas involved are usually statistical research on current production and sales and on long-range trends for future economic planning; commercial research to find wider and more profitable markets; and industrial research to find new or improved products or manufacturing techniques.

Most of the trade associations do not maintain laboratories of their own but sponsor outside research, often in the laboratories of one member. (Some of the industry institutes were organized by trade associations.) Another technique often used is cooperative work, with parts of the project being conducted in various laboratories. This approach is particularly effective when the association is seeking, through its research program, to establish standard testing methods for the industry.

Information about trade associations is available in the "Encyclopedia of Associations," Vol. 1, "National Organizations of the U.S.," published by Gale Research Company.

"Captive" Laboratories. It is generally realized by industry that suppliers of materials and equipment are usually good sources of technical information on the use of their products. When the potential for future business is great enough, suppliers will also often do a limited amount of development work to help find a solution to a problem. Such work will normally be oriented in the direction of making it possible to utilize the supplier's product rather than any other. It should also be realized that the amount of work done will be prescribed by the importance of the problem to the supplier rather than to the customer. Another important factor is that the solution to the problem, if found by the supplier, will then become available to the customer's competitors.

The most comprehensive directory of all the known research facilities operating in and for industry, including information about the staffs, scope of activities, and availability for outside work is entitled "Industrial Research Laboratories of the United States." The 16th edition, published in 1979, is available from R. R. Bowker Company, New York. This directory gives information on about 10,000 R&D facilities belonging to some 6,300 organizations. It also includes information on nonprofit or privately financed firms doing research, development, engineering, or behavioral research in support of and for industry. Not included are research programs conducted and supported totally by universities and/or government, nor are activities devoted entirely to quality control and testing.

Government Laboratories. *Federal Government.* Although the laboratories maintained by the U.S. Government are not available to industry to work on specific problems, good research management requires an intimate knowledge of the important research under way in these laboratories. Except where national security prevents it, almost all of this research is published and freely available, but it is often valuable to know what general areas are under investigation even before the results are published.

Each of the armed services has its own R&D complex. The Department of the Navy has several centers, such as the Naval Ship R&D Center and the Naval Surface Weapons Center, responsible for applied mission-oriented efforts. In addition there are laboratories such as the Naval Research Laboratory where more fundamental research is conducted. The Department of the Army and the Department of the Air Force also conduct their own R&D programs within major commands.

Additionally, the National Aeronautics and Space Administration (NASA) conducts a space-related program, including the Jet Propulsion Laboratory, operated by the California Institute of Technology under contract. Other Federal laboratories conducting large-scale research are the Sandra Laboratories, the Los Alamos Scientific Laboratory, the National Bureau of Standards, and the Oak Ridge National Laboratory.

Federal Contract Research Centers (FCRCs) are permanent facilities established to conduct studies for and render advisory and consulting service to their sponsoring agencies. There are some 75 such "captive" organizations, including well-known names such as RAND, Aerospace Corporation, MITRE, and Solar Energy Research Institute.

State Governments. Agricultural experiment stations, located at land-grant colleges and state universities, have extensive programs of research on problems relating to agriculture. The results of this research have contributed greatly to the agricultural economy. Facilities are maintained by all fifty states. These stations conduct a wide range of research projects and disseminate information on the development of higher-yield and disease-resistant crops, insecticides and fungicides, soil fertility and conservation, productive soil use, silviculture and forest management, plant and livestock breeding, livestock and dairy problems, and the preservation of foods. Activities are financed largely through state appropriations supplemented by Federal grants. Many of the experiment stations also cooperate with national, regional, state, or local trade associations and receive financial assistance for their research from these associations. A few undertake research projects supported by private companies and individuals, when the subject of the investigation is of public concern and is broad and basic in character.

Engineering research in these experiment stations is conducted in cooperation with Government agencies, individuals, firms, corporations, and trade associations, as well as by the station alone. Cooperative research is usually conducted under contract or grant.

Atomic Research Facilities. Irradiation services, often required in research programs, are not as widely available as other types of services. Research managers requiring the use of Cobalt-60 sources or Van de Graaff generators may find them available in outside laboratories. However, the widest range of services, including nuclear pile irradiation, is available through the Department of Energy, which has taken over much of the work of the former Atomic Energy Commission. Specifically: the Argonne National Laboratory (operated by the University of Chicago), the Brookhaven National Laboratory (operated by the Associated Universities, Inc.), the Oak Ridge National Laboratory (operated by Union Carbide Nuclear Co.), and Pacific Northwest Laboratories (of Battelle Memorial Institute).

Deciding on the Type of Organization. Traditionally, university laboratories have been considered the agency of choice for really basic research intended to open up a new area of knowledge without having any specific practical objective. To a certain extent, this is still true, but two factors have somewhat altered the situation:

(1) The tremendous growth of independent laboratories and research institutes has made it possible for them to attract scientists of high caliber who are capable of undertaking so-called "academic research."

(2) Many university laboratories have taken on so much applied research that they have lost a little of their atmosphere of complete freedom in research.

Accordingly, university laboratories should not be automatically chosen for basic research programs. The research institutes and the larger independent laboratories should also be investigated to see if they can offer scientists of the stature and reputation found in universities.

The research institutes and many of the independent laboratories are ideally suited for long-range research programs aimed at answering an industrial problem or learning more about an area of great practical interest. This type of project is often set up on an annual basis, but some of the research institutes prefer a contract of several years' duration.

Independent laboratories tend to have a greater flexibility, and for this reason are usually the best place to take a short-range problem of urgent, practical importance. Since an independent laboratory is a profit-making organization, it tends to appreciate the importance of timing, cost, and practicality in finding a solution. In general, independent laboratories have wide contacts in industry, keep in close touch with new industrial developments, and are alert to commercial possibilities, but these advantages are to a certain extent dependent on the size of the organization.

Where the objective of the project is product or process development, both the research institutes and the independent laboratories can often cooperate in later stages of the development by producing prototypes or large-scale samples, carrying on pilot-plant studies, designing machinery, conducting studies to delineate patent claims, doing market surveys, obtaining results to support advertising claims, and helping in publicizing the product or process by presenting research results at press conferences.

In general, an individual consultant is indicated when the requirement is for a specific viewpoint based on highly specialized knowledge, while a consultant group is often desirable when a broad evaluation involving the collection of much information is needed.

Deans and department heads in nearby universities will offer suggestions on faculty members qualified to serve as consultants in the field of interest. Members of the company's technical staff can suggest organizations or individuals who have outstanding reputations in the subject under consideration. A review of recent scientific and technical literature will reveal the names of those prominent in the field. (This path alone, however, cannot be relied upon to find all of those qualified, since results of most consulting work and independent laboratory research are never published.) Other sources include executives of other companies, fellow members of professional and trade associations, advertising agencies, customers, and suppliers.

Research projects intended to advance the industry in general or to promote public welfare are sometimes placed in state experiment stations, industry institutes, or trade association laboratories—either to take advantage of specialized talent, unusual skills, or unique facilities, or because it is felt that they will gain prestige from these locations. Such projects parallel in certain respects the support of basic research by grants to academic institutions.

Projects of a more confidential nature, intended for the specific benefit of the sponsor, are sometimes placed in state experiment stations or industry-supported laboratories, but this is a questionable practice unless the specific organization is truly unique in its ability to carry out the desired work. Since they are established as public or semipublic laboratories for the purpose of disseminating information, they are not as well geared to maintaining strictest confidence. Furthermore, by their very nature, they are a focal point for research personnel from many competing organizations—thus making it even more difficult to maintain the level of industrial secrecy usually desired.

Captive laboratories are usually called upon through their technical service departments to render assistance directly related to the supplier's products. Such assistance is usually at no cost, but if the investigation required becomes too extensive, it may no longer be possible for the supplier to provide the desired services. Under these circumstances and when it is desirable to utilize personnel intimately familiar with the supplier's products, it may be possible to arrange for the captive laboratory to continue the investigation as a sponsored project.

In addition, some companies have adopted the policy of seeking contract research for their captive laboratories. Such activities may be perfectly acceptable in many cases, but they are sometimes criticized on the basis that a captive laboratory may not always be completely unbiased.

Defining the Problem. The problem must be properly defined. Here lies one of the pitfalls of many outside research projects. A good working definition of the problem should be reached at preliminary conferences and during the preparation of the technical proposal. But a clear understanding of principles and purposes is most easily obtained when the client and the outside laboratory have achieved a smoothly operating team relationship.

It often becomes the job of the outside group to make the client back off from a preconceived notion and admit the possibility that an entirely different avenue might be worth consideration. A prospective client who looks upon his problem as a simple one of quality control is a typical example. He requests that a faster method of analysis be devised so that information can be fed back in time to control the product. While it is true that new instrumental methods and automation can accomplish a great deal in this direction, the outside group may consider it necessary to point out that the real problem is that the client does not know enough about the process to permit proper control. What he needs to achieve a better understanding of the process is a basic study of the reactions involved.

Contractual Arrangements. Unless the project is a sizable one, there is usually no necessity for any complicated legal document. Many outside laboratories will accept assignments of relatively small dollar amounts on the basis of a simple letter of authorization.

The following subjects are most frequently covered in outside research contracts:

Scope. The project should be described, preferably in enough detail to delineate the scope of the intended investigation.

Duration. The contract will often specify the starting date of the project, which may sometimes be the contract date. For extended projects, the duration of the contract will be specified. Shorter projects have more specific objectives, and it is usually preferable to have an informal understanding about estimated duration.

Cost. The contract should provide a maximum cost figure, requiring prior permission from the sponsor for any further rise. If the project is an extended one, the approximate rate of expenditure may also be specified.

Personnel. Personnel, if mentioned at all, is usually covered only in general terms, to permit the greatest flexibility.

Liaison. Relatively little mention of the important subject of liaison is made in most contracts. Occasionally, reference will be made to frequency of conferences, availability of results during working hours, or the establishment of a project committee consisting of representatives of both parties.

Reporting. Frequency of formal written reports is sometimes specified, usually to satisfy the sponsor's management requirements. From the scientific point of view, it is usually undesirable to break off the work at an arbitrary point for report purposes.

Secrecy. Independent laboratories, the major research institutes, and consultants will automatically maintain as high a degree of security as is found in any industrial laboratories. It is more important to have the precise degree of security spelled out in the contract when dealing with academic institutions, university-affiliated institutes, industry institutes, and state experiment stations, in view of the traditional modes of operation of such organizations.

Exclusivity. Contracts for projects of substantial size will usually specify that work on the same or closely related subjects will not be undertaken by the outside group while the contract is in force. This is usual with independent laboratories, research institutes, consultants, and even some of the university-affiliated institutes. It is less true of academic institutions, industry institutes, and state experiment stations.

Rights. Patent rights are almost invariably covered in the contract. When they are the property of the sponsor, the contract usually specifies that the employees of the outside laboratory have executed an agreement to assign all inventions to their employers. The laboratory, in turn, agrees to inform the sponsor of all inventions and assign all rights to him.

Independent laboratories and consultants normally agree to assign all inventions to the client.

Research institutes generally arrange to assign patents to sponsors, but some make special provisions, such as granting only an exclusive license or possibly an option for such a license. Here again, the institute may have had a prior interest in the subject and may have some rights that are subject to negotiation. Patent policies of research institutes are described in *Nonprofit Research and Patent Management in the United States* and *Nonprofit Research and Patent Management Organization,* both by Archie M. Palmer (published by the National Academy of Sciences-National Research Council, Washington, D.C.).

University patent policies vary widely. Patent policies of universities are reviewed in great detail in *University Research Patent Policies: Practices and Procedures* (1962), by Archie M. Palmer (also published by NAS-NRC).

Industry institutes tend to grant nonexclusive licenses to members of the industry, but some will assign all rights to the sponsor. Discoveries and inventions made in laboratories of state experiment stations are not frequently patented, and then only in the public interest. Usually non-exclusive, royalty-free licenses are granted to all qualified licensees.

Publication. Independent laboratories and consultants usually retain no publication rights in the contract, but are pleased to have the opportunity to publish results when the sponsor grants permission.

Most research institutes state in their standard contracts that they will not publish the results without prior approval of the sponsor.

It is the usual practice for educational institutions to retain control over the publication of all research conducted on the campus.

University-affiliated research institutes will sometimes permit the sponsor to delay publication for as long as three years.

Industry institutes and state experiment stations tend to publish more freely, since it is one of their functions to disseminate information.

Advertising. The results of research are frequently of value to the sponsor for advertising purposes, even when that has not been the objective of the project. Most outside research organizations feel that the results are the property of the client to use as he sees fit. However, the situation is very different if the sponsor wishes to associate the name of the research group with the results in any public manner. Virtually all contracts have a clause giving the laboratory the right to review all advertising, publicity, and sales promotional matter in which its name is mentioned. Permission to use the names of the major research institutes in actual advertising is rarely granted.

Legal Actions. Some contracts give the laboratory the right to review material prepared from the research results for presentation as evidence in disputes, litigation, or other legal action. However, most outside groups will cooperate, at the sponsor's expense, in supporting their results in legal actions or before government agencies. The contract restrictions are designed to prevent misuse of the information.

Responsibilities. In all basic research, in most applied research, and in much development work, there can be no guarantee that the desired results will be achieved. The closest that an outside group can come to it is to undertake the project on a "best efforts" basis. The contract should spell out responsibility for compliance with Federal, state, and municipal regulations. It should specify which party is to be responsible for public and personal liability and for property damage.

Maintaining Liaison. The member of the sponsor's technical staff who will be responsible for liaison should be chosen early—even before the outside group has been selected or proposals have been received. If the liaison person is involved from the start, he (she) can develop a better feeling for the problem and have the satisfaction of working with an organization that he or she has helped to select.

The proper frequency of personal contact and written reports is important, and should be adjusted to the nature of the project and the rate of activity. A long-range basic research project might warrant a conference only twice a year and a report once a year. A typical long-range applied research project might deserve a monthly conference, with the minutes of the conference serving as a progress report to be supplemented quarterly by a formal report. A long-range development project might rate a monthly summary or progress report, a monthly conference, and an annual or final formal report. A short-range project could be handled by a few conferences and a single final report. An emergency problem might require daily contact by phone or in person, with formal reporting of secondary importance.

Cost Considerations. It is a common mistake to compare costs of contract research with salaries of the sponsor's research staff. A realistic comparison should include all proper apportionment of indirect costs. The cost per "in-house" R&D scientist and/or engineer varies sharply by individual industry, depending on the type of R&D activity. The all-industry average for funds spent on R&D programs came to $76,400 per scientists or engineer in 1977, according to the National Science Foundation.

The system used for arriving at the charges of most outside research groups is to make an actual accounting of all costs, direct and indirect, properly assignable to the project. This obviously entails a great deal of bookkeeping. In a move to lower accounting costs and thus lower overhead, some independent laboratories have adopted a simplified method of computing charges. Each member of the technical staff is assigned a billing rate based on his salary plus a single factor designed to cover average overhead, taxes, materials, profit, and so on. These organizations have found that the only two items that cannot be satisfactorily included in such a system are special equipment and travel costs. Thus the only charges made to clients are for direct time applied to the project by technical personnel, and the two other items, when applicable. A further simplification of the method divides all technical personnel into classes according to salary, with one billing rate for each class.

MURRAY BERDICK, PH.D., formerly Director of Applied Research, Chesebrough-Pond's, Inc., Trumbull, Connecticut

Information References

Associations:

American Council of Independent Laboratories (contr. section on Independent Laboratories, above).
American Society for Engineering Education.
American Society for Testing Materials.
Association of Consulting Chemists.
National Academy of Sciences-National Research Council.
National Science Foundation.

Cross References: *Basic Research: Management Aspects; Industrial Research Accounting; Industrial Research Budgeting; Industrial Research and Development; Technological Forecasting.*

OVERHEAD ASSIGNMENT

Overhead Assignment is a two way process. One is to charge an appropriate amount of general expense to the business done in a period of time. The other is to assign a correct amount of overhead to a part or a product so as to know its total cost. The simplest, though somewhat incorrect, illustration of the latter is the mark-up method used by stores in setting prices. The difference between mark-up and overhead assignment is the percentage included in mark-up for profit.

Overhead assignment is necessary because only two of three general types of costs in industry are directly related to products—*direct labor* and *direct material.* Direct labor and direct material are charged directly to specific parts and products. All other costs incurred are classified as indirect or overhead. These expenses must be assigned one way or another to the business carried on so as to obtain its total cost. The same is true when computing the cost of a part or a product.

Before the advent of systematic cost accounting, profit was "the money left over in the cash drawer." It was the difference between the money taken in and the amounts paid out. That method of reckoning is still used by many small enterprisers. But today much more precision is required in most companies for two principal reasons: One is that they turn out many more products, and need to know what the potential profit or loss is on *each one.* The other stems from requirements for public accounting to stockholders and for taxes.

The "cash-drawer method" is not precise enough because the time of accounting rarely coincides with actual receipts and payments. Often, the largest amount of overlap is in the dollars represented by inventory. Some of these dollars are in finished goods not sold, some are in work-in-process, and some are in materials purchased but not used. Some overhead is ruled to be part of the cost of finished goods and of work-in-process. These amounts of overhead can be very large in companies that build up stocks in off-seasons to prepare for anticipated demands. In a like manner, large amounts accrue when complex products require months of time to complete.

Other examples of items of actual overhead expense out of phase with accounting periods are advertising, taxes, and insurance. These are paid for when due, but are not wholly assignable to that period's costs. Still another is the controversial expense of depreciation or depletion. The argument is about the time interval over which the cost shall be spread.

In the accounting-period profit and loss statement, overhead assignment is commonly done in two parts. One is the direct assignment of actual sales expense and administrative expenses to the goods sold during the period. These expenses show as a deduction from gross profit. The other part is in the portion of cost of goods sold that is built up of manufacturing overheads already assigned to the products as they were being made. Thus, usually, overhead is separated into two major categories primarily because of the time interval between making and selling the products. One part of overhead is termed Sales and Administrative, the other Manufacturing, Overhead, or Burden.

Generally, these two overheads are assigned differently, as the foregoing indicates. Usually, the total actual expense of Sales and Administrative for the period is charged against the actual sales income for that period. In contrast, most of Manufacturing Overhead is charged *pro-rata* through cost of sales by means of portions assigned to parts and products.

Manufacturing Overhead. Much of the attention to overhead assignment devolves upon computations of manufacturing overhead costs. This process was fairly simple in earlier times when the variety of products made was small. To illustrate with an oversimplification, when Henry Ford turned out only the Model T, he could get the overhead cost per car by simply dividing total overhead costs by total automobile production. Similarly shoe manufacturers computed overhead costs per dozen pairs. By reasoning that tons were finished products, steel mills and foundries assigned overhead costs by calculating overhead rates per ton. Textile mills computed overhead costs per yard.

The approaches used in the foregoing cases are methods of arriving at the objective of overhead costs per unit of product. But as companies developed more designs and acquired more products, they could no longer correctly use counts such as pieces, tons, yards or dozens as divisors. It became necessary to devise another method for assigning overhead. The newer method was based on choosing a common denominator that could be used to add together unlike products.

As a common denominator, many metal fabricators chose *machine hours.* Most companies selected *direct labor.* Some used both by assigning certain overheads to machine hours and others to direct labor. The term direct labor as used here includes four different denominators—*dollars* of labor, *actual* or *measured;* and *hours* of labor, *actual* or *measured.*

This procedure involves an intermediate step, namely to compute an *overhead rate* per unit of time or labor dollar. Then this rate is used to assign the overhead cost to the product made and sold. This common procedure consists of three basic steps:

(1) Determine amounts of production volume and overhead expenses that correspond.

(2) Divide expenses by volumes to obtain overhead rates.

(3) Multiply an overhead rate by the specific volume involved in a particular operation, part, assembly, or period to compute the overhead assigned.

Because Step 2 results in one or more overhead cost rates, there are many different approaches made in Step 1. The basic one goes back to the beginning of this discussion. It has to do with sorting *direct* from *indirect* labor. Whatever is called direct labor goes in the denominator (divisor) in Step 2. All other expenses related to the overhead rate go in the numerator. Therefore, there are many different interpretations of what is overhead and what is direct labor.

An early attempt at clarification defined direct labor as "that which changed the form or shape of the product." That definition had in it an important implication, namely that work done in converting material to some higher or more usable stage is the basic function of industry. Modern descriptions of our industrial process are stated in terms such as "conversion" and "value added."

However, the definition was lacking in two important aspects. One was that it excluded many operations that are actually direct labor. Examples are regularized inspection and packaging. The other was that it did not specify what was to be the measure of direct labor. Hence today, some accountants use labor dollars while others use labor hours. A further complication is that some accountants use dollars or hours accrued from *unmeasured* work, while others use similar bases resulting from *work measurement.* (The latter of course also has other uses when used with wage incentives.)

Consequently, the measures of direct labor (output) vary greatly from plant to plant. For instance, some treat material trucking and/or machine set-up as direct labor. In the same vein, it was common practice around 1918 for foremen to charge time to jobs going through their departments. On the other hand, some obviously direct costs like tumbling and heat-treating are deliberately put into overhead because their amounts are relatively insignificant. Some foundries charge the comparatively large direct cost of casting cleaning to overhead because they have not utilized convenient ways to charge costs to specific jobs.

In addition, there are mixed cases. Among these are *wait* and *extra work.* If separated, they may go into overhead. If buried in recorded times, piece work prices, or temporary rates, they go in direct labor. Similarly, there are mixed cases of materials. One example might be lumber. Boards used to make shipping boxes may be charged as direct material whereas other boards used to repair the roof are classified as indirect material and go into overhead. To summarize the effect of differing decisions about what is direct, Exhibit I shows an in-between section labelled *mixed.* Case 1 indicates an overhead percentage of 150 if all of the mixed is charged to overhead. Case 2 results in 100% when all mixed is classified as direct.

In Exhibit I, the divisor is some amount representing volume for the period used in calculating the overhead rate. For this purpose, some firms use the actual volume of the recent past. This is a carryover of the practice of computing actual or job costs. The method is convenient because, presumably, actual expenses correspond with actual volume.

But volume varies from year to year. Important causes are economic weather, competitive forces, and customer response. Changes in volume cause newly determined overhead rates to vary from those previously established. Consequently, newly computed costs appear different from those formerly used for comparisons with prices and for calculating profit or loss on sales.

The reason why changes in volume affect overhead rates is that most overhead costs are semi-variable. Exhibit II shows a typical overhead expense. It consists of a constant plus a variable. The same is true of total overhead, so that Exhibit II may be looked upon as representing total overhead. Thus, there is a major total overhead expense in a company that is fairly constant regardless of volume. This is the cost of the nucleus of the organization of a going concern. It includes expenses, such as depreciation, taxes, and insurance, commonly called *fixed.* The major portion, however, is made up of salaries and related costs. Because volume is divided into overhead to compute overhead rate, the amount taken as volume determines the proportion of constant cost to be assigned by the overhead rate. This is shown by Exhibit III, where the rate of constant cost is a reciprocal curve (1/x). To get around such variations, some accountants elect to use calculated actual rates as standards. Others choose a standard base for volume, as 80% of capacity. A better approach is to stop the changing cost in Exhibit III by establishing a normal or standard volume, and corresponding expenses. This method is suggested by point N and usually is adopted for the purpose of computing standard costs. (See STANDARD COSTING.)

It follows that variations in volume cause changes in costs and profits due simply to

EXHIBIT I

DIFFERING OVERHEAD RATES FROM IDENTICAL DATA

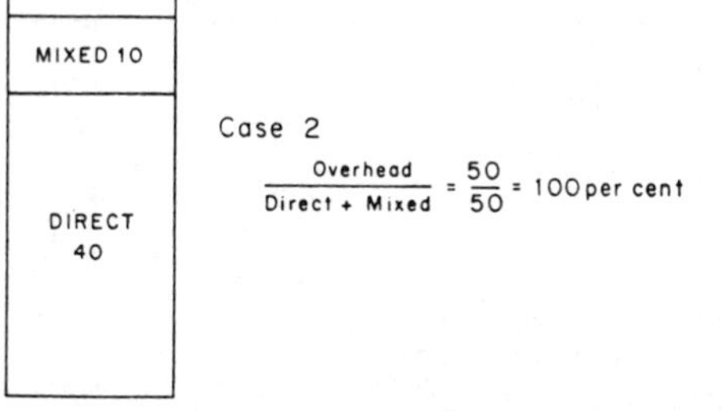

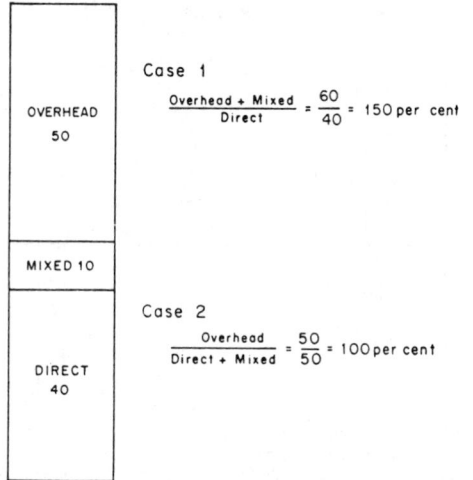

Examples of extremes in resulting overhead rates depending upon how certain expenses are classified.

EXHIBIT II

TOTAL OVERHEAD COST-VOLUME RELATIONSHIPS

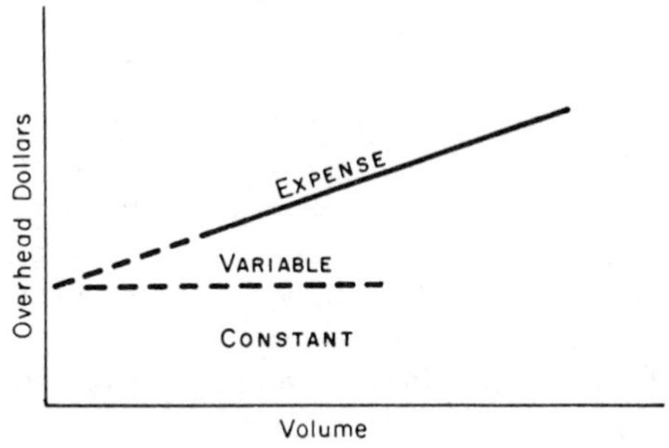

Most overhead expenses are semi-variable in that they contain constant amounts of cost.

EXHIBIT III

PER-UNIT OVERHEAD COST-VOLUME RELATIIONSHIPS

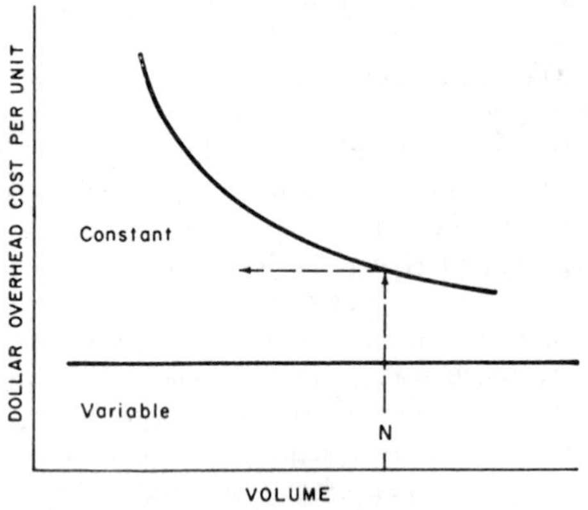

Overhead rates contain prorations of constant costs. That is one reason why actual costs change with volume.

bookkeeping under this method, which is known as *absorption costing.* Variations in performance and in control also affect the results.

Accounting Modifications. To separate the effects of bookkeeping from those of performance, accountants have devised several modifications. The simplest is that of adopting accounting periods of uniform length. A second way is similar in that it assigns the constant cost in relation to the proportion that one period's sales is of total anticipated annual sales. A third method is to show separately a variance due to volume.

Another relatively recent approach is DIRECT COSTING. It begins with a separation of *direct costs* from *period costs.* In principle, direct costs are material, labor, and those portions of overhead costs that vary with production. *Period* costs are those just described as constant. The direct costs are deducted from sales income to reveal a *contribution to profit.* Then the period costs are subtracted to determine the net profit [1].

The advantages of direct costing can be combined with the necessities of absorption costing in one accounting system [2]. The important reason for doing so is to determine the return on capital invested in the production and sale of each of a company's several products. This boils down to finding correct product costs.

It is in this process that there are so many variations in accounting procedures for assigning overhead costs. The reason is that a simple average overhead rate is incorrect for non-average products. The general types of errors are suggested by Exhibit IV. Instinctively recognizing probable errors, some managers have selected different overhead rates. Often, however, such decisions are prejudiced by desires to make costs compare more favorably with prices. (This tendency shows through when an estimate for price quotation is handed back with some comment like, "Sharpen your pencil.")

Cost Centers. The usual method of breaking up an average overhead rate is to establish departmental, cost, or burden center rates. The least subdivision in this procedure is a machine or a workplace. In this step, some accountants consider overhead departments as cost centers and assign to them expenses such as heat, light, and janitorial. Most, however, assign overhead costs to production centers only.

To each cost center chosen are assigned some or all of the factory expenses deemed applicable. In this sorting, some accountants separate general factory expenses from those more directly related to production. Some treat similarly any portion of a headquarters cost that is charged to a factory. Such general expenses are usually assigned to manufactured products by means of an average rate. If no such separation is made, then accountants using departmental or cost center rates charge factory expenses to those centers.

EXHIBIT IV

ERRORS IN OVERHEAD ASSIGNMENT

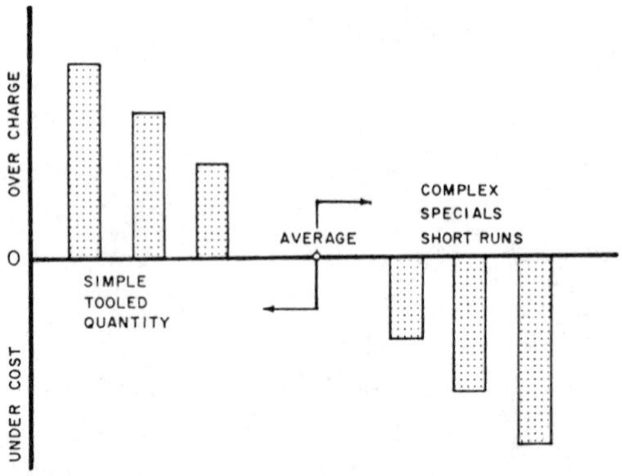

Average overhead rates tend to assign too much overhead cost to simple products, well-tooled operations, and quantity production and too little to complex products, special designs, and short runs. The more any of these differ from the average product, the greater are the errors in overhead assignment.

Interrelated Fundamentals. Underlying all of these approaches are two sets of interrelated fundamentals. These are (1) the types of costs and (2) the mechanics of overhead assignment. The types of costs are:

(a) *Cost of business done in a period of time.* This is concerned with past performance and usually is based on actual costs in that expenses such as sales and administrative, and variances from standard costs, where they exist, are written off.

(b) *Costs of existing and newly designed or proposed methods, parts, and products.* These are compiled as standard or estimated costs for predictive purposes. They are the costs managers need for comparison with current and probable prices and costs in planning the survival of the enterprise.

The mechanics of overhead assignment involve two fundamentals:

(a) *Volume used as the basis for assigning overhead costs.*

(b) *Factors chosen for making the cost assignments.*

Volume is disregarded, in effect, when a Profit & Loss statement is compiled for the recent past performance. But it has a very important bearing upon the calculation of overhead rates as portrayed in Exhibit III. Whether the volume used is the total output of a plant or a cost center, there may be errors in the resulting overhead rate because a total is used. In most companies, a total is a sum of parts that are not homogeneous. For example, sales dollars are mixtures of differing material contents, purchased or fabricated, as well as profit margins. Labor dollars are mixtures of unlike wage rates and productivities. Labor hours are mixtures of productivities and, often, times that are not direct labor, such as waiting and extra work mentioned earlier.

Further distortions in all such measures are caused by continuing changes in products, designs, methods and equipment. Such improvements, particularly those brought about by cost reduction efforts and work measurement installations, tend to reduce the volume of direct labor while increasing the related overhead expenses. All of these variations make the parts of a common denominator less alike. The basic premise of the common denominator is to obtain the equivalent of good salable pieces because the purpose is to get the overhead cost per piece.

The second method may compound the mixtures just described to the extent that volumes are used to assign overhead expense to products directly, or indirectly through cost centers. Examples are prorations made on the basis of labor dollars or hours.

Proration. To reduce both types of errors, a different approach should be used. It recognizes that many overhead expenses are related more to the several products themselves than to any type of cost center. This is about what Peter Drucker means when he writes, "The only realistic costing of a given product is one which assumes that costs other than raw material are total costs for a period of time divided by the number of items, without regard for the volume of each item" [3].

Therefore, generally, for complete realism, overhead costs should not be prorated on the assumption that each unit of volume is the same. Instead, each expense should be analyzed to determine its causes and their degrees. Each expense is then assigned to products according to the amounts used. For many expenses, this is done from counts or time records. As an example, the relatively large engineering costs of diversified products may be assigned to them by means of factors determined from engineering cost records. The effort is made to find a realistic way to assign each overhead expense to individual products as contrasted with using some single factor chosen as a compromise.

Thus expenses are assigned without regard to volume. This is important for two reasons. The first is that many overhead costs are like setups on production machines. They are relatively constant for a given type of sales or production order irrespective of quantity. For instance, it costs about the same to type an invoice for 35¢ as for $35.

Secondly, the total expense thus assigned to a product group can then be divided by the latter's own measure of volume. The conversion cost or overhead rate thus obtained would be correct for costing that product even if its measure of volume were inflated. In a simple example, suppose there are two products, A and B. Product A is made in large quantities, and its operations are on incentive. Product B is made in small lots, and, as is often the case, it is made on daywork. The productivity of Product A operations is double that of Product B operations. It takes 20 mins. to make one of A, and 40 mins. to make one item B. To keep out other variables, assume that the true overhead of either item is $1.00 each. With these figures, it is possible to build up the volume and overhead an accountant would have to start with. These are shown in the table given as Exhibit V. Common procedure is to divide the $450 total overhead by the 10,000 mins. total volume and get $.045 overhead cost per min. Overhead cost per piece is computed by multiplying $.045 by labor times as follows:

Product A: 20 mins. × $.045 = $.90 overhead assigned

Product B: 40 mins. × $.045 = $1.80 overhead assigned

If, instead, the overhead assigned to each product is divided by its measure of volume, the rate for Product A is $.050 per minute and for Product B $.025. When these product overhead rates are multiplied by their corresponding times, overhead costs are correctly assigned:

Product A: 20 mins. × $.050 = $1.00 overhead assigned

Product B: 40 mins × $.025 = $1.00 overhead assigned

The first set of overhead assignments reflects the error of using averages. Each error causes another. The overhead not assigned to one product is applied to another as illustrated by Exhibit IV. The second set of costs shows that when overhead expenses are assigned by analysis and then are divided by volumes that are more homogeneous, the resulting costs are more correct.

It should be evident from the foregoing that there are no accurate costs. All of the various approaches are but different ways to reduce the errors in overhead assignment. All but the final method have parts of the same three errors in common. One is the use of mixed units of volume added together as though they were all alike. The second is the assignment of overhead expenses in combinations to products or cost centers. The worst cases occur when combinations are total factory overhead or total sales and administrative. The third is the proration of overhead expense. Proration presupposes the value of each unit of measure to be the same. This method disregards both the existence of constant expenses earlier described as setups, and the different degrees of overhead cost that unlike products require.

Errors in overhead costing can be reduced by doing more assigning and less prorating. This approach is applicable to either absorption or direct costing. Regardless of costing plan, it is important to show the correct relation between the price of a product and its cost to make, sell, deliver, and service. Two reasons are vital. One is that ". . . the market price level of the product will tend to be set largely by the lowest cost arrived at by the different systems of overhead" [4].

The other is that the trend in industry is toward raising both constant and variable overhead costs by substituting better methods and equipment for some parts of direct labor. The extreme example is the completely automated plant where *everybody* is overhead. Each step taken in this direction can exaggerate errors made in overhead assignment unless more detailed analyses are used to replace simple prorations.

PHIL CARROLL, Industrial Engineer, Maplewood, New Jersey

EXHIBIT V

Prod.	*Quantity*	*Correct Overhead*	*Mins. Each*	*Volume Mins.*	*Overhead Cost/Min.*
A	400	$400	20	8,000	$.050
B	50	50	40	2,000	.025
		$450		10,000	$.045 Av.

Information References

Carroll, Phil, "How To Control Production Costs," New York, McGraw-Hill, 1953.

Carroll, Phil, "Profit Control—How To Plug Profit Leaks," Chap. 15, New York, McGraw-Hill, 1962.

Carroll, Phil, "Budgets and Cost Control," chap. in Heyel, Carl, ed., "The Foreman's Handbook," New York, McGraw-Hill, 4th ed., 1967.

References Cited

[1] Wright, Wilmer, "Direct Standard Costs," New York, McGraw-Hill, 1962.

[2] Kelley, Harry P., "A System Integrating Direct Cost in, Standard Costs, Flexible Budgets and Return on Investment," *Business Budgeting,* June 1959.

[3] Drucker, Peter, "Product Scatter," p. 101, *Nation's Business,* March 1962.

[4] Newman, Louis E., "Diseases That Make Whole Industries Sick," *Harvard Business Rev.,* March-April 1961.

Cross References: *Cost Accounting; Direct Costing; Flexible Budgeting; Standard Costing.*

OWEN, ROBERT

Robert Owen (1771–1858) was a textile mill employee who advanced to the position of managing director of a group of textile mills in

New Lanark, Scotland. During the years 1800–1828, as manager of these mills, he carried out an unprecedented experiment in industrial human relations which transformed the lives of the New Lanark textile workers. First, he set himself to improve the factory and domestic conditions of his employees, building streets and houses, and setting up workers' shops which sold necessities at cost price. The minimum working age for children was raised, and working hours were decreased. Facilities for meals were provided at the mills, and the surroundings of the mills themselves were made more attractive. Second, he undertook social reforms, creating a model community out of his mill town. The New Lanark schools, in which he instituted educational reforms, attracted many visitors from home and abroad. Owen emphasized that personnel management must not bear a "welfare" or "charity" label if it is to secure employee support. He also urged that the personnel function must not be a subordinate department of management, but must be identified with the purpose of good management itself. In 1828 he retired from executive work and devoted the remaining 30 years of his life to campaign in the press and in public speaking for the more general acceptance of his ideas of social reform. A representative selection of Owen's writing will be found in "A New View of Society," edited by G.D.H. Cole (London, Everyman, 1927).

Information Reference

Urwick, L., "The Golden Book of Management," edited for the International Committee of Scientific Management (CIOS), London, Newman Neame, Limited, 1956.

P

PACKAGING: Legal and Ethical Aspects

Today, more than ever before, it is necessary to understand the **Legal and Ethical Aspects of Packaging.** The legal concerns have become self-evident in the past few years. The ethical considerations are rapidly becoming legal factors too, and unless industry finds solutions for some of these problems, it will be faced with more and more "protective" legislation.

That more and more government control is being placed on industry is reflected in the statements of numerous authorities in business and education. Jesse S. Raphael sums it up in the foreword to his book on government regulations by pointing out that all those conducting or assisting in conducting business must be aware of the intensification of the power of government, especially the Federal Government, over the daily activities of private business [1]. This is further amplified by the editors of *Modern Packaging Encyclopedia* who state: "Now, as never before, packaging's decision makers will have to ponder the question of legality before starting any new packaging or surface-design program. To assume that what was acceptable last year will pass muster this year (or next) is to make, in the words of an unsung philosopher, 'the wrong mistake.' . . . Failure to measure up to the demands of packaging laws can be most expensive since the costs of legal defense and possible loss of reputation may have to be added to the expense of compliance. Definitely, the problems are such that they will not go away if ignored" [2]. This is as true today as when the Encyclopedia appeared a decade and a half ago.

It is not within the scope of this article to discuss the details of all the Federal, state, and local legislation that affects packaging. Such details can be found by consulting the pertinent laws as issued by the various governmental agencies. However, a brief description of important packaging regulation is given.

Background. One of the most controversial and most important pieces of legislation passed in recent years, as far as packagers are concerned, was the Fair Packaging and Labeling Act (Public Law (89–755). This was signed into law by President Johnson on November 3, 1966.

Although the Federal Meat Inspection Act of 1906 was one of the first laws requiring informative and truthful labeling, legislation with more widespread impact on packaging appeared later: The principal regulations concerning packaging of most consumer articles were contained in the Food, Drug, and Cosmetic Act of 1938, with the Food Additives Amendment of 1958; the Federal Trade Commission Act of 1914; and the Hazardous Substances Labeling Act of 1960. Other important legislation at the Federal level followed the Fair Packaging and Labeling Act.

The 1950s saw the start of agitation for new laws and amendments to old laws affecting packaging. This was intensified in the 1960s, and many diverse groups and individuals became self-proclaimed experts on protecting the consumer. Politicians, college professors, labor union officials, television stars, and magazine editors became authorities, and flooded communication media with stories about the need to protect the consumer from all sorts of malpractices, including packaging.

In 1959, the Food and Drug Administration cautioned that colored wrappings for produce were acceptable as long as they were not used to make the produce look better or more expensive than it really was.

In the early 1960s, Senator Phillip A. Hart of Michigan introduced legislation in the U.S. Senate to control the labeling and packaging of consumer products. This was promptly endorsed by the newly formed Consumer Advisory Council (1963), which had been instituted at the request of President Kennedy.

The pressure continued to mount, and, in the opinion of some observers, the packaging industry did not do a very convincing or effective job of defending itself. The Fair Packaging and Labeling Act was enacted, and many packagers are thankful that it is not more restrictive than it is. At the time, it appeared that the FPLA would only be the beginning, and the passage of time has seen much additional legislation. Today, the appeal for additional legislation is stronger than ever, and consumers activists are not satisified with the packaging legislation enacted so far.

The attitude of some public officials continues to be reflected by a statement made by

Senator Hart concerning the Fair Packaging and Labeling Act. He pointed out that his original bill stated that it was a policy of the United States to assist consumers in "facilitating price comparisons." He further pointed out that the word "price" was deliberately changed by the House to read "value." He went on to say that this meant that the policy of Congress has been enlarged to include "quality" comparisons. In his words, "This *'quality'* element has vastly greater implications than the more limited concept of 'price.' For instance, it opens the door to consideration of legislation such as grade labeling and governmental testing of consumer products." He ended his analysis with the observation that it was his belief that passage of the bill in its final form was a historic breakthrough. He further stated that this historic breakthrough was the beginning of a long and successful program of consumer-assistance legislation [3].

Recent Federal Packaging Legislation. Other, more recent Federal legislation with an impact on packaging is the Poison Prevention Packaging Act of 1970, which regulates packaging for various prescription and nonprescription drugs and household chemicals such as solvents and cleansers. This legislation, enforced by the Food and Drug Administration, requires safety closures or child-resistant flexible packaging for products that may harm a child should the product be ingested as a result of curiosity.

Safety closures are designed, in general, to frustrate attempts to open a package by young children—typically those under the age of five. Most safety closures operate in a way that takes advantage of a child's limited mechanical skills—such as the inability to push down, or to squeeze, while at the same time turning the closure. Or their inability (or unlikelyhood, randomly) to register or "line-up" two components in a closure, thus to open the container or actuate an aerosol valve.

Legislation of a generally similar nature, but applying more directly to products than to packaging, is embodied in the Child Protection and Toy Safety Act of 1969. In addition, the Consumer Product Safety Commission has authority to operate in the packaging arena if a question of consumer safety is involved.

The Department of Transportation has authority, under the Hazardous Materials Transportation Act (Public Law 93-633, published under Title 49 in the U.S. Code of Federal Regulations) to regulate packaging for a broad range of products that are classified (in the Code) as hazardous. Such products are listed by name, and include categories of items that are poisonous, explosive, corrosive, radioactive, flammable, or the like. Specific package sizes and types are required by this law, and quantities of products that may be shipped are prescribed.

Other packaging requirements are determined, not by legislative bodies, but by coming into effect under the power of contract. These are the packaging requirements established in freight classifications which set minimum standards for packaging materials, components, and structural design. The National Motor Freight Classification governs package requirements for goods shipped by common motor carrier, and the Uniform Freight Classification governs packaging for shipment by rail. These are published by respective freight classification committees. Other major areas of law that impact on packaging, but that are not "packaging law," per se, include patent law, trademark law, and copyright law. Much of what appears in package surface graphics is either trademarked or copyrighted, and some useful package design features can be patented. These practices are aimed at protecting unique features in packaging for exclusive use by a particular company. (See COPYRIGHT; TRADEMARKS; TRADEMARKS: INTERNATIONAL PROTECTION.)

State Laws. One major aspect of package compliance to regulatory standards does not come under Federal regulations: the conformance of the package to weights and measures standards. There is a model Federal law, after which some states pattern weights and measures regulations. Enforcement of "full packages" is left up to the individual states.

The area experiencing the most rapid change in terms of increasing regulation today has to do with attempts to control disposal of solid wastes and litter. Most of the legislation to date comes under the popular heading of "bottle laws." Effective control of waste and litter is one of the gravest problems facing our nation today, and all packaging suppliers and users must concern themselves with dealing with the problems. Not only do packagers have an ethical obligation to be concerned, but it is also a matter of good business. If they do not help eliminate or at least minimize the problem, they face the possibility of additional governmental regulation that could be far more restrictive to their operations than any voluntary program they could possibly formulate.

It was estimated in 1973 that some 42 million tons of used packaging materials had to be disposed of. Estimates of the proportion of packaging waste to the total solid-waste disposal problem range from 12% to 33%, depending on the source; however, nearly everyone agrees that the absolute tonnage will increase, based on current data. This will not be due to increased population alone. We will have used about 158 pounds more of packaging materials per capita in 1980 than were used in 1970. Chief among the factors contributing to this increase is the continuing rise in the demand for self-service merchandising of products.

Litter. Although the increase in waste from packaging materials alone has already presented a formidable collection and disposal task, a much greater problem is going to result if our present litter practices continue. It is not possible to tell how much packaging material, on a tonnage basis, becomes litter, but it is known that well over one half of the items in today's litter are packages or package components [4].

Evidence of the role that packaging plays in litter can be found in statistics that show that Americans must dispose of 48 billion cans, 25 billion bottles and jars, 65 billion metal and plastic caps and crowns, plus many billions of paper, paperboard, and plastic packages. A trade association studied a composite mile of highway in five states, finding 2,665 pieces of litter, the chief components being paper packages, cans, and bottles, in that order.

The fact that package manufacturers and users bear the brunt of the blame for litter is evident from a review of legislation which has been proposed recently. Each session of local, state, and even Federal legislatures seems to bring new bills which have a variety of potential impacts on packaging. One recent article indicates that some 1,200 bills, in nearly every state, are in various stages of the legislative process. However, as of this writing, only a few states have enacted laws which require deposits on beverage containers, or which ban the use of one-trip beverage containers—Oregon, Vermont, Michigan, and South Dakota.

A good deal of controversy is associated with legislation that restricts the use of particular types of containers. Although the Oregon law requiring a deposit on beverage containers has been in effect since late 1972, there is still much disagreement as to whether it has been effective in reducing litter, and whether there has been a loss of jobs within the state because of the bill.

As municipalities continue to struggle with problems of waste disposal and litter, it seems inevitable that further legislation will be proposed to limit the use of, or ban outright, certain kinds of containers, or that will restrict, in some way, the manufacture of containers that work against convenient recycling of materials, or that do not lend themselves to convenient methods of disposal.

Ethical Considerations. Finally, packaging for all kinds of products has an ethical or moral dimension. At the very least, this requires that packaging be done in a professional and competent manner. There are various written codes that indicate that the packaging professional is to ply his craft in a way that will not bring discredit to himself or his company.

Beyond this, however, it seems that the packaging professional should do all within his control to assure that the customer is not deceived. There is a continuing discussion of what constitutes deceptive packaging, and the Fair Packaging and Labeling Act is one attempt to make sure that the customer gets all that the package promises to deliver. Some products require large packages for small items—to help reduce pilferage, for example, but packages should not be designed to appear large while delivering small amounts of product. Nor should they appear to promise, say, in terms of package performance (or imply, on the package, product performance) more than can be delivered.

Almost anyone will buy almost anything one time. If the package (and/or product in it) does not do what is implied by graphics or structure, the customer will not return. So, even if it is only a matter of the economic preservation of business, good sense requires that packaging not be deceptive.

HAROLD J. RAPHAEL, PH.D., Director, and DAVID L. OLSSON, PH.D., Professor, Department of Packaging Science, Rochester Institute of Technology, Rochester, New York

Information References

Bierlein, L.W., "Red Book on Transportation of Hazardous Materials," Boston, CBI, 1977.

Burge, David A., "Patent and Trademark Tactics and Practice," New York, Wiley, 1980.

Buell, V.P. and Heyel, C., eds, "Handbook of Modern Marketing," Section 16, New York, McGraw-Hill, 1970.

Hicks, Lawrence D., "Coping With Packaging Laws," New York, American Management Associations,
Raphael, H.J. and Olsson, D.L., "Package Production Management," Westport, Conn., Avi, 2nd ed., 1976. (The above article, updated, follows the treatment in this book, by permission of the publishers.)
Sacharow, S., "Packaging Regulations," Westport, Conn., Avi, 1979.

References Cited

[1] Raphael, J.S., "Government Regulation in Business," New York, Free Press, 1966.
[2] *Modern Packaging Encyclopedia,* "Guide to Packaging Law," New York, McGraw-Hill, 1967.
[3] Hart, P.A., "Analysis of the Truth in Packaging Bill," (Washington, DC: Senate Office Building, Office of Senator Hart), undated.
[4] Darnay, A.J., Jr., "The Role of Packaging in Solid Waste," Statement before Subcommittee on Science, Research, and Development of the Committee on Science and Astronautics, U.S. House of Representatives, Feb. 2, 1968.

Cross References: *Packaging: Organizing for Package Development (and cross references there given).*

PACKAGING: Organizing for Package Development

The proper location of the **Package Development** function within a company will depend upon the type of business activity. Businesses predominantly in drugs, foods, and cosmetics are oriented more toward marketing and research than toward engineering, and find it logical to locate the package development function in Marketing or as a special staff operation. Package development for industrial products, hardware, appliances, and products which require protective shipping or have special use features, is often in Engineering or Production. Some companies have their Package Development Department located independently of other management functions (Marketing; Purchasing), and positioned at equal corporate stature.

Personnel. The handling of a package development program can range from a part-time job of a buyer, a limited function of an engineer, researcher, or graphic-arts expert, to the full-time responsibility of a Director of Package Development. A few companies have the individual in charge of the packaging function positioned as high as Vice President—Packaging.

Where the total responsibility is not delegated to one individual, the function is split among various departments. Often this means a Package Committee, composed of the heads of each department involved. The committee approach is being utilized less frequently. The trend now is to professionalization—requiring a Packaging Director or Coordinator of Packaging.

The qualifications necessary for the person responsible for the function will vary with each industry, but he or she must know packaging materials, components, methods, and equipment. In establishing personnel requirements, consideration should be given to the routine functions which may be conducted presently by other departments but which could be transferred to package development. For a rule of thumb, a company with 200 employees should have at least one person specializing in package development. With the use of a scheduling system, one trained individual can directly supervise many technicians in a packaging department.

Scope. A complete packaging program includes: (1) planning and coordination of package development activities throughout the organization; (2) conducting research in packaging materials properties, container performance, or marketing characteristics; (3) developing new packages for new products, or redesigning packaging for existing products, and engineering the technical performance of container systems; (4) testing materials and containers; (5) writing specifications; (6) assembling and storing of information, samples, etc.; and (7) analyzing packaging (return goods and value analysis). An effective initial procedure is to list current packaging activities, problems, and projects throughout the company. This list will help answer such questions as: How much duplication of effort occurs? Do any records of value exist? Are they organized for easy reference?

Planning and Coordinating Package Development. There is no established program for all industry, with respect to the functions to be mentioned here. However, a review of these functions will indicate the advantages of establishing a focal point for proper control.

Product Data. For a new product, product data must be obtained from Research (or, if necessary, produced by the package development group). A product-data checklist should be designed, covering all pertinent aspects of the product, including: special processing (if container and product are processed simultaneously); protection required by the product against light, oxygen, foreign odors, insects and rodents, shock and vibration, and the like, during the product's expected shelf life; and special packing protection, dispensing, and the like.

Package Data. Information to be sought here includes:

(1) Detailed description of the uses of the product, the conditions under which it is used, the type of user, and any supplementary devices used with the product.

(2) Sizes, possible combinations of packages, sample packages, special packages for particular markets, and the various put-ups required.

(3) Predicted volume: minimum order quantities for packaging components below which costs begin to soar, so that materials with prohibitive costs can be eliminated early.

(4) Processing of product and existing packaging facilities; special processing (sterilization, vacuum packaging, etc.); automated equipment and machine limitations.

(5) Channels of distribution: requirements for storage, shipping, handling, marketing, etc.

(6) Promotional requirements: The package should almost always be designed with features which will draw attention and please the consumer. Promotional requirements are dictated by the channel of distribution, advertising media, and type of consumer. Increasingly, consumer-convenience features are being incorporated in the package to provide an added factor for promotion, to extend penetration into new markets, and to encourage more effective product use.

(7) Legal requirements: legal aspects of the copy; patentable devices; Food and Drug Administration approval, deceptive packaging; etc. (See PACKAGING: LEGAL AND ETHICAL ASPECTS.)

(8) Research or pharmacological requirements, where applicable: sterility, design of anatomical devices, dosages, and similar aspects.

(9) Labeling, use directions, recipes. (Often these are the most important means of producing repeat use as well as intitial sales.)

Package Research. From information and samples it is possible to screen a new material or package for application in the product lines. Testing of all or even many new materials is, of course, not practical. By comparing the advantages and disadvantages of both the present material and a new candidate, many reasons why the material should or should not be tested will become obvious. Reasons for eliminating a new material from consideration include:

(1) It lacks one or more absolute requirements of the package, such as clarity, ease of tear, flexibility, rigidity, required barrier properties, capability of running on the production line, etc. However, one should determine whether modifications might not overcome the problem.

(2) While it has the required characteristics, it is more expensive than the present material.

(3) It offers all advantages of the present material and is less costly, but the yearly volume is so small that the cost of testing would not be justified.

(4) If accepted, it would require the purchase of new packaging equipment that could not be justified by anticipated volume.

Development and Engineering. Systematic procedures will simplify the determination of the right package from the great mass of materials, components, ideas, methods, and cost variations available. After it has been shown that necessary requirements will be satisfied, additional features can be incorporated.

Materials. From the product data covered previously, suitable materials must be determined. A review of files, catalogs, and published charts may produce a list of potential materials. However, it is sometimes necessary to search the supplier market (laminators, can, bottle, carton, or shipping container suppliers; liner manufacturers; basic plastic-resin manufacturers) for materials with particular characteristics. All potential materials must be further classified by advantages and disadvantages. For example, a transparent film may afford superior appearance (and eventual sales) but have a higher cost than a foil laminate. Materials with the greatest advantages must be tested under controlled simulated storage, shipping, use, and other important conditions. A similar process is used to determine the material for devices, intermediate packaging, and shipping containers.

Design. With the material selected, the type of packaging which may be manufactured is limited to available manufacturing processes (molding, extruding, laminating, etc.). Again, exploration, testing, and screening are necessary to determine which type of package—can, dish, tube, bottle or jar, carton, set-up box, flexible film or lamination, etc.—is best. Dimensional and design characteristics must be determined in relation to the requirements listed previously. Convenience features for dispensing or use should be investigated. Most package development departments have a collection of idea-stimulating sources. Visits to retail establishments (for consumer packaging ideas) are fruitful.

Available services of suppliers should be utilized, where possible, for preliminary tests and screening. It is sometimes necessary to obtain the services of commercial laboratories and consultants.

Copy. Sales promotion and research usually determine original copy for printed items. Package development must constantly check for size, color, copy, location of printing, and quality of workmanship.

Time. With experience, it is possible to estimate the time required to complete a development. Periodic recording of time needed to perform isolated development functions will furnish a valuable reference.

Testing. Package development performs two types of tests. First, performance claims made by suppliers must be verified. Second, functional tests determine whether a proposed package can withstand the rigors of processing, distribution, use, and environmental conditions of storage and retailing. Ideally, the entire life of the package should be simulated. However, experienced package development personnel can predict the durability and suitability of many materials and components under various conditions.

It is wise to permit the same individual to conduct all similar tests within one project. In this way, subjective values reported will be consistent and comparable.

Specifications. After development and approval, complete specifications must be prepared. At the minimum, the specifications should protect against use of packaging which does not meet the requirements in function, quality, or assurance of constant quality. Exacting, high-speed equipment, secondary processing (autoclaving, etc.), color matching of components, severe handling or storage conditions, and the like are common in today's large-scale packaging operations. Failure in any one of these can affect the others.

Each attribute of the material, component, or container listed in the specification should be labeled as *critical, major,* or *minor.* The acceptable quality level (AQL) can be established on this classification. Where many variations of one type of component are involved, it may be simpler to develop a manual which lists all similar specifications, with a supplemental sheet indicating the individual differences.

Color Standards. Color standards can be established by (1) accumulating present stock samples, (2) requesting a special run from a supplier, (3) requesting standards through the supplier's ink house, or (4) having them printed by a local printer. Northern daylight is the established light under which color matching is performed. Once color standards have been established, spectrophotometric readings can be obtained from the ink house for a small fee. This will enable a matching of the original colors, which are apt to change over extended periods of time. (The Container Corporation of America has developed a "Color Harmony Manual" to aid in color selection and control.

Pantone, Inc. also has a "coordinated matching system" of standardized and number-identified colors to facilitate designer/supplier/user communication.)

Information and Samples. Information files are set up under several broad categories: (1) basic materials; (2) type of component; (3) activities (e.g., testing, specification-writing, scheduling methods, etc.); (4) suppliers; (5) machinery and equipment; (6) specific subjects (color tables and charts, etc.). Samples may save thousands of words. Samples can be filed or stored in two categories: (1) materials; and (2) type of component.

Project files, test-report files, and specification files complete the major information aspects.

Packaging Analysis. The magnitude and complexity of package development call for constant vigilance. One barometer of packaging is the condition of returned goods. A periodic review of these will indicate necessary changes. A check with other companies will indicate a norm which should be expected in such things as bottle breakage, leakage of liquids, container failures, etc. High returns are, of course, danger signals. The general appearance and function of packaging should also be evaluated periodically. And occasional visits to retailers, wholesalers, distributors, and other segments of a distribution cycle will often uncover areas for improvement or cost reduction.

Value Analysis. A period review of each component of packaging in use will indicate many areas where substitution and change are possible. These include (1) material composition; (2)

size; (3) design; and (4) finish. Cost savings are often possible through standardization, and occasionally, by eliminating obsolete requirements. (See VALUE ENGINEERING.)

BERNARD F. MAJOR, formerly Manager, Package Development Laboratory, Ortho Pharmaceutical Corporation, Raritan, New Jersey, and, for third edition, DAVID L. OLSSON, PH.D, Professor, Department of Packaging Science, Rochester Institute of Technology, Rochester, New York

Information References

"The Kline Guide to the Packaging Industry," 4th ed., Fairfield, N.J., Charles H. Kline & Co., Inc., 1980.

Associations:

American Management Associations, Packaging Div.
Society of Packaging and Handling Engineers.
There is a thorough listing of trade associations in Section 10 of "The Kline Guide to the Packaging Industry," referenced above.

Texts:

Buel, Victor P. and Heyel, Carl, eds., "Handbook of Modern Marketing," Section 16, New York, McGraw-Hill, 1970.
Dichter, Ernest, "Packaging: The Sixth Sense?," Boston, Cahners Books, 1975.
Landsdale, David B., "The Vital Signs of Effective Packaging Management," AMA Briefing, New York, American Management Associations, 1978.
Leonard, Edmund A., "Managing the Packaging Side of the Business," AMA Briefing, New York, American Management Associations, 1977.
Raphael, Harold J. and Olsson, David L., "Package Production Management," Westport, Conn., Avi, 1976.

Cross References: *Copyright; Industrial Design; Packaging: Legal and Ethical Aspects; Packaging, Protective: The Systems Approach; Trademarks.*

PACKAGING, PROTECTIVE: The Systems Approach

With rare exceptions, commodities entering the physical distribution chain require at least some protection against the stresses they may expect to suffer en route to their point of consumption.

This is the fundamental function of **Protective Packaging:** to guard the goods against in-transit damage. Most frequently the damage feared is of a purely physical nature: breakage, dents, etc., due to buffeting and rough handling. There are, however, other types of damage which must be guarded against in specific circumstances. For example, foodstuffs and certain other products must be protected against spoilage, contamination, and the like.

A relatively new role for protective packaging relates to the increased incidence of crime in the public transportation system. Packaging techniques may be employed either to render theft-susceptible goods more difficult to steal (generally through unitization into large aggregates too cumbersome for the casual thief), or to disguise their nature. Manufacturers and vendors of television sets, radios, wristwatches, jewelry, electronic components, alcoholic liquors, tobacco products, automotive parts and accessories, etc.—traditionally among the most tempting goods to thieves—are increasingly marking their packages in codes, with all advertising removed, in an effort to thwart the criminals.

The degree and type of packaging needed depends almost totally on the nature of the goods being moved. Where the damage sought to be protected against is physical, industrial packaging engineers seek to determine impact points, areas of weakness, and other shipping characteristics in order to design the optimum packaging system. Among the materials available for use in containers are cardboard, corrugated paperboard, wood, wood-and-wire combinations, metal, plastic, styrofoam, etc. Numerous other commodities ranging from the traditional crumpled newspapers and excelsior to sophisticated (and reusable) cellulose and plastic foam substances, may be employed as dunnage, in order further to cushion the product against harm. Shrink-wrap and vacuum-pack systems are used to protect perishables where necessary.

Especially within the past decade, a new element has invaded the field of protective packaging. It has become widely recognized that packaging techniques may be employed to achieve significant economies in the physical distribution process. This function is exemplified by that most efficient of packages, the large intermodal container, which can travel as an unchanged unit from one carrier to another—truck to train to ship or plane.

From the standpoint of protection, the container is a highly utilitarian form of packaging. Its structural strength affords the most complete protection against physical damage; it may be refrigerated or subjected to atmospheric control to prevent contamination or spoilage of perishables, and its size and strength will deter all but the most ambitious and determined of thieves.

In addition to this, the container affords the

potential for major physical distribution economies. Its size and weight brings transportation economies-of-scale within reach, and the normal low loss-and-damage claims ratios provide a further economic incentive. For-hire transportation firms have generally recognized these advantages by establishing especially low rate levels on goods moving in containers, to the economic benefit of their customers as well as themselves.

Unfortunately, certain problems continue to beset containerization. Internecine conflicts within the transportation community, and outmoded legal restrictions imposed on that community, limit the use of containers in many cases. Theoretically, a containerized shipment is capable of portal-to-portal movement via any combination of rail, motor or water carriage; and the new "jumbo jet" aircraft are technologically capable of joining in this *de facto* consortium of modes. However, carrier or regulatory restrictions on container interchange, union insistence on needlessly unloading and repacking the containers in some cases, and similar occurrences deprive containerization of a good deal of its potential. Hopefully, these limitations will diminish in the course of time, permitting at least a closer approach to the full potential. Some gains have already been realized as a result of 1980 legislation that reduced or eliminated many impending regulatory restraints.

Containerization is actually just one aspect of a broader approach to the problem of packaging, which goes under the generic name "unitization." Pallets, airline "igloos," modular containers of various sorts, cargo nets, and other instrumentalities are also used to achieve similar objectives. Behind these developments runs the basic attitude that the larger and more enclosed a package becomes, the more easily, safely, and economically it may be shipped.

The same trend is visible in the handling of bulk commodities. Specially designed bulk carriers, of all modes, are growing increasingly larger and more sophisticated; at once they offer greater protection to the commodities being shipped, and a greater potential for consolidation into ever larger units of shipment. Among the more interesting developments in this area is the tendency to employ bulk-handling methods wherever possible, sometimes in instances where they would not appear on the surface to be applicable. Even that reputedly "perfect" natural package, the eggshell, has been discarded in the interests of bulk unitization; raw eggs are now shelled at or near their origin, and shipped on to destination in refrigerated liquid bulk vehicles.

Because of this broader role, packaging is becoming increasingly interwoven into the physical distribution management system. Packaging determinations are most often made within a company's physical distribution or traffic department, in recognition of the major role packaging can play with regard to physical distribution and transportation costs. In this systems approach, protective packaging is regarded as a physical distribution subsystem, which both affects and is affected by other subsystems such as traffic/transportation, material handling, warehousing, inventory control, and so forth.

As an example of how these factors are inseparably affiliated with protective packaging, it is clearly impossible to design or procure an efficient material handling system without reference to the form in which the company's goods are packaged. It is equally impossible to establish a warehouse operation without regard to packaging, or to effectuate inventory control procedures. To be sure, sales/marketing and production considerations enter into decisions concerning protective packaging, but for the majority of industrial concerns its most important affiliation is to the physical distribution area of operations.

COLIN BARRETT, Transportation Consultant, Reston, Virginia.

Cross References: *Packaging: Organizing for Package Development (and cross references there given).*

PATENTS

Patents secure potentially valuable property rights in inventions. It is essential that management have a good insight into the business and legal considerations affecting patents, so that sensible patent policies can be set and sensibly administered. Failure of communication where patents are involved is common. Deceptive over-simplification and imbalance of short-term and long-term goals can be costly. If the intertwined legal and business aspects of patents are to be profitably analyzed, management must be knowledgeable and perceptive in both areas.

Historical Perspective. The patent laws of the United States are the enactment of a remarkably stable Federal policy contemplated by the authors of the United States Constitution: "The Congress shall have power . . . To promote the progress of . . . useful arts, by securing for limited times to . . . inventors the exclusive right to their respective . . . discoveries."

Congress early availed itself of its power by a law enacted in 1790. The current statutes approached their present form by the general revision effected by the Patent Act of 1836. Present patent law is, specifically, embodied in Federal statutes collected and revised in 1952 as Title 35 of the United States Code. A Presidential Commission appointed in 1965 recommended statutory revisions having the effect of conforming the U.S. patent laws to a greater extent with those of foreign countries, but no such drastic changes were enacted. While minor statutory changes have been made since the Patent Act of 1952, the major changes have been made by the decisional law of the Federal courts, explaining and interpreting the patent statutes in the light of the constitutional purpose. The decisions are usually made in resolution of infringement litigation where patent validity is also an issue.

The U.S. Patent and Trademark Office, formerly entitled and still known as the Patent Office, is an agency in the Department of Commerce under the Commissioner of Patents. It has the duty of examining each application for a patent and granting the patent if the application meets the statutory requirements. Since the examination requires intensive expertise in the gamut of specialized technologies, the Patent Office function becomes more difficult to perform well with each order of magnitude accumulation of technological knowledge. Patent Office resistance to the examination of computer programs reflects concern over its ability to search out and apply prior-art evidence in a satisfactory manner. Criticisms of delays and uncertainty in both the Patent Office and the courts have been prevalent. The courts have invalidated over half of the patents before them, but usually on the basis of evidence unavailable to the Patent Office when it made a favorable patentability decision in granting the patent. Recent reform attempts have centered on measures for bringing more of the prior-art evidence to the attention of the Examiner during examination or re-examination.

The purpose and philosophy of the patent law remain as expressed in the Constitution. The patent law creates, as a property right in inventions, the right to exclude others for a limited period of years from the use of an invention. The basic rationale is that in return for publication of a new discovery or invention, the public undertakes to respect the inventor's exclusive rights for a limited time. Historically letters patent in England were exclusive trade privileges and monopolies granted to royal favorites. In 1623 the Statute of Monopolies abolished such privileges, although an exception was made under limited conditions where new manufacturers were involved. This heritage, in which patents for new inventions were a valued exception to a jealously enforced older tradition of freedom of commerce, gave rise to the patent system of the American Republic.

The definition or standard of patentable invention has been, and will continue to be, difficult and uncertain in application in view of the continuing concern with maintaining a proper line between "good" and "bad" monopolies. For over a century, the standard which has been most often applied recognizes new and useful contributions to an art as inventions only when they are beyond the usual skill to be expected of one familiar with and skilled in the art. It is frequently stated, with some semblance of statistical support, that the standard of patentable invention has been higher during the past several decades. Certainly the level of the expected or ordinary skill of the art increases as knowledge in that art increases and the difficulty of finding nonobvious improvements can be expected to increase with it. The difficulty of courts of general jurisdiction in comprehending technical fact issues in the many technologies likely to be involved can also be expected to increase.

Impact of Patent Laws. The patent system today provides incentive to continued investment in research. It serves to bring the fruits of research to market through the exclusivity offered by patent rights in recouping the cost and risk involved. Patent protection is also an incentive to public disclosure of new inventions, which might otherwise be secretly practiced. Whether or not secret use is a real alternative to patents in today's technology depends upon the situation; a head start of a few months may be adequate to recoup research costs in some cases and totally inadequate in others. The head start afforded by a patent rarely extends to the seventeen year patent term since most inventions in a changing technology do not have that long a useful life, but a head start need not be long to be profitable. It may sometimes operate usefully by causing competitors to design around the patented invention rather than copy it.

Inventions may be happy accidents, and their source is by no means confined to engineers and scientists, or to persons normally considered the most skilled or the most knowledgeable in the art involved. No pedigree is required. Nevertheless, most inventions are made by people who know enough of a problem at least to recognize an answer. Research and development departments must interact effectively with such people, and maintain follow-up effort in the more promising areas.

Much research simply is not patentable, no matter how useful. This may, of course, simply make it essential that the invention-bearing portion be all the more carefully examined as potential patent property. In most instances the costs of securing patents is only a small proportion of the research bill involved in making the invention, and in many instances the prospective patent rights offer the only likely basis for recovering R&D expense. Companies which do not move promptly to patent or otherwise publish inventions have no assurance that others with or without the benefit of research will not perfect patent rights in the same subject matter.

The Language of Patents. The patent literature contains meaningful words, which must be carefully employed, and jargon, which should be avoided. Important consequences may hang upon distinctions between terms.

Starting with the ultimate term, an *invention* is a thing newly created or discovered. *Discovery* is often employed as a synonym. Usually *patentable invention* is intended. An invention to be patentable in the United States must meet the three conditions of *utility, novelty,* and *unobviousness.* Satisfaction of the last-named condition is measured by the hypothetical *person skilled in the art.* That is, would the *new* and *useful* invention have been *obvious* to such a person, assuming he knew all the *prior art? Prior art* is the term for knowledge existing prior to the time the inventor made what he believed to be a new invention. Such knowledge is most readily proved when it is contained in a prior *printed publication,* such as a patent. Before the unobviousness condition was made statutory, the extra measure beyond utility and novelty required for patenting was called the *standard of invention.*

Less troublesome administratively than the *statutory conditions for patentability* are other statutory provisions for which resort to pertinent *decisional law,* representing adjudicated interpretations, usually furnishes a greater degree of guidance.

The *statutory classes* of patentable inventions are limited to *machine* or *manufacture* (i.e., apparatus), *process,* and *composition of matter.* These categories are broadly interpreted to cover technological improvements or, in the constitutional phrase, the *useful arts.* If the invention is useful only for further research, it may not qualify as patentable subject matter.

Outside of the discussion here of such "regular" (or *utility*) patents and generally of minor importance in their impact upon horticulture and the fine arts, are *patents* and *design* (i.e., ornamental design) *patents. Statutory* bars are legal conditions specified by the patent statutes and preclude patentability absolutely. For example, if the application for a patent is filed more than one year after the first date an invention is described in a *printed publication* anywhere or is placed in *public use* or *on sale* in this country, the patent is invalid. A statutory condition is that only the *inventor* may apply for a U.S. patent on an invention; however, the term *patentee* also includes the *assignee,* who is the successor in title of the inventor's patent rights.

The history of an invention and the procedure for patenting it bring several terms into focus. The birthdate of an invention is its *conception,* the complete mental realization of a workable solution to a problem or appraisal of a discovery. An invention is completed when it is *reduced to practice* by successfully demonstrating it under realistic conditions. *A disclosure* as a written or oral description of the invention is not necessarily a formal document. When a written disclosure meeting the various Patent Office requirements is filed in the United States Patent Office, it becomes an *application* identifiable by an official *serial number* and *filing date.* So long as the application is not *abandoned,* it is *pending.* A pending patent application cannot be *infringed,* even though claims are *allowed.* Only upon *issue* does the application become a *patent* or *letters patent* which can have legal force. It then bears a *patent number.* The *life* or *term* of the patent is seventeen years from issue, after which the patent *expires.*

The common parts of either a patent or an

application are the *specification,* which is the written disclosure; the *drawings,* not always necessary; and as the terminal portion of the specification, the very necessary *claim* or *claims,* which latter are the invention definition negotiated with the Patent Office. In recent patents, a short *abstract* precedes the specification.

Divisions, continuations, and *continuations-in-part* are names of applications stemming from a *parent* application. The relationship is significant. If they are filed while the parent application is pending so as to be *co-pending* with it, they are entitled to the benefit of the earlier filing date, except as to *new matter* not in the parent application.

The negotiations with the Patent Office during which the patent is pending is called the *prosecution.* The application is *examined* and the claims are usually initially rejected as reported in letters, prepared by an *Examiner* in the Patent Office, and called Patent Office *actions.* The examination includes the Examiner's *search* in the classified art files of his *art group* for prior art *references.* The Patent Office does not have knowledge of unpublished prior art acts such as *public use* or *sale* of the invention, and cannot reject the claims on suspicion that prior art exists. Failure of the applicant to call attention of the Examiner to pertinent prior art may give rise later to an infringement suit defense of *fraud on the Patent Office.*

Prior art examples called *references* are usually cited. The applicant's letters, responding to the actions, are usually called *amendments.* They are prepared by the applicant's patent attorney who is usually an *attorney-at-law* or *lawyer* specializing in patent practice, but registered, non-lawyer *agents* are also recognized by the Patent Office.

Usually in a few years after filing an application, it is either *allowed* or becomes *abandoned.* The prosecution of a patent application officially involves only the applicant and the *Commissioner of Patents,* and is termed an *ex parte* proceeding. The Patent Office maintains the *file wrapper* or *application file* secret until after the patent issues. The file becomes a public file after the patent issues. As a written record of the negotiations for a patent, it often has value in resolving ambiguities in the patent itself.

Minor corrections in an issued patent may be made by a *Certificate of Correction.* More significant corrections to a patent are sought by way of a *reissue application.* Re-examination is also available by way of a reissue application identifying further prior-art evidence not applied by the examiner to the initial application. Such reissue applications are not kept confidential, and members of the public may call pertinent prior art to the attention of the Patent Office in *opposition* to the maintenance of the original patent claims.

When contemporary inventors claim the same invention, an *inter partes proceeding* in the form of an *interference* is declared by the Patent Office. *Priority* of invention is the issue. While the inventor who is first both to *conceive* the invention and to *reduce it to practice* always wins, the time spans between these dates may differ to make significant sometimes the *diligence* of the inventor in completing his invention. The formidable problems of proof give substantial importance to crediting of the filing date as a date of *constructive reduction to practice.* The *senior party,* who is the first inventor to file, enjoys a very real advantage since the *junior party* must first shoulder the *burden of proof.*

Infringement is *making, using,* or *selling* the claimed invention without a *license* to do so from the patentee. The remedy is by a *civil action* for patent infringement in a Federal district court where the defendant or defendants can be reached under the appropriate *venue* statute. The principal legal remedy is the *injunction.* Sometimes *damages,* often computed as *reasonable royalties,* are awarded. If articles sold under a patent have not carried a *patent marking* identifying the patent, damages shall not be computed for infringements occurring before *notice of infringement* is given to the infringer sued. A party charged with infringement may take the initiative and file a *declaratory judgment* civil action against the patentee.

Royalties are a common form of return for the permitted or *licensed* sale of part or all of the patent rights.

Foreign Patents. U.S. patents are enforceable only within the United States. U.S. patentees doing business in foreign countries may find their marketing interests well served by developing a portfolio of corresponding patents in selected countries. Canada is often a first and easy choice. Beyond that, the complexity and expense of managing a useful portfolio in a large number of countries calls for careful selection of foreign filing decisions.

By treaty arrangements in effect for many

years, corresponding filings in most foreign countries can be deferred up to one year after filing in the United States and still maintain the benefit of the original filing date. A Patent Cooperation Treaty (PCT) and a European Patent Convention (EPC) have both recently gone into effect, and point the way toward international examination and grant of patents. PCT, to which the United States is a subscribing member, permits the use of a patent application format accepted by all countries for which patenting fees are paid, and involves only one prior-art search by an agreed-upon authority, followed by examinations in the selected countries. EPC is designed ultimately to consolidate the patent operations of most Western European nations to the point where a single patent effective within the boundaries of various designated European nations may be granted.

The patent laws of most European nations have also recently been brought into substantial conformance with one another and, to a large extent, with the laws of the United States, but the remaining differences are important. A seemingly minor formal difference having a large effect in practice attempts is the right of an inventor under U.S. law to defer filing a patent application up to a year after he has apparently put his invention into the public domain, whereas most other countries of the world require the initial application to be filed before the public has had an opportunity to learn about the invention.

The United States is almost unique among major countries in determining the right to a patent between contemporaneous inventors of the same invention by considering pre-filing invention dates. Most countries award the patent, if any patent is to be awarded, only to the first to file a patent application. The procedures for enforcing patents and the remedies available also vary greatly from country to country. In short, effective planning in this area needs to be based upon adequate information if the effort is to be worth the expense.

Patents in the Intellectual Property Spectrum. Patents are often associated with trademarks, copyrights, and trade secrets as different kinds of "intellectual property," and are often handled by the same legal department or law firm. But it should be noted that all stem from very different legal concepts and should not be confused with each other nor with the concept of property in land or tangible things.

Patents are granted solely by the Federal Government in return for the timely and complete disclosure of a patentable invention in some fields of technology. Patents are usually prepared and prosecuted by lawyers specializing in patent practice and having a scientific or technical background.

A trade secret in technology acquires its status as such by the pains taken not to divulge to the public or competitors the identity of the product or process involved. The owner's rights are rights against someone who must steal the secret to learn it, but once the secret has become publicly known, rights to its exclusive use are gone. Whether factory processes or other "buried" innovations can be long protected by maintaining secrecy is a matter of fact determination in each case. The owner cannot have it both ways, except to the extent the subject matter is kept in secrecy during the period of pendency of a patent application.

TRADEMARKS are an entirely different type of right based upon the use of a symbol or name in trade. The owner's right is one shared with the public in preventing confusing use of the symbol or name by others. Registration of a mark in the U.S. Patent and Trademark Office after it is used gives the owner access to the Federal courts and procedural advantages in pursuing infringers.

Somewhat similarly, COPYRIGHTS exist by reason of the creation of an original writing or artistic subject matter. They are a right against copying, and their registration by the Library of Congress facilitates subsequent enforcement in a Federal court proceeding.

Role of Patents in Exploiting Inventions. *(1) Protecting an Exclusive Market.* In this situation, the return from patents is measured as some portion of the company's profits. One patent alone might establish the commercial position of the owner and enable him to market a full line of products supplementing the patented product. Usually a patent represents but one of several ingredients of success in a profitable competitive situation. Several patents may be involved in the profits from any one product or process. These patents may include both basic and improvement patents, or may be patents covering different features of a product.

(2) Sharing a Present Market by Licensing. A cash return in the form of royalties from licensees often appears as an attractive supplement to the company's own marketing program. It

provides a direct and accountable reflection of the value of research and patent activities. This form of hedging on the research gamble, rather than seeking the entire profit by exclusive manufacture and sale, is usually preferable only when certain factors are present. Common ones are:

(a) Licensing others may help to establish and expand the market for the patented goods as well as distribute promotion expenses.

(b) A second source of supply may be a practical necessity for the licensing company's customers.

(c) The company may be unable to supply a demand which is too short-lived to justify expansion of the company's facilities. Otherwise such a demand would be filled by other products.

(d) The antitrust laws may require, in particular instances, that effective competition be established by licensing competitors.

(e) The prospects of a relatively quick return by licensing may help finance further research which is considered to be necessary to achieve more profitable results.

(f) A license may be a practical compromise in an infringement controversy where the cost and risk involved in litigation are not justified.

(3) Future Markets. Patents intended for later use by the company deserve careful scrutiny. Occasionally the subject matter of the patent is so broad in scope and revolutionary in concept that the lack of a presently profitable market is more than offset by the prospects of a very large future return, if followed up by further research and development. Until their commercial possibilities can be more definitely appraised, it would be folly to discount as merely speculative the value of pioneer patents associated with such a project.

The usual case is that the subject matter of a patent not presently worked or scheduled for working simply does not meet the market requirement more profitably than do other competitive goods. Only where the limiting market requirements can be reasonably expected to change is a value realistically based on prospects of future use. Reasonably foreseeable changes in limiting conditions include:

(a) Decreased cost of manufacturing under the patent.

(b) Increased cost of marketing the presently marketed goods.

(c) Prospective shortages of materials used in the present competitive market.

(d) Expansion of the market due to growth of a particular art or industry.

(e) Expiration of patent rights of others.

(4) Defensive or Insurance Patents. Sometimes the only value of a patent to a company is to establish priority of invention against later inventors. For example, an invention made by a manufacturing company may offer a certain economic advantage over available substitutes, but the total profits affected are too small to justify the expense of enforcing a patent obtained on such an invention against infringers. Once the company adopts the invention, however, it may be very expensive for the company to change its own manufacturing facilities or marketing commitments, should someone else be in a position to enforce a patent covering this invention. This situation is the justification for the insurance or defensive patent.

A promptly printed non-patent publication may serve, almost as well, the purposes of an insurance patent in forestalling the patenting of the invention by others. The difference between the two deserves careful analysis in order to be evaluated since it boils down to an opportunity to enter a patent interference.

Basically, a first inventor acquires no further rights to practice his invention by patenting it; he instead acquires the right to exclude others, including *second inventors* who independently but subsequently make the same invention. Because the patent system is designed to encourage prompt public disclosure, an inventor who files a patent application has an advantage in proving priority with respect to an inventor who does not file an application or files later. An insurance patent application, as contrasted with printed publicity or other printed publication of the same date, keeps the applicant in position to participate in a patent interference should another party claim the same invention. This enables each applicant claiming the same invention to submit proofs of facts showing that he made his invention earlier in time than his respective filing date and to contest the corresponding proofs of the other party. This interference procedure also affords close scrutiny of the patent claims before any award of priority is made, and forewarns the losing party of the basis of the subsequent infringement charge.

Enforceability of Patent Rights. The principal lever to settlement of differences is, on one side, the threat of an injunction against the infringer. In some instances the liability for damages may also be very high. On the other side, the number of available defenses which the accused infringer may raise is large, and the presumption of validity of a patent, being only a presumption, is overcome by facts showing that the Patent Office should not have granted the patent claims.

The cost and time involved in testing a patent by a law suit are large for both the plaintiff and defendant. This cost must be weighed carefully against expected profits from the invention. Because of its high cost and often far-reaching consequences, patent litigation has characteristically been a last resort.

The patentee and an accused infringer or prospective licensee are best guided by competent appraisals of the enforceability of a patent and the prospect and economic consequences of a court ruling that, on the facts of a particular situation, the patent rights involved are both valid and infringed.

Acquiring Potential Patent Rights in Employee Inventions. The rights to inventions may be acquired after the inventions are made, but the inventors in such instances are, almost by definition, "outside" inventors. No purpose of an industrial organization appears to be sensibly served by negotiating for rights in specific inventions with employees who have been paid to conduct research or who have access to the company's technical information.

In the absence of a specific agreement, and very generally speaking, the employer has a right to inventions made by employees on the employer's time or otherwise with his assistance at least when the invention relates to the business of the employer. Although the rights to an invention may be divided between the employer and employee, such an arrangement is usually not satisfactory from an administrative viewpoint. Death, resignation, or discharge of the employee greatly complicates the protection of the company's interest in inventions previously made.

A written agreement by the research or engineering employee to assign inventions made during his employment is a necessity. It is desirably executed at the time of hiring as part of the employment routine. Usually the terms of such an agreement can be recited in general language so that a uniform printed agreement form suffices for all research employees. The agreement may also be incorporated in a more extensive employment agreement. Typical covenants by the employee in such agreements are (1) to disclose inventions both during employment and for some stated reasonable period thereafter, and (2) to sign all papers and otherwise cooperate in connection with obtaining patent rights on such inventions and assigning them to the employer. An assignment, a separate document conveying the invention set forth in the application to the employer, is desirably executed at that time. Even in the absence of an initial agreement to assign inventions, a court will usually order an uncooperative inventor or a deceased inventor's executor to execute an application and assignment.

Employment agreements and patent assignments should be carefully preserved. The former is usually part of the personnel files; the latter is usually recorded in the U.S. Patent Office assignment records and preserved with the original of the patent granted as evidence of title until the patent has expired. Systematic review of agreements to assign is helpful and, if an employee's agreement cannot be located, a new one should be executed. Omissions are most likely to occur when the employees do not enter through usual Personnel Department channels. Acquisition of other companies, mergers, and transfer of retained outside research to regular employment status require follow-up on this point.

Preserving Potential Rights. A written record of inventions or innovations made in the course of research is important from both administrative and legal points of view. Two kinds of written records are usually involved. One is an original, permanent record, typically a bound notebook in which the entries are contemporaneous, or nearly so, with the ideas conceived or progress made. The other record is an *invention report,* often as a patent disclosure letter, written after the invention is sufficiently complete to enable management to evaluate its patent potential.

The original record is intended to contain data significant to proof of priority of invention in the event of a patent interference proceeding. Such data may also play a role in proving origin and date of invention in such instances as the defense of infringement suits, controversies involving submitted ideas, or claims to patent rights in contracted research. The earliest evidence usually considered by the Patent Office in an interference is (1) the earliest written description, (2) the earliest drawing,

(3) the earliest reduction to practice, and (4) the earliest disclosure to others.

As a matter of law, the inventor's own testimony, written or oral, is insufficient to prove invention dates earlier than the date his patent application is filed in the Patent Office. Corroboration by another is required. Reference in the record to other persons acquainted with the facts, initialing of the record by such other persons, and corroborating descriptive entries by such other persons are all helpful.

Generally, recent recollections of much earlier events carry little weight as compared with contemporaneous records of the events. Since opportunities for mistaken assumptions or fraud are great, any irregularities in the recorded data are viewed with suspicion. Anything less than comprehensive, specifically delineated, truly definitive, adequately witnessed records may prove in later years to be too fragmentary to be relied upon.

Because recording invention data is time-consuming and frequently irksome, establishment of routines and supervision are always desirable. A usual requirement is a bound notebook or diary assigned to each engineer or scientist involved in development or research activity. Dated entries are made by the person to whom the book is assigned. These entries should be a record of noteworthy ideas and should report work in developing and testing these ideas. Each entry should be signed, dated, and witnessed, as closely following the actual event as is practical.

Preparing an Invention Report for Evaluation. At some stage in the evolution of an apparent invention into patent property, a specific identity is attached to it. The invention report or disclosure letter usually marks this change of status. Such letters are forwarded to an office where they are numbered or docketed for evaluation as potential patents. Action or lack of action upon them becomes a matter of record from this point forward.

To achieve its purpose, the disclosure letter is preferably authored by the inventor, as a careful exposition of his contribution, the problem solved or the need fulfilled, and the advantages of the invention over prior approaches. This discipline so imposed on the inventor often assists in distinguishing objectives from results and otherwise clarifies the invention areas. The report or letter usually brings up to date the step by step progress recorded in the inventor's notebook. It is sometimes the first record of an invention, and often so if the inventor is not an employee to whom a notebook has been issued.

Evaluating Potential Patent Property. A systematic review and rating of disclosure letters or invention reports for appropriate patent action are essential to long-range success of a patent program. Decisions to file patent applications are based on estimates of the future value of the patent property, and the accuracy of such decisions may not be determinable for years, if ever. A keen appreciation of the limitations and implications of both the technical and legal definition of each invention is therefore the foundation of sound decision-making.

Decision to File. The decision to file or not to file a patent application is an economic one. The fact that a large amount of money has been expended on research does not itself determine the wisdom of spending more money in attempting to patent the research results. As a general rule, the desirability of filing increases with the sum of the two weighted factors: (1) the value of the invention; and (2) the prospects of patentability of claims of reasonably broad scope.

As a general policy, the further the prospective patent is from scheduled use by the company to protect an exclusive market, the more closely the basis of value must be examined. The particular forms in which an invention is most profitably commercialized are not reliably perceived at a distance. Likewise, the scope of the potentially allowable claims may be only generally envisaged. Partial reliance upon less commercially accountable grounds of value—such as prestige of the company and morale of the research inventor—should not replace knowledge of the merit of the research results. Decisions dominated by what a competitor is doing or not doing should be recognized as substituting the competitor's value judgment for that of the company. To the extent that research inventions are quite likely to represent substantial departure from known commercial practice, it is important to consider that the patentability and scope of the invention may be limited by other prior art available upon investigation.

Care should be taken that inventions are not branded as "impractical" because of economic limitations which are temporary or pertain only to certain forms of the invention. Doubts as to value are usually resolved in favor of filing where substantial breadth of claims is reasonably assured.

Time is almost always of the essence in patent matters, and this remains so in decisions to file a patent application. If the research project has received some publicity, or if competitors are suspected to have interests in the same research area, delay in filing applications on inventions made may lead to the inability to prove priority with respect to others who file earlier on the same invention. Printed publications disclosing the invention become an absolute bar, as does public use or sale, if they occur more than one year prior to the filing of a patent application on the invention. (If potential rights in certain foreign countries are to be preserved, no such publication, public use, or sale should occur before the U.S. patent is filed.) A priority classification, plus whatever absolute deadlines are known, becomes a significant part of each decision to file. The stated basis of the decision to file can usually guide the attorney charged with preparing the patent application as to the patent expense justified and the follow-up attention required.

Patent Counsel and Patent Activities. The preparation and prosecution of patent applications require highly specialized skills. This is the province of the patent attorney, and the description is beyond the purview of this article. More significantly, the development of the company's patent property is but one of the major functions assigned to patent personnel. Equally important are the employment of patent property after it has been acquired, and guidance of company management with respect to adversely held patents. Whatever the size of the company and its form of organization, these activities need to be carefully integrated, for they deal directly with assets and liabilities of the company as a whole.

Claims defining the invention in terms of its real distinctions over all prior art must be drawn and persuasively advocated. Avoidance of non-essential descriptive details or indefinite generalization in the claims requires a complete understanding of the invention by the patent attorney. The claims must find support in the patent specification, and both should anticipate and avoid rejections which might be raised by the Patent Office, or defenses which might be entered by an accused infringer. Continuing liaison with the inventor or other competent research representative is obviously needed, and is an important part of patent activities. All publications describing the invention should be brought to the attention of the patent attorney in order that filing at a timely date may be scheduled.

During the prosecution of the patent application (a process usually taking three or more years), the application claims may have to be revised in view of prior art cited by the Patent Office as negating invention or in view of other rejections. Assistance of technical personnel may be required for testing the invention or for analyzing the prior art. Further development of the invention or changes in its commercial form may require a shift of emphasis in the application claims. Filing of new and additional applications may be necessary as the research work and development of the invention progress. Only a very limited correction of the application drawings and specification is permitted once the application has been filed.

Several forms of contracts involve rights in inventions, patents, or both. The occurrence of such language in any proposed agreement is a signal that the patent counsel should be consulted. If the contract is principally a patent matter, patent counsel usually conducts the negotiations. Usual problem areas are defining the invention involved and examining the effect of the possible legal consequences of each contract on the company's interests.

Licenses under patents of others need careful scrutiny, particularly lest they bind the company to a greater liability for royalty or for greater periods than contemplated. Agreement stipulations that certain patents are valid and infringed deserve careful attention lest the party so agreeing be limited to a product design or committed to royalty levels which prevent it from competing effectively. Because of the public interest in patents, a licensee is permitted to challenge validity at almost any time, but the cost of doing so may itself be uneconomic.

Licenses under the company's patents to others are likewise of concern. They may be insufficiently limited to protect the overall value of the patent to the company. On the other hand, restrictions may run afoul of the antitrust laws and jeopardize enforceability of the patent, or expose the company to liability under the antitrust laws.

Development or supply contracts with the

Federal Government contain clauses affecting rights to patents on inventions made in the course of work under the contract. These rights are negotiable to some extent, depending upon the patent ownership policy of the Government agency involved and ultimately upon whether the contractor or the Government is subsidizing the cost of making the invention. Under such a contract, invention reports may be required from time to time from the contractor. Patent counsel can establish a routine to assure compliance with the contract terms.

Purchase orders and invoices may contain language affecting liability for patent infringement. The fact that they are printed forms does not remove the possibility of an unusually large liability.

Preventing Litigation. A most important responsibility of patent counsel is both to avoid suit by holders of adverse patent rights and at the same time to preserve a maximum freedom of action for his company. New products or processes destined for marketing are analyzed to deem what adversely-held patent right might be infringed, or what further patent rights need be acquired. Apparently infringed patents may be the subject of extensive validity investigations. When an adversely held patent is apparently infringed and not clearly invalid, a change of the product or process may be more economic than risking suit or purchasing rights. Close liaison between the patent counsel and research helps facilitate remedial changes before heavy commitments have been made.

Related Extra-Patent Responsibilities. Patent counsel may be responsible for preservation of the company's interest in non-patented ideas or proprietary information, or in preventing liability for infringing upon the interests of others. Technical "know-how" and trade secrets may be valuable assets of the company. The value of either of these is diminished by their disclosure in the company's patents or other publications. Realistic appraisal of asserted value in such unpatented information offered for sale to the company usually involves examination of patents and other published literature.

The control of liability for use of unsolicited unpatented ideas is of concern, since patentability or lack of it is not a controlling factor. Good intentions by a company employee receiving such ideas may be insufficient to prevent very large liability for an alleged breach of a confidential disclosure. Routines for referring all ideas submitted to the company, whether through the mails or by discussions with employees, to an office responsible for processing such suggestions are usually involved.

Patent Misuse and the Antitrust Laws. To the extent a patent or patent portfolio assures the owner a dominant position in a market segment, the more circumspectly and cautiously the patent rights need be exploited to avoid liability for restraining trade, monopolizing, or otherwise using the patents in ways offensive to the antitrust laws. (See ANTITRUST LEGISLATION.) The Sherman and Clayton Acts are the principal Federal antitrust laws which forbid a wide range of activities having anti-competitive effects, including activities involving patents. Antitrust litigation is not limited to civil and criminal actions brought by the Government, and private antitrust actions fueled by the prospects of treble damage recoveries are not uncommon. Acquisitions of patent portfolios, joint development projects, withholding of licenses under patents, and many other events or types of conduct entirely proper in one set of circumstances may give rise to liability in another. Competent counsel should be consulted.

Failure of management to appreciate antitrust consequences of activities of employees remote from the marketing activities usually associated with antitrust exposure may be expensive. For example, a patent judicially determined to have been improperly obtained—as, for example, by intentional failure of the patentee to have called pertinent prior art within its knowledge to the attention of the Patent Office during the examination—may be held to be in itself an illegal monopoly. Attempts to enforce such an inherently defective patent may themselves give rise to antitrust liability. Conventional wisdom of a generation ago to the contrary, an invalid patent may be a dangerous liability, not merely a dubious asset.

Anti-competitive use of a patent may also make it unenforceable in infringement litigation, quite apart from the validity and infringement issues or whether the antitrust laws are directly involved. For example, requiring a patent licensee to purchase unpatented components or ingredients may render the patent unenforceable.

In a similar vein, the courts have in recent years been concerned that the expense and business risks in defending infringement actions may force parties to accept licenses under invalid patents. As a result a patent licensee is at liberty after negotiating royalty terms to withhold royalties while contesting in court the validity of the patent rights on which the royalty obligation is based. One effect is more frequent resort to litigation for a judicial decree rather than to an out-of-court royalty agreement to settle disputes effectively.

HOMER J. SCHNEIDER, Attorney, Leydig, Voit, Osann, Mayer & Holt, Ltd., Chicago, Illinois; Adjunct Professor of Law, The John Marshall Law School, Chicago, Illinois

Information References

Statutes and rules are contained in the U.S. Department of Commerce booklets "Patent Laws" and "Rules of Practice of the United States Patent and Trademark Office in Patent Cases." From time to time, bar associations and the Department of Commerce issue leaflets on patents which might be suitable for distribution to research personnel. (Some companies print booklets explaining patents and their respective patent procedures for distribution to employees.)

Much general literature on the American patent system is oversimplified, and the critical literature should be carefully examined for its economic premises.

Cross References: *Copyright; New-Product Development (and accompanying entries with New-Product prefix); Trademarks; Trademarks: International Protection.*

PENSION PLANS. See Retirement Plans.

PERFORMANCE APPRAISAL (MERIT RATING)

Performance Appraisal or **Merit Rating** is the process of evaluating the performance and qualifications of the employee in terms of the requirements of the job for which he is employed, for purposes of administration, including placement, selection for promotion, providing financial rewards, and other actions which require differential treatment among the members of a group as distinguished from actions affecting all members equally.

In practice, the term *merit rating,* when applied to salary administration, has been used by many companies to cover almost all kinds of salary adjustments, including recognition of length of service, economic adjustments, and even general increases stemming from or preceding union contract negotiations as applied to non-union groups of employees, as well as for recognition of individual meritorious performance. Because of this broad use of the term, many managers prefer to use other terminology, such as *Performance Appraisal* or *Employee Appraisal* for purposes of identifying and recognizing individual differences among employees.

Value of Ratings. By means of a systematic rating procedure, management is enabled to maintain a record of the relative worth of its personnel and thereby be more able to make sound decisions regarding employment, placement, transfers, promotions, dismissals, and individual salary rewards related to worth. Despite their imperfections, appraisal records are relatively objective and provide information that often cannot be obtained in any other way.

Ratings replace subjective, general impressionistic opinions with judgments that are analytical and generally describable in quantitative terms. Based on observation over a period of time, they provide information that is valuable when critical decisions must be made in emergency situations. In general, ratings provide evidence that should serve as the bases for decisions. In addition, ratings, soundly developed and systematically administered, stimulate the person being appraised, especially when he is informed about his standing and has an opportunity to discuss ways and means of improving. They also cause the rater to be more analytical and objective, especially when he knows that he must be able to answer such questions as, "What is the evidence to support your rating of this employee?"

Rating records also provide a wealth of data for personnel research purposes. They are used, in addition to other purposes, to validate tests and other employment selection devices, to help establish training methods, and to clarify interrelationships among performance measures and other environmental conditions.

History and Methodology. Probably the first "scientific" or modern type of rating scale was one developed by Sir Francis Galton and described in his "Inquiry into Human Faculty and Its Development" [1]. His scale (in his example he describes the recollection of a breakfast table) presents nine degrees of "mental imagery," with a detailed description of each degree, ranging from *Highest*—brilliant, distinct, never blotchy," and *"First Suboctile*—the image once seen is perfectly clear and bright," through "*Middlemost*—fairly clear: brightness probably at least from half to two thirds of the original, one or two objects being much more distinct than others, but the latter comes out clearly if attention be paid to them," to "*Lowest*—my powers are zero, to my consciousness there is almost no association of memory with objective visual impressions, I recollect the table but do not see it."

A somewhat similar scale was developed by K. Pearson and reported in 1906 [2]. This describes seven degrees of Mental Ability, as follows:

(1) *Mentally Defective.* Capable of holding in the mind only the simplest facts, and incapable of perceiving or reasoning about relationships between facts.

(2) *Slow Dull.* Capable of perceiving relationship between facts in some few fields with long and continuous effort; but generally not without much assistance.

(3) *Slow.* Very slow in thought generally, but with time understanding is reached.

(4) *Slow Intelligent.* Slow generally, although possibly more rapid in certain fields; quite sure of knowledge when once acquired.

(5) *Fairly Intelligent.* Ready to grasp and capable of perceiving facts in most fields; capable of understanding without much effort.

(6) *Distinctly Capable.* A mind quick in perception and in reasoning rightly about the perceived.

(7) *Very Able.* Quite exceptionally able intellectually, as evidenced either by the person's career or by consensus of opinion of acquaintances, or by school record in case of children.

These scales point the way to the construction of valuable performance scales for use in industry. The basic material is the Position Description, and the performance scale is a series of statements to describe "essentially perfect performance," "intermediate between perfect and standard performance," "standard performance," "marginal performance," and "failing performance." Since such descriptive paragraphs are rather complex, intermediate steps, without description, can be used to indicate "better than a described level, but less than the next higher described level." Thus, given a nine-step scale, descriptions may be written for steps 9, 7, 5, 3, and 1. Steps 8, 6, 4, and 2 provide for the non-described in-between levels of performance.

Such scales are likely to be of more value when applied to incumbents of complicated positions of broad scope, such as managerial and professional, than when simpler, specialized job holders are being rated, but their values for all kinds of positions extend beyond the establishment of a performance index. Properly done they provide bases for analysis and identification of needs for development of the employee for improved performance.

The Order of Merit or *Rank Order* method of rating was developed originally by J. McKeen Cattell in connection with his studies of the prominence of scientists [3]. Each judge was requested to place a list of names of scientists in rank order from "best" to "least." Such a procedure is sometimes used within a relatively small group. It is effective for differentiating the extremes of ability, personal characteristics of other kinds, and performance, but it is not analytic or diagnostic, unless a number of rankings are made, one for each of a number of traits and performance characteristics. Furthermore, the use of such a technique requires that the ratings of people in a group must all be done at the same time.

The Paired Comparison method, [4] when applied under controlled conditions, probably is the soundest and most technically exact for the determination of individual differences. It requires a comparison of each person in the group with each other person and the recording of a judgment of *superior.* (Sometimes a judgment of *equal* may also be used.)

The number of *superior* judgments about each person establishes his relative standing in the group. The result may be a rank order, but degrees of difference will have been determined to a greater extent than by simple ranking.

Neither the Rank Order nor the Paired Comparison method is applicable when an appraisal of only one or of a few persons is undertaken at one time. Since many administrative decisions are required throughout a year, these methods cannot yield up-to-date ratings. For example, many companies have salary reviews on anniversary dates of employment, transfer, or promotion. Accordingly, if ratings are determined through ranking or paired comparison methods, requiring review of a considerable number of persons at the same time, they will not be "current" on most anniversary dates. Therefore, other reference points must be established. Such reference points should be related to job requirements. Thus, if "quantity of production" is a significant item for rating employees, quantitative criteria should be established. Such criteria are not revealed in Ranking or Paired Comparison and related methods of rating, except through statistical determinations of central tendency and variability.

The Army Man-to-Man Rating Scale is of

great historical significance, although it has been judged to be too cumbersome for use in industry. This method, stemming directly from the work of the Bureau of Salesmanship Research at Carnegie Institute of Technology, under the leadership of Walter Dill Scott, in 1916, can be briefly described as follows [5]: A five-step scale is constructed in which each step represents a known person. The highest step on the scale for *Leadership,* for example, is represented by that person who, in the opinion of the rater, possesses leadership qualities to the highest degree of any of his acquaintances in the type of activity engaged in by those to be rated. Other persons are selected to represent high level, middle level, low level, and lowest level possession of the trait. Persons to be rated are then slotted into the scale by comparing them in the trait in question with the individuals representing scale levels: hence the name, Man-to-Man Rating Scale.

As used in the Army, officers of a given rank were rated by this technique. In industry, such a method might be applicable to rating all general foremen, or foremen, or superintendents, or salesmen, but since each job even of the foreman type has its own characteristics, many scales, each covering relatively few people, would be needed, except as the ratees are to be judged and rated for their personal characteristics, regardless of their specific work assignments.

Other systems developed for performance appraisal or merit rating since World War I, include the following:

(1) *Graphic Rating Scales* [6], originally developed by the Scott Company Laboratory (Walter Dill Scott and associates), provide a series of traits and their definitions, opposite each of which the rater places a check mark on a line representing the full distance from "highest" to "lowest" rating. This approach, with variations, is one of the most commonly used rating forms in industry today. Variations include "boxes" to represent varying levels of quality or performance, and descriptive phrases under the graphic line or boxes to define degrees.

(2) *Lists* of descriptions of varying degrees of the characteristic or performance, to be checked by the rater.

(3) *Written* descriptions of the ratees' personal traits and performance characteristics, with or without a letter or number index (score) to represent the appraisal in quantitative terms. This method is used more often for appraising managerial personnel rather than clerical or manual personnel.

(4) *Forced-Choice* [7]. The rater selects from each of a number of groupings of generally unrelated "personal characteristics" statements, one that is *most like* and one that is *least like* the ratee. Numerical values are assigned on a statistical basis, and scores obtained. This method appears to improve objectivity and to reduce the effect of such pitfalls as the "halo" tendency, but it lacks face validity.

(5) *"Critical Incident"* [8]. The appraiser keeps a running record of activity incidents which were "critical" for successful and unsuccessful performance. This method, used over a period of time, identifies those types of activity which are characteristic of successful and of unsuccessful employees in specific types of jobs, and furnishes the basis for continuing appraisals of subordinates and for day-to-day discussions with them for corrective and development purposes.

(6) *Field Review.* Here a personnel specialist in appraisal and development work meets with supervisors and staff personnel and observes the persons to be appraised [9]. Following discussions with them, he writes out an analytic appraisal and reviews it with the supervisor for certification. This is an effective method, especially as applied to managerial personnel, when the specialist is properly qualified.

(7) *Performance Standards.* Appraising performance in relation to performance "standards" is not unlike the Graphic Rating Scale method in some respects. It tends to reduce the common tendency of many raters to rate high, because the basic reference point is "standard," and deviations are in terms of "above" or "better than," or "below" or "less than" standard. (This type of approach to appraising performance is described fully below, with examples of some forms in use in industry.)

(8) *Appraisal by Objectives.* This approach entails the preparation by the subordinate appraisee of written statements covering his understanding of the objectives of (a) his superior's job; (b) his own job; (c) the proper criteria of performance from his viewpoint; (d) the situation, including problems to be overcome; and (e) his plan of action to accomplish the objectives. This report is discussed with the supervisor for purposes of communication, analysis, modification or approval, and appraisal. The subordinate participates throughout and has largely *appraised himself* in the process. (See MANAGEMENT BY OBJECTIVES.)

Examples of Methods and Forms used for Merit Rating. Exhibit I presents a rating form for use with clerical and manual job holders. It is general rather than specific, and hence requires an indication by the rater, normally the supervisor (subject to review by *his* superior) of the relative importance to the job of the seven items listed on the form. The rater reports three determinations for each item, its relative importance, the level of performance by the employee, and the amount of evidence on which he bases his rating.

The reference point for the performance rating is "Standard," and nine degrees are available to the rater by use of the signs. A check mark (√) in the Standard box means that performance meets normal expectations (Standard). A plus (+) sign in the Standard box means that the performance is slightly better than Standard, but not sufficiently better to warrant a rating of Above Standard. Similarly, a minus (−) sign in the same box indicates some deficiency in performance, but not sufficient to warrant a Below Standard rating.

It is possible to compute a score for the ratings to obtain guidance in arriving at a Total Performance Rating by taking the Importance element into consideration. For example, if Standard (√) is given a value of zero, and each step down the scale from Standard (√) is given a minus value, such as −1, −2, −3, −4, and each step up the scale is given a plus value, such as +1, +2, +3, +4, these values, multiplied by the Importance degree (1, 2, or 3), totalled (algebraic total), and then divided by 7 (the number of items), provides an index number to be considered for purposes of giving a Total Performance Rating. This indexing process should be applied only to ratings of employees in the same type of job, or jobs which have the same total of weights assigned; otherwise, the final figure will vary because of differing total weights rather than different ratings.

It is obvious that a score obtained as described above must be interpreted in relation to other scores and the range of scores obtained in practice. It is clear, also, that ratings based upon "little" evidence should be discounted, usually by considering that actual performance is likely to be closer to "standard" than the rating given, unless the rater has made such a determination in the process of recording his judgment.

There are significant advantages in using "standard" performance rather than "average," "satisfactory," or "ideal" as the main point of reference for judging performance. It helps to avoid the pitfall tendency to rate higher or lower than the facts warrant. After all, if a supervisor rates all or most of his people as performing above standard, the performance of his department, which is likely to be measurable by other more objective means, should be above standard. Also, a new employee who is learning his job may be rated as performing "below standard" for the job, even though he is doing a very satisfactory job of learning. He may then be described as "not yet meeting job standards."

The establishment of standards of performance may or may not be expressible in quantitative terms. The supervisor, however, responsible for the work of his (her) department, is accountable to a superior for determining quantitative and qualitative acceptance criteria. Hence, it is appropriate to ask him or her to establish acceptable performance standards, subject to review by the superior. It then is the responsibility of management to achieve consistency among supervisors regarding performance standards. This may be accomplished most readily through periodic conference discussions, dry-run practice sessions, and occasional conference reviews of actual ratings, especially when performance reviews take place at the manager level.

Exhibit II presents a rating form similar in concept to that presented in Exhibit I. The form illustrated is one for use with employees in a specific job, that of Sales Representative. It is designed to reflect two aspects of rating, Results Obtained and Methods of Work. The Methods section may be regarded as being more diagnostic in nature, for training purposes, than the Results section, but both are pertinent for decisions about salary and related administrative matters.

Exhibit IIA presents the reverse sides of both forms.

Exhibit III shows one of four sections of a generalized form for appraising the performance of executive and professional personnel. It has features in common with the simpler forms just presented. The approach is primarily diagnostic, but it has been found to be effective for salary administration as well as for development. Questions asked in the other three sections, which are of similar format, are:

EXHIBIT I

RATING FORM FOR CLERICAL AND MANUAL JOB HOLDERS

PERFORMANCE REVIEW

NAME OF EMPLOYEE____________________ DATE__________

DEPARTMENT____________________ JOB TITLE__________

Instructions:

Ratings are made by the Supervisor, and reviewed by Department Heads. Three responses to each of the 7 items are required - a) Indicate relative importance for job performance by checking box 1, 2, or 3. (1 = less than average, 3 = more than average). - b) Indicate level of performance in relation to Standard (Std.), using a check ( ) mark, minus (—) sign, or a plus (+) sign to show small degrees of variation, especially in the Standard area. - c) Indicate, by checking the amount of evidence you have available or in mind to support the rating. Written comments or examples are requested.

Standard performance is that level of effectiveness on the job that the Supervisor considers to be sufficient for satisfactory results, that which can be reasonably expected from a normally qualified employee assigned to the job.

	Importance			Performance Level			Amount of Evidence		
How well does employee perform job duties?	1	2	3	Below	Standard	Above	Little	Adequate	Much
1. Quantity									
2. Quality and Accuracy									
3. Keeping Superior Informed									
4. Cooperating with Others									
5. Completing Tasks on Time									
6. Solving Problems, Making Suggestions									
7. Keeping Records and Orderliness									

Comments (after each item): ____________________

Attendance Record:

Number of days absent last 6 months:_____ Number of times late:_____

Rating		
Poor	Fair	Good

Total Performance: (Circle)

Below			Standard			Above		
1	2	3	4	5	6	7	8	9

EXHIBIT II

RATING FORM FOR EMPLOYEES IN A SPECIFIC POSITION (SALES REPRESENTATIVE)

PERFORMANCE REVIEW

NAME __________________________ DATE __________________

DEPARTMENT __________________ REGION __________ JOB TITLE ______________

Instructions:

These ratings are to be made by the employee's Supervisor. He will consider the amount of evidence available to him for appraising the employee's performance of each listed item, and will check the appropriate box to indicate Little, Adequate, or Much evidence. He then will indicate his appraisal of the employee's performance of each item, placing a check (✓) mark in the appropriate box, or a plus (+) sign, or a minus (—) sign to indicate degree distinctions within the appraisal steps of Standard, Above, or Below. Standard performance is that level of effectiveness on the job that the Supervisor considers "reasonably to be expected from a normally qualified employee," subject, of course, to review by the Sales Manager.

Section A

Results: How do results compare with objectives?

	Amount of Evidence: Little	Adequate	Much	Level of Performance: Below	Standard	Above
1. Balanced Product Sales						
2. New Customers						
3. Customer penetration						
4. Dealer relations						
5. Maintenance of quota of daily calls						
6. Supply of market information						
7. Control of expenses						
8. Promotion of "[redacted] Image."						

	BELOW			STANDARD			ABOVE		
Summary of Results	1	2	3	4	5	6	7	8	9

Section B

Methods: How well does he--

	Amount of Evidence: Little	Adequate	Much	Level of Performance: Below	Standard	Above
1. Plan and schedule work?						
2. Carry out work schedule?						
3. Interpret instructions?						
4. Establish and maintain contacts?						
5. Make decisions (accuracy, soundness, timing)?						
6. Solve problems and overcome obstacles?						
7. Express himself orally and in writing?						
8. Accept responsibility and carry through to completion?						
9. Recognize opportunities for improvement and initiate action?						
10. Keep superior and Home Office informed (reports, etc.)?						

	BELOW			STANDARD			ABOVE		
Summary of Methods	1	2	3	4	5	6	7	8	9

Over-all Performance

	BELOW			STANDARD			ABOVE		
How well does he carry out the total requirements of his position?	1	2	3	4	5	6	7	8	9

OBSERVATIONS AND COMMENTS: ____________________________

EXHIBIT IIA

(REVERSE OF FORMS IN EXHIBITS I AND II)

FUTURE ACTIONS

	Ratings		
	Fair	Good	Excellent
Health and Energy			
Requirement for job			

Promotability

To what job?____________________or not likely____________

When: Over 2 years________; From 1 to 2 years______; This year_______

Need for Training

In present job: Much____, Some____, None____

For next job: (What job?________________) Much___, Some___, None__

Plan for training: (Who will do what?)____________________

Date of conference with employee:________________ Comments:________

Initials of Supervisor________

Recommended Action

Job change__________________________Date____________

Pay change__________________________Date____________

Signature of Supervisor

________________Date______

Signature of Department Head

________________Date______

WORK PLANNING AND EXECUTION

How well does he (she):

1. Plan and schedule work in his area (long- and short-range)?
2. Make decisions (accuracy, soundness, timing)?
3. Solve problems and overcome obstacles?
4. Keep his superior and others informed of pertinent activities concerned with his work?
5. Establish and interpret objectives, policies, procedures, and practices?
6. Attain his objectives (quality, volume, cost, margin, etc.)?
7. Maintain essential records and effective operational controls?
8. Recognize opportunities for improvement and initiate action?
9. Accept responsibility and follow through to completion?

STUDY AND RESEARCH

How well does he (she):

1. Keep up to date in his required fields of study?
2. Recognize and identify needs for study and research?
3. Organize and apply his knowledge?
4. Analyze cause-and-effect relationships from the available information?

EXHIBIT III

SECTION OF FORM FOR APPRAISING EXECUTIVE AND PROFESSIONAL PERSONNEL

A. ORGANIZATION PLANNING, ADMINISTRATION, AND SUPERVISION

(This block to be used for supervisory positions only).
(Omit questions that do not apply)

How well does he:	Amount of Evidence: Little	Adequate	Much	Level of Performance: Below	Standard	Above
1. Plan and staff his organizational component?						
2. Establish and maintain clear-cut lines of communication?						
3. Prepare expense budgets and provide facilities for his component?						
4. Maintain work area and facilities?						
5. Administer Company personnel policies?						
6. Delegate appropriate responsibilities and authorities?						
7. Practice sound principles of human relations within his organization?						
8. Give instructions and assignments and follow thru to assure they are carried out?						
9. Appraise and develop (train) his subordinates?						
10. Exercise leadership with respect to his subordinates?						

Comments (strong points and needs) ____________________

Over-all Appraisal of Performance in
Organization Planning Administration and Supervision

1	2	3	4	5	6	7	8	9
BELOW			STANDARD			ABOVE		

5. Utilize available research and information facilities?

6. Provide information that is sound and reliable?

7. Maintain an objective viewpoint, open-mindedness, and broad perspective?

NON-SUPERVISORY RELATIONSHIPS

How well does he (she):

1. Establish and maintain contacts internally and externally?

2. Make available his special knowledge to others?

3. Coordinate his activities and service functions with work of others?

4. Utilize the services of others? (Does he follow proper channels?)

5. Represent and further the Company interests in his outside contacts?

6. Cooperate with others as "member-of-the team"?

7. Persuade others, sell ideas, and influence points of view?

8. Express himself orally and in writing?

9. Conduct or participate in conferences with associates?

When a generalized form is used, reference must be made to the position description, and each applicable question interpreted in terms of the job requirements. The various sections are "work sheets" for guidance in analyzing and judging performance, leading to the functional area appraisals and finally to an over-all Performance Appraisal. For this, a Summary Sheet is provided, for answers to such overall questions as, How well does this employee carry out the total requirements of this position? What are his or her principal strengths—what kinds of things does he or she do best? What are the obvious limitations that need attention to improve performance? Were there any unusual conditions or circumstances which influenced performance? In your opinion are the causes of the unfavorable conditions correctable?

Rating Indexes in Salary Administration. When salary ranges have been established and jobs have been classified into Salary Grades or Classes, if a Salary Grade is represented by a Position Rate (sometimes a mid-point is used), this rate of pay typically represents the worth of the work when performed in a "Standard" fashion. Therefore, an appraisal of "Standard" suggests a salary at the Position Rate. If length of service is also considered, the salary may be adjusted upward from Position Rate over an extended period of time by a limited amount, such as a maximum of 10% or 12%.

Exhibit IV offers some guide lines under a salary administration policy that illustrates this relationship between performance appraisals and salary rates in a company which deliberately recognizes length of service in addition to merit for salary determinations. In this situation a rating of 6 ("Meets all essential standards") on a nine-step scale is considered to warrant a salary at the Position Rate or Mode. Additional salary increments may be added on account of length of service. This approach has value in that performance ratings are less likely to be inflated because of upward pressures caused by long time intervals between salary increases, where performance continues to be relatively static.

Appraisal by Results. A basic procedure in the performance appraisal of managerial personnel is now being labelled "Appraisal by Results." This involves participational planning of work programs, with objectives, goals, or targets. At regular intervals, depending upon the plans, the employee and his superior review and appraise progress in relation to plan. The time span may vary up to a year and beyond. (This is the essence of MANAGEMENT BY OBJECTIVES.)

Since the plan or plans were developed jointly by the employee and his superior, agreed upon, and made a matter of record, the employee generally will be objective at the time of a progress review. He may, of course, rationalize deficiencies and failures, but the review process furnishes a wealth of evidence for arriving at a judgment of the employee's performance.

Obviously, the critical phases of this approach are the planning phase, the implementation phase, and the "audit" phase. If the planning is unrealistic, the implementation will be disappointing, and the appraisal may then be inadequately descriptive of the employee's qualities. Nevertheless, this approach is not only sound for appraisal purposes, it is or should be a standard operating procedure in fulfilling the management functions of planning, leading, and measuring. (See also EXECUTIVE APPRAISAL: DIAGNOSTIC PERFORMANCE APPRAISAL.)

Technical Problems. The preceding discussion of appraisal methods has not included any

EXHIBIT IV

RELATIONSHIPS OF PERFORMANCE RATINGS, LENGTH OF SERVICE, AND SALARY RATES

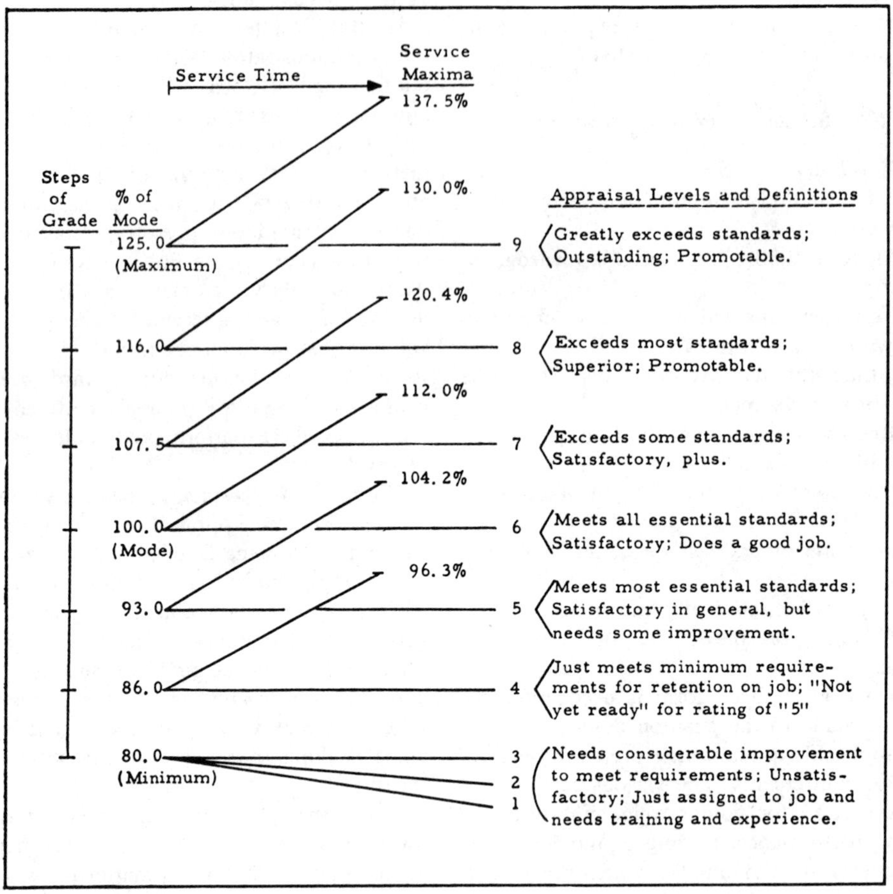

discourse on various technical problems such as corrections for "leniency tendency" or its opposite; overcoming the "halo" effect; and various statistical methods for determining the reliability and validity of ratings. These are matters for the technician, and text material is available in the literature of psychology and mental measurement, including textbooks on Personnel Administration.

THEOS A. LANGLIE, PH.D., Southbury, Connecticut

Information References

Lubben, Gary L., Thompson, Duane E., and Klasson, Charles R., "Performance Appraisal: The Legal Implications of Title VIII," *Personnel,* May-June, 1980.

Wilson, Jess E., "Employee Performance Appraisal," ch.6, sec.3, in Heyel, Carl, ed., "Handbook of Modern Office Management and Administrative Services," Huntington, N.Y., Krieger, repr. 1980.

Winstanley, N.B., "Legal and Ethical Issues in Performance Appraisal," *Harvard Business Review,* November-December, 1980.

(See also references given under EXECUTIVE APPRAISAL.).

References Cited

[1] Galton, Sir Francis, "Inquiry Into Human Faculty and Its Development," New York, Dutton, 1883.

[2] Pearson, Karl, "On the Relationship of Intelligence to Size and Shape of Head and to Other Physical and Mental Characters," *Biometrika,* 5, 1906–07.

[3] Cattell, J. McK., "A Statistical Study of American Men of Science," *Science,* N. S. 24, 1906. Also see: Guilford, J. P., "Psychometric Methods," Chap. VIII, New York, McGraw-Hill, 1936.

[4] Guilford, J. P., "Psychometric Methods," Chap. VII, New York, McGraw-Hill, 1936.

[5] Scott, W. D., Clothier, R. C., Mathewsen, and Spriegel, "Personnel Management," New York, McGraw-Hill, 1941; and Viteles, M. A., "Industrial Psychology," New York, Norton, 1931.

Cross References: *Assessment Centers; Executive Appraisal; Diagnostic Performance Appraisal: Executive Development: Selection Guide; Executive Traits; Job Evaluation; Management by Objectives.*

PERFORMANCE BUDGETING. See Public Administration section, Budgeting.

PERSONNEL ADMINISTRATION

Personnel Administration is best understood in terms of its three elements. First, it is a specialized body of knowledge developed primarily over the past 80 years. Second, it is a viewpoint, and hence expresses a philosophy or a value set. Third, it consists of specialized methods, tools, and techniques through which its viewpoint is implemented. A central principle is that people are an organization's most important asset.

Definition. Personnel administration may be defined as a well-rounded, planned, executed, and evaluated approach to employee recruitment, use, and development. It draws on a number of related disciplines (especially the behavioral sciences), psychology, sociology, anthropology, law, economics, education, and industrial engineering, to name a few. The role of personnel administration in a business organization has undergone historical change from that of mainly record keeping, to employment, to providing for the employee's welfare, to a comprehensive approach to human resource allocation and utilization.

Objectives. The overall task of personnel administration is to study and develop new ways in which human beings can be integrated effectively into the various organizations of our society. This requires that human resources be efficiently utilized, that positive working relationships be promoted among all members of the organization, and that maximum individual development be provided for and encouraged. Hence, its objectives are economic, social, and personal. It is not a series of human relations gimmicks, although admittedly in its earlier history, instances of exploitation, insincerity, and employee manipulation could be evidenced. Today, such questionable practices occur ever less frequently as the concept of human dignity increasingly influences personnel thinking.

Personnel administration contributes as much to profit as do other line activities. It is not a practice to be engaged in during times of profit making and full employment only to be discarded during difficult economic periods. On the contrary, good personnel practices can be even more advantageous to the organization when the profit squeeze is on.

Organizational Relationships. The term Personnel Manager is actually a misnomer. In a sense, all persons of management status are personnel managers (they manage people). Their results are achieved through the work of others. In small organizations, the personnel function is centralized. In large or geographically dispersed organizations, the personnel function is often decentralized from the parent organization but still locally centralized. In both, it will be a staff department activity, providing advice and expertise to line managers and top management.

This centralization of personnel activities has resulted from attempts to relieve line managers of some of the more routine chores, to utilize specialists in personnel who can advise and guide the line organization, and to assure a consistency and continuity in personnel practices. Early development and wide dissemination of good personnel policies by a company are ways of further ensuring consistency, but more important, they bring line management actively and with understanding into their personnel development role.

Personnel administration is a relatively late specialized area of general management, in contrast to production, engineering, marketing, and finance. But the need for it is as old as human organizations themselves. Thus, the owner and sole worker in a retail shop in the 1840s who, because of press of business, decided to employ one other person, had engaged in the following personnel activities. First, he had to determine what the new employee was to do and what type of person he wanted (job analysis and hiring specification). He perhaps put a sign in his window or ran an ad in the local paper (recruiting). Assuming he had more than one applicant for the position, he had to decide which applicant was to be employed (appraisal and selection). Starting wages had to be decided on (bargaining or wage surveying). Some training will have been needed for the new employee (on-the-job or apprenticeship training). As the new employee made progress, the owner will have had to evaluate his or her advancement in order to adjust wages and furnish further training (merit rating).

Approaches and Techniques. Personnel administration may be divided into three major areas. These are evaluation, motivation, and development of human resources.

Evaluation is made of the needs of the organization (organization charts and job analysis), of the human resources of an organization (performance appraisal and manpower inventory), and of how well the company is matching needs and resources (productivity indexes, employee attitude surveys, turnover ratios). It considers the company's long-range as well as immediate objectives (manpower/womanpower charts).

Motivation includes financial and non-financial incentives. It includes wage payment plans, both indirect as well as direct incentive plans. Fringe benefits and employee services are important indirect financial incentives. Non-financially, the establishment of an appropriate fit between the worker and the work, the worker and the work group, (group dynamics), and the work environment (safety and human engineering) are all basic to motivation.

Development would include, chronologically, presenting the job and orienting the new employee, on-the-job training, and preparation for advanced positions, managerial and technical. Day-to-day supervision and an open multi-directional employee communication system are important. Development will probably utilize intra-organizational, as well as external aids.

The above categories are somewhat artificial. In actual practice, an effective personnel program requires elements of all three. For example, good executive development programs require appropriate evaluation of what executives need and how well existing personnel are meeting these needs. It also must include a compensation structure which attracts and encourages the development of individuals who have the potential to assume executive positions. It involves, of course, continual training—both within, as in job rotation, and outside, as in attendance at formal educational institutions or management development institutes. Hence, personnel administration is best conceived and implemented as a total system [1].

Recent Developments. Personnel administration may be said to be conservative in contrast with marketing research, product development, and advertising. Effective personnel administration, however, results from the creativity we find in these other areas. It is appropriate and desirable that the most recent developments in personnel administration have derived from personnel research: research not only with respect to the effectiveness of internal personnel procedures, but in terms of the successful practices of other companies.

In the past two decades, large-scale changes have been taking place in personnel administration. In the area of philosophy and policy, a new emphasis on humanism and human resources has replaced the prior focus on human relations. The scope and areas of involvement of the personnel function have broadened considerably as new problem areas for resolution have emerged both in the organization and in its relationship to environment. There has been an increasing recognition among top managements of the vital role that personnel administration can and should play in the managing of change in organizations. A strong movement toward professionalization within the field has gathered momentum. And finally, the tools, methods, techniques, and approaches of the field have undergone important examination and refinement through increasing research, both from within the discipline and in response to pressures from state and Federal regulatory agencies. Each of these is considered in greater detail herein.

The prevailing value set of personnel administration during the 1950s was, simply, to keep the employee happy, an objective that was not too far out of context with the existing political, economic, and social climate of those years. Fair and considerate treatment of workers administered through the authority vested in managers and management was intended to create a work force that was both content and productive.

Technological advance, new social values and life styles, and a changing labor force have all combined to render the traditional value set of personnel administration increasingly inadequate to the challenge of the times. Thus, the challenge to today's personnel administration is not only fair treatment of employees, but the workers' expectation of *meaningful work* that uses their talents and interests and provides opportunity for individual advancement as well.

As a result of the changing business environment, new problem areas have emerged in the world of work to which personnel administration must now address itself. With the increasing number of multinational companies, personnel administration is increasingly extending its functions into areas of international operations, primarily in the staffing and compensation function. At home, our growing work force is rapidly changing in composition. Changes already under way include a growing proportion of young people in the labor force, greater numbers of female and minority group members, the fact that white collar workers now exceed blue collar workers, and the rapidly rising educational level of the work force.

Each of these developments presents new challenges and opportunities to personnel administration in its efforts to meet its objectives. In joint ventures with the Federal government, business organizations have increased their efforts to help solve the nation's social and economic problems. The National Alliance of Businessmen (NAB) and Job Opportunities in Business Sector (JOBS) are two examples of such partnerships. A more current example is the Comprehensive Employment and Training Act (CETA) program. (See HUMAN RESOURCES DEVELOPMENT, GOVERNMENT SPONSORED.) Personnel departments have a lead role in these types of programs.

Within organizations, personnel administration has expanded its role in such areas as management development, organization planning, manpower planning, communications, and personnel research. All of these activities have a common denominator, namely, the management of change in organizations. Accordingly, a new identity has emerged for personnel administration—agent of change in the corporation. To meet these new demands, effective personnel practice has increasingly required administrators with advanced levels of education and training, flexible and innovative minds, and men and women with broad understanding, insights, and interpersonal skills. The attainment of professionalization in the personnel function is clear.

Advances in personnel administration, as in all fields, depend on the continuing refinement of existing procedures and techniques and the development of new ones. The behavioral sciences—organizational psychology, sociology, and anthropology—continue to make important contributions toward this end. In employee selection, culture-free measures, work sample tests, and limitation on the content of the interview, are among the important contributors to enhance the accuracy of and reduce discrimination in employment decisions. Promising developments are under way using electronic data processing in the rapid matching of applicant profiles of skills, aptitudes, and interests with actual job requirements. At the managerial level, role playing, in-basket tests, the leaderless group conference are among the more widespread selection techniques in use. Against a background of increased test usage, however, the need continues for employers to demonstrate, in accordance with Title VII of the Civil Rights Act of 1964, that their job testing procedures are not discriminatory. (See EMPLOYMENT: ANTIDISCRIMINATION LEGISLATION.)

Behavioral scientists have offered important viewpoints to personnel administration in the areas of employee job satisfaction, motivation, and leadership. Paramount among these are Herzberg's dual factor theory of job satisfaction, Vroom's expectancy theory of motivation, the leadership concepts of Likert and Fiedler, and the viewpoints of Lawler and Adams on pay and compensation [2].

At the managerial level particularly, there has been a noticeable shift in emphasis from management training to management development. Essentially, the difference is one of moving from education in a narrow sense (training) to development, where the individual is prepared for a career in the firm rather than for a specific job. The term *organization development* represents the conceptual approach under which the total human resources of the firm are continually reviewed and renewed. Management games, programmed instruction, sensitivity training, systems-based supervisory training, behavior modeling, and assessment centers are examples of the newer approaches being taken. (See HUMAN RESOURCES DEVELOPMENT.)

In the 1980s personnel administration will be aggressively addressing itself to the problems of employee obsolescence, early retirement vs retirement at age 70, performance appraisal by objectives, alternate work schedules, drug use, alcoholism, and mental health, greater employee participation in organizational decision-making, cafeteria-style fringe benefit programs, career planning and change, and other quality of work life issues.

HRACH BEDROSIAN, PH.D., Professor of Management and Organizational Behavior, New York University, New York, New York

Information References

Associations:

American Psychological Association (Industrial and Organizational Psychology Division).
American Society for Personnel Administration
Society for Personnel Administration.
American Society for Training and Development.
Personnel Accreditation Institute.

Periodicals:
Publications of the Conference Board.
Harvard Business Review.
Human Resource Management.
Journal of Applied Psychology.
Personnel (American Management Associations).
Personnel Administrator.
Personnel Management Abstracts.
Personnel Psychology.
(For a complete listing, see "Dictionary of Personnel and Industrial Relations," Philosophical Library, New York.)

Texts:
French, Wendell, "The Personnel Management Process," Boston, Houghton Mifflin, 1978.
Heneman, Herbert G. et al., "Personnel/Human Resource Management", Homewood, Ill., Irwin, 1980.
Megginson, Leon C., "Personnel and Human Resources Administration." Homewood, Ill., Irwin, 1977.
Pigors, Paul and Myers, Charles A., "Personnel Administration, A Point of View and A Method," New York, McGraw-Hill, 1977.
Robbins, Stephen P. "Personnel: The Management of Human Resources," Englewood Cliffs, N.J., Prentice-Hall, 1978.
Strauss, George and Sayles, Leonard R., "Personnel: The Human Problems of Management," Englewood Cliffs, N.J., Prentice-Hall, 1980.

References Cited

[1] Glueck, William F., "Personnel: A Diagnostic Approach, Dallas, Texas. Business Publications, Inc., 1978, Chapter 1.
[2] Flippo, Edwin B., "Personnel Management," New York, McGraw-Hill, 1980, Chapters 12, 15, and 16.

Cross References: *Assessment Centers; Employee Attitude Research: Attitude Surveys; Employee Benefit Plans; Employment: Antidiscrimination Legislation; Employment Agencies; Executive Appraisal: Diagnostic Performance Appraisal; Executive Compensation; Executive Development: Away-From-Company Programs; Executive Development: Selection Guides; Executive Recruitment; Executive Selection; Guaranteed Annual Wage; Human Resources Development; Human Resources Requirements Planning; Incentive Systems; Job Evaluation; Labor Arbitration; Labor Relations Legislation; Labor Unions; Occupational Health; Occupational Safety and Health Act of 1970; Organization prefix entries; Performance Appraisal (Merit Rating); Personnel Counseling; Personnel Management: Pioneers; Personnel Testing; Safety and Health in the Workplace; Sensitivity Training; Suggestion Systems; Supervisory Training; Women in Management; Workers' Compensation.*

PERSONNEL COUNSELING

The term **Personnel Counseling** has both a general and a specific usage. In its general sense, the activities designated by the term resemble familiar industrial relations functions. These include such diverse activities as rendering direct assistance to the employee in meeting his problems, reducing turnover and absenteeism, investigating grievances, and improving the two-way flow of information between worker and management. In its specific sense, the term refers to the measures taken by an employer to facilitate the adjustment of the employee to his work situation. These measures are addressed to the mental and emotional state of the employee, his attitudes, feelings, and personal concerns. In its general sense, employee counseling is as old as management itself and designates functions traditionally performed by the employer, manager, supervisor, the industrial relations or medical staff. In its more restricted sense, the functions so designated are usually performed by a specialized staff.

History. Prior to World War II, there were only a few counseling programs in business, industry and government. Among the better known were those of the Metropolitan Life Insurance Company, R. H. Macy & Co., the Hawthorne plant of the Western Electric Company, and the Social Security Board.

The term *personnel counseling* entered the language of personnel management to designate a specific function as a result of the formal counseling program that developed from the HAWTHORNE EXPERIMENTS of the Western Electric Company. This program, which began as an experiment in 1936, and extended over a period of some twenty years, sought to extend to the general plant population some of the insights and findings concerning the beneficial effects of the nondirective interview [1].

Unlike most specialized counseling programs which have developed subsequently, and which utilize in varying degrees the concepts and methods developed in this research, the Hawthorne program was addressed not only to personal situations, but also to work-related problems and relationships. It was concerned with the worker in his work situation; and the problems arising from job assignment, supervisory relations, and informal group processes were of as central significance to the counselor as those of purely personal origin. While this program has been largely suspended, the basic concepts and techniques have found their way into general management and personnel practice within the company. Counseling theory and practice have also been incorporated in the

Western Electric Company's supervisory development programs [2].

Personnel counseling programs came into prominence during World War II to assist war industries in meeting the critical problems arising from an acute labor shortage. These programs were designed to keep the worker on the job, and the counselors were often charged with the responsibility of doing whatever was necessary to achieve this end. Such activities as assistance in finding housing, in establishing or finding day nurseries for children of working mothers, arranging car pools, and orienting the newcomer to the industrial environment, suggest the range of functions assigned to employee counselors during this period. Most of these programs were discontinued with the passing of the emergency which called them into being.

Approaches and Techniques. The methods and techniques used in employee counseling vary with the objectives of the program and the underlying assumptions as to how they may be best achieved. Approaches which depend upon guidance and advice may utilize various diagnostic techniques including interest, aptitude, and personality tests, case study, occupational history, and personal interviews. In the guidance phase, the counselor, through discussion of his findings with the employee, explores attitudes through directive or nondirective methods, seeks to improve self-understanding, impart broader or more objective perspectives, and stimulate motivation for achievement of goals [3].

In contrast to directive approaches, which focus on the skills of the counselor, nondirective approaches focus on the *interviewee* and stress the importance of the individual's thinking through his or her own situation, identifying sources of difficulty, and deciding upon and carrying through any changes felt to be desirable. Proponents of this approach contend that advice, however well intentioned, rarely accomplishes its objectives, and that ideas or decisions developed by the individual himself or herself are more useful in that they are related to the individual's particular level of development and to his or her total situation in all its complexity. Also, the process of thinking through a problem or situation is believed to encourage self-reliance and to strengthen ability to cope with future situations [4].

The Western Electric experience provides an example of the development of a nondirective approach. Under this program, counselors trained in interviewing and observation were assigned to territories comprising some 300 employees. Participation in the program was voluntary both for the organization and the individual. The program was formally introduced and explained to supervisors and employees through conferences and individual discussions.

The counselors had two types of contacts with the employee—on-the-job contacts and off-the-job interviews. The job contacts provided an opportunity to meet new employees, follow up on previous contacts, explain the program, build friendly relations, and make the counselor's services readily available. The formal interviews were held off the job in an interviewing room. Interviews could be initiated by the employee, the supervisor, or the counselor. All conversations with the counselor were confidential; the employee could talk freely about anything in any way he or she wished without fear of criticism, censure or violation of confidence.

The counselor functioned in a nonauthoritative capacity and refrained from giving advice or suggesting courses of action. These action-taking functions were regarded as being the responsibility of the employee and the employee's immediate supervisor. The counselor functioned somewhat as a catalytic agent in that he often stimulated change without becoming involved in it. The benefits of the program were chiefly those which derived from the counselor's type of interest in people and their free participation in the interview process. The program thus could be conceived as an organized way of extending to each individual a type of interest and understanding which research had demonstrated to be beneficial in improving employee attitudes and work relations.

Acceptance. It is difficult to estimate the extent to which the newer concepts of counseling have found their way into industrial application. In an early survey of sixty-one companies or governmental agencies reported by Helen Baker [5], it was found that in the main the various procedures evolving under the title of counseling were a re-assignment, under emergency conditions, of long recognized personnel functions and responsibilities. Yet the results suggested to a limited degree the growth of a new function. A survey made by the Bureau of National Affairs in 1961 [6] indicated that of the replies received from 136 executives participating in the Forum, 75% engaged in some kind of counseling but that most of the programs were informal. Forty-four percent of the reporting companies used nondirective counseling, 40% used a combination of directive and nondirective methods, and 16% were wholly directive.

While the results of these surveys are suggestive, they fail to indicate in any detail the respondent's conception of nondirective counseling or the extent to which the relationship of counselor to counselee is structured or perceived by the counselee as free from authoritative roles and functions. In an effort to isolate the truly nondirective programs from others which were said to be nondirective, Henry Eilbert [7], in 1955–56 surveyed 314 major American firms each employing over ten thousand employees. Of the 152 or 48.4% which gave usable replies, 93 or 61.2% provided counseling services by members of the staff who also performed other services, and 26 or 17.1% utilized special personnel employed for counseling functions. Of these 26, only a few indicated complete subscription to the nondirective method. While the others utilized "listening" techniques, they also gave advice or performed other services as well.

Eilbert indicates that the concepts and methods of counseling, as exemplified by the Western Electric program, have had a much wider impact on industrial management than these figures would indicate, especially in the field of executive development and training. In answer to a direct question, forty-seven of the large companies surveyed replied that they would use the non-directive approach if they were to institute a counseling program. Eilbert states that these responses suggest a receptive attitude toward this approach and should be regarded as indicating a theoretical acceptance that the nondirective approach is the proper, sound, and desirable practice.

Potentials. As to the further prospects of employee counseling, one can only point to current developments as being indicative:

(1) A growing understanding of the importance of the work situation, including job assignment, management climate, and associated social and psychological influences, to the individual's mental and emotional health, and the possible effects of these upon costs in terms of efficiency, absenteeism, turnover, and morale.

(2) A far less general agreement with respect to a company's responsibility for undertaking remedial or preventive measures and the particular form such measures should take.

(3) A continuing interest in general approaches which seek to equip the supervisor with the concepts, methods, and understanding to perform counseling functions as a normal supervisory responsibility.

(4) A continuing interest in and apparently a growing, but by no means general, acceptance of nondirective counseling as a specific approach. One might add here, more referrals to family service agencies, psychiatrists, and psychologists in private practice.

(5) A growing awareness of a company's responsibility to assist those employees whose job skills and knowledge, after many years of productive service, have become obsolete because of economic, social, and technological changes. The transition into new jobs and/or careers is very difficult for many and not possible for some, as it involves leaving the old, secure, and familiar and dealing with uncertainties and ambivalences associated with the new job and work conditions.

(6) A growing realization by management that the rapid development and implementation of those technological advances needed to remain competitive and viable may adversely impact on employees' expectations and personal feelings about the work situation—and the possible effects of these on the "bottom line." Counseling can provide employees the opportunity to resolve job conflicts and make appropriate adjustments to become more effective in a continuously changing work situation.

W. J. Dickson, Personnel Research, Western Electric Company, Inc., New York, New York

Information References

To place the foregoing in proper perspective as regards continuing research into human motivation and behavior in industry, the reader is referred to the entries, Motivation and Human Relations in Industry.

Association:

American Personnel and Guidance Association.

Periodicals:

Journal of Counseling Psychology, Ohio State University, Columbus, Ohio.

The Menninger Quarterly, Menninger Foundation, Topeka, Kans.

Studies in Personnel Policy, The Conference Board, New York.

Personnel, American Management Association, New York.

Texts:

Heyel, Carl, ed., see [2] below.

Levinson, Harry, "Emotional Health in the World of Work," New York, Harper & Row, 1964.
Roethlisberger, F. J. and Dickson, W. J., "Management and the Worker," Cambridge, Harvard Univ. Press, 1939 (esp. Chaps. XII, XIV, and XXVI).

References Cited

[1] "Twentieth-Century Beginnings in Employee Counseling," *The Business History Review,* Harvard University, Autumn, 1957.
[2] *Ed. note:* The basics of personnel counseling as set forth in this entry follow the treatment by the late Mr. Dickson in the first edition of *"The Encyclopedia of Management,"* and are conceptually valid today. Developments in the past decade have been to incorporate the skills of personnel counseling in the repertoire of skills required by first line supervision and to emphasize them in supervisory training. For a good overview of this approach to personnel counseling, see Drake, John D., chapter on "Employee Counseling" in Heyel, C., ed., "Handbook of Modern Office Management and Administrative Services," repr. Melbourne, Fla., Krieger, 1980.
[3] For a discussion of the directive approach see: Thorne, Frederic C., "Directive Psychotherapy: VII. Imparting Psychological Information," in "Readings in Modern Methods of Counseling" by Arthur H. Brayfield, ed., New York, Appleton-Century-Crofts, 1950.
[4] For a discussion of these two approaches and the assumptions underlying them see: Rogers, Carl R., "Counseling and Psychotherapy," Boston, Houghton Mifflin, 1942, esp. Chaps. I and II.
[5] Baker, Helen, "Employee Counseling, A Survey of a New Development in Personnel Relations," Industrial Relations Section, Princeton, N.J., Princeton University, 1944.
[6] Survey No. 63, Personnel Policies Forum, Washington, D.C., The Bureau of National Affairs, 1961.
[7] Eilbert, Henry, "A Study of Current Counseling Practices in Industry," *The Journal of Business,* University of Chicago, January, 1958.

Cross References: *Hawthorne Experiments; Motivation (and accompanying entries with Motivation prefix).*

PERSONNEL MANAGEMENT: Pioneers

Personnel Management is a multifaceted discipline to which distinguished individuals from a number of disciplines have made contributions. Therefore, no two observers of the personnel management scene probably would agree on just who meet the criterion of "outstanding." This lack of agreement is understandable when one considers that the past sixty years have been a period marked by movements and counter-movements, by diverse philosophies and great innovations. It thus is just as significant to include the pioneer of the GROUP DYNAMICS movement as it is to identify the most influential authority in the personnel testing field. Further, although personnel management is ordinarily conceived of as a staff function, two line managers whose work and thought have greatly influenced the personnel function seem also worthy of mention. (See **Chester I. Barnard** and **Charles P. McCormick,** below.)

When assessing "contribution," it is not always easy to assert categorically that an individual was the creator of an idea, the innovator of a technique, or the founder of a movement. Obviously ideas and techniques come from several sources. For example, Dr. Carl Rogers is considered to be the prime developer of the technique of nondirective counseling, but Freud's work in psychoanalysis is certainly basic to that technique. Also, authorities differ as to who was the father of a particular movement. An example is Kurt Lewin versus J. L. Moreno in group dynamics.

This article invites attention to various individuals who, many persons believe, have greatly influenced personnel management during this century.

In the early part of this period, **Dr. Walter Dill Scott** (1869–1955) educator and psychologist, was a long-time key figure in personnel management. He set up the World War I Army testing program, and was awarded the Distinguished Service Medal for "devising, installing, and supervising the personnel system in the U.S. Army." His work in testing influenced personnel management significantly in industry and government. He was also the joint author of an early textbook, "Personnel Management," 1923 [1].

Dr. Walter Van Dyke Bingham (1880–1952) is considered by many to have been the dean of American personnel psychologists. He worked with Walter Dill Scott and others in the testing field on the Army testing program in World War I. In that period Dr. Bingham was Executive Secretary, Committee on Classification of Personnel in the Army (1917–18), and then a Lieutenant Colonel, Personnel Branch, Army General Staff (1918–19). His "Aptitudes and Aptitude Testing," 1937 [2] and "How to Interview," 1931 [3], written with B. V. Moore, were long regarded as standard texts. He also was joint author of the widely used text, "Procedures in Employment Psychology," 1937 [4]. Toward the latter part of his long career, he was Chief Psychologist, Adjutant General's Office, U.S. War Department (1940–47).

Dr. Warner W. Stockberger (1872–1944) was the first Personnel Director (1925–38) of the U.S. Department of Agriculture and of the Federal Government. He was also the first president of the Society for Personnel Administration, Washington, D.C. (1937). An early pioneer in Federal personnel management, he had a keen appreciation of the human factor in management. His work, which included training of many personnel workers who utlimately moved on to other Federal agencies, influenced the character of Federal personnel management generally.

Dr. Leonard D. White (1891–1958) was an internationally recognized figure in public personnel administration. A teacher at the Univ. of Chicago, a scholar, writer, thinker, idealist, and practitioner, he is credited with many "firsts." He was the author of the first text on public administration, which also contained considerable information on personnel management; he was the first to teach public administration in a university classroom; he pioneered in starting the Junior Civil Service Examiner Examination, which attracted liberal arts and social science majors to careers in the Federal Government.

While in Washington with the Civil Service Commission in the 1930s, Dr. White taught a course in Public Personnel Administration at American University. In his class was born the idea which led to the establishment of the Society for Personnel Administration.

More recently, Dr. White served with distinction on the two Hoover Commissions which recommended improvements in Federal personnel management (1948–49, 1953–55). Some of his widely known works include "Introduction to the Study of Public Administration," (1926 [5], "The City Manager" 1927 [6]; and "Prestige Value of Public Employment," 1929 [7].

Dr. White's work on organization and personnel management was influenced by the SCIENTIFIC MANAGEMENT movement. (Some of his students, principally Herbert Simon, later challenged Dr. White's adherence to "principles" of organization [37]. The work of behavioral scientists presented many insights about management and organizational behavior, ones which Dr. White and others in his era had not explored.)

In retrospect, Dr. White's major contributions to personnel management lay in his support of the merit system; his having facilitated the entry of college graduates from *all* disciplines into the Federal service, rather than from the recognized professions only; his having encouraged the building of a personnel "profession"; and his concern with augmenting the prestige of the public service.

The first intensive human relations research study was the HAWTHORNE EXPERIMENTS conducted at the Hawthorne plant of the Western Electric Co. (1924–32) with the help (1927–32) of a research staff of the Harvard Graduate School of Business, directed by **Dr. G. Elton Mayo** (1880–1949). Whereas Frederick W. Taylor and his contemporaries in SCIENTIFIC MANAGEMENT viewed management and organization primarily from the standpoint of engineering, Dr. Mayo and his staff applied sociopsychological techniques to managerial problems. From this research, a new theory of human behavior in organizations was created.

The Hawthorne experiments led to, among other things, the creation of employee counseling programs in the 1930s, a phase of personnel management which is operative (albeit in a less elaborate form) in many organizations today. (See PERSONNEL COUNSELING.)

In his "The Human Problem of an Industrial Civilization," 1933 [8], and his "Social Problems of an Industrial Civilization," 1954 [9], Dr. Mayo has given a scholarly interpretation of the significance of human factors in our industrial culture. His thesis related to the advantages to be derived from involving the worker in the decision-making process. He questioned strongly the "rabble hypothesis"—that materialistic goals are the only motivating force and that authoritarian leadership is essential to get the lazy to work and to keep the grasping in line. For all of us, he said, the feeling of security and certainty derives always from assured membership in a group; if this is lost, no monetary gain, no job guarantee, can be sufficient compensation.

Another solid contributor to the personnel field is **Dr. Ordway Tead** (1892–1972). Dr. Tead taught personnel administration, and at Columbia, 1917–18, he was in charge of war emergency employment management courses of the War Department. He continued at Columbia as a lecturer in personnel administration during 1920–50, and from 1951–56 was Adjunct Professor of Industrial Relations. He was also a faculty member of the Department of Industry at the New York School of Social Work, 1920–29.

Dr. Tead's writings, which stress democratic principles of management, have not been dimmed by more recent research. His better known works are "The Art of Leadership," 1935 [10] and "The Art of Administration" 1951 [11]. He also co-authored with Henry C. Metcalf a pioneer personnel textbook, "Personnel Administration: Its Principles and Practices," 1920 [12].

Dr. Chester I. Barnard (1886–1961), an eminent industrialist, was president of the New Jersey Bell Telephone Co. and later of the Rockefeller Foundation. In his much-quoted classic, "The Functions of the Executive," 1938 [13], Dr. Barnard analyzed and stressed the sociopsychological and ethical aspects of managerial organization and functions. His book is an early, if not the first, recognition of the import of the informal as well as the formal organizational structure. He viewed organization as a social system.

This view necessitates a high degree of cooperation as opposed to emphasis upon authority and order-giving; the relegation of economic factors as motivators to a secondary role; the individual's identification with the organization based on a strong belief in its codes, as opposed to compliance imposed from without.

Dr. Barnard was also one of the first management authorities to stress the communication responsibilities of executives, to analyze the role of status in organizational endeavor, and to develop systematically an analysis of incentive systems in organizations.

Charles P. McCormick (1896–1970), late board chairman of McCormick and Co., Baltimore, was the founder of MULTIPLE MANAGEMENT, which involves the establishment of several boards—senior, junior, factory, and sales—as a means of securing employee participation and developing executives. Hundreds of companies now use this means of securing participation, manager development, problem solving, and morale building.

Among the leaders of the more current period, **Dr. Kurt Lewin** (1890–1947) is regarded by many social psychologists as the founder of contemporary GROUP DYNAMICS. Dr. Lewin tested his ideas about groups after he left Germany in 1932 and settled in the United States, carrying on his pioneer studies on group leadership at the University of Iowa, and later at M.I.T. and the University of Michigan. Results of his studies pointed up the direct relationship between production and participation in the decision-making process.

Dr. Lewin should be credited, too, with being the father of SENSITIVITY TRAINING. In this work he pioneered in the use of unstructured discussion groups which function without a leader and without procedures or agenda.

A distinguished disciple of Dr. Lewin, **Dr. Leland P. Bradford,** established in 1947 at Bethel, Maine, the first "sensitivity" or human relations laboratory. Since that time his efforts have spawned such training at many universities and other organizations. This development has been a significant contribution to group leadership, with a tremendous potential for organizational health. Dr. Bradford was Director, National Training Laboratories, National Education Assn., Washington, D.C. 1947–1970 (in 1967 renamed the NTL Institute for Applied Behavioral Science, located in Arlington, Va.; see SENSITIVITY TRAINING).

An early summation of the work at Bethel is contained in Bradford's "Explorations in Human Relations Training: An Assessment of Experience, 1947–53" [14]. A comprehensive account of laboratory training is given in a joint work with **Jack R. Gibb** and **Kenneth D. Benne** [15]. Dr. Bradford also launched for N.T.L. "The Journal of Applied Behavioral Science" in 1965.

Using sensitivity training concepts, **Robert R. Blake** and **Jane S. Mouton** developed a system of leaderless training laboratories in the early 1960s. Managers thus are enabled to receive feedback from their peers about their leadership style based on the MANAGERIAL GRID concepts [16]. Today, managers all over the world are being challenged through training to develop a 9–9 (team management) leadership style. Blake and Mouton also have developed a comprehensive system of organization development [17].

A long-time giant in the field is **Dr. Carl R. Rogers** (1902–). An internationally recognized psychotherapist, encounter group facilatator, and human relations theorist, he is credited with introducing the non-directive method of counseling and interviewing. In Roger's "person-centered" approach, the client is in charge of the pace, content, and direction of the interchange. The term "non-directive" is now used to refer to any similar approach used by any power figure: e.g., a teacher, counselor, consultant, manager, etc. To do this successfully, one must be willing (and able) really to listen to the other person, try to understand the other person's position without being judgmental, accept the other person as he/she is. Roger's work has also spawned the term "Rogerian" to indicate the non-directive, person-centered approach to interpersonal relations. A prolific and profound writer, his major works are "Counseling and Psychotherapy" (1942), "Client Centered Therapy," (1951), "On Becoming A Person" (1961), "On Encounter Groups," (1970), "Freedom to Learn" (1969), "Becoming Partners" (1972), and "On Personal Power" (1977). He is at this writing Resident Fellow at the Center For Studies of The Person, La Jolla, California.

Norman R. F. Maier (1901-1977), an industrial psychologist at the University of Michigan, was a prolific writer, researcher, teacher, trainer, lecturer, and consultant. His unusually creative work emphasized the importance of group decision, employee participation, problem solving and creativity, causation, motivation, and frustration. As a practical trainer of supervisors, Dr. Maier stimulated the wide use of "group-in-action" training methods (principally role-playing exercises) by training specialists. His "Principles of Human Relations," 1952 [18], "Psychology of Industry," 1946 [19], "Supervisory and Executive Development: A Manual for Role Playing," 1957 [20], "The Appraisal Interview," 1958 [21], "Creative Management," 1962 [22], and "Problem Solving Discussions and Conferences," 1963 [23] have enriched the personnel and training field.

Dr. Rensis Likert (1903-), Director, 1948-1972, of the Institute of Social Research, University of Michigan, conducted highly significant human relations research since the 1940s. He has pointed out that the concept of equating high morale with high productivity is much too simple. In fact many kinds of combinations are possible. Dr. Likert's research demonstrates the value to productivity of (1) "supportive" as opposed to threatening supervision and (2) "participative" as opposed to "hierarchically-controlled" management. In general, supervisory attitudes—that is, those which are "employee centered" as opposed to "production centered"—are basic to productivity. Dr. Likert's findings cast doubt on the long-range success of organizations which use people for short-range goals. His book, "New Patterns of Management," 1961 [24], reports his basic findings and conclusions. In "The Human Organization: Its Management and Value," 1967 [25], a direct link to the prior work, Likert looks at management systems and advocates that organizations use "System 4", or participative-group, for greater profitability and employee satisfaction.

We must also recognize that the contemporary scene can boast a good number of other top-flight thinkers, writers, and researchers. Examples are **Carroll Shartle** (Ohio State) who conducted highly significant studies in leadership [26], narrowing the description of a leader's behavior to two dimensions—"initiating structure" and "consideration." Later, **Fred E. Fiedler** (University of Illinois) developed a "Leadership Contingency Model" which emphasized the importance of the situation rather than the "best" leadership style [27].

Douglas McGregor (1906-1964) of M.I.T., is to be credited with having authored one of the most original, seminal, and quoted management books in the past quarter century—"The Human Side of Enterprise" [28]. Here he developed his ideas on leadership theory, motivation, and management by objectives, presented as "Theory X" and "Theory Y." (See MOTIVATION: MCGREGOR'S "THEORY X" and "THEORY Y.") He elaborated on his ideas in "The Professional Manager," 1967 [29], edited posthumously by Caroline McGregor and Warren G. Bennis, stressing the means of achieving the goals presented in the earlier work.

Warren G. Bennis, educator, trainer, consultant, and former President of the University of Cincinnati, was a close colleague of McGregor. He has drawn on the great mass of current behavioral science findings, and has developed ideas explaining causes and consequences of change in organizational behavior [30]. Bennis is a leading theorist in the field of organization development.

Chris Argyris (Harvard) advanced the "Immaturity-Maturity Theory," which suggests that organizations all too often keep workers passive and thus stunt their psychological growth [31]. Argyris, in general, has been concerned with making organizations "healthy" [32]. A significant book deals with "intervention theory," a behavioral science-consultant approach to helping organizations to diagnose better their ailments and thus to solve their problems in an in-depth way [33].

Frederick Herzberg (Case Western Reserve University and University of Utah) developed, while at Case, the popular and practical "Motivation-Hygiene Theory," i.e., hygiene factors depend on the environment and merely prevent job dissatisfaction whereas satisfiers or motivators derive from the job and produce positive effects on productivity [34, 35]. Herzberg's work forms an important support for the concept of job enrichment. (See JOB ENRICHMENT AND WORK EFFECTIVENESS.)

Melville Dalton (U.C.L.A.) is known for his sociological analysis of organizations and the men who manage them, including concern with line and staff conflict, power, status, influence, maneuvering, and the "implicit and the explicit" organization [36].

Herbert A. Simon (Carnegie) merits high recognition for his analysis of organizational behavior from the standpoint of decision-making, particularly its non-rational character [37, 38].

All these scholars and practitioners are representative of the continually expanding field of personnel administration, influenced markedly by behavioral science research.

Reference should also be made to **organizations** which pioneered in advancing the personnel art. First, on the *public* side of things, there was the **National Assembly of Civil Service Commissioners,** founded in 1906. Its first chairman was Charles S. Fowler, Civil Service Commissioner of New York State. That organization dropped the "National" in 1918 and later (1928) became the **Civil Service Assembly of U.S. and Canada,** headquartered in Chicago, Illinois. The first president of the CSA was Ellsworth Jeffrey. In 1957 the CSA became the **Public Personnel Association,** since 1973 known as the **International Personnel Management Association** with headquarters in Washington, D.C. The Association has both organizational and individual members, the former totalling 995 and the latter 4,305. IPMA is also organized into 49 chapters, all of them in the United States.

Another public personnel oriented group was founded in 1937, primarily for personnelists in the Federal Government, under the name of **Society for Personnel Administration,** Washington, D.C. (see reference above to Dr. Warner W. Stockberger). The SPA merged with the Public Personnel Association to become the **International Personnel Management Association** in 1973. Thus, the public personnel field is now represented by a single professional organization.

In reference to the *private* sector, the **American Society for Personnel Administration** (ASPA) was founded in 1949. It brought together numerous local personnel associations in the United States Headquartered in Berea, Ohio, ASPA now is a world-wide professional association of personnel and industrial relations practitioners, with more than 25,000 members and 300 chapters in 50 states. The Society also serves members in 39 foreign countries.

JULIUS E. EITINGTON, Director of Training and Research, BNA Communications Inc., Rockville, Maryland

References Cited

[1] Scott, Walter Dill, Clothier, Robert C., and Spriegel, William R., "Personnel Management," 5th ed., New York, McGraw-Hill, 1954.
[2] Bingham, Walter Van Dyke, "Aptitudes and Aptitude Testing," New York, Harper & Bros., 1937.
[3] ———, and Moore, Victor B., "How to Interview," 3rd. rev. ed., New York, Harper & Bros., 1941.
[4] ———, and Freyd, Max, "Procedures in Employment Psychology," Chicago, A. W. Shaw, 1937.
[5] White, Leonard D., "Introduction to the Study of Public Administration," 4th ed., New York, Macmillan, 1955.
[6] ———, "The City Manager," University of Chicago Social Science Studies No. 9., 1927.
[7] ———, "Prestige Value of Public Employment," University of Chicago Social Science Studies No. 14, 1929.
[8] Mayo, Elton, "The Human Problem of an Industrial Civilization," New York, Viking, 1933.
[9] ———, "Social Problems of an Industrial Civilization," Cambridge, Harvard University Press, 1945.
[10] Tead, Ordway, "The Art of Leadership," New York, McGraw-Hill, 1935.
[11] ———, "The Art of Administration," New York, McGraw-Hill, 1951.
[12] ———, and Metcalf, Henry C., "Personnel Administration: Its Principles and Practices," New York, McGraw-Hill, 1933.
[13] Barnard, Chester I., "The Functions of the Executive," Cambridge, Mass., Harvard University Press, 1938.
[14] Bradford, Leland P., "Explorations in Human Relations Training: An Assessment of Experience, 1947–1953," Washington, National Training Laboratories. (Now NLT Institute for Applied Behavioral Science, Arlington, Va.)
[15] Bradford, Leland P., Gibb, Jack R., and Benne, Kenneth D., "T-Group Theory and Laboratory Method," New York, Wiley, 1964.
[16] Blake, Robert R. and Mouton, Jane S., "The New Managerial Grid," Houston, Texas, Gulf, 1978. (The original work appeared in 1964, titled "The Managerial Grid." See entry, MANAGERIAL GRID.)

[17] Blake, Robert R. and Mouton, Jane S., "Corporate Excellence Through Grid Organization Development," Houston, Texas, Gulf, 1968.
[18] Maier, Norman F., "Principles of Human Relations," New York, Wiley, 1952.
[19] ———, "Psychology of Industry," rev. ed., New York, Houghton-Mifflin, 1955.
[20] ———, et al., "Supervisory and Executive Development: A Manual for Role Playing," New York, Wiley, 1957. (The book was revised and is now called "The Role-Play Technique: A handbook for Management and Leadership Practice," La Jolla, Calif., University Associates, 1978.)
[21 ———, "The Appraisal Interview: Objectives, Methods, and Skills," New York, Wiley, 1958.
[22] ———, and Hayes, John J., "Creative Management," New York, Wiley, 1962.
[23] ———, "Problem Solving Discussions and Conferences: Leadership Methods and Skills," New York, McGraw-Hill, 1963.
[24] Likert, Rensis, "New Patterns of Management," New York, McGraw-Hill, 1961.
[25] ———, "The Human Organization: Its Management and Value," New York, McGraw-Hill, 1967.
[26] Shartle, C. L., "Effective Performance and Leadership," Englewood Cliffs, N.J., Prentice-Hall, 1956.
[27] Fiedler, Fred E., "A Theory of Leadership Effectiveness," New York, McGraw-Hill, 1967.
[28] McGregor, Douglas, "The Human Side of Enterprise," New York, McGraw-Hill, 1960.
[29] ———, "The Professional Manager," McGraw-Hill, 1967.
[30] Bennis, Warren G., "Changing Organizations," New York, McGraw-Hill, 1966.
[31] Argyris, Chris, "Personality and Organization," New York, Harper & Row, 1957.
[32] ———, "Integrating the Individual and the Organization," New York, Wiley, 1964.
[33] ———, "Intervention Theory and Method: A Behavioral Science View," New York, Wiley, 1970.
[34] Herzberg, Frederick, Mausner, Bernard, and Synderman, Barbara, "The Motivation to Work," New York, Wiley, 1959.
[35] Herzberg, Frederick, "Work and the Nature of Man," New York, World, 1966.
[36] Dalton, Melville, "Men Who Manage," New York, Wiley, 1959.
[37] Simon, Herbert A., "Administrative Behavior," New York, Macmillan, 1947.
[38] ———, "Models of Man, Social and Rational," New York, Wiley, 1957.

Cross Reference: *Personnel Administration.*

PERSONNEL TESTING

Personnel Testing refers to the practice of administering psychological tests to personnel in order to secure information useful in their selection, placement, and career guidance. Thus, a major reason for personnel testing is to enhance the accuracy of personnel decisions relative to hiring, firing, promotion, transfer, training, and personnel development. Users of psychological tests believe that a carefully and professionally developed program of personnel testing can and does substantially reduce costly methods of trial and error in personnel administration and reduces the relative incidence of faulty decisions concerning personnel moves. Ideally, then, the end objective of personnel testing is to help in insuring a flow of the *right* people into the *right* jobs at the *right* times.

History. Broadly defined, personnel testing extends back at least as far as the early Greeks. References to the need for applying tests to determine latent capacities occur frequently in Plato's *Republic.* However, modern testing grew out of the work of Sir Francis Galton in England, Alfred Binet in France, and James McKeen Cattell in the USA. In 1894, Cattell administered early "mental tests" (tests of strength of grip, reaction time, memory for letters, etc.) to students at Columbia University. Working with school children in France, Alfred Binet was the first to demonstrate the usefulness of more complex tests (e.g. following directions, unscrambling words to make sentences, etc.) for the identification of mental retardation and the assessment of general mental ability. His series of tests, published in 1908, constituted the first intelligence test. By far the most successful translation and revision of Binet's tests for use in the United States was completed under the direction of Lewis Terman of Stanford University. First published in 1916, the Standford Binet Test of Intelligence has undergone two major revisions (1937 and 1960) and remains today the most widely used individually administered measure of intelligence in the world.

Personnel testing on a broad scale came of age during World War I when psychologists, under the direction of R. M. Yerkes, developed tests of intelligence which could be administered to groups rather than requiring individual administration. In the process of screening and assigning recruits during World War I, the Army tests were taken by over one and one-half million men. After the war, personnel testing expanded rapidly along many fronts. Scores of new tests were developed; test usage extended into a wide variety of educational and industrial settings; and, during the 1930s and 1940s, heavy emphasis was placed on developing vocational interest and personality tests. The 1950s and early 1960s were years of consolidation and further expansion and also witnessed the proliferation of large scale nationwide testing "programs."

As will be discussed later, the 1970s found personnel testing under attack from those who allege that many tests are discriminatory when used for selection or placement of minorities and women. As a consequence, more research emphasis has been given to issues growing from these charges than to development of new test instruments.

Rationale. A psychological test is best defined as *a sample of performance observed under standardized conditions.* A well developed test is one which presents a series of tasks to be performed under uniform conditions by each examinee. It is obvious that unless a test is carefully standardized, the behavior required by it will not be comparable from examinee to examinee. Thus, careful standardization is one of the most important attributes of a psychological test, and constitutes also one of the major advantages of testing over other more subjective personnel assessment procedures such as interviewing. The sampling concept is also important. A carefully developed test samples performance in order to be representative of broader areas of performance. Thus, a personality test designed to measure dominance should be representative of dominant behavior in a variety of situations and circumstances.

This leads to what is by far the most important concept in psychological testing: *validity.* In the broadest sense, the validity of a test refers to the *meaning* that may be attached to different levels of performance on the test. It should be apparent, then, that a test's validity cannot be expressed in a single index or in terms of a single item of information. Validity is *not* an either-or, all-or-none concept. Instead, the determination of the *validity* or the *meaning* of scores on a given test is a never-ending process based on the accumulation of research information over a lengthy period of time. Thus a test may be valid for some purposes and nonvalid for others. Management should ask the psychologist with whom it works to summarize for it the validity information available on the tests it is anticipating using. Armed with this information, management will be in a better position to judge whether or not the tests will be useful to the purpose it has in mind. The sole rationale for personnel testing rests on the nature and extent of validity information available about the tests management intends to use. The kinds of validity information necessary for various test uses are discussed in the following section.

Uses of Personnel Testing. Four major uses of personnel testing are listed and briefly discussed below:

(1) *Selection.* Personnel testing is most commonly used as an aid in selecting applicants. In using tests for selection, management will want to have evidence that they are valid for predicting job effectiveness defined in terms of such factors as supervisory ratings, productivity, sales volume, low turnover, etc.

(2) *Determining Training Needs.* Personnel testing may be used to establish the need for further training or specialized knowledge. Since knowledge or achievement examinations would normally be used for this purpose, management would want evidence that they sample content representative of the skills and or knowledge emphasized in its training programs.

(3) *Counseling.* Personnel testing is coming to play an increasingly important role in employee counseling. However, since the counseling would usually be undertaken by a professional counselor (e.g. a clinical psychologist), any decision concerning personnel testing would normally rest with him. In choosing tests, he would be somewhat less concerned about their validity for predicting job effectiveness and relatively more concerned about their validity for describing the major characteristics and personnel dynamics of the counselee.

(4) *Promotion and Transfer.* Personnel testing is widely used to aid in decisions concerning promotion and transfer. Since career guidance is an important part of such decisions, the tests must be useful not only in a selection sense but also in a counseling sense, and management will want evidence of their descriptive validity as well as their validity for predicting actual job performances.

It is apparent that different uses of personnel testing involve different kinds of decisions for management, and different kinds of information concerning the tests to be used. It is also obvious that management's use of personnel testing will nearly always involve *institutional* decisions in contrast to *individual* decisions. In other words, management's major purpose is to improve the quality of utilizing its human resources in order to enhance the over-all effectiveness of the organization or institution.

The usual purpose is to maximize accuracy or "batting odds" for selecting and placing persons on jobs in an organization. Management may desire 100% accuracy—all "hits." But it must accept the unfortunate necessity of occasional "misses"—some persons are rejected who could have been successful; others are hired who may actually fail. From the standpoint of the *institution,* management's purpose is to maximize the "hits" and to minimize the "misses." Personnel tests usually help achieve this purpose.

It should be noted, however, that this type of decision differs from what is involved in the typical *individual* decision. An individual may use psychological tests to help decide on a vocation or to make some other important lifetime decision. A person who has just made a decision about his (her) own future is proved in the light of time and experience to be either right or wrong, wise or unwise. For this person the "batting odds" are of little consequence if he or she is proven wrong. Testing may provide individuals with information that will make them more sure about the direction they should take, but they can take little comfort in population statistics or "odds" when faced with the necessity of choosing from among a number of practical alternatives which affect their own future.

Criticisms of Tests. Personnel testing in industry has often been criticized by those who dispute the use of personnel testing for making institutional decisions. However, most critics argue from the point of view of individual decision making and fail to realize that the "rightness" or "wrongness" of each individual decision must, of necessity, be secondary to the purpose of increasing the odds of accurate personnel decisions for the entire organization. Most critics of testing also choose to ignore or refuse to accept the fact that a carefully developed and validated program of personnel testing will, over the long run, increase relative numbers of correct individual decisions as well as increase the batting odds associated with institutional decisions.

In deciding whether to use testing or not to use testing, management should consider its potential *utility* to the organization. Personnel testing can be expensive. Management must weigh the costs of instituting and maintaining a testing program against the possible gain involved in making more accurate decisions.

One recent study of insurance salesmen showed that a personality test would increase the proportion of successful salesmen by a factor of only 3%. It would seem that such a modest increase in overall selective efficiency would hardly warrant the cost of the program.

We are not suggesting that personnel testing is not often useful; in actual fact, its relative utility is usually very great. We are suggesting, however, that management should diligently seek *evidence* of its utility for the specific uses and for making the kinds of decisions to be asked of it.

A more serious criticism of personnel testing has come to the fore since the passage of the Civil Rights Act of 1964. The Civil Rights Act, the work of the Equal Employment Opportunity Commission (EEOC), and that of the Office of Federal Contract Compliance (OFCC) have served to focus attention on personnel tests as potential instruments for discriminatory employment practices. The status of testing for a time was uncertain until in *Griggs vs. Duke Power Company* on March 8, 1971 the United States Supreme Court held:

> Nothing in the Act precludes the use of testing or measuring procedures; obviously they are useful. What Congress has forbidden is giving these devices and mechanisms controlling force unless they are demonstrably a reasonable measure of job performance. Congress has not commanded that the less qualified be preferred over the better qualified simply because of minority origins. Far from disparaging job qualifications as such, Congress has made such qualifications the controlling factor, so that race, religion, nationality, and sex become irrelevant. What Congress has commanded is that any tests used must measure the person for the job and not the person in the abstract.

The EEOC, Civil Service Commission, Department of Justice, and the Department of Labor have jointly set forth guidelines, particularly with respect to validation of personnel tests, in Title 29, Chapter XIV, Part 1607, *Guidelines on Employee Selection Procedures* (FR Vol. 43, no. 16, August 25, 1978).

The message of the Court and of the Federal Agencies concerned is very clear. *Management must be able to demonstrate the validity of tests and other selection procedures used.*

Institutional Considerations. It is obvious, then, that a program of personnel testing should not be undertaken without careful thought. In particular, a decision to use or not to use tests should *not* be based on fads, fashions, or personal opinions. Fortunately, a number of institutional considerations can be enumerated which should be taken into account in deciding whether or not to undertake a personnel testing program. These include:

(1) There should be evidence that the present selection program is not achieving maximum effectiveness; e.g. high turnover, low morale, or low job effectiveness may point up the need for "looking into" a testing program.

(2) Management should be able to define successful job performance and to specify explicitly the problems it wants to attack through personnel testing.

(3) Since testing will usually result in setting more rigorous selection and/or promotion standards, management should evaluate its source of supply of candidates. It will want to be assured of a sufficiently large supply to enable optimum use of the personnel testing program. Often, the use of personnel testing will need to be accompanied by improved recruiting methods and/or more effective and efficient personnel development programs.

(4) Management should confirm the availability of tests appropriate to the jobs and/or problem areas for which it hopes to use them. Ordinarily, the question of test availability will need to be answered by the psychologist with whom the company works.

(5) Management should lay the groundwork for the testing program. The program should not be instituted until everyone apt to be affected by it is fully informed and cognizant of the goals of testing, and the potential gains to be realized as a result of the program.

Types of Tests Available. Psychological tests may be classified into three broad types comprising *Aptitude* or *Ability, Vocational Interest,* and *Personality* measures. As has already been described, psychological testing had its beginning with the scales developed by Binet in France and by Terman in this country. These early tests were called intelligence tests because they were designed to measure so-called intelligent behavior, such abilities as imagination, memory, comprehension, attention, persistence, and problem solving facility. Neither Binet nor Terman believed that intelligence was a single entity nor an all-encompassing general factor. Instead, they believed that by measuring a number of different abilities and skills, they would be able to obtain a sort of sum total of an individual's mental status in comparison with other persons.

In order to express an individual's relative standing in comparison with other persons of the same age, Terman adopted a concept called the *Intelligence Quotient* (IQ). The IQ, roughly speaking, is the ratio between the number of questions answered correctly by an examinee and the average number of questions answered correctly by persons of the same age as he is. In order to avoid decimals, the ratio is multiplied by 100. Thus, an IQ of 100 suggests average mental status whereas IQ's above or below 100 indicate above and below average mental ability, respectively. Unfortunately, the IQ concept came to imply that intelligence was an entity or a single unitary quantity. This interpretation was, for a time, given theoretical support by the research and writings of Charles Spearman, an English statistician. One result of such theorizing was that the terms of *intelligence,* and *IQ* in particular, came to be bandied about, discussed and rediscussed, and widely misinterpreted.

Current informed usage recognizes (as Binet did) that intelligence is simply a grouping or summing of several more or less fundamental aptitudes and abilities. Thus *aptitude tests* are designed to measure relatively discrete traits or abilities which are indicative of a person's capacity to gain proficiency or to learn. The "abilities" measured by aptitude tests are extremely many and diverse; however, a useful and widely agreed upon classification includes eight major groupings: Spatial Relations Ability, Perceptual Speed and Accuracy (clerical aptitude), Numerical or Arithmetic Facility, Verbal Fluency, Word Knowledge, Memory, Inductive Thinking, and Deductive Thinking.

The "intelligence" tests of today are usually omnibus tests; in other words, they tap a number of abilities represented by the primary abilities outlined above. The IQ is, therefore, an outworn concept which is no longer particularly useful as a way of summarizing a person's mental status. It is particularly useless in business settings where we are much more intent on measuring an individual's major aptitudes than in assessing any general or overall factor. "Intelligence" tests most useful in business are those which are really measuring the vocabulary, word knowledge, and inductive reasoning abilities. Research has shown that these are the abilities which seem to be most closely associated with mental alertness: ability to learn, problem solving proficiency, and facility in collecting, integrating, and coordinating business information. Thus, the typical 'intelligence" test used in business today is simply an attempt to assess the above important information processing and managerial skills.

Vocational interest tests are designed to assess individual differences in likes and dislikes which are related to vocational persistence, and, by implication, vocational satisfaction. Interest tests may therefore be scored in terms of a variety of professional and skilled or semiskilled vocational dimensions. The better researched interest tests do possess validity for identifying the set of vocational activities most compatible with a person's likes and dislikes and may, therefore, be said to be measures of vocational motivation.

Personality tests attempt to assess individual traits which are related to the manner in which a person adjusts to the interpersonal and situational elements of his environment. Personality tests are only helpful in industry insofar as they give the user valid information concerning the manner in which an individual will adjust to the stresses, interpersonal contacts, and situational influences of his or her job.

Obviously a complete accounting of tests available cannot be attempted in these brief paragraphs. Detailed critical reviews of tests available and their uses can be found in the appended references: Buros, and Super and Crites. (See also PERSONNEL TESTING: TYPES OF TESTS.)

Because of the extremely large number and wide range of test materials available, it is also difficult to give examples of their format and item content. Aptitude tests are usually of the paper and pencil variety. Their content obviously depends upon the aptitude being measured. For example one widely used test of clerical aptitude requires the examinee, in a limited time, to scan two columns of numbers to detect differences:

3785778	3785778
6483225	6473225
7189161	7189161
4392845	4392845

Another test—of verbal reasoning ability—utilizes an analogy item and requires the examinee to complete the analogy with the correct alternative:

Rectangle is to *parallelogram* as *square* is to:
(1) *rhombus* _____ (2) *scalene* _____
(3) *quadrilateral* _____ (4) *cube* _____

A widely used test of inductive reasoning requires the examinee to discover a general principle from a sequence of numbers, words, or figures, and to apply this principle in order to designate the correct next item in sequence:

1 8 2 7 3 6 —
Should the next number be —
8; 4; 5; or 7?

Vocational interest tests are usually of the inventory type. The best measure of vocational interests, the *Strong Vocational Interest Blank*, utilizes a listing of 400 occupations, hobbies, school subjects, etc., and simply asks the examainee to express LIKE, INDIFFERENT, or DISLIKE with respect to each of the items. A sample from such a list is shown in Exhibit I.

A second well researched interest test, the *Minnesota Vocational Interest Inventory*, utilizes a "forced choice" format in which the examinee must choose, from among three activities, the one he likes best and the one he likes least, as shown in Exhibit II.

Personality tests cover a wider range of formats than the other types. A large number of tests use the inventory approach—that is, they request an examinee to indicate whether or not various statements do or do not apply to him (her), as shown in Exhibit III.

It should be emphasized that the scoring systems of the better personality and interest tests do *not* employ simple *a priori* judgments as the basis for their scoring weights. Instead, the scoring systems have been developed empirically by contrasting the actual answers of persons who belong to different groups (for example, occupational groups in the case of interest testing or groups defined in some way by

EXHIBIT I

SAMPLE QUESTIONS, STRONG VOCATIONAL INTEREST BLANK

Artist	L	I	D
Algebra	L	I	D
Stamp Collecting	L	I	D
Movies	L	I	D
Time Magazine	L	I	D

EXHIBIT II

EXAMPLES OF FORCED CHOICE QUESTIONS

	Like Best	*Like Least*
Sell pots and pans door to door		
Prepare a brochure describing use of pots and pans		
Set up equipment for manufacture of pots and pans		

EXHIBIT III

EXAMPLES OF INVENTORY QUESTIONS IN A PERSONALITY TEST

	Does Apply	Does Not Apply
1. I worry a great deal of the time		
2. My childhood was very happy		
3. I usually take charge in a group situation		
4. I am regarded as a leader by those who know me		
5. I am sick a great deal of the time		

their behavior, such as dominant, sociable, outgoing, etc. in the case of personality testing).

Other personality tests utilize so-called *projective techniques.* The examinee is asked to tell a story about or to tell what he sees in a series of ambiguous stimuli (such as pictures or ink blots). It is believed that the examinee, in so doing, will reveal aspects of his personality by "projecting" himself into the ambiguous situations. Psychologists do not agree among themselves on the relative usefulness of the projective methods. Such approaches are extremely difficult to score and they depend heavily on the ability of the examiner to develop adequate interpretations of the responses. The large majority of studies using projective methods of personality assessment cast grave doubts on the validity of such techniques for any purpose in business settings. Such techniques are much more appropriate to clinic, hospital, and psychiatric settings where they may possibly aid in the therapeutic process.

Securing a Personnel Testing Consultant. Personnel testing is an extremely technical and complex managerial tool. The typical manager is *not* appropriately trained to analyze his or her firm's potential needs, undertake the necessary research, and to develop and implement a program of personnel testing. He (she) will need to work with a qualified industrial psychologist. The reader can obtain names of qualified psychologists in his or her area by checking with the state psychological association or by writing to the American Psychological Association, 1200 Seventeenth St. NW., Washington, D.C., 20036, or The American Board of Professional Psychology, Inc., 1300 Midtown Tower, Rochester, N.Y., 14604.

MARVIN D. DUNNETTE, Professor of Psychology, University of Minnesota, Minneapolis, Minnesota

W. E. KENDALL, PH.D., Industrial Psychologist, Rye, New York

Information References

Anderson, Betty R. and Rogers, Martha P., eds., "Personnel Testing and Equal Employment Opportunity," Washington, D.C., U.S. Government Printing Office, 1970.

Buros, O. K., ed., "Mental Measurement Yearbook," Edison, N.J., The Gryphon Press, 8th ed., 1978.

Cronbach, L. J., "Essentials of Psychological Testing," 3rd ed., New York, Harper & Row, 1970.

Nunnally, Jum C., "Psychometric Theory," New York, McGraw-Hill, 1978.

Stone, C. H. and Kendall, W. E., "Effective Personnel Selection Procedures," Englewood Cliffs, N.J., Prentice-Hall, 1956.

Cross References: *Industrial Psychology; Personnel Testing: Types of Tests.*

PERSONNEL TESTING: Types of Tests

Personnel Tests may be *capacity or aptitude tests, proficiency or achievement tests,* or *personality and interest checklists or scales.* Aptitude tests serve to predict success of a person on a job in which he (she) had no (or very limited) experience. Proficiency tests measure skill or other occupational knowledge or ability. Interest and personality measures help to give insights into the kinds of work a person will find satisfaction in doing, and the type of behavior to be expected in his or her relations with other people. Interest and personality measures are usually considered separately from aptitude tests because of their special nature.

All tests mentioned here are available from established test publishers and have been tested in actual employment situations. Because of space limitations, a *selected list* is discussed here, illustrating types of tests found generally useful in selection and placement. Not included here are tests published for the sole use of clients. When such tests are offered to a firm, it is well to inquire into evidence of their validity and have such evidence evaluated by a competent personnel psychologist. The objective here is simply to indicate briefly the general nature of aptitudes and abilities shown by tests of different types and to provide examples of specific tests in each general test category.

Tests of Mental Ability. These measure general intelligence. They may be referred to as verbal ability tests, verbal-linguistic tests, intelligence tests, classification tests, personnel classification tests, or simply "personnel" tests. (It is recommended that the use of the term *intelligence test* be avoided in the employment situ-

EXHIBIT I

SAMPLE TEST PAGES

PERSONNEL CLASSIFICATION TEST

FORM A

Alexander G. Wesman

	Score	Percentile
Part I (V)		
Part II (N)		
Total		
Norms Used		

NAME____SEX__________
(Last) (First) (Middle)

ADDRESS____DATE__________
(Street) (City) (State)

EDUCATION: Circle the last school grade you completed: (Grade School) 1 2 3 4 5 6 7 8 (High School) 9 10 11 12 (College) Fr So Jr Sr

DO NOT OPEN THIS BOOKLET UNTIL YOU ARE TOLD TO DO SO.

This test has two parts. These are the directions for Part I. You will be told about Part II after you finish the first part.

Each question in Part I is a sentence with the first word and the last word left out. You are to pick out words to fill in the blanks so that the sentence will be true and sensible.

For the first blank, pick out a **numbered** word—1, 2, 3, or 4. For the blank at the end of the sentence, pick out one of the **lettered** words —A, B, C, or D. Then write the number and the letter you have picked on the line at the right.

Example 1. ..... is to water as eat is to 2C

1. continue 2. drink 3. foot 4. girl
A. drive B. enemy C. food D. industry

Drink is to water as eat is to **food. Drink** is numbered 2, and **food** is lettered C, so 2C has been written on the line at the right.

Now try the second example yourself.

Example 2. ..... is to one as second is to ..... ______

1. middle 2. queen 3. rain 4. first
A. two B. fire C. object D. hill

First is to one as second is to **two.** So you should have written **4A** on the line at the right.

Now do example 3.

Example 3. ..... is to night as breakfast is to ..... ______

1. flow 2. gentle 3. supper 4. door
A. include B. morning C. enjoy D. corner

Supper is to night as breakfast is to **morning.** So you should have written **3B** on the line at the right.

You are not expected to answer all the questions. Do as many as you can in the time allowed. Work quickly and accurately.

If you do finish Part I before time is called, do **not** turn to Part II. You will be told when to turn to the last page.

If you have any questions, ask them **before** you begin. No questions will be answered after you have begun the test.

Remember—work quickly but accurately.

DO NOT OPEN THIS BOOKLET UNTIL YOU ARE TOLD TO DO SO.

Above: Cover page of Personnel Classification Test, Form A. Reproduced by permission. Copyright 1945 by The Psychological Corporation, New York, N.Y. All rights reserved.

Fill in the requested information on your ANSWER SHEET.

Look at Sample X on this page. It shows two men carrying a weighted object on a plank, and it asks, "Which man carries more weight?" Because the object is closer to man "B" than to man "A," man "B" is shouldering more weight; so blacken the circle under "B" on your answer sheet. Now look at Sample Y and answer it yourself. Fill in the circle under the correct answer on your answer sheet.

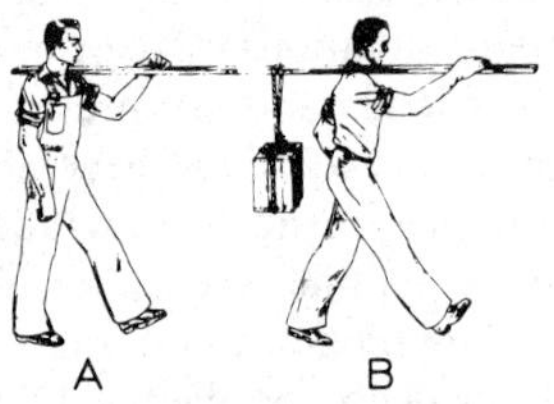

X

Which man carries more weight? (If equal, mark C.)

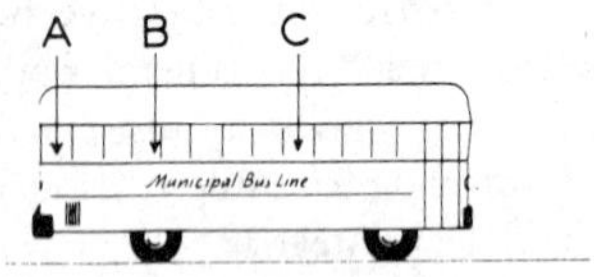

Y

Which letter shows the seat where a passenger will get the smoothest ride?

On the following pages there are more pictures and questions. Read each question carefully, look at the picture, and fill in the circle under the best answer on the answer sheet. Make sure that your marks are heavy and black. Erase completely any answer you wish to change. Do not make any marks in this booklet.

DO NOT TURN OVER THE BOOKLET UNTIL YOU ARE TOLD TO DO SO.

Left: Directions page and sample page for the Bennett Mechanical Comprehension Test, Form S. Reproduced by permission. Copyright 1940, renewed 1967; 1941, renewed 1969; 1942, renewed 1969, c. 1967, 1968, by The Psychological Corporation, New York, N.Y. All rights reserved.

ation. To many applicants, the idea of taking an "intelligence" test is upsetting.)

Briefly discussed below are some representative tests of mental ability in current use (for complete listing see the Buros 1978 reference at the end of this article):

Wesman Personnel Classification Text (PCT), alternate forms, The Psychological Corporation. Developed primarily for use in the employment situation, the PCT provides separate measures of verbal reasoning ability and facility in use of numerical concepts. It is suitable for use with older applicants or employees as well as with recent school graduates, since it is constructed to emphasize power rather than speed.

Adaptability Tests, alternate forms, Science Research Associates. This test attempts to furnish a quick estimate of "general mental ability" by means of a wide variety of items. Many terms used in the test items are relevant to an industrial situation.

Test of Learning Ability, alternate forms, Richardson, Bellows, Henry & Co., Inc. This follows the format of the Army General Classification Tests used and validated during World War II. Its design permits measurement of the three major components of what is commonly termed "general ability," or "intelligence"—vocabulary comprehension, arithmetic reasoning, and ability to perceive spatial relationships.

Fundamental Achievement Series, (FAS), alternate forms, The Psychological Corporation. FAS-Verbal and FAS-Numerical cover the ability range from basic literacy to somewhat above the eighth-grade level. The content taps the knowledge and competences that a job applicant may reasonably be expected to have acquired in the course of ordinary daily living and that will be relevant for actual job performance. Questions are based on experiences assumed to be familiar to both the disadvantaged and the advantaged.

Advanced Personnel Test, alternate forms, The Psychological Corporation. Distribution is restricted and test is administered only at specified licensed testing centers. This test was developed as an aid in selecting students for graduate work. Although not designed for industrial use, it is mentioned here since research in several large companies suggests that it is useful in identifying superior verbal ability among candidates for high-level executive and technical positions.

Tests of Clerical Aptitude. Extensive research indicates that two of the main components for success in clerical work are a minimum level of intelligence, and clerical aptitude—defined by speed and accuracy in perceiving numerical and verbal similarities and differences. For most jobs, the minimum level of mental ability is about the average level of the population as a whole. Where promotability is a factor, higher mental ability is often required. This can be determined from in-plant research.

Successful clerical workers form a highly selected portion of the population in terms of clerical aptitude. Illustrations may be found in norms from the Minnesota Clerical Test. The majority of men clerical workers (accountants, bookkeepers, bank tellers, etc.) have average clerical aptitude scores that exceed scores made by 90% of men in the general population. Average clerical aptitude scores for most women clerical workers indicate that the majority is drawn from the top 25% of women in this aptitude. Tests have been developed to identify levels of clerical aptitude quickly, easily, and with acceptable reliability, and thus their use has become more widespread than any other type of special aptitude test.

Minnesota Clerical Test, one form, The Psychological Corporation. This is a test of speed and accuracy of number checking and name checking. It is brief and easily administered. Since it is a measure of perceptual speed and accuracy, it has been found predictive of success in certain types of inspection, packing, and wrapping jobs.

General Clerical Test, one form, The Psychological Corporation. This is designed as a general and differential test for use in selecting and up-grading all types of clerical personnel. Three kinds of ability important in office work are measured: clerical (speed and accuracy in checking and alphabetizing), numerical (arithmetic computation, error location, and arithmetic reasoning), and verbal (spelling, reading comprehension, vocabulary, and grammar).

Short Tests of Clerical Ability, one form, Science Research Associates. Measures seven skills and aptitudes important in office jobs. Seven separate tests measure abilities in arithmetic, business vocabulary, checking, coding, understanding and following oral and written directions, filing and language (grammar, spelling, and punctuation).

The Short Employment Tests (SET), three forms, The Psychological Corporation. Three sub-tests in the battery are: word knowledge or vocabulary—essentially a short intelligence test; numerical ability or speed and accuracy in computations; and clerical speed and accuracy—applicant must locate and verify names in an alphabetic list and read and code the dollar balance associated with the name. The number and clerical sub-tests have shown acceptable validity in predicting success for several bank clerical positions. It has found use in establishing minimum levels of intelligence for such jobs.

Mechanical Aptitude Tests. In common usage, the term "mechanical aptitude" is applied rather generally to the ability to do any type of mechanical work. This somewhat loose usage has led to the false notion among some personnel managers that anyone they select with high mechanical aptitude, whether on the basis of a mechanical aptitude test or their own judgment, will be able to perform any mechanical job in the plant, given proper training. However, this overlooks both the widely varying nature of jobs labeled mechanical, and the fact that aptitude for mechanical work is apparently not a single trait. Mechanical aptitude also is frequently assumed to include a high amount of manual dexterity. Research has revealed that measures of mechanical aptitude are almost totally unrelated to measures of manual dexterity. Thus, results no better than chance may be expected if a mechanical aptitude test is used to predict success in semi-skilled assembly and operative jobs requiring superior manual dexterity. Because of this lack of relationship, tests of manual dexterity are treated separately from mechanical tests in this discussion.

A number of tests have been developed which have proved to be reasonably valid for various occupations requiring superior mechanical aptitude. The nature of mechanical aptitude has been clarified by a study of relationships among these tests. Studies indicate that mechanical aptitude is apparently a composite of spatial visualization, perceptual speed and acuity, and mechanical information. Because of these findings, spatial tests are included in the present category. However, it is desirable to try out several tests, tapping various factors of mechanical aptitude, in order to achieve maximum efficiency in prediction. Many companies following this procedure have materially improved their effectiveness in selection and differential placement through development of a battery of several mechanical aptitude tests.

Listed below are mechanical aptitude tests in most general use for which satisfactory validities have been reported for a variety of mechanical jobs. However, validation studies for specific jobs must be conducted before general application of any of the tests is made in selection and placement.

Mechanical Comprehension Test, alternate forms, The Psychological Corporation. This test is designed to measure ability to understand mechanical relationships. It consists of drawings with simply phrased questions about them. The test has been constructed to minimize the effects of special environment and rote memory of physical laws. The test has demonstrated validity for a variety of skilled mechanical jobs, in selection of trainees for skilled technical jobs, and for semiskilled jobs in which fairly complex equipment is used.

Revised Minnesota Paper Form Board Test, alternate forms, The Psychological Corporation. This test consists of eight practice items and 64 test items dealing with two-dimensional space perception. Each item consists of the disarranged parts of a geometrical figure, and five assembled geometrical figures. The task is to select the one figure which is made up of the correct combination of parts. The test has been used in selecting employees for such jobs as drafting, inspection, linotype operation, and packing, and in test batteries used to select mechanics, factory supervisors, and engineering and technical trainees.

Tests of Manual Dexterities. Research has demonstrated that two distinct types of manual dexterity can be measured by currently available tests—variously referred to as *gross* and *fine, manual* and *finger* dexterity, or *arm-and-hand* and *wrist-and-finger* dexterities. It also appears that these two types of dexterity are relatively discrete and unrelated to each other. As a result it cannot be assumed that workers who demonstrate skill in types of packing, wrapping, and sorting that require gross arm-and-hand dexterity are readily transferable to jobs requiring superior wrist-and-finger dexterity. By the same token, workers who may excel in the type of fine dexterity required for small-assembly work may do very poorly if placed on jobs requiring rapid gross dexterity.

Manual dexterities may not be used as indicators of mechanical aptitude. Studies show that manual dexterities are relatively independent of mechanical aptitude as measured by tests of mechanical comprehension and spatial visualization. Also, measures of dexterity have not been found valuable in the skilled trades, where understanding of the processes involved is more important than individual differences in the manual dexterity with which they are executed.

Arm-and-hand dexterity has been found important in such semi-skilled jobs as packing, wrapping, and inspection, and in gross-manual assembly and machine operation jobs. Fine-manual dexterity has been shown to be important in simple jobs which require rapid wrist-and-finger movements, such as power-sewing-machine operation and assembly of small electrical parts; in more complex assembly, requiring both speed and precision, such as watch assembly; and in other occupations in which rapid manipulation of small objects is involved, e.g. office-machine operator, bank teller, and typist. For the later jobs, tests of clerical aptitude and intelligence are generally more useful in selection.

Purdue Pegboard, Science Research Associates. This is a measure of wrist-and-finger dexterity. It consists of a rectangular board with four shallow cups or trays at one end and two rows of small holes perpendicularly down the center. Small metal pegs are provided for insertion in the holes in tasks involving measures of gross movements of arm, hand, and finger. Included also are metal collars and washers to fit the pins for tasks designed to measure finer finger dexterity and ability to perform different operations in a coordinated way with two hands simultaneously. Five scores are obtained with different sequences of left hand, right hand, and both hands together.

Bennett Hand-Tool Dexterity Test, The Psychological Corporation. This test measures proficiency in the use of wrenches and screw drivers. It combines measurements of achievement based on past experience in handling tools, and the dexterities required for such work. The apparatus is a U-shaped wooden frame with three sets of four bolts each in different sizes fastened with nuts and washers through holes bored in the left upright. The test involves removing each of the bolts from the left frame and rebolting them to the right frame in a prescribed order in the shortest possible time. A crescent wrench, two end wrenches, and a screwdriver are used.

Tests of Proficiency and Acquired Skill. Tests of aptitude may be used to assess the potential for work in which skill is claimed. More frequently it is desired to gauge the actual level of skill of an applicant in relation to present employees and other applicants. Here aptitude tests are not appropriate. Tests to measure job skills are actually achievement tests. They measure the level of skill and knowledge acquired by the applicant or employee prior to the time he is tested. Tests of this type are usually referred to as *proficiency tests* or *trade tests.* Proficiency tests may be primarily measures of job knowledge or information, and measures of *job skill.* Oral trade tests, merchandise knowledge tests, and measures of a nature similar to the Purdue tests referred to below are essentially job knowledge and information tests. Measures of job skill are usually work-sample tests such as those to measure proficiency in typing, shorthand, and various machine operations.

Tests of proficiency are of value in three main areas of personnel work: in hiring and assigning, in transferring and promoting, and in training. In selection, they readily disclose the "trade bluffers." In addition to detecting areas which can be remedied by training, proficiency tests are of value in measuring outcomes of training programs. Probably because many tests of job proficiency are tailor-made by companies using them (or perhaps because they are not as widely used as they should be), there is little published material describing them.

SRA Dictation Skills, Science Research Associates. This test is in two parts—speed and accuracy. Two 12-in. 78-rpm records are used for the accuracy test, and three 12-in. 78-rpm records comprise the speed test. The examinee takes dictation by any stenographic system and then inserts answers to questions on an answer pad.

Seashore-Bennett Stenographic Proficiency Tests, alternate forms, The Psychological Corporation. These recorded dictations provide measures of ability to take dictation at three levels of speed and transcribe shorthand notes into "mailable" business letters. Scoring is done for neatness and cleanness of typing, arrangement of letter, quality of stroke, typing errors, erasures and strike-overs, errors in English, and changes in wording and meaning.

Typing Test for Business, alternate forms, The Psychological Corporation. A test of typewriting proficiency for use with applicants for all kinds of typing jobs. May be used either as a short screening test, as a complete assessment of a variety of skills, or in combinations particularly adapted to specific jobs.

D.A.T. Language Usage Test, alternate forms, The Psychological Corporation. This is a two-part test measuring command of correct English. It is designed to predict effectiveness in secretarial and other jobs where correctness of expression is essential. The first part is a short spelling test; part two requires the examinee to locate errors in grammar, punctuation, etc.

Purdue Test for Electricians, alternate forms, Science Research Associates. This is designed to measure technical knowledge of electricity and electrical operations basic for plant electricians. As a measure of job information it is essentially a trade test.

Purdue Test for Machinists and Machine Operators, one form, Science Research Associates. This is a job-information test. In addition to a total score, five sub-scores are obtained for lathe, planer and shaper, milling machine, grinder, and general bench-work operations. The test was developed primarily for use by vocational teachers in public school systems, and may seem overly academic to some. It may have value in selecting apprentices and other applicants claiming vocational training or skill in machine-shop work.

Minnesota Engineering Analogies Test, alternate forms, The Psychological Corporation. This test, frequently referred to by the initials MEAT, combines features of an abstract reasoning test with those of a comprehensive engineering ability test which will identify high level engineering ability and be acceptable to engineers. It consists of multiple-choice problems in analogy form. In order to answer any one of the problems correctly, an engineer must not only know the subject matter, he must also be able to perceive and identify the appropriate relationships. Psychologists have known for a long time that this ability to perceive relationships is related in a subtle way to general intelligence and abstract reasoning ability. It is likely that MEAT is an effective measure not only of what the engineer knows but also of how well he can use the facts in his possession. It also helps to provide answers to two important questions: How do engineers performing different functions differ among themselves? Which differences are most important in determining success or failure on the job?

Vocational Interest Measures. In addition to aptitudes and proficiency, another factor presumed to be of importance is the basic interest of workers in the occupational field in which they are engaged. Studies have shown that successful workers in an occupation, particularly in the professions, have certain similarities of interests (a characteristic set of likes and dislikes) which can be measured and which differentiate them from other occupational groupings.

The majority of inventories of vocational interests have been developed for use in counseling and guiding students, and have wide use in high schools and colleges. Manuals of a number of published inventories suggest their usefulness in selection and placement, but supporting validation for most measures of interest is meagre or lacking. Thus prospective users of an interest measure should inquire into its research basis.

Research suggests that measures of interest are more useful in predicting job stability than in predicting levels of success. Interest apparently determines the "direction of effort," and ability the "level of achievement." There is evidence, however, that the Strong Vocational Interest Blank (below) predicts success in certain types of saleswork such as selling insurance, real estate, business machines, and vacuum cleaners. Measures of interest are probably of greatest value as supplemental information in transferring employees from one type of job to another.

Interest inventories are susceptible of "faking," and special care should be used in their administration. Applicants must be convinced that it is to their interest in the long run to answer all questions honestly.

Vocational Interest Blank for Men, Revised, Stanford University Press. This inventory provides ratings comparing the vocational interests of an individual with those of successful men in each of 50 occupations. Scores are also given for masculinity-femininity, occupational level (an indicator of level of aspiration), and interest-maturity.

Kuder Preference Record—Vocational, alternate seven forms, Science Research Associates. This questionnaire is designed to measure interests in ten broad job fields: mechanical, computational, scientific, persuasive, artistic, literary, musical, social service, clerical, and outdoor. Lists of occupations presumably related to inventory categories (mechanical, clerical, etc.) are given in the manual to aid in interpreting results for counseling and placement. Illustrative profiles are also presented for a variety of occupations.

Measures of Personality. The importance of

personality in job success is generally recognized. Most failures are due not to lack of ability, but rather to inadequacies of the person in his relationships with other people, in his attitude toward his work and toward society, in his motivations, and in his attitude toward himself.

Substantial advances have been made in recent years in the development of devices to aid in clinical diagnosis of personality deviations. But progress in development of personality measures for use in selection is still far behind that of aptitude measurement. Because of this, management will be wise to beware of any personnel consultant or test salesman who makes broad claims for his techniques of personality measurement, unless the data can be submitted to serious study and independent test by competent psychologists.

The majority of measures of personality currently published are of the questionnaire or inventory types, typically consisting of a series of questions of which the following are examples: Do you daydream frequently? Do you give money to beggars? Do you often feel just miserable? Do you ever have to fight against bashfulness?

The employment applicant answering such questions can be expected to give answers that will put him (her) in the best light in relation to the job for which he or she is applying, and may falsify answers. Primary uses of such tests at present seem to lie in screening out applicants most likely to be problem cases, and in assisting present employees to make more effective adjustments.

The Guilford-Marin Personnel Inventory, one form, Sheridan Supply Co. An inventory designed to aid in preventing the hiring of problem employees and to spot those already employed. It provides three scores: objectivity, agreeableness, and cooperativeness. It has the disadvantage of all such inventories that more intelligent applicants are likely to be shrewd enough to give the correct or "socially acceptable" answers.

Miscellaneous Tests. A number of tests are available which do not fit neatly into the previous classifications. Among these are single tests for which claims are made by the publishers as to values for selection and/or training. Examples are safety and supervisory tests. Test batteries represent another type of test (or combination of tests) which do not fit strictly into a functional classification.

How Supervise? alternate forms, The Psychological Corporation. This is a widely used supervisory test, designed for selecting candidates for supervisory training or upgrading, evaluating results of supervisory training programs, and counseling supervisors.

The Employee Aptitude Survey, alternate forms, Psychological Services, Inc., is one illustration of a test battery. The battery includes ten short tests which can be given singly or in combination, as appropriate. The tests are: Verbal, Comprehension, Numerical Ability, Visual Pursuit, Visual Speed & Accuracy, Space Visualization, Numerical Reasoning, Verbal Reasoning, Word Fluency, Manual Speed & Accuracy, and Symbolic Reasoning.

The Test Orientation Procedure, one form, The Psychological Corporation, is an interesting approach to the problem of dealing with people who are unfamiliar with test taking. This is a series of practice tests designed to help prepare a prospective job applicant to do his best on employment tests. A tape recording guides the examinee through a variety of easy test-like exercises. A second booklet, "Practice Tests," with similar material, is then provided for the prospective candidate for practice purposes.

W. E. KENDALL, PH.D., Industrial Psychologist, Rye, New York

Information References

Selected List of Test Publishers and Distributors (for complete listing, see Buros, below).

Bausch & Lomb Industrial Vision Service, Bausch & Lomb, Inc., Rochester, N.Y.

California Test Bureau, Del Monte Research Park, Monterey, Calif.

Cooperative Test Division, Educational Testing Service, Princeton, N.J.

Harcourt, Brace & Jovanovich, Inc., 757 3rd Ave., New York, N.Y.

Institute for Personality and Ability Testing, 1602 Coronado Drive, Champaign, Ill.

The Psychological Corporation, New York, N.Y.

Psychological Services, Inc., 4311 Wilshire Blvd., Los Angeles, Calif. 90005.

Science Research Associates, Inc., 259 E. Erie Street, Chicago, Ill.

Stanford University Press, Stanford, Cal.

Texts:

Buros, Oscar Krisen, ed., "The Seventh Mental Measurement Yearbook," Highland Park, N.J., Gryphon Press, 8th ed., 1978.

Stone, C. Harold and Kendall, William E., "Effective Personnel Selection Procedures," Englewood Cliffs, N.J., Prentice-Hall, 1956.

Cross References: *Industrial Psychology; Personnel Testing.*

PERT (PROGRAM EVALUATION AND REVIEW TECHNIQUE)

The advancing technology of the Space Age brought an explosive growth of a new family of planning and control techniques. Much of the development work was done in the defense industry, but the construction, chemical, and other industries have also played an important part. Perhaps the best known of all the new techniques is **Program Evaluation and Review Technique,** commonly referred to as **PERT.**

The new techniques have several distinguishing characteristics:

(1) They give management the ability to plan the best possible use of resources to achieve a given goal within overall time and cost limitations.

(2) They enable executives to manage "one-of-a-kind" programs, as opposed to repetitive production situations.

(3) They help management handle the uncertainties involved in programs where no standard time data of the Taylor-Gantt variety are available.

(4) They utilize a so-called "time network analysis" as a basic method of approach to determine manpower, material, and capital requirements.

Development of PERT. Project managers increasingly noted that the techniques of Frederick W. Taylor and Henry L. Gantt, introduced during the early part of the century for large-scale production operations, were inapplicable for a large portion of the industrial effort of the 1960s and 1970s, an era that has aptly been characterized as the "Age of Massive Engineering."

The Special Projects Office of the U.S. Navy, concerned with performance trends on large military development programs, introduced PERT on its Polaris Weapon System in 1958, after the technique had been developed with the aid of the management consulting firm of Booz, Allen & Hamilton. Since that time, PERT has spread rapidly throughout the U.S. defense and space industry. Currently almost every major government and military agency concerned with Space Age programs is utilizing the technique, as are large industrial contractors in the field. Small businesses wishing to participate in national defense programs have found it increasingly necessary to develop PERT capability.

At about the same time the Navy was developing PERT, the duPont company, concerned with the increasing costs and time required to bring new products from research to production, initiated a similar technique known as CRITICAL PATH METHOD (CPM) which has spread quite widely, and is particularly concentrated in the construction industry. (For an overview discussion of the various control techniques, see INTEGRATED PROJECT MANAGEMENT.)

What PERT Is. In the early 1960s, PERT was in practice restricted largely to the area of time. (Later extensions are described below.) The basic requirements of PERT/time as established by the Navy were as follows:

(1) All of the individual tasks to complete a given program must be visualized in a clear enough manner to be put down in a *network,* which is comprised of *events* and *activities.* An event represents a specified program accomplishment at a particular instant in time. An activity represents the time and resources which are necessary to progress from one event to the next. Emphasis is placed on defining events and activities with sufficient precision so that there is no difficulty in monitoring actual accomplishment as the program proceeds. Exhibit I shows a typical operating-level PERT network from the electronics industry. Events are shown by the circles in the network, and activities are designated by the arrows leading from one event to its successor event or events.

(2) Events and activities must be sequenced on the network under a highly logical set of ground rules which allow the determination of important critical and subcritical *paths.* These ground rules include the fact that no successor event can be considered completed until all of its predecessor events have been completed, and no "looping" is allowed, i.e., no successor event can have an activity dependency which leads back to a predecessor event.

(3) Time estimates are made for each activity of the network on a three-way basis, i.e., *optimistic, most likely,* and *pessimistic* elapsed-time figures are estimated by the person or persons most familiar with the activity involved. The three time estimates are required as a gauge of the "measure of uncertainty" of the activity, and represent full recognition of the probabilistic nature of many of the tasks in development-oriented and nonstandard programs. It is important to note, however, that, for the purposes of computation and reporting, the three time estimates are reduced to a single expected time (t_e) and a statistical variance (σ^2).

(4) *Critical path* and *slack times* are com-

EXHIBIT I

TYPICAL OPERATING-LEVEL PERT NETWORK.

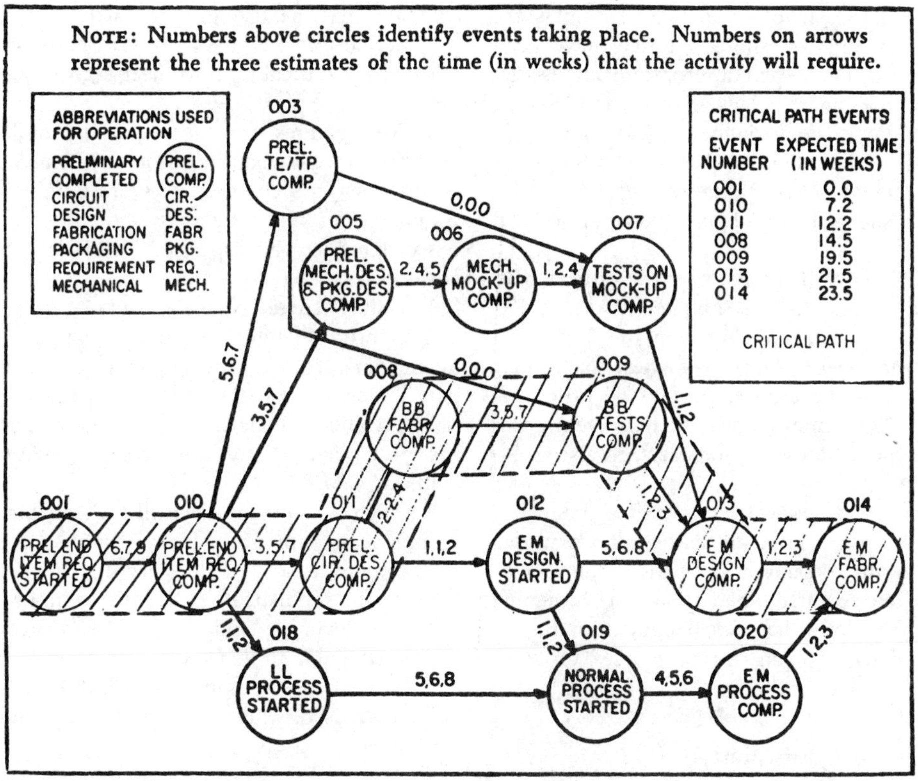

puted. The critical path is that sequence of activities and events which will require the *greatest expected time to accomplish.* Slack time is the difference between the total expected activity time required for any specific path and the total for the critical path. Thus for any event it is a measure of the spare time that exists at the moment in each of its subsequent sequence of events.

If the size and complexity of the network call for them, computer routines are available to calculate the critical path, as well as the amount of slack for all events and activities not on the critical path. If total expected activity time along the critical path is greater than the time available to complete the project, the program is said to have *negative slack.* Negative slack time is a measure of how much acceleration is required to meet the schedule objective dates.

Time Estimates. Interpretation of the concepts of optimistic, most likely, and pessimistic elapsed times has varied. The definitions which represent a useful consensus are as follows.

Optimistic—An estimate of the *minimum* time an activity will take, if unusual good luck is experienced and everything "goes right the first time."

Most likely—An estimate of the *normal* time an activity will take, a result which would occur most often if the activity could be repeated a number of times under similar circumstances.

Pessimistic—An estimate of the *maximum* time an activity will take, if unusually bad luck is experienced. It should reflect the possibility of initial failure and fresh start, but should not be influenced by such factors as "catastrophic events"—strikes, fires, power failures, and so on—unless these hazards are inherent risks in the activity.

Averaging formulas have been developed by which the three time estimates are reduced to a single expected time (t_e), variance (σ^2). and standard deviation (σ). Thus (approximately):

$$t_e = \frac{a + 4m + b}{6}$$

$$\sigma = \frac{b - a}{6}$$

where a is the most optimistic time, b is the pessimistic time, and m is the most likely time. The choice of probability distribution and the approximations involved in these formulas are subject to some question, but they have been widely used and seem appropriate enough in view of the inherent lack of precision of estimating data. The variance data for an entire network make possible the determination of the *probability of meeting an established schedule date,* as shown in the Appendix at the end of this article.

Exhibit II contains data on the critical path and slack times for the sample network of Exhibit I. The data are shown in the form of a *slack order report* (lowest to highest slack), perhaps one of the most important of PERT reports. Other output reports, such as event order and calendar time order reports, are also available.

Review and action by responsible managers, generally on a biweekly basis, are required, concentrating on important critical path activities. Where required, valid means of shortening lead times along the critical path must be determined by applying new resources or additional funds, obtained from those activities that can "afford" them because of their slack. Alternatively, sequencing of activities along the critical path may be changed. A final alternative may be, perforce, a change in the scope of the work of the critical path to meet a given schedule.

EXHIBIT II

SLACK ORDER REPORT

PERT SYSTEM

Airborne Computer—Slack Order Report

Date 7/12/73 Week 0.0 Time in Weeks Page 1

Event	T_E	T_L	T_L-T_E	T_S	*pr*	
001	0.0	0.0	0			T_E = Expected event date
010	7.2	7.2	0			T_L = Latest allowable event date
011	12.2	12.2	0			
008	14.5	14.5	0			T_L-T_E = Event slack
009	19.5	19.5	0			T_S = Scheduled event date
013	21.5	21.5	0			
014	23.5	23.5	0	23.5	.50	P_r = Probability of achieving T_S date
020	20.6	21.5	+ .9			
019	15.6	16.5	+ .9			
012	14.4	15.3	+ .9			
018	9.4	10.3	+ .9			
007	18.2	20.3	+2.1			
006	16.0	18.1	+2.1			
005	13.2	14.3	+2.1			
003	14.2	19.5	+5.3			

PERT requires constant updating and reanalysis, since the outlook for the completion of activities in a complex program is in a constant state of flux. Highly systematized methods of handling this aspect of PERT have been developed.

Benefits Gained. A big advantage of PERT is the kind of planning required to create a major network. Network development and critical path analysis reveal interdependencies and problem areas which are either not obvious or not well defined by conventional planning methods.

Another advantage, especially where there is a significant amount of uncertainty, is the three-way estimate. If the decision maker is statistically sophisticated, he can examine the standard deviation and probability of accomplishment data. If there is a minimum of uncertainty, the single-time approach may, of course, be used, while retaining the advantages of network analysis.

Finally, PERT allows a large amount of data to be presented in a highly ordered fashion, bringing the management-by-exception principle to an area of planning and control not hitherto readily susceptible to it. Additionally, many individuals in different locations can easily determine the total task requirements of a large program.

Implementation Techniques. When a well-thought-through network is developed in sufficient detail, the first activity time estimates made are as accurate as any, and these should not be changed unless a new application of resources or a trade-off in goals is specifically determined. Further, the first time estimates should not be biased by some arbitrarily established schedule objective, or by the assumption that a particular activity does not appear to be on a critical path. Schedule biasing of this kind, while it obviously cannot be prevented, clearly atrophies some of the main benefits of the technique—although it is more quickly discovered with PERT than with any other method.

In the case of common resource centers, it is generally necessary to undertake a loading analysis, making priority assumptions and using the resulting data on either a three-time or single-time basis for those portions of the network which are affected. It should be pointed out that the process of network development forces more problems of resource constraint or loading analysis into the open for resolution than do other planning methods.

Application to Production. It is sometimes viewed as a disadvantage of the PERT technique that it is not applicable to all manufacturing effort. PERT deals in the time domain only and does not contain the quantity information required by most manufacturing operations. Nevertheless, PERT can be, and has been, used very effectively through the preliminary manufacturing phases of production prototype or pilot model construction, and in the assembly and test of final production equipments which are still "high on the learning curve." After these phases, established production control techniques which bring in the quantity factor are generally more applicable.

It should be noted, however, that many programs of the Space Age never leave the preliminary manufacturing stage, or at least never enter into mass production. Therefore, a considerable effort is going forward to integrate the techniques of PERT within some of the established methods of production control, such as LINE-OF BALANCE or similar techniques that bring in the quantity factor.

PERT and Computers. There is a common impression that the technique is only applicable when large-scale data-processing equipment is available. This is certainly true for large networks, or aggregations of networks, where critical path and slack computations are involved for several hundred or more events.

However, several ingenious manual methods have been developed, ranging from simple inspection on small networks to more organized but clerically oriented routines for determination of critical path, subcritical path, and slack times on networks ranging from fifty to several hundred events. Exhibit I shows the network for a relatively small electronics program. Developed in less than a day, the whole network required only two hours for manual computation.

PERT Extensions. A considerable amount of research has been put into the extension of PERT into the areas of manpower, cost, and capital requirements. The ultimate objective is the determination of "trade-off" relationships between time, cost, and product or equipment performance objectives.

PERT/Cost. Most job-costing structures in industry on complex development programs need a great deal of interpretation to relate *actual costs* to *actual progress.* They are rarely, if ever, related in any explicit manner to the details of the scheduling plan. Yet cost constraints either in the form of manpower shortages or funding restrictions have a great deal to do with the program's success. For this reason, an approach called basic PERT/cost was developed. This involves establishing job cost estimates *directly from an activity or group of activities on a time network* [1]. The networks themselves are based upon the framework of a *work breakdown structure* for the complete program.

Regarding development of actual cost figures in basic PERT/cost, an estimate of manpower requirements, segregated by classification, is usually the easiest place to start, since these requirements were presumably known at the time the network was established. A single-valued scheduled time figure generally replaces t_e in the basic PERT/cost approach, as a matter of convenience in developing manpower leveling data. The summation of such data often reveals a manpower or funding restriction problem, and forces a replanning cycle if no alternatives are available. Also revealed may be inefficiencies in personnel loading, which can be removed by proper use of slack activities.

Nonlabor costs are often segregated in a manner quite different from that which would result from analysis of a time network. For example, there is a tendency to buy common materials on one purchase order for a number of different prototypes, each one of which represents a distinct phase of progress in the completion of the program.

Coordination and control efforts are often not indicated on time networks unless they result in specific outputs. For PERT costing, the network in all cases must be complete. This is an area of deficiency in many present-day networks, which must be overcome before an effective PERT/cost application can be made.

The ultimate objective in the area of PERT/cost is not only improvement in planning and control of time and cost, but also the opportunity to assess possibilities for "trading off" time and cost.

It is generally assumed that the fundamental relationships between time and costs are as

Exhibit III

Fundamental Relationships Between Time and Costs

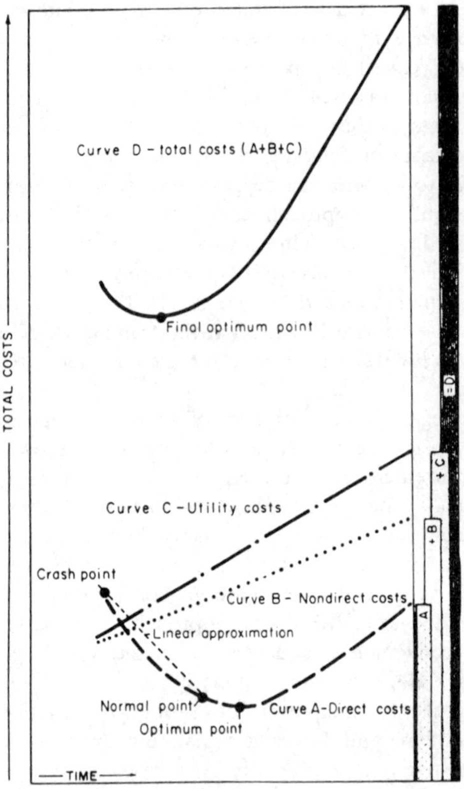

portrayed in Exhibit III. Curve A represents *total direct costs* versus time, and the "U" shape of the curve results from the assumption that there is an "optimum" time-cost point for any activity or job. It is assumed that total costs will increase with any effort to accelerate or delay the job away from this point.

In one application, in the construction industry, it is assumed that there is a normal job time (which might or might not coincide with the theoretical optimum), and that from this norm, costs increase linearly to a *crash* time (Exhibit III). Crash time represents the maximum acceleration the job can stand. With these assumptions, a complete mathematical approach and computer program have been developed which show how to accelerate progress on a job as much as possible for the lowest possible cost. This involves shortening the critical path or paths by operating on those activities which have the lowest time-cost slopes.

At the planning stage it is often difficult to determine time-cost relationships explicitly, either for individual or aggregates of activities. (There are often good arguments for characterizing time-cost relationships at this stage as nonlinear, flat, decreasing, or, more likely, as a range of cost possibilities.) If alternative equipment program objectives are added as a variable, the problem is further compounded. Solutions for the technical handling of such data, in whatever form they are obtained, have been developed.

Curve B of Exhibit III indicates *total nondirect costs,* which are assumed to increase linearly with time. Accounting practices will have to be reviewed to provide careful (and probably new) segregations of direct from nondirect costs for use in making valid time-cost trade-off evaluations.

Curve C is a representation of a *utility cost curve,* which is needed to complete the picture for *total time-cost* optimization (indicated as the final optimum point on Curve D). The utility cost curve represents a quantification of the penalty for *not accomplishing the job at the earliest possible time,* and is also shown as a linear function increasing with time.

The difficulties of determining such a curve for many programs, either in terms of its shape or dollar value, should be obvious. But it is significant to note that in certain industrial applications such utility cost data have already been developed, typically in the form of "outage" costs or loss-of-profit opportunities, and used as the basis for improved decision making.

APPENDIX

Expected Time Estimates. It is clear that the optimistic and the pessimistic time should occur least often, and the most likely time most often. Thus it is assumed that the most likely time is the peak or modal value of a probability distribution, although it can vary between the two extremes. These characteristics are described by the "Beta distribution" [2], shown in two different conditions in Exhibit IV, where:

a = optimistic time
m = most likely time
b = pessimistic time
M = mid-range $[(a+b)/2]$
t_e = expected time

As a result of approximation and analysis of the Beta distribution, the final equations for expected time (t_e), *variance* (σ^2), *and standard devi-*

EXHIBIT IV

BETA DISTRIBUTION

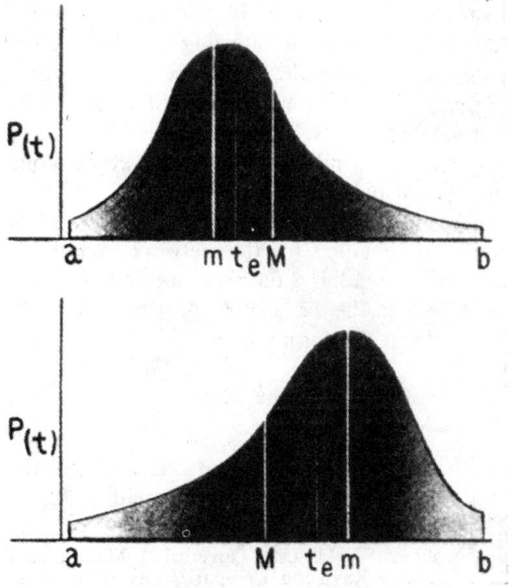

ation (σ) were written as follows for a given activity:

$$(1)\quad t_e = \tfrac{1}{3}(2m + M)$$

$$= \frac{1}{3}\left[2m + \frac{a+b}{2}\right]$$

$$= \frac{a + 4m + b}{6}$$

$$(2)\quad \sigma^2 = \left[\frac{b-a}{6}\right]^2$$

$$(3)\quad \sigma = \frac{b-a}{6}$$

The first equation indicates that t_e should be interpreted as the weighted mean of m (most likely) and M (mid-range) estimates, with weights of 2 and 1, respectively. In other words, t_e is located one third of the way from the modal to the mid-range values, and represents the 50% probability point of the distribution, i.e., it divides the area under the curve into two equal portions.

Probability of Meeting Schedule Times. On the basis of the Central Limit Theorem, one can conclude that the probability distribution of times for accomplishing a job consisting of a number of activities may be approximated by the normal distribution, and that this approximation approaches exactness as the number of activities becomes great (for example, more than 10 activities along a given path). Thus, we may define a curve which represents the probability of meeting an established schedule-end date, T_s, as shown in Exhibit V, where:

$$T_E = \Sigma\, t_{e_1} + t_{e_2} \cdots + t_{e_n}$$

$$\sigma^2(T_E) = \Sigma\, \sigma^2(t_{e_1}) + \sigma^2(t_{e_2}) + \cdots + \sigma^2(t_{e_n})$$

$$T_{E_1} = \text{Scheduled Time (earlier than } T_E)$$

$$T_{S_2} = \text{Scheduled Time (later than } T_E)$$

The probability of meeting the T_S date when given T_E and σ^2 for a chain of activities is defined as the ratio of (1) the area under the curve to the left of T_s, to (2) the area under the entire curve. The difference between T_S and T_E, expressed in units of σ, is:

$$\frac{T_S - T_E}{\sigma}$$

This will yield a value for the probability of accomplishing T_S by the use of the normal probability distribution table. Thus:

$$\frac{T_{S_1} - T_E}{\sigma} = -1.2\sigma$$

$$P_r \text{ (accomplishment of } T_{S_1}) = .12$$

$$\frac{T_{S_2} - T_E}{\sigma} = +1.2\sigma,$$

$$P_r \text{ (accomplishments of } T_{S_2}) = .88$$

EXHIBIT V

PROBABILITY OF MEETING AN ESTABLISHED SCHEDULE-END DATE

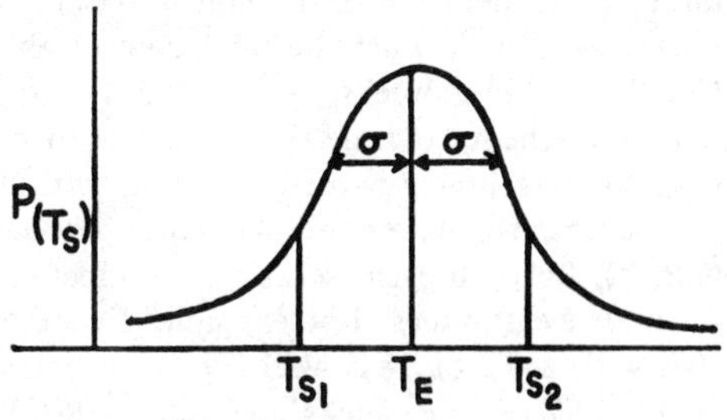

Determining Critical Path and Slack Times. The computation steps required to determine the critical path and slack times for the network shown in Exhibit I are as follows:

Step 1. Determine t_e for every activity on the network in accordance with the equation:

$$t_e = \frac{a + 4m + b}{6}$$

Step 2. Starting with Event No. 001, determine T_E (or cumulative T_E) for all succeeding events by summing small t_e's for each activity leading up to the event, *but choosing the largest value for the final T_E figure in those cases where there is more than one activity leading into an event.* For example, Exhibit I indicates three activities leading into Event No. 013 (EM design complete). The three preceding events are No. 007 (test on mock-up complete), No. 009 (breadboard tests complete), and No. 012 (EM design started). The cumulative T_E figures for these three preceding events, as can be seen from Exhibit II, are 18.2 weeks for Event No. 007, 19.5 weeks for Event No. 009, and 14.4 weeks for Event No. 012. Now, add the respective activity times between these three events and Event No. 013 and examine the results:

Event No.	T_E	*Activity Time t_e to Event No. .013*	*Total Weeks*
007	18.2	1.2	19.4
009	19.5	2.0	21.5
012	14.4	6.2	20.6

The largest figure, which represents the longest path or earliest time at which Event No. 013 can be completed, is 21.5 weeks, and this path leads through Event No. 009. As will be noted from Exhibit I, Events No. 009 and 013 are on the critical path, since the T_E values of all other paths leading into final Event No. 014 are smaller.

Step 3. Having determined the critical path through the network of Exhibit I to be 23.5 weeks, we can now set the final date of Event No. 014 at 23.5 weeks, or we can use some arbitrary scheduled time. The process covered in Step 2 is now reversed. Starting with the final event, we determine the *latest allowable time,* T_L, for each event so as not to affect critical path event times. For example, Event No. 007, with a T_E of 18.2 weeks, can be delayed up to a T_L of 20.3 weeks, before it will affect critical path Event No. 013.

Step 4. The difference between T_L and T_E, known as "slack," is next computed for each event. These computations are shown in Exhibit II in the form of a slack order report, i.e., in order of lowest to highest values of *positive* slack. Note that along the critical path there is zero slack at every event, since by definition there is no possibility of slippage along the critical path without affecting the final event date. In this example, if the end schedule date of Event No. 014 were set at 23.0 weeks rather than at 23.5 weeks, there would be 0.5 weeks of *negative* slack indicated for every event along the critical path.

Step 5. The computation of variance and of standard deviation for this network is optional and involves adding the variances for each activity along the critical path, which are obtained from the formula:

$$\sigma^2 = \left[\frac{b - a}{6}\right]^2$$

The interested reader may verify that the variance for final event No. 014, with a T_E of 23.5 weeks, is 1.46 weeks.

Robert W. Miller, Director of Management Sciences, Raytheon Company, Lexington, Massachusetts

Information References

Miller, Robert W., "How to Plan and Control with PERT," *Harvard Business Rev.,* Mar.–Apr., 1962. (The foregoing presentation largely follows this article, by permission of *Harvard Business Rev.* See also references cited, below.)

References Cited

[1] DOD and NASA PERT Cost Guide, Office of the Secretary of Defense, National Aeronautics and Space Administration, June, 1962, Government Printing Office, Washington.

[2] The Beta distribution and PERT are described in PERT Summary Report, Phase I, Special Projects Office, Department of the Navy, 1956, Governmental Printing Office, Washington.

Cross References: *Integrated Project Management (and cross references there given).*

PHYSICAL DISTRIBUTION MANAGEMENT

Physical Distribution Management is one of the "systems" disciplines of management wherein two or more functionally related, but previously unaffiliated, areas are conjoined to form a cohesive and unitized whole.

In its broadest sense, physical distribution management is concerned with the progress of a commodity from its point of initial production to its point of ultimate consumption. Between these two extremes there may lie several intervening stages of manufacture, processing, storage, etc.; these are not properly breaks in the physical distribution chain, but are interwoven in it, either through absorption or interdisciplinary coordination.

The nucleus around which physical distribution has evolved is transportation. Until quite recently, transportation was considered a discipline in and of itself. Gradually, however, there came a realization that transportation directly affected, and was affected by, many other functions of business management. As the "systems approach" to business management generally won favor, these functions became ever more closely associated with transportation, until the need for a new appellation—physical distribution—became apparent.

As presently conceived, physical distribution management embraces not only transportation (and its alter ego, traffic), but such other fields as material handling, material management, packaging, industrial site location, warehousing, inventory control, and order processing. It also overlaps into certain portions of the production and marketing/sales areas. Ideally, physical distribution engineers conceive of the management of a product-oriented company as divided into three basic functional areas—production, sales and physical distribution—each with somewhat indistinct borders relative to one another, and among them encompassing all of the firm's business activities.

This ideal is seldom realized in practice, however. The business community in general has adopted the concept of physical distribution to the extent of recognizing the interrelationship of its various components; but those components nevertheless usually continue to receive separate treatment in the organizational hierarchy. The reason is one of simple pragmatism: Sudden infusion of the physical distribution *gestalt* into a company traditionally oriented along more separatist lines could easily lead to contra-productive confusion—especially since, as a relatively new art (or science, according to one's preference), physical distribution's constraints are still too hazily defined for ready application to particular situations.

It is probable that, with the passage of time, the trend will be increasingly toward implementation of some form of physical distribution management in most types of business. As the new concept's parameters are more clearly defined through academic development and practical experience, this will become structurally and operationally more feasible. Indeed, to a substantial degree this has proven to be the case in the past two decades. Meanwhile, physical distribution management in practice will continue to stand for coordination of the several areas that make up its totality, without, in many cases, their organizational unification.

COLIN BARRETT, Transportation Consultant, Reston, Virginia

Information References

Ballou, Ronald L., "Business Logistics Management," Englewood Cliffs, N.J., Prentice-Hall, 1973.

Blanding, Warren, "Physical Distribution," Washington, D.C., Traffic Service Corp., 1978.

Cross References: *Materials Management; Shippers-Associations; Traffic Management.*

PLANNING-PROGRAMMING-BUDGETING SYSTEMS. See Public Administration.

PLANT ENGINEERING

Plant Engineering is a support and service function that exists in every industrial plant as well as in many commercial, institutional, and government facilities. Elements of it are as old as man's use of industrial machines. However, the plant engineer as a professional man, recognized as a specialist in plant construction, layout, maintenance, and all services to production, is a post World War II development—a development that is well advanced in this country, in England, and in Canada and Japan. It is emerging rapidly in Italy, Mexico, and many Latin American countries.

Title of the head of the department usually is Plant Engineer, but it may be any of several dozen ranging from Facilities Engineer or Manager, or Works Engineer, to Superintendent of Maintenance, Manager of Engineering, or Superintendent of Facilities and Utilities. The Plant Engineer may, depending on type of plant, report to the General Manager, Plant Manager, or Vice President, Operations.

Formal Definition. The American Institute of Plant Engineers, which has chapters in the United States and Canada, defines plant engineering as "that branch of engineering which embraces the installation, operation, maintenance, modification, modernization, and protection of physical facilities and equipment used to produce a product or provide a service. It requires the special competency to assume liaison or control responsibility for coordinating multidisciplinary engineering activities such as contractual engineering services, facility design, equipment selection and procurement, and construction."

History. There was some experimenting with improved production techniques and increased use of electric power during the period preceding World War I, but fundamentally there was little change in procedures from past generations. An industrial plant was built to operate without a major change until it fell to pieces. A millwright usually performed the function of plant engineer, although a few new specialists such as electrician, pipe fitter, and power-house operator were encroaching on his domain.

The new economic era between 1920 and 1930 was a period of boom and expansion. Mass production techniques were fully exploited. Labor-saving devices and use of electric power were investigated but not fully adopted—power costs were high and labor costs were low. Nevertheless, the plant engineer made a limited appearance on the scene. The growing complexity of industry demanded a technically trained man to direct and coordinate the essential activities of many different craftsmen performing non-production functions. Indirect labor costs were important, but quantity production had lowered prices and, with prosperous conditions generally, indirect costs were not closely watched.

In the depression period between 1930 and 1940—a rugged period of share-the-work, cut-costs, find-new-products—changes were made in plants, processes, and products. Plants failed and were reorganized with recognition given to the need for placing related, but miscellaneous plant service activities under one head. Critical examinations revealed that indirect costs were a great part of the total cost picture. The plant engineer took another step up the management ladder.

Beginning about 1940, and still continuing, production of diverse military and consumer products demonstrated that change, while expensive, was practical. Uncertainty about the future made plant flexibility essential. The value of good plant layout, low indirect costs, and continuity of operation was an accepted fact. Techniques of management and organization improved, and the plant engineer finally came into his own.

The nature of the plant engineering job has remained essentially unchanged since it reached a state of maturity in the 1940s. However, the importance of that job, and the status of the plant engineer, were given a dramatic upward boost during the 1970s. Early in that decade, Government applied the whip of regulatory legislation to environmental protection (EPA) and safety in the workplace (OSHA). (See ENVIRONMENTAL CONTROLS and OCCUPATIONAL SAFETY AND HEALTH ACT OF 1970.) The cost of manufacturing was rising and the war on indirect costs was intensified with special attention to the problems of reducing downtime, improving maintenance productivity, and training personnel to cope with the growing complexity and sophistication of increasing system automation.

Then, in 1976, the most serious threat to United States industry since the beginning of the industrial revolution was introduced by the infamous oil embargo, ushering in the era of restricted energy supplies. Effective management of energy usage through improved efficiency, conservation, and planning was no longer an option but a matter of survival. The plant engineer not only had come into his own but now was a valued and prominent member of the management team.

Scope of Responsibility. Basic domain of the plant engineer is all facilities and utilities of the industrial plant or of the physical plant of non-manufacturing establishments. Specifically, as defined by the American Institute of Plant Engineers, the practice of plant engineering at a professional level involves responsibility for various engineering activities, including, but not limited to, the following:

(1) Planning, development, and execution of maintenance programs and procedures for optimum economic benefits from physical facilities and equipment.

(2) Selection, installation, operation, maintenance, modification, and modernization of all plant utilities, including electric power, gas, water, fuel, waste-removal systems, and communications.

(3) Planning, selection, installation, operation, maintenance, modification, and modernization of environmental protection and resource recovery systems.

(4) Selection, installation, maintenance, modification, and modernization of equipment and techniques required to provide a comfortable, safe, and healthful working environment.

(5) Participation in the selection of plant sites and real estate, and the maintenance,

modification, and modernization of buildings and grounds.

(6) Provision of administrative services, program coordination, long-range planning and budgeting, and control of operating and capital expenditures in support of plant engineering.

(7) Selection, installation, maintenance, modification, and modernization of machinery and equipment that is an integral part of the physical plant and that is necessary to support the production or service process being performed, including material handling equipment, process heating and cooling systems, illumination, and compressed air systems.

Acceptance. The National Plant Engineering & Maintenance Show has become one of the major annual industrial equipment expositions in this country. Its companion national conference as well as several major regional Plant Engineering and Maintenance conferences and American Management Association Seminars all underscore the importance of this branch of engineering. The American Association of Engineering Societies, Inc., which replaced the Engineers Joint Council, has admitted the American Institute of Plant Engineers to full membership status, attesting to the repute and professional standing of the Institute's membership and admission requirements. The American Society of Mechanical Engineers has a separate Plant Engineering Division, recognizing the importance of this function.

A growing number of engineering schools have added plant engineering courses to their curricula. At least two degree programs are in the works, and a number of other schools have added, or are studying, plant engineering options as part of their regular engineering programs. In addition, acceptance by plant engineers, their employers, and engineers in other disciplines of the AIPE Plant Engineer Certification Program, which was initiated in the mid-1970s, has been steadily growing. These kinds of recognition are perhaps the strongest endorsement of the credentials of plant engineering as a full-fledged professional engineering discipline.

The importance of the plant engineer and the function he performs was perhaps best summed up by John P. Moser, Production Vice President, Lever Brothers Co.: "What can a plant engineering department contribute to a company? It can keep it from going broke!"

LEO SPECTOR, Editor, *Plant Engineering* Magazine, Barrington, Illinois

Information References

Associations:

American Institute of Plant Engineers.
American Management Association.
American Association of Engineering Societies, Inc.
International Maintenance Institute.

Periodicals:

Plant Engineering.

Texts:

Higgins, Lindley R. and Morrow, L. C., "Maintenance Engineering Handbook," 3rd ed., New York, McGraw-Hill, 1977.

Lewis, Bernard T. and Marron, J. P., "Facilities and Plant Engineering Handbook," New York, McGraw-Hill, 1973.

Lewis, Bernard T., "Management Handbook for Plant Engineers," New York, McGraw-Hill, 1977.

Rice, J. O. and Rosaler, R. C., "Standard Handbook for Plant Engineers," New York, McGraw-Hill, 1981.

Cross References: *Environmental Controls; Maintenance: Manufacturing Management.*

PLANT LOCATION

For many U.S. manufacturing industries, the location of plant facilities can effect a differential of 10% to 15% in total production and distribution costs. Geographic variations in return on investment—always an important consideration—have become even more critical as American companies seek to improve their share of maturing domestic markets and meet the competition of an increasingly industrialized world.

A poor locational choice involves a finality and costliness that can persist for many years. Conversely, a company's profitability can be enhanced and its competitive position strengthened through strategic location of manufacturing capacity.

When to Plan. The motivating force behind many new industrial facilities has been management's impromptu response to a "crisis," e.g., immediate need for more capacity, a lengthy strike, an inflationary union contract, a railroad abandonment, a pollution injunction, or new punitive tax legislation. Since inadequate time is available for a thorough exploration of alternatives, locational decisions made in meeting such emergencies can be hasty and ill-conceived.

Good management practice calls for more orderly and systematic planning for new and expanded capacity. Just as careful tracking of competitors' pricing, marketing, and new product development is now standard procedure in most firms, so it has become mandatory to monitor changing competitive relationships in production and distribution costs.

One early warning signal of such cost imbalance is a declining profit margin on the firm's major product lines. Rather than merely reacting to clever competition, management should have a long-term plan for progressive reductions in unit costs through (1) a program of modernization and (2) strategic positioning of its plants and warehouses.

Another continuous sounding must be made for the company's changing competitive position in its local labor market. Declining productivity, extended recruiting time to fill job openings, increased turnover, or excessive absenteeism should be viewed as precursory messages of future labor difficulties. Unless the firm can afford to adjust to inflationary aspects of the local external wage structure (perhaps caused by an influx of new plants), management should be preparing to shift production to lower-cost labor market areas.

Planning for plant location, therefore, must be viewed as a *constant* effort, rather than a response to immediate problems. Only this approach can enable the time-pressed executive to weigh his options and develop an effective production and distribution strategy.

How to Plan. Good planning for new production facilities begins with a "feasibility" phase in which management's philosophies, objectives, and assumptions are tested against the realities of economic geography. Simulation techniques can be employed to explore the possibilities for accomplishing cost reduction, increasing market share, etc. Use of a production/distribution model allows necessary adjustments to be made in the original specifications and constraints in response to regional cost variables.

In the feasibility phase, the following questions should be considered:

A What are the costs and competitive implications of the company's present configuration?
  1 Marketing penetration?
  2 Labor availability and cost?
  3 Raw material availability and cost?
  4 Utility supply and cost?
  5 Exposure to environmental controls?
  6 Total operating expense?
B What are the costs and competitive implications of a change in that configuration?
  1 Can economies be accomplished through
    a. Consolidation?
    b. Decentralization?
  2 If consolidation is indicated, should it be at the present location? At a new location?
  3 If decentralization is indicated, should it be by geographic division or by product line? Which product lines?
  4 What are the nonrecurring expenses associated with each of these alternatives? Is the cost/benefit ratio favorable?
C Can sales be increased through the addition of branch plants? Should such plants be located in order to
  1 Maximize market penetration?
  2 Neutralize competition?
  3 Minimize unit costs?
D Is the present physical distribution system yielding optimum results?
  1 Are the present warehouses efficient in number, location, capacity, inventory, and service level?
  2 What is the true interrelationship of plants and warehouses?
    a. Can additional branch plants replace distribution warehouses?
    b. Can additional distribution centers eliminate the need for more branch plants?

When goals and strategies are firmly established, management may proceed with confidence into the more advanced phases of site selection.

Selecting the Region. Modern analysis techniques can be readily applied to the traditional factors in location research, assisting in the determination of the most favorable region or subregion. The efficiency of computers not only permits a wider range of alternatives to be considered, but also narrows the geographic area which ultimately must be examined. While some of the examples which follow were developed as solutions to specific problems, they will serve to illustrate the use of mathematical concepts in selecting the optimal region for proposed facilities.

Transportation Costs. Comparative freight cost studies typically consist of extensive tables containing individual rates to and from representative locations, selected more or less at random. The expense of preparing these tables is quite high, and attempts to find the least-cost solution can be laborious. Moreover, quality of the result is highly dependent upon the skill of the researcher in selecting comparison points and his knowledge of territorial rate structures.

Adding to the complexity of the problem, use of published class rates may lead to erroneous conclusions. For any sizable plant, carriers can be expected to establish more favorable commodity rates on key inbound raw material movements and on volume shipments to major markets (or warehouses). While the carriers may be reluctant to commit themselves to lower rates prior to actual plant construction, a realistic estimate of comparative total freight cost is an essential element in the decision process.

A practical method of simplifying freight data has been developed which is useful in plant location analysis and related physical distribution problems. Basically, it permits freight rate trends to be expressed in terms of "best fit" for one of three empirical equations:

Type 1 $y = a + bx$
Type 2 $y = ax^b$
Type 3 $y = ax^b + \alpha$

Based upon tariff research, appropriate trends are identified for published rates, i.e., from raw material suppliers to existing plants in the study area and from regional manufacturers of similar products to their key markets. The computer program establishes the constants (a and b) and derives the adjustment factor (α). Given an input of the distance factor (x) and the total weight to be shipped, it can estimate rates (y) and costs for an infinite number of candidate locations.

Exhibit I illustrates how a computer program was used to determine the least-cost transportation point for a proposed branch plant in the Central States. The area under consideration was divided into 50-mile blocks and the computer established total shipping charges on a finished product to a 15-state market region from the center of each block. It also constructed isobars of inbound freight cost from six alternative raw material sources. On the final printout, block "38-H" was identified as the least-cost location, with annual charges of \$181,500. The range extended to \$322,000 within the study area, and the program defined the penalties in each of the 48 blocks for later

EXHIBIT I

BASE MAP—COMBINED TRANSPORTATION COSTS

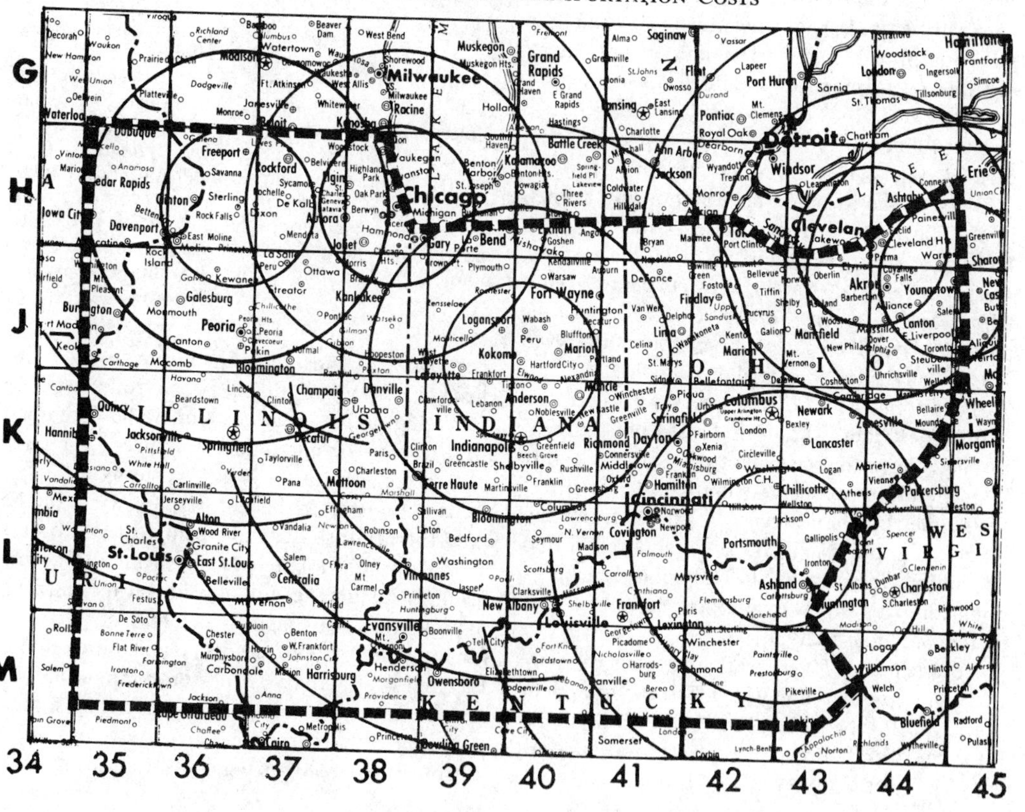

use in evaluating potential offsetting variations in other cost factors.

Still another plant location problem solved by computer techniques considered not only the optimum cost of serving present markets from alternate locations, but also programmed: (a) projected increases in the volume of sales and extent of market penetration through improved delivery schedules; (b) variations in growth rates among present and future customers; (c) anticipated inflation in freight rates; and (d) projected gradual changes in the unit weight and other characteristics of the product itself.

Warehouse Location. Attempts to apply usual Operations Research techniques to the warehouse location problem are frequently unsatisfactory. Since the primal-dual algorithms are designed for "allocation" situations, they cannot be correctly utilized in studies where the number of warehouse facilities, their size, and their geographic position are completely flexible. Configuration of physical distribution networks is best treated as a mathematical relationship between freight rates applying from origin plant(s) to service territories.

Exhibit II provides a graphic illustration of these relationships, which determine both the *size* and the *shape* of the area that can be economically served from any selected warehousing point. Contrary to common practice, distribution warehouses should not serve a circular territory.

Trend line A on the graph represents the carload rate on a given commodity from a Midwest plant to potential warehousing points in the East, and line B represents the trend of LTL rates from the origin plant to these same markets. Internal warehousing expense (rent, labor, taxes, interest on inventories, etc.) is plotted vertically as cents per 100 pounds at XY for any selected distribution point.

By shifting the LTL trend to Y as origin, the graph describes the full cost of delivery through the warehouse. Plotted as line C_1, this LTL trend from the distribution depot intersects line B (the direct LTL rate from the plant) at point Z_1. Thus, a warehouse located 400 miles east of the Midwest plant can economically ship stock to markets 825 miles east of the warehouse city.

Reversing the LTL trend line from point Y as origin, plotted line C_2 intersects line B at point Z_2. In the "blackhaul" direction, therefore, the warehouse can ship stock economically only for a distance of 40 miles.

EXHIBIT II

DETERMINING THE ECONOMICS OF WAREHOUSE DISTRIBUTION

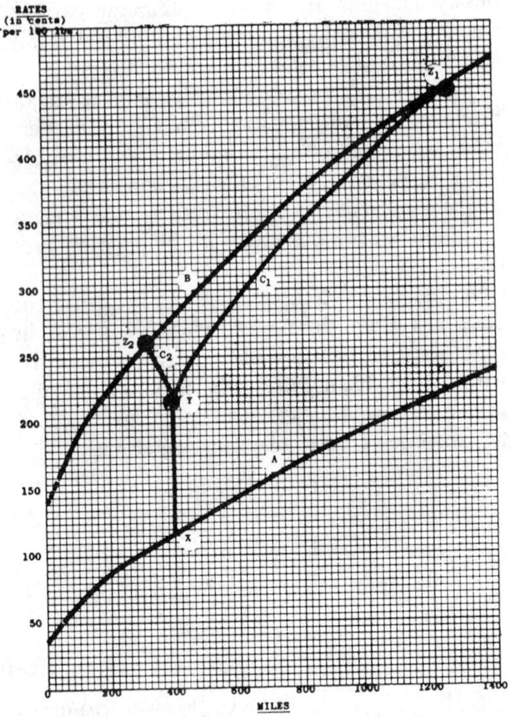

Line A shows carload rate on a given commodity from a Midwest plant to potential warehousing points in the East. Line B is the trend of LTL rates to eastern markets. Warehousing costs are plotted vertically as cents per 100 pounds. Line C_1 is the LTL line shifted to Y as origin. Line C_2 is reversed LTL trend line to determine backhauling costs. Z_1 is the eastern limit for economic shipments for a warehouse located at X, 400 miles east of the plant; Z_2 is the western limit for economical backhauling from a warehouse at X.

Labor. For most manufacturers in older industrial centers of the U.S., payroll costs are outpacing dollar inflation. Under the combined influence of strong union pressures and periodic labor shortages, wage patterns in these metropolitan areas have been distorted to the extent that unskilled and semiskilled workers have disproportionately high earnings. The net result is disturbing not only in terms of rising payroll costs, but also in the loss of incentive for individual employees to advance their skills. Lagging productivity is further compounded by resistance to improved machinery and manufacturing techniques.

Companies recognizing the situation have effectively minimized payroll costs by moving highly-repetitive fabrication and assembly operations out of their main plants to areas where wages are lower. Removal of simpler work has allowed the parent plant to concentrate on products requiring specialized labor. But, in the process of decentralization, management has frequently discovered that most so-called "skills" can actually be broken down into a series of less complicated tasks, and even highly complex products may be re-engineered to reduce or eliminate specialized labor needs.

Labor costs, of course, play an important role in determining the location for most decentralized operations. Management is seriously concerned, therefore, with the availability of most favorable wage patterns and their long-term stability.

Despite several decades of industrial migration, regional differentials in wage rates have persisted—and even show evidence of widening. Earnings of production workers in the Middle Atlantic and North Central States generally held parallel with the national average, rates throughout most of the South are lower, while the pattern in the West has exceeded the national average. Moreover, the prevalent practice of granting equal *percentage* increases in multiplant companies is reinforcing the persistence of differentials, as shown in Exhibit III.

Computer programs have been utilized to measure industry-by-industry and region-by-region trends in wage rates, fringe benefits, productivity, length of workweek, unionization, etc. These techniques permit the long-term outlook on payrolls to be directly compared with projected inflations among other cost factors and indicate shifting relationships, if any.

Computers have also aided companies to establish appropriate wage postures for new plants entering small communities or semi-rural areas where no comparable employment exists. If wages offered by the firm were too low, recruiting efforts might be unsuccessful in these environments, and dissident employees at the new facilities might resort to job action. If wages were too high, then profits might be unduly curtailed. Utilizing the "wage profile" approach, the computer program simulates the competitive position of the new facility under mature conditions in the local economy. Management is assured that it will be establishing appropriate internal differentials for various skill levels and that plantwide average earnings will be consistent with external conditions of the labor market.

Pollution. The basic premise of the ecologist is that, in order to survive, our economic system must be compatible with the environment. Business leadership must accept that premise, while being astute enough to recognize that compliance costs still show rather sizable geographic variation.

Fiscal attitudes also vary considerably among the states. Some provide partial allowances for costs of pollution abatement equipment. Others offer special amortization and tax credits. A substantial number of states exempt buildings and equipment devoted to air and/or water pollution treatment from ad valorem taxation.

Computers have been helpful in evaluating the alternatives of once-through systems and recirculation, considering the implications on capital investment, utility bills, taxes, etc. Computer-based risk analysis has also been applied to measure the advisability of installing pollution control equipment initially in the new plant or reacting to a threatened injunction at some future date.

Exhibit III

Persistence of Regional Differentials

	Plant #1 (Northeast)	*Plant #2* (South)	*Plant #3* (Far West)
Average Hourly Rate			
Prior to increase	$6.30	$4.55	$7.05
After 10% increase	6.93	5.01	7.76
Differential vs. Northeast (Plant #1)			
Prior to increase	—	−$1.75	+$0.75
After 10% increase	—	− 1.92	+ 0.83

Selecting the Community. In the subsequent site selection phase, the most likely candidates within the designated region are identified. Since this process involves numerous statisical and cost comparisons, the computer again can be a very useful analytical tool. No matter how extensive, however, such tabulations and rankings will have no real value without a comprehensive knowledge of the states and communities under consideration.

Personal field inspections are essential to the evaluation, and checklists are helpful in assuring that no key factors are overlooked. (See below, *Checklist for Site Selection.*) Yet, value judgments will still be necessary in appraising many of the tangible and intangible variables to reach a decision among the leading contenders.

In the field of taxation, for example, states typically apply allocation formulas based upon proportionate shares of property, sales, and payroll. But definition of even these elemental terms can differ radically. Consider the following interpretations of what constitutes "property" in two contiguous state (italics are ours):

State A: "The word 'value' as applied to property other than inventories, shall mean the *original cost* plus any additions or improvements, *without regard to deductions* for depreciation, amortization, write-downs, or similar charges."

State B: "The word 'value' as applied to property owned other than inventories shall mean *original cost* plus additions and improvements *less reserve for depreciation.*"

The interpretation by State A is obviously more beneficial to major multi-plant firms owning fully depreciated property in other states. The denominator of the property ratio will be larger, of course, by applying full original cost to all real estate, resulting in a lower state tax liability.

It is even more difficult to make meaningful comparisons of city and county fiscal data. In almost half of the states, local government accounting practices are not specified by law. Published tax rate tables fail to provide accurate information on local assessment practices and are usually silent on pending revaluation surveys. Most vague are the stipulations with respect to the levels of taxation on tangible and intangible personal property, where permissible by statute.

Similar data problems are encountered in the analysis of school systems. Once considered a reliable indicator of quality, "expenditures per pupil" figures are now distorted by the special needs of inner-city schools, support of court-imposed busing in rural areas to achieve racial balance, etc.

Personal judgment and objectivity are essential in evaluating such difficult intangibles as "life styles," labor stability, and ability to learn industrial disciplines. But even in such prosaic topics as utility rates, workers' compensation insurance, and unemployment benefits, the researcher must be prepared for hidden clauses that can adversely influence proposed operations.

Finally, the company must be aware of changing community attitudes toward industry. Some basic tenets are being shaken. Securing a new payroll was historically of paramount importance in most areas of the nation, and entire communities would enlist enthusiastically in campaigns to raise money for new plants. Today, citizens may vote just as fervently to eliminate an industry that is "polluting" the environment. In the past, a politician could achieve prominence through a "balance-agriculture-with-industry" platform. Today he may not be elected unless he promises to clean up or shut down these same plants. As a consequence of these changing attitudes, it is increasingly difficult to find communities that truly understand and are willing to provide for industry needs.

Some twenty-five years ago, in an article on plant location, Maurice Fulton, location consultant, prefaced his comments by two questions: "What makes for a good plant location? What criteria should management use in selecting a new site?"

He continued by saying: "It depends partly on whom you ask, because different executives have different views and prejudices. But it also depends on *when* you ask. The answer that XYZ Company would have given twenty-five years ago differs from the one it would give today. And the answer it would give today will probably be out of date ten years from now. Top executives who overlook this fact will cost industry hundreds of millions of dollars" [1].

These remarks have been more than confirmed. The contradictions, pressures, and ambiguities involved in the final location decision can be resolved only through constant and increasing research and through the intelligent application of the most modern techniques available.

CHECKLIST FOR SITE SELECTIONS

The following checklist can be used to develop a comparative analysis of candidate communities, sites, and available buildings. Detailed review is necessary to reach an informed decision among the leading contenders.

Community

(1) Population
(2) Location in state
(3) Distance to nearest major city
(4) Description of central business district
(5) Description of residential areas

Transportation

(1) Air access
(2) Rail services, including TOFC ramps
(3) Motor carrier services
(4) Water carrier services
(5) Parcel services
(6) Bus lines

Labor Market

(1) Size of the labor force
(2) Commuting patterns
(3) Labor availability
(4) Present employers
(5) Wage levels
(6) Fringe benefits
(7) Turnover and absenteeism rates
(8) Productivity levels
(9) Labor-management relations
(10) Vocational training facilities

Utilities

(1) Availability and cost of electric power
(2) Availability and cost of gas
(3) Price of alternate fuels
(4) Capacity of water system and rates
(5) Capacity of sewer system and rates
(6) Chemical analysis of water supply
(7) Regulations on waste disposal

Municipal Services

(1) Number of policemen and patrol cars
(2) Description of fire protection services
(3) Public schools, statistics and quality
(4) Hospitals and accreditation status

Taxes

(1) Current tax rates, city and suburbs
(2) Assessment practices
(3) State taxes, corporate and personal

Living Conditions

(1) Housing availability, purchase and rental
(2) Recreation facilities
(3) Cultural facilities
(4) Religious facilities (including parochial schools)
(5) Climate

Supporting Services

(1) Hotels and motels
(2) Restaurants
(3) Financial institutions
(4) Post office
(5) Telephone company
(6) Machine repair and industrial supply
(7) In-plant feeding services
(8) Continuing education courses

Incentives for Investment

(1) Financial assistance
(2) Tax moratoriums and credits
(3) Training assistance
(4) Site preparation, etc.

Sites

(1) Size and description
(2) Foundation conditions
(3) Flood hazards
(4) Zoning
(5) Road access
(6) Rail access
(7) Utility lines, size and position
(8) Tax rate
(9) Ownership
(10) Asking price

Available Buildings

(1) Size and description, including land area
(2) Ceiling clearance and bay size
(3) Floor, thickness and surface condition
(4) Zoning
(5) Truck loading facilities
(6) Rail siding capacity
(7) Utilities services, transformers, etc.
(8) Taxes
(9) Ownership
(10) Asking price or rental quotation

L. Clinton Hoch, Executive Vice President, The Fantus Company, South Orange, New Jesey

Information References

Association:

American Industrial Development Council

Government:

Chamber of Commerce of the United States, State Chamber of Commerce Department.

Publications:

Area Development, for periodic coverage.
Plant Engineering, for periodic coverage.
Plant Location.

Text:

Hoch, L. Clinton, "Community and Social Environment," in Howard, D., "Guide to Industrial Development," Englewood Cliffs, N.J., Prentice-Hall, 1972.

Reference Cited

[1] Fulton, Maurice, "Plant Location 1965," *Harvard Business Review,* March-April 1955.

Cross Reference: *Industrial Districts.*

PREDETERMINED MOTION TIMES

The concept of **Predetermined Motion Times** is not new. Frederick Taylor originally proposed it in the late nineteenth century. The emergence of usable predetermined motion-time systems, however, did not occur until the middle of the twentieth century. Five such systems accounted for virtually all of the applications made in a broad spectrum of industry in the early years.

Definition. A predetermined motion-times system is simply a list of all motions that a human being can or will perform in accomplishing factory or office tasks, and a standard performance time for making each of the motions. The five systems which fulfill the conditions of this definition in the order of their appearance are:

Motion Time Analysis (MTA)—A. B. Segur

Work Factor—Quick, Shea & Kohler

Methods-Time Measurement—Maynard, Stegemerten and Schwab

Basic Motion Times (BMT)—J. D. Woods & Gordon, Ltd. (Canada)

Dimensional Motion Times (DMT)—H. C. Gepinger.

Application. Of the five systems, Methods-Time Measurement is probably used as much as all of the others put together. MTM has been most widely accepted because from the very first, the authors chose to make their contribution a matter of public property (the text "Methods Time Measurement" [1], was published in 1948). In 1950, H. B. Maynard, G. J. Stegemerten, and J. L. Schwab, together with other consultants, industrialists, and university representatives formed the MTM Association for Standards and Research—a nonprofit corporation whose objectives are to continue research and to sustain quality among those using the system. It is located in Fair Lawn, New Jersey, and works in conjunction with the University of Michigan.

Of the remaining four systems, all except Work Factor have remained proprietary systems. Work Factor has received more recognition than the other three. It has been made generally available to industry since the publication of the text, "Work-Factor Time Standards" [2].

We shall confine our discussion of the principles of predetermined motion times to Methods-Time Measurement (MTM), since it is the most widely used system. Examples of representative MTM data appear in Exhibit I. These are the tables for the basic elements *Reach, Grasp,* and *Release.* Combinations of these three motions alone account for probably 50% of the work that human beings do. The time values are given in Time Measurement Units, "TMU," where one TMU = 1/100,000 of an hour, 0.0006 of a minute, or 0.036 of a second. In more familiar terms, a second is equivalent to about 28 TMUs. Tables for the other principal elements *Move, Position, Turn and Apply Pressure, Disengage, Eye and Body Motions,* complete the MTM data. To apply MTM as a direct measuring device, one is merely required to list the motions that an operator uses (or more appropriately *should* use) to perform his (her) job, assign the proper time value to each of the listed motions, and add up the times for the total motion pattern to arrive at an exact description of the method and an average or normal time in which it should be performed.

All predetermined motion times have run into difficulties with features that were at first considered a blessing. Each system required extreme detail and permitted a motion-by-motion study of method. This proved well worthwhile on short-cycled, highly repetitive operations. However, as industrial and office conditions changed, short-cycled highly repetitive operations became fewer and fewer in number. This led many to abandon predetermined motion times and revert to the stopwatch for measuring work. Also, it should be pointed out that many jobs exist that would be uneconomical to measure with any of the basic predetermined motion times.

Later Developments. A growing awareness by the industrial engineering profession of this limitation has somewhat altered the course of predetermined motion times. Where originally the tendency was to go into more and more detail and seek greater refinement (an attempt to be more "scientific"), the tendency in recent

Exhibit I

Examples of Methods—Time Measurement Application Data

TABLE I—REACH—R

Distance Moved Inches	Time TMU A	Time TMU B	Time TMU C or D	Time TMU E	Hand In Motion A	Hand In Motion B
¾ or less	2.0	2.0	2.0	2.0	1.6	1.6
1	2.5	2.5	3.6	2.4	2.3	2.3
2	4.0	4.0	5.9	3.8	3.5	2.7
3	5.3	5.3	7.3	5.3	4.5	3.6
4	6.1	6.4	8.4	6.8	4.9	4.3
5	6.5	7.8	9.4	7.4	5.3	5.0
6	7.0	8.6	10.1	8.0	5.7	5.7
7	7.4	9.3	10.8	8.7	6.1	6.5
8	7.9	10.1	11.5	9.3	6.5	7.2
9	8.3	10.8	12.2	9.9	6.9	7.9
10	8.7	11.5	12.9	10.5	7.3	8.6
12	9.6	12.9	14.2	11.8	8.1	10.1
14	10.5	14.4	15.6	13.0	8.9	11.5
16	11.4	15.8	17.0	14.2	9.7	12.9
18	12.3	17.2	18.4	15.5	10.5	14.4
20	13.1	18.6	19.8	16.7	11.3	15.8
22	14.0	20.1	21.2	18.0	12.1	17.3
24	14.9	21.5	22.5	19.2	12.9	18.8
26	15.8	22.9	23.9	20.4	13.7	20.2
28	16.7	24.4	25.3	21.7	14.5	21.7
30	17.5	25.8	26.7	22.9	15.3	23.2

CASE AND DESCRIPTION

- **A** Reach to object in fixed location, or to object in other hand or on which other hand rests.
- **B** Reach to single object in location which may vary slightly from cycle to cycle.
- **C** Reach to object jumbled with other objects in a group so that search and select occur.
- **D** Reach to a very small object or where accurate grasp is required.
- **E** Reach to indefinite location to get hand in position for body balance or next motion or out of way.

TABLE IV—GRASP—G

Case	Time TMU	DESCRIPTION
1A	2.0	Pick Up Grasp—Small, medium or large object by itself, easily grasped.
1B	3.5	Very small object or object lying close against a flat surface.
1C1	7.3	Interference with grasp on bottom and one side of nearly cylindrical object. Diameter larger than ½".
1C2	8.7	Interference with grasp on bottom and one side of nearly cylindrical object. Diameter ¼" to ½".
1C3	10.8	Interference with grasp on bottom and one side of nearly cylindrical object. Diameter less than ¼".
2	5.6	Regrasp.
3	5.6	Transfer Grasp.
4A	7.3	Object jumbled with other objects so search and select occur. Larger than 1" x 1" x 1".
4B	9.1	Object jumbled with other objects so search and select occur. ¼" x ¼" x ⅛" to 1" x 1" x 1".
4C	12.9	Object jumbled with other objects so search and select occur. Smaller than ¼" x ¼" x ⅛".
5	0	Contact, sliding or hook grasp.

TABLE VI—RELEASE—RL

Case	Time TMU	DESCRIPTION
1	2.0	Normal release performed by opening fingers as independent motion.
2	0	Contact Release.

(*From MTM Association for Standards and Research*)

years has been toward a more middle-of-the-road course—sacrificing some of the detail and methods description for considerably less clerical involvement, but with no appreciable loss of accuracy in the end result. This new use of predetermined motion times led to the development of new approaches for simplifying the application.

The five best known approaches to this objective are, in the order of their appearance:

(1) The present author's Master Standard Data (MSD).

(2) Universal Standard Data (USD), developed by H. B. Maynard Company.

(3) Ready Work Factor, developed by the Work Factor Company.

(4) General Purpose Data (GPD), developed by the U.S.-Canada MTM Association for Standards and Research.

(5) MTM-2 and MTM-3, developed by the Svenska MTM-Foreningen (Swedish MTM Association.)

To the credit of the industrial engineering profession, the developments have not stopped with these five. In recent years improvements have continued with the computer being introduced to facilitate the establishing and maintaining of standards. The most important developments in this area based on well-known predetermined time systems are:

(1) The computer software package known as 4M, offered by the U.S.-Canada MTM Association for Standards and Research.

(2) Maynard Operation Standard Times (MOST), developed by H. B. Maynard Company and available as both a manual and computer-aided system.

(3) MOD-II, a computer software package developed by the author's firm that is compatible with nearly all predetermined time systems.

(4) Computer-aided Work Factor, developed by Work Factor Company and compatible with nearly all predetermined time systems.

To be sure, others have also developed similar approaches or systems. However, most are either for a specialized use or adaptations of other systems [3].

MOST, MOD-II and computer-aided Work Factor have the capability of handling standards for direct and indirect labor in the factory as well as the work performed in the office. Since similarities exist in these approaches, the author here confines his remarks to the one he is most familiar with, MOD-II.

First came the simplification of predetermined times into easier-to-use elements that provided faster and thus more economical application. This resulted in the MTM motions listed on Exhibit II being combined into one element contained on the Master Standard Data (MSD) card reprinted as Exhibit III. The MTM motions on Exhibit II were combined into one MSD element that was symbolized by 012H2 and can be found on Exhibit III opposite "12" in the left-hand column and under

Exhibit II

MTM Analysis of Twelve-Inch Reaching Operation

RL1	2.0	RL1
R12C	14.2	(R11E)
G4B	9.1	
	3.6	R1C
	9.1	G4B
	38.0	

Exhibit III

Master Standard Data (MSD) (Simplification of MTM Data)

TABLE 1

OBTAIN — O				
Distance In Inches	Degree of Control			
	Some—S		High—H	
	1	2	1	2
2	8	8	17	30
6	13	13	21	34
12	17	17	25	38
18	21	21	30	42

TABLE 2

PLACE — P						
Distance In Inches	LOCATION					
	Other Hand	General	Exact			
			Loose—L		Close—C	
	O	G	1	2	1	2
2	7	5	11	26	21	47
6	11	9	16	31	27	52
12	15	13	21	36	31	57
18	19	17	26	41	37	62

TABLE 3

ROTATE R		
H	F	9
	W	15
C	S	17
	L	19

TABLE 4

USE U	
V	4
L	8
M	13
H	17

TABLE 5

FINGER SHIFT	
FS	6
EXERT FORCE	
EF	11

TABLE 6

BODY MOTIONS B		
A	Arise-Sit	108
F	Foot	9
V	Vertical	61
W	Walk	17

"2" in the extreme right-hand column. In MTM-2 (see Exhibit IV or the MTM-2 data card) this combination resulted in two codes and times as shown on Exhibit V. The difference in time of one unit in MTM-2 is probably due to the fact that the MTM-2 card is based on the metric system.

As work elements are combined into larger and larger units, it becomes uneconomical manually to define the method or methods they measure in detail. Using a computer-aided work-measurement approach will provide a detailed description of "how a job is to be done" as well as the time to do it, and it will do this economically.

Exhibit VI is a table for fastening threads, and values from this table are often included in the measuring of jobs. However, when it is

Exhibit IV

MTM II Data Card

MTM-2

CODE	GA	GB	GC	PA	PB	PC
– 5	3	7	14	3	10	21
– 15	6	10	19	6	15	26
– 30	9	14	23	11	19	30
- 45	13	18	27	15	24	36
– 80	17	23	32	20	30	41
GW: 1 per kg				PW: 1 per 5 kg		

A	R	E	C	S	F	B
14	6	7	•15	18	9	61

Warning: do not use this data unless you are properly trained

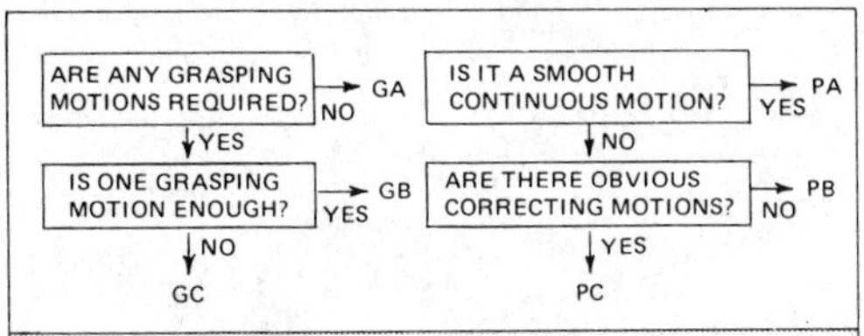

SVENSKA MTM FÖRENINGEN

Exhibit V

MTM II Analysis of Twelve-Inch Reaching Operation

GC-30	23	
	14	GC-5
	37	

Exhibit VI

Table of Fasten With Threads

Tool Used	Up To And Including 5 Threads: First Screw or Nut -A-	Up To And Including 5 Threads: Add'l Screws or Nuts -B-	Over 6 And Up To And Including 10 Threads: First Screw or Nut -C-	Over 6 And Up To And Including 10 Threads: Add'l Screws or Nuts -D-	
1. Power Tool	155	102	155	102	1
2. Yankee Screw Driver	173	120	201	148	2
3. Nut or Screw Driver—Loose	233	180	341	288	3
4. Nut or Screw Driver—Tight	287	234	467	414	4
5. Ratchet Wrench—Loose	255	202	291	238	5
6. Ratchet Wrench—Tight	376	323	664	611	6
7. Open End Or Box Wrench—Loose	325	272	361	308	7
8. Open End Or Box Wrench—Tight	596	543	1184	1131	8
9. "T" Wrench—Loose	217	164	253	200	9
10. "T" Wrench—Tight	255	202	375	322	10
11. Hold Nut With Tool	61	27	61	27	11

used, about all that appears is the code indicating the value used. For example, TFTA01 with a value of 155 multiplied by the number of occurrences merely tells you that it is fastened with power tool. Computerization of this table would also include a narrative description of TFTA01 that would printout. This narrative would appear as shown on Exhibit VII.

Each time this code is used we have the capability of having the narrative on Exhibit VII printed out to describe what is done. This is very valuable in explaining or auditing stan-

Exhibit VII

Narrative of Fasten Threads with Power Tool—First Screw or Nut

Get screw or nut, move to location, position screw or nut and start with fingers. Get power tool, place on screw or nut, run screw or nut down, and aside power tool.

Exhibit VIII

MCD-MOD II TASK CODING SHEET I

TASK NO. STEN-TBL-01 REV. NO. TRANS TYPE REPORT CODE

1 5 19 21 22

TASK NAME TYPE BUSINESS LETTER

23

INPUT TASK NO. REV.

63 77

HEADING INFORMATION

DEPARTMENT CORP. SERVICES

SECTION STENOGRAPHIC

JOB TYPIST II

ANALYST HWN

DATE CODED 10/9/99

EFFECTIVE DATE 11/1/99

ITEM COUNTED LETTER

BATCH SIZE 1

DAILY COUNT 40

HOW OFTEN DONE AS REQUIRED

EQUIPMENT 1 TYPEWRITER

EQUIPMENT 2

EQUIPMENT 3

MATERIALS 1 PAPER, CARBON SETS, ENVELOPES

MATERIALS 2

MATERIALS 3

SUPERSEDES

SUPERSEDED BY

ALLOWANCE (%)

RBL - 01/80

PAGE 1 OF 3

EXHIBIT IX

MCD-MOD II TASK CODING SHEET II

TASK NO STEN-TBL-01   REV NO   TRANS TYPE

STEP	LINE	Trans	TITLE/DESCRIPTION/OBJECT	MCD CODE	FREQUENCY
	00		PREPARE TO TYPE		
			GET ENVELOPE TO DESK,	GST	
			OPEN AND REMOVE LETTER.	MOUUO3	
			READ LETTER.	ERWA	198
			ASIDE BY TYPEWRITER.	GAT	
			COLLATE PAPER (ORIGINAL & 4 COPIES)	ACT	
				ACA	3
			AND ALIGN.	HSG	
				HJ501	3
				BST	
			PLACE PAPER IN TYPEWRITER.	TPP08	5
	00		TYPE LETTER		
			READ AND TYPE OPENING,	ERWA	18
			READ AND TYPE BODY	TOB01	
			OF LETTER,	ERWA	180
			AND TYPE CLOSING.	TCS	15
			MAKE CORRECTIONS.	TRI	3
				TEEC	10

RL 02/80

PAGE 2 OF 3

dards. As the reader will appreciate, when several elements such as TFTA01 are combined into a larger element, this capability becomes even more important. MOD-II has the capability of storing the time value of each element as well as a description of each element. In addition, the words, "screw or nut" contained in the narrative on Exhibit VII could be left blank and the word desired entered opposite the code TFTA01 when this code is used to create an element. Then this word—for example, nut—will become part of the narrative.

Of importance in a work measurement program are:

(1) The capability of easily locating the backup of each work element.

(2) The capability of economically revising or updating standards as changes are made in methods, equipment or materials.

(3) The capability of creating new standards from existing standards with full documentation of both the existing and new standards.

(4) The capability of having a permanent record relating to any revision or updating.

Often these features are difficult to attain in a manual work-measurement system. However, the correct use of the computer as an aid in work measurement makes all of these possible economically. MOD-II accomplished each of these goals as probably do other computerized approaches. This will be illustrated in the discussion below.

Other Areas. Thus far, this article has dealt only with predetermined times as they relate to

Exhibit X

Narrative of Fasten Threads with

EN–CAN MANUFACTURING CO.
555 INDUSTRIAL HWY.
HAROLD, SI 99900

TASK NO.—— STEN–TBL–01
REV. NO.——0
TYPE BUSINESS LETTER

DEPT.——CORP. SERVICES
SECTION——STENOGRAPHIC
JOB——TYPIST II

ANALYST——HWN
DATE CODED——10/09/99
EFFECTIVE DATE–11/01/99

ITEM COUNTED——LETTER
BATCH SIZE—— 1 DAILY COUNT—— 40
HOW OFTEN DONE——AS REQUIRED

SUPERSEDES——
SUPERSEDED BY——

EQUIPMENT——TYPEWRITER
MATERIALS——PAPER, CARBON SETS, ENVELOPES

TASK DESCRIPTION

STEP 1 – PREPARE TO TYPE

GET ENVELOPE TO DESK, OPEN AND REMOVE LETTER. READ LETTER. ASIDE BY TYPEWRITER. COLLATE PAPER (ORIGINAL & 4 COPIES) AND ALIGN. PLACE PAPER IN TYPEWRITER.

STEP 2 – TYPE LETTER

READ AND TYPE OPENING, READ AND TYPE BODY OF LETTER, AND TYPE CLOSING. MAKE CORRECTIONS.

REMOVE PAPER FROM TYPEWRITER. ASIDE TYPED COPIES FACE DOWN. BOTTOM COPY TO OTHER HAND, GET CONTROL OF CARBON, TEAR COPY FROM CARBON AND ASIDE CARBON TO WASTE BASKET. PLACE COPY IN FILE. CARBON COPIES TO OTHER HAND. TEAR CARBON FROM COPY AND ASIDE. PLACE ORIGINAL WITH COPIES. GET ORIGINAL AND COPIES AND ALIGN, GET ENVELOPE AND PLACE IN ENVELOPE. GET PEN AND ADDRESS ENVELOPE. ASIDE ENVELOPE TO OUT BASKET.

STANDARD TIME .18206
ITEMS PER HOUR 5.49

MCD–MOD II TASK CODING SYSTEM PAGE 1

manufacturing operations. The times developed for human motions performed in the factory will also work in the office. However, applying predetermined times to the office economically can only be done by combining the basic predetermined motions into larger elements tailored for office work. Several systems of predetermined times have been cataloged into clerical work elements and are in use today. However, only a few, to the present author's knowledge, are economical in both large and small offices. Many of the major systems in use today were tailored using the Serge A. Birn Company's Master Clerical Data (MCD) as a guide.

The latest version of MCD is known as MCD-MOD-II, as it utilizes the MOD-II computer software. The use of the computer eliminates detailed calculations and manual writing of task descriptions. The partial input for typing a letter from handwritten copy is shown on Exhibits VIII and IX, with Exhibit X being the task description and resulting standard. The step detail of this task can also be reproduced for use by the work measurement personnel.

In the establishment of the original standard, the computer only saves time in the detail preparation. However, once a standard is on file, updating or maintaining of standards becomes far easier than was ever possible manu-

Exhibit XII

MCD-MOD II TASK CODING SHEET II

TASK NO STEN-TBL-02 REV NO TRANS TYPE R

STEP	LINE	Trans	TITLE/DESCRIPTION/OBJECT	Cd	MCD CODE	FREQUENCY
1	2	R	OPEN AND REMOVE TAPE.			
1	3	S	PLACE TAPE IN TRANSCRIPTION MACHINE		GAP	
1	4	S	PULL LEVER TO THREAD TAPE AND		GMT	
			PUSH DOWN TRANSCRIPTION BUTTONS.		GMT	
2	1	S	TYPE LETTER FROM TRANSCRIPTION.		TOBO1	
2	2	S	WITH MAXIMUM OF 2 ERRORS	X	TLS	15
2	3	S	AND 3 PARAGRAPHS.	X	TEEC	10
2	4	S			TRI	3
2	5	S			TSAT	
2	6	D				

EXHIBIT XI

MCD-MOD II TASK CODING SHEET I

TASK NO. STEN-TBL-02 REV. NO. TRANS TYPE R REPORT CODE

TASK NAME TYPE BUSINESS LETTER FROM TRANSCRIPTION

INPUT TASK NO. STEN-TBL-01 REV.

HEADING INFORMATION

DEPARTMENT

SECTION

JOB

ANALYST

DATE CODED

EFFECTIVE DATE

ITEM COUNTED

BATCH SIZE

DAILY COUNT

HOW OFTEN DONE

EQUIPMENT 1 TYPEWRITER, TRANSCRIPTION MACHINE

EQUIPMENT 2

EQUIPMENT 3

MATERIALS 1

MATERIALS 2

MATERIALS 3

SUPERSEDES

SUPERSEDED BY

ALLOWANCE (%)

RBL - 01/80

PAGE 1 OF 2

EXHIBIT XIII

```
EN-CAN MANUFACTURING CO.                TASK NO.--     STEN-TBL-02
555 INDUSTRIAL HWY.                                     REV. NO.- - 0
HAROLD, SI 99900       TYPE BUSINESS LETTER FROM TRANSCRIPTION

DEPT.--CORP. SERVICES                   ANALYST--HWN
SECTION--STENOGRAPHIC                          DATE CODED--10/09/99
JOB--TYPIST II                              EFFECTIVE DATE -11/01/99

ITEM COUNTED--LETTER                      SUPERSEDES--
BATCH SIZE-- 1    DAILY COUNT -- 40   SUPERSEDED BY--
HOW OFTEN DONE--AS REQUIRED

EQUIPMENT--TYPEWRITER, TRANSCRIPTION MACHINE
MATERIALS--PAPER, CARBON SETS, ENVELOPES

                       TASK DESCRIPTION

STEP 1 - PREPARE TO TYPE

     GET ENVELOPE TO DESK, OPEN AND REMOVE TAPE. PLACE TAPE IN
TRANSCRIPTION MACHINE, PULL LEVER TO THREAD TAPE AND PUSH DOWN
TRANSCRIPTION BUTTONS. COLLATE PAPER (ORIGINAL & 4 COPIES) AND
ALIGN. PLACE PAPER IN TYPEWRITER.

STEP 2 - TYPE LETTER

     TYPE LETTER FROM TRANSCRIPTION.

STEP 3 - WRAP UP

     REMOVE PAPER FROM TYPEWRITER. ASIDE TYPED COPIES FACE DOWN.
BOTTOM COPY TO OTHER HAND, GET CONTROL OF CARBON, TEAR COPY FROM
CARBON AND ASIDE CARBON TO WASTE BASKET. PLACE COPY IN FILE.
CARBON COPIES TO OTHER HAND. TEAR CARBON FROM COPY AND ASIDE.
PLACE ORIGINAL WITH COPIES. GET ORIGINAL AND COPIES AND ALIGN, GET
ENVELOPE AND PLACE IN ENVELOPE. GET PEN AND ADDRESS ENVELOPE.
ASIDE ENVELOPE TO OUT BASKET.

                                   STANDARD TIME      .20435
                                   ITEMS PER HOUR      4.89

MCD-MOD II TASK CODING SYSTEM                    PAGE 1
```

ally. Also, existing standards form a data bank for establishing new standards.

Exhibits XI and XII would be the input needed to utilize the standard created in Exhibits VIII, IX and X to create a standard for typing this letter from dictation on a tape. The resulting task description with the new standard is on Exhibit XIII. Had the purpose been to update the standard for typing from dictation on a tape, then Task No. of Exhibits XI and XII would have been Sten-TBL-01, with no input task number on Exhibit XI. The result would have been the same as Exhibit XIII with the Task No. Sten-TBL-01 and Rev. No. 01.

The use of the computer for establishing and maintaining standards is only the beginning of the use that can be made of the information on file. The standards file will be useful in production planning and control, developing of standard costs, and in developing future as well as present staffing requirements. The real challenge in utilizing a work measurement computer-aided system is making sure the data bank contains the level of data that is most economical for your firm's specific needs.

H. W. NANCE, President, Serge A. Birn Company, Louisville, Kentucky

Information References

Associations:

American Institute of Industrial Engineers.
MTM Association for Standards and Research.

Texts:

Crossan, R. M. and Nance, H., "Master Standard Data—The Economic Approach to Work Measurement," Huntington, N.Y., Robert E. Krieger, 1980.

Nance, H. W. and Nolan, R. E., "Office Work Measurement," New York, McGraw-Hill, 1971.

References Cited

[1] Maynard, H. B., Stegemerten, G. J., and Schwab, J. L., "Methods-Time Measurement," New York, McGraw-Hill, 1948.

[2] Quick, J. H., Duncan, J. H. and Malcolm, J. A., Jr., "Work-Factor Time Standards," New York, McGraw-Hill, 1962.

[3] Karger, Delmar W. and Bayha, Franklin H., "Engineered Work Measurement," New York, Industrial Press, 1977.

Cross References: *Motion and Time Study (and cross references there given).*

PRICES: Statistics

The primary sources of **Price Data** are monthly publications of the Department of Labor, Bureau of Labor Statistics, which include: *Monthly Labor Review; Consumer Price Index; Estimated Retail Food Prices by Cities; Retail Prices and Indexes of Fuels and Utilities;* and *Producer* (formerly *Wholesale*) *Prices and Price Indexes.* The Bureau of Economic Analysis of the Department of Commerce is the source for the gross national product (GNP) implicit price deflator figures. The Department of Agriculture's Economics, Statistics, and Cooperatives Service (ESCS) prepared indexes of prices received and prices paid by farmers.

The Bureau of Labor Statistics prepares monthly indexes of producer prices for a large selection of commodities; monthly indexes of consumer prices for both commodities and services; and weekly indexes of spot market prices for 22 commodities.

Producer Price Index. This index (formerly the wholesale price index), dating from 1890, is the oldest continuous statistical series published by the Bureau of Labor Statistics. It is designed to measure average changes in prices of all commodities, at all stages of processing, produced or imported for sale in primary markets in the United States.

The index has undergone several revisions (see *Monthly Labor Review,* February 1962). It is now based on approximately 2,800 commodity price series instead of the approximately 1,900 included in the 1947–1960 period and the 900 included for the period prior to 1947. Prices used in constructing the index are collected from sellers, if possible, and generally apply to the first significant large-volume commercial transaction for each commodity—i.e., the manufacturer's or other producer's selling price, the importer's selling price, or the selling price on an organized exchange or at a central market.

The weights used in the index represent the total net selling value of commodities produced or processed in this country, or imported. Values are f.o.b. production point and are exclusive of excise taxes, interplant transfers, military products, and goods sold directly at retail from producing establishments. Effective January 1976, the weights are values of net shipments of commodities as derived from the industrial censuses of 1972 and other data. From January 1967 through 1975, weights were based on 1963 shipment values.

Consumer Price Indexes (CPIs). These indexes measure the average changes in the cost of fixed, or constant, "market baskets" of consumer goods and services purchased by all urban consumers and by urban wage earners and clerical workers. Weights, which reflect the relative importance of the components of the indexes (e.g. housing, food and beverages, entertainment) and which are used in calculating the indexes, are based on studies of actual expenditures by consumers. Quantities and qualities of items in the "market baskets" remain essentially the same between consecutive pricing periods (monthly for national data), so that the indexes measure the effect of price change only on the cost of living. They do not measure changes in the total amount families spend for living; geographic area indexes do not measure relative differences in prices or living costs between areas.

A study conducted during 1917–1919 provided the composition of the "market basket" and the weights used until 1935. Since then, this index has undergone several major revisions which involved bringing the "market basket" of goods and services up to date, revising the weights, and improving the sample and methodology. The most recent revision, initially issued with release of January 1978 data, is based on updated "market baskets" of goods

EXHIBIT I

PURCHASING POWER OF THE DOLLAR: 1940 TO 1979

1967 = $1.00. Producer prices prior to 1961, and consumer prices prior to 1964, exclude Alaska and Hawaii. Obtained by dividing the average price index for the 1967 base period (100.0) by the price index for a given period and expressing the result in dollars and cents]

Year	*Monthly Average as Measured by—*		*Year*	*Monthly Average as Measured by—*		*Year*	*Monthly Average as Measured by—*	
	Producer Prices	*Consumer Prices*		*Producer Prices*	*Consumer Prices*		*Producer Prices*	*Consumer Prices*
1940---------	$2,469	$2,381	1957---------	$1,072	$1,186	1969---------	$ .939	$ .911
1945---------	1.832	1.855	1958---------	1.057	1.155	1970---------	.906	.860
1947---------	1.307	1.495	1959---------	1.055	1.145	1971---------	.877	.824
1948---------	1.208	1.387	1960---------	1.054	1.127	1972---------	.840	.798
1949---------	1.271	1.401	1961---------	1.058	1.116	1973---------	.742	.752
1950---------	1.222	1.387	1962---------	1.055	1.104	1974---------	.625	.678
1951---------	1.098	1.285	1963---------	1.058	1.091	1975---------	.572	.621
1952---------	1.129	1.258	1964---------	1.056	1.076	1976---------	.546	.587
1953---------	1.144	1.248	1965---------	1.035	1.058	1977---------	.515	551
1954---------	1.142	1.242	1966---------	1.002	1.029	1978---------	.478	.512
1955---------	1.139	1.247	1967---------	1.000	1.000	1979---------		
1956---------	1.103	1.229	1968---------	.976	.960	May	.432	.467

SOURCE: U.S. Bureau of Labor Statistics. Monthly data in U.S. Bureau of Economic Anlaysis, *Survey of Current Business.*

and services and revised expenditure weights derived from a Consumer Expenditure Survey undertaken over the 1972–1973 period. This revision also established the second CPI representing all urban consumers (80% of the civilian noninstitutional population). For a discussion of the history and concepts of the CPI, see *Consumer Price Index,* report number 517, published by BLS.

Approximately 224 sets of items called item-strata are priced for the CPIs. These fairly broad categories of goods and services are exhaustively defined in checklists. The original selection of the specific items to be priced in a specific retail store is generally accomplished by a data collector using the checklist in systematic stages that take sales information provided by the respondent into account in each stage. After the initial selection, the same item (or a close substitute) is priced from period to period so that, as far as possible, differences in reported prices are measures of price change only. All taxes directly associated with the purchase or continued use of the items priced are included in the indexes.

The national indexes for the fifth revision of the CPI are based on prices collected in 85 primary sampling units which include central cities, suburbs, and urbanized places within 25 miles of a selected county or selected group of contiguous counties. Prices are also collected outside of the primary sampling units to represent out-of-town purchases. Foods, fuels, rents, and a few other items are priced monthly in all areas. Prices of most other commodities and services are obtained monthly in the five largest areas and bimonthly in the remaining areas. Between scheduled survey dates, prices are held at the level of their last pricing. Price data for the 85 areas are combined for the United States with weights based on the 1970 population of the areas represented by each sample area. Indexes are published for a wide variety of commodities and services, by region cross-classified by population size, and for 28 separate areas, usually consisting of the Standard Metropolitan Statistical Area (SMSA), exclusive of farms. L.A.-Long Beach, Anaheim, California is a combination of two SMSAs, and N.Y.-Northeastern N.J. and Chicago, Ill.-Northwestern Ind. are the most extensive Standard Consolidated Areas. Area definitions are those established by the Office of Management and Budget in 1973, except for Denver-Boulder, Colorado which does not include Douglas County. Definitions do not include revisions made since 1973.

Information References

Consult the current edition of the *Statistical Abstract of the United States for tables on* Producer prices and price index, consumer prices and price index, retail prices, etc.

Cross References: *Pricing: Legal Aspects; Pricing Policy; Statistical Abstract of the United States.*

PRICING: Legal Aspects

Preoccupation with the prevention of monopolies, restraints of trade, and their attendant abuses is neither a recent nor a uniquely American phenomenon. Nevertheless, though we find monopoly attacked in edicts of Emperor Zeno in the fifth century and again in the English statutes of the Elizabethan era, it is only here in America that we have made a free, dynamic, and competitive economy the cornerstone not only of our industrial supremacy but also of our political and social structure.

In the latter part of the nineteenth century, concentration in the fields of manufacturing and transportation reached a point where our citizens were threatened with, to quote the late Chief Justice Stone, "danger from another kind of slavery . . . the slavery that would result from the aggregation of capital in the hands of a few individuals and corporations controlling, for their own profit and advantage exclusively, the entire business of the country, including the production and sale of the necessaries of life." Congress responded by passing the Sherman Act in 1890. In essence, the law declares illegal every contract, combination, or conspiracy in restraint of trade or commerce and monopoly or attempts to monopolize trade. It also provides the Government with both civil and criminal sanctions to employ against violators and grants to the victims of such practices the right to recover their damages threefold. (See ANTITRUST LEGISLATION.)

The Sherman Act. With relation to pricing practices, the most obvious effect of the Sherman Act is to declare illegal any agreement among competitors concerning the prices at which they will sell their respective products. In order to violate the law, such an agreement does not have to be one to sell at identical prices. Agreements that specify that participants will not reduce prices below an established minimum or that fixed differentials in price will be maintained as between contracting parties are likewise condemned. It is the law's purpose to prohibit agreements or understandings which create an artificial rigidity of price, those designed to prevent prices from being fully responsive to the natural forces of a free competitive economy.

At one time it was not unusual to find such agreements reduced to writing. The modern, more sophisticated business man colludes in more subtle fashion. Price information may be exchanged through a trade association, whose minutes are carefully edited by its counsel. There may be a "gentleman's agreement" among the members of the association that price lists filed with it will not be changed without prior notification to the association. Less formally, agreements may be reached on the golf course or at the cocktail bar, where (if we are to give full faith and credit to the deductions claimed on income tax returns) so much of this country's business seems to be conducted. It makes no difference how or where the agreement is reached. Once it is established that there has been a meeting of the minds that prices will not be changed or will be held at or above a certain level, the participants are in direct and basic violation of the Sherman Antitrust Law.

This statute remains today at the foundation of national antitrust policy. However, the first twenty-four years of attempted enforcement demonstrated the need for supplementary legislation. The original statute provided no weapons for preventing monopoly in its incipient stage or for protecting victims of monopoly before their economic life had been destroyed.

The Clayton Act. In 1914 Congress, in response to a message from President Wilson, passed the Clayton Act. Section 2 of that Act declared discrimination in price to be illegal. This section was inserted especially in order to prevent territorial price discrimination, a practice by which a large national producer with extensive financial reserves could reduce prices in areas where local competition showed signs of developing strength and, at the same time, more than offset any loss involved by enjoyment of monopoly prices in other areas. This strategy was most effective since the smaller firm often had to reduce prices to a point below cost throughout the territory served by it while its larger rival could still operate profitably.

As originally drawn, Section 2 of the Clayton Act did not prove to be as effective as its authors intended. Its application was limited through judicial interpretation. For example, the statute made discriminations in price unlawful "where the effect of such discrimination may be to lessen competition substantially or tend to create a monopoly in any line of commerce." The courts held that in order to establish a violation, it was necessary to prove a tendency to restrain trade or create a monopoly in the entire line of commerce in which the seller was engaged. Therefore, a violation did not occur where it could be shown that the discrimination resulted in injury only to individual competitors without threatening ultimate monopoly, or where it could be demonstrated that the resulting monopoly or restraint was in the line of commerce of the customers rather than the seller. Further, the law contained the proviso that "nothing herein contained shall prevent discrimination in price between purchasers of commodities on account of difference in the grade, quality, or quantity of the commodity sold or that makes only due allowance for differences in the cost of selling or transportation." Thus, in order to establish a violation, it was necessary to show that the customers involved purchased identical quantities. If they did not, the fact that the difference in quantity did not produce any cost justification for the price differential was of no consequence.

The Robinson-Patman Act. With the astounding growth of mass-distribution outlets, a condition was reached in the mid-thirties where the large purchaser was able to exert such economic pressure that the seller was forced, through price concessions, to subsidize the very trade practices which were tending to destroy the independent retailer. A study made by the Federal Trade Commission at the direction of Congress demonstrated that chain stores were receiving price concessions. Some were open ones, given to large purchasers but wholly unjustified by any savings in cost to the seller. Others were concealed in the form of brokerage fees, advertising allowances, and preferential services and facilities. As a result, Congress in 1936 amended Section 2 of the Clayton Act by the passage of the Robinson-Patman Act. It is this statute which most directly affects the pricing of products today.

The basic provision is found in Section 2(a), which can be simply paraphrased as follows:

> It is unlawful for any person engaged in interstate commerce to discriminate in price in the course of that commerce, by charging different prices to different purchasers of commodities of like grade and quality, when the purchased goods are to be used, resold, or consumed within the United States, and where the effect of the price differential may be to substantially lessen competition, or may tend to create a monopoly, in any line of commerce.

The basic elements are: There must be (1) two or more completed sales; (2) by the same seller, (3) at around the same time, (4) of commodities, (5) of like grade and quality, (6) with a difference in price, (7) to two or more different purchasers, (8) for use, resale or consumption within the United States, (9) that may result in competitive injury and (10) the interstate commerce requirements of the Act must be satisfied.

Each of the foregoing ten elements must be present to constitute a violation of the Act.

The defenses provided in the statute are that (1) the difference in the price must reflect actual differences in the cost of manufacture, sale, or delivery arising from the differing quantities or methods of purchase; (2) the lower price must be made in good faith to meet an equally low price of a competitor; or (3) the price difference must result from a price change responsive to changing conditions affecting the market for the goods concerned or their marketability. Such conditions are the threatened obsolescence of seasonal goods, the deterioration of perishable goods, liquidation sales of distressed merchandise, or other abnormal conditions.

Competitive injury is one of the jurisdictional elements which must be present for there to be a violation of the Robinson-Patman Act. In determining whether competitive injury has occurred because of price discrimination, the courts will consider the size of the discrimination, its duration, the volume of business covered, the degree of competition in the relevant market, and the impairment of competition in said market. Losses suffered by individual competitors may be an indication of anticompetitive effects only when these losses are sufficient to distort and lessen the effectiveness of market forces.

Meeting competition is a distinct legal defense to a charge of price discrimination. It is in fact the most frequently asserted, and accepted defense. Any seller may meet in good faith an equally low, lawful price that is offered by a competing seller to a specific customer. The seller must not have substantial reason to believe that the offer or price that it is meeting is itself unlawful and discriminatory. Meeting competition must be based on individual competitive situations. Granting reduced prices to an entire class of customers may not be justified on grounds of individual competitive offers received by selected members of that class. A price reduction to an entire class may result in illegal discrimination with respect to other customer classes which are required to pay a higher regular price.

Special statutes exempt from the provisions of the Robinson-Patman Act all purchases of supplies for their own use by Federal and state governments, and by schools, churches, hospitals, and charitable institutions not operated for profit. These exemptions extend to various types of resale activity conducted in competition with private for-profit businesses, such as retail sales to qualified purchasers by military post exchanges and hospital pharmacies.

Private rights of action may be maintained for violations of the Robinson-Patman Act. In order to encourage private enforcement, Congress has provided that a successful litigant can recover three times the actual damages sustained by his business, as a result of the violation, plus a reasonable attorney's fee. Private action to enforce the Robinson-Patman Act may be brought only in the Federal District Courts.

Specific Pitfalls in Pricing. The manufacturer undertaking to establish a sound pricing policy must first determine what his method of distribution is going to be. Is he going to sell through wholesale distributors? Is he going to sell directly to retailers? Or is he going to sell to both?

Where his decision is to sell to only one class of buyer and thus to undertake but one distribution function, the foundation of a sound pricing plan is a uniform price to all customers. Upon that foundation he may provide for price differentials based upon variations in the size of individual orders for single shipment and delivery to one customer. However, such differences must be offered to all customers, and the seller must be able to assume successfully the burden of showing that the difference in price reflects no more than the actual difference in the cost of manufacture, sale, or delivery resulting from such variations in size.

"Price" includes a number of elements both monetary and nonmonetary. Discounts, returns, adjustments, and delivery or payment terms, may all be considered in determining whether a discriminatory price exists.

Advertising allowances, merchandising payments, services, or facilities furnished in connection with the resale of a commodity are not considered as a part of price discrimination. The granting of advertising allowances, merchandising payments, services, etc., by a manufacturer or supplier to a customer in connection with the resale of a commodity is covered in other provisions of the Robinson-Patman Act which require that such payments and services, if granted, be made on a proportionally equal basis to all competing customers.

Not every price difference is prohibited by the antitrust laws. The antitrust laws are designed to prevent and eliminate only anticompetitive business practices, especially price fixing and other unlawful lessening of price competition. Enforcement of price discrimination prohibited in Section 2(a) should not stifle pro-competitive price and marketing activities.

Many sellers like to offer what is, in effect, an incentive plan by providing a graduated scale of discounts or rebates based upon cumulative purchases over a period of time. They have been offered in some instances to individual customers and on other occasions to corporate or other chains and are computed upon the aggregate of purchases of all the units. On still other occasions they have been granted to loosely organized buying groups of otherwise independent firms joined together for the sole purpose of obtaining the maximum discount or rebate. Such plans are extremely vulnerable under the provisions of the Robinson-Patman Act and have been the subject of many Commission proceedings.

To say the least, such plans present almost insurmountable difficulties in the way of cost justification. By way of illustration, when we have one customer who at the start of a season places one firm order for delivery on a single date of $50,000 worth of a given commodity and another whose purchases in the course of a year total $100,000 but result from fifty calls by salesmen and fifty separate orders (each of which has to be separately processed and billed), the cost of sale and delivery per dollar of sales would be less to the first customer. Nevertheless, under a cumulative-discount or rebate plan, the second customer would enjoy a price advantage. It was to prevent such inequities that the Robinson-Patman Act was passed.

Where a manufacturer elects to establish a dual system of distribution by selling both to wholesalers and direct to retailers, he may encounter further difficulties. Normally, his price to the wholesaler must be less than it is to the retail customer, because the wholesaler must cover his expenses of warehousing, shipping, and selling, and still be in a position to offer merchandise to the retailer at the same price or at one not greatly in excess of the price charged by the manufacturer to his retailer customers.

The Robinson-Patman Act neither sanctions nor condemns the so-called functional discount given to the wholesaler. In the absence of cost justification, the test of legality of such a price differential is its competitive effect. If the wholesaler is solely engaged in the resale of the commodity to retailers and if the retailers are engaged exclusively in the sale to consumers, then, assuming all wholesalers purchase at the same discount and the cost to all retailers is the same, the discount extended to wholesalers would not have an adverse competitive effect and would therefore be legal.

Where the line of demarcation between the distribution functions of the two classes of customers is less clearly defined so that there are areas in which the so-called wholesaler sells direct to the consumer or where the so-called retailer actually resells to other retailers, then the likelihood exists that the difference in price will have a tendency and capacity to injure competition and thus be illegal. Illustrative of this point is the order of the Federal Trade Commission issued against Ruberoid Company and affirmed by the United States Supreme Court. In the sale of roofing materials, Ruberoid classified its customers as wholesalers, retailers, and contractors. The Commission found that the customers classified as wholesalers were allowed extra discounts and competed with others classified as contractors. The Commission therefore ordered Ruberoid to cease and desist from discriminating in price as between customers "who, in fact, compete," and this language was upheld by the court.

The Robinson-Patman amendment also attempted to close the loophole through which indirect price discriminations had managed to elude the prohibitions imposed by the original Section 2 of the Clayton Act. In a study of chain stores, the Federal Trade Commission found that the large grocery chains had required packers of canned goods to pay to their salaried purchasing agents the same brokerage fee normally paid by such packers to independent brokers negotiating the sale of canned goods on behalf of the packer. The proceeds were, of course, turned over by the purchasing agents to their principals.

Section 2(c) of the Robinson-Patman Act, in practical effect, makes illegal the payment by the seller—to the buyer, the buyer's agent, or anyone acting in behalf of the buyer or under his control—of a brokerage fee or commission, or a discount in lieu thereof, in connection with the buyer's own purchases.

After the passage of this section, one of the chain stores turned to the packers and said, "Under this section you can no longer pay our employee a brokerage fee. Therefore, you are now saving that amount. Consequently, you must charge us a net price equivalent to the market price, less the brokerage formerly paid." The Federal Trade Commission held that a net price arrived at in this fashion represented a discount in lieu of brokerage and was in violation of Section 2(c). This decision was also upheld by the courts.

Sections 2(d) and 2(e) also attempt to prevent the employment of subterfuge to disguise price discriminations and avoid the prohibitions of the basic statute. The law recognizes the value of cooperation in furnishing point-of-sale advertising and promotional services. It requires, however, that the seller desiring to compensate one customer for such services must afford to all competing customers the opportunity to provide similar services and to receive payment for them on proportionally equal terms. Where a seller furnishes a customer with services or facilities connected with the processing, handling, or sale of a commodity, he must also accord them to all who seek to purchase from him, on proportionally equal terms.

In marketing a product, the seller may be concerned not only with the price charged but with the image created for the product in the mind of the ultimate consumer. This may lead some to ascribe to the product a so-called list price grossly in excess of the usual and customary price at which it is sold at retail.

Under the provisions of Section 5 of the Federal Trade Commission Act, a retailer who employs fictitious comparative prices or value claims in his advertising violates the law. The manufacturer who aids and abets the retailer in such a practice by lending his prestige to create an atmosphere of authenticity through preticketing merchandise with fictitious and unrealistic prices is equally guilty.

JOHN F. O'BRIEN, Assistant Regional Director, New York Regional Office, Federal Trade Commission, New York, New York

Information References

Kintner, Earl W., "A Robinson-Patman Primer, 2nd ed., New York, Macmillan, 1979.

"Preparing an Application to the FTC for Robinson-Patman Complaint Concerning Alleged Price Discrimination," Washington, D.C., Bureau of Competition, Federal Trade Commission, 1980.

Cross References: *Marketing Strategy: Competitive Analysis; Prices: Statistics; Pricing Policy.*

PRICING POLICY

A price represents "the art of translating into quantitative terms (dollars and cents) the value of a product or service to customers at a point in time" [1]. The value of a product/service to a customer may involve both tangible (such as cost savings from a new machine) and intangible (such as pride of ownership) factors. A price may also refer to nonmonetary exchanges (such as barter). A price contains all the terms of purchase such as monetary and nonmonetary charges, discounts, handling and shipping fees, credit charges, and other forms of interest and late payment fees. From a broader perspective, price is the mechanism for rationing goods and services among purchasers and for ensuring competition among sellers.

Of the marketing mix components (price, product, distribution, and promotion), only price directly generates profits. Price is also the only element in every marketing transaction. A firm may not promote its products, require customers to pick up merchandise at a factory, or make undifferentiated commodities, yet it must determine a price strategy and **Pricing Policy.**

In 1964 and again in 1975, executives of 200 companies were asked to rank twelve aspects of marketing in terms of their importance in reaching marketing objectives. Pricing was ranked sixth in the 1964 study, behind product planning, marketing research, sale management, advertising, and customer service. Half of the executives did not consider pricing as one of the five most vital areas [2]. The results were quite different in the 1975 study. Pricing was named as the most vital marketing activity [3]. The rise in the relative importance of price may be attributed to rapid cost increases, more foreign competition for many products and services, greater price awareness on the part of consumers, and shortages leading to high prices in some product categories.

Two points must be stressed in connection with pricing policy: First, any company will be well advised to pursue a policy of "preventive maintenance" with respect to price. As with a building, if maintenance is deferred, when the test of undue stress and strain comes, there is always the temptation to patch things up—or alternatively, the necessity to rebuild. The one is unsatisfactory, the other costly.

Exhibit I lists common symptoms of problems with a firm's pricing policy.

Second, a pricing policy will pay off best if it is part of a more extensive procedure that comprehends the market-management structure of the company as a whole. There is need for an *integrated pricing policy for the firm:* of establishing one if none exists, and of maintaining such a policy once it has been established.

The objective of an integrated pricing policy for the firm requires equal emphasis upon its three concepts: First, by *pricing policy* we mean that body of doctrine on the subject which one is willing to live with. Second, it must be a policy for the *firm,* signifying that we should be concerned less with price-setting for an individual product, or a product line, or a technique, than with the policy involving all of these as they relate to the destiny of the business entity. Finally, the title requires us to consider an *integrated* policy: a word signifying the probability of many issues and decisions which must be reconciled each with the other—and all together—in terms of the objective of the company.

What must be done is to stake out, as comprehensively as possible, those questions which would provide a firm with a realistic evaluation of its pricing policy. Specifically:

(1) What are the factors, beyond the control of management, that limit or otherwise influence the effective zone within which price policy can be determined?

(2) What are proper objectives of pricing policy?

(3) What are the more commonly accepted pricing formulas that might be accepted or modified to meet the needs of the firm?

(4) What steps or systematic method can be followed to bring together all of these factors in such a perspective that an integrated policy can thereafter be developed?

Limiting Factors in Pricing Policy. No individual and no company can act as a free agent. Purely for purposes of summary, let us take account of the more important of these limiting factors:

(1) A marketer must understand the relationship between price and consumer purchases and perceptions. This relationship is explained by two economic principles: (1) the law of demand and price elasticity of demand, and (2) psychological pricing.

The *law of demand* states that consumers usually purchase more units at a low price than at a high price. The price elasticity of demand defines the sensitivity of buyers to price changes in terms of the quantities they will purchase.

When consumers are perceptually sensitive to certain prices and departures from these prices in either direction result in decreases in demand, they are responding to *psychological pricing.* Customary pricing (a price which a channel member seeks to maintain over an extended time period as in candy, gum, magazines), odd pricing (a price set at a level below even dollar values such as \$.49, \$4.95 and \$19.50), and prestige pricing (which assumes that consumers do not buy products or services at prices which are considered too low) are examples of psychological pricing.

(2) A second limiting factor is the effect of public laws, the more obvious of which include

EXHIBIT I

SYMPTOMS OF PROBLEMS WITH A FIRM'S PRICING POLICY

1. Price changes are made too frequently.
2. Pricing policy is difficult to explain to consumers.
3. Channel members complain that profit margins are inadequate.
4. Price decisions are made without adequate data and information.
5. Too many different price options are available.
6. Too much sales personnel time is spent in bargaining.
7. Price strategy is inconsistent with the target market.
8. A high proportion of goods are marked down or discounted late in the selling season.
9. Too high a proportion of customers are price-sensitive.
10. The firm has major problems conforming with pricing legislation.

anti-trust legislation, the Robinson-Patman Act, the Pure Food and Drug Act, the rules and regulations of the Interstate Commerce Commission, Federal Trade Commission advertising guidelines, state legislation (such as unfair-sales acts and unit pricing legislation) and price controls. Except for firms in intermittent contact with the Antitrust Department, few companies seem to provide themselves with a really thorough audit of their legal position with respect to price policy. A review of the company's legal position in all matters relating to price is suggested as an important step in the development of an integrated pricing policy. (See PRICING: Legal Aspects.)

(3) A third factor limiting the latitude for pricing policy is inherent in the nature of the product itself and the characteristics of the market within which it is sold. We refer here to products which tend to be standardized beyond the point of meaningful differentiation, such as sugar, salt, and cement; also to situations in which these or other products are set by formalized exchanges. The same thing is true of those industries subject to the complication of commodities which are sensitive and responsive to world conditions.

(4) A fourth limiting factor is the existence of some pronounced peculiarity which may be inherent in the relation of buyer to seller where, for example, the buyer may be able to negotiate on the basis of equal or perhaps even superior knowledge of the seller's costs, or in cases where the seller is likely to be inhibited by the ever-present threat of having the buyer undertake the production of the item himself.

(5) A fifth limiting factor is channel member relationships. To ensure channel cooperation, a manufacturer should first determine the final selling price consumers will pay and the profit margins required by wholesalers and retailers. Then, the manufacturer's price should be set. Common conflicts between manufacturers and channel members involve ultimate control over final selling prices, relative emphasis given to national brands and private label products by retailers, and the impact on price increases for goods with customary retail selling prices.

(6) A sixth limiting factor is competitive reactions. Since price strategies are relatively easy and quick to copy, the reaction of competition is predictable if the firm initiating price changes is successful. Accordingly, a marketer should view price from both short-run and long-run perspectives.

(7) Finally, the current stage of the business cycle is a factor outside the control of the company, directly influencing the degree of latitude which it can exercise in respect to price.

The Objectives of Pricing Policy. With these limitations in mind, we should next inquire what the objectives of pricing policy should be. There are three general pricing objectives from which a firm may select: sales-based, profit-based, and status-quo-based.

(1) A firm with a sales-based objective is oriented toward increasing sales volume or expanding its market share. Penetration pricing is an example of a sales-based strategy. A penetration price is a low price intended to capture the mass market for a product or service. It is a proper strategy when customers are highly sensitive to price, low prices discourage actual and potential competitors, there are economies of scale (per unit production and distribution costs decrease as sales increase), and a large consumer market exists. Penetration pricing also recognizes that a high price may make a product vulnerable to competition.

(2) A profit maximization objective is used when a firm sets a goal in terms of profits in dollars, return on investment, or early recovery of cash. Skimming pricing is an example of a profit maximizing strategy. A skimming price is a high price intended to attract the market segment that is more concerned with status than price. It is a proper strategy if competition can be kept out or minimized (through patent protection, brand loyalty, raw material control, or high capital requirements), funds are needed for early recovery of cash or further expansion, the market is insensitive to price or willing to pay a high initial price, and unit production and distribution costs remain equal or increase as sales increase (there are no economies of scale).

(3) Status-quo-based objectives are sought by a firm interested in stability of continuing a favorable climate for its operations. Pricing strategy is oriented toward avoiding declines in business and minimizing the impact of outside parties (such as government, competitors, and channel members).

A company may pursue more than one pricing objective at the same time, such as maximizing market share and earning at least $700,000 net profit before taxes. A firm may also set different short-run and long-run objectives.

Pricing Formulas. A pricing formula is much more than a device which management uses to make pricing decisions smoothly and mechanically. Pricing formulas should also be considered from the point of view of their effect on the level of prices of a firm and their effect on the differences between prices. Six commonly accepted pricing formulas are:

(1) *Prices equal to allocated total firm costs, plus a certain standard percentage markup.* Under this formula every product is presumed to contribute equally to the net profit of a firm.

(2) *Prices equal to a certain multiple of a major cost component.* This is the basic method of price determination in retail and wholesale trade. In certain manufacturing industries, where materials costs loom large, this method is easy to understand and calculate.

(3) *Prices equal to cost of purchases from other firms plus a certain multiple of remaining costs.* In this, the costs remaining after purchases from other firms constitute value-added by the firm.

(4) *Prices set to yield a given return on investment.* Under this formula prices are established based on determining costs and required investment at a standard volume level.

(5) *Prices proportional to size, weight, or service value.* When products in a line are numerous and when cost allocation is expensive or difficult, the setting of price differentials on the basis of relative product characteristics, with some rough adjustments for cost and demand considerations, often is desirable. Variations in measurable product characteristics often reflect variations in demand. Furthermore, informing customers of the variable that moves the price is a way of gaining customer acceptance of the price structure. Pricing according to service characteristics, such as the expected life or capacity, is likely to be particularly acceptable to customers. However, prices should be adjusted to encourage production or sales of the more profitable lines.

(6) *Prices set relative to competition.* In this, prices are set based on price changes of competitors. The firm decides as to whether it should meet or beat competitors' prices or to retain its current price level.

Research Toward an Integrated Pricing Policy. The measure of success of a firm's price making is the batting average of its pricing decisions, and only by an integrated price-making program can a firm enjoy a respectable average. An integrated price-making program utilizes, in a systematic fashion, several classes of facts. Whenever possible, facts about a company's operation should be compared with facts of competitors' or industry operation. The most relevant facts may be summarized as follows:

(1) *A complete write-up should be made of the company's price-making methods and policies.* The very act of making explicit that which has not been the subject of recent conscious attention tends to make apparent certain suggestions for change.

(2) *A complete list of present prices should be made and compared with competitors' prices, in as much detail as possible.* Included in this comparison should be the terms of trade of the firm and those of the industry. In those cases where prices are *higher,* management should make sure the premium is justified in the eyes of its customers in terms of better quality, design, or service. Where prices are *lower,* there should be a good reason for pricing lower than the market. (Sometimes raising a price will increase both unit and dollar sales because the consumer may have a better opinion of the commodity at a higher price.)

(3) *Production costs should not be neglected.* Good cost information shows which lines are most profitable, which lines should be dropped, and in which lines the greatest competition is likely to be felt; it gives insight into what competitors' future prices will be like, the likelihood of entry of new firms into the industry, the avenues where study is likely to yield the greatest cost reductions, and bases for setting discount schedules and special service charges.

(4) *Distribution costs should be considered if costs are considered at all in pricing.* When setting quantity discounts, class of customer discount, terms of sale discounts, and special service charges, a study of distribution costs is imperative. There are also many subsidiary benefits from distribution costing outside the realm of pricing policy: for example, discovery of profitable and unprofitable customers, distribution channels, and territories.

(5) *Pricing decisions should also be made in terms of the level and distribution of sales and those of competitors.* Examination of the price and sales structure in comparison with other firms in the industry would show up strengths and weaknesses in a company's own price structure. In times of falling prices, share of the market in conjunction with information on competitors' prices furnishes a good guide to pricing policy. *Assuming health on other fronts, prices should be lowered no faster than necessary to maintain share of the market.*

(6) *The final category of facts in price-making is the characteristics of the customer.* One needs

to know how good the customer's knowledge of prices is, and the extent to which he considers price in making a purchase. This is true whether one is selling consumer goods or industrial goods, and whether or not selling is done through intermediaries.

The Goal of an Integrated Pricing Policy. Pricing policy is not the exclusive province of any one department or executive group. It is the inescapable responsibility of the company's top management to establish pricing policy; but skillful top management will in turn see that the policy reflects the best judgment of sales and production heads, controller, and company counsel, and that their final judgment rests upon an objective analysis of the relevant facts.

An integrated pricing policy may be likened to the area within a triangle. One point of the triangle consists of production costs—assuming various levels of capacity operation. The second point concerns costs of sales and distribution—assuming various levels in intensity of selling effort. The third point consists of a volume of sales—assuming various levels of price. It is unfortunate that the systematic process of "triangulation" suggested here is all too rarely followed. The field of pricing policy is one in which there is no substitute for sound business judgment. What is here advocated is a foundation for such judgment based on fact, with a realistic regard for the current position of the firm and an optimistic eye toward the future.

BARRY BERMAN, PH.D., Professor of Marketing, Hofstra University, Hempstead, New York

JOEL R. EVANS, PH.D., Chairman, Marketing and International Business Department, Hofstra University, Hempstead, New York

Information References

Evans, Joel R. and Berman, Barry, "Marketing," New York, Macmillan, 1982.

"Flexible Pricing," *Business Week,* December 12, 1977.

Monroe, Kent B., "Pricing: Making Profitable Decisions," New York, McGraw-Hill, 1979.

Oxenfeldt, Alfred R. "A Decision Making Structure for Price Decisions," *Journal of Marketing,* January 1973.

"Pricing Strategy in An Inflationary Economy," *Business Week,* April 6, 1974.

References Cited

[1] Corey, E. Raymond, "Industrial Marketing: Cases and Concepts," Englewood Cliffs, New Jersey: Prentice-Hall, 1976.

[2] Udell, Jon G., "How Important Is Pricing in Competitive Strategy?" *Journal of Marketing,* January, 1964.

[3] Robincheaux, Robert A., "How Important Is Pricing in Competitive Strategy?" *Proceedings:* Southern Marketing Association, January 1976.

Cross References: *Marketing Strategy: Competitive Analysis; Prices: Statistics; Pricing: Legal Aspects.*

PROCESS ANALYSIS

Process Analysis is the act of studying the process used for producing a part or a product for the purpose of developing the lowest-cost, most efficient process which will yield products of acceptable quality.

The proper time to develop the correct method of performing a given piece of work is before it has been sent to the shop. This is usually practical, however, only when it is known at the outset that a given job will be produced in large quantities. Many jobs start out in insufficient quantities to justify advanced detailed study, and become highly repetitive through wide customer acceptance only after they have been in production for a period of time. In such cases, it is desirable to examine and analyze in detail the methods currently in use in the shop to correct any ineffective practices which may exist.

Improper or wasteful manufacturing methods exist in many cases only because no one realizes clearly that they are being used. Modern manufacturing is a complex procedure; it is almost impossible to carry a clear mental picture of all of the activities which are going on and their relation to one another. Many hidden inefficiencies are therefore likely to exist even in well-managed departments. As soon as the inefficiencies are discovered, it is usually a comparatively simple task to eliminate them. The major problem, therefore, is to locate the inefficiencies. This can be done fairly easily with the aid of a *Process Chart,* which is defined as follows:

A *Process Chart* is a graphic representation of events and information pertaining thereto occurring during a series of actions or operations.

The Process Chart forms a convenient means of presenting in a limited space information about a process. It can be used to show the relations among operations, the steps of a process, and any or all such factors as distance moved, operations performed, working and idle time, cost, production data, and time standards. It permits the quick visualization of a problem so that improvement can be undertaken systematically and in logical sequence.

Although a Process Chart can be drawn by anyone who learns a few simple principles of Process Chart construction, most often it is the industrial engineer who uses it as a tool of process analysis.

Three types of Process Charts are in general use for analyzing existing processes:

(1) Operation Process Chart
(2) Flow Process Chart
(3) Multiple Activity Process Chart

Process Chart Events and Symbols. For analytical purposes and to aid in detecting and eliminating inefficiencies, it is convenient to classify the events or actions which occur during a process into five classifications. These are known as *operations, transportations, inspections, delays,* and *storages.* The classifications are symbolized on process charts by the symbols shown in Exhibit I. The symbols are useful for distinguishing at a glance the classification of every event shown on the chart without reading the accompanying detailed information. (Practice is not altogether uniform regarding symbols; some industrial engineers use a smaller circle to designate transportation, and the inverted triangle to designate delay as well as storage.)

Inside each symbol, it is the practice to place identifying letters and numbers.

The following definitions cover the meaning of the classifications under the majority of conditions which will be encountered in process charting work [1].

An *operation* occurs when an object is intentionally changed in any of its physical or chemical characteristics, is assembled with or disassembled from another object, or is arranged or prepared for another operation, transportation, inspection, or storage. An operation also occurs when information is given or received or when planning or calculating takes place.

EXHIBIT I

STANDARD PROCESS CHART SYMBOLS

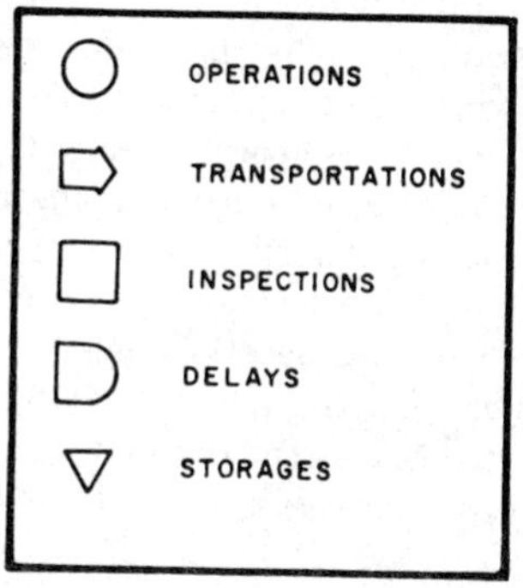

A *transportation* occurs when an object is moved from one place to another, except when such movements are caused by the process or by the operator at the work station during an operation or an inspection.

An *inspection* occurs when an object is examined for identification, verified for quality or quantity, or measured in any of its characteristics.

A *delay* occurs to an object when conditions except those of processing do not permit or require immediate performance of the next planned action.

A *storage* occurs when an object is kept and protected against unauthorized removal.

When unusual situations outside the range of the definitions are encountered, the intent of the definitions, summarized in the accompanying tabulation, is helpful.

CLASSIFICATION	PREDOMINANT RESULT
Operation	Produces or accomplishes
Transportation	Moves
Inspection	Verifies
Delay	Interferes
Storage	Keeps

The Operation Process Chart. The Operation Process Chart is a valuable means of showing clearly the operations performed on a given product, and it gives a quick understanding of the various operations in their relation to one another. It shows the flow of the process from the entering of the raw materials until the finished product emerges at the end. It is defined as follows:

> An *Operation Process Chart* is a graphic representation of the points at which materials are introduced into the process, and of the sequence of inspections and all operations except those involving material handling. It may include any other information considered desirable for analysis, such as time required and location.

The principles followed in constructing an Operation Process Chart are shown graphically in Exhibit II.

In addition to their use for the analysis of existing processes, Operation Process Charts are a great help in plant layout work. When an assembly requires a large number of detailed operations and involves enough bulk to present a handling problem, it is important to lay out

EXHIBIT II

GRAPHIC REPRESENTATION OF PRINCIPLES OF OPERATION PROCESS CHART CONSTRUCTION

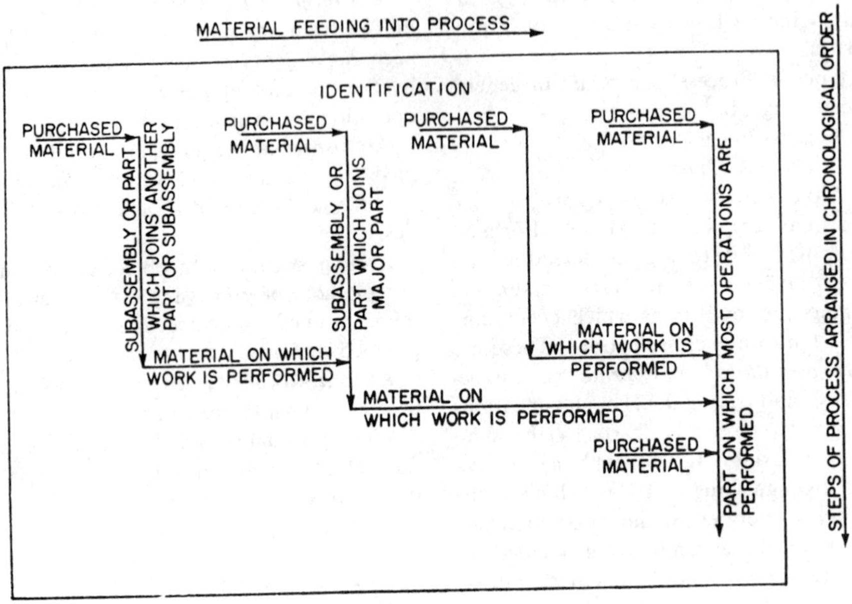

the plant so that material flows through the operations with a minimum of handling. It is comparatively easy to visualize the right hand side of the chart as a progressive assembly line. The horizontal material lines on the chart suggest feeder benches or sub-assembly lines feeding detail parts into the main assembly line. Exhibits III and IV illustrate this use of the Operation Process Chart.

The Flow Process Chart. In form, the Flow Process Chart is somewhat like the Operation Process Chart, but it gives more information. This is desirable on certain types of process studies, but on others the mass of detail would be too great for ready interpretation. On complex products, the Operations Process Chart presents the problem more clearly. If after a preliminary study more detailed information is desired, Flow Process Charts can be made for the various parts which make up the complete assembly. The formal definition is as follows:

> *A Flow Process Chart* is a graphic representation of the sequence of all operations, transportations, inspections, delays, and storages occurring during a process or procedure, and includes information considered desirable for analysis such as time required and distance moved.

There are two distinct types of Flow Process Charts, the *material* type and the *man* type. The first presents the process in terms of the events which occur to the material. The second presents the process in terms of the activities of the man. Care must be taken in making a Flow Process Chart to decide at the outset whether materials or men are to be followed. Otherwise the descriptions are likely to indicate the first one and then the other is being followed, which is confusing.

The Flow Process Chart shows the different steps or events of each process, time required for each step, and any other pertinent information which the one who is drawing it may wish to show. Flow Process Charts are used in industry chiefly to reduce distance traveled, to reduce time material spends in storage, to eliminate unnecessary operations and handling, and as a basis for improving plant layouts.

Because of the similarity in Flow Process Charts of single items, prepared forms are frequently used, although if more than one item is to be shown, or if it is desired to show alternative paths which a single item may take during processing, a prepared form is impracticable. Exhibit V shows a portion of a prepared form, and Exhibit VI shows a form prepared on plain paper, with the standard symbols.

In clerical analysis, paper usually takes the place of material as the object to be followed. Flow process charts are useful to show clearly

EXHIBIT III

OPERATION PROCESS CHART FOR TYPE K-02 FILTER BOX

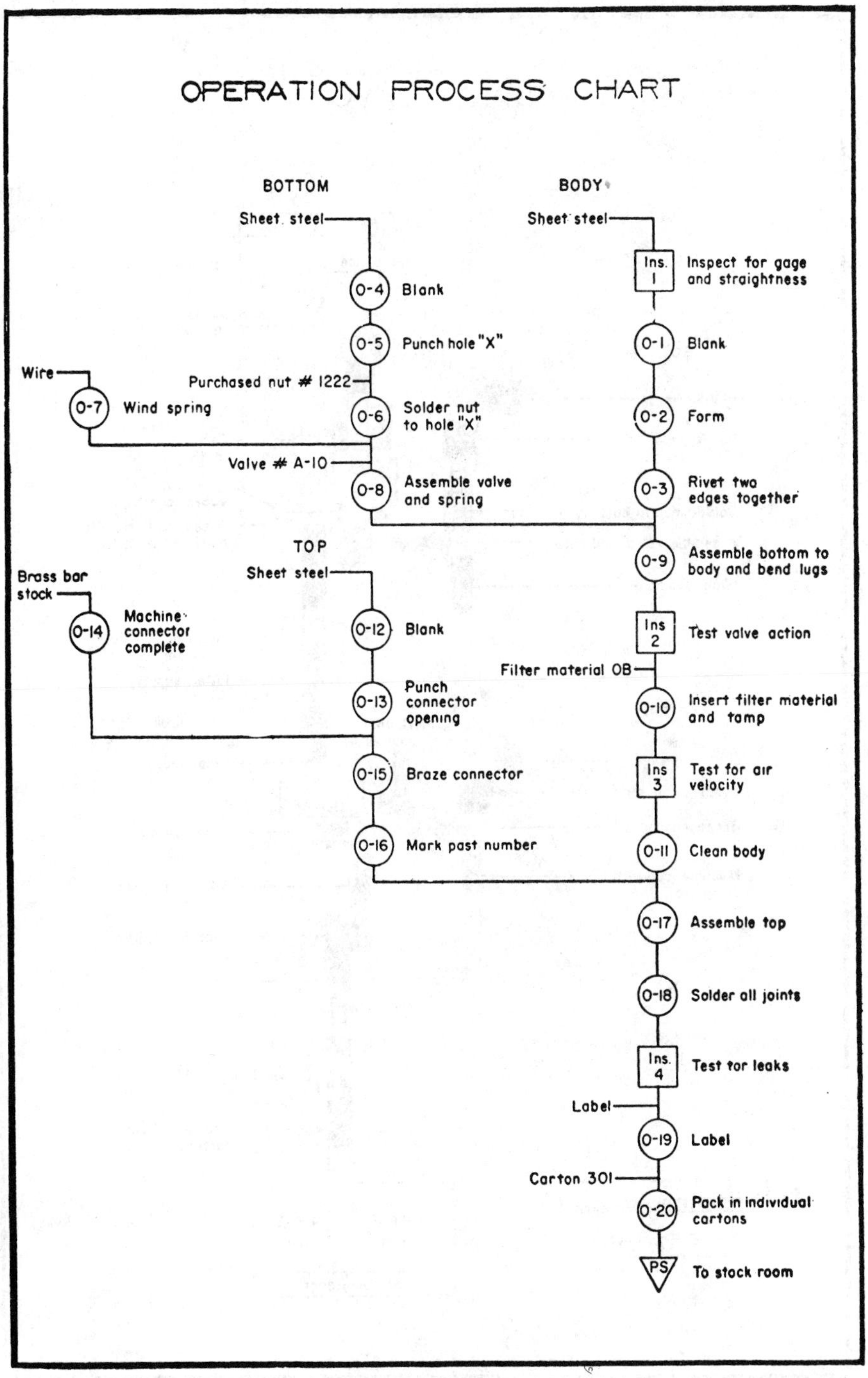

(*From Maynard, H. B., "Industrial Engineering Handbook"*)

EXHIBIT IV

PLANT LAYOUT PROCESS CHART FOR MANUFACTURE OF TYPE K-02 FILTER BOX

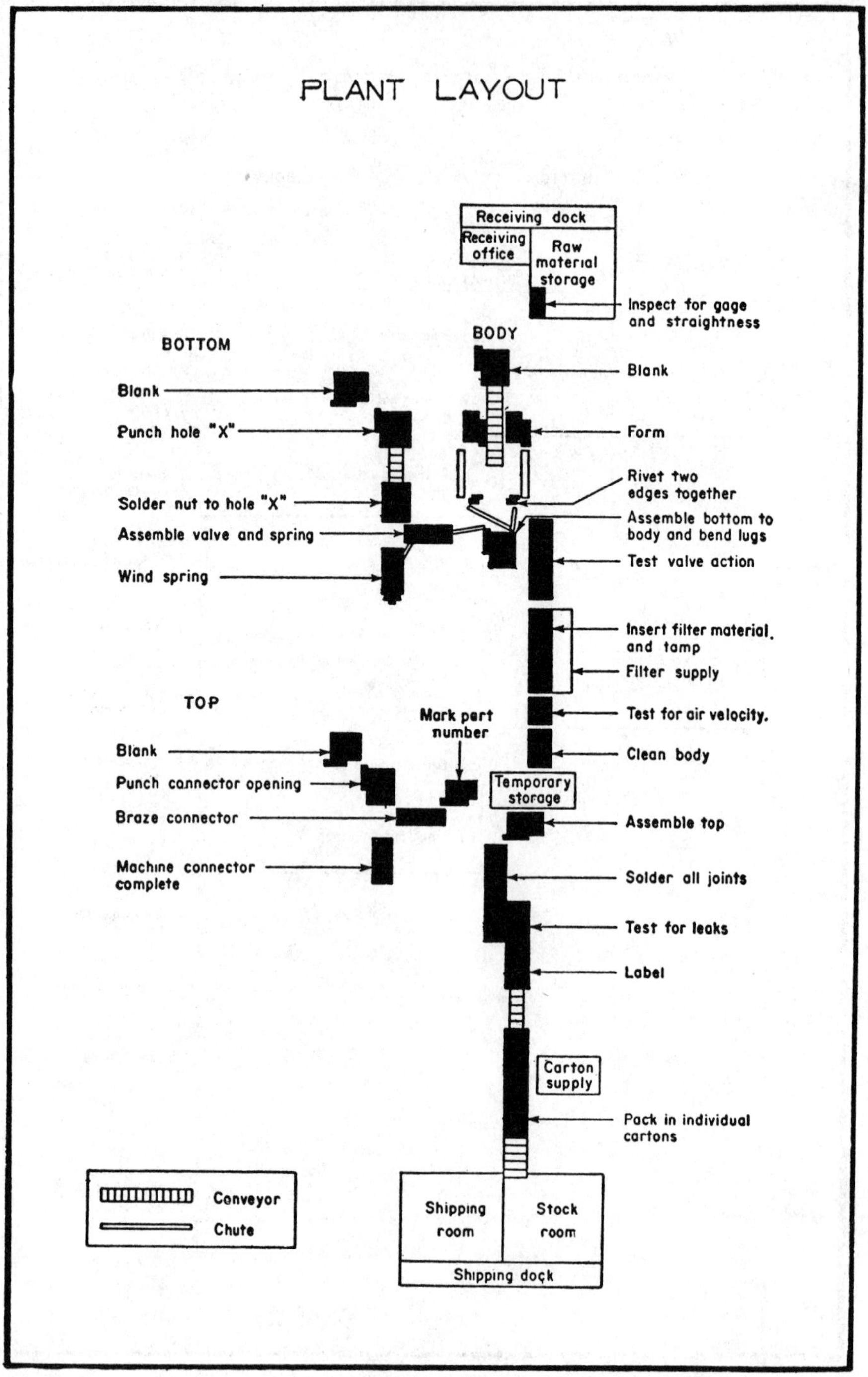

(*From Maynard, H. B., "Industrial Engineering Handbook"*)

EXHIBIT V

FLOW PROCESS CHART

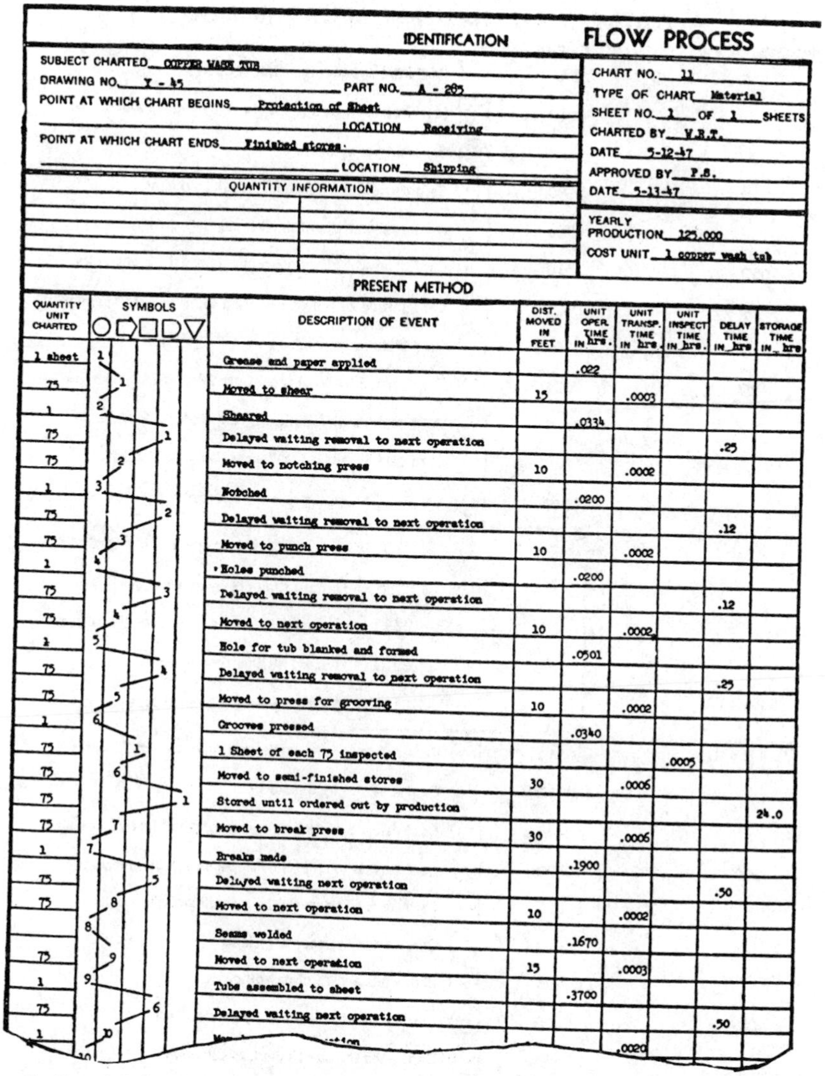

IDENTIFICATION	FLOW PROCESS
SUBJECT CHARTED COPPER WASH TUB	CHART NO. 11
DRAWING NO. X - 45 PART NO. A - 285	TYPE OF CHART Material
POINT AT WHICH CHART BEGINS Protection of Sheet	SHEET NO. 1 OF 1 SHEETS
LOCATION Receiving	CHARTED BY V.R.T.
POINT AT WHICH CHART ENDS Finished stores.	DATE 5-12-47
LOCATION Shipping	APPROVED BY P.S.
QUANTITY INFORMATION	DATE 5-13-47
	YEARLY PRODUCTION 125,000
	COST UNIT 1 copper wash tub

PRESENT METHOD

QUANTITY UNIT CHARTED	SYMBOLS ○ ⇨ □ D ▽	DESCRIPTION OF EVENT	DIST. MOVED IN FEET	UNIT OPER. TIME IN hrs.	UNIT TRANSP. TIME IN hrs.	UNIT INSPECT TIME IN hrs.	DELAY TIME IN hrs	STORAGE TIME IN hrs
1 sheet	○ 1	Grease and paper applied		.022				
75	⇨ 1	Moved to shear	15		.0003			
1	○ 2	Sheared		.0334				
75	D 1	Delayed waiting removal to next operation					.25	
75	⇨ 2	Moved to notching press	10		.0002			
1	○ 3	Notched		.0200				
75	D 2	Delayed waiting removal to next operation					.12	
75	⇨ 3	Moved to punch press	10		.0002			
1	○ 4	Holes punched		.0200				
75	D 3	Delayed waiting removal to next operation					.12	
75	⇨ 4	Moved to next operation	10		.0002			
1	○ 5	Hole for tub blanked and formed		.0501				
75	D 4	Delayed waiting removal to next operation					.25	
75	⇨ 5	Moved to press for grooving	10		.0002			
1	○ 6	Grooves pressed		.0340				
75	□ 1	1 Sheet of each 75 inspected				.0005		
75	⇨ 6	Moved to semi-finished stores	30		.0006			
75	▽ 1	Stored until ordered out by production						24.0
75	⇨ 7	Moved to break press	30		.0006			
1	○ 7	Breaks made		.1900				
75	D 5	Delayed waiting next operation					.50	
75	⇨ 8	Moved to next operation	10		.0002			
	○ 8	Seams welded		.1670				
75	⇨ 9	Moved to next operation	15		.0003			
1	○ 9	Tubs assembled to sheet		.3700				
75	D 6	Delayed waiting next operation					.50	
1	○ 10	[illegible]			.0020			

Portion of flow process chart on a prepared form. The connected numbers in the "Symbols" columns show the number of times each type of action is involved.

all of the steps followed by an order passing through the sales office, a time card through the shop and payroll department (Exhibit VI), or a material requisition through the stores and inventory control routine.

The Multiple Activity Process Chart. When it is necessary to study the activities of two or more men or machines in their relation to each other, the Multiple Activity Process Chart is a valuable aid. It may be used to show clearly the relation between man time, where the operation is under the control of the man, and machine or process time, where the man has no work to perform. This type of chart is used chiefly to uncover idle periods on the part of the man or the machine which might be used profitably if the job motion sequence could be rearranged to eliminate them. The formal definition of this chart is as follows:

> *A Multiple Activity Process Chart* is a synchronized graphic representation of operations performed simultaneously by two or more men, two or more machines, or any combination of men and machines.

EXHIBIT VI

FLOW PROCESS CHART

FLOW PROCESS CHART FOR DAILY TIME CARD

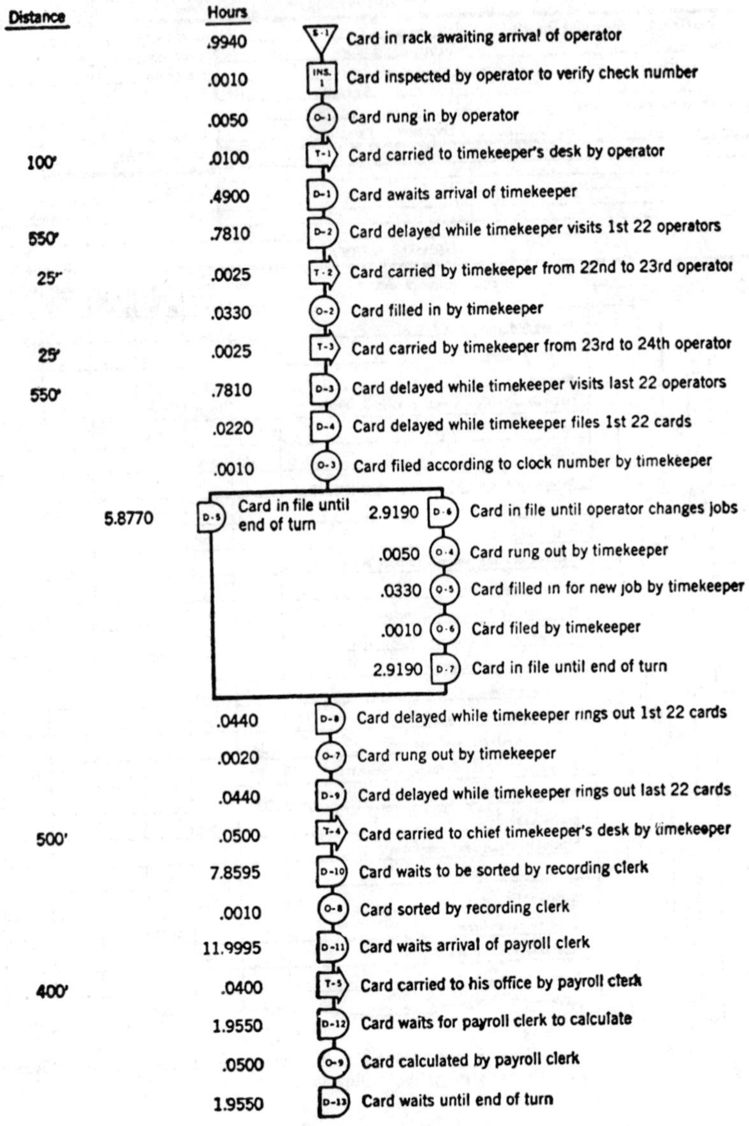
Distance
Hours
.9940 S-1 Card in rack awaiting arrival of operator
.0010 INS. 1 Card inspected by operator to verify check number
.0050 O-1 Card rung in by operator
100' .0100 T-1 Card carried to timekeeper's desk by operator
.4900 D-1 Card awaits arrival of timekeeper
550' .7810 D-2 Card delayed while timekeeper visits 1st 22 operators
25' .0025 T-2 Card carried by timekeeper from 22nd to 23rd operator
.0330 O-2 Card filled in by timekeeper
25' .0025 T-3 Card carried by timekeeper from 23rd to 24th operator
550' .7810 D-3 Card delayed while timekeeper visits last 22 operators
.0220 D-4 Card delayed while timekeeper files 1st 22 cards
.0010 O-3 Card filed according to clock number by timekeeper
5.8770 D-5 Card in file until end of turn
2.9190 D-6 Card in file until operator changes jobs
.0050 O-4 Card rung out by timekeeper
.0330 O-5 Card filled in for new job by timekeeper
.0010 O-6 Card filed by timekeeper
2.9190 D-7 Card in file until end of turn
.0440 D-8 Card delayed while timekeeper rings out 1st 22 cards
.0020 O-7 Card rung out by timekeeper
.0440 D-9 Card delayed while timekeeper rings out last 22 cards
500' .0500 T-4 Card carried to chief timekeeper's desk by timekeeper
7.8595 D-10 Card waits to be sorted by recording clerk
.0010 O-8 Card sorted by recording clerk
11.9995 D-11 Card waits arrival of payroll clerk
400' .0400 T-5 Card carried to his office by payroll clerk
1.9550 D-12 Card waits for payroll clerk to calculate
.0500 O-9 Card calculated by payroll clerk
1.9550 D-13 Card waits until end of turn

Flow process chart of a paper-work procedure, without use of special form.

Exhibit VII illustrates one sheet of a multiple activity process chart. It portrays what the operator of an engine lathe does in terms of man working, combined activity, and idleness. A similar chart for the machine would show the additional classification of machine running and would not include the man-working classification.

"Man working" occurs when a person performs an operation or any part of an operation independently of a machine or of another operator.

"Machine running" is defined as the time the machine operates, performing its work without requiring attention, so that the operator is free for other work.

"Combined activity" occurs during that part of a work cycle in which the man is working with a machine or with another man. It occurs, for example, when setting tools, in loading and

EXHIBIT VII

MULTIPLE ACTIVITY PROCESS CHART SHOWING ACTIVITIES OF ENGINE LATHE OPERATOR

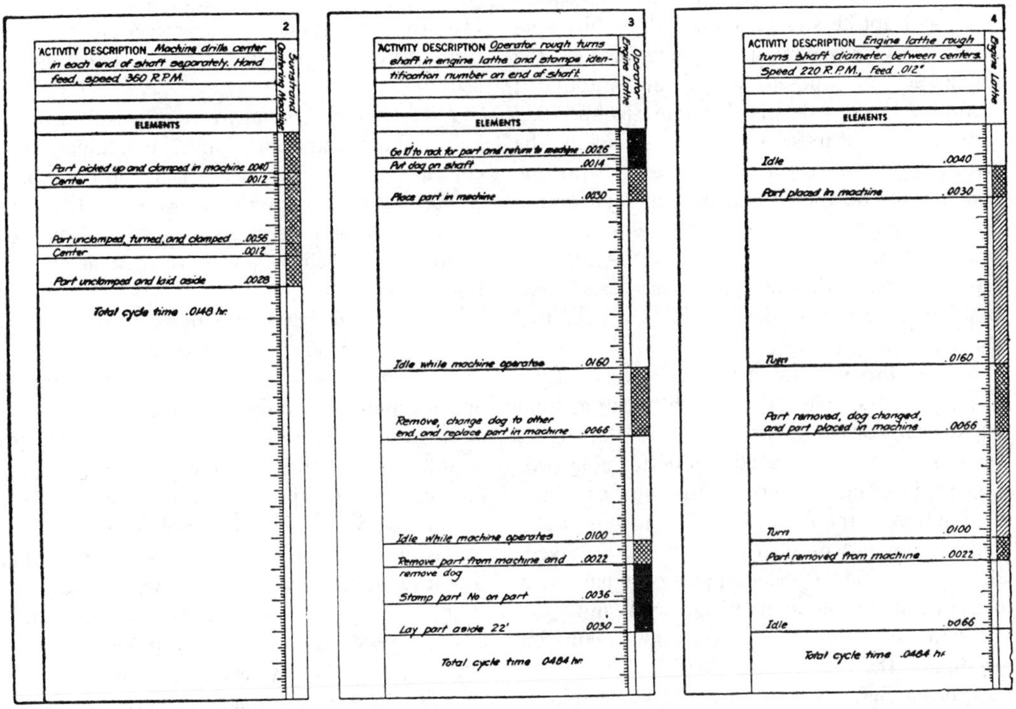

Shaded portions are color bars in the actual cnart, representing different classes of activity; actual length of form is 11 in.

unloading work where this ties up the machine, in machine running time when the attention of the operator is required (as when hand feed is used), and during the time when two or more men work together helping one another.

"Idleness" is complete inactivity on the part of a man or a machine. For the man, it usually occurs during the machine running time when there is nothing for him to do; for the machine, it occurs when the machine is stopped awaiting the attention of the operator. In this classification lie the greatest opportunities for quickly made improvements. By rearranging man elements, machine elements, and combined activity elements, it is often possible to develop a sequence of elements which reduces idleness periods considerably.

H. B. MAYNARD, formerly President, Maynard Research Council, Incorporated, Pittsburgh, Pennsylvania

Information References

Cook, Nathan H., "Manufacturing Analysis," Reading, Mass., Addison-Wesley, 1966.

Coughanowr, D. R., and Koppel, L. B., "Process Systems Analysis and Control," New York, McGraw-Hill, 1965.

Matthews, Lawrence M., "Manufacturing Cost Estimation," New York, Van Nostrand Reinhold, 1979.

Niebel, Benjamin W., "Operation Analysis," chaps. 3 and 4 in Niebel, B. W., ed., "Motion and Time Study," Homewood, Ill., Irwin, 1976.

Mullee, William Robert and David B., "Process Chart Procedures," sec. 2, chap. 3, in H. B. Maynard, ed., "Industrial Engineering Handbook," 3rd ed., New York, McGraw-Hill, 1971.

"Process Engineering," sec. 3, chap. 3, in H. B. Maynard, ed., "Handbook of Modern Manufacturing Management," New York, McGraw-Hill, 1970.

Riordan, Thomas S., "Processing and Operation Planning," sec. 2, chap. 2, in H. B. Maynard, ed., "Industrial Engineering Handbook, 3rd ed., New York, McGraw-Hill, 1971.

Cross References: *Method Improvement (and cross references there given).*

PROCESS ENGINEERING

Modern **Process Engineering** involves not only the selection of the most advantageous processes to be used in conjunction with a specific design, subject to quantity and cost constraints, but also the specification of the principal details related to the process. These details encompass the selection of the specific equipment to be employed. At times the equipment will not be standard, but will involve specially designed equipment such as in the application of semi-automated and automated facilities. Further details that must be specified as a function of process engineering include the selection of the tooling to be used with the equipment, and the specification of the locating points of the special tools with reference to the product component being processed. Also, time estimates of both the set-up and each-piece time are usually considered to be a function of process engineering.

When Process Engineering Should Take Place. Process engineering should begin as final engineering drawings are being developed for the design to be produced. By performing process engineering in concert with and before the completion of the final product drawings, much engineering and production time will be saved. It is only after process engineering has been carried out that equipment, material, and tooling can be ordered and production begun on producing the new design.

Process Selection. In the process selection to produce the design under study, the engineer will usually select one or more processes required to advance the product in its transformation from raw material into a finished product. Processes may generally be classified in six categories. These are:

(1) Basic processes.

(2) Secondary processes.

(3) Joining and assembly processes.

(4) Decorative and protective coating processes.

(5) Inspection, test, and quality control processes.

(6) Packaging processes.

Basic processes are those processes performed early in the sequence that identify the general form from which the finished product will be made and the physical and mechanical properties it will have. Typical basic processes include casting, forging, roll forming, extrusion, and the like.

Secondary processes include all those processes that take place after the basic processes that bring the work more closely to its final desired geometric configuration and size. Representative secondary processes are drilling, reaming, turning, boring, grinding, milling, lapping, threading, etc.

Joining and assembly processes involve those processes that bring together two or more components on either a temporary or permanent basis. These processes include stapling; stitching; riveting; spot, seam, projection welding; butt, lap electric welding; and nut and bolt assembly.

Decorative and protective coating processes include those temporary and permanent type coatings that are applied to give the product eye appeal or are applied to protect it from the elements. These processes include plating, painting, enameling, parkerizing, rust prevention dipping, etc.

Packaging processes are those processes that prepare the product for shipment to the customer. The package could be a plastic, metal, or cardboard container, or a wooden box.

It is quite helpful for the process engineer to maintain a card file that identifies all the process equipment within his company. This file should provide a separate card for each piece of equipment. Pertinent information that should be included would be the equipment description, capacity, limitations, special attachments, speed and feed capabilities, machine overhead rate, hourly rate of the operator usually assigned to the machine, location of the equipment, its age and state of repair, and typical part numbers produced on the equipment. For identifying purposes, a different colored card can be used for each class of equipment. Thus, equipment identified with basic processes would be inventoried on a different colored card from the card for equipment used in conjunction with secondary processes.

To select the most advantageous manufacturing method, process engineering must consider all applicable processes. Invariably there is more than one way to manufacture a part, although there is only one best way to produce a part under the constraints established. One way is best for a given set of conditions while another way is best for another set of conditions. Therefore, the process engineer should have information not only of available processes within his organizaion, but of competing processes located in other companies. Outside suppliers frequently provide a source of alternative processes that should be considered when planning the operations of a product. Modern process engineering encourages competition among divisions and encourages suppliers to bid in order to improve products and reduce costs.

In deciding what process to specify in the planning stages, the engineer will need to identify the principal constraints associated with each piece of equipment related to the process under study. The main contraints, for example, that must be considered in the selection of a given basic process to bring raw material more closely to the specifications of a functional design are:

(1) Type and condition of raw materials used.

(2) Geometrical and size limitations that the equipment can handle.

(3) Geometrical limitations that the equipment can impart to the work.

(4) Tolerance and surface finish capabilities of the equipment.

(5) Production capability of the process.

(6) Cost of operation of the process per unit of output.

Each of the aforementioned constraints will impose limitations on the acceptability of certain products to the process under consideration. For example, with reference to type and condition of raw materials used, die casting is at present limited to non-ferrous materials on a production basis, as is plaster mold casting.

Every process has a size or capacity constraint which can be on either a maximum basis, minimum basis, or both a maximum and minimum basis. Thus, every facility has a limitation where it would be impractical or impossible to use the equipment because the work is either too large or too small.

All processes have some limitations as to the geometry they can impart. For example, in drop forging, the hot plastic metal can be moved only a limited distance before folding or cracking will take place. The process of spinning is confined to symmetrical configurations, and powdered metal parts cannot be economically produced with undercuts or reentrant angles.

Every process has a limitation on the tolerance and surface finish that it is capable of achieving under normal operation. For example, a ½-in. drill will not consistently hold a 0.002-in. tolerance, whereas a ½-in reamer can consistently hold this tolerance. Again a 20-microinch finish is not consistently held by turning on a lathe; yet this finish may be consistently held by grinding.

The production capability of a process is an important factor in its choice as a method to produce a given design. Not only is the output potential important from the standpoint of meeting delivery requirements, but also the rate of production will have a bearing on the unit cost of the output.

Obviously the cost of operating the process has a most significant effect on its application for producing a given design. Three costs are of principal concern to the process engineer. These are (1) the tooling costs used in conjunction with the process; (2) the set-up and tear-down costs; and (3) the each-piece cost during the production run.

The selection of one process over another is based upon the six constraints outlined. The analyst must recognize that the factors influencing these constraints will change with time. Thus, a process that is advantageous today may not be tomorrow. A change in the cost of material, labor, quantity to be produced, or equipment available may make it economical to manufacture the part from another material or by a different process. Process engineering should be a continuing activity in every plant.

In simpler analyses where the number of alternative ways to produce a part is limited to but two or three possibilities, the use of a right-wrong form is helpful. This form provides for a statement of the problem under study. On the left side of the form all positive factors related to the process are shown, and to the right are listed the negative factors. If a certain process is not capable of holding a close tolerance, this should be indicated as a negative factor. The analyst should provide quantitative data when possible. Thus, he should not simply indicate that the process is not capable of holding close tolerances, but he should show how close a tolerance can be expected. After completing the right-wrong form, the analyst will usually be able to arrive at a decision either to accept the process for further consideration or reject it. Frequently one negative factor, such as cost, may outbalance all of the positive factors.

When the number of processes that should be considered is substantial, the analyst may find it desirable to use a more objective technique to select the most appropriate method. It is possible to identify the level or range of each of the aforementioned constraints that is suitable to a given process. For example, in the matter of size there is a range limitation (both high and low) that is characteristic of almost every process or the production facilities available. By comparing the required parameters of the design being studied with the characteristics of the available processes, it will be possible to eliminate many of the processes from further consideration. Thus, die castings larger than thirty pounds are seldom practical and die casting is limited for the most part to nonferrous metals; complex geometrical shapes cannot be forged; it seldom pays to set-up an automatic screw machine for less than 1,000 parts; and broaching is usually limited to "thru inside openings" (that is, the hole extends through), or to external surfaces. Numerical coding can be assigned to various levels of each parameter under consideration. Then by data processing techniques it is possible to sort out all applicable processes for performing a certain function on the design under study. These can be estimated on a cost-per-piece basis and then the most economical of the applicable processes may be selected. For example, the equation used to develop the computer program based on the major parameters shown in Exhibit I is:

$$D_t = A_{ijk} + N + B_{ij}$$

where

A is the coefficient of *N*, the number of units to be produced; *i* is the process to be considered, *j* is the size classification of the part being process planned, and *k* is the material specified. B_{ij} is the fixed element in the process.

This program will solve the cost equations for those processes that are applicable for producing a given design and print out their respective costs in ascending sequence.

Classifying the Secondary Operations and Related Operations. After the basic processes are performed, the process engineer must not only select the best secondary, joining, decorative, protective, and packaging operations, but specify their order. To assist in the assignment of the most logical order of all operations performed after the basic processes and before the final packaging for shipment operations, it is helpful to classify each of these operations into one of four categories. These are: critical operations, placement operations, tie-in operations, and protection operations.

Critical operations can easily be identified in one of the two following ways:

(1) The operation finishes a surface which will be used as a subsequent mastering or locating surface.

(2) The operation results in a close tolerance (less than 0.005 in.) or other rigid specification such as surface finish, flatness requirement, or squareness requirement.

Placement operations are those operations that either prepare the work to accept a critical operation, or correct or restore a part that has been undesirably changed or altered because of a previous operation. For example, to prepare a casting to fit in a fixture where an important slot will be milled, it may be necessary to perform a rough filing or snag grinding placement operation along the parting line, so that the casting will nest in the fixture. Again the placement operation of annealing might be necessary to soften a part that has been work-hardened by a series of press operations that were previously performed.

Tie-in operations are analogous to critical operations in that they are productive operations that advance the transformation of the work to its finished design. The sequence and method of performance of tie-in operations are determined principally by the geometry desired, since they do not result in a locating surface nor are they produced to exacting tolerance requirements and surface specifications. Most decorative operations would be classed as tie-in operations.

Protection operations are those operations that are performed to protect the product from the environment and handling as it is processed through the plant and shipped to the customer. All inspection and quality-control operations are considered to be protection type operations. Broadly speaking, these operations include: application of protective coatings, inspections and tests, and packaging for shipment.

Determining the Operation Sequence. In determining the best sequence of all the operations that need to be performed, several guidelines will prove helpful. These include the following:

(1) Critical operations that establish locating or mastering points should be accomplished early in the operation sequence.

(2) Critical operations that establish exacting tolerances and specifications should be performed late in the operation sequence.

(3) Internal work is usually done in advance of external work.

(4) The logical sequence of internal work is: drilling, boring, recessing, reaming, and tapping.

(5) The logical sequence of external work is: turning, facing, grooving, forming, threading.

(6) Rough work involving heavy cuts and liberal tolerances should be performed early in the sequence.

(7) Operation sequence should give consider-

EXHIBIT I

PORTION OF GUIDE SHEET FOR SELECTION OF OPTIMUM BASIC PROCESS ON SIZE RANGE

Process	*Applicable Geometry*	*Intricacy of Geometry*	*Applicable Materials*	*Minimum Lot Size For Which Process Is Economical*	*Secondary Operation Cost*	*Cost Decision Equation For Order of N Units*	*Expected Rate of Production*	*Time In Weeks To Get Into Production*
Die casting	1,2,3,4,5,6,7,8,9	x	t	3000	1	$D_t = 1.623\ N + 1515$	200 to 500 injections/hr	12
Investment casting	1,2,3,4,5,6,7,8,9	x	s, t	100	5	$D_t = 2.370\ N + 320$ $D_s = 1.000\ N + 320$	10 to 20 molds/hr	5
Permanent molding	1,2,3,4,5,6,7,8	y	s, t	500	9	$D_t = 0.770\ N + 465$ $D_s = 0.335\ N + 465$	20 to 30 molds/hr	10
Plaster mold casting	1,2,3,4,5,6,7,8,9	x	t	100	5	$D_t = 2.160\ N + 320$	15 to 28 molds/hr	5
Shell molding	1,2,3,4,5,6,7,8,9	x	s, t	300	6	$D_t = 1.965\ N + 320$ $D_s = 0.595\ N + 320$	35 to 45 molds/hr	5

ation to the physical location and scheduled work of existing equipment.

In planning complex work, it is often helpful for the analyst to record on 3- by 5-in. operation cards all the operations to be performed on a part. He should use a separate card for each operation, and each card should identify the part number being planned, the proposed operation number, a description of the operation, the operation class, the facility used for the operation, the location of the equipment, the mastering or locating surface, and time or cost information related to the operation. Exhibit II illustrates an operation process planning card. These cards can then be arranged in a sequence that will provide satisfactory results. Exhibit III illustrates such a planned sequence. A review of this sequence indicates that Operation 2 is probably a placement type operation to prepare the work for a critical location type operation—Operation 3. A protective operation (such as rust inhibitor) is then applied to protect the product in its flow through the plant. Close tolerance or specification operations are probably the result of critical Operations 8 and 9. A decorative operation is indicative of tie-in Operation 10. Protection Operation 11 is probably related to quality control, and Protection Operation 12 is related to packaging the product for final shipment.

Providing the Special Tooling. As has been stated, process engineering also involves the provision of all special tooling used in conjunction with each specified process. Once the manufacturing operations have been decided upon, the process engineer will need to determine how the work should be located and held in position while the various operations are being performed. Thus, when ordering the special tooling, he should indicate the most favorable locating or mastering surface of the work. He will usually indicate a plane surface because it is easier to maintain control from a large plane surface than from a curved, irregular, or small surface. In addition to indicating the locating surface, he should identify that portion of the workpiece that is suited to supporting or holding it while it is being processed, and that area that is best suited for clamping it.

The process engineering function does not usually involve the design of the special tooling, but it does include the responsibility of procuring it. When ordering the design and construction of all durable tools (from either within or outside of the plant) as much information as possible should be provided.

Making the Time Estimates. The provision of both set-up and each-piece time estimates may also be the responsibility of Process Engineering. While estimating the required times, the process engineer will need to consider three classes of time that will be utilized in performing the work. These are:

(1) Machine time (this will apply only to the each-piece time estimates).

(2) Effort time (this will apply to the set-up and tear-down elements which will comprise the total set-up time and also the effort time that will apply to each cycle of the production time).

EXHIBIT II

OPERATION PROCESS PLANNING CARD

Part No. BA-1692-1 Drawing No. BA-1692 Operation No. 9
Operation Description Straddle mill two 3/4" slots in base of forging

Operation Class Tie-in
Performed On #2 Hor. Cincinnati Mill Location Dept 46
Locate From Flange end of forging Use three points of location on this surface, two on base & one point on back
Outside Supplier No
Estimated Set-up Time 1.5 hrs Special Tool Cost $300
Estimated Each Piece Time 6 min By BWH
Remarks None

EXHIBIT III

SEQUENCE OF PLANNED OPERATIONS

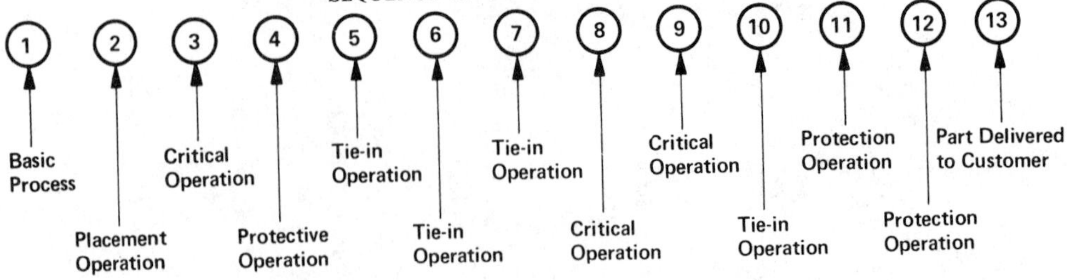

(3) Delay time: (a) unavoidable delays; (b) avoidable delays; and (c) personal delays.

It should be noted that machine time and effort time are usually estimated through the application of standard data. Standard data are elemental time values taken from time studies or calculated from proven previous studies. These elemental values are classified and coded so that they can be readily retrieved and accumulated in order to determine an equitable standard on an operation without having to measure the time required to perform that operation. The term standard data refers not only to tabulated data, but algebraic expressions, curves, alignment charts, and tables that allow the rapid determination of an elemental time value. Exhibit IV provides standard data applicable to effort times in a given plant for drilling operations performed on an Allen 17-inch vertical single-spindle drill press. All delays are usually handled by providing an adequate allowance to the effort time and the machine time.

Place of Process Engineering Within the Organization. In the majority of manufacturing industries, the process engineering function should report to the manager of manufacturing engineering, who in turn reports to the general manager of the plant or division. A typical organization chart illustrating the place of process engineering is shown in Exhibit V.

The principal responsibilities of Process Engineering include:

(1) Determination of the manufacturing feasibility of new functional designs.

(2) Identification of the most favorable processes for producing a given product design subject to both product and sales engineering constraints.

(3) Using group technology concepts, work with product engineering in order to simplify new functional designs.

(4) Determination of the operation sequence in the manufacture of all products.

(5) Determination of durable and nondurable tool requirements used in conjunction with new product designs.

(6) Applying group technology concepts in connection with tooling and set-ups for new products.

(7) The specification of the facilities to be used for each operation.

(8) Preparation of manufacturing operational instructions including recommended feeds, speeds, depth of cut, tool angles, etc.

EXHIBIT IV

Application: Allen 17-inch verticle single-spindle drill.

Work size: Small work—up to four pounds in weight and such that two or more parts can be handled in each hand.

Setup elements:	*Minutes*
A. Study drawing.	1.25
B. Get material and tools and return to place ready for work	3.75
C. Adjust height of table	1.31
D. Start and stop machine	0.09
E. First-piece inspection (includes normal wait time for inspector)	5.25
F. Tally production and post on voucher	1.50
G. Clean off table and jig	1.75
H. Insert drill in spindle	0.16
I. Remove drill from spindle	0.14
Each piece elements:	
1. Grind drill (prorate)	0.78
2. Insert drill in spindle	0.16
3. Insert drill in spindle (quick-change chuck)	0.05
4. Set spindle	0.42
5. Change spindle speed	0.72
6. Remove tool from spindle	0.14
7. Remove tool from spindle (quick-change chuck)	0.035
8. Pick up part and place in jig	
a. Quick-acting clamp	0.070
b. Thumbscrew	0.080
9. Remove part from jig	
a. Quick-acting clamp	0.050
b. Thumbscrew	0.060
10. Position part and advance drill	0.042
11. Advance drill	0.035
12. Clear drill	0.023
13. Clear drill, reposition part, and advance drill (same spindle)	0.048
14. Clear drill, reposition part, and advance drill (adjacent spindle)	0.090
15. Insert drill bushing	0.046
16. Remove drill bushing	0.035
17. Lay part aside	0.022
18. Blow out jig and part and lay part aside	0.081
19. Plug gauge part	0.12 per hole

SOURCE: Niebel, B. W., "Motion and Time Study," 6th ed., Homewood, Illinois, Irwin, 1976.

EXHIBIT V

ORGANIZATION CHART SHOWING PATHS OF AUTHORITY RELATED TO PROCESS ENGINEERING

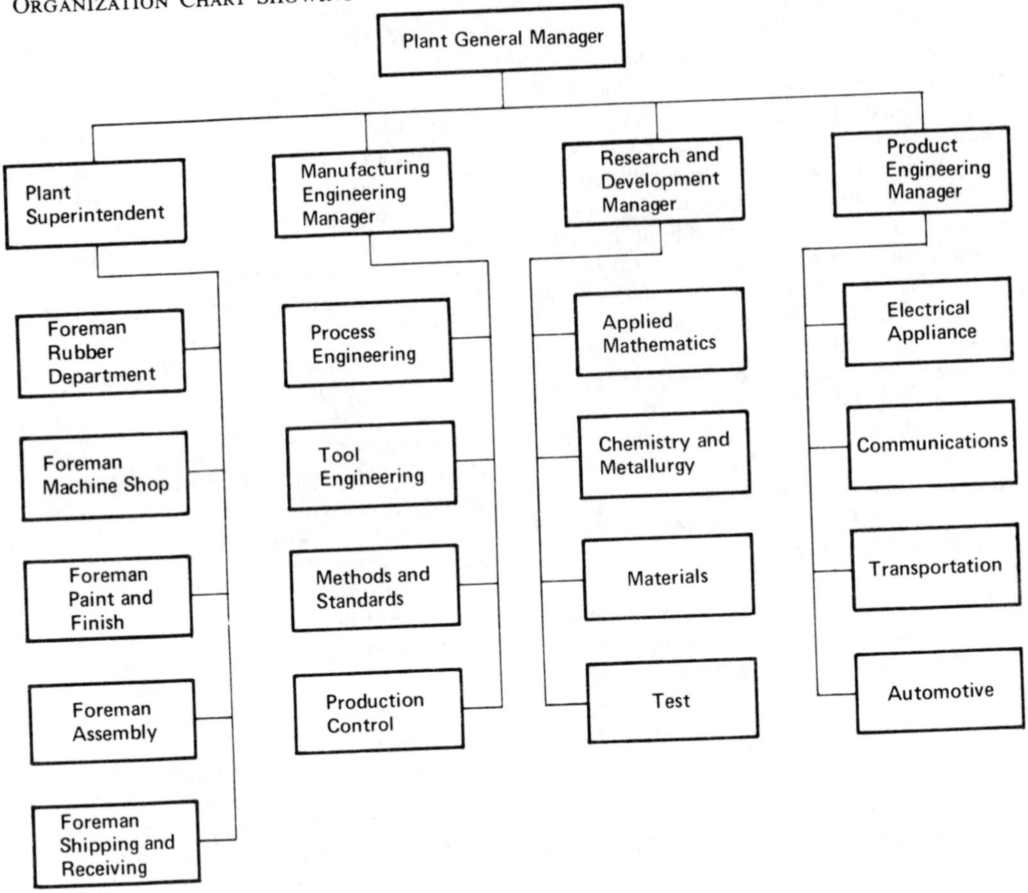

(9) Making time estimates, both set-up and each-piece times from existing standard data.

(10) Preparing and issuing in-process drawings for semifinished parts.

(11) Reviewing engineering deviations or change requests.

(12) Assisting in the identification and correction of manufacturing difficulties.

(13) Providing guidance and assistance to purchasing of vendor items such as special jigs, dies, gauges, and fixtures.

(14) Specifying and identifying inspection frequencies and in-process quality control methodology.

(15) Requesting machine tool and other process facility capability studies and review results.

(16) Developing data for make-or-buy determination.

(17) Maintaining equipment capability records.

(18) Assisting quality control in resolution of quality problems.

(19) Providing for disposition of obsolete special tools.

BENJAMIN W. NIEBEL, Professor Emeritus of Industrial Engineering, The Pennsylvania State University, University Park, Pennsylvania

Information References

American Society of Tool and Manufacturing Engineers, "Fundamentals of Tool Design," Englewood Cliffs, N.J., Prentice-Hall, 1962.

Eary, Donald F. and Johnson, Gerald E., "Process Engineering for Manufacturing," Englewood Cliffs, N.J., Prentice-Hall, 1962.

Niebel, Benjamin W. and Baldwin, Edward N., "Designing for Production," Homewood, Ill., Irwin, 1963.

Niebel, Benjamin W. and Draper, Alan B., "Product Design and Process Engineering," New York, McGraw-Hill Book Co., 1974.

Niebel, Benjamin W., "Process Engineering," in "Encyclopedia of Science and Technology," 5th ed., New York, McGraw-Hill, 1980.

Ostwald, Philip F., "Cost Estimating for Engineering and Management," Englewood Cliffs, N.J., Prentice-Hall Inc., 1974.

Cross References: *Method Improvement (and cross references there given).*

PRODUCTION: Large Scale

Mass Production is not to be confused with SCIENTIFIC MANAGEMENT, although successful mass-production industries are scientifically managed. The outstanding characteristic of mass production is, of course, high volume of output, whereas scientific management was developed in relatively small plants where products were not necessarily standardized, and were produced not on high-speed single-purpose machines, but on machines that could be used for many jobs—and not necessarily by highly routinized workers performing one task over and over again.

By the same token, mass production is not characterized by quantity of output alone. Its essential elements include: (1) high volume, as stated; (2) product simplification for maximum economy in production; (3) standardization of parts and components; (4) maximum use of automatic equipment, often in the form of high-speed single-purpose machines; (5) arrangement of production lines and material flow for continuous production, often including assembly conveyors on which the work is held fixed in exact alignment; and (6) careful planning and coordination of all elements in the production chain, from plants of suppliers to receiving docks of ultimate destination for the maximum degree of *total* production, with minimum tie-up of work in process or materials and finished goods in transit.

Since continuous production, as in automobile assembly, is at the heart of mass production, highly precise synchronization of all contributing operations is required to mesh in with the requirements of uninterrupted final assembly. Thus a continuous production line in end assembly will depend upon preplanned continuous production lines in the manufacture of parts and components which themselves may be produced in feeder plants many miles away.

History. What is commonly understood as mass production dates from 1798 when Eli Whitney originated interchangeable parts manufacture in his arms factory in New Haven, Conn. The principle became applicable to industry in general when Carl Johansson standardized measurement in 1885 by creating "Joblocks," gauges which may be used as standards of measure with minute error (see METHOD IMPROVEMENT). However, even before that time, many of the planning and control techniques associated today with mass production (as well as with scientific management) were applied in an early form by Boulton and Watt at the Soho Engineering Foundry near Birmingham, England in the early nineteenth century (see BOULTON, MATTHEW ROBINSON).

In popular imagination, and justifiably so, the name of Henry Ford is associated with the first dramatic implementation of mass production in the modern grand manner (although he himself had observed the use of sequential steps in production and the movement of assemblies in railroad-car manufacturing in Detroit as early as 1879). The first complete application of all of the elements of mass production was realized in 1912–13 at the Highland Park, Detroit, plant of the Ford Motor Company. There moving conveyor lines were first used for assembly, with parts and materials fed to the lines from overhead conveyors. From this effective demonstration the concept spread rapidly to other plants in automobile manufacturing and allied industries.

Automation. In automated mass production (for the pioneering of which the Ford Motor Company is also given credit), production operations are melded with control operations to tie separate pieces of automatic equipment into continuous automatic production through a series of operations, an entire line, or a complete plant (see AUTOMATION). Parts are automatically transferred to, into, and out of a series of machines which perform successive operations on a part. The transfer mechanisms successively position the part being worked on for each operation.

Rationalization. This term connotes the merging of all the plants in a given industry, with a view to increasing efficiency and lowering costs. It is associated with European philosophies of production, and involves governmental regulation of production to balance consumption. Rationalization thus runs necessarily into price control, standardization of methods and materials, stabilization of wages, and the like, which in the American tradition is acceptable only in times of great stress, such as war, or other national emergency situations.

Cross References: *Automation; Manufacturing Management.*

PRODUCTION PLANNING AND INVENTORY MANAGEMENT

(The Introduction and following five sections in this entry have been prepared by the designated contributors for the American Production and Inventory Control Society.)

INTRODUCTION

Ever since the stock-market crash of 1929 and the resulting depression of the thirties, increasing attention has been given by top management to **inventory** and **production levels.**

During World War II, production scheduling and inventory controls received particular emphasis because of the priorities systems of allocating materials. In the years since the war, business management has further developed the techniques and equipment for controlling inventories and production, and economists have recognized that continued increases in the national total of industrial inventories is one of the early-warning signs of a potential economic sag in the near future. The Federal Government recognizes that the cumulative effect of the management of individual inventories, and particularly inventory accumulations, is an economic influence that affects the business cycle.

Approximately one-third of the assets of the average manufacturing company are invested in inventories which are controlled by production and inventory managers. Their goal is to maintain stable levels of inventories, production, and employment. The manager of materials, production, and inventories is a person who is thoroughly familiar with the latest developments in equipment and techniques. He (she) is a manager with a broad point of view and the good judgment to select the proper tools for collecting information and balancing the factors which enter into decisions that accomplish the best results.

HENRY F. SANDER, Executive Director, American Production and Inventory Control Society, Inc., Washington, D.C.

CONCEPTS AND OBJECTIVES

Production is the process of transforming raw materials or purchased components into finished products for sale. Where products are not manufactured to customers' specifications, however, they are produced and held in inventory in anticipation of customer demand. Thus, production and sales during a given period of time are not necessarily equivalent; rather, the product output of a plant is the amount of goods sold *plus or minus the net change in finished goods inventory* during that period.

Inventories as "Reservoirs." Essentially, finished goods inventories are "reservoirs" which permit continuous flow of the product to customers. The minimum level of each reservoir, or inventory, is dependent upon two factors: It varies directly with (1) product demand, and (2) production lead time, or the time required to replenish the inventory. The most variable and unpredictable of these factors is product demand, which may have wide seasonal variation and which is subject to general economic conditions or forces beyond the control of management.

A rise in the level of finished goods inventories to meet increased product demand can result only from a rise in the level of production and in the level of work-in-process inventories. Similarly, a rise in the level of production and work-in-process inventories requires a corresponding rise in the level of raw materials inventories. The latter inventories must be at levels sufficiently high to permit the continuous flow of raw materials to the factory. These minimum levels vary directly both with (1) production demand (as derived from product demand) and (2) purchasing lead time.

Production management and inventory management are "Siamese twins" in that decisive action in one area cannot be made independently of the other.

Management Objectives. (1) *Customer Service.* Profits and growth depend upon serving more customers better. Where a product is built to a customer's own specifications, it must be delivered to him as promised at the time he needs it. In the case of a standard or branded product, current (and oftentimes future) income is lost to the company if the finished goods reservoir runs dry and customers' immediate demand cannot be satisfied. In addition to the satisfaction of customers' demand for existing products, progressive managements are ever alert to create demand through the development and introduction of new or improved products.

(2) *Uninterrupted Material Flow.* Costs rise if planned production schedules are interrupted for lack of materials or for any other reason. Thus, it is equally important that the raw materials reservoir not run dry.

(3) *Optimum Inventory Levels.* The minimum

inventory levels to assure continuous flow of materials and products may not be the most economic levels. The most economic quantity to purchase or manufacture at one time often results in average inventory levels which are higher than necessary for this purpose alone. As purchase and production order quantities increase (demand factors and lead times remaining unchanged), ordering costs are decreased but inventory carrying costs are increased. To the extent that the decrease in ordering cost is greater than the increase in inventory carrying costs, optimum inventory levels will rise.

(4) *Increased Productivity.* Work-in-process must be so planned and controlled that production time and cost will be held at or below predetermined limits. To the extent that normal production lead times are reduced, at any given level of production and sales demand, work-in-process inventory is reduced and the minimum inventory level needed to assure continuous flow of the products to customers is also lowered.

The uninterrupted and effective flow of work through the factory requires the coordinated efforts of many departments in the organization. Materials must be received from stores, primary and assembly operations and their sequences must be planned, tools must be available on requisition, inspection points must be established, semifinished materials must be moved to subsequent operations, and finished goods must be delivered to stock. Production control is essentially a coordinative function.

(5) *Production and Employment Stabilization.* In addition to its function in satisfying immediate customer and factory demand, inventories make it possible for production to proceed at a steadier rate. The absorption of weekly, period, and seasonal fluctuations to achieve production (and therefore, employment) stabilization is made possible by planned changes in the normal level of inventories throughout the year.

To the extent that production and employment stabilization is achieved and maintained, production costs are lowered. Labor costs are reduced through elimination or reduction in overtime, shift premiums, call-in pay, rehiring, and training costs, and in the reduction in required plant capacity which permits lower unit overhead costs.

It is to be noted, however, that production and employment stabilization may often conflict with plans to hold inventories at optimum levels. The extent to which both of these objectives can be attained simultaneously is dependent, of course, upon the balance of costs.

Role in Business Cycles. Economists point out that business inventories are cyclical in nature. Each initial forecasted demand is amplified many times as it travels along the distribution chain from the ultimate consumer to the retailer, wholesaler, and manufacturer, and finally to the raw material supplier. Each distribution channel, of course, is a customer for the next preceding one, and the series of derived demands become increasingly optimistic when original demand is on the rise, and increasingly pessimistic when original demand is declining. The resulting wide fluctuations in inventory investment become increasingly more serious as the gross national product continues to expand and the long-term level of inventories continues to rise.

Management is thus concerned with the role of inventories in business cycles, and inventory adjustments are themselves greatly influenced by cyclic factors. Inventory fluctuations and business cycles are each both a cause and an effect. Production and inventory management can make a large contribution to a stable economy by the reduction of inventory accumulations, and at the same time receive many benefits from such action.

Functional Responsibilities. Production and inventory management encompasses a wide gamut of functions which are commonly differentiated by the terms, *production planning, production control,* and *inventory control.* Each of these concepts is explained as follows [1]:

(1) *Production Planning* is the function of "setting the limits or levels of manufacturing operations in the future, consideration being given to sales forecasts and the requirements and availability of men, machines, materials and money." Stated in another way, it is the coordination, or balancing, of all contributions to production throughout the entire organization. Such planning is in reference not only to existing products of the company, but to new products as well.

Production planning is of several types, distinguishable by how far into the future the production (and inventory) plan is projected. Such plans include short- and long-term "production programs" and current "master schedules" of production. The latter govern the release of production orders to the production control department.

(2) *Production Control* is the function of "directing or regulating the orderly movement of goods through the entire manufacturing cycle, from the requisitioning of raw materials to the delivery of the finished product, to meet the objectives of customer service, minimum inventory investment, and maximum manufacturing efficiency."

Whereas the purpose of production planning is to set the requirements for production, the purpose of production control is to keep production within these requirements. In the former case, the term "planning" is used in the *determinative* sense, and in the latter instance it is used in the *regulative* sense. "Planning for control" includes not only the maintenance of production in accordance with *predetermined* quantitative and over-all time limits, but also the departmental routing and scheduling of specific production orders in accordance with *predetermined* process specifications. Production control is primarily a matter of "detailed" scheduling (the breakout of master schedules) and the preparation of factory directives (subsidiary production orders). Dispatching and the follow-up or expediting of these production orders are the "action" phase of production control.

(3) *Inventory Control* in many plants is organized as a department, though it is a common element in production planning and production control. Functionally it embraces all the techniques employed in maintaining inventories at predetermined levels consistent with planned production schedules and forecasted sales requirements.

CLIFFORD M. BAUMBACK, Professor of Production Management, University of Iowa, Iowa City, Iowa

Reference Cited

[1] The definitions used in this section are those prepared by the Nomenclature Committee of the American Production and Inventory Control Society, as contained in the third edition of its *Dictionary*.

PRODUCTION PLANNING

(MANUFACTURING RESOURCE PLANNING)

Production Planning is a broad term that has been used in the past to describe the management function of establishing levels or limits of manufacturing operations applicable to some future time period. The definition has been modified and changed as the science and technology of the profession of production and inventory control have become increasingly sophisticated. **Manufacturing Resource Planning** is a newer term used to cover the broader aspects of production planning as well as the higher level business planning, and the lower levels of master production scheduling, materials requirement planning, and capacity requirement planning. Production planning, as used here, is the broader interpretation of the definition to bridge the gap between the very high-level business planning and the master schedule.

The management decisions, incorporated in a production plan, are made after various factors and forces, both internal and external, have been considered. These factors include:

(1) Forecast of sales.

(2) The requirements for labor, raw material, production equipment and machinery, facilities, and warehousing.

(3) Financial requirements and the availability of financial resources.

Facets of Production Planning. The first step in the sequence of developing any production plan is the sales forecast or prediction. The sales forecast must extend through a planning horizon that is sufficient in length to determine the requirements for labor, facilities, equipment, material, and financing. In the final analysis, the sales forecast may be modified because of the lack of compatibility between the forecast and the available physical assets and material resources, or a combination of all. A production plan, in its truest sense, depicts the optimum utilization of all resources to accomplish a realistic and acceptable sales forecast.

A variety of planning horizons may be used for determining different resource requirements within any given industry and within individual companies. This means that the sales forecast may be very broad and general in nature or very specific and detailed, depending on the time span of the horizon.

At the highest level within a company, the chief planning officer may be primarily concerned with the requirement for capital related to equipment and facilities, and the current asset requirements of the company (cash, accounts receivable, and inventory). At this level in the organization, the planning horizon with the required sales forecasts most likely will be at least three to five years out, or even greater.

Sales forecasts which are used to develop these plans, and the related capacity requirements, are stated in the broadest of terms (i.e., product groups or product families).

At the next lower level of production planning, the time span of the forecast and the planning horizon is usually shortened, probably in the range of 18 to 30 months.

Concomitantly, the details of the sales forecast related to production groups or families are more clearly defined. At this level, the timing of capacity additions can be more specific, an analysis can be given to the capability of suppliers to meet material requirements, a better analysis of general logistics can be performed, the adequacy of physical distribution requirements for servicing the market can be studied, and a more precise definition of capital requirements throughout all phases of the horizon can be made.

Production planning, as the term is most commonly used today, also relates to still a shorter time horizon, somewhere in the 6 months to 18 months time frame. The objective of the production plan at this lower level is to establish operating levels and production rates that will achieve the management objectives in terms of meeting the demands of the marketplace, raising or lowering of inventories of finished products, or raising or lowering of backlogs of orders. Planning at this level will establish labor force requirements, and the need for overtime or short work weeks in critical operations.

Materials requirements over the planning horizon may continue to be general in nature but detailed enough to analyze suppliers' immediate capabilities and to negotiate purchasing contracts. Although many definitions of production planning do not include the sales forecast as part of the production plan, a complete production plan should include the sales forecast, related to the production output and the resulting finished inventories as part of the overall program, particularly in those industries where production is scheduled in anticipation of demand, rather than on a "to-order" basis.

A production plan must ultimately be translated into a Master Production Schedule. The time horizon for this will depend on the industry, the company, and the traditions of the plant. The master production schedule is a detailed statement of what the company or plant expects to manufacture. A master production schedule will become the basis for resource requirements planning, and will be used to determine such specifics as labor hours, machine hours, storage requirements, and production load profiles.

The master production schedule will be a detailed schedule denoting what to produce, when to produce it, and how much to produce for each individual finished product. The master production schedule will also be the basis for capacity requirements planning which is a detailed review of output requirements at various work centers. Finally, the master production schedule will be the basis for developing a materials requirements plan. The latter is a system which uses a bill of material, inventory status, open-order data, and the master production schedule, to calculate time phase requirements for material deliveries.

Functions and Responsibilities of Production Planning. It should be recognized that in any individual company, the functions and responsibilities of production planning may be divided among various departments or individuals and will not necessarily be organized into a production planning organization. Centralization of the planning function into a production planning organization facilitates a coordinated and properly executed planning operation. The trend throughout industry today is in this direction.

The functional duties of production planning will generally include: (1) sales forecasting, or at least active participation in sales forecasting, (2) the determination of production requirements to accomplish the sales forecast, (3) the determination of raw material requirements, (4) inventory management, both raw material and finished stock, (5) establishment or assisting in the establishment of labor requirements based on planned operating levels. Additional duties may include (1) customer order processing, (2) order promising, (3) the issuance of production orders to the production department, and (4) the releasing of shipments to customers. If the functions also include purchasing and physical distribution, the organization unit may most likely be called Materials Management Department.

Sales Forecasting. Sales forecasting should be divided into two phases, major product or commodity group forecasting for planning purposes, and individual item forecasting for master schedule purposes.

A major product group or commodity may be established for forecasting purposes because of significant differences in the production process, the location of production operations, or manpower requirements for the product. A major product group may also be established solely because a product is sold through different markets or to different types of users or a combination of both. From a production standpoint, significant product differences necessitate separate sales forecasting in order to establish a sound production plan that considers equipment, manpower, and raw materials. Where only marketing methods or ultimate users differ, the reason for separate forecasts may be only to make possible an accurate sales forecast that considers market trends, seasonal factors, etc.

Forecasts by major market groups must take into consideration all external factors affecting sales. This would include (1) cyclical patterns or general business conditions and the general economic climate that is anticipated; (2) secular trends of the product and competing commodities; (3) seasonal patterns; (4) short-range or irregular influences including price changes or adjustments, labor negotiations, promotional campaigns, etc. (See BUSINESS FORECASTING); and (5) distributor or wholesaler inventory positions of the product. Forecasting for major products or groups is an integral part of inventory control, but it concerns itself more with anticipation stocks and overall planned inventory programs that stabilize labor, avoid capacity shortages, and cover unusual changes in demand, etc.

Sales forecasts for individual items that are included in a major product group require less attention to external and internal forces as listed above, and will generally be a proportion or breakdown of the major product group based on past trends or anticipated changes in demand. Item forecasting is a necessary part of effective finished inventory control, since it determines the establishment of reorder points and economic order quantities as explained under INVENTORY CONTROL, below.

Determining Production Requirements. After the establishment of a sales forecast, production requirements must be established which will give the optimum utilization of equipment, facilities, labor, and inventory investments.

Capacities and output capabilities of equipment, availability of inventory space, and adequacy of the labor force are an integral part of the production requirement program. The alternatives in the process of optimization are numerous, and range from the extremes of limiting sales, to the opposite extreme of acquiring new production facilities. The areas in between include, among others, adjusting manpower levels, overtime utilization, major inventory changes, additional warehouse facilities, and changes in distribution methods. In these areas, the Production Planning Department carries its greatest responsibility. To carry out the responsibility, overall knowledge of the business, including the peculiarities and limiting factors, is required.

New Product Introduction. New product introduction is so closely related to production planning and can have such a direct influence on established plans that production planning organizations should be active participants in any new product introduction or new product planning. (See NEW PRODUCT entries.)

Sales Order Processing. Whether the Production Planning Department becomes involved in sales order processing depends, to a large degree, on the type of business involved. With job order products or specific customer products, Production Planning must process, plan, and schedule these special or specific products. Where sales orders cover only standard items carried in stock, Production may not become involved in the order processing at all and may receive only general or summary information relative to shipments or releases. However, this should not be interpreted as meaning that Production Planning should not be closely associated with the sales organization. Sales programs, promotional efforts, price adjustments, field service requirements, etc., all influence sales and must be a part of any forecast and plan.

Issuing Production Orders. Production planning and production control dovetail at the point of the production orders. Production orders are a direct result of establishing current and routine production plans. The issuance of production orders to Production Control begins the production process. However, Production Planning's function and responsibility do not end until assurance is received that the production orders have been properly executed.

Organization. Effective production planning depends to a large degree upon the organizational structure under which it functions. It is quite obvious that production planning is a function that influences and is influenced by production, sales, and financial positions. It is an optimizing function that necessitates compromise of conflicting desires and objectives. Since it can have a direct effect on costs and sales volume, it must be managed by persons capable of exercising sound judgment as well as being technically proficient. Organizationally, consideration should be given to establishing production planning as a staff function that reports to the management level that has the responsibility for both sales and production.

FREDRIC E. BULLEIT, Vice-President and Director, Materials Management, Armstrong Cork Company, Lancaster, Pennsylvania; past International President, American Production and Inventory Control Society; past Chairman, Curricula and Certification Council, APICS

Information References

Greene, James H., "Production and Inventory Control Handbook," New York, McGraw-Hill, 1970.
Brown, R. G., "Materials Management Systems," New York, Wiley, 1977.
Wheelwright, Steven C. and Makridakis, Spyros, "Forecasting Methods for Management, 2nd ed.," New York, Wiley, 1977.
Greene, James H., "Production and Inventory Control: Systems and Decisions," Homewood, Ill., Irwin, 1978.

PRODUCTION CONTROL

Production Control is the purposeful concentration of responsibility and authority for the control of all activity leading up to the production and eventual shipment of the finished product. Considerable thought and planning must precede the manufacture of any product, event the simplest. A long-term or master production forecast must be made, to serve as a procurement guide and to inform all departments of the manufacturing goal; and based on this, a master schedule must be developed.

Preparation of the master schedule is normally the responsibility of Production Control, but it is usually based upon an outlook of market requirements, which Marketing must provide in the form of a sales forecast for each finished product. In its final form, approved by management, the master schedule represents management's plan of operation for the coming year, and therefore becomes a guide to the entire organization. The Master Schedule is the input document containing the master data for the generation of Materials Requirements Planning (M.R.P.) [2]. It is "exploded" into detail schedules reflecting requirements for procurement, shop processing, and assembly operations. "Make or buy" decisions, tool planning, facilities planning, facilities loading, and routing are thus an orderly outgrowth of the master production forecast and master schedule.

Master Scheduling. Master scheduling [1] is the assignment of due dates to customer orders, or for the completion of specific quantities of specific products. Achievement of the scheduling task requires some basic tools of production control, a knowledge of the specific manufacturing process, and an appreciation of customer and Marketing Department demands. Essentials are:

(1) Inventory policy and position.

(2) Procurement lead times (including subcontract.

(3) Product manufacture lead times and cycle times.

(4) Manufacturing department capacities.

(5) Manufacturing department loads.

(6) Detail schedule.

(7) Operations required and operations sequence.

(8) Specific operations presenting critical path or imbalance of production flow.

(9) Special tools and tool planning.

(10) Production plan, including quantitative data and demand rates.

(11) Learning curve analysis.

(12) Production standards.

(13) Specific customer demands or delivery requirements.

(14) Alternate delivery schedules acceptable, though not desirable.

(15) Marketing service level policy.

(16) Demand curve for finished products.

(17) Sales forecast.

The information needed for the above should be available in the required detail as a result of production planning, detail scheduling, manufacturing engineering, marketing, and the policy-making segment of Production Management.

Precision of an absolute sort far out into time is not required or attainable—but detail schedules must still be made up with care and accuracy, and properly adjusted as required. The effectiveness of the ultimate detail schedule can be directly related to the skill with which the master schedule has been formulated.

Master schedules and detail schedules are frequently combined and, as a result, often confused, one for the other. Such combination is usually practiced in job shops (sometimes called "functional shops" or "contract shops"). The reason for this is that the lack of repetitiveness in the job shop offers little or no previous product or manufacturing data usable to the maker of the master schedule. Hence the items for consideration must be worked out in detail as part of the development of the master schedule. (Although techniques are available for minimizing the need for this practice, they will not be elaborated in the present discussion.)

Exhibit I shows a sales forecast for an electric motor company, reflecting a fairly linear distribution for one year. A simple evaluation of manpower requirements is shown in Exhibit II. The hours required for each of the motor models are tabulated and totalled by schedule period. Next, available assembly department hours adjusted by variance from standard, vacation periods, absentee rates, etc. are tabulated by schedule period. A comparison of the hours by period reflects the usual problems and indicates that an adjustment must be made.

In the development of a proposed master schedule, the scheduler must make note of certain factors which vary from company to company, depending upon management philosophy, industry climate, inventory policy, and product line. In this case the following considerations are important:

(1) Delivery in accordance with the sales forecast must be satisfied in order to maintain a competitive position within the industry.

(2) The product line is comprised of precision electric motors used in manned aircraft and missiles. Therefore, a high degree of quality and reliability must be maintained.

(3) The operators of the assembly department are long-service men with exceptional skills, and can be used to produce all models interchangeably.

(4) Motors reflected in the sales forecast are current production models, and all operators are at the high point of the learning curve.

(5) All assembly department operators are represented by a labor union. The contract provides for recall of all laid-off personnel prior to subcontract.

(6) Management strongly desires to stabilize the work force, and to minimize fluctuations in load from period to period.

(7) Historically, variances from standard have decreased with load leveling or stabilization, and conversely increased when fluctuation existed.

(8) Costs of "having," or inventory carrying charges, are historically 25%. Set-up time is very low.

(9) Management expressed a willingness to trade off inventory carrying charges for quality improvement and decrease in variance from standard decreases.

(10) The plant shuts down for half the schedule period of August.

One solution is shown in Exhibit III. Obvi-

EXHIBIT I

SALES FORECAST—MOTOR DIVISION

	Jan	*Feb*	*Mar*	*Apr*	*May*	*Jun*	*Jul*	*Aug*	*Sep*	*Oct*	*Nov*	*Dec*
Model "A"	250	250	250	300	300	300	350	350	350	300	250	200
Model "B"	1,000	1,000	1,000	750	750	750	750	750	750	750	750	750
Model "C"	250	250	350	350	450	450	500	500	500	500	500	500
Monthly Totals	1,500	1,500	1,600	1,400	1,500	1,500	1,600	1,600	1,600	1,550	1,500	1,450
Totals Accumulated	1,500	3,000	4,600	6,000	7,500	9,000	10,600	12,200	13,800	15,350	16,850	18,300

EXHIBIT II

SALES FORECAST—MANPOWER EVALUATION

	Jan	*Feb*	*Mar*	*Apr*	*May*	*Jun*	*Jul*	*Aug*	*Sep*	*Oct*	*Nov*	*Dec*
Model A-Hrs	5,000	5,000	5,000	6,000	6,000	6,000	7,000	7,000	7,000	6,000	5,000	4,000
Model B-Hrs	10,000	10,000	10,000	7,500	7,500	7,500	7,500	7,500	7,500	7,500	7,500	7,500
Model C-Hrs	5,000	5,000	7,000	7,000	9,000	9,000	10,000	10,000	10,000	10,000	10,000	10,000
Total Hours	20,000	20,000	22,000	20,500	22,500	22,500	24,500	24,500	24,500	23,500	22,500	21,500
Ass'y Dept Avail Hours	23,530	23,530	23,530	23,530	23,530	23,530	23,530	11,790	23,530	23,530	23,530	23,530

EXHIBIT III

PRELIMINARY MASTER SCHEDULE—MOTOR DIVISION

	Jan	*Feb*	*Mar*	*Apr*	*May*	*Jun*	*Jul*	*Aug*	*Sep*	*Oct*	*Nov*	*Dec*
Model "A"												
Std. Hrs. 20												
Units Month Sched	250	250	250	300	300	300	612	88	350	300	250	200
Units Acc'l Sched	250	500	750	1,050	1,350	1,650	2,262	2,350	2,700	3,000	3,250	3,450
Month Hours	5,000	5,000	5,000	6,000	6,000	6,000	12,240	1,760	7,000	6,000	5,000	4,000
Acc'l Hours	5,000	10,000	15,000	21,000	27,000	33,000	45,240	47,000	54,000	60,000	65,000	69,000
Model "B"												
Std. Hrs. 10												
Units Month Sched	1,353	1,353	1,153	1,053	853	853	129	3	750	750	750	750
Units Acc'l Sched	1,353	2,706	3,859	4,912	5,765	6,618	6,747	6,750	7,500	8,250	9,000	9,750
Month Hours	13,530	13,530	11,530	10,530	8,530	8,530	1,290	30	7,500	7,500	7,500	7,500
Acc'l Hours	13,530	27,060	38,590	49,120	57,650	66,180	67,470	67,500	75,000	82,500	90,000	97,500
Model "C"												
Std. Hrs. 20												
Units Month Sched	250	250	350	350	450	450	500	500	500	500	500	500
Units Acc'l Sched	250	500	850	1,200	1,650	2,100	2,600	3,100	3,600	4,100	4,600	5,100
Month Hours	5,000	5,000	7,000	7,000	9,000	9,000	10,000	10,000	10,000	10,000	10,000	10,000
Acc'l Hours	5,000	10,000	17,000	24,000	33,000	42,000	52,000	62,000	72,000	82,000	92,000	102,000
Total Units	1,853	1,853	1,753	1,703	1,603	1,603	1,241	591	1,600	1,550	1,500	1,450
Total Hours	23,530	23,530	23,530	23,530	23,530	23,530	23,530	11,790	24,500	23,500	22,500	21,500

ously, the first step in the scheduling process is to reduce the problem to a common unit of measure—in this case, hours [3]. From this point forward, loading principles apply. It must be noted that the forecast requirements for the plant shut-down period stand firm. Therefore, leveling production is automatically a function of inventory, and the impact of carrying charges must be measured. However, the carrying charges are not the only element of inventory computation. More frequently than not, the risk element will carry more weight in the final conclusion than will all other elements. For example, Model B in the master schedule reflects almost 100% of the inventory. An evaluation of the three models, by Marketing, indicated that the highest confidence factor was placed on Model B. A further evaluation by Engineering indicated that of the three models, Model B reflected itself as least probable to be changed.

Frequently, Production Control is called upon to provide master schedules without benefit of sales forecasts, or at best with only inaccurate forecasts. In these cases the scheduler and production management must provide their own forecast. This is not recommended because usually historic data are used, and these do not have the benefit of marketing intelligence, and the inventory risk factor is very high. Where these conditions exist, the development of a planned rate is substituted for a sales forecast. The planned rate method requires constant surveilance and must respond to changes rapidly.

A sample Master Schedule is shown in Exhibit IV. The format is designed so that progress may be posted by schedule period as well as specific assignments of due dates to customer orders. This combination of data in a single format often provides a check against future schedules as well as current schedules.

For purposes of illustration, the results of the prior eight months scheduling are shown, through August. Acceptable practice in scheduling is to project a schedule for twelve months. This is done each schedule period (or month) by dropping the earliest period and adding the sequential period not shown previously. Changes as required are made with each publication. However, these must be made so that the effective data of the change provides ample lead time; for example, in Exhibit IV, a schedule increase of significant value can only be incorporated three months (or periods) after the current period.

Machine Loading and Detail Scheduling. Detail scheduling [1] is the process of breaking down the master schedule into departmental operations in order to synchronize the flow of

Exhibit IV

Master Schedule Control, Motor

Drawing #789012 Lead Time: 3 Months
Department #71 Standard Hours: 11.2

	Jan		Feb		Mar		Apr		May		Jun		Jul		Aug		Sep		Oct		Jul		Aug	
	Mo.	*Cum.*	*Mo.*	*Cum.*	*Mo.*	*Cum.*	*Mo.*	*Cum.*	*Mo.*	*Cum.*	*Mo.*	*Cum.*	*Mo.*	*Cum.*	*Mo.*	*Cum.*	*Mo.*	*Cum.*	*Mo.*	*Cum.*	*Mo.*	*Cum.*	*Mo.*	*Cum.*
Planned Rate	650	650	650	1,300	675	1,975	700	2,675	700	3,375	750	4,125	775	4,900	400	5,300	800	6,100	800	6,900	600	13,900	600	14,500
Assignments	650	650	650	1,300	675	1,975	700	2,675	575	3,250	750	4,000	775	4,775	400	5,175	750	5,925	750	6,675				
Production Output	640	640	650	1,290	690	1,980	710	2,690	700	3,390	710	4,100	750	4,850	350	5,200								
Sales Order #77999	650	650	350	1,000																				
Qty—1,000																								
Completions	640	640	350	990	10	1,000																		
Sales Order #78000			300	300	200	500																		
Qty—500																								
Completions			300	300	200	500																		
Sales Order #78001					475	475	275	750																
Qty—750																								
Completions					475	475	275	750																
Sales Order #78002							425	425	575	1,000														
Qty—1,000																								
Completions							425	425	575	1,000														
Sales Order #78003											500	500	300	800										
Qty—800																								
Completions											500	500	300	800										
Sales Order #78004											250	250	250	500	250	750	250	1,000	250	1,250				
Qty—2,000																								
Completions											250	250	250	500	250	750								
Sales Order #78005													225	225	150	375	500	875	500	1,375				
Qty—3,000																								
Completions													225	225	150	375								

work through the several manufacturing departments. Time allowances are determined from master route sheets or files of standard time data. Frequently, manufacturing cycle time estimates, based upon historic data, are used where standards resulting from operation study and analysis are not available.

Scheduling may better be defined as "the assignment of work to a facility and the specification of the time and the sequence in which the work is to be done." The time dimension of detail scheduling must be coordinated realistically to the master schedule of the end product [3]. This may be accomplished through the plotting of Lead-Time Chart. This technique is commonly used in the job shop, or when introducing new products into the factory. (See Exhibit V.)

Detail explosions of the flow of work through a department or departments is usually acquired through the use of Route Sheets or Operation Sheets (sometimes called Sequence Sheets.) Exhibit VI demonstrates this procedure. The Route Sheet provides the sequential listing of operations to be performed. The following information is essential for detail scheduling and machine loading: (1) Part Number and Description; (2) Quantity of Order; (3) Sequential Operations (4) Machines or Machine Centers; (5) Set up time per Operation; (6) Production Standard.

Optional information, depending upon systems and procedures, include: (7) Manufacture Order Number; (8) Material Specification; (9) Material Requirement per unit or 1,000 units.

Provision must be made for inserting schedule dates and load hours, as per Exhibit VI. With the Route Sheet method of detail scheduling, specific dates may be assigned to each operation, including inspection. A common

EXHIBIT V

LEAD-TIME CHART

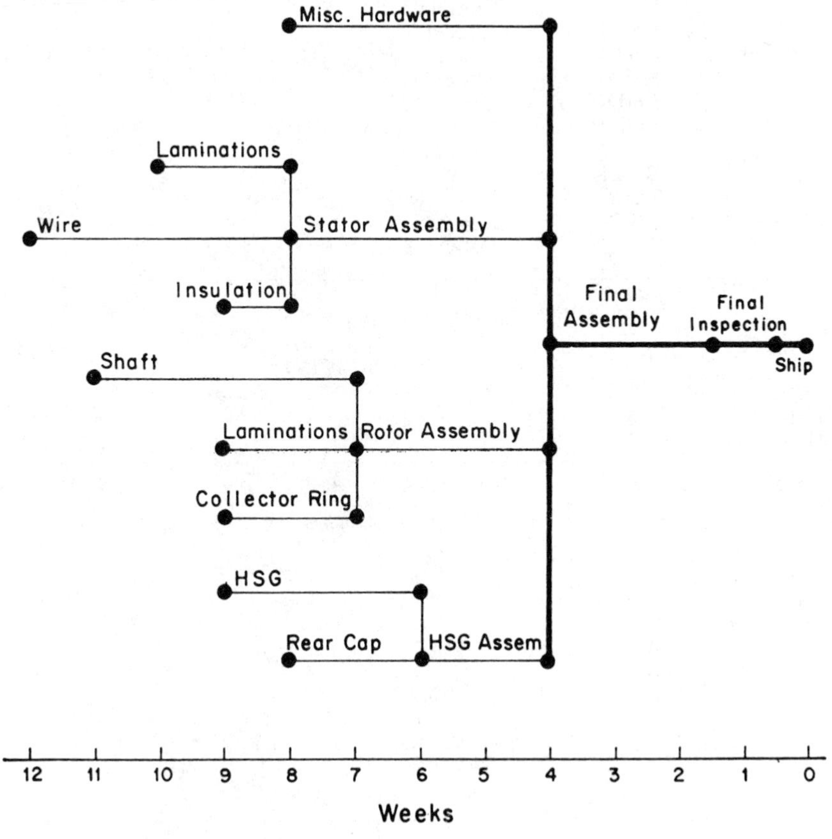

technique used is to "reverse schedule" [4]. This means that the required date is assigned to the last operation, and then scheduling proceeds in the reverse direction of operation sequence, with schedule dates assigned to each operation. Ultimately, a start date for the first operation is computed. It is important to note that in the process of computing schedule dates for each operation, transportation time as well as available load hours in a given machine center must be known.

Frequently, a Load Center Summary report is used to determine specific loads [5]. An example of this summary is shown in Exhibit VII.

The solution may appear in the development of production forecasts exploded in detail, load center by load center, as far into the future as possible. These operations plans may require a re-evaluation of the make-or-buy policy [6], and some reconsideration of facilities planning integrating the labor union contractual obligations. Indeed, these are management policies to be resolved before the scheduler seeks to attempt the solution via the route of systems and procedures. The application of MATHEMATICAL

EXHIBIT VI

ROUTE SHEET

Part Name: Front Cap
Material Specification: Stainless Steel
Type 303

Part No. —12345
M.O. No. —10754
Qty. —2,750
Start Date—7/3
Due Date —9/2

Oper. No.	*Load Center*	*Mach.*	*Operation Description*	*Set Up Std.*	*Load Hrs.*	*Sched. Date*
3	01	5 SPDL	First Turn	20	58	7/14
5		BNCH	Inspect			7/16
7V		V	Tumble			7/23
9		BNCH	Inspect			7/25
10	013	HRCH	Second Turn	1.5	63	8/1
12	013	HRCH	Third Turn	1.5	46	8/7
20	030	LGDR	Drill (2) Holes	.4	55	8/14
30	030	LGDR	CNTR SINK (2) Holes	.3	12	8/18
40	035	HSK	Tap (2) Holes	.4	25	8/21
50		BNCH	Inspect			8/25
60		Tank	Passivate			8/27
70		BNCH	Inspect			9/1
		TRANS	Deliver To Stores			9/2

EXHIBIT VII

LOAD CENTER SUMMARY

MACHINE CENTER
Drill Press
Avail. Hrs/wk *1,000*

Job #	*Week #1*		*Week #2*		*Week #3*		*Week #4*		*Week #5*		*Week #6*	
	Assigned	*Open*	*Assigned*	*Open*	*Assigned*	*Open*	*Assigned*	*Open*	*Assigned*	*Open*	*Assigned*	*Open*
1	50	950										
2	300	650										
3	300	350										
4	350	0										
5			100	900								
6			700	200								
7			200	0	100	900						
8					500	400						
9					400	0	400	600				
10									600	400		
11											300	700

PROGRAMMING should be considered in severe cases.

The Load Center Summary as shown assumes a fixed capacity, and therefore can present serious problems. Should the scheduler be confronted with a customer requirement in Week #3, the requirement could obviously not be satisfied, unless additional capacity were made available. This could be accomplished by (1) authorizing overtime, (2) subcontracting, (3) rescheduling other jobs, or (4) adding more machines. Usually, one or more of these solutions will solve the problem.

Often the suggested solutions may introduce further problems, for example:

(1) Time or sufficient load may not be available to warrant adding machines.

(2) Subcontracting cannot always be assumed practical for several reasons:

- (a) Subcontract capability is not available.
- (b) Multiple usage of tools or fixtures prevents subcontracting.
- (c) Complexities of labor union contracts prevents subcontract and sometimes overtime.

(3) Overtime may be prohibitive where close margins of profit are involved.

(4) Rescheduling other jobs will sometimes warrant severe administrative costs in view of the reaction and interaction of other load centers. This may appear like a never ending chain reaction.

The ultimate solution to ease detail scheduling and shop-floor control is in capacity planning. Capacity Planning and Control is the function of establishing, measuring, and adjusting the limits or levels of capacity that are consistent with the production plan and or Master Schedule [1].

The use of a computer-oriented M.R.P. (Materials Requirements Planning) system will provide the input to a Capacity Planning system. The Capacity Requirements Planning system will provide the projection into the future (13 to 52 weeks) of the individual work center loads. It should be clearly understood that while modern computerized Shop Floor Control and Dispatching systems provide the tools for timely collection of Shop Floor Data, the Shop Floor Control system in itself will not provide the solution to overload or underload problems as they occur. The combination and interaction of M.R.P., Capacity Planning, and Shop Floor Control Systems is essential for effective Production Control [7].

Dispatching. Dispatching [1] is the assignment of work to machines, machine centers, or workers. Dispatching considers preplanned schedules, machine loads, and replanned priorities. Often the required corrective action decisions in connection with delays, overloads, and underloads are made by or at Dispatching.

Serious consideration should be given to the establishment of organizational lines of authority and responsibility in connection with the dispatching function. The establishment of decentralized instead of centralized dispatching or vice versa, will depend largely upon the nature of product line and the characteristics of the manufacturing process. Where machine or machine center operations are dependent upon other centers, the centralized dispatching for overall control is mandatory. Conversely, work centers whose operations are somewhat autonomous, might well use decentralized dispatching.

Usually where centralized dispatching is practiced, the dispatcher is a member of the Production Control staff. The dispatch station is of necessity a nerve center, a communication center, where schedule and load information can be transmitted rapidly. Data processing equipment is available which can tie the activities of the shop directly to the computer or data processing center. Manufacturers of equipment can supply detailed proposals engineered to fit specific needs.

Where electronic data collection equipment cannot be economically installed, some manual methods can successfully be employed.

Progress Reporting. It is mandatory that production plans and schedules be monitored to ensure that the action called for has been taken. Unfortunately, one cannot predict all of the causes for delay, or the sequence and timing in which they will occur. Provisions for corrective action must therefore be made, and these call for reports and follow-up.

Reports of schedule or production progress can be developed to include actual production in each operation by job, or can reflect exceptions only. Using the exception rule will, in most cases, provide the necessary controls. Machine loading and unloading will require specifically defined reporting. Exhibit VIII reflects this kind of reporting.

Follow-up of schedules and projects frequently requires expediting. Although the amount of expediting required may sometimes reflect upon planning and scheduling, it does not follow that good planning will eliminate

EXHIBIT VIII

MACHINE LOAD REPORT

Load Center #021		*Load Center Name: Turret Lathe #3*		*Report Date: Dec. 1, 19—*		*Capacity: 1,000*		*% of Capacity:*
		Load				*Load Transactions*		
Load Center	*Load Peroid*	*Live*	*Potential*	*New Orders*	*Adj. Potential*	*Transferred Potential to Live*	*Adj. to Live*	*Completions*
	1	900	100					
	2	800	200	100	50	50	25	
	3	500	300					
	4	600	300	300		100		
	5	400	200					
	6	400	300					

expediting entirely. It must be remembered that although we are planning and scheduling machines, materials, and money, we are also scheduling manpower—and people are less predictable than machines. Expediting is that function of Production Control that insures the procurement, movement, and delivery of all parts, materials, and tools essential for meeting production schedules. It is the corrective action superimposed upon the entire manufacturing control system. It "makes things happen" when delays would otherwise occur [7].

A. V. SANTORA, CMfgE., Vice President, Operations, Visual Graphics Corp. Tamarac, Florida

References Cited

[1] "Dictionary of Production and Inventory Control Terms" Washington, D.C., American Production and Inventory Control Society, 1979, revised.

[2] "Master Scheduling Reprints" Washington, D.C., American Production and Inventory Control Society, 1978.

[3] "Certification Study Guides," Washington, D.C., American Production and Inventory Control Society, 1979.

[4] Greene, J. H., "Production and Inventory Control Handbook," New York, McGraw-Hill, 1969.

[5] "COPICS" I.B.M. Corporation, 1978, revised.

[6] Plossl, G. W. and White, O. W., "Production and Inventory Control," Englewood Cliffs, N.J., Prentice Hall, 1975, revised.

[7] Santora, A. V. "Shop Orientation and Discipline," *Production and Inventory Management Journal*, Third Quarter, 1976. Washington, D.C., American Production and Inventory Control Society.

INVENTORY CONTROL

Approximately one third of America's industrial capitalization is in inventory, and yet industry clings to traditional rules of thumb to control this investment, such as the rule of "turnover." When sales go up, most managements permit inventories to become inflated; when sales go down, they stress inventory reduction. The only policy directive given to inventory managers in many companies is simply, "Keep your inventory down but don't run out of stock."

It is the purpose of this section to acquaint managers with some of the newer, scientific methods of **Inventory Control.**

Certainly, there is still much to be done in the study of the means for evaluating and controlling inventories, but the methods to be discussed here are well tested and tried and have proven their value. However, no formula is a substitute for judgment, and it is well to remember that the following approaches are offered as guides only.

Scientific Inventory Control. The inventory manager must make two decisions as he (she) runs inventory. To begin with, he has a dwindling supply of stock on hand: He must decide *when* to replenish on reorder his stock. Secondly, he must decide *how much* to order. These two decisions, *when* and *how much* determine the size of his inventory, and are illustrated in Exhibit I.

In Exhibit I, we start with a given stock position on January 1, and gradually the stock drops lower and lower until, finally, we must reorder or face a stock-out. This is the *reorder point.* The determination of the reorder point determines the *cushion.*

Every inventory has a cushion. The average checking account for example, probably has no less then three cushions. Few people reduce their account to zero for fear of error in the

EXHIBIT I

TYPICAL INVENTORY RELATIONSHIPS

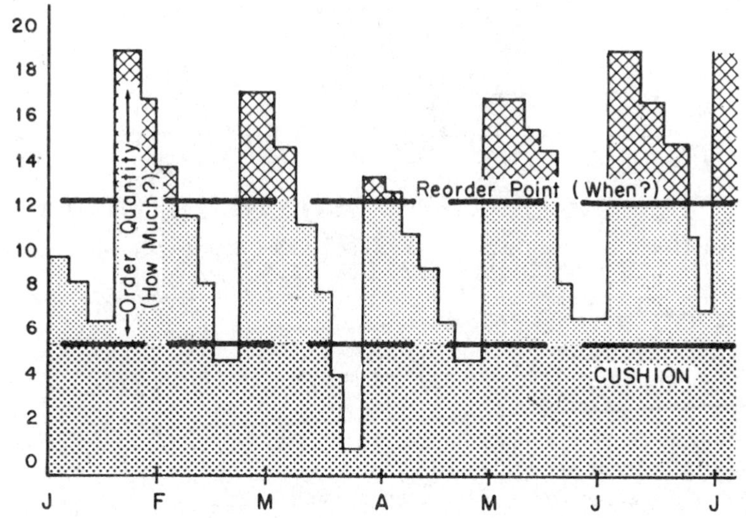

figures. This gives one cushion, or "protective stock." Secondly, there is a two to three-day period from the time a check is written until it is deducted from the account. This delay provides a second cushion. Thirdly, many people put $25 in their account but do not record it in their balance. This $25 represents a third, or "safety" cushion.

Cushion or safety stock arises in industrial inventory from the fear of overdrawing or stocking out.

It is apparent from Exhibit I that if we use an average of six units every two weeks (the normal length of time to get this particular item), then we dare not wait until stocks get down to six units to reorder. If we did, we would find ourselves overdrawn or out of stock *half the time,* since it probably would be just as likely as not that goods would move faster or more slowly than anticipated during the time between reorder and actual receipt of new supplies. Hence, as a matter of protection, we must reorder sooner. The question of just when to reorder will be discussed in detail later. Suffice to say here, that the problem of *when* is the problem of delivery. The more effectively we control our reorder point, the better we control our stock-outs, and, hence, our ability to deliver when needed.

The question of *how much* is an economic problem. In Exhibit I, we ordered twelve units at a time. We could have ordered one at a time (more frequently of course). Or we could have ordered 100 at a time (less frequently). The question of how much to order is a question of economic order quantities.

Space will not permit a fully detailed discussion of economic order quantities or reorder points, but we can explore them to provide an understanding of their meaning and use. (A more detailed approach is given in the writer's "Production Control," Prentice-Hall, Inc., 1963).

Economic Order Quantities. Two factors or variables affect the decision of how much to order. In any company, these factors are clearly defined and brought into sharp conflict on the one side by the foremen and on the other by the controller.

The foreman sees before him on every machine the costs of setup. He sees numerous examples of jobs that are set up and then set up again and again each year. A setup may be broken down for a new job and two weeks later the original job is back on the machine. To him, setups represent losses in capacity and costs. They are actually controlled in the office and can be increased at will by decreasing the size of the production lot. The solution in the mind of the foreman is to plan better: to make long runs—for example, to run a year's supply at a time and thus pay for only one setup a year.

This cost of setup is the *cost of getting.* (Where items are purchased, it is the cost of going through the motions of procurement.)

EXHIBIT II

COSTS OF VARIABLE PORTION* OF INVENTORY OF A VALVE BODY

	Order Quantity in Months' Usage					
	1	*2*	*3*	*6*	*12*	
					Costs	
A. Annual Cost of Getting	$192	$96	$64	$32	$16	($16 × frequency of ordering per year)
Average Variable Inventory	$128	$256	$384	$768	$1536	(½ of amount put into inventory)
B. Annual Cost of Having	$21	$43	$64	$128	$256	(17% of average inventory)
Total Cost	$213	$139	$128	$160	$272	

"Givens" on Valve Body
Cost of Getting—$16
Cost of Having—17%
Monthly Usage—$256
* These are the costs over and above the cost of carrying the cushion, or safety stocks.

The cost of getting is actually a whole family of costs, and can be more precisely defined as follows: The *costs of getting* are those costs that we pay for twice when we produce an order in two lots instead of one. Upon reflection, we can see by this definition that many costs are increased when we produce two small lots instead of one larger one: the setup costs of the foreman; expediting, scheduling and paperwork costs; some inspection and scrap costs; and so on. In sum, from the shop's point of view an economic run is to make a long run—possibly a year's supply.

In the office, the controller must meet increasing demands for money. Methods improvements cost money and pay off later. New machinery may pay a high return but it takes years to recover the investment. Better plant and facilities, pay raises, increased expenditures on advertising, sales, marketing, larger payrolls, more research and staff positions, all require funds. The controller wants to get money *from* inventory, not put more money *in* it! Inventory not only drains off money, but also costs money to store it. These are the *costs of having*—the inventory carrying charges.

The carrying charges include the following: interest on money, taxes, insurances, storage space, clerical and physical inventorying, deterioration, and obsolescence. There are, in fact, over 200 items that can be listed in the cost of carrying inventory. These factors can be computed as a per cent of the average inventory. For example, a 25% cost of having could mean that a $1,000,000 inventory costs $250,000 per year to carry.

In recent years, the industrial average cost of having has increased from about 18% to about 25%. This increase may reflect a reinterpretation of the interest figure: 6% at one time was a common figure. Today, many companies use return on investment (for example, 15%).

These two variables, the costs of getting and the costs of having, determine the economic order quantity. Note that the annual costs of getting go down as the variable portion of inventory goes up, since larger order quantities mean fewer orders per year. The carrying charges, however, go up as average inventory increases. These relationships are illustrated in the cost analysis table, Exhibit II.

The lowest total cost in this example occurs when we order three months' supply of the item. At that time, our costs are $128. Note, that although the costs go up as we deviate from the economic order quantity (three months), they increase less rapidly when we over order than under order. Hence, it is better to err on the high side than the low side.

If the data in the table are plotted, they become a curve as shown in Exhibit III. The data

EXHIBIT III

TOTAL INVENTORY COST VS. ORDER QUANTITY

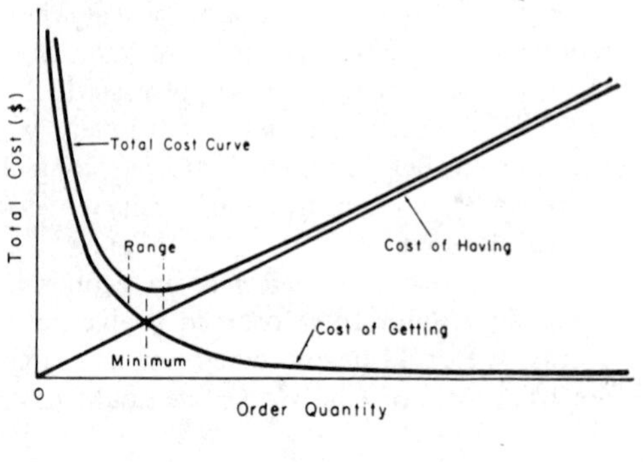

can be generalized to develop a formula as follows: using G for cost of getting, M for monthly usage in dollars and H for cost of having, and EOQ for economic order quantity in months' usage, we get:

A. Annual Cost of Getting $= \dfrac{12G}{EOQ}$

B. Annual Cost of Having

$$= \frac{(M \times EOQ \times H)}{2}$$

Solving for minimum total cost (i.e., finding the trough or bottom point of the total cost curve A + B, by setting its derivative equal to zero and solving for EOQ), we get:

$$EOQ = \sqrt{\frac{G}{M} \times \frac{24}{H}}$$

This is the formula for economic order quantities in months.

Using the data of the previous example, we get:

$$EOQ = \sqrt{\frac{16}{256} \times \frac{24}{\frac{1}{6}}} = 3.$$

This is the classic Economic Lot Formula. Numerous variations of it will be found in the literature. For example, by slight changes in the components, it is possible to get the answer in terms of dollars, weeks, periods, pieces, and so on. It is often given in terms of units, rather than months' supply, viz:

$$EOQ\ (pieces) = \sqrt{\frac{2U(S + O)}{HC}}$$

Here U is usage in pieces per year, C is the cost per piece, H is the cost of having, or carrying charges, per year, expressed as a percentage, and the expression (S + O) is the getting costs in terms of "set up and order" costs.

For purchased items, the same formula is used as for manufactured items, but the S in the expression (S + O) drops out, since there is no set-up cost, and the O becomes the cost of processing the order (such as paperwork, cost of receiving, etc.).

It can be seen from Exhibit III, without resort to calculus, that the optimum order quantity occurs at the point where the linearly rising carrying charges cross the decreasing curve of procurement or "getting" costs—i.e., where the annual carrying cost equals the annual cost of getting.

The formula is cumbersome in practice, despite its relative simplicity, since it does require numerous calculations. For this reason, it is usually best to reduce the formula to a slide rule or graphic solution as illustrated in Exhibit IV.

Using the original example again, with a $16 cost of getting, $256 monthly usage and 17% cost of having, we read from the chart an EOQ of three months. The chart offers great flexibility, permitting a wide selection of costs and usages in determining the EOQ. For example, a $10 cost of getting, $10 monthly usage, at 17%, gives us an EOQ of twelve months, whereas, a $10 cost of getting, a $1,000 monthly usage, at 17%, gives an EOQ of 1.2 months.

Obviously it does make a difference whether we order 1.2 months' supply or a year's supply at a time. In fact, it makes a very great difference as is illustrated by the comparison in Exhibit V.

By means of the formula (or chart) it is almost always possible to keep our base costs within 3% of the optimum. This is true despite great errors that are inherent in the rough data that must go into the formula. For example, it is not uncommon to encounter wide variations of thinking relative to carrying charges. In the same company, depending on the interpretation of the basic data in the carrying charges, one individual may favor 17% while another favors 24%. The lack of agreement loses significance when we compare one view against the other in the chart. At 24%, the EOQ becomes 2.6 months compared to three months at 17%. This is a variation of about 12% and is well within the "ball-park area" of a 3% base cost increase.

It will also be found that wide ranges of errors are possible in the forecast with similar results. For example, if we had used $384 instead of $256 as the monthly usage in the original example, our order quantity would become (from the chart) about 2.5 months. This is certainly an acceptable error according to our ball park analysis, and such deviations in forecasts are common.

How well could we do without the formula in estimating the proper order quantity? The chances of good results would be slim. For any company stressing turnover as the basis for running an inventory the chances favor great errors. Thus, an attempt to order everything four times a year (not uncommon in industry) would result in the correct EOQ in our original example, but would produce only 1/4 of the EOQ in the second example just cited, and would order 3.33 times the correct amount in the third example.

The only conclusion that can be reached is that even though we are not able to forecast precisely, or estimate our costs of having or getting, we are nevertheless much safer with the formula than hunch. *The formula will almost always put us within 3% of the base cost.* Hunch may, but usually will not. Studies by the present writer, using actual company cost data, forecasts, and usage figures, where order quantities have been selected without formula, have revealed order quantities ranging from one piece all the way up to 100, on the same item.

The "ABC" Analysis. The EOQ formula is applicable to in-process stores as well as to finished goods. (For purchased items, separate computations are required for quantity discounts, to see whether buying the larger quantitiy would save more than would be involved in carrying the additional inventory.) However, applying a formula to a company with thousands upon thousands of items, even when the formula is reduced to a chart or a computer is used, is a time-consuming task, and a simplifying set of rules must be developed.

If we take an inventory, forecast the annual usage of each item, and convert this to total dollar usage per item, we can then list the items in descending order, with the biggest seller at the top. The top 20% of this listing will usually cover about 80% of the total dollars involved. If we control this 20%, we control most of the dollars. These items must therefore be controlled tightly. The bottom 60% of the items in the listing will usually account for only about 10% of the dollars. Minimum control here will lower operating costs while sacrificing little by way of excess inventory costs. This method of trisecting an inventory is frequently referred to as the "ABC" method of inventory control.

Returning to the EOQ formula, we can spot-check a few C items. If these C items end up with EOQs in excess of 12 months, the rule then becomes to order all C items annually. (Most companies place a ceiling on orders that exceed a year's supply.) Checking a few C items (using the formula sparingly) reduces the whole C category to a sound set of rules which do not violate the principles discussed. In addition, it is frequently more expensive to gather

Exhibit IV

Economic Order Quantity Chart

ECONOMIC ORDER QUANTITY CHART

TO USE CHART:

Lay a straight-edge on the two outer variables, and read order quantity where straight-edge intersects inner scale.

COMPUTATION OF CARRYING CHARGES

(Yearly Cost Charged Against Value of Inventory)

Interest Rate on Investment ______%

Insurance Rate = $\dfrac{\text{Insurance Cost} \times 100}{\text{Ave. Inventory (\$)}}$ ______%

Storage Rate = $\dfrac{\text{All Storage Costs} \times 100}{\text{Ave. Inventory (\$)}}$ ______%

Obsolescence Rate = $\dfrac{\text{Obsolescence Losses (\$)} \times 100}{\text{Ave. Inventory (\$)}}$ ______%

Deterioration Rate = $\dfrac{\text{Deterioration Costs} \times 100}{\text{Ave. Inventory (\$)}}$ ______%

Taxes, Miscellaneous ______%

Total Yearly Carrying Charge ______%

CONVERSION TO YOUR OWN CARRYING CHARGE

To convert chart to your own yearly carrying charge, multiply figures on 24% side of vertical line by conversion factor, determined by following formula:

Conversion Factor = $\sqrt{\dfrac{24}{\text{Your Yearly Carrying Charge (\%)}}}$

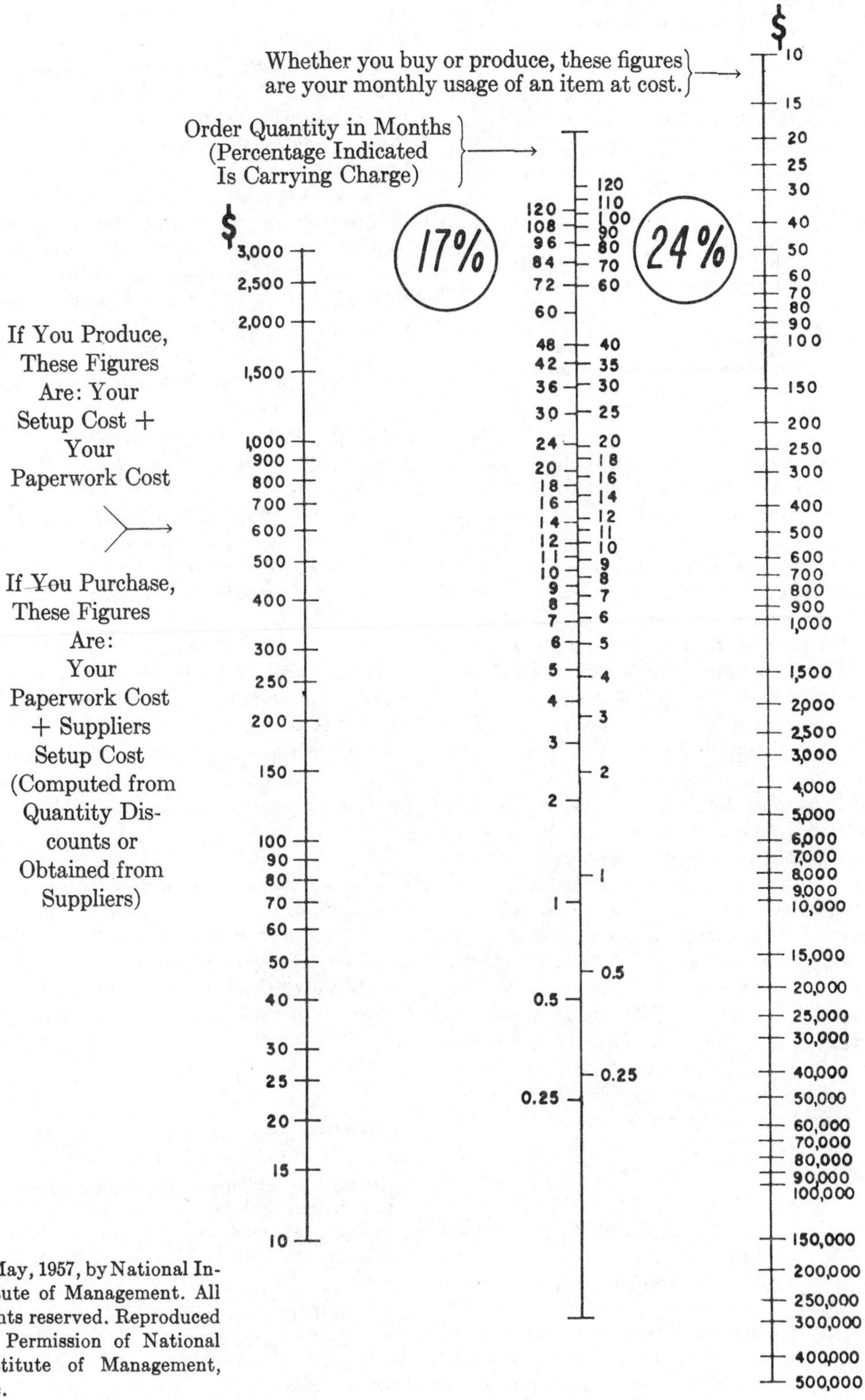

Whether you buy or produce, these figures are your monthly usage of an item at cost.
Order Quantity in Months (Percentage Indicated Is Carrying Charge)
17%
24%
If You Produce, These Figures Are: Your Setup Cost + Your Paperwork Cost
If You Purchase, These Figures Are: Your Paperwork Cost + Suppliers Setup Cost (Computed from Quantity Discounts or Obtained from Suppliers)
$

EXHIBIT V

COST EFFECT OF DEPARTING FROM ECONOMIC ORDER QUANTITY

If you produce (or buy) only this part of the proper order quantity	*Then your base costs will increase by this amount*
10%	405%
20%	160%
33%	67%
50%	25%
80%	3%
100%	0%
125%	3%
200%	25%
300%	67%
500%	160%
1000%	405%

facts on costs of getting for C items than the expected savings. Hence, indirectly, the classification procedure actually saves money two ways.

Applying the formula to the A and B group involves only 40% of the work had we applied it to the whole inventory.

Reorder Points. The preceding discussion determined *how much* to order. We still face the question of *when*—the question of delivery.

Studies begun in 1923 at the Bell Telephone Laboratories under the direction of R. H. Wilson show that inventories tend to follow the "Poisson distribution." In other words, their random fluctuations are definable by probability. (Poisson distribution is discussed in STATISTICS.)

When an item is on order, there are three things that vary, creating the total fluctuations in usage: first, the length of the lead time varies. Lead times which average two weeks, may frequently vary, in practice, from one to four weeks. In a typical study made of one vendor over a period of one year involving 67 orders, the vendor took an average of 61.2 days to give delivery. *He was promising delivery in three weeks!* Secondly, the size of the orders will vary. One customer buys two pieces, another 300. Thirdly, the number of orders varies. One week we may have ten customers, another thirty.

Because the true inventory usage has three variables, it involves a so-called "tri-variate Poisson distribution." Because of the cost of solving such a formula, practice dictates simplification to something more workable. In a commonly used procedure where these advanced techniques are applied, the length of the lead time is averaged; the size of the order is averaged; and the Poisson is applied only to the number of orders. Tests and comparisons between the two procedures shows that the simplified approach is practical and reasonable. This simplified procedure will be discussed here.

Exhibit I showed an item in which the usage is about twelve per month. For a two week lead time *(average),* we would expect to use about six units. However, we would not wait until we reached six units in inventory before reordering. If we did, we would stock-out half the time. By means of the Poisson formula, we can predict our chances of stock-outs for *any* given reorder point.

Or to invert the thinking, we can use the Poisson to establish the reorder point, if we will state *how many stock-outs we will accept.*

Policy on Stock-Outs. If we do not stock-out, we are carrying too much. For example, a study by R. H. Wilson at the Bell Telephone Laboratories revealed requirements as shown in Exhibit VI.

The "never" is in quotes, because theoretically, at least, there is always some slight chance of stock-outs even with a very large inventory. Note that the $200,000 increase in inventory is really an increase in cushion or protective stocks. The cost of carrying such protective inventory at 25% would be $50,000 a year!

It is clear that the real decision to be made is a policy decision on stock-outs. Naturally, this policy will vary with companies and products. A common policy is to permit stock-out once every two years on all items except highly critical ones. Critical items may call for a "never" policy and hence should be carefully

EXHIBIT VI

INVENTORY REQUIREMENTS AS AFFECTED BY ACCEPTABLE STOCK-OUTS

Accepting 1 stock-out a year required an inventory of only $76,000

Accepting 1 stock-out every 2 years increased the required inventory to $100,000

Accepting 1 stock-out every 5 years increased the required inventory to $134,000

Accepting 1 stock-out every 10 years increased the required inventory to $167,000

"Never" out of stock increased the required inventory to $276,000

selected. In other words, cars can be delivered without a fifth tire, but not without engines.

In the following discussion, we shall assume a policy of once every two years.

The Relation Between EOQ and Policy. For an EOQ of three months' usage, there are four times a year in which a stock-out can occur (i.e., such an item will be on order four times a year). Hence, if this item stocked-out 25% of the time, it would stock-out once a year. To stock-out once every two years, would be to stock-out 12.5% of the time.

With a one-month EOQ, we could permit stock-outs only 4% of the time, to achieve a stock-out every two years.

The Poisson Solution. The formula for the Poisson is:

$$\mathbf{P}\,[c] = (a^c e^{-a})/c!.$$

By this formula, we can compute the probability of using c units, when our *average* usage is a. Fortunately, we do not have to solve such a formula to get the reorder point, but can read directly from a chart, as shown in Exhibit VII (see following two pages).

The top of the chart gives the per cent of stock-outs we will accept. For a one-month EOQ, this was found to be 4%, if we permit one stock-out every two years. From the left, we read our usage during the lead time. Let us assume a usage of six during the lead time, such as does occur in Exhibit I.

Coming down from the top of the chart and in from the side, lines drawn from the 4% and the figure 6 meet at the (interpolated) curve reading about 11. This is the reorder point.

Cost of Stock-Out. A further extension of the Poisson may be made by using cost figures in place of company policy to get the percentage figure at the top of Exhibit VII. This approach is possible if we can develop figures showing how much it costs to stock-out. In some cases, for example, it costs very little to run across the street to the hardware store and buy an item. This cost could be the basis for such an approach.

The formula for determining the proper per cent of stock-outs when we know the cost, is

$$\% = \frac{100 \times \text{EOQ} \times \text{H} \times \text{C}}{12 \times \text{M} \times \text{K}}$$

Where the EOQ is in dollars, H is cost of having in per cent, C is cost per piece in dollars, M is monthly usage in dollars, and K is cost of stock-out in dollars.

Example: EOQ = \$308
H = 25%
C = \$ 22
M = \$308
K = \$ 14

$$\frac{100 \times 308 \times \frac{1}{4} \times 22}{12 \times 308 \times 14} = 3.3\%$$

Hence, 3.3% would be the figure to read from the top of Exhibit VII.

Conclusion. There is still much work to be done in the field of inventory control. There is need for research and greater interest on the part of industry. However, the methods described in the foregoing are in general use where advanced practice is followed. Scientific management of inventory can free significant capital for use elsewhere in the business. The two keys are economic order quantities for the variable portion of inventory, and a policy of cushions or safety stocks based on the application of mathematical probability, so that an exorbitant price will not be paid for an unnecessarily low (or "never") acceptable stockout percentage.

NYLES V. REINFELD, Director, National Institute of Management, Inc., Bath, Ohio

Information References

Associations:

American Production and Inventory Control Society.

Texts:

Drucker, Peter F., "Management Tasks, Responsibilities, Practices," New York, Harper & Row, 1973.

Mann, Rolad, ed., "The Arts of Top Management: A McKinsey Anthology," New York, McGraw-Hill, 1971.

Plossl, G. W., "Manufacturing Control: The Last Frontier for Profits," Reston, Va., Reston Publishing, 1973.

——— and Mather, H. F., "The Master Production Schedule: Managements Handle on the Business," Reston, Va., Reston Publishing, 1975.

——— and Welch, W. Evert, "The Role of Top Management in the Control of Inventory," Reston, Va., Reston Publishing, 1979.

Reinfield, Nyles V., "Production Control," Englewood Cliffs, N.J., Prentice-Hall, 1963

———, "Survival Management for Industry," Reston, Va., Reston Publishing, 1981.

Articles:

Reinfeld, Nyles V., "The Ghosts of Rome," *Commodities,* December, 1979.

———, "Turnaround or Bankruptcy," *Buckeye Business Journal,* February, 1980.

———, and Meddor, Ron, "Release Scheduling and Allocation, *Tooling & Production,* January, 1975.

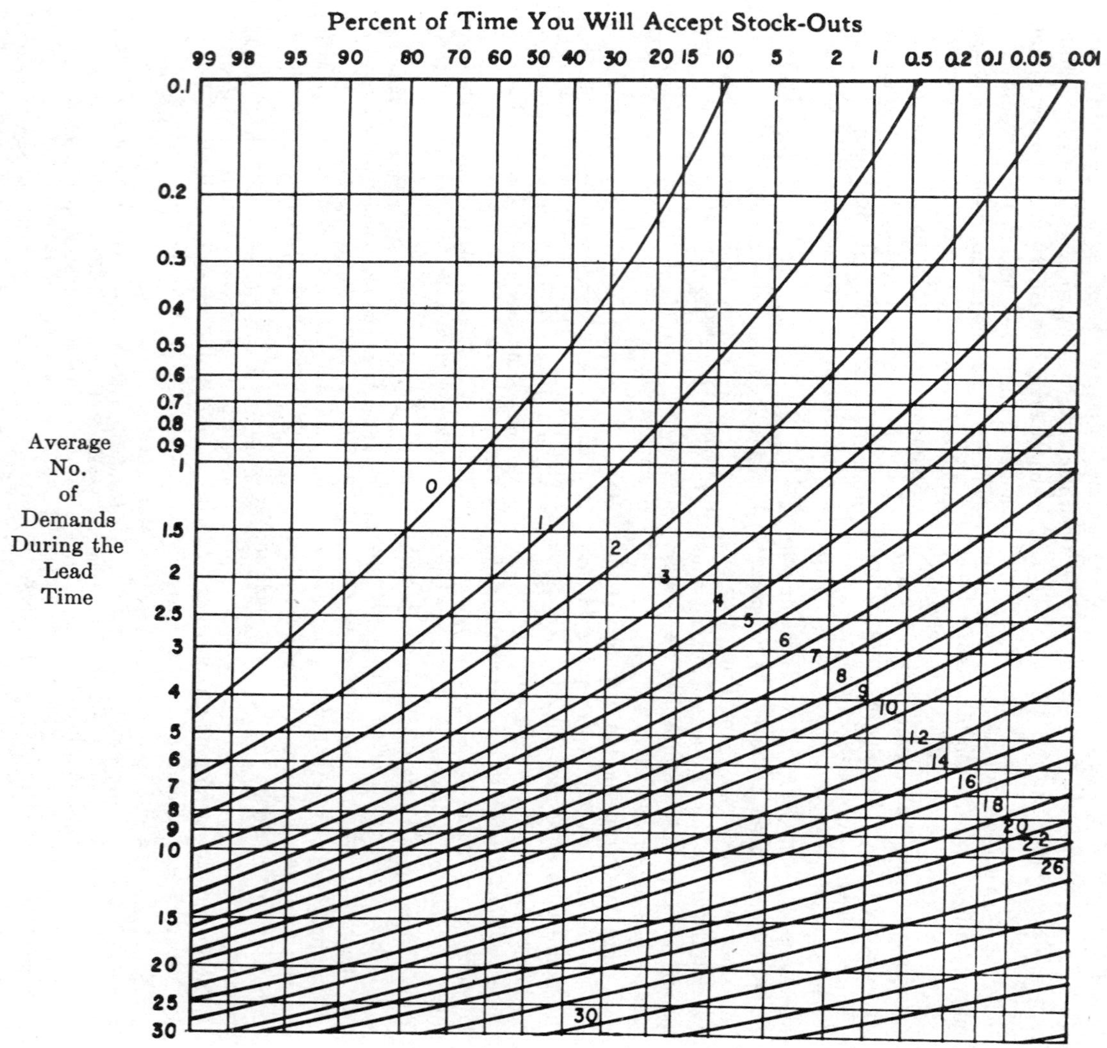

Exhibit VII

REORDER POINT CHART

TO USE CHART:

1. Select correct usage figure for item to be protected.
2. Select percent of stock-outs you will accept.
3. Find point where 1 and 2 intersect: Read reorder point from curves at intersection.

IF GREATER ACCURACY IS DEMANDED, or where usage during lead time exceeds the chart, the reorder point can also be calculated directly as follows:

1. Determine "Factor" from table below based on percent of time you will accept stock-outs.
2. Take the square-root of the usage during the lead time. (This can be gotten from a table of square-roots.)
3. Multiply square-root of usage by "Factor."
4. Add usage during lead time to product found in 3.
5. Answer is the reorder point.

Average
No.
of
Demands
During the
Lead
Time

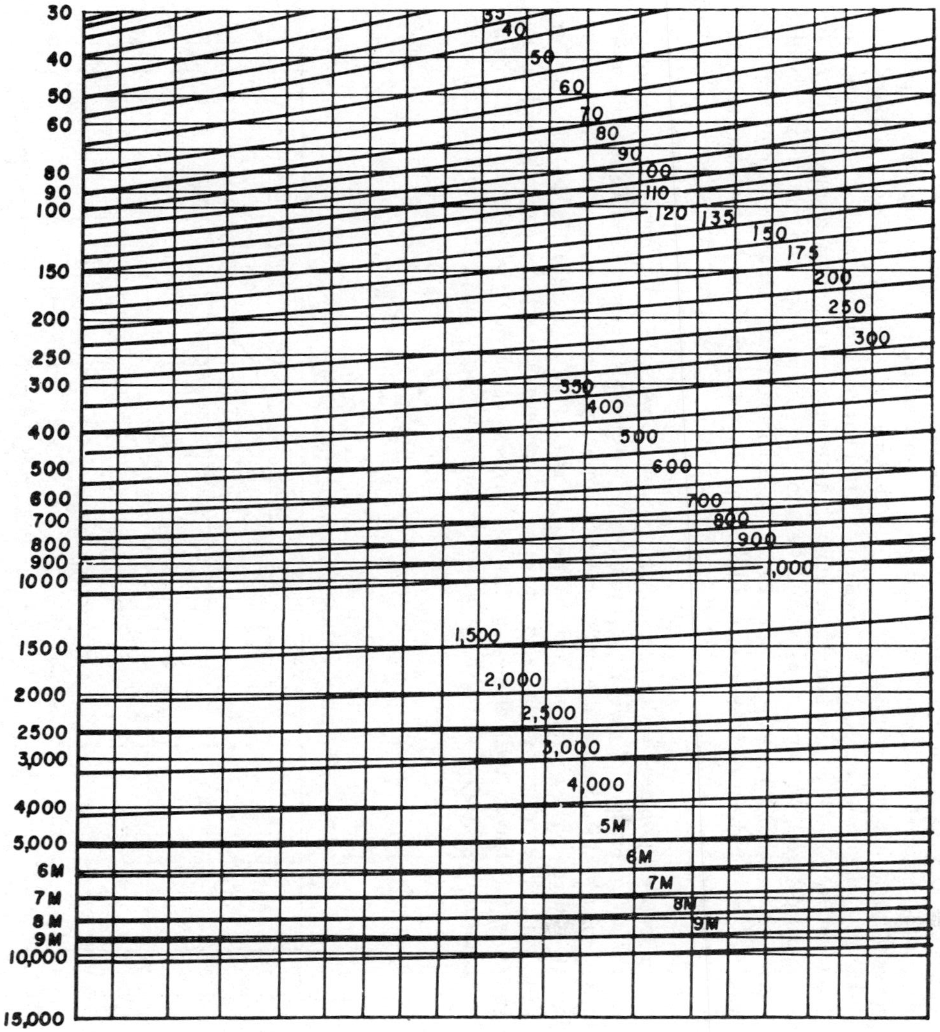

Factors	Acceptable % of Stock-outs
4.0	"Never"
3.5	.023
3.0	.135
2.8	.26
2.6	.47
2.5	.62
2.4	.82
2.33	1.00
2.17	1.50
2.06	2.00
1.96	2.50
1.89	3.00
1.82	3.50
1.76	4.00
1.65	5.00
1.56	6.00
1.48	7.00
1.41	8.00
1.35	9.00
1.29	10.00
1.16	12.50
1.04	15.00
1.00	15.87
0.85	20.00
0.68	25.00
0.53	30.00
0.39	35.00
0.26	40.00
0.13	45.00
0.00	50.00

EXAMPLE

1. 1% stock-outs: Factor = 2.33.
2. Assume usage during lead time is 100.
   $\sqrt{100} = 10$
3. $10 \times 2.33 = 23.3$
4. $100 + 23 = 123$
5. Reorder point is 123

MEASUREMENT OF EFFECTIVENESS

There is no magic formula for evaluating the effectiveness of production and inventory management, since to a large extent, evaluation depends upon the point of view. There are however, many indexes useful for comparative purposes which cover the five major areas of interest to all segments of management.

On-Schedule Performance is the cornerstone of good operations. It is the measure of a well-coordinated organization, customer satisfaction, and usually, a reasonable and controllable work-in-process inventory.

There are a number of ways in which performance to schedule can be measured: (1) the amount of work, orders, or items behind schedule (Exhibit I); (2) aging of work behind schedule; (3) the per cent of schedule met; and (4) per cent of on-time shipments.

Records of performance should be made for direct comparison to the schedule. In addition to tabulated forms, key operations should be charted to emphasize relative performance to plan. Where improvement is necessary, dotted line projections on the chart are effective in stimulating progress.

Competitive Customer Service is essential in any business. Certainty of delivery to promise is not enough—the interval is equally important. If efficient plant operations are obtained at the expense of being over-regulated and too deliberate, the delivery interval may no longer be reasonably competitive and result in loss of business. Comparison of the length of time between receipt of order and shipment (not delivery promises) of competitors is the best measure but it is usually difficult to obtain accurate information. Promises and performance of vendors in related fields will prove helpful for comparative purposes and may be obtained from the Purchasing Department.

Lead-time charts which detail the time required to process an order and perform the manufacturing operations will provide revealing information on the total interval (Exhibit II). Almost invariably the preparation of such charts results in the telescoping of operations and shortening of time allowances to conform to management policies.

An analysis of performance to quoted intervals sometimes reveals differences between the planned interval and that which is quoted. This difference may be the amount in excess of truly competitive service, depending upon sales and management ethics. And finally, a comparison to previous practice and performance within the company will show whether or not there has been improvement in this area. The extent and rate of improvement together with some knowledge of the reason therefor, will help determine whether further progress is possible.

Inventory Investment and Turnover is an important factor in financial management. Turnover is the accepted index of inventory management. It reflects not only proportional investment but how well the stock is moving. The ratio varies widely from industry to indus-

EXHIBIT I

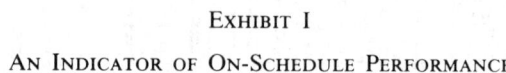

AN INDICATOR OF ON-SCHEDULE PERFORMANCE

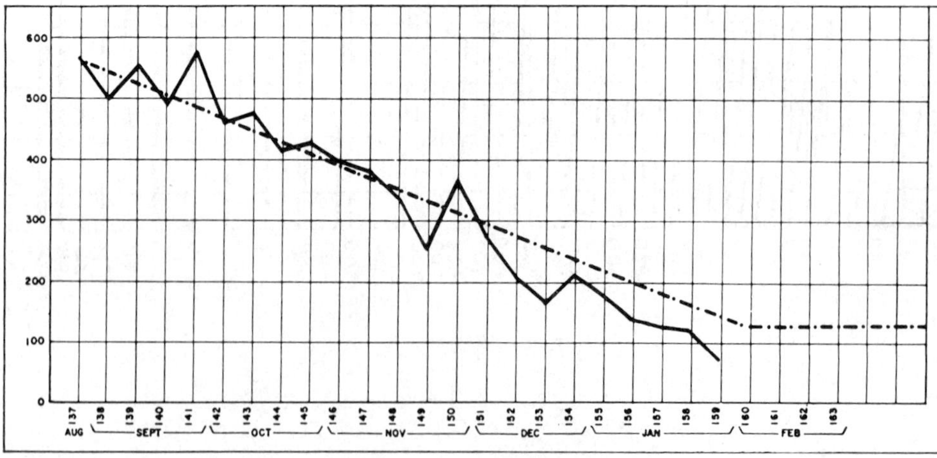

Graphic portrayal of items behind schedule, with projection indicating acceptable level.

Exhibit II

Lead-Time Chart

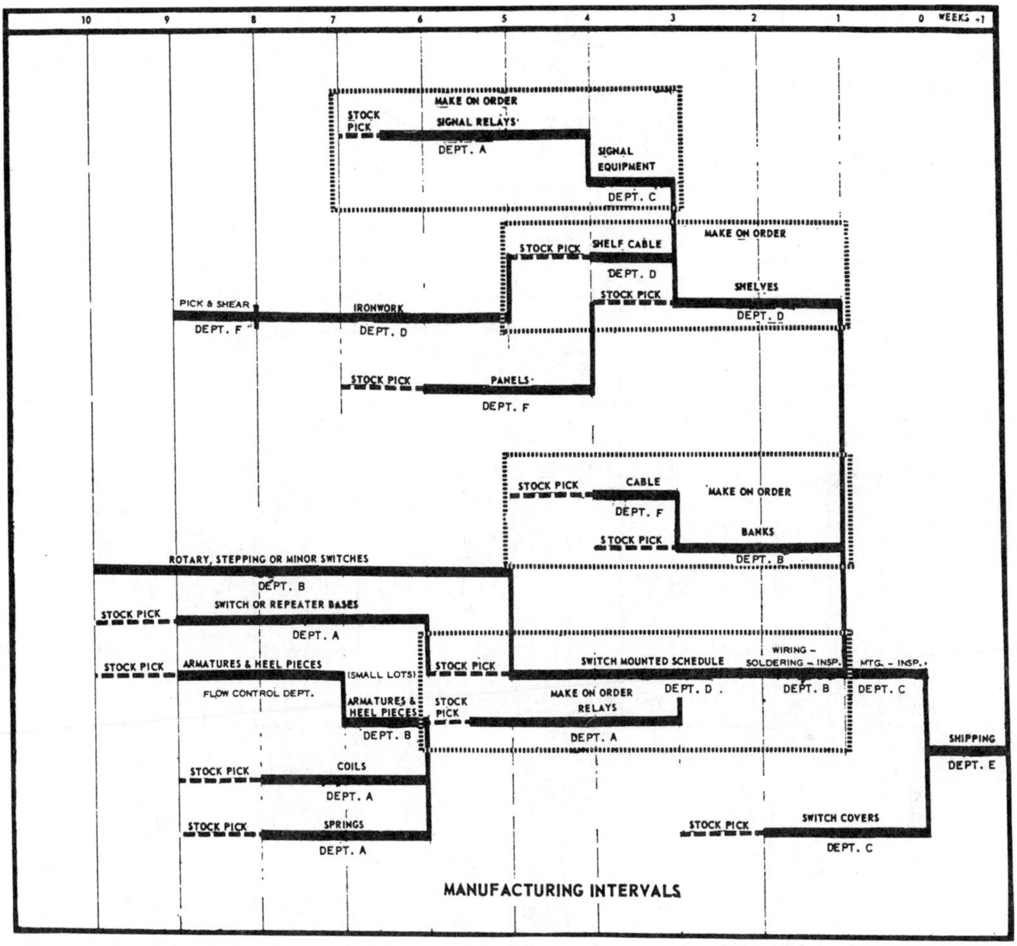

try since it is dependent upon the length of manufacturing and procurement intervals, competitive conditions, predictability of sales, perishability of the product, and financial considerations (Exhibit III.)

Historical precedence is a valuable guide and is usually the starting point in evaluation. There are frequently strong policy reasons which establish ordering and stocking practices, which in turn determine the basis for turnover. Operations research techniques and tighter control can bring about improvement, but for a specific period, turnover is largely influenced by the size of the starting inventory, ordering policies, and sales volume.

A convenient but less accurate ratio is used by Dun & Bradstreet, called, "Net Sales to Inventory Ratio." Net sales are defined as, "The dollar volume of business transacted for 365 days net after deductions for returns, allowances, and discounts from gross sales." The quotient obtained by dividing the annual net sales by the statement inventory does not represent the actual physical turnover, but it does provide a means of comparison from commonly available figures. (See Financial Ratios.)

Any evaluation of inventory control should take into consideration the methods and records used. Manual versus electronic data processing, perpetual or periodic audit methods, identification of obsolete materials, non-productive usage, and type of status reporting, may provide clues to the degree of sophistication and depth of understanding which exist.

Efficient Production Operation can be greatly affected by production control through ordering and scheduling. Planning is the basis

Exhibit III

Comparisons for Inventory Control *

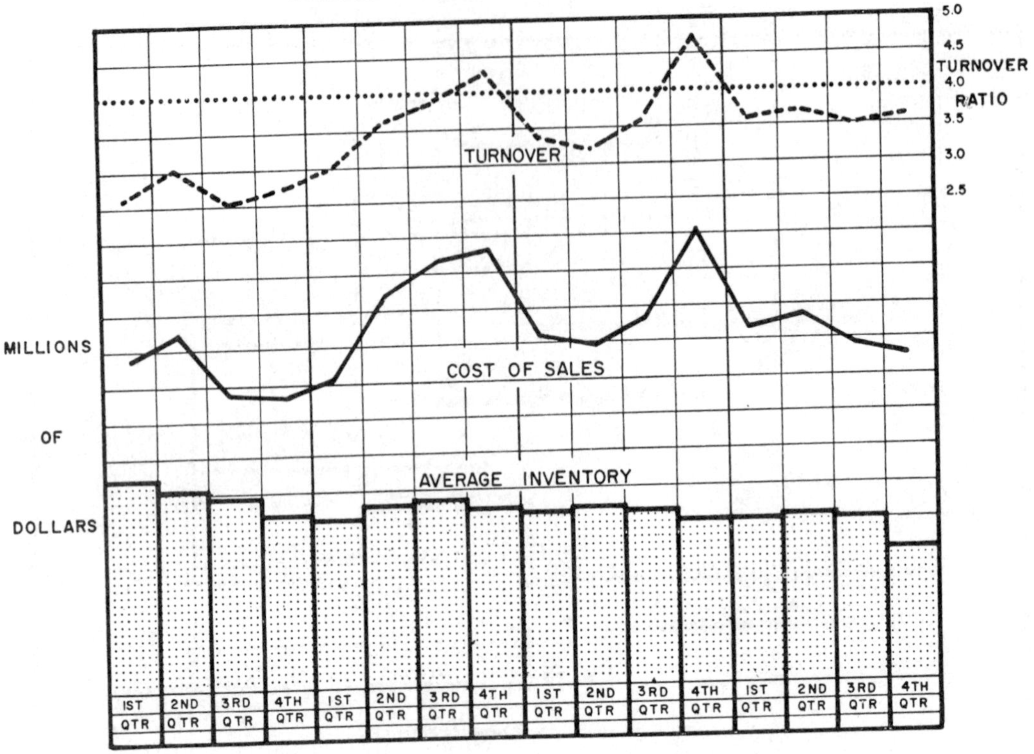

* *(Dollar figures omitted at request of subject company.)*

Exhibit IV

Actual vs. Planned Production

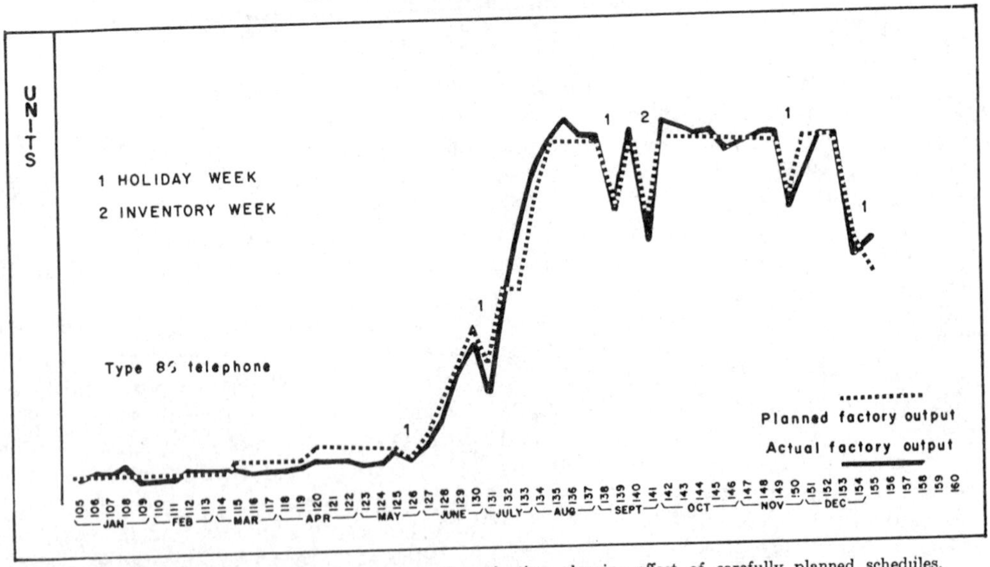

Graphic presentation of actual versus planned production, showing effect of carefully planned schedules. On "Inventory Week," physical inventory is taken, with no production on Friday of that week. Sequential numbering is used for the weeks, for the convenience of handling on data processing equipment.

of control (Exhibit IV). Equipment and labor capacities should be balanced against requirements and loaded accordingly. The sales forecast is an essential element and, depending upon its degree of accuracy, will mimimize fluctuations in employment levels and permit maximum utilization of plant.

Scheduling should be based upon known manufacturing intervals, which should be in an organized and usable form such as charts, listings, or computer memory. They should be accurate but provide reasonable allowance for contingencies. Clearly understood policies should be established on the amount of emergency or supplementary load which may be added to an existing schedule, and provision made therefor.

There are many yardsticks for evaluation in this area. Overtime, while not necessarily an indication of poor planning or scheduling, may be the only way to meet overloaded schedules. While some idle time is normal, wide fluctuations in the amount are usually danger signals. Interrupted production as evidenced by unfinished work set aside, layoffs, or excessive shifting of labor, should be noted.

Shortages as measured in frequency and volume are the most obvious and common index of inefficiency. A summary report showing number and distribution is extremely helpful in evaluating the degree and causes. The tolerance level varies widely from company to company, depending upon the complication of the product, technical development, and whether lead times are ample or tight. Historical averages help to judge, but observation on the amount of effort expended to relieve shortages is the best guide.

The Production Control Department varies in size and cost according to type of industry, complication of product, degree of control desired, and methods used. The volume of work in production control for a job shop is considerably greater than in a straight line production plant or process industry. The proportion of repetitive to special parts and whether the product is engineered to the customer's requirement or a standard manufacturer's design make a great deal of difference in the size and cost of the control group.

Some yardsticks prove useful either on an historical comparison within a company or for comparison to similar businesses: A common measure is the ratio of the number of production control employees to direct factory labor, or total employment. A similar ratio of production control employees to cost of sales is useful. Another measure is the percentage of production control burden to cost of sales. It is important when using such measures, to make certain that comparisons are on the same basis; that employees performing the functions of planning, scheduling, ordering, dispatching, and expediting, are counted whether they are in the department or not. There is a direct relationship between the amount of work in Production Control and the volume of paperwork. Simple measures such as the number of shop orders issued can be helpful, but any system of work measurement of basic paperwork would be more effective. Allowances must be made for certain fixed staff functions and supervision which are affected only by major changes in work level.

Summary. In the final analysis, it is total performance that counts. Sometimes this is somewhat intangible, but is felt nonetheless. Top management must be convinced the scheduling and inventory are under good control, efficiently administered, using modern techniques, and cooperating well with other departments. The sales organization expects sufficient flexibility to allow consideration of customer's special problems. A stiff, inflexible system and attitude will fail in this important area. It also wants prompt receipt of information on the status of an order and confidence in the accuracy of such information. Other departments likewise, expect certain standards of performance.

To satisfy all of these factors, or to make reasonable compromises where all cannot be satisifed, Production Control must know what is going on in Manufacturing, Sales, and Engineering Development. Sufficient control points and a reporting procedure must be established which will give a clear picture of factory operations. Communications in other areas depend upon personal contact and regular review of operations reports to be continuously informed. In the important area of human relations, technical perfection alone will not do the job. To perform its task successfully, Production Control must function well in all areas.

PHILIP A. LINK, Production Control Manager, Automatic Electric Company, Northlake, Illinois

Cross References: *(all sections): Business Forecasting; Cost Accounting (Managerial Accounting); FIFO/LIFO Inventory Accounting; Financial Ratios; Gantt Chart; Industrial Engineering; Line of Balance (LOB); Line of Balance: Day-Control;*

Manufacturing Management; Materials Management; Production: Large Scale; Purchasing; Standard Costing; Vendor Rating; Warehousing; Warehousing: The Public Warehouse.

PRODUCTIVITY: Concepts and Measures

Productivity refers to the relative efficiency or effectiveness with which resources are used in the production of goods or the delivery of services. When the same quantity of input yields more or "better" goods or services in one time period than in another, or when the same quantity of output is produced with less input, we say that productivity is higher, or has increased.

Since resources are always scarce compared with people's wants, managers in every economic system concentrate on increasing their yield. The productivity problem is to determine various feasible alternative combinations of labor, capital, materials, land, and energy, and to select the combination that yields the optimal ratio of output to these inputs. "Productivity," writes Peter Drucker, "is a difficult concept, but it is central. Without productivity objectives, a business does not have direction. Without productivity measurements, it does not have control."

The productivity concept applies to any level of activity, and measures may be made for a cost center or individual product up to a whole plant, company, industry, or even the economy. It is applicable to the productivity of services, as well as goods, in the public as well as the private sector.

Output/Input Ratios. A variety of output/input ratios fit the productivity definition. Each measure is designed to answer different questions. The best known concept—labor productivity—traces the change in quantity of output per unit of work input. Thus, it can be used to compare output per hour in one period with that of an earlier period characterized by a different scale of output or method of production. Furthermore, output per hour of work can be compared across countries which operate under different systems of management of resources and technology.

There are many other single-factor ratios of interest. Thus, instead of confining attention to labor input, we may measure output per dollar of capital input, or per BTU of energy consumed or per square or cubic foot of space, and, in agriculture, we may focus on yield per acre of land. All of these measures are plausible and valid indicators of productivity, and the selection depends on the purpose intended.

A more complex variant—composite or "multifactor productivity"—relates output to a combination of resources used in production, each appropriately weighted. Multifactor productivity, combining labor and capital, tells how efficiently both factors are employed jointly in production. It is useful for reflecting changes in productivity of a combination of inputs, especially when one of them may be substituted in some degree over time, as in the case of substitution of capital, in the form of machinery, for labor.

Since each ratio deals with a different facet of productive activity, they are not interchangeable. They may show different rates of change over time. Moreover, no one ratio can be said to be the single true measure of productivity. To avoid confusion, it is always important to make clear which specific ratio is being used. A family of consistent ratios for any given firm or process can be particularly useful to a manager interested in determining areas or operations requiring improvement.

Measuring output and input often involves many complex, methodological problems. The output of an industry or firm may be defined as gross or net of materials and supplies purchased from other industries. Productivity based on a net output measure would be less affected by changes in the integration of operations than a measure based on gross output. Another issue is handling radical changes in the quality or design of products such as autos, computers, or refrigerators. Measures of the quantity of output must therefore be adjusted to include these changes in order to assure valid comparisons. In the construction industry, measurement deals with the output of custom-made goods which might be best handled by a "sub-product" or "sub-activity" approach rather than the usual end-product measurement.

Quantifying some of the less tangible outputs of banks, insurance companies, hospitals, hotels and motels, and other service industries and government may require special interpretation. Managers in these industries can often identify common "sub-product" or "sub-activities" that when combined result in the successful delivery of their service.

The desire for a single measure of output for different products of an individual company or industry requires the selection of an appropriate weighting system to represent their importance in the aggregate. Theoretically, in measuring labor productivity, unit labor requirements are preferred as weights; in practice, unit values or prices are usually employed as weights of product classes.

The measurement of input also involves various conceptual choices. For example, labor input may be measured as the total number of hours worked, or paid, or the total number of persons employed. Total hours spent in production take account of differences between two periods in the average length of the work week or work year. Furthermore, hours may be aggregated without any distinction regarding the hours worked by employees of different levels of skill. Or instead, they may be weighted by wages or salaries to take account of differences in their quality.

The measurement of capital input involves many conceptual challenges. Apart from the choice between capital stock and capital services, there is a need to decide between gross capital and capital net of depreciation. Also, the scope of capital is not self-evident. It may be measured in terms of tangible capital invested in plant, equipment, tools and rolling stock, land, and mines; it may also include all kinds of inventories; or it could be extended further to include intangible capital invested in education, training, and health for the improvement of the quality of labor. Finally, even a measure limited to the quantity of tangible capital input involves many complex decisions regarding the treatment of items of different age, price, model, size, and technology, and the estimation of depreciation according to various tax and accounting conventions.

For a manager interpreting changes in output/input ratios, whether labor productivity or the composite or multifactor productivity, it is important not to impute to the denominator the entire responsibility for the level of productivity or its increase or decrease. The effort of labor contributes to the changes in measured labor productivity, but many other variables are pertinent too—for example, work-force skills, production techniques and capital equipment, managerial knowledge and ability, the rate of capacity utilization, the scale of operations, materials flow, product mix, the state of industrial relations, the level of technology employed, the weather, and other factors that cannot readily be quantified, if at all. Any composite measure, too, fails to account exhaustively for all the inputs. For example, a measure of labor and capital input may not cover the input of entrepreneurship, nor does it cover the contribution of government. Those factors that cannot be included in the measure of input can, however, be discussed in the interpretation of the change in the ratio.

Important Distinctions. Although the concept of productivity is generally familiar to managers, it is sometimes confused with production, i.e., the quantity of goods and services produced without regard to the quantity of resources used. It is also sometimes mistakenly equated with profitability, or return on sales or assets, a standard financial measure for judging the progress of a company or industry, which is influenced by productivity but does not necessarily reflect changes in the ratio of quantities of inputs and outputs.

It is important to distinguish "productivity" from conditions affecting it and methods of improving it, such as reduction of absenteeism, turnover, grievances, or the acquisition of a new piece of machinery. Productivity can be improved by correction of counterproductive behavior and the implementation of new technology, but its measure still relates output to resources used. The tendency to use "productivity" loosely as a synonym for other concepts can create confusion and mis-direct improvement efforts.

Statistics. Statistics on national productivity are published regularly by the U.S. Bureau of Labor Statistics (BLS). The output measure is based on U.S. Department of Commerce estimates of the constant dollar market value of final goods and services produced by the sector. These estimates are derived by deflating (i.e., adjusting for price changes) current dollar values reported in the national income accounts.

Quarterly and annual indexes of output per hour are published for the private business sector, as well as for nonfarm business, corporate, and manufacturing sectors. The input of hours covers all persons producing the output, including proprietors, employees, self-employed, and unpaid family workers. Series are also prepared covering only employees. In addition, annual indexes of output per hour are published for about 100 individual industries. Special series are prepared for the Federal Government, and for 28 different functions. The BLS also publishes comparative series on output per hour in manufacturing for the U.S.

and major industrialized nations in western Europe, Canada, and Japan.

Productivity series based on the multifactor concept have been developed for the private business sector by Dr. John W. Kendrick and Dr. Elliott S. Grossman. These series are updated annually and published by the American Productivity Center.

National productivity measures are useful to managers for understanding the economic environment of the firm. They are vital to explanation of inflation, international competitiveness, and the standard of living. Exhibit I depicts the annual rates of change in output per hour in major sectors of the U.S. economy in different periods since 1947. The figures highlight the slowdown in the U.S. that began after 1965 and which became more acute after 1973.

The significance of recent productivity trends for persistent inflation is examined in Exhibit II, showing the annual rates of change in output per hour, compensation per hour, unit labor cost, and prices. Compensation per hour (all persons) includes wages and salaries plus supplemental payments such as employer contribution to Social Security and private health and pension funds; also, an estimate of salaries for the self-employed and proprietors. Unit labor cost (representing the cost of labor to produce a unit of output) is derived by adjusting the change in hourly compensation by changes in output per hour. Exhibit II shows hourly compensation increasing much more rapidly than output per hour after 1965. Rising unit labor cost, the major component of price, contributed significantly to the sharp rise in prices which, in turn, created pressures for increased hourly compensation.

EXHIBIT I

RATES OF CHANGE IN OUTPUT PER HOUR, UNITED STATES PRIVATE BUSINESS SECTOR & MAJOR DIVISIONS, SELECTED PERIODS, 1947–1979.

	Average Annual Rate of Change		
Sector	1947–65	1965–73	1973–79
Private business sector	3.4	2.3	0.6
Farm	5.7	5.3	3.1
Non-farm	2.4	1.8	1.0
Manufacturing	3.2	2.5	1.5

SOURCE: U.S. Bureau of Labor Statistics

EXHIBIT II

RATES OF CHANGE IN OUTPUT PER HOUR, HOURLY COMPENSATION, UNIT LABOR COST, AND PRICES, PRIVATE BUSINESS SECTOR, SELECTED PERIODS, 1950–1979.

	Average Annual Rate of Change			
Item	1950–60	1960–65	1965–73	1973–79
Output per hour	2.6	3.9	2.1	1.2
Compensation per hour	5.2	4.3	6.9	8.9
Unit Labor Cost	2.5	0.4	4.6	7.6
Prices	2.1	1.1	4.2	7.3

SOURCE: U.S. Bureau of Labor Statistics

The productivity figures for recent years show a slowdown that has aroused deep concern among businessmen about the lagging competitiveness of American industry and the possible need for basic readjustments in managerial practices. Exhibit III shows comparative

EXHIBIT III

OUTPUT PER HOUR AND UNIT LABOR COSTS IN MANUFACTURING, 11 COUNTRIES, 1960–79, AVERAGE ANNUAL RATES OF CHANGE.

	Average Annual Rate of Change	
Country	*Output per hour*	*Unit labor cost (U.S. Dollar Basis)*
United States	2.5	3.9
Canada	4.0	4.1
Japan	8.3	9.1
Belgium (1)	7.3	7.1
Denmark	6.8	6.8
Federal Republic of Germany	5.4	9.2
France	5.6	6.1
Italy	6.1	7.5
Netherlands (1)	7.3	8.6
Sweden	5.5	7.4
United Kingdom	3.2	6.0

(1) Data related to period ending 1978 only.
SOURCE: U.S. Bureau of Labor Statistics

international data on productivity and unit labor costs in manufacturing, estimated by U.S. Bureau of Labor Statistics. U.S. output per hour grew more slowly than the rates for other industrialized countries. Unit labor costs (measured in U.S. dollar terms to take account of relative changes in exchange rates) also increased at a lower rate. The level of U.S. productivity, not shown here, however, still exceeds that of other countries, but the gap is closing.

Implementation. Productivity according to Drucker, "is the first test of management's competence." Special programs are being introduced in many companies to improve productivity performance. In some large companies, productivity coordinators, reporting to the top manufacturing manager, the comptroller or other high-level executives, have been appointed, with responsibility to plan corporate-wide efforts.

An important step in planning an effective improvement program is establishing a system for measuring productivity. Many different types of organizations, ranging from manufacturing firms to insurance companies and government agencies, monitor their performance periodically to heighten interest in improvement efforts, locate problem areas, and devise correctional steps. Labor productivity ratios or work measurements are used to discover cases of underperformance and overstaffing. Group wage incentive systems (e.g., SCANLON, EDDY-RUCKER-NICKELS, Improshare) involve calculation of productivity or labor cost as a basis for determining bonus payments. Measurement is indispensable in appraising the effectiveness of remedial action.

If a firm can compare its performance with that of other firms in the same industry, as well as monitor its performance over time, it can greatly enhance the usefulness of its measurment program. Some companies construct their productivity indexes so that they can be compared with the BLS index for their industry. More elaborate interfirm comparison systems have been developed by trade associations. For example, in the wholesale grocery industry, the trade association collects data on 63 different productivity ratios covering various warehousing operations and compiles the data into industry averages for comparative purposes. These data are reported to participants for use in analyzing their relative standing and determining operations needing improvement.

Productivity measurement at the plant level was encouraged by the National Center for Productivity and Quality of Working Life as a useful and inexpensive tool for improving productivity. Assistance in establishing a productivity measurement program is now obtainable from the American Productivity Center, state productivity centers such as those established at universities in Utah, Maryland, Oklahoma, and Georgia, and private consultants. (See Encyclopedia Appendix A.)

Outside the United States, national productivity centers which operate in Western European, Japan, and other market economies, sponsor interfirm productivity comparison programs as a tool of industrial strategy. The Canadian government assists firms in various industries through a voluntary program of interfirm comparisons of productivity and profitability. On the basis of a firm's operating performance, government-paid consultants advise managers on remedial action to improve its performance.

Productivity improvements are achievable through action at the plant level in three major areas: plant and equipment, organization and control of production, and personnel and industrial relations. Selected examples of possible actions are briefly presented in the following paragraphs.

Modernization of plant and equipment, either through installation of the latest technological processes and machinery or through modification of existing equipment, reduces the amount of labor, energy, materials, or capital to produce a unit of output. Faster, larger, more powerful, more reliable and more accurate tools and equipment, more integrated and automatic production machinery, mechanized materials handling, automatic inspection—all of these improve the effectiveness with which operations are carried out. Computer-aided design, computer-aided manufacture, robots, and automated assembly are new advances in automation that may significantly increase productivity in the future. (See AUTOMATION AND ROBOTS IN INDUSTRY.)

Even when substantial changes in capital equipment cannot be made, it is possible to use more fully and efficiently the available means of production through better planning, organization, and production control. Productivity gains can be achieved through changes in plant layout, standardization, simplification, and specialization of products, scheduling materials flow to minimize inventory, downtime, and overtime, and coordination of specialized activities. Group technology, which is designed to identify and code various existing part characteristics to reduce handling and to rationalize new parts design, will also facilitate automation. Management science provides many computerized approaches to optimize production control for productivity gains.

Mangers are increasingly concerned with enhancing the contribution of all employees to improving productivity and the overall performance of the enterprise. Considerable attention is given to ON-THE-JOB TRAINING, skill apprenticeship, employee career development, and professional education, to upgrade the quality of the work force. Some companies concentrate on involving employees in improving performance at the individual's work station through use of WORK SIMPLIFICATION, ZERO DEFECTS techniques, VALUE ANALYSIS, and comparative cost analysis. To reward higher performance, some companies have established one of several available INCENTIVE SYSTEMS, including: sales commissions, bonuses, suggestion system rewards, etc. Techniques of PERFORMANCE APPRAISAL, MANAGEMENT BY OBJECTIVES, and effective feedback communication are a few of the behavioral science programs being used to improve performance.

Newer concepts of participatory problem-solving, focus on QUALITY CIRCLES, joint labor-management consultation or committees, and QUALITY OF WORKING LIFE projects. Some companies are using employee stock ownership as a means of stimulating employee interest in the organization's goals. As the productivity slowdown becomes an increasingly serious challenge to U.S. competitiveness, management and labor are coming to the conclusion that they may need to cooperate more closely for their mutual survival.

There is no simple formula for productivity improvement that fits all firms or governmental operations. Each enterprise must study its own situation and adopt the improvement techniques most suitable to its circumstances.

GEORGE H. KUPER, Associate, Production Resources Staff, General Electric Company, Bridgeport, Conn.; formerly Director, National Center for Productivity and Quality of Working Life, Washington, D.C.

EDGAR WEINBERG, Consulting Economist, Bethesda, Md., formerly Assistant Director, National Center for Productivity and Quality of Working Life

Information References

Drucker, Peter F., "Management: Tasks, Responsibilities, Practices," New York, Harper & Row, 1974.

Fabricant, Solomon, "A Primer on Productivity," New York, Random House, 1969.

Greenberg, Leon, "A Practical Guide to Productivity Measurement," Washington, Bureau of National Affairs, 1973.

Hinrichs, John R., "Practical Management for Productivity," (Work in America Institute Series), New York, Van Nostrand Reinhold, 1978.

Kendrick, John W., "Understanding Productivity, an Introduction to the Dynamics of Productivity Change," Baltimore, Johns Hopkins University Press, 1977.

"Measurement and Interpretation of Productivity," Washington, D.C., Nat'l. Acad. of Sciences, 1980.

Rosow, Jerome M., ed., "Productivity: Prospects for Growth," New York, Van Nostrand Reinhold, 1981.

Siegel, Irving H., "Company Productivity: Measurement for Improvement," Kalamazoo, Mich., Upjohn Institute for Employment Research, 1980.

U.S. Government Publications:

U.S. Bureau of Labor Statistics:

Productivity and Costs, quarterly.

Productivity Indexes for Selected Industries, annual.

Productivity: A Selected Annotated Bibliography, 1976–78, *Bulletin 2051,* 1980.

International Comparisons of Manufacturing Productivity and Labor Costs, annual.

Stein, Herbert and Mark, Jerome A., "The Meaning and Measurement of Productivity," *Bulletin 1714,* 1971.

"Improving Productivity: A Description of Selected Company Programs," 1975.

"Improving Productivity Through Industry and Company Measurement," 1976.

PROFIT SHARING

Profit-Sharing programs are currently being initiated in American industry at the rate of more than 125 every working day. Executives are finding the incentives, versatility, and flexibility inherent in profit sharing advantageous in gaining greater employee cooperation, reducing labor turnover, raising productivity, cutting costs and providing retirement security.

Formal Definition. *Profit sharing* is an adaptable organizational incentive program under which an employer pays to employees, in addition to prevailing wages, special current or deferred sums based on the profits of the business. Quite distinct from individual incentive pay, small group production bonuses, and pension plans, it is a means of giving employees a direct stake in profitability—a common venture with a common gain.

John H. Leslie, Chairman of Signode Corp., Chicago (a medium-sized manufacturer sharing its profits since 1941) described profit sharing as a system of industrial partnership which fills a fundamental human need in modern corporations: "In a little over a hundred years, Americans have moved from an agricultural, small-craft economy where most people were motivated and rewarded by profits to one where millions of our fellow citizens are wage-earning employees who are not so motivated or rewarded. . . . Millions are divorced from the profit motive of our economic system. . . . During this country's transition to our present-day corporate form of organization, a vital and traditional element in our society was largely lost—*the personal involvement of the individual in the fortunes of the enterprise.* Profit sharing fills this void by restoring to each individual that element of personal involvement in the fortunes of his company and by making him realize that he is a responsible, appreciated member of the corporate group" [1].

Profit sharing means much more than mere "money-sharing"—it means "sharing the caring" in the business. It is a way of developing an atmosphere in which employees want the business to succeed as much as management does. A partnership evolves, out of which flows appropriate information sharing, responsibility sharing, participation, a sense of belonging. Money-sharing then becomes the essential outward sign and vital cohesive force of this partnership.

True profit sharing is not a *static* concept—a redistribution of existing profits, but rather a *dynamic* concept—a creation of "efficiency earnings" (extra profits) in which all can share. It provides an extra reward for added cooperative activity over and above the regular line of duty.

Types of Programs. There are three basic types of profit-sharing programs:

Cash (Current): where profit shares are paid out directly (immediately) in cash (or stock) to employees.

Deferred: where profit shares are paid into a trust fund on behalf of individual employees and distributed to them at a later date or contingency—e.g., retirement.

Combination: where part of the profit share is paid out directly in cash and part is deferred into a trust fund.

It should be emphasized that profit sharing is not a substitute for other well-conceived personnel and industrial relations programs. Fair wages based on adequate job evaluation and wage survey programs, an opportunity to increase individual earnings through properly administered wage incentive and merit rating programs, and sound promotion policies are only a few of the many industrial practices that have an important role to play in the total corporate picture. Profit sharing builds on these other programs and partially depends on them for its success. For example, inequities in the wage structure would only be compounded if profit sharing were allocated on inequitable wages.

History. Profit sharing was quite prevalent in primitive fishing and farming economies. The whaling industry in this country in the nineteenth century used profit sharing, and it still persists among fishermen in many parts of the world today. Thus, profit sharing is not a new idea, but its practical application on any wide scale to a highly scientific-technical society is new.

Albert Gallatin, Secretary of the Treasury under Presidents Jefferson and Madison, introduced profit sharing into his New Geneva, Pennsylvania, glassworks in the 1790s. However, the idea grew slowly in this country, in starts and stops. Some of earliest, best-conceived profit-sharing programs still in successful operation at the present time are: Procter & Gamble Co. (1887), Eastman Kodak Co. (1912), Harris Trust and Savings Bank (1916), Sears, Roebuck and Co. (1916), S. C. Johnson & Son, Inc. (1917), Sanborn, now a division of Hewlett-Packard Company (1918), and Joslyn Manufacturing and Supply Co. (1918).

During the Depression of the 1930s, interest in profit sharing was at a low ebb. However, in 1939, new interest was sparked by Senator Arthur H. Vandenberg's Senate Finance Subcommittee study of profit sharing [2]. At that time there were only 37 qualified deferred profit-sharing programs and a few hundred cash programs in operation. After intense examination and extensive hearings, the Senate Subcommittee concluded that profit sharing can be "eminently successful, when properly established, in creating employer-employee relations that make for peace, equity, efficiency and contentment," and went so far as to declare profit sharing "essential to the ultimate maintenance of the capitalistic system."

Tax Advantages. Subsequent to the Senate report, encouragement was given to companies through favorable tax legislation to initiate deferred profit-sharing plans for employees. These tax advantages benefit all participants whether higher-paid or lower-paid employees. Briefly, IRS regulations permit the deductibility of the employer's profit-sharing contributions as a business expense (up to 15% of payroll of participants) and allow the deferral of this money into a trust without any current tax liabilities on employee participants. This means that participants do not pay any current tax on their respective profit shares and that trust investment earnings and appreciation are not currently taxable. Tax is paid only when participants actually or constructively receive benefits (usually at retirement, disability, death, severance of employment, or under withdrawal provisions) and then normally at a lower tax rate, due to lower income and/or through use of a ten-year averaging technique.

Growth of Plans. Through a combination of many factors, including tax benefits, as well as the increasing success companies were having with well administered programs, profit-sharing plans of all types (cash, deferred, and combination) dramatically grew in number over the last three decades. This growth can be most accurately illustrated with respect to deferred profit-sharing plans, as compared to pension plan growth in Exhibit I. More new deferred profit-sharing plans were started in the last eight years of the period depicted than in all previous years combined, despite the adverse effects of the Employee Retirement Income Security Act of 1974 (ERISA) on plan approvals.

By December 31, 1980, there were over 285,000 qualified plans in operation. Much of this growth is attributable to the movement of smaller companies into retirement programs; another factor is the ascending position of deferred profit sharing in retirement planning. This ascending position is illustrated in the pie charts of Exhibit II, where the shaded sections represent profit sharing, and the white, pensions.

Today, deferred profit-sharing programs and pensions (including both money purchase and defined benefit) are increasing at very nearly a one-to-one pace. Smaller companies frequently choose deferred profit sharing rather than pensions, while large companies often choose both, supplementing basic fixed-benefits pensions with flexible profit sharing.

On September 2, 1974, the Employee Retirement Income Security Act (ERISA) was signed into law. The intent of ERISA was to protect employee rights under qualified retirement income plans (i.e., corporate pensions, deferred profit sharing, and stock bonus) and welfare plans. ERISA does not require any company to establish a plan, nor does it set any minimum benefit levels. ERISA laid down many complicated provisions with respect to participation, vesting, funding, fiduciary standards, reporting/disclosure, and plan termination insurance. These provisions of the law impacted on all qualified plans, but most adversely on corporate-defined benefit pension programs.

Governmental procedures, dual administration of plans by the U.S. Department of Labor and the U.S. Treasury Department, and excessively slow issuance of clarifying regulations choked the growth of new plans and caused many companies to terminate their pension and/or profit-sharing programs. For almost two years, plan administrators treaded water without sufficient information to bring their existing plans into compliance with ERISA. By mid-1977, however, profit-sharing administrators learned to cope with ERISA, most existing plans were brought into compliance, and a favorable turnaround in new plan approvals began.

Much debate ensued after ERISA as to whether the act would trigger a move toward defined contribution plans (i.e., profit sharing, thrift, stock bonus, and money purchase pensions) or toward defined-benefit pension programs. Cross currents flowed, with some companies terminating their profit-sharing programs in favor of pensions, others terminating their pensions in favor of profit sharing. Certain companies opted for both. Treasury data on new plan approvals suggests that a trend may be taking place toward defined contribution plans, although there still are cogent arguments in favor of defined-benefit pension plans. Both types of plans have their advantages and shortcomings [3].

The growth data in Exhibits I and II represent only deferred (and combination) profit-sharing programs for corporate employees and do not include the 85,000–100,000 cash profit-sharing plans in operation. Approximately 16 million employees participate in these one-third of a million U.S. corporate profit-sharing plans—around 20% of private, nonfarm employment.

Profit sharing has applicability to many different kinds of businesses. One out of five

EXHIBIT I

CUMULATIVE GROWTH IN NUMBER OF QUALIFIED DEFERRED PROFIT-SHARING PLANS AND PENSIONS IN THE UNITED STATES 1939 THROUGH 1980 (APPROVALS MINUS TERMINATIONS)

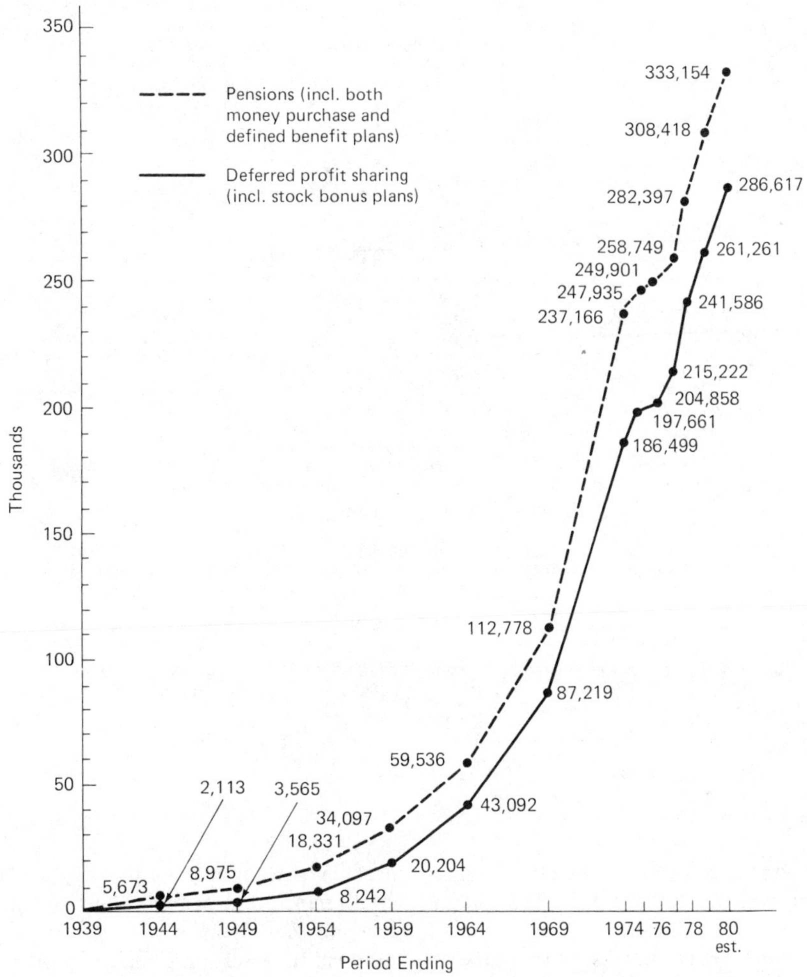

SOURCE: Profit Sharing Research Foundation calculations based on U.S. Treasury Dept. Reports.

EXHIBIT II

ASCENDING ROLE OF DEFERRED PROFIT-SHARING PLANS IN RETIREMENT INCOME PROVISION (NUMBER OF PLAN APPROVALS IN DESIGNATED PERIOD)

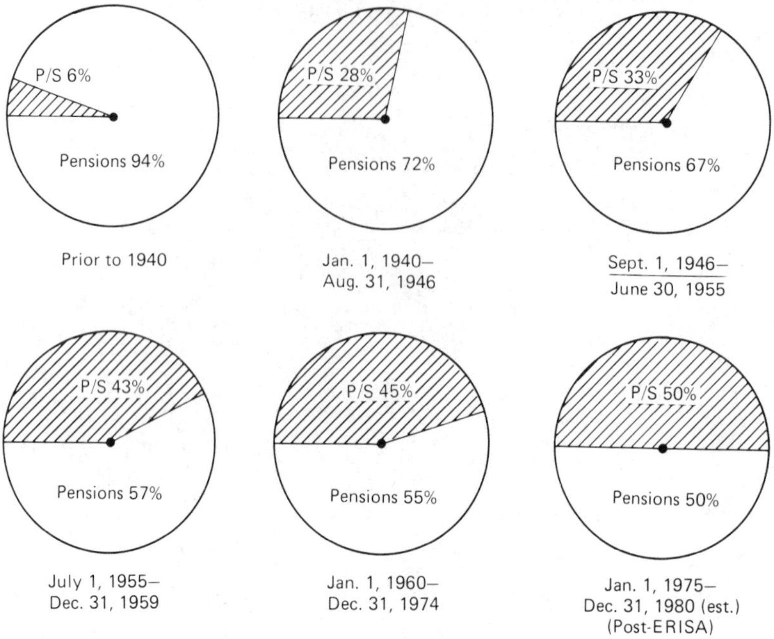

Source: Profit Sharing Research Foundation calculations based on U.S. Treasury Department reports. Profit sharing plans include stock bonus plans; pensions include money purchase and defined benefit plans.

insurance companies, one out of four manufacturing companies, one out of three retail firms/wholesale distributors, and two out of five banks now share profits with workers. Even more significant than the growth rate is the fact that the profit-sharing concept is being utilized successfully in large and small companies, in labor-intensive and capital-intensive industries, in mass production and job shop situations, in industries with fluctuating profits as well as those with stable profits.

Depending on the design of the plan, profit sharing can reward employee performance, seniority, or thrift. However, the theory of profit sharing and its recent growth should not cloak the fact that it does not always work out. It takes work to make profit sharing work. It is a "total-system incentive" that has worked remarkably well for many companies, fairly well for others, and not at all for some.

Currently, around 2% of the deferred plans are being terminated annually, while the discontinuance rate of cash plans is unknown but probably somewhat higher. Some plans are terminated as a result of mergers; others are discontinued when businesses are liquidated or sold. The higher discontinuance rate of cash plans is partly due to the higher mortality rate among smaller companies where most cash profit-sharing plans are found.

The annual rate of discontinuance due to the inappropriateness of profit sharing in a given company is even lower. These terminations tend to occur after a string of unprofitable years, where cash payments are anticipated by employees and then fail to materialize, where investment performance has been poor, or where ineffective communication has resulted in employee lack of understanding, appreciation, and interest.

Profit Sharing in Large Companies [4]. One common misconception about profit sharing is that it works well only in small companies where workers can more easily see the connection between their greater efficiency and the desired increased company profit-sharing contributions. Actually, profit sharing has been practiced successfully for many years in some of America's largest companies of which a small sampling is given here:

Largest soap company	Procter & Gamble Co.
Largest wax manufacturer	S. C. Johnson & Son, Inc.
Largest magazine publisher	Time, Inc.
Largest department store and mail order house	Sears, Roebuck and Co.
Largest photographic manufacturing company	Eastman Kodak Co.
Largest copy machine company	Xerox, inc.

A list of other large companies with effective profit-sharing programs would include:

American Brands, Inc.
Burlington Industries, Inc.
Carter Hawley Hale Stores, Inc.
DeLuxe Check Printers, Inc.
Farmers Insurance Group
Hallmark Cards, Inc.
Jewel Companies, Inc.
McGraw-Edison Co.
J. C. Penney Company, Inc.
Quaker Oats Co.
Standard Oil Co. of California
Tektronix, Inc.
Texas Instruments, Inc.

Profit Sharing as an Organizational Incentive. The greatest challenge management faces today is to achieve a fusion, a unity of purpose among stockholders, management, and employees. This may well necessitate a rethinking and reshaping of a number of organizational and motivational principles.

Managements have organized corporations as "pyramids" from top to bottom in the interests of efficiency, and then have in many ways thwarted this efficiency. Communication up and down within this pyramid is not very effective and, by and large, a common language has not developed.

Either by design or default, a fragmented approach to motivation has evolved. Corporate pyramids have been carefully stratified, and horizontal modes of motivating each employee group have developed. Artificial wedges have been driven between this group and that, and then managements wonder why alienation, lack of cohesion, and loss of employee identification with the firm plague corporations. Beyond that, the work process has been broken down into its smallest possible components, jobs have been fitted into this rigid structure, and a percentage of the work force has been put on individual incentives which gear pay to output on the particular job.

There is little doubt that these individual financial incentives have contributed to the increase in productivity experienced over the years in business, but along the way important values have been needlessly sacrificed. This "scientific management" approach has tended to link each individual to his ever more narrow task, giving him positive financial reasons for restricting his interests, and no incentive at all to think beyond his immediate work environment or to place his own performance in the context of the total operation.

Challenge of Behavioral Sciences. The newer behavioral science approach emphasizes the vital need in industry today for a new breed of incentives (to supplement or substitute for individual incentives) that:

(1) Cut *vertically* through the organization and strengthen organizational bonds.

(2) Focus on the *qualitative* aspects of work—on new ideas and more effective teamwork.

(3) Appeal not only to the financial needs but also to the *social* and *ego-fulfillment* needs of employees.

(4) *Facilitate change,* the introduction of new techniques, processes, equipment, and products.

(5) *Relate people* to the common goal of improving organizational effectiveness.

In short, organizational incentives are needed today which can simultaneously motivate and unite all factors of production (distribution)—all those contributing to corporate growth—namely, stockholders, management, and employees at all levels.

Total System Incentives. Profit sharing is one of the new breed of incentives called "total system incentives." Such incentives link all individuals in a company together in pursuit of organizational goals. These total system incentives take various forms, e.g., cost-savings sharing, sales-value sharing (see SCANLON PLAN OF GROUP INCENTIVES), production-value sharing (see RUCKER PLAN OF GROUP INCENTIVES), profit-sharing plans, and employee stock-ownership plans (ESOPs).

Profit-sharing and stock-ownership programs are really the "ultimate" in the total-system approach because they link employee self-interests to the final measure of corporate success (efficient satisfaction of human needs as evidenced by profits). Profit sharing also reflects the "test of the market," paying rewards only when they can be afforded. These system incentives work together well in tandem, mutually supportative.

Inflation, Productivity, and Profit Sharing. To curb inflation, to promote domestic economic growth, to make American products once again competitive in world markets, it is imperative that management and labor collaborate to boost productivity, cut costs, and share resultant gains with all factors of production. Up to the present, however, this "sharing" has largely taken the form of higher wages and fringe benefits. These fixed costs have been structured into the price of American products, gradually pricing them out of world markets, opening domestic doors to foreign imports, and leading to job exportation abroad and high unemployment at home.

"Productivity bargaining" supplemented by soundly conceived profit-sharing programs constitute flexible reward mechanisms through which employees can get their fair share without creating inflationary pressures, structuring high rigid costs into the price of U.S. products, undermining labor's own job security, or penalizing stockholders and consumers.

Profit Sharing and Stockholders. A frequently voiced feeling about profit sharing is that such programs are unfair to stockholders—if labor gets more, stockholders get less. In order to evaluate the incentive impact of profit sharing and to measure the effects of such programs on stockholder interests, the Profit Sharing Research Foundation compared the financial performance of a group of large department store chains with profit sharing against a similar group without profit sharing over the period 1952–1969 [5].

The profit sharers outperformed the nonprofit sharers (based on growth since 1952) by 35% on sales, 47% on net worth, 88% on earnings per share, 68% on dividends per share, and 97% on market price per share. Other studies of more recent vintage point in the same direction:

Bion Howard, of the Graduate School of Management, Northwestern University, studied the financial performance of profit-sharing companies and nonprofit-sharing companies in six industries [6]. Sixteen comparisons were made for each industry—i.e., operating ratios and growth measures. The results revealed that the performance of the profit-sharing companies was clearly superior to the non-profit sharers for the six industries as a group. However, the superiority of the profit sharers lay in their *level* of performance and not in their *trend* (which tended to run parallel to that of nonprofit-sharing companies). The profit sharers were above average in two-thirds of the cases and below average in less than one-fifth.

Michael Conte and Arnold S. Tannenbaum, of the Survey Research Center, Institute for Social Research, The University of Michigan, in a study of 98 firms, found that employee ownership, in one form or another, may be associated with better employee attitudes toward the job and higher productivity and profitability than comparable sized companies in their respective industries [7].

Donald V. Nightingale, Associate Professor, School of Business, Queen's University at Kingston, examined 83 firms with profit sharing, using a 124-item questionnaire [8]. Because most of the firms in the sample were small and privately held, documented evidence was not available from audited statements for return on invested capital, growth in sales, and the like. However, executives were asked to evaluate the effectiveness of their profit-sharing plans. Overall, profit sharing was rated as most effective in attracting and holding desirable employees, followed sequentially by providing economic security for employees, increasing productivity, improving teamwork and cooperation, rewarding individuals, giving employees a better understanding of factors entering into business success, and facilitating the introduction of new plant and equipment. Sixty-four per cent of the respondents reported that turnover in their companies is lower than their industry average. Only 6% reported higher than average turnover rates. Executives also reported high levels of employee satisfaction with their profit-sharing plans.

A survey of 72 companies with ESOPs (Employee Stock Ownership Plans) by The ESOP Association of America showed significant corporate gains post-ESOP compared with pre-ESOP [9].

Profit Sharing Research Foundation in its study, "Profit Sharing in 38 Large Companies," found that 23 profit-sharing industrials outperformed *Fortune's* 500 largest industrials, and 10 profit-sharing retailers achieved higher results than *Fortune's* 41 retailers on measures of return on sales and return on equity [10].

While none of these studies "prove" the efficacy of profit sharing and/or employee stock ownership, they do establish positive correlations between system incentive programs and superior corporate performance. This should not come as a surprise. It makes sense that employees, individually and as a team, will more likely strive for excellence if they have a direct stake in the results.

Profit Sharing and Employees. The benefits of profit sharing from the employee's point of view can be substantial, particularly if the plan has been in existence for some time and the company has done well. The Profit Sharing Research Foundation recently studied actual profit-sharing benefits which were paid out to long-term, nonmanagement employees to determine if these benefits equalled or exceeded those which would have been generated by a typical "pension standard" [11]. The pension standard was defined as "1.3 per cent of final average pay times years of service."

Out of 33 companies studied, only six provided profit-sharing benefits which fell below the pension standard, and these six also had separate pension programs for their people. The other 27 provided profit-sharing benefits which amounted to 102% to 1,011% of the pension standard (and thirteen of these latter also had separate pension programs).

At DeLuxe Check Printers, Inc., for example, an employee with 26 years of service and final average pay at retirement of $12,966 had a profit-sharing account balance of $99,625, which provided him with profit-sharing benefits amounting to 273% of the pension standard (or $11,955 per year rather than $4,383 which he would have received under the pension).

At Signode Corporation, an employee with 35 years of profit-sharing participation, who retired at a final average pay of $14,466 received $127,752 in profit sharing—233% of the pension standard (or $15,300 per year rather than $6,582 from the standard pension).

This is not to assert that all profit-sharing participants end up as well. It does imply that if the company on average contributes 8% to 12% of pay into a profit-sharing trust, and investment returns over the years fall at least in the 6% to 10% range, employees should receive enough in profit sharing to fund adequately their retirement programs and/or build up sizable "capital accumulation" accounts.

Hewitt Associates, in cooperation with the Profit Sharing Council of America, surveyed 522 profit-sharing companies in 1979 and discovered that the average employer profit-sharing contribution as a percentage of pay was 9.89% [12]. This percentage varied considerably from company to company. At Worthington Industries in Columbus, Ohio, for example, the average production worker received just under $10,000 in cash in 1978 under the company's cash profit-sharing program. This was in addition to an average of approximately $12,000 in base pay. Worthington also has a deferred profit-sharing program [13].

Profit Sharing and Consumers. Benefits for the consumer are at the heart of the profit-sharing philosophy. A profit-sharing company executive expressed this aptly: "Progress sharing means an equitable division of economic progress among consumers, stockholders, employees at all levels, and with business associates, dealers, and suppliers. Overriding consideration must be given to sharing progress with consumers—because unless you give your customers the kind of genuine product value . . . that attracts them to you, there will be no progress to share with anyone else."

A profit-sharing company like Lincoln Electric Company in Cleveland, Ohio has consistently followed this philosophy. Since 1934, the year Lincoln started its profit-sharing incentive bonus program, the cost of labor, copper, steel and chemicals (all cost elements going into Lincoln's products) has increased manyfold. Yet the cost of welding machines and electrodes has increased in most cases only very slightly. This remarkable stability in prices has been achieved through individual and collective employee efforts to cut costs and increase productivity. Lincoln has shared not only with its employees but also with its consumers. (See LINCOLN INCENTIVE MANAGEMENT PLAN.)

Profit Sharing and Labor Unions. Union attitudes toward profit sharing historically have been hostile or indifferent. In the early days of business unionism, higher wages, better working conditions, and union security were chief labor goals. They wanted their gains "in the pay envelope." To a large extent, this is still true today. Union leaders were suspicious of profit-sharing programs because they felt managements were using profit sharing to avoid paying decent wages, to keep the unions out, and/or to undermine collective bargaining.

Organized labor has gradually modified its position. Developments, such as the acceptance of collective bargaining as national policy, the improvement in wages and working conditions, the attainment by and large of union security, the plethora of guaranteed fringe benefits already won, and the increasing numbers of unionized employees participating in satisfactory profit-sharing programs, have interacted to change union attitudes toward profit sharing in a somewhat more positive direction, at least in some union circles. However, there is no universal union attitude toward profit sharing. Attitudes vary among individuals, unions, and levels (local or international). Attitudes depend a great deal on the particular experiences encountered by union people with specific profit-sharing programs.

In the study "Profit Sharing in 38 Large Companies" previously referred to, 24 of the 38 companies were unionized to some extent—i.e., some of the employees within these enterprises were represented by unions. Unionized employees participated in the profit-sharing programs in 19 out of the 24 companies. In 10 out of 11 companies, where 11% of more of the employees were unionized, the union people participated in the profit-sharing plan. This included retail clerks, meat cutters, restaurant employees, grain millers, machinists, electrical workers, steel workers, teamsters, brewery workers, oil, chemical and atomic workers, and many others. While many companies with unions share profits, most very large unionized companies do not.

Walter P. Reuther, then President of the UAW, became keenly aware of the limitations of collective bargaining in the years immediately preceding his death:

> The stress in collective bargaining . . . stems in large part from the fact that neither management nor labor really knows what the true equity of the workers will be over the full term of the contract. . . . Each party, therefore, is sparring in a kind of twilight zone of incomplete knowledge of the economic circumstances that will affect the profitability of the corporation and hence the equity of executives, stockholders, and workers alike. . . .
>
> If a contract is negotiated at the peak of prosperity, the workers may be able to obtain gains that will impose heavy costs on the firm if the market for its products slackens. Conversely, a contract negotiated at the trough of a recession may saddle the workers for three years with wage and fringe benefit gains far smaller than those the company will actually be able to afford, and should in justice and reason provide. . . . Profit Sharing would resolve the conflict between management apprehensions and worker expectations on the basis of solid economic facts as they materialize rather than on the basis of speculation as to what the future might hold. . . . [14].

The UAW position on profit sharing today, at least at the international level, is the same as enunciated by Reuther.

The adversarial role of unions may be anachronistic. There is a time to fight and a time to cooperate. The inordinate cost of labor-management conflict can/will no longer be borne by consumers or society. The principal victims in the struggle—whether they recognize it or not—are the parties themselves (management and labor) who suffer lost markets and jobs as conflict drives costs up, up, up. Organized labor should have an important role to play in the future—along constructive, collaborative lines. The "credibility gap" must be closed, and management needs labor's help to accomplish this. The management-labor relations between the American Velvet Company, Stonington, Conn. and Local 110, Textile Workers Union of America, shows that profit sharing can help create such a climate of understanding, with rewards to both labor and management. [15]

Capital Property Ownership through Profit Sharing. Karl Marx claimed that there was a basic, inevitable conflict between the proletariat and the capitalist, caused by the fact that the few were owners of the capital goods of society and the many were not. Marx's solution was to eliminate this private property ownership through the transference of the capital goods of society to a supreme administrator—the government. Experience has shown, however, that this system leads to man's loss of both political and economic freedom and justice.

A German economist, Johann Heinrich Von Thunen (1783–1850), felt that there was another solution which would solve the economic problem in the economic sphere, not the political sphere. He based his idea upon the retention of private property ownership and a broadening of the base of such ownership. Make everyone an owner, he asserted, and then described deferred profit sharing as one of the best ways of doing this [16].

Von Thunen worked his system out on his agricultural estate in Germany by paying his employees "going wages" and then, in addition, by giving them a share in the profits of the estate. He reinvested the worker's share of profits in the estate in the worker's name and paid him earnings on the investment each year in cash. As the deferred principal grew each profitable year, the annual cash payout of earnings increased proportionately. When the worker retired or quit, he received the equity which had accumulated in his account.

Many companies with deferred profit sharing, particularly those investing in whole or in part in its own company securities, are implementing the basic principles in Von Thunen's

EXHIBIT III

PROFIT-SHARING "MODELS"

Plan Features	Galveston–Houston Co.	Signode Corp.	Fisher–Price Toys
Type of plan:	Deferred	Deferred	0–100% cash-deferred option plan
Coverage:	Broad	Broad	Broad
Started:	1976	1941	1936
Eligibility:	1 year of service; no age requirement	6 months and 870 hours of service; no age requirement	8 weeks of service; no age requirement
Employee contributions:	None	Voluntary between 1% and 10% of pay	None
Company contributions:	Discretionary. Determined by board of directors annually—up to 15% of compensation	30% of profits after taxes but not less than 5% of aggregate salaries of participants—up to 15% of compensation	22% of pre-tax profits—up to 20% of compensation
Prior reservation for capital:	None	None	None
Allocation:	In relation to pay	In relation to pay	In relation to pay
Vesting rights:	After 1 year, 10%; 10% annual increments to 100% after 10 years	50% immediate with 5% annual increments after 5 years employment to 100% after 15 years of service	100% immediate
Loans/ withdrawals:	None	No loans, but partial withdrawals for purchase of home, mortgage reduction, home improvement, education or medical expenses	Withdrawals permitted for purchase of primary residence, education beyond secondary school level, or extraordinary financial hardship arising from sickness or illness

EXHIBIT III (Continued)

Plan Features	Galveston-Houston Co.	Signode Corp.	Fisher-Price Toys
Investments:	Employee investment options. Three funds are available: Fund A (fixed income fund), Fund B (an equities fund) and Fund C (insured savings accounts). Participant may divide his/her share among two or more funds in 25% amounts	No employee investment options, except that a participant who has completed 10 years participation may have up to 75% of his vested account balance invested in a deferred annuity. Diversified portfolio of investments with approximately 15% in Signode common stock	Employee investment options. Two funds are available: a diversified fund and a guaranteed interest fund. A participant may elect to invest the company contribution into either or both funds in 25% amounts
Transfer of balances privilege:	A participant can transfer his/her share from one account to another once in three years	None, except transfer into deferred annuity	A participant can transfer from one fund to another in 25% increments once a year
Pass-through voting:	No own company stock	Participants individually vote the Signode common stock in their profit-sharing accounts	No own company stock
Management:	Administrative Committee appoints investment manager to invest assets in Funds A and B. Corporate trustee manages Fund C	Three individual trustees and a corporate trustee administer the fund. Individual trustees may select investment managers to invest trust assets within guidelines	Administration is handled by the company. Fund managers invest the diversified fund. A corporate trustee invests the guaranteed fund with an insurance company
Disbursements:	Lump sum, installments, or annuity	Lump sum, annual or monthly installments up to 30 years or life expectancy (whichever is greater), annuity, or combination	Lump sum or installments
Pension plan:	None. Thrift and Stock Purchase Plan initiated in October, 1979	Special guarantees and a "floor" pension	Defined benefit pension with funding taken out of profit-sharing contribution

theory. Most of these companies reinvest fund earnings as well as principal, so that the compounding effect will result in a greater accumulation.

Profit Sharing and Loss Sharing. Many people feel that workers should not share profits unless they are also willing to share losses. A response to this is that workers share losses in a bad year through layoffs and/or reduced hours, and that this is usually loss-sharing enough. However, some companies include a provision in their plans that losses must be made up in subsequent profitable years before profit-sharing contributions resume.

How to Set Up a Profit-Sharing Plan. Four conditions are highly important, if not essential, to the success of a profit-sharing plan:

(1) Confidence of most of the employees in the honesty, good intentions, and ability of management.

(2) A management with a friendly attitude toward employees and a respect for them as individuals and as contributing members of a productive team.

(3) The payment of wages, salaries, and basic fringe benefits equal to those prevailing in the industry or locality.

(4) A profit-sharing formula that has a good chance of producing significant results.

The first step in establishing a profit-sharing plan should be the preparation of a list of objectives for the plan. This will aid the formulation of a statement of policy (preferably written) answering the "why" behind the program.

The type of plan chosen (cash, deferred or combination), as well as the specific variants within plan provisions, will depend on many factors, such as the nature of the particular business, presence or absence of other incentive or retirement progams, the make-up of the work force (age, sex, and the like), management objectives, employee attitudes, and union relations (if any).

Decisions will have to be made on who will share, how much will be shared, how individuals will share, how vesting rights will be handled, and several other features. Competent profit-sharing advisers can be very helpful in this area.

Some plans have failed because too small a percentage was shared to make for a substantial employee reward; others may have failed because too much was allotted to profit sharing and too little retained for growth of the business and for stockholders. The most successful plans have been those which, on the average, produced credits of 8% or more of participating payroll. Great flexibility is possible (see Exhibit III) [17].

The major thrust in profit-sharing developments today is in the direction of broader coverage and greater flexibility in plans to meet the individual needs of participants. A range of options is being incorporated into plans so that the individual has an important say on how the plan will function on his or her behalf: voluntary employee contributions, cash-deferred options, partial withdrawal provisions, employee investment options, and disbursement elections.

If enough flexibility is built into the plan, the individual can select the options that will make the plan meet his or her needs now, change options to make the plan relevant to needs ten years from now, and change the options again to meet the employee's needs during the years immediately preceding retirement.

Communication and Employee Involvement. A thorough presentation of the plan to employees at the start is not enough. The philosophy of profit sharing should be emphasized often to generate understanding and enthusiasm. Group meetings, articles in the house organ, letters from the president—all can bring the profit-sharing message of "cooperative effort leading to cooperative reward" home to employees. It is important to get across from the beginning the concept that shares of profits are quite distinct from regular pay, and must never be taken for granted.

Profit *making* must always precede profit *sharing.* Management's real challenge is its ability to create or intensify "pro-profit" attitudes among employees through profit sharing, and to modify the organization so as to enlist employee support in reducing costs, raising quality, and furthering all profit-productivity improvement programs. This does not mean that innermost corporate financial secrets must be divulged, but it does mean that enough cost and profit information should be presented so that employees can respond in a meaningful fashion. An environment must be created conducive to the growth of both human beings and profits [18].

BERT L. METZGER, President, Profit Sharing Research Foundation, Evanston, Illinois

Information References

Profit Sharing Research Foundation.
Profit Sharing Council of America.

References Cited

[1] Leslie, John H., "The Importance of Profit Sharing to a Capitalistic Economy," Chicago, Signode Corp., 1962.
[2] Subcommittee of the Committee on Finance, United States Senate, "Survey of Experiences in Profit Sharing and Possibilities of Incentive Taxation," Washington, D.C., U.S. Government Printing Office, 1939.
[3] Metzger, Bert L. "Advantages and Limitations of Pension and Deferred Profit Sharing Programs," Evanston, Ill., Profit Sharing Research Foundation, 1979.
[4] Metzger, Bert L. "Profit Sharing in 38 Large Companies: Piece of the Action for 1,000,000 Participants," vol. II, Evanston, Ill., Profit Sharing Research Foundation, 1978.
[5] Metzger, Bert L. and Colletti, Jerome A., "Does Profit Sharing Pay?" Evanston, Ill., Profit Sharing Research Foundation, 1971.
[6] Howard, Bion B. "A Study of the Financial Significance of Profit Sharing 1958-1977," Chicago, Ill., Profit Sharing Council of America, 1979.
[7] Conte, Michael and Tannenbaum, Arnold S. "Employee-owned Companies: Is the Difference Measurable?" *Monthly Labor Review*, July, 1978.
[8] Nightingale, Donald V., "Does Profit Sharing Really Make Any Difference?" Ottawa, The Conference Board in Canada, January 17, 1980.
[9] "The Performance of ESOP Companies," San Francisco, Calif., The ESOP Association of America *Newsletter*, September, 1979.
[10] Metzger, "Evidence of Superior Performance," in "Profit Sharing in 38 Large Companies," Evanston, Ill., Profit Sharing Research Foundation, 1978.
[11] *Ibid.* "Benefits for Long-term Participants."
[12] Hewitt Associates, "1979 Profit Sharing Survey (1978 Experience)," Chicago, Ill., Profit Sharing Council of America, 1979.
[13] Metzger, Bert L., "Increasing Productivity through Profit Sharing," Evanston, Ill., Profit Sharing Research Foundation, 1980.
[14] Reuther, Walter P., Presentation before Joint Economic Committee, February 20, 1967; and UAW statement to General Motors, July 28, 1967.
[15] Metzger, Bert L., "Sharing at American Velvet Company," in "Sharing a Business: Prescription for Growth," Evanston, Ill., Profit Sharing Research Foundation, 1975.
[16] Dempsey, Bernard J., "The Frontier Wage—The Economic Organization of Free Agents," Chicago, Loyola University Press, 1963.
[17] Metzger, Bert L. "Evolution of the Profit Sharing/Share Ownership Philosophy Worldwide," Evanston, Ill. Profit Sharing Research Foundation, May 22, 1980.
[18] Metzger, Bert L., "How to Motivate with Profit Sharing," Evanston, Ill., Profit Sharing Research Foundation, 1978.

Cross References: *Guaranteed Annual Wage; Incentive Systems; Lincoln Incentive Management Plan; Rucker Plan of Group Incentives; Scanlon Plan of Group Incentives; Standard Minute System.*

PROGRAMMED LEARNING. See Teaching Machines, Programmed Instruction, and Computer-Aided Instructions.

PROJECT MANAGEMENT

In new and expanding fields, such as electronics, nucleonics, astronautics, etc., a new type of manager has evolved. Although he (she) has many titles, the one most generally used is **Project Manager.** His business is to create a *product*—a piece of advanced-technology hardware—or to generate a *service* that requires a set of advanced-technology programs generally termed *software*. His primary tool is the brainpower of professional specialists in diverse fields, and he uses this tool in all phases of his product, from concept through initial test and final implementation.

A *project* is an organization unit dedicated to the attainment of a goal—the successful completion of a developmental product or service on time, within budget, in conformance with predetermined performance specifications.

The project staff will be a "mix" of brainpower, varying with the project's mission. Thus a project involving a high degree of development, such as one devoted to a practical demonstration of ionic propulsion that can later be applied in rocketry, will have a high proportion of scientists to engineers and a high proportion of theoretically inclined personnel. In contrast, a project committed to a successful demonstration of a synfuel concept utilizing proven theories will have relatively more engineers.

Projects are typically organized by task (vertical structure) instead of by function (horizontal organization). The relative advantages of "project" and "systems" organizations have been the subject of widespread controversy, and it is not the intent here to elaborate on this issue. The obvious organizational goal is to seek the advantages of both—the vertical structure in which the control and performance associated with autonomous management are maintained for a given project, and the horizontal in which better continuity, flexibility, and use of scarce talents may be achieved in a technical group.

In the more or less autonomous project, "real" management and personnel responsibility reside with the project manager. This autonomy is in contrast to the organization in which the project function is maintained by a "project engineer," who often is relegated to a staff position with responsibilities far outweighing his authority, and who must pursue tenuous relationships and a great deal of skill and persistence to achieve even modest performance goals.

During the later 1970s, the critical importance of the project manager and project organization became widely realized in the data processing and information systems industries. Frederic G. Withington, in a *Harvard Business Review* article [1], illuminates the role of project management in implementing distributed computing responsibility within the large organization.

Approaches. How does the job of the advanced-technology project manager differ from the picture of the conventional manager in industry? For one thing, he (or she) is managing a higher proportion of *professionals,* from the working level of the journeyman engineer or programmer, up through the subordinate managers. Even in manufacturing operations on advanced-technology products, it is often necessary to introduce engineers and scientists to the laboratory floor in large numbers. Even purchasing groups for these projects are likely to be staffed by a substantial proportion of engineers. In view of this, the project manager needs a different attitude regarding the classic management functions of control, coordination, communication, and the setting of performance standards.

In learning to manage a group of professional employees, the usual boss-subordinate relationship must be modified. Of especial importance, the *how*—the details or methods of work performance by a professional employee—should be established *by the employee.* It follows that he (she) must be given the facts needed to permit the employee to develop a rational understanding of the *why* of tasks assigned. Such an employee may be granted the prerogatives of a professional—independence of detailed supervision, freedom from administrative routine where feasible, and working quarters which afford privacy and comfort. But at the same time he must never be excused from the responsibility of having to *produce* in accordance with the exacting requirements of a profession.

Another unique aspect of the project manager's job is that the task is finite in duration. He or she is managing a group of advanced specialists; the professional mix of the group is tailored specifically for the accomplishment of an assigned mission. If the manager and the group are successful, they will complete all facets of their job, and so work themselves out of a job, as quickly as possible. This may be a year or less in some projects, and may run to five years and upward for long-range, high-budget projects.

In any case, the project manager must trust corporate management, implicitly in most cases, to provide the project group with continuity of work on successive projects. Needless to say, the record of top management in achieving this continuity will affect the peace of mind, if not the performance, of the project manager and his or her entire staff.

Another feature of the project manager's job is the absence of feedback information during the early stages and often other stages of the project. Under the servomechanism analogy of management control, a manager establishes a closed loop in which the performance output of the group is fed back to be compared with performance standards. Corrective control action is then directed into the system. However, in advanced-technology work, during the design phase of a project and before test results are available, the project manager often is in the position of a pilot flying blind, relying on a relatively unproven set of instruments. His experience, judgment, and faith must carry him through until early test results become available; from this first feedback he can modify the design approach in a direction most likely to meet the acid requirements of further proof tests. Meanwhile, during these periods of blind flying, he may be forced to make long-term decisions which commit substantial funds.

A feature of advanced-technology projects is that *late changes* must perforce be accepted, both on the drawing boards and in the shops, and in components being procured for the system. In short, the project staff must expect to live through periods of "technological crises." However, it must always be realized that each of these crucial periods leaves residual effects throughout the remaining course of the project. The resolution of such a crisis generally involves a sacrifice of engineering principle for expediency, which may in turn lead to subsequent crises. Further, each crisis, with its resultant need for immediate solution, erodes the constructive attitude of the project's engineers and scientists, particularly the theoreticians.

Clearly, therefore, the more that can be done to avoid or alleviate these situations in advance, the better. Thus, advance planning is vital in a project.

Authority and Responsibility. Essential to

the project management concept is a clear delineation of authority and responsibility. The project manager knows that his basic responsibilities are to deliver his end product (1) in accordance with performance requirements, (2) within the limitations of his budget, and (3) within the time schedule that his company or customer has specified. In general, the project manager will delegate by tasks, so that subordinate managers in his group will have these same three responsibilities for subprojects. Here success or failure may well hinge on the manager's ability to discern fine variations in emphasis among performance, budget, and time schedule needs and to resolve the continuous apparent conflicts which occur among them.

The first-line supervisors—the "supervising engineers"—are by definition the ones who play the key roles in guiding the day-by-day progress of a project toward its goals. Such a supervisor bears a wide range of burdens; demands on his time can easily be overpowering if the project manager does not act to shield him from diversionary requirements.

At the same time it should be borne in mind that in attempting to shield a supervisor, to free him to concentrate chiefly on the vital technical job at hand, the project manager can unknowingly deal a severe blow to the supervisor's advancement potential. The supervisor is at a critical point in his career, at which leadership capability and administrative potential can blossom or be blighted. A general and basic tenet of management—the training of individuals for leadership—must not be shelved merely because the pace of an advanced-technology project seems at times to be overpowering.

In pursuing his objective of maintaining momentum, the project manager must be constantly aware of the apparent disdain for time commitments which prevails on the part of the more theoretically inclined scientists, engineers, and systems analysts. While this attitude is a rather deep study in itself, one part of it that must be understood is the drive for perfection that so often characterizes the professional mind. Any kind of promised delivery date inevitably involves a compromise with perfection. The tendency to finish the job "to a T," if allowed to run rampant, can result in continuous postponements of output and reduce the productivity of the project as a whole.

Organizational Planning. In advanced-technology industries, sound organization planning requires adroitness in recruiting scarce talent both from within and without the parent organization. It also involves the ability to utilize engineers and scientists who in some cases do not measure up to reasonable requirements for the project—the ability to shape a team which can "play over its head" when it has to. Sound organization planning in a project cannot be done without a thorough understanding of the personalities, the characteristics, and the attitudes of all the technologists, both as individuals and as members of their particular professional methodologies.

At any time during the course of the project, the manager may be called on to act as "front man" to help shape or reshape the policies that affect his project relative to the corporate structure and the company's development objectives. "Selling" is a never-ending job of a project manager, as it is of most other senior managers in the corporate organization. In the matters of acquiring scarce funds, people, and materials, the project manager must always be able to make an effective presentation, often on short notice. Many project managers have suddenly found themselves, in mid-course, fighting for the very existence of their project.

The project manager needs a modicum of what has been termed "projectitis" to generate the necessary drive and momentum to spark the project to success. However, when dealing with his engineers and scientists, he must not suffer, or appear to suffer, from any blind or extreme case of it in establishing schedular aims and policy objectives. If he does, at least two adverse results may occur: (1) technological advancement in the development of his product will suffer; (2) the human resources of the project will be reduced in efficiency and productivity.

Communication. Vannevar Bush, in his book "Modern Arms and Free Men," noted the distinctly different reactions to communication which he observed among military men and academicians:

> In the military there is vigorous and open debate on proposed actions before the decision. But when an office with clearly constituted authority makes the decision, the antagonists, acting under a basic doctrine of their profession, swing around to support actively the idea they had opposed.
>
> In contrast, under the customs which prevail in academic circles, the duly established decision signals the *start* of the fight. In this environment, it is very difficult to learn the nature

of the opposition to administrative planning, since academicians are not inclined to communicate freely in such matters. Consequently, after decisions are drawn there tends to be considerable passive and sometimes active resistance in the execution of the ideas.

The lessons here for the project manager are plain. He must expend considerable active effort in learning to communicate adequately with his scientists and in developing the communicative attitudes of his engineers. It has been clearly demonstrated that scientists and systems engineers who work in the operating environment *can* adapt their output to mesh with corporate schedules and budgets, if they are *adequately informed* regarding corporate policies and objectives.

In the case of research administration, it may be unwise to burden a research team by requiring from it regular status reports on a periodic basis. Rather, it may be preferable to require the team to submit a report only when it has something to report, since research advances do not come by regular increments of the calendar. However, in the advanced-technology project, periodic status reports are appropriate and valuable. A report showing the absence of advance during a reporting period is an important indicator of trouble to project management.

The Next Project. The temporal aspect of a project manager's task may strain his capacities in dealing with people. Because the duration of a project is well defined, it is only human for the scientists and engineers who work on it to come to anticipate their next assignment, even though it may be a year or more away. This can result in a kind of divided allegiance, in which the engineers look to others outside the project who may be able to help them in gaining their next assignment.

The project manager must counter this tendency to cast about for the next task, for it will diminish his effective control of the present task. In this effort he must be bulwarked by a potent company sales policy that has provided and will continue to provide new products for professional employees. When he has this backing, the manager then need only follow a basic rule of managerial conduct—that of letting his people know where they stand.

Thinkers and Doers. There has been generated an impressive indictment of the smothering of individuality and inhibition of creativity resulting from the integration of scientists and engineers with organized corporate groups. While most of this criticism has validity, it should not be interpreted to reflect adversely on the project method in advanced technology.

The project method has proved to be an effective way of *utilizing* the scientific output of the thinkers in the laboratories. The project—i.e. group, organization, team, task force, or whatever name it may go by—has piled up an impressive record of accomplishment since the days of the famed Manhattan Project.

PAUL O. GADDIS, Dean, School of Management and Administration, The University of Texas at Dallas, Texas

Information References

Gaddis, Paul O., "The Project Manager," *Harvard Business Review,* May-June 1959. The above entry, updated by the author, follows the treatment of that article.

Kerzner, Harold, "Project Management: A Systems Approach to Planning, Scheduling, and Controlling," New York, Van Nostrand Reinhold, 1979.

Reference Cited

Withington, Frederic G., "Coping with Computer Proliferation," *Harvard Business Review,* May-June, 1980.

Cross References: *Organization Theory (and cross references there given).*

PUBLIC ADMINISTRATION

By the early 1980s, the discipline of **Public Administration** had passed through a period of introspection, and was seeking reorientation in response to social turmoil that had massive and unforeseen impact on conventional governmental activities. In a relatively short period, administrators had to readjust to a rapidly expanding body of knowledge, to altered perceptions of government-citizen relations, to the formidable rise of unionism in government, to new technologies, to changing concepts of fairness in the employment of groups hitherto only sparsely represented in governmental ranks, and to the growing "mix" of the public and private sectors.

The new knowledge that entered the discipline fell into various general groupings: (1) it was mathematical and quantitative; (2) it was concerned with the inter-relationships and conduct of people in group context; (3) it dealt with revised theories of management and decision making, many of them clashing with the formerly held concepts of administrative hierarchies and management formats; (4) the term *communication* took on startlingly new meaning, as meetings, files, memoranda, and formerly hidden materials were opened to public view, and (5) citizen participation became a burgeoning fact of governmental life, particularly at municipal governmental levels.

The term *public administration* itself came under scrutiny. By the 1980s, it was clear that no simple definition could adequately contain it. Involved is an inexact and expanding field of information, an academic discipline, an occupational activity comprising subsidiary segments of activities, and a group of yet unsettled relationships in a grey area that can only be defined as politics/government. Indeed, some political scientists have argued that no separate entity exists entitled to such a term as *public administration*.

Nevertheless, there it is. People in government are making budgets, manipulating the economy, preparing civil service tests, devising plans for everything from the national defense to local school buildings, arguing court cases, preparing legislation, advising elected officials on policy, heading large organizations called agencies, supervising scientific tests, organizing sanitation routes, carrying out mandates imposed by the national and local legislatures, building water supply networks, providing assistance to the poor, running schools and jails, monitoring the ways of private business. The men and women who do these things are known as *public administrators,* sometimes by the pejorative term "bureaucrats." Management of the services they perform is known collectively as *public administration*.

Public administrators play major roles in both the formulation and execution of public policies. In this, they participate in the political process.

Concerned with technical managerial procedures, public administrators act to give effect to the government's laws. In the sense that public administration affects private rights and obligations, when law is implemented through administrative rule-making and orders, public administrators are involved in legal procedures.

The administrative process and activities utilize virtually every type of expertise: lawyers, accountants, economists, statisticians, engineers, educators, psychologists, mathematicians, policy and program analysts, planners, systems analysts, physicians, nutritionists, writers, every kind of scientist, among others. They are engaged in the broad task of building individuals into organizations, and managing and directing those organizations.

Organization, however, is only the prelude to integrating individuals and functions into productive relationships. An effective administrator must have the ability to ascertain objectives, comprehend and define the problems he or she must solve, weave policies into workable plans, make efficient utilization of resources, and take actions calculated to achieve the desired goals.

The Philosophic Base. Alexander Hamilton first defined the subject matter of public administration in *Federalist Paper No. 72,* wherein he developed a remarkable philosophy of administration whose key element was an "energetic executive" possessed of "unity," "duration," and "competent powers."

In a famous essay, "The Study of Public Administration," published in 1887, Woodrow Wilson defined public administration as the "detailed and systematic execution of public law." Wilson presented a basic postulate: the determination of law (policy) was the special province of the statesman (politician) while the execution of the law was within the realm of administration.

Frank J. Goodnow in 1900 followed with a book titled "Politics and Administration," which amplified the idea that administration is a "technical process" concerned with executing the will of the state. This essentially legalistic view of administration remained dominant during the first two decades of the twentieth century.

A major shift from this legalistic strand emerged in the first textbook in the field, "Introduction to the Study of Public Administration," by Leonard D. White, published in 1926. White visualized administration as "the management of men and materials to accomplish the purposes of the state." He continued to recognize the politics-administration dichotomy posited by Wilson and elaborated by Goodnow, but suggested that the *study* of administration should be rooted in management rather than law.

Wilson earlier had characterized administration as a "field of business." He suggested that the executive be rescued from the unbusiness-like methods in use and urged the scientific study of administrtion, with the civil service reforms then in progress being the prelude to more comprehensive administrative reform. White's book in 1926 continued to reflect a common view that business was more efficient because it was compelled by competition constantly to improve, and thus would serve as a good model for government to emulate.

Prior to White's textbook, the ideas expressed by Goodnow and others had won sufficient support to trigger establishment of the New York Bureau of Research, whose aim was to conduct "scientific research" into the organization and administration of government and to seek the practical implementation of its findings. As Wallace S. Sayre stated, the first textbooks "were based upon premises and concepts about the executive branch and its administrative agencies which had been at least a half century in the making." The Taft Commission on Economy and Efficiency studies of 1910–1912, the City Manager Movement promoted in 1910 by Richard Childs of the National Municipal League, reports on administrative reform in Illinois and New York, as well as other studies, helped to provide the raw materials for the texts and codified the premises, the concepts, and the data for the emerging study of public administration.

Within a year of the publication of White's text, W. F. Willoughby's "Principles of Public Administration" appeared. Willoughby argued that the threefold classification of the separation of powers (legislative-executive-judicial) was a confusing oversimplification. He suggested that there was a distinct "administrative function" which must be recognized.

Administration was "The function of actually administering the law" as declared by the legislature and interpreted by the judiciary—the "work proper" of putting policies and programs into execution. Contrariwise, the "executive function" represented the government as a whole, was distinctly "political" in character, and involved seeing that the laws and adopted policies were duly enforced and carried into effect.

Willoughby suggested that certain fundamental principles and practices must obtain if efficiency and economy in governmental operation were to be secured. Perhaps administration was still an "art" rather than a "science," but it was surely a subject for study to which the scientific method could be applied.

While Goodnow, White, Willoughby and others had focused their efforts primarily on public sector administration, they were influenced by a contemporaneous movement flourishing in the private sector—the "scientific management" movement. FREDERICK W. TAYLOR'S "Principles of Scientific Management" had advocated careful observation and analysis of the work process, time and motion studies, and a reorganization of supervision along functional lines. An effort was made to install the system in Army arsenals. Federal employees resisted, strikes occurred, and Congress soon prohibited by law the use of the system's essential features. (See SCIENTIFIC MANAGEMENT: "TAYLORISM.")

HENRI FAYOL, a French industrialist, espoused views which complemented some aspects of "Taylorism," but presented his ideas from a different vantage point. Taylor had concentrated on the work process at the base of the hierarchy to measure efficiency on a scale constructed according to input-output calculations. He was interested in the cost per unit of production, and emphasized tasks rather than structure, stating that it was the "duty" of management to find "the one best way."

Fayol, on the other hand, was interested in the view of the top manager. He advocated a "body corporate" which characterized the entire organization, with all parts fitting into the broader scheme. He attempted to develop "principles of administration" directed primarily to top administrators.

In 1937 a volume called "Papers on the Science of Administration" appeared. Edited by Luther Gulick and Lyndall Urwick, the book was a collection of classic papers prepared by leading students of administration, public and private, in the United States and Europe. Gulick's paper, "The Theory of Organization" was a noteworthy attempt to deal with the central factors around which an organization is formed, namely: purpose, place, clientele, or process. The paper considered the nature of hierarchy, staff and line, span of control, and the functions of the executive set forth in the acronym POSDCORB, i.e., planning, organizing, staffing, directing, coordinating, reporting, and budgeting. The Gulick and Urwick "Papers," along with the "Report of the President's Committee on Administrative Management," were acclaimed as representing the "high noon of orthodoxy" in public administration theory in the United States.

The Behavioral Approach. There were dissenters who rejected the *a priori* approach of some of the writers on prescriptive principles, or who scorned the aura of infallibility ascribed to Taylorism. They spawned psychological and sociological studies which became the basis of a behavioral approach to administration.

The HAWTHORNE EXPERIMENTS (1927–32), conducted by Elton Mayo, F. J. Roethlisberger and others, constituted a series of such experiments, focusing upon work groups at the Hawthorne plant of the Western Electric Co. These experiments tended to show the importance of the internal social organization in the motivation and morale of workers, and the limitations implicit in reliance upon scientific management's stress on monetary rewards and the physical aspects of a work situation. The studies pointed out the existence of an "informal organization," which influenced the real practices in a given work situation, and signaled a human relations approach to management.

The writings of MARY PARKER FOLLETT served as a bridge to the later behavioral approach. She brought "power" into the literature of administration, distinguishing power from authority. By analyzing the nature of consent, she argued that the authority of command is an "illusion," and stressed the authority of ideas as distinct from chain of command in an organization. Espousing the conference technique as creative and imaginative, she emphasized the application of psychological insight and social science findings to industry.

Two additional pioneering works from the private sector deserve mention. In 1938 Chester I. Barnard published "The Functions of the Executive," acclaimed by some academicians as the most important book of organization theory of its decade. Barnard's "Functions" was a reasoned exposition of formal organization as the process by which social action is largely accomplished. Organization was conceived as necessary cooperation among individuals, arising out of the limited capacities and choices of humans. Purpose became the coordinating principle. The success of the organization is its effectiveness in carrying out the purpose, and efficiency was the ability to secure continued contribution from individuals. Ultimately conscious, purposeful and deliberate cooperation rests upon the "character" and acceptance of *communication.* In essence, the functions of an executive are to formulate and define the purpose, communicate that purpose, and secure the cooperation of individuals. Barnard envisioned the dangers of mechanistic solutions and perceived the interrelationships between leadership, communication, and coordination.

Post-War Developments. A hiatus in the intellectual evolution of public administration as an academic discipline occurred during World War II. It ended abruptly with the publication of several noteworthy articles and books. Resumption of dissent took several directions simultaneously. Politically conscious political scientists vigorously questioned the politics-administration dichotomy allegedly enshrined by Goodnow. In 1946 Fritz Moorstein-Marx edited a volume titled "Elements of Public Administration," which supported the proposition that public administration is a political process, since administrators participate in the shaping of public policy through formal policy and through their widespread use of informal discretionary powers.

Norton E. Long provided a classic article, "Power and Administration" (1949), which bluntly stated: "The lifeblood of administration is power." He propounded the thesis that the attainment and retention of political power was a necessary precondition for the accomplishment of all other objectives, and suggested that a realistic science of administration would teach administrative behavior appropriate to the existing political situation. The same year Paul H. Appleby's monograph "Policy and Administration" also pronounced administration to be a political process. Indeed, said Appleby, it is its political character which distinguishes public from business administration. He noted that in government, political efficiency was the final criterion. Appleby also held that executive agencies did perform a "certain representative function," and an agency could swing politically without necessarily being partisan.

In 1948 Dwight Waldo published his now classic study, "The Administrative State: A Study of the Political Theory of American Public Administration." Waldo's incisive analyses portrayed how value-loaded, how political were the premises and concepts of the orthodox theorists.

Harold Stein's casebook titled "Public Administration and Policy Development" (1952) depicted the political roles played by administrators.

Near the end of the decade Wallace S. Sayre, in "Premises of Public Administration: Past and Emerging," suggested several premises as major components of a reformulation: public administration is one of the major political processes; organization theory in public administration is a problem in political strategy; and public administration is ultimately a problem in political theory.

A parallel thrust challenged the claims of the prewar traditionalists. As early as 1947, Robert A. Dahl's article, "The Science of Administration," challenged the pretentions to principles implicit in the writings of Willoughby, Urwick, and others, concluding that "we are a long way from a science of public administration." He contended that even the discovery of general principles of wide but not necessarily universal applicability was handicapped by three basic problems—values, the individual personality, and the social framework.

Perhaps the most influential and controversial attack on the prewar principles was contained in Herbert Simon's massive work, "Administrative Behavior: A Study of Decision-Making Processes in Administrative Organizations" (1947). Simon's stated purpose was to develop linguistic and conceptual tools to describe realistically an administrative organization. The creation of operational concepts was stated to be the first task of theory.

Simon charged that the so-called "principles" of administration were ambiguous, inconsistent, and contradictory, constituting little more than proverbs. But he went beyond criticizing the past neglect of decision making, and constructed a theory of "rational choice" to understand the influences that bear upon decision making in an organizational environment. Finally, Simon rejected as outmoded the politics-administration dichotomy, proposing instead a "fact-value" dichotomy. He argued that decisions stemmed from two kinds of premises: factual premises, which could be empirically tested and validated, and value premises, which could not be tested and validated. Decision-makers should keep the two sets of premises analytically distinct. Since the task of "deciding" prevades the entire organization and is integrally tied in with "doing," his decision-making schema is virtually the heart of the administrative process.

The book generated a host of rejoinders. Simon was accused of being the prophet of a new science of administration rooted in logical-positivism (facts must be separated from values). Critics insisted that values, philosophy, and human judgment were vital elements, and the logical-positivist had little to contribute save logic. Simon's concept of "authority" was scorned as not being useful to distinguish a "stick-up man" from a boss.

Clearly, scientific method has a place in public administration, and scientific research will continue to be germane to the problems of public administration. If for no other reason, Simon's challenge to the earlier doctrines evoked a response which compelled the traditionalists to reexamine their assumptions.

During the 1950s and 1960s a flood of literature was produced by psychologists, sociologists, and cultural anthropologists interested in organization. They focused on organization as a social system or social process: leadership, authority, decision-making, conflict, the behavior of the individual in the organization, and the character and behavior of bureaucracy.

Kenneth Boulding's "The Organizational Revolution" (1953), propounded a "growing complexity" thesis. Organizations have "inner necessities," and the larger the size the greater the inner fluctuations. William H. Whyte's "The Organization Man" (1956) queried whether the organization was being deified as an end in itself, rather than a means to a useful end. Contrasting individualistic pretensions and collectivistic behaviors, he posited the desirability of "conflict" between the individual and the organization. Conformity became the culprit.

Simon teamed with James C. March to write "Organizations" (1958), analyzing interactions and interrelationships. Investigating subjects such as decision making, communication, and cooperation, they considered the cognitive limits on rationality and set forth hypotheses related to human behavior in organizations. Peter M. Blau and W. Richard Scott produced "Formal Organizations" (1962), dealing with the nature and types of organizations and their publics, as well as the social structure of work groups and group dynamics.

The literature was prodigious in quantity. Outstanding contributors included Philip Selznick, Robert K. Merton, Chris Argyris, Robert V. Presthus, Robert Golembiewski, Rensis Likert, Kurt Lewin, James D. Thompson, Amitai Etzioni, Daniel Katz, Robert Kahn, Victor A. Thompson, and Charles A. Perrow.

The significance of the contributions is substantial, although critics have questioned what they regard as excessive detachment and esotericism in a practical and applied discipline. Skeptics asked whether organization theory was at best "an unnecessary elaboration or at worst a positive obfuscation."

As we entered the 1980s, we were still confronted with basic problems and controversial issues. Organization remains integrally related to policy, planning and decision making. The implications of Watergate led to a call for re-examination of American systems of authority and control. Structure continues to reflect the distribution of political power.

"Behavioralism" became a catch-all phrase; and some of the behavioralists insisted that there were discoverable regularities in organizations. They tended to use the methodological assumptions of the natural sciences and sought techniques to verify the regularities by reference to relevant behavior, which would be observed, analyzed, and recorded. Method became basic, and precision required measurement. This tenet bred a whole new generation of "quantifiers." Following the lead of Simon, ethical evaluation and empirical evaluation were to be kept analytically distinct. The studies were generally limited in scope, interdisciplinary in nature, and, hopefully for its advocates, one giant step toward the long-sought goal of a science of administration.

Beginning in the 1960s a splinter group of academics studying organizations concentrated upon a specialty referred to as *organization development* (OD). The conceptual approach was essentially socio-psychological in orientation. Authority was viewed as based on expertise, and collaboration was favored over competition. The basic assumption was: if you revise the value structure within an organization, structural modification will inexorably follow.

The crux of OD was planned, guided change as a long-range process organization-wide, in contrast to still another specialization called *management development.* The latter focused on the individual manager. Triggered by gaps in organizational performance, the basic goals of OD are to alter the values, beliefs, and attitudes prevalent within an organization. This is to be achieved by creating an "organizational capacity to solve problems on an ongoing basis," galvanizing both adaptiveness and self-renewal.

The methodology encompasses: (1) problem recognition, (2) data collection, analysis, and feedback, (3) intervention programs to effect change, (4) assignment of a "change-agent" role, (5) the collaborative development of norms, policies, and procedures, and (6) training which is participatory and experience-based.

Critics charged OD with being one more gimmick that actually stimulated conflict.

The New Public Administration. During the late 1960s and early 1970s, a so-called "new public administration" evolved. The period since 1960 had been characterized by deep unrest and accelerating protest, verbal and active, against established social arrangements and traditional authority. Virtually no segment of society was untouched by the civil rights movement, the urban crisis, "opening the windows" of the church by Pope John XXIII, and campus unrest triggered by the Vietnam war.

In September of 1968 a group of young professors and public administration professionals convened at Minnowbrook, N.Y. to exchange ideas. The conference papers were collected and published in a volume edited by Frank Marini titled "Towards A New Public Administration—The Minnowbrook Perspective." Several of the young scholars posited "social equity" as the overriding norm. Since administrators were morally bound to counter the existing inequities, they were urged to shed the mantle of "administrative value neutrality," and to assume a posture of advocacy to promote better services to those in lower social, economic, and political circumstances. Administrators could support and should be more responsive to the development of the impoverished racial minorities. In emotional terms, the Minnowbrook group called for a greater concern with the individual. The client should be the focus; the organization existed to serve the client.

The ripple effect of Minnowbrook burgeoned into what was characterized as the "Post-Behavioral Period" during the mid-1970s. Some writers even wrote in terms of "the new revolution in political science." In summary form, the characteristics were: public administration should be future-oriented; substance was more important than technique, and "technical excesses" were to be deplored; "behavioral science" had concealed the brute realities of politics and protected ideological conservatives; intellectuals had an obligation to promote humane, equitable values and a duty "to break the barriers of silence" and act individually and through their professional associations. Relevancy and advocacy moved to center stage.

Dr. Sterling D. Spero, a distinguished commentator on public administration, noted that the Minnowbrook papers showed little concern for the welfare and rights of rank-and-file civil employees. Nor was much interest shown regarding the problems growing out of the unionization of public employees, despite the fact that no development had so shaken established assumptions and modes of operation as had unionism. The question remained: Is there a failure to distinguish between analysis and advocacy which would replace one form of dogmatism with another under subtle and elusive new labels?

As public administration moved into the 1980s, concern with techniques re-emerged. The sub-specialties of what is broadly termed "management engineering"—work-sampling, work distribution analysis, work flow-charting, layout analysis, and queuing theory. Closely related is the older technique known as operations research, with quantitative techniques such as linear programming. In essence, considerable progress has been made in applying these aspects of management science to the public sphere. The computer and more recently the "electronics revolution," have exercised increasing impact on public administration techniques, particularly in the flow of information and, on the opposite side, the performance of "drudge" work like payroll processing. (See MANAGEMENT SCIENCES and ELECTRONIC DATA PROCESSING.)

Largely stemming from the Watergate crisis, the 1980s are witnessing attention to an age-old problem: how can we assure a responsive, responsible, and accountable bureaucracy? As part of the move toward greater accountability, program evaluation has received a heavier impetus. Finally, subdivisions of administration are becoming established. They include court management, health and hospital administration, transportation administration, and policy analysis, among other specializations.

Policy Analysis. Public policy analysis, under the rubric of "policy science," has received abundant attention, spawned by concern for urban life, the interface between society and technology, and the ever-increasing interdependency of the public and private sectors of the economy. In particular, the economic analysis of public policy has generated a thrust to revive "political economy" as a specialty. Economics is crucial to public budgeting and finance, as economic theories, analytical techniques, and even economic language pervades the process. Both COST-BENEFIT AND COST-EFFECTIVENESS ANALYSIS and systems approaches are rooted in economics, and have been introduced into administration.

Putting aside academic dialectics, it is clear that the many expressions of public policy extend beyond laws enacted by legislatures. It is equally clear that public policy encompasses social choices related to decision making. Public policy also consists of the general principles by which government is guided in the management of its affairs. All governmental institutions are best perceived as "interrelated producers" of public policies, and policy includes the determination of means by which legal mandates are effectuated.

While academics are attempting to describe policy analysis, and differing among themselves about it, public officials are making use of it, formally and informally. The President of the United States has designated individuals who, though not named policy analysts, perform the policy-analysis function. In New York City, the Mayor in 1977 named a Deputy Mayor for Policy. As the complexities of government increase, it is likely that elected officials will with increasing frequency call upon individuals capable of "asking the right questions" and formulating the possible consequences of current proposals. The interrelationship between policy and politics is clear.

The Budgetary Process. The United States Constitution vests the "power of the purse" in Congress; and the appropriations process is the keystone of legislative participation in control of administration. During the nineteenth century and the first two decades of the twentieth century, bureau chiefs in the Executive Branch prepared and sent budgetary estimates to the Secretary of Treasury, who submitted the estimates unchanged to the Congress. On June 27, 1912 President Taft sent a message to Congress, based on the work of the Taft Commission on Economy and Efficiency, suggesting that the President, as the constitutional head of administration, lay before the Congress "a definite business and financial program."

Congress failed to act on the Taft Commission's budgetary recommendations, but in 1921 finally enacted the Budget and Accounting Act. This legislation recognized the principle of an executive budget, and created a Bureau of the Budget as an agency within the Treasury Department.

The budgeting concept in vogue during this period was referred to as *line-item budgeting.* Each line of the budget designated an object of expenditure and the corresponding amount of money allocated to the item on the same line. Every employee's title and salary were listed.

The basic orientation was fiscal accountability. Detailing by line-item enabled greater legislative control. Reformers who had pushed for administrative integration were happy with the fact that responsibility for preparation was now in executive hands. Other reformers, primarily interested in administrative honesty, were pleased that Congress had enhanced its ability to control.

As a result of recommendations by Franklin D. Roosevelt's Committee on Administrative Management (the Brownlow Committee), FDR issued Executive Order 8248 in 1939, designating a greater managerial role for the Bureau of the Budget after its transfer from Treasury to the newly established Executive Office of the President.

The broad movement for greater management efficiency in the post-World War II years introduced a concept called "performance budgeting." Its concern was efficiency (performance), and the scope of budgeting was extended to "outputs," not merely the "inputs" characteristic of line-item budgeting. By 1949 the Hoover Commission popularized the term *performance budgeting.*

In 1960, Robert McNamara became Secretary of Defense, and, with the help of Charles J. Hitch, introduced a new dimension which came to be known as Planning-Programming-Budgeting-System Analysis (PPB). Hitch characterized PPB as a "new management and decision-making technique which attempted to introduce scientific method into these processes."

In some ways PPB is a systematic method of making budgetary decisions. The immediate objective is a cost-effective multi-year fiscal plan for agency management. PPB requires the existence in each agency of an analytic capability to provide continuing analyses of an agency's objectives and programs for attaining those objectives. PPB necessitates a multi-year planning and programming process, utilizing an information system to throw up data in meaningful terms essential to decision-making.

Planning becomes an instrument to analyze needs, formulating appropriate goals government should seek by testing old assumptions, filling informational gaps, integrating new information, and re-evaluating continuously. Programming relates the planned goals to concrete alternative programs that are categorized into program packages and further subdivided into program elements. The budgeting phase relates the programs to specific resources, the budgeted dollars being projected several years ahead. System analysis subsequently aids in quantifying the comparative costs and benefits of alternative programs. Ostensibly, such "quantitative common sense," aided by the prodigious ability of computers, can analyze and present in a rational way a multiplicity of options.

President Johnson was so impressed that in 1965 he ordered PPB to be used throughout the Federal government, and by 1968 some 28 states and 60 local governments indicated they were in the process of implementing PPB. Proponents argued that finally agencies had more explicit information, better techniques to measure performance, more alternatives, and information on total systems costs. Agencies reconsidered their missions, coordination was enhanced, and a note of rationality had been introduced.

Mere economy was not the objective; instead, get "the biggest bang for a buck" put in the right place for the right purpose. Despite the ascribed advantages, PPB met with resistance. Critics suggested that it was a case of "seduction by technique," it overstressed quantification, it did not consider values adequately, it was one more manifestation of a "centralizing bias," and it potentially undercut Congress' ability and right to control. Both at the national and local levels there was protest against the avalanche of paper required by PPB.

By 1970 President Nixon had reorganized the Bureau of the Budget, renaming it the Office of Management and Budget (OMB). A newly formed Domestic Council was established to be concerned with *what* to do, and the OMB was to focus its efforts on *how* it should be done, and how well it was done. In March, 1973, Allen Shick, who closely followed the progress of PPB, authored an article in the *Public Administration Review* announcing that PPB drowned in an avalanche of paper-work and suffered increased opposition from agency heads. By the early 1970s many state and local units had also largely abandoned its use.

During the early 1970s a variant of budgeting, MANAGEMENT BY OBJECTIVES, enunciated by Professor Peter Drucker, came into vogue. Its origins were in private industry, and its central theme was that objectives must be made operational before one can manage efficiently and effectively. In order to make objectives operational, you had to convert them into specific work assignments. Second, you had to ascertain priorities and select out what could be postponed or abandoned. The third step was to establish specific goals and designate specific targets, timetables, and strategies to fulfill the goals. Finally, it was essential to determine how results could be measured or judged.

MBO is concerned with inputs, outputs, and effects. The policy-making is more participative and decentralized than in PPB, and it does not stress economic analysis and a plethora of alternatives. In theory, the "decision flow" in MBO was up, while PPB's decision flow was down.

In 1975, OMB issued *Circular A-11,* requiring the submission of agency objectives along with budget estimates. While President Ford also made use of MBO, the accession to the Oval Office of Jimmy Carter effectively eliminated its use in the Federal Government. In 1977 OMB issued a bulletin marking the introduction of a "new" budgetary concept, ZERO-BASE BUDGETING.

Under ZBB, each program is challenged for its very existence in each budget cycle; program objectives are re-examined "as if we are to start all over again." The first step involves describing and analyzing all current or proposed programs in documents usually called "decision packages." This process of identification, analysis, and formulation assists an evaluation in terms of: purposes, consequences, performance measures, alternatives, and costs and benefits. Decision units i.e., the meaningful elements, "are the lowest-level program or organizational entity for which budgets are prepared."

The second phase involves the ranking of decision packages along with documents in support of those packages. During the third phase, resources are allocated in accordance with the ranking.

Those who favor ZBB insist that it identifies not only the costs and benefits of specific packages but also reveals duplicate efforts. They contend that there are benefits derived from greater participation by middle managers, and that the process assures continuous evaluation of programs.

Critics aver, however, that like PPB, ZBB tends to ignore political realities and administrator biases. They claim that in reality ZBB persists in perpetuating the mindless "mountains of paperwork," not to mention the massive methodological problems that are implicit in the procedures.

Although some experienced budget-watchers proclaim ZBB as "a solid concept," its utility cannot be assessed definitively as of this writing. The burden of proof is on the proponents who will have to answer the key questions: Has it changed budgetary behavior in such a way that efficiency, economy, and effectiveness have been promoted? Have the planning and policy-making been improved? Has it changed budgetary behavior for the better?

As of March, 1980 a report published by the National Association of State Budget Officers (NASBO) and the Urban Institute noted that ZBB had been installed in twenty states, and had aided in the identification of program initiatives and improvements. But the report concluded that it had not substantially reduced state expenditure growth. Although ZBB has not encountered the passionate opposition engendered by PPB, a declining growth rate seems probable.

The recent clamor for increased accountability spurs once again a return to the control orientation of line-item budgeting, which proved to be a hardy animal, while coexisting with a succession of budgetary innovations. Reversion to simple line-item budgeting is not in the cards in the 1980s; but fiscal accountability is never outdated, as proven by the passage of Proposition 13 in California (sharply limiting the real estate taxes that may be imposed by local governments), and the fact that a majority of states have enacted "sunset laws," requiring periodic re-examination of a program's and even an agency's right to exist.

Perhaps the most significant piece of budgetary legislation enacted since the Act of 1921 is the Budget Control and Impoundment Act of 1974. Basically, the Act is an attempt by Congress to reassert its control of the purse through revamped budgetary procedures; the prime goal is to achieve more orderly scrutiny of spending. It provides both substantive and procedural changes: (1) new House and Senate Budget Committees were established; (2) a new Congressional Budget Office (CBO) was established; (3) a new fiscal year was adopted, October 1 to September 30; (4) limits on "backdoor spending" were put in place; (5) a new budgetary timetable was adopted; and (6) the ability of the President to impound appropriated funds was circumscribed.

Audit and Control. The Budgeting and Accounting Act of 1921 went beyond the legal recognition of the concept of an executive budget and the creation of a Bureau of the Budget. The Act also established the General Accounting Office (GAO) headed by a Comptroller-

General as a "watchdog agency" over executive expenditures. The CG was appointed by the President for a non-renewable fifteen-year term of office.

Among the most important provisions of the statute was Section 312, vesting the CG with broad authority to investigate all matters relating to the "receipt, disbursement, and application of funds." Thus, the intent was not to create an accountant or bookkeeper, but a nonpartisan, independent arm of the legislature "to be our will, our eyes, and our own ears, to study and determine and enforce economy."

During the post World War II period, the administrative management movement entered its heyday. The new-found thrust of the GAO's audits was "managerial accountability." In the late 1960s and 1970s Congress gave to the GAO a constantly increasing stream of investigative and auditing directives, among them: to examine the extent to which Office of Economic Opportunity programs achieved statutory objectives; to analyze grant-in-aid programs; to develop and recommend to Congress methods for reviewing and evaluating government programs carried out under existing laws; and to audit certain nonappropriated funds. The Ethics in Government Act of 1978, the Civil Service Reform Act of 1978, and the Amtrak Reorganization Act of 1979 imposed additional responsibilities on the GAO.

In sum, upon entrance into the 1980s, it was evident that the importance of internal auditing and systems of control within agencies was being increasingly recognized. Audit reviews have focused on program accountability. Finally, the legal and other assistance that the GAO provides to Congress with regard to its legislative and "oversight" activities has increased.

At the local level of government, financial stringencies have compelled a re-examination of the way funds are calculated, received, and expended. One result has been the development of integrated financial management systems, which permit a jurisdiction to know at any time precisely where it stands financially, and diminishes the possibility of fiscal gimmickry.

Independent Regulatory Commissions (IRCs). Beginning with the establishment of the Interstate Commerce Commission in 1887, a new type of government agency was established to regulate major elements within the economy, including labor, trade, banking, securities, electric power, etc. The regulatory agencies evolved out of practical need to cope with increasingly complex social and economic problems. These agencies appeared to violate the traditional notion that legislative, executive, and judicial powers were to be kept separate. They resembled miniature governments, possessing quasi-legislative, quasi-judicial, and executive powers.

The IRCs comprise agencies such as the Civil Aeronautics Board which tend to focus on particular industries, and others such as the OCCUPATIONAL SAFETY AND HEALTH ADMINISTRATION, whose focus is largely functional. Among the most prominent are the National Labor Relations Board, the Securities and Exchange Commission, the Federal Communications Commission, the Federal Trade Commission, the Federal Power Commission, the Food and Drug Administration, and the Environmental Protection Agency.

Basically, the regulatory agencies promulgate rules and regulations to effectuate statutory policies, and enforce such policies by a variety of formal and informal actions, ranging from suasion to sanctions. Legislatures did not have the time or the capability to enact detailed rules on such a variety of subjects.

Why were they made "independent"? Although the primary reason varied from agency to agency, the legislation aimed to isolate such agencies from the blandishments of economic and political centers of power, including the Presidency, and to a lesser extent the legislative branch. Congress also felt that such agencies should be, in part, freed from the highly restrictive legal trappings of the judiciary.

For decades critics have inveighed against the IRCs. At least five separate commissions have recommended curbing their powers. During the late 1970s the media reported an accentuating drumfire of criticism as to the "regulation mess," the "rage over rising regulation," and "runaway regulation." The objectives of the present-day critics are: (1) to deemphasize the 90-year trend of ever-increasing regulation; (2) to end the duplicative efforts, and reduce the complexity and costs of regulation that, it is argued, contribute to the inflationary spiral; and (3) to alter the functions of some agencies and increase the efficiency of necessary regulation.

Business views the IRCs as a formidable "Big Brother" who not only overregulates but can harass, fine, or deny Federal aid. And all this with an attitude ranging from insensitive to arrogant. The plethora of rules and regulations is held to be excessive, and the personification of bureaucracy lacking in clarity and bewildering in quantity. Because of the rapidity of changes, the substantive changes required, case delays, and the reporting requirements, costs have skyrocketed. Conservatives see the IRCs as being run by ideological "do-gooders" trying to "eliminate all evil from the world."

Simultaneously, the IRCs are attacked as captives of the regulated, not diligent enough, unable to respond, and deficient from a technological standpoint. Defenders say the regulatory agencies are essential protectors of the consumer against the excesses and greed of corporate power.

In 1980, several measures before Congress sought to rein in the regulatory agencies, particularly the Federal Trade Commission. One of the earliest policy determinations of the Reagan administration, in 1981, was to set the stage and establish the framework for reducing the powers of the independent agencies. The concept of independence always has been a myth. Presidents have demonstrated they cannot be ignored. Congressional oversight is far from minuscule. The courts still continue to assure the rule of law through judicial review. The true question is not whether we shall have regulation, but what kind and to what degree.

Administrative Discretion. The significance of the wide-ranging activities of regulatory agencies is their enormous discretionary powers, from rule-making to investigation to adjudication. Whether a local housing inspector or an office of the Food and Drug Administration, the public administrator, in a hundred ways, exercises enormous influence over the day-to-day activities of citizens. Thus, Kenenth C. Davis notes that in a single year, 1974, the Social Security Administration made 1,250,000 determinations in disability claims. The Occupational Health and Safety Administration that same year visited 78,082 workplaces, issued 45,960 citations, alleging nearly 23,000 violations. The significance of these illustrative figures is that "eighty to ninety percent of the impact of the process comes from informal action that is not reviewed" by the courts, nor protected by formal procedures.

Discretion includes not only the choice to act or not to act, but against whom, when, where, how, and to what extent. Administrators decide whether to negotiate, settle, or investigate further. The decisions may be interim or final. Somebody must, in accordance with law, perform these tasks. But the power is, in fact, formidable; it is an administrative power, with significant economic, social, and political overtones.

Personnel Management. Public personnel administration in the United States has developed in stages. The bureaucratic beginnings (1789–1829) are perceived as the "guardian period." George Washington set the tone, and the system was one of character, competence, elitist, and government by gentlemen.

With the onset of Jacksonian democracy, there was ushered in the so-called *spoils system*, characterized by patronage under the rationale "to the victor belong the spoils." The spoils period is usually dated 1829–1883, and patronage in varying degrees and forms remains with us today.

The excesses of patronage, machine politics, and corruption generated a reform period (1883–1906). Actually, the civil service and moral reform movement had begun after the Civil War. Industrialization, corporate power, and bossism had led to the concentration of inordinate power in the hands of a few. Widespread agrarian and labor unrest further spurred reform.

Principles and oratory were not enough. It took the assassination of President Garfield to obtain enactment of the Pendleton Act in 1883, which brought civil service reform into the national government. The twin goals were to achieve "merit" and "political neutrality." There was rapid spillover into the states, which adopted their own personnel reform measures.

In 1919 a Congressional Joint Commission on the Reclassification of Salaries sought to bring order out of the chaotic salary situation in the Federal work force. In part due to the efforts of the National Federation of Federal Employees, Congress enacted legislation in 1923 that represented an application of the principles of scientific management and a further extension of the merit system, with the aim of assuring fair and equal treatment of all employees.

In 1935 the Commission of Inquiry on Public Service Personnel urged adoption of a career system in all levels of government and the further extension of the merit system to positions exempt from the requirements of civil service. The Brownlow Committee Report added its voice favoring extension of the merit system "upward, outward, and downward" to include all government positions except a few higher policy-making posts.

The period of 1937–1955 has been described as one of "administrative management." The first Hoover Commission in 1949, the second Hoover Commission in 1955, and the so-called Watson Report of the National Civil Service League, all generated minor improvements in the civil service. The Hatch Acts of 1939 and 1940 placed sharp limitations on the permissible political activities of public employees. The reports of the Hoover Commissions for Reorganization of the Executive Branch dealt with the latter's structure, organization, and functions. They argued that efficient operation requires a direct chain of command from the President to the lowest rungs of the Bureaucracy.

Since 1955, further efforts have been undertaken to advance the professionalism and developmental nature of public personnel administration. The second Hoover Commission advanced the concept of a senior civil service, to strengthen top management by providing "non-political executives." The Government Employees Training Act of 1958 enunciated a government-wide policy of training. A new philosophy and practice of personnel management was triggered, mainly by the changed manpower needs stemming from a complex and technological society. The training of public employees occupied an important place in the approach. The Municipal Manpower Commission Report of 1962 pointed up the need. Studies by the Brookings Institution recommended enlarging the potential capacity of civil servants to acquire greater skills and assume greater responsibilities.

Enactment of the Intergovernmental Personnel Act in 1971 extended Federal aid and expertise to train personnel in state and local government. In 1970, a task force had already been created to prepare a comprehensive plan to establish a coordinated system of job evaluation and rank of civilian positions in the Executive Branch.

In October, 1978, Congress completed a major effort to reorganize and reform the Federal personnel management system. The Civil Service Reform Act sought to make the civil service more responsive to public needs and civil servants more accountable. The Act also aimed to provide greater efficiency and competence within the pesonnel system. The legislation was hailed as the "centerpiece" of President Carter's pledge, in his 1976 campaign, to reorganize the bureaucracy in the interests of economy and efficiency.

The existing Civil Service Commission was split into two bodies: an Office of Personnel Management (OPM) and a Merit Systems Protection Board (MSPB). The OPM provides leadership, acting as a central personnel agency, and the MSPB oversees and safeguards the merit principles enumerated in the statute.

The legislation also created an Office of the Special Counsel to investigate and prosecute actions by agencies that might constitute violations of the Act. There is an intent to protect against reprisal the "whistle-blowers" who publicize waste or illegal activities. The Act also makes provision for a senior executive service, incentive pay tied to performance rather than longevity, and speedier and fairer procedures in the hiring, disciplining, or firing of employees. The new law also modified the existing labor-management relations program and created the Federal Labor Relations Authority to administer the program.

A variety of challenges currently beset personnel administrators. Since the enactment of the Civil Rights Act of 1964 and the Equal Employment Opportunity Act of 1972, administrators at all governmental levels are confronted not only by the ethical aspects of hiring and promoting individuals who do not meet the traditional standards required by merit system, but also by technical and legal problems. In a 1971 decision (Griggs *v* Duke Power Co.) the Supreme Court indicated that if job selection requirements have an adverse effect in terms of race, sex, religion, or national origins, those requirements must be altered. Civil Service examinations must be job-related: if not job-related, there has been illegal discrimination, even where there is no intent to discriminate. In essence, the court focused on the consequences of an employer's conduct, rather than his subjective intent.

A 1976 decision (Mayor of Washington, D.C. *v.* Davis) of the Supreme Court reversed a Circuit Court of Appeals case, which appeared to rely on the reasoning of the Griggs decision. Despite the views of dissenters, who said the majority ignored Griggs, the court rejected the notion that a law or action was unconstitutional solely on the grounds that it had a racially disproportionate impact, regardless of an intent to discriminate.

Personnel administrators continue to be plagued by court challenges contesting the validity and bias of tests and the legitimacy of affirmative action programs, even when instituted voluntarily. A number of Supreme Court cases have dealt with patronage aspects and restrictions on the political activities of public employees. Elrod *v.* Burns (1976) held a patronage system inimical to our system of government to the extent that it compels or restrains beliefs or association. U.S. Civil Service Commission *v.* National Association of Letter Carriers (1973) reaffirmed the constitutionality of the Hatch Act restrictions on political activities of Federally funded employees. At the local level, at least one court has mandated appointment of employees on a strict quota ethnic basis.

In sum, the issues of the political neutrality of public employees, race, quotas, and affirmative action are still in a state of flux in the 1980s.

Unionism and Collective Bargaining. Since the mid-1950s and especially since the early 1960s, union membership of public employees in all levels of government has expanded at an unprecedented rate. This growth has been accompanied by demonstrations of militancy akin to those accompanying the organization drives of workers in the mass production industries in the 1930s. One result has been the movement away from established unilateral determination of working conditions by the public employer. The determination of working conditions in public employment by legislative or administrative action is being rapidly replaced by collective bargaining between employee organizations and the employing authorities.

Perhaps the most publicized event in public employment relations in the post World War II years was the issuance in 1962 of President John F. Kennedy's Executive Order on Employee-Management Cooperaton in the Federal services. The order provided for the official recognition of employee organizations by employing agencies. It allowed exclusive agreements with organizations representing the majority of the employees in recognized bargaining units. The scope of the agreements was necessarily confined to issues falling within the limits of administrative discretion over personnel matters, since, in the Federal service, basic conditions of work, including wages and hours, are fixed by Congressional action. Many states, counties, and cities, reacting to growing union power, also mandated bargaining with their employees.

Having secured the right to bargain. unions attempted to expand the scope of bargaining during the early 1970s, and sought to achieve the "right to strike" accorded to private sector employees since the Wagner Act in 1935. As of 1980, eight states have granted some or most of their employees a limited right to strike. Unions also attempted to enhance their security through the use of devices such as the "agency shop" concept.

Attempts to resolve impasses in the public sector spawned a new class of professional mediators, fact-finders, and arbitrators. Administrative machinery such as public employment relations boards and offices of labor relations evolved to administer the law or participate in the bargaining process.

During the late 1970s, the strike issue remained as confused as it was dramatic. The claims of sovereignty failed to deter union strikes, and the efficacy of strike bans was doubtful. During the decade 1966–1976, more than 3,500 work stoppages took place in the public sector. Doubts about the injunctive process grew as the Michigan Supreme Court refused in the Holland Case (157 N.W. 2d. 210, 1968) to affirm a lower court injunction in the absence of a showing of violence, irreparable injury, or breach of the peace in a school teacher strike. Some public employers, however, attempted to convince unions they would not achieve their goals through illegal strikes. A 1977 decision of the U.S. Supreme Court sustained the Hortonville, Wisconsin School district's discharge of strikers. Courts increasingly imposed fines when unions violated injunctions, and in some cases union leaders received jail sentences.

Several trends are now discernible: (1) Employee groups continue to lobby for legislation which enhances their right to bargain. (2) The scope of bargaining has perceptibly widened. (3) More states are legislatively acceding to their employees' right to strike, once certain statutory requirements have been complied with. (4) During the mid-1970s, urban fiscal crises compelled a toughened stance on the part of some employers, and unions found themselves in a defensive posture as new "actors" were introduced into or affected the parties bargaining. Experiences in New York City and San Francisco spurred greater caution on the part of unions. (5) More coalition bargaining and multitier bargaining was taking place. (6) The issue of whether the scope of negotiations had intruded too far into the policy-making prerogatives of elected public officials remains controversial. (7) More attention is being directed to the increasingly autonomous role of organized bureaucracies in public affairs. (8) Public employee unions tend to place more stress on legislative or political action to get what they cannot achieve through collective bargaining. And (9) the unions and the employing agencies are beginning, in the early 1980s, to examine ways of increasing employee productivity. "Sitting around the table together" has evoked glimmers of possible other fruitful relationships between management and labor in government.

Legislative Oversight and Judicial Control. The misuse and abuse of administrative power has ancient roots; and although the environment in which transgressions have taken place has changed, the nature of the problems and issues has not. The wide-ranging functions of government and concomitant discretionary powers have converged, however, to pose threats to individual rights unforeseen in the pre-industrial age.

Considering the subject of responsible bureaucracy, one is immediately faced with the semantic problems. The term "responsibility" encompasses a complex of values (e.g., probity, prudence, accountability, candor, etc.) having moral, social, professional, and legal aspects. "Accountability," however, is often used to denote the legal locus of responsibility and denotes "answerability" (e.g., A is accountable to B for C).

The practical question remains: to what extent have Congress and the courts succeeded in controlling and overseeing the use of administrative power? Oversight and control are intended to assure that power is used only for purposes authorized by Congress and in conformity with the constitutional rights, privileges, and immunities of individuals. The dilemma is how to vest sufficient power in the bureaucracy to fulfill the legislative intent, and avoid excessive legislative control which cripples administration.

Decentralization: The social turmoil of the 1960s, together with the rising expectations of America's deprived groups and the recognition that citizens were often alienated from their governments, led to a push for *decentralization,* at local levels of government. The burgeoning demand was for greater access to the instruments of governmental power. The movement assumed a variety of names, "community control," "citizen participation," "neighborhood power." The Federal government assisted the movement, making citizen participation a significant element of various Federal aid programs. Long enshrined principles of public administration, e.g. that authority must be commensurate with responsibility, and that larger units work more efficiently than smaller ones, were questioned. The movement led to greater governmental sensitivity to citizen grievances, to the establishment of complaint-receiving centers and "little city halls," and to efforts to provide some form of community involvement into the governmental process.

The most advanced form of local governmental decentralization in the United States occurred in New York City. A charter enacted in 1975 provided for community boards (59 were created) having specific roles in: the determination of land use; authority to monitor the services of central government agencies; the establishment of co-terminality, a scheme mandating the agencies of government to realign their field operations to coincide with the borders of the new communities; and the establishment of geographic budgeting, which was designed to inform each community of the amount of funds being expended within its area for each local government service.

The decentralization issue had aroused furious debate, but by the early 1980s the system was in place and public administrators adjusted to the fact that their work-lives now contained a new element—formal consultation with the city's communities. The system of decentralization was "catching on" in other American cities as well, although nowhere had decentralized government reached the status it holds in London, where each of 32 districts elects its own local officials, collects its own taxes, and performs a variety of services which in the United States are within the province of the central city governments.

Also, as government moved into the 1980s, there was rising discussion about "contracting out" of services. Thus, San Francisco does not collect garbage; that function is contracted out to private firms. In Los Angeles County, cities may "buy" services from the county or from private sector purveyors, at their option. The financial difficulties being encountered by cities was accentuating this trend, in the face of strong opposition from the public employee unions.

Biology and Administration. While no definition of public administration adequately covers its many facets, the practitioners and academics within that discipline are constantly alert to technological, scientific, and social developments that might affect them or help explain what they do and why they do it. Lynton Caldwell, professor of public and environmental affairs at Indiana University, has laid open to question all of the assumptions "upon which modern government and bureaucracy has been based." He argues that "The theories of human behavior which underlie modern government have been derived through deductive reasoning from pre-scientific premises; governmental institutions, laws, and programs based upon these theories are thus founded upon propositions that are not demonstrably valid." That is why they don't answer the persisting social questions. The problem-solving records of most governments are impressive by their failures. He opts for the new science of *sociobiology*. If present assumptions regarding criminality, mental health and breakdown, old age, family relations, education, are based on incorrect evidence, then the government agencies and bureaucracies dealing with these matters inevitably must fail. There is needed, suggests Caldwell, "a conceptual revolution," with recognition that the confluence of biology and sociology are necessary, and that government and bureaucracy will be formidably influenced by the resulting accretion of understanding about the human species. "With some aid from sociobiological analysis, political reformers and public administrators might improve their realism and the probabilities of achieving desired results while avoiding undesired consequences."

That new vistas face public administration in the 1980s is clear. The reorientation period is far from over.

MAXWELL LEHMAN, Professor of Political Governmental Communication, Fairfield University, Fairfield, Connecticut; formerly City Administrator, City of New York

JOHN CAPOZZOLA, Professor of Public Administration, New York University, New York, New York

Information References

Advisory Commission on Intergovernmental Relations.
American Academy of Political and Social Science.
American Political Science Association.
American Society for Public Administration.
Council of State Governments.
Council on Graduate Education in Public Administration.
Institute of Public Administration
International City Management Association.
International Institute of Administrative Sciences.
International Personnel Management Association.
National Institute of Public Management.
National Municipal League.
Public Administration Service.
Royal Institute of Public Administrative Sciences.
Urban Institute.

Periodicals

Administrative Science Quarterly.
American Political Science Review.
Annals of the American Academy of Political and Social Science.
GAO Review.
International Review of Administrative Sciences.
National Civic Review.
Policy Analysis.
Policy Sciences.
Public Administration (Journal of the Royal Institute of Public Administration, London, Eng.).
Public Administration Review.
Public Management.
Public Personnel Mangement.

Texts and Readers

Barnard, Chester I., "The Functions of the Executive," Cambridge, Mass., Harvard University Press, 1938.
Charlesworth, James C., ed., "Theory and Practice of Public Administration," American Academy of Political and Social Science and the American Society for Public Administration, October, 1968.
Davis, Kenneth Culp, "Administrative Law: Cases, Text, Problems," 6th ed., St. Paul, Minn., West Publishing Co., 1977.
Dimock, Marshal E., and Gladys O., "Public Administration," New York, Holt, Rinehart & Winston, 4th ed., 1969.
Gulick, Luther and Urwick, L., "Papers on the Science of Administration," Institute of Public Administration, New York, 1937.
Harris, Joseph P., "Congressional Control of Administration," Washington, D.C., Brookings, 1964.
Hawley, Claude E., and Ruth G. Weintraub, "Administrative Questions and Political Answers," Princeton, N.J., D. Van Nostrand Co., 1966.
Henry, Nicholas, "Public Administration and Public Affairs," 2nd ed. Englewood Cliffs, N.J., Prentice-Hall, 1980.
Jones, Charles O., "An Introduction to the Study of Public Policy," 2nd ed., Belmont, CA, Wadsworth, 1977.
Mailick, Sidney and Van Ness, Edward H., eds., "Issues in Administrative Behavior," Englewood Cliffs, N.J., Prentice-Hall, 1962.
March, James G., and Simon, Herbert A., "Organizations," New York, Wiley, 1960.
Marini, Frank, ed., "Toward a New Public Administration: The Minnowbrook Perspective," Scranton, Pa., Charles Publishing Co., 1971.
Mosher, Frederick C., ed., "Basic Documents of American Public Administration," N.Y. Holmes & Meier, 1976.
Nigro, Felix A. and Lloyd G. Nigro, "Modern Public Administration," 5th ed., New York, Harper & Row, 1980.
Pois, Joseph, "Watchdog on the Potomac," Wash., D.C., University Press of America, 1979.

Presthus, Robert V., "Public Administration," 6th ed., N.Y., Ronald Press, 1975.
Rourke, Francis E., ed., "Bureaucratic Power in National Politics," 3rd ed., Boston, Little, Brown & Co., 1978.
Shafritz, J.M., and A.C. Hyde, eds., "Classics of Public Administration," Oak Park, Ill., Moore Publishing, 1978.
Simon, Herbert A., "Administrative Behavior, Study of Decision-Making Processes in Administrative Organization," 2nd ed., New York, Macmillan, 1957.
Spero, Sterling D., and John M. Capozzola, "The Urban Community and Its Unionized Bureaucracies," N.Y. Dunellen Co., 1973.
Van Riper, Paul P., "History of the United States Civil Service," Evanston, Ill., Row, Peterson & Co., 1958.
Waldo, Dwight, "The Administrative State," New York, Ronald, 1948.
White, Leonard D., "Introduction to the Study of Public Administration," 4th ed., New York, Macmillan, 1955.
Wildavsky, Aaron, "The Politics of the Budgetary Process," 3rd ed., Boston, Little, Brown & Co., 1979.

Cross Reference: *Public Authorities.*

PUBLIC AUTHORITIES

The **Public Authority** in the United States is a unique form of governmental organization whose primary purpose is the expeditious delivery of public services. It combines the techniques of public administration with the managerial practices of the modern corporation. The public authority may be defined as a public-enterprise corporate instrumentality created by general-purpose governments to perform specialized public functions. It is usually of a revenue-producing and often self-supporting character, and its bonds are exempt from most taxes. It is estimated that state and local public authorities have raised between $7 and $12 billion annually through the municipal bond market. Authorities are operated along business-type lines with substantial autonomy, subject to the ultimate control of the governments which created them. Authorities typically lack power to levy taxes.

A correlative form of organization, termed special district, frequently has capacity to levy taxes, as in the case of fire or school districts, but the two forms otherwise are difficult to distinguish and the terms often are used interchangeably (the U.S. Census of Governments uses "special districts" as a generic term encompassing the public authority). A public authority may be established to overcome fiscal restrictions of general-purpose governments, as in the case of public building authorities; its main thrust is in the development of public enterprises to operate in efficient, businesslike ways. A case in point is the Washington (State) Public Power Supply System which is contructing five nuclear plants. Another was the New York State Urban Development Corporation, created in 1968 to combat massive housing shortages, which later became the center of controversy over its financial policies.

The authority is popular because it avoids financial limits, red tape, civil service bureaucracy, and jurisdictional restrictions of general-purpose government. Conversion of line departments of governments to a public corporate form has not always met expectations, however. Examples include the U.S. Postal Service (1970), at the Federal level; and the New York City Health and Hospitals Corporation (1969) at the municipal level. Controversy has surrounded both of these institutions reflecting managerial and financial concerns and accomplishments. Overall, a high record of managerial success has supported the belief that the public authority is more effective for specified public services than general governments. Some students of local and state government feel that the centralization of tremendous resources and powers in autonomous entities is inimical to democratic principles, since such autonomy inhibits governments from planning comprehensively, particularly for large metropolitan regions and from efficient allocation of scarce resources.

Historical Development. Authorities can be traced to remote origins, including chartered enterprises in medieval and Renaissance times. One scholar suggests that authorities were developed by medieval city-states of Genoa and Venice to handle the movement of ships and cargoes in their harbors [1].

Corporations in the modern sense were originally quasi-public, with earlier ones chartered to construct canals, railroads, and other transportation or utility enterprises, often with governmental support. During the nineteenth century in the United States, many of these enterprises became increasingly devoted to private gain at public expense, and public trust and confidence declined. State constitutions were amended to prohibit aid to private corporations, including railroads and others dealing with "internal improvements." Often these amendments also barred state governments and municipalities from engaging directly in or using public credit for internal improvements. (Under the judicial "special fund" doctrine, accepted in most states, public corporations may borrow money, provided their bonds or other obligations are to be liquidated from the use of special funds, that is, from revenues derived from the corporation's own activities, without constituting a state debt.)

The public authority as it is typically portrayed today has its immediate prototypes in two British enterprises. One is the Mersey Docks and Harbour Board, established in 1858 as a port agency for Liverpool. The other is the Port of London Authority, created in 1909. The first American authority—the Port Authority of New York and New Jersey, created in 1921—used the London experience as a model and is itself the most cited model in the United States.

During the depression years of the 1930s, state and local governments found it increasingly difficult to finance needed activities through general taxation, and turned to the public authority to avoid state debt limitations. Revenue bonding not involving the credit of general-purpose governments proved attractive. Authorities also received financial support from relief programs of the Federal Government. Between 1933 and 1936, nineteen states established authorities to finance revenue-producing activities, and 25 states authorized their subdivisions to do the same. After World War II, the public authority experienced a new wave of popularity as a means of meeting the wartime public works backlog and the new demand for added public services. Combined with the special-district form, the authority form today is endemic in the subnational governmental machinery, and it has developed a distinctive life style.

Functions. Authorities perform a variety of functions with a predominant role in transportation. Turnpike authorities were responsible for the construction and operation of express toll roads in Pennsylvania, New Jersey, New York, the New England States, Ohio, West Virginia, Indiana, and others. Public authorities finance, construct, and operate bridges, tunnels, and parking facilities, and manage major port and transport facilities. The latter include the New York Metropolitan Transportation Authority, Delaware River Port Authority, Port Authority of New York and New Jersey, Board of Harbor Commissioners of the Port of New Orleans, South Carolina State Ports Authority, and the Massachusetts Port Authority. There are navigation agencies with responsibility for the navigable channels of the state or jurisdiction involved.

Authorities manage airports and other transportation facilities. Many of these operate on a local level. Metropolitan transit systems are operated by authorities, as in New York, Atlanta, Washington, D.C., Chicago, Boston, Los Angeles, and the Bay Area Rapid Transit District in San Francisco.

Power and water plants also are among the specialized functions of public authorities, as well as electric power distribution facilities, including nuclear and solar energy. There are local housing and redevelopment authorities in most states. Miscellaneous facilities operated, and functions performed, by authorities are those dealing with parks and recreation, conservation, ferries, hospitals, regional and local markets, industrial promotion, air and water pollution control, grain terminals, and a host of other activities [2]. Many of these authorities were created to deal with a single function of limited dimension, but not infrequently have assumed other areas of responsibility.

Classification in the Governmental Scheme. The Bureau of the Census has noted that "in addition to the widely recognized pattern of Federal, state, county, municipal, and township governments, there exist many offshoots from the structure in the form of single-function and multiple-function districts, authorities, commissiones, boards, and other entities that have varying degrees of autonomy. The basic pattern differs widely from state to state. Moreover, various classes of local units within a particular state also differ in their characteristics" [3].

The Census Bureau has established three criteria which must exist before an activity will be classified as a government unit: (1) existence as an organized entity with evidence of corporate powers or designation in law as "municipal corporation," "public corporations," "bodies corporate and politic," or the like; (2) governmental character, including election of officers or appointment by public officials, high degree of public responsibility, public accountability, power to levy property taxes, or authorization to issue bonds or other obligations which pay interest exempt from Federal taxation; and (3) substantial autonomy, that is, considerable fiscal and administrative independence.

The authority also differs from general-purpose governments in that its functions are limited, often to a single activity or group of activities. The geographical jurisdiction of authorities may transcend local, state, or even international boundaries. The board of directors or other governing body of an authority rarely is publicly elected. The authority possesses no inherent sovereign authority or home rule powers. Its power is derived completely from its enabling statute.

In the narrow definitional sense, the authority is distinguished from other public corporations (mostly special districts) in that it rarely possesses independent taxing power. Nonetheless, the Bureau of the Census includes authorities with special districts. The actual number of public authorities is small relative to the total number of special districts. As of 1978, one scholar estimated that of 23,885 special districts (Census of Governments data), nearly 60% have no debt and that 74% are not involved in major investment in public facilities from *independently* raised capital as are the public authorities. It was estimated . . . "that no more than 5,000 to 6,000 of the entities are public authorities" [4].

Classes of Authorities. At the Federal level are wholly owned government corporations and mixed ownership corporations. While not all of these are authorities in the strict sense of the word, many possess sufficient characteristics as development enterprises to be classed as authorities. There are also state and interstate authorities, municipal and intermunicipal authorities, and single and multifunction authorities. The Port Authority of New York and New Jersey is both interstate and multifunctional, its latest enterprise being the World Trade Center in lower Manhattan—the subject of considerable controversy and litigation.

Characteristics. Only a few authorities issue certificates of stock to their parent government to evidence ownership. In this respect they differ from the private corporation. Authorities invariably possess corporate identity and the power to sue and be sued, to adopt a seal, to make contracts in their own names, to appoint their principal officers and employees, to issue obligations (usually revenue bonds), and to collect fees and rentals for the sale or use of their services. They do not pay most Federal, state and local taxes. Although the traditional concept of an authority is one which is entirely self-supporting, there is increasing recognition that this characteristic is not crucial. An important characteristic is that authorities do not rely on general-purpose governments to guarantee their obligations. (The use of moral obligation bonds was popular for a period of time but has declined in popularity and use.)

A primary characteristic of authorities is the use of business-type procedures and budgeting arrangements. They are relatively free to decide how best to utilize financial resources available to them, including capacity to compete for top executives without the salary level constraints typical of general-purpose governments. The Government Corporation Control Act subjects Federal corporations to budgetary supervision by the U.S. Office of Management and Budget and by Congress. But funds of most of the twenty wholly owned Federal corporations are not subject to fiscal-year limitations. Authorities at the state and local government level generally enjoy a favorable bond market. Bonds of many authorities are highly attractive investments offering significant tax savings.

Method of Creation and Appointment. Public authorities are created by specific legislative act of a state, without public approval at a referendum. Certain types of authorities performing municipal services may be created locally, pursuant to general enabling legislation. Less frequently, an authority is created by incorporation under a state's general corporation law. Federal corporations are created by or under authority of Acts of Congress. Interstate authorities require concurrent legislation of the states involved, and the consent of Congress, pursuant to Article 1, Section 10 of the Federal Constitution. Once a compact is in effect, it becomes binding on the parties. Authorities created by a state or the Federal government can be abolished by act of the legislature or the Congress, respectively.

Authority board members generally are appointed by the chief executive of the parent government. Other methods of selection include *ex officio* membership and, less frequently, representation of economic interests, or even direct election, but this is atypical. There are many variations.

The President of the United States appoints members of the boards of wholly owned Federal corporations. He may also appoint their principal officials. Appointments are subject to Senate confirmation. The President appoints the Administrator and Deputy Administrator of the St. Lawrence Seaway Development Corporation. The Corporation is supervised by the

Secretary of Transportation. The multipurpose Tennessee Valley Authority is governed by a three-man board of directors appointed by the President. The principal executive officer is a general manager.

Management. Internal policy of an authority is determined by its governing board. Most authority boards have smaller memberships than the average private corporation, but there is considerable variation. The authority's board determines the major details concerning its operations and financing. However, the extent of its powers may be quite restricted, with little opportunity to make important policy, when the enabling legislation determines the basic functions (such as to build a bridge located at a specified spot and financed in a designated manner).

Day-to-day management is the responsibility of an executive director or general manager, who usually is appointed by the board to serve at its pleasure. Other officers, such as comptroller, counsel, director of public relations, personnel manager, and heads of the operating divisions often are recruited in the same manner as are top corporate executives. Many authorities are free from civil service requirements and have developed their own merit systems for hiring and promoting personnel. Large authorities have an enviable record in recruiting and retaining managerial personnel. They boast of high salary scales, attractive pensions, and considerable opportunity for advancement.

Criticism of Authorities. As thriving public enterprises, public authorities, Federal, state, and local, often have succeeded beyond original expectations. At the state and local levels, the Port Authority of New York and New Jersey and similar agencies are contributing to the economic well-being of metropolitan communities. But this record is dotted with failures and controversy. Several turnpike authorities, including the West Virginia Turnpike Commission, have had financial difficulties, and some authorities have never gotten off the ground.

A charge often leveled at authorities is that public controls are inadequate. Authorities, it is argued, frequently operate outside of the mainstream of public affairs; they tend to ignore emerging public needs. Authority boards, it is asserted, are more concerned with the marketability of their bonds and their self-perpetuation than with the overall public interest.

Proponents of the authority device reply that attempts to interfere unduly with the internal management and fiscal operations of authorities will hamper their effectiveness and fiscal integrity. They assert that public controls are adequate. Controls include the power of appointment and removal for cause of board members, independent or state audit of the books of authority, strict interpretation of the authority's jurisdiction and powers, veto power of the governor over the authority's actions (as in the case of the Port Authority of New York and New Jersey), local government approval before acquisition of property through purchase or condemnation, requirement of annual reports, and political pressure by state and local officials, and by the public.

Critics of the authority device retort that these controls are insufficient or ineffectual. Charges have been made that authorities often impose tolls or other charges on what are clearly monopolistic services beyond what is necessary to recover extant capital and operating expenses. The ability of the governor of New York or New Jersey to control actions of the Port Authority of New York and New Jersey by disapproving minutes of the authority's formal actions rarely has been asserted. One exception was the veto of the action of the Authority to include a hotel within the World Trade Center complex, an action taken by Governor Cahill of New Jersey in July 1971 (the matter was resolved; the hotel was built). Since Congressional consent is required to create most interstate authorities, Congressional influence over interstate bodies may be a point of control, but the constitutional extent of such influence is not fully defined.

Public and Intergovernmental Relations. The public authority device is subject to one overriding criticism stemming from the fact that it is a highly self-contained unit with considerable independence. The ability of elected public officials of general-purpose governments to decide public policy for the community at large and to make full use of resources within the public sector of the economy often is effectively constrained by powerful and autonomous public corporations. Such criticisms are tempered by the pervasive need to overcome the constraints of traditional governmental forms and the fragmentation of local authority in metropolitan areas, river basins, and valleys.

The Advisory Commission on Intergovernmental Relations has argued that "in the absence of compelling conditions that make it impractical, local public services should be provided through multipurpose units of general government. Assignment of responsibility for some services to independent specialized units tends to reduce the public's effective control over local government, to interfere with an orderly evaluation and reconciliation of competing demands for the local revenue dollars, and to hamper coordination of interrelated services" [5]. Walsh has argued that while public authorities generally are successful in management and operations, the system ". . . has been generally unsuccessful at planning and allocating resources equitably" [6].

Future of Authorities. In years ahead, the authority will continue to play an important role in developing public enterprises. However, the traditional or orthodox authority may become somewhat less easily recognizable, and may be replaced by bodies whose policy position is more strictly limited by parent governments, as well as by more complex forms.

An important development is the partnership of the Federal government and the states in sponsoring public authorities involving regional development activities. The Delaware River Basin Commission, in which four states and the Federal government are partners, is the prototype of such a model. Compare too the French Regie Autonome des Transports, which provides transit service in the Paris urban region and is run by an intergovernmental board. The Washington Public Power Supply System is a joint operating agency of the State of Washington whose *ex officio* board is comprised of representatives of local power districts and municipal power departments. For specific nuclear power projects, non-member participants are represented by participant committees.

The creation of the National Railroad Passenger Corporation (AMTRAK) in 1970 by an Act of Congress represents use of a mixed corporate approach, in which public and private investment and controls are combined to deal with public enterprises—in this case intercity rail passenger service. New York State's Metropolitan Transportation Authority is an umbrella agency under which several other authorities exist and are controlled: the New York City Transit Authority, Triborough Bridge and Tunnel Authority, Long Island Railroad, *et al.* The creation of MTA as a central body was not without substantial growing pains. A full-time executive director was not appointed until 1979 and the autonomy of the Transit Authority has not been fully tempered.

The concept of a wholly self-supporting, autonomous enterprise may give place to mutually interdependent agencies, contributing to broad programs of public planning and action, and aided by grants or other means of financial support from Federal sources and from state or local governments. In the future, public authorities may find competition in private for-profit corporations, if the latter become major deliverers of public services, traditionally the province of state and local governments, under "contracting out" or "privatization" arrangements. In any event, the public authority has clearly become established as a vital tool for public enterprise, and is as much a part of subnational government as are the states, counties, and cities.

HOWARD N. MANTEL, Director of Government Programs, Institute of Public Administration, New York, New York

Information References

Cape, William H., Graves, Leon B., and Michaels, Burton M., "Government by Special Districts," Lawrence, Kansas, University of Kansas, 1969.

Goldberg, Sidney D. and Seidman, Harold, "The Government Corporation: Elements of a Model Charter," Chicago, Public Administration Service, 1953.

Grad, Frank P., "Federal-State Compact—A New Experiment in Cooperative Federalism," *Columbia Law Review,* May 1963.

"Public Authorities," *Law and Contemporary Problems,* Autumn 1961.

Smith, Robert G., "Ad Hoc Governments: Special Purpose Transportation Authorities in Britain and the United States," Beverly Hills, California, Sage Publications, 1974.

References Cited

[1] Gerwig, Robert, "Public Authorities: Legislative Panacea?" *Journal of Public Law,* Fall 1956.

[2] "Public Authorities in the States," p. 35, Chicago, The Council of State Governments, 1953.

[3] U.S. Bureau of the Census, "Census of Governments: 1967, Vol. I, Governmental Organization," pp. 12–15, Washington, D.C., U.S. Government Printing Office, 1969.

[4] Walsh, Annmarie H., "The Public's Business: The Politics and Practices of Government Corporations," Cambridge, Massachusetts, MIT Press, 1978.

[5] "Advisory Commission on Intergovernmental Relations, Urban America and the Federal System," p. 87, Washington, D.C., U.S. Government Printing Office, 1969.

[6] Walsh, *op. cit.*

Cross Reference: *Public Administration.*

PUBLIC RELATIONS

Public Relations is the management function which attempts to create good will for an organization and its products, services, or ideals, with groups of people which can affect its present and future welfare. The most advanced type of public relations not only attempts to create good will for the organization as it exists, but also helps formulate policies, if needed, which will of themselves result in a favorable reaction. For a corportion, the groups which are the concern of the Public Relations Department include employees, customers, potential customers, stockholders, governments at all levels, communities in which the firm operates, suppliers, distributors, educational institutions, and all media.

History. Public relations activity has been practiced on a formal basis since around 1900, and some of its elements have been utilized almost since recorded history. Rulers and leaders have always used various PR techniques to keep themselves dramatically in the public eye or to help sell an idea or philosophy. The type of public relations that has evolved as a business management tool developed when leading U.S. industrialists began to recognize that their own interests were inextricably tied with the general public interest. As early in 1883, T. N. Vail, head of the American Bell Telephone Company (now A.T.&T.) raised searching questions about the relationships between local Bell companies and the public. A.T.&T. was one of the first to retain outside counsel for PR. Among professional pioneers are Pendleton Dudley, who organized the firm of Dudley, Anderson, Yutzy in 1906, around the same time that the famed Ivy Lee established a public relations counseling agency, now known as T. J. Ross and Associates, Inc. (However, it should be pointed out that the term "Public Relations" was not used until the late 1920s.) Another pioneer was Edward L. Bernays, who set up his public relations firm in 1919 after having served on the U.S. Committee on Public Information at the Paris Peace Conference.

With respect to recent developments, a 1979 *Business Week* special report on public relations had this to say: [1].

> The corporate public relations business, which had its ups and downs in the past few decades, is enjoying a new boom. Record sums are being spent on a wide spectrum of activities that loosely fit under the umbrella of "public relations." Companies that slashed budgets during the 1974 recession are resurrecting their programs, many are increasing expenditures and expanding the scope of PR operations, and others are elevating the PR function to a loftier rung in their organizational hierarchies. . . .
>
> The primary reason for the revival is that the corporation, more than ever, is operating in what David I. Margolis, president of Colt Industries, Inc., calls a "pressure-cooker" environment. It is under seige from consumerists, environmentalists, women's liberation advocates, the civil-rights movement, and other activist groups. . . .
>
> The corporation also faces intensified competition in the marketplace, the growing threat of takeover by outsiders, and new challenges in employee relations. And all the while, the corporate community continues to be plagued by a negative public image. Only 22% of the general population has confidence in business leadership, down from 55% at the beginning of the decade [1970], according to Pollster Louis Harris.

Prior to World War II, relatively few people were involved in professional public relations; as of 1981 there are an estimated 130,000. Authoritative estimates place the amount spent on public relations at $2 billion annually. Most major business firms have some type of organized PR program or department. New departments are being established at the rate of approximately 100 each year. Existing departments are constantly being expanded and revamped as techniques improve and PR personnel become more qualified. Public relations agencies are also experiencing a rapid growth. There are about 1,400 such agencies today, ranging from one-man shops to large organizations with world-wide operations employing several hundred persons.

Scope. While public relations is not the answer to all corporate problems, if can, if incorporated into the total management philosophy, be very useful as both a defensive and an aggressive tool. PR programs which operate on a long-range, continuing basis are usually more effective. But public relations often can be of great assistance in helping solve immediate and short-range problems, such as strikes, anti-trust investigations, and negative publicity of any type. It has also become a basic part of any good marketing program.

However, a word of caution is necessary for those who are unfamiliar with public relations: The activity cannot do more on a long-range basis than the material with which it has to work. It cannot prop up an outmoded product merely by saying that the product represents an advance over competitive items. It cannot clear a polluted river merely by saying that the river is not polluted. It can, however, add some glamour and interest to a product which is basically sound. It can help convince the public that the river is no longer polluted when this is true. It can be immense help in getting across the company's side of the story when the firm and some of its officials are unjustly accused of anti-trust violations. It can forcefully help put forth the company's side during a Congressional investigation. It can successfully tell the company's story and future prospects to those individuals who may want to become shareholders. It can help create a greater feeling of security among employees. It can help attract top talent to an organization.

The executive who is uninitiated in the field of public relations may confuse it with related activities. Public Relations is not ADVERTISING or SALES PROMOTION, although it can be used to support these activities. Public relations is different from advertising, for example, in that it is not usually concerned with purchase of space or time from the media to sell specific products. Some companies, however, do consider institutional advertising a public relations function.

Trends. Although public relations techniques have become relatively standardized in recent years, there have been some dramatic trends in the manner of their use. Among them, of course, is very widespread utilization of the audiovisual arts. The age of "flip charts" and "chalk talks" has virtually given way to closed-circuit television programs, some of which use very large projection systems, automated slide shows, motion pictures, and, increasingly, systems that utilize all of these in the same presentation, interspersed sometimes with live participants. Some of these very elaborate and highly effective presentations utilize many slide projectors, several motion picture projectors, and several TV tape players and monitors. All the mechanical equipment is controlled by a computerized program, and the total impact can be extraordinarily effective. Within a very short time, a monumental amount of information can be provided in this manner in an interesting and dramatic format. Some firms are also using television widely for communications with employees in cafeterias, work areas, and in plants distant from headquarters. Some even go so far as to produce daily television programs which present news of the company, along with general news and weather and, in some cases, even some light entertainment.

Another notable trend, used sparingly until a few years ago but now becoming widespread, particularly among the larger companies, is the "advocacy editorial." This is an editorial for which the company buys advertising space to present its point of view on a subject which may have no immediately apparent relationship to its business. The message may defend against an unfair concept ("X industry is gouging the public," etc.), or it may express a strongly held management belief. An example is the editorial reproduced as Exhibit I, published on October 15, 1980, in Connecticut newspapers by Hartford based United Technologies.

The same firm also conducted one of the most spectacular print public relations advertising campaigns in recent times, via *The Wall Street Journal.* It periodically published a full-page ad devoted to one of a miscellaneous series of topics. Clever and terse writing, and a great deal of white space characterized the format. Results were phenomenal. One of the most successful ads was entitled "Let's Get Rid of 'The Girl,' " urging executives to stop referring to their secretaries as "the girl" ("If I'm not here, just leave word with the girl.")

Reprints of the ads were offered. The "Girl" ad drew requests for more than 58,000 reprints. Additionally, national newspapers published stories and editorials about the ad, and the company received a special award from the National Secretaries Association. Importantly, a survey showed that there was a sharply increased awareness of United Technologies, even among non-*Journal* readers.

Another important trend in public relations is the widespread support of the arts by corporations. Practically ever since American business began, firms have to some extent provided support to educational institutions, libraries, and the like. And, of course, wealthy persons have individually endowed museums and other cultural institutions and projects. In recent years, however, there has been a phenomenal increase in corporate support in these areas. Moreover, this support has been essentially free of attached strings. Nevertheless, it has been offered because it is considered to be good business. *Advertising Age* reported: [3]

> Corporate investment in cultural causes . . . is now a full-blown movement. For business it means having opportunities to present itself in an impeccable environment; for the arts it means having a flow of important cash which has made

EXHIBIT I

GOALS FOR AMERICANS

Goals for Americans

How do these principles strike you as a guide for America in the 1980s?

• *The status of the individual must remain our primary concern.*

• *Vestiges of religious prejudice, handicaps to women, and, most important, discrimination on the basis of race must be recognized as morally wrong, economically wasteful, and in many respects dangerous.*

• *The vastly increased demands upon the federal government require at the higher levels more public servants equal in competence and imagination to those in private business and professions.*

• *The development of the individual and the nation demand that education at every level and in every discipline be strengthened and its effectiveness enhanced.*

• *Knowledge and innovation must be advanced on every front.*

• *Government participation in the economy should be limited to those instances where it is essential to the national interest and where private individuals or organizations cannot adequately meet the need.*

• *The economy should grow at the maximum rate consistent with primary dependence upon free enterprise and the avoidance of marked inflation.*

• *Technological change should be promoted and encouraged as a powerful force for advancing our economy.*

• *The healthiest world economy is attained when trade is at its freest.*

Most Americans would readily embrace these precepts for the new decade. Actually, they were set forth two decades ago. They were some of the objectives expressed in 1960 by the President's Commission on National Goals. This was a non-partisan group of distinguished citizens who were challenged by President Eisenhower to stimulate the democratic process by defining a framework of aspirations within which national, state, and local governments could work together for a better America.

There were other goals, too: a strengthening of our military forces; a tightening of NATO; aid to less developed nations; a search for effective world disarmament.

Goals for Americans was published as a 372-page book. It's all but forgotten today. Yet it is just as pertinent in 1980 as it was in 1960. It is a reminder of aspirations unfulfilled, objectives unachieved. It could well serve as a guide for America in the turbulent times now at hand.

UNITED TECHNOLOGIES

Pratt & Whitney Aircraft • Carrier • Otis • Essex • Inmont • Sikorsky
Hamilton Standard • Mostek • Elliott • Jenn-Air • Norden • Research Center

the U.S. a leader in many art fields . . . Philanthropic contributions to the arts and humanities are increasing steadily, according to the American Association of Fund-Raising Counsel. For example, $2.49 billion went to the arts and humanities in 1978, an 8% increase over the $2.31 contributed in 1977.

Painting and photograph exhibits comprise only a portion of the activities benefiting from the new trend toward arts support. Companies are also sponsoring such activities as theatrical productions, rock concerts, and other events.

Approaches. For maximum success, a PR program must be carefully thought out in advance, and a great deal of preparation made. The techniques to reach the desired goals must be designated.

Best results are obtained when public relations is looked upon by management as an activity which starts internally and reaches outward. The very first concern of a management is its employees. That employees want more out of life than a paycheck has been demonstrated time and again. Public relations can help keep employees satisfied by translating to them their benefits, publicizing their achievements, recognizing their special contributions, interpreting management policies to them and reporting to them the firm's progress. Many techniques are utilized for this purpose. Basic among them are the employee newspapers and magazines and similar publications. (See HOUSE MAGAZINES.)

The next area of concern is communities in which a firm has plants. The firm wants to be known as a good neighbor. It wants to attract the best employees available in the area. It wants to prevent as much restrictive legislation as possible. Public relations can help a company to be known as a good neighbor by publicizing the economic contribution the firm makes to the community, by offering executives as speakers before civic groups, by making affordable financial gifts to worthy local charities, and by encouraging its employees to do the same. A firm can engender a greater understanding of itself by maintaining frequent contact with city and state officials, inviting them to the plant and visiting them at their offices. Also, a company can make itself better understood by encouraging its employees to take part in civic and political activities of their choice.

Public relations can be of assistance in marketing. If the company develops a new product, the Public Relations Department can publicize its availability, describing its advantages and advancements over previous similar products. Practically all media consider genuinely new products newsworthy. Such publicity can bring in many enquiries and give initial marketing efforts a good boost. When a trade publication does an in-depth article on how the product is made, describing quality control and listing the advantages of the product, the article can usually be reprinted and distributed to potential customers with excellent effect. Feature stories telling the consumer how-to-do something and listing the manufacturers of the product as the authority often are used widely by the media, and assist in sales. The stories,of course, have to offer some genuinely helpful suggestions.

Relations with the state and Federal governments are becoming an essential corporate activity. Corporate executives should make it a point to know personally the congressmen and senators from their areas. These officials should be invited to facilities to make speeches or at least to take tours. Corporate executives should in turn communicate their views to them in writing and in person. Visits to Washington for an informal chat with a senator or a congressman are considered good PR practice by both the astute business manager and the elected official. Employees should be encouraged to communicate their private views about the burning issues of the day to the congressmen and senators who represent them in the national and state governments.

Communications with the company's owners, that is its shareholders, be they a few hundred or many thousands, can be enhanced with PR techniques. Although publicly-held companies are encouraged to communicate fully with the financial community, the basic requirements by law and rule do not nearly go far enough. Many companies are leaning today toward annual meetings that are accessible to great numbers of shareholders. The annual meeting presents an opportunity to give this large number a first-hand review of past progress and future plans. Public relations personnel can provide valuable assistance in every phase of such meetings. Public relations techniques are also useful in helping produce annual reports that will graphically communicate a company's character and potential. Quarterly statements, dividend inserts, and other shareholder communiques have become a PR function in many firms. Presentations before security analysts and arranging individual interviews with the analysts are necessary components of a good financial PR program. When a company goes public, PR techniques can be invaluable in helping create interest in its stock. Another word of caution: ethical PR practitioners are not "stock touters." PR techniques can be used to inflate a company's stock but unless continued company performance bears out the stock price, a sudden plunge creating irrevocable ill will is likely. FINANCIAL PUBLIC RELATIONS is perhaps the most sensitive area of public relations, and should not be undertaken except by the most knowledgeable and experienced practitioners.

Evaluation. Evaluation of public relations activity is difficult in most instances. One exception involves some cases of product publicity. If a news conference is held and a press kit serviced announcing a new product and the subsequent publicity brings in several thousand enquiries, many of which result in sales, there is no problem in making an evaluation. However, most PR results are less tangible. No one, for example, can prove that a union strike would have occurred if employees had not been receiving the company publication for five years; no one can prove that the firm's stock would be selling for $10 per share instead of $50 were it not for a good financial PR program. No one can prove that a company would have been indicted on anti-trust charges if it had not created a clear understanding of its operations among Federal Government officials. And even when good PR programs exist all of these and worse disasters can befall a company.

However, there are many small indications, which taken together, can help in evaluation. Some of these involve competitive comparisons which may be distasteful to some PR people and corporate managements but which must be taken into account. For example, is a company's stock selling at a price level in line with similar firms within the same industry: Does Firm X have a great deal more labor trouble than Firm Z, even though they are comparable firms in many other ways? Did Firm Y get a big contract when Firm X actually is better equipped to handle it? Many factors other than public relations, of course, would enter into any such incidents. But, taken cumulatively, these questions and hundreds of others sometimes add up to a picture indicating the need for PR or at least a different type of PR program.

Additional help in evaluation of PR effectiveness may be obtained from public opinion research. The organizations which perform this function have made great advances in recent years in their methods. Sometimes this type of research, if done properly, is prohibitively expensive, but if it is affordable it should be utilized. Such research projects can often disclose the source of discontent among employees, can turn up previously unthought-of reasons for lagging sales of a good product, can discover why in some cases a good stock is stuck at a certain point when it should be moving higher. Using this information, a PR director can decide whether or not to reorient his program, what to stop doing, and what new elements to introduce. (See PUBLIC RELATIONS RESEARCH.)

Organization. The type of PR organization needed to carry out these and the many other functions of public relations varies widely. Some firmes depend entirely on staff personnel. Large companies may employ groups of specialists headed by an experienced PR professional who ranks close to top management. Others merely employ one or two people to put out the company newspaper, appointments and earnings stories, and have them report to the Personnel Manager or Advertising Manager. Still others employ the outside agencies to do the complete PR job for them. Perhaps a majority of the most successful corporate PR programs utilize a staff of specialists in various fields, combined with outside counsel. The outside counsel, if it is a good one and compatible with the corporation, offers an objective approach and diverse experience with many companies that can be of great value.

Of all the corporate functions that demand to report directly to the company's chief executive officer, public relations should be among those receiving top priority. Particularly in this time of increasing government control, antitrust indictments, and the like, it has never been more true that a corporate chief executive needs a lawyer on one side and a PR man on the other. In many of the large firms, the top PR executive holds the rank of vice president, giving him reasonable access to the company's top decision makers and policy formulators. It is essential, if maximum success is to be achieved, that the PR head know of all major company decisions and new policies while they are in the formulation stage. There are still many firms in which public relations is an adjunct to the marketing or personnel department. However, for best results on a long-range basis, the individual responsible for public relations should be a professional in the field and should have the support of top management.

PAUL W. BURTON, Director of Public Relations, Norden Systems, Inc., a subsidiary of United Technologies Corporation, Norwalk, Connecticut

Information References

Association:

Public Relations Society of America.

Texts:

Bernays, Edward L., "Public Relations," University of Oklahoma Press, 1977.

Black, Sam., ed., "Public Relations in the 1980's" (World Congress Proceedings), Elmsford, N.Y., Pergamon, 1980.

Burton, Paul, "Corporate Public Relations," New York, Van Nostrand Reinhold, 1966.

"Dartnell Public Relations Handbook," Chicago, Dartnell, 1980.

Lesly, Philip, "Lesly's Public Relations Handbook," Englewood Cliffs, N.J., Prentice-Hall, 1978.

Nolte, L.W., "Fundamentals of Public Relations," Elmsford, N.Y., 1979.

Reilly, R., "Public Relations in Action," Englewood Cliffs, N.J., Prentice-Hall, 1981.

References Cited

[1] *Advertising Age,* Jan. 5, 1981.

[2] *Business Week,* Jan. 22, 1979.

[3] *Advertising Age,* June 16, 1980.

Cross References: *Annual Reports; Financial Public Relations; House Magazines; Public Relations Research; Publicity.*

PUBLIC RELATIONS RESEARCH

Today business enterprises recognize that one result of effective management is public acceptance. Corporate managers have come to know that public opinion in a democracy has become a vital force, a power, that can and does influence sales and profits. The men and women who direct the successful organizations realize that the product must be well designed, well made, honestly advertised, fairly priced, and promptly delivered, because customer opinion will choose from among many competing brands. Managements also realize that the corporate policies must be carefully weighed in the balance of private and public interest, because the government's opinion influences such policies with increasing frequency. A company's interests must coincide, not collide, with community interests, with supplier interests, with employee interests—these are all separate and important "publics" with a significant influence on corporate success.

Increasingly, business managers are turning to **Public Relations Research** to study and understand public opinion—a process that is referred to as "environmental monitoring." A survey in 1978 found that 68% of *Fortune* 1,000 industrial corporations use research to guide their public relations planning. The Public Relations Measurement Project at American Telephone & Telegraph Co. developed procedures to assess six functions: employee publications, media relations, advertising, community relations, educational relations, and administrative processes. James Tirone, director of the project, says, "I think we have proved, factually and decisively, that it is possible to measure some aspects of public relations performance" [1].

The problems in understanding public opinion are persistent, and ever-changing. Therefore the nature and depth of these problems have to be defined carefully. Once this definition is obtained the researchers can then estimate the possible outcome of the problem, and how this outcome would influence management's decision if it proved correct or incorrect. In effect the researcher proceeds when a hypothesis or estimated outcome is established and its verification or refutation is sought.

Objectives. Usually the spelling out of objectives begins with a statement of the problem followed by a listing of all the items of data the survey will collect. If, for example, the survey is purposed to determine trends of thought among stockholders, the research is designed so that the stockholders, or a sample of them, are selected and interviewed at specific intervals of time. The data gathered alert management to an appreciation of what Cornelius Du Bois calls "a company's share of mind," similar to a company's share of market so often measured by marketing reserch.

A second objective of PR research is found in what management has to say to its publics. Comparisons are made of contrasting messages or presentations to determine whether certain words are more effective than others in influencing public opinion. (Examples of effective words and phrases: "democratic," "leader," "manager," "social responsibility," "the switch is to —.")

A third objective could be the measurement of cause and effect relationships. This is accomplished by choosing similar groups and to one of these showing a message not shown to the other, and then measuring the effect, if any, on the group to which the message was shown.

Surveys. There are many problems in connection with designing the surveys and securing the information related to the problem under study. The nature of the group to be studied (employees, stockholders, community, and others) must be carefully defined. If the group is unwieldy numerically, a sample must be selected. The problem of loss of reliability of this sample is created by bias. The question of how many persons to include often depends upon the amount of time and money available for the study.

The questionnaires structured to secure the data can create problems for several reasons. Some questionnaires do not include all possible choices and, as a result, precise data are difficult to obtain. In others, words are poorly chosen and either mislead or confuse. The use of "prestige words" or other "emotionally toned" words may materially affect the responses to a question. ("Prestige" words: "chief executive," "opinion leader"; emotionally toned words: "social activist," "enviromentalist.")

Just as important as the questionnaires are the interviewers who are hired to ask the questions. Difficulties arise when these persons are improperly trained, inexperienced, or unprepared. Answers that are influenced by an interviewer can invalidate the data secured. The failure to ask related and dependent questions also weakens the quality of the responses.

Implementation of Results. Understanding

public opinion is the primary area of public relations research. The results that this research reveals leads students of PR logically to a second area, viz., how to improve the communications used in influencing the public's opinion after the opinions are obtained. If, for example, public distrust of an enterprise is revealed by research, the enterprise quite naturally seeks the causes of such distrust. Most frequently the explanation is poor communications, things unsaid or said badly, so that misunderstanding and distrust result. Fortunately, the explanation indicates the corrective measures needed—sharpened efforts to close the communications gap. Research may suggest: add a house magazine, hold meetings, keep the public informed, and listen to their opinions so that the distrust may be dissipated. This solution concerns itself with improving the effectiveness of the media and frequency of saying whatever is necessary.

Many public relations managers have used the results of their opinion research to build programs that, like those developed in the advertising function, attempt to influence public opinion so that greater public understanding of the enterprise, its products, policies, and people, is achieved. These programs include strategies and tactics that are carefully chosen to prove effective at a given time and in a particular climate of opinion. The research that measures these programs is referred to as the "public relations audit."

Research must also reveal the "climate of opinion" which indicates how receptive the public will be to whatever the corporation may say. A decision to publish a house magazine, for example, may be faulty because the climate of public distrust carries over to such an extent that any information printed under the company's name is prejudged and disbelieved. Choice of media, choice of words, timing of the message, the attempts to influence and propagandize, are all aspects of the problem that follow from a determination of what opinion the public holds of an enterprise at any time. The choice of a solution is neither quick nor easy, because at any given time the public may base its opinions on its perception of an industry rather than on the knowledge it has of a particular organization. Certainly the petroleum industry has experienced a crisis in social responsibility since the OPEC boycott in 1974, although any individual corporation in that industry may not deserve the bad press that it may have received. The research calculated to measure how corporations are meeting their social responsibilities is called the "social audit." (See SOCIAL AUDIT.)

This latter factor is a logical explanation of why research is a necessity in public relations. The research will always include the area of polling opinion. But, as the knowledge of behavior and group dynamics increases, the research specialists find it increasingly necessary to know not only what the public senses, but also how it perceives the corporation. It cannot be said that because 10,000 copies of a house magazine are printed that 10,000 good impressions are made on public opinion. The corporation and the public relations officers will want to know how well the messages were read, understood, and believed. And when these data are interpreted carefully and thoroughly, their meaning can clearly indicate to the enterprise the character of the opinion which the public holds.

While the need for this kind of research is clear, it has not been sufficiently met even by public relations practitioners. The search for data that reveal the depth of understanding sought for is expensive and time-consuming. Moreover, the methods for securing such facts are not entirely scientific. But, more importantly, the public which is polled and questioned always retains the right to withhold the real reason for an opinion, or the ways by which that opinion was reached. It is acknowledged that many opinions held by the public are the result of no thinking at all, that they stem from the rumors and hearsay so widespread about "Big Business" and specific corporations.

Potentials. The future use of public relations research will grow. It will grow because of the continuing development of scientific techniques for determining data. Problems in relationships will be more predictable. More and more business policies will be based on the findings of research because many companies now believe in testing new policies and products in the court of public opinion before introducing them in the marketplace. In the future, public relations research will help reduce the risk of doing business in a growingly complex economy, and will provide more accurate data for decision making and for the establishment of worthwhile business objectives.

The growing importance of understanding public opinion is recognized by many corporations. In his article "Hunches No Longer Suffice" Walter K. Lindenmann, senior vice president, Attitude and Program Research, Hill and Knowlton, Inc., has stated clearly and didactically: "Research and evaluation, quite simply, mean that the days of relying exclusively on hunches for communications planning are over: No longer will you be allowed to guess, or to rely on your gut feelings, to develop plans and programs aimed at communicating with your organization's internal and external publics" [2].

DR. STANLEY H. MULLIN, Vice President, University Alumni Relations, Pace University, New York, New York

Information References

Texts and Journals:

Lesly, Philip, ed., "Lesly's Public Relations Handbook," Englewood Cliffs, N.J., Prentice-Hall, 2nd ed., 1978.

"Measuring Public Relations Effectiveness," *Public Relations Journal,* July 1979.

Foundation for Public Relations Research and Education, "Measuring the Effectiveness of Public Relations," special issue, *Public Relations Review,* 1977.

References Cited

[1] Jacobson, Harvey K., "Guidelines for Evaluating Public Relations Programs," *Public Relations Quarterly,* Summer 1980.

[2] Lindenmann, Walter K., "Hunches No Longer Suffice," *Public Relations Journal,* June 1980.

Cross References: *Public Relations (and cross references there given).*

PUBLICITY

For far too many top executives, **Publicity,** other than annual gifts to the United Way, Scouts, or community hospital, is to be avoided. At best, those at the top grudgingly concede to releasing SEC required financial data, executive appointments and promotions, and the briefest possible description of products/services/processes.

In an age of aggressive journalism, these top executives have witnessed the results of "bad publicity" following press reports of an industrial accident, pollution, recalls, or layoffs. Faced with reduced sales or falling stock prices, these executives tend to blame the media and, naturally, seek to avoid any contact that might result in additional unfavorable publicity.

But by following this course, management is not avoiding bad publicity, but fostering it, for the lack of public information will cause a company far more headaches than any professionally planned and monitored publicity campaign conducted in conjunction with a company's complete corporate communications program. (See PUBLIC RELATIONS and ADVERTISING.)

When the media do not have, and cannot gain, access to information, they will base their reports on rumor, unreliable third parties, or attacks by critics, all guaranteed to be unfavorable to a company. Any firm with a publicity organization that has functioned in close harmony with the local, national, trade, and financial media will be in a far better position to counter "bad publicity" than a company that hides behind the crumbling walls of "no comment."

Definition. In its basic form, publicity is the release of information through the communications media. There must be an immediate differentiation between publicity and advertising, for publicity is not "free advertising." Advertising is paid for and can carry the company's message exactly as the advertiser wants it to appear. Publicity, on the other hand, must earn its way into print or onto the airways. Therefore, a publicity item must have genuine news value. It may carry the connotation of self-interest, but the item itself must be legitimate news.

Numerous company activities qualify as legitimate news, including new products, promotions, capital improvements, new processes, company milestones, civic and philanthropic activities, and opinions of company policy makers either in the form of speeches and articles or interviews. Just as there are numerous activities that qualify as legitimate news, so, too, are there numerous ways to make this news public, beginning with the press release and ranging through feature articles, press conferences, one-on-one interviews, and even trade shows.

Regardless of the news item or technique selected to publicize it, the first rule of any public relations professional is to have an objective in mind and make any release of information fit a plan for reaching that objective, whether the objective be image building, product support, or community awareness.

Techniques. As a general rule, institutions lag behind events, and public relations/publicity is no exception. The professional must be constantly aware of the general media situation and what the media needs. Certainly it is hopelessly out-of-date to be oriented to the "objective reporting" code of the newspaper-dominated world in which the mimeograph machine, mats, and measurement of inches were primary. Traditional methods of dealing with the press are often obsolete. In today's world of mass communications, the press release and quiet event will not suffice. The true professional must adapt to meet today's challenges brought on by the ever-expanding electronic media.

While methods may change, the first dictum remains: *never lie to the media.* You have the right to reserve comment, but be truthful.

While, by itself, the press release is of little practical use to television and of limited use to radio, it remains the primary weapon in the publicist's arsenal. The terse, well-written press release distributed to all the print and electronic media still serves two purposes. First, those publications with a general interest in the company or product will publish the release, often without significant change or amplification. Secondly, those publications with a special interest, and also the electronic media, will likely seek to secure more data or a taped interview.

When issuing a press release, the company should be prepared to supply photographs and other supporting material. The advance preparation of a press kit along with the general release, a kit containing a fact sheet on the company and photographs, is often a time saver. Never overlook the needs of the electronic media during the preparation of material for general release. For television, the advance production of a film clip and script will help get an item onto the station's news program, as will a taped presentation for radio.

In the preparation of a press release or tape recording or film clip, the following are some key rules to follow: know the audience of the media outlet; meet editors' deadlines; don't badger already harried editors about using your material; don't try to dictate how the item is to be used; make sure the item is accurate and complete; and only issue material when the event warrants it.

Most news media, either electronic or print, are always eager to secure feature material; thus "soft" news stories are usually an ideal vehicle for securing publicity. The feature may be specifically prepared for a newspaper or radio/television station or be general enough for universal distribution.

If the news a company wants publicized is important enough to warrant something more than a general press release, a news conference can be employed. The spokesman at the conference should be the chief executive officer or a very high ranking company executive to add importance to the event.

To be successful, the conference must be preceded by good planning. The media must be notified and convinced an important announcement will be made. Press kits, film clips, and tape recordings must be prepared to support the announcement, and the executive who will be making the announcement must be totally prepared. Not only should the spokesman know the subject matter, but he should be prepared, and briefed, on possible questions that will come from the floor.

It should be kept in mind that a press conference can be a two-edged sword. The live announcement of a major breakthrough, new product, plant expansion, acquisition, or the like, can easily be lost if the spokesman is not well prepared to handle any situation. The media representatives are not limited to asking questions about the scheduled announcement and may probe into other areas.

A well meaning, but unprepared spokesman, can easily make a major blunder. A classic example occurred several years ago in New York City when a press conference was called by a construction company to extol the opening of a new, high quality, but low-rent apartment complex. The company president was asked how his firm managed to build the complex, but keep rents down. He replied, (jokingly, we must presume): "Easy, we just add more water to the cement."

Smaller, less formal meetings between executives and the media often work better than massive press conferences. And, in certain instances, one-on-one interviews between reporters and company executives can be extremely effective mechanisms for disseminating a company's story.

In fact, an interview with one, or several key members of the media can add importance to a routine announcement, enhance a firm's prestige, strengthen company relations, and explain a company's position on controversial issues.

Like a press conference, an interview can backfire unless the spokesman is well prepared. A few tips include: know what the interviewer writes, for whom he writes, and what his opinions are; keep the subject of the interview firmly in hand and stick to it; be noncommercial, give facts, not a "pitch"; if you don't want to see it in print, don't say it—there is no such thing as "off the record"; welcome all questions, even "naive" ones; be specific or admit not knowing an answer; and when you're through, stop. And throughout the interview, remember that the interviewer is working for a publication or other news outlet, and his first responsibility is to the audience, not the source.

Strategy. There is no way for a public relations professional to prevent the occasional publication/broadcast of information unfavorable to his or her company. However, a well-planned, continuing publicity campaign can certainly lessen the impact of much bad publicity, and eventually, counter it. In fact, a skillful campaign can easily turn initially poor impressions into much more positive ones.

Any publicity campaign must begin in the offices of top management. Without the complete cooperation of this management, a publicity campaign cannot work. This cooperation involves more than the approval to release good news about a company or the willingness of top executives to meet with reporters. The public relations professional must be included in the decision-making process that will impact the company's position in the outside world. When the company spokesman hears about a company problem from a reporter, there is little that that individual can do. But with foreknowledge and consultation, there is much that can be done.

The first duty of the publicity professional, then, is to be informed about the company. Next, he or she must make it a policy to release bad news to the media in the same way that good news is released. This does not mean that all the company's secrets must be revealed to every reporter who calls. A company has the right to privacy. But a policy of never ignoring an inquiry should be followed.

By being open and accessible, a public relations professional can do much to avoid a media "hatchet job." Responsible reporters will seek both sides of an issue, and, if the company has been straight with the media in the past, it can expect a fair hearing of the company's position.

A simple denial usually is not enough to counter a damaging report. For example, if a firm is charged with violating air pollution laws, it should try bringing the press into the plant to show what it is doing to stop the pollution. It is important to follow up the first visit—the media should be brought back when scrubbers are installed or when the firm passes the next pollution test. The policy should be always to try to create a positive position.

There are numerous vehicles for creating positive and favorable publicity. One often overlooked is the trade show. Media tend to flock to these events and a close relationship with members of the press can often be built. Trade shows present the press with an opportunity to see a company's products firsthand, and so a press kit should always be kept handy.

The sponsorship of a special award can be very effective. The company's participation should be limited to instituting the award and hosting, usually at a neutral site, the presentation ceremony. The recipient of the award should be selected by an objective group such as a trade association. The company may also want to underwrite a musical or choral group that appears during the ceremony at no charge.

Finally, a good maxim is, "Don't forget your employees." They are often the best ambassadors a company can have, especially in the local community. The policy should be to keep them informed through company publications, video newsreels, and bulletin boards.

Summarizing strategy, a publicity campaign that is begun merely in reaction to unfavorable publicity is unlikely to have the desired results. However, a planned, continuing program that develops mutual respect between media and publicity personnel will do much to create a positive company image that will continue regardless of occasional "bad publicity."

Staffing for Publicity. Publicity is commonly practiced by today's business organization in one of three ways. First, publicity specialists may be employed directly and full time by the company, working ordinarily under the director of public relations, the advertising manager, or possibly the product marketing managers.

Second, many other companies maintain small internal staffs, or even assign the responsibility for supervising publicity to an officer with other duties (advertising manager or possibly sales manager). As a general rule, however, the bulk of the actual publicity work will be performed by outside specialists.

The third, and ordinarily the ideal structure for companies large enough to afford it, is an inside staff coordinating the activities of outside counsellors. The often-needed objectivity in analyzing the company's publicity objectives and programs is supplied by the outside counsel who also maintains contacts with editors on a more efficient basis.

Evaluation. It is often impossible to measure in specific terms the net results in newly won approvals of a company and its products. Some measure of results can be garnered from the number and relative importance of publicity placements made. Two cautions should be observed: first, the relative value of individual placements must be considered. A single article placed with a news syndicate may appear in 300 newspapers throughout the country. Another article on a similar subject, but much different in depth and details, may appear in only one business publication. Both have a place in a well-rounded publicity program, but one may contribute more to the company's aims than the other.

The second caution concerns a practice scorned by publicity men but nevertheless practiced by some managements. This involves actual measurements of columns of publicity appearing in newspapers and magazines, and evaluation of that number of column inches in terms of the cost of identical advertising space. Two fallacies are inherent in such a practice. The first is the comparison of unequal factors. The second lies in the reader reaction to printed publicity versus advertising. Publicity printed in a publication carries at least the implied endorsement of the publication's editor. Much less credibility is accorded to straight advertising. Therefore, such measurement that compares the two might measure costs but never effects.

Benefits and Shortcomings. Publicity is a versatile and agile technique of communications. It can cover markets broadly, by either geography or industry. It can likewise be aimed directly at specific audiences in the same categories. Intelligently used, it can cover the publications in an industry that cannot be reached by advertising budgets. Publicity is used, though not frequently enough, as an economical method of determining interest for a product in a new market. It may assist greatly in developing for a product new applications not originally recognized by a manufacturer.

On the negative side, it is inherent in the nature of publicity that the distributing source has little control over its use. Publicity is subject to the judgment and discretion of an editor. The person in charge of company publicity does not control the length or time of appearance of a company release in print or on view. When it does appear, the publicity may not say as strongly the points which company officers might like it to emphasize, but rather, may stress the points that are of interest to readers or viewers, as determined by the media editor.

While publicity would never pretend to be the only technique of communications a company should employ, it has become in recent years an important one, and a particularly effective one for the organizations that practice it skillfully.

RICHARD C. SMITH, Manager-Public Affairs, Norden Systems, Norwalk, Connecticut

Information References

Associations:

Public Relations Society of America.

Texts:

Carlson, R., "Communications and Public Opinion," New York, Praeger, 1975.

Gompertz, Rolf, "Promotion and Publicity Handbook for Broadcasters," Blue Ridge, Pa., Tab, 1977.

Jefkins, Frank, "Planned Press and Public Relations," London, Intertext, 1977.

Leidig, "Layman's Guide to Successful Publicity," Bala Cynwyd, Pa., Ayer, 1979.

Wagner, "Publicity Forum," New York, R. Weiner, 1978.

Services:

PR Newswire, a subsidiary of Western Union, links major news media across the country with private teletype lines.

Bacon's Publicity Checker: Magazines/Newspapers, Chicago. Up-to-date listing of media outlets, addresses, and key personnel.

Cross References: *Advertising (and related entries with Advertising prefix); Annual Reports; Financial Public Relations; House Magazines; Public Relations; Public Relations Research.*

PURCHASING

In any commercial transaction, however primitive, there is always a buyer and a seller. Thus **Purchasing** is one of the basic functions in any economy. The buyer requires certain goods and materials to satisfy his wants. He seeks a seller who can and is willing to supply him with what he needs. Together they negotiate a mutually satisfactory price and the deal is completed.

Industrial Purchasing is a highly refined, highly specialized version of this activity. Modern manufacturing firms spend, on the average, more than half their sales income on materials, goods, and services purchased from other companies. They assign this buying job to specialists who have the authority to select suppliers and commit company funds.

Purchasing's responsibilities have a direct effect on the company's financial and competitive position. The buyer, in addition to investing his company's money prudently, must satisfy the demands of the operating departments. Thus the "best" price that he constantly seeks involves much more than selection of the lowest quotation.

In selecting a supplier and negotiating a price, the buyer must also be certain that what he is buying will (1) meet specifications and quality standards; (2) arrive in the plant on time to meet production schedules; and (3) be stocked in amounts sufficient to meet manufacturing requirements without causing excessive carrying expense. He (she) must see that the supplier gives prompt and adequate service.

Individual purchases can range from simple to highly complex. The buyer of an intricate electronic subassembly for a space rocket obviously faces greater problems than the buyer of No. 2 fuel oil. The electronic unit involves advanced engineering and exotic materials. Nothing like it may have ever been made before; neither the buyer nor the supplier has any real cost data to go on in negotiating a price. No. 2 fuel oil, on the other hand is a standard product, with basic specifications. The market price can be found on the business page of the morning newspaper.

More complex purchases obviously require buying experts. It is in the relatively simple purchases, however, that justification for a specialized, centralized purchasing department can be found. An expert buyer of any commodity will do much more than check current prices. He (she) will study market trends in an attempt to anticipate price changes. He will analyze his supplier's shipping and his own company's storage methods for possible improvements that will reduce costs. He will, for example, study the long-range supply outlook and possibilities of substituting competitive fuels. In such studies, he will work closely with the plant engineer.

Definition. The broad scope of Purchasing's interest and authority makes inadequate the classic definition: "Purchasing is the activity responsible for getting the right material to the right place, at the right time, in the right quantity, at the right price."

Purchasing—or more precisely, procurement—can be called that function responsible for the phase of the materials cycle from the time an item is requisitioned until it is delivered to the user. This includes direct responsibility for selection of vendor, negotiation of price, and assurance of quality and delivery; it can also include direct or indirect responsibility for transportation, receiving, inspection, and inventory control.

Background. Until the turn of the century, the concept of a separate, independent buying function did not exist in American industry. In most cases, company owners did their own buying. As companies grew larger, the buying job was delegated to engineering or manufacturing managers on the premise that those who specified and used materials naturally knew best how to buy them.

As industry expanded, however, and mass production dominated the industrial scene, functional specialization became a necessity. Purchasing agents were named to handle the paperwork of buying. With the advent of World War I, the advantages of having a strong, specialized purchasing department became obvious. With production and engineering managers hard pressed to carry out their own duties, buying was left to buying experts and they performed creditably.

As purchasing personnel recognized the potential in the function and their own opportunities, they saw the need for making an organized effort toward self-improvement and education. In 1915, a number of local purchasing groups formed the National Association of Purchasing Agents (now the National Association of Purchasing Management). N.A.P.M. has grown steadily since then to a membership of almost 24,000 in some 125 affiliated chapters in all parts of the country. The association sponsors a broad range of educational programs through its numerous committees, climaxed by the annual convention each year. The monthly report of its Business Survey Committee on economic and market conditions is widely printed throughout the business press and is used by the U.S. Department of Commerce as a leading economic indicator.

The purchasing function went through another growth cycle in the twenties and thirties, climaxed by developments in World War II. The advance of mass production and industrialization led to greater emphasis on management of the materials function. The mad scramble for materials during World War II and the period immediately following spotlighted Purchasing's important role in finding and developing supply sources. The return of fierce competitive conditions in the late fifties and early sixties spotlighted its unique abilities in cost reduction. And throughout both periods, management learned that Purchasing was an integral part of the manufacturing team, along with Engineering and Production. Good purchasing, it was realized, was something more than a mere service function, called in to perform a more or less clerical task after important material decisions were made elsewhere. Purchasing was, in the words of one prominent procurement executive, becoming a "profit-making function."

Modern Concept. John H. Hill, president of Air Reduction Company, Inc., speaking before the National Association of Purchasing Agents, put the development of Purchasing in these terms [1]:

"Purchasing traditionally has been considered a service function, a place where money was spent, not made . . . Recent developments have shaken this point of view. Good purchasing is essential to good profits. The difference between good purchasing and poor purchasing can be the difference between outstanding results and mediocre performance. Modernized purchasing departments have shown that skillful procurement can cut 5 to 10% from the total cost of goods purchased.

"A saving of 5% to 10% in the cost of purchases (in a company where purchases absorb 50% to 60% of the sales dollar) is equivalent to 2½% to 5% of the sales dollar."

This concept of procurement stands today as it did when it was first enunciated some three decades ago, and serves to define the objectives of a modern well-run purchasing department with broad responsibility. These may be listed as follows: Low prices for purchased materials and services; high inventory turnover; low cost of acquisition and possession; continuity of supply; consistency of quality; low payroll costs; favorable relations with suppliers.

Other objectives of the department include: new materials and products; greater standardization and interchangeability; product improvement and simplification; good relations with other departments; long and short term economic forecasts; reduction of transportation costs; favorable reciprocal relations.

Value Analysis and Pre-Production Purchase Analysis. VALUE ENGINEERING (VALUE ANALYSIS) as an organized effort to reduce costs on purchased parts and materials was originated in the purchasing department of the General Electric Company in the late forties. A parallel development was taking place in Ford Motor Company purchasing at the same time. Basically, it involved a study of every part and service to determine how much of its cost could be reduced without impairing its function. This included a search for alternate materials or manufacturing processes; elimination of unnecessary features; location of specialty suppliers who could make the part for less; substitution of standards for specials.

Purchasing's success with Value Analysis (the first major G.E. project resulted in savings of $300,000) led to extension of the technique to other departments. Value Analysis or Value Engineering is now a team effort involving Engineering, Production, and Purchasing in thousands of plants.

Purchasing has moved up its analytical efforts in many companies to the design stage of a product. At this point it is able to recommend, on the basis of its market experience, changes in design or materials to take advantage of new developments or new techniques available from suppliers. In one major television company, for example, an engineer from the purchasing department participates in design engineering discussions of new or improved products. Thus Purchasing gets involved in the design-manufacturing cycle long before prints are made and handed to it with requisitions.

Vendor Evaluation. With greater demands and greater responsibilities being placed on it, Purchasing has in turn taken a closer look at the most important link in the materials cycle, the supplier. Both new and established vendors are coming in for a more critical review of their plant and capabilities, financial condition, and performance. Regular physical inspection of suppliers' facilities by teams from Purchasing, Engineering, and Production are not unusual.

Statistical measurement of vendor performance on price, delivery, and quality has become standard practice in hundreds of industrial purchasing departments. The techniques used vary from the relatively rough approach of asking buyers and using departments to rate suppliers on certain factors, to developing index numbers of performance from data taken from computers. In the latter case, weights are assigned to each category (e.g., Price—40%; Quality—30%; Delivery—30%). Index numbers are calculated for each factor, as well as for overall performance. (See VENDOR RATING.)

Inventory Control. Although stores are not always directly under the control of the purchasing department, Purchasing has an important stake in inventory control policy. How well inventory is controlled affects material shortages, the number of purchase orders that must be placed, possibilities of obtaining quantity discounts, expediting, and supplier relations—all Purchasing responsibilities.

Inventory control systems range from relatively simple to very elaborate, depending on the nature, variety, volume, and value of the items involved. A basic step in any system is the segregation of items into three classes: high value, medium value, and low value. (Critical items, regardless of dollar value, are generally placed in the high value category.)

Control procedures are then developed for each category, the stricter controls naturally being placed on the higher value items. This would include frequent review of future requirements, lead time, quantity on hand, quantity on order, safety stock, etc.

The basic objective is to have the right part or material on hand when it is needed. But it is also important to keep average inventory at a minimum, so that carrying costs are kept down and money which could be used productively elsewhere is not tied up in inventory. On the other hand, frequent ordering boosts administrative costs. Purchasing agents therefore try to order in quantities in which ordering costs and inventory carrying costs are in balance, thereby giving them lowest over-all costs. This quantity—calculated through the use of standard formulas—is known as the Economic Ordering Quantity, or EOQ. (See PRODUCTION PLANNING AND INVENTORY MANAGEMENT.)

In the past few years, Purchasing has developed a number of techniques to shift some of the responsibility for carrying inventory on to the supplier. These include contract purchasing, blanket orders, "stockless purchasing" programs, and commitment buying. Excluding minor variations, they all involve the same basic approach: to assure a given vendor a certain amount of business in a given period if he will maintain a stock of the item and release it as needed by the customer. This enables Purchasing to avoid piling up an inventory of the item, cut its ordering paperwork, and generally obtain a lower price on the basis of increased volume.

Reduction of Administrative Costs. Since the generation of paper is inherent in the purchasing function, close control of administrative costs is of continuing concern to the purchasing agent.

Purchasing has developed a number of procedures and methods designed to reduce clerical effort and costs and free personnel for more creative buying. These range from the universally used traveling requisition to punched card and punched tape systems to handle paperwork involved in repetitive purchasing.

Today Purchasing is also using integrated data processing systems to tie together purchasing, inventory, and production data. Computers are used to store purchase histories, price records, inventory figures, data on suppliers, engineering specifications, accounting records, and receiving information. The machines are being used to write purchase orders, produce expediting documents, make vendor payments, figure cost data, and measure supplier performance.

As the administrative side of purchasing becomes more automated, its managerial and technical responsibilities will be broadened. Purchasing agents and buyers will have to have greater knowledge of manufacturing operations, materials and processes, and general economics. They will require greater skill in negotiating complex contracts with suppliers. They will have to possess a certain degree of skill in both financial and engineering analysis to evaluate vendors—or have that skill available to them in their own departments. All this in turn will increase the demand for purchasing executives who have a broad concept of the materials function, and the ability to manage every phase of it.

JOHN F. O'CONNOR, Editorial Director, *Purchasing* Magazine, Boston, Massachusetts

Information References

Association:

National Association of Purchasing Management.

Periodicals:

Associated Purchasing Publications.
Industrial Purchasing Agent.
Purchasing Magazine.
Purchasing World.

Texts:

Aljian, G.W., ed., "Purchasing Handbook," New York, McGraw-Hill, 3rd ed., 1973.

Corey, E. Raymond, "Procurement Management: Strategy, Organization, and Decision-Making," Boston, CBI, 1978.

Dowst, Somerby R., "Basics for Buyers," Boston, CBI, 1971.

Dowst, Somerby R., "More Basics for Buyers," Boston, CBI, 1979.

Karass, Chester L., "Give and Take," New York, Crowell, 1974.

Monczka, Robert M., and Carter, Phillip L., "Purchasing Performance Measurement and Control," Lansing, Mich., Michigan State Univ. Grad. Schl. of Bus. Admin., 1979.

Reference Cited

[1] Address to the 38th International Convention, National Association of Purchasing Agents, Los Angeles, Calif., May 25, 1953.

Cross References: *Production Planning and Inventory Management, section, Inventory Control; Value Engineering (Value Analysis); Vendor Rating.*

Q

QUALITY CONTROL AND QUALITY ASSURANCE

Quality Control is one of the advanced mathematical tools of modern management, which, like OPERATIONS RESEARCH, gained its early impetus from the pressures of World War II. Unlike operations research, which began immediately as a decision-making tool at the management level, quality control got its start on the shop floor. As a practical technique for applying the principles of statistics and probability to every-day production problems, quality control today is being successfully applied to many levels and types of decision-making problems.

Quality Assurance is an activity that has evolved over the last three decades as a management function. It was originally conceived in the Bell Telephone Laboratories as an auditing function to assure that the quality control activities were effectively carried out. In the 1950s, a broader concept of quality management responsibility was enunciated by Feigenbaum as **Total Quality Control** [1]. This integrated the quality-development, quality-maintenance, and quality-improvement efforts of the various groups in an organization to provide the most economic levels of production and service that allow for full customer satisfaction. This concept of quality has evolved from subjective relative quality statements to a more precise view, used in quality control, known as "conformance to specification," to an even broader view, described by Juran [2] as "fitness for use." This latter concept includes all areas of quality including quality of design, quality of conformance to design specifications, and quality of installation and field service, all of which contribute to ultimate customer satisfaction.

The work elements that comprise the functions of quality assurance and quality control in an enterprise are collectively called the *quality system.* The elements of a broad-based total quality system are described in American National Standard ANSI/ASQC Z1.15-1980 "A Generic Guidelines for Quality Systems" [3], developed by the American Society for Quality Control.

Definitions. This evolutionary development of the quality discipline has been captured in standard definitions developed by the ASQC and approved as American National Standards by the American National Standards Institute (ANSI) [4, 5, 6].

Objective. Virtually every problem in human experience can be described in terms of cause and effect. What we see is effect; what we usually do not see are the underlying causes. Our decision-making problem, therefore, is to observe the effects that we can see and from these observations do something that will produce future effects we want—in other words, control the effect. To do this we must determine (1) the causes that produce the effect we observe; (2) the relative importance of each cause; (3) the magnitude of the effect of each cause on the result; and (4) which causes are controllable, which are not.

Many intelligent business managers, department heads, supervisors, foremen, and shop personnel have in the past made excellent decisions through the informal application of the above principles. But two things are wrong with the informal approach. In the first place, the methods are usually laborious and time-consuming, with no great assurance that the solution is correct. Secondly, even the astute decision-maker will soon discover many problems which no amount of informal technique will solve. A quality system provides a much faster and more reliable technique for solving the easy problems; for the difficult problems it provides the varying levels of sophistication needed to derive solutions that would not otherwise be possible. In either case, quality systems also provide estimates of the risks of wrong decisions. This view of quality control and assurance as decision-making tools is helpful for understanding all the various branches and applications of such a system.

All manufacturing has in common a basic difficulty: it is physically impossible to make all items, units, or systems exactly alike. There is always variability in the product. With precision manufacturing the variability may be difficult to see, but it is there nevertheless. More often the variability is disconcertingly obvious, resulting in scrap, rework, and warranty losses with their attendant high costs. Modern quality control attacks this problem primarily by statistical means—through use of the Shewhart Control Chart and numerous other techniques.

The function of the quality system is to reduce this variability to an economical minimum. It does so through controls for Purchasing and Receiving to assure uniform incoming materials and parts, controls for Production to enable the operators "to make it right the first time," controls for Inspection which are generally grouped under quality control and assurance activities, and design controls over complete systems not only as they leave the plant but in the hands of satisfied customers. This last activity is known as Reliability (see RELIABILITY ENGINEERING).

In addition to controlling the *product variability,* the quality control function also participates with management in establishing the *levels of quality.* On this point there is a major misconception. Many people associate quality control only with very high-quality product. This is not the case. Quality control assures management that outgoing product quality meets the *desired* quality level, regardless of where that level might be. The desired quality level is, of course, a management decision which is based on costs, desired profits, etc., but which ultimately depends on the quality the customer wants and is willing to pay for. As a matter of fact, quality control may well be more useful to the profitable manufacture of a medium-quality, low-price item than it is to that of a high-quality item which has been priced high enough to absorb the various production costs usually associated with top quality.

Objective. In any case, quality control's objective is the economical production of a greater quantity of more uniform product at the quality level the customer wants. Each part of this objective is important, because only when all phases of the objective are realized will a true quality control program be achieved.

For example, greater uniformity can be realized if inspection simply sorts out the bad product from the good. This, of course, is one way to get top quality product, and it is a procedure that industry has been using ever since the introduction of the inspection function. While many people still regard such inspection sorting as quality control, it actually is not. It results in very uneconomical production costs, waste of material and labor in scrap losses, and less rather than greater quantity of output.

It should be apparent that quality control properly applied has many beneficial consequences. By reducing variability and increasing product uniformity, a greater quantity of good product is produced. Scrap and rework losses are minimized. Raw material costs are reduced. Both productive and non-productive labor costs are reduced. And these savings can be utilized (1) for profit improvement, (2) for product quality improvement, or (3) for price reductions to the customer. Beyond these direct benefits to manufacturers are the longer term economic benefits of conservation of the nation's manpower and resources.

A third viewpoint useful for describing quality control is by analogy. Just as engineering is the bridge between the theories of science and the practical application of these theories to the development of useful products, so quality control bridges the gap between the theories of statistics and probability and their practical application to industrial decision-making problems.

Definition of Quality Control. This discussion of what quality control is and does is necessarily quite brief and restricted to the statistical discipline on which it is based. In the actual application to the practical industrial situation, quality control must also draw together many other disciplines.

Quality control is a growing activity in the industrial scene, and definitions based on today's scope are obsolete tomorrow. Because of both the broad scope and the growth, it is doubtful that all authorities would agree on a single definition.

But the principal difficulty in formulating a single, formal definition lies in the interaction of quality control as an industrial function with quality control as a technical discipline. Therefore quality control is best defined separately in three areas:

(1) *Quality System: The collective plans, activities, and events that are provided to ensure that a product, process, or service will satisfy given needs.*

Comment: The *quality system* encompasses all of the elements of *quality assurance* and *quality control.* The term *quality system* refers to the "total quality system" whereas the terms "quality assurance system" and "quality control system" refer to the systems associated with the functions of *quality assurance* and *quality control*, respectively.

Note: Past practice has used the terms *quality system, quality program,* and *quality plan* virtually interchangeably.

(2) *Quality Assurance: All those planned or systematic actions necessary to provide adequate confidence that a product or service will satisfy given needs.*

Comment: Quality assurance involves making sure that *quality* is what it should be. This includes a continuing evaluation of adequacy and effectiveness with a view to having timely corrective measures and feedback initiated where necessary. For a specific product or service, *quality assurance* involves the necessary plans and actions to provide confidence through verifications, audits, and the evaluation of the quality factors that affect the adequacy of the design for intended applications, specification, production, installation, inspection, and use of the product or service. Providing assurance may involve producing evidence.

Note: When *quality assurance* is used in the total system sense, as it normally is without a restrictive adjective, it has to do with all aspects of *quality*. When it is used in a more restricted sense for a particular phase or function within the total quality assurance system, the phrase *quality assurance* is modified by an adjective or used as an adjective to restrict some other operation. For example, "conformance quality assurance."

(3) *Quality Control: The operational techniques and the activities which sustain a quality of product or service that will satisfy given needs; also the use of such techniques and activities.*

Comment: The aim of *quality control* is to provide *quality* that is satisfactory; (e.g., safe, adequate, dependable, and economical). The overall system involves integrating the quality aspects of several related steps including: the proper *specification* of what is wanted; *design* of the product or service to meet the requirements; *production* or *installation* to meet the full intent of the specification; *inspection* to determine whether the resulting product or service conforms to the applicable specification; and *review of usage* to provide for revision of specification. Effective utilization of these technologies and activities is an essential element in the economic control of *quality*.

Note: To some, *quality assurance* is a staff operation while *quality control* is a line operation.

History. The birth of quality control is generally recognized as having occurred in 1924 when Dr. Walter A. Shewhart developed the control chart as a means of distinguishing between the normal variation introduced by chance causes and the excess variation introduced by assignable causes. His first chart was designed as a new method for presenting "percent defective" inspection data. The first published book on quality control appeared in 1931, Shewhart's "Economic Control of the Quality of Manufactured Product" [7].

Shewhart's development came as the result of a request from Western Electric engineers who had for some time been investigating quality problems at the Hawthorne Works. One of the better known members of this group was J.M. Juran. The group was interested in getting the maximum amount of information from a minimum amount of inspection data, and their request to Bell Laboratories was for assistance in developing a method of data presentation and analysis. An inspection engineering group was thereupon set up at the Bell Laboratories.

During most of the depression years of the 1930s, statistical quality control was little more than a scientific curiosity with very little industrial cognizance of it outside of the Bell System, let alone acceptance. However this period was marked by extensive development of the new technique, much of it sparked by Dr. Shewhart as Chairman of the Joint Committee on the Development of Applications of Statistics in Engineering and Manufacturing (American Society for Testing Materials and American Society of Mechanical Engineers).

In 1933, the *ASTM Manual on Presentation of Data* was published under the direction of Harold F. Dodge, the Manual Committee Chairman. This was followed in 1938 by *Supplement A,* "Presenting $\pm$ Limits of Uncertainty of an Observed Average" and *Supplement B,* "Control Chart Method of Analysis and Presentation of Data." Subsequent revisions of the ASTM Manual have been conducted by Committee E-11 on Statistical Methods.

As originally conceived by Shewhart, the process control chart was in two parts—$\bar{X}$ for observing the average level about which it was desired to control the results, and σ, or standard deviation, for observing the variability of the results. (For the σ concept, see STATISTICS.) The problem was that the statistical concept of the standard deviation as a measure of the dispersion is not readily grasped by the layman nor is the calculation of σ simple—certainly not a procedure that the average inspector or machine operator could do easily.

In England, Leonard H.C. Tippett suggested the use of a Range Chart instead of the σ chart as the measure of variability. His first work on the range appeared in 1925 and his subsequent development of the range conversion factors for the control limits for both the average and range ($\bar{X}$, R) charts appeared in 1935 as part of British Standard 600, "The Application of Statistical Methods to Industrial Standardization and Quality Control," by E.S. Pearson of the British Standards Institution [8]. His work greatly simplified the calculations required to maintain a control chart, but in spite of these simplifications acceptance did not really become widespread until after the War.

With the great production demands of World War II, it soon became apparent that pre-war manufacturing procedures of American industry were quite inadequate. While Manufacturing and Production were by no means blameless (it was not uncommon to have scrap losses of 50–76%), it was Inspection that generally constituted the biggest bottleneck. Chief inspectors necessarily adopted all kinds of work speed-up methods—some good; many bad. Operations previously inspected 100% were cut to a "spot check"—popularly 10%. Critical operations were still nominally checked 100%, but in practice, backlogs would force "sample" checking every second or third piece, or less. The rework sections of many inspection departments became almost as large as the inspection forces. Substandard parts and lots frequently had to be accepted over everyone's objections simply to meet production quotas.

It was in this atmosphere of wartime problems that quality control was born as an industrial function, and there came into being as a recognized industrial specialist, the quality engineer, or quality technician. Industrial and government leaders realized the impossible situation and took steps to get quality control worked into the industrial picture quickly.

They drew heavily upon the earlier work of that inspection engineering group at Bell Laboratories which included such notables as Dr. Shewhart, George D. Edwards, Donald A. Quarles, Harold F. Doge, and Harry G. Romig. Several publications resulted, chief of which was the Dodge and Romig "A Method of Sampling Inspection," first published in the October, 1929, *Bell System Technical Journal.* Later they published "Single Sampling and Double Sampling Inspection Tables" in the January, 1941 issue of the same journal. These articles led to the publication in 1944 of the famous Dodge-Romig "Sampling Inspection Tables" [9].

A key outgrowth of this work was the development of MIL-STD-105, "Sampling Procedures and Tables for Inspection by Attributes," and MIL-STD-414, "Sampling Procedures and Tables for Inspection by Variables for Percent Nonconformity." Both documents were later introduced into the ANSI system as American National Standards Z1.4–1971 [10] and Z1.9–1980 [11], respectively. They are employed world-wide today as sampling inspection systems—the standard in quality technology. Shortly before his death in 1976 Dr. Dodge summarized the theories and developmental steps leading to these documents in "Notes on the Evolution of Acceptance Sampling" [12].

As a first step, Dr. Shewhart, Professors Holbrook Working and Edwin G. Olds and other pioneers of quality control were released by their companies to work with the War Production Board and ESMWT in setting up training courses in quality control. These were eight-day short courses offered at various colleges and universities around the country to which companies were urged to send their chief inspectors and other key inspection personnel.

Having tasted the excitement of this new field, classes of students at these institutions continued to meet and began to form local societies. Adding others, thirteen local groups organized the Society of Quality Engineers in October, 1945. Meanwhile, the Buffalo Society of Quality Engineers (seeded by the University of Buffalo course) was formed, and published the first U.S. journal on quality control, *Industrial Quality Control,* edited by Dr. M.A. Brumbaugh. Soon thereafter four other local societies formed the Federation of Quality Control Societies to foster mutual interests and to assist in the development of *IQC.* Finally, in February, 1946, the two groups federated into what is now known as the American Society of Quality Control, with George Edwards as its first president, and *IQC* the official "spokesman." Later *IQC* was revamped into today's *Quality Progress* as the official ASQC monthly journal, while the quarterly *Journal of Quality Technology (JQT)* covers more technical applications.

Secondly, the American Standards Association (now ANSI; cf. INDUSTRIAL STANDARDIZATION) in December, 1940, was requested by the War Department to initiate a project on the application of statistical methods to the quality control of materials and manufactured products. This it did through an Emergency Technical Committee under the chairmanship of Dodge. Other pioneering members of the Committee were Prof. W. Edwards Deming, then with the Bureau of the Census, Major General (ret.) Leslie E. Simon, then with the Army Ordnance Department, and Ralph E. Wareham, then with General Electric Co. The Committee's work culminated in publication of American War Standards Z1.1, Z1.2 in May, 1941 and Z1.3 in April, 1942 [13, 14] (later ANSI/ASQC standards B-1, B-2, and B-3, respectively).

Finally, the Army and Navy procurement agencies provided further impetus to quality by specifying that quality control clauses be included in all purchase contracts.

Acceptance. The postwar spread of quality sciences has been marked by a spirit of cooperation. Companies which otherwise carefully guard proprietary information have been generous in giving permission to their quality personnel to exchange experiences with others in the field. It has been this free interchange of knowledge that has led to rapid and widespread growth.

Under the sponsorship of the State Department and UNESCO, and through the cooperation of organizations such as the International Statistical Institute and the International Academy for Quality, quality control exists in most major countries of the world. While early action resulted in Japan and Mexico Sections of ASQC, the recent policy of the Society has been to foster national societies in their respective countries. Today, the European Organization for Quality Control (EOQC) includes 23 East and West European nations. Other quality organizations have been formed in India, Singapore, Israel, Australia, and New Zealand, as well as certain countries in South America.

Quality science has had to prove itself both to management and shop personnel every step of the way. Failures, of which there are always some with the introduction of any new field, have been very few. In the long run there has been a vastly greater percentage of successes, as evidenced in part by the growth of the American Society for Quality Control which was founded on February 16, 1946 with 1,100 members, and which today numbers over 36,000 in 179 Sections and 12 Divisions and 26 Technical Committees.

Statistical Quality Control by Variables. While the foregoing has described and defined quality control, the best understanding of how quality control works is obtained by looking at a specific control problem. One could pick an inspection problem, an inventory problem, an engineering design problem, an experimental analysis problem, or any one of a dozen others, but for purposes of illustration let us consider a process control problem, since one of the main objectives of quality control is to make things right the first time.

For simplicity, let us examine the elementary problem of grinding a bearing shaft to a diameter of 0.500 in. $\pm$ 0.001 in., and for proper perspective let us look first at the usual procedure used for this kind of an operation.

Customarily, the operator or setup man will set up the grinder, run a piece, and measure it with a micrometer or dial indicator. If the piece is O.K., the operator will go ahead and run; if not he will readjust the machine up or down as needed, run another piece, and check it. Usually this setting-up procedure is continued through several pieces until one measures as close to the center value of 0.500 in. as possible and then the run is started. Perhaps a dozen pieces or so later the operator will measure one to verify that he is still within specifications. If the particular piece he measures is getting a little too close to the limits—e.g., 0.5008 in. or 0.4992 in.—he will reset the stops on his grinder, checking the next piece to be sure that the resetting has actually reduced or increased the diameter the proper amount. Being conscientious, the operator will do this several times during the run and will finally release his completed lot to Inspection, confident that every piece is as close to perfect as it is humanly possible to make it. *The trouble is Inspection will reject the lot because almost 25% of the diameters are over the high specification limit!*

The first step to understanding this problem is to recognize that variability is ever-present. Variability is introduced by a number of things, but typical examples are these: variability in the physical properties of the stock used for the bearings; looseness or backlash in the gears and screw threads of the grinder; if the ground diameter depends on some prior machined dimension, then variability from the previous machining operation; variability from the wear of the grinding wheel; and, of course, variability from the continual re-adjustment of the process by the operator. Because of all these causes and others acting on the process, no two bearings will come out exactly alike.

The quantitative effect of all these individual variabilities can be easily demonstrated by the simple procedure of actually measuring a large number of pieces as they are made on the grinder. For sake of illustration let us assume that 100 such pieces were measured and classified as to size category in intervals of 0.0002 in. on each side of the 0.500 in. dimension. Let us further assume that the number of pieces falling into each category are distributed according to Exhibit I. The pattern formed by this dispersion is called a *frequency distribution* and it is depicted visually in a graph called a *histogram,* as shown in Exhibit II.

EXHIBIT I

CLASSIFICATION OF PIECES BY SIZE CATEGORIES

Size Category, Inches	*No. of Pieces*
0.5020–0.5018	2
5018– 5016	3
5016– 5014	4
5014– 5012	6
5012– 5010	9
5010– 5008	11
5008– 5006	13
5006– 5004	14
5004– 5002	11
5002– 5000	12
5000– 4998	7
4998– 4996	4
4996– 4994	3
4994– 4992	1

The particular pattern shown in Exhibit I is the pattern that is most often encountered in practice. Because of this it is known mathematically as a "normal" frequency distribution, which is depicted by the solid curve superimposed over the tops of the bars. (See STATISTICS.)

While this "normal distribution" is instructive from the standpoint of understanding the effect of variability, and while it does form the basis for the process control chart, it is not something the operator needs to know about, because the control chart itself is quite different.

Before describing the control chart, however, let us look at certain conclusions about the grinder problem that we can draw directly from the histogram—things that a quality control engineer would do, for example if this were a process capability study. First, twenty-four

EXHIBIT II

QUALITY-CONTROL HISTOGRAM OF DATA FROM EXHIBIT I

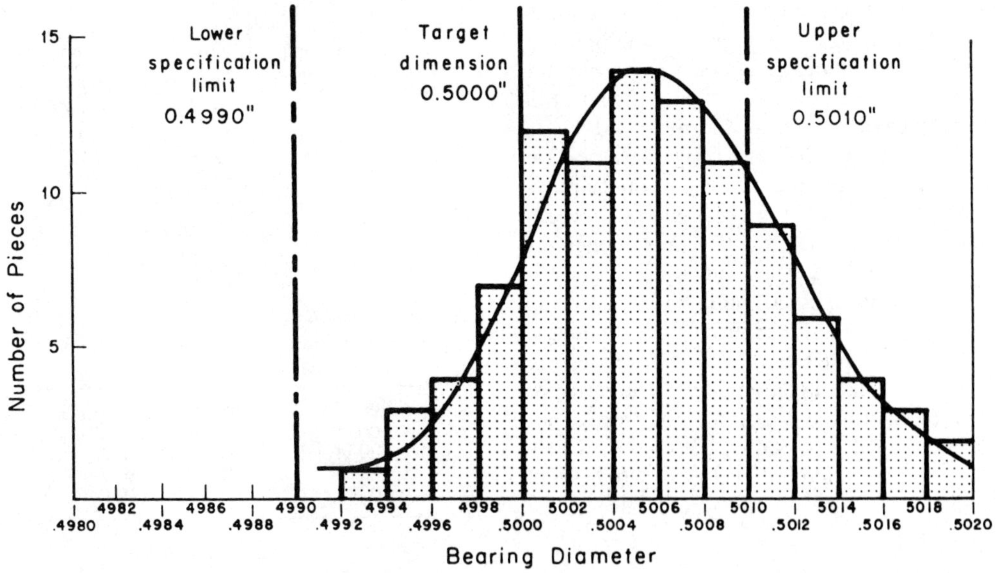

pieces (or 24%) are above the upper specification limit of 0.5010 in. This of course is why Inspection rejected the lot. Second, the first thing the operator can do is to center the average of the process, which now falls at 0.5006 in., back down to 0.5000 in. If this were done, the shape of the distribution would not change, but each bar of the distribution would move three units to the left. The third thing to observe is that even if the process were properly centered on the specifications in this way, both "tails" would still fall slightly beyond the specification limits. Specifically the first two and last two bars, for a total of nine pieces or 9%, would still fall outside the high or low limits.

The significance of this last fact is that the *inherent variability* of the grinding operation is greater than the *specification limits,* which means simply that the operation as it now stands cannot possibly produce all parts to specifications. It was mentioned in the original statement of the problem that the operator conscientiously reset his machine every time he found a part getting too close to the limits. This in itself introduced variability which is contributing to the overall spread of the distribution. If the operator is more carefully instructed when to reset, the chances are the spread will reduce so that none of the pieces will fall outside the limits.

If they still should, however, then there are only a few things that can be done. One would be to check the grinder to see if an overhaul would tighten it up sufficiently to eliminate that factor as a source of variability. Another would be for Production Control to schedule this particular operation on a different unit. A third might be to check back into the previous machining operation for closer control over the variability of the dimension used for control of the grinding diameter. A fourth would be to work with the vendor supplying the stock for closer control over the variability of its physical properties. Failing in these efforts or in addition to them, the quality control engineer would go back to Design Engineering to see if the specifications could safely be opened up from ± 0.001 in. to ± 0.0015 in. If so the process will produce parts satisfactorily; if not there is only one, last alternative. The operator would be instructed to center his process not on 0.500 in. but on 0.504 in. This would assure that no parts would fall below 0.490 in. and become scrap. But all lots would have to be 100% inspected so that the oversize pieces, which will now run 15%, can be sorted out and reworked.

The setting up of chart control for the grinder is quite different from the histogram study, even though the normal distribution curve revealed by the histogram is used as the basis. To set up a control chart, an initial set of readings from the process is needed. For our example, the same 100 readings used in the histogram study will suffice, but in this case instead of bulking all 100 readings together in size categories, they are taken in chronological sequence as the parts were produced on the grinder. Let us assume the first 25 readings were as shown in Exhibit III.

Rather than a plotting of individual values as was done for the histogram, the control chart is a plotting of the *average* and *range* of a *series of subgroups.* The subgroups may vary in size from two pieces on up, but five is commonly used, which is why the readings in Exhibit III are grouped by fives. The average is well known; the range is simply the smallest value of a subgroup subtracted from the largest. The averages, $\bar{X}$, and ranges, R, for the five subgroups shown in Exhibit III are given in

EXHIBIT III

FIRST 25 READINGS OF PIECES PORTRAYED IN EXHIBIT I

1	.5001	14	.5011
2	.5007	15	.5006
3	.5006		
4	.5003	16	.5005
5	.5008	17	.4994
		18	.5004
6	.5009	19	.5009
7	.5001	20	.4998
8	.5014		
9	.4997	21	.5005
10	.5005	22	.5018
		23	.5002
11	.5008	24	.5012
12	.4999	25	.5007
13	.5003		

EXHIBIT IV

AVERAGES OF SUBGROUPS FROM EXHIBIT III

$\bar{X}$	R
.50050	.0007
.50052	.0017
.50054	.0012
.50020	.0015
.50088	.0016

Exhibit IV. These values are plotted in Exhibit V. Actually about 20 to 25 such average and range points are needed to start a chart. Let us assume that all 100 of the grinder readings have been plotted, giving a total of 20 points.

The next step is to compute an overall or grand average of all the averages. This gives us the central value around which all the readings will tend to cluster. This is identified in quality control as $\bar{\bar{X}}$, and for our example we have assumed it will come out at 0.50065 in.

Next we need the control limits for both the Range Chart and the Average Chart. Since the control limits define the spread of the readings, they must be calculated from the ranges which we are using as the measure of spread. To do this the average range ($\bar{R}$) of the 20 readings is calculated. Let us assume this value is 0.0012 in. Without going into the actual calculations here, suffice it to say that factors have been computed and tabulated which can be used

Exhibit V

$\bar{X}$, R Control Chart Plotted from Exhibit IV

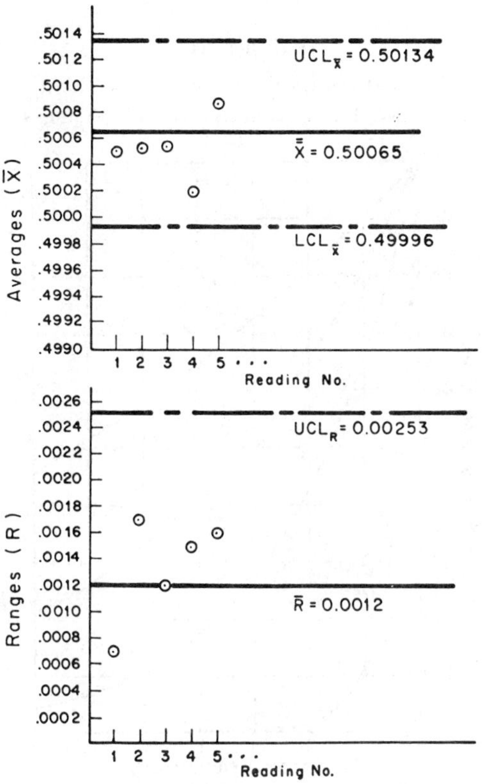

with $\bar{R}$ to compute the upper and lower control limits for the Average Chart (UCL$_{\bar{X}}$ and LCL$_{\bar{X}}$) and the upper control limit for the Range Chart (UCL$_R$), all of which are shown as dotted lines in Exhibit V. The lower control limit for range is zero, unless the subgroup size has been chosen at 7 or more, in which case other tabulated values can be used to find it.

This is all there is to the development of an $\bar{X}$, R Chart. Once the control limits have been established from the initial readings, they are extended to the right across the chart to serve as guides for future production. The grinder operator then periodically measures *five successive* pieces of future production, computes their average and range, and plots these values on the chart. As long as both points fall within their respective control limits, then only chance causes are acting on the process and he need do nothing about resetting. If either one or the other of the points falls out-of-control, then an immediate search is made for an assignable cause and the cause when found is corrected.

It should be pointed out that the $\bar{X}$, R Chart for the grinder example points up the same difficulties (though not as directly apparent) that the histogram study showed. These problems need correcting first to obtain new control limits before an extension to the right is warranted. Also, by making his plottings in chronological order, the operator will find that the averages follow a trend which he can use as a guide to know when to dress the grinding wheel. This will save him wasted production time of dressing the wheel too often, or the risk of producing bad pieces by waiting too long between dressings.

The main advantage of the average ($\bar{X}$) chart is that once it has been set up and the proper control limits established by the quality control engineer, further plottings on the chart can be easily handled by the machine operator. He can then monitor his own work and catch trouble right when it occurs. It has one disadvantage from the operator's standpoint, and that is that the specification limits given on a blueprint for the individual parts cannot be placed directly on the chart and compared to the control limits—which one has a natural tendency to do. The reason, of course, is that the chart plots averages rather than individual values, and while the control limits for averages can be converted to control limits for individual pieces, it involves a calculation that most operators normally do not understand or want to do.

The slight disadvantage of this particular drawback is more than offset by the two technical reasons for using a chart of averages. First, it is much more sensitive than a chart of individuals, which means that it will signal trouble faster. Secondly, the formulas used in calculating control limits are based on the assumption that the values being plotted follow a normal distribution. While this is true in many industrial situations, there are enough situations when the distribution is non-normal to make the calculation of control limits by the usual methods invalid. However it is known that even though the distribution of *individuals* is non-normal, the distribution of *averages of small samples* from the group will still be normal. For this reason the control limits for averages will be valid even in these situations.

We have, of course, done nothing more than scratch the surface with this example simply to give a general idea of how statistical quality control works. For a thorough discussion, the Grant-Levenworth text, "Statistical Quality Control" [15] is suggested.

Statistical Quality Control by Attributes. We have already discussed the average and range ($\bar{X}$, R) Control Chart and pointed out its application to a grinding operation. It can be used in any situation where the quality characteristic is measurable in terms of variable readings. When the characteristic is not numerically measurable but must be expressed in terms of attributes—that is, it is either "good" or "bad" with little or no degrees of good and bad—then a *percent defective* p-Chart or *number of defects* Np-Chart is used. This type of inspection charting is used for parts which are simply checked with a "Go; No-go" gage.

Another chart is the *defects per unit,* or *c*-Chart, to be used when the number of possible defects is very large but the expected occurrence is small. Such a condition would be the number of surface blemishes or nicks on a refrigerator or stove. Here it is possible that there could be several thousand on any one unit but not very likely. The *c*-Chart is also used for process control of the number of blemishes per unit area of paper coming off a paper calendar or the number of weaving defects per unit area of cloth coming off a loom. It is also useful in controlling typing errors or printer's typos, in which the quality characteristic would be the number of errors per letter, or galley, or page. Mail-order houses use the *c*-Chart to control the number of errors per order processed, or per 10 orders processed, or per 100 orders processed—the size of the base unit being increased as the quality improves.

In the example, the frequency distribution or histogram was used to illustrate the phenomenon of variability. This is a valuable QC technique, one of whose applications is the *process capability analysis.* It is also useful in the analysis of measuring instruments to determine their precision and error distribution. Frequency distribution studies—especially non-normal distributions—are also useful in accelerated life-testing of products and reliability studies.

Sampling procedures were referred to in our discussion of historical background. In judging various acceptance sampling plans, their performance is compared over a range of possible quality levels of submitted product. A picture of this performance is given by the *operating characteristic curve,* commonly referred to as an OC curve. Exhibit VI is an example of the OC curves of a number of single sampling plans. For any given fraction defective p in a submitted lot, the OC curve shows the probability P_a that such a lot will be accepted by the given

EXHIBIT VI

COMPARISON OF OC CURVES FOR FOUR SAMPLING PLANS INVOLVING 10% SAMPLES

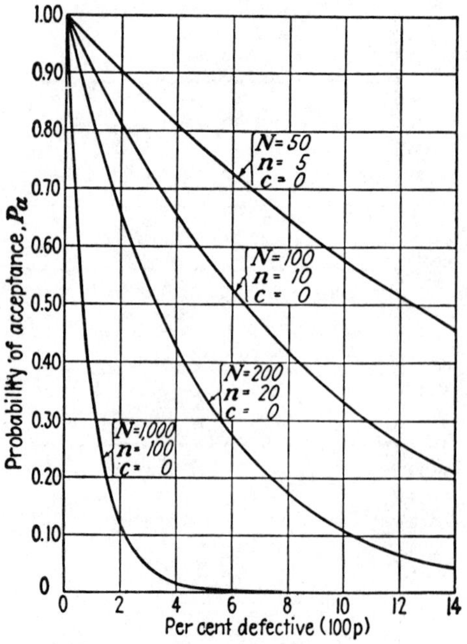

SOURCE: Grant, "Statistical Quality Control."

sampling plan. Or, the OC curve shows the long-run percentage of submitted lots that would be accepted if a great many lots of any stated quality were submitted for inspection. In most cases, OC curves may also be thought of as showing the probability of accepting lots from a stream of products having a fraction defective p.

These are only a few of the methods and applications of quality control. It is hoped the listing is sufficient to indicate the large number of different problems in all departments and types of companies for which quality control can yield more reliable decisions.

Organization of the Quality Function. The American Society for Quality Control has not stated that any one form of quality organization is preferable, since different forms can be successful in different industries. However, as the Secretariat for American National Standards Committee Z1 on Quality Assurance, ASQC has published "Generic Guidelines for Quality Systems" (ANSI/ASQC Z1.15-1980) which speaks to quality policy, the quality function, scope of authority, and systems evaluation. In this regard, Z1.15 states that "a quality policy should be adopted to describe explicitly management's specific intentions with respect to quality."

A quality policy, approved by the chief executive officer, should address an organized approach for achieving quality objectives with "provisions for periodic organizational audits to assure adherence to quality policy." Further, "clear lines of authority should be established to administer the quality system." Also, "responsibility for reporting to higher management performance against stated quality objectives should rest with functions independent of those responsible for the attainment of those objectives." Finally, to provide assurance, "a periodic audit of the quality system should be made by an organizational element independent of the unit being audited, or by a qualified third party." Audits should be made of product, process, policy, and system to assure compliance.

Within the Quality Assurance umbrella, quality technology has applications in Purchasing, Research & Development, Engineering, Design, Manufacturing, Process Control, Inspection (receiving, in-process, and final shipping), Test Engineering, Marketing (sales, field services, and advertising). (See Exhibit VII.)

Of course, not every company that has a quality program has as extensive a one as described herein. A key quality aim is to help companies provide a better product/service, with more reliability, safety, and at lower costs commensurate with the customer's willingness to pay the price determined by the economics of quality of design and manufacture. The increase in government regulation and consumerist pressure makes concern for product safety and quality cost programs essential. (See CONSUMER PROTECTION.)

Another aim is the development of appropriate quality programs for small businesses, where the maintenance cost of the quality function and specialized staff may take longer to recover than is the case with large companies. However, most firms experience quality costs of nonconformance (rework, scrap, field problems, warranty returns, etc.). These can be reduced by appropriate quality technologies using a quality cost program for discovery and prevention—easily repaying the investment in quality personnel.

Still another objective is to extend the applications of quality assurance to new groups of industries and businesses. Today, with the trend of U.S. business to service orientation, banks, insurance companies, health care facilities, mail order houses, fast food restaurants, printing firms, and the like are introducing formalized quality programs staffed by quality professionals. Many of the latter are certified by ASQC in one of its three programs of professional development for quality practitioners. At the same time, the quality function is being accepted into the Boardroom, with a growing number of "directors of quality." A corporate vice-president of quality assurance, unheard of ten to fifteen years ago, is today an increasingly common position.

In many cases, the quality function may not resemble that of the older manufacturing quality control department. New forms are being developed to meet new requirements and activities. However, the basic principles are finding ever expanding applications to products, services, and administrative activities. Further research must continue to explore the types of problems to which quality technology and the assurance sciences can be successfully applied.

ROBERT A. ABBOTT, Director, Technical Services, American Society for Quality Control, Milwaukee, Wisconsin

DAVID C. LEAMAN, Director, Professional Development, American Society for Quality Control, Milwaukee, Wisconsin

EXHIBIT VII

QUALITY PROGRAM APPLICATIONS

1. *Purchasing*
   Vendor analysis and certification
   Specifications and contracts, and vendor quality and systems review
   Vendor-customer relations
2. *Engineering-Research and Development*
   Design of Experiments—Latin square, factorial, random balance
   Tests of significance and confidence intervals—t-test, F-tests, χ^2 tests
   Correlation and regression
   Analysis of data
   Analysis of variance and covariance
   Response surface methodology
3. *Engineering—Design*
   Specifications and tolerances
   Materials and parts selection
   Standardization
   Probability and prediction theory
   Reliability of design
   Design review
   Value analysis and classification of quality characteristics
4. *Manufacturing Planning*
   Process capability studies
   Configuration control
   Reliability assurance of production
5. *Manufacturing*
   Process Control—variables and attributes discrete unit, batch and continuous processes
   Automation control (design of QC principles into feed-back control systems)
   Frequency distribution studies—histograms
   Evolutionary operations (EVOP)
   Production measurement & gaging—narrow limit gaging
6. *Inspection (Receiving, In-process, Final)*
   Variables ($\bar{X}$ R) (median and mid-range) plans
   Attributes (p, Np, c) plans
   Single-, double-, multiple-sampling plans
   Continuous and chain sampling . . . Lot-Plot plans . . . theory of lotting . . . discovery sampling
   Frequency distribution studies—normal, skewed, triangular, binomial, and Poisson
   Classification and measurement of quality characteristics
   Instrumentation and gaging
   Packaging and shipping
7. *Test Engineering*
   Test planning
   Procedures and control
   Non-destructive testing and destructive testing
   Organoleptic testing—visual, taste, smell
   Environmental test
   Life test theory
   Failure modes
   Reliability distribution functions—exponential, Weibull
8. *Sales & Service*
   Field service failure analysis
   Customer complaint analysis . . . feedback to design engineering
9. *Individual Engineering*
   Inventory control analysis
   Sampling & distribution theory for time & motion studies—work sampling and measurement
   Quantity-quality incentive wage plans
   Frequency distributions for equipment maintenance schedules and replacement
   Production control and materials handling
10. *Quality Control*
    In-plant quality training . . . quality motivation and human factors
    Reports of quality
    Quality-cost analyses
    Quality information systems
    Developing new applications
11. *Quality Assurance*
    Quality systems planning
    Quality charter and manuals, and quality auditing
    Product safety and product liability prevention
    Qualify information feedback and corrective action
12. *Administrative Applications*
    Clerical and filing . . . typing
    Sales forecasting
    Audit sampling of income tax returns
    Error reduction in filing mail orders
    Invoice control

Information References

Associations:

American Society for Quality Control

Periodicals:

Quality Progress, monthly news magazine of the American Society for Quality Control.

Journal of Quality Technology, quarterly journal of the American Society for Quality Control.

Technometrics, quarterly published jointly by the American Statistical Association and the American Society for Quality Control.

Texts:

Dodge, H.F. and Romig, H.G., "Sampling Inspection Tables," 2nd ed., Somerset, N.J., Wiley, 1959.

Duncan, A.L., "Quality Control and Industrial Statistics," 4th ed., Homewood, Ill., Irwin, 1974.

Feigenbaum, A.V., "Total Quality Control," New York, N.Y., McGraw-Hill, 1961.

Grant, Eugene L. and Leavenworth, Richard S., "Statistical Quality Control," 5th ed., New York, N.Y., McGraw-Hill, 1980.

Juran, J.M., "Quality Control Handbook," 3rd ed., New York, N.Y., McGraw-Hill, 1974.

Juran, J.M. and Gryna, P., "Quality Planning and Analysis," 2nd ed., New York, N.Y., McGraw-Hill, 1980.

Schewhart, Walter A., "Economic Control of Quality of Manufactured Product," 50th anniversary commemorative edition, Milwaukee, Wisc., American Society for Quality Control, 1980.

*ANSI/ASQC Standards:**

ANSI/ASQC-A1-1978, "Definitions, Symbols, Formulas and Tables for Control Charts."

ANSI/ASQC-A2-1978, "Terms, Symbols and Definitions for Acceptance Sampling."

ANSI/ASQC-A3-1978, "Quality Systems Terminology."

ANSI/ASQC-B1/B2-1958, "Guide for Quality Control"/"Control Chart Method of Analyzing Data."

ANSI/ASQC-B3-1969, "Control Chart Method for Controlling Quality During Production.".

ANSI/ASQC-C1-1968, "Specification of General Requirements for a Quality Program."

ANSI/ASQC-Z1.15-1980, "Generic Guideline for Quality Systems."

* Available through American Society for Quality Control

References Cited

[1] Feigenbaum, A.V., "Total Quality Control," New York, N.Y., McGraw-Hill, 1961.

[2] Juran, J.M., "Quality Control Handbook," 3rd ed., New York, N.Y., McGraw-Hill, 1974.

[3] ANSI/ASQC-Z1.15-1980, "Generic Guidelines for Quality Systems," Milwaukee, Wisc., American Society for Quality Control.

[4] ANSI/ASQC-A1-1978, "Definitions, Symbols, Formulas and Tables for Control Charts," Milwaukee, Wisc., American Society for Quality Control.

[5] ANSI/ASQC-A2-1978, "Terms, Symbols and Definitions for Acceptance Sampling," Milwaukee, Wisc., American Society for Quality Control.

[6] ANSI/ASQC-A3-1978, "Quality Systems Terminology," Milwaukee, Wisc., American Society for Quality Control.

[7] Shewhart, W.A., "Economic Control of Quality of Manufactured Product," 50th anniversary commemorative edition, Milwaukee, Wisc., American Society for Quality Control, 1980.

[8] Pearson, E.S., "The Application of Statistical Methods to Industrial Standardization and Quality Control," B.S. 600:1935, British Standards Institution, London, 1935.

[9] Dodge, Harold F. and Romig, Harry G., "Sampling Inspection Tables," 2nd ed., New York, N.Y., Wiley, 1959.

[10] ANSI/ASQC-Z1.4-1971, "Sampling Procedures and Tables for Inspection by Attributes," (MIL-STD-105D), Milwaukee, Wisc., American Society for Quality Control.

[11] ANSI/ASQC-Z1.9-1980, "Sampling Procedures and Tables for Inspection by Variables for Percent, Non Conforming," (MIL-STD-414 adapted), Milwaukee, Wisc., American Society for Quality Control.

[12] Dodge, Harold, F., "Notes on the Evolution of Acceptance Sampling," Milwaukee, Wisc., American Society for Quality Control, 1973.

[13] ANSI/ASQC-B1/B2-1958, "Guide for Quality Control"/"Control Chart Method of Analyzing Data," Milwaukee, Wisc., American Society for Quality Control.

[14] ANSI/ASQC-B3-1969, "Control Chart Method for Controlling Quality During Production," Milwaukee, Wisc., American Society for Quality Control.

[15] Grant, Eugene L., and Leavenworth, Richard S., "Statistical Quality Control," 5th ed., New York, N.Y., McGraw-Hill, 1980.

Cross References: *Consumer Protection; Quality Control Circles; Reliability Engineering; Statistics; Zero Defects.*

QUALITY CONTROL CIRCLES

The **Quality Control Circle** is a management style that involves workers in quality analysis and quality improvement. The concept originated in Japan in the early 1960s. Japan had a critical economic need to overcome a reputation as the source of cheap, poorly made goods. "Made in Japan" had a definite and pejorative meaning in the 1950s and 1960s. It goes without saying that a dramatic change in that image occurred in the late 1960s. Japanese products have become synonymous with superior quality and highly productive labor. We continually marvel at their ability to remain so competitive in world markets despite their extremely high cost of living. *Quality and produc-*

tivity is the answer one receives from any Japanese manager, and most will state that quality circles are a way of life in the typical Japanese plant.

It is estimated that four out of five Japanese production workers are members of a quality control circle. The ratio of inspectors to workers provides the most dramatic example of the effect of this process. At Honda, for instance, there are only 50 inspectors for every 10,000 workers. The ratio in the United States is nearly four times that, and in some locations, over twenty times. In addition to the improved quality, the Japanese have demonstrated a remarkable ability to increase productivity year after year.

Dr. Ishakawa, formerly of the Tokyo University and considered one of the originators of the concepts, has stated the purpose of QC circles to be the following:

- Developing oneself and others.
- Increasing quality awareness.
- Encouraging the creativity and brain power of the work force.
- Improving worker morale.
- Developing managerial ability of circle leaders.
- Implementing and managing accepted ideas.

What Is a QC Circle? A QC circle is a voluntary group of workers who have a shared area of responsibility. They meet together weekly to discuss, analyze, and propose solutions to quality problems. They are taught group communication process, quality strategies, and measurement and problem-analysis techniques. They are encouraged to draw on the resources of the company's management and technical personnel to help them solve problems. In fact, they take over the responsibility for solving quality problems, and they generate and evaluate their own feedback. In this way, they are also responsible for the quality of communications. The supervisor becomes the leader in the circle and is trained to work as a group member and not as a "boss."

W.S. Rieker, formerly of Lockheed and now president of Quality Control Circles, Inc., has been credited with introducing the QC circle concept in the United States, bringing it from Japan. He defines a QC circle as follows [1]:

> A small group of employees doing similar work voluntarily meet for an hour each week to discuss their quality problems, investigate causes, recommend solutions, and take corrective actions . . .

Rieker makes several important points about this definition. One is that a circle is primarily a normal work crew—a group of people who work together to produce a part of a product or service. This is not a program in which a few are selected from various parts of the organization to solve problems for those who are not present. The key to QC circles is that people represent themselves—no one else speaks for them.

A second point is that it is a voluntary program. This is probably the single most unique feature, one that is absolutely necessary. Such a factor assures the workers that this is not "just another management program."

The next point is that there is nothing sacred about the one-hour meeting, or meeting every week, but generally it has been found that this represents the best plan. The meetings should be regularly scheduled and not just held when there is some problem. Holding a meeting provides the opportunity for members to bring up problems that aren't necessarily apparent to the supervisor.

Finally, QC circles are not just another suggestion program where employees come up with complaints or ideas for others to investigate and implement. Rather, it is a process whereby the group identifies a problem, sets priorities for working on it, finds causes, proposes solutions and, where possible, goes ahead and implements those solutions. The key is involvement—involving the employees in every aspect of the prospect wherever this is feasible.

Organization. The organization of a QC circle is somewhat standard from one company to another. With the exception of a *company facilitator* who organizes, trains, and works with circles, no new positions or superstructures are added, for the process typically uses the present management and union structure. The facilitator plays a key role in training circle leaders and in helping these leaders to train their members. The facilitator also plays a major role in helping circle members and leaders communicate the results of their efforts to senior management and to other circles.

Entire sets of materials—including manuals, films, forms, etc.—for training the facilitator, the circle leader, and the circle members are available from a number of consulting firms around the country. The circle leaders go through training in leadership skills, adult learning techniques, motivation, and communication techniques. The QC circle itself is trained in the use of various measurement techniques and quality strategies, including cause and effect diagrams, "pareto diagrams," histograms, and various types of check sheets and graphs. More advanced circles move on in their training to learn sampling, data collection, data arrangement, control charts, stratification, scatter diagrams, and other techniques. (See QUALITY CONTROL AND QUALITY ASSURANCE.)

A typical quality circle includes five to ten members. If the department requires more than one circle, then a second leader is trained, and a second circle is formed. The circles then call on technical experts to assist in solving problems. The facilitator again plays a key role here, assuring that the experts learn to serve as consultants and do not take over the group through their superior technical knowledge.

Management must be firmly committed to the process to realize its full potential. If the circle members feel that they are being manipulated, or that the formation of the circle is in management's interest and not in their own and that management does not truly delegate its responsibility for quality, then the process will die.

Circle meetings are held on company time and on company premises. Once or twice a year, management meets with the circle and its leaders to listen to summary presentations of progress, results, and actions in progress. This recognition is a key element of the success of the program.

Union Attitude. Where companies have unions, the union members and leaders are encouraged to take an active role in the circle, to attend leader training, and to become fully aware of circle principles. The writer is not aware of any union problems caused by the circle concept. In fact, union reactions tend to be very positive.

Problems and Potential Problems. J.F. Beardsley, [2] outlines the following problems which will be encountered and must be resolved. He also outlines potential problems which must be addressed.

- Failure to involve the peripheral organization.
- Failure to emphasize technical aspects.
- Not keeping management informed.
- Lack of publicity (programs work under a low profile).
- Program grows too fast (or too slow).
- Inadequate leader preparation.
- Lack of visible management support.
- Perception of management manipulation.
- Failure to keep members informed of progress.
- Starting to work on problems too soon.
- Interruption/takeover by other groups.
- Overemphasis on quick financial return or productivity increase.

Potential difficulties include the following:

- Working out details with existing suggestion or quality control program.
- Labor/union relationships.
- Failure of previous programs.
- Poor management response to the suggestions.
- Impatience on the part of either management or the circle members.
- Selecting problems which are too difficult for the circle.
- Scheduling problems.
- Too much or too little publicity.

There are answers to all of these problems, based on the writer's experience and that of other companies and circles. Some need to be worked out or developed for each individual organization. They are seldom unusual problems, but simply those that need to be addressed carefully, with a great deal of sensitivity for those who are involved.

Results. Results have been dramatic. Lockheed, for example, documented savings of $2,844,000 in the first two years with only fifteen circles in operation. In one operation alone, the company reduced rejects from 25 to 30 per 1,000 hours to less than 6 per 1,000 hours. Ninety-seven percent of those who have participated in circles have indicated a strong desire to continue with the program.

Numerous studies in other companies have demonstrated dramatic reductions in tardiness, absenteeism and work disruption. Typically, the break-even or payback point on the installation of a quality control circle runs somewhere between three and five months, and most companies are finding a six or eight to one ratio to payback after the first year of operation.

ED. YAGER, President, Consulting Associates, Inc., Novi, Michigan

Information References

Gregerman, Ira B., "Introduction to Quality Circles: An Approach to Participative Problem-Solving," *Industrial Management,* September-October 1979.

Juran, J.M., "Japanese and Western Quality: A Contrast in Methods and Results," *Management Review,* November 1978.

Yager, Ed., "Examining the Quality Control Circle," *Personnel Journal,* October, 1979. (The above entry is based on this article, by permission of *Personnel*

Journal, Costa Mesa, Calif., copyright October 1979.)

References Cited

[1] Rieker, W.S., "Quality Control Circles, The Key to Employee Performance Improvement," Saratoga, Calif., W.S. Rieker Quality Circles, Inc. (undated).
[2] Dewar, D.L., Beardsley, W.S., et al., "Quality Circles," New York, International, 1977.

Cross Reference: *Zero Defects.*

QUALITY OF WORKING LIFE

"How do we accentuate the positive performance of people—'turn them on' to the organization? And how do we minimize the negative actions that turn them off? The answer lies in addressing the target of improving the quality of life at work, which in turn results in better performance and higher productivity on the job"[1].

The term **Quality of Working Life** is perceived by many as implying improved management of human resources, leading to overall improvement in organizational effectiveness. The concept of quality of working life is seen as encompassing work place democracy, increased worker participation, and, at the same time, productivity improvement through optimized or refined human input. Quality of working life is generally seen as an outgrowth of the "human relations" movement of the fifties and sixties.

History. While the origins of quality of working life would appear to lie in the human-relations concept, its most direct predecessor was the socio-technical systems approach. Conceptualized at Tavistock Institute in England during the 1960s, this approach promoted the optimal design of work organizations through a balanced meld of human needs and goals with the technical needs and goals of the organization.

In recent years, an increasing volume of attention and discussion has centered on the concept of quality of working life. The concept, together with its initials QWL, has come to represent ideas born of the so-called youth counter-culture revolution of the late sixties and early seventies. This era in American history represented a rejection of traditionally held values and beliefs and the pursuit of an improved environment, consumer interests, and an end to the war in Vietnam. Together, these were recognized as quality of life issues. Consequently, it was not surprising that the concern for overall improvement in the quality of life spilled over to the arena of work, leading inevitably to the concept of quality of working life.

Quality of working life represents the ultimate expression of concern for human values because (1) individuals devote the greater part of their mature lives to their occupations, expending time, energy, and physical and mental resources in these endeavors; (2) the individual's freedom, growth, and self-respect, as well as his or her standard of living, depend upon earned income; (3) the role of breadwinner is fundamental to the family and to society; (4) both the individual and society benefit from the full utilization of human resources, the only plentiful natural resource; and, most important of all; (5) production, industrial growth, and technological advances are not ends in themselves, but simply means to an end—namely, the improvement of quality of life for all.

The 1960s was a period of growing difficulty in the labor-management relations of the automobile industry. This was evidenced by the increased grievance filing, absenteeism, turnover, wildcat strikes, and ultimately plant sabotage. Media attention was focused on the General Motors plant in Lordstown, Ohio, as the outstanding example of this disharmony and "blue collar blues."

"Lordstown" came to symbolize a G.M. attempt to avoid or by-pass labor-management difficulties through increased mechanization or "automated speed-up." The labor reaction to this approach was flat-out rejection bordering upon violence. While the media tended to overplay the Lordstown difficulties, there can be little doubt about the impact which such problems had in steering G.M. and the U.A.W. toward new directions.

The first push for a national QWL agreement was initiated by Irving Bluestone, vice president of the U.A.W., during 1970 contract negotiations. This was refined, negotiated, and signed into the 1973 national contract between G.M. and the U.A.W., as mentioned later herein.

Aspects of QWL. A wide variety of terms and definitions has been employed to describe the concept of the quality of working life. The first comprehensive definition of QWL was provided by Richard Walton in the *Harvard Business Review,* May–June 1974. More recently, Jerome M. Rosow, president of Work in America Institute, a nonprofit organization devoted to the advancement of productivity and quality of working life, has redefined and expanded Walton's definition into a ten-part approach to QWL. It includes these elements:

1. *Adequate and fair pay.* Equal pay for equal work and fair and equitable pay relationships. "Adequate and fair pay" means pay that is linked to responsibility and that recognizes and regards service, skill, performance, and individual accomplishment; pay that is internally consistent between occupations and across organization lines; and pay that is competitive with the external labor market of the community and the industry, and is responsive to prevailing practices and changing economic conditions.

2. *Benefits.* Provision of an adequate and competitive package of employee benefits that reflect prevailing practice. A benefits program that protects the employee and the employee's family against illness, accidents, old age, and death in conjunction with benefits provided by state and federal law. Leisure time for rest, recreation, and self-renewal through adequate holidays, vacations, and opportunities for educational leave.

3. *A safe and healthy environment.* Working conditions that are clear, reasonably safe, and that do not unduly endanger the health or safety of the worker or the worker's family. An environment that meets all minimum national standards and that minimizes risk to individual workers in regard to its own unique conditions regarding dangerous chemicals, materials, equipment, and work conditions.

4. *Job security.* Employment that provides for continuity so that the employee is reasonably secure about the future. Recognition of past service and performance, with formal rules and policies regarding retention, layoffs, and removals. A set of policies and practices that do not place the entire burden and cost of change on the individual worker. Opportunities for retraining, reassignment, and transfer in lieu of separation. Early warning systems to alert employees to economic changes in the organization, with advance notification and severance pay graduated with service. Early pension vesting and pension portability as critical factors in long-term economic security for employees facing relocation.

5. *Free collective bargaining.* The right of all employees to organize in unions, professional associations, or other organizations that represent employees as a group or a profession. This right should apply equally to all and should include the right to refrain from membership.

6. *Growth and development.* Personnel systems that consider the individual employee as a growing, developing human asset. Opportunities for employees to compete for training, development, recognition, and promotion. Career paths providing for upward mobility and professional growth and advancement. Work assignments that are diverse, varied, and challenging enough to expand skills, abilities, and knowledge. Programs to prevent skill obsolescence and to provide normal facilities for self-renewal and learning on the job, to help the employee keep pace with the organization.

7. *Social integration.* A work place where the employee has a feeling of belonging and is a meaningful part of the entire organization. A climate that encourages openness, a sense of community, freedom from prejudice, and personal equality, regardless of rank in the hierarchy. An organization that encourages teamwork and group cooperation within and across organization units.

8. *Participation.* Linkage of employee participation to the productive goals of the enterprise. The recognition of individual creativity, initiative, and talent in order to open the channels of communication and to encourage the free and easy flow of ideas through the organization. In such an organization, participation is rewarded by a ready response to ideas; when decisions must be made to reject ideas, these decisions are explained.

9. *Democracy at work.* Recognition that the modern organization is a total society in microcosm and that employees deserve rights and privileges compatible with their voluntary membership in the organization. This includes the right to free speech, the right to privacy, the right to dissent, the right to fair and equitable treatment, and the right to due process in all work-related activities. The work place requires an executive, legislative, and judicial system, administered by appointed officials, which is compatible with the rights of free men and women living in a democratic society.

10. *Total life space.* Since the work place interacts with its own employees, their families, the community, and the society, it should do so as a positive force for itself and for the other people and institutions that it affects. Work should be a balanced part of the entire lifestyle, with work schedules, travel demands, career pressures, and overtime balancing reasonably well with the needs and responsibilities for family, leisure, recreation, and self-renewal [2].

Organizational Advantages. Efforts to improve the quality of working life offer intrinsic benefits for the entire organization as well as for the individual worker. Most visible among such benefits are: increased individual and group commitment to the organization and its goals; greater self-esteem for individual workers as well as production groups; increased involvement on the job; strengthened ties to the work group and to the organization; and enhanced personal dignity.

Ideally, comprehensive quality of working-life efforts will incorporate all ten elements of the definition discussed. In actual practice, however, most such efforts begin with an initial focus on increased worker participation in job-related decisions.

An Expanding Idea. At present General Motors represents the largest American, if not international, ongoing quality-of-working-life effort. QWL at General Motors began on paper with a national agreement between the United Auto Workers union and the company in 1973. Practically speaking, however, the company's successful experience began at the GM assembly plant in Tarrytown, New York, in 1973, where a quality of working-life experiment resulted in some dramatic changes. The experiment's success resulted in improved labor-management relations, improved productivity, and transformation of product quality from the worst in the company to the best—clearly signifying important gains in organizational effectiveness.

The success of the Tarrytown experience has precipitated QWL activity in every General Motors production facility in the United States, with paired gains in organizational effectiveness and quality of working life taking place throughout the company. This commitment and its scope are most clearly evidenced by the latest development at General Motors—the full participation of assembly-line workers in the design of production facilities, manufacturing equipment, and assembly lines in new plants. In effect, General Motors is presently attempting to move full circle from the initial experiment in participation at Tarrytown to a full socio-technical systems approach to the design of new plants.

This evolutionary process, in perhaps the largest manufacturing organization in the world, provides insights into the rationale for quality of working life as well as some inkling of what the future holds for QWL in the United States. General Motors' success in this area has spurred growing attention to the quality-of-working-life movement by Ford, Chrysler, and numerous other American organizations, which have begun to seek the same results through the introduction of full-scale employee participation programs.

Finally, a significant industry-wide development has resulted from the 1979 steel industry negotiations. These culminated in a national agreement between the United Steelworkers and the largest companies to establish labor-management participation teams in each operating unit of selected plants within each company. This agreement is viewed by both parties as a step toward a broad-based participative effort aimed at making jobs more meaningful for workers and more effective for the companies. It represents the first national industry-wide agreement to experiment with shop-floor participation.

The ten aspects of improved quality of working life listed above have a second and equally important object: productivity. As organizations direct their policies to the achievement of QWL for their employees, they are also bolstering the level of employee productivity. For productivity and quality of working life are both parts of the same equation—the human equation.

Whether in capital-intensive or in labor-intensive industries, the human equation, represented by the twin goals of productivity and quality of working life, is inescapable. At the organizational level, it is the basic key to survival, growth, and profitability. For society as a whole, it means more jobs, more investment in capital and equipment, lower prices, an improved real standard of living, and greater opportunity for all Americans.

DR. MICHAEL ROSOW, Director, The Productivity Forum, Work in America Institute, Inc., Scarsdale, New York

Information References

"Productivity and the Quality of Working Life," Scarsdale, N.Y., and other publications of Work In America Institute.

References Cited

[1] Rosow, J.M. "Solving the Human Equation in the Productivity Puzzle" *Management Review,* August 1977, pp. 40–43.

[2] *Ibid.,* pp. 40–43.

Cross References: *Employee Attitude Research: Attitude Surveys; Hawthorne Experiments; Human Relations in Industry; Job Enrichment and Work Effectiveness; Motivation, and entries with Motivation prefix; Personnel Counseling.*

R

RATIO DELAY

Ratio-Delay, more latterly designated by the term *Work Sampling,* is a random-sampling method of accumulating information about the activities of workers and the utilization of machines. It permits gathering facts inexpensively and with a high degree of accuracy about an operation, process, or any other activity for the purpose of improving manpower effectiveness.

The ratio of delays and elements of work to the total process time are obtained by random observations. Thus an observer visits a machine location a predetermined number of times a day, say ten. This would *not* mean every forty-eight minutes, since that would not be *random* sampling. The ten random samples should follow no set pattern. The observer records which element is occurring *at the instant of each visit,* e.g., Operation, Setup, Maintenance, and Delay. The percentage distribution of the various elements, as they occurred during the random observations, tends to equal the exact percentage of these activities that would be found by continuous observation.

Information Reference

Brisley, C.L., "Work Sampling," Chap. 4, Sect. 3, in Maynard, H.B., ed., "Industrial Engineering Handbook," New York, McGraw-Hill, 3rd ed., 1971.

Cross References: *Work Measurement (and cross references there given).*

RECORDS MANAGEMENT

Despite continued growth in the use of the computer as a management tool, electronic data processing has not eliminated or materially reduced the need for effective administration of organizational records. Computers have not produced paperwork-free management. In too many instances, the computer has done little more than change the size, shape, and volume of the paperwork produced—but has not materially reduced its overall mass. And under careful analysis it becomes evident that many of the techniques used in design and development of computer management information systems involve **Records Management** functions. For instance, data base management really is an improved approach to file organization.

Nature and Function of the Records Management Program. A properly developed records management program is a comprehensive and orderly effort to control the creation, maintenance, and final disposition of all of the organization's records—without regard to the form or manner in which they are created and retained, or to the circumstances of their creation or accumulation. The program has several basic goals. It seeks to assure that (1) only essential records are created or retained, (2) records are maintained in a manner that facilitates reference to and timely retrieval of necessary information, (3) vital records and information are properly safeguarded, (4) nonessential and no longer current records are promptly and properly disposed of, and (5) measures of cost effectiveness and operating efficiency are applied continually to each of these activities. (This sort of program has recently been called by some, *information resource management.* While some of the terms used in the latter are a bit different from those used in *records management,* the concepts, processes, and interrelations are essentially the same.)

Creation or use of any record reflects an investment of organizational assets in the communication process. Realistic but strong management techniques are needed to assure the greatest possible return for that investment. In short, information handling activities should be subject to the same return-on-investment criteria to which other company expenditures are subject. For the records manager this will involve periodic challenging of the need for every record item. And, it will involve placing a current and realistic price tag on the handling and use of every record item. In the latter instance, a dollar value will be attached to each report—one that expresses the true organizational investment in the report, not just the cost of operating the computer printer or copying machine that brings that particular report or copy into existence.

The records manager is a staff specialist who monitors every organizational function that involves accumulation, arrangement, and use of information resources. This person does not compete with the data processor or systems specialist; he is their partner. Records management is not concerned with the techniques and facilities for data manipulation; however, it is concerned with captured data and the means and methods for its efficient capture and later exploitation.

The records manager should be a skilled professional whose experience will permit him to function at the same organizational level as the senior internal auditor, the data processing manager, the chief purchasing agent, the senior staff accountant, and others in similar positions. If the records manager reports to an executive in charge of systems or management information, then the programming and computer operations managers should report to the same person. It is important that the records manager not be placed in some line segment of the organization—such as Finance or Operations—or in some incidental executive staff, such as Law.

A program for certification of records management professionals has been maintained since 1976 by the Institute of Certified Records Managers. Examinations are given annually at various locations by the Institute.

An adequate records management program deals with three aspects of organizational records (or, if one prefers, *information*) handling: creation, maintenance, and disposition. The records manager provides certain administrative services to the organization such as forms design and noncurrent records storage. However, the record manager's efforts should emphasize comprehensive planning, development, and application of standards for each records handling function, as well as periodic monitoring of the way in which operating management is applying those standards.

Most records management programs do not begin with a concern for controlling records creation. Rather, they begin to take shape when management discovers that it needs an orderly program for disposing of excess records accumulations. From this point, management concern expands to seek effective controls over the way in which records are created and maintained; eventually a full records management program evolves. However, the contribution of records management to organizational effectiveness is best understood when it is considered functionally.

Records Creation Control. This involves management of the administrative functions that bring into existence correspondence, forms, reports, and directives. Often these functions interrelate; thus, a report may be submitted on a standard form. In some instances the records manager works closely with the data processor, as when he participates in the design of forms for computerized information systems or deals with the problems of source data automation. And, the records manager shares the concerns of others for avoiding excessive use of copiers. Creation control is the crucial records management area: The record that is *not* created does not need to be maintained or disposed of.

Control of correspondence requires far more than guiding secretaries and stenographers in the correct use of letter formats and grammar. It touches on both repetitious letters—such as acknowledgments, transmittals, notifications, and responses to routine inquiries—as well as individually composed communications. Every effort is made to assure that what is written is necessary and that it is stated in the simplest and clearest fashion possible in order to avoid communications confusion and the need for later clarifying correspondence. Individually composed and typed repetitious letters are replaced with preprinted form letters. Where routine communications must be personalized and typed rather than mechanically reproduced, patterned paragraphs and guide letters, as well as automated typewriters, are used to speed processing and to reduce per-letter production costs. The records manager plays an important role in planning and appraising "word processing." (See WORD PROCESSING.)

Control of forms has three elements: (1) efficient arrangement of form data items, (2) improvement of the circumstances of form use, and (3) systematic planning for economical and orderly production and distribution of the form. The form is designed to be an accurate information processing tool—easy to understand, complete, process, and extract or transcribe information from. Care is taken to assure that it performs a necessary function in the information-processing systems of which it is a part. Adequate—but not excessive—stocks are made available when and where they are needed. Functional classification and other analytical techniques are used to avoid creating unnecessary forms and to relate forms properly to formal directives and information-handling activities generally in the organization. Efforts to control forms use will increasingly involve the records manager in source data automation problems. Entry of data into computer systems mainly involves transcription by humans or machines of data already entered on forms. Increased use of optical character recognition technology will make the use of efficient forms and the proper application of source data automation techniques of steadily greater value. (See FORMS CONTROL and FORMS DESIGN.)

Control of reports has many of the same goals as forms control and uses many of the same analytical control methods. Every effort is made to avoid preparation and handling of unnecessary reports and to assure that those reports that are prepared are easy to understand and use. The goal is to assure that those in the organization who must make key decisions have the current and particular information that they need to make the right ones.

Control of directives completes an organizational communications loop: reports tell management what has been done; directives tell what management wants done—and how it is to be done. Directives are related through indexes and other analytical devices to forms, reports, and various information handling routines. They are subjected to all of the communications clarity standards used to improve correspondence quality and employ all of the available techniques for improving graphic display of information.

Records Maintenance Control. This involves management of the administrative functions that require collection, analysis, classification, arrangement, and retrieval of essential organization information. This second phase of records management deals with selecting appropriate information classification or filing systems, assuring that they are properly used, and that the records with which they are used are easily accessible to those requiring the information that they contain. Among other things, records managers will be involved in selection of appropriate equipment: design and installation of manual, computerized, or microfilm-based INFORMATION STORAGE AND RETRIEVAL systems, and continuing audit appraisal of reference services.

Records Disposition Control. The final phase of records management involves the systematic and orderly disposal of noncurrent nonessential records, identification and protection of essential operating records, low-cost mass storage of essential noncurrent records, and preservation of basic legal and historical documents.

Legal Requirements. While a relatively small volume of records must be maintained to meet the organization's clear legal obligations, there is no reason to keep indefinitely *every* copy of *every* record created. Records retention schedules are formal documents that (1) describe related groups of organization records, (2) identify the functions performed by these records, and (3) specify the organization policy on the length of time they are to be retained. In most instances management needs will set this retention policy; in other instances this policy is determined by existing legal requirements. A general "Guide to Federal Records Retention Requirements" is published annually in the *Federal Register.* State government records retention requirements are published in various forms. Companies in regulated industries can secure retention guidelines published by pertinent regulatory agencies. And, in many industries, guidance on records retention practices is provided by trade associations.

Records retention schedules are used—usually annually—to identify those groups of records that may safely be destroyed or moved to low-cost records-storage-center maintenance. Noncurrent records of continuing value do not have to be retained in high-cost office filing equipment, or necessarily in high-cost office space. On-site file space is thus made available for retention and retrieval of newly created records.

The Company's Own Experience. In this connection, it should be pointed out that legal requirements are not the only considerations in establishment of retention schedules. The company's own administrative experience must be a consideration in the decision to keep or destroy a specific record. For example, the legal requirements may show a six-year statute of limitations on a document involving accounts receivable, but on the basis of past experience and actual practice, the company may take a calculated risk and discard the record within two, three, or four years. It may go even further and establish a monetary limit for retention periods. For example, accounts receivable documents under $50 may be destroyed after two years, while those under $100 may be held for three to four years.

There are many records that have no direct relation to the various statutes or regulations. These records will require a study of actual usage—the frequency of reference and the purpose of reference. Once these important factors have been analyzed, a retention schedule can be established for records without a legal retention period.

Comparable Company Data. It is helpful for management to obtain records retention information from comparable companies, but it is important to remember that such information should be used as only *one* of the guides for assisting in deciding on the retention of specific records. It is also important to realize that such information often represents what is *being* done—not what *should* be done.

It is of paramount importance that management avoid any decision about the disposition of a record until all three factors have been carefully considered. Applying a "canned" solution to specific problems in a particular company may give some results, but it will not realize the full potential of scientific records management.

Records Storage Center. The records storage center provides for low-cost high-volume retention and retrieval of noncurrent records of value. These records are placed in standard corrugated containers that will hold a cubic foot of legal or letter size documents. In turn, these record-filled containers are placed on steel shelving arranged to secure the highest possible ratio of cubic feet of records to square feet of center floor space. A cubic foot of records can be retained in a records storage center for a fraction of the cost of keeping the same records in regular office filing equipment. Exhibit I sets forth acceptable records-center steel-shelving specifications. Exhibit II outlines the storage container specifications. This container will hold up to thirty pounds of records. It can be erected and handled easily by a single person.

When proper air-conditioning and humidity controls are installed, the records storage center may be used also to maintain noncurrent data processing magnetic tapes and similar materials, as well as microfilm, motion picture film, and other audio-visual materials. Where operation of a company records center is not economically feasible, records storage space may be leased in a commercial storage facility; or a records-storage service firm may be engaged which will do filing and retrieval in addition to storage.

BELDEN MENKUS, C.R.M., Management Consultant, Middleville, New Jersey.

EXHIBIT I

SPECIFICATIONS FOR STEEL SHELVING UNITS FOR RECORDS STORAGE

1. Each unit to be 42" wide by 32" deep by any multiple of 23" high (depending on ceiling height).
2. Each unit to have four single uprights, as high as determined in (1) above.
3. Each unit to have shelves 23" on center, so that each unit will have one less opening than shelves with 22" clearance for each opening. (i.e., if 5 shelves, then there will be 4 openings between shelves).
4. Reinforcing angles for each unit; each shelf to be reinforced along the 42" width front and rear.
5. Angle sway braces for each unit; the second and fourth shelves of each unit to be tied to each upright by angle sway braces.
6. Side sway braces for each unit (1 pair).
7. All units to have a closed 3" base on the front only.
8. No sides or back required.
9. Uprights to be 11 guage steel.
   Shelves to be 18 guage steel.
   Bases to be 18 guage steel.
   Reinforcing angles to be 11 guage steel.
   Angle sway braces to be 11 guage steel.
   Side sway braces to be 11 guage steel.

EXHIBIT II

SPECIFICATIONS FOR RECORDS STORAGE CONTAINERS

Inside Dimensions

	High	*Wide*	*Deep*
Box	10"	12"	15"
Cover	2"	12⅜"	15⅜"

Both case and cover to be made from 200 lb. test Kraft-lines B flute corrugated paper. Box is double-walled.

Grip hole on front and back of box (10" × 12" sides) 3" from top of box. Grip hole to be 3" wide and 1" high.

Information References

Associations:

Association for Systems Management.
Society of American Archivists.

Periodicals:

Information and Records Management.
Records Management Quarterly.

Texts:

Greenwood, Frank and Mary M., "Information Re-

sources in the Office of Tomorrow," Cleveland, Association for Systems Management, 1979.
Horton, Forest W., "Information Resources Management, Concepts and Cases," Cleveland, Association for Systems Management, 1979.
Johnson, Mina and Kallaus, Norman, "Records Management," Cincinnati, South Western, 2nd. ed., 1974.
Moskowitz, George Jerome, "Records Management and Control," Ch. 8, Sec. 4, in Heyel, Carl, ed., "Handbook of Modern Office Management and Administrative Services," New York, McGraw-Hill, 1972.
Place, Irene and Popham, Estelle, "Filing and Records Management," Englewood Cliffs, N.J., Prentice-Hall, 1966.
"Records Management Handbooks," a series of monographs, Washington, D.C., National Archives and Records Service, General Service Administration.

Cross References: *Forms Control; Forms Design; Information Storage and Retrieval (non computer); Records Protection; Systems Management.*

RECORDS PROTECTION

When a company has established a RECORDS MANAGEMENT program, the next logical step is **Records Protection** in the event of a natural, sabotage-induced, or wartime (even nuclear) disaster. Depending upon the size of the company, the protection plan can range from a very expensive and elaborate program to a comparatively inexpensive, but effective, safeguarding of important documents and business records.

There are, of course, thousands of records to screen before a decision is made as to the "vital" status of any of them. What documents are vital and require extra protection attention? What are the guidelines for determining what are vital records? What factors determine the importance of a document?

Guidelines for Priority. While the importance of some documents will vary according to the nature of the business, a number of important guidelines can be applied to determine the priority of protection. The key factors in the measurement of records "vitality" are as follows:

(1) Information needed to resume company operations.

(2) Data required to reestablish the legal and financial status of the company.

(3) Records that fulfill obligations to stockholders, employees, and outside interests, including regulatory agencies.

(4) Records that involve products, prices, inventories, and the technical know-how related to products.

All of the above are related to the over-riding consideration of assuring the continuity of the business in the event of a natural or manmade disaster, civil disorder, or other disturbance of normal operations. In most instances, an effective records protection program will be an integral part of a larger program for systematic protection of company premises.

The Functional Approach. In the "functional method," records are identified by analyzing the major operations of the business. Major operations are then divided into basic functions to determine the information needed to carry out these functions. When this has been done, the records containing information vital to the discharge of the functions can be easily identified.

Usually, a company has five or six major operations. For a manufacturing company the major operations may be these five areas: (1) Treasury, (2) Sales, (3) Engineering, (4) Production, and (5) Administration.

To illustrate the "functional method," the Treasury operation may be broken down into the following functions: receiving, paying, bookkeeping, and costing. Let us now take a specific function such as receiving and examine the factors involved.

First, the company must have the monthly accounts receivable trial balance, listing all outstanding receivables. It must also have the accounts receivable invoices showing additional accruals between trial balances. Then it must have the credit slips showing what customers have paid against their bills in the period between trial balances. With only these records the company's entire accounts receivable structure can be reconstructed if the need arises. This functional approach can be applied to any type of business. The process of determining which records are "vital" is complicated when an organization is making significant use of a computer. In some instances, changes in administrative procedures make it difficult to relate computer data files clearly to conventional records that serve the same purpose. However, these problems can be alleviated and the success of the vital records program assured if one thinks of the need to protect *information* in whatever form it is gathered, processed and retained, rather than merely of the need to protect records as physical entities. Examples of information types most frequently designated as vital are shown in Exhibit I.

The truly vital records of a given company usually constitute only one or two per cent of the total records. The protection program must assure that this small percentage is given top priority. The less important records may then be considered in the order of their importance to the continuity of the business.

Transfer of Authority Records. Special consideration must be given to the documents pertaining to the following elements of the business: assignments, powers of attorney, and legal authorizations required to reconstitute the board of directors, officers, operating committees, etc. Usually, key executives and technicians cannot be personally dispersed from the central office or plant. The documents specifying their substitutes must be dispersed instead. Here again the continuity of the business is the vital element. The chain of command in the event of casualties among key personnel must be firmly established and protected by the documents that give authority for management succession.

Hazards. Most business managements place the hazard of nuclear explosion in the top priority bracket when they consider protective devices or the dispersal of records. Nuclear explosion is, of course, one of the most devastating disaster hazards, and it does warrant special attention. At the same time, statistics show that each year two other disaster hazards take a dreadful toll of human lives and destroy millions of dollars of property: *fire* and *flood*. These must be given equal consideration with a nuclear disaster in the design of any Records Protection program. However, because nuclear disaster occupies the "glamour" spot in disaster circles, it will be discussed first.

Nuclear Disaster. There was a time when charts could be developed to show the relative damage to people and property in a nuclear explosion. These statistics were based on the early A-bombs and their effect upon Hiroshima and Nagasaki. However, since Hiroshima and Nagasaki, there have been tremendous advances in the size and type of nuclear weapons. In addition, the secrecy surrounding the development of these weapons here and abroad has

EXHIBIT I

VITAL RECORDS

- I. Treasury Operation
  - A. Receiving Function
    1. Invoices
    2. Credit Memos
    3. Trial Balances
    4. Shipping Orders
  - B. Paying Function
    1. Vouchers Payable List
    2. Check Register
    3. Payroll Register
    4. Payroll Summary
    5. Employees' Earnings Records
    6. Tax Returns
  - C. Bookkeeping Function
    1. General Ledger
    2. General Ledger Trial Balance
    3. Deeds
    4. Leases
    5. Insurance Policy Index (or Policies)
    6. Monthly Financial Statement
    7. Deposit Slips
- II. Sales Operation
  - A. Contracting Function
    1. Contracts
    2. Price Lists
    3. License and Royalty Agreements
  - B. Service Function
    1. Service Manuals
- III. Engineering Operation
  1. Drawings
  2. Specifications
  3. Notebooks
  4. Patents, Trade-marks, Copyrights
  5. Laboratory Reports
  6. Manuals
- IV. Manufacturing Operation
  - A. Purchasing Function
    1. List of Vendors
    2. Vendors' Prices
  - B. Producing Function
    1. Operation Sheets
    2. Tool Designs
    3. Tool Specifications
    4. Plant Layout Drawings
    5. Manuals
  - C. Testing Function
    1. Test Procedure Sheets
    2. Test Drawings & Specifications
    3. Manuals
- V. Administrative Operation
  1. Organization Manual
  2. Monthly Activity Reports
  3. Minutes
  4. Vital Records Manual
  5. Employee Insurance Records
  6. Union Contracts
  7. Seniority Lists
  8. Job Description Manuals
  9. Procedure Manuals
  10. Computer Program Documentation

made it virtually impossible to determine the probable effects upon people and property. Latest thinking indicates that the fallout-shelter technique will protect some human life from the initial blast and the subsequent radiation danger. For records, current opinion favors storage outside of key target areas.

The most common practice is to store the records in specially designed locations within a reasonable distance from the company's headquarters. Storage facilities employed include vaults well below ground level or in the side of a mountain. In addition, vaults of banks in small towns well away from a prime target are being used for the storage of vital records. Some companies have adopted the practice of microfilming selected vital records to reduce the storage space required. In summary, then, the philsophy seems to be "dig deep or disperse widely, away from prime target areas."

Fire. In designing any protection against fire, the primary consideration is simple—keep the temperature of the material below its combustion point. Means to accomplish this vary from elaborate water sprinkler systems to specially constructed safes with added insulation protection. There are some records, however, that cannot be stored in insulated safes or vaults. These must of necessity be stored in the open, as it were, and special precautions must be taken to insure the best protection possible.

If these records are stored in a warehouse, or in any normal building, water sprinkler systems can be installed. Here, of course, consideration must be given to possible damage from water. Where information is maintained on microfilm or on computer magnetic tapes and disks, it may be advisable to consider installation of "dry" extinguishing systems, employing carbon dioxide, Halon 1301, or high-expansion foam extinguishing agents.

Conventional insulated records storage containers are suitable for protection of paper records since they are designed to keep the temperature of their contents below the 350°F "flash point" of paper during a fire. However, microfilm and computer magnetic tapes and disks can be damaged by temperatures above 150°F. Thus, when they contain vital information, it is preferable that they be stored in special insulated containers designed to maintain their contents at the lower temperature during a fire.

Tests have shown that documents kept in uninsulated metal containers are literally baked to cinders under intense heat. Wood of course is extremely combustible. On the other hand, laboratory tests have demonstrated that double-thickness corrugated cardboard cartons, protected by watchmen and a sprinkler system, are about as good a protective container as any practicably available. Their resistance to combustion and ability to withstand water damage rate high. A water test of corrugated cardboard cartons conducted in the New York Operations Office of the Nuclear Regulatory Commission revealed that under a flow of 180 gallons of water an hour the following conditions prevailed: (a) after one hour there was evidence of dampness inside the box but no damage to records; (b) after two hours the contents of the box were still virtually unchanged; (c) after three hours there was still no substantial damage to the records.

Flood. Here the damage is due to the destructive forces of continuous water soaking. Water-tight compartments are of course available for vital records, and there usually are some storage areas available on very high ground away from the headquarters location. But some records cannot be stored in compartments or moved from headquarters, and some means must be devised to protect them.

In determining safe storage points that will most likely remain above flood level, the company can be guided by past history of floods in the area. The experience of other communities will also serve as a guide.

In recent flood disasters, some companies, forewarned, moved file cabinets to upper levels of their buildings. Others, thinking the water would not rise more than a few feet, simply took the bottom file drawers out and put them on top of the cabinets—only to find that flood waters completely submerged the lower floors by evening.

When the waters have receded, many companies find that all materials within file cabinets are salvageable to a certain extent. Paper is smudged and the ink has spread to other documents in the same drawer. Documents are stuck together, but can be spread apart and dried. File drawers are difficult to open because the documents have absorbed water and have expanded, jamming the drawers.

All loose material is usually lost. Binders are swept away by the flood waters. In some cases the loss can be serious because the material was the only documentation of current management thinking on important policies and projects. Magnetic media used in DP operations recovered from flood waters may prove unstable after submersion, or require lengthy drying and cleaning.

Civil Disturbance. Demonstrations over real or imagined social and economic grievances have mounted since the mid-1960s. Often they have included assaults on the plants and operations of related business enterprises. (Overseas operations of U.S. firms have proven particularly vulnerable targets.) Bombings of computer installations, burning of files, and various acts of malicious mischief have emphasized the potential dangers to organization records. Generally, it is necessary to develop and implement special emergency procedures for protecting vulnerable vital records in the event of disorders.

Industrial Espionage. Increasingly information about company products and processes, current operations, and future plans has become one of the most important assets the company possesses. This information is proving to be a tempting target for disgruntled employees and unscrupulous competitors. (In one instance, a major company's entire projected advertising budget was offered to its principal competitor in circumstances reminiscent of foreign intelligence operations. In another situation, employees openly sold customer mailing lists to the company's competitors.) Management must control employee and customer access to this vital information with the establishment of procedures somewhat similar to those employed in protecting Department of Defense security classified information. Contact with this information must be limited to a *need-to-know* basis.

Protection Methods. The basic methods for protecting vital records are variations or combinations of evacuation and duplication. There are four reliable means for protecting vital records. Threee of them require the establishment of a special storage location or Vital Records Center.

Built-in Dispersal. This method does not require the establishment of a special storage location or Vital Records Center. It makes certain that duplicate copies of records are kept in two or more separate and dispersed locations. For example, in a multiplant company, a plant may retain an original record and send a copy to the home office. There are many other records with duplicate copies in company files. There is no need to keep other copies as long as management knows that the record is kept at a sufficiently distant location, that it is retained for the necessary length of time, and that adequate safeguards have been established.

Designed Copy Dispersal. This method involves evacuation of an existing copy of a vital record to a Vital Records Center. For example, the fourth copy of each invoice can be sent out daily from the Sales Contract Department and sorted only for the period between trial balances.

Evacuation or Vaulting of the Original. When records have been designated as vital but have infrequent reference use, the most economical and effective protection is to send the original to a Vital Records Center. This eliminates the cost of reproduction and maintenance of duplicates. Records of historical value lend themselves especially well to this treatment.

Duplication of Original Records. This calls for making a copy of a record after it has been produced, in addition to the copies needed for business purposes, by microfilm, or photostatic reproduction. This is the most expensive method of the four and should be limited to records that cannot be protected by the other three methods. A cost analysis should be made to determine the most economical method of reproduction and storage.

Vital Records Center. Selection of the Records Center location depends upon the needs and circumstances of the individual company. There are not many areas that can be termed "completely safe" from nuclear or natural disasters. Selection must be made with utmost care to ensure the greatest possible protection within the means available.

Management should guard against converting the Records Center into an unwieldy collection of material. The type of data for storage should be carefully selected. Turnover is as necessary in the Vital Records Center as it is in any records storage area. When data are replaced by new information, the old records should be destroyed or removed from the Records Center.

Blank forms required for the continuity of the business need not be stored in vast stocks of individual forms. A master copy of selected or key forms used should be kept at the Records Center. This will enable the company to reproduce any form in the number of copies required if the basic stock in the home office or plant is destroyed.

Lowest Possible Cost. It is difficult to put a target price on the protection of vital records that are of inestimable value. Actual cost will vary in each company according to the number of records, the method of protection, and the size and scope of operations. One way to keep down excessive costs is to examine the various reproduction methods available. It may be cheaper to microfilm a large quantity of records rather than store the original copies in a Records Center.

Another way to cut costs is for companies to pool their resources for mutual protection. Group action can spread the expense and can, in some instances, eliminate "double protection" for the same records when they are kept by different companies or government agencies. When a group program is considered, the confidential status of the individual company's records must be preserved. This calls for the establishment of controls that will limit the access to a company's records to authorized personnel.

BELDEN MENKUS, C.R.M., Management Consultant, Middleville, New Jersey

Information References

Associations:

Association of Records Managers and Administrators.

Naremco Services, National Records Management Council. (The above entry, updated, follows the treatment by Naremco in previous editions of the Encyclopedia.)

Texts:

"Protection of Vital Records," Special Report by the Association of Records Managers and Administrators, prepared for the Office of Civil Defense, Department of Defense, Washington, July 1966.

"Protection of Records" (Standard 232), Boston, National Fire Protection Association, 1975.

Carroll, John, "Computer Security," Woburn, Mass., Butterworth, 1977.

Hoffman, Lance, "Modern Methods for Computer Security and Privacy," Englewood Cliffs, N.J., 1977.

Pritchard, J.A., "Security in On-Line Systems," Manchester, England, National Computing Centre, 1979.

Cross References: *Computer Security/Automated Office Security; Records Management.*

RECRUITMENT AND SELECTION. See Employment: Antidiscrimination Legislation; Employment Agencies; Executive Recruitment; Executive Selection; Human Resources Requirements; Personnel Testing; Personnel Testing: Types of Tests; Temporary Personnel Services.

RELIABILITY ENGINEERING

Reliability Engineering is a combination of management and technical disciplines which has as its objective the assurance of maximum time stability of a product's specified performance. It is, essentially, a formalized overall approach to the problem of achieving optimum product reliability, embracing an organized and oriented collection of management, engineering, mathematical, and statistical elements and concepts. It deals with every area of corporate activity which can influence the ultimate reliability of the product. The individual elements and concepts are not new, although many of them have been re-oriented to the reliability problem.

Although reliability engineering received its original impetus from military requirements, it has in recent years been increasingly applied in commercial manufacturing operations, specifically in automobile and television-set manufacturing, and in the manufacture of other complex products.

History. With the rapid advances in the design and development of highly complex equipment in the missiles and space fields, beginning around 1950, and the use of such equipment under high stress conditions and relatively unknown exotic environments, the problems of performance failures began to require increasing attention. The formation of the Ad Hoc Group on Reliability of Electronic Equipment by the Department of Defense through the Research and Development Board in 1950 marks the formal beginning of current reliability thinking. The initial work of this group led to the AGREE report in 1957 on "Reliability of Military Electronic Equipment," by the Advisory Group on Reliability of Electronic Equipment. This report forms the basis for numerous military specifications and documents providing the basis for organized reliability effort by equipment contractors. It led also to the publication in 1960 of PSMR-1, "Parts Specification

Management for Reliability," by another group formed under the Department of Defense, dealing with specific recommendations for the improvement of the reliability and specifications of electronic parts. The major recommendations of these groups are currently being implemented by the Department of Defense.

Many persons from both industry and the Department of Defense contributed to the numerous surveys, studies, and documents which form the basic current thinking in the reliability area. Foremost among these were the late R. R. Carhart of the Rand Corporation, C. R. Knight of Aeronautical Radio, Inc., Robert Lusser while with Army Redstone Arsenal, and C. M. Ryerson while with Radio Corporation of America.

Underlying Definitions and Concepts. *Product reliability* is defined as the probability of a product's performing a specified function, under given conditions, for a specified time, without failure. The reliability of any product, then, will be dependent on the level of performance required, as indicated, for example, by the position, speed, size, etc., of the target for a guided missile; on the levels of the numerous internal and external stresses which it must endure during operation; and on the length of time that the product must perform continuously without a failure.

For precisely specified performance and levels of environmental stress, product reliability becomes a function of time, R(t). Under certain conditions, R(t) may be the *exponential life function,* $e^{-t/m}$ or the Weibull life function, exp $[-(t/\alpha)^{\beta}]$,

t = time
e = natural logarithm base
m, β, α are parameters

—or some other less frequently used life function. (See Exhibit I.)

EXHIBIT I

TYPICAL LIFE FUNCTION

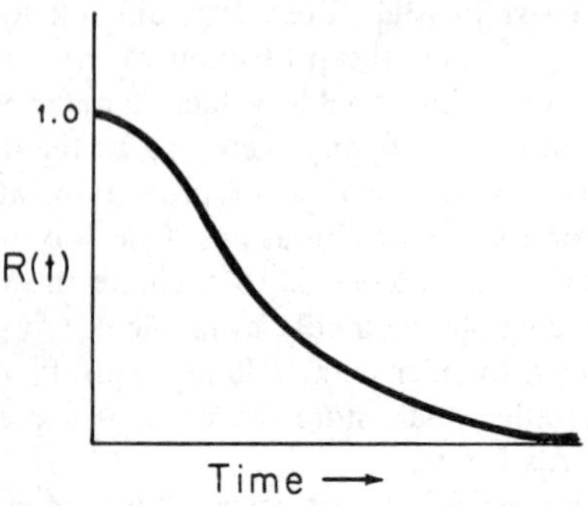

The necessary condition which leads to the more frequent application of the exponential life function is that the *failure rate* (sometimes called "hazard rate"), λ, remains relatively unchanged during the entire normal operating life of the product. The time span of this normal operating life is referred to as the *longevity* of the product, beginning at some point after the "debugging" period has been concluded and ending when an anticipated increase in wearout of the product begins. This says that when the product has been fully debugged, the frequency or likelihood of failure at the end of the normal operating phase will be substantially the same as it was at the beginning of the phase. In other words, there is substantially no wearout effect during this period. Because of its shape, the graphic representation has come to be known as the "bathtub" curve (Exhibit II).

The *constant failure rate,* λ, is the reciprocal of the mean, m, in the expression $R(t) = e^{-t/m}$. Thus $R(t) = e^{-\lambda t}$.

The *mean life,* m, is more commonly referred to as MTBF, *mean time between failures,* for repairable equipment, or MTTF, *mean time to failure,* for unrepairable parts or equipments. Thus, a specification of a reliability of 0.99 for a mission time of two hours leads to:

$0.99 = e^{-\lambda(2)}$, so that $\lambda = 0.005$, and m, or MTBF, or MTTF = 1/0.005, or 200 hours.

Associated with a reliability specification such as given above may be a numerical value of *confidence,* such as 80% or 90%. Such a confidence statement means that actual demonstration of the reliability of the equipment is part of the contractual requirement. The 80% or 90% confidence expresses the required degree of certainty that the product meets its minimum reliability specification. The complement of the confidence (1 − C), when confidence is designated by C, expresses the *degree of risk* that the customer is willing to take that the product is not better than the minimum reliability requirement. Thus, 80% confidence means a 20% risk to the purchaser that the product in our foregoing example has the minimum 200 hour MTBF, or less. This risk to the purchaser is commonly referred to as the *consumer's risk,* and together with the *minimum reliability specification* provides part of the basis for determination of the number of required test hours and the number of permissible fail-

EXHIBIT II

NORMAL OPERATING LIFE—THE "BATHTUB" CURVE.

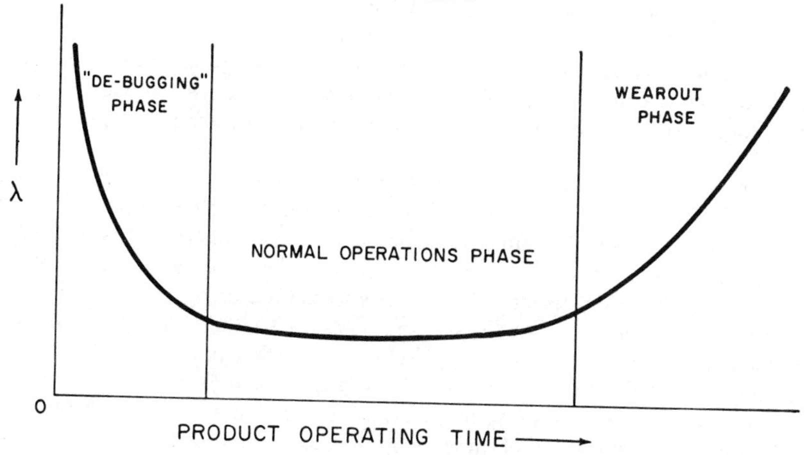

ures which make up the criteria for acceptability in the demonstration of reliability.

Following the accumulation of some number of test hours with some number of failures, an MTBF or failure rate may be estimated from the data. For example, if two failures had occurred in 500 hours of test, the estimated MTBF would be 500/2, or 250 hours. The estimated failure rate would be 2/500, or 0.004 failures per hour. The *true* MTBF or λ could be either greater or smaller than these values, and a confidence statement can be made to establish limits within which the true MTBF or λ actually lies.

For the example given above (by reference to the statistician's so-called Chi-Square Tables), we can be 90% confident that the true MTBF is at least 94 hours, allowing for a 10% risk that it may be less. We can similarly be 90% confident that the true MTBF is at most 940 hours. Or we can be 80% confident that the true MTBF lies between 94 and 940 hours.

In general such confidence limits will be closer together when these limits are based on a lower degree of confidence or when the calculations are based on a larger number of test hours and failures.

A special relationship between reliability, confidence, and the number of units to be tested for a given number of hours each is

$$R^n = 1 - C$$

where R = reliability, n = number of units, and C is confidence. This relationship applies only to the particular case in which the number of failures is zero.

Thus, if it is required to demonstrate a reliability of 0.8 for a specified time, with a confidence of 90%, then $0.8^n = 1 - .90 = .10$, and n (to the nearest whole number) is computed to be 23. Then if 23 units were tested without failure for the time specified, we would be 90% confident that R was *at least* 0.8. It should be noted that the formula can be used to obtain any one of the three variables, as long as the other two are given. Thus if 23 units had been tested for the specified time without failure, we could compute the reliability for any given confidence limit, or we could ascribe a confidence limit to any stated reliability.

Frequently associated with questions of reliability are the additional considerations of *maintainability* and *availability.* The former relates to the ease of maintenance and repair which has been designed into the equipment. The latter reflects both the reliability and the maintainability, since together they determine the proportion of time that the equipment will be available for use.

The reliability which has been designed and manufactured into the product is *inherent reliability,* reflecting basic design, parts and their application, manufacturing techniques, and workmanship. It assumes idealized use of the equipment. *Operational reliability* is the reliability which takes into consideration the inherent reliability and the added effects of use, such as the operating and maintenance equipment and personnel, auxiliary and supporting equipment, installation environment, deterioration in storage, effects of shipping and handling, etc.

Management Considerations. The responsibilities of management lie in:

(1) Developing a definite capability to assess the current state of performance of company operations and product as they relate to reliability.

(2) Setting forth specific reliability objectives.

(3) Organizing a well-defined and effective program to eliminate current deficiencies and to meet reliability objectives. A truly effective program must return many times its basic cost through the reduction of wasteful engineering effort, through minimization of the time required to reach an optimum design during development, and through minimization of time required to debug the prototype models, the early production models, and the manufacturing processing.

(4) Providing the personnel, funds, authority, and time schedules necessary for the program.

(5) Constantly monitoring the program with a critical evaluation of its effectiveness; modifying the program or existing procedures, policies, and organization as may be necessary.

Technical Aspects. In the initial consideration of a product, prior to full-scale design activities, it is essential to determine that the reliability objectives are consistent with the state of the art. The techniques of *systems analysis,* using mathematical analysis, particularly the calculus of probabilities, will yield an estimate of the expected reliability which may be possible with alternate design configurations, and an estimate of the reliability requirements which may have to be placed on individual units of the total equipment.

During the engineering design activity, the techniques of *reliability prediction* are continuously applied to get some estimate of the reliability of the design which has been formulated to this point; to compare reliabilities of alternate designs; and to determine weak links of the reliability chain. This reliability prediction approach is based on part-failure rates which may come from many alternative sources, and which may, in fact, not be completely appropriate for the application at hand. However, for the objectives given above, the prediction techniques do serve as an invaluable design guide, and become more precise as additional test information and experience are generated as the hardware itself becomes available for engineering tests.

The techniques of derating of parts, redundancy, and trade-offs are available to the engineer in modifying his design to achieve his reliability objectives. As already noted, the reliability prediction techniques measure the relative merits of alternative modifications. *Derating* is the use of parts at lower than manufacturer's specified stress levels. For example, a resistor rated at 1 watt might be derated to a ½-watt application. *Redundancy* refers to the use of parallel systems or portions of a system so that one of the branches will take over the function should a failure occur in the other. *Trade-offs* involve giving up certain complex functions to achieve higher reliability through, say, reduced number of parts and simpler over-all design, or the foregoing of lower costs for achieving higher reliability, say by use of more expensive components.

To bring the total resources of experience and highly developed skills of such personnel as the parts specialists, stress analysts, environmental test specialists, human engineering specialists, packaging specialists, manufacturing spcialists, etc., into the design, a formalized plan of design reviews at appropriate points of design progress becomes necessary. Formal design-review practice will employ prepared checklists on both electronic and mechanical aspects of any design. It will involve written reports on recommended modifications with justification for them. And it will provide for a follow-up of the implementation of recommended modifications when they have been approved by appropriate personnel.

As the engineering design becomes translated into actual hardware, the earlier paperwork efforts to determine modes of failure and their likelihood must be replaced by appropriate methods of revealing actual modes of failure and the weakest points on the reliability chain, using the actual hardware. The tolerances which had been specified on the drafting-board design must be evaluated realistically on the breadboard design to determine with assurance that they are neither so wide that the resulting outputs are seriously affected, nor so unnecessarily tight that they will lead to avoidable manufacturing problems and avoidable increased costs.

As an alternative to the tremendously high costs of accumulating enormous numbers of part and component hours of test, at specified environmental stress levels, to determine the part and component reliabilities, it makes sense to apply judiciously the philosophy of Robert Lusser. He urged that the parts, components, and larger units be tested under increasing stresses to their points of failure, thus generating the picture of the distribution of strength (resistance to stress) of the population of such units as are tested. In this way the probability of failure at any given level may be determined for any unit. By increasing resistance to stress wherever the probabilities of failure are too marginal, higher over-all reliabilities may be achieved.

By appropriate statistical planning and experimental design, the numbers of units tested to failure under increasing stress may be kept at a minimum. Under the philosophy that the predominant modes of failure must be discovered quickly, it may frequently be sufficient to stress-test only two or even one unit to study the types of failure which occur first, and the level of stress at which they occur.

With the understanding that variation itself is the best indicator of its cause, carefully planned techniques of variation analysis provide the means for identifying the causes of variation, and thus for their control or elimination as a critical problem. The indicated technique may be a multivariable screening type of study in which the important few sources of variation are sorted out from among the inconsequential many sources, in a relatively small number of tests. It may be a "Latin square" design in which only two units differing in performances are disassembled and reassembled several times, with planned interchange of elements so that the resulting tests point directly toward the source of the initial differences.

Applying the Latin square technique to a generator, for example, two supposedly identical generators might be giving unacceptably different outputs. Targeting in on the causes of the difference would be done by the evaluation of three components, say, "armature," "brush assembly," and "the remainder." First the two generators would be disassembled and reassembled as they were, and tested again, to be sure that the difference was not due to some fault in the assembling process. Next, the two generators would be tagged, respectively, "high" and "low." Identifying the selected components as A for armature, B for brush assembly, and R for remainder, the two units would be repeatedly disassembled and reassembled and tested in various combinations, as follows:

A-High with B-Low and R-High
A-Low with B-Low and R-Low
A-High with B-High and R-Low
A-Low with B-High and R-High

Tests would be run on each combination twice, giving eight test runs in all. (These eight runs would be performed in random sequence.) Next, the two readings for each test run would be entered on the Latin square diagram shown in Exhibit III, i.e., two readings in each box. Then by averaging the four readings in each vertical *column*, the effects of "A-High" and "A-Low" would be measured. (It will be noted that the *other* effects cancel themselves out.) By averaging the four readings in each horizontal *row*, the effects of "B-Low" and "B-High" would be measured. By averaging the four readings *diagonally* each way, the effects of "R-High" and "R-Low" would be measured. Thus the combination providing the most significant difference would point to the location of the cause. It can be seen that if the cause is isolated as lying within "the remainder," further targeting could readily be done by using the Latin square technique on the remainder, choosing three logical component breakdowns.

Similarly, a number of statistically engineered techniques applied throughout the development activity and into early production can provide an effective route to optimizing both the design and the production processes to higher product reliability.

The contractual requirement for demonstration of reliability will be fulfilled through reliability tests which are based on a fixed number of equipment hours of operation with an allowable number of failures, or on a sequential test procedure in which the number of equipment hours of tests are not precisely predetermined, but will not exceed some established upper limit. Instead, the number of accumulated fail-

EXHIBIT III

LATIN SQUARE TEST DESIGN

	A-High	A-Low
B-Low	R-High	R-Low
B-High	R-Low	R-High

ures is constantly paired with the accumulated equipment hours of test, so that predetermined criteria will indicate that the equipment tested passes the test, fails, or must be tested further before a conclusion can be reached.

The actual test criteria for acceptance or rejection are statistically calculated from the initially specified minimum reliability with the associated confidence (or consumer's risk), and a predetermined higher acceptable reliability level with an associated producer's risk (usually 5% or 10%) that the equipment will fail to pass the test when it is actually at this higher acceptable reliability level. This higher acceptable reliability level would normally be the reliability target during design.

Field-Failure Reporting. The final element of an effective reliability program is the field-failure reporting and evaluation system. It remains impossible to eliminate completely the normal system of evolution any product goes through as a result of actual operating experience. Previous considerations will have substantially reduced the traditional degree of dependence on the evolutionary process.

The worth of any failure reporting system is measured by its effectiveness in using actual field experience to achieve maximum product reliability improvement in the least time. This means the organization of a system in which the data from the field contain the most useful form of information and are themselves reliable. It may require a system of sampling to monitor the data reliability, or the data flow itself may be only a carefully controlled sample of all possible data. The analysis of these data must be based on a well-planned system of identifying the most critical problems with sufficient information to lead directly to the corrective action required. Routine follow-up on the implementation of corrective action is vital.

An essential element of this field-failure evaluation system is the physical analysis of the failed parts themselves. Through such analysis, true causes for failure which are frequently mistakenly identified are often determined. It is essential that information on identified deficiencies in the materials and manufacture of parts be channeled to the sources of such parts so that the necessary corrective and preventive action will be taken.

The future of higher reliability rests on the organization of effort which relentlessly seeks for the basic causes of failure and variation, so that these causes can be eliminated as problems for the future. The effort, originating with the systems manufacturer, must be extended to the parts manufacturer and then to his processed-materials suppliers and ultimately to the raw-material sources. When at each level of material supply the important causes of variation have been identified and controlled, unreliability will cease to be a major problem.

THOMAS A. BUDNE, Statistical Engineering Consultant, Great Neck, New York

Information References

Government:

"Reliability of Military Electronic Equipment," *AGREE Report,* Office of Assistant Secretary of Defense, Research & Engineering, U.S. Government Printing Office, Washington, June, 1957.

"Parts Specification Management for Reliability, PSMR-1," Office of Assistant Secretary of Defense, Supply & Logistics, U.S. Government Printing Office, Washington, May, 1960.

Lusser, R., "Reliability Through Safety Margins," *Redstone Arsenal Report,* Oct., 1958.

Associations:

American Society for Quality Control: Annual National Convention *Transactions;* "Journal of Quality Technology" (quarterly journal of methods applications and related topics); "Quality Progress" (monthly news magazine); "Production and Field Reliability" (selected papers, Electronics Division, February, 1959); "Research and Development Reliability," February, 1961.

Institute of Electrical and Electronic Engineers: "IEE Transactions on Reliability" (quarterly journal which also serves as the journal of the Electronics Division of ASQC); *Proceedings* of annual symposia on reliability (jointly sponsored with ASQC); "Reliability Group Newsletter;" Ryerson, C. M., "The Reliability and Quality Control Field from Its Inception to the Present," *Proceedings of the IRE,* May, 1962 (IRE became part of IEEE in 1963).

Texts:

Barlow, R. and Proschan, F., "Mathematical Theory of Reliability," New York, Wiley, 1965.

Barlow, R. and Proschan, F., "Statistical Theory of Reliability and Life Testing," New York, Holt, 1974.

Jorgensen, D.W., McCall, J.J., and Radner, R., "Optimal Replacement Theory," New York, North Holland, 1967.

Kalbfleisch, J.D., "The Statistical Analysis of Failure Time Data," New York, Wiley, 1980.

Mann, Nancy R. et al., "Methods for Statistical Analysis of Reliability and Life Data," New York, Wiley, 1974.

Tillman, Frank A., Hwang, Ching-Lai, and Kwo, Way, "Optimization of Systems Reliability," New York, Marcel Decher, 1980.

Cross References: *Quality Control and Quality Assurance; Statistics.*

RESEARCH AND DEVELOPMENT. See Industrial Research and Development.

RESPONSIBILITY REPORTING

Responsibility Reporting is a term used to describe accounting and management reporting systems that are directed toward controlling costs at basic supervisory levels. It is a primary management control tool and an essential companion to the delegation of authority by management.

Formal Definition. Responsibility reporting involves a grouping and defining of the responsibilities within an organization structure, the determination and assignment of costs to appropriate levels and activities, and a strong emphasis on cost controllability. Effective responsibility reporting systems depend on the same sound principles and practical methods as used in organization planning, cost accounting, operations budgeting, and cost control.

Approaches and Techniques. Responsibility reporting does not introduce new techniques to accounting practice. It does, however, provide a convenient means of presenting to management an important concept of accounting. Under responsibility reporting, the organization of responsibilities, the accounting for costs, and the budgetary control operations are integrated into one overall program to serve management.

Decentralization and delegation of management authority and responsibility create the need for developing a responsibility reporting system. Decentralization also provides a real though not insurmountable obstacle to the design of the system. The problem is that true decentralization of responsibility requires parallel authority, which often extends to freedom in internal organization. Responsibility reporting seeks to establish a reporting structure directly related to the organization structure. If each level has authority to define its own internal organization, the organization structure tends to become both nonuniform and nonstatic. Under such circumstances it is not practical to attempt a standardization of the system of accounts, responsibilities for accounts, and management reports.

In many cases involving decentralized management, the only workable approach to responsibility reporting (other than a company reorganization) is to develop a system for general application by each subdivision of the organization to its own operations. *Each level of management defines and assigns responsibilities and reporting systems for the next lower level only.* The definition of content and the application of the chart of accounts, aside from determining responsibilities, can and should be standardized and controlled at the top level of management. However, such a chart of accounts should not be prepared in a way that would force a particular type of organization on each subdivision.

In some situations, a well defined and standardized organization exists at all levels of management. Here the system design can be specific. Responsibilities for accounts can be definitely assigned and standard reports can be prepared for all positions of responsibility.

In any case, whether or not the organization is standardized, certain principles of good organization must be followed. Those principles which are important to the responsibility reporting program are: (1) every necessary function is assigned to a unit of the organization; (2) the assignment of responsibilities is specific and understood; (3) overlapping of responsibilities must not exist; (4) each position of an organization reports to one and only one supervisor; and (5) a supervisory position over each logical grouping (either geographic or functional) of activities at each management level must be assigned.

For economy and personality reasons, no actual organization follows the ideal. Situations where one person occupies several different positions of responsibility are handled by separately identifying each position. It is then established that the one person has several separate and distinct official positions. For example, in one division a manager may be responsible for both sales and advertising, while in another division a manager may head up each of these functional areas. These positions are reported as separate responsibilities, and the flow of reports for summarization purposes follows its own separate functional responsibility channel. Thus, in the one case the manager might receive two summary reports—one for the sales area and the other for advertising. In the second case the two reports would be separately directed to the two managers. By focusing attention on functions and functional organization, flexibility of application is retained to fit the actual organization and assignment of responsibilities.

Relation to Cost Accounting. Responsibility reporting is closely associated with COST ACCOUNTING. Certainly a cost accounting system which is to be used as a managing tool must first assign responsibility for expenses. This is particularly true in standard cost systems. Knowledge of variances in performance has little meaning if responsibility for these variances is not established. While it is entirely possible to establish a responsibility reporting system which is not intended to produce product costing, a good all-purpose system will incorporate the essential principles of product cost accounting.

The design of responsibility reporting systems should be guided by the same rules applied to cost accounting. Some of the more significant principles are: (1) appropriate accounts should be established so that cost items can be readily recorded in the proper account without detailed analysis, cost items can be kept intact, and each account represents a homogeneous, well defined, and readily analyzed expense grouping without reconstruction of accounts; (2) all items of expense should be recorded according to the lowest level or area of operations to which they can be directly related and assigned; (3) no items should be split to a lower classification requiring allocation or proration on any basis, however appropriate; and (4) any desired information which requires cost allocations or other arbitrary assignment of costs to lower levels of classification should be provided only by special analytical reports prepared from basic accounting records.

Relation to Budgeting. Responsibility reporting is essential to the most effective use of budgetary control. A definition of responsibilities for the budget is the first step in preparing a budget. If the budget performance is to be reported and measured, the accounting system must coincide with established budgetary responsibilities. While it is possible to have responsibility reporting without a budget program, an effective budget cannot be practically established without a responsibility reporting system.

A necessary requirement of a responsibility reporting system designed to support a budget program is complete coordination of the two. Responsibility reporting system design should be guided by the following budgeting rules: (1) budget (and all types of responsibility) performance accounting and reporting should be tied directly to actual financial accounting without memo adjustments or additions; (2) budgets should be directed toward the control of expenditures at the point of disbursements approval; and (3) budgets should be simple and confined to the main purpose.

Sample Reports. The following sample reports illustrate how some of the key features of responsibility reporting work in a typical manufacturing company. Each executive and supervisor in the company's organization has his or her own report, reflecting items of income and expense over which that executive has control.

Exhibit I shows the costs chargeable to the foreman of the Punch-Press Department for the current month and for the year to date, as well as variances above and below the foreman's budget. Associated reports for each succeeding higher level of organizational responsibility are also shown in Exhibits II, III, and IV.

The Punch-Press foreman is held fully responsible for the costs given in his report, since they represent the usage of labor, materials, and supplies over which he has authority. The designation "supervision" refers to his own salary and the salaries of supervisors under him.

It should be noted that both fixed and variable costs are included in this report without distinction. The test is whether they are controllable by the foreman. He has, for example, the power to decide how many people to keep on his department's payroll and how much overtime is needed to get the work done on time. Even if these decisions must be reviewed at higher levels, the basic authority and respon-

EXHIBIT I

THE TYPICAL COMPANY

PUNCH PRESS DEPARTMENT

O. A. Belforth, Foreman May, 1980

COST REPORT

Year to Date			*Current Month*	
Actual	*Gain (Loss)*		*Actual*	*Gain (Loss)*
$ 87,500	$ (7,000)	Direct Labor	$15,600	$(1,200)
4,000	(400)	Rework Labor	900	(150)
14,800	(2,700)	Indirect Labor	2,500	(500)
22,900	(4,050)	Overtime Premium	1,300	(100)
3,400	50	Supervision	650	—
5,100	1,100	Operating Supplies	1,000	200
7,000	500	Spoilage	1,400	100
3,500	(2,000)	Other	650	(350)
$148,200	$(14,500)	Total	$24,000	$(2,000)

EXHIBIT II

THE TYPICAL COMPANY
PRODUCTION DEPARTMENT
D. F. Colhart, Superintendent May, 1980
COST REPORT

Year to Date: Actual	Year to Date: Gain (Loss)		Current Month: Actual	Current Month: Gain (Loss)
$ 8,200	$ 1,300	Superintendent's Office	$ 1,500	$ 200
78,600	5,100	Shearing and Slitting	16,300	1,000
49,500	1,100	Screw Machine	9,600	200
58,000	2,100	Drill Press	11,800	400
148,200	(14,500)	Punch-Press	24,000	(2,000)
34,800	2,100	Welding	6,800	400
93,000	(2,200)	Finishing	18,000	(700)
96,500	(6,200)	Assembly	20,000	1,400
$566,800	$(11,200)	Total	$108,000	$ 900

sibility are his. (If they are not, these expenses should not be charged to his account, but to the account of the executive who actually has the decision-making power in each case.)

For consistency throughout the reporting structure, the heading "Gain (Loss)" is used instead of the more common "Over (Under) Standard" or "Increase (Decrease)." "Gain" always means a variation that is favorable to profits; "Loss" always means a variation that is unfavorable.

In Exhibit II, the totals for the Punch-Press Department—both actual and variance from the budget—are carried to the report for the foreman's immediate supervisor, the production superintendent. This report also shows total expenses for which each of the other foremen supervised by the superintendent are responsible. Normally, the superintendent will also receive copies of the more detailed reports given to his subordinates; he also receives a complete statement of the expenses chargeable directly to his own department (supervision, secretarial, space, etc.), broken down like those for the organizational units under him.

The Manufacturing Vice-President's Report (Exhibit III) summarizes the results reported to the Production Department and the other departments for which he is responsible, as well as the expenses of his own office that cannot be fairly assigned to any of those subordinates.

Exhibit IV, the income and expense statement, is the President's Report. It summarizes the costs incurred by the Manufacturing, Sales, Engineering, Finance, and Personnel groups, plus the president's own costs.

EXHIBIT III

THE TYPICAL COMPANY
MANUFACTURING
G. N. Horner, Vice-President,
Manufacturing May, 1980
COST REPORT

Year to Date: Actual	Year to Date: Gain (Loss)		Current Month: Actual	Current Month: Gain (Loss)
$ 14,700	$ 700	Vice-President's Office	$ 2,650	$ 150
32,000	2,500	Plant Maintenance	6,000	450
32,000	900	Tool and Die Shop	7,200	200
10,000	(1,200)	Production Control	2,500	(200)
566,800	(11,200)	Production	108,000	900
22,500	50	Inspection and Quality Control	4,900	160
10,000	350	Purchasing	2,100	60
22,500	1,000	Receiving, Stores, and Shipping	3,800	250
$710,500	$ (6,900)	Total	$137,150	$ 1,970

Installation. The design and installation of a responsibility reporting program represents a major undertaking, requiring competence in solving problems in organization, cost accounting, budgeting, and cost control. But more important than technical competence is the participation of general management. This participation must begin immediately with a clarification of the organization and assignment of responsibilities, and continue through the installation and administration of the program. In doing this, general management must be extremely careful not to assume the roles of the accountant or systems designer. Each decision must be examined in relation to good accounting practice and practical system operation. By emphasizing the part that the operating manager and the accountant play, the program makes necessary a team effort.

Financial management is ordinarily assigned the responsibility for the technical development of the system. This includes conducting detailed field surveys, designing a coding system for a chart of accounts and responsibility iden-

EXHIBIT IV

THE TYPICAL COMPANY
INCOME AND EXPENSE STATEMENT

May, 1980

Year to Date			Current Month	
Actual	*Gain (Loss)*		*Actual*	*Gain (Loss)*
$1,610,000	$(20,000)	Net Sales	$340,000	$(3,000)
1,243,500	(9,000)	Cost of Sales	277,200	(6,200)
6,900	(6,900)	Manufacturing Cost Variances	(1,970)	1,970
$ 359,600	$(35,900)	Gross Profit	$ 64,770	$(7,230)
		SELLING, GENERAL AND ADMINISTRATIVE		
$ 60,100	500	Engineering	$ 12,500	$ 300
190,600	(1,300)	Sales	21,050	100
43,000	900	Finance	8,300	100
14,500	400	Personnel	3,500	180
15,500	1,100	President's Office	3,600	250
233,700	1,600	Total	48,950	930
$ 125,900	$(34,300)	Net Profit—Before Income Taxes	$ 15,820	$(6,300)

tification, preparing a manual of accounts, designing detailed procedures, issuing a manual of instructions, and accomplishing the installation of the system. It further includes calling to the attention of general management organizational inconsistencies that come to light during the study.

A thorough understanding of the operations as conducted in the field is essential to designing the system. This is gained from an extensive survey of all areas of operating and administrative activity. In this survey, emphasis must be placed on identifying costs, origins of costs, authority for approval of expenditures, management responsibilities for operations, and organization structures for responsibilities. This information must be sufficient to describe the organization structure as to chain of command, groupings of responsibilities and levels of management; to prepare a chart and descriptive manual of accounts; to develop management reports; and to develop necessary procedures and instructions.

Applicability of Responsibility Reporting. Over the years, management's attention has been increasingly directed toward the refinement and usage of accounting and financial tools as operating tools. Organization principles, cost accounting systems, and budgetary cost controls were developed to a highly useful state. With these techniques already developed, whenever the need for accounting controls is recognized, it is now possible to integrate them into a single package under the title of responsibility reporting.

The concept of responsibility reporting is extremely important for the control of all types of organized effort. It has been applied with great success in every type of business activity. Responsibility reporting is a basic tool for effective management control in all companies.

K.S. AXELSON, Executive Vice President, J.C. Penney Company, Inc., New York, New York

Information References

Axelson, K.S., ed., "Responsibility Reporting," Peat, Marwick, Mitchell & Co., New York, 1961.

Dew, R. Beresford and Gee, Kenneth P., "Management Control and Information," New York, Wiley, 1973.

Lorsch, Jay W., Baughman, James P., Reece, James, and Mintzberg, Henry, "Understanding Management," New York, Harper & Row, 1978.

Patz, Alan L. and Rowe, Alan J., "Management Control and Decision Systems," Santa Barbara, Calif., Wiley, 1977.

Cross Reference: *Management Accounting.*

RETIREMENT PLANS

An important personnel problem is posed by older employees whose physical and mental capabilities have begun to decline. It is inefficient to keep them on in their present capacity. It is bad for employee morale and public relations to dismiss them arbitrarily, and it is usually not satisfactory to transfer them to less responsible positions. A better solution is to encourage or require them to leave active employment, with the employer undertaking to provide them with an income for the rest of their lives.

Corporate management has very generally adopted the last of the above approaches. Instead of attempting to judge the time at which the individual employee has passed the peak of usefulness, employment is generally terminated upon fulfillment of a set of conditions, one of which is almost without exception the attainment of a specified age. The Age Discrimination in Employment Act (ADEA) amendments of 1978, however, make it illegal to terminate an individual's employment prior to age 70 *solely* on account of the individual's age, even if such termination is pursuant to the terms of a bona fide plan or arrangement. The body of rules governing the termination of employment and the payment of a specified income to superannuated employees is referred to as a **Retirement Plan** or a **Pension Plan.**

The earliest plans were informal, with the amount and continuance of a retirement benefit dependent upon the promise (often oral) of one person to another. However, this type has now given way to the formal plan, with the terms and conditions contained in a written document. From 1875, when the American Express Company adopted the first formal retirement plan in this country [1], the number of formal plans has increased, slowly at first, rapidly in recent years. At the end of 1975, an estimated 45 million persons were covered by private formal retirement plans—15 million persons under insured plans, and 30 million under non-insured plans [2]. In addition, there are public plans covering employees of various Federal, state, and local governmental units.

The principal reasons for a formal plan are (1) the plan is easier to administer if it is written down and can be referred to by interested parties; (2) employees will have greater confidence in the permanence of benefits provided by a written plan which has been adopted by the corporate directors; (3) employees can count on definite benefits at retirement as a matter of right (subject to the ability of the corporation to pay for them); and (4) employees are assured more uniform treatment than if the plan were informal. Furthermore, there are important tax advantages to a plan which qualifies under Section 401 of the Internal Revenue Code of 1954. One requirement for qualification is that the plan be contained in a written document [3].

Essential Features. The establishment of a retirement plan (insured or trust fund) requires the services of an actuary and an attorney. The actuary designs a benefit formula, makes cost calculations, and consults with the attorney on technical details. The attorney drafts the plan or contract, advises of the applicable laws, and takes care of qualifying the plan with the Internal Revenue Service (IRS). Actual provisions may vary, but certain essential features may be recognized:

(1) The plan should have an official title so that it may be readily identified.

(2) Eligibility requirements should be clearly stated.

(3) The normal retirement date, that is the date on which retirement benefits begin, should be stated. This is generally the first of the month coincident with or next following the 65th birthday. Provision may also be made for early or late retirements, if desired.

(4) The formula for calculating normal retirement benefits should be unequivocably set forth.

(5) Provision should be made for financing the plan. Often, regular periodic contributions of an amount within the minimum and maximum limits prescribed by Regulations of the IRS are specified. Frequently, too, especially in plans covering salaried employees, the corporation simply promises to maintain the fund in a sound actuarial condition. Contributions by the employees may or may not be required.

(6) The right to terminate the plan should be reserved, and provision should be made for the disposition of the assets of the plan in the event of termination.

(7) The responsibility for carrying out the terms of the plan should be fixed. This duty is generally assigned to a committee, almost invariably composed of executives with or without employee representatives.

Benefits. The purpose of a retirement plan is to provide a stated regular income, usually for life, to an employee who has retired, though disability benefits and incidental death benefits may also be provided. The stated regular income must be calculated by a definite formula. While space does not permit a detailed discussion of the various formulas found in practice, certain general types may be recognized:

(1) *Formula Based on Final Average Earnings and Years of Service.* "Final average earnings" means average compensation over a period of years (often five) just prior to retirement. This type is often used in plans covering executives and other salaried personnel where final salaries are usually much higher than starting salaries. From the employee's point of view, this type has definite advantages. The transition from final earnings to retirement benefits is smoother if the two are connected by a percentage relationship than if benefits are independent (or partially independent) of final salary. Inflation is taken into consideration to a greater extent than in other formulas.

The benefit is often computed by a formula which applies one accrual rate to that portion of earnings up to a stated amount, or "bend point," and a higher accrual rate to earnings in excess of the bend point. If a single accrual rate is used, total benefits, including Social Security, will be a smaller percentage of earnings for higher-paid personnel than for the lower-paid. A higher accrual rate above the bend point is designed to mitigate this situation.

As an example, the annual benefit might be years of service times a benefit unit composed of 1% of the first $10,000 of final average earnings, and 1¾% of earnings in excess of $10,000. Higher bend points may be expected in the future because of recent substantial increases in the Social Security tax base. In fact, bend points which move up automatically with increases in the Social Security tax base are common.

Another type of formula which takes Social Security benefits into account is the "offset" type, the benefit from the plan being defined in terms of an accrual rate less a portion of the "primary insurance amount." One such formula, for example, might provide an annual benefit equal to years of service times a benefit unit composed of 2% of final average earnings less 2% of the primary insurance amount in effect at termination of actual service.

When a "bent" or "offset" formula is used, particular care must be taken to see that the benefits "integrate" with Social Security benefits if the plan is to qualify for favorable tax treatment. Briefly, this means that total benefits, including Social Security benefits, must not enable higher-paid personnel to receive a higher percentage of final average earnings than lower-paid personnel. One requirement for a "bent" formula is satisfied if the bend point is not in excess of the "average maximum taxable earnings" for Social Security benefits. Integration requirements are not limited to final average formulas, but apply to other formulas for basic income benefits and for certain other benefits, such as disability and early retirement [4].

(2) *Formulas Based on Career Average Earnings.* The benefit formula is applied to each year's earnings separately, the pension being the total of the units which have accrued each year. Benefits for service prior to the effective date may be based on earnings at the effective date and years of prior service rather than on historical year-by-year earnings. It is typical to "update" benefits periodically under career average plans, in order to base benefits for service prior to the effective date of the update on pay just prior to such effective date.

(3) *Money Purchase Formulas.* A fixed percentage of salary or other stated sum is set aside each year to purchase a deferred annuity beginning at retirement. The benefit at retirement is the sum of the separate units purchased.

(4) *Flat Amounts.* The formula may provide a fixed dollar amount for each year of service; for example, $10 per month per year of service, or simply a flat amount, such as $200 per month on retirement, this latter often subject to a minimum service requirement.

(5) Combinations of two or more of the four previous types.

In addition to the basic income benefit, other benefits may be provided. Certain examples may be cited:

(1) *Benefit on Total and Permanent Disability.* Although IRS regulations rule out temporary disability benefits, they permit permanent disability benefits. This is logical. A person permanently incapacitated to the extent that he can no longer perform the duties of his occupation presents a management problem—often more acute than a person who qualifies for normal retirement by normal age and service. Most plans, therefore, provide that after some minimum period of service (usually ten years) and attainment of a minimum age (though the age requirement is disappearing, probably because of the influence of the Social Security disability benefit), an employee who is totally and permanently disabled may retire on pension. The latter is usually the normal pension

accrued to date of disability if integration rules permit. Disability pensions are payable until normal retirement date, when the regular benefit becomes payable.

The typical disability benefit in a pension plan provides rather small benefits unless disability occurs after relatively long service, and it often provides no benefit at all for disability occurring before ten years of service. Furthermore, disability must be total and permanent. This leaves many disabilities uncovered or covered inadequately. In recent years, "long term disability" (LTD) plans, separate from the pension plan, have been developed to meet these needs. A long term disability plan will generally provide a benefit which, with Social Security benefits, will be equal to a stated percentage (e.g., 60%) of salary at disability for incapacity which prevents the employee from performing the duties of his occupation. If the incapacity has continued for two years (or in some plans, one year) benefits may continue if the employee is unable to perform the duties of any occupation for which he may be fitted by reason of education or training.

Where long term disability plans are in effect, care should be taken to avoid duplication with disability benefits from the retirement plan. One approach is to remove disability benefits from the retirement plan, leaving disabilities before normal retirement date to be covered by the long term disability plan. Credit for service with the employer is often given for the period during which long term disability benefits are paid. At normal retirement date, the regular retirement benefit becomes payable.

(2) *Early Retirement.* Many plans provide that the employee may elect to retire early, usually at any time within ten years of his normal retirement date. The benefit payable is the normal pension accrued to date of early retirement, reduced actuarially because it begins at an age younger than the normal retirement age.

More recently, there has been a trend away from actuarial reduction. Some plans now provide full benefits at age 62 with 30 years of service, or at the point where age and service total 85, or some other specified number. Other plans, especially plans covering executives, deliberately encourage early retirement by subsidizing early retirement benefits, especially after age 55. Any departure from exact actuarial reduction adds to the theoretical cost of the plan, but may be rationalized on the ground that the extra cost may be less than that of keeping an inefficient employee until normal retirement date.

(3) *Vesting.* Although one purpose of a retirement plan is to hold employees, there has been a growing feeling that they should not be chained to the job, and that if they wish to change employers, they should not lose accrued retirement benefits. Accordingly, most plans now provide for some form of "vesting." Typically, after a specified period of service, such as ten years, any accrued retirement pension will be payable at age 65. The Employee Retirement Income Security Act of 1974 (ERISA) requires all plans to have a vesting provision at least as liberal as one of three alternatives specified in the law, all of which require full 100% vesting after no more than fifteen years of service.

(4) *Death Benefits.* The IRS regulations permit the payment of "incidental" death benefits "through insurance or otherwise." Although the meaning of "incidental" is not too clear in the event a plan provides a lump-sum benefit, benefits of the type described in (5), (6), and (7) below are permitted without question. While many corporations prefer to have a group life insurance program separate from the retirement plan, an increasing number provide substantial death benefits as part of the plan.

(5) *Joint and Survivor Benefits.* Many plans now provide that an employee may elect, in advance of retirement, that his benefit will be paid during the joint existence of himself and his wife and will continue to the death of the survivor. The amount of the monthly benefit will be reduced from that payable during his lifetime only. ERISA requires all plans to provide that married employees are assumed to elect a joint and survivor benefit, unless they specifically choose some other form of payment.

(6) *Annuity—Payable for a Period Certain and Life Thereafter.* An option found in many plans is an annuity payable for a definite period of years (such as ten) immediately after retirement and so long thereafter as the pensioner may live. The amount is somewhat less than if the provision for the period certain were not included.

(7) *Surviving Spouse Pension.* ERISA also requires that all plans provide a pension payable to the surviving spouse of an employee who dies while eligible to retire, but before actual retirement. This benefit can either be provided to the employee at no cost, or the employee

can be required to pay for this protection by means of a percentage reduction in his or her pension when retirement does take place, which reflects the cost of the employee's having been provided this protection.

Typically, the benefit provided is a specified percentage of the benefit which the employee has accrued up to date of death, or it may be the benefit the employee's spouse would have received if the employee had retired first and then died.

(8) *Lump-Sum Option.* Although defeating the primary purpose of a retirement plan, which is to provide an income for life to the retiring employee, a number of plans pay the lump-sum equivalent of the future benefit payments at the election of the employee. Under present statutes, the portion of the lump-sum attributable to employer conditions made prior to 1974 is subject to capital gains tax, and the portion resulting from employer contributions made in 1974 and later is taxed as regular income, subject to special 10-year averaging.

(9) *Medical Benefits.* Under Section 401(h) of the Internal Revenue Code, medical benefits for retired persons may be provided and funded in advance. Benefits must be subordinate to retirement benefits and contributions must be reasonable and ascertainable and made to an account other than the fund from which retirement benefits will be paid.

(10) *Miscellaneous.* There are other benefits besides those mentioned, and new types are constantly being developed, limited only by the imagination of the corporate executive or the union bargaining team and the ability of the Corporation to finance them. However, it must be remembered that each new benefit adds something to the cost of the plan. In recent years, there has been a great interest in a benefit which would compensate for inflation. One attempt to meet the problem is the "variable annuity" under which part of the pension assets is invested in equities, with payments adjusted as the value of the equities varies. Another is a direct cost-of-living adjustment, reflecting changes in the Consumer Price Index of the Bureau of Labor Statistics, or some other recognized index. Few employers, at present, are willing to commit themselves to a full, open-end adjustment. Rather, the adjustment has taken the form of a periodic ad hoc increase in the benefits to employees already retired, the amount often depending on the number of years which have elapsed since the date of retirement.

Funding. There are three principal approaches to funding:

(1) *Pay-as-You-Go.* As the name implies, no advance provision is made for meeting the obligations of the plan. As each monthly pension payment falls due, funds are provided from corporate assets. This method is not widely used at present, principally because by postponing pension outlay, an organization may be building up an obligation which cannot conveniently be met. Secondly, money set aside for a qualified plan will earn tax-free interest, so that fewer employer dollars will be required to pay a specified benefit with advance funding.

(2) *Terminal Funding.* As each employee retires, the single premium, or single sum, necessary to provide his retirement benefits on the basis of assumed mortality and interest rates (with or without provision for administrative expenses) is contributed to the fund implementing plan. This method has certain disadvantages. Since retirements may not occur evenly, the required annual outlay may fluctuate widely and the variation may be sufficient to produce irregular corporate earnings. Furthermore, funding in advance of retirement is less costly because more interest can be earned. ERISA prohibits the use of either pay-as-you-go or terminal funding for private formal pension programs; however, many Federal, state, and local government plans, as well as Social Security, still utilize pay-as-you-go funding.

(3) *Advance Funding.* Modern corporate plans are financed by making regular periodic payments during the employee's working years for the purpose of building up a fund from which benefits will be provided on his retirement. The periodic payments are usually referred to as "contributions," and there are two principal funding agencies with which the contributions may be deposited—the trust fund and the insurance company.

Choice of Funding Medium. There is no general agreement as to which of the two funding media mentioned above is the better method. Under a trust fund, all contributions are received by a bank, trust company, or other custodian of the fund, and benefit payments are withdrawn from the same fund as they fall due. Full advantage may be taken of investment opportunities; there has been, consequently, an opportunity to invest in equities to a greater extent than an insurance company is permitted to do under the laws of most states. (However, insurance companies in most states are permitted to operate "separate accounts" with investment freedom comparable to that of a trust fund.) Moreover, greater flexibility in the matter of contributions and benefits is generally considered possible under a trust fund plan because the employer is limited only by restrictions of the IRS. Under an insured plan, the introduction of a new type of benefit or a change in amount or frequency of contributions would also require the consent of the insurance company. On retirement, the continuation of benefit payments depends on the continuing sufficiency of the fund which, in turn, depends on the continuing financial ability of the employer. Given proper investment and actuarial advice, a trust fund plan can be perfectly sound. Trust fund plans are also sometimes called "self-insured," "self-administered," or "uninsured" plans.

Proponents of the insured plan point to certain advantages, chief of which are the guarantees which only an insurance company can give. Once benefits are "purchased," their payment is absolutely guaranteed by the insurance company. (By "purchase" is meant the setting up of a definite reserve liability by the insurance company against the retirement benefit payment accrued for a specified individual.)

Also, the typical "deposit administration group annuity" provides that even before benefits are purchased, funds deposited with the insurance company are guaranteed a minimum interest return, and the fund is guaranteed against capital losses. However, the rate may be changed annually, after some specified initial period such as five years, and the employer loses a certain investment flexibility since, generally, he cannot withdraw funds once contributions have been made, except at a sacrifice.

Insurance companies offer four types of contracts, in addition to the "separate accounts" (where permitted by law) and "split funding":

(1) *Deposit Administration Group Annuity.* This contract consists of two parts: an active life fund and a retired life fund. Contributions are made by the employer to the active life fund in an amount calculated by a consulting actuary or the insurance company as necessary to provide the benefits promised. The fund is credited with interest each year.

The fund is charged with administrative expense and contributions toward general and special contingency reserves. On retirement, a transfer is made from the active life fund to the retired life fund of an amount necessary to purchase the accrued benefit for the retiring employee, such benefit being fully guaranteed from this point (but not before) by the insurance company. Because contributions are not definitely allocated to individuals until actual retirement, the deposit administration plan is quite versatile and adaptable to a wide variety of benefits.

Deposit administration contracts are usually subject to experience rating or dividend action by the insurance company. If the group covered is large, a variation known as "immediate participation guarantee" may be offered by the insurer. Under this method, each group stands squarely on its own experience as regards benefit payments and overhead expense—there is no pooling or risk sharing as in other insured plans. There are no guarantees; the insurance company simply manages the fund, receiving contributions, investing money, and making benefit payments. (However, "purchases" of guaranteed benefits for retired lives may be made if the fund becomes "thin.") The plan is usually restricted to groups large enough to have a fairly stable experience from year to year.

(2) *"Conventional" Group Annuity.* The employer's contributions (and the employee's, if required by the plan) are applied immediately on receipt or at the end of the contract year to purchase a deferred retirement benefit for each individual employee. This type of contract, while well suited to some of the older retirement plans, has largely given way to the deposit administration group annuity because of the greater flexibility and economy of this newer form.

(3) *Individual Policy Plan.* A separate individual contract is required for each covered employee, and one or more additional contracts for each employee may be required if benefits increase after the original issue. The contract often provides life insurance benefits in addition to retirement benefits, and this is its chief advantage. However, if insurance benefits are provided, the individual employees must meet the applicable underwriting requirements of the insurance company. The plan is relatively expensive, cumbersome, and inflexible, and is now generally recommended only when the group to be covered is too small to qualify for a group plan.

(4) *Group Permanent Plan.* Group permanent insurance combines life insurance and annuity benefits in one group contract. It is similar, therefore, to combining in one contract the individual contracts under an individual policy plan. This type retains many of the dis-

advantages of the individual policy plan with few advantages. From the employer's point of view, the plan is relatively expensive in comparison with the cost of providing annuity and insurance benefits under a deposit administration plan and group term life insurance.

(5) *Separate Accounts.* As the name indicates, funds deposited in separate accounts are segregated from the regular assets of the insurance company. The laws of some states require that funding by a separate account be limited to retirement plans qualified under Sections 401 and 404 of the Internal Revenue Code. This requirement must also be met if the Separate Account is to be exempt from regulation by the Securities and Exchange Commission. Upon the retirement of an employee, benefits are purchased by transferring the amount of the necessary single premium from the Separate Account to the General Account of the company. From this point on, the benefit to the employee is fully guaranteed.

There are no guarantees prior to retirement; in this respect it differs from the deposit administration funds which have guarantees of a minimum interest return and no impairment of capital. The principal difference from the "immediate purchase guarantee" is that the latter is subject to state laws restricting investment to media specified for other regular insurance company funds.

Investment-only separate accounts are also available which, although they allow for the purchase of annuities at retirement, are usually not used for that purpose and instead are used only for the investment of funds.

(6) *Split Funding.* Sometimes a combination of trust fund and insurance company is used. One such arrangement is to have employer contributions go to a trust fund but, on retirement, a sum is withdrawn from the fund to purchase an annuity from an insurance company. Or, a trust fund may be used to supplement a conventional group annuity or individual policy plan in the event that the plan provides "final average," disability, or special benefits.

Funding Techniques. Because the liability for retirement plan benefits is often very large, most corporations prefer to set aside money currently, usually annually or more frequently. It is of the greatest importance to decide on a definite funding program and to determine periodically the sum which should be contributed annually.

The calculation of the required contribution is highly technical, and requires the services of an actuary. The pension payments have a "present value," that is, although they are deferred to normal retirement date, a one-sum dollar value can be calculated by use of assumed mortality and interest rates. Similarly, the amount of the required future contributions to the fund implementing the plan can be determined as that amount which will make the present value of contributions equal to the present value of the pension payments.

The calculation may or may not include an assumed rate of withdrawal other than by death, and should, in a "final average" plan, make some attempt to estimate final average salaries. The latter is usually done by projecting current salaries on the basis of certain assumed rates of salary increase. Without such a projection, there is a strong possibility that benefits (dependent on final salaries) will be understated, and as a result, the annual contributions actually required will be underestimated initially, leaving more to be made up in later years.

An important consideration in funding, once the assumptions have been decided upon, is the treatment of prior service. This generally means service with the employer before the plan was established, but for which pension credit is given. It can also mean service prior to the date on which a benefit increase became effective, or service prior to the date of valuation. Prior service may be calculated separately and funded separately, or it may be considered as an integral part of the total cost of the benefits (i.e., under an "aggregate method"). An advantage of funding methods which treat prior service separately is that it is possible to introduce flexibility into the funding program. Briefly, some of the more common funding methods are:

(1) *Entry-Age-Normal-Cost.* The age at which service credit begins for each employee is recorded and a level annual contribution, level either as a percent of salary or as a dollar amount, is calculated, payable from "entry age" to normal retirement age, in an amount sufficient to provide his prospective benefit at retirement on the basis of the valuation assumptions. The level annual contribution is the "normal cost." The valuation is carried out at the attained age, thus creating an "actuarial deficiency" if service begins before the effective date, or if there have been increases in benefits,

because the normal cost has been calculated at the entry age (i.e., an earlier age). This "actuarial deficiency" may be treated in several ways. It may be amortized over a stated period of years from the effective date of the plan (or from the date of a subsequent increase), or it may be funded at a specified rate (maximum rate, for purposes of Federal income tax is over ten years). Alternatively, interest only may be paid, in which case there is no reduction of the unfunded deficiency except through gains arising if actual experience is better than expected. ERISA does not allow private plans to pay interest only; generally, all benefits added to the plan must be funded over no more than 30 years.

(2) *Frozen Initial Liability Method.* As of the effective date of the plan, a calculation similar to entry age normal cost is made and an initial deficiency (or liability) is obtained. Later valuations are made on the basis of keeping this initial liability constant, and varying the current cost. The initial deficiency may be adjusted if there are later benefit increases.

(3) *Single-Premium Method.* Single premium funding is adapted to benefit forms such as "career average," "unit purchase," and "money purchase." Each year benefits are purchased as they accrue, and "prior service" may be funded as in (1) above.

(4) *Level Annual Premium Method.* A level annual premium is payable from date of entry. On a benefit increase, a new level annual premium for the increase is payable based on the attained age at date of increase. There is, consequently, no deficiency as in the entry-age-normal-cost method. The method is cumbersome and little used at present except with individual policies.

(5) *Aggregate Method.* The present value of future pensions is found, less any assets in the fund, and less present value of future salaries expected to be paid to normal retirement date or prior death or termination. An annual accrual rate is determined as the ratio of unfunded future pensions to future salaries. The annual contribution is the accrual rate times present salaries.

Federal and State Regulation. *Internal Revenue Service.* Because of the favorable tax treatment given to advance contributions by an employer in a plan qualifying under the Internal Revenue Code and implementing Regulations, and to distributions from the plan either to an employee or his beneficiary, modern corporate plans are almost always submitted to the IRS for formal approval.

The Regulations, Sec. 1.401-1(a)(2)(i) and Sec. 1.401-1(b)(1)(i), define a plan somewhat more narrowly than the definition of a retirement plan given earlier herein. A pension plan is "a definite written program and arrangement which is communicated to the employees and which is established and maintained by the employer . . . to provide for the livelihood of the employees or their beneficiaries after the retirement of such employees through the payment of benefits determined without regard to profits," and further, "a plan established and maintained by an employer primarily to provide systematically for the payment of definitely determinable benefits to his employees over a period of years, usually for life, after retirement."

The Regulations, Sec. 1.401-1(a)(3), give eight tests which a trust forming part of a pension plan must meet if it is to qualify:

(1) It must be created or organized and maintained at all times as a domestic trust in the United States.

(2) It must be part of a plan established by an employer for the exclusive benefit of his employees or their beneficiaries.

(3) It must be formed or availed of for the purpose of distributing to the employees or their beneficiaries the corpus and income of the fund accumulated by the trust in accordance with the plan.

(4) It must be impossible under the trust instrument, at any time before the satisfaction of all liabilities under the trust, for any part of the corpus or income to be used for or diverted to purposes other than for the exclusive benefit of the employees or their beneficiaries.

(5) It must be part of a plan which benefits prescribed percentages of the employees, or which benefits such employees as qualify under a classification set up by the employer and found by the Commissioner not to be discriminatory in favor of certain specified classes of employees.

(6) It must be part of a plan under which contributions or benefits do not discriminate in favor of certain specified classes of employees.

(7) It must provide that in the event of its termination, the rights of the employee shall vest.

(8) It must provide that forfeitures will not be used to increase benefits for remaining employees.

Amendments to the Internal Revenue Code

made by ERISA also established minimum requirements for eligibility, vesting, spouse's benefits, and funding of qualified plans, as well as imposing maximum limitations on benefits and contributions to qualified plans.

Self-employed individuals can establish qualified plans to which they can contribute and deduct up to $7,500, or 15% of earned income, if less, annually.

Common law employees not covered by a qualified plan may contribute and deduct up to $1,500, or 15% of compensation, if less, annually to an Individual Retirement Account. A Company may establish a group IRA for its employees.

Department of Labor. ERISA also established certain minimum reporting, disclosure, and fiduciary standards for all employee benefit plans, which are subject to enforcement primarily by the Department of Labor. A report on each plan must be filed annually, and a summary of the annual report must be distributed to plan participants. Employees must also be furnished with a summary description in layman's terms of each employee benefit plan in which they are eligible to participate.

Pension Benefit Guaranty Corporation. The Pension Benefit Guaranty Corporation (PBGC) guarantees the payment of certain vested benefits under employee pension plans. For this coverage, employee pension plans must pay an annual premium per participant to the PBGC.

Revision of Plans. Retirement plan provisions should be reviewed periodically to determine whether or not revision is needed. Changes in economic conditions may make a change in the benefit level advisable. Changes in income, capital gains, or estate tax laws may make it necessary to amend the plan if it is to continue effectively to serve the employer, employee, or other beneficiary. Changes in Social Security or other public benefits should also be considered from the standpoint of compatibility with existing benefit levels. In addition to the duty of administering the plan, retirement committee members have the responsibility of seeing to it that the plan is kept up to date.

FRANCIS M. SCHAUER, JR., Fellow, Society of Actuaries; Actuary, The Wyatt Company, Washington, D.C.

Information References

McGill, Dan M., "Fundamentals of Private Pensions," Homewood, Ill., Irwin, 1975.

"1980 Corporate Pension Plan Study," New York, Bankers Trust Company.

"Guides for Qualification of Pension, Profit-Sharing, and Stock Bonus Plans," Washington, D.C., Internal Revenue Service, U.S. Government Printing Office.

Internal Revenue Code, Sections 401–415 and Applicable Regulations.

"Survey of Retirement, Thrift, and Profit Sharing Plans Covering Salaried Employees of the 50 Largest U.S. Industrial Companies as of January 1, 1980," Washington, D.C., The Wyatt Company, 1980.

References Cited

[1] Wyatt, Birchard E., "Private Group Retirement Plans," published by the author, Washington, 1936.

[2] "Pension Facts," 1980, p. 6, prepared and published by the American Council of Life Insurance, New York.

[3] Income Tax Regulations Section 1.401-1(a)(2).

[4] Revenue Ruling 71-446.

Cross References: *Employee Benefit Plans; Executive Compensation.*

RETURN ON CAPITAL

Rate of Return on Capital (also referred to as "rate of return on investment") is widely used to appraise the effectiveness of management performance, to select the contents of an investment portfolio, and to make decisions regarding new product development and acquisition of plant and equipment. Unfortunately, the term means different things to different people.

Definition. Return on capital is the relationship, usually expressed as a ratio or percentage, between the income (or "profit" or "interest") from an enterprise or undertaking and the related investment or capital commitment.

History. While ratios between interest and principal have been computed as long as man has loaned money (return on capital consciousness is particularly evident in discussions of usury and "just price" in the Middle Ages), modern applications of this concept may be divided into three historical periods. The first of these periods used the ratio between the income as displayed on the contemporary income statement and divided it by the assets or equity as shown on the balance sheet. This computation developed in the nineteenth century, predominated in security analysis during the first half of the twentieth century, and may still in the 1980s be seen in connection with regulation of public utilities and analyses made in connection with the purchase and sale of shares of common stock. It is referred to here as the *mercantile rate of return.*

A second approach to capital budgeting reflects the time preference concepts of the bond and money markets. It was not until 1951—partly as a result of trail-breaking books by Dean [1] and the Lutzes [2] that were published in that year—that the method began to be used by financial management in connection with capital budgeting decisions (decisions involving the long-term commitment of capital). For capital budgeting decisions involving bonds and bank loans, the "arithmetic" of discounted cash flow computations and present value computations had been in use centuries earlier. But the attempt to apply the same kind of arithmetic that had been used for fixed-obligation bonds to the wider class of problems involving uncertain cash flows may be identified with the two decades following the publication of the Dean and Lutz books. During the fifties, the use of this approach to capital budgeting was more common in business literature than in the corporate board room, but the method became increasingly popular during the sixties, and is widespread in the seventies. It is referred to here as the *industrial rate of return.*

Over the years, a technique widely used has been the estimation of the time that would elapse before the cash inflows (or the reduction in outflows) resulting from an initial outlay of cash will equal that outlay. This is known as the *pay-back period,* or "payout" or "pay-in" period. While not strictly speaking a return-on-capital computation, the reciprocal of the pay-back period will often be an excellent approximation to the rate of return on capital computed by the industrial method, and this is considered later in the discussion of the various methods.

Beginning with an article by Charnes, Cooper, and Miller [3] in 1959, there has been a trend toward a third approach to the solution of capital budgeting problems by the use of LINEAR PROGRAMMING techniques. During the 1960s, several publications appeared on this approach; see particularly the powerful capital budgeting models developed by H. Martin Weingartner [4].

While this approach does not yet seem to have played a major role in actual capital budgeting decisions, it is certain to do so in connection with large industrial projects and military and space procurement expenditures. This linear programming approach selects the best projects and the best courses of action in terms of some stated objective (say to maximize equity at some later date). While it does not usually involve a direct computation of return on capital, it does permit the capital analyst to detect the binding constraints or bottlenecks to his maximization efforts, and it may thereby permit an indirect computation of a "quasi-" return on capital. It is here termed the *bottleneck rate of return,* and is discussed in some detail in the concluding section of this entry, under the head, *Emerging Techniques.*

WIDELY USED TECHNIQUES COMPARED

The Mercantile Rate of Return. *The mercantile rate of return is the ratio (expressed in percentage form) between some figure appearing on the contemporary income statement and some figure appearing on the contemporary balance sheet.* For illustrative purposes, a simplified income statement for a hypothetical company for the year ending December 31, 1980 and the related balance sheets at the beginning and end of the year are presented in Exhibits I and II respectively. Referring to the figures given there, the mercantile rate might be computed as follows:

$$\text{Rate of Return} = \frac{\text{Income}}{\text{Average Assets}} \times 100$$

$$= \frac{1330}{(4982 + 6312)/2} \times 100$$

$$= 24\%.$$

This mercantile method of computing rate of return on capital has also been referred to as the "accountant's method" (a lamentable libel on a proud profession!) and the "financial-statement method."

Assets are chosen as the base when it is desired to measure the performance of manage-

EXHIBIT I

MERCANTILE ACCOUNTING INCOME STATEMENT

Year Ending December 31, 1980

Revenues			$4,200
Less:	Cost of sales	$2,500	
	Depreciation	370	2,870
INCOME			1,330

EXHIBIT II

MERCANTILE ACCOUNTING BALANCE SHEET
December 31

	1980	*1979*
Cash	$1,000	$1,000
Receivables	4,200	
Inventory		2,500
Equipment	1,852	1,852
Accumulated depreciation	(740)	(370)
ASSETS	6,312	4,982
Contributed capital	5,352	5,352
Retained income (loss)	960	(370)
EQUITY	6,312	4,982

ment in using the total amount of property entrusted to its control. Thus, for internal management purposes and from the point of view of the entity as a whole, the important thing may be the effectiveness with which management makes use of the total assets of the company. In contrast, stockholders' equity may be the base of the computation when appraising not only the overall use of the assets, but also the extent to which financing methods were advantageous from the point of view of the stockholders.

The two approaches may be distinguished by the terms "return on assets" and "return," or "yield," on "equity."

To illustrate the distinction, suppose the corporation had been partly financed by the issue of 10% bonds and that the liabilities and equity section of the balance sheet was as follows:

	12/31/80	*12/31/79*
Bonds payable	$2,000	$2,000
Contributed capital	3,352	3,352
Retained income	960	(370)
LIABILITIES AND EQUITY	6,312	4,982

Let the concluding part of the income statement be the following:

Income before interest expense	$1,330
Less: Interest expense	200
INCOME	1,130

The computation of return on assets would be identical to the previous computation. It would be the ratio of total income ($1,330) earned from the use of all assets (averaging $5,647) without considering the amounts of that income available for the different types of investors and without considering the extent to which those assets had been financed by particular classes of investors. In contrast, emphasizing the interests of stockholders, it would be necessary to relate the net income available to stockholders with the stockholders' equity, specifically:

$$\text{Return on Equity} = \frac{1130}{(2982 + 4312)/2} \times 100 = 31\%$$

Trading on the Equity. Return on assets and return on equity may be used to understand the effect of "trading on the equity." Where bondholders are paid a lower rate of return on their investment than the rate of return earned on total assets, stockholders will benefit. Stockholders, in effect, will receive the benefit on the extra return earned on the assets financed by bondholders. The following *leverage factor* may be computed to assess the extent to which return on equity is improved over return on assets as a result of trading on the equity:

$$\text{Leverage Factor} = \frac{\text{Rate of Return on Equity}}{\text{Rate of Return on Assets}}$$

$$= \frac{0.31}{0.24} = 1.3$$

Where this leverage factor is greater than 1 (as in the example), the stockholders may have benefited through use of the funds supplied by bondholders at a lower rate of return than that earned on the assets. To determine whether stockholders have really benefited, however, it is further necessary to assess or attempt to weigh the greater risk that may be incurred by the company as a result of the greater fixed obligation imposed by the interest and principal on the bonds.

Some companies use gross assets (that is, assets before deducting the depreciation taken on these assets in prior years) instead of net assets in computing return on assets. Such companies justify their use of gross assets by their desire to prevent the rate of return from rising as the net book value of depreciable assets is reduced by depreciation. Undepreciated cost provides an unchanging base and, so long as annual income is constant, the rate of return is stable.

This viewpoint involves certain preconceptions not only about the stability of future earnings but also about what rate of return ought to be: Should the figure for rate of return be stable from year to year because it is stable or because the accountant expects it to be stable and therefore adopts conventions that make it stable? Some accountants have argued that the relevant investment base should instead be assets net of accumulated depreciation allowances, since it seems inconsistent to compare a profit figure from which depreciation *has* been deducted with an investment figure from which the accumulated depreciation *has not* been deducted. There are also many other variations regarding the rate base and dealing with matters such as whether the assets should include excess or idle assets, assets still in construction, assets financed by short-term sources of credit, etc.

There are also many variations in the income figure employed for the mercantile rate of return. Thus some companies do not deduct taxes because they are anxious to measure those things under the control of management, and they feel that taxes, while somewhat subject to managerial control (tax planning), are more under the control of Congress than of management. There are also variations in practice regarding the inclusion of dividend income, interest income, and "other income" and "other expenses" in computing net income for the rate of return calculation.

Whatever variations exist with regard to the capital base and the return on that capital, certain common features seem to be evident in the mechanics of computation. Thus, most companies attempt to get a "representative" figure for the capital base in the sense that it is the average of the relevant balance sheet magnitude at the beginning and end of the year, or it is a thirteen-point average of the balance sheet magnitude at the beginning of the year and at the end of the following twelve months. Furthermore, most companies "annualize" their income statement figure; thus, net income for two months would be multiplied by 12/2 to get its annual equivalent.

"Du Pont Analysis" of Return on Capital and Sales. Some companies make use of the "du Pont analysis" of return on capital, named after the company that pioneered in its use. While income and capital determine the rate of return on capital, the du Pont analysis intro-

EXHIBIT III

DU PONT ANALYSIS OF RETURN ON CAPITAL

Relationships in the du Pont analysis of return on capital. Arithmetic calculations proceed from right to left.

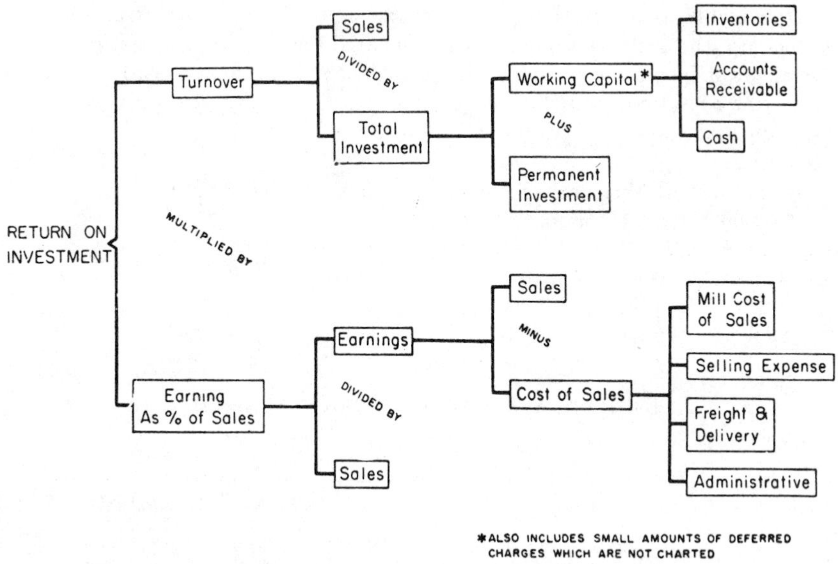

SOURCE: Watson, Alfred M., "Operations Research and Financial Planning," *Financial Management Series No. 102*, American Management Associations, New York, 1952.

duces a third factor—sales—that may be used to assist in judging the adequacy of income and capital. Note from Exhibit III that:

$$\frac{\text{Income}}{\text{Capital}} = \frac{\text{Income}}{\text{Sales}} \times \frac{\text{Sales}}{\text{Capital}}$$

The first factor on the right-hand side of the above equation may be referred to as the *profit margin* and the second as *turnover.* Such a breakdown of return on capital into two factors permits introduction into the analysis of the very important element of sales volume. Further, it permits the breakdown of return on capital to be handled in ratio terms.

If this ratio approach is not taken, then the analysis takes place in terms of total investment and total income and, because of differences in the scale of business, these total dollar figures are not comparable from business to business. By introducing sales, both income and investment are reduced to ratios, and these ratios are somewhat comparable.

To illustrate this du Pont approach, consider the three companies for which certain information is summarized in Exhibit IV. Assuming all three companies are in the same industry, why is it that companies B and C have earned only 1% on capital when company A has earned 20%? Income and investment figures alone shed little light on the question because of disparities in size between company A and the other two companies. Thus it is impossible to say whether B's low rate of return in comparison with A's is attributable to its larger capital or to its lower income. The fact that companies B and C have identical income and capital suggests that the same conditions underlie the low rate of return, but, as shown below, this conclusion is erroneous.

Introducing sales to measure level of operations helps to disclose areas for more intensive investigation. For example:

Company B does as well as company A in terms of profit margin, for both earn 10% on sales. But B has a much lower turnover of capital than does A. Whereas a dollar of capital in A supports two dollars in sales each period, a dollar in company B supports only ten cents in sales. Perhaps the analyst should look carefully at B's investment. Is the company keeping inventory larger than necessary for its sales volume? Are receivables being collected promptly? On the other hand, company C's turnover is as high as that achieved by company A, but C's margin on sales in much lower. If A can earn ten cents of profit on a dollar of sales, why does C earn only half a cent? Are its operations inefficient, its material costs too high, or does its location entail high transportation costs? The du Pont analysis will not categorically answer these questions, but it may point the investigator in the right direction.

Industrial Rate of Return. The industrial approach to the computation of return on capital examines the relationships among the cash inflows and outflows relating to long-term commitments of capital. It has two main varieties: the *rate of return* approach and the *net present value* approach.

Using the rate of return approach, the analyst designates as the industrial rate of return *that rate of interest which will discount or accumulate the cash inflows and outflows from a project or undertaking to zero at some particular reference date.* Designating the cash flows of year i as R_i (where R may be positive if it is a cash inflow or negative if an outflow), the industrial rate of return is that interest rate r (expressed in decimal form) which solves the following equation for given R_i:

$$0 = \frac{R_0}{(1+r)^0} + \frac{R_1}{(1+r)^1} + \frac{R_2}{(1+r)^2} + \cdots + \frac{R_n}{(1+r)^n}$$

EXHIBIT IV

DU PONT ANALYSIS OF RETURN ON CAPITAL

	Company A	*Company B*	*Company C*
1. Sales	$1,000,000	$ 500,000	$10,000,000
2. Income	100,000	50,000	50,000
3. Capital	500,000	5,000,000	5,000,000
4. Income as a % of sales (line 2/line 1, × 100)	10%	10%	0.5%
5. Turnover (line 1/line 3)	2	.1	2
6. Return on investment (line 4 × line 5)	20%	1%	1%

where the cash flows commence at time 0 and continue through time n.

To illustrate this approach using actual numbers, suppose a new company is formed to carry out an industrial undertaking that requires it to make the following disbursements and cash commitments at time 0:

Required minimum cash balance	$1,000
Purchase of initial inventory	2,000
Purchase of depreciable assets	1,852
DISBURSED AND COMMITTED AT TIME 0	4,852

At time 1 there will be a further disbursement of $500 in connection with an additional purchase of inventory. While there will be various receipts in the next few years they will be promptly reinvested in inventory. At time 6 the equipment will be worn out and the project completed and the company will be able to withdraw from the venture with $9,400. (These are the same cash flows implicit in the illustration of the mercantile rate of return and the reader should have no difficulty in relating the cash flows at time 0 and at time 1 with the 12/31/1979 balance sheet previously presented.) It will be found that these cash flows can be discounted to zero through use of a 10% discount factor, as verifiable by substitution in the foregoing equation, as follows:

$$0 = \frac{(4.852)}{1.1^0} + \frac{(500)}{1.1^2} + \frac{9,400}{1.1^6}$$

(The 10% is arrived at by trial-and-error use of percentages obtained from financial tables mentioned in connection with the discussion of *Net Present Value,* below.)

An accounting interpretation consistent with this rate of return approach can be had through industrial accounting. (For further information about industrial accounting, see [5], [6] and [7].)

Designating time 1 as the year ending December 31, 1980, the relevant operating statement or statement of receipts and disbursements appears in Exhibit V. Over the life-span of the project or undertaking, the net income from the project will be the same—$4,048—whether one considers mercantile accounting and the mercantile rate of return or whether one considers industrial accounting and the industrial rate of return. The manner in which that income will be considered to have been realized or earned will, however, differ. In mercantile accounting and the mercantile rate of return, income is earned when a sale is made. In industrial accounting and the industrial rate of return, income is assumed to be earned through the passage of time in the same manner that interest is earned on a savings and loan account. The earning of income in years 1 and 2 may be computed as follows using the industrial approach:

EXHIBIT V

INDUSTRIAL ACCOUNTING STATEMENTS OF RECEIPTS, DISBURSEMENTS AND CASH COMMITMENTS

Years Ending December 31
(Drafted As Of December 31, 1980)

1984	expected future net receipts and released cash commitments	$9,400
1980	net disbursements	(500)
1979	Net disbursements and cash commitments	(4,852)
ANTICIPATED INCOME		4,048

Year 1 income: 10% of 4,852	$485
Year 2 income: 10% of (4,852 + 500 + 485)	584
TOTAL EARNED IN YEARS 1 AND 2	1,069

These figures may readily be related to the balance sheets drafted at the end of year 1 and 2 as seen in Exhibit VI.

As in the case of the mercantile rate of return, the industrial rate of return may be employed either to assist in making decisions ("capital budgeting") or to assist in appraising

EXHIBIT VI

INDUSTRIAL ACCOUNTING BALANCE SHEET

	12/31/80	*12/31/79*
Expected future net receipts	$9,400	$9,400
Less: Unearned income	(2,979)	(3,563)
ASSETS	6,421	5,837
Contributed capital	5,352	5,352
Retained income	1,069	485
EQUITY	6,421	5,837

the past performance of management in reaching goals ("control"). But note the perils of using one method for the accept or reject decision with regard to a particular project, and using another to post-audit that decision and to assess its desirability once the project has been chosen. Using the discounted cash flow approach to capital-budgeting, for example, management might be led to expect a 10% return on this project and a postaudit of the decision at the end of year 2 might, even if the project is exactly on target, suggest that the project is actually earning 24% if the mercantile approach is employed. If capital budgeting relies on the discounted cash flow approach, then a meaningful appraisal of past performance in implementing capital budgeting decisions can only be had through the type of numbers generated by industrial accounting.

Net Present Value. As an alternative to the rate of return approach discussed above, many capital analysts prefer the *net present value* approach. The net present value approach relies in part upon determining a "cost of capital" rate. This cost of capital may be defined as the rate at which the company would be disposed to finance the additional projects. It may also be defined in alternative opportunity cost terms. Suppose, in the present case, that those who provide the capital to finance this project could easily earn at least 8% on their money in several other ventures of comparable risk.

Using 8% for discounting purposes, the net present value of the project may be computed as follows:

9,400	discounted 6 years at 8% has a present value of	$5,924
(500)	discounted one year at 8% has a present value of	(463)
(4,952)	expended or committed at time 0 has a present value of	(4,852)
	NET PRESENT VALUE AT 8%	609

Whereas the rate of return approach leads to acceptance of projects if they have an industrial rate of return greater than the cost of capital, the cost of capital approach leads to acceptance of those projects for which the net present value is positive when the cash flows are discounted through use of the cost of capital rate. (Both approaches usually lead to acceptance and rejection of the same projects.)

Industrial accounting may again be employed to give an effective postaudit of capital budgeting decisions implemented by the net present value approach. The operating statement would be identical to that already shown in Exhibit V. One version of the appropriate balance sheet is shown in Exhibit VII. In this version, assets are carried at the amount of the initial disbursements and capital commitments when compounded two years at the cost of capital rate:

Investment at time 0	$4,852
Earned income in year 1 = .08×4,852	388
Investment in year 2	500
	5,740
Earned income in year 2 = .08×5,740	459
ASSETS AT END OF YEAR 2	6,199

This version, a conservative one, does not recognize the net present value as being earned until the sixth year, at which time its compound amount at 8% (namely $966) will be considered earned income. Another and less conservative approach would be to consider the net present value of $609 as earned income when the project is commenced. While the conservative approach shows the assets at the compound amount of the past investment, the less conservative approach carries the assets at the present value of future expected receipts when discounted by use of the cost of capital rate.

In the above discussion and illustrations, it has been assumed that all cash flows occur at a moment or point in time and that interest is compounded once a year. While these assumptions simplify the arithmetic and comport well with the bond and banking markets where coupons are clipped once a year and interest may be added to the account at December 31, they depart from the more general world of business where money flows in and out continously and

EXHIBIT VII

INDUSTRIAL ACCOUNTING BALANCE SHEET
December 31, 1980

Expected future net receipts	$9,400
Less: Unearned income	3,201
ASSETS	6,199
Contributed capital	5,352
Retained income	847
EQUITY	6,199

is immediately available for reinvestment. For decisions involving capital budgeting in this more general world of business, it is often useful to use instead tables which assume continuous cash flows and continuous compounding. Exhibit VIII is a portion of extensive tables of the present value of $1 assuming continuous cash inflows and continuous compounding, prepared by The Atlantic Refining Company, and published in National Association of Accountants Research Study No. 35, "Return on Capital," 1959. (See Appendix A to this entry.) Tables for periodic compounding are available in standard texts, e.g., Bierman, Harold, Jr., and Smidt, Seymour, "The Capital Budgeting Decision," 4th ed., New York, Macmillan, 1975.

To illustrate the use of such a table, suppose a company is considering making a large initial investment in a project which is expected to require a further net cash disbursement during its first year of $10,000 and which should then result in a net cash inflow of $100,000 during the second year, a further cash inflow of $200,000 during the third year, and no further cash flows thereafter. Assuming the company's cost of capital is 15% compounded continuously, then the present value of these cash flows (before considering the initial cash disbursement) would be computed as follows:

$200,000 × .6879	$137,580
100,000 × .7993	79,930
	217,510
10,000 × .9286	9,286
PRESENT VALUE	208,224

If the project requires an initial disbursement of less than $208,224 it may be worth considering.

While past discussions have tended to treat the expectations of future cash flows as single-valued expectations, there has been an increasing tendency to treat these expectations as a probability distribution. With this interpretation in mind, the figures appearing in Exhibits V, VI, and VII may be thought of as "expected values," given perhaps by the arithmetic mean or the mode or the median. These expected values may than be "surrounded" by confidence limits, and the distance of these confidence limits from the expected values may be used to indicate the degree of risk. See [8] for an accounting interpretation.

Pay-Back. The *pay-back period,* as stated earlier, is the period of time that will elapse before the cash inflows (or the reduction in outflows) resulting from an initial outlay of cash will equal that outlay. For example, if a company will have to disburse $1,449,480 for the purchase of a plant and if the net cash inflows from the operation of that plant will be $600,000 per year, then it will take about 2.4 years before the cash inflows from the operation of the plant will "return" the initial investment. In this case, the pay-back period, or pay-back, is 2.4 years.

The reciprocal of the pay-back period will often be an excellent approximation to the rate of return on capital computed by the industrial method. If, for example, the cash inflows of $600,000 were expected to continue into the indefinite future, the rate of return computed by the industrial method would be 41%. The reciprocal of the pay-back period is, in this case, 1/2.4, or also 41%. This reciprocal of the pay-back period will only serve as a good approximation to the industrial rate of return if the cash inflows will continue for considerably longer than the pay-back period—say twice as long. If the cash inflows of $600,000 were only expected to continue for three years, then the

EXHIBIT VIII

CONTINUOUS INTEREST TABLE
DISCOUNTING PERFORMANCE AFTER REFERENCE POINT
WHICH OCCURS UNIFORMLY OVER INDIVIDUAL YEARS

	10%	*15%*	*20%*	*25%*	*30%*
From 0 to 1 year	.9516	.9286	.9063	.8848	.8640
From 1 to 2 years	.8611	.7993	.7421	.6891	.6400
From 2 to 3 years	.7791	.6879	.6075	.5367	.4741
From 3 to 4 years	.7050	.5921	.4974	.4179	.3513
From 4 to 5 years	.6379	.5096	.4072	.3255	.2602
From 5 to 6 years	.5772	.4386	.3334	.2535	.1928

industrial rate of return would be only 15%, computed by the method previously described. The reciprocal of the pay-back period, 41%, would here be a very poor approximation to this industrial rate of return. The pay-back approximation of 41% is, however, an excellent approximation to the industrial rate of 40% that applies if the cash inflows continue for 8½ years.

Another requirement for a meaningful use of the pay-back approximation is that the expected cash inflows must be relatively uniform in amount from year to year; thus, where the cash inflows during the initial year or two of a project are very low but the cash inflows in later years are very high, the pay-back approximation would not be a reliable guide to rate of return.

Given these limitations, pay-back is to the industrial rate of return what a slide rule is to a computer. Pay-back is a quick, convenient calculation that may be used for small and incidental capital budgeting decisions (say the decision to buy a bookkeeping machine) whereas the industrial rate of return should be used for the big decisions.

Pay-back is also frequently used as a measure of the risk or uncertainty involved in a particular investment. However, while it is true that the pay-back period is an estimate of the period during which the initial outlay of cash is expected to be recovered, this period tells little about risk. It may well be true that the shorter the period of capital commitment, the less the risk of loss on that capital commitment. Risk should be measured by the extent to which future cash inflows may differ from their expected values. Since the pay-back period is an estimate of the period of capital commitment and since it is based on expected (possibly arithmetic mean) values, it cannot be used as a reliable indicator of the dispersion of future expectations around that mean value.

Emerging Techniques

Linear Programming. Linear Programming offers new and powerful insights into the capital budgeting process and into the concept of rate of return. In particular, models developed by Charnes, Cooper, and Miller [3] and [9], and by Weingartner [4] are particularly directed toward the capital budgeting process and result in the computation of a type of rate of return.

A simple example of the Charnes, Cooper and Miller linear programming model appears in Exhibit IX. A company has a large warehouse (more than ample to take care of any inventory it might stock in the next few periods), and it knows (or thinks it knows, based on good information about the present market and various trends developing in that market) that the prices for the only product it buys and sells will be:

Product	*Buying Price*	*Selling Price*
1	$25	$20
2	25	35
3	25	30
4	35	25
5	45	50

Its purpose is to buy and sell in such a manner as to maximize the cash inflow from this product over the next five periods. It might, for example, buy large quantities in period 1 at $25 per unit, and sell them at $50 per unit in period 5. The company's objective is to pick a pattern of purchases and sales that will maximize the net cash inflow. Designating the number of units purchased in period i by x_i and the number sold in period i by y_i, the purpose is to:

$$\text{Maximize } -25x_1-25x_2-25x_3-35x_4-45x_5 \\ +20y_1+35y_2+30y_3+25y_4+50y_5$$

In accomplishing such an objective, the company must operate within certain marketing and financial constraints. It has an initial inventory of 100 units, and it cannot therefore sell more than 100 in the first period. This constraint is represented by

$$y_1 \leq 100$$

in Exhibit IX. Assuming that the quantities purchased in one period are not available for resale until the following period, then the most the company can sell in the second period is the 100 units plus whatever was purchased in the first period less whatever was sold in the first period or

$$y_2 \leq 100 + x_1 - y_1$$

This inequality—with the variables moved to the left hand side—appears as the second marketing constraint in Exhibit IX. The next three inequalities denote similar limitations on the quantities that can be sold in the following three years.

There are also certain financial constraints which limit the amount that can be purchased in the various years. Stockholders had made a contribution to the capital of this company of \$5,352 in the prior year and had indicated to management that they would contribute no more and wanted management to keep out of debt.

The company has spent \$1,852 of this amount in the first year to acquire certain materials-handling equipment for use in its warehouse, and has spent \$2,000 in the purchase of an initial 100 units of inventory. By the end of the initial period, the company still has \$1,500 but believes that the nature of its operations is such that it will need to maintain a minimum amount of cash of \$1,000 on deposit with the bank. Accordingly, as it goes into the first of the five planning periods, it finds itself with \$500 that can be used for the purchase of inventory. Since a unit of inventory costs \$25 in the first period, the most it can buy in that first period is 20 units as indicated by the first financial constraint:

$$25x_1 \leq 500$$

Implicit in this constraint is that purchases are on a cash and carry basis. By contrast, sales are on an "accrual" basis, with collection coming in the period following the sale. The amount that can be purchased in the second period is therefore limited to the initial cash balance of \$500, less whatever has been expended on purchases in the first period, plus whatever is collected in the second period as a consequence of the units sold in the first period. Thus:

$$25x_2 \leq 500 - 25x_1 + 20y_1$$

Moving the unknowns to the left hand side, the second financial constraint in Exhibit IX is derived. The other financial constraints are derived in like manner for the third, fourth and fifth years.

The optimal solution appears at the bottom of Exhibit IX. The best course of action is to purchase 20 units in the first planning period, to sell all 120 units in the second period, to use the proceeds from these sales to buy 168 units in the third period, and to sell all of these 168 units in the fifth and final period. Linear programming may thus be employed to determine an optimum plan of action, given a complicated situation with various limitations on the decision-maker's course of action.

But what has this model to do with the concept of rate of return and how does it relate to the capital budgeting process?

To answer this question, first note that the cash flows implicit in this model are identical

EXHIBIT IX

LINEAR PROGRAMMING FORMULATION OF CASH FLOW PROBLEM

Maximize $-25x_1 - 25x_2 - 25x_3 - 35x_4 - 45x_5 + 20y_1 + 35y_2 + 30y_3 + 25y_4 + 50y_5$

Subject to

$$\begin{array}{lllllllllll}
 & & & & & y_1 & & & & & \leq 100 \\
-x_1 & & & & & +y_1 & +y_2 & & & & \leq 100 \\
-x_1 & -x_2 & & & & +y_1 & +y_2 & +y_3 & & & \leq 100 \\
-x_1 & -x_2 & -x_3 & & & +y_1 & +y_2 & +y_3 & +y_4 & & \leq 100 \\
-x_1 & -x_2 & -x_3 & -x_4 & & +y_1 & +y_2 & +y_3 & +y_4 & +y_5 & \leq 100
\end{array}$$

$$\begin{array}{lllllllllll}
25x_1 & & & & & & & & & & \leq 500 \\
25x_1 & +25x_2 & & & & -20y_1 & & & & & \leq 500 \\
25x_1 & +25x_2 & +25x_3 & & & -20y_1 & -35y_2 & & & & \leq 500 \\
25x_1 & +25x_2 & +25x_3 & +35x_4 & & -20y_1 & -35y_2 & -30y_3 & & & \leq 500 \\
25x_1 & +25x_2 & +25x_3 & +35x_4 & +45x_5 & -20y_1 & -35y_2 & -30y_3 & -25y_4 & & \leq 500
\end{array}$$

Solution

$x_1 = 20$ $\quad$ $y_2 = 120$

$x_3 = 168$ $\quad$ $y_5 = 168$

Other variables zero.

Exhibit A–1

Continuous Interest Table*

Compounding Performance Before Reference Point which Occurs:	*5%*	*10%*	*15%*	*20%*	*25%*	*30%*	*35%*	*40%*	*45%*	*50%*
A. In an Instant										
1 month before	1.0042	1.0084	1.0126	1.0168	1.0211	1.0253	1.0296	1.0339	1.0382	1.0425
2 months “	1.0084	1.0168	1.0253	1.0339	1.0425	1.0513	1.0601	1.0689	1.0779	1.0869
3 “ “	1.0126	1.0253	1.0382	1.0513	1.0645	1.0779	1.0914	1.1052	1.1191	1.1331
6 “ “	1.0253	1.0513	1.0779	1.1052	1.1331	1.1618	1.1912	1.2214	1.2523	1.2840
9 “ “	1.0382	1.0779	1.1191	1.1618	1.2062	1.2523	1.3002	1.3499	1.4014	1.4550
12 “ “	1.0513	1.1052	1.1618	1.2214	1.2840	1.3499	1.4191	1.4918	1.5683	1.6487
1½ years before	1.0779	1.1618	1.2523	1.3499	1.4550	1.5683	1.6905	1.8221	1.9640	2.1170
2 “ “	1.1052	1.2214	1.3499	1.4918	1.6487	1.8221	2.0138	2.2255	2.4596	2.7183
2½ “ “	1.1331	1.2840	1.4550	1.6487	1.8682	2.1170	2.3989	2.7183	3.0802	3.4903
3 “ “	1.1618	1.3499	1.5683	1.8221	2.1170	2.4596	2.8577	3.3201	3.8574	4.4817
B. Uniformly Until Reference Point										
From 3 Months Before to 0	1.0063	1.0126	1.0190	1.0254	1.0319	1.0385	1.0451	1.0517	1.0584	1.0652
“ 6 “ “ “ 0	1.0126	1.0254	1.0385	1.0517	1.0652	1.0789	1.0928	1.1070	1.1214	1.1361
“ 9 “ “ “ 0	1.0190	1.0385	1.0584	1.0789	1.0999	1.1214	1.1435	1.1662	1.1895	1.2133
“ 12 “ “ “ 0	1.0254	1.0517	1.0789	1.1070	1.1361	1.1662	1.1973	1.2296	1.2629	1.2974
From 2 years before to 0	1.0517	1.1070	1.1662	1.2296	1.2974	1.3702	1.4482	1.5319	1.6218	1.7183
“ 3 “ “ “ 0	1.0789	1.1662	1.2629	1.3702	1.4893	1.6218	1.7692	1.9334	2.1166	2.3211
Discounting Performance After Reference Point: Which Occurs:										
C. In an Instant										
1 year later	.9512	.9048	.8607	.8187	.7788	.7408	.7047	.6703	.6376	.6065
2 years “	.9048	.8187	.7408	.6703	.6065	.5488	.4966	.4493	.4066	.3679
3 “ “	.8607	.7408	.6376	.5488	.4724	.4066	.3499	.3012	.2592	.2231
4 “ “	.8187	.6703	.5488	.4493	.3679	.3012	.2466	.2019	.1653	.1353
5 “ “	.7788	.6065	.4724	.3679	.2865	.2231	.1738	.1353	.1054	.0821
10 “ “	.6065	.3679	.2231	.1353	.0821	.0498	.0302	.0183	.0111	.0067
15 “ “	.4724	.2231	.1054	.0498	.0235	.0111	.0052	.0025	.0012	.0006
20 “ “	.3679	.1353	.0498	.0183	.0067	.0025	.0009	.0003	.0001	—
25 “ “	.2865	.0821	.0235	.0067	.0019	.0006	.0002	—	—	—
30 “ “	.2231	.0498	.0111	.0025	.0006	.0001	—	—	—	—
35 “ “	.1738	.0302	.0052	.0009	.0002	—	—	—	—	—
40 “ “	.1353	.0183	.0025	.0003	—	—	—	—	—	—
45 “ “	.1054	.0111	.0012	.0001	—	—	—	—	—	—
50 “ “	.0821	.0067	.0006	.0000	—	—	—	—	—	—
D. Uniformly over Individual Years										
From 0 to 1 year	.9754	.9516	.9286	.9063	.8848	.8640	.8438	.8242	.8053	.7869
“ 1 “ 2 years	.9278	.8611	.7993	.7421	.6891	.6400	.5946	.5525	.5135	.4773
“ 2 “ 3 “	.8826	.7791	.6879	.6075	.5367	.4741	.4190	.3703	.3274	.2895
“ 3 “ 4 “	.8395	.7050	.5921	.4974	.4179	.3513	.2953	.2482	.2088	.1756
“ 4 “ 5 “	.7986	.6379	.5096	.4072	.3255	.2602	.2081	.1664	.1331	.1065
“ 5 “ 6 “	.7596	.5772	.4386	.3334	.2535	.1928	.1466	.1115	.0849	.0646
“ 6 “ 7 “	.7226	.5223	.3775	.2730	.1974	.1428	.1033	.0748	.0541	.0392
“ 7 “ 8 “	.6874	.4726	.3250	.2235	.1538	.1058	.0728	.0501	.0345	.0238
“ 8 “ 9 “	.6538	.4276	.2797	.1830	.1197	.0784	.0513	.0336	.0220	.0144
“ 9 “ 10 “	.6219	.3869	.2407	.1498	.0933	.0581	.0362	.0225	.0140	.0087
“ 10 “ 11 “	.5916	.3501	.2072	.1227	.0726	.0430	.0255	.0151	.0089	.0053
“ 11 “ 12 “	.5628	.3168	.1783	.1004	.0566	.0319	.0180	.0101	.0057	.0032
“ 12 “ 13 “	.5353	.2866	.1535	.0822	.0441	.0236	.0127	.0068	.0036	.0020
“ 13 “ 14 “	.5092	.2593	.1321	.0673	.0343	.0175	.0089	.0045	.0023	.0012
“ 14 “ 15 “	.4844	.2347	.1137	.0551	.0267	.0130	.0063	.0030	.0015	.0007

EXHIBIT A-1 (Continued)

Discounting Performance After Reference Point Which Occurs:	5%	10%	15%	20%	25%	30%	35%	40%	45%	50%
E. Uniformly Over 5 Year Periods										
From 0 to 5 years	.8848	.7869	.7035	.6321	.5708	.5179	.4721	.4323	.3976	.3672
" 5 " 10 "	.6891	.4773	.3323	.2325	.1635	.1156	.0820	.0585	.0419	.0301
" 10 " 15 "	.5367	.2895	.1570	.0855	.0469	.0258	.0143	.0079	.0044	.0025
" 15 " 20 "	.4179	.1756	.0742	.0315	.0134	.0058	.0025	.0011	.0005	.0002
" 20 " 25 "	.3255	.1065	.0350	.0116	.0038	.0013	.0004	.0001	—	—
" 25 " 30 "	.2535	.0646	.0165	.0043	.0011	.0003	.0001	—	—	—
" 30 " 35 "	.1974	.0392	.0078	.0016	.0003	.0001	—	—	—	—
" 35 " 40 "	.1538	.0238	.0037	.0006	.0001	—	—	—	—	—
" 40 " 45 "	.1197	.0144	.0017	.0002	—	—	—	—	—	—
" 45 " 50 "	.0933	.0087	.0008	.0001	—	—	—	—	—	—
F. Declining to Nothing at Constant Rate										
From 0 to 5 years	.9216	.8522	.7906	.7358	.6867	.6428	.6033	.5677	.5355	.5063
" 0 " 10 "	.8522	.7358	.6428	.5677	.5063	.4555	.4131	.3773	.3468	.3205
" 0 " 15 "	.7906	.6428	.5355	.4555	.3945	.3468	.3088	.2779	.2525	.2311
" 0 " 20 "	.7358	.5677	.4555	.3773	.3205	.2779	.2449	.2188	.1975	.1800
" 0 " 25 "	.6867	.5063	.3945	.3205	.2689	.2311	.2026	.1800	.1620	.1472
" 0 " 30 "	.6428	.4555	.3468	.2779	.2311	.1975	.1723	.1528	.1372	.1244
" 0 " 35 "	.6083	.4131	.3088	.2449	.2026	.1723	.1499	.1327	.1189	.1078

* This table was prepared by The Atlantic Refining Company (now Atlantic Richfield Co.) Philadelphia, Pa., and is reproduced here with permission

to those underlying the extended illustration appearing in Exhibits I, II, V, VI, and VII. Before the decision maker who posited the model in Exhibit IX took over, there had already been certain initial cash flows taken here as given, which corresponded to those at time zero in previous paragraphs. During period 1 there is a $500 disbursement to buy 20 units of inventory at $25 per unit, and that $500 agrees with the amount used in the previous computations of industrial rate of return and net present value.

The 120 units sold at $35 in period 2 will result in collections of $4,200 in the third period, but there will be no net cash inflow in that period because the full $4,200 will immediately be expended in the purchase of 168 units of inventory at a cost of $25 each. These 168 units will be sold at $50 each in period 5, with a consequent collection of $8,400 in period 6. That $8,400 plus the minimum cash balance of $1,000 (which is no longer required because the project is completed) gives the $9,400 used in the previous example of time-adjusted rate of return. Linear programming may therefore be used to define the optimal operating plan of action to optimize the cash flows in a capital budgeting situation.

In the above analysis, time preference—the idea that a dollar today is superior to a dollar tomorrow—has not been explicitly introduced. Time preference considerations may however readily be introduced. Instead of maximizing the total net cash flows as is done with the present "objective function" given in Exhibit IX:

$$-25x_1 - 25x_2 - 25x_3 - \cdots + 50y_5$$

the effort might instead be to maximize the present value of those cash flows through use of the following objective function:

$$-\frac{525x_1}{(1+r)^0} - \frac{25x_2}{(1+r)^1} - \frac{25x_3}{(1+r)^2} - \cdots + \frac{50y_5}{(1+r)^5}$$

where r is an appropriately defined interest rate used for discounting purposes.

The previous objective function may then be regarded as that special case where r, the rate of time preference, is zero. Assume the various constraints are unaffected by this introduction of time preference into the analysis. (Thus, suppose that while there may be a positive rate of time preference, there is no required periodic interest payment so that the financial constraints in Exhibit IX are unaffected.) By allowing r to vary from 0% to 20%, it will be found that the purchase and sale pattern presented in Exhibit IX remains optimal, although the present value of the future receipts and disbursements will diminish as the rate of time preference increases. Above 20% it will be found that better patterns of receipts and disbursements are available from a time-preference point of view.

That branch of linear programming known as "parametric linear programming" may be employed in this manner to test the "sensitivity" of a particular operating plan to changed assumptions with regard to the relevant "cost of capital" rate. Suppose a particular pattern of receipts and disbursements is optimal from a time-preference point of view, using an 8% cost of capital rate. Would that pattern still be optimal if the relevant cost of capital rate were really 10%? Linear programming may therefore not only help to define the optimum pattern of receipts and disbursements in a given capital budgeting situation, but it may also be used to test the "sensitivity" of the decisions to possible errors in the assumed figures with regard to cost of capital, expected receipts and disbursements, etc.

The "Bottleneck Rate of Return." But there is another and possibly more significant manner in which this model and comparable models may throw light on capital budgeting problems. For every direct or "primal" problem in linear programming, there is another derived or "dual" problem. Without dwelling on the mathematical aspects of the dual problem, it is worth noting that the dual problem results in the calculation of "shadow prices" or "dual evaluators." These "dual evaluators" may be considered "price tags" which measure the severity of the primal constraints and help to identify which primal constraints are "binding" or "bottleneck" constraints.

Thus the "price tag" relating to the first financial constraint is $0.80, and it suggests that if the company had $1 less available for purchase of inventory in the first period (that is, if purchases in the first year were limited to what could be purchased with $499 rather than $500), then the total net cash inflow would be less by not only the $1, but also by a further $0.80. Again without going into the rather detailed manner in which the receipts and disbursements would change, it should be noted that the $0.80 may be thought of as the incremental or marginal "profit" from the 500th dollar. It may then be argued that the $0.80 is somewhat akin to an interest rate and that the $0.80 plus the 500th dollar may be thought of as a compounded amount. Charnes, Cooper and Miller have said that such dual evaluators have the "dimensions of compound interest" and have referred to these rates and amounts as "compounded rates of accumulation," "compound internal yield rates," and "internal discount factors." [10]

While neither the linear programming approach to capital budgeting problems nor the "bottleneck" rate of return seems to have been used extensively in practice as yet, nevertheless they offer such penetrating insights into the funds allocation process that their future in the practical world of capital budgeting seems secure.

APPENDIX

Because *continuous* interest tables as discussed in this entry have not had widespread treatment, the 0–50% portion of the Atlantic Refining table is reproduced here as Exhibit A–1.

In computing rate of return, each cash flow is discounted from the time it occurs to a common reference point in time. The year in which income or savings start is usually the zero point on the time scale, although any date can be used if consistency is observed. Some project expenditures are made before this date because time is required for construction. Interest accumulated on these outlays increases the amount of capital invested by the time operations begin. Section A in Exhibit A–1 shows, for various rates of interest, the accumulated amount of $1 invested for periods of from one month to three years.

Expenditures and revenues after the reference date must be discounted to ascertain their present value on the reference date. Section C in Exhibit A–1 gives, for various interest rates, the present worth of $1 received at times ranging from one to 50 years into the future.

Tables in use are based on differing assumptions with respect to the timing of cash flows during a year. For example, the assumption may be that the cash flow occurs (1) at the end of the year, (2) in uniform monthly installments during the year, and (3) continuously during the year. When relatively large cash flows occur at one time (for example, a large lump-sum payment for a building or piece of equipment) it may be desirable to compound or discount such items from the instant at which the cash flow occurs, or from the nearest period for which the discount factor can be read from the tables available. However, operating expenses and revenues tend to constitute fairly uniform flows. In Exhibit A–1, Sections B, D, E, and F assume that cash flows occur continuously. Sections A and C assume that the cash flow occurs in a lump sum at the times given in the table.

John Coughlan, CPA, Partner, La France, Walker, Jackley, and Saville, Washington, D.C.; Adjunct Professor, Loyola College, Washington, D.C.

References Cited

[1] Dean, Joel, "Capital Budgeting," New York, Columbia University Press, 1951.

[2] Lutz, Friedrick and Vera, "The Theory of Investment of the Firm," Princeton University Press, 1951.

[3] Charnes, A. and Cooper, W.W. and Miller, M.H. "Application of Linear Programming to Financial Budgeting and the Costing of Funds," *Journal of Business,* January 1959 as reproduced in Ezra Solomon, ed., "The Management of Corporate Capital," Glencoe, Illinois, The Free Press, 1959, pp. 229–255.

[4] Weingartner, H. Martin, "Mathematical Programming and the Analysis of Capital Budgeting Decisions," Englewood Cliffs, Prentice-Hall, 1963.

[5] Coughlan, John, "Industrial Accounting," *Accounting Review,* July 1959, pp. 415–428.

[6] Coughlan, John, "Guide to Contemporary Theory of Accounts," Prentice-Hall, 1965, Chapter XI.

[7] Coughlan, John, "Accounting and Capital Budgeting," *The Business Quarterly,* Winter 1962, pp. 39–48.

[8] Coughlan, John, "Profit and Probability," *Advanced Management Journal,* April 1968, pp. 53–69.

[9] Charnes, A. and Cooper, W.W. "Management Models and Industrial Applications of Linear Programming," Vol. II, New York, Wiley, 1961, Chapter XV.

[10] Charnes, Cooper and Miller, *op. cit.,* pp. 234, 245, 238, and 242. Others (including Weingartner) have also used the dual to compute similar "quasi" rates of return.

Cross References: *Fixed-Asset Investment Analysis; Leasing of Industrial Equipment; Long-Range Planning: Financial Aspects; Mergers and Acquisitions; New-Product Planning: Profitability Projections.*

RISK MANAGEMENT

Risk Management is concerned with the conservation of a firm's assets, earning power, and people against risks of accidental loss. The duties of the executive or outside professional consulting firm charged with this function encompass seeking out potential loss-producing hazards and their elimination or avoidance, and the scientific prevention of loss that could result from non-removable or non-avoidable hazards. To the extent that the proper use of insurance to transfer non-avoidable risk to a professional risk carrier (insurance company) is one method (among several) of treating a firm's exposure to risk, INSURANCE MANAGEMENT also falls within the scope of risk management.

Formal Definition. Risk management is that branch of management concerned with:

(1) Conservation of already acquired assets against erosion or total destruction through accident.

(2) Safeguarding the firm's continued ability to earn in the face of possible accidental loss that could curtail or prevent continued earnings. This includes protection of a company's personnel.

(3) Overall responsibility for the astute buying of only necessary insurance, at favorable terms.

(4) The planning and supervision of non-insurance treatment of risk: i.e., outright intentional non-insurance, funded self-insurance programs and captive insurance programs; contractual transfer via non-insurance contracts (hold-harmless idemnity contracts, bills of lading, net-net leases, etc.) and post-loss financing arrangements.

(5) When losses occur, minimizing their effects, within the insurance function, by supervising prompt and proper settlement or defenses; and outside of the insurance function, by supervision of previously planned emergency and catastrophe programs.

In the case of multinational operations, not the least important aspect of such a disaster plan includes plans for evacuation of United States and other foreign nationals and their families should there be a political, social, medical, geological, or other life-threatening emergency; and, for injured employees or injured members of their families, arrangements for repatriation to where they can get proper medical treatment.

(6) Pre-loss and post-loss engineering and analysis to prevent future losses.

Background. At the first meeting concerning insurance sponsored by the American Management Association in 1930, Dr. Solomon Huebner of the University of Pennsylvania, considered by many to be the sage of American insurance, emphasized that "prevention of loss in the first instance constitutes the greatest insurance of all." Although he did not specifically use the term, he was speaking of what is now considered a major function of risk management.

By 1940, only a relatively few firms had an insurance manager on their staff, concerned with problems that had grown out of the neglect of the insurance function: over-insurance, under-insurance, overlapping and gaps in coverage, and excessive premium and loss costs. Fewer had risk managers who approached their jobs broadly, insurance buying being but a part of their responsibilities, with a communication line directly to top management. During the five-year period after World War II, and especially under the impetus given by the commercial aviation business (whose leaders' recognition of the importance of risk management was not clouded by precedents), it became more and more apparent that insurance management was not adequate to meet the demands of modern business. Thus the position and function of *risk management* became more accepted and utilized. Since about 1950, the function of the risk manager has become fully accepted with a priority place in the management scheme.

The Risk and Insurance Management Society, Inc., counted over 3,200 members as of mid-1980. It is estimated that some 3,000 professional risk managers are on the payroll of American corporations (although all may not carry that specific title), and by the beginning of the 1980s it was becoming more and more evident that industry was granting risk managers officer status. In addition to on-staff risk managers, there are about 60 recognized independent non-insurance-selling management consulting firms specializing in risk management in the United States, Canada, and abroad. About half of these firms belong to and subscribe to the standards of the Insurance Consultants' Society, a professional society established to further the education of its members and to enforce a strict ethical code. In 1975, another consultants' professional society, the Institute of Risk Management Consultants, was formed. There is no substantial difference between the goals and ethical and professional standards of the two organizations.

The professional risk manager today—be he a corporate officer, a corporate staff member, or an independent professional consultant—has a knowledge of law, finance, management, accounting, shipping, loss-prevention engineering, loss adjusting, banking, and the technical aspects of insurance.

Approaches. Since risk is encountered from the moment a firm does something and continues until long after it ceases to do anything, the complexity of risk exposure is vast and yet often hidden, obvious and yet unpredictable. Hence, the initial step in any risk management program is the thorough analysis, by qualified analysts, of every activity and asset of the firm, to seek out possible risks of accidental loss. This analysis must be extensive and intensive and repeated periodically. It must be concerned with but not necessarily limited to:

(1) Examination of physical assets by those qualified, such as engineers and safety specialists, under the general supervision of the risk manager.

(2) Examination, from the risk viewpoint, of contracts, leases, warranties, etc., in conjunction with the firm's attorneys.

(3) Evaluation of future earning power in conjunction with top management, the firm's accountants, economists, and research and development people.

(4) Evaluation—and where necessary, ultimately, development—of the firm's risk-abatement and loss-prevention program.

(5) Analysis of the firm's risk-treatment program (transfer and other financial devices). Though a substantial portion of every firm's risk treatment is its formal insurance (risk transfer) program, more and more firms—in view of unstable insurance markets, new insurance exposure problems, and increasing premium costs—are turning to economically more advantageous methods of treating some of their risk exposures. Examples are intentional noninsurance, self-insurance (funded retention of risk), and the development and utilization of captive insurers. The risk manager's responsibilities extend to the planning, execution, and review stages of these alternatives.

Historically, risk treatment has been attempted almost entirely through insurance. Modern risk-management concepts do not recommend that insurance is the only or even the best answer to risk exposure. A firm with financial stability should self-insure wherever economically feasible.

On risks treated by insurance, there are two general areas where firms self-insure (more correctly noninsure) in conjunction with insurance. One area which is not acceptable is having inadequate insurance in relation to value, where, by the workings of co-insurance penalties or the differentials between actual cash value and replacement values, or too low limits, companies share their losses with the insurance company on what is originally a non-determinable basis. This is often to their considerable detriment and frequently to their considerable surprise.

The other area of frequent noninsurance of part of the risk while insuring another part is through deductibles. This is *intentional* noninsurance, and is good risk management. The amount of risk intentionally assumed must be accurately measurable at the time of assumption, and must be readily financially bearable. However, in addition to arriving at the proper deductible measured against the premium advantage of having it, there is also the question of corporate philosophy. (See *Risk Aversion,* below.) It is strongly recommended that all self-assumption of exposure be predicated on the bottom through the use of deductibles, and not on the top through inadequate coverage, improperly written coverage, or co-insurance liabilities.

A firm's true exposure to loss at all locations should be determined by examination, analysis, and evaluation. "Real" exposure to loss is replacement cost (though not necessarily from an accounting point of view). From the standpoints of contents, the real loss in case of destruction is as follows:

(1) Where items would be replaced with substantially similar types, albeit of more modern manufacture, the real loss is the cost of that replacement if the location is going to be used again (repaired or rebuilt) and if, had there been no loss, the items would have continued to be used.

(2) Where the location, if destoyed, would not be rebuilt at the same or another location, the real loss of contents is replacement cost less *real* depreciation for the time the company had use of the now damaged or destroyed contents.

The next step in proper risk management progression would then be to analyze the treatment to be given to this exposure to "real" loss. Values at this writing are increasing at an inflationary rate, and insurance premiums are generally increasing even more rapidly. Therefore businesses should insure only those real exposures to loss that they cannot readily and properly bear themselves. This determination should be based on:

(1) The extent that exposure to loss is known (destruction of property is indeed such an exposure) and readily measurable.

(2) The extent to which the loss is financially bearable. In general, if a firm operates under tight cash-flow conditions, it should insure. Where, in case of loss, access to funds would be expensive if available at all, the firm should insure. Even if the cost of funds is manageable, if the money would not be available in time to rebuild or restore, the firm should insure. And obviously if a firm is not financially sound and a loss would impair its financial position even further, possibly even leading to its demise, it should insure.

Trade-offs. Where the discounted value of the rate of return on the premiums paid for exposure reduction (insurance) is less than the discounted value of the rate of return the company normally gets from the use or investment of its funds, it should not insure *to that extent.* Conversely, if the discounted value of the rate of return on the premiums exceeds what the company normally expects from the use of its funds, the company should insure. The reasoning is the same as that normally followed in making capital investment decisions. (See RETURN ON CAPITAL.)

However, there may be other reasons for a company to resist self-assumption of loss, and to insure. These include:

(1) Stockholder criticism of noninsured losses.

(2) Demands of lenders.

(3) Desire for a nonaffiliated buffer (the insurance company) between the company and the public (especially in cases of liability suits), as well as between the company and its employees (in cases of workers compensation, dependent hospitalization, and medical claims, etc.).

(4) The value of the insurance company's specialized knowledge in claims handling, not only in liability suits (e.g., products liability), but also in officers and directors suits by stockholders or in kidnap or extortion situations.

(5) Statutory compliance.

(6) Deductibility of premiums for tax purposes. Generally, noninsurance expenses (including reserves for losses) are not deductible until there is an incurred claim, and then only for the amount paid.

(7) Desirability of other specialized insurance company services, such as the engineering and inspection services provided to boiler and machinery insurance policyholders.

Conversely, there may be exposure to risk for which insurance is desirable, but where the risk is either uninsurable or only uneconomically insurable (e.g., war, strikes, nuclear contamination). In such cases, other risk treatment alternatives must be developed.

Risk Aversion. The motive any firm has for insuring is its aversion to risk. The greater the aversion to risk, the greater the willingness to pay for insurance. Generally speaking, larger companies have a smaller risk aversion level than do smaller ones. There is no universally correct level of risk aversion, although every company has such a level, usually arrived at intuitively. However arrived at, the risk aversion level changes as conditions and people change. For each risk profile (exposure to loss) and premium combination there is a risk aversion threshold at which company management or the risk manager is indifferent as to insuring or not insuring.

To the extent practicable, all exposures to loss in excess of the risk aversion threshold should be insured to the full extent of the real exposure to loss. It is good risk management practice for every firm to have a consciously arrived at risk aversion threshold.

Scope. The risk-management function extends farther today than it has ever done before. It now includes loss prevention planning in the building stages—e.g. the isolation of hazardous processes and equipment, floor drainage (including palletization of merchandise), and construction material from a loss prevention standpoint; floor loading limitations, etc., the planning and implementation of catastrophe programs—e.g., provisions for alternate headquarters, safeguarding of vital records, the availability of alternate or temporary operating funds, alternate raw material sources, standby electronic data processing facilities, etc.; risk accounting (the procedural aspects of risk management); supervision of often diverse insurance management programs in foreign countries emanating from a firm's foreign operations or foreign subsidiaries; and safety program administration

In many companies risk management input permeates the entire corporate management process, including but not limited to: security (physical as well as informational), product testing, advertising planning (to preclude suits for plagiarism, libel, slander, etc.), accounting (to avoid computer and other types of fraud, as well as to assure compliance with new S.E.C. and Financial Standards Board rules regarding published financial information, e.g., reflection of current replacement values of physical assets, and pending claims and their offsetting insurance), product labeling (to comply with statutes and to help prebuild litigation defense against suits alleging injuries due to products or improper warnings and operational instructions), and the like.

With the astronomical growth of employee benefit programs in the last twenty years, employers are today more interested than ever before in the financing of these programs. More often than not, the supervision of such internally financed programs falls under the management of the Risk Management Department.

In many firms, the risk manager—especially if he is a corporate officer—reports directly to the president. Commonly, however, the risk manager reports to a financial vice-president or a management or executive committee. In a decentralized operation, the function of risk management (including insurance management) should be centralized, including overseas operations. This is becoming especially important in view of the growth of American firms' interests in overseas operations, the complex—and often nationalistic—insurance regulations in foreign countries, the general lack of interest in most foreign countries in risk management, and the very complex tax problems that can emanate from premium expenditure and loss receipts, as regards the foreign countries' tax regulations as well as those of the United States.

The Future of Risk Management. Risk management is, ultimately, a money-control program, involving so vast a corporate spectrum that modern management is increasingly recognizing it as a vital corporate function. Several universities are now providing formal risk-management curricula and degrees. The Insurance Institute of America now awards a diploma in Risk Management, and the professionals earning this recognition are authorized to use the title "Associate in Risk Management" (ARM).

The American Institute of Property and Liability Underwriters has awarded the C.P.C.U. designation (Chartered Property-Casualty Underwriter) to over 13,500 candidates since 1945. This is regarded by many as the insurance profession's highest professional distinction. The Institute now includes risk management (beyond insurance concepts) in its curricula and examinations.

LEONARD J. SILVER, C.P.C.U., ARM, President, First Risk Management Company, Wyncote, Pennsylvania, and First Risk Management (P.R.) Inc., San Juan, Puerto Rico.

Information References

Associations:

American Society of Insurance Management, Inc.
American Institute of Property and Liability Underwriters.
Insurance Institute of America.
Risk and Insurance Management Society, Inc.

Texts

"Commercial Liability Risk Management and Insurance," Malvern, Pa., American Institute for Property and Liability Underwriters, 1978.

"Commercial Property Risk Management and Insurance," Malvern, Pa., American Institute for Property and Liability Underwriters, 1978.

Green, Mark R. and Serbein, Oscar N., "Risk Management: Text & Cases," Reston, Va., Reston, 1978.

Lentz, Matthew Jr., "Risk Management Manual," Santa Monica, Calif., Merritt, 1976.

Pearce, Alan M. and Nutt, Fred A., "Practical Self Insurance," Nashville, Tenn., Corroon and Black Corporation, 1978.

"Principles of Risk Management and Insurance," Malvern, Pa., American Institute for Property and Liability Underwriters, 1978.

"Readings in Risk Management," Bryn Mawr, Pa., Insurance Institute of America, 1980.

Silver, Leonard and Sleeper, Richard, "EDP Risk Management and Insurance," AMA Bulletin #131, New York, American Management Associations, 1969.

Williams, C.A. Jr., "Risk Management & Insurance," 3rd ed., New York, McGraw-Hill, 1976.

Cross Reference: *Insurance Management.*

ROBOTS IN INDUSTRY

Industrial Robots are a highly flexible and versatile form of automation. They have internal memory systems, and give and receive information from computers. More technically, they have been defined as "programmed controlled manipulators" [1] and are to be distinguished from manipulators which do not perform true robot functions. These industrial robots bear no resemblance to the anthropoid robots or "androids" of science fiction which have captured the popular mind in films, books, TV, and the theater, and have been depicted as sometimes aiding and sometimes threatening humankind (aspects of the subject which are beyond the scope of this article). Instead, they have been described as looking more like overgrown fire hydrants with telescoping arms holding grippers or tools.

For example, the "Unimate" mentioned below is a programmed mechanical manipulator whose motions simulate those of waist, shoulder, elbow, wrist, and fingers—with many "hands" to suit different jobs. These "hands" are taken slowly through the job, one time, so that the robot's "brain" may assimilate the operations it must perform. Subsequently, the robot will go through a series of up to 2,000 or more separate steps to do this operation at a controlled speed, and for a given period of time.

Similarly, at an Ingersoll Rand Compressor installation, a large metal-sheathed arm of a robot welder rises out of a stocky floor-anchored torso, goes through complex motions as dictated by a nearby computer, and searches for the 31 locations it will weld in 11 minutes. When it has finished the job, it pivots and begins work on a second unit while a human coworker replaces the first unit.

In more precise technical terms, robots are mechanical devices, with multiple modes or degrees of freedom and motion—each such mode being under separate control with multiple-axis motion, in a spatial reference system not unlike that inherent in human beings. Most true robots have digital memories and can interface with computer-control systems. Their mechanical movement is hydraulically or electrically driven, and robots are designed for continuous duty cycles. Weight-handling capacity at present ranges from ounces to hundreds of pounds.

Flexibility. Robots have numerous advantages over specialized production stations. One in particular is that data on products produced in the past can be stored in the robot's memory banks. With proper robot "hands" and proper tooling of the production process, such products may be placed again into production with minimal time and expense as compared with traditional tooling up.

History. The word *robot* entered our language with the production of the play "R.U.R." (Rossum's Universal Robots) in 1922, by Czechoslovakian author and dramatist Karel Capek. "Robot" is a variant of the Czech word for work, *robota,* and in the play, R.U.R. is the name of a firm that developed and manufactured a line of artificial "people." In the intervening years, robots moved out of the laboratory and off the stage, and into industry, and recent estimates (although definitional boundaries are not precise) place the number now installed in U.S. factories at 5,000. The modern industrial robot dates from 1954, when the first unimate robot, designed and patented by the present author, was installed in the Trenton, N.J., plant of General Motors to perform die-casting operations.

Applications. The main reason for using robots in industry is to achieve automatic production at lowest cost without the need for a large number of expensive, specialized machines at sequential work stations. Generally, robots have been identified with the taking over of jobs that are dangerous, tiring, or boring for human workers, with the robot doing the jobs faster and more accurately.

The greatest number of robots are currently employed in the automotive industry, with body welding the No. 1 application to date for the more complex and expensive installations. Other heavy-industry uses include handling of forgings, loading and unloading of machine tools, automatic unloading of die castings and plastic-molding machines, processing of investment casting shells, auto body painting, automatic assembly of complex parts, palletizing, and transfer and handling of foundry molds and castings.

Ranked by number of robots installed, the most popular uses [2] are:

Materials Handling. For so-called pick-and-place work—moving parts to and from conveyors, pallets, and containers, relatively simple and inexpensive ($10,000 to $25,000 as of 1981) are adequate.

Welding. In auto plants, car bodies are spot-welded on lines at which a dozen or more robots may be lined up. Such models currently cost about $60,000. The fastest-growing application is arc welding, where robots costing roughly $80,000 can join a seam by moving the torch along a continuous path.

Spray Painting. Manufacturers are spending about $80,000 for robots to spray paint coatings and adhesives. Doing such work by traditional methods in the confinement of a spray booth is unpleasant and potentially hazardous.

Assembly. There is an enormous potential for robots that can do the repetitive jobs on assembly lines. But until artifical-vision systems are perfected (see below), parts must be fed to assembly robots in a very precise manner.

Future Applications. Future applications of industrial robots may be anticipated in the nuclear power industries, in naval and military applications where their current low utilization is surprising, and in mining and other hazardous occupations. Robots are also being used in the exploration of space.

The universal flexibility around mutually independent axes will remain the hallmark of the industrial robot. Increased memory capability, linked to advances in computer technology, will vastly extend its usefulness.

A current constraint is limited or no "sight" for most robots. TV and camera "eyes" have been employed on experimental and some production models, but at this writing there are design problems which have not yet been overcome. The sight constraint makes the design and processing of the product on which the robot is to work of utmost importance, a point which is frequently overlooked by engineers and managements. The situation is analogous to the problem of the blind: if an object is precisely where it is supposed to be, and correctly oriented in space, it may easily be grasped and processed. However, the slightest error in positioning may greatly tax a sightless individual—or a sightless robot.

For example, if a part is removed from a die-caster and placed immediately into an adjacent drill jig by a robot, the whole sequence may be automated and easy to perform. However, if the part is first placed at random on a conveyor and carried to a new work station, it then becomes more difficult to sense its arrival, pick it up, orient it, and place it in the jig. For this reason, it is critical that product parameters be such as to utilize robot configurations fully and promote easy interface with the robot.

Cost Factors. Steadily rising labor, start-up, and tooling costs have stimulated use of robots worldwide. As an example, the median cost of a robot in 1981 U.S. dollars is about $50,000. Annual maintenance and operating costs run around $3,000. In the automotive industry, basic labor plus fringe benefits is now up to about $16 an hour. On a normal two-shifts-per-day basis, the annual cost of operating a robot is thus about $20,000 on a three-year amortized schedule. This is to be compared with $61,000 for human labor. Further, a robot makes possible three shifts a day where that is indicated, at no drop in quality or rate of production. With labor, three-shift production is often difficult to obtain at reasonable costs.

In the near future we shall see the emergence of a rental-robot industry which will permit manufacturers with limited capital to avail themselves of robot production techniques.

A favorable cost aspect of owning and operating robots is that to a certain extent they never wear out. Many robots over fifteen years old have been refurbished and placed again into production. This capacity for long production life is tied to further development of a spare-parts industry for robots, and ready availability of components for rebuilding.

Implementation. In-house engineering staffs

may be unable to supply special data to their managements upon which to make an appropriate decision as to a commitment for robots, because of the specialized technology involved. To meet the need for the expertise called for, a specialized consultant, the robotics consultant, has emerged, who can provide professional counsel on evaluation of needs and definition of goals, and oversee actual robot installation and "run-in" where that is required.

Robots of the Future. The next generation of industrial robots will be what has been termed "smart robots." These units will be able to "see" and to determine shape and position of random parts on conveyors and in machines. Breakthrough developments in the controls industry are making this possible.

One coming development, requisite to release the full potential in robots, is a tactile sensor. Other sensors will detect distance between the robot and the object it is to manipulate; detect heat and particle radiation; permit the robot to follow a curve (analogous to a human finger tracing an object); and permit voice control of robots by their partners in robot/human work teams.

Presently, most industrial robots are fixed units; in the future it may be advantageous to have them move about over a considerable distance to perform their functions and to interface with other machines, and other robots.

GEORGE C. DEVOL, President, Devol Research Associates, Fort Lauderdale, Florida

Information References

Periodicals:

Robotics Age.

Robotics Today.

Associations:

International Institute for Robotics.

Robot Institute of America.

Japan Industrial Robot Association.

Society of Manufacturing Engineers.

Texts:

Gabor, Dennis, "Innovations," New York, Oxford University Press, 1970.

Engelberger, Joseph F., "Robotics in Practice," New York, American Management Associations, 1980.

Various *Abstracts* from meetings of the Robot Institute of America, Dearborn, Mich. meetings.

References Cited

[1] Robot Institute of America (Society of Mechanical Engineers).

[2] "The Most Popular Jobs for 'Steel-Collar' Workers," *Business Week,* February 9, 1981.

Cross References: *Automation; Production: Large-Scale; Technological Change: Union-Management Agreements.*

ROWNTREE, B. SEEBOHM

Benjamin Seebohm Rowntree (1871–1954) is considered the British management movement's greatest pioneer. His early work was directed towards improving industrial welfare, when in 1897 he became labor director of Rowntree & Co., Ltd., the chocolate and confectionery manufacturers of York. (He succeeded his father in 1923 as Chairman of Rowntree & Co., Ltd., but retained the post of labor director until 1936.) He established provisions for employee welfare far in advance of the practice of his time. During World War I he founded at the Ministry of Munitions a new Welfare Department, offering advisory services to employers in difficulties over the unfamiliar human problems arising out of war production. Through Rowntree's work and influence, an interest in industrial welfare and in human aspects of work became firmly established in British industry. After the war, his work for industrial welfare within his own firm expanded. "As early as 1904 he had established a Medical Department. Then, in 1905, there was established a day continuation school. In 1919 there was introduced a 44-hour, 5-day week . . . (and) in 1919 a comprehensive system of Works Councils. Many pioneering measures introduced into the Cocoa Works in the 1920s included family allowances, unemployment pay, higher education, the employment of trained industrial psychologists, and further provisions for health, canteens, and recreation. In 1919 he had put in hand a comprehensive investigation of all profit-sharing experience up to that time, and as a result . . . introduced in 1923 a profit-sharing scheme which was widely regarded as a model. Beyond the confines of his own firm he gave substantial support to the foundation of the Industrial Welfare Society and the National Institute of Industrial Psychology" [1].

From 1923 on, the Rowntree Works were systematically reorganized according to the new principles of Scientific Management. (MARY PARKER FOLLETT chose the Rowntree Works as one of her "cases" for her study of the social philosophy of business.) In 1919 Rowntree founded the conferences for works directors, managers, and foremen which became the annual "Oxford Management Conferences." In 1926 he founded the Management Research Groups for the exchange of confidential management information for mutual benefit among senior executives from noncompeting firms. These two movements are credited with being virtually the inception of the study of Scientific Management in Great Britain [1]. Rowntree led the way in the York Works toward a new conception of successful joint consultation in industry, as set forth in his book, "The Human Factor in Business: Experiments in Industrial Democracy," 1921 (Longmans Green, London). Innovations here included a full-time company-paid shop steward; a works council; a joint appeal committee for disciplinary matters; and the regular dissemination of management information to employees.

Major published works by Rowntree include: "Poverty: A Study of Town Life," 1901 (Macmillan, London); "Unemployment: A Social Study," 1911 (with Bruno Lasker; Macmillan, London); "How the Labourer Lives," 1913 (with May Kendall; Thos. Nelson, London); "The Responsibility of Women Workers for Dependants," "English Life and Leisure: A Social Study," 1951 (with G.R. Lavers; Longmans Green, London).

Reference Cited

[1] Urwick, L., ed., "The Golden Book of Management," London, Newman Neame, Ltd. 1956.

RUCKER PLAN OF GROUP INCENTIVES

The **Rucker Plan** is a program for group incentives that uses day-to-day employee participation and broad coverage to develop cost reductions and improve profits. It is backed by a precise measurement of productivity gains in money terms (not physical units). It recognizes and reinforces those gains with an equitable, automatic method of sharing them between the participants (added pay) and the company (added margin).

Measure of Productivity. The measure used is called *economic productivity*—the output of *value added by manufacture* for each dollar of input of *payroll costs.* Value added by manufacture is the difference between sales income from goods produced and the costs of the materials, supplies, and outside services consumed in the production and delivery of that output. Payroll costs are all employment costs paid to, because of, or on behalf of the employee group measured.

Thus, economic productivity may measure the financial effectiveness of a plant's hourly-rated employees, its total employment, or some blend of hourly and salaried people. Flexible extra pay programs may be designed, using the principles described here for plant people only, for a mixture of plant and office people, for office people only, or for managers only.

History. Studies of data published in U.S. Censuses and Surveys of Manufacturers by Allan W. Rucker in 1932–33 showed that the economic productivity of U.S. factory employment had been extremely stable from 1899 through 1929, varying narrowly about an average of $2.54 [1]. Continuing analyses [2] [3] of comparable data by Rucker's organization have shown that the pattern still continues. (A similar consistent relationship, despite certain statistical and reporting differences, was reported in 1969 by P. J. Loftus, Director of the Statistical Office of the United Nations, regarding the economies of seventeen "developed" nations, including Russia and Japan. He also found that twenty-five other national economies are approaching the same balance as their economies mature [4].)

Continuing his research, Rucker found similar consistent patterns for various broad industry segments, such as chemicals, food, leather, furniture, and non-electrical machinery, and that the same type of economic productivity balance held true in nearly all subsegments, with only the following few exceptions:

(1) Oil refining, publishing, and certain other situations with highly capitalized and semi-automated operations where employment does not rise and fall in direct proportion to values produced. Many of these, however, have "fixed-variable" patterns similar to the wholly variable situation of the overall economy.

(2) Extractive and certain other natural resource industries where market prices fluctuate widely, correlated more with world demand than with industrial efficiency.

Exhibit I shows long-term averages for a few such industrial sub-segments and actual ratios at specific plants. The various industries do not all show economic productivities of plant employment costs close to the combined national average, but they have their own patterns. They range from very high (with high capital commitments per job, high research and development costs, or considerable selling expenses) to

EXHIBIT I

ECONOMIC PRODUCTIVITY DATA FOR SELECTED U.S. INDUSTRIAL CATEGORIES AND SPECIFIC PLANTS

Product	S.I.C. Code	Industry Average (1) Value Added per $1.00 Plant Payroll Average 1972–1976	Corresponding Ratio (2) at a Specific Plant Within the Same Industry
Grey Iron Castings	3321	$1.76	$2.49
Wood Household Furniture	2511	2.16	2.04
Metal Partitions & Fixtures	2542	2.82	4.11
Bolts, Nuts, Rivets & Washers	3452	2.75	2.75
Transformers	3612	2.46	2.69
Blowers and Fans	3564	3.30	2.95

(1) From *Industry Profiles* 1972–1976; published by U. S. Dept. of Commerce.
(2) From records of studies conducted by The Eddy-Rucker-Nickels Company for specific companies.

very low (with low capital commitments per job, little research and development, and modest selling expenses). Industry patterns remain relatively stable through both the peaks and the troughs of the business cycle.

Investigation of comparable data for single companies led to the practical applications of what had otherwise been simply a new economic discovery. In about 90% of the instances studied, a competitive and profitable manufacturing plant has its own stable pattern. There is a broad range of economic productivity relationships for plants whose data are reported under a single segment by the Census.

Specific plant ratios in Exhibit I are both above and below their industry averages. Thus, while industry data often serve as a useful check against a plant's performance in, say, wire drawing or extruded rubber goods, the economic productivity measure has to be developed for each specific plant.

The first practical application of these individual plant or company patterns was as a guide to wage increases during 1936–39 when companies were able gradually to restore the severe rate reductions imposed during 1931–34. Thus it first became a management guide for overall wage and salary administration and cost control. The second practical application of these findings was as the basis of "productivity bonuses." A few programs were installed prior to World War II and others were authorized under Federal wage-control regulations during World War II. Since prices were similarly frozen, the gains in economic productivity were an approved non-inflationary basis for determination of added wages. (The same basis was again approved by Federal authorities during the Korean Conflict and during the "Phase 2" controls of 1971–72.)

As the economy first compressed after World War II and then began its upward growth in the 1950s, this measurement of economic productivity was tested by Rucker for many companies. Some of those with necessary stability of economic productivity began trying to develop faster gains through coordinated efforts of their employees; and gradually, several thousand plant years of experience were accrued. By review of what has happened in both successful and unsuccessful companies, the following criteria have been developed as guides to where the program is most apt to show significant accomplishments:

(1) Situations where the plant people can actually make substantial contributions to improved productivity through conservation of materials, supplies, and time, as well as through improved quality, output, and job methods.

(2) Plants employing between 50 and 800 people. Those that are smaller generally have more rigid employment costs, and less formal programs than this can work very effectively. Those that are larger have a hard time obtaining the overall understanding and "team cohesiveness" that this program requires for best results.

(3) Broad enough end-use markets, products, or customers—or some blend of all three elements—so that no single market product, contract, etc. can create chaos if it is lost.

(4) Evidence of past and probable future commitments of both managerial talents and capital to keep the physical productivity (units per manhour) rising sufficiently fast to balance wage escalation less marketplace inflation.

(5) Reasonable human relationship between people in the company at all levels, together with what is sometimes called "leader" management as opposed to "driver" management.

(6) Sufficient short-term volume potential so that people wil not fear job loss; and long-term growth potential so that employment can likely be expanded.

Development of Standard(s). Since each plant has its own individual pattern of economic productivity, the first step in the installation of a Rucker Plan, whether as an executive control guide or as the basis of flexible added pay, is a study of historical accounting data to develop that specific pattern. This involves a consistent determination for a period of years of the net sales value of the output of the plant, the costs of the materials, supplies and services used, and of the payroll costs (including all fringe benefit items) incurred. The data can first be tested in a rough but consistent manner so that the detailed study necessary for actual application is only done where the desired goal can be achieved. This quickly eliminates the one case in ten which does not fit the expected pattern. The detailed study will then exactly derive the economic productivity pattern in a comparable and consistent manner so that a standard can be recommended and applied.

The study may show that some amount of fixed payroll must be taken into account in setting the standard. It may also show that the various product lines of the plant are sufficiently different in nature as to require their own individual standards. In the majority of cases, however, the relationship will be found to be directly variable. (See Exhibit II.)

Since the standard is determined from independently audited accounting information no question of fact is involved. The standard has not been set on the basis of a company official's judgment, rather it is the end result of thousands of negotiated agreements between the plant and its customers, its suppliers, and its employees. The full attention of both the employees and the management can then be concentrated not on how to measure or on how to split up the gain, but on how to *obtain* and *increase* that gain to their mutual benefit.

EXHIBIT II

DETERMINATION OF VALUE-ADDED STANDARD

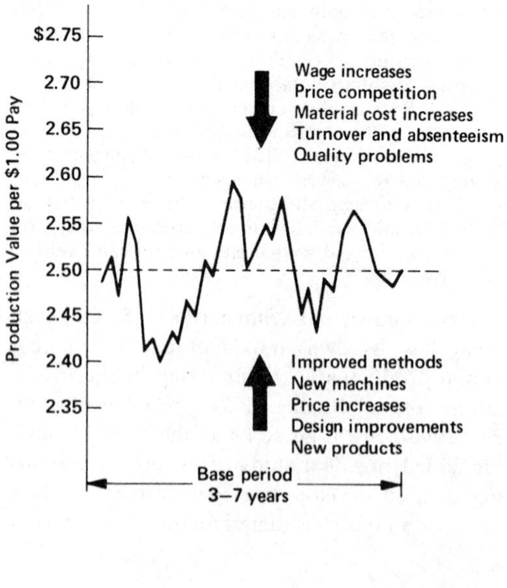

Development of Monthly Operating Basis. Although the plan itself is based on annual figures after audit, and future operations will also be reconciled to annual audit reports, experience has given convincing proof that monthly separate extra checks provide the best reinforcement and are a key element of success with the entire program. It is therefore necessary also to analyze at least two full years by months and to study the month-to-month profile of economic productivity. Seasonal factors may require provisions or adjustments; certain benefits such as vacations must be accrued, at least in memorandum form; wide swings in either work in process or finished goods inventory must be properly valued for plan purposes to avoid large deficits or payoffs due to inventory cycles; and actual performance of accounting practices must be tested. Further refinement will yield worksheets for month-to-month calculations, including provisions for a reserve, which can then be used during a dummy run period before actual initiation of a formal pay program.

Source of Gains. Since the objective of the Rucker Plan is to maximize the output of value added for a given payroll input, opportunity for added earnings to the participants and added margin to the company comes from the following:

Improved use of materials.
Improved use of supplies.
Improved output per man-hour.
Improved product quality.
Improved production methods.
Improved machinery and equipment.
Improved service to customers.
Reduced absenteeism and turnover.
Better training of new employees.
Skill upgrading for older employees.
Improved safety performance.

Whereas the usual "piecework" or "standard hour" type of individual or small group incentive based on physical productivity usually covers only 40–65% of a plants workforce, this program is intended to cover *everyone* [5]—including indirect plant people, supervision, planning and scheduling people, etc.

Start-Up Procedures. Once designed, a Rucker Plan is an economically sound and equitable plant-wide incentive plan. But at that point it is only a tool; it does not work by itself, any more than does any other incentive program. It must be made to work by the people involved, and this can be accomplished only by a thorough and continuing process of training, paralleled by an effective program of upward and downward communication about both day-to-day plant operations and month-to-month plan results [6]. The basic steps at the time a Rucker Plan is begun at a plant are as follows:

(1) A visual presentation of the plan's history and success, how the particular plant's standard was determined, what improvements will help create bonuses, how the results are to be computed, and how each person will participate. This visual presentation is made to:

(a) Top management of the plant.
(b) Middle-management and supervisory personnel.
(c) All participants, preferably at one mass showing so that there is no question that all saw and heard the same thing.

(2) Distribution of an explanatory booklet with the same exhibits and text to reinforce what was seen and heard at the visual presentation.

(3) A series of small group meetings, so that all participants may get answers to specific questions. These meetings are also used to start the waste identification and elimination program.

(4) Thorough development of an "Ideas, Problems and Wastes Campaign," so that the thoughts of participants which may lead to improvements are recorded, investigated, publicized, resolved, and acted on—constructively, carefully, and promptly.

(5) Establishment of plant productivity groups to improve communication about everything affecting the plan's results. These groups should have rotating membership from all plant areas and meet at least monthly with key management people to review, analyze, and discuss progress and plans.

Continuing Procedures. These start-up procedures must be backed up by continuing programs of education and individual involvement. Following are samples of the methods used:

(1) Rotation of the productivity group members so that in time all interested persons have the opportunity to serve.

(2) "Guest speakers" at the productivity group meetings, perhaps a salesman, or someone from Purchasing or Plant Engineering, to describe specific future plans or give an explanation of current problems in one of these areas.

(3) A continuing flow of information on easily accessible bulletin boards. Include monthly results and uncomplicated explanations from a thorough analysis of them. Frequently revise the list about all ideas, problems, and wastes being investigated. Post minutes of group meetings in summary form. Develop special displays about customer applications of plant products. Let people know about good orders received and compliments as well as customer complaints. (Too few managers understand the thirst for information their plant people have or how constructively they will accept both good news and bad news when it is received in a constant, straightforward flow.)

(4) Pay check stuffers on a variety of subjects at intervals.

(5) A quiz with prizes to check understanding of the plan. Or, one about specific material costs, to help plan further explanations or training.

(6) An idea contest, with awards for the most items during a week, the best idea, etc. Also, waste identification contests.

There are many other means, but the aim is always the same: to get people emotionally and mentally *involved* in their jobs and *committed* to the overall goals of both productivity and income improvement, with growth and improved security of their own jobs in a competitive environment. Most plant jobs today, especially if they require routine and repetitive work, demand only 5–8% of a typical worker's mental and emotional capacities. The other 92–95% is a great *unused resource* and thus a tremendous waste of motive power for industrial progress. The economic productivity can be increased by 10–30% with the normal short-term fluctuations occurring at a higher level (see Exhibit III).

EXHIBIT III

INCREASE IN PRODUCTIVITY OVER TIME

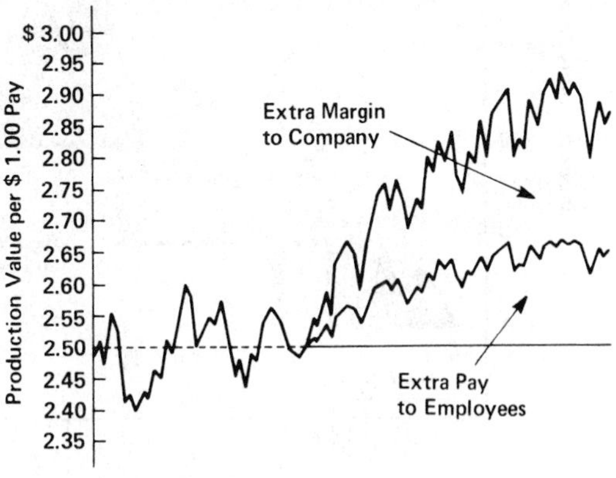

Results. Almost all Rucker Plans are set up to provide results on a monthly basis. The important points here are:

(1) All of the necessary figures are readily available from the normal accounting statements.

(2) For a payoff, there must first be a gain in productivity beyond that which simply offsets fixed wage and benefit increases. The gain is determined by multiplying the payroll times the economic productivity standard to get the standard value added, and comparing that with the actual value added. If there is no such gain for a particular month, then there is no payoff in that month.

(3) In months when there is a gain, it is shared in accordance with the predetermined standard. The company gets its share of the gain as increased margin whenever the employees get their share as bonus. For example, if the standard is $2.50, the company gains $1.50 as *added* margin (toward reinvestment, working capital or dividends) for each $1.00 of added pay just as had held true before.

(4) Generally, two-thirds of the bonus shown by a monthly calculation is paid out in cash, and one-third is held as a memorandum reserve until the end of the fiscal year. This is a cushion against any year-end adjustments to accounting data, and against any month in which performance is not up to standard. In such a month, the deficit in performance is charged against the memorandum reserve. The intention is that, over the course of a fiscal year, the amount received by the participants in the form of regular pay plus monthly bonuses will not be more nor less than their established share of the created value added (40% in the example discussed above). The adjusted reserve is distributed as an additional bonus check after the audit is completed. Any negative reserve is usually wiped out and the next year begun with a "clean slate."

(5) The bonus is generally distributed as a

EXHIBIT IV

TYPICAL RESULTS PROFILE

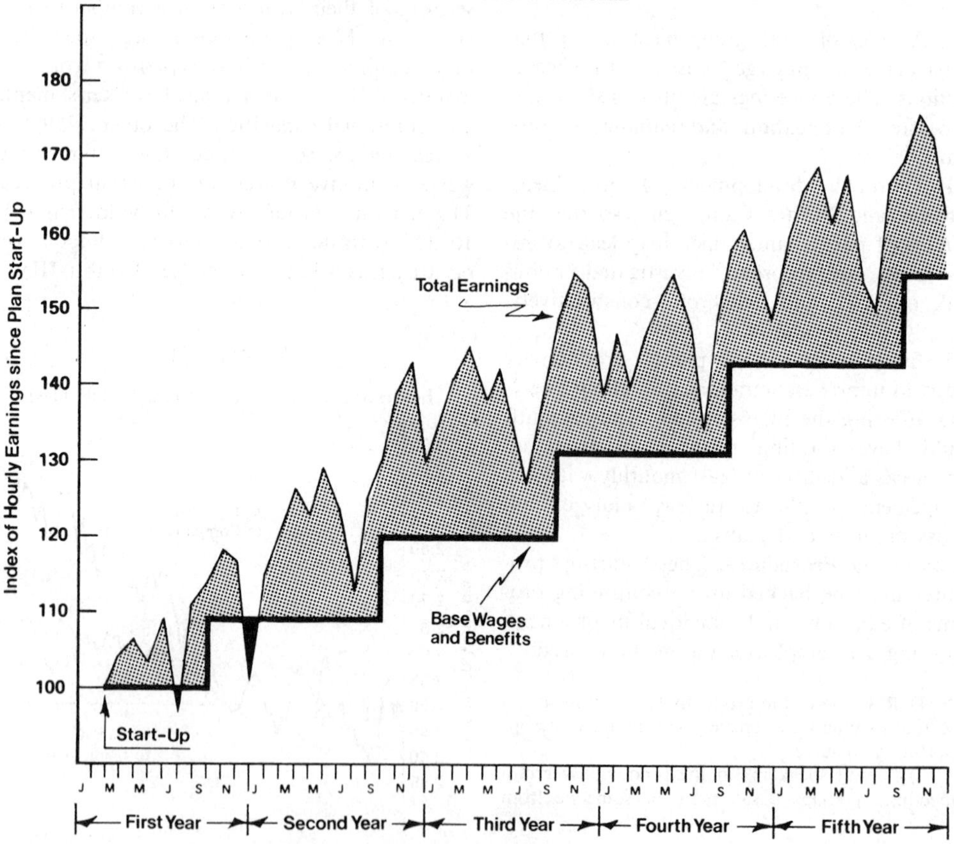

percentage of participants' monthly earnings. This preserves the differentials set between jobs by contract, skill, job evaluations, or past practices. In the United States it is necessary to include overtime premium in the monthly earnings to satisfy Federal Wage and Hour regulations (pertaining to bonus as it affects overtime premium rates).

A page of notes on the month's results is equally important. This is an analysis of those factors that helped create bonus earnings or hurt the results. It might, for example, include mention of extraordinary customer returns, an increase in overtime necessary to meet delivery schedules, a drop in cost of a particular supply item, start-up of new equipment, and so forth.

End Achievement. A selectively applied, properly designed, well installed and conscientiously administered program should keep the company using it well ahead of its competition by consistently producing 12–17% more net margin per hour of people's time than could be expected without the program. Exhibit IV is a typical case profile. With current normal yearly increases in wage rates and productivity, organizations without this program can expect to have both employee earnings and company margin increase by an average of 8–10% a year, largely through managerial talents, added capital investments, and inflation. The achievement of a Rucker Plan program is that by involving *everyone* in the organization those increases can be accomplished several years *before* they would normally occur at small marginal cost for design, adoption, and operation. This inexpensive but significant gain on competition represents extra pay, extra profit, and extra growth opportunity—and the lead can be maintained over long years of operation.

Although business cycles with periods of both good and bad conditions have occurred and been well documented since the late 1700s, all too few managers and employee representatives seem to understand the importance to *both* of them of partial wage flexibility. A company which has 12–17% or more of its employment costs flexible with its own marketplace economics is in a much stronger position to compete for business and has a far better chance of weathering downside conditions without laying off people, or with smaller workforce reductions. It can temporarily give its customers part of its economic productivity improvement through special services or price concessions. By attracting work away from others, and keeping its own force fully scheduled, it has an extremely potent tool to protect the job security of everyone in the organization [7].

R.C. Scott, Vice President, Eddy-Rucker-Nickels Company, Cambridge, Massachusetts

Information Reference

Zollitsch, Herbert G. and Langsner, Adolph, "Wage and Salary Administration," Cincinnati, South-Western, 1970. (Chapters 17–21 contain material on compensation, motivation, individual incentives, and plant-wide incentives, including checklists for selection, installation, and maintenance, as well as economic comparisons.)

References Cited

[1] Rucker, A.W., "Labor's Road to Plenty," Boston, Page, 1937.
[2] "Progress in Productivity and Pay," Cambridge, Mass., The Eddy-Rucker-Nickels Co., 1952. (Updates the research of [1] for the entire U.S. economy.)
[3] Rucker, A.W., "Gearing Wages to Productivity," Cambridge, Mass., The Eddy-Rucker-Nickels Co., 1962.
[4] Loftus, P.J., "Labor's Share in Manufacturing," *Lloyds Bank Review,* London, April 1969.
[5] Scott, R.C., "Incentives in Manufacturing," Vols. 1, 2, and 3, Cambridge, Mass., The Eddy-Rucker-Nickels Co. (Reprinting a series of 18 articles by R. C. Scott in *Circuits Manufacturing* magazine during 1965–1967.)
[6] Scott, R.C., "Plant-wide Incentives—How to Make Them Work." *Automatic Machining,* August-September 1979.
[7] Scott, R.C., "Protecting Jobs and Profits with Automatic Cost Reduction," *Journal of Systems Management,* Cleveland, Ohio, Association for Systems Management, March 1979.

Cross References: *Guaranteed Annual Wage; Incentive Systems; Lincoln Incentive Management Plan; Profit Sharing; Scanlon Plan of Group Incentives; Standard Minute System.*

S

SAFETY AND HEALTH IN THE WORKPLACE

At the turn of the century, work accidents were one of industry's most severe problems. More than 50 out of every 100,000 workers were killed annually as a result of work injuries. Some accident prevention efforts were undertaken, and workers' compensation laws were put into effect. (See WORKERS' COMPENSATION.) But there was no national organized effort to reduce the accidental death toll until 1912, when a small group of safety minded individuals met under the auspices of the American Iron and Steel Institute to lay plans for an all-out war on work accidents. This resulted in the formation of the National Council for Industrial Safety in 1913, which became a clearing-house for all available **Safety** information, and a promoter of further safety technology and education. Its scope was soon broadened to encompass all accidents, wherever they occurred—home, work, highway or public place—but the roots and prime support of the National Safety Council (as it is now known) are in industry.

Although a half-century of organized accident prevention has reduced industry's problem by two-thirds, making the workplace the safest place of all, accidents remain a major concern and responsibility of management, with employee involvement. In 1979, 13,300 workers were killed in on-the-job accidents. An additional 2,300,000 suffered injuries disabling beyond the day of the accident (see Exhibit I). The cost to the nation was an estimated $27.3 billion, comprised of both direct and indirect costs which included wage loss, medical expense, insurance costs, and production and time losses, among others.

Those losses were shared by management and labor. But the most significant point is that none of the loss of life, limb, or capital was necessary. Accidents can be prevented through programmed safety.

A great number of companies of all sizes and in all industries have found that accident prevention is an important economic factor in the success of their businesses and an invaluable aid in building good employee and public relations. Nevertheless, there remains a lack of universal accomplishment through programs based upon a sustained, organized approach, especially in companies with 100 to 250 employees.

It is a fallacy to think the work place is safe because laws and regulations are complied with, or that risks are covered because they are insured. State and Federal laws as well as municipal codes and ordinances usually provide only minimal criteria for safety. Insurance costs cover only workers' compensation and medical costs. They do not cover equipment damage, production delays, lost customers, and a host of other uninsurable losses.

Accident prevention can seldom be justified on the basis of savings in workers' compensation insurance alone. The critical loss for a company from work injuries, occupational illness, and accidents is in the loss of key employees, delays in production, and in additional and nonproductive work required of supervisors, foremen, and levels of management beyond the foremen.

The Hidden Costs. The computation of total time taken away from production by all the unnecessary, almost entirely controllable first-aid, medical, and disability cases reported to the Council reveals misused production time of staggering proportions. Here is a typical example of how the hidden costs of accidents can penalize a company. If an employee is injured, he continues to draw his base pay while he goes to the first-aid room or to the physician. During this time, generally, the worker's press or operation is shut down and produces nothing. Other employees direct their attention to the accident scene, provide help for the injured, discuss how the accident happened, respond as witnesses during the accident investigation process—all of which costs money and degrades productivity. However, the overhead in the plant goes on just the same. It includes the cost of power, light, heat, truckers, clerks, depreciation, fringe benefits, and other items.

Production and accident prevention cannot be separated but must be considered parts of the same activity. Progressive companies have found that it takes less time and costs less money to prevent accidents than to pay for them.

Management's Responsibility. There are three compelling reasons why management must accept the responsibility for protecting its employees against accidents and against exposure to unhealthful working conditions.

First, management must meet certain legal obligations. Federal and state regulations require employers not only to pay for injuries suffered by their workers under state workers' compensation laws, but also to conform to reasonable standards for safety in their operations.

Second, safe operation is a social and moral obligation imposed by modern society and demanded by the obligation and privileges of owning and managing business enterprises and Federal agencies. The trend to increasing emphasis on accident prevention has been evident for many years and has led to Federal presence in safety.

Third, the acceptance of financial responsibility for a share of the economic loss which accidents cause workers has led companies to realize that a large proportion of injuries and occupational illnesses are preventable, and that industry can and should utilize a share of its technical brain power for their prevention. Industry discovered, at almost the beginning of the modern period, that concern for safety produced efficiency, and that concern for efficiency must include concern for safety.

As evidence that accidents can be controlled, from 1926 to 1976, the last year records were kept under the ANSI Z16 standard, the combined frequency rate for all companies reporting to the National Safety Council dropped from 31.87 to 10.87. In other words, about two out of every three disabling injuries that would have occurred in 1926 were prevented in 1976 in the concerns reporting to the Council. During the same period both the severity rate and the number of accidental deaths and total disabilities in relation to man-hours worked declined by some two-thirds.

These figures represent over 12,000 units of companies in all industries, members of the Council, and participants in the work of the organized safety and health movement. They cannot be considered special cases or merely a handful of firms with a high level of safety enthusiasm.

The Occupational Safety and Health Act. New national policy was established on December 29, 1970, when President Nixon signed into law the Occupational Safety and Health

EXHIBIT I

PART OF BODY INJURED IN WORK ACCIDENTS

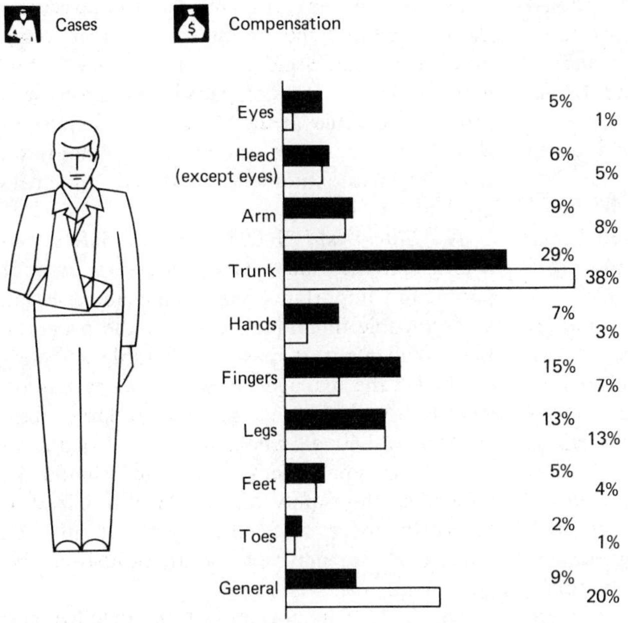

Disabling work injuries in the entire nation totalled approximately 2,300,000 in 1979. Of these, about 13,200 were fatal and 80,000 resulted in some permanent impairment.

Injuries to the trunk occurred most frequently, with thumb and finger injuries next, according to State Labor Department reports.

Eyes	110,000
Head (except eyes)	140,000
Arms	210,000
Trunk	670,000
Hands	160,000
Fingers	340,000
Legs	300,000
Feet	110,000
Toes	50,000
General	210,000

The chart shows for each body part, per cent *in black* of all injuries and per cent *in white* of all compensation paid.

Source: State Labor Departments, 1978–1979; cases — 18 States, compensation — 11 States.

Act of 1970 (Public Law No. 91-596). The Congressionally declared purpose of OSHA is "to assure so far as possible every working man and woman in the nation safe and healthful working conditions and to preserve our human resources." The Act took effect on April 28, 1971.

OSHA grants the OSHA Administration, U.S. Department of Labor, the authority, among other things, to (1) promulgate, modify, and revoke safety and health standards; (2) conduct inspections and investigations and issue citations, including proposed penalties; (3) require employers to keep records of safety and health data; (4) petition the courts to restrain imminent danger situations; and (5) approve or reject state plans for programs under the Act. (For a detailed discussion of OSHA, see OCCUPATIONAL SAFETY AND HEALTH ACT OF 1970.)

The Occupational Safety and Health Review Commission established under OSHA is a quasi-judicial board of three members appointed by the President. The principal function of the Commission, which is not a part of the Department of Labor, is to adjudicate cases resulting from OSHA Administration's enforcement action when such action is contested by the employer.

The National Institute for Occupational Safety and Health (NIOSH), a part of the Department of Health and Human Services, is the principal Federal agency engaged in research, education, and training related to occupational safety and health. One of the principal functions of NIOSH is to develop and establish recommended occupational safety and health standards for the OSHA Administration.

Initially, the OSHA Administration focused its efforts on the safety aspects of the Act. However, recently more attention is being given to eliminating exposure to occupational illnesses. (See OCCUPATIONAL HEALTH.)

The jury is still out in determining OSHA's effectiveness in preventing occupational injuries and illnesses. Incidence rates (number of recordable injuries or illnesses per 200,000 person-hours worked) for all recordable injuries has decreased slightly, while the more serious injuries—incidence of lost work-day cases—has increased slightly. OSHA has had no measurable effect on work fatalities.

There is no doubt the Act has given new visibility to the whole realm of occupational safety and health. However, to rely on mere compliance with OSHA standards is to invite disaster, since the residual risk after compliance remains unacceptable.

The Safety Program Elements. The first step in planning an accident prevention program is *organization,* and this step must be taken by the highest management official. The safety and health organization must be designed to enlist and maintain the support of all personnel in an organization.

An analysis of safety organizations in companies of all sizes with outstanding safety records shows that invariably the program includes seven basic elements:

(1) *Management Leadership:* assumption of responsibility; declaration of policy.

(2) *Assignment of Responsibility:* to operating officials, safety and health directors, supervisors, committees.

(3) *Maintenance of Safe Working Conditions:* involving safety and health inspections, engineering revisions, purchasing.

(4) *Safety and Health Training:* for management, for supervisors, for workers.

(5) *Accident Investigation and Accident and Illness Record System:* accident analysis; reports on injuries; measurement of results.

(6) *Medical and First-Aid Systems:* placement examinations; treatment of injuries; and occupational illnesses, first-aid services; periodic health examinations.

(7) *Acceptance of Personal Responsibility by Employees:* training; maintenance of interest.

To initiate the program, the top executive must determine the extent to which an organized attack on accidents is to become a permanent part of the company's operations and procedures. This determination is important and it must be made known to all employees. If the top man is not sold on safety, few others are likely to be.

The Safety and Health Director. Safety and health activities must have leadership. It is of paramount importance that management assign a responsible individual to direct the program. In a small plant, it may be advisable and necessary for the manager himself to carry this responsibility. In a medium-sized or large plant another individual, whose duties and qualifications determine whether he (she) should be known as the Safety and/or Health Director, Safety Engineer, or Safety Supervisor, may be selected. There may also be an Industrial Hygiene Director.

The S&H Director must keep detailed and accurate accidents data, not only for workers' compensation purposes of making reports to the Workers' Compensation Board and the insurance company, and to satisfy the requirements of the Occupational Safety and Health Act, but also because such data are the best tools for determining the causal factors of each accident so that preventive measures can be taken. Study of accident records may also reveal additional hazards which can be corrected before they cause accidents.

S&H Committees. The basic function of all S&H committees is to create and maintain an active interest in safety and health and to reduce the number of accidents. The committees may perform the following basic functions:

(1) Meet on a monthly or quarterly basis to discuss and formulate S&H policies and recommend their adoption by management.

(2) Discover hazardous conditions and practices through inspections, determine remedies, and make recommendations to management.

(3) Investigate serious accidents, review accident reports, and make recommendations to management.

(4) Review hazardous conditions and practices reported by employees.

(5) Endeavor to have its management-approved recommendations put into practice.

(6) Relay safety and health information to the entire personnel of the company.

Inspection. Before control measures can be set up, the extent and nature of existing and potential hazards must be ascertained through an inspection of the entire plant. This initial inspection can best be made by a group composed of production representatives, a maintenance man, the individual to whom safety and health responsibilities have been assigned, and one or more representatives of the workers.

The importance of the first inspection and of the steps taken to eliminate as many hazards as possible cannot be over-emphasized. This activity gives the workers their first specific indication of management's sincerity with regard to accident prevention. It is difficult to persuade workers to do what is proper if a company is unwilling to authorize the expenditure of time and money needed to eliminate observable hazardous working conditions.

Safety and Health Training. S&H training is not difficult if it is handled as a part of ordinary production training. It is always easier to train employees to form new and safe habits while they are learning their job than it is to correct established, unsafe habits later.

Training Supervisors. When an accident prevention program is first organized, it is to be expected that few supervisors will have enough information to supervise it with maximum effectiveness. A training program for supervisors can be of tremendous help to them. Since they will carry the principal responsibility for conditions and work practices in their departments, supervisory training is best given as soon as the accident and occupational illness prevention program has been set up.

Accident and Occupational Illness Records. To eliminate guesswork with regard to accident and occupational illness experience and costs, a record system should be set up. Such records can also be used for the isolation and cure of "sore spots" in a plant, such as recurrent bad practices or hazardous conditions of a specific kind, and departments with high accident and/or illness rates. Standard forms which request enough information to make the reports useful in the investigation of accident and occupational illness causes, and in planning subsequent preventive measures, are available from insurance companies. OSHA requires special reporting forms and the posting of records that must be posted and available when a compliance officer makes an inspection. Information and forms can be obtained from OSHA area offices.

Medical and Health Service. Health maintenance for employees, through prevention as well as treatment, is the purpose and goal of modern industrial (occupational) health programs (see OCCUPATIONAL HEALTH.)

Report Forms. Since the completeness and accuracy of the entire accident/illness record system depend upon the information in the individual reports, simple report forms which can contain all essential data must be used. Two types of report forms are recommended: the *first-aid form* for reporting every injury or occupational illness and the *supervisor's* (or investigator's) *report form* to be completed after each injury, illness, or accident investigation.

Monthly Summary of Injuries and Illnesses. First-aid reports and supervisors' accident reports should be summarized monthly so that injury/illness rates can be determined. If possible, these rates should be secured for individual departments, as well as for the entire company.

Injury and illness incidence rates relate the number of cases or the number of lost workdays to the number of employee-hours worked. These rates, established by the Occupational

Safety and Health Act, are easy to compute and understand, and are accepted as the standard for all industries. They automatically adjust for differences in the size of companies and for variations in employment within a company.

Incidence Rates. Rates can be calculated for different kinds of cases or lost workdays, but the basic formula is the same; it uses 200,000 employee-hours as the equivalent of 100 full-time workers. Thus the rates may be interpreted as the percentage of workers liable to incur the degree of injury or illness represented in the rate. The formula is:

$$\text{Incidence rate} = \frac{(\text{Number of cases or days}) \times 200{,}000}{\text{Total employee hours}}$$

The number of cases or days is taken from the OSHA form 200 Log and Summary of Occupational Injuries and Illnesses and usually involves total recordable cases, lost workday cases (actual time away from work and restricted work), nonfatal cases without lost workdays, total lost workdays, or days away from work.

When an establishment has calculated its own incidence rates, the S&H director can then compare the company's experience to that of other companies in the same industry, and he (she) can keep track of the trend in the company's experience over time.

Federal Regulations on Occupational Injury and Illness Records. Under the Occupational Safety and Health Act, new injury and illness reporting requirements have been developed. After July 1, 1971, establishments subject to the Act were required to maintain records as follows:

(1) A log and summary of occupational injuries and illnesses.

(2) A supplementary record of each occupational injury and illness.

Definitions of occupational injuries and illnesses under the new Act differ from those in American National Standard Z16.1, and may differ from state worker's compensation requirements and other records systems.

Injuries and illnesses are to be recorded separately with three different categories, as follows:

(1) *Fatalities,* regardless of the time between the injury and death, or the length of the illness.

(2) *Lost Workday Cases,* other than fatalities, that result in lost workdays (actual time away from work and restricted work cases).

(3) *Nonfatal Cases Without Lost Workdays,* which result in transfer to another job or termination of employment, or require medical treatment, or involve loss of consciousness or restriction of work or motion. This category also includes any diagnosed occupational illnesses which are reported to the employer, but are not classified as fatalities or lost workday cases.

Some organizations continue to use both frequency and severity rates, in addition to the reports required under OSHA.

Compliance under the Act is administered through forty-odd area offices of OSHA. These offices are under ten regional offices. The National Institute of Occupational Safety and Health also maintains regional offices, but their main concern is with toxic materials and harmful environments. They maintain a laboratory for long- and short-term exposures to harmful materials. NIOSH publishes annual lists of toxic materials.

Any employee can register a complaint to an area OSHA office and request an inspection if he believes that a condition exists that threatens physical harm or imminent danger. The name or names of the complainants need not be furnished to the employer by OSHA. The OSHA office will respond if it considers that a valid complaint has been registered.

Compliance officers may enter establishments without warning for inspections. Employer and employee representatives can accompany the OSHA representative.

When an investigation reveals a violation, the employer will be issued a written citation and a reasonable time will be given to bring about compliance. The citation for the violation must be posted at or near where the violation occurred. At the same time, the OSHA office will notify the employer of the penalty to be assessed for the violation. If the employer wishes to contest the citation or the penalty, notification must be made to the OSHA office within fifteen days. The OSHA office will then notify the Occupational Safety and Health Review Commission which will set up a hearing date and assign a hearing officer. Hearing will be scheduled in the regional area of the employer contesting the complaint.

Citation penalties can be up to $1,000, and willful or repeated violations can be up to $10,000. Willful violation that results in death is punishable by a fine of $10,000 or imprisonment for up to six months.

The Act encourages states to assume the responsibilities of the Act and provides grants both for planning for such responsibility and also for the continued administration of the provisions of the Act if their plans meet the criteria set up by OSHA.

Accident Analysis. Within a relatively few years, accident prevention has progressed from a hit-or-miss affair to a technique closely approaching the scientific method. In earlier years humanitarian appeal to management and workers was the primary means used in attempts to reduce accident rates. Today, methods which isolate and identify the causes of accidents and which permit direct and positive action to prevent recurrence are employed.

IRVIN B. ETTER, Director, Occupational Safety & Loss Control Consultant, National Safety Council, Chicago, Illinois

Information References

Associations:

American Industrial Hygiene Association.
American National Red Cross.
American Society of Safety Engineers.
American National Standards Institute.
Industrial Hygiene Foundation.
National Fire Protection Association.
National Safety Council.
National Society for the Prevention of Blindness.

Government:

Occupational Safety and Health Administration.
National Institute for Occupational Safety and Health.

Periodicals:

Industrial Supervisor (NSC).
Professional Safety (ASSE).
National Safety News (NSC).
OSHA Up To Date (NSC).

Texts published by National Safety Council, Chicago:

Accident Prevention Manual for Industrial Operations, 8th ed., "Engineering and Technology" Vol. II, 1980 and "Administration and Programs" Vol. I, 1981.
Fundamentals of Industrial Hygiene, 2nd ed., 1979.
Handbook of Occupational Safety and Health, 1976.
Supervisor's Safety Manual, 5th ed., 1975.
Industrial Noise and Hearing Conservation, 1975.
MORT—Safety Assurance Systems, 1980.

Cross References: *Fire Loss Prevention; Occupational Health; Occupational Safety and Health Act of 1970; Office Safety.*

SALARY AND WAGE ADMINISTRATION: See Employee Benefit Plans; Executive Appraisal: Diagnostic Performance Appraisal; Executive Compensation; Guaranteed Annual Wage; Incentive Systems; Job Evaluation; Lincoln Incentive Management Plan; Performance Appraisal (Merit Rating); Profit Sharing; Retirement Plans; Rucker Plan of Group Incentives; Scanlon Plan of Group Incentives; Standard Minute System

SALES FORECASTING: See Business Forecasting; Production Planning and Inventory Management; Sales Statistics

SALES MANAGEMENT

Sales Management is the planning of a company's sales strategies and the hiring, training, supervision, and motivation of salesmen to carry out those strategies. As such, it is the key function of the MARKETING process. Without it, most companies would revert to the simplicities of a hundred years ago, when the emphasis was on manufacturing, and it was considered somewhat immoral for people to buy more than necessary to meet their daily needs.

There are four major branches (all interrelated) in successful sales management: (1) *Top Level Policy Planning,* which establishes a framework of policy within which the sales objectives of a company or institution may be achieved, depending on an individual company's particular situation; (2) *Line and Staff Operational Planning,* through which procedures are established in advance, against which the quality and quantity of work may be controlled; (3) *Organization,* the setting up of a structure of responsibilities and normal interrelations—charting the organization, assigning responsibility, delegating authority, tracing accountability, and clarifying the character of collaboration; and (4) *Administration,* by which management meets planned objectives through guidance and evaluation of activity, including SALES TRAINING, *Motivation, Coordination,* and *Execution.*

Sales management methods are conditioned by the nature of individual products or product lines, and by the channels through which selling moves. Quite dissimilar problems develop in the sale of industrial and consumer goods, for instance, and within each field there are many variations depending upon whether sales are made to consumers or middlemen. There is also a wide variety in personal preference among sales managers with regard to methods and techniques of organization, motivation, and planning.

Thus the way in which the sales management function is organized differs from industry to industry, and even among firms selling the same type of product. Organization becomes more and more complex as the company size and diversity increase. Many firms have hundreds of salesmen, and a few have thousands. Some firms (such as those selling technical products) have sophisticated sales personnel requiring less supervision than do less sophisticated representatives (such as route salesmen).

The relative emphasis placed on order-getting versus order-taking varies among different selling jobs. However, all salespersons must sell aggressively in some situations and in others need only take orders coming their way. Thus the driver-salesman for a soft drink bottler is mainly an order-taker since the product has been presold to consumers and dealers reorder automatically. The salesman of aluminum siding calling on homeowners is much more of an order-getter, and his main goal is demand stimulation. If a manufacturer's selling strategy relies heavily upon advertising to attract business and build demand, marketing channels are likely to include several layers of middlemen, and the manufacturer's salesmen may primarily be order-takers, and only incidentally order-getters. When advertising is used mainly to back up personal selling, marketing channels contain fewer layers of middlemen, and salespeople concentrate more on order-getting.

What makes sales management challenging and difficult is that personnel in the field are pretty much on their own, with relatively little close supervision. Their hours are usually irregular and working time is hard to conserve because of waiting for interviews, broken appointments, and other problems of dealing with customers, each of whom may have different needs and different buying motives. Moreover, each territory has different potential and characteristics, making norms of performance more difficult to set up than in other activities of the business.

Thus the sales manager's most important functions are to find salespeople who are likely to be productive self-starters, train them, assign them to the right territories, motivate them, and keep track of their efforts. In short, sales management is a people-oriented profession. To be successful, a sales manager must know not only what makes people buy, but also what keeps salespeople happy and productive. Additionally, the successful sales manager must be a good organizer. He or she must determine how the total selling job should be set up—by geographical areas, by product lines, by type of customer, consumer or industrial, and the like.

Scope. The scope of the sales manager's job is indicated by the following listing of typical problem-questions with which he or she is continually confronted:

Shall distribution be through middle men or direct to buyers? Shall the emphasis be on new business or maintaining and developing present customers—or both?

What is the potential market for the product or service? What is a reasonable sales forecast for the periods ahead? What is the company's main sales goal—more volume, a bigger share of the market, greater profits? What size sales staff is needed to meet the forecast and achieve the company's sales goals? What budget is needed to carry out the sales task? Is top management aware that the payout for some investments in the sales function may be several years ahead?

What advertising and sales promotion support are needed? Are those responsible for those functions kept informed of the changing nature and needs of the market as seen from the field?

What arrangements have been made for recruiting and interviewing new salesmen? Have minimum requirements been established for recruits? Are aptitude tests to be used in the selection process? Have accurate job descriptions been put on paper?

What sort of training, and how much, will be given? Does selling your product or service require only a short training period (as in the case of some consumer goods items) or a more extended period (as is common with technical industrial products)? Has a program of continuous training been organized, usually through sales meetings, pesonal conferences, special seminars, sales staff bulletins and the like?

Have territories been assigned that will be fair to the salesmen and adequate to get the job done? Have supervisors and regional managers been selected and trained to control local selling activities? Have call frequencies been established for classes of customers or specific accounts? Have quotas been determined for each division, territory, and salesman, and have those affected been involved in setting up those quotas?

Has a system of rating activities of salespeople been set up, with written reports indicating sales performance in relation to quota, number of calls made, number of sales in relation to number of calls, average size of orders received, travel and entertainment expenses incurred, and other details considered important to the particular type of selling? Is a computer being used to assimilate this information quickly, pinpoint trouble spots, and give the district managers and salespersons prompt feedback?

Has a compensation and incentive program been created that is fair and that really motivates? Shall it be straight commission, salary, salary plus commission or bonus, or a combination? Shall it be based on sales volume, gross profit, or sales in excess of quota? For better control, should there be different rates of commission or bonus to encourage the selling of certain more profitable or slower-moving items or to get more action on preferred classes of accounts? How much leeway will be allowed the salesman in cutting prices and should there be a bonus for selling at the regular price? To what extent will sales contests be used, when will they be used, and what will be the method of scoring and the prizes?

Has the competition been studied to see how your benefits, prices and sales methods compare and how you might meet or beat them?

The above are some of the questions that most sales managers must consider and answer to do an effective job. Considering the importance and growing complexity of the task, it is no wonder that the sales manager must have a special kind of organizing and managerial talent. No longer can the top salesman be rewarded by promotion to management if he or she does not have these talents. To do that is often to lose a good salesman and acquire a poor sales manager.

HARRY R. WHITE, formerly Executive Director, Sales Executives Club of New York, New York

Information References

Associations:

National Society of Sales Training Executives.
Sales and Marketing Executives International.

Periodicals:

Industrial Marketing.
Journal of Marketing.
Sales and Marketing Management.

Texts:

Buell, V.P. and Heyel, C., eds, "Handbook of Modern Marketing," New York, McGraw-Hill, 1970.
Hartley, Robert F., "Sales Management," New York, Houghton-Mifflin, 1979.
Jolson, Marvin A., "Contemporary Readings in Sales Management," New York, Van Nostrand Reinhold, 1977.
Jolson, Marvin A., "Sales Management: A Tactical Approach," New York, Van Nostrand Reinhold, 1977.

Cross References: *Marketing (and cross references there given).*

SALES PROMOTION

Sales Promotion used to be considered an inconsequential branch of advertising, and few organizations attempted to distinguish between the two. Sales promotion was perceived as something for "emergencies only." This mistaken notion still persists among those who refer to sales promotion as "gimmickry." That so much unclarity exists concerning the subject is mainy because it so often functions as a "catchall" promotion tool.

Definition. Many marketers perceive sales promotion as everything within the realm of promotion that is not clearly identifiable as either advertising, publicity, or personal selling. This negative approach "by default" can easily be detected in the formal definition of sales promotion as offered by the Definitions Committee of the American Marketing Association [1]: "those marketing activities other than personal selling, advertising, and publicity that stimulate consumer purchasing and dealer effectiveness, such as display, shows and distribution, demonstrations and various non-recurrent selling efforts not in the ordinary routine." Besides showing a lack of consideration for the broad area of non-profit marketing, which also uses sales promotion, albeit so far only in limited form, the American Marketing Association definition does not really clarify what sales promotion is. A definition which takes a positive approach and which also clearly states its nature is the one proposed by Runyon [2]. Sales promotion is: (1) A relatively short-term activity. (2) Directed towards the sales force, distribution channels, or consumers, or towards some combination of these groups. (3) Used in order to stimulate some specific action.

This conceptualization also clearly deals with sales promotion as encompassing a wide variety of promotional tools of a strategic type, with short term incentive objectives. These objectives are also specific in nature (e.g., a stronger initial target market response).

Types of Sales Promotion Audiences. The promotional tools can be differentiated according to the specific type of audience considered. Thus:

(1) *Sales Force Promotions.* There is some controversy with respect to promotions directed to the company sales force, questioning whether it is acceptable to consider promotions aimed at generating motivation among salespeople as part of sales promotion. Yet when promotion involves short-term incentives in which sales personnel are motivated and stimulated to do a better job of contacting consumers it is clearly a case of sales promotion. To this end, the promo-tools to be considered include the following:

(a) *Sales meetings* to present to the salesforce new products, marketing strategies, and sales stimulation.

(b) *Sales manuals and portfolios* to provide sales personnel with the necessary data and references when making presentations. They allow for a better understanding of the company's products and also help emphasize important sales points.

(c) *Product models* to help in the presentation of the products to prospective clients. Scale models are easily carried to a sales call and they are often supplemented if not supplanted by color slides or video films, the latter especially if the product has to be shown in use.

(d) *Special Rewards* offered for achieving sales volume goals, as well as gaining special in-store displays or getting cooperative advertising support.

(2) *Promotions to the Trade.* When distributors and dealers are in the producer's channel of distribution, they should be receiving promotional aid. Quite often this takes the form of special promo-tools which are part of the manufacturer's sales promotion. To be considered here are:

(a) *Stocking allowances,* among the most often used promotion devices. This short-term inducement gives a retailer an allowance for each case on initial orders or on all orders for a specified period of time (e.g., a month). *Loading* is the term employed to refer to allowances used to increase inventories of products already stocked.

(b) *Consignment selling,* when possession but not ownership is given to distributors. This hidden form of financing dealers is a clear sales promotion tactic when it is used to gain new distribution outlets.

(c) *Retailer contests,* similar to the special rewards offered to company sales personnel, except that in this case the incentive and prizes are awarded by the manufacturer to sales personnel belonging to distributors and dealers.

(d) *Retail training,* such as sales seminars held for retail sales personnel in order to provide them with technical product information as well as suggestions concerning sales techniques.

(e) *Push money (PM),* involving paying sales personnel a bonus (or commissions) to "push" a particular brand.

(f) *Cooperative advertising,* considered part of the sales promotion effort when it is a clear case of a short-term stimulation of sales to be achieved by having manufacturer and distributor share the advertising costs.

(g) *Dealer-listed promotion,* a special form of cooperative advertising when the manufacturer's promotion mentions the distributor.

(h) *Merchandising the advertising,* a special form of sales promotion which involves the selling of the promotional activities conducted by the manufacturers to channel intermediaries. This includes presentation of the promotional plans of the manufacturer and the delivery of merchandising kits (clear summaries of the planned strategies, including, for example, story-boards of product commercials). This is done to bring about enthusiasm for the producer's promotional activities.

(i) *Point-of-purchase (P.O.P.) displays,* to be used in the retailer's stores. These include items such as counter top racks, posters, displays, and mechanized stands.

(j) *Nonbranded promotions,* consisting of a wide variety of free nonidentified promotional material offered by the manufacturer to establish a good relationship with the retailer. This nonidentified promotional material consists of items to decorate the retailer's store, and includes items such as window signs, display cards, price stickers, and seasonally themed store decorations.

(k) *Trade shows and exhibits* which allow the manufacturers to display their products. Several thousand trade shows, conventions and expositions take place annually and they provide a great opportunity to demonstrate new products and develop a relationship with prospective buyers. (See TRADE SHOWS AND EXHIBITS.)

(3) *Consumer Promotions.* Consumer promotions are primarily used to (1) attract new consumers, and (2) increase the consumption by old consumers. Additionally, consumer promotions serve to generate an aura of excitement and enthusiasm around the products, and also help to lower inventory levels. Special promotools used in consumer promotions are:

(a) *Product samples,* which help to induce trial of products by the consumer. This is an expensive form of sales promotion, but it is of tremendous value especially in the case of new products if the product sampled is clearly superior to competitive products of a relevant dimension.

(b) *Coupons and price-off offers,* enabling the manufacturer of new products to propose an inducement to trial as well as a temporary price reduction which does not lower the perceived quality of the product. Couponing has become big business in the United States. The claim has been made that the usage of cut-out coupons in this country has increased from 20.3 billion in 1972 to 60 billion in 1977 (in other words, approximately 280 coupons for every man, woman and child in the United States) [3].

(c) *Premiums,* merchandise offered free as a gift or at low cost as an award to purchasers of specific products. The three major types of premiums are: In-pack (premium enclosed in package), Near-pack (item can be picked up at the dealer's location), and Mail-in. The latter requires the consumer to send in a request and proof of purchase.

(d) *Combination offers,* a special kind of premium which involves the offer to consumers that upon purchase of product X they can get product Y free or at a greatly reduced price.

(e) *Trading stamps,* a bonus given for the purchase from a particular retail outlet. Trading stamps collected by a consumer may be redeemed for merchandise by catalog or through special redemption centers.

(f) *Contests,* involving the consumer's competing for prizes on the basis of some skill displayed by the entrant (i.e. writing a jingle).

(g) *Sweepstakes,* differing from contests primarily in the way they are used to award prizes. In sweepstakes, entrants are awarded prizes purely by chance, requiring only the submission of the consumer's name on the proper form. By law, all prizes *offered* on both contests and sweepstakes must be *awarded.* The main point to be considered by the manufacturer is to avoid having the contest or sweepstake considered as a lottery since that would be illegal.

(h) *In-Store demonstrations,* a high-cost sales promotion tool which allows the demonstration of the product in the presence of consumers. In-store demonstrations also provide a good environment to supply consumers with samples. Overall, they can be considered a sampling device.

(i) *Brochures and leaflets,* to supplement the sampling notion. They are often considered as advertising, and would probably classify as sales promotion especially in those cases when they point out sales which are in effect for short periods of time.

Applications. Sales promotion, as can be seen from the forgoing, is quite diverse and complex. It lends itself particularly well to breaking through buyer inertia, especially where consumers are economy minded. In the main, its intentions are short-term and limited in objective. Sales promotion provides supplements to the other components (advertising, publicity, and personal selling) of promotion and can be seen as providing the connecting factor with the other components of the marketing mix (product, distribution, and price).

Expenditures for sales promotion have followed a rising pattern, and some experts even estimate these expenditures to have been over $30 billion in 1976 [4]. This indicates that sales promotion has come of age and should be considered seriously. Nonetheless, research in this area is still relatively rare, especially in regrd to the evaluation in terms of profitability. This again is probably because of its limited nature as a supplementary marketing activity, which has not been sufficiently recognized as distinct from other forms of promotion.

BENNY BARAK, PH.D., Assistant Professor of Marketing, Baruch College, City University of New York, New York, New York

Information References

Associations:

Direct Mail Advertising Association
Marketing Communications Executives International (formerly Sales Promotion Executives Association)
Point-of-Purchase Advertising Institute
Premium Advertising Association of America
Trading Stamp Institute of America

Texts:

Enis, B.M., "Marketing Principles," 3rd ed., Santa Monica, Calif., Goodyear Publishing Co., 1980.

Kotler, P., "Marketing Management," Analysis, Planning and Control, 4th ed., Englewood Cliffs, N.J., Prentice Hall, 1980.

Luick, J.F. and Ziegler, W.L., Sales Promotion and Modern Merchandising," New York, McGraw-Hill, 1968.

Mandell, M.I., "Advertising," 3rd ed., Englewood Cliffs, N.J., Prentice Hall, 1980.

Nickels, W.G., "Marketing, Communication and Promotion," 2nd ed., Columbus, Ohio: Griel Publishing, 1980.

Runyon, K.E., "Advertising and the Practice of Marketing," Columbus, Ohio: Charles E. Merrill, 1980.

Stanley, R.E., "Promotion, Advertising, Publicity, Personal selling, sales promotion," Englewood Cliffs, N.J., Prentice Hall, 1977.

References Cited

[1] Committee on Definition, "Marketing Definitions: A Glossary of Marketing Terms," Chicago, American Marketing Association, 1060, p. 20.

[2] Runyon, K.E., "Advertising and the Practice of Marketing," Columbus, Ohio: Charles E. Merrill, 1980, p. 363.

[3] Haugh, L.J., "New Marketing Woe; It's Coupon Clutter", *Advertising Age,* December 26, 1977, p. 1.

[4] Strang, R.A., "Sales Promotion—Fast Growth, Faulty Management", *Harvard Business Review,* July-Augut, 1976, p. 115-124.

Cross References: *Marketing; Sales Management; Trade Shows and Exhibits.*

SALES STATISTICS

Sales Statistics denotes that branch of business statistics concerned with the statistical problems of the collection, analysis, and presentation of sales data. It is characterized by the area of application rather than type of statistics, primarily with regard to volume-cost-price relationships (see COST-VOLUME-PROFIT ANALYSIS), and the four dimensions of sales volume: *actual, future, potential,* and *desirable* sales.

The application of statistical methods to actual sales is often called *sales analysis* in a narrow sense of the term. Statistical methods employed in the problem of future sales involve *sales forecasting.* Possible sales on a geographic basis are measured by *geographic sales potentials.* Desirable sales find their expression in *sales quotas.* Some of these terms are used interchangeably, a practice which hampers precise communications on the subject. The four dimensions are distinct concepts.

Actual sales are the observed sales, and their study has aptly been called "anatomy of sales." They are the only one of the four dimensions referring to the past, and involve observed rather than computed data.

Future sales estimates are obtained basically by statistical forecasting and usually modified by nonstatistical considerations. The distinction is emphasized in the development of mathematical models and techniques. A sales forecast represents the expected sales of a specific product or service to a specific consumer group over a specified period of time. It is realistic.

Sales potential represents the maximum sales a company could achieve for the sales of a specific product or service to a specific consumer group over a specified period of time if the firm performs optimally. Sales potential defines the upper limit for a company if it maximizes advertising, production, and other factors. It is rarely achieved.

A useful distinction is one between geographic sales potentials and aggregate sales potentials. The territorial distribution of potential sales, once these have been determined on a national basis, is commonly considered part of sales statistics. Basic estimates of total "size of market" are usually considered a function of market research. Possible sales may be reflected in geographic sales potentials merely as an abstract measurement without a dollar value necessarily attached. For example, the geographic sales potential in a district may be 3% of the possible sales of a product in the entire United States.

Desirable sales are sales goals. Their quantitative expression is the sales quota, which is not always a statistical measure. Although sales statistics and their interpretation are an important aid, the goals themselves are a decision by management, taking into account all pertinent factors.

The four dimensions of sales volume may differ from one another. The actually achieved sales of a product may be exceeded by the sales anticipated for the next year which, however, may not completely realize the sales opportunities. The sales goal, reflecting management policy, takes the other three dimensions into consideration.

Scope and Organization. Sales statistics is concerned with sales transactions and closely related items, e.g., orders, returns, and salesmen's calls. The scope of sales statistics is usually restricted to the sales of a company or its sub-divisions. However, nondirect sales of a company's products, such as those by a retail customer to the consumer, are often also included. There are substantial variations between companies regarding the "sophistication" of statistical sales analysis, depending upon the type and size of the firm. Problems of sales statistics, differ somewhat for manufacturing, wholesaling, and retailing firms, and for consumer-goods and industrial-goods manufacturing, because of differences in amounts, types, ease of availability, and predictability of data. Some industries, such as department-store retailing, steel, paper manufacturing, and others are reported upon in great detail in regularly appearing trade-association and governmental reports. In others, the bases for industry comparisons are difficult to ascertain precisely.

The place of sales statistics in the firm's organization varies. Typically, statistical activities having to do with sales are carried on in several departments, such as Marketing Research, Accounting, and Sales. These groups must thus often collaborate, for example in the analysis of distribution costs. However, sales statistics as a recognized, separate function is in most cases "housed" in the Marketing Department, as a unit of the Sales Department (where the organizational form has a broad marketing function overseeing sales, sales promotion, market research, and related activities); in some cases it is a unit of the Market Research Department. In any case, its function is to supply information and interpretations for marketing management, identifying problems for further marketing research, and sometimes serving management outside the marketing area, e.g., in production and finance.

Techniques. Most techniques in use may be characterized as descriptive statistics of an elementary nature. Electronic data processing has brought the use of some hitherto tedious statistical methods into the realm of practicality, making it possible to process large masses of sales data in a short time, with great accuracy. Electronic tape techniques and advanced card methods make possible many groupings of data with great flexibility. Nonroutine analysis of sales data is greatly facilitated. See ELECTRONIC DATA PROCESSING.)

In the *collection* of sales information, sales statisticians contribute the planning and design for complete enumerations and for samples. Statistical considerations must enter into the scientific selection of sample records for detailed study and into sample surveys to obtain information on buying patterns and expectations. Useful preliminary data are available through the annual "Survey of Buying Power" by *Sales & Marketing Management, Editor & Publisher Market Guide,* trade publications, and government documents. Internal company records also provide excellent information on sales, customers, product lines, etc. Sales personnel provide an important link with the market.

The *analysis* of sales involves comparisons, establishing relations, and providing estimates of future or theoretical sales. The following procedures are frequently employed: classification of sales by relevant characteristics, as well as cross-classification and summarization, by averages or indexes, with the determination of trends and the removal of the effects of seasonality. Statistical techniques involved are:

- *Simple trend analysis,* which graphically plots the evolution of sales over time.
- *Market share analysis,* which examines the company's sales relative to competition.
- *Jury of company executive opinion,* whereby managers assess sales data based on their expertise and experience.
- *Sales-force surveys,* whereby consumer research is conducted and analyzed. (See also CONSUMER BEHAVIOR RESEARCH and MARKETING RESEARCH.)
- *Chain-ratio method,* with which sales potential is estimated by weighting a series of general and specific market factors.
- *Market build-up method,* with which sales potential is estimated by aggregating data from several small, separate market areas.
- *Index of buying power,* a measure showing purchasing power in given markets. (See INDEX OF BUYING POWER.)
- *Simulation,* whereby sales data are entered into a computer-based model under varying market conditions, and outcomes are then evaluated. (See SALES STATISTICS: Case Example.)
- *Complex trend analysis (time-series analysis),* a sophisticated method that examines the evolution of sales, and takes into account sales fluctuations and cyclical factors. (See BUSINESS FORECASTING.)
- *Regression and correlation,* which explore the mathematical relationships between sales and market factors. (See STATISTICS.)

In addition, sales ratios comparing sales with various items in the balance sheet are widely used. Indexes, usually expressed in percents, are often compiled. Frequency distributions are important tools, in their simple as well as cumulative form. Their representation by summary expressions, especially averages and measures of dispersion, is widely used in sales statistics. In time series analysis, electronic computers have found fruitful application, especially for the analysis of seasonal patterns and for sales forecasting.

Some specialized techniques have been developed recently, which have proven useful in sales statistics. For example, "exponential smoothing" a special kind of weighted moving average useful in scientific inventory control, is a valuable aid in sales forecasting. The "principal component" analysis, which is similar to factor analysis, is an effective method of computing geographic sales potentials.

Where appropriate, sales statisticians will estimate the error involved in making generalizations from samples, and will test the statistical significance of observed differences in survey and test results.

OPERATIONS RESEARCH has brought some of its techniques to statistical problems in sales analysis. For example:

- *Allocation models* may be used for developing territories and assigning sales personnel.
- *Competitive strategy models* may be used to anticipate reactions to changes in selling tactics.
- *Critical path models* may be used in coordinating the components of team selling for complex, expensive items. (See CRITICAL PATH METHOD (CPM) and INTEGRATED PROJECT MANAGEMENT.)
- *Queueing models* may be used to determine the proper size of the sales force during peak periods. (See WAITING LINE THEORY (QUEUEING THEORY.)
- *Linear Programming* may be used to determine the best mix of selling and advertising expenditures. (See also OPERATIONS RESEARCH IN MARKETING DECISIONS.)

Applications of Sales Statistics. The following four examples show how sales statistics may be utilized:

(1) The product mix is to be compared in terms of the sales of individual salesmen. *Percentaging* is used to relate each man's sales of a product to his entire sales during a given time period. Thus, the sales of a certain product may constitute 8% of one salesman's sales and 12% of another's. Generally, the importance of each product for each salesman is ascertained. Or, the importance of each salesman in the results of each product may be shown. Thus, the sales of one salesman may constitute 2% of one product's sales, and that of another, 3%. The effectiveness of this type of analysis is illustrated by the case example following this entry.

(2) The invoice size is to be studied, and regional differences are to be observed. *Frequency distributions* of invoice size are obtained for one class of customers, separately for each sales region. A computation of the mean invoice size may reveal that it is $50 in one region, and $30 in another. Since there are often a few very large invoices, a *median* invoice size is ascertained, which is not affected by extreme values. The uniformity of invoice values in the various regions may be compared through a measure of dispersion, such as the *standard deviation* (see STATISTICS). Finally, the proportion of small invoices may be ascertained and compared in the various regions.

(3) The growth pattern of a company's sales is to be investigated. The decision as to the most appropriate way to *fit a trend line* to the historical sales data is made by the sales statistician. Trends, seasonal variations, and long-term cyclical variations, determined from past data, must then be interpreted in terms of foreseeable economic factors and special sales, merchandising, and advertising pressures to determine projections, yielding a long-range sales forecast as a benchmark for short-range projections.

(4) Various determinants of sales are to be studied to establish their relative importance. *Partial correlation* is applied to provide an estimate. Data such as population, income, and number of outlets by state are correlated with sales per state. The influence upon sales of each of these determinants separately may be obtained, while allowing for the fact that the other determinants are also operative.

Acceptance. A large percentage of companies perform most of the major sales statistics activities here discussed, although with varying degrees of statistical sophistication. Despite this broad acceptance, sales statistics has achieved only limited recognition as a professional field.

JOEL R. EVANS, PH.D., Chairman, Marketing and International Business Departments, Hofstra University, Hempstead, New York

BARRY BERMAN, PH.D., Professor of Marketing, Hofstra University, Hempstead, New York

Information References

Gross, C. and Peters, R., "Business Forecasting," Boston, Houghton-Mifflin, 1976.

Kotler, P., "From Sales Obsession to Marketing Effectiveness," *Harvard Business Review,* November–December 1977.
Stanton, F. and Buskirk, R., "Management of the Sales Force," 5th ed., Homewood, Ill, Irwin, 1978.
Articles in *Sales and Marketing Management.*

Cross References: *Marketing Research; Operations Research in Marketing Decisions; Sales Management.*

SALES TRAINING

Sales Training becomes more and more an essential tool of sales management because of the changing nature of selling, which is shifting from mere product or service selling to the study and satisfaction of customer's needs. Added to that are the growing pressures of competition, which require that every salesman, from cub to veteran, continually be brought up to date on new market conditions, rehearsed in productive selling methods, and inspired to meet or beat quota.

But there are two more reasons why sales training is growing in importance. One is the ever-escalating cost of recruiting, equipping, and supervising a salesman before he or she becomes productive—estimated by *Sales & Marketing Management* in 1979 to be $19,025 for industrial products, $13,173 for consumer products, and $9,918 for service companies (and that does not include the cost of recruiting and interviewing). The other reason is the risk a company takes by exposing a recruit to prospects and customers before he or she is ready, endangering the company's competitive image and undermining the morale of other salespeople on the staff.

Traditionally, sales training consisted of studying the product and its merits, reading a book on how to sell, and getting some coaching from the sales manager or supervisor in the field. In many small firms, this is still the way it is done. But in larger and more progressive companies, the emphasis is on a more formal and scientific approach, with psychological and technical training, practice selling under simulated conditions, and continuing appraisal of training results.

Perhaps in no other field of business administration is there such a welter of "new" techniques, courses, outside services, and bulletins. This is because even a small increase in the productivity of each salesman can sometimes spell the difference between profit and loss, so that sales managers are ever on the lookout for ways to get their salesmen to "sell smarter." But there are two basic principles of sales training that never change: (1) it must follow the classic method of teaching, testing, and grading; and (2) the training program must be continuous. Many companies now prefer that sales recruits have a college degree because they are considered more receptive to the disciplines of learning.

The more sophisticated training programs have these features:

(1) A customer-oriented approach to the learning process rather than the old system of rules and rote that spawned the "canned" presentations.

(2) Division of trainees into small groups to encourage active participation and independent thinking.

(3) Simulation of selling encounters with coaching, role-playing, and sometimes videotaping, so that the trainees can observe and correct their faults.

(4) Frequent use of such teaching materials as programmed instruction, by use of which the trainee must master each step before going on to the next (see TEACHING MACHINES, PROGRAMMED INSTRUCTION, AND COMPUTER-AIDED INSTRUCTION); games, often with computer assistance to show quickly the results of decisions (see MANAGEMENT GAMES); and sales films and bulletins available from numerous consulting and service organizations.

One relatively new development in sales training is instruction in the art of listening. Most salesmen are by nature talkative and inclined to dominate the sales interview, with the result that they often miss the prospect's real objections, buying motives, and needs. Training them to "shut up and listen" is no easy task, but it is being done with gratifying results.

Another recent development is training in the use of the telephone as a sales tool. With the cost of a sales call continuing to soar skyward in recent years, the telephone can be used more effectively to make and confirm appointments, reducing travel and waiting time. It can also be used as the primary selling tool, especially with smaller accounts. Some companies have achieved marked success in selling *only* by telephone. Courses and materials on telephone selling are available from the Long Lines Division of American Telephone & Telegraph Co.

Who does the training? In small companies, it is the sales manager. Large companies usually have sales training specialists to do the job of teaching company policies and procedures, product knowledge, selling methods, territory orientation, and work organization. Formal training is usually done at company headquarters or in a hotel or training facility where trainees can better concentrate. Training in the field is generally done by the branch managers, who occasionally accompany the salesmen on regular calls and give them "curb-side" advice, but never interfering with the salesman's presentation in the presence of the prospect unless absolutely necessary.

Before organizing a sales training program, it is wise to make a survey of the sales force to find out any weak areas. Are these product knowledge, mastery of selling techniques, use of time on the job, knowledge of company advertising and promotions, how to keep records? This review should be done at least once a year, so that sales management may know what areas to emphasize in its training. The review can be by the sales manager in smaller companies, or by field managers or outside consulting firms in larger companies.

There is one more rule that every successful sales trainer keeps in mind: Conduct the training program for a profit-oriented reason—to lower selling costs, raise sales volume, reduce expenses, get more active accounts, reduce salesman turnover. This not only keeps the training on target but is impressive to top management if the value received for money spent on training should come up for question.

HARRY R. WHITE, formerly Executive Director, Sales Executives Club of New York, New York

Information References

Associations:

American Society of Training Directors.
National Society of Sales Training Executives.
Sales and Marketing Executives International.

Periodicals:

Industrial Marketing.
Journal of Marketing (American Marketing Association).
Sales and Marketing Management.

Texts:

Buell, V.P. and Heyel, Carl, eds., "Handbook of Modern Marketing," New York, McGraw-Hill, 1970.
"The Sales Manager as a Trainer," Orlando, Fla., National Society of Sales Training Executives, 1977.
Smith, Homer, "Salesman's Guide to More Effective Selling," New York, *Sales and Marketing Management,* 1979.

Cross Reference: *Sales Management.*

SCANLON PLAN OF GROUP INCENTIVES

The Scanlon Plan is a system of group incentives on a company-wide or plant-wide basis, now in current use in a number of small to medium-sized companies. It was originally conceived by the late Joseph N. Scanlon of the Massachusetts Institute of Technology, who prior to joining MIT's faculty in 1946 was an official of the United Steelworkers of America. After his death in 1956, his work was carried on at MIT by his close colleague and friend, Frederick G. Lesieur. Lesieur had been the local president of the union at Lapointe Machine Tool Company, and came to MIT to work with Scanlon, remaining until 1962.

Universal Standards. The Scanlon Plan meets the problem of universal standards by setting up one measure that reflects the results of all efforts. This measure is the sales value of a company's production. In effect, the plan says that if production sales values are increased with no change in labor costs, productivity rises and unit costs are lowered. The universal standard, then, is the ratio of labor costs to sales value added by production.

A feature of the Scanlon Plan is the use of historical data on labor costs and production sales values to determine this standard. A labor cost "norm" is computed according to past accounting records, and a formula is devised for giving employees the benefit of anything saved under the norm. The overall company performance is considered in computing the norm, which is expressed as a ratio between output—units, dozens, ounces, pounds, tons, or dollars of sales value—and the cost of the output in terms of wages and salaries paid. The ratio may be computed as an average, taking into account factors such as vacations, seasonal fluctuations in demand, and price fluctuations.

How this works can be seen in the case of a company producing $200,000 worth of goods during each month. According to past accounting records, the average paid in wages and salaries to produce the goods equals $60,000. This ratio becomes the norm. During another month, following the installation of the Scanlon Plan, the company produces $235,000 worth of goods with the wage and salary bill not exceeding the $60,000 figure. The extra

$35,000 in production, less material and other costs, is distributed, in part, on a prorated basis to employees covered by the plan.

Once the relationship between total payroll and the sales value produced by it is established, a bonus pool is created for any month when labor costs are below the norm. To protect against deficit months, a reserve of 25% is set aside from the pool. If anything is left in this reserve at the end of the year, an extra payment is made. After the reserve has been taken out for a given month, the balance of the bonus is split, with 25% usually going to the company and the remaining 75% to employees.

A majority if not all employees on direct and indirect labor may participate in a Scanlon Plan. Even nonexempt white collar employees are included in some plans. And a few companies extend participation to exempt supervisors and executives.

Proponents of individual and small-group incentives say such "universal treatment" is unfair to individual employees. They feel individual performance is diluted or lost sight of in the large group and therefor all covered employees are treated no better or worse than the "group average." Perhaps more importantly, many professional industrial engineers who advocate individual incentive plans contend that by use of plans such as the Scanlon, *management control* is in large measure relinquished. They particularly take issue with group plans that allow employees to set their own pace, "police themselves," and to share on a broad over-all basis in savings in manufacturing costs over some "historical normal" labor cost. Their objection is that management is simply abdicating its right and duty to manage. They support this view on three grounds: (1) a so-called "historical norm" will in all likelihood be far above what would reasonably be established by sound engineering studies; (2) much of the gain over the norm is frequently due not to employee effort but rather to improvements in methods and technology, the effects of which may not be allowed for at all under the plan, or if so, by a formulation which is far from precise; and (3)—growing out of (2)—such plans too often share increases in productivity with labor that to a significant degree should rightfully accrue to the consumer.

However, advocates of the Scanlon Plan and other types of large-group incentive plans favor the idea since it embodies a cooperative goal: to receive their incentive pay, employees work for the good of the whole group. The proponents of the plan believe the company's total production is the result of group action and the coordination of efforts and interests of all employees, rather than the efforts of just a selected few.

CARL HEYEL, Management Counsel, Manhasset, New York.

Cross References: *Guaranteed Annual Wage; Incentive Systems; Lincoln Incentive Management Plan; Profit Sharing; Rucker Plan of Group Incentives; Standard Minute System.*

SCIENTIFIC MANAGEMENT

The title "Father of Scientific Management" has been bestowed affectionately upon Frederick W. Taylor, and has been inscribed on his tombstone. However, he was not present when the term **Scientific Management** was coined by Louis D. Brandeis at a meeting of engineers in the home of H. L. Gantt in October, 1910. Shortly thereafter, Brandeis used the term in his brief as counsel for the Traffic Committee of the Trade Organizations of the Atlantic Seaboard. The occasion was the famous Eastern Rate Case hearings before the Interstate Commerce Commission, and Brandeis seized upon "Scientific Management" as the clearest and most effective expression to describe the heart of the case he wished to present. The Eastern railroads had raised wages that spring, and had petitioned the Interstate Commerce Commission for a general advance in freight rates. They were vehemently opposed by the shippers affected.

"Scientific management" received tremendous publicity in the newspapers and magazines as a result of the testimonies given in the hearings during 1910–11, and in the subsequent hearings, before the Special Committee of the House of Representatives in 1912. As counsel for the shippers, Brandeis produced eleven engineers as witnesses, who testified that it was possible to raise wages and at the same time reduce costs in railroad operations through the practices of this new set of philosophies and techniques. One witness, Harrington Emerson, gave as his estimate that $300,000,000 a year, or $1,000,000 a day could be saved in this way. He successfully demonstrated how he had arrived at his conclusions, and it was his testimony that made the headlines.

The management concepts and practices which the engineers had innovated and introduced had previously been identified by several different names, such as "efficiency engineering," "rationalism," "Taylorism," and "the science of management." *Scientific Management,* however, became the accepted term which identified the new concept of management in the MANAGEMENT MOVEMENT, and which distinguished the progressive management practices from the traditional practices known as "conventional management," or "systematic management."

Climate for Scientific Management. Management thought and practices underwent some revolutionary developments early in the twentieth century, as the influences of the management movement began to penetrate the growing economy. In 1900, the national population consisted of almost 76 million people of whom around 27 million made up the work force. In industry, the work week averaged over sixty hours. Both the population and the work force had been expanding rapidly. An increasing domestic market resulted from the growing population. Factories grew into large-scale enterprises which decentralized their operations and diversified their products. As the basic industries expanded, the communication and transportation systems developed throughout the nation. The innovators, the scientists, and the engineers had made important technological contributions to the economy. The economic climate had the factors which could contribute to prosperity and plenty.

However, in spite of the many favorable factors in the environmental situation, the economy suffered from low productivity and low wages. Industrial operations, which were characterized by craft traditions of work, were crude and wasteful in actuality as compared with potential. Employees were used in jobs for which they were poorly prepared or suited. The employers of industrial workers had little knowledge about the effects of fatigue, the sequence of work, and the tempo of work upon employees and their productivity. Little attention was given to the proper methods for establishing the standards or determining the efficiency of operations. The function of management had not developed sufficiently to utilize intelligently the fruits of technology and the available economic factors for the benefits of society.

Genesis of Scientific Management. The practices of so-called *conventional management* and *systematic management* were not adequate for the demands of the changing economic, social, and technological environment after the turn of the century. (The distinguishing feature of *conventional management* is the acceptance of practices already in existence and the choosing, by guess, from among those methods which have been developed by others. *Systematic management* is distinguished by the collection and classification of the records of past practices to determine the relative value of methods of work for choosing the most suitable alternative.)

A few pioneering engineers and industrial managers reacted to the demands of the changing climate and began to inquire about the reasons for inefficiency in the operations of shops, mills, and factories. They began a series of experiments with the hope of finding better methods of employing human effort in manufacturing activities. The scope of the experiments embraced better methods for machining metals, enlightened understanding of the effects of fatigue on human work, and an approach to devising equitable wage systems. These experiments led to scientific methods for determining work standards, for planning work methods, and for establishing control procedures to maintain the standards.

Improved methods were found for establishing the relationships among work assignments, employees with better tools, and the work environment. From the basic experiments in work methods a system of management thought developed which came to be known as scientific management.

Scientific management was conceived and developed as a way of resolving problems which stood in the path of managerial objectives and industrial progress. Its methodology was aimed at the careful investigation of every operating problem in the industrial world in order to determine the best solution or "the one best way." It did not rely merely upon systematic records or upon the judgment of the most experienced manager. It aided and facilitated the work of management with all the resources of science that were known to the pioneering engineers of the time.

In essence, scientific management was distinguished by the application of the scientific methods of research to the managerial problems which were generated by the growing industrial economy. Every possible method of performing work was carefully analyzed and the best elements of all the methods were combined to form a new method in search of "the one best" method. Upon the establishment of the best methods of work, scientific management required that workmen be instructed in how best to perform their tasks, and that they be offered incentives to accomplish their tasks by the methods prescribed.

Scientific Management as a Philosophy and a Process. Scientific management was not an "invention." It was a discovery of the use of the application of the scientific method of attack upon a new set of problems. The concept of scientific management involves a *way of thinking* about management; it entails a *philosophy* which establishes a mental attitude and a logic of effective problem solving for managers of enterprises. The correct concept of scientific management was often misunderstood or misinterpreted when the pioneering engineers and industrial managers were introducing its methods to the industrial world and the public.

On October 12–13–14, 1911, the Amos Tuck School of Administration and Finance at Dartmouth College sponsored the first Conference on Scientific Management "to enable businessmen and manufacturers of New Hampshire and New England to meet the organizing engineers who have applied SCIENTIFIC MANAGEMENT and the manufacturers in whose plants it is in operation, in the hope that they may carry away from the conference an understanding of its principles . . ." Explanations of the concept and principles of scientific management given at that conference are as follows:

Frederick W. Taylor: "I want to tell you as briefly as I can what Scientific Management is. It certainly is not what most people think it to be. It is not a lot of efficiency expedients. It is not the printing and ruling of a lot of pieces of blank paper and spreading them by the ton about the country. It is not any particular system of paying men. It is not a system of figuring costs of manufacture. It is none of the ordinary devices which unfortunately are going by the name of Scientific Management. It may in its essence be said in the present state of industry to involve a complete mental revolution, both on the part of the management and of the men. It is a complete change in the mental attitude of both sides towards their respective duties and towards their opponents. That is what constitutes Scientific Management.

"Let me repeat briefly these four principles of Scientific Management. . . . They are the development of a science to replace the old rule-of-thumb methods; the scientific selection and then the progressive teaching and development of the workmen; the bringing of the scientifically selected workmen and the science together; and then this almost equal division of the work between the management and the men."

Henry L. Gantt: "The high-sounding term Scientific Management should not be allowed to mislead anybody. It is not something that can be bought wholesale and utilized retail, but simply means: Study your problem according to scientific methods, eliminating guess, setting each man a proper task, and allowing suitable rewards for the accomplishment of these tasks. This done, increased efficiency is bound to follow."

Harrington Emerson: "What is the aim of Scientific Management? It is intelligently to use all the available resources and knowledge of the universe in order to realize definite ideals. The ideals are: to use incarnate and uncarnate energy and incarnate intelligence, to decrease toil, to lessen costs that wages and profits may be increased; and so to distribute the loot of uncarnate energy and of the infinite possibilities of incarnate intelligence as to lessen the friction between man and man, thus raising moral, mental and physical standards, but at the same time lessening the destructive strain of living."

These explanations of scientific management all place the emphasis on its concept of mental attitude, and warn against confusing the techniques with the aims.

Taylor spoke out against the prevalent tendency of uninformed people to grasp at some of the techniques which he employed and then expecting the techniques to solve management problems. He complained that many had "mistaken the mechanism for the true essence," and placed heavy emphasis upon the distinction between, as well as the relationship of, the mechanisms and the philosophy of scientific management. He contended that mechanisms "will lead to failure and disaster if accompanied by the wrong spirit of those who are using it."

Although Taylor and his associates thus made much of the primary importance of the underlying philosophy, the augmenting mechanisms and techniques developed revolutionary practices of planning and control based upon measurements of work.

Planning in advance was the essence of scientific management. Planning was separated from performance. Analytical study and preparedness were demanded before the start of operations. Standardized equipment and methods were essential. New relationships between management and workers were created.

Early Work. In determining the best way to perform jobs previously taken for granted under conventional or systematic practices, Taylor and other pioneers used the scientific approach of investigation and experiment. Typical is the early work Taylor did at the Bethlehem Steel Company (1898–1901) to answer the question, "Is there a science of shoveling?" By first selecting two or three first-class shovelers and paying them extra wages for doing reliable work, Taylor found by careful experiment that a first-class man would do his biggest day's work with a shovel of about twenty-one pounds. As a result, some eight to ten different kinds of shovels were provided, each one appropriate for a given type of material, to enable the man to handle an average load of twenty-one pounds—a small shovel for ore, and a large one for ashes.

Similarly, in his early days at the Midvale Steel Company (1878–1890), Taylor undertook his classic experiments on cutting metals. Using a skilled worker, he studied every conceivable variation in the operation of a particular machine—belting, shafting, tools, speeds, materials, methods, motions, etc. His objective was the combination that would permit best use of existing facilities.

Unit time study, an important Taylor development, was applied to industries other than metalworking and became the basis for all planning and scheduling, leading to better methods of inventory control, functional control, scientific cost accounting, production control, and quality control. Later came micromotion study, now a widely accepted tool of modern industrial engineering.

Classic examples of the results of applying motion and time measurement in the early stages of scientific management are:

(1) The performance of the individual worker increased from 12½ to 47 tons per day in the simple operation of hand-loading a railroad car with pig iron.

(2) The performance of bricklayers increased from 1,000 to 2,700 bricks laid per day.

(3) Increases in production of certain operations of machine shop work ranged from 400% to 1,800%.

(4) In the shovelling of coal, workers' performance doubled and sometimes trebled.

(5) The output in the manufacture of cotton goods increased 100%.

These demonstrations of the advantages of scientific management to workers, managers, and the public gradually brought about the acceptance of its principles and methods.

Sound work procedures, techniques, and management-worker organizational relationships developed from the underlying principles and philosophy. These were described by Taylor, Gantt, and Barth in papers before the American Society of Mechanical Engineers as follows:

(1) The task idea in management with a bonus for successful achievement of the task.

(2) The management function of planning.

(3) Time study under standard conditions and methods for setting time standards of work.

(4) Standardization of tools and implements used on the job.

(5) Motion study for standardizing the acts and movements of workers for each class of work.

(6) Instruction cards for workmen.

(7) The "differential rate" for piece work.

(8) Modern cost estimating and accounting.

(9) Routing systems for the movement of work in process.

(10) Slide rules and other time-saving implements.

(11) Visual techniques for the planning and control of work such as GANTT CHARTS, flow charts, and assembly sequence diagrams.

(12) Mnemonic systems for classifying manufactured products.

These applications of scientific management were designed to increase productivity through the elimination of waste and inefficiency. The savings realized were to be distributed among all concerned under its philosophy so as to soften the struggle for existence by improving the productivity and increasing the happiness of workers.

Scope and Concepts of Scientific Management. The founders and developers of scientific management not only revolutionized management thought and practice, but also contributed a body of knowledge in their publications. Representative basic published work may be summarized as follows:

(1) Frederick W. Taylor's major publications are "A Piece Rate System" (1895); "Shop Management," (1903); "On the Art of Cutting Metals" (1906); and "The Principles of Scientific Management" (1911). "Shop Management" is an expansion of his earlier paper on piece rates. The emphasis is on the importance of "the coupling of high wages for the workman with low labor cost for the employer" and the resulting public benefits from lower prices. The following principles are listed as guides for the best type of management:

(a) *A Large Daily Task.* Each man in the establishment, high or low, should daily have a clearly defined task laid out before him.

(b) *Standard Conditions.* The workman should be given such standardized conditions and appliances as will enable him to accomplish his task with certainty.

(c) *High Pay for Success.* The workman should be sure of high pay when he accomplishes his task.

(d) *Loss in Case of Failure.* When the workman fails he should be sure that sooner or later he will be the loser for it.

"The Principles of Scientific Management" in a slightly different way develops the same ideas. In the later book, Taylor lists the new duties for management as:

First—The development of a true science.

Second—The scientific selection of workmen.

Third—His scientific education and development.

Fourth—Intimate friendly cooperation between management and the men.

(2) Harrington Emerson's major publications are "Efficiency as a Basis for Operation and Wages" (1911), and "The Twelve Principles of Efficiency" (1913). The major portion of his latter book is devoted to a description and illustration of his principles of efficiency which are: (a) a clearly defined ideal; (b) common sense; (c) competent counsel; (d) discipline; (e) the fair deal; (f) reliable, immediate, adequate, and permanent records; (g) dispatching; (h) standards and schedules; (i) standardized conditions; (j) standardized operations; (k) written standard-practice instructions; (l) efficiency reward.

(3) Henry L. Gantt's major publications are: "Work, Wages and Profits" (1911); "Industrial Leadership" (1916); and "Organizing for Work" (1919).

A selection of some of the most lasting and useful contributions to management thought from Gantt are:

(a) *Man is Goal Oriented.* The most effective method of stimulating interest in people in general is to set a task, an objective. This concept provided the basis for his task and bonus plan.

(b) *Training Is the Responsibility of Management.* It is management's responsibility because it can increase productivity.

(c) *Task Setting Is Essential.* It is superior to driving or urging men to more strenuous toil without any well measured standards of how much work is reasonable under the conditions present.

(d) *Authority and Responsibility.* The *authority* to issue an order involves the *responsibility* of seeing that it is properly executed.

(e) *Planning and Control.* These provide proper methods, and proper results will follow proper methods. Fact must be substituted for opinion. This concept is the basis for the principle of the Gantt Charts for which Gantt is best remembered.

(4) Alexander H. Church's most influential book is "The Science and Practice of Management" (1914). He was the first to analyze the basic functions essential to any manufacturing activity. His organic functions of manufacturing are:

(a) *Design,* which originates.

(b) *Equipment,* which provides physical conditions.

(c) *Control,* which specifies duties, and which orders.

(d) *Comparison,* which measures, records, and compares.

(e) *Operation,* which makes.

Church's principles of effort to be applied to the organic functions are (a) experience must be systematically accumulated, standardized, and applied; (b) effort must be economically regulated; and (c) personal effectiveness must be promoted.

(5) Frank B. Gilbreth's major publications are: "Concrete System" (1908); "Bricklaying System" (1909); "Motion Study" (1911); and "Primer of Scientific Management" (1912). "Applied Motion Study" was written with Lillian Gilbreth in 1917. His contributions to manufacturing management are in the area of motion and time study. He stated that "the aim of motion study is to find and perpetuate the scheme of perfection." Motion Study was explained by him as having three stages: (a) discovering and classifying the best practice; (b) deducing the laws; and (c) applying the laws to standardize practice, either for the purpose of increasing output or decreasing hours of labor, or both. Gilbreth devised a system of dividing work into its most elementary elements which were called "Therbligs." His goal was the development of methods of least waste. (See GILBRETH PRINCIPLES OF MOTION ECONOMY.)

These basic concepts of the representative pioneers of scientific management serve to illustrate that they did not put their faith entirely in systems or mechanisms. They considered scientific management to be a way of thinking about the process of achieving objectives or tasks and the elimination of wastes through efficiency methods which can be measured.

Scientific Management in Europe. While the concepts of scientific management were augmenting the management movement in the United States, a similar movement was emerging in Poland, Russia, France, and England. In Europe, a developing industrial economy generated problems which required new concepts of management thought and practices. Representatives of the pioneers of modern management thought in Europe and their contributions to the literatue of management follow:

(1) Karol Adamiecki's major book is "Harmonizacja Pracy" (Harmonization of Labor). He published "Principles of Collective Work" (1903) and "The Graphical Method of Organization of Work in Rolling Mills," (1909). He presented the concept of the harmonogram before the Society of Russian Engineers in 1903, the same year that Taylor's Shop Management appeared. The harmonogram concept was similar to the principles of the Gantt Chart.

(2) Henri Fayol's major publication is "Administration Industrielle et Generale" (1916). The first English edition appeared in 1929. Fayol is noted for his divisionalization of all industrial undertakings into six groups which are: (a) Technical activities; (b) Commercial activities; (c) Financial activities; (d) Security activities; (e) Accounting activities and (f) Managerial activities. He was the first person to present a breakdown of the functions of management which he listed as: planning, organizing, command, coordination, and control. He also formulated several principles as guides to managerial actions.

(3) In England, Oliver Sheldon's book, "The Philosophy of Management" (1923) was the first publication to present management as a philosophy. He conceived of administration as the function for the determination of corporate policy and management as the function for the execution of corporate policy. Organization was the process of combining work and individuals or groups. His divisionalization of the functions of a business firm consisted of: (a) Preparation (design and equipment); (b) Production (manufacture); (c) Facilitation (transport, planning, comparison, labor); (d) Distribution (sales planning, sales execution).

The basic concepts of scientific management emerged in Europe in the same period as in the United States. This suggests a chronological relationship to the development of the economic and industrial climate of the countries where it evolved. However, scientific management arose in different parts of the world independently. In the United States, it was in the area of operative work; in Europe, it originated in the administrative level of general or executive management.

Original Aims of Scientific Management. As the concept of scientific management was developing in the early part of the twentieth century, the following aims were stated:

(1) Industrial processes can be reduced to units for scientific observations and experiments. The operations of workmen can be reduced to fundamental motions to ascertain the longest, shortest, and average time required for each motion. From experimentation, data can be obtained to derive a standard time for the performance of each operation.

(2) The standard time established for each operation can be used as the task for each workman to achieve. Each unit of product can be produced at a designated standard of efficiency and at a standard cost.

(3) The workmen can be instructed in the best methods for achieving the standard. The responsibility for training and providing standard working conditions must be accepted by the foremen or supervisors.

(4) The workmen can be relieved of the responsibility for determining how a process is to be performed and thereby concentrate on the development of their manual dexterities. The managerial functions of planning and controlling must be responsible for determining the process and the routing of work. Workmen do not need to plan; they can concentrate on performance. (However, for modifications of this concept by later insights of the behavioral sciences, the reader is referred to the entries JOB ENRICHMENT, MOTIVATION, and related cross references.)

(5) The workmen can be inspired to accept new methods and to acquire dexterity in carrying out the specifications to achieve performance standards. The inspiration for the workmen can be provided by wage systems which permit them to share the benefits from increased productivity.

The emphasis was on maximum output with optimum human effort through the methods of separating waste and inefficiency from human work at the level of operative performance. The scientific management approach to the utilization of human efforts in work assignments embodied these concepts which became central to management: (1) an objective; (2) a managerial process for achieving the objective such as planning, organizing, motivating or directing, and controlling; and (3) the intelligent use of people for the performance of work projects.

Continuing Trend of Scientific Management. The basic concepts of Scientific Management have endured and developed into modern management theories, philosophies, and expanded conceptual frameworks for managerial problem solving.

Although Scientific Management in the United States emerged from operating management, its values and basic concepts are now applied universally to all levels of management and fields of industrial enterprise. A process of management has developed that can be applied to the firm as a whole or any divisionalized or functional segment of it. Thus:

(1) Goals or objectives must be set which are compatible with the economic, social, technological, and political environment.

(2) Policies as guides to managerial decision making and behavior must be formulated.

(3) Planning is essential to the efficient and effective achievement of the objectives.

(4) Organizing is needed to effect the plans by establishing the relationship of work, people, and work environment.

(5) Motivating or directing the people in the organization to effect the plans is required to realize the objectives.

(6) Controlling the performance of the people in the organization is essential to achieve the objectives in conformance with the plans.

As the concept of identifiable functions of management that could be combined and integrated into a process of management for the achievement of predetermined results became established, contributions from other disciplines furthered the developing MANAGEMENT MOVEMENT. Contributions from the economists, mathematicians, and engineers are in the clarified areas of decision making, strategies of planning and controlling, MANAGEMENT SCIENCES, GAME THEORY, AND SYSTEMS MANAGEMENT. Psychologists, sociologists, and behavioral scientists are contributing to management knowledge and skills through research findings in the areas of human motivation, organizational relationships, alternative organizational structures, and comparative theories of leadership.

The mental approach and methods of scientific management that sparked the MANAGEMENT MOVEMENT in the early 20th century continue to augment management science and philosophy as the 21st approaches.

JOHN F. MEE, PH.D. LL.D., Mead Johnson Professor Emeritus of Management, Indiana University, Bloomington, Indiana

Information References

Brandeis, Louis D., "Scientific Management and Railroads," *The Engineering Magazine,* 1911.

Drury, Horace B., "Scientific Management: A History and Criticism," New York, Columbia University Press, 1915.

George, Claude S., Jr., 'The History of Management Thought," Englewood Cliffs, N.J., Prentice Hall, 1968.

Hunt, Edward E., "Scientific Management Since Taylor," New York, McGraw-Hill, 1924.

Merrill, H. F., "Classics in Management," New York, American Management Associations, 1960.

Taylor, F. W., "Principles of Scientific Management, New York, Harper & Bros., 1911.

"Scientific Management" (Tuck School Conference). Hanover, New Hampshire, Amos Tuck School of Administration and Finance, Dartmouth College, 1912.

Urwick, Lyndall, ed., "The Golden Book of Management," New York, Arno Press, repr. 1979.

Cross References: *Barth, Carl; Emerson, Harrington; Gayol, Henri; Follett, Mary Parker Gantt, H.L.; Gilbreth, F.B. and Lillian, E.M.; Hathaway; H.K.; Management Movement; Management Movement: Leaders in Thought; Scientific Management: "Taylorism"; Taylor, Frederick W.*

SCIENTIFIC MANAGEMENT: "Taylorism"

Near the end of a long period of depression in 1878, when it was virtually impossible for many mechanics to get work in their trades, **Frederick W. Taylor** joined the Midvale Steel Company as a day laborer. Through good fortune and ability, he became gangboss of the lathes section several months later. For the next three years he took part in a bitter struggle with his men which undoubtedly left a vivid imprint on him for the remainder of his life.

Taylor was convinced that the machinists, who were paid on a piece work basis, were holding back on production. In his words, he ". . . used every expedient to make them do a fair day's work, such as discharging or lowering the wages of the more stubborn men who refused to make an improvement, and such as lowering the piece work price, hiring green men, and personally teaching them how to do the work, with the promise from them that when they had learned how, they would then do a fair day's work. . . . No one who has not had this experience can have an idea of the bitterness which is gradually developed in such a struggle. In a war of this kind the workmen have one expedient which is usually effective. They use their ingenuity to contrive various ways in which the machines which they are running are broken . . . and this they always lay at the door of the foreman, who has forced them to drive the machine so hard that it is overstrained and is being ruined" [1].

After three years of such struggle, Taylor was made foreman. He had been loyal to the company probably out of a sense of duty and social obligation far more than a feeling that the company had been fair. He knew, and had had to admit to his workers, that under their piece work system they would not be allowed to earn more despite increased output.

But this is a glimpse of the character of the man. His Quaker background and dominant mother had helped to make him tireless, self-demanding in his work, and a person of unquestioned integrity, but he was often arrogant and tactless in his dealing with employers, and often autocratic and overly quick with fines in his dealings with employees [2]. As a result, his relations with organizational members were typically strained and unrewarding. This was probably a leading cause of the two or three nervous breakdowns he reported having suffered, in a letter to a friend [3].

It is not surprising, then, that he would seek security, acceptance from others, and justice for workers through a concrete, predictable system of SCIENTIFIC MANAGEMENT, rather than through the development of warm close personal relations with workmen and others. Seemingly, his sense of confidence rested more upon his intellectual than his social skills.

Soon after being made foreman, Taylor decided to make a determined effort to change the system of management, so that the interests of the workmen and the management would become less antagonistic. He felt that the greatest obstacle to harmonious relations between labor and management lay in management's ignorance as to what really is a proper day's work for a workman. Partly as a reward for having made good as foreman of the shop in getting more work out of the men, the president of the Midvale Steel Company permitted him to spend some money for a systematic study of the time required to do various kinds of work. Thus was started the first of his pioneering studies.

Before leaving the Midvale Steel Works in 1890, Taylor rose to the rank of chief engineer. He had obtained a degree in engineering in 1883 through evening study, and had given his first paper, "The Relative Value of Water-gas and Gas from the Siemens Producer for Melting in the Open-Hearth Furnace," before the American Society of Mechanical Engineers at a meeting in 1886. This Society, the ASME, was to become the principal forum through which Taylor would present his developing ideas.

The New Concept. Acceptance by ASME of management as a legitimate field of study for its members did not come readily. Not until 1907 did it recognize the subject of management engineering, and beyond 1915 an influential section of its membership continued to deny that there could ever be a science of management. In 1886 Henry Towne, President of the Yale and Towne Manufacturing Company, presented a paper before the Society on "The Engineer as an Economist." His continuing plea that shop management was as important as engineering in industry and his support for Taylor's work did much to enlist the prestige and support of the Society for the scientific management movement. And, of course, there were others who were closely associated with Taylor: who played important roles in the development of scientific management. They included H.K. HATHAWAY, CARL BARTH, HENRY GANTT, and Morris Cooke.

Horace Hathaway, the youngest of the close associates, worked his way up from apprentice to tool-room foreman at the Midvale Steel Company after Taylor's departure, and in 1902 was made superindendent of a manufacturing company at the age of 24. In 1905 he was engaged to assist in the installation of the Taylor System in the Philadelphia plant of the Link Belt Company by James Dodge, its president, who was a strong Taylor disciple.

Later, he was requested by Taylor, on loan from the Link Belt Company, to help install scientific management in the Tabor Manufacturing Company of Philadelphia. So successful was his work, that he was made works manager and vice-president of this company in 1907. There is little question that these two companies, Link Belt and Tabor, became the most celebrated "demonstration ground" for the scientific management movement. Taylor gave

Hathaway the ultimate compliment by referring to him as the best all-round man in the movement.

Carl Barth, according to H. S. Person, was one of the two greatest management engineers that the United States had produced. . . . When Barth became Taylor's assistant at the Bethlehem Steel Company in 1899, the latter was in possession of a vast accumulation of experimental data relating to machine operations which no one had been able to analyze successfully. Taylor had submitted the data to several university professors of mathematics who had been unsuccessful in getting anything of value out of them. Taylor submitted them to Barth who soon developed the famous formula of twelve variables described in Taylor's "Shop Management." On the basis of this formula he then developed the Barth slide-rule [4].

Barth continued to assist Taylor with the installation of scientific management in various plants until Taylor's death in 1915. Barth was the man who convinced the dean of the new Harvard School of Business Administration in 1908 that it should accept the Taylor System as the standard of modern management. Taylor had broad vision and ideals, but he very much needed men like Carl Barth to translate them into specific realities.

Henry Gantt and Morris Cooke were the other two close associates of Taylor. Gantt had been Taylor's assistant when Taylor was Chief Engineer at the Midvale Steel Company; later, Gantt became superintendent of the casting department. He is well known for his "task and bonus" system and the GANTT CHART. But among the pioneers of the scientific management movement, probably, he was the best known for the emphasis he placed upon the role of *good industrial relations* and *leadership* in successful management. Cooke was distinguished by his introduction of scientific management into the printing field, and his attempt to apply it to university administration. There were many others in America who made significant contributions to the scientific management movement. Among them were such men as Harrington Emerson, Sanford Thompson and FRANK GILBRETH who did so much to develop the art of time and motion study in the building trades.

Significant Foreign Contributors. Concepts and techniques similar to those of Taylor and his associates evolved independently and almost simultaneously in England, Poland, and France, as comparable industrial and economic pressures developed in those countries [5].

Joseph S. Lewis, while employed as general manager of a rolling mill in England wrote a book, "The Commercial Organization of Factories," which was published simultaneously in London and New York in 1896 [6]. As Taylor did later, Lewis stressed the importance of separating planning from doing. Two of his articles, "Works Management for the Maximum of Production," and "The Mechanical and Commercial Limits of Specialization," were published in *American Engineering Magazine* in 1899 and 1901. Among other things, these stressed the use of flow charting to trace the progress of work through the factory, and the systematic development and training of employees.

Karol Adamiecki of Poland was another who independently and simultaneously developed concepts and techniques similar to those of Taylor. Drawing upon his experiences and observations in Polish and Russian rolling mills, he developed several principles of organization. The introduction of his graphic "harmonogram," a Gannt-Chart-like means for coordinating the performance of activities (developed in 1896), caused increases in output ranging from 100% to 400% in factories in various industries in Poland and elsewhere [7].

The Michelin Brothers of France, before they had heard of scientific management, applied similar concepts and techniques to the manufacture of tires at the turn of the century. After the First World War they joined Henri LeChatelier and his collaborator, Charles de la Poix de Freminville, in enthusiastically "spreading the word" about scientific management throughout the French-speaking world [8].

Taylor's Basic Approach. Taylor recognized the need to separate the *planning* of work from its *execution*. He made it clear that management must first systematically study its work for the purpose of identifying and defining various principles. Then, it must develop adequate procedures for applying them. He indicated that to work according to scientific laws, management would have to take over and perform much of the work which was currently being performed by the men; that almost every act of the workman would be preceded by one or more preparatory acts of management which would enable him to do his work better and quicker than he could otherwise do it.

Taylor stated that scientific management comprises a combination of four great underlying principles of management: *First,* the development of a true science. *Second,* the scientific selection of workmen. *Third,* the scientific education and development of workmen. *Fourth,* intimate friendly cooperation between management and the men.

He listed various tools to serve these principles such as time study, functional foremanship, standardization of tools and movements of workmen for each class of work, planning rooms or departments, the "exception principle" in management, slide-rules, and other time-saving devices, instruction cards for workmen, the task idea in compensation with bonuses for above-average performance, the mnemonic classification system, routing systems, and cost accounting techniques.

In a specific situation, say a metal working plant, the introduction of the Taylor System would entail the following steps: *First,* the development and introduction of standards throughout the works and office. *Second,* the scientific study of unit times on several different kinds of work. *Third,* a complete analysis of the pulling, feeding power, and the proper speeding of the various machine tools throughout the place with the view of making a slide rule for properly running each machine. *Fourth,* the work of establishing the system of time cards by means of which ultimately all of the desired information would be conveyed from the men to the planning room. *Fifth,* overhauling the stores issuing and receiving system so as to establish a complete running balance of materials. *Sixth,* ruling and printing the various forms that would be required for shop returns and reports, time cards, instruction cards, expense sheets, cost sheets, pay sheet, and balance records; and preparing other forms which would be required in the store-room, for the tickler file, and for the maintenance of standards throughout the plant.

Functional Foremanship. In large plants, Taylor wanted the man in charge of introducing the system to appoint a special assistant in charge of each of the above functions. He felt that the most important and difficult task of the organizer would be that of selecting and training the various "functional foremen" who would lead and instruct the workmen.

Eight of these "functional foremen" or specialist bosses replaced the single foreman when the Taylor System was installed. Taylor's idea was to introduce the advantages of division of labor and of specialized training and experience at the supervisory level. He regarded four of the eight as "executive functional bosses" who handled the active work of the shop. These were: the gang boss, the speed boss, the inspector, and the repair boss. The other four "functional bosses" were located in the planning room. They were: the order of work and route clerk, the instruction card clerk, the time and cost clerk, and the shop disciplinarian.

Of the innovations which Taylor introduced, the use of "functional foremen" was the least successful. His work did emphasize the glaring need for more specialized study and skill in industry, and it did stress the usefulness of providing staff specialists with more than advisory authority under certain conditions. Unfortunately, he selected the least desirable way of dealing with these matters.

"Functional foremen" were skilled specialists, but they were also *human.* Because the approach fragmented the foreman's job, certain matters could more easily "fall through the cracks," and no one person was responsible for effective integration of effort and adaptation to changing circumstances and opportunities. Also, established foremen resented the functional approach because it reduced their authority and status. Interpersonal friction within the group was virtually assured by the impossibility of accurately defining where one man's jurisdiction ended and another's began. And one can only imagine the bewilderment of the worker confronted with eight bosses!

However, Taylor's idea of functional foremanship did lead to the use of staff specialists in the framework of the "line and staff" form or organization. Harrington Emerson was one of the early leaders in the scientific management movement who recognized and advocated the superiority of this "line and staff" approach.

Many examples of the striking successes achieved during the early years of the scientific management movement could be cited. However, perhaps the most important long-range value was not the amazing advance in efficiency, but the provision of a basis for the development of professional pride on the part of business leaders. By supplying them with a growing body of principles and professional techniques, by challenging them to develop these further and for the right purposes, scientific management gave business leaders a sense of direction, achievement, and worthwhileness in the eyes of society.

Taylor understood this, and never stopped pointing out that the mechanisms of management must not be mistaken for its essence or underlying philosophy. (See SCIENTIFIC MANAGEMENT.)

Ideals and Practice. Generally, Taylor and the other pioneers did not know how to translate effectively their ideals into practice. Their first error was in claiming that theirs was an "exact science." In 1916, in his book "Industrial Leadership," Gantt wrote that "The substitution of fact for opinion is the basis of modern industrial progress, and rate of this progress is controlled by the extent to which the methods of scientific investigation supplant the debating society methods in determining a basis for action" [9].

In his testimony before a Congressional Committee in 1912, Taylor pointed out that "both sides must recognize as essential the substitution of exact scientific investigation and knowledge for the old individual judgment or opinion, either of the workman or the boss, in all matters relating to the work done in the establishment" [10].

These are typical of the comments made by many of the early leaders. Even if restricted to the more specific procedures such as time and motion study, methods analysis, and job evaluation, such statements are quite misleading, for these activities are far from being based upon "exact science." Collaborative judgment plays an important role in the development and implementation of these procedures for any particular application. Modifying them to meet organizational needs, allowing for the human element in their operation, and preparing the organization for their introduction, are hardly matters of exact procedure.

Nevertheless, many of these leaders felt that exactness could be achieved in all areas of activity. They felt, for example, that compromise and negotiation could be entirely discarded in labor management relations. This conviction rested upon the assumption that the worker was essentially an "economic man." If the employer could scientifically determine a fair day's pay; if the employee were told the best way to do his work and permitted to earn a bonus for above-average performance; and if the employer's intentions were honorable, then "What more could the worker want?"

Frank Gilbreth claims that Taylor told him that the "instruction card can be depended upon to carry the word of the master or the manager without a line of translation in the way of the human element" [11]. The logics of this approach suggest that as long as management wishes to be fair, unions are superfluous; that the complexities of the "science" dictate that it be *unilaterally* developed and administered by experts; that any grumbling or discontent on the part of workers under well planned scientific management is due solely to a misunderstanding on their part as to the "objectives" of the movement. Recognition of the human element usually took the form of pointing out the pride and stimulation the worker derived from competing with and outdoing his fellow-workers.

Again, there can be little question as to Taylor's sincerity when he wrote that "No system of management, however good, should be applied in a wooden way. The proper personal relations should always be maintained between the employers and men. . . . The employer who goes through his works with kid gloves on, and is never known to dirty his hands or clothes, and who either talks to his men in a condescending or patronizing way, or else not at all, has no chance whatever of ascertaining their real thoughts or feelings. . . . The opportunity which each man should have of airing his mind freely, and having it out with his employers, is a safety-valve; and if the superintendents are reasonable men, and listen to and treat with respect what their men have to say, there is absolutely no reason for labor unions and strikes."

Motivation. But despite these insights, Taylor held to an overly simplified view of motivation. For example, he explained in a paper read before the American Society of Mechanical Engineers in 1903 that "loafing or soldiering proceeds from two causes. First, from the natural instinct and tendency of men to take it easy, which may be called natural soldiering. Second, from more intricate second thought and reasoning caused by their relations with other men, which may be called systematic soldiering" [1].

And what was the solution? In Taylor's view it was the *unilateral* determination of a fair day's work, the *unilateral* development of a fair incentive pay system, and the swift application of stern discipline to those who failed to "see the light" and respond properly. In this scheme of things there was little basis for employees participation in or identification with the work of the organization. And the need for participation became more pronounced as the planning room displaced the worker as the custodian of job knowledge—knowledge which was "returned" to the worker only piecemeal. Taylor's ideal of mutuality stressed only increased material rewards for labor rather than cooperation based upon shared influence. Paradoxically, as the unilateral approach of Taylor and other proponents of the movement threatened and alienated union leaders, the consultative-participative approach of one disciple, gained their support and cooperation [12].

Cooke's approach was not representative; consequently, the scientific management movement gave impetus to "selfish paternalism" in industry: the giving of benefits, bonuses, and gifts by employers with the expectation that they would get unquestioning obedience, hard work, and nonunion shops in return. If a worker grumbled openly, he was to be sternly disciplined or dismissed, for after all, the rationale of scientific management assured the satisfaction and well-being of "normal" employees. Many unscrupulous employers hired "experts" to "engineer" (manipulate) work standards so as to exploit their workers. Organized labor was not strong enough to combat them. Labor legislation at that time gave little protection. And the public of that day embraced the *laissez-faire* philosophy with the notion that if an employee did not like a particular situation, he could move on to another or set up shop for himself.

There is ample evidence that many employers took full advantage of the opportunity to exploit their employees. One common way was through the "speed-up," a procedure of repeated production quota revisions upward whereby the worker must get out more and more work to obtain the same pay. Under legitimate scientific management, the rate was never cut unless there was some absolute change in the duties or tools of the job which would permit greater output with the same effort from the worker. In practice, it was not too difficult ostensibly to alter the job to "justify" higher output requirements.

Labor Opposition. Undoubtedly, fear of the "speed-up" and rate-cutting was a prime reason for organized labor's opposition to scientific management. There were other objections too. The best compilation of these was made in 1914 when Professor Robert Hoxie made an investigation of scientific management in its relations to labor for the United States Commission on Industrial Relations.

The Commission had spent four days in April of 1914 taking testimony on scientific management. When it developed that representatives of organized labor stood in almost unqualified opposition to what they understood to be scientific management, the Commission authorized a more exhaustive study to be conducted by Professor Hoxie. His book, "Scientific Management and Labor," which reports the findings of this investigation, is undoubtedly the most comprehensive and carefully documented criticism of the subject available [13].

Professor Hoxie submitted his compilation of "Labor Objections to Scientific Management" to the American Federation of Labor for editing. Following are representative criticisms from the revised compilation: "Scientific Management—not, necessarily science in management—is a device employed for the purpose of increasing production and profits; and tends to eliminate consideration for the character, rights, and welfare of the employees." "It looks upon the worker as a mere instrument of production and reduces him to a semi-automatic attachment to the machine or tool." "It puts into the hands of employers at large an immense mass of information and methods which may be used unscrupulously to the detriment of the workers, creates the possibility of systematic blacklisting, and offers no guarantee against the abuse of its professed principles and practices."

And there were earlier expressions of hostility on the part of organized labor. In the spring of 1911 an attempt was made to introduce at the Rock Island Arsenal the methods which had proved successful at the Watertown Arsenal. Rock Island employees, backed by President Gompers of the A.F. of L. and President O'Connell of the International Association of Machinists, vigorously opposed the move.

As a result, hearings were arranged before the House Committee on Labor and when an attempt was made to introduce the bonus system in the Watertown foundry in the summer of 1911, the entire force walked out. In June, 1913, Watertown employees petitioned for the abolition of the Taylor System. However, in January, 1915, several hundred employees of the Frankfort Arsenal petitioned for its *continuance.*

In March 1915, the House forced an unwilling Senate to agree to provisions in both Army and Navy appropriations bills forbidding the use of funds for time study work or the payment of bonuses on Government work. In 1916 "anti-efficiency" riders were attached to the Fortifications, Army, Navy, Post Office, and Sundry Civil bills.

This kind of reaction to scientific management often has been blamed upon those practitioners who openly "perverted" the essential philosophy and intent of Frederick W. Taylor, and upon them only. This is not entirely accurate. Frequently distrust of the system and perversion of its goals were the result of the failure of its sincerest advocates to consider adequately the human factors involved.

The Human Job of the Manager. The HAWTHORNE EXPERIMENTS begun in 1927 and the post-World War II research in GROUP DYNAMICS and HUMAN RELATIONS IN INDUSTRY served to reject the over-simplified notion that economic incentives largely explain employee behavior. But even before, in 1924, Oliver Sheldon, the Englishman, wrote "The Philosophy of Management" which was widely adopted as a textbook in both Great Britain and the United States. His theme was that though Taylorism had helped greatly in the development of a science of management, such work had in no way detracted from the predominantly human job of the manager to manage.

MARY PARKER FOLLETT, a well known business philosopher of the time, agreed with Sheldon as to the need for emphasizing human factors in management, but disagreed in stating that a science of co-operation could be developed. She saw in her "Law of the Situation" a means for bridging the gap between the ideal of scientific management and the unilateral practice of it. In a paper delivered in 1925, she explained this law as a means for depersonalizing order-giving and uniting all concerned in a study of the situation to discover the "Law of the Situation" and obey that. In effect, she proposed the development of objectives, plans, and "facts" through the same kind of collaborative effort between leaders and their subordinates as usually takes place between leaders of the same rank. She went even further to say that, "From one point of view, one might call the essence of Scientific Management the attempt to find the 'Law of the Situation'."

In 1926, Sam Lewisohn wrote "New Leadership in Industry" which provided a new view of the responsibility of personnel specialists for the maintenance of good human relations in an organization. The worker, he contended, wants "justice, status, and opportunity." And a specialist should not be given the chief role in meeting these needs: "The manager cannot delegate this responsibility, even to a personnel officer; it remains his alone."

Scientific Management at Ford. In many respects, the finest expression of the early scientific management movement occurred in an organization which produced none of its acknowledged leaders or official spokesmen: The Ford Motor Company. The quality of leadership at the company was very uneven, but during the early days, around 1905, there was an informality and spirit of mission that permeated the entire factory. Henry Ford would spend much of his time walking through the various departments—chatting here, and taking off his coat to help a mechanic solve a job there. He was much like Taylor in his basic idealism and his strong sense of mission. He kept saying that he had to build a better and better car at an ever decreasing price so that cars would eventually be within the reach of every family.

As Allan Nevins points out in his monumental work, "Ford: The Time, the Man, the Company," the introduction of scientific management at the company began in earnest as early as 1908. In June of that year, one car was assembled and tested in fourteen minutes. This demonstrated the degree to which production of interchangeable parts had been developed and the efficiency with which the assembly line was being supplied with components in proper time and order. In 1910 the Highland Park Plant was opened. Its design and machinery were hailed as being in advance of anything in the industry. Only with the introduction of scientific management could the Ford Motor Company have kept up with the swelling demand as its Model T became the most popular vehicle in the history of mankind [14].

Ford felt that the going-rate wages he paid were not in line with his profits—net income of more than $27 million was realized in 1913. Thus, in 1914, he made an announcement which shook Detroit and, for that matter, the world: the five-dollar day. Probably the most dramatic result of the wage increase was its impact upon productivity. Though the average wage per hour rose 105%, the labor cost per car rose only 35%!

In those years, men were proud to be Ford employees and regarded themselves as members of an industrial elite. One manifestation of this pride was the wearing of work badges to social functions. Despite its paternalism, the company represented a uniquely successful blending of scientific management with effective "human management." As Nevins points out: "The factory in those years of swift expansion from 12,000 to nearly 33,000 workers might have been content to pay ordinary wages, fight ordinary labor battles, and thus join other automotive plants in fostering the growth of slums already too large. It was much to the credit of John Lee, James Couzens, and Henry Ford—the younger, more idealistic Ford of this era—that they took a different attitude. They had caught the spirit of the new progressive impulse."

It is difficult for people today, so much better acquainted with the Ford of the 1920s and 1930s, to realize that there really were "two" Fords: that there existed the younger, more idealistic Ford of this earlier period.

Scientific Management Today. During the 1940s and early 1950s the technical phases were largely displaced from the limelight by clamor over group dynamics and human relations in industry. Now, with the advent of highspeed computers, automation, and OPERATIONS RESEARCH techniques, we are in the midst of a new managerial revolution and the technical phases of management are again gaining ascendancy. But there is little danger of the kind of extremism which characterized the early days of the scientific management movement. Management has learned many things since the early days of "Taylorism." Few industrial leaders now question the inadequacy of the "economic man" approach to behavior or the essential need for employee participation at all levels in the organization.

They recognize that participation is necessary to provide the basis for identification with company goals and a feeling of worthwhileness on the part of employees. Also, they realise that workers as well as themselves will resist and fight changes which they feel threaten their security, regardless of how these changes may appear to others.

The work of men like Einstein, Planck, and Heisenberg has helped to explode the mechanical-deterministic view of the universe which nurtured the dogmatism of many of the pioneers in the scientific management movement. Today, the evolution of a statistical-probability concept has done much to discourage claims for absolutism in any field of study.

WILLIAM M. FOX, PH.D., Professor of Industrial Relations and Management, University of Florida, Gainesville, Florida

Information References

Aitken, Hugh J., "Taylorism at Watertown Arsenal," in "Scientific Management in Action, 1908–1915," Cambridge, Mass., Harvard University Press, 1960.

Drury, Horace B., "Scientific Management: A History and Criticism," New York, Columbia University Press, 1922.

Hoxie, Robert F., "Scientific Management and Labor," New York, Appleton, 1915.

Taylor, Frederick W., "Scientific Management Comprising Shop Management, the Principles of Scientific Management," Testimony Before Special House Committee, New York, Harper & Bros., 1947. For a full discussion of Taylor's system, see his "Shop Management" (1903) and "The Principles of Scientific Management" (1911). Fortunately, these, along with his "Testimony Before the Special House Committee" (1912) are printed in one volume, "F. W. Taylor, 'Scientific Management,' " New York, Harper & Bros., 1947.

Thompson, Clarence B., ed., "Scientific Management, A Collection of the More Significant Articles Describing the Taylor System of Management," Cambridge, Mass., Harvard University Press, 1914.

References Cited

[1] Taylor, Frederick W., "The Principles of Scientific Management," New York, Harper & Bros., 1911.

[2] Krakar, Sudhie, "Frederick Taylor: A Study in Personality and Innovation." Cambridge, Mass., M.I.T. Press, 1970.

[3] Ibid.

[4] Person, H.S., *Advanced Management,* vol. iv, No. 5, Sect. 1, 1939.

[5] Urwick, L., "The Golcen Book of Management," London, Newman Neame Ltd., 1956.

[6] Lewis, Joseph S., "The Commercial Organization of Factories," London, 2nd ed. FN Spon, 1896.

[7] Urwick, *op. cit.*

[8] Urwick, *op. cit.*

[9] Gantt, Henry, "Industrial Leadership," New York, Associated Press, 1916.

[10] "Hearings before Special Committee of the House of Representatives to Investigate the Taylor and Other Systems of Shop Management," 1912, H. Res. 90, Vol. III, 1377–1508.

[11] Quoted in Brandeis, Louis D., "Scientific Management and Railroads" (part of a brief submitted to the Interstate Commerce Commission), *The Engineering Magazine,* 1911. (This reference is to a book published by the magazine.)

[12] Wren, Daniel, "The Evolution of Management Throught," New York, Ronald, 1972.

[13) Hoxie, see Information References.

[14] Nevins, Allan, "Ford: The Time, The Man, The Company," New York, Scribner, 1954.

Cross References: *Scientific Management (and cross-references there given).*

SECURITIES AND EXCHANGE COMMISSION

The **Securities and Exchange Commission,** created under the authority of the Securities and Exchange Act of 1934, provides the fullest possible disclosure to the investing public and protects the interests of the public and investors against malpractices in the securities and financial markets. The Commission also serves as adviser to United States district courts in connection with reorganization proceedings for debtor corporations in which there is a substantial public interest.

The Commission is vested, inter alia, with quasi-judicial functions. Persons aggrieved by its decisions in the exercise of those functions have a right of review by United States courts of appeals.

Full and Fair Disclosure. The Securities Act of 1933 requires issuers of securities making public offerings of securities in interstate commerce or through the mails, directly or by others on their behalf, to file with the Commission registration statements containing financial and other pertinent data about the issuer and the securities being offered. A similar requirement applies to such offerings on behalf of a controlling person of the issuer. Unless a registration statement is in effect with respect to such securities, it is unlawful to sell the securities in interstate commerce or through the mails. (There are certain limited exemptions, such as Government securities, nonpublic offerings, and intrastate offerings, as well as offerings not exceeding $1,500,000 in amount which comply with the Commission's Regulation A.)

The effectiveness of a registration statement may be refused or suspended after a public hearing, if the statement contains material misstatements or omissions, thus barring sale of the securities until it is appropriately amended. Registration of securities does not imply approval of the issue by the Commission or that the Commission has found the registration disclosures to be accurate. It does not insure investors against loss in their purchase, but serves rather to provide information upon which investors may make an informed and realistic evaluation of the worth of the securities.

Persons responsible for filing false information with the Commission subject themselves to the risk of fine or imprisonment or both; and persons connected with the public offering may be liable in damages to purchasers of the securities if the disclosures in the registration statement and prospectus are materially defective. Also, the above act contains antifraud provisions which apply generally to the sale of securities, whether or not registered.

Regulation. The Securities Exchange Act of 1934 assigns to the Commission broad regulatory responsibilities over the securities markets, the self-regulatory organizations within the securities industry, and persons conducting a business in securities. The Commission is directed to facilitate the establishment of a national market system for securities and a national system for the clearance and settlement of securities transactions. Securities exchanges and certain clearing agencies are required to register with the Commission, and associations of brokers or dealers are permitted to register with the Commission.

The Securities Exchange Act also provides for the establishment of the Municipal Securities Rulemaking Board to formulate rules for the municipal securities industry. The Commission oversees the self-regulatory activities of the national securities exchanges and associations, registered clearing agencies, and the Municipal Securities Rulemaking Board. In addition, the Commission regulates industry professionals, such as securities brokers, and dealers, certain municipal securities professionals, and transfer agents.

The Securities Exchange Act authorizes national securities exchanges, national securities associations, clearing agencies, and the Municipal Securities Rulemaking Board to adopt rules which are designed, among other things, to promote just and equitable principles of trade and to protect investors. The Commission is required to approve or disapprove most proposed rules of these self-regulatory organizations and has the power to abrogate or amend existing rules of the national securities exchanges, national securities associations, and the Municipal Securities Rulemaking Board.

In addition, the Commission has broad rulemaking authority over the activities of brokers, dealers, municipal securities dealers, securities information processors, and transfer agents. The Commission may regulate such securities trading practices as short sales and stabilizing transactions. It may regulate the trading of options on national securities exchanges and the activities of members of exchanges who trade on the trading floors and may adopt rules governing broker-dealer sales practices in dealing with investors. The Commission also is authorized to adopt rules concerning the financial responsibility of brokers and dealers and reports to be made by brokers and dealers. The Securities Exchange Act also empowers the Board of Governors of the Federal Reserve System to prescribe rules relating to the extension of credit by brokers and dealers for securities transactions. Such rules include the establishment of minimum margin requirements with respect to securities registered on national securities exchanges and certain securities traded over-the-counter.

The Securities Exchange Act also requires the filing of registration applications and annual and other reports with national securities exchanges and the Commission by companies whose securities are listed upon the exchanges, by companies which have assets of $1 million or more and 500 or more shareholders of record, and by companies which distributed securities pursuant to a registration statement declared effective by the Commission under the Securities Act of 1933. Such applications and reports must contain financial and other data prescribed by the Commission as necessary or appropriate for the protection of investors and to ensure fair dealing.

In addition, the solicitation of proxies, authorizations, or consents from holders of such registered securities must be made in accordance with rules and regulations prescribed by the Commission. These rules provide for disclosures to securities holders of information relevant to the subject matter of the solicitation.

Disclosure of the holdings and transactions by officers, directors, and large (10%) holders of equity securities of companies is also required, and any and all persons who acquire more than 5% of certain equity securities are required to file detailed information with the Commission and any exchange upon which such securities may be traded. Moreover, any person making a tender offer for certain classes of equity securities is required to file reports with the Commission, if as a result of the tender offer, such person would own more than 5% of the outstanding shares of the particular class of equity security involved. The Commission also is authorized to promulgate rules governing the repurchase by a corporate issuer of its own securities.

Regulation of Mutual Funds and Other Investment Companies. The Investment Company Act of 1940 provides for the registration with the Commission of investment companies, and subjects their activities to regulation to protect investors. The regulation covers sales and management fees, composition of boards of directors, and capital structure. Also, various transactions of investment companies, including transactions with affiliated interests, are prohibited unless the Commission first determines that such transactions are fair. Under the act, the Commission may institute court action to enjoin the consummation of mergers and other plans of reorganization of investment companies if such plans are unfair to security holders. It also may impose sanctions by administrative proceedings against investment company managements for violations of the act and other Federal securities laws, file court actions to enjoin acts and practices of management officials involving breaches of fiduciary duty involving personal misconduct, and to disqualify such officials from office.

Regulation of Companies Controlling Electric or Gas Utilities. The Public Utility Holding Company Act of 1935 provides for regulation by the Commission of the purchase and sale of securities and assets by companies in electric and gas utility holding company systems, their intrasystem transactions, and service and management arrangements. It limits holding companies to a single coordinated utility system and requires simplification of complex corporate and capital structures and elimination of unfair distribution of voting power among holders of system securities.

The issuance and sale of securities by holding companies and their subsidiaries, unless exempt (subject to conditions and terms which the Commission is empowered to impose) as an issue expressly authorized by the state commission in the state in which the issuer is incorporated, must be found by the Commission to meet statutory standards, namely: that the new security is reasonably adapted to the security structure and earning power of the issuer; that the proposed financing is necessary and appropriate to the economical and efficient operation of the company's business; that the consideration received, and fees, commissions, and other remuneration paid, are fair; and that the terms and conditions of the sale are not detrimental to investors, consumers, or the public.

The purchase and sale of utility properties and other assets may not be made in contravention of rules, regulations, or orders of the

Commission regarding the consideration to be received, maintenance of competitive conditions, fees and commissions, accounts, disclosure of interest, and similar matters. In passing upon proposals for reorganization, merger, or consolidation, the Commission must be satisfied that the objectives of the act generally are complied with and that the terms of the proposal are fair and equitable to all classes of security holders affected.

Regulation of Investment Counselors and Advisers. The Investment Advisers Act of 1940 provides that persons who, for compensation, engage in the business of advising others with respect to their security transactions must register with the Commission. The act prohibits certain types of fee arrangements, makes unlawful practices of investment advisers involving fraud or deceit, and requires, among other things, disclosure of any adverse interests the advisers may have in transactions executed for clients. The act authorizes the Commission to issue rules proscribing acts and practices which may operate as a fraud or deceit upon investors.

Rehabilitation of Failing Corporations. Chapter X of the Bankruptcy Act provides for Commission participation as adviser to Federal courts in proceedings for the reorganization of insolvent corporations. An important aspect of this activity is the advice rendered to the parties and the court with respect to the fairness and feasibility of proposed plans of reorganization.

Interests of Holders of Debt Securities. The interests of purchasers of publicly offered debt securities issued pursuant to trust indentures are safeguarded under the provisions of the Trust Indenture Act of 1939. This act, among other things, requires the exclusion from such indentures of certain types of exculpatory clauses and the inclusion of certain protective provisions. The independence of the indenture trustee, who is a representative of the debt holder, is assured by proscribing certain relationships which might conflict with the proper exercise of his duties.

Enforcement. The Commission's enforcement activities are designed to secure compliance with the Federal securities laws administered by the Commission and the rules and regulations adopted thereunder. These activities include measures (1) to compel obedience to the disclosure requirements of the registration and other provisions of the acts, (2) to prevent fraud and deception in the purchase and sale of securities, (3) to obtain court orders enjoining acts and practices which operate as a fraud upon investors or otherwise violate the laws, (4) to revoke the registrations of brokers and dealers and investment advisers who willfully engage in such acts and practices, (5) to suspend or expel from national securities exchanges or the National Association of Securities Dealers, Inc., any member or officer who has violated any provision of the Federal securities laws, (6) and to prosecute persons who have engaged in fraudulent activities or other willful violations of those laws.

In addition, attorneys, accountants, and other professionals who violate the securities laws face possible loss of their privilege to practice before the Commission. To this end, private investigations are conducted into complaints or other evidences of securities violations. Evidence thus established of law violations is used in appropriate administrative proceedings to revoke registration or in actions instituted in Federal courts to restrain or enjoin such activities. Where the evidence tends to establish criminal fraud or other willful violation of the securities laws, the facts are referred to the Attorney General for criminal prosecution of the offenders. The Commission may assist in such prosecutions.

Investor Information and Protection. Complaints and inquiries may be directed to the home office or to any regional office. Registration statements and other public documents filed with the Commission are available for public inspection in the public reference room at the home office. Much of the information also is available in its New York, Chicago, and Los Angeles regional offices, and to a lesser extent in the other regional offices of the Commission. Reproduction of the public material may be purchased from the Commission at prescribed rates.

SOURCE: United States Government Manual.

Information References

Inquiries on the following information should be directed to the specified office, Securities and Exchange Commission, 500 North Capitol Street, Washington, D.C. 20549:

Consumer Activities

Publications detailing the Commission's activities, which include material of assistance to the potential investor, are available from the Publications Unit. In addition, the Office of Consumer

Affairs answers questions from investors, assists investors with specific problems regarding their relations with broker-dealers, companies, and advises the Commission and other offices and divisions regarding problems frequently encountered by investors and possible regulatory solutions to such problems.

Contracts

Contact the Office of Records and Service.

Small Business Activities

Information on security laws which pertain to small businesses in relation to securities offerings may be obtained from the Commission.

Publications

Subscriptions to the following publications are available through the Superintendent of Documents, Government Printing Office, Washington, D.C. 20402.

SEC Docket—A weekly compilation of the full texts of SEC releases under the following acts: Securities Act, Security Exchange Act, Public Utility Holding Company Act, Trust Indenture Act, Investment Advisers Act, and Investment Company Act. Also included are the full texts of Accounting Series releases, corporate reorganization releases, and litigation releases.

News Digest—A daily report of Commission announcements, decisions, orders, rules and rule proposals, current reports and applications filed, and litigation developments.

Statistical Bulletin—A weekly publication containing data on odd lot and round lot transactions, block distributions, working capital of U.S. corporations, assets of noninsured pension funds, Rule 144 filings, and 8K reports.

Official Summary—A monthly summary of securities transactions and holdings of officers, directors, and principal stockholders.

Cross References: *Antitrust Legislation; Corporate Capitalization.*

SECURITY

An increasing attention to **Security,** which in larger companies takes the form of appointing a full-time executive responsible for implementation, is necessary because of rapidly rising crime throughout the nation. Crime, which according to the American Society for Industrial Security, costs U.S. business more than $40 billion a year, takes at least eight major forms: (1) white collar crime; (2) organized crime; (3) internal pilferage and embezzlement; (4) computer-related crime; (5) external attack, including robbery, hijacking, and shoplifting; (6) vandalism; (7) terrorism; and (8) industrial espionage. Not included in the aforementioned estimated $40 billion in business crime costs is an additional $25 to $35 billion in fraud, theft, and waste in Government programs such as welfare, social security, job corps, medical programs, and the like.

The job of maintaining security is very much complicated by the fact that these eight forms are often interrelated; losses ascribed to one factor are actually due to another. In other words, the true threat is not recognized. For example, high inventory losses, which are often blamed on shoplifters, may actually be due to employee pilferage. On the other hand, measures instituted to prevent one form of attack can also help deter other forms of criminal behavior.

Other complications are public corruption, escalating cost of crime insurance, and the need for greater care in selecting suppliers of security equipment and personnel. The revelations of the Knapp Commission in New York (1971–1973) showed that businessmen must worry about thieves in uniform. Further indications of depredations by "servants of the people" were the 1977 disclosure of widespread corruption in the Federal Government's General Services Administation and the 1978–1979 announcements concerning $5 to $7 billion in fraud associated with the programs administered by the then Department of Health, Education, and Welfare. The Abscam revelations of 1980 showed that the highest segments of Government are subject to compromise. And, of course, the private sector is not without fault—some 500 firms, including some of the largest in the country, have acknowledged making secret payments (bribes) both in the United States and around the world.

The ever-increasing reliance on computer systems provides an ever-increasing exposure to criminal activity. (As one outstanding example, a data processing consultant was able to execute an undetected illegal wire transfer of $10.2 million involving the Security Pacific National Bank in 1978. His crime was only discovered after he was apprehended trying to slip $8 million worth of industrial diamonds past U.S. customs.) A respected authority on computer-related crime has conservatively estimated that such crime approximated between $1.2 and $1.8 billion in 1980. The projection was based on an assumption that only 15% of computer-related crimes were reported to appropriate authorities. (However, Judge William Webster, Director of the FBI, stated in 1980 that the FBI estimated that not more than 1%

of all computer-related crimes were ever discovered, and of those, not more than 12% were reported for investigation and prosecution.)

The above magnitude of crime losses makes even more necessary the concept of "self protection," especially because "self insurance" has been stimulated by the rapid rise in premiums for crime insurance and ever higher deductibles on losses. The problem of security equipment specification is complicated by the fact that unscrupulous persons have invaded the security field, and by the high mortality rate among suppliers.

It is obvious that the greatest threat comes not from professional criminals, but from one's own employees, who account for 75% or more of the routine crime losses and probably 80% to 90% of all computer-related crime. The external theft, which takes the form of shoplifting, larceny, burglary, and robbery probably accounts for 5% or 6% of the total non-computer-related crime losses. Another 5% is generally attributed to vandalism.

The losses associated with organized crime and industrial espionage are exceedingly difficult to estimate, since very limited factual data pertaining to these crimes are available. Terrorism, a relative recent crime category, is rapidly becoming costly. For example, one study involving 232 kidnappings indicated that corporations paid more than $146 million in ransom to secure the release of employees. Terrorist bombings and facility takeovers resulted in payments exceeding $125 million in 1980.

The Security Program. Objectives of any security program are manifold. First comes protection of employees. Goods and cash can be replaced, but a life cannot. And a maiming injury cannot be made up. As great as the damage done to the persons of attacked employees is the loss of morale among all other employees. Next, of course, is protection of company assets, merchandise, and property. Finally, property of employees on company premises must be protected, as much for its own sake as for maintaining employee morale.

Any security program must begin with the employees—choosing them, indoctrinating them, and training them. The simplest and least costly way to handle a dishonest employee is not to hire him in the first place. This means checking all references carefully, down to the lowliest employee. Obviously any employee with a criminal record has to be considered with special care. To reject automatically all applicants with criminal records may not only be unfair but unwise. Since 40% of all males now alive in the U.S. will be arrested at least once during their lives for a non-traffic offense, to reject all those with criminal records could result in overlooking good material. Reformed criminals may indeed make good employees, but at least initially they must not be placed in sensitive operations, such as those handling cash or in the computer room (the wide availability of programming courses in prisons means that some ex-convicts will inevitably apply for EDP jobs). Of course, those with known criminal records cannot be bonded.

Before a program can be set up properly to screen, train, and motivate employees, some executive has to be prepared to handle this responsibility, on a full-time basis in large companies, or on a part-time basis in smaller companies. Large companies quite routinely hire former "peace officers" for the job of security officer or "director of security." Commonly, these men are former policemen, FBI agents, or retired military officers with experience in security or investigation. Obviously, a smaller company must select some present executive who can take on the added responsibilities of security. The personnel director is often a good choice, since he is already involved in hiring and training. Because cash is the chief target of dishonest employees, the chief financial officer should be involved in security, if not directly, then in an advisory capacity.

Responsibilities of the security officer, in addition to screening personnel, are extensive: hiring or contracting for guards; selecting electronic security systems and arranging for their maintenance; setting up procedures to handle fire, civil disturbance, or bomb threats (often a series of bomb threats causes greater losses through disruption than an actual bombing); liaison with local police; and keeping up with the state of the art in security devices. If the company has EDP facilities, the security officer should work closely with the EDP manager to insure the physical security of the computer and tape library, guard against misappropriation of computer time for non-company purposes, and make sure that the computer is not employed for embezzlement or fraud.

Procedures. Security procedures for the entire company must be set up and enforced. These should include:

(1) Inspection of outgoing parcels where

valuable merchandise, tools, or material are handled.

(2) Badging for all employees if the facility is large enough so that the guard could not recognize all who enter.

(3) Rigid visitor controls after-hours and on weekends to make sure that only those employees authorized for other than regular hours are present—and then checked out.

(4) Inspection of trash baskets and bins to make sure that valuable materials or parts are not being slipped out by this means.

Alarm Systems. A disciplined work force is the first step. However, while the employees are being trained and motivated to accept the simple rules that make for good security, certain security devices are required for after-hours when no one, or at most a few guards, are on the premises. By far the most common of all security systems is that installed by a central-station alarm company, of which the best known are American District Telegraph (ADT) and Holmes. The equipment and the installation are approved by the Underwriters' Laboratories, a non-profit testing service set up by the insurance industry. If certain levels of burglary insurance are sought, then the matching level in central-station service is required. These services generally charge a large initial fee to cover most of the cost of installation, then a monthly fee. They also monitor fires, flooding, and other emergencies.

Large companies with their own 24-hour guard service frequently install their own "proprietary" alarm systems in which any emergencies are reported on a console at which a guard is stationed.

Because of the high false-alarm rate associated with central-station service (most of the false alarms are due to improper setting by the company's own employees), some companies are turning to a comparatively new central-station service based on sound monitoring. Microphones are mounted throughout the premises to be protected, while a monitor at the central station listens in via leased phone lines. Because of the low incidence of alarms, a single man can monitor over 150 establishments. By experience, the monitor can differentiate between the sound of animals, wind and rain storms, or trucks passing—and a real intrusion.

To provide even more protection, many companies concentrate high-value merchandise or materials in one room and install a "space detector" in this room. Space detectors operate by creating ultrasonic or radio-wave fields that can detect any movement. These detectors are particularly effective against the "lie-in" burglar who hides at closing time to emerge later.

Defrauders and Embezzlers. The purpose of the above measures is defense against intrusion, but intruders cause only a fraction of the loss caused by the defrauder and embezzler on the payroll. The target of the embezzler is cash, while the defrauder is more often a thief who diverts company property to his advantage. The defrauder often uses company equipment such as metal-working machinery, computers, trucks or printing gear to perform work for others for his own account. In one such instance, computer-room workers were taking in so much unauthorized outside work that they asked management to add to computer capacity at great cost. Blocking defrauders calls for supervisory vigilance, with frequent inspections of facilities at unannounced, irregular times. Tell-tale signs are workers who habitually work overtime and on weekends, who turn down promotions, and never take vacations. (See also COMPUTER SECURITY/AUTOMATED OFFICE SECURITY and SECURITY: PROTECTION OF TRADE SECRETS AND PROPRIETARY INFORMATION.)

The same telltale signs apply to embezzlers. But the most effective way to prevent embezzling is by division of responsibilities in all fiscal matters. For example, the person who approves invoices should obviously not be the one to make out checks. At least once a year, an outside auditor should be brought in not only to check the books but aso to spot-check against embezzlement. These skilled auditors make many checks, such as: reports of returned goods test-checked against records of actual entries into stock; counts of inventory conducted on a surprise basis; sources of supply spot-checked to verify information on purchase orders, etc. Such outside checking is essential because the most damaging of all embezzlers are long-term employees who are trusted.

Because so much vital data are now stored in computers, the embezzler now either has to work in the computer room or obtain the cooperation of computer-room employees. One of the simplest ways to prevent such cooperation is to ban *everyone* from the computer room except those who actually operate the machines. This means no visitors, delivery personnel, customers, or other employees, even programmers (programmers can do their work in separate rooms). This "no visiting" policy also helps protect the computer itself against the fanatic vandals and arsonists who have been attacking computers in universities and banks. So far, they have not turned their wrath against computers in small and middle-size companies. Another deterrent is an "instant termination" policy for unsatisfactory computer-room workers, with appropriate severence, of course.

Bomb Threats. Although bombings have declined sharply since the March 1970 self-destruction of a bomb factory in Manhattan's Greenwich Village, and the highly-destructive bombing at the University of Wisconsin in early 1971, the level of *bomb threats* has not declined. Recognizing that they cannot possibly evacuate a building fast enough in the event of a real bomb is planted, many companies are now adopting the policy of making intense, rapid searches of the premises rather than evacuating all employees, which generally disrupts the rest of the work day. In addition to guards, maintenance personnel and younger executives are mobilized and trained for this special effort. If these volunteer searchers find no suspicious objects, which is nearly always the case, they report this fact, and no evacuation takes place. Many managements may be discouraged from following this "no-evacuation" practice because most local police officials still counsel evacuation in the event of a phoned-in bomb threat.

Guard services. To hire guard services or contract out for them is a problem for the security director. Obviously, it is simpler to contract with one of the established guard services to provide any guards required: the company does not have to cope with overtime and vacation scheduling, a real headache if only a few guards are required. Sometimes it is even cheaper to contract out, because no training period is involved. On the other hand, many companies have been dissatisfied with contract guard services. They have found that after the initial "honeymoon" period, the service may send guards of poorer and poorer quality. Some companies work out a satisfactory compromise arrangement in which the contract guard service only provides men for special occasions and during vacation periods.

Security Equipment Suppliers. Selecting and evaluating suppliers of security equipment is another big responsibility of the security director. Unfortunately, the field has attracted a swarm of sharpsters, fly-by-nights, inexperienced franchisees, and some outright frauds. Turnover among suppliers of security equipment is high, with some giant corporations backing out of the business after only a year's experience. To make sure that the company is getting good value, the director should make the following checks:

(1) Look for UL approval, a mark of good workmanship.

(2) Check with prior customers and the local police department on the qualifications and reputation of any supplier considered.

(3) As much as possible, use only those local suppliers close enough to provide quick service.

(4) Check the financial resources of any supplier to help make sure he will be around in future years when spare parts or service are needed.

(5) Ask for competitive bids if more than one supplier is available. List prices have little significance in the security field, which is characterized by high markups.

(6) Avoid overly sophisticated gear. Try to select the least complicated system that will do the job. The more complicated a system, the more likely it is to fail.

(7) Plan ahead for the eventual obsolescence of any equipment purchased. In time the criminals learn how to defeat the latest and cleverest of security systems, which means they have to be replaced or modernized even if functioning properly.

ARNOLD GOLDBERGER, Security Consultant, Great Neck, New York; and LINDSAY L. BAIRD, JR., Management Consultant, Mountain Lakes, New Jersey, for American Society for Industrial Security (for third edition)

Information References

Association:

American Society for Industrial Security.

Periodicals:

Security Management.
Security World.

Cross References: *Computer Security/Automated Office Security; Security: Protection of Trade Secrets and Proprietary Information; Terrorism: Protective Measures.*

SECURITY: Protection of Trade Secrets

In pursuing marketing strategies, companies are becoming more and more diligent in gathering commercial intelligence about competitors' marketing strategies and new product plans. A recent *Harvard Business Review* article [1] has outlined specific means by which even small companies can effectively monitor their competitors' activities and project their progress in certain areas. It points out that much potentially valuable information is publicly available. Some of the information is free; most may be obtained with minimum expenditure of time and effort.

That is good news for those seeking competitive marketing data. However, it is not so good for those who are charged with **Protecting Proprietary Information.** As managements learn to cultivate reliable sources of information about competitors, they must also learn to protect what should be their property alone. Safeguarding trade secrets and other sensitive data is the other side of the competitive vigilance coin. No company can afford to ignore it.

Trade Secrets. For legal purposes, the term *trade secret* has been defined as: "Any formula, pattern, device, or compilation of information which is used in one's business and which gives one an opportunity to obtain an advantage over competitors who do not know how to use it. . . . It may be a formula for a chemical compound, a process of manufacturing, a list of customers, a code for determining discounts, or a method of bookkeeping or office management " [2].

Two recent case histories, involving companies that learned too late about protecting proprietary information, are illuminating:

> One large manufacturing company aggressively pursued both civil redress and criminal prosecution after a longtime employee was caught selling secrets to Japanese competitors. It was a textbook case of industrial espionage—"cloak and dagger" intrigue. The trusted employee, a plant manager, led surreptitious after-hours tours of his manufacturing facility, and sold microfilm records containing literally thousands of engineering drawing, manufacturing reports, and test results. The manager was sentenced to a stint in the Federal penitentiary, the Japanese firm was fined $300,000, and the American company lost information worth millions of dollars.
>
> In a less dramatic incident, the chief of menu development for a well-known hamburger chain left the company to accept a marketing position with a fast-food pizza firm. Unfortunately, he allegedly took "crateloads" of marketing information along with him. The restaurant rivals are at this writing doing battle in a Kansas court. The menu man was charged with removal of trade secrets and confidential documents. And his new employer is reportedly considering several "menu extensions."

Obviously, whether management is dealing with hamburgers or high-technology magnetic tape, trade secrets such as these can mean big money as long as they are secrets—and big trouble the moment they are not.

Consider the first example. Up to a point, the theft and duplication of vital microfilm records is a physical security problem. Items such as lists, formulas, design specifications, financial statements, blueprints, manuscripts, and advertising schedules are tangible entities that can be protected by locks, alarms, and uniformed guards. But when a piece of transactional paper or part or all of a reel of magnetic tape holds vital information, how should it be protected? It is important that whoever is responsible for security consider the physical setup first. He (she) may wish to consult with a specialist in risk analysis—someone who can review security needs objectively.

To establish priorities for safeguarding vital documents, or information stored by whatever means, management should seek answers to the following questions:

From whom is the information being protected? Who might pose a threat to the information site? Not just the obvious competitor. Whoever it is, one can't expect him to identify himself at the front door. What about employees? Visitors? Deliverymen? Intruders posing as maintenance or housekeeping personnel?

It is important to establish strict ingress and egress controls for all areas of a facility: Require use of identification badges for employees and visitors, vendors, repairmen and other maintenance and janitorial personnel, and issue specially coded badges for tracking them. Within limits of local laws, search packages and briefcases. Extend diligence after hours. Institute continuous patrols of sensitive areas by uniformed security personnel.

What is the nature of the material being safeguarded? Where is the material being kept? Competent consultants are well-versed in state-of-the-art security hardware. Depending on needs, they can help select a storage area and equip it with appropriate locks, alarms, motion detectors, photographic and recording equipment, or other monitoring devices. Make sure any security survey includes checks for electronic intrusion or "bugging" devices. Check the computer system to see if unauthorized access can be detected.

Consider establishing a "safe room" where the company's important information is protected from fire as well as from intrusion.

The safe room recommendation is one that surfaces with increasing frequency. Fire safety experts can advise about proper storage facilities for microfilm and other heat-sensitive materials. Consider the threat posed by other natural disasters—including floods, earthquakes, and (remember Mt. St. Helens) even volcanic eruption. (See DISASTER CONTROL.) One prominent FBI official advises executives to design safe rooms with personal protection in mind also. A properly equipped safe room could serve as a holding area in the event of a terrorist activity or a hostage situation.

The priority assigned to the material will dictate the nature of the protective measures to surround it. But in any case, management should limit information about and access to sensitive materials and their storage to the smallest possible number of employees.

Computer Security. The extend of computer crime being committed today can only vaguely be defined. But there is no question that it is huge: estimates of losses from high-technology criminals have ranged from at least $2 billion to more than $40 billion a year.

The extensive use of computer equipment has made it impossible for supervisors to look over the shoulder of every employee who has to access potentially sensitive information. Physically limiting access to the computer protects the machine, but the information itself is still vulnerable. Operators at terminals thousands of miles from the corporate data center have access to the data at their fingertips.

Security software controls provide the most important kind of protection against unauthorized access. The prevalence of electronic crime has forced many data processing users to focus their attention on more stringent internal controls. Programs are being written to increase the number and complexity of electronic barriers that must be crossed by passwords and secret-number combinations to enter important data banks.

Above all, there should be safeguards against human error. Computer security consultants say the biggest problem they encounter is the sloppy procedures prevalent in some companies. In some work areas, computer passwords or other important numerical codes are simply taped on the wall or on the equipment itself. That makes the computer sign-on procedure easy for potential thieves as well as for employees.

Theft of important information is not the only price paid for unauthorized access to computer equipment. Tampering may also result in alteration or elimination of vital data, and falsification of existing programs.

"Intangible" Information. The foregoing concerns the protection of tangible proprietary assets—information that is committed to paper or computer data banks. What is more difficult to safeguard is intangible information stored only in the minds of employees or of not-so-casual observers. Certainly stories about daring thefts and sophisticated industrial espionage schemes do surface. And the latest electronic wizardry makes eavesdropping a real threat to confidential telecommunications. But it is far more common for company trade secrets and proprietary information to leak out through careless or corruptible employees.

To prevent losses of this type, it is necessary to begin at the beginning—while about-to-become employees are still applicants. The company's protective attitude should penetrate the hiring, training, and assignment processes. Start with pre-employment screening. What a company doesn't know about job applicants can hurt it. Institute and enforce a system of extensive background checks to make sure applicants are everything they say they are.

When vital information is involved, an applicants reliability and moral integrity are just as important as his or her technical ability. Reference checks and employment histories are important tools. It is recommended that checks cover a ten-year period, with explanations of any gaps or irregularities. Psychological testing and personality inventories are also helpful in evaluating an applicants acceptability for a sensitive position.

Before new employees are officially added to the payroll, many companies require them to sign a legal document assigning rights to any inventions or processes they may develop to the company. The document also limits employees' use of confidential job-related information.

A fairly standard agreement form for a researcher on the staff of a chemical manufacturing firm reads:

> Employee will use confidential professional information obtained by him while in the employ of the corporation only as directed by the corporation and will not disclose any formulas or processes, in whole or in part, to a third party without the written consent of the corporation either during, or subsequent to, his term of employment.

Complementary provisions may allow for instructions that employees surrender all materials relating to trade secrets to the employer before they leave the company. Other agreements prohibit "moonlighting" and preclude the company's outgoing employees from accepting jobs with competitors for a specific number of months or years.

Noncompetitive agreements should be discussed with the company's attorneys. Follow their guidelines for establishing—and enforcing—employee agreements that will effectively inhibit the outflow of confidential information. Companies with business and technical information that is not patentable may have the additional legal protection of an official "trade-secret" designation. If the conditions defining a "trade secret" are met, the information may be disclosed to employees as necessary. But the company is obligated to clarify the highly confidential nature of the disclosure. In these instances, pre-employment secrecy pacts or noncompetitive agreements may establish a pattern of "due diligence" by the company in protecting confidential information.

Before the hiring process is complete, it should be determined whether prospective employees are bound by secrecy agreements with previous employees. If they do not appear to take a previous commitment seriously, it is doubtful that they will respect a similar pact with the employing company.

Once employees have officially signed on, attention should turn to the training process. Specific information of a confidential nature should be treated with care at every stage of its evolution. Be sure that training materials do not reveal more than necessary. Do not expose new recruits to information which could be subjected to unnecessary risk. By the same token, a security-conciousness should be instilled from the beginning. The training process for new employees should include conditioning to the company's attitudes toward and rules about all security procedures.

About duties and responsibilities: Assignment of access to confidential information should be made only after careful consideration of the employee's capability and dependability. Access to proprietary information should be granted strictly on a "need-to-know" basis. How important is it that a given individual be privy to certain policy decisions, planning sessions and reports? Establishing "need-to-know" priorities gives an element of control over the distribution of information and limits the risks of leaks.

Importance of "Little Things." Even when careful controls are exercised over selection, training, and assignment, "little things" can make a big difference—and carelessness is often the culprit. Whether one is collecting sensitive marketing data or handling details for a new product release, steps should be taken to make sure that pertinent information reaches the intended receiver and is not intercepted along the way. Thus:

(1) Have telephones, data transmission systems, and dictating equipment checked for monitoring or recording devices on a routine basis.

(2) Watch the trash. Office wastebaskets are gold mines for discarded drafts of important documents. Obtain shredders and instruct your staff to use them.

(3) Destroy old typewritter ribbons. Cassette-type ribbons may be adjusted to be read as clearly as an actual letter or finished document.

(4) Watch your desk. Careless handling of routine paper flow can pose a threat. A few simple memos, when pieced together, can provide valuable clues about company operations.

(5) For legal purposes, make sure that documents or data of any sort that is considered "company confidential" is clearly marked. A simple rubber stamp or preprinted label should be used on every page or portion of the material. If documents are stolen, these markings may prove helpful in the pursuit of legal redress.

(6) Be diligent about locking desks, credenzas, file cabinets, and other storage areas. All too often, keys to important drawers or files are left in the unlocked top drawer of a secretary's desk. That may be convenient, but it is certainly not secure!

(7) Consider auxiliary personnel. Top management executives are carefully screened . . . how about the custodial staff? The mainte-

nance crews? Even the security guards? Rigorous standards are a must. In sensitive positions, consider administration of pre-employment polygraph examinations. Periodic polygraph testing may be a deterrent to illicit activities once an individual is on the job.

As a matter of policy, managers should make sure that "company confidential" information is not a subject for discussion anywhere outside the company. Casual conversation with friends or relatives, customers or suppliers, could have serious implications.

Carefully consider information to the Federal Government . . . . the Freedom of Information Act may make it possible for competitors—including foreign citizens—to obtain copies of vital materials.

Also consider information supplied to market researchers, pollsters, or others armed with apparently harmless questionnaires.

Public relations is another sensitive area. Everything from glowing stories in the big magazines to what is said in the "Help Wanted" section of the local newspaper has the potential of saying more than was intended. Avoid needless detail in sales and promotional brochures, and limit the information released to public relations personnel. What they don't know they can't circulate.

In the broad area of employee relations, many considerations will enhance the security of sensitive information. A sense of job security in key positions is important; so is adequate compensation. Satisfied employees are less likely to be tempted by competitive offers for employment. They are also more resistant to bribery and scheming for extracurricular profits. Study existing compensation plans and consider incentive arrangements and rewards for special developments—designs, packaging concepts, research projects, market strategies.

Of course, even the best efforts often fall short. In the event of an employee's termination or defection to another company, an "exit interview" should be conducted. The employee should be reminded of legal obligations with respect to confidential information and future employment elsewhere. In addition, employees who announce their intentions to leave should do just that—rather than spending two weeks collecting information that might benefit their new employers.

IRA A. LIPMAN, Chairman of the Board, and President, Guardsmark, Inc., Memphis, Tennessee

References Cited

[1] Hershey, Robert, "Commercial Intelligence on a Shoestring," *Harvard Business Review*, September–October, 1980.

[2] "How Smaller Companies Protect Their Trade Secrets," New York, The Conference Board, 1971, re. Section 757 of the restatement of the law of torts.

Cross References: *Computer Security/Automated Office Security; Security.*

SELECTION: See Recruitment and Selection, entries given there.

SENSITIVITY TRAINING

Sensitivity Training, also referred to as "Laboratory Training," or "T-Group" training, and as "the laboratory approach to human relations training" has increasingly become an important approach to executive and managerial development, although it is by no means limited in application to the improvement of an individual's behavioral skills in the business setting alone.

Formal Definition. Sensitivity training is an intensive experience, usually residential and extending over a number of days (commonly at least one or two weeks), in which the content for learning how to behave more effectively in interpersonal situations is not *outside* the learners, but is their *own* behavior, the transactions among them as they struggle to create a productive work group and as they learn to help one another to learn and to change. A basic assumption is that involving experiences are a necessary condition for learning. An equally necessary condition is a process of inquiry by which the learners examine, analyze, learn from, and eventually generalize from their experiences to back-home situations.

Broadly, the goal of sensitivity training has been defined as helping trainees improve the quality of their membership and participation in human affairs. Three of the founders of laboratory training, Benne, Bradford, and Lippitt [1], list specific areas of learning stressed as:

(1) Increased sensitivity to emotional reactions and expressions in oneself and in others.

(2) Greater ability to perceive and to learn from the consequences of one's actions through attention to feelings, one's own and others.

(3) Clarification and development of personal values and goals consonant with a democratic and a scientific approach to problems of social and personal decision and action.

(4) Development of concepts and theoretical insights as tools in linking personal values, goals, and intentions to actions consistent with these "inner" factors and with situational requirements.

(5) Development of behavioral skills to support better integrations of intentions and actions.

(6) Ability to transfer laboratory learnings to back-home situations.

(7) Learning how to learn—to continue to be an analyst of one's own behavior and to become the kind of self the learner is seeking to become.

History. The origins of sensitivity training are generally traced to Kurt Lewin's experimental work in GROUP DYNAMICS, specifically to a conference of community leaders called in 1946 by the Connecticut Interracial Commission. The conference was seen as "an experiment designed to reveal effective ways of teaching individual and group skills required for harmonious and productive living in modern society" [2]. Partly adventitiously and partly as the result of planning, the staff and participants discovered the training potential of a group in which the content for learning is the processes by which members learn to work together.

The Connecticut experiment was carried further by the same training staff and others in 1947 when the National Training Laboratories (originally the National Training Laboratory for Group Development) conducted its first summer sessions at Bethel, Maine, the first program of sensitivity or laboratory training in the area of human behavior. Since 1947, programs utilizing sensitivity training have expanded both geographically, as training centers have been established across the country, and as to occupational and organizational interest.

"Target populations" for sensitivity training have come to include the supervisor, manager, or administrator whose job is to work with and through people to get work done; the growing number of professional helpers who have educational and consultative responsibilities in community, industrial, educational, governmental organizations; and the total membership of an organization with training groups composed of persons who customarily work together (in distinction to the early training groups composed of strangers who might never see one another again). A recent development involves training for children, youth, and college students, including an emphasis on cross-generational relations. Another recent and growing application is for persons coming from different cultural or national backgrounds. Sensitivity or laboratory training thus assumes that there are generic characteristics of learning experiences that are common for all clients [1].

Since the early 1960s there has been a great proliferation of types of programs under the general heading of Sensitivity Training, ranging from "encounter groups," "personal growth groups" and "human potential groups," to a variety of programs created for therapeutic purposes. The rapid spread of this approach, with an estimated one million persons having participated in some form of sensitivity training, has inevitably produced some questionable programs led by untrained and inexperienced trainers. The International Association of Applied Social Scientists has been formed with the express purpose of accrediting trainers so that the public may be better protected.

A third change has been the growing realization of the importance both of pre-laboratory efforts to create receptivity to change within the organization and of follow-up efforts to support continuing change efforts.

Approaches and Techniques. The primary setting for sensitivity training has been the residential training laboratory, and the specific medium has been the training group (widely known as the "T Group"). In describing sensitivity training, it is thus necessary to describe these two educational innovations.

The term "laboratory" is deliberately descriptive. The laboratory is a special, constructed environment where it is possible to observe forces that operate in the field (the job situation of the trainees), but to observe them under advantageous conditions—well-contained, free from distractions, and under circumstances where trying new things and making mistakes are not too costly. The laboratory, and specifically the T Group, were invented to provide these conditions for training.

A sensitivity training group is the central

training unit within a laboratory. It is an initially *unstructured group* in which individuals participate as learners. The rationale for the lack of structure may be summarized thus: The ambiguity of a situation in which normal "givens" (e.g. stated agenda, established roles of membership and leadership, standards of performance, norms of behavior) are absent creates in most persons anxieties and tensions. Efforts to relieve the tension either by withdrawing from active participation or by attempting to provide the missing elements (by taking leadership, gathering support, making assumptions about goals, assigning roles, setting up an agenda, making ground rules) reflect the individual's normal ways of behaving under stress. In normal, on-the-job situations, however, such behavior may be resented or may be unproductive but still be accepted without comment by associates, whether peers, subordinates, or superiors. Or there may be comments, but the individual may be unable to hear them or to make use of them. There is a lack of awareness of and skill in testing and learning from the consequences of one's own behavior.

There is no "typical way" in which a sensitivity training session gets under way. Depending upon the nature of the group and the assessment of the training director, the opening session may be literally and completely unstructured, with the group assembling and doing nothing until one member breaks the ice by an opening remark related to the problems of interpersonal relations. After that, the group "takes it from there" by pursuing whatever line of discussion is thus triggered. On the other hand, the leader may open the session with perhaps a form of role playing by suggesting a hypothetical situation and letting the group carry on with its own discussion and the ramifications thereby opened up.

A controversial aspect of sensitivity training has been the frustration and interpersonal animosity which may occur in T-group sessions. The following example from one group's experiences is provided by Marrow [3]:

> *Phil:* "George, that last comment is typical of your attitude toward all of us. You're sharp and you know it. But here's something you don't know; you don't know why you need to have your own way all the time, why you argue over every trifle. The rest of us don't act that way. We feel the group is too important to waste our time arguing about insignificant items. Personally I feel that we've put up with your attitude long enough."
>
> *George:* "I'm tired of you people leaning on me. Everyone has an equal chance to be heard and to influence the rest, and if you are that easily persuaded, heaven help your companies. I'd hate to have a bunch of rubber stamps like you working for me!"
>
> *Sam:* "I wonder if you really know the kind of yes men you must have on your staff. You have a blind spot on this subject that keeps you from seeing how obnoxious your manner is. I'm not talking about your ability; you've got plenty. And you're an able speaker, the most articulate member of the group. But you don't seem to realize how you bulldoze everyone else by your manner. I think you'd be a great success in a one-man company. But in a big outfit the only men who would work with you and not resign would be the weak ones—those who were willing to let somebody else do all the thinking."
>
> *George* (answering with impatience): "Do you think you've said anything constructive—all you want to do is to find a scapegoat."

The above interchange illustrates the highly personal, no-holds-barred interaction which may arise in a T-group session. Such interplay among members, if uncontrolled, may result in emotional traumas that are not easily healed. This underscores the importance of the point previously made about the need for properly accredited trainers.

A basic requirement, according to Bradford et al [4], is "that persons entering a course of professional development as trainers should have a well-developed background of training, academic and professional, in one of the behavioral sciences, preferably perhaps in social or clinical psychology. But understanding and appreciation of sociological, anthropological, and philosophical approaches to human behavior are also important. In addition, the prospective trainer should have a concern for developing his skills in processes of application to human affairs. He should be committed to the growth of individuals, groups, and organizations, and to improving his understandings and skills in the helping role. He should be further committed to the continuing development of laboratory methodologies of education through theory building, research, and scholarship."

Effectiveness. How much each member can learn in the training group is determined in large part by the extent to which he is able to become personally involved in the learning group and its processes, i.e., by how much of himself he is able and willing to invest. The trainer and the group members cannot help an individual member change and improve his ways of behaving unless they have opportunity to see and react to what is to be changed. Willingness to expose one's behavior, however, requires a high level of trust. Creating a climate in which "exposure" is safe thus becomes an important task in a training group—one which has implications for work groups back on the job. With skillful help from the trainer—through his interventions, sometimes by his example—and from one another, training groups do learn how to create a climate where it is safe to expose characteristic ways of behaving, to react freely, to express feelings in ways that can be helpful, to ask for reactions to one's own behavior, to try out other ways of behaving. Members can learn how to listen more keenly to cues about their own impact on others. And they can become more skillful and sensitive as they try to help others. Many experience, often for the first time, the "remarkable release of individual and group creativity which sometimes appears upon the reduction of socially-induced defensiveness" [5].

Through an opportunity to experiment in an ambiguous situation, members are learning how to establish processes of inquiry, of giving and receiving help ("feedback"), of creating conditions in which they can learn and work colaboratively. The very ambiguity seems to enable members to "start over again," to *re*-learn things about human behavior and human relations that have been poorly learned or mislearned. From an initial lack of structure, the training group moves toward workable structure which it has itself created. In the process each member may learn about his own motives, feelings, and strategies for dealing with other persons, and about their consequences.

In the processes of helping to build a work group, each member may learn also about other groups. He may develop skills of membership and leadership and skills for changing and improving his organization as well as himself. Since critical decisions are increasingly made in small groups, improvement here may be reflected in total organization improvement. Of greatest importance, the member may learn what in his behavior causes distrust in others and what he may do to create trust and openness back on the job.

The training group in a deeply involving experience. As such it generates the motivating energy for learning from other activities of the total laboratory. These activities are designed, broadly, to help "make sense" of the training group experiences. Generally, they include sessions for the presentation of behavioral and organizational theory—the "cognitive map" for learning about human behavior—and activities (e.g. role playing, participative cases, simulation exercises, problem analysis, consultation) designed to provide practice in testing and using new approaches and new ways of behaving.

Acceptance and Spread. In 1975 the NTL Institute for Applied Behavioral Science reorganized as a professional member organization. The 345 professional members staff the wide variety of NTL programs which range from the basic Human Interaction (T Group) laboratory to training of trainers and organization development consultants. NTL sponsors approximately 130 programs around the United States and at the conference center at Bethel, Maine. At the same time there has been an emergence of many other organizations here and in other parts of the world which sponsor and conduct a variety of sensitivity training programs. In Europe in 1964 the European Institute for Transnational Studies in Group and Organizational Development was founded to give focus to the various approaches and to such training in many of the Western European countries.

In many universities in the United States as well as abroad, laboratory methods of learning in the area of human behavior are utilized. A large variety of organizations—industrial, educational, governmental, health, community, social service, youth groups—have made use of sensitivity training resources or have built such programs into their own organizations.

Particularly noticeable has been the vast increase of literature concerning sensitivity training that has appeared during the last decade. One portion of this writing has been the increase in professional and scholarly articles and books. The *Journal of Applied Behavioral Science,* at this writing in its sixteenth annual volume, is published by NTL Institute for Applied Behavioral Science.

A second area of writing comprises the articles appearing in many lay magazines, some supporting and some opposing sensitivity training. But all are evidence of the continuing spread and appropriate modification of the basic premises of laboratory training.

Leland P. Bradford, former Executive Director and Dorothy J. Mial, former Director, Education Division, National Training Laboratories (now NTL Institute); and Harold L. Hodgkinson, President, NTL Institute

Information References

Associations

International Association of Applied Social Scientists.
NTL Institute for Applied Behavioral Science.

Texts

Dyer, William G., "Modern Theory and Method in Group Training," New York, Van Nostrand Reinhold, 1972.

Golembiewski, Robert T. and Blumberg, Arthur, eds., "Sensitivity Training and the Laboratory Approach," 35d ed., Itasca, Ill., Peacock, 1977.

References Cited

[1] Benne, Kenneth D., Bradford, Leland P., and Lippitt, Ronald, "The Laboratory Method," in "T-Group Theory and Laboratory Method," Leland P. Bradford, Jack R. Gibb, and Kenneth D. Benne, eds., New York, Wiley, 1964.

[2] Lippitt, Ronald, "Training in Community Relations," New York, Harper & Bros. 1949.

[3] Marrow, Alfred J., "Behind the Executive Mask," New York, American Management Association, 1964.

[4] Bradford, Leland P., Gibb, Jack R., and Benne, Kenneth D., "A Look at the Future," from "T Group Theory and Laboratory Method" (see Ref. 1 above).

[5] Horwitz, Murray, "Training in Conflict Resolution," from "T Group Theory and Laboratory Method" (see Ref. 1 above).

Cross References: *Executive Development: "Away-from-Company" Programs (and cross references there given).*

SHIPPERS' ASSOCIATIONS

Cooperative Shipping by industrial firms under certain circumstances can be a significant method of reducing transportation costs. Since transportation involves the public interest, Congress considered it wise in 1942 to add Section 402(c)(1) to the Interstate Commerce Act, to permit manufacturers or other commercial enterprises which ship goods interstate to band together and arrange volume shipments. Group shipping was practiced before 1942 however, and began to expand in 1937 when the railroads published an all-commodity rate (carload mixture of different articles) to encourage volume shipping. This liberalization of rail tariffs helped large retail department store companies particularly because of their steady flow of traffic to their scattered outlets. The rapid growth of associations in the late 1950s and the 1960s was aided by the introduction of rail "piggyback" services and "freight all kinds" rates.

At the outset of this shipping innovation some companies held back using them for fear of revealing customer names and sales volume to competitors in the pool. But when distant markets were cut off by freight costs and minimum shipments became prohibitive, potential users joined in pursuit of a common goal—sales at low delivery prices.

This arrangement is advantageous for companies shipping less-than-carload lots between metropolitan areas more than approximately 600 miles apart, where carload rates offer sizeable economies—sometimes half the less carload rates.

The **Shippers' Association** operates like a freight forwarder in assembling small shipments, consolidating them into carload or truckload lots, and distributing the individual shipments to the proper destinations. But the similarity ends there because the freight forwarder (1) is an independent firm, (2) is in business for profit, (3) is a common carrier subject to Federal regulation, (4) collects less-than-carload rates and minimum charges from the shipper and pays the railroad carload rates for its transportation service on the long haul, and (5) generally covers a wider area. (See FREIGHT FORWARDERS.)

When freight rates began to increase rapidly after World War II, new associations spread quickly and now number well over 100. The American Institute for Shippers' Associations, Inc., was organized to coordinate the activities of its members as well as act to preserve and protect their rights.

Some shippers' associations have failed, mainly because of insufficient tonnage and poor planning. Regularity of car forwarding is important, because sacrifice of service to members may jeopardize sales, thereby defeating the original marketing purpose.

Some associations become involved in investigations of—and even prosecutions for—ICC violations or improper practices. Shippers or associations and carriers are equally liable to many of the penalty provisions of the Act.

Generally the nature or classification of merchandise for shipment is not restricted, provided the commodity is packed well and can be loaded without danger of damage to other lading. Associations are usually formed by companies shipping similar merchandise. Membership is not limited in number, since tonnage must be sufficient to ship full cars to a central point as a practical matter.

The ICC has recommended various amendments to Congress to tighten exempt provision relating to shippers' associations to eliminate from operation other than bona fide, non-profit shipper groups. Legislators have turned a deaf ear to such suggestions primarily because of heavy shipper opposition.

Advantages gained through successful group shipping are: reduced total freight costs; fast and reliable delivery service; no penalty for small shipments; minimum stocks because of constant flow of merchandise from manufacturers to stores; shipments pinpointed through manifest tracing; and in most cases, reduced claims through systematic freight handling.

Local chambers of commerce or trade groups in most large cities will usually assist in organizing shippers' associations. However, no company without a full-time trafic manager or the help of a transportation consultant should attempt to form one.

STEPHEN TINGHITELLA, Editorial Director, *Traffic Management,* New York, New York

Information Reference

For a list of nonprofit shipper associations and their consolidators and distributors in the U.S., and for related information: New York Chamber of Commerce and Industry, Transportation Department, New York, N.Y.

Cross References: *Freight Forwarders; Physical Distribution Management; Traffic and Transportation: Structure of the Transportation Industry; Traffic Management.*

SIMULATION. See Management Games; Operational Gaming and Monte Carlo Simulation.

SMALL BUSINESS ADMINISTRATION

The **U.S. Small Business Administration** is a small, independent Federal agency, created by Congress in 1953 to assist, counsel, and champion the millions of American small businesses which are the backbone of this country's competitive free-enterprise economy.

The mission of SBA, is to help people get into business and to stay in business. To do this, SBA acts as an advocate for small business; it espouses the cause of small business, explains small business's role and contributions to society and the economy, and advocates programs and policies that will help small business. The Agency acts in close coordination with other Federal agencies, with Congress, and with financial, education, professional and trade institutions and associations. SBA also provides prospective, new, and established persons in the small business community with financial assistance, management counseling, and training. Additionally, SBA helps get a share of government procurement contracts for small firms.

The Agency has about 4,400 permanent employees and more than 100 offices throughout the nation. To provide quick service, it has delegated decision-making authority to its field offices in most of the program areas. (See listing of cities at end of this article.)

What Is a Small Business? SBA defines a small business as one which is independently owned and operated and is not dominant in its field. To be eligible for SBA loans and other assistance, a business must meet a size standard set by the Agency. For many years, this standard was based on annual receipts, assets, net worth, and/or number of employees, depending on type of industry and SBA program. Early in 1980, SBA proposed a new and simple standard, based solely on total number of employees per firm. The number-of-employee standard would vary by industry; in some cases, companies would be considered "small" if they had fifteen or fewer workers and in other cases the "small" standard would be as high as 2,500 employees. Specific size-standard information is available through any SBA office.

Eligibility for Assistance. Most small, independent businesses are eligible for SBA assistance. Under the Disaster Loan Recovery Program, owners of both small and large businesses are eligible for SBA Disaster Loan Assistance. Homeowners, renters, and nonprofit organizations are also eligible.

Advocacy. Congress in recent years has reemphasized the Advocacy function of SBA to bring about visible, substantive changes in both Federal and public policy toward small business. To champion more effectively the causes of small business and to help it survive in the economic marketplace, Congress created the post of Chief Counsel for Advocacy within SBA. The Chief Counsel is appointed by the President and confirmed by the Senate.

Congress specified five basic, statutory duties for SBA's advocacy office:

(1) Serve as a focal point for the receipt of complaints, criticisms, and suggestions concern-

ing the policies and activities of any part of the Executive Branch of the Federal Government which affect small business.

(2) Counsel small businesses on how to resolve their problems in dealing with the Federal Government.

(3) Develop proposals for changes in the Executive Branch to carry out better the mandate of the Small Business Act that the Government "aid, counsel, assist, and protect . . . the interest of small business concerns in order to preserve free competitive enterprise . . ." and to communicate such proposals to the appropriate Federal agencies;

(4) Represent small businesses before other Federal agencies whose actions affect small business.

(5) Enlist the help of Government and private groups to disseminate information about the programs and services of the Federal Government and how small businesses can use these for their benefit.

To carry out these statutory duties, the Chief Counsel for Advocacy, subject to the approval of the SBA Administrator, can: consult with private business, economic, financial, legal, and regulatory experts . . . use the services of SBA's National Advisory Council and appoint other advisory boards or committees as needed . . . hold hearings on matters affecting small business . . . and submit reports to Congress along with recommendations for improving the climate for small business.

All offices within SBA—not just the Advocacy operation—have an advocacy function as they carry out their particular assistance programs in financial, procurement, and management aid. Because of that emphasis, much of the Agency's day-to-day service consists of advocacy case work. Advocacy also performs both general and specific research. It helps in gathering small business data on which the Federal government can make sound policy decisions on matters affecting small business. Other research efforts concentrate on continually assessing the relative position of small business in the economy.

Help For Women Entrepreneurs. Women, of course, are eligible for all SBA loan and assistance programs and counseling services. But helping women become successsful entrepreneurs is a stated major goal of SBA. Women make up more than half of America's population, but they own fewer than 5% of its businesses. Since 1977, SBA has had an on-going nationwide women's business ownership campaign. In 1980, as a result of the President's and SBA's increasing commitment to women, an SBA Assistant Administrator for Women's Business Enterprise was appointed and staff and programs were expanded.

All areas of SBA are involved in helping women entrepreneurs. A "women's representative" has been designated in each SBA office. Workshops and seminars are held around the country to teach women how to get into business, how to improve their basic business skills, and how SBA can help them expand an existing business.

A woman-owned business is defined as a "business that is at least 51% owned by a woman or women who also control and operate it."

Financial Assistance. *Regular Business Loans.* SBA offers a variety of loan programs to eligible small business concerns which cannot borrow on reasonable terms from conventional lenders without Government help. There are two types of regular business loans: *direct loans* from SBA; and *guaranty loans,* under which SBA guarantees up to 90% of the loan which a bank or other private lender agrees to make.

Under law, SBA cannot consider making a direct loan unless a private lender (usually a bank) refuses to make a loan itself or take part in an SBA guaranty loan. In any case, the funds which SBA has for direct loans are limited, and the demand for direct loans exceeds the supply of funds. Therefore, most business loans are of the bank-guaranty type. (In the Fiscal Year ending September 30, 1979, for example, Congress authorized SBA to make direct loans totaling $220 million but guaranty loans totaling $3.3 billion.) Direct business loans are for not more than $350,000 and guaranteed loans are for not more than $500,000. Maturity may be up to ten years (twenty for acquiring real property or construction of facilities). The average size of an SBA business loan is $115,000 and the average maturity is eight years.

In late 1979, SBA began offering a new "mini-loan" program for women, under which small firms owned by a woman or women could be eligible for loans of up to $20,000. Regular business loans may be used for: business construction, expansion, or conversion; purchase of machinery, equipment, facilities, supplies or materials; and working capital.

Special Loan Programs. In the general area of financial assistance, SBA also offers a variety of special loan programs:

Economic Opportunity Loans, to low-income persons and those who are socially or economically disadvantaged, wanting to start their own firms or expand existing ones. Military service in the Vietnam years may be a contributing factor in determining a person's socially or economically disadvantaged status.

Local Development Company Loans, to groups of local citizens whose aim is to improve the economy in their area. The funds may be used by the development company to assist specific small businesses for the purpose of plant acquisition, construction, conversion, or expansion, including acquiring land, machinery, and equipment.

State Development Company Loans, to state development companies chartered by special state legislation to promote state-wide business growth. Loan proceeds may be used by the development company to provide small firms within a state with long-term loans and equity capital.

Pool Loans, to corporations formed and capitalized by groups of eligible small firms. Loan proceeds may be used to assist firms in the pool.

Small General Contractor Loans, to assist small construction firms with short-term financing. Loan proceeds can be used to finance residential or commercial construction or rehabilitation of property for sale. Proceeds cannot be used for owning and operating real estate for investment purposes.

Contractors Line of Credit Guarantees, to assist small firms in the short-term financing of labor and material costs of an assignable contract.

Seasonal Line of Credit Guarantees, to provide short-term financing for small firms having a seasonal loan requirement due to seasonal increase in business activity.

Energy Loans, to firms engaged in manufacturing, selling, installing, servicing, or developing specific energy measures.

Displaced Business Loans, to small firms suffering substantial economic injury caused by federally (or state or locally) assisted construction contracts.

Handicapped Assistance Loans, to physically handicapped small business owners and private nonprofit organizations which employ handicapped persons and operate in their interest.

Product Disaster Loans, to small firms engaged in processing or marketing products for human consumption. The loans are made when such firms suffer substantial economic injury because of disease or toxicity resulting from natural or undetermined causes.

Base Closing Economic Injury Loans, to small firms suffering substantial economic injury caused by the closing of a major military installation or severe reduction in the size and scope of operations at a major military installation.

Strategic Arms Economic Injury Loans, to small firms suffering substantial economic injury as a result of international strategic arms limitation treaties.

Emergency Energy Shortage Loans, to small firms suffering substantial economic injury as a result of shortages of energy or fuel.

Regulatory Economic Injury Loans, to small firms suffering substantial economic injury caused by new Federal law or regulation. Examples of laws which might injure small firms are the Federal Mine Safety and Health Amendments Act, the Occupational Safety and Health Act (OSHA), the Clean Air Act, and the Federal Water Pollution Control Act.

Economic Dislocation Loans, to small business concerns suffering substantial economic injury which are located in certain regions or business sectors designated by the SBA Administrator as suffering from any extraordinary severe, and temporary natural or other condition which is not associated with regular business occurrences.

Disaster Assistance. Natural disasters, such as hurricanes, floods, tornados, etc., often cause hardship to businesses and individuals. Homes and businesses may be damaged or destroyed. When the President or the Administrator of the Small Business Administration declares a specific area to be a disaster area, two types of loans are offered by SBA:

Physical Damage Natural Disaster Recovery Loans. They are made to homeowners, renters, businesses (large and small), and nonprofit organizations within the disaster area. Loan proceeds can be used to repair or replace damaged or destroyed homes, personal property, and businesses.

Economic Injury Natural Disaster Loans. They are made to small businesses which suffer economic losses because of the disaster. Loan proceeds may be used for working capital and to pay financial obligations which the small business owners could have met had the disaster not occurred. SBA establishes on-site offices with experienced personnel to help with loan information, processing, and disbursement.

Pollution Control Financing. SBA assists highly qualified small businesses to finance pollution control facilities through the use of Federal tax-exempt industrial revenue bonds. Terms are up to 30 years and rates are as low as 5½%. Up to $5 million per small business may be obtained through the bond markets with a 100% guarantee from SBA.

Surety Bonds. SBA is committed to making the bonding process accessible to small and emerging contractors who, for whatever reasons, find bonding unavailable to them. The Agency is authorized to guarantee to a qualified surety up to 90% of losses incurred under bid, payment, or performance bonds issued to contractors on contracts valued up to $1 million. The contracts may be used for construction, supplies, or services provided by either a prime or subcontractor for government or non-government work.

Loan Administration. After a loan has been made, SBA personnel in district offices service the loan to help assure borrower success in every case possible. In its participation loans, SBA works with banks in troublesome situations. In the instance of direct loans. Agency personnel work directly with borrowers.

When loan repayment difficulties develop, SBA attempts to mitigate losses, both to the government and borrowers, by such means as counseling by SCORE (see below), remedial loan adjustments or, in the event of business failure, disposition of the business assets and other collateral security or through reliance on the pledge of any guarantors.

Small Business Investment Companies (SBICs). Money for "venture" or "risk" investments is difficult for small businesses to obtain. SBA licenses, regulates, and provides financial assistance to privately owned and operated Small Business Investment Companies (SBICs). Their major function is to make "venture" or "risk" investments by supplying equity capital and extending unsecured loans and loans not fully collateralized to small enterprises which meet their investment criteria. SBICs are privately capitalized and obtain financial leverage from SBA. They are intended to be profit-making corporations. Because of their own economics, most SBICs do not make very small investments.

SBICs finance small firms in two general ways—by straight loans and by equity-type investments which give the SBIC actual or potential ownership of a portion of a small business' equity securities. Many SBICs provide management assistance to the companies they finance.

SBA also licenses a specialized type of SBIC solely to help small businesses owned and managed by socially or economically disadvantaged persons. Military service in the Vietnam years may be a contributing factor in determining a person's socially or economically disadvantaged status. This type of SBIC is a Section 301(d) SBIC, formerly referred to as a MESBIC (Minority Enterprise SBIC).

The administration of the SBIC program is handled by SBA's central office in Washington, D.C.

Minority-Owned Small Business. Americans who are members of minority groups, such as Blacks, Native Americans, and Hispanics, long have had difficulty entering the nation's economic mainstream. Raising money to open their small businesses has not been easy for them, and they often lack adequate training. Minority business persons also have had trouble finding, keeping, and expanding sales markets. Members of minority groups, of course, are eligible for all SBA programs. But SBA offers special programs to assist members of minority groups who want to start small businesses or expand existing ones. In this effort, SBA has combined its own programs with those of private industry, banks, local communities, and other Federal agencies.

Efforts to help minority-owned businesses were expanded in 1978, when Congress approved a capital ownership development program for minorities and placed this effort under the direction of SBA's Associate Administrator for Minority Small Business and Capital Ownership Development.

The office of Minority Small Business and Capital Ownership Development, located in the Agency's central office, is assisted by Minority Business Development field representatives in SBA's regional and district offices. Minority Small Business staff members cooperate with local business development organizations and explain to potential minority entrepreneurs how SBA's services and programs can help them become successful business owners.

Under one section of the Small Business Act, Section 8(a), SBA, working with procurement officials in other agencies, serves as prime contractor for Federal goods and service purchases, and then subcontracts this Federal work to small firms owned by socially and economically disadvantaged persons—minority persons, in effect. SBA also is empowered to provide management, technical and bonding assistance to firms holding 8(a) contracts.

Management Assistance. SBA places special emphasis on improving the management ability of small business owners and managers.

The Agency's Management Assistance program includes free individual counseling, courses, conferences, workshops, problem clinics, and a wide range of publications. Counseling is provided through programs established by SBA's Management Assistance staff; the Service Corps of Retired Executives (SCORE); its corollary organization of active business men and women, the Active Corps of Executives (ACE); and numerous professional associations. SBA tries to match the need of a specific business with the expertise available through its counseling programs. The following is a brief summary of what these programs include:

SCORE and *ACE* help small business executives solve their operating problems through a one-on-one counseling relationship. Counseling is not limited to small businesses that have a problem. It is available as well to managers of successful firms who wish to review their objectives and long-range plans for expansion and diversification.

Small Business Institutes (SBIs) have been organized through SBA on almost 500 university and college campuses as another way to help small business. At each SBI, senior and graduate students at schools of business administration, and their faculty advisors, provide on-site management counseling. Students are guided by the faculty advisors and SBA management assistance experts and receive academic credit for their work.

Small Business Development Centers (SBDCs) draw from resources of local, state, and Federal Government programs, the private sector, and university facilities to provide managerial and technical help, research studies, and other types of specialized assistance of value to small business. These university-based centers provide individual counseling and practical training for small business owners.

Business management courses in planning, organization, and control of a business—as distinguished from administration of daily activities—are co-sponsored by SBA in cooperation with educational institutions, Chambers of Commerce, and trade associations. Courses generally take place in the evening and last from six to eight weeks. In addition, conferences covering such subjects as working capital, business forecasting, and marketing are held for established businesses on a regular basis. SBA conducts Pre-Business Workshops, dealing with finance, marketing assistance, types of business organization, and business site selection, for prospective business owners. Clinics on particular problems of small firms in specific industrial categories are held on an as-needed basis.

International trade counseling and training is available to managers of small businesses considering entering the overseas marketplace as well as those desiring to expand current export operations. SBA works closely with the U.S. Department of Commerce and other Government agencies, and with private organizations, to help develop programs to aid small firms in doing business abroad.

Management, marketing, and technical publications issued by SBA on hundreds of topics are available to established and prospective managers of small firms concerned about specific management problems and various aspects of business operations. Most of these publications are available from SBA free of charge. Others can be obtained for a small fee from the U.S. Government Printing Office. In addition to management assistance publications, brochures describing the Agency's programs are available at all SBA offices.

Procurement Assistance. Each year, the Federal Government contracts with private companies for billions of dollars in goods and services. SBA helps small businesses obtain a fair share of this Government business, as required by law.

In helping implement that law, SBA:

Helps federal agencies to direct government subcontracts to small businesses.

Helps private contractors to direct Federal subcontracts to small businesses.

Refers qualified small businesses to Federal prime contractors.

Monitors the granting of Federal contracts to small firms by Federal agencies.

Federal procurement specialists in SBA offices throughout the country counsel small businesses on how to prepare bids and obtain prime contracts and subcontracts, direct them to Government agencies that buy the products or services the small firms supply, help them get their names placed on bidders' lists, and assist in obtaining drawings and specifications for proposed purchases. These procurement experts also offer many related services, including supplying leads on research and development projects, new technology, and assistance in technology transfer.

Government purchasing offices set aside some contracts or portions of contracts for exclusive bidding by small business. SBA Procurement Center Representatives stationed at major military and civilian procurement installations recommend additional "set-asides," refer small businesses to Federal contracting officers, assist small concerns with contracting problems, and recommend relaxation of unduly restrictive specifications.

SBA develops subcontracting opportunities for small business by maintaining close contact with prime contractors and referring qualified small firms to them. The Agency has developed agreements and close working relationships with the majority of the nation's top 100 prime contractors, who cooperate by offering small firms opportunities to compete for their subcontracts.

If a small firm is the low bidder on a Federal contract, and the contracting officer questions the firm's ability to perform the contract, the firm may ask SBA for a Certificate of Competency (COC). When a firm applies for a COC, SBA makes an on-site study of the firm's facilities, management, performance record, and production capacity in relationship to the contract in question. If SBA determines that the firm is capable of performing the contract within the required time period, the Agency issues a COC attesting to that fact. The contacting officer must then award the contract to the small firm.

To make available a master list of small companies capable of performing work on Federal contracts and subcontracts, SBA has developed the Procurement Automated Source System (PASS). This computerized system lists the names of small companies and their capabilities, to assist Federal procurement officers and procurement officials at private contractors assign Federal work to the small business community. SBA Regional Offices and major purchasing centers at the Department of Energy are equipped with PASS computer terminals. Terminals also are being made available to other Federal agencies and to SBA's procurement representatives at selected Department of Defense installations.

Each year, the Federal Government sells surplus real and personal property and natural resources, such as timber. SBA works with Government agencies which are selling the property and resources to assure that small businesses have an opportunity to buy a fair share of them. The Agency also ensures that small firms operating in energy-related industries obtain an equitable portion of Federal energy-related mineral lease contracts.

SBA also aims to win for small businesses a fair share of Federal research and development contracts. Technology Assistance Officers (TAOs) are responsible for the conduct of the Technology Assistance Program in SBA Regional Offices. The TAOs use a variety of resources and data banks to identify appropriate technology and make it available to small firms that have requested assistance in solving a problem, improving a process, or developing a new product.

In a cooperative agreement with the National Aeronautics and Space Administration. SBA has established technology assistance projects with selected NASA Industrial Application Centers, and is under contract to serve the technology needs of small businesses in the four-state area of Missouri, Kansas, Iowa, and Nebraska.

How to Get Help from the SBA. The Small Business Administration is organized into three operational levels:

(1) The Central Office in Washington, D.C. The Central Office determines Agency policy, works with the White House, other Executive Branch agencies and departments, and Congress to provide management and direction of SBA programs nationwide. The Central Office, while receptive to inquiries from the small business community and the public in general, does not make loans or offer assistance to specific companies or to individuals wanting to start a small business. The SBIC Program, however, is administered by Central Office.

(2) Regional Offices, located in ten major cities around the country—Boston, New York, Philadelphia, Atlanta, Kansas City, Dallas, Denver, Chicago, Seattle, and San Francisco. Each Region encompasses several states (the New York Region has jurisdiction over Puerto Rico, the San Francisco office has jurisdiction over Guam and American Samoa), and directs

a number of District Offices within the Region. Again, Regional Offices do not make individual loans or offer specific assistance to individuals or companies.

(3) District Offices, located throughout the country. Each District Office is staffed by a team of experts in the lending and assistance areas, who have the responsibility to consider loan applications, to offer individual management assistance, and to coordinate other small business services. District Offices are the real contact point for small businesses needing information or assistance. A District Director, appointed by the Regional Administrator, is in charge.

There is no charge for any SBA service. However, interest in small business today is high, and the demand for SBA assistance is great. Applicants for information and assistance can help by familiarizing themselves with SBA programs through the Agency's brochures and other literature, determining as precisely as possible what they need—and what they are eligible for—and bringing complete information when they meet with an SBA representative.

A. Vernon Weaver, Administrator, Small Business Administration, Washington, D.C.

Information References

For a complete list of SBA publications, and to order any SBA publication, a toll-free number has been established: 800/433-7212. Field offices are located in principal cities in all 50 states and in the District of Columbia, Guam, Puerto Rico, and the Virgin Islands.

SMITH, ADAM

Adam Smith (1723–1790), Scottish economist and philosopher, is most widely known for his *magnum opus,* "The Wealth of Nations" (full title, "Inquiry into the Nature and Causes of the Wealth of Nations"), published in 1776. This recognized masterpiece, a "first" in political economy, examined in detail the consequences of economic freedom, such as division of labor, the function of markets and mediums of exchange, and their international implications. He attacked the theories of mercantilism, the economic system of the major trading nations during the 16th, 17th, and 18th centuries which were based on the premise that national wealth and power depended upon increasing exports over imports and thus collecting precious metals by virtue of the "favorable balance." (For a further discussion of Smith's contribution to modern economic theory of an industrialized society, see the section, *Historic Development of Economics,* in the entry, Economics.)

Smith's earlier work was in philosophy. In 1751 he was elected professor of logic at Glasgow and in 1752 succeeded to the chair of moral philosophy, a position he held for some twelve years. While teaching there he wrote his "Theory of Moral Sentiments," which gave him the beginning of an international reputation.

Information References

Hollander, Samuel, "Economics of Adam Smith," Toronto, University of Toronto Press, 1973.

Cross Reference: *Economics.*

SOCIAL AUDIT

The business corporation is an integral part of the functioning of our nation. As such, in return for the privileges and rights granted it by the state, increasingly the corporation is being expected to assume responsibility toward the society in which it operates.

Business corporations themselves have changed, and at the same time have become so massive that they exercise important influences on the communities in which they exist. Often they strongly influence the laws to which they are required to conform. The entire private sector has become all mixed up with the public sector, private rights-of-way crossing public thoroughfares.

There is ample evidence that corporate managements are recognizing the importance of their actions on the social well-being of our nation, and increasingly are reporting this aspect of their operations in annual reports. Thus, in 1976, of the Fortune 500 companies, 456 or 91% made some kind of social disclosures in their annual reports to stockholders, as compared to 286 or 57% in 1973. [1]

The manner of reporting social actions, however, varies considerably, ranging from observations within the body of a President's Letter to Shareholders to a structured separate report. Only seven of the Fortune 500 corporations, however, reported their social actions in a separate report.

A Ford Foundation-supported study found that 57% of institutional investors take social considerations into account in the selection of investments. In addition, they review the social aspects of their investment policy on a current basis [2]. A U.S. Chamber of Commerce study a number of years ago recommended that wherever possible, each business firm should quantify costs and benefits of its social performance in order to help plan and measure its social action programs. It further urged business firms to develop a **Social Audit** procedure. [3].

In an attempt to determine the current business practices in assessing the social activities of corporations, the Committee for Economic Development conducted a survey of 880 companies. Replies were received from 284 companies. Three-fourths of the companies reported that they had performed a form of social audit during the preceding year. A question designed to establish whether executives thought that corporations would be required in the future to make social audits revealed that 44% thought such audits would be required. [4].

To implement a social audit program successfully, a company must be organizationally geared to the effort. It must arrange to set into motion corporate machinery to:

(1) Evaluate, quantitatively where possible, the social environment in which it functions.

(2) Establish improvement objectives.

(3) Make resource allocations in response to identified needs.

However formidable this may seem, it is no more complicated than setting up the planning and support organization for a new product line, or a marketing or manpower development program.

It can be argued that the time has come for a social exhibit to be prepared along with a business organization's traditional Income Statement and Statement of Financial Condition. Such a social exhibit or Socio-Economic Operating Statement (SEOS) [5] could be a tabulation of those expenditures made voluntarily by a business aimed at improving the welfare of its employees and the public, the safety of the product, and conditions of the environment. Expenditures required by law or union contract need not be included, inasmuch as these are mandatory and thereby necessary costs of doing business.

Offset against these "pro bono publico" expenditures could be those costs of socially beneficial items which have been brought to the attention of management, and which a "reasonably prudent socially aware management" would be expected to undertake, but this management chooses to ignore.

The statements themselves could be prepared by an internal interdisciplinary team. Members of the team might include a seasoned business executive, sociologist, accountant, public health administrator, economist, or members of other disciplines whose specific expertise would apply to a particular industry or circumstance. To give such statement credibility, they would be audited by an outside independent interdisciplinary team, headed by a certified public accountant.

An example of the type of statement referred to here is the Socio-Economic Operating Statement (SEOS) shown as Exhibit I [6].

Typical basic guidelines for the preparation of such a statement are:

(1) If a socially beneficial action is required by enforceable law or union regulations, it is not included in the SEOS.

(2) If a socially beneficial action is required by law but is ignored, the cost of such item is a "detriment" for the year. The same treatment is given an item if postponed, even with government approval.

(3) A prorated portion of salaries and related expenses of personnel who spend time in socially beneficial actions or with social organizations is included.

(4) Cash and product contributions to social institutions are included.

(5) The cost of setting up facilities for the general good of employees or the public, if done voluntarily without union or government mandate, is included.

(6) Expenditures made voluntarily for the installation of safety devices on the premises or in products and not required by law or other contract are included.

(7) Neglecting to install safety devices to protect employees or the public, where available at reasonable cost, is a "detriment."

(8) The cost of voluntarily building a playground or nursery facility for employees and/or neighbors is included. Operating costs of the unit are also included for each succeeding year applicable.

(9) The costs of relandscaping strip-mining sites or other environmental eyesores, if not required by law, are included.

(10) Extra costs of designing and building business facilities to upgrade health, beauty or safety standards are included.

There have been suggestions that Congress should consider enacting legislation allowing

EXHIBIT I

CHEM PRODUCTS MANUFACTURING CO., INC.
SOCIO-ECONOMIC OPERATING STATEMENT FOR THE YEAR ENDING DECEMBER 31, 19--.

I		
Social Actions—People-Related		
A—IMPROVEMENTS		
1. Minority enterprise technical assistance program	$ 4,000	
2. Emergency flood relief	3,000	
3. Training program for handicapped workers	8,000	
4. Executive time—hospital trusteeship	5,000	
5. Minority hiring program—extra training and turnover costs	6,000	
6. Day-care center for children of employees—set-up and maintenance cost; voluntarily established	11,000	
Total Improvements		$37,000
B—LESS DETRIMENTS		
1. Postponed installation of hydraulic safety control system—cost of unit	16,000	16,000
C—PEOPLE-RELATED ACTIONS—NET IMPROVEMENT FOR THE YEAR		$21,000
II		
Social Actions—Environment-Related		
A—IMPROVEMENTS		
1. Cost of installing water quality monitoring system to control pollution	22,000	
2. Cost of clearing and landscaping company-owned ravaged area and dump	41,000	
3. Executive time—free consulting service to state environmental protection agency	4,000	
Total Improvements		67,000
B—LESS DETRIMENTS		
1. Deferral of liquid waste treatment facility	60,000	
2. Postponed installation of higher smoke stacks to reduce air pollution	19,000	
Total Detriments		79,000
C—ENVIRONMENT-RELATED ACTIONS—NET DEFICIT FOR THE YEAR		($12,000)
III		
Social Actions—Product-Related		
A—IMPROVEMENTS		
1. Voluntarily discontinued alkaline product judged unsafe for home use—projected annual net income	23,000	
2. Salary of chemical engineer on loan to government product safety committee	21,000	
Total Improvements		44,000
B—LESS DETRIMENTS		
1. Cost of process redesign to reduce manufacturing hazard—recommended by Safety Council, but implementation deferred	36,000	36,000
C—PRODUCT-RELATED ACTIONS—NET IMPROVEMENT FOR THE YEAR		$8,000
Total Socio-economic Improvements for the Year Ending December 31		$17,000
Add: Net Cumulative Socio-Economic Improvements as at January 1		$176,000
GRAND TOTAL NET SOCIO-ECONOMIC IMPROVEMENTS TO DECEMBER 31		$193,000

companies a deduction against taxable income for the total Socio-Economic Improvements for the year as shown on the Socio-Economic Operating Statement which exceeds a percentage of the taxpayer's net worth.

The undersigned would recommend that such net socio-economic expenditures which exceed 1% of the net worth of a company be allowed as a full deduction from taxable income. This would be in addition to all other expense and depreciation allowances already made for these same items. Such a tax allowance would consciously assert the collective responsibility for our environmental and social problems by having government and the citizen-consumer indirectly share in the costs.

Other than the Socio-Economic Operating Statement, among the various efforts at constructing models for a social audit are the work of Raymond A. Bauer and Don H. Fenn, Jr. [7], Clark C. Abt [8], David H. Blake, William C. Fredrick, and Mildred S. Myers [9], and the analyses and model by John J. Corson and George A. Steiner in the Committee for Economic Development's "Measuring Business's Social Performance" [10].

Bauer and Fenn do not attempt to create a comprehensive model for the social audit. They write:

> Our goal is not to prescribe or predict a single form of audit. This is premature. We assume that if the concept has a future, its form or forms will

> evolve largely out of experience of people and institutions in doing audits, out of reactions of others to those audits, and out of the mores of the community as the audits develop.

Although the above authors do not present a comprehensive social audit, they nevertheless present a detailed analysis of the goals and problems of the social audit, and the need for greater research and development of social audit theories and models.

The Abt approach is to audit the total social impact of the company, and not simply its social programs. The financial equivalents are given in extreme detail, with elaborating notes as to methodology. This quantified social statement has been criticized as not fulfilling the real need of management, namely, an assessment of the cost and performance of specific social programs, and on the grounds that not much realism can be attached to the dollar-equivalents arrived at by arbitrary formula, to say nothing of the cost and effort of assembling the figures.

In 1974 the Committee for Economic Development published "Measuring Business's Social Performance" by John J. Corson and George A. Steiner. In addition to a survey of the extent and nature of corporate social disclosures in the early 1970s, the work presents a model for social auditing and reporting. This model is another example of the "process approach" to social auditing. It requires management to set up specific goals and objectives for identified social activities, and to prepare a quantitative statement. Although a model is proposed for auditing and reporting social information, the specific methods of auditing and the form of disclosure are not presented.

A more comprehensive model of the social audit was developed in 1976 by David H. Blake, William C. Frederick, and Mildred S. Myers of the University of Pittsburgh in "Social Auditing: Evaluating the Impact of Corporate Programs." Their social process audit "is designed to evaluate specific social programs established by management. Moreover, it evaluates the programs, in the light of managerial or corporate goals and objectives. [It] does not access the overall social impact of the corporation nor does it judge management according to some preconceived notion of what is good or correct behavior." Their social audit process is presented in much detail for management's internal use. [9]

It does not offer a comprehensive statement to be used to present the information in a concise, easy-to-read manner, but rather recommends a long, prose-form report which might be developed for each social program adopted by management.

Stockholders, enlightened business executives, and society in general would benefit by encouraging the implementation of a standardized reporting procedure for the social actions and non-actions of a business organization. Those responsible for directing the affairs of these mammoth institutions cannot be expected to initiate and expand activities which because of their costs would have an adverse impact on the income statement, thereby reflecting adversely on an incumbent management's stewardship. Another element in reporting the results of operations of a corporation is needed. The Socio-Economic Operating Statement, or other appropriate social exhibit would fill that need.

DAVID F. LINOWES, Boeschenstein Professor of Political Economy and Public Policy, University of Illinois, Urbana, Illinois

Information References

Bradshaw, Thornton, and Vogel, David, "Corporations and Their Critics," New York, McGraw-Hill, 1980.

Brown, Courtney, "Beyond the Bottom Line," New York, Macmillan, 1979.

Committee on Social Measurement of A.I.C.P.A., "The Measurement of Corporate Social Performance: Determining the impact of Business Actions on Areas of Social Concerns," New York, American Institute of Certified Public Accountants, 1977.

Dierkes, Meinolf and Bauer, Raymond A., "Corporate Social Accounting, New York, Praeger, 1973.

Estes, Ralph W., "Accounting and Society," Los Angeles, Melville Publishing Co., 1973.

Hay, Robert D. and Gray, Edmund R., "Business and Society," Cincinnati, South-Western, 1981.

Heyel, Carl, "The Social Audit," Madison, N.J., The Anderson Group, 1974.

Linowes, David F., "Strategies for Survival," New York, AMACOM Div., American Management Associations, 1973.

References Cited

[1] Beresford, Dennis R., "Social Responsibility Disclosure: 1977 Survey of Fortune 500 Annual Reports, New York, Ernst & Ernst, 1977.

[2] Ford Foundation, "Corporate Social Responsibility and the Institutional Investor—The Long-Streth Report," New York, Praeger, 1973.

[3] U.S. Chamber of Commerce, "The Corporation in Transition: Redefining Its Social Charter," Washington, 1973.

[4] Corson, John J. and Steiner, George A., "Measuring Business's Social Performance," Washington, Council on Economic Development, 1974.

[5] Linowes, David F., "The Corporate Conscience," New York, Hawthorn, 1974.
[6] *Ibid.*
[7] Bauer, Raymond A. and Feen, Dan H., Jr., "The Corporate Social Audit," New York, Russel Sage Foundation, 1972.
[8] Abt, Clark C., "The Social Audit for Management," New York, AMACOM Div., American Management Associations, 1977.
[9] Blake, David H., Frederick, William C., and Myers, Mildred S., "Social Auditing: Evaluating the Impact of Social Programs," New York, Praeger, 1976.

Cross References: *Financial Public Relations; Management Audit; Public Relations.*

STANDARD COSTING

Standard Costing refers to the establishment of cost standards and their application to problems of management, particularly those problems relating to product costs and departmental cost control.

Standard costs consist of allowed amounts of various cost factors, such as: materials, direct labor, manufacturing overhead, marketing, and administrative cost, as well as subdivisions of these, expressed in a variety of terms such as: pounds, tons, hours, invoice lines, and salesman's calls, all weighted by dollars. Although the overwhelming practice is to apply these standards in the course of operations, daily, weekly, and monthly, standards are sometimes established and applied at the conclusion of relatively long periods of operations, for example, a year.

There are three distinguishing characteristics of standard costs: (1) they are based upon objective experimentation or a careful study of past experience, or upon a combination of both procedures; (2) the nature, quality, and makeup of a product in terms of materials, labor, and facility requirements are carefully established; and (3) the productive or functional processes through which the product moves are carefully studied for integration and standardization.

Uses of Standard Costs. Standard costs:

(1) Provide a basis against which actual costs may be compared, and deviations from standards expressed in quantitative terms for ready use in the evaluation of efficiency at some level of an organization's operations.

(2) Provide for the assignment of costs representative of the actual costs on a consistent basis to production inventories and cost of goods sold.

(3) Expedite the ascertainment of profits during the interim on a product, departmental, or plant level.

(4) Are utilized in the preparation of budgets and in planning.

(5) Are useful as a guide to pricing present and prospective products or services.

(6) Provide data useful to a study of alternatives, particularly where the problem calls for a knowledge of activity costs by specified operations.

(7) Add to convenience in accounting routine, particularly in connection with raw materials, work in process, and finished goods accounting.

Considerable controversy raged in the late 1920s and during the 1930s concerning the proper interpretation of standard costs of manufacturing: Should they be considered simply units of measure to be employed entirely on a statistical basis outside the accounts proper, or as having a value representative of actual costs and capable of recording in the accounts?

By and large, the latter interpretation won out, and most accountants interpret standard manufacturing costs as costs representative of actual costs ideally suited to measure the flow of manufacturing costs through work in process, finished goods, and cost of goods sold accounts. For a great many purposes, greater reliance will be placed upon these figures during the course of a fiscal period than upon the accumulating historical cost data. For example, in the interim, standard costs take precedence over the recorded historical costs for most reporting purposes. A similar concensus concerning the integration of standard marketing costs into the formal accounts has not taken place, largely because it is generally assumed that most marketing costs are not applicable to product units. In contrast to practice with respect to standard manufacturing costs, standard marketing costs are widely used both on an independent statistical basis and on an integrated account basis.

Concepts. Standard costs may be established upon the basis of: (1) the best or average costs incurred in the past; (2) what costs are expected to be for the period under consideration under ordinary conditions of control; (3) the level of costs attainable under optimum conditions of control but not necessarily ideal with respect to efficiency of workers and equipment; and (4) what costs would be under ideal conditions of control and efficiency.

Standard costs of the nature of (1), above, should be used with considerable caution. The best costs of the past may have been entirely accidental in nature and not attainable in the future, or represent extremely poor performance relative to what is possible under good conditions of both good and bad experience weighted by the contingencies under which they took place. In general, because the very objective of standard costing is to improve upon past performance, standard costs based entirely upon past experience neither provide an incentive for improvement, nor are representative of the actual costs if the desired improvements take place.

Standard costs commonly referred to as "current" tend to partake of concepts indicated in points (2) and (3). When standard costs are established on the basis of what costs are expected to be under ordinary conditions of control, point (2), they tend to be attainable in nature and quite representative of accumulating actual costs. In the construction of such standards, allowance is made for the fact that it is difficult to maintain maximum efficiency continuously over extended periods of time. Sizable variances arising when such standards are employed indicate serious deviations from anticipated costs.

When standards are established on the basis of the level of costs attainable under optimum conditions of control, point (3), they become less attainable on a day-to-day basis. Such standards may be achieved sporadically over short periods of time, particularly toward the close of an operating period after considerable experience has been had in attempting to meet them. Although these higher but attainable standards provide more of a stimulus to cost reduction than standards of the order of (2), above, they will be less representative of accumulating actual costs. Because of this, sizable variances may be less serious in nature than variances arising in connection with the expected cost type of standard. When best attainable standards are used, variances will tend to be the rule rather than the exception.

Ideal standards, point (4), signify standards not currently attainable with present facilities and personnel. Although students of modern behavioral psychology point on occasion to situations where some people perform more efficiently when a goal is placed beyond their attainment, the concensus is that standards of the ideal type frustrate rather than stimulate improvement. Consequently, such standards are ordinarily useless for day-to-day performance control purposes. Because ideal standard costs are hypothetical, they have no place in the inventory and cost-of-goods-sold accounts. Their use would give rise continuously to significant variances. Ideal standard costs, however, are pertinent to certain comparisons made on a statistical basis. For example, the differences in cost obtained when these standards are applied to output as contrasted to an application of current standard costs provide an excellent measurement of the opportunity costs of not utilizing the most efficient equipment and personnel.

Current Cost Standards. When standard costs are computed on a current basis, the immediate future for the most part becomes the concern of the accountant. Forecasts of material prices, for example, may be used to determine material price standards; labor rates will emanate from union contracts or rates expected to prevail. Similarly, with respect to the price aspect of other costs factors, reference will be made to circumstances expected in the forthcoming fiscal period.

The establishment of usage standards varies, depending upon the "tightness" of standards contemplated. Where standards tending toward the ideal are utilized, physical quantities indicated by engineering drawings, weighing, or measuring of a model of the product to be produced, provide the basis for the usage aspect of the material cost standard. Similarly, time and motion studies may be employed to establish labor usage studies. At the other extreme, past experience may be brought to bear to allow for expected over-use of materials and labor time. In between these two divergent concepts of tightness or looseness, a range of attainable standards is employed in the construction of current cost standards calling for varying exertion upon the part of management and employees to reach standards established.

Standard Product Cost Card. Although a variety of business forms may be utilized in connection with standard costing, the standard product cost card or sheet is basic to the operation of a standard cost system on either a statistical or integrated account basis. The standard product cost card first shows physical quantities of materials allowed per unit of a particular product with quantities extended at standard prices. Subsequent sections of the card display in similar detail standard labor and overhead costs, as shown in Exhibit I.

All of the data shown on the standard product cost card will be supported by a great variety of complementary business forms, in which productive activity may be broken down by operations, and supervisory responsibility subdivided by cost centers. Thus, in addition to the standard product card illustrated, there may be:

An *operational standard cost sheet* detailing the variable standard costs of an operation.

A *cost center standard fixed cost sheet* showing all the fixed costs of a center on a flexible budget basis and including a computation of the center's normal overhead rate. (See FLEXIBLE BUDGETING.)

A *cost center control form* used to display actual and standard costs deemed controllable by the cost center supervisor.

Setting Standard Costs. *Materials.* Standard material prices are best established upon the

EXHIBIT I

STANDARD PRODUCT COST CARD

Product Name——————— Product Code No.———————

Material Costs				*Total Cost Per Unit*
Code No.	*Quantity Allowed Per Unit*	*Price Per Lb./Item*	*Total Cost Per Unit*	
B-225X	1/2	$0.50	$0.25	
L-217	2	1.00	2.00	
W-257	1	.20	.20	
			Total Material Cost Per Unit	$2.45
Direct Labor Costs				
Dept. and Op. No.	*D.L. Hrs. Allowed Per Unit*	*Labor Rates*	*Total Cost Per Unit*	
105	.10	$2.00	$0.20	
107	.20	2.00	.40	
210	.50	1.50	.75	
			Total Direct Labor Cost Per Unit	1.35
Manufacturing Overhead Costs				
Dept. and Op. No.	*D.L. Hrs. Allowed Per Unit*	*Overhead Rates*	*Total Cost Per Unit*	
105	.10	$3.00	$0.30	
107	.20	3.00	.60	
210	.50	2.00	1.00	
			Total Manufacturing Overhead Cost Per Unit	1.90
			TOTAL STANDARD COST PER UNIT	$5.70

basis of budgeting and forecasting, where possible looking forward to actual contractss for materials placed. When this is done, the material price standard for a particular item of material may be obtained by (1) adding together costs of anticipated purchases of the item and the current standard cost of the expected opening inventory, and (2) dividing the total cost of the two by the number of units involved. Alternatively, current invoice prices or vendor price lists adjusted for anticipated movements in prices may be relied upon as a basis for the material price standard.

Standard material quantities are best determined by reference to engineering drawings, weighing, measuring, and calculating, or by using experience gleaned from test runs. Standard allowances for waste or spoilage are similarly computed, and their sale value is used to diminish gross standard material cost. Alternatively, standard material usage may be based upon a careful analysis and study of past experience concerning material usage.

Labor. Standard labor rates are established by reference to union contracts or prevailing rates of pay, taking into consideration their possible incorporation into wage incentive plans. For purposes of standard costing, the labor rate is best established by setting rates by tasks to be accomplished rather than on an individual employee basis. With regard to a particular department or operational area, the labor rate is often computed by taking a total of standard payments made for a variety of tasks in an area and dividing this total by the standard hours of work.

Standard labor allowances are developed by (1) past experience, (2) simple observation, (3) TIME AND MOTION STUDIES, (4) PREDETERMINED MOTION TIMES standards such as "motion time measurement" (MTM) where tables are available indicating the time values of various physical motions, and (5) generalizing and tying together random observations by means of statistical methods. Standard labor allowances per unit of product priced at standard labor rates are shown by departments on the standard product cost card in Exhibit I.

Manufacturing Overhead. Standard overhead rates are established by a computation which divides the standard budgeted overhead costs of an area by an appropriate quantitative expression of operating activity. Keeping in mind the relationship between materiality and the cost and convenience of accounting, the most useful expression of the overhead costs of an area on an activity unit basis results from basing the rate on the costs of a carefully delimited single operational area or on the costs of a related group of operations. Conversely, the larger area for which overhead rates are constructed, the less validity do the resulting unit costs have to problems of costing a variety of products undergoing divergent processing.

A center of controversy in standard manufacturing accounting since 1920 has been the appropriate concept of the denominator of the standard fixed costs overhead formula: whether it should express maximum potential use of facilities, average use, or some attainable level of capacity. The term "normal overhead" is often applied to such concepts of the denominator of the standard overhead rate formula. Standard rates based on average use of capacity or an attainable level of capacity tend to channel fixed overhead costs which approximate actual fixed costs to products produced over a series of years. Where a maximum capacity measurement of the denominator of the overhead formula is employed, fixed costs attached to products during protracted periods of idleness become less representative of the actual fixed costs taking place. However, the resulting idle capacity variance provides a rather absolute measure of inability to operate at maximum capacity.

The denominator of the manufacturing overhead formula is customarily measured by such activity bases as: direct labor hours, direct labor cost, machine hours, and prime cost. Needless to say, such bases ought to be representative of the activity of the area to which they are applied. It may be noted that in automated industries, labor hours or labor cost have in fact become auxiliary to the operation of machinery. Rather than use a labor basis of overhead allocation, it can be argued that use of a machine hour basis and the inclusion of labor cost of tenders in the numerator of the overhead formula would result in a more useful method of tracing costs to product.

Once a quantity expressive of the normal level of output has been established, the standard overhead rate may be computed by dividing budgeted overhead costs of an area by this quantity. For example, referring to Dept. No. 16, Exhibit II, if normal output were defined as 70,000 direct labor hours, the normal overhead rate for the area would be established as follows:

EXHIBIT II

FLEXIBLE BUDGET SHOWING COST BY LEVELS OF OUTPUT
Department No. 16

	Direct Labor Hours					
Expense	*40,000*	*50,000*	*60,000*	*70,000*	*80,000*	*90,000*
Indirect Materials	$1,000	$1,250	$1,500	$ 1,750	$ 2,000	$ 2,250
Power	400	500	600	700	800	900
Indirect Labor	1,800	2,200	2,600	3,000	3,400	3,800
Maintenance	300	350	400	450	500	550
Supplies	550	650	750	850	950	1,050
Miscellaneous	950	1,100	1,250	1,400	1,550	1,700
Depreciation	500	500	500	500	500	500
Space Occupancy	400	400	400	400	400	400
Supervision	1,000	1,000	1,000	1,000	1,000	1,000
Totals	$6,900	$7,950	$9,000	$10,050	$11,100	$12,150

$$\frac{\text{Budgeted Overhead Cost at 70,000 DLH}}{\text{Normal Capacity in DLH}}$$

$$= \frac{\$10{,}050}{70{,}000} = \$0.1435 \text{ per DLH}$$

Alternatively, referring to the data given in Exhibit III, the rate for Dept. No. 16 may be subdivided into a fixed and variable rate and expressed as follows:

$$\frac{\text{Budgeted Fixed Overhead Cost}}{\text{Normal Capacity in DLH}} =$$

$$\frac{\$2{,}700}{70{,}000} = \$0.0385$$

Fixed Overhead Rate per DLH =	$0.0385
Variable Overhead Rate per DLH (from Exhibit III) =	0.1050
Total Overhead Rate per DLH =	0.1435

EXHIBIT III

FLEXIBLE BUDGET SHOWING COSTS BY FIXED AND VARIABLE ELEMENTS
Department No. 16

	Fixed Amount (if any)	*Variable Rate*
Indirect Materials		$0.025
Power		.010
Indirect Labor	$ 200	.040
Maintenance	100	.005
Supplies	150	.010
Miscellaneous	350	.015
Depreciation	500	
Space Occupancy	400	
Supervision	1,000	
	$2,700	$0.105

Standard Cost Variances Defined. Variances in standard costing refer to differences between actual and standard costs for specified areas of operational activity and are usually expressed in dollars. Brief descriptions of common variances follow.

Material Price Variance. Difference between actual and standard material costs because actual material prices differ from standard material prices.

Material Usage Variance. Difference between actual and standard material cost because actual quantities consumed differ from standard quantities allowed.

Labor Rate Variance. Difference between actual and standard labor cost, because actual labor rate differs from standard labor rate.

Labor Usage Variance. Difference between actual and standard labor cost because actual labor hours employed to produce the output differ from the standard labor hours allowed for that output.

Overhead Capacity Variance. Difference between actual and standard overhead costs due ordinarily to the fact that operating activity (hours facilities were used) has been above or below normal activity on which standards were based. The measure of operating activity may be standard time allowed for good product achieved under the "2-variance method" or actual time operated under the "3-variance method." (Refer to foregoing discussion, "Setting Standard Costs: Manufacturing Overhead"; see also FLEXIBLE BUDGETING.)

Overhead Budget Variance. Under the 3-variance method, the difference between actual and standard overhead cost because of above- or below-standard efficiency relative to expense incurrence. Under the 2-variance method, this variance is also expressive of the standard variable cost of time misused. (See FLEXIBLE BUDGETING.)

Overhead Efficiency Variance. Difference between actual and standard overhead cost due to above- or below-standard efficiency in the time required to produce the output.

Computation of Variances. A difference between actual and standard costs may be subdivided in innumerable ways preparatory to further analysis into the cause of the variance. For example, the fact that $5,100 was spent for 1,200 hours of labor when a standard $4,000 should have been spent for 1,000 hours may be explained as indicated in Exhibit IV.

Keeping the foregoing in mind, a conventional computation of variances is shown in Exhibits V and VI.

Common methods of constructing variances have been criticized unfavorably from time to time. Considerations advanced in this connection are as follows:

(1) They lump together in one or more figures differences between actual and standard costs, some of which may be controllable at the operating level for which drawn, some of which may not. (See FLEXIBLE BUDGETING.)

(2) They represent in one amount so many causes of variances that further analysis is necessary. For example, a material usage variance may be due to: inferior materials, excessive application of materials (paint), excessive scrap,

EXHIBIT IV

COMPUTATION OF VARIANCES

Labor Usage Variance, 200 additional hours taken at the $2.00 standard hourly rate	$400	Labor Usage Variance
Labor Rate Variance, 1,200 hours of labor paid for at 25¢ per hour in excess of the standard hourly rate	300	Labor Rate Variance
Total Labor Variance	$700	

Alternatively, the $700 variance may be subdivided into:

Payment for delays while waiting for work, 100 delay hours at $2.00 standard rate	$200	Labor Delay Variance
Inefficient use of 100 hours of labor	200	Labor Usage Variance
Money paid because of failure to earn $1.50 an hour guaranteed	240	Make-Up Money Variance
Payment of 5¢ an hour in excess of standard labor rate	60	Labor Rate Variance
	$700	

EXHIBIT V

COMPUTATION OF MANUFACTURING OVERHEAD VARIANCE
(2-Variance Method)

	(1)	*(2)*	*(3)*	*(4)*	*(5)* *Variance*	*(6)*
	Quantity Allowed at Std. Prices or Rates	*Actual Quantity at Std. Prices or Rates*	*Actual Quantity at Actual Pr. or Rate*	*(1) − (3) Total*	*(1) − (2) Usage*	*(2) − (3) Pr. or Rate*
Materials:	2 × 700 × $1 = $1400	1500 × $1 = $1500	1500 × $1.10 = $1650	$250	$100	$150
Labor:	1 × 700 × $2 = $1400	800 × $2 = $1600	800 × $2.05 = $1640	$240	$200	$ 40

SOURCE: Adapted from Schiff and Benninger, "Cost Accounting."

EXHIBIT VI

COMPUTATION OF MANUFACTURING OVERHEAD VARIANCE
(3-Variance Method)

(1) Hours Allowed at Std. Rate	(2) Budget Allowed For Std. Hours in Product	(3) Budget Allowed For Actual Hrs. Worked	(4) Actual Overhead	(5) Total (1) − (4)	(6) Capacity (1) − (2)	(7) Efficiency (2) − (3)	(8) Budget (3) − (4)
	(700)	(800)					
700 × $6	Fixed $2000	Fixed $2000					
	Var. 2800	Var. 3200					
$4200	$4800	$5200	$5300	$1100	$600	$400	$100

SOURCE: Adapted from Schiff and Benninger, "Cost Accounting."

loss of materials because of machine break-down, and spoilage of product containing materials. Also, all the cost of excess usage may not be included in the material usage variance amount (see next item).

(3) The content of variances which are isolated are not mutually exclusive. Excess material usage may aggravate a materials price variance by calling for a greater consumption of materials at above standard prices. A portion of the material price variance may therefore be caused by excess material consumption. A similar problem exists with labor and overhead variances, in the case of the latter particularly in connection with the 2-variance method of overhead analysis.

Disposition of Variances. When a standard cost system is utilized, variances may be occasioned by:

(1) Errors in the construction of standards.

(2) Inefficiency of expenditure or in the use of labor time and facilities.

(3) Purposely setting standards beyond what is currently attainable as a stimulus to increased productivity.

(4) Failure to utilize capacity as anticipated in the computation of the normal overhead rate.

(1) Errors in the construction of standards may represent simply a mistake in estimating price, rates, or the attainable level of performance. The necessary information was available at the time standards were established. Had standards been properly computed, they would have been valid throughout the period in question. Variances in this instance are the responsibility of the standard setter. On the other hand, errors may be due to a change in circumstances: higher prices occasioned by shortages brought on by a war or below-standard performance resulting from unexpected orders and the necessity of hiring relatively unskilled labor. In this latter case, it is assumed that the change, under the circumstances, could not have been known at the time standards were established, and, consequently, no one in the organization may be held responsible for ensuing variances. Regardless of whether the error giving rise to variances was due to a mistake in judgment or to changing conditions, if the error is significant in amount, and if feasible, accounts misstated because of the error need to be modified by the amount of the variance or variances. If the variance is nominal in amount, it is closed out as a periodic item.

(2) If there is excess expenditure or if labor time and facilities have been misused, variances should be tied to their cause: defective materials, machine break-downs, unnecessary delays, or simply shoddy performance. They should then be brought to the attention of the supervisor responsible. Where there is *under-absorbed* fixed overhead cost due to the fact that overhead rates have been premised on good production attainable and such production has not been attained because of inefficiency, the variance again should be charged to the supervisor responsible. Some authorities hold that variances due to inefficiency are losses, not costs, and favor their showing as period deductions on the income statement. Others argue that, in any event, these variances represent additional costs and should therefore be prorated as applicable to inventories and cost of goods sold. Again, if the variance is insignificant in amount, it is summarily disposed of to profit and loss.

(3) When standards are purposely set higher than is attainable on a continuous basis, resulting variances become a mixture of "losses" and

figures representing the cost of inability to achieve presently unattainable goals. If the attainable level of performance is known, variances due to inefficiency should be separated out and treated as in (2), above. The portion of such variances which measure the opportunity cost of utilizing present personnel and facilities is disposed of, following proper reporting to planning administration, much like variances in (1), above.

(4) Where fixed overhead costs remain under- or overabsorbed because of anticipated fluctuations in the use of facilities, theoretically the variance, debit or credit, should be deferred. However, it is common to allocate such variances when significant to inventories and cost of goods sold; otherwise to dispose of them simply as a period deduction.

Standard Costing Applied to Marketing Activities. Standard manufacturing cost accounting stresses relating manufacturing costs to products and departments and the importance of comparing actual and standard costs on these levels. From its very beginnings, marketing cost accounting has been less concerned with product costs, in part because of the tracing and allocation difficulties involved, and has instead attempted to effect other tracings and allocations useful to cost control and analyses of special interest to management. Standard marketing costing is employed to determine the marketing costs of a wide range of objects of managerial interest, such as: function, responsibility level, district operation, channel of trade, class of customer, salesman, and product.

In contrast to what is commonly found in manufacturing cost accounting, namely that direct costs often make up a significant portion of total manufacturing cost, marketing costs capable of direct tracing to the ultimate object of interest, such as district, salesman, or channel of trade, may be quite small relative to the total of such costs. Consequently, an initial analysis attempting to subdivide marketing costs between those which are capable of direct tracing to the object or objects of interest and those which are not, ordinarily ends with a sizable group of unallocated costs.

In manufacturing cost accounting, costs termed "indirect" to product are commonly taken to departmental classifications prior to product application. Similarly, "indirect" marketing costs are customarily traced to functional classifications such as storing, packing and shipping, order processing and billing, and advertising. Once such a tracing has been accomplished, the parallel between manufacturing cost accounting and marketing cost accounting tends to end, partly because the ensuing object of managerial interest in marketing cost accounting analysis may not be products, and partly because of the difficulties of relating a large body of marketing costs to products even through management may be interested in such an association.

In general, there are three levels of standardization in marketing cost accounting. The first level is the establishment of standard costs for a marketing function with the sole objective of subsequently allocating the functional cost to some object of interest. A second level is where standardization accomplishes both the allocation of cost as in the first level, but also aids in the control of the cost of the function. A third level of standardization occurs where functional marketing costs are directly traceable without allocation to the ultimate object of interest, but standardization aids in the control of the costs of the function. (See also MARKETING COST ANALYSIS.)

The real significance of marketing cost accounting lies in the value of information derived from attempts at direct tracing, functional analyses, standard setting, and the application of flexible budgeting technique. Standard marketing cost accounting serves best in aiding management to control marketing costs and in providing data useful to managerial decision making in the marketing area.

Estimated vs. Standard Costs. Sometimes an attempt is made to distinguish between standard costs and a related, term *estimated costs.* Cost estimates of varying degrees of accuracy and reliability may be employed intermittently as desired, outside the formal accounting structure. Where the estimates are incorporated in the accounts and the accounts themselves are made to show differences between actual and estimated costs, cost accounting of the estimated type may be said to exist. Used this way, estimated costs assigned to work in process and finished goods inventories are substituted for an analysis and allocation of currently incurred historical costs. An estimated cost system may be defined therefore as one in which estimated unit costs of a product are used to price inventories of work in process and finished goods shown in the ledger accounts.

An important advantage in the use of estimates within the formal accounting system is that burdensome detail and paper work inherent in a cost accounting system dealing entirely with actual costs is reduced or eliminated when an estimated cost system is employed. Work in process and finished goods control accounts as well as their supporting detail are kept in terms of estimates. Differences between estimated and actual costs are abstracted and isolated in variation accounts.

When estimated costs differ from actual costs, the usual assumption is that the estimates were incorrectly computed. This is in sharp contrast to the understanding which exists when a standard cost system is employed, where when variances arise it is generally assumed that the actual costs are wrong. Consequently, when it is ascertained periodically that actual costs differ from estimated costs, there is a strong impetus to correct estimated data contained in inventory and cost of goods sold accounts. However, since the strength of estimated cost systems rests upon their convenience, complex and precise procedures for the allocation of variations will ordinarily not be followed, and when tenable, the variance will be closed out to the income account as a period charge. Estimated costs serve only incidentally and then rather poorly as a medium for cost control. Where it is desired to secure variances expressing differences between actual and "should be" costs by *causes,* it is much more satisfactory to adopt a thoroughgoing standard cost system.

Probabilistic Standards. Much interest has been displayed in recent years concerning the use of probabilistic control standards either of the quality control type or of types which are more subjective in nature as suggested by modern decision theory. Advocates of the use of probabilistic models argue that considerable time and effort are spent in traditional standard costing, in investigating variances which, in fact, represent operations within the bounds of normal performance. Further, they argue that the cost of investigation in the traditional standard costing model often exceeds the savings achieved.

L. J. Benninger, Ph.D., Professor Emeritus of Accounting, University of Florida, Gainesville, Florida

Information References

Association:

National Association of Accountants.

Texts:

Horngren, Charles T., "Cost Accounting, a Managerial Emphasis," Englewood Cliffs, N.J., Prentice-Hall, 4th ed., 1977.

Neuner, John J. and Deakin, Edward B., "Cost Accounting: Principles and Practice," Homewood, Ill., Irwin, 9th ed., 1977.

Cross References: *Cost Accounting (and references there given).*

STANDARD INDUSTRIAL CLASSIFICATION SYSTEM (S.I.C.)

The Standard Industrial Classification System, (S.I.C.) is a numerical system devised by the Federal Bureau of the Budget (now Office of Management and Budget in the Executive Office of the President), and available from the Superintendent of Documents, U.S. Government Printing Office.

The Classification is highly useful in many types of industrial and commercial marketing research and existing and potential sales analyses. Its objective is the classification of establishments by type of activity in which engaged for purposes of facilitating the collection, tabulation, presentation, and analysis of data relating to establishments, and for promoting uniformity and comparability in the presentation of statistical data collected by various agencies of the United States Government, state agencies, trade associations, and private research organizations.

Scope of the Classification. The Classification is intended to cover the entire field of economic activities: agriculture, forestry, and fisheries; mining; construction; manufacturing; transportation, communication, electric, gas, and sanitary services; wholesale and retail trade; finance, insurance, and real estate; services; and public administration. A single volume, "Standard Industrial Classification Manual—1972," contains all industry titles and descriptions, as well as an alphabetic index of principal products, processes, and services. A "1977 Supplement" to the Manual was issued by the newly created Office of Federal Statistical Policy and Standards in the Department of Commerce. The 1972 Manual represented the first revision since 1957. At this writing, a second revision is scheduled for 1982.

Principles of the Classification. The Classification was prepared by the *Technical Committee on Standard Industrial Classification,* assisted by a number of special committees of experts in various fields of business under the sponsorship and general supervision of the Office of Statistical Standards of the then Bureau of the Budget.

The Technical Committee was guided by the following general principles:

(1) The Classification should conform to the existing structure of American industry.

(2) The reporting units to be classified are establishments, rather than legal entities or companies.

(3) Each establishment is to be classified according to its major activity.

(4) To be recognized as an industry, each group of establishments must have significance from the standpoint of the number of persons employed, volume of business, and other important economic features, such as the number of establishments. (An exception to this principle is found in the grouping of establishments into industries described as "not elsewhere classified.")

Definition of Establishment. An "establishment" is an economic unit which produces goods or services—for example, a farm, a mine, a factory, a store. In most instances, the establishment is at a single physical location; and it is engaged in only one, or predominately one, type of economic activity for which an industry code is applicable.

Where a single physical location encompasses two or more distinct and inseparate economic activities for which different industrial classification code seem applicable, such activities are treated as separate establishments and classified in separate industries, provided it is determined that: (1) such activities are not ordinarily associated with one another at common physical locations; (2) no one industry description in the Standard Industrial Classification includes such combined activities; (3) the employment in each such economic activity is significant; and (4) reports can be prepared on the number of employees, their wages and salaries, and other establishment type data.

An establishment is not necessarily identical with a business concern or firm, which may consist of one or more establishments. Also, it is to be distinguished from organizational subunits, departments, or divisions within an establishment. Supplemental interpretations of the definition of an establishment are included in the industry descriptions of the Standard Industrial Classification.

Auxiliary Units. The activity of an establishment under consideration may have some, but not all, of the characteristics of individual industries. The activities of these establishments are subordinate to, and operated for the use of, some other establishment(s) of the same concern and are generally at locations separate from the establishment(s) served. Such establishments are called "*auxiliary units.*" The more important types of such auxiliary units are:

(1) A separate research laboratory operated for manufacturing plants of the same concern.

(2) A warehouse operated by another establishment primarily for its own use and not for public storage; counted as auxiliary to establishment for which operated. Thus, warehouses may be auxiliary to manufacturing, wholesaling, or retailing operations.

(3) Trading stamp redemption stores.

(4) An automotive repair shop or storage garage operated by a department store or transportation company primarily for its own use and not for the public repair or storage of vehicles.

(5) A separate repair shop serving various manufacturing plants of the same concern primarily for the maintenance and repair of plant machinery and equipment.

Exhibit I lists other typical auxiliary establishments.

Mines and manufacturing plants operated primarily for the use of other establishments of the same firm are not considered auxiliary units, but are classified on the basis of their primary activity. Important types are:

(1) A coal mine operated by a steel company for its own use is classified as a coal mine.

(2) A tin can manufacturing plant operated by a canning company for its own use is classified as a tin can manufacturing plant.

(3) A printing plant operated primarily for the use of another establishment(s) of the same company is classified as a printing plant.

Central and District Administrative Offices. A central or district administrative office is an establishment primarily engaged in general administrative, supervisory, purchasing, accounting, and other management functions performed centrally for other establishments of the same company.

Auxiliary units and central and district administrative offices, when separately reported, are classified on the basis of the most appropriate Major Group representing the primary activity of the establishments served.

Code Assignment. Each establishment is assigned an industry code on the basis of its major activity, which is determined by the product or group of products produced or handled, or services rendered. Ideally, the principal products or service is determined by reference to "value added." In practice, however, it is rarely possible to obtain this information for individual products or services, and it becomes necessary to adopt some other criteria which may be expected to give approximately the same results. As far as possible, the characteristics shown in Exhibit II are used for each of the major economic sections.

Occasionally in cases of mixed businesses, the above characteristics cannot be determined or estimated for each product or service, and less frequently a classification based upon the recommended characteristics will not represent adequately the process or activity of the establishment. In such cases, if employment information is available, the major activity is determined by the activity in which the greatest number of employees work.

Code Structure. Major Groups represent the primary activity of establishments, and are assigned the first two digits of the code (01 through 89) with further refinements of classification calling for additional digits up to four. Establishments are thus classified by industry on either a two-digit, three-digit, or four-digit basis, according to the degree of detail of information provided. In compilation of data, comparability with the Classification may be maintained on a two-digit basis by combining groups or industries within a Major Group; similarly, comparability may be maintained by combining industries within a three digit group.

In the collection of industrial census data, a zero may be used temporarily on the third-digit-position for coding reports on which available information is inadequate for proper allocation to a specific three-digit group. For example, Major Group 25—Furniture and Fixtures—is divided into the following groups:

251 Household Furniture
252 Office Furniture
253 Public Building and Related Furniture
254 Partitions, Shelving, Lockers, and Office and Store Fixtures
259 Miscellaneous Furniture and Fixtures

If an establishment is described as engaged in manufacturing furniture, the report should be coded as "250" until sufficient information is obtained to assign the establishment to the appropriate group. But if complete detail is available, an establishment may be classified as 2522—Metal Office Furniture.

Exhibit I

Other Auxiliary Establishments

Examples of separate auxiliary establishments performing supporting services for other establishments of the same company:

1. Product display showrooms in which sales do not take place.
2. Milk receiving stations for dairies.
3. Field engineering support activities.
4. Separate establishments engaged in news collection, editorial work, or advertising sales for a publishing activity of the same company.
5. Recreational facilities such as bowling alleys or swimming pools, maintained by a company for the benefits of its employees.
6. Computing, tabulating, or data processing establishments operated for own use are auxiliary to the central administrative office served.
7. Purchasing offices of multi-unit firms.
8. Accounting and billing facilities operated for company use are auxiliary to the central administrative office served.

Exhibit II

Criteria Used in Code Assignment

Economic Section	*Characteristics*
Agriculture, forestry, and fisheries (except agricultural services)	Value of production.
Mining	Value of production.
Construction	Value of work done.
Manufacturing	Value of production.
Wholesale and retail trade	Value of sales.
Finance, insurance, and real estate	Value of receipts or revenues.
Services (including agricultural services)	Value of receipts or revenues.
Public Administration	Employment or payroll.

For manufacturing industries the S.I.C. System combines and classifies all manufacturing into twenty major industry groups (designated by a two-digit code—example: No. 20, Food and Kindred Products).

Each group is subdivided into about 150 industry groups (designated by a three-digit code—example: No. 202, Dairy Products).

A further breakdown reveals approximately 450 individual industries (designated by a four-digit code—example: No. 2021, Creamery Butter). Thus, each industry has a classification number—the more digits, the finer the classification.

Classifications

Division A—Agriculture, Forestry, and Fisheries

Major Group 01.—Agricultural production—crops
Major Group 02. Agricultural production—livestock
Major Group 07.—Agricultural services and hunting and trapping
Major Group 08.—Forestry
Major Group 09.—Fisheries

Division B.—Mining

Major Group 10.—Metal mining
Major Group 11.—Anthracite mining
Major Group 12.—Bituminous coal and lignite mining
Major Group 13.—Ore & Gas extract
Major Group 14.—Mining and quarrying of nonmetallic minerals, except fuels

Division C.—Construction

Major Group 15.—Building construction—general contractors
Major Group 16.—Construction other than building construction—general contractors
Major Group 17.—Construction—Special trade contractors

Division D.—Manufacturing

Major Group 20.—Food and kindred products
Major Group 21.—Tobacco manufacturers
Major Group 22.—Textile mill products
Major Group 23.—Apparel and other finished products made from fabrics and similar materials
Major Group 24.—Lumber and wood products, except furniture
Major Group 25.—Furniture and fixtures
Major Group 26.—Paper and allied products
Major Group 27.—Printing, publishing, and allied industries
Major Group 28.—Chemicals and allied products
Major Group 29.—Petroleum refining and related products
Major Group 30.—Rubber and miscellaneous plastic products
Major Group 31.—Leather and leather products
Major Group 32.—Stone, clay, and glass products
Major Group 33.—Primary metal industries
Major Group 34.—Fabricated metal products, except machinery, and transportation equipment
Major Group 35.—Machinery, except electrical
Major Group 36.—Electrical machinery, equipment and supplies
Major Group 37.—Transportation equipment
Major Group 38.—Measuring, analyzing, and controlling instruments; photographic, medical, and optical goods; watches, and clocks
Major Group 39.—Miscellaneous manufacturing industries

Division E.—Transportation, Communication, Electric, Gas, and Sanitary Services

Major Group 40.—Railroad transportation
Major Group 41.—Local and suburban transit and interurban highway passenger transportation
Major Group 42.—Motor freight transportation and warehousing
Major Group 44.—Water transportation
Major Group 45.—Transportation by air
Major Group 46.—Pipe line transportation
Major Group 47.—Transportation services
Major Group 48.—Communication
Major Group 49.—Electric, gas, and sanitary services

Division F.—Wholesale Trade

Major Group 50.—Wholesale trade—durable goods
Major Group 51.—Wholesale trade—nondurable goods

Division G.—Retail Trade

Major Group 52.—Retail trade—building materials, hardware, and farm equipment
Major Group 53.—Retail trade—general merchandise
Major Group 54.—Retail trade—food stores

Major Group 55.—Automotive dealers and gasoline service stations
Major Group 56.—Retail trade—apparel and accessories stores
Major Group 57.—Retail trade—furniture, home furnishings, and equipment stores
Major Group 58.—Retail trade—eating and drinking places
Major Group 59.—Retail trade—miscellaneous retail stores

Division H—Finance, Insurance, and Real Estate

Major Group 60.—Banking
Major Group 61.—Credit agencies other than banks
Major Group 62.—Security and commodity brokers, and dealers, exchanges, and services
Major Group 63.—Insurance carriers
Major Group 64.—Insurance agents, brokers, and service
Major Group 65.—Real estate
Major Group 66.—Combinations of real estate, insurance, loans, law offices
Major Group 67.—Holding and other investment companies

Division I—Services

Major Group 70.—Hotels, rooming houses, camps, and other lodging places
Major Group 72.—Personal services
Major Group 73.—Business services
Major Group 74.—Automobile repair, automobile services, and garages
Major Group 75.—Automotive repair, services, and garages
Major Group 76.—Miscellaneous repair services
Major Group 78.—Motion pictures
Major Group 79.—Amusement and recreation services, except motion pictures
Major Group 80.—Health services
Major Group 81.—Legal services
Major Group 82.—Educational services
Major Group 84.—Museums, art galleries, botanical and zoological gardens
Major Group 86.—Membership organizations
Major Group 88.—Private households
Major Group 89.—Miscellaneous services

Division J.—Public Administration

Major Group 91.—Executive, legislative, and general government, except finance
Major Group 92.—Justice, public order, and safety
Major Group 93.—Public finance, taxation, and monetary policy
Major Group 94.—Administration of human resources programs
Major Group 95.—Administration of environmental quality and housing
Major Group 96.—Administration of Economic programs
Major Group 97.—National security and international affairs

Division K.—Nonclassifiable establishments

Major Group 99.—Nonclassifiable establishments

Cross References: *Marketing Research; Sales Statistics; Standard Metropolitan Statistical Areas.*

STANDARD METROPOLITAN STATISTICAL AREAS

The concept of **Standard Metropolitan Statistical Areas,** which number 276, has been developed to meet the need for the presentation of general-purpose statistics by agencies of the Federal Government, in accordance with specific criteria. On the basis of these criteria, definitions of the areas in terms of geographic boundaries are established by the Office of Management and Budget.

SMSAs are valuable to management in the conduct of marketing analyses, in the setting of sales and operating areas, in making determinations for plant loction, and the like. Standard definitions of Metropolitan Statistical Areas were first issued in 1949, as "Standard Metropolitan Areas." They were developed to replace four different sets of definitions then in use for various statistical series—"metropolitan districts," "metropolitan counties," "industrial areas," and "labor market areas." Because of the use of these different definitions, it was not possible to relate the statistics on population, industrial production, labor force, and other series for the area in question, since each series included a slightly different territory.

The primary objective in establishing standard definitions of metropolitan areas was thus to make it possible for all Federal statistical agencies to utilize the same boundaries in publishing statistical data useful for analyzing metropolitan problems. The term "Standard Metropolitan Area" has been changed to "Standard Metropolitan Statistical Area" to describe more accurately the objective of the definitions.

Information reported in a census taken by the Bureau of the Census is the usual basis for designating a standard metropolitan statistical area. Population estimates prepared by the Bureau of the Census which have been accepted for use in the distribution of Federal benefits are also used.

All standard metropolitan statistical areas include the county or counties in which the qualifying population resides. Other counties may be added to the SMSA definition provided that information from a census shows that they meet certain criteria of metropolitan character and integration. In New England, cities and towns are used to designate and define SSMAs.

The criteria used to designate standard metropolitan statistical areas are subject to continuing review, and changes are made as appropriate. They represent a reasoned judgment as to how metropolitan areas may be defined statistically in a uniform manner, using data items that are (1) widely recognized as indicative of metropolitan character (population, urban character, nonagricultural employment, population density, commuting ties); and (2) available from a body of Federal statistics which has been collected at the same time in all parts of the country and processed and tabulated according to consistent standards. Further changes in the criteria may be expected in the future as additional statistical data become available and as the nature and structure of metropolitan areas themselves become better understood.

Criteria Followed in Establishing Standard Metropolitan Statistical Areas. A standard metropolitan statistical area always includes a city (cities) of specified population which constitutes the central city and the county (counties) in which it is located. It also includes contiguous counties when the economic and social relationships between the central and contiguous counties meet specified criteria of metropolitan character and integration. An SMSA may cross State lines.

A standard metropolitan statistical area is generally designated on the basis of population statistics reported in a census conducted by the Bureau of the Census. An area designated on the basis of a census does not lose its designation except as provided for in criterion 5, below.

An SMSA is sometimes designated on the basis of population estimates published by the Bureau of the Census which have been accepted for use in the distribution of Federal benefits. An area designated on the basis of such estimates loses its designation, if it does not quality for designation on the basis of population statistics reported in the next succeeding census conducted by the Bureau of the Census.

(1) *Population Criteria.* Each standard metropolitan statistical area must include at least:

(a) One city with 50,000 or more inhabitants, *or*

(b) A city with at least 25,000 inhabitants, which, together with those contiguous places (incorporated or unincorporated) having population densities of at least 1,000 persons per square mile, has a combined population of 50,000 and constitutes for general economic and social purposes a single community, provided that the county or counties in which the city and contiguous places are located has a total population of at least 75,000.

(2) A contiguous county will be included in a standard metropolitan statistical area if:

(a) At least 75% of the resident labor force in the county is in the nonagricultural labor force, *and*

(b) At least 30% of the employed workers living in the county work in the central county or counties of the area.

(3) A contiguous county which does not meet the requirements of criterion 2 will be included in a standard metropolitan statistical area if at least 75% of the resident labor force is in the nonagricultural labor force and it meets two of the following additional criteria of metropolitan character and one of the following criteria of integration.

(a) Criteria of metropolitan character:

(i) At least 25% of the population is urban.

(ii) The county had an increase of at least 15% in total population during the period covered by the two most recent Censuses of Population.

(iii) The county has a population density of at least 50 persons per square mile.

(b) Criteria of integration.

(i) At least 15% of the employed workers living in the county work in the central county or counties of the area, *or*

(ii) The number of people working in the

county who live in the central county or counties of the area is equal to at least 15% of the employed workers living in the county, *or*

(iii) The sum of the number of workers commuting to and from the central county or counties is equal to 20% of the employed workers living in the county.

(4) *Area Titles.* The following guidelines are used for determining titles SMSAs:

(a) The title of the standard metropolitan statistical area always includes the name of the largest city.

(b) There shall be no more than three city names in the title of any standard metropolitan statistical area. The addition of up to two city names may be made in the area title on the basis of the following:

(i) For those area where the largest city has a population of 50,000 or more inhabitants (criterion 1(a)), the additional city or cities must have a population equal to one-third or more of that of the largest city and a minimum population of 25,000, provided that the name of each additional city having a population of at least 250,000 will be included in the title.

(ii) For those areas where the largest city has a population of at least 25,000 but less than 50,000 (criterion 1(b)), the additional city or cities must have a population equal to one-third or more of that of the largest city and a minimum population of 15,000.

(c) Area titles which include the names of more than one city shall start with the largest city and list other cities in order of their size according to the most recent census, except that the names of cities qualifying an area as an SMSA under criterion 1(b) shall precede those of any other qualifying city.

(d) In addition to city names, the area titles will contain the name of the State or States included in the area.

(5) *Loss of Designation.* A standard metropolitan statistical area shall lose such designation if it fails to meet the criteria for defining an SMSA as measured by information reported in two successive censuses. A contiguous county (city or town in New England) included in a standard metropolitan statistical area shall be excluded from that area if it fails to meet the criteria for inclusion in an SMSA as measured by information reported in two successive censuses.

Information Reference

For complete listings of the 276 areas, with breakdowns by counties and cities making them up, see the latest "Standard Metropolitan Statistical Areas," published by the Executive Office of the President, Office of Management and Budget, obtainable from the Superintendent of Documents, U.S. Government Printing Office.

STANDARD MINUTE SYSTEM

The **Standard Minute** is a unit of measure widely used in systems of engineered performance standards and individual wage incentives. Where the work measurement is coupled with an incentive payment plan, it is a great improvement over older piecework systems. (Systems of the same type use the hour, and a percentage subdivision of the hour, as a basis of calculation, and are called "standard hour" or "unit hour" systems. However, the mathematical relationships, with suitable conversion, work out the same as with the standard minute system). It should be emphasized that the standard minute concept is not limited to incentive payment plans, although it has proved extremely effective where individual incentives are coupled with it. Where no incentives are used, engineered performance standards are highly desirable, and these may be effectively based on the standard minute.

The standard minute system makes it possible to separate the money question—which can be made the subject of separate wage negotiations—from the factual determination of just how much work constitutes a *fair day's work.* By stopwatch measurements or by PREDETERMINED MOTION TIMES, the timestudy man arrives at the standard amount of time which should be taken to produce a certain piece, perform a certain operation, and the like. Then all work can be expressed in terms of standard minutes of production instead of so many pieces or pounds or other measures. The common denominator, time, measures the employee's output, no matter what he is producing—machined parts, assembled units, typed invoices—in any kind of business. The standard minute should be thought of as the *amount of work* which the employee is *expected to do,* as a *minimum,* in *one minute by the clock.*

If the employee is on incentives, he receives, on the basis of his hourly wage rate, one minute's worth of pay for every standard minute's worth of work he produces, even if by working faster he produces it in less than a minute. Thus in an hour he may produce 75 standard minutes' worth of work and therefore be paid

75/60 times his hourly rate. On the other hand, if standard practice is followed, if he produces *less* than 60 standard minutes' worth of work he is not penalized. This is a protection to the worker, although, of course, if he consistently averages below standard, he may be admonished, or given more training if required, or transferred, or perhaps even dismissed.

The standard time is so calculated that, with due allowances for unavoidable delays and for normal fatigue and personal requirements, the average employee, without undue strain or fatiguing speed-up, should be able to produce, on the average, 20% to 30% more standard minute's worth of work per hour than 60. In most applications he is expected to average 75, thus netting him a bonus of 25% over his base pay. Under this system, the direct benefits of increased output above standard are not shared with the company. The employee's earnings increase in direct proportion to his production above standard. This is known as "100% premium," and offers high monetary motivation. Another advantage to the employee is that he can always be sure that he is getting the agreed upon bonus without resort to formulas that may be difficult for him to understand.

In developing the standards, time studies must be taken of specific workers doing specific jobs (presupposing no predetermined motion times). These workers must be "rated" in terms of what the *normally qualified* employee would do, and for this a "grading factor" is used. This factor permits an adjustment when the observed employee is a fast worker, doing the job in less time than the average normally experienced operator would take, or when he is working at a slower than average pace.

The need for inserting a grading factor has led to the charge that the system is far from scientific, and only depends upon the idea of the time study person as to what the normal pace should be. Aside from the fact that the seasoned time study professionals have observed different types of operations, it should be pointed out that much has been done by the industrial engineering profession to assure consistent ratings by different observers. Exhaustive research by the Society for Advancement of Management [1] has led to the development by SAM of its performance rating films, used in the training of time study men. Moreover, reliance is not placed on a single reading by a rater to determine standards. In a well run installation *standard data* are compiled by grouping and analyzing many time studies, to provide reliable time measures of specific elements going into many jobs.

Exhibit I shows schematically the derivation of a Standard Minute measure. The operator here made one piece in 1.20 minutes. However, he is a fast worker and does the job in less time than the average normally experienced operator would take, even when working at "incentive pace." Accordingly, the time study man applied a grading factor of 1/6, adjusting the time to 1.40 minutes for "adjusted time study time at incentive pace." (Had the observed worker been slower than average, the grading factor would have worked in the reverse direction.) An allowance is then added for delays: personal time, fatigue, and unavoidable delays. These three factors are usually lumped into an allowance of 15%, here adding another 0.21 minutes. The unavoidable delays are those necessary operations which are bound to occur during the day, but not regularly. This factor allows for time a machinist, say, would require every day now and then to grind a drill or change a cutting angle, or for a bench worker to move a new supply of components into position.

After the delay allowances have been added, the total is called the optimum, or *incentive time,* because an operator working at this rate is considered to be working at incentive pace. In our example this comes to 1.61 minutes.

EXHIBIT I

DERIVATION OF A STANDARD-MINUTE MEASURE

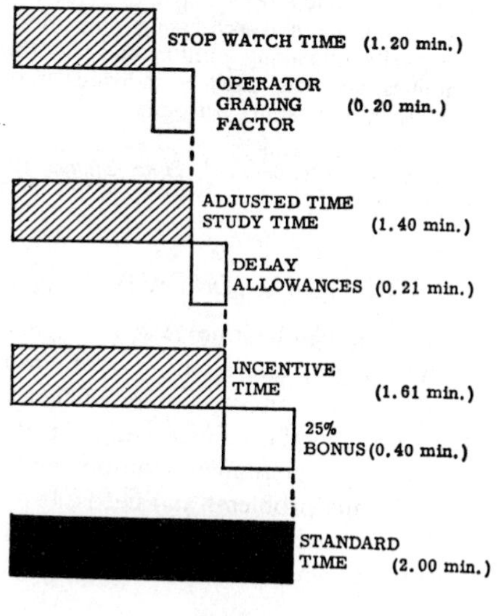

If the incentive system provides for 25% bonus, this amount (here, 0.40 minutes) is added to the incentive time to arrive at the *standard time,* or 2 standard minutes for the operation in the example. Thus even though it would take the worker only 1.61 minutes to produce the piece, he is *paid* for 2.00 minutes.

In many plants, daily production reports are posted on departmental bulletin boards. These list employees by name, giving the standard minutes per hour produced during the previous day, and ranking them with the highest producers at the top. This adds the incentives of competition and personal pride to the purely monetary one of dollar bonuses. The average standard minute performance of a department can also be used as the basis for bonus compensation to departmental supervision.

CARL HEYEL, Management Counsel, Manhasset, New York

Information References

Consult standard industrial engineering reference works, e.g., Maynard, H. B., ed., "Industrial Engineering Handbook," 3rd ed., New York, McGraw-Hill, 1971, for detailed discussions of time measurements, rating of operator performance, etc. For a more general discussion, developing the basic concepts involved, see Heyel, Carl, "Management for Modern Supervisors," Ch. 9, New York, American Management Association, 1962. The above entry is based on the booklet, "Got a Minute?" produced by Dale, Elliott & Company, Inc., New York.

References Cited

[1] "A Fair Day's Work," a publication of the Research Division of the Society for Advancement of Management, New York, 1954. The research project, interrupted by the war, extended from 1941 to 1950 and covered 181 companies, representing 38 manufacturing and processing industries, as well as retailing, banking, printing and publishing, and utilities, and was based on individual ratings by over 1,200 time study personnel.

Cross References: *Motion and Time Study; Work Measurement; Work Measurement in the Office.*

STANDARDIZATION, COMPANY

Company Standardization is a management tool for encouraging and securing optimum utilization of resources and maximum efficiency of operations through formal establishment of the most suitable, predetermined solutions and answers to recurring problems and needs. It is the systematic formulation, adoption, application, and revision of *company standards.* A company standard is an authoritative and preferably consentaneous expression of the requirements to be met for the most efficient realization of a recurrent company object. It is thus a coordinate specification of qualities or other characteristics, or of actions essential to optimum company performance of repetitive operations. It is intended for utilization by all units of the company wherever and whenever applicable.

Company standards might be formulated, for example, to govern the selection of threaded fasteners and their performance. Sizes, threads, head styles, lengths, base materials, and corrosion-preventive finishes for certain exposures could all be specified. Metal alloys, resin compounds, and all other raw materials regularly used by the company can be standardized as can all other procurement items. Likewise, standards can be prepared for soldered connections, for electrodeposited metallic coatings, for machined finishes, and for the thousands of other processes and operations comprising modern industry. Every such company standard then is intended for utilization by all units of the company wherever and whenever applicable.

Company standards may be technical specifications of particular value in design, procurement, production, and control; or administrative specifications of particular value in supervision and management. They may deal with products, processes, methods, materials, parts, inspection, tests, procedures, or other types of requirements. Such standards may for example serve as purchase specifications for all materials and items regularly procured by the company. They provide the purchasing agent with clear, precise, complete definitions of the materials or items which will most economically satisfy all of the company requirements. The purchasing agent is thus relieved of the need for extensive comparison and negotiation. He is left free to concentrate on his specific function of procurement with the most favorable quality, quantity, price, and delivery. He is enabled to effect savings through the purchase of larger quantities of fewer items, the issuance of fewer orders, the reduction of procurement time and inventories, the establishment of better vendor relations and elimination of misunderstandings and disputes, and the development of multiple sources of supply on a more competitive basis.

Standard specifications and test methods form a basic requirement for satisfactory inspection and effective quality control. Standards of many types are indispensable tools of engineering. Vast amounts of development and design time can be saved through reliance on the reuse of proven designs, components, and materials, and through the elimination of duplicate and unnecessary individual activity. Standard processes, methods, operations, patterns, jigs, fixtures, dies, and tools can mean significant economies in the factory. Standard forms, procedures, and policies can be very helpful in administration. Every department thus can benefit from a company standardization program, and the company as a whole can realize important savings.

History. Organized company standardization antedates World War II. As is always the case, however, attention to standardization in general was again brought into sharp focus by the exigencies of the war period. In the postwar period and subsequently, the essentiality and value of company standardization have been still further emphasized by the increasing complexity of industrial operations caused by continued growth, diversification, and decentralization of industry, by the rapid advance in technology, and by the intensified problem of maintaining communication and coordination as the character of industrial projects and activities becomes more and more interdisciplinary.

In its simplest form, modern standardization has been recognized and used since the advent of the mass production technique to which it is a necessary adjunct. As dramatically demonstrated by Eli Whitney in connection with his 1793 government contract for 10,000 "stand of arms," the standardization of component parts to assure interchangeability is essential to mass production on an assembly line basis. In its broader concept of applicability to all repetitive company operations and problems, however, standardization has been recognized and utilized only in modern times.

Modern Practice. A few of the larger American companies initiated standardization programs as a result of their own and of the national experience during World War I and of the economic situation which obtained thereafter. The effectiveness, through standardization, of the German war machine had considerable influence to that end. Between the wars the movement continued to advance, but slowly. In World War II the situation faced by the country, and the responsibility of its industrial machine, were such that standardization could not be ignored. Standardization attained urgency status at every level and in every activity related to national safety: allied, national, military, industrial, technical, professional, company, and even departmental and individual. To supply the armed services with their needs at maximum efficiency, to conserve human and natural resources, and to realize the potential of industrial resources, it was essential that every step be taken which would contribute to coordination of the national effort. It was imperative that capabilities be concentrated on the single best answer to any need and that the costs and confusing penalties of multiplicity and duplication be eliminated. Along with increased participation in military, industrial, and national programs, therefore, many more companies of all sizes initiated their own corporate programs. With the value of standardization clearly demonstrated, the movement continued in the postwar period, although the favorable economic climate deemphasized the need for standards and evoked mixed reaction from management to organized company activity.

In some cases during this period, standardization was seen as an additional expense which simply was unnecessary while market conditions were favorable and profits were high. In other cases a strong financial position was seen as providing the opportunity to undertake standardization efforts at least on an experimental basis and without penalty from an expense standpoint. That standardization thus was not fully understood was demonstrated by discontinuation or reduction of the activity in some companies during the subsequent recession periods. Standardization as a tool for effecting continued improvement of company efficiency is not a luxury or extravagance to be indulged in periods of prosperity and quickly dropped in periods of austerity, but an instrument of increasing importance as competition heightens and as profits are squeezed by rising costs. Despite some misunderstanding, however, more and more company managements have instituted standardization programs, and its benefits are being more widely appreciated.

Savings. The savings realized from standardization are admittedly difficult to evaluate, since there is no simple method for their calculation, and the additional cost of obtaining actual figures usually seems unwarranted. A good part of the saving is intangible in any case. The value of standardization should be acceptable on the basis of its demonstrated and obvious benefits, some of which are: simpler and faster engineering development; simplified, more accurate, and faster product design, production engineering and drafting; fewer materials and smaller variety of parts to purchase, stock, handle, and assemble—greater interchangeability and less rejection; greater flexibility in purchasing—larger quantities of fewer items, larger discounts, increased sources of supply, better competitive situation, and less paperwork; reduced inventories in factory and distributor or dealer locations, and reduced obsolescence; longer production runs and greater uniformity of operation; better plant layout and increased mechanization; better control of inventory, production, and quality—more reliable inspection; simplified and faster training; more efficient materials handling, packaging, and distribution; greater safety; faster and better understood communication—less confusion and fewer mistakes.

Organization. A formal company standards program is required to coordinate activities and supervise the application of standards. Company needs and overall structure will determine how the program is organized and administered. As a basic minimum, the following principles should be followed to ensure success of the program:

(1) The program should apply to all company functions.

(2) The program should be established by, report to, and have the active support of top management.

(3) Standards approved for company use should be acceptable to all affected departments.

In large companies the general responsibility for standardization activities may reside in an independent standards department having coequal rank with other functional departments. Smaller companies may assign the responsibility to a department or division involved, for example, in engineering or design. Some companies establish a standards policy committee composed of department heads, chaired by a corporate-level executive, and with a standards department serving as secretariat.

Procedures. Implementation of a company standards program proceeds through three phases. First, identify the problem that application of standards will solve. Next, locate existing standards or develop new standards that will meet these needs and be acceptable to the affected departments. Finally, promulgate the standards for company use.

A search and evaluation should be made to determine if existing national consensus standards meet the stated needs, either as promulgated or with modifications. Multinational companies or companies engaged in import/export may find that international standards or, on occasion, the national standards of other countries will satisfy their requirements. If no applicable national or international standard can be found, a search should be made for industry standards that might apply.

Development of a company standard should be started if the search for existing applicable standards proves fruitless. As an alternative, and if time permits, a national or international coordinating organization can be asked to initiate a standards development project. This approach must be taken if the proposed standard will affect more than one company, industry, or sector.

Before initiating a standards writing project, the company should obtain answers to such questions as: Is the standard technically feasible? Is the development effort timely? What will be the overall cost to develop the standard, maintain it, convert it, and implement it? Will the standard be useful within the scope of company operations? What will be the long-term benefits of the standard?

Once a standards writing project is initiated, the group responsible for standardization activities should consult with all affected departments and enlist their cooperation in the development process, reconciliation of differences, and final acceptance of the standard for company use. General acceptance is essential no matter what the standard's origin—whether it was developed internally or adopted or adapted from those available from outside sources.

Distribution of accepted standards is usually carried out by the standards department, which serves as a clearinghouse for all company standards. Complete sets should be placed in as many locations as necessary for easy access by departments or individuals having use for them. Ensuring that standards are kept up-to-date is another responsibility of the standards department. Supervising application of standards within a company may be assigned to the standards department or may be handled through the company's normal management system.

Sources of Standardization Help. The greatest contribution to the company through standardization also will be made when every possible advantage is taken of standards already developed at higher levels. At the industrial or technical level many thousands of standards have been prepared, such as those published by the American Society for Testing and Materials, the Society of Automotive Engineers, the National Electrical Manufacturers Association, etc. The standards are inexpensive, and their use is encouraged. They will frequently fit the exact needs of the company, and company purposes are best served by their adoption as company standards.

At the national level, more than 11,000 standards have been approved as American National Standards by the American National Standards Institute. ANSI serves as the national standards coordinating body, and on the principle of consensus approves as "American National Standards" the standards of other organizations. It also provides the means by which entirely new work may be undertaken for the development of American Standards on a cooperative basis by all national organizations concerned. The adoption of American National Standards as company standards is encouraged, since in view of their truly national character, they can be used with greatest assurance and benefit. All American National Standards are available from ANSI.

A large proportion of voluntary international standards are developed through the world's two major nongovernmental standardizing bodies, the International Organization for Standardization (ISO) and the International Electrotechnical Commission (IEC). More than 5,000 international standards have been issued. These, too, are available from ANSI, the United States member of both ISO and IEC.

ANSI, which serves as the clearinghouse for information on national and international standards and standardization activities, promulgates standards catalogs and publishes two biweekly periodicals. The *ANSI Reporter,* a newsletter, provides information on policy-level actions of the Institute, international organizations to which it belongs, and government agencies involved in standardization. *Standards Action* lists for public review and comment proposed new and revised standards that ANSI is considering for approval. It also reports on final actions on standards.

DOROTHY HOGAN, Director, Communications, American National Standards Institute, Inc., New York, New York

STATISTICAL ABSTRACT OF THE UNITED STATES

The **Statistical Abstract of the United States,** published since 1878, is the standard summary of statistics on the social, political, and economic organization of the United States. It is designed to serve as a convenient volume for statistical reference and as a guide to other statistical publications and sources. The latter function is served by the introductory text to each section, the source notes below each table, and an Appendix which comprises the Guide to Sources of Statistics and the Guide to State Statistical Abstracts.

The volume includes a selection of data from many statistical publications, both governmental and private. Publications cited as sources usually contain additional statistical detail and more comprehensive discussions of definitions and concepts. Data not available in publications issued by the contributing agency but obtained from unpublished records are identified in the source notes. More information on subjects so noted may generally be obtained from the source.

Although emphasis is given primarily to national data, many tables present data for regions and individual states, and a small number for metropolitan areas and cities. Statistics for the Commonwealth of Puerto Rico and for outlying areas of the United States are included in many state tables and are supplemented by additional information. Additional information for cities, counties, metropolitan areas, congressional districts, and other small units, as well as more historical data, are available in various supplements to the Abstract.

A "Recent Trends" section is available separately in a reprint, "Recent Social and Economic Trends." "USA Statistics in Brief" is also available separately.

In the 1979 edition, a new section, "Selected Current Topics," was introduced, covering subjects of important national interest for which only a minimum of data can be shown in the Abstract sections.

Cross Reference: *Business Intelligence: Sources of Information, and references there given.*

STATISTICAL ACCOUNTING

Statistical Accounting denotes the application of probability theory and statistical sampling techniques to the general area of accounting. Clerical accounting operations have become a costly activity in many businesses because of the large masses of data which must be processed. Statistical accounting techniques provide a means of reducing such costs significantly by developing the necessary accounting information through projections of results obtained from processing only selected samples of the basic accounting data, while still providing the required degree of reliability with a known degree of risk. In appropriate applications, with proper planning, the results achieved may be as reliable, if not more so, as those obtained through other means.

Formal Definition. Statistical accounting is the application of the concepts of probability theory and the techniques of statistical sampling to the development of prime accounting data and/or the verification, authentication, and audit of accounting data prepared by other means.

History. The use of statistical sampling and probability theory in quality control obtained its major impetus during World War II (see QUALITY CONTROL AND QUALITY ASSURANCE). Subsequent thereto, the same concepts and techniques were applied to quality control of clerical operations and gradually extended during the late 1950s to include the development of prime accounting data. During this same period, the techniques also began to receive increasing attention in connection with internal and independent public auditing procedures.

Approaches and Techniques. The applications of statistical accounting may be classified into two groups. The first involves the development of prime accounting data. One of the earliest and most widely publicized applications involves the taking of physical inventories. Using statistical sampling, only selected items (perhaps less than 10% of the total number of items) are counted, priced, and extended. The results are projected to obtain the value for the total inventory. Results obtained are frequently within 1% or 2% tolerance limits, with 95% or greater reliability. A comparable degree of error may exist in a 100% physical inventory taken at considerably greater cost. Other examples of applications in use today are the interline settlement of ticket revenues between various airlines, the aging of accounts receivable, the establishment of warranty reserves, and the development of price indices for LIFO inventory valuations. In each of these cases, the dollar amounts of business transactions and accounting entries are based on a projection of results obtained from a statistical sample of the total data.

The second area of application is in the verification, authentication, and audit of accounting data originally compiled by some other means. Typical accounting applications involve the verification of vendors' invoices before payment, the rechecking of payroll computations, and the checking of customer billings. In each case, the statistical approach is used in lieu of 100% checking to establish the degree of error existing in the data. If an unsatisfactory condition is detected, special corrective action, including perhaps a complete reprocessing of the data, can be undertaken. Internal and independent external auditors also use statistical techniques in order to ensure that their audit tests provide the desired degree of assurance. When audit tests are made using statistical sampling techniques, the degree of reliability and precision of the results can be evaluated mathematically. When such tests are made solely on the basis of judgment sampling, their reliability cannot be evaluated objectively. Typical audit applications include the confirmation of accounts receivable and payable, the vouching of cash receipts and disbursements, and the checking of inventory pricings.

The successful application of statistical accounting techniques requires a fairly sophisticated analysis of the problem area, the objectives to be attained, and the characteristics of the accounting data involved. After business management has established risk and reliability tolerances, trained statisticians can prepare working plans for sample size, selection, and analysis, based on mathematical formulae, to obtain the desired results. The results obtained may be subjected to further statistical tests to assure that the desired degree of reliability and risk have been obtained. (See STATISTICS.)

Acceptance. While the use of statistical accounting varies greatly among companies, certain applications such as statistical LIFO (last-in, first-out inventory accounting) conversions are widespread. The companies that have utilized the technique have found the results very satisfactory and are extending their applications. In the area of auditing, various public accounting firms, internal audit staffs, and governmental audit agencies have found many useful applications.

The techniques have not yet been adopted as standard auditing procedures by the American Institute of Certified Public Accountants, though their use has been recognized as being in conformance with generally accepted auditing standards. Auditors who have used statistical techniques believe they are reliable and effective, and continue to expand their use.

C.E. Graese, CPA, Partner, Peat, Marwick, Mitchell & Co., New York, New York

Information References

American Institute of Certified Public Accountants: "An Auditor's Approach to Statistical Sampling," a set of programmed learning texts covering statistical concepts and estimation of dollar values (Vol. I), sampling for attributes (Vol. II), stratified random sampling (Vol. III), and discovery of sampling (Vol. IV).

American Institute of Certified Public Accountants, "Codification of Statements on Auditing Standards," Appendix A: "Relationship of Statistical Sampling to Generally Accepted Auditing Standards." Appendix B: "Precision and Reliability for Statistical Sampling in Auditing." New York, AICPA, 1977.

Arkin, Herbert, "Handbook of Sampling for Auditing and Accounting," Vol. I—Methods, New York, McGraw-Hill, 2nd ed., 1974.

Federal Government Accountants Association, "Sampling Techniques and Regression Analysis for Accounting and Auditing Information—A Practical Approach," special supplement to *The Federal Accountant,* November 1967.

Leslie, Donald A., Teitlebaum, Albert D., and Anderson, Rodney J., "Dollar Unit Sampling, A Practical Guide for Auditors," Toronto, Capp Clark Pitman, 1979.

Roberts, Donald M., "Statistical Auditing," American Institute of Certified Public Accountants, New York, 1978.

Slonim, Morris James, "Sampling in a Nutshell," New York, Simon & Schuster, 1966.

Springer, Clifford H., Herlithy, Robert E., Mall, Robert T., and Beggs, Robert I., "Statistical Inference," Vol. III of "Mathematics for Management Series," Homewood, Ill., Irwin, 1966.

Spurr, William A. and Bonini, Charles P., "Statistical Analysis for Business Decisions," Homewood, Ill., Irwin, 1973.

Cross References: *Management Accounting (and cross references there given).*

STATISTICS

In modern management practice, the most important use of **Statistics** is as a tool of decision-making. Decisions may be required in either of two situations: (1) when there is certainty of all elements of the problem; or (2) when risk or uncertainty exists, either in terms of informational hiatuses or through the limitations implicit in sampling procedures. In either case, statistics contributes to action, but it is in the second instance that its fullest effectiveness is realized.

Indeed, a recent definition of statistics describes the subject as "a body of methods for making wise decisions in the face of uncertainty." This is to say, in short, that statistics deals with problem solving and consequently lies within the established bounds of scientific method.

Three principal methodological areas comprise the main body of statistics used for management actions: *Description, Inference,* and *Decision-Making.* In many instances, these three branches of statistics comprise logical, sequential stages in the ultimate approach to problem solving but each may independently serve many purposes.

Description. In the statistical sense, *description* departs from the literary concept of the term. In statistics, description deals with the collection, tabulation, and summarization of numerical data. These may involve the arithmetic mean, standard deviation, coefficient of correlation, and other summary measures (to be described later).

In the absence of uncertainty, description may in itself provide the full solution of a problem, as, for example, the stock market pages do in reflecting the activity of the stock market. In the above instance, all of the relevant data are available, and description simply digests, summarizes, and presents them in useful form. The description function was, in fact, the first statistical area to be investigated and developed, and still comprises a large share of all present-day statistical activity.

Inference. When description is applied to conditions of certainty, as in stock market tables in which a *census* of traded stocks is shown, it becomes a methodological entity. In most present-day statistical problems, however, a sample rather than a census is used, and description then becomes merely a preparation for the next branch of statistics: *inference.*

When we engage in inference, we arrive at a conclusion or formulate a statement under some condition of uncertainty. Uncertainty, itself, may arise from the condition of randomness implied in dealing with any sample, or from lack of knowledge of those precise laws of randomness that are applicable to the specific situation. In conclusion theory, however, the aspect of uncertainty of the correctness of the statement made or the conclusion drawn is made simply in terms of the probability of its occurrence.

Two major categories of problems are dealt with by inference. These are *estimation* and *tests of hypotheses.* Estimation deals with the measurement of some *parameter of a universe, within a known range of error at some known cofidence level, through statistical induction from a sample finding.* For example, a sample survey among dealers or consumers to establish the market share owned by a particular product brand or a laboratory test of samples of a product flowing from a production line to establish a measure of some physical characteristic would both fall within the terms of the foregoing statement.

The second area of inference deals with the *test of hypothesis.* Any hypothesis is *an assumption which, on the basis of some experimental findings, may be rejected or allowed to stand.* When the experiment is based on a sampling technique, the question arises as to whether or not the particular finding is, in truth, a measure of the entire population from which the sample was drawn, within known and acceptable limits of random error. Rejection or acceptance of the hypothesis, then, rests upon some statistical determination of the facts of the case, generally called a *test of significance.* Many such tests are available, each more or less useful in particular circumstances, some of which will be dealt with in following sections. In every test of significance, however, the hypothesis under test is rejected or not as it exceeds or falls within some predetermined level of the probability of its occurrence through chance alone.

Decision Making. Implicit in any test of a hypothesis, and a logical consequence of the process of inference, is the expectation that some management action will be taken in the form of selecting one of two or more alternative courses. This is *decision making,* and around this function has been developed *decision theory,* embodying much of the advanced work in statistics undertaken within the past few decades.

Decision theory, in addition to dealing with alternative courses of action *per se,* takes into account three other factors:

(1) Possible states of nature or events or outcomes to which, in some manner, probabilities of occurrence may be assigned.

(2) Some method of assessment of the correctness of actions or events and their consequences in terms of profitability or utility.

(3) Some criterion or criteria for the determination of the best or "optimum" act.

Obviously, it is important that the data upon which decisions are based have maximum application to the subject as well as adequate reliability. Whether in the laboratory or in the factory or field, this demands the development of some experimental design that will produce the most and best information possible within limits of time and budget available. Both these latter criteria properly enter into the final efficiency of the design of the total experiment.

Among more recent developments in statistical decision theory has been the entry of the *Bayesian Theorem* to the field, with its concept of personalistic or subjective probability of events as a basis for the maximization of expected profit or utility through the act or decision taken.

ORIGINS OF STATISTICS

As compared with the main stream of mathematics from which it evolved, statistics has always been an applied science.

The earliest use of statistics was in its descriptive function. In this sense, statistics was in use at least 4,000 years ago as a tool of government, employed to enumerate and describe populations. Records exist of a census conducted in Judea in 2030 B.C. The registration, for tax purposes, that brought about the birth of Jesus in Bethlehem, was a statistical device, as was the Golden Book in Medieval Venice and the Domesday Book in early England. These latter works, incidentally, were the direct antecedents of modern vital statistics compilations by municipal health departments.

William Petty is generally credited, through his "Essays on Political Arithmetick" (1690), with stimulating thought and research in political science that eventually gave rise to economics in the modern sense as an independent scientific discipline. It is however in the aspects of inference or conclusion theory that statistics is of most interest to management, and the birth of this branch of science is attributable to the concept and development of the theory of probability.

"What are the odds?" has always been a reasonable question when money is about to be risked; it is essentially the question that initiated a correspondence, circa 1654, between Chevalier de Méré, an amateur mathematician and gambler, and Blaise Pascal, theologian and mathematician. Certainly it must have been in his latter capacity that Pascal, fascinated with the problems of chance suggested by de Méré, entered into his now celebrated exchange of letters with Pierre de Fermat, concerning the "Problems of Points" from which probability theory began to emerge.

The spark struck by Pascal and Fermat lighted fire in the mind of Jacques Bernoulli, first of nine mathematicians of greater or lesser stature, all members of the same family. Bernoulli was quick to perceive the applicability of "odds" to problems far removed from cards or dice. In his "Ars Conjectandi" published posthumously in 1713, he showed the application of probability to civil, moral, and economic affairs, discoursed on permutations and combinations, and laid other important groundwork for those who followed. Their names were legion, since these were basic concepts that captured the imagination of the whole eighteenth-century scientific community. Outstanding among them were, certainly, Abraham DeMoivre (1667–1754), Pierre Simon Marquis de La Place (1749–1827), and Karl Friedrich Gauss (1777–1855). Each of these independently produced the idea of the normal curve from which arose the whole theory of errors, without which modern statistics could not serve those who depend on it.

Bridging the eighteenth and nineteeth centuries Adolph Quetelet (1796–1874), perhaps the first person to whom the term "statistician," in its present-day sense, could be applied, merged the work of his predecessors in the fields of description, government, and probability into a working tool for the investigation of social phenomena. He was an organizer in the fullest sense, exercising great influence on such contemporaries as Florence Nightingale and Francis Galton, and assuming a leading role in the founding of the International Statistical Congress in 1853—the first international gathering of statisticians as professional scientists in their own right.

The modern statistical movement generated by Quetelet gained continuing momentum during the second half of the nineteenth century. This was a burgeoning period in the natural and physical sciences, and the need for statistical methods and techniques threatened to outdistance their development. The last of the forerunners of statistics as we recognize the subject today was Sir Francis Galton, who, with the publication of "Natural Inheritance" in 1889, linked the work of all earlier theoreticians with the present, and stimulated Karl Pearson, "father of statistics," to the revolution in statistical thinking that launched the first of four great modern movements, beginning about 1890 and still in exciting progress.

It will be the purpose of later sections of this entry to define and discuss many of the terms coined by and identifying the men whose names are synonymous with each of the four aforesaid movements. For our present purpose, it is only necessry to name them and the stages of the science associated with them.

Karl Pearson was the first, and perhaps greatest, of these giants of intellectual attainment. Beginning with his four lectures on "The Scope and Concepts of Modern Science" and his "Mathematical Contributions to the Theory of Evolution," it is doubtful if a year passed between 1890 and his death at age 79 in 1936, without some significant contribution to statistical science emerging from his inventive and prolific mind.

To Karl Pearson, statistics is indebted for virtually all of the techniques for dealing with large samples; for the invention of the correlation coefficient and other methods for measuring association; for the invention of Chi-Square Distribution, and perhaps most important of all from the viewpoint of service to the entire statistical fraternity, for the construction and publication of a whole literature of tables needed and used by every statistician. He, it may truly be said, launched the first great movement in modern statistics.

The second movement, characterized by the investigation and development of methods appropriate to small samples, rather than the large aggregates of data with which Karl Pearson dealt, belongs to R. A. Fisher and, to a lesser degree, to William S. Gossett (who published under the pseudonym of "Student"). Here began the great concepts of the design of experiments and the testing of hypotheses, the theory of multivariate analysis, multiple correlation, and the analysis of variance.

In the interim between the great world wars, Jerzy Neyman and Egon Pearson (son of Karl Pearson) set in motion the third wave of statistical development through further expansion of the logic of statistical inference. This, too, was a period of great technical and theoretical advances, with many men engaged in the develvopment of new ideas. Great emphasis began to be laid on techniques for sample surveys. Tests of hypotheses were refined and their criticality improved by the introduction of new tests for confidence limits, risks, and error functions, and the power of tests. In the 1940s, statistical methods in quality control began to emerge, and non-parametric statistics found enthusiastic acceptance by many.

Out of these stirring times emerged the late Abraham Wald, who, with his sweeping innovations in decision theory (1942), began the last of the four discernible movements of twentieth century statistics.

Future historians of science may find in the past two decades the beginnings of still another well-marked stage in the maturation of statistics. These years have been marked by a surprisingly rapid development of another approach to decision theory: that of the Bayesian school. Rejecting Wald's "minimax principle" for selection of the "best" act, the Bayesian approach substitutes the criterion of maximization of expected utility. Application of this concept requires the inclusion of a premise of personal or subjective probability and, for the first time in statistical history, integrates management experience and judgment with statistical models in the decision-making function.

As mathematics has been called the handmaiden of all other sciences, so statistics, today, may well be adjudged the servant of science and the humanities alike, with special and unique applicability to the problems of business management.

Sample surveys, designed to elicit market and marketing information, are routine in marketing research. Product quality is maintained through the establishment of statistical standards. Forecasts of sales, economic expectations, plant and equipment needs, and rates of obsolescence are based on sampling and other statistical techniques, and these find additional applications in the selection of personnel, in accounting and auditing functions, and, indeed, in virtually every phase of design, production, distribution, advertising, and selling of products and services.

DESCRIPTIVE STATISTICS

Descriptive statistics deals with numerical data. These data represent observations obtained either through counting or through some measurement process. They may define an entire population or universe or they may be simply representative of a universe and be derived through some sampling procedure. In either event, they represent the raw materials of any subsequent statistical processing and may, in some cases, be sufficient by themselves to answer particular questions or solve particular problems.

If all populations and universes were alike in all their components, it would not be necessary to collect data at all. Any single observation would be the same as any other or all others. But there is no such thing in nature as absolute homogeneity or identity. All things vary, in some manner and to some degree, from all others. It is for the purpose of discovering the range and pattern and extent of such variables that data are collected.

Variables may be of two distinct classes: purely *quantitative,* as for example, physical measurements of height or weight; or *qualitative,* such as sex or color of hair or economic status. For convenience, a purely quantitative variable is termed a *variate*; a qualitative variable is called an *attribute.* Both are susceptible of arithmetic aggregation and analysis.

Variates are of two kinds: *continuous* or *discrete.* Continuous variates are those in which every value within some given range may occur, as, for example in the heights of men or the life expectancy of an electric lamp bulb. Discrete variates have no such continuum, but represent points selected along some scale, frequently to the nearest whole number or integer. An example might be ages in terms of years, number of children per household, or number of defective units per lot in a manufacturing process.

The characteristics of data may be dealt with one at a time or in groups of two or more.

Univariate data, in which only a single characteristic is measured, would be sufficient to determine the range of heights of men in some population group and to find such measurements as average weight, the distribution of weights, or other descriptive analysis. *Bivariate* or *multivariate* data, treating two or more characteristics simultaneously, such, for example as weight and height, or weight, age and shoe sizes, would permit analysis in associative terms.

Dealing with Univariate Data. Man's mind is not equipped to evaluate meanings simply by viewing large masses of raw data. Merely to list size of family as reported by a city census, for example, in the order of street address, would be confusing and would tell us little.

Data then, must be organized to be useful. A simple first step for treating the foregoing example might be to array the data from largest to smallest family size encountered. This would, at least, indicate the range of variability. Next, it would be easy to group the arranged data into classes or class intervals, and thus learn something about the relative incidence of 1-, 2-, 3-, or more member households in the area. (Such an analysis is called a *frequency distribution.*) Or the data might be graphically portrayed by means of a *histogram* or a *frequency polygon.*

For purposes of illustration, the following data are extrapolated from a much larger body of observations, dealing with the life tests of 417 lamp bulbs. Exhibit I shows the raw data, as collected. Even though the number of observations is small, it is easy to see how difficult it is to derive real knowledge of bulb life from the observations in this form.

Exhibit II presents the data in an array, in terms of life hours. The variability of bulb life is now easily discernible, as is the range of hours over which it extends.

From a practical standpoint, we should now like to know what percentage of all these bulbs have given maximum, minimum, or some intermediate term of useful performance. Exhibit III, by grouping the data into class intervals, tells us this.

Finally, to visualize the importance of these analyses, Exhibit IV is given. Here, the pattern of bulb life distribution emerges. Ranges, fluctuations within the extremes and the central tendency, and general symmetry of the distribution become clear.

EXHIBIT I

LIFE IN HOURS OF 417 INCANDESCENT LAMPS

1,067	919	1,196	785	1,126
936	918	1,156	920	948
855	1,092	1,162	1,170	929
950	905	972	1,035	1,045
1,157	1,195	1,195	1,340	1,122
938	970	1,237	956	1,102
1,022	978	832	1,009	1,157
1,151	1,009	765	958	902
923	1,333	811	1,217	1,085
896	958	1,311	1,037	702
521	933	928	1,153	946
858	1,071	1,069	830	1,063
.	.	.	.	.
.	.	.	.	.
.	.	.	.	.
1,109	827	1,209	1,202	1,229
1,079	1,176	1,173	769	905

SOURCE: Extracted from Bowker, Albert H., and Lieberman, Gerald J., "Engineering Statistics," Prentice Hall, Englewood Cliffs, N.J., 1959.

In this instance, the histogram presents a fairly symmetrical distribution. But this is not always the case. Skewed patterns of all forms may just as well result from other types and degrees of variations within a population.

Reduction of Data by Single Measures. The types of descriptions just discussed are, of course, useful and meaningful measures of collected data. For many purposes, however, it may be desirable to find some unique terms, descriptive of the entire body of observations. There are many such simple measurements,

EXHIBIT II

AN ARRAY OF LIFE IN HOURS OF 417 INCANDESCENT LAMPS

225	521	525	529	609
610	612	621	623	653
658	666	675	699	702
704	705	709	709	716
730	732	744	759	760
765	765	769	773	775
.	.	.	.	.
.	.	.	.	.
.	.	.	.	.
1,438	1,461	1,470	1,485	1,490
1,550	1,555	1,562	1,635	1,690

SOURCE: Extracted from Bowker, Albert H., and Lieberman, Gerald J., "Engineering Statistics," Prentice Hall, Englewood Cliffs, N.J., 1959.

EXHIBIT III

FREQUENCY TABLE FOR LENGTH OF LIFE OF INCANDESCENT LAMPS

Class Interval (100 hr.)	*Frequency f*	*Relative Frequency, Per Cent*
201–300	1	0.2
301–400	—	—
401–500	—	—
501–600	3	0.7
601–700	10	2.4
701–800	21	5.0
801–900	45	10.8
901–1,000	91	21.8
1,001–1,100	85	20.4
1,100–1,200	80	19.2
1,201–1,300	44	10.6
1,301–1,400	23	5.5
1,401–1,500	9	2.2
1,501–1,600	3	.7
1,601–1,700	2	.5
	417	100.0

SOURCE: Bowker, Albert H., and Lieberman, Gerald J., "Engineering Statistics," Prentice Hall, Englewood Cliffs, N.J., 1959.

some of the most useful of which will now be discussed.

In general, measurements of univariate data may be directed to the determination of central tendencies or to variabilities from some central focus; that is, of nearness of measures to or distance from an average or median attained for all the data presented.

The first unique measurement of a central tendency applicable to any group of numerical data is their *aggregate* or *total.* How many or how much of anything is obviously an important function of data, and to the process of summation by which this measurement is obtained the symbol Σ is given. It means to add. Statisticians usually denote an observation from sample data with the symbol "x_i," the number of such observations as "n" and the number of possible observations within the entire universe or population as "N." Thus, to determine the aggregate "a" of a sample, the statistician would employ the formula:

$$a = \sum x_i .$$

where i ranges from 1, 2, . . . , n.

EXHIBIT IV

LIFE LENGTH HISTOGRAM FOR INCANDESCENT LIGHT BULBS

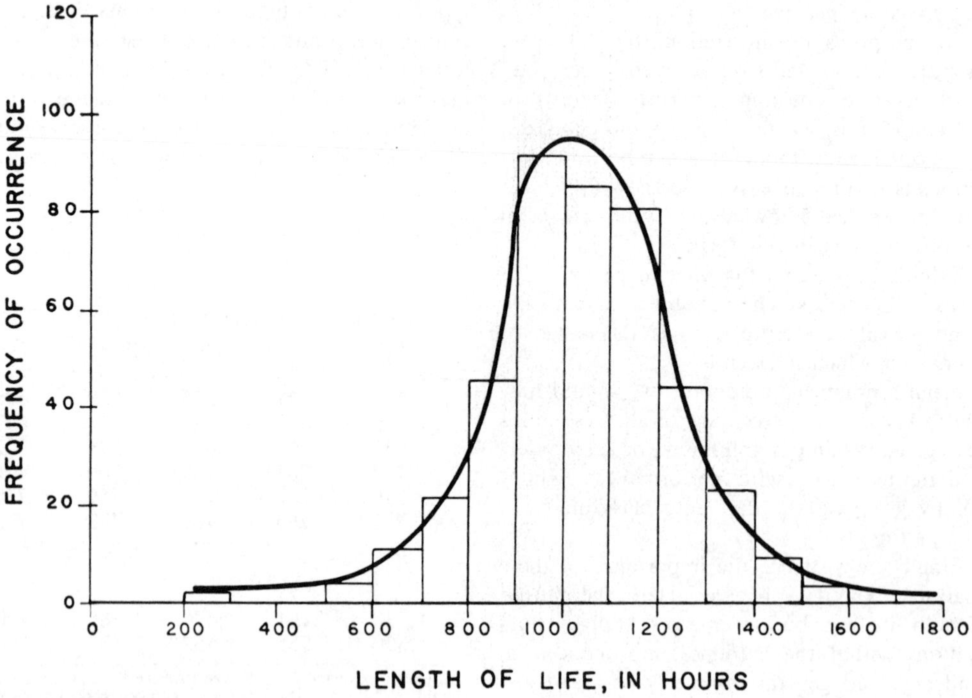

SOURCE: Exhibit III

A simple illustration of the use of an aggregate would be to measure the total dollar sales produced by a sales force during some period. Such a figure, when compared with one for some similar preceding period or following period would be adequate to determine a rudimentary sales trend. Or, to utilize the data already presented for illustration, the total life-hours inherent in the 417 incandescent lamp bulbs may be given as 435,921 hours.

A second measure, also of central tendency, that is of great utilitarian value is the *proportion* or *ratio* of some characteristic of a part of the data to the whole. For example, what proportion of men in some designated area or in some period of time smoke cigarettes? What is the ratio of blue-eyed blondes to all women over 18 years of age in Brooklyn, N.Y. this afternoon? Or, if the manufacturer of the light bulb we have been discussing considers a life span of less than 800 hours as evidence of a manufacturing defect, what proportion of those shown in our illustration is defective? The formula for computing this proportion is:

P (proportion of light bulbs defective)

$$= \frac{\text{Number of defectives found}}{\text{Number of light bulbs tested}} = \frac{35}{417} = 0.084$$

Probably the most common single measure applied to data is the *arithmetic mean* or average. Its computation makes use of every datum collected, and it is descriptive of the central character of the whole body of data. The arithmetic mean may be likened to the center of gravity of a mass or to the fulcrum of a lever system, such as a see-saw or a pharmacist's balance scales. Everything in the system clusters around it. It is an every-day concept in every area of life: the average man, his average income, average rental are terms of common currency.

Computation of the arithmetic mean is half done when the aggregate, previously discussed, has been determined. The rest of the process consists merely of dividing this number by the number of observations yielding it. The complete designation is

$$\frac{\sum x_i}{N}$$

and it is indicated by the Greek letter μ when it is applied to a total population (*complete count* or *census*) and by $\bar{X}$ when it is derived from a sample:

$$\bar{X} = \frac{\text{Aggregate or total hours of all light bulbs tested}}{\text{Number of light bulbs tested}}$$

$$= \frac{a}{n} = \frac{\sum x_i}{n}$$

From Exhibit III, this becomes:

$$= \frac{435{,}921}{417} = 1{,}045 \text{ hours} = \bar{X}, \text{ the arithmetic mean.}$$

Computing the arithmetic mean from grouped data is slightly more cumbersome but is identical in principle.

In addition to the aggregate and the arithmetic mean, there are other measures of central tendency applicable to any body of observations. Among them may be mentioned the *geometric mean,* the *harmonic mean,* the *median,* and the *mode.* The geometric mean, representing the nth root of the product of all observations, is useful as an average of index numbers, prices, and various ratios. The *harmonic mean,* computed from the *reciprocals* of observations, is principally used when it is desired to view various ratios in inverse terms: for example, as "hours per mile" when "miles per hour" are given.

The *median,* as contrasted with any form of mean, is a fixed point representing the exact mid-point of a series of observations. It is a number that neither exceeds, nor is exceeded by more than half of the observations. When distributions include open-ended values or are skewed, the median is often a more reliable measure of the norm than is any other measure of central tendency.

The *mode* is the value of the variable having the greatest frequency of occurrence. It is the *most representative* value in any set of observations—the one which occurs most frequently. When two values occur with equally great frequency, the distribution is said to be *bimodal*; with three equal values: *tri-modal*; etc.

Measures of Dispersion. In addition to measures of central tendency, there are also measurements of the *dispersion* or *variability* of data. Knowledge of how observations are scattered throughout the range of their occurrence is of extremely practical value—as witness the oft-quoted example of the man who went over his head in a pond averaging only two feet in depth.

Any manufacturer concerned with such factors as interchangeability of parts knows the importance of variability. If he has a quality control program, it is certain to be aimed at minimizing the number of items exceeding some acceptable range of variability. On the other hand, the sample surveyor may wish to *increase* dispersion or scatter of his observations to insure maximum representativeness of his universe. In either case, it is important that reliable measures of variability be available.

It should be noted that the best and most commonly used techniques for measuring variability are similar in nature to those used in measuring central tendency: the computation of various types of averages.

Variation may be expressed in terms of *average or mean* deviation, which is simply the average variation, without regard to direction, from the mean or median of all observations. However, the most important and most frequently-used measure of variability is the *standard deviation,* also called the *root mean square deviation,* represented by the Greek letter σ. It is expressed in the following formula:

$$\sigma = \sqrt{\frac{\sum (x_i - \bar{X})^2}{N - 1}}$$

Referring to the data in our light-bulb example,

$$\sigma = \sqrt{\frac{(1{,}065 - 1{,}045)^2 + (936 - 1{,}045)^2 + \cdots + (905 - 1{,}045)^2}{(417 - 1)}}$$
$$= 190.57$$

The standard deviation has great versatility in its functions, as will be seen, for example, in following sections dealing with the normal curve and with sample distributions. The standard deviation is also of great importance in statistical inference, where it is used as a measure of sampling error or reliability. It is worth noting now that, in a normal distribution, to be discussed later, virtually all observations fall within the limit of plus or minus three σ around the arithmetic mean.

In descriptive statistics, however, the greatest usefulness of the standard deviation is as an indicator of the dependability of a mean as a summary measure. An example of this use, based on the lamp bulb illustration already cited, is given in Exhibit V.

Note that in this example, virtually all of the observations obtained fall within a *range* of 3σ on either side of the mean.

The square of the standard deviation (σ^2) is a measure of the *variance* of a set of data. It is used in correlation problems, the analysis of variance, and in the design of experiments.

When the standard deviation is divided by the mean and the resultant quotient is multiplied by 100, the result is called the *coefficient of variation.* It expresses σ as a percentage of the mean, and makes possible comparison between sets of observations. If, for example, the average weight of cats is found to be four pounds, with a standard deviation of one pound, the coefficient of variation is 25%. If, on the other hand, the average weight of dogs is found to be 10 pounds, with a standard deviation of one pound, the coefficient of variation is 10%. A logical conclusion is not merely that cats are different from dogs, but that they are far more different from other cats, than dogs are from other dogs.

Mathematical Probability. From the preceding discussion, it is evident that statistical description may deal with subjects or areas about which *everything* is known or about which only *some* things are known. Statistically, these two states are identified as *certainty* or *uncertainty.* A census, for example, would represent certainty about the universe it measures; a sample of the universe, on the other hand, would embody some elements of uncertainty.

As stated earlier, statistical inference and decision-making are aspects of statistics upon which management is most apt to call when some uncertainty of events or information exists. When data are, in some measure, incomplete there must be some means of evaluating or reducing the uncertainty thus engendered if they are to be used at all. What is needed, then, is knowledge and application of the principles of one of the most fascinating areas of mathematics: *probability.*

Probability or, to give it another name, *mathematical chance*, is the most pervasive force we know. Its implications are evident in everything we do or know or think. "What are the chances . . .?" is a question asked not

EXHIBIT V

NORMAL CURVE SUPERIMPOSED UPON LIFE-LENGTH HISTOGRAM FOR LIGHT BULBS

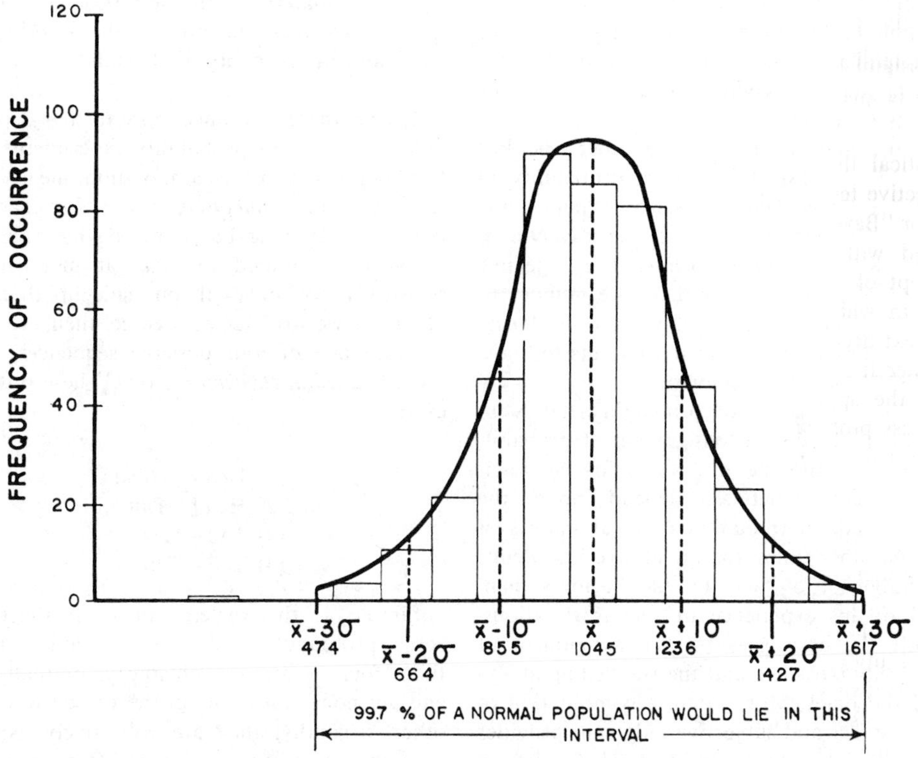

SOURCE: Exhibit IV

merely about whether it would be profitable to add a square lamp bulb to a manufacturer's line or to bet on a horse with a good record in mud, or against the throw of the dice in craps. It is also applicable to the question of whether our next space vehicle will collide with a meteor, or whether next season's corn crop will germinate and grow to harvest, or if the atoms of the reader's hand, as he holds this page, may suddenly merge and intermix with those of the paper itself!

Anything may, indeed happen. It is because we can assign probability values to the event that we are able to draw conclusions and make our decisions. QUEUING, or WAITING LINE THEORY, uses probability to determine such questions as how many servers or facilities should be available at what points and at which times to meet the variations in arrival and waiting times of customers; to plan dial telephone exchange capacities; to establish stacking patterns at airports; to provide acceptable solutions to any problem of handling *uncertain* situations.

While the uses of probability are myriad, there are three basic axioms or laws governing its applicability in any situation, as follows:

(1) The probability of any event or occurrence can be stated as some number ranging from 0 to 1, both included.

(2) The probability of an event consisting of two or more mutually exclusive events is expressed as the sum of the individual probabilities (addition rule).

(3) One event consisting of two or more collectively exhaustive and mutually exclusive events has a probability of 1.

From these basic rules of probability, all other functions and theorems of chance are derived or deduced. A *probability measure* is an assignment of real numbers to events in such a manner that these three basic principles of mathematical chance or probability are followed.

There is virtually universal agreement on these axioms of probability, but there is by no means similar unanimity of agreement on their use. One school of statistics, characterized as "objective," holds that probability is properly applicable only to events that can be repeated *ad infinitum*: to the tossing of a coin, the operation of a production line, or the random variation of life-hours of our lamp bulb, for example. To the objective probabilist, the idea of assigning probability values to a unique event is anathema.

On the other hand, there is another school of statistical thought which views probability in subjective terms. The "subjective," "personalistic" or "Bayesian" viewpoint is specifically concerned with individual events. The objective concept of probability predicts the number of days in which precipitation will occur during the next decade; the subjectivist wants to know whether it may rain tomorrow.

In the application of probability theory to business problems, the assignment of probability measures and the analysis of logical possibilities may sometimes depend upon the analysis and interpretation of great masses of data. At other times, the qualitative knowledge and judgment of facts by the business man, based on his experience in similar situations, provide the best basis for the assignment of probability measures and the succeeding analysis of outcomes. More often, a combination of objective fact and subjective judgment provides the optimum approach to the final decision in business problems.

Basic to the employment of probability theory for any purpose are of course, the three axioms given, all of which are dependent on the ability to assign some measure of likelihood to each possible event or occurrence. The same basic rules apply whether we are dealing with such a simple situation as assigning a measure to the probability of heads appearing half the time after repeated tosses of a fair coin, or to the result of subjective judgment applied to the solution of a business problem.

The most prevalent form of applying probability measures is through the use of the "ideal or long-run relative frequency." This conforms with the objective view of probability, limiting the "proper" application of probability to events that can be repeated endlessly. How the tools of probability theory develop from this viewpoint will be seen through examples which follow.

For all its versatility and universality of applications, the working tools of probability are, essentially, as simple in concept as the three axioms on which the whole theory rests. Its use, ranging from the determination of "odds" relating to the occurrence of *elementary events* to the assessment of probabilities in highly complex situations is simple and logical. It requires only the following of the step-by-step development of easily understandable principles.

Let us, then, turn once more to that dependable trial horse of probability experiments: the fair coin. (Fair, in this connotation, means only that the coin is *unbiased;* is not, for example, double-headed and has not been mechanically designed or altered to make it more likely, physically, to land with one side up than the other.) If we toss our coin twice, then, we *must* produce one of four possible sequences, each identified as an *elementary event.* These possible events are:

(1) Head—Head
(2) Head—Tail
(3) Tail—Head
(4) Tail—Tail

Simple as this experiment is, it illustrates some profoundly important principles. First, these four events are, obviously, mutually exclusive: none can occur in the presence of any other. Secondly, they are collectively exhaustive: they represent *every* possible event attendant upon the experiment of tossing one coin twice. Finally, in total, they represent an important aspect of any experiment in that they constitute the concept of *sample space:* that is, the limits within which *any* result of the experiment must fall.

It is easy to see why, in the foregoing example, each possible experimental result is called an *elementary event.* If the *order of tosses of the coin* is considered to be a fixed dimension, it is impossible to decompose the content of any of the four possible events. However, there are also such outcomes as *compound events,* one of whose criteria is that they *can* be decomposed. Thus, if the order of the tosses is *not* a criterion of the experiment, the appearance of one head and one tail actually comprises two of the *elementary events* listed above. Thus *an elementary event may constitute a special class of a compound event.* A compound event may also include more than one event or, on occasion even no event at all! (In our present experiment, it might consist of the chance of three heads, for example, which is not within the prescribed *sample space.*)

We have seen how the four elementary events possible in the sample space of our experiment are mutually exclusive. In treating of conpound events, it is only necessary to remember that when two compound events have *no* elementary events in common, they are also mutually exclusive events.

A sample space may contain an infinite or a finite number of elementary events or outcomes, or it may consist of all possible measurements of a *continuous* quantity, such as body weight, or the life hours of electric bulbs, or, perhaps, of discrete sample points. If the sample space is finite and if a set of events, elementary or compound, includes *all* the points of the sample space, the set is called *collectively exhaustive.*

Remember that a probability measure is merely an assignment of real numbers to events in such a way that the numbers obey the three basic axioms of mathematical probability. In a sample space comprising the four events defined by our example of two tosses of a single coin, we have seen that the elementary events can be only four: HH, HT, TH, TT. It is easy to see that, as a matter of sheer chance, each of the four combinations has an equally likely opportunity to occur, and we might therefore assign probability measures of $1/4$ to each. However, should we have some *a priori* information on the likelihood of different events occurring, then under Bayesian Theory, the actual probability measures we *do* assign would be a question of probability *assessment.* In passing, it may be noted that subjective judgment based on experience may very well play a role in such assessment.

As one can see, probability theory is simply common sense, applied to a specialized area. Because that specialized area happens to be mathematical as well as logical, it is usual to apply the universal shorthand of mathematical notation to facilitate manipulation. Thus, if we denote the events with which we have been dealing (or any events, in any set of circumstances) as $A, B, C \ldots$, then the probability, P, assigned to the events is designated by $P(A)$, $P(B)$, $P(C) \ldots$ etc.

In addition to the simple probability of the occurrence of an independent event, there are, of course, other situations in which more complex factors give rise to *joint, conditional,* and *marginal* probabilities. Such situations often arise in business, and an example may be found in a typical marketing experiment in which it is desired to learn something of the relationship between viewing of a television commercial and purchasing of the product it advertises.

Let us assume, then, that we are dealing with a set of 400 observations, which we find to be distributed as shown in Exhibit VI.

The values shown in the cells of the body of this exhibit can be called, collectively, a *joint frequency distribution.* We must classify any observation in this set jointly by the criteria of viewing and purchase to determine to which cell it is to be assigned. The total column, then, gives the total frequency of purchase or nonpurchase, regardless of viewing, while the total row gives the frequency of viewing or nonviewing, regardless of purchase. Because the total row and column occur in the margins outside the body of the table, or matrix, they are called *marginal frequencies.*

Most people have difficulty in seeing the real proportional relationship among sets of whole numbers. Rather, we are all conditioned to the evaluation of parts of a whole in such familiar terms as percentages. The preceding data in percentage terms, with every cell and margin value divided by the total of 400 observations, are presented in Exhibit VII.

Technically, what we now have is a table of *joint relative frequencies,* which total to 1, and whose *marginal relative frequencies* also total to 1. If we are willing to assess probabilities objectively on the basis of these relative frequencies, the table can also be regarded as a table of joint and marginal probabilities. In the notation of mathematics, they are expressed as shown in Exhibit VIII.

EXHIBIT VI

TYPICAL MARKETING EXPERIMENT DETERMINING THE RELATIONSHIP BETWEEN ADVERTISING EXPOSURE AND SALES

	Viewed Commercial (A)	*Did Not View Commercial* ($\bar{A}$)	*Total*
Purchased Product (B)	140	20	160
Did Not Purchase ($\bar{B}$)	140	100	240
Total	280	120	400

EXHIBIT VII

MARKETING EXPERIMENT IN PERCENTAGE FORM

Event	*Viewed Commercial (A)*	*Did Not View Commercial ($\bar{A}$)*	*Total*
Purchased Product (*B*)	.35	.05	.40
Did Not Purchase ($\bar{B}$)	.35	.25	.60
Total	.70	.30	1.00

EXHIBIT VIII

PROBABILITY TABLE FOR MARKETING EXPERIMENT

	Viewed Commercial (A)	*Did Not View Commercial ($\bar{A}$)*	*Marginal Probability*
Purchased Product (*B*)	$P(A, B)$	$P(\bar{A}, B)$	$P(B)$
Did Not Purchase ($\bar{B}$)	$P(A, \bar{B})$	$P(\bar{A}, \bar{B})$	$P(\bar{B})$
Total	$P(A)$	$P(\bar{A})$	1

When we come to the use of these values for the purpose for which the experiment was designed, however, we are perhaps more interested in knowing the probability of *B* (purchase) given *A* (viewing). In mathematical terms, this is expressed as $P(B/A)$. For this purpose, it is customary to percentage the data shown in Exhibit VI by dividing each entry by its column total. The results are shown in Exhibit IX.

EXHIBIT IX

CONDITIONAL DISTRIBUTION

	Viewed Commercial (A)	*Did Not View Commercial ($\bar{A}$)*	*Marginal Distribution*
Purchased Product (*B*)	.50	.167	.40
Did Not Purchase ($\bar{B}$)	.50	.833	.60
Total	1.00	1.00	1.00

Now we can see that, conditioned upon viewing the commercial, the relative frequency or probability of purchasing the product is 50%, and in this instance the likelihood of not purchasing has the same value. If the commercial is *not* viewed, however, the probability of purchase is only 16.7%, while the probability of non-purchase rises to 83.3%. These are, then, *conditional probabilities,* since they represent one factor being conditional upon another—in this case, purchase conditional upon commercial viewing.

Obviously, we can reverse the direction of our computation, dividing each entry by its row total, to obtain the conditional probability (in this instance) of viewing conditional upon purchase.

As a matter of course we can also assess conditional relative frequency as probability, and we have, therefore, now explained each of these terms with which we began: joint, marginal, and conditional probability.

There is, evidently, a general relationship here and it is in the form of:

$$\text{Conditional Probability} = \frac{\text{Joint Probability}}{\text{Marginal Probability}}$$

$$P(B|A) = \frac{P(A, B)}{P(A)}$$

where $P(B|A)$ reads, "the probability of *B*, given that *A* has occurred."

This equation can be rearranged into the form $P(A, B) = P(A) \cdot P(B|A)$. In this form, it is used to calculate a joint probability from a marginal and conditional probability.

This is the *multiplication rule* which is used often in probability calculations. It leads to the basic concept of *independence,* which holds that events *A* and *B* are independent, if $P(B|A) = P(B)$.

The multiplication rule then becomes:

$$P(A, B) = P(B) \cdot P(A)$$

In other words the probability of two or more independent events is equal to the probability of occurrence of the first event multiplied by the probability of the other or others.

An extension of the multiplication rule formed the basis of a short paper by the Reverend Thomas Bayes, published posthumously in 1764. Generally acknowledged as one of the most famous memoirs in the library of science, it has also become one of the most controversial since, in effect, it merges subjective with objective statistics in a predictive tool to evaluate the likelihood of future events.

What the Bayes theorem advances is the assignment of probability measures to both *a priori* and *a posteriori* events: that is, to information available *prior* to the performance of an experiment as well as to that obtained from it. This concept will come in for some illustration when we discuss decision-making. For the present, let it merely be noted that the Bayes Theorem is expressed in mathematical notation as:

$$P(A_1|B) = \frac{P(A_1)\cdot P(B|A_1)}{P(A_1)P(B|A_1) + P(A_2)P(B|A_2) \cdots P(A_n)P(B|A_n)}$$

Random Variables and Probability Distributions. Backgrounded as we now are, we are prepared to experiment on a more sophisticated level than repetitive tosses of a single coin. Let us, instead, simultaneously toss three coins. Now, how many show heads?

Knowing something about the notion of sample space, we know that the number of heads may be 0, 1, 2, or 3. While we cannot predict exactly what outcome will occur, we can determine the associated probabilities for all possible outcomes if we were to perform the actual experiment, as indicated in Exhibit X.

EXHIBIT X

OUTCOMES OF THREE TOSSES OF A COIN

Event in Point in Sample Space	*Number of Heads*	*Probability*
H H H	3	$\frac{1}{8}$
H H T	2	$\frac{1}{8}$
H T H	2	$\frac{1}{8}$
T H H	2	$\frac{1}{8}$
H T T	1	$\frac{1}{8}$
T H T	1	$\frac{1}{8}$
T T H	1	$\frac{1}{8}$
T T T	0	$\frac{1}{8}$

Note that each of the eight possible elementary events shown in the table has an equal chance of occurring: they are, then *equiprobable.* Since each event may be comprised of the occurrence of from none to three heads, the probability of any of these possible values of heads actually occurring is determined by the rules of addition. The number of heads is a variable, and, since it is determined by the outcome of an experiment, it is called a random variable and is denoted by x.

If we summarize the information from the preceding table, letting the variable x, represent the number of heads, a new table can be set up, as shown in Exhibit XI.

The probability measures appearing in connection with the number of heads is the *probability distribution* or, more precisely, the *probability function* of x.

The random variable, then, as seen in Exhibit XI, is simply a *rule* or *system* by which real numbers can be assigned to elementary events. And any listing of the probabilities assigned to all the possible values of a random variable is a probability (or relative frequency) distribution of that random variable.

In practice, it is more convenient, and equally valid, to show the probability function by means of a formula for the function of the random variable, $P(x)$.

Random Processes. In any business operation we are, of course, accustomed to deal with many variables: seasons, for example, or absenteeism, or container sizes. A random variable is like any other variable except in one important respect: we get to know more about it through being able to assess the probability of each of its possible values.

Think what this means! When we set up the probability distribution of a series of possible outcomes or events we have actually constructed a mathematical model that is a predictive tool. With it, we can know in advance the precise likelihood of any occurrence in a given state of nature and we can plan to take action accordingly.

EXHIBIT XI

PROBABILITY OF NUMBER OF HEADS IN THREE TOSSES OF A COIN

Number of heads: x	0	1	2	3
Probability of x	$\frac{1}{8}$	$\frac{3}{8}$	$\frac{3}{8}$	$\frac{1}{8}$

When we speak of the values of random variables, we mean those occurring without assignable causes. Anyone who has ever been concerned with a manufacturing process, for example, knows that there is no such thing as absolute reproducibility of whatever is manufactured. We build "interchangeable" parts, for example, to *tolerances* which may be extremely minute; but the mere fact that we accept or reject on the basis of *any* tolerance is a recognition of the concept of variability.

Random variable values then, assume homogeneity and occur *within* that assumption.

Now, an interesting and useful thing about the values generated by random variables, whether in nature or in some industrial or commercial process, is that while they are the result of many uncontrollable, independent causes, the *nature* of these causes tends to produce predictable patterns of variations, called *random processes.*

Bernoulli Process and Binomial Distribution. An infinite number of random processes are encountered in practical business problems. Many of these can be described in terms of separate, distinct trials, each of which embodies one of two possible outcomes. Our electric lamp bulb manufacturer, for example, may classify his bulbs, in the course of repeated, distinct trials, as "good" or "defective." Or, a sample of voters in an election may be classified as votes for Candidate A or for Candidate B. In all dichotomous processes of this kind, each trial or outcome may be classified as a "success" or "failure" for one of its components.

The simplest processes of this kind are those in which the trials are independent of each other. In these cases, the occurrence of success or failure is without a pattern of interdependence. A process that meets this condition is called a Bernoulli process, and the long-run fraction of successes characterizing a Bernoulli process and imparting stability to it is called the *parameter of the process.*

The most frequent use businessmen are likely to make of probabilistic models is as predictive devices. In illustration of the foregoing discussion of random processes and their application, then, let us assess the probability that exactly three aces will occur in five successive rolls of a die. The probability that an ace will occur on any single roll is 1/6. That probability is constant for any single roll, regardless of the outcome of any of the others. We have, then, the two conditions of independence and stability and we may thus safely assume that the die behaves as a Bernoulli process in generating random values.

If we specify the order of occurrence of the three aces as A A A N N, where A represents an ace and N a non-ace, the multiplication rule for probability of independent events gives the following:

$$P = 1/6 \times 1/6 \times 1/6 \times 5/6 \times 5/6 = 25/7{,}776.$$

Obviously, since the occurrence of three aces out of five rolls will *always* involve these values, the probability of the relative frequency for any other order is also 25/7,776.

Examining the number of possible orders, which comprise mutually exclusive occurrences, we find that there are only ten ways in which three aces may appear. This is shown in Exhibit XII.

Recalling our earlier experiment with three coins, it is evident from the exhibit that as soon as we cease to demand a specified *order* of occurrence for the three aces, the existence of compound events increases the probability of their occurrence by the number of ways in which they may occur.

In this case,

$$P(x=3,\ n=5) \ = \ 10 \times 25/7{,}776 \ = \ 250/7{,}776.$$

From this example, we can now generalize a formula for assessing the probability of any number of successes in any number of trials, thus:

The probability of x successes and $(n - x)$ failures in a specified order is:

$$(p \times p \times \cdots p)\,(q \times q \times \cdots q), \text{ or } p^x q^{n-x}$$

EXHIBIT XII

TEN WAYS IN WHICH THREE ACES MAY APPEAR IN FIVE SUCCESSIVE ROLLS OF A DIE

A A A N N	A N N A A
A A N A N	N A A A N
A A N N A	N A A N A
A N A A N	N A N A A
A N A N A	N N A A A

The number of possible orders in which x successes can occur in n trials is denoted by the symbol C_x^n, which means merely the number of combinations of x possible successes in n trials.

$$C_x^n = \frac{n!}{x!\,(n-x)!}$$

$$\text{where } n! = 1 \times 2 \times 3 \ldots \times n$$

and is read "n factorial." (Note: It is accepted in mathematics that $0! = 1$.)

Thus, the probability of exactly x successes in n trials, *regardless of order,* is defined by the Bernoulli or binomial distribution:

$$P(x/n) = C_x^n p^x q^{n-x}$$

By substituting the values found in our illustration in the Bernoulli probability distribution, we find:

$$P(x = 3/n = 5)$$

$$= \left(\frac{5!}{3!\,2!}\right)(1/6)^3(5/6)^2 = 250/7{,}776 = 3.2\%.$$

In terms of frequencies, the mean of the expected number of successes of the binomial distribution is $E(x) = np$, where $E(x)$ is the expected value of the random variable x. Again, using the values from our sample:

$$E(x) = 5(1/6) = 5/6 \text{ of a success in 5 rolls.}$$

To simplify the visualization of $E(x)$ as the mean, consider 24 rolls of the die and substitute

$$E(x) = 24\ (1/6) = 4 \text{ successes in 24 tosses}$$

—exactly what one would expect!

Incidentally, the formula $P(x) = C_x^n p^x q^{n-x}$ is not limited to the definition of only *one* distribution of X, but defines a whole family of distributions, embracing every combination of n and p; n and p are called parameters of the binomial distribution.

A mean is, of course, a descriptive function. Another useful descriptive function in dealing with distributions is the standard deviation, as stated earlier.

The standard deviation of the binomial distribution is:

$$\sigma = \sqrt{npq}$$

While coins and dice are extremely handy devices for demonstrating probabilistic functions, it must be admitted that they are somewhat extraneous to the content of real life business situations, except of course to the professional gambler or croupier. But the principles illustrated by our use of them are universal in their application.

Exhibit XIII, for example, shows the fitting of a theoretical binomial distribution to an actual Bernoulli process. It is a mathematical model providing a theoretical framework for predicting the expected number of successes to be achieved in the germination of Pima cotton seeds, planted six seeds to a hill (n), in 1,120 hills (N).

The distribution shown in the exhibit was derived from the knowledge that two weeks after planting, the 6,720 seeds planted had, in fact produced 3,220 seedlings. Thus:

$$p = 3{,}220/6{,}720 = 0.47917$$

$$q = (1 - p) = 0.52043$$

EXHIBIT XIII

FITTED BINOMIAL DISTRIBUTION FOR THE NUMBER OF SEEDLINGS PER HILL

Number of Seedlings Per Hill x	$C_x^n p^x q^{n-x}$	*Probabilities*	*Expected Frequency* $NC_x^n p^x q^{n-x}$
0	$1\,p^0q^6$	0.01996	22.4
1	$6\,p^1q^5$	0.11017	123.4
2	$15\,p^2q^4$	0.25341	283.8
3	$20\,p^3q^3$	0.31087	348.2
4	$15\,p^4q^2$	0.21451	240.3
5	$6\,p^5q^1$	0.07894	88.4
6	$1\,p^6q^0$	0.01210	13.6
		0.99996	1,120.1

SOURCE: Treloar, Alan E., "Elements of Statistical Reasoning," p. 175, John Wiley & Sons, Inc. (New York, 1939).

Assuming that this experimental planting was, indeed, representative of the results to be expected from sowing six seeds per hill under any set of like circumstances, the exhibit now makes it possible for the cotton farmer to plan his future operations with the knowledge that approximately 48% of the seed he sows will germinate; that in about 1% of the hills planted, all six seeds will produce seedlings, while in nearly 2% no seedlings will be produced at all, and that in 31% of the hills, three out of the six seeds will germinate.

Poisson Process and Poisson Distribution. We have noted that the Bernoulli process embodies the two conditions of independence and stability, and is characterized by the probability of success or failure in any trial. Sometimes, however, the data with which we are dealing in business problems are not generated by such dichotomies, and then some other process or distribution is better suited to the development of probabilistic models for our purposes.

When, to the two factors of independence and stability, we add the criterion of expected number of successes in a unit of *space* or *time,* we find that the *Poisson Process* and the *Poisson Distribution* better describe the random process.

The Poisson process actually is best described as a measure of the probability of an occurrence in a unit of space or time. In a Poisson process, the expected or average number of successes is considered to be the sole parameter and is often called the *intensity* of the process.

Typical instances in which a Poisson process might generate probability measures include such cases as the number of surface defects in a sheet of photographic film, or the number of breakdowns in a given length of insulated wire subjected to a test voltage; the distribution of the number of arrivals of cars at a toll station; or the number of appointments to the Supreme Court during a given Presidential term.

As one can see, in all of these cases, and in practically all others to which a Poisson distribution applies, one of the distinguishing features is that the average number of successes or defects is low in relationship to a high number of possible events.

The photographic film manufacturer, for example, might know from simple descriptive statistics that an average of three surface defects per sheet of film will occur. What are the probabilities, then, of producing film sheets with *no* defects, or with fewer than 3 defects or, for that matter, with a dozen defects per sheet?

It is to this kind of problem that the Poisson process, (discovered and named for its discoverer in 1837) best applies. It is expressed in the mathematical formula:

$$P(x) = \frac{e^{-m} m^x}{x!}$$

where e = a constant, the natural logarithm base, approximately equal to 2.71828 and m = average number of defects. (See Molina, E. C., "Poisson's Exponential Binomial Limit," New York: D. Van Nostrand Co., 1942 for tables of cumulative probabilities.)

The *mean* of the Poisson distribution is equal to the mean of the Binomial Distribution, $E(x) = np = m$, and the *variance* of the distribution is equal to its mean, $\sigma^2 = m$. The Poisson distribution is therefore considered to be a "one parameter distribution," since only the single parameter, m, needs to be known to compute the probabilities of all values of the random variable.

Applied to the example of film surface defects the probabilities of any number of defects occurring, from 0 to 10, are as shown in Exhibit XIV.

The important thing to remember about the Poisson Process is that the events described by it never occur simultaneously: that is, there is always a measurable interval of space or time between any pair of events.

EXHIBIT XIV

FITTED POISSON DISTRIBUTION TO THE NUMBER OF FILM SURFACE DEFECTS

Number of Defects x*	$P(x) = \frac{e^{-3}\, 3^x}{x!}$	*Probabilities*
0	$e^{-3}\, 3^0/0!$	0.049787
1	$e^{-3}\, 3^1/1!$	0.149361
2	$e^{-3}\, 3^2/2!$	0.224042
3	$e^{-3}\, 3^3/3!$	0.224042
4	$e^{-3}\, 3^4/4!$	0.168031
5	$e^{-3}\, 3^5/5!$	0.100819
6	$e^{-3}\, 3^6/6!$	0.050409
7	$e^{-3}\, 3^7/7!$	0.021604
8	$e^{-3}\, 3^8/8!$	0.008102
9	$e^{-3}\, 3^9/9!$	0.002701
10	$e^{-3}\, 3^{10}/10!$	0.000801

* m = average number of defects = 3.

The Poisson distribution might almost be viewed as a special case of the Binomial Distribution, when n increases while p decreases in such a way that the expected number of successes, np, is left unchanged.

Exponential Distribution. Still another distribution, the *Exponential Distribution,* deals with the length of intervals between adjacent Poisson events. This distribution has had wide application in the area of WAITING LINE THEORY and RELIABILITY ENGINEERING. Unlike the Poisson distribution which deals with discrete data, the random variable assessed by the Exponential process is continuous.

Normal Process and the Normal Distribution. Generally speaking, both the Bernoulli and Poisson distributions deal with discrete data and, for their respective purposes can achieve close to exact fitness of the data to which they are applied.

However, as every manufacturer of men's shirts, for example, knows, while it may be desirable to manufacture shirts for such specific purposes as formal evening wear in neck bands of quarter sizes, for all-round sports use, small, medium, and large give close enough appoximation to meet practically every need.

The *normal process* and the *normal distribution* to which it gives rise is, in fact, not quite as precise as those we have previously been discussing, but it is so close an approximation to so many of the natural and industrial phenomena with which we constantly deal that it is, perhaps, the most useful of all the probabilistic devices we know.

While the normal distribution can in fact be applied in certain instances to discrete data, it is a continuous distribution with probability given by the formula:

$$P(x_i \text{ given } \mu \text{ and } \sigma) = \frac{1}{\sigma\sqrt{2\pi}} e^{-[(x_i-\mu)^2/2\sigma^2]}$$

where

where

e = the mathematical constant, approximately 2.71828

π = approximately 3.1416

μ = a parameter, the mean of the population

σ = a parameter, the standard deviation of the population

x_i = any value of a random variable

The quantities μ and σ (the mean and standard deviation) are the parameters of the normal distribution, just as n and p are the parameters of the binomial distribution; every possible combination of numerical values of μ and σ give rise to a separate and different normal distribution.

When a normal distribution is plotted in graph form, it assumes a bell shape, its dispersion being measured by σ. As the normal curve declines in either direction from its peak, its descent is gradual at first, automatically becomes steeper, and, at a certain point, changes direction and begins to level off. This point is called the "point of inflection" and its distance from the mean, μ, in either direction along its horizontal base is equal to σ.

The normal curve is symmetrical, and about 68% of all observations in any normal distribution always occur between the two points of inflection—i.e., within 1 σ from the mean. Approximately 95% fall within 2 σ of the mean, and virtually all (99.73%) within 3 σ. These characteristics of the normal curve are readily seen in Exhibit XV.

The most striking characteristic of the normal curve is, of course, its perfect symmetry, with the right-hand half of the curve the mirror image of the left-hand half. The curve always has only one mode which occurs at μ.

Note that as the distance from μ increases, the probabilities generated by this distribution constantly decline, *but never reach zero.* The area under the curve is unity, and the range of the random variable it generates is infinite extending from $-\infty$ to $+\infty$.

EXHIBIT XV

NORMAL CURVE

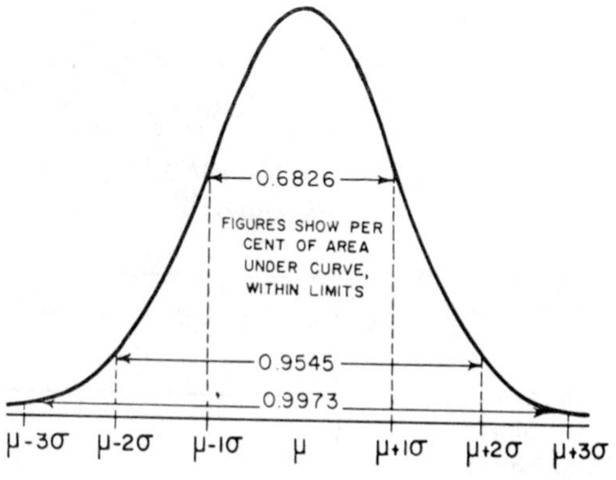

The normal process is described by a two-parameter function, with the parameters μ and σ distinguishing one normal distribution from any other. To avoid the impossible task of providing separate tables of probabilities for each possible μ and σ, the device of the *standardized normal distribution* has been developed to obtain the heights and tail areas for *any* normal distribution.

The relationship between the standardized normal distribution and the non-standard normal distribution is geometrical. By relabeling the horizontal axis in terms of standard deviation units, the application of the distribution becomes universal. This procedure is illustrated in Exhibit XVI.

One means of visualizing probabilities generated by normal distributions is through speciication of areas under a normal curve. Exhibit XVII shows probabilities, or areas under the Standard Normal Curve from 0 to a specified point along the Z-axis. (This illustration is adapted from F. Mosteller, R.E.D. Rourke and G. B. Thomas, Jr., "Probability Statistical Applications," Addison-Wesley Publishing Co., Inc., Reading, Mass. 1970.)

Random Sampling and Sampling Distribution. In every area of statistical thought and practice two basic concepts exist: *population* and *sample*. Population (or universe), in the statistical sense, need not signify people—although, indeed, it may; it is simply a fixed body of numbers—a totality of objects. A group selected from a population, giving rise to information through some number of observations, is called a sample.

Any summary measure of a population is called a *parameter*; the same measure, generated by a sample, is called a *statistic*. These are terms which will occur frequently in discussions of sampling.

Many different samples can be derived from a single population. At any moment in time, the population is stable, but samples taken from it vary. Indeed, another definition of a population is that it represents the totality of values of a random variable generated by a random process. In statistics, *random* is a technical word with a meaning different from "haphazard," which is its connotation in popular usage. *Unrestricted random sample*, as used statistically, does not describe the data in the sample, but rather the *process by which the sample was obtained.*

A sample is random when each possible set of n values in the population has the same probability of being included in the sample. This is a tremendously important concept because if a sample is random, the mathematical laws of probability are applicable to it. It is then possible to know the patterns of sampling variability in terms of what the sample must interpret.

To achieve randomness, in the statistical sense, is no easy task. Pure, mathematical chance is the only criterion of randomness. When human judgment or control, even unconscious, is permitted to play any part in sample selection, randomness is destroyed. As a practical statistical tool, tables of random numbers, generated by chance and subjected to exhaustive tests for bias, have been developed. Early tables were the product of the laborious process of tossing dice or spinning an unbiased wheel. Modern tables, such as the Rand Corporation's volume, "A Million Random Digits," are electronically generated.

The type of random sample we have been discussing is *unrestricted* or, as it is sometimes called, *simple random* sampling. As a practical matter, more elaborate sampling procedures are sometimes used, such as stratified, systematic,

EXHIBIT XVI

HORIZONTAL AXIS OF THE NON-STANDARDIZED AND STANDARDIZED NORMAL DISTRIBUTION

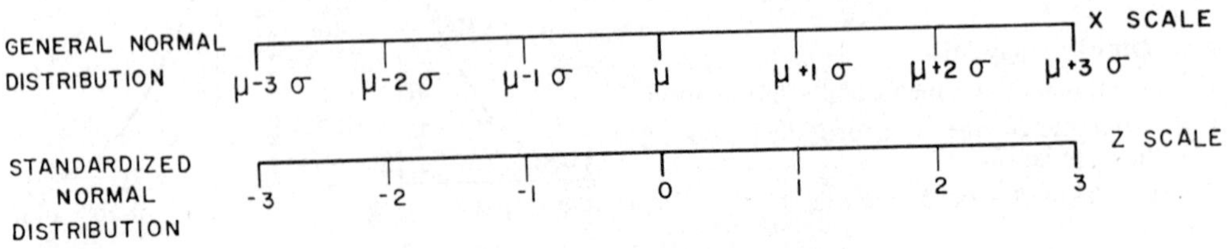

EXHIBIT XVII

STANDARDIZED NORMAL CURVE AREAS

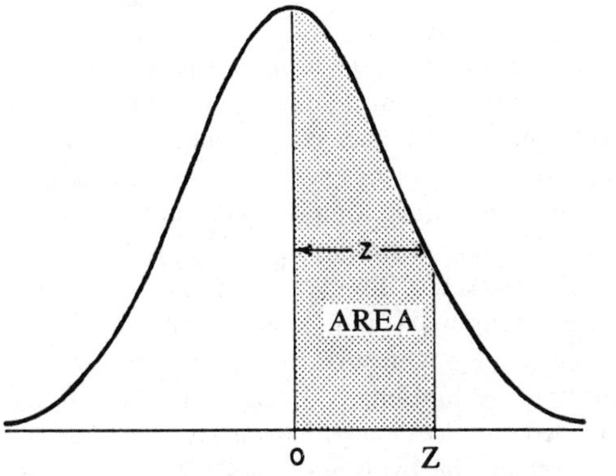

Z In Standard Units*	*Area or Probability*	*Z*	*Area or Probability*	*Z*	*Area or Probability*
0.0	.0000	1.0	.3413	2.0	.4772
0.1	.0398	1.1	.3643	2.1	.4821
0.2	.0793	1.2	.3849	2.2	.4861
0.3	.1179	1.3	.4032	2.3	.4893
0.4	.1554	1.4	.4192	2.4	.4918
0.5	.1915	1.5	.4332	2.5	.4938
0.6	.2257	1.6	.4452	2.6	.4953
0.7	.2580	1.7	.4554	2.7	.4965
0.8	.2881	1.8	.4641	2.8	.4974
0.9	.3159	1.9	.4713	2.9	.4981
				3.0	.4987

* *Z* represents the distance of the specified point on the standardized scale from zero in terms of standard units.

and cluster samples. In general, such samples substitute "known chance" for "equal chance" of inclusion, and provide statistical methods for compensating for this departure from unrestricted random sampling. However, ultimately all such variations are based on samples that are random in the sense described.

It is customary, in describing samples based on "known" rather than "equal" probabilities, to use the broader term *probability sample of size n.*

Any sample is a device for inferring information about the population from which it is drawn. Since many samples can be drawn from any population, the fact that we usually rely upon a single sample as a means of eliciting information means that we acknowledge that the same chance which yielded the sample we are using might, in another sample, produce statistics at some variance from those in hand. Since, were we to draw repetitive samples by the same method from a population, such fluctuations known as *sampling errors* could not be attributed to the selection process, it is obvious that they must arise out of the operation of chance, itself.

When we draw conclusions about a population from a sample, it is always in full recognition of the fact that the statistics it yields form probability distributions such as have previously been discussed.

Just as a theoretical distribution of individual items is called a probability distribution, the distribution of any statistic yielded by a sample is called a *random sampling distribution* of that statistic for a sample of size *n*.

When we considered the probability distributions of individual observations, we were able to assign values to the random variables attaching to the observations. In dealing with sampling distributions, we also assign probability values to variations of the statistics yielded by different samples.

Three factors are necessary to specify any random sampling distribution. These are: (1) the character of the original distribution; (2) the size of the sample; and (3) the particular statistic under consideration.

Each summary measure, or statistic, obtained from a sample will have its own sampling distribution. For example, the random sampling distribution of means of samples of size *n* obtained from a normal population will be a normal distribution. However, just as probability distributions may be of different kinds, so, too, the sampling distributions generated by various statistics may assume different forms, such as the normal, binomial, chi-square or, in the case of small samples, the distribution developed by "Student," as well as many other types.

The normal distribution, as mentioned earlier, provides a reasonably good fit for data resulting from many different random processes, and is adequate to the handling of most of the frequently encountered problems of statistical inference. It is important to note that *even when the population itself is not a normal distribution, the distribution of means and sums generated by samples of the population tends to be normal.* This fact has been proved mathematically, and is called the *central limit theorem,* which states, principally, that sampling distributions of most means tend to be normal and so permit the use of this simple pattern of variability in the solution of an extremely wide range of problems.

It has already been mentioned that the random sampling distribution of means will be a normal distribution. It can also be proved mathematically that the mean of the sampling distribution of means equals the mean of the original population from which the sample was drawn. The standard deviation from the mean, in the case of sample distributions, is no longer termed standard deviation, but is called the *standard error of the sample statistic.* Its computation consists of dividing the standard deviation of the population by the square root of the sample size:

$$\sigma_{\bar{x}} = \frac{\sigma}{\sqrt{n}}$$

The standard deviations of the distributions of all other statistics generated by samples, such as medians, variances, correlation coefficient, and other summary measures, are also called standard errors of the statistic and are similarly computable with appropriate formulas.

With the statistical tools thus far described, we are in a position to proceed with two of the most fruitful areas of statistics in modern management practice: *statistical inference* (also termed *conclusion theory*) and *decision making.*

STATISTICAL INFERENCE

Statistical inference (or conclusion theory) deals with two important statistical areas: tests of hypotheses and estimation.

Tests of Hypotheses. Two questions may properly be raised: "*Why* should it be necessary to develop a hypothesis to test?" "*How* can a hypothesis be tested statistically?"

In statistics, as in the physical sciences, knowledge is gained through the use of experiements. And what is an experiment? It is, simply, a means of testing an idea under controlled conditions.

A child, haphazardly combining the contents of a chemistry set to see what will happen, is not performing an experiment; he is merely playing with a toy. A chemist, perhaps using precisely the same materials, will combine them in accordance with a preconceived plan to obtain empirical confirmation or rejection of a theoretical concept, or hypothesis.

A test of a hypothesis, then, is a means of determining the validity of some prediction or expectation. Establishing a working hypothesis is an important step in planning any investigation. It suggests, in the first place, the kinds of data which will be needed and how they should be arranged and classified; and it establishes the basis on which judgments concerning the hypothesis can be made.

The manufacturer of a consumer product, for example, might wonder about the sales effectiveness of his package. He might, of course, on the basis of prior experience and the actions of his competitors, simply take a chance on either changing it or not changing it. If he is a sound marketer, however, he is likely to want some preliminary indication of the likelihood of success for whichever course he elects before committing himself to it. If he has tentatively decided not to change his package, he has, in fact set up the hypothesis that a change would not improve sales. Now, by preparing an appropriate sampling experiment, he can confirm or reject that hypothesis and proceed accordingly.

Before subjecting his prejudgment to test, he will find it necessary to formalize the terms of his hypothesis. He might do this in any of several ways, as, for example:

Statement A: Package Design "A" and Package Design "B" are equally effective in producing sales.

Statement B: Package Design "A" is more effective in producing sales than Package Design "B."

Statement C: Package Design "A" is less effective than Package Design "B" in producing sales.

Statement D: Package Design "B" is equally as or less effective than Package Design "A" in producing sales.

Present day tests of hypotheses generally follow the formal procedure contributed to Statistics by Jerzy Neyman and Egon Pearson. This involves several separate steps, as follows:

Step 1. Formulation of the Hypothesis

Two or more alternative hypotheses, based on the formal statement of the problem, are established. The *first*, called the *null hypothesis,* is that *no* action will be required, that the experiment will confirm the *status quo.* The truth of this hypothesis is assumed and is the subject of the experiment.

If the experiment gives grounds for its acceptance, we behave as if it were true and take no steps to change the situation. If on the other hand, it must be rejected on the experimental evidence, an *alternative hypothesis* must be accepted. In mathematical terms, the null hypothesis is identified as H_0, and the alternative hypotheses as H_a, or H_1, etc.

In the present example, as given above, statement D is the null hypothesis to be tested. It assumes package "A" to be the present package design against which proposed package "B" is to be assessed. If the results of the experiment indicate that the effectiveness of package "B" is either the same as or less than the effectiveness of package "A," no action will be required and the null hypothesis will be accepted. If package "B" is demonstrated to be a sales producer better than package "A," the null hypothesis must be rejected and an alternative hypothesis accepted; mathematically, these ideas are expressed as:

$$H_0: \quad \mu_b \leq \mu_a$$

$$H_1: \quad \mu_b > \mu_a$$

where

μ_a = Average sales of package A (the standard)
μ_b = Expected sales of package "B".

(Most often the null hypothesis is stated as H_0: $\mu_b = \mu_a$. However in terms of management action, when $\mu_b < \mu_a$, the *status quo* is, of course, not changed.)

Step 2. Establishment of Test Criteria for Acceptance or Rejection of the Hypothesis

In an ideal situation, there would be no doubt in the mind of the experimenter that his experimental results were completely true and definitive and his actions would be taken accordingly. Since experiments are based on sampling procedures, however, it is known that some risk of error is always implicit in the findings. This fact gives rise to the probability of committing one of two types of error in judgment in the interpretation of experimental findings.

If the null hypothesis is in fact true, but the sampling results cause the experimenter to reject it, he commits an error. If, on the other hand, the null hypothesis is false, and the results of the experiment lead the experimenter to accept the hypothesis, he has also committed an error. In the former case, the error is said to be an error of the *Class I* type, represented by the Greek letter α; in the second instance the error is denominated *Class II* type, represented by the Greek letter β.

Confronted with this dilemma, the experimenter must obviously make some preliminary decision as to how large an error he can afford to risk in rejecting a hypothesis which is, in fact, true. If the decision resting upon the hypothesis is one of great criticality (as, for example, in a question of the lethal effects of a pharmaceutical product) the probability of an error must be kept very small. If, on the other hand, the decision involves risks of lesser import, less critical measurements may be acceptable.

The term "probability" in relationship to the error is used in its technical sense, as in the previous dicussion of distributions and random processes. If we determine to accept a probability of an error of 5%, for example, we have, in fact, established a *critical region* lying under a curve, as seen in Exhibit XVIII.

The region of rejection of the null hypothesis is shown in the shaded area. If the sample value falls within the unshaded area the hypothesis is accepted. The region of rejection is equivalent to the probability of rejecting the null hypothesis if it is true. The α error, or the critical region, is also termed the *level of significance* of the test.

We can, of course, set the level of significance at any value we wish, but it should be noted that as the critical region is reduced, the probability of incurring the risk of a β error is likely to be increased.

In common practice it is usual to set the risk of a Class I error at either 0.05 or 0.01, and to term a value found significant with an error of the lower magnitude simply "significant," and, in the second instance, "highly significant." This is, of course, an arbitrary procedure: there is nothing to preclude us from establishing a critical region with a probability of 0.08 or 0.005, if we wish, depending upon our evaluation of the problem.

Unfortunately, experimenters frequently direct their attention to setting the appropriate level of significance to restrict the Class I type error and fail to recognize the risk of incurring a Class II type error, which may well be equally serious when translated into action terms.

In the preceeding exhibit, for example, 70 is the value of μ, which is the null hypothesis. If we set a probability of 5%, we will reject the hypothesis $\mu = 70$ if the value found exceeds 76.58.

The critical value of 76.58 which would reject H_0 is obtained by the following expression:

$$\mu_c = \mu + Z\sigma_{\bar{x}} = 70 + 1.645 \cdot 4 = 76.58$$

where

μ = critical level or level of significance is the standardized normal deviate.
Z = 1.645, which corresponds to the .05 probability level.
$\sigma_{\bar{x}}$ = standard error of the mean.

Observe that a β error can only occur when H_0 is false. The size of the β error depends on what is the *true* hypothesis if the null hypothesis is, in fact, false and that the true value of μ is for example, 78.

The risk of a Class II error is shown in the shaded portion of the second curve in Exhibit XVIII, and we may proceed to identify the whole area as β. A value above 76.58 based on experimental findings rejects $\mu = 70$, and the probability of its rejection when it is false (as, in this case when the true value of μ is 78) is equal to the unshaded area, which is expressed statistically as $(1 - \beta)$. This is an extremely important measure since it defines, and is called, the *power of the test.* In the example, it can be computed that the value of β is 36% and $(1 - \beta)$ is 64%.

The values of β and $(1 - \beta)$ will, of course, change with each possible true value of μ, but the value of $(1 - \beta)$ is always the probability of rejecting a false hypothesis.

By setting up in advance possible values of μ, we can plot the resultant $(1 - \beta)$s as a curve. Such curves are called *power curves.* Their complementary curves, based on the corresponding values of β, are called *operating characteristic curves.* The practical value of these curves lies in their ability to indicate the necessary size of the sample n to reduce risk of error to useful limits and to enable the experimenter to strike an acceptable balance of probabilities of α and β errors.

EXHIBIT XVIII

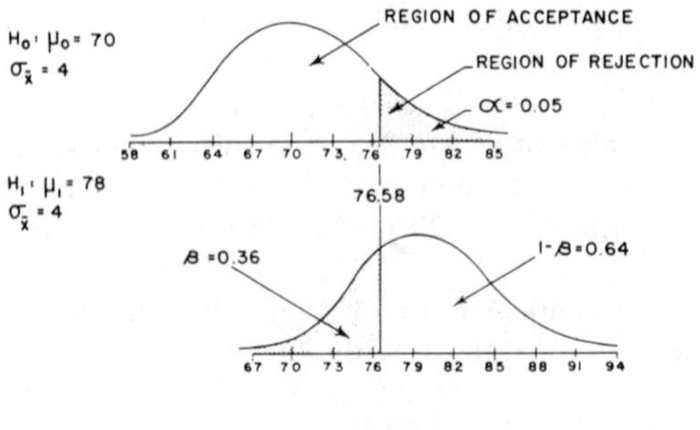

Step 3. Selection of a Statistical Technique for Testing H_0

To determine whether or not to reject the null hypothesis we have set up, some test statistic must be selected for later generation by a sampling procedure.

In the illustration we are using, H_0 postulates that Package Design "B" is less than or equally effective as Package Design "A," as a sales producer; i.e., that $\mu_1 < \mu_0$, and that, therefore, no action will be required. The statistic to use for this test is stated mathematically as

$$Z = \frac{\bar{x}_b - \bar{x}_a}{\sqrt{\dfrac{\sigma_b^2}{n_b} + \dfrac{\sigma_a^2}{n_a}}}$$

The numerator of this fraction is the difference, d, between the average value of Package "A" and the average of Package "B," as sample findings. This is, in essence, an estimate of the real difference between the packages in the total population. What we are concerned with, mainly, is whether this estimated difference is adequate to the rejection of the null hypothesis. In repeated independent sampling, values of d will be normally or nearly normally distributed and, if the real difference, D, in the total universe is zero, the mean of the sampling distribution will be zero.

Since the values obtained for d are subject to sampling error, the magnitude of that error is the square root of the sum of the squares of the standard error of Package "A" and Package "B," which is the denominator of the fraction. The quotient of this fraction is the *normal deviate* in *standardized units,* and is conventionally symbolized by "Z."

For each hypothesis tested, there is some appropriate statistic and an appropriate formula for the computation of its standard error.

While the normal distribution is an adequate sampling distribution for establishing probabilities for most statistics, there are some that do not fit it. In such cases, other distributions, such as chi-square or, for small sample sizes, "Student's" distribution, or the analysis of variance ratios, or others may be used.

Step 4. Obtaining Experimental Data

Having determined the statistic to be employed, a sample of observations relating to both products must be taken to produce that statistic. The size of the sample can be determined by reference to the power curve appropriate to an acceptable probability of wrong decision at the level of significance we have selected.

Step 5. Reaching the Conclusion

On the basis of the preceding steps, we decide whether to reject the hypothesis or not, depending upon whether the statistic falls within the critical region.

Perhaps the simplest way to illustrate how compactly the preceding steps are reduced to a working statistical tool is to recapitulate them in a practical manufacturing problem.

Let it be assumed, then, that a tire manufacturer is offered two types of synthetic cord, both designed for passenger car tire construction. Type A is priced somewhat below Type B and the manufacturer would, of course, like to use it unless there is statistical evidence to support the contention of the supplier of Type B that his product is significantly better than Type A in terms of tensile strength, which is central to the tire manufacturer's problem.

From considerable past experience, the manufacturer knows that the standard deviation of the tensile strength of both Type A and Type B is 1.20 ounces. An experiment performed with 9 strands of Type A gives a mean tensile strength of 6.52 ounces, while a sample of 16 strands of Type B gives a mean tensile strength of 7.20 ounces. Is this difference significant and does it justify using Type B cord at its higher cost?

Applying the five steps necessary to test the hypothesis that the mean of one population is less than or equal to the mean of the second population when σ is known, the hypothesis is first stated, as:

Step 1:

$$H_0 : \mu_b \leq \mu_a$$
$$H_1 : \mu_b > \mu_a$$

A criterion for acceptance or rejection of the hypothesis is established as:

Step 2:

$$\alpha = .05$$

A statistical technique for testing $\mu_b \leq \mu_a$ is selected by assuming that the statistic Z has a normal distribution, as stated in

Step 3:

$$Z = \frac{\bar{X}_b - \bar{X}_a}{\sqrt{\frac{\sigma_b{}^2}{n_b} + \frac{\sigma_a{}^2}{n_a}}}$$

The experimental data have supplied numerical values for the terms shown in the formula, and are substituted in:

Step 4:

$$\frac{6.52 - 7.20}{\sqrt{\frac{(1.20)^2}{9} + \frac{(1.20)^2}{16}}} = -1.36$$

Finally, a conclusion is reached by consulting the standardized normal table for the probability value corresponding to Z = 1.36, to perform

Step 5:

$$P(z = -1.36) = .0869.$$

This is larger than $\alpha = .05$ as established in Step 2 and is thus attributable to chance. The manufacturer, already beset by labor troubles, regulating bodies and rapidly deteriorating molds, at least does not have to pay more for his cord since the null hypothesis is not rejected and there is no reason to conclude that Type B cord is, on the average, superior to Type A.

Student's Distribution. In the foregoing example, it was specified that σ was known. This is a prerequisite for the use of a normal distribution as the basis for testing the statistics relating to the hypothesis. Often, however, in practical laboratory work, no data exist beyond those yielded by a small number of observations. In such cases, the standard deviation must be obtained from the sample itself, and is subject to its inherent sampling error.

One of the most useful contributions to inferential theory was developed by a statistician, Wm. A. Gosset, employed by the famous Guiness Brewery of Dublin, who found himself constantly faced with precisely this problem of deriving tests of hypotheses from very small samples. Publishing under the pseudonym of "Student," he described the distribution that now bears his name (also sometimes called the *t-distribution*), which requires a table of standarized probability measures for each value of "degrees of freedom" which in turn is dependent on sample size.

Degrees of freedom is one of the most frequently encountered terms in statistics—and one of the most important. It means, simply, the number of *unrestricted variables* available from a set of observations; and it is important because only *free* variables provide information relating to the variations of the universe. Fixed values do not define movement; only those which *contribute* to movement can aid in measuring it.

The Student Distribution is used when sample size is small (under 30 observations) and σ is unknown. As sample size increases, the Student Distribution approaches the Normal Distribution. In common with the Normal Distribution the t-distribution is most usefully applied to hypotheses about means, regressions, and correlation coefficients.

Estimation. When management is concerned with problems of production or marketing, it needs to know not merely that a given decision should be taken but, also, what to expect from that decision. It is not enough to be satisfied that one course of action will produce more results than another; it is also necessary to know *how much more.* Estimation, the second area treated by conclusion theory, deals with that question. It is, in short, a means of predicting quantities or proportions.

In practice, two types of estimation are used: *point estimates* and *interval estimates.* Differing in basic concept, each recognizes that a statistic derived from a sample may not, in fact, be an exact measure of the parameter it represents.

There are four principal, recognized procedures for determining point estimates: (1) The analogue method, or method of moments, originally developed by Karl Pearson; (2) the maximum likelihood method, contributed by R. A. Fisher; (3), the strategies based on the work of the Reverend Thomas Bayes, and (4) minimum variance of unbiased estimates, by Jerzy Neyman.

Pearson's *method of moments* consists simply of estimating some parameter of a universe from values obtained by a sample drawn from that universe. It is primarily applicable to large samples and its reliability increases as sample size is increased.

The *maximum likelihood estimate* proceeds from a different theoretical approach. It first takes into consideration every possible value that a given parameter *might* have and then determines for each value the probability that the sample finding was generated from a universe having that parametric value. The value yielding the highest probability is accepted as the maximum likelihood estimator of the parameter of the universe.

In the following example, a sample of ten transistors from a production line was found to yield six defective units. What is the best estimator of the proportion of defective units in the universe from which the sample was taken? The probabilities and the maximum likelihood estimator are as shown in Exhibit XIX.

The probability of six defective units in a sample of ten is greatest at p = parameter value = 0.60. Therefore, 0.60 is selected as the estimate of the universe proportion defective.

Bayesian strategies, while of equally classic origin, have in recent years undergone a great revival, especially in the field of decision theory. They will be discussed at greater length in that section of this entry. For the moment, it is sufficient to say that they represent the maximum exploitation of continuously revised information.

EXHIBIT XIX

PROBABILITY OF SIX DEFECTIVE TRANSISTORS IN A SAMPLE OF 10

Population Proportion (defectives) p	*Probability of 6 defectives in a sample of 10 given the values of the parameter*
0.00	0.0000
0.10	0.0001
0.20	0.0055
0.30	0.0367
0.40	0.1114
0.50	0.2051
0.59	0.2503
0.60	0.2508
0.61	0.2503
0.70	0.2001
0.80	0.0881
0.90	0.0112
1.00	0.0000

Interval Estimation. As has been shown, a point estimate is usually simply a useful approximation of the parameter. While point estimates have many applications in business problems, their use is generally limited to areas in which conclusions are based on some value either exceeding or falling below some critical level.

There are many more problem areas, however, in which it is important that an estimator's margin of error be known before a conclusion can be drawn or a decision taken. Determining such a margin of error is usually accomplished by specifying, in advance, some interval within which it may be stated with confidence that the parameter does lie; hence, the term "confidence interval" and, descriptive of the objective probability attaching to confidence in such an interval, the "confidence coefficient."

The upper and lower limits that bound a confidence interval are statistics and, as such, are subject to sampling error. Just as in any other application of a sample of a population, the higher the confidence coefficient used, the wider the confidence interval will be. In other words, the more certain of inclusion of the parameter within the confidence interval, the less useful that knowledge becomes.

The techniques in computing confidence intervals or confidence limits are closely related to those used in tests of hypotheses. Just as in the latter case, the process may be stated in steps. However, instead of establishing, prior to test, two or more alternative hypotheses, in estimation it is assumed that all possible hypotheses of the value of the parameter will fall into one of two groups: those which are included in the confidence interval and those which are excluded, based upon the sample information.

Step 1. Establishment of Confidence Coefficient

The first step to be taken in finding an interval estimate is to determine the degree of reliability required of it. This is expressed in terms of the *confidence coefficient.* A confidence coefficient of 95%, for example, states that in long-run, repeated sampling, the limits of the interval computed from the confidence coefficient will include the true value of the parameter 95% of the time, and obviously, would fail to include it in the remaining 5%.

Just as in testing a hypothesis, there are two kinds of risks associated with establishing a confidence coefficient. First, the width of the interval it produces may fail to include the true value of the parameter: secondly, it may be so broad as to include too many false values to be useful.

Step 2. Establishment of Upper and Lower Limits of the Confidence Interval

Precisely as in the case of testing hypotheses, some assumptions must be made relating to the possible values of the parameter being tested. In dealing with means, for example, a normal distribution may be assumed, while other parameters may require other types of distributions.

For an estimate of μ (the arithmetic mean of the universe) the confidence interval and its upper and lower limits are formulated as:

$$\left(\bar{X} - Z\frac{\sigma}{\sqrt{n}} < \mu < \bar{X} + Z\frac{\sigma}{\sqrt{n}}\right)$$

A confidence coefficient of 95% is equivalent to a Z value of 1.96, in terms of normal standardized units. A 99% level produces a Z value of 2.58 standardized units. It will be seen from the formula that the interval becomes wider as σ increases, wider as the confidence coefficient approaches 1.00, and grows narrower as n becomes larger.

Step 3. Obtain Experimental Data

Once the statistic to be employed has been determined, (as, for example, the arithmetic mean in the above formula), it is computed from a sample designed to yield it. If σ is not known in advance, it is estimated from the sample, whose size also determines the value of σ_x (the standard error of the mean).

Step 4. Reaching the Conclusion

One now draws the appropriate conclusion that the mean is included in the confidence interval on the assumption that this confidence is of the same order as that of the confidence coefficient.

Estimates are useful and often essential preliminaries to solving many marketing and production problems. In illustration of the application of the technique just discussed, for example, assume that a cold cereal manufacturer has conducted a survey to determine purchase of his own and competitive products per

U.S. household. His sample survey has indicated an annual purchase of an average of 240.0 ounces per year. How good is that figure as an estimate for marketing purposes? The estimating formula shown above will answer the question.

Assuming that the survey was designed and executed on the basis of an unrestricted random sample, size 900, with a standard deviation of 150 ounces, numerical values to yield upper and lower confidence limits are computed as follows:

Upper Limit:

$$\bar{X} + 1.96\frac{\sigma}{\sqrt{n}} = 240 + 1.96\frac{150}{\sqrt{900}} = 249.8$$

Lower Limit:

$$\bar{X} - 1.96\frac{\sigma}{\sqrt{n}} = 240 - 1.96\frac{150}{\sqrt{900}} = 230.2$$

It can now be stated, with 95% confidence, that the *true* annual purchase of cold cereals lies somewhere between 230.2 and 249.8 ounces.

DECISION THEORY

In our earlier discussion of the decision processes, it was pointed out that when there is no choice of action, no decision is necessary; that the need for making any decision only occurs when some uncertainty as to outcome exists.

For a good many years, there was a growing tendency in statistics to assume that because all decisions require some form of evaluation of the results likely to accrue from them, the most completely "objective" methods were likely to be the most valid and, therefore, most useful. Judgment, experience, management skill were deemed to be intrusions upon rather than adjunctive to good decision-making practice since they introduce a personalistic factor into the objectivity of the process.

In recent years, however, many statisticians have recognized the need to re-evaluate decision theory to introduce more realistic utilization of evidential material. In the works of the 18th century English clergyman to whom we have previously referred, the Reverend Thomas Bayes, such a "new" approach to the problem was found to exist. Bayes' original theorem, based on the use of observed evidence to modify prior judgment, was subjected to new scrutiny and modified and developed under the general term of *Bayesian Analysis,* to include the work of a great many modern contributors to the area.

As currently practiced, decision theory comprises the critical analysis of all possible alternate actions and their outcomes, when the effects of the decision are uncertain. (See also the entry DECISION THEORY) Four basic elements are involved in this process: (1) "acts" or strategies available for choice by the decision maker; (2) "states of nature" indicating the possible conditions with which the decision elected may meet; (3) "payoff," meaning the consequences of the decision, either in monetary terms or some equivalent; and (4) a "criterion" for the choice of the "best" act or decision.

The first subject for consideration by the decision maker is the range of acts possible in the situation. These acts will comprise a series of relevant actions or procedures that might be taken. "Increase advertising budget by a million dollars," or "withdraw from a presently unprofitable location," for example, might be among the acts considered in a marketing problem. The experience and judgment of the decision maker can and should contribute to the creative formulation of the decisional act.

Obviously, any act elected may be expected to produce varying results depending upon the situation in which it is taken. If an increased advertising budget catches competition unaware and makes the decision maker's company the dominant voice in his field, its effect will be quite different from that likely to occur if it is only a lesser increment than his competitors have already determined to add. Withdrawal from an unprofitable location may be a wise decision if its potential remains static, a foolish one if an upsurge in population is about to take place.

Theoretically, every possible *outcome* or state of nature must be identified for each possible act, even though the same state of nature may apply to several or all acts under consideration. The essential criterion is that all *relevant* states of nature be identified and, again, the decision maker's experience, knowledge, and skill are of prime importance for this purpose.

For any given act in any given state of nature, the "*payoff*" can be computed in terms of the preferences or needs of the decision maker. The form the payoff usually takes is in monetary terms or in some qualitative measure, such as utility. (The determination of utility values is a complex problem. A widely employed technique for the purpose is the "Standard Gamble" method of scaling individual utilities developed by John von Neumann and Oskar Morgenstern.)

In any of the statistical procedures previously discussed, whenever uncertainty was encountered, the probability attaching to each uncertainty was assessed. Here, it is in the states of nature that uncertainty exists and the assignment of probabilities of the occurrence of each possible state is central to the decision.

When a large body of experimental data is available, as the result of repetitive decisions, for example, relative frequencies already known may be used as the "prior" probabilities. In most cases, however, determination of probability for the relevant states is a difficult and imprecise procedure. But even limited past experience can provide some sort of guide, and even a crude approximation of probability for the states affecting a decision is better than none. For this purpose, personalistic or subjective probabilities have been usefully applied to assessing possible actions.

It is extremely important to the Bayesian decision maker that probability measures be assigned to each possible outcome or state of nature which may confront each possible act, because it is the *weighting* of this act by *all* outcomes and the computation, by this means, of *net expected payoff* for each act, that supplies, ultimately, the criterion for action. Other decision making methods employ various and different criteria; some, such as those of Wald and Hurwicz, do not require the use of probabilities at all, but all are aimed at providing some criterion for action.

An Application of "Bayesian" Decision Theorem. Because of its nearly unique use of subjective or personalistic probability as a formal element of its basic concept, the "Bayesian" Decision Theorem promises to have particularly wide application for management decision problems. It can best be understood by example, and for that purpose a problem formulated by R. Schlaifer, in "Probability and Statistics for Business Decisions," will be informally discussed.

A commercial photographic company uses 100,000 flash bulbs per year and, to obtain the best possible price, orders a full year's supply at one time. It is preparing to place its order for the coming year and has been informed that a new type of bulb, reported to be more reliable than the present type, has just been announced.

Experience has shown that each time a bulb fails to fire, the company's loss in film and labor averages \$2.50.

The old type bulb has a known reliability of 99.0%. Management subjectively assigns the probabilities of reliability of the new type, as shown in Exhibit XX.

EXHIBIT XX

RELIABILITY TABLE

Reliability of New Bulb	*Defective Bulbs*	*Probability*
0.995	0.005	
0.990	0.010	1/3
0.980	0.020	1/3
		1/3
		1

Here, in the absence of experience with the new bulb and with a skeptical view of the manufacturer's claims, the decision maker has assigned equal probabilities to the likelihood of the new bulb either matching the old bulb or varying slightly from it, one way or the other. These are called "prior probabilities" because they are postulated in advance of "objective" new experimental evidence. (Obviously, he has *not* considered *all* possible states of nature, taking only those he thinks will be relevant.)

Simply on the basis of the values in the table, the Bayesian decision maker can take *some* action. He knows he is faced with only two relevant acts: to purchase the new bulbs or to re-purchase the old. What will the net payoff be for each of each possible outcome?

It is easy to compute these values. For event 0.005 and act II (the purchase of the new bulb), the conditional costs are 100,000 p (\$2.50) = 100,000 (.005) (\$250) = \$1,250 where p = (1 − the reliability expected). All other conditional costs are computed in the same way and summarized in a payoff table (Exhibit XX-A)—a two-way table in which the new readings are possible events, the column headings possible acts, and the cell entries the conditional or incremental costs (profits, losses, or utilities).

EXHIBIT XX-A

PAYOFF TABLE

State of Nature	Conditional Cost	
p	Old*	New
0.005	$2,500	$1,250
0.010	2,500	2,500
0.020	2,500	5,000

* p for the old bulb is 0.01.

same way and summarized in a payoff table (Exhibit XX) which is a 2-way table in which the new readings are possible events, the column headings possible acts, and the cell entries the conditional or incremental costs (profits, losses or utilities).

At this point, a criterion already exists for taking some action, since the Bayesian principle states, "Choose that act for which the expected cost is lowest or expected net revenue, or utility, is highest."

If the decision maker does elect to take action at this point, he can do so on the basis of the expected values shown in the terminal action table he will prepare as in Exhibit XXI.

Now it can be seen that the expected cost of the new bulb due to defective bulbs is $2,916.67, as compared with $2,500 by staying with the old. Unless the decision maker is infatuated with the idea of change at any price, he will, of course, re-order the old bulb. Statistically, there is a long-run justification for acceptance of this decision criterion since, if he repeatedly made decisions in this way and conditions remained indefinitely static, his costs would always average $2,916.67 − $2,500 = $416.67 less by continuing to use the old-type bulb.

Suppose, however, that the decision maker decides to try some of the new bulbs for experimental use before making his decison, and arbitrarily decides to purchase and try 500 bulbs. If the decision maker discovers three defective bulbs in the sample of 500 bulbs, how does he now revise his original assignment of probabilities and what, if any, different action should be taken?

He is now armed with experimental data gained from a sample. Recognizing that he is dealing with a very small fraction defective, he assumes that a Poisson distribution applies and, by reference to the appropriate table, determines the probability of three defective bulbs in a sample of 500 to be 0.2138 when $p = 0.005$. Such a probability is called a *likelihood* and can be obtained for each state of nature. It can be seen that the likelihood that the sample originated in a universe of 0.995 reliability is 28 times as great as the likelihood of its originating from a universe with a reliability of 0.980.

An important function of these sample likelihoods is to revise prior probabilities to obtain "posterior" probabilities. *It is this specific procedure that is known as Bayes Theorem* and it is illustrated in Exhibit XXII.

In Exhibit XXII, column 4 is the *joint probability,* obtained by multiplying column 2 (prior probability) by column 3 (likelihood). The summation of joint probabilities here = 0.1206, (which is actually the marginal probability) and, in long-run terms, indicates that approximately 12% of all samples of size 500 selected from the states of nature shown, will yield three defective bulbs.

To convert these values to posterior probabilities where the sum = 1.0, each joint probability is divided by the total and the results are shown in the final column.

Expressed algebraically, the table takes the form as shown in Exhibit XXIII, whose final

EXHIBIT XXI

TERMINAL ACTION BEFORE SAMPLING

State of Nature "p"	Prior Probabilities	Cost of Old Bulb		Cost of New Bulb	
		Conditional	Expected	Conditional	Expected
0.005	$\frac{1}{3}$	$2,500	$833.33	$1,250	$416.67
0.010	$\frac{1}{3}$	2,500	833.33	2,500	833.33
0.020	$\frac{1}{3}$	2,500	833.33	5,000	1,666.67
	1		$2,500.00		$ 2,916.67

EXHIBIT XXII

REVISION OF PRIOR PROBABILITIES

(1) State of Nature "p"	(2) Prior Probability	(3) Likelihood	(4) = (2) × (3) Joint Probability	(5) Posterior Probability
0.005	$\frac{1}{3}$	.2138	0.0713	0.591
0.010	$\frac{1}{3}$	.1404	0.0468	0.388
0.020	$\frac{1}{3}$	.0076	0.0025	0.021
	1		0.1206	1.000

EXHIBIT XXIII

REVISION OF PRIOR PROBABILITIES

(1) State of Nature	(2) Prior Probabilities $P(A_i)$	(3) Likelihood $P(B/A_i)$	(4) = (2) × (3) Joint Probability $P(A_i, B) = P(A_i)\,P(B/A_i)$	(5) Posterior Probabilities $P(A_i/B)$
A_1	$P(A_1)$	$P(B/A_1)$	$P(A_1, B)$	$P(A_1/B)$
A_2	$P(A_2)$	$P(B/A_2)$	$P(A_2, B)$	$P(A_2/B)$
A_3	$P(A_3)$	$P(B/A_3)$	$P(A_3, B)$	$P(A_3/B)$
	marginal probability		$P(B)$	1

statement is the Bayes Theorem, as shown in the section on Probability, where

$$P(A_1/B) = \frac{P(A_1, B)}{P(B)}$$

= Conditional Probability

$$= \frac{\text{Joint Probability}}{\text{Marginal Probability}}$$

$$= \frac{P(A_1)P(B/A_1)}{P(A_1)P(B/A_1) + P(A_2)P(B/A_2) + P(A_3)P(B/A_3)}$$

= Bayes Theorem

In exactly the same manner in which decision would have been taken when only prior probabilities were available, it is now possible to establish a criterion for terminal action after sampling, by weighting the posterior probability by conditional costs.

Now, with the decision-maker's judgment refined with experimental evidence, it becomes clear that his investment in the sample was justified: for the expected cost of the old-type bulb is still $2,500 but the new bulb will cost only $1,813.75. (Exhibit XXIV).

The decision-maker now orders the new bulbs.

EXHIBIT XXIV

TERMINAL ACTION AFTER SAMPLING

State of Nature "p"	Posterior Probability	Cost of New Bulb	
		Conditional	Expected
0.005	0.591	$1,250	$738.75
0.010	0.388	2,500	970.00
0.020	0.021	5,000	105.00
			$1,813.75

Linear Regression and Correlation Analysis. Early in the sections dealing with descriptive statistics, the terms "univariate," "bivariate," and "multivariate" data were used to distinguish between the variations occurring within the distribution of a single characteristic and those of two or more characteristics acting or occurring together.

Throughout the subsequent discussion of distributions, tests of hypotheses, conclusion theory, and decision-making, the techniques were illustrated in terms of their application to univariate data. However, in all areas of statistical practice, and particularly in industrial and marketing situations, it is often necessary to base predictions and estimations on the behavior of bi- or multi-variates.

From the statistician's viewpoint, there are basically two kinds of problems which occur in industry: linear regression problems and correlation problems. *Linear regression analysis* is used to measure the relationship of frequency distributions of some selected variable at controlled levels of another variable. The latter, called the "independent" or "X" variable, is held fixed at predetermined levels, and the random frequency distributions of the "Y" or "dependent" variable are observed in relationship to those levels.

Linear regression analysis is used when it is desired to estimate or predict the value of one variable *with relation* to another: weight gain at levels of vitamin intake; crop yields with fertilizers of varying nitrogen content; concentration of Strontium 90 in milk by TNT megaton equivalents of A-Bomb tests; levels of noise with thickness of material; surface hardness of high carbon steel tempered at different temperature levels; sales of household detergents in relationship to supermarket shelf facings—all of these are examples of problems susceptible of treatment with linear regression.

Correlation analysis treats of the covariation of two variables, neither of which is controllable by the experimenter. It examines the degree of relationship between such variables as they occur in nature. Examples of such bivariation might be heights and weights of males in the population; IQ measures and school grades; blood pressure rates and basal metabolism; heights of mates; or in fact, any pair of variables, neither of which can logically be considered as independent.

Regression analysis is primarily a predictive or estimating device. When a regression can be postulated for bivariates, it is perfectly logical to inquire what will be the effect on the dependent variable if, in practice, the independent variable is restricted to stated levels.

The basic mathematical purpose of regression analysis is to develop a means of measurement descriptive of the relationship between the variables by some functional equation, and to determine the degree of confidence attaching to that estimating equation. The equation might be represented by a straight line; if that is not descriptive of the data, some non-linear function might be used in the analysis.

In any regression analysis, it is the *dependent variable* whose changes are being studied. The independent variable is deemed to be directly associated with these changes. No mathematical assumptions are made for the independent variable (also called the "X" variable, and plotted along the horizontal axis in graph form). The dependent or "Y" variable, however, is assumed to comprise an independent normal distribution for each selected point in the X axis, and the standard deviation of each distribution is assumed to be equal.

In most business problems, data are generated by samples. This is true, also, in problems of regression analysis and the treatment of sampling data by this technique is closely related to that of univariate data, with a "best line" rather than a "best point" describing the relationship that exists between the two variables.

Customarily, the data relating to the dependent variable are converted to graphic form by plotting them along the Y axis, or *ordinate,* of a graph whose X axis, or *abscissa,* is the distribution of the independent variable. The result of the independent variable. The result is a "scatter diagram" and initial test of a line visualizing the relationship of the data is generally accomplished empirically. The equation expressing a line is

$$Y_c = a + bX,$$

where

Y_c = estimated or computed value of the dependent variable,

X = value or level of the independent variable,

"a" indicates where the line intercepts the "Y" axis and is called the "Y intercept," (it is the average value of "Y" when the "X" value is 0) and

"b," the regression coefficient, represents the slope of the line. It indicates the change in "Y" with a unit change in "X".

The constants "a" and "b" are estimates of the population parameter, α and β, and can be computed through the "least squares" or "best line" method. By this method, the sum of the squares of the deviations from the actual observations to that line is smaller than that of any other line.

The formula for the least squares estimate of the slope is

$$b = \frac{\sum (X - \bar{X})(Y - \bar{Y})}{\sum (X - \bar{X})^2}$$

where $(Y - \bar{Y})$ = deviation of observed data from the mean of the Y values

The estimated Y intercept is computed as:

$$a = \bar{Y} - b\bar{X}$$

In the same way that a standard deviation measures the variation about a mean, the *standard error of estimate* is a measure of scatter about a *best line* or *curve,* and is denoted by the symbol $\sigma_{y/x}$. Its estimate from a sample $(S_{y/x})$ is measured by a formula which considers the deviation of each observation from the computed *best line* as follows:

$$S_{Yc} = S_{y/x}\sqrt{\frac{1}{n} + \frac{(x - \bar{x})^2}{\sum (x - \bar{x})^2}}$$

where Y_c represents the computed values. (The denominator, $n - 2$, indicates degrees of freedom with two restrictions imposed by the fixed constants a, b.)

Since the best line is an estimate derived from a sample, it is subject to sampling variation. Its confidence limits (or confidence band) can be computed by multipying the standard error of estimate (S_{Yc}) by t. The S_{Yc} can be obtained by the formula:

article 281; insert equation 41

The values of Y_c will be normally distributed around the population value of Y for a given

X. As the formula indicates, the width of the band increases as it is removed from the mean, since errors in the slope are magnified in relationship to the distance they are projected. Sample size and degree of scatter are also contributors to the width of the confidence level.

The decision maker is not particularly concerned with the confidence interval of the best line, but rather with the degree of confidence attaching to the estimate of an individual Y for a given value of X. This requires the imposition of another standard error, and the formula used is:

$$S_{Y-Yc} = S_{y/x}\sqrt{1 + \frac{1}{n} + \frac{(X - \bar{X})^2}{\sum (X - \bar{X})^2}}$$

The actual use of linear regression analysis is easy to explain in terms of a problem. Such a problem arises in the brewing industry, in which it is desired to predict what the metal content of canned beer will be at a given time by use of a laboratory test of samples of the can before use. The test is conducted by measuring conductivity to an electric current (which can only occur in uncoated areas of the can lining) in milliamperes.

In the problem cited, a sample of seven observations was used. The conductivity ratings (the independent variable) and the metal content in terms of parts per million (the dependent variable) are shown in Exhibit XXV.

The data were plotted in the form of a scatter diagram which indicated that a linear relationship did exist. Based on the above formulae, the Y intercept, $a = 0.0865$; $b=0.00611$; and the best line was expressed as

$$Y_c = 0.0865 + 0.00611\ X$$

When $X = 20$, then $Y_c = 0.2087$

EXHIBIT XXV

CONDUCTIVITY RATINGS AND METAL CONTENT OF CANNED BEER

Conductivity Ratings	X	5	15	25	30	45	55	70
Metal Content	Y	0.15	0.10	0.25	0.35	0.30	0.45	0.50

The standard error of estimate was computed as

$$S_{y/x} = \sqrt{\frac{\sum (Y - Y_c)^2}{n - 2}} = 0.0608 \text{ parts per million}$$

Now, to predict the metal content of the beer at a conductivity rating of 20 milliamperes, with a confidence level of 95%, the estimated value of Y_c is first computed from the equation $Y_c = 0.0865 + 0.00611 \times 20$, which gives a Y_c of 0.2087.

The standard error of that estimate is then determined through use of the formula

$$S_{Y-Y_c} = 0.0608\sqrt{1 + \frac{1}{7} + \frac{225}{3{,}150}} = 0.067$$

and the 95% confidence level for the specified point =

$$Z(.05)\ S_{Y-Y_c} = (2.571)(0.067) = 0.1723$$

From the above, the confidence level is given by

$$0.2087 - 0.1723 \leq \mu \leq 0.2087 + 0.1723$$
$$0.0364 \leq \mu \leq 0.38101$$

For conductivity of size 20, it is concluded that metal content will fall between 0.0364 and 0.381 parts per million with a confidence of 95%.

Exhibit XXVI is a scatter diagram of the data used in the example, showing the line of regression and the confidence band for the best line.

Other problems may be best solved through a non-linear or curvilinear function or by using several independent variables to estimate the value of the dependent variable. The latter procedure is called multiple regression analysis.

Correlation Analysis. When there is no independent variable that the experimenter can control, it is still possible to test whether two variates vary together. The *coefficient of correlation* is the device used for this purpose. It mea-

EXHIBIT XXVI

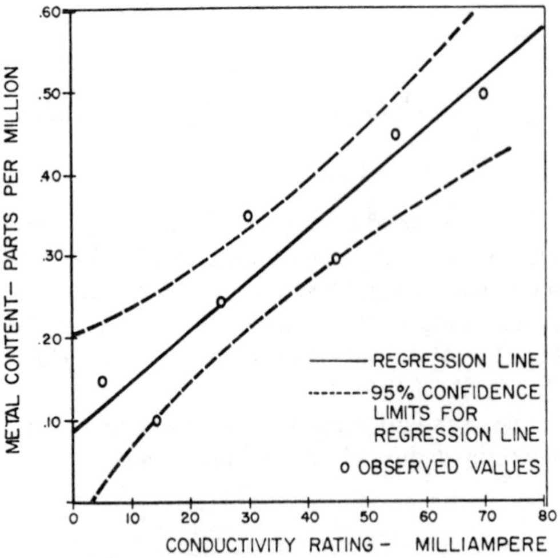

sures, in relative numbers, the degree or intensity of the covariation. A perfect positive correlation would have a coefficient of correlation $= +1$; a completely negative correlation $= -1$; and no correlation at all would have a value of zero. (Incidentally, a negative coefficient of correlation would occur from a relationship that would also produce a negative regression coefficient in linear regression analysis.)

The coefficient of correlation is denominated by "r". It is usually computed by Pearson's product moment formula:

$$r = \frac{\sum XY}{N\sigma_x\sigma_y}$$

$$= \frac{N\sum XY - (\sum X)(\sum Y)}{\sqrt{[N\sum X^2 - (\sum X)^2][N\sum Y^2 - (\sum Y)^2]}}$$

This formula assumes that a linear relationship between the variables exists in the population; that the sample has, in fact, been drawn from a bivariate normal distribution. The coefficient of correlation is not a particularly useful measurement for small sample sizes, since its sampling error tends to have a wide range in such cases.

As the formula indicates, r is simply a ratio of the covariance of X and Y to the square root of the product of the variances of the individual variables; r can also be used in regression problems to measure the relative variation of X on Y, where the regression coefficient, b, measures the absolute variation of X on Y.

Another useful measure derived from the computation of r is the *coefficient of determination,* which is simply r^2. This measures the proportion of the total variation of the dependent variable which has been explained by the regression equation.

OTHER STATISTICAL TECHNIQUES

Less universally used than the methods of analysis already discussed are others now coming into broader use by business decision makers. Some of these are discussed at length in other entries of this encyclopedia. Among such methods and techniques are: Analysis of Variance, Design of Experiments, Chi-Square, Nonparametric Tests, Time Series, Markov Processes, Factor Analysis, Multiple Discriminant Analysis, and Computer Statistical Packages, as well as other techniques implicit in Operations Research and Simulation procedures beyond the scope of this article.

Analysis of Variance. Among the most useful of the statistical devices introduced by the late R. A. Fisher in 1923, is the Analysis of Variance. This, like many of the other techniques we have discussed in brief, is essentially a test of significance. But, whereas other tests of significance deal with two treatments (or levels) of variables, Fisher's technique was designed to handle more than two levels for simultaneous test.

The Analysis of Variance has extremely widespread application throughout the whole general area of statistics. In business and management problems, however, it is most often used to assess the contributions of identifiable or *assignable* causes to the variations encountered in some characteristic or attribute. Any number of suspected associated components and their interactions, provided only that they are relevant to the problem, may be tested simultaneously for their significance.

Two basic models of Analysis of Variance are recognized: *fixed* and *random.* In business problems, elements of each often enter into a problem and the solution is then to be found in a mixed model.

Although identical methods of computation are involved in the use of a fixed or random model, the interpretation of results is different for each.

As its name implies, the fixed model of Analysis of Variance is concerned with testing the significance of fixed treatments or levels of a selected factor of some variable as compared with the random variation in the process. If, on the other hand, the same treatments are regarded as a random sample of an entire universe of treatments, the random model is applicable.

If a textile mill engineer were concerned with warpage breaks occurring among three specific looms, he would wish to test for any significant differences among those three looms only. They would, in fact, comprise the total universe for his experiment and his observations of warpage breaks, obtained through any sampling process, would be analyzed in terms of a fixed model.

On the other hand, if an engineer were concerned with the contribution of looms to warpage breaks, he might still confine his observations to the same three looms as a random sample of *all* looms. He would now be testing the components of variance in warpage breaks arising from looms. In this case, his analysis would be by means of a random model.

As in many other tests of significance, Analysis of Variance measures observed effects against the null hypothesis and ultimately yields a Variance Ratio whose value is identified by the term "*F*":—a contribution of the eminent statistician George Snedecor, who used the letter to honor R. A. Fisher. Tables of "*F*" values are available, and references to them reveals the significance of the value at various probability levels for any number of degrees of freedom *within* and *between* sample findings.

Design of Experiments. It seems incredible that, prior to 1936 and the publication of "Design of Experiments" by R. A. Fisher, the formalized procedures for establishing the framework of statistical experimentation had been largely limited to work in the agricultural areas by Fisher and his followers.

All research data, whether in the physical sciences or in the area of decision making, have in common the factor of variability. As the range of variability increases and when it is not feasible to take many observations, it becomes necessary to design effective and efficient experiments for the test of the hypotheses involved.

Experiments have been devised to cover an extremely wide range of situations, from simple comparisons to the evaluation of many variables, their interactions and the differences among them at many different levels.

An efficient experimental design will embody four essential criteria:

1. Randomization in the selection of observations for each factor under investigation.
2. Replication of the experiment to insure reproducibility.
3. Inclusion of a mathematical basis for the evaluation of each of the variables and their interactions.
4. The design of a control mechanism against which to measure or compare findings.

Although Fisher was concerned with agricultural experiments, his principles of design were quickly introduced into laboratory research and industrial research and now, increasingly, are used in research for management decision making.

Chi-Square. Another of the extremely useful statistical tests arising from the agricultural and biological areas is the *Chi-square* test, introduced by Karl Pearson in 1890. It has enormously wide application in statistics, particularly as a test of significance. As contrasted with tools for analyzing *measurements,* χ^2 (Chi-square) deals essentially with *counts.* It is, thus, especially useful in the study of attributes and to test the hypothesis that characteristics or principles of classification are independent. It is also used to determine *goodness of fit* between distributions of experimental data with theoretical random sampling distributions.

Nonparametric Tests. Classical procedures of statistical inference presented so far are frequently called "parametric" methods, since their efficient use in estimation and tests of hypotheses involves explicit assumptions about the population distributions and parameters. In general, these parametric methods deal with observations measured on an interval scale.

When, as is frequently the case in industrial and marketing problems, the above criteria are not valid, "nonparametric" or, alternatively, "distribution-free" tests can be applied. These tests require only mild assumptions with respect to the form of the population distribution, and these assumptions do not specify the parameters of the population sampled.

These procedures are frequently based simply on classification, or *nominal data,* but they also often use as their data the ranking or order of observations.

Time Series Analysis. Time series analysis infers the future by examining past changes, a process known as extrapolation. Trends and periodical or seasonal movements, as well as cyclical patterns oscillating about trends, are measured from observations taken over different periods in time. Time series analysis, long used in solving business problems, has gained greater acceptance as a guide to managerial planning and control of forecasting. One technique is exponential smoothing which uses exponentially weighted moving averages to predict market potential, sales, and costs. (Cf. *Exponential Smoothing,* in BUSINESS FORECASTING.) Another technique, the Box-Jenkins approach, uses computer procedures to test several extrapolative methods in order to determine which one provides the best forecast.

Markov Processes. In recent years, there has been a revival of interest in the system of chain analysis developed in 1907 by the Russian mathematician, A. Markov, to deal with a study of the physical phenomena of gas particle movements in a closed system.

As a parametric estimating device, used to determine best strategies, the Markov process requires:

(1) A physical system capable of characterization in one of several possible states at a given point in time.

(2) Random changes (or stochastic processes) affecting the state of the system.

(3) The association of each possible change in the system with a measure of probability.

(4) The establishment of *transition* or *switching* of conditional probabilities on the basis of some empirical evidence.

In a stationery system, Markov Chain Analysis is based on two assumptions:

(1) Changes in the state of a system are solely dependent on its state in an immediately preceding period.

(2) Transitional probabilities are stationery and remain constant over time.

The process is frequently used in predicting brand-to-brand switching in marketing problems and to plan appropriate tactical responses to such movements.

Factor Analysis. During the past two decades, a revolution in the technology of problem solving has taken place. Under the broad head of multivariate methods, new statistical techniques and procedures have emerged almost as rapidly as the development of new computer facilities has provided practical means of their utilization.

Multivariate analysis deals with those statistical procedures concerned with the summarization, representation, and analysis of the relationship of measurements of multiple variables made on a number of individuals. *Factor analysis* represents an important class of multivariate techniques involved with data reduction and summarization. An important application of factor analysis is to determine a smaller set of dimensions or "latent" variates called *factors,* which can best represent the observable or "manifest" variates.

Factor analysis was originally developed by Charles Spearman in 1904. He sought to clarify an underlying factor of intelligence that was common to tests of human abilities.

Principal components analysis, developed principally by Harold Hotelling (1933), is an extremely useful factor analytic procedure applied when the problem involves the extraction of a set of independent dimensions or "components" needed to explain most of the variance in the original set of variables. Components are extracted sequentially, so that the first component represents the maximum variance explained by a single factor, the second, the maximum variance yet to be explained, and so on.

While factor analytic techniques were developed largely by psychologists, their usefulness as a statistical tool extends to problems arising in marketing, sociology, management, and education.

Multiple Discriminant Analysis. Another multivariate test important to business researchers is *Multiple Discriminant Analysis,* introduced by R. A. Fisher, as a method of classifying and assigning an individual into one of several groups or populations. By use of multiple measures to discriminate between two or more groups, the technique enables the statistician to construct a *linear discriminant function* consisting of the best combination of variables that will achieve maximum difference among groups. Discriminant analysis, as distinguished from multiple regression, is an appropriate method when the *criterion,* or dependent variable, is represented on a *categorical* or *nominal* scale (heavy vs. light, or good vs. bad), and the *predictor* or independent variables are measured on an interval scale.

Discriminant analysis has been used in such widely different problem areas as the classification of potential sales areas as good or bad, the analysis of coal samples to determine source by vein, and, in semantics, for example, to establish authorship of the *Federalist Papers* when the problem of ascribing them to Hamilton or Madison had not been resolved.

Computer Packages in Statistics. Finally, statistical analysis was greatly aided by the development of the first commercial mainframe computers in the late 1950s. However, the benefits of increased speed of performing calculations, greater accuracy of results, and the ability to undertake large-scale analyses were soon offset by the costs of developing, debugging, and maintaining the necessary statistical programming.

It was such costs that led Wilfrid J. Dixon, of the Health Sciences Computer Facility of the University of California at Los Angeles, to develop Biomedical Programs, the first *standardized* statistical applications software. BMD and other similar software that followed became known as "statistical packages," for, when implemented on a computer, such packages provided the business decision maker with a simple, all-inclusive means of instructing a computer to perform various types of analyses.

While some of the earlier packages, such as CROSSTABS, were capable of performing only a limited number of statistical procedures, packages today are generally capable of performing many different types of statistical analysis. These analyses range from simple frequency distributions, cross-tabulations, and other descriptive statistices to such advanced—and in some cases relatively new—methods as analysis of variance and covariance, multiple regression, discriminant and factor analysis, canonical correlation, multidimensional scaling, exploratory data analysis, and multivariate discrete data analysis.

Widely used multipurpose packages include the Statistical Package for the Social Sciences (SPSS), the Statistical Analysis System (SAS), MINITAB, DATATEXT, and BMDP (the successor to Dixon's original effort). The choice of which package to use depends upon the nature of the business decision-maker's particular problem or the computer system available.

Although some packages initially contained errors which resulted in allowing a statistically naive user to perform invalid analyses, newer versions of such packages contain routines that either disallow or flag such an occurrence. Because of this and an increasing use of the interactive mode, as well as improved documentation (which not only explains how to use a package, but also the statistical theory behind the programming), a business decision-maker with guidance from a professional statistician can perform the most complex statistical analyses, confident that the results will be correct. Computer statistical packages are thus an increasingly important management tool.

RECENT DEVELOPMENTS

Every scientific discipline undergoes constant change as old concepts and techniques are modified and new ones emerge. Statistics is no exception. More powerful computers perform analyses that were heretofore humanly impossible. Information gathering and retrieval systems create ever larger sets of data. In response, Statistics has changed to answer today's more complex questions in decision making.

Changes have been most strongly felt in the areas of multivariate analysis and the body of techniques characterized by their "statistical robustness" (the latter term will become clear in what follows). The increasing application to business problems of methods gleaned from these areas warrants their further discussion.

Multivariate analyses, defined within, includes techniques far too numerous to mention individually. Two multivariate techniques, factor analysis, and multiple discriminant analysis, have already been discussed. Three others which have gained prominence recently are discrete multivariate analysis and the two principal classification schemes, cluster analysis and multidimensional scaling.

Discrete multivariate analysis depends upon cross-classified tables of counts, commonly referred to as contingency tables. These tables contain each subject cross-referenced according to each of several categorical variables or sets of categories. In this way, this type of analysis would aid a market research in, say, discovering the effect of sex (or more specifically gender: male-female) and television habits (viewing, not viewing) upon a consumer's purchase preferences (purchased Product A, did not purchase Product A). The examination of several categories simultaneously in effect leads to the formulation of a multidimensional contingency table, with each variable corresponding to one dimension of the table. Analyzing these tables would be virtually impossible without a computer.

Classification schemes are techniques which determine the natural patterns in a set of data. In cluster analysis, subjects are grouped in a modicum of homogeneous classes, based upon measured characteristics of each subject. Multidimensional scaling creates a spatial representation of subjects in order to determine the variables most responsible for similarities between them. As examples, cluster analysis would be used by a market researcher concerned with product positioning, whereas multidimensional scaling would be used to identify consumers' perceptions and preferences concerning brands and products.

Statistically robust processes are those which yield valid analyses regardless of whether departure from classifical assumptions have occurred. For example, the package design problem discussed earlier used a non-robust classical model, which employed assumptions of normality and the equality of variances, among others. Had these assumptions been incorrect, as is frequently the case when dealing with large sets of data, the resulting analysis would have been invalid. However, a robust analysis employing no such assumptions would have resulted in a suitable solution.

By their nature, robust processes resist the effects of extreme values. In this sense, the median (but not the mean) is a robust measure of location. Locational measures such as the median are not the only type of robust processes. Others include outlier analysis, which examines the extreme variations from a pattern in a set of data, certain non-parametric techniques, and exploratory data analysis—the robust process perhaps of more interest to the business decision maker.

Exploratory Data Analysis. Intrinsically interactive and iterative, exploratory data analysis uses intensive numerical manipulation and visual displays to examine data for both unanticipated patterns and deviations from these patterns. The underlying philosophy of these methods is that the more one discovers the salient data characteristics and hidden relationships, the more effectively data can be used to develop appropriate classical models for inferential purposes.

In a sense, exploratory data analysis is not entirely new, for like descriptive statistics it attempts to present data in summary form. However, unlike the formal descriptive procedures, exploratory data analysis seeks to obtain the most information to be gleaned from the data by following the principles of skepticism and openness. Skepticism allows an analyst to assume that descriptive summarization of data may hide or even misrepresent the true nature of the data. A willingness to be "open," unencumbered by suppositions about the nature of the data, allows the analyst to discover unanticipated structure and anomalies in the data.

Exploratory data analysis begins by examining the data and identifying a dominant gross pattern (graphs and plots of the data facilitate this identification process). The dominant pattern is then eliminated by removing the data which produced it, and another, underlying pattern is determined. The process is repeated as many times as necessary in order to produce a residue that appears patternless. Then the entire analysis is reviewed in order to ascertain which relationships and variables should be candidates for further inferential study. As such, exploratory analysis has been labeled by the statistician John W. Tukey as "numerical detective work." Tukey is author of "Exploratory Data Analysis" (Reading, Mass., Addison-Wesley, 1977), which codifies the techniques of this process. Tukey has devised many innovative techniques applicable to exploratory analysis, including the "stem and leaf display" and the "box and whisker plot." The former illustrates the distribution of a single variable and is analogous to a histogram. The latter summarizes information concerning one or both tails of such a distribution. These techniques, among others, easily lend themselves to graphical presentation by a computer, an important consideration in this interactive process.

Exploratory data analysis is not an end in itself, only a means by which one can uncover clues pointing to the further statistical path to take. As such, its importance to a business decision maker cannot be overestimated.

CONCLUSION

When it is realized that literally millions of words dealing with statistics and statistical techniques are written each year in books and papers, it is obvious that this entry could do no more than touch on some of the more basic statistical tools available to management. Those mentioned were selected on the basis of their high frequency of application to business.

Tomorrow may bring other and better methods and procedures, adding new dimensions or improving, still further, the precision and reliability of the measurements employed by the decision-maker. Karl Pearson and Fisher, Neyman and Wald and the other pioneers who drove across statistical frontiers and widened statistical horizons will be succeeded by others who will carry knowledge forward another inch—a foot—a giant step.

Geniuses appear when they are needed. The paths of science lead ever onward and upward; today's statistics are adequate for today's problems; tomorrow's problems will bring their own techniques for solution as they appear.

DR. DAVID VALINSKY, Professor of Statistics, and Chairman, Department of Statistics and Computer Information Systems, Bernard N. Baruch College, City University of New York, New York, New York

Information References

Associations:

American Society for Quality Control.
American Statistical Association.
Institute of Mathematical Statistics.
Royal Statistical Society (London).
Operations Research Society of America.
The Institute of Management Sciences.

Periodicals:

Applied Statistics (London).
Biometrics
Industrial Quality Control.
Journal of the American Statistical Association.
Journal of the Royal Statistical Society (London).
Management Science
Operations Research
The Annals of Mathematical Statistics.

Statistical Computing Packages:

Dixon, W.J. and Brown, M.B., ed., "BMDP Biomedical Computer-Programs P-Series 1977," Berkeley, Calif., University of California Press, 1977.

Ryan T., Joiner, B.L., and Ryan, B.F., "MINITAB—Student Handbook," North Scituate, Mass., Duxbury, 1976.

Nie, N.H., Hull, C.H., Jenkins, J.G., Steinbrenner, K., and Hunt, D.G., "SPSS Statistical Package for the Social Sciences," 2nd ed., New York, McGraw-Hill, 1975.

Texts:

Arkin, Herbert, "Handbook of Sampling for Auditing and Accounting, vol. 1, Methods," New York, McGraw-Hill, 2nd ed., 1973.

Berenson, Mark L. and Levine, David M., "Basic Business Statistics—Concepts and Applications," Englewood Cliffs, N.J., Prentice-Hall, 1979.

Bowker, Albert H. and Lieberman, Gerald J., "Engineering Statistics," Englewood Cliffs, N.J., 1969.

Deming, W. Edwards, "Sample Design in Business Research," New York, Wiley, 1960.

Gibbons, J.D., "Nonparametric Methods for Quantitative Analysis," New York, Holt, 1976.

Green, Paul E. and Tull, Donald S., "Research for Marketing Decisions," 4th ed., Englewood Cliffs, N.J., Prentice-Hall, 1978.

Hartwig, Frederick and Dearing, Brian E., "Exploratory Data Analysis," Beverly Hills, Calif., Sage, 1979.

Hays, W.L., "Statistics for the Social Sciences," 2nd ed., New York, 1973.

Kish, L., "Survey Sampling," New York, Wiley, 1965.

Mosteller, F. and Tukey, J.W., "Data Analysis and Regression: A Second Course in Statistics," Reading, Mass., Addison-Wesley, 1977.

Neter, J. and Wasserman, W., "Applied Linear Statistical Models," Homewood, Ill., Irwin, 1974.

Owen, D.B., "Handbook of Statistical Tables," Reading, Mass., Addison-Wesley, 1962.

Pearson, E.S. and Kendall, M.G., eds., "Studies in the History of Statistics and Probability," Darien, Conn., Hafner, 1970.

Raiffa, H., "Decision Analysis," Reading, Mass., Addison-Wesley, 1968.

RAND Corporation, "A Million Random Digits with 100,000 Normal Deviates," New York, Free Press, 1955.

Schlaifer, Robert, "Probability and Statistics for Business Decisions," New York, McGraw-Hill, 1959.

Tanur, J., Mosteller, F., Kauskal, W.H., Link, R.F., Pieters, R.S., and Rising, G.R., eds., "Statistics: A Guide to the Unknown," San Francisco, Holden-Day, 1972.

Tukey, John W., "Exploratory Data Analysis," Reading, Mass., Addison-Wesley, 1977.

SUGGESTION SYSTEMS

Alert management recognizes the benefits to be derived from any system which can draw out and apply the best thinking of individuals at all levels in an organization. New ideas put into practice are a necessity if a company is to succeed in today's world-wide, highly competitive economy. A well-designed and properly administered **Suggestion System** provides the incentive and the organization around which this thinking on the part of all employees can be developed. Training in creativity and work simplification is naturally associated.

One suggestion-system director defined his program as ". . . a formalized approach to creative effort designed to encourage fresh, original thinking by all employees and provide positive recognition for those making worthwhile contributions . . . it is actually a philosophy of life that utilizes the widely varying skills of each individual to the maximum capacity he (she) is able to fulfill and willing to undertake. It keeps top management alert to improvements which enhance the profits through increased productivity and, at the same time, gives the individual the needed outlet for the expression of his ideas. A creative idea receives recognition according to its demonstrated value in the market place. This is private enterprise in action . . . The program, properly administered, demonstrates the interdependence of all groups of workers."

History. Formal suggestion systems in industry started prior to the turn of the century, but first received widespread application during World War II, when manpower and productivity became extremely critical. Ezra S. Taylor of the Pullman Company and the first president of the National Association of Suggestion Systems (organized in 1942) was called in by Henry L. Stimson, Secretary of War, to direct the development of a formal suggestion program for civilian personnel in the War Department. Mr. Taylor also served as Chairman of the Government Civilian Award Board. The comparable Navy program, initiated by an act of Congress in 1918, was also given special emphasis during World War II under the direction of then Lieutenant Commander Francis W. McMenimen (a past president of NASS). Today, all departments of the Federal Government conduct active suggestion programs.

In industry, substantial growth followed the war, with the greatest increase in both quality of results and coverage of programs after 1950. During this same period, suggestion systems expanded rapidly in Canada and Europe.

The excerpt (Exhibit I) from the National Association of Suggestion Systems' statistical reports indicates growth of systems in this country between 1950 and 1980.

EXHIBIT I

GROWTH OF SUGGESTION SYSTEMS

Year	Mbr. Orgs. Reporting	Elig. Empl. (in millions)	Suggestions Rec'd per 100 Empl. (Avg.)	% Adopted	Average Award ($)
1950	177	4.3	15.5	27	22
1980	*229	9.0	14.5	24	159

*The 229 reporting organizations represent about 1,000 plants or local units in industries and businesses plus about 5,000 Federal government units.

The figures are national *averages.* A good suggestion system should produce at least one idea from about 35 out of every 100 eligible employees each year. On the average, one out of every four suggestions submitted will be adopted. The award for an adopted suggestion varies widely, from 15% to 25% of net is a common practice.

Level of achievement in an important industry is illustrated by a General Motors Corporation News Release of February 27, 1980, concerning highlights of 1979. In that year, awards to employees in the United States and Canada were more than $21.1 million for 99,618 adopted suggestions out of 368,985 suggestions submitted by eligible employees. From the time the plan was established on a corporate-wide basis in 1942, through December 31, 1979, more than 15,750,000 suggestions have been submitted by employees of which more than 4 million have been adopted. The total awards paid to the employees was over $274 million. . . . IBM Corporation, in recent years, has had several maximum awards of $75,000 and, in 1978, increased their maximum award to $100,000.

The Federal Government's Office of Personnel Management (successor to the Civil Service Commission) reported $3,888,190 paid in awards for reported first-year savings of $147,721,814 in fiscal year 1979. Since the establishment of the Government-wide suggestion program in 1954, benefits to the Government have exceeded $2.7 billion, and have earned employees more than $92 million in awards. A recent award of $25,000 was granted by the President to a Navy engineer whose work in the development of an orifice and filter assembly that replaced conventional steam traps on navy ships saved over $10.2 million in fuel and maintenance costs.

Objectives. The following are the more commonly accepted objectives to be considered in designing and administering a suggestion system.

Economic Objectives and Benefits

(1) Obtain tangible cash savings. Each employee, being closest to the problems encountered, is in the best position to recommend improvements which will generate these savings.

(2) Ensure objective appraisal of ideas advanced. Constructive thought processes are required to answer a written suggestion.

(3) Obtain maximum utilization of ideas. A formal system can transmit good ideas to all other potential applications within the organization.

(4) Identify for management areas which need improvement.

(5) Obtain employee ideas regarding new uses for existing products, new products, and wider markets.

(6) Emphasize the need for quality improvement.

(7) Accumulate a reservoir of ideas with potential.

(8) Improve competitive position through increased efficiency, production, and profits.
(9) Save energy.

Employee Relations Objectives

(1) Develop in employees an attitude of loyalty and a voluntary desire to bring about improvements.

(2) Provide an opportunity for individual expression. The employee is made to feel that he has a part in contributing to the success of the business.

(3) Give personal recognition for specific accomplishment, even though the activity may normally be a group effort.

(4) Enhance the dignity of the individual. Offset the philosophy that the interest of the individual is subordinate to that of the group and that improvement reduces jobs. Emphasize achievement in contrast to wages paid for time spent on the job.

(5) Provide a natural environment for training in creativity and work simplification.

(6) Identify the individuals who are creative thinkers and employees who are potential supervisory material or promotable to more responsible jobs.

(7) Provide two-way communications channel—especially upward.

(8) Improve safety and other working conditions.

(9) Develop a spirit of teamwork among all employees, in a competitive atmosphere.

(10) Reduce grievances by providing a channel for an individual to propose a corrective solution to his problem.

(11) Add to employee's job knowledge by providing an opportunity for the supervisor when declining a suggestion to explain the reasons for not using the idea.

(12) Improve supervisor-employee relations by building mutual understanding and trust.

(13) Provide an additional indicator of supervisory performance in terms of suggestion program accomplishment.

(14) Give management personnel a better knowledge of specific problems and accomplishments within their areas of responsibility as a result of their reviewing some or all of the ideas considered in the program.

Designing a Program. Thorough initial research and careful planning are imperative. Sufficient time must be allowed and sufficient funds provided to develop a potentially effective and high quality program. If some halfway measure is contemplated, it is usually better to drop the subject entirely; a partial or poorly operated program can do more harm than good.

Organizational Features. The success of any program is dependent upon full and continuous top management support. After management determines the objectives in their relative order of importance, the plan can be tailored to meet these objectives and to fit into the various plans and policies of the organization. The following organizational features are important:

(1) A suggestion system will function best if its administration is placed in a top staff position independent of line organization.

(2) A well-qualified individual, with adequate budget and clerical assistance, should be assigned full time to study the subject and develop a program. This development should not be rushed; a schedule of at least six months is recommended.

(3) To obtain complete support of the entire organization in the administration of the suggestion system, it is preferable to involve representation from all segments in its initial planning. A typical Special Review Committee would include a high level representative from Personnel, Finance, Engineering, Manufacturing, Sales, and Legal to work with the designated administrator.

Introducing a Program. The method of introduction of a new plan to the organization is important to its initial success. When all operational details are established and the plan is fully organized with personnel, office procedures, forms, etc., introduction to the organization can be scheduled and announced. The preferred method is to introduce through successive echelons, by presentations appropriate to each level. Distribution of booklets explaining the plan can be made at this time so that the various levels will be clearly informed as to what part they are to play in administering the program.

The first suggestions received should be given prompt processing as well as unusually thorough consideration in order not to develop employee antagonism. After the employees understand the program, they will be more willing to wait a reasonable time for a decision and reply on their proposals.

Through the early years of a suggestion system in particular, some supervisors will view every successful suggestion by others (especially their subordinates) relating to their operations as a reflection on themselves. Therefore, it is essential that supervisors, both individually and as a group, be convinced from the beginning that good suggestions are a compliment to the leadership given by a supervisor.

Mechanical Features

(1) Develop specific, written statement regarding minimum and maximum awards. (See *Policy Features,* No. 1, below, re. award limits.)

(2) Provide authority to a committee or to specific individuals to approve awards.

(3) Establish reporting requirements to permit evaluation of system achievement in light of objectives established for operating the program.

(4) Clearly delineate employee and employer rights to the suggestion.

Policy Features

(1) Adopt a liberal award policy. Concerning minimum and maximum awards, over the years the tendency has been to increase both limits. Most popular minimum is $15, based on the philosophy that rewards should be liberal to gain more employee relations benefit, even though the savings are minor. Some companies establish a higher minimum such as $25. Maximum limits range from $2,500 to $75,000, although many companies do not establish a maximum limit. From a legal point of view, a maximum limit will control the extent of financial responsibility for an idea.

Most plans pay a percentage of the savings for the first full year in which the idea is used. This percentage generally ranges between 10 and 25.

(2) Process ideas rapidly, and keep suggester advised of status.

(3) Designate responsibility for making decisions on adoption of proposals. The decision on an idea should normally be the responsibility of the line organization where the improvement applies. Placing this authority outside the line organization may split the responsibility for the function. This can result in conflict and can easily alienate many in the line organization.

(4) Present awards in a manner which will give the suggester appropriate recognition. Awards are generally presented by the supervisor who also deserves credit for maintaining an atmosphere conducive to improvement. Award presentations can have more value than any other type of promotion undertaken. Large awards are often made by the company president at a special luncheon or dinner. The affair is then given broad publicity in the house organ, local newspapers, etc. Some organizations, including the National Association of Suggestions Systems, promote the idea of annual suggester-of-the-year dinners.

(5) Make a decision regarding centralized control versus decentralization by placing full control at the department or plant level. In small organizations, control will normally be centralized. In large organizations, either policy can be followed, but experience indicates that central control is preferable. Benefits from using central control are:

(a) Uniform practices which give equal treatment to all employees.

(b) Full exchange and application of all usable ideas submitted.

(c) Composite reporting to keep management informed on performance of all segments of organization related to an average, midpoint, or goal. Opportunity for top management to take appropriate action where segments are not meeting expectations.

(d) Justification of an administrator with a higher degree of competency.

(e) Evaluation and exchange of suggestion system experience and know-how.

(6) Establish rules clearly stating eligibility of various types of employees. Many organizations exclude professionals, such as engineers and research personnel who are exempt under the Fair Labor Standards Act, upper levels of management, and technical personnel from eligibility. However, these higher paid people make decisions which have a greater impact upon the business, and react to incentives much the same as the non-exempt personnel. A few companies have successful plans for this group which exclude monetary awards but retain the other features. When upper-level or professional employees develop proposals which are patentable, change well-established practices, initiate new business ventures, or bring about significant economies through ingenious concepts, many managements believe a substantial award will give proper recognition and produce a continuing incentive.

(7) A fair, honest, and liberal administration is necessary. The employee must feel he is receiving the full extent of consideration offered in the system. Otherwise, his reaction will be negative.

(8) A supervisor or foreman must not try to take full or partial credit for an employee's idea. However, many firms provide additional

recognition and award to supervisors who encourage suggestions from their subordinates.

(9) A proposal must be considered as a serious personal contribution important to the individual. Each deserves careful consideration and a reasonable reply, either an award or a full explanation of the reason it is not being used.

(10) Supervisors or professionals often consider suggestions as a criticism of their decisions causing them to react adversely. This action discourages team spirit and builds up relations barriers. Management can explain that an improved end result reflects credit on the supervisor or responsible professional who encourages ideas from all who are involved with the work. It is their responsibility, therefore, to promote ideas which will benefit the total organization.

(11) A suggestion may be declined by an individual authorized to do so. Later this individual or someone else unaware of the suggestion may decide to carry out the idea. The suggester then may see it in use and naturally will be unhappy, since he will believe that his suggestion brought about the action. The suggestion plan should make it clear that employees are free to reopen any suggestion at any time for reconsideration. The situation is then re-evaluated, and if the idea is adopted, the employee is given proper consideration. The right to the idea after non-award notice can be extended indefinitely. Most plans will establish a one- or two-year "equity" period after which no award will be paid for adoption unless the suggester resubmits his suggestions. The equity period is necessary also to establish the right to an idea in case someone else submits the same idea some time later.

(12) As a result of publicizing larger awards to individuals, complaints may arise from associates who have assisted in the development or adoption of the basic idea. It must be clearly understood that the originator of the idea receives full credit even though others may have helped with its formulation and adoption, unless in the judgment of the administrator or suggestion committee the added contribution is in itself awardable.

(13) A suggester will be justifiably critical if pertinent data upon which the award decision is based are not factual. He generally knows the facts. To obtain the facts, there should be no reluctance to contact the suggester directly.

(14) Arbitrary decisions on the amount of award, particularly on the low side, can have bad effects. A stated policy uniformly applied is acceptable to employees when they are informed beforehand and understand what to expect.

(15) Most plans require the signature of the suggester, recognizing that a contractual relationship exists within a suggestion system. They also wish to identify the suggester at the time his idea is being evaluated. If the supervisor-employee relationships are good, this is the preferred practice. Many companies process suggestions after receipt without the suggester's name to preserve anonymity. Most of the employees, however, are signing their suggestions.

Maintaining a Successful Program.

(1) Make special effort to communicate full management support for the program, using the normal channels of communication in a dignified manner.

(2) Maintain appropriate continuous promotion. Periodic special campaigns are also effective. Training programs for employees on how to be creative and how to find quality ideas for improvements have been used successfully by suggestion administrators.

(3) Train supervision to understand properly and carry out their responsibilities in this area.

(4) Expect and demand a high level of performance from the program.

Certification. The National Association of Suggestion Systems has established a professional certification program for qualified suggestion administrators.

OLIVER S. HALLETT, Executive Secretary, National Association of Suggestion Systems, Chicago, Illinois

Information Reference

National Association of Suggestion Systems.

Cross References: *Method Improvement (and cross references there given).*

SUPERVISORY TRAINING

Supervisory Training continues to receive high priority in modern industrial practice. Advanced management puts as much emphasis on the selection and development of supervisors as it does on the development of higher-level executives.

In the present discussion, the terms *supervisor* and *foreman* are synonymous. Frequently the former is associated with office supervision and the latter with the supervision of hourly-rated production employees. The first official attempt to identify the supervisor was made in the Taft-Hartley Act of 1947. It defines supervisors as those having authority to exercise independent judgment in hiring, discharging, disciplining, rewarding, and taking other actions of a similar nature with respect to employees.

It has always been recognized that first-line supervisors perform a vital and indispensable management function. But in many companies, their status has been unclear and often confused. Contributing to this uncertainty of status have been the controversy over whether supervisors should be allowed to join unions, or form unions of their own, the uncertainty about authority and about whether they are really a part of management, the myriad petty tasks with which they have been saddled, the exclusion of first-line supervisors from management development programs, shortcomings in selection and training, and the failure to treat supervisors as part of the management team. However, in well managed companies a serious attempt is made to clarify the supervisor's status, to include him in appropriate management activities, to restore some of the authority that has been siphoned out of his job, and to give him status symbols and financial incentives commensurate with the responsibilities he is asked to assume.

History. General Motors, Western Electric, Westinghouse, A.T&T., Alcoa, Armco, Standard Oil Company (N.J.), and many others have had supervisor-training programs dating back to the early 1920s. But the real beginnings of widespread training came with the War Manpower Commission's Training Within Industry programs (the "J" courses of World War II; see TRAINING-WITHIN-INDUSTRY PROGRAMS), and the Armed Forces programs for civilian supervisors prior to and during the war. The U.S. Airforces programs in which some 40,000 supervisors were trained, the U.S. Navy programs, and the TWI programs formed the basis for countless supervisor training programs. Many of the books on supervisory training since the war were based upon the programs mentioned, written by men and women who were conference leaders or administrators in them. For some years after World War II the conference method was the usual approach to the training of supervisors.

Recent Developments. The trend today is to select the supervisor for leadership and management ability, rather than for superior performance as a technician, mechanic, or production worker. (True, this emphasis in selection had long been piously advocated in professional journals and from management-society platforms; but it is only in the past several decades that it has been widely implemented in practice.) The tendency is also to delegate more responsibility and authority in selection, merit rating, and wage and salary administration to the supervisor. Development programs concentrate on performance-centered training, and on increasing the supervisor's decision-making ability and communication skills.

The objectives of supervisory training have usually been stated as (a) to improve present performance, and (b) to prepare for greater responsibility. Most programs today focus on training needs of the supervisor to do a superior job *now*. As a result, the training is performance-oriented, rather than future-promotion oriented.

An earlier assumption was that no training in the technical aspects of the supervisor's job was required, since he was selected because he was generally the outstanding performer in the group. Present emphasis is that leadership ability is the determining factor. Thus the person is selected for leadership potential, and therefore may require training in the technical side of the job. Provision is made for this need in the better programs, so that they include technical as well as leadership or management training.

A significant trend in supervisory training is the underlying philosophy of modern programs, best expressed by a quotation from Galileo: "You cannot teach a man anything; you can only help him to find it within himself." There is a shift away from neatly packaged courses to programs especially designed to meet individual and group needs. The stress on what the supervisor needs to perform effectively on the present job has resulted in greater emphasis upon on-the-job training and job-related training.

Newer supervisor-appraisal systems have been developed, minimizing and even eliminating personality traits, and rating heavily on performance. The supervisor himself participates in his appraisal, exploring such questions as Exactly what is my job? What is required of me? What training do I need to meet the requirements of my job? What can I, myself, do to improve my performance? What can my superior do to help me? What can the company do? The result of this approach is that the supervisor himself has become involved in designing his training program.

In addition to in-company programs, extensive use is being made of outside-the-company programs—conferences, seminars, workshops, training laboratories, and the like.

Finally, there has been increased attention to the evaluation of supervisor training. Experience has shown that the immediate reaction of participants in well planned programs is generally one of interest, enthusiasm, and appreciation. However, while this is important, it does not in itself prove that the program will be translated into improved performance on the job. Such positive results depend not only on how the course was conducted and the degree of involvement of participants, but also on the follow-up activities taken to reinforce the learning. (This point is discussed in further detail at the conclusion of this article.)

Supervisory Training Methods. Following are brief descriptions of methods and techniques in common use:

Lecture. This method, involving a minimum of audience participation, is best used for presentation of straight factual material, e.g., the company's annual report, the organization chart, implications of new plant layout or facilities. Illustrative material should be large enough to be clearly seen in the back row, and should be professionally prepared. Use of slides or motion pictures should be limited to about twenty minutes, and the lecture period itself to an hour at the most.

The advantage of the lecture is its direct approach. Material can be presented in a logical predetermined order, placing emphasis exactly where it is wanted. And the per-capita cost of a lecture is the lowest of all techniques.

The disadvantage of the lecture is the possible lack of communication between leader and group. Experienced speakers can usually feel the audience reaction, but many leaders are not able to do this.

The Conference Method. As practiced after World War II, the supervisor conference was as a rule highly controlled by the leader, who followed a set, pre-planned outline from which there was little freedom to vary. Most conferee responses were anticipated and written into the instructions. The leader was usually directed to "stick to your outline," and to attempt to get the desired responses from the group. In such a controlled conference, the leader was not supposed to express his or her own ideas, nor to lecture, nor to assume the role of instructor. The leader knew the answers and was expected, by leading questions and other conversational gambits, to get the group to arrive at the desired conclusion. The following list of "don'ts" from a manual for conference leaders illustrates this delimited role:

"Don't set yourself up as an authority or expert in anything."

"Don't lecture."

"Don't tell a member of the group that he is wrong."

"Don't tell the members of the group that they ought to do anything."

"Don't take sides."

Today the conference is still widely employed, but it is generally *member-centered*—i.e., the needs and problems of the group are of paramount importance (see GROUP DYNAMICS). The approach will vary. Depending upon the training objectives, it may involve a combination of methods—instructing, lecturing, pooling ideas, presentations, and any or several of the methods that follow. Extensive use is made of audio and visual aids. The advantage of today's conference method is the active involvement of the participants, stimulating them to apply the developed ideas to their individual job situations.

The Case Study (Case History). In a case study, the student analyzes and discusses a written description of a specific business situation. This approach was first introduced at the Harvard Business School where students currently work on about one thousand cases in their two years of study. Case studies are said to be effective in analyzing complex problems and in framing solutions to them, and reducing snap judgments by exposure to other viewpoints. Interpretation of a variety of realistic situations is also considered to broaden the scope of the participant and to stimulate interest which motivates further investigation.

Critics of the case-study approach point to its inability to provide objective feedback, to the fact that it ignores the elements of timing and dynamic change in business decision making, and to its weakness in teaching principles of management. Furthermore, cases often are expensive to prepare and occasionally lack focus.

Case Problem. This method is identical to that of the case history, but the material ends with an unsolved situation. The relevant facts are given in detail, and the participants are asked to determine the course of action called for. The problems are usually much shorter in narrative than case histories. However, irrelevant facts are often included to provide the challenge of separating the meaningful from the trivial. The advantage of case problems over case histories is largely one of focus.

As cited by Derby [1], in recent years a substantial number of case problems have been filmed so that participants can see, as well as read about, the situation. Two excellent sources for well-made filmed cases are Round Table Films, Beverly Hills, Calif., and B.N.A. Films, Rockville, Md.; the American Management Associations, New York, also has filmed cases available as part of its course in supervisory management.

The Critical Incident Process. This technique was developed by Paul Pigors, at M.I.T. An incident is described, and the conferees are required to feret out as much additional information as they may require for a solution to the problem(s) it poses. The leader is usually the "resource person" from whom the information can be obtained. The conferee decides for himself what information he requires and keeps coming back to the resource until he feels he has enough.

The Action Maze. This relatively recent training technique is a combination of the case problem and critical incident methods [1]. The total group is divided into smaller groups of six or seven. All groups are given the same initial situation in the form of a short case problem. At the end of the description, three or four possible actions are indicated, from among which each group makes its choice. Each choice leads to a second situation which is the result of the first choice of action. This, too, ends with several possible actions, and again each small group must choose the one it believes is best.

The groups thus progress through the maze by selecting one of the suggested actions at the end of each situation. Eventually the maze leads to a suitable situation with which to end. Often there are two or even more possible endings. At certain stages of the decision making, each group records its reasons for its selection. After about an hour and a half, the total group assembles to examine and discuss the differing points of view causing each group to follow the path it chose. Involvement of each member is almost automatic, and the pace of each group improves as the maze continues.

The cost of a maze lies in the preparation of the material, which requires the skill to put together several trails of realistic situations. However, the technique is so effective that experimentation seems to be worth the effort involved in creation.

Role Playing. Here a few "actors" chosen from the group play out a situation in front of the group. It is entirely unrehearsed, with no script. Advocates say that role playing enables the participant to gain insight into human relations situations by experimenting with various roles in a safe learning environment. Because it is spontaneous, flexible, and action-oriented, it provides a valuable bridge between principle and practice. It can be used to demonstrate the effects of misunderstanding, to assist in self-analysis, to develop self-reliance, and to enable the participant to observe his effect on others in different circumstances. The critics of role playing say that it may lead to embarrassment or appear puerile, and that the participants sometimes forget the subject or problem areas in the general theatrical involvement.

The In-Basket Exercise. The participant is given some correspondence and asked to deal with it as though he had found it in his "in-basket." He is asked to take whatever action he considers appropriate, such as immediate disposal of certain items, request for further information, delegation, etc. Included are letters, memoranda, reports, complaints, suggestions, documents for approval, and the like. Much of the material is inter-related, so that effective action on one item depends on information contained in another.

Simulation Exercises, or Management Games. A management game is a training exercise utilizing a model of a business situation. Executives are grouped into competing companies. Using a set of mathematical relationships built into a model, the decisions of the group are made under simulated operating conditions. The decisions are processed to produce periodic performance reports, as a result of which further decisions are made. In some of the more complex games the model is programmed into an electronic computer. (See MANAGEMENT GAMES.)

In management games, the concentration on decision making produces many of the same advantages as do case studies. In both, there is great emphasis on the effective selection of information from a large mass of data, and its subsequent organization and analysis which result in the framing of alternate problem solutions. Both can be used to illustrate decision making under uncertainty or conditions of inadequate information. Both can be employed to give the trainee practice in the use of certain accounting or analytical tools such as budgeting and statistical analysis. Both require consideration of the possible responses which might be made by competitors to certain decisions, and expose the student to the different viewpoints of his classmates. However, management games add two extremely important elements to the case-study approach—the objectivity of the feedback and the new use of the time dimension—and these two factors are the key to the great potential effectiveness of this technique.

Disadvantages of management games are that they cost more, both in money and in time of personnel, than other training techniques; and where a computer is involved, expense of computer time and problems in scheduling the computer are involved. Some questions have been raised as to the validity of games, since it cannot be proven that the simulation used actually does produce the same kind of decisions as would real-life experience. However, their increasing use would argue that experience has been favorable.

Exhibit I, by Derby [1], compares the characteristics of the training techniques discussed above.

Obviously, all conceivable methods in supervisory training have not been covered in the above. Other techniques and devices include:

Pre-Program and Post-Program Assignments. Participants are required to prepare themselves before attending the course by reading certain materials, preparing a list of supervisory functions, posing several on-the-job problems, and the like. After the course has been concluded, or between sessions, the participants are given assignments which relate to day-to-day supervision and which must be checked with the immediate superior.

Communications Exercise. One person gives instructions to another—first "one-way," where the recipient is not allowed to ask questions; second, "two-way," where the recipient may ask questions at will for clarification.

Sub-Grouping Within the Conference Group. The group is divided into several smaller

EXHIBIT I

CHARACTERISTICS OF PRINCIPAL SUPERVISORY AND MANAGEMENT TECHNIQUES

Method	Trainee activity	Group size	Required leadership skill	Appropriate subject matter	Special material needed	Source of material	Relative cost of program
Lecture	None	Practically unlimited	High	Factual material	Charts, pictures, etc.	Purchase or self-prepared	Low
Conference	Fairly active	10–25	High	Policies, plans, problems	None	—	Low
Case history	Fairly active	10–40 (divided)	Medium	Business policy	Prepared case	Purchase	Medium
Case problem	Active	10–40 (divided)	Medium	Administrative problems	Prepared case	Purchase	Medium
Critical incident	Personally involved	10–25	High	Immediate decisions	Incident description or film	Self-develop or purchase	Low
Action maze	Very active	10–40 (divided)	Medium	Decision making	Prepared maze	Purchase or self-develop	High
Role playing	Personally involved	10–25	High	Interpersonal relations	Prepared situation	Self-develop or purchase	Low
In-basket	Personally involved	10–40	Medium	Daily problems	Prepared in-basket	Self-develop or purchase	Medium
Simulation	Personally involved	10–60 (divided)	Medium	Operating decisions	Prepared decision model	Purchase	High

From the chapter "Supervisory Training," by Elles M. Derby, in Heyel, Carl, ed., "Handbook of Modern Office Management and Administrative Services," repr. Krieger, Melbourne, Fla., 1980.

groups (two to ten members) which are given similar assignments for fifteen minutes to one hour. They then reconvene for reporting and discussion.

Projects. Assignments to study and report on a specific problem—data gathering, cost-reduction studies, production studies, etc.

Programmed Instruction. Units or entire courses are prepared in frame or item form for self-instruction. The material may be prepared in textbook form, in which case it is arranged into a so-called "scrambled text." Or a masking device may be used to expose only one item or frame at a time. Answers are written on a separate sheet or in the text itself. The material may also be prepared for use in a teaching machine, which may be simple and inexpensive or complex and electronically operated. (See TEACHING MACHINES, PROGRAMMED INSTRUCTION, AND COMPUTER-AIDED INSTRUCTION.)

Matrix Logic Training. This is a modern approach to improve employee communication developed by Perpetual Systems Management, San Diego, California around 1970 and used successfully by various Government contractors and private industry. The program delineates the functional or working relationships among various documents, supplies, materials, equipment, and specific jobs within the supervisor's province, permitting him (her) to gain quick and thorough understanding of the relationships and needs of component units. The program also makes possible quick and efficient assimilation of new requirements and work procedures, even including computer and robot technologies.

Evaluation. To be meaningful, evaluation of supervisory training must be made against realistic objectives expressed in terms of *specific performance improvement expected on the job.* For example, if training is designed to teach general management principles and does it well, that does not mean that knowledge of principles of management will, *per se,* help on the job. It will be important to measure not only whether the participants learned the principles, but also to what extent this knowledge had direct application on the job and resulted in improved performance.

It is therefore obvious that the starting point of evaluation must begin with clearly defined objectives. Measurement of results can then yield data which can serve as a basis for relating training to performance requirements, and pinpointing areas of the job where special or additional help is needed.

Specific Yardsticks

(1) Increased production (the most convincing yardstick).

(2) Reduction in numbers of employees required to perform the work of a unit, section, or department.

(3) Reduction in absenteeism.

(4) Reduction in labor turnover.

(5) Reduction in costs of operation.

(6) Reduction in numbers and types of grievances, and improvements in handling them.

(7) Greater effectiveness of appraisals of subordinates.

Methods and Techniques of Measurement

(1) Interviews with participants sixty to ninety days after training; also with participants' superiors.

(2) Questionnaires to participants.

(3) Before- and after-training studies and tests. Quentin File's "How to Supervise" [2] has been effective in evaluating supervisor training.

(4) Survey teams. Surveys are conducted at periodic intervals and reports made to plant or office management for remedial action or further training.

(5) Subordinate rating of supervisors before and after training.

(6) Evaluation and reports by consultants or departments of colleges or universities.

(7) Appraisals by the immediate superior. The superior must certify in writing that his subordinate is practicing the principles learned in the supervisor training course sixty days after termination of the training.

(8) Control groups. One group is given training while another is not. Studies and comparisons are then made of results.

(9) Evaluation by key people. Many companies use operating management groups for this purpose, such as a central training committee, audit teams, steering committees, or temporary committees for a given program.

In general, it is safe to say that managements are examining supervisor training activities much more critically than in the past, and demanding that they produce results on the job in terms of tangible improved supervisory performance.

CARL HEYEL, Management Counsel, Manhasset, New York
ANITA LOEBER, Consultant to Management, San Diego, California

Information References

Texts:

Broadwell, Martin M., "Moving Up to Supervision," Boston, CBI Pub., 1978.

Burby, Raymond J., "Introduction to Creative Supervision," Cambridge, Mass., Addison-Wesley, 1980.

Fournies, Ferdinand F., "Coaching for Improved Work Performance," New York, Van Nostrand Reinhold, 1978.

Heyel, Carl, ed., "The Foreman's Handbook," 4th ed., New York, McGraw-Hill, 1967.

Maxwell-Towers, J., "Role Playing for Managers," Elmsford, N.Y., Pergamon, 1975.

Wilson, Howard, "Improving Supervisory Skills," ARA Research Papers, Irvine, Calif., Administrative Research Associates, 1978–1979.

Periodicals:

Personnel Journal.
Supervision.
Supervisory Management.

Associations and Service Organizations:

Administrative Management Society.
American Management Associations.
American Society for Training and Development.
Clemprint, Incorporated (specif. *Successful Supervision* and *The Better-Work Supervisor* and plant poster services).
National Foreman's Institute.

References Cited

[1] Derby, Elles, "Supervisory Training," in Heyel, Carl, ed., "Handbook of Modern Office Management and Administrative Services," repr. ed., Melbourne, Fla., Krieger, 1980.

[2] File, Quentin, "How to Supervise," 1971, a test distributed by The Psychological Corporation, New York, N.Y.

Cross References: *Human Resources Development (and cross references there given); Work Simplification.*

SYSTEMS MANAGEMENT

Systems concepts and techniques have always been tools of the manager to help organize and administer resources, and to develop improved methods of operation which will enhance the internal operating efficiency of his organization. While each manager still exercises these tools, the growth in size and complexity of modern organizations and of the load of paperwork has gradually evolved the Systems staff, formerly called the Systems and Procedures staff, to aid management in developing and maintaining an effective framework of systems and procedures to satisfy the specific needs of the organization.

Definitions. A *system* is an orderly arrangement of interdependent activities and related procedures which implements and facilitates the performance of a major activity of an organization.

A *policy* is a basic precept which guides administrative action and defines the authority and respective relationships required to accomplish the organization's objectives. (Policies are more fluid or changeable than objectives since they are subject to external and internal changes in conditions, they exist in all levels of the organization, and are the product of managerial decision making.)

A *procedure* is a series of logical steps by which all repetitive business action is initiated, performed, controlled and finalized. A procedure establishes what action is required, who is required to act, and when the action is to take place. (Its essence is chronological sequence and its implementation is translated into results or actions.)

A procedure is also a medium for communicating managerial policy decisions applying to routine or repetitive areas of operations to all parties concerned.

History. Systems concepts and techniques have existed from the beginning of organized human effort. But as an organized field in itself, present-day concepts and techniques of systems stem largely from the efforts of the early SCIENTIFIC MANAGEMENT pioneers—of Frederick W. Taylor, Frank and Lilian Gilbreth, Henri Fayol, and their associates. There is thus a close similarity between the application of WORK SIMPLIFICATION and measurement concepts by Systems personnel to clerical operations in the office and by Industrial Engineering to the work of the shop. This accounts also for the affinity of interest between the office manager and the systems function in techniques for controlling the flow of paperwork and measuring clerical work.

The basic responsibilities of the systems function cover a spectrum of tasks from reducing clerical costs, improved timeliness for management reports, and meeting new and more sophisticated management information requirements.

The scope of the systems function today, however, goes far beyond simply systemizing clerical office operations and preparing procedures to govern them. It concerns itself with the overall complex interrelationship of organization structure, functional divisions of responsibility, and the optimum flow of management information—in fact, with the dynamics of the total administrative process in modern organizations.

The electronic computer (see ELECTRONIC DATA PROCESSING), modern DATA COMMUNICATIONS, and the techniques of OPERATIONS RESEARCH, provide additional powerful systems tools to the systems function. These enhance its challenging role in treating an organization and its administrative process as an organic whole, and in developing integrated management information systems for improved managerial decision-making and control. Accompanying these developments is also the current trend for far closer organizational ties between the systems, electronic data processing, and operations research staffs. In some companies, these staffs are, in fact, being merged into a single function.

Present State of the Systems Function. Many systems staffs perform all or most of the following functional responsibilities:

Organizational Analysis. The development of close interrelationships between organization structure, effective administrative systems, and optimum management information flow. This may include developing the organizational structure for new functions, reviewing the existing organizational structure in the light of changing organizational objectives, and preparing and issuing of organization charts and functional statements of responsibilities.

Systems Analysis and Design. Periodic surveys of functional activities and study of administrative problems; the application of concepts and techniques of work simplification to the design of systems which will facilitate integration of business data flow throughout the organization and assure accurate feedback of information to management; and conducting feasibility studies on the application of new techniques and equipment ranging from office reproduction equipment to more intricate data transmission equipment and electronic computers.

Management Audits. A combination of organizational analysis and systems surveys to determine the effectiveness of specific operating functions. (See MANAGEMENT AUDIT.)

Development of Written Policies and Procedures. The development of written administrative guidelines for operating personnel, including the initiation, coordination, maintenance and classification of them into appropriate manuals. These may include broad policy statements, interfunctional procedures crossing departmental lines, intra-functional procedures applicable only within a single department, and special supplementary managerial bulletins of a more temporary nature. In some companies, the systems staff is also responsible for the preparation of supplementary job instructions for major tasks involved in a procedure.

Forms Design and Control. The design of appropriate formats to assist in proper transmission of data, and forms control measures to eliminate excess clerical data handling, with the recognition that forms are one of the main media for transmitting business data. (See FORMS CONTROL.)

Reports Analysis and Control. The design of reports to assure accurate and timely feedback of the relevant information in the form and detail needed by various levels of operations and the elimination of redundant reporting.

Records Management. The development of records retention schedules and records storage facilities, to assure protection of vital records and to facilitate information retrieval from stored records. (See RECORDS MANAGEMENT.)

Work Measurement. The analysis and measurement of clerical work and development of clerical work standards. (See WORK MEASUREMENT IN THE OFFICE.)

Office Equipment Selection. The selection of optimum office tools for use in systems designed to optimize the efficiency of office operations. This includes conducting feasibility studies on applications of electronic data processing equipment and data transmission devices. (See ELECTRONIC DATA PROCESSING.)

Office Layout. The best grouping of related and interdependent functions commensurate with optimum space utilization. (See OFFICE SPACE PLANNING: The "Open Plan.")

Systems Specialization. Some of the above functions, such as organization, work measurement, and forms control, may form sub-fields of specialization within the systems department, or may even form the basis of separate staffs. Other forms of specialization may be in particular types of systems applications, e.g., accounting systems, production control systems, engineering administration systems, computer programming, etc.

Impact of New Developments. The last two decades have seen the rise of powerful new systems tools for processing, storing, and transmitting masses of business data. The application of electronic computers, data communication devices, and new developments in concepts and techniques of information storage and retrieval now make possible far greater integration of business functions. It is now possible to automate much of the routine clerical data processing, and provide economical means for transmitting and safeguarding masses of vital data and guarantee their rapid and accurate retrieval for improved managerial decision-making. However, implementation of such techniques requires even greater stress on good systems design and maintenance.

The modern systems man must thoroughly understand electronic data processing and data transmission concepts and techniques. He must be able to lead effective EDP feasibility studies, design and modify systems to integrate data flow and make effective use of machine operations, assist in eliminating communication barriers between systems work and computer programming, and, where they are organized separately, assure optimum coordination between the systems and EDP departments.

There is now a rising trend for merging systems and electronic data processing departments, and with the widespread use of English-language computer programming languages, for merging systems and programming staffs. Thus systems analysts can be trained to carry the complete job of systems survey and design through the cycle of systems installation, including the computer programming, where applicable.

Since World War II there has also been a steady rise in business application of the quantitative analysis methods of OPERATIONS RESEARCH. Thus a highly sophisticated systems staff includes at least one knowledgeable operations research analyst. The modern systems man must know how to apply the operations research concepts and techniques, and must assure proper coordination among systems, operations research, and EDP staffs where they are organizationally separate.

Conceptual Approaches to Systems Work. Much of the systems work of the past few decades has tended to be oriented toward resolving specific operational problems. This has given an aura of "fire-fighting" or trouble-shooting to all of systems work, and has often produced a patchwork of systems and procedures that may not necessarily be compatible with each other. Office automation applications, especially the use of electronic computers, have similarly followed specific problem orientation that has not permitted its optimum utilization as a powerful systems tool. This has also added the problem of narrow technical orientation and inflexible manual-machine relationships, and an erroneous assumption that mechanization, *per se,* provides maximum efficiency. Systems analysts have also tended to concentrate on one facet of systems work, such as procedure writing, forms control, or on specific types of systems, such as those for accounting or inventory control.

Management is now beginning to recognize that neither continuous fire-fighting nor narrow specialized approaches can provide the dynamic systems to solve the real administrative problems. Thus, there is a growing acceptance of the new systems concepts which recognize an organization as an organic system composed of many interdependent subsystems; concepts which call for the determination of the real management information needs, and which will utilize fully the unique capabilities of the computer and other new tools to produce better, more accurate and more timely information, and more integrated administrative processes. This means that the systems analyst must not only be fully versed in all systems techniques, but also a management generalist who fully comprehends the functions and problems of his organization.

This dynamic newer approach is sometimes referred to as "the total systems concept" or by such terms as *Integrated Systems, Management Information Systems, Integrated Information Systems,* etc.

Acceptance and Potentials. Some type of systems staff exists in most large and medium size companies in all industries in American business and in most government agencies. According to a 1981 survey by the Association for Systems Management, 46% of the heads of the systems function reported to the president or vice president, and, in a sharp decline from earlier findings, only 12% reported to the controller. The frequency with which systems activities transcend internal organizational boundaries is, of course, the reason that systems departments so often report to top corporate executives. And as stated earlier herein, the importance of systems work has been further enhanced by the increased utilization of electronic computers.

Much of the acceptance of systems personnel, as widespread as it is, has been on the basis of a specialized technician. However, the potential for acceptance as valuable members of management and not simply technicians, is increasing rapidly as the full potentialities of a "total systems" philosophy are recognized, and as systems personnel themselves evidence their mastery of this concept. This will also hasten the merger of the systems, electronic data processing, and operations research staffs into a single, dynamic systems function, a trend which can be seen in many modern organizations.

Many organizations are coming to realize that their systems staff can materially assist in management development. Companies frequently rotate managerial prospects through the systems department to acquaint them with an overall company approach. Similarly, through such rotation, members of the systems department develop greater knowledge of their company's total operations and are, therefore, more valuable as potential managers.

A. JAMES ANDREWS, Director of Publications, Association for Systems Management, Cleveland, Ohio

Information References

Associations:

The Association for Systems Management is concerned with the entire field. Other professional organizations covering various aspects of systems work include: Administrative Management Society, Data Processing Management Association, National Records Management Association, Operations Research Society of America, and the Special Interest Group on Business Data Processing of the Association of Computing Machinery.

Periodicals:

The Journal of Systems Management.
Systemation.
Systems Management.

Texts:

Association for Systems Management, Cleveland:
"Business Systems," 1975.
"Information Resources Management in the Office of Tomorrow," 1980.
"Forms Design and Management," 1979.
"Peopleware in Systems," 1978.
Haslett, J.W., "Business Systems Handbook," New York, McGraw-Hill, 1979.
Mathies, Leslie H., "The Management System," New York, Wiley, 1979.
Ramsgard, William C., "Making Systems Work," New York, Wiley, 1979.
Taggart, William M., "Information Systems," Boston, Allyn and Bacon, 1980.

Cross References: *Forms Control; Forms Design; Office Automation; Office Management and Administrative Services; Records Protection; Word Processing; Work Measurement in the Office.*

T

TAXATION

Taxation is a science, and the techniques and niceties of tax systems have long been and will continue to be subjects for study and debate among professional economists. But there are some broad principles which are fundamental and which every executive must understand, not only in regard to the immediate burden on his company, but because as a citizen he must make the decisions regarding the services he desires from the Federal, state, and local governments, and the amount he is willing to pay for these services.

Taxation is in a constant state of flux. The economy of this nation is dynamic and ever changing. New areas of tax revenue are needed to meet burgeoning governmental budgets, and old avenues of escape or relief are constantly being closed. It is the purpose of this discussion to expose the business executive to the general aspects of taxation, since awareness of applicable law often opens avenues of legitimate tax avoidance. Presented here are a brief history and description of business taxes which may be considered as comprising the minimum basic tax knowledge required by the ordinary corporate executive.

The total taxes paid by publicly owned corporations are frequently equal to, and sometimes many times larger than, the net income of the organizations. To increase, therefore, the net income available for dividends, the most fertile ground is frequently to be found in the probability of reducing taxes rather than in increasing sales or performing some other managerial function. Postwar costs of maintaining the Federal Government have rocketed upward with the speed of modern space vehicles.

The annual Federal budget has in recent fiscal years exceeded $700 billion. To enable states and municipalities to expand needed public services, sales taxes have been increased sharply in the last few years. State and local public expenditures are now keeping pace proportionately with Federal expenditures. Increasing demands for major social welfare improvements, as well as constant increases in other operating costs, have resulted in a transmission of these costs to both business units and individuals. Various pledges have been made to cut tax rates, and while some rates have been held on a comparatively level plane, the increased costs have been transferred to the taxpayer by indirect means, such as licensing fee increases, additional excise taxes, and changes in classification of business units.

Federal Taxation—General Considerations

In its report on the Revenue Act of 1916 (the first to reflect the demands for arming for the First World War), the House Ways and Means Committee said:

> Up to the present time, our revenue system, in order to meet the increased demands on the Treasury, has passed through three stages. For over fifty years the National Government depended for its necessary revenue almost exclusively upon one system of indirect taxation, namely, customs revenue. During the Civil War the shortcomings of this system became apparent. . . . Thus the second permanent method of taxation was added, namely, internal revenue. Up to the enactment of the tariff act of August 5, 1909, our revenues were almost entirely collected from these two sources, both being taxes upon consumption. The increasing demands of the Treasury made it necessary to incorporate into the tariff act of August 5, 1909, a provision imposing a special excise tax on corporations. The tariff act of October 3, 1913, imposed a permanent and comprehensive tax on the net incomes of corporations and individuals.

It should be noted that this statement, written over 65 years ago, refers to new and permanent taxes—there is no suggestion that adoption of a new tax should result in abandonment of an old tax. Since that time, corporations have, along with almost all other business entities, borne an increasing burden of excise taxes—that is, commodity or service taxes.

At the present time there is no capital stock tax levied by the Federal Government, but there has been on different occasions a capital stock tax which might be considered the charge for the Federal Government's franchise. The Federal Government does not grant corporate franchises (except for the Federal District and some semi-government corporations such as FDIC), and a student of taxation must have it driven home to him that neither excise taxes nor franchise taxes mean what the dictionary definition would imply. They are simply two means of raising revenue employed by the Federal Government.

Before the adoption of the Sixteenth Amendment (the beginning of our present income tax procedure) these excise taxes were, in a sense, nothing less than a subterfuge to tax income under a misnomer. The Sixteenth Amendment to the Federal Constitution was adopted February 28, 1913. Prior to its adoption, the Constitution gave the Federal Government the right to collect taxes, duties, imposts, and excises. The Federal Government was not permitted to impose a capitation or other direct tax, except in proportion to population. Had such direct taxes been collected, they would, in accordance with the Constitution, have been required to be apportioned to the various states. During the Civil War days an income tax law was passed; in 1894 this tax was declared to be a direct tax, and therefore held to be unconstitutional. Thus, March 1, 1913, is a notable date in the financial history of the United States. On the day prior thereto (February 28) the last state required to validate the Constitutional Amendment had given its approval. Prior to the adoption of the Sixteenth Amendment, the Federal Government was required, if it imposed a direct tax, to do so in proportion to population, and to allocate the proceeds to the states. The Federal Government could then collect vast sums from comparatively few taxpayers, while collecting nothing, or relatively small amounts, from vast numbers of individuals.

Progressive Tax Rates and Expense Allowances. With the adoption of the income tax law there has developed a new theory of tax assessment in this country, viz., progressive tax rates allegedly based upon ability to pay. The theory of ability to pay led to staggering rates on high personal incomes, and, to a certain extent, high rates on corporations. Some in Congress, when imposing income taxes on corporations, have doubtless looked upon corporations as the instruments of wealthy individuals, when as a matter of fact the corporation itself has no ability to pay taxes. The corporation is only a medium through which business transactions are carried on, and its tax burden must fall upon one or the other, or all, of (a) stockholders, (b) employees, and (c) customers.

That we may better understand that which is being taxed and how it can be taxed, it is appropriate to consider the exact wording of the Sixteenth Amendment, which reads as follows:

> The Congress shall have power to lay and collect taxes on incomes, from whatever source derived, without apportionment among the several States, and without regard to any census or enumeration.

It will be noted from this quotation that ". . . incomes, from whatever source derived . . ." are the monies on which Congress is empowered to assess taxes. Nothing is said about graduation, and nothing is said about either gross income or net income. The average person is inclined to think in terms of corporate net income because there is some similarity between taxable net income as defined in our statutes and the ordinary bookkeeping net income of the corporation. Seldom are the two exactly the same, but they are fairly close. It must be borne in mind that, with the passage of the first income tax law together with minor changes that have crept into statutory concept, the congressional definition of "taxable net income" has been "gross income" less certain specific deductions, such as interest, officers' salaries, depreciation, etc., and a basket clause (originally known as Section 23 and now known as Section 162) allowing a deduction for ordinary and necessary expenses in connection with a trade or business.

Generally speaking, ordinary and necessary expenses would include salaries, traveling expenses, rents, and items of that nature. The term "in connection with trade or business," however, limited these deductions to a taxpayer engaged in trade or business in an ordinary sense. With the passage of the Higgins Amendment in the 1942 Act, permission was granted for deduction of such similar expenses by taxpayers not actually engaged in a trade or business, if related to the production or collection of income; or for the management, conservation, or maintenance of property held for the production of income. Some judicial decisions and an interpretation by the Regulations have added a "reasonableness" test to the statutory concept of "ordinary and necessary" expense.

The taxpayer, because of a lack of sufficient evidence to substantiate travel and entertainment expenses, usually invoked the usage of the "Cohan Rule," which resulted in an allowance by the Internal Revenue Service of a portion of the expenses incurred. George M. Cohan, theatrical producer, manager, and entertainer, was unable to substantiate certain travel and entertainment expenses. The Board of Tax Appeals denied his claim for these deductions in their entirety, but was reversed by the Court of Appeals. This tribunal—in *Cohan v. Comm.*, 39F2(d) 540, 544, (CCA-2, 1930)—stated ". . . absolute certainty in such matters is usually impossible and it is not necessary; the Board should make as close an approximation as it can, bearing heavily if it chooses upon the taxpayer whose inexactitude is of his own making. But to allow nothing at all appears to us inconsistent with saying that something was spent. . . ."

During the 1950s the Internal Revenue Service attempted to curtail the allowance for expense accounts. Public indignation rose to new heights as a result of the exposure of so-called abuses by corporate executives in the use of expense accounts. The Executive Department of the Government set out to curb these abuses and the President recommended drastic reductions on certain types of business expenses, especially in the area of entertainment where certain substantial tax free benefits were conferred upon corporate executives.

These highly controversial matters were partly resolved by Congress in the Revenue Act of 1962. Section 274 of the Code was added which placed new restrictions on expense accounts. The Section disallowed, in whole or in part, expenses which were fully deductible under the old law. In addition to the necessity for greater substantiation of expenditures incurred (the Cohan Rule has been eliminated), entertainment, amusement, or recreation expenses must now be directly related to the active conduct of the trade or buisness. If an entertainment facility such as a yacht, a hunting lodge, or a country club is used, then an additional requirement states that the facility must be used primarily for the furtherance of the taxpayer's trade or business. Dues and fees to country clubs fall under the general category of facilities.

Only a loose-leaf tax service published by a concern constantly in touch with all current changes, rules and regulations, court decisions, and legal interpretations, can furnish the tax specialist up-to-date authoritative information on the every-day application of tax law. However, certain phases of corporate tax procedure have developed over a period of years which are likely to remain significant factors in current and future tax laws, and which can be safely presented without too much danger of being out-of-date before publication of the present article. A few of the more important of these considerations are dealt with in the following paragraphs. These may be regarded as outlining the minimum basic tax data with which the average business executive should have a "nodding acquaintance."

Elective Provisions of Federal Income Tax Laws. Throughout the period of corporation income tax procedure in America, taxpayers have been permitted many elective provisions whereby they can choose the procedure they think most favorable, and the law generally contemplates that the taxpayer will be permitted to take advantage of whatever procedure will involve the lowest tax liability. Elections discussed here are specific and technical, not including the much more important election to accelerate or defer consummation of a transaction to a time deemed more advantageous taxwise by the taxpayer. Since in the accounting sense (which is the criterion for a constitutional decision) income or loss can result only from a completed transaction, and since our system of taxation of income is built upon an annual, separable, accounting period, every taxpayer has a real election as to when to arrive at the "completed" stage of a transaction which will result in the creation of income or a loss.

However, the specific elections which taxpayers may make include:

(a) The business year.

(b) Bad debts—may be charged through a system of reserves or the actual write-off of specific items known to be lost.

(c) Cash or accrual basis of accounting.

(d) Method of valuing inventories.

The Business Year. In the case of a new business, the selection of the business year is, of course, of paramount importance, not only from a tax standpoint, but from a normal accounting point of view. If the business is such as to involve definite annual cycles, the end of its business year might best be established at the end of the month during which inventories and production will be at the lowest ebb.

Regardless of the method of valuing inventories, it is obvious that the lower the inventory at the close of a period, the less likely it will be that the income report will include uncertain inventory valuations which may, in reality, affect the profit and loss of another year. The law regarding calendar and fiscal years is very definite. Where the taxpayer does not keep books and does not have a regularly established fiscal year, other than the calendar year, the tax return must be made on a calendar year basis. The law is also clear that, for companies operating on a fiscal year (other than a calendar year), the year must end on the last day of the calendar month, or an annual accounting period varying from 52 to 53 weeks if an election is made to use that type of accounting period. Failure to keep books on a basis of an accounting year that will end on the last day of a specific calendar month may give the Commissioner grounds for asserting that the tax liability should be computed on the basis of a calendar year.

It sometimes happens that, with a change of tax laws in the middle of a year, a concern operating on a fiscal year basis may have a tax advantage. In this situation, the Commissioner is almost certain to insist on a calendar year tax computation if the books are not kept so as to reflect clearly a fiscal year closing at the end of a particular month, or an annual accounting period varying from 52 to 53 weeks, if an election is made to use that type of accounting period. This fiscal period will be recognized only if it is established as the annual accounting period of the taxpayer, and only if the books of the taxpayer are kept in accordance with such fiscal year. The election of a fiscal year by a taxpayer consisting of 52 to 53 weeks is permitted if the period varies from 52 to 53 weeks, and ends always on whatever date the same day of the week last occurs in a calendar month or whatever date this same day of the week falls which is nearest to the last day of the calendar month. The 52-53 week accounting period is used by many concerns for comparative purposes and simplification of cost accounting.

Cash or Accrual. The choice of cash or accrual basis of accounting is perhaps to be governed more by accounting requirements than by tax considerations. It is obvious that in some instances, when the tax rates are changed in successive years, a concern operating under either cash or accrual basis will have certain advantages at certain times. Since our system of taxation is based on graduated rates and an annual accounting period, inequities can result from bunching "cash received" income in one year in cases where it can be shown to have accrued over more than one year.

Valuing Inventories. The method of valuing inventories to be elected requires considerable study before an election is made. For simplification of cost accounting, inventories always valued at cost would keep the income account as reported for tax purposes more nearly in accordance with the cost accounting records of the company. However, the election of cost or market, whichever is lower, gives the taxpayer the right to accrue, when the market is lower than cost, certain inventory losses which otherwise would be deferred until the goods were sold at some future period.

In connection with the election of valuing inventory at cost or market, whichever is lower, the law and regulations require the computation of end-of-year inventories, on the theory that the goods on hand at the time represent the most recently purchased or produced. In other words, regardless of how the actual sales are made, the theoretical sales are invariably treated as though the first goods received were the first goods sold. However, another elective provision has been added to the Code whereby the taxpayer may secure permission from the Commissioner to adopt the reverse of this rule, which places the taxpayer in the theoretical position of always having on hand the oldest stock. Under this procedure, the taxpayer is permitted to charge against current sales the cost of most recently acquired merchandise. In a period of rising markets, especially if the income during that period is higher than normal, it is distinctly to the advantage of the taxpayer in many instances to secure the privilege of valuing inventories on the basis of last in first out. In common terminology among tax practitioners, the abbreviated term of last in first out, is LIFO. If LIFO is used, the basis of valuation must be cost only. (See FIFO/LIFO INVENTORY ACCOUNTING.)

In all elective provisions there is perhaps nothing more important for the general run of merchandising corporations than the selection of the proper type of inventory electives. No businessman should ever attempt to solve this problem without the aid of a good accountant who is familiar with both his business methods and the tax technicalities.

Current Income and the Effects of Taxation. There are many technicalities regarding the particular time that a certain deduction is valid, or the particular time when certain income becomes taxable. Every businessman should know something about the statute of limitations, i.e., the number of years the tax return remains open and is subject to change either by the taxpayer or the Government. This statute may work in favor of the Government or the taxpayer. If there is doubt within the meaning of the tax law whether income has been earned in one year or another, it is to the taxpayer's advantage to accrue that income in the latest year for which there seems reasonable grounds; and the reverse is so for deductions about which there may be dispute as to when they became valid.

If there is any possibility that the corporate income tax will be reduced significantly, the timing of expenditures that must be made in one year or the other, so that they will be deducted in the current year, may save the corporation a considerable amount of money.

While the foregoing concerns items upon which there is doubt of the date applicable within the meaning of the tax law, it is important that the businessman constantly keep in mind the timing of events. Once a thing has happened, it is neither honest nor good tax policy to try to make it appear that it happened in a different period, in order to gain a tax advantage. The danger of being charged with fraud or placed in a prejudicial position with the Internal Revenue Service is serious. However, the businessman can, in numerous instances, time the transaction so that it will fall in the period desired.

Through a cycle of years there are innumerable necessary items of maintenance, special expenses, etc., which must be incurred if the business is to be run successfully. It often happens, however, that a fairly heavy maintenance item, as well as many other items which are not necessarily required each year, can be contracted for or actually acquired at such a time that the deduction will be most advantageous from the standpoint of corporate taxation. Businessmen should know enough about their probable income and effect of taxes to determine whether the liability for some of these extraordinary charges should be incurred in the current year or postponed to a succeeding year. Even though it looks as if there is to be good income in the current year and in all probability there will be good income in a succeeding year, much can be gained if the businessman keeps abreast of the probability of tax reduction. Consider the difference in profit-after-taxes resulting from the payment of a bonus in 1945, with a 95% excess profits tax rate, rather than in 1946, with a corporate tax rate of only 38%, or even in 1979 with a corporate income tax of 46%.

One of the important results of our annual accounting period principle in income tax reporting is an emphasis on the time of accrual of income or deduction items. It is not uncommon for corporations to have in effect some kind of bonus, or profit-sharing plan, which is based primarily on the success, profitwise, of the corporation. Suppose the management has in mind paying a certain bonus if the profits of the year are equal to, or greater than, a predetermined amount. The management may not know until after the books are closed that the profit standard will be met. Then, some few weeks after the books are closed and the profit results are found to be favorable, the management authorizes a distribution of $100,000 to certain key employees. The payment of this $100,000 is definitely within the period of the succeeding year. Obviously, if the corporation is on an accrual basis, it would like to be able to accrue this $100,000 as a deductible item in determining the tax liability for the prior year.

The rules with respect to such an accrual state clearly the deductibility in the year prior to actual payment is not valid for tax purposes unless the liability has been established before the close of the fiscal year in question. Therefore, if the accounting department is notified by the management prior to the close of the year in question that such a liability for the bonus expenditures is definitely planned, to be contingent only upon the profits of the year, and further, if there has been an election whereby it is known that such a plan is in operation, little question can be raised concerning the correctness of the accrual of the liability when closing the books of the year in question. On the other hand, if the management, with no previously established plan, reviews the favorable earnings of the corporation after the earnings have been fully determined, and then pays a bonus based upon the earnings of the year just ended, deduction of that bonus can be made only in the year of payment.

It would be quite unusual if in the affairs of the average corporation there were not many items similar to the foregoing that could, by knowledge of tax law and regulations, be so handled as to afford a distinct advantage from the standpoint of tax liability.

The Tax Benefit Rule. It frequently happens that a cost is incurred in one year and either all or part of that cost is recovered in some future year. These recoveries are generally regarded as taxable in the year of actual receipt (not the recovery of an income tax in which there has been no deduction in the first instance); but there has been enunciated by court dictum, and it is now part of the law and regulation, that certain recoveries are non-taxable in the year of receipt if it can be shown that the deduction of the item when first paid, or the cost first charged, gave the corporation no tax benefit. For example, under an ordinary and reasonable system of charging off bad debts, an item is charged off in a year in which there is no taxable income and, say, five years hence part or all of it is collected. The recovery in this instance, up to the extent that it did not exceed the net loss in the year first charged off, would be a non-taxable item.

This Tax Benefit Rule applies to bad debts, state and local taxes, delinquency charges, and to expenses and losses, with the exception of depreciation, depletion, amortization, and bond premiums. Correction of the items listed as "exceptions," giving effect to having overcharged therefor in prior years, cannot be so handled as to compensate tax-wise for the lack of tax benefits resulting from previous overcharges. As an example, let us assume that a 10% rate had been used in depreciation, and that it is later determined that only 5% should have been the proper allowance. Let us assume also that during all the years when the 10% rate was in effect the company was operating at a loss. Later, when the item has been 50% depreciated, at the 10% rate, it is determined that this item should have had a twenty-year life (which would have justified only 5%); instead of going back and correcting the depreciation for prior years, the corporation is required then to charge off the remaining undepreciated balance over a corrected fifteen year remaining life, which would give it the effective rate of $3\frac{1}{3}$% depreciation for future years instead of permitting a deduction of the correct 5% rate throughout the succeeding years.

There is no easier way of actually making money than by being able to tabulate correctly the items that apply under the Tax Benefit Rule and prove that the correction for the overcharge in the previous year should be excluded from taxable income in the future years. Bad debts are perhaps the best example. Many companies charge off bad debts during a loss year in such a manner that they are unable to identify a specific item of recovery in a later profitable year, although it should be excluded from taxable income of a taxable year. It is of the utmost importance that the corporation procedure for charging bad debts and for recording recoveries thereof, should establish easily and unquestionably all the tax benefits to which the concern is entitled.

Carryback and Carryover of Net Operating Losses. Under current law, corporations are allowed to reduce taxable income by the amount of net operating losses. A net operating loss occurring in any taxable year ending after 1957 can be carried back to the immediately preceding taxable years to the extent that the loss of a given year may exceed the income of the first, second, and third years immediately prior to that loss. The balance may be carried forward as an offset against taxable income of the next seven succeeding years. The corporation may at its election forego the carryback, and carry forward the entire loss.

Some taxpayers, knowing that this rule exists, have felt that such a rule would inevitably guarantee their receiving all deductions over say, a nine year period. However, they overlook the fact that a deduction taken in a year when the tax rate is low, when it could have been taken in a year when the tax rate was high, cannot be adjusted by manipulation of carry-forward or carry-backward of losses. The most important thing for the businessman to remember is that in prior laws there was a provision for the carry-forward of net losses, but that this portion of the tax law was repealed immediately after the depth of the 1932 Depression, when most corporations had sustained heavy losses. Corporations were deprived of the right to offset prior losses from the days of the Depression until a provision was enacted in the law of 1942, and this right has been revised frequently.

Admittedly, income measured by a single year is not a fair standard for paying income tax, and some such adjustment as carry-backward and carry-forward losses is necessary to avoid payment of taxes over a long period of time on an income considerably higher than the corporation actually realized. Busnessmen should be on guard against any attempt to repeal this provision in the future, and, certainly they should not overlook the opportunity, in such ways as the law permits, to deal currently with each item of expense to their own advantage.

Ordinary and Necessary Expenses. Congress, in passing all the various revenue acts since the date of the Sixteenth Amendment, has set forth its own concept of "taxable net income." This concept has invariably defined certain specific items that were deductible in determining net taxable income, and through what might be called the "basket clause" (at present Section 162 of the law) Congress has provided that, in addition to certain specified deductions, there shall be allowed reasonable deductions for all other ordinary and necessary expenses paid or incurred in carrying on a trade or business. This broad classification included numerous items, such as rents, salaries, pensions, advertising, traveling expenses, entertaining, and such miscellaneous matters.

For a long time, these general items were not carefully scrutinized by the Treasury Department, and many taxpayers were not sufficiently impressed with the fact that an item to be deductible under this broad classification must be ordinary and necessary. To be "ordinary and necessary" it must be fair and reasonable; it must have a business purpose that can be fully justified in connection with the business affairs of the corporation. Throughout World War II when corporations were enjoying unusually high income, subject to the highest rates of taxation ever known in this country, and furthermore, subject to renegotiation of war-contract income if the profit seemed unreasonably high, various taxpayers began to look upon the so-called "ordinary and necessary" expenses as costing the corporation very little money. "Ten-cent dollars," "fifteen-cent dollars," and "twenty-five cent dollars" became the talk of the day among the ordinary businessmen engaged in entertaining and traveling. And, even though it is a sad commentary on the businessmen, extravagances were readily condoned.

It is important to note that any deduction which is, directly or indirectly, in the nature of compensation, must pass all of the following tests:

(1) The item must have accrued or been paid.

(2) It must be ordinary and necessary for the corporation.

(3) It must be reasonable in amount.

The requirement of reasonableness is specifically in the law. As noted above, lack of substantiating records can be costly; the courts have evolved the theory that, even when they recognize the propriety of a deduction, inadequate support requires leaning heavily against the taxpayer. As mentioned previously, Section 274 of the Revenue Act of 1962 drastically restricts the abuse of corporate expenses for travel, entertainment, and business gifts. Flagrant abuses of corporate expenditures were curbed by the Act in four major areas: Entertainment activities and facilities must be shown as being directly related to the business activity and must be used primarily to further the trade or business of the taxpayer. (With the abolition of the Cohan Rule, a new era of strict record keeping and substantiation of expenses has been ushered in.) If an executive travels, definite allocations must be made between business and pleasure parts of the trip. Strict record keeping of time will be necessary. Finally in the area of business gifts, a deduction will be allowed for business gifts with a maximum amount of $25 per person per year.

Corporations which still persist in the loose handling of entertainment and traveling expenses and miscellaneous items of that nature, despite the provisions of Section 274, are almost certain to have a sad awakening when their tax returns are examined. To the present date, it has been a not uncommon occurrence for the corporate executives, especially of smaller concerns, to incur certain expenses for which they do not seek reimbursement from the company, but deduct the expenses from their own personal tax returns. There have been decisions that such deductions by the individual cannot be sustained unless it be proved that the individual was working under a fixed compensation that contemplated the spending of part of that compensation on behalf of the company.

Travel and entertainment accounts of corporations have always been an object of careful scrutiny and review by the field agent. It is in this area that many tax-free benefits were bestowed upon the corporate executive. In certain small closed corporations, disallowances by agents of so-called travel and entertainment expenses have resulted in a tax higher than the amount actually deducted as expense. In these situations, when considering combined Federal and state taxes, both the executive-stockholder and corporation are in a bracket above 50%. Disallowance of the expense to the corporation and a concomitant declaration by the Internal Revenue Service of the amount as a constructive dividend to the executive stockholder, result in a tax dollar assessment higher than the amount originally deducted as an expense.

One way to circumvent this "double tax" is to elect to have the closely held corporation treated as a "Subchapter S" corporation. Since all net income in a "Subchapter S" corporation is taxed to the shareholders, the Internal Revenue Service is automatically estopped from duplicating this charge when an item is disallowed.

It is incumbent upon the management of every corporation to insist that reasonable rules for detailed accounts are observed by everyone, in order that deduction of legitimate expenses truly incurred and necessary in the business may not be jeopardized. Maintenance of a system of internal control and audit, and proof to sustain the ordinary and necessary expenses of the corporation, are factors in connection with the management of any business that cannot be over-emphasized. Inventory valuations, determination of depreciation, allowance for bad debts, and similar major items, none of which can be defined with precise accuracy, are too important to be jeopardized by any looseness in the handling of ordinary and necessary expenses that might in themselves cast suspicion on the integrity of the entire bookkeeping system of the corporation.

Under this caption, attention must be directed to what is a fair and reasonable compensation for the individual. In years gone by, officers' salaries, especially when they appeared high in relation to the size of the business, have frequently been challenged by the Internal Revenue Service. More recently, it has extended this challenge to the amounts paid to lower officers and sometimes to the ordinary salaried clerk. It is necessary, therefore, that a reasonably good basis of appraising salaries be established, and that proof can be furnished showing that no person in the organization is paid compensation higher than can be truly justified. Small concerns that pay high salaries only during periods when making high incomes, which are subject to high tax rates, are extremely vulnerable in this regard. If higher salaries are to be paid during periods of proportionately higher profits, then reasonable care should be exercised to show that the procedure followed is in keeping with tax regulations. (See EXECUTIVE COMPENSATION.)

For the deduction of ordinary and necessary expenses, and for other deductions specifically authorized by statute, it must be borne in mind that one who claims a deduction for tax purposes must bring himself within the precise terms of the statutory provision and consistent regulations relating thereto.

It frequently happens that failure to meet some minor provisions in the law or regulations disqualifies a deduction of major importance. Thus, the man in charge of taxation for the corporation must see to it that other executives are properly informed regarding all special requirements in connection with tax deductions.

Company payments to pension trusts and retirement plans are deductible as ordinary and necessary expenses, upon compliance with regulations, even though the employee is not required to pay income tax on the amount deposited in the retirement plans at the time of deposit.

FEDERAL TAXATION—IMPORTANT SPECIFIC PHASES

The penalty tax on improper accumulation of surplus has received widespread attention from businessmen.

Surtax on Corporations Improperly Accumulating Surplus. I.R.C. Section 531, Surtax on Corporations Improperly Accumulating Surplus, and its counterpart in prior Federal income tax legislation back to 1913, were enacted for the sole purpose of discouraging the unnecessary retention of accumulated earnings in the hands of the corporation in cases where it is obvious that retention is motivated by a desire to avoid the imposition of income tax on dividends to the shareholders. Earnings are retained by permitting earnings (profits) to accumulate instead of being distributed to shareholders as taxable dividends. The penalty tax rates provided in this section are 27½% of the accumulated taxable income not in excess of $100,000, plus 38½% of the accumulated taxable income in excess of $100,000.

The tax law does not, and perhaps could not, define the term "improper accumulation of surplus" in any other than a very broad sense. It does set up a certain legislative presumption; namely, that in the absence of proof to the contrary, any accumulation in excess of the apparent needs of the corporation shall be deemed to be for the purpose of preventing the imposition of taxes upon the shareholders. However, it is clear that, even though the amount of the surplus is such as to cause the legislative presumption to apply, the corporation is not subject to the penalty tax if it proves that the accumulation is not for the purpose of gaining a tax advantage for the shareholders.

Many corporations resort to elaborate "window dressing" in the way of verbose statements in the minutes and the adoption of numerous resolutions, etc., altogether out of keeping with the common practice of such corporations. It would seem that this may in itself act as a boomerang, in that, by laboring the point of proof and the establishment of so-called documentary evidence, those corporations may find themselves in a prejudicial position. Thus, it would seem that any corporation justifiably retaining profits and earnings in order to finance its plans for the future should find some simple and easy method of preserving the necessary proof. However, the necessity for unostentatious proof cannot be overemphasized. In many cases, the minutes act as a silent witness for and against the company.

Numerous schemes are suggested for legal methods that might avoid the imposition of the tax on accumulated surplus. It has been suggested that, in organizing a new company which would normally be financed by common stock, the stockholders might take a limited amount of common stock, some debenture bonds, some preferred stock, etc., and then establish a financial program for the redemption of bonds and preferred stock out of accumulated surplus. Such a program might leave little or no surplus available for ordinary dividends. It should not be overlooked that the law specifically relates to a corporation which "created or organized, is formed or availed of for the purpose of preventing the imposition of the surtax upon its shareholders," and, further, that the word "purpose" is emphasized in the regulations. While it is true that it is legal, as well as good management, so to handle the affairs of the taxpayer as to incur the lowest tax liability, it must not be overlooked that, under current regulations, supported by court decisions, whatever is done requires justification by business reasons.

Whether the corporation operates on a cash basis or an accrual basis is a matter of election. Here it may appropriately be stated that, so far as Section 531 is concerned, it would seem that a corporation operating on an accrual basis would have a distinct advantage in establishing that its distributions meet the requirements of Section 531.

A new and growing company should find it less difficult to prove the necessity for retained earnings than the old and well-established concern. Of the companies of the latter type, those having a steady earning record should perhaps find it more difficult to establish the need for retaining a significant portion of earnings than those subject to cyclical conditions.

Retirement Plans. Formalized retirement plans of mutual advantage to employees and employer alike must rest upon a solid foundation of basic business considerations. If the plan can be justified by advantage-expectancies without any thought of tax savings, it is most likely to survive the usual run of business uncertainties. Given the premise that a retirement plan involving a definite formula for predetermining some precise retirement allowance and procedure can be justified by sound business consideration, then and then only, should the integration of tax considerations come into play in determining what details and what formal procedure will best serve the combined interest of the employer and employees.

Most corporations have sufficient resources and expect to remain in business long enough to show a proper economic justification for adopting a formal plan providing financial security for superannuated employees under a procedure that calls for current funding (or current cost) out of the business results from current employment. A reservation, in a formal plan, that permits change or discontinuance when future conditions so require will not signify lack of performance from the Treasury Department's point of view if it is clearly indicated that the change or discontinuance will not cause payments previously made for the account of employees to be diverted for the use of the employer. The effects of the Employee Retirement Income Security Act of 1974 (ERISA) must be considered prior to the implementation of a retirement plan or any employee benefit plan. (See RETIREMENT PLANS.)

The Depreciation Recapture Rule. In 1942, Section 117(j), now known as Section 1231, was enacted which provided that if a taxpayer realized a net gain from sales or exchanges of certain depreciable property used in his trade or business, such net gain would be treated as a long term capital gain, so long as the property was owned for more than the time period necessary to qualify for long-term capital gain treatment. However, if the taxpayer realized a net loss, the net loss would be treated as an ordinary loss. The Treasury Department has felt for many years that this was a means of tax avoidance and that consequently it should be eliminated. It was Treasury Department's belief that gain on the disposition of real and personal depreciable property should be taxed as ordinary income to the extent of the depreciation deducted by the taxpayer in prior periods.

A portion of this proposal was accepted by Congress and enacted in the Revenue Act of 1962, and is now called Section 1245. This Section considerably restricts the application of Section 1231 with the exception of Real Property.

A general examination of this Section indicates that if any 1245 property is disposed of in any manner, the gain up to the amount allowed or allowable previously as a deduction for depreciation or authorization will be classified as ordinary income (but not over the amount realized).

Two facts immediately become evident. Amounts which previously were taxed as capital gains via Section 1231, now may be converted into ordinary income. Basically it affects depreciation or amortization claimed after December 31, 1961, and it includes all personal property tangible and intangible, and also includes certain other tangible property which under certain state laws may have been considered a part of realty. Secondly, it superimposes its powers over other Sections of the Code which provide for non-recognition of gain. This is evident in Section 333, on one month corporate liquidations where in certain situations distributions by corporations previously would not result in taxable income to the corporation or the shareholders. By virtue of this new Section any property distributed classified as Section 1245 property would thus be considered as creating taxable income to the corporation. Other non-recognition of gain Sections, such as 311 and 336, are also affected.

This depreciation recapture rule in effect prevents corporate taxpayers from quickly writing off an asset at high income tax rates of 46% and then selling the property and reporting the gain at a lower capital gain rate. Under this rule, for all property acquired after 1961, and depreciated, any gain on its disposition will, up to the amount of depreciation taken, automatically result in ordinary income.

The Revenue Act of 1964 enacted Code Section 1250, which prevented the conversion of ordinary income into capital gains by taking accelerated depreciation on commercial real property. At the time of sale the accelerated portion of depreciation over straight line depreciation is considered ordinary income. Different formulas for computing the accelerated portion of depreciation are found in the Internal Revenue Code based on the holding period of the property disposed of. In addition, if the real property was held for less than one year, the entire amount of depreciation taken was considered as ordinary income.

Public Law 91-172, the Tax Reform Act of 1969, dealt a tremendous financial blow to investors involved in commercial real property. Congress severely restricted the use of accelerated depreciation on commercial real property and greatly increased the amounts of depreciation to be recaptured. A Senate report indicated that this avenue of "a fast buck" should be closed. The new act permits the use of 200% declining balance and the sum of the years digits method by those investors involved in new residential property. In addition, to provide a stimulant for low income rental housing, Congress further provided that depreciation based on a straight line writeoff of sixty months could be used in this area. All other new real property was limited to a maximum of 150% declining balance method. (See DEPRECIATION.)

Other Changes Re. Depreciation. The corporate executive should realize that every effort is under way by the Treasury Department to close loopholes which provide for the loss of revenue. An example of this is evidenced in Revenue Ruling 62–92, which provided that if the adjusted basis of a depreciable asset at the beginning of the taxable year is lower than the sale price of this asset at any time during the year, then the depreciation in the year of the sale will be disallowed. In effect an automatic adjustment is made for a change in salvage value, which the Department says should be adjusted annually to conform with current market values.

Revenue Procedure 62-21 represents one of the most significant developments in Federal income tax law. It embodies basic reforms in the standards and procedures used for the determination of depreciation for tax purposes. Guidelines have been established for broad classes of assets, in an effort to liberalize depreciation by shortening the useful lives of such classes. These guidelines replace Bulletin F, now obsolete, which formerly covered some 5,000 separate items.

Business units, if they choose to use a guideline class life, must now include in that class all of the items which are covered by the description of that class, irrespective of the differences in useful lives among those items covered. Strong emphasis is laid on the broad class approach rather than the utilization of an item-by-item measurement.

A common example used to amplify the broad class approach is that of the hotel industry. All hotel equipment is now covered by a guideline term of ten years, whereas under Bulletin F, there were eighteen specified lives for equipment used in hotels, ranging from six years on blankets and spreading to twenty years for fire alarm and prevention equipment.

The business executive should be aware of the fact that the use of these guidelines is optional. Justification of a shorter useful life period will permit a quicker writeoff by the corporation than the time limit set up by the guidelines. It is therefore, incumbent upon the firm to maintain accurate depreciation records in order to set an experience factor which may provide a shorter life than the guidelines.

As usual, whenever the economy slows down, the Executive Branch of the Government attempts to fill the vacuum partially with additional tax incentives. New depreciation regulations were filed on June 22, 1971, which give businessmen a very unusual opportunity greatly to increase their depreciation writeoffs and consequently reduce taxes. It represents a brand new theory of depreciation. These new regulations pertain to machinery and equipment that is physically placed into service during 1971 and future years.

Many tax advantages appear to flow from these new regulations, which are keyed into the guidelines mentioned above. Whatever the guideline may be for a particular class of machinery, the taxpayer will have the chance of electing from a range of 20% above to 20% below the guideline established by the Service. This choice may be teamed with the use of a full year's writeoff if the asset was put into service during the first half of the year, or a one-half year writeoff if the asset is placed into use during the last half of the year.

A further advantage gained is that if the taxpayer elects to utilize the Asset Depreciation Range System (ADR), the taxpayer will not be questioned by the Service for the duration of the asset's useful life. Benefits are also available when repairs of considerable magnitude occur. If the taxpayer elects to use the Guideline Repair allowance percentage for computation of his repairs, he is also protected from challenge by the Service.

The Tax Reform Act of 1969. This Act has been called by many people the most complicated tax act in the history of our country. Effective dates of the Act's provisions range from the early part of 1969 to 1975.

Controlled corporations lost major benefits inasmuch as multiple surtax exemptions and multiple accumulated earnings credits were phased. The compression for tax purposes of controlled corporations into a single corporation after 1974 greatly reduces the desirability of establishing additional corporations within a controlled group. In addition, the Act for the first time made the provision for a carryback of capital losses by a corporation to the three preceding years prior to the loss year. The five year carryforward provision for capital losses was not changed.

The law greatly affected shareholders of Subchapter S corporations, as new restrictions were placed on employee benefit plans of these types of corporations. Contributions made on behalf of shareholder employees owning more than 5% of the corporation's stock were limited. In addition, any forfeitures arising from the termination of employment of any covered employee cannot inure to the benefit of such shareholder employee.

Time of Deductibility of Contested Taxes. In computing tax liability, corporations are entitled to deduct state and local taxes, and, in fact, almost all taxes other than Federal income tax itself. However, the deductibility of any item of expense, if accrued but not paid, hinges entirely upon whether or not the liability for the payment definitely existed in the year in which the deduction is taken. The Supreme Court has held that unpaid state tax may not be accrued and deducted on a Federal income tax return as long as liability for such tax is being contested. If a corporation is assessed a certain state or local tax and it believes the assessment to be invalid and decides to contest payment, the mere step taken to avoid payment of the tax at time of assessment is regarded by the Treasury Department as indicative of indefiniteness. Therefore, if the taxpayer should fight the case for three years and lose and then pay the tax, the liability would be deductible only in the year in which it was definitely settled.

Payments Against Public Policy. In determining whether or not an item is deductible as an ordinary and necessary expense, the corporation must recognize the dangers inherent in connection with an expenditure which might be viewed as contrary to public policy.

In securing or carrying out business contracts with a governmental agency, even though in normal times competitive bidding is required, it is not uncommon to pay commissions to the person who procures the contract. During World War II, several deductons for such commissions were disallowed, the contention of the Commissioner being that the person to whom the commissions were paid used his personal influence with the Government; and that, in itself, is contrary to public policy. Where it is clear that the agent receiving commissions used no improper influence but does render a service, of course, the expense is an allowable deduction. It is in connection with these, however, that the taxpayer should be extremely careful.

Under current law, certain donations are deductible to a limited extent out of the corporation's income, and it seems quite clear that contributions are prohibited for any activity to influence the enactment of specific legislation, unless it appears that the contributions are not made for the purpose of, or with a reasonable expectation of, deriving business benefit therefrom. Obviously, contributions and dues to trade associations and, in general, to organizations that specifically benefit the corporation fall within the definition of "ordinary and necessary" expenses. These may be deducted, regardless of the limitation placed on contributions for charitable purposes, if it can be demonstrated that the expenditure falls within the rule of a reasonable expectation of a specific benefit accruing to the corporation.

By statutes other than those relating to taxation, contributions by a corporation to political campaigns are expressly prohibited. Political contributions and other questionable payments and slush funds maintained by corporations have been high on the Internal Revenue Service's audit list.

Minimum Taxes on Tax Preference Add-on Minimum Tax. The new add-on minimum tax on items of tax preferences has proved to be a vehicle for the Internal Revenue Service's attack on tax shelters. This new tax affects both individuals and the business taxpayer. If the taxpayer has items of tax preference, he (or a business) can pay an income tax even though the results from the business operations for the accounting period was a loss. Items of tax preference include certain portions of accelerated depreciation, and percentage depletion in excess of cost depletion, to name two.

In addition to the add-on minimum tax discussed above, individuals, estates, and trusts may be liable for an additional minimum tax called the "alternative minimum tax." This additional tax is imposed only to the extent that it exceeds the sum of (1) the taxpayer's income tax liability and (2) the taxpayer's add-on minimum tax.

These new taxes have made consultation with the company's tax department ever more important.

Employer's Withholding of Employees' Taxes. Since Social Security legislation has been in effect, the employees' tax in this respect has been required to be withheld by the employer and periodically paid over the Federal Treasury. Beginning with the "pay-as-you-go" tax act in 1943, employers have been required to withhold, at regular prescribed percentage rates, a portion or all of the employees' current Federal income tax liability. There are minor exceptions wherein no withholding is required for certain types of employment and certain sizes of organizations, but these will not be detailed here.

It is clear that any amounts withheld from employees' salaries or wages are held in trust, pending the time those amounts are paid by the employer to the Federal Treasury. Such amounts of money definitely do not belong to the employer. However, the average concern allows this money to become commingled with the general funds of the organization. There is no specific requirement that the amount withheld be deposited in a separate fund, for the account of the Government. Unless these funds, however, are kept in a separate account, it is absolutely necessary that the treasurer of the corporation have up-to-date information at all times as to the amount of his cash balance that actually represents employees' funds payable to the Federal Government.

Originally the quarterly reports and the payroll tax monies were remitted to the Government at the end of the first month following the close of the calendar quarter. The law was changed after the Treasury Department suffered large losses because many companies used these trust funds for payment of regular business liabilities and subsequently entered bankruptcy.

Today, businesses are required to remit employment taxes to the Government periodically. In some instances, remittances are required weekly. By this method, the Treasury Department has checked to a large degree the losses suffered in previous periods. The Treasury now receives the money much earlier, and this procedure in many cases has prevented any further loss on the Treasury's part. Failure to comply with this rule results in a penalty and the possibility of a monthly reporting form on wages, in addition to early remittances.

Many states have also adopted a withholding procedure similar to the one instituted by the Treasury. However, in most cases, the employer does not remit any funds until the last day of the first month following the end of the calendar quarter. Evidence is rapidly gathering that many of the states soon will switch over to the Federal method to ensure an early receipt of the funds and also to preclude possible losses.

State and Local Taxation

States are primary sovereign bodies with inherent taxing powers limited only by the prohibitions of the Constitution of the United States, plus the limitations established by each of the state constitutions. The prohibitions imposed by the law have been generally summarized by authorities as follows:

(1) The states may not exact import or export duties.

(2) The states may not collect tonnage taxes.

(3) Federal treaties cannot be interfered with by state taxes.

(4) The states may not impose tax laws impairing contractual obligations.

(5) The states may not impose tax laws interfering with privileges and immunities guaranteed to citizens of all states.

(6) The states may not pass tax laws having the effect of depriving any person of life, liberty, or property without due process of law.

(7) No state tax shall deny to any person the equal protection of the laws.

(8) The states may not tax property or instrumentalities of the Federal Government.

(9) The states may not, through taxation, burden or regulate interstate commerce.

Only the first two of the foregoing limitations are expressly stated in the actual wording of the Constitution. The remaining prohibitions are largely the outgrowth of case law and legal interpretation, and it seems appropriate to mention that for a period of years extreme confusion has existed, primarily because the courts have shifted their position several times.

To the average businessman, prohibition 5 is significant. Section 2 of Article 4 of the Constitution of the United States provides in substance that citizens of each state shall be entitled to all the privileges and immunities of the citizens of the several states—the United States. For instance, an individual may go into a state in which he is a nonresident to sell his wares, and the state is prohibited from taxing his activities at any higher rate than would apply to the same activity if carried on by a local resident. However, a corporation does not enjoy the same protection as individuals in states other than the particular state in which it is incorporated. Thus, states are not prohibited from taxing foreign corporations differently or at higher rates than their laws may prescribe for domestic corporations.

Situs. A vast amount of legislation has resulted from the wording of the 14th Amendment to the Constitution, which, in effect, provides that no state shall deprive any person of life, liberty, or property, "without due process of law." The legal interpretation that has been placed upon this limitation (prohibition 6) clearly defines a tax to be confiscatory if, for instance, local property (ad valorem taxes) is subject to a higher basis of assessment, or to a higher rate of taxation, in case of the nonresident, than is applicable to the resident.

However, when it comes to levying a tax on intangible assets, the courts have been compelled to establish a legal fiction of *situs.* Situs, as defined by the courts, is merely the court's own interpretation of "legal location" of the particular intangible property in question, and the result is that an intangible item may have more than one situs, meaning that it may be legally situated in more than one taxing jurisdiction, and, as a result, subject to more than one tax. Double situs is common, and in the case of a corporation's capital stock it is possible that the stock may be subject to a triple tax because:

(1) The corporation is subject to a taxable situs in the state where organized.

(2) The owner of the share capital is subject

to situs at the place of his domicile for the particular capital stock.

(3) To the extent that the business assets (underlying the capital stock of the corporation) are situated in another state they may be thus taxed as local property in a third state.

With regard to tangible property, the courts hold that only one situs—the state wherein it is located and permanently used in business—is the controlling factor.

Interstate and Intrastate Commerce. It is Item 9, "interstate and foreign commerce limitations," that concerns the businessman more than any other. State governments are constitutionally forbidden to impose a burden on interstate commerce, but what becomes a burden as a matter of law, will be developed later on. It should be borne in mind that the doctrine of the division of Federal and state powers, as interpreted by the Federal courts, has implied considerable limitations upon the rights of states to tax in this area. It would seem that any state or local tax law is unconstitutional which directly or indirectly effects a discrimination against interstate or foreign commerce as a business, or against goods brought in from another state. Furthermore, it would seem that there are limitations on the levying even of non-discriminating taxes upon interstate commerce or property used in interstate commerce. Articles of interstate commerce not yet having arrived at final destination, even though temporarily located in the state, are not subject to local property taxes in the state unless the corporation is a resident thereof.

In regard to state taxation of income resulting from interstate business, as distinguished from a direct tax on the business activity, the income derived is held to be too far removed from the act of commerce for a state income tax thereon to be considered a burden on interstate commerce. However, income taxation on a multiple or interstate and intrastate business may be imposed by a state provided there is some intrastate business or that the state in question has given the particular corporation the right to do business. Thus, no state is empowered to tax the income of out-of-state corporations unless there is some intrastate business or the corporation has qualified to do business in the state and is subject to the tax laws of the state. More will be said later on about the danger that results from actually "doing business" in a state without having qualified and without having paid the entrance fees as well as other required taxes resulting from "doing business."

Further discussion under this heading divides itself into two main categories: (1) income, sales, license, and miscellaneous taxes that result from business transactions; and (2) property taxes that result from having taxable property with a taxable situs within a given taxable jurisdiction. There are comparatively few problems in the latter category, other than the proper determination of the assessed value of the property, and what is not subject to the tax rates.

Miscellaneous taxes that result from business transactions, as distinguished from ad valorem taxes, present a great maze of complexities, depending upon the states, or the number of states, in which the product or service of the corporation is produced and sold. There are literally thousands of state and local tax statutes affecting everyday business transactions conducted on a national scale. In order that the businessman may have an elementary concept of this problem, he should understand that in the matter of sales which may involve any one of the numerous state or local taxes, it is necessary to distinguish between those sales referred to as Interstate Commerce, and those referred to as Intrastate Commerce.

Interstate commerce means commerce between two or more states, where goods may be shipped from one state to a customer in another state; *intrastate commerce* means sales transactions that are completed, or substantially completed, within the bounds of the particular state involved. The courts have taken into consideration numerous factors concerning intrastate sales, to determine whether or not the transaction is substantially completed within the state. A fundamental consideration here, previously referred to in brief, is the limitation of taxes on interstate commerce by the Constitution itself. The immunity normally granted to interstate commerce is based upon the "commerce clause" (Article 1, Section 8) of the Constitution, which gives to Congress the power to "regulate commerce with foreign nations and among the several states" and which, in effect, places interstate business beyond the control or regulation of the state.

Difficulty with respect to taxation arises in connection with the courts' decisions concerning a burden on interstate commerce, or a regulation of interstate commerce by any state or local taxing jurisdiction. Some years ago, it was commonly thought that any state or local tax on an interstate sale would be a burden on that sale by the local jurisdiction, which is plainly prohibited by the Constitution. However, the courts have held, for instance, that a sales tax imposed by a local government under certain conditions on an interstate shipment is not a burden in a broad sense of the word.

For example, it has been held that a sales tax might be imposed upon an interstate shipment and not be a burden on interstate sale, provided the tax burden is by statute imposed upon the customer. If it can be demonstrated, therefore, that the customer does not suffer through having the particular interstate transaction taxed, the immunity guaranteed by the "commerce clause" is not involved. A customer in New York City purchasing goods from a supplier in Pennsylvania might be required to pay a tax on that purchase (a sales tax) equal to the tax the customer would have to pay were he buying from a local New York City distributor. Furthermore, it has been held that the out-of-state supplier may be required to collect the tax from the customer and to pay it to the New York City tax authorities. This, of course, is not a tax on the supplier, and therefore, is not a tax on interstate commerce. It would seem that the fine distinction drawn here depends upon whether the burden of the tax legally falls on the buyer or the seller.

Many states that have local sales-tax laws also have enacted use-tax laws as compensatory to the tax burden on local buyers from local suppliers, and, for administrative purposes, have required that the out-of-state sellers collect the tax and remit it to the local collector. These statutes have been contested by out-of-state suppliers on the ground that the trouble of collection is a burden on interstate commerce. So far the courts have not considered that burden (trouble of collection) of sufficient consequence to classify the particular taxing statute as being prohibited by the limitation of the "commerce clause."

The question of inter- and intrastate sales, however, has far greater significance in connection with:

(1) Subjecting the selling corporation to state income or franchise taxes.

(2) Subjecting the selling corporation to the necessity of qualifying to do business in the particular state where the customer resides.

(3) Subjecting the corporation to various license taxes.

(4) Subjecting the corporation to unemployment taxes, compensation insurance, etc., to the extent that agents or traveling employees may be involved.

"Doing Business." What constitutes doing business in the state is extremely vague. It is impossible to lay down any general rule that would serve as a guide in this determination. However, there are some broad considerations that usually serve as guides in connection with normal business. For instance, the mere solicitation of orders by a traveling salesman in a state to which the goods are to be shipped from a point without the state, the orders being accepted at a point without the state, is not generally regarded as "doing business." However, if the salesman has power to complete binding contracts, or if the salesman makes collections, or if there are carried into the state certain stocks or merchandise from which the orders may be shipped, then, of course, the corporation is getting close to the borderline of "doing business." It is extremely dangerous to continue such procedure without having the peculiar statutes of the state thoroughly examined, and receiving competent tax advice upon the necessity of qualifying and paying the local tax required or possibly modifying the method of business activity.

Perhaps one of the most difficult matters to determine is the amount of business done in a state under the concept of "doing business" when a company has qualified to do business there and does maintain, say, a branch or a warehouse within the state. Obviously, if a corporation has a branch in that state (other than that of its home office) it will be considered to be doing business there. The usual procedure in connection with state income and franchise taxes is the allocation of a portion of the income, or a portion of the net worth (whichever is the basis of the tax to the state involved) based on numerous considerations, such as the amount of property in the state, the amount of wages and salaries paid within the state, and similar matters. It is impossible to outline here the peculiar requirements, generally known as the allocating factors, which are applied in the various states. However, it should be pointed out that the maintenance of adequate records to prove what falls within and without the factor allocating to the particular state is a major consideration.

Many years ago, when tabulating and mechanical bookkeeping devices were first used extensively, it was found by a number of corporations that the ease of tabulating and proving the categories of all sales saved enough franchise, income, and local sales taxes to pay the entire cost of the tabulating equipment. The developments in electronic equipment present even greater advantages.

Many of the states have sales-tax laws applicable to retail transactions, and many corporations that do engage primarily in wholesale transactions have some transactions falling within the definition of a retail sale. Here it is necessary to analyze and prove which transaction came within which category; not infrequently, when the tax returns are properly filed, the actual amount of retail taxes owed by the corporation are of less consequence than the cost of labor involved in preparing the tax return in the first instance. The immediate question arises: Why do this unnecessary work when there is such a small amount of tax involved? The answer to this is clear: Without doing the work to prove that the sales were not subject to tax, the taxing authorities could proceed on the assumption that *all* of the sales are subject to tax, under which condition there might be a staggering burden of retail taxes to be paid.

Those in a corporation charged with meeting the requirements of various taxing jurisdictions should be sufficiently familiar not only with company business, but also with the actual operation of the everyday company business, so as to lay out a procedure for management to follow that would enable securing maximum business with minimum taxes. Certainly, the tax department should not stifle business; if it knows enough about the business, it can usually offer many suggestions to keep taxes to a minimum without seriously interfering with what would normally be the usual method of doing business.

There are a few important factors, however, for corporate executives, other than tax specialists, to keep constantly in mind:

Traveling Salesmen. If the salesman exercises power over and above the mere solicitation of business, such as making a binding contract, collecting cash, or rendering a particular type of service to the customer beyond merely offering to make a direct sale, these transactions could be construed as "doing business." Sometimes the salesman may carry samples and actually fill an order from his sample stock, or he may sell samples, and these activities also may bring the company seriously close to the definition of "doing business." When the salesman follows the goods into the state and renders a service in the way of helping the customer dispose of them, or matters of that kind, he is again treading on dangerous ground.

Consignment Shipments. Where a corporation consigns its goods to an independent dealer in a state other than that of its home office, and the dealer sells the goods to his own customers and remits the price, such transactions are usually held to be strictly interstate commerce. However, if the selling corporation exercises an unusual amount of control over the activities of the consignee, it may be held that the customer is an agent of the corporation and the agent's activities constitute "doing business" on the part of the corporation.

Conditional Sales. Many of the states impose peculiar laws regarding the enforcement of conditional sales; any company engaging in national business with conditional sales contracts should make certain that the peculiar state laws are complied with, or it may find itself subject to taxes and penalties, to say nothing of its being denied the use of the courts for the purpose of enforcing its contracts.

General. For the new corporation starting to engage in a national business wherein its products will be sold through its own selling force in several states, it is imperative that the corporation receive competent advice about the peculiar statutes of the various states, and that it determine in advance the safest course of procedure with respect to taxes that might be imposed by reason of its distribution methods. Furthermore, in the event that the corporation already established in a national business does not have a tax department continually looking after every phase of its tax matters, it should have its entire business procedure reviewed occasionally by competent tax advisors, to see whether or not it should alter its business procedure in the light of newly enacted state tax laws, or new court decisions changing the concept with respect to old statutes. A thorough investigation of this kind once every four or five years might well turn out to be very cheap insurance.

ELI WERLIN, CPA, Professor and Chairman of Accounting, Russell Sage College, Troy, New York; Partner, Urbach, Kahn & Werlin, Certified Public Accountants, Albany, New York.

STEVEN N. FISCHER, CPA, Adjunct Professor, Russell Sage College, Troy, New York; Shareholder, Urbach, Kahn & Werlin, Albany, New York

Information References

(The foregoing discussion follows the treatment in Oliver, J. W., "Taxation—A Management Problem," in "Reading Course in Executive Technique," Heyel, C., ed., New York, Funk & Wagnalls, 1948, reviewed and revised by Mr. Werlin for the first and second editions of the Encyclopedia, and reviewed and revised by Mr. Fischer for this edition.

Tax Services:

"Standard Federal Tax Reporter," Commerce Clearing House, New York.
"Federal Tax Service," Prentice-Hall, New York.
"Tax Ideas," Prentice-Hall, New York.

Periodicals:

Taxes—The Tax Magazine (Commerce Clearing House, New York)

Cross References: *Taxation: Organization for; Tests for Employment.*

TAXATION: Organization for

The question as to when a corporation is large enough to justify a separate tax department cannot be answered, except in small degree and in generalities, and certainly the matter of size is not always the determining factor. A corporation doing business from a single plant, handling all of its executive and sales activities from the plant, and not having to meet the requirements of other than one state (Federal tax matters being understood) may be several times as large in actual size, that is, in capital, output, and volume, than some other corporation which must have a separate tax department devoted exclusively to handling tax problems and keeping management properly informed of the alternative methods of doing business that may entail the lowest tax liability. However, the smaller the business, the more important it is that its tax problems be reviewed by professional accountants or lawyers. It is obvious that the employee of the small firm who handles tax matters as a side issue is so burdened with other duties as to prevent his keeping well posted on tax law and regulations.

As for the single-plant corporation with all transactions being consummated in the state where the head office is located, it may be that the treasurer, the controller, or some other corporate official will understand the operation of tax law sufficiently to handle the major portion of routine matters, but here again it must be emphasized that, for the same reason applicable to the small business, there is greater necessity for the outside adviser, lawyer, or accountant to review carefully the returns and procedure with respect to the handling of tax matters.

To the extent that the corporation is larger, or more involved in various Federal and state tax requirements, a separate tax department is justified; but in no instance does the corporation ever reach the point where it will have a tax department headed by such a staff of experts as never to require outside assistance.

The outside lawyer or accountant whose advice is being sought can usually render better service to the corporation through contact with a properly established tax department than would be the case if the consultations were between the lawyer or accountant and the president, treasurer, controller (assuming that these men are not tax students) or such other officials as might see fit to discuss these problems.

To whom should the head of the tax department report in the ordinary management chart? This, again, is unanswerable, except in general terms. It is absolutely mandatory for the success of the corporation and the tax department that the person in charge of the tax procedure of the corporation should either be a part of top management or report to one of the principal officers of the company. In some corporations, the head of the tax department reports directly to the president. In many instances, the tax department is a separate division of the accounting department, and reports to the controller. This is ideal only if the controller himself is a man who takes a considerable interest in taxes, or has had training in that field. To ensure that the management is kept constantly abreast of the tax situation and that the man charged with administering tax procedure is kept abreast of the corporation, the most nearly ideal situation is for the head of the tax department to be not only one of the top management but actually a member of the board of directors.

Tax Department Functions. The function of the tax department differs in various corporations. In some of the larger concerns in America, the tax department has complete jurisdiction over the handling of all tax matters, from the assessment of local property taxes upon every taxable item of the corporation throughout the country up to and including the handling of corporate Federal income tax returns. In others, the tax department concerns itself primarily with income taxes and business taxes as distinguished from *ad valorem* taxes, leaving to the local operating manager in residence the problems of contact with the local accessor and such discussions as result from proposed assessments for local property taxes. With the passage of time, however, the tendency has been more and more for the successful corporations to have all tax matters handled exclusively by one department at executive headquarters, where there is no divided responsibility and there is no room for passing the buck.

In connection with local property taxes, some companies have found that their *ad valorem* tax problems are so varied and so great as to require a separate department that does nothing but handle that type of tax problem. Where the properties are widely distributed, it may be that the *ad valorem* tax problems are so extensive that an *ad valorem* tax department is justified because there is enough work to keep a certain number of property tax specialists busy with that problem alone, and this specialization more definitely fixes responsibility among those most capable of looking after the peculiar phases of the situation. The routine of tax assessment and the protesting of tax assessments prior to definite dates when *ad valorem* returns will be established is so different from that of handling normal income tax procedure as to justify under certain conditions an *ad valorem* tax department.

In reviewing the procedure of several of the leading corporations, it has been found that the one item of taxation which in many cases is an exception to the foregoing relates to payroll taxes, such as social security and unemployment. It is not infrequent that those in charge of payrolls, personnel divisions, etc., will look after these details and, with the help of the accounting department, file the necessary reports.

Whether the tax department be simply a division of the accounting department or a self-contained department with a separate staff head, it is necessary that its personnel be made up of students of taxation who have the proper personal characterisitcs to deal with public officials. In negotiations leading to the settlement of tax liabilities, the problems of the tax department are somewhat akin to the problems of public relations. Most of the advantageous tax settlements are made through negotiations around the conference table, and seldom by court action. A corporate representative who can sell his ideas to the local assessor or to the tax examiner (assuming, of course, that he has a reasonable amount of facts and law in his favor) can, in the initial stage, accomplish more than a dozen lawyers. This is not to belittle the lawyer. This same corporate representative, when he reaches the point where he must litigate, must turn to the lawyer for assistance, but some of the most important tax cases won in the courts result from the excellent prehandling of the material and the preparation of the facts, which a good corporate tax representative can do most successfully.

Whether a lawyer or an accountant should head a tax department depends on a number of factors. If it is largely a matter of income tax (which is based on accounting results) that takes up the time of the department, it would seem that an accountant well trained in income tax procedure might be better suited to head the department than a lawyer. On the other hand, with a corporation whose activities spread to so many fields that there is a maze of legal complexities with which the tax department must deal, perhaps the lawyer is the one better suited to head the tax department. In the very large corporations, tax departments may consist of lawyers, accountants, engineers, actuaries, and economists—all of whom are aided by an array of technical assistants.

It is necessary that a regular tax calendar be established to indicate the dates when the various types of returns are to be filed, when the liabilities are to be paid, and when work invariably should be started in order to meet these deadlines. This calendar should also show dates for filing claims for refunds, protests on assessment of additional taxes, etc. Without such a calendar constantly kept before all members of the tax department, there is grave danger that some return, possibly insignificant with respect to the time required to prepare it, may be overlooked, with a severe penalty imposed upon the corporation as a result of the omission. The controller's department should be provided with the complete tax calendar, and it should receive progress reports at least every quarter showing the status of all unsettled taxes. No matter how good the tax department, the controller is never relieved of his duty in this respect.

The tax department should prepare an unnual budget in detail, based upon its best advance determination of the tax outlays for the ensuing year.

As an aid to management, correct settlement

of current tax liabilities is not in itself the sole basis of judging the effectiveness of a tax department. Pretesting of all future business proposals involving new sales, new production, expansion, creation of subsidiaries, etc., to see that business planning is done on a basis that will involve the least tax liability, is a most important function of the tax department.

Liaison. That the tax department should cooperate with all other departments of the corporation is, of course, axiomatic. However, it is sometimes overlooked that the tax department should take an active part in establishing the particular type of accounting records to be kept and prescribing the kinds of reports which the accounting department must prepare, matters which are commonly regarded as the controller's duties. If the tax department is not consulted in this respect, the controller, who may not be a tax-minded person, may set up the entire accounting procedure in such a way that the required tax information is not obtainable with the minimum accounting effort. Furthermore, the tax department should be in constant touch with other departments so as to help with public speeches, advertising, and similar matters, with the aim of preventing the appearance of statements in the press or in public addresses that might give rise to some tax dispute or to misunderstanding by a government agent.

To ensure best results for the corporation, the tax department, and business in general, the head of a corporation tax department should be active on various tax committees. No tax department head can be successful unless he rises above what would at first glance appear to be problems peculiar to his (her) company. Separate tax laws, complete in themselves, are not written for each of the industries. Thus, a decision in the case of an insurance company may apply with equal advantage to a mining company, and bank tax decisions may govern in deciding a tax problem of an ordinary manufacturing concern. Finally, tax department heads of all companies should recognize their responsibilities in educating the public regarding sound tax laws, and should help in formulating and promoting the type of tax law that will best serve the interest of the country. Corporations that severely restrict their tax departments in this respect are not ensuring the development of tax advisers capable of rendering the most effective aid in the management of the corporation's affairs.

One of the most important functions of the tax department is that of preventing unnecessary tax liabilities. This can be accomplished by pretesting all proposed business procedures as they may relate to taxation before the procedures are made effective. Pretesting embraces selling and manufacturing methods in general, where and when transactions are to take place, as well as proposed corporate rearrangements, acquisitions, disposition of corporate properties, and like matters. A tax dollar saved in the initial state by wise counsel with the operating departments is worth considerably more to the corporation than potential savings that may result from overpaid taxes upon which claims for refund must later be filed. It frequently happens that the tax department can suggest changes which will ensure the lowest tax liability without serious interferences with the intended business objective. And it by no means infrequently happens that certain tax liabilities result solely from technicalities where the tax loss cannot be regained by claims for abatement or for refund. Thus, significant amounts may be irretrievably lost through failure of the tax department to carry out its proper function in the formulation of business policy, details, and plans in connection with the business activity of the corporation.

JOHN W. OLIVER, formerly Senior Vice President, The Linen Thread Company, Inc., New York, New York

Cross References: *Taxation.*

TAYLOR, FREDERICK W.

Frederick Winslow Taylor (1856–1915) American management engineer, "Father of Scientific Management," abandoned plans to study law to begin work as a machine shop apprentice and laborer (1875–78) at the Enterprise Hydraulic Works in Philadelphia. He later joined the Midvale Steel Works, Philadelphia (1878–90), rising to the position of Chief Engineer. After a period (1890–93) as General Manager, Manufacturing Investment Company, Philadelphia, he worked principally as a consulting engineer in management, although he was associated with Bethlehem Steel Company for three years (1898–1901). He spent the last fourteen years of his life working without pay to further scientific management. (For details of his extensive contributions to management, see SCIENTIFIC MANAGEMENT, and SCIENTIFIC

MANAGEMENT: "TAYLORISM.") Most of Taylor's writings were in the form of papers delivered before the American Society of Mechanical Engineers, a monumental contribution being "On the Art of Cutting Metals," 1906. His widely known book, "Principles and Methods of Scientific Management" (Harper & Bros.) appeared in 1911.

Cross References: *Barth, Carl; Emerson, Harrington; Gantt, H. L., Gilbreth, F. B. and Lillian, E. M.; Hathaway, H. K.; Scientific Management; Scientific Management: "Taylorism."*

TEACHING MACHINES, PROGRAMMED INSTRUCTION, AND COMPUTER-AIDED INSTRUCTION

Teaching-Machines, Programmed Instruction, and **Computer-Assisted Instruction (CAI),** represent a major stage in the development of teaching and human learning. They combine traditional learning theory, an advancing engineering technology, and an increasing acceptance of man-machine relationships by business and governmental managements. While much of previously known adult learning theory is involved, the introduction of the "non-human instructor," the teaching machine, programmed text, and computer program brought the application of a number of unused principles. Machine instruction is an evolutionary development for the improvement of employee performance on the job.

Formal Definition. Teaching-machine technology, programmed learning, and CAI are techniques of instructing employees without the presence of a human instructor. The teaching machine is a mechanism or apparatus, possibly a computer system, which presents a lesson consisting of information, actions, or objects in a prescribed sequence. The lesson is understood, learned, and retained by an employee completely without the presence of a human instructor. The *criteria* that distinguish this technology are:

(1) Instruction is provided for without the presence of a human instructor.

(2) The employee learns at his own rate.

(3) The employee receives immediate knowledge of his progress through feedback, and this controls his behavior.

(4) There is a participative, overt interaction or two-way communication between the learner and the machine or program.

(5) The sequence of the lesson is carefully controlled and consistent.

(6) Reinforcement is used to strengthen learning.

The valid statement is often made that the mechanism is not of prime significance, but that the "program" or lesson plan which constitutes the step-by-step teaching points is. However, as computers are utilized, it may be necessary to add an additional criterion to the list:

(7) The teaching machine *software and hardware mix* shapes and controls employee behavior.

History. One of the most important outgrowths of training experience during World War I was the realization that to train effectively, it was first necessary to determine by a careful *analysis* of the work to be done, the skills and information which the employee must be taught [1]. Charles R. Allen is credited with two extremely significant contributions to training methodology which rank with the history-making efforts of Pressey and Skinner. Both of these techniques form the foundation for what is now called "instructional programming." In 1910, Dr. Allen began to formulate a systematic approach to vocational education and training. It was not until 1917 that, as director of education and training of Emergency Fleet Corporation, he could implement his methods of job analysis and the principles of instruction incorporating preparation, presentation, application, and test. In 1918, Dr. Allen's book, "The Instructor, The Man, and The Job," not only established analysis as a necessary prerequisite to effective instruction, but also stated the principles which, in World War II, became known as the "Four-step Method." Of these steps, "presentation" is most interesting because it was generalized in 1941 as ". . . instruct slowly, clearly, completely, and patiently, one point at a time . . . question and repeat . . . make sure the learner really learns" [1]. (See TRAINING-WITHIN-INDUSTRY PROGRAM; ON-THE-JOB TRAINING.)

The Job Instructor Training Program called for one employee or learner to be instructed step-by-step by one supervisor or instructor. This constituted a "man-man" relationship. Industry soon found that the efficiency of the human instructor's communication could be improved by the use of such familiar curriculum materials as the textbook, workbook, and text-workbook which in the trade areas included the operation sheet, job sheet, information sheet, and assignment sheet. Further improvement resulted from the judicious utilization of audiovisual aids or training devices. They were fundamentally *instructor-centered* in the sense that they were aids to the human instructor's communication.

Beginning in 1920, Dr. Sidney L. Pressey developed what became known as teaching machine technology. In 1926, he described the first teaching machine which he used at Ohio State University [2].

An influential voice was added to that of Pressey's in favor of the teaching machine, when in 1954 Dr. Burrus F. Skinner published his famous paper, "The Science of Learning and the Art of Teaching" [3]. Both Pressey and Skinner visualized teaching machine technology as a *method,* a curriculum method in which the device was important but incidental to the curriculum. One might say that the "what" or subject-matter was the content, the "how" or psychological technique was method, and the "way" or machine was the mechanism. This is a *learner-centered* concept, particularly since there is no human instructor, but more significantly because the curriculum is designed around the learning needs of the learner rather than upon the communication needs of the instructor.

The Movement Today. The first published collection of information on teaching machines was in 1956 by Silvern, at which time he referred to them as "pseudo-simulators" [4]. He created this term in an effort to establish an appropriate vocabulary to suit the "total or radical change in thought about training devices." "Pseudo-simulator" applied to "devices which presume to train the learner in skills and knowledge as required by the actual equipment on the job but which . . . [do not] . . . assume the appearance of the man-machine relationship . . . What then can this device be named? It presumes to satisfy the most essential feature of the simulator without resembling the original object." However, it was Galanter's book [5] in 1959 which actually overcame inertia by focusing attention upon the experimental phase and caused the teaching machine and programmed learning movement to pick up momentum. Lumsdaine and Glaser were the first to formalize the movement as editors of the compendium, "Teaching Machines and Programmed Learning" in 1960 [6].

Subsequently, teaching machines and programmed learning emerged from the relative obscurity of the research laboratory and developed into a permanent, reliable method of employee training.

Unfortunately, premature decisions to form companies or to establish divisions or subsidiaries of existing firms to exploit the new technology led to the marketing of untried programs and machines. As a result, by 1962, the mortality rate of program and machine producers was in balance with or slightly in excess of the conception-birth rate.

To introduce an element of stability into the movement by establishing guidelines for producers of materials and users, a Joint Committee on Auto-Instructional Devices and Programs was formed in 1961 by the American Psychological Association, American Educational Research Association, and DAVI-National Education Association. The American Society of Training Directors (now known as the American Society for Training and Development) became affiliated with the Committee in the fall of 1961. The Joint Committee directed its efforts largely to the academic community and, in 1965, published a set of guidelines for the effectiveness of materials [7]. While researchers in human learning tended to accept these recommendations, the publishers who represented commercial interests studiously ignored them. Consequently, a large number of unvalidated or poorly validated programs were marketed. Then, during the period 1964–1966, many firms which had rushed in to capitalize on the market potential sold their divisions and subsidiaries as unprofitable.

The Joint Committee was disbanded upon publication of its recommendations [7], and the National Society for Performance and Instruction (NSPI) now maintains standards for validation.

The Man-Machine Relationship. The fact that a human may learn as the result of exposure to any machine does not attest to the efficacy of a teaching machine environment. A teaching machine is not merely a machine which teaches or communicates—it must operate according to the criteria established for it. Important here is the interaction between man and machine. Overt responses by the learner fall into these modes in the general-purpose teaching machine: (1) multiple-choice (recognition); (2) written-completion (recall); (3) oral-completion (recall). The constructed response in manual form known as the "written-completion" frame or step is a direct outgrowth of Skinner's original work. The constructed response in oral form is referred to as the "oral completion" frame or step and is an outgrowth of early language laboratory experience, coupled with the marriage of the laboratory and the pure teaching machine in 1960 by Silvern.

Exhibit I shows a man-machine model which describes a general-purpose teaching machine. This entire process is characteristic of the man-machine or, better, the learner-teaching machine relationship. Unlike traditional instructor-centered environments, the learner is the only human in the man-machine system, and the system, therefore, is obviously "learner-centered."

A programmed text may be substituted for the machine in the model, and the five steps, with some modification, continue to describe the same fundamental relationship. Because the text format is relatively inexpensive, and publishing houses traditionally have served training and education needs faithfully, a major emphasis was placed on the Crowderian "scrambled book" and various text versions of linear-like Skinnerian programs.

A programmed text may be substituted for the machine in the model, and the five steps, with some modification, continue to describe the same fundamental relationship. Such a text is organized into a *program* or sequence of carefully written, small, logical steps. Each step gives the learner a new piece of information, and may also review instruction given in previous steps. Then it poses a question that calls for a *response* from the learner.

Each step of a programmed text (also called a *frame*), in addition to giving substantive information, asks a question and provides space for the learner to write his response. The step may refer the learner to a page in a supplementary workbook or manual, or to other material, such as film, kit of parts, etc.

Programmed instruction texts conceal the correct answer from the learner until he either turns the page as directed, or slides a masking device with a "window" in it along the page (see Exhibit II). The window is the size of the step, and, when it moves to a new step, it reveals at the same time the correct response to the question posed by the preceding step. This immediately tells the learner whether he is right or wrong. Success reinforces learning; and if he is wrong, the error can quickly be isolated.

Programmed texts using a masking device which reveals one step after another going down a page are said to be "segment vertical."

EXHIBIT I
GENERAL-PURPOSE TEACHING MACHINE (SCHEMATIC)

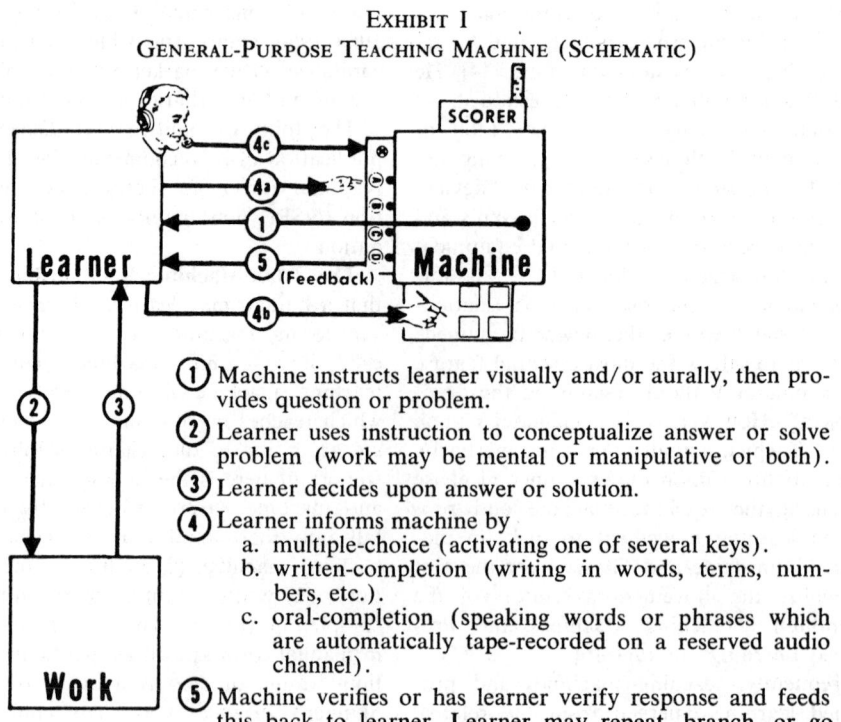

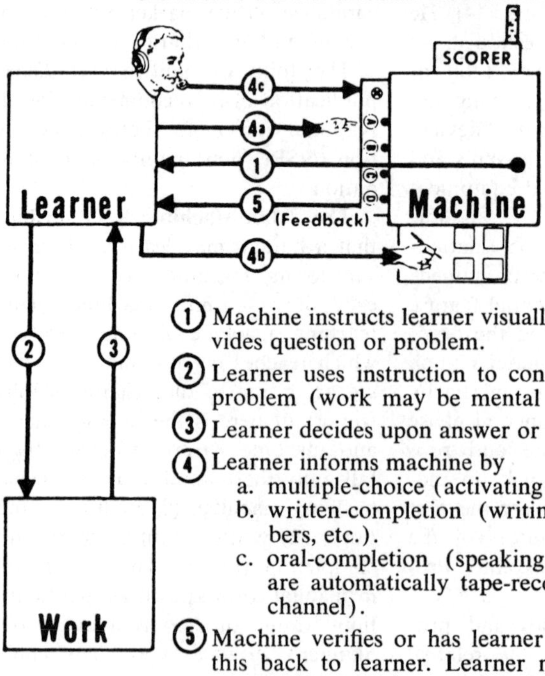

(1) Machine instructs learner visually and/or aurally, then provides question or problem.
(2) Learner uses instruction to conceptualize answer or solve problem (work may be mental or manipulative or both).
(3) Learner decides upon answer or solution.
(4) Learner informs machine by
   a. multiple-choice (activating one of several keys).
   b. written-completion (writing in words, terms, numbers, etc.).
   c. oral-completion (speaking words or phrases which are automatically tape-recorded on a reserved audio channel).
(5) Machine verifies or has learner verify response and feeds this back to learner. Learner may repeat, branch, or go on to the next incremental instruction depending upon curriculum design.

EXHIBIT II

81. The final part of a job is the "put away." This could be:	time spent cleaning up a machine.	finishing the last of the do part.
A	BOTH | A	B | NEITHER

82. John is assigned Job #16. His supervisor spends 4 minutes explaining the job to him. It takes him 8 minutes to go to the tool crib and get a special lathe chuck he needs for Job #16. The chuck takes 3 minutes to install and then he spends the next hour doing the job. When he finishes, John takes the same time to remove the chuck and return it to the tool crib. What is the makeready time for Job #16? __________ What is the do time? __________ What is the putaway time? __________

15 minutes
1 hour, 11 minutes

83. When scheduling any job, a supervisor should break the job down into __________, __________, and __________ time.

make ready, do, put-away

Break each job down into make-ready, do, and put-away time. (2.3)

84. Long make-ready and put-away times can greatly affect a schedule. Time gained by using a fast machine may be offset by a long make-ready or put-away time. Which machine should be used for Job #78?	Machine #9 requires 10 minutes for make-ready, 35 minutes to do the job, and 8 minutes for put-away.	Machine #13 requires 19 minutes for make-ready, 25 minutes to do the job, and 11 minutes for put-away.
A	BOTH | A	B | NEITHER
85. Another important point to watch when scheduling jobs is the number of *change-overs* from job to job. Fewer change-overs mean fewer setups and, therefore, less unproductive time. Which is the more productive schedule?	An employee doing 3 different jobs with setups during an 8-hour shift.	An employee doing the same job with only one setup during an 8-hour shift.
B	BOTH | A	B | NEITHER

2-17

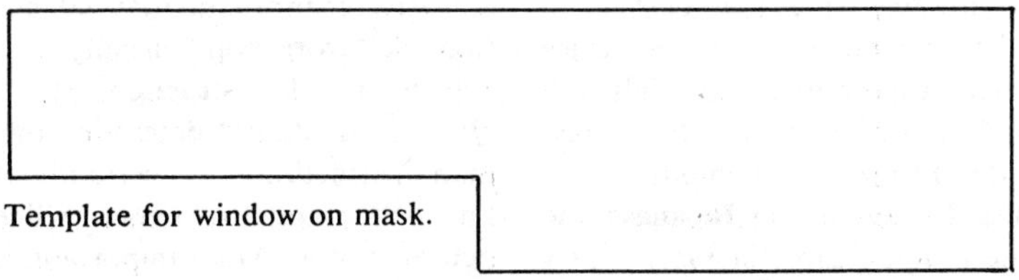

Template for window on mask.

A representative set of steps from PRIME IX—*How to Plan and Organize Work,* a text published by the American Management Associations, 1968 (reprinted by permission). AMA's format uses a plastic flap, or mask, with a clear window in it of the shape shown beneath the page reproduction. As the window is slid down the page, it reveals one step at a time. The correct response to a step is disclosed when the succeeding step is opened up. The reader can see how this works by cutting a window in a sheet of paper, the exact size of the template, and moving the paper downwards, over the illustration. In the PRIME text, the pages are 8½ by 11 in. The circled figure 2.3 refers to supplementary materials provided with the text.

Some texts are "segment sequential," and require no mask. Instead, for a given set of pages, the learner proceeds horizontally by reading step No. 1 at the top of page 1, step No. 2 at the top of page 3, step No. 3 at the top of page 5, and so on for the given number of pages. After this he returns to page 1 again and reads, say step No. 6, which appears second from the top of page 1, then step No. 7, which appears second from the top of page 3, and so on. The advantages claimed for the vertical type is that it is less confusing and, more importantly, that by concealing *everything* else on the page, the masking forces the learner to concentrate on the step without distraction.

A text programmed as above, whether vertical or sequential, is said to be a *linear* program. In a *branching* program, the learner reads a step and answers a question which provides for a multiple-choice response. The next step he reads is determined by his answer. If correct, he moves on to more advanced material, but if incorrect, the next piece of information is designed to clear up his misunderstanding. The branching programs generally have fallen into disfavor as being too simplistic, especially when instructing complex subject matter, and written-completion programs in linear format constitute most of the programmed texts produced in the United States today. Laboratory research supports this trend.

Introduction of the tape cassette has liberated the audio tape device and encouraged its utilization in audiovisual programmed instruction. The microprocessor-controlled slide-cassette device has afforded foolproof synchronization of projected image and audio, thus poularizing the AV teaching machine, but the response mechanism remains as multiple-choice.

Time-shared computer systems have also contributed by providing languages which the lesson planner or instructional programmer can use with ease. However, the low cost of a printed text and the mobility of such a device make it clear that programmed materials will continue to roll off an offset press or letterpress rather than a video recorder or computer.

Introducing the Technology in Business and Government. The training director faces a new and somewhat unusual technology when he considers programmed instruction. This is true because trainers as a rule rise from the ranks, and there has been little experience of this kind within companies of small and moderate size—and indeed not a significant amount in larger companies. There are four possible alternatives:

(1) *Purchase* generalized courses on the open market as "off-the-shelf" items.

(2) *Contract* for specialized courses with companies established for custom programming or curriculum development.

(3) *Borrow* or otherwise obtain general and special courses through membership in a "user's group."

(4) *Produce* courses by training selected employees within the company's training organization.

Guidelines published by the APA-AERA-DAVI Joint Committee, assisted by ASTD, are invaluable to management in examining programs for purchase or borrowing, and will strengthen any specifications set forth in contracts for the acquisition of custom courses [7]. However, the production of programs within a company presents problems normally associated with any new technology. The training director must equip his training specialists with the skills and knowledge which result in workable programmed teaching machine curricula. His first thoughts will be toward a *training program for his training specialists.*

Management choices in training the training specialist range from sending him to a one to three day seminar, to a two or three week "institute" or "workshop," or to a local or distant university for a regularly scheduled course. Other alternatives are to invite a consultant to set up a "workshop" on the premises, or to apprentice the training specialist for at least three months to an experienced organization. The specialist should also, of course, steep himself in articles, technical papers, and local meetings on the subject [8].

It is generally agreed by experienced curriculum developers that a one to three day "seminar" is not training, but merely an exposure to this technology. A three-unit university course consists of approximately 40 hours of instruction. A "workshop" usually consists of 80 to 120 hours of instruction. It is obvious that hours alone do not determine the quality of human instruction . . . certainly the instructor's knowledge and experience will enter into this determination. More important, however, is the *course content,* its *organization* and the *method of instruction.* The general rules of shaping *learner* behavior through teaching machine technology should be applied in the very course which will shape the *trainer's* behavior.

Only a few university departments of business administration offer courses in instructional programming. Occasionally, the extension division or general-studies college will offer an introductory course. There has been a decline since 1965 in the one-to three-day seminar offerings on an institutional or itinerant basis. As of 1981 the University of

Michigan continued to offer workshops designed particularly for business and industry [9].

Potential. The real strength of the technology lies in the recognition by management that human performance must be improved. The need is to identify precisely *standards* for job performance and make detailed *job analyses* for training purposes. With these completed, or nearly so, the development of a training program—for human-instruction or machine-instruction—can proceed.

If the great need in American business and industry will be for competent leadership characterized by first-line supervisory and middle management positions, then this technology should be called upon to produce results in the area of supervision and management. Some authorities thought that the union would take place only on factual material at first, then in subject areas requiring more interpretation, and finally in the field of human relations. Experience has revealed that management competence can be improved by this technology [9]. Sophisticated teaching machine environments including computer simulation and computer-assisted instruction (CAI) are now being developed, after twenty years of research.

CAI had to await the development of time-sharing computer systems (see ELECTRONIC DATA PROCESSING) before it could be used in business and industrial settings. The formative years of 1958–1966 saw one student per computer, then two . . . six . . . twelve . . . and eventually forty, when the Silverns handled that number of trainees simultaneously, using a General Electric 265 computer. Today, most computers servicing up to 2,000 terminals which have appropriate executive software can use instructional programmer languages such as COURSEWRITER (IBM), PLATO (CDC), or DECAL (DEC). Most other instructional programmer languages are on university campuses where they are tied to special-purpose systems. Computer programmer (not instructional programmer) languages such as APL, BASIC, COBOL, FORTRAN, PASCAL, and PL/1, and their subsets, can be used, but only with considerable difficulty and expense.

Exhibit III shows a typical CAI-student-computer interaction. A stimulus is printed out by the computer and the computer halts, awaiting the learner's response. Some stimuli have blanks inserted in the question, while others are open-ended, terminating with a question mark. The computer signals the learner that a response is requested by returning to the left margin printing ?, and then halting.

The learner can type in his answer, in one character, one word, or a group of words constituting a sentence. When the learner has completed his response, he strikes the proper key and the computer analyzes his response. It then provides feedback as shown in the exhibit. In the system illustrated, slides are rear-screen projected and automatically changed by the computer. The computer can change to any slide, going either forward or backward, and can provide remedial instruction if the response is inappropriate. The multiple-choice question illustrated has six possible answers.

The reordering of national priorities in the 1970s temporarily reduced interest in CAI, simply by reducing expenditures for developing or procuring CAI courses. The emphasis was on programmed *texts* because they are cheaper—not because they necessarily do a better job.

By 1975, the introduction of the microcomputer had made possible its use as a stand-alone CAI teaching machine, so long as the system satisfied the seven criteria stated earlier. However, the same kinds of problems and marketing solutions which plagued the programmed instruction movement during 1960–1966 are serving to confound the use of microcomputers for CAI in the 1980s. Computer programmers largely untrained and unskilled in *instructional programming* are generating CAI software which is unvalidated. This exposes the training director to more complex decision making than he would normally face in selecting or even developing a programmed instruction text.

The term stand-alone means that the complete computer system is used by one learner, and, except for electric power, is not connected in any way to another device or system. In contrast, a *time-shared* CAI system accommodates many learners simultaneously, with learner terminals remotely connected to a central computer. Time-sharing can at the same time process hundreds of learners separated by thousands of miles. Stand-alone CAI is less costly than time-sharing, since telephone interconnections are not necessary, and it is likely that training directors will tend to favor this mode.

DR. LEONARD C. SILVERN, President, Education and Training Consultants Co., Sedona, Arizona

EXHIBIT III

```
   (NEXT SLIDE --> 47)

WE HAVE ALREADY REFERRED TO THE INTERSECTION OF THE CROSS-
HAIRS AS THE CIRCLE.  IT IS MORE ACCURATE TO CALL IT:  IRIS

   (NEXT SLIDE --> 48)

BEFORE PRESSING THE LOCK-ON SWITCH, THE PILOT MUST BE SURE
THE TARGET IS INSIDE THE -----.

? IRIS
YOU'VE GOT YOUR EYE ON THE BALL.  (GET IT?)

THE TARGET APPEARS IN THE IRIS. THE PILOT PRESSES THE LOCK-
ON SWITCH.  THE LASER IS MOUNTED INSIDE A LARGE GYROSCOPE.
AT THIS MOMENT, THE GYRO IS 'UNCAGED'....MEANING IT IS FREE
TO MOVE IN ALL FORWARD-LOOKING DIRECTIONS.  THE LASER IS
LOOKING DIRECTLY AT THE TARGET.  IF THE AIRCRAFT SHOULD
MOVE A LITTLE OFF TARGET, THE LASER WOULD BE LOCKED-ON THE
TARGET AND SWING AS THE AIRCRAFT TURNS AWAY.

SO, YOU CAN SAY THAT THE LASER WILL LOOK AT THE TARGET EVEN
IF THE AIRCRAFT IS LOOKING IN A SLIGHTLY DIFFERENT DIRECTION.
THE LASER, MEANING EYBOL, IS TRACKING THE TARGET.

FOR THE GYRO TO BE 'UNCAGED' AND TRACKING, WHAT ACTION BY
THE PILOT MUST HAVE OCCURRED AN INSTANT BEFORE?

? HE ACQUIRED THE TARGET VISUALLY
TRY AGAIN. FOR THE GYRO TO BE 'UNCAGED' AND TRACKING, WHAT ACTION BY
THE PILOT MUST HAVE OCCURRED AN INSTANT BEFORE?

? AN INSTANT BEFORE --  HE PRESSED THE LOCK-ON SWITCH
ROGER.

      (NEXT SLIDE --> 49)

WHILE TRACKING WITH EYBOL, THE PILOT IS ALLOWED SOME
VARIATION IN AIRCRAFT ATTITUDE.  WITHIN THESE LIMITS, AND
FOR ANY COMBINATION OF THESE MOVEMENTS, THE LASER WILL
TRACK AND KEEP LOCK-ON.  IF HE EXCEEDS THESE LIMITS, HE WILL
LOSE LOCK-ON.  WHAT WILL HAPPEN IF HE YAWS 3 DEGREES?

? SINCE HE EXCEEDED THE LIMIT --  HE WILL LOSE HIS LOCKON
GOOD THINKING.  HE LOSES LOCK-ON.
```

Portion of a typical CAI student-computer interaction. The computer halts after each ? at the left margin and awaits the student's response. Slides are changed automatically under computer control. This course was written in LYRIC language. (Reproduced by permission of Education and Training Consultants Co.)

Information References

Associations:

American Society for Training and Development.
Association for Educational Communications & Technology.
Association for Computing Machinery.
Association for Educational Data Systems.
Association for Media-Based Continuing Education for Engineers.
National Society for Performance and Instruction.
Society for Applied Learning Technology.

Texts:

DeGreene, K., "Systems Psychology," New York, McGraw-Hill, 1970.

"Control Data PLATO-System Overview," Document 97406700, Minneapolis, Control Data Education Co., 1977.

Silvern, L.C., "Principles of Computer-Assisted Instruction Systems," Los Angeles, Education and Training Consultants Co., 1970.

Silvern, L.C., "Computer-Aided Education," in The Diebold Group, eds., "Automated Data Processing Handbook," New York, McGraw-Hill, 1977.

Waldman, H., ed., "Automated Education Handbook," Detroit, Automated Education Center, 1977.

References Cited

[1] War Manpower Commission, "The Training Within Industry Report, 1940–1945," Bureau of Training, WMC, September 1945.

[2] Pressey, S. L., "Simple Apparatus Which Gives Tests and Scores and Teaches," *School and Society*, **23**, 373–376 (1926).

[3] Skinner, B. F., "The Science of Learning and the Art of Teaching," *Harvard Educational Rev.*, 86–97 (Spring 1954).

[4] Silvern, L. C., "Textbook in Methods of Instruction," Culver City, Calif, Hughes Aircraft Co., January 1, 1957; 2nd ed. 1962.

[5] Galanter, E., "Automatic Teaching: The State of the Art," pp. 1–198, New York, Wiley, 1959.

[6] Lumsdaine, A. A., and Glaser, R., eds., "Teaching Machines and Programmed Learning: A Source Book," Washington, D.C., DAVI, National Education Association, July 1960.

[7] Joint Committee on Programmed Instruction and Teaching Machines, AERA-APA-DAVI, "Recommendations for Reporting the Effectiveness of Programmed Instruction Materials, *AV Communications Review,* XIV, Spring 1966, 117–123; XIV, Summer 1966, 243–258.
[8] Silvern, L. C., "Fundamentals of Teaching Machines and Programmed Learning Systems," Los Angeles, Education and Training Consultants, 1964.
[9] Ofiesh, G. D., "Programmed Instruction—a Guide for Management," New York, American Management Associations, 1965.

Cross References: *Human Resources Development (and cross references there given.)*

TECHNOLOGICAL CHANGE: Union-Management Agreements

Automation and technological change often raise fears among employees of loss of jobs, income, pensions, health and other fringe benefits, and fears of downgrading, involuntary retirement, relocation, and other readjustment problems. Many union-management agreements contain provisions designed to ease the transition to new technologies and to cushion the disemployment effects of technological innovations. The nature of these agreements is strongly influenced by the structure, technology, and market conditions of the particular firm and industry and by the special characteristics and needs of the workers in terms of age, sex, skill levels, education, mobility, and geography.

Efforts to protect workers against negative effects of progress in automation and technology have included guarantees against job or income loss and in some cases protection against the loss of supplementary benefits. Other measures taken here included severance pay compensation or early retirement benefits for workers losing their jobs, income guarantees for workers required to take lower-paying jobs, retraining provisions, transfer rights, and relocation allowances to help displaced workers move to another plant. Commonly, agreements include advance notice to unions and workers of plant closings or other major company changes affecting employees' welfare, and joint labor-management committees to discuss and negotiate plans for easing the transition and cushioning the impact of technological change.

Job-security provisions have included attrition as a way of making sure that current employees affected by technological change will be assured of continued employment while unneeded jobs will be eliminated as workers quit voluntarily, retire, or die. Kennecott Copper Company and the United Steelworkers have attrition provisions in their contracts. However, attrition has remained a controversial issue between railroad unions and railroad management. More common than attrition provisions are "no layoff" provisions, which are, in effect, the same as attrition protections for currently employed workers. For example, the New York City–Transit Workers Union contract and the Pacific Maritime Association–International Longshoremen's and Warehousemen's Union agreements provide for no layoffs.

Wage-employment guarantees have been included in many major contracts, often with seniority provisions for displaced workers to "bump out" other less senior workers in the same or other plants of the company.

Severance-pay plans were included in 490 out of 1,570 major labor-management agreements in 1976, with greatest coverage in the primary metal, transportation equipment, and communications industries. A typical severance-pay plan may call for one week's pay for each year of service. Early retirement benefits and incentives for displaced workers have been negotiated in a number of industries, including meat-packing, petroleum refining and chemicals, and West Coast longshoring.

Income guarantees for workers moved into lower-paying jobs usually take the form of "red circle" protections that hold the employee at his previous pay rate, even when he is required to take a lower-rated job.

The right to training or retraining for new jobs has been written into contracts between Motors and the Auto Workers and between *The New York Times* and the Newspaper Guild. Campbell Soup Company and the Food-Commercial Workers have a tuition-aid plan for retraining.

The right to transfer to another job in the same plant or in another plant and the right to preferential hiring after layoff, either in the same plant or in another plant, were assured in 425 major 1976 labor-management agreements, the greatest number of these being in transportation equipment, primary metals, transportation, communications, and retail trade. Interplant transfer arrangements with seniority and preferential hiring have been negotiated by General Motors and the Auto Workers. Relocation allowances were provided for in 170 major 1976 contracts covering 1,000 or more workers, with the same industry concentration. Moving-expense reimbursement allowances ranged up to a maximum of $1,450 in Steelworkers agreements with U.S. Steel and American Can.

Advance notice of prospective layoffs, plant shutdown, or plant relocation was specified in more than 780 major 1976 contracts, with a heavy industry concentration in transportation equipment, communications, and non-electrical machinery. The required advance notice period in 1979 ranged from seven days in a General Electric contract with the International Union of Electrical Workers to twelve months in an American Can Company agreement with the Steelworkers union.

Joint labor-management committees on industrial relations issues, including technological change, work transfer, and plant closings are heavily concentrated in the primary metal and transportation equipment industries. Such committees, specifically charged with dealing with technological change, have been set up by General Motors and the Auto Workers, Armour and the Food-Commercial Workers, the Bituminous Coal Association and the United Mine Workers, and the New York Nursing Home Association and the Service Employees International Union.

Among the best known labor-management attempts to deal with automation and technological change are the 1959–1960 agreement between the Pacific Maritime Association and the International Longshoremen and Warehousemen's Union which set up a jointly administered fund to help maintain workers' income and finance early retirement as cargo handling on the West Coast docks was modernized and mechanized; the 1959 Armour "automation fund" with tripartite administration to help provide training and new job opportunities for displaced workers; and the 1963 Kaiser Steel-Steelworkers "progress sharing" plant-wide plan at Fontana, Calif., which encouraged workers to accept costcutting efficiencies by giving them a share of the savings based on the proportion of labor costs to total costs. However, serious problems emerged over the years in all three plans, due in part to economic conditions, including high unemployment.

The technology factor in international trade and capital movements is raising increased concern among economists and among workers affected by technology exports and relocation of production abroad by U.S. corporations [1]. It seems likely that labor-management negotiations will increasingly deal with these issues. The labor unions have also urged action by the Congress.

Thus, private labor-management arrangements to deal with automation and technological change must be set in a wider context of industry conditions and general national and world economic conditions. The 1966 Automation Commission report [2] points out that government fiscal, monetary and manpower policies are needed to supplement private efforts to ease adjustments to new technology. Its conclusions are still valid today.

MARKLEY ROBERTS, Economist, Department of Research, American Federation of Labor and Congress of Industrial Organizations, Washington, D.C.

Information References

AFL-CIO Department for Professional Employees, "Silicon, Satellites and Robots: The Impacts of Technological Change on the Workplace," Washington, D.C., 1979.

AFL-CIO Industrial Union Department, "Comparative Survey of Major Collective Bargaining Agreements: Manufacturing and Non-Manufacturing, March, 1979," Washington, D.C., 1979.

Levinson, Harold, Rehmus, Charles, Goldberg, Joseph P., and Kahn, Mark, "Collective Bargaining and Technological Change in American Transportation," Evanston, Ill., Transportation Institute of Northwestern University, 1972.

National Commission on Technology, Automation, and Economic Progress, "Technology and the American Economy," Washington, D.C., 1966.

Roberts, Markley, "Harnessing Technology: The Workers' Stake," AFL-CIO American Federationist, April, 1979.

Schlichter, Sumner H., Healy, James J., and Livernash, E. Robert, "The Impact of Collective Bargaining on Management," Washington, D.C., Brookings Institution, 1960.

Somers, Gerald G., Cushman, Edward L., and Weinberg, Nat, eds., "Adjusting to Technological Change," New York, Harper & Row, 1963.

U.S. Department of Labor, Bureau of Labor Statistics, "Characteristics of Major Collective Bargaining Agreements, July 1, 1976," BLS *Bulletin 2013,* 1979.

U.S. Department of Labor, Bureau of International Labor Affairs, "The Impact of International Trade and Investment on Employment," Washington 1978.

References Cited

[1] U.S. Department of Labor, "The Impact of International Trade and Investment on Employment."

[2] National Commission on Technology, Automation, and Economic Progress, Washington, D.C., 1966.

Cross References: *Automation; Labor Unions.*

TECHNOLOGICAL FORECASTING

Technological Forecasting is a term that has attained increasing currency over the past decade and a half to denote a formalized set of procedures and techniques designed to bridge the gap between administrative, marketing, and financial policy makers, and the "far out" thinking of science. The assumption is that the latter, seen in the proper perspective of current and impending state-of-the-art and foreseeable economic, social, and political developments, will (under varying degrees of inevitability) evolve into realities that will react upon a firm's markets, mode of operation, competitive climate, and perhaps upon its chances for economic survival.

Utilizing technological forecasting, an awareness of over-the-horizon technological developments can be tied into a master plan covering broad types of products, markets, and processes toward which to aim. Responsibility for this input into planning is lodged in a small analysis group or in a single knowledgeable individual.

Definition. James R. Bright, of the Graduate School of Business, University of Texas, an authority on technological innovation, has defined the activity as follows [1]: "Technological forecasting means systems of logical analysis that lead to common quantitative conclusions (or a limited range of possibilities) about technological attributes and parameters, as well as technical-economic attributes. Such forecasts differ from opinions in that they rest upon an explicit set of quantitative relationships and stated assumptions; and they are produced by a logic that yields relatively consistent results." The essence of the concept is that it should provide quantitative predictions within a realistic time frame regarding future technology or foreseeable extensions of currently developed technology.

Technological forecasting is both *exploratory* (i.e., trying to see what is likely to become technically feasible given the present state of knowledge) and *normative* (setting goals or anticipating specific future needs, and working backward to see how and through what stages and time frames they might be attained). Time horizons may vary from five to twenty years, with some forecasts of a general nature for longer periods ahead. The oil industry, for example, may look as far ahead as 50 years into the future, and the planning for such projects as water supplies for a large metropolitan area may make it necessary to peer ahead even farther.

While technical forecasting as a discipline is hardly out of its infancy (Bright [1] stated that as of his writing, 1968, it stood where economic forecasting stood circa 1910), a large body of literature on the subject has developed. It would appear, however, that as of this writing, despite the increased interest in formal forecasting methods in recent years, the practice of long-range technological forecasting has not yet refined into a uniform methodology, and many companies are attempting a systematic approach for the first time. For a run-down of significant books on technological forecasting that appeared in the three-year period prior to 1979, the reader is referred to a review and commentary by Professor Brian C. Twiss [2]. The Bright book [1], a compilation of contributions by 28 authors, contains a comprehensive and partially annotated bibliography as of 1968.

Approaches and Techniques. A distinction should be drawn between technological *forecasting* and business *planning*. Technological forecasting, as pointed out by Philip Francis [3] differs from planning in that it does not imply a commitment to allocate resources. It may include an analysis of the resources needed to achieve the capabilities projected, but the decision to allocate resources belongs to the planning process. Management as part of its planning function must translate the technological forecast information into the goals, policies, programs, and procedures of the organization.

Thus, the purpose should be to provide the broad background information about foreseeable trends and their implications, on the basis of which more intelligent strategic planning and investment decisions can be made. In an early article on the subject, Brian Quinn [4] observed that a sophisticated manager would not expect market forecasts to be made with decimal accuracy, yet could reasonably ask his market analyst to estimate the most likely size of market and to evaluate the probabilities and implications of other sizes. Similarly, competent persons suitably organized for the task can predict "expected" future technological developments and analyze the probabilities and implications of variations around these. Such "scenarios" can help to identify and assess *opportunities* and *threats* in the company's environment so that management can act more effectively to improve the company's future position.

Exploratory Forecasts. Following are salient categories of exploratory technological forecasting identified in the literature.

Individual or "Genius" Forecasting. It may be acknowledged that there is considerable merit in a forecast made by a single individual who is expert in his (her) special area and has both depth in the underlying scientific disciplines or technologies as well as a synoptical view of the functional area to which his or her expertise has direct application. One should, however, note the caveats provided by some historical wrong pronouncements by such experts. The dangers here were cited by Milton Harris on the occasion of his being awarded the Priestley Medal (March 24, 1980) by the American Chemical Society [5]:

> The record of our peers is pretty dismal. Just 25 years ago, for example, a group of eminent Americans—leaders in government, industry, and education—recorded their prophecies for 1980 in a book entitled "The Fabulous Future, America in 1980." Here are a few of their predictions: Cancer would be cured; the national debt would be slashed; transcontinental mail would travel by guided missile; there would be a terrible surplus of oil . . . energy would be virtually free—enterprising real estate developers probably would advertise "free electricity with a $20,000 house"; and the average family's income would be $8,000. Obviously things didn't work out exactly according to those predictions.

The Consensus Approach. A lessening of the hazards of predictions cited above is offered by combining the judgments of several individuals active in a given field. The so-called *Delphi technique* is an interesting variant on which detailed comment is deferred to a separate heading below.

Trend Analysis. The simplest form here is to assume *constant trends,* namely, that the future will be different from the present, but broadly predictable; trends now evident will be maintained, and adequate forecasts for planning can be derived from the simple extrapolation of historical data. It is obvious that this approach has significant shortcomings if extended beyond the immediate short term. Even if sophisticated mathematical techniques of correlation and trend projections are used to arrive at projections of individual devices or technologies that enter into the broader technology being forecast, the upsetting factor will be breakthroughs in a given technology, or the substitution of a new technology for one that has reached the end of its rapid advance.

Use of *modified constant trends* seeks to take account of emerging new trends and events that can introduce abrupt changes. A sophisticated technique here is the use of *envelope curve forecasting.* Ayers [6] describes the concept by means of an illustration involving high-energy particle accelerators (atom smashers): Typically each new type of machine (d.c. generator, electrostatic generator, cyclotron, betatron, electron synchrotron, proton synchrotron) takes the lead for a short period and then, because of inherent limitations, it reaches the end of its phase of rapid improvement while a newer invention escalates to a higher level. The "envelope" is a curve which approximates the general trend and is tangent to the individual performance trends. At any given moment, particle accelerator designers are tempted to think that the particular machine then in vogue is the "ultimate" and that future progress will be controlled by its particular constraints. A forecaster from the traditional school almost automatically projects a future curve which "saturates" and levels off rapidly, following the familiar S curve. In other words, even though aware that inventions have been occurring at a regular rate in the past, he assumes that in the future there will be no more. The envelope curve thesis is that projecting the envelope itself is the safest thing to do, because it assumes a continuation of the past rate of invention.

A considerable body of additional mathematical techniques has been developed for measuring and taking account of uncertainty in technological forecasting, based on the probability theory. These techniques permit the build-up of uncertainty distribution of total projects from the distribution of individual parameters. It is obvious, however, that no matter how refined the mathematical techniques, a high judgmental factor remains, especially in matters of estimating the timing of expected breakthroughs and the speed with which one technology may be expected to substitute for another.

Normative Forecasting. In the normative forecast, goals, needs, objectives, or desires are specified, and the forecast works backward to the present to see what capabilities now exist or could be extrapolated to meet future goals. In some cases, the goals may force technology—in other words, "make the future happen."

An approach useful here is the so-called *rel-*

evance tree. This is an analytical device to assure that all feasible options leading to a specified goal have been considered and evaluated. The approach is to lay out all of the paths which can possibly lead to a technological objective, permitting an organized study of areas needing improvement or upgrading. For example, if the objective were the commercial production of solar energy, two paths would lead, respectively, from *direct conversion* and *indirect conversion.* Direct conversion would be possible alternatively from photovoltaic cells (on buildings or on space stations to be beamed to earth by microwave), or from solar thermal units. Indirect conversion could also proceed from solar thermal units, or from the utilization of ocean thermal differences, ocean tides, or by the production of fuels by growing plants or utilizing wastes. (Plants would include not only trees, but also grasses, algae, and water plants; it is stated that a modest use of the total land and water area of the United States could meet the entire electrical energy needs of the country.) [7].

Costs and time elements involved in each of the levels of the relevance tree can be projected, and return-on-capital computed for the investment required, using conventional financial analytical methods. (See RETURN ON CAPITAL.)

The Delphi Technique. Widely discussed in the literature as an effective method to structure intuitive thinking and produce "scenarios" for exploratory technological forecasting is the so-called Delphi technique developed by the RAND Corporation. It can be used for the systematic collection and collation of informed judgments obtained individually from members of a selected group of experts (possibly representing various disciplines) on any specific issue, and, while preserving anonymity, the refinement of these judgments by an iterative process to arrive at a "best possible" decision.

In the first feedback, the judgments of the individuals are collected, digested or perhaps formulated as a group response, and fed back. Each individual then considers whether he wants to contribute more information, or to modify his earlier views. This iteration is continued until a reasonable consensus is obtained. All responses may be fed back anonymously, to ensure objectivity.

In the words of Dr. Olaf Helmer, who with collaborators from Douglas Aircraft developed the technique at the RAND Corporation [8]:

> The traditional method of achieving a consensus of experts has been to conduct a round-table discussion and ask for a statement of a group position. The outcome is apt to be a compromise between divergent views, arrived at, all too often, under the undue influence of certain psychological factors such as specious persuasion by the member with the greatest supposed authority, or even merely the loudest voice; the unwillingness to abandon publicy expressed opinions; and the bandwagon effect of majority opinion. The Delphi technique . . . eliminates committee activity among the experts altogether, and replaces it with a carefully designed program of sequential, individual interrogation (usually best conducted by questionnaires). These are interspersed with information and opinion feedback.

A sophisticated form of Delphi conferencing was developed by Dr. Murray Turoff while serving as a senior operations research analyst in the Office of Emergency Preparedness, Washington [9]. By using a time-shared computer with terminals available to all participants (who may be widely dispersed), Turoff completely computerizes the entire communication and feedback process, achieving a totally new and expanded type of interaction. The computer-based communication allows participants to "talk" (by typing in remarks) or "listen" (by reading printouts of remarks of others) as they choose. The computer stores remarks until someone indicates he (she) is ready to read more of the conversation, so the participant controls his rate of interaction. When he inputs, his remarks are added at the end of the conversation list supplied to all participants, and will be received by others when they have reached that point. (Remarks can be edited before input.)

Additionally, the sorting capability of the computer can be used to regroup the discussions into separate threads by utilizing unique identifiers, such as the sequence numbers or key words used in the discussion itself to define a particular topic. Any individual may write private messages to any other individual, unbeknownst to the other members, although they may be "carboned" to any subgroup. Such "whispered" discussions lead to more rapid resolution of some issues. (Private messages are eliminated from the file after delivery.)

Despite a tremendous body of literature on Delphi applications, some controversy persists about the technique. A quite critical editorial by Samuel Eilon, chief editor of OMEGA, the international journal of management science, appeared in the December 1978 issue of that publication [10]. His main criticism is the implicit assumption in accounts about Delphi projects that the truth about the future is lurking somewhere, and that the Delphi opinion consensus will home in on that target. "It is quite possible," he says, "for an expert under these conditions [Delphi] to be cowed into submission by sequential feedback (even under the protection of anonymity), abandon what may turn out in retrospect to have been an excellent forecast, and gravitate towards a common median which is nevertheless far off the mark."

Twiss, previously cited [2], also characterizes Delphi as a highly controversial approach to long-range forecasting, although he points out that the problem may be that many Delphi programs have been poorly conducted. (For the interested reader, one of the books his commentary cites, "The Delphi Method" [11], contains 33 articles by major contributors to the technique.)

Technical Assessment. Activities subsumed under this head are related to technological forecasting, but with a different end in view. As the term is used in the literature [12], it has to do with forecasting the impact of future processes upon the political, social, and economic environment of the firm. It is obvious that the approaches and techniques of technological forecasting related to the firm's profit-making operations are applicable here, too. In view of increasing environmental concerns (see ENVIRONMENTAL CONTROLS), it is clear that this aspect of the subject must be incorporated in the charter and agenda of technological forecasting.

Acceptance. Despite the large and growing body of literature on technological forecasting, and the attention now being given to the subject in the curricula of engineering and business schools, it appears that formalized programs are not yet widespread in industry. Establishing the worth of technological forecasting techniques has proven difficult because of the very nature of the activity, which deals in long-range projections that cannot be put to the test of actual experience until a considerable time has elapsed. William Ascher, in his book "Forecasting: An Appraisal for Policy Makers and Planners" [13], which appeared in 1978, devotes a chapter to technological forecasting. He found only a "limited range" of technical forecasting efforts which were amenable to appraisal, and for those forecasts which could be appraised, "evaluation reveals that technical forecasting is quite erratic."

Ascher's finding was that the earlier enthusiasms of technological forecasters has given way to a more sober outlook. While the technological forecasters of the 1960s displayed a rather remarkable confidence that their methods work, there is a realization now that the accuracy of forecasting depends more on the validity of the core assumptions rather than on the elaboration of method.

Experts in the field are the best source of core assumptions, but the caveat sounded is that even with the most thorough analysis of directions and trends of specific technologies, the ultimate constraints will not be those of the technologies involved, but rather those imposed from the outside, viz., political, social, and ecological.

Twiss [2] points out that although literature containing speculations about the future of the world goes back as far as Jules Verne, H. G. Wells, and some earlier writers, it is only during the past decade that attention has been focused on a systematic approach to world futures, ranging from the gloomy predictions of the Club of Rome ("Limits to Growth" [14]) to the technological optimism of Herman Kahn ("The Year 2000" [15]). Whatever the merits of these alternative features, he says, they have encouraged many managements to consider the environment in which their organizations will be working in the long-range term, in some cases as far ahead as 50 years.

CARL HEYEL, Management Counsel, Manhasset, New York

References Cited

[1] Bright, James R., "Technological Forecasting for Industry and Government," Englewood Cliffs, N.J., Prentice-Hall, 1968.
[2] Twiss, Brian C., "Recent Trends in Long-Range Forecasting for Technology-Based Organizations—Book Review Article," *Long Range Planning*, April 1979.
[3] Francis, Philip H., "Principles of R&D Management," New York, AMACOM, 1977.
[4] Quinn, James Brian, "Technological Forecasting," *Harvard Business Review*, March-April 1967.
[5] Harris, Milton, "Science and Technology in the 1980's," *Chemical & Engineering News*, March 31, 1980.
[6] Ayres, Robert U., "Envelope Curve Forecasting," in [1].
[7] Peters, E. Bruce, "Technological Forecasting: An Investment Analysis Aid," *Managerial Planning*, July-August 1978.
[8] Helmer, Olaf, "Analysis of the Future: The Delphi Method," in [1]. (See also North, Harper Q. and Pyke, Donald L., "'Probes' of the Technological Future," *Harvard Business Review*, May-June 1969.)

[9] Turoff, Murray, "Human Communications via Data Networks," *Computer Decisions,* January 1973.
[10] Eilon, Samuel, "Better than the Oracle?" *OMEGA,* December 1978.
[11] Linstone, H. A. and Turoff, M., eds, "The Delphi Method: Techniques and Applications," Reading, Mass., Addison-Wesley, 1975.
[12] Oberkampf, Volker, "Technology Assessment: Need and Motivation of Industry," *Long Range Planning,* August 1978.
[13] Ascher, William, "Forecasting: An Appraisal for Policy Makers and Planners," Baltimore, Johns Hopkins University Press, 1978.
[14] Meadows, D. et al., "The Limits to Growth," Wolf City, Tex., University Press, 1972.
[15] Kahn, H., Brown, W., and Martel, L., "The Year 2000," New York, Macmillan, 1967.

Cross References: *Basic Research: Management Aspects; Brainstorming; Creativity Training; Industrial Research and Development; Long-Range Corporate Planning.*

TEMPORARY PERSONNEL SERVICES

Supplying **Temporary Help** is big business. Estimates put current domestic sales (1980) of such services at close to $3 billion annually, compared with $50 million in 1958. Counting all local suppliers, there are several thousand firms in the business in the United States and Canada, although only a handful of large contractors, operating regionally, nationally, and in some cases internationally, account for slightly below half the volume. Well known names in the field are Manpower, Inc., The Olsten Corp., and Kelly Services.

Use of temporary services emerged as a significant source of employees just after World War II. In the early years of the industry, the temporary help contractor was viewed as a short-range resource to meet emergency situations. Today, however, these services are built into long-range planning as well as emergency situations. Some supplying firms have now reached the point where they can provide the entire staff, workers and supervisors, for a given project. Some contractors also do "in-house" work, supplying the personnel, equipment, and space when the client is not equipped to do the job himself. Additionally, such firms are increasingly contracting to do specialized jobs or services, in much the same way as maintenance or security services are provided. The range of temporary employees available today covers virtually every kind of permanent job in the economy.

Mode of Operation. Temporary personnel are the employees of the service firm, and the using firm is usually billed 35% to 50% over the worker's rate of pay, which is generally the going rate in the area. (For the difference between salaries paid and the client billing, the temporary service is responsible for all taxes, insurances, and withholdings required by law.)

Actually, the real cost of permanent employees may significantly exceed that of temporaries, if one counts fringe benefits, recruiting, and related expenses (see Exhibit I).

The client company pays only for the actual time put in by the temporary worker. If the temporary does not show up, no matter what the reason, there is no charge. Nor will most reputable firms charge for unsatisfactory work by a temporary if the client notifies them of the situation within a reasonable time.

It must be kept in mind that a temporary service is very different from an employment agency. The latter simply acts as a go-between for worker and employer, and is paid for filling a job opening. The temporary service is the legal employer of the temporary worker, and the client company is not hiring an employee but is buying the use of his time and skills.

While office workers constitute the bulk of the temporary employees today, the services of temporary-personnel contractors is not limited

EXHIBIT I

TYPICAL FRINGE COSTS AS A PER CENT OF AN EMPLOYEE'S SALARY

Federal unemployment insurance State unemployment insurance Social security State disability Compensation insurance	11.24%
Recruiting, hiring Bookkeeping and records	6.5%
Health and life insurance Average severance pay Pension plans Non-working time Holiday pay Vacation pay Sick pay Average Christmas bonus Misc. benefits	24.40%
	42.14%

to them by any means, and especially not to the lower skills. Although, basic office needs, such as secretaries, typist, keypunch operators, bookkeepers, clericals, receptionists, and the mailroom personnel continue to be the greatest number of skill categories requested, other areas are increasing constantly. Temporary employees from supervisors to clerks are called on to take inventories, work on long-term records management conversions, on short-term file purging assignments, and operating data processing, word processing, and microfilming equipment. Draftmen, engineers, designers, and even pharmacists are furnished at various times. Many types of industrial employees can be provided, including packers, loaders, cleaners, assemblers, and inventory takers. A wide variety of marketing jobs include selling, sales supervision, convention assistants, exhibit aids, trade-show attendants, store product and service demonstrators, comparison shoppers, survey and questionnaire takers, telephone marketers, and scores of other non-office white-collar jobs.

In addition, there are situations where complete staffs of temporary personnel, including supervisors, are called in to handle a basic company function. Mailrooms, billing departments, bill payment operations, and similar functions are handled by the "permanent temporary" team for the company.

Advantages. In addition to the cost aspects mentioned, a big advantage of using temporaries is flexibility. For rush-order demands, foreseeable peak periods, vacation seasons, emergency situations, staffing new departments, and special one-time projects, the temporary can fill in for part of a day or for several months, on a one-time basis, occasionally, or regularly, full time or part time. Moreover, properly planned use of temporaries will reduce the personnel problems attendant upon layoffs of permanent employees in periods of slack business.

Disadvantages. There are possible disadvantages that the intelligent user should be aware of. Permanent employees who welcome occasional overtime pay may complain if this extra income is eliminated. There are also situations where the work itself is not conducive to the effective use of temporaries: the job may be based on such in-depth knowledge of procedure and background that it may be more economical to pay a regular employee overtime.

Selecting the Temporary Employee. To use temporary personnel correctly, companies must have the correct person report for the specific job. Many of the more advanced personnel service companies conduct a client survey in which service representatives explore and record a client's needs, department by department, together with observations on the total company environment. A similar profile of the applicant is taken at the time of registration, and every effort is made to match experience, aptitudes, proven skills, and other qualifications of the temporary employee to the equipment, skill, needs, and environment of the client's work place.

Choice of a Contractor. Because of the wide choice available, the temporary service user should carefully scrutinize the kinds of companies and nature of their services. Some contractors specialize in certain job categories. The "Yellow Pages" will give a good listing of the firms in any area, and the user might then check with his local chamber of commerce, attorney, accountant, and, of course, companies that have used the services of a particular supplier. It is well to check into how long the temporary help contractor has been in business, what is behind its claims regarding training programs, whether it uses adequate testing in its hiring, and whether it has proper insurance coverage, including personal and general liability, blanket bonds, etc. If the relationship promises to be a long one, it is good policy for an executive of the contractor and using companies to visit each other's offices. A personal meeting will give the temporary personnel firm a better understanding of the client's operations and particular needs, which will lead to better service.

WILLIAM OLSTEN, Chairman and Chief Executive Officer, The Olsten Corporation. Westbury, L.I., New York; Past President, Institute of Temporary Services, Inc., New York, New York

Information References

Association:

Institute of Temporary Services, Inc.
National Association of Temporary Services.

Publications:

"For Rent—Secretaries, Salesmen, and Physicists," *Fortune,* October 1978.
"How to Get the Most from Temporary Employees," *Nation's Business,* March 1978.
Olsten William, "Use of Temporary Help Contractors," Sec. 3, Chap. 7, in Heyel, Carl, "Handbook of Modern Office Management and Administrative Services," Melbourne, Fla., Krieger, repr. 1980.

Small Business Administration, "Small Marketeers Aid," Pub. #106, Washington, D.C.

Cross Reference: *Human Resources Requirements.*

TERRORISM: Protective Measures

The decade of the Seventies saw a sharp rise in acts of terrorism throughout the world by political and criminal groups. Over 5,000 attacks were recorded, ranging from bombing and hijacking to kidnapping and assassination. Nearly one-half of this total were business-connected incidents and 11% were directed against United States corporations.

Over one-half of the kidnappings during this period involved businessmen and 20% were American nationals.

In the earlier years of the decade, terrorist attacks concentrated primarily on government facilities, personnel, and police. When these efforts met with stiffening resistance, the attacks shifted to diplomatic establishments and personnel. As these hostile ventures were also answered by stronger countermeasures and official reluctance to meet demands, the focus swung in mid-decade to more vulnerable business organizations and personnel.

The majority of terrorist attacks took place in Europe and Latin America. In the last half of the decade the greatest number of incidents in Europe occurred in Italy, Spain, Germany, and Northern Ireland, in that order. In Latin America in the first half of the decade Argentina and Uruguay were the most active, while in more recent years Columbia, El Salvador, Mexico, Nicaragua, and Guatemala, especially the first three countries, were the most active in the kidnapping of foreign business personnel.

Of some small comfort, the current trend has been toward kidnappings of executives for ransom rather than outright assassination. Only 13% of the recorded assassinations since 1970 involved business personnel: 2% were U.S. nationals, 2% foreign personnel, and 8% domestic personnel. (By contrast, 42% of the victims were police officers and 18% diplomatic/government personnel.) The prime reason for this trend is that the terrorists are more interested in seeking additional funds to support their activities rather than in deliberate vengeance against corporations.

Types of Terrorism. Modern terrorism is of two general types: criminal and political. Criminal terrorism is staged by individuals who are seeking immediate personal gain. They have no political interests or connections with ideological terrorists. For this reason, they are usually easier to deal with, negotiate with, and handle successfully.

Political terrorism generally falls into one of five types:

(1) Resistance to political rule, e.g., Cyprus, Algeria, Palestine.

(2) National separatism, e.g., Eritrea, Puerto Rico.

(3) Internal political (power takeover), e.g., Northern Ireland, mainland China, Cuba.

(4) Ideological political (system destruction), e.g., Tupamaros in Uruguay, Baader-Meinhof in West Germany, Weather Underground in America.

(5) Support of an external takeover, e.g., Vietnam.

Left-wing political terrorists seek out business organizations as targets primarily because they view multinational businesses as representatives of capitalism, allies of their ideological enemy: political and economic imperialism.

Business Corporation Countermeasures. Countermeasures by corporations against terrorism should include a series of specific steps: analysis of global, country, corporation, and executive threats and vulnerabilities; development of a corporate policy toward terrorism; implementation of a security survey and protective measures; and establishment of a *crisis management operating plan.* Private security consultant firms will provide professional counsel and assistance in undertaking these steps and manpower to implement any measures desired.

Global Analysis. Assessment of terrorism on a worldwide level would focus on the following points: the general level of political/social instability; terrorist activities; success of specific terrorist tactics and incidents; activity and public statements of governments friendly to terrorist activity; and relationship of the activity of corporations to the aims of terrorists and "friendly" governments.

Country Analysis. On the national level, an analysis would include: past and current political/social problems and incidents; specific terrorist actions; number, structure and capabilities of national security forces; status of the corporation in relation to the government and influence on its political/social activity; other related factors such as crime rates, attitude toward violence, and public opinion.

Corporation Analysis. Analysis of corporate vulnerability would cover a wide range of elements:

(1) Product: environmental impact, military usage, large use of natural resources, manufacture in underdeveloped areas.

(2) Services: profitability for governments which are dictatorial or repress minorities.

(3) Public dissemination of profits.

(4) Degree of dissemination of corporate political views.

(5) Degree of "hardness" and public dissemination of corporate security policy toward terrorism.

(6) Monopoly position of corporation in its own industry.

(7) Employment of foreign nationals in host country.

(8) Efforts to further national goals of host country.

Executive Analysis. On the individual executive level, some of the points to consider are:

(1) Acts or public statements demeaning to the host country's government, workers, or customs.

(2) Displays of wealth and status considered ostentatious by host country.

(3) Provocative political statements about terrorists, their causes or supporting groups.

Development of a Corporate Policy. Once an assessment has been made, corporate policy covering administration, organization, and operations should be established.

Administrative Policy. Administrative policy should define the degree of protection for various levels of executive positions, assignments of responsibility for the executive protection plan, extortion insurance coverage, criteria for engaging in negotiation with terrorists, representatives to handle negotiations, and criteria for compliance with terrorist demands.

Organizational Policy. Organizational policy should clarify the size and nature of the security force established for executive protection, its organizational structure, liaison with law enforcement and related agencies.

Operations Policy. Operations policy should establish specific counteraction during terrorist incidents, including security force response, law enforcement agencies notification, insurance company notification, and liaison treatment of hostage's relatives, etc.

Security Survey and Implementation of Protective Measures. A comprehensive survey of the existing security features of corporation facilities and, especially overseas, of executive activity is essential for the highest practical degree of protection. This should include travel, office, vehicles used, home, and social. Although no security system is completely invulnerable, a greater degree of security reduces the risk of terrorist action by reducing the chance of success.

Private security firms are experienced in providing an in-depth review of corporate security systems, detecting weaknesses, recommending corrective steps, improving existing features and, where required, providing necessary manpower and equipment.

For industrial organizations, an effective security system provides job applicant background investigation, positive employee identification, visitor and vendor control, shipping and receiving area control, parking lot and grounds control, lighting and power equipment control, door locks and key supervision, fire and intruder alarm systems, and where feasible, closed-circuit television surveillance systems installation and operation.

For business offices in urban high-rise or suburban buildings, public access to executive areas should be limited structurally. Office facilities should have exterior doors that lock internally and can be monitored visually; an interior door leading to executive areas should be remotely controlled by both outer perimeter and interior areas and, if possible, linked with local law enforcement agencies. After-hours access to restrooms, offices, maintenance closets, etc., should also be strictly controlled. A "safe room," equipped with emergency communication equipment and food supplies, provides an added measure of protection in areas of high incidence of terrorists attacks.

A highly sensitive business organization should also consider maintaining a low public profile through minimal public identification of its location and operational functions.

Executive Protection. Generally speaking, the most effective principle to practice in executive protection is: *keep a low public profile.* This covers primarily corporate news releases (with photographs) on promotions, transfers, awards, conference participation, travel plans, club memberships, and even social activities.

For example, business and personal travel plans should be kept private and revealed only to those with "a need to know." Executives should also know how to recognize signs that they may be under hostile surveillance. While traveling or commuting, an executive can also carry a normally functional briefcase with a bullet-resistant construction similar to body armor which provides emergency protection against terrorist weapon attacks. The pros and cons of commercial versus corporate aircraft travel should be thoroughly discussed and a firm corporate policy established.

The other major area to consider is the home. While an executive may understandably be reluctant even to be compelled to consider this aspect of protection, the safety of family members is inextricably woven with his own. Therefore, their well-being must also be a primary goal of an effective executive protection plan. A core of procedures and training is available from security professionals in handling unfamiliar visitors, suspicious pretext phone calls, and unusual mail packages; also as regards securing residence doors, locks, lighting, windows, and fire and intruder detection alarms. Here, too, a residence "safe room," especially in high-risk areas, should be given serious consideration.

Crisis Management. If an executive is kidnapped, coordinated response between the crisis management team, executives, security professionals, and hostage negotiator is vital. The key is a well-established emergency plan devised in advance, with definite responsibilities assigned to personnel in a crisis management team who have been thoroughly trained in their specific duties.

In forming a crisis management team, the smaller the group the more effective the response. As a minimum, the team should include a coordinator to supervise operations and deal directly with corporate executives, security consultants, law enforcement personnel, hostage negotiator, insurance company, and the victim's relatives. A legally authorized corporate executive should be designated to make corporate decisions on ransom payments and other matters. (Several alternates should also be selected, since top executives are the most attractive targets for terrorist actions.) A financial officer should be added to handle internal fund transactions and a legal advisor named to counsel on any jurisdictional matters, especially foreign country laws. While a kidnapping should be kept as confidential as possible, news media interest may inadvertently arise and a press officer should be included on the team.

The crisis management plan should specify the conditions under which payment of ransom will be made, and how requests for transportation, supplies, publicity, release of political prisoners, cessation of local corporate operations, etc., will be handled. It should also include emergency biographical data on all corporate executives and the names, addresses, and telephone numbers of all groups involved such as law enforcement agencies, security consultants, hostage negotiators, and crisis management team members. A central meeting place with adequate communications equipment and supplies, should be designated. *The plan should be reviewed periodically by team members.*

While terrorism has not yet occurred on a large scale in the United States, it is becoming increasingly obvious that the nation will not be immune forever. While most terrorist groups have concentrated primarily on bombings of property rather than attacks on individuals, there is no guarantee that these actions will not escalate to kidnappings and assassinations in the future. As a result, the American business community must be prepared by instituting positive prevention measures which will reduce the intensity of this threat.

EDWARD PATROSKI, Director of Investigations, Pinkerton's, Inc., New York, New York

Information References

Hancock, W.A., "Sample Crisis Management Plan," Cleveland, Ohio, Business Laws, Inc.

McClure, Brooks, "The Dynamics of Terrorism," Gaithersburg, Md., International Association of Chiefs of Police, 1976.

Private Security Advisory Council to the Law Enforcement Assistance Administration, U.S. Department of Justice, "Prevention of Terroristic Crimes: Security Guidelines for Business, Industry and Other Organizations," Washington, D.C., Superintendent of Documents, U.S. Government Printing Office, May 1976, Stock No. 027-000-00515-2.

Shaw, Paul D., "Planning for Executive Protection," Gaithersburg, Md., International Association of Chiefs of Police, 1976.

Cross Reference: *Security.*

TESTS FOR EMPLOYMENT. See Personnel Testing: Types of Test.

TIME STUDY. See Motion and Time Study; Predetermined Motion Times; Ratio Delay; Standard Minute System; Work Measurement; Work Measurement in the Office.

TRADE SHOWS AND EXHIBITS

Trade Shows and Exhibits have become an essential marketing tool for virtually all sizeable companies in the United States and for many smaller ones. Although each such exposition tends to have its own characteristics, shows may be divided into three general classifications.

The first is an *industrial exposition* at which manufacturers buy products not for resale but for use in their companies. Such purchases might be equipment for warehousing, such as forklift trucks, or new types of lubricants for maintenance, or components such as original equipment to be used in the making of end products.

Industrial expositions, in turn, are divided into two types. One is *vertical* in that it serves a single industry only, and all exhibits are directed to an audience involved in that industry. The other is *horizontal*—one which is directed to a single function, such as plant engineering, or packaging, or design engineering, or information processing. In short, it is addressed to all types of industries.

Trade shows are a second classification. Exhibits here are of merchandise intended for either retailers who sell directly to the public, or wholesalers and distributors who sell to retailers. These shows exhibit finished merchandise, such as shoes, toys, or furniture, and buyers for retailers or wholesalers attend them. They are usually held seasonally.

The third type of exhibition is a *public show* where exhibitors sell directly to the public. Public shows vary in size from a huge World's Fair to local affairs in small city arenas.

Industrial and trade shows have grown substantially in size, variety, and importance since World War II and seem headed upward still. Dollar figures for the exhibition industry are notoriously hard to come by because there is no single standard by which they may be measured. Does one include the cost of the rental of space only, or the cost of constructing an exhibit background, or the cost of hauling the products to the show site, or the preliminary promotion, or the cost or printed matter or souvenirs, or the salaries of the personnel and their travel and maintenance away from home, or the cost of travel by visitors to and from the show site, or the cost of follow-up work? Since figures for even these single elements are unavailable on any reliable basis, it is idle to try to construct a single figure for the entire industry.

On the other hand, it appears indisputable that exhibiting is one of the most effective, and economical, elements in the marketing mix. A single salesperson's call is currently reckoned at approximately $135, and this is a general average. In some industries, it runs higher. Selling at shows often results in substantial savings.

Shows as Selling Media. Two aspects of shows make them unique as selling media. One is the fact that the item to be sold may be seen in its three dimensions. It may be tried, tested, examined, and used. No printed description, with or without pictures, and no word-of-mouth detailing can be quite as convincing as a real-life demonstration. Obviously, too, it is impossible to carry a motorized sweeper or a huge computer in a salesperson's briefcase.

Second, and perhaps even more important, is the fact that the buyer is coming to the seller, rather than the other way around. This makes for an ideal selling situation. Buyers wear badges which identify them by name, title, and company. Exhibit attendants are trained to use a few specific questions to determine the nature of the visitor's interests.

Many companies find, too, that visitors' questions often will mention unfilled needs and thus reveal potentials for new products. This type of market research, along with expressed dissatisfaction with either the exhibitor's or competitor's products, can often be as valuable as sales.

From the buyer's standpoint, the show offers the wide range of products needed to make an informed decision on a purchase. One sees, in one visit, all that the market has to offer. A prospect may speak to one exhibitor, then move a few feet down the aisle and hear a competitor outline the advantages of his product and the shortcomings of the initial product. After speaking to five or six such exhibitors, the visitor is sufficiently educated to return to the first and hear an informed rebuttal. It is not unusual at this point to call for colleagues to come to the show and, together, make a buying decision.

Shows are produced by either entrepreneurs, called show managements, or by nonprofit associations in a particular trade or business. Shows are international, national, or regional in nature, depending for their character on the audience appealed to. The designation given to a show by its sponsor is not, of course, always indicative of the scope of its audience. As travel expenses rise, however, more attention is being given to regional offshoots of national shows and it is generally believed to be an important trend. Often in regional shows, exhibits are conducted by regional distributors whose expenses are sometimes met, in whole or in part, by a national manufacturer.

Rentals. Exhibit space is rented on the basis of a specified cost per square foot. These costs vary widely from show to show but they are relatively minor compared with the total cost which may include salaries of booth personnel, transportation and living costs, shipment of products to be demonstrated, cost of designing and building booth backgrounds, printing, cost of samples, rental of furniture, hiring demonstrators and receptionists, entertaining customers and the like. On the other hand, a small exhibitor may rent a booth for less than one thousand dollars, (which usually includes a suitable background drape and a sign carrying the name of his company), hand-carry the products he expects to exhibit, do no entertaining, and use previously printed materials. Although costs for large exhibitors, which may also include advertising and promotion to attract visitors, can run into the high six figures, it is not uncommon to see small booths, individually staffed by owner-executives, do a thriving business.

Effectiveness of Participation. Exhibiting companies should carefully examine their objectives when they plan their exhibit. A company must know what it hopes to accomplish, direct every effort toward that goal, and analyze carefully the results after the show closes.

Selling at a show is measurably different from other forms of selling and the booth staff must be trained to recognize the differences. Considerable study must be given to the nature of the products to be demonstrated, the booth background, the number of booth attendants to be present, the amount of floor space required, the type of printed materials to distribute, and the type of demonstration to be used.

By far the most important element in the latter grouping is the need for an effective demonstration. A demonstration which is both eye-catching and self-explanatory of the virtues of the product is, of course, best. This dual-purpose demonstration is not always easy to achieve, but care should be taken not to substitute shallow, eye-catching devices.

Women in skimpy attire, often the first-resort of the unimaginative exhibitor, may draw a crowd of interested men but do little to sell a product. On the other hand, a man in a shop coat actually using the product will sometimes draw an even larger group, because business executives at a show are earnest about seeking answers to their problems. Sometimes, of course, a graceful woman operating what is assumed to be a difficult machine may emphasize ease of operation. In short, knowing one's objectives and executing the exhibit plan to achieve them will make show-going profitable.

Selection of the right show to attend is probably the most important element of all. If the show is well-established, the task is simplified. A conscientious show management will provide a prospective exhibitor with an analysis of the attendance, broken down among several approaches. Among the data provided should be the total number of those who attended, from what geographical areas they came, the types of industries (in the case of horizontal industrial expositions), the titles of the visitors, and the like.

The reputation of the show management or the sponsoring organization is paramount because figures can be falsified. Some show managements will provide a serious exhibitor with the name, title, company, and address of every single visitor. This may be the most precise proof needed. Other reputable show managements provide totals which are audited by an independent agency.

What the Show Management Offers. The most valuable element the show management offers is the audience. Without a good audience, there is no show. A prospective exhibitor should inquire, therefore, about management's activities to produce this audience. To what extent will it advertise the show, how many pieces of direct mail does it plan to distribute, what promotional aids will it offer the exhibitor, how extensive will its publicity activities be? Given a good, solid audience of prospects, an exhibitor should have a successful show if he has planned his demonstration carefully. Show management's responsibility ends, however, when the audience passes through the show's doors. It is up to the exhibitor to be certain that part of that audience stops at his booth.

While a good demonstration is, as stated, fundamental, there are supplementary methods, which will ensure that the exhibitor gets its fair share of the audience. Advertising, promotion, and publicity provide the answer. A careful exhibitor will consult with its advertising agency to ensure that its participation in an important show is mentioned prominently. It will distribute promotional materials, such as advance registration cards, conference programs, discount tickets when these are provided, and show guides through the mails and through its sales force and distributors. It will send special letters of invitation to customers and prospects and will include mention of its participation in external house organs, on mailing machine imprints, and by inserts and stick-on labels in its mail.

Some shows are accompanied by conferences. When they are, conference registrants often are identified by special badges. Since conference registrants pay substantially higher fees, spend more time at the show, and are generally of a higher echelon, a careful exhibit staff will look closely for such badges. In selecting a show, it is a good idea to ask if there will be a conference, what its scope is, and how well attended the sessions are expected to be.

Follow-through. Trade shows for retailers and wholesalers usually concentrate on immediate sales, and there is considerable order-taking right in the booth. At industrial expositions, because products purchased often have to be used in a larger system, extensive further conversations at the prospect's plant may be required. Accordingly, the concentration is in obtaining qualified inquiries.

Inquiries should be immediately classified according to the nature of the interest. Immediate or deferred, intense or casual interest should be noted. The value of the show may easily be lost if inquiries are not followed promptly and carefully. The system for such follow-up should be in place long before the show opens. It can be just as ineffective to ask sales personnel or distributors to spend time with those who have only casual interest as to fail to meet with those whose interest is real and immediate.

SAUL POLIAK, President, Clapp & Poliak, Inc.
New York, New York

Information References

Associations:

American Assn. of Association Executives.
Association of National Advertisers (Shows & Exhibits Committee).
Business/Professional Advertising Assn.
Exhibit Designers & Producers Assn.
Exposition Service Contractors Assn.
International Assn. of Auditorium Managers.
International Assn. of Convention & Visitors Bureaus.
International Assn. of Fairs & Expositions.
National Assn. of Exposition Managers.
National Trade Show Exhibitors Assn.
Professional Convention Management Assn.
Trade Show Bureau.

Periodicals:

Association & Society Manager.
Association Management.
Canadian Sales Meetings & Conventions.
Industrial Marketing.
Medical Meetings.
Meetings & Expositions.
Sales & Marketing Management.
Successful Meetings (also publishes a full calendar of expositions).
Tradeshow Convention Guide.
Tradeshow Week.
World Convention Dates.

Texts:

"The Exhibit Medium," Philadelphia, *Successful Meetings.*
Hanlon, Al, "Creative Selling through Trade Shows," New York, Hawthorn, 1977.
Konikow, Robt., "How to Participate Profitably in Trade Shows," Chicago, Dartnell, 1977.
"The Invisible Line: A Motion Picture for Training Booth Personnel," New York, Clapp & Poliak, Inc.
"Key to an Effective Industrial Exhibit," New York, Banner & Greif, Ltd.
"Pre-Show Promotion," New York, Banner & Greif, Ltd.
"Reducing Exhibit Costs," New York, Clapp & Poliak, Inc.
Trade Show Bureau Reports and Studies.

Cross References: *Advertising Media; Sales Promotion.*

TRADEMARKS

Trademarks are words or other symbols used to identify a particular company's goods and to distinguish them from the goods of others. Although the development, promotion, and protection of trademarks is an important facet of modern business, the use of a distinguishing mark of the maker dates back to Ancient Greece and Egypt. Today, almost half a million trademarks are on file at the United States Patent and Trademark Office, and about 50,000 new applications are filed every year.

Usually valued at one dollar on corporate balance sheets, trademarks can become property of exceptional value. A company that has earned a reputation for the quality and integrity of its trademarked products, that has made a substantial investment in promoting and merchandising them so that the particular brand is in demand, may well find the trademark to be worth millions of dollars. The courts have recognized this fact and sizable sums of money often are involved in infringement litigation.

Laws that protect trademarks in the United States include the Federal registration statute known as the Lanham Act, common law, individual registration statutes in the fifty states, and criminal laws covering counterfeiting, etc. in most of the states, and in foreign countries by local statutes, and throughout the world by convention or treaty. Since World War II, significant progress in establishing and protecting the rights of the trademark owner was made through the adoption of the Lanham Act which became effective in July of 1947.

It is generally understood that the more successful a trademark becomes the greater is the need to protect it. The danger is not only infringement. There is the possibility of losing the trademark by default. If it is not used properly and consistently, if a competitor is allowed to use a similar mark without challenge, if it is allowed to degenerate into generic use, the trademark can be lost.

Formal Definitions. A trademark or brand is a word, a symbol, a device, a name, a design or a combination of these used to designate the product of a particular manufacturer or merchant (in much the same terms as a rancher's brand on his cattle) and to distinguish it from the products of competitors. *Trademark* and *brand name* are synonymous terms. A *trade name* is not a trademark, but rather the company name under which the company does business. Some companies, however, use the same term both as a trademark and as a trade name, e.g., "Ford" and "Chrysler." The trademark essentially is used as identification: it is the brand name for a single product or a line of products, but never the generic term for a product; it may often double as a symbol for the company itself in doing business (e.g., GE, IBM, ALCAN); it provides a legal means of protecting the consumer, the company, and the product from deceptive imitations.

The trademark is used on goods, in packaging, on business documents, in advertising, display, and promotion. It is the company's "calling card" to the trade and to the public in stores, on radio, or television, or billboards, in newspapers, and in magazines. The trademark is always used with a capital letter. If a trademark is federally registered, it may carry with it a registration mark or notice. (® or Reg. U.S. Pat. and Tm. Off.)

History. The first recorded trademark is 4,000 years old. It is the emblem of the maker of a piece of pottery discovered in the ruins of Corinth. The sign or identification of the maker has been found on many artifacts uncovered among ancient Grecian ruins and in Egyptian tombs. In the Middle Ages, goldsmiths and silversmiths were required to mark their wares for the protection of the public. In England, the marks were filed at Goldsmiths' Hall and some of these "hallmarks" have survived to this day. An account dating back to the reign of Elizabeth I tells of one of the earliest examples of trademark litigation on record: "A clothier of Gloucestershire sold very good cloth, so that in London if they saw any cloth of his mark they would buy it without searching thereof; and another who made ill cloth put his mark on it without privity; and an action was brought by him who bought the cloth, for this deceipt; and adjudged maintainable." In France in the 16th century false labelling was punishable by death. In the United States, common law established the right of a trademark originator since Colonial times.

Modern Practice. The first broad, truly-effective statute for registration of trademarks on a national level was enacted in 1905. The Federal Trademark Act (Lanham Act of 1946) provides extensive legal protection through registration on the so-called "principal register." After five years of continuous use (subject to certain limitations and exceptions) a trademark so registered becomes "incontestable." The Act also provides for the registration of "service marks" (for services), "certification marks" (to certify origin, quality, etc.), and "collective marks" (for members of a cooperative, collective group or organization, etc.). It also provides for the registration of labels, packages, and configurations of goods on a "supplemental register." To increase understanding of trademarks, protect the interests of the public in the use of trademarks, and to promote the interests of trademark owners generally in the use of their trademarks, The United States Trademark Association was founded in 1878. Today, many major corporations interested in the future of their trademarks are members.

A good trademark performs three key functions: it distinguishes the product from those of competitors; it serves as a guarantee of consistency of quality; it helps to advertise and sell the product. Selecting a useable, acceptable, and marketable trademark requires the advice and assistance of specialists among whom should be included legal trademark counsel, as well as specialists from Public Relations, Advertising, Design, Market Research, Sales, and other areas of the company which may be particularly affected. The U.S. Patent and Trademark Office (PTO) has rejected hundreds of applications which have overlooked certain prohibitions. A new mark should not resemble another already in use in a similar field. It should not be descriptive of the product on which it is used, although it may be suggestive. Geographical terms and family surnames used as trademarks create special problems which should be thoroughly explored with legal counsel before adoption.

Registration of a mark is absolutely prohibited if it comprises immoral, deceptive, or scandalous matter; matter which may disparage or falsely suggest a connection with persons, institutions, beliefs, or national symbols; or matter that uses the flag or coat of arms of the United States, any state, municipality, or foreign nation. The name of a living person may not be used without consent. Sometimes, an established "house mark" of a company (such as AMF, GE, IBM) or a derivative of an existing trademark of the company (e.g. Kodachrome from Kodak) is used on a new product. A new brand name generally is selected from the following categories: an invented, arbitrary or coined word; a word that is suggestive of the article; a business or family name or derivative of them; a portrait, picture, symbol, or other illustration which may be accompanied by a word or phrase.

Although it is not required that a company register its mark in the Patent and Trademark Office, doing so does provide advantages for the owner. Registration gives public notice of rightful ownership and exclusive right to use. It may represent conclusive evidence of the right to exclusive use and it may be used as the basis for obtaining registration in foreign countries. In the United States a trademark must be in use in interstate commerce before it can be federally registered. The owner of the mark may then submit a written application to the Patent Office setting forth the goods on which it is currently being used, accompanied by a drawing of the mark, five specimens or facsimilies, the date of its first use, and a nominal fee established by law.

Under the Lanham Act, registration is permitted for collective marks (used by members of a union, association, cooperative, or other group to indicate membership), certification marks (used by others beside the owner to certify origin or quality, such as seals of approval), and service marks (a symbol, name or slogan used in advertising or sale of services to identify them). If the application is approved, the trademark will be published in the *Official Gazette* of the PTO to enable anyone who feels that he would be damaged by registration of that mark to file his opposition within thirty days. The renewal term for registration in the U.S. Patent and Trademark Office is twenty years, and registrations are renewable indefinitely, as long as the marks are in use.

Trademarks also may be registered in each of the fifty states and in most foreign countries. (See TRADEMARKS: International Protection.) State registration fees range from $1 to $50; the official fees for registering in all states amounts to about $750. Marks are registered in perpetuity in one state (West Virginia); in others they are renewable after ten or twenty years.

To prevent the loss of a trademark through misuse, a continuous effort usually is made by the owners to "police" the mark. Courts take cognizance of the way a mark is used by its owner as well as the manner in which it is reproduced in print by others. To maintain his exclusive right to the mark, the owner must exercise due diligence by seeking out and correcting misuse, whether in the press, radio, or television, or by a competitor, a dealer or a distributor. These issues are relevant in any judicial determination of whether or not a trademark has become generic. Proper use contributes to the maintenance of the mark. Improper use can lead to the loss of the mark.

Enforcement. In most instances, regular use of the statutory notice (e.g., ®) and proper use of the registered mark will be all that is necessary to put competitors and the public on notice of the company's trademark rights. In some situations, such as where a mark is threatened with genericness, or being made part of the general language, it may be advisable to undertake a "trademark advertising" campaign to educate the public of the value and proper use of the particular mark. Instances of truly innocent misuse of a mark by competitors, distributors, or others usually can be corrected by a simple letter or some other informal approach.

Any successful business may, however, see imitators and pirates in the marketplace who intend to appropriate or share unfairly in that market success.

Copying a successful trademark and related activities such as copying the trade dress (label, packaging, etc.), advertising, product shapes and colors, and the like, are typical devices of the unfair competitor. In such situations, the Lanham Act provides extensive relief.

Moreover, even fair-minded persons may disagree strongly whether or not use of a particular mark in certain circumstances is an infringement.

Trademark litigation can be expensive and time-consuming, and requires the involvement of a trademark attorney who is well-versed in the intricacies of the trademark laws and the psychology of the marketplace.

There are a number of basic questions to be answered in most trademark infringement cases, such as: (1) Does the plaintiff (trademark owner), have a valid trademark? (2) Is the trademark registration valid and is the plaintiff's title good? (3) Are the plaintiff's rights prior in time to the defendant's (accused infringer's) use? (4) Are the plaintiff's rights sufficiently strong (nature of the mark and its use; extent of advertising and sales; secondary meaning; incontestability of registration; etc.)? (5) Is the defendant's use of the accused mark likely to cause confusion, mistake, or deception (requiring consideration of the appearance, pronunciation, and connotation of the respective marks; the products or services involved and their relationship in marketing and in use; the likely degree of care exercised in purchasing decisions; the defendant's intent; and other factors)? No infringement will be found where the mark is invalid or where there is no finding of a likelihood of confusion.

Relief. Remedies which are available to a trademark owner under the Lanham Act include: injunctions against future infringements; recovery of the infringer's profits, the trademark owner's damages, and the costs of the lawsuit; a possible award of three times the actual damages or such other additional monetary award as is found to be just; in "exceptional cases," an award of reasonable attorney's fees; surrender and destruction of labels, advertisements, and other objects bearing the infringing mark; cancellation of conflicting registrations; and other relief.

DOROTHY FEY, Executive Director, The United States Trademark Association, New York, New York

LAWRENCE S. WICK, Leydig, Voit, Osann, Mayer & Holt, Ltd., Chicago, Illinois

Information References

(The foregoing text represents a guide in the general areas of trademarks. It is recommended that trademark counsel be consulted on all specifics.)

Associations:

The United States Trademark Association.
Patent law associations throughout the United States.

Periodicals:

The Trademark Reporter (USTA).

Texts:

"Handbook for the Executive as a Witness," 1980.
"Trademarks in Advertising & Selling," 1966.
"Trademarks in the Marketplace," 1964.
"Trademark Licensing." 1962.
"Trademark Management," 1981.
"Trademark Problems in Acquisitions and Mergers," 1968.
"Trademarks and Brand Management: Selected Annotations," 1976.
(Above published by United States Trademark Association).

Cross References: *Copyright; Industrial* Design; *Franchising: Legal Aspects; Patents; Trademarks: International Protection.*

TRADEMARKS: International Protection

Protection of the **Trademarks** of United States companies in foreign markets is a matter of growing importance not only to major multinational corporations, but also to businesses of all sizes that are now selling their products and services abroad or are contemplating doing so. Adequate attention to foreign trademark protection is important in order to ensure that future market expansion is not impeded by some enterprising foreign "trademark entrepreneur" or as a natural result of competition abroad.

Unfortunately, as of 1981 there is no single procedure by which a United States company may obtain trademark protection worldwide, or even in all major industrialized and developing markets. A large company with major foreign markets may proceed to obtain worldwide trademark protection as a matter of course in the 200 or more foreign trademark jurisdictions, prior to any new market entry. But for many companies, such protection necessarily will be limited to existing and planned expansion markets, or a selection of the most important markets, even though the cost of acquiring such protection may be comparatively low. Reliance upon local foreign distributors or the like for such protection frequently leads to unfortunate conflicts, such as involvement in undesired local litigation, or a belated discovery that the foreign company has acquired the local rights.

Preliminary Planning. Adequate time for choosing a trademark for use in domestic and foreign markets may be an unavailable luxury, particularly where a mark already is in use. Where there is an opportunity for such considerations, selection of a mark should involve essentially two questions, whether they are to be answered by a company's owners, senior executives, marketing, advertising, sales or other personnel, outside consultants, trademark counsel, or a combination of them: (1) What is the anticipated value of the mark as a marketing and advertising tool? (2) Is the mark available for use and registration in the intended markets?

In considering the availability of the mark for use and registration, trademark counsel can be of assistance to businessmen in offering preliminary advice and conducting any necessary searches. Certain kinds of marks generally are not registrable or cannot be used in many or all jurisdictions. For example, most countries restrict or prohibit the use of government or other official names, flags, and symbols; marks which are contrary to local political, moral and/or religious precepts; and other such marks [1]. Many countries also restrict or prohibit the registration of descriptive or generic marks; personal or geographic names; colors, letters or numbers; or the like [2]. The strength of the mark also ought to be considered. (See TRADEMARKS.) Not only the English pronunciation and meaning of the mark, but also the relevant foreign pronunciations, meanings, and translations ought to be reviewed.

Once one or more potential marks have been selected, it is often advisable to have a trademark search made in the selected countries, in order to discover potential conflicts or other problems. Most countries prohibit registration of marks which are confusingly similar to or otherwise resemble previously registered marks, and an effective search is designed to uncover those problems, although no search can be infallible.

Armed with these results, management should be in a position to select its new mark with greater certainty and awareness of the relative business and legal risks which may be involved.

Registration. In most countries, trademark rights are secured simply by registration, whether or not the mark has been used. The United States is one of the few countries which requires that a mark be used on the products or for the services before an application for registration may be filed.

In some countries, generally including most of what are known as the "civil law" or "code" countries, the national laws provide that a trademark is actually acquired by registration, not by use, whether or not someone else already may have been using the mark in that country. The first to obtain the registration acquires all of the exclusive rights. These countries include France, West Germany, Japan, Mexico, Brazil, Egypt, most of the other countries of Europe and South America, much of Asia and Africa, most of the Communist world, excluding Albania, and others.

In many other countries, including the "common law", "British law" and some code countries, the first to use a mark generally is entitled to a trademark registration. Virtually all of these countries (excluding the United States and a few others) permit an application to be filed without first using the mark, on the basis of intent or a declaration that use of the mark will begin in the particular country. These countries include the United Kingdom, Canada, Australia, Ireland, Israel, Liechtenstein, Panama, Switzerland, most of the former British colonies in Africa and Asia, and others.

In many situations where filing priorities must be assigned for economic or other reasons, it may be more important for a company to acquire trademark registrations first in countries where the rights are based on registration, rather than on actual use, because as a general rule it is easier and more effective in those countries for competitors or others to obtain the exclusive rights in the particular mark.

Except in some convention countries, a United States company may acquire trademark registrations only by filing written applications in each individual country. In typical situations, powers of attorney, a description of the goods (or services, where service marks may be registered), copies of the trademark, and a limited number of other formal papers simply are supplied to a trademark attorney or agent, who handles the details of the registration. Some countries require a U.S. company to submit a copy of a U.S. registration for the mark; and in those situations, advance planning is essential because it may take several years to obtain a U.S. registration. Nearly all countries have an examination or review procedure, which sometimes is no more than a determination that the papers are in proper form. In some countries, procedures are available for interested parties to oppose or object to applications, and all provide for the cancellation of registrations for various reasons, such as failure to use the mark, or another's proof of superior local rights. Trademark registrations are effective for as little as five years (as in Mexico) to as long as 60 years (as in Lebanon), and are renewable.

Treaties and Conventions. A U.S. company may file a single trademark application for registration in Belgium, the Netherlands, and Luxembourg under the terms of the Benelux Trademark Treaty of 1971. A similar procedure has been available for certain French-speaking countries in Africa. These are the only procedures now available for U.S. companies to acquire a registration in multiple countries from a single application, although in certain situations it may be possible to make international filings through foreign subsidiaries or by other arrangements.

The United States is a member of the International Convention of Paris (1883) which allows a U.S. company to claim rights in foreign applications based upon an earlier U.S. trademark filing date, and provides other reciprocal benefits, but no provision is made for multiple-country registrations. Both the Paris Convention and the Pan American Convention (1929) also protect U.S. interests to some extent against unfair competition and trademark infringement in some countries. The Trademark Registration Treaty, which has been signed by the United States but not ratified by the U.S. Senate as of early 1981, would provide U.S. companies with a procedure for obtaining trademark registrations in many countries by filing a single international application at a United Nations agency in Switzerland, called the International Bureau of the World Intellectual Property Organization. Supporters claim that the Treaty would simplify worldwide trademark protection procedures and cut costs. Opponents insist that the Treaty would obstruct internal U.S. trademark procedures and increase costs.

Ownership Rights. As in the United States, the U.S. owner of a foreign-registered trademark can license, sell, or otherwise transfer the rights, and generally can prevent others from using the same or confusingly similar marks in the marketplace. Registration of a mark therefor plays an important role in an orderly marketplace, in creating demand for the owner's products and services, and in curtailing poaching, piracy, and other forms of unfair competition.

Some countries require licensees to file as "registered users," and assignments generally must be recorded. In some countries, failure to record may invalidate the registration. The national law of many countries contemplates trademark licensing in franchising and similar market distribution arrangements. (See FRANCHISING: Legal Aspects.)

LAWRENCE S. WICK, Attorney, Leydig, Voit, Osann, Mayer & Holt, Ltd., Chicago, Illinois

Information References

The United States Trademark Association
Greene, A.M., "Trademarks Throughout the World" New York, Trade Activities, Inc., 3rd ed., 1980. (Digests of trademark laws of various countries; periodic subscription supplements.)

References Cited

[1] The United Kingdom, for example, restricts, among other things, the use of representations of Her Majesty, any member of the Royal Family, the words "Red Cross," "Geneva Cross," "Red Crescent," "Red Lion and Sun," the Royal or Imperial Arms, among others; in the People's Republic of China, every country's national flags, emblems, or medals, the markings of the "Red Cross" or "Red Cresent," and marks which have an "ill effect politically," such as Nazi emblems, are barred from registration.

[2] In Brazil, as an example, an isolated letter, numeral or date is unregistrable, unless it has been displayed in a distinctive manner. Brazil also prohibits registration of, among other things: generic names, including words commonly used to indicate weight, value, quality, nationality, etc.; colors and names of colors, unless used in an original combination; geographic names; and product packages and shapes.

Cross References: *Copyright; Franchising: Legal Aspects; Industrial Design; Patents; Trademarks.*

TRAFFIC AND TRANSPORTATION: Structure of the Transportation Industry

The **Transportation Industry** is fundamentally structured according to the technologies employed in the physical movement of goods and passengers. There are five basic technological forms, each comprising a separate **mode of transportation.** These modes are *rail, highway, pipeline, water,* and *air.*

Legal Forms. In addition to the basic technological groupings, there is a second type of subdivision of the transportation industry based on the legal forms of individual carriers. To a greater or lesser extent, these different legal forms cut across the five basic transportation modes as a secondary striation of the industry.

The *common carrier* is, in legal form, the cornerstone of the transportation industry, offering its services for hire to the general public. By law it is obliged to make its services publicly available on a non-discriminatory basis; this is the traditional "common carrier obligation" which, although somewhat weakened by deregulatory legislation in the 1976–80 period, remains a significant limitation on the ability of common carriers to pick and choose the business they will handle.

The *contract carrier* is akin to the common carrier in that it offers its services for hire on a commercial basis; but, unlike the common carrier, it deals only with those customers it chooses on a contractual basis. The only obligation that devolves upon it is that which is imposed by the contract(s) into which it enters.

The *private carrier* is, as the name implies, strictly proprietorial in terms of its transport operations. It provides transportation service only for itself, as an adjunct to its other non-transportation business activities. A 1980 change in the law also allows enterprises that are 100% affiliated (through common ownership, parent-subsidiary relationship, etc.) to provide private carriage for one another on a compensated basis; previously, private carriage had been limited to a single business entity with all other transportation considered for-hire in nature.

Railroads. Railroads are the oldest form of mechanized transportation, the first commercial rail transport operations having been initiated well over 150 years ago. They provide principally common carriage to the shipping public, although beginning in the late 1970s they were permitted to enter into extended-term contracts with individual shippers, and there are also a few industrial (proprietorial) rail services.

In terms of ton-miles, railroads still provide a greater share of the nation's freight transportation service than does any other mode, although the percentage of freight traffic moving by rail has fallen from 70+% as recently as the World War II era to only about one-third of total volume today. Rail passenger service has suffered a much more precipitous decline because of the growing role of automobile, airline and, to some extent, bus travel. Today the only long-haul rail passenger service of any consequence is provided by the National Rail Passenger Corp. (Amtrak) on a government-subsidized basis; and there also remains a limited, diminishing amount of rail commuter service in a few major metropolitan areas.

Rail carriers are unique in the transportation industry (except for pipeline) in that they operate over privately owned and maintained rights of way. This imposes on the railroad industry a major investment requirement not shared by other modes; coupled with equipment and terminal expenses, it produces the highest ratio of fixed to total costs in the transportation industry.

Railroads' energy consumption per unit of service is among the lowest in the transporation industry, because of the technological and operating considerations that encourage maximum utilization of motive power. The railroads' ability to alter the makeup of trains by adding or subtracting both payload cars and locomotive units, plus the relatively gentle grading of railroad tracks and the lower coefficient of friction where steel wheel turns on steel rail, allows great energy efficiency, especially on longer hauls. As energy costs increase, this factor may give railroads a significant competitive boost and help them recover at least a portion of their dwindling market share.

Labor is a long-standing railroad industry problem. Rail carriers have been rigidly unionized for many years, and operate under strict, often technologically archaic work rules that produce serious cost inefficiencies in this area. The labor situation is proving one of the most serious impediments to the carriers' efforts to improve their economic and competitive posture; union leaders are extremely reluctant to make concessions in work rules (which in extreme cases guarantee a worker a full day's pay for as little as two or three hours' actual work) or accept reductions in labor force even by attrition.

Another major problem confronting the railroads is the antiquity and inefficiency of their gigantic capital plant, much of which (trackage, terminals, yards, etc.) was originally built half a century or more ago when socioeconomic conditions were vastly different. Much of the existing rail plant is redundant and/or underutilized, while at the same time the high costs and difficulties of building new plants have kept the carriers from exploiting new or changed markets.

Legislation enacted in 1976 (the Railroad Revitalization and Regulatory Reform—"4-R"—Act) and 1980 (the Staggers Rail Act) has gone far toward reducing the rail industry's problems. Basically, these acts grant railroads much greater pricing freedom by removing many regulatory constraints, and encourage them to rationalize their operating plant to attain greater operating efficiencies.

Notwithstanding the new legislation, the railroad industry remains in serious trouble in certain geographic regions. As of mid-1981, Conrail—the amalgam of a number of once-proud railroads serving the northeast which plummeted into bankruptcy in the late 1960s—continued to struggle with heavy red ink, kept afloat only by Federal financial aid. In the north central region, the Chicago, Rock Island & Pacific (the storied "Rock Island Line") was liquidated in the late 1970s, and the Chicago, Milwaukee, St. Paul & Pacific declared bankruptcy in the same period.

Elsewhere, however, there were signs of health among the railroads. Especially encouraging were a number of mergers of major carriers in the late 1970s and early 1980s, spurred in part by legeslative relaxations, which promised greater operating efficiencies and elimination of redundant plants for the carriers involved.

Highway. Commercial motor carriage, although in existence for almost the entire twentieth century, did not rise into real prominence as a mode of transportation (freight or passenger) until after World War II. Today motor carriers provide large measures of common, contract, and private carriage of freight, and a significant volume of common carriage of passengers.

In terms of ton-miles, truck transportation of freight still lags behind the railroad sector, with a market share of approximately 25%. Because of the different distance-related economies of scale for the two modes, however, trucks actually haul considerably more tonnage than do railroads—40% as against the railroads' 25%—with the trucks' much shorter average haul responsible for the spread. In terms of passenger-miles, buses account for 11%–12% of all commercial intercity travel (leaving aside private automobile travel); while local-transit bus operations provide varying proportions of local transportation service in different metropolitan areas.

Major road-building programs, culminating in the construction of the Interstate Highway System (begun in the 1950s and essentially completed by the mid-1970s), afford motor carriers of both freight and passengers enormous flexibility. Funding for these construction programs was provided by the Federal and, to a much smaller extent, state and local governments, out of user-charge collections in the form of fuel and various other automotive taxes; however, since this tax burden is shared by the huge number of private automobiles, commercial carriers have not had to bear anything like the full amount of the economic load.

Accordingly, fixed costs of commercial motor carriers are relatively quite low—especially since the greatest proportion of the user-type taxes is based on fuel purchases, and is in consequence treated as operating and not capital costs. Fixed capital investment in the motor transportation sector is mainly in operating equipment (truck, trailers, buses, etc.) and terminal buildings and other facilities.

Because of the wide range of services provided by motor carriers, energy efficiency in this sector of the transportation industry varies widely. For long-haul transportation of heavy lading, it can approach the level achieved by the railroad sector; whereas for other types of operations (particularly "peddle run" pickup-and-delivery transportation in short-haul markets, involving short distances and many stops) it is quite poor. The upsurge in energy costs during the 1970s produced significant technological advances in terms of engines, aerodynamic design, etc., aimed at reducing fuel consumption per unit of service. However, the level of improvement in fuel efficiency was much smaller during this era than was the increase in fuel costs.

Labor accounts for the preponderance of motor carrier costs—as much as 70% of total costs for some carriers. This is occasioned by both the relative labor-intensity of motor carriage as compared to other transportation modes and the importance of the powerful Teamsters Union, which has driven wage rates to among the highest in the country.

Among motor carriers of freight, there are basically three categories:

(1) The "supermarket" type of carrier that provides a wide range of service to its customers on a standardized, mass-production-type basis. For the most part these are common carriers, the largest of which have revenues approaching half a billion annually (although there are also many much smaller carriers of this basic type). Some carriers also provide contract-carrier services to some customers under a recent regulatory liberalization that permits such "dual" (common and contract carriage) services.

(2) Specialized carriers which, because of the type of equipment they have and/or their own operating abilities and limitations, serve only limited market sectors. Among these are carriers that specialize in transportation of unusually heavy and/or bulky commodities ("heavy haulers"), or perishable items that must move under temperature-controlled conditions, or small package freight, etc. This category includes both common and contract carriers as well as a limited number of private carriers, and runs the gamut from extremely large to extremely small operators.

(3) "Boutique"-type carriers, that limit their services (usually geographically) to small market segments for managerial, rather than operational, reasons. These carriers include most of the smaller firms in this sector of the transportation industry, in all three legal forms of carriage (or some blend of two or more such forms).

The Motor Carrier Act of 1980 sharply reduced Federal regulation of motor carriage, allowing relatively free entry into the business and granting carriers much greater flexibility in rate and service areas. Its purpose was to introduce a greater element of competition into the industry in order to stimulate innovation and efficiency. While it is too early, as of mid-1981, to assess the effects of this legislation, likely results appear to be a sharp reduction in the total number of carriers (estimated at over 15,000 regulated carriers, and a great many more unregulated, as of 1980), a greater range of competitive options in major market areas, and some reduction in service (or increase in rates) for smaller markets.

Pipelines. Although in both form and operations a mode of transportation, the pipeline industry is to some degree a breed apart from the other modes of transportation. The basic distinction is that, because of technological limitations, pipelines transport only two products—oil and natural gas.

Despite these limitations, pipelines account for a high proportion of total transportation in the United States. Oil pipelines provide nearly a quarter of the total transportation service, in terms of ton-miles, in the country. (Natural gas is not included in the figures measuring volume of freight transportation.)

Like railroads, pipeline carriers own their own rights of way—the underground pipes through which the oil and natural gas move. Fixed costs are thus extremely high relative to total costs—higher even than the railroads,' since operating costs are of course quite low.

Historically, oil pipelines were regulated by the Interstate Commerce Commission, while natural gas pipelines were under the aegis of the Federal Power Commission. These jurisdictions were combined in the 1970s into the Federal Energy Regulatory Commission, which now has both economic and safety jurisdiction.

The extreme high energy efficiency and low operating costs of pipelines ensures their continuation as prime carriers of oil and natural gas; indeed, both sectors of the industry are in the process of expansion to serve the newly developing domestic sources of these fuels. There are also proposals for development of new pipeline networks to transport "slurries" (particles suspended in water) of coal and metal ores, although economic and political problems have thus far held up progress in this area.

Water. Relative to the three modes thus far discussed, water carriage is of lesser importance in the total United States transportation picture. Nevertheless, it is of great importance in those areas accessible to navigable waterways—principally the coastal markets, the Mississippi-Missouri system, and the Great Lakes.

Domestically, water transportation accounts for about 16% of total freight movements in ton-mile terms—a third along the Great Lakes, and the remainder on the Mississippi-Missouri and the Intracoastal Waterways. Nearly as much traffic again, in ton-miles, moves in oceanborne commerce, accounting for the vast preponderance of import/export freight transportation.

Ocean carriers pay little or nothing for the thoroughfares over which they operate, since they provide service on the high seas; their only fixed costs, except for terminals and vessels, are limited tax assessments to cover port dredging. Until the late 1970s, domestic water carriers were in the same situation; currently, however, they must pay user charges, in the form of fuel taxes, to cover a limited proportion of waterway improvements.

Because of this cost situation, and the fact that water transportation is not especially labor-intensive and has extremely good energy efficiency, water carriers have been able to compete domestically with other modes of transportation quite well. The carriers' markets, however, are of course quite limited because of the need for navigable waterways, which has greatly restricted their impact on the transportation industry.

In international ocean commerce, the U.S. merchant marine for decades operated at an almost insuperable disadvantage *vis-á-vis* the ocean transport fleets of other nations. High construction costs and high labor costs made U.S.-flag carriers non-competitive. Had it not been for both government construction subsidies and legislation requiring that much U.S. cargo be transported aboard U.S.-flag vessels, the American merchant marine would have virtually vanished in the 1955–1975 era.

Changing world economic relationships, however, may herald something of a comeback for the U.S. merchant marine in the 1980s. Relatively speaking, American construction and labor costs are no longer out of proportion by comparison with other major industrialized nations. American-flag vessels must still contend with heavy government subsidization of foreign fleets (especially where Iron Curtain countries are involved), and also with "flag-of-convenience" vessels operating out of tiny nations whose major attraction is ease of vessel registration and lack of safety and other restrictions. Nevertheless, the outlook is appreciably brighter for the American fleet today.

Ocean transportation, by both U.S.-flag vessels and foreign-flag ships that call at U.S. ports or carry U.S. cargoes, is regulated by the Federal Maritime Commission. Domestic water transportation is under the jurisdiction of the Interstate Commerce Commission under increasingly loose regulatory standards.

Air. Commercial aviation did not become of significance as a mode of transportation until the advent of the jet age in the 1950s. Today it has carved out a major share of the common carrier passenger transportation sector, and lesser shares of common, contract, and even private carriage of freight.

In terms of ton-miles, relatively little freight transportation is performed by air carriers—about two-tenths of 1% of total domestic movements, and not a great deal more internationally. In passenger transportation, however, airlines have become the predominant public mode (again leaving aside automobile travel), with a market share of about 80% in passenger-miles.

Airlines enjoy relatively low fixed costs, since they are not responsible for construction or maintenance of their own terminals; these are paid for out of public funds collected through user-charge taxes that generally fall into the category of operating costs for the airlines. Even so, airline fixed costs are not negligible; a single commercial aircraft can cost upward of $20 million (some run as high as $100 million or more), and some ground installations are also required.

Fuel accounts for the preponderance of airline operating costs, since aircraft, despite technological advances of the past few years that have somewhat improved energy efficiency, are extremely fuel-intensive. Labor costs are likewise high; unionization pressures, plus the high level of skill required in many areas, make airline employees among the highest paid in any industry.

In the late 1970s, Congress acted to deregulate substantially all aspects of the air transportation industry (although phasing out of preexisting regulations, and some residual jurisdiction, will leave the Civil Aeronautics Board in existence until at least the middle of the 1980s). Initially the results have been intensification of competition among major carriers in the bigger markets, and establishment of a number of new (or greatly enlarged) carriers to serve both small and large markets. In major markets, passenger fares and freight rates have in some cases been sharply reduced, and service improved, because of the new competitive pressures—particularly where such actions appear likely to attract new business to this sector of the transportation industry. Service has somewhat diminished, however, and fares and rates have (relatively) risen, in many smaller markets. This is the industry sector where the results of the deregulatory legislation that was enacted in the 1976–80 period are most clearly visible, and those results appear to be fairly mixed (at least as of mid-1981).

Freight Forwarders. A sixth so-called "mode" of transportation is freight forwarding, although in technological terms it is not a separate mode of transportation at all but rather an administrative subdivision of the industry.

FREIGHT FORWARDERS provide service to shippers through use of the services of "underlying" carriers by rail, highway, water, and air. The freight forwarder accepts shipments and then moves them under arrangements with one or more carriers of these modes. In essence, the forwarder is a middleman whose main functions are (1) to relieve shippers of the need to deal directly with other carriers, and (2) where possible, to consolidate or combine smaller shipments in order to develop service improvements.

In the same basic category are SHIPPERS' ASSOCIATIONS (basically freight forwarders that provide service only to shippers enrolled in their memberships), *brokers* (who arrange for transportation services but never, as do forwarders, take physical custody of or responsibility for the goods), *consolidating agents* (who consolidate shipments for transportation but don't assume responsibility or liability for them in transit), etc.

Intermodal Transportation. Of increasing importance in the transportation industry is the growing trend toward intermodal service—coordinated transportation provided by carriers of more than one mode in connection with a single movement of freight. Examples are *piggyback* (also known as "trailer on flat car," or TOFC, service, where a truck trailer is loaded aboard a railroad flat car), *fishyback* (truck trailer loaded aboard water vessel) and, especially, *containerization.*

The basic concept of containerization is a type of packaging that permits freight to be transloaded readily from one vehicle or vessel to another, regardless of the mode of transportation. In its ultimate form the container is a structurally reinforced truck trailer with removable "bogeys" (wheel and undercarriage assemblies), transportable by rail, water or highway with equal facility. Other types of intermodal containers are also used, especially the so-called "igloo" airline containers which are extremely lightweight (in recognition of the need to reduce air cargo weight as much as possible), but have enough structural strength and integrity to withstand limited movement via other modes as well.

The chief advantage of all forms of intermodal transportation is that it allows shippers to combine the advantages of more than one mode of transportation without extensive transloading, repackaging, etc. Many carriers also combine to offer administratively coordinated intermodal services under a single set of shipping papers at a single rate, etc.

Although it would appear that the next logical step would be modal combinations through mergers, consolidations, etc., this has generally not happened. Save for a certain amount of railroad and truck service within a single corporate structure, virtually all transportation companies specialize in a single mode of transportation. Because of the vastly different operational expertise required for each mode—and because, too, of various legal restrictions and inhibitions against multi-modal transportation "supermarkets"—it is unlikely that such conglomerate transportation companies will come into being significantly in the foreseeable future.

COLIN BARRETT, Transportation Consultant, Reston, Virginia

Information References

Associations:

American Society of Traffic and Transportation.
Railway Systems and Management Association.

Periodicals:

Distribution Worldwide.
Handling & Shipping.
National Defense Transportation Journal.
Traffic Management.
The Transportation Journal.
Traffic World.

Cross References: *Traffic Management (and cross references there given).*

TRAFFIC MANAGEMENT

Traffic Management concerns itself with the totality of the transportation that is required by a company during the course of its business activities. An indication of the importance of this function may be gleaned from the fact that fully 20% of the U.S. gross national product is annually spent on transportation.

Traffic management is primarily cost-oriented. This is not to demean the importance of the service factor, pertaining to such questions as promptness, reliability, consistency, etc. However, the principal aim of the industrial traffic manager is cost control—an objective of increasing importance due to the inflationary trend in transportation and other costs.

The traffic manager is normally responsible

for both proprietary and purchased transportation services. With respect to the former, he must oversee administration of the company's private trucking operation (if any), as well as utilization of any private railroad cars it may own or lease. With respect to the latter, he must involve himself in such matters as negotiation of rates with for-hire carriers of all modes, handling of loss-and-damage claims, litigation before state and Federal transport regulatory agencies, the conduct of rate research, the selection of carriers and routes, etc.

In addition to these line functions, the traffic manager also has certain duties in a staff capacity. Foremost among them is formulation of the company's transportation policy, which must set forth the company's basic approach to its procurement of transportation services. Besides setting forth the criteria which will determine the company's stand on its rate, route, and service relationships with for-hire carriers (including the circumstances under which it will seek governmental regulatory intervention), such a policy will spell out the basic criteria for determining division of the company's traffic among potential modes of carriage. The fundamental question whether a company will use common or private carriage, for example, will be an integral part of such a policy.

Further staff functions include the conduct of, or at least participation in, site location studies involving coordination with the purchasing, production, and marketing departments to select the most advantageous geographic areas (from a transportation standpoint) for the conduct of company activities, determination of the most desirable units of purchase and sales as relates to transportation constraints, etc. The pervasiveness of transportation throughout the operations of most industrial concerns means that the industrial traffic manager must be consulted, if optimum cost control in this area is to be realized, with regard to virtually every important business decision made by the company.

The traffic manager will also have at least some voice—and often full managerial control—in such areas as warehousing, material management, material handling, protective packaging, inventory control, order processing, and other related fields. In the most sophisticated administrative structures, all of these disciplines, in addition to the traffic management function itself, are brought together under the generic term, PHYSICAL DISTRIBUTION MANAGEMENT. However, the concept of physical distribution management is relatively new to the business world, and many companies continue to function without this added hierarchical layer. In any event, the increased breadth of responsibility given to the traffic manager often gives him the authority, if not the title, of physical distribution manager.

The traffic manager's duties with regard to the company's personnel must not be overlooked. He or she usually handles arrangements concerning the transfer of company personnel from one location to another, including the formulation of expense reimbursement policies. Business travel arrangements will also commonly be made by the traffic department, which in some cases also reviews travel expense accounts of personnel traveling on company business.

Freight Transportation. The main part of traffic management concerns itself with freight transportation. In this regard, the highly specialized nature of transportation rate structures, routing and service arrangements, governmental regulation, etc., make centralized planning mandatory for efficient management. This means that a relatively few individuals will exercise basic company-wide control over its transportation activities.

An important management tool in this effort is the traffic manual—what amounts to a "routing guide" to be used by lower-echelon employees in the traffic department and by employees in other departments who must involve themselves in purchasing transportation services. Such a manual is a particularized extension of the transportation policy; whereas the policy specifies the ends to be achieved, the manual discusses specific means of accomplishing those ends.

Routing guides often give the names of specific carriers that must be used for the various types of transportation in which the company engages, and are highly detailed and restrictive in their application. They are also under almost continuous review because of fluctuations in the company's transportation needs and the availability of service to fulfill those needs.

Traffic department review of all invoices for transportation services is the way management ensures adherence to the standards set forth in the policy and the manual. This will not amount to a full-fledged audit—the traffic department will not normally be equipped to handle such an audit—but will be limited to a check to make certain the standardized instructions have been followed. The traffic department will also normally have charge of certifying freight bills for payment, and this requires institution of and adherence to basic control procedures.

Computer applications have in recent years helped to extend the scope of the traffic department's control over the company's transportation. Card, tape, and other automated systems have in some companies more or less supplanted the traffic manual as a management tool, furnishing full rate, routing, and service data on a "real-time" basis. Indeed, the potential of computerization in this field is enormous and still largely untapped. Of recent note are highly sophisticated vehicle- and shipment-location systems developed independently by a number of sources, as well as software advances that permit computerized modeling of the company's entire transportation program to facilitate cost optimization. Progress in this area continues, but to date has been somewhat limited because of the inability of programmers and present-generation hardware to handle full transportation rate computerization. The disorganized for-hire transportation rate structure continues to defy efforts at full-scale computerization—a necessary step to the advent of full automation in traffic management.

It is worth noting that only the most myopic of traffic departments will restrict its activities solely to transportation services which are paid for directly by the company. Whether or not they are identified separately as such, transportation charges will be included in the price of every item purchased by the company f.o.b. its own plants. It behooves the traffic department to oversee, and if necessary assume control of, transportation arrangements on these shipments as well if it is to avoid deleterious cost effects.

An example cited by the Aerospace Industries Association is an aerospace firm which in one year purchased more than $92 million worth of goods and services from some 4,800 small business firms. The same company placed over 200,000 individual contracts—about three-quarters of its subcontracts—with small business firms employing fewer than 500 persons. In the majority of cases, these small subcontractors were without expert traffic personnel, and proper cost-control procedure in this situation virtually required management of the traffic function by the prime contractor, which alone had the capability to do so in optimum fashion.

Organization of the Industrial Traffic Department. The traffic department of a major industrial firm may have as many as hundreds of employees, and may function under one of several organizational patterns. Generally, the traffic department will have two major divisions, one designated "Services," the other "Rates and Research." On occasion, there will be a third section for warehousing and a fourth for personnel administration, and an Export Traffic Manager if circumstances warrant. Exhibit I depicts such a traffic department.

The General Traffic Manager (or Vice President—Traffic, as is often the case) is the operating head of the department, with principal operating authority delegated to the Traffic Manager and the various Assistant Traffic Managers in line functions.

There is little consistency among companies as to where the General Traffic Manager reports. If he is of vice presidential rank—and often he is not—he usually reports to the president or to a senior vice president. And in many cases where he is not a vice president he still reports directly to the president. In other companies he reports to vice presidents of Manufacturing, Purchasing, Marketing, or Finance.

Although the background of industrial traffic executives varies, the largest proportion worked their way up from clerical positions as rate clerk or tariff clerk, receiving specialized training at one of the various traffic management colleges or academies in major metropolitan areas. In the larger companies, it is a general policy to send junior traffic employees to these schools at company expense; where there are executive development programs within traffic departments, the policy is to hire college graduates and then send them to the specialized traffic schools.

Other Departments. It has been noted that the management of transportation is almost exclusively in the province of the industrial traffic manager and his chief assistants, but there are a few exceptions. These are primarily cases where the nature of the product and its method of sale are tied closely to the type of transportation and the specific transport equipment used.

An example would be bulk chemicals, where very often the customer's receiving and production facilities will have a considerable bearing

EXHIBIT I

TRAFFIC MANAGEMENT ORGANIZATION

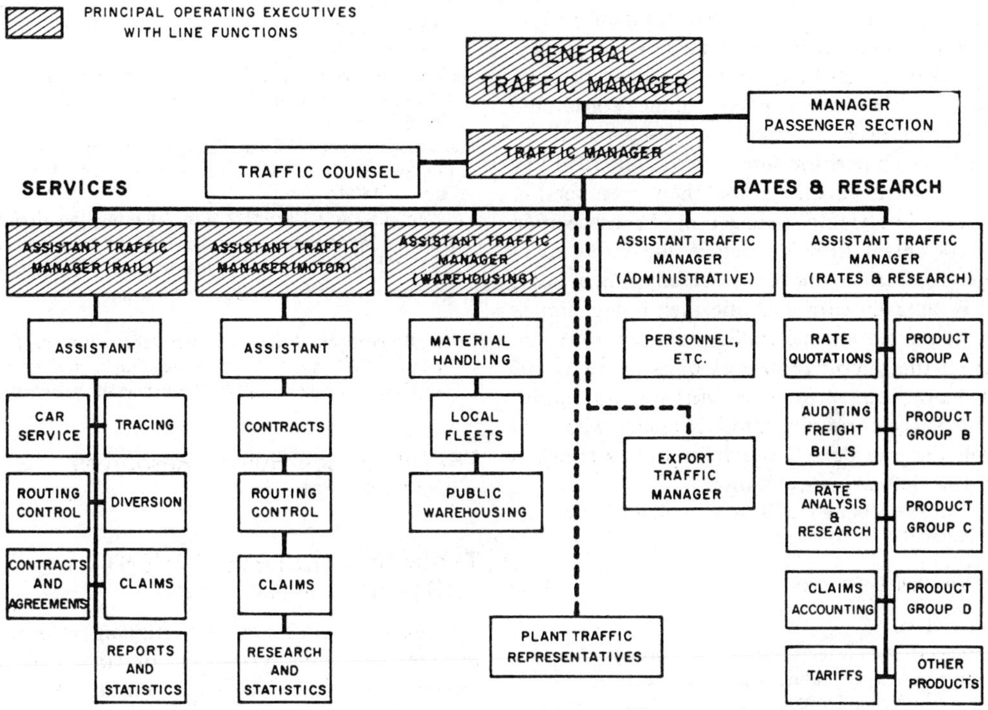

on how the product is shipped. Since the producer's own production, storage and handling facilities would also be involved, these personnel would become involved in transportation decisions: Traffic Manager; Sales Manager; Plant or Production Manager; Material Handling Engineer or Plant Engineer; Warehouse Manager; and Packaging Engineer.

On inbound shipments of raw materials, the alignment would be similar, with the Purchasing Agent replacing the Sales Manager. The Traffic Manager would still be the prime mover in this group, however, inasmuch as the actual transportation cost is usually 50% or more of the total costs in the procurement or distribution operation. Cases of this type will usually involve bulk commodities or large volume shipments of uniform goods.

Transportation Management in Smaller Companies. There is a marked difference between the larger companies and the smaller companies in transportation-buying practices. The larger companies—about 4,000—have highly organized traffic departments and strict rules of procedure, and in this respect there is very little difference between one company and another. In smaller companies, however, the transportation management function is seldom formally organized, with the result that the "principal influence" (if there is one) may be anybody from the shipping clerk to the office manager or even the company president himself.

It has already been noted that many of these smaller companies handle routing and carrier selection in accordance with specific instructions furnished them by traffic departments of larger companies to whom they sell. The use of automation for purchase order-writing by these larger companies almost always encompasses automatic print-out on the purchase order of pre-programmed shipping instructions to the supplier. In one not abnormal case, the general traffic department of a major retail chain furnishes such shipping instructions to some 4,000 vendors and will not accept merchandise shipped otherwise.

Similarly, these smaller companies will usually have their inbound shipments routed by larger companies from whom they buy because the larger companies make every effort to give them the lowest delivered price, and employ special skills not available in the smaller companies.

The other principal method of traffic management employed by smaller companies is to delegate these functions to an outside agency: a SHIPPERS' ASSOCIATION, a chamber of commerce, or an independent traffic consultant. These agencies maintain professional traffic staffs which perform almost all standard traffic management functions for their members or clients. The traffic manager of the association or consultant firm is in effect the traffic manager for each of the firms served, and in some cases actually carries a title identifying him as such; there are some traffic managers who represent the shipping interests of as many as 100 or more smaller firms, a situation not unlike that of the corporate traffic manager who controls the transportation activities of as many as 300 or 400 company plants.

COLIN BARRETT, Transportation Consultant, Reston, Virginia

Information References

Associations:

American Society of Traffic & Transportation (the professional certifying organization).

Delta Nu Alpha Transportation Fraternity (a shipper-carrier group with primary focus on education.

The National Council of Physical Distribution Management.

The National Industrial League (an all-shipper group with primary focus on legislative and regulatory matters).

National Defense Transportation Association.

Traffic Clubs International (the parent organization of the 200-plus traffic clubs located in all major U.S. cities, with a business and educational focus).

Periodicals:

The Delta Nu Alphian (monthly except July and August, published by Delta Nu Alpha Transportation Fraternity).

Distribution

Handling & Shipping Management.

ICC Practitioner's Journal.

National Defense Transportation Journal.

Traffic Bulletin.

Traffic Management.

Traffic World.

Transportation Journal (published quarterly by American Soc. of Traffic & Transportation).

Texts:

Augello, William J., "Freight Claims in Plain English," Huntington, N.Y., Shippers National Freight Claim Council, Inc., 1979.

Barrett, Colin, "Shippers, Truckers, and the Law—1980," Reston, Va., Colin Barrett, Transportation Consultant, 1980.

Blanding, Warren, "Blanding's Physical Distribution," Washington, D.C., The Traffic Service Corp., 1978.

Morse, Leon Wm., ed., "Practical Handbook of Industrial Traffic Management," 6th ed., Washington, D.C., Traffic Service Corp., 1980.

Murr, Alfred, "Export/Import Traffic Management and Forwarding," 6th ed., Centerville, Md., Cornell Maritime Press, Inc., 1979.

Newbourne, Malcolm J., "A Guide to Freight Consolidation for Shippers," Washington, D.C., The Traffic Service Corp., 1976.

Sigmon, Richard, "Miller's Law of Freight Loss and Damage Claims," 4th ed., Dubuque, Ia., Wm. C. Brown, 1974.

Traunig, J.S. and Barrett, Colin, "Paying the Freight Bill—A Management Approach," 2nd ed., Reston, Va., Colin Barrett, Transportation Consultant, 1979.

Cross References: *Freight Forwarders; Physical Distribution; Shippers' Association; Traffic and Transportation: Structure of the Transportation Industry.*

TRAINING. See Human Resources Development.

TRAINING AND DEVELOPMENT (Government Sponsored)

Numerous programs for human resources development are sponsored by the Federal Government, or by the states through Federal grants. This article presents highlights of those government-sponsored training programs of direct interest to the private sector. Further information on these, and information on all employment and training programs may be obtained from the U.S. Department of Labor, Employment and Training Administration.

Apprenticeship. Apprenticeship programs are authorized by the National Apprenticeship Act of 1937, as amended. Apprenticeship is a combination of on-the-job training and related technical instruction in which workers learn the practical and theoretical aspects of a skilled occupation, craft, or trade. Programs are conducted by employers, often jointly with labor and management. (See APPRENTICESHIP PROGRAMS.)

Comprehensive Employment and Training Programs. All states and cities, counties, and combinations of local units with populations of 100,000 or more receive direct Federal grants under the Comprehensive Employment and Training Act (CETA). The purpose of the grants is to help them design and administer comprehensive employment and training programs to serve the needs of their areas. These 475 state and local units, called "prime sponsors," operate projects themselves, or contract with other groups to provide services. Generally, states are responsible for programs in areas that do not meet the population criterion to receive Federal funds directly.

Following are some of the kinds of services (by no means inclusive) that prime sponsors may choose to make available to eligible participants: classroom and on-the-job training, practical work experience, basic education, and support services such as child care and health aid. They may target some programs to specific groups: youth, ex-offenders, persons with limited English-speaking ability, and veterans. And they may decide to use CETA funds to finance activities such as affirmative action programs, revising local merit system procedures, and developing labor market information.

The law requires every sponsoring government to have a planning council whose members represent clients, labor, business, education, and community organizations, among other groups. Councils make recommendations to government on the services that will best fit the needs of their communities, and monitor and evaluate ongoing programs.

Unemployed, underemployed, and economically disadvantaged persons are eligible to participate. Over 1.5 million were enrolled in locally operated CETA programs in the year ending October 30, 1980.

Authorization for the foregoing is the Comprehensive Employment and Training Act of 1973, as amended. Persons seeking to take advantage of the opportunities offered can contact the agency in their areas designated to run the CETA program. Such an agency may be called the Manpower Office, the Human Development Department, or the Employment and Training Administration. Further information may be obtained from the Employment and Training Administration, U.S. Department of Labor, Washington, D.C. or any of the ten regional offices of the Department of Labor in Boston, New York, Philadelphia, Atlanta, Chicago, Dallas, Kansas City, Mo., Denver, San Francisco, and Seattle.

The Private Sector Initiative Program (PSIP), established under Title VII of the CETA Reauthorization Act of 1978, is designed to increase the involvement of the business community in employment and training activities, and to increase private sector opportunities for the economically disadvantaged. Keystone of PSIP is the establishment, by the individual prime sponsors, of Private Industry Councils. The "PICs" participate with the prime sponsors in developing a wide variety of in-school, on-the-job, and other programs under Title VII aimed at involving the private sector. With majority business representation, the PICs advise the prime sponsors to help them coordinate all their programs with training requirements and opportunities in the private sector.

The Job Service Improvement Program (JSIP) is a new effort to improve the effectiveness of the U.S. Employment Service at the local level. Employer Committees work with local Employment Service offices to improve service delivery. The local office responds to the specific recommendations of the employer committee with a "plan of Action," which describes the steps that will be taken to implement the recommendations. As of October, 1980, there were 637 employer committees nationwide, involving over 15,000 employers.

U.S. Employment Service. The U.S. Employment Service and affiliated state agencies operate over 2,400 local offices to serve those seeking employment and those providing it. General services include outreach, interviewing, testing, counseling, and referral to placement, training, and other services in readying individuals for employment. Special services such as the following are provided:

Veterans. By law and regulation, veterans receive priority treatment (with preference for disabled) in all services leading to employment and training.

Youth. This group receives such services as counseling, testing, referral to training and other agencies, job development, and placement. The services are geared both to high school dropouts, 16 to 22, and to graduates entering the labor market.

Older Workers. These workers receive specialized job counseling, job development, referral to training or health and social services, and job placement. The services are directed to those 45 and older.

Handicapped. The handicapped benefit by special placement techniques that seek to match the physical and mental demands of a job to the capabilities of a worker. Such services are given in cooperation with other community agencies, and include special employment counseling and placement assistance, both for physically and mentally handicapped.

Rural Residents and Workers. In addition to the full range of employment services, workers in this group also receive special services in the areas of recruitment and placement in farm and woods occupations. Growers receive assistance in meeting critical seasonal labor needs and moving workers from supply to demand areas.

Disadvantaged Individuals. This group receives such services as testing, counseling, referral to training and other supportive services, job search and development, job placement, and follow-up. This help is for the poor and unemployed or underemployed persons handicapped by race, age, lack of education, or physical or mental disabilities.

Employers. Employers receive help in obtaining workers for their workforce needs, help in filling jobs with special skills or other requirements, development of personnel management tools, and assistance in identifying and resolving internal workforce problems. The last-named includes problems such as turnover, absenteeism, and special recruitment difficulties. Auxiliary services include comprehensive information on employment, unemployment, and other labor market activity on a local, state, regional, and national basis. In addition, in virtually every major urban area and 43 entire states, the Employment Service operates a computerized job bank, updated daily to list local job openings.

Authorization for the foregoing is the Wagner-Peyser Act of 1933, as amended. Further information may be obtained from the Employment and Training Administration, U.S. Department of Labor, or any of the ten regional offices, as previously listed.

Job Corps. A national system of 60 residential centers in 31 states and Puerto Rico provides basic education, vocational training, counseling, health care, and similar renewal services for young men and women, 16 through 21.

Enrollees in Job Corps residential centers receive room and board, clothing for work and dress, books and other learning supplies, and a cash allowance, part of which is paid on leaving the program after satisfactory participation. A few of the centers can also accommodate young people who do not live on center but take training during the day. Enrollees may stay in Job Corps as long as two years, and at the end of their stay are given assistance in finding a job.

Training, often by skilled union workers, is given in such occupations as heavy equipment operation, auto repair, carpentry, painting, masonry, nursing and other health care jobs, clerical and office work, and electronic assembly. Basic education includes reading, mathematics, social studies, and preparation for the General Education Development (GED) high school equivalency examination. Job Corps enrollees also receive instruction in general living skills, such as hygiene and grooming, getting along in the world of work, and constructive use of leisure time. For eligibility, young men and women, 16 through 21, must be classified as disadvantaged as defined by Federal poverty criteria (i.e., at this writing, a family of four with $5,010 annual income or less).

Authorization is Title IV of the Comprehensive Employment and Training Act of 1973, as amended. Contact is through a local office of any State employment Service, and applicants must have permission to join from parents or guardians. Further information may be obtained from the Employment and Training Administration, U.S. Department of Labor, or any of the ten regional offices, as previously listed.

Worker Adjustment Assistance Programs. Workers making a number of products—color television sets, shoes, electronic parts, steel, and other goods—have in recent years been laid off or forced to go on short workweeks because of foreign trade competition. The Worker Adjustment Assistance Program gives such workers substantial weekly allowances and a variety of help in preparing for and finding new employment. Workers may also receive grants to look for work outside their home areas, and money to pay for moving to new jobs.

This assistance is reserved for workers whose unemployment in linked to increased imports of foreign-made products. The law requires the Department of Labor to determine whether imports contributed importantly to job reductions in a particular company or unit. The Labor Department makes this determination in response to petitions from workers who have been laid off or threatened with layoffs from their plant.

Petitions of group eligibility may be filed by a group of three or more workers, their union, or an authorized representative. Copies of the petition form are available from State employment security agencies, any of the ten regional offices of the Employment and Training Administration, or the Office of Trade Adjustment Assistance, Bureau of International Labor Affairs, U.S. Department of Labor, Washington,

D.C. Once a group is certified, each worker in the group is eligible to apply for benefits.

Authorization for the foregoing is the Trade Act of 1974.

DONALD J. KULICK, Associate Regional Administrator, U.S. Department of Labor, Employment and Training Administration, New York, New York

Cross References: *Human Resources Development (and cross references there given).*

TRAINING WITHIN INDUSTRY PROGRAM (TWI)

The **Training Within Industry Program** was an activity designed to teach foreman and key men, during the World War II years, how to teach a job or a specific task to totally inexperienced workers. The training was done on the job (see ON-THE-JOB TRAINING), and the techniques developed were so effective that the basic approach has become a classic.

History. In 1940, the Federal Government and industry were greatly concerned over production in defense industries. At a meeting of The National Defense Council's Committee on Industrial Training held in Washington, July 24, 1940, it was agreed that there was great and growing need for more skilled supervisors and workers in defense plants, and that the solution would have to be a training *within* industry, a "learn by doing" activity.

The resulting Training Within Industry program was authorized in August 1940 by the National Defense Advisory Commission, and was continued under the Office of Production Management and then the War Production Board. By Presidential order on April 18, 1942, TWI functions were made part of the War Manpower Commission.

TWI functioned from 1940 through 1945 on a nationwide basis as a Government service, performing the biggest industrial training job in history. By September 1945, its four national directors had trained 22 regional field representatives who had trained 200 TWI institute conductors. Through this multiplier method, 23,000 trainers were trained, who in turn trained 1,750,000 supervisors in 16,500 plants.

The program was terminated at the close of the war. However, it was continued under private auspices through the Training-Within-Industry Foundation (see below).

Supervision and training had previously often been regarded as separate functions. TWI's concept was that they were actually concurrent with management, and its work dealt exclu-

ten been regarded as separate functions. TWI's concept was that they were actually concurrent with management, and its work dealt exclu-

sively with what management itself could do to train its supervisors.

On September 24, 1940, TWI issued its first bulletin which stated:

> The underlying purpose of this activity is to assist defense industries to meet their manpower needs by training within industry each worker to make the fullest use of his best skill up to the maximum of his individual ability . . . It is the intention of this organization to render specific advisory assistance to defense industries in inaugurating programs which they will carry on within their own plants at their own expense. The availability of this service will be made known, but will not be compulsory. There will be no authority to go into a plant on any basis other than at their request.

Throughout the war effort, TWI policy did not change—the real job had to be done *by* industry, *within* industry. Industry's own men collected, standardized, streamlined, and developed techniques for industry itself to use.

The TWI effort was handled from the very start by industrial management personnel. Four experts in personnel and training were chiefly responsible for the program—C. R. Dooley of Socony Vacuum Co., Walter Dietz of Western Electric Co., M. J. Kane of American Telephone and Telegraph Co., and William Conover of U.S. Steel Co. They organized Training-Within-Industry as a clearing house for up-to-the minute methods in improving supervision at the job level. Advisors from both management and labor served throughout the war.

While TWI started out in 1940 as a dollar-a-year organization, paid staff members were added until the paid staff in 1944 reached a peak of over 400, on loan from their companies. At TWI Headquarters in Washington was a small group which reached a peak of forty-five in 1943, with ten additional technical men who were on the Headquarters payroll but who were stationed in the field.

From the beginning TWI operated as a decentralized service. In September 1940, it divided the country into twenty-two geographical districts according to the main industrial areas. In each an informal group was headed by a prominent local production executive or industrial personnel man who gave TWI part-time service as a "dollar-a-year" man.

T.W.I. Program. The demands of war production placed emphasis on products, materials, and methods, many of which were new to industry. It was necessary to discover a way of talking about supervisory needs that would prove useful in outlining what TWI was prepared to do, and making clear the fields in which the plant, itself, would have to develop its own programs. An early statement of TWI proved effective in discussing the special needs of a plant and made "our business is different" concepts clear in relation to basic needs of all supervisors. The statement, which became a standard part of TWI thinking and publications emphasized that every supervisor has five basic needs, as shown in Exhibit I.

TWI's job was to get top management to accept the responsibility; to get executives to back their program through the line organization; to help the training director and operating supervisors plan and operate an adequate program; and to coach supervisors in the three skills—instructing, improving methods, and leading. The company job consisted of establishing policy, giving executive backing, operating the program, and making supervisors available for training.

An intensive method of presentation was developed, designed for ten men in five two-hour sessions. These covered scheduling of timetables to meet their own training needs, making job breakdowns, and giving instructions through a standard four-step method (see ON-THE-JOB TRAINING).

This presentation evolved out of the initiative and research of Glenn Gardiner, then with Forstmann Woolen Company. Using the original World War I steps of Charles R. Allen, a vocational training pioneer, he proposed a standard ten-hour program on "How to Instruct." The activity adopted as a standard training demonstration was the tying of the Fire Underwriter's knot. This was a dramatic example of something easy to do, *once the learner knew how,* but which could be confusing to the learner unless the four definite training steps were followed. It built confidence in the usefulness of the method when applied to local needs.

Training was done entirely by solving problems by members of a group and discussion of principles and procedures involved. There were no prepared lectures, no text books, no illustrative or entertaining pictures. The principles were not new. The entire time was spent in practice in the use of principles until there had been some changes in habits and attitudes. The same basic approach was developed in skills in improving *methods of improving jobs* and in doing pioneering work to present the problems of *human relationships* at the job level in a way that gave supervisors confidence in meeting their responsibility in getting results through people. In most cases this was new to them.

The presentations were so organized that a summary of the discussions and the four steps used could be issued as pocket cards. The J.I.T. (Job Instruction Training), J.M.T. (Job Methods Training), and J.R.T. (Job Relations Training) cards were used as reference reminders by supervisors. (For the text of the cards, see ON-THE-JOB TRAINING.)

Other Uses of TWI. The program spread to the Armed Forces and was used by the Federal Government in various agencies.

During the war, wide use was made of TWI programs outside American industry. Hospitals and many service organizations used the techniques to meet pressing manpower needs.

Training Within Industry Foundation. After the war, proposals were advanced that the TWI activities be carried on as a U.S. Government Service, either in the Department of Labor or the Department of Education. However, many industrial managers felt that if this work was

EXHIBIT I

Two Knowledges Specific for each plant	1. *Knowledge of the Work*—materials, tools, processes, operations, products and how they are made and used. 2. *Knowledge of Responsibilities*—policies, agreements, rules, regulations, schedules, interdepartmental relationships.
Three Skills Universally used	3. *Skill in Instructing*—increasing production by helping supervisors to develop a well trained work force which will get into production quicker; have less scrap, rework and rejects, fewer accidents, and less tool and equipment damage. 4. *Skill in Improving Methods*—utilizing materials, machines, and manpower more effectively by having supervisors study each operation in order to eliminate, combine, rearrange, and simplify details of the job. 5. *Skill in Leading*—increasing production by helping supervisors to improve their understanding of individuals, their ability to size up situations, and their ways of working with people at the job level.

worthwhile, it should not be another Government service but should be carried on within industry and by industrial people. Sufficient financial backing was secured to launch a modest non-profit foundation to carry on under the guidance of the same directors who were loaned by industry for the wartime effort. The Training Within Industry Foundation was incorporated in 1946.

Since 1946, the staff and associated field men have worked with more than 125 companies and organizations, some at several locations. An increasing number of plants are using TWI techniques, integrated into their own programs. Universities are promoting instruction in the programs.

During the years since the war, under sponsorship of the British Ministry of Labor, TWI programs have gone to more than thirty foreign countries. The International Labour Organization of Geneva has granted fellowships for men from developing countries to come to Britain for intensive coaching. TWI activity has been introduced into Mexico, Italy, Ceylon, India, Trinidad, Nepal, Indonesia, Cyprus, and New Zealand. The job instruction program was widely used in South America by American oil companies. The program has been promoted and carried out under the auspices of consulting engineering firms in Canada, Australia, France, Holland, and Belgium. [See editor's note below.]

J. Walter Dietz, formerly President, Training Within Industry Foundation, Summit, New Jersey

Information Reference

The late Mr. Dietz was one of the principles in launching and guiding the highly successful TWI programs during World War II. After the war he was instrumental in the formation of The Training Within Industry Foundation, which made the significant contributions he describes. Upon Mr. Dietz's death the Foundation became inoperative, but the results of its work still greatly and constructively influence industrial training activities. ED.

Cross References: *Human Resources Development; On-the-Job Training.*

TRANSACTIONAL ANALYSIS IN MANAGEMENT

Transactional Analysis, also known as TA, is an observable and verifiable system of human behavior and human communications. In management, TA offers both concepts and methods for the improvement of human interactions on the job. It has been taught to thousands of managers, sales people, public contact personnel, and other employees in business and government.

TA means the system itself and also one of the components of the system. These parts are *Structural Analysis, Life Script Analysis, Transactional Analysis,* and *Game Analysis.*

Structual Analysis divides personality into three ego states: Parent, Adult, and Child. An ego state is a system of feelings accompanied by a related set of behavior patterns [1]. The Parent part is authoritative, judgmental, nurturing, and caring. It represents the attitudes of a parent or parent-figures such as teachers or ministers. The Adult part is objective and has the capacity for decision-making and problem-solving in much the fashion of a computer. The Child part is creative, fun-loving, intuitive, and impulsive and/or mischievous. It reflects the feeling part of the personality.

Life Script means a life plan based on decisions made in childhood that is carried forward into adulthood and continues even though it proves to be nonfunctional. Outside of awareness it moves people forward to the destiny decided on in childhood.

Transactional Analysis provides a means of predicting human behavior by the observation of the transactions occurring between people. Such observation will identify the ego states influencing the transaction, and such transactions can be diagrammed to facilitate the understanding of TA and improve communication methods.

Game Analysis refers to transactions that are nonproductive and disruptive in nature.

History. Like some of the other behavioral sciences used in management, TA has its roots in psychotherapy. In the Fifties, Eric Berne, a psychiatrist, noted that people responded to each other in consistent ways. They demonstrated the ego states of Parent, Adult, and Child in their interactions. Penfield [2] had earlier demonstrated that memories can be retained in ego states and re-experienced when appropriately stimulated; feelings and responses learned in childhood may then influence adult attitudes and behavior. Berne noted that despite the influence of memories activated in the Parent and Child ego states, people had the capacity to use their Adult ego state to sort out the realities of the present.

After five years of teaching TA, Berne published "Transactional Analysis in Psychotherapy" in 1961, a book meant for therapists [3].

When "Games People Play" came out in 1964 [4], the public seized on it and it became a best-seller. Later "I'm OK—You're OK" by Harris [4] and "Born To Win" by James and Jongeward [5] also became best-sellers and the public acceptance of TA encouraged its use in non-therapy fields such as management and education. The International Transactional Analysis Association created a Special Fields membership for non-clinical people attainable by those who completed a professional training program.

Management Applications. The goal of the TA specialist in management is to help people understand themselves and others, and to use that understanding to become more individually and organizationally effective. TA programs can be designed for a variety of management needs: improved communications, management development, sales, personal growth, public contact, supervisory training, and teambuilding. TA training has also been offered to the spouses of employees as part of an employee relations program.

Basic to any TA program is the understanding of ego states. An ego state is simply a set of memories and/or feelings connected with a childhood experience that may be reactivated in later life by an appropriate stimulus. For example, a compulsively punctual project manager assigned to a group of creative design people might destroy any hope of teamwork by his irrational reaction to any tardiness among team members. When anyone is late, the project manager's Parent ego state is flooded with Parent messages reminding him of the dire consequences when he was late as a boy, and he gets unduly irritated.

Another example concerns a woman who aspires to an executive spot in her organization. She is thoroughly qualified for the position, but has a terrible fear of speaking up in staff meetings. Her Child messages about "Silence is golden" and "Speak when you are spoken to" immobilize her when she needs to speak to groups.

Both people project responsibility for stressful situations on others. In avoiding responsibility for their attitudes and actions, they frequently become involved in *Games*—disruptive transactions that reinforce their life scripts. For example, an employee may play a Game of "Kick Me" by making the same mistake repeatedly until he/she is fired, reinforcing a life script that calls for being a loser.

TA focuses on the ability of people to function from their Adult ego state and engage in Adult-to-Adult (objective) transactions. It also emphasizes that each person is responsible for himself (herself) and is expected to act autonomously rather than to react to situations. This means deciding on attitudes and behavior appropriate to the situation. When this is done, the manager and the employee, or the sales person and prospect, implicitly or explicitly contract for performance. A performance contract on an ongoing Adult-to-Adult basis has been found to lead to much better results than the average performance appraisal system.

Life positions simplify the classification of people by their outlook on life, and the classification of organizations by their managerial style.

"I'm OK—You're OK" typifies a person who is comfortable with himself and comfortable to be with. It also describes a "Theory Y" management style. (See MOTIVATION: MCGREGOR'S "THEORY X" AND "THEORY Y.")

"I'm OK—You're Not OK" signifies a person who feels superior to others and treats them in an authoritarian or demeaning manner. It also describes a "Theory X" style of management.

"I'm Not OK—You're OK" represents a person who is a follower and is submissive. It could describe on organization that lets employees and customers dictate policies even though they might not be in the best interests of the company.

"I'm Not OK—You're Not OK" indicates a person who doesn't think much of himself or his employer. It is difficult to imagine a profit-making organization surviving in this position, but it aptly describes some nonprofit and Government agencies.

Life Script information deals with Winners, Nonwinners, and Losers [6]. It also suggests three roles in life that affect on-the-job behavior: *Persecutor, Rescuer,* or *Victim.*

A Persecutor is an overly bossy type and plays games of "Now I've Gotcha." A Rescuer type frequently offers unsolicited advice, and plays games of "I'm Only Trying To Help." A Victim type will cover up incompetence by manipulating others into helping him out, and plays games of "Why Does This Always Happen To Me?" if things go wrong. When people flip-flop or switch their roles, disruptive transactions result [7].

The influence of a script on job performance is related to the injunctions and counterinjunctions (DO and DON'T messages) learned in childhood. In adulthood these messages can unconsciously affect thought and action in a counterproductive manner.

For example, a boy's father constantly exhorts him "Do Try Hard," but when the boy finishes a task he never gets any praise. Gradually he concludes that trying hard is more important than accomplishment. On the job he has difficulty finishing his assignments, and when he is criticized he says, "Well, look how hard I tried." If he gets fired he feels like a Victim. If he does not change his working habits he ends up a Victim and a Loser.

A little girl is told over and over by her mother that she must be polite to people and never hurt anyone's feelings or they won't like her. Her message is "Do Please People," and she becomes a people-pleaser. Being competent and charming she easily wins a promotion on her first job. When she must do performance appraisals of her employees she asks for a demotion because she cannot bring herself to be critical of her friends.

Some TA writers call these influences "drivers," and list five: Be Perfect, Try Hard, Please Me (Please everyone), Be Strong (Don't show your feelings), and Hurry Up [8]. Hurry-Up people rush through life without taking time to enjoy themselves. A compulsive response to a Hurry-Up driver and Try-Hard driver typifies the behavior of workaholics, and can lead to the disruption of a career because of negative effects on health.

Organizations also have scripts, observable as company policy, written and unwritten. Sometimes the organizational script is a carry-forward of the founder's dreams, and sometimes it is a representation of the collective scripts of the governing body. When a script negatively influences an organization's capacity to make constructive change, organizational survival is threatened [9].

Implementation. Any management considering implementation of a TA program needs to have clearly in mind what payoff is expected from such a program. TA is not a panacea, but it can be extremely helpful in solving problems that arise from lack of understanding of human behavior. It has been used to resolve communication problems and to improve production, work output, and sales. It is a valuable method in team building, planning, and the selection of personnel for promotion. Supervisors have found it helpful in relieving the stress of doing performance appraisal interviews. Safety programs have become more effective when employees were taught TA. It is an excellent tool, emphasizing objectivity in individual or group problem-solving and decision-making. Career counselors, manpower development and human resources management people, and organization development people have incorporated TA into numerous personal growth programs in business, industry, and government.

However, care must be taken when considering the implementation of a TA program. An unskilled, inexperienced, or improperly trained person may create more problems than she/he is asked to solve. The International Transactional Analysis Association can provide the names of Special Field Members who have undergone rigorous training in the application of TA in management.

Advantages. Because TA is primarily an intellectual presentation, employees find it less threatening than some of the other behavioral sciences such as SENSITIVITY TRAINING and encounter groups.

The results of TA training can be evaluated, and have been reported on in a number of journals and texts. Thus:

An investment sales firm reported a 55% increase in sales by TA-trained sales people compared with an untrained group. Great care was taken to eliminate any unequal variables in the quality of the prospects.

The local operations manager of a large financial institution underwent two years of TA training and applied it to his management practices. The result: a 28% increase in human effectiveness; a 6% decrease in personnel turnover; and an 18% savings annually in personnel costs.

A government manager said, "Since the TA training, we can have a meeting in twenty minutes that used to take two hours."

Caution. A TA program may not be cost effective if used as a first-aid approach to problems without commitment on the part of management. When employees know they are becoming more productive and effective, they expect their supervisors and managers to "practice what they preach." When that doesn't happen, morale can suffer.

The competent TA trainer will warn trainees that the use of TA jargon can turn off employees who have not attended a TA session, or would prefer not to be involved in amateur analysis.

Joe Alexander, Consultant to Management, Aptos, Calif.

Information References

Associations

International Transactional Analysis Association.

Periodicals

Transactional Analysis Journal.

Texts

Alexander, Joe, "Transactional Analysis for Executives," Mahwah, New Jersey, Roy W. Walters & Associates, Inc., 1980.

James, Muriel, "The OK Boss," Reading, Mass. Addison-Wesley, 1975.

Jongeward, Dorothy and contributors, "Everybody Wins: Transactional Analysis Applied to Organizations," Reading, Mass., Addison-Wesley, 1973.

Meininger, Jut, "Success Through Transactional Analysis," New York, Grosset & Dunlap, 1973.

Morrison, J. H. and O'Hearne, J. J., "Practical Transactional Analysis in Management," Reading, Mass., Addison-Wesley, 1977.

Novey, Theodore B., "TA for Management," Sacramento, Calif., Jalmar Press, 1980.

References Cited

[1] Berne, Eric, M.D., "Games People Play," New York, Grove, 1964.

[2] Penfield, W., "Memory Mechanisms," *Archives of Neurology and Psychiatry,* 1952.

[3] Berne, Eric, M.D., "Transactional Analysis in Psychotherapy," New York, Grove Press, 1961.

[4] Harris, Thomas A., "I'm OK—You're OK," New York, Harper & Row, 1969.

[5] James, Muriel and Jongeward, Dorothy, "Born To Win," Reading, Mass., Addison-Wesley, 1971.

[6] Berne, Eric, M.D., "What Do You Say After You Say Hello?" New York, Grove, 1972.

[7] Karpman, Stephen B., M.D., "Fairy Tales and Script Drama Analysis," *Transactional Analysis Bulletin,* April, 1968.

[8] Kahler, Taibi, Ph.D with Capers, Hedges, "The Miniscript," *Transactional Analysis Bulletin,* Jan. 1974.

[9] Jongeward, Dorothy and contributors, "Everybody Wins: Transactional Analysis Applied to Organizations," Reading, Mass., Addison-Wesley, 1973.

Cross References: *Human Resources Development (and references there given).*

TREASURERSHIP

Treasurership is the function of business management which combines the responsibility for the custody and investment of money, the granting of credit and collection of accounts, the provision of capital, the maintenance of a market for the company's securities, and related areas. Although essentially charged with all of the duties which fall under the heading of "money management," perhaps the most challenging aspect of treasurership today is creating maintaining the company's capital structure. Included in this activity is borrowing, both long and short term, and the sale of capital stock issues, as well as the cultivation, through financial public relations, of a market for such securities. The function is typically performed by an executive with the title of Treasurer (frequently augmented by designation as vice president), but is sometimes assigned to a financial vice president, or to a controller, Treasurership is closely allied to Controllership, but whereas the latter is purely a staff type function, the treasurer is generally endowed with broad authority to take action with respect to banking, disbursement of cash, borrowing, and investing.

Formal Definition. An authoritative definition is published by Financial Executives Institute. The Institute's concept of the function of treasurership is:

(1) *Provision of Capital.* To establish and execute programs for the provision of the capital required by the business, including negotiating the procurement of capital and maintaining the required financial arrangements.

(2) *Investor Relations.* To establish and maintain an adequate market for the company's securities, and, in connection therewith, to maintain adequate liaison with investment bankers, financial analysts, and shareholders.

(3) *Short-term Financing.* To maintain adequate sources for the company's current borrowings from commercial banks and other lending institutions.

(4) *Banking and Custody.* To maintain banking arrangements, to receive, have custody of, and disburse the company's monies and securities and to be responsible for the financial aspects of real estate transactions.

(5) *Credits and Collections.* To direct the granting of credit and the collection of accounts due the company, including the supervision of required special arrangements for financing sales, such as time payment and leasing plans.

(6) *Investments.* To invest the company's funds as required, and to establish and coordinate policies for investment in pension and other similar trusts.

(7) *Insurance.* To provide insurance coverage as required.

History. The function of the treasurer is almost as old as recorded history, examples being plentiful in the Bible and other ancient writings. The financial management function has always been recognized as a well defined necessity in business enterprise, requiring specialized training and skills. In recent times, various local treasurers' clubs and associations have been organized, but a milestone in the development of the techniques of treasureship through organization occurred in 1962 when Controllers Institute of America, recognizing its already large representation among the treasurers in the United States, Puerto Rico, and Canada, adopted the name Financial Executives Institute, published the foregoing definition of treasureship duties, and began the conscious dedication of its energies to development of that area along with controllership.

Related Techniques. Treasureship is closely related to accounting, to controllership, and, in a broader sense, to economics as applied in the field of corporate finance and investment. Specialized phases of corporate activity frequently assigned to the treasurer are insurance, leasing, time payment plans and, sometimes, tax administration. Credit and collection practice is almost universally his direct responsibility. Some of these subjects have their own literature and professional organizations.

FINANCIAL EXECUTIVES INSTITUTE, New York, New York

Information References

Associations:

Financial Executives Institute (formerly Controllers Institute of America).

American Management Association (Finance Division).

Periodicals:

Financial Executive (a monthly magazine published by FEI); and various research studies, in book and paper cover form, published by Financial Executives Research Foundation. Various studies and papers published by AMA. Bibliography available from Financial Executives Institute, New York.

Cross References: *Controllership; Corporate Capitalization; Financial Analysis: Earnings; Financial Public Relations.*

U

UNEMPLOYMENT: Concepts and Measurement

Employment and Unemployment data are among the most important indexes of the nation's economic well-being. The most used and most important labor-market statistics are the Labor Force-Employment and Unemployment figures derived from the Current Population Survey (CPS).

Employment and Unemployment Trends, 1970–1979. Statistics on the employment status of workers are published each month. Exhibit I shows the main labor-force components for 1970 and 1979 (annual averages) and for May 1980.

The civilian labor force grew from 82.7 million in 1970 to 102.9 million in 1979, an increase of 20.2 million for the period, or 2.2 million a year. During the same period, employment advanced from 78.6 million to 96.9 million, a gain of 23.3%, or about 2.6% a year—a very strong growth rate. However, unemployment showed a much faster growth from a 4.1 million average in 1970 to 6.0 million in 1979, an increase of 1.9 million or 46%. Thus, unemployment increased about 5% a year in the decade of the 1970s [1].

EXHIBIT I

POPULATION, LABOR FORCE, EMPLOYMENT AND UNEMPLOYMENT IN THE UNITED STATES—16 YEARS AND OVER
(In thousands)

Labor Force Item	1980 May (1)	1979 Annual Avg. (2)	1970 Annual Avg. (3)
Non-institutional Population	**165,886**	**163,620**	**140,182**
Labor force	107,230	104,996	85,903
Labor force % of population	64.6%	64.2%	61.3%
Civilian labor force	105,142	102,908	82,715
Civilian labor force—% of Population	63.4%	62.9%	59.0%
Employed	**96,988**	**96,945**	**78,627**
Non-agricultural industries	93,609	93,648	75,165
Agricultural	3,379	3,297	3,462
Unemployed	**8,154**	**5,963**	**4,088**
Unemployment rate (% of civilian labor force)	7.8%	5.8%	4.9%

SOURCE: **Employment and Earnings,** June 1980, Table A-1, (Household Survey Data), U.S. Department of Labor, Bureau of Labor Statistics.

The unemployment rate was 4.9% in 1970 and reached a high point of 8.5% in 1975. It declined to an average of 7.7% in 1976, 7.0% in 1977, 6.0% in 1978, and 5.8% in 1979, only to soar to 7.8% in May, 1980 [1].

The actual monthly rates of unemployment are seasonally adjusted, although the Bureau of Labor Statistics method of calculating the seasonal adjustments have been severely criticized as over-adjustments during periods of major cyclical movements [2]. Also, unemployment rates vary substantially for different categories of workers. For instance, although the official unemployment rate for all workers sixteen years and over was 7.8% as of May, 1980, the rate for blacks and other minority groups in the same age bracket was 13%, and the rate for blue-collar workers was about three times that of white-collar workers [1].

Sources and Methods. In order to understand and interpret various statistical data relating to the labor force, and unemployment in particular, an understanding of the source and methods used is critical. There are four primary sources of labor force or labor market data. These, discussed herein in some detail are: (1) The Current Population Survey (CPS); (2) The Establishment Survey (of Non-Agricultural Establishments); (3) Unemployment Insurance Reports; and (4) State and Local Area Unemployment Statistics (LAUS).

(1) Current Population Survey (CPS), conducted and tabulated by the Bureau of the Census for the Bureau of Labor Statistics, is the cornerstone of the nation's labor market information system. Household interviews are made monthly from a sample survey of 65,000 households on the employment status of each member of the household 16 years of age and over. This survey provides comprehensive data on the labor force, the employed, and the unemployed, including such characteristics as age, sex, race, family relationship, marital status, occupation and industry attachment. Data on the characteristics and past work experience of those not in the labor force are also provided [1].

The Bureau of Labor Statistics issues a monthly Press Release, and *News* summarizing the data from the CPS. It also publishes monthly the *Employment and Earnings* report which regularly carries about 50 tables, the A Series, on Employment Status, Characteristics of the Employed and Unemployed, and special groups, and tables of annually adjusted data, and numerous charts. These tables include information on unemployment by reason, job search methods used, duration of unemployment, industry and occupation, as well as the demographic characteristics of age, sex, race, and other characteristics.

All the CPS results for a given month become available simultaneously and are based on returns from the entire panel of respondents. There are no subsequent adjustments to independent benchmark data on the labor force, employment or unemployment. Therefore historical data are not revised. The CPS series are used in making estimates of population statistics for the nation, by state, standard metropolitan areas, urban, rural non-farm, and rural farm estimates.

(2) *Establishment Survey.* This is conducted by the U.S. Bureau of Labor Statistics in cooperation with state agencies. A schedule, Form 790, is shuttled monthly by mail to and from the respondent establishments and the cooperating state agency, usually the State Employment agency. Participation in the 790 program is voluntary [1].

The sample of establishments employ over 30 million, or about 40% of the total of all non-agricultural wage and salary workers. The data relate to all workers (full and part-time) who received pay during the payroll period which includes the 12th of the month.

This survey provides industry information on non-agricultural wage and salary employment, average weekly hours, average hourly and weekly earnings for the nation, 50 States, and 233 areas including most STANDARD METROPOLITAN STATISTICAL AREAS (SMSAs).

The BLS monthly *News* includes a national summary of employees on non-agricultural payrolls by two-digit industry classification, and weekly hours and earnings data. *Employment and Earnings* reports these data monthly in about twenty detailed tables. Also contained in this publication is "Labor Force and Unemployment by State and selected Metropolitan Areas." [1]

(3) *Unemployment Insurance Reports.* Employers subject to state and Federal unemployment insurance laws must make mandatory reports quarterly on their employment, total and taxable wages and the amount of tax or "contributions" they owe for each employee. From these reports the ES-202 Series is tabulated by all states. In addition, the administration of the Unemployment Insurance program requires the tabulation and report on claims for unemployment, weeks claimed and compensated, and benefit costs. These reports provide a substantial amount of information as to the number and characteristics of "insured" unemployed persons. These data are published by the U.S. Department of Labor, Employment and Training Administration in a weekly report *Unemployment Insurance Claims* for the U.S. and by states.

(4) *State and Local Area Unemployment Statistics (LAUS).* Employment and unemployment figures are among the few current economic measures available to some states and many local areas. Local labor force data are used to anticipate unemployment insurance claim loads, plan job development and placement efforts, formulate training programs, and guide economic development [3].

By far the most controversial use of state and local data is the allocation of Federal funds. Several laws enacted in the 1960s and 1970s for employment and training, area development, countercyclical revenue sharing, and extension of unemployment benefits have relied on local unemployment statistics in determination of how much assistance to grant each area. These data are also used for granting of Federal contracts. The amount of such aid distributed by these programs has risen from under $1 billion a year in the early 1970s to over $10 billion by 1980, with allocations based largely on state and local estimates of total unemployment rates, insured unemployment rates, or the total number of unemployed [3].

Measures of Unemployment. The official unemployment figure (CPS) is defined as comprising: all persons who did not work during the survey week, who made specific efforts to find a job within the past four weeks, and who were available for work during the survey week (except for temporary illness). Also included as unemployed are all those who did not work at all, were available for work, and (a) were waiting to be called back to a job from which they had been laid off, or (b) were waiting to report to a new wage or salary job within 30 days [1].

Unemployed persons are divided by reasons

for their unemployment into four major groups. These are:

(1) *Job losers:* persons whose employment ended involuntarily who immediately began looking for work, and persons on layoff.

(2) *Job leavers:* persons who quit or otherwise terminated their employment voluntarily and immediately began looking for work.

(3) *Reentrants:* persons who previously worked at a full-time job lasting two weeks or longer but were out of the labor force prior to beginning to look for work.

(4) *New-entrants:* persons who never worked at a full-time job lasting two weeks or longer.

Included in any of the above categories may be *job seekers:* all unemployed persons who made specific efforts to find a job, sometime during the four-week period preceding the survey week. Job seekers do not include persons unemployed because they: (a) are waiting to be called back to a job from which they have been laid off, or (b) were waiting to report to a new wage or salary job within 30 days. Job seekers are grouped by methods they use to seek work—going to a public or private employment agency, to employers directly, answering ads, assistance from friends or relatives, or from union registers, or other methods [1].

Discouraged workers are persons sixteen years and over who want a job but are not actively seeking work because they believe no suitable work is available. Since 1967, they have been tabulated separately by the CPS but *not included* in the labor force or as unemployed. The interest in this group is that they, like the unemployed, represent unutilized human resources, and that information on them is necessary for a full measure of slackness or tightness in the labor marked [3].

The Unemployment Rate as an Economic Indicator. The unemployment rate is a reliable and useful indicator of overall conditions in the labor market, and of the level of economic activity. As the demand for goods and services slackens, the unemployment rate rises as the demand for labor slows. As Gross National Product (GNP), an overall measure of economic activity, declines, the rate of unemployment shows a rising trend. However, as economic recovery occurs and GNP rises, the unemployment rate continues high and lags slightly behind recovery in business conditions. The BLS has published since 1976 six measures of labor market tightness, in addition to the official unemployment rate as shown in Exhibit II.

Exhibit II

Published Unemployment Measures, First Quarter 1979 (1)

		Rate %
U 1	Persons unemployed 15 weeks or longer, as % of civilian labor force.	1.2
U 2	Job losers as % of civilian labor force	2.4
U 3	Unemployed persons 25 years and over, as % of civilian labor force 25 years and over	3.9
U 4	Unemployed full-time job seekers, as % of full time labor force.	5.2
U 5	*Official Rate*—persons 16 years and over, as % of all civilian labor force 16 years and over.	5.7
U 6	Full time job seekers plus 1/2 part-time job seekers plus 1/2 total on part-time for economic reasons, as % of civilian labor force less 1/2 of part-time labor force.	7.2
U 7	(Unpublished): Numerator of U 6 *plus* discouraged workers as % of civilian labor force, less 1/2 of part time Labor Force	7.2

SOURCE: U.S. Dept. of Labor Bureau of Labor Statistics "The Employment Situation" *News Release* Table A-7, June 1, 1979.

The range of unemployment rates shown for U1 through U6 for the first quarter of 1979 indicates the spread in rates (from 1.2% to 7.2%) resulting from various concepts of what constitutes "unemployment." The official unemployment rate is U5, with a rate of 5.7% for the first quarter of 1979, and with a rate of 7.8% as of June 1980 [1]. Four of these rates, U2, U3, U4, and U5 (the official rate) are shown regularly in the BLS *Employment and Earnings.*

Meeting Full Employment Goals. Since the end of World War II, full employment, increasing productivity, and a stable price level have been the major objectives of economic policy in the United States. The Employment Act of 1946 placed a statutory requirement upon the Government to pursue policies to achieve full employment, and each year the Joint Economic Committee appraises the President's program for promoting "maximum employment, production, and purchasing power" [4].

The Full Employment and Balanced Growth Act of 1978 (The Humphrey-Hawkins Act) established goals of 4% unemployment and 3% inflation by the end of calendar year 1983. This act also provided for revision of the timetable for achieving these goals, if necessary, stated in the 1980 Economic Report of the President.

Based on the performance of the economy during 1979, and its projected performance during 1980 and 1981, it is apparent that these goals of the Full Employment Act cannot be achieved in the timetable originally presented. As a result, the long-range economic projection presented in President Carter's Fiscal Year 1981 Budget were revised consistent with a new schedule for attaining the goals of the 1978 Act.

The achievement of the 4% unemployment rate goal has at this writing been postponed by the Administration to two years later, or 1985, and the 3% inflation goal is postponed to 1988. These are ambitious goals and will require effective long-run policies to reduce both unemployment and inflation.

Monetary and fiscal restraint alone will not be sufficient to reduce the rate of inflation to an acceptable rate. Braking the momentum of inflation will require continued compliance by business and labor with voluntary pay and price standards in addition to other policies to hold down price increases.

How to achieve full employment or control unemployment is a central part of economic theory. Basicly the economic theory is that the growth in GNP has to equal the increase in the labor force, plus the increase in productivity, to ensure a constant rate of employment. When there is a high rate of unemployment, there is need to increase the level of GNP to create more jobs. However, as employment grows, more people enter the labor force and work hours lengthen. This means the level of GNP has to increase sufficiently to absorb the "original unemployed," and also absorb the addition to the labor force that results from population growth and from higher labor force participation rates [5, 6].

Arthur Okun, former chairman of the Council of Economic Advisors, has estimated that it takes a 2½% increase in GNP just to hold the unemployment rate constant, and a 3½% increase in GNP to bring about a one percentage point drop in unemployment [7]. Then the sum of these, 6%, would be required to reduce unemployment by one percentage point. But the difficulty with revving up GNP to eliminate unemployment is that inflationary bottlenecks occur. When unemployment drops to a 5% to 6% level, inflationary pressures increase. At this point in time we know how to reduce unemployment by raising aggregate demand, but do not know how to do so without creating unacceptable levels of inflation [5]. Lack of aggregate demand is the prime cause of unemployment, but not the only cause.

Technological Unemployment. The joblessness caused by the introduction of new machines and processes plays a role in adding to unemployment. The technology of automation will increase the productivity of labor. However, the crucial aspect for the 1980s is whether the computer, the transitor, and major new possibilities in feed-back engineering and other new inventions and processes will give rise to a new flow of investment which will open new fields for a demand for labor [5].

Technical development upsets equilibria. The macro-economic optimum growth models show technical change as an uncomplicated and trouble-free phenomenon—a picture that does not fully correspond to reality, as it ignores effects of technical development, such as the changes in market power of companies, and the changes in the employment situation. Thus the active guidance and control of technical development by the central government is seen by many as justified by the effects of technical change on employment and the environment [8].

Structural Unemployment. Structural unemployment is the unemployment that results from a mismatch between existing skills and required skills. The remedy for it requires the individual worker to acquire new skills, more education, or adopt to different types of work as the demand for workers shifts to specific occupations and becomes more specialized. The cost of remedying structural unemployment will be substantial as programs to hire and train "employables," and to raise educational standards are introduced. [5] The most difficult aspect of structural unemployment is: for what jobs shall the unemployed be trained? Unless the future demand for workers in specific occupations can be determined corrrectly, workers may be prepared for jobs that no longer exist or for new types of jobs that do not materialize.

Frictional Unemployment. This is the "normal" unemployment that occurs when workers voluntarily leave one job in search of another. Reducing the period of frictional unemployment can be accomplished by making job-vacancy information more easily available to job searchers. This can be accomplished to some extent through improving the nation-wide public employment service, giving access to job listings and dissemination of job opportunities to workers, providing relocation assistance, and stimulating more active private recruitment efforts by employers.

The Hardship Index. Unemployment today is less closely associated with hardship than up through the 1950s when a large percentage of the families had only one wage earner. In 1978, more than half of the unemployed lived in families where the household head is working. In 1976, about one in six unemployed persons had an inadequate family income. The increase in government income-support programs (unemployment insurance, public assistance, food stamps, medical benefits for low income families) has raised the income for many unemployed persons [2].

The National Commission on Employment and Unemployment Statistics recommended that the Bureau of Labor Statistics prepare an annual report containing measures of different types of labor-market-related economic hardship data resulting from low wages, unemployment, and insufficient participation in the labor force—presented in conjunction with household income status and family relationships for individuals affected. A conclusion reached by several commission members was that a composite hardship index would lose too much informative detail, and that multiple measures were preferable [3].

A hardship measure requires simultaneous consideration of labor force status and income derived from that status. A person would be counted in the measure of labor market hardship if: (1) the worker earns less than the poverty threshold during the calendar year and is also a member of a household whose total income is less than twice the poverty standard, and (2) the worker has demonstrated a significant amount of labor market activity by either working or seeking work for 40 weeks during the calendar year. Such a measure of hardship would not replace, but rather would complement, the unemployment rate.

ESTHER E. ESPENSHADE, Manager, Employment Security Research, Illinois Bureau of Employment Security, Chicago, Illinois

Information References

Controller General of the U.S., *Report to Congress,* "Reliable Local Unemployment Estimates: A Challenge for Federal and State Cooperation," 1979.

Dayun, Estela B., "On the Seasonal Adjustment of Economic Time Series Aggregates: A Case Study of the Unemployment Rates," *Background Paper* No. 31, Arlington, Va., National Commission on Employment and Unemployment Statistics, April, 1979.

Fishman, Betty G. and Leo, "Employment and Unemployment," New York, Crowell, 1969.

Ruggles, Richard, "Employment and Unemployment Statistics as Indexes of Economic Activity and Capacity Utilization," *Background Paper No. 28,* Arlington, Va., National Commission on Employment and Unemployment Statistics, April, 1979.

References Cited

[1] U.S. Department of Labor, Bureau of Labor Statistics, *Employment and Earnings,* Vol. 27, No. 6, June 1980, "Explanatory Notes" and "Monthly Household Data," Tables A-1 through 41.

[2] Meadows, Edward, "Why the Unemployment Rate is Out of Touch with the Real World," *Fortune,* May 8, 1978.

[3] National Commission on Employment and Unemployment Statistics, "Counting the Labor Force," Arlington, Va., 1979.

[4] Burns, Arthur F., "Full Employment, Guideposts and Economic Stability," Washington, D.C., American Enterprise Institute for Public Policy, 1967.

[5] Heilbroner, Robert L. and Thurow, Lester C., "Understanding Macroeconomics," 6th ed., Ch. 17, "The Problems of Unemployment," Englewood Cliffs, N.J., Prentice-Hall, 1978.

[6] Averitt, Robert T., "The Dual Economy—the Dynamics of American Industry Structure." New York, Norton, 1968.

[7] Okun, Arthur M., "The Gap Between Actual and Potential Output," in "The Battle Against Unemployment," New York, Norton, 1965.

[8] Heertje, Arnold, "Economic and Technological Change," New York, Wiley, 1973.

Cross References: *Statistical Abstract of the United States; Unemployment Insurance.*

UNEMPLOYMENT INSURANCE

Unemployment Insurance is a social program designed to compensate workers for part of their wage loss caused by involuntary joblessness.

Voluntary plans date back to the mid nineteenth century in Europe and in the United States when trade unions and some fraternal societies assessed their members to pool funds from which benefit payments to their members were made. Some European cities provided additional subsidies to such private plans. The world's first national compulsory unemployment insurance system was established by Great Britain in 1911. Italy followed in 1919, and seven other countries had compulsory laws before 1930. [1] [2]

Early U.I. History in the United States. From the time the first bill on unemployment insurance was introduced in Massachusetts in 1916, numerous bills and study committees had proposed unemployment insurance legislation. With the Depression of the 1930s, activity accelerated and 52 bills were introduced in seventeen states in 1931, and 68 bills in 25 states in 1933 [1].

Wisconsin was the first State to enact an

Unemployment Insurance Act, in 1932. No other state passed an unemployment insurance law until it was certain that the Federal Government would act. Then in 1935, six states—Utah, Washington, New York, New Hampshire, California, and Massachusetts—enacted laws before the Social Security Act was passed by Congress. After the Social Security Act was enacted in August 1935, state legislation was rapidly enacted. By 1937, all the states had approved unemployment insurance laws [2].

Basic Federal Legislation. The Federal-state unemployment insurance system was embodied in the Social Security Act of 1935, in Title III, "Grants to States for Unemployment Compensation Administration," and Title IX, "Tax on Employers of Eight or More." With later amendments, its provisions are codified in separate parts of the U.S. Code [3].

FUTA. The Federal Unemployment Tax Act (FUTA) levies a Federal excise tax on every covered employer based on wages paid during the calendar year. In 1978, this tax was increased to 3.4% of the first $6,000 of each employee's annual earnings [3, 4].

The tax-credit provision works as follows: An employer who contributes a state payroll tax to an approved State UI program offsets against his Federal unemployment tax an amount equal to that contribution, but not more than 2.7% of Federal taxable wages. Moreover, an employer may take the full 2.7% credit even if he pays at a rate below 2.7% on the basis of his experience rating. All states tax their employers in such a manner as to qualify them for the full tax credit.

Beginning in 1977, employers pay an effective Federal tax of 0.7% after offsetting the 2.7% against the current 3.4% rate. However, in states having an outstanding unpaid Federal loan balance, employers have their Federal tax credit reduced by 0.3% (i.e., from 2.7% to 2.4%) in the first year after which the loan is required to be paid, and a further 0.3% reduction for each succeeding year in which an unpaid balance remains.

The FUTA tax is used: (1) to finance half the cost of extended benefits during periods of high unemployment; (2) to provide repayable loans to the states to continue payment of benefits when their own funds become exhausted.

The Federal Unemployment Trust Fund and its various accounts function as a bank for the entire unemployment insurance system. The fund contains four separate accounts. The Employment Security Administative Account receives all FUTA revenues. These are used to pay the administrative costs of state programs. The excess goes to the Federal Unemployment Account which is used for loans to the states to meet the cost of benefit payments, and to the Extended Unemployment Compensation Account used to help finance the Federal-State extended benefit programs.

The State Unemployment Fund Accounts consist of the proceeds from the employer contributions under the various state unemployment compensation laws. A separate account is maintained for each state, which may be used by the state solely for the payment of unemployment insurance benefits [3].

FUTA Debt. As a result of the 1974–1975 recession, substantial sums are owed to the U.S. Treasury to be repaid from future revenues from FUTA, [4].

In the 1970s, Federal loans were made to 22 states (and the District of Columbia and Puerto Rico) totaling $6.2 billion. In August 1980, nearly $4.4 billion was owed by 15 states and about $1.9 billion had been repaid.

The recession of 1980 resulted in states again having to borrow to continue paying benefits. It is estimated that at least twelve states are likely to be in serious financial difficulties in 1980–1983. In the Federal Fiscal Year 1981, states possibly will have to borrow $3.7 billion, and $4.6 billion in FY 1982 [5].

State Unemployment Insurance Financing. As a result of the Federal unemployment tax on employers and the tax credit allowed, all states enacted their own UI laws. Employer contributions have been regarded as the major source of benefits, and currently only three states (Alabama, Alaska, and New Jersey) also require contributions of employees. All states now pool the proceeds of the tax into a common fund although this procedure is not required by the Federal law [4].

At the time the Social Security Act was passed, it was expected that it would require about 3% of payrolls to finance the unemployment insurance program, with a tenth of that being for administrative costs. The 2.7% Federal tax credit induced the states to tax employers initially at that rate. At least three years of experience was required as the basis for an employer's reduction below 2.7%. In 1941, a third of the states adopted experience rating and reduced some employers rates. By

1948, the practice of experience rating had become universal [4].

There are four types of *Experience Rating* systems of which the reserve-ratio method, used by 31 states, is the most popular. These are:

(1) *Reserve Ratio.* This sets up a bookkeeping account for each employer to which the taxes he pays are credited, and against which benefits "charged" are debited. An employer's account balance is brought forward each year. The balance ordinarily represents the difference between the employer's total accumulated taxes paid and the total benefits charged to the account since the law became effective, or since some other date as specified by the state law. The employer's reserve ratio must be built to a specified level before his tax rate is reduced below the standard rate according to a tax schedule based on specific ranges of reserve ratios. In all states, there is a maximum tax rate and minimum rate as well. In some states, employers are also assigned a uniform subsidiary rate, the proceeds of which are credited to a common account to absorb benefits not specifically charged to an individual account.

(2) *Benefit Ratio.* The Benefit-Ratio type of experience rating is used by eleven states (Connecticut, Florida, Maryland, Michigan, Minnesota, Mississippi, Oregon, Pennsylvania, Texas, Vermont, and Wyoming). In these states the ratio of benefits paid to taxable payrolls for a given period is the index for rate variation used to determine the basis for experience rating of each employer.

(3) *Benefit-Wage Ratio.* Used in five states (Alabama, Delaware, Illinois, Oklahoma, and Virginia), this is a more complex system. Instead of charging benefits paid directly to an employer, the base-period wages against which the benefits were paid are recorded on each employer's account as "benefit-wages." The employer's ratio of "benefit-wages" to total taxable payrolls on which contributions are paid provides the index to establish relative experience used to determine the employer's tax rate in accordance with a tax schedule based on a "State Experience Factor." The formula for the "State Experience Factor" is the ratio of total benefit payments in the state to total benefit wages, usually for a three-year period, which is designed to assess variable rates which will raise the equivalent of the amount paid out in benefits.

(4) *The Payroll Variation.* This method, used by three states (Alaska, Utah, and Washington) measures the decline in the employer's payrolls from quarter-to-quarter or from year-to-year, expressed as a percentage of payrolls in the preceding period. If the payroll shows no decline or a small percentage decline, the employer will be eligible for the lowest rates. A variety of methods are used to assign rates—such as classification or arrays of employers.

It is to be noted that Experience Rating for individual employers is a departure from usual insurance policy in setting rates [6]. Experience (or merit) rating was originally designed to serve as an incentive for employers to stabilize their employment, but other objectives have emerged. One that has been most stressed is to secure proper allocation of the costs of the program. More recently, it has fostered employers' active interest and participation in the program, especially in policing the system to contest claims and broaden the law's disqualification system [1], [6].

The range between the minimum and maximum rates is the most important determinant of a program's degree of experience rating. UI contains, however, a strong element of subsidy reallocation. About 20% of all employers pay more in UI taxes than their employees withdraw in benefits, while another 20% predictably have benefit-tax ratios greater than one.

Experience rating's allocative effect makes the cost of maintaining an (unemployed) labor reserve a variable cost of doing business. Such costs are subject to market pressures, which are presumed in America to be optimal resource allocators. The stabilization effect of experience rating is slight, possibly because the maximum UI taxes are insufficient to encourage more costly employment stabilization measures [6].

U.I. Taxes. The unemployment insurance taxable wage base and tax rates vary widely between states. The taxable wage base in the states ranged from $6,000 to $11,200 in Hawaii [7, 8].

Insolvency. Insolvency of U.I. Trust funds have been a problem during recessions. In the 1957–1958 recession and its aftermath, six states became eligible for Federal loans, but only Alaska and Pennsylvania had to use borrowed funds to pay benefits in this period. Each of these six states had been maintaining reserve ratios of at least one and one-half times their highest twelve month benefit cost rate [4].

Between 1972 and 1978, 22 States had to borrow over $6.2 billion from the Federal Unemployment Account. As of August 1980, fifteen states still had loans outstanding of nearly

$4.4 billion, and $1.9 billion had been repaid by states. Four large industrial states—Pennsylvania ($1.2 billion), Illinois $946.5 million, New Jersey $694.9 million, and Michigan $624.0 million—accounted for about two thirds of the loans outstanding in 1979 [4].

State Unemployment Insurance Benefits. *Eligibility* for benefits is a most pressing issue in unemployment insurance. Who should draw benefits? Eligibility for unemployment insurance benefits is primarily based on a record of recent and substantial covered employment and a continuing attachment to the labor force during unemployment as shown by ability and availability for work.

The first test of eligibility is the qualifying requirement of a certain amount of employment or wages with a covered employer. This requirement relates to the worker's attachment to the labor force and to whether his earnings in covered employment have been sufficient to justify payment of benefits. States may set their own qualifying requirements and consequently the provisions vary widely from state to state. Some states require a qualifying amount of wages and others a specified number of weeks of employment, and some a combination of these requirements.

A worker's benefit rights are determined on the basis of his employment in covered work over a prior period, called the *base period.* Benefit rights remain fixed for a period called the *benefit year* [7].

Base periods are individual in all states except New Hampshire, and depend on when the worker first applies for benefits or begins drawing benefits. In 33 states, the base period is the first four of the last five quarters [7].

Benefit year is usually a one-year period, or a 52-week period, during which a worker may receive his benefits. Nearly all states have an individual benefit year whose beginning relates to the date of the claimant's unemployment and filing for benefits [7].

Qualifying Wages or Employment. All states require that an individual must have earned a specified amount of wages, or worked for a certain time within the base period, or both, to qualify for benefits. Forty-three states require that some earnings must be in more than one quarter. Fourteen states require a specified period of employment during the base period—in six of these states twenty weeks is required, two states require as little as fourteen weeks.

Weekly Benefit Amount. Most States use a formula which bases benefits on wages in the worker's high quarter of his base period. In thirteen states, the fraction of the high quarter is 1/26. This fraction gives workers with thirteen full weeks of employment in the high quarter 50% of their full-time wages, between fixed minimum and maximum benefit limits. Several states compute the weekly benefit amount as a percentage of annual wages, some as a percentage of the claimant's average weekly wage in the base period, and other methods are also used by some states [7].

Thirty-three states provide for a flexible maximum benefit by annual or semi-annual computation of the *maximum* weekly benefit amount based on statewide average wages. Twenty of these states have a maximum weekly benefit of 60% or more of the statewide average weekly wage, with 70% the maximum in one state (West Virginia). The lowest maximum is 50% in five States [7].

All states provide for payment of benefits when under-employment reaches a certain stage, and the amount of the benefit is usually the weekly benefit amount less some part of the wages earned [7].

Dependent's allowances are provided in only twelve States and all of these states include dependent children. Non-working wives or husbands may be dependents in eight states. Three states provide for a dependent parent or brother or sister [7].

Duration of Benefits. The *maximum* potential duration of regular benefits is 26 weeks in 42 States, and eight states have a higher maximum duration, up to 36 weeks in Utah. In 29 States a claimant's benefits are limited to a fraction of the base-period wages. In several states maximum potential benefits are limited to a fraction of weeks worked. *Minimum* annual benefits result from the minimum qualifying wage and the duration fraction, or from a schedule [7].

Federal-State Extended Benefits. This program, financed equally from Federal and state funds, pays extended benefits to workers during periods of high unemployment. The Omnibus Budget Reconciliation Act of 1981 repealed the national trigger operational since January 1972, so that extended benefits would be payable only in states with insured employment rates as provided in the Federal-State Unemployment Compensation Act. For the state EB trigger, the insured unemployment rate (IUR) calculation include only claimants for the regular state UI program, effective after August 1981. After September 25, 1982, extended benefits are payable in any state in which the IUR is at least 5% and is 20% higher than the average of the same 13-week period in the two previous years. Optionally, a state may pay EB when its IUR reaches 6%, regardless of the IUR in previous years. A claimant may receive extended benefits equal to one half the total of his/her regular benefits, including dependent's allowances; or 13 times weekly benefit amount, with overall limit of 39 weeks on regular extended benefits [7].

Disqualification for Benefits. Each state established its requirements which an unemployed worker must meet to receive benefits. All states require the claimant to be able to work and to be available for work or benefits will be denied. One evidence of the ability to work and availability for work is registration for work at a public employment office and active job search. Nonavailability may be evidenced by refusal of a referral to suitable work.

Special provisions relating to availability of trainees and students are included in many state laws. FUTA requires that all states provide that compensation shall not be denied to an otherwise eligible individual for any week he or she is attending a training course with the approval of a state agency [7].

The major causes for disqualification from benefits are voluntary separation from work (quitting), discharge for misconduct, refusal of suitable work, and unemployment resulting from a labor dispute. Disqualifications imposed for these causes may include: a postponement of benefits for some prescribed period, ordinarily in addition to the required waiting period; a cancellation of benefit rights; or a reduction of benefits otherwise payable. Disqualification means benefits denied for a specified period [7].

Voluntary leaving without good cause can result in disqualification in all states. In some states, "good cause" is not explicitly restricted to good cause related to employment, thus permitting interpretation to include good personal cause. Some states specify various circumstances that constitute good cause for voluntary leaving, such as to accept other work, to join the armed forces, illness, etc. [7].

Discharge for misconduct is defined variously in state laws in such terms as "willful misconduct," "failure to obey orders, rules and instructions," or "failure to discharge duties for which he (she) was employed." Interpretations of what constitutes misconduct have been developed in each state's benefit decisions [7].

Some states provide for "gross misconduct" resulting in heavier disqualification. Included are discharge for dishonesty, or a crime or felony in connection with the claimant's work, unlawful misconduct, willful violation of safety rules, assault, theft, sabotage, arson, negligence, and wanton disregard of employer's interest.

Labor Disputes. Usually a worker is not disqualified unless the dispute is in the establishment in which the worker was last employed. The term "labor dispute" is not defined in the state laws (except in three states) and different terms are used such as "strike," and "bona fide labor dispute." Some states exclude lockouts and strikes resulting from the employer's failure to conform to the provisions of a labor contract, or to conform to laws on wages, hours, or working conditions. In most states the disqualification ends whenever the stoppage of work due to the labor dispute ends [7].

Fraudulent misrepresentation to obtain benefits result in administrative penalties in all states, such as provision for repayment of benefits, fines, and imprisonment for willfully misrepresenting or concealing facts [7].

Adequacy of U.I. Benefits. *Coverage.* One measure of adequacy is the completeness of UI coverage. In 1979, over 92 million workers in the United States were covered by U.I. programs. Covered workers were about 95% of the 96.9 million employed workers in the United States in 1979. Covered workers included 88,281,000 under state U.I. programs, and 2,958,000 Federal workers in the Unemployment Compensation Program for Federal employees and railroad workers insured under the Railroad Unemployment Insurance program [9].

Only some domestic workers and agricultural workers, not included in those covered in 1978, employees of small establishments in some states, self-employed and family workers are not now covered by state U.I. programs.

During 1979, an average of 86.5 million persons were covered under state unemployment insurance laws, representing about 92% of all employees in nonagricultural industries. (Only a small proportion of agricultural workers were eligible.)

Only approximately 10% of the covered workers received a "first payment," and about 27% of these beneficiaries exhausted their benefit entitlements during the year, indicating that some 73% either found jobs or were dropped from the unemployment rolls for other reasons before exhausting entitlement. Unemployment benefits totaling nearly $7.8 billion were paid in 1979 under these state programs [9].

The *maximum weekly benefit amount* including dependents' allowances ranged from a high of $202 in Ohio and $201 in Connecticut to a low of $90 in Alabama, Arizona, Georgia, and Mississippi as of January 1980 [10]. The *average* weekly benefit for all states averaged $89.54 in 1979, and was only 39% of average weekly earnings in covered employment.

Duration of Benefits. The average *potential* duration of benefits for regular programs in 1978, ranged from 36 weeks in Utah to 17.5 weeks in Wyoming. The average *actual* duration ranged from 19.6 weeks in Alaska, to only 6.9 weeks in New Hampshire in 1978, and in nineteen states the actual duration was from eleven to thirteen weeks [10].

State unemployment systems primarily are designed to assist workers for relatively short periods of unemployment, such as seasonal layoffs, and relatively short periods for adjustment of production and inventories. In recession periods, the maximum of 39 weeks for the Regular and Extended Benefits programs is scarcely sufficient for workers, as the recession periods usually run twelve to fifteen months [11].

Exhaustees. The exhaustion ratio for all state U.I. Regular programs for twelve months ending in 1979 was 26.6% [9].

For twelve months ending in June 1979, the per cent of recipients exhausting benefit rights in all states combined was 26.1%. The proportion of workers exhausting benefits exceeded 26.0% in twenty states, with a high of 39.5% for New Jersey. [9] These high exhaustion rates prevailed in a year of peak employment. In recession years, much higher exhaustion rates occur.

Benefit Cost Rates. The average seven-year cost rate from 1970–1977 of regular state programs for all states averaged 1.24% of total wages, ranging from only 0.35% in Texas to 2.02% in Connecticut.

UI in the 1980s. The National Commission on Unemployment Compensation issued its Final Report to Congress in July, 1980. Its recommendations can be summarized under seven main areas:

(I) Removal of unemployment compensation accounts from the unified Federal Budget.

(II) Putting the program on a sound financial footing by:

A Increasing the FUTA taxable wage base, and providing that as wages increase, the base will increase automatically, beginning with 50% in 1983 and increasing 5% each two years to 65% in 1989.

B Reducing employer payroll taxes for past debts under state laws.

C Strengthening requirements for borrowing from loan.

D Providing protection to states against unusually heavy benefit costs through reinsurance.

E Establishing a Board of Trustees for UI trust funds.

F Increase funds for state costs of administration.

G Making recommendations to the states on financing.

(III) Removal of unemployment benefits from being subject to Federal income tax.

(IV) Ensuring a sound benefit structure, including increased basic Federal minimum benefit standards providing greater protection during periods of heavy unemployment and to older workers.

(V) Income initiatives for longer-term unemployed, through job programs and employment assistance.

(VI) More efficient administration, including improved processing of interstate claims and appeals and improvement of United States Employment Service.

(VII) Special employee protection programs should not be paid concurrently or be a supplement to U.I., but should be paid from general revenues.

Management Functions. Employers and managers should become familiar with the provisions of their state U.I. law, and the forms and notices they are required to file or reply to. The most important forms are the *Contribution Report* and the *Employer's Report of Wages Paid to Each Worker,* required quarterly and used to compute the tax or contribution required to be paid. These forms with the check or money order for the tax due should be mailed so as to be received by the due dates, usually the last day of April, July, October, and January. An employer should check the tax rates assigned from his own tax report, payroll records, and notice of claims and benefits charged to him.

When a former worker files a claim for unemployment benefits the *Notice of Claim* or *Notice of Additional Claim* is sent to his last employer, and *Notice to Base-Period Employers* is also sent. An employer who receives these forms and believes the claimant may be ineligible for benefits for any reason must file a *Notice of Possible Ineligibility* if he wishes to appeal the claims, stating why he believes the claimant is ineligible, within the time limit specified. The employer should be informed of the determination, and if he wishes to appeal he must file his appeal within the stated time limit.

Other forms are *Report to Determine Liability* required of all newly created employing units, and *Notice of Change* required whenever an employer goes out of business, or transfers or sells his business.

Employers are generally required to serve *Notice of Separation* if a mass separation of employees is planned. If there is a labor dispute the employer should file *Notice of Labor Dispute.*

Persons authorized to sign forms and certify to the accuracy of these reports are generally limited to the owner if the employer is a sole proprietorship, a partner of a partnership, or duly authorized officer if the employer is a corporation or trust.

Employer's Responsibilities to Worker. Employers are required to inform their workers concerning rights to unemployment benefits, usually by posting the Notices sent to him for that purpose. When the worker quits, or is discharged, or laid off for a duration of week, the employer is required to give the worker information on "What the Worker Should Know about Unemployment Insurance," furnished by the U.I. agency. This informs the worker of conditions under which he is eligible for benefits.

Management or personnel functions should include developing employment policies to minimize labor turnover. Good personnel policies to stabilize employment and reduce or minimize unemployment tax costs include: careful selection of workers, adequate on-the-job training, a promotion policy to encourage workers to seek and expect advancement, competitive wage policies, proper supervision and recognition for good work, and nondiscriminatory policies as to race or sex and other personal characteristics.

A goal of management should be to even out production schedules so there is as stable a level of work force as possible throughout the year. Unpreventable unemployment then becomes a necessary business expense and the periods of unemployment for workers are reduced.

ESTHER E. ESPENSHADE, Manager of Employment Security Research, Illinois Bureau of Employment Security, Chicago, Illinois

References Cited

[1] Haber, William, "Unemployment Insurance in the American Economy—An Historical Review and Analysis," Homewood, Ill., Irwin, 1966.
[2] Colorado Department of Labor and Employment, "Four Decades of Unemployment Insurance," Pubinfo, Denver, Colo. March, 1976.
[3] "Legal Services Guide to Federal Unemployment Compensation Law and Issues," New York, National Employment Law, Inc., 1977.
[4] Mackin, Paul J., "Benefit Financing in Unemployment Insurance: A Problem of Balancing Responsibilities." Kalamazoo. Mich., Upjohn Institute for Employment Research, 1978.
[5] National Commission on Unemployment Compensation, "Policy Decisions—Preliminary," June 30, 1980, and "Final Report," July 1980.
[6] Malisoff, Harry, "The Insurance Character of Unemployment Insurance," Kalamazoo, Mich., Upjohn Institute for Employment Research, 1961.
[7] U.S. Bureau of Employment Security, "Comparison of State Unemployment Insurance Laws," published since 1948, latest update January 1980, Washington, D.C.
[8] U.S. Dept. of Labor, Employment and Training Administration, U.I. Service, "Significant Provisions of State Unemployment Insurance Laws," July 6, 1980, Washington, D.C.
[9] U.S. Dept. of Labor, Employment and Training Administration, *Unemployment Insurance Statistics,* December 1979; also *Unemployment Insurance Claims,* weekly, Washington, D.C.
10 Ohio Bureau of Employment Security, charts on unemployment benefits, August 1980, Columbus, Ohio.
11 Blaustein, Saul J., "Principles and Objectives of Unemployment Insurance," Kalamazoo, Mich., Upjohn Institute for Employment Research, 1978.

Cross References: *Statistical Abstract of the United States; Unemployment: Concepts and Measures; Workers' Compensation.*

UNIFORM COMMERCIAL CODE

The **Uniform Commercial Code** is a body of law governing the rights and obligations incurred by individuals and business entities with respect to a broad range of commercial transactions. Included in its coverage are all aspects of commercial transactions or sale of tangible personal property, including sales of goods, express warranties and implied warranties of merchantability and fitness in sales contracts, rules regarding negotiable instruments (commercial paper), bank deposits and collections, bulk transfers, letters of credit, warehouse receipts, bills of lading and other documents of title, investment securities, secured transactions, sales of accounts, contract rights, chattel papers, and unconscionable contract clauses (to be defined by the courts). National regulatory legislation dealing with contract warranties of sellers and manufacturers was enacted in 1975 under the title, Magnuson-Moss Warranty–Federal Trade Commission Improvement Act.

The Code was promulgated and sponsored in 1951 by the National Conference of Commissioners on Uniform State Laws and the American Law Institute after many years of study and numerous changes in drafting. In 1953 Pennsylvania was the first state to enact the Code as promulgated. As the several states began to enact the Code, they proceeded to make amendments. However, since uniformity was one of the chief purposes of the Code, the sponsors created a Permanent Editorial Board to sift amendments and issue official recommendations. At this writing, all of the states except Louisiana, as well as the District of Columbia, Puerto Rico, and the Virgin Islands have enacted the Code.

Information References

Associations:

American Law Institute, New York.

National Conference of Commissioners on Uniform State Laws, Chicago. (Judges, law school deans and professors, and practicing attorneys appointed by state governors to promote uniformity in state law on all subjects where uniformity is deemed necessary.)

Texts:

Anderson, Ronald A., "Uniform Commercial Code," 4 vols., 2nd ed., Rochester, N.Y., Lawyers Co-Op, 1970.

Quinn, Thomas M., "Uniform Commercial Code Commentary & Law Digest," Boston, Warren, 1978.

Raphael, J.S., "Uniform Commercial Code Simplified," New York, Ronald, 1967.

U.S. CENSUS OF MANUFACTURES

The 1977 **Census of Manufactures** is the thirtieth and, as of this writing, the most recent such census of the United States. (The previous census covered the year 1972.) Data from it are scheduled for issuance in 1981 in some 60 industrial and 50 area publications, for later issuance as five volumes comprising the 1977 results.

The first census of manufactures covered 1809 as part of the 1810 decennial census, and (with the exception of 1829) a census was taken at ten-year intervals in connection with the Decennial Census of Population up to and including 1899. It was conducted at five-year intervals from 1904 through 1919, and every other year from 1921 through 1939. The census was suspended during World War II, but it was resumed for 1947. New legislation subsequently provided for a Census of Manufactures every five years, with annual sample surveys authorized for interim years.

The five-year censuses cover the years ending in 2 and 7; thus, at this writing the latest year covered by the interim Annual Survey of Manufactures is for 1976. Key measures of manufacturing activity (value added by manufacture, employment, plant hours, payrolls, capital expenditures, etc.), by industry and geographic area, are thus maintained continuously in an annual time series. The industrial statistics program also provides for coverage, on an annual, quarterly, or monthly basis, of the production or shipments of important commodities in separate commodity surveys. The product class information collected in the Annual Survey of Manufactures fills important gaps in the Bureau's commodity survey program.

The annual survey is designed to yield estimates of general statistics (number of employees, payrolls, number of production workers, production worker plant-hours and wages, value of shipments, value added, cost of materials, new capital expenditures; and inventories) for industry groups, individual industries, States, STANDARD METROPOLITAN STATISTICAL AREAS (SMSAs), large industrial countries, and selected cities. It also provides broad industrial and geographic totals for gross assets, rental payments, supplemental labor costs, and cost of fuels and electric energy, as well as United States totals for the more important classes of products shipped by manufacturing establishments. For states and SMSAs industry group totals are provided while only total manufacturing estimates are available for countries and cities.

To meet the needs for small-area manufacturing data, comparable county-by-industry-group employment figures have been developed for annual survey years in the *County Business Patterns* series published by the Bureau of the Census. This overall program meets the needs of industry and government for industrial statistics at a considerably lower cost than the previous program in which a complete census of manufactures was taken every second year.

Definition of Manufacturing Establishments. Following previous census procedures, annual survey data are collected on reports received from individual manufacturing establishments. The term "establishment" denotes a single plant or factory in which manufacturing operations are performed. A company that operates in more than one location is required to submit a separate establishment report for each location. In some instances, companies engaged in distinctly different lines of activity at one location are requested to submit separate reports for these activities if the plant records permit such a separation and the operations are substantial in size.

For single-establishment companies, the reporting establishment is identical with the company. Some 251,000 of the approximately 312,000 manufacturing establishments in the United States are operated by single-establishment companies. In addition, there are approximately 16,000 multi-unit companies that operate one or more manufacturing establishments. These multi-establishment firms operate somewhat more than 70,000 manufacturing establishments.

The Annual Survey of Manufactures and the five-year censuses of manufactures include only establishments with one or more employees at any time during the year. Thus, manufacturing establishments operated by individual proprietors or partners with no paid employees are excluded. Current information on the economic significance of manufacturing in plants with no paid employees is not available. A special study in 1958 revealed that there were over 52,000 establishments with no paid employees, but that they accounted for less than 1% of the total value of shipments of all manufacturing industries in that year.

The Annual Survey of Manufactures follows the definitions of manufacturing industries contained in the 1972 edition of the *Standard Industrial Classification Manual* published by the Office of Management and Budget. A full description of each of approximately 450 separate industries is published in the 1972 Census of Manufactures volumes. (See STANDARD INDUSTRIAL CLASSIFICATION.)

The SIC Manual defines manufacturing as the mechanical or chemical transformation of inorganic or organic substances into new products. The assembly of component parts or intermediate products is also considered to be manufacturing if the resulting product is neither a structure nor other fixed improvement. These activities are usually carried on in plants, factories, or mills, which characteristically use power-driven machines and materials-handling equipment.

No single classification system will satisfy all possible uses of the data to be classified. Accordingly, users of data frequently regroup detailed SIC industries into broad classifications different from the SIC two- and three-digit categories. The Federal Reserve Board, for example, for many years has made combinations to put emphasis on such classifications as durable, nondurable, consumers, producers, finished, and intermediate goods. Its Industrial Production Index contains tables which present regroupings of the industry statistics based on categories developed by the Federal Reserve Board.

Industry Classification of Establishments. Each of the establishments covered in the Annual Survey of Manufactures was classified in one of approximately 450 manufacturing industries in accordance with the industry definitions embodied in the SIC system. The product groupings, from which industry classifications of establishments are derived, are based on such considerations as whether they are typically produced by the same establishment, require similar manufacturing processes or materials, or are sold to the same types of customers, and the like. The group of products typical of an industry is said to be "primary" to that industry. Accordingly, an establishment is classified in a particular industry on the basis of its major activity, that is, if its shipments of the primary products of that industry exceed in value its shipments of products of any other industry. In a few instances, however, the industry classification of an establishment is determined not only by the products it makes but also by the processes employed in making those products.

While some establishments produce only the primary products of the industry in which they are classified, it rarely happens that all the establishments in an industry specialize to this extent. The general statistics (employment, inventories, value added by manufacture, etc.) shown for an industry, therefore, reflect not only the primary activities of the establishment in the industry in which it is classified but also its activities associated with manufacture of secondary products and, in some instances, auxiliary activities as well (sales of scrape, receipts for repair, resales).

In some of the borderline areas between manufacturing and other major divisions of the Standard Industrial Classification system, such as retail trade, wholesale trade, or construction, manufactured products are often made by establishments primarily engaged in these nonmanufacturing activities. Examples of such products are venetian blinds, awnings, millwork, dried fruit, ice, prepared feed, poultry dressing, housefurnishings, canvas products, and dairy products. Since no reports were obtained in the annual survey from establishments primarily engaged in nonmanufacturing activities, national totals for these products as published are understated to the extent of exclusion of the products of such nonmanufacturing production.

Product Classes. The annual survey product classes are grouped according to the industry primarily responsible for their output. Thus, the five-digit class of product numbering system relates the product class to the industry to which the products "belong," the first four digits representing the industry. The fifth digit distinguishes the particular product class from other product classes of the industry. Under this system of classification, each product can be assigned a unique five-digit code.

The product-class numbering system also recognizes the distinctions in products which stem from the fact that the SIC system on occasion defines an industry on the basis of the manufacturing process employed or kind of materials used rather than the specific products made. Products produced in such industries may, therefore, be "primary" to more than one industry.

Estimating Procedures Used in the 1975 and 1976 Annual Surveys. Most of the Annual Survey of Manufactures estimates were computed by the "difference estimate formula." For each item, linear estimates of the totals for both the most recent Census of Manufactures year and the current year were developed by multiplying each sample establishment's data by its sample weight (the reciprocal of its probability of selection) and summing the weighted values to publication levels. Then the difference between the two linear estimates was added to the complete total for the census year to produce the current estimate. Estimates developed by the difference estimate formula usually are far more reliable than the comparable linear estimates developed from the current sample data alone.

Information References

U.S. Department of Commerce, Washington, D.C.: "Annual Survey of Manufactures;" "Census of Manufactures;" Statistical Abstract of the United States."

Cross References: *U.S. Economic and Business Censuses (and cross references there given).*

U.S. DEPARTMENT OF COMMERCE

The **Department of Commerce** was established by the act of March 4, 1913 which reorganized the Department of Commerce and Labor (created by the act of February 14, 1903) by transferring all labor activities into a new, separate Department of Labor. The Department is composed of the Office of the Secretary and the operating units, as charted in Exhibit I.

The Department of Commerce encourages, serves, and promotes the nation's economic development and technological advancement, providing a wide variety of programs. It offers assistance and information to domestic and international business; provides social and economic statistics and analyses for business and government planners; assists in the development and maintenance of the U.S. merchant marine; provides research for and promotes the increased use of science and technology in the development of the economy; provides assistance to speed the development of the economically underdeveloped areas of the nation; seeks to improve understanding of the earth's physical environment and oceanic life; promotes travel to the United States by residents of foreign countries; and assists in the growth of minority businesses.

The principal organizational units in the Department of Commerce are as follows:

International Trade Administration. This unit, formerly the Industry and Trade Administration, was established in January, 1980 to promote world trade and to strengthen the international trade and investment of the United States. It is headed by the Undersecretary for International Trade, with day-to-day management by the Deputy Undersecretary for International Trade. Activities include programs

EXHIBIT I

DEPARTMENT OF COMMERCE

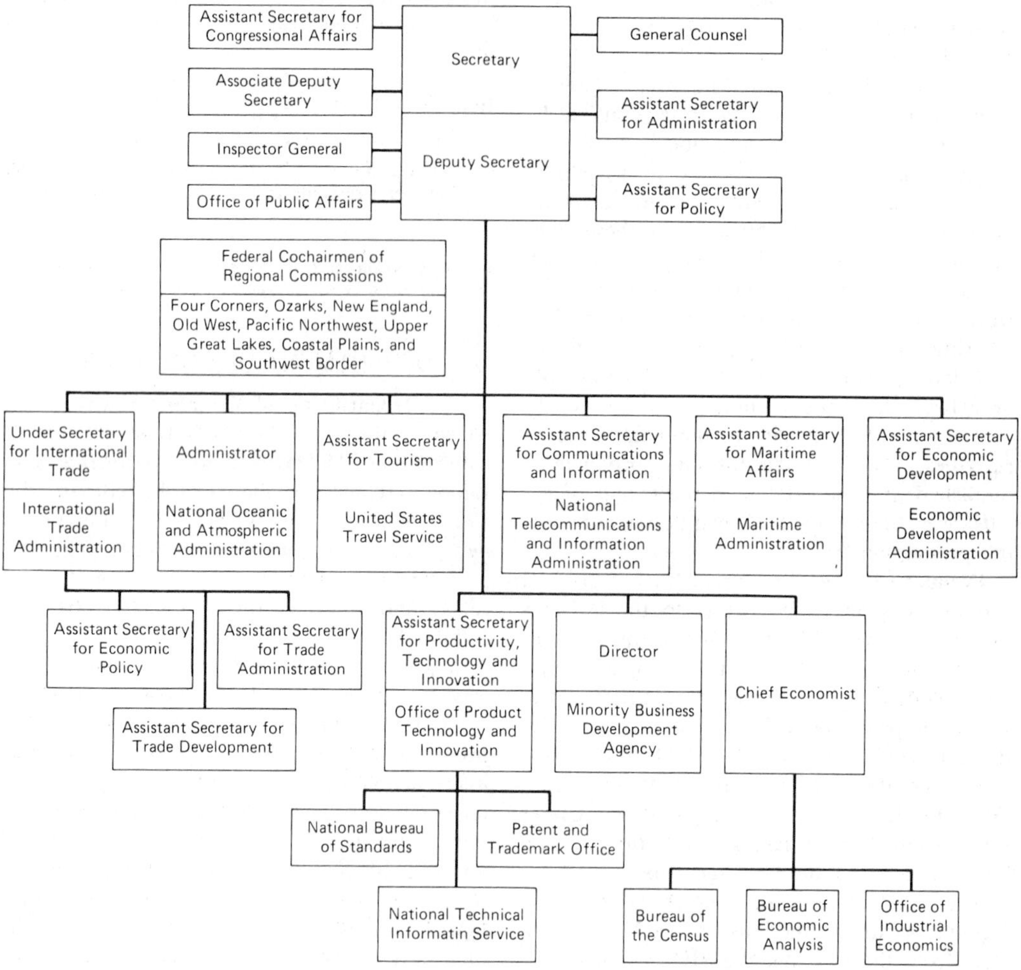

dealing with import and export issues, including industrial mobilization and foreign boycotts. Policies and programs are implemented at the local level through District Offices located in principal cities throughout the United States and Puerto Rico. ITA publishes the *Commerce Business Daily* and *Business America* magazine.

Economic Development Administration. The primary function of EDA, established in 1965, is the long-range development of areas with several unemployment and low family income problems. It aids in the development of public facilities and private enterprise to help create new, permanent jobs. Programs include public works grants and loans; economic adjustment assistance grants; business loans for industrial and commercial facilities and working capital; guarantees of leases for private industry and of private loans for industrial and commercial facilities and working capital; and technical, planning and research assistance for areas designated as Redevelopment Areas by the Assistant Secretary.

Maritime Administration. Established in 1950, the Maritime Administration administers programs to aid in the development, promotion, and operation of the U.S. merchant marine. It is also charged with organizing and directing emergency merchant ship operations. The EDA administers subsidy programs, through the Maritime Subsidy Board, under which the Federal Government pays the difference between certain costs of operating ships under the United States flag and foreign competitive flags on essential services, and the difference between the costs of constructing ships in United States and foreign shipyards. It also administers a War Risk Insurance program which insures operators and seamen against losses caused by hostile action if domestic commercial insurance is not available.

Minority Business Development Agency. The MBDA, formerly the Office of Minority Business Enterprise, was established in 1969. Its purpose is to develop and coordinate a national program for minority business enterprise. Management and technical assistance is provided to minority firms on request, primarily through a network of local business development organizations funded by the Agency. Specialized business assistance is available to firms exhibiting growth potential or involved in growth or high-technology sectors of the economy.

National Bureau of Standards. The overall goal of this Bureau, established in 1901, is to strengthen and advance the nation's science and technology, and to facilitate their effective application for public benefit. To this end, the Bureau conducts research and provides a basis for the nation's physical measurement system, scientific and technological services for industry and government, a technical basis for equity in trade, and technical services to promote public safety.

National Oceanic and Atmospheric Administration. The mission of NOAA is to explore, map, and chart the global ocean and its living resources, to manage, use, and conserve those resources, and to describe, monitor, and predict conditions in the atmosphere, ocean, sun, and space environment, issue warnings against impending destructive natural events, develop beneficial methods of environmental modification, and assess the consequences of inadvertent environmental modification over several scales of time. NOAA reports the weather of the United States and its possessions and provides weather forecasts to the general public.

National Technical Information Service. NTIS was established in 1970 to simplify and improve public access to Department of Commerce publications and to data files and scientific and technical reports sponsored by Federal agencies. It is obligated to recover its costs from sales to users. The Service is the central point in the United States for the public sale of Government-funded research and development reports and other analyses prepared by Federal agencies, their contractors, or grantees. The public may quickly locate abstracts of interest from among the 650,000 Federally sponsored research reports completed and published from 1964 on, by using the Agency's on-line computer search service (NTISearch). Copies of the research reports are sold in paper or microfiche.

Patent and Trademark Office. The PTO examines applications for design patents, plant patents, and utility patents. It also processes international applications for patents under the provisions of the Patent Cooperation Treaty. More than 70,000 patents are issued annually which provide inventors with exclusive rights to the results of their creative work, for specified periods of time. (See PATENTS.) About 30,000 trademarks are registered each year, and about 7,000 are renewed. (See TRADEMARKS.)

Bureau of the Census. The major functions of the Bureau of the Census, established in 1902, are authorized by the Constitution, which provides that a census of population shall be taken every ten years. The Bureau is a general-purpose statistical agency which collects, tabulates, and publishes a wide variety of statistical data about the people and the economy of the nation. (See U.S. CENSUS OF BUSINESS; U.S. CENSUS OF MANUFACTURES; and STATISTICAL ABSTRACT OF THE UNITED STATES.)

Bureau of Economic Analysis. The Bureau of Economic analysis, formerly Office of Business Economics, was established in 1953. Its objective is to provide a clear picture of the United States economy through the preparation, development, and interpretation of the national income and product accounts, summarized by the gross national product (GNP); the wealth accounts, which show the business and other components of national wealth; the input-output accounts, which trace the interrelationships among industrial markets; personal income and related economic series by geographic area; the United States balance of payments accounts and associated foreign investment accounts; and measures relating to environmental change and to welfare within the framework of the national economic accounts. The data and analyses prepared by BEA are disseminated mainly through its monthly publications, the *Survey of Current Business* (including periodic supplements) and *Business Conditions Digest.*

Bureau of Industrial Economics. The Bureau of Industrial Economics (latest successor to the earlier **Bureau of Domestic Commerce**), was established in January 1980. The mission of the Bureau is to provide government and business decision-makers with the data and objective analytical support needed to assess the individual industry implications of major policy decisions and worldwide economic developments. The Bureau engages in industry forecasting, and conducts studies on important issues related to the industrial sector, such as productivity developments, impact of Government regulations, capacity and capital formation needs, energy conservation trends, and international competitive developments.

National Telecommunications and Information Administration. NTIA was formed in 1978, combining the resources of the Office of Telecommunications within the Department of Commerce and the Office of Telecommunications Policy from the Executive Office of the President. NTIA's broad goals include formulating policies to support the development, growth, and regulation of telecommunications, information, and related industries; providing policy for the use of the electromagnetic spectrum; and providing telecommunications facilities grants to public service users.

United States Travel Service. This Service stimulates and facilitates travel to the United States by residents of foreign countries.

Office of Product Standards Policy. The mission of OPSP is to ensure that the United States public interest is adequately promoted and protected in domestic and international product standardization activities, both private and governmental.

Regional Action Planning Commissions. Authorized in 1965, the Commissions promote and manage development of multi-state regions designated by the Secretary of Commerce upon a finding of economic and social need. The Commissions are composed of the governors of the states in the region and a Federal member. They are required by statute to develop long-range regional development plans which serve as a framework for program and project funding. In general, the principal program categories of the Commissions include industrial development, human resource development, energy conservation and development, natural resource development, and tourism and recreation development.

Information References

"United States Government Manual, 1980–1981," available from U.S. Government Printing Office, Washington, D.C. 20402.

U.S. DEPARTMENT OF LABOR

The purpose of the **Department of Labor** is to foster, promote, and develop the welfare of the wage earners of the United States, to improve their working conditions, and to advance their opportunities for profitable employment. It administers more than 130 Federal labor laws guaranteeing workers' rights to safe and healthful working conditions, a minimum hourly wage and overtime pay, freedom from employment discrimination, unemployment insurance, and workers' compensation. The Department also protects workers' pension rights; sponsors job-training programs; helps workers find jobs; works to stengthen free collective bargaining; and keeps tract of changes in employment, prices, and other national economic measurements.

The Secretary of Labor is the head of the Department of Labor and the principal adviser to the President on the development and execution of policies and the administration and enforcement of laws relating to working conditions and employment opportunities.

The Wage Appeals Board acts on behalf of the Secretary in deciding appeals on questions of law and fact, taken in the discretion of the Board from wage determinations issued under the Davis-Bacon Act and its related prevailing wage statutes.

The Office of the Inspector General (OIG) provides an independent audit and investigations program to identify and report program deficiencies and improve the effectiveness of operations.

The Director of Information, Publications, and Reports advises the Secretary on Public Information matters and provides overall direction to the Department's public information and publications programs.

The Women's Bureau is responsible for standards and policies that promote the welfare of wage-earning women and advance their opportunities for professional employment. It has regional offices in ten areas throughout the United States.

The Undersecretary of Labor is the principal advisor to the Secretary, and serves as Acting Secretary in his absence.

The Employees' Compensation Appeals Board consists of three members appointed by the Secretary of Labor. The Board considers and decides appeals from final decisions in cases arising under the Federal Employees' Compen-

EXHIBIT I

DEPARTMENT OF LABOR

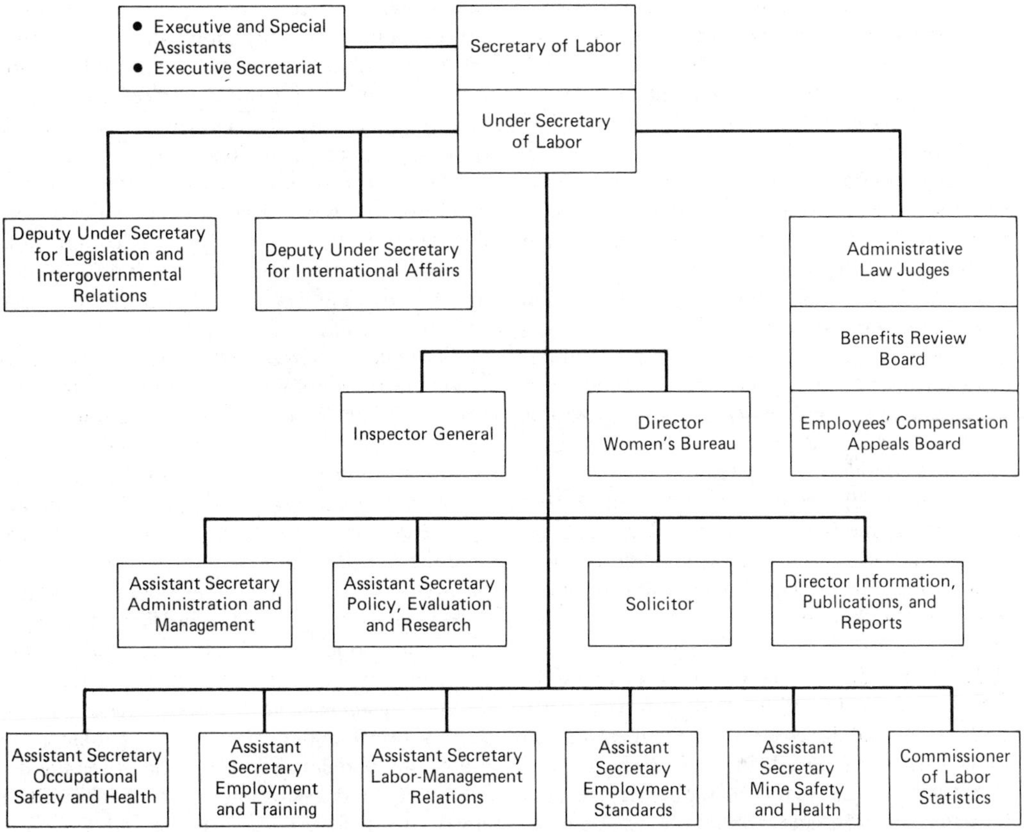

sation Act. Its decisions are final and not subject to court review.

Administrative Law Judges preside over formal hearings to determine violations of minimum wage requirements, overtime payments, compensation benefits, employee discrimination, grant performance, alien certification, employee protection, and health and safety regulations set forth in numerous statutes and various Executive orders. The Office of Administrative Law Judges also has a permanent Board of Contract Appeals for the Department and provides the hearings and appeals system required by the Talmadge Amendments to the Social Security Act.

The Benefits Review Board is a three-member quasi-judicial body with exclusive jurisdiction to consider and decide appeals raising substantion questions of law or fact from decisions of Administrative Law Judges.

The Solicitor of Labor is responsible for all the legal activities of the Department and its legislative program, and serves as legal adviser to the Secretary other officials of the Department. With a staff of attorneys in Washington and sixteen field offices, he directs a broad-scale litigation effort pertaining to the many statutes administered by the Department.

The Assistant Secretary for Administration and Management is responsible for administrative policy; centralized management staff support and services to the Department's agencies in the areas of financial, organization, and personnel management; program review; labor-management relations; ADP systems development and services; and equal employment opportunity.

The Assistant Secretary for Policy, Evaluation, and Research coordinates and provides leadership to the Department's activities in policy and program planning, program evaluation, and economic and social research bearing on the welfare of all workers.

The Deputy Undersecretary for Legislation and Intergovernmental Relations coordinates and directs all legislative activities of the Department, including contacts with the Congress and liaison with Federal, state, and local officials and with community, labor, and minority business groups. Regional representatives are located in the ten standard Federal regions.

International Responsibilities of the Department are carried out under the direction of the *Deputy Undersecretary for International Affairs* and the *Bureau of International Labor Affairs* which he supervises. The Bureau assists in formulating international economic and trade policies affecting American workers and helps represent the United States in multilateral and bilateral trade negotiations.

Employment and Training Administration (ETA) encompasses a group of offices and services established to implement responsibilities assigned to the Department for the conduct of work-experience and work-training programs conducted under the provisions of the Comprehensive Employment and Training Act of 1973 as amended, by states and other authorized sponsors; administration of the Federal-State Employment Security System; and the conduct of a continuing program of research, development, and evaluation.

The United States Employment Service (USES) provides assistance to states in establishing and maintaining a system of nearly 2,500 local public employment offices in the states and territories. USES efforts have been directed in recent years to improving the performance of state employment service agencies as labor market intermediaries, through such programs as computerized job matching, local office relocation and redesign, establishment of local employer committees, and improvement of linkages with CETA (see below) and other employment and training programs. Special programs are directed to veterans, rural area workers, and youth between the ages of 16 and 24. The USES also provides subsidiary services that include certifying aliens who seek to enter the United States for permanent or temporary employment and providing employment services and adjustment assistance to U.S. workers adversely affected by foreign trade imports.

The Office of Comprehensive Employment Development (OCED) provides leadership in nationwide work and training programs for economically disadvantaged, unemployed, and underemployed persons. The OCED has major responsibility for implementation of titles, I, II, VI, and VII of the Comprehensive Employment and Training Act (CETA) Amendments of 1978, and the Work Incentive Program (WIN). Under CETA, the Secretary of Labor makes grants to about 460 state and local units of government, which serve as prime sponsors under the act, and consortia of such units. Prime sponsors identify employment and training needs in their areas and plan and provide the job training and other services required to meet those needs. (See TRAINING AND DEVELOPMENT (Government Sponsored.)

The Work Incentive Program (WIN) is jointly administered by the Department of Labor and the Department of Health, Education, and Welfare. It is designed to help persons receiving Aid to Families with Dependent Children (AFDC) become self supporting.

The Office of National Programs (ONP) is responsible for employing and training programs which, by law or reason, must be administered directly from the Employment and Training Administration's headquarters in Washington.

Apprenticeship and Training. The National Apprenticeship Act was passed in 1937 to enable the Department of Labor to formulate and promote the furtherance of labor standards necessary to safeguard the welfare of apprentices, and cooperate with the states with respect to them. (See APPRENTICESHIP PROGRAMS.)

The Unemployment Insurance Service (UIS) provides leadership and policy guidance to State Employment Security agencies for the development and operation of the Federal-State employment insurance program and related wage-loss income maintenance programs.

The Office of Policy, Evaluation, and Research formulates and recommends ETA policies, plans, and resource allocations.

The Assistant Secretary for Labor-Management Relations is responsible for the Department's labor-management relations activities. The Labor-Management Services Administration (LMSA) administers three laws and section 7120 of the Civil Service Reform Act of 1978. It also provides assistance to collective bargaining negotiations, and keeps the Secretary posted on developments in labor-management disputes of national scope.

The Labor-Management Reporting and Disclosure Act calls upon labor organizations to file with LMSA copies of their constitutions and bylaws and annual financial reports of their transactions for public view. The act also prescribes rules for election of union officers, administration of trusteeships by labor organizations, and rights of union members, and the handling of union funds.

The Assistant Secretary for Employment

Standards has responsibility for administering employment standards programs dealing with minimum wage and overtime standards; registration of farm labor contractors; determining prevailing wage rates on Government contracts and subcontracts; nondiscrimination and affirmative action for minorities, women, veterans, and handicapped workers on Government contracts and subcontracts; and workers' compensation programs for Federal and certain private employers and employees.

The Wage and Hour Administrator is responsible for planning, directing, and administering programs dealing with a variety of Federal labor legislation. These programs are designed to increase and protect low-wage incomes as provided by the Fair Labor Standards Act; and otherwise safeguard the health and welfare of workers by discouraging excessively long hours of work. Regional offices are maintained in ten areas throughout the United States.

The Office of Federal Contract Compliance Programs establishes policies and goals, and coordinates the Government's program to achieve nondiscrimination in employment by Government contractors and subcontractors and federally assisted construction programs. Regional offices are maintained in ten areas throughout the United States.

The Office of Workers' Compensation Programs is responsible for the administration of the basic Federal workers' compensation laws. (See WORKERS' COMPENSATION.)

The Assistant Secretary for Occupational Safety and Health has responsibility for occupational safety and health activities. OSHA offices are established in ten areas throughout the United States. (See OCCUPATIONAL SAFETY AND HEALTH ACT OF 1970.)

The Assistant Secretary for Mine Safety and Health is responsible for safety and health in the nation's mines. The Mine Safety and Health Administration (MSHA), formerly the Mining Enforcement and Safety Administration in the Department of the Interior, was established by the Federal Mine Safety and Health Administration Act of 1977, which consolidates all provisions for mine safety and health under a single Federal law applicable to all types of mines.

The Bureau of Labor Statistics (BLS) is the Government's principal factfinding agency in the field of labor economics, particularly with respect to the collection and analysis of data on labor requirements, labor force, employment, unemployment, hours of work, wages and employee compensation, prices, living conditions, labor-management relations, productivity and technological developments, and international aspects of certain of these subjects. The information collected is issued in monthly press releases, in special publications, and in the Bureau's official publications, the *Monthly Labor Review.* Other major periodicals of the Bureau include: the *Consumer Price Index, Producer Prices and Price Indexes, Employment and Earnings, Current Wage Developments, Occupational Outlook Handbook,* and *Occupational Outlook Quarterly.*

SOURCE: United States Government Manual, 1980–1981.

U.S. ECONOMIC AND BUSINESS CENSUSES

The **Economic Censuses** are comprehensive and periodic canvasses of the Nation's **Industrial and Business Activities.** Taken by the Census Bureau, a part of the U.S. Department of Commerce, the censuses provide a detailed statistical profile of a large segment of the national economy.

The first economic census of the United States was conducted as part of the 1810 decennial census, when inquiries on manufacturing were included with the census of population. All other decennial censuses through 1900, except in 1830, contained questions on manufacturing. In 1904 the quinquennial U.S. CENSUS OF MANUFACTURES began. It was conducted every fifth year until 1920 and every second year from 1921 to 1939. Although some distributive trade data were collected in the decennial census of 1840, the first census of business was taken in 1929. It covered only retail and wholesale trades, but beginning with the second business census in 1933 and in succeeding censuses various services also have been included. Business censuses were subsequently taken for 1935 and 1939 and after a wartime interruption were resumed in 1948. Beginning in 1954, and continuing in the censuses of 1958, 1963, 1967, and 1972, the business censuses have been conducted concurrently with the censuses of manufactures and mineral industries. Beginning with the 1967 censuses, Congress authorized the economic censuses to be taken at five-year intervals covering years ending in "2" and "7".

Uses of the Economic Censuses. The economic censuses are the primary source of facts about the structure and functioning of the economy and, therefore, provide information essential for both government and business. The censuses furnish an important part of the framework for such composite measures as the national accounts. In forecasting and planning, they are especially useful in analyzing the national product in terms of the transactions that determine its size and composition. The economic censuses also provide weights and benchmarks for indexes of the industrial production, productivity, and price, all of which are essential for understanding current economic developments.

Manufacturers and distributors make widespread use of the economic censuses in establishing measures of their potential markets by areas, kinds of businesses, and kinds of products. Management in various industries and trades get facts from them for use in economic or sales forecasting, analyzing sales performance, laying out sales territories, allocating advertising budgets, and locating plants, warehouses, and stores. Trade organizations use census statistics for insight into changes in the structure of industry. State and local governments use the geographic detail that describes the patterns of economic change in individual communities. Local business organizations and research groups do too.

Following every census, reports are purchased by thousands of businesses and other users; likewise, census facts are widely disseminated by trade associations, business journals, and the daily press. Volumes containing census statistics are available in most major public and college libraries.

Census of Retail Trade. The 1977 Census of Retail Trade, part of the 1977 Economic Censuses, covered retail trade as defined in the STANDARD INDUSTRIAL CLASSIFICATION SYSTEM (SIC) Manual. It included all establishments primarily engaged in selling merchandise for personal or household consumption and rendering services incidental to the sale of the goods. It excluded governmental organizations classified in the covered industries except for liquor stores operated by state and local governments. It also excluded data for direct sellers with no paid employees and post exchanges, ship stores, and similar establishments operated on military posts by agencies of the Federal Government. In the Major Retail Center series of reports only, data for nonstore retailers were excluded.

For the 1977 Census of Retail Trade, large- and medium-size firms, plus all firms known to operate more than one establishment, were sent questionnaires to be completed and returned to the Bureau by mail. For most very small firms, including those with no paid employees, data from existing records of the Internal Revenue Service (IRS) and the Social Security Administration (SSA) were used instead. The two sources produced basic information on location, kind of business, volume of sales and payrolls, and number of employees. In addition, more detailed information for selected kinds of business was obtained on the various questionnaires.

Central Business District. A "central business district," as defined by the Bureau, is the defined downtown retail area of an SMSA central city, or other SMSA city of 50,000 or more persons. A CBD is an area of very high land valuation; high concentration of retail businesses, offices, theaters, hotels, and "service" businesses; and high traffic flow. It is defined by existing census tract boundaries and consists of one or more whole census tracts. Census tracts are small, relatively permanent areas into which large cities and adjacent areas have been divided to show comparable small-area statistics. Data for CBD's are published only in reports of the census of retail trade.

In 1972, CBDs were enumerated only for SMSA cities with 100,000 inhabitants or more. The CBD definition for 1977 was changed so that areas defined as downtown business areas (DBAs) in the 1972 censuses became CBDs for the 1977 censuses.

Major Retail Center. A "major retail center" is a concentration of at least 25 retail stores located inside an SMSA but outside a CBD. At least one of the 25 stores must be a general merchandise store with a minimum of 100,000 square feet of total under-rock floor space. MRCs include planned suburban shopping centers as well as unplanned centers such as older "string streets" (continuous businesses along a thoroughfare with few cross streets containing any businesses) and combinations of planned and unplanned centers.

In 1972, MRC's were defined by the Bureau as those concentrations of retail stores (located inside the standard metropolitan statistical area but outside the CBD) having at least $5 million in retail sales and at least ten retail establishments, one of which was classified as a department store (SIC 531).

Census of Wholesale Trade. The 1977 Census of Wholesale Trade, part of the 1977 Economic Censuses, covered wholesale trade as defined in the Standard Industrial Classification (SIC) Manual. It included all establishments with one or more paid employees primarily engaged in selling merchandise to retailers; to industrial, commercial, institutional, farm, or professional users; or to other wholesalers; or acting as agents or brokers in buying merchandise for or selling merchandise to such persons or companies. It excluded governmental organizations classified in the covered industries, except for wholesale liquor establishments operated by state and local governments.

As in the past, wholesale firms without employees were excluded from the census. In the censuses of retail trade and service industries, the sales/receipts of firms with no paid employees are derived from reports filed with the Internal Revenue Service (IRS) rather than from a direct canvass. However, this source proved impractical for wholesale firms without paid employees. The census sales figure for wholesale trade represents the gross volume of business conducted. Firms which operate wholly or partly on a commission basis must provide both gross volume of business conducted and commission receipts on the census form, but only one figure for IRS records. Moreover, administrative records make no distinction between reports submitted by the various types of wholesale operation. No reliable estimates of the dollar volume accounted for by wholesale firms with no employees are available, but this undercoverage is believed to be relatively minor.

Microfiche and Computer Tapes. Microfiche reports are sold by the Subscriber Services Section (Publications), Bureau of the Census, Washington, D.C. 20233. Computer tapes are sold by the Customer Services Branch, Data User Services Division, Bureau of the Census, Washington, D.C. 20233.

Special Tabulations. Special tabulations of data collected in the 1977 Census of Wholesale Trade may be obtained on computer tape or in tabular form. The data are in summary form and subject to the same rules prohibiting disclosure of confidential information (including name, address, kind of business, or other data for individual business establishments or companies) as are the regular publications. Special tabulations are prepared on a cost basis. A request for a cost estimate, as well as exact specifications on the type and format of the data to be provided, should be directed to the Chief, Business Division, Bureau of the Census, Washington, D.C. 20233.

Census of Service Industries. The 1977 Census of Service Industries, part of the 1977 Economic Censuses, covered services as defined in the Standard Industrial Classification (SIC) Manual, except Religious Organizations, Private Households, and governmental organizations classified in the covered industries. The scope of the census also included Arrangement of Passenger Transportation, a component of Transportation Services. The series of reports comprises two segments:

Selected Service Industries (SC77-A-1 through SC77-A-52) Data are presented for establishments subject to Federal income tax in the following classifications:

Hotels, motels, trailering parks, and camps.
Personal services.
Business services.
Automotive repair, services, and garages.
Miscellaneous repair services.
Amusement and recreation services, including motion pictures.
Dental laboratories.
Legal services.
Engineering, architectural, and surveying services.

Other Service Industries. Data are also presented for establishments and organizations within the following classifications:

Arrangement of passenger transportation.
Rooming and boarding houses and membership lodging.
Health services, except dental laboratories.
Educational services.
Social services
Museums, art galleries, botanical and zoological gardens (noncommercial).
Membership organizations, except religious organizations.
Miscellaneous services, except engineering, architectural, and surveying services.

Microfiche and Computer Tapes. Microfiche reports are sold by the Subscriber Services Section (Publications), as is done for Wholesale Trade.

Special Tabulations. Special Tabulations of the data collected in the 1977 Census of Service Industries may be obtained on computer tape or in tabular form. The data will be in summary form and subject to the same rules prohibiting disclosure of confidential information (including name, address, kind of business, or other data for individual business establishments or companies) as are the regular publications. Special tabulations are prepared on a cost basis. A request for a cost estimate, as well as exact specifications on the type and format of the data to be provided, should be directed to the Chief, Business Division, Bureau of the Census, Washington, D.C. 20233.

Cross References: *Business Intelligence: Sources of Information; Statistical Abstract of the United States; U.S. Census of Manufactures.*

V

VALUE ADDED TAX (VAT)

The **Value Added Tax (VAT)** is a form of indirect tax introduced by France in 1954 to meet a serious fiscal crisis. It is a levy on the "value added" to goods at each stage of production and distribution. The tax worked so well that its base was gradually expanded and the rates were raised. It was introduced throughout the Common Market and became the world's fastest-growing revenue producer. As of 1972 it was estimated [1] that the revised French VAT accounted for about 52% of France's $30-billion tax revenues, and one quarter of Germany's $51 billion of taxes; in Belgium, in its first year, VAT accounted for 33% of the 1971 tax revenues, and 26% in Holland.

The question of whether the United States should adopt a VAT is an extremely difficult one. Arguments have been advanced both for and against it, and Richard M. Hammer, National Director of International Tax Services for Price Waterhouse, has pointed out [2] that "serious disagreement continues to remain among the nation's leading economists regarding the precise impact of a VAT on such diverse considerations as the United States balance of payments and the incentive toward savings." Comments made by witnesses during the hearings on the proposed Tax Restructuring Act of 1980 made it clear that further study is required before an informed decision can be made to adopt or reject the tax.

Both the proposed Restructuring Act of 1979 and that of 1980 failed of enactment, and as of 1981 there are no prospects of such legislation in the near future. Nevertheless, while ultimate implementation of a VAT system in the United States may be a number of years away, the move for a European-style value added tax has gained significant momentum in this country.

How VAT Works. VAT is an indirect tax imposed on each sale starting from the beginning of the production and distribution cycle and culminating with the sale to the ultimate consumer. The tax is usually imposed at a flat rate in the same manner as a sales tax, but the rates are generally much higher. Each seller in the chain collects the VAT from the purchaser at the time of sale (the VAT is added to the sales price but must be separately stated except on the final sale to the consumer), deducts from this amount any VAT he himself has paid on his purchases, and remits the balance to the government. The net effect of offsetting purchases and sales is to impose the tax at each stage of production on the sum of wages, interest, rents, profits and other factors of production not furnished by suppliers subject to the tax at the previous stage of production—hence, a tax on value added.

The seller sustains no economic burden on his purchases, since he receives a credit from the government for any VAT paid to his suppliers. Instead, the effect of the credit mechanism operates to push the VAT forward through the production and distribution chain to the final consumer. Upon each sale, the government collects a tax on the incremental value added to the product during the preceding stage of production or distribution. The consumer absorbs the VAT as part of the sales price but receives no credit. Thus, VAT is in reality a consumption tax borne by the final consumer.

In operation, a federal VAT differs from sales taxes currently imposed in the United States at the state and local levels, and from single-stage turnover taxes which were popular in Europe, in that the government collects a part of the revenue at each stage of the production and distribution cycle. However, the total tax ultimately collected by the government is the same regardless of the number of intermediate producers [3].

The example in Exhibit I is a simple illustration of VAT as applied to the apparel industry with an assumed rate of tax of 20%. Most discussion of VAT for America has been in terms of a single-rate tax, rather than different rates for different types of products, as is the case in Europe.

In addition to its broad base and high level of revenue generation, VAT has the advantage of being largely self-enforcing. The manufacturer submits to the Government, along with his own tax payment, a claim for credit for the taxes included in his suppliers' prices, thus discouraging attempts by the latter to avoid pay-

EXHIBIT I

ILLUSTRATION OF VAT [3]

	Purchase				Sale				
	Price paid for goods	VAT	Total	"Value Added"	Price charged	VAT collected	Total	Credit for VAT paid	Net to gov't
Cotton grower & Processor	—	—	—	10	10	2	12	—	2
Textile producer	10	2	12	30	40	8	48	2	6
Clothing manufacturer	40	8	48	60	100	20	120	8	12
Clothing distributor	100	20	120	20	120	24	144	20	4
Retailer	120	24	144	30	150	30	180	24	6
Consumer	150	30	180	—	—	—	—	—	—
Totals				150		84		54	30

Note: that the total collected by the government is 16.67 percent of the final selling price (30/180) and that this amount is borne completely by the ultimate consumer who receives no credit.

ment of their VAT. Disadvantages claimed by opponents of VAT are that it bears more heavily on low-income people, and that it is inflationary, particularly if introduced in an economy that is already under inflationary pressure. On the other hand, advocates seek to tie VAT in with a reduction in increasingly onerous local property taxes.

References Cited

[1] "How Value-Added Works in Europe," *Business Week,* February 26, 1972.

[2] Remarks in connection with the publication by Price Waterhouse of the April, 1980 Supplement to its Information Guide, "Value Added Tax, below.

[3] Information Guide, "Value Added Tax," New York, Price Waterhouse & Co., November 1979.

VALUE ENGINEERING (VALUE ANALYSIS)

During the years since World War II, **Value Engineering** (also known as Value Analysis) has emerged as an effective cost-reduction discipline in defense, space, and consumer products industries.

Origin and Development. The genesis of value engineering can be traced to 1947 when the General Electric Company launched an intensive effort to identify the essential functions of their consumer products, and to attain these functions at lowest cost. The term was coined by H. A. Winne, Vice President, Engineering for General Electric, to describe the original set of techniques created for this purpose. Lawrence D. Miles, Manager of Value Services, was given the prime responsibility for the value analysis program, and is credited with its successful development at GE.

The growth pattern of value engineering can be traced to a number of compelling factors. In the defense industry, the cost-plus-fixed-fee contracting environment virtually ignored cost effectiveness in the mad scramble for superior performance and rapid delivery of weapon systems. Ultimately, the cost spiral reached such proportions that more and more individuals and agencies within the Department of Defense became preoccupied with the task of arresting this trend.

Within the DOD, the Navy Bureau of Ships was the first military establishment to evince an interest in this new approach to cost reduction. In 1952, the Bureau sent a task team to GE to examine at close range the what, when, and how of value analysis. Results of this survey were sufficiently encouraging to warrant the initiation of a similar effort in 1954 within the Bureau of Ships. The driving force was Rear Admiral Richard S. Mandelkorn, who organized the first Navy value engineering program. A formal value engineering activity was established early in 1954, and by 1956 all Naval shipyards had a value engineering program under way. For his contribution to this undertaking, the Navy awarded the Navy Distinguished Public Service Award to Miles in 1958.

The development of an effective value engineering program, together with attractive contractual inventives, has enabled the Department of Defense and many of its prime contractors to realize substantial savings. Within non-defense industry, value engineering emerged initially as an effective answer to the cost/price squeeze. More recently it has become an integral cost-reduction discipline in the space program, civil systems, hospitals, construction, and a wide variety of other industries and activities.

Value engineering has a fundamental difference from the more traditional approaches to design, cost reduction, INDUSTRIAL ENGINEERING, and production engineering. The key difference is that value engineering is a deliberate effort to identify and select the lowest cost method, from many alternative methods, *to satisfy the proper functional needs.* A single idea that is generated resulting in a lower cost to meet a design requirement is not value engineering. Although the idea probably represents a better value, it probably enbodies no attempt to determine whether the idea represents the *best* value from a selection of alternatives or whether the design requirement being satisfied *represents the real problem.* It is within this context that value engineering adds another dimension to good engineering. VE has been applied to systems, equipment, facilities, procedures, methods, software, and support services, to name a few.

Formal Definitions. Value engineering is defined as: "An organized effort directed at analyzing the functions of goods or services for the purpose of achieving the ncessary functions and essential characteristics at the lowest cost, consistent with the business objectives."

The key terms in this definition are:

An organized effort: Value engineering utilizes a methodology that was developed for problem-solving over 30 years ago.

. . . *analyzing the functions:* achieving the necessary function. It is a deliberate effort to identify what is being furnished and what the market *needs,* as opposed to wants and desires. This analysis involves engineering and marketing to define the priority requirements from the point of view of the *customer,* and includes the target selling price, margins, and market shape.

. . . *and essential characteristics:* In addition to achieving the product functions, other requirements must be satisfied, such as reliability, maintainability, and quality.

. . . *lowest overall cost:* The lowest cost is determined by generating and evaluating a range of alternatives including new concepts, reconfiguration, eliminating or combining items, and process or procedure changes. The lowest overall cost also considers the operation and maintenance of the product. This element interfaces engineering with manufacturing.

. . . *consistent with the business objectives:* The end results must satisfy the intended business purpose, such as timeliness of development, compatibility with other product lines, resources, market environment, and the after market. The disciplines of marketing, engineering, and manufacturing, as well as other disciplines, working together, maintain a focus on the requirements, design, and cost.

In simplest terms, value engineering is the systematic use of techniques that identify the required function, establish a value for the function, and finally provide the function at the lowest overall cost. It differes from pre-existing cost-reduction activities in that it is *function-oriented,* involving a searching analysis of the function of a product or service as opposed merely to seeking lower costs in methods and processes to produce the same item. Obviously, value engineering involves the use of many known cost-cutting techniques. Organization of these techniques in a manner which permits systematic application to function represents, in part, the "newness" of value engineering.

DOD accepts studies performed prior to the existence of hardware, or "before the fact," as value engineering. Cost reduction on existing products is identified as "value analysis." Commercial industry will distinguish the difference (if at all) by the nature of the problem to be solved. If the problem requires the physical sciences as the principal discipline in arriving at a solution, it is value engineering. If the nature of the problem is non-product oriented, or "Software" it is Value Analysis. However, it is a more common practice to use the terms interchangeably.

Methodology. The Job Plan is considered the essential element in performing value engineering. Each market, agency, or company uses job plan variations which contain from four to eight or more distinct phases. However, the following five basic phases of the value engineering program will generally be included in all value engineering job plans:

(1) Item selection.
(2) Information and analysis of function.
(3) Development of alternatives.
(4) Analysis of alternatives.
(5) Proposal development.

Item Selection. An item selected for value engineering study may be hardware, software, a system, or any type of product or service. Carefully considered are such factors as the production quantity, unit cost, timeliness of change in the production cycle, implementation costs (which include not only production-line modifications, tooling, and procedures, but also the effect on spare parts, manuals, field maintenance, etc.) and others.

Where the Government contractor uses the contractor unit cost as a value standard, commercial industry uses its market dynamics. Margins can be improved in only two ways: increase price, or reduce cost (or a combination of both). Therefore it is the erosion of margins, the loss of sales, the growth of the market and a company's share that will determine the selection of a candidate's value study project.

Once that product category is identified, priority of selection is then based largely upon (1) production quantity, current and future; (2) present status with respect to design and/or production; (3) present item value; and (4) implementation costs.

Information and Analysis of Function. In this phase, the objectives are (1) to collect all pertinent information available about the item (e.g., specifications, design criteria, costs, quantity, manufacturing methods, and the like); (2) to determine the item's basic (required) and secondary functions; and (3) to determine the cost of the item and the "worth" of the functions involved.

To accomplish these objectives, the following basic questions must be answered:

(1) What is the item?
(2) What is its function?
(3) What is its present cost?
(4) What is the "worth" of its function?
(5) What else will perform the function?
(6) What will that cost?

If a product is the case study, it is reviewed with the cognizant design engineer from a standpoint of determining the item's "engineering history"—what approaches were taken; what failed; what succeeded. Marketing and Sales are brought in to assess competitive factors, product life, market growth, price limits or sensitivities, and margin objectives. Management reviews charters, capital availability, resources, and any organizational impacts. Manufacturing and purchasing personnel are consulted on the same basis. Finally a complete assessment of the information obtained leads to the determination of required or essential function(s).

In this phase of the study a number of "tests for value" are applied. The following are typical in hardware analysis:

(1) Does its use contribute value?
(2) Is its cost proportional to its usefulness?
(3) Does it need all of its features?
(4) Is there anything better for the intended use?
(5) Can a usable part be made by a lower cost method?
(6) Can a standard product be found which will be usable?
(7) Is it made on proper tooling—considering quantities used?

Development of Alternatives. This represents the speculative or creative phase of the job plan. Having defined the required function, the next step is to examine the methods used to provide this function and to explore alternate approaches. Again the emphasis is on *function,* a ground rule which allows complete freedom of thought—as opposed to conventional cost reduction efforts which are basically directed toward producing essentially the same item at lower cost.

Analysis of Alternatives. The value engineer now begins to make cost comparisons and other comparative analyses. The lowest cost method is tentatively selected, subject to verification that it will provide the required function and will lead to net reduction in overall cost without degradation of any other essential design parameters, e.g., reliability, safety, maintainability, etc.

Proposal Development. The economically promising alternative approaches are next subjected to intensive evaluation to assure feasibility. In some cases, technical adequacy is easily demonstrated; in others, proof of feasibility demands considerable effort, often involving hardware testing and verification of results. Finally, a Value Engineering Proposal is generated which presents all data necessary for final evaluation by the cognizant management authority. A typical proposal would include design sketches, material and labor cost estimates, tooling requirements, investments in capital, payback, and all other cost consequences associated with the change. (See RETURN ON CAPITAL.)

To meet the needs of sophisticated industrial environments, as in defense production, which may involve low production quantities, rapid state-of-the-art changes, high complexity, and high reliability, value engineering has undergone changes which have placed emphasis "up the stream" in the specification, design, and production processes. Each case represents an amalgam of value engineering technology, comprising:

Function Analysis System Technique (FAST). Developed by C.W. Byetheway, FAST builds upon traditional "random function determination" methods by systematically analyzing each function as it affects other functions, directing creative attention to the root problem rather than its symptoms.

Market Analysis. Marketing identifies a need expressed in terms of performance specifications and price goals, so that Design Engineering can conceptualize a product that satisfies both market and business objectives. (See MARKETING RESEARCH and related entries.)

Specification Analysis. VE identifies and eliminates areas of overspecification. Check lists are employed which place emphasis on the cost consequences of each specified requirement.

Design Review. Periodic design reviews enable the value engineer to influence the design before it is turned over to production. The objective is optimum trade-offs to reduce overall cost while maintaining "value" characteristics.

Value Engineering Task Forces. As previously described, value engineering uses marketing to define the customer requirements (including price); engineering to define the product; and manufacturing to define the production. Other expert resources are used further to fine-tune the product—Purchasing, sales, finance, quality control. (See pertinent entries.)

Recognizing that cost avoidance techniques are seldom completely effective, a "second look" can often produce significant savings. For this purpose *VE task forces* are organized to implement the VE job plan on specific low-value items. Each element of cost is challenged from a function/worth viewpoint, and alternative approaches are developed in each case where value is considered low.

Target Cost. For value engineering program purposes, a cost target is defined as the cumulative average standard product cost goal necessary to achieve the sales and margin objective of the product offering.

The selling price is established by a management decision and includes cost elements that are not directly influenced by the design (profit, taxes, corporate expenses, and marketing and selling expenses). The cost elements that are directly influenced by a design are the inventory costs consisting of direct labor, burden, and direct material. All cost elements are in some way affected by the design, but inventory cost is immediately visible to the designer for assessing the economic consequences of design decisions. The cost elements used are those that make up inventory costs. A simplified version of the cost elements are displayed in Exhibit I.

In the company's earnings plans, the inventory cost as a percent of sales is one of the specified goals. Using these data as a cost-to-price ratio (CPR), a target inventory cost can be established as a percent or ratio of the target selling price.

$$\text{Target Cost} = \text{Selling Price} \times \text{CPR}$$

The VE program has as an objective the stimulation of cost consciousness in all individ-

EXHIBIT I

COST ELEMENTS

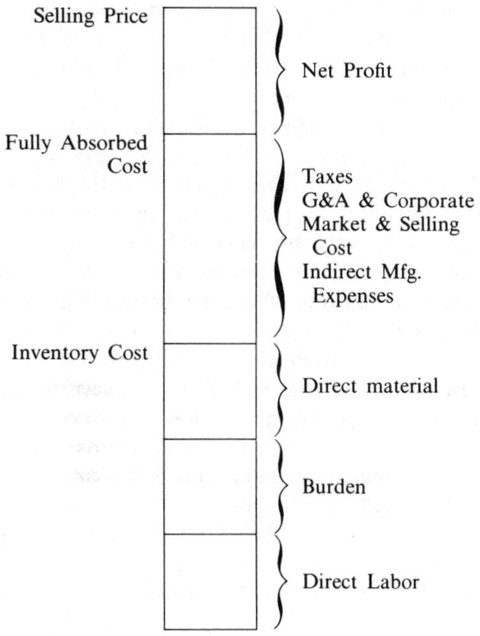

uals who contribute to product cost. A cost target provides a goal for the designer and a continuous assessment of cost performance against that goal.

Organization. Organization for value engineering generally involves both line and staff functions. The staff role is primarily one of planning, coordination, assuring compliance with company policy, customer interface, etc. The line activity is mainly concerned with the actual "doing" of value engineering. As a staff function, value engineering is often found as an element of corporate Product Assurance (which may include Reliability, Quality Control, Specifications, and Standards) or as a separate function reporting at the vice president level.

As a line function, the value engineering focal point is normally located within the engineering organization, particularly in defense industry where the value engineering emphasis is on design.

Over the years, a number of mutually supportive and interdependent cost-oriented disciplines have been developed, especially in the defense industry. These include, in addition to value engineering, ZERO DEFECTS (DOD), Awareness Programs (NASA), and plant SUGGESTION SYSTEMS, special cost reduction programs, and others. Many industrial firms and government agencies have found it advantageous to combine two or more of these programs in one organizational entity, thereby eliminating redundancy and maximizing their synergistic effect. In many cases, this organizational amalgam has been identified as "Performance Improvement," normally a staff function.

The Value Engineer. Basically, two types of personnel are involved in a value engineering program: those having prime responsibility for the design of a product, and those providing the focal point for cost reduction and cost avoidance as a full-time endeavor. One of the essential elements of a good value engineering program is the establishment of a comparatively small group of individuals whose *prime* responsibility involves value engineering actions which assure management that cost considerations are systematically factored into the decision-making process. This is the role of the professional value engineer.

The position of the *Value Engineer,* the director of the VE program, requires a professional background in the physical sciences and a strong knowledge of manufacturing techniques. Further professional level competency is required in such quantitative and qualitative analysis techniques as are utilized in market, economic, and operational evaluation. The job also requires a sound knowledge of business economics such that the incumbent is aware of the implications of value program reports and recommendations. And it is, of course, important that the incumbent be trained in the value disciplines on a professional level. Further, because of the heavy interdisciplinary nature of this activity, plus the fact that the results of these efforts depend upon motivating individual team members, the director requires a high degree of human relations skills in order to help assure a continuing level of managerial and employee involvement. Given the fact that VE efforts are often seen as competing for the limited time available to daily operational tasks, there is a requirement for "salesmanship" and persuasiveness in order to maintain a high and productive level of effort on the part of project personnel.

Professional Activity. The Society of American Value Engineers was organized in 1959. The Society is dedicated to the advancement of the theory and practice of value engineering and the promotion of professional standards of ethics. Its activities include conferences, seminars, publications, and the work of various technical committees at both the chapter and national level.

In recent years the Society has structured a professional competence recognition program called "Certified Value Specialist" (CVS). After fulfilling academics and practical prerequisites, the Candidate is given an examination. After successfully complying with all standards and reviews by a Board of Judges, he or she is certified for four years. Continued certification is predicated upon maintaining proficiency.

ANTHONY R. TOCCO, Manager, Manufacturing Engineering, TRW Mission Mfg. Company, Houston, Texas; Past National President, Society of American Value Engineers (SAVE).

JOSEPH KAUFMAN, Manager, Value Programs, Cooper Industries, Houston, Texas; Past National President Society of American Value Engineers (SAVE).

Information References

Association:

Society of American Value Engineers (SAVE).

Periodicals:

Performance Magazine.
Value Engineering Digest.
Value World.

Texts:

Fallon, Carlos, "Value Analysis", New York, Triangle Press, 2nd rev., 1978.
Miles, Lawrence D., "Techniques of Value Analysis and Engineering," New York, McGraw-Hill, 1972, rev.
Mudge, Arthur E., "Value Engineering: A Systematic Approach," New York, McGraw-Hill 1971.
"SAVE Proceedings, 1980," Irving, Texas, Society of American Value Engineers.

Cross References: *Purchasing; Vendor Rating.*

VENDOR RATING

Vendor Rating is an integral part of most QUALITY CONTROL AND QUALITY ASSURANCE programs. Vendor-rating schemes have evolved over a ten- to fifteen-year period from strictly numerical indices to the current practice of using descriptive evaluation.

High-Technology Applications. The original numerical rating schemes of the kind described in the "Procurement Quality Control Handbook" published by the American Society for Quality Control (ASQC) were developed for use in the restricted spheres of aerospace industries and other high-technology manufacturing. The schemes are useful and successful where the vendor and vendee are at comparable levels of sophistication and operate to common standards specifications and practices. In those circumstances where conformity to performance specifications is the overriding consideration, numerical rating of compliance is a preferred method of supplier control.

Exhibit I illustrates the rating formula suggested in the ASCQ "Procurement Quality Control" handbook of recommended practices, 2nd edition. Starting with a perfect rating of 100, departures from say, acceptable quality levels, price, delivery service, or other elements would each subtract a specified value, resulting in the final rating. Emphasis must be placed on the need to adjust these point values for different products even within the same industry and market. For example, a high-quality requirement item such as a critical component may be purchased from a vendor at the same time the vendee is buying from that vendor a nonfunctional part with very little quality needs.

Broadened Applications. The rapid expansion of quality assurance requirements in many industries has broadened the application of

EXHIBIT I

ELEMENTS AND SUGGESTED DEMERIT POINT VALUES

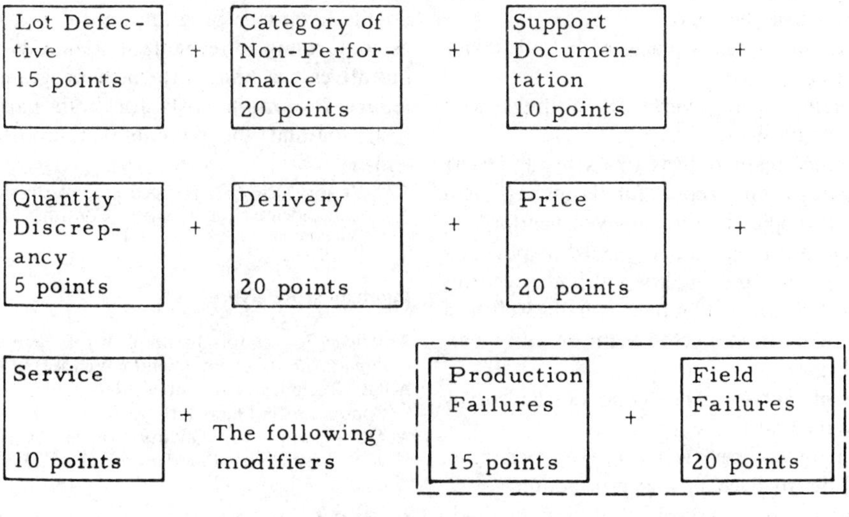

From American Society for Quality Control, "Procurement Quality Control," 2nd ed.

vendor rating concepts from high-technology industries to industry in general. This trend has been spurred by the current climate of consumer demands for protection, supported by the courts in terms of major damage payments and massive recall programs.

The intent of vendor evaluation is to determine, usually by pre-contract survey, if the intended vendors have "in place" the basic quality control procedures which will enable them to deliver products within specifications in a timely and cost-effective manner. Such an investigation is desirable because the vendor is probably in a completely different industrial stream from that of the vendee.

A history of previous contract performance is a useful base to start from, but is actually not essential in the evaluation process. In most industries the evaluation process has become a team action, with members from purchasing, engineering, and quality assurance of the vendor and vendee companies meeting to exchange pertinent information. (Specific team make-up varies with the industry involved.) A typical evaluation would proceed as follows:

(1) Vendee evaluation team meets at its work location to plan the evaluation.

(2) Vendee's purchasing representative contacts potential vendors and arranges for visits.

(3) Visit sequence is confirmed and vendor and vendee teams make final preparation for actual visits. Relevant documents, drawings, specifications, etc., are exchanged for study.

(4) Vendee team arrives at vendor plant or work location and briefs vendor management on the scope of the survey.

(5) The survey takes place, with both teams participating.

(6) Vendee team reviews its findings with vendor management.

(7) Vendee team returns to its headquarters and prepares a final report for its management group, with copies to the surveyed vendor.

(8) Vendor ratings are confirmed in purchasing, engineering, and quality assurance records.

The above sequence applies equally well to a complete five- or six-person team or a two-person work party.

Scope of Survey. The scope of the survey normally includes:

(1) Personnel: Review of the key personnel who will be involved in any transaction.

(2) Engineering: Review of design methods and product integrity control.

(3) Production: Materials and inventory control, machine set-up and loading, control of scrap, surplus, or obsolete materials.

(4) Finance: Account systems, financial ratings, etc.

(5) Labor: Degree of unionization, strike history, etc.

(6) Quality Control: Manufacturing inspection and control procedures, instrument calibration procedures, engineering change control.

(7) Marketing: Business profile—military, aerospace involvement.

Evaluation. Survey results are tabulated, and the observations form the subject matter for a vendee conference to explore all possible good and bad points of (usually) three potential suppliers. A decision is then made as to which supplier will be the most economical and logical choice (perhaps with upgrading) to meet contract requirements.

Exhibit II shows a representative comparison summation of three vendors, on the basis of which the final choice can be made.

The foregoing account highlights the significant difference between the numerical schemes and present practices. Vendee companies are now prepared to change process cycles to meet vendor capabilities, and are also prepared to assist vendors to restructure their production and quality assurance system to meet vendee needs.

Most vendee teams regard the survey and its subsequent follow-up as an educational process, and are encouraged by their management to cooperate with the vendor in improving his quality assurance program until it is acceptable as conforming to recognized standards. Various incentives are built into most programs which reduce inspection costs for both parties and foster mutual understanding of product problems.

VENDOR-VENDEE TECHNICAL COMMITTEE, American Society for Quality Control, Milwaukee, Wisconsin

Information References

American Society for Quality Control, *Technical Conference Transactions* (Vendor-Vendee), 1979–1980.

ASQC Technical Committee Report 107, "How to Conduct a Supplier Survey.

ASQC "Procurement Quality Control: A Handbook of Recommended Practices," 2nd ed., 1976.

Cross References: *Purchasing; Reliability Engineering; Value Engineering (Value Analysis).*

EXHIBIT II

REPRESENTATIVE COMPARISON SUMMATION

Vendor 1	Vendor 2	Vendor 3
Design staff professionally trained. Some experience in producing similar components.	Staff technically qualified, but not well organized. No experience in similar components.	First class staff, well trained and organized. New plant. Relevant production experience.
Design staff not current. Little use of computer-assisted design. Adequate control of drawings and specs. Acceptable material evaluation facilities and staff.	Young staff: good potential but needs more work experience in this field. Drawings and specifications control marginal. Excellent materials evaluation lab and staff.	Professional staff well directed and very businesslike. Excellent drawing and spec control. Engineering change formalized and well executed.
Materials control: acceptable, depends on local communication, not documentation; possible problem. Inventory control: manual with stock cribs; cumbersome. Machine set-up and loading very well organized and responsive to engineering. Control of scrap and surplus goods: well organized.	Materials control: excellent, directly responsible to the Materials Lab. Inventory control automated, first class system. Production control well organized with experienced staff directly on the plant floor. Present production looks good. Scrap control effective, excellent feedback to Engineering.	Manufacturing not responsive to Engineering. Incoming inspection and inventory control not emphasized in production cycle, so frequent production held up for material. Machine set-up acceptable but suffering from material supply fluctuation. Scrap well controlled.

VENTURE CAPITAL

Venture Capital is the name given to money invested in business enterprises that do not have access to conventional sources of capital such as the stock market, banks, or near banks (such as leasing companies or commercial factors). These businesses usually fall into three categories:

(1) Start-ups.

(2) Growing young businesses which need additional capital to continue their growth.

(3) Leveraged buy-outs. This is a phenomenon that has been particularly prevalent in recent years, in which a management group is assisted by venture capitalists to acquire a business—usually from a large public company or a private individual.

The key ingredient in all of these situations is an entrepreneurial team. The entrepreneurs generally prepare a detailed business plan that describes the nature of the business and forecasts the future activity and future incomes. This business plan is used to attract venture capital. Venture capital investors are interested in and will only invest in situations that will ultimately produce sizeable capital gains. Because the investments are made in unproven situations, or with large amounts of debt, venture capital investing is risky and very dependent on the ability of the entrepreneurs to turn their ideas into a successful company.

The investment in the enterprise is made by buying stock (generally from the treasury) or by lending it money, or combinations of both. Debt instruments such as direct notes or convertible debentures are often the mode of investment, but "sweeteners" in the form of warrants or stock are invariably part of such arrangements, so that capital gains can be realized when the investor ultimately "unlocks" his investment. Venture capital investments are often described as "lock-ups" because of the long time between investment and realization.

The extent of the possible capital gains is indicated by the outcome of the investment of AR&D—American Research & Development Corporation—in Digital Equipment Corporation, the company that created the minicomputer. AR&D, which is one of the most successful professional venture capital organizations operating in the United States and (until it was merged with Textron) one of the four listed on the New York Stock Exchange, saw its original $70,000 investment in DEC in 1957 reach a peak value of over $500 million by 1968. In a similar way, F. S. Smithers & Co., Inc. invested in IBM back in 1911. The appreciation of its initial investment in IBM substantially exceeds that of AR&D's in DEC, although over a longer time.

Until a few decades ago, the primary sources of venture capital were wealthy families or partnerships of affluent individuals looking for capital gains. For example, the Rockefeller family has funded several venture capital pools. There is one venture-capital group based on the private fortune of a wealthy European family that has been operating for centuries. Currently, the fifth generation has funds in venture-capital pools operating in several countries outside of the parent country where the fortune was founded. This particular venture-capital investment group has the interesting philosophy that it is investing for the benefit of the next generation. To its members, the common problem of venture capital—the long lock-up—obviously presents no problem.

In the past, only a few investment banks and brokerage houses were involved in venture capital. However, the activity of brokerage houses in venture capital has in recent years been stimulated by the enormous interest in new issues. At the beginning of the 1960s, and again during the extraordinary bullish period of 1968–69, new issues of untried companies enjoyed unparalleled market acceptance. Realizing that the capital appreciations prior to going public were often the greatest, many brokerage houses became interested in grooming companies and investing in them before they went public. The venture-capital route of investing in new or very young companies was a logical consequence of this desire to become involved at a much earlier stage of growth. However, this source of venture capital tends to be extremely volatile and follows the same cycles as the new issue over-the-counter market. When this market is "hot," plenty of risk money seems to be available. When the over-the-counter market is in the doldrums, the brokerage world becomes a very poor source of venture capital [1].

Growing Sophistication. Beginning after World War II, a variety of professional institutions were established specifically to invest in venture capital. These new groups changed the original frontier character of the industry to a sophisticated, institutionalized, professionally-managed network of organizations whose fulltime activity is the investigation, analysis, and investment in venture capital situations. This movement began in 1946 when American Research & Development Corporation was founded, with a capital of about $4 million. AR&D was the brain-child of Senator Ralph Flanders when he was still president of the Federal Reserve Bank of Boston. New England was in an economic decline at that time, primarily as a result of the shrinking of the textile industry and the loss of some traditional machine industries directly involved with textiles. Flanders, believing that the region's trouble was not the loss of old industries but the lack of new ones, came to the conclusion that the area's birthrate for new enterprises was too low. He concluded that this low birthrate was due to the lack of capital for new enterprises, in spite of the fact that the region had enormous technical resources in the world-famous educational institutions located in and around Boston. He felt that the large reserves of capital available in Boston, which traditionally were invested in Government bonds and in the securities of blue-chip corporations, had to be tapped, and sums set aside for the support of new enterprises.

One of the landmark policies was the creative and unorthodox decision to establish a policy that AR&D would willingly consider minority positions in its investments. The policy made it possible for AR&D to make investments in a company at a much later stage of the company's growth without the need for capital reorganizations to the disadvantage of the founders and original investors. The policy also opened up the possibility of joint ventures (while not a regular practice of AR&D). This became a common practice of other organizations, particularly the private venture-capital partnerships. Unless they were prepared to take minority positions, two or more venture capital organizations obviously could not jointly invest in one company. AR&D's first investment was in a company called Tracerlab (now part of LFE). It did not make its famous investment in DEC until 1957, nearly twelve years after it was founded.

The U.S. Government entered the picture in 1958 with financial support for organizations giving loans to small businesses through SBIC (Small Business Investment Corporation) operating under the auspices of the SMALL BUSINESS ADMINISTRATION.

Recent Developments. During the late 1960s and early 1970s, there was a rapid growth of venture capital companies, paralleled by a growth in internal venture departments of large corporations. This growth became particularly rapid after the lowering of capital gains tax rates in 1978.

The largest of the venture-capital organizations at this writing is the Chicago-headquartered Heizer Corporation. Launched in December, 1969, with a capitalization of $81 million supplied by 35 institutional backers, it now has approximately $300 million in assets. Running close second is Citicorp's venture capital group with assets of over $200 million.

Formal venture-capital organizations with professional management and significant capital pools are also springing up in Europe [2]. An example is Technical Development Capital Ltd. which has branch offices in many of the major cities of England and regularly advertises its desire to invest in companies with a technological base. In France, there is European Enterprises Development, which is patterned after AR&D. Scienta, which is headquartered in Brussels, is a consortium of several European industrial companies. As with the two previous groups. Scienta is primarily interested in investments in technical companies.

A noteworthy development is the establishment of internal and external venture capital operations by many of the largest corporations in the United States, with a sprinkling of the same activity by some Canadian and U.K. companies. These corporate venture activities take two very distinct and separate forms. One is the independent operation which is strategically (and sometimes geographically) independent of the parent. The second is the venture operation within the framework of the parent corporation, in effect operating as a captive activity. In both instances, the objective is to promote the diversified growth of the parent.

The corporate venture capital activities usually operate relatively independently of their corporate sponsors. Generally, they have their own charter, their own company-supplied pool of investment capital, and their own personnel—a small group of "bright young people" presenting an independent cluster of marketing, technical, and financial skills. The use of a supracorporate team for corporate venturing has the prime virtue of liberating the venture team from the limits of the sponsoring corporation's capabilities. This frees the venture group from having to operate within the constraints of the corporate resources of technology, market research, personnel, plant facilities, and probably most important of all, the self image of the company. A maker of synthetic fibres, for example, generally does not present a good environment to develop an activity in disposable paper garments.

Two other interesting variations of venturing can occur within the corporate framework. First is the intra-corporate team or department. This venture group functions largely as an internal operating unit. This approach is often termed VENTURE MANAGEMENT. The second is the intercorporate team or joint-venture where a company double-teams with another corporation to explore and perhaps enter a new era. The Bunker-Ramo Corporation is an outgrowth of this type of approach.

Limited Partnerships. A quite recent significant development has been a large growth in limited partnerships for venture capital.

Through the centuries, investment groups have been formed to invest in specific ventures. This indeed was how West Indies Tea Company, which had so important an effect on the development of the American Colonies, was started—as was the Hudson's Bay Company, which led to the development of Canada. However, these investment groups were *ad hoc* in nature; that is, they were brought together for the one investment, and there was no continuity in their investment actions.

A later development was the creation of pools of capital for investment in a *series* of risk situations. These venture-capital groups were generally formed as limited partnerships. The limited partners would be wealthy individuals interested in providing capital for venture situations. Management of the pool would rest in the hands of one or two general partners who were responsible for making investment decisions and monitoring the investments. The limited partners would be passive investors.

This method of investment has been refined

and there are several very well known partnerships operating in the United States now. Customarily the general partners form a separate management organization which receives a management fee commonly reckoned as a percentage of the assets. Additionally, as an incentive they receive a portion of the capital gains. In some partnerships the annual management fee is equal to 3½% of the invested assets at the commencement of the partnership. All of the limited partnerships generally have a specific life period, often seven or ten years. At the end of this time, the limited partnership is dissolved and the assets—cash and stock—are distributed to all partners.

Probably the most famous such partnership was the Davis & Rock partnership which was founded in 1962 and was terminated in 1969. The original investment was $3.4 million and at the conclusion of the partnership's life, $76 million was distributed. The most successful investment of the partnership was in Scientific Data Systems, which was its first investment. Davis & Rock saw SDS grow until it was acquired by Xerox for $940 million of Xerox stock.

Small Business Investment Companies (SBICs). These are companies qualified to borrow money with the guarantee of the Small Business Administration (SBA) of the U.S. Government with the mandate to invest their funds in operations defined as small businesses. The fundamental purpose of the Government-supported SBIC program was to create a system that would provide risk capital to smaller companies. Although the investments in their companies was generally in the form of a loan, the risk attached to the loan exposed it to virtually the same jeopardy as equity in the common stock of the company.

The basic concept of the SBIC legislation was that private capital could be induced to invest in small companies with Government backing leading to high leverage. In effect, the Government realized that small companies needed venture capital, which would not be forthcoming without special incentives, Spurred by studies that showed that the equity financing gap for small companies might be as high as $500 million per year, Congress passed the Small Business Investment Act in August 1958, twenty-five years after the initial effort for such legislation. Probably the unique aspect of this remarkable legislation was that it did not propose direct Government subsidization or a Government administered capital bank. Instead, it proposed the creation of a series of completely new sources of capital to be called SBICs. (See also discussion of SBICs under SMALL BUSINESS ADMINISTRATION.)

The newly organized industry suffered through the usual early growing pains encountered by any new type of financial industry. From their inception, the number of active SBICs rose to a peak of 649 in 1964, then sank to 248 in 1973 before rising to 350 at the end of 1980. More significantly, the private capital and total assets of the industry rose to record levels of $625 million and $1.375 billion, respectively. Total financing disbursements also attained a new high of $295 million. Now coming into maturity, SBICs have proven to be of great assistance to smaller businesses in the United States, investing over $3 billion in 43,000 small businesses in the 21 years of their existence. There are also numerous MESBICs (Minority Enterprise SBICs) which specialize in financing minority businesses owned and run by minority groups.

Preparation of a Business Plan. The most important preliminary step in organizing a new venture is the preparation of a business plan. This should describe the market for the proposed product or service, the capabilities of the team constituting the original entrepreneurs, the production, marketing, and financial program of the new company, and finally what type of deal the entrepreneurs are seeking. One of the best guides for the preparation of a business plan for a new business was prepared by Kley [3] shown as Exhibit I.

EXHIBIT I

GUIDE FOR THE PREPARATION OF A BUSINESS PLAN

1. Provide a one-page summary of the venture idea.
2. Describe the key goals and objectives. Specify what you are setting out to achieve, particularly your sales and profitability goals.
3. Provide an in-depth market analysis. If you can support your own probe with some solid numbers from a recognized research institution such as Stanford Research Institute or Arthur D. Little, Inc., so much the better.
4. List the names of close competitor firms, and briefly analyze their strengths and weaknesses.
5. List the anticipated selling, lease, and maintenance price to your ultimate consumer for each product in the projected line. Include also a brief summary of comparison prices.

6. Provide a list of potential customers, particularly indicating those who have expressed an interest in your projected products.
7. Provide a one-page summary of the functional specifications of each product in your overall spectrum. Cover the total line, but don't get down to individual models.
8. Show the physical forms of the products, with photographs of prototypes if possible, or art renderings.
9. Provide a profile of key patents (where and when and what device is being covered).
10. List and categorize the key technologies and skills required to develop and manufacture the products. Indicate which fronts of the art are being pushed hardest.
11. Describe the alternative channels of sales distribution; indicate whether you intend to sell direct, through manufacturers' representatives, or to original-equipment manufacturers.
12. Describe the basis for determining if your products will be typically "lease" or "buy" items. This will depend upon the propensities of your potential customers, who must be sorted out.
13. Describe the type and geographical distribution of your anticipated field service organization.
14. Tell how you can modularize your product line with changeable subassemblies. This is critical from an inventory point of view, and can mean tremendous cost savings.
15. Show cost-volume curves for each module, with breakdown for material, labor, and factory burden.
16. Describe the manufacturing process involved, and illustrate it with block diagram.
17. Describe the types and quantities of capital equipment needed and when.
18. Present a flow-event-logic feedback chart, illustrating achievement milestones and showing stepped levels of when and how additional funds should go into the venture.
19. Project staff and plant space requirements over a five-year period.
20. Describe the rationale for choosing any single manufacturing plant location.
21. Present cash flow projections, monthly for the first twelve months, and then quarterly for the next three years.
22. Provide pro-forma balance sheets for five years.
23. Provide pro-forma P&Ls for five years.
24. Present your position on the degree of ownership control you and the other founders seek, and the limits to which these can be varied with time and profitability.

EMANUEL BATLER, President, Glentech Instruments, Ltd., Toronto, Ontario, Canada

To raise expansion capital for an existing business, or purchase capital for a leveraged buyout, the information can be simpler, but should definitely include:

(1) A one- or two-page summary.

(2) Background of the key people involved in the venture.

(3) History of the company.

(4) Description of the product or products.

(5) Description of the market and the competitors.

(6) Historical financial information.

(7) Pro forma P&L and Balance Sheet information for three to five years.

(8) Amount of financing needed, and how it will be used.

ARTHUR D. LITTLE, Chairman of the Board, Narragansett Capital Corporation, Providence, Rhode Island

Information References

Associations and Journals:

National Venture Capital Association.
Venture, The Magazine for Entrepreneurs.

Texts:

Little, Royal, "How I'm Deconglomerating the Conglomerates," *Fortune,* July 16, 1979.

"The Evolution of an Industry: Venture Capital Redefined for the 1980s," *Venture Capital,* January 1980.

SBIC Digest, February 1980.

References Cited

[1] Mandell, Melvin, "When Venture Capital Dries Up," *Innovation,* No. 19, 1971.

[2] Pratt, Stanley, ed., "Guide to Venture Capital Sources," 5th ed., Wellesley, Mass., Capital Publishing Co., 1981.

[3] "Guide for the Preparation of a Business Plan," Ann Arbor, Mich., Robert Kley Associates, 1971.

Cross Reference: *Venture Management.*

VENTURE MANAGEMENT

Venture Management is a corporate strategy for building new businesses. It places primary emphasis on the use of internal resources as the means to grow, rather than on mergers and acquisitions. While it is currently being used only by a small number of large U.S. industrial companies, its applications may increase in the future as the natural advantages of venture management become more important to the success of large organizations.

Venture management is different from venture capital investments in that the initiating company usually has 100% ownership of the venture and supplies significant management and technical assistance. It is also different from new-product development because it is concerned with the building new businesses rather than the extension or modification of existing product lines.

Being venturesome is not new to American business. What is relatively new is that this venturesomeness is being channeled and directed by these organizations in formal organization structures. (A 1970 survey of venture management functions in 36 corporations revealed that twenty-six of these had organized their functions within the prior two years.) Venture departments are established, usually at the corporate level, as separate organizational units. The central concept of venture management is that responsibility for initiating new business is separated from responsibility for operating existing businesses.

Reasons for Venture Management. Common reasons cited for venture management are:

1. *To help reach long-term growth objectives.* If growth projections from existing operations do not meet company growth objectives, a planning gap exists. Companies turn to venture management to help fill this gap.

2. *As a major alternative to acquisitions.* The diversification movement continues strong in American industry. In past years the major vehicle for diversification has been mergers or acquisitions. However, a number of changes in the accounting, tax, financial, and anti-trust aspects of acquisitions have made this route more expensive and less certain. (See MERGERS AND ACQUISITIONS.)

3. *To aid diversification in new areas.* Some companies use venture management to enter attractive new business areas where there may not be any good acquisition candidates, or, if there are, they may be too expensive. A related objective is helping the large company respond to segmented, small, or temporary markets that may be highly profitable but not worth the disruption of its existing operations.

4. *To improve the effectiveness of a company's research and development expenditures.* It is well known that a number of companies are disenchanted with the output of their laboratories in relation to the funds being expended. Several companies are using venture management to increase this output by commercializing new research discoveries that do not quite fit into existing markets and hence might not be fully exploited.

5. *To overcome organizational constraints to entering new business areas.* Most large organizations are set up on a divisionalized, decentralized basis. This model is effective for managing existing operations, but it does not facilitate the development of new business areas. That is why responsibility for new ventures is most often lodged at the corporate level under the chief executive officer, even though successful new ventures may be transferred to divisional responsibility at a later point. Overall, venture management represents a split in the organization. One part runs today's businesses; the other builds new businesses for the divisions of the future. This can cause resentment and conflict between divisional executives (who are responsible for producing current income) and the venture function, which is viewed as a risky and expensive proposition, at least in the early years.

6. *To provide entrepreneurial opportunity to employees within the large-firm setting.* Many talented younger managers are somewhat disenchanted with large organizations and would prefer to work in smaller organizations where their efforts are more visible and have more impact and where they have more independence. One of the reasons cited for venture management is to overcome this advantage of small companies in the attraction and retention of talented employees.

There are situations where venture management may not be appropriate. These include companies whose long term growth objectives can be fully met by expansion of existing divisions, who do not have adequate capital or management resources to invest in new business, and whose management climate is not conducive to the innovativeness required to succeed in venture management.

How Venture Functions Can Be Organized. There are three different ways of organizing for venture management: (1) Task force or project management approach, (2) venture management division or department, and (3) venture management company.

The *task force approach* is the most informal of all the methods employed. There is no staff assigned full-time to investigate and develop new ventures. One person in the organization, perhaps the head of corporate planning, is responsible for establishing and managing task-force investigations into new venture areas. Employees assigned to task forces usually have other responsibilities in the organization and are only on loan to the venture function. The task force leader should be an individual highly interested and knowledgeable in the product concept of the potential venture. The members of his team should be carefully chosen for the skills they bring to the project. Some may work on the project full time; others on an as-needed basis. Members of the task force could change as the skill needs of the project change. Under the task-force approach, projects are handled as they come along rather than on a planned basis. A fixed budget for task-force investigations may not exist.

The *venture management division or department* is a more formal structure. There are usually more individuals involved on a full-time basis than in the task-force concept. There also tends to be an established budget and criteria for evaluating new ventures. The department itself might be composed of a number of venture analysts. Their job is to investigate new venture ideas generated internally or brought to the corporation's attention. As ideas are translated into new ventures, the venture managers would also be assigned to the department, usually until the venture reaches or passes its commercialization stage. As such, a venture management department tends to have both line and staff attributes: staff in that it investigates new business opportunities for corporate decisions, and line in that it manages new ventures until they are ready to take their place in the existing organization structure.

The *venture management company* is the most formally structured of the three approaches. It is a separate legal entity, wholly owned by the parent organization. Its major responsibility is to investigate, build, and manage new business ventures for the parent.

Each of the three types of venture organizations can be effective for a particular company. The chosen structure needs to reflect a particular company's objectives, current situation, and commitments to new ventures. Those organizations using the task-force approach to venture management tend to be process-manufacturing oriented, functionally organized and fairly centralized in their decision-making processes, interested in new business ventures that are closely allied to their existing businesses and which tend to be offshoots of their R&D efforts, and only interested in exploring a small number of potentially large ventures, after which the function could be disbanded.

Organizations using the venture management department or company approach tend to be highly decentralized, already engaged in a wide variety of new business areas, interested in exploring a still broader spectrum of new businesses, many of which could be fairly limited in potential size, concerned with the need to maintain a separate environment conducive to new ventures, and fairly certain that the need for venture management will be long.

How the Venture Process Works. Building a new venture can be visualized as a six-step process: (1) idea search, (2) idea screening, (3) idea investigation, (4) venture development, (5) venture commercialization, and (6) venture disposition.

The venture process begins with the *idea search.* One individual in the organization may be designated as the person to whom all new business ideas are sent. He gathers new ideas from a variety of sources, both internal and external.

The second step is *idea screening.* Broad criteria are used to avoid rejecting a venture which does not look promising at first but which may, in the long run, have great potential. A sample of the criteria used at this stage is: (1) compatibility with existing technology and resource strength; (2) market needs; (3) uniqueness of product and patentability; and (4) economic considerations (investment required, sales and earnings potential). New venture ideas that pass screening may be ranked in terms of priority and placed in a "pool" from which they are drawn for further analysis and investigation as time and funds permit.

The *idea investigation* stage involves the gathering and analyzing of information necessary to determine whether the organization should enter a particular business area. Many companies have developed specific criteria (strategic, financial, marketing, and technological) against which all new ventures are measured. The existence of such criteria helps guide the venture staff in their collection and evaluation of potential ventures. Some examples of criteria employed at this stage are: "compatibility with long-range plan;" "capital intensive;" "20% return on investment;" "fifth-year sales volume: $50 million;" "fifth-year profit contribution: $5 million;" "market growth rate: 20% annually;" "minimum share of market: 30%;" "proprietary product."

In most companies, the return-on-investment (ROI) criterion for new ventures is higher than returns from existing operations. This compensates for the risk involved in a new venture.

Some companies have developed quite elaborate computer models to help in evaluating potential ventures. In some cases, the ROI requirement may vary in proportion to the risk involved. (See RETURN ON CAPITAL.)

The end result of the investigation stage is a report to senior management recommending that the idea should proceed into development as a venture, or be dropped, shelved, sold, or licensed. A venture development plan, evaluating the potential venture in terms of all the pre-established criteria, may be presented. The decision for entering a new business area is usually made by the chief executive officer, by a committee of senior executives, or by the board of directors if major funding or a reorientation of business activity is required. The decision at this stage is not a final one—it merely authorizes development of the venture.

In *venture development,* a venture team is formed with a venture manager in charge. The team may be the group that originally investigated the idea. Likewise, the venture manager may be the person who headed the investigation. It is important that the venture manager be carefully selected for his skills, experience, and interest in the venture.

All necessary steps are now taken to build the venture: product refinement and testing, prototypes, consumer and market research, pilot plant, test marketing, pricing, advertising campaign, production, distribution, and sales facilities. The development process is guided by the venture plan, which is modified as additional factors become known. The process of venture development is reported to the chief executive periodically. Funding may be on a short-term basis, with additional funding dependent on progress. The development stage may take a long time and be quite expensive, especially if a new area of technology is involved.

In the fifth step, *venture commercialization,* the success of the venture should be apparent rather quickly. The business is usually run by the same venture team that brought the venture through the development phase, and it continues to report to the head of the venture function.

The final step in the venture process is *disposition of the venture.* Successful ventures may either join an existing division, become a new, independent division, join a special division composed of other successful ventures, or be sold to another company or to the public. New ventures that fail may either be dropped or sold, the technology could be licensed, or the company could seek a partner for a joint venture in a further effort to gain success.

The venture process is far easier to explain than to carry out. In most cases the time and funds required are great, and the outcome is risky because by definition the company is entering an area with which it is somewhat unfamiliar. If a company does not recognize and accept this in advance, it should steer clear of the concept.

The Venture Manager. The venture manager performs the classic entrepreneurial function of combining ideas, resources, and people to form new enterprises, but he does so within the large-company setting. However, the typical individual described in the literature as a classical entrepreneur probably will not be an effective venture manager: he would be stifled by the somewhat restrictive atmosphere of the large firm. What is needed is a person who has both the skill and drive necessary to build a business on his own, and the ability to put up with the requirements placed on him by the parent company.

The process by which companies select their venture managers is not scientific, nor is it ever likely to be. There are no systematic testing and selection mechanisms for venture managers. Such mechanisms would undoubtedly be helpful even though the criteria for selecting venture managers are likely to vary from company to company in response to different organizational structures, operating environments, and objectives.

Deciding how to pay venture managers is a problem for any company. The key question is, Should the compensation arrangements for the venture manager differ from the arrangements for other managers in the company? Some companies say "no," citing the disruption it would cause in the management ranks. They also feel the recognition and speed of advancement that can come from building a successful new venture are sufficient motivation. Other companies say "yes," special compensation is appropriate and supportable by the economics of the situation, but have not instituted such programs, again for fear of disrupting the other managers. Others say special compensation arrangements are vital to the success of the venture process and have instituted them.

Requirements for Success in Venture Management. Companies that are successful in venture management seem to exhibit the following attributes:

1. *Top management support.* Such support on a continuing basis is essential because of the long time and high risk involved in building new businesses.

2. *Clear relation to planning.* Tie-in between corporate planning and venture selection helps insure that the venture function fulfills corporate ends.

3. *Clear organizational lines.* Clear definition of responsibilities and authority helps overcome the conflicts likely to be generated by an active venture function.

4. *Strong management control.* Such control helps insure objectivity and minimize losses.

5. *Proper climate.* A free environment (within mandated controls) conducive to new ventures is essential. The separate department and company venture approaches help create and maintain this environment.

6. *Capable people.* The head of the venture function and the venture managers are keys to the success of the venture function.

7. *Good estimates.* While ventures always seem to take longer and cost more than originally estimated, every attempt should be made to secure estimates that are as close to the work as possible.

8. *Adequate funding.* Sufficient capital over the venture development period helps insure continuity of the venture. Several companies have run into problems here and have had to curtail otherwise successful ventures. A few companies have established separate capitalizations for their ventures. These funds can be committed at the discretion of the head of the venture function within specified limits.

The success requirements for new ventures are not unique to venture management—they are required in operating any business. However, costs of mistakes in venture management are large. But then so is the payoff from successful new ventures.

Conclusion. Unless a company has a highly innovative environment and a flexible structure, a separate organization for new ventures would seem to be called for. This permits the major portion of the organization to concentrate on managing and improving today's businesses, while in another part of the company, a separate unit is evaluating and building new businesses that may be the operations of tomorrow. The two functions are joined together and coordinated at the top through corporate planning, other staff functions, and top executive control.

Venture management activity to date has been concentrated in large industrial companies. Other types of organizations as well could benefit from applying the concept. These include banks, railroads, insurance companies, utilities, foundations, schools, medical institutions, and government units. In fact, any type of organization that wants or needs to undertake new activities—activities that are not direct extensions of current operations—might find venture management applicable as a means of accomplishing this objective.

FREDERIC W. COOK, Frederic W. Cook & Co., Inc., New York, New York.

Cross Reference: *Venture Management.*

W

WAGE PAYMENT PLANS. See Salary and Wage Administration, entries given there.

WAITING-LINE THEORY (QUEUEING THEORY)

Waiting Lines or **Queues** are commonly encountered in everyday life; for example, shoppers waiting for service at a grocery store checkstand. In the case of the grocery store, customers will tend to go to another store if they are required to wait too long for service, thus costing the store profits because of lost sales. On the other hand, too many clerks will result in idle time with a resulting loss due to an excessive payroll. The store manager would like to have the number of clerks on duty that will minimize the losses due to lost sales and clerks' idle time.

Waiting-line theory can be used as an aid to management decision making in solving many similar types of problems. Applications have occurred for the most part since the end of the second World War. Other examples of waiting lines are airplanes waiting in a stack to land, factory workers waiting for service at a tool crib, automobile drivers waiting to pay at a toll gate, and the flow of stock in and out of a warehouse.

Formal Definition. Waiting-line theory is the theory of efficiently servicing arrivals at a service facility. Waiting-line problems arise when there is either too much demand on a service facility with a resulting excessive waiting time for service, or there is too little demand, in which case there is too much idle facility time. The objective of waiting-line analysis is generally to balance the costs associated with waiting time and idle time.

The primary characteristics of a waiting-line facility are *arrivals, servicing,* and *queue discipline.*

Arrivals. Units arrive at a service facility from some statistical population according to a frequency distribution which describes the number of arrivals during a particular interval of time. The time between arrivals is also important, and this may be constant, predetermined (as at a doctor's office), or of random length. In the random case, the most commonly used assumption is that the number of arrivals is described by the so-called "Poisson Distribution." The Poisson distribution often occurs in applications when a large number (n) of identical "experiments" occur and the probability (p) of success on each experiment is small (np less than 5). In practice it is necessary to know only the product $M = np$, where M is the average number of successes observed. (See STATISTICS.)

In mathematical terms, the probability of exactly x arrivals during a time period of t is given by the Poisson Distribution as

$$P(x) = \frac{(\lambda t)^x}{x!}e^{-\lambda t}, \qquad x = 0, 1, 2, \ldots$$

where λ is the average arrival rate per unit time, and e is the familiar Naperian, or natural, logarithm base. In this notation $M = \lambda t$.

The distribution of the time between arrivals in this case follows a negative exponential distribution:

$$f(t) = \lambda e^{-\lambda t}, \quad t \geq 0$$

The graphic representation of these expressions is shown in Exhibits I and II.

These processes have the important property that the probability of an event is the same for all intervals of length t, regardless of where the interval is situated. Incoming telephone calls, failures of many types of equipment due to random causes (not wearout), and other arrival situations have been found by experience to be described very well by the Poisson process. Other distributions are also used where applicable.

Servicing. Servicing is characterized by such things as the number of service channels and the distribution of the service time of each channel. Service time can be constant (as often occurs at a toll gate) or be of random length. The negative exponential distribution fits many service time distributions, and in other cases a service time can be represented by the Erlangian distribution, a sequence of independent operations, each operation time having a negative exponential distribution. Service lines may

EXHIBIT I

THE POISSON DISTRIBUTION

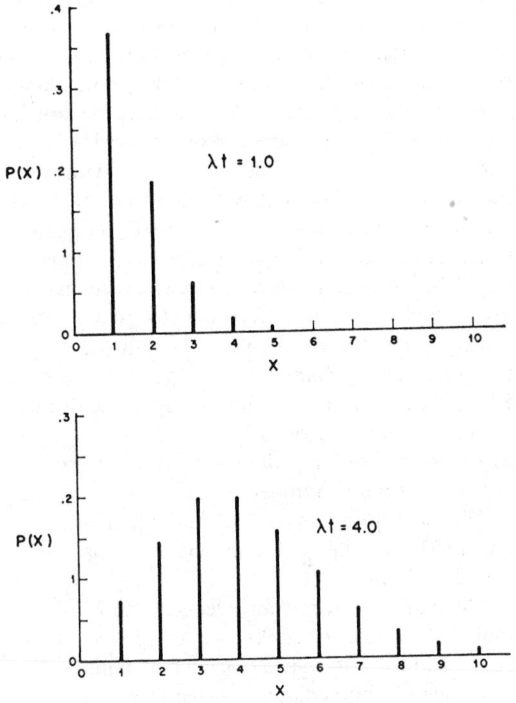

also be characterized by other probability distributions.

Queue Discipline. Queue discipline is characterized by such things as the number of waiting lines, the maximum possible queue length, and the method of selecting a specific waiting item for service. Maximum queue lengths will vary from problem to problem, varying from zero to those having no restriction on length. Items can be selected for service on a first come-first served basis, on a random basis, according to priority, and so forth.

History. E. K. Erlang, a Danish telephone engineer, first began research on the theory of waiting lines in 1905 in connection with the design of automatic telephone exchanges. T. C. Fry, an American, also developed much of the theory independently of Erlang. In his book [1] published in 1928, Fry recognized that waiting line problems arise in many phases of industrial activity. However, applications of the theory were limited almost entirely to telephone problems until the advent of OPERATIONS RESEARCH in the 1940s. E. C. Molina, G. F. O'Dell, and others also made important contributions.

The early research assumed Poisson inputs from unlimited resources, and either constant or exponential service times. Since that time, theory has been extended to include many other assumptions concerning arrivals, service, and queue discipline. Important contributions to the theory and applications have been made by a group of people much too large to give credit to here. Included in this group must be P. M. Morse [2], W. Feller [3], and T. L. Saaty [4]. More recent publications on the theory are by Gross and Harris [5] and White, Schmidt, and Bennett [6].

Approach and Techniques. A waiting-line system is described at any instant of time by the number waiting for service and the number in service. The various possible descriptions (that is, number waiting and number in service) are referred to as *states of the system.* Associated with each state is the *probability* of being in that state, since in general no regularity exists. The central problem in the mathematical solution of a queueing problem is the solution of the state probabilities, from which are calculated average values of the quantities of interest (such as average queue length, average waiting time and average facility idle time) and cumulative probabilities (such as the probability that a queue exceeds a certain length). Many queueing problems have been solved and the results made available in the published literature on queues. Mathematical solutions become impossible if the waiting-line system is very complicated, and this can occur commonly in real-life situations. In some cases it is valid to make simplifying assumptions, allowing use of known theoretical results. Otherwise solutions are found using Monte Carlo techniques. (See OPERATIONAL GAMING AND MONTE CARLO SIMULATION.)

Starting with the initial conditions of a system, one can observe the states of the system as a function of time. These time-dependent states are referred to as *transient states.* As time increases, the effects of the initial conditions tend to become negligible, and with most systems the same state probabilities exist at one instant of time as at another. The system is then said to be in *equilibrium* or *steady state* with associated *steady state probabilities.* Usually it is sufficient in the analysis of a waiting-line problem to use steady state solutions.

The usual procedures in the solution of a waiting-line problem are as follows: The waiting-line system is described in terms of *arrivals, service,* and *queue discipline.* If possible, and if

Exhibit II

Negative Exponential Distribution

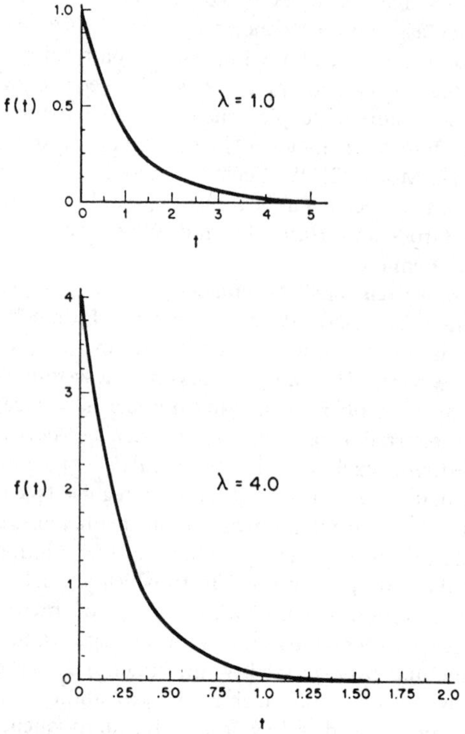

not already known, samples of arrival times and service times are obtained and analyzed to determine the respective distributions. When not possible, distributions may have to be assumed on the basis of known characteristics of comparable systems. A measure of facility effectiveness is selected, which will vary from problem to problem. For example, in a factory tool crib problem one may wish to balance the cost of mechanics waiting for service against the cost of idle time of the tool crib clerks. For highway toll booths one may want the probability that the waiting line of cars does not exceed a certain length. A system of simultaneous equations is set up based on the system characteristics, and these are solved if possible to yield the state probabilities. The characteristics of interest that are required for the measure of effectiveness are then calculated from these probabilities.

The following illustrates the typical approaches and techniques. (The reader is referred to the classic and still useful articles cited under *Information References* at the conclusion of this entry and to [5], chapter 9, [7], chapters 9 through 15, and [8], chapter 4, for detailed discussions of actual case studies.)

An Example. The mechanics at a production department of the Ace Aerospace Company go to a tool crib to obtain special tools as required for their work. The department manager has observed that at many times during the day one or more mechanics are waiting at the tool crib for service. There is a single clerk on duty, who, when no mechanics require service, has various other jobs to do associated with the tool crib; thus the total work load at the tool crib is sufficient to keep one clerk busy full time. However, the manager reasons that it might be more economical to have two or more extra clerks on duty in order to reduce the waiting time for mechanics since the average pay rate for mechanics is \$40 per day versus \$25 per day for clerks. The manager decides to obtain the services of an operations analyst to assist him in studying the problem of determining the optimum number of clerks.

The operations analyst formulates a waiting line model of the tool crib operation as illustrated in Exhibit III.

Mechanics arrive at an average rate λ at the tool crib where *k* clerks are employed. If a clerk is free (not waiting on a mechanic), service begins immediately, otherwise the mechanic must wait. Service is on a "first-come, first-served" basis. The measure of effectiveness of the facility is the average cost per day resulting from the idle time of clerks and mechanics.

Average cost per day = (average queue length) · (cost per day per mechanic) + (average fraction of time clerks are idle) · (number of clerks) · (cost per day per clerk). (1)

The optimum number of clerks is that number which results in the minimum average cost

Exhibit III

Waiting Line Model of the Tool Crib Operation

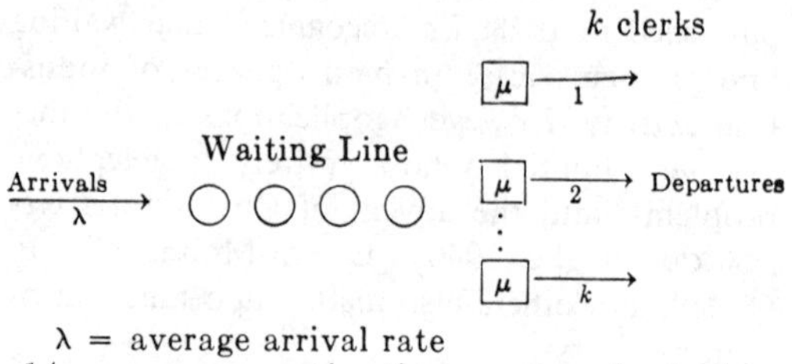

λ = average arrival rate
$1/\mu$ = average service time once service begins

per day. The facility characteristics which must be calculated are the average queue length and the average fraction of time the clerks are idle.

Samples were taken to determine the distributions of arrival and service time. The statistician's Chi-square test was used to show that the Poisson distribution with an average arrival rate (λ) of 20 mechanics per hour is a good fit for the arrival distribution. The Chi-square test was also used to show that negative exponential distribution with an average service time ($1/\mu$) of 2 minutes is a good fit for the service time distribution.

Exhibits IV and V show the probabilities involved. (Statistical justification is given below; let us concentrate on the results here.)

EXHIBIT IV

COMPARISON OF SAMPLE AND POISSON ARRIVALS OF MECHANICS AT A TOOL CRIB

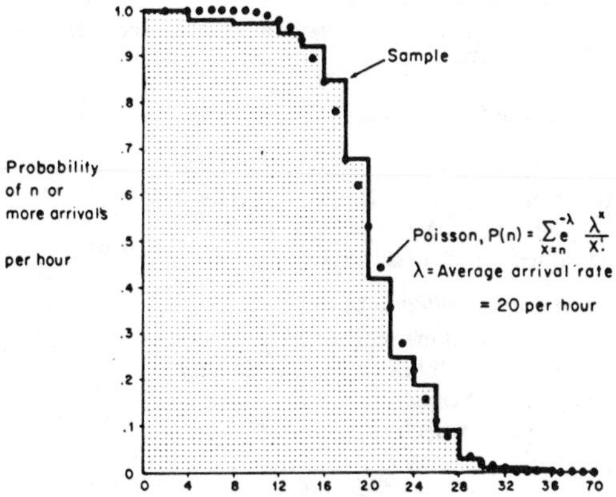

EXHIBIT V

COMPARISON OF SAMPLE AND NEGATIVE EXPONENTIAL SERVICE TIMES AT A TOOL CRIB

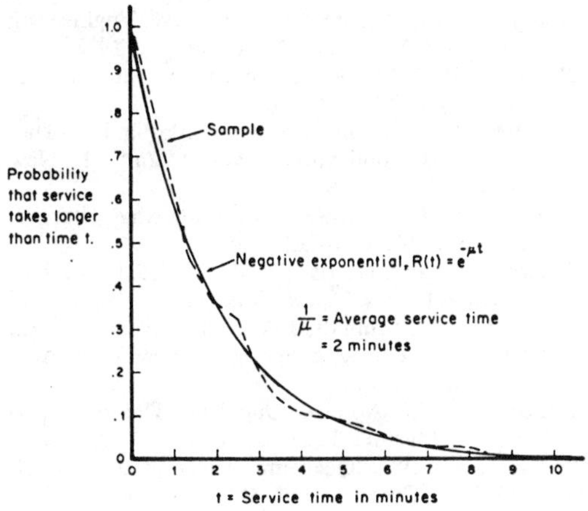

Application of statistical theory results in the numerical calculations of Exhibit VI. P_0, P_1, and P_2 are the probabilities of having for each value of K (total number of clerks) respectively 0, 1, and 2 mechanics at the tool crib. While of interest in their own right, they have been used in this example only to obtain $E(s)$ and $E(m)$ (the latter derivation is not shown). $E(s)$ is the average fraction of time during which the K clerks are not waiting on mechanics; thus, the average number of idle clerks per day is $KE(s)$. It is assumed for purposes of calculating costs that one-third day of clerks' time is utilized for various duties other than waiting on mechanics. $E(m)$ is the average queue length at the crib including queues of zero length. $E(C)$ is the average cost per day for the combined idle time of mechanics and clerks.

Minimum cost is obtained with two clerks, the savings amounting to \$25.00 per day. Note that even though a single clerk can do the job and have sufficient work to be occupied for the entire day, it would still be more economical to have three clerks than one. A manager's decision will of course depend upon other subjective considerations in addition to costs. More general (parametric) forms of analysis will be found in the references.

Mathematical Probabilities. The model illustrated in Exhibit III can now be described as follows:

1. Poisson arrivals.
2. K identical clerks (or servers) with exponential service time.
3. First come-first served queue discipline.

The derivation of the probabilities and averages that describe the system are too extensive for this article (for mode of proof see Reference 4), and only the necessary results are shown. The required results are the average queue length and the probability that there are exactly n mechanics at the tool crib (in queue plus in service). The latter is used to calculate the average fraction of clerks idle.

EXHIBIT VI

RESULTS OF CALCULATIONS

K	P_0	P_1	P_2	$E(s)$	$E(m)$	$E(C)$*
1	0.333	0.222	0.148	0.333	1.333	\$53.34
2	0.500	0.333	0.111	0.667	0.0825	28.34
3	0.512	0.342	0.114	0.778	0.0093	50.33

* Cost calculations exclude $\frac{1}{3}$ day of clerks' idle time that is required for duties other than serving mechanics. $E(C)$ = average cost per day.

Let

K = total number of clerks
m = number of mechanics in queue
n = number of mechanics at the tool crib (waiting plus in service)
$x = \lambda/\mu$ = (mean arrival rate/mean service rate), $(\lambda/\mu < K)$
s = fraction of clerks idle.

Then

P_n = probability of exactly n mechanics in the system at any instant of time

$$= \frac{1}{n!}x^n P_0 \qquad 0 \le n \le K$$

$$= \frac{1}{K!\,K^{n-K}}x^n P_0 \quad n \ge K \tag{2}$$

where

$$P_0 = \left(\sum_{n=0}^{K-1} \frac{x^n}{n!} + \frac{x^K}{K!}\frac{1}{1 - x/K}\right)^{-1} \tag{3}$$

$$E(m) = \text{average number in queue}$$
$$= \frac{\lambda\mu x^K}{(K-1)!\,(K\mu - \lambda)^2} P_0 \tag{4}$$

Results for substitution into Equation 1, the average total cost per day, are calculated for K = 1, 2 and 3. $E(m)$ is calculated directly using Equations 3 and 4. $E(s)$, the average fraction of clerks idle, is calculated by noting that for $K = 1$, if there are zero mechanics in the system, then the clerk is idle, otherwise busy. Thus,

$$E(s) = P_0 \qquad \text{for } K = 1.$$

Similarly

$$E(s) = P_0 + \tfrac{1}{2}P_1 \qquad \text{for } K = 2$$

$$E(s) = P_0 + \tfrac{2}{3}P_1 + \tfrac{1}{3}P_2 \qquad \text{for } K = 3$$

Assumptions in this case study are single units arriving for service, a single waiting line, and one or more service channels. More generally, units may also arrive in groups, such as a box of parts to be inspected, diners at a restaurant, or a tour group arriving at a hotel check-in desk. These are referred to as bulk or batch models. One may also find multiple, parallel waiting lines. The operation of these are usually assumed to be independent for purposes of analysis, but there can be compelling factors which would have to be considered, such as people jumping from line to line, the flow of traffic tending to direct people to particular waiting lines, and so forth.

The single-service channel with exponential service time is the simplest case, and the models rapidly become very complicated mathematically as one considers multiple channels and nonexponential service times. It is also assumed in the case study that the arrival and service distributions are sufficiently well fitted by the Poisson and exponential distributions. (See STATISTICS.) It is also assumed that there is independence between interarrival times and also between arrivals and features of the waiting-line system. It is not possible in this article to discuss solutions to all of these conditions; fortunately, however, the references cited contain excellent discussions of the theory involved and of various types of case histories.

Acceptance and Potentials. The acceptance of waiting line theory is well demonstrated by the many applications of the types described. It has been applied extensively to other major fields; including reliability, maintainability, and inventory control.

H. H. PETERSON, President, OSR, Inc., Honolulu, Hawaii

Information References

Associations:

Operations Research Society of America.
The Institute of Management Sciences.
The American Statistical Association.

Professional Publications:

Journal of the American Statistical Association.
Journal of the Royal Statistical Society.
Management Science.
Operations Research.

Articles:

Brigham, Georges, "On a Congestion Problem in an Aircraft Factory," *Operations Research,* Nov., 1955.
Edie, L. C., "Traffic Delays at Toll Booths," *Operations Research,* May, 1954.

References Cited

[1] Fry, T. C., "Probability and Its Engineering Uses," New York, Van Nostrand Co., 1928.
[2] Morse, P. M., "Queues Inventory and Maintenance," New York, J. Wiley, 1958.
[3] Feller, W., "An Introduction to Probability Theory and Its Applications," vol. 1, 2nd ed., New York, J. Wiley, 1959.
[4] Saaty, T. L., "Elements of Queueing Theory," New York, McGraw-Hill, 1961.
[5] Gross, D. and Harris, C. M., "Fundamentals of Queueing Theory," New York, Wiley, 1974.
[6] White, J. A., Schmidt, J. W., and Bennett, G. K., "Analysis of Queueing Systems," New York, Academic Press, 1975.
[7] Lee, A. M., "Applied Queueing Theory," New York, St. Martin's Press, 1968.
[8] Panico, J. A., "Queueing Theory," Englewood Cliffs, N.J., Prentice-Hall, 1969.

Cross References: *Management Sciences (and cross references there given).*

WAREHOUSING

In the last few years, **Warehousing**—the storage and protection of raw materials and/or finished goods—has come to be regarded as a key element in marketing strategy.

Most industrial firms include both company-owned (private) and public warehouses in their distribution systems. A few companies use all private or all public warehouses, and there are some that use a single public warehouse as a "control" on the cost/service performance of their own system of privately operated warehouses.

The prime purpose of warehousing activity is of course strategic deployment of marketable goods in such a way as to minimize total distribution costs and maximize customer service. Determining the optimum number, location and size of warehouses for any given company is a highly complex matter, however, involving a great deal more than cheap land and a proximity to markets. In fact, some companies have found it practical to do away with regionalized warehousing altogether and switch to premium transportation, air or truck, to render a level of customer service comparable to that offered by an extensive network of warehouses.

One reason in particular why many managements make careful studies of their companies' warehousing patterns goes even beyond the cost of the warehousing operation itself; this is the cost of carrying inventory, both the actual physical handling costs and the costs of invested capital. These inventory costs have been found to run as high as 25% of the value of the finished goods; where goods have a high per-pound value or where there is infrequent customer demand, these costs can eat deeply into potential profits.

Traditionally, warehouses have been located to serve areas conforming with sales territories, often as the direct responsibility of the regional sales managers. This picture has largely changed, as the increasing use of OPERATIONS RESEARCH analysis shows that territories which are good from a sales management point of view are often inefficient and costly from a distribution point of view. Moreover, there is a definite trend to relieve sales management personnel of warehousing responsibilities which may conflict with their primary duties.

Where the distribution center concept has been adopted, warehousing operations tend to be under the central control of a warehousing/transportation/inventory control executive who may be head of a distinct warehousing department (particularly true in companies with several hundred or more warehouses) or at the head of warehousing activities within a distribution department. In many companies, the warehousing function—both private and public—is placed in the traffic department because of the close relationship between the transportation and warehousing functions, with numerous transportation privileges like "storage in transit," "processing in transit," free switching, etc., having a direct bearing on warehousing operation.

The fact that use of warehouses enables companies to take advantage of volume transportation rates for long-haul shipments has long been at the heart of the entire warehousing operation, but current thinking places it on the same level with inventory costs and competitive advantage. In exploration of total costs, for example, companies have found that it is more practical to increase the speed of order processing (through teletype, telephone, and data processing systems) and eliminate various of their warehouses, while continuing to render the same level of customer service. A major company, Westinghouse, took this approach some years ago, and reduced inventory in one item alone from $5 million to $2 million, at the same time closing a number of its field warehouses. If order time could be reduced by twenty-four hours, the company reasoned, customers could be served from warehouses twenty-four hours more distant and the problem of maintaining complete stocks at numerous locations could be more easily solved.

While it is true that sales and marketing management still tend to feel that opening new warehouses is a good competitive tool, and usually resist warehouse closings and relocations, it is rapidly being demonstrated by many companies that competitive advantage and customer service improve with scientific management of warehouses as part of a complete system.

There are numerous points of view as to the relative merits of private warehouses vs. public. While the direct charges for public warehousing space are generally found to be higher than those involved in private warehousing, public warehousing offers a good deal more flexibility and contains no fixed charges. At the same time, private warehousing offers the advantage of special tailoring of equipment and facilities to a company's products, something that is not always possible with public warehouses. On the other hand, a number of public warehousing companies are adopting the "distribution center" concept for their own operations and in addition to using highly sophisticated order-picking and handling equipment, also have data processing systems for order processing, inventory control, and even customer billing on behalf of their clients. In some cases these warehouses perform such finishing operations as unit packaging of bulk materials, labeling, pricing, etc., and furnish display and office space for their clients. (See WAREHOUSING: The Public Warehouse.)

As a management function, responsibility for warehousing operations is rapidly becoming of major importance in total marketing and distribution. Although it is doubtful that many companies will create executive posts for this single operation, it is likely that whoever is responsible for the function will carry considerable weight in all major distribution decisions.

COLIN BARRETT, Transportation Consultant, Reston, Virginia

Cross References: *Materials Management; Materials Management: Material Handling Equipment Types; Physical Distribution; Warehousing: The Public Warehouse.*

WAREHOUSING: The Public Warehouse

Warehousing, in the general sense, is the storage of goods pending consumption or other use. Business has always required this, but as trade and commerce broadened, there developed the opportunity and need for facilities in which someone will take care of property *for others,* temporarily. Thus we have the business of **Public Warehousing.**

It is an old business. Public warehousing transactions took place in the Middle Ages at Venice and Genoa. Wherever there is trade and commerce, there is need for public warehousing, and the service is now provided in every country.

Warehouses in Modern Distribution. In the United States, with its free flow of trade and intense competition, manufacturers and distributors bid for sales in markets throughout the nation. To meed competition, both price-wise and service-wise, alert and efficient distribution is a prime necessity. As to service, no method of shipping can improve on having goods already in the market—the maintenance of "spot stocks" at diversified and strategic locations.

The manufacturer is, therefore, faced with the need of determining whether he will build, buy, or lease a branch warehouse for operation by his own personnel, or whether he will use a public warehouse. For many companies the latter has been found to have numerous pronounced advantages. Perhaps the most important of these is flexibility. But before discussing this factor, six other specific advantages are briefly listed here:

(1) *Space-Cost Economy.* Year-round maintenance costs, heat, light, taxes, etc., that apply to company-owned facilities regardless of degree of utilization are of no concern to the user of public warehouses. Storage charges are made on a per package, per hundredweight, or other unit basis per month.

(2) *Labor Economy.* Trends toward guaranteed pay plans create a serious situation where wide seasonal variations are inherent in either production or sales. The manufacturer must maintain level production, and, as later explained, the public warehouseman helps him accomplish this. Handling charges are "per unit" in a public warehouse, thereby assessing labor costs only as they are actually incurred.

(3) *Transportation Efficiency.* Shipping in carload or truckload quantity to public warehouses and distributing to local and nearby areas from warehouse stocks saves the shipper the difference between LCL and carload rates, an appreciable transportation cost factor.

(4) *Reduced Investment.* Even where only the bare essentials are provided, capital investment in a company-owned warehouse building is substantial. The user of a public warehouse avoids tying up large sums in fixed assets.

(5) *Accurate Cost Prediction.* The warehouseman's tariff or quotation permits accurate prediction and budgeting of distribution cost for each unit of merchandise.

(6) *Sales Efficiency.* Often a salesman located at a branch house finds himself tied down with the administrative detail of running the establishment. The public warehouse provides office space and services for the salesman but frees him from all non-selling detail.

Flexibility. Some companies have small amounts of merchandise to store and distribute; others find that in a given area their need may run to the storage and handling of hundreds of carloads. Usually these needs vary widely throughout the year. Use of public warehouse facilities can exactly match the needs of the moment.

Shifting population, and decentralization of merchandising centers and a industrial facilities create a need for a mobile distribution system. The volume handled through a given distribution point may drop in favor of another. The public warehousing industry, represented in every marketing center of the United States, provides the immediate mobility necessary.

Another need for flexibility is found in changing transportation requirements. Whatever mode of transportation is necessary for a particular shipment, the warehousing industry is located and equipped to adapt itself to its customers' needs.

Finally, efficient warehousing demands a versatility of types of space. Some storage needs are best served in multi-story buildings, others in single-story facilities. Some commodities need controlled conditions of temperature or humidity. The public warehouseman is able to furnish or arrange for the facility most suited to the storage, handling, and distribution of each product.

The Production Function and Warehousing. The public warehouse is of importance to others than those directly concerned with distribution. Advantageous purchases of raw materials and components can be made, and the items can be held, pending use, in a public merchandise warehouse local to the factory; subassemblies and component parts can be delivered to the assembly line by the local warehouseman as needed; and elimination of other than immediate daily storage needs at both ends of the production line can free up additional area for new production facilities.

Blending of Peaks and Valleys. The historical association of production and consumption with periods of peaks and valleys does not fit in with the modern business concept of optimum use of productive facilities. In steps taken to alleviate this situation, the necessity of providing customer service at minimum cost cannot be overlooked. It is here that public warehousing blends the fluctuating requirements of many manufacturers into a reasonably constant volume, allowing maximum utilization of facilities.

Distribution. Two basic conditions inherent in public warehousing make for efficiency in distribution:

(1) The ability to pool the distribution needs of many companies makes it possible to eliminate pronounced peaks and valleys.

(2) The large-scale storage and handling operation permits the economic utilization of specialized facilities and personnel.

A graphic, though simplified, exposition of the dovetailing process used is shown in Exhibit I. Each company's varied requirements for storage space are combined in the public warehouse. Company A, for example, would need 25,000 square feet of storage space for March and October peaks, and during June would use less than 5,000 square feet. Operation of its own storage and distribution facilities would require building, equipment, and personnel geared to the maximum requirement. Comparable variations exist in the distribution needs of the other companies. In June, Company B needs 37,500 square feet; in December, Company C uses 40,500 square feet; and in March, Company D requires 50,000 square feet. The public warehouseman meets all of these needs with a physical plant of 100,000 square feet, yet individually operated storage and distribution facilities would require a total of 153,000 square feet to meet separate company peak requirements.

Public warehousing services are available to small and large users. From a pick-up truckload to a trainload, the warehouseman handles the requirements of each of his customers, and it is the combination of small and large needs that enables him to operate at a high degree of efficiency. Similarly, comparable savings accrue in labor and equipment costs.

Lest there be any misunderstanding of the term "blending," it is emphasized that the public warehouseman keeps the goods of each customer separate, provides the individual care required by each commodity, and maintains exact stock records on every item in his custody. His responsibility under the law is to exercise, with regard to goods in his custody, the same care "as a reasonably careful owner of similar goods would exercise."

Additional Services. In conjunction with the services of storage and handling, the public warehouseman performs numerous "branch house" and "branch office" functions for his customers. These include such services as supplying office and display space; special clerical and telephone service; traffic information rates

EXHIBIT I

BLENDING THE PEAKS AND VALLEYS IN PUBLIC WAREHOUSING

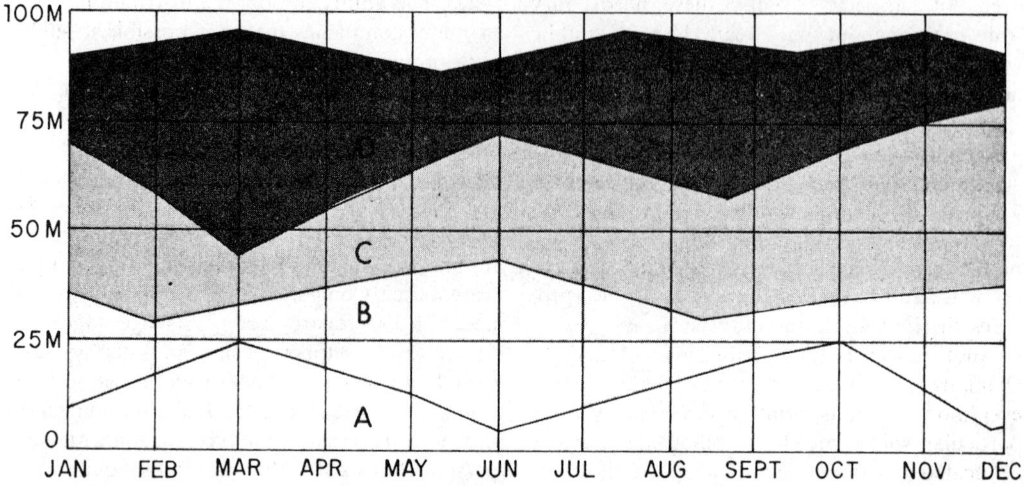

on all transportation, and handling and distribution of pool cars and consolidated shipments; break-bulk operations, including packaging and assembly; physical inventories; C.O.D. collections; maintenance of and delivery to accredited customer lists; prepaying of freight bills; and loans on stored commodities.

Warehouse Receipts as Collateral. When inventories are made up of marketable commodities and cash is needed to finance increased purchases or production, *warehouse receipts* issued by responsible warehousemen provide acceptable collateral for loans to reliable principals. Under the UNIFORM COMMERCIAL CODE, this type of financing is a well established business procedure.

Bonded Warehouses. In the terminology relating to the warehousing industry, the words "bonded warehouse" probably are least understood by the general public, and by many businessmen. Despite continuing educational efforts by bankers and warehousemen, the erroneous belief persists that only warehouse receipts issued by a "bonded" warehouse are acceptable as collateral, or that a bonded warehouse, *per se,* affords some special security not afforded by an unbonded warehouse.

There are two types of United States bonded warehouses: *Customs Bonded* and *Internal Revenue Bonded* houses, neither of which affords any bonded protection to the depositor of the goods. The bond in each of these instances is to the Federal Government to protect it against nonpayment of duties or taxes.

In twenty-two states, warehousemen may be "bonded" or licensed under state regulation. In some, the bonding or licensing requirement is little more than a revenue producing measure, while in others the existence of the bonding statute and the posting of a bond by the warehouseman may mean that some degree of inspection is undertaken by state authorities.

A third classification of bonded warehouses are those for agricultural products, licensed under the United States Warehouse Act. This is a category that is of little concern to the business community and is therefore not discussed here.

It may be said that in the selection of a public warehouse, the individual integrity of the operator and his established reputation as a capable warehouseman are the important considerations to the customers or to the holder of a warehouse receipt.

JERRY LEATHAM, President, American Warehousemen's Association, Chicago, Illinois

Information References

American Warehousemen's Association (see Appendix B) provides a "Director of Public Merchandise Warehousemen," a brochure, "The New World of Public Warehousemen," and other publications. The Association's Physical Distribution Research Center is a non-profit subsidiary conducting research and educational programs, and its library is open to all with a legitimate interest in warehousing and physical distribution.

National Association of Refrigerated Warehouses provides a "Directory of Public Refrigerated Warehouses," detailing services and facilities of members.

(See also references under MATERIALS MANAGEMENT.)

Cross References: *Materials Management; Materials Management: Material Handling Equipment Types; Physical Distribution: Warehousing.*

WOMEN IN BUSINESS AND INDUSTRY

Women's contribution to the economic life of the nation has undergone many changes in this century. In earlier times, women produced at home a large part of the goods, such as food, clothes, and household furnishings for their families' needs. As the industrial revolution proceeded and migration from farms to urban areas took place, women's contribution to the nation's economy shifted from employment in the home to employment in industry—mostly into factories and low-paying jobs. In more recent decades, rising expectations of what constitutes a good life and the desire for a higher standard of living—the need to contribute to family income, fewer children and smaller families, and new job opportunities in expanding retailing and service industries—brought more women into the labor market. In the words of Eli Ginzberg, former director of the National Commission on Manpower Policy, "The rapid entry of women into the labor market is the single most outstanding phenomenon of the century [1].

During the past decade, more compelling social and economic forces have accelerated this trend. Most important has been the changing role and status of women. Women are setting their educational and career goals, planning their life cycles for careers and family: seeking to achieve equality with men in job opportunities, advancement, and earnings [2], [11].

I. WOMEN IN THE LABOR FORCE

Labor Force Growth. At the turn of the century, only 5 million women were in the labor force, and fewer than 14 million in 1940 before World War II. By 1967, women in the labor force doubled to 28.4 million and their participation rate reached 41.1% [3]. Unprecedented numbers of women, over a million a year, entered (or reentered) the labor force during the 1970s—more than in any other decade. The gain of 1.9 million women during 1978 set a record. During 1979, an average of 43.4 million women were in the work force. Most of the record gain in the women's labor force participation in the 1970s occurred among women under 35 years of age. They provided new workers for the burgeoning white-collar and service jobs.

Women in the labor force topped the 44 million mark in January 1980. Their participation rate—the proportion of women sixteen years old and over in the labor force—reached 51.6% [3]. The Bureau of Labor Statistics estimates that by 1990, about 52 million women will be working—or 55% of all women sixteen years and over [4].

Thus, from the beginning of the twentieth century to the end of the decade of the 1980s, the number of women in the U.S. labor force will have multiplied eleven times, from 5 million to 55 million.

Employment. In January, 1980, women comprised over 42% of all employed workers 16 years old and over, totaling 41.3 million. This compared with 36% and 26.9 million in 1967 [3].

Unemployment. Women have a higher incidence of unemployment than men. In every year from 1967 through 1979, women's unemployment rate exceeded that of men, generally by nearly two points [3]. During 1979, both women and men averaged 3 million unemployed workers. Women's rate of unemployment averaged 6.8%, compared to 5.1% for men. In January 1980, men's unemployment rose to 5.7% while women's was 6.8% [3].

For those unemployed in January 1980 who had lost their jobs, the duration of women's unemployment was similar in length to men's. However, women who were reentrants or new entrants had a considerably shorter period of unemployment than men reentering or new to the labor market [5].

Occupations. Women are moving into some of the occupations traditionally held by men. While the total number of women employed increased 25% between 1972 and 1978, the growth of women in three major occupation groups was significantly greater. The increase was 67% for managers and administrators, 81% as craftworkers, and 84% as laborers. Female accountants, engineering and science technicians, bank officers, and financial managers have increased beyond the general increase in employed women [6].

In January 1980, of the 40.9 million employed women shown by occupation in the Bureau of the Census monthly survey, 26.8 million, or 65.6% were in white-collar occupations. Included were 14.4 million clerical workers, or 35% of all employed women. Next, were the professional and technical occupations in which 6.9 million women, or 17% were employed, mostly as teachers and health workers. Over 2.8 million women were employed as sales workers, or 6.9%. Nearly as many, 2.7 million, or 6.7% were employed as managers and administrators [7].

Service occupations employed 7.9 million women or 19%. A substantial number, 2.9 million of these women, were employed in food services. Women in blue-collar occupations totaled 5.8 million or 14% of the total. Most of these women were employed as operatives (in manufacturing industries) [7]. Most teen-age women, totaling 3.5 million, were employed as clerical workers, 1.3 million; service workers, 1.2 million, sales works, 427,000; and operatives, 228,000 [7].

Industry Distribution. As of January, 1980, over 81% of employed women, or some 31 million, were in service industries, and only less than 19% in goods-producing industries. Of the former group, 10.2 million were in health services, including education, personal services, and business and repair services (SIC classifications). Retail trade employed 7.5 million, and the same number were in government. Over 3 million were in finance, insurance, and real estate. Manufacturing employed 6.5 million, of whom over a million were in apparel manufacturing [7].

Women-Owned Businesses. Female-owned businesses are increasing but still are fairly rare. Data from the U.S. Department of Commerce Survey taken in 1977 showed that there were 702,000 businesses owned by women, an increase of 30% from the 1972 Survey. Receipts of women-owned businesses totaled $41.5 billion in 1977, up 72% from 1972. Still, women-owned businesses represented only 7% of all business firms in the nation, excluding large corporations, and 6.6% of all receipts. Women are likely to be first-time entrepreneurs. Almost half of the businesswomen worked in their own homes, and only about one-third had part-time or full-time employees [8]. Most of women-owned businesses are in retail trade or the services [6].

Women on Corporate Boards. Women are now found as directors on corporate boards. The women's movement, affirmative action legislation, Government pressure on corporations to increase the number of outside directors, the fact that 12 million women entered the labor force in the last decade, and the growing number of women in management and executive ranks have created a climate receptive to the woman director. Of the 1,300 major companies listed by *Fortune* in 1980, nearly a third, or 427 companies, have at least one woman serving on their boards. Each of the top ten industrial corporations had a woman director. Of the top 100, 48 had a woman director [9]. With fewer than 500 women on corporate boards compared to 15,000 men, it will be some time before women can have an important role in shaping U.S. corporate policy.

Women do not sit on corporate boards to represent women: they are there to represent the interest of the stockholders, and should be selected on the same basis as male members—on their professional and business credentials—and not as tokenism. Women directors have to be well informed. As corporate boards assume greater involvement in company policy making and management (see DIRECTORS and DIRECTORS: Legal Duties and Responsibilities), women members will have an expanded role in bringing women's and consumer issues to the attention of boards, and thus have an increasing impact on U.S. corporate policies.

Marital and Family Characteristics of Women Workers. The rising number of multi-earner families was one of the most important socioeconomic developments of the 1970s. In March 1979, three out of every five married-couples families reported having at least two members who were earners during the previous year. Since 1970, the number of such families has increased by more than 3 million, reaching 28.4 million in 1979 [10]. Wives in the work force have increased by one-third since March 1970, rising from 18.4 million to nearly 24 million by March 1979. More than half of this gain was among wives 25–34 years old [2].

Working wives made substantial contributions to their families' economic welfare. Wives who worked 50–52 weeks full-time contributed an average of 40% to family income. In 1978, all working wives contributed about 26% to family income. Working wives had lower unemployment rates than single or divorced women [2], [10].

Over 6 million women in the labor force had children under six years of age. Over 3 million had children under three years old. Nearly 10.6 million women in the labor force had children between six and seventeen years old [10].

Public concern about special problems of women who are the main source of support for their families and themselves is increasing. Women headed one-fourth of all households in 1978. Of the 8.2 million women who are heads

II. LAWS GOVERNING WOMEN'S EMPLOYMENT STATUS

Discrimination and Equal Opportunity. Three Federal laws have been enacted which protect women from discrimination.

The Equal Pay Act of 1963, an amendment to the *Fair Labor Standards Act,* went into effect in June 1964. The law is administered by the Equal Employment Opportunity Commission (EEOC). (See EMPLOYMENT: Anti-Discrimination Legislation.)

Employers are prohibited from paying women and men different wages when they do jobs that are the same or similar in skill, effort, and responsibility, and that are performed under similar working conditions. The act covers employers and unions in industries engaged in interstate commerce [12].

Title VII of the Civil Rights Act of 1964 (420 SC) 2000(e)) as amended in 1972, resulted in the creation of the Equal Employment Opportunity Commission (EEOC). The legislation bans discrimination on the basis of race, color, religion, sex, or national origin in hiring, referral, classification, membership in labor organizations, admission to apprenticeship, and other terms and conditions of employment. Also prohibited are advertisements that indicate discriminatory preferences.

The legislation covers public as well as private employers of fifteen or more workers, employment agencies, labor organizations, and joint-labor-management apprenticeship committees [12]. Discrimination on the basis of pregnancy was prohibited by section 701k effective April 30, 1979 [13].

The Age Discrimination in Employment Act of 1967, effective in June 1968, is administered also by EEOC. This law prohibits discrimination against people between the ages of 40 and 65 years in hiring, referral, classification, compensation, and other terms and conditions of employment (and related advertising) on the part of employers with twenty or more workers, employment agencies, and labor organizations [12], [13].

The Executive Order 11246, issued in 1965, as amended by Executive Order 11375 in 1968, covers employers with Federal contracts or subcontracts of more than $10,000. This law not only bans discrimination against applicants on the basis of race, color, religion, sex, or national origin, but it also requires that employers, "take affirmative action" to ensure the provision of equal opportunity. Further, employers must state in all advertising that they are affirmative-action and equal-opportunity employers [13].

According to Revised Order 4, employers with over $50,000 in Federal contracts and 50 or more workers must file affirmative-action plans with goals and timetables with the Office of Federal Contract Compliance (OFCCP) [12].

The EEOC in its report "Guidelines on Discrimination because of Sex," issued in March 1972, set forth general principles to assist employers in complying with Title VII of the Civil Rights Act. Employers could not refuse to hire a woman because they believed women in general have a higher job turnover rate than men do. Nor could they refuse to hire a woman because of the assumption that women as a group are less capable at certain tasks than men are. Nor could employers cite the preferences of coworkers or customers in excluding women (or men) from consideration for employment [12].

These Guidelines provide clarification as to illegality of separate seniority systems by sex, discrimination against married women, sex-separated advertising, discriminatory practices by employment agencies, preemployment inquiries by sex, provision of unequal fringe benefits, providing discriminatory benefits for temporary disabilities such as those related to pregnancy and childbirth [12], [13].

The Guidelines also provide the useful information that *Title VII supersedes state laws that treat women workers differently from men* [12].

The Federal laws require not only that employers stop any illegal discriminatory practices, but also that they take positive action. For example, that they make a special effort to include women and minorities among those who are reached by their job advertisements. To be in compliance with the law, employers must make a good-faith effort to seek out, hire, and promote women and minority groups on the same basis that majority members are sought, hired, and promoted. "Equal pay for work of comparable worth" has became the policy of EEOC. Affirmative Action practice is to move away from quotas and establish goals instead [12], [13].

Employers should respond completely and carefully to required forms used to determine their degree of compliance with affirmative-action goals. Failure to do so can bring loss of Government contracts, close surveillance, and citations for failure to comply [12].

Labor Standards. The *Fair Labor Standards*

Act enacted in 1938 and amended many times since, often called the Wage-Hour Law, has had and will continue to have an important impact on women's employment terms. It is a complex piece of legislation, containing provisions on miminum wage, overtime pay, child-labor restrictions, sex discrimination, age discrimination, executive, administrative and professional and outside salesmen's exemptions, and enforcement [14]. The FLSA attempts to eliminate labor conditions that are detrimental to health, efficiency, and well-being of workers and to eliminate any unfair competition based on these conditions [15]. The law applies to over a million industrial and business establishments, and about 75% to 80% of all U.S. workers.

The law provides overtime pay of at least one and a half times the regular rate for all hours worked in excess of 40 hours each week by employees—male and female—of employers covered under the Act [14], [15].

The minimum wage effective January 1, 1980 was $3.10, and was scheduled to be $3.35 an hour effective January 1, 1981 for both women and men. In general, the minimum age for employment is sixteen years. However, eighteen years is the minimum age for occupations defined as hazardous. Children fourteen to fifteen may be employed outside of school hours in a limited number of jobs (such as office and sales positions).

Occupational Safety and Health. The *Occupational Safety and Health Act* of 1970 sets specific standards for the maintenance of safe and healthful working conditions which must be observed by employers. Covered under the Acts, are employers engaged in businesses affecting interstate commerce, which covers almost all workers in the United States.

This Act preempted from the states jurisdiction of responsbility for safety and health in most of the nation's work places for issues covered by the thousands of standards promulgated under the provisions of the Act. Standards appeared in the January 1976 *Federal Register* which also carried announcements of new standards or revisions. Information on these Standards (safety and health requirements) may be obtained from the National or Regional Offices for the Occupational Safety and Health Administration known as OSHA [16]. (See OCCUPATIONAL SAFETY AND HEALTH ACT OF 1970.)

What do the OSHA provisions have to do with women workers? They may save their lives and health (and those of men as well), and help create and maintain a more healthful work environment. No longer are accidental injuries and plant disasters the overriding concerns in work place safety. Today, it is invisible contaminants—anesthetics in the hospital operating room; asbestos dust, vinyl chloride, the compound of the plastics industry; pesticides, benzene widely used; beta-naphthylamine used in rubber factories; and numerous other chemical substances—that are the major hazards of the work place [17].

State Laws. States enacted various protective laws for women beginning in the 1890s to help mitigate the miserable working conditions of long hours, low wages, and unsafe working environment. At the peak in 1967, laws or regulations on hours of employment for women were in effect in 46 States. These included standards on weekly and daily hours, limitation in night work, and rest and meal periods [18], [19]. In 1970, 40 jurisdictions had minimum wage provisions of which seven applied to women (or minors) only, and seven others had some provisions applying to women [20].

Other protective legislation governed industrial homework, regulations on employment before and after childbirth, prohibiting of employment of women in some occupations (for example coal mining), establishing requirements for seating, and imposing restrictions on weight-lifting [18], [19].

The more than 60-year tradition of protective laws for women was challenged by the Civil Rights Act of 1964, Title VII, The Equal Rights Amendment which became effective in July 1965. Since 1965, the pressing question was how states could reconcile their protective laws for women with Title VII. After several changes in policy, the EEOC issued "Guidelines" in August 1969 and March 1972, that clearly stated that Title VII superseded state laws that treat women workers differently from men.

A Task Force on Labor Standards, created in the Federal government to study the issues, recommended that states with minimum wage provisions, hours of work limitations, meal and rest-period requirements, weight-lifting limits, and other provisions for women, extend the same regulations to men. Many states have repealed, or amended, such protective legislation to apply to both women and men [18] [20]. Any state laws which remain applicable only to women are probably unenforceable. However, the U.S. Supreme Court may have to determine whether the abolition of female protective legislation, as the EEOC contends, is final.

Unless there are statutes enacted on a Federal or state level to limit hours of work per day and per week and make overtime work for both men and women voluntary, many women will be disadvantaged by the removal of protection from long daily and weekly hours. Women not covered by the Federal Fair Labor Standards Act minimum wage provisions will lose the right to be paid at least a minimum amount under state laws which are repealed or become unenforceable [18].

Some states have passed Fair Employment and Equal Pay laws which are more specific on the "no discrimination" principle than the Federal laws, and are establishing legal precedents as to what constitutes compliance with their provisions in relation to women's issues. State labor legislation on minimum wages and hours of work have largely been preempted by the Federal Fair Labor Standards Act (Wage and Hour Law).

State occupational safety laws have generally been replaced by OSHA standards which in most states are enforced by the Federal Occupational Safety and Health Administration. Only 22 states have state plans in effect to enforce these Federal standards as of June 1980 [21].

The states administer Workers Injury Compensation Laws that have various provisions of importance to both men and women workers injured on the job, as to their rights for compensation for work-related injuries and illnesses. Unemployment insurance laws, which provide weekly benefits to qualified workers who become unemployed, and which provide for the collection of taxes from employers to provide those benefits, are administered by the states. (See WORKERS' COMPENSATION.)

State Labor Departments have to be contacted to determine the status of labor standards and women's rights acts and the interpretations which are currently in effect, as well as the provisions of other state labor laws, because legislation and court decisions are in a state of flux.

III. SPECIAL PROBLEMS CONCERNING WOMEN WORKERS

Equal Pay. The concept of equal pay for work of comparable value is foremost among issues for women workers. Work comparability is not to be confused with the totally separate concept of equal pay for equal work. Jobs are rated on a point system based on skill, responsibility, education and experience requirement, etc., and evaluated for pay scales commensurate with the rated level of the job. Work comparability attempts to compare the value of large classifications of workers [22]. (See JOB EVALUATION.)

The Gap in Women's Earnings. Women's median earnings were only 58.9% of men's earnings in 1977, having declined from the 63.9% in 1955, according to a comprehensive study of year-round full-time workers, from data of the U.S. Department of Commerce studied by the U.S. Bureau of Labor Statistics. Women's median earnings were $8,618 compared to $14,626 for men during 1977 in this study. Men's earnings exceeded women's by 69.7% [15].

Occupational comparisons showed women health workers (except physicians and dentists) earned 90.5% of men's earnings—the highest ratio of the 33 occupations in this study. The lowest ratio was of women farm workers, 25.5% of men's earnings; next lowest was for self-employed women 34.3%; then sales workers at 42.3% of men's wages.

For other studies on the differences between women's and men's earnings, the reader is referred to references [23], [24], and [25].

Opening Job Opportunities to Women in Non-traditional Jobs. Women are making slow but steady gains in managerial and professional jobs. Women held only 23% of manager jobs, and were 43% of professional workers in 1977 [18]. (See WOMEN IN MANAGEMENT.)

Women have made few gains in the skilled crafts. By 1975, women held only 2% of the jobs in male-intensive industries where most of the craft jobs are located [26]. Women are beginning to enter apprenticeship programs. Women were apprenticed in 1977 in about 200 of the 450 occupations recognized as apprenticeable by the U.S. Department of Labor. In 53 trades, in which 95% of all apprentices are employed, there were 4,819 women, or 2% of the total of 244,591 apprentices registered in June 1977 [27]. (See APPRENTICESHIP PROGRAMS.)

In the next decade, women will enter all types of jobs in increasing numbers, and will follow career ladders to promotion to supervisors and to management and executive jobs, and into technical and professional occupations, on relatively equal terms with men [25].

Maternity, Pregnancy, Child Birth, and Child Care. Some of the more important issues for women are related to pregnancy and childbirth, such as coverage under medical and health insurance provided to workers, company policy on leaves of absence, and reinstatement after childbirth, a woman's right to draw unemployment benefits if she loses her job during pregnancy and is able and actively seeking work. These issues will be resolved in the framework of no discrimination. Under the "Guidelines" issued by EEOC, a job applicant or employee may not be discriminated against because of pregnancy [25], [28].

Disabilities caused or contributed by pregnancy, miscarriage, abortion, or childbirth and recovery should be considered *temporary disabilities* and treated as such under any health or temporary disability insurance or sick-leave plans of the employer. Accrual of seniority, reinstatement, and payment under a sick leave plan or temporary disability insurance should be applied to disability due to pregnancy or childbirth [29].

A variety of maternity leave provisions exist in the United States, but availability of maternity leave is growing very slowly. An important issue in many private firms and public-sector institutions is the possible loss of job security or consideration for promotion because of short absence for maternity leave [25], [29].

Child Care. The question as to who should bear the cost of providing day care for children remains unanswered. Most child-care arrangements are in the child's family home, and care is provided by relatives. Institutional care of children is obviously much more expensive than at-home care. Although licensed day-care facilities more than doubled in capacity between 1960 and 1973, the space available could only accommodate one out of every six preschool children of mothers in the work force [25].

Providing good care for children at day-care centers will be a major challenge for public policy during the 1980s. By 1990 there will be an estimated 10.5 million children under six years who will need day-care facilities because their mothers are working [4]. The financial burden of child care is reduced somewhat by the reduction in income taxes for "employment related expenses" of up to $400 a month for household services for dependents under fifteen years [28].

Alternative Work Schedules. Flexi-time and alternative work schedules or job sharing are ways working mothers can adapt their schedules to meet the need for being with their young children outside of school hours and hold jobs. Flexible hours are gaining acceptance with employers. Private employers with flexible hours include insurance companies, banks, electronic firms, airlines, manufacturers, utilities, retailers, and publishers [30]. (See ALTERNATIVE WORK SCHEDULES.)

Job sharing is where two women share one job, perhaps working on alternate days, or weeks, or three or four days (or nights) each week. The four-day week would help some working women. Managers and supervisors should give consideration as to how the work schedule variations needed by many working women can be met.

Sexual Harassment at Work. Recent studies have revealed that sexual harassment is a much more serious problem than previously thought [31]. Sexual harassment takes place as unsolicited staring at, commenting upon, or touching a woman's body; repeated non-reciprocated propositions for dates, sexual favors or demand for sexual intercourse, or rape. A woman has a right to be free from demands for a trade-off of sex for employment or promotion. Surveys have indicated that 70% of women experience sexual harassment at one time or another [32].

Some court decisions suggest that sexual harassment is illegal. Other decisions are specific in considering that such sexual behavior is beyond the purview of the current law. One judge went to great pains to make it clear that Title VII cannot be interpreted to include grievances involving sexual harassment [33]. Complaints regarding sexual harassment can be filed with both state and Federal agencies (EEOC) [28].

The EEOC has taken the position that sexual harassment constitutes sex discrimination under Title VII and that it guarantees female employees a work environment free of (discriminatory) intimidation. The Department of Labor has revised equal-employment opportunity regulations to require Federal contractors "ensure and maintain a working environment free of sexual harassment, intimidation, and coercion at all sites" [28].

IV. OTHER ASPECTS OF WOMEN AND WORK

Women and Union Membership. Some 6.7 million women were members of labor unions and employee associations in 1978, with 5.1 million of these belonging to unions. About 15% of the women in the labor force were union or association members, as compared to nearly 30% of men. Women members made up about 27% of all organized workers. Unions gained 455,000 women members between 1976 and 1978; and associations lost 231,000 women members [34].

Through the years many women have been active leaders in labor unions, and have spearheaded crusades to secure better working conditions. However, many women-employing industries are not union-organized. In none of the nine industries in which women constitute 40% of the total employment was the share of workers organized as high as 75%. In five of these nine industries, union membership was less than 25% of the workers [22].

The Coalition of Labor Union Women (CLUW) was founded in 1974 to promote women's issues, and to aid in organizing women workers [35]. In January 1980 the CLUW joined the Industrial Union Department in co-sponsoring a conference on organizing women, and their activities included establishing permanent organizing committees in each of 22 CLUW chapters. In its booklet, "Effective Contract Language for Women," the CLUW says the contract of the 1980s should be one that spells out the rights of female workers to help women break out of the poorly paid "women's jobs," secure comparable pay for work of equal value, and go beyond provisions of the law in pregnancy coverage. The CLUW has developed a manual to help union women move into leadership roles [22].

Lane Kirkland, president of the AFL-CIO, has announced that he wants more women to have policy-making jobs in unions.

The more aggressive union policy to organize more women and take greater interest in pursuing their interests may stimulate more unionization among women in the 1980s. Women will need the assistance of labor to obtain ratification of the Equal Rights Amendment, and so there may be more interest on the part of women in joining unions. Contract negotiations will then include more women-related issues such as opening all jobs to women equally, with equal pay.

Women and Absenteeism. Wage and salary workers had an incidence of *absence* from work of 6.6% in May 1978. This was the percent of all workers who had an absence during a typical week. The absentee incidence was 5.4% for men and 8.6% for women. Thus, the absence rate for women was 60% higher than for men. Wage and salary workers who normally worked full-time lost an average of 3.5% of their usual hours in May 1978. The proportion of time lost by married men was 3.1%, and the time lost by married women was 4.3%, or 39% greater [36].

The question is asked, are women's absenteeism rates really worse than men's? Despite the higher rates of absenteeism shown for women, factors other than sex have to be considered in comparing time lost by men and women. Women are more likely to be new hires and employed in lower-skilled, lower-paid occupations—two factors associated with higher rates of absence. Sex difference in absence rates narrow when comparisons are made within a particular occupation group, even though men occupy the better paying jobs [37], [38].

The attendance records of women compare more closely with those of men when compared to similar job levels and similar situations. The skill level of the worker, the age of the worker (younger workers have poorer attendance), the worker's length of service with the employer, and the worker's job stability, give better clues to understanding absenteeism than whether the worker is a man or a woman [39].

Counseling and discipline methods generally used to reduce absenteeism may not reduce the absence of women as their family responsibilities may have to take precedence over their job responsibilities [40], [41].

Job Safety, Work Injuries, and Illnesses. Job safety for women workers (as well as for men) is a major concern in many industries and occupations. Providing a "safe work place" is an important legal responsibility of management mandated by the Federal Occupational Safety and Health Act of 1970.

The potential for staggering financial liability for long-time effects of industry-produced illnesses, especially from various chemical compounds and substances in use in many industries today—hazards which have only recently been recognized—require higher management priority and new approaches to job safety. A much higher level of technical and scientific skill will be needed to evaluate and control the hazards in the work environments of the 1980s.

A new problem in women's health and safety is protective discrimination. Fearing damage to the unborn child, employers may deny certain jobs to women, thus closing off an employment opportunity without adequate knowledge of the substances posing a potential risk. Federal equal-employment officials estimate that at least 100,000 jobs involving contacts with potential teratogens (any substance that may interfere with the development of a fetus after conception) are now closed to women, either because of corporate policies or through channeling women away from these positions [22]. Exclusionary procedures circumvent the new Pregnancy Discrimination Act, which went into effect April 29, 1979, as an amendment to Title VII. This Act requires employers to give pregnant employees the same benefits they give all other workers with temporary disabilities and other benefits [17], [22].

The exclusion of women from a certain job can be a violation of both OSHA and Title VII. The OSHA section protects employees' reproductive health by requiring that health standards be set so "no employee will suffer material impairment of health or functional capacity."

Banning women from jobs known to be hazardous to their reproduction systems is no answer to the need to provide a safe work place. In many cases where lead, for example, has been found to be dangerous to both men and women, men have stayed on the job [17], [22]. EEOC resolved in 1978 that "exclusionary employment actions taken hastily or without regard for vigorous adherence to acceptable scientific processes may be viewed as unlawful discrimination."

Every establishment should have a well-developed health and safety program, including education and training of employees to know and recognize hazardous conditions and substances, and knowledge of OSHA standards and other safety precautions. Supervising staffs should include responsibility for assuring that the work environment is safe and free of hazards, and that employees obey safety rules and know how to perform their regular work and any special assignments safely.

Inexperienced workers, or those new to the job, contribute greatly to the number of accidents that occur at the worksite. Thus, increases in injury rates during periods of rising unemployment are attributable largely to newly hired workers. Women, as stated earlier, are frequently new employees and inexperienced.

A comprehensive safety program should be in effect in every establishment. Included should be instruction in safety practices. Employees should be taught how to lift without straining their backs, by using their leg muscles. Women may be less familiar with industrial tools and machinery than men, and may need special instruction on how to use them. For a complete outline of a safety program, see the National Safety Council's "Action Prevention Manual of Industrial Operations." (See also SAFETY AND HEALTH IN THE WORK PLACE.)

* * *

A review of "women in industry," and women's concerns, has revealed how women's contribution to the nation's production has increased in the past decade—how their status has improved under the principle of equal rights and equal treatment, even though many avenues of discrimination still exist—and what issues are of current importance to working women. Many of the concerns of women workers in the 1980s are the age-old problems of better working conditions, but with a new perspective.

ESTHER E. ESPENSHADE, Manager, Employment Security Research, Illinois Bureau of Employment Security, Chicago, Illinois

References Cited

[1] *Working Women,* March 1980.

[2] Norwood, J.L. and Waldman, E., "Women in the Labor Force: Some New Data Series," U.S. Dept. of Labor, Bureau of Labor Statistics, *Report 575* 1979.

[3] U.S. Dept. of Labor, "Employment and Earnings," February 1980, Tables A-1 and A-2 (Household Data).

[4] "Women in the Labor Force—A Revolution in the Making," *Viewpoint,* Spring 1980, AFL-CIO, Washington, D.C.

[5] *Op. cit.* [3], Table A-13.

[6] U.S. Dept. of Commerce, Bureau of the Census, "A Statistical Portrait of Women in the United States, 1978," Chap. 8, "Occupation, Industry, and Women-Owned Businesses."

[7] *Op. cit.* [3] Table A-21 (Household Data).

[8] U.S. Dept. of Commerce, "1977 Survey of Women-Owned Businesses," Release, June 1980.

[9] Curran, Ann, "The New Look of Corporate Boards: Women Directors," *Working Women,* February 1980.

[10] Johnson, Beverly L., "Marital and Family Characteristic, of the Labor Force, March 1979," *Monthly Labor Review,* April 1980; also "Labor Force Patterns of Single Women," August 1979, and "Working Mothers in the 1970s," October 1979.

[11] U.S. Dept. of Labor, Women's Bureau, "Facts About Women Heads of Families," December 1979.

[12] Farley, Jennie, "Affirmative Action and the Woman Worker," New York, American Management Associations, 1979.

[13] Rozmarin, George C., "Employment Discrimination Laws and Their Applications," *Barrister,* Spring 1980, American Bar Association.

[14] Patten, Thomas H. Jr., "Pay: Employee Com-

pensation and Incentive Plans," New York, Free Press, 1977.
[15] "Earnings Gap Between Women and Men," U.S. Dept. of Labor, Women's Bureau, 1979; also "Fair Labor Standards Act: Changes of Four Decades," *Monthly Labor Review,* July 1979.
[16] "Accident Prevention Manual for Industrial Operations," 7th ed., 1974, also 8th ed., 1980, Chicago, National Safety Council.
[17] "Is Your Job Dangerous to Your Health?" *U.S. News and World Report,* February 5, 1979.
[18] Jewell, Donald O., ed. "Women and Management: an Expanding Role, Chap. 3, Munts, Raymond and Rice, David C., "Women Workers: Protection or Equality," Atlanta, Ga., Georgia State University College of Business Administration, 1977.
[19] U.S. Dept. of Labor, "Summary of State Labor Laws for Women," March 1969.
[20] U.S. Dept. of Labor, Bureau of Labor Standards, "State Minimum Wage Laws," February 1979.
[21] Occupational Safety and Health Administration, "Status of State Plans, July 1980."
[22] Jacobson, Carolyn, "New Challenges for Women Workers," *AFL-CIO Federationist,* April 1980.
[23] Henle, Peter and Ryscavage, Paul, "Distribution of Earnings Among Men and Women," *Monthly Labor Review,* April 1980; and Brown, Gary D., "Discrimination and Pay Disparities Between White Men and Women," *Monthly Labor Review,* March 1978.
[24] "Annual Average Statistics," *Monthly Labor Review,* August 1979.
[25] "Changing Economic Role of Women," 1975 Manpower Report of the President.
[26] Conference Board Study of 265 Major U.S. Companies.
[27] "A Woman's Guide to Apprenticeship," U.S. Dept. of Labor, Women's Bureau, 1978.
[28] "A Working Woman's Guide to Her Job Rights," U.S. Dept. of Labor, Women's Bureau, Leaflet 55, December, 1978; also, "Maternity Standards," 1976.
[29] U.S. Dept. of Labor, Women's Bureau, "Maternity Standards," 1976.
[30] Commission on the Status of Women, State of Illinois, Report to the Governor and General Assembly, February 1979.
[31] Kovis, Sally, "Sexual Shakedown: Author Claims Women Are Suffering Physical Harassment," *Los Angeles Herald Tribune,* January 27, 1980.
[32] Hamilton, Mildred, "Working Women and Sexual Harassment," *San Francisco Examiner,* January 8, 1979.
[33] Farley, Lin, "Sexual Shakedown: The Sexual Harassment of Women on the Job," New York, McGraw-Hill, 1978.
[34] U.S. Bureau of Labor Statistics, "Labor Union and Employee Association Membership, 1978," Release September 3, 1979.
[35] Hubbell, Sue, "State of the Unions for Women," *Working Women,* June 1980; also, "Women and Unions," *Working Women,* April 1980.
[36] U.S. Bureau of Labor Statistics, "Absences from Work Remain Steady," Release March 12, 1979; also "Absent Workers and Lost Work Hours," *Monthly Labor Review,* August 1979.
[37] "Absenteeism—Missing Employees Mean 100 Million Man-Hours Lost," *The Better-Work Supervisor,* January 5, 1976.
[38] U.S. Dept. of Labor, Bureau of Labor Statistics, "Absence from Work—Measuring Hours Lost 1973–1976," Special Labor Force Report 207.
[39] Lewis, Edwin C., "Developing Women's Potential," Ames, Ia. Iowa State University Press, 1968.
[40] U.S. Dept. of Labor, Manpower Administration, "Suggestions for Control of Turnover and Absenteeism," 1972.
[41] George, Claude S., "Supervision in Action: The Art of Managing Others, Reston, Va., Reston, 2nd ed., 1979.

Cross Reference: *Women in Management.*

WOMEN IN MANAGEMENT

Women in Management comprised more than 2.9 million of the 11 million managers and administrators in the United States in July 1980. Thus, one in every four managers and administrators were women [1].

This represented substantial progress for women. Twenty years earlier, in 1960, there were only 1.1 million women managers and administrators—an increase of 1.8 million or 164% over the two decades [1], [2]. This contrasted with an increase of 2.3 million or 38% for male managers and administrators [1].

The proportionate gain of women as managers and administrators was even more marked during the decade of the 1970s. Nearly 1.6 million more women were managers or administrators in 1980 than in 1970—a gain of 120%. During the 1970s, 1.3 million male managers and administrators were added—up only 18% [1], [2].

These figures showing the rapid increase in the number of women as managers and administrators reflect the impact of the Equal Employment Opportunity Commission's Guidelines issued in 1972 to enforce Title VII of the Civil Rights Act of 1964, and the affirmative action plans which required employers to open job opportunities at all job levels to minorities.

Still, in 1980 women managers and administrators were only 7% of all employed women, while male managers and administrators were 14% of all employed men [1]. Although women comprised 42% of the work force in 1980, only 26% of the managers and administrators were women [1]. For women to obtain their proportionate representation in management many positions will have to be opened to them in the 1980s.

What Are the Managerial and Administrative Occupations? Occupations described as managerial and administrative are those classified in the "Dictionary of Occupational Titles" in Code 16, "Occupations in Administrative Specializations." These include: descriptions of 144 specific occupations classified within such categories as accountants and auditors, budget and management system analysts, purchasing, sales, and advertising management occupations, public relations, personnel administration, inspectors and investigators, public service managerial occupations, and administrative specializations [3].

Also, included are 346 specific occupations of "Managers and Officials" in Code 18 classified within three-digit industries [3]. These positions are managerial occupations which require the management and operation of an organization, rather than a scientific, technical, or administrative specialty. Generally speaking, these are the "line management" occupations in contrast to the "staff" and specialist occupations included in Code 16.

Code 18 includes such occupations as officers and executives of corporations, nonprofit organizations and government. These are the positions sometimes thought of in a narrower concept as "managers and executives."

General managers, general foremen, department heads and their assistants in industrial and business establishments are also occupations in Code 18 [3].

The nearly 500 descriptions of these management and administrative occupations reveal the diversity of the task elements, and the knowledge, education and training, and professional competence needed to perform adequately the duties of these occupations. Care must be taken to classify and think of occupations according to duties and requirements rather than an incumbent's education and experience [3].

Women's Path into Management Jobs. "The managerial and executive field is an ideal one for women today, . . . the doors are opening," says Carmen R. Maymi, Director of the Women's Bureau of the U.S. Department of Labor, who strongly urges young women to look beyond the routine clerical jobs and the familar professions of education, social work, nursing, and library science to these new job opportunities [4]. Women entering the field now will be the managers of tomorrow. In the past few years, far greater numbers of women have been majoring in business administration and engineering and earning graduate degrees. Many more women are working as accountants, bankers, securities dealers, marketing managers, purchasing directors, and in supervisory positions in corporations and nonprofit organizations which can lead to promotions into management positions.

Although many women (and men) have become managers as the result of on-the-job training in the past, modern management has become a highly specialized skill involving many scientific and technical disciplines. Modern management is not something one can dabble in or pick up casually.

Certain traits are associated with those who are more likely to become managers. Stashower [4] points out that the successful manager (see also EXECUTIVE TRAITS) is:

- Career minded, future oriented, with ambitions and goals.
- Likes to take on responsibilities and leadership roles.

Thinks logically and finds satisfaction in solving problems.

- Is energetic, hard-working, and a self-starter.
- Enjoys competing, and the feeling of accomplishment that comes from performing well.
- Is a good organizer who can plan and oversee a project from start to finish.
- Works well in a group situation, and gets along well with other people.

Education. The following points are emphasized by Stashower:

The educational foundation should begin in high school—a college preparatory course with adequate preparation in English, social studies, science, and math (the last-named being essential). Many high schools and junior colleges offer courses in economics, business law, bookkeeping, and computer science.

Part-time jobs and work-study programs and career internships are ways to catch a glimpse of different areas of management, even if it is from the mailroom, or a kitchen of a restaurant. Selling in a local retail store, typing in a business office, or clerking in a bank can offer useful on-the-scene experience.

For doors to open to women in the management field, at least a bachelor's program in business administration in an accredited college is seen as a necessity. Most state universities have a School of Business Administration that offers both a bachelor and an MBA program; and many private colleges have such programs. The required core curriculums include: economics, statistics, computer science and data processing, business organization, management procedures and theory, personnel management, public communications, law, marketing, and finance. Most schools require students to take the Graduate Management Admissions Test (GMAT). For women, the Master's degree can be a sign of career commitment that helps employers view a woman more seriously as a future executive.

In 1969–1970, women nationally comprised less than 5% of the registrations in the MBA programs. By the 1976–1977 academic year, many schools reported that women made up 25% to 30% of their enrollments. Current projections are that by 1985, the nation's graduate schools of business expect to award 60,000 such degrees, with women making up at least 20% of the total.

Stashower emphasizes that women need a superior education to be able to compete with men for management positions. Therefore adding a specialty, such as management systems and strategies, budgeting and financing, public relations and communications, for example, will open up better job offers.

The Way up the Ladder. Skill in interpersonal relationships is important for women managers (as indeed it is for all managers). This requires thinking through situations, assessing needs and wants of subordinates, and developing a style of supervising to motivate them to move ahead in their own careers. A subordinate's skills are highly important to a woman manager who wants to move ahead, and she must be surrounded by people who can contribute to her job achievement [5].

Women need experience in decision making. Since many of their professional activities are in supportive roles, they generally have less experience in problem solving that leads to executive decision making. Women should seek and be given management training in problem solving.

Women must set definite goals for promotion and advancement, and develop strategies to achieve these goals. They must make their superiors aware of their aspirations, and affirm their interest in career development by seeking opportunities for training programs, and applying for higher level jobs when vacancies occur. They should make higher level managers aware that they are just as eager—or more so—as any man, and are willing to undertake the work challenges and risks and sacrifices necessary to move upward—all the way to the top [5], [6], [8], [9].

Stead [8] reports that the experience of successful women managers is that sexual relationships with business associates should be avoided. The ambitious woman must accept, as men do, that her career will have to come first. She may marry and have a family but the family will have to fit in around the demands of her career. This is difficult, especially while the children are young, but many women are succeeding in this accomplishment.

The fundamental change in family roles which is rapidly taking place in America will make it possible for women to assume the greater responsibilities required of managers. As more wives pursue careers and work outside the home, more husbands are sharing household management and nurturing tasks.

Company Policies on Women in Management. The fulfillment of affirmative action programs to meet the EEOC Guidelines will require active recruitment policies to bring women and other minorities into management-level positions in the 1980s. Schaeffer and Lynton [7] make the following points as regards company policy:

In the early stages of a company's efforts to increase the representation of women in both professional and managerial categories, most of the women will typically be employed as individual contributors—as staff specialists such as assistant engineers, beginning market analysts, and in accounting, personnel, and communications. Such individual contributors will typically be college graduates. Most will be considered low-level administrators or managers. Some with technical degrees are likely to be considered as professional employees.

Substantial movement of women into the higher echelons of management may be expected to occur in the 1980s, following the entrance of many women into lower management jobs in the 1970s, since the policy of many large companies has traditionally been to fill key managerial positions by promotion from lower-level professional or managerial ranks.

For the 1980s, a much more comprehensive approach to affirmative action programs must be corporate policy. Ekberg-Jordon [10] outlines the process in fifteen steps:

(1) Formulation of the company's written *affirmative* action program and distribution and discussion of the policy among employees.

(2) Appointment of an affirmative action officer who reports to top management. In most organizations this should be a woman.

(3) Recruitment and hiring of qualified women, through on-campus recruiting programs and using the services of an executive search firm that specializes in finding women for all levels of management jobs.

(4) Reassessment of career paths. Analysis of existing positions so that upward mobility will be possible from a larger number of positions. Salary schedules for all positions should be equal for both men and women.

(5) Career counseling for women employees. Company career ladders can help women learn what career options exist and define long-range career goals.

(6) Informal meetings for new women in management. The experienced women will serve as role models and offer advice and share experiences.

(7) Encouragement of women to improve their knowledge. Information should be provided about credit courses and MBA programs, as well as conferences and professional meetings.

(8) Development of an assessment technique to measure progress made by women in different departments. The department manager should be held responsible for the development of women within the department, and evaluated on how well the women have been counseled and given the professional exposure they need.

(9) Public posting of all open positions, and access to personnel representatives with whom to discuss the openings.

(10 Establishment of a Women's Advisory Committee to recommend programs and policies to the affirmation action officer and senior management.

(11) Sponsorship of sensitivity workshops for men and women at managerial levels.

(12) Development of a sponsorship procedure for women managers.

(13) Establishment of flexible hours and part-time positions to allow women with children to work different schedules.

(14) Revaluation of policies regarding maternity leaves and paternity leaves.

(15) Review of relocation policies as regards women managers.

Assessment centers to evaluate managerial ability and potential by placing a candidate in a standardized performance situation where behavior can be observed and rated, is another strategy to bring about fuller utilization of women within a short period [8]. (See ASSESSMENT CENTERS.)

Stead [8] advocates that the potential woman manager be asked to identify what she sees as her next two jobs within the company. A program should then be tailored to help her prepare for her desired future.

Sex stereotyping, she adds, should be eliminated by dropping the suffix "men" and substituting worker or generic terms such as manager and supervisor. Semantics should be utilized to equalize the perception of the roles of the sexes.

Women at the Top. A 1980 study by Heidrick and Struggles, Inc. [11] showed that women executives in United States companies had made some significant career gains in recent years, but that their levels of compensation and responsibility still did not approach those of their male counterparts. The number of women officers continues to grow—to 497 in 1980, compared to 325 in 1977, as counted in a sample of annual reports of 1,300 companies. However, the survey of women officers of the nation's 1,000 largest industrial companies and 50 leading financial and retailing concerns showed that the typical female business executive earned less than $50,000 a year in cash compensation. Thus the gap between the salaries paid male and women executives is still very wide.

According to the survey, the typical woman officer is married, in her 40s, and white. She holds at least one college degree. Women officers typically had three different employers during their careers. About a fourth had worked fewer than six years for their current employers, and 22% had devoted 26 or more years to the same company.

More than one-fourth of the women officers surveyed had a graduate degree. Advanced degree holders constituted nearly half of those who earned more than $50,000 a year. Most women officers believed that an MBA degree would prove most helpful in accelerating the progress of a woman just starting her career.

Progress Report. Stead [8] reports that, when asked to evaluate women managers' competence at decision making, handling of emotions, and response to criticism (three areas in which women are frequently stereotyped as being inferior to men) both male and female executives rated women managers high.

Many of the male managers sampled indicated that women have brought a long-needed balance to the organization—that women bring a degree of sensitivity that allows a broader perspective in a determining the course of action and decision making.

Male managers were optimistic that women can effectively handle the management positions they are assuming. The problems women have are perceived as primarily due to lack of experience. The men reported having to help women overcome their initial insecurity, gain confidence, and assume an active and not a passive role.

* * *

Whenever qualified women make their way to higher positions in management, the worst of the struggle is over. Once there, the tensions, feeling of threat, and apprehension rapidly disappear.

In the 1980s, the question of how women are working out in management will be replaced by how are *men and women* working out as managers? The sexist attitude that gender is an important attribute to success will disappear and managers will be evaluated impartially on their accomplishments and performance.

ESTHER E. ESPENSHADE, Manager of Employment Security Research, Illinois Bureau of Employment Security, Chicago, Illinois

Information References

Connor, Patrick E., "Dimensions in Modern Management," Boston, Houghton Mifflin, 1979.

Crawford, Jacquelyn S., "Women in Middle Management," Ridgewood, N.J., Forkner, 1977.

Lumsden, George J., "Impact Management: Personal Power Strategies for Success," New York, AMACOM Div., American Management Association, 1979.

References Cited

[1] *Employment and Earnings,* August 1980, U.S. Department of Labor, Bureau of Labor Statistics, Table A-1, A-2 and A-21.

[2] "Statistical Abstract of the United States," U.S. Department of Commerce, Bureau of the Census, 1979 Edition, Table 685.

[3] "Dictionary of Occupational Titles," 1977, U.S. Department of Labor, Employment and Training Administration, Government Printing Office, Washington, D.C.

[4] Stashower, Gloria, "Careers in Management for the New Woman," New York, Franklin Watts, 1978.

[5] Hennig, Margaret and Jardim, Anne, "The Managerial Woman," Garden City, N.Y., Anchor Press/Doubleday, 1977.

[6] Higginson, Margaret V. and Quick, Thomas, "The Ambitious Woman's Guide to a Successful Career," New York, AMACON, American Management Association, 1980.

[7] Shaeffer, Ruth Gilbert, and Lynton, Edith F., "Corporate Experiences in Improving Women's Job Opportunities," New York, The Conference Board, 1979.

[8] Stead, Bette Ann, "Women in Management," Prentice Hall, Inc., Englewood Cliffs, N.J. 1978. (An excellent compilation of 38 articles giving a comprehensive view with an excellent annotated bibliography.

[9] Lynch, Edith M. "Woman's Guide to Management—How To Get To The Top and Stay There," New York, Cornerstone Library, 1979.

[10] Ekberg-Jordon, Sandra, "Preparing for the Future: Commitment and Action," *Atlanta Economic Review* (March-April 1976; pp. 47–49); also in (8).

[11] Allen, Frank, "Women Managers Get Paid Less than Males Despite Career Gains," *Wall Street Journal,* October 7, 1980. (Report on study by Heidrick and Struggles, Inc., New York, N.Y.)

Cross Reference: *Women in Business and Industry.*

WORD PROCESSING

For many years, administrative office procedures for producing correspondence and handling routine chores involved a one-on-one secretary/principal relationship. With the introduction of text-editing machines, managers interested in automating the work flow installed new equipment, separated personnel into typing (word processing) and non-typing (administrative support) functions, and standardized procedures. The resulting operation became known as **Word Processing.**

History. The idea for the new office technique was developed in Germany after the end of World War II, when reconstruction of office space gave impetus to the open "office landscape" concept (cf. OFFICE SPACE PLANNING: THE "OPEN PLAN."), and the shortage of workers made the efficient handling of office tasks a top priority. The revolution manifested itself more dramatically in the mid-1960s, with the introduction of the IBM Magnetic Tape Selectric Typewriter (MT/ST) developed along the principles of the Autotypist, a technically advanced machine introduced in the 1930s which assisted the secretary in producing routine, repetitive letters. Ulrich Steinhilper, who served as manager for IBM Germany during the 1960s and early 1970s, is given credit for coining the term *word processing* (originally *Textverarbeitung* in German). His concrete ideas helped make word processing visible as an independent work area within administration.

Throughout the 1970s, more advanced text-editing machines were introduced. Typically, these contain a keyboard and printing mechanism (similar to those employed by standard electric typewriters), and a magnetic media storage device, and may also include a display window or screen.

Operations. With the installation of text-editing equipment, management often finds it necessary to reorganize its office systems in order to obtain maximum efficiency and productivity. Equipment may be centralized (located in a common area accessible to all principals) or decentralized (grouped in small clusters, each serving several executives).

Because a skilled word-processing operator can produce at least two or three (and often much more) times the correspondence generated by a secretary using a standard electric typewriter, by keeping machines active, organizations can offset the relatively high cost of automated typing equipment. Therefore, firms often divide typing and non-typing tasks between equipment operators and administrative support personnel. The word-processing support group is usually dedicated to typing, revising, and printing office correspondence. On the other hand, administrative support secretaries generally answer telephones, schedule appointments, perform proofreading/filing/copying activities, relieve principals of routine dictation, and may even conduct research.

Work may be presented to the word-processing operation in the form of machine dictation, long-hand notes, or typewritten/printed copy. Typing is performed much as it is on a standard typewriter. Typographical errors are corrected in almost all instances by a simple backspace/strikeover process. Alternatively, material can be prepared on standard electric typewriters equipped with OCR (Optical Character Recognition) readable type elements. Hard copy is then read into a text-editing machine via an optical scanner. This frees the latter unit to handle more revision work. In either case, digitally encoded keystrokes and page format codes (such as space, tab, carriage return, center, underscore) are stored on magnetic media, in the form of cards, tapes, or disks.

Documents to be revised are read from the medium into machine memory. Characters, words, and blocks of text can be inserted into or deleted from the original text using keys provided for these functions. A final document is then printed at speeds ranging from 15.5 to 55 characters per second or more, depending upon the model and sophistication of the printer.

As the firm's needs expand, a text-editing machine can often be connected to other electronic office machines by means of cable or communications interface. This enables material prepared on a text-editing machine to be transmitted to another electronic office machine, such as a high-speed printer, "intelligent" copier/printer, photocomposition unit, or computer, and vice versa, thus eliminating the need to retype information for entry into each unit in the system. Firms employing communicating devices can further exchange documentation with remotely located offices having compatible equipment, or access to a computer data base for research purposes.

Designing a large information system requires a great deal of expertise to implement correctly. Minimally, a knowledge of word processing, data processing, and digital data communications must be combined with skill in developing personnel policies, training programs, and operational procedures.

Implementation. Word-processing operations are implemented primarily in paper-intensive organizations, including medical, banking, insurance, legal, and educational institutions. Documents handled include "boilerplate" (standard paragraphs), repetitive correspondence, standard forms, light to extensively revised multi-page documents, and statistical material. Text-editing machines accepting special applications software programs can also perform mathematical calculations (to prepare invoices) and sorting routines (to create management records). Efficiency in producing documents depends upon skilled personnel and standardized procedures.

Because text-editing machines utilize a keyboard with standard typewriter keys plus special function keys—sometimes used alone and sometimes in combination with other keys (the method varies from model to model)—office personnel must receive special instruction in machine operation. Training programs are generally available from text-editing equipment manufacturers, educational institutions, independent word-processing training organizations, and businesses that have developed in-house training courses. In order to produce quality materials, operators should also possess good grammar, spelling, and proofreading skills. Realizing how valuable highly skilled operators are in increasing productivity, many companies offer well-defined career paths—from operator to supervisory and management levels, through which personnel can progress in the word-processing operation—as an incentive for employees to remain with the organization.

Standard procedures also contribute to increased efficiency. Therefore, companies often develop procedures manuals for word-processing/administrative support personnel (describing uniform methods for performing work) as well as for principals (informing them how to utilize word-processing services). Manuals often incorporate or are accompanied by form books containing sample correspondence and specifying formats and variables to be used.

Costs. The bulk of the expense in establishing a word-processing operation involves hardware and people. At the end of the 1970s, low-end electronic typewriters, which perform a few repetitive functions, cost between $1,700 and $5,000. Blind units (without a display), used for assembling boilerplate paragraphs and merging variables into standard text, ranged from $5,000 to $10,000. Linear display machines providing a window into memory for verifying characters and instruction codes typed and capable of handling short to medium-length documents with light to medium revisions were priced between $7,000 and $13,000. Stand-alone text-editing machines with keyboard/video-display screen, storage unit, and separate printer, widely used for editing lengthy and heavily revised documents, averaged $10,000 to $18,000 (although some were available for as little as $5,000 and others for up to $27,000). Work stations clustered around and sharing the resources of peripheral equipment (such as a computer, storage device, or printer) cost substantially less on per terminal basis than comparable stand-alone units.

Staffing the word-processing operation will require paying salaries commensurate with individual skill levels. Salaries offered are generally higher than those commanded by ordinary secretaries. The exact pay scale is determined by the company's geographical location and personnel policies.

Although the initial expenses in providing word-processing services are greater than establishing a typing pool, extensive savings can be realized as more work is generated by fewer people.

Possibilities for the Future. Word-processing industry leaders anticipate a growing need for automating office procedures to speed the flow of information. In the future, systems that combine word/information/data processing and electronic document distribution will be developed (either on one set of hardware or utilizing a multiple-vendor approach whereby intelligent text-editing machines that are software programmable, expandable, and have communicating capabilities are interfaced with a growing number of office machines). Such systems will provide virtually instantaneous access to stored information (including correspondence, management records, financial data, and equipment usage reports) whether it is within the system or in another remotely situated system.

Willoughby Ann Walshe, Executive Editor, *Word Processing Systems,* Geyer-McAllister Publications Inc., New York, New York

Information References

Associations:

International Word Processing Association.
Word Processing Society Inc.

Periodicals:

The Word.
Word Processing Report.
Word Processing Systems.
Words.

Texts:

Kleinschrod, Walter, "Management's Guide to Word Processing," Chicago, Dartnell, 1976.

Kleinschrod, Walter, Kruk, Leonard, and Turner, Hilda, "Word Processing: Operations, Applications, and Administration," Indianapolis, Bobbs-Merrill, 1980.

Cross Reference: *Office Automation.*

WORK MEASUREMENT

Work Measurement, or "time study" as it is often called, originated with the Scientific Management movement at the turn of century. It develops operation times used in scheduling, estimating, labor incentives, method studies, and economic studies. Recent work has been characterized by an increased interest in Predetermined Motion Times, improved methodology, the application of statistical techniques, and computer-assisted recording and processing of times observed.

Formal Definition. Work measurement (time study) is a collection of techniques used to determine the time required by a qualified and well trained person working at a normal pace to do a specific job. An alternate definition views work measurement as a method for estimating production times for an operator who is working under stable conditions using consistent methods. (See MOTION AND TIME STUDY.)

History. While an instance of the application of work measurement is recorded in 1760, [1], it was not widely used until this century, and its introduction into industry was largely due to the writing of FREDERICK W. TAYLOR. The technique was significantly changed in the late 1920s when Lowry, Maynard, and Stegemerten introduced the idea of rating—adjusting observed times to the observer's concept of what the times would be if they had been performed at a "normal" pace [2]. Various devices such as rating films have since been developed which are used to train observers to make rating judgments—judgments that are consistent with those made by engineers whose judgment of the "correct" ratings of the operations filmed or demonstrated is considered sound. Systems of predetermined times—tabulated times for basic body motions such as MTM ("Methods Time Measurement") began appearing in the 1930s, but were not widely used until after World War II.

In the late 1940s, interest was focused on some of the shortcomings of time study by the searching work of William Gomberg. This led to the development of procedures employing modern statistical techniques, particularly the statistical control chart [3]. (See QUALITY CONTROL AND QUALITY ASSURANCE.)

Approaches and Techniques. *Contemporary Work Measurements.* The time study aimed at determining the time required to perform a job at a *normal pace* is accomplished through timing the conduct of the job through several performances, or *cycles* of the job. A stopwatch is generally used and the job cycle is broken into *elements*—arbitrary but logical segments of a cycle characterized by not being too short to be timed, having easily distinguished beginnings, and short enough to be compared with similar elements in other jobs and to be used in constructing predetermined times for new operations. The observed data are adjusted through rating and adding time allowances to provide recovery from fatigue, allow for unavoidable delays, and make provisions for body functions. The result is time to perform one cycle of the job and hence the time to produce a unit of product. This time if expressed in minutes is termed the *standard minutes* per unit provided for the operation to be performed, or if expressed in hours, the time is termed "standard hours." (See STANDARD MINUTE SYSTEM). The timing may be preceded by a study of the operation to improve the method used. The *labor standard* thus developed often becomes part of the data used in standard cost accounting.

Stability Studies. When the purpose of a study is to determine the time required to perform a job under stable conditions using consistent methods, rating is omitted. The data observed are subjected to examination using the statistical control chart—a device originated in quality control—to see if consistent conditions and stable methods are present or if method changes to obtain these conditions are possible. While studies made under this procedure cannot be used for setting incentives, they offer opportunities for uncovering subtle but perhaps fruitful method changes. Other statistical techniques, such as the determination of the number of cycles to be observed, are used both in stability studies and in contemporary work measurement.

Contemporary work measurement, as described here, establishes the time that management would like the work cycle to take. Stability studies establish the time that the cycle *will* take if the conditions during which the observations were taken were consistent and if they remain that way in the future. While few engineers make stability studies today, the technique seems to some to offer the answer to persistent and difficult questions regarding the place of rating in work measurement.

Predetermined Times. Systems of predetermined times usually have been developed from extensive work measurement data (using rating) where the timing is sometimes done using instruments more precise than the conventional stop-watch. Many systems are in use, in addition to MTM already mentioned, including: MTA (Motion Time Analysis), MTS (Motion Time Standards), Work Factor, BMT (Basic Motion Time), DMT (Dimensional Motion Times), and numerous private systems developed from a firm's time study data. Predetermined times are particularly useful where an operation has not been started and an estimated time is required. (See PREDETERMINED MOTION TIMES.)

Considerable controversy exists as to whether the times for motions in predetermined times may be meaningfully summed. It is believed by some investigators that the elements in a work cycle are not independent and that the correct time value for an element depends upon the element preceding and following it.

Work Sampling. Instants of time are sampled through work sampling in somewhat the same way that units of product are sampled in product inspection. The time samples allow an estimate to be made of the way a worker or group of workers spend periods of work. The work sampling technique is sometimes used to establish *delay allowances* to be used in setting labor time standards of performance. Work sampling has also been recommended as an alternative to timing work cycles; however, this method in many cases requires a great many observations. (See RATIO DELAY.)

Potential. Work measurement is likely to be extended in two directions in the future: (1) to the study of more clerical jobs and indirect factory jobs such as maintenance and material handling; (2) to the study of vigilance tasks—jobs associated with automated systems that mainly require keeping watch over the systems. As the degree of automation is increased and jobs where workers directly control productivity decrease, time study as commonly practiced will be less frequently employed. The statistical design and analysis of work measurement procedures is likely to find increasing use as statistical concepts and their advantages become more evident to management.

DANIEL J. DUFFY, Professor of Business Administration, Loyola College, Baltimore, Maryland

Information References

Associations and Periodicals: See Industrial Engineering.

Texts:

Mundel, Marvin E., "Motion and Time Study," 5th ed., Englewood Cliffs, N.J., Prentice-Hall, 1978.

Niebel, Benjamin W., "Motion and Time Study," 6th ed., Homewood, Ill., Irwin, 1976.

References Cited

[1] Morrow, R. L., "Time Study and Motion Economy," New York, Ronald Press, 1946.

[2] Davidson, H. O., "Functions and Bases of Time Standards," Cleveland, American Institute of Industrial Engineers, 1957.

[3] Gomberg, William, "A Trade Union Analysis of Time Study," 2nd ed., Englewood Cliffs, N.J., Prentice-Hall, 1955.

Cross References: *Motion and Time Study (and cross references there given); Work Measurement in the Office.*

WORK MEASUREMENT IN THE OFFICE

The increasing ratio of indirect or administrative work, in proportion to direct or factory production, points to the more extensive use of scientific devices to determine the adequacy of clerical and other office output. Although many cost-conscious companies have installed and are maintaining effective **Office Work Measurement** systems in their administrative operations, this area of measurement has not nearly reached the widespread coverage to which industrial work utilizes it.

Definition. Work measurement is the method of determining the proper ratio of manpower used to results obtained—the energy input versus the work output. Whether measurement is applied to industrial operations or to clerical and administrative activities of the office, its definition is the same. It is composed of two basic factors: *man-hours* and *volume.* Work measurement could also be defined as the process by which relatively objective criteria, usually called standards, are substituted for subjective judgment. Although a certain degree of subjectivity may be present in all standards, work measurement may be considered a scientific approach to establishing what a fair day's work should be.

History. The application of scientific methods to manufacturing had led, by the close of the last century and the early years of the present one, to the development of work measurement in industrial operations and to the payment of work based on measured output. However, it was to be a number of decades later, during and after World War II, before widespread attempts would be made to apply these techniques to white collar operations. The first of these, the historical method and the use of employee reports, were fairly readily acceptable by office employees. Later, when stop watch timing was attempted in the office, it met with a great deal of resistance. So much so, that for years its use was strictly prohibited in any department of the Federal Government.

The use of *predetermined data* was just as skeptically viewed when first suggested for office activities, but its success, especially following the publication of "Method-Time Measurement" by Maynard, Stegemerten, and Schwab in 1948 [1], led to the gradual experimentation and acceptance of this technique in office work. The first uses of this tool of measurement came at a time when the use of *micromotion* was also found to be fairly successful in office work. However, the high expense of micromotion (which employs the use of motion picture analysis), practically prohibited its use in small companies. As a result, the use of standard data was given further impetus. During the 1950s, numerous modifications of the industrial predetermined time data were developed by consulting and professional groups. (See PREDETERMINED MOTION TIMES.)

The application of *work sampling* to the measurement of work in the office gained its popularity during the mid 1950s. This technique, based on the industrial "ratio delay" method of observing work, was stimulated by the books of Ralph Barnes [2] and Heiland and Richardson [3] in 1957, and B. L. Hanson in 1960 [4]. A modification of this approach to measurement and evaluation of employee output is evident in "PACE," as used by the Northrup Aircraft Corp. (PACE—*P*erformance *A*nd *C*ost *E*valuation—is essentially work sampling, in which the items observed are limited to "Work," "Idle," and "Away." However, it does introduce the rated value of employees observed to be working, based on a standard value of 100 for a 3-miles-per-hour work pace. The total net rated value, or actually rate of speed, of the workers, offset by number of idle and away employees of the group, provides the PACE rate. This is always expressed for the group of workers rather than for the individual.)

Objectives of Measuring Office Work. The five principal objectives for undertaking a program of office work measurement are listed below.

(1) *To provide management with the means of evaluating and appraising performance.* The larger an organization grows, the more necessary it becomes to delegate authority and responsibility; yet in doing so, management must still retain control. Without measurement, management has no control, for it has no means of evaluating the progress and performance of its employees; it has no standard against which to gauge its direction or rate of achievement.

(2) *To permit the programming and scheduling of work.* With sound measurement data, it is possible to plan for normal or widely fluctuating work, to establish and control backlogs. With it, management can determine the most practical time to undertake special work, when to shift personnel, to reassign or re-train in advance of pressure periods.

(3) *To permit more effective budgeting and cost control.* To operate at a profit, a company must establish a realistic budget, and must know, with relative certainty, what costs (especially personnel costs) are going to be, so as not to price itself out of business. Measurement permits the development of realistic costs of proposed programs and projects which can then be evaluated and scheduled on a priority basis. Cost control is also facilitated by measurement data.

(4) *To assist in achieving work reduction and increased effectiveness.* The close scrutiny of work required by most techniques of measurement serves to highlight duplications of work effort, cumbersome work processes, and needless operations. A reduction in the actual amount of work required almost inevitably results from measurement.

(5) *To provide greater motivation of employees.* Repeated experience with measurement programs has affirmed that employees produce their best work when they are given a definite task to be performed in a definite way, and are informed of the expected time standard for its completion. The knowledge of a fair day's work stimulates the employee to compete against the standard, even of his or her own making. Measurement has repeatedly produced increases in production, even without work changes.

Approaches and Techniques. Five major groupings of office work measurement techniques may be cited, namely: Historical Measurement, Employee Reporting Data, Stop Watch or Time Study Data, Predetermined or Standard Data, and Work Sampling Data.

Historical Measurement. Historical work measurement is the calculated correlation of data, using the records of work completed in some period in the past, and the time spent on its performance. Very often regular employee time cards or payroll time sheets are used, selecting as reliable or typical a period of working time that is available for the basic information. The time data are analyzed in conjunction with production records for the same period to develop very simple time factors for each of certain broad types of work.

In developing simple standards such as these, the key units of work most indicative of the work effort are identified and used as the central index of work output. Standards set by this method sometimes lack objectivity since the quality or difficulties of the work may fluctuate widely, or the conditions of the work may vary. Yet even such broad guides can be extremely useful.

Employeee Reporting Approach. This approach of having employees keep records of current input and output of work, and using current reports for the development of data, is a technique which is partcularly applicable to the office areas. It is basically simple and relatively inexpensive. Each employee reports his (her) time distribution in terms of previously defined and categorized work items. These are related to the work units completed for the same period, adjusting the data for supervision, training, etc. From such correlations, standards of performance are developed. These are fairly objective and meaningful, since they contain extensive detail and can be adjusted for special or distorting factors occurring during the current periods of work, whereas in historical standards, the distortion is often no longer possible to define or adjust. Numerous simple tally forms are used for recording and reporting the data by the employees. One such form is shown on Exhibit I.

Stop Watch Time Standards. Undoubtedly the best known device for measuring work is the simple stop watch. The stop watch is designed to indicate fractions of seconds (some as fine as a thousandth of a second), and to start and stop instantaneously at finger pressure. The work to be measured is divided into its operational cycles. Because of the complexity of most operations, and the occurrence of delay factors, it is common practice to break the operational cycles into elements. These elements are usually groups of the basic motion elements and are long enough to be conveniently timed—usually at least .5 minute. Timing can either be developed on the individual components, or on the total cycle of work, depending on the variables, length of cycle, etc.

The rating or evaluation of the work effort, which is an accepted part of time study in industrial areas (see WORK MEASUREMENT and STANDARD MINUTE SYSTEM), is not frequently employed in measuring clerical operations, although some adjustment is normally made for overly slow or fast production. The high-speed camera filming the short cycle work operation with a clock in the background (see MOTION AND TIME STUDY) is seldom used in measuring office work. The exception would be only where the operation is a very critical one which is highly repetitive and of sufficient importance to warrant the added cost and effort.

Predetermined or Standard Time Measurement. The system of measurement is based on the use of time values which have previously been obtained (by stop watch or micromotion camera) for motions or elemental parts of work identical to those in the work to be measured. The elements may be grouped differently in the new work, but have nevertheless been validly timed and measured in the hundreds of previ-

EXHIBIT I

WEEKLY EMPLOYEE REPORT OF DISTRIBUTION OF TIME

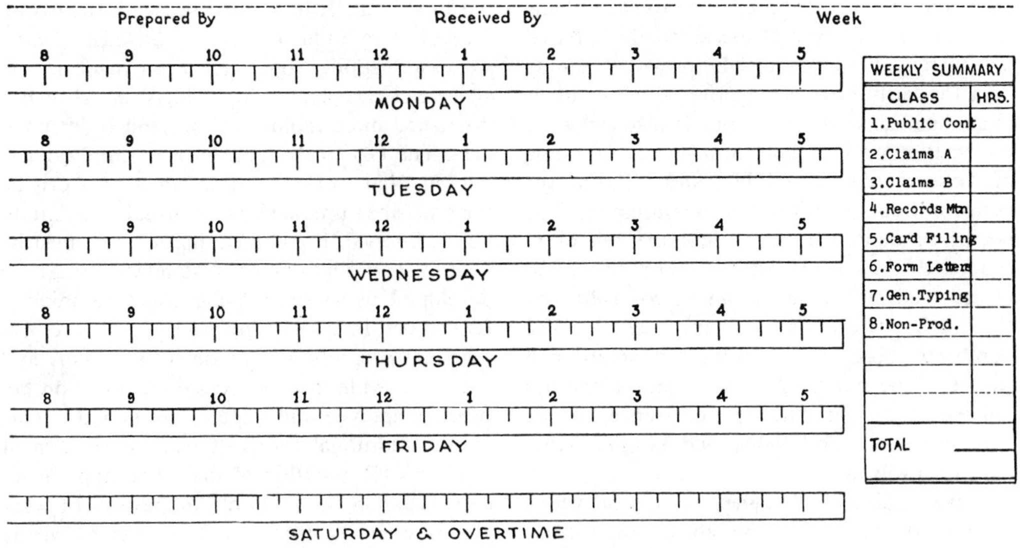

ously observed basic items. By the careful definition and identification of the items, and their calculated frequency of occurrence, the accurate and reliable measurement for the new operation can be achieved without the use of further stop watch timing.

Tables of established time values have been developed by numerous consulting firms and become available by using the services of the consultants for the planning, training, or other phases of the program. Some sets of time values are also available in published texts in summary form.

The principal difference in the various systems of such timings now in use lies in the grouping of the elemental data. Any simple clerical task is composed of numerous individual motions. The measurement of the task can be accomplished by adding each of the elementary motions or by adding the totals of the several groups of motions in sequence which compose the whole. Obviously, the more the motions can be reliably grouped, the more simple will be the measurement of the whole. Since this type of measurement requires careful verification of the individual steps in the work operation, it uncovers many operations which can be simplified or eliminated, and leads to the reduction of the work itself. Changes in work processes can be adjusted in the measurement without great difficulty.

Work Sampling. Here truly random observations are used to obtain a tally of the frequency of each type of work being performed. The number and percentage of observations in each category of work are then related to the total time, and this is distributed back to each of the work items. This type of measurement is based on current performance. It provides timing data for fairly broad categories of work rather than detailed work units, but it also provides information on lost time through the recording of observations of "Idle" and "Put-away" items, not obtained in other measurement. The degree of desired accuracy and the reliability can be determined in advance, and the speed of the total measurement can be controlled by the number of observations taken per day. The number of observations required is determined by use of the statistical formula, and is directly influenced by the rate of occurrence of the items observed. Probability and sampling theory are involved.

Other Office Techniques. In recent years, several adaptations of the above basic techniques have been refined and practiced with varying degrees of popularity. Two in particular have gained favor and achieved frequency of application: *Modapts* and *Short-Interval Scheduling.*

Modapts stands for Modular Arrangement of Predetermined Time Systems. The system is based on the concept that since all body movements are similar or modular, all movements in a typical operation can be measured in terms of multiples (or modules) of finger movement. The result is a system that has been found easy to learn and to use and remarkably accurate. Its application does not require the variety or degree of technical capability required to apply some of the other standards systems. It recognizes sixteen different activities and assigns basic values to them. By appropriate combinations, measurement can be made of almost any likely work situation. All work values are expressed in terms of a module, which is a simple finger movement having a value of one-seventh of a second. The system can normally be applied without reference to any table of values and without a stopwatch [5]. This system of measurement was developed and used extensively by Price Waterhouse & Co. during the 1970s.

Strictly speaking, *Short-Interval Scheduling* is not a separate measurement technique in itself, but since it is quite frequently referred to as a separate approach, it justifies inclusion. Simply stated, it is a method for assigning a planned quantity of work to be completed by a specific time, and a means to determine that the assigned quantity of work is completed within the time limit. It has been used with increasing frequency in industry and in business. Many successful applications have been made in the general clerical and office field, although it has flourished most rapidly in the mail order business. The key to this approach is simply determining what work and how much of it can be done at what time and place, usually within an hour's interval. For this, units of work must be defined and measurement standards must be developed using one of the usual techniques. Its "short interval" approach to assure on-schedule progress and to detect problems and delays, provide more direct communication between employee and supervisor than do some of the traditional forms of work measurement programs [6]. (Neither of these two approaches is included in the table of comparison of techniques since the first is still not yet as widely used as the more basic approaches, and the second is not in itself a separate and different way of determining the measurements.)

Comparison of Measurement Techniques. The markedly divergent methods of measurement indicate that while no strong controversy may exist, proponents of each of the methods emphasize the advantages of their favorite technique. Each technique is best in its own individual situation, and the proper technique for a given area of work or circumstances can only be determined after a careful analysis of the special factors influencing the situation. Where broad measurements are adequate, Work Sampling, Employee Reporting, or even Historical Measurement permit the development of standards without undue costs or lengthy delays. Where more detailed and accurate measurements are required, Stop Watch Timing or the use of Standard Data is preferable. A table of comparison of the techniques on the basis of the major criteria of most programs is shown as Exhibit II. It is offered only as a general guide, since under certain circumstances, any of the shown ratings may vary materially. Frequently the type of measurement used in a company progresses from the very simplest, the use of Historical Data, to the more detailed and comprehensive, Stop Watch or Standard Data. The two approaches which have grown most rapidly in usage and application are Work Sampling and the numerous types of

EXHIBIT II

EVALUATION OF OFFICE WORK MEASUREMENT TECHNIQUES

Criteria	*Work Sampling*	*Predetermined Time Standards*	*Stop Watch Timing*	*Employee Reporting*	*Historical*
1. *Speed:* Time required to measure and establish standards	Average to fast	Slow to average	Average	Average	Fast
2. *Training and Skill Required:* Technicians, Supervisors	Low to moderate	High	Moderate to high	Low	Low
3. *Cost:* Technician, employee time, equipment, etc.	Average	Fairly high	Average	Low	Minimal
4. *Assistance in Methods Improvement*	Low to moderate	High	Good	Very little	No
5. *Accuracy:* Subjective vs. objective; degree of distortion	Fair to good	Very high	Good to high	Fair	Low
6. *Acceptability:* Employee, Supervisor	Fair	Good	Fair to good	Fair to good	Fair to good
7. *Interruption of Work Operations*	Moderate	Low	Fairly high	Fairly high	None
8. *Applicability:* For physical, clerical, professional work	Very good	Average	Average	Very good	Good
9. *Savings:* How quickly; how much	Average to high	High	Average to high	Fair to good	Fair
10. *Usability:* In scheduling production; evaluating performance	Average to high	High	High	Fair to good	Fair
11. *Reporting Requirements:* Difficulty of furnishing data	Average	Average	Average	Fair	Simple

Standard Data systems. Modifications of any of the approaches are still to be expected.

Acceptance and Potentials. Although work measurement and standards in the office were not widely accepted or used before 1950, they are rapidly being introduced in business today. The most obvious paperwork businesses, notably insurance, banking, investments, etc., have probably been the pioneering leaders, and their successes have given added impetus to others. The fact that the ratio of indirect to direct costs has continued to rise in the past twenty-five years, indicates that the potential for measurement is very great in office or administrative areas. The measurement of the work and the establishment of standards most frequently provide at least a 20% saving in the work measured. This saving is for the most part still unrealized in American business today.

ANITA P. LOEBER, Consultant to Management, San Diego, California

Information References

Associations:

Administrative Management Society.
American Institute of Industrial Engineers.
American Management Association.
American Statistical Association.
Association For Systems Management.
The Institute of Management Sciences.

Periodicals:

Journal of Systems Management.
Management Methods.
Management Review.
Systems Management.
The Office.
Journal of Industrial Engineering.
Time and Motion Study.

Selected Publications:

Budde, James F., "Measuring Performance in Human Service Systems," New York, AMACOM, 1979.
Cochran, W. G., "Sampling Techniques," New York, Wiley, 1977.
Loeber, Anita P., "Work Reduction and Measurement Techniques," in "Ideas for Management," Cleveland, Association for Systems Management, 1979.
Moch, Theodore and Groves, Hugh, "Measurement, Accounting, and Organizational Information," New York, Wiley, 1978.
Reed, Emma A., "Time-Sheet Accounting," *Journal of Systems Management,* January 1979.
Stevens, Robert I., "Ratio-delay Study," *Journal of Systems Management,* February 1979.

References Cited

[1] Maynard, H. B., Stegemerten, G. J., and Schwab, J. L., "Methods-Time Measurement," New York, McGraw-Hill, 1948.
[2] Barnes, Ralph M., "Work Sampling," Melbourne, Fla., Krieger, repr. 1979.
[3] Heiland, Robert E., and Richardson, Wallace J., "Work Sampling," New York, McGraw-Hill, 1957.
[4] Hanson, B. L., "Work Sampling for Modern Management," Englewood Cliffs, N.J., Prentice-Hall, 1960.
[5] Colbert, Bertram A., "Introducing a New Tool for Planning and Controlling Work," New York, Price Waterhouse & Co., *The Price Waterhouse Review,* Spring, 1970.
[6] Smith, Martin R., "Principles of Short-Interval Scheduling," in Handbook of Modern Office Management and Administrative Services, Carl Heyel, ed., Melbourne, Fla., Krieger, repr. 1980.

Cross References: *Motion and Time Study (and cross references there given); Work Measurement.*

WORK SIMPLIFICATION

Work Simplification is a way of getting something done, step by step, by breaking a problem down into simple segments. It is an organized, commonsense attack upon the way in which work is done now, with a view of doing it better. It makes use of the techniques of METHOD IMPROVEMENT, but it goes beyond a series of techniques. Work simplification "stretches the mind" by introducing and solidifying the concept of what is useful work. It changes habits of thinking about what must be considered waste work.

The heart of any work simplification program is the recognition by management of the *foreman* and *supervisor* as a vital part of the company's methods improvement team, and through them tapping the enthusiasm of everyone at the working level to ship a *better product,* (or perform a *better service*) at a *lower price,* at the *right time.* It should be noted that work simplification is not limited to manufacturing operations. While it began in the factory, it is now applied wherever work is done: in offices, in governmental operations, in retailing, in construction, and even in the medical profession in the streamlining of surgical techniques.

The basic premise of work simplification is that once a person really sees how a job is done, asks why it is done that way, and attacks the job with the desire to improve the present method, possibilities for improvement will inevitably occur to him (her). In this statement there are three key words: "*really* sees," "asks *why,*" and "*inevitably* occur."

History. The expressive term *work simplification* was coined by Professor Erwin H. Schell of the Massachusetts Institute of Technology, who inspired several generations of students in his classes in engineering and industrial management. But it was Allan H. Mogensen, an industrial engineer and a former editor on the staff of *Factory,* and director of the now famous Work Simplification Conferences held annually at Lake Placid, New York, since 1937, who put the techniques and philosophy together into a unified program that can be implemented by supervisors and other key personnel, and through them brought to the working force. Associated with him in this pioneering work were Lillian Gilbreth, Erwin Schell, David Porter, and Herbert Goodwin.

The graduates of the Mogensen Work Simplification Conferences have initiated programs in their plants, "bringing the religion" to their own supervisory forces. Conferences in work simplification are now held at leading universities, and in-plant training in work simplification is offered as part of the services available from management consulting firms.

Emphasis on Reducible Waste. A fundamental premise of work simplification is that any work that does not add value to material, does not plan or calculate, does not give or receive essential information, is *reducible waste.* There are four types of reducible waste:

(1) *Transportation, by any means, any distance, in any situation.* This can be moving a tote pan from a storage area to a work area; walking from one work area to another; the body movement of an operator to get his hands in position to work; the movement of a hand to grasp or release or manipulate a tool; the travel of part in a conveyor. Whatever the reason for such transportation, it *adds no value to the product.*

(2) *Delay-storage-idle in any situation for any reason.* Examples are the momentary hesitation of a hand in an intricate assembly; an idle hand for lack of something to do; a man waiting for a machine to finish a cut; a machine idle while it is being set up; a piece of material waiting in a tote pan for its turn to be worked on; a major assembly in a stores bin waiting to be scheduled for the final assembly operation; a typist idle while carbon paper is being brought from the storeroom.

(3) *Inspection to verify for quantity or dimension or a quality characteristic.* Every inspection is a costly, constant reminder that sufficient quality has not been built into the product. The inspection, necessary though it may be, adds no value to the product.

(4) *Falure to use known faster devices.* Mechanization and its ultimate goal, automation, are simply the reduction of the transportation, the delay-storage-idle, and the inspection of a subject to the minimum. But there are countless opportunities for the supervisor to apply relatively simple faster devices; and, once his eyes are opened, the search will be extremely rewarding. Where, in all handling, can slide-grasp bins, gravity feed chutes, pegboards, and the like be used? Where can a holding hand be relieved by a foot treadle or an air chuck? How can time be saved by using something that is helpful on another job?

It is by concentrating the supervisor's attention to the elimination of waste wherever it occurs that management can achieve a substantial total of individual "little" savings which only he has time to bring about, since the full-time methods man will be out "catching bigger fish." Especially on short-run jobs, waste will keep on going unnoticed. The way they were set up in the first place to get them done somehow will be the way they will be done until the supervisor takes the initiative to make what improvements he can. (But this is not to say that numerous large-scale savings may not be accomplished. Company work simplification programs have been known to result in individual improvements representing first-year savings of $20,000 and more.)

The foreman's role is thus four-fold: (1) to be an alert observer, with eyes newly opened to waste; (2) to be a cooperative assistant to fulltime methods personnel, after indoctrination with the elementary principles of the industrial engineer's techniques of charting and analysis; (3) to develop improved methods of his or her own; and (4)—and this is highly important—to motivate everyone in his (her) department to be *waste-conscious* and come up with suggestions for improvements.

The Questioning Attitude. The method of attack is to instill in every supervisor a continuing, hard-headed, insatiable questioning attitude, which takes nothing for granted. Its fundamental requirement is an *open mind* that approaches an improvement problem without any preconceived ideas, without bias, and without prejudice. To be effective, however, the questions cannot be haphazard. They must be channeled toward four possible results, as follows:

(1) *What can we eliminate?* This could be a process, a value-adding or a non-value-adding

operation, a delay or storage or idle or inspection. To eliminate is to improve!

(2) *What can we combine?* The use of known faster devices often provides the answer. If two operations cannot be combined, it may be possible to combine a transportation with an operation.

(3) *Should the sequence be changed?* Changes in sequence may eliminate or reduce non-value-adding operations, transportations, delays, storages, and inspections. Again, the use of known faster devices will often make this possible.

(4) *What can we simplify?* The time to start to think about ways to simplify is when the processes and operations have been reduced as much as possible through elimination, combination, and/or change of sequence.

In this purposeful channeling the six basic questions of work simplification are used over and over again: *What? Why? Where? When? Who? How?* The way in which these can be pin-pointed to locate improvement possibilities is illustrated in Exhibit I.

The Written Record. Work simplification emphasizes the analysis of work by means of a written record made by the supervisor, of just how a particular job or process is done. The mere making of such a record will of itself generate ideas for improvement. The written record is made by means of simple charting techniques, with each element of work marked with its own symbol. Such charting shows in clear relief the wastes that constantly occur when a man uses his hands; when material is processed, operation by operation, part by part, to the completed product. The work simplification definition and symbol for each element in a written record are shown in Exhibit II. (Some programs use ⇨ for a transportation, and add a symbol D for delay.)

Three basic charts are used, making use of the symbols, along with terse descriptive phrases: the *Process Analysis,* the *Man-Machine Analysis,* and the *Operation Analysis.*

(1) *The Process Analysis* is the written record in chronological sequence of all the elements of work in the series of operations in a process to change a subject in any of its physical or chemical characteristics or to assemble it or disassemble it from another object. Note that a *single subject* is followed; there are never two or more subjects to this analysis. A process analysis could follow a *man* as well as a part. When the man walks, it is a "transportation" (he is "transporting" himself).

The *transportation* of parts in a process is made with a container or holder of some kind; or the part is of sufficient size or weight or is

EXHIBIT I

WORK SIMPLIFICATION'S SIX BASIC QUESTIONS

Key Question	*Idea Kickers*	*Improvement Possibilities*
WHAT is done?	What is its purpose? Does it do what it is supposed to do?	Eliminate
WHY is it done?	Should it be done at all? Can as good a result be obtained without it? Is it an absolute must?	Eliminate
WHERE is it done?	Why is it done there? Why should it be done there? Where should it be done? Can it be done easier by changing the location of person or equipment?	Combine and/or change sequence
WHEN is it done?	Why is it done then? Is it done in right sequence? Can all or part of it be done at some other time?	Combine and/or change sequence
WHO does it?	Why does this person do it? Is the right person doing it? Is it logical to give it to someone else?	Combine and/or change sequence
HOW is it done?	Why should it be done this way? Can it be done better with different equipment or different layout? Is there any other way to do it?	Simplify

EXHIBIT II

WORK SIMPLIFICATION DEFINITIONS AND SYMBOLS

○ *Operation:* An *operation* occurs when the subject is changed in any of its physical or chemical characteristics, or is assembled with or disassembled from another object, or is arranged or prepared for another operation, transportation, delay or storage, or inspection. An operation occurs when information is given or received, or when planning or calculating is done.

○ *Transportation:* A *transportation* occurs when the subject is moved from one place to another.

▽ *Delay-Storage-Idle:* A *delay* occurs when the subject is prevented by any condition from having the next operation performed on it, or the next planned operation does not require immediate performance. A *storage* occurs when the subject is kept and protected against unauthorized removal. *Idle* is the delay of a man or a machine; that is, when the subject remains in one place awaiting further action.

□ *Inspection:* An *inspection* occurs when the subject is verified for quality or quantity, or checked in any of its specified physical or chemical characteristics; that is, when the subject is checked or verified, but not changed.

so delicate that it is moved part by part. In any case there is always a "pick-up" waste operation before and a "place" waste operation after a transportation.

A part cannot begin a *delay* or *storage* until it or its container is placed in some particular spot, to wait there until it is needed again. It cannot end a delay or storage until it or its container is picked up. Hence, there are always a "place" waste operation before a delay and a "pick-up" waste operation after a delay.

An *inspection* is almost always made part by part. There is always a "delay" before and a "delay" after an inspection.

In many procedures, a value-adding operation is shown on a process analysis by shading in the symbol. This makes the few value-adding-operations stand out starkly. There is always a "delay" before and after an operation.

Forms are usually provided for convenience in charting. A fragment of such a form is shown in Exhibit III. (For details, see PROCESS ANALYSIS.) The foreman is admonished to be terse, but to put down *all* information of the process as he sees it. After he improves the process, his new chart usually shows a dramatic reduction in operations, distance moved, and time.

When a foreman observes a work situation and records all the elements in chronological order as they occur, he is impressed by the large amount of work that must be done preparatory to, and after, the small amount of work that adds value to the subject, or gives or receives essential information, or plans or calculates. The small amount of *value-adding* work stands out as tiny islands in a huge sea of waste. Writing about the wastes as separate elements makes them stand apart from the elements of work that get something done.

(2) *The Man-Machine Analysis.* * As soon as it has been determined that an operation in a process must be performed (after we have asked, "Why must it be done at all?") the Man-Machine Analysis comes into play. In general, an operation will fall into one of the following two groups: (1) Those operations in which a machine controls the rate of production, such as a milling machine operation. This is termed a "Man-Machine Operation." (2) Those in which the effort of the operator controls the rate of production, such as a hand assembly operation. This is termed a "man-controlled operation."

In a Man-Machine Analysis the transportation includes the body motion of the man. This is because the subjects of the analysis are the *man* and the *machine.* There is no transportation by the machine. It is the transportation of the man, by himself, that is the waste of transportation here.

The man-machine analysis separately records each element of work done by the man and each element of work done by the machine, with the machine elements placed in proper time sequence with the man elements. Special forms are provided here also. Exhibit IV shows a fragment of a Man-Machine Analysis chart.

(3) *The Operation Analysis* is the observation of the activity of the operator himself, and it concerns the use the man makes of his hands and the assistance rendered to the hands by other members of the body, such as the use of a foot to push a pedal. The Process Analysis does not look inside any of the value-adding operations and the Man-Machine Analysis is a broad, over-all look at the man's activity to re-

* In deference to embedded usage, we retain here the masculine locution as applying to men and women operators. ED.

EXHIBIT III

PROCESS ANALYSIS

○ AN OPERATION o A TRANSPORTATION ▽ A DELAY-STORAGE-IDLE □ AN INSPECTION

WHAT IS BEING DONE? WHERE IS IT BEING DONE? WHEN IS IT DONE? WHO IS DOING IT? HOW IS IT BEING DONE? WHY IS IT DONE?

ELEMENT NO.	DESCRIPTION — GIVE ALL DETAILS ALL YOU WILL KNOW ABOUT THE PROCESS FOR YOUR IMPROVEMENT ANALYSIS ARE THE FACTS YOU RECORD HERE WHILE ACTUALLY OBSERVING THE PROCESS	SYMBOL	DISTANCE in feet	TIME in minutes	NOTES - DATA - SKETCHES Things To Check For IMPROVEMENT POSSIBILITIES
1	Regular Pork Trimmings (40%) in truck in Cooler No. 21, where it had been placed in storage by trucker during hog cut operation	▽			Tub 28 X 57 X 23 deep Capacity 1000 lb. approx.
2	Truck grasped by grinder and grinder-helper from Dept. 15 - Sausage.	○			Why not taken directly to cooler No. 9?
3	Truck pushed to grinder in meat preparation room of Sausage Department. Two men needed on account of the unevenness of the floors and weight of truck.	o	375		Grinder secures pork when needed. Two tubs are ground ahead of the frankfurter emulsion grinding operation.
4	Truck released by grinder and helper in position at grinder work area.	○			Will not a tub each of Regular and Jowl Trimmings do just as well, and grind as needed?
5	Till forked into grinder.	▽			Grinder head has 3/16" grid. Grinder is Buffalo 78B, John E. Smith's Sons Co.
6	Pork Trimmings forked from truck and tossed into bowl of grinder by grinder Jowl Pork Trimmings forked simultaneously into the bowl by grinder helper. The two pork trimmings are thus mixed by the grinding operation. The ground fresh pork falls directly into a truck, and it is leveled in the tub as needed. The truck is turned end for end when about two-thirds full	●		9	Grinder bowl is a bit too high--making the forking a bit awkward. Can machine be lowered with little cost? Why not chop directly into tubs?
7	Till trucks of regular pork and jowl trimmings have been all ground, and grinder and helper are ready to move it.	▽			The grinder cannot grind the two pork items as fast as the two men can fork them into the bowl -- hence there is IDLE TIME in this man-machine combination
8	Truck of ground fresh pork grasped by the two men.	○			
9	Truck pushed into Cooler No. 9.	o	55		

Portion of a process analysis of an ingredient, regular pork trimmings, in the manufacture of a frankfurter.

duce idle time, handling time, and value-adding time. The Operation Analysis, to give complete coverage of all phases of work, centers in detail on the right- and left-hand activities of the operator.

In the Operation Analysis an *operation* occurs when a hand is changing material in any of its characteristics or is assembling or disassembling one object from another; or when a hand is used to prepare material, machine, tools, jigs, fixtures, holders, or appliances; and to dispose of the material after the value-adding work.

A transportation occurs when an empty hand is moved to be in position to be used effectively or is moved to a position to become idle, or when a hand is transporting something. Here *inches count,* because of the sheer number of hand movements.

Idle-hold occurs when the hand is idle or is merely holding something.

Exhibit V shows a fragment of a typical Operation analysis.

Motion Economy. After all major wastes under prevailing conditions have been eliminated, the supervisor is ready to study the operator in detail. He will want to be sure that the operator is using his hands properly and that all his actions are performed with a minimum of fatigue and waste motion. To achieve this objective, he must apply the principles of motion economy. Work simplification programs drill the supervisor in the basics of motion economy without going into the refinements of micromotion study and other advanced techniques of the industrial engineer. (See MOTION AND TIME STUDY.)

Motion economy is the last technique to employ, since it is obvious that it will be difficult to get a worker to cooperate by changing his habitual way of doing something if he himself sees all sorts of glaring opportunities for making substantial improvements in planning, handling, and flow of work. His attitude will understandably be, "Why pick on me?" Moreover, the supervisor would be red-faced if he went to a lot of trouble to improve an individual operation only to have it eliminated when purposeful thought is applied to the process as a whole!

EXHIBIT IV

MAN-MACHINE ANALYSIS

○ AN OPERATION   o A TRANSPORTATION   ▽ IDLE   □ AN INSPECTION

MAN							MACHINE
		NAME Luther W______, Jr.	CYCLE TIME 20 Sec.				TYPE Grinding Machine SPECIFICATIONS 12" Wheel, Bonded TOOL-JIG-FIXTURE DATA 12" Level Plate
ELEMENT NO.	DISTANCE	WHAT - HOW - WHY RECORD HERE THE FACTS AND THE KEY POINTS OF WHAT YOU ACTUALLY SAW THE MAN DO	ELEMENT SYMBOL	VALUE ADDING TIME MAN	VALUE ADDING TIME MACHINE	ELEMENT SYMBOL	RECORD HERE WHAT THE MACHINE DID
1		Turns body to left	o			▽	Idle
2		Picks up Casting	○				
3	18"	Carries casting to level plate	o				
4		Checks casting legs on plate	○				
5	12"	Carries casting to grinding machine	o				
6		Grinds casting legs	●	2	2	●	Grind
7	12"	Carries casting to level plate	o			▽	Idle
8		Checks casting legs on level plate	○				
9	12"	Carries casting to machine (grinding)	o				
10		Grinds gates off casting	●	4	4	●	Grind
11		Turns body to right	o			▽	Idle
							Cycle Time - 20 Sec.
12		Tosses ground casting into tote barrel	○				Machine Effectiveness - 30%
							Man Effectiveness - 30%

Portion of a Man-Machine Analysis showing present method, grinding legs and grinding gates on loader casting.

Management Opportunities. Once top management and manufacturing management are themselves convinced of the profit potentials of work simplification, their biggest opportunity for implementing the philosophy is through those in direct charge of the work—the foremen, the first-line supervisors. But the inspiration and gospel must be carried *to* these people. The new (to them) concepts about waste work and useful work, and the techniques of method improvement must be taught to them. They do not come by themselves. (It should be emphasized that the philosophy, techniques, and applications of work simplification are as effective in office work, sales, engineering, or any other activity as they are in manufacturing.)

The foreman who has been properly motivated and who has been given the chance to master the techniques will begin to produce money-saving, profit-increasing ideas almost immediately. He will have the means for a two-pronged attack: first, since he is in daily contact with the way work is being done, he can apply the purposeful thought and methods of analysis to specific departmental operations, and thus directly and in a very practical way complement the professional methods people whose full-time job it is to make improvements.

Second, the foreman who is properly inspired will also carry the spark to the people working for him, and will draw out their suggestions for improvements. Then, if management supports the foremanship program with a system of rewarding rank-and-file employees for suggestions, it will, so to speak, get "compound interest" on its investment.

W. CLEMENTS ZINCK, P.E., Industrial Engineering, formerly Vice President—Operations, Arbogast & Bastion, Inc., Allentown, Pennsylvania

Information Reference

"Dynamic Work Simplification," by W. Clements Zinck, New York, N.Y., Reinhold, 1962), covers the application of work simplification to the foreman on his production job and indicates how top management can develop the necessary climate for a successful program. An early classic is Allan H. Mogensen's "Common Sense Applied to Motion and Time Study," (McGraw-Hill, New York,

EXHIBIT V

OPERATION ANALYSIS

DIE MAKER FILE

LEFT HAND					RIGHT HAND				
ELE-MENT	DIS-TANCE	DESCRIPTION OF ELEMENT	SYMBOL	VALUE ADD'G TIME	VALUE ADD'G TIME	SYMBOL	DESCRIPTION OF ELEMENT	DIS-TANCE	ELE-MENT
1		Picks up insert	○			▽	Holds file		1
2	12"	To filing position	o			o	To insert	12"	2
3		Holds insert	▽		20	●	Files insert at hole to remove rough edge		3
4		Rotates insert	○			▽	Holds file		4
5		Holds insert	▽		20	●	Files at hole		5
6		Rotates insert	○			▽	Holds file		6
7		Holds insert	▽		20	●	Files at hole		7
8	12"	To container	o			o	To relaxed position	12"	8
9		Places insert in container	○			▽	Idle - Holds file		9
		To pick up next insert	o						
		Repeat					Repeat		

Operation Cycle Time - 64 Seconds

Left-Hand Effectiveness - 0%

Right-Hand Effectiveness - 94%

Operation Analysis of filing a hole in a plastic clothes line insert, showing imbalanced use of hands.

1932). Industrial engineering texts treat the subject under "Methods engineering." Case histories of work simplification and articles on phases of it appear frequently in industrial publications.

Cross References: *Method Improvement (and cross references there given).*

WORKERS' COMPENSATION

Workers' Compensation is the statutory system under which an employer is made liable, regardless of fault, for medical care and definite monetary benefits to employees injured in its employment to compensate for loss of wages or earning capacity. It embodies the concept, now generally accepted, that economic loss due to such injury is part of the cost of production and should be incorporated in the price structure. In exchange for this definite liability, for which management can make provision through the purchase of insurance or through self-insurance, the employer is relieved of liability at law with no limit on the amount of damages that may be recovered for such injuries which may be caused by the company's negligence or that of its agents.

History. Prior to the enactment of workers' compensation laws, the employer was faced with extensive and expensive litigation if an employee were injured at work. On the other hand, the employee was faced with a slow and uncertain remedy and with the necessity of paying medical bills and living expenses in the meantime. While one injured employee might eventually obtain a substantial judgment, another might be unable to obtain any recovery at all. Even if a judgment were obtained, it might not be possible to collect it. The uncertainty of the result was increased by the existence of certain common law defenses which the employer could assert: assumption of risk, contributory negligence, and the negligence of a fellow servant. However, even before the enactment of workers' compensation laws, courts and legislatures had begun to limit the application of such defenses.

Dissatisfaction with this situation, by both employers and employees, caused a search for a better remedy. This was found in workers' compensation which provided prompt payment of definite benefits regardless of the question of negligence. The first valid state workers' compensation law was enacted in 1911. Ten states enacted workers' compensation laws in that year. The Federal Government had previously enacted a law covering Government employees engaged in hazardous operations in 1908. A few crude attempts to provide compensation, very limited in scope, were enacted by one or two states about the same time, but most of them were held invalid.

In those days the concept of making an employer liable for an injury where he was not at fault was controversial, and the constitutionality of such laws was often attacked. A law enacted in New York in 1910 providing for compulsory compensation in certain hazardous employment, Chapter 674 Laws of 1910, was held unconstitutional in the case of *Ives v. South Buffalo Railroad Company,* 201 N.Y. 271. Some states adopted constitutional amendments to make certain of the validity of compensation acts. Others adopted elective statutes. Now such laws have gained general acceptance both by employers and labor, and have usually been upheld by the courts. Most of the early workers' compensation acts in this country were patterned somewhat after the British Compensation Act enacted in 1897.

Today there are workers' compensation laws in every state, the District of Columbia, and Puerto Rico, and in some form in most of the countries in the world.

Development of these laws in this country was somewhat curtailed by economic conditions prevailing during the Great Depression of the 1930s, followed by World War II. With the removal of wartime wage and price controls, a sharp escalation of wages and prices occurred. However, workers' compensation benefits, dependent on legislative action, did not keep pace with the wage-price spiral, and Congressional concern developed.

In 1971, President Richard Nixon, pursuant to act of the Congress, appointed a National Commission on State Workmen's Compensation Laws, on which the undersigned had the privilege to serve. The Commission's report aroused a great deal of interest among legislators, administrators, and business and labor groups. Benefit and coverage improvements were recommended, but these were conditioned on other recommendations relating to administration.

Great legislative activity followed submission of the report, directed primarily at benefit and coverage aspects of the problem. Recommendations covering improvements in the operations of the system remained largely unimplemented. At the same time, the courts, as they have in other areas of liability during this period, greatly broadened the concepts of what injuries, illnesses, and disabilities were compensable under those laws. The effect of these developments has had a substantial cost impact. Benefit payments increased from somewhat over $3.5 billion dollars in 1971 to over $10 billion in 1979. The cost of workers' compensation is presently (1980) causing some concern.

Compulsory or Elective. As indicated above, a number of state laws were at one time elective. Today, the laws in all but three states are compulsory. In these states, employers and employees subject to the Act must comply with its provisions. In two additional states, for constitutional reasons, employees but not employers may elect not to be covered. Because of the generally accepted view that coverage under workers' compensation laws is desirable, the right of election is seldom if ever exercised.

Scope and Coverage. It has been estimated that about 88% of employees today are covered by compensation laws. Two large classes of employees that are not fully covered are agricultural employees and domestic servants. Railroad employees engaged in interstate commerce are covered by the Federal Employers' Liability Act. In some states, specific employment, e.g., recipients of charitable aid, professional athletes, executive officers, etc., are excluded. The present trend is to bring practically all employments under the acts. Fourteen states still have numerical exemptions, but in seven, only companies with two or less employees are excluded. The highest exemption is five, in Missouri. Thirty-nine jurisdictions have no numerical exemption provisions for covered employments. In nearly all states an employer can elect voluntarily to bring exempted employments under the act.

Security. Nearly all laws require that an employer subject to the Act must insure or otherwise secure his liability to his employees. This can usually be done through the purchase of insurance from a company authorized to do business in the state. Most states also will permit large employers, who are of sufficient financial stability, to "self-insure" upon making a substantial deposit of money, security, or bonds and assuming the obligation to pay all compensation claims directly. In some states, a form of reciprocal co-insurance known as "group self-insurance" is permitted. In six states and Puerto Rico insurance must be obtained from a monopolistic state compensation fund. These funds were created in the early days of compensation, before the advantages of competitive insurance became apparent. The last of such funds was created 1919. In twelve other states, there are state funds which operate in competition with insurance companies. Most employers obtain coverage from insurance companies rather than from a state fund.

Rates for workers' compensation insurance are scientifically calculated and subject to regulation by the various state insurance commissioners under rate regulatory laws. Early in the operation of workers' compensation laws, it was recognized that the pooling of experience would be of great value in the determination of proper rates. At the request of the National Association of Insurance Commissioners, a national rate making organization, the National Council on Compensation Insurance (One Penn Plaza, New York, N.Y. 10119), was organized in 1922. In some states, however, there are individual state rating bureaus. Presently (1980), increasing attention is being given to the feasibility of allowing greater interplay of competition under such laws, while maintaining the necessary data base.

Rating plans and methods are constantly being reviewed and improved to give the insured the benefit of improved experience. These are designed to give an employer an incentive to maintain effective safety programs. Insurance companies have been among the leaders in the field of safety. They are in a position to assist employers in making such programs effective, to their joint advantage. As a result of cooperative efforts among employers, employees, government, and insurance companies, countrywide, the frequency rate of industrial injuries was reduced between 1926 and 1972 by 68% and the severity rate by 73%. There was a further improvement of 14% between 1972 and 1977 in the new rate of recordable injuries under the system instituted under OSHA (Occupational Safety and Health Act).

Even though many factors have increased workers' compensation costs, overall premiums for workers' compensation amount to only about 2% of payroll, largely because of effective safety work. The security features are a vital part of the compensation system because they assure that the employee will receive all benefits due him or her in the event an injury occurs, and at the same time enable the employer to know or accurately estimate in advance the cost of this protection.

Injuries Covered. Worker's compensation laws of all states cover accidental injuries arising out of and in the course of employment. This has been liberally construed to apply to injuries resulting from a variety of situations related to employment activity. In some states the reference to "accidents" is omitted. In addition, in all states, there is broad coverage of occupational diseases. Formerly, in some states only specifically listed occupational diseases were covered.

The tendency has been constantly to broaden coverage of injuries in workers' compensation laws. This subject is presently (1980) receiving increased attention. Industry is concerned that it may be held liable for conditions which are not causally related to the employment. Others contend that employees are not receiving compensation for disabilities due to exposures which have not been recognized and may be long past. Current laws provide broad coverage for present exposures. Equitable solutions for the effects of long-past exposures which antedate current laws may be more difficult to achieve. This has been attempted in the Federal Black Lung Benefits Act for coal miners under which financing and other problems have developed with costs to the Federal Government, now being transferred in part to private industry, exceeding one billion dollars a year.

Medical Benefits. In all states the employer is

obliged to provide unlimited medical benefits. (At one time a number of states had limitations on such benefits.)

The emphasis in workers' compensation today is on rehabilitation rather than indemnity. It is obviously far preferable to restore the injured employee, if possible, to useful employment than to compensate for any wage loss. The quality of medical and physical care plays a very important part in reaching these results. In most states it is the obligation of the employer and the insurance carrier to supply such care, but in a number of states the employee can obtain such care at the expense of the employer. In actual practice it has been found that some guidance in obtaining the best medical care available is beneficial to the employee.

Indemnity Benefits. Monetary benefits, usually referred to as "compensation," are payable under workers' compensation laws for the following disabilities:

(1) *Temporary Total Disability.* This is the most frequent type of disability. It covers cases where an employee is unable to engage in employment for a limited period of time because of a work-connected injury. Compensation in such cases is usually payable at the rate of 66⅔% of the employee's average weekly wages, subject to a specified weekly maximum and minimum.

In many states, the maximum for injuries occurring in a particular year is adjusted annually to reflect changes in the average state wage. In 30 states, such maximum must equal 100% or more of the state average weekly wage. In some states, the weekly benefit, once established, is adjusted in the future to reflect changes in wage levels or the cost of living in long-term disability and death cases. The maximum applicable in the different states ranges from $650 a week in Alaska to $98 a week in Mississippi. As of July 1, 1980, in forty-two state jurisdictions, the weekly maximum amounted to $150 or more and the average countrywide was $219.82. In some states the weekly maximum is increased if there are dependents.

(2) *Permanent Total Disability.* This is intended to cover cases where the injury is so severe that the employee is permanently unable to return to employment. Fortunately, these cases are infrequent. In some states, certain disabilities such as blindness or loss of two major members are presumed to constitute permanent total disability either conclusively or rebutably. Through remarkable advances in rehabilitation, persons who previously would have been disabled for life are today increasingly returning to useful employment, or at least, they become able to take care of their personal needs without assistance.

Concepts of what constitutes disability are constantly being broadened. Factors other than physical ability to perform work are taken into consideration. In some states, compensation must be paid without a formal finding of permanent total disability where the employee has a considerable degree of earning capacity.

Compensation for permanent total disability is usually payable at the same rate as temporary total disability, but in some states the weekly amount of such compensation is reduced after a certain period of time. As of January 1, 1980, in 45 jurisdictions such benefits were payable for life. In others, there is a monetary overall limit ranging from $42,000 to $120,624.

(3) *Temporary Partial Disability.* This covers cases where an employee temporarily suffers partial wage loss as a result of an injury. This may be due to inability for a time to perform full-time work, or temporarily having to perform lighter duties at a reduced rate. Usually compensation in such cases is payable on the basis of a percentage of the loss in earning capacity subject again to a specified weekly maximum. In one state (Massachusetts), compensation is payable for the full difference in earnings subject to a maximum of $45,000. In a few states a minimum as well as a maximum is specified, but this sometimes causes inequitable results where the difference in earnings happens to be less than the minimum specified.

(4) *Permanent Partial Disability.* This category covers cases where the injury results in a permanent condition which is partially disabling. In most cases, compensation for such conditions is payable for a period specified in a schedule listing such disabilities. These usually refer either to complete or to partial loss or loss of use of specified members. The weekly amount of compensation is usually subject to the maximum and minimum applicable to cases of temporary total disability. The scheduled payments are intended to compensate for possible future loss of earning capacity even though no loss of earnings may be suffered after the healing period. Usually the amount of payment under such a schedule constitutes the full remedy for such injuries, but in a few states additional compensation is payable if

there is actual wage loss. In a few states, benefits for permanent partial disability are based primarily on wage loss.

Naturally, it is not possible to list all permanent partial disabilities in this schedule. Many laws, therefore, provide that in "other cases" compensation is payable on a basis of percentage of loss of earning capacity, subject again to a specified maximum. In some states compensation is payable in such cases on the basis of a percentage of a person as a whole.

Waiting Period. In all states a waiting period of a few days is provided before compensation is payable. In 23 states it is three days, in 22, one week. This is intended to eliminate cases involving very minor injuries for which a very limited amount of compensation would be payable. The loss of wages for this period presents no serious hardship and the administrative cost of providing such benefits would outweigh the benefits which the employee would receive. In all states, if disability extends beyond a specified time (in many states two weeks), benefits become payable from the first day of disability.

Death Benefits. In the event of death due to an injury, payment of funeral expenses and compensation for dependents of the worker are provided in all states. Benefits to children are usually paid until they reach eighteen years of age, or over that age if they are physically incapacitated. In a number of states, the age limit is somewhat extended while a child is a full-time student. Compensation to the widow is usually paid during widowhood. In some states a lump sum payment is made upon remarriage. Usually, death benefits, subject to a weekly maximum, are based on a percentage of the employee's earnings. Subject to this maximum, provisions is usually made for payments to other dependents such as brothers or sisters or parents.

In fourteen states an overall maximum is provided as to either time or amount.

Third Party Actions. Most workers' compensation laws provide for a right of subrogation (i.e., some method of reimbursement for compensation and medical benefits) to the employer and his insurer against the employee's right of action against a third party who may have caused a compensable injury. In the past, these presented no serious problem, being applicable usually to motor vehicle accidents and the like. Under the broadened rules of liability established by the courts with respect to products in recent years, there has been increased litigation involving either machinery or other products used in the employment where the rights of the different parties are more difficult to determine.

Administration. Workers' compensation laws are usually administered by a board or commission or by an individual administrator. In five states such laws are administered by the courts. However, since this is a specialized field, administration by persons who devote full time to this work is generally deemed preferable.

Payment is made in about nine out of ten of the cases without controversy. The relatively simple remedy and the avoidance of litigation are an important feature of the workers' compensation system.

Information on the operation of the law in a particular state may be obtained from the appropriate administrative agency.

ANDREW KALMYKOW, Consultant, American Insurance Association, New York, New York

Information References

Associations:

International Association of Industrial Accident Boards and Commissions.
Alliance of American Insurers.
American Insurance Association.
American Bar Association, Section of Insurance, Negligence and Compensation Law, American Bar Center, Chicago.

Publications:

Report, National Commission of State Workers' Compensation Laws, Superintendent of Documents, U.S. Government Printing Office, Washington, D.C.
Proceedings, and Newsletter, International Association of Industrial Accident Boards and Commissions.
Workers' Compensation Bulletins, U.S. Department of Labor, U.S. Government Printing Office, Washington, D.C.
"Compensation Laws" (annotated), American Insurance Association, New York.
"Analysis of Workers' Compensation Laws," in chart form, published annually, Chamber of Commerce of the United States, Washington, D.C.

Texts:

Larson, Arthur, "The Law of Workmen's Compensation, New York, Matthew Bender & Co., 1952, with annual supplements.
Millus, Albert J. and Gentile, Willard J., "Workers' Compensation Law and Insurance," New York, Roberts Publishing Co., 1976.
Schneider, W. R., "Schneider's Workers' Compensation," St. Louis, Mo., Schneider Publishing Co., permanent edition with annual supplements.

Cross References: *Employee Benefit Plans; Occupational Health; Occupational Safety and Health Act of 1970; Safety and Health in the Workplace.*

Z

ZERO-BASE BUDGETING

Zero-Base Budgeting became a "buzzword" in management circles ever since President Carter, upon assuming office in January of 1977, announced that he was setting the future Federal budgeting process on the concepts set forth in "Zero-Base Budgeting: A Practical Management Tool for Evaluating Expenses," by Peter A. Pyhrr [1]. Actually, the book was published in 1973, and the term and technique were introduced by Pyhrr, a management consultant, in an article in *Harvard Business Review* for November-December 1970 [2]. Fortunately for the author, Mr. Carter read that article, and, in 1971 when he was governor of Georgia, he hired the consultant to install the system in that state. As of this writing, estimates of ongoing installations vary from 30 to 100, including states and cities and a number of companies in the private sector. Organizational impacts and effects are discussed in a recent American Management Associations Survey Report [3].

One commmercial user reporting pronounced success with the system is Florida Power and Light Company. In March of 1977, the process was adopted for all FPL General Office staff departments. The essence of the program as reported by the company's director of Management Control, Ben Dady, is that managers start with "zero" budget dollars each year, then prove the case—activity by activity or project by project—for all the dollars they propose to spend. New and existing problems are placed on an equal footing, since both are being rated according to their relative effectiveness. Each manager or supervisor activity is thoroughly identified and then evaluated by considering (1) better alternative ways, and (2) different levels of performing that same function. Then a ranking plan establishes relative priorities.

While much of the publicity attending zero-base budgeting has given the impression that it is a revolutionary new technique, that is not the case. The process has many similarities to PPBS (Planning-Programming-Budgeting System), introduced in many governmental agencies and jurisdictions in the 1960s. (See PUBLIC ADMINISTRATION.) Both concepts involve analyzing the inputs and outputs for specific programs, rather than relying exclusively on the traditional line-item format.

As described by Pyhrr, the philosophy and procedures used to install zero-base budgeting in industry and government are almost identical, with the mechanics differing slightly to fit the needs of each user. The process requires each manager to justify his entire budget request in detail, and puts the burden of proof on him to justify why he should spend *any* money.

Each manager must prepare a "decision package" for each activity or operation, and this package includes an analysis of cost, purpose, alternative courses of action, measures of performance, consequences of not performing the activity, and benefits. The analysis of alternatives as required by zero-base budgeting introduces a new concept to typical budgeting techniques. Managers must first identify different ways of performing each activity—such as centralizing versus decentralizing operations, or evaluating the economy of in-house print shops versus commercial printers.

In addition, zero-base budgeting requires that managers identify different levels of effect for performing each activity. They must identify a minimum level of spending—often about 75% of their current operating level—and then identify in *separate* decision packages the costs and benefits of additional levels of spending for that activity. This analysis forces every manager to consider and evaluate a level of spending lower than his current operating level; gives management the alternative of eliminating an activity or choosing from several levels of effort; and allows substantial tradeoffs and shifts in expenditure levels among organizational units.

Once the decision packages have been developed, they must be ranked or listed in order of importance. The ranking process allows each manager to identify his priorities explicitly, merges decision packages for ongoing and new programs into one ranking, and allows top management to evaluate and compare the relative needs and priorities of different organization units to make funding decisions.

Advantages. Advantages of zero-base budgeting as enumerated by Pyhrr are as follows: It provides top management with detailed information concerning the money needed to accomplish desired ends. It spotlights redundancies and duplication of effort among departments, focuses on dollars needed for programs rather than on the percentage increase or decrease from the previous year, specifies priorities within and among departments and divisions, allows comparisons across the organizational lines as to the respective priorities funded, and allows a performance audit to determine whether each activity or operation has performed as promised.

Changes in desired expenditure levels do not require the recycling of budget inputs, but the decision package ranking identifies those activities and operations (decision packages) to be added or deleted to produce the budget change. The list of ranking packages can also be used during the operating year to identify activities to be reduced or expanded if allowable expenditure levels change or actual costs vary from the budget. The process also gives top management a good tool with which to judge the performance of managers and employees, and gives managers a greater sense of responsibility for their budgets.

Evaluation. A recent issue of *Harvard Business Review* [4] reports upon a thorough review of the burgeoning literature on zero-base budgeting, giving equal attention to the cons as well as the pros. The authors' review shows that many organizations have tried the technique in one form or another but found that it did not work. Properly implemented, however, zero-base budgeting can be a considerable improvement over the typical budgeting approach. It is noted that the number and nature of decision packages will vary from organization to organization. For example, the school district of Greece, N.Y., identified approximately 150 packages for the elementary, junior high, and senior high schools. The State of Georgia identified approximately 11,000 packages for its 1972–1973 fiscal year. It seems logical that any large organization can expect to have several thousand packages.

Setting priorities on the basis of the decision packages is not easy, since it is almost impossible for a group of executives in a large organization to have the expertise and the time to rank and establish priorities for thousands of packages. One solution, says the HBR article, is to have each manager rank his own packages, and then each senior executive rank the packages of all managers who report to him. This is the approach used by Texas Instruments, a zero-base budgeting pioneer. Another approach is to let each level of management approve given amounts or percentages of those packages within its own area of responsibility. Thus the first level of review can rank and fund up to 50% of the proposed expenditures. The next level(s) may handle funding in the 50% to 80% range. Finally, top management only has to concentrate on the remaining part of the budget.

There appears to be general agreement that zero-base budgeting requires a lot of time, money, and paperwork. Developing decision packages takes a great deal of time. And a big problem is the review process. "Reviewing thousands of decision packages," says the HBR report, "is a monumental burden; reviewing them each year is a boring, not-too-productive Herculean task." The authors' final summation: "If you are dissatisfied with your present budgeting system, or are uneasy about the magnitude of some of your administrative programs, you will find that zero-base budgeting provides you with a systematic method of addressing your problems . . . It requires training, lots of time, lots of paperwork and measurements that enable every decision package to be ranked. . . . There is good and bad in zero-base budgeting."

Carl Heyel, Management Counsel, Manhasset, New York

References Cited

[1] Pyhrr, Peter A., "Zero-Base Budgeting: A Practical Management Tool for Evaluating Expenses," New York, Wiley, 1973.

[2] Pyhrr, Peter A., "Zero-Base Budgeting," *Harvard Business Review,* November-December 1970.

[3] Austin, L. Allan, "Zero-Base Budgeting: Organizational Impacts and Effects," An AMA Survey Report, New York, American Management Associations, AMACOM Div., 1977.

[4] Suver, James D. and Brown, Ray L., "Where Does Zero-Base Budgeting Work?,"*Harvard Business Review,* November-December 1977.

Cross References: *Budgeting (and cross references there given).*

ZERO DEFECTS

In recent years, American industry has made intensive efforts aimed at *perfect* performance—100%, not 95% or 90%. To achieve such excellence, the Martin Company of Orlando, Fla. in 1962 launched its so-called **Zero De-**

fects program, the focal point of which was *employee motivation.* Its success on an Army weapon system led to its adoption by the Army Missile Command, and early in 1964 the Assistant Secretary of Defense for Installations and Logistics gave it the full impetus of the Department of Defense. Since then, copies or variations of the Martin program have been adopted by industry in general. Successful programs have been reported by General Electric's Flight Propulsion Division, Litton Industries, Thiokol Chemical, Autonetics Div. of North American Aviation, Westinghouse, and many other companies.

By the end of 1966 there were an estimated 7,500 plants with Zero Defects types of programs. The vast majority of these were in plants not linked to the aerospace and defense industries where the movement got its start—plants ranging in size from small (under 250 employees) to operations of large corporations. Most of the programs use Martin's popular "Zero Defects" title; many have variations of their own: Autonetics Division of North American Aviation calls its program PRIDE, for Personal Responsibility in Daily Effort. Westinghouse calls its program, reported to be somewhat wider in scope than most, EFP, for Error Free Performance.

Westinghouse described its quality-motivation concept and program in its first anniversary report on EFP in the following manner:

> It is a program designed to instill in every employee a more conscientious *attitude* toward the day-to-day performance of his work. It is a concept built around a simple theme—*to do the job right the first time.*
>
> In the past we have placed most of the emphasis on a comprehensive system of detecting errors to insure a quality product. EFP does not eliminate defect detection systems; they will always be needed. The EFP program stresses the principle of *prevention.*
>
> EFP simply emphasizes the individual's contribution to the quality of work, the importance of individual responsibility, and the need to develop to a greater degree a sense of pride in workmanship.
>
> Until now employees have had less reason to shoot for error-free performance because they have known that an elaborate system to detect errors would catch any slips. The basic inconsistency in our previous approach to employees should be obvious. We asked them to produce a quality product, but because we expected them to fail, we developed an elaborate system to find the mistakes!
>
> This program is not confined to the manufacturing departments. It embraces all areas, for errors can occur at any level in every department in all divisions. Every employee, regardless of his position, must recognize the simple truth that his output is someone else's input. A seemingly small error committed at one level can produce a monumental and expensive catastrophy.

Publicity. Hard-hitting internal and external publicity help assure the success of a Zero Defects program—with a special bang on kick-off day. Westinghouse, for example, in its initial dramatization asked employees to sign a large, prominently placed EFP scroll, or a pledge book or cards, pledging themselves to strive for error-free performance in their daily work. The scrolls and books, exhibited in each plant, soon included the names of thousands of employees.

Goals. Realistic, achievable goals are the essence of a successful ZD program. Focus is on the identification and elimination of the *causes* of errors. Beyond specific causes of specific errors, workable objectives spelled out in the Westinghouse program include: (1) general job performance factors such as cost and schedule control and improvement, adherence to procedures, documented departures from standards, response to requests for information and assistance, etc., and (2) individual performance as evidenced by punctuality, safety consciousness, housekeeping, material handling, thoroughness in documenting agreements and technical information, etc.

Classifying Errors. The following Westinghouse check list classifying errors will serve as a practical guide for supervisory forces in any company:

(1) Failure to do things according to plans.
(2) Work that for any reason requires rework before delivery.
(3) Work that is acceptable in all respects except that it could have been done for less cost.
(4) Work to quality standards below those required by customers or by the Company.
(5) Work to quality standards above those required by the customer in all cases where there has been a determination that the customer's standards are sound and practical.
(6) Failure to perform detailed tasks as required by schedule.
(7) Failure to preplan work in detail, and failure to instruct each worker in these details. Failure to maintain surveillance and follow-through while work is in progress, so that necessary corrective action can be taken before the work is completed.
(8) Failure to manage costs effectively.
(9) Work that is otherwise acceptable, but in some way encourages the commission of errors by others or results in higher costs or in late delivery.

(10) Items in cost estimating that lead to higher quotations than are actually justifiable.
(11) Omission of items from cost estimates.
(12) Failure to meet budget.

Error-Rate Measurements. In the Westinghouse program, every supervisor is required to determine those functions in his area which should be measured for improvement. The next step is to establish a reviewing or counting method. Certain operations have a review function naturally assigned, and the location of this review function may give an automatic mode of counting errors. Other methods of counting errors may involve sampling.

Performance can be computed by the following formula:

$$\text{Performance} = 100 - \frac{\text{error-containing items}}{\text{error-free items}} \times 100$$

In some plants using EFP, each foreman is required to establish a goal for the quarter ahead. The ultimate goal, of course, is 100%. The interim goal can be halfway between the first reading and 100. This goal is changed each quarter to the half-way point between the best performance of the past quarter and 100. Results are charted and posted for all to see.

Final evaluation for Error Free Performance is made by the following formula:

$$\text{Performance for the current month} + \frac{\text{performance for current month}}{\text{average performance for previous 3 months}} \times 100$$

It will be noted that the above formula emphasizes improvement as well as actual performance. Thus a foreman could select an area where performance is almost perfect and have a high first factor, but he would not have as good an improvement factor as he would with an area where errors had been common.

Recognition and Awards. In ZD programs, employees and supervisory personnel can win awards either as groups or individuals. Types of awards and the basis for granting them can be worked up by an Awards Committee. Full publicity should be given through recognition in employee publications, bulletin-board postings, presentations at special employee gatherings, and the like.

Results. Critics of ZD have called such programs and similar programs relying heavily on exhortation and propaganda as "gimmicks"—transient fads soon to be replaced with other highly publicized programs with a "catchy" title. As was to be expected, there has been a decline in discussion of and publicity about ZD since the initial fanfare. However, most programs achieved constructive initial impact, and often quite substantial gains. EFP at Westinghouse turned in an admirable record for the first year of operations, covered in its 1965 report. In that year, fourteen divisions adopted the program, and at year's end sixteen more were actively planning similar programs. Annualized savings of $1.8 million were directly attributed to ZD, and it was estimated that $8 million per year in savings would be attainable if all Westinghouse divisions adopted EFP.

The following commentary by one critic [1] provides a balancing appraisal:

> Unfortunately, some managements allowed Zero Defects to replace sound analytical quality control procedures, and inevitably this proved to be detrimental to quality and profits. Underemphasis of study and analysis resulting from overemphasis of propaganda under such circumstances sets the stage for neglect in correction of management-controllable causes of trouble. Complete dependence should not be placed on the employees to correct causes of trouble, most of which are not really employee-controllable. If this is done, negative motivation results, and the programs tend to decline in effectiveness.

CARL HEYEL, Management Counsel, Manhasset, New York

Information References

Heyel, Carl, "Zero Defects," Part 3 of Chap. 3 in Heyel, Carl, ed., "The Foreman's Handbook," 4th ed., New York, McGraw-Hill, 1967.

Jones, Warren E., "Error Control in Office Operations," Chap. 10 in Sec. 5, in Heyel, Carl, ed., "Handbook of Modern Office Management and Administrative Services," Melbourne, Fla., Krieger, repr. 1980.

Ludmer, Henry, "Zero Defects," *Industrial Management,* April 1969.

"Zero Defects Workshop for Supervisors," Washington. D.C., Army Materiel Command.

Reference Cited

[1] Jones, Warren E., as given above.

Cross References: *Quality Control Circles; Quality Control and Quality Assurance.*

APPENDIX A

UNIVERSITIES AND COLLEGES

AACSB Accredited

*Universities and Colleges Offering Programs in Business Administration**

University of Akron, Akron, Ohio 44325 (UM)
University of Alabama, University, Alabama 35486 (UM)
University of Alabama in Birmingham, Birmingham, Alabama 35294
University of Alberta, Edmonton, Alberta, Canada (UM)
Appalachian State University, Boone, North Carolina 28608 (U)
University of Arizona, Tucson, Arizona 85721 (UM)
Arizona State University, Tempe, Arizona 85281 (UM)
University of Arkansas, Fayetteville, Arkansas 72701 (UM)
University of Arkansas at Little Rock, Little Rock, Arkansas 72204 (U)
Arkansas State University, State University, Arkansas 72467 (U)
Atlanta University, Atlanta, Georgia 30314 (M)
Auburn University, Auburn, Alabama 36830 (U)
Stephen F. Austin State University, Nacogdoches, Texas 75962 (U)

Babson College, Babson Park, Massachusetts 02157 (U)
Ball State University, Muncie, Indiana 47306 (U)
The Bernard M. Baruch College, the City University of New York, New York, New York 10010 (U)
Baylor University, Waco, Texas 76706 (UM)
Boise State University, Boise, Idaho 83725 (U)
Boston College, Chestnut Hill, Massachusetts 02167 (UM)
Boston University, Boston, Massachusetts 02215 (UM)
Bowling Green State University, Bowling Green, Ohio 43403 (UM)

* Accredited by the American Assembly of Collegiate Schools of Business, 11500 Olive Street Road, Suite 142, St. Louis, Missouri 63141. U = Undergraduate; M = Masters. (See also MANAGEMENT EDUCATION: Professional Degrees.)

Bradley University, Peoria, Illinois 61625 (U)
University of Bridgeport, Bridgeport, Connecticut 06602 (U)
Brigham Young University, Provo, Utah 84602 (UM)

University of California, Berkeley, California 94720 (UM)
University of California at Los Angeles, Los Angeles, California 90024 (M)
California State College at Bakersfield, Bakersfield, California 93309 (U)
California State University at Chico, Chico, California 95929 (UM)
California State University at Fresno, Fresno, California 93740 (UM)
California State University at Fullerton, Fullerton, California 92634 (UM)
California State University at Hayward, Hayward, California 94542 (U)
California State University at Long Beach, Long Beach, California 90840 (UM)
California State University at Los Angeles, Los Angeles, California 90032 (UM)
California State University at Northridge, Northridge, California 91140 (U)
California State University at Sacramento, Sacramento, California 95819 (UM)
Canisius College, Buffalo, New York 14208 (U)
Carnegie-Mellon University, Pittsburgh, Pennsylvania 15213 (M)
Case Western Reserve University, Cleveland, Ohio 44106 (UM)
University of Central Florida, Orlando, Florida 32816 (UM)
University of Chicago, Chicago, Illinois 60637 (M)
University of Cincinnati, Cincinnati, Ohio 45221 (UM)
Clarkson College, Potsdam, New York 13676 (U)
Clemson University, Clemson, South Carolina 29631 (U)
Cleveland State University, Cleveland, Ohio 44115 (UM)

University of Colorado, Boulder, Colorado 80309 (UM)
Colorado State University, Fort Collins, Colorado 80523 (UM)
Columbia University, New York, New York 10027 (M)
University of Connecticut, Storrs, Connecticut 06268 (UM)
Cornell University, Ithaca, New York 14853 (M)
Creighton University, Omaha, Nebraska 68178 (U)

Dartmouth College, Hanover, New Hampshire 03755 (M)
University of Delaware, Newark, Delaware 19711 (U)
University of Denver, Denver, Colorado 80208 (UM)
Depaul University, Chicago, Illinois 60604 (UM)
University of Detroit, Detroit, Michigan 48221 (UM)
Drake University, Des Moines, Iowa 50311 (UM)
Drexel University, Philadelphia, Pennsylvania 19104 (UM)
Duke University, Durham, North Carolina 27706 (M)
Duquesne University, Pittsburgh, Pennsylvania 15219 (UM)

East Carolina University, Greenville, North Carolina 27834 (UM)
East Texas State University, Commerce, Texas 75428 (U)
Eastern Michigan University, Ypsilanti, Michigan 48197 (U)
Eastern Washington University, Cheney, Washington 89004 (U)
Emory University, Atlanta, Georgia 30322 (UM)

University of Florida, Gainesville, Florida 32611 (UM)
Florida Atlantic University, Boca Raton, Florida 33432 (UM)
Florida State University, Tallahassee, Florida 32306 (UM)
Fordham University, New York, New York 10023 (U)
Fort Lewis College, Durango, Colorado 81301 (U)

The George Washington University, Washington, DC 20052 (U)
University of Georgia, Athens, Georgia 30602 (UM)
Georgia Institute of Technology, Atlanta, Georgia 30332 (UM)
Georgia Southern College, Statesboro, Georgia 30458 (U)
Georgia State University, Atlanta, Georgia 30303 (UM)

Harvard University, Boston, Massachusetts 02163 (M)
University of Hawaii, Honolulu, Hawaii 96822 (UM)
Hofstra University, Hempstead, New York 11550 (U)
University of Houston, Houston, Texas 77004 (UM)
Howard University, Washington, DC 20059 (UM)

Idaho State University, Pocatello, Idaho 83209 (UM)
University of Illinois at Chicago Circle, Chicago, Illinois 60680 (U)
University of Illinois at Urbana-Champaign, Urbana, Illinois 61801 (UM)
Indiana State University, Terre Haute, Indiana 47809 (U)
Indiana University, Bloomington, Indiana 47405 (UM)
University of Iowa, Iowa City, Iowa 52242 (UM)

John Carroll University, Cleveland, Ohio 44118 (U)

University of Kansas, Lawrence, Kansas 66045 (UM)
Kansas State University, Manhattan, Kansas 66506 (UM)
Kent State University, Kent, Ohio 44242 (UM)
University of Kentucky, Lexington, Kentucky 40506 (UM)

Lamar University, Beaumont, Texas 77710 (U)
Lehigh University, Bethlehem, Pennsylvania 18015 (UM)
Louisiana State University, Baton Rouge, Louisiana 70803 (UM)
Louisiana Tech University, Ruston, Louisiana 71272 (UM)
Loyola University, Chicago, Illinois 60611 (UM)

Loyola University, New Orleans, Louisiana 70118 (UM)

University of Maine at Orono, Orono, Maine 04469 (U)
Marquette University, Milwaukee, Wisconsin 53233 (UM)
University of Maryland, College Park, Maryland 20742 (UM)
University of Massachusetts, Amherst, Massachusetts 01003 (UM)
Massachusetts Institute of Technology, Cambridge, Massachusetts 02139 (UM)
Morris State University, Memphis, Tennessee 38152 (UM)
University of Miami, Coral Gables, Florida 33124 (UM)
Miami University, Oxford, Ohio 45056 (UM)
The University of Michigan, Ann Arbor, Michigan 48109 (UM)
Michigan State University, East Lansing, Michigan 48824 (UM)
Middle Tennessee State University, Murfreesboro, Tennessee 37132 (U)
University of Minnesota, Minneapolis, Minnesota 55455 (UM)
University of Mississippi, University, Mississippi 38677 (UM)
Mississippi State University, Mississippi State, Mississippi 39762 (UM)
University of Missouri at Columbia, Columbia, Missouri 65211 (UM)
University of Missouri at Kansas City, Kansas City, Missouri 64110 (UM)
University of Missouri at St. Louis, St. Louis, Missouri 63121 (UM)
University of Montana, Missoula, Montana 59801 (U)
Murray State University, Murray, Kentucky 42071 (U)

University of Nebraska at Lincoln, Lincoln, Nebraska 68588 (UM)
The University of Nebraska at Omaha, Omaha, Nebraska, 68101 (U)
University of Nevada at Reno, Reno, Nevada 89557 (UM)
The University of New Mexico, Albuquerque, New Mexico 87131 (UM)
New Mexico State University, Las Cruces, New Mexico 88003 (U)
University of New Orleans, New Orleans, Louisiana 70122 (UM)
New York University at Washington Square, New York, New York 10003 (U)
New York University Graduate School of Business Administration, 100 Trinity Pl., New York, New York 10006 (M)
State University of New York at Albany, Albany, New York 12222 (UM)
State University of New York at Buffalo, Buffalo, New York 14214 (UM)
University of North Carolina, Chapel Hill, North Carolina 27514
North Carolina A&T State University, Greensboro, North Carolina 27411 (U)
University of North Florida, Jacksonville, Florida 32216 (U)
North Texas State University, Denton, Texas 76203 (UM)
Northeast Louisiana University, Monroe, Louisiana 71209 (UM)
Northeastern University, Boston, Massachusetts 92115 (UM)
Northern Arizona University, Flagstaff, Arizona 86011 (UM)
Northern Illinois University, DeKalb, Illinois 60115 (UM)
Northwestern University, Evanston, Illinois 60201 (M)
University of Notre Dame, Notre Dame, Indiana 46556 (UM)

Ohio State University, Columbus, Ohio 43210 (UM)
Ohio University, Athens, Ohio 45701 (UM)
University of Oklahoma, Norman, Oklahoma 73019 (UM)
Oklahoma State University, Stillwater, Oklahoma 74074 (UM)
Old Dominion University, Norfolk, Virginia 23508 (UM)
University of Oregon, Eugene, Oregon 97403 (UM)
Oregon State University, Corvallia, Oregon 79331 (UM)

Pacific Lutheran University, Tacoma, Washington 98447 (UM)
Pan American University, Edinburg, Texas 78539 (U)
University of Pennsylvania, Philadelphia, Pennsylvania 19104 (UM)
The Pennsylvania State University, University Park, Pennsylvania 16802 (UM)
University of Pittsburgh, Pittsburgh, Pennsylvania 15260 (UM)
University of Portland, Portland, Oregon 97203 (U)

Portland State University, Portland, Oregon 97207 (U)

Purdue University, West Lafayette, Indiana 47907 (UM)

Rensselaer Polytechnic Institute, Troy, New York 12181 (U)

University of Rhode Island, Kingston, Rhode Island 02881 (UM)

University of Richmond, Richmond, Virginia 23173 (U)

University of Rochester, Rochester, New York 14627 (M)

Roosevelt University, Chicago, Illinois 60605 (U)

Rutgers—The State University of New Jersey, Newark, New Jersey 07102 (M)

St. Cloud State University, St. Cloud, Minnesota 56301 (U)

St. John's University, Jamaica, New York 11439 (U)

Saint Louis University, St. Louis, Missouri 63108 (UM)

University of San Diego, San Diego, California 92110 (U)

San Diego State University, San Diego, California 92182 (UM)

University of San Francisco, San Francisco, California 94117 (U)

San Francisco State University, San Francisco, California 94132 (UM)

San Jose State University, San Jose, California 95192 (UM)

University of Santa Clara, Santa Clara, California 96053 (UM)

Seattle University, Seattle, Washington 98122 (UM)

Seton Hall University, South Orange, New Jersey 07079 (U)

University of South Alabama, Mobile, Alabama 36688 (UM)

University of South Carolina, Columbia, South Carolina 29208 (UM)

University of South Dakota, Vermillion, South Dakota 57069 (UM)

University of South Florida, Tampa, Florida 33620 (UM)

University of Southern California, Los Angeles, California 90007 (UM)

Southern Illinois University at Carbondale, Carbondale, Illinois 62901 (UM)

Southern Illinois University at Edwardsville, Edwardsville, Illinois 62026 (UM)

Southern Methodist University, Dallas, Texas 75275 (UM)

University of Southern Mississippi, Hattiesburg, Mississippi 39401 (UM)

Stanford University, Stanford, California 94305 (M)

Syracuse University, Syracuse, New York 13210 (UM)

Temple University, Philadelphia, Pennsylvania 19122 (UM)

University of Tennessee at Knoxville, Knoxville, Tennessee 37916 (UM)

Tennessee Technological University, Cookeville, Tennessee 38501 (U)

The University of Texas at Arlington, Arlington, Texas 76019 (UM)

The University of Texas at Austin, Austin, Texas 78712 (UM)

University of Texas at San Antonio, San Antonio, Texas 78285 (UM)

Texas A&M University, College Station, Texas 77843 (UM)

Texas Christian University, Fort Worth, Texas 76129 (UM)

Texas Southern University, Houston, Texas 77004 (U)

Texas Tech University, Lubbock, Texas 79409 (U)

The University of Toledo, Toledo, Ohio 43606 (UM)

Tulane University, New Orleans, Louisiana, 70118 (M)

University of Tulsa, Tulsa, Oklahoma 74104 (UM)

University of Utah, Salt Lake City, Utah 84112 (UM)

Utah State University, Logan, Utah 84322 (U)

Vanderbilt University, Nashville, Tennessee 37203 (M)

Villanova University, Villanova, Pennsylvania 19085 (U)

University of Virginia, Colgate Darden Graduate School, Charlottesville, Virginia 22906 (M)

University of Virginia, McIntire School of Commerce, Charlottesville, Virginia 22903 (U)

Virginia Commonwealth University, Richmond, Virginia 23284 (U)

Virginia Polytechnic Institute and State University, Blackburg, Virginia 24061 (UM)

University of Washington, Seattle, Washington 98195 (UM)
Washington and Lee University, Lexington, Virginia (U)
Washington State University, Pullman, Washington 99164 (UM)
Washington University, St. Louis, Missouri 68130 (UM)
Wayne State University, Detroit, Michigan 48202 (U)
West Virginia University, Morgantown, West Virginia 26506 (UM)
Western Illinois University, Macomb, Illinois 61455 (U)
Western Michigan University, Kalamazoo, Michigan 49008 (U)
Wichita State University, Wichita, Kansas 67208 (UM)
College of William and Mary, Williamsburg, Virginia 23185 (UM)
Winthrop College, Rock Hill, South Carolina 29730 (U)
University of Wisconsin—Eau Claire at Eau Claire, Wisconsin 54701 (U)
University of Wisconsin at Madison, Madison, Wisconsin 53706 (UM)
University of Wisconsin at Milwaukee, Milwaukee, Wisconsin 53201 (UM)
University of Wisconsin at Oshkosh, Oshkosh, Wisconsin 54901 (UM)
University of Wisconsin at Whitewater, Whitewater, Wisconsin 53190 (UM)
Wright State University, Dayton, Ohio 45435 (UM)
University of Wyoming, Laramie, Wyoming 82071 (U)

APPENDIX B

SOURCES OF INFORMATION

*Associations, Societies, Special Services, and Publishers Mentioned in Text**

ACADEMIC PRESS, 111 Fifth Ave., New York, N.Y. 10003

ACADEMY OF MANAGEMENT, Mississippi State University, Mississippi State, Miss. 39762

ACADEMY OF POLITICAL SCIENCE, 619 W. 114th St., New York, N.Y. 10025

ADDISON-WESLEY PUBLISHING COMPANY, INC., Jacob Way, Reading, Mass. 01867

ADMINISTRATIVE MANAGEMENT SOCIETY, Willow Grove, Pa. 19090

ADULT EDUCATION ASSOCIATION OF THE U.S.A., 1810 18th St. N.W., Washington, D.C. 20006

ADVERTISING PUBLICATIONS, INC., 740 Rush St., Chicago, Ill. 60611

AIR FREIGHT ASSOCIATION OF AMERICA, 1730 Rhode Island Ave. N.W., Suite 607, Washington, D.C. 20036

AIR FREIGHT FORWARDERS ASSOCIATION, now AIR FREIGHT ASSOCIATION OF AMERICA

ALCOHOLICS ANONYMOUS, 468 Park Ave. South, New York, N.Y. 10016

ALDINE PUBLISHING COMPANY, 200 Saw Mill River Road, Hawthorne, N.Y. 10532

ALFRED PUBLISHING CO., INC., 15335 Morrison St. Sherman Oaks, Calif. 91403

ALLIANCE OF AMERICAN INSURERS, 20 N. WACKER DRIVE, CHICAGO, ILL. 60606

ALLYN AND BACON, INC., 470 Atlantic Ave., Boston, Mass. 02210

AMERICAN BUSINESS COMMUNICATION ASSOCIATION (ABCA), 317b David Kinley Hall, University of Illinois, Urbana, Ill. 61801

AMERICAN ACADEMY OF OCCUPATIONAL MEDICINE, 150 N. Wacker Drive, Chicago, Ill. 60606

AMERICAN ACADEMY OF POLITICAL AND SOCIAL SCIENCE, 3937 Chestnut St., Philadelphia, Pa. 19104

AMERICAN ACCOUNTING ASSOCIATION, 5717 Bessie Dr., Sarasota, Fla. 33577

AMERICAN ADVERTISING FEDERATION, 1225 Connecticut Ave. N.W., Washington, D.C. 20036

AMERICAN ARBITRATION ASSOCIATION, 140 W. 51st St., New York, N.Y. 10020

AMERICAN ASSEMBLY OF COLLEGIATE SCHOOLS OF BUSINESS, 11500 Olive Street Road, Suite 142, St. Louis, Mo., 63141

AMERICAN ASSOCIATION FOR THE ADVANCEMENT OF SCIENCE, 1515 Massachusetts Ave., N.W. Washington, D.C. 20005

AMERICAN ASSOCIATION OF ADVERTISING AGENCIES, 200 Park Ave., New York, N.Y. 10017

AMERICAN ASSOCIATION OF COLLEGIATE SCHOOLS OF BUSINESS, now AMERICAN ASSEMBLY OF COLLEGIATE SCHOOLS OF BUSINESS

AMERICAN ASSOCIATION OF ENGINEERING SOCIETIES, 345 E. 47th St., New York, N.Y. 10017

AMERICAN ASSOCIATION OF INDUSTRIAL EDITORS, now INTERNATIONAL ASSOCIATION OF BUSINESS COMMUNICATORS

AMERICAN ASSOCIATION OF INDUSTRIAL MANAGEMENT, 7425 Old York Road, Philadelphia, Pa. 19126

AMERICAN ASSOCIATION OF INDUSTRIAL NURSES, now AMERICAN ASSOCIATION OF OCCUPATIONAL HEALTH NURSES

AMERICAN ASSOCIATION OF OCCUPATIONAL HEALTH NURSES, 575 Lexington Ave., New York, N.Y. 10022

AMERICAN ASSOCIATION FOR PUBLIC OPINION RESEARCH, P.O. Box 17, Princeton, N.J. 08540

AMERICAN BAR ASSOCIATION, 1155 E. 60th St., Chicago, Ill. 60637

AMERICAN BUSINESS COMMUNICATION ASSOCIATION, University of Illinois, Urbana, Ill. 61801

AMERICAN BUSINESS PRESS, 205 E. 42nd St., New York, N.Y. 10017

AMERICAN CHEMICAL SOCIETY, 1155 16th St. N.W., Washington, D.C. 20036

* Certain consulting firms, manufacturers, and academic institutions are included when they have been cited in the text as sources of published material.

AMERICAN COLLECTORS ASSOCIATION, 4040 W. 70th St., Minneapolis, Minn. 55435

AMERICAN CONFERENCE OF GOVERNMENTAL INDUSTRIAL HYGIENISTS, P.O. BOX 1937, CINCINNATI, OHIO 45201

AMERICAN COUNCIL OF INDEPENDENT LABORATORIES, INC., 1725 K St. N.W., Washington, D.C. 20006

AMERICAN COUNCIL OF LIFE INSURANCE, 1850 K St. N.W., Washington D.C. 20006

AMERICAN DEFENSE PREPAREDNESS, 1700 N. Moore St., Suite 900, Arlington, Va. 22209

AMERICAN ECONOMIC ASSOCIATION, 1313 21st Ave. S., Nashville, Tenn. 37212

AMERICAN ENTERPRISE INSTITUTE FOR PUBLIC POLICY, 1150 17th St. N.W., Washington, D.C. 20036

AMERICAN FEDERATION OF INFORMATION PROCESSING SOCIETIES, 1815 Lynn St., Suite 800, Arlington, Va. 22209

AMERICAN FEDERATION OF LABOR AND CONGRESS OF INDUSTRIAL ORGANIZATIONS, 815 16th St. N.W., Washington, D.C. 20006

AMERICAN INDUSTRIAL DEVELOPMENT COUNCIL, 1207 Grand Ave., Suite 845, Kansas City, Mo. 64106

AMERICAN INDUSTRIAL HYGIENE ASSOCIATION, 475 Wolf Ledge Pkwy., Akron, Ohio 44311

AMERICAN INSTITUTE OF CERTIFIED PUBLIC ACCOUNTANTS, 1211 Ave. of the Americas, New York, N.Y. 10036

AMERICAN INSTITUTE OF GRAPHIC ARTS, 1059 Third Ave., New York, N.Y. 10021

AMERICAN INSTITUTE OF INDUSTRIAL ENGINEERS, 25 Technology Park, Atlanta, Ga. 30092

AMERICAN INSTITUTE OF PLANT ENGINEERS, 3975 Erie Ave., Cincinnati, Ohio 45208

AMERICAN INSTITUTE FOR PROPERTY & LIABILITY UNDERWRITERS, Providence and Sugartown Roads, Malvern, Pa. 19355

AMERICAN INTERNATIONAL GROUP, 70 Pine St., New York, N.Y. 10005

AMERICAN INSURANCE ASSOCIATION, 85 John St., New York, N.Y. 10038

AMERICAN INTERNATIONAL GROUP, INC., 70 Pine St., New York, N.Y. 10005

AMERICAN LAW INSTITUTE, 4025 Chestnut St., Philadelphia, Pa. 19104

AMERICAN MANAGEMENT ASSOCIATIONS, 135 W. 50th St., New York, N.Y. 10020

AMERICAN MARKETING ASSOCIATION, 222 S. Riverside Plaza, Chicago, Ill. 60606

AMERICAN MATERIAL HANDLING SOCIETY, now INTERNATIONAL MATERIAL MANAGEMENT SOCIETY

AMERICAN MATHEMATICAL SOCIETY, P.O. BOX 6248, Providence, R.I. 02904

AMERICAN MEDICAL ASSOCIATION, 535 N. Dearborn St., Chicago, Ill. 60610

AMERICAN MUTUAL INSURANCE ALLIANCE, now ALLIANCE OF AMERICAN INSURERS

AMERICAN NATIONAL RED CROSS, 17 and D Sts., N.W., Washington, D.C. 20006

AMERICAN NATIONAL STANDARDS INSTITUTE, 1430 Broadway, New York, N.Y. 10018

AMERICAN NEWSPAPER PUBLISHERS ASSOCIATION, 11600 Sunrise Valley Dr., Reston, Va. 22091

AMERICAN OCCUPATIONAL MEDICAL ASSOCIATION, 150 N. Wacker Drive, Chicago, Ill. 60606

AMERICAN PERSONNEL AND GUIDANCE ASSOCIATION, Two Skyline Place, Suite 400, 5203 Leesbury Pike, Falls Church, Va. 22041

AMERICAN PETROLEUM INSTITUTE, 2101 L St. N.W., Washington, D.C. 20037

AMERICAN PHILOSOPHICAL ASSOCIATION, University of Delaware, Newark, Del. 19711

AMERICAN POLITICAL SCIENCE ASSOCIATION, 1527 New Hampshire Ave. N.W., Washington, D.C. 20036

AMERICAN PRODUCTION AND INVENTORY CONTROL SOCIETY, Washington Bldg., Suite 504, Washington, D.C. 20037

AMERICAN PRODUCTIVITY CENTER, 1700 West Loop South, Suite 210, Houston, Tex. 77027

AMERICAN PSYCHOLOGICAL ASSOCIATION, 1200 17th St. N.W., Washington, D.C. 20036

AMERICAN PUBLIC HEALTH ASSOCIATION, 1015 15th St. N.W., Washington, D.C. 20036

AMERICAN RECIPROCAL INSURERS, now AMERICAN INTERNATIONAL GROUP

AMERICAN RECORDS MANAGEMENT ASSOCIATION, now ASSOCIATION OF RECORDS MANAGERS AND ADMINISTRATORS

AMERICAN SOCIETY OF APPRAISERS, Dulles International Airport, P.O. Box 17265, Washington, D.C. 20041

AMERICAN SOCIETY OF ASSOCIATION EXECUTIVES, 1575 Eye St. N.W., Washington, D.C. 20005

AMERICAN SOCIETY OF CORPORATE SECRETARIES, One Rockefeller Plaza, New York, N.Y. 10020

AMERICAN SOCIETY FOR ENGINEERING EDUCATION, 1 Dupont Circle, Washington, D.C. 20036

American Society for Engineering Management, 301 Harris Hall, University of Missouri—Rolla, Rolla, Mo. 65401

American Society of Insurance Management, now Risk and Insurance Management Society

American Society of Mechanical Engineers, 345 E. 47th St., New York, N.Y. 10017

American Society for Performance Improvement, 790 Broad St., Newark, N.J. 07102

American Society of Personnel Administration, 52 E. Bridge St., Berea, Ohio 44017

American Society for Public Administration, 1225 Connecticut Ave. N.W., Washington, D.C. 20036

American Society for Quality Control, 161 West Wisconsin Ave., Milwaukee, Wisc. 53203

American Society of Safety Engineers, 850 Busse Highway, Park Ridge, Ill. 60068

American Society for Testing & Materials, 1916 Race St., Philadelphia, Pa. 19103

American Society of Traffic and Transportation, Box 33095, Louisville, Ky. 40232

American Society for Training and Development, Box 5307, Madison, Wisc. 53705

American Sociological Association, 1722 N St. N.W., Washington, D.C. 20036

American Statistical Association, 806 15th St. N.W., Washington, D.C. 20006

American Warehousemen's Association, 222 W. Adams St., Chicago, Ill., 60606

Amos Tuck School of Administration and Finance, Dartmouth College, Hanover, N.H. 03755

Anchor Press/Doubleday & Co., 501 Franklin Ave., Garden City, N.Y. 11530

The Anderson Group, P.O. Box 508, Madison, N.J. 07928

Appleton-Century-Crofts, 222 Madison Ave., New York, N.Y. 10017

Armed Forces Management Association, now American Defense Preparedness Association

Arno Press, 3 Park Ave., New York, N.Y. 10016

Associated Credit Bureaus, 6767 Southwest Freeway, Houston, Texas 77036

Associated Factory Mutual Fire Insurance Companies, now Factory Mutual System

Associated Press, 50 Rockefeller Plaza, New York, N.Y. 10020

Association for Computing Machinery, 1133 Ave. of the Americas, New York, N.Y. 10036

Association of Consulting Chemists & Chemical Engineers, 50 E. 41st St., New York, N.Y. 10016

Association of Data Processing Service Organizations (ADAPSO), 1925 N. Lynn St., Arlington, Va. 22209

Association for Educational Communications & Technology, 1126 16th St. N.W., Washington, D.C. 20036

Association for Educational Data Systems, 1201 16th St. N.W., Washington, D.C. 20036

Association of Executive Recruiting Consultants, 10 Rockefeller Plaza, New York, N.Y. 10020

Association of Internal Management Consultants, Box 472, Glastonbury, Conn. 06033

Association of Labor Mediation Agencies, now Association of Labor Relations Agencies

Association of Labor Relations Agencies, 1215 Western Ave., Albany, N.Y. 12203

Association of Management Consultants (AMC), 331 Madison Ave., New York, N.Y. 10017

Association of Management Consulting Firms (ACME), 230 Park Ave., New York, N.Y. 10017

Association of National Advertisers, 155 E. 44th St., New York, N.Y. 10017

Association of Records Executives and Administrators, now Association of Records Managers and Administrators

Association of Records Managers and Administrators (ARMA), 4200 Somerset, Suite 215, Prairie Village, Kans. 16208

Association for Systems Management, 2487 Bagley Road, Cleveland, Ohio 44158

Auerbach Publishers, Inc., 6560 N. Park Drive, Pennsauken, N.J. 08109

Avi Technical Books Inc., 250 Post Road East, Westport, Conn. 06880

Ayer Press, 1 Bala Ave., Bala Cynwyd, Pa. 19004

Ballinger Publishing Co., 17 Dunster St., Harvard Square, Cambridge, Mass. 02138

Bank Administration Institute, 303 S. Northwest Highway, Park Ridge, Ill. 60068

Bankers Trust Co., 16 Wall St., New York, N.Y. 10005

BANNER & GREIF, LTD., 110 E. 42nd St., New York, N.Y. 10017

BARNES & NOBLE, INC., 110 E. 53rd St., New York, N.Y. 10022

BASIC BOOKS, INC., 10 E. 53rd St., New York, N.Y. 10022

BAUSCH & LOMB, INC., One Lincoln First Square, Rochester, N.Y. 14601

BECKMAN PUBLISHERS, P.O. Box 20081, Cincinnati, Ohio 45219

BENDER, MATTHEW & CO., 235 E. 42nd St., New York, N.Y. 10017

BIBLIOGRAPHIC RETRIEVAL SERVICES, INC., , Corporation Park, Bldg. 702, Scotia, N.Y. 12302

BNA FILMS, Division of BUREAU OF NATIONAL AFFAIRS

BOBBS-MERRILL COMPANY, INC., 4300 W. 62nd St., Indianapolis, Ind. 46208

BOWKER CO., R.R., 1180 Ave. of the Americas, New York, N.Y. 10036

BRADFORD'S DIRECTORY OF MARKETING RESEARCH & MANAGEMENT, P.O. Box 276, Dept. B-15, Fairfax, Va. 22030

BRITISH COMPUTER SOCIETY, 13 Mansfield St., London Wl, England

BRITISH PUBLISHING CO., Box 188, South Chatham, Mass. 02659

BRITISH STANDARDS INSTITUTION, 2 Park St., London W1A 2B5, England

BROOKINGS INSTITUTION, 1775 Massachusetts Ave., N.W., Washington, D.C. 20036

BROWN, WM. C. & CO., 2460 Kerper Blvd., Dubuque, Ia. 52001

BUREAU OF LABOR STATISTICS, U.S. Dept. of Labor, 14th St. and Constitutional Ave., Washington, D.C. 20210

BUREAU OF NATIONAL AFFAIRS, INC., 1231 25th St. N.W., Washington D.C. 20037

BUSINESS EQUIPMENT MANUFACTURERS ASSOCIATION, now COMPUTER AND BUSINESS EQUIPMENT MANUFACTURERS ASSOCIATION

BUSINESS/PROFESSIONAL ADVERTISING ASSOCIATION, 205 E. 42nd St., New York, N.Y. 10017

BUSINESS PUBLICATIONS AUDIT BUREAU OF CIRCULATION, 100 Park Ave. S., New York, N.Y. 10010

BUTTERWORTH & CO. PUBLISHERS, LTD., 10 Office Tower Park, Woburn, Mass. 01801

CAHNERS PUBLISHING CO., 270 St. Paul St., Denver, Colo. 80206

CALIFORNIA TEST BUREAU (CTB-MCGRAW-HILL), Monterey, Calif. 93940

CANADIAN CIRCULATION AUDIT BOARD, 44 Eglinton, Toronto, Ontario, Canada

CAPITAL PUBLISHING CORP., P.O. Box 348, Two Laurel Ave., Wellesley Hills, Mass. 02181

CARNEGIE INSTITUTE OF TECHNOLOGY, now CARNEGI-MELLON UNIVERSITY

CARNEGIE-MELLON UNIVERSITY, Pittsburgh, Pa. 15213

CBI PUBLISHING, INC., 51 Sleeper St., Boston, Mass. 02210

CENSUS, BUREAU OF, Dept. of Commerce, Washington, D.C. 20233

CENTER FOR BUSINESS ETHICS, Bentley College, Waltham, Mass. 02154

CENTER FOR THE STUDY OF PRODUCTIVITY MOTIVATION, Graduate School of Business, University of Madison, Madison, Wisc. 53706

CHAMBER OF COMMERCE OF THE UNITED STATES, 1615 H St., Washington, D.C. 20062

CHANDLER PUBLISHING CO., see CHANDLER & SHARP PUBLISHERS, INC.

CHANDLER & SHARP PUBLISHERS, INC., 11A Commercial Blvd., Novato, Calif. 99567

CHARLES PUBLISHING CO., INC., 21125 Riverside Drive, North Hollywood, Calif. 91607

CHASE MANHATTAN BANK, 1 Chase Manhattan Plaza, New York, N.Y. 10005

CHEMICAL PUBLISHING CO., 155 W. 19th St., New York, N.Y. 10011

CIOS (COMITÉ INTERNATIONAL DE L'ORGANIZATION SCIENTIFIQUE), c/o Nederlandse Vereniging Voor Management, Van Alkemadelaan 700, NL 2019 The Hague, Nether-lands

CITIBANK N.A., Citicorp Center, Lexington Ave. and 53rd St., New York, N.Y. 10022

CLAPP & POLIAK, INC., 245 Park Ave., New York, N.Y. 10017

CLEARING HOUSE FOR PUBLIC ADMINISTRATION, c/o Public Administration Service, 1313 E. 60th St., Chicago, Ill. 60616

COLUMBIA UNIVERSITY BUREAU OF PUBLICATIONS, 116th St. and Broadway, New York, N.Y. 10027

COLUMBIA UNIVERSITY PRESS, 562 W. 113th St., New York, N.Y. 10025

COMMERCE CLEARING HOUSE, INC., 4025 W. Peterson Ave., Chicago, Ill. 60646

COMMERCE AND INDUSTRY ASSOCIATION OF NEW YORK, now NEW YORK CHAMBER OF COMMERCE AND INDUSTRY

COMMITTEE FOR ECONOMIC DEVELOPMENT

(C.E.D.), 477 Madison Ave., New York, N.Y. 10022

COMMUNICATIONS CHANNELS, INC., 185 Madison Ave., New York, N.Y. 10016

COMPUTER AND BUSINESS MANUFACTURERS ASSOCIATION, 1828 L St. N.W., Washington, D.C. 20036

COMPUTER SECURITY INSTITUTE, 43 Boston Post Road/W. Main St., Northboro, Mass. 01332

CONFERENCE BOARD, THE, 845 Third Ave., New York, N.Y. (Canadian headquarters, 25 McArthur Rd., Suite 100, Ottowa, Montreal, KIL 6R3, Canada

CONGRESSIONAL INFORMATION SERVICE, 7101 Wisconsin Ave., Washington, D.C. 20014

CONNECTICUT GENERAL LIFE INSURANCE CO., Hartford, Conn. 06152

CONSUMERS UNION, 256 Washington St., Mount Vernon, N.Y. 10550

CONTROL DATA EDUCATION CO., Box O, Minneapolis, Minn. 55440

CONTROLLERS CONGRESS, now NATIONAL RETAIL MERCHANTS ASSOCIATION

CONVEYOR EQUIPMENT MANUFACTURERS ASSOCIATION, 1000 Vernon Ave. N.W. Washington, D.C. 20005

CORNELL UNIVERSITY, Ithaca, N.Y. 14853

CORNERSTONE LIBRARY, INC., 1230 Ave. of the Americas, New York, N.Y. 10020

COUNCIL OF BETTER BUSINESS BUREAUS, 1150 17th St. N.W., Washington, D.C. 20036

COUNCIL OF GRADUATE EDUCATION IN PUBLIC ADMINISTRATION, now NATIONAL ASSOCIATION OF SCHOOLS OF PUBLIC AFFAIRS AND ADMINISTRATION

COUNCIL OF MANAGEMENT CONSULTING ORGANIZATIONS, 230 Park Ave., New York, N.Y. 10017

COUNCIL OF PROFIT-SHARING INDUSTRIES, 20 N. Wacker Drive, Chicago, Ill. 60606

COUNCIL OF STATE GOVERNMENTS, Ironworks Pike, Lexington, Ky. 40505

CRAIN BOOKS, 740 Rush St., Chicago, Ill. 60611

CREDIT UNION NATIONAL ASSOCIATION, P.O. Box 431, Madison, Wisc. 53701

CRONER PUBLICATIONS, 211-03 Jamaica Ave., Queens Village, N.Y. 11428

CROWELL, THOMAS Y., PUBLISHERS, 10 E. 53rd St. New York, N.Y. 10022

DARTNELL CORP., 4660 Ravenswood Ave., Chicago, Ill. 60640

DATA PROCESSING MANAGEMENT ASSOCIATION, 505 Busse Highway, Park Ridge, Ill., 60068

DECKER, MARCEL, INC., 270 Madison Ave., New York, N.Y. 10016

DELTA NU ALPHA TRANSPORTATION FRATERNITY, 1040 Woodcock Rd., Orlando, Fla. 32803

DIALOG, 3251 Hanover St., Palo Alto, Calif. 94304

DICKENSON PUBLISHING CO., 10 Davis Drive, Belmont, Calif. 94002

DIRECT MAIL ADVERTISING ASSOCIATION now DIRECT MAIL MARKETING ASSOCIATION

DIRECT MAIL MARKETING ASSOCIATION, 6 E. 43rd St., New York, N.Y. 10017

DISTRIBUTION BY DESIGN, 25 The Loch, Roslyn, N.Y. 11576

DOW JONES-IRWIN, INC., 1818 Ridge Rd., Homewood, Ill. 60430

DRYDEN PRESS, 901 N. Elm St., Hindsdale, Ill. 60521

DUN & BRADSTREET, INC., 99 Church St., New York, N.Y. 10007

DUPONT DE NEMOURS, E.I. & CO., Wilmington, Dela. 19898

DUTTON, E.P. & CO., INC. 2 Park Ave., New York, N.Y. 10016

DUXBURY PRESS, 6 Bound Brook Ct., N. Scituate, Mass. 02060

ECONOMETRIC SOCIETY, Dept. of Economics, Northwestern University, Evanston, Ill. 60201

ECONOMICS INDEX AND SURVEYS, now PREDICASTS, INC.

EDUCATION AND TRAINING CONSULTANTS, Box 2085, Sedona, Ariz. 86366

EDUCATIONAL TESTING SERVICE, Rosedale Rd., Princeton, N.J. 08541

ELECTRONIC INDUSTRIES ASSOCIATION, 200 Eye St. N.W. Washington, D.C. 20006

EDDY-RUCKER-NICKELS CO., 4 Brattle St., Cambridge, Mass. 02138

ELLIOTT SERVICE, INC.

ENGINEERS JOINT COUNCIL, now AMERICAN ASSOCIATION OF ENGINEERING SOCIETIES

EXHIBIT DESIGNERS AND PRODUCERS ASSOCIATION, 521 Fifth Ave., New York, N.Y. 10017

FACTORY INSURANCE ASSOCIATION, now INDUSTRIAL RISK INSURERS

FACTORY MUTUAL RESEARCH CORPORATION, 1151 Providence Highway, Norwood, Mass. 02062

FEDERAL RESERVE BANK OF KANSAS CITY, Kansas City, Mo., 64198

FEDERAL RESERVE SYSTEM, 20th St. and Constitutional Ave. N.W., Washington, D.C. 20551

FEDERAL TRADE COMMISSION, Pennsylvania Ave. at Sixth St. N.W., Washington, D.C. 20580

FEDERATION OF MUTUAL FIRE INSURANCE COMPANIES, now ALLIANCE OF AMERICAN INSURERS

FINANCIAL ACCOUNTING STANDARDS BOARD, High Ridge Park, Stamford, Conn. 06905

FINANCIAL EXECUTIVES INSTITUTE, 633 Third Ave., New York, N.Y. 10017

FINANCIAL EXECUTIVES RESEARCH FOUNDATION, 633 Third Ave., New York, N.Y. 10017

FIRST NATIONAL CITY BANK, now CITIBANK N.A.

FOUNDATION PRESS, P.O. Box 3056, St. Paul, Minn. 55165

FOUNDATION FOR PUBLIC RELATIONS, 845 Third Ave., New York, N.Y. 10022

FREE PRESS OF GLENCOE, now THE FREE PRESS, 866 Third Ave., New York, N.Y. 10022

FREIGHT FORWARDERS INSTITUTE, Suite 410, 1055 Thomas Jefferson St. N.W., Washington, D.C. 20007

FUNK & WAGNALLS, 10 E. 53rd St., New York, N.Y. 10022

GALE RESEARCH CO., Book Tower, Detroit, Mich. 48226

Geyer-McAllister Press, Inc., 51 Madison Ave., New York, N.Y. 10010

GOODYEAR PUBLISHING CO., INC., 1640 Fifth St., Santa Monica, Calif. 90401

GORDON AND BREACH SCIENCE PUBLISHERS, INC., 1 Park Ave., New York. N.Y. 10016

GOVERNMENT PRINTING OFFICE, Washington, D.C. 20402

GOWER PRESS, LTD., c/o Unipub, 345 Park Ave. S., New York, N.Y. 10010

GRADUATE MANAGEMENT ADMISSION COUNCIL, Princeton, N.J. 08541

GRAPHICS INSTITUTE, INC., 42 W. 39th St., New York, N.Y. 10018

GREENWICH RESEARCH ASSOCIATES, 115 E. Putnam Ave., Greenwich Conn. 06830

GREENWOOD PRESS, 88 Post Road West, Westport, Conn., 06881

GRIESINGER, FRANK K., AND ASSOCIATES, Suite 1412, Superior Bldg., 815 Superior Ave. E., Cleveland, Ohio 44114

GROSSMAN PUBLICATIONS, INC., 625 Madison Ave., New York, N.Y. 10022

GROUP & ORGANIZATION STUDIES, 7596 Ends Ave., LaJolle, Calif. 92037

GROVE PRESS, INC., 196 W. Houston St., New York, N.Y. 10014

GRYPHON PRESS, 220 Montgomery St., Highland Park, N.J. 08904

GULF PUBLISHING CO., Box 2608, Houston, Tex. 77001

HAFNER PRESS, 866 Third Ave., New York, N.Y. 10022

HAMILTON PUBLISHING CO., 563 W. Westfield, Indianapolis, Ind. 46203

HARCOURT, BRACE & JOVANOVICH, INC., 757 Third Ave., New York, N.Y. 10017

HARDWARE AFFILIATED REPRESENTATIVES, 520 Pleasant St., St. Joseph, Mich. 49085

HARPER & BROTHERS, now HARPER & ROW PUBLISHERS, INC.

HARPER & ROW PUBLISHERS, INC., 10 E. 53rd St., New York, N.Y. 10022

HARVARD GRADUATE SCHOOL OF BUSINESS ADMINISTRATION, Boston, Mass. 02163

HARVARD UNIVERSITY PRESS, 79 Garden St., Cambridge, Mass. 02138

HATINGS CENTER, INSTITUTE OF SOCIETY, ETHICS, AND LIFE SCIENCES, 360 Broadway, Hastings-on-Hudson, N.Y. 10706

HAWTHORN BOOKS, 2 Park Ave., New York, N.Y. 10016

HEALTH INSURANCE INSTITUTE, 1850 K St. N.W., Washington, D.C. 20006

HEALTH PHYSICS SOCIETY, 4720 Montgomery Lane, Bethesda, Md. 20014

HEAVY DUTY REPRESENTATIVES ASSOCIATES, INC., 520 Pleasant St., St. Joseph, Mich. 49085

HOLDEN-DAY, INC., 500 Sansome St., San Francisco, Calif. 94111

HOLT, RINEHART AND WINSTON, INC., 383 Madison Ave., New York, N.Y. 10017

HOUGHTON MIFFLIN CO., 2 Park St., Boston, Mass. 02107

HUGHES AIRCRAFT CO., CULVER CITY, CALIF. 90230

HUMAN FACTORS SOCIETY, Box 1369, Santa Monica, Calif. 90406

HUMAN RELATIONS LABORATORY, University of Colorado, Boulder, Colo. 80302

ILLINOIS DEPARTMENT OF LABOR, 160 N. LaSalle St., Chicago, Ill. 60601

IMPROVED RISK INSURERS, 85 Woodland St., Hartford, Conn. 06102

IMPROVED RISK MUTUALS, 15 N. Broadway, White Plains, N.Y. 10601

INDUSTRIAL MARKETING ASSOCIATES, INC., 520 Pleasant St., St. Joseph, Mich. 49085

INDUSTRIAL MEDICAL ASSOCIATION, now AMERICAN OCCUPATIONAL MEDICAL ASSOCIATION

INDUSTRIAL PRESS, INC., 200 Madison Ave., New York, N.Y. 10016

INDUSTRIAL RELATIONS RESEARCH ASSOCIATION, Social Science Bldg., University of Wisconsin, Madison, Wisc. 53706

INDUSTRIAL RESEARCH INSTITUTE, 100 Park Ave., Suite 2209, New York, N.Y. 10017

INDUSTRIAL RISK INSURANCE, 85 Woodland St., Hartford, Conn. 06102

INFORMATION INDUSTRY ASSOCIATION, 316 Pennsylvania Ave. S.E., Suite 502, Washington, D.C. 20003

INSTITUTE OF COST AND WORKS ACCOUNTANTS, see next entry.

INSTITUTE OF COST & MANAGEMENT ACCOUNTANTS, 63 Portland Place, London Wl, England

INSTITUTE OF ELECTRICAL AND ELECTRONIC ENGINEERS, 345 E. 47th St., New York, N.Y. 10017

INSTITUTE OF INTERNAL AUDITORS, 249 Maitland Ave., Altamonte Springs, Fla. 32701

INSTITUTE OF LIFE INSURANCE, now AMERICAN COUNCIL OF LIFE INSURANCE

INSTITUTE OF MANAGEMENT CONSULTANTS (IMC), 19 W. 44th St., New York, N.Y. 10036

INSTITUTE OF MANAGEMENT SCIENCES, THE (TIMS), 146 Westminster St., Providence R.I., 02903

INSTITUTE OF MATHEMATICAL STATISTICS, Statistical Laboratory, Michigan State University, East Lansing, Mich. 48824

INSTITUTE OF NEWSPAPER CONTROLLERS AND FINANCE OFFICERS, 66 E. Main St., Moorestown, N.J. 08057

INSTITUTE OF OUTDOOR ADVERTISING, INC .485 Lexington Ave., New York, N.Y. 10017

INSTITUTE OF PERSONALITY AND ABILITY TESTING, 1602 Coronado Dr., Champaign, Ill. 61822

INSTITUTE OF PROFESSIONAL ACCOUNTING, Graduate School of Business, University of Chicago, 1101 East 58th St., Chicago, Ill. 60637

INSTITUTE OF PUBLIC ADMINISTRATION, 55 W. 44th St., New York, N.Y. 10036

INSTITUTE OF RADIO ENGINEERS, now INSTITUTE OF ELECTRICAL AND ELECTRONIC ENGINEERS

INSTITUTE OF RISK MANAGEMENT CONSULTANTS, c/o S.B. Ackerman Associates, 500 Fifth Ave., New York, N.Y. 10036

INSTITUTE OF TEMPORARY SERVICES, INC., now NATIONAL ASSOCIATION OF TEMPORARY SERVICES

INSURANCE CONSULTANTS' SOCIETY, 835 Glenside Ave., Wyncote, Pa. 19095

INSURANCE INSTITUTE OF AMERICA, P.O. Box 314, Malvern, Pa. 19355

INTERNATIONAL ACADEMY OF MANAGEMENT, The Hague, Netherlands

INTERNATIONAL ACCOUNTING STANDARDS COMMITTEE, 3 St. Helens Place, London EC3a 6DN, England

INTERNATIONAL ASSOCIATION OF APPLIED SOCIAL SCIENTISTS, Box 1625, Sta. B., Nashville, Tenn. 37235

INTERNATIONAL ASSOCIATION OF AUDITORIUM MANAGERS, 111 E. Wacker Drive, Room 620, Chicago, Ill. 60601

INTERNATIONAL ASSOCIATION OF BUSINESSMEN AND PROFESSIONALS, 1710 Connecticut Ave. N.W., Washington D.C. 20009

INTERNATIONAL ASSOCIATION OF CHIEFS OF POLICE, 11 Fairfield Rd., Gaithersburg, Md. 20760

INTERNATIONAL EXECUTIVES ASSOCIATION, INC., 122 E. 42nd St., New York, N.Y. 10017

INTERNATIONAL FEDERATION OF INFORMATION PROCESSING SOCIETIES, now INTERNATIONAL FEDERATION OF INFORMATION PROCESSING, 32 Rue de Marche, CH1204, Geneva, Switzerland

INTERNATIONAL FRANCHISE ASSOCIATION, 1025 Connecticut Ave. N.W., Washington, D.C. 20036

INTERNATIONAL INSTITUTE OF ADMINISTRATIVE SCIENCES, 25 Rue de la Charite, Brussels 4, Belgium

INTERNATIONAL INSTITUTE FOR ROBOTICS, affiliate of SOCIETY OF MANUFACTURING ENGINEERS

INTERNATIONAL MANAGEMENT COUNCIL, 291 Broadway, New York, N.Y. 10007

INTERNATIONAL MATERIAL MANAGEMENT SOCIETY, 3310 Bardaville Dr., Lansing, Mich. 48906

INTERNATIONAL ORGANIZATION FOR STANDARDIZATION, One Rue de Varembe, CH 1121, Geneva 20, Switzerland

INTERNATIONAL PUBLICATIONS SERVICE, 114 E. 32nd St., New York, N.Y. 10016

INTERNATIONAL TELECOMMUNICATION UNION,

Place des Nations, CH 1211, Geneva 20, Switzerland

INTERNATIONAL TEXTBOOK CO., Oak St. and Pawnee Ave., Scranton, Pa. 18515

INTERNATIONAL TRANSACTION ANALYSIS ASSOCIATION, 1772 Valejo St., San Francisco, Calif. 94123

INTERNATIONAL WORD PROCESSING ASSOCIATION, INC., Willow Grove, Pa. 19090

INTEXT EDUCATIONAL PUBLISHERS, Oak St. and Pawnee Ave., Scranton, Pa. 18515

INVESTMENT INDEX COMPANY, now PREDICASTS, INC

IOWA STATE COLLEGE PRESS, Iowa State University, Ames, Ia. 52203

IRWIN, RICHARD D., INC., 1818 Ridge Rd., Homewood, Ill. 60430

IRWIN-DORSEY, 1818 Ridge Rd., Homewood, Ill. 60430

JAI PRESS, INC., 165 W. Putnam Ave., Greenwich, Conn. 06830

JALMAR, INC., 6501 Elvas Ave., Sacramento, Calif. 95819

JAPAN INDUSTRIAL ROBOT ASSOCIATION, Jihai Shinko Bldg., 3-5-8 Shiba Koen, Minato-Ku, Tokyo 105, Japan

KEMPER INSURANCE COMPANIES, Long Grove, Ill. 60049

KLINE, CHARLES H & CO., INC., 330 Passaic Ave., Dept. 39, Fairfield, N.J. 07006

KLUWER BOSTON, INC., 160 Old Derby St., Hingham, Mass. 02043

KNOPF, ALFRED A., INC., 201 E. 50th St., New York, N.Y. 10022

KRIEGER PUBLISHING COMPANY, INC., P.O. Box 9542, Melbourne, Fla. 32901 (change from Huntington, N.Y. shown in text references)

LABOR AND INDUSTRIAL RELATIONS CENTER, Michigan State University, East Lansing, Mich. 48823

LAWYERS COOPERATIVE PUBLISHING CO., Aqueduct Bldg., Rochester, N.Y. 14694

LEADERSHIP RESOURCES, INC., 1750 Park Ave. N.W., Washington, D.C. 20018

LEXINGTON BOOKS, 125 Spring St., Lexington, Mass. 02173

LINCOLN ELECTRIC CO., 22801 St. Clair Ave., Cleveland, Ohio 44117

ARTHUR D. LITTLE, INC., 25 Acorn Park, Cambridge, Mass. 02140

LITTLE, BROWN AND CO., 34 Beacon St., Boston, Mass. 02106

LOCKHEED INFORMATION SYSTEMS, see DIALOG

LONGMAN'S, GREEN & CO., LTD., now LONGMAN GROUP

LONGMAN GROUP LTD., LONGMAN HSE., Burnt Mill, Harlow CM20 2JE, London WC2, England

LOYOLA UNIVERSITY PRESS, 3441 N. Ashland Ave., Chicago, Ill. 60657

MACHINERY AND ALLIED PRODUCTS INSTITUTE (MAPI), 1200 18th St. N.W., Washington, D.C. 20036

MACMILLAN COMPANY, 866 Third Ave., New York, N.Y. 10017

MACMILLAN & CO. LTD., 4 Little Essex St., London WC2, England

MAGAZINE ADVERTISING BUREAU, now Marketing Div. of MAGAZINE PUBLISHERS ASSOCIATION

MAGAZINE PUBLISHERS ASSOCIATION, 575 Lexington Ave., New York, N.Y. 10022

MANAGEMENT PUBLISHING CORP., now MANAGEMENT PUBLISHING GROUP, 866 Third Ave., New York, N.Y. 10022

MANAGEMENT PUBLISHING TRUST, 5 Winsley St., London, W1 England

MANUFACTURING AGENTS NATIONAL ASSOCIATION, 2021 Business Center Dr., P.O. Box 16878, Irvine, Calif. 92713

MARKETING COMMUNICATIONS EXECUTIVES INTERNATIONAL, 1831 Chestnut St., Philadelphia, Pa. 19103

MARKETING SCIENCE INSTITUTE, 14 Story St., Cambridge, Mass. 02138

MASSACHUSETTS INSTITUTE OF TECHNOLOGY PRESS (M.I.T. PRESS), 28 Carleton St., Cambridge, Mass. 02143

MATERIAL HANDLING INSTITUTE, 1326 Freeport Rd., Pittsburgh, Pa. 15238

MATERIALS MARKETING ASSOCIATES, INC., 520 Pleasant St., St. Joseph, Mich. 49085

MAYNARD RESEARCH COUNCIL, INC., 300 Alpha Dr., Pittsburgh, Pa. 15238

MCGRAW-HILL BOOK CO., 1221 Ave. of the Americas, New York, N.Y. 10020

MEAD CORPORATION, Courthouse Plaza N.E., Dayton, Ohio 45463

MERRILL, CHARLES E. PUBLISHING CO., 1300 Alum Creek Dr., Columbus, Ohio 43216

METCUT RESEARCH ASSOCIATES, INC., 3980 Rosylyn Dr., Cincinnati, Ohio 43209

M.I.T. SCHOOL OF MANAGEMENT, Massachusetts Institute of Technology, Cambridge, Mass. 02139

MOODY'S INVESTORS SERVICE, INC., 99 Church St., New York, N.Y. 10007

MTM ASSOCIATION FOR STANDARDS AND RE-

SEARCH, 1601 Broadway, Fair Lawn, N.J. 07410

NATIONAL ACADEMY OF ARBITRATORS, 4335 Cathedral Ave. N.W., Pittsburgh, Pa. 20016

NATIONAL ACADEMY OF SCIENCE—NATIONAL RESEARCH COUNCIL, 2101 Constitutional Ave. N.W., Washington, D.C. 20418

NATIONAL ALLIANCE OF BUSINESSMEN, 1730 K St. N.W., Washington, D.C. 20006

NATIONAL ARCHIVES AND RECORDS SERVICE, General Service Administration, 18th and F St. N.W., Washington, D.C. 20405

NATIONAL ASSOCIATION OF ACCOUNTANTS, 919 Third Ave., New York, N.Y. 10022

NATIONAL ASSOCIATION FOR BANK AUDIT CONTROL AND OPERATIONS, now BANK ADMINISTRATION INSTITUTE

NATIONAL ASSOCIATION OF BROADCASTERS, 1771 N St. N.W., Washington, D.C. 20036

NATIONAL ASSOCIATION OF CORPORATE DIRECTORS, 1800 K St. N.W., Washington, D.C. 20006

NATIONAL ASSOCIATION OF COUNTIES, 1735 New York Ave. N.W., Washington, D.C. 20006

NATIONAL ASSOCIATION OF CREDIT MANAGEMENT, 475 Park Ave. S., New York, N.Y. 10010

NATIONAL ASSOCIATION OF EXPOSITION MANAGERS, c/o AMERICAN SOCIETY OF ASSOCIATION EXECUTIVES

NATIONAL ASSOCIATION OF MANUFACTURERS (NAM), 1776 F St. N.W., Washington, D.C. 20006

NATIONAL ASSOCIATION OF PERSONNEL CONSULTANTS, now NATIONAL PERSONNEL CONSULTANTS

NATIONAL ASSOCIATION OF PURCHASING AGENTS, now NATIONAL ASSOCIATION OF PURCHASING MANAGEMENT, 11 Park Place, New York, N.Y. 10007

NATIONAL ASSOCIATION OF REFRIGERATED WAREHOUSES, 7315 Wisconsin Ave., Washington, D.C. 20014

NATIONAL ASSOCIATION OF PUBLIC AFFAIRS AND ADMINISTRATION (NASPAA), 1225 Connecticut Ave. N.W., Washington, D.C. 20036

NATIONAL ASSOCIATION OF TEMPORARY SERVICES, 1001 Connecticut Ave. N.W., No. 932, Washington, D.C. 20036

NATIONAL ASSOCIATION OF WHOLESALERS, now NATIONAL ASSOCIATION OF WHOLESALER-DISTRIBUTORS, 1725 K St. N.W., Washington, D.C. 20006

NATIONAL BEUREAU OF ECONOMIC RESEARCH, 261 Madison Ave., New York, N.Y. 10016

NATIONAL CABLE AND TELEVISION ASSOCIATION, 918 16th St. N.W., Washington, D.C. 20006

NATIONAL CLEARING HOUSE FOR ALCOHOL AND DRUG ABUSE INFORMATION, Box 2345, Rockville, Md. 20852

NATIONAL COUNCIL ON ALCOHOLISM, INC., 733 Third Ave., New York, N.Y. 10017

NATIONAL COUNCIL OF PHYSICAL DISTRIBUTION MANAGEMENT, 2803 Butterfield Rd., Oak Brook, Ill. 60521

NATIONAL CREDIT UNION ADMINISTRATION, 1325 K St. N.W., Washington, D.C. 20456

NATIONAL DEFENSE TRANSPORTATION ASSOCIATION, 910 17th St. S.W., Washington, D.C. 20006

NATIONAL EDUCATION ASSOCIATION, 1201 16th St. N.W., Washington, D.C. 20036

NATIONAL EMPLOYMENT ASSOCIATION, now ASSOCIATION OF PERSONNEL CONSULTANTS

NATIONAL EMPLOYMENT LAW PROJECT, 475 Riverside Dr., New York, N.Y. 10027

NATIONAL FIRE PROTECTION ASSOCIATION, 470 Atlantic Ave., Boston, Mass. 02210

NATIONAL FRANCHISING ASSOCIATION, Box 366, Fox Lake, Ill. 60020

NATIONAL HOME STUDY COUNCIL, 1601 18th St. N.W., Washington, D.C. 20009

NATIONAL INDUSTRIAL TRAFFIC LEAGUE, 1909 K St. N.W., Washington, D.C. 20006

NATIONAL INSTITUTE FOR APPLIED BEHAVIORAL SCIENCE, now NTL INSTITUTE

NATIONAL INSTITUTE OF CREDIT, 3000 Marcus Ave., Lake Success, N.Y. 11032

NATIONAL INSTITUTE OF MANAGEMENT, Suite 7A Ghent Square, Bath, Ohio 44210

NATIONAL INSTITUTE OF MENTAL HEALTH, now NATIONAL MENTAL HEALTH ASSOCIATION

NATIONAL INSTITUTE FOR OCCUPATIONAL SAFETY AND HEALTH, NOW OCCUPATIONAL HEALTH INSTITUTE

NATIONAL INVESTOR RELATIONS INSTITUTE, 1629 K St. N.W., Washington, D.C. 20006

NATIONAL MENTAL HEALTH ASSOCIATON, 1800 N. Kent St., Rosslyn, Va. 22209

NATIONAL MICROGRAPHICS ASSOCIATION, 8719 Colesville Rd., Silver Springs, Md. 20910

NATIONAL MANAGEMENT ASSOCIATION, 2210 Arbor Blvd., Dayton, Ohio 45439

NATIONAL PERSONNEL CONSULTANTS, 1012 14th St. N.W., Washington, D.C. 20003

NATIONAL PLANNING ASSOCIATION, 1606 New

Hampshire Ave. N.W., Washington, D.C. 20009

NATIONAL RECORDS MANAGEMENT COUNCIL, 60 E. 42nd St. New York, N.Y. 10017

NATIONAL RETAIL MERCHANTS ASSOCIATION (NRMA), 100 W. 31st St., New York, N.Y. 10001

NATIONAL SAFETY COUNCIL, 444 N. Michigan Ave., Chicago, Ill. 60611

NATIONAL SCIENCE FOUNDATION, 122 G St. N.W., Washington, D.C. 20550

NATIONAL SOCIETY FOR PERFORMANCE AND INSTRUCTION, 1126 16th St. N.W., Suite 315, Washington, D.C. 20036

NATIONAL SCIENCE FOR PROGRAMMED INSTRUCTION, now NATIONAL SOCIETY FOR PERFORMANCE AND INSTRUCTION

NATIONAL SOCIETY FOR THE STUDY OF EDUCATION, 5835 Kimbark Ave., Chicago, Ill. 60637

NATIONAL SOCIETY OF SALES TRAINING EXECUTIVES, 104 Woodcock Rd., Orlando, Fla. 32803

NATIONAL TECHNICAL SERVICES ASSOCIATION, 111 E. Wacker Dr., Suite 600, Chicago, Ill. 60601

NATIONAL TOOL, DIE, AND PRECISION MACHINERY ASSOCIATION, now TOOLING AND MACHINERY ASSOCIATION, 9300 Livingston Rd., Washington, D.C. 20022

NATIONAL TRADE SHOW EXHIBITORS ASSOCIATION, 4300-L Lincoln Ave., Rolling Meado, Ill. 60008

NATIONAL TRAINING LABORATORIES, now NTL INSTITUTE

NATIONAL UNDERWRITER CO., 99 John St., New York, N.Y. 10038

NATIONAL UNIVERSITY EXTENSION ASSOCIATION, 1 DuPont Circle, Suite 360, Washington, D.C., 20036

NATIONAL VENTURE CAPITAL ASSOCIATION, 2030 M St. N.W., Washington, D.C. 20036

NEW YORK CHAMBER OF COMMERCE AND INDUSTRY, 65 Liberty St., New York, N.Y. 10005

NEW YORK CONSUMER ASSEMBLY, INC., 465 Grand St., New York, N.Y. 10002

NEW YORK STATE SCHOOL OF INDUSTRIAL AND LABOR RELATIONS, Cornell University, Box 1000, Ithaca, N.Y. 14853

NEW YORK STOCK EXCHANGE, 11 Wall St., New York, N.Y. 10005

NEW YORK UNIVERSITY PRESS, 113-15 University Place, New York, N.Y. 10003

NEWMAN BOOKS LTD., 48 Poland St., London W1V 4PP, England

NEWMAN NEAME, LTD., now Newman Books Ltd.

NEWSPAPER ADVERTISING BUREAU, INC., 485 Lexington Ave., New York, N.Y. 10017

NORTH AMERICAN SOCIETY FOR CORPORATE PLANNING, 1406 Third National Bldg., Dayton, Ohio 45402

NORTHWESTERN UNIVERSITY, Evanston, Ill. 60201

NTL INSTITUTE, P.O. Box 9155, Rosslyn Sta., Arlington, Va. 22201

NORTON, W. W. & CO., INC., 500 Fifth Ave., New York, N.Y. 10036

OCCUPATIONAL HEALTH INSTITUTE, 150 N. Wacker Dr., Chicago, Ill. 60606

OCCUPATIONAL SAFETY AND HEALTH ADMINISTRATION, U.S. Dept. of Labor, 200 Constitutional Ave. N.W., Washington, D.C. 20210

OFFICE TECHNOLOGY RESEARCH GROUP, Box 65, Pasadena, Calif. 91102

OLIVER & BOYD, Robert Stevenson Hse. 1/3 Baxter's Place Leith Walk, Edinburgh EH1,3BB Scotland

OPERATIONAL RESEARCH SOCIETY, Neville House, Water 100 St., Birmingham B2 STX, England

OPERATIONS RESEARCH SOCIETY OF AMERICA, 428 E. Preston St., Baltimore, Md. 21202

OPINION RESEARCH CORPORATION, North Harrison St., Princeton, N.J. 08540

OUTDOOR ADVERTISING ASSOCIATION OF AMERICA, 1899 L St. N.W., Suite 403, Washington, D.C. 20036

OXFORD UNIVERSITY PRESS, 200 Madison Ave., New York, N.Y. 10016

PACKAGE DESIGNERS COUNCIL, P.O. Box 3753, Grand Central Sta., New York, N.Y. 10017

PACKAGING INSTITUTE, 342 Madison Ave., New York, N.Y. 10017

PEACOCK, F.E. PUBLISHERS, INC., 401 West Irving Park Rd., Itasca, Ill. 60143

PEAT, MARWICK, MITCHELL, 345 Park Ave., New York, N.Y. 10022

PENTON PUBLISHING CO., Penton Plaza, Cleveland, Ohio 44114

PERGAMON PRESS, INC., 226 E. College Ave., Appleton, Wisc. 54911

PETROCELLI BOOKS, 1101 State Rd., Princeton, N.J. 08540

PHILOSOPHICAL LIBRARY, INC., 200 W. 57th St., New York, N.Y. 10019

PITMAN, SIR ISAAC & SONS, 39/41 Parker St., London, WC2, England

PLANNING EXECUTIVES INSTITUTE, 5500 College Corner Pike, Oxford, Ohio 45056

PLIMPTON PRESS, Lennox Ave., Boston, Mass. 02062

POINT-OF-PURCHASE ADVERTISING INSTITUTE, 60 E. 42nd St., New York, N.Y. 10017

POTOMAC PRESS, INC., Box 31086, Washington, D.C. 20031

PRACTICING LAW INSTITUTE, 810 7th Ave., New York, N.Y. 10019

PRAEGER PUBLISHERS, 383 Madison Ave., New York, N.Y. 10017

PREDICASTS, INC., 1101 Cedar Ave., Cleveland, Ohio 44106

PREMIUM ADVERTISING ASSOCIATION OF AMERICA, now PROMOTION MARKETING ASSOCIATION, 420 Lexington Ave., New York, N.Y. 10019

PRENTICE-HALL, INC., Englewood Cliffs, N.J. 07632

PRICE WATERHOUSE & CO., 1251 Ave. of the Americas, New York, N.Y. 10019

PRINCETON UNIVERSITY PRESS, Princeton, N.J. 08540

PROFESSIONAL MANUFACTURERS' AGENTS, INC., Sheppard-Benning Bldg., St. Joseph, Mich. 49085

PROFIT SHARING COUNCIL OF AMERICA, 20 N. Wacker Dr., Chicago, Ill. 60606

PROFIT SHARING RESEARCH FOUNDATION, 1718 Sherman Ave., Evanston, Ill. 60201

PSYCHOLOGICAL CORPORATION, 304 E. 45th St., New York, N.Y. 10017

PSYCHOLOGICAL SERVICES, INC., 3450 Wilshire Blvd., Los Angeles, Calif. 90005

PUBLIC ADMINISTRATION SERVICE, 1776 Massachusetts Ave. N.W., Washingtion, D.C. 30036

PUBLIC AFFAIRS INFORMATON SERVICE, 11 W. 40th St., New York, N.Y. 10018

PUBLIC RELATIONS SOCIETY OF AMERICA, 845 Third Ave., New York, N.Y. 10022

RADIO ADVERTISING BUREAU, 85 Lexington Ave., New York, N.Y. 10017

RAILWAY SYSTEMS AND MANAGEMENT ASSOCIATION, P.O. Box 330, Ocean City, N.J. 08226

RAND CORPORATION, 1700 Main St., Santa Monica, Calif. 90406

RAND-MCNALLY & COMPANY, Box 7600, Chicago, Ill. 60680

REIHOLD PUBLISHING COMPANY, now VAN NOSTRAND REINHOLD COMPANY

RESEARCH INSTITUTE OF AMERICA, 589 Fifth Ave., New York, N.Y. 10017

RINEHART & COMPANY, INC., now HOLT, RINEHART & WINSTON, INC.

RESTON PUBLISHING CO., INC., 11480 Sunset Hill Rd., Reston, Va. 22090

ROBERTS PUBLISHINGCORP., 45 John St., New York, N.Y. 10038

ROBOTICS INSTITUTE OF AMERICA, affiliated with SOCIETY OF MANUFACTURING ENGINEERS

RONALD PRESS CO., 605 3rd Ave., New York, N.Y. 10016

ROUGH NOTES COMPANY, INC., 1200 N. Meridian St., Indianapolis, Ind. 46204

ROW, PETERSON & CO., now HARPER & ROW PUBLISHERS, INC.

ROYAL INSTITUTE OF PUBLIC ADMINISTRATION, Hamilton House, Mableton Pl., London WC1, England

ROYAL STATISTICAL SOCIETY, 25 Enford St., London W1, England

RUSSELL SAGE FOUNDATION, 633 Third Ave., New York, N.Y. 10017

SAGE PUBLICATIONS, INC., 275 S. Beverly Drive, Beverly Hills, Calif. 90212

SALES AND MARKETING EXECUTIVES INTERNATIONAL, 380 Lexington Ave., New York, N.Y. 10017

SALES PROMOTION EXECUTIVES ASSOCIATION, now MARKETING COMMUNICATIONS EXECUTIVES ASSOCIATION

SAUNDERS, W.B. CO., 218 W. Washington Square, Philadelphia, Pa. 19105

SCHNEIDER PUBLISHING CO., 1627 Locust St., St. Louis, Mo. 63103

SCIENCE RESEARCH ASSOCIATES, 155 N. Wacker Dr., Chicago, Ill. 60606

SCOTT, FORSTMAN AND COMPANY, PUBLISHERS, 1900 E. Lake, Glenview, Ill. 60025

SCRIBNERS, CHARLES, SONS, 597 Fifth Ave., New York, N.Y. 10017

SDC SEARCH SERVICE, Systems Development Corporation, 2500 Colorado Ave., Santa Monica, Calif., 90406

SECURITIES AND EXCHANGE COMMISSION, 500 N. Capitol St., Washington, D.C. 20549

SIGNODE CORPORATION, 3600 W. Lake Ave., Glenview, Ill. 60025

SIMMONS-BOARDMAN PUBLISHING CORP., 1809 Capitol Ave., Omaha, Neb. 68102

SIMON & SCHUSTER, INC., 1230 Ave. of the Americas, New York, N.Y. 10020

SMALL BUSINESS ADMINISTRATION, 1441 L St. N.W., Washington, D.C.

SMITHERS, CHRISTOPHER D. FOUNDATION, Oyster Bay Rd., Millneck, N.Y. 11765

SOCIETY FOR THE ADVANCEMENT OF MANAGE-

MENT, now a div. of AMERICAN MANAGEMENT ASSOCIATIONS

SOCIETY OF AMERICAN ARCHIVISTS, 330 S. Wells St., Chicago, Ill. 60609

SOCIETY OF AMERICAN VALUE ENGINEERS, P.O. Box 210887, Dallas, Tex. 75211

SOCIETY OF AUTOMOTIVE ENGINEERS, 400 Commonwealth Dr., Warrendale, Pa. 15096

SOCIETY FOR BUSINESS ETHICS, Loyola University of Ill., Chicago, Ill. 60611

SOCIETY OF CHARTERED PROPERTY AND CASUALTY UNDERWRITERS, Kahler Hall, Providence Rd., Malvern, Pa. 19355

SOCIETY OF INDUSTRIAL ACCOUNTANTS OF CANADA, 154 Main St., E. Hamilton, Ontario, Canada L8N 169

SOCIETY OF INSURANCE AND RISK MANAGEMENT CONSULTANTS, c/o First Insurance Management Co., 855 Glenside Ave., Wyncote, Pa. 19095

SOCIETY OF LOGISTICS ENGINEERS, 3222 S. Memorial Parkway, Huntsville, Ala. 35801

SOCIETY FOR MANAGEMENT INFORMATION SYSTEMS, 111 E. Wacker Drive, Chicago, Ill. 60611

SOCIETY OF MANUFACTURING ENGINEERS, P.O. Box 930, Dearborn, Mich. 48128

SOCIETY OF NATIONAL ASSOCIATION PUBLICATIONS, 820 Davis St., Suite 400, Evanston, Ill. 60201

SOCIETY OF PACKAGING AND HANDLING ENGINEERS, Reston Internatonal Center, Reston, Va. 22901

SOCIETY FOR PERSONNEL ADMINISTRATION, 485 National Press Bldg., 14th and F Sts. N.W., Washingtion, D.C. 20004

SOCIETY OF PROFESSIONAL MANAGEMENT CONSULTANTS, 205 W. 89th St., New York, N.Y. 10036

SOCIETY OF REAL ESTATE APPRAISERS, 645 N. Michigan Ave., Chicago, Ill. 60611

SOCIETY OF TYPOGRAPHIC ARTS, 54 E. Erie St., Chicago, Ill. 60611

SOUTH-WESTERN PUBLISHING CO., 5101 Madison Rd., Cincinnati, Ohio 45227

SPENCER, CHARLES D. ASSOCIATES, 222 W. Adams St., Chicago, Ill. 60606

SPRINGER PUBLISHING CO., INC., 200 Park Ave. S., New York, N.Y. 10003

ST. MARTIN'S PRESS, 175 Fifth Ave., New York, N.Y. 10010

STANDARD & POOR'S, 25 Broadway, New York, N.Y. 10004

STANDARD RATE & DATA SERVICE, 5201 Old Orchard Rd., Skokie, Ill. 60076

STANFORD RESEARCH INSTITUTE, Menlo Park, Calif. 94025

STANFORD UNIVERSITY PRESS, Stanford, Calif. 94305

STATION REPRESENTATIVES ASSOCIATION, 230 Park Ave., New York, N.Y. 10017

STATISTICAL INDICATORS ASSOCIATES, North Egremont, Mass. 01252

STEELCASE INC., 1120 36th St., Grand Rapids, Mich. 49508

SUPERINTENDENT OF DOCUMENTS, Government Printing Office, North Capitol and H Sts. N.W., Washington, D.C. 20401

SYSTEMS AND PROCEDURES SOCIETY, now ASSOCIATION FOR SYSTEMS MANAGEMENT

TAB BOOKS, Blue Ridge Summit, Pa. 17214

TAYLOR SOCIETY, now SOCIETY FOR ADVANCEMENT OF MANAGEMENT (AMERICAN MANAGEMENT ASSOCIATIONS)

TECHNIMETRICS, INC., Citicorp Center, 153 E. 53rd St., New York, N.Y. 10022

TECHNOLOGY PRESS, INC., P.O. Box 125, Fairfax Sta., Va. 22039

TELEVISION BUREAU OF ADVERTISING, 1345 Ave. of the Americas, New York, N.Y. 10019

TEMPLE UNIVERSITY PRESS, Philadelphia, Pa. 19122

TEXAS TECHNOLOGICAL UNIVERSITY, Lubbock, Tex. 79409

THOMAS PRINTING & PUBLISHING CO. and THOMAS PUBLICATIONS, LTD., Desnoyer St., Kaukana, Wisc. 54130

TIMS, see THE INSTITUTE OF MANAGEMENT SCIENCES

TJM CORPORATION, 5500 Florida Blvd., Baton Rouge, La. 70806

TRADE ACTIVITIES, INC., 815 Washington Bldg., Washington, D.C. 20005

TRADE SHOW BUREAU, 49 Locust St., New Canaan, Conn. 06840

TRADING STAMP INSTITUTE OF AMERICA, 1600 Route 22, Union, N.J. 07083

TRAFFIC AUDIT BUREAU, INC., 708 Third Ave., New York, N.Y. 10017

TRAFFIC CLUBS INTERNATIONAL, 1040 Woodstock Rd., Orlando, Fla. 82803

TRAFFIC SERVICE CORP., 1435 G St. N.W., Washington, D.C. 20005

TRANSIT ADVERTISING ASSOCIATION, 1725 K St. N.W., Washington, D.C. 20006

TRANSPORTATION ASSOCIATION OF AMERICA, 1100 17th St. N.W., Washington, D.C. 20036

TRANSPORTATION INSTITUTE, 923 15th St. N.W., Washington, D.C. 20005

TRIANGLE PUBLICATIONS INC., 4 Radnor Corporate Center, Radnor, Pa. 19088

TWENTIETH CENTURY FUND, 41 E. 70th St., New York, N.Y. 10021

UNDERWRITERS' LABORATORIES, INC., 333 Pfingston Rd., Northbrook, Ill. 60062

UNIPUB, 345 Park Ave. S., New York, N.Y. 10010

UNITED NATIONS STATISTICAL OFFICE, United Nations, New York, N.Y. 10017

UNITED STATES TRADEMARK ASSOCIATION, 6 E. 45th St., New York, N.Y. 10017

UNIVERSITY OF ALABAMA PRESS, Box 2877, University, Ala. 35486

UNIVERSITY ASSOCIATES, 8517 Production Ave., San Diego, Calif. 92121

UNIVERSITY OF BUFFALO, Buffalo, N.Y. 14214

UNIVERSITY OF CALIFORNIA PRESS, 2223 Fulton St., Berkeley, Calif. 94720

UNIVERSITY OF CHICAGO, Chicago, Ill. 60637

UNIVERSITY OF CHICAGO PRESS, 5801 Ellis Ave., Chicago, Ill. 60637

UNIVERSITY OF DELAWARE, Newark, Del. 19711

UNIVERSITY OF KANSAS, Lawrence, Kans. 66044

UNIVERSITY OF KENTUCKY, Lexington, Ky. 40506

UNIVERSITY OF MICHIGAN PRESS, Box 1104, Ann Arbor, Mich. 48106

UNIVERSITY MICROFILMS, INC., 300 B, Zeeb Rd., Ann Arbor, Mich. 48106

UNIVERSITY OF NEBRASKA PRESS, 901 N. 17th St., Lincoln, Nebr. 68508

UNIVERSITY OF OKLAHOMA PRESS, 1005 Asp Ave., Norman, Okla. 73069

UNIVERSITY OF PENNSYLVANIA PRESS, 3933 Walnut St., Philadelphia, Pa. 19104

UNIVERSITY PRESS, 302 Fifth Ave., New York, N.Y. 10001

UNIVERSITY OF UTAH PRESS, Salt Lake City, Utah 84112

UNIVERSITY OF VIRGINIA, DARDEN SCHOOL OF BUSINESS, Charlottesville, Va. 22903

UPJOHN INSTITUTE, 300 S. Westnedge Ave., Kalamazoo, Mich. 49007

THE URBAN INSTITUTE, 2100 M St. N.W., Washington, D.C. 20037

U.S. CHAMBER OF COMMERCE, see CHAMBER OF COMMERCE OF THE UNITED STATES

U.S. DEPARTMENT OF AGRICULTURE, 14th St. and Independence Ave. S.W., Washington, D.C. 20250

U.S. DEPARTMENT OF COMMERCE, Washington, D.C. 20230

U.S. DEPARTMENT OF LABOR, Washington, D.C. 20102

U.S. GOVERNMENT PRINTING OFFICE, Washington, D.C. 20402 (For U.S. Government agencies and departments, see latest ed., "United States Government Manual," Office of the Federal Register, National Archives and Records Service, General Service Administration, Washington, D.C. 20408.)

VAN NOSTRAND REINHOLD COMPANY, 135 W. 50th St., New York, N.Y. 10020

VANDERBILT UNIVERSITY, Nashville, Tenn. 37203

VETERANS ADMINISTRATION, Alcohol and Drug Dependent Service, 810 Vermont Ave. N.W., Washington, D.C. 20420

VIKING PRESS, 625 Madison Ave., New York, N.Y. 10022

WADSWORTH PUBLISHING CO., INC., Belmont, Calif. 94002

WALTERS, ROY & ASSOCIATES, Whitney Road, Whitney Industrial Park, Mahwah, N.J. 07430

WARREN, GORHAM & LAMONT, INC., 210 Fifth St., Boston, Mass. 02111

WARREN, S.D. CORPORATION, 225 Franklin, Boston, Mass. 02176

WAYNE STATE UNIVERSITY PRESS, 5959 Woodward Ave., Detroit, Mich. 48202

WEST PUBLISHING CO., 50 W. Kellogg Blvd., St. Paul, Minn. 55102

WILEY, JOH & SONS, INC., 605 Third Ave., New York, N.Y.

WILSON, H.W. CO., 950 University Ave., Bronx, N.Y. 10452

WORD PROCESSING SOCIETY, INC., P.O. Box 92533, Milwaukee, Wisc. 53202

WORK IN AMERICA INSTITUTE, 200 White Plains Rd., Scarsdale, N.Y. 10583

WORLD PUBLISHING CO., 1400 Sterlin Rd., Mountain View, Calif. 94043

WRIGHT-ALLEN PRESS, 238 Main St., Cambridge, Mass. 02142

THE WYATT COMPANY, Suite 500, 1990 K St. N.W., Washington, D.C. 20006

YALE UNIVERSITY PRESS, 302 Temple St., New Haven, Conn. 06520

YANKELOVICH SKELLY AND WHITE, INC., 575 Madison Ave., New York, N.Y. 10002

YOUNG PRESIDENTS ORGANIZATION, 201 E. 42nd St., New York, N.Y. 10017

APPENDIX C

SOURCES OF INFORMATION

*Periodicals Mentioned in the Text**

Abitare, Editrice Segesta S.P.A. Milano, 15 Corso Monforte, 20122 Milano, Italy

Academy of Management Journal, Academy of Management

Accounting Review, American Accounting Association

Administrative Management, 51 Madison Ave., New York, N.Y. 10010

Administrative Science Quarterly, Cornell Graduate School of Business Administration, Ithaca, N.Y. 14850

Advanced Management Journal, Society for the Advancement of Management

Advanced Management-Office Executive, now *Advanced Management Journal*

Advanced Management Review, now *Advanced Management Journal*

Advertising Age, 740 Rush St., Chicago, Ill. 60611

Advertising & Publishing News, Adult Education Association of the U.S.A.

AFL-CIO Federationist, American Federation of Labor and Congress of Industrial Organizations

AIEE Transactions, American Institute of Industrial Engineers

American Banker, 525 W.W. 42nd St., New York, N.Y. 10036

American Behavioral Scientist, Sage Publications, Inc.

American Economic Review, Oxford House, 1313 21st Ave., Nashville, Tenn. 37212

American Industry, Box 4AA, Anchorage, Alaska

American Machinist, 1221 Ave. of the Americas, New York, N.Y. 10020

American Political Science Review, American Political Science Association

American Psychologist, American Psychological Association

* Where a periodical is published by an association or professional society, address is as given in Appendix B, unless otherwise shown here.

American Salesman, 424 N. 3rd St., Burlington, Ia. 52601

American Sociological Review, American Sociological Association

Annals of Mathematical Statistics, California State College at Hayward, Hayward, Calif. 94542

ANSI Reporter, American National Standards Institute

Annals of Occupational Hygiene, Fairview Park, Elmsford, N.Y. 10523

Applied Ergonomics, 205 E. 42nd St., New York, N.Y. 10017

Applied Statistics, Royal Statistical Society

Arbitare, Via Guerrazzi 1, Milan, Italy

Arbitration Journal, American Arbitration Association

Archives of Environmental Health, 4000 Albermarle St., N.W., Washington, D.C. 20016

Archives of Neurology and Psychology, American Medical Association

Area Development, 432 Park Ave., New York, N.Y. 10016

ARMA Quarterly, American Records Management Association

Associated Purchasing Publications, 1518 Walnut St., Philadelphia, Pa. 19102

Association Management, American Society of Association Executives

Atlantic Economic Journal, Box 100, Southern Illinois University, Edwardsville, Ill. 62026

Australian Accountant, 49 Exhibition St., Melbourne 3000, Australia

Automatic Machining, 65 Broad St., Rochester, N.Y. 14614

Automation, Penton Bldg., Cleveland, Ohio 44113

AV Communications Review, Association for Educational Communications and Technology

Barrister, American Bar Association

Behavioral Science, Society for General Systems Research, P.O. Box 1055, Lousiville, Ky. 40201

Best's Review, A.M. Best Co., Oldwick, N.J. 08858

Better-Work Supervisor, Clement Communications Inc., Concord Industrial Park, Concordville, Pa. 19331

Billboard, 9000 Sunset Blvd., Los Angeles, Calif. 90069

Biometrics, Biometric Society, 806 15th St. N.W., Washington, D.C. 20005

Biometrika, University College, Gower St., London WC1E, England

British Journal of Industrial Medicine, British Medical Association, Tavistock Square, London WC1H, England

Broadcasting Magazine, 1746 DeSales St., Washington, D.C. 20036

Budgeting, now *Managerial Planning*, Planning Executives Institute

Business Automation, now *Infosystems*, Hitchcock Bldg., Wheaton, Ill. 60187

Business Budgeting, formerly published by National Society for Business Publishing, Cincinnati, Ohio; disc.

Business Forms Reporter, 401 N. Broad St., Philadelphia, Pa. 19108

Business Forms Management, Box 569, Florissant, Mo. 63033

Business History Review, Harvard Graduate School of Business, Soldiers Field, Boston, Mass. 02163

Business Horizons, Indiana University Graduate School of Business, Bloomington, Ind. 47401

Business and Professional Ethics Newsletter, Rennselaer Polytechnic Institute, Troy, N.Y. 12181

Business Quarterly, University of Western Ontario School of Business Administration, London, Ontario, Canada

Business Week, 1221 Ave. of the Americas, New York, N.Y. 10020

California Law Review, University of California School of Law, Berkeley, Calif. 94720

California Management Review, University of California, Berkeley, Calif. 94720

Canadian Sales Meetings and Conventions, 1450 Don Mills Road, Don Mills, Ontario M3B 1X7, Canada

Chain Store Age, 425 Park Ave., New York, N.Y. 10022

Chemical Engineering, 1221 Ave. of the Americas, New York, N.Y. 10020

Circuits Manufacturing Magazine, 1050 Commonwealth Ave., Boston, Mass. 02215

Collector, The, American Collectors Association

Columbia Journal of World Business, 407 Uris Hall, Columbia University, New York, N.Y. 10027

Columbia Law Review, 425 W. 116th St., New York, N.Y. 10027

Commentary, 165 E. 56th St., New York, N.Y. 10022

Commodities, 219 Parkdale, Cedar Falls, Ia. 50613

Computer Decisions, 50 Essex St., Rochelle, N.J. 07662

Computer Journal, British Computer Society

Computer Operations Journal, British Computer Society

Computerworld, 797 Washington St., Newton, Mass. 02160

Conference Board Record, The Conference Board

Connecticut Bar Journal, 15 Lewis St., Hartford, Conn. 06103

Consultants News, Templeton Road, Fitzwilliam, N.H. 03447

Consumer Reports, Consumer Union

Control Engineering, 1301 S. Grove Ave., Barrington, Ill. 60010

Cost and Management, Society of Industrial Accountants of Canada

Data Processor, IBM, 1133 Westchester Ave., White Plains, N.Y. 10604

Data Processing Digest, 6020 LaTijera Blvd., Los Angeles, Calif. 90045

Datamation, 1801 S. La Cienega Blvd., Los Angeles, Calif. 90035

Decision Sciences, American Institute for Decision Sciences, University Plaza, Atlanta, Ga. 30303

Design (U.S.), 1100 Waterway Blvd., Indianapolis, Ind. 46202

Design (British), Design Center, 28 Haymarket, London S.W. 1, England

Design Industrie, 38 Boulevard Raspail, Paris, (7e), France

Distribution World Wide, Chilton Way, Radnor, Pa. 19089

Domus, Via A Grandi 5/7 20089 Rozzano/Milano, Italy

Dun's Review, 666 Fifth Ave., New York, N.Y. 10019

Econometrica, Department of Economics, Northwestern University, Evanston, Ill. 60201

EDP Weekly, Little Rock Turnpike, Annandale, Va. 22003

Engineering Economist, American Society for Engineering Education
Emory Law Journal, Emory University, School of Law, Atlanta, Ga., 30322
Engineering Magazine, 33-39 Bowling Green Lane, London EC1PAH, England
Engineering Management International, Aspirana Ave Private Bag, Glenn Innes, Aukland, New Zealand
Engineering Management Review, Institute of Electrical and Electronic Engineers
Environmental Control & Safety Management, A. M. Best Co., Oldwick, N.J. 08858
Esthetique Industrielle, now *Design Industrie*, 38 Boulevard Raspail, Paris (7e) France

Factory, disc.
Federal Accountant, now *Government Accountant's Journal*
Federal Register, National Archives and Records Center, Washington, D.C. 20402
Federal Reserve Bulletin, Federal Reserve System, Washington, D.C. 20551
Financial Analysis Journal, Financial Analysts Federation, 219 E. 42nd St., New York, N.Y. 10017
Financial Executive, Financial Executives Institute
Financial Management, Financial Management Association, Indiana University, Graduate School of Business, Bloomington, Ind. 47401
Financial World, 919 Third Ave., New York, N.Y. 10017
Form, Verlag form GmbH, Ernsthöfer Str. 12, D-6104 Seeheim-Jugenheim 3, West Germany
Fortune, Time Life Bldg., New York, N.Y. 10020

Geyer Dealer Topics, 51 Madison Ave., New York, N.Y. 10010
Group & Organization Studies, 7596 Ends Ave., La Jolle, Calif. 92037

Handling and Shipping Management, 614 Superior Ave., West Cleveland, Ohio 44113
Harvard Business Review, Soldiers Field, Boston, Mass. 02163
Health Physics Journal, Health Physics Society
Human Behavior, 12031 Wilshire Blvd., Los Angeles, Calif. 90025
Human Factors Journal, Human Factors Society
Human Relations, Tavistock Centre, 120 Belsize Lane, London NW3 5BA, England

ICC Practitioners Journal, Association of Interstate Commerce Practitioners, 1000 16th St., Washington, D.C. 20036
ID, 130 E. 59th St., New York, N.Y. 10022
Industrial Design, now ID
Industrial Distributor News, 1 Olney Ave., Philadelphia, Pa. 19120
Industrial Labor Relations Review, New York State School of Industrial and Labor Relations
Industrial Laboratories, Instrument Society of America, 400 Stanwix St., Pittsburgh, Pa. 15222
Industrial Maintenance and Plant Operations, 1 West Olney Ave., Philadelphia, Pa. 19120
Industrial Management, Industrial Management Society
Industrial Marketing, 740 Rush St., Chicago, Ill. 60611
Industrial Marketing Management, 52 Vanderbilt Ave., New York, N.Y. 10017
Industrial Purchasing, Agent, 21 Russell Woods Road, Great Neck, N.Y. 11021
Industrial Research/Development, 1301 S. Grove Ave., Barrington, Ill. 60010
Industrial Supervisor, National Safey Council
Infosystems, Hitchcock Bldg., Wheaton, Ill. 60187
Innovation, 300 E. 42nd St., New York, N.Y. 10017
Institutional Investor, 488 Madison Ave., New York, N.Y. 10022
Instruments and Control Systems, Chilton Way, Radnor, Pa. 19089
Internal Auditor, Institute of Internal Auditors
Instrumentation Technology, Instrument Society of America, 400 Stanwix St., Pittsburgh, Pa. 15222
International Journal of Physical Distribution, MCB Publications Ltd., 198/200 Keighley Road, Bradford, West Yorkshire England BD9 4JQ6
ISA Journal, now *Instrumentation Technology*
International Management, 1221 Ave. of the Americas, New York, N.Y. 10020
International Review of Administrative Sciences, International Institute of Administrative Sciences

Journal of Abnormal and Social Psychology, American Psychological Association
Journal of the Academy of Management, Academy of Management
Journal of Accounting, Auditing, and Finance, 210 South St., Boston, Mass. 02111

Journal of Accounting Research, Institute of Professional Accounting

Journal of Advertising Research, Advertising Research Foundation

Journal of the American Statistical Association, American Statistical Association

Journal of Applied Psychology, American Psychological Association

Journal of the Association for Computer Machinery, Association for Computer Machinery

Journal of Business, University of Chicago, Chicago, Ill. 60637

Journal of Business Communication, American Business Communication Association

Journal of Business Strategy, Warren, Gorham & Lamont, Inc., 210 South St., Boston, Mass. 02111

Journal of Commerce, 110 Wall St., New York, N.Y. 10005

Journal of Conflict Resolution, 275 S. Beverly Dr., Beverly Hills, Calif. 90212

Journal of Counseling Psychology, American Psychological Association

Journal of Creative Behavior, State University College at Buffalo, N.Y. 14222

Journal of Economic Literature, American Economic Association

Journal of Engineerng Psychology, Research International, Box 2137, Ventnor, N.J. 08406

Journal of Industrial Engineering, American Institute of Industrial Engineers

Journal of Management Studies, 108 Cowley Rd., Oxford OX4 1JF, England

Journal of Marketing, American Marketing Association

Journal of Marketing Research, American Marketing Association

Journal of Occupational Medicine, Industrial Medical Association

Journal of Political Economy, 5801 S. Ellis Ave., Chicago, Ill. 60637

Journal of Public Law, now *Emory Law Journal*

Journal of Quality Technology, American Society for Quality Control

Journal of Retailing, New York University Institute of Retail Management, Commerce Bldg., N.Y. 10003

Journal of Social Issues, Society for the Study of Social Issues, Box 1248, Ann Arbor, Mich. 48106

Journal of Systems Management, Association for Systems Management

Labor Law Journal, 4025 W. Peterson Ave., Chicago, Ill. 60646

Labor Law Reporter, Bureau of National Affairs

Law and Contemporary Problems, Duke University School of Law, Durham, N.C. 27706

Lloyd's Bank Review, 71 Lombard St., London, England

Long Range Planning, Pergamon Press, Inc., Journals Dept., Maxwell House, Fairview Park, Elmsford, N.Y. 10523

Machine Design, Penton Plaza, Cleveland, Ohio 94414

Magazine of Standards, The, American National Standards Institute

Management, Associated Credit Bureaus

Management Accounting, National Association of Accountants

Management Adviser, American Institute of Certified Public Accountants

Management of Personnel Quarterly, University of Michigan Bureau of Industrial Relations, Graduate School of Business, Ann Arbor, Mich. 48104

Management Review, American Management Associations

Management Science, The Institute of Management Sciences (TIMS)

Managerial Planning, Planning Executives Institute

Manufacturing Engineering, Society of Manufacturing Engineers

Material Handling Engineering, 614 Superior Ave., W. Cleveland, Ohio 44113

Materials Handling News, Quadrant House, The Quadrant, Sutton, Surrey SM2 5A5, England.

Mechanical Handling, now *Materials Handling News.*

Media Decisions, 342 Madison Ave., New York, N.Y. 10077

Medical Meetings, 750 Third Ave., New York, N.Y. 10017

Medical World News, 1221 Ave. of the Americas, New York, N.Y. 10020

Meetings and Expositions, 22 Pine St., Morristown, N.J. 07960

Menninger Quarterly, now *Menninger Perspective,* Menninger Foundation, Box 829, Topeka, Kans. 66601

Modern Materials Handling, 28 St. Paul St., Denver, Colo. 80206

Modern Office Procedures, 614 Superior Ave. W., Cleveland, Ohio 44113

Modern Packaging, now *Package Engineering*

Monthly Economic Letter, Citibank NA., Citicorp Center, 153 E. 53rd St., New York, N.Y. 10022

NAFM News, National Association of Furniture Manufacturers, 8401 Connecticut Ave., Suite 911, Washington, D.C. 20015

National Defense Transportation Journal, National Defense Transportation Association

National Safety News, National Safety Council

National Public Accountant, 1717 Pennsylvania Ave. N.W., Washington, D.C. 20006

Nation's Business, Chamber of Commerce of the United States

Naval Research Logistics Quarterly, G.P.O., Washington, D.C. 20402

National Law Review, University of Nebraska, College of Law, Lincoln, Nebr. 68508

New Equipment Digest, Penton Plaza, Cleveland, Ohio 44114

New York Certified Public Accountant, New York State Society of Certified Public Accountants, 600 Third Ave., New York, N.Y. 10009

Occupational Hazards, National Safety Council

Occupational Health Nursing, American Association of Occupational Health Nurses

Occupational Health and Safety, 4901 Bosque Blvd., Box 7573, Waco, Tex. 76710

Office, The, 1200 Sumner St., Stamford, Conn. 06904

Operational Research Quarterly, Operations Research Society of America

Organizational Dynamics, American Management Associations

Package Engineering, 5 S. Wabash Ave., Chicago, Ill. 60603

Performance Magazine, American Society for Performance Improvement

Personnel, American Management Associations

Personnel Administrator, American Society for Personnel Administration

Personnel Journal, 866 W. 18th St., Costa Mesa, Calif. 92627

Personnel Management Abstracts, University of Tulsa Information Services, 1133 N. Lewis St., Tulsa, Okla. 74110

Personnel Psychology, Box 6965 College Sta., Durham, N.C. 27708

Plant Engineering, 1301 S. Grove Ave., Barrington, Ill. 60010

Production, Box 101, Bloomfield Hills, Mich. 48103

Professional and Business Ethics Newsletter, Rensselaer Polytechnic Institute, Troy, N.Y. 12181

Professional Safety, American Society of Safety Engineers

Psychological Bulleting, American Psychological Association

Psychological Review, American Psychological Association

Public Administration, Royal Institute of Public Administration

Public Administration Review, American Society for Public Administration

Public Relations Journal, Public Relations Society of America

Purchasing Magazine, 205 E. 42nd St., New York, N.Y. 10017

Purchasing World, 35 Mason St., Greenwich, Conn. 06833

Quality Progress, American Society for Quality Control

Quarterly Journal of Economics, 605 Third Ave., New York, N.Y. 10016

Records Management Journal, Association of Records Executives and Administrators

Records Management Quarterly, American Records Management Association

Research/Development, 1301 S. Grove Ave., Burlington, Ill. 60010

Research and Education, now *Resources in Education*

Resources in Education, 4833 Rugby Ave. South, Suite 303, Bethesda, Md. 20014

Review of Economics and Statistics, Box 211, 1000 AE Amsterdam, Netherlands

Rutgers Law Review, Rutgers University School of Law, 180 University Ave., Newark, N.J. 07102

Safety Maintenance and Production, changed to *Environmental Control & Safety Management*

Sales Management, now *Sales & Marketing Management*, 633 Third Ave., New York, N.Y. 10017

Saturday Review, 150 E. 58th St., New York, N.Y. 10155

School and Society, now *USA Today*

Science, American Association for the Advancement of Science

Security Management, American Society for Industrial Security, 2000 K St. N.W., Suite 651, Washington, D.C. 20006

Security World, 2630 S. La Cienega Blvd., Los Angeles, Calif. 90034

Social Psychology, 1722 N St. N.W., Washington, D.C. 20036

Sociometry, now *Social Psychology*

St. John's Law Review, St. John's University, School of Law, Grand Central and Utopia Parkway, Jamaica, N.Y. 11439

Standards Action, American National Standards Institute

Statistical Journal, American Statistical Association

Stores, National Retail Merchants Association

Strategic Management Journal, John Wiley & Sons Ltd., Buffins Lane, Chichester Sussex, PO 19 1UD, England

Studies in Business Administration, University of Chicago, School of Business, Chicago, Ill. 60637

Successful Meetings, 1422 Chestnut St., Philadelphia, Pa., 19102.

Supervision, 424 N. Third St., Burlington, Ia. 52607

Supervisory Management, American Management Associations

Systemation, The Foundation of Administrative Research, c/o Ross-Martin Co., 6504 E. 44th St., Tulsa, Okla. 74145

Systems and Procedures, now *Journal of Systems Managmement*

Tax Review, Tax Foundation, Inc., 1875 Connecticut Ave. N.W., Washington, D.C. 20009

Taxes—The Tax Magazine, 4025 W. Peterson Ave., Chicago, Ill. 60646

Technology Review, Massachusetts Institute of Technology, Cambridge, Mass. 02139

Technometrica, American Statistical Association and American Society for Quality Control (jointly)

Television Factbook, 1836 Jefferson Plaza, Washington, D.C. 20036

Television/Radio Age, 1270 Ave. of the Americas, New York, N.Y. 10020

Time and Motion Study, now *Work Study*

Tooling and Production, 5821 Harper Rd., Solon, Ohio 44139

Trademark Reporter, United States Trademark Association

Tradeshow Convention Guide, P.O. Box 7, New York, N.Y. 10004

Tradeshow Week, 8687 Melrose Ave., Los Angeles, Calif. 90069

Traffic Bulletin, 815 Washington Bldg., Washington, D.C. 20005

Traffic Management, 205 E. 42nd St., New York, N.Y. 10017

Traffic World, 815 Washington Bldg., Washington, D.C. 20005

Training in Business and Industry, now *Training*, 731 Hennepin Ave., Minneapolis, Minn. 55403

Transactional Analysis Bulletin, now *Transaction Analysis Journal*, Transaction Analysis Association

Transactions in Engineering Management, Institute of Electrical and Electronic Engineers

Transportation and Distribution Management, 815 Washington Bldg., Washington, D.C. 20005

Transportation Journal, American Society of Traffic and Transportation

U.S. News & World Report, 200 N St. N.W., Washington, D.C. 20037

USA Today, Society for Advancement of Education, 1860 Broadway, New York, N.Y. 10023

Value Engineering Digest, now *Value Engineering and Management Digest/Defense Contract Guide*, 986 National Press Bldg., Washington, D.C. 20004

Value World, 20 W. 14th St., New York, N.Y. 10011

Vending Times, 211 E. 43rd St., New York, N.Y. 10017

Venture, The Magazine for Entrepreneurs, 35 W. 45th St., New York, N.Y. 10036

Venture Capital, Box 348, Wellesley Hills, Mass., 02181

Viewpoint, American Federation of Labor and Congress of Industrial Organizations

Wall Street Journal, The, 22 Cortland St., New York, N.Y. 10004

Weltwirtschafliches Archiv (Review of World Economics), Wilhelmstrasse 18, Postfach 2040, 7400 Tübingen, West Germany

Word Processing Report, 51 Madison Ave., New York, N.Y. 10010

Word Processing Systems, 51 Madison Ave., New York, N.Y. 10010

Working Woman, 600 Madison Ave., New York, N.Y. 10022

World Convention Dates, 79 Washington St., Hempstead, N.Y. 11550

INDEX